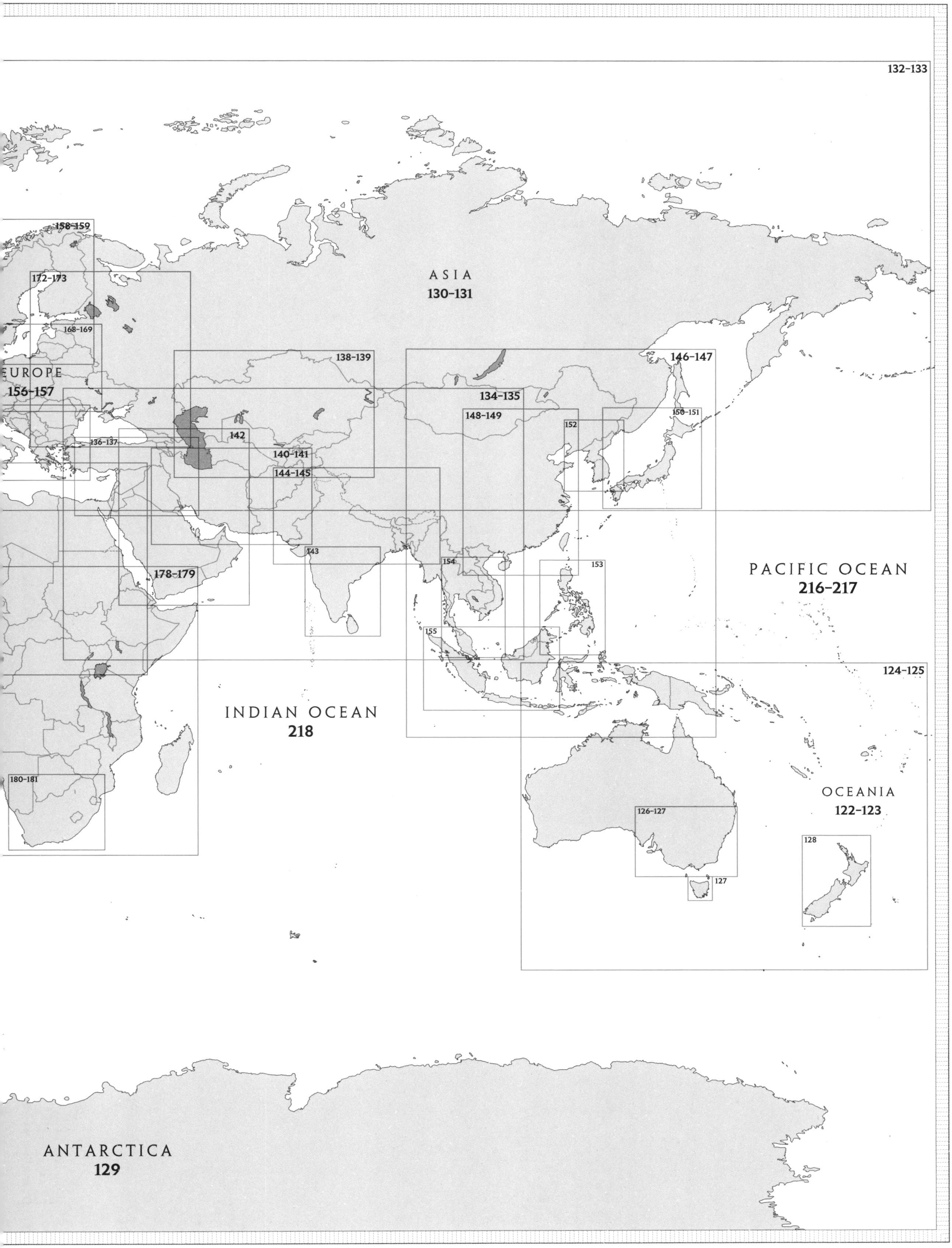
132–133
ASIA
130–131
158–159
172–173
168–169
EUROPE
156–157
138–139
146–147
134–135
148–149
152
150–151
136–137
142
140–141
144–145
143
154
153
178–179
PACIFIC OCEAN
216–217
155
124–125
INDIAN OCEAN
218
180–181
OCEANIA
122–123
126–127
128
127
ANTARCTICA
129

# THE TIMES REFERENCE ATLAS OF THE WORLD

Times Books, 77–85 Fulham Palace Road, London W6 8JB

First published 1995
Published as The Times Atlas of the World New Generation Edition 1997
Second Edition 2002
Third Edition 2005
Fourth Edition 2008
Fifth Edition 2010

Sixth Edition 2013



Printed and bound in Hong Kong

British Library Cataloguing in Publication Data
A catalogue record for this book is available from the British Library

ISBN 978 0 00 749821 5
Imp 001

All mapping in this atlas is generated from Collins Bartholomew digital databases. Collins Bartholomew, the UK's leading independent geographical information supplier, can provide a digital, custom, and premium mapping service to a variety of markets.
For further information:
Tel: +44 (0) 208 307 4515
e-mail: collinsbartholomew@harpercollins.co.uk

or visit our website at: www.collinsbartholomew.com

If you would like to comment on any aspect of this atlas, please write to
Times Atlases, HarperCollins Publishers, Westerhill Road, Bishopbriggs, Glasgow G64 2QT
e-mail: timesatlas@harpercollins.co.uk

or visit our website at: www.timesatlas.com

Follow us on twitter: @timesatlas

The world's most authoritative and prestigious maps and atlases

**www.timesatlas.com**

THE TIMES

REFERENCE

# ATLAS OF THE WORLD

TIMES BOOKS
LONDON

| Pages | Title | Scale |
|---|---|---|
| | **IMAGES OF EARTH** | |
| 4–5 | INTRODUCTION TO IMAGES OF EARTH | |
| 6–7 | OCEANIA | |
| 8–9 | ASIA | |
| 10–11 | EUROPE | |
| 12–13 | AFRICA | |
| 14–15 | NORTH AMERICA | |
| 16–17 | SOUTH AMERICA | |
| 18–19 | ANTARCTICA | |
| 20–21 | MATANGI ISLAND, FIJI | |
| 22–23 | UVS NUUR, MONGOLIA | |
| 24–25 | ROME, ITALY | |
| 26–27 | ASWAN HIGH DAM, EGYPT | |
| 28–29 | MACKENZIE RIVER DELTA, CANADA | |
| 30–31 | AKIMISKI ISLAND, CANADA | |
| 32–33 | NAZCA LINES, PERU | |
| 34–35 | ICE FIELDS, ANTARCTIC PENINSULA, ANTARCTICA | |
| | **HISTORICAL MAPPING** | |
| 36–37 | INTRODUCTION TO HISTORICAL MAPPING | |
| 38–39 | THE WORLD ON MERCATOR'S PROJECTION 1858 | |
| 40–41 | POLITICAL MAP OF THE WORLD 1914 | |
| 42–43 | WORLD POLITICAL DIVISIONS 1936 | |
| 44–45 | WORLD ROUTES OF COMMERCE 1950 | |
| 46–47 | WORLD POLITICAL CHART 1963 | |
| 48–49 | STATES OF THE WORLD 1982 | |
| 50–51 | NEW ZEALAND 1879 | |
| 52–53 | UNITED STATES OF AMERICA 1879 | |
| 54–55 | NORTH POLAR REGIONS AND SOUTH POLAR REGIONS 1898 | |
| 56–57 | AUSTRALIA 1898 | |
| 58–59 | AFRICA POLITICAL 1895 | |
| 60–61 | THE FAR EAST 1907 | |
| 62–63 | TURKEY IN ASIA, PERSIA, &c. 1914 | |
| 64–65 | EUROPE POLITICAL 1922 | |
| 66–67 | CHINA 1922 | |
| 68–69 | WORLD POWERS 1957 | |
| | **GEOGRAPHICAL INFORMATION** | |
| 70–89 | STATES AND TERRITORIES | |
| 90–91 | EARTHQUAKES AND VOLCANOES | |
| 92–93 | CLIMATE I | |
| 94–95 | CLIMATE II | |
| 96–97 | POPULATION | |
| 98–99 | COMMUNICATIONS | |
| 100–101 | PHYSICAL FEATURES | |
| | **CITY PLANS** | |
| 102 | Auckland, Melbourne, Sydney, Jakarta | |
| 103 | Singapore, Bangkok, Hong Kong, Beijing, Shanghai, Seoul | |
| 104–105 | Tōkyō | |
| 106 | Karachi, Delhi, Mumbai, Tehrān, Jerusalem, İstanbul | |
| 107 | Athens, Moscow, St Petersburg, Berlin, Brussels, Amsterdam | |
| 108–109 | London | |
| 110–111 | Paris | |
| 112 | Rome, Milan, Madrid, Barcelona, Cairo, Cape Town | |
| 113 | Montréal, Toronto, Chicago, Washington D.C., Los Angeles, San Francisco | |
| 114–115 | New York | |
| 116 | Mexico City, Lima, Rio de Janeiro, São Paulo, Buenos Aires, Caracas | |
| | **ATLAS OF THE WORLD** | |
| 117 | MAP SYMBOLS | |
| | **WORLD** | |
| 118–119 | WORLD Physical | 1:80 000 000 |
| 120–121 | WORLD Political | 1:80 000 000 |
| | **OCEANIA** | |
| 122–123 | OCEANIA | 1:32 000 000 |
| 124–125 | AUSTRALASIA and SOUTHWEST PACIFIC | 1:20 000 000 |
| 126–127 | AUSTRALIA Southeast | 1:5 000 000 |
| | Tasmania | 1:5 000 000 |
| 128 | NEW ZEALAND | 1:5 000 000 |
| 129 | ANTARCTICA | 1:32 000 000 |
| | **ASIA** | |
| 130–131 | ASIA | 1:28 000 000 |
| 132–133 | RUSSIAN FEDERATION | 1:21 000 000 |
| 134–135 | ASIA Central and South | 1:20 000 000 |
| 136–137 | THE MIDDLE EAST | 1:5 000 000 |
| 138–139 | ASIA Central | 1:7 000 000 |
| 140–141 | THE GULF, IRAN and AFGHANISTAN | 1:7 000 000 |
| 142 | ARABIAN PENINSULA | 1:12 500 000 |

| Pages | Title | Scale |
|---|---|---|
| 143 | INDIA South and SRI LANKA | 1:7 000 000 |
| 144–145 | INDIA North and BANGLADESH | 1:7 000 000 |
| 146–147 | ASIA East and Southeast | 1:20 000 000 |
| 148–149 | CHINA Central and East | 1:7 500 000 |
| | Hong Kong | 1:750 000 |
| 150–151 | JAPAN | 1:5 000 000 |
| 152 | CHINA Northeast, NORTH KOREA and SOUTH KOREA | 1:5 000 000 |
| 153 | PHILIPPINES | 1:7 000 000 |
| 154 | THAILAND, CAMBODIA and PENINSULAR MALAYSIA | 1:7 500 000 |
| | Singapore | 1:550 000 |
| 155 | INDONESIA West | 1:10 000 000 |
| | **EUROPE** | |
| 156–157 | EUROPE | 1:17 500 000 |
| 158–159 | SCANDINAVIA and THE BALTIC STATES | 1:5 000 000 |
| | Iceland | 1:5 000 000 |
| | Faroe Islands | 1:5 000 000 |
| 160–161 | ENGLAND and WALES | 1:2 000 000 |
| 162 | SCOTLAND | 1:2 000 000 |
| | Shetland Islands | 1:2 000 000 |
| 163 | IRELAND | 1:2 000 000 |
| 164–165 | BELGIUM, NETHERLANDS and GERMANY North | 1:2 000 000 |
| 166 | FRANCE | 1:5 000 000 |
| 167 | SPAIN and PORTUGAL | 1:5 000 000 |
| 168–169 | EUROPE North Central | 1:5 000 000 |
| 170–171 | ITALY and THE BALKANS | 1:5 000 000 |
| 172–173 | RUSSIAN FEDERATION West | 1:7 000 000 |
| | **AFRICA** | |
| 174–175 | AFRICA | 1:28 000 000 |
| 176–177 | AFRICA North | 1:16 000 000 |
| | Cape Verde | 1:16 000 000 |
| 178–179 | AFRICA Central and South | 1:16 000 000 |
| 180–181 | REPUBLIC OF SOUTH AFRICA | 1:5 000 000 |
| | **NORTH AMERICA** | |
| 182–183 | NORTH AMERICA | 1:32 000 000 |
| 184–185 | CANADA | 1:17 000 000 |
| 186–187 | CANADA West | 1:7 000 000 |
| 188–189 | CANADA East | 1:7 000 000 |
| 190–191 | THE GREAT LAKES | 1:3 500 000 |
| 192–193 | UNITED STATES OF AMERICA | 1:12 000 000 |
| 194–195 | USA West | 1:7 000 000 |
| 196–197 | USA Southwest | 1:3 500 000 |
| | Hawai'ian Islands | 1:6 000 000 |
| | O'ahu | 1:5 000 000 |
| 198–199 | USA Central | 1:7 000 000 |
| 200–201 | USA East | 1:7 000 000 |
| 202–203 | USA Northeast | 1:3 500 000 |
| 204–205 | CENTRAL AMERICA and THE CARIBBEAN | 1:14 000 000 |
| 206–207 | MEXICO and CENTRAL AMERICA | 1:7 000 000 |
| | **SOUTH AMERICA** | |
| 208–209 | SOUTH AMERICA | 1:32 000 000 |
| 210–211 | SOUTH AMERICA North | 1:15 000 000 |
| | Galapagos Islands | 1:15 000 000 |
| 212 | SOUTH AMERICA South | 1:15 000 000 |
| | South Georgia | 1:15 000 000 |
| 213 | VENEZUELA and COLOMBIA | 1:7 500 000 |
| 214 | BRAZIL Southeast | 1:7 500 000 |
| 215 | CHILE Central, ARGENTINA Central and URUGUAY | 1:7 500 000 |
| | **OCEANS** | |
| 216–217 | PACIFIC OCEAN | 1:58 000 000 |
| 218 | INDIAN OCEAN | 1:58 000 000 |
| 219 | ATLANTIC OCEAN | 1:58 000 000 |
| 220 | ARCTIC OCEAN | 1:32 000 000 |
| | **INDEX AND ACKNOWLEDGEMENTS** | |
| 221 | INTRODUCTION TO THE INDEX | |
| 222–271 | INDEX | |
| 272 | ACKNOWLEDGEMENTS | |

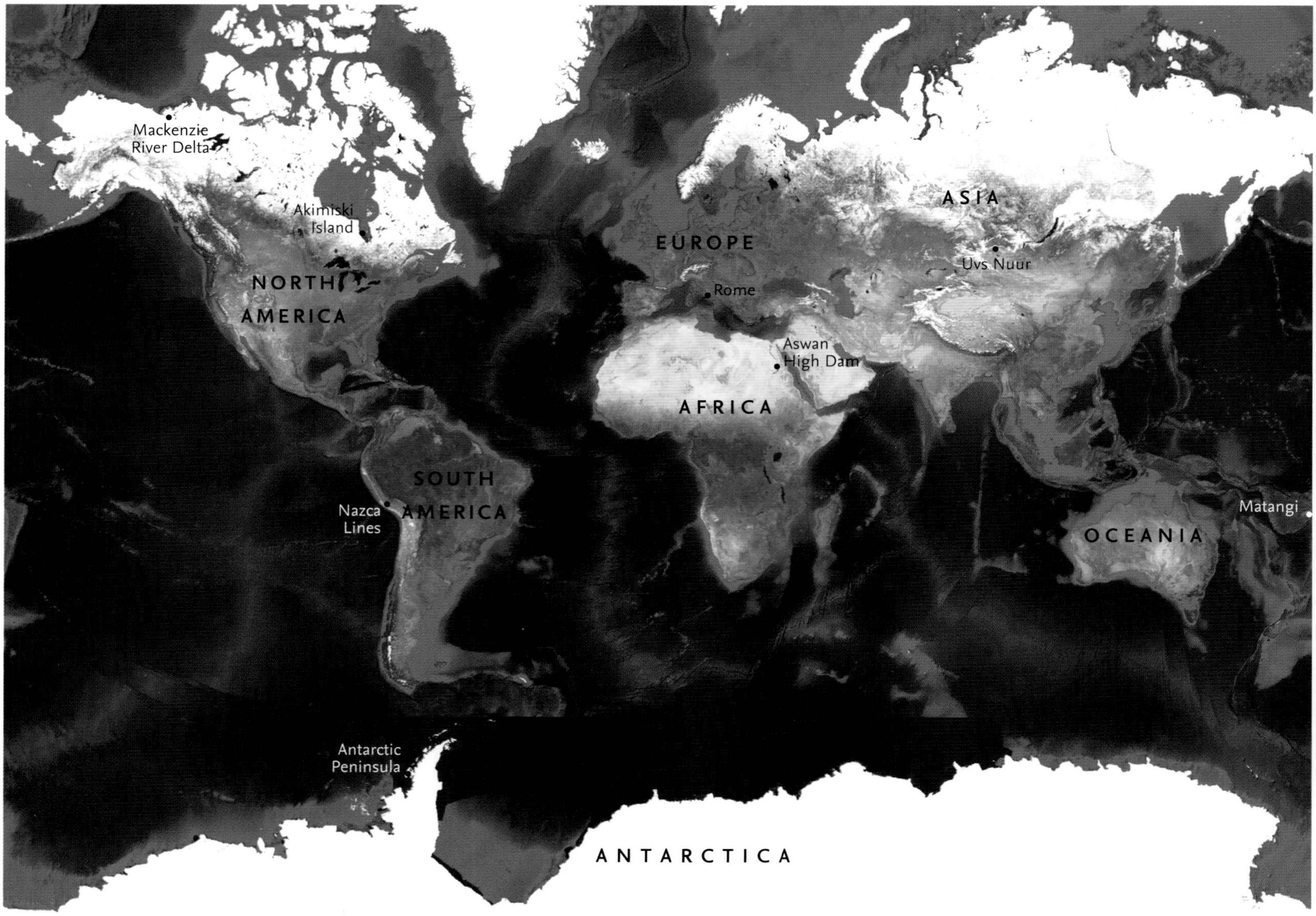


## 6–7 OCEANIA

The continent of Oceania comprises Australia, New Guinea, New Zealand and the islands of the Pacific Ocean. The main Pacific island groups of Melanesia, Micronesia and Polynesia sit amongst the complex of ridges and troughs which make up the Pacific seafloor. Notable among these, and visible extending northwards from New Zealand, are the Kermadec and Tonga trenches – the latter reaching a depth of 10 800 m (35 424 ft) at Horizon Deep. Australia itself appears largely dry and barren, its vast interior consisting of several deserts, with brighter salt lakes in the low artesian basin of the east central area. The east coast of Australia, separated from the interior by the Great Dividing Range – the source of the continent's longest rivers the Murray and the Darling – is more densely vegetated. New Guinea is covered by dense tropical forest, while New Zealand displays a great variety of land cover types, most prominent being the snow-capped Southern Alps on South Island.

## 8–9 ASIA

This vast continent – the world's largest – covers an enormous area and contains a great variety of landscapes, evident on this image. It stretches from the Mediterranean Sea in the west to the far east of the Russian Federation and Japan, and from arctic Siberia in the north to the tropical islands of Indonesia. The Caspian Sea – the world's largest lake – is prominent in the west. The snow-capped Caucasus mountains stretching from the Caspian Sea to the Black Sea clearly mark the divide between Asia and Europe. Just east of the Caspian Sea lies the complex shape of the Aral Sea. This was once the world's fourth largest lake, but is now drastically reduced in size because of climate change and the extraction of water for irrigation. In the centre of the image, the long arc of the mountain ranges of the Himalaya, Karakoram, Hindu Kush and Tien Shan circle the featureless Tarim Pendi basin and the lake-riddled Plateau of Tibet.

## 10–11 EUROPE

The generally densely vegetated continent of Europe contains some dramatic geographical features. Its northern and western limits are marked by the complex coastlines of Iceland, Scandinavia and north-western Russian Federation, while the British Isles sit on the flat, wide continental shelf. Europe's mountain ranges divide the continent – in the southwest, the Pyrenees separate France from the drier Iberian Peninsula, the wide arc of the Alps separates Italy from the rest of western Europe, the Carpathian Mountains, appearing as a dark curve between the Alps and the Black Sea, mark the edge of the vast European plains, and the Caucasus, stretching between the Black Sea and the Caspian Sea, create a prominent barrier between Europe and Asia. Two of Europe's greatest rivers are also clearly visible on this image – the Volga, Europe's longest river, flowing south from the Ural Mountains into the Caspian Sea and the Dnieper flowing across the plains into the northern Black Sea.

## 12–13 AFRICA

This image of Africa clearly shows the change in vegetation through the equatorial regions from the vast, dry Sahara desert covering much of the north of the continent, through the rich forests of the Congo basin – the second largest drainage basin in the world – to the high plateau of southern Africa. Lake Victoria dominates central east Africa and the Nile and its delta create a distinctive feature in the desert in the northeast. The path of the Great Rift Valley can be traced by the pattern of linear lakes in east Africa, to Ethiopia, and along the Red Sea. The dark fan-shaped feature in central southern Africa is the Okavango Delta in Botswana – one of the world's most ecologically sensitive areas. To the east of the continent lies Madagascar, and in the Indian Ocean northeast of this is the Mascarene Ridge sea feature stretching from the Seychelles in the north to Mauritius and Réunion in the south.

## 14–15 NORTH AMERICA

Many well-known geographical features are identifiable on this image of North America, which also illustrates the contrasts in landscapes across the continent. Greenland, the world's largest island, sits off the northeast coast while the dramatic chain of the Aleutian Islands in the northwest stretches from Alaska across the Bering Sea to the Kamchatka Peninsula in the Russian Federation. Further south in the Pacific Ocean, at the far left of the image, lie the Hawai'ian Islands and their very distinctive ocean ridge. There is a strong west-east contrast across the continent. The west is

dominated by the Rocky Mountains, which give way to the Great Plains. In the east, the Great Lakes, the largest of which, Lake Superior, is second in size only to the Caspian Sea, the valley of the Mississippi and the Coastal Plain are prominent.

## 16–17 SOUTH AMERICA

The Andes mountains stretch along the whole length of the west coast of South America, widening into the high plains of the Altiplano in Bolivia and Peru in the centre of the continent. Lake Titicaca, the world's highest large navigable lake, lies on the Altiplano, straddling the Bolivia–Peru border. Running parallel to the Andes, just off the west coast, is the Peru–Chile Trench which marks the active boundary between the Nazca and South American tectonic plates. Movement between these plates gives rise to numerous volcanoes in the Andes. The Amazon river runs across almost the whole width of the continent in the north, meeting the Atlantic Ocean in its wide delta on the northeast coast. The vast Amazon basin is one of the most ecologically diverse areas of the Earth. In the south, the wide continental shelf stretches eastward from the tip of the continent to the Falkland Islands and South Georgia on the bottom edge of the image.

## 18–19 ANTARCTICA

Protected by the Antarctic Treaty, implemented in 1959, from commercial exploitation and from the realization of territorial claims, Antarctica is perhaps the world's greatest unspoilt, and relatively unexplored, wilderness. This image combines bathymetric data (incomplete in some black areas) with a mosaic of over a thousand Landsat ETM+ scenes to show the extent of the continental ice sheet in an austral summer.
Floating sea ice is not shown. The Antarctic Peninsula – home to numerous scientific research stations – in the top left of the image reaching towards South America, the huge Ronne and Ross ice shelves, and the Transantarctic Mountains – dividing the continent into West and East Antarctica – are the dominant physical features.

## 20–21 MATANGI ISLAND, FIJI

Matangi could be described as a tropical island paradise. On this image individual trees can be seen, spread all across the unusual horseshoe-shaped hilly island. There is an obvious visual difference between trees in their natural self-set positions, as contrasted with areas where they have been planted and carefully spaced. In this image, the reef around the island is shown in pale blue, giving a good impression of the detailed topography in the shallow water. Some shallow-water vegetation shows as dark green patches. White sandy beaches fringe parts of the coastline. Matangi is a privately-owned island, used as a resort, and is one of the smaller of the many Fijian islands, covering only 97 hectares (240 acres).
Not surprisingly, the bay is called Horseshoe Bay. The characteristic shape is derived from an old volcano, half of which has been eroded away – many islands in Fiji are of volcanic origin.

## 22–23 UVS NUUR, MONGOLIA

This large salt lake – nuur being the local word for a lake – is about 80 km (50 miles) across and lies in an inland or 'endorheic' drainage basin in an upland region of northwest Mongolia, touching the borders of Tuva in the Russian Federation. The edges of the body of water are defined sharply, sometimes by steep mountainsides, while the left-hand edge consists of a broad alluvial fan brought down by the main river that feeds it. The bright green indicates vegetation, most prominently on the delta itself, but also in a lowland zone in the upper right and in thin lines along the rivers. The highly arid mountains also show extensive fans of erosion debris across much of the picture. Thin straight lines of roads or tracks become very evident on closer inspection, especially across the salt flats, although otherwise the influence of people is minimal in this hostile environment. Partly for that reason a vast surrounding area is classed as a World Heritage Site, noted for its diverse and unspoiled natural fauna as well as for numerous undisturbed archaeological remains.

## 24–25 ROME, ITALY

This is a close-up aerial view of the centre of Rome, taken almost vertically and looking due south. Views of city centres from above can often look rather similar to each other, perhaps needing some research, foreknowledge or personal experience to identify them positively; houses, tower blocks and streets can look alike from the air. However, absolutely unmistakeable in this case is the dominant presence of the large oval shape at the top left. This can only be Rome: the Coliseum, or Colosseum, is a uniquely-preserved amphitheatre, designed in the first century AD for mass public events. Some of them were bloodthirsty to a degree perhaps never seen anywhere, either before or since. It could even be flooded, to stage battles involving boats, and 50 000 people could watch the entertainments. At the top right of the picture a bend of the river Tiber shows up, bright green, with an island in the middle. In the bottom centre (north) appears a well-known edifice, the controversial white-marble Victor Emmanuel II Monument, built in the 1930s but commemorating the nineteenth century king who first presided over a unified Italy. Covering extensive grounds to the southeast of it are significant Roman remains, notably the Forum, which included a large open meeting place and numerous temples. The wooded areas are the Palatine Hill and the Capitoline Hill, two of the famous Seven Hills of Rome. The Vatican City (an independent country since the 1920s) is contained entirely within the city, but lies off the picture to the right.

## 26–27 ASWAN HIGH DAM, EGYPT

This aerial view shows the Aswan High Dam (Khazzān Aswān), an embankment dam, which is just north of the border between Egypt and Sudan, on the river Nile. The British built the Low Dam, 6 km (3.7 miles) downstream, in 1902; at the time it was the largest dam in the world. But it was later judged inadequate to hold back the very highest floodwaters, and so construction on the High Dam took place, between 1950 and 1960. The dam is over 3 800 m (12 500 ft) long and 110 m (360 ft) tall and is considered to be one of the greatest engineering projects ever accomplished. The resulting reservoir, Lake Nasser, is the largest artificial lake in the world. Most of Egypt's population lives along the Nile and depends on it for survival. The dam prevents the annual flooding that used to occur, damaging homes and crops and bringing down sediment in quantity. Lake Nasser's water is used instead for hydroelectricity production and irrigation. However, damming the Nile has proved to be a mixed blessing – many thousands of people had to be relocated to make way for the dam, and farmers now have to use artificial fertiliser as a substitute for the previous annual supply of natural nutrients.

## 28–29 MACKENZIE RIVER DELTA, CANADA

Canada's longest river, the Mackenzie, runs from Great Slave Lake just north of the Alberta-Northwest Territories border, to the Beaufort Sea north of the Arctic Circle. This image shows a section of the Mackenzie Delta in August, with the Middle Channel of the river clearly visible just left of centre. The main channel of the river is running from south to north and where it leaves the top of the image, it still has around 75 km (47 miles) to travel before reaching the coast. In winter months, most of this area is blanketed by ice and snow, but in the summer the whole of the delta region is awash with small lakes and swamps, showing blue on the image; vegetation is green. Human habitation is very sparse in the delta region. Inuvik (population 3 586 in 2009), just off the top right of the image, is the administrative centre for the region and Fort McPherson the next nearest place around 50 km (31 miles) to the southwest. An oxbow lake is clearly forming off the middle channel (centre-top). Although now almost complete, previous images of the area have shown that the process of creating the oxbow has taken twenty years to get to this point. The channel which leaves the main one about one third up from the bottom and then heads off to the left represents the start of what will become the West Channel of the Mackenzie River Delta. This channel will eventually join the sea at Shallow Bay, more than 70 km (43 miles) along the coast from the river's eastern-most major channel at Kugmallit Bay.

## 30–31 AKIMISKI ISLAND, CANADA

Akimiski Island in James Bay, at the southern end of Hudson Bay, is rich with vegetation in this stunning satellite image taken at the height of the Canadian summer. This has not always been the case, as in the last ice age Akimiski was entirely buried under thousands of metres of ice. Since the retreat of the ice, Akimiski's previously bare surface has been reclaimed by trees and plants, while the island's elevation has increased with the removal of the heavy ice. Beaches can be identified especially on the northern shore, and new streams and lakes have formed in the island's interior. At 3 000 sq km (1 159 sq miles), Akimiski is the largest island in James Bay. It is currently uninhabited. To the bottom left of the image, the river mouths of the Ontario coast have deposited a light brown sediment which has been allowed to build up due to the island sheltering this part of the bay.

## 32–33 NAZCA LINES, PERU

Located on an arid coastal plain 400 km (249 miles) south of Lima, this is one of a series of lines and geoglyphs covering 450 sq km (174 sq miles) of desert up to the edge of the Andean foothills. Believed to have been scratched onto the ground between 500 BC and AD 500 by the local people, they represent one of archaeology's greatest and most impressive mysteries. The questions of how and why they were created are both fascinating and as yet, still partially unexplained. The quality of the geometry and full impression of the shapes can only really be appreciated from the air. The shapes differ in complexity from individual lines and simple geometric shapes to stunning images of creatures including spiders, lizards, fish and birds. The image shown is believed to be a hummingbird, wings outstretched with its head pointing left. The whole area was designated a UNESCO World Heritage Site in 1994, due to its depiction of human creative genius amongst other criteria.

## 34–35 ICE FIELDS, ANTARCTIC PENINSULA, ANTARCTICA

These ice fields are near Adelaide Island, which lies at the north end of Marguerite Bay on the west coast of the Antarctic Peninsula. The image was captured in April 2012 at the start of the Antarctic winter. The island, which can be seen to the left, is the location of the British Antarctic Survey Research Station Rothera. The station is involved in several areas of research including glacial retreat, taking ice cores for study of the chemistry of the atmosphere and the climate, and collecting geological data to assist computer modeling of past movements of the ice sheets. The Bonner Laboratory at the station is a biology centre that includes a year-round diving programme. In the winter divers cut holes in the sea ice to enter the water. Antarctica is almost completely covered in ice that averages at least a mile (1.6 km) in thickness, but the Antarctic Peninsula is one of the places on the earth that is warming the fastest, so the information collected here will help to identify the effects of climate change.

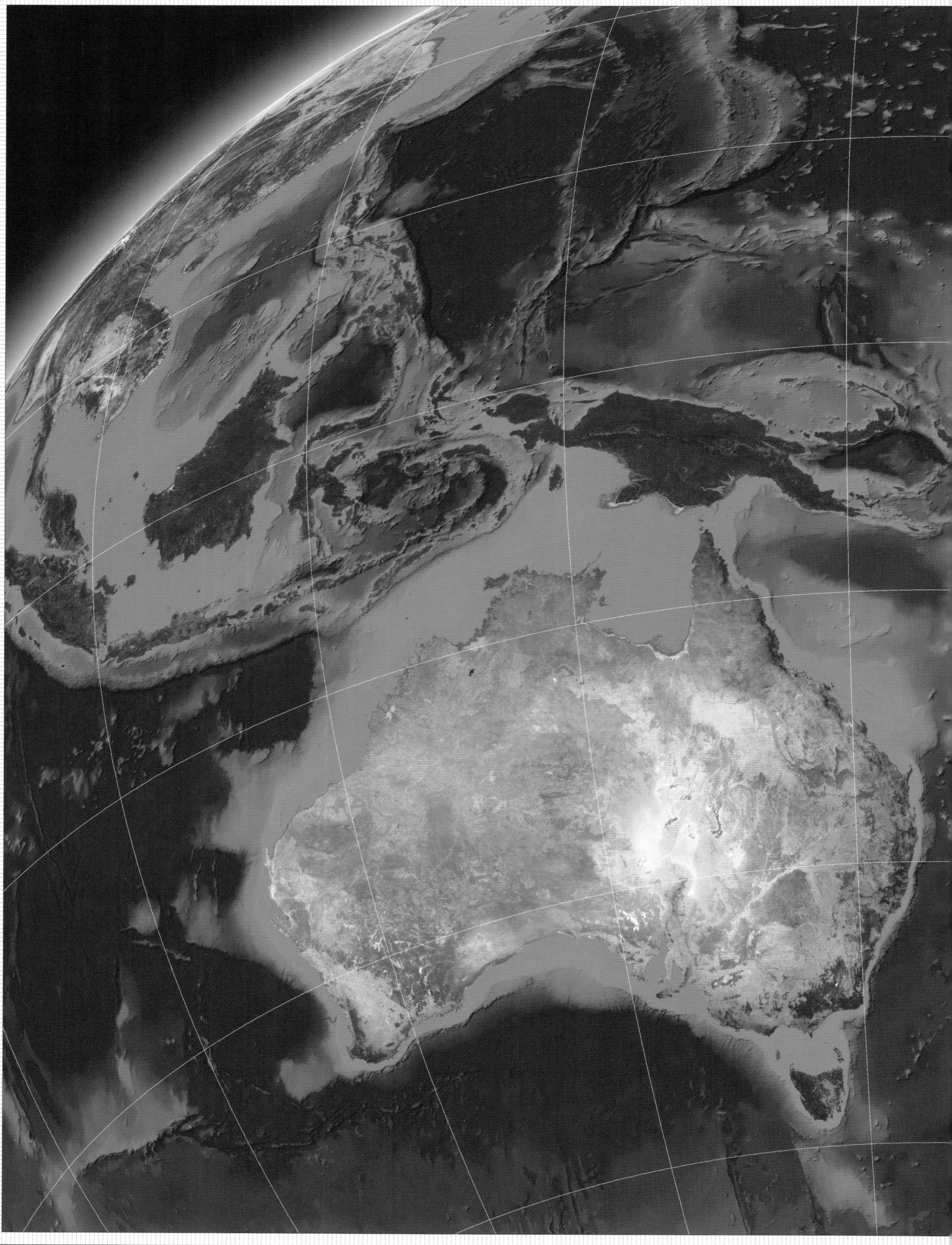

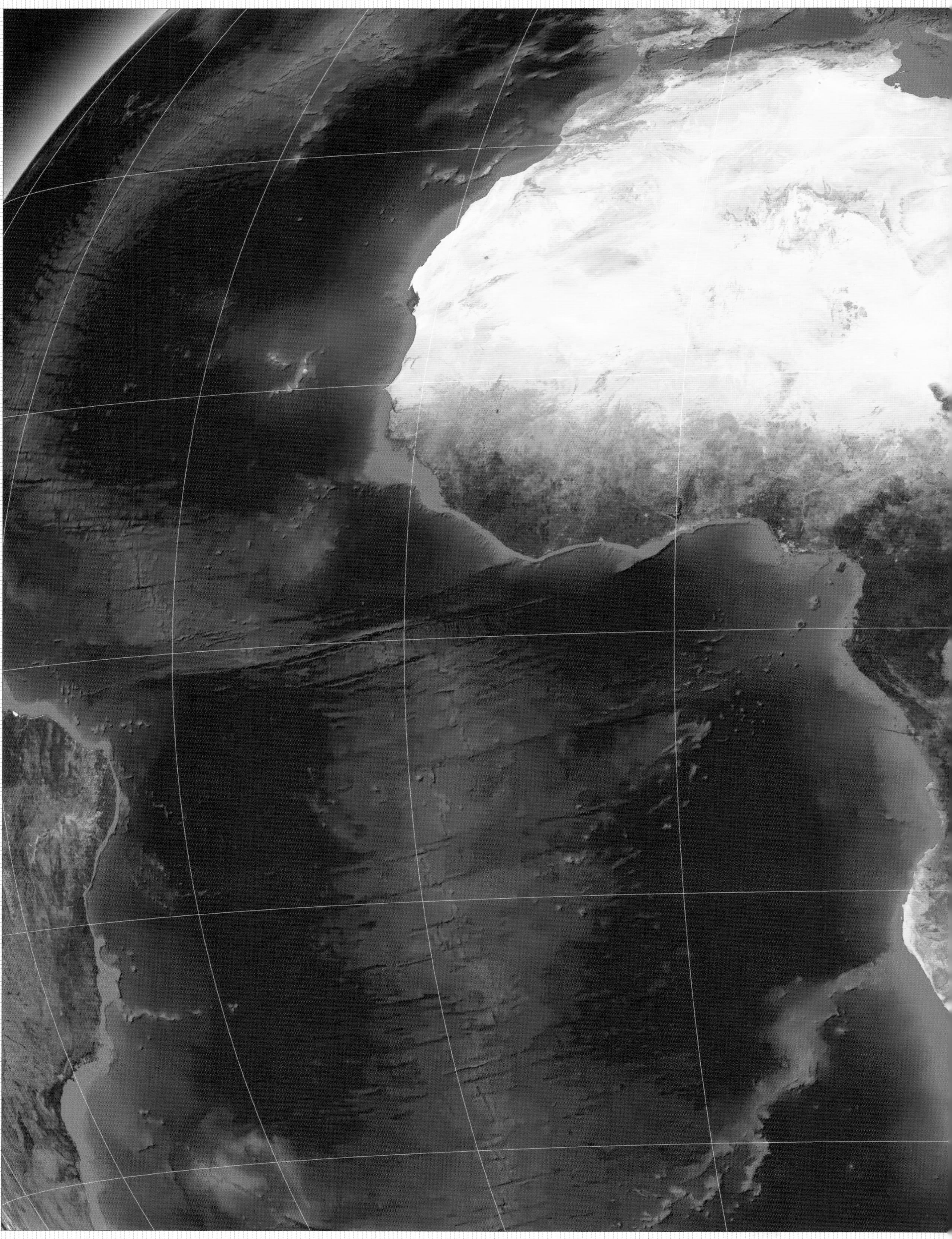

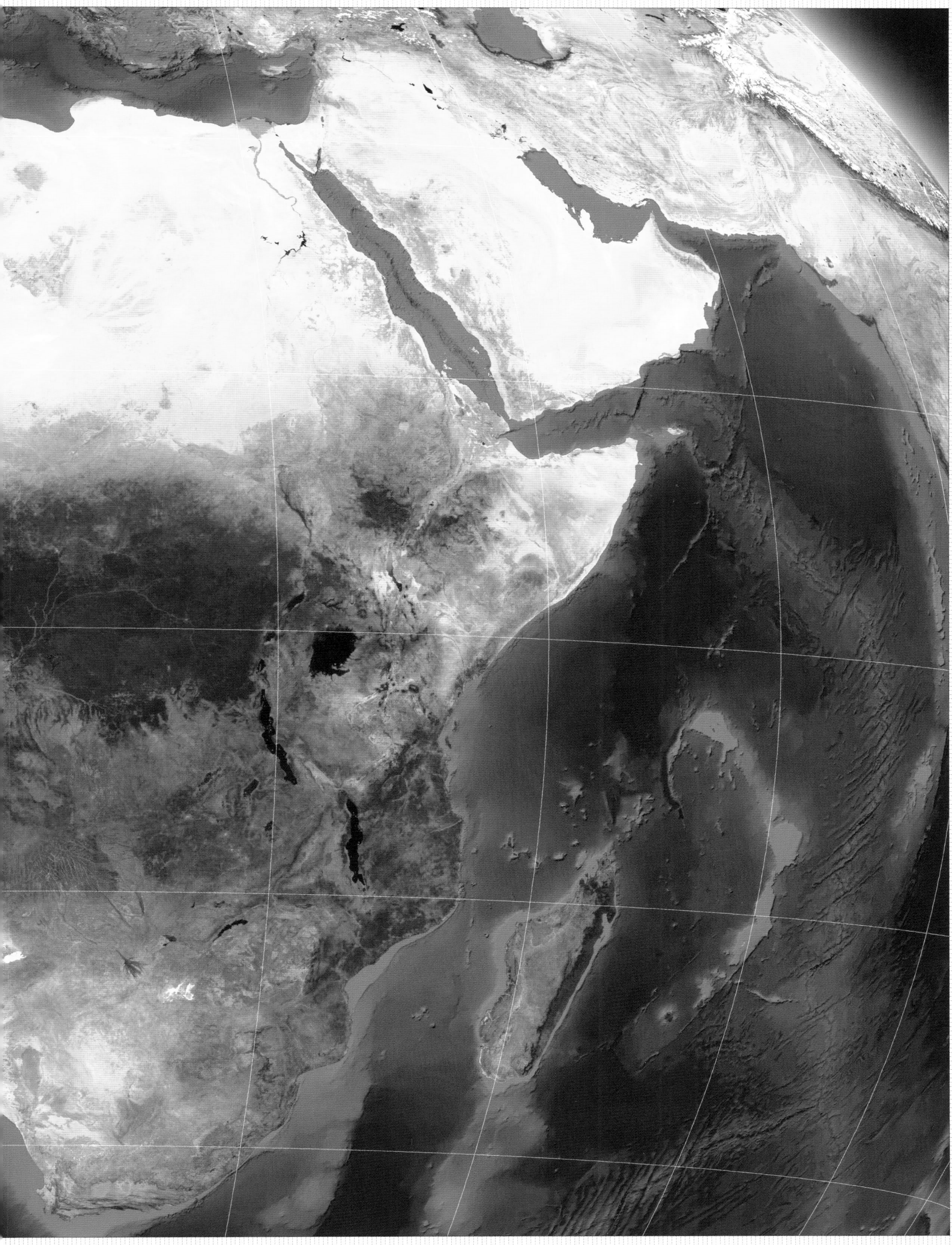

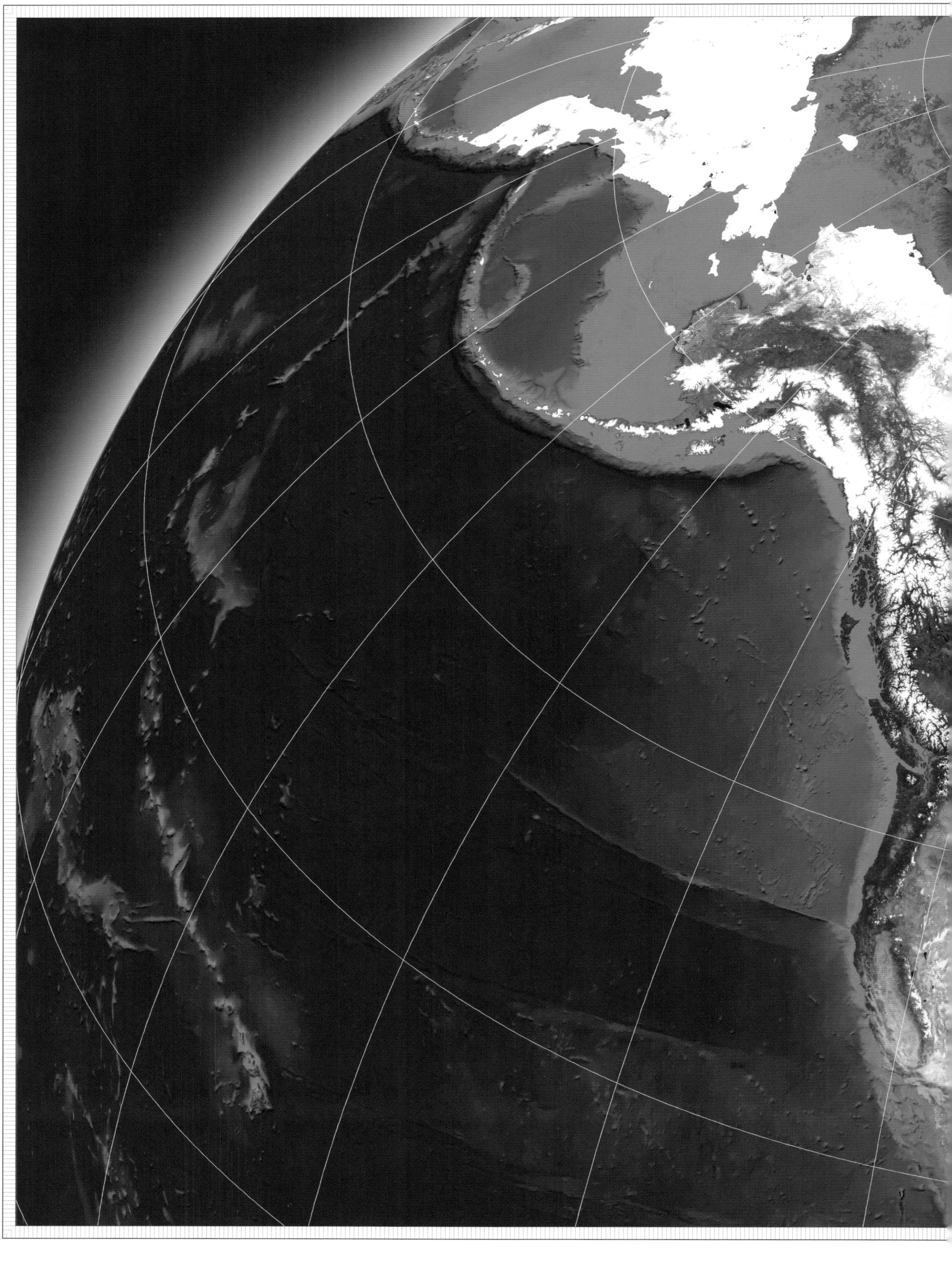

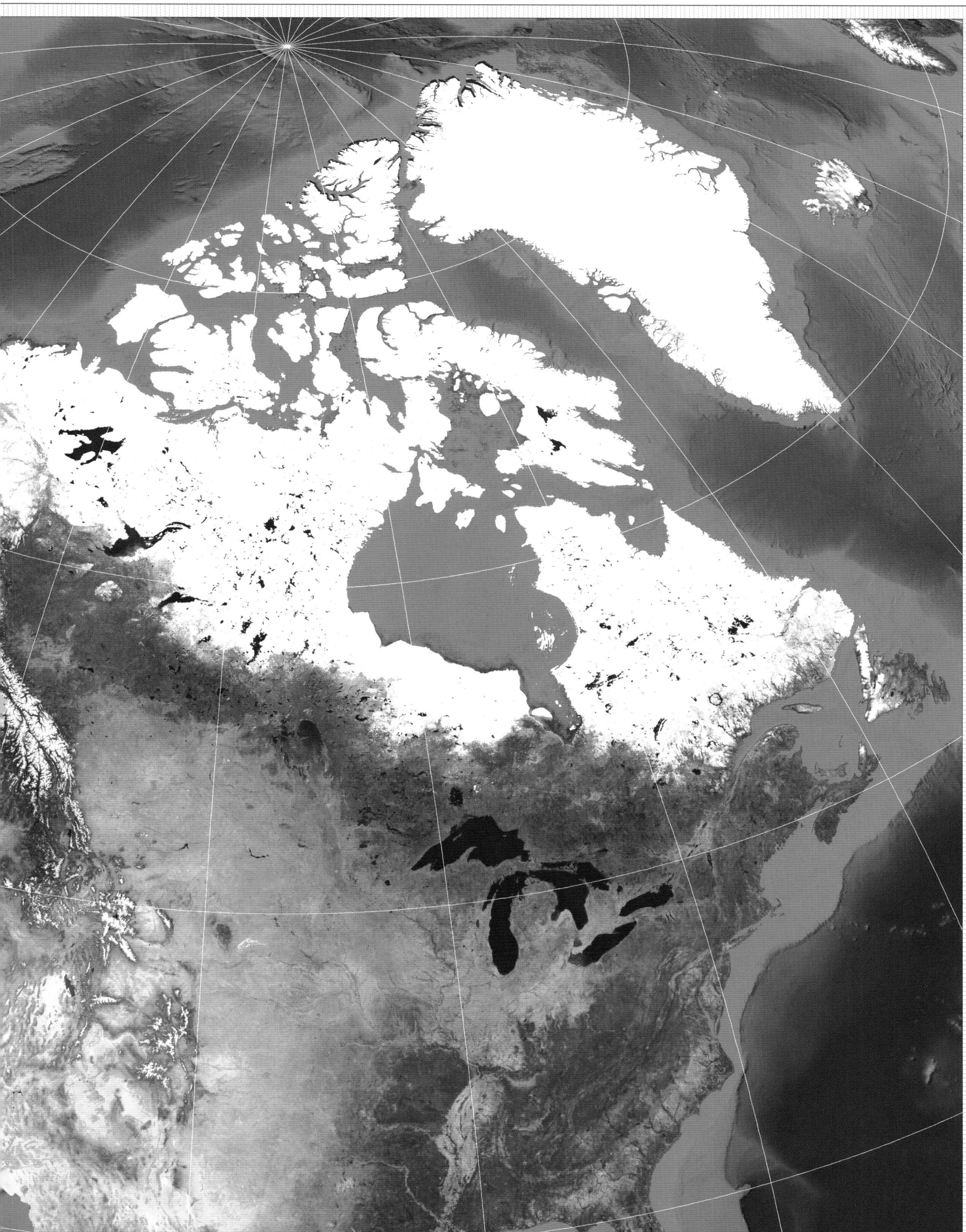

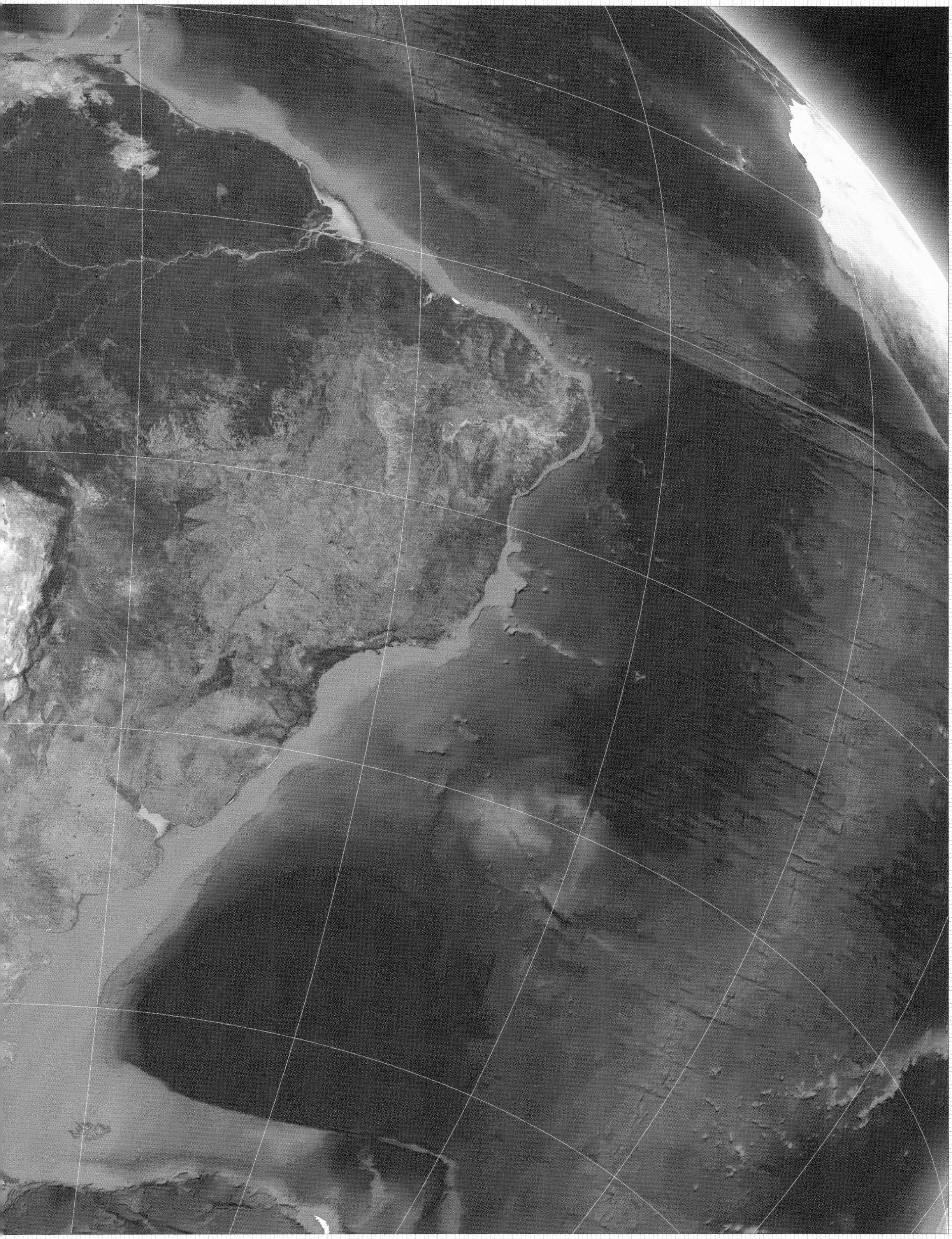

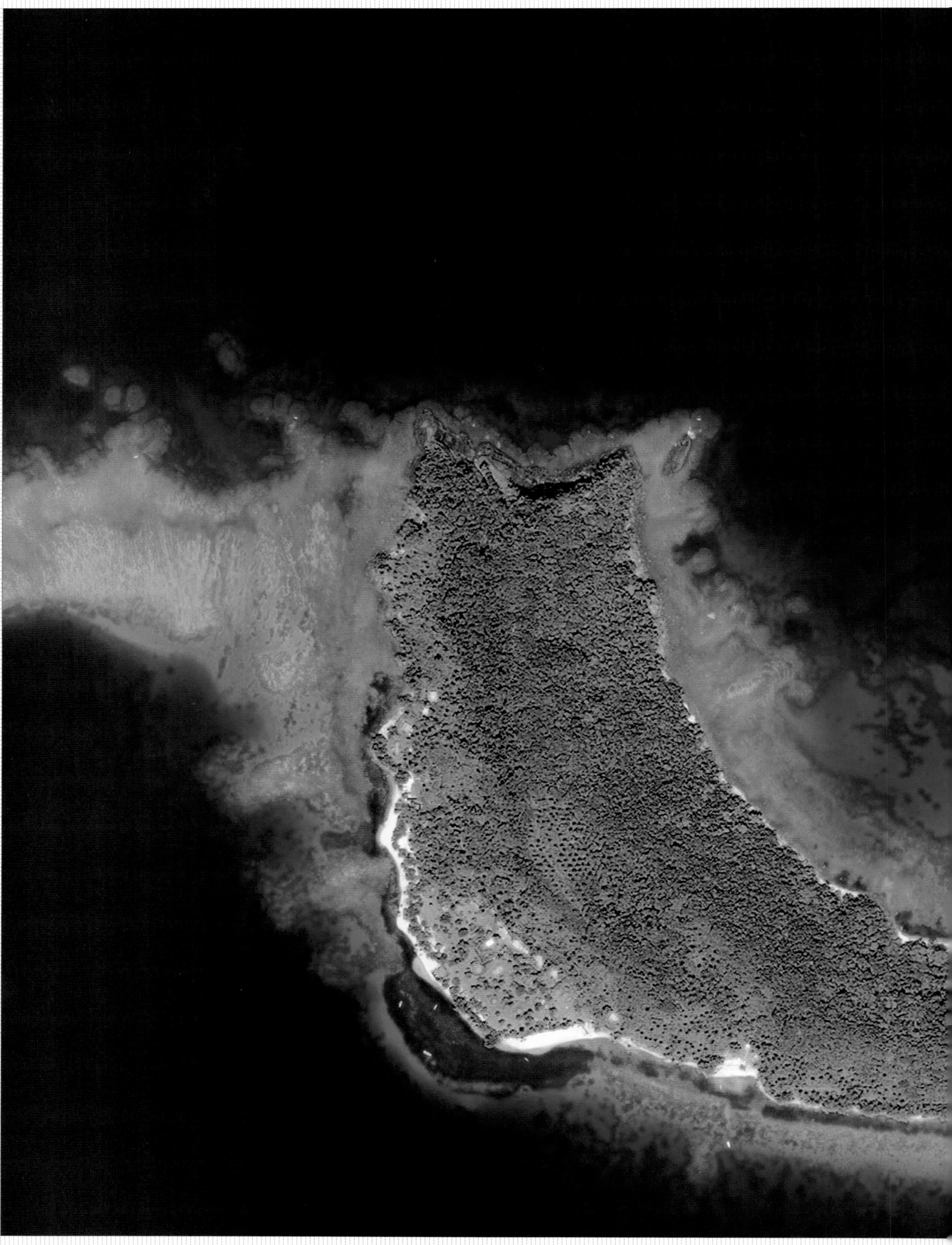

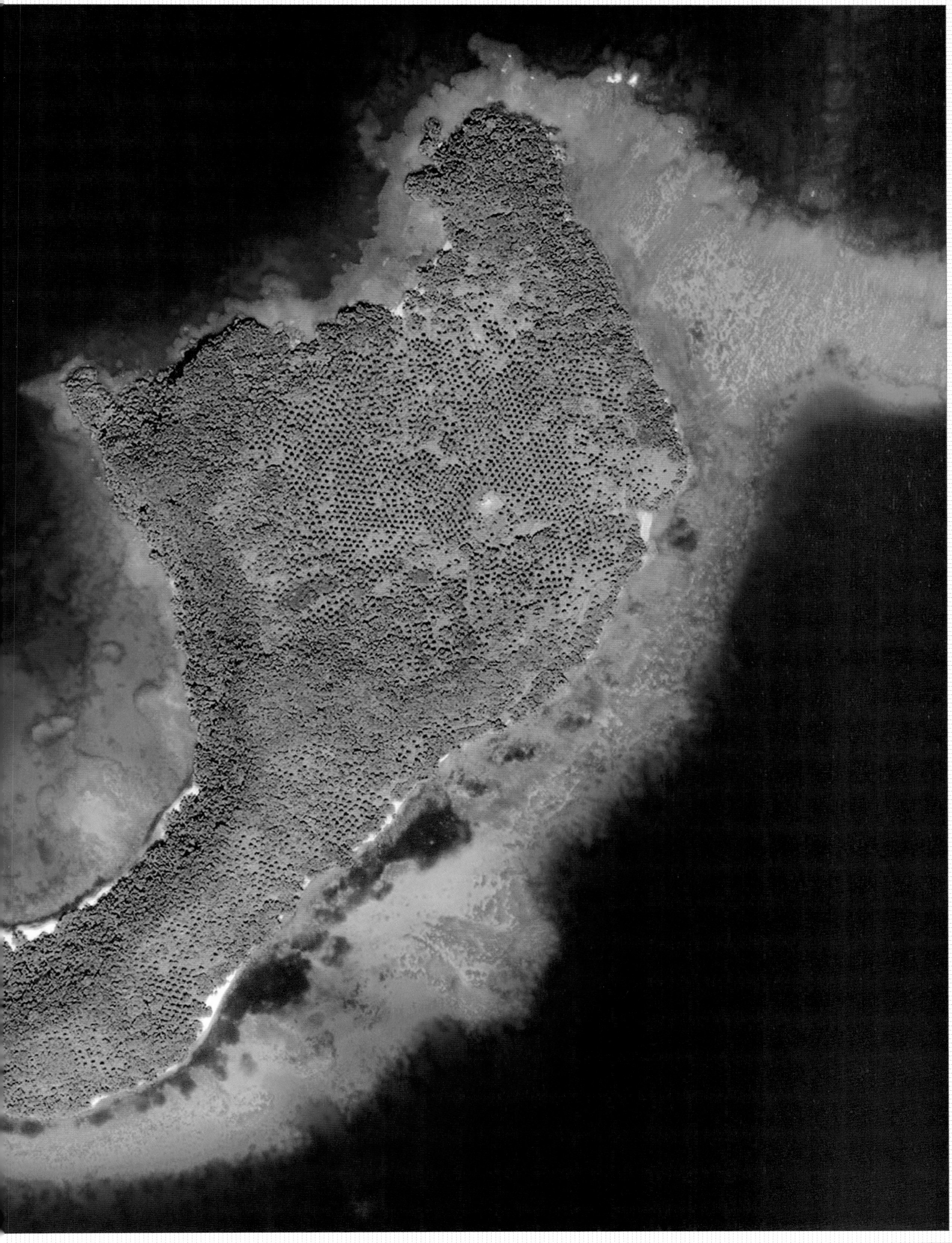

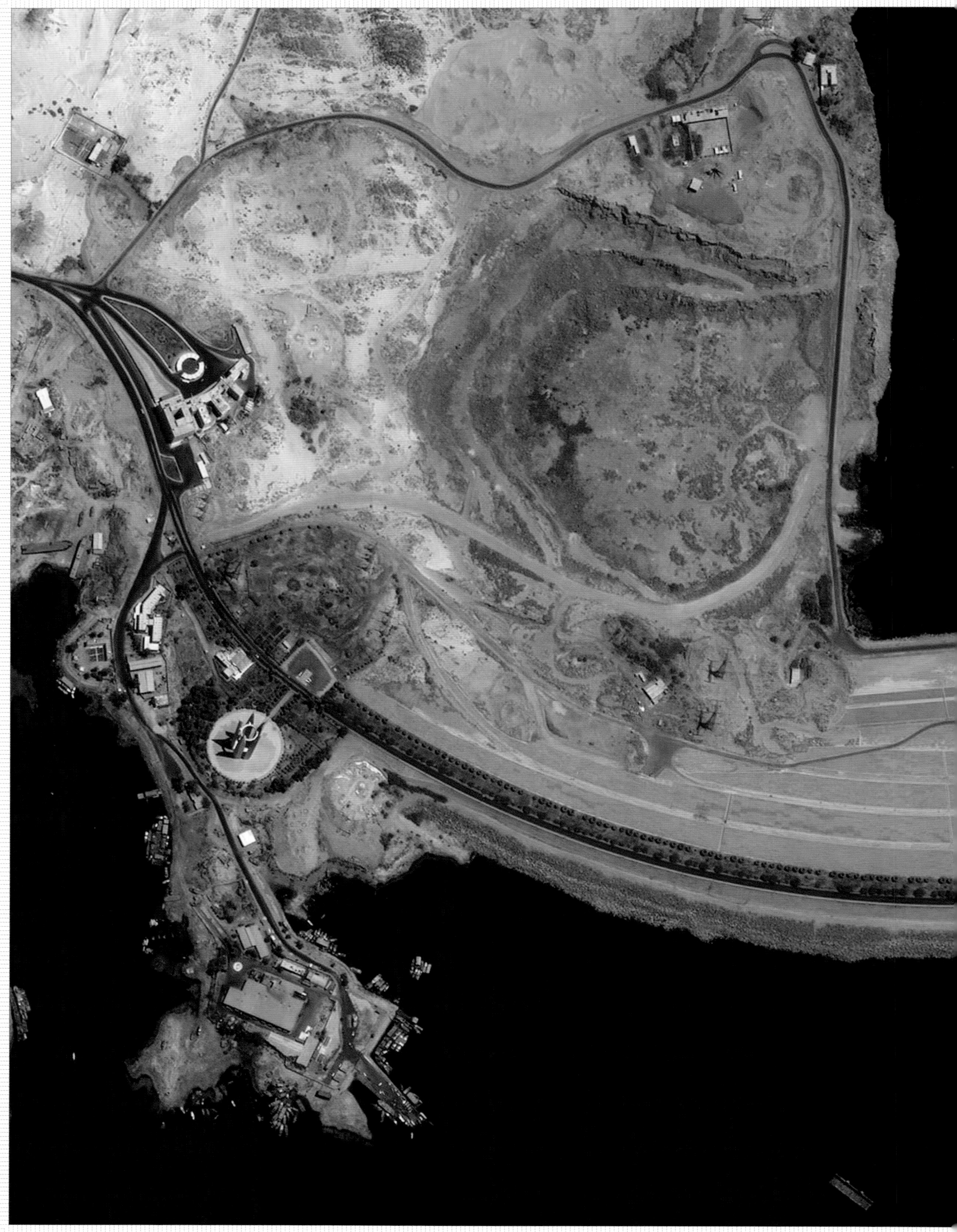

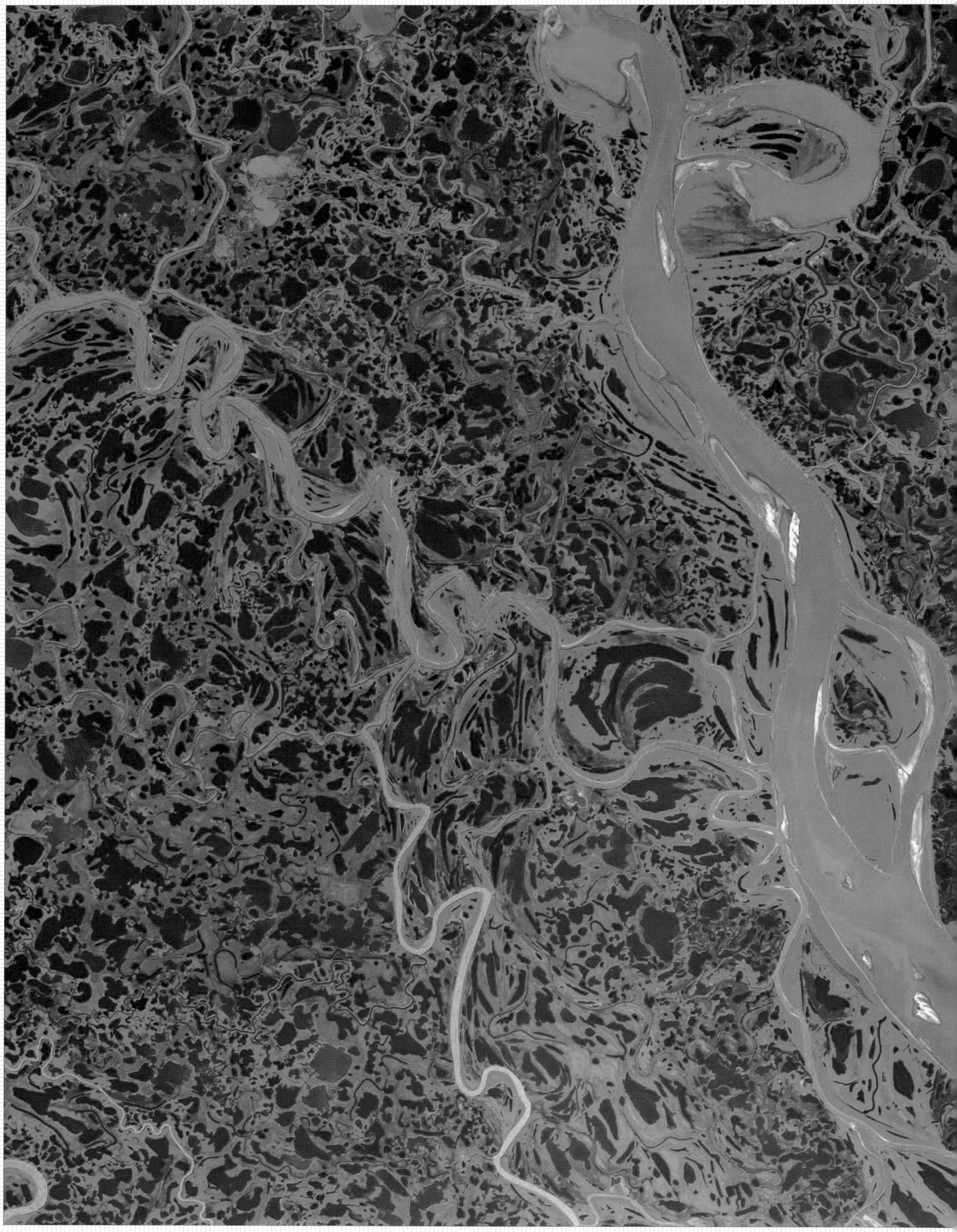

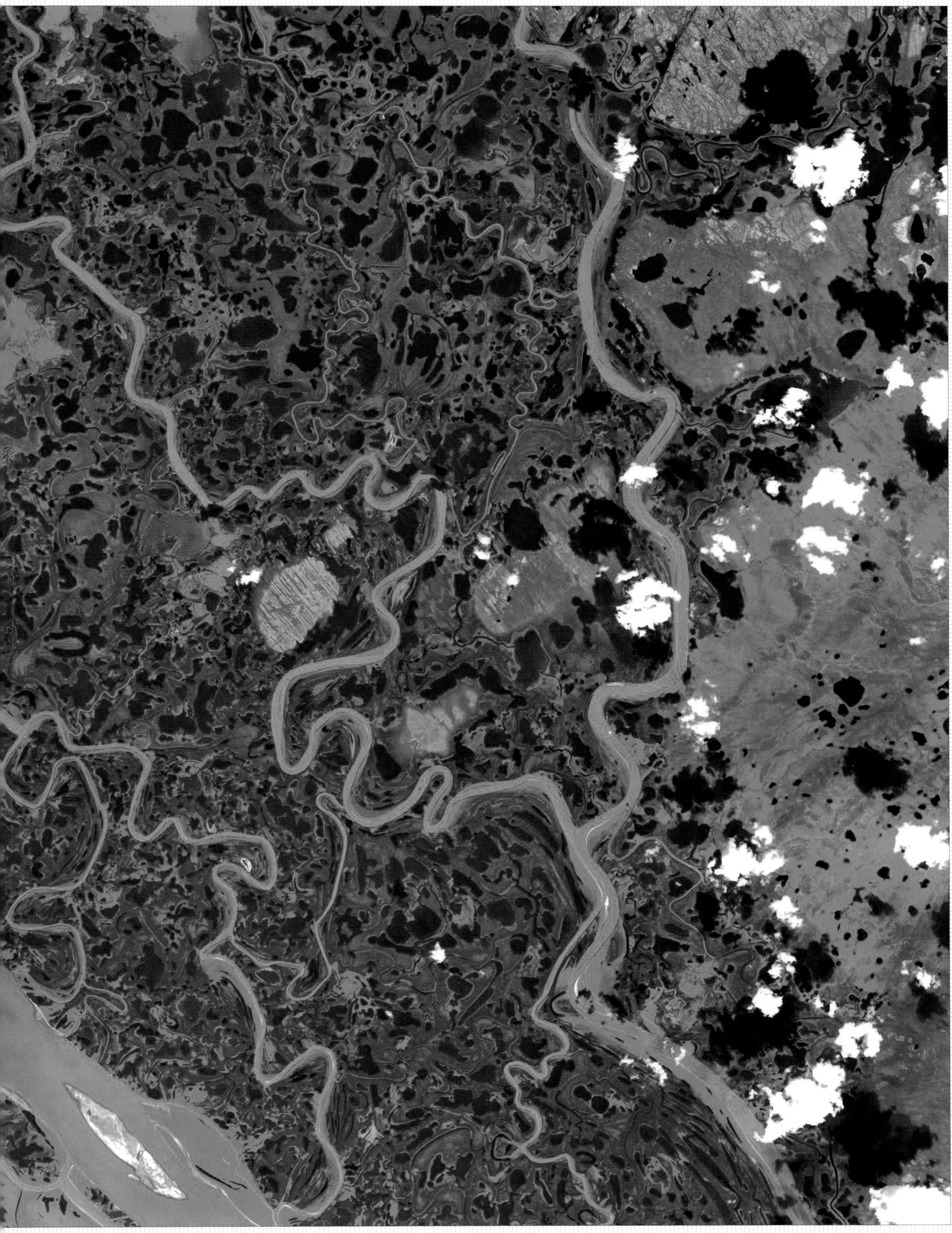

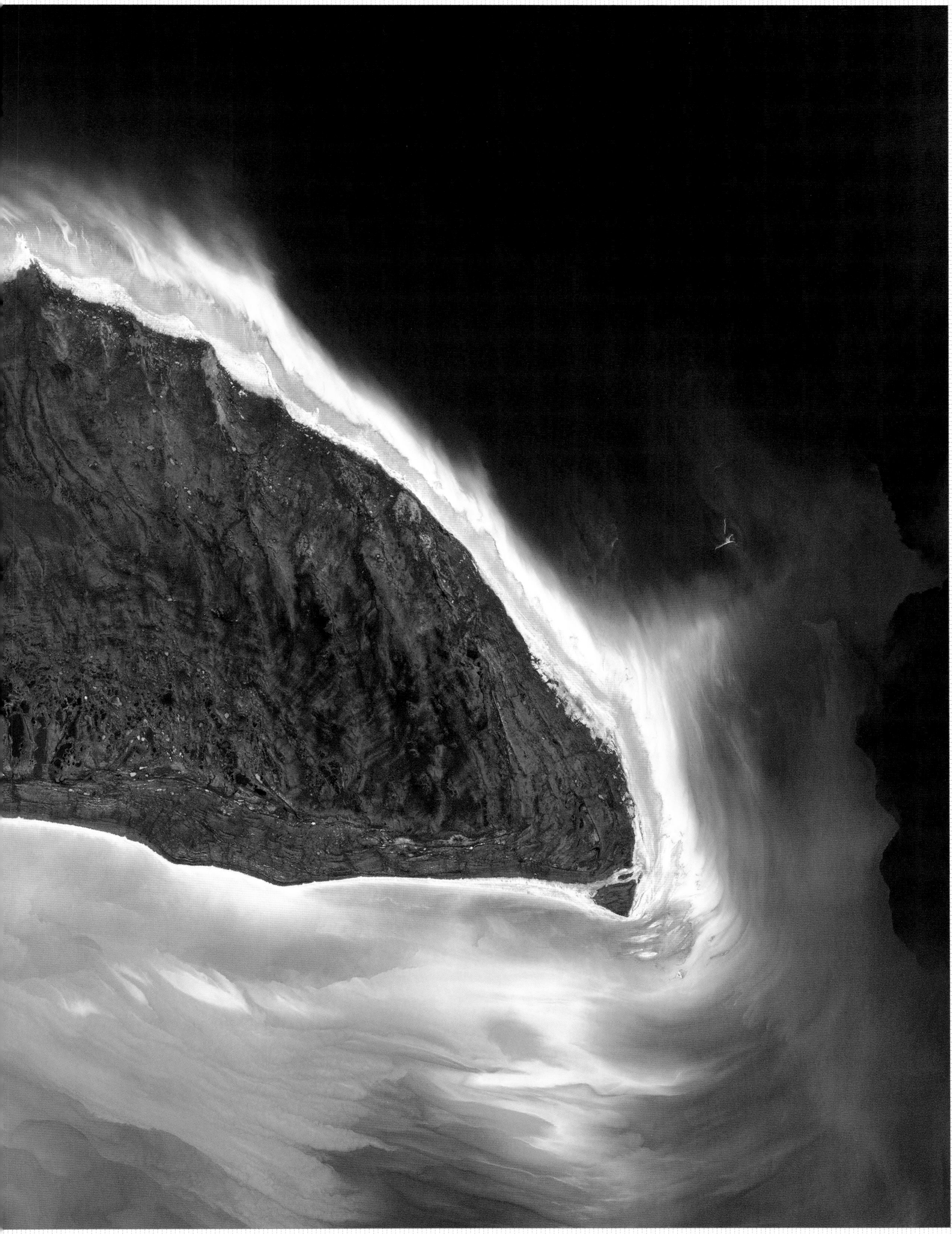

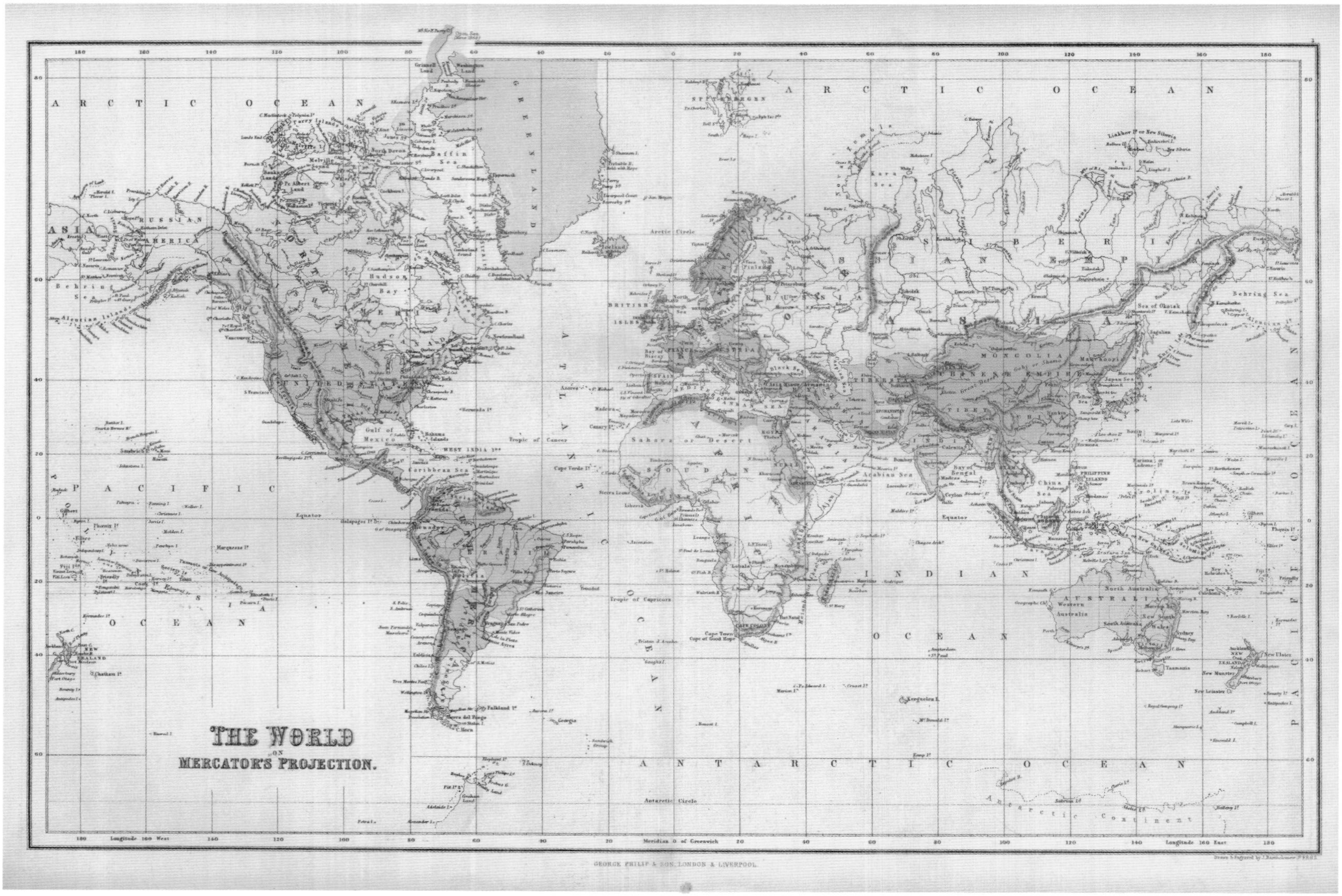


## 38–39 THE WORLD ON MERCATOR'S PROJECTION 1858

From the *Family Atlas of Physical, General and Classical Geography*. Drawn and engraved by J. Bartholomew Jr, F.R.G.S.

The nineteenth century was known as the 'Age of Empire', when all the major European powers harboured imperial ambitions and used their commercial and military might to extend their influence. In the first half of the century, the process had been gradual. Britain had emerged as the pre-eminent overseas power, extending the boundaries of her established colonial possessions in North America, India and Australia. In the second half of the century, the pace of imperial expansion increased markedly and the world depicted here was on the cusp of a dramatic change.

## 40–41 POLITICAL MAP OF THE WORLD 1914

From the *International Reference Atlas of the World*. Cartography by J. G. Bartholomew, LL.D., F.R.G.S., Cartographer to the King.

This map shows the imperial divisions of the world at the onset of the First World War in 1914. European colonial empires had grown rapidly over the past century and by now the Great Powers of Europe had engrossed nine-tenths of Africa and much of Asia. Prior to 1914, Europe had been run on balance-of-power politics, where a status quo was maintained between the major powers, often with unofficial agreements and alliances.

## 42–43 WORLD POLITICAL DIVISIONS 1936

From the *Advanced Atlas, Fifth Edition*. Cartography by John Bartholomew, M.C., M.A., F.R.S.E., F.R.G.S., Cartographer to the King.

The political situation of the world three years before the outbreak of the Second World War can be seen from this map. The power of empires had waned significantly after the First World War, and a number of treaties and pacts were signed between countries to safeguard against military attacks. Growing political and social conflict was leading to nationalist uprisings, while both communism and fascism were on the rise in Europe.

## 44–45 WORLD ROUTES OF COMMERCE 1950

From the *Advanced Atlas of Modern Geography*. Cartography by John Bartholomew, M.C., Director, the Geographical Institute, Edinburgh.

Just as the First World War had acted as a catalyst for massive change to the existing world order, so too the fallout from the Second World War brought significant political, territorial and economic upheaval across the globe. The most significant development in world politics post-1945 was the emergence of the USA and USSR as hostile superpowers, and the ideological alignment of other nations with each respective camp. The armed stand-off which emerged between the two power blocs became known as the Cold War and lasted until the fall of Soviet communism in the early 1990s.

## 46–47 WORLD POLITICAL CHART 1963

From the *Edinburgh World Atlas, Fifth Edition*. Cartography by John Bartholomew, C.B.E., M.C., LL.D., F.R.S.E., F.R.G.S.

Almost twenty years on from the end of the Second World War, the 'Age of Empire' was close to its end. International politics had instead become dominated by two superpowers – the United States and the Union of Soviet Socialist Republics (USSR) – who were opposed to each other during the lengthy Cold War. Significant changes affected French and British possessions worldwide at this time. After the war, European powers no longer had the military strength to defend against nationalist movements, nor the economic strength to enforce their rule. Decolonisation in Africa increased.

## 48–49 STATES OF THE WORLD 1982

From the *Bartholomew World Atlas, Twelfth Edition*. Cartography by John Bartholomew, M.A., F.R.S.E., Director, the Geographical Institute, Edinburgh.

This map represents a transition between one extensive series of changes and another – beforehand, the decolonisation which had gone on, especially in Africa; and afterwards, the collapse of communist regimes in the 1990s. One of the inset maps plots the many changes of sovereignty that had occurred since 1939. Britain sought to maintain association with its former colonies through the Commonwealth. The changes that came after this map was published mostly resulted from political changes in the Soviet Union and its Warsaw Pact allies.

## 50–51 NEW ZEALAND 1879

From the *Collins New Complete Atlas.*

To forestall growing French interest in the islands and control the increasingly lawless trading settlements there, the British Government had signed the Treaty of Waitangi with the indigenous Maori chieftains in 1840, as a first step to claiming full sovereignty over New Zealand. The following year, it became a colony in its own right, having previously been administered as part of the Australian colony of New South Wales.

European colonisation then began in earnest, with most immigrants opting to settle on South Island. However, on North Island, where the Maoris were greatest in number, a steady influx of settlers led to intense competition for land with the indigenous tribes. Disputes over territory were exacerbated by disagreements over the precise terms of the Waitangi treaty and these boiled over into outright war in the mid-1840s and throughout much of the 1860s. Following the latter of these Land Wars, large tracts of land were confiscated from the local Maori by the government, a source of resentment that continues to the present day.

## 52–53 UNITED STATES OF AMERICA 1879

From the *Handy General Atlas of America, Philip's.* Cartography by John Bartholomew, F.R.G.S.

This 1879 map of the United States of America depicts the country at a particularly interesting time in its history. Following the Union victory in the civil war in 1865 the southern states were very slow to re-build. The northern states by comparison, driven by an unprecedented influx of immigrants from Europe, forged ahead with rapid urbanization, infrastructure development and economic growth.

One of the main barriers to westward expansion into California was the Sierra Nevada mountain range. Emigrants attempting to cross the range by wagon faced a long and dangerous journey that many did not survive. In 1844 a party travelling westward into the mountains followed the Truckee River. This led them to what is now called the Donner Pass at 2 160 m (7 085 ft). This low narrow pass became the gateway west into California for thousands of emigrants. A direct rail connection came in 1869 with the completion of the First Transcontinental Railroad through the Donner Pass. While the pass is not named on the map, the railroad can be seen crossing the Nevada/ California state boundary and then the Sierra Nevada mountains to the northwest of Carson City.

## 54–55 NORTH POLAR REGIONS AND SOUTH POLAR REGIONS 1898

From the *Citizen's Atlas.* Cartography by J. G. Bartholomew, F.R.G.S.

These maps of the polar regions allow a variety of interesting comparisons to be drawn about these extremes of the Earth and how they were being explored.

Far from being homogeneous ice masses, the northern and southern polar regions are physically very different. The North Pole is at the centre of the Arctic Ocean and is an almost landlocked body of water largely composed of drifting pack ice; the South Pole, by contrast, lies on a continental land mass.

The motivations of those who ventured into these unexplored regions were different. For many northern polar explorers, the intention was to find a navigable passage through the ice to open up a trade route to link the Atlantic and Pacific Oceans – the so-called Northwest Passage. Unlike the northern polar region, the physical boundaries of the southern polar region were very poorly understood, as is evident from the map. It was not until the 1820s that Antarctica was first actually sighted, probably by the Russian explorer, Bellingshausen. From the 1830s a series of national expeditions embarked for Antarctica.

## 56–57 AUSTRALIA 1898

From the *Citizen's Atlas.* Cartography by J. G. Bartholomew, F.R.G.S.

This map records the geopolitical make-up of Australia immediately prior to the ending of British colonial rule. Three years after it was drawn, the federal Commonwealth of Australia came into being, holding Dominion status under the British Crown. The political boundaries depicted here had been established during the course of the nineteenth century, and with minor exceptions have remained unchanged to the present day. A particularly striking feature of the map is the pattern of settlement. The temperate and subtropical climates of the southwestern and eastern coastal areas attracted the original European settlers and 60 per cent of the Australian population still lives there. The drive inland was accelerated by a series of goldrushes beginning in the 1850s.

## 58–59 AFRICA POLITICAL 1895

From *The Times Atlas, First Edition.*

The African continent was parcelled up between competing European powers in the late nineteenth century and this map illustrates those divisions. Before then, little of Africa was ruled directly by Europeans, with the exceptions of the British Cape Colony, French Algeria and some smaller coastal footholds. But the work of explorers such as Livingstone, Stanley, Burton and Speke revealed the vast resources that lay in what was then the unknown 'Dark Continent'.

The imperial 'Scramble for Africa' began in the 1880s, fuelled by strategic rivalries, national ambitions and a commercial imperative to find new markets and new materials. Britain was the chief beneficiary, spurred on by the desire to secure communication channels with India, keystone of the empire. For this reason, Egypt was effectively annexed in 1882 to protect the strategically vital Suez Canal; and neighbouring Sudan would be annexed in 1898. But Britain would shortly face its sternest African military test from the Dutch Boers who from 1899–1902 would fight to re-establish the autonomy of their southern African republics.

## 60–61 THE FAR EAST 1907

From *The Atlas of the World's Commerce, George Newnes.* Edited by J. G. Bartholomew, F.R.G.S.

One of the most striking features of this map of the Far East from 1907 is the web of activity around the coasts and inland. Shipping lines, railways and, to a lesser extent, canals and navigable rivers all form a network of connections designed to facilitate movement. Lines of communication, notably undersea cables and consular offices, back up the mass of transport links, all together painting a picture of a mercantile system whose very density portrays a vibrant energy.

By the early twentieth century, trade and economic activity spanned the globe, connecting people on opposite sides of the world. A nation's trade was not just with its neighbours a packhorse ride away, but was across seas and international boundaries. The industrialized nations opened up new markets in the Far East, buying raw materials and foods for manufacture, driving new industries and inventions and benefitting buyers and sellers alike.

## 62–63 TURKEY IN ASIA, PERSIA, ARABIA, &c. 1914

From the *International Reference Atlas of the World.* Cartography by J. G. Bartholomew, LL.D., F.R.G.S., Cartographer to the King.

The late nineteenth and early twentieth centuries had seen a dramatic contraction of the Ottoman Empire, particularly in the Balkans but also in North Africa, where Algeria and Tunisia had been ceded to France, and Libya to Italy. Although never formally invaded, Persia was economically dependent on Europe, and as a result, Britain and Russia effectively divided the country between them from 1907 into two spheres of economic interest in which each power could exert its influence.

In October 1914, Turkey entered the First World War on Germany's side, setting in motion the train of events that would bring about the final dissolution of the Ottoman Empire and the ultimate creation of the modern Turkish republic.

## 64–65 EUROPE POLITICAL 1922

From *The Times Survey Atlas of the World,* Prepared at "The Edinburgh Geographical Institute" under the direction of J. G. Bartholomew, LL.D., F.R.S.E., F.R.G.S., Cartographer to the King.

The aftermath of the First World War and the Treaty of Versailles in 1919 redrew the world map and brought an end to the centuries of dynastic power in central and eastern Europe. The new separate states of Austria, Hungary, Czechoslovakia and Yugoslavia emerged after the demise of the Habsburg dynasty. At this time, ethnic nationalism was threatening European colonial empires with ideas of democracy and social reform.

Following the Russian Revolution in 1917,the Russian Empire lost much of its western frontier – the new Baltic states of Estonia, Latvia and Lithuania successfully fought independence and were recognised as independent countries in 1920. The map, however, shows these states during only a brief spell of independence.

## 66–67 CHINA 1922

From *The Times Survey Atlas of the World,* prepared at "The Edinburgh Geographical Institute" under the direction of J. G. Bartholomew, LL.D., F.R.S.E., F.R.G.S., Cartographer to the King.

The map shows how English-speakers were used to seeing Chinese place names long before modern 'Pinyin' spellings, which are characterised by frequent occurrences of q, x, y and z. Most obviously, some main names are in English – eg Inner Mongolia – and some are partly English – eg Gulf of Liao-tung. Hyphens are used in the old Wade-Giles spelling system to show sounds that come from separate characters.

The inset map from 1958 shows how the cartographer's view of Chinese names had evolved in the meantime: the names look somewhat more familiar to the modern eye, the hyphens have mostly gone, and some spellings are simpler. The most noticeable difference between the two maps is that the important places are in much bigger type, aiding clarity and legibility.

## 68–69 WORLD POWERS 1957

From *The Times Atlas of the World, Mid-Century Edition 1958.* Cartography by John Bartholomew, M.C., LL.D.

The most striking feature of this map is its unusual viewpoint (or projection). Devised in 1948 by John Bartholomew, the Atlantis Projection abandons the common atlas convention of showing the Arctic at the top and the Antarctic at the bottom. Here the projection is tilted to focus on the Atlantic Ocean. In this instance it is particularly effective in conveying the combative nature of relations between the United States and the Soviet Union, the two 'superpowers' which emerged to dominate the new world order following the Second World War.

Within a few short years of this particular map being drawn, significant colour changes would be required for a number of countries: Alaska would become a full member state of the USA (1959); Fidel Castro would establish a Marxist government on America's doorstep in Cuba (1959), and the process by which many African nations would shake off the last remnants of European colonialism would begin in earnest.

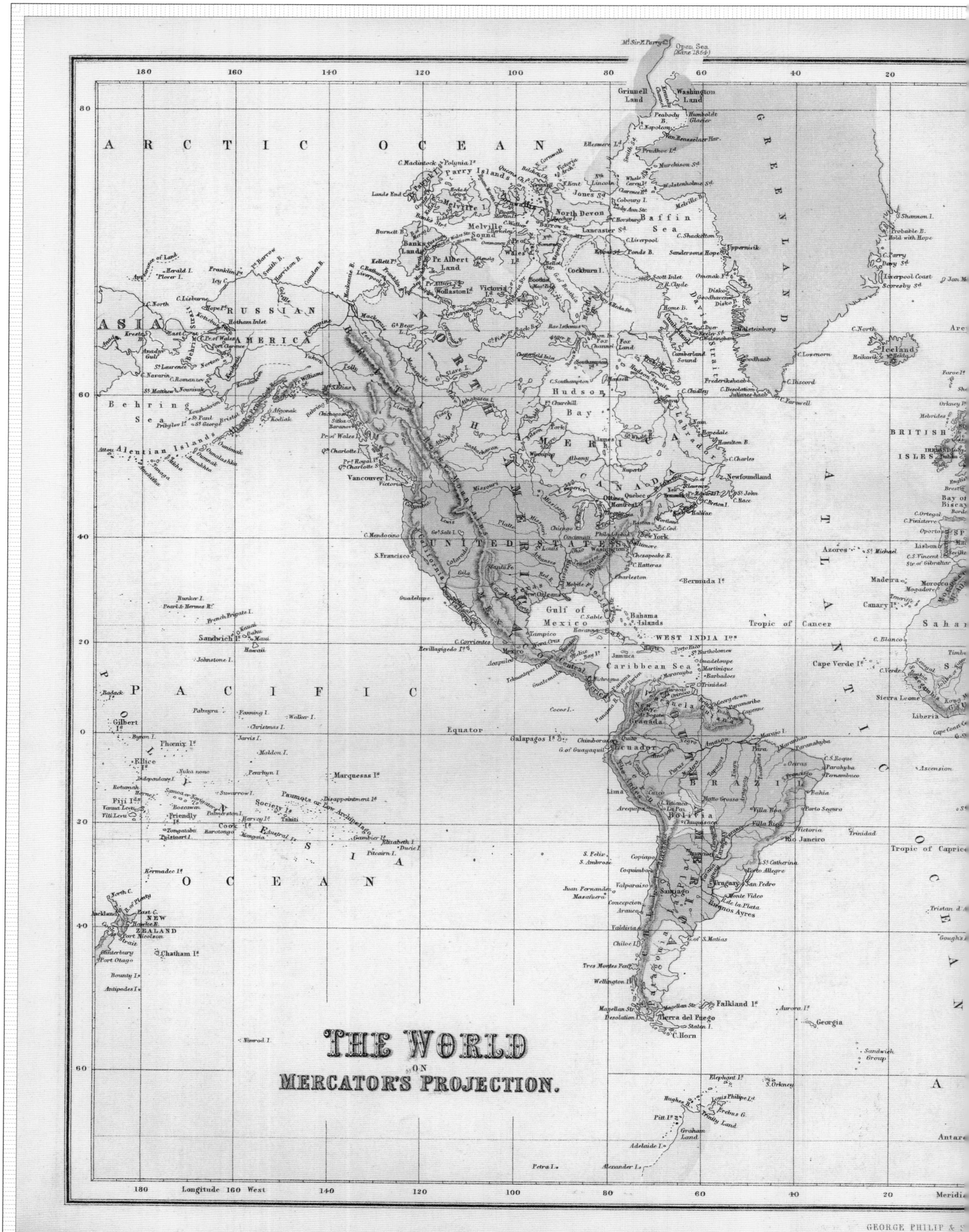
THE WORLD
ON
MERCATOR'S PROJECTION.
ARCTIC OCEAN
PACIFIC
OCEAN
POLYNESIA
ATLANTIC
OCEAN
GREENLAND
ASIA
RUSSIAN
AMERICA
NORTH
AMERICA
CANADA
UNITED STATES
Hudson
Bay
Baffin
Sea
Behring
Sea
Aleutian Islands
Gulf of
Mexico
Caribbean Sea
WEST INDIA Is.
Tropic of Cancer
Equator
Tropic of Capricorn
BRAZIL
Bolivia
Ecuador
Granada
Sandwich Is.
Marquesas Is.
Society Is.
Fiji Is.
Friendly
NEW
ZEALAND
Chatham Is.
Galapagos Is.
Bermuda Is.
Bahama
Islands
Falkland Is.
Tierra del Fuego
C. Horn
Georgia
Iceland
BRITISH
ISLES
Azores
Madeira
Canary Is.
Cape Verde Is.
Sahara
Newfoundland
Vancouver I.
S. Francisco
New Orleans
New York
Quebec
Rio Janeiro
Buenos Ayres
Valparaiso
Lima
Quito
Graham
Land
Petra I.
Alexander I.
Longitude 160 West
Meridian
180
140
120
100
80
60
40
20
GEORGE PHILIP & S

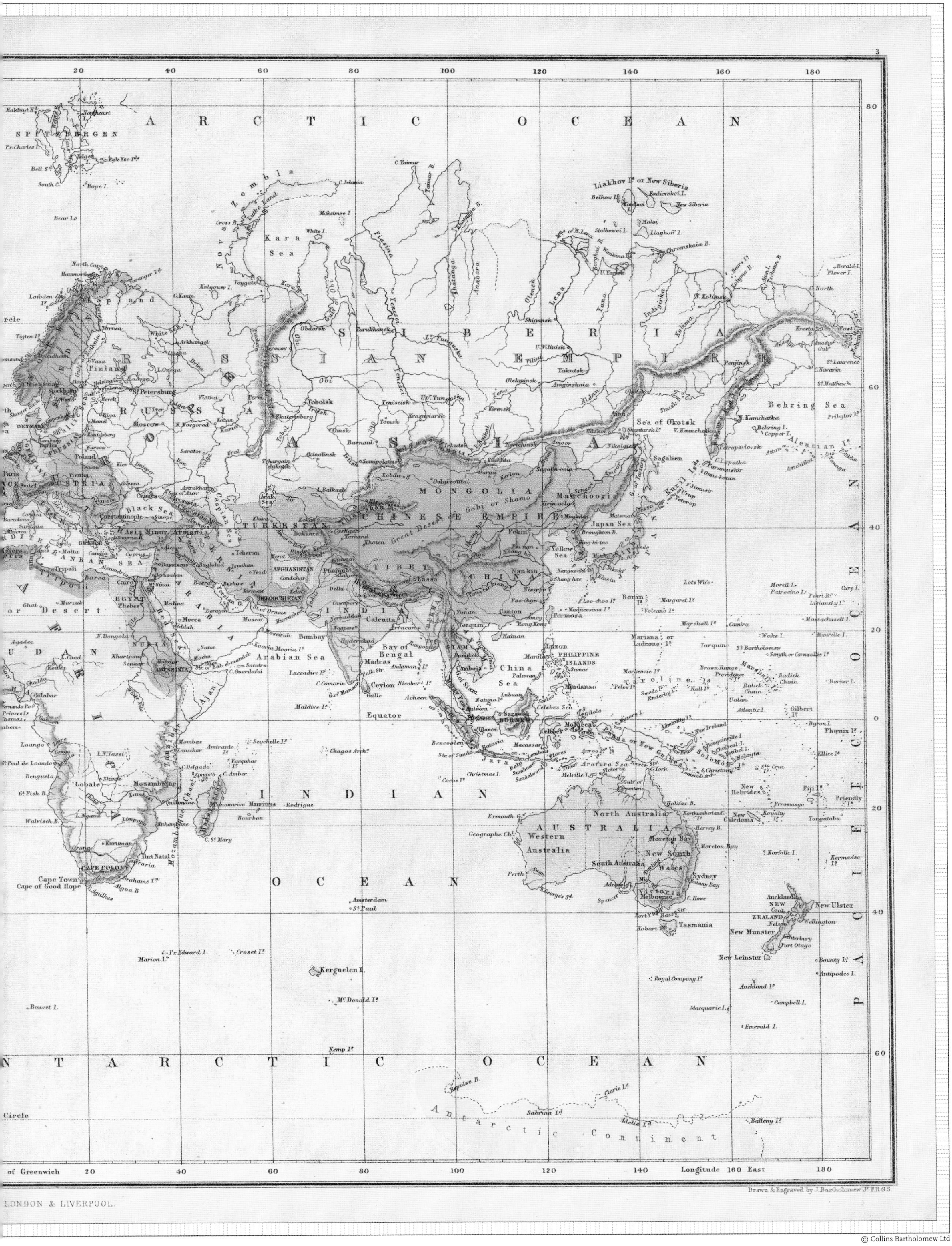
ARCTIC OCEAN
SPITZBERGEN
Nova Zembla
Kara Sea
SIBERIA
RUSSIAN EMPIRE
ASIA
RUSSIA
Lapland
Finland
St Petersburg
Moscow
Black Sea
Caspian Sea
TURKESTAN
MONGOLIA
Manchooria
CHINESE EMPIRE
Great Desert of Gobi or Shamo
TIBET
CHINA
Japan Sea
Yellow Sea
Sea of Okotsk
Behring Sea
Aleutian Is
Kuril Is
AFGHANISTAN
BELOOCHISTAN
Persian G.
ARABIA
Red Sea
EGYPT
NUBIA
ABYSSINIA
Arabian Sea
Bay of Bengal
INDIA
Calcutta
Bombay
Madras
Ceylon
SIAM
China Sea
PHILIPPINE ISLANDS
Borneo
Java
Caroline Is
Equator
Papua or New Guinea
INDIAN OCEAN
Mozambique
Madagascar
Mauritius
CAPE COLONY
Cape Town
Cape of Good Hope
AUSTRALIA
North Australia
Western Australia
South Australia
New South Wales
Victoria
Sydney
Melbourne
Tasmania
NEW ZEALAND
New Ulster
New Munster
New Leinster
New Caledonia
New Hebrides
Fiji Is
Kerguelen I.
ANTARCTIC OCEAN
Antarctic Continent
PACIFIC OCEAN
Longitude 160 East
of Greenwich
LONDON & LIVERPOOL.
Drawn & Engraved by J. Bartholomew Jr F.R.G.S.

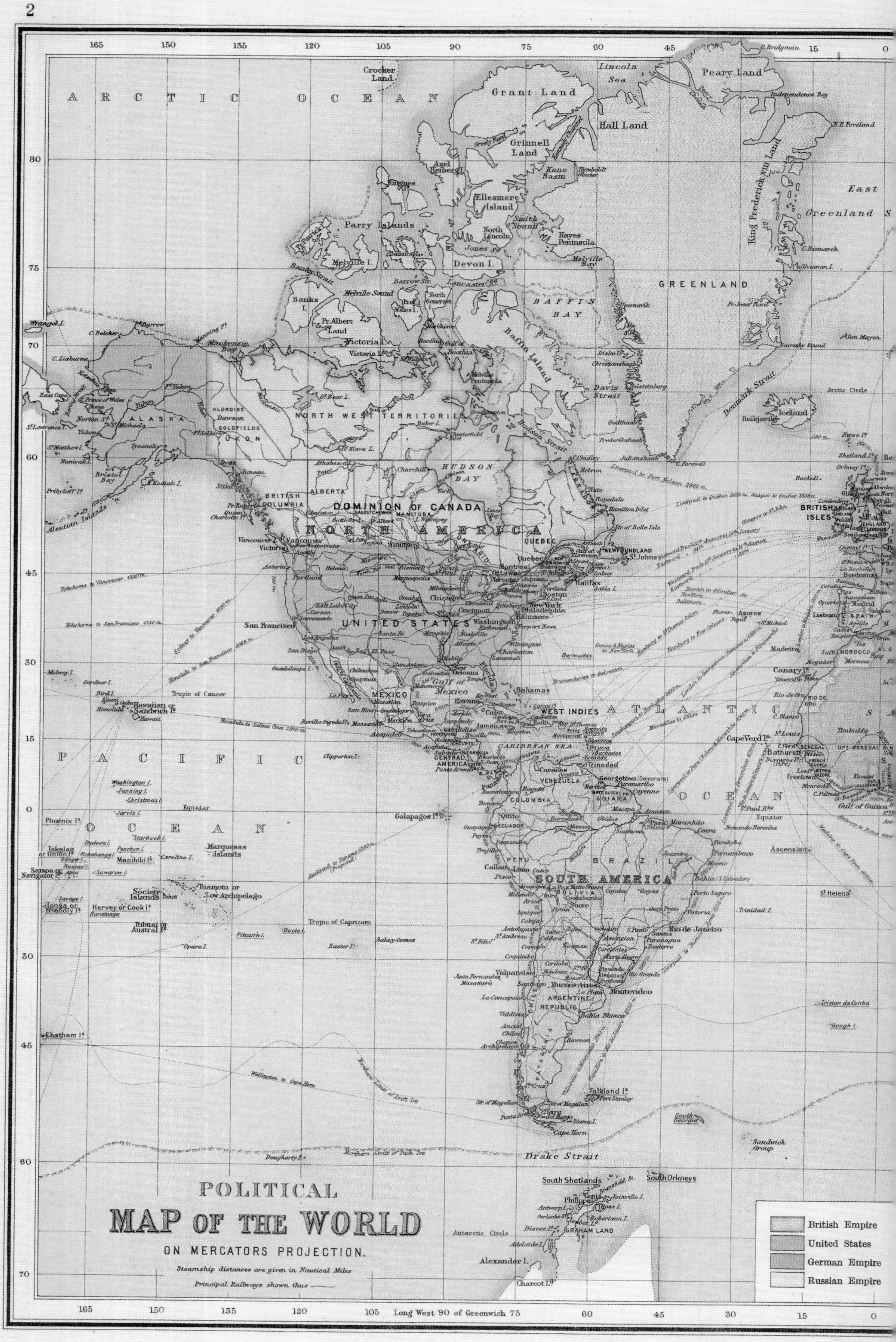
2
POLITICAL
MAP OF THE WORLD
ON MERCATORS PROJECTION.
Steamship distances are given in Nautical Miles
Principal Railways shown thus
British Empire
United States
German Empire
Russian Empire
ARCTIC OCEAN
PACIFIC OCEAN
ATLANTIC OCEAN
Long West 90 of Greenwich 75
Grant Land
Peary Land
Hall Land
GREENLAND
East Greenland
BAFFIN BAY
HUDSON BAY
NORTH WEST TERRITORIES
ALASKA
YUKON
DOMINION OF CANADA
NORTH AMERICA
BRITISH COLUMBIA
ALBERTA
QUEBEC
NEWFOUNDLAND
UNITED STATES
MEXICO
WEST INDIES
Gulf of Mexico
CARIBBEAN SEA
VENEZUELA
COLOMBIA
ECUADOR
PERU
BOLIVIA
BRAZIL
SOUTH AMERICA
ARGENTINE REPUBLIC
PATAGONIA
Drake Strait
South Shetlands
South Orkneys
GRAHAM LAND
Alexander I.
Antarctic Circle
Tropic of Cancer
Tropic of Capricorn
Equator
Arctic Circle
BRITISH ISLES
Iceland
SPAIN
MOROCCO
San Francisco
New York
Vancouver
Quebec
Montreal
Boston
Philadelphia
Chicago
Rio de Janeiro
Buenos Ayres
Montevideo
Valparaiso
Lima
Hawaiian or Sandwich Is.
Galapagos Is.
Marquesas Islands
Society Islands
Falkland Is.
Cape Horn
Ascension
St. Helena
Tristan da Cunha
Canary Is.
Cape Verd Is.
Azores

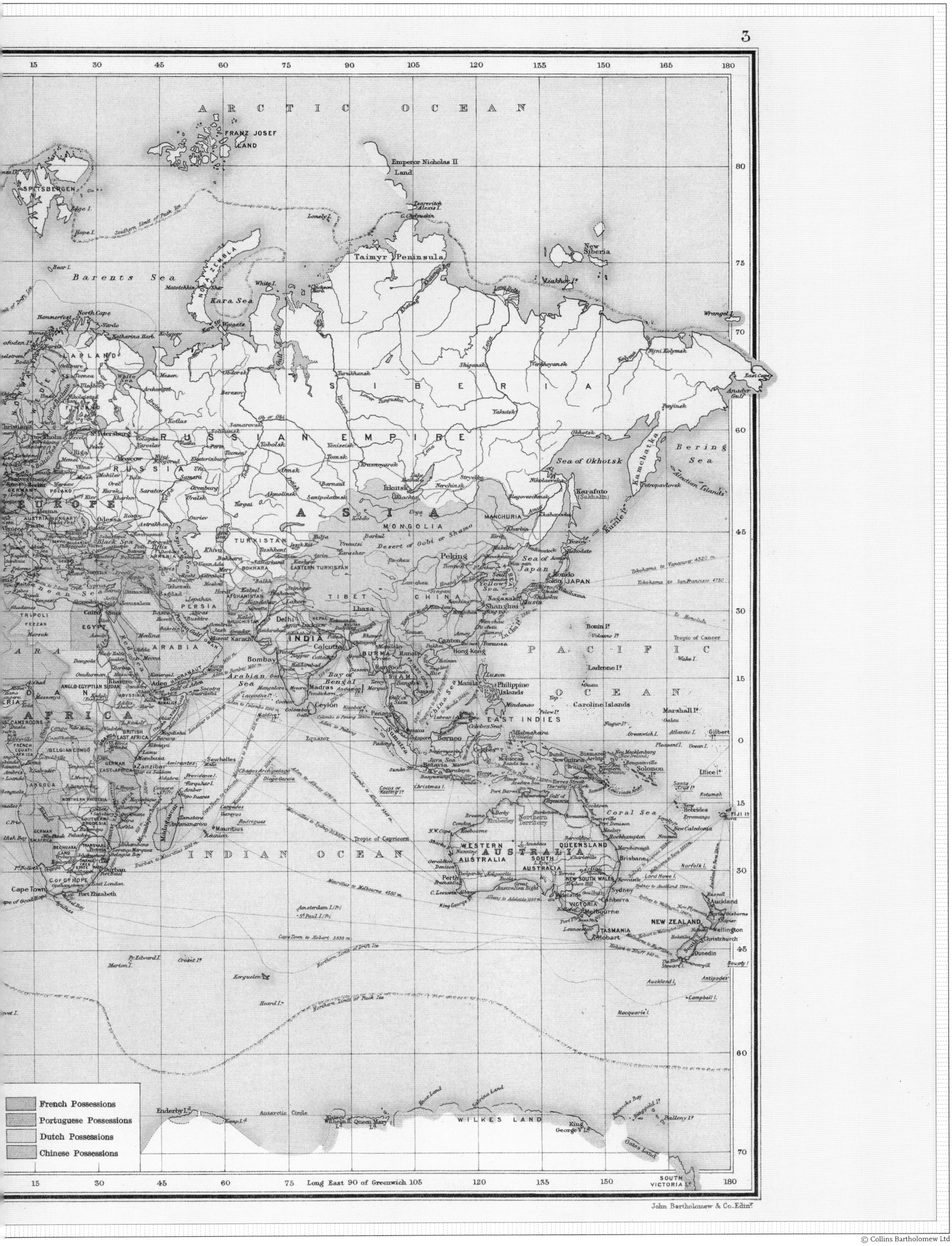
3
ARCTIC OCEAN
FRANZ JOSEF LAND
Emperor Nicholas II Land
SPITSBERGEN
NOVA ZEMBLA
Barents Sea
Kara Sea
Taimyr Peninsula
New Siberia
LAPLAND
SIBERIA
RUSSIAN EMPIRE
RUSSIA
EUROPE
ASIA
MONGOLIA
Desert of Gobi or Shamo
MANCHURIA
Sea of Okhotsk
Kamchatka
Bering Sea
Aleutian Islands
Karafuto (Sakhalin)
Sea of Japan
JAPAN
TURKISTAN
EASTERN TURKISTAN
PERSIA
TIBET
CHINA
Peking
Shanghai
Yellow Sea
Hong Kong
ARABIA
EGYPT
INDIA
Bombay
Calcutta
Delhi
Madras
Ceylon
Arabian Sea
Bay of Bengal
BURMA
SIAM
Manila
Philippine Islands
Borneo
EAST INDIES
PACIFIC OCEAN
Caroline Islands
Marshall Is.
Tropic of Cancer
AFRICA
ANGLO-EGYPTIAN SUDAN
ABYSSINIA
BRITISH EAST AFRICA
BELGIAN CONGO
GERMAN EAST AFRICA
Zanzibar
ANGOLA
NORTHERN RHODESIA
SOUTHERN RHODESIA
Madagascar
Mauritius
Cape Town
Durban
INDIAN OCEAN
Tropic of Capricorn
WESTERN AUSTRALIA
SOUTH AUSTRALIA
Northern Territory
QUEENSLAND
NEW SOUTH WALES
VICTORIA
AUSTRALIA
Perth
Brisbane
Sydney
Canberra
Melbourne
TASMANIA
Hobart
Coral Sea
NEW ZEALAND
Auckland
Wellington
Christchurch
Dunedin
FIJI Is.
New Caledonia
Solomon Is.
Kerguelen I.
Macquarie I.
Enderby Ld.
Antarctic Circle
WILKES LAND
King George V Ld.
Oates Land
SOUTH VICTORIA Ld.
French Possessions
Portuguese Possessions
Dutch Possessions
Chinese Possessions
Long East 90 of Greenwich 105
John Bartholomew & Co. Edinr.

20 WORLD POLITI

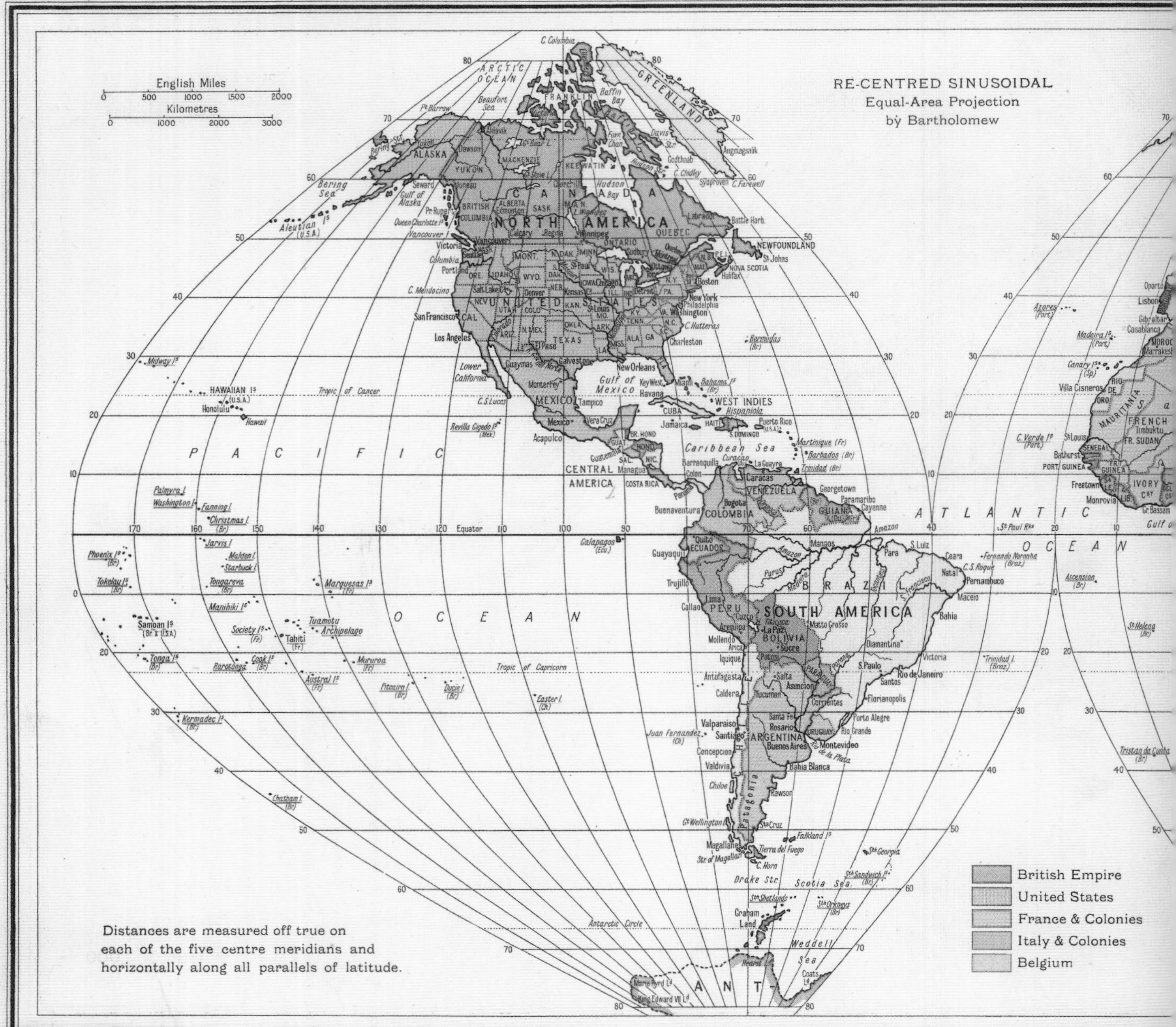


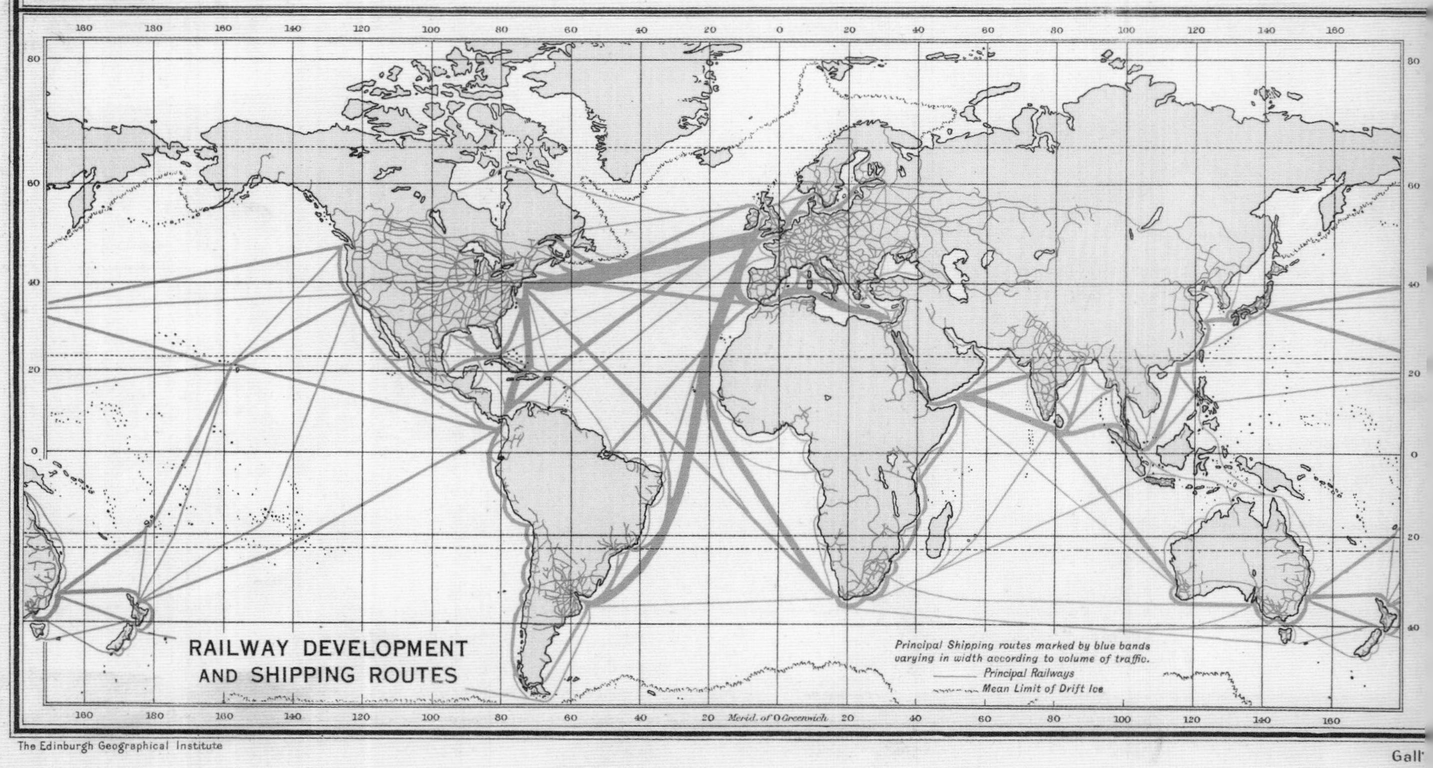


The Edinburgh Geographical Institute

Gall

CAL DIVISIONS 21

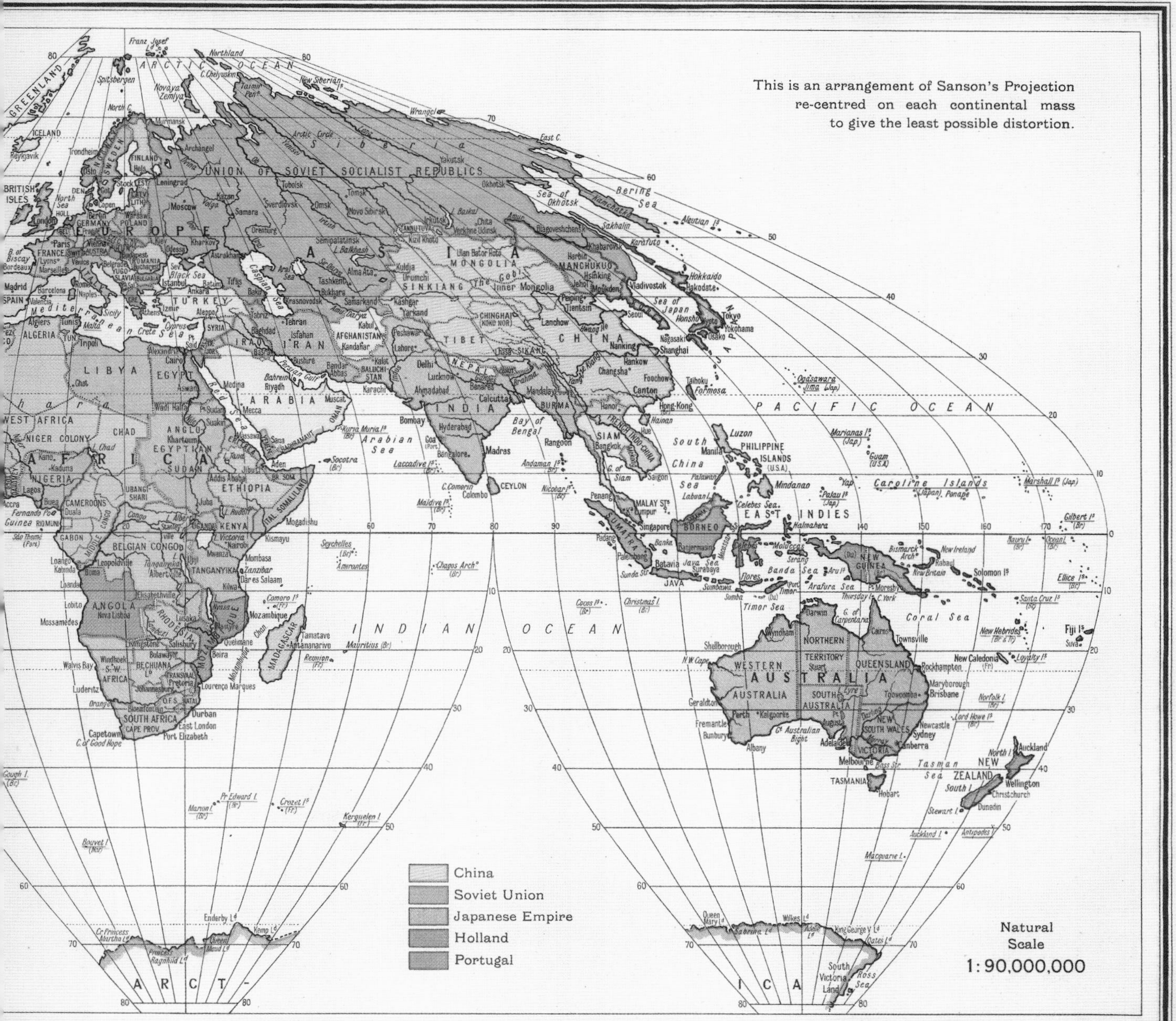


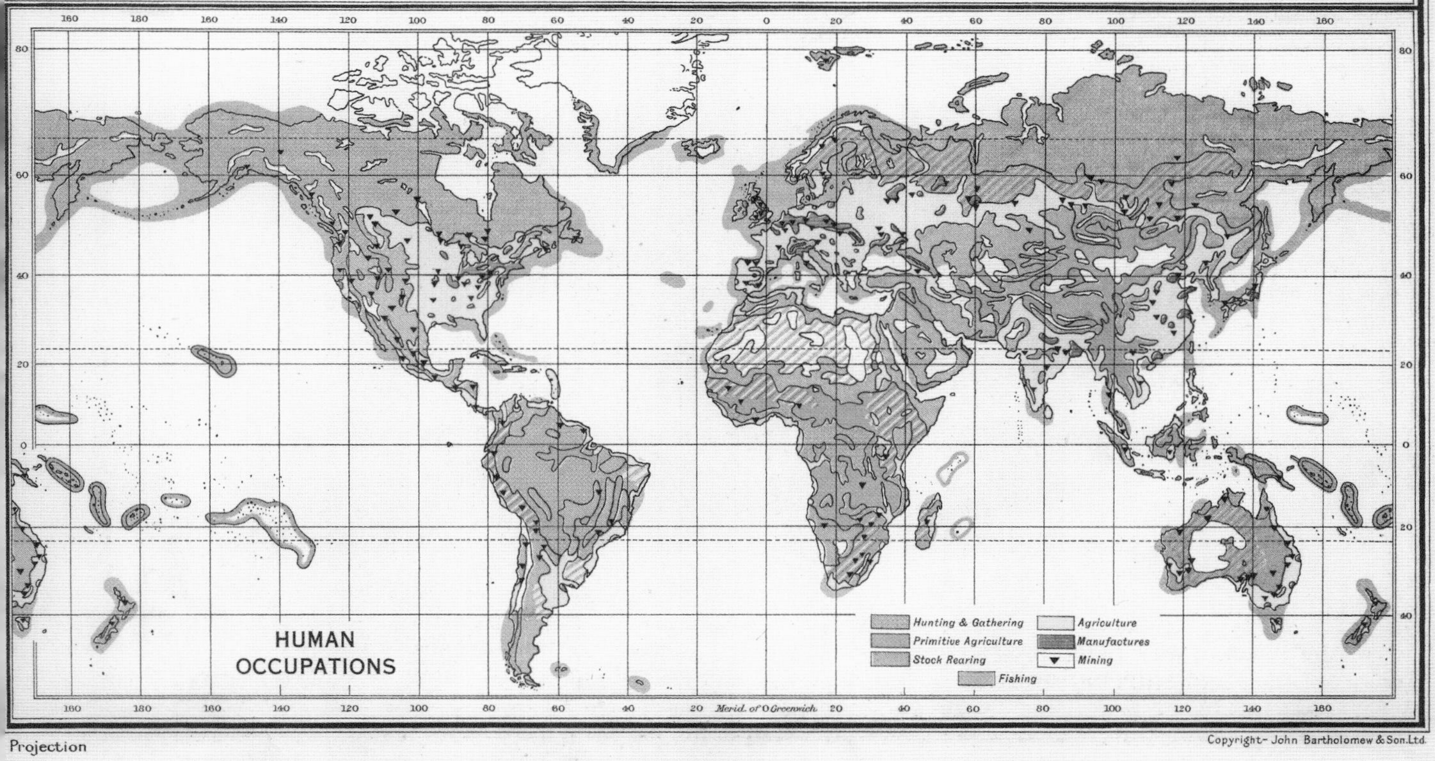


Projection

Copyright- John Bartholomew & Son.Ltd.

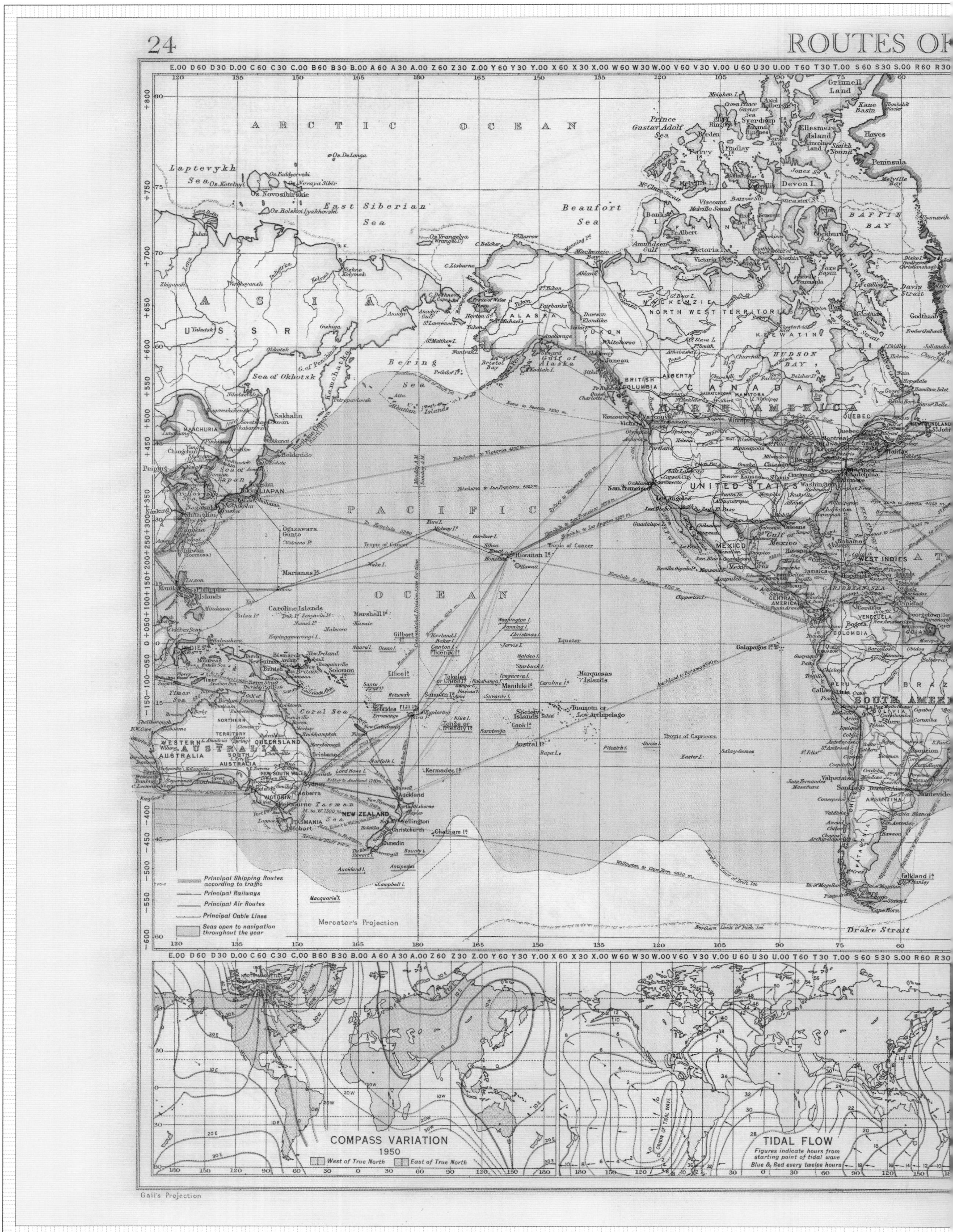
24
ROUTES OF
ARCTIC OCEAN
PACIFIC OCEAN
ASIA
U S S R
NORTH AMERICA
CANADA
UNITED STATES
MEXICO
SOUTH AMERICA
AUSTRALIA
NEW ZEALAND
Principal Shipping Routes according to traffic
Principal Railways
Principal Air Routes
Principal Cable Lines
Seas open to navigation throughout the year
Mercator's Projection
COMPASS VARIATION
1950
West of True North
East of True North
TIDAL FLOW
Figures indicate hours from starting point of tidal wave
Blue & Red every twelve hours
Gall's Projection

COMMERCE
25
ARCTIC OCEAN
UNION OF SOVIET SOCIALIST REPUBLICS
INDIAN OCEAN
PACIFIC OCEAN
British Commonwealth
United States of America
French Territories
Netherlands Territories
W. European States
Latin American States
Middle East States
Soviet Russian Group
Far Eastern Group
African States
STANDARD TIME
Red and Blue areas are based on standard differences in hours from G. M. T., Yellow areas on half-hourly differences, e.g. India is 5½ hours fast on Greenwich.
LANGUAGES OF COMMERCE
English
French
Spanish
Portuguese
Other European
Arabic Group
Slavonic
Mongolian
Other Languages
Copyright- John Bartholomew & Son.Ltd.Edinburgh

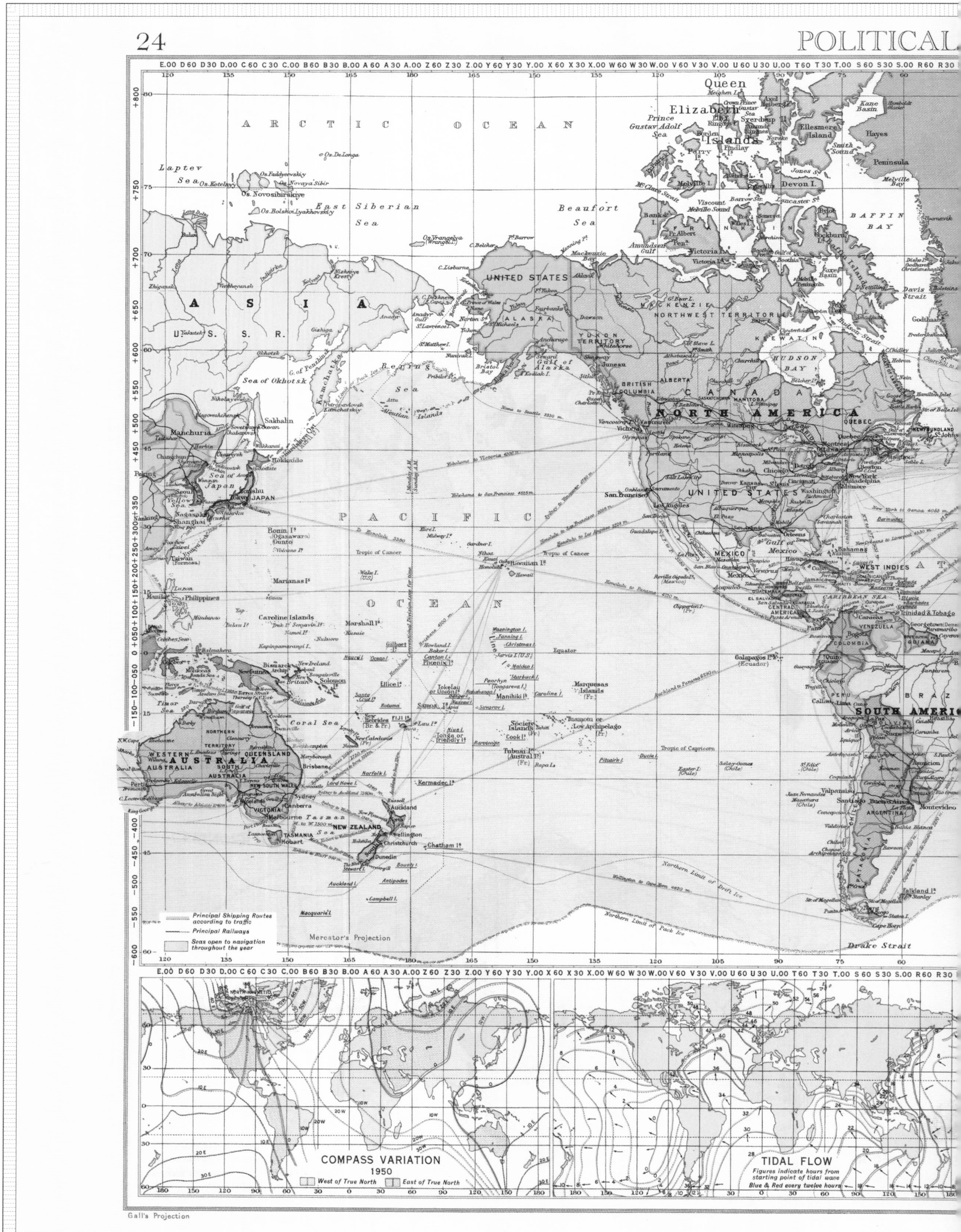
24
POLITICAL
ARCTIC OCEAN
Laptev Sea
East Siberian Sea
Beaufort Sea
Queen Elizabeth Islands
Prince Gustav Adolf Sea
Ellesmere Island
BAFFIN BAY
Davis Strait
ASIA
U. S. S. R.
Sea of Okhotsk
Bering Sea
Aleutian Islands
UNITED STATES (ALASKA)
YUKON TERRITORY
NORTHWEST TERRITORIES
KEEWATIN
HUDSON BAY
BRITISH COLUMBIA
ALBERTA
CANADA
NORTH AMERICA
QUEBEC
NEWFOUNDLAND
UNITED STATES
Manchuria
Sea of Japan
JAPAN
Yellow Sea
PACIFIC OCEAN
Tropic of Cancer
Hawaiian Is
Marianas Is
Caroline Islands
Marshall Is
Philippines
Equator
Gilbert Is
Phoenix Is
Marquesas Islands
Society Islands
Tuamotu or Low Archipelago
MEXICO
Gulf of Mexico
WEST INDIES
CARIBBEAN SEA
CENTRAL AMERICA
VENEZUELA
COLOMBIA
Galapagos Is (Ecuador)
PERU
SOUTH AMERICA
New Guinea
Coral Sea
AUSTRALIA
WESTERN AUSTRALIA
NORTHERN TERRITORY
QUEENSLAND
SOUTH AUSTRALIA
NEW SOUTH WALES
VICTORIA
TASMANIA
Tasman Sea
NEW ZEALAND
Tropic of Capricorn
ARGENTINA
Falkland Is
Drake Strait
Northern Limit of Drift Ice
Northern Limit of Pack Ice
Principal Shipping Routes according to traffic
Principal Railways
Seas open to navigation throughout the year
Mercator's Projection
COMPASS VARIATION 1950
West of True North
East of True North
TIDAL FLOW
Figures indicate hours from starting point of tidal wave
Blue & Red every twelve hours
Gall's Projection

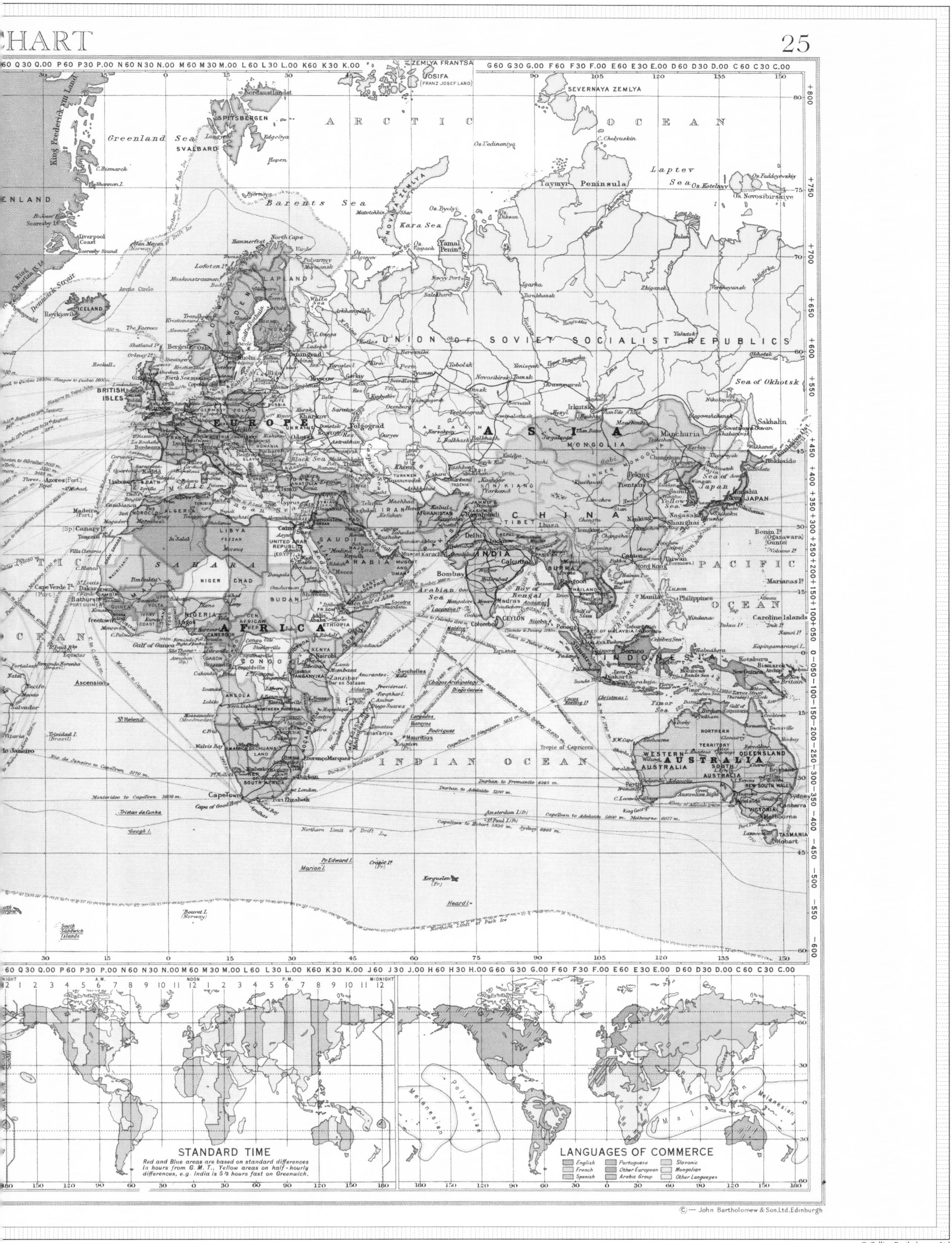
CHART
25
ARCTIC OCEAN
SEVERNAYA ZEMLYA
ZEMLYA FRANTSA IOSIFA (FRANZ JOSEF LAND)
SPITSBERGEN
SVALBARD
Greenland Sea
Barents Sea
Kara Sea
Laptev Sea
Taymyr Peninsula
ICELAND
BRITISH ISLES
EUROPE
UNION OF SOVIET SOCIALIST REPUBLICS
Sea of Okhotsk
ASIA
MONGOLIA
Manchuria
CHINA
INDIA
JAPAN
PACIFIC OCEAN
AFRICA
SAHARA
LIBYA
SUDAN
NIGERIA
CONGO
ANGOLA
SOUTH AFRICA
ARABIA
Arabian Sea
Bay of Bengal
INDIAN OCEAN
Philippines
Borneo
AUSTRALIA
WESTERN AUSTRALIA
QUEENSLAND
SOUTH AUSTRALIA
NEW SOUTH WALES
VICTORIA
TASMANIA
Tropic of Capricorn
Northern Limit of Drift Ice
Northern Limit of Pack Ice
STANDARD TIME
Red and Blue areas are based on standard differences in hours from G. M. T., Yellow areas on half-hourly differences, e.g. India is 5½ hours fast on Greenwich.
LANGUAGES OF COMMERCE
English
French
Spanish
Portuguese
Other European
Arabic Group
Slavonic
Mongolian
Other Languages
Melanesian
Polynesian
Malayan
©— John Bartholomew & Son,Ltd.,Edinburgh

24

# STATES OF

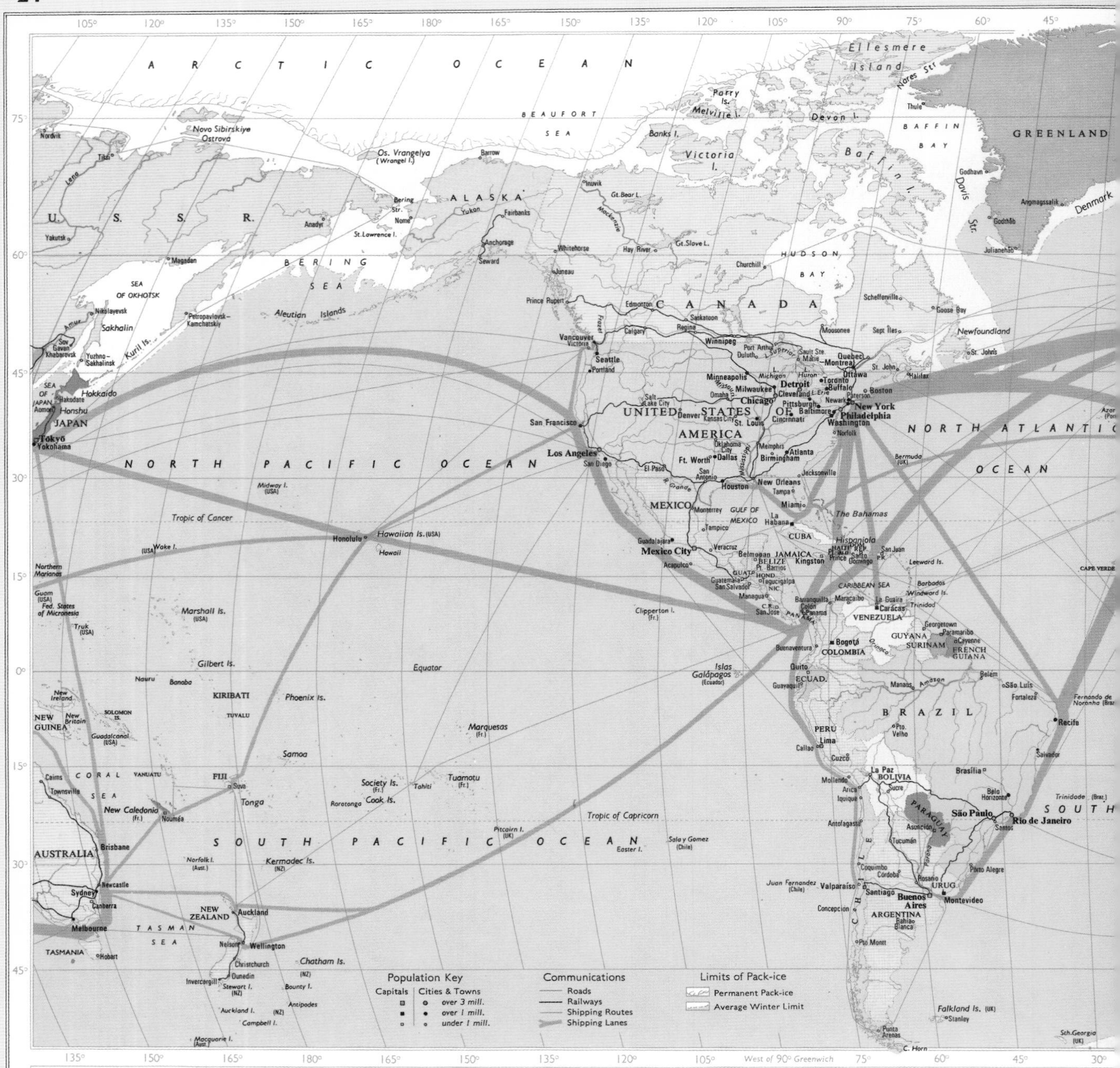


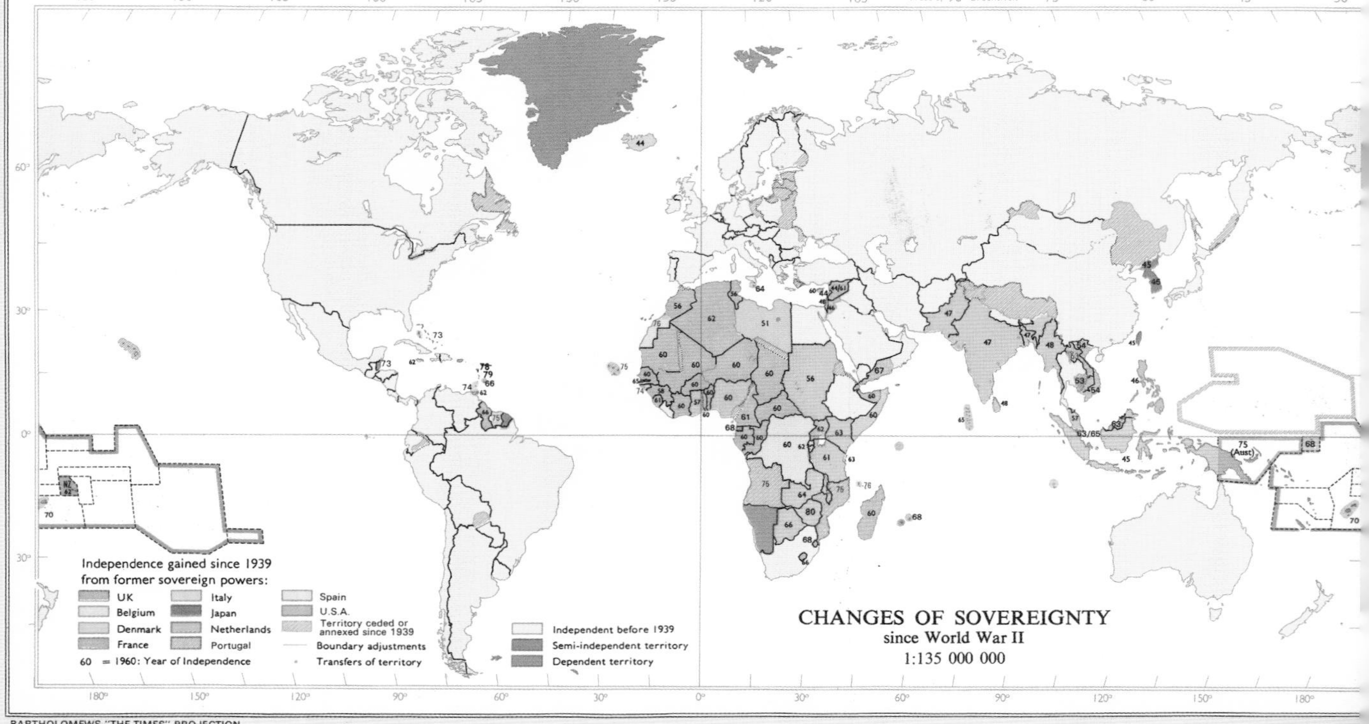


CHANGES OF SOVEREIGNTY
since World War II
1:135 000 000

BARTHOLOMEWS "THE TIMES" PROJECTION

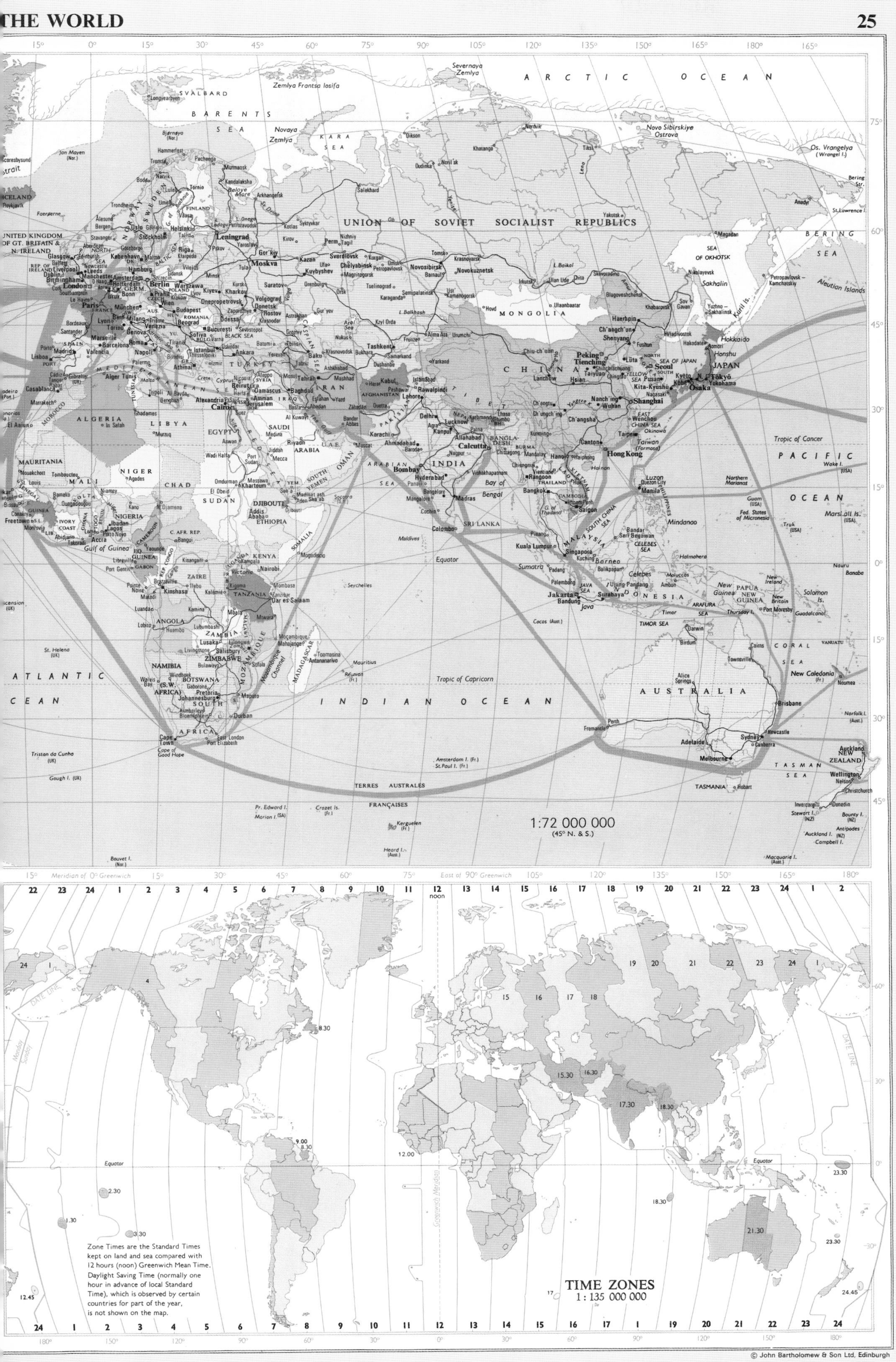
THE WORLD
25
ARCTIC OCEAN
BARENTS SEA
KARA SEA
UNION OF SOVIET SOCIALIST REPUBLICS
SEA OF OKHOTSK
BERING SEA
MONGOLIA
CHINA
JAPAN
TURKEY
IRAN
AFGHANISTAN
PAKISTAN
INDIA
TIBET
SAUDI ARABIA
EGYPT
LIBYA
ALGERIA
NIGER
CHAD
SUDAN
MALI
MAURITANIA
NIGERIA
ETHIOPIA
KENYA
ZAIRE
TANZANIA
ANGOLA
ZAMBIA
NAMIBIA
BOTSWANA
SOUTH AFRICA
MADAGASCAR
INDONESIA
AUSTRALIA
NEW ZEALAND
PACIFIC OCEAN
ATLANTIC OCEAN
INDIAN OCEAN
CORAL SEA
TASMAN SEA
Tropic of Cancer
Tropic of Capricorn
Equator
TERRES AUSTRALES FRANÇAISES
1:72 000 000
(45° N. & S.)
Meridian of 0° Greenwich
East of 90° Greenwich
Zone Times are the Standard Times kept on land and sea compared with 12 hours (noon) Greenwich Mean Time. Daylight Saving Time (normally one hour in advance of local Standard Time), which is observed by certain countries for part of the year, is not shown on the map.
TIME ZONES
1 : 135 000 000
© John Bartholomew & Son Ltd, Edinburgh

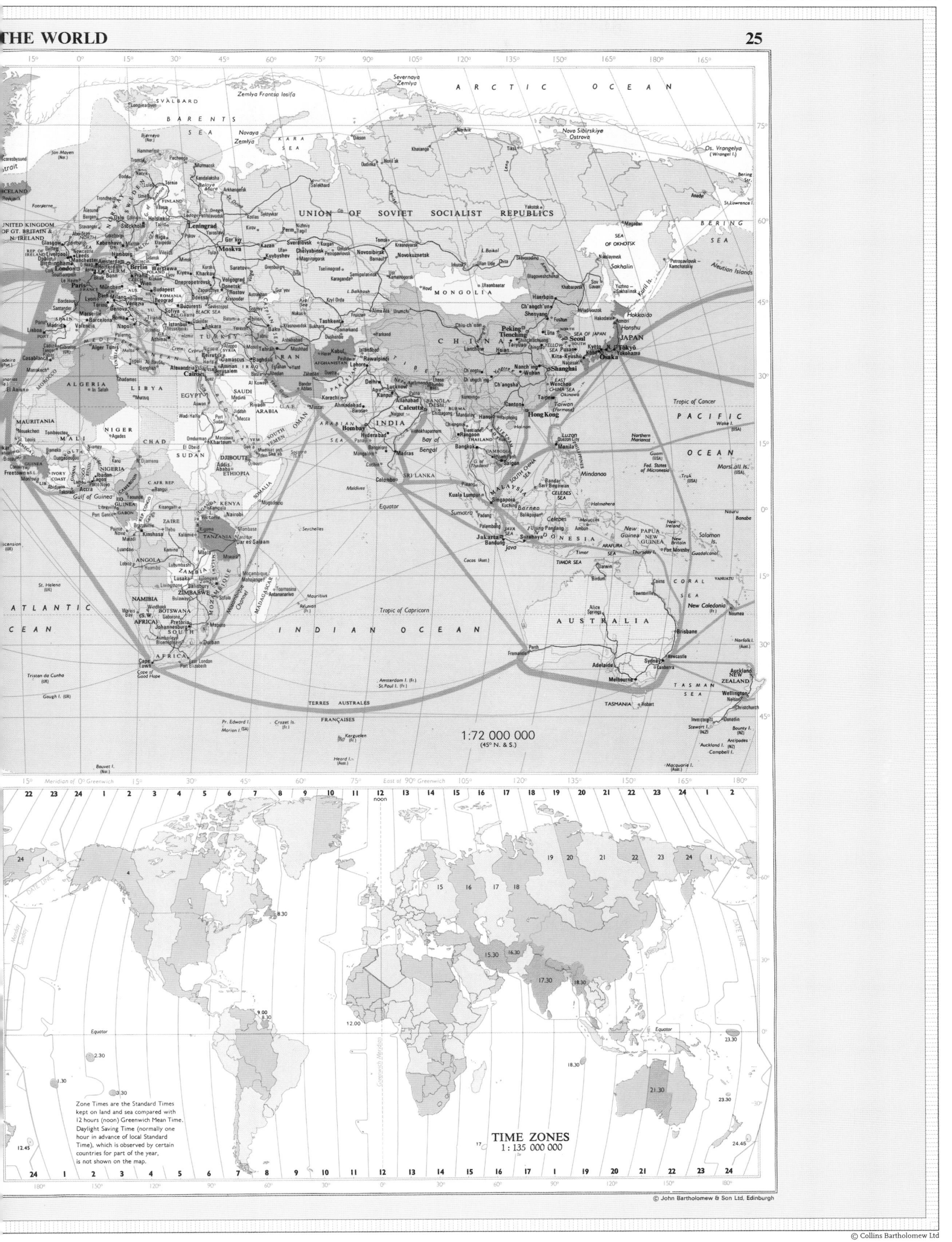

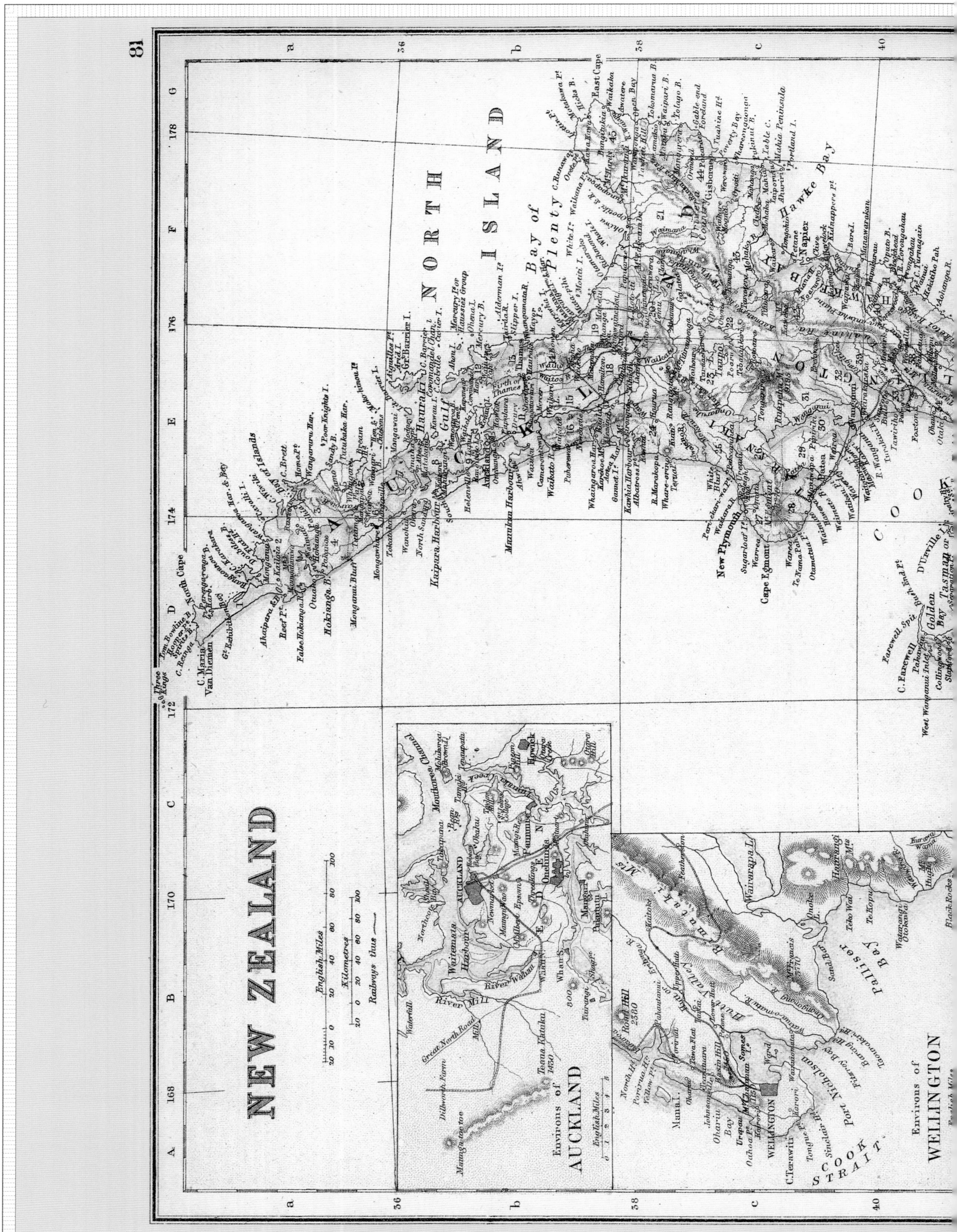
81
NEW ZEALAND
English Miles
Kilometres
Railways thus
NORTH ISLAND
Bay of Plenty
Hawke Bay
COOK
Environs of AUCKLAND
Environs of WELLINGTON
COOK STRAIT

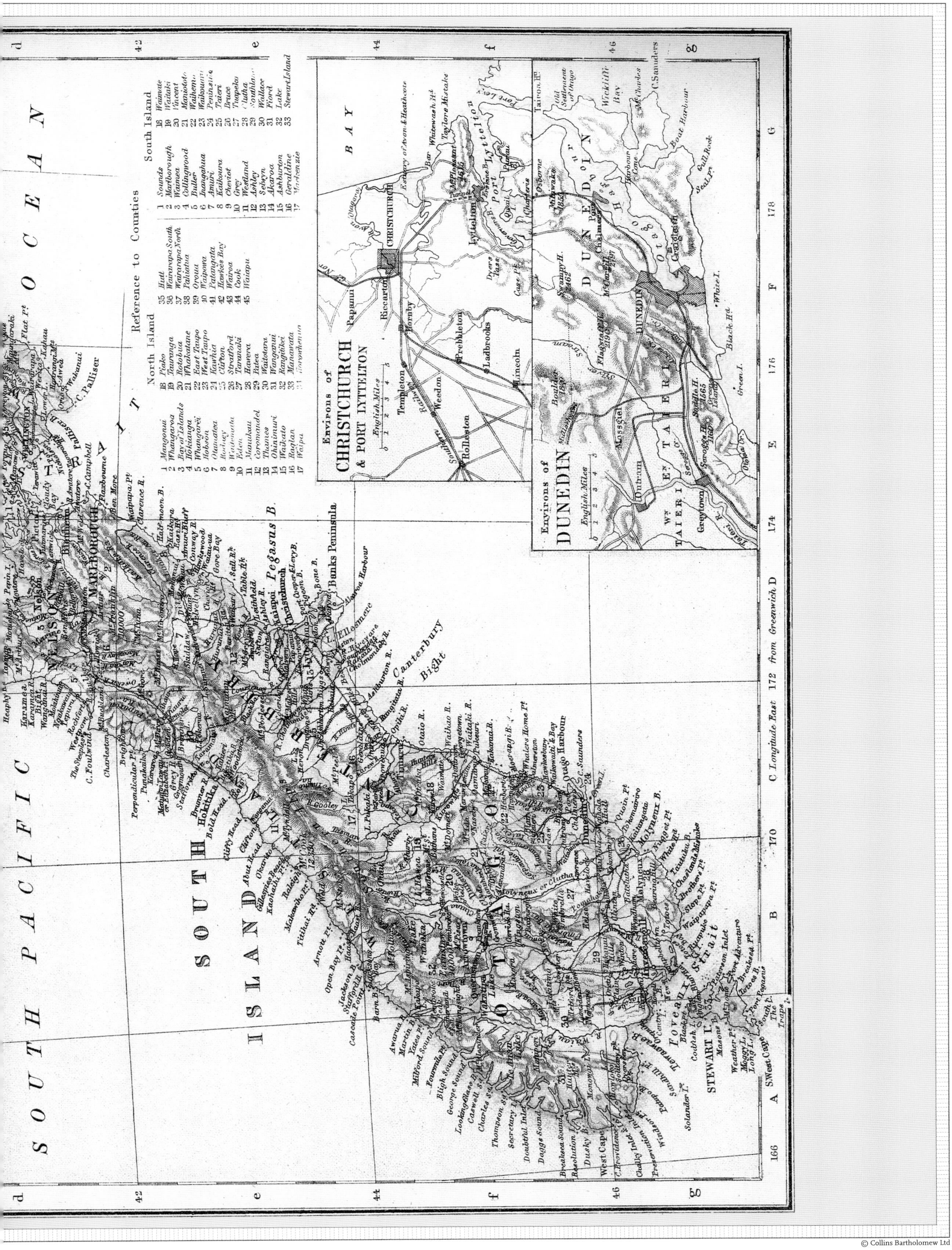
SOUTH PACIFIC OCEAN
SOUTH ISLAND
Reference to Counties
Environs of CHRISTCHURCH & PORT LYTTELTON
Environs of DUNEDIN
Canterbury Bight
Pegasus B.
Banks Peninsula
STEWART I.
Foveaux Strait
OTAGO
Longitude East 172 from Greenwich

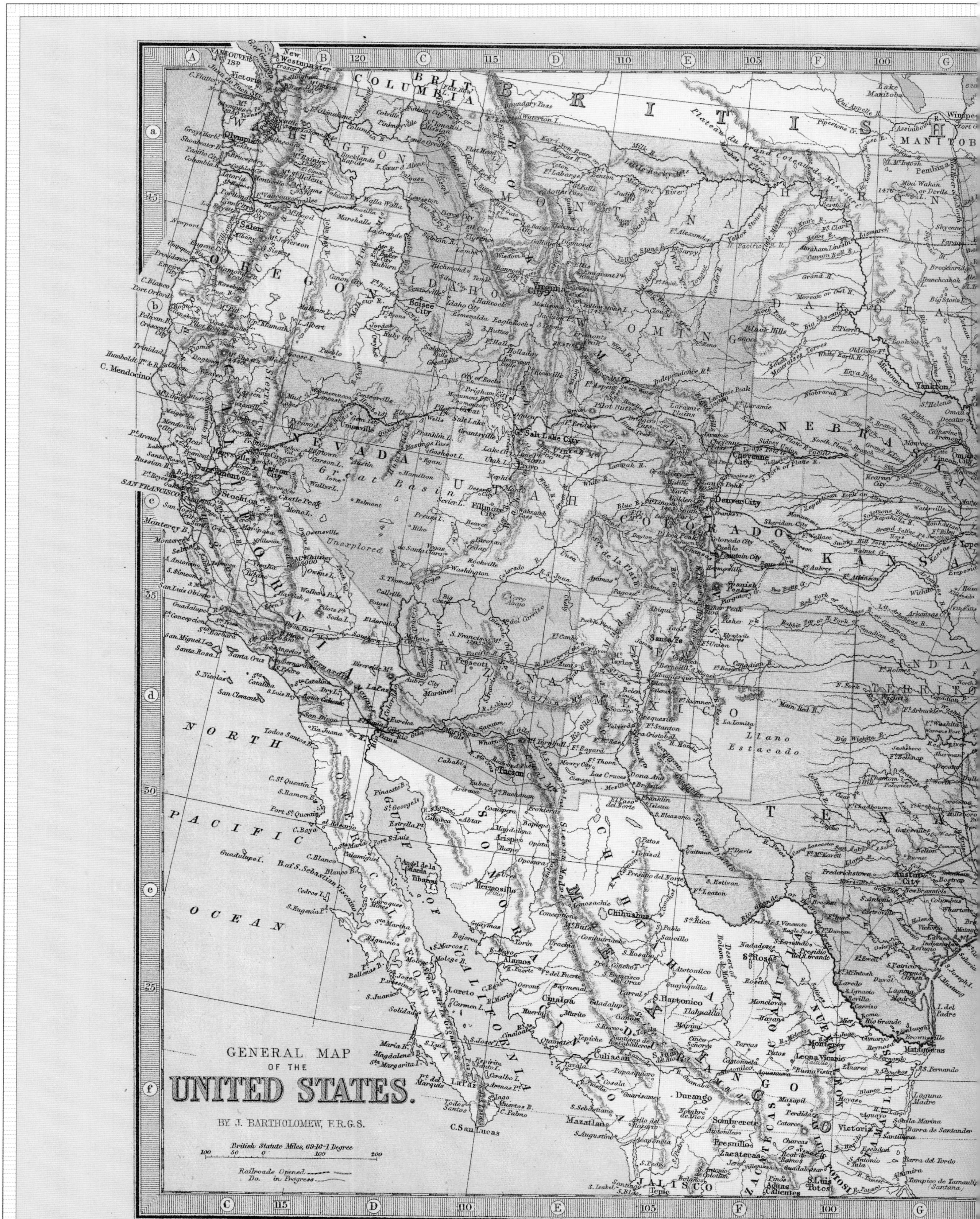
GENERAL MAP
OF THE
UNITED STATES.
BY J. BARTHOLOMEW, F.R.G.S.
British Statute Miles, 69·10=1 Degree
100 50 0 100 200
Railroads Opened
Do. in Progress
Engraved & Printed in Colours
GEORGE PHILIP & S
NORTH
PACIFIC
OCEAN
OREGON
NEVADA
UTAH
COLORADO
KANSAS
NEBRASKA
WYOMING
DAKOTA
MONTANA
IDAHO
ARIZONA
TEXAS
CHIHUAHUA
SONORA
Unexplored
Llano Estacado
Salt Lake City
Denver City
Sacramento
Santa Fe
Chihuahua
Durango
Monterey
SAN FRANCISCO

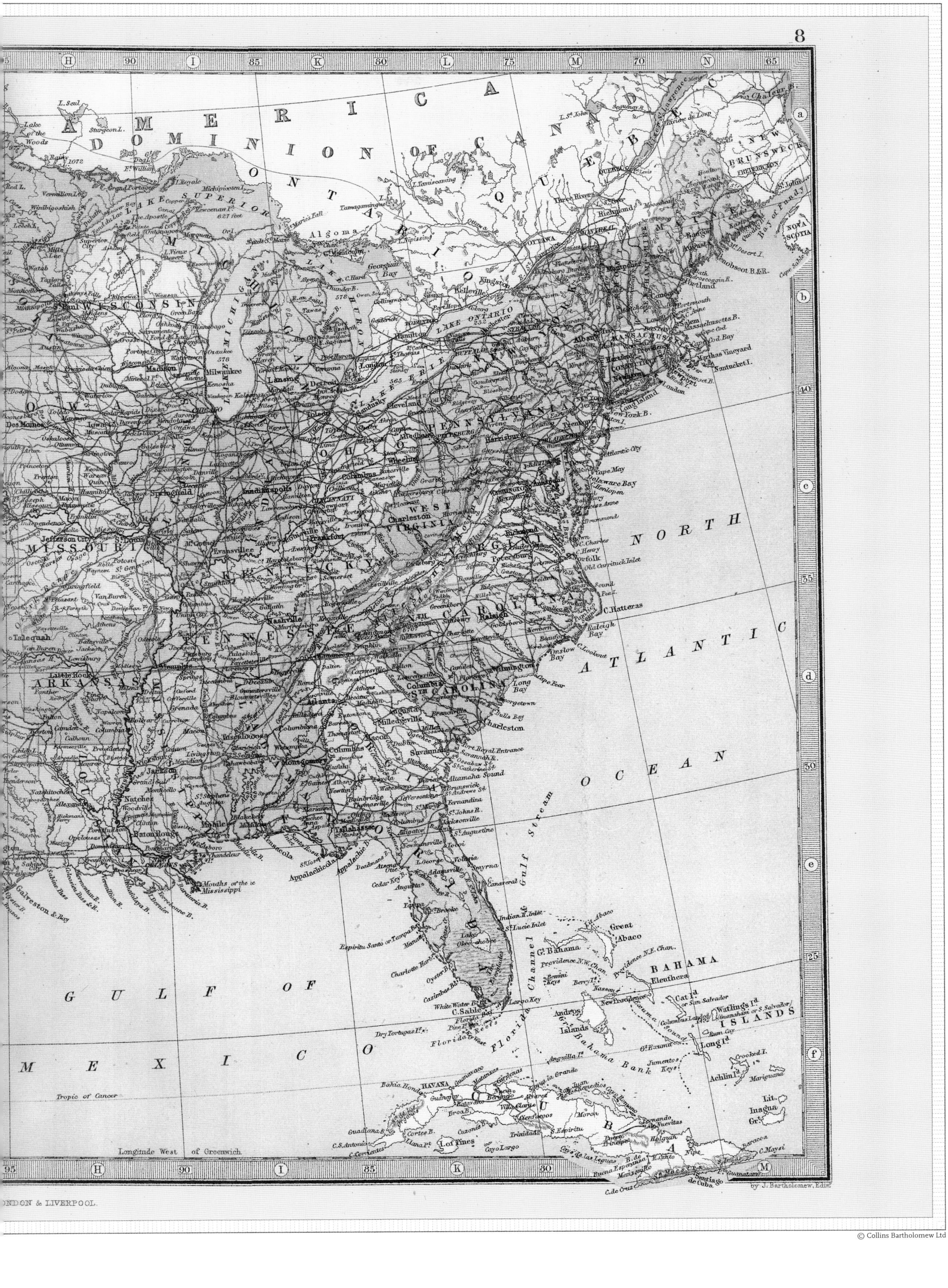
8
DOMINION OF CANADA
AMERICA
ONTARIO
QUEBEC
NEW BRUNSWICK
NOVA SCOTIA
LAKE SUPERIOR
LAKE MICHIGAN
LAKE HURON
LAKE ONTARIO
LAKE ERIE
WISCONSIN
MICHIGAN
IOWA
MISSOURI
KENTUCKY
TENNESSEE
ARKANSAS
OHIO
PENNSYLVANIA
WEST VIRGINIA
VIRGINIA
NORTH CAROLINA
STH CAROLINA
MASSACHUSETTS
CONNECTICUT
NORTH ATLANTIC OCEAN
GULF OF MEXICO
Gulf Stream
Florida Channel
BAHAMA ISLANDS
CUBA
Great Abaco
Eleuthera
Andros Islands
Gt. Bahama Bank
HAVANA
Tropic of Cancer
Longitude West of Greenwich
Madison
Milwaukee
Lansing
Detroit
Cleveland
Toledo
Indianapolis
Springfield
Columbus
Frankfort
Nashville
Harrisburg
Charleston
Richmond
Raleigh
Atlanta
Savannah
Wilmington
Tallahassee
Jacksonville
St. Augustine
Mobile
Baton Rouge
Natchez
Jackson
Memphis
Little Rock
Jefferson City
Des Moines
Kingston
Ottawa
Quebec
Montreal
Portland
Boston
New York
Trenton
Albany
C. Hatteras
Raleigh Bay
Long Bay
Cape Fear
Cape May
Delaware Bay
Bay of Fundy
Nantucket I.
Martha's Vineyard
Long Island
C. Sable
Cedar Key
Appalachicola
Pensacola
Mouths of the Mississippi
Galveston B.
Dry Tortugas Is.
Florida Reefs
by J. Bartholomew, Edin.
ONDON & LIVERPOOL.

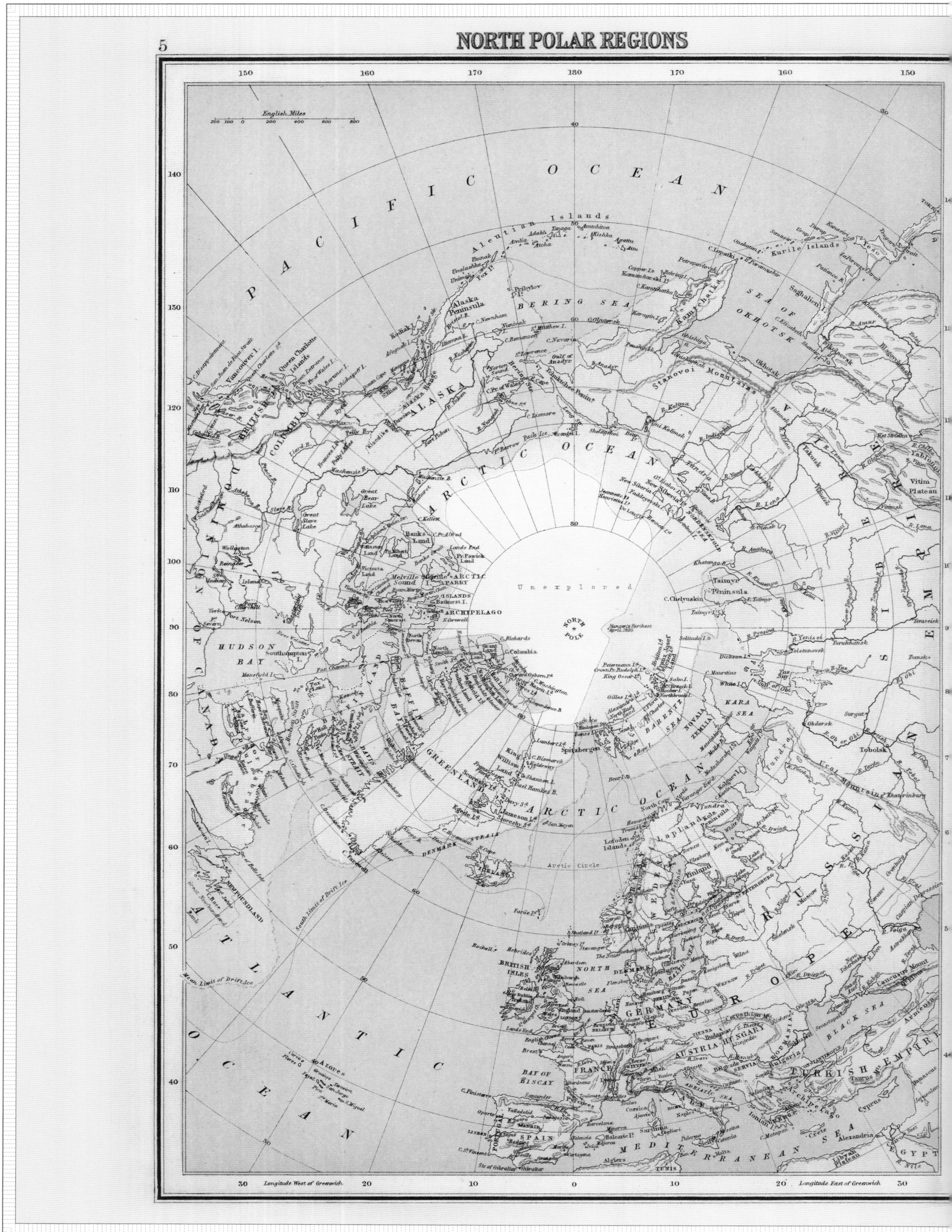
5
NORTH POLAR REGIONS
English Miles
PACIFIC OCEAN
Aleutian Islands
BERING SEA
SEA OF OKHOTSK
Kurile Islands
Kamtchatka
Stanovoi Mountains
ALASKA
BRITISH COLUMBIA
DOMINION OF CANADA
ARCTIC OCEAN
Unexplored
NORTH POLE
ARCTIC ARCHIPELAGO
HUDSON BAY
BAFFIN BAY
DAVIS STRAIT
GREENLAND
DENMARK STRAIT
ICELAND
Spitzbergen
NOVAIA ZEMLIA
BARENTZ SEA
KARA SEA
Taimyr Peninsula
Lapland
Arctic Circle
SIBERIA
Ural Mountains
RUSSIA
EUROPE
NORTH SEA
BRITISH ISLES
GERMANY
FRANCE
BAY OF BISCAY
SPAIN
AUSTRIA HUNGARY
BLACK SEA
TURKISH EMPIRE
MEDITERRANEAN SEA
ATLANTIC OCEAN
Azores
Longitude West of Greenwich
Longitude East of Greenwich

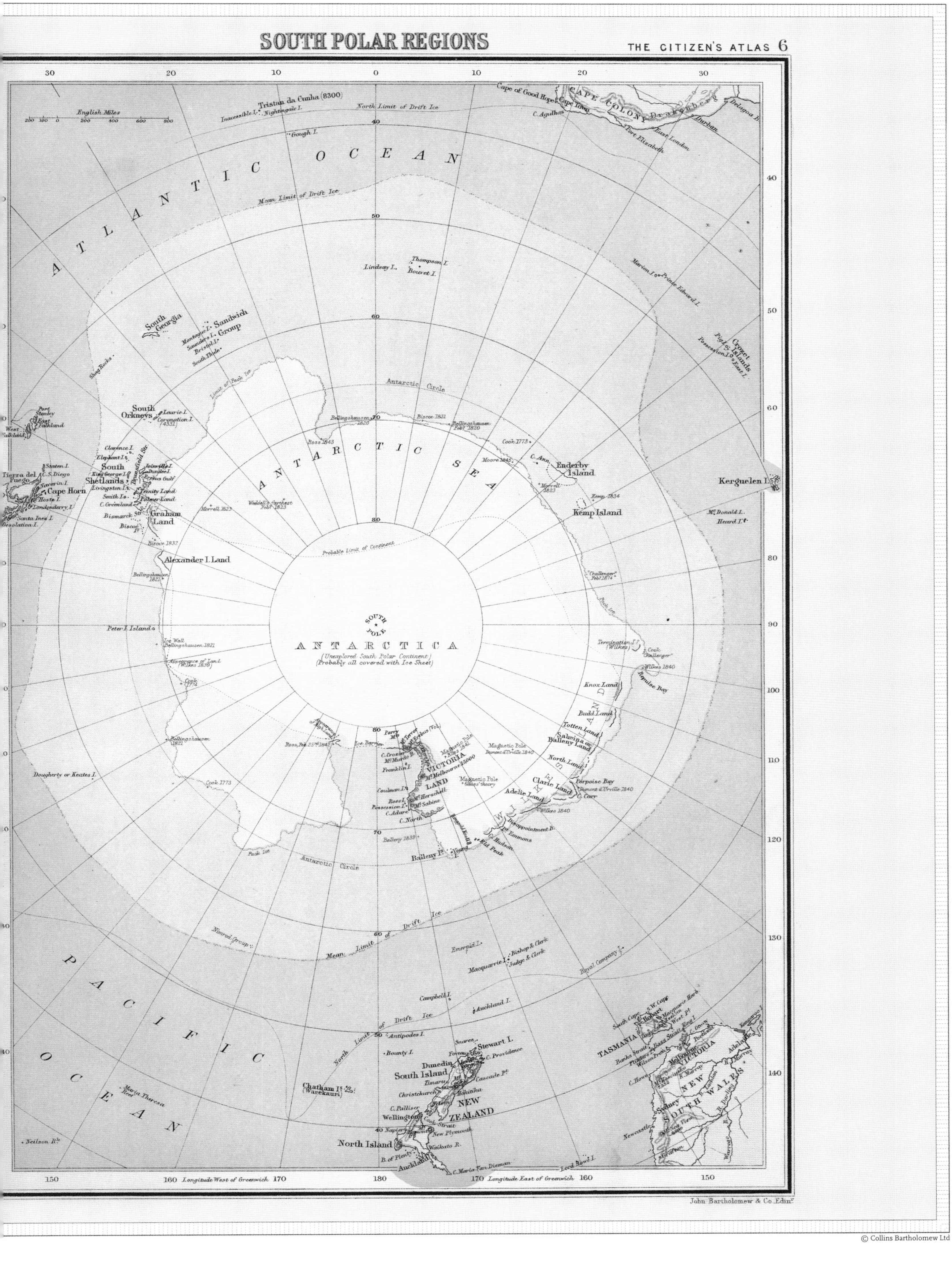
SOUTH POLAR REGIONS
THE CITIZEN'S ATLAS 6
ATLANTIC OCEAN
PACIFIC OCEAN
ANTARCTIC SEA
ANTARCTICA
(Unexplored South Polar Continent)
(Probably all covered with Ice Sheet)
SOUTH POLE
Tristan da Cunha (8300)
Gough I.
Bouvet I.
South Georgia
Sandwich Group
South Orkneys
South Shetlands
Cape Horn
Tierra del Fuego
Graham Land
Alexander I. Land
Peter I. Island
Enderby Island
Kemp Island
Kerguelen I.
Knox Land
Budd Land
Totten Land
Sabrina or Balleny Land
North Land
Clarie Land
Adelie Land
VICTORIA LAND
Balleny Is.
Antarctic Circle
Mean Limit of Drift Ice
North Limit of Drift Ice
Probable Limit of Continent
CAPE COLONY
Cape of Good Hope
Cape Town
Port Elizabeth
East London
Durban
Crozet Islands
Macquarie I.
Auckland I.
Campbell I.
Antipodes I.
Bounty I.
Chatham Is. (Warekauri)
Stewart I.
South Island
North Island
NEW ZEALAND
Wellington
Dunedin
Christchurch
Auckland
TASMANIA
Hobart
VICTORIA
Melbourne
NEW SOUTH WALES
Sydney
Newcastle
Adelaide
English Miles
Longitude West of Greenwich
Longitude East of Greenwich
John Bartholomew & Co. Edin.

113
AUST
CITY OF PERTH
Burswood Estate
MELVILLE WATER
SOUTH PERTH
FREMANTLE
NORTH FREMANTLE
TIMOR
TIMOR SEA
Sumba
INDIAN OCEAN
WESTERN AUSTRALIA
Great Sandy Desert
Great Victoria Desert
Unexplored
Kimberley Division
Glenelg District
Proclaimed Goldfields
Tropic of Capricorn
Nullarbor Plain
GREAT AUSTRALIAN BIGHT
Eucla Division
South West Div
Victoria District
Gascoyne Div
Murchison Division
Eastern Division
Shark Bay
Dirk Hartog I.
Geraldton
PERTH
Albany
King George Sound
Recherche Archipelago
Esperance
Coolgardie
Kalgoorlie
Broome
Dampier Land
Collier Bay
Bedout I.
Monte Bello Is.
Barrow I.
Houtman Rocks or Abrolhos
C. Leeuwin
C. Naturaliste
Lake Austin
KING GEORGE SOUND
PRINCESS ROYAL HARBOUR
Frenchman Bay
North Channel
Middle Channel
South Channel
Oyster Bay
British Statute Miles 69·16 = 1 Degree
Railways
Telegraphs
Longitude East 130 of Greenwich
15
20
25
30
115
120
125
130

RALIA
THE CITIZEN'S ATLAS 114
ARAFURA SEA
TORRES STRAIT
NEW GUINEA (British Territory)
PAPUA OR NEW GUINEA
Louisiade Archipelago
GULF OF CARPENTARIA
Cape York Peninsula
CORAL SEA
QUEENSLAND
NEW SOUTH WALES
VICTORIA
SOUTH PACIFIC OCEAN
BASS STRAIT
Great Barrier Reef
SYDNEY
BRISBANE
MELBOURNE
ADELAIDE
John Bartholomew & Co. Edin.

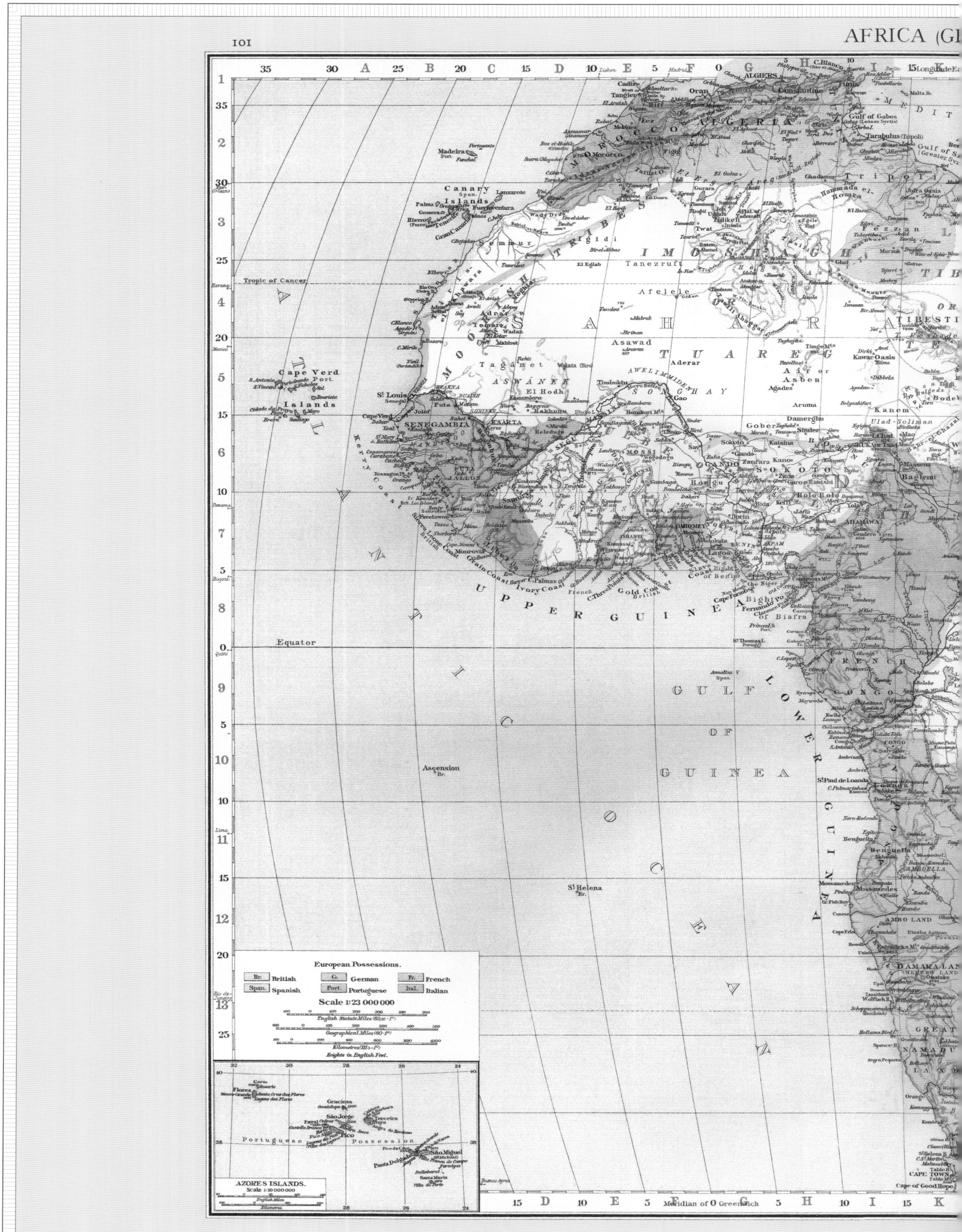
101
AFRICA (GE
Tropic of Cancer
Equator
ATLANTIC OCEAN
GULF OF GUINEA
UPPER GUINEA
LOWER GUINEA
SAHARA
Canary Islands
Cape Verd Islands
Madeira
Ascension Br.
St Helena Br.
St Louis
Senegambia
Sierra Leone
Monrovia
Grain Coast
Ivory Coast
Gold Coast
Slave Coast
Bight of Benin
Bight of Biafra
Timbuktu
Sokoto
Bagirmi
Congo
Angola
Benguela
Mossamedes
Damaraland
Great Namaqualand
Cape Town
Cape of Good Hope
Algiers
Oran
Constantine
Tunis
Tangier
Morocco
Algeria
Fezzan
European Possessions.
Br. British
Span. Spanish
G. German
Port. Portuguese
Fr. French
Ital. Italian
Scale 1:23 000 000
English Statute Miles
Geographical Miles
Kilometres
Heights in English Feet.
AZORES ISLANDS.
Scale 1:10 000 000
Portuguese Possession
Flores
Graciosa
São Jorge
Terceira
Pico
São Miguel
Ponta Delgada
Santa Maria
Meridian of Greenwich

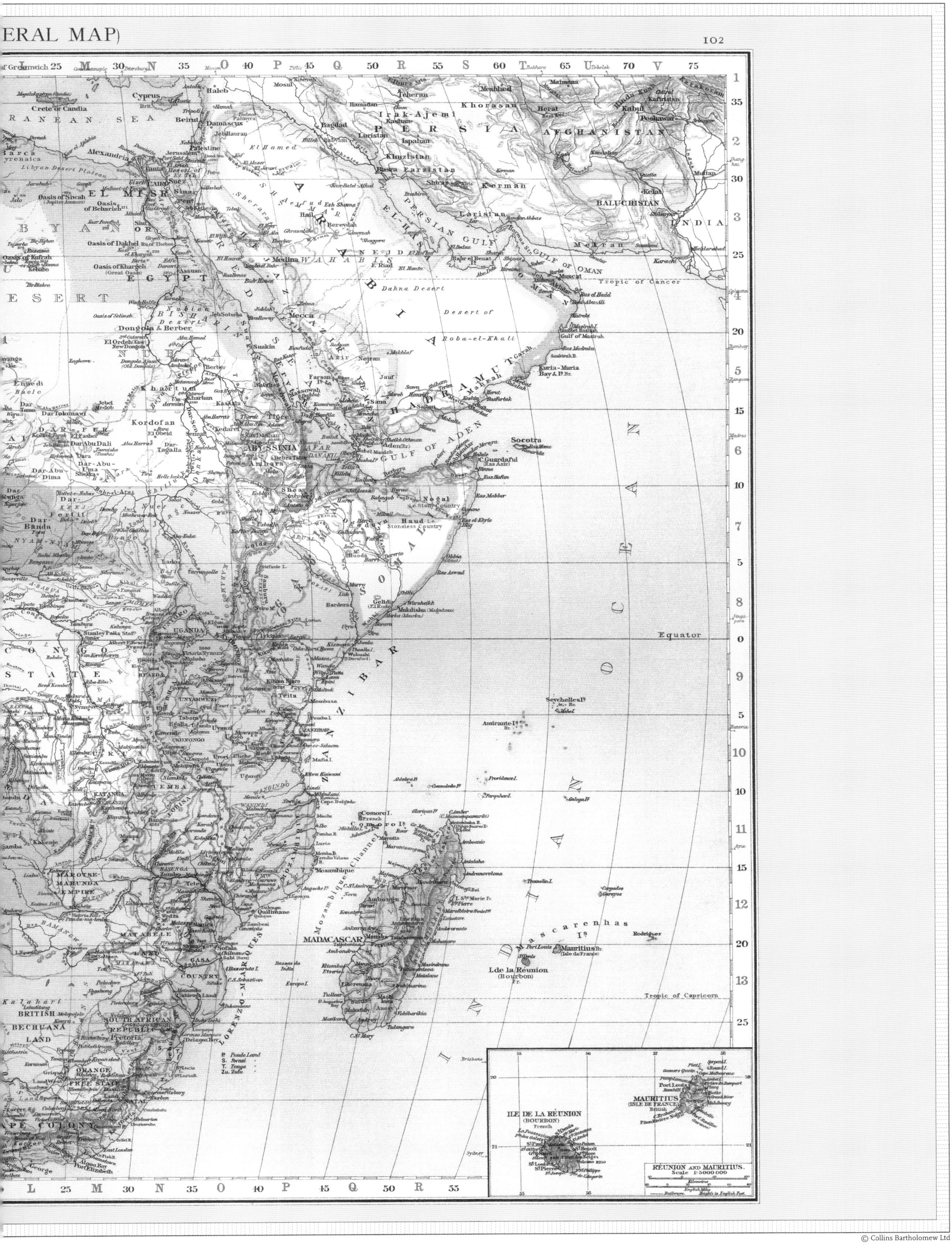
ERAL MAP)
102
Cyprus
Crete or Candia
Alexandria
Damascus
Beirut
Jerusalem
Bagdad
Teheran
Irak-Ajemi
P E R S I A
Ispahan
Khorasan
Meshhed
Herat
Kabul
Peshawar
A F G H A N I S T A N
BALUCHISTAN
I N D I A
Kerman
Shiraz
Laristan
PERSIAN GULF
GULF OF OMAN
Muscat
Tropic of Cancer
Mekran
Karachi
Oasis of Siwah
Oasis of Dakhel
Oasis of Khargeh
E G Y P T
Assuan
Medina
Mecca
A R A B I A
Dahna Desert
Desert of
Roba-el-Khali
Dongola & Berber
Suakin
Kordofan
Khartum
ABYSSINIA
Aden
GULF OF ADEN
Socotra
C. Guardaful
Berbera
Harar
Nogal
Haud
Stoneless Country
Mukdishu
Equator
UGANDA
C O N G O
S T A T E
Mombasa
ZANZIBAR
Seychelles Is
Amirante Is
Comoro I.
Mozambique Channel
Mozambique
MADAGASCAR
Mascarenhas Is
Mauritius
I. de la Réunion (Bourbon)
Rodriguez
Tropic of Capricorn
MAROTSE-MABUNDA EMPIRE
MATABELE
GASA COUNTRY
SOUTH AFRICAN REPUBLIC
Pretoria
BRITISH BECHUANA LAND
ORANGE FREE STATE
NATAL
CAPE COLONY
East London
Port Elizabeth
George
Delagoa Bay
P. Ponde Land
S. Swazi
T. Tonga
Zu. Zulu
I N D I A N O C E A N
ILE DE LA RÉUNION (BOURBON) French
MAURITIUS (ISLE DE FRANCE) British
RÉUNION AND MAURITIUS.
Scale 1: 5000 000

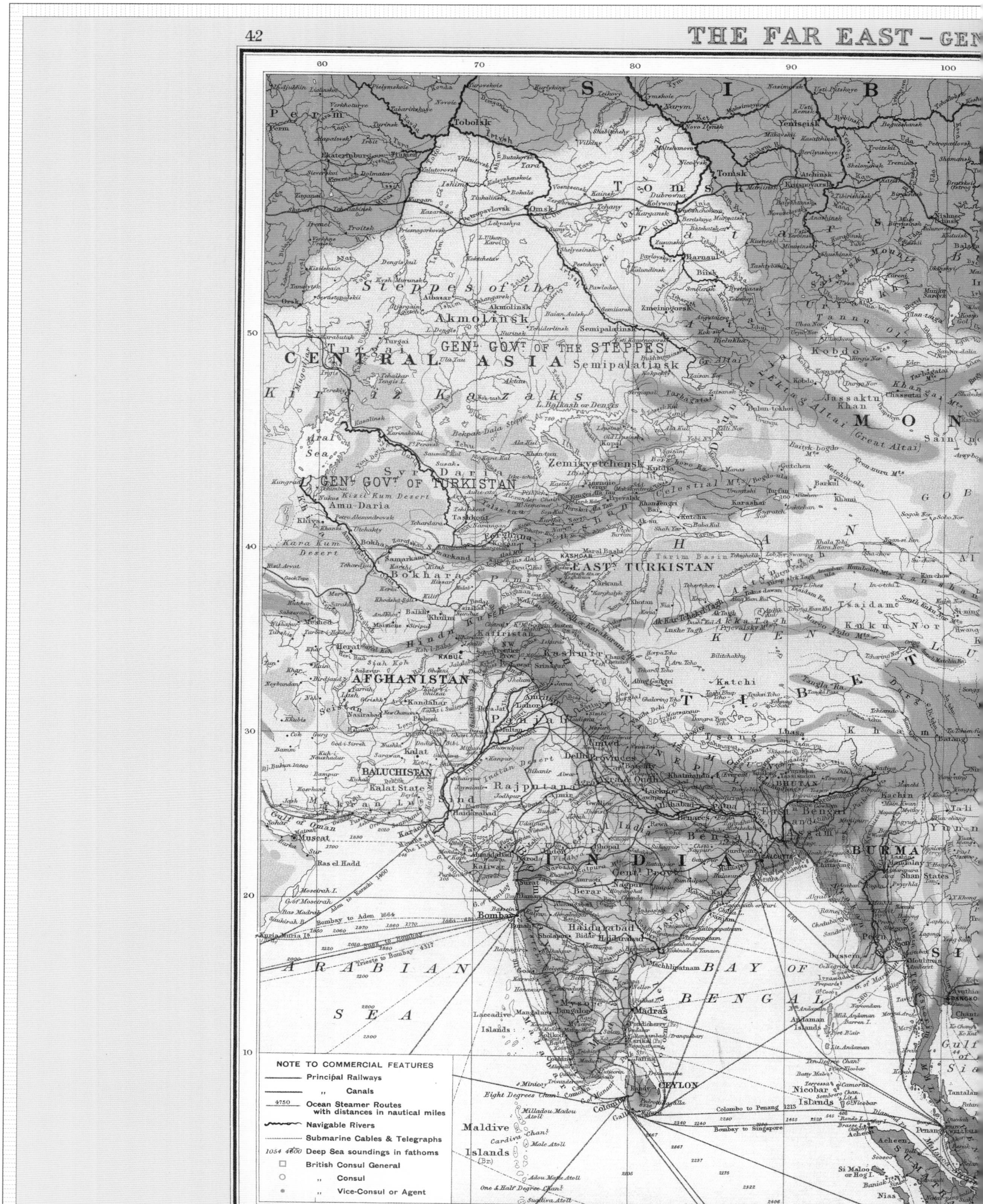
42
THE FAR EAST - GEN
NOTE TO COMMERCIAL FEATURES
Principal Railways
,, Canals
4750 Ocean Steamer Routes with distances in nautical miles
Navigable Rivers
Submarine Cables & Telegraphs
1054 4600 Deep Sea soundings in fathoms
British Consul General
,, Consul
,, Vice-Consul or Agent
CENTRAL ASIA
AFGHANISTAN
BALUCHISTAN
INDIA
BURMA
CEYLON
ARABIAN SEA
BAY OF BENGAL
EAST TURKISTAN
GEN^L GOV^T OF THE STEPPES
GEN^L GOV^T OF TURKISTAN

RAL COMMERCIAL CHART
ATLAS OF WORLD'S COMMERCE 43
SEA OF OKHOTSK
GEN^L GOV^T OF THE AMUR
Amur Prov.
SAKHALIN OR KARAFUTO
Transbaikalia
MANCHURIA
MONGOLIA
SHAMO
KOREA
SEA OF JAPAN
YELLOW SEA
CHINA
JAPAN (DAI NIPPON)
YEZO
HONDO
Kurile Is.
Liu Kiu Islands
EASTERN SEA
PACIFIC OCEAN
Magelhaes Archipelago (mostly uninhabited)
Bonin I^s.
Volcano I^s.
PHILIPPINE ISLANDS (United States)
Luzon
Mindanao
SULU SEA
SOUTH CHINA SEA
Formosa
Hong-kong (Brit.)
Canton
Shanghai
Peking
Vladivostock
Yokohama to Victoria 4320
S. Francisco 5280
Yokohama to Honolulu 3445
BORNEO
Singapore
NOTE TO VEGETATION COLOURING
Tropical Forests
Forests, chiefly coniferous
Trees, Grassland & Cultivation
Prairies and Steppes
Barren Desert
High Mountain Flora
VERTICAL DISTRIBUTION OF VEGETATION
HIMALAYAS
M^t Everest
THIAN SHAN
KUEN LUN
ALTAI
Alpine Region
Mosses & Lichens
Mountain Grassland, Steppe and Desert
Temperate Forest
Sub-Tropical Savanna
Siberian Tundra
Savanna
Siberian Forest
PLAINS OF INDIA
John Bartholomew & Co. Edin^r

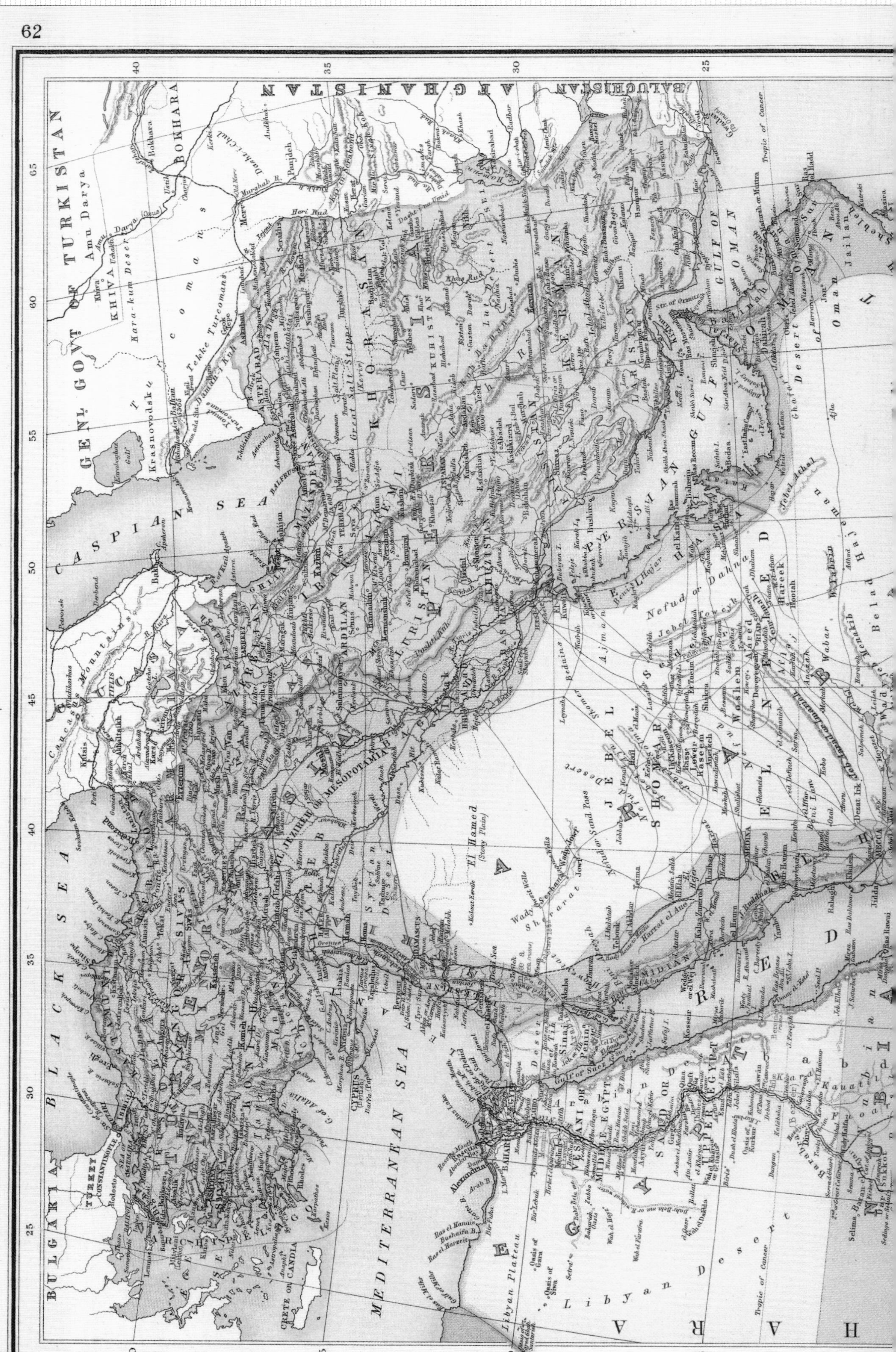
62
CASPIAN SEA
BLACK SEA
MEDITERRANEAN SEA
GENL GOVT OF TURKISTAN
AFGHANISTAN
BALUCHISTAN
BOKHARA
KHIVA
GULF OF OMAN
Libyan Desert
Tropic of Cancer
CYPRUS
CRETE OR CANDIA
DAMASCUS
BULGARIA

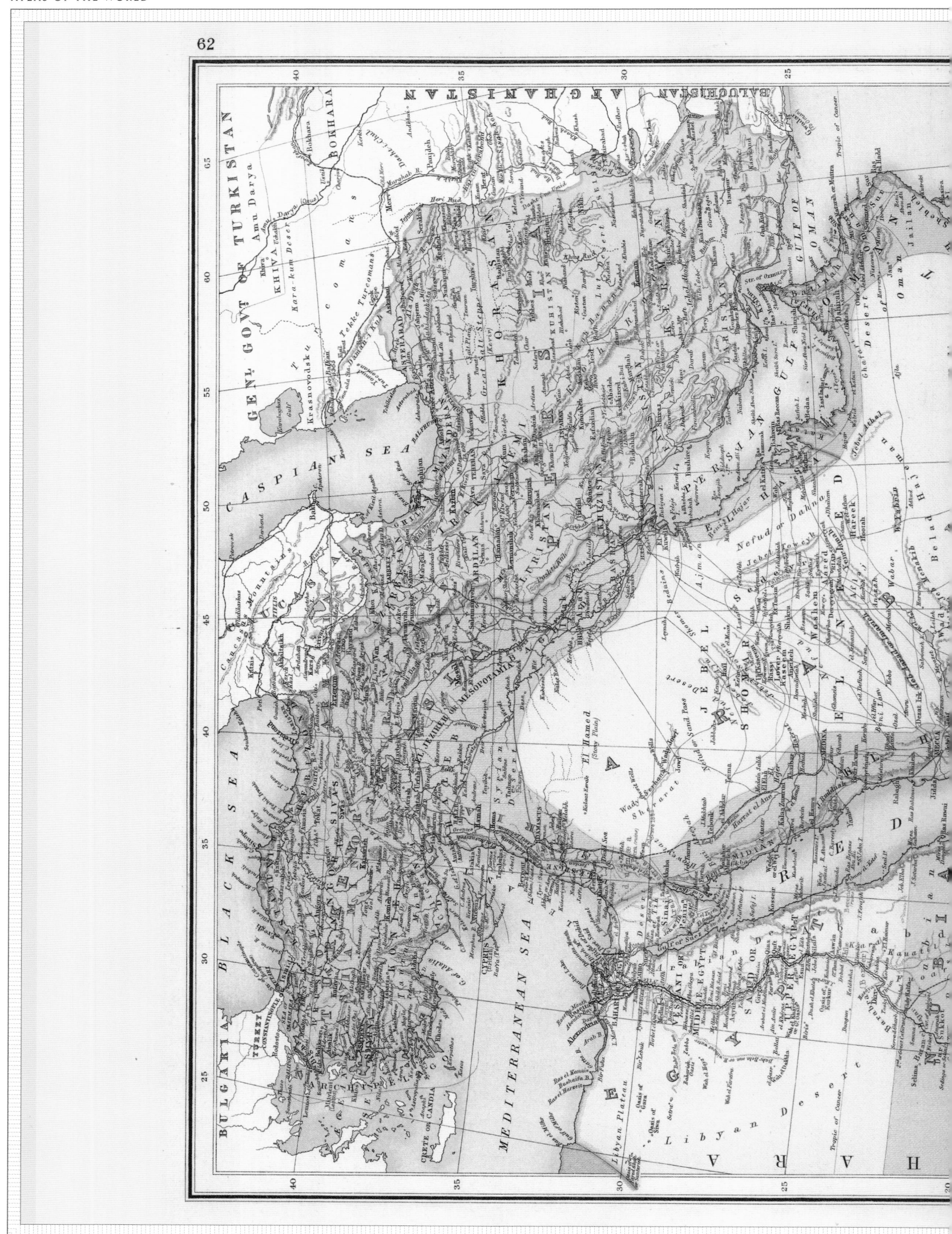

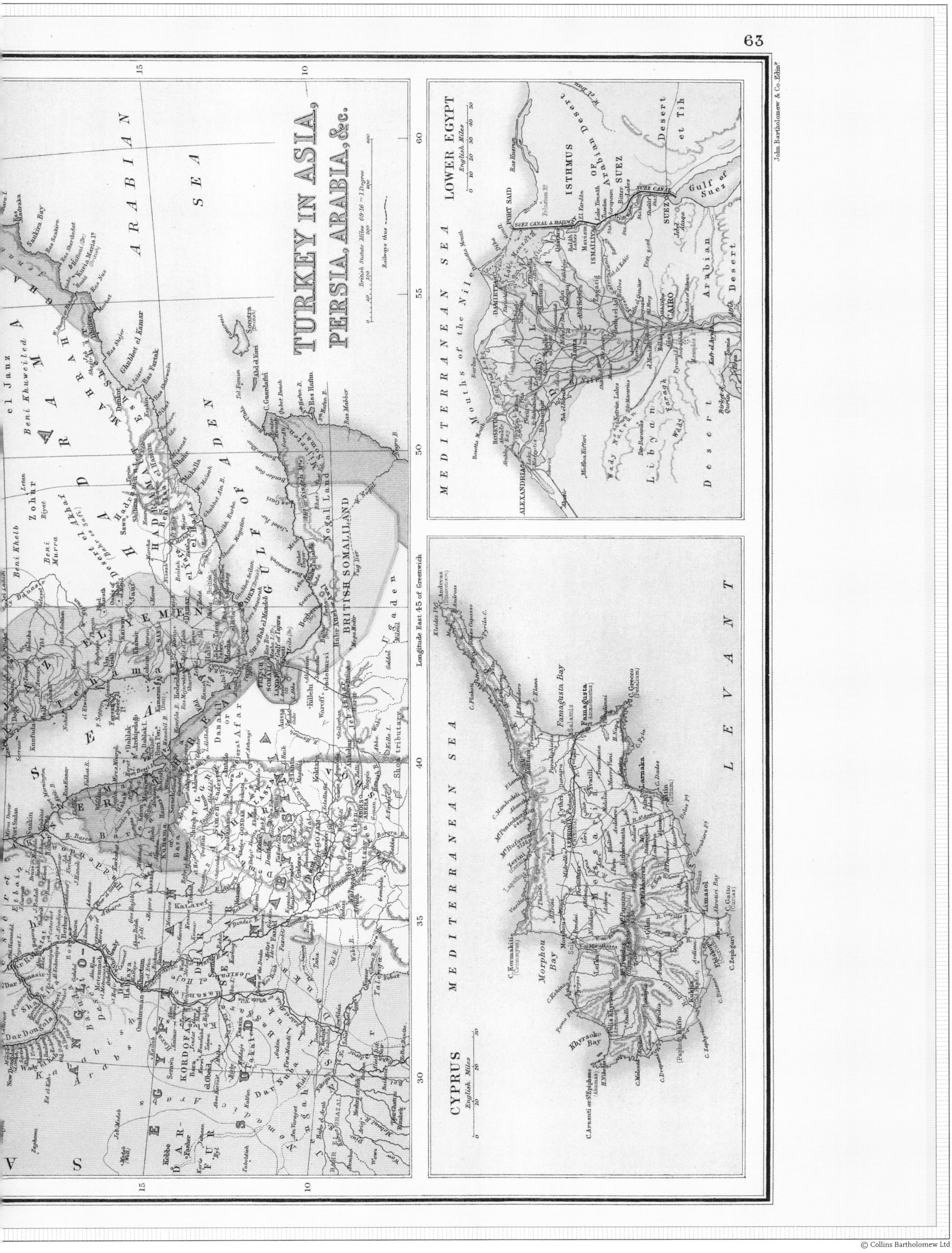
63
TURKEY IN ASIA, PERSIA, ARABIA, &c.
LOWER EGYPT
CYPRUS
MEDITERRANEAN SEA
LEVANT
ARABIAN SEA
GULF OF ADEN
BRITISH SOMALILAND
Longitude East 45 of Greenwich
John Bartholomew & Co. Edinʳ

"The Times" ATLAS
EUROP
Scale 1: 10,000,000
English Miles
Kilomètres
ARCTIC
Arctic Circle
ICELAND
Faroes
Shetland Is.
Orkney Is.
BRITISH ISLES
SCOTLAND
IRELAND
ENGLAND
IRISH SEA
NORTH SEA
ATLANTIC OCEAN
ENGLISH CHANNEL
BAY OF BISCAY
FRANCE
SPAIN
GERMANY
SWITZERLAND
AUSTRIA
DENMARK
CORSICA
SARDINIA
Balearic Islands
TYRRHENIAN SEA
IONIAN SEA
SICILY
MEDITERRANEAN SEA
MOROCCO
ALGERIA
TUNIS
PARIS
AMSTERDAM
Bergen
Edinburgh
Dublin
Barcelona
Marseilles
Longitude East 20 of
THE EDINBURGH GEOGRAPHICAL INSTITUTE

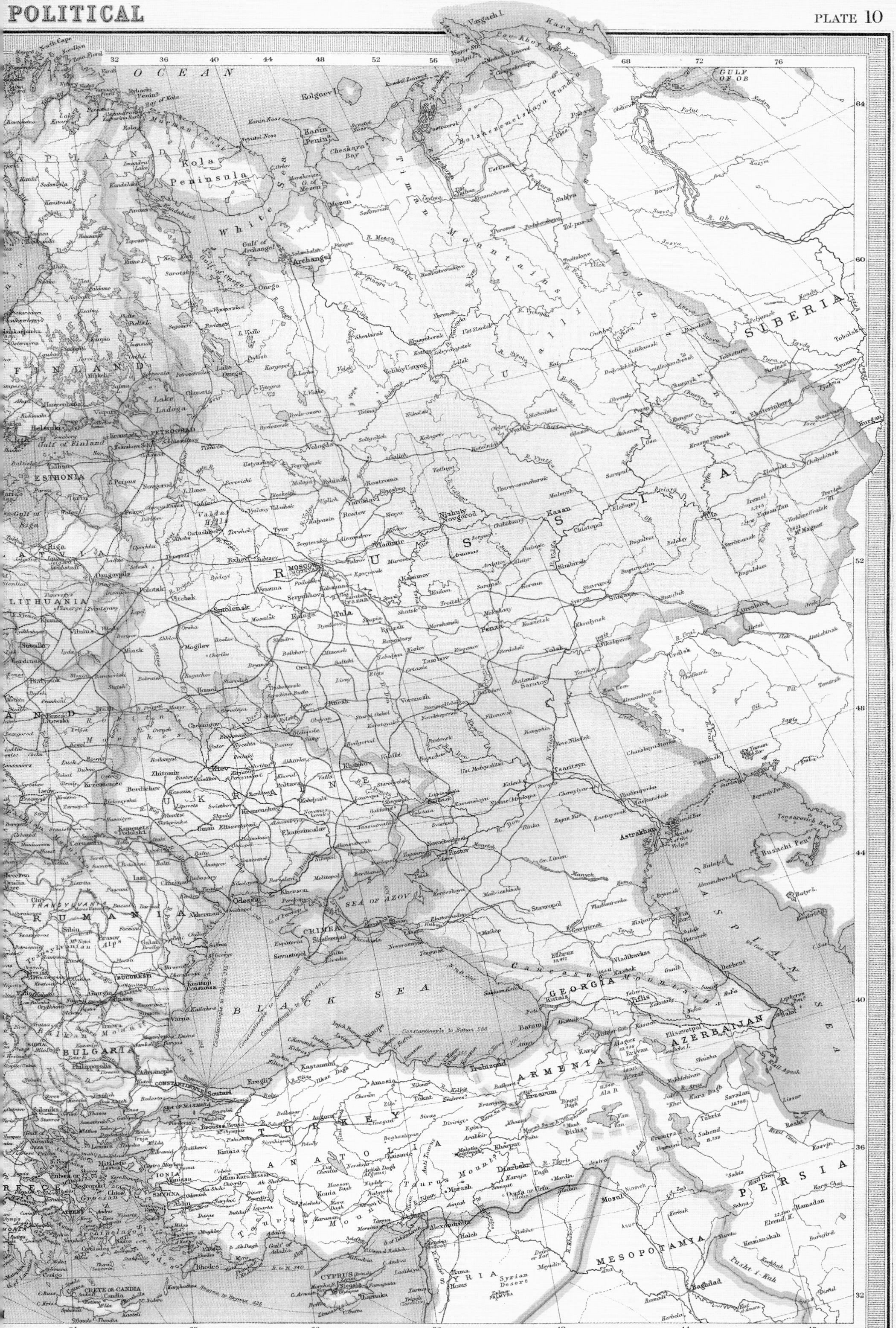
POLITICAL
PLATE 10
OCEAN
Kolguev I.
Kanin Penin.
Kola Peninsula
White Sea
Archangel
Timan Mountains
Ural Mountains
SIBERIA
GULF OF OB
R. Ob
Tobolsk
Ekaterinburg
FINLAND
Lake Ladoga
Lake Onega
Petrograd
Gulf of Finland
ESTHONIA
Gulf of Riga
LITHUANIA
Vilnius
Smolensk
Moscow
Tula
Nizhniy Novgorod
Kazan
Simbirsk
Samara
Penza
Saratov
Voronezh
Kursk
Orel
Kharkov
Kiev
Poltava
Ekaterinoslav
Tsaritsyn
Astrakhan
Rostov
RUSSIA
UKRAINE
RUMANIA
Odessa
Kherson
Sevastopol
CRIMEA
SEA OF AZOV
BLACK SEA
Bucharest
Varna
BULGARIA
Adrianople
Constantinople
Sea of Marmara
Smyrna
Athens
Rhodes
CRETE OR CANDIA
CYPRUS
Caucasus Mountains
Elbruz
Kasbek
Vladikavkas
Tiflis
Batum
Trebizond
GEORGIA
AZERBAIJAN
ARMENIA
Erivan
Erzerum
Baku
Apsheron Pen.
CASPIAN SEA
TURKEY
ANATOLIA
Taurus Mounts.
Kharput
Diarbekr
Aleppo
Alexandretta
SYRIA
Syrian Desert
Mosul
Tabriz
PERSIA
Hamadan
Kermanshah
Baghdad
MESOPOTAMIA
JOHN BARTHOLOMEW & SON, LTD.

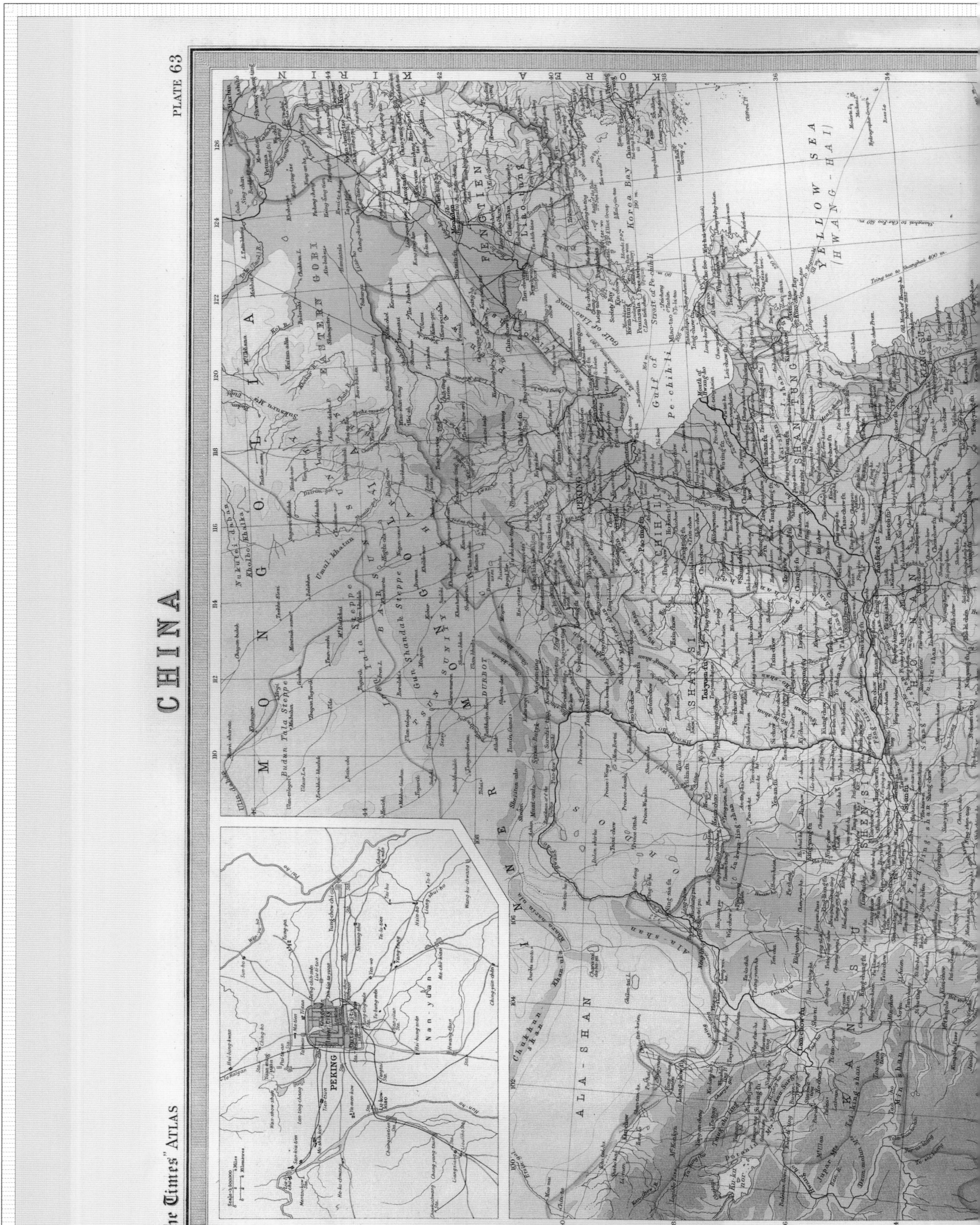

PLATE 63
CHINA
"The Times" ATLAS
PEKING
YELLOW SEA
(HWANG-HAI)
Gulf of Pe-chih-li
KOREA BAY
EASTERN GOBI
FENGTIEN
CHIH-LI
SHAN-TUNG
SHAN-SI
SHEN-SI
HO-NAN
KAN-SU
KIANG-SU
ALA-SHAN

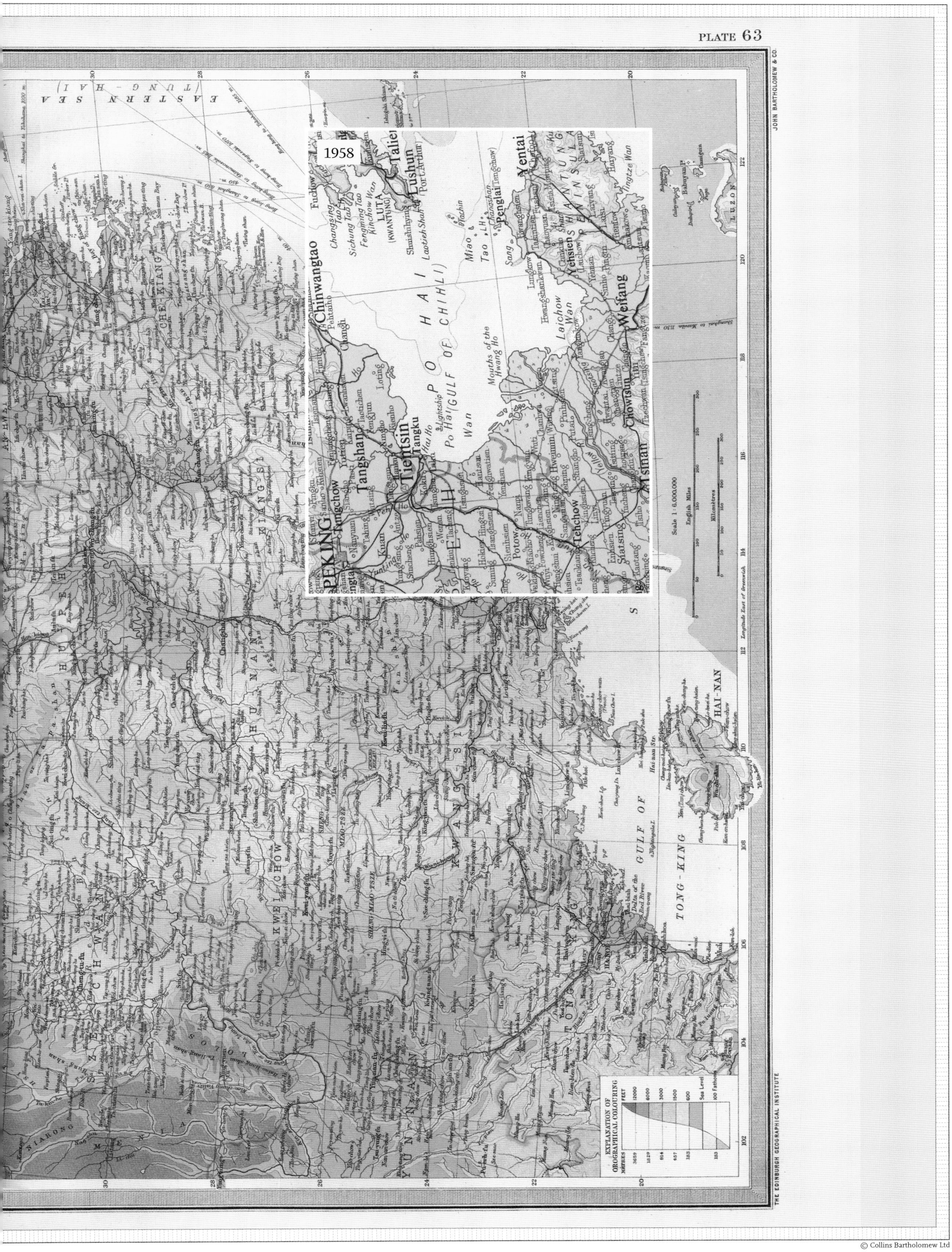
PLATE 63
1958
PEKING
Tientsin
Tangshan
Chinwangtao
Lushun
Yentai
Weifang
PO HAI (GULF OF CHIHLI)
EASTERN SEA
HAI-NAN
GULF OF TONG-KING
KWEI-CHOW
EXPLANATION OF OROGRAPHICAL COLOURING
JOHN BARTHOLOMEW & CO.
THE EDINBURGH GEOGRAPHICAL INSTITUTE

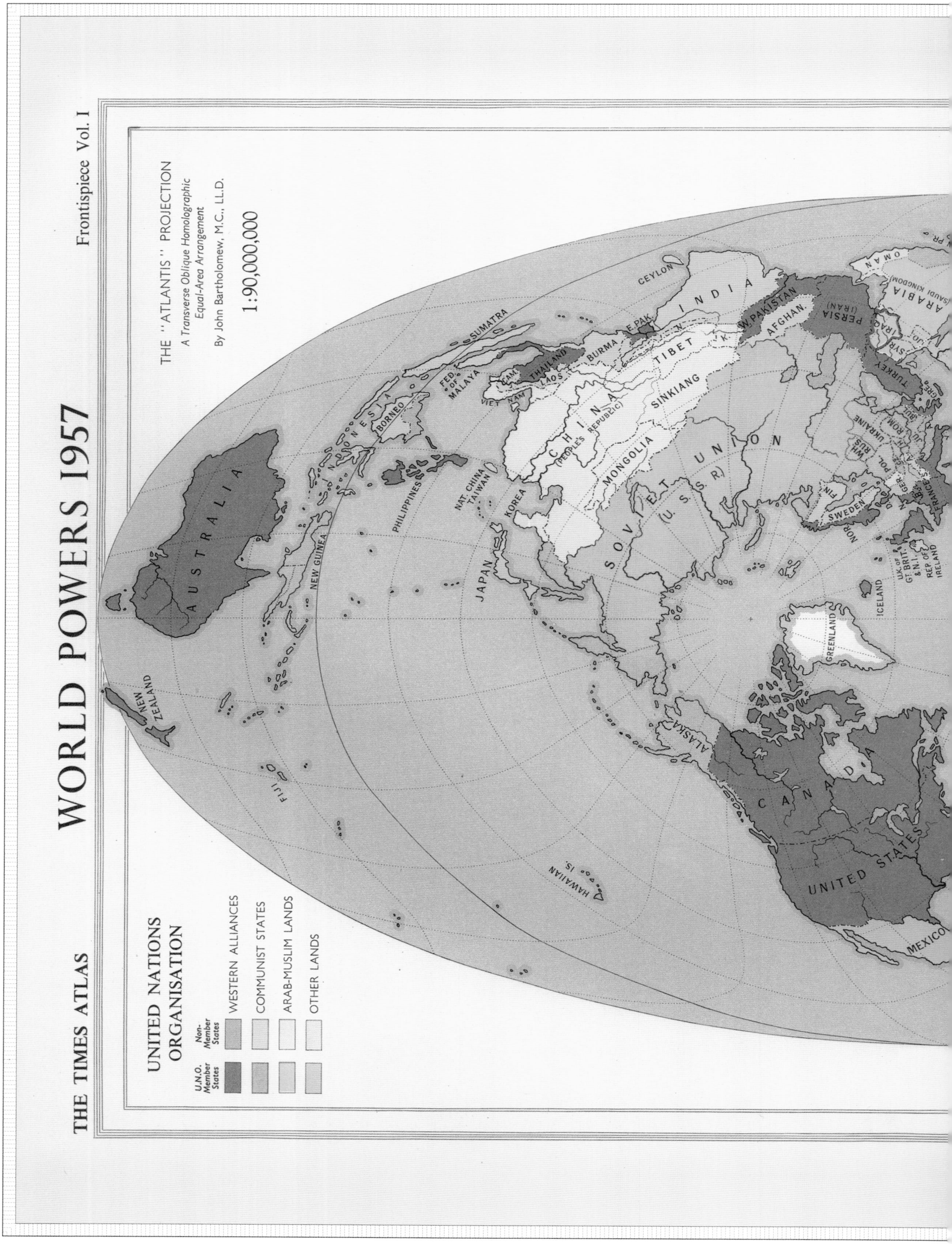
THE TIMES ATLAS
WORLD POWERS 1957
Frontispiece Vol. I
THE "ATLANTIS" PROJECTION
A Transverse Oblique Homolographic Equal-Area Arrangement
By John Bartholomew, M.C., LL.D.
1:90,000,000
UNITED NATIONS ORGANISATION
U.N.O. Member States
Non-Member States
WESTERN ALLIANCES
COMMUNIST STATES
ARAB-MUSLIM LANDS
OTHER LANDS
AUSTRALIA
NEW ZEALAND
FIJI
HAWAIIAN IS.
NEW GUINEA
PHILIPPINES
INDONESIA
BORNEO
SUMATRA
FED. OF MALAYA
THAILAND
LAOS
VIET NAM
BURMA
E.PAK.
CEYLON
INDIA
W.PAKISTAN
AFGHAN.
PERSIA (IRAN)
ARABIA (SAUDI KINGDOM)
OMAN
TURKEY
TIBET
SINKIANG
CHINA (PEOPLE'S REPUBLIC)
MONGOLIA
NAT. CHINA TAIWAN
KOREA
JAPAN
SOVIET UNION (U.S.S.R.)
FIN.
SWEDEN
NOR.
POL.
UKRAINE
ROM.
FRANCE
U.K. OF GT. BRIT. & N.I.
REP. OF IRELAND
ICELAND
GREENLAND
ALASKA
CANADA
UNITED STATES
MEXICO

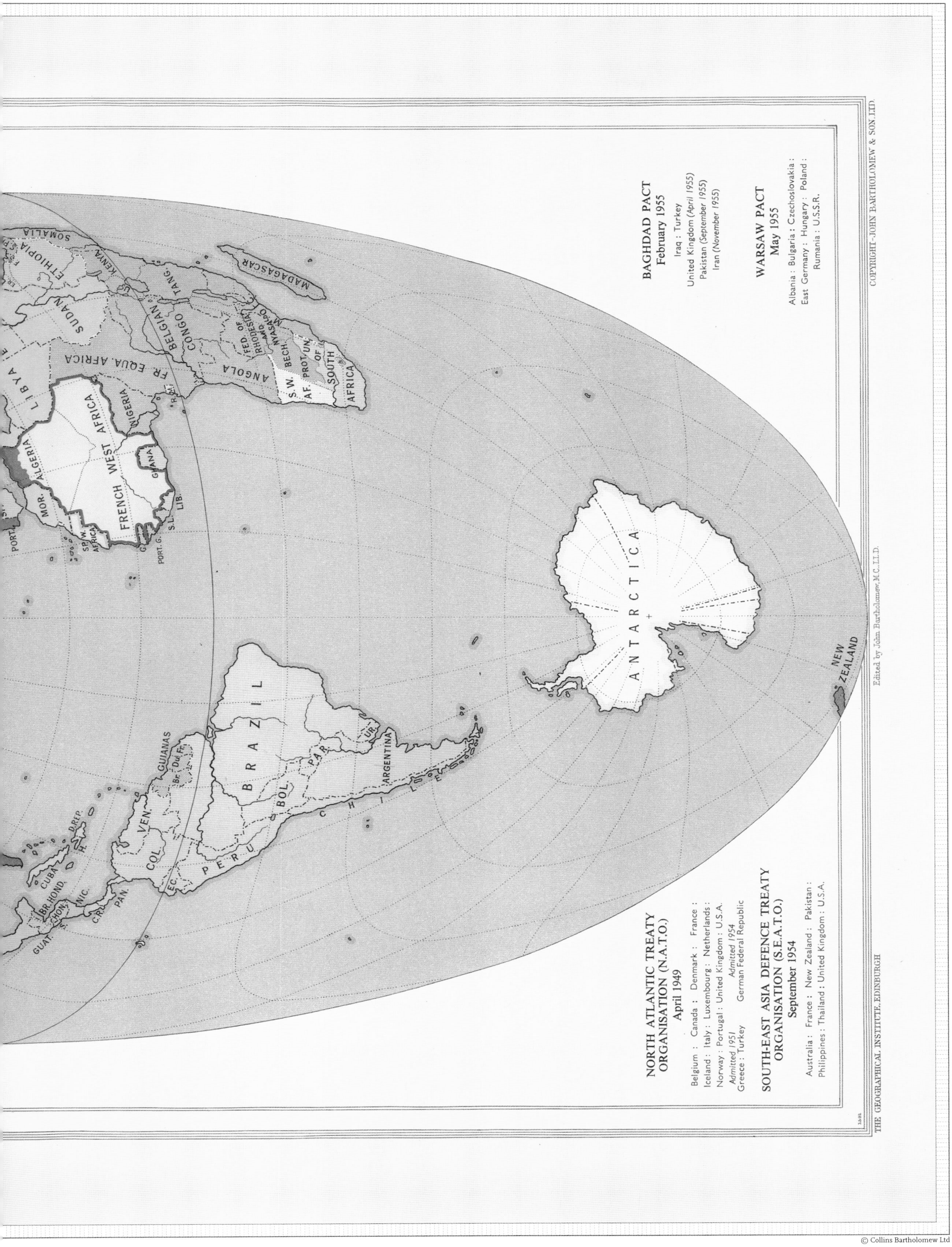
BAGHDAD PACT
February 1955
Iraq : Turkey
United Kingdom (April 1955)
Pakistan (September 1955)
Iran (November 1955)
WARSAW PACT
May 1955
Albania : Bulgaria : Czechoslovakia :
East Germany : Hungary : Poland :
Rumania : U.S.S.R.
NORTH ATLANTIC TREATY
ORGANISATION (N.A.T.O.)
April 1949
Belgium : Canada : Denmark : France :
Iceland : Italy : Luxembourg : Netherlands :
Norway : Portugal : United Kingdom : U.S.A.
Admitted 1951 Admitted 1954
Greece : Turkey German Federal Republic
SOUTH-EAST ASIA DEFENCE TREATY
ORGANISATION (S.E.A.T.O.)
September 1954
Australia : France : New Zealand : Pakistan :
Philippines : Thailand : United Kingdom : U.S.A.
COPYRIGHT-JOHN BARTHOLOMEW & SON, LTD.
Edited by John Bartholomew, M.C., LL.D.
THE GEOGRAPHICAL INSTITUTE, EDINBURGH
SOMALIA
ETHIOPIA
KENYA
MADAGASCAR
SUDAN
TANG.
BELGIAN CONGO
FED. OF RHODESIA AND NYASA.
FR. EQUA. AFRICA
ANGOLA
S.W. AF.
BECH. PROT.
UN. OF SOUTH AFRICA
LIBYA
NIGERIA
ALGERIA
FRENCH WEST AFRICA
GHANA
MOR.
SP. W. AFRICA
LIB.
S.L.
PORT. G.
ANTARCTICA
NEW ZEALAND
BRAZIL
GUIANAS
BOL.
PAR.
UR.
ARGENTINA
CHILE
PERU
VEN.
COL.
EC.
CUBA
BR. HOND.
NIC.
PAN.
GUAT.

# STATES AND TERRITORIES

All 196 independent countries and all populated dependent and disputed territories are included in this list of the states and territories of the world; the list is arranged in alphabetical order by the conventional name form. For independent states, the full name is given below the conventional name, if this is different; for territories, the status is given. The capital city name is given in conventional English form with selected alternative, usually local, form in brackets.

Area and population statistics are the latest available and include estimates. The information on languages and religions is based on the latest information on 'de facto' speakers of the language or 'de facto' adherents of the religion. This varies greatly from country to country because some countries include questions in censuses while others do not, in which case best estimates are used. The order of the languages and religions reflects their relative importance within the country; generally, languages or religions are included when more than one per cent of the population are estimated to be speakers or adherents.

## ABBREVIATIONS

CURRENCIES

| | |
|---|---|
| **CFA** | Communauté Financière Africaine |
| **CFP** | Comptoirs Français du Pacifique |

Membership of selected international organizations is shown by the abbreviations below; dependent territories do not normally have separate memberships of these organizations.

ORGANIZATIONS

| | |
|---|---|
| **APEC** | Asia-Pacific Economic Cooperation |
| **ASEAN** | Association of Southeast Asian Nations |
| **CARICOM** | Caribbean Community |
| **CIS** | Commonwealth of Independent States |
| **Comm.** | The Commonwealth |
| **EU** | European Union |
| **GCC** | Gulf Cooperation Council |
| **NATO** | North Atlantic Treaty Organization |
| **OECD** | Organisation for Economic Co-operation and Development |
| **OPEC** | Organization of the Petroleum Exporting Countries |
| **SADC** | Southern African Development Community |
| **UN** | United Nations |

### Abkhazia
Disputed territory

| | | | |
|---|---|---|---|
| **Area Sq Km** | 8 700 | **Languages** | Abkhaz, Russian, Georgian |
| **Area Sq Miles** | 3 359 | **Religions** | Abkhaz Orthodox Christianity, Sunni Muslim |
| **Population** | 180 000 | | |
| **Capital** | Sokhumi (Aq"a) | **Currency** | Russian rouble, Abkhaz apsar |

**Map page 173** An autonomous republic within Georgia, Abkhazia has an active separatist movement seeking independence from Georgia. Although it is de jure part of Georgia, it effectively currently functions as an independent state with backing from the Russian Federation. This dispute has led to intermittent, but serious, armed conflict over the last twenty years. Abkhazia voted to separate from Georgia in 1992, a move rejected by Georgia and prompting a Georgian invasion. Abkhazian and Russian forces ousted Georgia and a cease-fire was established in 1994.

### AFGHANISTAN
Islamic Republic of Afghanistan

| | | | |
|---|---|---|---|
| **Area Sq Km** | 652 225 | **Languages** | Dari, Pashto, Uzbek, Turkmen |
| **Area Sq Miles** | 251 825 | **Religions** | Sunni Muslim, Shi'a Muslim |
| **Population** | 32 358 000 | **Currency** | Afghani |
| **Capital** | Kābul | **Organizations** | UN |

**Map page 141**

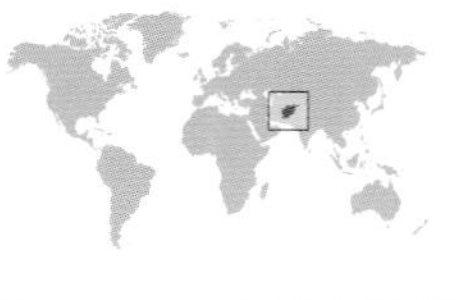

A landlocked country in central Asia with central highlands bordered by plains in the north and southwest, and by the mountains of the Hindu Kush in the northeast. The climate is dry continental. Over the last thirty years war has disrupted the economy, which is highly dependent on farming and livestock rearing. Most trade is with the former USSR, Pakistan and Iran.

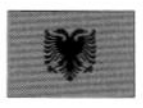

### ALBANIA
Republic of Albania

| | | | |
|---|---|---|---|
| **Area Sq Km** | 28 748 | **Languages** | Albanian, Greek |
| **Area Sq Miles** | 11 100 | **Religions** | Sunni Muslim, Albanian Orthodox, Roman Catholic |
| **Population** | 3 216 000 | | |
| **Capital** | Tirana (Tiranë) | **Currency** | Lek |
| | | **Organizations** | NATO, UN |

**Map page 171**

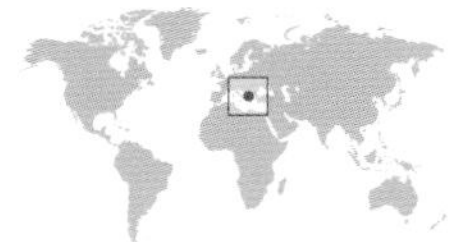

Albania lies in the western Balkan Mountains in southeastern Europe, bordering the Adriatic Sea. It is mountainous, with coastal plains where half the population lives. The economy is based on agriculture and mining. Albania is one of the poorest countries in Europe and relies heavily on foreign aid.

### ALGERIA
People's Democratic Republic of Algeria

| | | | |
|---|---|---|---|
| **Area Sq Km** | 2 381 741 | **Languages** | Arabic, French, Berber |
| **Area Sq Miles** | 919 595 | **Religions** | Sunni Muslim |
| **Population** | 35 980 000 | **Currency** | Algerian dinar |
| **Capital** | Algiers (Alger) | **Organizations** | OPEC, UN |

**Map page 176**

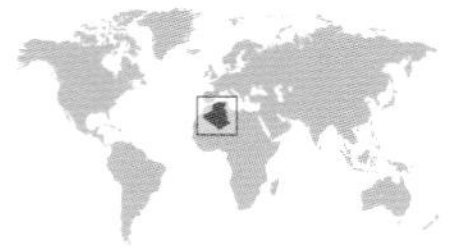

Algeria, the largest country in Africa, lies on the Mediterranean coast of northwest Africa and extends southwards to the Atlas Mountains and the dry sandstone plateau and desert of the Sahara. The climate ranges from Mediterranean on the coast to semi-arid and arid inland. The most populated areas are the coastal plains and the fertile northern slopes of the Atlas Mountains. Oil, natural gas and related products account for over ninety per cent of export earnings. Agriculture employs about a quarter of the workforce, producing mainly food crops. Algeria's main trading partners are Italy, France and the USA.

### American Samoa
United States Unincorporated Territory

| | | | |
|---|---|---|---|
| **Area Sq Km** | 197 | **Languages** | Samoan, English |
| **Area Sq Miles** | 76 | **Religions** | Protestant, Roman Catholic |
| **Population** | 70 000 | **Currency** | United States dollar |
| **Capital** | Fagatogo | | |

**Map page 123**

Lying in the south Pacific Ocean, American Samoa consists of five main islands and two coral atolls. The largest island is Tutuila. Tuna and tuna products are the main exports, and the main trading partner is the USA.

### ANDORRA
Principality of Andorra

| | | | |
|---|---|---|---|
| **Area Sq Km** | 465 | **Languages** | Catalan, Spanish, French |
| **Area Sq Miles** | 180 | **Religions** | Roman Catholic |
| **Population** | 86 000 | **Currency** | Euro |
| **Capital** | Andorra la Vella | **Organizations** | UN |

**Map page 167**

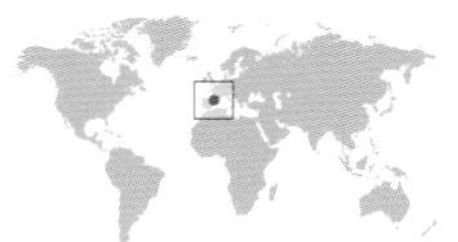

A landlocked state in southwest Europe, Andorra lies in the Pyrenees mountain range between France and Spain. It consists of deep valleys and gorges, surrounded by mountains. Tourism, encouraged by the development of ski resorts, is the mainstay of the economy. Banking is also an important economic activity.

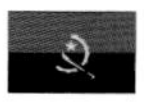

### ANGOLA
Republic of Angola

| | | | |
|---|---|---|---|
| **Area Sq Km** | 1 246 700 | **Languages** | Portuguese, Bantu, local languages |
| **Area Sq Miles** | 481 354 | | |
| **Population** | 19 618 000 | **Religions** | Roman Catholic, Protestant, traditional beliefs |
| **Capital** | Luanda | | |
| | | **Currency** | Kwanza |
| | | **Organizations** | OPEC, SADC, UN |

**Map page 176–177**

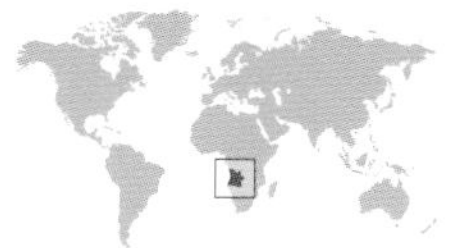

Angola lies on the Atlantic coast of south central Africa. Its small northern province, Cabinda, is separated from the rest of the country by part of the Democratic Republic of the Congo. Much of Angola is high plateau. In the west is a narrow coastal plain and in the southwest is desert. The climate is equatorial in the north but desert in the south. Over eighty per cent of the population relies on subsistence agriculture. Angola is rich in minerals (particularly diamonds), and oil accounts for approximately ninety per cent of export earnings. The USA, South Korea and Portugal are its main trading partners.

### Anguilla
United Kingdom Overseas Territory

| | | | |
|---|---|---|---|
| **Area Sq Km** | 155 | **Languages** | English |
| **Area Sq Miles** | 60 | **Religions** | Protestant, Roman Catholic |
| **Population** | 16 000 | **Currency** | East Caribbean dollar |
| **Capital** | The Valley | | |

**Map page 205** Anguilla lies at the northern end of the Leeward Islands in the eastern Caribbean. Tourism and fishing form the basis of the economy.

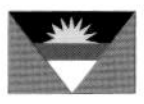

### ANTIGUA AND BARBUDA

| | | | |
|---|---|---|---|
| **Area Sq Km** | 442 | **Languages** | English, Creole |
| **Area Sq Miles** | 171 | **Religions** | Protestant, Roman Catholic |
| **Population** | 90 000 | **Currency** | East Caribbean dollar |
| **Capital** | St John's | **Organizations** | CARICOM, Comm., UN |

**Map page 205**

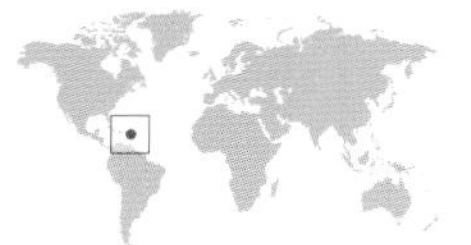

The state comprises the islands of Antigua, Barbuda and the tiny rocky outcrop of Redonda, in the Leeward Islands in the eastern Caribbean. Antigua, the largest and most populous island, is mainly hilly scrubland, with many beaches. The climate is tropical, and the economy relies heavily on tourism. Most trade is with other eastern Caribbean states and the USA.

### ARGENTINA
Argentine Republic

| | | | |
|---|---|---|---|
| **Area Sq Km** | 2 766 889 | **Languages** | Spanish, Italian, Amerindian languages |
| **Area Sq Miles** | 1 068 302 | | |
| **Population** | 40 765 000 | **Religions** | Roman Catholic, Protestant |
| **Capital** | Buenos Aires | **Currency** | Argentinian peso |
| | | **Organizations** | UN |

**Map page 212**

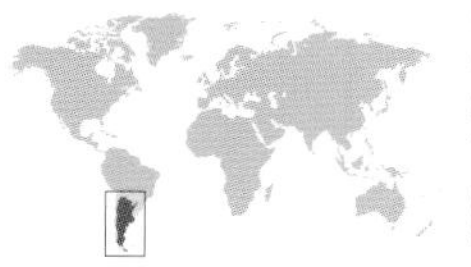

Argentina, the second largest state in South America, extends from Bolivia to Cape Horn and from the Andes mountains to the Atlantic Ocean. It has four geographical regions: subtropical forests and swampland in the northeast; temperate fertile plains or Pampas in the centre; the wooded foothills and valleys of the Andes in the west; and the cold, semi-arid plateaus of Patagonia in the south. The highest mountain in South America, Cerro Aconcagua, is in Argentina. Nearly ninety per cent of the population lives in towns and cities. The country is rich in natural resources including petroleum, natural gas, ores and precious metals. Agricultural products dominate exports, which also include motor vehicles and crude oil. Most trade is with Brazil and the USA.

### ARMENIA
Republic of Armenia

| | | | |
|---|---|---|---|
| **Area Sq Km** | 29 800 | **Languages** | Armenian, Yezidi |
| **Area Sq Miles** | 11 506 | **Religions** | Armenian Orthodox |
| **Population** | 3 100 000 | **Currency** | Dram |
| **Capital** | Yerevan (Erevan) | **Organizations** | CIS, UN |

**Map page 137**

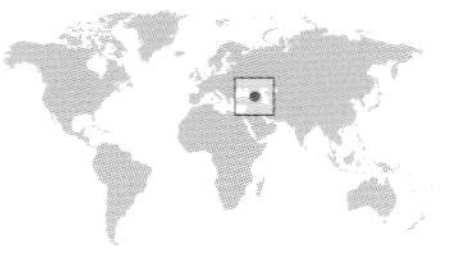

A landlocked state in southwest Asia, Armenia lies in the south of the Lesser Caucasus mountains. It is a mountainous country with a continental climate. One-third of the population lives in the capital, Yerevan. Exports include diamonds, scrap metal and machinery. Many Armenians depend on remittances from abroad.

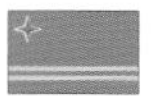

### Aruba
Self-governing Netherlands Territory

| | | | |
|---|---|---|---|
| **Area Sq Km** | 193 | **Languages** | Papiamento, Dutch, English |
| **Area Sq Miles** | 75 | **Religions** | Roman Catholic, Protestant |
| **Population** | 108 000 | **Currency** | Aruban florin |
| **Capital** | Oranjestad | | |

**Map page 213** The most southwesterly of the islands in the Lesser Antilles in the Caribbean, Aruba lies just off the coast of Venezuela. Tourism, offshore finance and oil refining are the most important sectors of the economy. The USA is the main trading partner.

### AUSTRALIA
Commonwealth of Australia

| | | | |
|---|---|---|---|
| **Area Sq Km** | 7 692 024 | **Languages** | English, Italian, Greek |
| **Area Sq Miles** | 2 969 907 | **Religions** | Protestant, Roman Catholic, Orthodox |
| **Population** | 22 606 000 | | |
| **Capital** | Canberra | **Currency** | Australian dollar |
| | | **Organizations** | APEC, Comm., OECD, UN |

**Map page 124**

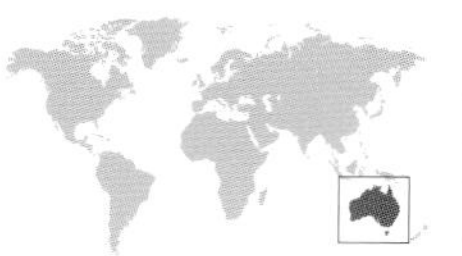

Australia, the world's sixth largest country, occupies the smallest, flattest and driest continent. The western half of the continent is mostly arid plateaus, ridges and vast deserts. The central eastern area comprises the lowlands of river systems draining into

Lake Eyre, while to the east is the Great Dividing Range, a belt of ridges and plateaus running from Queensland to Tasmania. Climatically, more than two-thirds of the country is arid or semi-arid. The north is tropical monsoon, the east subtropical, and the southwest and southeast temperate. The majority of Australia's highly urbanized population lives along the east, southeast and southwest coasts. Australia has vast mineral deposits and various sources of energy. It is among the world's leading producers of iron ore, bauxite, nickel, copper and uranium. It is a major producer of coal, and oil and natural gas are also being exploited. Although accounting for less than five per cent of the workforce, agriculture continues to be an important sector of the economy, with food and agricultural raw materials making up most of Australia's export earnings. Fuel, ores and metals, and manufactured goods, account for the remainder of exports. China, Japan and the USA are Australia's main trading partners.

**Australian Capital Territory (Federal Territory)**
**Area Sq Km (Sq Miles)** 2 358 (910) **Population** 359 700 **Capital** Canberra

**Jervis Bay Territory (Territory)**
**Area Sq Km (Sq Miles)** 73 (28) **Population** 611

**New South Wales (State)**
**Area Sq Km (Sq Miles)** 800 642 (309 130) **Population** 7 253 400 **Capital** Sydney

**Northern Territory (Territory)**
**Area Sq Km (Sq Miles)** 1 349 129 (520 902) **Population** 230 200 **Capital** Darwin

**Queensland (State)**
**Area Sq Km (Sq Miles)** 1 730 648 (668 207) **Population** 4 532 300 **Capital** Brisbane

**South Australia (State)**
**Area Sq Km (Sq Miles)** 983 482 (379 725) **Population** 1 647 800 **Capital** Adelaide

**Tasmania (State)**
**Area Sq Km (Sq Miles)** 68 401 (26 410) **Population** 508 500 **Capital** Hobart

**Victoria (State)**
**Area Sq Km (Sq Miles)** 227 416 (87 806) **Population** 5 567 100 **Capital** Melbourne

**Western Australia (State)**
**Area Sq Km (Sq Miles)** 2 529 875 (976 790) **Population** 2 306 200 **Capital** Perth

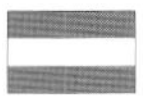

## AUSTRIA
Republic of Austria

| | | | |
|---|---|---|---|
| **Area Sq Km** | 83 855 | **Languages** | German, Croatian, Turkish |
| **Area Sq Miles** | 32 377 | **Religions** | Roman Catholic, Protestant |
| **Population** | 8 413 000 | **Currency** | Euro |
| **Capital** | Vienna (Wien) | **Organizations** | EU, OECD, UN |

**Map page 168**

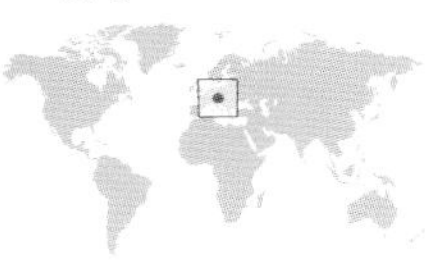

Two-thirds of Austria, a landlocked state in central Europe, lies within the Alps, with lower mountains to the north. The only lowlands are in the east. The Danube river valley in the northeast contains almost all the agricultural land and most of the population. Although the climate varies with altitude, in general summers are warm and winters cold with heavy snowfalls. Manufacturing industry and tourism are the most important sectors of the economy. Exports are dominated by manufactured goods. Germany is Austria's main trading partner.

## AZERBAIJAN
Republic of Azerbaijan

| | | | |
|---|---|---|---|
| **Area Sq Km** | 86 600 | **Languages** | Azeri, Armenian, Russian, Lezgian |
| **Area Sq Miles** | 33 436 | **Religions** | Shi'a Muslim, Sunni Muslim, Russian and Armenian Orthodox |
| **Population** | 9 306 000 | **Currency** | Azerbaijani manat |
| **Capital** | Baku | **Organizations** | CIS, UN |

**Map page 137**

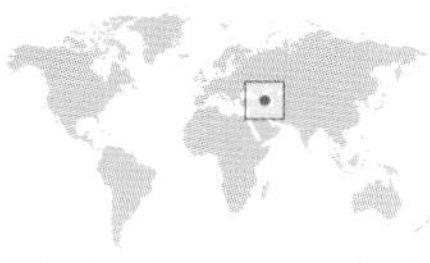

Azerbaijan lies to the southeast of the Caucasus mountains, on the Caspian Sea. Its region of Naxçıvan is separated from the rest of the country by part of Armenia. It has mountains in the northeast and west, valleys in the centre, and a low coastal plain. The climate is continental. It is rich in energy and mineral resources. Oil production, onshore and offshore, is the main industry and the basis of heavy industries. Agriculture is important, with cotton and tobacco the main cash crops.

## THE BAHAMAS
Commonwealth of The Bahamas

| | | | |
|---|---|---|---|
| **Area Sq Km** | 13 939 | **Languages** | English, Creole |
| **Area Sq Miles** | 5 382 | **Religions** | Protestant, Roman Catholic |
| **Population** | 347 000 | **Currency** | Bahamian dollar |
| **Capital** | Nassau | **Organizations** | CARICOM, Comm., UN |

**Map page 205**

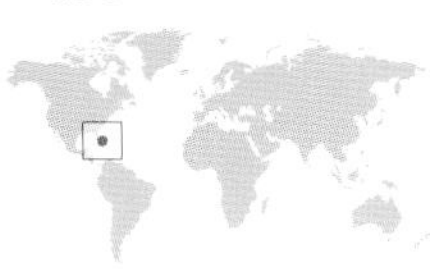

The Bahamas, an archipelago made up of approximately seven hundred islands and over two thousand cays, lies to the northeast of Cuba and east of the Florida coast of the USA. Twenty-two islands are inhabited, and two-thirds of the population lives on the main island of New Providence. The climate is warm for much of the year, with heavy rainfall in the summer. Tourism is the islands' main industry. Offshore banking, insurance and ship registration are also major foreign exchange earners.

## BAHRAIN
Kingdom of Bahrain

| | | | |
|---|---|---|---|
| **Area Sq Km** | 691 | **Languages** | Arabic, English |
| **Area Sq Miles** | 267 | **Religions** | Shi'a Muslim, Sunni Muslim, Christian |
| **Population** | 1 324 000 | **Currency** | Bahraini dinar |
| **Capital** | Manama (Al Manāmah) | **Organizations** | GCC, UN |

**Map page 140**

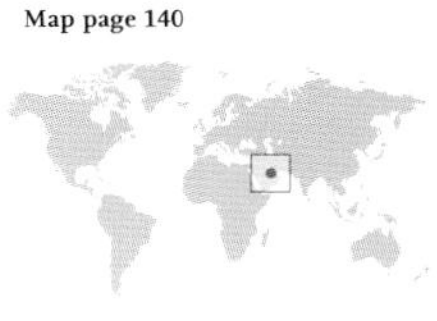

Bahrain consists of more than thirty islands lying in a bay in The Gulf, off the coasts of Saudi Arabia and Qatar. Bahrain Island, the largest island, is connected to other islands and to the mainland of Arabia by causeways. Oil production and processing are the main sectors of the economy.

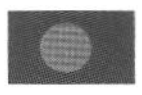

## BANGLADESH
People's Republic of Bangladesh

| | | | |
|---|---|---|---|
| **Area Sq Km** | 143 998 | **Languages** | Bengali, English |
| **Area Sq Miles** | 55 598 | **Religions** | Sunni Muslim, Hindu |
| **Population** | 150 494 000 | **Currency** | Taka |
| **Capital** | Dhaka (Dacca) | **Organizations** | Comm., UN |

**Map page 145**

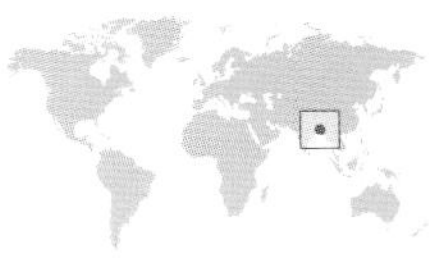

The south Asian state of Bangladesh is in the northeast of the Indian subcontinent, on the Bay of Bengal. It consists almost entirely of the low-lying alluvial plains and deltas of the Ganges and Brahmaputra rivers. The southwest is swampy, with mangrove forests in the delta area. The north, northeast and southeast have low forested hills. Bangladesh is one of the world's most densely populated and least developed countries. The economy is based on agriculture, though the garment industry is the main export sector. Storms during the summer monsoon season often cause devastating flooding and crop destruction. The country relies on large-scale foreign aid and remittances from workers abroad.

## BARBADOS

| | | | |
|---|---|---|---|
| **Area Sq Km** | 430 | **Languages** | English, Creole |
| **Area Sq Miles** | 166 | **Religions** | Protestant, Roman Catholic |
| **Population** | 274 000 | **Currency** | Barbados dollar |
| **Capital** | Bridgetown | **Organizations** | CARICOM, Comm., UN |

**Map page 205**

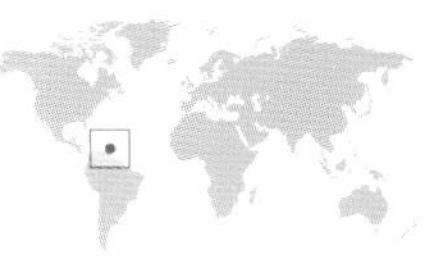

The most easterly of the Caribbean islands, Barbados is small and densely populated. It has a tropical climate and is subject to hurricanes. The economy is based on tourism, financial services, light industries and sugar production.

## BELARUS
Republic of Belarus

| | | | |
|---|---|---|---|
| **Area Sq Km** | 207 600 | **Languages** | Belorussian, Russian |
| **Area Sq Miles** | 80 155 | **Religions** | Belorussian Orthodox, Roman Catholic |
| **Population** | 9 559 000 | **Currency** | Belarus rouble |
| **Capital** | Minsk | **Organizations** | CIS, UN |

**Map page 169**

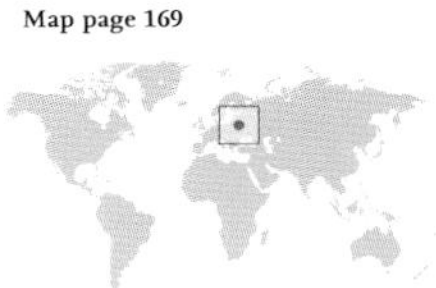

Belarus, a landlocked state in eastern Europe, consists of low hills and plains, with many lakes, rivers and, in the south, extensive marshes. Forests cover approximately one-third of the country. It has a continental climate. Agriculture contributes one-third of national income, with beef cattle and grains as the major products. Manufacturing industries produce a range of items, from construction equipment to textiles. The Russian Federation and Ukraine are the main trading partners.

## BELGIUM
Kingdom of Belgium

| | | | |
|---|---|---|---|
| **Area Sq Km** | 30 520 | **Languages** | Dutch (Flemish), French (Walloon), German |
| **Area Sq Miles** | 11 784 | **Religions** | Roman Catholic, Protestant |
| **Population** | 10 754 000 | **Currency** | Euro |
| **Capital** | Brussels (Bruxelles) | **Organizations** | EU, NATO, OECD, UN |

**Map page 164**

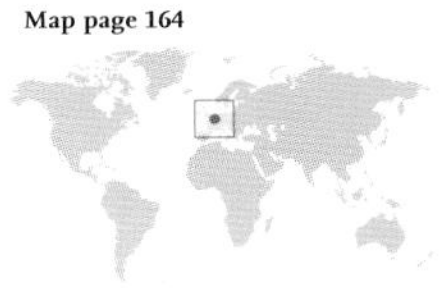

Belgium lies on the North Sea coast of western Europe. Beyond low sand dunes and a narrow belt of reclaimed land, fertile plains extend to the Sambre-Meuse river valley. The land rises to the forested Ardennes plateau in the southeast. Belgium has mild winters and cool summers. It is densely populated and has a highly urbanized population. With few mineral resources, Belgium imports raw materials for processing and manufacture. The agricultural sector is small, but provides for most food needs. A large services sector reflects Belgium's position as the home base for over eight hundred international institutions. The headquarters of the European Union are in the capital, Brussels.

## BELIZE

| | | | |
|---|---|---|---|
| **Area Sq Km** | 22 965 | **Languages** | English, Spanish, Mayan, Creole |
| **Area Sq Miles** | 8 867 | **Religions** | Roman Catholic, Protestant |
| **Population** | 318 000 | **Currency** | Belize dollar |
| **Capital** | Belmopan | **Organizations** | CARICOM, Comm., UN |

**Map page 207**

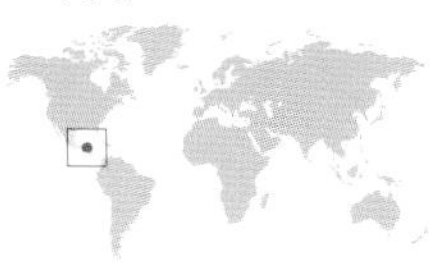

Belize lies on the Caribbean coast of central America and includes numerous cays and a large barrier reef offshore. The coastal areas are flat and swampy. To the southwest are the Maya Mountains. Tropical jungle covers much of the country and the climate is humid tropical, but tempered by sea breezes. A third of the population lives in the capital. The economy is based primarily on agriculture, forestry and fishing, and exports include raw sugar, orange concentrate and bananas.

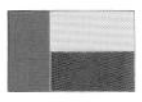

## BENIN
Republic of Benin

| | | | |
|---|---|---|---|
| **Area Sq Km** | 112 620 | **Languages** | French, Fon, Yoruba, Adja, local languages |
| **Area Sq Miles** | 43 483 | **Religions** | Traditional beliefs, Roman Catholic, Sunni Muslim |
| **Population** | 9 100 000 | **Currency** | CFA franc |
| **Capital** | Porto-Novo | **Organizations** | UN |

**Map page 176**

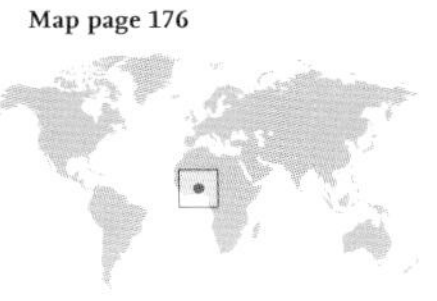

Benin is in west Africa, on the Gulf of Guinea. The climate is tropical in the north, equatorial in the south. The economy is based mainly on agriculture and transit trade. Agricultural products account for two-thirds of export earnings. Oil, produced offshore, is also a major export.

## Bermuda
United Kingdom Overseas Territory

| | | | |
|---|---|---|---|
| **Area Sq Km** | 54 | **Languages** | English |
| **Area Sq Miles** | 21 | **Religions** | Protestant, Roman Catholic |
| **Population** | 65 000 | **Currency** | Bermuda dollar |
| **Capital** | Hamilton | | |

**Map page 205** In the Atlantic Ocean to the east of the USA, Bermuda comprises a group of small islands with a warm and humid climate. The economy is based on international business and tourism.

## BHUTAN
Kingdom of Bhutan

| | | | |
|---|---|---|---|
| **Area Sq Km** | 46 620 | **Languages** | Dzongkha, Nepali, Assamese |
| **Area Sq Miles** | 18 000 | **Religions** | Buddhist, Hindu |
| **Population** | 738 000 | **Currency** | Ngultrum, Indian rupee |
| **Capital** | Thimphu | **Organizations** | UN |

**Map page 145**

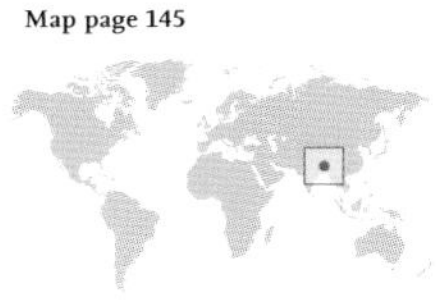

Bhutan lies in the eastern Himalaya mountains, between China and India. It is mountainous in the north, with fertile valleys. The climate ranges between permanently cold in the far north and subtropical in the south. Most of the population is involved in livestock rearing and subsistence farming. Bhutan is a producer of cardamom. Tourism is an increasingly important foreign currency earner, and hydroelectric power is also sold to India from the Tala site in the southwest.

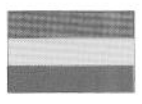

## BOLIVIA
Plurinational State of Bolivia

| | | | |
|---|---|---|---|
| **Area Sq Km** | 1 098 581 | **Languages** | Spanish, Quechua, Aymara |
| **Area Sq Miles** | 424 164 | **Religions** | Roman Catholic, Protestant, Baha'i |
| **Population** | 10 088 000 | **Currency** | Boliviano |
| **Capital** | La Paz/Sucre | **Organizations** | UN |

**Map page 210**

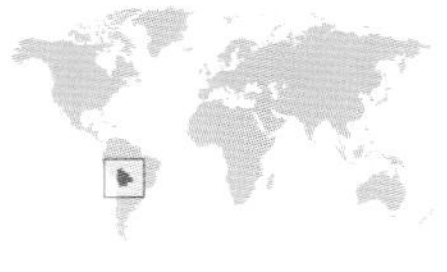

Bolivia is a landlocked state in central South America. Most Bolivians live on the high plateau within the Andes mountains. The lowlands range between dense rainforest in the northeast and semi-arid grasslands in the southeast. Bolivia is rich in minerals (zinc, tin and gold), and sales generate approximately a quarter of export income. Natural gas, timber and soya beans are also exported. Brazil is the main trading partner.

## BOSNIA-HERZEGOVINA
Republic of Bosnia and Herzegovina

| | | | |
|---|---|---|---|
| **Area Sq Km** | 51 130 | **Languages** | Bosnian, Serbian, Croatian |
| **Area Sq Miles** | 19 741 | **Religions** | Sunni Muslim, Serbian Orthodox, Roman Catholic, Protestant |
| **Population** | 3 752 000 | **Currency** | Marka |
| **Capital** | Sarajevo | **Organizations** | UN |

**Map page 170–171**

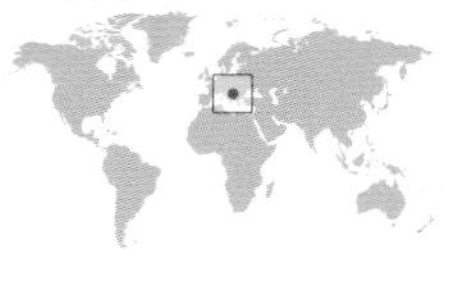

Bosnia-Herzegovina lies in the western Balkan Mountains of southern Europe, on the Adriatic Sea. It is mountainous, with ridges running northwest-southeast. The main lowlands are around the Sava valley in the north. Summers are warm, but winters can be very cold. The economy relies heavily on overseas aid.

## BOTSWANA
Republic of Botswana

| | | | |
|---|---|---|---|
| **Area Sq Km** | 581 370 | **Languages** | English, Setswana, Shona, local languages |
| **Area Sq Miles** | 224 468 | **Religions** | Traditional beliefs, Protestant, Roman Catholic |
| **Population** | 2 031 000 | **Currency** | Pula |
| **Capital** | Gaborone | **Organizations** | Comm., SADC, UN |

**Map page 179**

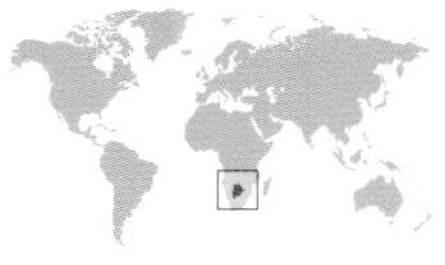

Botswana is a landlocked state in southern Africa. Over half of the country lies within the Kalahari Desert, with swamps to the north and salt-pans to the northeast. Most of the population lives near the eastern border. The climate is subtropical, but drought-prone. The economy was founded on cattle rearing, and although beef remains an important export, the economy is now based on mining. Diamonds account for seventy per cent of export earnings. Copper-nickel matte is also exported. The main trading partners are South Africa and the UK.

## BRAZIL
Federative Republic of Brazil

| | | | |
|---|---|---|---|
| **Area Sq Km** | 8 514 879 | **Languages** | Portuguese |
| **Area Sq Miles** | 3 287 613 | **Religions** | Roman Catholic, Protestant |
| **Population** | 196 655 000 | **Currency** | Real |
| **Capital** | Brasília | **Organizations** | UN |

**Map page 210–211**

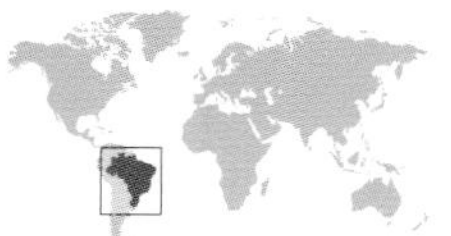

Brazil, in eastern South America, covers almost half of the continent, and is the world's fifth largest country. The northwest contains the vast basin of the Amazon, while the centre-west is largely a vast plateau of savanna and rock escarpments. The northeast is mostly semi-arid plateaus, while to the east and south are rugged mountains, fertile valleys and narrow, fertile coastal plains. The Amazon basin is hot, humid and wet; the rest of the country is cooler and drier, with seasonal variations. The northeast is drought-prone. Most Brazilians live in urban areas along the coast and on the central plateau. Brazil has well-developed agricultural, mining and service sectors, and the economy is larger than that of all other South American countries combined. Brazil is the world's biggest producer of coffee, and other agricultural crops include grains and sugar cane. Mineral production includes iron, aluminium and gold. Manufactured goods include food products, transport equipment, machinery and industrial chemicals. The main trading partners are the USA, China and Argentina. Economic reforms in Brazil have turned it into one of the fastest growing economies.

## BRUNEI
State of Brunei Darussalam

| | | | |
|---|---|---|---|
| **Area Sq Km** | 5 765 | **Languages** | Malay, English, Chinese |
| **Area Sq Miles** | 2 226 | **Religions** | Sunni Muslim, Buddhist, Christian |
| **Population** | 406 000 | **Currency** | Brunei dollar |
| **Capital** | Bandar Seri Begawan | **Organizations** | APEC, ASEAN, Comm., UN |

**Map page 155**

The southeast Asian oil-rich state of Brunei lies on the northwest coast of the island of Borneo, on the South China Sea. Its two enclaves are surrounded by the Malaysian state of Sarawak. Tropical rainforest covers over two-thirds of the country. The economy is dominated by the oil and gas industries.

## BULGARIA
Republic of Bulgaria

| | | | |
|---|---|---|---|
| **Area Sq Km** | 110 994 | **Languages** | Bulgarian, Turkish, Romany, Macedonian |
| **Area Sq Miles** | 42 855 | **Religions** | Bulgarian Orthodox, Sunni Muslim |
| **Population** | 7 446 000 | **Currency** | Lev |
| **Capital** | Sofia (Sofiya) | **Organizations** | EU, NATO, UN |

**Map page 171**

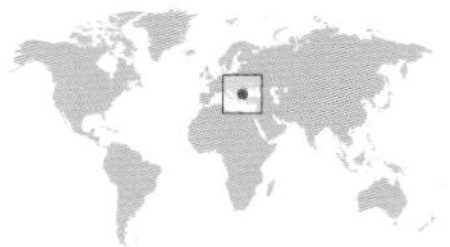

Bulgaria, in southern Europe, borders the western shore of the Black Sea. The Balkan Mountains separate the Danube plains in the north from the Rhodope Mountains and the lowlands in the south. The economy has a strong agricultural base. Manufacturing industries include machinery, consumer goods, chemicals and metals. Most trade is with the Russian Federation, Italy and Germany.

## BURKINA FASO
Democratic Republic of Burkina Faso

| | | | |
|---|---|---|---|
| **Area Sq Km** | 274 200 | **Languages** | French, Moore (Mossi), Fulani, local languages |
| **Area Sq Miles** | 105 869 | **Religions** | Sunni Muslim, traditional beliefs, Roman Catholic |
| **Population** | 16 968 000 | **Currency** | CFA franc |
| **Capital** | Ouagadougou | **Organizations** | UN |

**Map page 176**

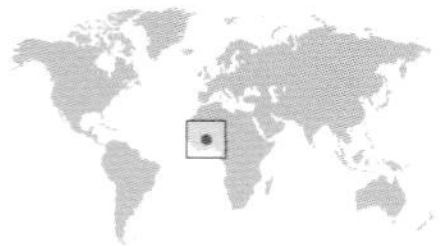

Burkina Faso, a landlocked country in west Africa, lies within the Sahara desert to the north and semi-arid savanna to the south. Rainfall is erratic, and droughts are common. Livestock rearing and farming are the main activities, and cotton, livestock, groundnuts and some minerals are exported. Burkina Faso relies heavily on foreign aid, and is one of the poorest and least developed countries in the world.

## BURUNDI
Republic of Burundi

| | | | |
|---|---|---|---|
| **Area Sq Km** | 27 835 | **Languages** | Kirundi (Hutu, Tutsi), French |
| **Area Sq Miles** | 10 747 | **Religions** | Roman Catholic, traditional beliefs, Protestant |
| **Population** | 8 575 000 | **Currency** | Burundian franc |
| **Capital** | Bujumbura | **Organizations** | UN |

**Map page 178**

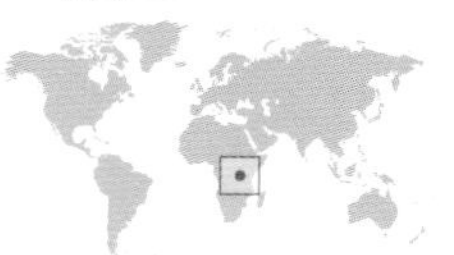

The densely populated east African state of Burundi consists of high plateaus rising from the shores of Lake Tanganyika in the southwest. It has a tropical climate and depends on subsistence farming. Coffee is its main export, and its main trading partners are Germany and Belgium. The country has been badly affected by internal conflict since the early 1990s.

## CAMBODIA
Kingdom of Cambodia

| | | | |
|---|---|---|---|
| **Area Sq Km** | 181 035 | **Languages** | Khmer, Vietnamese |
| **Area Sq Miles** | 69 884 | **Religions** | Buddhist, Roman Catholic, Sunni Muslim |
| **Population** | 14 305 000 | **Currency** | Riel |
| **Capital** | Phnom Penh (Phnom Pénh) | **Organizations** | ASEAN, UN |

**Map page 154**

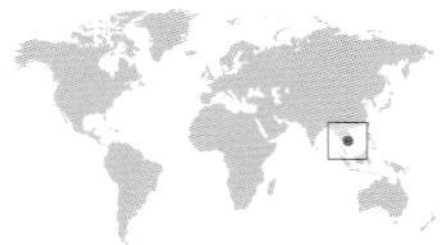

Cambodia lies in southeast Asia on the Gulf of Thailand, and occupies the Mekong river basin, with the Tônlé Sap (Great Lake) at its centre. The climate is tropical monsoon. Forests cover half the country. Most of the population lives on the plains and is engaged in farming (chiefly rice growing), fishing and forestry. The economy is recovering following the devastation of civil war in the 1970s, with rapid progress since 2000. Mineral resources are starting to be identified for development.

## CAMEROON
Republic of Cameroon

| | | | |
|---|---|---|---|
| **Area Sq Km** | 475 442 | **Languages** | French, English, Fang, Bamileke, local languages |
| **Area Sq Miles** | 183 569 | **Religions** | Roman Catholic, traditional beliefs, Sunni Muslim, Protestant |
| **Population** | 20 030 000 | **Currency** | CFA franc |
| **Capital** | Yaoundé | **Organizations** | Comm., UN |

**Map page 176–177**

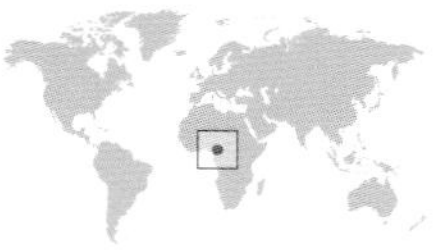

Cameroon is in west Africa, on the Gulf of Guinea. The coastal plains and southern and central plateaus are covered with tropical forest. Despite oil resources and favourable agricultural conditions Cameroon still faces problems of underdevelopment. Oil, timber and cocoa are the main exports. France is the main trading partner.

## CANADA

| | | | |
|---|---|---|---|
| **Area Sq Km** | 9 984 670 | **Languages** | English, French |
| **Area Sq Miles** | 3 855 103 | **Religions** | Roman Catholic, Protestant, Eastern Orthodox, Jewish |
| **Population** | 34 350 000 | **Currency** | Canadian dollar |
| **Capital** | Ottawa | **Organizations** | APEC, Comm., NATO, OECD, UN |

**Map page 184–185**

The world's second largest country, Canada covers the northern two-fifths of North America and has coastlines on the Atlantic, Arctic and Pacific Oceans. In the west are the Coast Mountains, the Rocky Mountains and interior plateaus. In the centre lie the fertile Prairies. Further east, covering about half the total land area, is the Canadian Shield, a relatively flat area of infertile lowlands around Hudson Bay, extending to Labrador on the east coast. The Shield is bordered to the south by the fertile Great Lakes-St Lawrence lowlands. In the far north climatic conditions are polar, while the rest has a continental climate. Most Canadians live in the urban areas of the Great Lakes-St Lawrence basin. Canada is rich in mineral and energy resources. Only five per cent of land is arable. Canada is among the world's leading producers of wheat, of wood from its vast coniferous forests, and of fish and seafood from its Atlantic and Pacific fishing grounds. It is a major producer of nickel, uranium, copper, iron ore, zinc and other minerals, as well as oil and natural gas. Its abundant raw materials are the basis for many manufacturing industries. Main exports are machinery, motor vehicles, oil, timber, newsprint and paper, wood pulp and wheat. Since the 1989 free trade agreement with the USA and the 1994 North America Free Trade Agreement, trade with the USA has grown and now accounts for around fifty per cent of imports and around seventy-five per cent of exports.

**Alberta (Province)**
**Area Sq Km (Sq Miles)** 661 848 (255 541) **Population** 3 742 753 **Capital** Edmonton

**British Columbia (Province)**
**Area Sq Km (Sq Miles)** 944 735 (364 764) **Population** 4 554 085 **Capital** Victoria

**Manitoba (Province)**
**Area Sq Km (Sq Miles)** 647 797 (250 116) **Population** 1 243 653 **Capital** Winnipeg

**New Brunswick (Province)**
**Area Sq Km (Sq Miles)** 72 908 (28 150) **Population** 753 232 **Capital** Fredericton

**Newfoundland and Labrador (Province)**
**Area Sq Km (Sq Miles)** 405 212 (156 453) **Population** 509 148 **Capital** St John's

**Northwest Territories (Territory)**
**Area Sq Km (Sq Miles)** 1 346 106 (519 734) **Population** 43 554 **Capital** Yellowknife

**Nova Scotia (Province)**
**Area Sq Km (Sq Miles)** 55 284 (21 345) **Population** 943 414 **Capital** Halifax

**Nunavut (Territory)**
**Area Sq Km (Sq Miles)** 2 093 190 (808 185) **Population** 33 303 **Capital** Iqaluit (Frobisher Bay)

**Ontario (Province)**
**Area Sq Km (Sq Miles)** 1 076 395 (415 598) **Population** 13 282 444 **Capital** Toronto

**Prince Edward Island (Province)**
**Area Sq Km (Sq Miles)** 5 660 (2 185) **Population** 143 481 **Capital** Charlottetown

**Québec (Province)**
**Area Sq Km (Sq Miles)** 1 542 056 (595 391) **Population** 7 942 983 **Capital** Québec

**Saskatchewan (Province)**
**Area Sq Km (Sq Miles)** 651 036 (251 366) **Population** 1 052 050 **Capital** Regina

**Yukon (Territory)**
**Area Sq Km (Sq Miles)** 482 443 (186 272) **Population** 34 306 **Capital** Whitehorse

## CAPE VERDE
Republic of Cape Verde

| | | | |
|---|---|---|---|
| **Area Sq Km** | 4 033 | **Languages** | Portuguese, Creole |
| **Area Sq Miles** | 1 557 | **Religions** | Roman Catholic, Protestant |
| **Population** | 501 000 | **Currency** | Cape Verde escudo |
| **Capital** | Praia | **Organizations** | UN |

**Map page 176**

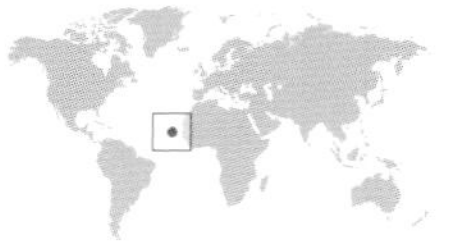

Cape Verde is a group of semi-arid volcanic islands lying off the coast of west Africa. The economy is based on fishing, subsistence farming and service industries. Windfarms on four islands supply around a quarter of all electricity.

## Cayman Islands
United Kingdom Overseas Territory

| | | | |
|---|---|---|---|
| **Area Sq Km** | 259 | **Languages** | English |
| **Area Sq Miles** | 100 | **Religions** | Protestant, Roman Catholic |
| **Population** | 57 000 | **Currency** | Cayman Islands dollar |
| **Capital** | George Town | | |

**Map page 205** A group of islands in the Caribbean, northwest of Jamaica. There are three main islands: Grand Cayman, Little Cayman and Cayman Brac. The Cayman Islands are one of the world's major offshore financial centres. Tourism is also important to the economy.

## CENTRAL AFRICAN REPUBLIC

| | | | |
|---|---|---|---|
| **Area Sq Km** | 622 436 | **Languages** | French, Sango, Banda, Baya, local languages |
| **Area Sq Miles** | 240 324 | **Religions** | Protestant, Roman Catholic, traditional beliefs, Sunni Muslim |
| **Population** | 4 487 000 | **Currency** | CFA franc |
| **Capital** | Bangui | **Organizations** | UN |

**Map page 177**

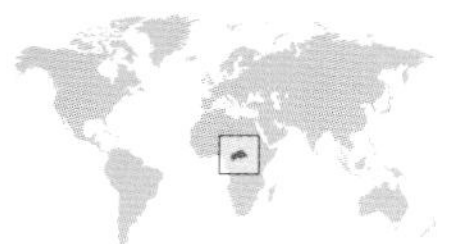

A landlocked country in central Africa, the Central African Republic is mainly savanna plateau, drained by the Ubangi and Chari river systems, with mountains to the east and west. The climate is tropical, with high rainfall. Most of the population lives in the south and west, and a majority of the workforce is involved in subsistence farming. Some cotton, coffee, tobacco and timber are exported, but diamonds account for over sixty per cent of export earnings.

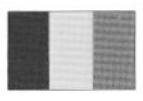

## CHAD
Republic of Chad

| | | | |
|---|---|---|---|
| **Area Sq Km** | 1 284 000 | **Languages** | Arabic, French, Sara, local languages |
| **Area Sq Miles** | 495 755 | **Religions** | Sunni Muslim, Roman Catholic, Protestant, traditional beliefs |
| **Population** | 11 525 000 | **Currency** | CFA franc |
| **Capital** | Ndjamena | **Organizations** | UN |

**Map page 177**

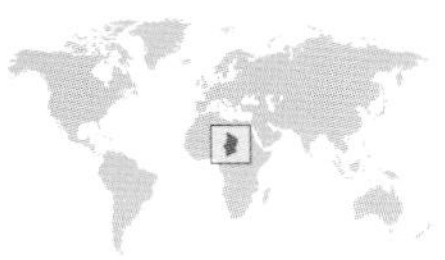

Chad is a landlocked state of north-central Africa. It consists of plateaus, the Tibesti mountains in the north and the Lake Chad basin in the west. Climatic conditions range between desert in the north and tropical forest in the southwest. With few natural resources, Chad relies on subsistence farming, exports of raw cotton, and foreign aid. The main trading partners are France, Portugal and Cameroon.

## CHILE
Republic of Chile

| | | | |
|---|---|---|---|
| **Area Sq Km** | 756 945 | **Languages** | Spanish, Amerindian languages |
| **Area Sq Miles** | 292 258 | **Religions** | Roman Catholic, Protestant |
| **Population** | 17 270 000 | **Currency** | Chilean peso |
| **Capital** | Santiago | **Organizations** | APEC, OECD, UN |

**Map page 212**

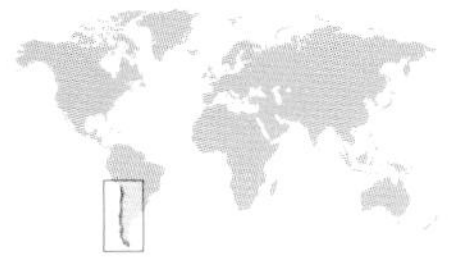

Chile lies along the Pacific coast of the southern half of South America. Between the Andes in the east and the lower coastal ranges is a central valley, with a mild climate, where most Chileans live. To the north is the arid Atacama Desert and to the south is cold, wet forested grassland. Chile has considerable mineral resources and is a major exporter of copper. Nitrates, molybdenum, gold and iron ore are also mined. Agriculture (particularly viticulture), forestry and fishing are also important to the economy.

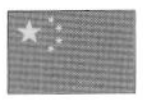

## CHINA
People's Republic of China

| | | | |
|---|---|---|---|
| **Area Sq Km** | 9 584 492 | **Languages** | Mandarin (Putonghua), Wu, Cantonese, Hsiang, regional languages |
| **Area Sq Miles** | 3 700 593 | **Religions** | Confucian, Taoist, Buddhist, Christian, Sunni Muslim |
| **Population** | 1 332 079 000 | **Currency** | Yuan, Hong Kong dollar, Macao pataca |
| **Capital** | Beijing (Peking) | **Organizations** | APEC, UN |

**Map page 146**

China, the world's most populous and fourth largest country, occupies a large part of east Asia, borders fourteen states and has coastlines on the Yellow, East China and South China Seas. It has a huge variety of landscapes. The southwest contains the high Plateau of Tibet, flanked by the Himalaya and Kunlun Shan mountains. The north is mountainous with arid basins and extends from the Tien Shan and Altai Mountains and the vast Taklimakan Desert in the west to the plateau and Gobi Desert in the centre-east. Eastern China is predominantly lowland and is divided broadly into the basins of the Yellow River (Huang He) in the north, the Yangtze (Chang Jiang) in the centre and the Pearl River (Xi Jiang) in the southeast. Climatic conditions and vegetation are as diverse as the topography: much of the country experiences temperate conditions, while the southwest has an extreme mountain climate and the southeast enjoys a moist, warm subtropical climate. Around fifty per cent of China's huge population lives in rural areas, and agriculture employs over forty per cent of the working population. The main crops are rice, wheat, soya beans, peanuts, cotton, tobacco and hemp. China is rich in coal, oil and natural gas and has the world's largest potential in hydroelectric power. It is a major world producer of iron ore, molybdenum, copper, asbestos and gold. Economic reforms from the early 1980s led to an explosion in manufacturing development concentrated on the 'coastal economic open region'. The main exports are machinery, textiles, footwear, toys and sports goods. Japan and the USA are China's main trading partners.

### Anhui (Province)
**Area Sq Km (Sq Miles)** 139 000 (53 668) **Population** 61 350 000 **Capital** Hefei

### Beijing (Municipality)
**Area Sq Km (Sq Miles)** 16 800 (6 487) **Population** 16 950 000 **Capital** Beijing (Peking)

### Chongqing (Municipality)
**Area Sq Km (Sq Miles)** 23 000 (8 880) **Population** 28 390 000 **Capital** Chongqing

### Fujian (Province)
**Area Sq Km (Sq Miles)** 121 400 (46 873) **Population** 36 040 000 **Capital** Fuzhou

### Gansu (Province)
**Area Sq Km (Sq Miles)** 453 700 (175 175) **Population** 26 280 000 **Capital** Lanzhou

### Guangdong (Province)
**Area Sq Km (Sq Miles)** 178 000 (68 726) **Population** 95 440 000 **Capital** Guangzhou (Canton)

### Guangxi Zhuangzu Zizhiqu (Autonomous Region)
**Area Sq Km (Sq Miles)** 236 000 (91 120) **Population** 48 160 000 **Capital** Nanning

### Guizhou (Province)
**Area Sq Km (Sq Miles)** 176 000 (67 954) **Population** 37 930 000 **Capital** Guiyang

### Hainan (Province)
**Area Sq Km (Sq Miles)** 34 000 (13 127) **Population** 8 540 000 **Capital** Haikou

### Hebei (Province)
**Area Sq Km (Sq Miles)** 187 700 (72 471) **Population** 69 890 000 **Capital** Shijiazhuang

### Heilongjiang (Province)
**Area Sq Km (Sq Miles)** 454 600 (175 522) **Population** 38 250 000 **Capital** Harbin

### Henan (Province)
**Area Sq Km (Sq Miles)** 167 000 (64 479) **Population** 94 290 000 **Capital** Zhengzhou

### Hong Kong (Special Administrative Region)
**Area Sq Km (Sq Miles)** 1 075 (415) **Population** 6 978 000 **Capital** Hong Kong

### Hubei (Province)
**Area Sq Km (Sq Miles)** 185 900 (71 776) **Population** 57 110 000 **Capital** Wuhan

### Hunan (Province)
**Area Sq Km (Sq Miles)** 210 000 (81 081) **Population** 63 800 000 **Capital** Changsha

### Jiangsu (Province)
**Area Sq Km (Sq Miles)** 102 600 (39 614) **Population** 76 770 000 **Capital** Nanjing

### Jiangxi (Province)
**Area Sq Km (Sq Miles)** 166 900 (64 440) **Population** 44 000 000 **Capital** Nanchang

### Jilin (Province)
**Area Sq Km (Sq Miles)** 187 000 (72 201) **Population** 27 340 000 **Capital** Changchun

### Liaoning (Province)
**Area Sq Km (Sq Miles)** 147 400 (56 911) **Population** 43 150 000 **Capital** Shenyang

### Macao (Special Administrative Region)
**Area Sq Km (Sq Miles)** 17 (7) **Population** 552 000 **Capital** Macao

### Nei Mongol Zizhiqu Inner Mongolia (Autonomous Region)
**Area Sq Km (Sq Miles)** 1 183 000 (456 759) **Population** 24 140 000 **Capital** Hohhot

### Ningxia Huizu Zizhiqu (Autonomous Region)
**Area Sq Km (Sq Miles)** 66 400 (25 637) **Population** 6 180 000 **Capital** Yinchuan

### Qinghai (Province)
**Area Sq Km (Sq Miles)** 721 000 (278 380) **Population** 5 540 000 **Capital** Xining

### Shaanxi (Province)
**Area Sq Km (Sq Miles)** 205 600 (79 383) **Population** 37 620 000 **Capital** Xi'an

### Shandong (Province)
**Area Sq Km (Sq Miles)** 153 300 (59 189) **Population** 94 170 000 **Capital** Jinan

### Shanghai (Municipality)
**Area Sq Km (Sq Miles)** 6 300 (2 432) **Population** 18 880 000 **Capital** Shanghai

### Shanxi (Province)
**Area Sq Km (Sq Miles)** 156 300 (60 348) **Population** 34 110 000 **Capital** Taiyuan

### Sichuan (Province)
**Area Sq Km (Sq Miles)** 569 000 (219 692) **Population** 81 380 000 **Capital** Chengdu

### Tianjin (Municipality)
**Area Sq Km (Sq Miles)** 11 300 (4 363) **Population** 11 760 000 **Capital** Tianjin

### Xinjiang Uygur Zizhiqu Sinkiang (Autonomous Region)
**Area Sq Km (Sq Miles)** 1 600 000 (617 763) **Population** 21 310 000 **Capital** Ürümqi

### Xizang Zizhiqu Tibet (Autonomous Region)
**Area Sq Km (Sq Miles)** 1 228 400 (474 288) **Population** 2 870 000 **Capital** Lhasa

### Yunnan (Province)
**Area Sq Km (Sq Miles)** 394 000 (152 124) **Population** 45 430 000 **Capital** Kunming

### Zhejiang (Province)
**Area Sq Km (Sq Miles)** 101 800 (39 305) **Population** 51 200 000 **Capital** Hangzhou

**Taiwan:** The People's Republic of China claims Taiwan as its 23rd Province

## Christmas Island
Australian External Territory

| | | | |
|---|---|---|---|
| **Area Sq Km** | 135 | **Languages** | English |
| **Area Sq Miles** | 52 | **Religions** | Buddhist, Sunni Muslim, Protestant, Roman Catholic |
| **Population** | 1 403 | **Currency** | Australian dollar |
| **Capital** | The Settlement (Flying Fish Cove) | | |

**Map page 147** The island is situated in the east of the Indian Ocean, to the south of Indonesia. The economy was formerly based on phosphate extraction, although the mine is now closed. Tourism is developing and is a major employer.

## Cocos Islands (Keeling Islands)
Australian External Territory

| | | | |
|---|---|---|---|
| **Area Sq Km** | 14 | **Languages** | English |
| **Area Sq Miles** | 5 | **Religions** | Sunni Muslim, Christian |
| **Population** | 621 | **Currency** | Australian dollar |
| **Capital** | West Island | | |

**Map page 147** The Cocos Islands consist of numerous islands on two coral atolls in the eastern Indian Ocean between Sri Lanka and Australia. Most of the population lives on West Island or Home Island. Coconuts are the only cash crop, and the main export.

## COLOMBIA
Republic of Colombia

| | | | |
|---|---|---|---|
| **Area Sq Km** | 1 141 748 | **Languages** | Spanish, Amerindian languages |
| **Area Sq Miles** | 440 831 | **Religions** | Roman Catholic, Protestant |
| **Population** | 46 927 000 | **Currency** | Colombian peso |
| **Capital** | Bogotá | **Organizations** | UN |

**Map page 213**

A state in northwest South America, Colombia has coastlines on the Pacific Ocean and the Caribbean Sea. Behind coastal plains lie three ranges of the Andes mountains, separated by high valleys and plateaus where most Colombians live. To the southeast are grasslands and the forests of the Amazon. The climate is tropical, although temperatures vary with altitude. Only five per cent of land is cultivable. Coffee (Colombia is the world's third largest producer), sugar, bananas, cotton and flowers are exported. Coal, nickel, gold, silver, platinum and high-quality emeralds are mined. Oil and its products are the main export. Industries include the processing of minerals and crops. The main trade partner is the USA. Internal violence – both politically motivated and relating to Colombia's leading role in the international trade in illegal drugs – continues to hinder development.

## COMOROS
United Republic of the Comoros

| | | | |
|---|---|---|---|
| **Area Sq Km** | 1 862 | **Languages** | Shikomor (Comorian), French, Arabic |
| **Area Sq Miles** | 719 | **Religions** | Sunni Muslim, Roman Catholic |
| **Population** | 754 000 | **Currency** | Comoros franc |
| **Capital** | Moroni | **Organizations** | UN |

**Map page 179**

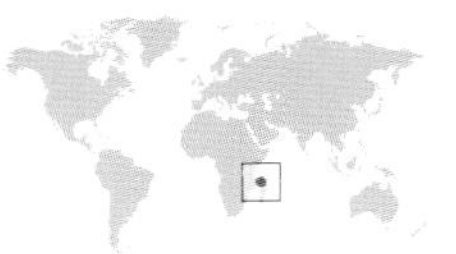

This state, in the Indian Ocean off the east African coast, comprises three volcanic islands of Ngazidja (Grande Comore), Nzwani (Anjouan) and Mwali (Mohéli), and some coral atolls. These tropical islands are mountainous, with poor soil and few natural resources. Subsistence farming predominates. Vanilla, cloves and ylang-ylang (an essential oil) are exported, and the economy relies heavily on workers' remittances from abroad.

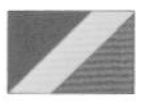

## CONGO
Republic of the Congo

| | | | |
|---|---|---|---|
| Area Sq Km | 342 000 | Languages | French, Kongo, Monokutuba, local languages |
| Area Sq Miles | 132 047 | Religions | Roman Catholic, Protestant, traditional beliefs, Sunni Muslim |
| Population | 4 140 000 | Currency | CFA franc |
| Capital | Brazzaville | Organizations | UN |

Map page 178

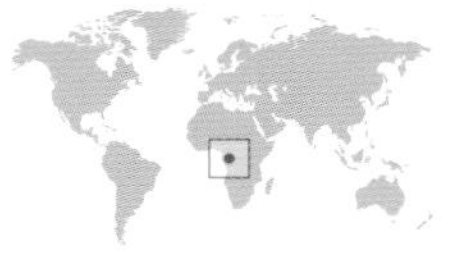

Congo, in central Africa, is mostly a forest or savanna-covered plateau drained by the Ubangi-Congo river systems. Sand dunes and lagoons line the short Atlantic coast. The climate is hot and tropical. Most Congolese live in the southern third of the country. Half of the workforce are farmers, growing food and cash crops including sugar, coffee, cocoa and oil palms. Oil and timber are the mainstays of the economy, and oil generates over two-thirds of the country's export revenues.

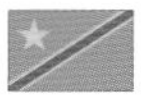

## CONGO, DEMOCRATIC REPUBLIC OF THE

| | | | |
|---|---|---|---|
| Area Sq Km | 2 345 410 | Languages | French, Lingala, Swahili, Kongo, local languages |
| Area Sq Miles | 905 568 | Religions | Christian, Sunni Muslim |
| Population | 67 758 000 | Currency | Congolese franc |
| Capital | Kinshasa | Organizations | SADC, UN |

Map page 178–179

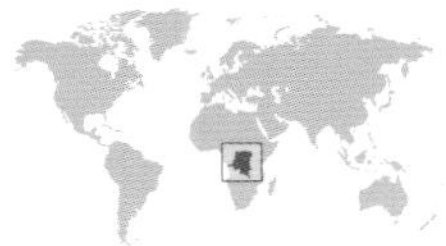

This central African state, formerly Zaire, consists of the basin of the Congo river flanked by plateaus, with high mountain ranges to the east and a short Atlantic coastline to the west. The climate is tropical, with rainforest close to the Equator and savanna to the north and south. Fertile land allows a range of food and cash crops to be grown, chiefly coffee. The country has vast mineral resources, with copper, cobalt and diamonds being the most important.

## Cook Islands
Self governing New Zealand Overseas Territory

| | | | |
|---|---|---|---|
| Area Sq Km | 293 | Languages | English, Maori |
| Area Sq Miles | 113 | Religions | Protestant, Roman Catholic |
| Population | 20 000 | Currency | New Zealand dollar |
| Capital | Avarua | | |

Map page 123 These consist of groups of coral atolls and volcanic islands in the southwest Pacific Ocean. The main island is Rarotonga. Distance from foreign markets and restricted natural resources hinder development.

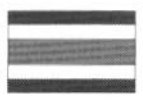

## COSTA RICA
Republic of Costa Rica

| | | | |
|---|---|---|---|
| Area Sq Km | 51 100 | Languages | Spanish |
| Area Sq Miles | 19 730 | Religions | Roman Catholic, Protestant |
| Population | 4 727 000 | Currency | Costa Rican colón |
| Capital | San José | Organizations | UN |

Map page 206

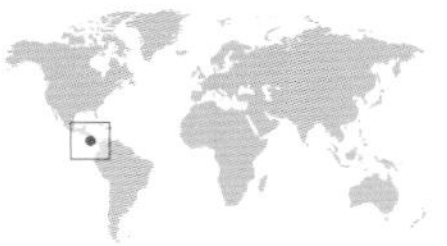

Costa Rica, in central America, has coastlines on the Caribbean Sea and Pacific Ocean. From tropical coastal plains, the land rises to mountains and a temperate central plateau, where most of the population lives. The economy depends on agriculture and tourism, with ecotourism becoming increasingly important. Main exports are textiles, coffee and bananas, and the USA is the main trading partner.

## CÔTE D'IVOIRE (Ivory Coast)
Republic of Côte d'Ivoire

| | | | |
|---|---|---|---|
| Area Sq Km | 322 463 | Languages | French, Creole, Akan, local languages |
| Area Sq Miles | 124 504 | Religions | Sunni Muslim, Roman Catholic, traditional beliefs, Protestant |
| Population | 20 153 000 | Currency | CFA franc |
| Capital | Yamoussoukro | Organizations | UN |

Map page 176

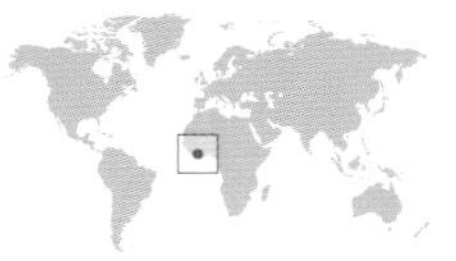

Côte d'Ivoire (Ivory Coast) is in west Africa, on the Gulf of Guinea. In the north are plateaus and savanna; in the south are low undulating plains and rainforest, with sand-bars and lagoons on the coast. Temperatures are warm, and rainfall is heavier in the south. Most of the workforce is engaged in farming. Côte d'Ivoire is a major producer of cocoa and coffee, and agricultural products (also including cotton and timber) are the main exports. Oil and gas have begun to be exploited.

## CROATIA
Republic of Croatia

| | | | |
|---|---|---|---|
| Area Sq Km | 56 538 | Languages | Croatian, Serbian |
| Area Sq Miles | 21 829 | Religions | Roman Catholic, Serbian Orthodox, Sunni Muslim |
| Population | 4 396 000 | Currency | Kuna |
| Capital | Zagreb | Organizations | NATO, UN |

Map page 170

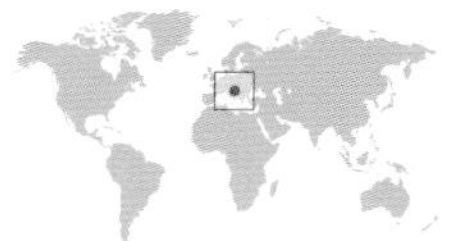

The southern European state of Croatia has a long coastline on the Adriatic Sea, with many offshore islands. Coastal areas have a Mediterranean climate; inland is cooler and wetter. Croatia was once strong agriculturally and industrially, but conflict in the early 1990s, and associated loss of markets and a fall in tourist revenue, caused economic difficulties from which recovery has been slow.

## CUBA
Republic of Cuba

| | | | |
|---|---|---|---|
| Area Sq Km | 110 860 | Languages | Spanish |
| Area Sq Miles | 42 803 | Religions | Roman Catholic, Protestant |
| Population | 11 254 000 | Currency | Cuban peso |
| Capital | Havana (La Habana) | Organizations | UN |

Map page 205

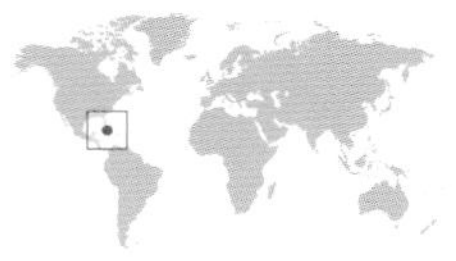

The country comprises the island of Cuba (the largest island in the Caribbean), and many islets and cays. A fifth of Cubans live in and around Havana. Cuba is slowly recovering from the withdrawal of aid and subsidies from the former USSR. Sugar remains the basis of the economy, although tourism is developing and is, together with remittances from workers abroad, an important source of revenue.

## Curaçao
Self-governing Netherlands territory

| | | | |
|---|---|---|---|
| Area Sq Km | 444 | Languages | Dutch, Papiamento |
| Area Sq Miles | 171 | Religions | Roman Catholic, Protestant |
| Population | 142 180 | Currency | Caribbean guilder |
| Capital | Willemstad | | |

Map page 213 Situated in the Caribbean Sea off the north coast of Venezuela, Curaçao was previously part of the Netherlands Antilles until they were dissolved in October 2010. It consists of the main island and the smaller uninhabited Klein Curaçao and is the largest and most populous of the Lesser Antilles. Oil refining and tourism form the basis of the economy.

## CYPRUS
Republic of Cyprus

| | | | |
|---|---|---|---|
| Area Sq Km | 9 251 | Languages | Greek, Turkish, English |
| Area Sq Miles | 3 572 | Religions | Greek Orthodox, Sunni Muslim |
| Population | 1 117 000 | Currency | Euro |
| Capital | Nicosia (Lefkosia) | Organizations | Comm., EU, UN |

Map page 136

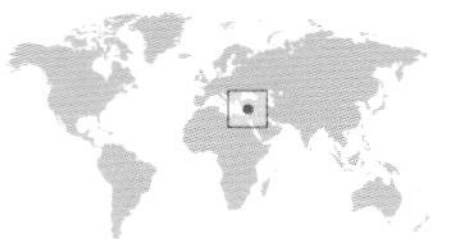

The eastern Mediterranean island of Cyprus has effectively been divided into two since 1974. The economy of the Greek-speaking south is based mainly on specialist agriculture and tourism, with shipping and offshore banking. The ethnically Turkish north depends on agriculture, tourism and aid from Turkey. The island has hot dry summers and mild winters. Cyprus joined the European Union in May 2004.

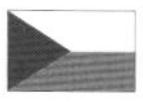

## CZECH REPUBLIC

| | | | |
|---|---|---|---|
| Area Sq Km | 78 864 | Languages | Czech, Moravian, Slovakian |
| Area Sq Miles | 30 450 | Religions | Roman Catholic, Protestant |
| Population | 10 534 000 | Currency | Koruna |
| Capital | Prague (Praha) | Organizations | EU, NATO, OECD, UN |

Map page 168

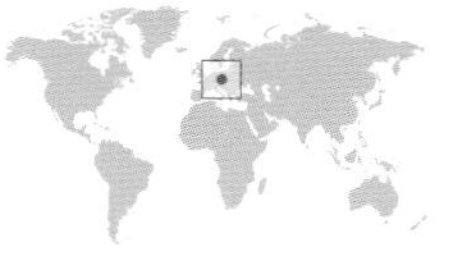

The landlocked Czech Republic in central Europe consists of rolling countryside, wooded hills and fertile valleys. The climate is continental. The country has substantial reserves of coal and lignite, timber and some minerals, chiefly iron ore. It is highly industrialized, and major manufactured goods include industrial machinery, consumer goods, cars, iron and steel, chemicals and glass. Germany is the main trading partner. The Czech Republic joined the European Union in May 2004.

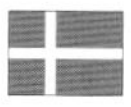

## DENMARK
Kingdom of Denmark

| | | | |
|---|---|---|---|
| Area Sq Km | 43 075 | Languages | Danish |
| Area Sq Miles | 16 631 | Religions | Protestant |
| Population | 5 573 000 | Currency | Danish krone |
| Capital | Copenhagen (København) | Organizations | EU, NATO, OECD, UN |

Map page 159

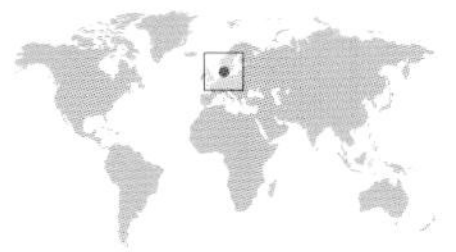

In northern Europe, Denmark occupies the Jutland (Jylland) peninsula and nearly five hundred islands in and between the North and Baltic Seas. The country is low-lying, with long, indented coastlines. The climate is cool and temperate, with rainfall throughout the year. A fifth of the population lives in and around the capital, Copenhagen (København), on the largest of the islands, Zealand (Sjælland). The country's main natural resource is its agricultural potential: two-thirds of the total area is fertile farmland or pasture. Agriculture is high-tech, and with forestry and fishing employs only around six per cent of the workforce. Denmark is self-sufficient in oil and natural gas, produced from fields in the North Sea. Manufacturing, largely based on imported raw materials, accounts for over half of all exports, which include machinery, food, furniture and pharmaceuticals. The main trading partners are Germany and Sweden.

## DJIBOUTI
Republic of Djibouti

| | | | |
|---|---|---|---|
| Area Sq Km | 23 200 | Languages | Somali, Afar, French, Arabic |
| Area Sq Miles | 8 958 | Religions | Sunni Muslim, Christian |
| Population | 906 000 | Currency | Djibouti franc |
| Capital | Djibouti | Organizations | UN |

Map page 178

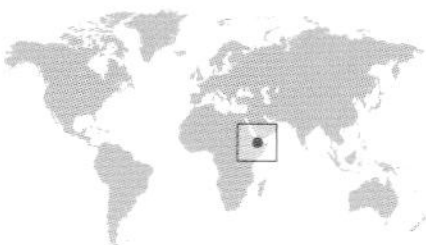

Djibouti lies in northeast Africa, on the Gulf of Aden at the entrance to the Red Sea. Most of the country is semi-arid desert with high temperatures and low rainfall. More than two-thirds of the population live in the capital. There is some camel, sheep and goat herding, but with few natural resources the economy is based on services and trade. Djibouti serves as a free trade zone for northern Africa, and the capital's port is a major transhipment and refuelling destination. It is linked by rail to Addis Ababa in Ethiopia.

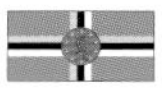

## DOMINICA
Commonwealth of Dominica

| | | | |
|---|---|---|---|
| Area Sq Km | 750 | Languages | English, Creole |
| Area Sq Miles | 290 | Religions | Roman Catholic, Protestant |
| Population | 68 000 | Currency | East Caribbean dollar |
| Capital | Roseau | Organizations | CARICOM, Comm., UN |

Map page 205

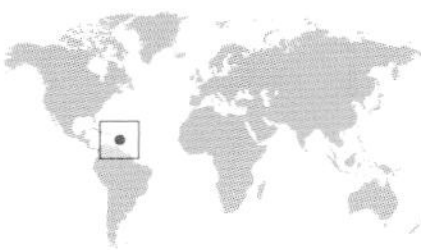

Dominica is the most northerly of the Windward Islands, in the eastern Caribbean. It is very mountainous and forested, with a coastline of steep cliffs. The climate is tropical and rainfall is abundant. Approximately a quarter of Dominicans live in the capital. The economy is based on agriculture, with bananas, coconuts and citrus fruits the most important crops. Tourism is a developing industry.

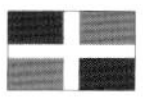

## DOMINICAN REPUBLIC

| | | | |
|---|---|---|---|
| Area Sq Km | 48 442 | Languages | Spanish, Creole |
| Area Sq Miles | 18 704 | Religions | Roman Catholic, Protestant |
| Population | 10 056 000 | Currency | Dominican peso |
| Capital | Santo Domingo | Organizations | UN |

Map page 205

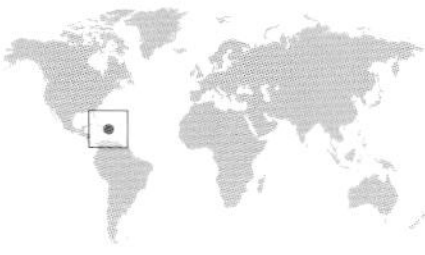

The state occupies the eastern two-thirds of the Caribbean island of Hispaniola (the western third is Haiti). It has a series of mountain ranges, fertile valleys and a large coastal plain in the east. The climate is hot tropical, with heavy rainfall. Sugar, coffee and cocoa are the main cash crops. Nickel (the main export), and gold are mined, and there is some light industry. The USA is the main trading partner. Tourism is the main foreign exchange earner.

## EAST TIMOR (Timor-Leste)
Democratic Republic of Timor-Leste

| | | | |
|---|---|---|---|
| Area Sq Km | 14 874 | Languages | Portuguese, Tetun, English |
| Area Sq Miles | 5 743 | Religions | Roman Catholic |
| Population | 1 154 000 | Currency | United States dollar |
| Capital | Dili | Organizations | UN |

Map page 147

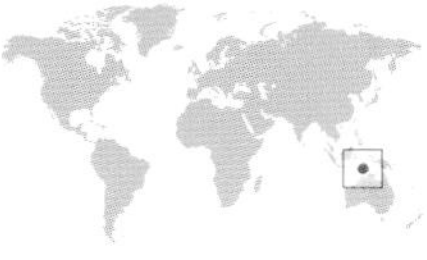

The island of Timor is part of the Indonesian archipelago, to the north of western Australia. East Timor occupies the eastern section of the island, and a small coastal enclave (Ocussi) to the west. A referendum in 1999 ended Indonesia's occupation, after which the country was under UN transitional administration until full independence was achieved in 2002. The economy is in a poor state and East Timor is heavily dependent on foreign aid.

## ECUADOR
Republic of Ecuador

| | | | |
|---|---|---|---|
| **Area Sq Km** | 272 045 | **Languages** | Spanish, Quechua, and other Amerindian languages |
| **Area Sq Miles** | 105 037 | **Religions** | Roman Catholic |
| **Population** | 14 666 000 | **Currency** | United States dollar |
| **Capital** | Quito | **Organizations** | OPEC, UN |

Map page 210

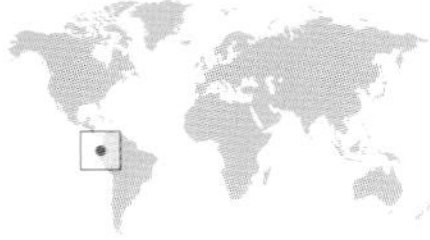

Ecuador is in northwest South America, on the Pacific coast. It consists of a broad coastal plain, high mountain ranges in the Andes, and part of the forested upper Amazon basin to the east. The climate is tropical, moderated by altitude. Most people live on the coast or in the mountain valleys. Ecuador is one of South America's main oil producers, and mineral reserves include gold. Most of the workforce depends on agriculture. Petroleum, bananas, shrimps, coffee and cocoa are exported. The USA is the main trading partner.

## EGYPT
Arab Republic of Egypt

| | | | |
|---|---|---|---|
| **Area Sq Km** | 1 001 450 | **Languages** | Arabic |
| **Area Sq Miles** | 386 660 | **Religions** | Sunni Muslim, Coptic Christian |
| **Population** | 82 537 000 | **Currency** | Egyptian pound |
| **Capital** | Cairo (Al Qāhirah) | **Organizations** | UN |

Map page 177

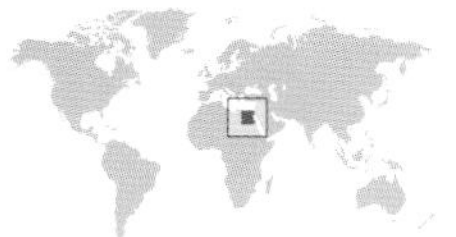

Egypt, on the eastern Mediterranean coast of north Africa, is low-lying, with areas below sea level in the Qattara depression. It is a land of desert and semi-desert, except for the Nile valley, where ninety-nine per cent of Egyptians live. The Sinai peninsula in the northeast of the country forms the only land bridge between Africa and Asia. The summers are hot, the winters mild and rainfall is negligible. Less than four per cent of land (chiefly around the Nile floodplain and delta) is cultivated. Farming employs about one-third of the workforce; cotton is the main cash crop. Egypt imports over half its food needs. There are oil and natural gas reserves, although nearly a quarter of electricity comes from hydroelectric power. Main exports are oil and oil products, cotton, textiles and clothing.

## EL SALVADOR
Republic of El Salvador

| | | | |
|---|---|---|---|
| **Area Sq Km** | 21 041 | **Languages** | Spanish |
| **Area Sq Miles** | 8 124 | **Religions** | Roman Catholic, Protestant |
| **Population** | 6 227 000 | **Currency** | El Salvador colón, United States dollar |
| **Capital** | San Salvador | **Organizations** | UN |

Map page 207

Located on the Pacific coast of central America, El Salvador consists of a coastal plain and volcanic mountain ranges which enclose a densely populated plateau area. The coast is hot, with heavy summer rainfall; the highlands are cooler. Coffee (the chief export), sugar and cotton are the main cash crops. The main trading partners are the USA and Guatemala.

## EQUATORIAL GUINEA
Republic of Equatorial Guinea

| | | | |
|---|---|---|---|
| **Area Sq Km** | 28 051 | **Languages** | Spanish, French, Fang |
| **Area Sq Miles** | 10 831 | **Religions** | Roman Catholic, traditional beliefs |
| **Population** | 720 000 | **Currency** | CFA franc |
| **Capital** | Malabo | **Organizations** | UN |

Map page 176

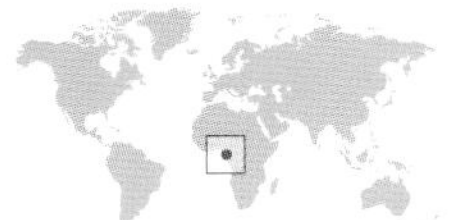

The state consists of Rio Muni, an enclave on the Atlantic coast of central Africa, and the islands of Bioko, Annobón and the Corisco group. Most of the population lives on the coastal plain and upland plateau of Rio Muni. The capital city, Malabo, is on the fertile volcanic island of Bioco. The climate is hot, humid and wet. Oil production started in 1992, and oil is now the main export, along with timber. The economy depends heavily on foreign aid.

## ERITREA
State of Eritrea

| | | | |
|---|---|---|---|
| **Area Sq Km** | 117 400 | **Languages** | Tigrinya, Tigre |
| **Area Sq Miles** | 45 328 | **Religions** | Sunni Muslim, Coptic Christian |
| **Population** | 5 415 000 | **Currency** | Nakfa |
| **Capital** | Asmara | **Organizations** | UN |

Map page 178

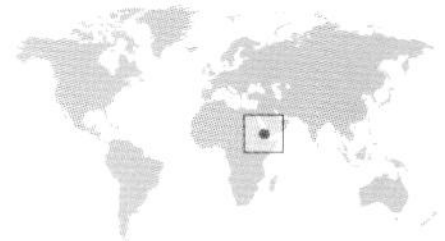

Eritrea, on the Red Sea coast of northeast Africa, consists of a high plateau in the north with a coastal plain which widens to the south. The coast is hot; inland is cooler. Rainfall is unreliable. The agriculture-based economy has suffered from over thirty years of war and occasional poor rains. Eritrea is one of the least developed countries in the world.

## ESTONIA
Republic of Estonia

| | | | |
|---|---|---|---|
| **Area Sq Km** | 45 200 | **Languages** | Estonian, Russian |
| **Area Sq Miles** | 17 452 | **Religions** | Protestant, Estonian and Russian Orthodox |
| **Population** | 1 341 000 | | |
| **Capital** | Tallinn | **Currency** | Euro |
| | | **Organizations** | EU, NATO, OECD, UN |

Map page 159

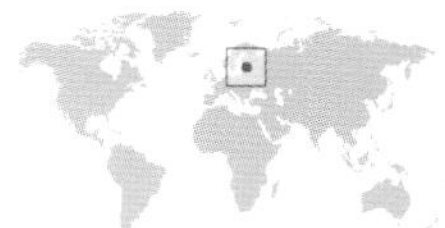

Estonia is in northern Europe, on the Gulf of Finland and the Baltic Sea. The land, over one-third of which is forested, is generally low-lying with many lakes. Approximately one-third of Estonians live in the capital, Tallinn. Exported goods include machinery, wood products, textiles and food products. The main trading partners are the Russian Federation, Finland and Sweden. Estonia joined the European Union in May 2004.

## ETHIOPIA
Federal Democratic Republic of Ethiopia

| | | | |
|---|---|---|---|
| **Area Sq Km** | 1 133 880 | **Languages** | Oromo, Amharic, Tigrinya, local languages |
| **Area Sq Miles** | 437 794 | **Religions** | Ethiopian Orthodox, Sunni Muslim, traditional beliefs |
| **Population** | 84 734 000 | | |
| **Capital** | Addis Ababa (Ādīs Ābeba) | **Currency** | Birr |
| | | **Organizations** | UN |

Map page 178

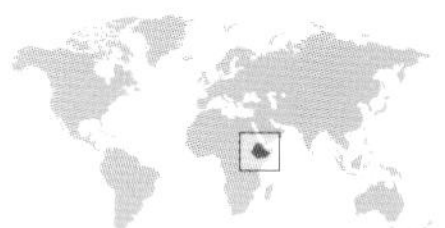

A landlocked country in northeast Africa, Ethiopia comprises a mountainous region in the west which is traversed by the Great Rift Valley. The east is mostly arid plateau land. The highlands are warm with summer rainfall. Most people live in the central–northern area. In recent years civil war, conflict with Eritrea and poor infrastructure have hampered economic development. Subsistence farming is the main activity, although droughts have led to frequent famines. Coffee is the main export and there is some light industry. Ethiopia is one of the least developed countries in the world.

## Falkland Islands
United Kingdom Overseas Territory

| | | | |
|---|---|---|---|
| **Area Sq Km** | 12 170 | **Languages** | English |
| **Area Sq Miles** | 4 699 | **Religions** | Protestant, Roman Catholic |
| **Population** | 2 955 | **Currency** | Falkland Islands pound |
| **Capital** | Stanley | | |

Map page 212 Lying in the southwest Atlantic Ocean, northeast of Cape Horn, two main islands, West Falkland and East Falkland and many smaller islands, form the territory of the Falkland Islands. The economy is based on sheep farming and the sale of fishing licences.

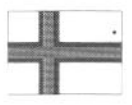

## Faroe Islands
Self-governing Danish Territory

| | | | |
|---|---|---|---|
| **Area Sq Km** | 1 399 | **Languages** | Faroese, Danish |
| **Area Sq Miles** | 540 | **Religions** | Protestant |
| **Population** | 49 000 | **Currency** | Danish krone |
| **Capital** | Thorshavn (Tórshavn) | | |

Map page 158 A self-governing territory, the Faroe Islands lie in the north Atlantic Ocean between the UK and Iceland. The islands benefit from the North Atlantic Drift ocean current, which has a moderating effect on the climate. The economy is based on deep-sea fishing.

## FIJI
Republic of Fiji

| | | | |
|---|---|---|---|
| **Area Sq Km** | 18 330 | **Languages** | English, Fijian, Hindi |
| **Area Sq Miles** | 7 077 | **Religions** | Christian, Hindu, Sunni Muslim |
| **Population** | 868 000 | **Currency** | Fiji dollar |
| **Capital** | Suva | **Organizations** | UN |

Map page 125

The southwest Pacific republic of Fiji comprises two mountainous and volcanic islands, Vanua Levu and Viti Levu, and over three hundred smaller islands. The climate is tropical and the economy is based on agriculture (chiefly sugar, the main export), fishing, forestry, gold mining and tourism.

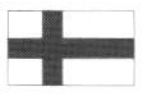

## FINLAND
Republic of Finland

| | | | |
|---|---|---|---|
| **Area Sq Km** | 338 145 | **Languages** | Finnish, Swedish |
| **Area Sq Miles** | 130 559 | **Religions** | Protestant, Greek Orthodox |
| **Population** | 5 385 000 | **Currency** | Euro |
| **Capital** | Helsinki (Helsingfors) | **Organizations** | EU, OECD, UN |

Map page 158–159

Finland is in northern Europe, and nearly one-third of the country lies north of the Arctic Circle. Forests cover over seventy per cent of the land area, and ten per cent is covered by lakes. Summers are short and warm, and winters are long and severe, particularly in the north. Most of the population lives in the southern third of the country, along the coast or near the lakes. Timber is a major resource and there are important minerals, chiefly chromium. Main industries include metal working, electronics, paper and paper products, and chemicals. The main trading partners are Germany, Sweden and the UK.

## FRANCE
French Republic

| | | | |
|---|---|---|---|
| **Area Sq Km** | 543 965 | **Languages** | French, Arabic |
| **Area Sq Miles** | 210 026 | **Religions** | Roman Catholic, Protestant, Sunni Muslim |
| **Population** | 63 126 000 | | |
| **Capital** | Paris | **Currency** | Euro |
| | | **Organizations** | EU, NATO, OECD, UN |

Map page 166

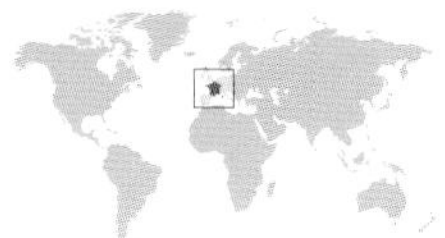

France lies in western Europe and has coastlines on the Atlantic Ocean and the Mediterranean Sea. It includes the Mediterranean island of Corsica. Northern and western regions consist mostly of flat or rolling countryside, and include the major lowlands of the Paris basin, the Loire valley and the Aquitaine basin, drained by the Seine, Loire and Garonne river systems respectively. The centre-south is dominated by the hill region of the Massif Central. To the east are the Vosges and Jura mountains and the Alps. In the southwest, the Pyrenees form a natural border with Spain. The climate is temperate with warm summers and cool winters, although the Mediterranean coast has hot, dry summers and mild winters. Over eighty per cent of the population lives in towns, with almost a sixth of the population living in the Paris area. The French economy has a substantial and varied agricultural base. It is a major producer of both fresh and processed food. There are relatively few mineral resources; it has coal reserves, and some oil and natural gas, but it relies heavily on nuclear and hydroelectric power and imported fuels. France is one of the world's major industrial countries. Main industries include food processing, iron, steel and aluminium production, chemicals, cars, electronics and oil refining. The main exports are transport equipment, plastics and chemicals. Tourism is a major source of revenue and employment. Trade is predominantly with other European Union countries.

## French Guiana
French Overseas Department

| | | | |
|---|---|---|---|
| **Area Sq Km** | 90 000 | **Languages** | French, Creole |
| **Area Sq Miles** | 34 749 | **Religions** | Roman Catholic |
| **Population** | 237 000 | **Currency** | Euro |
| **Capital** | Cayenne | | |

Map page 211 French Guiana, on the north coast of South America, is densely forested. The climate is tropical, with high rainfall. Most people live in the coastal strip, and agriculture is mostly subsistence farming. Forestry and fishing are important, but mineral resources are largely unexploited and industry is limited. French Guiana depends on French aid. The main trading partners are France and the USA.

## French Polynesia
French Overseas Country

| | | | |
|---|---|---|---|
| **Area Sq Km** | 3 265 | **Languages** | French, Tahitian, other Polynesian languages |
| **Area Sq Miles** | 1 261 | **Religions** | Protestant, Roman Catholic |
| **Population** | 274 000 | **Currency** | CFP franc |
| **Capital** | Papeete | | |

Map page 123 Extending over a vast area of the southeast Pacific Ocean, French Polynesia comprises more than one hundred and thirty islands and coral atolls. The main island groups are the Marquesas Islands, the Tuamotu Archipelago and the Society Islands. The capital, Papeete, is on Tahiti in the Society Islands. The climate is subtropical, and the economy is based on tourism. The main export is cultured pearls.

## GABON
Gabonese Republic

| | | | |
|---|---|---|---|
| Area Sq Km | 267 667 | Languages | French, Fang, local languages |
| Area Sq Miles | 103 347 | Religions | Roman Catholic, Protestant, traditional beliefs |
| Population | 1 534 000 | Currency | CFA franc |
| Capital | Libreville | Organizations | UN |

Map page 178

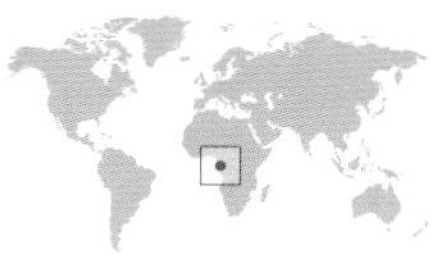

Gabon, on the Atlantic coast of central Africa, consists of low plateaus and a coastal plain lined by lagoons and mangrove swamps. The climate is tropical and rainforests cover over three-quarters of the land area. Over eighty per cent of the population lives in towns. The economy is heavily dependent on oil, which accounts for over eighty per cent of exports; manganese, uranium and timber are the other main exports. Agriculture is mainly at subsistence level.

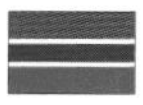

## THE GAMBIA
Republic of The Gambia

| | | | |
|---|---|---|---|
| Area Sq Km | 11 295 | Languages | English, Malinke, Fulani, Wolof |
| Area Sq Miles | 4 361 | Religions | Sunni Muslim, Protestant |
| Population | 1 776 000 | Currency | Dalasi |
| Capital | Banjul | Organizations | Comm., UN |

Map page 176

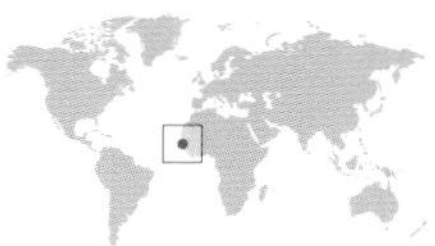

The Gambia, on the coast of west Africa, occupies a strip of land along the lower Gambia river. Sandy beaches are backed by mangrove swamps, beyond which is savanna. The climate is tropical, with most rainfall in the summer. Over seventy per cent of Gambians are farmers, growing chiefly groundnuts (the main export), cotton, oil palms and food crops. Livestock rearing and fishing are important, while manufacturing is limited. Re-exports, mainly from Senegal, and tourism are major sources of income.

## Gaza
Disputed territory

| | | | |
|---|---|---|---|
| Area Sq Km | 363 | Languages | Arabic |
| Area Sq Miles | 140 | Religions | Sunni Muslim, Shi'a Muslim |
| Population | 1 535 120 | Currency | Israeli shekel |
| Capital | Gaza | | |

Map page 136 Gaza is a narrow strip of land on the southeast corner of the Mediterranean Sea, between Egypt and Israel. This Palestinian territory has limited autonomy from Israel, but hostilities between Israel and the indigenous Arab population continue to restrict its economic development.

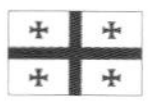

## GEORGIA
Republic of Georgia

| | | | |
|---|---|---|---|
| Area Sq Km | 69 700 | Languages | Georgian, Russian, Armenian, Azeri, Ossetian, Abkhaz |
| Area Sq Miles | 26 911 | Religions | Georgian Orthodox, Russian Orthodox, Sunni Muslim |
| Population | 4 329 000 | Currency | Lari |
| Capital | T'bilisi | Organizations | UN |

Map page 173

Georgia is in the northwest Caucasus area of southwest Asia, on the eastern coast of the Black Sea. Mountain ranges in the north and south flank the Kura and Rioni valleys. The climate is generally mild, and along the coast it is subtropical. Agriculture is important, with tea, grapes, and citrus fruits the main crops. Mineral resources include manganese ore and oil, and the main industries are steel, oil refining and machine building. The main trading partners are Turkey, Ukraine and Azerbaijan.

## GERMANY
Federal Republic of Germany

| | | | |
|---|---|---|---|
| Area Sq Km | 357 022 | Languages | German, Turkish |
| Area Sq Miles | 137 849 | Religions | Protestant, Roman Catholic |
| Population | 82 163 000 | Currency | Euro |
| Capital | Berlin | Organizations | EU, NATO, OECD, UN |

Map page 168

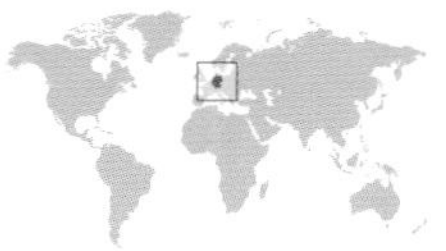

The central European state of Germany borders nine countries and has coastlines on the North and Baltic Seas. Behind the indented coastline, and covering about one-third of the country, is the north German plain, a region of fertile farmland and sandy heaths drained by the country's major rivers. The central highlands are a belt of forested hills and plateaus which stretch from the Eifel region in the west to the Erzgebirge mountains along the border with the Czech Republic. Farther south the land rises to the Swabian Alps (Schwäbische Alb), with the high rugged and forested Black Forest (Schwarzwald) in the southwest. In the far south the Bavarian Alps form the border with Austria. The climate is temperate, with continental conditions in eastern areas. The population is highly urbanized, with nearly seventy-five per cent living in cities and towns. With the exception of coal, lignite, potash and baryte, Germany lacks minerals and other industrial raw materials. It has a small agricultural base, although a few products (chiefly wines and beers) enjoy an international reputation. Germany is the world's fourth ranking economy after the USA, China and Japan. Its industries are amongst the world's most technologically advanced. Exports include machinery, vehicles and chemicals. The majority of trade is with other countries in the European Union, the USA and Japan.

### Baden-Württemberg (State)
Area Sq Km (Sq Miles) 35 752 (13 804) Population 10 758 000 Capital Stuttgart

### Bayern (State)
Area Sq Km (Sq Miles) 70 550 (27 240) Population 12 538 000 Capital Munich (München)

### Berlin (State)
Area Sq Km (Sq Miles) 892 (344) Population 3 456 000 Capital Berlin

### Brandenburg (State)
Area Sq Km (Sq Miles) 29 476 (11 381) Population 2 505 100 Capital Potsdan

### Bremen
Area Sq Km (Sq Miles) 404 (156) Population 661 000 Capital Bremen

### Hamburg (State)
Area Sq Km (Sq Miles) 755 (292) Population 2 834 221 Capital Hamburg

### Hessen (State)
Area Sq Km (Sq Miles) 21 114 (8 152) Population 6 071 000 Capital Wiesbaden

### Mecklenburg-Vorpommern (State)
Area Sq Km (Sq Miles) 23 173 (8 947) Population 1 645 000 Capital Schwerin

### Niedersachsen (State)
Area Sq Km (Sq Miles) 47 616 (18 385) Population 7 922 000 Capital Hannover

### Nordrhein-Westfalen (State)
Area Sq Km (Sq Miles) 34 082 (13 159) Population 17 851 000 Capital Düsseldorf

### Rheinland-Pfalz (State)
Area Sq Km (Sq Miles) 19 847 (7 663) Population 4 006 000 Capital Mainz

### Saarland (State)
Area Sq Km (Sq Miles) 2 568 (992) Population 1 019 000 Capital Saarbrücken

### Sachsen (State)
Area Sq Km (Sq Miles) 18 413 (7 109) Population 4 152 000 Capital Dresden

### Sachsen-Anhalt (State)
Area Sq Km (Sq Miles) 20 447 (7 895) Population 2 339 000 Capital Magdeburg

### Schleswig-Holstein (State)
Area Sq Km (Sq Miles) 15 761 (6 085) Population 2 834 221 Capital Kiel

### Thüringen (State)
Area Sq Km (Sq Miles) 16 172 (6 244) Population 2 237 000 Capital Erfurt

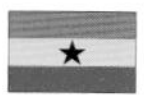

## GHANA
Republic of Ghana

| | | | |
|---|---|---|---|
| Area Sq Km | 238 537 | Languages | English, Hausa, Akan, local languages |
| Area Sq Miles | 92 100 | Religions | Christian, Sunni Muslim, traditional beliefs |
| Population | 24 966 000 | Currency | Cedi |
| Capital | Accra | Organizations | Comm., UN |

Map page 176

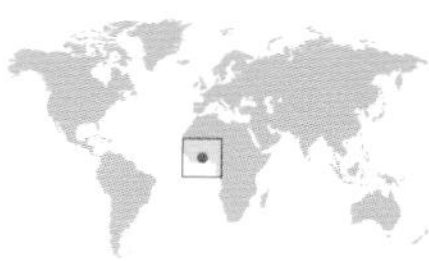

A west African state on the Gulf of Guinea, Ghana is a land of plains and low plateaus covered with savanna and rainforest. In the east is the Volta basin and Lake Volta. The climate is tropical, with the highest rainfall in the south, where most of the population lives. Agriculture employs around fifty per cent of the workforce. Main exports are gold, timber, cocoa, bauxite and manganese ore.

## Gibraltar
United Kingdom Overseas Territory

| | | | |
|---|---|---|---|
| Area Sq Km | 7 | Languages | English, Spanish |
| Area Sq Miles | 3 | Religions | Roman Catholic, Protestant, Sunni Muslim |
| Population | 29 000 | Currency | Gibraltar pound |
| Capital | Gibraltar | | |

Map page 167 Gibraltar lies on the south coast of Spain at the western entrance to the Mediterranean Sea. The economy depends on tourism, offshore banking and shipping services.

## GREECE
Hellenic Republic

| | | | |
|---|---|---|---|
| Area Sq Km | 131 957 | Languages | Greek |
| Area Sq Miles | 50 949 | Religions | Greek Orthodox, Sunni Muslim |
| Population | 11 390 000 | Currency | Euro |
| Capital | Athens (Athina) | Organizations | EU, NATO, OECD, UN |

Map page 171

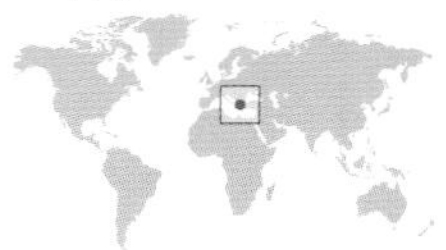

Greece comprises a mountainous peninsula in the Balkan region of southeastern Europe and many islands in the Ionian, Aegean and Mediterranean Seas. The islands make up over one-fifth of its area. Mountains and hills cover much of the country. The main lowland areas are the plains of Thessaly in the centre and around Thessaloniki in the northeast. Summers are hot and dry while winters are mild and wet, but colder in the north with heavy snowfalls in the mountains. One-third of Greeks live in the Athens area. Employment in agriculture accounts for approximately twenty per cent of the workforce, and exports include citrus fruits, raisins, wine, olives and olive oil. Aluminium and nickel are mined and a wide range of manufactures are produced, including food products and tobacco, textiles, clothing, and chemicals. Tourism is an important industry and there is a large services sector. Most trade is with other European Union countries.

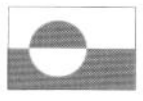

## Greenland
Self-governing Danish Territory

| | | | |
|---|---|---|---|
| Area Sq Km | 2 175 600 | Languages | Greenlandic, Danish |
| Area Sq Miles | 840 004 | Religions | Protestant |
| Population | 57 000 | Currency | Danish krone |
| Capital | Nuuk (Godthåb) | | |

Map page 185

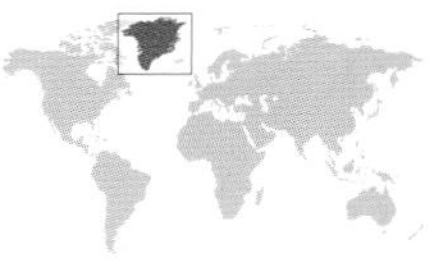

Situated to the northeast of North America between the Atlantic and Arctic Oceans, Greenland is the largest island in the world. It has a polar climate and over eighty per cent of the land area is covered by permanent ice cap. The economy is based on fishing and fish processing.

## GRENADA

| | | | |
|---|---|---|---|
| Area Sq Km | 378 | Languages | English, Creole |
| Area Sq Miles | 146 | Religions | Roman Catholic, Protestant |
| Population | 105 000 | Currency | East Caribbean dollar |
| Capital | St George's | Organizations | CARICOM, Comm., UN |

Map page 213

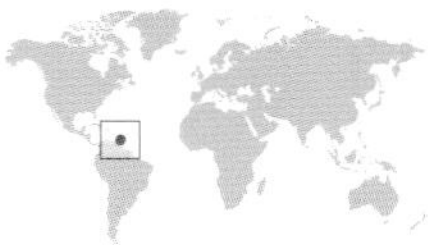

The Caribbean state comprises Grenada, the most southerly of the Windward Islands, and the southern islands of the Grenadines. Grenada has wooded hills, with beaches in the southwest. The climate is warm and wet. Agriculture is the main activity, with bananas, nutmeg and cocoa the main exports. Tourism is the main foreign exchange earner.

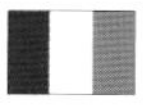

## Guadeloupe
French Overseas Department

| | | | |
|---|---|---|---|
| Area Sq Km | 1 780 | Languages | French, Creole |
| Area Sq Miles | 687 | Religions | Roman Catholic |
| Population | 463 000 | Currency | Euro |
| Capital | Basse-Terre | | |

Map page 205 Guadeloupe, in the Leeward Islands in the Caribbean, consists of two main islands (Basse-Terre and Grande-Terre, connected by a bridge), Marie-Galante, and a few outer islands. The climate is tropical, but moderated by trade winds. Bananas, sugar and rum are the main exports and tourism is a major source of income.

## Guam
United States Unincorporated Territory

| | | | |
|---|---|---|---|
| Area Sq Km | 541 | Languages | Chamorro, English, Tagalog |
| Area Sq Miles | 209 | Religions | Roman Catholic |
| Population | 182 000 | Currency | United States dollar |
| Capital | Hagåtña | | |

Map page 147 Lying at the south end of the Northern Mariana Islands in the western Pacific Ocean, Guam has a humid tropical climate. The island has a large US military base and the economy relies on that and on tourism.

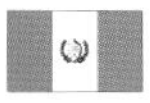

## GUATEMALA
Republic of Guatemala

| | | | |
|---|---|---|---|
| **Area Sq Km** | 108 890 | **Languages** | Spanish, Mayan languages |
| **Area Sq Miles** | 42 043 | **Religions** | Roman Catholic, Protestant |
| **Population** | 14 757 000 | **Currency** | Quetzal, United States dollar |
| **Capital** | Guatemala City | **Organizations** | UN |

**Map page 207**

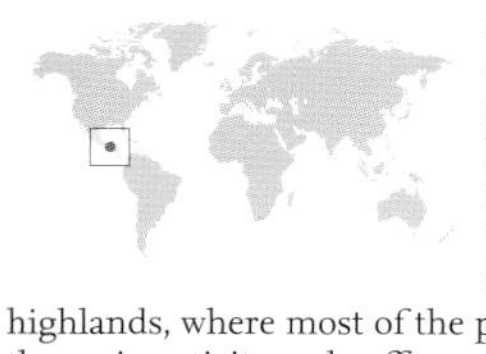

The most populous country in Central America after Mexico, Guatemala has long Pacific and short Caribbean coasts separated by a mountain chain which includes several active volcanoes. The climate is hot tropical in the lowlands and cooler in the highlands, where most of the population lives. Farming is the main activity and coffee, sugar and bananas are the main exports. There is some manufacturing of clothing and textiles. The main trading partner is the USA.

## Guernsey
United Kingdom Crown Dependency

| | | | |
|---|---|---|---|
| **Area Sq Km** | 78 | **Languages** | English, French |
| **Area Sq Miles** | 30 | **Religions** | Protestant, Roman Catholic |
| **Population** | 65 264 | **Currency** | Pound sterling |
| **Capital** | St Peter Port | | |

**Map page 166** Guernsey is one of the Channel Islands, lying off northern France. The dependency also includes the nearby islands of Alderney, Sark and Herm. Financial services are an important part of the island's economy.

## GUINEA
Republic of Guinea

| | | | |
|---|---|---|---|
| **Area Sq Km** | 245 857 | **Languages** | French, Fulani, Malinke, local languages |
| **Area Sq Miles** | 94 926 | **Religions** | Sunni Muslim, traditional beliefs, Christian |
| **Population** | 10 222 000 | **Currency** | Guinea franc |
| **Capital** | Conakry | **Organizations** | UN |

**Map page 176**

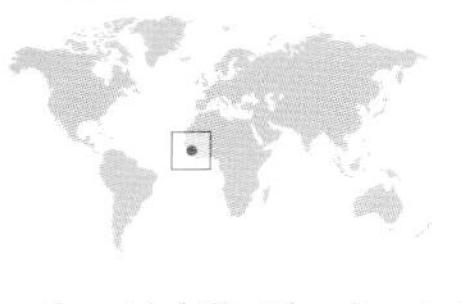

Guinea is in west Africa, on the Atlantic Ocean. There are mangrove swamps along the coast, while inland are lowlands and the Fouta Djallon mountains and plateaus. To the east are savanna plains drained by the upper Niger river system. The southeast is hilly. The climate is tropical, with high coastal rainfall. Agriculture is the main activity, employing nearly eighty per cent of the workforce, with coffee, bananas and pineapples the chief cash crops. There are huge reserves of bauxite, which accounts for more than seventy per cent of exports. Other exports include aluminium oxide, gold, coffee and diamonds.

## GUINEA-BISSAU
Republic of Guinea-Bissau

| | | | |
|---|---|---|---|
| **Area Sq Km** | 36 125 | **Languages** | Portuguese, Crioulo, local languages |
| **Area Sq Miles** | 13 948 | **Religions** | Traditional beliefs, Sunni Muslim, Christian |
| **Population** | 1 547 000 | **Currency** | CFA franc |
| **Capital** | Bissau | **Organizations** | UN |

**Map page 176**

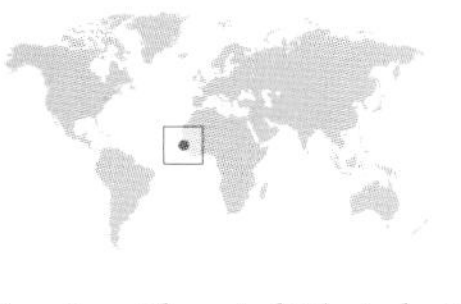

Guinea-Bissau is on the Atlantic coast of west Africa. The mainland coast is swampy and contains many estuaries. Inland are forested plains, and to the east are savanna plateaus. The climate is tropical. The economy is based mainly on subsistence farming. There is little industry, and timber and mineral resources are largely unexploited. Cashews account for seventy per cent of exports. Guinea-Bissau is one of the least developed countries in the world.

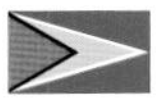

## GUYANA
Co-operative Republic of Guyana

| | | | |
|---|---|---|---|
| **Area Sq Km** | 214 969 | **Languages** | English, Creole, Amerindian languages |
| **Area Sq Miles** | 83 000 | **Religions** | Protestant, Hindu, Roman Catholic, Sunni Muslim |
| **Population** | 756 000 | **Currency** | Guyana dollar |
| **Capital** | Georgetown | **Organizations** | CARICOM, Comm., UN |

**Map page 210–211**

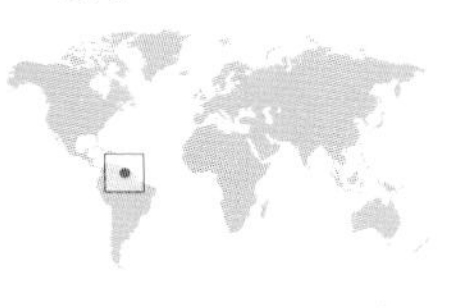

Guyana, on the northeast coast of South America, consists of highlands in the west and savanna uplands in the southwest. Most of the country is densely forested. A lowland coastal belt supports crops and most of the population. The generally hot, humid and wet conditions are modified along the coast by sea breezes. The economy is based on agriculture, bauxite, and forestry. Sugar, bauxite, gold, rice and timber are the main exports.

## HAITI
Republic of Haiti

| | | | |
|---|---|---|---|
| **Area Sq Km** | 27 750 | **Languages** | French, Creole |
| **Area Sq Miles** | 10 714 | **Religions** | Roman Catholic, Protestant, Voodoo |
| **Population** | 10 124 000 | **Currency** | Gourde |
| **Capital** | Port-au-Prince | **Organizations** | CARICOM, UN |

**Map page 205**

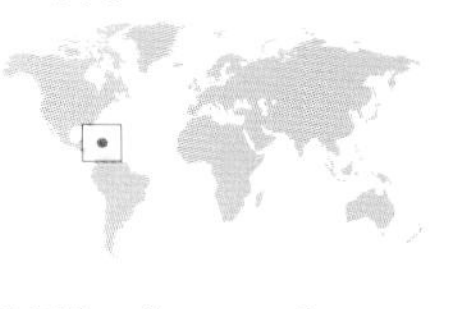

Haiti, occupying the western third of the Caribbean island of Hispaniola, is a mountainous state with small coastal plains and a central valley. The Dominican Republic occupies the rest of the island. The climate is tropical, and is hottest in coastal areas. Haiti has few natural resources, is densely populated and relies on exports of local crafts and coffee, and remittances from workers abroad. The country has not yet recovered from the 2010 earthquake.

## HONDURAS
Republic of Honduras

| | | | |
|---|---|---|---|
| **Area Sq Km** | 112 088 | **Languages** | Spanish, Amerindian languages |
| **Area Sq Miles** | 43 277 | **Religions** | Roman Catholic, Protestant |
| **Population** | 7 755 000 | **Currency** | Lempira |
| **Capital** | Tegucigalpa | **Organizations** | UN |

**Map page 206**

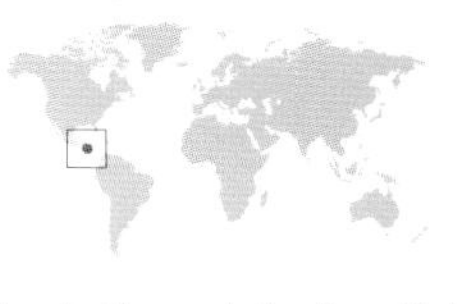

Honduras, in central America, is a mountainous and forested country with lowland areas along its long Caribbean and short Pacific coasts. Coastal areas are hot and humid with heavy summer rainfall; inland is cooler and drier. Most of the population lives in the central valleys. Coffee and bananas are the main exports, along with shellfish and zinc. Industry involves mainly agricultural processing.

## HUNGARY

| | | | |
|---|---|---|---|
| **Area Sq Km** | 93 030 | **Languages** | Hungarian |
| **Area Sq Miles** | 35 919 | **Religions** | Roman Catholic, Protestant |
| **Population** | 9 966 000 | **Currency** | Forint |
| **Capital** | Budapest | **Organizations** | EU, NATO, OECD, UN |

**Map page 168–169**

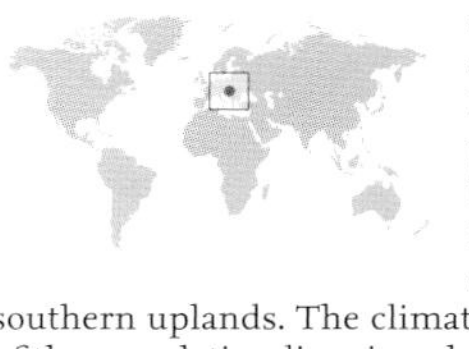

The Danube river flows north-south through central Hungary, a landlocked country in eastern Europe. In the east lies a great plain, flanked by highlands in the north. In the west low mountains and Lake Balaton separate a smaller plain and southern uplands. The climate is continental. Sixty per cent of the population lives in urban areas, and one-fifth lives in the capital, Budapest. Some minerals and energy resources are exploited, chiefly bauxite, coal and natural gas. Hungary has an industrial economy based on metals, machinery, transport equipment, chemicals and food products. The main trading partners are Germany and Austria. Hungary joined the European Union in May 2004.

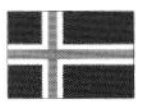

## ICELAND
Republic of Iceland

| | | | |
|---|---|---|---|
| **Area Sq Km** | 102 820 | **Languages** | Icelandic |
| **Area Sq Miles** | 39 699 | **Religions** | Protestant |
| **Population** | 324 000 | **Currency** | Icelandic króna |
| **Capital** | Reykjavík | **Organizations** | NATO, OECD, UN |

**Map page 158**

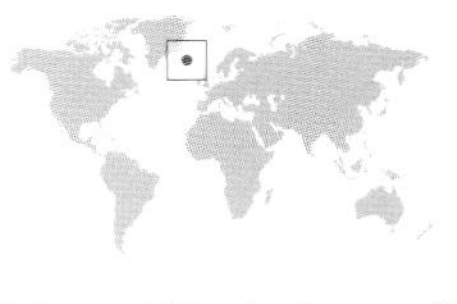

Iceland lies in the north Atlantic Ocean near the Arctic Circle, to the northwest of Scandinavia. The landscape is volcanic, with numerous hot springs, geysers, and approximately two hundred volcanoes. One-tenth of the country is covered by ice caps. Only coastal lowlands are cultivated and settled, and over half the population lives in the Reykjavik area. The climate is mild, moderated by the North Atlantic Drift ocean current and by southwesterly winds. The mainstays of the economy are fishing and fish processing, which account for a third of export earnings. Agriculture involves mainly sheep and dairy farming. Hydroelectric and geothermal energy resources are considerable. The main industries produce aluminium, ferro-silicon and fertilizers. Tourism, including ecotourism, is growing in importance.

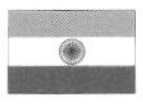

## INDIA
Republic of India

| | | | |
|---|---|---|---|
| **Area Sq Km** | 3 064 898 | **Languages** | Hindi, English, many regional languages |
| **Area Sq Miles** | 1 183 364 | **Religions** | Hindu, Sunni Muslim, Shi'a Muslim, Sikh, Christian |
| **Population** | 1 241 492 000 | **Currency** | Indian rupee |
| **Capital** | New Delhi | **Organizations** | Comm., UN |

**Map page 134–135**

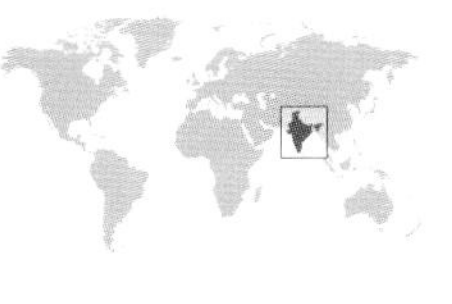

The south Asian country of India occupies a peninsula that juts out into the Indian Ocean between the Arabian Sea and Bay of Bengal. The heart of the peninsula is the Deccan plateau, bordered on either side by ranges of hills, the western Ghats and the lower eastern Ghats, which fall away to narrow coastal plains. To the north is a broad plain, drained by the Indus, Ganges and Brahmaputra rivers and their tributaries. The plain is intensively farmed and is the most populous region. In the west is the Thar Desert. The mountains of the Himalaya form India's northern border, together with parts of the Karakoram and Hindu Kush ranges in the northwest. The climate shows marked seasonal variation: a hot season from March to June; a monsoon season from June to October; and a cold season from November to February. Rainfall ranges between very high in the northeast Assam region to negligible in the Thar Desert. Temperatures range from very cold in the Himalaya to tropical heat over much of the south. Over seventy per cent of the huge population – the second largest in the world – is rural, although Delhi, Mumbai (Bombay) and Kolkata (Calcutta) all rank among the ten largest cities in the world. Agriculture, forestry and fishing account for a quarter of national output and two-thirds of employment. Much of the farming is on a subsistence basis and involves mainly rice and wheat. India is a major world producer of tea, sugar, jute, cotton and tobacco. Livestock is reared mainly for dairy products and hides. There are major reserves of coal, reserves of oil and natural gas, and many minerals, including iron, manganese, bauxite, diamonds and gold. The manufacturing sector is large and diverse – mainly chemicals and chemical products, textiles, iron and steel, food products, electrical goods and transport equipment; software and pharmaceuticals are also important. All the main manufactured products are exported, together with diamonds and jewellery. The USA, Germany, Japan and the UK are the main trading partners.

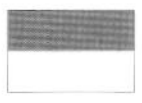

## INDONESIA
Republic of Indonesia

| | | | |
|---|---|---|---|
| **Area Sq Km** | 1 919 445 | **Languages** | Indonesian, local languages |
| **Area Sq Miles** | 741 102 | **Religions** | Sunni Muslim, Protestant, Roman Catholic, Hindu, Buddhist |
| **Population** | 242 326 000 | **Currency** | Rupiah |
| **Capital** | Jakarta | **Organizations** | APEC, ASEAN, UN |

**Map page 147**

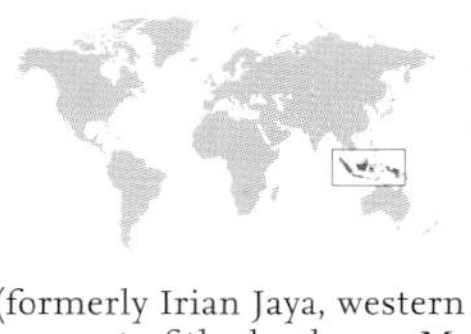

Indonesia, the largest and most populous country in southeast Asia, consists of over thirteen thousand islands extending between the Pacific and Indian Oceans. Sumatra, Java, Sulawesi (Celebes), Kalimantan (two-thirds of Borneo) and Papua (formerly Irian Jaya, western New Guinea) make up ninety per cent of the land area. Most of Indonesia is mountainous and covered with rainforest or mangrove swamps, and there are over three hundred volcanoes, many active. Two-thirds of the population lives in the lowland areas of the islands of Java and Madura. The climate is tropical monsoon. Agriculture is the largest sector of the economy and Indonesia is among the world's top producers of rice, palm oil, tea, coffee, rubber and tobacco. Many goods are produced, including textiles, clothing, cement, tin, fertilizers and vehicles. Main exports are oil, natural gas, timber products and clothing. Main trading partners are Japan, the USA and Singapore.

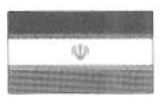

## IRAN
Islamic Republic of Iran

| | | | |
|---|---|---|---|
| **Area Sq Km** | 1 648 000 | **Languages** | Farsi, Azeri, Kurdish, regional languages |
| **Area Sq Miles** | 636 296 | **Religions** | Shi'a Muslim, Sunni Muslim |
| **Population** | 74 799 000 | **Currency** | Iranian rial |
| **Capital** | Tehrān | **Organizations** | OPEC, UN |

**Map page 140–141**

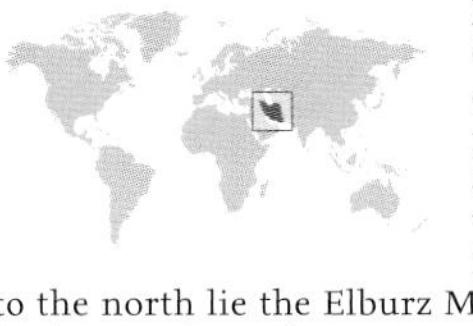

Iran is in southwest Asia, and has coasts on The Gulf, the Caspian Sea and the Gulf of Oman. In the east is a high plateau, with large salt pans and a vast sand desert. In the west the Zagros Mountains form a series of ridges, and to the north lie the Elburz Mountains. Most farming and settlement is on the narrow plain along the Caspian Sea and in the foothills of the north and west. The climate is one of extremes, with hot summers and very cold winters. Most of the light rainfall is in the winter months. Agriculture involves approximately a quarter of the workforce. Wheat is the main crop, but fruit (especially dates) and pistachio nuts are grown for export. Petroleum (the main export) and natural gas are Iran's leading natural resources. Manufactured goods include carpets, clothing, food products and construction materials.

## IRAQ
Republic of Iraq

| | | | |
|---|---|---|---|
| **Area Sq Km** | 438 317 | **Languages** | Arabic, Kurdish, Turkmen |
| **Area Sq Miles** | 169 235 | **Religions** | Shi'a Muslim, Sunni Muslim, Christian |
| **Population** | 32 665 000 | **Currency** | Iraqi dinar |
| **Capital** | Baghdād | **Organizations** | OPEC, UN |

Map page 137

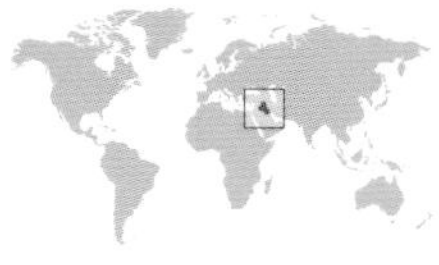

Iraq, in southwest Asia, has at its heart the lowland valley of the Tigris and Euphrates rivers. In the southeast, where the two rivers join, are the Mesopotamian marshes and the Shaṭṭ al 'Arab waterway leading to The Gulf. The north is hilly, while the west is mostly desert. Summers are hot and dry, and winters are mild with light, unreliable rainfall. The Tigris-Euphrates valley contains most of the country's arable land. One in five of the population lives in the capital, Baghdad. The economy has suffered following the 1991 Gulf War and the invasion of US-led coalition forces in 2005. The latter resulted in the overthrow of the dictator Saddam Hussein, but there is continuing internal instability. Oil is normally the main export.

## IRELAND

| | | | |
|---|---|---|---|
| **Area Sq Km** | 70 282 | **Languages** | English, Irish |
| **Area Sq Miles** | 27 136 | **Religions** | Roman Catholic, Protestant |
| **Population** | 4 526 000 | **Currency** | Euro |
| **Capital** | Dublin (Baile Átha Cliath) | **Organizations** | EU, OECD, UN |

Map page 163

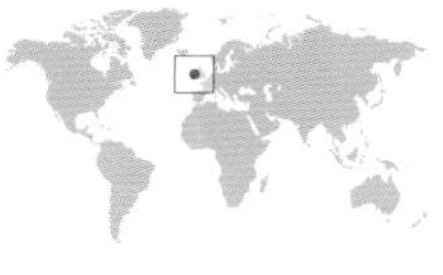

The Irish Republic occupies some eighty per cent of the island of Ireland, in northwest Europe. It is a lowland country of wide valleys, lakes and peat bogs, with isolated mountain ranges around the coast. The west coast is rugged and indented with many bays. The climate is mild due to the modifying effect of the North Atlantic Drift ocean current and rainfall is plentiful, although highest in the west. Nearly sixty per cent of the population lives in urban areas, Dublin and Cork being the main cities. Resources include natural gas, peat, lead and zinc. Agriculture, the traditional mainstay, now employs less than six per cent of the workforce, while industry employs nearly thirty per cent. The main industries are electronics, pharmaceuticals and engineering as well as food processing, brewing and textiles. Service industries are expanding, with tourism a major earner. The UK and USA are the main trading partners.

## Isle of Man
United Kingdom Crown Dependency

| | | | |
|---|---|---|---|
| **Area Sq Km** | 572 | **Languages** | English |
| **Area Sq Miles** | 221 | **Religions** | Protestant, Roman Catholic |
| **Population** | 83 000 | **Currency** | Pound sterling |
| **Capital** | Douglas | | |

Map page 160

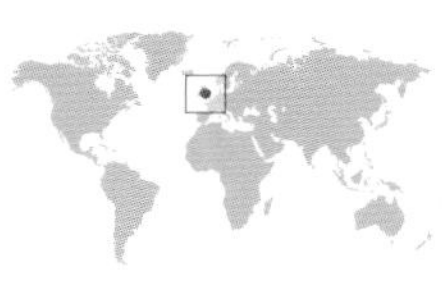

The Isle of Man lies in the Irish Sea between England and Northern Ireland. The island is self-governing, although the UK is responsible for its defence and foreign affairs. It is not part of the European Union, but has a special relationship with the EU which allows for free trade. Eighty per cent of the economy is based on the service sector, particularly financial services.

## ISRAEL
State of Israel

| | | | |
|---|---|---|---|
| **Area Sq Km** | 20 770 | **Languages** | Hebrew, Arabic |
| **Area Sq Miles** | 8 019 | **Religions** | Jewish, Sunni Muslim, Christian, Druze |
| **Population** | 7 562 000 | **Currency** | Shekel |
| **Capital** | Jerusalem (Yerushalayim) (El Quds) De facto capital. Disputed. | **Organizations** | OECD, UN |

Map page 136

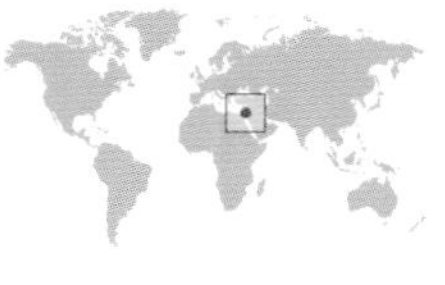

Israel lies on the Mediterranean coast of southwest Asia. Beyond the coastal Plain of Sharon are the hills and valleys of Samaria, with the Galilee highlands to the north. In the east is a rift valley, which extends from Lake Tiberias (Sea of Galilee) to the Gulf of Aqaba and contains the Jordan river and the Dead Sea. In the south is the Negev, a triangular semi-desert plateau. Most of the population lives on the coastal plain or in northern and central areas. Much of Israel has warm summers and mild, wet winters. The south is hot and dry. Agricultural production was boosted by the occupation of the West Bank in 1967. Manufacturing makes the largest contribution to the economy, and tourism is also important. Israel's main exports are machinery and transport equipment, software, diamonds, clothing, fruit and vegetables. The country relies heavily on foreign aid. Security issues relating to territorial disputes over the West Bank and Gaza have still to be resolved.

## ITALY
Italian Republic

| | | | |
|---|---|---|---|
| **Area Sq Km** | 301 245 | **Languages** | Italian |
| **Area Sq Miles** | 116 311 | **Religions** | Roman Catholic |
| **Population** | 60 789 000 | **Currency** | Euro |
| **Capital** | Rome (Roma) | **Organizations** | EU, NATO, OECD, UN |

Map page 170–171

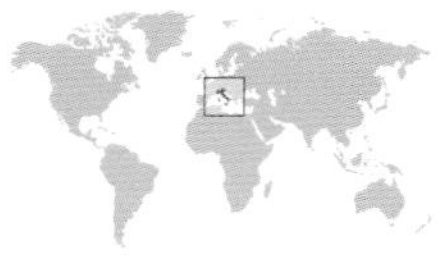

Most of the southern European state of Italy occupies a peninsula that juts out into the Mediterranean Sea. It includes the islands of Sicily and Sardinia and approximately seventy much smaller islands in the surrounding seas. Italy is mountainous, dominated by the Alps, which form its northern border, and the various ranges of the Apennines, which run almost the full length of the peninsula. Many of Italy's mountains are of volcanic origin, and its active volcanoes are Vesuvius, near Naples, Etna and Stromboli. The main lowland area, the Po river valley in the northeast, is the main agricultural and industrial area and is the most populous region. Italy has a Mediterranean climate, although the north experiences colder, wetter winters, with heavy snow in the Alps. The economy is fairly diversified. Some oil, natural gas and coal are produced, but most fuels and minerals used by industry are imported. Agriculture is important, with about a third of the land under cultivation and cereals, vines, fruit and vegetables are the main crops. Italy is the world's second largest wine producer. The north is the centre of Italian industry, especially around Turin, Milan and Genoa. Leading manufactures include industrial and office equipment, domestic appliances, cars, textiles, clothing, leather goods, chemicals and metal products. There is a strong service sector, and with over forty-three million visitors a year, tourism is a major employer and accounts for five per cent of the national income. Finance and banking are also important. Most trade is with other European Union countries.

## JAMAICA

| | | | |
|---|---|---|---|
| **Area Sq Km** | 10 991 | **Languages** | English, Creole |
| **Area Sq Miles** | 4 244 | **Religions** | Protestant, Roman Catholic |
| **Population** | 2 751 000 | **Currency** | Jamaican dollar |
| **Capital** | Kingston | **Organizations** | CARICOM, Comm., UN |

Map page 205

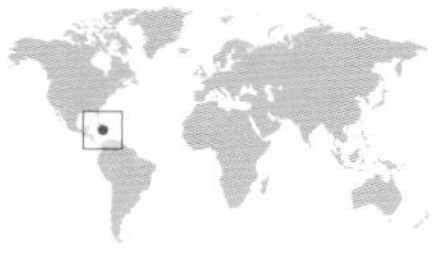

Jamaica, the third largest Caribbean island, has beaches and densely populated coastal plains traversed by hills and plateaus rising to the forested Blue Mountains in the east. The climate is tropical, but cooler and wetter on high ground. The economy is based on tourism, agriculture, mining and light manufacturing. Bauxite, aluminium oxide, sugar and bananas are the main exports. The USA is the main trading partner. Foreign aid is also significant.

## JAPAN

| | | | |
|---|---|---|---|
| **Area Sq Km** | 377 727 | **Languages** | Japanese |
| **Area Sq Miles** | 145 841 | **Religions** | Shintoist, Buddhist, Christian |
| **Population** | 126 497 000 | **Currency** | Yen |
| **Capital** | Tōkyō | **Organizations** | APEC, OECD, UN |

Map page 150–151

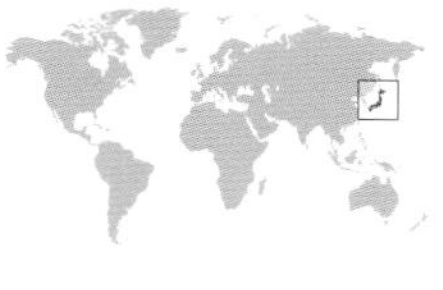

Japan lies in the Pacific Ocean off the coast of eastern Asia and consists of four main islands – Hokkaidō, Honshū, Shikoku and Kyūshū – and more than three thousand smaller islands in the surrounding Sea of Japan, East China Sea and Pacific Ocean. The central island of Honshū accounts for sixty per cent of the total land area and contains eighty per cent of the population. Behind the long and deeply indented coastline, nearly three-quarters of the country is mountainous and heavily forested. Japan has over sixty active volcanoes, and is subject to frequent earthquakes and typhoons. The climate is generally temperate maritime, with warm summers and mild winters, except in western Hokkaidō and northwest Honshū, where the winters are very cold with heavy snow. Only fourteen per cent of the land area is suitable for cultivation, and its few raw materials (coal, oil, natural gas, lead, zinc and copper) are insufficient for its industry. Most materials must be imported, including about ninety per cent of energy requirements. Yet Japan has the world's second largest industrial economy, with a range of modern heavy and light industries centred mainly around the major ports of Yokohama, Ōsaka and Tōkyō. It is the world's largest manufacturer of cars, motorcycles and merchant ships, and a major producer of steel, textiles, chemicals and cement. It is also a leading producer of many consumer durables, such as washing machines, and electronic equipment, chiefly office equipment and computers. Japan has a strong service sector, banking and finance being particularly important, and Tōkyō has one of the world's major stock exchanges. Owing to intensive agricultural production, Japan is seventy per cent self-sufficient in food. The main food crops are rice, barley, fruit, wheat and soya beans. Livestock rearing (chiefly cattle, pigs and chickens) and fishing are also important, and Japan has one of the largest fishing fleets in the world. A major trading nation, Japan has trade links with many countries in southeast Asia and in Europe, although its main trading partner is the USA.

## Jersey
United Kingdom Crown Dependency

| | | | |
|---|---|---|---|
| **Area Sq Km** | 116 | **Languages** | English, French |
| **Area Sq Miles** | 45 | **Religions** | Protestant, Roman Catholic |
| **Population** | 92 500 | **Currency** | Pound sterling |
| **Capital** | St Helier | | |

Map page 166 One of the Channel Islands lying off the west coast of the Cherbourg peninsula in northern France. Financial services are the most important part of the economy.

## JORDAN
Hashemite Kingdom of Jordan

| | | | |
|---|---|---|---|
| **Area Sq Km** | 89 206 | **Languages** | Arabic |
| **Area Sq Miles** | 34 443 | **Religions** | Sunni Muslim, Christian |
| **Population** | 6 330 000 | **Currency** | Jordanian dinar |
| **Capital** | 'Ammān | **Organizations** | UN |

Map page 136–137

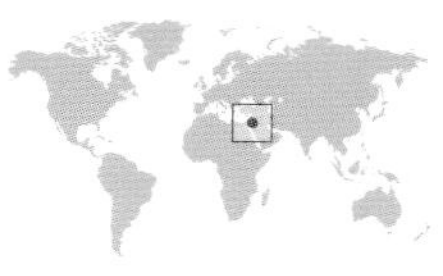

Jordan, in southwest Asia, is landlocked apart from a short coastline on the Gulf of Aqaba. Much of the country is rocky desert plateau. To the west of the mountains, the land falls below sea level to the Dead Sea and the Jordan river. The climate is hot and dry. Most people live in the northwest. Phosphates, potash, pharmaceuticals, fruit and vegetables are the main exports. The tourist industry is important, and the economy relies on workers' remittances from abroad and foreign aid.

## KAZAKHSTAN
Republic of Kazakhstan

| | | | |
|---|---|---|---|
| **Area Sq Km** | 2 717 300 | **Languages** | Kazakh, Russian, Ukrainian, German, Uzbek, Tatar |
| **Area Sq Miles** | 1 049 155 | **Religions** | Sunni Muslim, Russian Orthodox, Protestant |
| **Population** | 16 207 000 | **Currency** | Tenge |
| **Capital** | Astana (Akmola) | **Organizations** | CIS, UN |

Map page 138–139

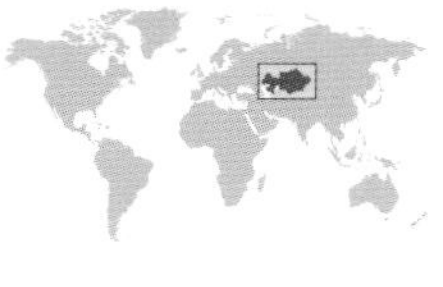

Stretching across central Asia, Kazakhstan covers a vast area of steppe land and semi-desert. The land is flat in the west, with large lowlands around the Caspian Sea, rising to mountains in the southeast. The climate is continental. Agriculture and livestock rearing are important, and cotton and tobacco are the main cash crops. Kazakhstan is very rich in minerals, including coal, chromium, gold, molybdenum, lead and zinc, and has substantial reserves of oil and gas. Mining, metallurgy, machine building and food processing are major industries. Oil, gas and minerals are the main exports, and the Russian Federation is the dominant trading partner.

## KENYA
Republic of Kenya

| | | | |
|---|---|---|---|
| **Area Sq Km** | 582 646 | **Languages** | Swahili, English, local languages |
| **Area Sq Miles** | 224 961 | **Religions** | Christian, traditional beliefs |
| **Population** | 41 610 000 | **Currency** | Kenyan shilling |
| **Capital** | Nairobi | **Organizations** | Comm., UN |

Map page 178

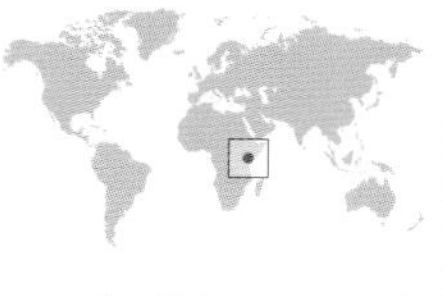

Kenya is in east Africa, on the Indian Ocean. Inland beyond the coastal plains the land rises to plateaus interrupted by volcanic mountains. The Great Rift Valley runs north-south to the west of the capital, Nairobi. Most of the population lives in the central area. Conditions are tropical on the coast, semi-desert in the north and savanna in the south. Hydroelectric power from the Upper Tana river provides most of the country's electricity. Agricultural products, mainly tea, coffee, fruit and vegetables, are the main exports. Light industry is important, and tourism, oil refining and re-exports for landlocked neighbours are major foreign exchange earners.

## KIRIBATI
Republic of Kiribati

| | | | |
|---|---|---|---|
| **Area Sq Km** | 717 | **Languages** | Gilbertese, English |
| **Area Sq Miles** | 277 | **Religions** | Roman Catholic, Protestant |
| **Population** | 101 000 | **Currency** | Australian dollar |
| **Capital** | Bairiki | **Organizations** | Comm., UN |

**Map page 123**

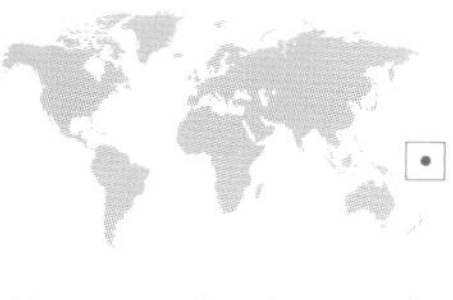

Kiribati, in the Pacific Ocean, straddles the Equator and comprises coral islands in the Gilbert, Phoenix and Line Island groups and the volcanic island of Banaba. Most people live on the Gilbert Islands, and the capital, Bairiki, is on Tarawa island in this group. The climate is hot, and wetter in the north. Copra and fish are exported. Kiribati relies on remittances from workers abroad and foreign aid.

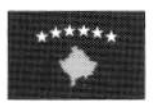

## KOSOVO
Republic of Kosovo

| | | | |
|---|---|---|---|
| **Area Sq Km** | 10 908 | **Languages** | Albanian, Serbian |
| **Area Sq Miles** | 4 212 | **Religions** | Sunni Muslim, Serbian Orthodox |
| **Population** | 2 180 686 | **Currency** | Euro |
| **Capital** | Prishtinë (Priština) | | |

**Map page 171**

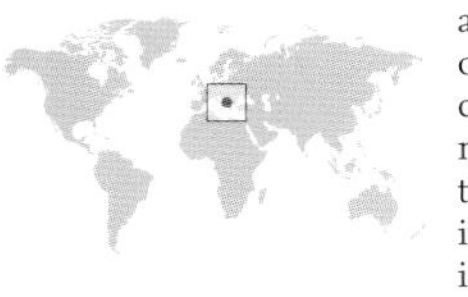

Kosovo, traditionally an autonomous southern province of Serbia, was the focus of ethnic conflict between Serbs and the majority ethnic Albanians in the 1990s until international intervention in 1999, after which it was administered by the UN. Kosovo declared its independence from Serbia in February 2008. The landscape is largely hilly or mountainous, especially along the southern and western borders.

## KUWAIT
State of Kuwait

| | | | |
|---|---|---|---|
| **Area Sq Km** | 17 818 | **Languages** | Arabic |
| **Area Sq Miles** | 6 880 | **Religions** | Sunni Muslim, Shi'a Muslim, Christian, Hindu |
| **Population** | 2 818 000 | **Currency** | Kuwaiti dinar |
| **Capital** | Kuwait (Al Kuwayt) | **Organizations** | GCC, OPEC, UN |

**Map page 137**

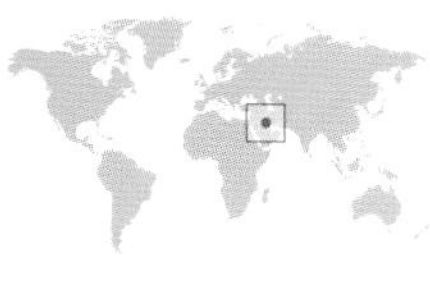

Kuwait lies on the northwest shores of The Gulf in southwest Asia. It is mainly low-lying desert, with irrigated areas along the bay, Kuwait Jun, where most people live. Summers are hot and dry, and winters are cool with some rainfall. The oil industry, which accounts for ninety per cent of exports, has largely recovered from the damage caused by the Gulf War in 1991. Income is also derived from extensive overseas investments. Japan and the USA are the main trading partners.

## KYRGYZSTAN
Kyrgyz Republic

| | | | |
|---|---|---|---|
| **Area Sq Km** | 198 500 | **Languages** | Kyrgyz, Russian, Uzbek |
| **Area Sq Miles** | 76 641 | **Religions** | Sunni Muslim, Russian Orthodox |
| **Population** | 5 393 000 | **Currency** | Kyrgyz som |
| **Capital** | Bishkek (Frunze) | **Organizations** | CIS, UN |

**Map page 139**

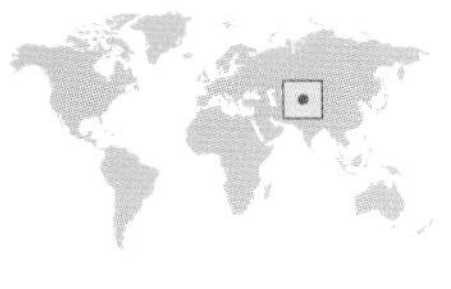

A landlocked central Asian state, Kyrgyzstan is rugged and mountainous, lying to the west of the Tien Shan mountain range. Most of the population lives in the valleys of the north and west. Summers are hot and winters cold. Agriculture (chiefly livestock farming) is the main activity. Some oil and gas, coal, gold, antimony and mercury are produced. Manufactured goods include machinery, metals and metal products, which are the main exports. Most trade is with Germany, the Russian Federation, Kazakhstan and Uzbekistan.

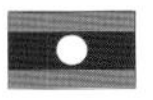

## LAOS
Lao People's Democratic Republic

| | | | |
|---|---|---|---|
| **Area Sq Km** | 236 800 | **Languages** | Lao, local languages |
| **Area Sq Miles** | 91 429 | **Religions** | Buddhist, traditional beliefs |
| **Population** | 6 288 000 | **Currency** | Kip |
| **Capital** | Vientiane (Viangchan) | **Organizations** | ASEAN, UN |

**Map page 147**

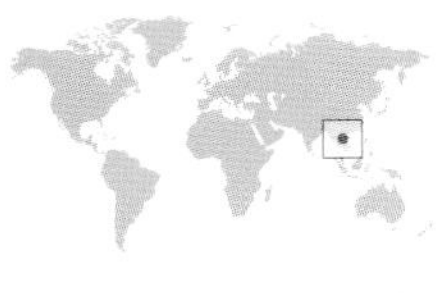

A landlocked country in southeast Asia, Laos is a land of mostly forested mountains and plateaus. The climate is tropical monsoon. Most of the population lives in the Mekong valley and the low plateau in the south, where food crops, chiefly rice, are grown. Hydroelectricity from a plant on the Mekong river, timber, coffee and tin are exported. Laos relies heavily on foreign aid.

## LATVIA
Republic of Latvia

| | | | |
|---|---|---|---|
| **Area Sq Km** | 64 589 | **Languages** | Latvian, Russian |
| **Area Sq Miles** | 24 938 | **Religions** | Protestant, Roman Catholic, Russian Orthodox |
| **Population** | 2 243 000 | **Currency** | Lats |
| **Capital** | Riga | **Organizations** | EU, NATO, UN |

**Map page 159**

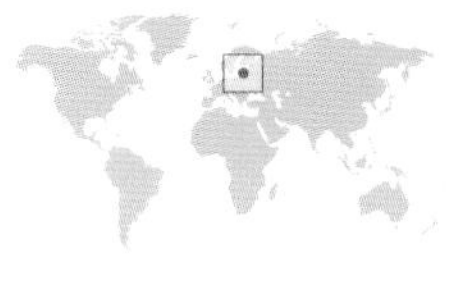

Latvia is in northern Europe, on the Baltic Sea and the Gulf of Riga. The land is flat near the coast but hilly with woods and lakes inland. The country has a modified continental climate. One-third of the people live in the capital, Rīga. Crop and livestock farming are important. There are few natural resources. Industries and main exports include food products, transport equipment, wood and wood products and textiles. The main trading partners are the Russian Federation and Germany. Latvia joined the European Union in May 2004.

## LEBANON
Republic of Lebanon

| | | | |
|---|---|---|---|
| **Area Sq Km** | 10 452 | **Languages** | Arabic, Armenian, French |
| **Area Sq Miles** | 4 036 | **Religions** | Shi'a Muslim, Sunni Muslim, Christian |
| **Population** | 4 259 000 | **Currency** | Lebanese pound |
| **Capital** | Beirut (Beyrouth) | **Organizations** | UN |

**Map page 136**

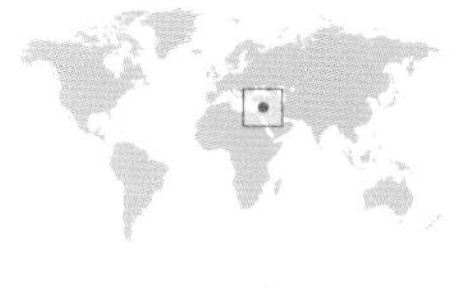

Lebanon lies on the Mediterranean coast of southwest Asia. Beyond the coastal strip, where most of the population lives, are two parallel mountain ranges, separated by the Bekaa Valley (El Beq'a). The economy and infrastructure have been recovering since the 1975–1991 civil war crippled the traditional sectors of financial services and tourism. Switzerland, the USA, France and the UAE are the main trading partners.

## LESOTHO
Kingdom of Lesotho

| | | | |
|---|---|---|---|
| **Area Sq Km** | 30 355 | **Languages** | Sesotho, English, Zulu |
| **Area Sq Miles** | 11 720 | **Religions** | Christian, traditional beliefs |
| **Population** | 2 194 000 | **Currency** | Loti, South African rand |
| **Capital** | Maseru | **Organizations** | Comm., SADC, UN |

**Map page 181**

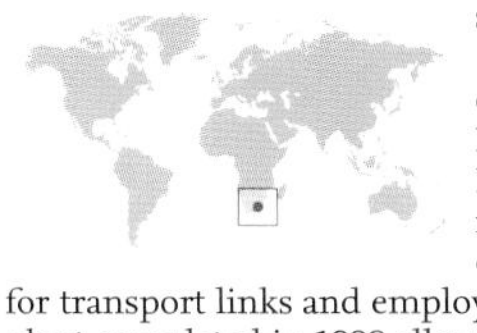

Lesotho is a landlocked state surrounded by the Republic of South Africa. It is a mountainous country lying within the Drakensberg mountain range. Farming and herding are the main activities. The economy depends heavily on South Africa for transport links and employment. A major hydroelectric plant completed in 1998 allows the sale of water to South Africa. Exports include manufactured goods (mainly clothing and road vehicles), food, live animals, wool and mohair.

## LIBERIA
Republic of Liberia

| | | | |
|---|---|---|---|
| **Area Sq Km** | 111 369 | **Languages** | English, Creole, local languages |
| **Area Sq Miles** | 43 000 | **Religions** | Traditional beliefs, Christian, Sunni Muslim |
| **Population** | 4 129 000 | **Currency** | Liberian dollar |
| **Capital** | Monrovia | **Organizations** | UN |

**Map page 176**

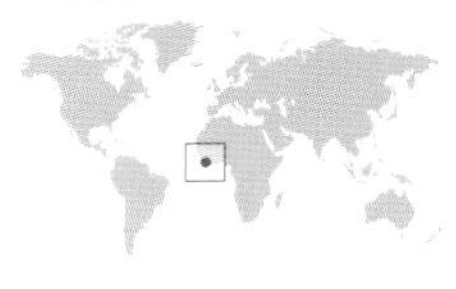

Liberia is on the Atlantic coast of west Africa. Beyond the coastal belt of sandy beaches and mangrove swamps the land rises to a forested plateau and highlands along the Guinea border. A quarter of the population lives along the coast. The climate is hot with heavy rainfall. Liberia is rich in mineral resources and forests. The economy is based on the production and export of basic products. Exports include diamonds, iron ore, rubber and timber. Liberia has a huge international debt and relies heavily on foreign aid.

## LIBYA

| | | | |
|---|---|---|---|
| **Area Sq Km** | 1 759 540 | **Languages** | Arabic, Berber |
| **Area Sq Miles** | 679 362 | **Religions** | Sunni Muslim |
| **Population** | 6 423 000 | **Currency** | Libyan dinar |
| **Capital** | Tripoli (Țarābulus) | **Organizations** | OPEC, UN |

**Map page 176–177**

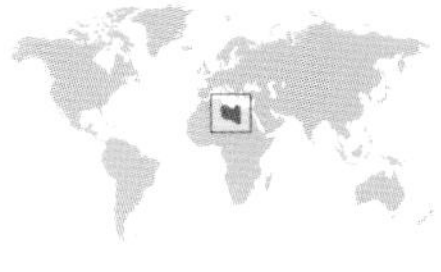

Libya lies on the Mediterranean coast of north Africa. The desert plains and hills of the Sahara dominate the landscape and the climate is hot and dry. Most of the population lives in cities near the coast, where the climate is cooler with moderate rainfall. Farming and herding, chiefly in the northwest, are important but the main industry is oil. Libya is a major producer, and oil accounts for most of its export earnings. Italy and Germany are the main trading partners. As a result of the civil war in 2011 oil exports were disrupted and there was severe damage to the infrastructure of the country.

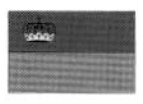

## LIECHTENSTEIN
Principality of Liechtenstein

| | | | |
|---|---|---|---|
| **Area Sq Km** | 160 | **Languages** | German |
| **Area Sq Miles** | 62 | **Religions** | Roman Catholic, Protestant |
| **Population** | 36 000 | **Currency** | Swiss franc |
| **Capital** | Vaduz | **Organizations** | UN |

**Map page 166**

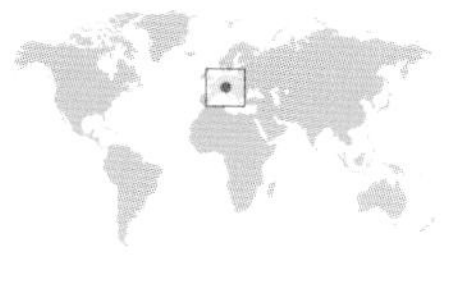

A landlocked state between Switzerland and Austria, Liechtenstein has an industrialized, free-enterprise economy. Low business taxes have attracted companies to establish offices which provide approximately one-third of state revenues. Banking is also important. Major products include precision instruments, ceramics and textiles.

## LITHUANIA
Republic of Lithuania

| | | | |
|---|---|---|---|
| **Area Sq Km** | 65 200 | **Languages** | Lithuanian, Russian, Polish |
| **Area Sq Miles** | 25 174 | **Religions** | Roman Catholic, Protestant, Russian Orthodox |
| **Population** | 3 307 000 | **Currency** | Litas |
| **Capital** | Vilnius | **Organizations** | EU, NATO, UN |

**Map page 159**

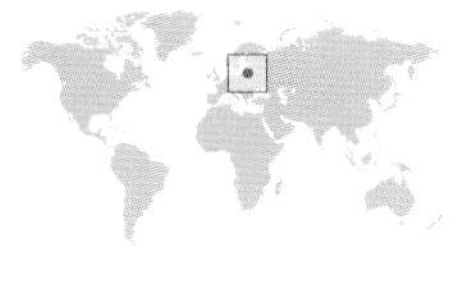

Lithuania is in northern Europe on the eastern shores of the Baltic Sea. It is mainly lowland with many lakes, rivers and marshes. Agriculture, fishing and forestry are important, but manufacturing dominates the economy. The main exports are machinery, mineral products and chemicals. The Russian Federation and Germany are the main trading partners. Lithuania joined the European Union in May 2004.

## LUXEMBOURG
Grand Duchy of Luxembourg

| | | | |
|---|---|---|---|
| **Area Sq Km** | 2 586 | **Languages** | Letzeburgish, German, French |
| **Area Sq Miles** | 998 | **Religions** | Roman Catholic |
| **Population** | 516 000 | **Currency** | Euro |
| **Capital** | Luxembourg | **Organizations** | EU, NATO, OECD, UN |

**Map page 164**

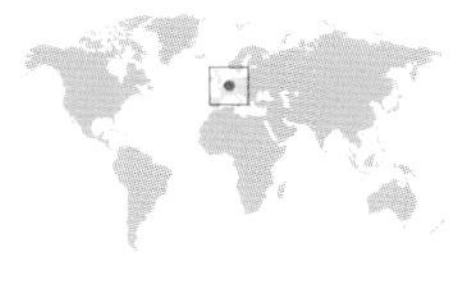

Luxembourg, a small landlocked country in western Europe, borders Belgium, France and Germany. The hills and forests of the Ardennes dominate the north, with rolling pasture to the south, where the main towns, farms and industries are found. The iron and steel industry is still important, but light industries (including textiles, chemicals and food products) are growing. Luxembourg is a major banking centre. Main trading partners are Belgium, Germany and France.

## MACEDONIA (F.Y.R.O.M.)
Republic of Macedonia

| | | | |
|---|---|---|---|
| **Area Sq Km** | 25 713 | **Languages** | Macedonian, Albanian, Turkish |
| **Area Sq Miles** | 9 928 | **Religions** | Macedonian Orthodox, Sunni Muslim |
| **Population** | 2 064 000 | **Currency** | Macedonian denar |
| **Capital** | Skopje | **Organizations** | NATO, UN |

**Map page 171**

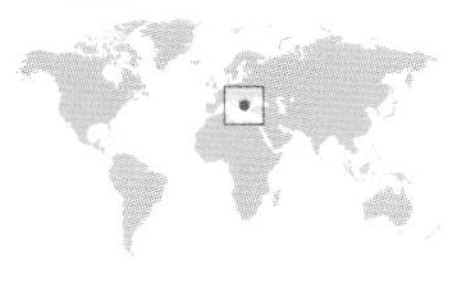

The Former Yugoslav Republic of Macedonia is a landlocked state in southern Europe. Lying within the southern Balkan Mountains, it is traversed northwest-southeast by the Vardar valley. The climate is continental. The economy is based on industry, mining and agriculture, but conflicts in the region have reduced trade and caused economic difficulties. Foreign aid and loans are now assisting in modernization and development of the country.

## MADAGASCAR
Republic of Madagascar

| | | | |
|---|---|---|---|
| **Area Sq Km** | 587 041 | **Languages** | Malagasy, French |
| **Area Sq Miles** | 226 656 | **Religions** | Traditional beliefs, Christian, Sunni Muslim |
| **Population** | 21 315 000 | **Currency** | Malagasy franc |
| **Capital** | Antananarivo | **Organizations** | SADC, UN |

**Map page 179**

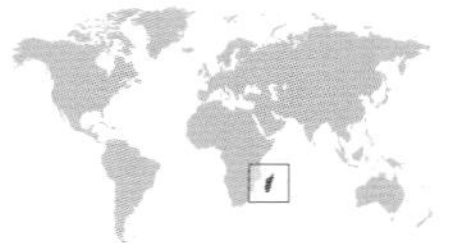

Madagascar lies off the east coast of southern Africa. The world's fourth largest island, it is mainly a high plateau, with a coastal strip to the east and scrubby plain to the west. The climate is tropical, with heavy rainfall in the north and east. Most of the population lives on the plateau. Although the amount of arable land is limited, the economy is based on agriculture. The main industries are agricultural processing, textile manufacturing and oil refining. Foreign aid is important. Exports include coffee, vanilla, cotton cloth, sugar and shrimps. France is the main trading partner.

## MALAWI
Republic of Malawi

| | | | |
|---|---|---|---|
| **Area Sq Km** | 118 484 | **Languages** | Chichewa, English, local languages |
| **Area Sq Miles** | 45 747 | **Religions** | Christian, traditional beliefs, Sunni Muslim |
| **Population** | 15 381 000 | **Currency** | Malawian kwacha |
| **Capital** | Lilongwe | **Organizations** | Comm., SADC, UN |

**Map page 179**

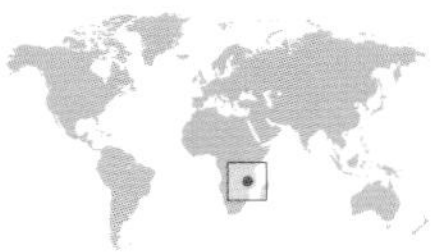

Landlocked Malawi in central Africa is a narrow hilly country at the southern end of the Great Rift Valley. One-fifth is covered by Lake Nyasa. Most of the population lives in rural areas in the southern regions. The climate is mainly subtropical, with varying rainfall. The economy is predominantly agricultural, with tobacco, tea and sugar the main exports. Malawi is one of the world's least developed countries and relies heavily on foreign aid. South Africa is the main trading partner.

## MALAYSIA
Federation of Malaysia

| | | | |
|---|---|---|---|
| **Area Sq Km** | 332 965 | **Languages** | Malay, English, Chinese, Tamil, local languages |
| **Area Sq Miles** | 128 559 | **Religions** | Sunni Muslim, Buddhist, Hindu, Christian, traditional beliefs |
| **Population** | 28 859 000 | **Currency** | Ringgit |
| **Capital** | Kuala Lumpur/ Putrajaya | **Organizations** | APEC, ASEAN, Comm., UN |

**Map page 155**

Malaysia, in southeast Asia, comprises two regions, separated by the South China Sea. The western region occupies the southern Malay Peninsula, which has a chain of mountains dividing the eastern coastal strip from wider plains to the west. East Malaysia, consisting of the states of Sabah and Sarawak in the north of the island of Borneo, is mainly rainforest-covered hills and mountains with mangrove swamps along the coast. Both regions have a tropical climate with heavy rainfall. About eighty per cent of the population lives in Peninsular Malaysia. The country is rich in natural resources and has reserves of minerals and fuels. It is an important producer of tin, oil, natural gas, rubber and tropical hardwoods. Agriculture remains a substantial part of the economy, but industry is the most important sector. The main exports are transport and electronic equipment, oil, chemicals, palm oil, wood and rubber. The main trading partners are Japan, China, the USA and Singapore.

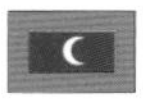

## MALDIVES
Republic of the Maldives

| | | | |
|---|---|---|---|
| **Area Sq Km** | 298 | **Languages** | Divehi (Maldivian) |
| **Area Sq Miles** | 115 | **Religions** | Sunni Muslim |
| **Population** | 320 000 | **Currency** | Rufiyaa |
| **Capital** | Male | **Organizations** | Comm., UN |

**Map page 130**

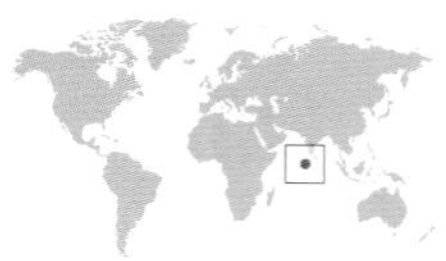

The Maldive archipelago comprises over a thousand coral atolls (around two hundred of which are inhabited), in the Indian Ocean, southwest of India. Over eighty per cent of the land area is less than one metre above sea level. The main atolls are North and South Male and Addu. The climate is hot, humid and monsoonal. There is little cultivation and almost all food is imported. Tourism has expanded rapidly and is the most important sector of the economy.

## MALI
Republic of Mali

| | | | |
|---|---|---|---|
| **Area Sq Km** | 1 240 140 | **Languages** | French, Bambara, local languages |
| **Area Sq Miles** | 478 821 | **Religions** | Sunni Muslim, traditional beliefs, Christian |
| **Population** | 15 840 000 | **Currency** | CFA franc |
| **Capital** | Bamako | **Organizations** | UN |

**Map page 176**

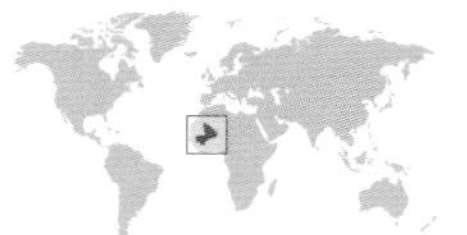

A landlocked state in west Africa, Mali is low-lying, with a few rugged hills in the northeast. Northern regions lie within the Sahara desert. To the south, around the Niger river, are marshes and savanna grassland. Rainfall is unreliable. Most of the population lives along the Niger and Falémé rivers. Exports include cotton, livestock and gold. Mali is one of the least developed countries in the world and relies heavily on foreign aid.

## MALTA
Republic of Malta

| | | | |
|---|---|---|---|
| **Area Sq Km** | 316 | **Languages** | Maltese, English |
| **Area Sq Miles** | 122 | **Religions** | Roman Catholic |
| **Population** | 418 000 | **Currency** | Euro |
| **Capital** | Valletta | **Organizations** | Comm., EU, UN |

**Map page 170**

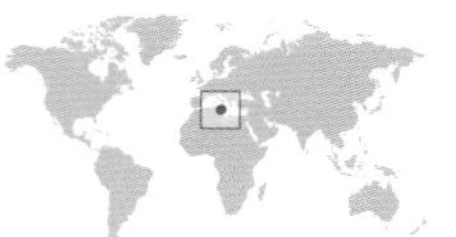

The islands of Malta and Gozo lie in the Mediterranean Sea, off the coast of southern Italy. The islands have hot, dry summers and mild winters. The economy depends on foreign trade, tourism and the manufacture of electronics and textiles. Main trading partners are the USA, France and Italy. Malta joined the European Union in May 2004.

## MARSHALL ISLANDS
Republic of the Marshall Islands

| | | | |
|---|---|---|---|
| **Area Sq Km** | 181 | **Languages** | English, Marshallese |
| **Area Sq Miles** | 70 | **Religions** | Protestant, Roman Catholic |
| **Population** | 55 000 | **Currency** | United States dollar |
| **Capital** | Delap-Uliga-Djarrit | **Organizations** | UN |

**Map page 123**

The Marshall Islands consist of over a thousand atolls, islands and islets, within two chains in the north Pacific Ocean. The main atolls are Majuro (home to half the population), Kwajalein, Jaluit, Enewetak and Bikini. The climate is tropical, with heavy autumn rainfall. About half the workforce is employed in farming or fishing. Tourism is a small source of foreign exchange and the islands depend heavily on aid from the USA.

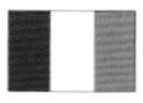

## Martinique
French Overseas Department

| | | | |
|---|---|---|---|
| **Area Sq Km** | 1 079 | **Languages** | French, Creole |
| **Area Sq Miles** | 417 | **Religions** | Roman Catholic, traditional beliefs |
| **Population** | 407 000 | **Currency** | Euro |
| **Capital** | Fort-de-France | | |

**Map page 205** Martinique, one of the Caribbean Windward Islands, has volcanic peaks in the north, a populous central plain, and hills and beaches in the south. Tourism is a major source of foreign exchange, and substantial aid is received from France. The main trading partners are France and Guadeloupe.

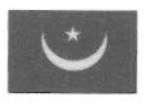

## MAURITANIA
Islamic Arab and African Republic of Mauritania

| | | | |
|---|---|---|---|
| **Area Sq Km** | 1 030 700 | **Languages** | Arabic, French, local languages |
| **Area Sq Miles** | 397 955 | **Religions** | Sunni Muslim |
| **Population** | 3 542 000 | **Currency** | Ouguiya |
| **Capital** | Nouakchott | **Organizations** | UN |

**Map page 176**

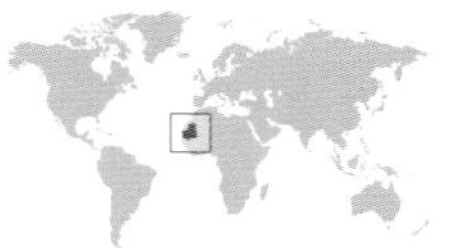

Mauritania is on the Atlantic coast of northwest Africa and lies almost entirely within the Sahara desert. Oases and a fertile strip along the Senegal river to the south are the only areas suitable for cultivation. The climate is generally hot and dry. About a quarter of Mauritanians live in the capital, Nouakchott. Most of the workforce depends on livestock rearing and subsistence farming. There are large deposits of iron ore which account for more than half of total exports. Mauritania's coastal waters are among the richest fishing grounds in the world. The main trading partners are France, Japan and Italy.

## MAURITIUS
Republic of Mauritius

| | | | |
|---|---|---|---|
| **Area Sq Km** | 2 040 | **Languages** | English, Creole, Hindi, Bhojpurī, French |
| **Area Sq Miles** | 788 | **Religions** | Hindu, Roman Catholic, Sunni Muslim |
| **Population** | 1 307 000 | **Currency** | Mauritius rupee |
| **Capital** | Port Louis | **Organizations** | Comm., SADC, UN |

**Map page 175**

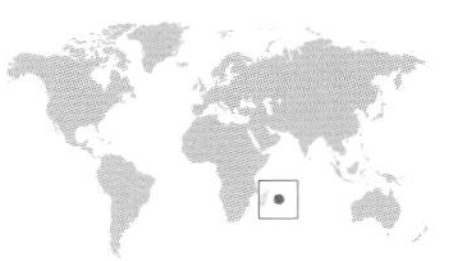

The state comprises Mauritius, Rodrigues and some twenty small islands in the Indian Ocean, east of Madagascar. The main island of Mauritius is volcanic in origin and has a coral coast, rising to a central plateau. Most of the population lives on the north and west sides of the island. The climate is warm and humid. The economy is based on sugar production, light manufacturing (chiefly clothing) and tourism.

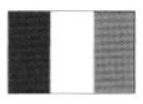

## Mayotte
French Overseas Department

| | | | |
|---|---|---|---|
| **Area Sq Km** | 373 | **Languages** | French, Mahorian (Shimaore), Kibushi |
| **Area Sq Miles** | 144 | **Religions** | Sunni Muslim, Christian |
| **Population** | 211 000 | **Currency** | Euro |
| **Capital** | Dzaoudzi | | |

**Map page 179**

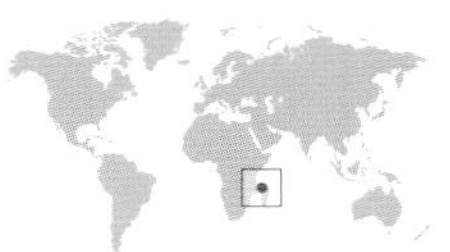

Lying in the Indian Ocean off the east coast of central Africa, Mayotte is geographically part of the Comoro archipelago. The economy is based on agriculture, but Mayotte depends heavily on aid from France.

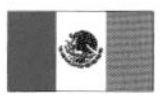

## MEXICO
United Mexican States

| | | | |
|---|---|---|---|
| **Area Sq Km** | 1 972 545 | **Languages** | Spanish, Amerindian languages |
| **Area Sq Miles** | 761 604 | **Religions** | Roman Catholic, Protestant |
| **Population** | 114 793 000 | **Currency** | Mexican peso |
| **Capital** | Mexico City (México) | **Organizations** | APEC, OECD, UN |

**Map page 206–207**

The largest country in Central America, Mexico extends south from the USA to Guatemala and Belize, and from the Pacific Ocean to the Gulf of Mexico. The greater part of the country is high plateau flanked by the western and eastern ranges of the Sierra Madre mountains. The principal lowland is the Yucatán peninsula in the southeast. The climate varies with latitude and altitude: hot and humid in the lowlands, warm on the plateau and cool with cold winters in the mountains. The north is arid, while the far south has heavy rainfall. Mexico City is the fifth largest conurbation in the world and the country's centre of trade and industry. Agriculture involves thirteen per cent of the workforce; crops include grains, coffee, cotton and vegetables. Mexico is rich in minerals, including copper, zinc, lead, tin, sulphur, and silver. It is one of the world's largest producers of oil, from vast reserves in the Gulf of Mexico. The oil and petrochemical industries still dominate the economy, but a variety of manufactured goods are produced, including iron and steel, motor vehicles, textiles, chemicals and food and tobacco products. Tourism is growing in importance. Over three-quarters of all trade is with the USA.

## MICRONESIA, FEDERATED STATES OF

| | | | |
|---|---|---|---|
| **Area Sq Km** | 701 | **Languages** | English, Chuukese, Pohnpeian, local languages |
| **Area Sq Miles** | 271 | **Religions** | Roman Catholic, Protestant |
| **Population** | 112 000 | **Currency** | United States dollar |
| **Capital** | Palikir | **Organizations** | UN |

**Map page 122–123**

Micronesia comprises over six hundred atolls and islands of the Caroline Islands in the north Pacific Ocean. A third of the population lives on Pohnpei. The climate is tropical, with heavy rainfall. Fishing and subsistence farming are the main activities. Fish, garments and bananas are the main exports. Income is also derived from tourism and the licensing of foreign fishing fleets. The islands depend heavily on aid from the USA.

## MOLDOVA
Republic of Moldova

| | | | |
|---|---|---|---|
| **Area Sq Km** | 33 700 | **Languages** | Romanian, Ukrainian, Gagauz, Russian |
| **Area Sq Miles** | 13 012 | **Religions** | Romanian Orthodox, Russian Orthodox |
| **Population** | 3 545 000 | **Currency** | Moldovan leu |
| **Capital** | Chişinău (Kishinev) | **Organizations** | CIS, UN |

**Map page 173**

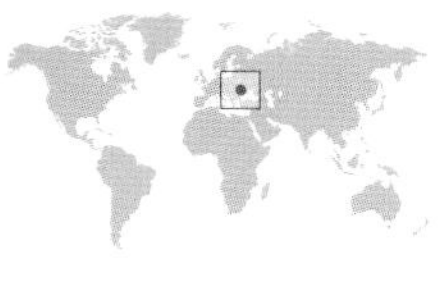

Moldova lies between Romania and Ukraine in eastern Europe. It consists of hilly steppe land, drained by the Prut and Dniester rivers. Moldova has no mineral resources, and the economy is mainly agricultural, with sugar beet, tobacco, wine and fruit the chief products. Food processing, machinery and textiles are the main industries. The Russian Federation is the main trading partner.

## MONACO
Principality of Monaco

| | | | |
|---|---|---|---|
| **Area Sq Km** | 2 | **Languages** | French, Monégasque, Italian |
| **Area Sq Miles** | 1 | **Religions** | Roman Catholic |
| **Population** | 35 000 | **Currency** | Euro |
| **Capital** | Monaco-Ville | **Organizations** | UN |

**Map page 166**

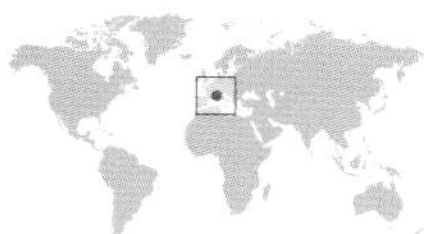

The principality occupies a rocky peninsula and a strip of land on France's Mediterranean coast. Monaco's economy depends on service industries (chiefly tourism, banking and finance) and light industry.

## MONGOLIA

| | | | |
|---|---|---|---|
| **Area Sq Km** | 1 565 000 | **Languages** | Khalka (Mongolian), Kazakh, local languages |
| **Area Sq Miles** | 604 250 | **Religions** | Buddhist, Sunni Muslim |
| **Population** | 2 800 000 | **Currency** | Tugrik (tögrög) |
| **Capital** | Ulan Bator (Ulaanbaatar) | **Organizations** | UN |

**Map page 146**

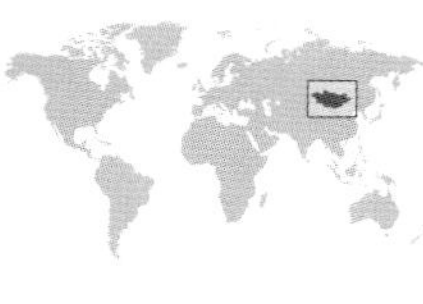

Mongolia is a landlocked country in eastern Asia between the Russian Federation and China. Much of it is high steppe land, with mountains and lakes in the west and north. In the south is the Gobi Desert. Mongolia has long, cold winters and short, mild summers. A quarter of the population lives in the capital, Ulaanbaatar. Livestock breeding and agricultural processing are important. There are substantial mineral resources. Copper and textiles are the main exports. China and the Russian Federation are the main trading partners.

## MONTENEGRO

| | | | |
|---|---|---|---|
| **Area Sq Km** | 13 812 | **Languages** | Serbian (Montenegrin), Albanian |
| **Area Sq Miles** | 5 333 | **Religions** | Montenegrin Orthodox, Sunni Muslim |
| **Population** | 632 000 | **Currency** | Euro |
| **Capital** | Podgorica | **Organizations** | UN |

**Map page 171**

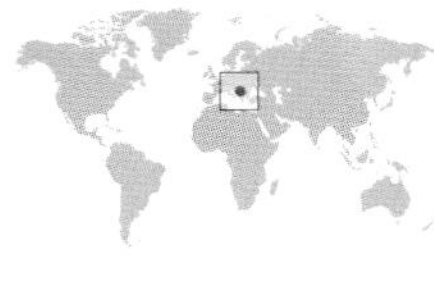

Montenegro was the last constituent republic of the former Yugoslavia to become an independent nation, in June 2006. At that time it opted to split from the state union of Serbia and Montenegro. Montenegro separates the much larger Serbia from the Adriatic coast. The landscape is rugged and mountainous, and the climate Mediterranean.

## Montserrat
United Kingdom Overseas Territory

| | | | |
|---|---|---|---|
| **Area Sq Km** | 100 | **Languages** | English |
| **Area Sq Miles** | 39 | **Religions** | Protestant, Roman Catholic |
| **Population** | 4 655 | **Currency** | East Caribbean dollar |
| **Capital** | Brades (temporary capital) | **Organizations** | CARICOM |

**Map page 205**

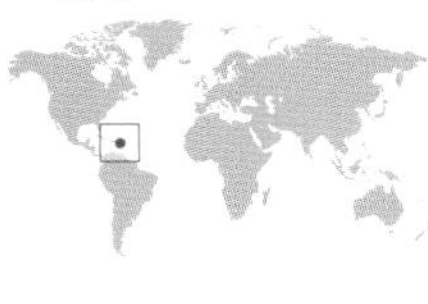

An island in the Leeward Islands group in the Lesser Antilles, in the Caribbean. From 1995 to 1997 the volcanoes in the Soufrière Hills erupted for the first time since 1630. Over sixty per cent of the island was covered in volcanic ash and Plymouth, the capital was, virtually destroyed. Many people emigrated, and the remaining population moved to the north of the island. Brades has replaced Plymouth as the temporary capital. Reconstruction is being funded by aid from the UK.

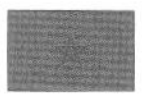

## MOROCCO
Kingdom of Morocco

| | | | |
|---|---|---|---|
| **Area Sq Km** | 446 550 | **Languages** | Arabic, Berber, French |
| **Area Sq Miles** | 172 414 | **Religions** | Sunni Muslim |
| **Population** | 32 273 000 | **Currency** | Moroccan dirham |
| **Capital** | Rabat | **Organizations** | UN |

**Map page 176**

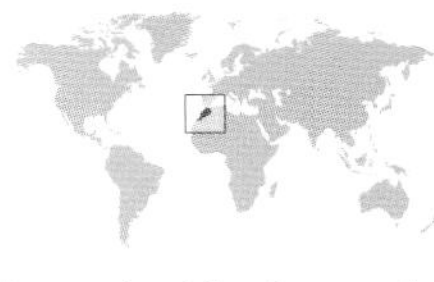

Lying in the northwest of Africa, Morocco has both Atlantic and Mediterranean coasts. The Atlas Mountains separate the arid south and disputed region of western Sahara from the fertile west and north, which have a milder climate. Most Moroccans live on the Atlantic coastal plain. The economy is based on agriculture, phosphate mining and tourism; the most important industries are food processing, textiles and chemicals.

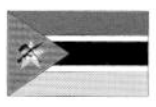

## MOZAMBIQUE
Republic of Mozambique

| | | | |
|---|---|---|---|
| **Area Sq Km** | 799 380 | **Languages** | Portuguese, Makua, Tsonga, local languages |
| **Area Sq Miles** | 308 642 | **Religions** | Traditional beliefs, Roman Catholic, Sunni Muslim |
| **Population** | 23 930 000 | **Currency** | Metical |
| **Capital** | Maputo | **Organizations** | Comm., SADC, UN |

**Map page 179**

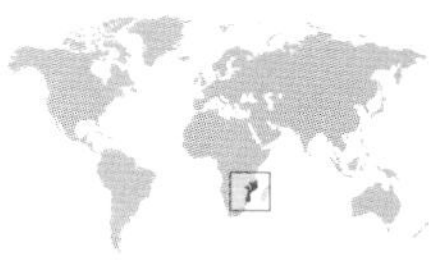

Mozambique lies on the east coast of southern Africa. The land is mainly a savanna plateau drained by the Zambezi and Limpopo rivers, with highlands to the north. Most of the population lives on the coast or in the river valleys. In general the climate is tropical with winter rainfall, but droughts occur. The economy is based on subsistence agriculture. Exports include shrimps, cashews, cotton and sugar, but Mozambique relies heavily on aid, and remains one of the least developed countries in the world.

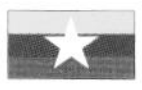

## MYANMAR (Burma)
Republic of the Union of Myanmar

| | | | |
|---|---|---|---|
| **Area Sq Km** | 676 577 | **Languages** | Burmese, Shan, Karen, local languages |
| **Area Sq Miles** | 261 228 | **Religions** | Buddhist, Christian, Sunni Muslim |
| **Population** | 48 337 000 | **Currency** | Kyat |
| **Capital** | Nay Pyi Taw | **Organizations** | ASEAN, UN |

**Map page 147**

Myanmar (Burma) is in southeast Asia, bordering the Bay of Bengal and the Andaman Sea. Most of the population lives in the valley and delta of the Irrawaddy river, which is flanked by mountains and high plateaus. The climate is hot and monsoonal, and rainforest covers much of the land. Most of the workforce is employed in agriculture. Myanmar is rich in minerals, including zinc, lead, copper and silver. Political and social unrest and lack of foreign investment have affected economic development.

## Nagorno-Karabakh (Dağlıq Qarabağ)
Disputed territory

| | | | |
|---|---|---|---|
| **Area Sq Km** | 6 000 | **Languages** | Armenian |
| **Area Sq Miles** | 2 317 | **Religions** | Armenian Orthodox |
| **Population** | 140 000 | **Currency** | Armenian dram |
| **Capital** | Xankändi (Stepanakert) | | |

**Map page 137** Established as an Autonomous Region within Azerbaijan in 1923, Nagorno-Karabakh is a disputed enclave of Azerbaijan. It is legally part of Azerbaijan, but is populated largely by ethnic Armenians who have established what amounts to a separatist de facto republic operating with support from Armenia. In 1991, the local Armenian population declared independence and Azerbaijan abolished the area's autonomous status. As a result of conflict, Nagorno-Karabakh/Armenia occupies approximately twenty per cent of Azerbaijan. A Russian-brokered cease-fire has been in place since 1994, with the cease-fire line enclosing the territory of Nagorno-Karabakh and the additional parts of Azerbaijan, up to the Armenian border, seized by Karabakh Armenians during the fighting. The area between the cease-fire line and the boundary of Nagorno-Karabakh is effectively a 'no-go' area.

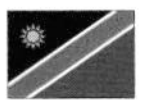

## NAMIBIA
Republic of Namibia

| | | | |
|---|---|---|---|
| **Area Sq Km** | 824 292 | **Languages** | English, Afrikaans, German, Ovambo, local languages |
| **Area Sq Miles** | 318 261 | **Religions** | Protestant, Roman Catholic |
| **Population** | 2 324 000 | **Currency** | Namibian dollar |
| **Capital** | Windhoek | **Organizations** | Comm., SADC, UN |

**Map page 179**

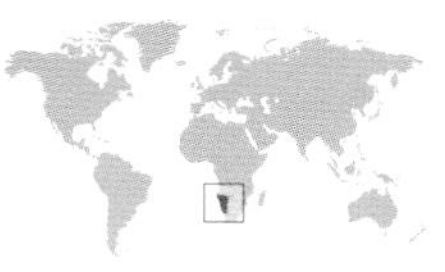

Namibia lies on the southern Atlantic coast of Africa. Mountain ranges separate the coastal Namib Desert from the interior plateau, bordered to the south and east by the Kalahari Desert. The country is hot and dry, but some summer rain in the north supports crops and livestock. Employment is in agriculture and fishing, although the economy is based on mineral extraction – diamonds, uranium, lead, zinc and silver. The economy is closely linked to the Republic of South Africa.

## NAURU
Republic of Nauru

| | | | |
|---|---|---|---|
| **Area Sq Km** | 21 | **Languages** | Nauruan, English |
| **Area Sq Miles** | 8 | **Religions** | Protestant, Roman Catholic |
| **Population** | 10 000 | **Currency** | Australian dollar |
| **Capital** | Yaren | **Organizations** | Comm., UN |

**Map page 125**

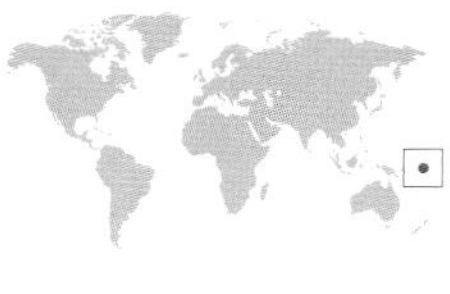

Nauru is a coral island near the Equator in the Pacific Ocean. It has a fertile coastal strip and a barren central plateau. The climate is tropical. The economy is based on phosphate mining, but reserves are near exhaustion and replacement of this income is a serious long-term problem.

## NEPAL
Federal Democratic Republic of Nepal

| | | | |
|---|---|---|---|
| **Area Sq Km** | 147 181 | **Languages** | Nepali, Maithili, Bhojpuri, English, local languages |
| **Area Sq Miles** | 56 827 | **Religions** | Hindu, Buddhist, Sunni Muslim |
| **Population** | 30 486 000 | **Currency** | Nepalese rupee |
| **Capital** | Kathmandu | **Organizations** | UN |

**Map page 144–145**

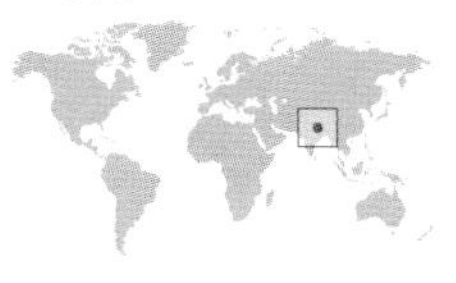

Nepal lies in the eastern Himalaya mountains between India and China. High mountains (including Everest) dominate the north. Most people live in the temperate central valleys and subtropical southern plains. The economy is based largely on agriculture and forestry. There is some manufacturing, chiefly of textiles and carpets, and tourism is important. Nepal relies heavily on foreign aid.

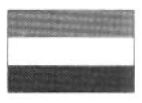

## NETHERLANDS
Kingdom of the Netherlands

| | | | |
|---|---|---|---|
| **Area Sq Km** | 41 526 | **Languages** | Dutch, Frisian |
| **Area Sq Miles** | 16 033 | **Religions** | Roman Catholic, Protestant, Sunni Muslim |
| **Population** | 16 665 000 | **Currency** | Euro |
| **Capital** | Amsterdam/ The Hague | **Organizations** | EU, NATO, OECD, UN |

**Map page 164**

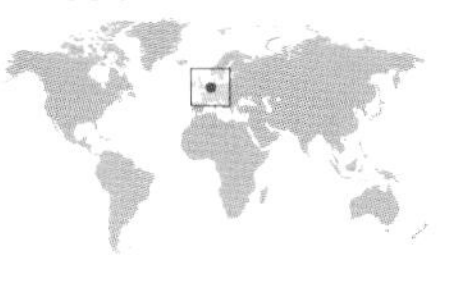

The Netherlands lies on the North Sea coast of western Europe. Apart from low hills in the far southeast, the land is flat and low-lying, much of it below sea level. The coastal region includes the delta of five rivers and polders (reclaimed land), protected by sand dunes, dykes and canals. The climate is temperate, with cool summers and mild winters. Rainfall is spread evenly throughout the year. The Netherlands is a densely populated and highly urbanized country, with the majority of the population living in the cities of Amsterdam, Rotterdam and The Hague. Horticulture and dairy farming are important activities, although they employ less than three per cent of the workforce. The Netherlands ranks as the world's third agricultural exporter, and is a leading producer and exporter of natural gas from reserves in the North Sea. The economy is based mainly on international trade and manufacturing industry. The main industries produce food products, chemicals, machinery, electrical and electronic goods and transport equipment. Germany is the main trading partner, followed by other European Union countries.

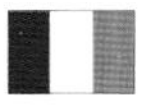

## New Caledonia
French Overseas Collectivity

| | | | |
|---|---|---|---|
| **Area Sq Km** | 19 058 | **Languages** | French, local languages |
| **Area Sq Miles** | 7 358 | **Religions** | Roman Catholic, Protestant, Sunni Muslim |
| **Population** | 255 000 | **Currency** | CFP franc |
| **Capital** | Nouméa | | |

**Map page 125**

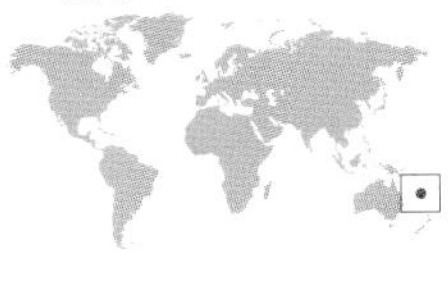

An island group lying in the southwest Pacific, with a sub-tropical climate. New Caledonia has over one-fifth of the world's nickel reserves, and the main economic activity is metal mining. Tourism is also important. New Caledonia relies on aid from France.

## NEW ZEALAND

| | | | |
|---|---|---|---|
| **Area Sq Km** | 270 534 | **Languages** | English, Maori |
| **Area Sq Miles** | 104 454 | **Religions** | Protestant, Roman Catholic |
| **Population** | 4 415 000 | **Currency** | New Zealand dollar |
| **Capital** | Wellington | **Organizations** | APEC, Comm., OECD, UN |

**Map page 128**

New Zealand comprises two main islands separated by the narrow Cook Strait, and a number of smaller islands. North Island, where three-quarters of the population lives, has mountain ranges, broad fertile valleys and a central plateau with hot springs and active volcanoes. South Island is also mountainous, with the Southern Alps running its entire length. The only major lowland area is the Canterbury Plains in the centre-east. The climate is generally temperate, although South Island has colder winters. Farming is the mainstay of the economy. New Zealand is one of the world's leading producers of meat (beef, lamb and mutton), wool and dairy products; fruit and fish are also important. Hydroelectric and geothermal power provide much of the country's energy needs. Other industries produce timber, wood pulp, iron, aluminium, machinery and chemicals. Tourism is the fastest growing sector of the economy. The main trading partners are Australia, China, the USA and Japan.

## NICARAGUA

Republic of Nicaragua

| | | | |
|---|---|---|---|
| **Area Sq Km** | 130 000 | **Languages** | Spanish, Amerindian languages |
| **Area Sq Miles** | 50 193 | **Religions** | Roman Catholic, Protestant |
| **Population** | 5 870 000 | **Currency** | Córdoba |
| **Capital** | Managua | **Organizations** | UN |

**Map page 206**

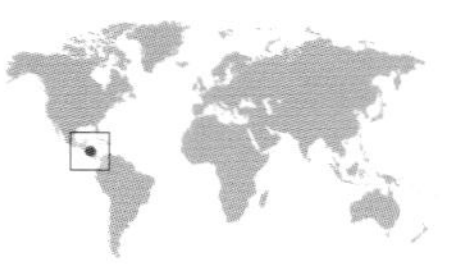

Nicaragua lies at the heart of Central America, with both Pacific and Caribbean coasts. Mountain ranges separate the east, which is largely rainforest, from the more developed western regions, which include Lake Nicaragua and some active volcanoes. The highest land is in the north. The climate is tropical. Nicaragua is one of the western hemisphere's poorest countries, and the economy is largely agricultural. Exports include coffee, seafood, cotton and bananas. The USA is the main trading partner. Nicaragua has a huge national debt, and relies heavily on foreign aid.

## NIGER

Republic of Niger

| | | | |
|---|---|---|---|
| **Area Sq Km** | 1 267 000 | **Languages** | French, Hausa, Fulani, local languages |
| **Area Sq Miles** | 489 191 | **Religions** | Sunni Muslim, traditional beliefs |
| **Population** | 16 069 000 | **Currency** | CFA franc |
| **Capital** | Niamey | **Organizations** | UN |

**Map page 176–177**

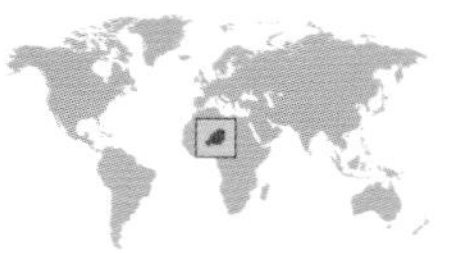

A landlocked state of west Africa, Niger lies mostly within the Sahara desert, but with savanna in the south and in the Niger valley area. The mountains of the Massif de l'Aïr dominate central regions. Much of the country is hot and dry. The south has some summer rainfall, although droughts occur. The economy depends on subsistence farming and herding, and uranium exports, but Niger is one of the world's least developed countries and relies heavily on foreign aid. France is the main trading partner.

## NIGERIA

Federal Republic of Nigeria

| | | | |
|---|---|---|---|
| **Area Sq Km** | 923 768 | **Languages** | English, Hausa, Yoruba, Ibo, Fulani, local languages |
| **Area Sq Miles** | 356 669 | **Religions** | Sunni Muslim, Christian, traditional beliefs |
| **Population** | 162 471 000 | **Currency** | Naira |
| **Capital** | Abuja | **Organizations** | Comm., OPEC, UN |

**Map page 176–177**

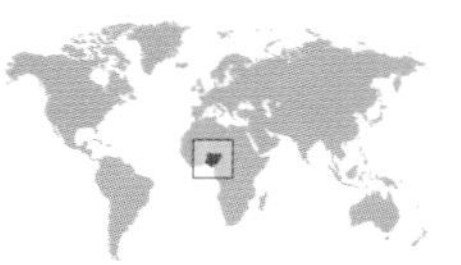

Nigeria is in west Africa, on the Gulf of Guinea, and is the most populous country in Africa. The Niger delta dominates coastal areas, fringed with sandy beaches, mangrove swamps and lagoons. Inland is a belt of rainforest which gives way to woodland or savanna on high plateaus. The far north is the semi-desert edge of the Sahara. The climate is tropical, with heavy summer rainfall in the south but low rainfall in the north. Most of the population lives in the coastal lowlands or in the west. About half the workforce is involved in agriculture, mainly growing subsistence crops. Agricultural production, however, has failed to keep up with demand, and Nigeria is now a net importer of food. Cocoa and rubber are the only significant export crops. The economy is heavily dependent on vast oil resources in the Niger delta and in shallow offshore waters, and oil accounts for over ninety per cent of export earnings. Nigeria also has natural gas reserves and some mineral deposits, but these are largely undeveloped. Industry involves mainly oil refining, chemicals (chiefly fertilizers), agricultural processing, textiles, steel manufacture and vehicle assembly. Political instability in the past has left Nigeria with heavy debts, poverty and unemployment.

## Niue

Self-governing New Zealand Territory

| | | | |
|---|---|---|---|
| **Area Sq Km** | 258 | **Languages** | English, Nivean |
| **Area Sq Miles** | 100 | **Religions** | Christian |
| **Population** | 1 496 | **Currency** | New Zealand dollar |
| **Capital** | Alofi | | |

**Map page 125**

Niue, one of the largest coral islands in the world, lies in the south Pacific Ocean about 500 kilometres (300 miles) east of Tonga. The economy depends on aid and remittances from New Zealand. The population is declining because of migration to New Zealand.

## Norfolk Island

Australian External Territory

| | | | |
|---|---|---|---|
| **Area Sq Km** | 35 | **Languages** | English |
| **Area Sq Miles** | 14 | **Religions** | Protestant, Roman Catholic |
| **Population** | 2 523 | **Currency** | Australian dollar |
| **Capital** | Kingston | | |

**Map page 125**

In the south Pacific Ocean, Norfolk Island lies between Vanuatu and New Zealand. Tourism has increased steadily and is the mainstay of the economy and provides revenues for agricultural development.

## Northern Mariana Islands

United States Commonwealth

| | | | |
|---|---|---|---|
| **Area Sq Km** | 477 | **Languages** | English, Chamorro, local languages |
| **Area Sq Miles** | 184 | **Religions** | Roman Catholic |
| **Population** | 61 000 | **Currency** | United States dollar |
| **Capital** | Capitol Hill | | |

**Map page 147**

A chain of islands in the northwest Pacific Ocean, extending over 550 kilometres (350 miles) north to south. The main island is Saipan. Tourism is a major industry, employing approximately half the workforce.

## NORTH KOREA

Democratic People's Republic of Korea

| | | | |
|---|---|---|---|
| **Area Sq Km** | 120 538 | **Languages** | Korean |
| **Area Sq Miles** | 46 540 | **Religions** | Traditional beliefs, Chondoist, Buddhist |
| **Population** | 24 451 000 | **Currency** | North Korean won |
| **Capital** | P'yŏngyang | **Organizations** | UN |

**Map page 152**

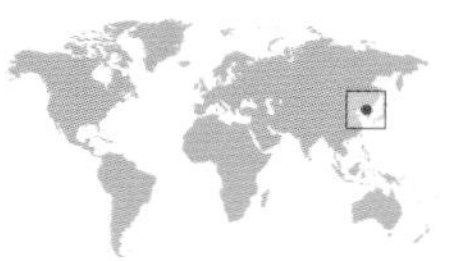

Occupying the northern half of the Korean peninsula in eastern Asia, North Korea is a rugged and mountainous country. The principal lowlands and the main agricultural areas are the plains in the southwest. More than half the population lives in urban areas, mainly on the coastal plains. North Korea has a continental climate, with cold, dry winters and hot, wet summers. Approximately one-third of the workforce is involved in agriculture, mainly growing food crops on cooperative farms. Various minerals, notably iron ore, are mined and are the basis of the country's heavy industries. Exports include minerals (lead, magnesite and zinc) and metal products (chiefly iron and steel). The economy declined after 1991, when ties to the former USSR and eastern bloc collapsed, and there have been serious food shortages.

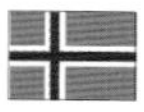

## NORWAY

Kingdom of Norway

| | | | |
|---|---|---|---|
| **Area Sq Km** | 323 878 | **Languages** | Norwegian |
| **Area Sq Miles** | 125 050 | **Religions** | Protestant, Roman Catholic |
| **Population** | 4 925 000 | **Currency** | Norwegian krone |
| **Capital** | Oslo | **Organizations** | NATO, OECD, UN |

**Map page 158–159**

Norway stretches along the north and west coasts of Scandinavia, from the Arctic Ocean to the North Sea. Its extensive coastline is indented with fjords and fringed with many islands. Inland, the terrain is mountainous, with coniferous forests and lakes in the south. The only major lowland areas are along the southern North Sea and Skagerrak coasts, where most of the population lives. The climate is modified by the effect of the North Atlantic Drift ocean current. Norway has vast petroleum and natural gas resources in the North Sea. It is one of western Europe's leading producers of oil and gas, and exports of oil account for approximately half of total export earnings. Related industries include engineering (oil and gas platforms) and petrochemicals. More traditional industries process local raw materials, particularly fish, timber and minerals. Agriculture is limited, but fishing and fish farming are important. Norway is the world's leading exporter of farmed salmon. Merchant shipping and tourism are major sources of foreign exchange.

## OMAN

Sultanate of Oman

| | | | |
|---|---|---|---|
| **Area Sq Km** | 309 500 | **Languages** | Arabic, Baluchi, Indian languages |
| **Area Sq Miles** | 119 499 | **Religions** | Ibadhi Muslim, Sunni Muslim |
| **Population** | 2 846 000 | **Currency** | Omani riyal |
| **Capital** | Muscat (Masqaṭ) | **Organizations** | GCC, UN |

**Map page 142**

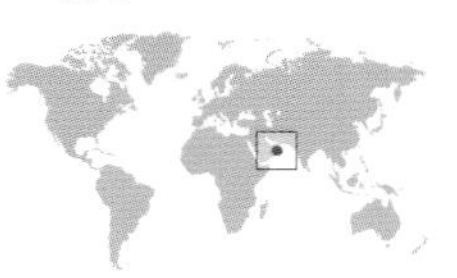

In southwest Asia, Oman occupies the east and southeast coasts of the Arabian Peninsula and an enclave north of the United Arab Emirates. Most of the land is desert, with mountains in the north and south. The climate is hot and mainly dry. Most of the population lives on the coastal strip on the Gulf of Oman. The majority depend on farming and fishing, but the oil and gas industries dominate the economy with around eighty per cent of export revenues coming from oil.

## PAKISTAN

Islamic Republic of Pakistan

| | | | |
|---|---|---|---|
| **Area Sq Km** | 803 940 | **Languages** | Urdu, Punjabi, Sindhi, Pashto (Pashtu), English, Balochi |
| **Area Sq Miles** | 310 403 | **Religions** | Sunni Muslim, Shi'a Muslim, Christian, Hindu |
| **Population** | 176 745 000 | **Currency** | Pakistani rupee |
| **Capital** | Islamabad | **Organizations** | Comm., UN |

**Map page 141**

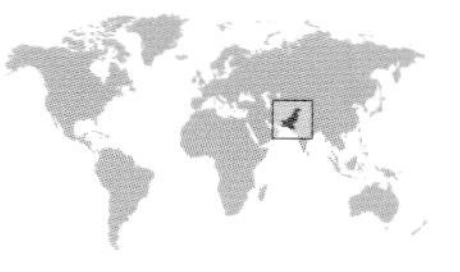

Pakistan is in the northwest part of the Indian subcontinent in south Asia, on the Arabian Sea. The east and south are dominated by the great basin of the Indus river system. This is the main agricultural area and contains most of the predominantly rural population. To the north the land rises to the mountains of the Karakoram, Hindu Kush and Himalaya mountains. The west is semi-desert plateaus and mountain ranges. The climate ranges between dry desert, and arctic tundra on the mountain tops. Temperatures are generally warm and rainfall is monsoonal. Agriculture is the main sector of the economy, employing over forty per cent of the workforce, and is based on extensive irrigation schemes. Pakistan is one of the world's leading producers of cotton and a major exporter of rice. Pakistan produces natural gas and has a variety of mineral deposits including coal and gold, but they are little developed. The main industries are textiles and clothing manufacture and food processing, with fabrics and ready-made clothing the leading exports. Pakistan also produces leather goods, fertilizers, chemicals, paper and precision instruments. The country depends heavily on foreign aid and remittances from workers abroad.

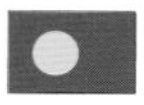

## PALAU

Republic of Palau

| | | | |
|---|---|---|---|
| **Area Sq Km** | 497 | **Languages** | Palauan, English |
| **Area Sq Miles** | 192 | **Religions** | Roman Catholic, Protestant, traditional beliefs |
| **Population** | 21 000 | **Currency** | United States dollar |
| **Capital** | Melekeok | **Organizations** | UN |

**Map page 147**

Palau comprises over three hundred islands in the western Caroline Islands, in the west Pacific Ocean. The climate is tropical. The economy is based on farming, fishing and tourism, but Palau is heavily dependent on aid from the USA.

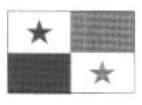

## PANAMA
Republic of Panama

| | | | |
|---|---|---|---|
| **Area Sq Km** | 77 082 | **Languages** | Spanish, English, Amerindian languages |
| **Area Sq Miles** | 29 762 | **Religions** | Roman Catholic, Protestant, Sunni Muslim |
| **Population** | 3 571 000 | **Currency** | Balboa |
| **Capital** | Panama City (Panamá) | **Organizations** | UN |

**Map page 206**

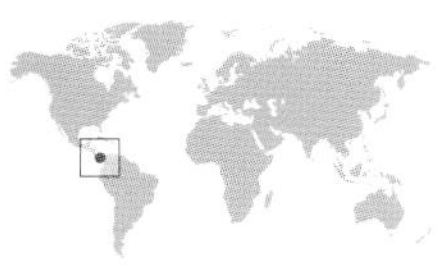

Panama is the most southerly state in central America and has Pacific and Caribbean coasts. It is hilly, with mountains in the west and jungle near the Colombian border. The climate is tropical. Most of the population lives on the drier Pacific side. The economy is based mainly on services related to the Panama Canal: shipping, banking and tourism. Exports include bananas, shrimps, coffee, clothing and fish products. The USA is the main trading partner.

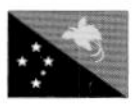

## PAPUA NEW GUINEA
Independent State of Papua New Guinea

| | | | |
|---|---|---|---|
| **Area Sq Km** | 462 840 | **Languages** | English, Tok Pisin (Creole), local languages |
| **Area Sq Miles** | 178 704 | **Religions** | Protestant, Roman Catholic, traditional beliefs |
| **Population** | 7 014 000 | **Currency** | Kina |
| **Capital** | Port Moresby | **Organizations** | APEC, Comm., UN |

**Map page 124**

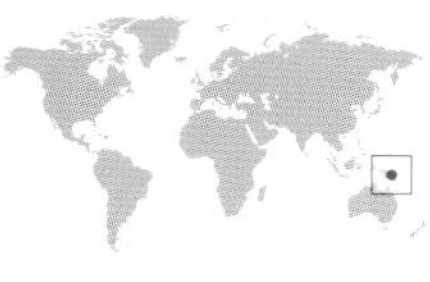

Papua New Guinea occupies the eastern half of the island of New Guinea and includes many island groups. It has a forested and mountainous interior, bordered by swampy plains, and a tropical monsoon climate. Most of the workforce are farmers. Timber, copra, coffee and cocoa are important, but exports are dominated by minerals, chiefly gold and copper. The country depends on foreign aid. Australia, the USA and Singapore are the main trading partners.

## PARAGUAY
Republic of Paraguay

| | | | |
|---|---|---|---|
| **Area Sq Km** | 406 752 | **Languages** | Spanish, Guaraní |
| **Area Sq Miles** | 157 048 | **Religions** | Roman Catholic, Protestant |
| **Population** | 6 568 000 | **Currency** | Guaraní |
| **Capital** | Asunción | **Organizations** | UN |

**Map page 212**

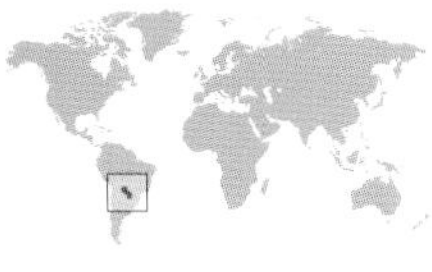

Paraguay is a landlocked country in central South America, bordering Bolivia, Brazil and Argentina. The Paraguay river separates a sparsely populated western zone of marsh and flat alluvial plains from a more developed, hilly and forested region to the east and south. The climate is subtropical. Virtually all electricity is produced by hydroelectric plants, and surplus power is exported to Brazil and Argentina. The hydroelectric dam at Itaipú is one of the largest in the world. The mainstay of the economy is agriculture and related industries. Exports include cotton, soya bean and edible oil products, timber and meat. Brazil and Argentina are the main trading partners.

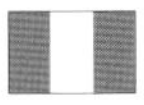

## PERU
Republic of Peru

| | | | |
|---|---|---|---|
| **Area Sq Km** | 1 285 216 | **Languages** | Spanish, Quechua, Aymara |
| **Area Sq Miles** | 496 225 | **Religions** | Roman Catholic, Protestant |
| **Population** | 29 400 000 | **Currency** | Sol |
| **Capital** | Lima | **Organizations** | APEC, UN |

**Map page 210**

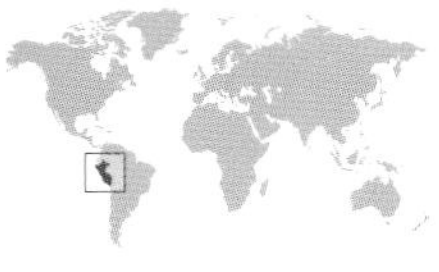

Peru lies on the Pacific coast of South America. Most Peruvians live on the coastal strip and on the plateaus of the high Andes mountains. East of the Andes is the Amazon rainforest. The coast is temperate with low rainfall while the east is hot, humid and wet. Agriculture involves one-third of the workforce and fishing is also important. Agriculture and fishing have both been disrupted by the El Niño climatic effect in recent years. Sugar, cotton, coffee and, illegally, coca are the main cash crops. Copper and copper products, fishmeal, zinc products, coffee, petroleum and its products, and textiles are the main exports. The USA and China are the main trading partners.

## PHILIPPINES
Republic of the Philippines

| | | | |
|---|---|---|---|
| **Area Sq Km** | 300 000 | **Languages** | English, Filipino, Tagalog, Cebuano, local languages |
| **Area Sq Miles** | 115 831 | **Religions** | Roman Catholic, Protestant, Sunni Muslim, Aglipayan |
| **Population** | 94 852 000 | **Currency** | Philippine peso |
| **Capital** | Manila | **Organizations** | APEC, ASEAN, UN |

**Map page 153**

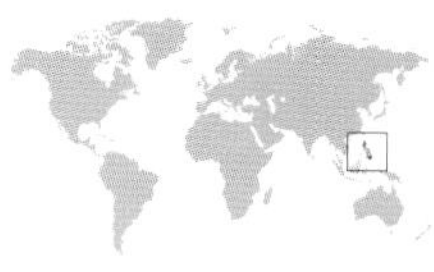

The Philippines, in southeast Asia, consists of over seven thousand islands lying between the South China Sea and the Pacific Ocean. The main islands are mountainous and forested. Volcanoes are active, and earthquakes and tropical storms are common. Most of the population lives on the plains or the coastal strips. The climate is hot and humid with monsoonal rainfall. Rice, coconuts, sugar cane, pineapples and bananas are the main crops, and fishing is important. Exports include electronic and transport equipment and machinery, clothing, and coconuts. Foreign aid and remittances from workers abroad are important to the economy. The USA and Japan are the main trading partners.

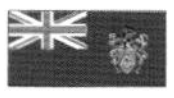

## Pitcairn Islands
United Kingdom Overseas Territory

| | | | |
|---|---|---|---|
| **Area Sq Km** | 45 | **Languages** | English |
| **Area Sq Miles** | 17 | **Religions** | Protestant |
| **Population** | 48 | **Currency** | New Zealand dollar |
| **Capital** | Adamstown | | |

**Map page 123**

An island group in the southeast Pacific Ocean consisting of Pitcairn Island and three uninhabited islands. It was originally settled by mutineers from HMS *Bounty* in 1790.

## POLAND
Polish Republic

| | | | |
|---|---|---|---|
| **Area Sq Km** | 312 683 | **Languages** | Polish, German |
| **Area Sq Miles** | 120 728 | **Religions** | Roman Catholic, Polish Orthodox |
| **Population** | 38 299 000 | **Currency** | Złoty |
| **Capital** | Warsaw (Warszawa) | **Organizations** | EU, NATO, OECD, UN |

**Map page 168–169**

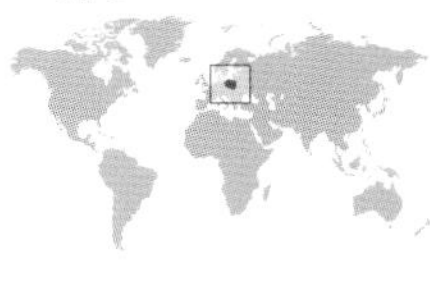

Poland lies on the Baltic coast of eastern Europe. The Oder (Odra) and Vistula (Wisła) river deltas dominate the coast. Inland, much of the country is low-lying, with woods and lakes. In the south the land rises to the Sudeten Mountains and the western part of the Carpathian Mountains, which form the borders with the Czech Republic and Slovakia respectively. The climate is continental. Around a quarter of the workforce is involved in agriculture, and exports include livestock products and sugar. The economy is heavily industrialized, with mining and manufacturing accounting for over thirty per cent of national income. Poland is one of the world's major producers of coal, and also produces copper, zinc, lead, sulphur and natural gas. The main industries are machinery and transport equipment, shipbuilding, and metal and chemical production. Exports include machinery and transport equipment, manufactured goods, food and live animals. Germany is the main trading partner. Poland joined the European Union in May 2004.

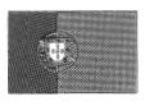

## PORTUGAL
Portuguese Republic

| | | | |
|---|---|---|---|
| **Area Sq Km** | 88 940 | **Languages** | Portuguese |
| **Area Sq Miles** | 34 340 | **Religions** | Roman Catholic, Protestant |
| **Population** | 10 690 000 | **Currency** | Euro |
| **Capital** | Lisbon (Lisboa) | **Organizations** | EU, NATO, OECD, UN |

**Map page 167**

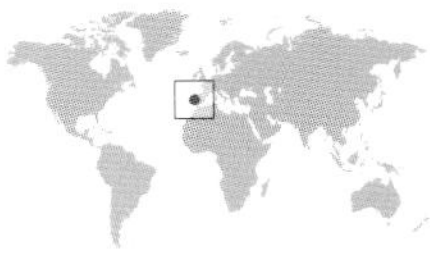

Portugal lies in the western part of the Iberian peninsula in southwest Europe, has an Atlantic coastline and is bordered by Spain to the north and east. The island groups of the Azores and Madeira are parts of Portugal. On the mainland, the land north of the river Tagus (Tejo) is mostly highland, with extensive forests of pine and cork. South of the river is undulating lowland. The climate in the north is cool and moist; the south is warmer, with dry, mild winters. Most Portuguese live near the coast, and more than one-third of the total population lives around the capital, Lisbon (Lisboa). Agriculture, fishing and forestry involve approximately ten per cent of the workforce. Mining and manufacturing are the main sectors of the economy. Portugal produces kaolin, copper, tin, zinc, tungsten and salt. Exports include textiles, clothing and footwear, electrical machinery and transport equipment, cork and wood products, and chemicals. Service industries, chiefly tourism and banking, are important to the economy, as are remittances from workers abroad. Most trade is with other European Union countries.

## Puerto Rico
United States Commonwealth

| | | | |
|---|---|---|---|
| **Area Sq Km** | 9 104 | **Languages** | Spanish, English |
| **Area Sq Miles** | 3 515 | **Religions** | Roman Catholic, Protestant |
| **Population** | 3 746 000 | **Currency** | United States dollar |
| **Capital** | San Juan | | |

**Map page 205**

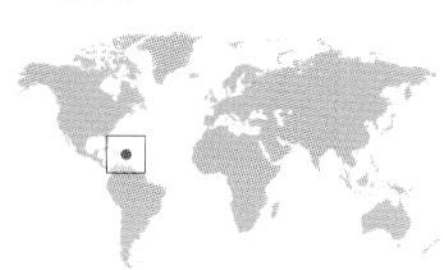

The Caribbean island of Puerto Rico has a forested, hilly interior, coastal plains and a tropical climate. Half of the population lives in the San Juan area. The economy is based on manufacturing (chiefly chemicals, electronics and food), tourism and agriculture. The USA is the main trading partner.

## QATAR
State of Qatar

| | | | |
|---|---|---|---|
| **Area Sq Km** | 11 437 | **Languages** | Arabic |
| **Area Sq Miles** | 4 416 | **Religions** | Sunni Muslim |
| **Population** | 1 870 000 | **Currency** | Qatari riyal |
| **Capital** | Doha (Ad Dawḩah) | **Organizations** | GCC, OPEC, UN |

**Map page 140**

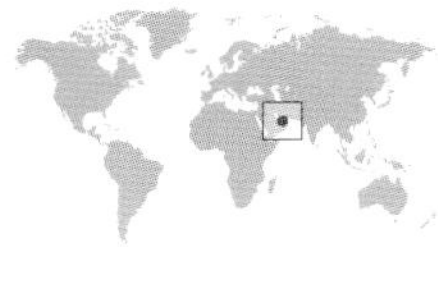

Qatar occupies a peninsula in southwest Asia that extends northwards from east-central Saudi Arabia into The Gulf. The land is flat and barren with sand dunes and salt pans. The climate is hot and mainly dry. Most people live in the area of the capital, Doha. The economy is heavily dependent on oil and natural gas production and the oil-refining industry. Income also comes from overseas investment. Japan is the largest trading partner.

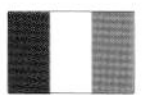

## Réunion
French Overseas Department

| | | | |
|---|---|---|---|
| **Area Sq Km** | 2 551 | **Languages** | French, Creole |
| **Area Sq Miles** | 985 | **Religions** | Roman Catholic |
| **Population** | 856 000 | **Currency** | Euro |
| **Capital** | St-Denis | | |

**Map page 175**

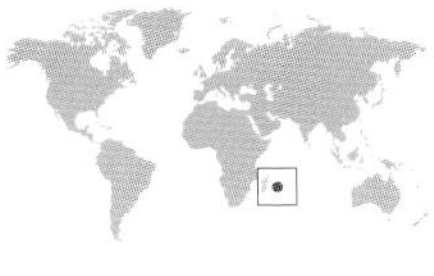

The Indian Ocean island of Réunion is mountainous, with coastal lowlands and a warm climate. The economy depends on tourism, French aid, and exports of sugar. In 2005 France transferred the administration of various small uninhabited islands in the seas around Madagascar from Réunion to the French Southern and Antarctic Lands.

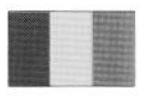

## ROMANIA

| | | | |
|---|---|---|---|
| **Area Sq Km** | 237 500 | **Languages** | Romanian, Hungarian |
| **Area Sq Miles** | 91 699 | **Religions** | Romanian Orthodox, Protestant, Roman Catholic |
| **Population** | 21 436 000 | **Currency** | Romanian leu |
| **Capital** | Bucharest (București) | **Organizations** | EU, NATO, UN |

**Map page 171**

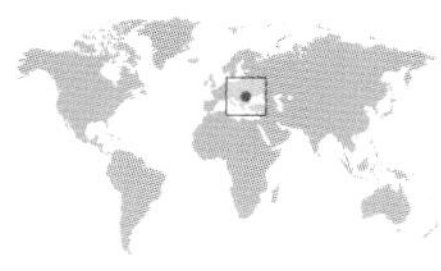

Romania lies in eastern Europe, on the northwest coast of the Black Sea. Mountains separate the Transylvanian Basin in the centre of the country from the populous plains of the east and south and from the Danube delta. The climate is continental. Romania has mineral resources (zinc, lead, silver and gold) and oil and natural gas reserves. Economic development has been slow and sporadic, but measures to accelerate change were introduced in 1999. Agriculture employs over one-third of the workforce. The main exports are textiles, mineral products, chemicals, machinery and footwear. The main trading partners are Germany and Italy.

## RUSSIAN FEDERATION

| | | | |
|---|---|---|---|
| **Area Sq Km** | 17 075 400 | **Languages** | Russian, Tatar, Ukrainian, local languages |
| **Area Sq Miles** | 6 592 849 | **Religions** | Russian Orthodox, Sunni Muslim, Protestant |
| **Population** | 142 836 000 | **Currency** | Russian rouble |
| **Capital** | Moscow (Moskva) | **Organizations** | APEC, CIS, UN |

Map page 132–133

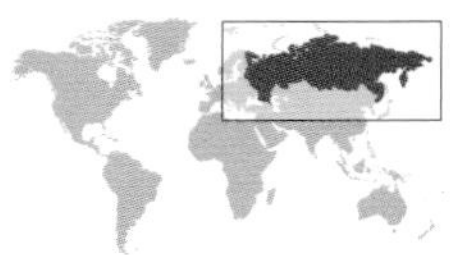

The Russian Federation occupies much of eastern Europe and all of northern Asia, and is the world's largest country. It borders fourteen countries to the west and south and has long coastlines on the Arctic and Pacific Oceans to the north and east. European Russia lies west of the Ural Mountains. To the south the land rises to uplands and the Caucasus mountains on the border with Georgia and Azerbaijan. East of the Urals lies the flat West Siberian Plain and the Central Siberian Plateau. In the south-east is Lake Baikal, the world's deepest lake, and the Sayan ranges on the border with Kazakhstan and Mongolia. Eastern Siberia is rugged and mountainous, with many active volcanoes in the Kamchatka Peninsula. The country's major rivers are the Volga in the west and the Ob', Irtysh, Yenisey, Lena and Amur in Siberia. The climate and vegetation range between arctic tundra in the north and semi-arid steppe towards the Black and Caspian Sea coasts in the south. In general, the climate is continental with extreme temperatures. The majority of the population (the eighth largest in the world), and industry and agriculture are concentrated in European Russia. The economy is dependent on exploitation of raw materials and on heavy industry. Russia has a wealth of mineral resources, although they are often difficult to exploit because of climate and remote locations. It is one of the world's leading producers of petroleum, natural gas and coal as well as iron ore, nickel, copper, bauxite, and many precious and rare metals. Forests cover over forty per cent of the land area and supply an important timber, paper and pulp industry. Approximately eight per cent of the land is suitable for cultivation, but farming is generally inefficient and food, especially grains, must be imported. Fishing is important and Russia has a large fleet operating around the world. The transition to a market economy has been slow and difficult, with considerable underemployment. As well as mining and extractive industries there is a wide range of manufacturing industry, from steel mills to aircraft and space vehicles, shipbuilding, synthetic fabrics, plastics, cotton fabrics, consumer durables, chemicals and fertilizers. Exports include fuels, metals, machinery, chemicals and forest products. The most important trading partners include Germany, the USA and Belarus.

## RWANDA
Republic of Rwanda

| | | | |
|---|---|---|---|
| Area Sq Km | 26 338 | Languages | Kinyarwanda, French, English |
| Area Sq Miles | 10 169 | Religions | Roman Catholic, traditional beliefs, Protestant |
| Population | 10 943 000 | Currency | Rwandan franc |
| Capital | Kigali | Organizations | Comm., UN |

Map page 178

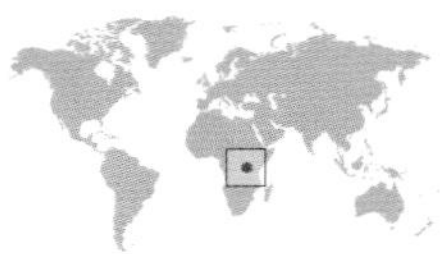

Rwanda, the most densely populated country in Africa, is situated in the mountains and plateaus to the east of the western branch of the Great Rift Valley in east Africa. The climate is warm with a summer dry season. Rwanda depends on subsistence farming, coffee and tea exports, light industry and foreign aid. The country is slowly recovering from serious internal conflict which caused devastation in the early 1990s.

## St-Barthélemy
French Overseas Collectivity

| | | | |
|---|---|---|---|
| Area Sq Km | 21 | Languages | French |
| Area Sq Miles | 8 | Religions | Roman Catholic |
| Population | 8 823 | Currency | Euro |
| Capital | Gustavia | | |

Map page 205

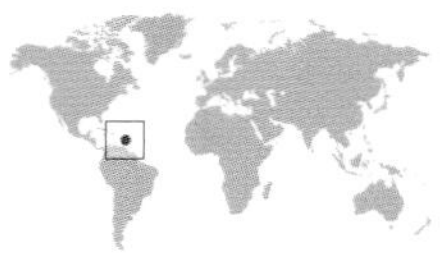

An island in the Leeward Islands in the Lesser Antilles, in the Caribbean south of St-Martin. It was separated from Guadeloupe politically in 2007. Tourism is the main economic activity.

## St Helena, Ascension and Tristan da Cunha
United Kingdom Overseas Territory

| | | | |
|---|---|---|---|
| Area Sq Km | 410 | Languages | English |
| Area Sq Miles | 158 | Religions | Protestant, Roman Catholic |
| Population | 5 404 | Currency | St Helena pound, Pound sterling |
| Capital | Jamestown | | |

Map page 174 St Helena and its dependencies Ascension and Tristan da Cunha are isolated island groups lying in the south Atlantic Ocean. St Helena is a rugged island of volcanic origin. The main activity is fishing, but the economy relies on financial aid from the UK. Main trading partners are the UK and South Africa.

## ST KITTS AND NEVIS
Federation of St Kitts and Nevis

| | | | |
|---|---|---|---|
| Area Sq Km | 261 | Languages | English, Creole |
| Area Sq Miles | 101 | Religions | Protestant, Roman Catholic |
| Population | 53 000 | Currency | East Caribbean dollar |
| Capital | Basseterre | Organizations | CARICOM, Comm., UN |

Map page 205

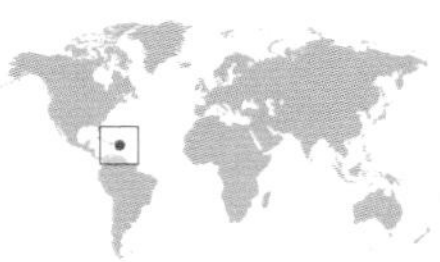

St Kitts and Nevis are in the Leeward Islands, in the Caribbean. Both volcanic islands are mountainous and forested, with sandy beaches and a warm, wet climate. About three-quarters of the population lives on St Kitts. Agriculture is the main activity, with sugar the main product. Tourism and manufacturing (chiefly garments and electronic components) and offshore banking are important activities.

## ST LUCIA

| | | | |
|---|---|---|---|
| Area Sq Km | 616 | Languages | English, Creole |
| Area Sq Miles | 238 | Religions | Roman Catholic, Protestant |
| Population | 176 000 | Currency | East Caribbean dollar |
| Capital | Castries | Organizations | CARICOM, Comm., UN |

Map page 205

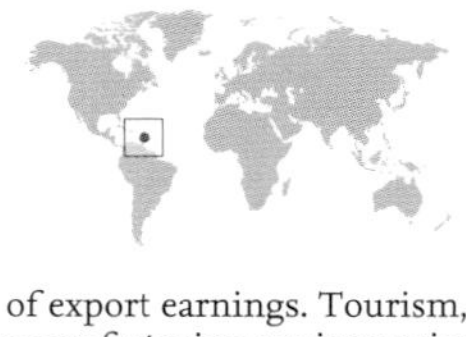

St Lucia, one of the Windward Islands in the Caribbean Sea, is a volcanic island with forested mountains, hot springs, sandy beaches and a wet tropical climate. Agriculture is the main activity, with bananas accounting for approximately forty per cent of export earnings. Tourism, agricultural processing and light manufacturing are increasingly important.

## St-Martin
French Overseas Collectivity

| | | | |
|---|---|---|---|
| Area Sq Km | 54 | Languages | French |
| Area Sq Miles | 21 | Religions | Roman Catholic |
| Population | 37 163 | Currency | Euro |
| Capital | Marigot | | |

Map page 205

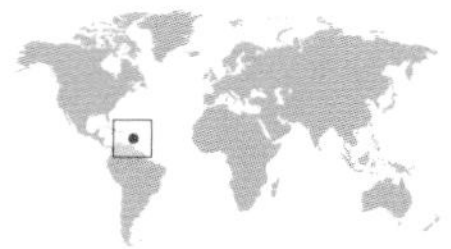

The northern part of St-Martin, one of the Leeward Islands, in the Caribbean. The other part of the island is part of the Netherlands Antilles (Sint Maarten). It was separated from Guadeloupe politically in 2007. Tourism is the main source of income.

## St Pierre and Miquelon
French Territorial Collectivity

| | | | |
|---|---|---|---|
| Area Sq Km | 242 | Languages | French |
| Area Sq Miles | 93 | Religions | Roman Catholic |
| Population | 6 290 | Currency | Euro |
| Capital | St-Pierre | | |

Map page 185

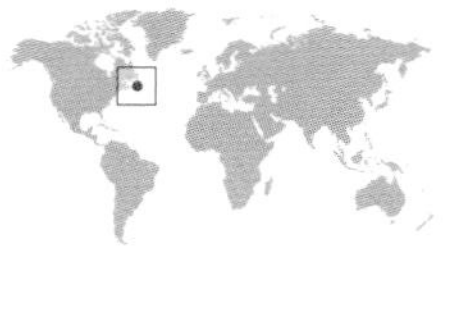

A group of islands off the south coast of Newfoundland in eastern Canada. The islands are largely unsuitable for agriculture, and fishing and fish processing are the most important activities. The islands rely heavily on financial assistance from France.

## ST VINCENT AND THE GRENADINES

| | | | |
|---|---|---|---|
| Area Sq Km | 389 | Languages | English, Creole |
| Area Sq Miles | 150 | Religions | Protestant, Roman Catholic |
| Population | 109 000 | Currency | East Caribbean dollar |
| Capital | Kingstown | Organizations | CARICOM, Comm., UN |

Map page 205

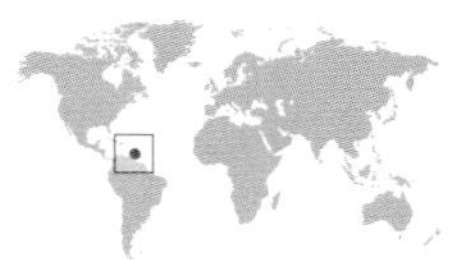

St Vincent, whose territory includes islets and cays in the Grenadines, is in the Windward Islands, in the Caribbean. St Vincent itself is forested and mountainous, with an active volcano, Soufrière. The climate is tropical and wet. The economy is based mainly on agriculture and tourism. Bananas account for approximately one-third of export earnings and arrowroot is also important. Most trade is with the USA and other CARICOM countries.

## SAMOA
Independent State of Samoa

| | | | |
|---|---|---|---|
| Area Sq Km | 2 831 | Languages | Samoan, English |
| Area Sq Miles | 1 093 | Religions | Protestant, Roman Catholic |
| Population | 184 000 | Currency | Tala |
| Capital | Apia | Organizations | Comm., UN |

Map page 125

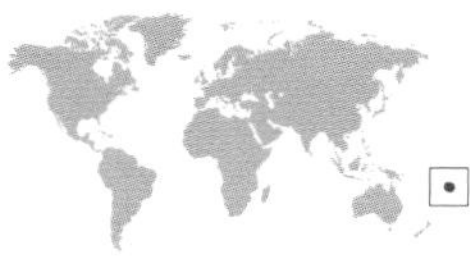

Samoa consists of two larger mountainous and forested islands, Savai'i and Upolu, and seven smaller islands, in the south Pacific Ocean. Over half the population lives on Upolu. The climate is tropical. The economy is based on agriculture, with some fishing and light manufacturing. Traditional exports are coconut products, fish and beer. Tourism is increasing, but the islands depend on workers' remittances and foreign aid.

## SAN MARINO
Republic of San Marino

| | | | |
|---|---|---|---|
| Area Sq Km | 61 | Languages | Italian |
| Area Sq Miles | 24 | Religions | Roman Catholic |
| Population | 32 000 | Currency | Euro |
| Capital | San Marino | Organizations | UN |

Map page 170

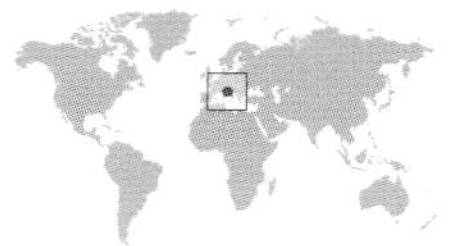

Landlocked San Marino lies in northeast Italy. A third of the people live in the capital. There is some agriculture and light industry, but most income comes from tourism. Italy is the main trading partner.

## SÃO TOMÉ AND PRÍNCIPE
Democratic Republic of São Tomé and Príncipe

| | | | |
|---|---|---|---|
| Area Sq Km | 964 | Languages | Portuguese, Creole |
| Area Sq Miles | 372 | Religions | Roman Catholic, Protestant |
| Population | 169 000 | Currency | Dobra |
| Capital | São Tomé | Organizations | UN |

Map page 176

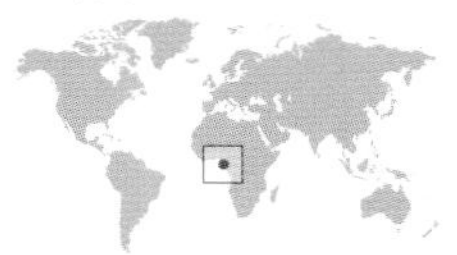

The two main islands and adjacent islets lie off the coast of west Africa in the Gulf of Guinea. São Tomé is the larger island, with over ninety per cent of the population. Both São Tomé and Príncipe are mountainous and tree-covered, and have a hot and humid climate. The economy is heavily dependent on cocoa, which accounts for around ninety per cent of export earnings.

## SAUDI ARABIA
Kingdom of Saudi Arabia

| | | | |
|---|---|---|---|
| Area Sq Km | 2 200 000 | Languages | Arabic |
| Area Sq Miles | 849 425 | Religions | Sunni Muslim, Shi'a Muslim |
| Population | 28 083 000 | Currency | Saudi Arabian riyal |
| Capital | Riyadh (Ar Riyāḑ) | Organizations | GCC, OPEC, UN |

Map page 142

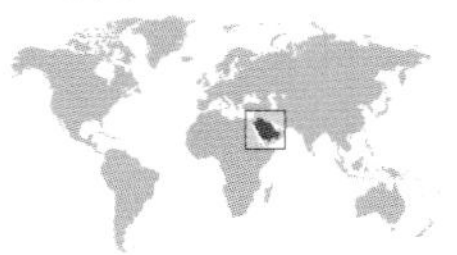

Saudi Arabia occupies most of the Arabian Peninsula in southwest Asia. The terrain is desert or semi-desert plateaus, which rise to mountains running parallel to the Red Sea in the west and slope down to plains in the southeast and along The Gulf in the east. Over eighty per cent of the population lives in urban areas. There are over five million foreign workers in Saudi Arabia, employed mainly in the oil and service industries. Summers are hot, winters are warm and rainfall is low. Saudi Arabia has the world's largest reserves of oil and significant natural gas reserves, both onshore and in The Gulf. Crude oil and refined products account for over eighty per cent of export earnings. Other industries and irrigated agriculture are being encouraged, but most food and raw materials are imported. Saudi Arabia has important banking and commercial interests. China and the USA are the main trading partners.

## SENEGAL
Republic of Senegal

| | | | |
|---|---|---|---|
| Area Sq Km | 196 720 | Languages | French, Wolof, Fulani, local languages |
| Area Sq Miles | 75 954 | Religions | Sunni Muslim, Roman Catholic, traditional beliefs |
| Population | 12 768 000 | Currency | CFA franc |
| Capital | Dakar | Organizations | UN |

Map page 176

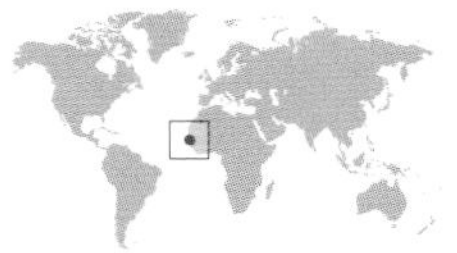

Senegal lies on the Atlantic coast of west Africa. The north is arid semi-desert, while the south is mainly fertile savanna bushland. The climate is tropical with summer rains, although droughts occur. One-fifth of the population lives in and around Dakar, the capital and main port. Fish, groundnuts and phosphates are important exports. France is the main trading partner.

## SERBIA
Republic of Serbia

| | | | |
|---|---|---|---|
| Area Sq Km | 77 453 | Languages | Serbian, Hungarian |
| Area Sq Miles | 29 904 | Religions | Serbian Orthodox, Roman Catholic, Sunni Muslim |
| Population | 7 306 677 | Currency | Serbian dinar |
| Capital | Beograd (Belgrade) | Organizations | UN |

Map page 171

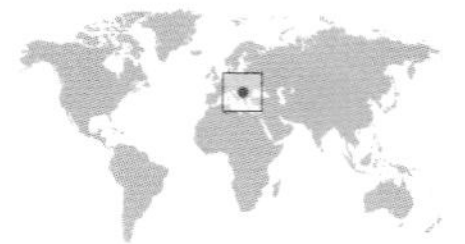

Following ethnic conflict and the break-up of Yugoslavia through the 1990s, the state union of Serbia and Montenegro retained the name Yugoslavia until 2003. The two then became separate

independent countries in 2006. The southern Serbian province of Kosovo declared its independence from Serbia in February 2008. The landscape is rugged, mountainous and forested in the south, while the north is low-lying and drained by the Danube river system.

## SEYCHELLES
Republic of Seychelles

| | | | |
|---|---|---|---|
| Area Sq Km | 455 | Languages | English, French, Creole |
| Area Sq Miles | 176 | Religions | Roman Catholic, Protestant |
| Population | 87 000 | Currency | Seychelles rupee |
| Capital | Victoria | Organizations | Comm., SADC, UN |

Map page 175

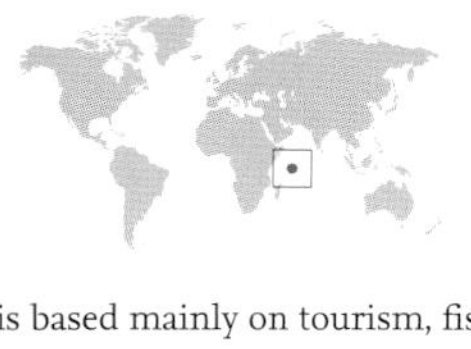

The Seychelles comprises an archipelago of over one hundred granitic and coral islands in the western Indian Ocean. Over ninety per cent of the population lives on the main island, Mahé. The climate is hot and humid with heavy rainfall. The economy is based mainly on tourism, fishing and light manufacturing.

## SIERRA LEONE
Republic of Sierra Leone

| | | | |
|---|---|---|---|
| Area Sq Km | 71 740 | Languages | English, Creole, Mende, Temne, local languages |
| Area Sq Miles | 27 699 | Religions | Sunni Muslim, traditional beliefs |
| Population | 5 997 000 | Currency | Leone |
| Capital | Freetown | Organizations | Comm., UN |

Map page 176

Sierra Leone lies on the Atlantic coast of west Africa. Its coastline is heavily indented and is lined with mangrove swamps. Inland is a forested area rising to savanna plateaus, with mountains to the northeast. The climate is tropical and rainfall is heavy. Most of the workforce is involved in subsistence farming. Cocoa and coffee are the main cash crops. Diamonds and rutile (titanium ore) are the main exports. Sierra Leone is one of the world's poorest countries, and the economy relies on substantial foreign aid.

## SINGAPORE
Republic of Singapore

| | | | |
|---|---|---|---|
| Area Sq Km | 639 | Languages | Chinese, English, Malay, Tamil |
| Area Sq Miles | 247 | Religions | Buddhist, Taoist, Sunni Muslim, Christian, Hindu |
| Population | 5 188 000 | Currency | Singapore dollar |
| Capital | Singapore | Organizations | APEC, ASEAN, Comm., UN |

Map page 150

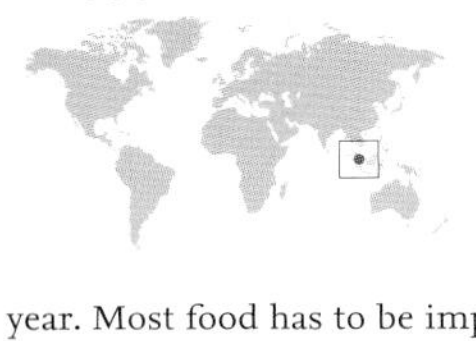

The state comprises the island of Singapore and over fifty others, at the tip of the Malay Peninsula in southeast Asia. Singapore is generally low-lying and includes areas of reclaimed land. The climate is hot and humid, with heavy rainfall all year. Most food has to be imported. Singapore lacks natural resources; industries and services have fuelled the nation's economic growth during recent decades. Main industries include electronics, oil refining, chemicals, pharmaceuticals, ship repair, food processing and textiles. Singapore is also a major financial centre. Its port is one of the world's largest and busiest. Tourism is also important. Japan, the USA and Malaysia are the main trading partners.

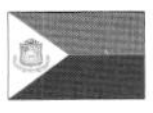

## Sint Maarten
Self-governing Netherlands territory

| | | | |
|---|---|---|---|
| Area Sq Km | 34 | Languages | Dutch, English |
| Area Sq Miles | 13 | Religions | Roman Catholic, Protestant |
| Population | 37 429 | Currency | Caribbean guilder |
| Capital | Philipsburg | | |

Map page 205 The southern part of one of the Leeward Islands, in the Caribbean; the other part of the island is a dependency of France. Sint Maarten was previously part of the Netherlands Antilles until they were dissolved in October 2010. Tourism and fishing are the most important industries.

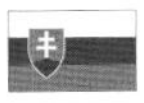

## SLOVAKIA
Slovak Republic

| | | | |
|---|---|---|---|
| Area Sq Km | 49 035 | Languages | Slovak, Hungarian, Czech |
| Area Sq Miles | 18 933 | Religions | Roman Catholic, Protestant, Orthodox |
| Population | 5 472 000 | Currency | Euro |
| Capital | Bratislava | Organizations | EU, NATO, OECD, UN |

Map page 168–169

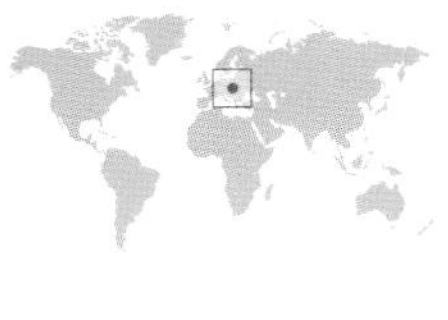

A landlocked country in central Europe, Slovakia is mountainous in the north, but low-lying in the southwest. The climate is continental. There is a range of manufacturing industries, and the main exports are machinery and transport equipment, but in recent years there have been economic difficulties and growth has been slow. Slovakia joined the European Union in May 2004. Most trade is with Germany, the Russian Federation and Poland.

## SLOVENIA
Republic of Slovenia

| | | | |
|---|---|---|---|
| Area Sq Km | 20 251 | Languages | Slovene, Croatian, Serbian |
| Area Sq Miles | 7 819 | Religions | Roman Catholic, Protestant |
| Population | 2 035 000 | Currency | Euro |
| Capital | Ljubljana | Organizations | EU, NATO, OECD, UN |

Map page 170

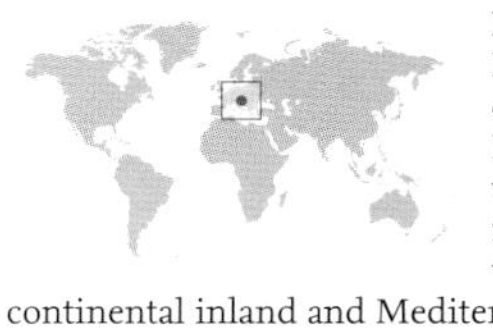

Slovenia lies in the northwest Balkan Mountains of southern Europe and has a short coastline on the Adriatic Sea. It is mountainous and hilly, with lowlands on the coast and in the Sava and Drava river valleys. The climate is generally continental inland and Mediterranean nearer the coast. The main agricultural products are potatoes, grain and sugar beet; the main industries include metal processing, electronics and consumer goods. Trade has been re-orientated towards western markets and the main trading partners are Germany and Italy. Slovenia joined the European Union in May 2004.

## SOLOMON ISLANDS

| | | | |
|---|---|---|---|
| Area Sq Km | 28 370 | Languages | English, Creole, local languages |
| Area Sq Miles | 10 954 | Religions | Protestant, Roman Catholic |
| Population | 552 000 | Currency | Solomon Islands dollar |
| Capital | Honiara | Organizations | Comm., UN |

Map page 125

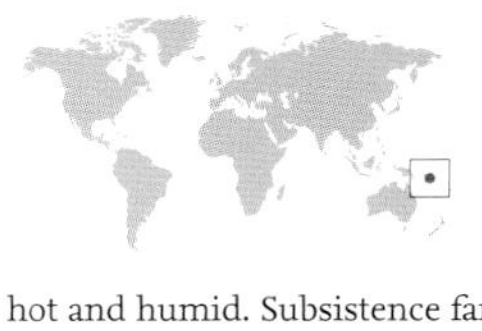

The state consists of the Solomon, Santa Cruz and Shortland Islands in the southwest Pacific Ocean. The six main islands are volcanic, mountainous and forested, although Guadalcanal, the most populous, has a large lowland area. The climate is generally hot and humid. Subsistence farming, forestry and fishing predominate. Exports include timber products, fish, copra and palm oil. The islands depend on foreign aid.

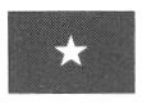

## SOMALIA
Somali Republic

| | | | |
|---|---|---|---|
| Area Sq Km | 637 657 | Languages | Somali, Arabic |
| Area Sq Miles | 246 201 | Religions | Sunni Muslim |
| Population | 9 557 000 | Currency | Somali shilling |
| Capital | Mogadishu (Muqdisho) | Organizations | UN |

Map page 178

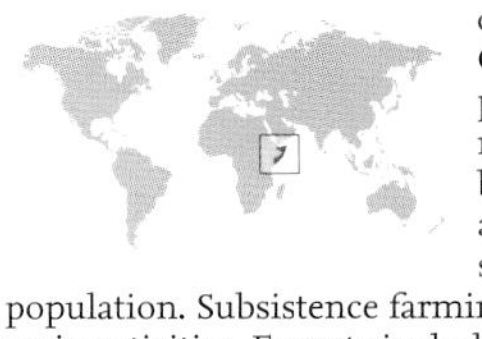

Somalia is in northeast Africa, on the Gulf of Aden and Indian Ocean. It consists of a dry scrubby plateau, rising to highlands in the north. The climate is hot and dry, but coastal areas and the Jubba and Webi Shabeelle river valleys support crops and most of the population. Subsistence farming and livestock rearing are the main activities. Exports include livestock and bananas. Frequent drought and civil war have prevented economic development. Somalia is one of the poorest, most unstable and least developed countries in the world.

## Somaliland
Disputed territory

| | | | |
|---|---|---|---|
| Area Sq Km | 140 000 | Languages | Somali, Arabic, English |
| Area Sq Miles | 54 054 | Religions | Sunni Muslim |
| Population | 3 500 000 | Currency | Somaliland shilling |
| Capital | Hargeysa | | |

Map page 178 After the collapse of the central Somali government in 1991 and at the start of the civil war, Somaliland, in the northwest of the country, covering the area of the former British Protectorate of Somaliland, declared its independence from Somalia as the Republic of Somaliland.A referendum in 2001 saw a majority vote for secession, and Somaliland currently operates as a de facto independent country, with fairly close relations with Ethiopia. The Transitional Federal Government of Somalia does not recognize its independence and conflicts still arise between Somaliland and the neighbouring region of Puntland over ownership of the administrative regions of Sanaag and Sool.

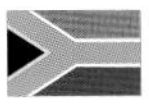

## SOUTH AFRICA, REPUBLIC OF

| | | | |
|---|---|---|---|
| Area Sq Km | 1 219 090 | Languages | Afrikaans, English, nine other official languages |
| Area Sq Miles | 470 693 | Religions | Protestant, Roman Catholic, Sunni Muslim, Hindu |
| Population | 50 460 000 | Currency | Rand |
| Capital | Pretoria (Tshwane)/ Cape Town | Organizations | Comm., SADC, UN |

Map page 180–181

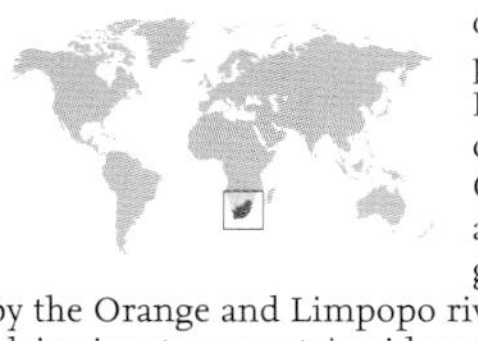

The Republic of South Africa occupies most of the southern part of Africa. It surrounds Lesotho and has a long coastline on the Atlantic and Indian Oceans. Much of the land is a vast plateau, covered with grassland or bush and drained by the Orange and Limpopo river systems. A fertile coastal plain rises to mountain ridges in the south and east, including Table Mountain near Cape Town and the Drakensberg range in the east. South Africa has warm summers and mild winters. Most of the country has the majority of its rainfall in summer, but the coast around Cape Town has winter rains. South Africa has the largest economy in Africa, although wealth is unevenly distributed and unemployment is very high. Agriculture employs approximately one-third of the workforce, and produce includes fruit, wine, wool and maize. The country is the world's leading producer of gold and chromium and an important producer of diamonds. Many other minerals are also mined. The main industries are mineral and food processing, chemicals, electrical equipment, textiles and motor vehicles. Financial services are also important.

## SOUTH KOREA
Republic of Korea

| | | | |
|---|---|---|---|
| Area Sq Km | 99 274 | Languages | Korean |
| Area Sq Miles | 38 330 | Religions | Buddhist, Protestant, Roman Catholic |
| Population | 48 391 000 | Currency | South Korean won |
| Capital | Seoul (Sŏul) | Organizations | APEC, OECD, UN |

Map page 152

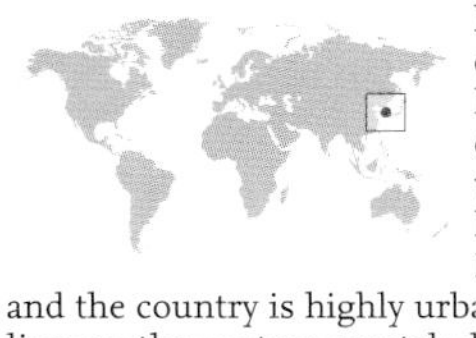

The state consists of the southern half of the Korean Peninsula in eastern Asia and many islands lying off the western and southern coasts in the Yellow Sea. The terrain is mountainous, although less rugged than that of North Korea. Population density is high and the country is highly urbanized; most of the population lives on the western coastal plains and in the river basins of the Han-gang in the northwest and the Naktong-gang in the southeast. The climate is continental, with hot, wet summers and dry, cold winters. Arable land is limited by the mountainous terrain, but because of intensive farming South Korea is nearly self-sufficient in food. Sericulture (silk) is important, as is fishing, which contributes to exports. South Korea has few mineral resources, except for coal and tungsten. It has achieved high economic growth based mainly on export manufacturing. The main manufactured goods are cars, electronic and electrical goods, ships, steel, chemicals and toys, as well as textiles, clothing, footwear and food products. The USA, China and Japan are the main trading partners.

## South Ossetia
Disputed territory

| | | | |
|---|---|---|---|
| Area Sq Km | 4 000 | Languages | Ossetian, Russian, Georgian |
| Area Sq Miles | 1 544 | Religions | Eastern Orthodox |
| Population | 70 000 | Currency | Russian rouble |
| Capital | Tskhinvali | | |

Map page 173 The formerly autonomous region of South Ossetia seeks independence from Georgia and looks to the Russian Federation, which recognizes its independence, as its principal ally. South Ossetia's autonomous status was removed in 1990. Violent conflicts followed between Georgia and the separatists, supported by Russia, who wished to unite with Russian North Ossetia. A cease-fire was agreed in 1992. Elections in 1996 were not recognized by Georgia, nor were elections and an independence referendum, voting in favour of independence, in 2006. Russian interference and interest in the area has continued to cause tensions with the Georgian government, the most recent conflict was in 2008 when Georgian troops attacked separatists. Russia responded and a week of fighting was ended by a cease-fire and resulted in Russia recognising South Ossetia's independence.

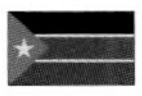

## SOUTH SUDAN
Republic of South Sudan

| | | | |
|---|---|---|---|
| Area Sq Km | 644 329 | Languages | English, Arabic, Dinka, Nuer, local languages |
| Area Sq Miles | 248 775 | Religions | Traditional beliefs, Christian |
| Population | 8 260 490 | Currency | South Sudan pound |
| Capital | Juba | Organizations | UN |

Map page 177

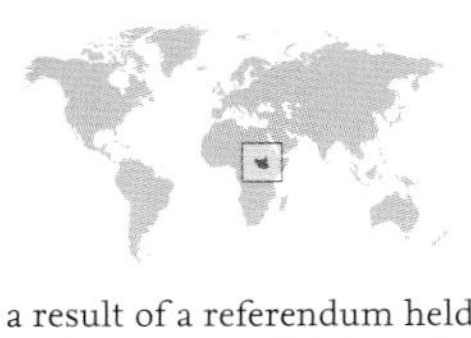

South Sudan in northeast Africa has grasslands, tropical forests and swamps in the north with higher lands in the south. The equatorial climate has moderate temperatures, high humidity and heavy rainfall. Independence from Sudan was gained in July 2011 as a result of a referendum held as part of the agreement which ended decades of civil war between north and south. The government plan to move the capital from Juba to Ramciel in the centre of the country. The economy is mostly agricultural, but the vast natural resources, including huge oil-reserves, are now being exploited.

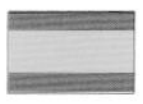

## SPAIN
Kingdom of Spain

| | | | |
|---|---|---|---|
| **Area Sq Km** | 504 782 | **Languages** | Spanish (Castilian), Catalan, Galician, Basque |
| **Area Sq Miles** | 194 897 | **Religions** | Roman Catholic |
| **Population** | 46 455 000 | **Currency** | Euro |
| **Capital** | Madrid | **Organizations** | EU, NATO, OECD, UN |

**Map page 167**

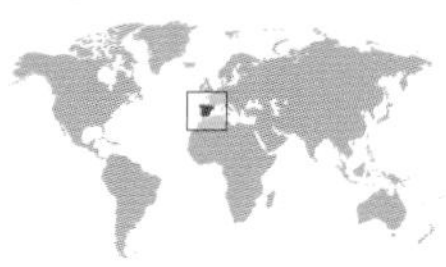

Spain occupies most of the Iberian peninsula in southwest Europe. It includes the Canary Islands, and two enclaves in north Africa. Much of the mainland is a high plateau, and the Pyrenees form the border with France. Summers are hot and winters cool, especially in the north. Most of the population is urban, and agriculture involves only a tenth of the workforce. Fruit, vegetables and wine are exported. Mineral resources include lead, copper, mercury and fluorspar. Some oil is produced, but Spain has to import energy. Manufacturing industries include machinery, transport equipment, vehicles and food products. Fishing, tourism and financial services are also important. Most trade is with other EU countries.

## SRI LANKA
Democratic Socialist Republic of Sri Lanka

| | | | |
|---|---|---|---|
| **Area Sq Km** | 65 610 | **Languages** | Sinhalese, Tamil, English |
| **Area Sq Miles** | 25 332 | **Religions** | Buddhist, Hindu, Sunni Muslim, Roman Catholic |
| **Population** | 21 045 000 | **Currency** | Sri Lankan rupee |
| **Capital** | Sri Jayewardenepura Kotte | **Organizations** | Comm., UN |

**Map page 143**

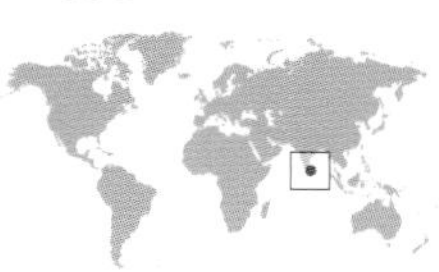

Sri Lanka lies in the Indian Ocean off the southeast coast of India in south Asia. It has rolling coastal plains, with mountains in the centre-south. The climate is hot and monsoonal. Most people live on the west coast. Manufactures (chiefly textiles and clothing), tea, rubber, copra and gems are exported. The economy relies on foreign aid and workers' remittances. The USA and the UK are the main trading partners.

## SUDAN
Republic of the Sudan

| | | | |
|---|---|---|---|
| **Area Sq Km** | 1 861 484 | **Languages** | Arabic, Dinka, Nubian, Beja, Nuer, local languages |
| **Area Sq Miles** | 718 725 | **Religions** | Sunni Muslim, traditional beliefs, Christian |
| **Population** | 36 371 510 | **Currency** | Sudanese pound (Sudani) |
| **Capital** | Khartoum | **Organizations** | UN |

**Map page 177**

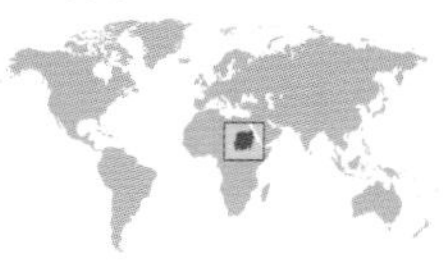

The Sudan is in the northeast of the continent of Africa, on the Red Sea. It lies within the upper Nile basin, much of which is arid plain but with swamps to the south. Mountains lie to the northeast, west and south. The climate is hot and arid with light summer rainfall, and droughts occur. Most people live along the Nile and are farmers and herders. Cotton, gum arabic, livestock and other agricultural products are exported. The government is working with foreign investors to develop oil resources, but the independence of South Sudan in July 2011 after civil war, and ethnic cleansing in Darfur continue to restrict the economy. Main trading partners are Saudi Arabia, China and Libya.

## SURINAME
Republic of Suriname

| | | | |
|---|---|---|---|
| **Area Sq Km** | 163 820 | **Languages** | Dutch, Surinamese, English, Hindi |
| **Area Sq Miles** | 63 251 | **Religions** | Hindu, Roman Catholic, Protestant, Sunni Muslim |
| **Population** | 529 000 | **Currency** | Suriname guilder |
| **Capital** | Paramaribo | **Organizations** | CARICOM, UN |

**Map page 211**

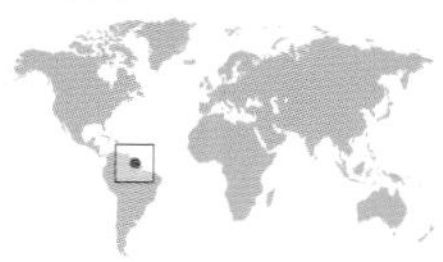

Suriname, on the Atlantic coast of northern South America, consists of a swampy coastal plain (where most of the population lives), central plateaus, and highlands in the south. The climate is tropical, and rainforest covers much of the land. Bauxite mining is the main industry, and alumina and aluminium are the chief exports, with shrimps, rice, bananas and timber also exported. The main trading partners are the Netherlands, Canada and the USA.

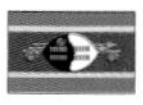

## SWAZILAND
Kingdom of Swaziland

| | | | |
|---|---|---|---|
| **Area Sq Km** | 17 364 | **Languages** | Swazi, English |
| **Area Sq Miles** | 6 704 | **Religions** | Christian, traditional beliefs |
| **Population** | 1 203 000 | **Currency** | Emalangeni, South African rand |
| **Capital** | Mbabane | **Organizations** | Comm., SADC, UN |

**Map page 181**

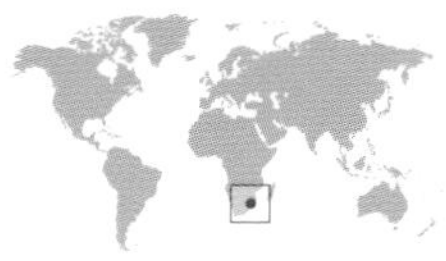

Landlocked Swaziland in southern Africa lies between Mozambique and the Republic of South Africa. Savanna plateaus descend from mountains in the west towards hill country in the east. The climate is subtropical, but temperate in the mountains. Subsistence farming predominates. Asbestos and diamonds are mined. Exports include sugar, fruit and wood pulp. Tourism and workers' remittances are important to the economy. Most trade is with South Africa.

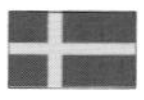

## SWEDEN
Kingdom of Sweden

| | | | |
|---|---|---|---|
| **Area Sq Km** | 449 964 | **Languages** | Swedish |
| **Area Sq Miles** | 173 732 | **Religions** | Protestant, Roman Catholic |
| **Population** | 9 441 000 | **Currency** | Swedish krona |
| **Capital** | Stockholm | **Organizations** | EU, OECD, UN |

**Map page 158–159**

Sweden occupies the eastern part of the Scandinavian peninsula in northern Europe and borders the Baltic Sea, the Gulf of Bothnia, and the Kattegat and Skagerrak. Forested uplands cover the northern half, which extends beyond the Arctic Circle. The south is a lowland lake region where most of the population lives. Sweden has warm summers and cold winters, severe in the north. Natural resources include forests, minerals and water. Dairy products, meat, cereals and vegetables are produced. Iron and copper are mined, and also zinc, lead, silver and gold. Exports include machinery and transport equipment, chemicals, forest products, furniture and telecommunications equipment. Most trade is with other EU countries.

## SWITZERLAND
Swiss Confederation

| | | | |
|---|---|---|---|
| **Area Sq Km** | 41 293 | **Languages** | German, French, Italian, Romansch |
| **Area Sq Miles** | 15 943 | **Religions** | Roman Catholic, Protestant |
| **Population** | 7 702 000 | **Currency** | Swiss franc |
| **Capital** | Bern | **Organizations** | OECD, UN |

**Map page 166**

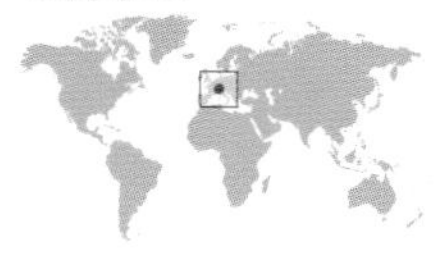

Switzerland is a mountainous, landlocked country in west-central Europe. The southern half lies within the Alps, and the Jura mountains are in the northwest. The rest is a high plateau, where most of the population lives. Climate varies depending on altitude, but in general summers are mild and winters are cold. Switzerland has a very high living standard, yet it has few mineral resources, and most food and raw materials are imported. Manufacturing (especially precision instruments and heavy machinery, chemicals and pharmaceuticals) and financial services are the mainstay of the economy. Tourism, and international organizations based in Switzerland, are also major foreign currency earners. Germany is the main trading partner.

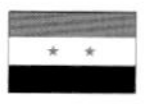

## SYRIA
Syrian Arab Republic

| | | | |
|---|---|---|---|
| **Area Sq Km** | 185 180 | **Languages** | Arabic, Kurdish, Armenian |
| **Area Sq Miles** | 71 498 | **Religions** | Sunni Muslim, Shi'a Muslim, Christian |
| **Population** | 20 766 000 | **Currency** | Syrian pound |
| **Capital** | Damascus (Dimashq) | **Organizations** | UN |

**Map page 136–137**

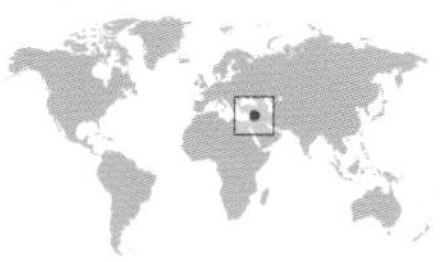

Syria is in southwest Asia, has a short coastline on the Mediterranean Sea, and stretches inland to a plateau traversed northwest-southeast by the Euphrates river. Mountains flank the southwest borders with Lebanon and Israel. The climate is Mediterranean in coastal regions, hotter and drier inland. Most Syrians live on the coast or in the river valleys. Cotton, cereals and fruit are important products, but the main exports are petroleum and related products, and textiles.

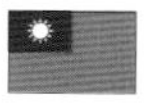

## TAIWAN
Republic of China

| | | | |
|---|---|---|---|
| **Area Sq Km** | 36 179 | **Languages** | Mandarin (Putonghua), Min, Hakka, local languages |
| **Area Sq Miles** | 13 969 | **Religions** | Buddhist, Taoist, Confucian, Christian |
| **Population** | 23 164 000 | **Currency** | Taiwan dollar |
| **Capital** | T'aipei | **Organizations** | APEC |

**Map page 149**

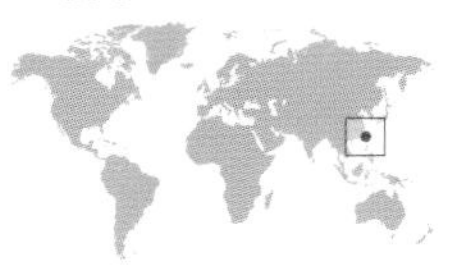

The east Asian state consists of the island of Taiwan, separated from mainland China by the Taiwan Strait, and several much smaller islands. Much of Taiwan is mountainous and forested. Densely populated coastal plains in the west contain the bulk of the population and most economic activity. Taiwan has a tropical monsoon climate, with warm, wet summers and mild winters. Agriculture is highly productive. The country is virtually self-sufficient in food and exports some products. Coal, oil and natural gas are produced and a few minerals are mined, but none of them are of great significance to the economy. Taiwan depends heavily on imports of raw materials and exports of manufactured goods. The main manufactures are electrical and electronic goods, including television sets, personal computers and calculators, textiles, fertilizers, clothing, footwear and toys. The main trading partners are the USA, Japan and Germany. The People's Republic of China claims Taiwan as its 23rd Province.

## TAJIKISTAN
Republic of Tajikistan

| | | | |
|---|---|---|---|
| **Area Sq Km** | 143 100 | **Languages** | Tajik, Uzbek, Russian |
| **Area Sq Miles** | 55 251 | **Religions** | Sunni Muslim |
| **Population** | 6 977 000 | **Currency** | Somoni |
| **Capital** | Dushanbe | **Organizations** | CIS, UN |

**Map page 139**

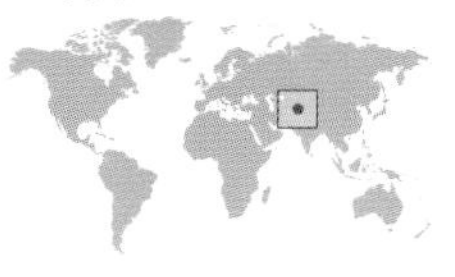

Landlocked Tajikistan in central Asia is a mountainous country, dominated by the mountains of the Alai Range and the Pamir. In the less mountainous western areas summers are warm, although winters are cold. Agriculture is the main sector of the economy, chiefly cotton growing and cattle breeding. Mineral deposits include lead, zinc, and uranium. Processed metals, textiles and clothing are the main manufactured goods; the main exports are aluminium and cotton. Uzbekistan, Kazakhstan and the Russian Federation are the main trading partners.

## TANZANIA
United Republic of Tanzania

| | | | |
|---|---|---|---|
| **Area Sq Km** | 945 087 | **Languages** | Swahili, English, Nyamwezi, local languages |
| **Area Sq Miles** | 364 900 | **Religions** | Shi'a Muslim, Sunni Muslim, traditional beliefs, Christian |
| **Population** | 46 218 000 | **Currency** | Tanzanian shilling |
| **Capital** | Dodoma | **Organizations** | Comm., SADC, UN |

**Map page 178–179**

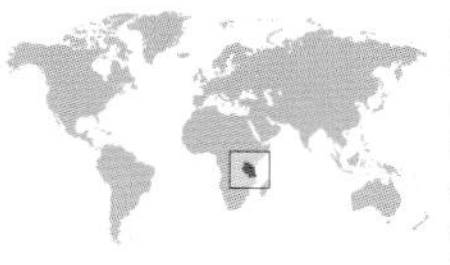

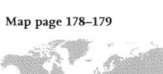

Tanzania lies on the coast of east Africa and includes the island of Zanzibar in the Indian Ocean. Most of the mainland is a savanna plateau lying east of the Great Rift Valley. In the north, near the border with Kenya, is Kilimanjaro, the highest mountain in Africa. The climate is tropical. The economy is predominantly based on agriculture, which employs about three-quarters of the workforce. Agricultural processing and gold and diamond mining are the main industries, although tourism is growing. Coffee, cotton, cashew nuts and tobacco are the main exports, with cloves from Zanzibar. Most export trade is with India, China and Switzerland. Tanzania depends heavily on foreign aid.

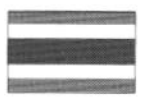

## THAILAND
Kingdom of Thailand

| | | | |
|---|---|---|---|
| **Area Sq Km** | 513 115 | **Languages** | Thai, Lao, Chinese, Malay, Mon-Khmer languages |
| **Area Sq Miles** | 198 115 | **Religions** | Buddhist, Sunni Muslim |
| **Population** | 69 519 000 | **Currency** | Baht |
| **Capital** | Bangkok (Krung Thep) | **Organizations** | APEC, ASEAN, UN |

**Map page 154**

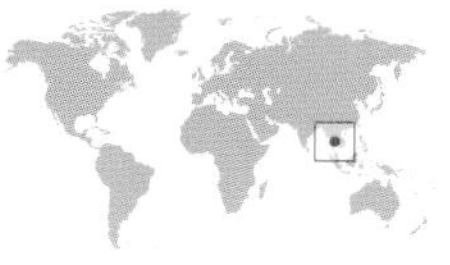

Thailand lies between the Gulf of Thailand and the Andaman Sea and includes the northern Malay Peninsula and many islands lining the coast. To the east of the extensive Chao Phraya basin is a plateau drained by the Mekong, while much of the rest is forested upland. The climate is hot, humid and monsoonal. Half the workforce is involved in agriculture, and fishing is also important, but tourism is the major earner. Minerals include gas, oil, lignite, tin, tungsten and baryte, and gemstones, and manufacturing includes electronics, clothing and food processing. Thailand is a leading exporter of rice, rubber, palm oil and cassava. Japan and the USA are the main trading partners.

## TOGO
Republic of Togo

| | | | |
|---|---|---|---|
| Area Sq Km | 56 785 | Languages | French, Ewe, Kabre, local languages |
| Area Sq Miles | 21 925 | Religions | Traditional beliefs, Christian, Sunni Muslim |
| Population | 6 155 000 | Currency | CFA franc |
| Capital | Lomé | Organizations | UN |

Map page 176

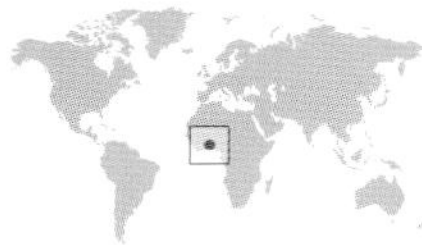

Togo is a long narrow country in west Africa with a short coastline on the Gulf of Guinea. The interior consists of plateaus rising to mountainous areas. The climate is tropical, and is drier inland. Agriculture is the mainstay of the economy. Phosphate mining and food processing are the main industries. Cotton, phosphates, coffee and cocoa are the main exports. Lomé, the capital, is an entrepôt trade centre.

## Tokelau
New Zealand Overseas Territory

| | | | |
|---|---|---|---|
| Area Sq Km | 10 | Languages | English, Tokelauan |
| Area Sq Miles | 4 | Religions | Christian |
| Population | 1 466 | Currency | New Zealand dollar |

Map page 125

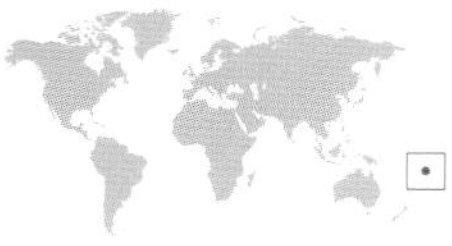

Tokelau consists of three atolls, Atafu, Nukunonu and Fakaofa, lying in the Pacific Ocean north of Samoa. Subsistence agriculture is the main activity, and the islands rely on aid from New Zealand and remittances from workers overseas.

## TONGA
Kingdom of Tonga

| | | | |
|---|---|---|---|
| Area Sq Km | 748 | Languages | Tongan, English |
| Area Sq Miles | 289 | Religions | Protestant, Roman Catholic |
| Population | 105 000 | Currency | Pa'anga |
| Capital | Nuku'alofa | Organizations | Comm., UN |

Map page 125

Tonga comprises some one hundred and seventy islands in the south Pacific Ocean, northeast of New Zealand. The three main groups are Tongatapu (where sixty per cent of Tongans live), Ha'apai and Vava'u. The climate is warm and wet, and the economy relies heavily on agriculture. Tourism and light industry are also important to the economy. Exports include squash, fish, vanilla beans and root crops. Most trade is with New Zealand, Japan and Australia.

## Transnistria
Disputed territory

| | | | |
|---|---|---|---|
| Area Sq Km | 4 200 | Languages | Russian, Ukrainian, Moldovan |
| Area Sq Miles | 1 622 | Religions | Eastern Orthodox, Roman Catholic |
| Population | 520 000 | Currency | Transnistrian rouble, Moldovan leu |
| Capital | Tiraspol | | |

Map page 173 Transnistria, the area of Moldova mainly between the Dniester river and the Ukrainian border, is a predominantly ethnic Russian, and Russian-speaking region. Campaigns for Transnistrian autonomy and independence led to civil war between Moldovan forces and separatists who had proclaimed the self-styled 'Dniester Republic', aligned to Russia, in 1990. A peace agreement with Russia in 1992 ended this war, granted Transnistria special status and established a security zone along its border with Moldova, controlled by Russian, Moldovan and Transnistrian troops. An agreement between Moldova and Transnistria in 1996 stated that Transnistria would remain a part of Moldova, but the campaign for independence continues and the status of the region remains to be resolved. It currently functions as a (predominantly Russian) de facto autonomous republic, separate from Moldova – the Pridnestrovian Moldavian Republic.

## TRINIDAD AND TOBAGO
Republic of Trinidad and Tobago

| | | | |
|---|---|---|---|
| Area Sq Km | 5 130 | Languages | English, Creole, Hindi |
| Area Sq Miles | 1 981 | Religions | Roman Catholic, Hindu, Protestant, Sunni Muslim |
| Population | 1 346 000 | Currency | Trinidad and Tobago dollar |
| Capital | Port of Spain | Organizations | CARICOM, Comm., UN |

Map page 213

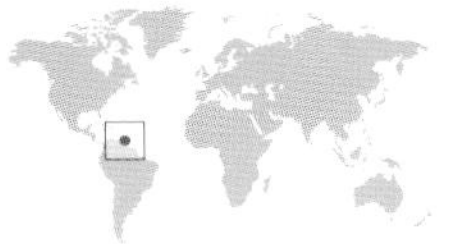

Trinidad, the most southerly Caribbean island, lies off the Venezuelan coast. It is hilly in the north, with a central plain. Tobago, to the northeast, is smaller, more mountainous and less developed. The climate is tropical. The main crops are cocoa, sugar cane, coffee, fruit and vegetables. Oil and petrochemical industries dominate the economy. Tourism is also important. The USA is the main trading partner.

## TUNISIA
Republic Tunisian

| | | | |
|---|---|---|---|
| Area Sq Km | 164 150 | Languages | Arabic, French |
| Area Sq Miles | 63 379 | Religions | Sunni Muslim |
| Population | 10 594 000 | Currency | Tunisian dinar |
| Capital | Tunis | Organizations | UN |

Map page 176

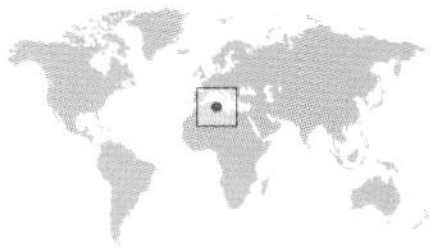

Tunisia is on the Mediterranean coast of north Africa. The north is mountainous with valleys and coastal plains, has a Mediterranean climate and is the most populous area. The south is hot and arid. Oil and phosphates are the main resources, and the main crops are olives and citrus fruit. Tourism is an important industry. Exports include petroleum products, textiles, fruit and phosphorus. Most trade is with European Union countries.

## TURKEY
Republic of Turkey

| | | | |
|---|---|---|---|
| Area Sq Km | 779 452 | Languages | Turkish, Kurdish |
| Area Sq Miles | 300 948 | Religions | Sunni Muslim, Shi'a Muslim |
| Population | 73 640 000 | Currency | Lira |
| Capital | Ankara | Organizations | NATO, OECD, UN |

Map page 136–137

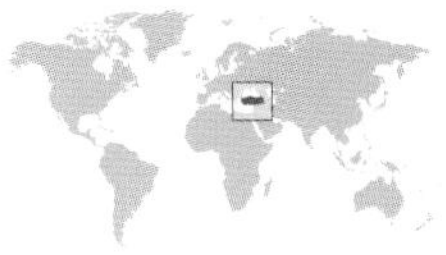

Turkey occupies a large peninsula in southwest Asia. It includes eastern Thrace, in southeastern Europe. The Asian mainland consists of the semi-arid Anatolian plateau, flanked to the north, south and east by mountains. The coast has a Mediterranean climate, but inland conditions are more extreme, with hot, dry summers and cold, snowy winters. Cotton, grains, tobacco, fruit, nuts and livestock are produced, and minerals include chromium, iron ore, lead, tin, borate, baryte, and some coal. Manufacturing includes clothing, textiles, food products, steel and vehicles. Tourism is a major industry. Germany and the Russian Federation are the main trading partners. Remittances from workers abroad are important to the economy.

## TURKMENISTAN
Republic of Turkmenistan

| | | | |
|---|---|---|---|
| Area Sq Km | 488 100 | Languages | Turkmen, Uzbek, Russian |
| Area Sq Miles | 188 456 | Religions | Sunni Muslim, Russian Orthodox |
| Population | 5 105 000 | Currency | Turkmen manat |
| Capital | Aşgabat (Ashkhabad) | Organizations | UN |

Map page 138

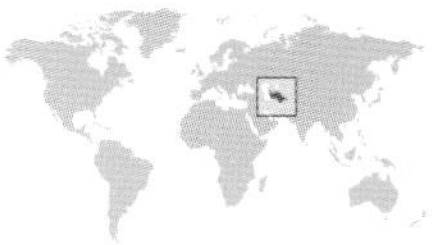

Turkmenistan, in central Asia, comprises the plains of the Karakum Desert, the foothills of the Kopet Dag mountains in the south, the Amudar'ya valley in the north and the Caspian Sea plains in the west. The climate is dry, with extreme temperatures. The economy is based mainly on irrigated agriculture (chiefly cotton growing), and natural gas and oil. Main exports are natural gas, oil and cotton fibre. Ukraine, Iran, Turkey and the Russian Federation are the main trading partners.

## Turks and Caicos Islands
United Kingdom Overseas Territory

| | | | |
|---|---|---|---|
| Area Sq Km | 430 | Languages | English |
| Area Sq Miles | 166 | Religions | Protestant |
| Population | 39 000 | Currency | United States dollar |
| Capital | Grand Turk (Cockburn Town) | | |

Map page 205 The state consists of over forty low-lying islands and cays in the northern Caribbean. Only eight islands are inhabited, and two-fifths of the people live on Grand Turk and Salt Cay. The climate is tropical, and the economy is based on tourism, fishing and offshore banking.

## TUVALU

| | | | |
|---|---|---|---|
| Area Sq Km | 25 | Languages | Tuvaluan, English |
| Area Sq Miles | 10 | Religions | Protestant |
| Population | 10 000 | Currency | Australian dollar |
| Capital | Vaiaku | Organizations | Comm., UN |

Map page 125

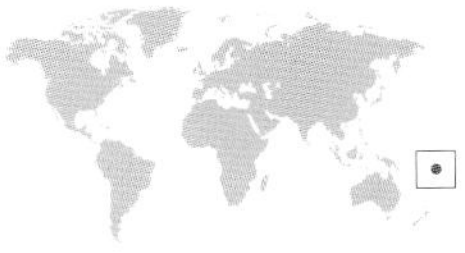

Tuvalu comprises nine low-lying coral atolls in the south Pacific Ocean. One-third of the population lives on Funafuti, and most people depend on subsistence farming and fishing. The islands export copra, stamps and clothing, but rely heavily on foreign aid. Most trade is with Fiji, Australia and New Zealand.

## UGANDA
Republic of Uganda

| | | | |
|---|---|---|---|
| Area Sq Km | 241 038 | Languages | English, Swahili, Luganda, local languages |
| Area Sq Miles | 93 065 | Religions | Roman Catholic, Protestant, Sunni Muslim, traditional beliefs |
| Population | 34 509 000 | Currency | Ugandan shilling |
| Capital | Kampala | Organizations | Comm., UN |

Map page 178

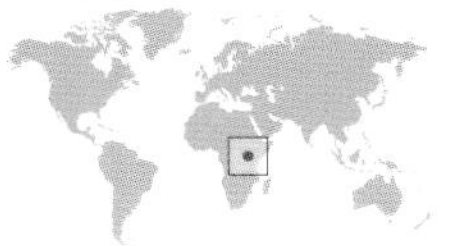

A landlocked country in east Africa, Uganda consists of a savanna plateau with mountains and lakes. The climate is warm and wet. Most people live in the southern half of the country. Agriculture employs over two-thirds of the workforce and dominates the economy. Coffee, tea, fish and fish products are the main exports. Uganda relies heavily on aid.

## UKRAINE

| | | | |
|---|---|---|---|
| Area Sq Km | 603 700 | Languages | Ukrainian, Russian |
| Area Sq Miles | 233 090 | Religions | Ukrainian Orthodox, Ukrainian Catholic, Roman Catholic |
| Population | 45 190 000 | Currency | Hryvnia |
| Capital | Kiev (Kyiv) | Organizations | UN |

Map page 173

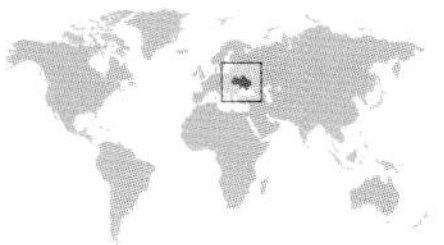

The country lies on the Black Sea coast of eastern Europe. Much of the land is steppe, generally flat and treeless, but with rich black soil, and it is drained by the river Dnieper. Along the border with Belarus are forested, marshy plains. The only uplands are the Carpathian Mountains in the west and smaller ranges on the Crimean peninsula. Summers are warm and winters are cold, with milder conditions in the Crimea. About a quarter of the population lives in the mainly industrial areas around Donets'k, Kiev and Dnipropetrovs'k. The Ukraine is rich in natural resources: fertile soil, substantial mineral and natural gas deposits, and forests. Agriculture and livestock rearing are important, but mining and manufacturing are the dominant sectors of the economy. Coal, iron and manganese mining, steel and metal production, machinery, chemicals and food processing are the main industries. The Russian Federation is the main trading partner.

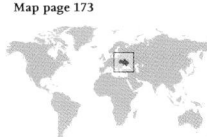

## UNITED ARAB EMIRATES
Federation of Emirates

| | | | |
|---|---|---|---|
| Area Sq Km | 77 700 | Languages | Arabic, English |
| Area Sq Miles | 30 000 | Religions | Sunni Muslim, Shi'a Muslim |
| Population | 7 891 000 | Currency | United Arab Emirates dirham |
| Capital | Abu Dhabi (Abū Ẓaby) | Organizations | GCC, OPEC, UN |

Map page 140

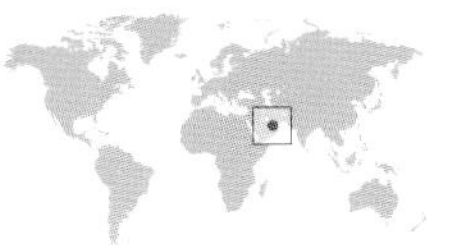

The UAE lies on the Gulf coast of the Arabian Peninsula. Six emirates are on The Gulf, while the seventh, Fujairah, is on the Gulf of Oman. Most of the land is flat desert with sand dunes and salt pans. The only hilly area is in the northeast. Over eighty per cent of the population lives in three of the emirates - Abu Dhabi, Dubai and Sharjah. Summers are hot and winters are mild, with occasional rainfall in coastal areas. Fruit and vegetables are grown in oases and irrigated areas, but the Emirates' wealth is based on hydrocarbons found in Abu Dhabi, Dubai, Sharjah and Ras al Khaimah. The UAE is one of the major oil producers in the Middle East. Dubai is an important entrepôt trade centre The main trading partners are India, Iran, Iraq and China.

### Abu Dhabi (Emirate)
Area Sq Km (Sq Miles) 67 340 (26 000) Population 1 628 000 Capital Abu Dhabi (Abū Ẓaby)

### Ajman (Emirate)
Area Sq Km (Sq Miles) 259 (100) Population 250 000 Capital 'Ajman

### Dubai (Emirate)
Area Sq Km (Sq Miles) 3 885 (1 500) Population 1 722 000 Capital Dubai (Dubayy)

### Fujairah (Emirate)
Area Sq Km (Sq Miles) 1 165 (450) Population 152 000 Capital Fujairah

### Ra's al Khaymah (Emirate)
Area Sq Km (Sq Miles) 1 684 (650) Population 241 000 Capital Ra's al Khaymah

### Sharjah (Emirate)
Area Sq Km (Sq Miles) 2 590 (1 000) Population 1 017 000 Capital Sharjah (Ash Shāriqan)

### Umm al Qaywayn (Emirate)
Area Sq Km (Sq Miles) 777 (300) Population 56 000 Capital Umm al Qaywayn

## UNITED KINGDOM
United Kingdom of Great Britain and Northern Ireland

| | | | |
|---|---|---|---|
| **Area Sq Km** | 243 609 | **Languages** | English, Welsh, Gaelic |
| **Area Sq Miles** | 94 058 | **Religions** | Protestant, Roman Catholic, Muslim |
| **Population** | 62 417 000 | **Currency** | Pound sterling |
| **Capital** | London | **Organizations** | Comm., EU, NATO, OECD, UN |

**Map page 160–163**

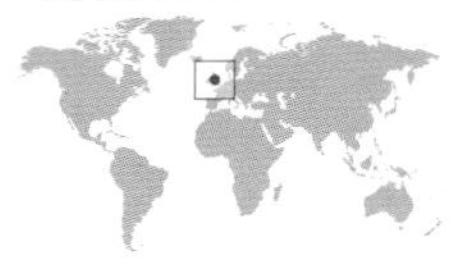

The United Kingdom, in northwest Europe, occupies the island of Great Britain, part of Ireland, and many small adjacent islands. Great Britain comprises England, Scotland and Wales. England covers over half the land area and supports over four-fifths of the population, at its densest in the southeast. The English landscape is flat or rolling with some uplands, notably the Cheviot Hills on the Scottish border, the Pennines in the centre-north, and the hills of the Lake District in the northwest. Scotland consists of southern uplands, central lowlands, the Highlands (which include the UK's highest peak) and many islands. Wales is a land of hills, mountains and river valleys. Northern Ireland contains uplands, plains and the UK's largest lake, Lough Neagh. The climate of the UK is mild, wet and variable. There are few mineral deposits, but important energy resources. Agricultural activities involve sheep and cattle rearing, dairy farming, and crop and fruit growing in the east and southeast. Productivity is high, but approximately one-third of food is imported. The UK produces petroleum and natural gas from reserves in the North Sea and is self-sufficient in energy in net terms. Major manufactures are food and drinks, motor vehicles and parts, aerospace equipment, machinery, electronic and electrical equipment, and chemicals and chemical products. However, the economy is dominated by service industries, including banking, insurance, finance and business services. London, the capital, is one of the world's major financial centres. Tourism is also a major industry, with approximately thirty million visitors a year. International trade is also important, equivalent to one-third of national income. Main trading partners are the USA and other European Union countries.

### England (Constituent country)
**Area Sq Km (Sq Miles)** 130 433 (50 360) **Population** 51 809 700 **Capital** London

### Northern Ireland (Province)
**Area Sq Km (Sq Miles)** 13 576 (5 242) **Population** 1 788 900 **Capital** Belfast

### Scotland (Constituent country)
**Area Sq Km (Sq Miles)** 78 822 (30 433) **Population** 5 194 000 **Capital** Edinburgh

### Wales (Principality)
**Area Sq Km (Sq Miles)** 20 778 (8 022) **Population** 2 999 300 **Capital** Cardiff

## UNITED STATES OF AMERICA
Federal Republic

| | | | |
|---|---|---|---|
| **Area Sq Km** | 9 826 635 | **Languages** | English, Spanish |
| **Area Sq Miles** | 3 794 085 | **Religions** | Protestant, Roman Catholic, Sunni Muslim, Jewish |
| **Population** | 313 085 000 | **Currency** | United States dollar |
| **Capital** | Washington D.C. | **Organizations** | APEC, NATO, OECD, UN |

**Map page 192–193**

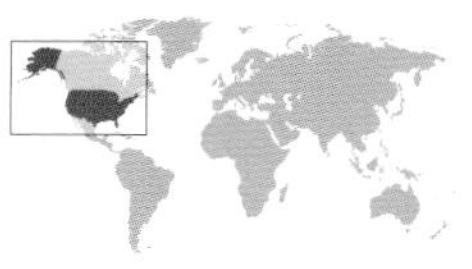

The USA comprises forty-eight contiguous states in North America, bounded by Canada and Mexico, plus the states of Alaska, to the northwest of Canada, and Hawaii, in the north Pacific Ocean. The populous eastern states cover the Atlantic coastal plain (which includes the Florida peninsula and the Gulf of Mexico coast) and the Appalachian Mountains. The central states occupy a vast interior plain drained by the Mississippi-Missouri river system. To the west lie the Rocky Mountains, separated from the Pacific coastal ranges by intermontane plateaus. The Pacific coastal zone is also mountainous, and prone to earthquakes. Hawaii is a group of some twenty volcanic islands. Climatic conditions range between arctic in Alaska to desert in the intermontane plateaus. Most of the USA has a temperate climate, although the interior has continental conditions. There are abundant natural resources, including major reserves of minerals and energy resources. The USA has the largest and most technologically advanced economy in the world, based on manufacturing and services. Although agriculture accounts for approximately two per cent of national income, productivity is high and the USA is a net exporter of food, chiefly grains and fruit. Cotton is the major industrial crop. The USA produces iron ore, copper, lead, zinc, and many other minerals. It is a major producer of coal, petroleum and natural gas, although being the world's biggest energy user it imports significant quantities of petroleum and its products. Manufacturing is diverse. The main industries are petroleum, steel, motor vehicles, aerospace, telecommunications, electronics, food processing, chemicals and consumer goods. Tourism is a major foreign currency earner, with approximately sixty million visitors a year. Other important service industries are banking and finance, Wall Street in New York being one of the world's major stock exchanges. Canada and Mexico are the main trading partners.

### Alabama (State)
**Area Sq Km (Sq Miles)** 135 765 (52 419) **Population** 4 708 708 **Capital** Montgomery

### Alaska (State)
**Area Sq Km (Sq Miles)** 1 717 854 (663 267) **Population** 698 473 **Capital** Juneau

### Arizona (State)
**Area Sq Km (Sq Miles)** 295 253 (113 998) **Population** 6 595 778 **Capital** Phoenix

### Arkansas (State)
**Area Sq Km (Sq Miles)** 137 733 (53 179) **Population** 2 889 450 **Capital** Little Rock

### California (State)
**Area Sq Km (Sq Miles)** 423 971 (163 696) **Population** 36 961 664 **Capital** Sacramento

### Colorado (State)
**Area Sq Km (Sq Miles)** 269 602 (104 094) **Population** 5 024 748 **Capital** Denver

### Connecticut (State)
**Area Sq Km (Sq Miles)** 14 356 (5 543) **Population** 3 518 288 **Capital** Hartford

### Delaware (State)
**Area Sq Km (Sq Miles)** 6 446 (2 489) **Population** 885 122 **Capital** Dover

### District of Columbia (District)
**Area Sq Km (Sq Miles)** 176 (68) **Population** 599 657 **Capital** Washington

### Florida (State)
**Area Sq Km (Sq Miles)** 170 305 (65 755) **Population** 18 537 969 **Capital** Tallahassee

### Georgia (State)
**Area Sq Km (Sq Miles)** 153 910 (59 425) **Population** 9 829 211 **Capital** Atlanta

### Hawaii (State)
**Area Sq Km (Sq Miles)** 28 311 (10 931) **Population** 1 295 178 **Capital** Honolulu

### Idaho (State)
**Area Sq Km (Sq Miles)** 216 445 (83 570) **Population** 1 545 801 **Capital** Boise

### Illinois (State)
**Area Sq Km (Sq Miles)** 149 997 (57 914) **Population** 12 910 409 **Capital** Springfield

### Indiana (State)
**Area Sq Km (Sq Miles)** 94 322 (36 418) **Population** 6 423 113 **Capital** Indianapolis

### Iowa (State)
**Area Sq Km (Sq Miles)** 145 744 (56 272) **Population** 3 007 856 **Capital** Des Moines

### Kansas (State)
**Area Sq Km (Sq Miles)** 213 096 (82 277) **Population** 2 818 747 **Capital** Topeka

### Kentucky (State)
**Area Sq Km (Sq Miles)** 104 659 (40 409) **Population** 4 314 113 **Capital** Frankfort

### Louisiana (State)
**Area Sq Km (Sq Miles)** 134 265 (51 840) **Population** 4 492 076 **Capital** Baton Rouge

### Maine (State)
**Area Sq Km (Sq Miles)** 91 647 (35 385) **Population** 1 318 301 **Capital** Augusta

### Maryland (State)
**Area Sq Km (Sq Miles)** 32 134 (12 407) **Population** 5 699 478 **Capital** Annapolis

### Massachusetts (State)
**Area Sq Km (Sq Miles)** 27 337 (10 555) **Population** 6 593 587 **Capital** Boston

### Michigan (State)
**Area Sq Km (Sq Miles)** 250 493 (96 716) **Population** 9 969 727 **Capital** Lansing

### Minnesota (State)
**Area Sq Km (Sq Miles)** 225 171 (86 939) **Population** 5 266 214 **Capital** St Paul

### Mississippi (State)
**Area Sq Km (Sq Miles)** 125 433 (48 430) **Population** 2 951 996 **Capital** Jackson

### Missouri (State)
**Area Sq Km (Sq Miles)** 180 533 (69 704) **Population** 5 987 580 **Capital** Jefferson City

### Montana (State)
**Area Sq Km (Sq Miles)** 380 837 (147 042) **Population** 974 989 **Capital** Helena

### Nebraska (State)
**Area Sq Km (Sq Miles)** 200 346 (77 354) **Population** 1 796 619 **Capital** Lincoln

### Nevada (State)
**Area Sq Km (Sq Miles)** 286 352 (110 561) **Population** 2 643 085 **Capital** Carson City

### New Hampshire (State)
**Area Sq Km (Sq Miles)** 24 216 (9 350) **Population** 1 324 575 **Capital** Concord

### New Jersey (State)
**Area Sq Km (Sq Miles)** 22 587 (8 721) **Population** 8 707 739 **Capital** Trenton

### New Mexico (State)
**Area Sq Km (Sq Miles)** 314 914 (121 589) **Population** 2 009 671 **Capital** Santa Fe

### New York (State)
**Area Sq Km (Sq Miles)** 141 299 (54 556) **Population** 19 541 453 **Capital** Albany

### North Carolina (State)
**Area Sq Km (Sq Miles)** 139 391 (53 819) **Population** 9 380 884 **Capital** Raleigh

### North Dakota (State)
**Area Sq Km (Sq Miles)** 183 112 (70 700) **Population** 646 844 **Capital** Bismarck

### Ohio (State)
**Area Sq Km (Sq Miles)** 116 096 (44 825) **Population** 11 542 645 **Capital** Columbus

### Oklahoma (State)
**Area Sq Km (Sq Miles)** 181 035 (69 898) **Population** 3 687 050 **Capital** Oklahoma City

### Oregon (State)
**Area Sq Km (Sq Miles)** 254 806 (98 381) **Population** 3 825 657 **Capital** Salem

### Pennsylvania (State)
**Area Sq Km (Sq Miles)** 119 282 (46 055) **Population** 12 604 767 **Capital** Harrisburg

### Rhode Island (State)
**Area Sq Km (Sq Miles)** 4 002 (1 545) **Population** 1 053 209 **Capital** Providence

### South Carolina (State)
**Area Sq Km (Sq Miles)** 82 931 (32 020) **Population** 4 561 242 **Capital** Columbia

### South Dakota (State)
**Area Sq Km (Sq Miles)** 199 730 (77 116) **Population** 812 383 **Capital** Pierre

### Tennessee (State)
**Area Sq Km (Sq Miles)** 109 150 (42 143) **Population** 6 296 254 **Capital** Nashville

### Texas (State)
**Area Sq Km (Sq Miles)** 695 622 (268 581) **Population** 24 782 302 **Capital** Austin

### Utah (State)
**Area Sq Km (Sq Miles)** 219 887 (84 899) **Population** 2 784 572 **Capital** Salt Lake City

### Vermont (State)
**Area Sq Km (Sq Miles)** 24 900 (9 614) **Population** 621 760 **Capital** Montpelier

### Virginia (State)
**Area Sq Km (Sq Miles)** 110 784 (42 774) **Population** 7 882 590 **Capital** Richmond

### Washington (State)
**Area Sq Km (Sq Miles)** 184 666 (71 300) **Population** 6 664 195 **Capital** Olympia

### West Virginia (State)
**Area Sq Km (Sq Miles)** 62 755 (24 230) **Population** 1 819 777 **Capital** Charleston

### Wisconsin (State)
**Area Sq Km (Sq Miles)** 169 639 (65 498) **Population** 5 654 774 **Capital** Madison

### Wyoming (State)
**Area Sq Km (Sq Miles)** 253 337 (97 814) **Population** 544 270 **Capital** Cheyenne

## URUGUAY
Oriental Republic of Uruguay

| | | | |
|---|---|---|---|
| **Area Sq Km** | 176 215 | **Languages** | Spanish |
| **Area Sq Miles** | 68 037 | **Religions** | Roman Catholic, Protestant, Jewish |
| **Population** | 3 380 000 | **Currency** | Uruguayan peso |
| **Capital** | Montevideo | **Organizations** | UN |

**Map page 215**

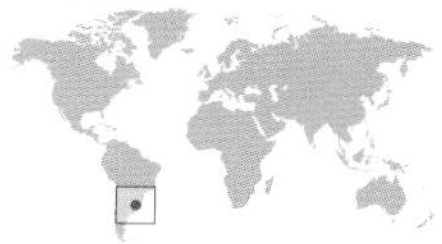

Uruguay, on the Atlantic coast of central South America, is a low-lying land of prairies. The coast and the River Plate estuary in the south are fringed with lagoons and sand dunes. Almost half the population lives in the capital, Montevideo. Uruguay has warm summers and mild winters. The economy is based mainly on cattle and sheep ranching, and the main industries produce food products, textiles, and petroleum products. Meat, wool, hides, textiles and agricultural products are the main exports. Brazil and Argentina are the main trading partners.

## UZBEKISTAN
Republic of Uzbekistan

| | | | |
|---|---|---|---|
| **Area Sq Km** | 447 400 | **Languages** | Uzbek, Russian, Tajik, Kazakh |
| **Area Sq Miles** | 172 742 | **Religions** | Sunni Muslim, Russian Orthodox |
| **Population** | 27 760 000 | **Currency** | Uzbek som |
| **Capital** | Toshkent (Tashkent) | **Organizations** | CIS, UN |

**Map page 138–139**

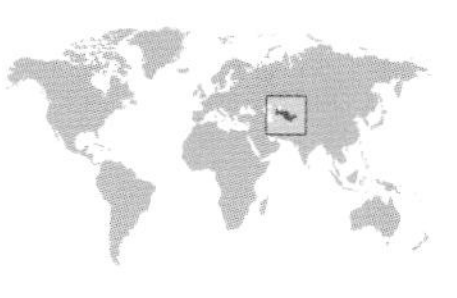

A landlocked country of central Asia, Uzbekistan consists mainly of the flat Kyzylkum Desert. High mountains and valleys are found towards the southeast borders with Kyrgyzstan and Tajikistan. Most settlement is in the Fergana basin. The climate is hot and dry. The economy is based mainly on irrigated agriculture, chiefly cotton production. Uzbekistan is rich in minerals, including gold, copper, lead, zinc and uranium, and it has one of the largest gold mines in the world. Industry specializes in fertilizers and machinery for cotton harvesting and textile manufacture. The Russian Federation is the main trading partner.

## VANUATU
Republic of Vanuatu

| | | | |
|---|---|---|---|
| **Area Sq Km** | 12 190 | **Languages** | English, Bislama (Creole), French |
| **Area Sq Miles** | 4 707 | **Religions** | Protestant, Roman Catholic, traditional beliefs |
| **Population** | 246 000 | **Currency** | Vatu |
| **Capital** | Port Vila | **Organizations** | Comm., UN |

**Map page 125**

Vanuatu occupies an archipelago of approximately eighty islands in the southwest Pacific. Many of the islands are mountainous, of volcanic origin and densely forested. The climate is tropical, with heavy rainfall. Half of the population lives on the main islands of Éfaté and Espíritu Santo, and the majority of people are employed in agriculture. Copra, beef, timber, vegetables, and cocoa are the main exports. Tourism is becoming important to the economy. Australia, Japan and Germany are the main trading partners.

## VATICAN CITY
Vatican City State or Holy See

| | | | |
|---|---|---|---|
| **Area Sq Km** | 0.5 | **Languages** | Italian |
| **Area Sq Miles** | 0.2 | **Religions** | Roman Catholic |
| **Population** | 800 | **Currency** | Euro |
| **Capital** | Vatican City (Città del Vaticano) | | |

**Map page 170**

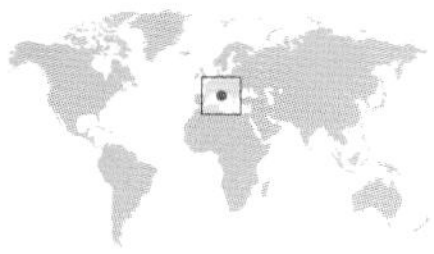

The world's smallest sovereign state, the Vatican City occupies a hill to the west of the river Tiber within the Italian capital, Rome. It is the headquarters of the Roman Catholic church, and income comes from investments, voluntary contributions and tourism.

## VENEZUELA
Bolivarian Republic of Venezuela

| | | | |
|---|---|---|---|
| **Area Sq Km** | 912 050 | **Languages** | Spanish, Amerindian languages |
| **Area Sq Miles** | 352 144 | **Religions** | Roman Catholic, Protestant |
| **Population** | 29 437 000 | **Currency** | Bolívar fuérte |
| **Capital** | Caracas | **Organizations** | OPEC, UN |

**Map page 213**

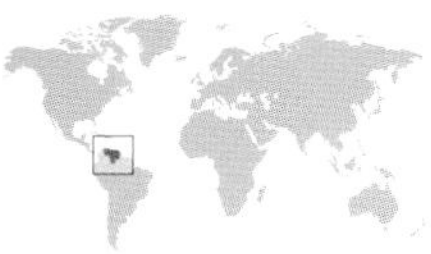

Venezuela is in northern South America, on the Caribbean. Its coast is much indented, with the oil-rich area of Lake Maracaibo at the western end, and the swampy Orinoco Delta to the east. Mountain ranges run parallel to the coast, and turn southwestwards to form a northern extension of the Andes. Central Venezuela is an area of lowland grasslands drained by the Orinoco river system. To the south are the Guiana Highlands, which contain the Angel Falls, the world's highest waterfall. Almost ninety per cent of the population lives in towns, mostly in the coastal mountain areas. The climate is tropical, with most rainfall in summer. Farming is important, particularly cattle ranching and dairy farming; coffee, maize, rice and sugar cane are the main crops. Venezuela is a major oil producer, and oil accounts for about seventy-five per cent of export earnings. Aluminium, iron ore, copper and gold are also mined, and manufactures include petrochemicals, aluminium, steel, textiles and food products. The USA, China and Brazil are the main trading partners.

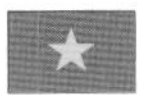

## VIETNAM
Socialist Republic of Vietnam

| | | | |
|---|---|---|---|
| **Area Sq Km** | 329 565 | **Languages** | Vietnamese, Thai, Khmer, Chinese, local languages |
| **Area Sq Miles** | 127 246 | **Religions** | Buddhist, Taoist, Roman Catholic, Cao Dai, Hoa Hao |
| **Population** | 88 792 000 | **Currency** | Dong |
| **Capital** | Ha Nôi (Hanoi) | **Organizations** | APEC, ASEAN, UN |

**Map page 147**

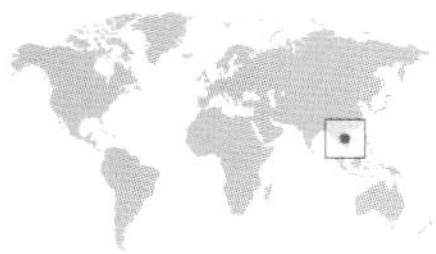

Vietnam lies in southeast Asia on the west coast of the South China Sea. The Red River delta lowlands in the north are separated from the huge Mekong delta in the south by long, narrow coastal plains backed by the mountainous and forested terrain of the Annam Highlands. Most of the population lives in the river deltas. The climate is tropical, with summer monsoon rains. Over three-quarters of the workforce is involved in agriculture, forestry and fishing. Coffee, tea and rubber are important cash crops, but Vietnam is the world's second largest rice exporter. Oil, coal and copper are produced, and other main industries are food processing, clothing and footwear, cement and fertilizers. Exports include oil, coffee, rice, clothing, fish and fish products. Japan and Singapore are the main trading partners.

## Virgin Islands (U.K.)
United Kingdom Overseas Territory

| | | | |
|---|---|---|---|
| **Area Sq Km** | 153 | **Languages** | English |
| **Area Sq Miles** | 59 | **Religions** | Protestant, Roman Catholic |
| **Population** | 23 000 | **Currency** | United States dollar |
| **Capital** | Road Town | | |

**Map page 205** The Caribbean territory comprises four main islands and over thirty islets at the eastern end of the Virgin Islands group. Apart from the flat coral atoll of Anegada, the islands are volcanic in origin and hilly. The climate is subtropical, and tourism is the main industry.

## Virgin Islands (U.S.A.)
United States Unincorporated Territory

| | | | |
|---|---|---|---|
| **Area Sq Km** | 352 | **Languages** | English, Spanish |
| **Area Sq Miles** | 136 | **Religions** | Protestant, Roman Catholic |
| **Population** | 109 000 | **Currency** | United States dollar |
| **Capital** | Charlotte Amalie | | |

**Map page 205**

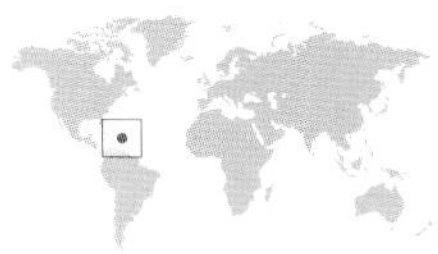

The territory consists of three main islands and over fifty islets in the Caribbean's western Virgin Islands. The islands are hilly, of volcanic origin, and the climate is subtropical. The economy is based on tourism, with some manufacturing, including a major oil refinery on St Croix.

## Wallis and Futuna Islands
French Overseas Collectivity

| | | | |
|---|---|---|---|
| **Area Sq Km** | 274 | **Languages** | French, Wallisian, Futunian |
| **Area Sq Miles** | 106 | **Religions** | Roman Catholic |
| **Population** | 13 000 | **Currency** | CFP franc |
| **Capital** | Matā'utu | | |

**Map page 125**

The south Pacific territory comprises the volcanic islands of the Wallis archipelago and the Hoorn Islands. The climate is tropical. The islands depend on subsistence farming, the sale of licences to foreign fishing fleets, workers' remittances from abroad and French aid.

## West Bank
Disputed territory

| | | | |
|---|---|---|---|
| **Area Sq Km** | 5 860 | **Languages** | Arabic, Hebrew |
| **Area Sq Miles** | 2 263 | **Religions** | Sunni Muslim, Jewish, Shi'a Muslim, Christian |
| **Population** | 2 513 283 | **Currency** | Jordanian dinar, Israeli shekel |

**Map page 136**

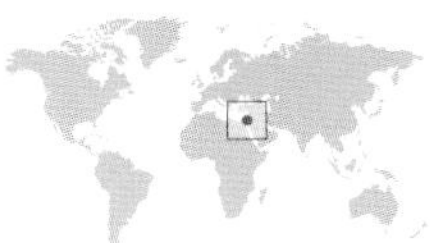

The territory consists of the west bank of the river Jordan and parts of Judea and Samaria. The land was annexed by Israel in 1967, but some areas have been granted autonomy under agreements between Israel and the Palestinian Authority. Conflict between the Israelis and the Palestinians continues to restrict economic development.

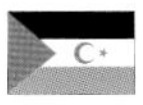

## Western Sahara
Disputed territory

| | | | |
|---|---|---|---|
| **Area Sq Km** | 266 000 | **Languages** | Arabic |
| **Area Sq Miles** | 102 703 | **Religions** | Sunni Muslim |
| **Population** | 548 000 | **Currency** | Moroccan dirham |
| **Capital** | Laâyoune | | |

**Map page 176**

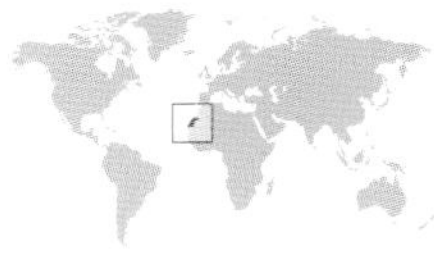

Situated on the northwest coast of Africa, the territory of the Western Sahara is now effectively controlled by Morocco. The land is low, flat desert with higher land in the northeast. There is little cultivation and only about twenty per cent of the land is pasture. Livestock herding, fishing and phosphate mining are the main activities. All trade is controlled by Morocco.

## YEMEN
Republic of Yemen

| | | | |
|---|---|---|---|
| **Area Sq Km** | 527 968 | **Languages** | Arabic |
| **Area Sq Miles** | 203 850 | **Religions** | Sunni Muslim, Shi'a Muslim |
| **Population** | 24 800 000 | **Currency** | Yemeni riyal |
| **Capital** | Şan'ā' | **Organizations** | UN |

**Map page 142**

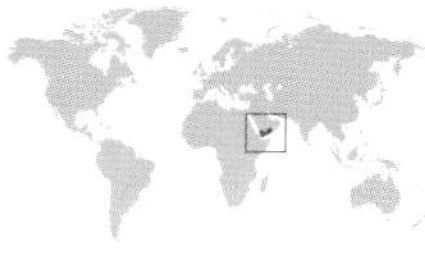

Yemen occupies the southwestern part of the Arabian Peninsula, on the Red Sea and the Gulf of Aden. Beyond the Red Sea coastal plain the land rises to a mountain range and then descends to desert plateaus. Much of the country is hot and arid, but there is more rainfall in the west, where most of the population lives. Farming and fishing are the main activities, with cotton the main cash crop. The main exports are crude oil, fish, coffee and dried fruit. Despite some oil resources Yemen is one of the poorest countries in the Arab world. Main trading partners are Thailand, China, South Korea and Saudi Arabia.

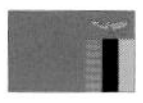

## ZAMBIA
Republic of Zambia

| | | | |
|---|---|---|---|
| **Area Sq Km** | 752 614 | **Languages** | English, Bemba, Nyanja, Tonga, local languages |
| **Area Sq Miles** | 290 586 | **Religions** | Christian, traditional beliefs |
| **Population** | 13 475 000 | **Currency** | Zambian kwacha |
| **Capital** | Lusaka | **Organizations** | Comm., SADC, UN |

**Map page 179**

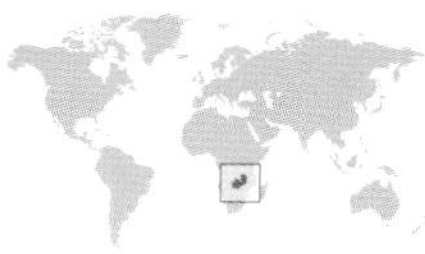

A landlocked state in south central Africa, Zambia consists principally of high savanna plateaus and is bordered by the Zambezi river in the south. Most people live in the Copperbelt area in the centre-north. The climate is tropical, with a rainy season from November to May. Agriculture employs over seventy per cent of the workforce, but is mainly at subsistence level. Copper mining is the mainstay of the economy, although reserves are declining. Copper and cobalt are the main exports. Most trade is with South Africa.

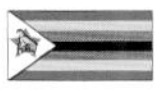

## ZIMBABWE
Republic of Zimbabwe

| | | | |
|---|---|---|---|
| **Area Sq Km** | 390 759 | **Languages** | English, Shona, Ndebele |
| **Area Sq Miles** | 150 873 | **Religions** | Christian, traditional beliefs |
| **Population** | 12 754 000 | **Currency** | Zimbabwean dollar (suspended) |
| **Capital** | Harare | **Organizations** | SADC, UN |

**Map page 179**

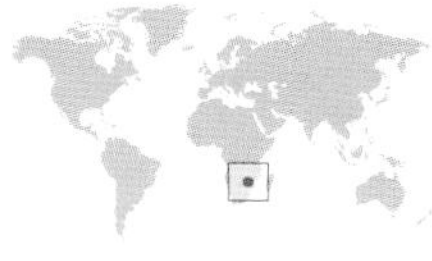

Zimbabwe, a landlocked state in south-central Africa, consists of high plateaus flanked by the Zambezi river valley and Lake Kariba in the north and the Limpopo river in the south. Most of the population lives in the centre of the country. There are significant mineral resources, including gold, nickel, copper, asbestos, platinum and chromium. Agriculture is a major sector of the economy, with crops including tobacco, maize, sugar cane and cotton. Beef cattle are also important. Exports include tobacco, gold, ferroalloys, nickel and cotton. South Africa is the main trading partner. The economy has suffered recently through significant political unrest and instability.

# EARTHQUAKES AND VOLCANOES

## DISTRIBUTION OF EARTHQUAKES AND VOLCANOES

- Deadliest earthquake
- Earthquake of magnitude >=7.5
- Earthquake of magnitude 5.5 – 7.5
- Major volcano
- Other volcano

Winkel Tripel Projection
scale approximately 1:95 000 000

## DEADLIEST EARTHQUAKES 1900–2011

| Year | Location | Deaths |
|---|---|---|
| 1905 | **Kangra,** India | 19 000 |
| 1907 | west of **Dushanbe,** Tajikistan | 12 000 |
| 1908 | **Messina,** Italy | 110 000 |
| 1915 | **Abruzzo,** Italy | 35 000 |
| 1917 | **Bali,** Indonesia | 15 000 |
| 1920 | **Ningxia Province,** China | 200 000 |
| 1923 | **Tōkyō,** Japan | 142 807 |
| 1927 | **Qinghai Province,** China | 200 000 |
| 1932 | **Gansu Province,** China | 70 000 |
| 1933 | **Sichuan Province,** China | 10 000 |
| 1934 | **Nepal/India** | 10 700 |
| 1935 | **Quetta,** Pakistan | 30 000 |
| 1939 | **Chillán,** Chile | 28 000 |
| 1939 | **Erzincan,** Turkey | 32 700 |
| 1948 | **Aşgabat,** Turkmenistan | 19 800 |
| 1962 | northwest **Iran** | 12 225 |
| 1970 | **Huánuco Province,** Peru | 66 794 |
| 1974 | **Yunnan** and **Sichuan Provinces,** China | 20 000 |
| 1976 | central **Guatemala** | 22 778 |
| 1976 | **Tangshan,** Hebei Province, China | 255 000 |
| 1978 | **Khorāsān Province,** Iran | 20 000 |
| 1980 | **Ech Chélif,** Algeria | 11 000 |
| 1988 | **Spitak,** Armenia | 25 000 |
| 1990 | **Manjil,** Iran | 50 000 |
| 1999 | **İzmit (Kocaeli),** Turkey | 17 000 |
| 2001 | **Gujarat,** India | 20 000 |
| 2003 | **Bam,** Iran | 26 271 |
| 2004 | **Sumatra,** Indonesia/Indian Ocean | >225 000 |
| 2005 | northwest **Pakistan** | 74 648 |
| 2008 | **Sichuan Province,** China | >60 000 |
| 2010 | **Léogâne,** Haiti | 222 570 |
| 2011 | **Tōhoku,** Japan | 14 500 |

The capital city of Port-au-Prince in Haiti was destroyed by a massive 7.0 magnitude earthquake in January 2010. It was estimated that 222 570 people died and more than one million people lost their homes.

## RICHTER SCALE

The scale measures the energy released by an earthquake. The scale is logarithmic – a quake measuring 4 is 30 times more powerful than one measuring 3, and a quake measuring 6 is 27 000 times more powerful than one measuring 3.

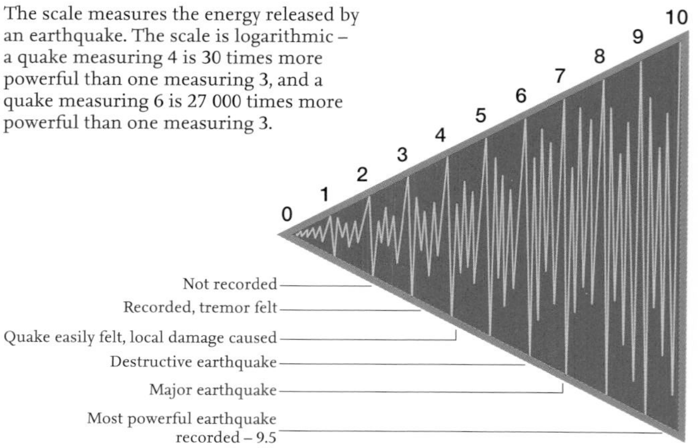

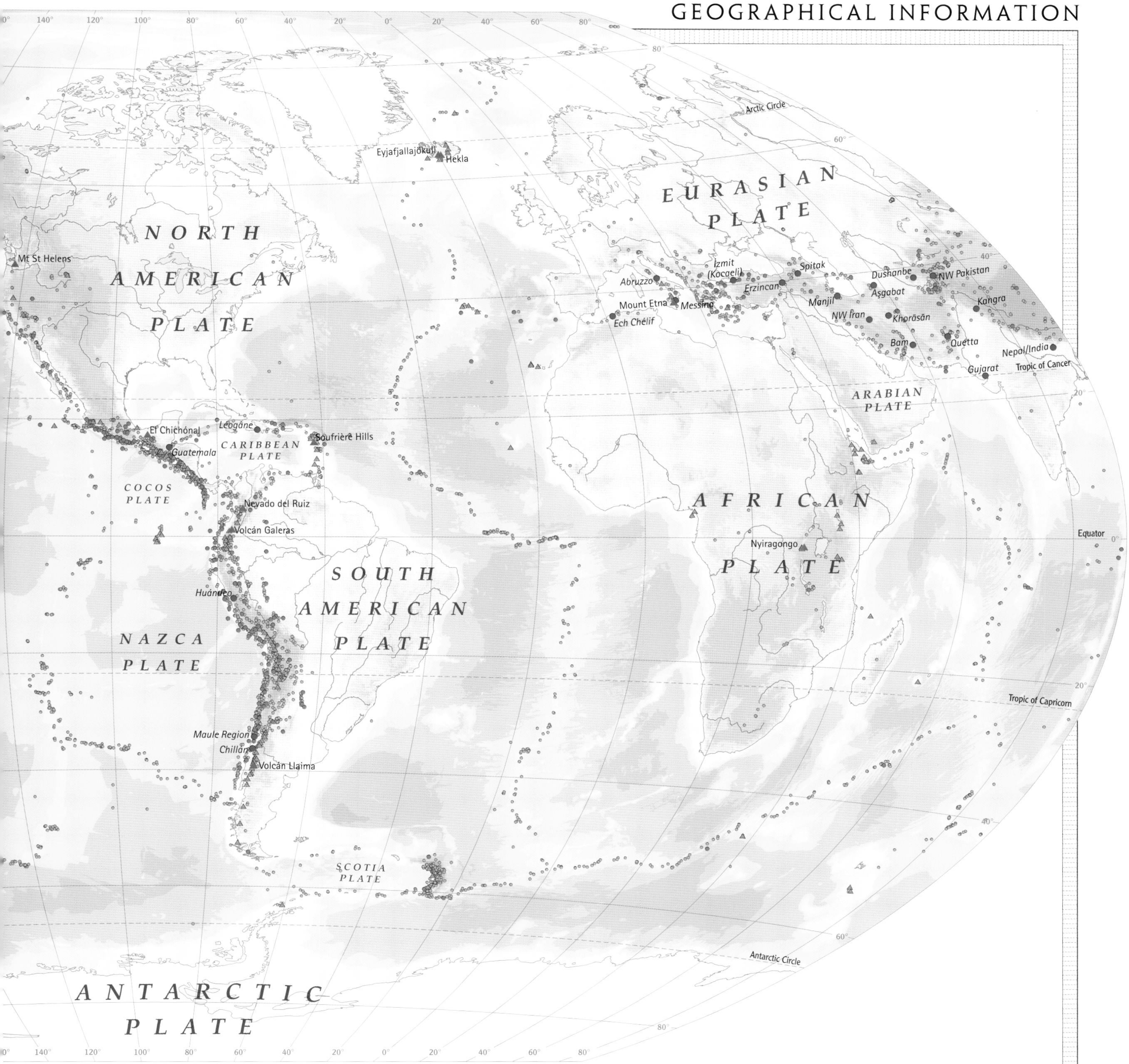


## MAJOR VOLCANIC ERUPTIONS 1980–2011

| Year | Volcano | Country |
|---|---|---|
| 1980 | **Mt St Helens** | USA |
| 1982 | **El Chichónal** | Mexico |
| 1982 | **Gunung Galunggung** | Indonesia |
| 1983 | **Kilauea** | Hawaii, USA |
| 1983 | **Ō-yama** | Japan |
| 1985 | **Nevado del Ruiz** | Colombia |
| 1991 | **Mt Pinatubo** | Philippines |
| 1991 | **Unzen-dake** | Japan |
| 1993 | **Mayon** | Philippines |
| 1993 | **Volcán Galeras** | Colombia |
| 1994 | **Volcán Llaima** | Chile |
| 1994 | **Rabaul** | Papua New Guinea |
| 1997 | **Soufrière Hills** | Montserrat |
| 2000 | **Hekla** | Iceland |
| 2001 | **Monte Etna** | Italy |
| 2002 | **Nyiragongo** | Democratic Republic of the Congo |
| 2010 | **Eyjafjallajökull** | Iceland |

Mount Bromo, Java, Indonesia, one of the many active volcanoes that have formed around the edge of the Pacific Ocean.

# CLIMATE I

## MAJOR CLIMATIC REGIONS AND SUB-TYPES

Köppen classification system
Winkel Tripel Projection
scale 1:110 000 000

• Climate graph location
o Weather extreme location

| Polar | | Cooler humid | | Warmer humid | | Dry | | Tropical humid | |
|---|---|---|---|---|---|---|---|---|---|
| EF | Ice cap | Dc Dd | Subarctic | Cb Cc | Temperate | BS | Steppe | Aw As | Savanna |
| ET | Tundra | Db | Continental cool summer | Ca | Humid subtropical | BW | Desert | Af Am | Rain forest |
| | | Da | Continental warm summer | Cs | Mediterranean | | | | |

A Rainy climate with no winter: coolest month above 18°C (64.4°F).

B Dry climates; limits are defined by formulae based on rainfall effectiveness:
**BS** Steppe or semi-arid climate.
**BW** Desert or arid climate.

*C Rainy climates with mild winters: coolest month above 0°C (32°F), but below 18°C (64.4°F); warmest month above 10°C (50°F).

*D Rainy climates with severe winters: coldest month below 0°C (32°F); warmest month above 10°C (50°F).

E Polar climates with no warm season: warmest month below 10°C (50°F).
**ET** Tundra climate: warmest month below 10°C (50°F) but above 0°C (32°F).
**EF** Perpetual frost: all months below 0°C (32°F).

a Warmest month above 22°C (71.6°F).
b Warmest month below 22°C (71.6°F).
c Less than four months over 10°C (50°F).
d As 'c', but with severe cold: coldest month below -38°C (-36.4°F).
f Constantly moist rainfall throughout the year.
*h Warmer dry: all months above 0°C (32°F).
*k Cooler dry: at least one month below 0°C (32°F).
m Monsoon rain: short dry season, but is compensated by heavy rains during rest of the year.
n Frequent fog.
s Dry season in summer.
w Dry season in winter.

*** Modification of Köppen definition**

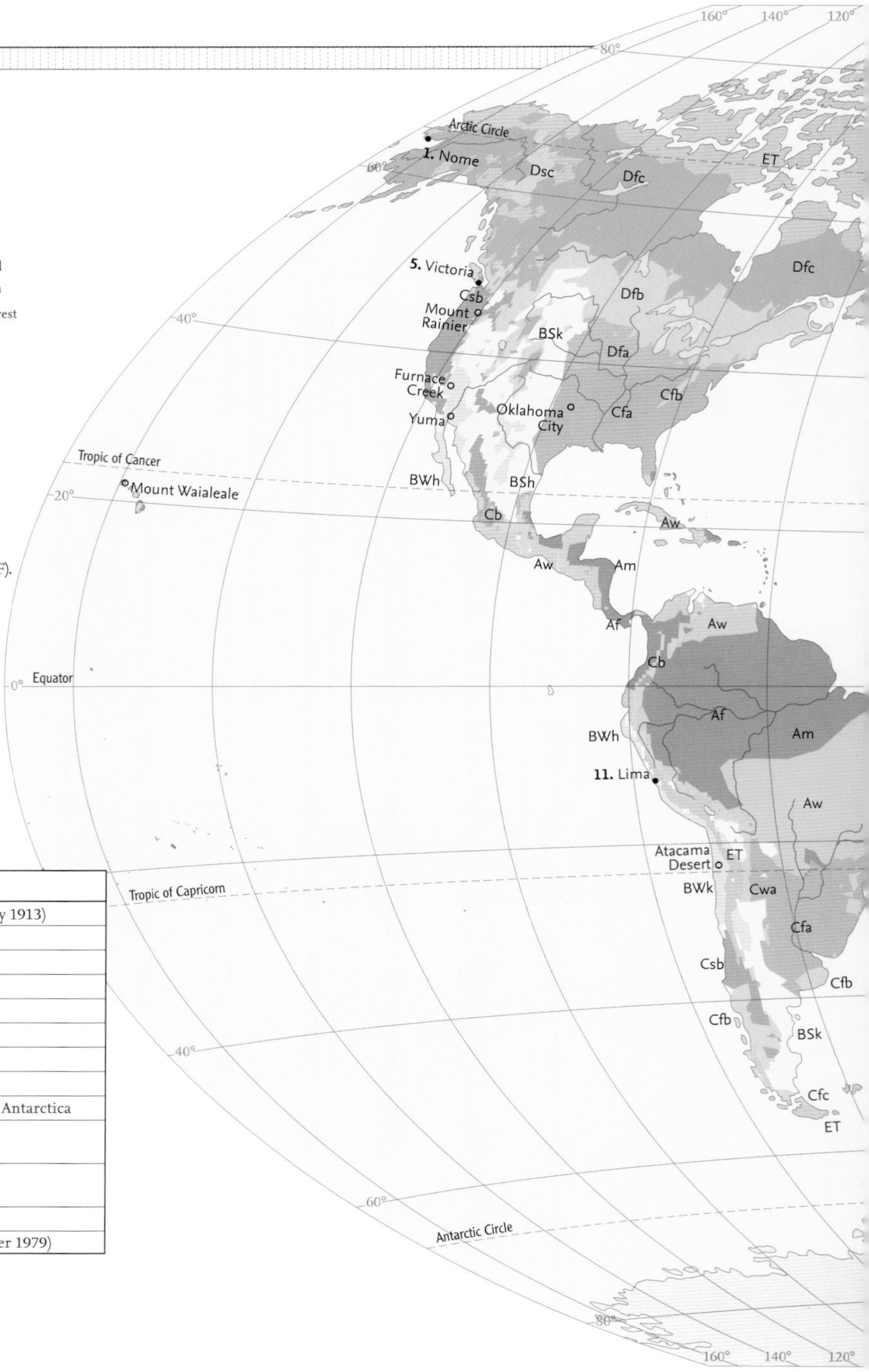


## WORLD WEATHER EXTREMES

| | Location |
|---|---|
| **Highest shade temperature** | 56.7°C / 134°F Furnace Creek, Death Valley, California, USA (10th July 1913) |
| **Hottest place – Annual mean** | 34.4°C / 93.9°F Dalol, Ethiopia |
| **Driest place – Annual mean** | 0.1 mm / 0.004 inches Atacama Desert, Chile |
| **Most sunshine – Annual mean** | 90% Yuma, Arizona, USA (over 4 000 hours) |
| **Lowest screen temperature** | -89.2°C / -128.6°F Vostok Station, Antarctica (21st July 1983) |
| **Coldest place – Annual mean** | -56.6°C / -69.9°F Plateau Station, Antarctica |
| **Wettest place – Annual mean** | 11 873 mm / 467.4 inches Meghalaya, India |
| **Most rainy days** | Up to 350 per year Mount Waialeale, Hawaii, USA |
| **Windiest place** | 322 km per hour / 200 miles per hour in gales, Commonwealth Bay, Antarctica |
| **Highest surface wind speed** | 512 km per hour / 318 miles per hour in a tornado, Oklahoma City, Oklahoma, USA (3rd May 1999) |
| **Greatest snowfall** | 31 102 mm / 1 224.5 inches Mount Rainier, Washington, USA (19th February 1971 – 18th February 1972) |
| **Highest barometric pressure** | 1 083.8 mb Agata, Siberia, Russian Federation (31st December 1968) |
| **Lowest barometric pressure** | 870 mb 483 km / 300 miles west of Guam, Pacific Ocean (12th October 1979) |

Hurricane Sandy made the news headlines around the world as it approached the heavily populated east coast of the USA. This image was taken on 28 October 2012, one day before before it made landfall, when it caused widespread disruption including a storm surge in New York city. The line of clouds from another weather system runs north-south along the Appalachian Mountains, approaching from the west to meet Sandy, leading to it being dubbed the "Frankenstorm".

## TRACKS OF TROPICAL STORMS

(wind speeds often over 160 km per hour)
scale 1:247 000 000

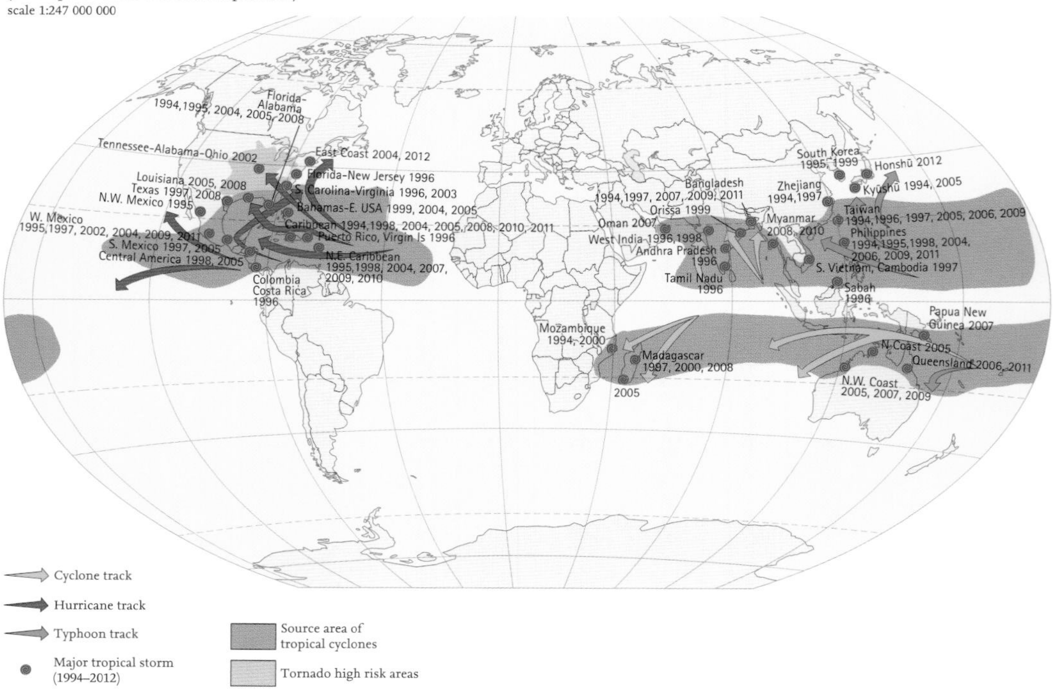

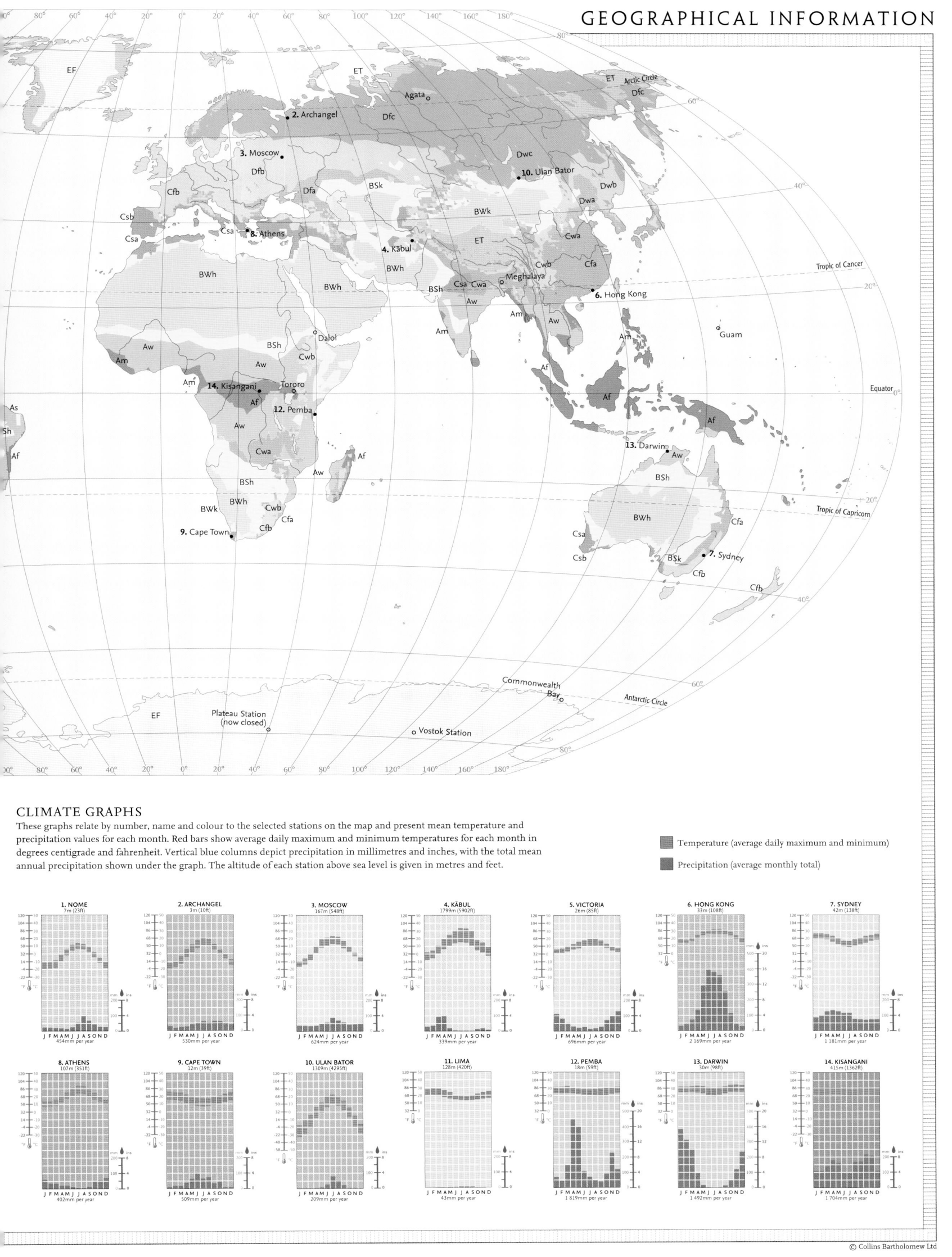

## CLIMATE GRAPHS

These graphs relate by number, name and colour to the selected stations on the map and present mean temperature and precipitation values for each month. Red bars show average daily maximum and minimum temperatures for each month in degrees centigrade and fahrenheit. Vertical blue columns depict precipitation in millimetres and inches, with the total mean annual precipitation shown under the graph. The altitude of each station above sea level is given in metres and feet.

Temperature (average daily maximum and minimum)

Precipitation (average monthly total)

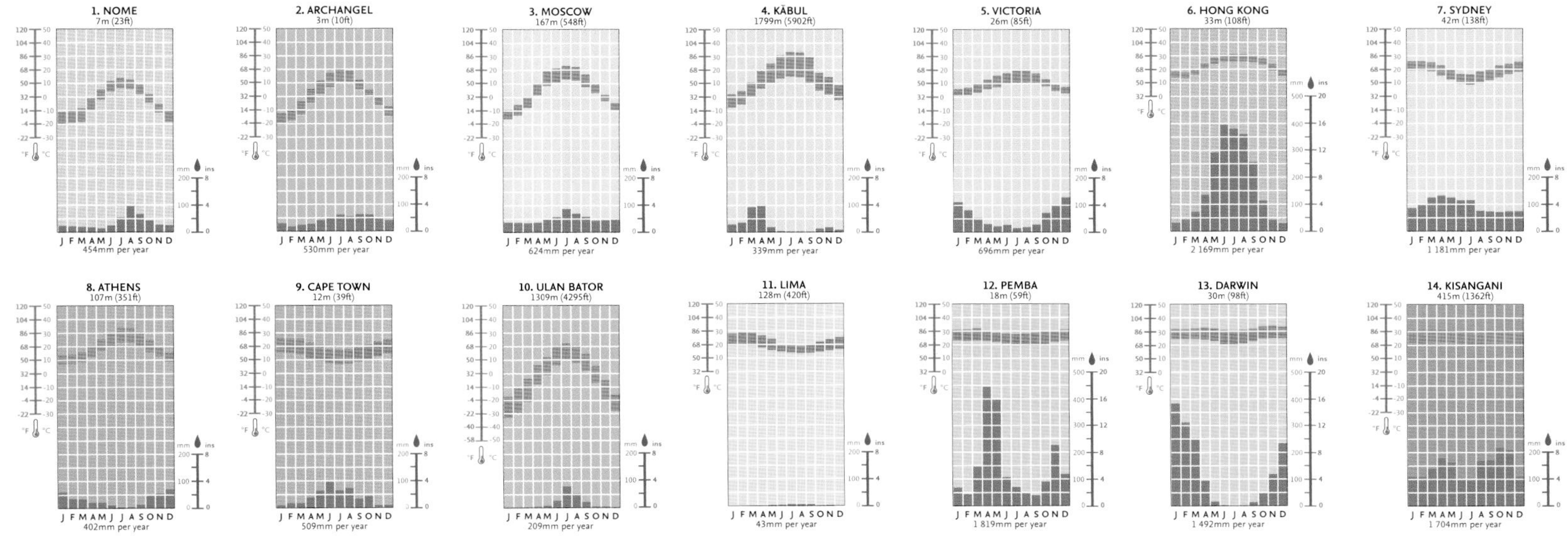

# CLIMATE II

## CLIMATE CHANGE

Climate records show that the global average temperature has risen by approximately 0.7°C since the end of the nineteenth century. Most of this warming is caused by human activities which result in a build-up of greenhouse gases, mainly carbon dioxide, allowing heat to be trapped within the atmosphere. Carbon dioxide emissions have increased since the beginning of the industrial revolution due to burning of fossil fuels, increased urbanization, population growth, deforestation and industrial pollution.

Annual climate indicators such as number of frost-free days, length of growing season, heat wave frequency, number of wet days, length of dry spells and frequency of weather extremes are used to monitor climate change. The map below shows how future changes in temperature will not be spread evenly around the world. Some regions will warm faster than the global average, while others will warm more slowly.

The McCarty Glacier in the Kenai Peninsula in Alaska is a tidewater glacier which has retreated around 16 km between 1909 (top) and 2004 (bottom).

## PROJECTION OF GLOBAL TEMPERATURE CHANGE 2090–2099

Average of all IPCC models for emissions IPCC scenario A1B. Annual average change in June-July-August relative to 1980–1999.

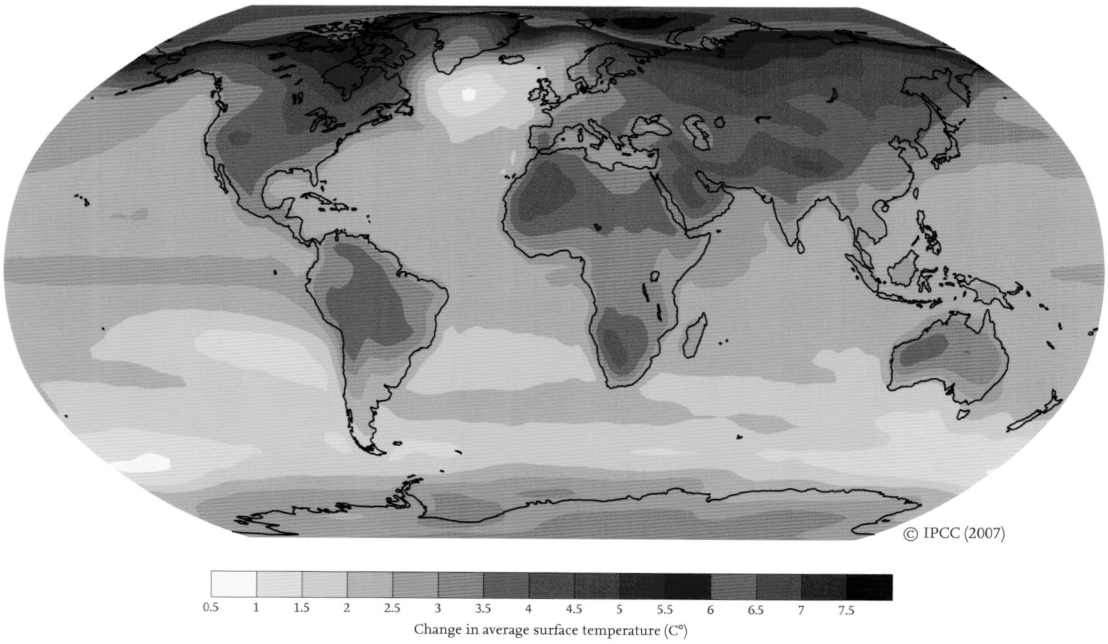


Faster warming is expected near the poles, as the melting snow and sea ice exposes the darker underlying land and ocean surfaces which then absorb more of the sun's radiation instead of reflecting it back to space in the way that brighter ice and snow do.

## THREAT OF RISING SEA LEVEL

It has been suggested that further global warming of between 1.0 and 6.4 C° may occur by the end of the 21st century. Sea level is projected to rise by between 28 cm and 58 cm, threatening a number of coastal cities, low-lying deltas and small islands. Larger rises are predicted in some locations than others.

## AREAS AT RISK OF SUBMERSION

- Major cities
- Coastal areas at greatest risk
- Islands and archipelagos
- Areas of low-lying islands

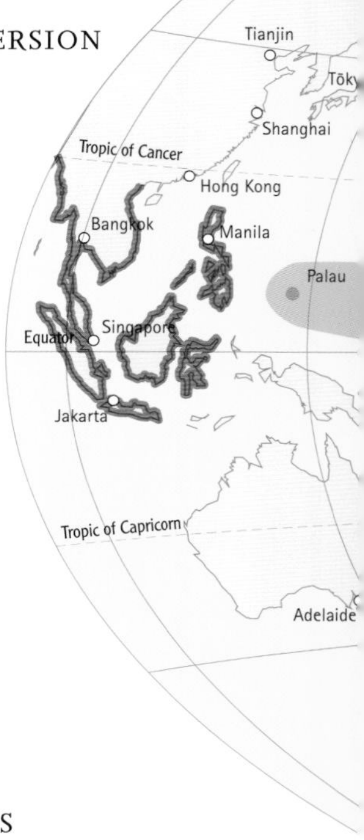


## LOWEST PACIFIC ISLANDS

| Location | Maximum height above sea level | Land area sq km | Land area sq miles | Population |
|---|---|---|---|---|
| Kingman Reef | 1 m (3 ft) | 1 | 0.4 | 0 |
| Palmyra Atoll | 2 m (7 ft) | 12 | 5 | 0 |
| Ashmore and Cartier Islands | 3 m (10 ft) | 5 | 2 | 0 |
| Howland Island | 3 m (10 ft) | 2 | 1 | 0 |
| Johnston Atoll | 5 m (16 ft) | 3 | 1 | 0 |
| Tokelau | 5 m (16 ft) | 10 | 4 | 1 466 |
| Tuvalu | 5 m (16 ft) | 25 | 10 | 10 000 |
| Coral Sea Islands Territory | 6 m (20 ft) | 22 | 8 | 0 |
| Wake Island | 6 m (20 ft) | 7 | 3 | 0 |
| Jarvis Island | 7 m (23 ft) | 5 | 2 | 0 |

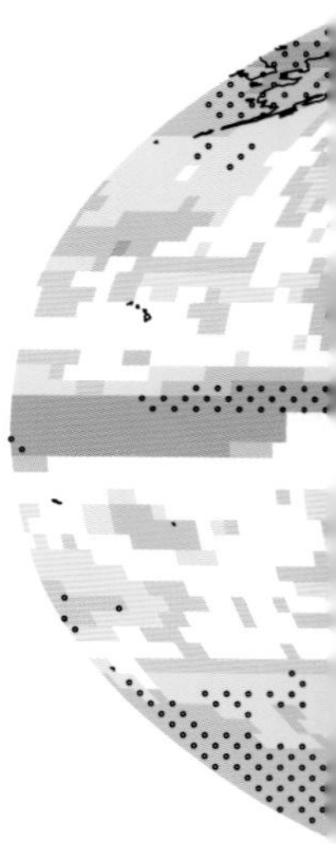

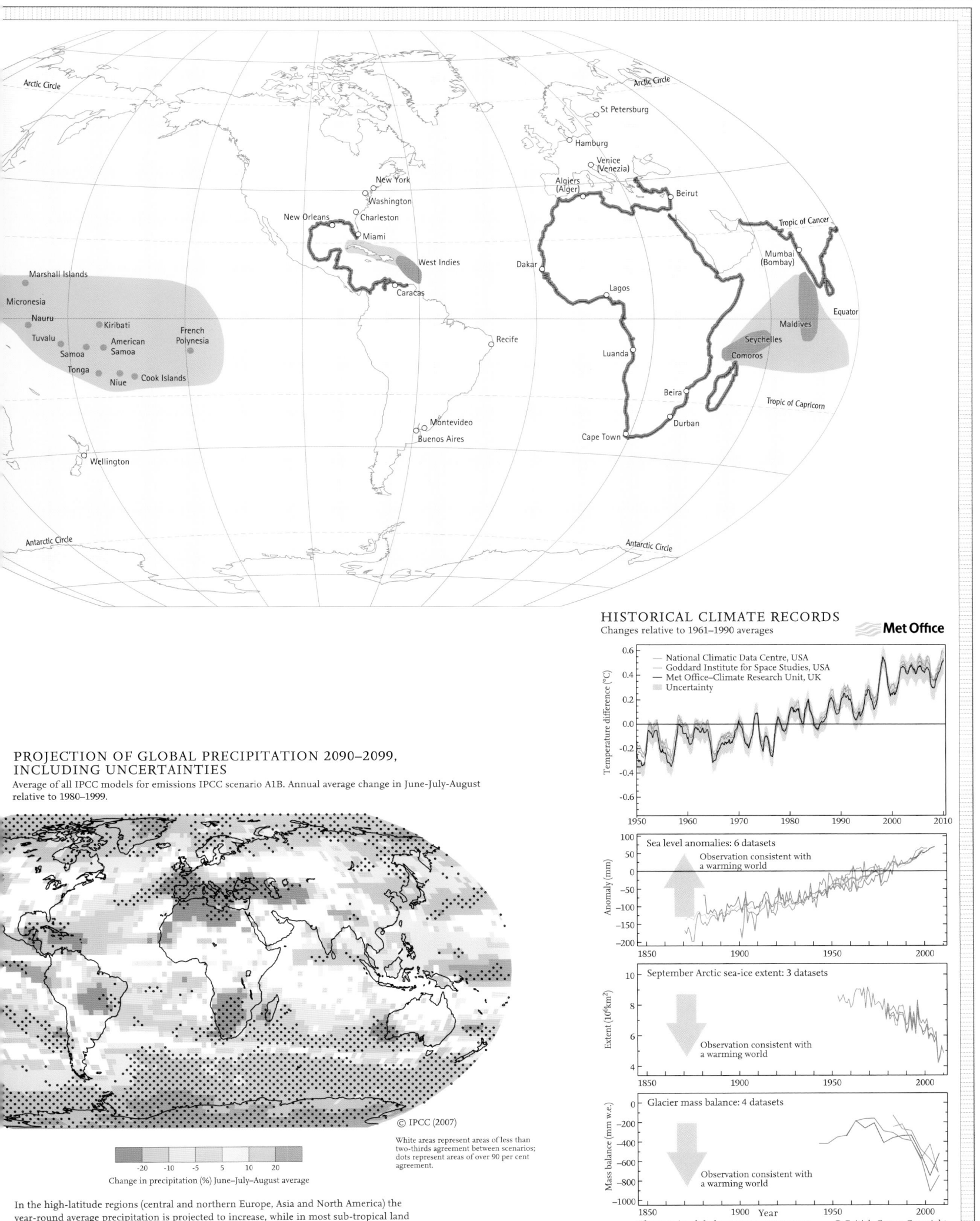

## HISTORICAL CLIMATE RECORDS

Changes relative to 1961–1990 averages

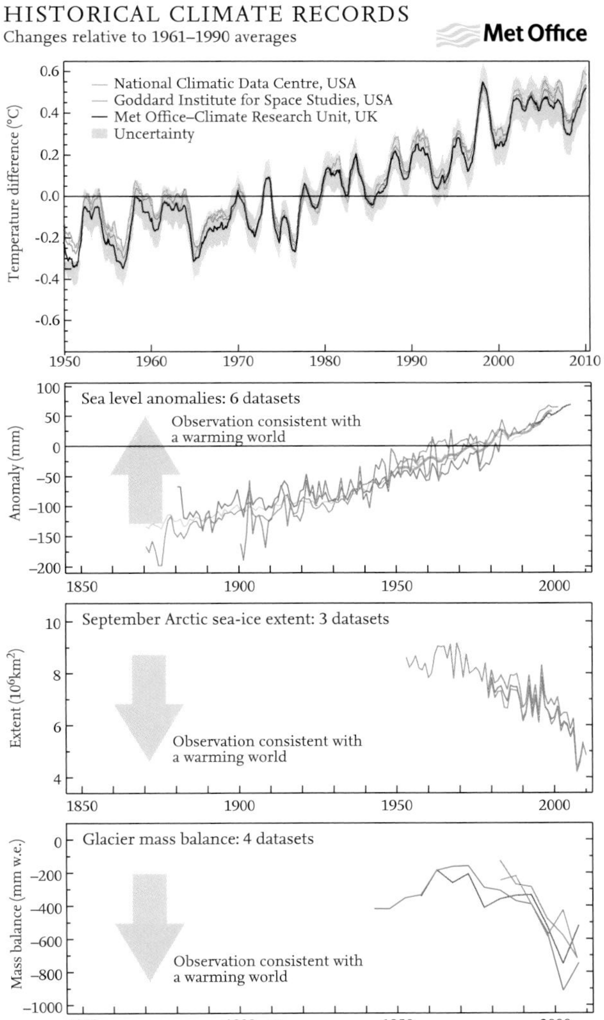


Changes in global average temperature, sea level, sea ice and glacier mass balance, from different datasets.



## PROJECTION OF GLOBAL PRECIPITATION 2090–2099, INCLUDING UNCERTAINTIES

Average of all IPCC models for emissions IPCC scenario A1B. Annual average change in June-July-August relative to 1980–1999.

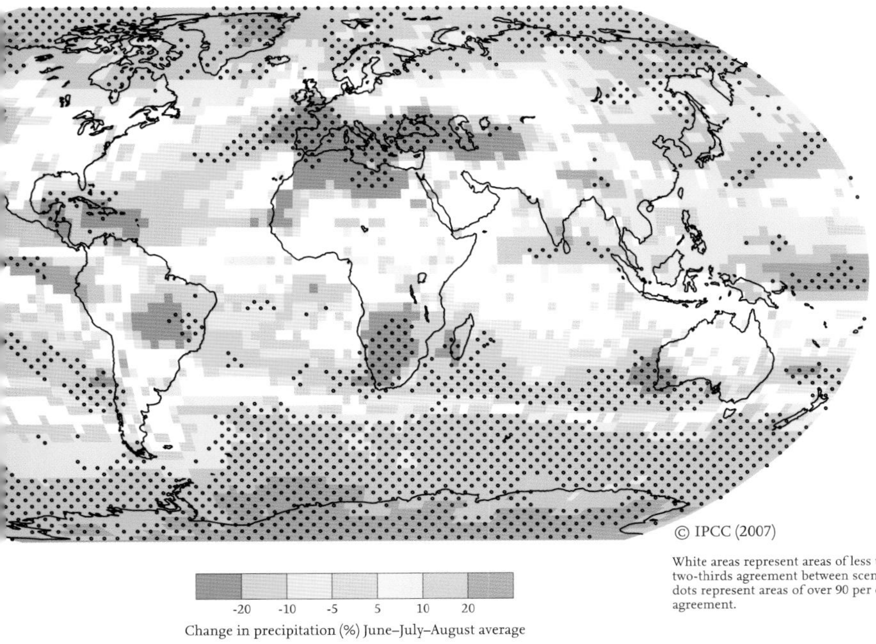




White areas represent areas of less than two-thirds agreement between scenarios; dots represent areas of over 90 per cent agreement.

In the high-latitude regions (central and northern Europe, Asia and North America) the year-round average precipitation is projected to increase, while in most sub-tropical land regions it is projected to decrease by as much as 20 per cent. This would increase the risk of drought and, in combination with higher temperatures, threaten agricultural productivity.

# POPULATION

## TOP TWENTY COUNTRIES BY POPULATION AND POPULATION DENSITY 2011

| Total population | Country | Rank | Country* | Inhabitants per sq mile | Inhabitants per sq km |
|---|---|---|---|---|---|
| 1 332 079 000 | China | 1 | Bangladesh | 2 707 | 1 045 |
| 1 241 492 000 | India | 2 | Taiwan | 1 658 | 640 |
| 313 085 000 | United States of America | 3 | South Korea | 1 262 | 487 |
| 242 326 000 | Indonesia | 4 | Rwanda | 1 076 | 415 |
| 196 655 000 | Brazil | 5 | India | 1 049 | 405 |
| 176 745 000 | Pakistan | 6 | Netherlands | 1 039 | 401 |
| 162 471 000 | Nigeria | 7 | Haiti | 945 | 365 |
| 150 494 000 | Bangladesh | 8 | Belgium | 913 | 352 |
| 142 836 000 | Russian Federation | 9 | Japan | 867 | 335 |
| 126 497 000 | Japan | 10 | Sri Lanka | 831 | 321 |
| 114 793 000 | Mexico | 11 | Philippines | 819 | 316 |
| 94 852 000 | Philippines | 12 | Vietnam | 698 | 269 |
| 88 792 000 | Vietnam | 13 | United Kingdom | 664 | 256 |
| 84 734 000 | Ethiopia | 14 | Germany | 596 | 230 |
| 82 537 000 | Egypt | 15 | Pakistan | 569 | 220 |
| 82 163 000 | Germany | 16 | Dominican Republic | 538 | 208 |
| 74 799 000 | Iran | 17 | Nepal | 536 | 207 |
| 73 640 000 | Turkey | 18 | North Korea | 525 | 203 |
| 69 519 000 | Thailand | 19 | Italy | 523 | 202 |
| 67 758 000 | Democratic Republic of the Congo | 20 | Nigeria | 456 | 176 |

*Only countries with a population of over 10 million are considered.

## WORLD POPULATION DISTRIBUTION

Winkel Tripel Projection
scale approximately 1:112 000 000

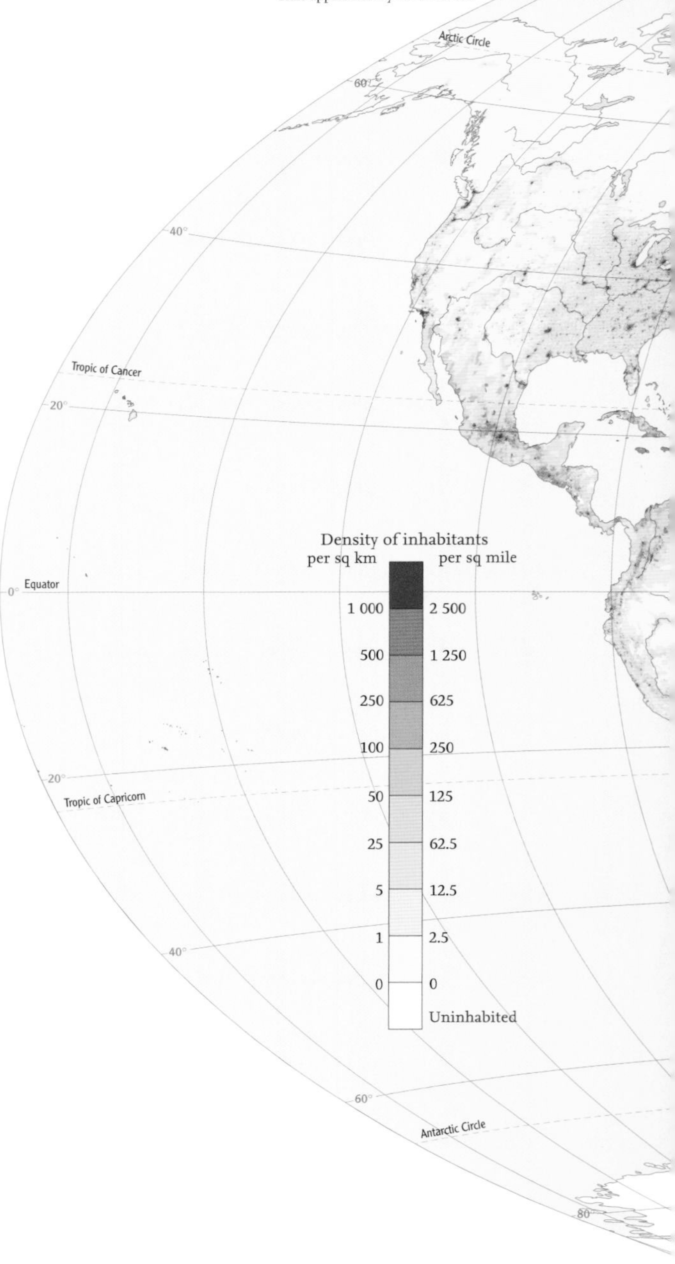


## AGE PYRAMIDS

World population by five-year age group and sex.

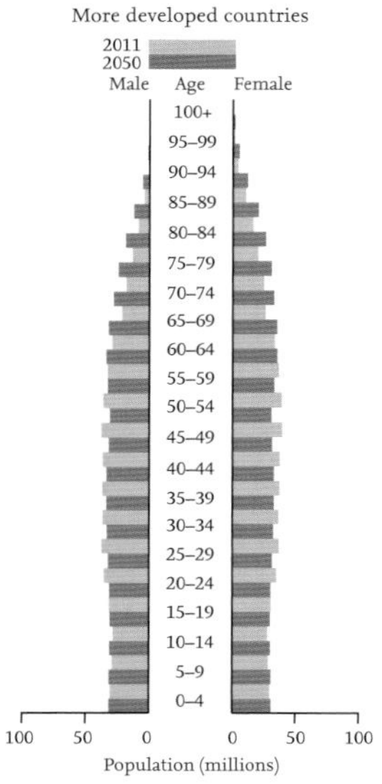


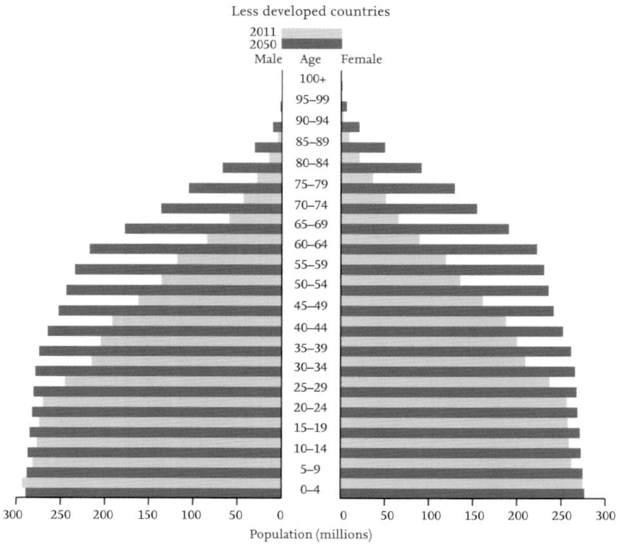


## KEY POPULATION STATISTICS FOR MAJOR REGIONS

| | Population 2011 (millions) | Growth (per cent) | Infant mortality rate | Total fertility rate | Life expectancy (years) | % aged 60 and over 2010 | % aged 60 and over 2050 |
|---|---|---|---|---|---|---|---|
| World | 6 974 | 1.1 | 42 | 2.45 | 69 | 11 | 22 |
| More developed regions[1] | 1 240 | 0.3 | 6 | 1.7 | 78 | 22 | 32 |
| Less developed regions[2] | 5 774 | 1.3 | 46 | 2.6 | 67 | 8 | 20 |
| Africa | 1 046 | 2.3 | 71 | 4.4 | 55 | 6 | 10 |
| Asia | 4 207 | 1.0 | 37 | 2.2 | 70 | 10 | 24 |
| Europe[3] | 739 | 0.1 | 6 | 1.6 | 77 | 22 | 34 |
| Latin America and the Caribbean[4] | 597 | 1.1 | 19 | 2.2 | 75 | 10 | 25 |
| North America | 348 | 0.9 | 6 | 2.0 | 79 | 19 | 27 |
| Oceania | 37 | 1.5 | 19 | 2.5 | 78 | 15 | 24 |

Except for population and % aged 60 and over figures, the data are annual averages projected for the period 2010–2015.

1. Europe, North America, Australia, New Zealand and Japan.
2. Africa, Asia (excluding Japan), Latin America and the Caribbean, and Oceania (excluding Australia and New Zealand).
3. Includes Russian Federation.
4. South America, Central America (including Mexico) and all Caribbean Islands.

Population growth in the 20th century was rapid and continued growth carried the world's population past seven billion in 2011.

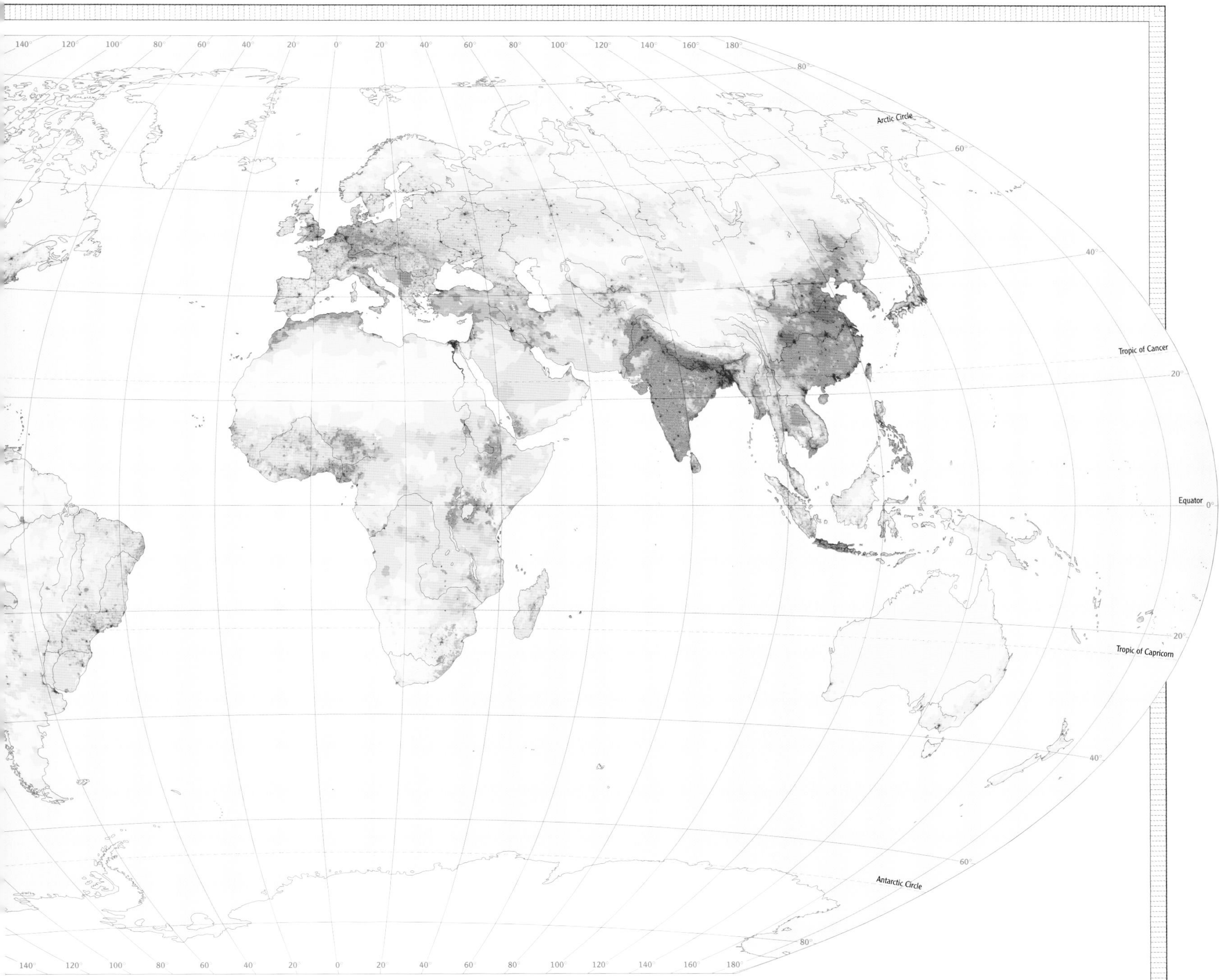


## POPULATION CHANGE 2010–2015

Average annual rate of population change (per cent) and the top ten contributors to world population growth (net annual addition).

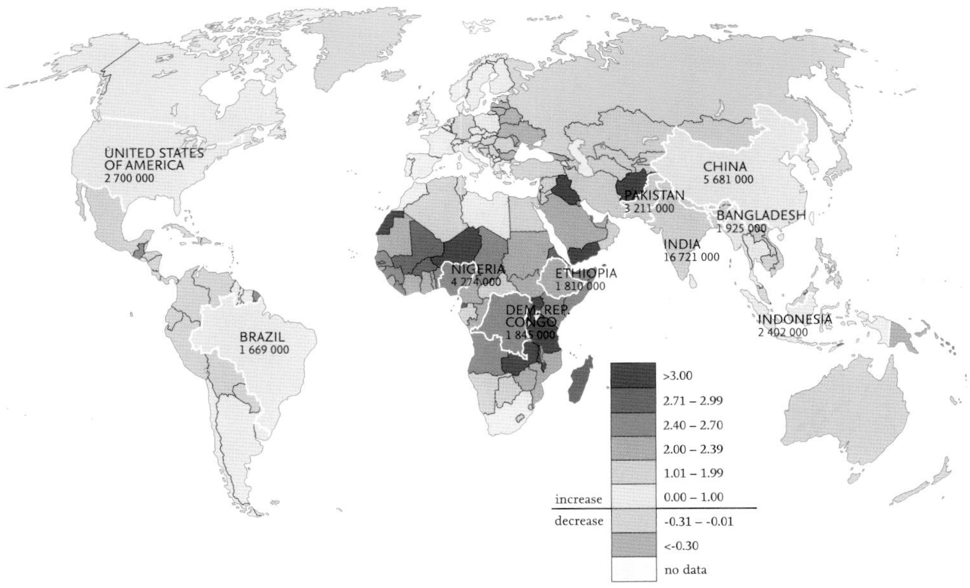


## WORLD POPULATION GROWTH 1750–2050

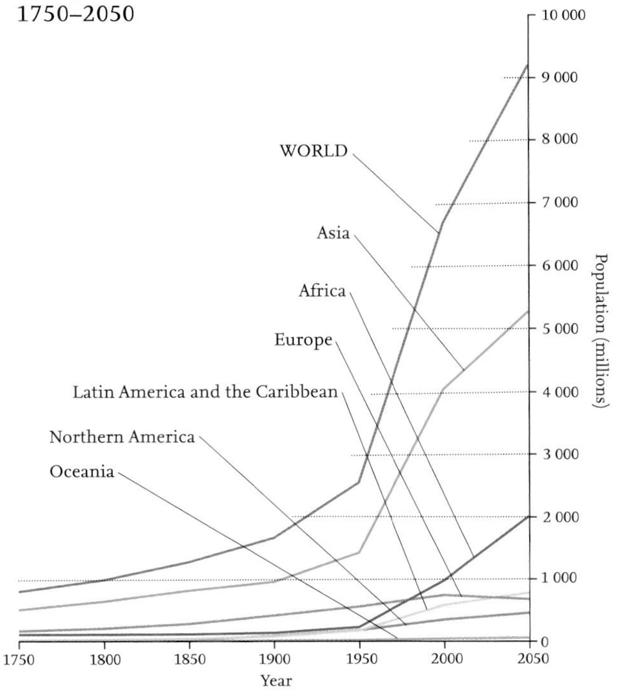

# COMMUNICATIONS

## WORLD COMMUNICATIONS EQUIPMENT 1996 – 2011

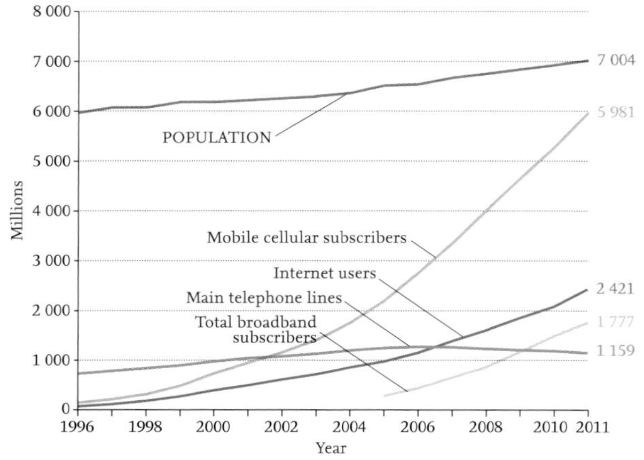


## TOP BROADBAND ECONOMIES 2011

Countries with the highest broadband penetration rate – subscribers per 100 inhabitants

| Top Economies | Fixed Broadband rate | | Top Economies | Mobile Broadband rate |
|---|---|---|---|---|
| Netherlands | 38.1 | 1 | South Korea | 91.0 |
| Switzerland | 37.9 | 2 | Japan | 87.8 |
| Denmark | 37.7 | 3 | Sweden | 84.0 |
| South Korea | 35.7 | 4 | Australia | 82.7 |
| Norway | 35.3 | 5 | Finland | 78.1 |
| Iceland | 34.1 | 6 | Hong Kong, China | 74.5 |
| France | 33.9 | 7 | Portugal | 72.5 |
| Luxembourg | 33.2 | 8 | Luxembourg | 72.1 |
| Sweden | 31.8 | 9 | Singapore | 69.7 |
| Germany | 31.7 | 10 | Austria | 67.4 |

## INTERNATIONAL TELECOMMUNICATIONS INDICATORS BY REGION 2011

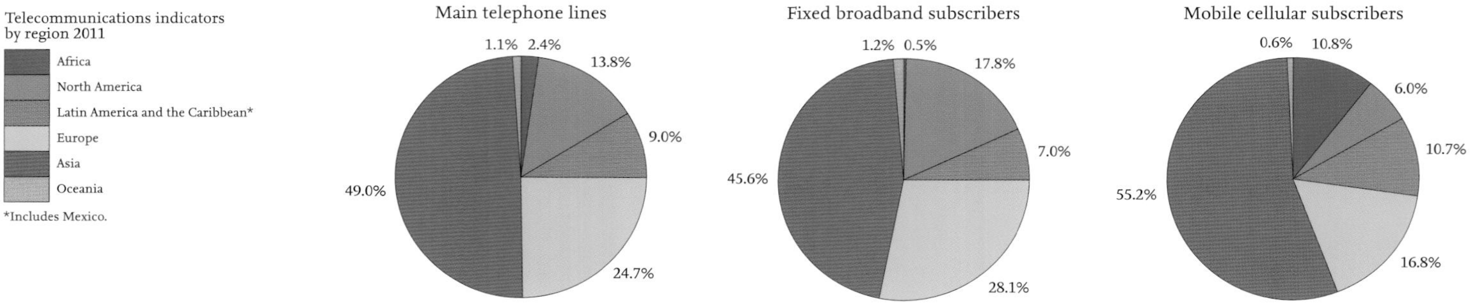


## FIXED TELEPHONE SUBSCRIBERS 2011

Winkel Tripel Projection

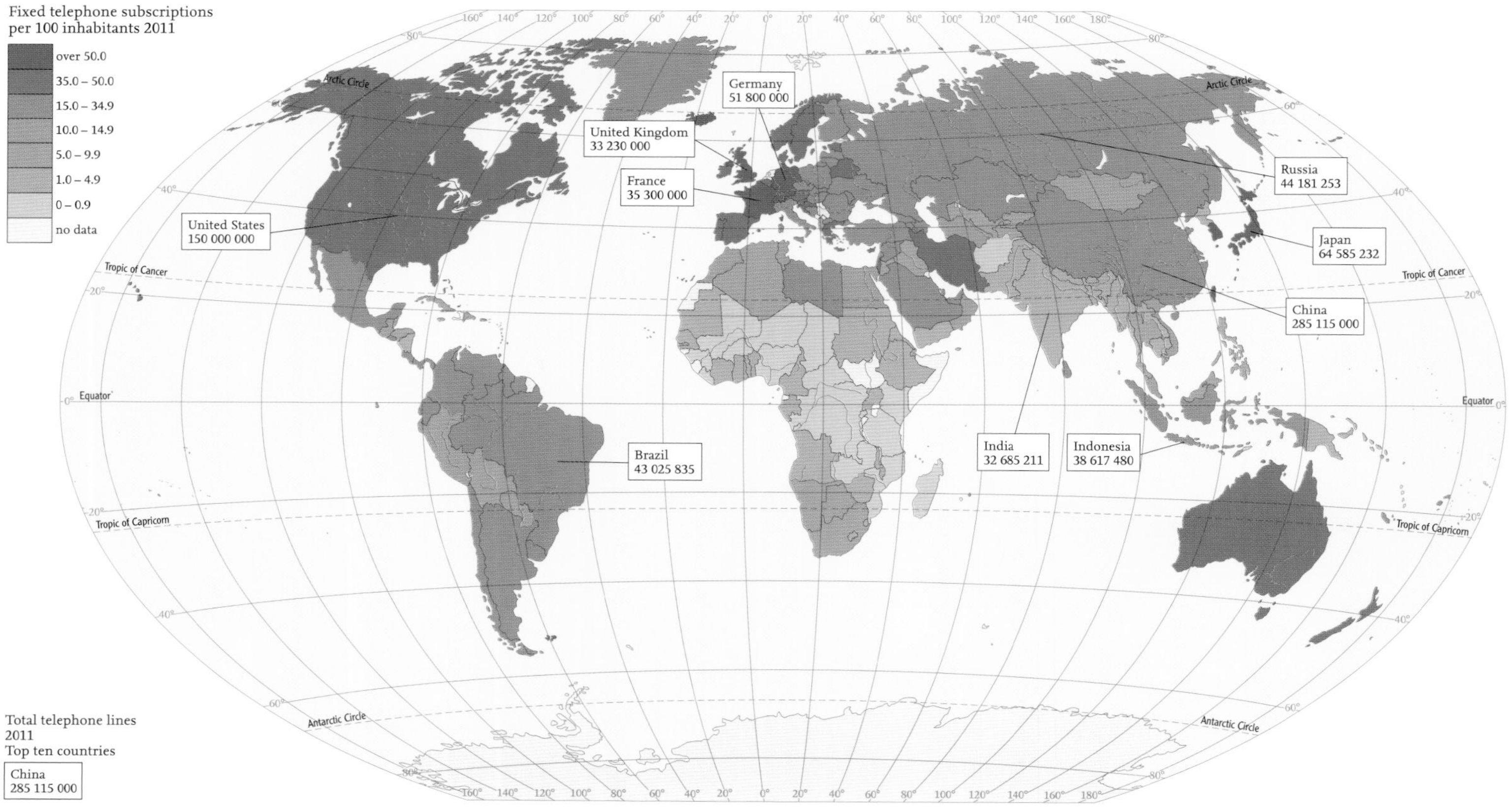

## FIXED BROADBAND SUBSCRIBERS 2011

Winkel Tripel Projection

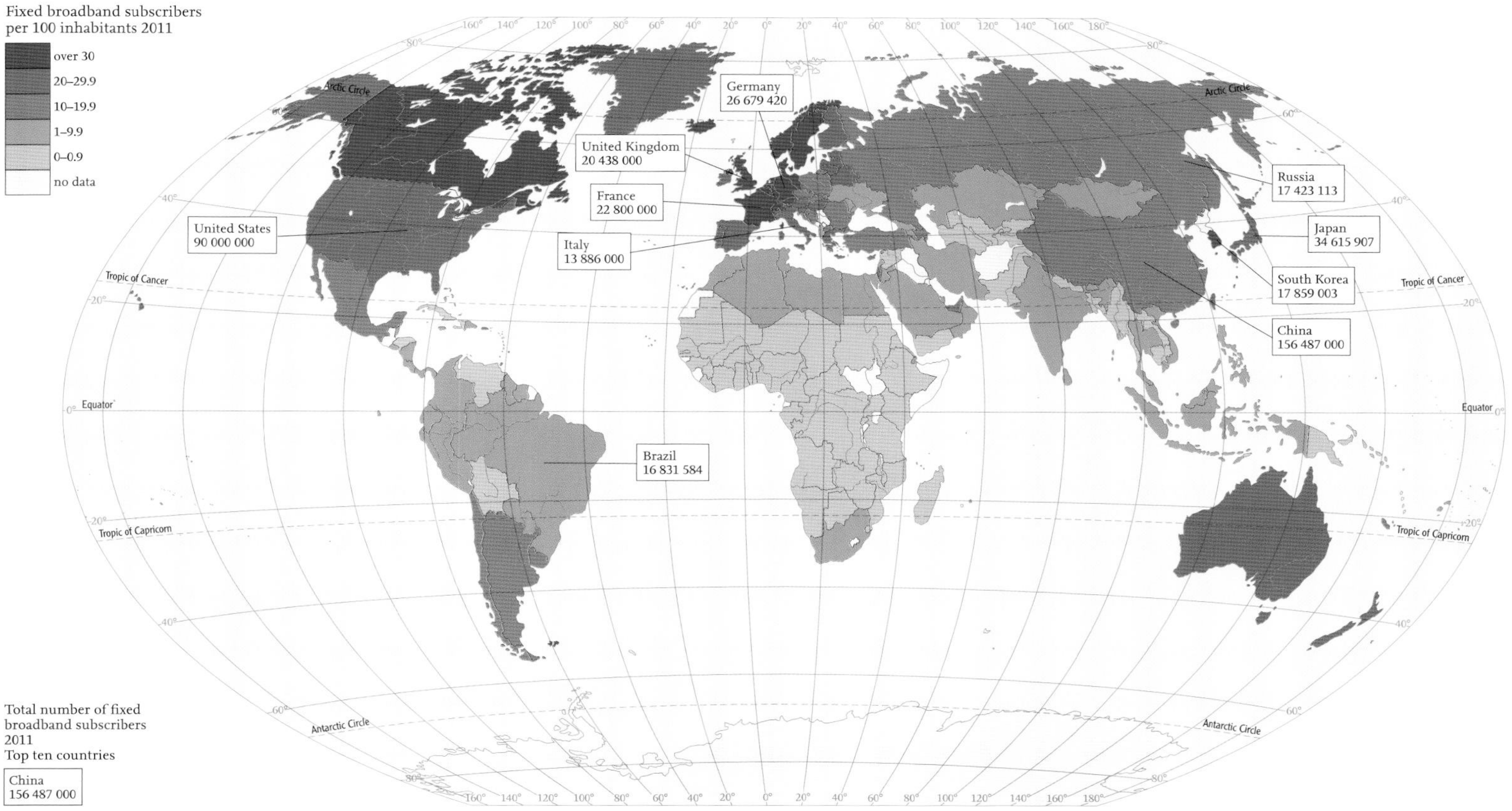


## MOBILE CELLULAR SUBSCRIBERS 2011

Winkel Tripel Projection

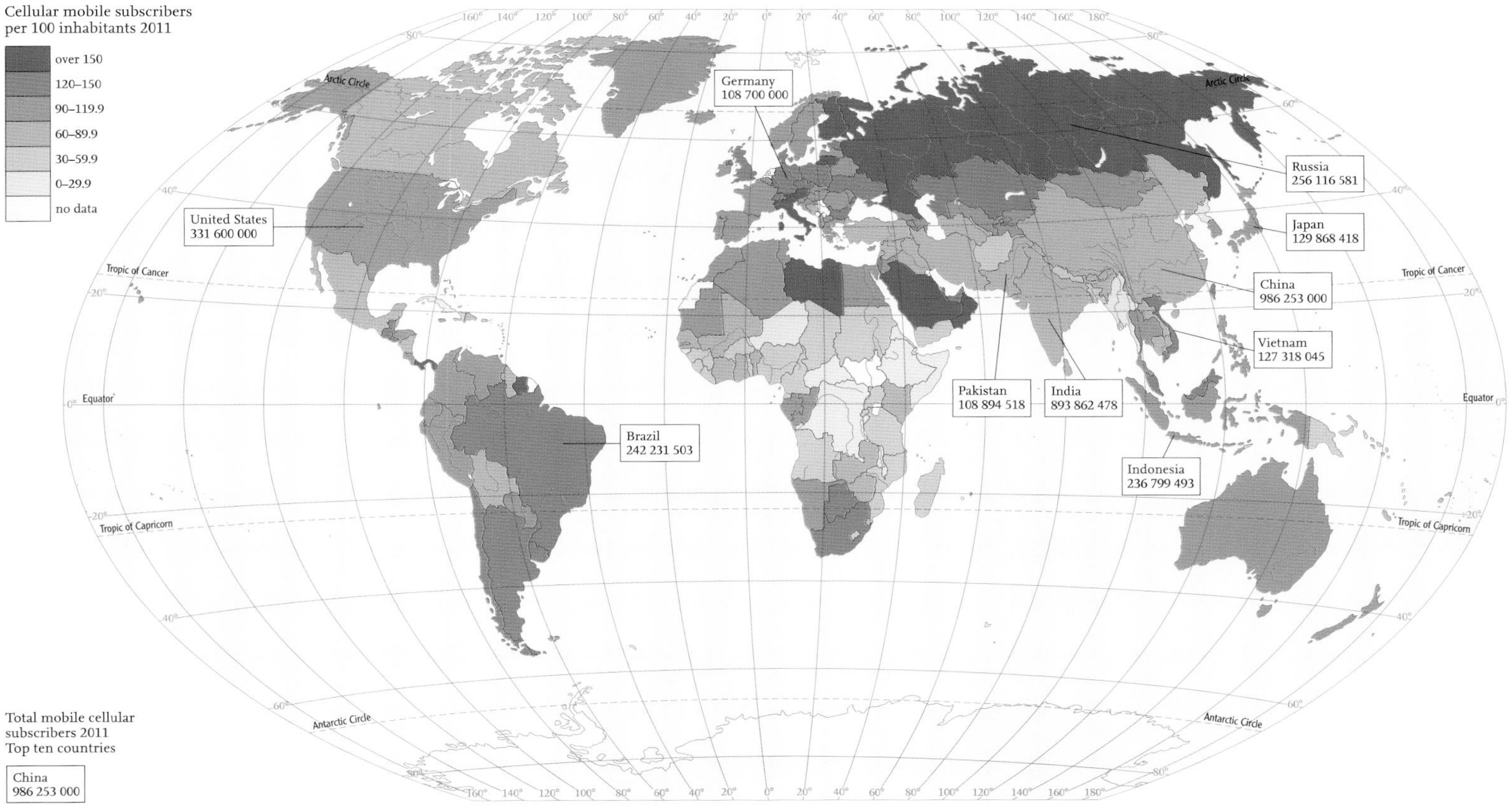

# PHYSICAL FEATURES

The images below illustrate some of the major physical features of the world.

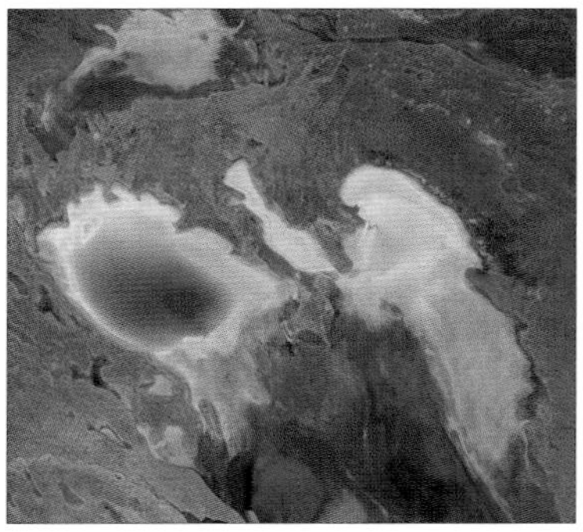

Lake Eyre, South Australia

Mississippi-Missouri, United States of America

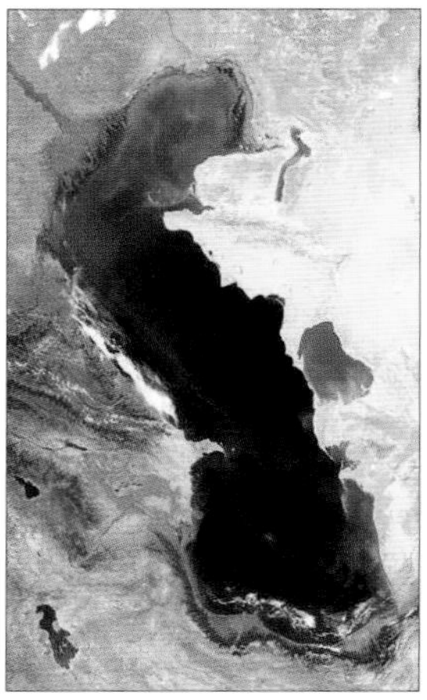

The Caspian Sea

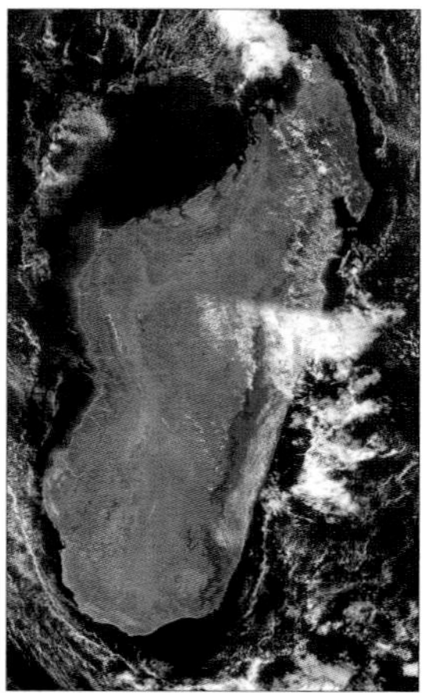

The island of Madagasgar

## ANTARCTICA Total Land Area 12 093 000 sq km / 4 669 107 sq miles (excluding ice shelves)

| HIGHEST MOUNTAINS | metres | feet |
|---|---|---|
| Vinson Massif | 4 897 | 16 066 |
| Mt Tyree | 4 852 | 15 918 |
| Mt Kirkpatrick | 4 528 | 14 855 |
| Mt Markham | 4 351 | 14 275 |
| Mt Jackson | 4 190 | 13 747 |
| Mt Sidley | 4 181 | 13 717 |

| LARGEST KNOWN SUBGLACIAL LAKES | metres | feet |
|---|---|---|
| Lake Vostok | 15 690 | 6 058 |
| 90°East Lake | 2 000 | 772 |
| Sovetskaya Lake | 1 600 | 618 |

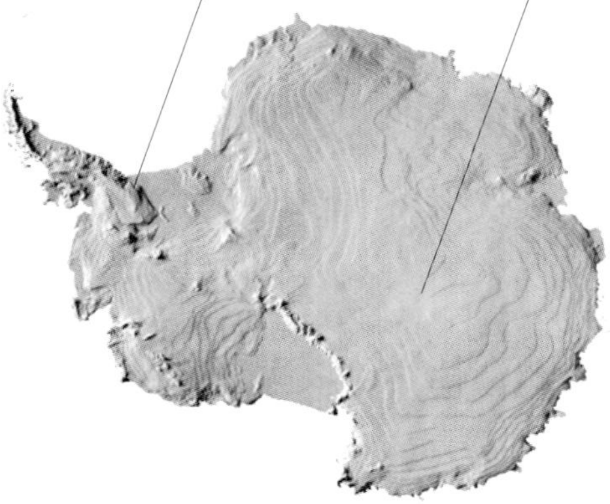


## OCEANIA Total Land Area 8 844 516 sq km / 3 414 868 sq miles

| HIGHEST MOUNTAINS | metres | feet |
|---|---|---|
| Puncak Jaya, Indonesia | 5 030 | 16 502 |
| Puncak Trikora, Indonesia | 4 730 | 15 518 |
| Puncak Mandala, Indonesia | 4 700 | 15 420 |
| Puncak Yamin, Indonesia | 4 595 | 15 075 |
| Mt Wilhelm, Papua New Guinea | 4 509 | 14 793 |
| Mt Kubor, Papua New Guinea | 4 359 | 14 301 |

| LONGEST RIVERS | km | miles |
|---|---|---|
| Murray-Darling | 3 672 | 2 282 |
| Darling | 2 844 | 1 767 |
| Murray | 2 375 | 1 476 |
| Murrumbidgee | 1 485 | 923 |
| Lachlan | 1 339 | 832 |
| Cooper Creek | 1 113 | 692 |

| LARGEST ISLANDS | sq km | sq miles |
|---|---|---|
| New Guinea | 808 510 | 312 166 |
| South Island, New Zealand | 151 215 | 58 384 |
| North Island, New Zealand | 115 777 | 44 701 |
| Tasmania | 67 800 | 26 178 |

| LARGEST LAKES | sq km | sq miles |
|---|---|---|
| Lake Eyre | 0–8 900 | 0–3 436 |
| Lake Torrens | 0–5 780 | 0–2 232 |

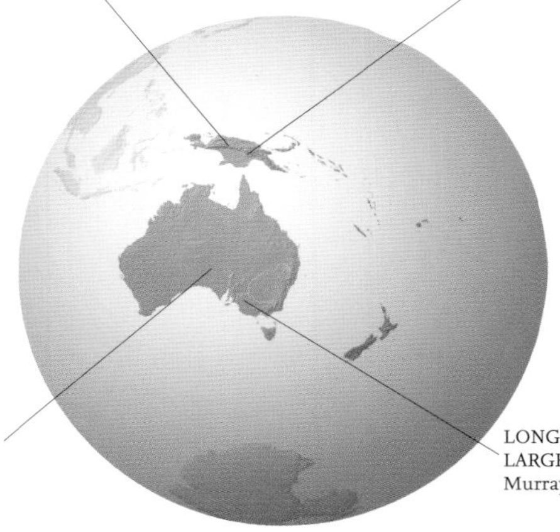


## ASIA Total Land Area 45 036 492 sq km / 17 388 589 sq miles

| HIGHEST MOUNTAINS | metres | feet |
|---|---|---|
| Mt Everest (Sagarmatha/ Qomolangma Feng), China/Nepal | 8 848 | 29 028 |
| K2 (Chogori Feng), China/Pakistan | 8 611 | 28 251 |
| Kangchenjunga, India/Nepal | 8 586 | 28 169 |
| Lhotse, China/Nepal | 8 516 | 27 939 |
| Makalu, China/Nepal | 8 463 | 27 765 |
| Cho Oyu, China/Nepal | 8 201 | 26 906 |

| LONGEST RIVERS | km | miles |
|---|---|---|
| Yangtze (Chang Jiang) | 6 380 | 3 965 |
| Ob'-Irtysh | 5 568 | 3 460 |
| Yenisey-Angara-Selenga | 5 550 | 3 449 |
| Yellow (Huang He) | 5 464 | 3 395 |
| Irtysh | 4 440 | 2 759 |
| Mekong | 4 425 | 2 750 |

| LARGEST ISLANDS | sq km | sq miles |
|---|---|---|
| Borneo | 745 561 | 287 861 |
| Sumatra (Sumatera) | 473 606 | 182 859 |
| Honshū | 227 414 | 87 805 |
| Celebes (Sulawesi) | 189 216 | 73 056 |
| Java (Jawa) | 132 188 | 51 038 |
| Luzon | 104 690 | 40 421 |

| LARGEST LAKES | sq km | sq miles |
|---|---|---|
| Caspian Sea | 371 000 | 143 243 |
| Lake Baikal (Ozero Baykal) | 30 500 | 11 776 |
| Lake Balkhash (Ozero Balkash) | 17 400 | 6 718 |
| Aral Sea (Aral'skoye More) | 17 158 | 6 625 |
| Ysyk-Köl | 6 200 | 2 394 |

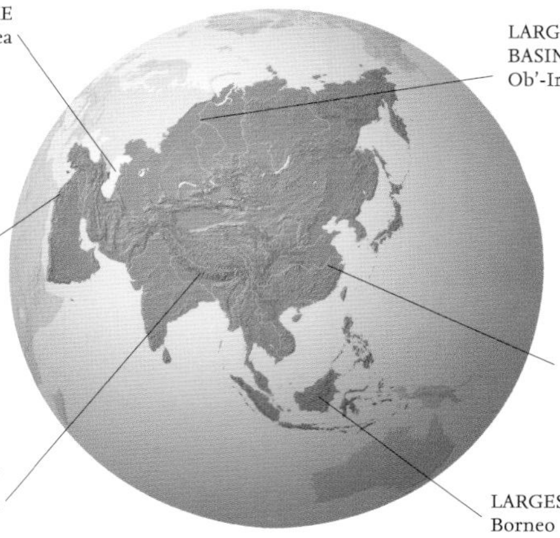

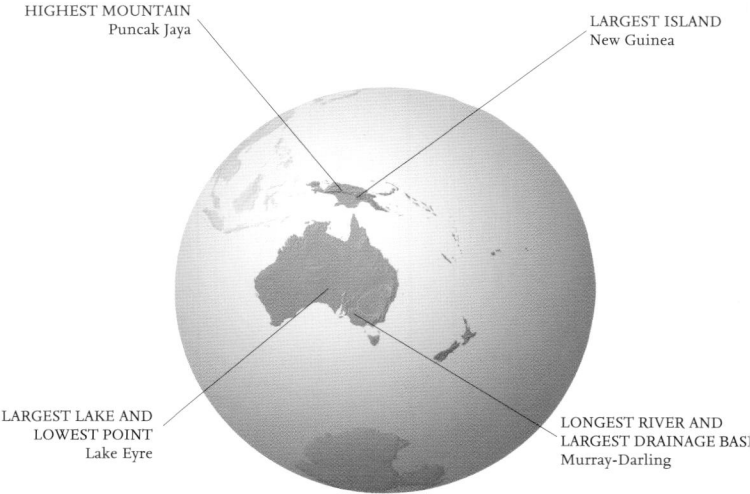

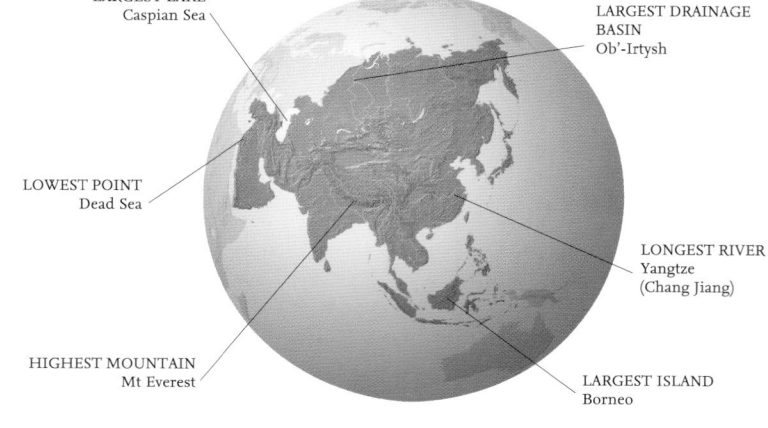

## EUROPE Total Land Area 9 908 599 sq km / 3 825 710 sq miles

| HIGHEST MOUNTAINS | metres | feet |
|---|---|---|
| **El'brus,** Russian Federation | 5 642 | 18 510 |
| **Gora Dykh-Tau,** Russian Federation | 5 204 | 17 073 |
| **Shkhara,** Georgia/Russian Federation | 5 201 | 17 063 |
| **Kazbek,** Georgia/Russian Federation | 5 047 | 16 558 |
| **Mont Blanc,** France/Italy | 4 810 | 15 781 |
| **Dufourspitze,** Italy/Switzerland | 4 634 | 15 203 |

| LONGEST RIVERS | km | miles |
|---|---|---|
| **Volga** | 3 688 | 2 292 |
| **Danube** | 2 850 | 1 771 |
| **Dnieper** | 2 285 | 1 420 |
| **Kama** | 2 028 | 1 260 |
| **Don** | 1 931 | 1 200 |
| **Pechora** | 1 802 | 1 120 |

| LARGEST ISLANDS | sq km | sq miles |
|---|---|---|
| **Great Britain** | 218 476 | 84 354 |
| **Iceland** | 102 820 | 39 699 |
| **Ireland** | 83 045 | 32 064 |
| **Ostrov Severnyy** | 47 079 | 18 177 |
| **Spitsbergen** | 37 814 | 14 600 |
| **Ostrov Yuzhnyy** | 33 246 | 12 836 |
| **Sicily (Sicilia)** | 25 426 | 9 817 |

| LARGEST LAKES | sq km | sq miles |
|---|---|---|
| **Caspian Sea** | 371 000 | 143 243 |
| **Lake Ladoga (Ladozhskoye Ozero)** | 18 390 | 7 100 |
| **Lake Onega (Onezhskoye Ozero)** | 9 600 | 3 707 |
| **Vänern** | 5 585 | 2 156 |
| **Rybinskoye Vodokhranilishche** | 5 180 | 2 000 |

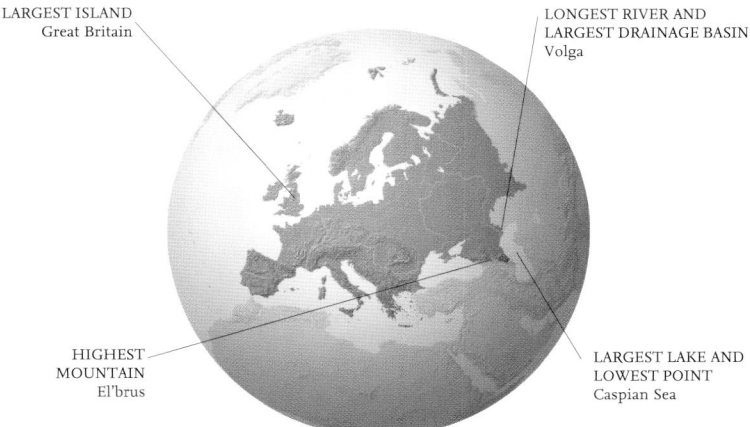

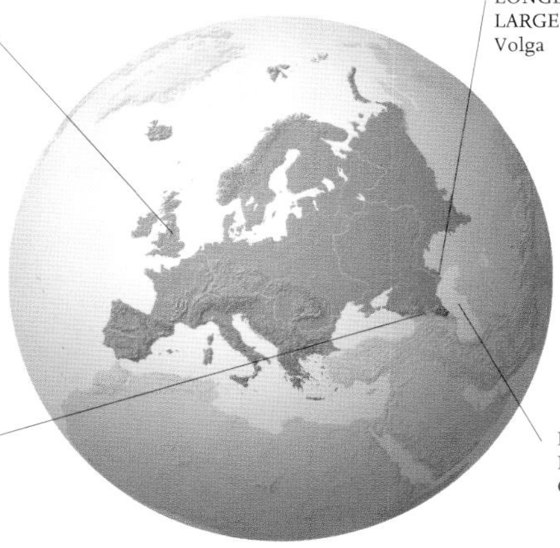


## NORTH AMERICA Total Land Area 24 680 331 sq km / 9 529 076 sq miles

| HIGHEST MOUNTAINS | metres | feet |
|---|---|---|
| **Mt McKinley,** USA | 6 194 | 20 321 |
| **Mt Logan,** Canada | 5 959 | 19 550 |
| **Pico de Orizaba,** Mexico | 5 610 | 18 405 |
| **Mt St Elias,** USA | 5 489 | 18 008 |
| **Volcán Popocatépetl,** Mexico | 5 452 | 17 887 |
| **Mt Foraker,** USA | 5 303 | 17 398 |

| LONGEST RIVERS | km | miles |
|---|---|---|
| **Mississippi-Missouri** | 5 969 | 3 709 |
| **Mackenzie-Peace-Finlay** | 4 241 | 2 635 |
| **Missouri** | 4 086 | 2 539 |
| **Mississippi** | 3 765 | 2 340 |
| **Yukon** | 3 185 | 1 979 |
| **St Lawrence** | 3 058 | 1 900 |

| LARGEST ISLANDS | sq km | sq miles |
|---|---|---|
| **Greenland** | 2 175 600 | 839 999 |
| **Baffin Island** | 507 451 | 195 927 |
| **Victoria Island** | 217 291 | 83 896 |
| **Ellesmere Island** | 196 236 | 75 767 |
| **Cuba** | 110 860 | 42 803 |
| **Newfoundland** | 108 860 | 42 031 |
| **Hispaniola** | 76 192 | 29 418 |

| LARGEST LAKES | sq km | sq miles |
|---|---|---|
| **Lake Superior** | 82 100 | 31 699 |
| **Lake Huron** | 59 600 | 23 012 |
| **Lake Michigan** | 57 800 | 22 317 |
| **Great Bear Lake** | 31 328 | 12 096 |
| **Great Slave Lake** | 28 568 | 11 030 |
| **Lake Erie** | 25 700 | 9 923 |
| **Lake Winnipeg** | 24 387 | 9 416 |
| **Lake Ontario** | 18 960 | 7 320 |

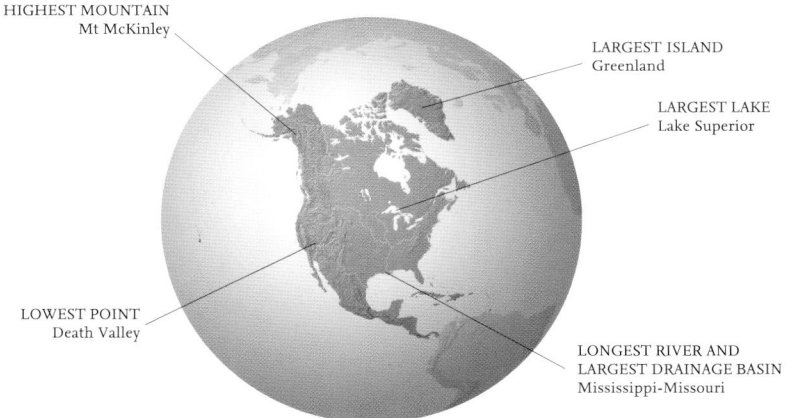

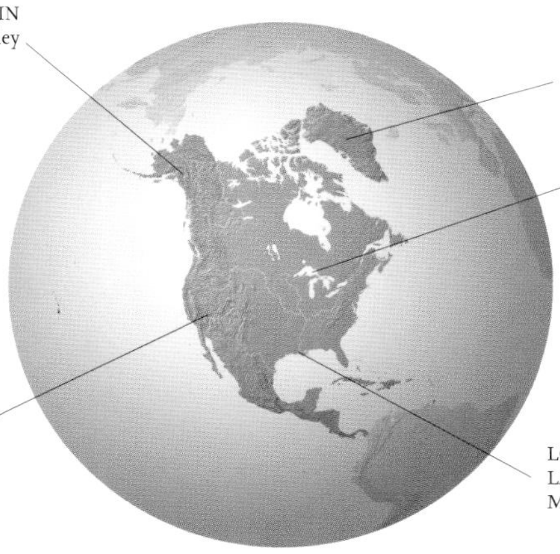


## AFRICA Total Land Area 30 343 578 sq km / 11 715 655 sq miles

| HIGHEST MOUNTAINS | metres | feet |
|---|---|---|
| **Kilimanjaro,** Tanzania | 5 892 | 19 330 |
| **Mt Kenya (Kirinyaga),** Kenya | 5 199 | 17 057 |
| **Margherita Peak,** Democratic Republic of the Congo/Uganda | 5 110 | 16 765 |
| **Meru,** Tanzania | 4 565 | 14 977 |
| **Ras Dejen,** Ethiopia | 4 533 | 14 872 |
| **Mt Karisimbi,** Rwanda | 4 510 | 14 796 |

| LONGEST RIVERS | km | miles |
|---|---|---|
| **Nile** | 6 695 | 4 160 |
| **Congo** | 4 667 | 2 900 |
| **Niger** | 4 184 | 2 600 |
| **Zambezi** | 2 736 | 1 700 |
| **Webi Shabeelle** | 2 490 | 1 547 |
| **Ubangi** | 2 250 | 1 398 |

| LARGEST LAKES | sq km | sq miles |
|---|---|---|
| **Lake Victoria** | 68 870 | 26 591 |
| **Lake Tanganyika** | 32 600 | 12 587 |
| **Lake Nyasa (Lake Malawi)** | 29 500 | 11 390 |
| **Lake Volta** | 8 482 | 3 275 |
| **Lake Turkana** | 6 500 | 2 510 |
| **Lake Albert** | 5 600 | 2 162 |

| LARGEST ISLANDS | sq km | sq miles |
|---|---|---|
| **Madagascar** | 587 040 | 226 656 |

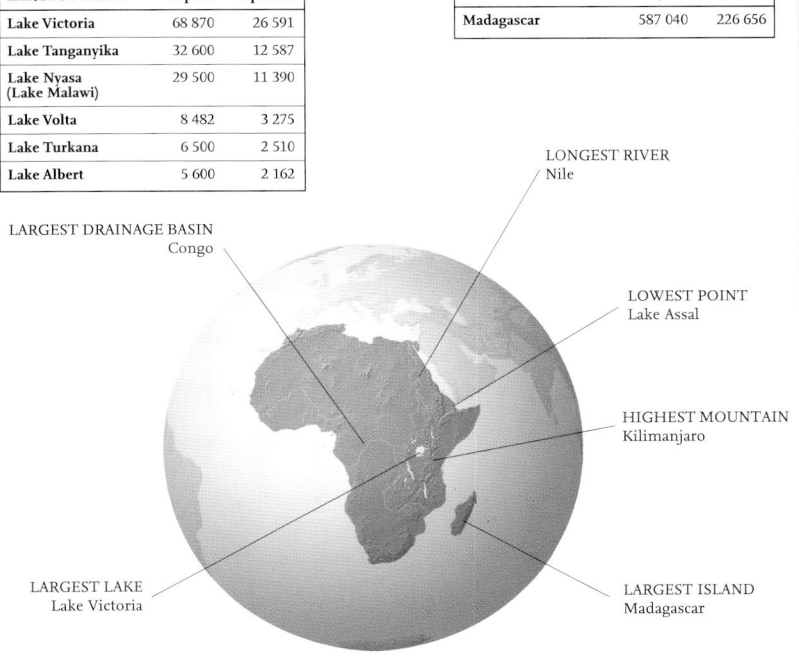

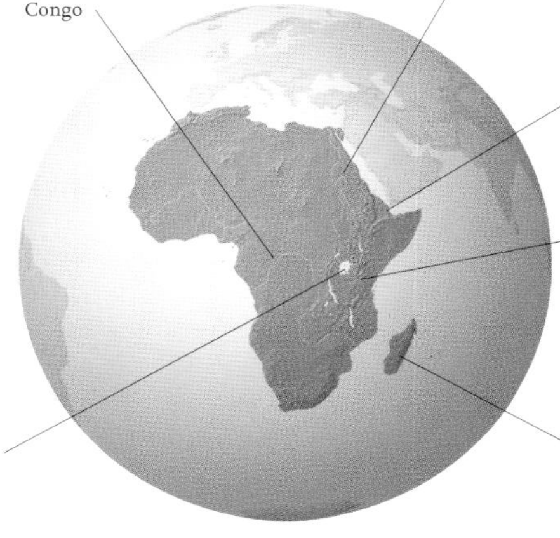


## SOUTH AMERICA Total Land Area 17 815 420 sq km / 6 878 534 sq miles

| HIGHEST MOUNTAINS | metres | feet |
|---|---|---|
| **Cerro Aconcagua,** Argentina | 6 959 | 22 831 |
| **Nevado Ojos del Salado,** Argentina/Chile | 6 908 | 22 664 |
| **Cerro Bonete,** Argentina | 6 872 | 22 546 |
| **Cerro Pissis,** Argentina | 6 858 | 22 500 |
| **Cerro Tupungato,** Argentina/Chile | 6 800 | 22 309 |
| **Cerro Mercedario,** Argentina | 6 770 | 22 211 |

| LONGEST RIVERS | km | miles |
|---|---|---|
| **Amazon (Amazonas)** | 6 516 | 4 049 |
| **Río de la Plata-Paraná** | 4 500 | 2 796 |
| **Purus** | 3 218 | 2 000 |
| **Madeira** | 3 200 | 1 988 |
| **São Francisco** | 2 900 | 1 802 |
| **Tocantins** | 2 750 | 1 709 |

| LARGEST ISLANDS | sq km | sq miles |
|---|---|---|
| **Isla Grande de Tierra del Fuego** | 47 000 | 18 147 |
| **Isla de Chiloé** | 8 394 | 3 241 |
| **East Falkland** | 6 760 | 2 610 |
| **West Falkland** | 5 413 | 2 090 |

| LARGEST LAKES | sq km | sq miles |
|---|---|---|
| **Lake Titicaca** | 8 340 | 3 220 |

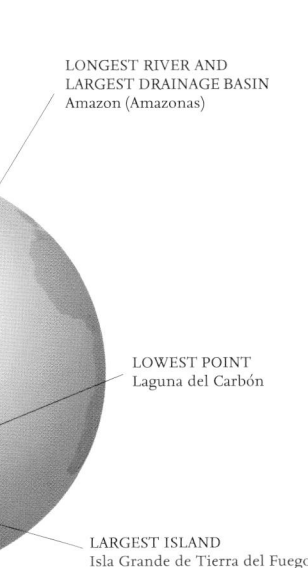

# WORLD CITIES


| City | Page |
|---|---|
| AMSTERDAM *Netherlands* | **107** |
| ATHENS *Greece* | **107** |
| AUCKLAND *New Zealand* | **102** |
| BANGKOK *Thailand* | **103** |
| BARCELONA *Spain* | **112** |
| BEIJING *China* | **103** |
| BERLIN *Germany* | **107** |
| BRUSSELS *Belgium* | **107** |
| BUENOS AIRES *Argentina* | **116** |
| CAIRO *Egypt* | **112** |
| CAPE TOWN *South Africa* | **112** |
| CARACAS *Venezuela* | **116** |
| CHICAGO *U.S.A.* | **113** |
| DELHI *India* | **106** |
| HONG KONG *China* | **103** |
| İSTANBUL *Turkey* | **106** |
| JAKARTA *Indonesia* | **102** |
| JERUSALEM *Israel* | **106** |
| KARACHI *Pakistan* | **106** |
| LIMA *Peru* | **116** |
| LONDON *United Kingdom* | **108-109** |
| LOS ANGELES *U.S.A.* | **113** |
| MADRID *Spain* | **112** |
| MELBOURNE *Australia* | **102** |
| MEXICO CITY *Mexico* | **116** |
| MILAN *Italy* | **112** |
| MONTRÉAL *Canada* | **113** |
| MOSCOW *Russia* | **107** |
| MUMBAI *India* | **106** |
| NEW YORK *U.S.A.* | **114-115** |
| PARIS *France* | **110-111** |
| RIO DE JANEIRO *Brazil* | **116** |
| ROME *Italy* | **112** |
| ST PETERSBURG *Russia* | **107** |
| SAN FRANCISCO *U.S.A.* | **113** |
| SÃO PAULO *Brazil* | **116** |
| SEOUL *South Korea* | **103** |
| SHANGHAI *China* | **103** |
| SINGAPORE | **103** |
| SYDNEY *Australia* | **102** |
| TEHRĀN *Iran* | **106** |
| TŌKYŌ *Japan* | **104-105** |
| TORONTO *Canada* | **113** |
| WASHINGTON D.C. *U.S.A.* | **113** |


## KEY TO CITY PLANS

Built-up area · Cemetery · Marsh · Road · Administrative boundary · General place of interest · Academic/Municipal building

Park/Open space · Water · River/Canal · Railway · Airport · Place of worship · Transport location

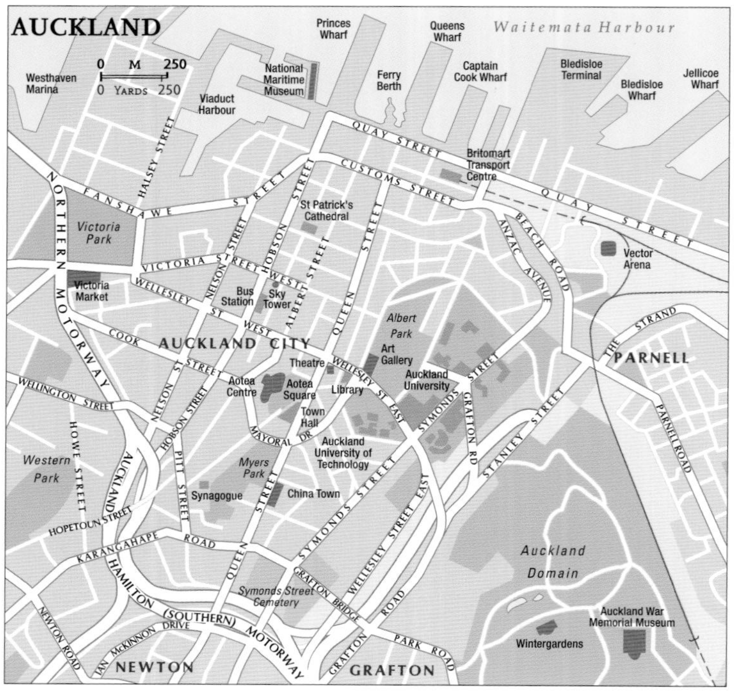


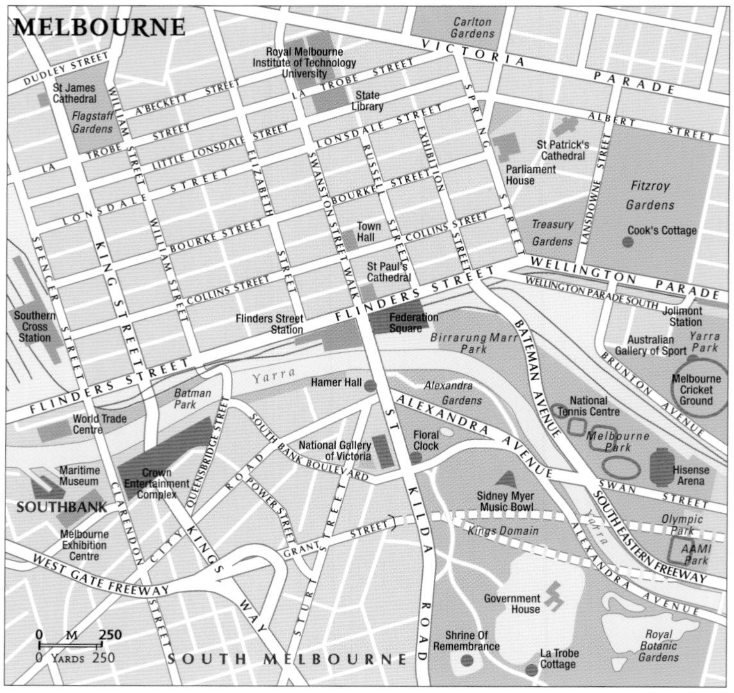


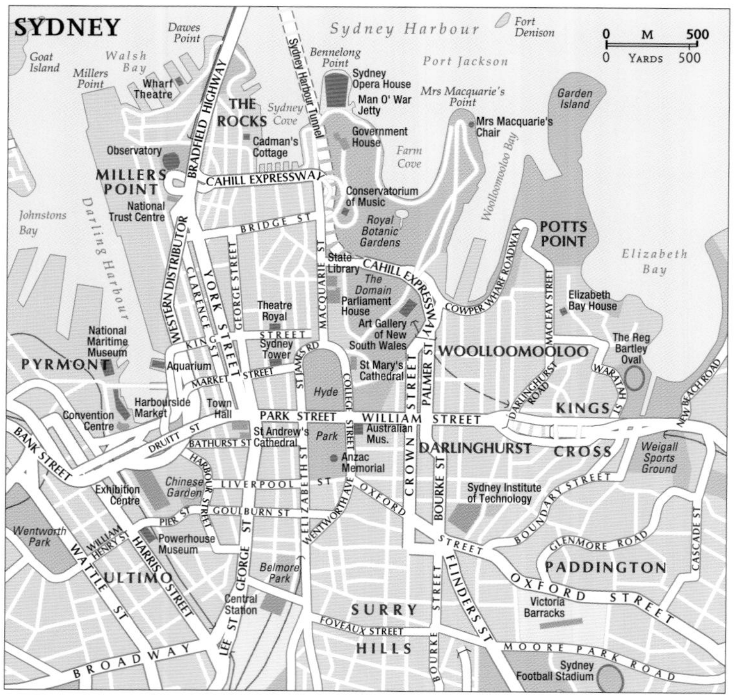


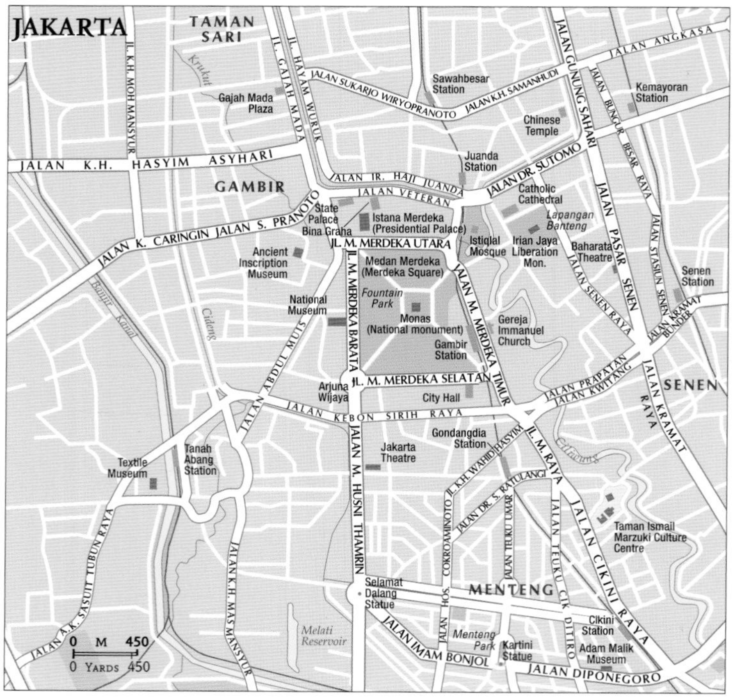

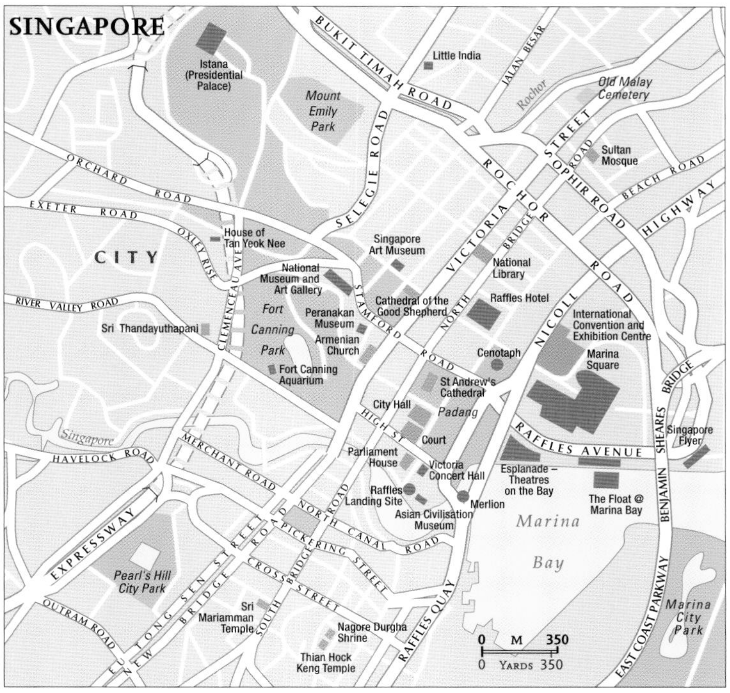
SINGAPORE
Istana (Presidential Palace)
Mount Emily Park
Little India
Old Malay Cemetery
Sultan Mosque
BUKIT TIMAH ROAD
ORCHARD ROAD
EXETER ROAD
CITY
House of Tan Yeok Nee
National Museum and Art Gallery
Singapore Art Museum
National Library
Raffles Hotel
Peranakan Museum
Armenian Church
Cathedral of the Good Shepherd
Fort Canning Park
Fort Canning Aquarium
Sri Thandayuthapani
RIVER VALLEY ROAD
International Convention and Exhibition Centre
Marina Square
Cenotaph
St Andrew's Cathedral
City Hall
Padang
Court
Parliament House
Victoria Concert Hall
Raffles Landing Site
Asian Civilisation Museum
Merlion
Esplanade – Theatres on the Bay
The Float @ Marina Bay
Singapore Flyer
RAFFLES AVENUE
HAVELOCK ROAD
MERCHANT ROAD
NORTH CANAL ROAD
PICKERING STREET
CROSS STREET
EXPRESSWAY
Pearl's Hill City Park
Sri Mariamman Temple
Nagore Durgha Shrine
Thian Hock Keng Temple
OUTRAM ROAD
NEW BRIDGE ROAD
RAFFLES QUAY
EAST COAST PARKWAY
BENJAMIN SHEARES BRIDGE
Marina Bay
Marina City Park
0 M 350
0 YARDS 350

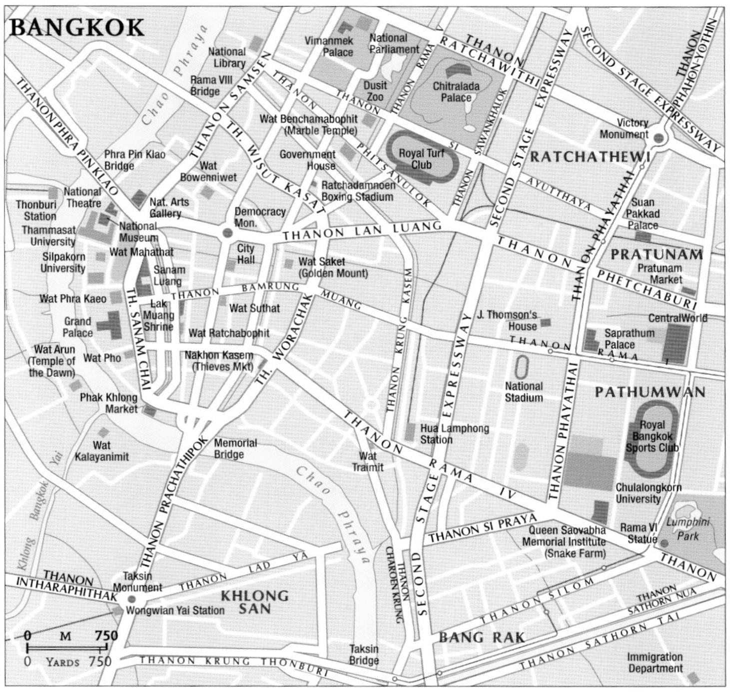
BANGKOK
National Library
Vimanmek Palace
National Parliament
Dusit Zoo
Chitralada Palace
Rama VIII Bridge
Chao Phraya
THANON SAMSEN
Wat Benchamabophit (Marble Temple)
Phra Pin Klao Bridge
Wat Bowonniwet
Government House
Royal Turf Club
Victory Monument
RATCHATHEWI
Ratchadamnoen Boxing Stadium
Thonburi Station
National Theatre
Nat. Arts Gallery
Democracy Mon.
THANON LAN LUANG
Thammasat University
National Museum
Wat Mahathat
Silpakorn University
City Hall
Wat Saket (Golden Mount)
Suan Pakkad Palace
PRATUNAM
Pratunam Market
THANON PHETCHABURI
Sanam Luang
Wat Phra Kaeo
Lak Muang Shrine
Wat Suthat
Grand Palace
Wat Ratchabophit
J. Thomson's House
Saprathum Palace
CentralWorld
Wat Arun (Temple of the Dawn)
Wat Pho
Nakhon Kasem (Thieves Mkt)
National Stadium
PATHUMWAN
Phak Khlong Market
Royal Bangkok Sports Club
Wat Kalayanimit
Memorial Bridge
Hua Lamphong Station
Wat Traimit
Chulalongkorn University
THANON RAMA IV
THANON SI PRAYA
Queen Saovabha Memorial Institute (Snake Farm)
Rama VI Statue
Lumphini Park
Taksin Monument
THANON INTHARAPHITHAK
Wongwian Yai Station
KHLONG SAN
THANON SILOM
THANON SATHORN NUA
BANG RAK
THANON SATHORN TAI
Taksin Bridge
THANON KRUNG THONBURI
Immigration Department
0 M 750
0 YARDS 750

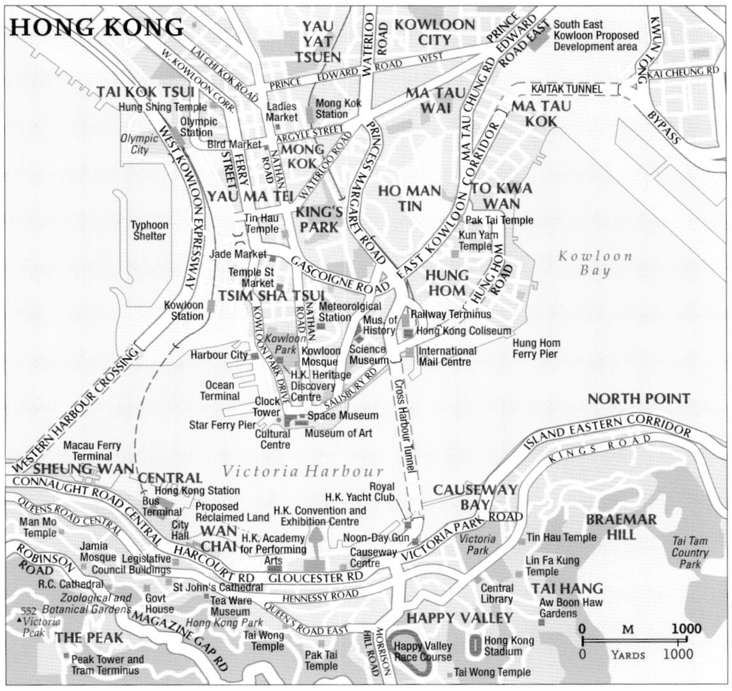
HONG KONG
YAU YAT TSUEN
KOWLOON CITY
South East Kowloon Proposed Development area
KAITAK TUNNEL
TAI KOK TSUI
Hung Shing Temple
Olympic Station
Olympic City
Ladies Market
Mong Kok Station
MA TAU WAI
MA TAU KOK
Bird Market
MONG KOK
HO MAN TIN
TO KWA WAN
YAU MA TEI
KING'S PARK
Pak Tai Temple
Typhoon Shelter
Tin Hau Temple
Kun Yam Temple
Jade Market
Temple St Market
Kowloon Bay
HUNG HOM
TSIM SHA TSUI
Kowloon Station
Meteorological Station
Mus. of History
Railway Terminus
Hong Kong Coliseum
Kowloon Park
Kowloon Mosque
Science Museum
Harbour City
H.K. Heritage Discovery Centre
International Mail Centre
Hung Hom Ferry Pier
Ocean Terminal
Clock Tower
Space Museum
Star Ferry Pier
Cultural Centre
Museum of Art
Cross Harbour Tunnel
NORTH POINT
WESTERN HARBOUR CROSSING
ISLAND EASTERN CORRIDOR
Macau Ferry Terminal
SHEUNG WAN
CENTRAL
Victoria Harbour
Hong Kong Station
Bus Terminal
Proposed Reclaimed Land
H.K. Convention and Exhibition Centre
Royal H.K. Yacht Club
CAUSEWAY BAY
Man Mo Temple
City Hall
WAN CHAI
Noon-Day Gun
Tin Hau Temple
BRAEMAR HILL
Jamia Mosque
Legislative Council Buildings
H.K. Academy for Performing Arts
Causeway Centre
Victoria Park
Tai Tam Country Park
ROBINSON ROAD
R.C. Cathedral
St John's Cathedral
GLOUCESTER RD
HENNESSY ROAD
Lin Fa Kung Temple
Central Library
TAI HANG
Zoological and Botanical Gardens
Govt House
Tea Ware Museum
Hong Kong Park
Aw Boon Haw Gardens
552 Victoria Peak
HAPPY VALLEY
THE PEAK
MAGAZINE GAP RD
Tai Wong Temple
Pak Tai Temple
Happy Valley Race Course
Hong Kong Stadium
Peak Tower and Tram Terminus
Tai Wong Temple
0 M 1000
0 YARDS 1000

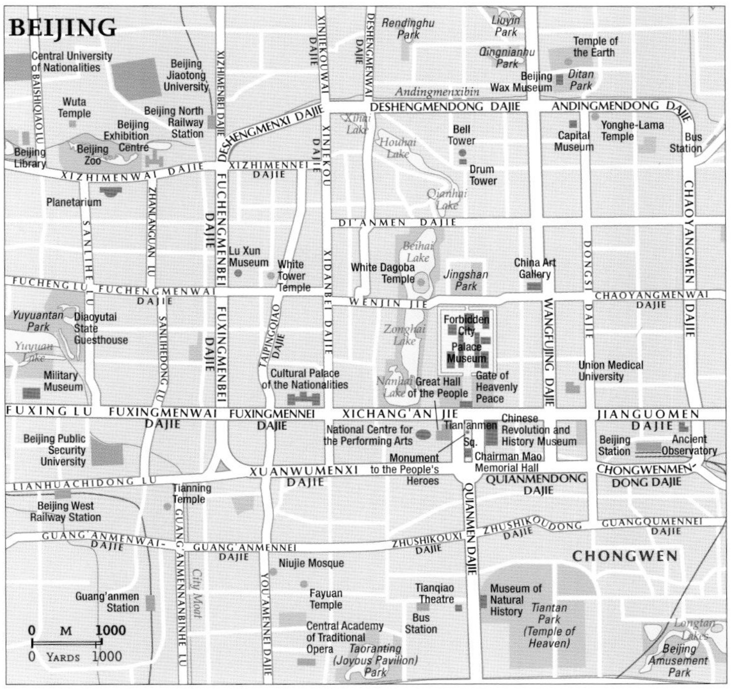
BEIJING
Rendinghu Park
Liuyin Park
Qingnianhu Park
Temple of the Earth
Ditan Park
Central University of Nationalities
Beijing Jiaotong University
Andingmenxibin
Beijing Wax Museum
DESHENGMENDONG DAJIE
ANDINGMENDONG DAJIE
Wuta Temple
Beijing North Railway Station
Beijing Exhibition Centre
Xinjiekou
Houhai Lake
Bell Tower
Capital Museum
Yonghe-Lama Temple
Bus Station
Beijing Library
Beijing Zoo
XIZHIMENWAI DAJIE
XIZHIMENNEI DAJIE
Drum Tower
Qianhai Lake
Planetarium
DI'ANMEN DAJIE
CHAOYANGMEN
Lu Xun Museum
White Tower Temple
White Dagoba Temple
Beihai Lake
Jingshan Park
China Art Gallery
FUCHENGMENWAI DAJIE
CHAOYANGMENWAI DAJIE
WENJIN JIE
Yuyuantan Park
Diaoyutai State Guesthouse
Zhonghai Lake
Forbidden City Palace Museum
WANGFUJING DAJIE
Union Medical University
Military Museum
Nanhai Lake
Cultural Palace of the Nationalities
Great Hall of the People
Gate of Heavenly Peace
FUXINGMENWAI DAJIE
FUXINGMENNEI DAJIE
XICHANG'AN JIE
Tian'anmen Sq.
JIANGUOMEN DAJIE
Beijing Public Security University
National Centre for the Performing Arts
Monument to the People's Heroes
Chinese Revolution and History Museum
Chairman Mao Memorial Hall
Beijing Station
Ancient Observatory
XUANWUMENXI DAJIE
QIANMENDONG DAJIE
CHONGWENMEN DONG DAJIE
Tianning Temple
Beijing West Railway Station
GUANG'ANMENWAI DAJIE
GUANG'ANMENNEI DAJIE
ZHUSHIKOUXI DAJIE
ZHUSHIKOUDONG DAJIE
GUANGQUMENNEI DAJIE
Niujie Mosque
CHONGWEN
Guang'anmen Station
City Moat
Fayuan Temple
Tianqiao Theatre
Museum of Natural History
Tiantan Park (Temple of Heaven)
Central Academy of Traditional Opera
Bus Station
Taoranting (Joyous Pavilion) Park
Longtan Lake
Beijing Amusement Park
QIANMEN DAJIE
0 M 1000
0 YARDS 1000

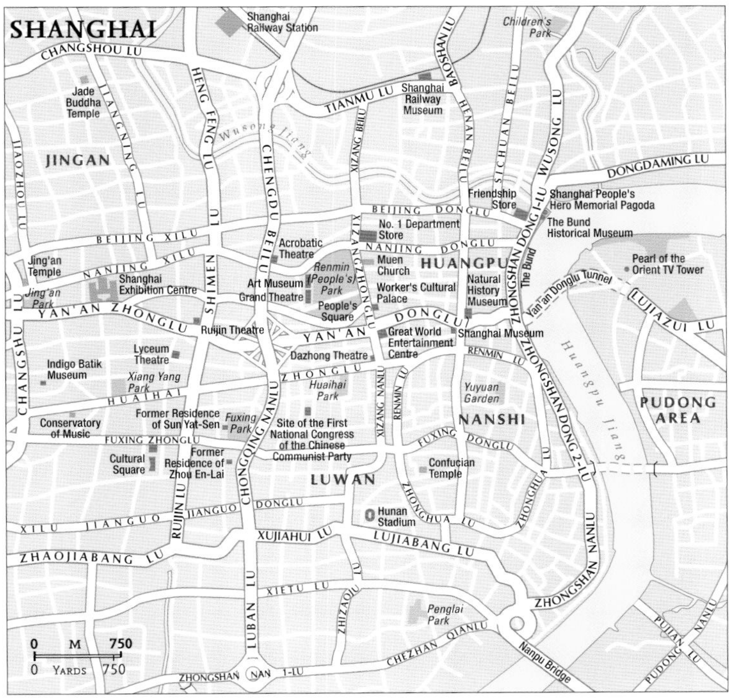
SHANGHAI
Shanghai Railway Station
Children's Park
CHANGSHOU LU
Jade Buddha Temple
TIANMU LU
Shanghai Railway Museum
Wusong Jiang
JINGAN
DONGDAMING LU
Friendship Store
Shanghai People's Hero Memorial Pagoda
BEIJING DONGLU
No. 1 Department Store
The Bund Historical Museum
BEIJING XILU
NANJING XILU
Acrobatic Theatre
NANJING DONGLU
Pearl of the Orient TV Tower
HUANGPU
Jing'an Temple
Shanghai Exhibition Centre
Art Museum
Renmin (People's) Park
Muen Church
Worker's Cultural Palace
Natural History Museum
Jing'an Park
Grand Theatre
People's Square
Yan'an Donglu Tunnel
LUJIAZUI LU
YAN'AN ZHONGLU
Ruijin Theatre
YAN'AN DONGLU
Great World Entertainment Centre
Shanghai Museum
Huangpu Jiang
Lyceum Theatre
Dazhong Theatre
Indigo Batik Museum
Xiang Yang Park
Huaihai Park
Yuyuan Garden
PUDONG AREA
HUAIHAI
Former Residence of Sun Yat-Sen
Fuxing Park
Site of the First National Congress of the Chinese Communist Party
NANSHI
Conservatory of Music
FUXING ZHONGLU
Cultural Square
Former Residence of Zhou En-Lai
Confucian Temple
LUWAN
Hunan Stadium
XILU JIANGUO
ZHAOJIABANG LU
XUJIAHUI LU
LUJIABANG LU
ZHONGSHAN NANLU
XIETU LU
Penglai Park
Nanpu Bridge
CHANGSHU LU
RUIJIN LU
LUBAN LU
CHEZHAN QIANLU
ZHONGSHAN NAN 1-LU
0 M 750
0 YARDS 750

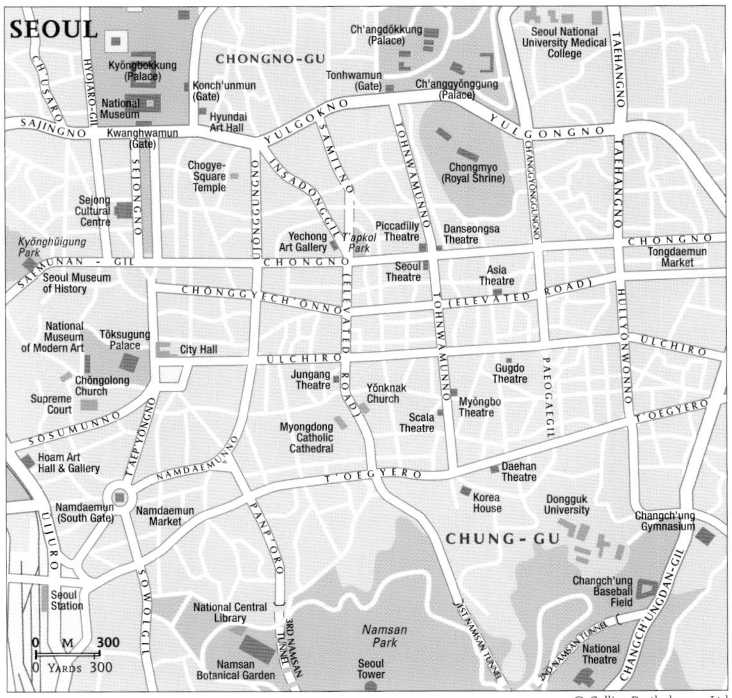
SEOUL
Ch'angdŏkkung (Palace)
Seoul National University Medical College
Kyŏngbokkung (Palace)
CHONGNO-GU
Konch'unmun (Gate)
Tonhwamun (Gate)
Ch'anggyŏnggung (Palace)
National Museum
Hyundai Art Hall
SAJIKNO
Kwanghwamun (Gate)
YULGOKNO
YULGONGNO
Chogye-Square Temple
Chongmyo (Royal Shrine)
Sejong Cultural Centre
Yechong Art Gallery
T'apkol Park
Piccadilly Theatre
Danseongsa Theatre
Kyŏnghŭigung Park
CHONGNO
Tongdaemun Market
Seoul Museum of History
Seoul Theatre
Asia Theatre
CHONGGYECH'ONNO (ELEVATED ROAD)
National Museum of Modern Art
Tŏksugung Palace
City Hall
ULCHIRO
Jungang Theatre
Gugdo Theatre
Chŏngdong Church
Yŏnknak Church
Myŏngbo Theatre
Supreme Court
Scala Theatre
Myongdong Catholic Cathedral
T'OEGYERO
Hoam Art Hall & Gallery
Daehan Theatre
Korea House
Dongguk University
Namdaemun (South Gate)
Namdaemun Market
Changch'ung Gymnasium
CHUNG-GU
Seoul Station
National Central Library
Changch'ung Baseball Field
Namsan Park
National Theatre
Namsan Botanical Garden
Seoul Tower
3RD NAMSAN TUNNEL
0 M 300
0 YARDS 300

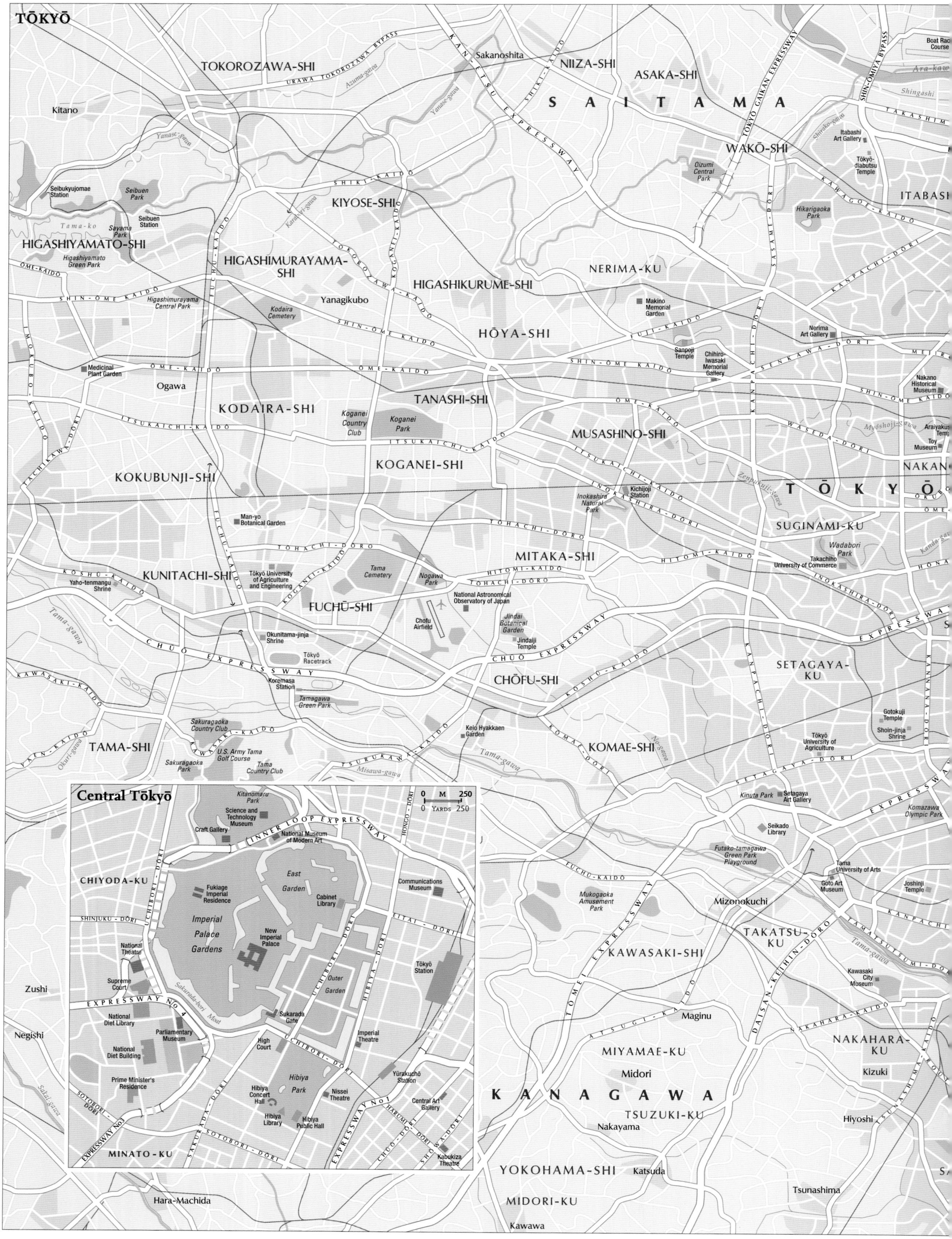
TŌKYŌ
Sakanoshita
TOKOROZAWA-SHI
NIIZA-SHI
ASAKA-SHI
SAITAMA
Kitano
WAKŌ-SHI
Oizumi Central Park
Itabashi Art Gallery
Tōkyō-diabutsu Temple
ITABASHI
Seibukyujomae Station
Seibuen Park
Seibuen Station
Tama-ko
Sayama Park
HIGASHIYAMATO-SHI
Higashiyamato Green Park
KIYOSE-SHI
HIGASHIMURAYAMA-SHI
Hikarigaoka Park
NERIMA-KU
HIGASHIKURUME-SHI
Higashimurayama Central Park
Kodaira Cemetery
Yanagikubo
Makino Memorial Garden
HŌYA-SHI
Nerima Art Gallery
Sanpoji Temple
Chihiro-Iwasaki Memorial Gallery
Medicinal Plant Garden
Ogawa
Nakano Historical Museum
KODAIRA-SHI
TANASHI-SHI
Koganei Country Club
Koganei Park
MUSASHINO-SHI
Araiyakushi Temple
Toy Museum
KOKUBUNJI-SHI
KOGANEI-SHI
NAKANO
Kichijoji Station
Inokashira Natural Park
TŌKYŌ
Man-yo Botanical Garden
SUGINAMI-KU
Wadabori Park
MITAKA-SHI
Takachiho University of Commerce
KUNITACHI-SHI
Yaho-tenmangu Shrine
Tōkyō University of Agriculture and Engineering
Tama Cemetery
Nogawa Park
National Astronomical Observatory of Japan
FUCHŪ-SHI
Chofu Airfield
Jindai Botanical Garden
Jindaiji Temple
Okunitama-jinja Shrine
Tōkyō Racetrack
SETAGAYA-KU
Koremasa Station
CHŌFU-SHI
Tamagawa Green Park
Gotokuji Temple
Sakuragaoka Country Club
Keio Hyakkaen Garden
Shoin-jinja Shrine
TAMA-SHI
U.S. Army Tama Golf Course
KOMAE-SHI
Tōkyō University of Agriculture
Sakuragaoka Park
Tama Country Club
Central Tōkyō
Kitanomaru Park
Science and Technology Museum
Craft Gallery
National Museum of Modern Art
0 M 250
0 Yards 250
CHIYODA-KU
Fukiage Imperial Residence
East Garden
Cabinet Library
Communications Museum
Imperial Palace Gardens
New Imperial Palace
National Theatre
Outer Garden
Tōkyō Station
Supreme Court
National Diet Library
Parliamentary Museum
Sukarada Gate
National Diet Building
High Court
Imperial Theatre
Prime Minister's Residence
Hibiya Park
Hibiya Concert Hall
Nissei Theatre
Yūrakuchō Station
Hibiya Library
Hibiya Public Hall
Central Art Gallery
MINATO-KU
Kabukiza Theatre
Kinuta Park
Setagaya Art Gallery
Komazawa Olympic Park
Seikado Library
Futako-tamagawa Green Park Playground
Tama University of Arts
Goto Art Museum
Joshinji Temple
Mukogaoka Amusement Park
Mizonokuchi
TAKATSU-KU
KAWASAKI-SHI
Kawasaki City Museum
Zushi
Maginu
Negishi
NAKAHARA-KU
MIYAMAE-KU
Midori
Kizuki
KANAGAWA
TSUZUKI-KU
Hiyoshi
Nakayama
YOKOHAMA-SHI
Katsuda
Tsunashima
Hara-Machida
MIDORI-KU
Kawawa

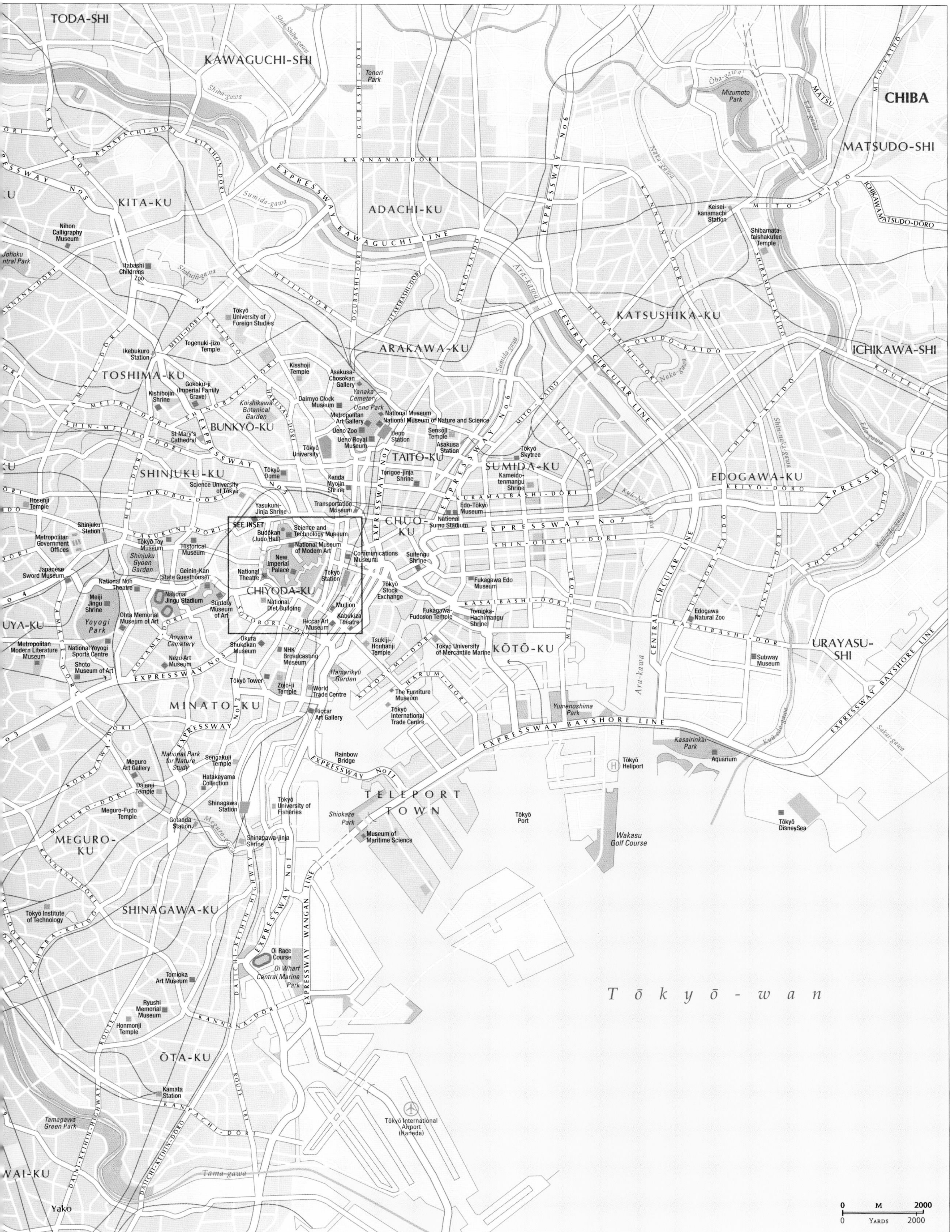
TODA-SHI
KAWAGUCHI-SHI
CHIBA
MATSUDO-SHI
KITA-KU
ADACHI-KU
KATSUSHIKA-KU
ARAKAWA-KU
ICHIKAWA-SHI
TOSHIMA-KU
BUNKYŌ-KU
TAITŌ-KU
SUMIDA-KU
SHINJUKU-KU
EDOGAWA-KU
CHŪŌ-KU
CHIYODA-KU
KŌTŌ-KU
URAYASU-SHI
MINATO-KU
TELEPORT TOWN
MEGURO-KU
SHINAGAWA-KU
ŌTA-KU
Tōkyō-wan
Tōkyō Skytree
Ueno Zoo
Tōkyō Station
New Imperial Palace
Tōkyō Tower
Tōkyō DisneySea
Tōkyō International Airport (Haneda)
SEE INSET
0 M 2000
0 YARDS 2000

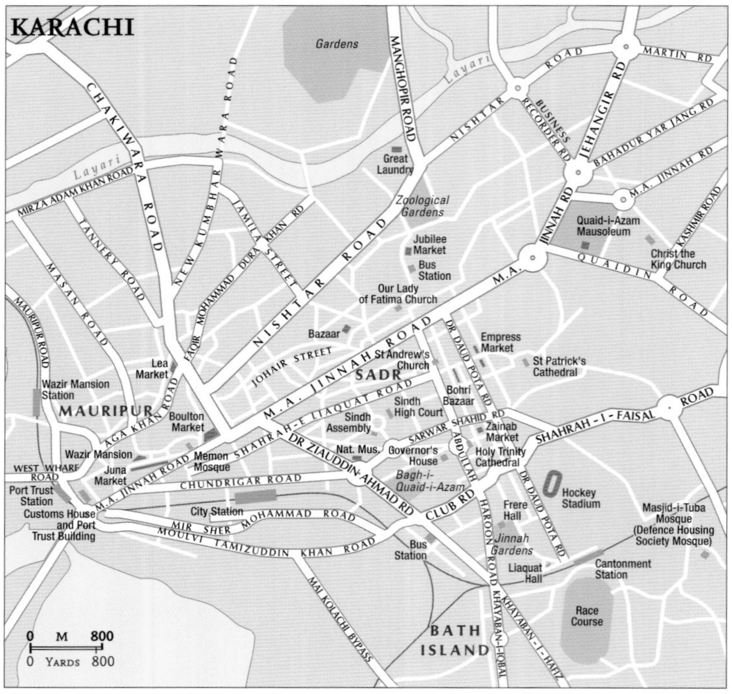
KARACHI
Gardens
Great Laundry
Zoological Gardens
Quaid-i-Azam Mausoleum
Jubilee Market
Bus Station
Christ the King Church
Our Lady of Fatima Church
Bazaar
Lea Market
Empress Market
St Andrew's Church
SADR
St Patrick's Cathedral
Wazir Mansion Station
MAURIPUR
Boulton Market
Sindh Assembly
Sindh High Court
Bohri Bazaar
Zainab Market
Wazir Mansion
Memon Mosque
Nat. Mus.
Governor's House
Holy Trinity Cathedral
Juna Market
Bagh-i-Quaid-i-Azam
Hockey Stadium
Port Trust Station
Customs House and Port Trust Building
City Station
Frere Hall
Jinnah Gardens
Masjid-i-Tuba Mosque (Defence Housing Society Mosque)
Bus Station
Liaquat Hall
Cantonment Station
Race Course
BATH ISLAND
WEST WHARF
CHAKIWARA ROAD
NISHTAR ROAD
M.A. JINNAH ROAD
SHAHRAH-I-FAISAL
CHUNDRIGAR ROAD
CLUB RD
MARTIN RD
0 M 800
0 YARDS 800

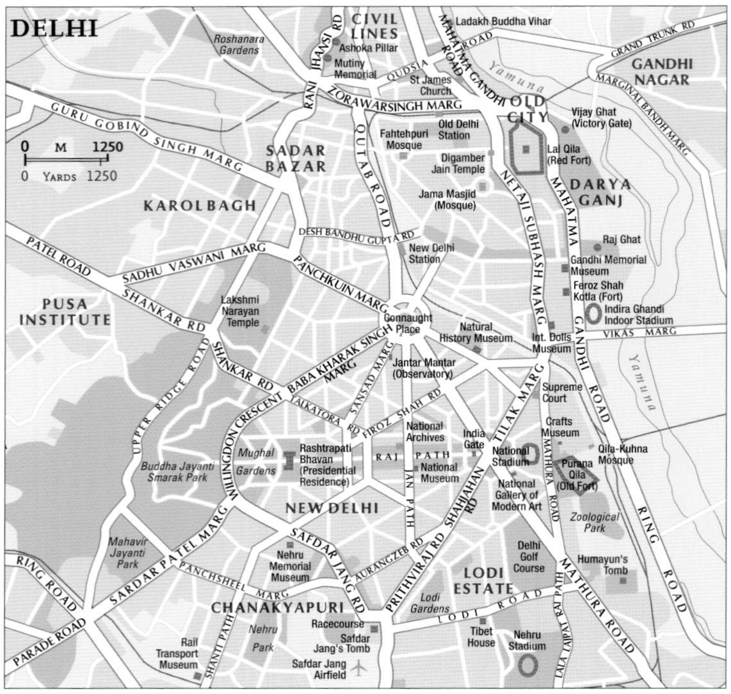
DELHI
Roshanara Gardens
CIVIL LINES
Ashoka Pillar
Mutiny Memorial
Ladakh Buddha Vihar
St James Church
OLD CITY
GANDHI NAGAR
Vijay Ghat (Victory Gate)
SADAR BAZAR
Fahtehpuri Mosque
Old Delhi Station
Digamber Jain Temple
Lal Qila (Red Fort)
DARYA GANJ
KAROLBAGH
Jama Masjid (Mosque)
Raj Ghat
New Delhi Station
Gandhi Memorial Museum
Feroz Shah Kotla (Fort)
Indira Ghandi Indoor Stadium
PUSA INSTITUTE
Lakshmi Narayan Temple
Connaught Place
Natural History Museum
Int. Dolls Museum
Jantar Mantar (Observatory)
Supreme Court
Crafts Museum
Rashtrapati Bhavan (Presidential Residence)
National Archives
India Gate
Qila-Kuhna Mosque
National Museum
National Stadium
Purana Qila (Old Fort)
National Gallery of Modern Art
Buddha Jayanti Smarak Park
Mughal Gardens
NEW DELHI
Zoological Park
Mahavir Jayanti Park
Nehru Memorial Museum
Delhi Golf Course
LODI ESTATE
Humayun's Tomb
CHANAKYAPURI
Lodi Gardens
Nehru Park
Racecourse
Safdar Jang's Tomb
Tibet House
Nehru Stadium
Rail Transport Museum
Safdar Jang Airfield
RING ROAD
0 M 1250
0 YARDS 1250

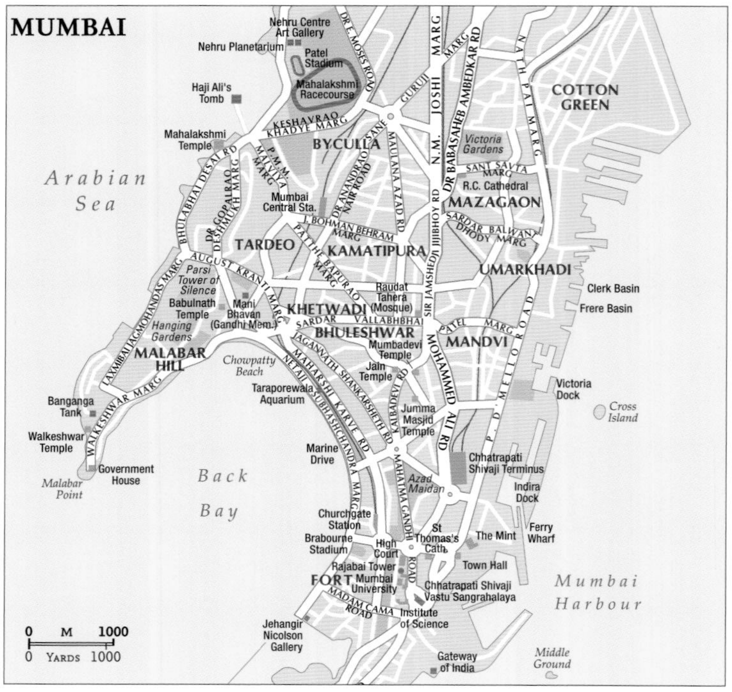
MUMBAI
Nehru Centre Art Gallery
Nehru Planetarium
Patel Stadium
Haji Ali's Tomb
Mahalakshmi Racecourse
Mahalakshmi Temple
COTTON GREEN
BYCULLA
Victoria Gardens
Arabian Sea
R.C. Cathedral
MAZAGAON
Mumbai Central Sta.
TARDEO
KAMATIPURA
UMARKHADI
Clerk Basin
Parsi Tower of Silence
Babulnath Temple
Mani Bhavan (Gandhi Mem.)
KHETWADI
Raudat Tahera (Mosque)
Frere Basin
Hanging Gardens
BHULESHWAR
Mumbadevi Temple
MANDVI
MALABAR HILL
Chowpatty Beach
Jain Temple
Victoria Dock
Banganga Tank
Taraporewala Aquarium
Jumma Masjid Temple
Cross Island
Walkeshwar Temple
Marine Drive
Government House
Chhatrapati Shivaji Terminus
Malabar Point
Back Bay
Azad Maidan
Indira Dock
Churchgate Station
Brabourne Stadium
High Court
St Thomas's Cath.
The Mint
Ferry Wharf
Rajabai Tower
Town Hall
FORT
Mumbai University
Chhatrapati Shivaji Vastu Sangrahalaya
Mumbai Harbour
Jehangir Nicolson Gallery
Institute of Science
Gateway of India
Middle Ground
0 M 1000
0 YARDS 1000

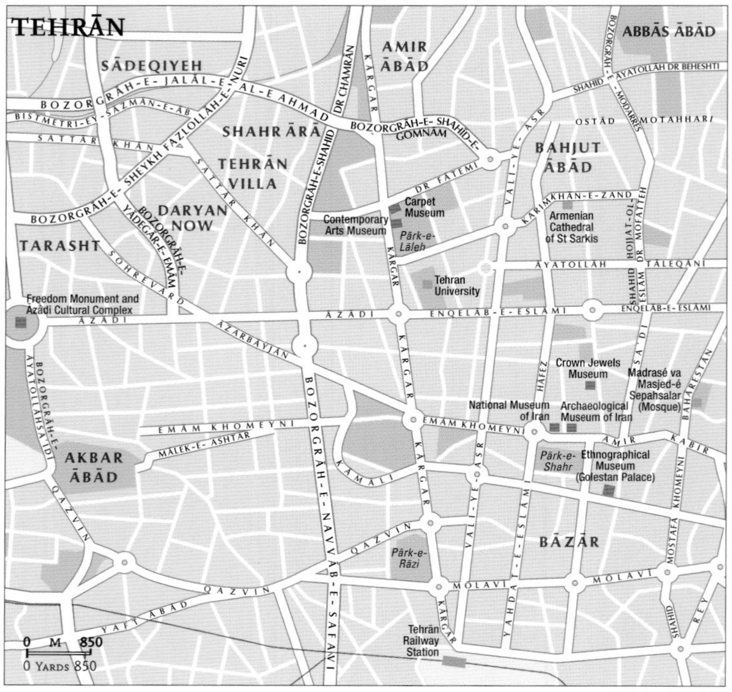
TEHRĀN
ABBĀS ĀBĀD
SĀDEQIYEH
AMIR ĀBĀD
SHAHR ĀRĀ
TEHRĀN VILLA
BAHJUT ĀBĀD
DARYAN NOW
Carpet Museum
Contemporary Arts Museum
Pārk-e-Lāleh
Armenian Cathedral of St Sarkis
TARASHT
Tehran University
Freedom Monument and Āzādi Cultural Complex
Crown Jewels Museum
Madrasé va Masjed-é Sepahsalar (Mosque)
National Museum of Iran
Archaeological Museum of Iran
AKBAR ĀBĀD
Pārk-e-Shahr
Ethnographical Museum (Golestan Palace)
BĀZĀR
Pārk-e-Rāzi
Tehrān Railway Station
0 M 850
0 YARDS 850

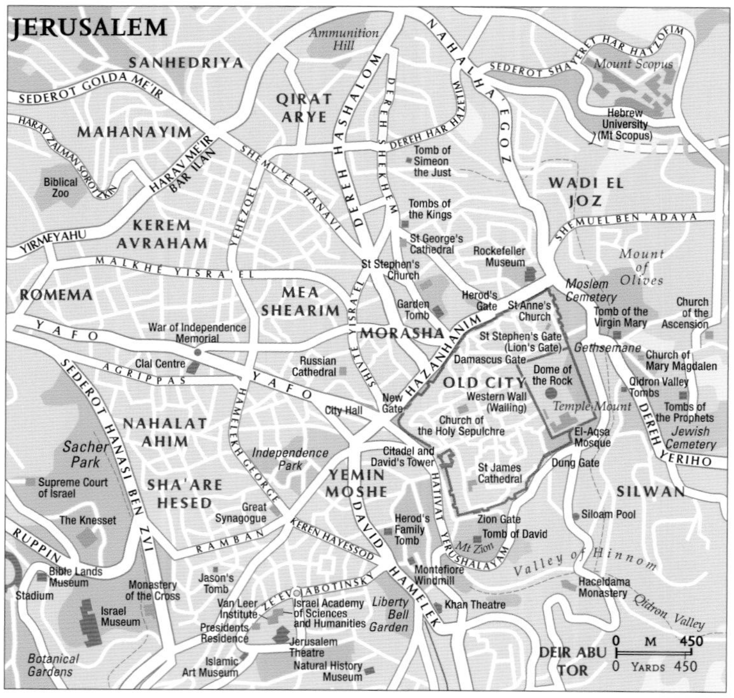
JERUSALEM
Ammunition Hill
SANHEDRIYA
Mount Scopus
QIRAT ARYE
Hebrew University (Mt Scopus)
MAHANAYIM
Tomb of Simeon the Just
Biblical Zoo
WADI EL JOZ
KEREM AVRAHAM
Tombs of the Kings
St George's Cathedral
Rockefeller Museum
Mount of Olives
St Stephen's Church
ROMEMA
MEA SHEARIM
Garden Tomb
Herod's Gate
St Anne's Church
Moslem Cemetery
Tomb of the Virgin Mary
Church of the Ascension
War of Independence Memorial
MORASHA
St Stephen's Gate (Lion's Gate)
Damascus Gate
Dome of the Rock
Church of Mary Magdalen
Clal Centre
Russian Cathedral
OLD CITY
Western Wall (Wailing)
Gethsemane
Kidron Valley Tombs
Temple Mount
Tombs of the Prophets
Jewish Cemetery
NAHALAT AHIM
City Hall
New Gate
Church of the Holy Sepulchre
El-Aqsa Mosque
Sacher Park
Independence Park
Citadel and David's Tower
Dung Gate
Supreme Court of Israel
SHA'ARE HESED
YEMIN MOSHE
St James Cathedral
SILWAN
The Knesset
Great Synagogue
Herod's Family Tomb
Zion Gate
Tomb of David
Mt Zion
Siloam Pool
Valley of Hinnom
Bible Lands Museum
Monastery of the Cross
Jason's Tomb
Montefiore Windmill
Haceldama Monastery
Stadium
Israel Museum
Van Leer Institute
Israel Academy of Sciences and Humanities
Liberty Bell Garden
Khan Theatre
Kidron Valley
Presidents' Residence
Jerusalem Theatre
DEIR ABU TOR
Botanical Gardens
Islamic Art Museum
Natural History Museum
0 M 450
0 YARDS 450

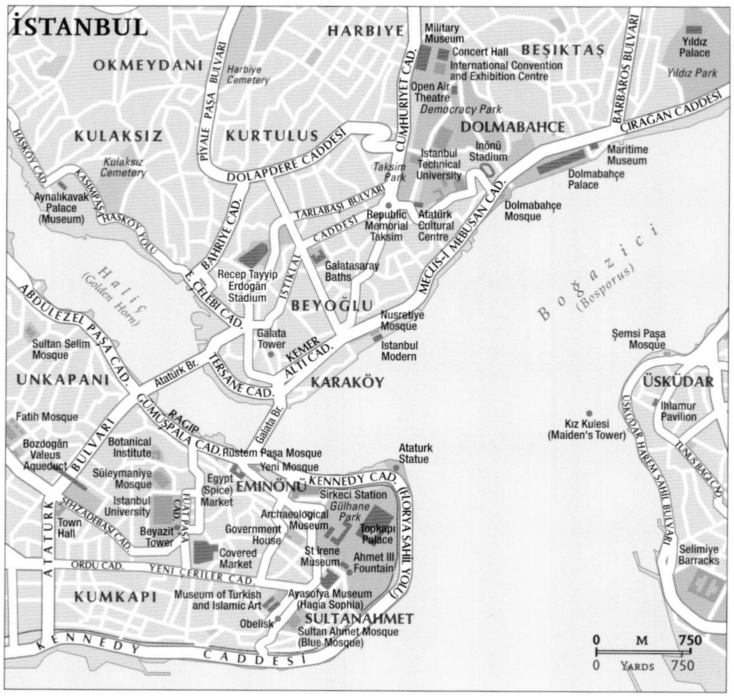
İSTANBUL
HARBIYE
Military Museum
Concert Hall
BEŞIKTAŞ
Yıldız Palace
OKMEYDANI
Harbiye Cemetery
International Convention and Exhibition Centre
Yıldız Park
Open Air Theatre
Democracy Park
DOLMABAHÇE
KULAKSIZ
KURTULUS
Inönü Stadium
Maritime Museum
Kulaksız Cemetery
Istanbul Technical University
Taksim Park
Dolmabahçe Palace
Aynalıkavak Palace (Museum)
Republic Memorial Taksim
Atatürk Cultural Centre
Dolmabahçe Mosque
Haliç (Golden Horn)
Recep Tayyip Erdoğan Stadium
Galatasaray Baths
Boğaziçi (Bosporus)
BEYOGLU
Nusretiye Mosque
Şemsi Paşa Mosque
Sultan Selim Mosque
Galata Tower
Istanbul Modern
ÜSKÜDAR
UNKAPANI
Atatürk Br.
KARAKÖY
Galata Br.
Fatih Mosque
Ilıamur Pavilion
Bozdoğan Valeus Aqueduct
Botanical Institute
Rüstem Paşa Mosque
Yeni Mosque
Atatürk Statue
Kız Kulesi (Maiden's Tower)
Süleymaniye Mosque
Egypt (Spice) Market
EMINÖNÜ
Sirkeci Station
Istanbul University
Gülhane Park
Town Hall
Beyazit Tower
Government House
Archaeological Museum
Topkapı Palace
Covered Market
St Irene Museum
Ahmet III Fountain
Selimiye Barracks
KUMKAPI
Museum of Turkish and Islamic Art
Ayasofya Museum (Hagia Sophia)
Obelisk
SULTANAHMET
Sultan Ahmet Mosque (Blue Mosque)
KENNEDY CADDESI
0 M 750
0 YARDS 750

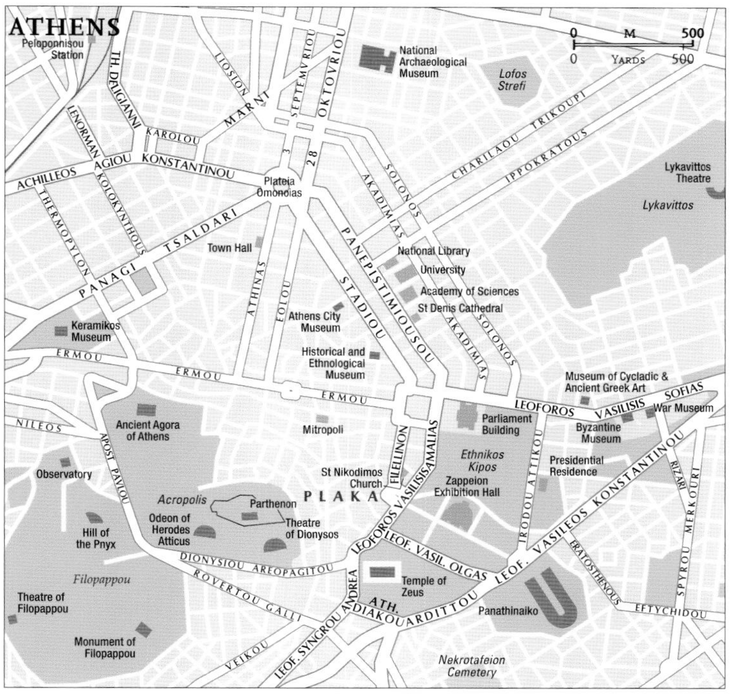
ATHENS
0 M 500
0 Yards 500
Peloponnisou Station
National Archaeological Museum
Lofos Strefi
Lykavittos Theatre
Lykavittos
Plateia Omonias
Town Hall
National Library
University
Academy of Sciences
St Denis Cathedral
Keramikos Museum
Athens City Museum
Historical and Ethnological Museum
Museum of Cycladic & Ancient Greek Art
War Museum
Byzantine Museum
Parliament Building
Ethnikos Kipos
Zappeion Exhibition Hall
Presidential Residence
Ancient Agora of Athens
Mitropoli
St Nikodimos Church
Observatory
PLAKA
Acropolis
Parthenon
Odeon of Herodes Atticus
Theatre of Dionysos
Hill of the Pnyx
Filopappou
Theatre of Filopappou
Monument of Filopappou
Temple of Zeus
Panathinaiko
Nekrotafeion Cemetery
ACHILLEOS
AGIOU KONSTANTINOU
PANAGI TSALDARI
ERMOU
LEOFOROS VASILISIS SOFIAS
PANEPISTIMIOU
STADIOU
AKADIMIAS
OKTOVRIOU
DIONYSIOU AREOPAGITOU
ATH. DIAKOU
VASILEOS KONSTANTINOU

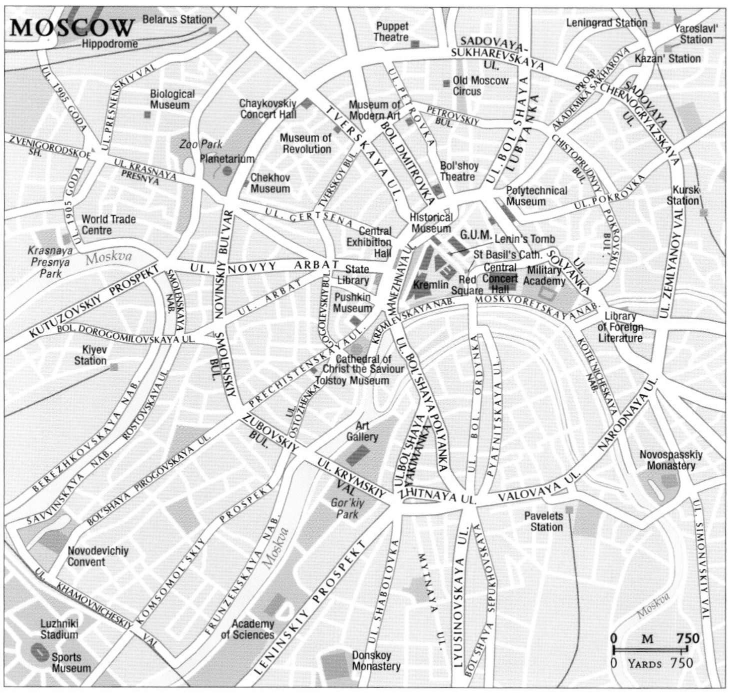
MOSCOW
Belarus Station
Hippodrome
Puppet Theatre
Leningrad Station
Yaroslavl' Station
Kazan' Station
SADOVAYA-SUKHAREVSKAYA UL.
Old Moscow Circus
Biological Museum
Chaykovskiy Concert Hall
Museum of Modern Art
Museum of Revolution
Zoo Park
Planetarium
Chekhov Museum
Bol'shoy Theatre
Polytechnical Museum
Kursk Station
World Trade Centre
Krasnaya Presnya Park
Moskva
Central Exhibition Hall
Historical Museum
G.U.M.
Lenin's Tomb
St Basil's Cath.
Central Concert Hall
Military Academy
Red Square
Kremlin
State Library
Pushkin Museum
NOVYY ARBAT
KUTUZOVSKIY PROSPEKT
Library of Foreign Literature
Kiyev Station
Cathedral of Christ the Saviour
Tolstoy Museum
Art Gallery
Gor'kiy Park
Novospasskiy Monastery
Pavelets Station
Novodevichiy Convent
Luzhniki Stadium
Sports Museum
Academy of Sciences
Donskoy Monastery
LENINSKIY PROSPEKT
0 M 750
0 Yards 750

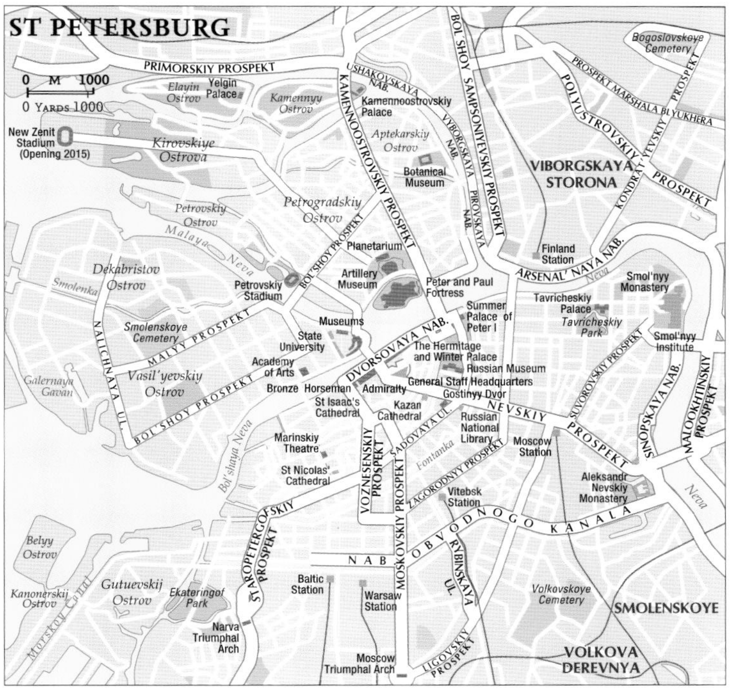
ST PETERSBURG
0 M 1000
0 Yards 1000
PRIMORSKIY PROSPEKT
Yelagin Palace
Elagin Ostrov
Kamennyy Ostrov
Kamennoostrovskiy Palace
New Zenit Stadium (Opening 2015)
Kirovskiye Ostrova
Aptekarskiy Ostrov
Botanical Museum
VIBORGSKAYA STORONA
Bogoslovskoye Cemetery
Petrogradskiy Ostrov
Petrovskiy Ostrov
Malaya Neva
Dekabristov Ostrov
Planetarium
Artillery Museum
Finland Station
Petrovskiy Stadium
Peter and Paul Fortress
Summer Palace of Peter I
Tavricheskiy Palace
Tavricheskiy Park
Smol'nyy Monastery
Smol'nyy Institute
Smolenskoye Cemetery
Museums
State University
The Hermitage and Winter Palace
Russian Museum
General Staff Headquarters
Admiralty
Gostinyy Dvor
Academy of Arts
Vasil'yevskiy Ostrov
Galernaya Gavan
Bronze Horseman
St Isaac's Cathedral
Kazan Cathedral
Russian National Library
Moscow Station
NEVSKIY PROSPEKT
Mariinskiy Theatre
St Nicolas' Cathedral
Vitebsk Station
Aleksandr Nevskiy Monastery
Neva
Belyy Ostrov
Kanonerskii Ostrov
Gutuevskii Ostrov
Ekateringof Park
Baltic Station
Warsaw Station
Narva Triumphal Arch
Volkovskoye Cemetery
SMOLENSKOYE
VOLKOVA DEREVNYA
Moscow Triumphal Arch

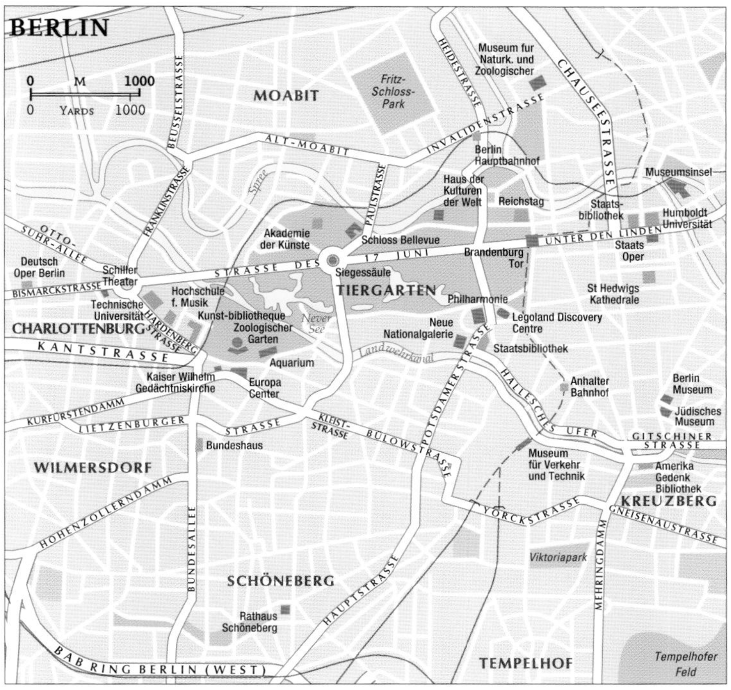
BERLIN
0 M 1000
0 Yards 1000
MOABIT
Museum fur Naturk. und Zoologischer
Fritz-Schloss-Park
ALT-MOABIT
INVALIDENSTRASSE
Berlin Hauptbahnhof
Haus der Kulturen der Welt
Reichstag
Museumsinsel
Staatsbibliothek
Humboldt Universität
Akademie der Künste
Schloss Bellevue
Siegessäule
STRASSE DES 17 JUNI
Brandenburg Tor
UNTER DEN LINDEN
Staats Oper
Deutsch Oper Berlin
Schiller Theater
TIERGARTEN
Hochschule f. Musik
Kunst-bibliotheque
Zoologischer Garten
Technische Universität
Philharmonie
St Hedwigs Kathedrale
Legoland Discovery Centre
Neue Nationalgalerie
Staatsbibliothek
CHARLOTTENBURG
KANTSTRASSE
Aquarium
Kaiser Wilhelm Gedächtniskirche
Europa Center
Anhalter Bahnhof
Berlin Museum
Jüdisches Museum
KURFÜRSTENDAMM
Bundeshaus
Museum für Verkehr und Technik
Amerika Gedenk Bibliothek
KREUZBERG
WILMERSDORF
SCHÖNEBERG
Rathaus Schöneberg
Viktoriapark
BAB RING BERLIN (WEST)
TEMPELHOF
Tempelhofer Feld

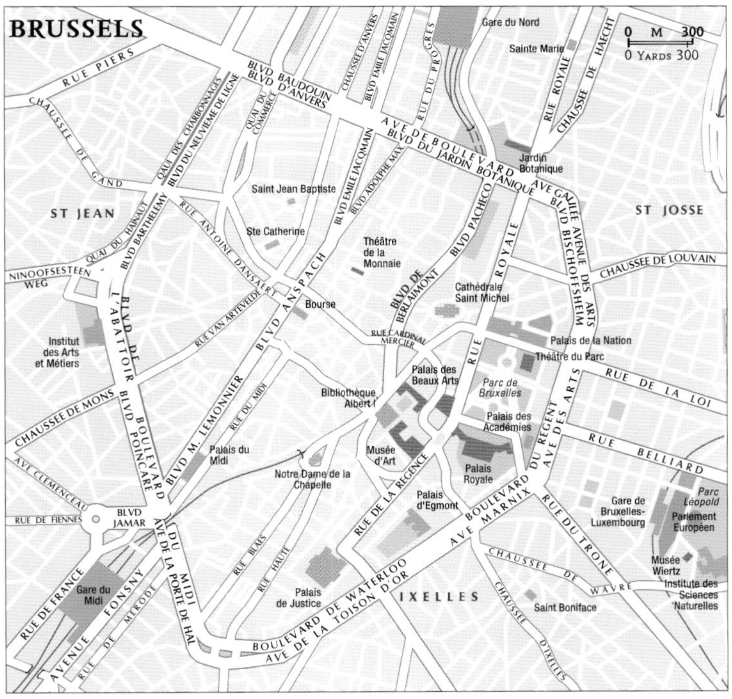
BRUSSELS
Gare du Nord
Sainte Marie
0 M 300
0 Yards 300
RUE PIERS
CHAUSSÉE DE GAND
Jardin Botanique
Saint Jean Baptiste
ST JEAN
ST JOSSE
Ste Catherine
Théâtre de la Monnaie
CHAUSSÉE DE LOUVAIN
Cathédrale Saint Michel
Bourse
Institut des Arts et Métiers
Palais de la Nation
Théâtre du Parc
Palais des Beaux Arts
Parc de Bruxelles
Bibliothèque Albert I
Palais des Académies
RUE DE LA LOI
RUE BELLIARD
CHAUSSÉE DE MONS
Palais du Midi
Musée d'Art
Palais Royale
Notre Dame de la Chapelle
Palais d'Egmont
Gare de Bruxelles-Luxembourg
Parc Léopold
Parlement Européen
Musée Wiertz
Institute des Sciences Naturelles
Gare du Midi
Palais de Justice
IXELLES
Saint Boniface
BOULEVARD DE WATERLOO
AVE DE LA TOISON D'OR

AMSTERDAM
Het IJ
PRINS HENDRIKKADE
DE RUIJTERKADE
Centraal Station
PIET HEINKADE
JORDAAN
Anne Frankhuis
Westerkerk
Museum Amstelkring
Oude Kerk
New Metropolis
Nieuwe Kerk
CENTRUM
Nationaal Monument
Koninklijk Paleis
Waag
Nieuw-Markt
Nederlands Scheepvaart Museum
Madame Tussaud
Amsterdams Historisch Museum
Allard Pierson Museum
Rembrandthuis
Mozes-en Aaronkerk
Stadhuis en Muziektheater
Joods Historisch Museum
Hortus Botanicus
Geologisch Museum
Planetarium
Natura Artis Magistra
Bijbels Museum
AMSTELSTRAAT
Paleis van Justitie
Theater Carré
OOST
Oosterpark
Vondelpark
Rijksmuseum
Van Gogh Museum
Stedelijk Museum
OUD ZUID
STADHOUDERSKADE
0 M 500
0 Yards 500

LONDON
Central London
British Museum
Dominion Theatre
HIGH HOLBORN
Holborn
The Wigmore Hall
Lincoln's Inn Fields
Lincoln's Inn
OXFORD STREET
REGENT STREET
Palladium
CHARING CROSS ROAD
KINGSWAY
Royal Courts of Justice
Soho
Royal Opera House
Theatre Royal
ALDWYCH
STRAND
NEW BOND STREET
SHAFTESBURY AVE
London Transport Museum
King's College
Royal Academy of Arts
PICCADILLY CIRCUS
National Gallery
Somerset House
HAYMARKET
WATERLOO BR
Mayfair
PICCADILLY
TRAFALGAR SQUARE
Charing Cross Station
EMBANKMENT
Royal National Theatre
St James's
Admiralty Arch
Queen Elizabeth Hall
ST JAMES'S ST
PALL MALL
HUNGERFORD BRIDGE
Marlborough House
Royal Festival Hall
St James's Palace
THE MALL
Government Buildings
EDF Energy London Eye
WATERLOO RD
Green Park
WHITEHALL
VICTORIA
Thames
Waterloo Station
St James's Park
DOWNING ST
County Hall
CONSTITUTION HILL
PARLIAMENT STREET
London Aquarium
Treasury
Buckingham Palace
BIRDCAGE WALK
PARLIAMENT SQUARE
WESTMINSTER BR
LAMBETH
Big Ben
WESTMINSTER BRIDGE ROAD
GROSVENOR PLACE
WESTMINSTER
Houses of Parliament
Westminster Abbey
Lambeth Palace Gardens
VICTORIA STREET
0 M 500
0 YARDS 500
Victoria Station
Westminster Cathedral
Lambeth Palace
Hatch End
Pinner Park
Belmont
Burnt Oak
RAF Museums
A1
GREAT N. WAY
Holders Hill
EDGWARE ROAD
Queensbury
Kingsbury
Hendon
Bayhurst Wood Country Park
Golders Green
HENDON
Fryent Country Park
M1
FRYENT WAY
Northwick Park
Brent Reservoir
A41
NORTH CIRCULAR ROAD
Wembley Park
Dollis Hill
Ickenham
BRENT
Cricklewood
Wembley Arena
Wembley Stadium
Gladstone Park
Wembley
Willesden
A406
Sunbury Golf Course
EALING ROAD
Willesden Green
North Hillingdon
Alperton
Harlesden
Kilburn
Perivale
Grand Union Canal
Park Royal
HARROW ROAD
Hillingdon
Ealing Golf Course
North Acton
WESTERN AVENUE
Wormwood Scrubs
Hayes End
HANGER LANE
EALING
Ealing
North Kensington
Brent
WESTWAY
A40
Notting Hill
A3220
Hayes
Acton
East Acton
Yiewsley
Shepherd's Bush
Southall
THE VALE
A402
Hanwell
Holland Park
Gunnersbury
HAMMERSMITH
West Drayton
Norwood Green
Olympia
Grand Union Canal
Gunnersbury Park
M4
AND FULHAM
CHISWICK HIGH ROAD
A4
North Hyde
Earls Court Exhibition Centre
Chiswick
Hammersmith Bridge
Earls Court
Osterley Park
Brentford
Castelnau
Harlington
Chiswick House
BATH ROAD
Heston
Osterley
Royal Botanic Gardens Kew
Syon House
A316
WWT London Wetland Centre
Football Stadium
GREAT WEST ROAD
Cranford
KEW ROAD
Syon Park
FULHAM ROAD
Barnes
Heathrow Airport (London)
Hounslow West
Mortlake
Isleworth
A30
Putney Bridge
SOUTH CIRCULAR ROAD
A205
Hounslow
GREAT SOUTH WEST ROAD
Richmond
ROEHAMPTON LANE
Putney
HOUNSLOW
Hounslow Heath
Rugby Ground
Putney Heath
Southfields
Stanwell
East Bedfont
RICHMOND UPON
Twickenham
Thames
Richmond
Feltham
Crane
THAMES
Park
A3
All England Lawn Tennis and Croquet Club
Wimbledon Common
Ashford
Hanworth
Wimbledon Park
Teddington
Coombe Hill Golf Course
KINGSTON HILL
KINGSTON
Wimbledon
A308
Queen Mary Reservoir
Kempton Park Racecourse
Bushy Park
COOMBE LANE
KINGSTON ROAD
Hampton
BYPASS
Norbiton
Sunbury
New Malden
Molesey Reservoirs
M3
Hampton Court Palace
Hampton Court Park
Kingston Upon Thames
Bushy Mead
West Molesey
East Molesey
A307
KINGSTON UPON THAMES
West Barnes
Morden Park
Baitul Futuh Mosque
Shepperton
Queen Elizabeth II Reservoir
Island Barn Reservoir
Mole
A309
Thames Ditton
Motspur Park
A24
Surbiton
0 M 800
0 YARDS 800
Long Ditton
Walton-on-Thames
Old Malden

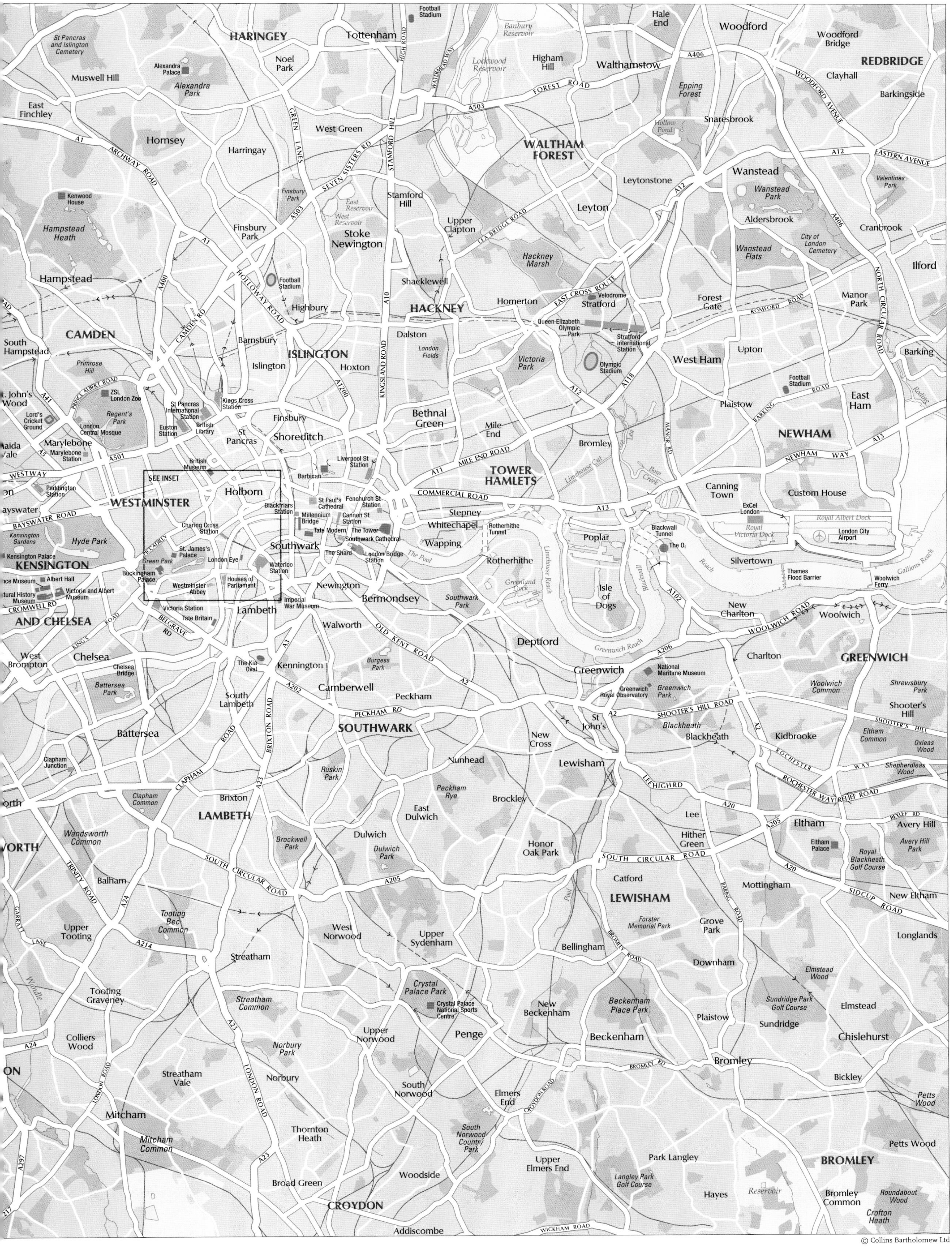
HARINGEY
Tottenham
Football Stadium
Hale End
Woodford
Banbury Reservoir
St Pancras and Islington Cemetery
Alexandra Palace
Noel Park
Lockwood Reservoir
Higham Hill
Walthamstow
A406
Woodford Bridge
REDBRIDGE
Muswell Hill
Alexandra Park
HIGH ROAD
WALTHAMSTOW WAY
FOREST ROAD
Epping Forest
Clayhall
Barkingside
East Finchley
GREEN LANES
A503
West Green
STAMFORD HILL
Hollow Pond
Snaresbrook
WOODFORD AVENUE
A1
ARCHWAY ROAD
Hornsey
Harringay
SEVEN SISTERS RD
WALTHAM FOREST
A12
EASTERN AVENUE
Wanstead
Leytonstone
Valentines Park
Kenwood House
Finsbury Park
East Reservoir
West Reservoir
Stamford Hill
Wanstead Park
Hampstead Heath
Finsbury Park
Stoke Newington
Upper Clapton
LEA BRIDGE ROAD
Leyton
Aldersbrook
A406
Cranbrook
City of London Cemetery
Wanstead Flats
Hackney Marsh
Ilford
Hampstead
A400
HOLLOWAY ROAD
Football Stadium
A10
Shacklewell
EAST CROSS ROUTE
Velodrome
Stratford
Forest Gate
ROMFORD ROAD
Manor Park
NORTH CIRCULAR ROAD
CAMDEN RD
Highbury
HACKNEY
Homerton
CAMDEN
Queen Elizabeth Olympic Park
Stratford International Station
South Hampstead
Barnsbury
Dalston
ISLINGTON
London Fields
Victoria Park
Olympic Stadium
West Ham
Upton
Barking
Primrose Hill
Islington
Hoxton
KINGSLAND ROAD
A1200
A12
A118
Football Stadium
PRINCE ALBERT ROAD
ZSL London Zoo
St. John's Wood
A41
Lord's Cricket Ground
Regent's Park
London Central Mosque
St Pancras International Station
Kings Cross Station
Euston Station
British Library
Finsbury
Bethnal Green
Plaistow
BARKING ROAD
East Ham
Roding
Maida Vale
Marylebone
Marylebone Station
St Pancras
Shoreditch
Mile End
Bromley
MANOR RD
Lea
NEWHAM
A5
A501
British Museum
Liverpool St Station
MILE END ROAD
A11
TOWER HAMLETS
Limehouse Cut
Bow Creek
NEWHAM WAY
A13
WESTWAY
Paddington Station
SEE INSET
Barbican
COMMERCIAL ROAD
Canning Town
Custom House
Bayswater
BAYSWATER ROAD
WESTMINSTER
Holborn
Blackfriars Station
St Paul's Cathedral
Fenchurch St Station
A13
ExCel London
Royal Albert Dock
Millennium Bridge
Cannon St Station
Stepney
Kensington Gardens
Charing Cross Station
Tate Modern
The Tower
Whitechapel
Rotherhithe Tunnel
Blackwall Tunnel
Poplar
Royal Victoria Dock
London City Airport
Hyde Park
PICCADILLY
St. James's Palace
Southwark
Southwark Cathedral
Wapping
The O2
Kensington Palace
Green Park
London Eye
The Shard
London Bridge Station
The Pool
Limehouse Reach
Reach
Silvertown
Gallions Reach
KENSINGTON
Buckingham Palace
Waterloo Station
Rotherhithe
Thames Flood Barrier
Woolwich Ferry
Science Museum
Albert Hall
Westminster Abbey
Houses of Parliament
Newington
Greenland Dock
Blackwall
Isle of Dogs
Natural History Museum
Victoria and Albert Museum
Imperial War Museum
Bermondsey
Southwark Park
A102
New Charlton
CROMWELL RD
Victoria Station
Lambeth
Woolwich
AND CHELSEA
Tate Britain
Walworth
OLD KENT ROAD
WOOLWICH ROAD
BELGRAVE RD
KING'S ROAD
Deptford
Greenwich Reach
A206
West Brompton
Chelsea
The Kia Oval
A3
Kennington
Burgess Park
Greenwich
National Maritime Museum
Charlton
GREENWICH
Chelsea Bridge
A2
Battersea Park
Camberwell
A202
Greenwich Royal Observatory
Greenwich Park
Woolwich Common
Shrewsbury Park
South Lambeth
Peckham
PECKHAM RD
A2
St John's
SHOOTER'S HILL ROAD
Shooter's Hill
SHOOTER'S HILL
SOUTHWARK
Blackheath
Battersea
New Cross
Blackheath
Kidbrooke
Eltham Common
Oxleas Wood
BRIXTON ROAD
Clapham Junction
Ruskin Park
Nunhead
Lewisham
ROCHESTER
WAY
Shepherdleas Wood
CLAPHAM ROAD
Peckham Rye
ROCHESTER WAY RELIEF ROAD
Clapham Common
Brixton
A23
Brockley
LEE HIGH RD
A20
East Dulwich
Lee
BEXLEY RD
LAMBETH
Eltham
Avery Hill
A205
Wandsworth Common
Brockwell Park
Dulwich
Honor Oak Park
Hither Green
Eltham Palace
Avery Hill Park
Royal Blackheath Golf Course
SOUTH CIRCULAR ROAD
Dulwich Park
SOUTH CIRCULAR ROAD
A20
TRINITY ROAD
Balham
A205
Catford
BARING ROAD
Mottingham
SIDCUP ROAD
New Eltham
LEWISHAM
A24
Tooting Bec Common
Pool
GARRATT LANE
Upper Tooting
West Norwood
Upper Sydenham
Forster Memorial Park
Grove Park
Longlands
A214
BROMLEY ROAD
Bellingham
Streatham
Downham
Wandle
Elmstead Wood
Tooting Graveney
Crystal Palace Park
Streatham Common
Crystal Palace National Sports Centre
New Beckenham
Beckenham Place Park
Sundridge Park Golf Course
Elmstead
Plaistow
A23
Sundridge
Colliers Wood
Upper Norwood
Penge
Beckenham
Chislehurst
A24
Norbury Park
BROMLEY RD
Bromley
Streatham Vale
LONDON ROAD
Norbury
LONDON ROAD
Bickley
South Norwood
Elmers End
CROYDON ROAD
Petts Wood
Mitcham
Thornton Heath
South Norwood Country Park
Mitcham Common
Petts Wood
A297
A23
Upper Elmers End
Park Langley
BROMLEY
Woodside
Langley Park Golf Course
Broad Green
Hayes
Reservoir
Bromley Common
Roundabout Wood
CROYDON
Crofton Heath
Addiscombe
WICKHAM ROAD

PARIS
Boisemont
Neuville-s.-Oise
Éragny
Pierrelaye
Beauchamp
St-Leu-la-Forêt
Montlignon
Andilly
Conflans-Ste-Honorine
Herblay
Le Plessis-Bouchard
Eaubonne
Soisy-sous-Montmorency
Montmorency
Maurecourt
Montigny-lès-Cormeilles
Franconville
Ermont
Port-Maron
Verneuil-s.-Seine
Triel-s.-Seine
Chanteloup-les-Vignes
Andrésy
Cormeilles-en-Parisis
Sannois
St-Gratien
Enghien-les-Bains
Vernouillet
Forêt de St-Germain
Achères
Carrières-sous-Poissy
Médan
Maisons-Laffitte
Argenteuil
Epinay-sur-Seine
Sartrouville
Villennes-s.-Seine
Poissy
Le Mesnil-le-Roi
Gennevilliers
Villeneuve-la-Garenne
Orgeval
Houilles
Bezons
Colombes
Bois-Colombes
Asnières-s.-Seine
Béthemont
Montesson
Carrières-s.-Seine
La Garenne-Colombes
Clichy
Chambourcy
Aigremont
Le Vésinet
Chatou
Courbevoie
Levallois-Perret
St-Germain-en-Laye
Le Pecq
NANTERRE
Neuilly-s.-Seine
Fourqueux
Mareil-Marly
Le Port-Marly
Croissy-s.-Seine
Rueil-Malmaison
Puteaux
Feucherolles
St-Nom-la-Bretèche
L'Étang-la-Ville
Marly-le-Roi
Bougival
HAUTS-DE-SEINE
Suresnes
Louveciennes
La Celle-St-Cloud
Garches
St-Cloud
Boulogne
Auteuil
Chavenay
Noisy-le-Roi
Bailly
Vaucresson
Villepreux
Rocquencourt
Boulogne-Billancourt
Rennemoulin
YVELINES
Le Chesnay
Marnes-la-Coquette
Ville-d'Avray
Vanves
Malakoff
Issy-les-Moulineaux
Les Clayes-sous-Bois
Fontenay-le-Fleury
Sèvres
Montrouge
VERSAILLES
Meudon
Bois d'Arcy
St-Cyr-l'École
Chaville
Viroflay
Châtillon
Clamart
Arcueil
Bagneux
Fontenay-aux-Roses
Vélizy-Villacoublay
Le Plessis-Robinson
Trappes
Montigny-le-Bretonneux
St Quentin-en-Yvelines
Guyancourt
Buc
Jouy-en-Josas
Sceaux
Châtenay-Malabry
Voisins-le-Bretonneux
Les Loges-en-Josas
Bièvres
Verrières-le-Buisson
Antony
Le Mesnil-St-Denis
Magny-les-Hameaux
Toussus-le-Noble
Châteaufort
Igny
Massy
St-Lambert
Saclay
Milon-la-Chapelle
Villiers-le-Bâcle
Palaiseau
Chevreuse
Rhodon
Chevincourt
St-Aubin
Champlan
0 M 1200
0 Yards 1200

Piscop
Chauffour
Villiers-le-Bel
le Puits-les Carreaux
la-Marlière
Cité de la Fauconnière
St-Brice-sous-Forêt
Miraville
les Marronniers
AL-D'OISE
les Thioux
Sarcelles
Groslay
les Alluets
le Mont-de-Gif
la Madeleine
Arnouville-lès-Gonesse
les Hauts-du-Roi
Bel-Air
Montmagny
Barrage
Cité Bousselin
Bonneuil-en-France
Deuil-la-Barre
la Butte-Pinson
Pierrefitte-s.-Seine
Garges-lès-Gonesse
les Pieds-Humides
Aéroport de Paris-le-Bourget
Villetaneuse
le Colombier
la Cerisaie
le Parc
Pont-Yblon
Stains
le Clos-St-Lazare
Dugny
Musée de l'Air et de l'Espace
le Globe
Parc départemental de la Courneuve
la Mutualité
St-Denis
la Comète
l'Economie
Cathédrale
les Six-Routes
le Bourget
le Château
Cité Jardin
Nonneville
Fort de l'Est
la Courneuve
Paris-Campagne
les Quatre-Routes
Drancy
le Petit-Groslay
la Muette
Montfort
Aubervilliers
Fort d'Aubervilliers
BOBIGNY
Nouveau-Village
la Nove-Caillet
la Poudrette
les Pavillons-sous-Bois
Cimetière parisien de St-Ouen
la Plaine-St-Denis
St Ouen
Cimetière parisien de Pantin-Bobigny
les Quatre-Chemins
Pantin
Canal de l'Ourcq
SEINE
ST-DENIS
Vieux-Pays
la Talmouse
le Thillay
Roissy-en France
Vaudherland
Gonesse
Patte-d'Oie de Gonesse
le Mesnil-Amelot
Aéroport Charles-de-Gaulle
Thieux
les Trois-Villes
Compans
Tremblay-Vieux-Pays
Circuit moto
Parc des expositions
Villepinte
Mitry-Mory
Mory
les Acacias
Mitry-le-Neuf
Gressy
le Petit-Vert-Galant
Tremblay-en-France
Clos de Montceleux
Sevran
la Rose-des-Vents
le Gros-Saule
Ambourget
Le Blanc-Mesnil
Aulnay-Sous-Bois
Parc forestier de Sevran
le Vert Galant
Villeparisis
Morfonde
Bois de Claye
la Rosée
Souilly
la Closerie
Mauperthuis
le Bois-Fleuri
les Petits Bois
Freinville
Vaujours
Bois de Bernouille
Coubron
Courtry
Villevaude
Bois de Montjay
Livry-Gargan
les Couronnes
le Coteau
le Pin
Clichy-sous-Bois
Parc forestier de Bondy
Montjay-la-Tour
la Bazoche
Bondy
le Raincy
la Vallée-des-Angers
les Coudreaux
Montfermeil
Aérodrome Chelles-le-Pin
Chantereine
Franceville
Brou-s.-Chantereine
Bois de Brou
la Pomponnette
Pomponne
la Villeneuve
Noisy-le-Sec
Merlan
Fort de Romainville
Romainville
Le Pré-St-Gervais
Cité des Sciences et de l'Industrie
la Chapelle
Gare du Nord
Montmartre
Sacré-Coeur
Parc des Buttes Chaumont
Belleville
Gare de l'Est
Synagogue de Paris
PARIS
Les Lilas
Fort de Noisy
les Marnaudes
Villemomble
Gagny
la Boissière
Rosny-sous-Bois
le Plateau-d'Avron
Maison-Blanche
Chelles
Vaires-Triage
St-Thibault-des-Vignes
Place de la République
Ménilmontant
Malassis
les Sept-Chemins
St-Antoine
Fort de Rosny
Neuilly-Plaisance
Pointe-de-Gournay
Canal de Chelles
Vaires-s.-Marne
Bagnolet
Centre G. Pompidou
Palais Royal
Hôtel de Ville
Cimetière du Père-Lachaise
Charonne
Montreuil
Tillemont
la Maltournée
Gournay-s.-Marne
Neuilly-s.-Marne
Parc de Champs
Parc de Noisiel
Noisiel
Torcy
Place de la Bastille
Place de la Nation
Notre-Dame
Panthéon
Vincennes
Fontenay-sous-Bois
Fort de Nogent
les Rigollots
Parc de Villeflix
les Pyramides
Val-Maubuée
St-Germain-des-Noyers
Palais du Luxembourg
Jardin des Plantes
Gare d'Austerlitz
Gare de Lyon
Reuilly
Bry-s.-Marne
Noisy-le-Grand
Champs-s.-Marne
Marne-la-Vallée
Hameau de Rentilly
Grande Mosquée de Paris
Gare de Paris-Bercy
Bercy
Fort de Vincennes
St-Mande
Château de Vincennes
Parc floral
Parc Zoologique
Bois de Vincennes
Lac des Minimes
Le Perreux-s.-Marne
Nogent-s.-Marne
Pave-Neuf
la Butte-Verte
les Hautes-Noues
les Richardets
Bois de la Grange
Lognes
Collégien
Gare Denfert Rochereau
Place d'Italie
Bibliothèque National de France
Lac Daumesnil
Hippodrome
le Tremblay
Villiers-s.-Marne
les Yvris
Malnoue
Bois du Boulay
Aérodrome Lognes-Emerainville
Étang de Croissy
Cité Universitaire
Charenton-le-Pont
St-Maurice
Joinville-le-Pont
Champigny-sur-Marne
la Fourchette
le Bois-Gaumont
le Kremlin-Bicêtre
Gentilly
Fort de Bicêtre
Cimetière parisien d'Ivry
Ivry-s.-Seine
Cité des Baux
Maisons-Alfort
Fort de Charenton
Pasteur
Fort d'Ivry
Alfortville
le Parc
St-Maur-des-Fossés
les Monts Cuchets
les Malassis
Mons-Ivry
Villejuif
les Hautes-Bruyères
le Moulin-de-Saquet
Vitry-s.-Seine
Créteil
la Varenne-St-Hilaire
la Pie
Marne
les Vaux-de-Rome
Petit-Vitry
le Closeau
Mont-Mesly
L'Haÿ-les-Roses
VAL-DE-MARNE
Chevilly-Larue
Cité du Moulin-Vert
les Gondoles
Parc municipal des sports
Bonneuil-sur-Marne
les Petits-Carreaux
Marché d'intérêt national de Rungis
Cimetière parisien de Thiais
Thiais
Choisy-le-Roi
Parc dépt. des sports
Val Pompadour
Brévannes
Grignon
les Antes
les Graviers
Valenton
Limeil-Brévannes
Rungis
Orly
le Fer-à-Cheval
la Faisanderie
Villeneuve-le-Roi
le Bois-Matar
Château de la Grange
Bois de la Grange
Villeneuve-St-Georges
Ablon-s.-Seine
Aéroport de Paris-Orly
Cité de l'Air
Crosne
le Maroc
le Cottage
Athis-Mons
Paray-Vieille-Poste
Yerres
le Bois-Prie-Dieu
Villecresnes
les Mardelles
Cercay
Servon
Chevry-Cossigny
Beauverger
Bois d'Attilly
la Doutre
Ozoir-la-Ferrière
l'Avenir de Roissy
le Prieuré
Parc de Croissy
Forêt de Ferrières
Place de Lamirault
Central Paris
Bibliothèque Nationale de France (Richelieu)
Palais de la Bourse
LES HALLES
Porte St-Denis
Porte St-Martin
Conservatoire National des Arts et Métiers
Place de la République
Planète Magique
Saint Roch
Saint Nicolas des Champs
Palais Royal
Saint Eustache
Musée Instruments de Musique Mécanique
Jardin des Tuileries
Arc de Triomphe du Carrousel
Musée du Louvre
Palais du Louvre
Forum des Halles
Archives Nationales
Musée Picasso
Centre Georges Pompidou
Seine
Musée d'Orsay
Théâtre du Châtelet
Tour St-Jacques
Musée Cognacq-Jay
Musée Carnavalet
École des Beaux Arts
Institut de France
Hôtel des Monnaies
Pont Neuf
Palais de Justice
Conciergerie
Sainte-Chapelle
Théâtre de la Ville
Hôtel de Ville
BASTILLE
ST-GERMAIN DES PRÉS
Musée Delacroix
Saint Germain des Prés
ÎLE DE LA CITÉ
Saint Gervais
Saint-Paul St-Louis
Notre-Dame
ÎLE ST-LOUIS
Saint-Séverin
St-Louis en l'Île
Bibliothèque de l'Arsenal
Saint Sulpice
Théâtre Europe Odéon
Musée de Cluny
Pont de Sully
Institut du Monde Arabe
Palais du Luxembourg
Sorbonne
QUARTIER LATIN
Universités de Paris VI et VII
Pierre et Marie Curie
Saint Etienne du Mont
Panthéon
Jardin du Luxembourg
0 M 500
0 YARDS 500

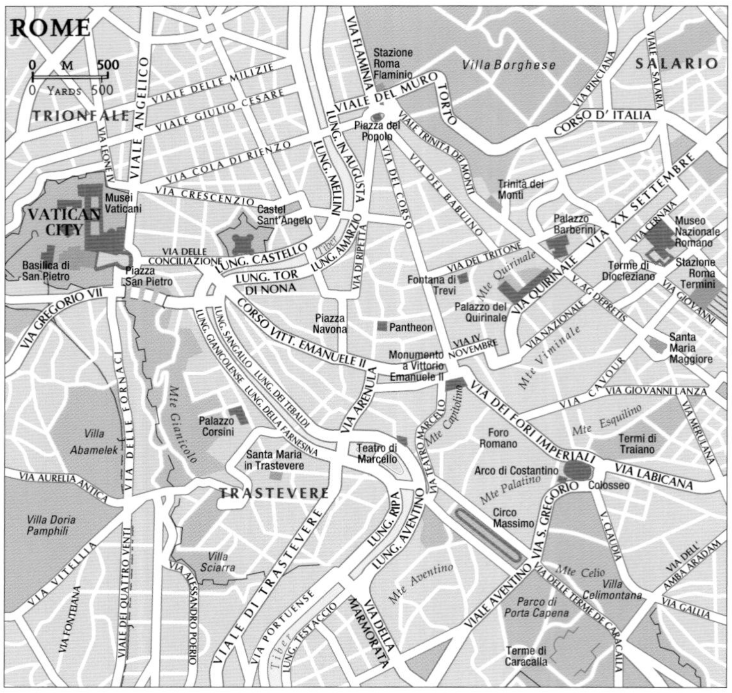
ROME
0 M 500
0 YARDS 500
TRIONFALE
SALARIO
VATICAN CITY
Musei Vaticani
Basilica di San Pietro
Piazza San Pietro
Castel Sant'Angelo
Stazione Roma Flaminio
Villa Borghese
Piazza del Popolo
Trinità dei Monti
Palazzo Barberini
Museo Nazionale Romano
Stazione Roma Termini
Terme di Diocleziano
Fontana di Trevi
Palazzo del Quirinale
Mte Quirinale
Mte Viminale
Santa Maria Maggiore
Piazza Navona
Pantheon
Monumento a Vittorio Emanuele II
Palazzo Corsini
Mte Gianicolo
Villa Abamelek
Santa Maria in Trastevere
TRASTEVERE
Teatro di Marcello
Mte Capitolino
Foro Romano
Mte Esquilino
Termi di Traiano
Arco di Costantino
Colosseo
Mte Palatino
Circo Massimo
Villa Doria Pamphili
Villa Sciarra
Mte Aventino
Mte Celio
Villa Celimontana
Parco di Porta Capena
Terme di Caracalla
VIALE DEL MURO TORTO
CORSO D' ITALIA
VIA XX SETTEMBRE
VIA CRESCENZIO
VIA COLA DI RIENZO
VIALE GIULIO CESARE
VIALE DELLE MILIZIE
VIALE ANGELICO
VIA DELLA CONCILIAZIONE
LUNG. CASTELLO
LUNG. TOR DI NONA
CORSO VITT. EMANUELE II
VIA GREGORIO VII
VIA AURELIA ANTICA
VIA DEL CORSO
VIA DEL BABUINO
VIA NAZIONALE
VIA QUIRINALE
VIA CAVOUR
VIA GIOVANNI LANZA
VIA DEI FORI IMPERIALI
VIA LABICANA
VIA ARENULA
VIALE DI TRASTEVERE
VIA PORTUENSE
LUNG. AVENTINO
VIALE AVENTINO
VIA SAN GREGORIO
VIA MARMORATA
VIA DELLA MARMORATA
VIALE DELLE TERME DI CARACALLA
VIA GALLIA
VIA VITELLIA
VIA FONTEIANA
VIA DELLE FORNACI
VIALE DEI QUATTRO VENTI
VIA ALESSANDRO POERIO
LUNG. TESTACCIO
Tevere

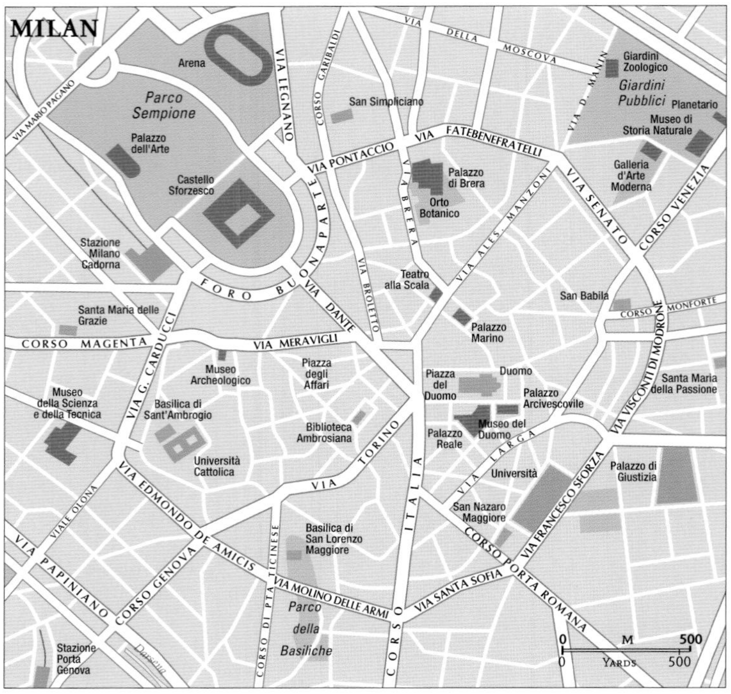
MILAN
Arena
Parco Sempione
Palazzo dell'Arte
Castello Sforzesco
San Simpliciano
Giardini Zoologico
Giardini Pubblici
Planetario
Museo di Storia Naturale
Galleria d'Arte Moderna
Palazzo di Brera
Orto Botanico
Stazione Milano Cadorna
Teatro alla Scala
San Babila
Palazzo Marino
Santa Maria delle Grazie
Museo Archeologico
Piazza degli Affari
Duomo
Piazza del Duomo
Palazzo Arcivescovile
Santa Maria della Passione
Museo della Scienza e della Tecnica
Basilica di Sant'Ambrogio
Biblioteca Ambrosiana
Museo del Duomo
Palazzo Reale
Università Cattolica
Università
Palazzo di Giustizia
San Nazaro Maggiore
Basilica di San Lorenzo Maggiore
Parco della Basiliche
Stazione Porta Genova
VIA LEGNANO
VIA MOSCOVA
VIA PONTACCIO
VIA FATEBENEFRATELLI
VIA SENATO
CORSO VENEZIA
FORO BUONAPARTE
VIA DANTE
CORSO MAGENTA
VIA MERAVIGLI
VIA G. CARDUCCI
VIA TORINO
CORSO MONFORTE
VIALE OLONA
VIA EDMONDO DE AMICIS
VIA PAPINIANO
CORSO GENOVA
CORSO ITALIA
VIA MOLINO DELLE ARMI
VIA SANTA SOFIA
CORSO PORTA ROMANA
VIA FRANCESCO SFORZA
VIA VISCONTI DI MODRONE
0 M 500
0 YARDS 500

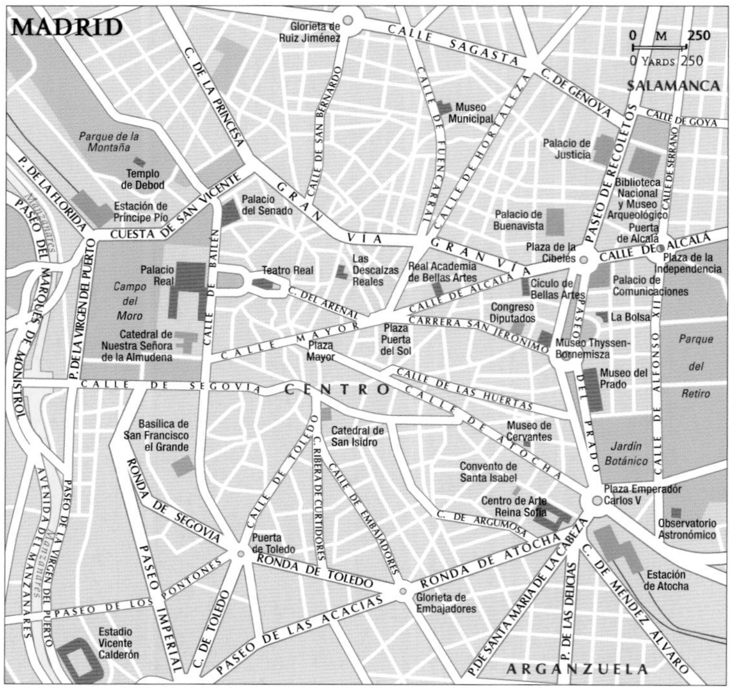
MADRID
0 M 250
0 YARDS 250
Glorieta de Ruiz Jiménez
CALLE SAGASTA
SALAMANCA
C. DE GÉNOVA
CALLE DE GOYA
Museo Municipal
Palacio de Justicia
Parque de la Montaña
Templo de Debod
Estación de Príncipe Pío
Palacio del Senado
Biblioteca Nacional y Museo Arqueológico
Puerta de Alcalá
Palacio de Buenavista
Plaza de la Cibeles
Plaza de la Independencia
CUESTA DE SAN VICENTE
GRAN VÍA
CALLE DE ALCALÁ
Palacio Real
Campo del Moro
Teatro Real
Las Descalzas Reales
Real Academia de Bellas Artes
Círculo de Bellas Artes
Palacio de Comunicaciones
La Bolsa
Congreso Diputados
Museo Thyssen-Bornemisza
Plaza Puerta del Sol
Plaza Mayor
Catedral de Nuestra Señora de la Almudena
CALLE MAYOR
CARRERA SAN JERÓNIMO
Museo del Prado
Parque del Retiro
CALLE DE SEGOVIA
CENTRO
CALLE DE LAS HUERTAS
Basílica de San Francisco el Grande
Catedral de San Isidro
Museo de Cervantes
Convento de Santa Isabel
Jardín Botánico
Centro de Arte Reina Sofía
Plaza Emperador Carlos V
Observatorio Astronómico
Puerta de Toledo
RONDA DE SEGOVIA
RONDA DE TOLEDO
RONDA DE ATOCHA
Estación de Atocha
Glorieta de Embajadores
PASEO DE LAS ACACIAS
PASEO IMPERIAL
Estadio Vicente Calderón
ARGANZUELA
PASEO DEL PRADO
PASEO DE RECOLETOS
C. DE LA PRINCESA
P. DE LA FLORIDA
PASEO DE LA VIRGEN DEL PUERTO
C. DE TOLEDO
C. DE MÉNDEZ ÁLVARO
P. DE LAS DELICIAS
P. DE SANTA MARÍA DE LA CABEZA

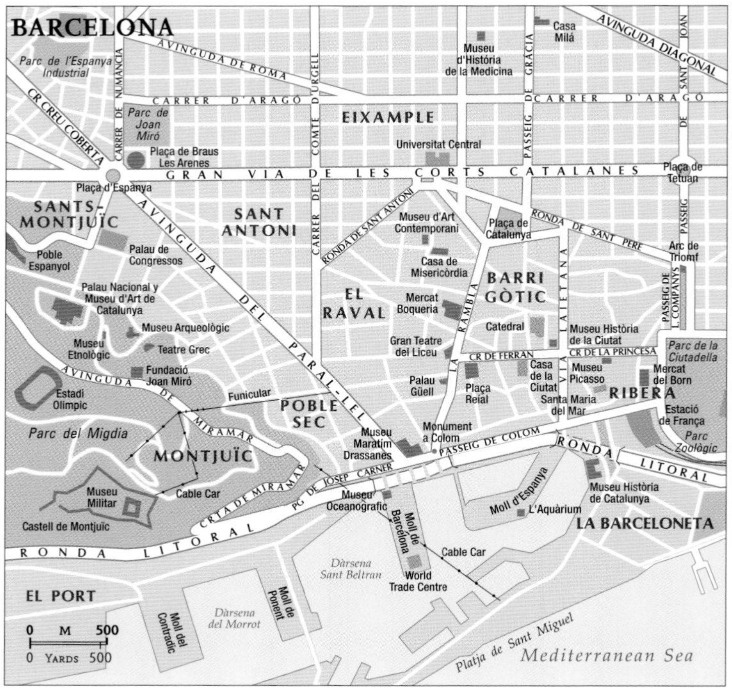
BARCELONA
Casa Milà
AVINGUDA DIAGONAL
Museu d'Història de la Medicina
AVINGUDA DE ROMA
Parc de l'Espanya Industrial
CARRER D'ARAGÓ
EIXAMPLE
Parc de Joan Miró
Plaça de Braus Les Arenes
Universitat Central
Plaça d'Espanya
GRAN VIA DE LES CORTS CATALANES
Plaça de Tetuan
SANTS-MONTJUÏC
SANT ANTONI
Museu d'Art Contemporani
Plaça de Catalunya
RONDA DE SANT PERE
Arc de Triomf
Poble Espanyol
Palau de Congressos
Casa de Misericòrdia
BARRI GÒTIC
EL RAVAL
Palau Nacional y Museu d'Art de Catalunya
Mercat Boqueria
Museu Arqueològic
Catedral
Museu Història de la Ciutat
Teatre Grec
Gran Teatre del Liceu
Museu Etnològic
Fundació Joan Miró
Palau Güell
Casa de la Ciutat
Museu Picasso
Parc de la Ciutadella
Mercat del Born
Estadi Olímpic
Funicular
POBLE SEC
Plaça Reial
Santa Maria del Mar
RIBERA
Estació de França
Parc Zoològic
Parc del Migdia
MONTJUÏC
Museu Marítim Drassanes
Monument a Colom
PASSEIG DE COLOM
RONDA LITORAL
Museu Militar
Cable Car
Museu Oceanogràfic
Moll d'Espanya
L'Aquàrium
Museu Història de Catalunya
Castell de Montjuïc
LA BARCELONETA
EL PORT
Dàrsena Sant Beltran
World Trade Centre
Moll del Contradic
Dàrsena del Morrot
Moll de Ponent
Platja de Sant Miquel
Mediterranean Sea
0 M 500
0 YARDS 500

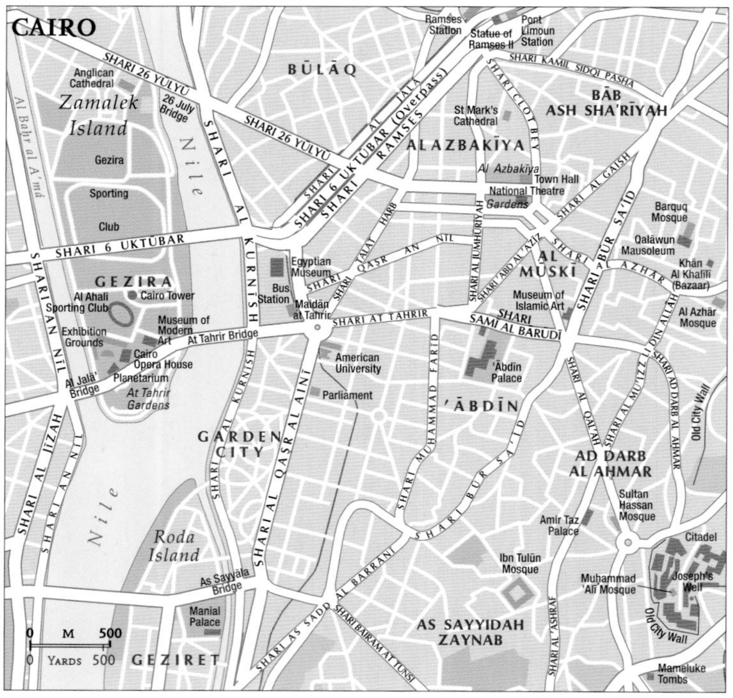
CAIRO
Ramses Station
Statue of Ramses II
Pont Limoun Station
BŪLĀQ
Anglican Cathedral
Zamalek Island
26 July Bridge
SHARI 26 YULYU
Al Bahr al A'mā
Nile
BĀB ASH SHA'RIYAH
St Mark's Cathedral
ALAZBAKĪYA
Gezira
Sporting Club
Al Azbakīya Gardens
Town Hall
National Theatre
Barquq Mosque
Qalāwūn Mausoleum
SHARI 6 UKTUBAR
GEZIRA
Al Ahali Sporting Club
Cairo Tower
Egyptian Museum
Bus Station
Maidān at Tahrīr
AL MUSKI
Khān Al Khalīlī (Bazaar)
Museum of Islamic Art
Al Azhar Mosque
Exhibition Grounds
Museum of Modern Art
At Tahrir Bridge
Cairo Opera House
Planetarium
At Tahrir Gardens
Al Jalā' Bridge
American University
Parliament
'Ābdīn Palace
'ĀBDĪN
GARDEN CITY
AD DARB AL AHMAR
Sultan Hassan Mosque
Amir Taz Palace
Citadel
Roda Island
Ibn Tulūn Mosque
Muhammad 'Ali Mosque
Joseph's Well
As Sayyala Bridge
Manial Palace
AS SAYYIDAH ZAYNAB
Old City Wall
Mameluke Tombs
GEZIRET
SHARI AL KURNISH
SHARI AL QASR AL AINI
SHARI RAMSES
SHARI AT TAHRIR
SHARI BUR SA'ID
SHARI AL JIZAH
0 M 500
0 YARDS 500

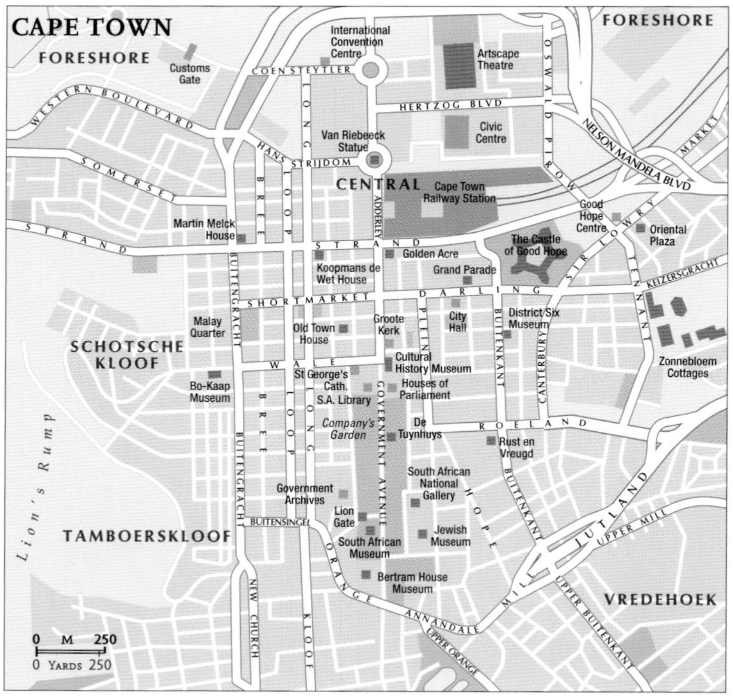
CAPE TOWN
FORESHORE
International Convention Centre
Customs Gate
Artscape Theatre
HERTZOG BLVD
Civic Centre
WESTERN BOULEVARD
Van Riebeeck Statue
NELSON MANDELA BLVD
CENTRAL
Cape Town Railway Station
Good Hope Centre
Oriental Plaza
Martin Melck House
STRAND
The Castle of Good Hope
Golden Acre
Grand Parade
Koopmans de Wet House
KEIZERSGRACHT
SHORTMARKET
DARLING
Malay Quarter
Old Town House
Groote Kerk
City Hall
District Six Museum
SCHOTSCHE KLOOF
Bo-Kaap Museum
St George's Cath.
S.A. Library
Cultural History Museum
Houses of Parliament
Zonnebloem Cottages
Company's Garden
De Tuynhuys
ROELAND
Rust en Vreugd
Lion's Rump
South African National Gallery
Government Archives
Lion Gate
Jewish Museum
TAMBOERSKLOOF
South African Museum
Bertram House Museum
ORANGE
ANNANDALE
UPPER MILL
VREDEHOEK
LONG
LOOP
BREE
BUITENGRACHT
GOVERNMENT AVENUE
ADDERLEY
PLEIN
BUITENKANT
HOPE
CANTERBURY
SIR LOWRY
JUTLAND
OSWALD PIROW
NEW CHURCH
KLOOF
0 M 250
0 YARDS 250

## MONTRÉAL

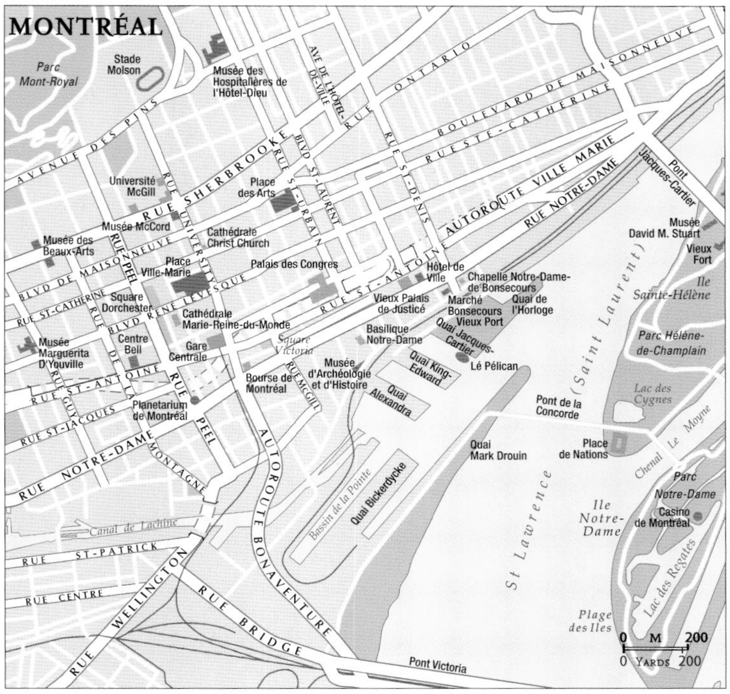


## TORONTO

## CHICAGO

## WASHINGTON D.C.

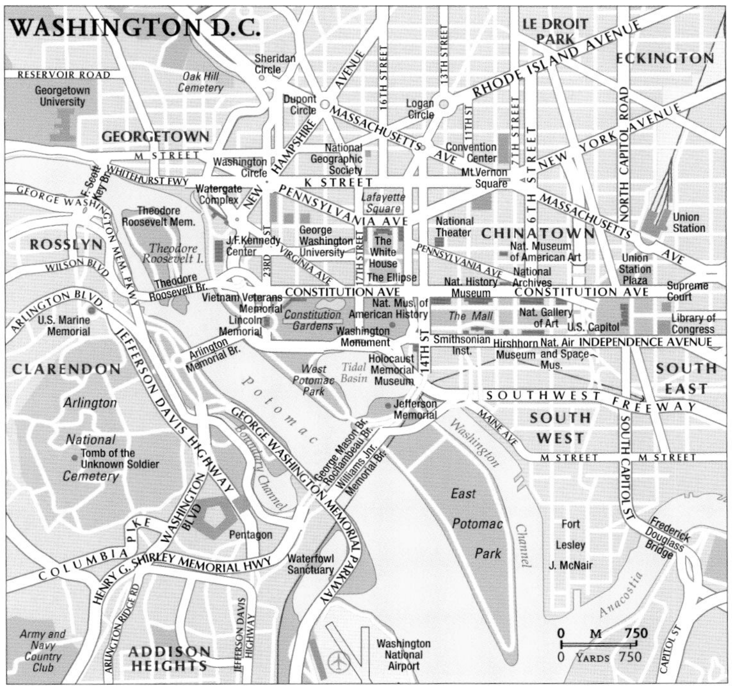


## LOS ANGELES

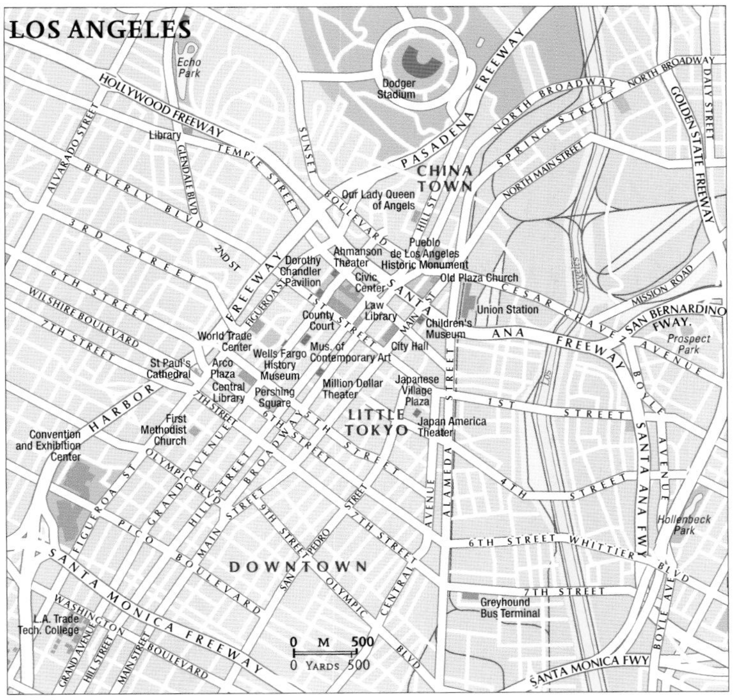


## SAN FRANCISCO

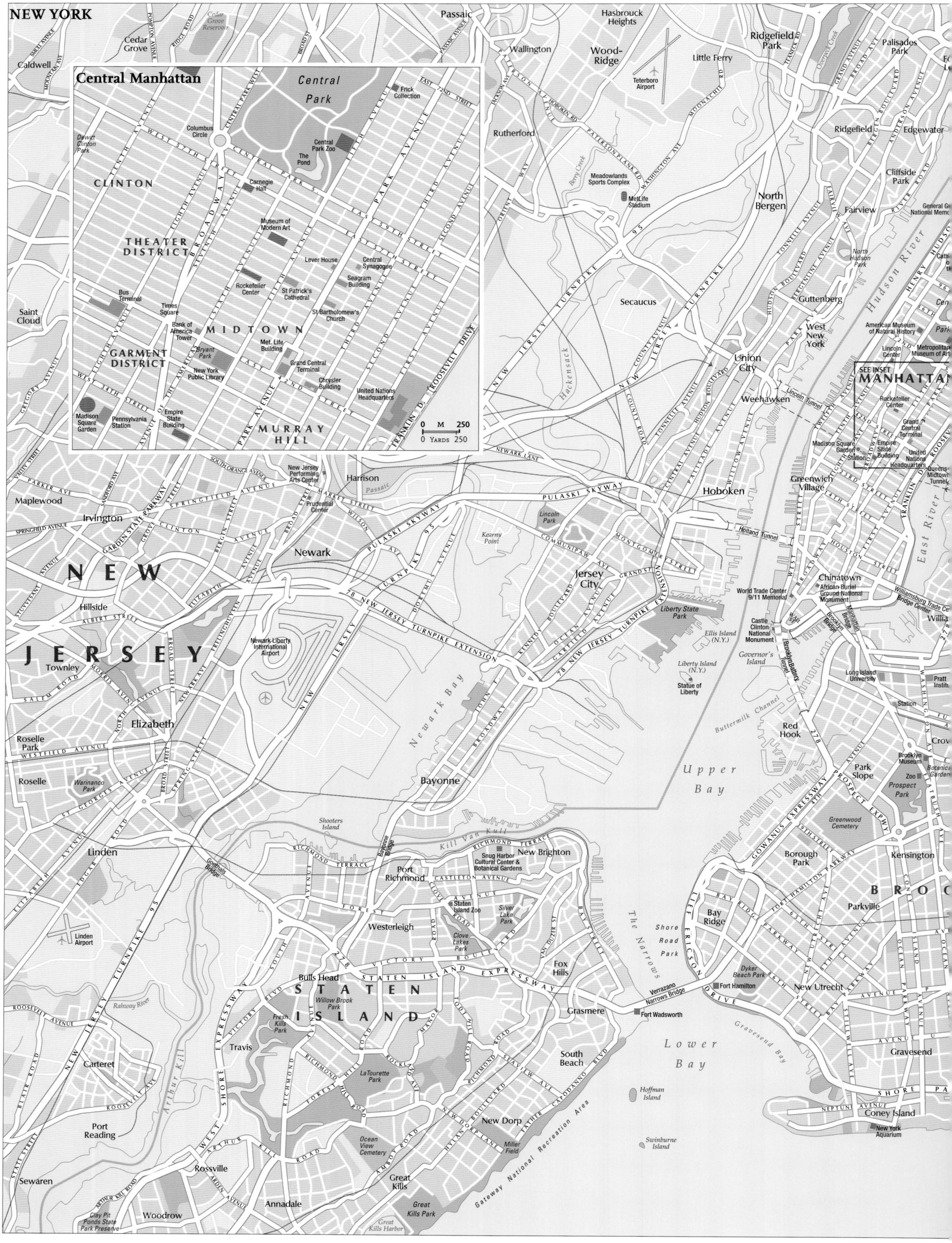
NEW YORK
Central Manhattan
Central Park
CLINTON
THEATER DISTRICT
MIDTOWN
GARMENT DISTRICT
MURRAY HILL
NEW JERSEY
STATEN ISLAND
Passaic
Caldwell
Cedar Grove
Wallington
Wood-Ridge
Hasbrouck Heights
Little Ferry
Ridgefield Park
Palisades Park
Ridgefield
Edgewater
Rutherford
Cliffside Park
Fairview
North Bergen
Secaucus
Guttenberg
West New York
Union City
Weehawken
Hoboken
Saint Cloud
Maplewood
Irvington
Harrison
Newark
Hillside
Townley
Elizabeth
Roselle Park
Roselle
Linden
Jersey City
Bayonne
Port Richmond
New Brighton
Westerleigh
Bulls Head
Travis
Carteret
Port Reading
Sewaren
Rossville
Woodrow
Annadale
Great Kills
New Dorp
South Beach
Grasmere
Fox Hills
Greenwich Village
Chinatown
Red Hook
Park Slope
Borough Park
Kensington
Parkville
Bay Ridge
New Utrecht
Gravesend
Coney Island
Upper Bay
Lower Bay
Newark Bay
Hudson River
East River
SEE INSET MANHATTAN
Teterboro Airport
Newark Liberty International Airport
Linden Airport
Liberty State Park
Statue of Liberty
Ellis Island (N.Y.)
Governor's Island
Verrazano Narrows Bridge
Fort Wadsworth
Fort Hamilton
Gateway National Recreation Area
0 M 250
0 Yards 250

BRONX
NEW YORK
QUEENS
Long Island Sound
East River
Eastchester Bay
Manhasset Bay
Hempstead Harbor
Flushing Bay
Little Neck Bay
Jamaica Bay
Head of Bay
Grassy Bay
Hewlett Bay
Rockaway Inlet
East Rockaway Inlet
Sheepshead Bay
ATLANTIC OCEAN
Fordham
Baychester
Hunters Island
Pelham Bay Park
Botanical Garden
Tremont
Belmont
Bronx Zoo
West Farms
Crotona Park
Yankee Stadium
Melrose
Harlem
City College
Mott Haven
Soundview
Sound view Park
Hunts Point
Throgs Neck
Ferry Point Park
Brother Islands
Hunts Point
Clason Point
Rikers Island
Wards Island
Icahn Stadium
Museum of the City of New York
Guggenheim Museum
College Point
Whitestone
Bronx Whitestone Bridge
Throgs Neck Bridge
Maritime College
Fort Totten
Astoria
La Guardia Airport
Flushing Airport
Long Island City
Broadway
Bayside
Flushing
City Field Stadium
Jackson Heights
Sunnyside
Woodside
Elmhurst
New York Hall of Science
USTA National Tennis Center
Queen's Zoo
Flushing Meadows Corona Park
Kissena Park
Corona
New Calvary Cemetery
Cedar Grove Cemetery
Queens College
Fresh Meadows
Oakland Gardens
Alley Pond Park
Cunningham Park
Laurel Hill
St John's University
Bellaire
Queens Village
Belmont Park Race Track
Floral Park
Forest Hills
Kew Gardens
Jamaica
Hillside
Glendale
Richmond Hill
Mt Carmel Cemetery
Forest Park
Bushwick
Cypress Hills Nat. Cemetery
Cemetery of the Evergreens
Highland Park
Wood Haven
Bedford-Stuyvesant
St Albans
Cambria Heights
Elmont
Beth David Cemetery
Franklin Square
West Hempstead
North Valley Stream
Ozone Park
Aqueduct Race Track
Montefiore Cemetery
Springfield Gardens
Valley Stream
Valley Stream State Park
Malverne
Hempstead Lake State Park
East New York
Brooklyn Children's Museum
Brownsville
New Lots
Howard Beach
Flatbush
Laurelton
Rosedale
Brookville Park
South Valley Stream
Lynbrook
John F. Kennedy International Airport
Spring Creek Park
Canarsie
Canarsie Beach Park
North Woodmere Park
Woodmere
Hewlett
Cedarhurst
Woodsburgh
Bay Park
Green Sedge
Flatlands
Gateway National Recreation Area
Jamaica Bay Wildlife Refuge
Bergen Beach Park
Inwood
Lawrence
Marine Park
Floyd Bennett Field
Mill Basin
Rockaway Park
Far Rockaway
Sheepshead Bay
The Raunt
Broad Channel
Island Park
Garrett Marsh
Edgemere
Lawrence Marsh
Reynolds Channel
Rockaway Park
Silver Point Beach Park
Long Beach
Atlantic Beach
Jacob Riis Park
Rockaway Beach
Fort Tilden
Breezy Point
Rockaway Point
Prospect Point
Sands Point
Hart Island
Sands Point Park
Mott Point
Garvies Point Preserve
Manorhaven
Port Washington North
City Island
Kings Point
Port Washington
Hempstead Harbor Park
U.S. Merchant Marine Academy
Kings Point Park
Flower Hill
Plandome
Saddle Rock
Great Neck
Manhasset
Harbor Hills
Thomaston
Douglaston
Little Neck
Lake Success
Glen Oaks
North New Hyde Park
New Hyde Park
Garden City Park
0 M 1000
0 Yards 1000

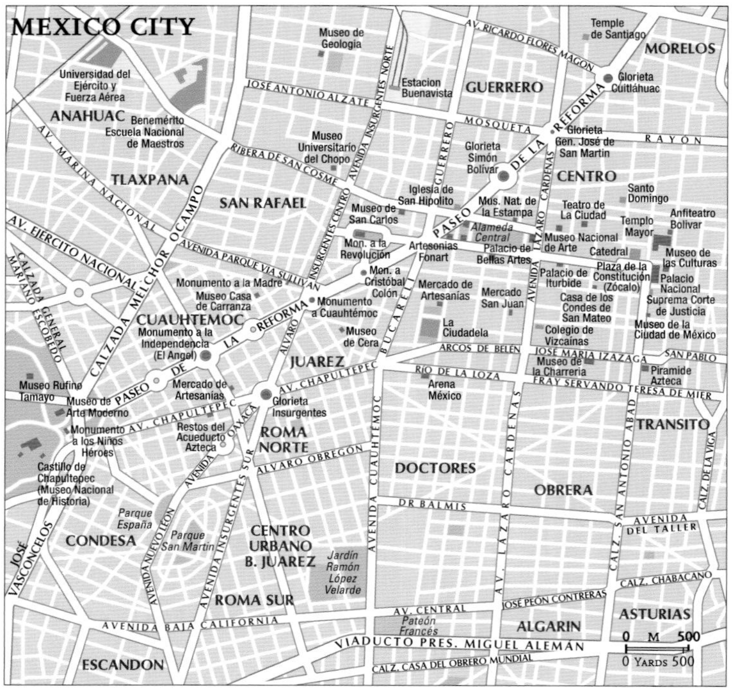
MEXICO CITY
Museo de Geología
Temple de Santiago
MORELOS
Glorieta Cuitláhuac
Universidad del Ejército y Fuerza Aérea
Estacion Buenavista
GUERRERO
ANAHUAC
Benemérito Escuela Nacional de Maestros
Museo Universitario del Chopo
Glorieta Gen. José de San Martín
Glorieta Simón Bolívar
RAYON
TLAXPANA
CENTRO
SAN RAFAEL
Iglesia de San Hipolito
Mus. Nat. de la Estampa
Santo Domingo
Teatro de La Ciudad
Museo de San Carlos
Alameda Central
Templo Mayor
Anfiteatro Bolivar
Mon. a la Revolución
Artesonias Fonart
Palacio de Bellas Artes
Museo Nacional de Arte
Catedral
Museo de las Culturas
Monumento a la Madre
Mon. a Cristobal Colón
Mercado de Artesanías
Palacio de Iturbide
Plaza de la Constitución (Zócalo)
Palacio Nacional
Museo Casa de Carranza
Monumento a Cuauhtémoc
Mercado San Juan
Casa de los Condes de San Mateo
Suprema Corte de Justicia
CUAUHTEMOC
Monumento a la Independencia (El Angel)
Museo de Cera
La Ciudadela
Colegio de Vizcainas
Museo de la Ciudad de México
JUAREZ
Museo Rufino Tamayo
Mercado de Artesanías
Museo de la Charrería
Arena México
Pirámide Azteca
Museo de Arte Moderno
Glorieta Insurgentes
Monumento a los Niños Heroes
Restos del Acueducto Azteca
ROMA NORTE
TRANSITO
Castillo de Chapultepec (Museo Nacional de Historia)
DOCTORES
OBRERA
Parque España
Parque San Martín
CONDESA
CENTRO URBANO B. JUAREZ
Jardín Ramón López Velarde
ROMA SUR
Panteón Francés
ALGARIN
ASTURIAS
ESCANDON
AV. RICARDO FLORES MAGON
JOSE ANTONIO ALZATE
MOSQUETA
PASEO DE LA REFORMA
AV. INSURGENTES NORTE
AV. MARINA NACIONAL
AV. EJERCITO NACIONAL
RIBERA DE SAN COSME
AVENIDA PARQUE VIA SULLIVAN
CALZADA MELCHOR OCAMPO
CALZADA GENERAL MARIANO ESCOBEDO
AV. CHAPULTEPEC
ARCOS DE BELEN
JOSE MARIA IZAZAGA
SAN PABLO
RIO DE LA LOZA
FRAY SERVANDO TERESA DE MIER
ALVARO OBREGON
DR BALMIS
AVENIDA DEL TALLER
CALZ. CHABACANO
JOSE PEON CONTRERAS
AV. CENTRAL
AVENIDA BAJA CALIFORNIA
VIADUCTO PRES. MIGUEL ALEMAN
CALZ. CASA DEL OBRERO MUNDIAL
JOSÉ VASCONCELOS
0 M 500
0 YARDS 500

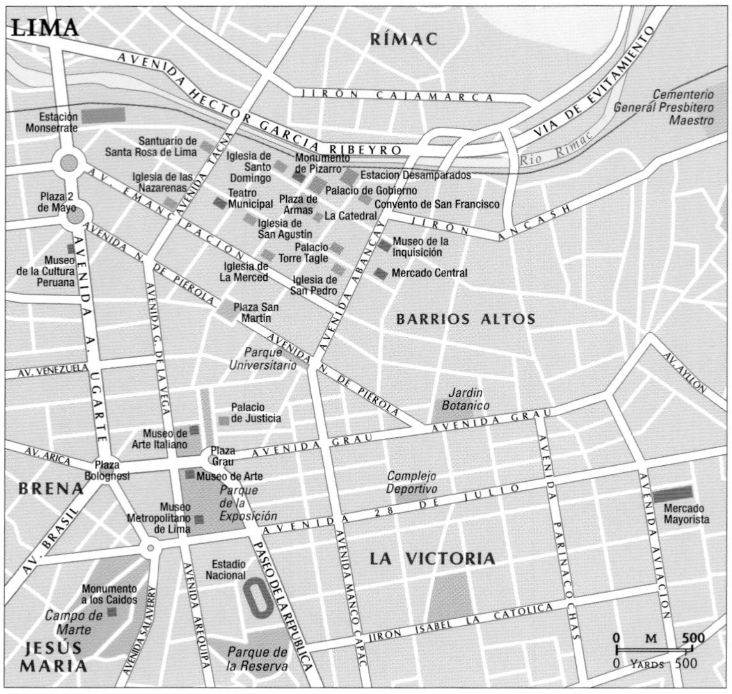
LIMA
RÍMAC
AVENIDA HECTOR GARCIA RIBEYRO
JIRON CAJAMARCA
VIA DE EVITAMIENTO
Cementerio General Presbitero Maestro
Estacion Monserrate
Santuario de Santa Rosa de Lima
Iglesia de Santo Domingo
Monumento de Pizarro
Estacion Desamparados
Río Rímac
Iglesia de las Nazarenas
Palacio de Gobierno
Convento de San Francisco
Plaza 2 de Mayo
Teatro Municipal
Plaza de Armas
La Catedral
JIRON ANCASH
Iglesia de San Agustín
Palacio Torre Tagle
Museo de la Inquisición
Museo de la Cultura Peruana
Iglesia de La Merced
Iglesia de San Pedro
Mercado Central
Plaza San Martín
BARRIOS ALTOS
Parque Universitario
AV. VENEZUELA
Jardín Botanico
Palacio de Justicia
Museo de Arte Italiano
Plaza Grau
AVENIDA GRAU
Museo de Arte
AV. ARICA
Plaza Bolognesi
BREÑA
Complejo Deportivo
Parque de la Exposición
Museo Metropolitano de Lima
AVENIDA 28 DE JULIO
Mercado Mayorista
Estadio Nacional
LA VICTORIA
Monumento a los Caidos
Campo de Marte
JESÚS MARÍA
Parque de la Reserva
AV. BRASIL
AVENIDA AREQUIPA
PASEO DE LA REPUBLICA
AVENIDA MANCO CAPAC
AVENIDA AVIACION
JIRON ISABEL LA CATOLICA
AV. AYLLON
0 M 500
0 YARDS 500

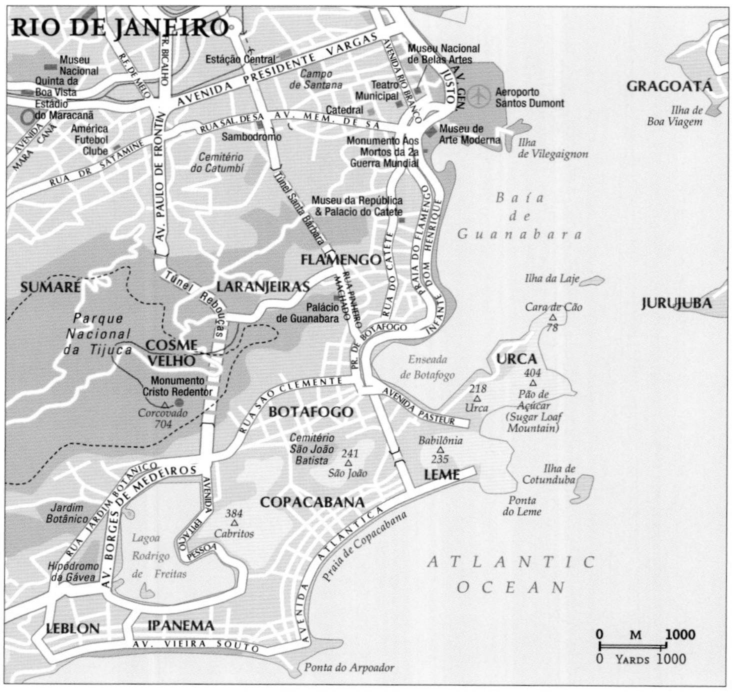
RIO DE JANEIRO
Museu Nacional
Quinta da Boa Vista
Estádio do Maracanã
América Futebol Clube
Estação Central
AVENIDA PRESIDENTE VARGAS
Campo de Santana
Museu Nacional de Belas Artes
Teatro Municipal
Aeroporto Santos Dumont
GRAGOATÁ
Ilha de Boa Viagem
Catedral
Sambódromo
Museu de Arte Moderna
Monumento Aos Mortos da 2a Guerra Mundial
Ilha de Vilegaignon
Cemitério do Catumbi
Baía de Guanabara
Museu da República & Palacio do Catete
FLAMENGO
Ilha da Laje
SUMARÉ
LARANJEIRAS
JURUJUBA
Palácio de Guanabara
Cara de Cão 78
Parque Nacional da Tijuca
COSME VELHO
Enseada de Botafogo
URCA
404
Pão de Açúcar (Sugar Loaf Mountain)
Monumento Cristo Redentor
Corcovado 704
218 Urca
BOTAFOGO
Babilônia 235
Cemitério São João Batista
241 São João
LEME
Ilha de Cotunduba
Ponta do Leme
Jardim Botânico
COPACABANA
384 Cabritos
Lagoa Rodrigo de Freitas
Praia de Copacabana
Hipódromo da Gávea
ATLANTIC OCEAN
LEBLON
IPANEMA
AV. VIEIRA SOUTO
Ponta do Arpoador
AV. PAULO DE FRONTIN
RUA SÃO CLEMENTE
AVENIDA PASTEUR
AV. BORGES DE MEDEIROS
AVENIDA ATLANTICA
Túnel Rebouças
0 M 1000
0 YARDS 1000

SÃO PAULO
Aerodromo de Marte
AVENIDA PRESIDENTE CASTELO BRANCO
AVENIDA ASSIS CHATEAUBRIAND
Rio Tietê
DIAS FIGUEIREDO
0 M 500
0 YARDS 500
Estação do Barra Funda
BARRA FUNDA
BOM RETIRO
AV. MARQUEZ DE SÃO VICENTE
PARI
AVENIDA TIRADENTES
AVENIDA CRUZEIRO DO SUL
AVENIDA DO ESTADO
AV. PACAEMBU
Parque da Luz
Estação da Luz
SANTA CECÍLIA
Igreja Santa Cecília
SANTA EFIGÊNIA
AVENIDA SÃO JOÃO
Mercado de Flores
Mercado Municipal
Basílica São Bento
Estação Roosevelt
Praça da República
Teatro Municipal
Santa Casa de Misericórdia
Praça Buenos Aires
Biblioteca Municipal
Igreja de Santo Antonio
Patio do Colégio
Parque Dom Pedro II
CONSOLAÇÃO
BRÁS
Cemitério da Consolação
Igreja NS de Consolação
SÉ
Igreja São Francisco de Assis
Catedral Metropolitana
AV. ALCÂNTARA MACHADO
Igreja São Gonçalo
BELA VISTA
Igreja das Almas
MOÓCA
Igreja NS Achiropita
AVENIDA 9 DE JULHO
AVENIDA 23 DE MAIO
AVENIDA RANGEL PESTANA
RUA DA CONSOLAÇÃO
CERQUEIRA CÉSAR
Museu Memórias do Bixiga
LIBERDADE
Parque 9 de Julho

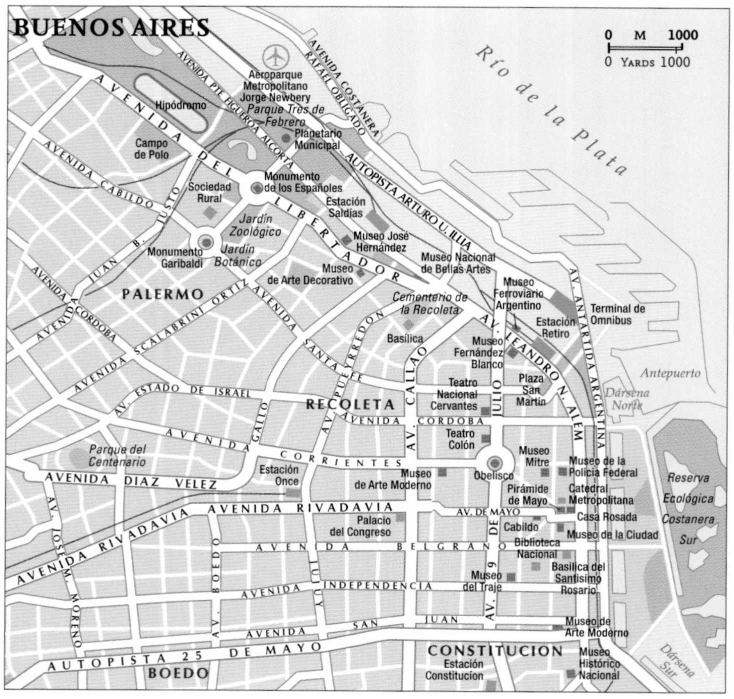
BUENOS AIRES
0 M 1000
0 YARDS 1000
Río de la Plata
Aeroparque Metropolitano Jorge Newbery
Hipódromo
Parque Tres de Febrero
Planetario Municipal
Campo de Polo
AVENIDA DEL LIBERTADOR
AVENIDA COSTANERA RAFAEL OBLIGADO
AUTOPISTA ARTURO U. ILLIA
Sociedad Rural
Monumento de los Españoles
Estación Saldías
Jardín Zoológico
Jardín Botánico
Monumento Garibaldi
Museo José Hernández
Museo Nacional de Bellas Artes
Museo de Arte Decorativo
PALERMO
Museo Ferroviario Argentino
Terminal de Omnibus
Cementerio de la Recoleta
Basilica
Estación Retiro
Museo Fernández Blanco
Antepuerto
Teatro Nacional Cervantes
Plaza San Martín
Dársena Norte
RECOLETA
AVENIDA CORDOBA
Teatro Colón
Museo Mitre
Museo de la Policía Federal
Parque del Centenario
AVENIDA CORRIENTES
Estación Once
Museo de Arte Moderno
Obelisco
Pirámide de Mayo
Catedral Metropolitana
Reserva Ecológica Costanera Sur
AVENIDA DIAZ VELEZ
AVENIDA RIVADAVIA
Palacio del Congreso
Casa Rosada
Cabildo
Museo de la Ciudad
Biblioteca Nacional
AVENIDA BELGRANO
Basílica del Santísimo Rosario
Museo del Traje
INDEPENDENCIA
SAN JUAN
Museo de Arte Moderno
AVENIDA 9 DE JULIO
AV. CALLAO
AV. LEANDRO N. ALEM
AVENIDA CABILDO
AVENIDA SCALABRINI ORTIZ
AV. ESTADO DE ISRAEL
AVENIDA SANTA FE
AV. PUEYRREDON
AV. BOEDO
CONSTITUCION
Estación Constitucion
Museo Histórico Nacional
Dársena Sur
AUTOPISTA 25 DE MAYO
BOEDO

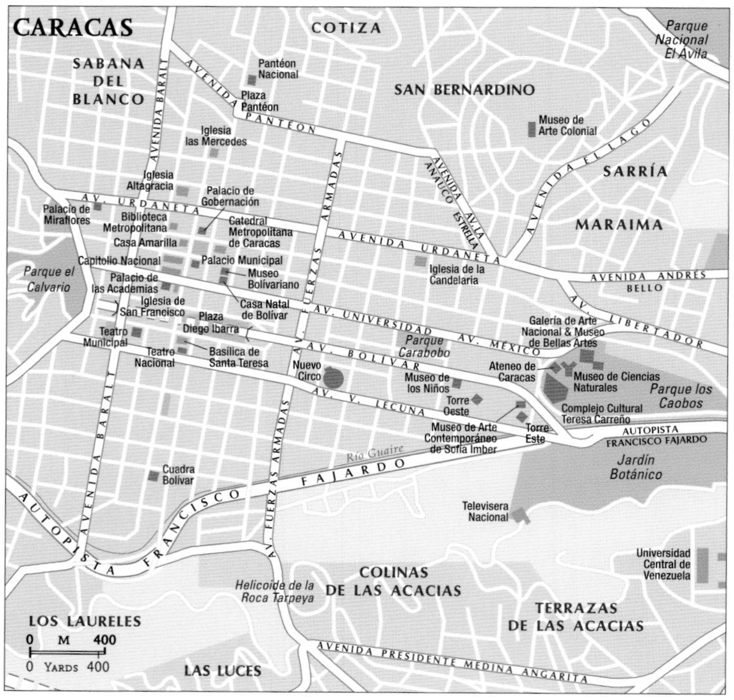
CARACAS
COTIZA
Parque Nacional El Avila
SABANA DEL BLANCO
Panteón Nacional
Plaza Panteón
SAN BERNARDINO
Iglesia las Mercedes
Museo de Arte Colonial
Iglesia Altagracia
Palacio de Gobernación
SARRÍA
Palacio de Miraflores
Biblioteca Metropolitana
Catedral Metropolitana de Caracas
MARAIMA
Casa Amarilla
Capitolio Nacional
Palacio Municipal
Museo Bolivariano
AVENIDA URDANETA
Iglesia de la Candelaria
Parque el Calvario
Palacio de las Academias
Iglesia de San Francisco
Casa Natal de Bolivar
AVENIDA ANDRES BELLO
Plaza Diego Ibarra
AV. UNIVERSIDAD
Galería de Arte Nacional & Museo de Bellas Artes
Teatro Municipal
Parque Carabobo
AV. MEXICO
AV. LIBERTADOR
Teatro Nacional
Basilica de Santa Teresa
Nuevo Circo
Ateneo de Caracas
Museo de Ciencias Naturales
Museo de los Niños
Parque los Caobos
AV. BOLIVAR
AV. LECUNA
Torre Oeste
Complejo Cultural Teresa Carreño
Museo de Arte Contemporáneo de Sofia Imber
Torre Este
AUTOPISTA FRANCISCO FAJARDO
Río Guaire
Jardín Botánico
Cuadra Bolivar
Televisera Nacional
AUTOPISTA FRANCISCO FAJARDO
Universidad Central de Venezuela
Helicoide de la Roca Tarpeya
COLINAS DE LAS ACACIAS
LOS LAURELES
TERRAZAS DE LAS ACACIAS
0 M 400
0 YARDS 400
AVENIDA PRESIDENTE MEDINA ANGARITA
LAS LUCES
AVENIDA BARALT
AVENIDA FUERZAS ARMADAS
AVENIDA EL LAGO

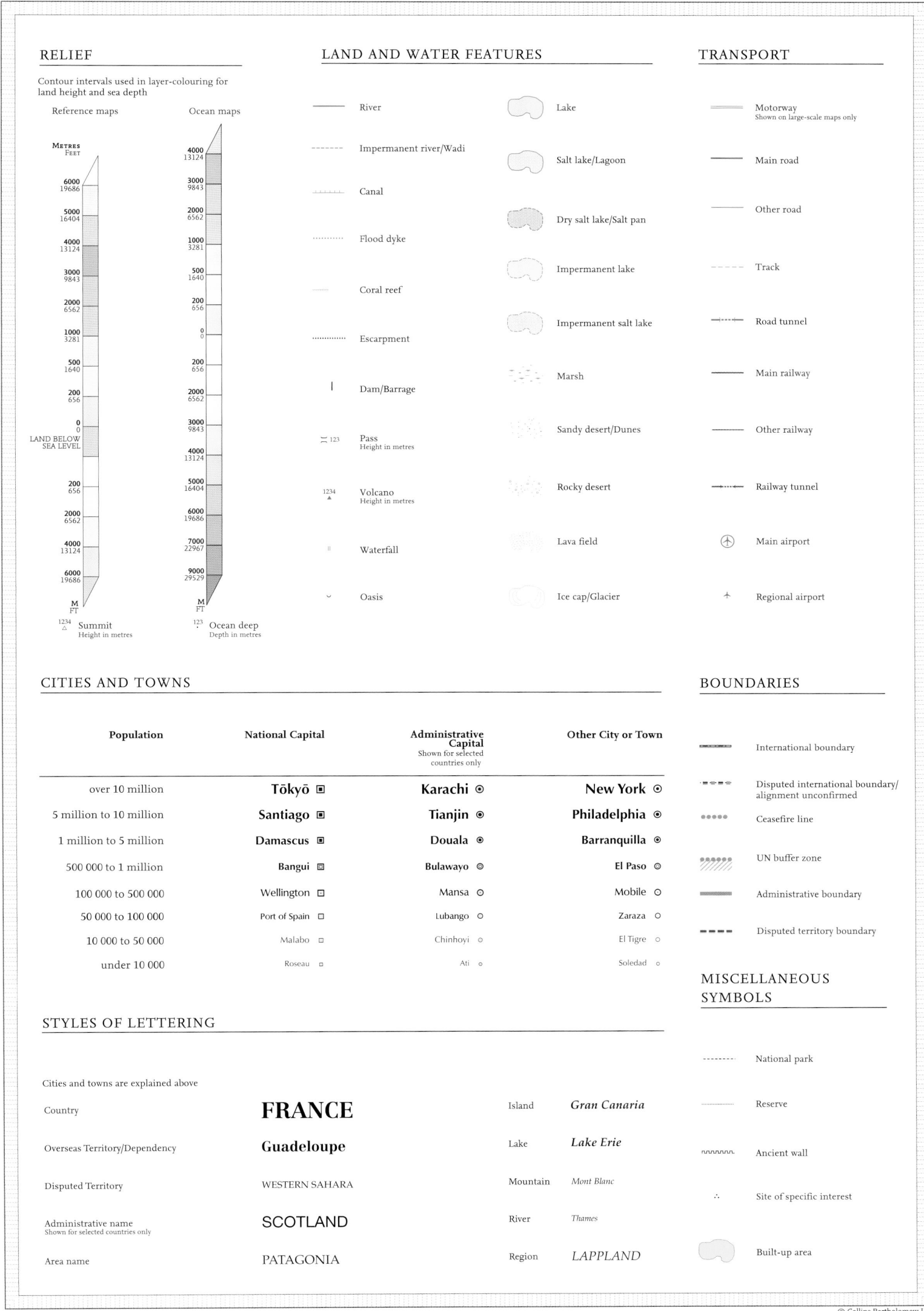

## RELIEF

Contour intervals used in layer-colouring for land height and sea depth

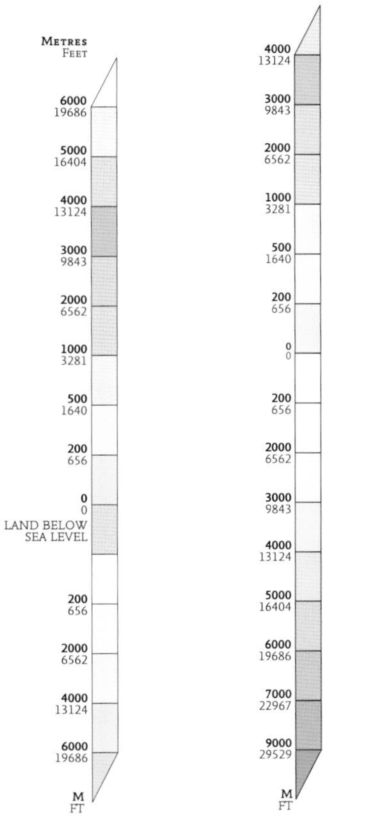
Reference maps
Ocean maps
METRES
FEET
6000 19686
5000 16404
4000 13124
3000 9843
2000 6562
1000 3281
500 1640
200 656
0 0
LAND BELOW SEA LEVEL
200 656
2000 6562
4000 13124
6000 19686
M
FT
4000 13124
3000 9843
2000 6562
1000 3281
500 1640
200 656
0 0
200 656
2000 6562
3000 9843
4000 13124
5000 16404
6000 19686
7000 22967
9000 29529
M
FT

1234 △ Summit
Height in metres

123 · Ocean deep
Depth in metres

## LAND AND WATER FEATURES

- River
- Impermanent river/Wadi
- Canal
- Flood dyke
- Coral reef
- Escarpment
- Dam/Barrage
- Pass 123
  Height in metres
- Volcano 1234 ▲
  Height in metres
- Waterfall
- Oasis
- Lake
- Salt lake/Lagoon
- Dry salt lake/Salt pan
- Impermanent lake
- Impermanent salt lake
- Marsh
- Sandy desert/Dunes
- Rocky desert
- Lava field
- Ice cap/Glacier

## TRANSPORT

- Motorway
  Shown on large-scale maps only
- Main road
- Other road
- Track
- Road tunnel
- Main railway
- Other railway
- Railway tunnel
- Main airport
- Regional airport

## CITIES AND TOWNS

| Population | National Capital | Administrative Capital<br>Shown for selected countries only | Other City or Town |
|---|---|---|---|
| over 10 million | **Tōkyō** ▣ | **Karachi** ⊙ | **New York** ⊙ |
| 5 million to 10 million | **Santiago** ▣ | **Tianjin** ⊙ | **Philadelphia** ⊙ |
| 1 million to 5 million | **Damascus** ▣ | **Douala** ⊙ | **Barranquilla** ⊙ |
| 500 000 to 1 million | **Bangui** ⊡ | **Bulawayo** ◎ | **El Paso** ◎ |
| 100 000 to 500 000 | Wellington ⊡ | Mansa ○ | Mobile ○ |
| 50 000 to 100 000 | Port of Spain □ | Lubango ○ | Zaraza ○ |
| 10 000 to 50 000 | Malabo □ | Chinhoyi ○ | El Tigre ○ |
| under 10 000 | Roseau □ | Ati ○ | Soledad ○ |

## BOUNDARIES

- International boundary
- Disputed international boundary/alignment unconfirmed
- Ceasefire line
- UN buffer zone
- Administrative boundary
- Disputed territory boundary

## MISCELLANEOUS SYMBOLS

- National park
- Reserve
- Ancient wall
- ∴ Site of specific interest
- Built-up area

## STYLES OF LETTERING

Cities and towns are explained above

| | | | |
|---|---|---|---|
| Country | **FRANCE** | Island | ***Gran Canaria*** |
| Overseas Territory/Dependency | **Guadeloupe** | Lake | ***Lake Erie*** |
| Disputed Territory | WESTERN SAHARA | Mountain | *Mont Blanc* |
| Administrative name<br>Shown for selected countries only | SCOTLAND | River | *Thames* |
| Area name | PATAGONIA | Region | *LAPPLAND* |

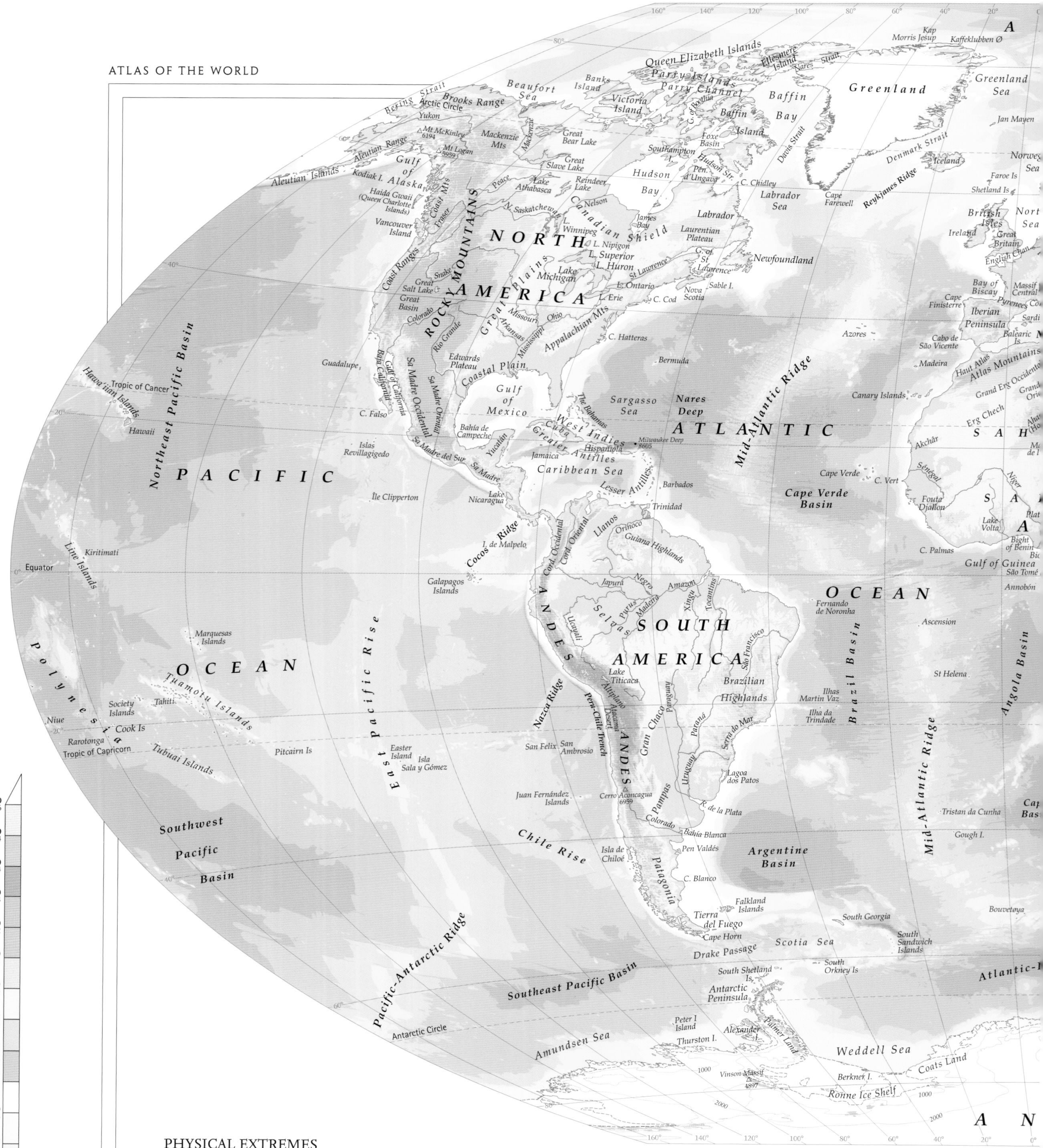


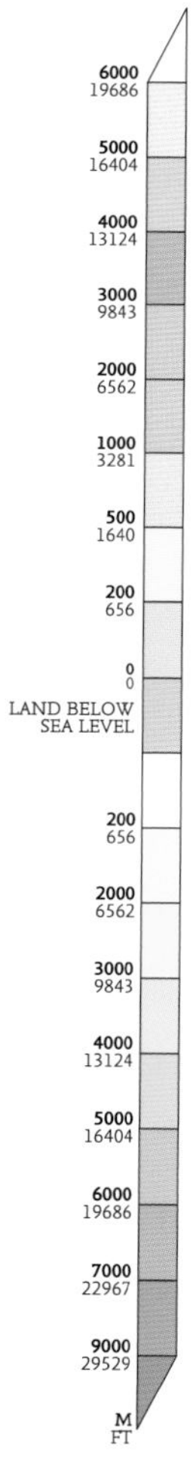


## PHYSICAL EXTREMES

### EARTH'S DIMENSIONS

| | |
|---|---|
| **Mass** | 5.974 x $10^{21}$ tonnes |
| **Volume** | 1 083 207 x $10^6$ cu km / 259 911 x $10^6$ cu miles |
| **Total area** | 509 450 000 sq km / 196 698 645 sq miles |
| **Land area** | 149 450 000 sq km / 57 702 645 sq miles |
| **Water area** | 360 000 000 sq km / 138 996 000 sq miles |
| **Water volume** | 1 389 500 x $10^3$ cu km / 333 405 x $10^3$ cu miles |
| **Equatorial diameter** | 12 756 km / 7 927 miles |
| **Polar diameter** | 12 714 km / 7 900 miles |
| **Equatorial circumference** | 40 075 km / 24 903 miles |
| **Meridional circumference** | 40 008 km / 24 861 miles |

### HIGHEST MOUNTAINS

| HIGHEST MOUNTAINS | metres | feet |
|---|---|---|
| **Mt Everest,** China/Nepal | 8 848 | 29 028 |
| **K2,** China/Pakistan | 8 611 | 28 251 |
| **Kangchenjunga,** India/Nepal | 8 586 | 28 169 |
| **Lhotse,** China/Nepal | 8 516 | 27 939 |
| **Makalu,** China/Nepal | 8 463 | 27 765 |
| **Cho Oyu,** China/Nepal | 8 201 | 26 906 |
| **Dhaulagiri,** Nepal | 8 167 | 26 794 |
| **Manaslu,** Nepal | 8 163 | 26 781 |
| **Nanga Parbat,** Pakistan | 8 126 | 26 660 |
| **Annapurna I,** Nepal | 8 091 | 26 545 |

### LONGEST RIVERS

| LONGEST RIVERS | km | miles |
|---|---|---|
| **Nile,** Africa | 6 695 | 4 160 |
| **Amazon,** South America | 6 516 | 4 049 |
| **Yangtze,** Asia | 6 380 | 3 965 |
| **Mississippi-Missouri,** North America | 5 969 | 3 709 |
| **Ob'-Irtysh,** Asia | 5 568 | 3 460 |
| **Yenisey-Angara-Selenga,** Asia | 5 550 | 3 449 |
| **Yellow,** Asia | 5 464 | 3 395 |
| **Congo,** Africa | 4 667 | 2 900 |
| **Río de la Plata-Paraná,** South America | 4 500 | 2 796 |
| **Irtysh,** Asia | 4 440 | 2 759 |

Winkel Tripel Projection

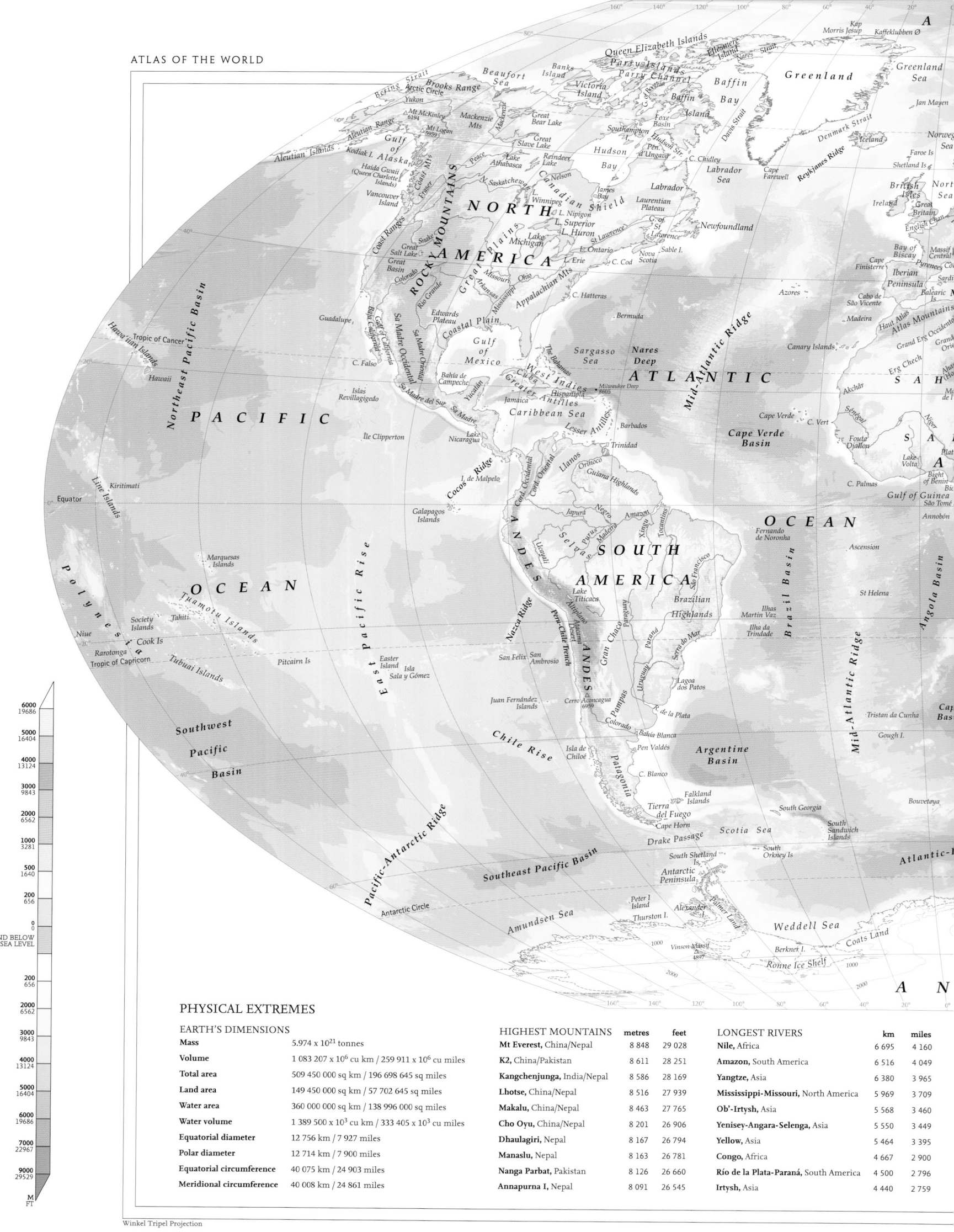

# WORLD PHYSICAL

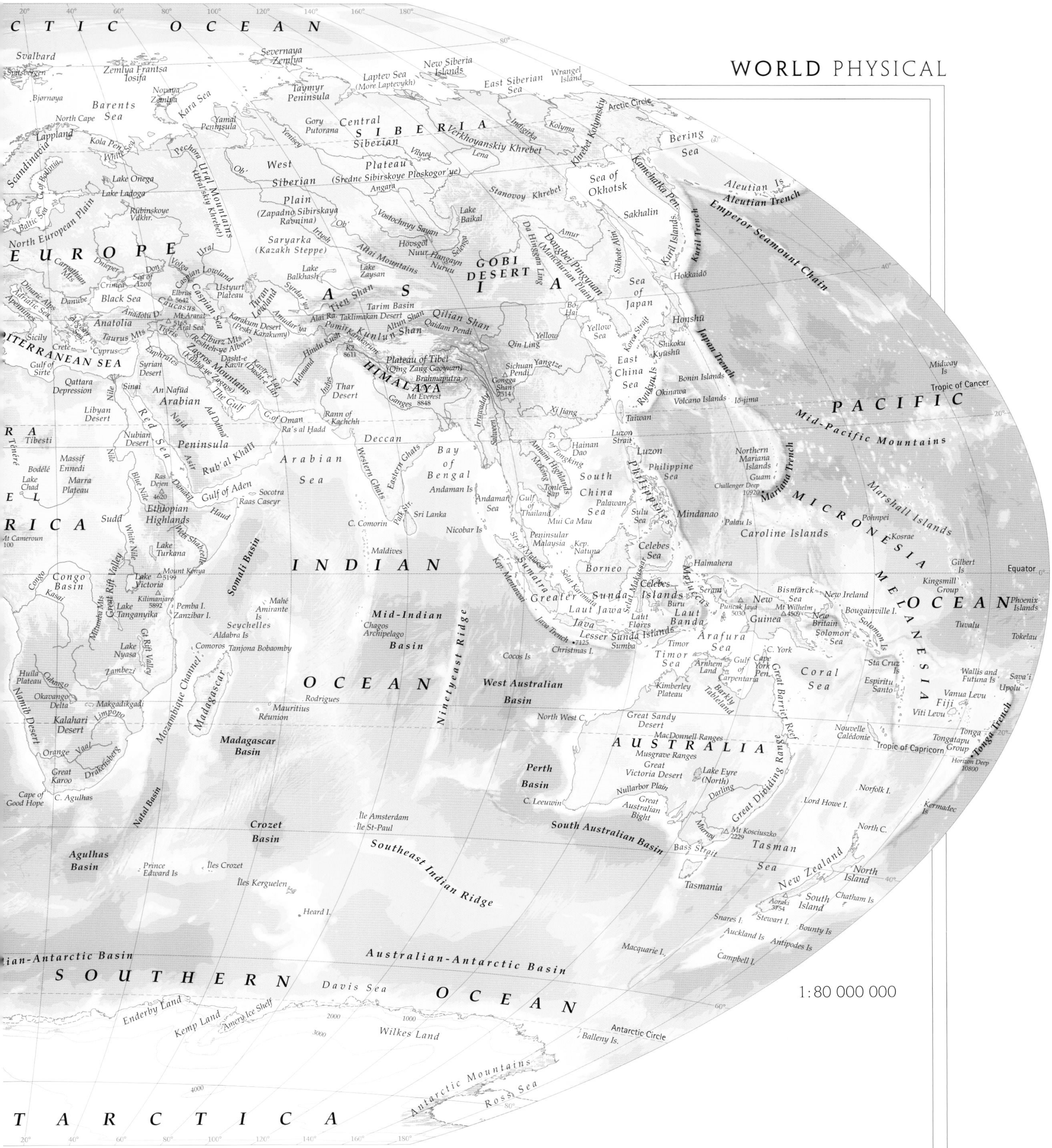


| LARGEST ISLANDS | sq km | sq miles |
|---|---|---|
| **Greenland,** North America | 2 175 600 | 839 999 |
| **New Guinea,** Oceania | 808 510 | 312 166 |
| **Borneo,** Asia | 745 561 | 287 861 |
| **Madagascar,** Africa | 587 040 | 266 656 |
| **Baffin Island,** North America | 507 451 | 195 927 |
| **Sumatra,** Asia | 473 606 | 182 859 |
| **Honshū,** Asia | 227 414 | 87 805 |
| **Great Britain,** Europe | 218 476 | 84 354 |
| **Victoria Island,** North America | 217 291 | 83 896 |
| **Ellesmere Island,** North America | 196 236 | 75 767 |

| LARGEST LAKES | sq km | sq miles |
|---|---|---|
| **Caspian Sea,** Asia/Europe | 371 000 | 143 243 |
| **Lake Superior,** North America | 82 100 | 31 699 |
| **Lake Victoria,** Africa | 68 870 | 26 591 |
| **Lake Huron,** North America | 59 600 | 23 012 |
| **Lake Michigan,** North America | 57 800 | 22 317 |
| **Lake Tanganyika,** Africa | 32 600 | 12 587 |
| **Great Bear Lake,** North America | 31 328 | 12 096 |
| **Lake Baikal,** Asia | 30 500 | 11 776 |
| **Lake Nyasa,** Africa | 29 500 | 11 390 |
| **Great Slave Lake,** North America | 28 568 | 11 030 |

| OCEANS AND SEAS | Area | | Deepest point | |
|---|---|---|---|---|
| | sq km | sq miles | metres | feet |
| **Pacific Ocean** | 166 241 000 | 64 185 650 | 10 920 | 35 826 |
| **Atlantic Ocean** | 86 557 000 | 33 419 658 | 8 605 | 28 231 |
| **Indian Ocean** | 73 427 000 | 28 350 165 | 7 125 | 23 376 |
| **Arctic Ocean** | 9 485 000 | 3 662 159 | 5 450 | 17 880 |
| **South China Sea** | 2 590 000 | 999 999 | 5 514 | 18 090 |
| **Caribbean Sea** | 2 512 000 | 969 883 | 7 680 | 25 197 |
| **Mediterranean Sea** | 2 510 000 | 969 111 | 5 121 | 16 801 |
| **Bering Sea** | 2 261 000 | 872 972 | 4 150 | 13 615 |
| **Bay of Bengal** | 2 172 000 | 838 609 | 4 500 | 14 764 |
| **Gulf of Mexico** | 1 544 000 | 596 138 | 3 504 | 11 496 |

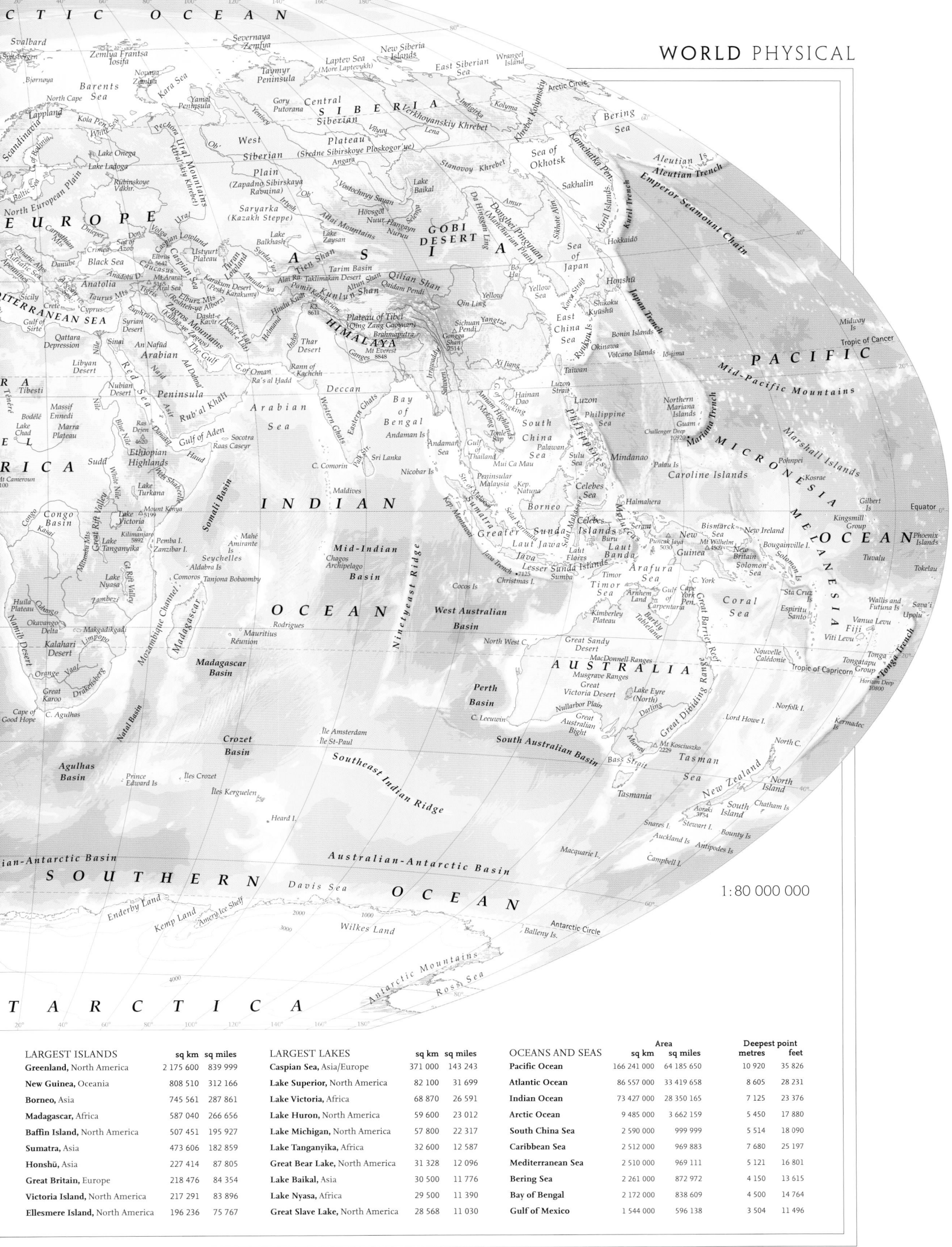

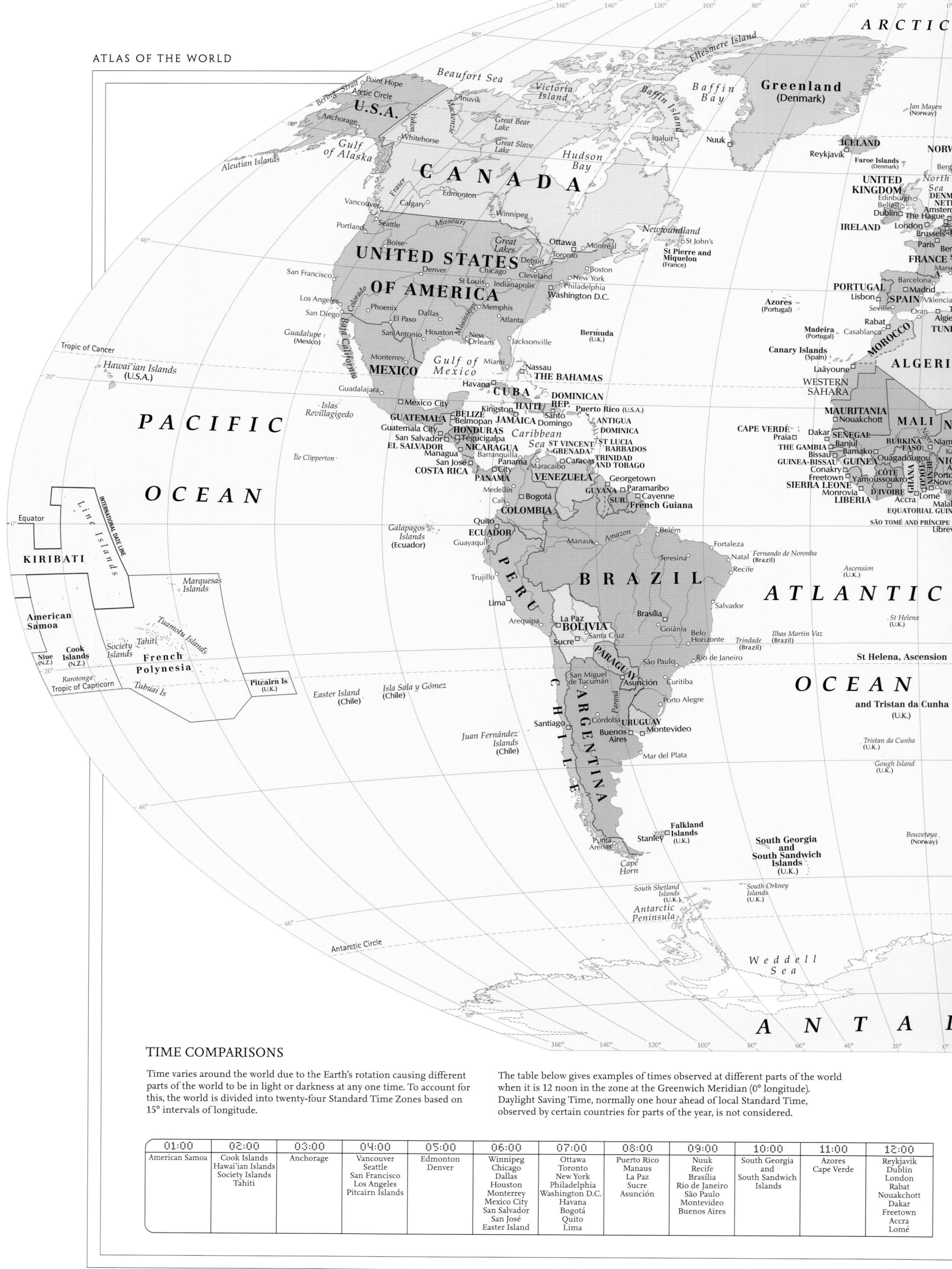

## TIME COMPARISONS

Time varies around the world due to the Earth's rotation causing different parts of the world to be in light or darkness at any one time. To account for this, the world is divided into twenty-four Standard Time Zones based on 15° intervals of longitude.

The table below gives examples of times observed at different parts of the world when it is 12 noon in the zone at the Greenwich Meridian (0° longitude). Daylight Saving Time, normally one hour ahead of local Standard Time, observed by certain countries for parts of the year, is not considered.

| 01:00 | 02:00 | 03:00 | 04:00 | 05:00 | 06:00 | 07:00 | 08:00 | 09:00 | 10:00 | 11:00 | 12:00 |
|---|---|---|---|---|---|---|---|---|---|---|---|
| American Samoa | Cook Islands<br>Hawai'ian Islands<br>Society Islands<br>Tahiti | Anchorage | Vancouver<br>Seattle<br>San Francisco<br>Los Angeles<br>Pitcairn Islands | Edmonton<br>Denver | Winnipeg<br>Chicago<br>Dallas<br>Houston<br>Monterrey<br>Mexico City<br>San Salvador<br>San José<br>Easter Island | Ottawa<br>Toronto<br>New York<br>Philadelphia<br>Washington D.C.<br>Havana<br>Bogotá<br>Quito<br>Lima | Puerto Rico<br>Manaus<br>La Paz<br>Sucre<br>Asunción | Nuuk<br>Recife<br>Brasília<br>Rio de Janeiro<br>São Paulo<br>Montevideo<br>Buenos Aires | South Georgia and South Sandwich Islands | Azores<br>Cape Verde | Reykjavik<br>Dublin<br>London<br>Rabat<br>Nouakchott<br>Dakar<br>Freetown<br>Accra<br>Lomé |

Winkel Tripel Projection

# WORLD POLITICAL

## MAP ABBREVIATIONS

| | | | | | | | | | | | | | |
|---|---|---|---|---|---|---|---|---|---|---|---|---|---|
| A. | ANDORRA | BEL. | BELGIUM | GEOR. | GEORGIA | LAT. | LATVIA | MOL. | MOLDOVA | S. | SERBIA | TAJIK. | TAJIKISTAN |
| AL. | ALBANIA | B.H. | BOSNIA-HERZEGOVINA | HUN. | HUNGARY | LEB. | LEBANON | NETH. | NETHERLANDS | SL. | SLOVENIA | TURKM. | TURKMENISTAN |
| ARM. | ARMENIA | BULG. | BULGARIA | ISR. | ISRAEL | LITH. | LITHUANIA | R. | RWANDA | SLA. | SLOVAKIA | U.A.E. | UNITED ARAB EMIRATES |
| AUST. | AUSTRIA | CR. | CROATIA | JOR. | JORDAN | M. | MACEDONIA | R.F. | RUSSIAN FEDERATION | SUR. | SURINAME | U.S.A. | UNITED STATES OF AMERICA |
| AZER. | AZERBAIJAN | CZ.R. | CZECH REPUBLIC | K. | KOSOVO | MO. | MONTENEGRO | ROM. | ROMANIA | SW. | SWITZERLAND | UZBEK. | UZBEKISTAN |
| B. | BURUNDI | EST. | ESTONIA | L. | LUXEMBOURG | | | | | | | | |

| 13:00 | 14:00 | 15:00 | 16:00 | 17:00 | 18:00 | 19:00 | 20:00 | 21:00 | 22:00 | 23:00 | 00:00 |
|---|---|---|---|---|---|---|---|---|---|---|---|
| Oslo<br>Berlin<br>Paris<br>Madrid<br>Rome<br>Algiers<br>Abuja<br>Kinshasa<br>Luanda | Helsinki<br>Kiev<br>Ankara<br>Jerusalem<br>Cairo<br>Kigali<br>Harare<br>Pretoria<br>Cape Town | St Petersburg<br>Moscow<br>Baghdād<br>Qatar<br>Riyadh<br>Addis Ababa<br>Mogadishu<br>Dodoma<br>Antananarivo | T'bilisi<br>Yerevan<br>Baku<br>Abu Dhabi<br>Muscat<br>Seychelles<br>Mauritius | Yekaterinburg<br>Asgabat<br>Bishkek<br>Tashkent<br>Islamabad<br>Karachi | Omsk<br>Astana<br>Bhutan<br>Dhaka | Ha Nôi<br>Vientiane<br>Bangkok<br>Phnom Penh<br>Ho Chi Minh City<br>Jakarta | Ulan Bator<br>Beijing<br>T'aipei<br>Hong Kong<br>Manila<br>Kuala Lumpur<br>Singapore<br>Perth | P'yŏngyang<br>Seoul<br>Tōkyō<br>Ōsaka<br>Palau | Port Moresby<br>Brisbane<br>Sydney<br>Canberra<br>Melbourne | Magadan<br>Solomon Islands<br>Vanuatu<br>New Caledonia | Marshall Islands<br>Tuvalu<br>Fiji<br>Auckland<br>Wellington<br>Samoa |

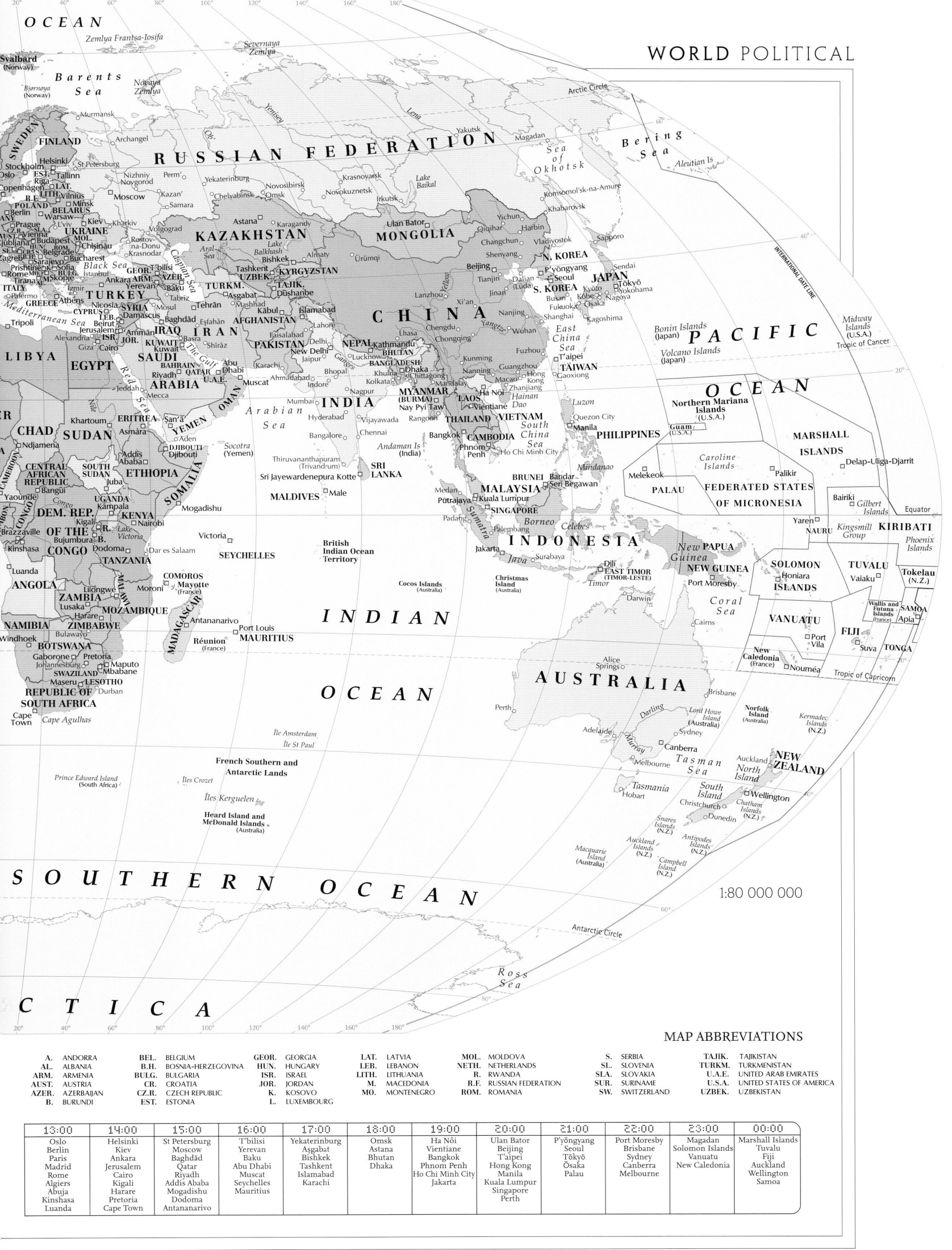

Orthographic Projection

F
G
H
I
J
1
2
3
4
5
6
7
Hawaiian Islands
Kure Atoll
Midway Islands
Pearl and Hermes Atoll
Lisianski Island
Laysan Island
Gardner Pinnacles
Necker Island
Kaua'i
O'ahu
Maui
Hawai'i
Tropic of Cancer
INTERNATIONAL DATE LINE
Wake Island (U.S.A.)
MARSHALL ISLANDS
Bikini
Ralik Chain
Ratak Chain
Kwajalein
Maloelap
Delap-Uliga-Djarrit
Mili
Palikir
Pohnpei
Kosrae
OF MICRONESIA
PACIFIC OCEAN
Johnston Atoll (U.S.A.)
Gilbert Islands
Tarawa
Bairiki
Aranuka
Yaren
NAURU
Banaba
Nonouti
Tabiteuea
Onotoa
Tamana
Beru
Nikunau
Kingsmill Group
Arorae
Howland Island (U.S.A.)
Baker Island (U.S.A.)
Kingman Reef (U.S.A.)
Palmyra Atoll (U.S.A.)
Line Islands
Teraina
Tabuaeran
Kiritimati
Jarvis Island (U.S.A.)
Phoenix Islands
McKean
Kanton
Nikumaroro
Orona
Rawaki
Manra
KIRIBATI
Bougainville Island
Nukumanu Islands
Ontong Java Atoll
Choiseul
Santa Isabel
New Georgia
Malaita
SOLOMON ISLANDS
Guadalcanal
Honiara
San Cristobal
Rennell
Duff Islands
Santa Cruz Islands
Nanumea
Nanumanga
Niutao
TUVALU
Nui
Vaitupu
Nukufetau
Funafuti
Vaiaku
Nukulaelae
Niulakita
Banks Islands
Espiritu Santo
VANUATU
Maéwo
Malakula
Ambrym
Épi
Port Vila
Éfaté
Erromango
Tanna
Anatom
Îles Chesterfield (France)
New Caledonia (France)
Nouméa
Îles Loyauté (France)
Île des Pins
Hunter I.
Cato Island and Bank
Rotuma (Fiji)
Wallis and Futuna Islands (France)
Îles Wallis
Matā'utu
Île de Hoorn
Yasawa Group
Viti Levu
Vanua Levu
Suva
Koro
FIJI
Kadavu
Totoya
Ono-i-Lau
Ceva-i-Ra
Nukunono
Atafu
Tokelau (New Zealand)
Fakaofo
Swains Island
SAMOA
Savai'i
Apia
Upolu
American Samoa
Tutuila
Manu'a Is
Fagatogo
Niuafo'ou
Tafahi
Vava'u Group
Tofua
TONGA
Nuku'alofa
Tongatapu Group
Ata
Alofi
Niue (New Zealand)
Pukapuka
Nassau
Rakahanga
Manihiki
Penrhyn
Suwarrow
Malden Island
Starbuck Island
Vostok Island
Flint Island
Caroline Island (Millennium Island)
Equator
Palmerston
Aitutaki
Cook Islands (New Zealand)
Rarotonga
Mangaia
Mauke
Motu One
Papeete
Society Islands
Tahiti
Rangiroa
Fakarava
Anaa
Îles du Roi-Georges
Tuamotu Islands
French Polynesia
Raroia
Hao
Nuku Hiva
Hiva Oa
Marquesas Islands
Îles du Désappointement
Pukapuka
Maria
Îles du Duc de Gloucester
Hereheretue
Rurutu
Tubuai
Tubuai Islands
Raivavae
Mururoa
Groupe Actéon
Îles Gambier
Rapa
Marotiri
Adamstown
Pitcairn Islands (U.K.)
Henderson I.
Ducie I.
Pitcairn Island
Tropic of Capricorn
Norfolk Island (Australia)
Kingston
Lord Howe Island (Australia)
Raoul Island
Kermadec Islands (New Zealand)
TASMAN SEA
Cape Maria van Diemen
Whangarei
Great Barrier Island
North Island
Auckland
Manukau
Hamilton
New Plymouth
NEW ZEALAND
Gisborne
Napier
Palmerston North
Nelson
Wellington
Greymouth
Blenheim
South Island
Aoraki 3754
Southern Alps
Christchurch
Cape Providence
Timaru
Oamaru
Dunedin
Stewart Island
Invercargill
Chatham Islands (New Zealand)
Pitt Island
Snares Islands (New Zealand)
Bounty Islands (New Zealand)
Antipodes Islands (New Zealand)
Auckland Islands (New Zealand)
Campbell Island (New Zealand)
Macquarie Island (Australia)
MILES
KM
1200
800
400
0
2000
1600
1200
800
400
0

1:32 000 000

147

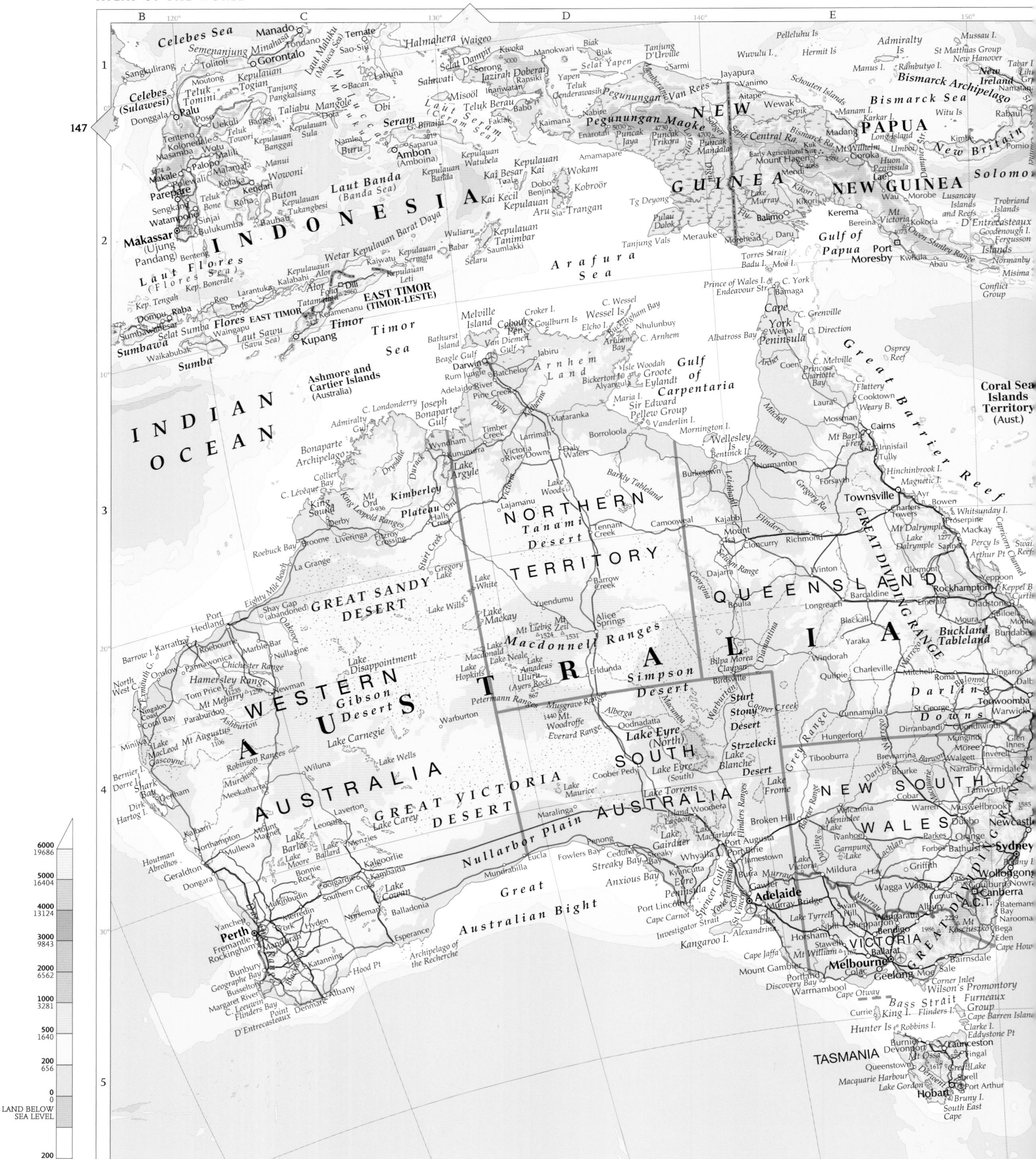


Lambert Azimuthal Equal Area Projection

F
G
H
I
160°
170°
180°
1
2
3
4
5
6
Equator
Tropic of Capricorn
NAURU
Yaren
Banaba
Aranuka
Nonouti
Gilbert Islands
Tabiteuea
Beru
Nikunau
Onotoa
Kingsmill Group
Tamana
Arorae
Howland Island (U.S.A.)
Baker Island (U.S.A.)
KIRIBATI
Phoenix Islands
Kanton
McKean
Phoenix Islands Protected Area
Nikumaroro
Manra
Orona
Nanumea
Niutao
Nanumanga
Nui
Nukufetau
Vaitupu
TUVALU
Funafuti
Fongafale
Nukulaelae
Niulakita
Atafu
Nukunonu
Fakaofo
Tokelau (N.Z.)
Lyra Reef
Tanga Is
Nuguria Is
Feni Is
Kilinailau Is
Takuu Is
Nukumanu Is
St George
Buka I.
Sohano
Bougainville Island
Ontong Java Atoll
Roncador Reef
Arawa
Choiseul
Treasury Is
SOLOMON ISLANDS
Vella Lavella
New Georgia Sound
Santa Isabel
Kolombangara
Buala
Malu'u
New Georgia Is (Solomon Is)
New Georgia
Florida Is
Malaita
Stewart Is
Rendova
Russell Is
Woodlark I.
Honiara
Maramasike
Guadalcanal
Avuavu
Ulawa I.
Kirakira
Duff Is
San Cristobal
Nupani
Swallow Is
Louisiade Arch.
Rossel I.
Santa Ana
Nendo
Santa Cruz Islands
Tagula I.
Rennell
Utupua
Vanikoro Is
Cherry Island
Tikopia
Mitre Island
Indispensable Reefs
Rotuma
CORAL SEA
Torres Islands
Ureparapara
Banks Islands
Vanua Lava
Santa Maria I.
Espiritu Santo
Tabwémasana 1879
Aoba
Maéwo
VANUATU
Pentecost I.
Malo
Norsup
Ambrym
Malakula
Épi
Émaé
Shepherd Is
Éfaté
Port Vila
Îles Chesterfield (France)
Récifs D'Entrecasteaux
Grand Passage
Erromango
Îles Belep
Grand Récif de Cook
Récif des Français
Tanna
Aniwa
Futuna
Anatom
Ouvéa
Îles Loyauté (Fr.)
Koumac
New Caledonia (France)
Nouvelle-Calédonie
Lifou
Tadine
Yaté
Maré
Nouméa
Cato Island and Bank
Grand Récif du Sud
Î. des Pins
Hunter I. (Fr.)
Ceva-i-Ra (Conway Reef)
Wallis and Futuna Islands (Fr.)
Îles Wallis
Matā'utu
Îles de Hoorn
Savai'i
SAMOA
Apia
Upolu
Tutuila (U.S.A.)
Great Sea Reef
Yasawa Group
Labasa
Vanua Levu
Bligh Water
Niuatoputapu
Lautoka
Tomanivi
Koro
Viti Levu
1324
Ovalau
Koro Sea
Suva
Tafahi
FIJI
Beqa
Gau
Kadavu Passage
Moala
Kadavu
Matuku
Vava'u Group
Ono-i-Lau
Tofua
TONGA
Niue (N.Z.)
Alofi
Nuku'alofa
Tongatapu Group
Ata
Horizon Depth 10882
Sandy Cape
Hervey Bay
Fraser Island
Maryborough
Gympie
Tewantin
Nambour
Caboolture
Brisbane
Beenleigh
Gold Coast
Byron Bay
Ballina
Casino
Grafton
Coffs Harbour
Macksville
Port Macquarie
Taree
Norfolk Island (Aust.)
Lord Howe Island (Aust.)
PACIFIC OCEAN
Raoul Island (N.Z.)
Kermadec Islands (N.Z.)
Three Kings Is
Cape Maria van Diemen
North Cape
Whangarei
Great Barrier Island
Kaipara Harbour
Takapuna
Auckland
Manukau
NORTH ISLAND
TASMAN SEA
Hamilton
Tauranga
Bay of Plenty
Tokoroa
North Taranaki Bight
New Plymouth
Mt Taranaki
Lake Taupo
East Cape
1752
Hikurangi
Gisborne
Mt Ruapehu
2797
South Taranaki Bight
Wanganui
Napier
Wairoa
Mahia Peninsula
Hawke Bay
Hastings
Cape Farewell
Palmerston North
Karamea Bight
Nelson
Cook Strait
Masterton
Westport
Blenheim
Lower Hutt
Wellington
NEW ZEALAND
Greymouth
Cape Palliser
Hokitika
Aoraki (Mt Cook) 3754
Southern Alps
Mt Aspiring
3030
Christchurch
Pegasus Bay
Banks Peninsula
Lake Te Anau
Lake Wanaka
Timaru
Canterbury Bight
Resolution Island
Lake Wakatipu
Oamaru
Cape Providence
SOUTH ISLAND
Otago Peninsula
Foveaux Strait
Dunedin
Invercargill
Stewart Island
South West Cape
Snares Is
Chatham Islands (N.Z.)
Pitt Island
Bounty Islands
Auckland Is
J
K
Miles
KM
0
200
400
600
800
1000
1200
1400
1:20 000 000

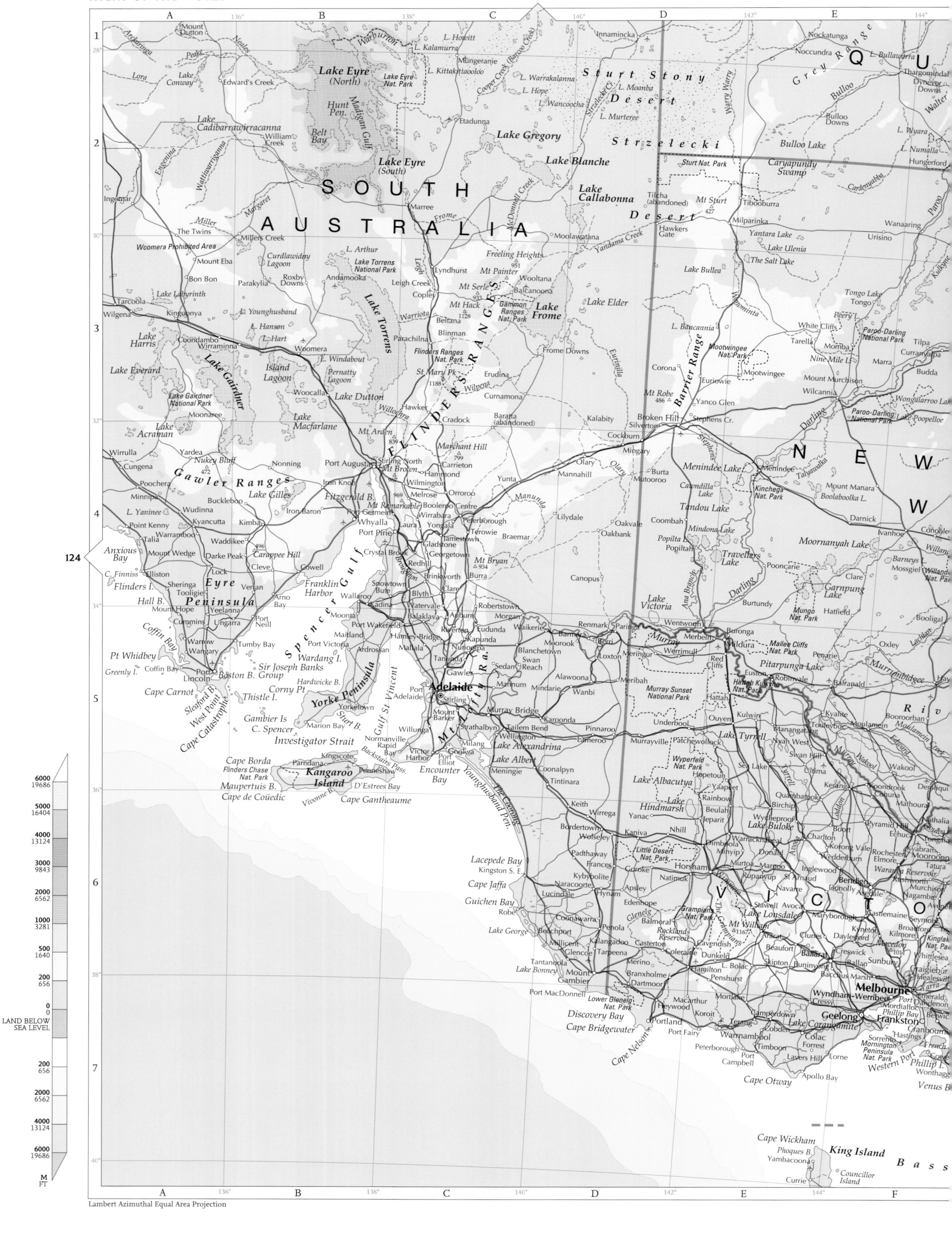


Lambert Azimuthal Equal Area Projection

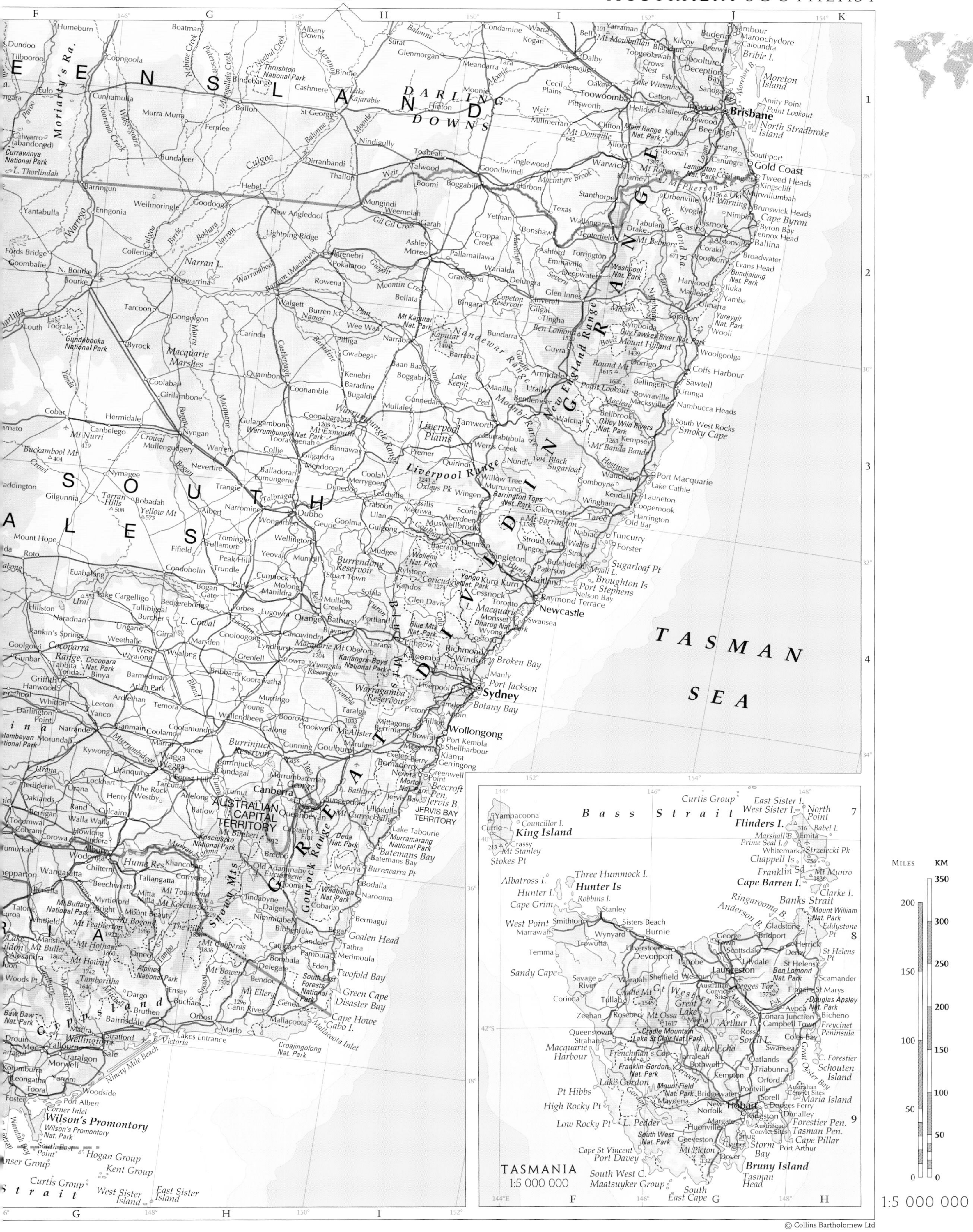
124
QUEENSLAND
NEW SOUTH WALES
DARLING DOWNS
GREAT DIVIDING RANGE
TASMAN SEA
AUSTRALIAN CAPITAL TERRITORY
JERVIS BAY TERRITORY
Brisbane
Gold Coast
Toowoomba
Newcastle
Sydney
Wollongong
Canberra
Port Macquarie
Coffs Harbour
Tamworth
Dubbo
Orange
Bathurst
Wagga Wagga
Albury
Griffith
Bourke
Liverpool Plains
Liverpool Range
Blue Mts
Snowy Mts
Kosciuszko National Park
Wilson's Promontory
Bass Strait
TASMANIA
1:5 000 000
King Island
Flinders I.
Launceston
Hobart
Devonport
Burnie
Bruny Island
Maria Island
Tasman Pen.
MILES
KM
1:5 000 000

# NEW ZEALAND

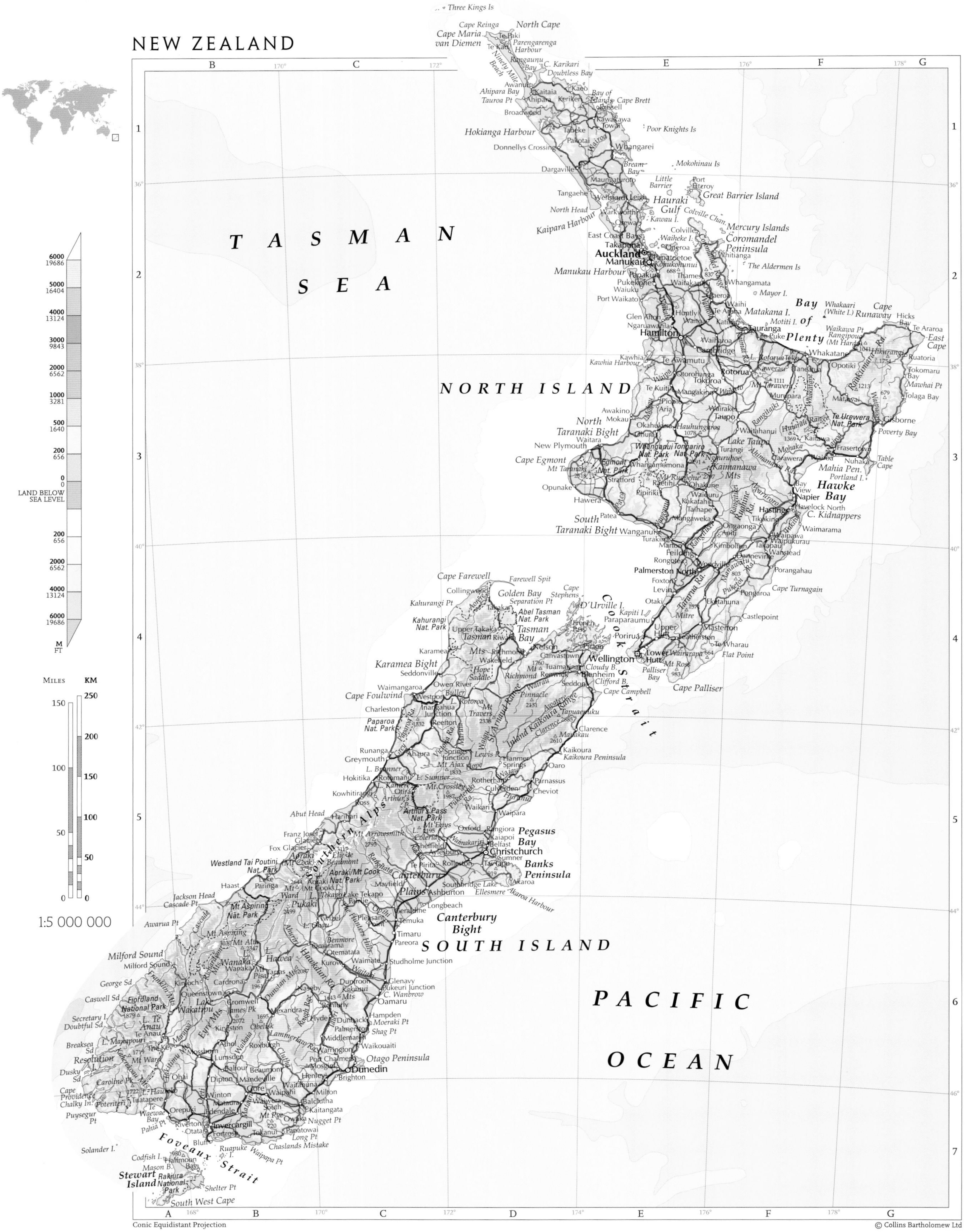


Conic Equidistant Projection

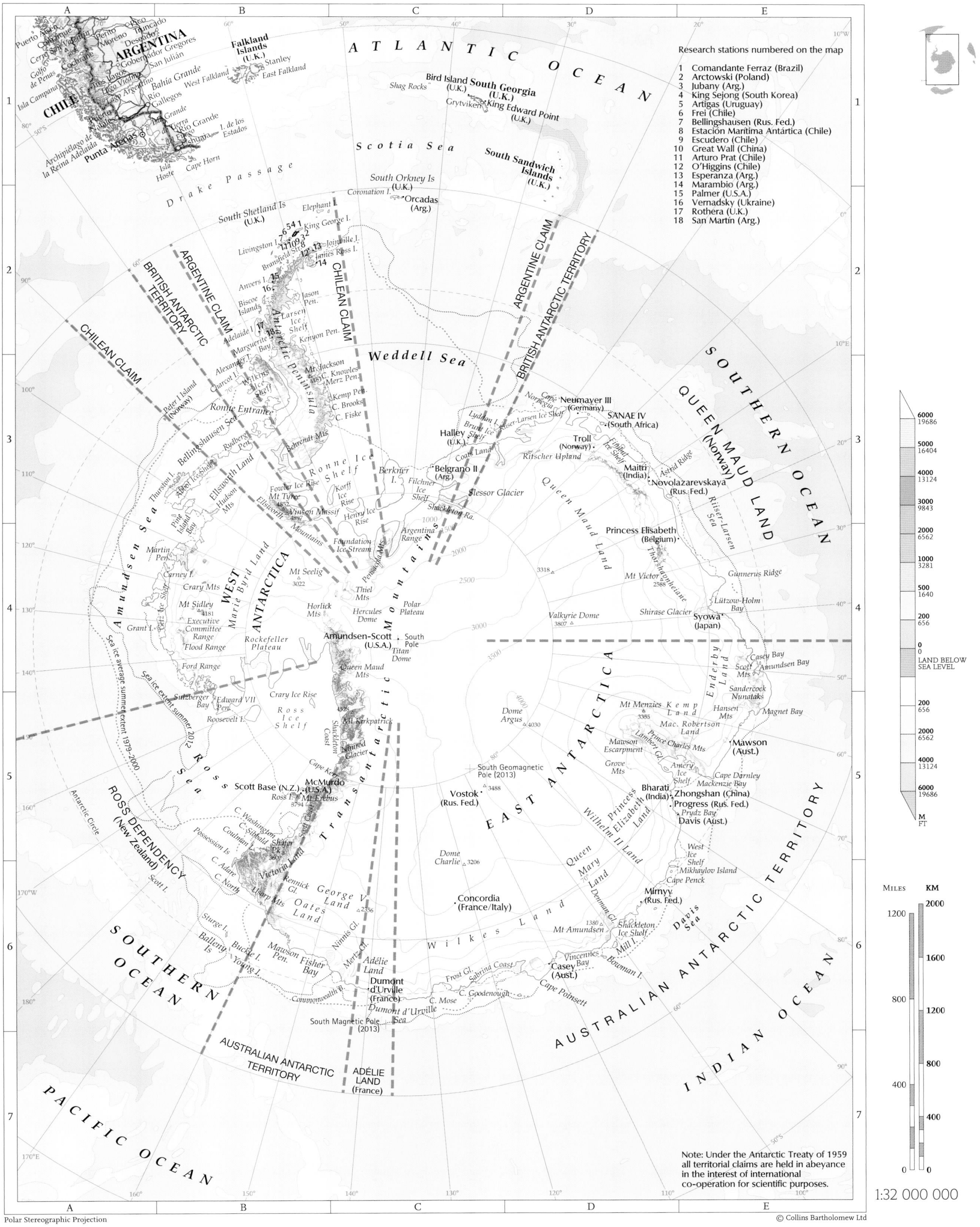
ATLANTIC OCEAN
Research stations numbered on the map
1 Comandante Ferraz (Brazil)
2 Arctowski (Poland)
3 Jubany (Arg.)
4 King Sejong (South Korea)
5 Artigas (Uruguay)
6 Frei (Chile)
7 Bellingshausen (Rus. Fed.)
8 Estación Marítima Antártica (Chile)
9 Escudero (Chile)
10 Great Wall (China)
11 Arturo Prat (Chile)
12 O'Higgins (Chile)
13 Esperanza (Arg.)
14 Marambio (Arg.)
15 Palmer (U.S.A.)
16 Vernadsky (Ukraine)
17 Rothera (U.K.)
18 San Martín (Arg.)
ARGENTINA
CHILE
Falkland Islands (U.K.)
Stanley
East Falkland
West Falkland
Punta Arenas
Drake Passage
Scotia Sea
South Georgia (U.K.)
Bird Island (U.K.)
King Edward Point (U.K.)
Grytviken
Shag Rocks
South Sandwich Islands (U.K.)
South Orkney Is (U.K.)
Orcadas (Arg.)
Coronation I.
South Shetland Is (U.K.)
Elephant I.
King George I.
Livingston I.
Joinville I.
James Ross I.
Anvers I.
Biscoe Islands
Adelaide I.
Alexander I.
Charcot I.
Jason Pen.
Larsen Ice Shelf
Kenyon Pen.
Antarctic Peninsula
Marguerite Bay
Mt Jackson
C. Knowles
Merz Pen.
Kemp Pen.
C. Brooks
C. Fiske
Wilkins Ice Shelf
Peter I Island (Norway)
Ronne Entrance
Bellingshausen Sea
Rydberg Pen.
Thurston I.
Ellsworth Land
Hudson Mts
Fowler Ice Rise
Mt Tyree 4852
Vinson Massif 4897
Ellsworth Mountains
Ronne Ice Shelf
Korff Ice Rise
Henry Ice Rise
Berkner I.
Filchner Ice Shelf
Weddell Sea
Halley (U.K.)
Belgrano II (Arg.)
Coats Land
Slessor Glacier
Shackleton Ra.
Foundation Ice Stream
Pensacola Mts
Argentina Range
Neumayer III (Germany)
SANAE IV (South Africa)
Troll (Norway)
Maitri (India)
Novolazarevskaya (Rus. Fed.)
Riiser-Larsen Ice Shelf
Ritscher Upland
Astrid Ridge
Riiser-Larsen Sea
QUEEN MAUD LAND (Norway)
Queen Maud Land
Princess Elisabeth (Belgium)
Mt Victor 2588
Gunnerus Ridge
Lützow-Holm Bay
Syowa (Japan)
Shirase Glacier
Valkyrie Dome 3807
SOUTHERN OCEAN
BRITISH ANTARCTIC TERRITORY
ARGENTINE CLAIM
CHILEAN CLAIM
Amundsen Sea
Pine Island Bay
Martin Pen.
Carney I.
Crary Mts
Mt Sidley 4181
Executive Committee Range
Flood Range
Grant I.
Getz Ice Shelf
Ford Range
Sulzberger Bay
Edward VII Pen.
Roosevelt I.
WEST ANTARCTICA
Marie Byrd Land
Mt Seelig 3022
Thiel Mts
Horlick Mts
Hercules Dome
Polar Plateau
Rockefeller Plateau
Amundsen-Scott (U.S.A.)
South Pole
Titan Dome
Queen Maud Mts
Crary Ice Rise
Ross Ice Shelf
Mt Kirkpatrick 4528
Shackleton Coast
Nimrod Glacier
Transantarctic Mountains
Cape Kerr
Scott Base (N.Z.)
McMurdo (U.S.A.)
Ross I.
Mt Erebus 3794
Ross Sea
ROSS DEPENDENCY (New Zealand)
Sea ice average summer extent 1979–2000
Sea ice extent summer 2012
Antarctic Circle
C. Washington
C. Sibbald
Coulman I.
Possession Is
Shafer Pk 3600
Victoria Land
C. Adare
C. North
Scott I.
Rennick Gl.
Usarp Mts
George V Land
Oates Land
Sturge I.
Balleny Is
Buckle I.
Young I.
Mawson Pen.
Fisher Bay
Ninnis Gl.
Mertz Gl.
Adélie Land
Dumont d'Urville (France)
Dumont d'Urville Sea
Commonwealth B.
South Magnetic Pole (2013)
Dome Argus 4030
Mt Menzies 3355
Kemp Land
Mac. Robertson Land
Mawson Escarpment
Lambert Gl.
Prince Charles Mts
Mawson (Aust.)
Grove Mts
Amery Ice Shelf
Cape Darnley
Mackenzie Bay
Bharati (India)
Zhongshan (China)
Progress (Rus. Fed.)
Prydz Bay
Davis (Aust.)
South Geomagnetic Pole (2013)
Vostok (Rus. Fed.) 3488
EAST ANTARCTICA
Princess Elizabeth Land
Wilhelm II Land
West Ice Shelf
Mikhaylov Island
Cape Penck
Queen Mary Land
Dome Charlie 3206
Concordia (France/Italy)
Mirnyy (Rus. Fed.)
Denman Gl.
Mt Amundsen 1380
Shackleton Ice Shelf
Mill I.
Davis Sea
Wilkes Land
Vincennes Bay
Bowman I.
Casey (Aust.)
Sabrina Coast
Frost Gl.
C. Goodenough
C. Mose
Cape Poinsett
Enderby Land
Casey Bay
Amundsen Bay
Scott Mts
Sandercock Nunataks
Hansen Mts
Magnet Bay
AUSTRALIAN ANTARCTIC TERRITORY
ADÉLIE LAND (France)
PACIFIC OCEAN
INDIAN OCEAN
Note: Under the Antarctic Treaty of 1959 all territorial claims are held in abeyance in the interest of international co-operation for scientific purposes.
M FT
6000 19686
5000 16404
4000 13124
3000 9843
2000 6562
1000 3281
500 1640
200 656
0 0
LAND BELOW SEA LEVEL
200 656
2000 6562
4000 13124
6000 19686
MILES KM
1200 2000
1600
800 1200
800
400 400
0 0
1:32 000 000
Polar Stereographic Projection

Orthographic Projection

OCEAN
Bering Strait
Tiksi
CENTRAL SIBERIAN PLATEAU
Verkhoyanskiy Khrebet
Arctic Circle
Anadyr'
Ugol'nyye Kopi
Khrebet Kolymskiy
Kolyma
Lena
Vilyuy
Aldan
Nizhnyaya Tunguska
Susuman
Mirnyy
Yakutsk
FEDERATION
BERING SEA
Pribilof Islands
Magadan
Sea of Okhotsk
Kamchatka Peninsula
Petropavlovsk-Kamchatskiy
Aleutian Islands
Angara
Aldan
Lena
Vitim
Bodaybo
Stanovoy Khrebet
Bratsk
Ust'-Kut
Kansk
Tynda
Lake Baikal
Amur
Heilong Jiang
Amgun'
Sakhalin
Irkutsk
Chita
Ulan-Ude
Komsomol'sk-na-Amure
Blagoveshchensk
Argun'
Hövsgöl Nuur
Hulun Buir
Hulun Nur
Da Hinggan Ling
Khabarovsk
Yuzhno-Sakhalinsk
Korsakov
Kuril Islands
Darhan
Uliastay
Ulan Bator
Buir Nur
Qiqihar
Daqing
Jiamusi
MONGOLIA
Matad
Harbin
Wakkanai
GOBI DESERT
Lake Khanka
Hokkaidō
Changchun
Jilin
Vladivostok
Sapporo
Dalandzadgad
INNER MONGOLIA
Hakodate
Ch'ŏngjin
Shenyang
Fushun
Anshan
Sea of Japan (East Sea)
Akita
Hohhot
NORTH KOREA
P'yŏngyang
Honshū
Sendai
Laojunmiao
Wuhai
Baotou
Yellow (Huang He)
Datong
Beijing
Tianjin
Dalian
Niigata
Qilian Shan
Yinchuan
Shijiazhuang
Bo Hai
Korea Bay
Seoul
Kanazawa
Tōkyō
Taiyuan
Jinan
Zibo
Yantai
SOUTH KOREA
Daejeon
Daegu
Kyōto
Yokohama
Qinghai Hu
Xining
Handan
Gwangju
Busan
Kōbe
Ōsaka
JAPAN
Gyaring Hu
Lanzhou
Jining
Qingdao
Kita-Kyūshū
Hiroshima
Shikoku
Zhengzhou
Xuzhou
Yellow Sea
Fukuoka
Nagasaki
Kumamoto
Xi'an
Huainan
Nanjing
Kagoshima
Kyūshū
CHINA
Suizhou
Wuxi
Shanghai
Chengdu
Nanchong
Wuhan
Hefei
East China Sea
Mekong (Lancang Jiang)
Neijiang
Chongqing
Yangtze (Chang Jiang)
Hangzhou
Ningbo
Yibin
Yueyang
Quzhou
Bonin Islands (Japan)
Changsha
Nanchang
Wenzhou
PACIFIC
Tropic of Cancer
Okinawa
Ryukyu Islands
Panzhihua
Guiyang
Hengyang
Fuzhou
Volcano Islands (Japan)
Myitkyina
Qujing
T'aipei
Kunming
Xun Jiang
Liuzhou
Meizhou
Xiamen
Taiwan Strait
TAIWAN
Salween
Nanning
Guangzhou
Shantou
T'aitung
OCEAN
Macao
Hong Kong
MYANMAR (BURMA)
Ha Nôi
Hai Phong
Zhanjiang
Batan Islands
Pagan
Louangphabang
Gulf of Tongking
Haikou
Luzon Strait
Northern Mariana Islands
LAOS
VIETNAM
Hainan Dao
Aparri
Chiang Mai
Mae Nam Nan
Vientiane
Luzon
PHILIPPINES
Saipan
Tinian
Rota
Mawlamyaing
Huê
Da Năng
Paracel Islands
Quezon City
Guam
THAILAND
Mekong
SOUTH CHINA SEA
Manila
Nakhon Ratchasima
Naga
Bangkok
Tonle Sap
Mindoro
Samar
Myeik
CAMBODIA
Nha Trang
Masbate
Yap
Phnom Penh
Panay
Gulf of Thailand
Ho Chi Minh City
Iloilo
Cebu
Surigao
Caroline Islands
Chuuk
Sihanoukville
Spratly Islands
Palawan
Negros
PALAU
Melekeok
Nakhon Si Thammarat
Malay Peninsula
Dapitan
Sulu Sea
Mindanao
Davao
Mortlock Islands
Zamboanga
Kota Bharu
Kota Kinabalu
Sandakan
Sulu Archipelago
George Town
BRUNEI
Bandar Seri Begawan
SABAH
Kepulauan Talaud
Ipoh
MALAYSIA
Kepulauan Sangir
Kuala Lumpur
Celebes Sea
Equator
Putrajaya
SARAWAK
Laut Maluku
Strait of Malacca
Medan
Kuching
Sibu
Sri Aman
Manado
Halmahera
Singapore
Nias
Sumatra
Borneo
Manokwari
Bismarck Archipelago
Jazirah Doberai
Jayapura
Siberut
Kepulauan Lingga
Pontianak
Balikpapan
Selat Makassar
Palu
Kepulauan Sula
Maluku
Bismarck Sea
Padang
Laut Seram
Seram
New Britain
Kepulauan Mentawai
Bangka
Ketapang
Barito
Celebes
Puncak Jaya 5030
New Guinea
Palembang
Banjarmasin
Buru
Solomon Sea
Bengkulu
Parepare
Buton
Laut Banda
Digul
Laut Jawa
Makassar
Kepulauan Aru
Bandar Lampung
INDONESIA
Gulf of Papua
Enggano
Selat Sunda
Jakarta
Madura
Kepulauan Tanimbar
Semarang
Surabaya
Laut Bali
Laut Flores
Wetar
Dili
Torres Strait
Bandung
Java
Bali
Raba
Flores
EAST TIMOR (TIMOR-LESTE)
Arafura Sea
Yogyakarta
Lombok
Sumbawa
Laut Sawu
Timor
Cape York Peninsula
CORAL SEA
Sumba
Kupang
F
G
H
I
J
1
2
3
4
5
6
7
MILES
KM
1000
750
500
250
0
1500
1250
1000
750
500
250
0
1:28 000 000

Conic Equidistant Projection

169

134

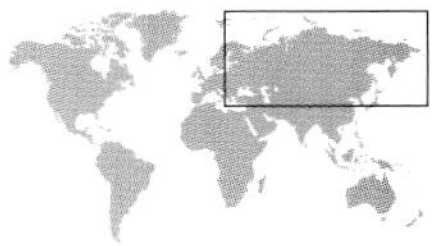

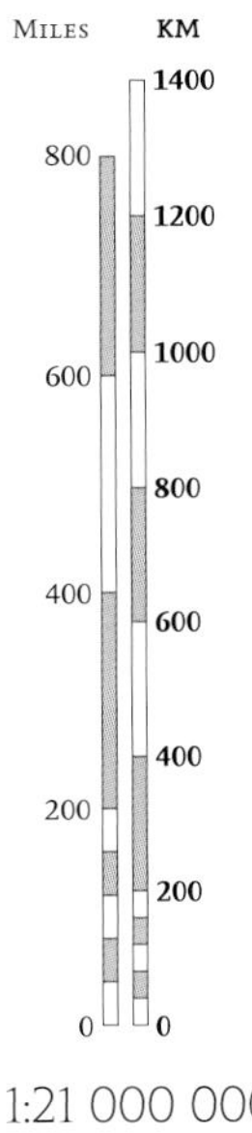


1:21 000 000

135

132

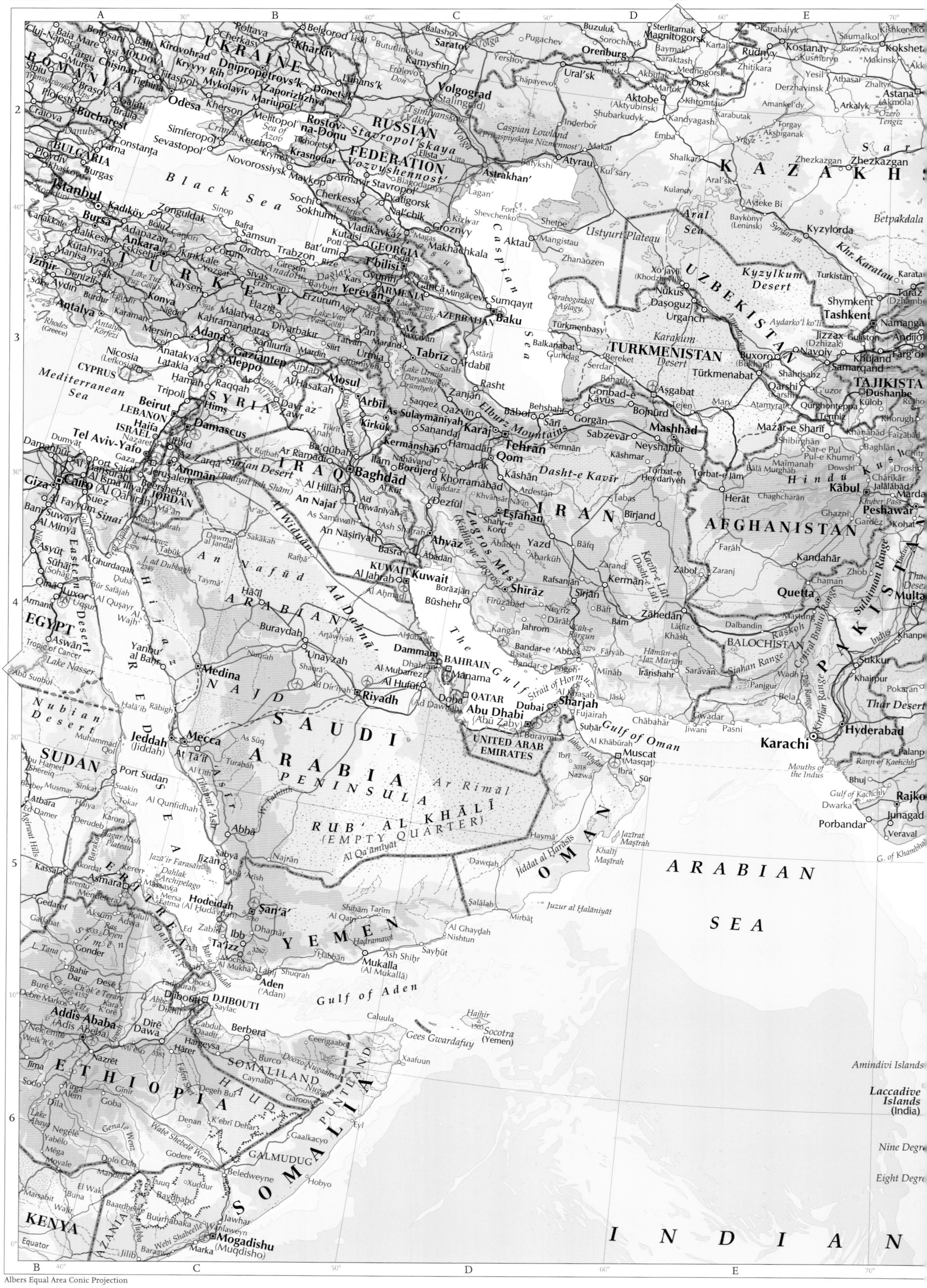


177

6000 19686
5000 16404
4000 13124
3000 9843
2000 6562
1000 3281
500 1640
200 656
0 0
LAND BELOW SEA LEVEL
200 656
2000 6562
4000 13124
6000 19686
M FT

Albers Equal Area Conic Projection

133
146
147
155
RUSSIAN FEDERATION
MONGOLIA
GOBI DESERT
ALTAI MOUNTAINS
INNER MONGOLIA
KYRGYZSTAN
Lake Balkhash
TIEN SHAN
XINJIANG
Tarim Basin
(Tarim Pendi)
Taklimakan Desert
(Taklimakan Shamo)
KUNLUN SHAN
Plateau of Tibet
(Qingzang Gaoyuan)
TIBET
CHINA
Qaidam Pendi
Tanggula Shan
HIMALAYA
NEPAL
BHUTAN
BANGLADESH
INDIA
MYANMAR
(BURMA)
LAOS
THAILAND
CAMBODIA
VIETNAM
PENINSULAR MALAYSIA
MALAYSIA
SINGAPORE
INDONESIA
SRI LANKA
MALDIVES
BAY OF BENGAL
Andaman Sea
OCEAN
Gulf of Thailand
Strait of Malacca
Deccan
Coromandel Coast
Malabar Coast
Eastern Ghats
Western Ghats
Hainan Dao
Andaman Islands
(India)
Nicobar Islands
(India)
Ulan Bator
(Ulaanbaatar)
Ürümqi
Almaty
Bishkek
Kashi
Lhasa
Kathmandu
Thimphu
Delhi
Kolkata
(Calcutta)
Dhaka
Mumbai
(Bombay)
Chennai
(Madras)
Bangalore
Hyderabad
Colombo
Sri Jayewardenepura Kotte
Rangoon
(Yangon)
Nay Pyi Taw
Mandalay
Bangkok
(Krung Thep)
Vientiane
Ha Nôi
Phnom Penh
Ho Chi Minh City
Kuala Lumpur
Beijing
(Peking)
Tianjin
Chongqing
Chengdu
Xi'an
Lanzhou
Kunming
Wuhan
MILES
KM
1:20 000 000

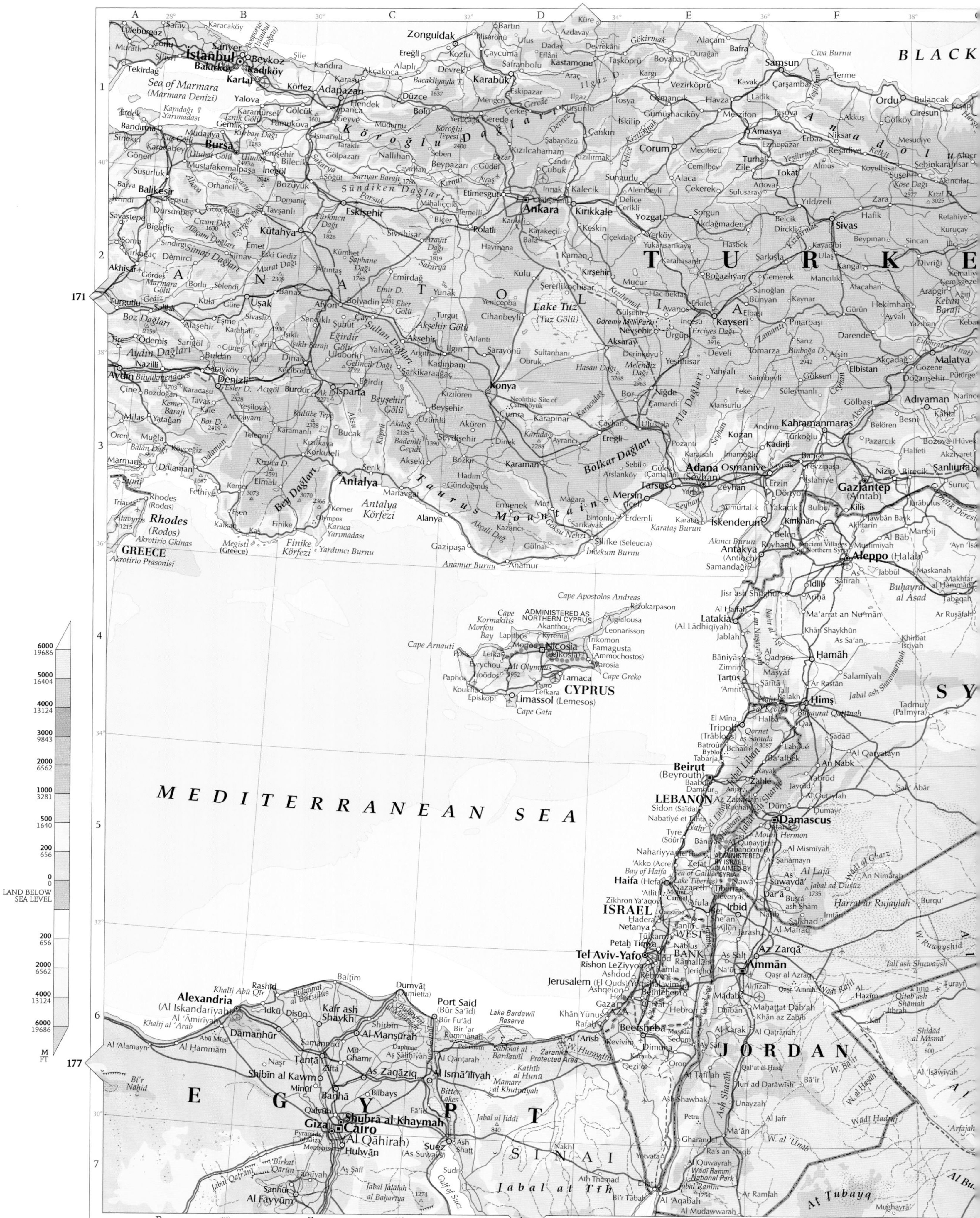


Conic Equidistant Projection

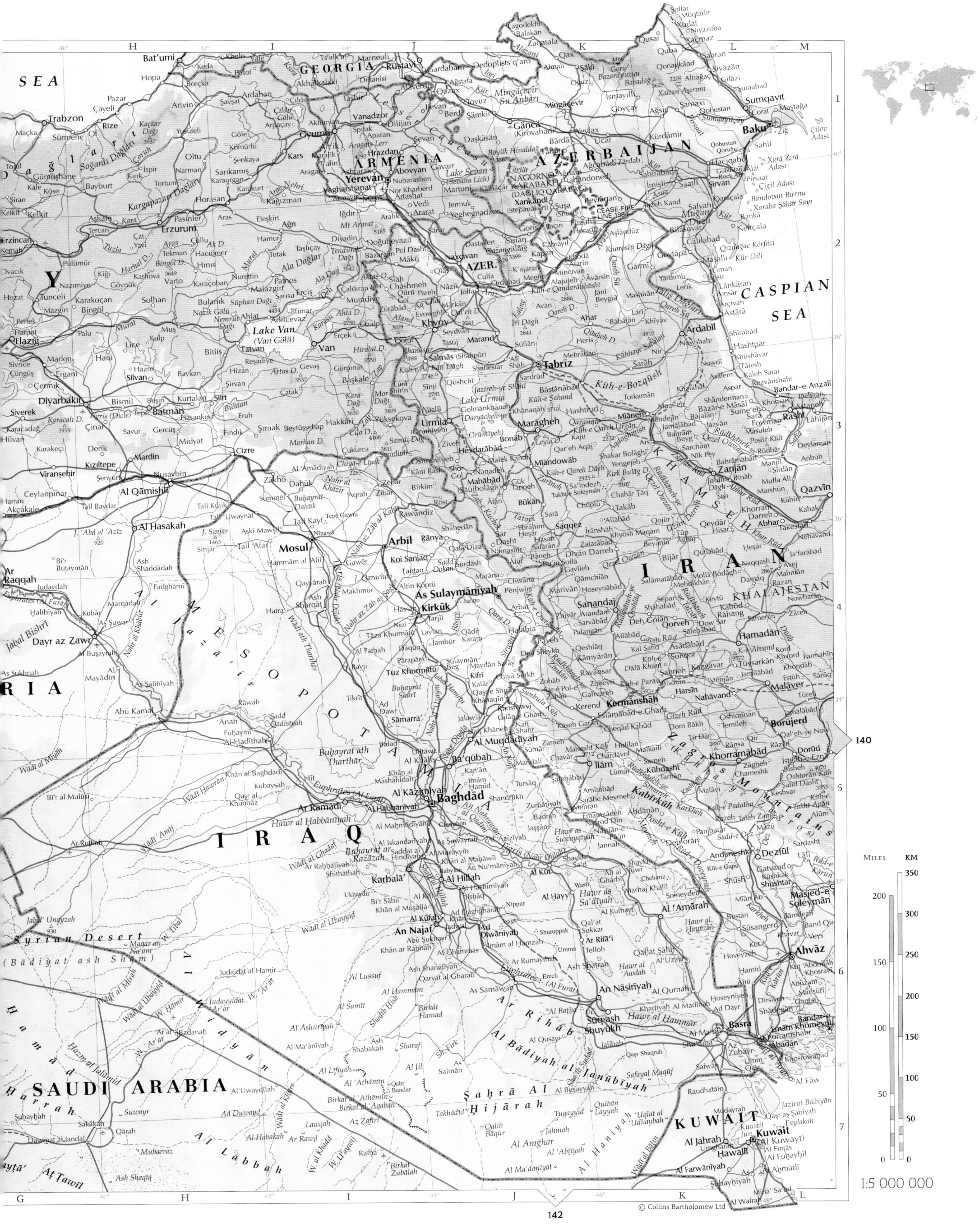
GEORGIA
ARMENIA
AZERBAIJAN
AZER.
IRAN
IRAQ
KUWAIT
SAUDI ARABIA
MESOPOTAMIA
CASPIAN SEA
SEA
Syrian Desert
(Bādiyat ash Shām)
Al Jazīrah
Al Widyān
Al Bādiyah al Janūbīyah
Şaḩrā Al Ḩijārah
Zagros Mountains
KHAMSEH
KHALAJESTAN
Lake Van
(Van Gölü)
Lake Urmia
Yerevan
Baku
Tabrīz
Baghdād
Mosul
Kirkūk
Arbīl
As Sulaymānīyah
Basra
Kuwait
(Al Kuwayt)
Ahvāz
Hamadān
Kermānshāh
Zanjān
Qazvīn
Rasht
Ardabīl
Erzurum
Trabzon
Diyarbakır
Urmia
Karbalā'
An Najaf
Al Ḩillah
Ar Ramādī
Dezfūl
Khorramābād
Sanandaj
Al 'Amārah
An Nāşirīyah
Sumqayıt
Gəncə
Gyumri
Rustavi
Tigris (Dicle)
Euphrates (Al Furāt)
NAGORNO KARABAKH
CEASE-FIRE LINE 1994
Hawr al Ḩammār
Hawr al Ḩabbānīyah
Mt Ararat
5165
140
142
1:5 000 000
MILES
KM
© Collins Bartholomew Ltd

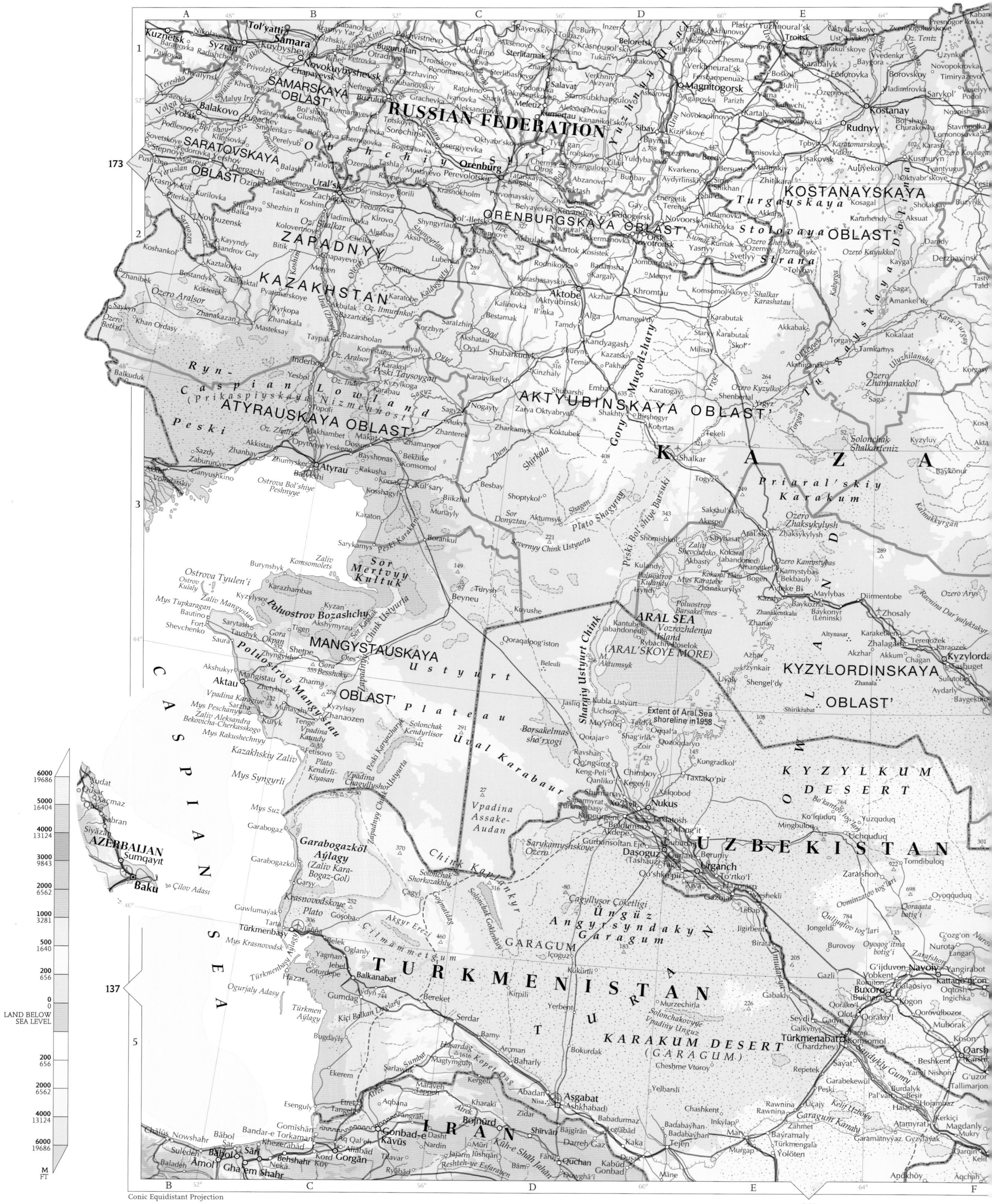
RUSSIAN FEDERATION
SAMARSKAYA OBLAST'
SARATOVSKAYA OBLAST'
ORENBURGSKAYA OBLAST'
KOSTANAYSKAYA OBLAST'
ZAPADNYY KAZAKHSTAN
AKTYUBINSKAYA OBLAST'
ATYRAUSKAYA OBLAST'
MANGYSTAUSKAYA OBLAST'
KYZYLORDINSKAYA OBLAST'
KAZAKHSTAN
UZBEKISTAN
TURKMENISTAN
AZERBAIJAN
IRAN
CASPIAN SEA
ARAL SEA (ARAL'SKOYE MORE)
Extent of Aral Sea shoreline in 1958
Caspian Lowland (Prikaspiyskaya Nizmennost')
Ustyurt Plateau
KYZYLKUM DESERT
KARAKUM DESERT (GARAGUM)
Turgayskaya Stolovaya Strana
Obshchiy Syrt
Priaral'skiy Karakum
Samara
Tol'yatti
Orenburg
Ural'sk
Aktobe (Aktyubinsk)
Kostanay
Magnitogorsk
Atyrau
Aktau
Nukus
Dasoguz
Urganch
Kyzylorda
Buxoro
Navoiy
Türkmenbaşy
Balkanabat
Asgabat (Ashkhabad)
Türkmenabat (Chardzhev)
Baku
Sumqayit
Gorgān
Conic Equidistant Projection
6000 19686
5000 16404
4000 13124
3000 9843
2000 6562
1000 3281
500 1640
200 656
0 0
LAND BELOW SEA LEVEL
200 656
2000 6562
4000 13124
6000 19686
M FT
173
137
141

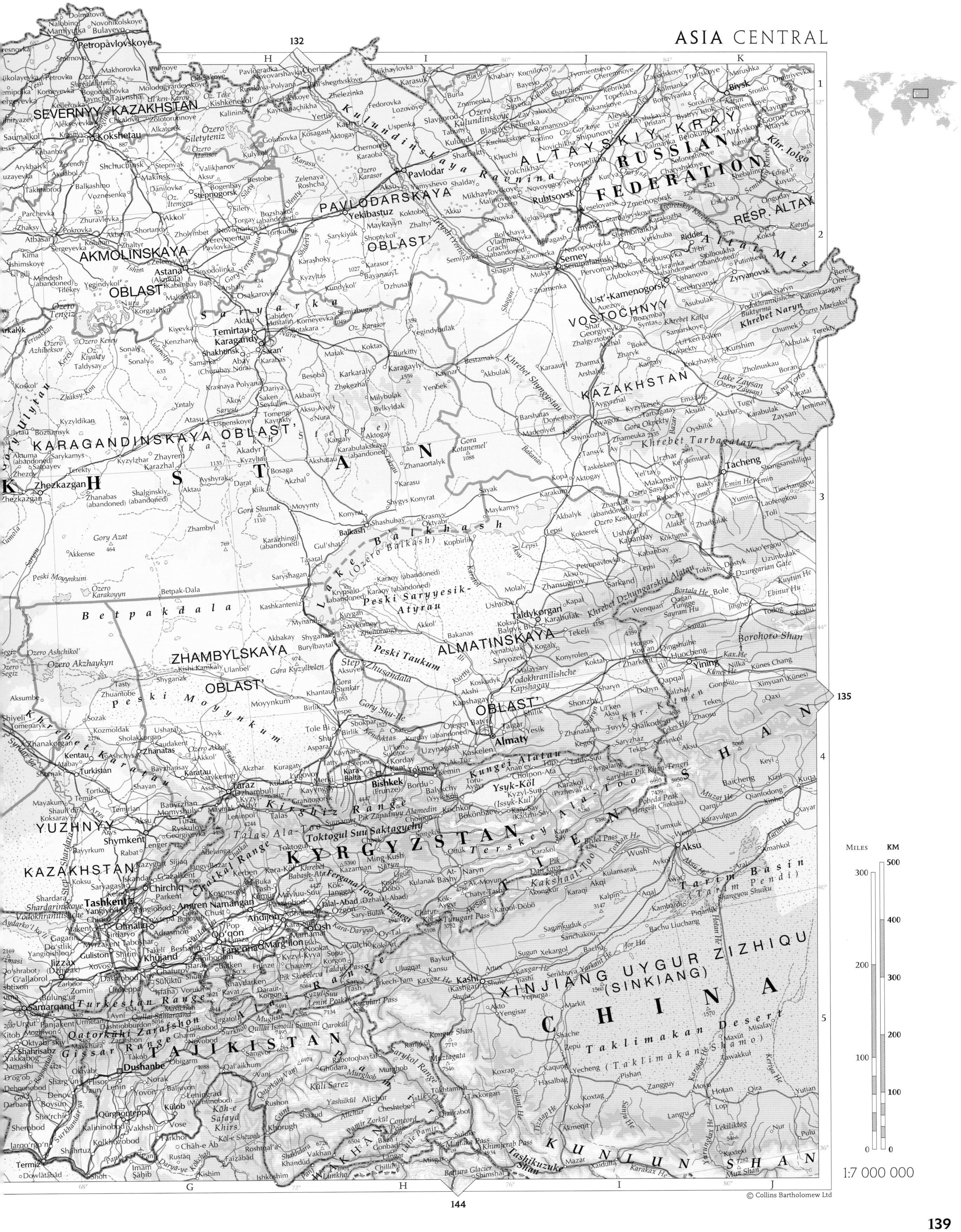
132
135
144
SEVERNYY KAZAKHSTAN
AKMOLINSKAYA OBLAST'
PAVLODARSKAYA OBLAST'
ALTAYSKIY KRAY
RUSSIAN FEDERATION
RESP. ALTAY
KARAGANDINSKAYA OBLAST'
VOSTOCHNYY KAZAKHSTAN
KAZAKHSTAN
ZHAMBYLSKAYA OBLAST'
ALMATINSKAYA OBLAST'
YUZHNYY KAZAKHSTAN
KYRGYZSTAN
TAJIKISTAN
XINJIANG UYGUR ZIZHIQU (SINKIANG)
CHINA
TIEN SHAN
KUNLUN SHAN
Taklimakan Desert
Taklimakan Shamo
Tarim Basin
Tarim Pendi
Lake Balkhash
Ozero Balkhash
Betpakdala
Peski Moyynkum
Saryarka
Kazakh Stepe
Petropavlovskoye
Kokshetau
Astana
Pavlodar
Karagandy
Temirtau
Semey
Ust'-Kamenogorsk
Rubtsovsk
Biysk
Zhezkazgan
Balkash
Taldykorgan
Almaty
Bishkek
Taraz
Shymkent
Tashkent
Andijon
Namangan
Osh
Samarqand
Dushanbe
Kashi
Aksu
Yining
Tacheng
Hotan
Termiz
Lake Zaysan
Ysyk-Köl
Pik Pobedy
Pik Khan-Tengri
Turkestan Range
Altai Mts
Pamir
Gissar Range
Zhungarian Gate
1
2
3
4
5
G
H
I
J
K
MILES
KM
0
100
200
300
400
500
1:7 000 000
© Collins Bartholomew Ltd

137

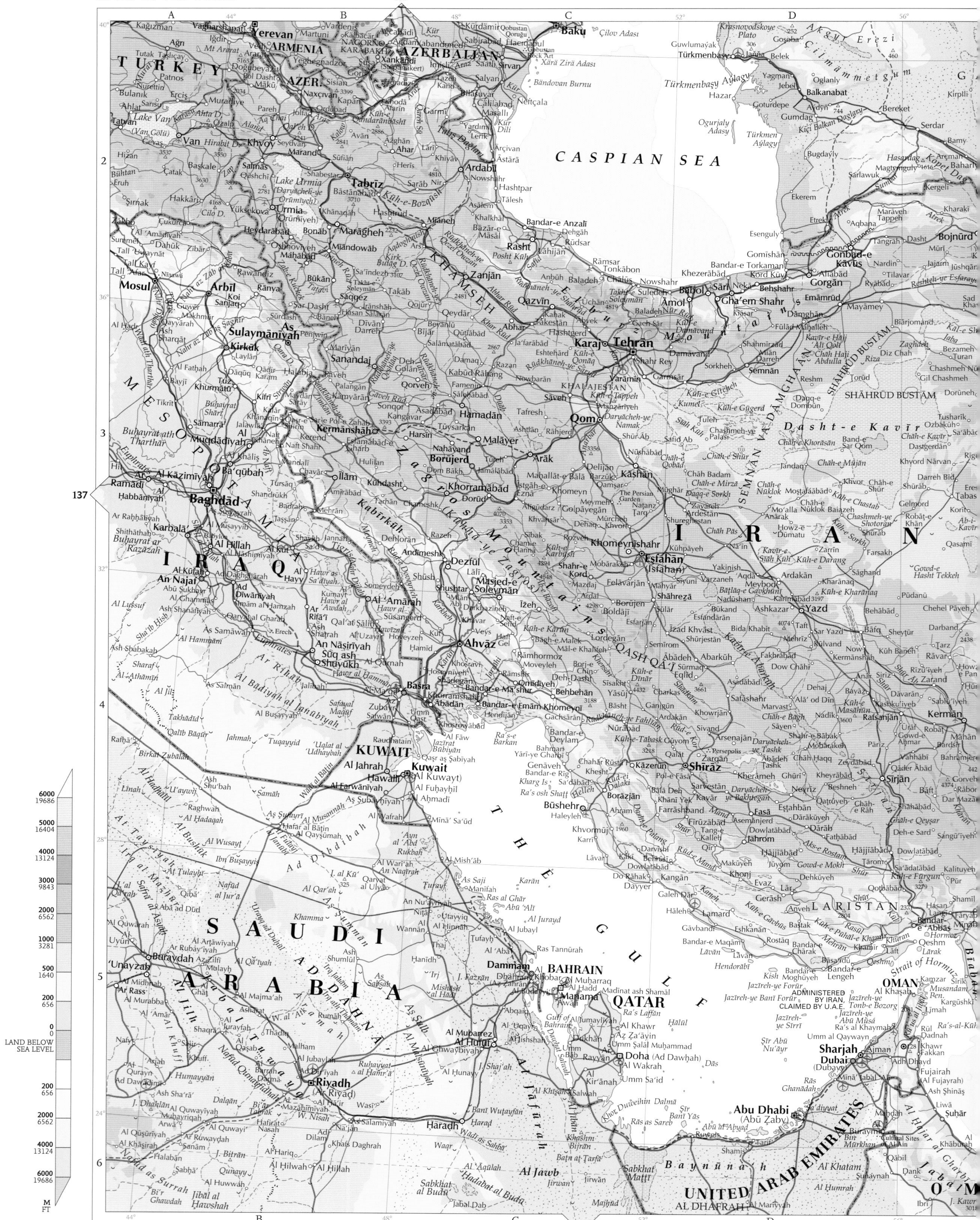


Conic Equidistant Projection

142

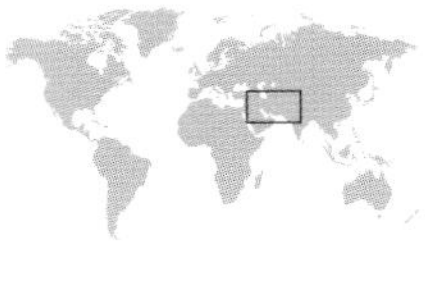

138

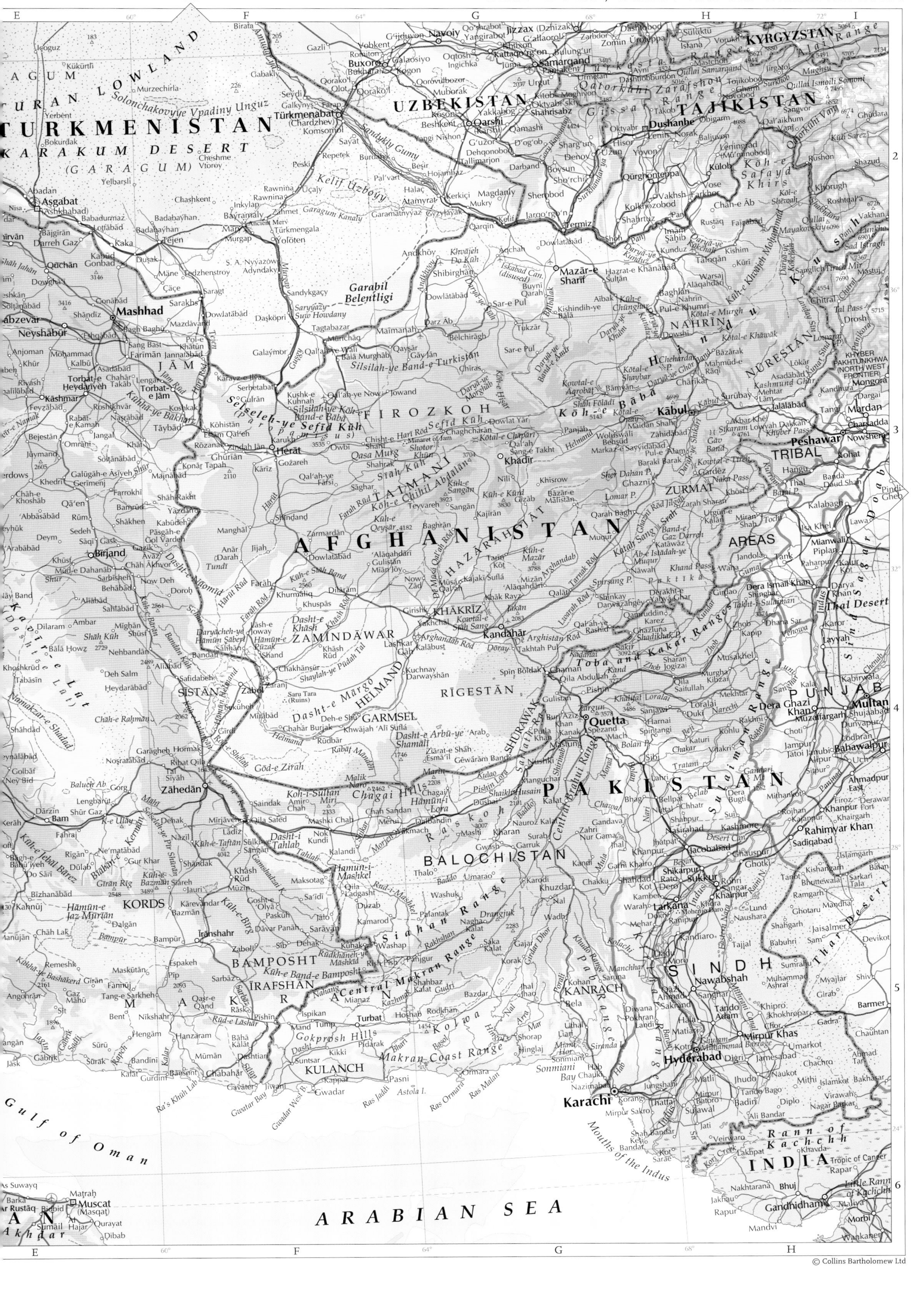


144

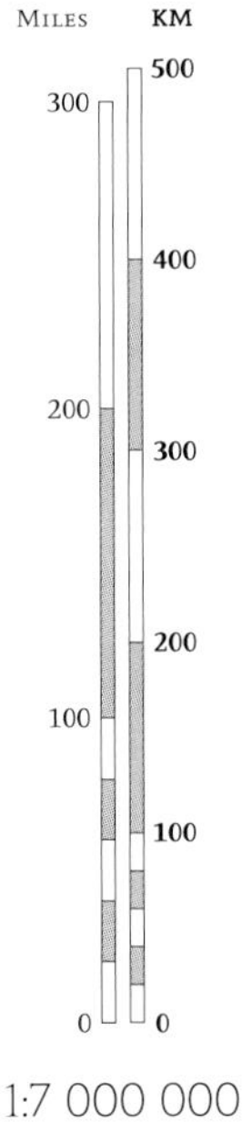


1:7 000 000

# ARABIAN PENINSULA

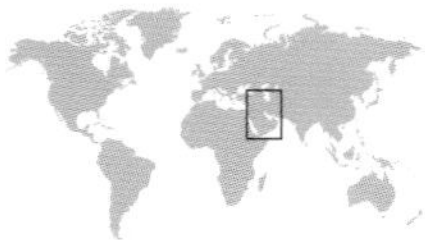

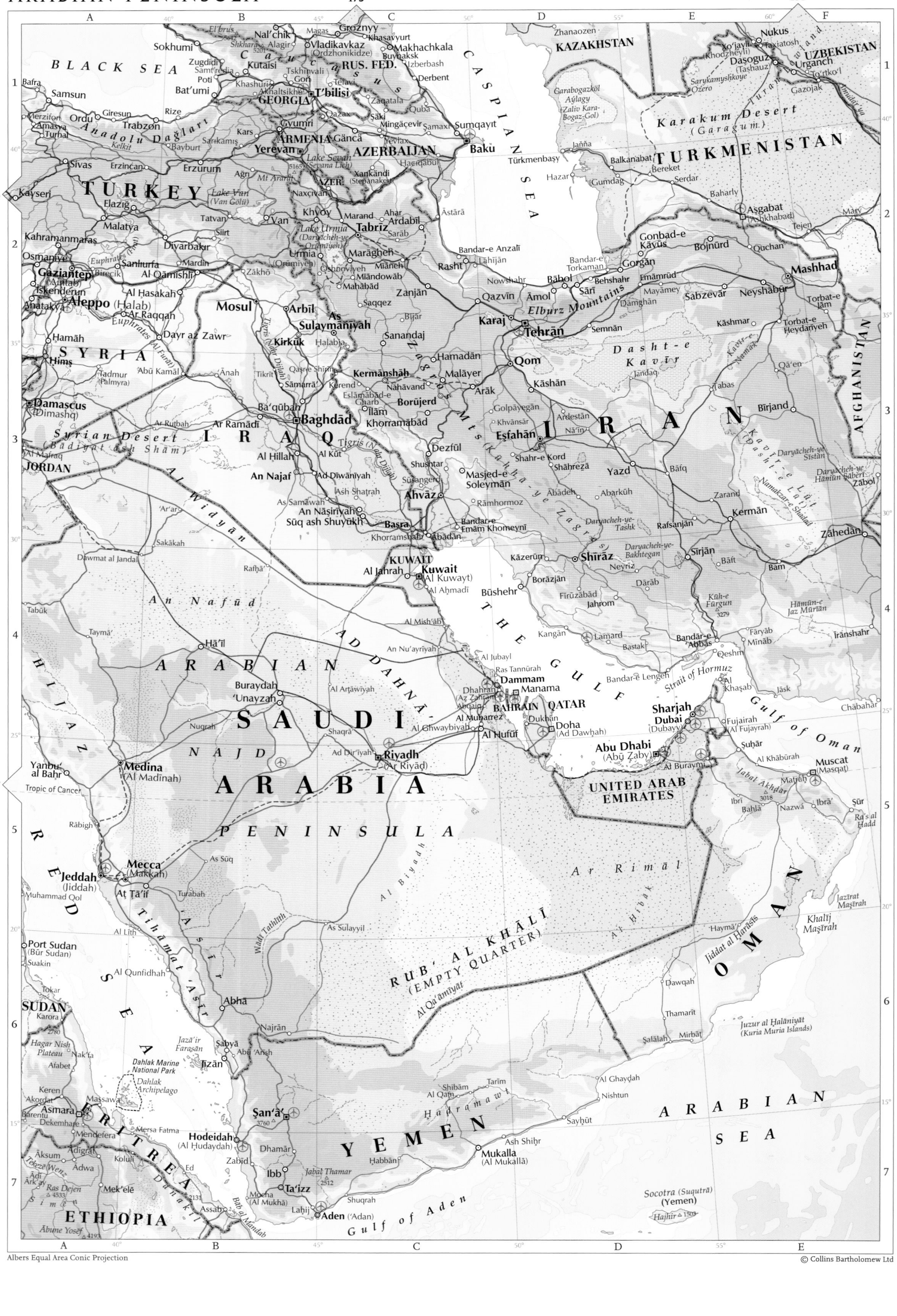


Albers Equal Area Conic Projection

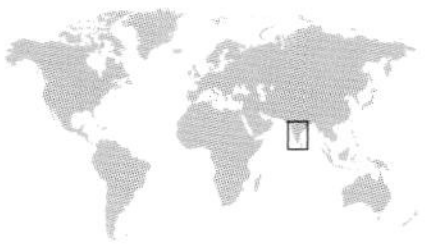

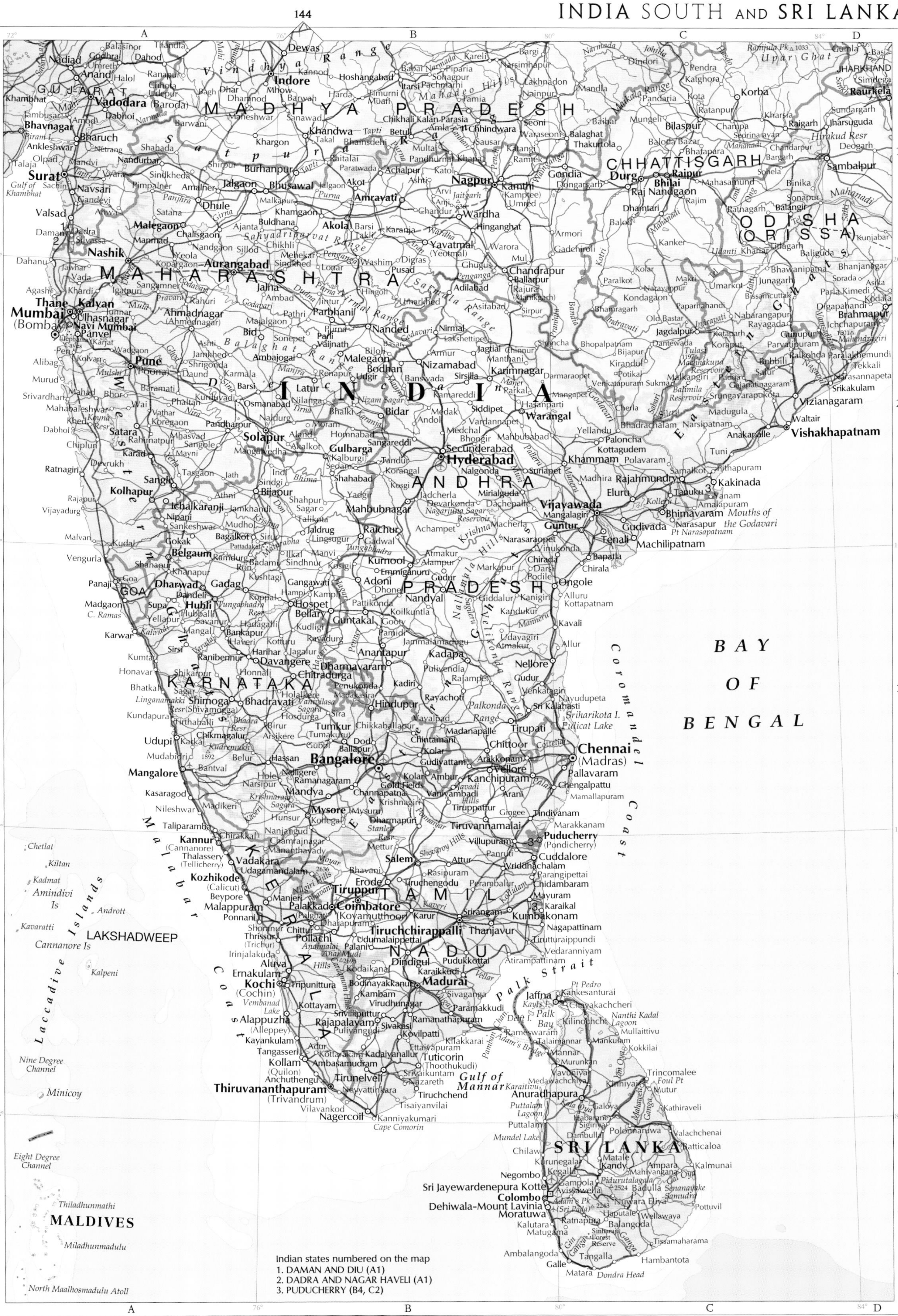


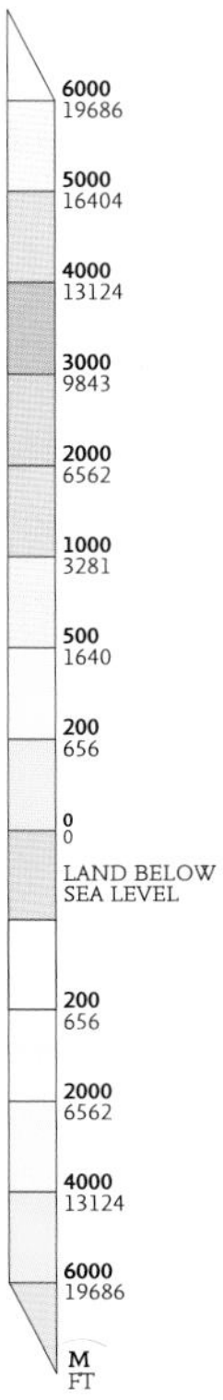


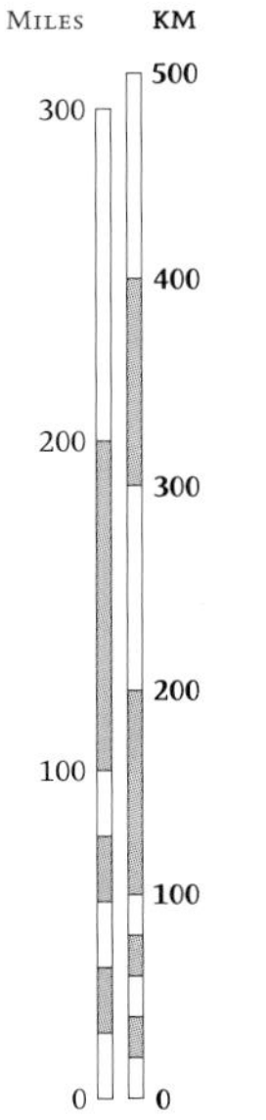


1:7 000 000

Conic Equidistant Projection

139

141

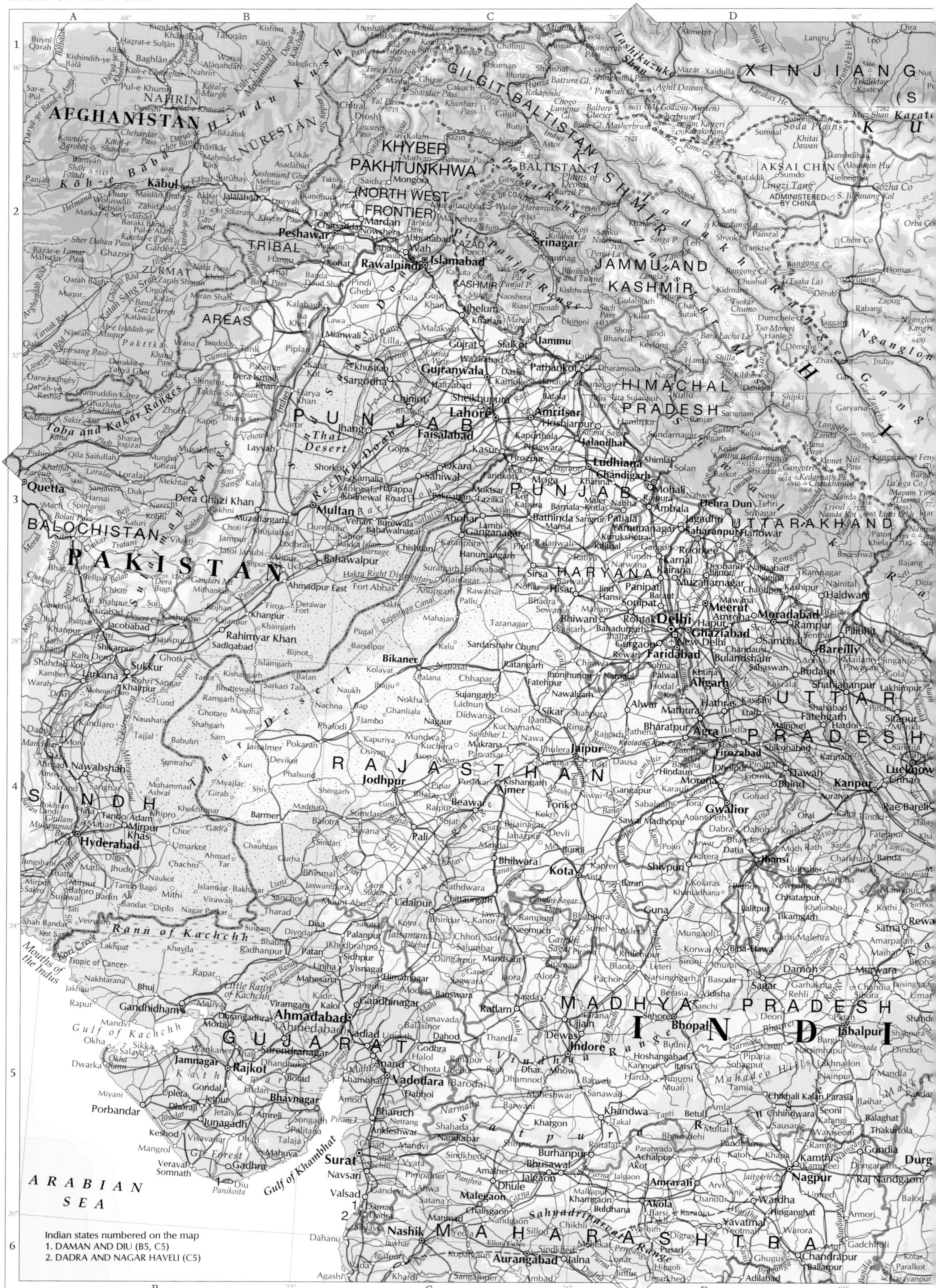
A
B
C
D
1
2
3
4
5
6
AFGHANISTAN
Kābul
Hindu Kush
NURESTĀN
KHYBER PAKHTUNKHWA (NORTH WEST FRONTIER)
TRIBAL AREAS
Peshawar
Islamabad
Rawalpindi
GILGIT BALTISTAN
KASHMIR
AZAD KASHMIR
Srinagar
JAMMU AND KASHMIR
XINJIANG
AKSAI CHIN
ADMINISTERED BY CHINA
HIMACHAL PRADESH
PUNJAB
Lahore
Faisalabad
Multan
Amritsar
Ludhiana
Chandigarh
UTTARAKHAND
HARYANA
Delhi
New Delhi
Quetta
BALOCHISTAN
PAKISTAN
SINDH
Hyderabad
Sukkur
Thar Desert
RAJASTHAN
Jaipur
Jodhpur
Bikaner
Ajmer
Kota
Udaipur
UTTAR PRADESH
Agra
Kanpur
Lucknow
Gwalior
Jhansi
MADHYA PRADESH
Bhopal
Indore
Jabalpur
GUJARAT
Ahmadabad
Rajkot
Vadodara
Surat
Gulf of Kachchh
Gulf of Khambhat
Rann of Kachchh
MAHARASHTRA
Nagpur
Nashik
Aurangabad
ARABIAN SEA
INDIA
Indian states numbered on the map
1. DAMAN AND DIU (B5, C5)
2. DADRA AND NAGAR HAVELI (C5)

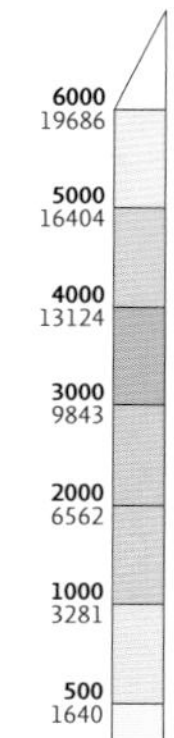
6000
19686
5000
16404
4000
13124
3000
9843
2000
6562
1000
3281
500
1640
200
656
0
0
LAND BELOW SEA LEVEL
200
656
2000
6562
4000
13124
6000
19686
M
FT

Conic Equidistant Projection

143

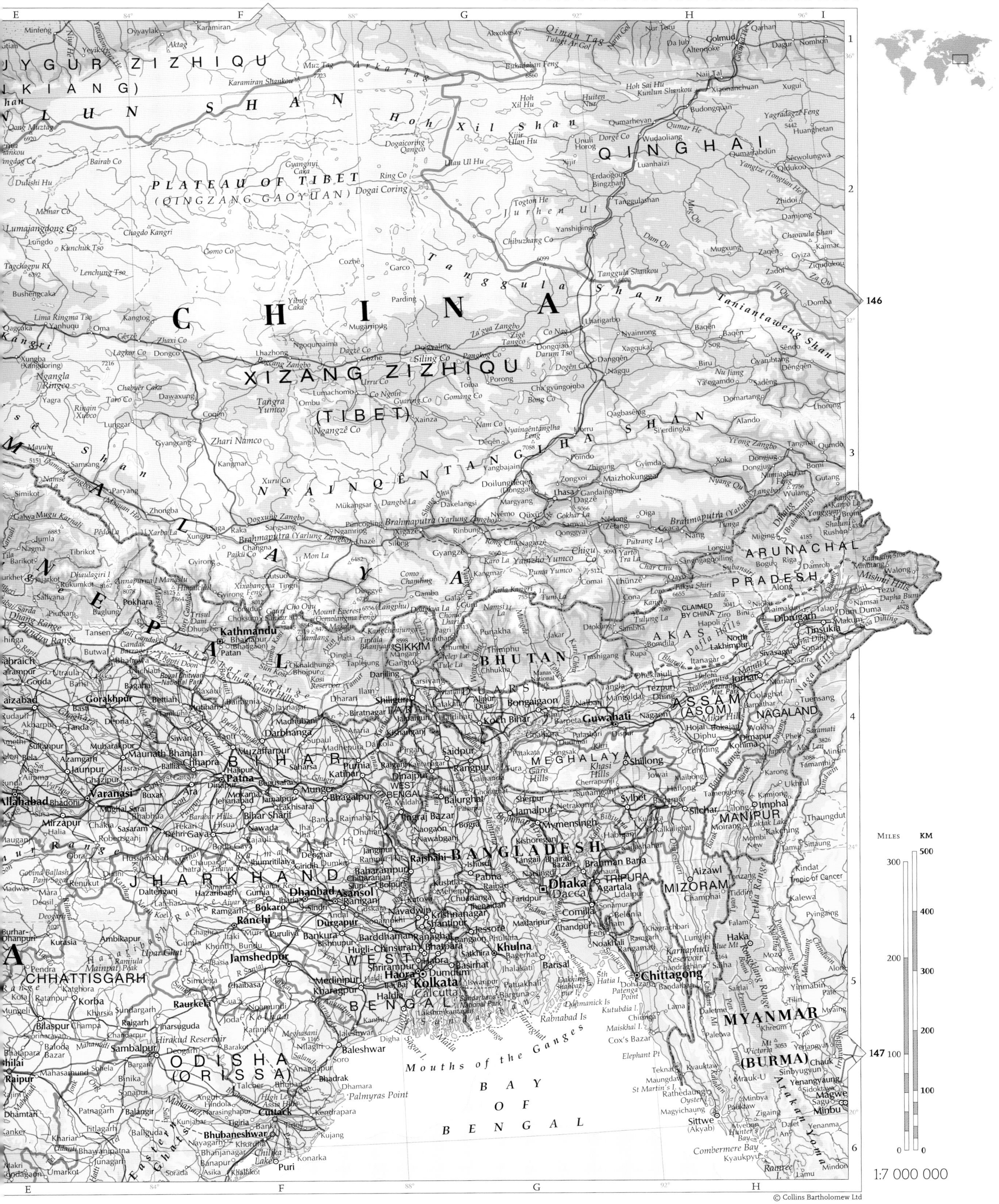
135
146
147
CHINA
XIZANG ZIZHIQU
(TIBET)
QINGHAI
PLATEAU OF TIBET
(QINGZANG GAOYUAN)
NEPAL
BHUTAN
SIKKIM
ARUNACHAL PRADESH
ASSAM (ASOM)
NAGALAND
MANIPUR
MIZORAM
MEGHALAYA
TRIPURA
BANGLADESH
WEST BENGAL
BIHAR
JHARKHAND
ODISHA (ORISSA)
CHHATTISGARH
MYANMAR (BURMA)
BAY OF BENGAL
Mouths of the Ganges
Kathmandu
Lhasa
Thimphu
Dhaka (Dacca)
Kolkata (Calcutta)
Patna
Guwahati
Shillong
Chittagong
Bhubaneshwar
Ranchi
Varanasi
Allahabad
Imphal
Agartala
Aizawl
Kohima
Sittwe (Akyab)
CLAIMED BY CHINA
Miles
KM
1:7 000 000
© Collins Bartholomew Ltd

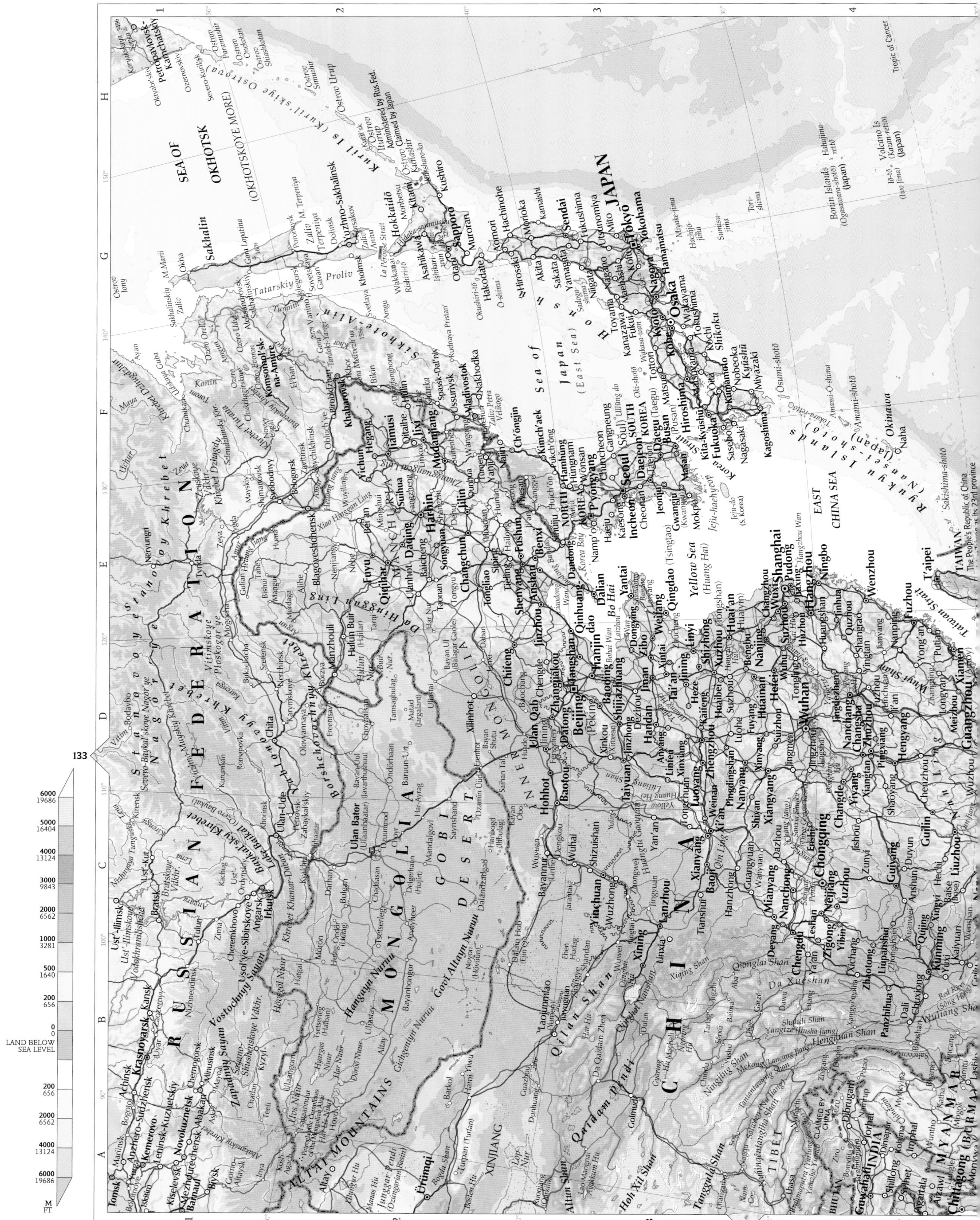


Conic Equidistant Projection

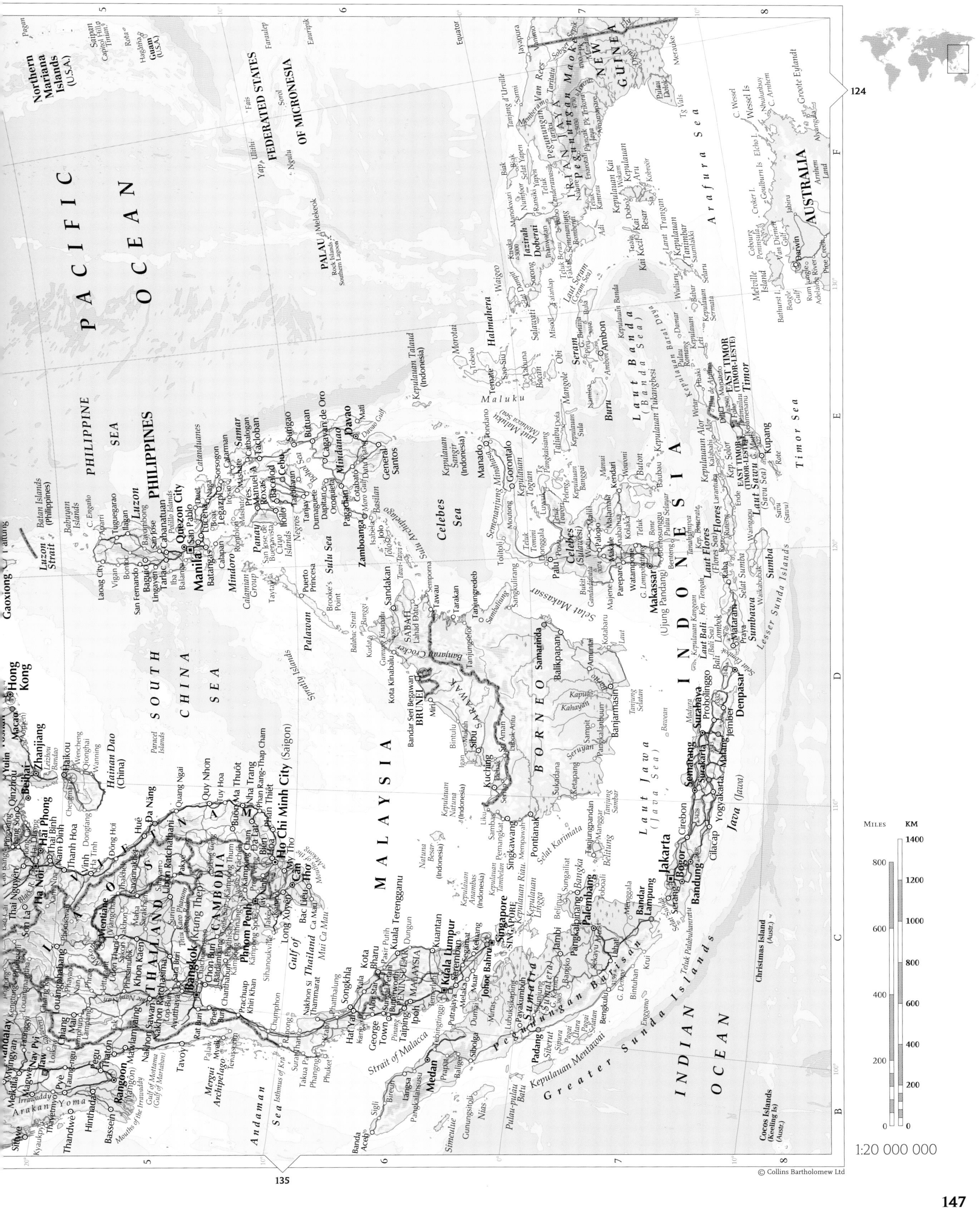
PACIFIC OCEAN
PHILIPPINE SEA
PHILIPPINES
SOUTH CHINA SEA
MALAYSIA
INDONESIA
INDIAN OCEAN
BORNEO
Celebes Sea
Timor Sea
Arafura Sea
AUSTRALIA
NEW GUINEA
FEDERATED STATES OF MICRONESIA
PALAU
THAILAND
CAMBODIA
Gulf of Thailand
Andaman Sea
Hong Kong
Manila
Bangkok
Singapore
Jakarta
Ho Chi Minh City (Saigon)
Kuala Lumpur
Phnom Penh
Quezon City
Rangoon (Yangon)
Makassar (Ujung Pandang)
Darwin
Guam (U.S.A.)
Northern Mariana Islands (U.S.A.)
Christmas Island (Austr.)
Cocos Islands (Keeling Is) (Austr.)
EAST TIMOR (TIMOR-LESTE)
Equator
124
135
Miles
KM
1:20 000 000

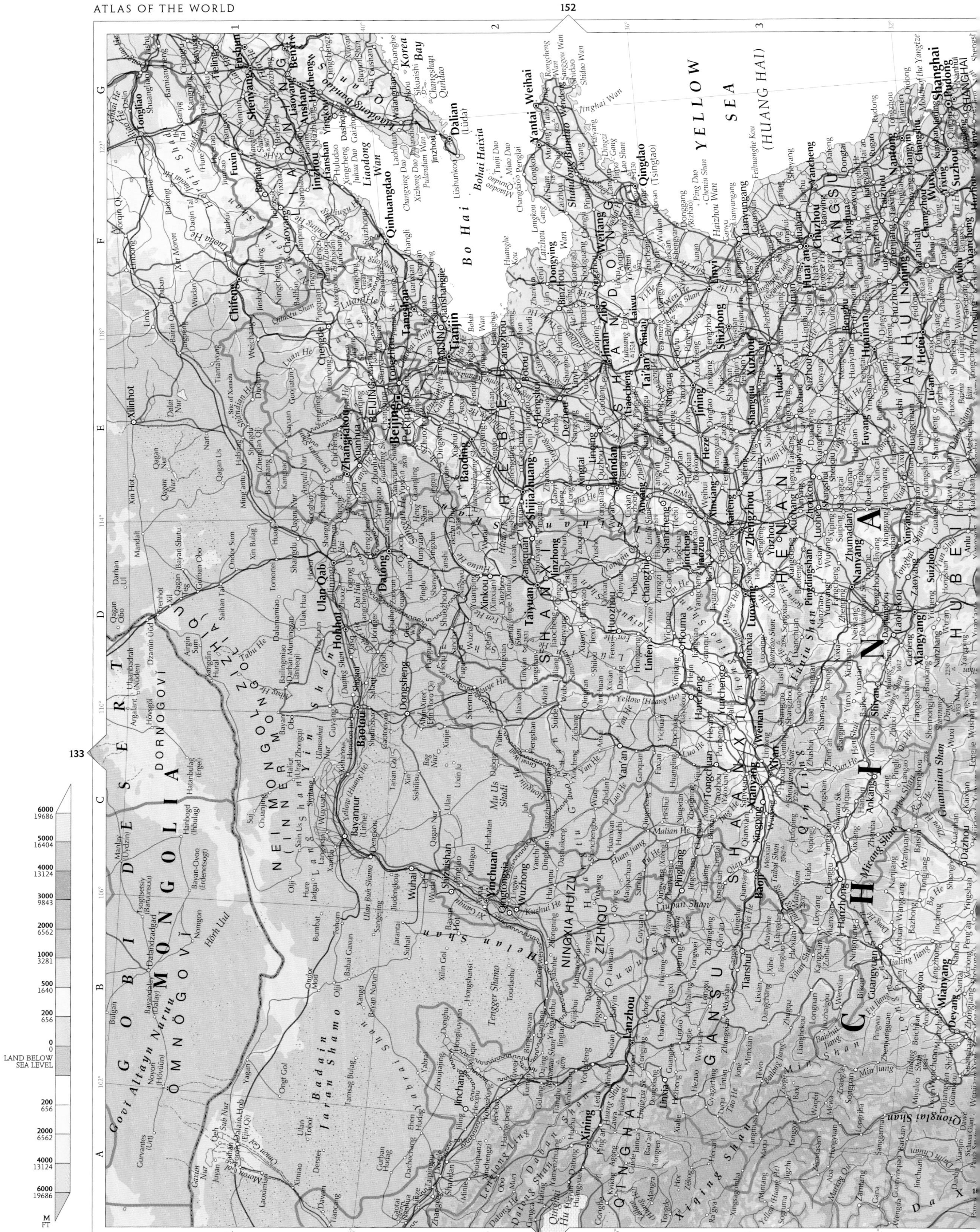
152
135
133
6000
19686
5000
16404
4000
13124
3000
9843
2000
6562
1000
3281
500
1640
200
656
0
0
LAND BELOW
SEA LEVEL
200
656
2000
6562
4000
13124
6000
19686
M
FT
MONGOLIA
GOBI DESERT
NEI MONGOL (INNER MONGOLIA)
NINGXIA HUIZU ZIZHIQU
GANSU
QINGHAI
SHAANXI
SHANXI
HEBEI
HENAN
HUBEI
ANHUI
JIANGSU
SHANDONG
LIAONING
BEIJING
TIANJIN
SHANGHAI
CHINA
YELLOW SEA (HUANG HAI)
Bo Hai
Liaodong Wan
Korea Bay
Beijing
Tianjin
Shanghai
Dalian
Qingdao
Lanzhou
Xining
Yinchuan
Hohhot
Baotou
Taiyuan
Shijiazhuang
Zhengzhou
Xi'an
Jinan
Nanjing
Hefei
Shenyang

Conic Equidistant Projection

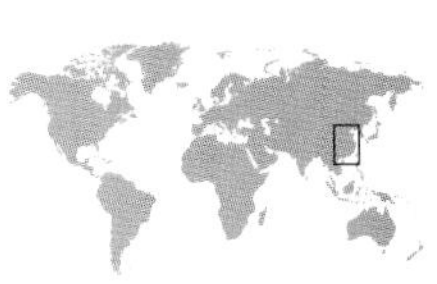

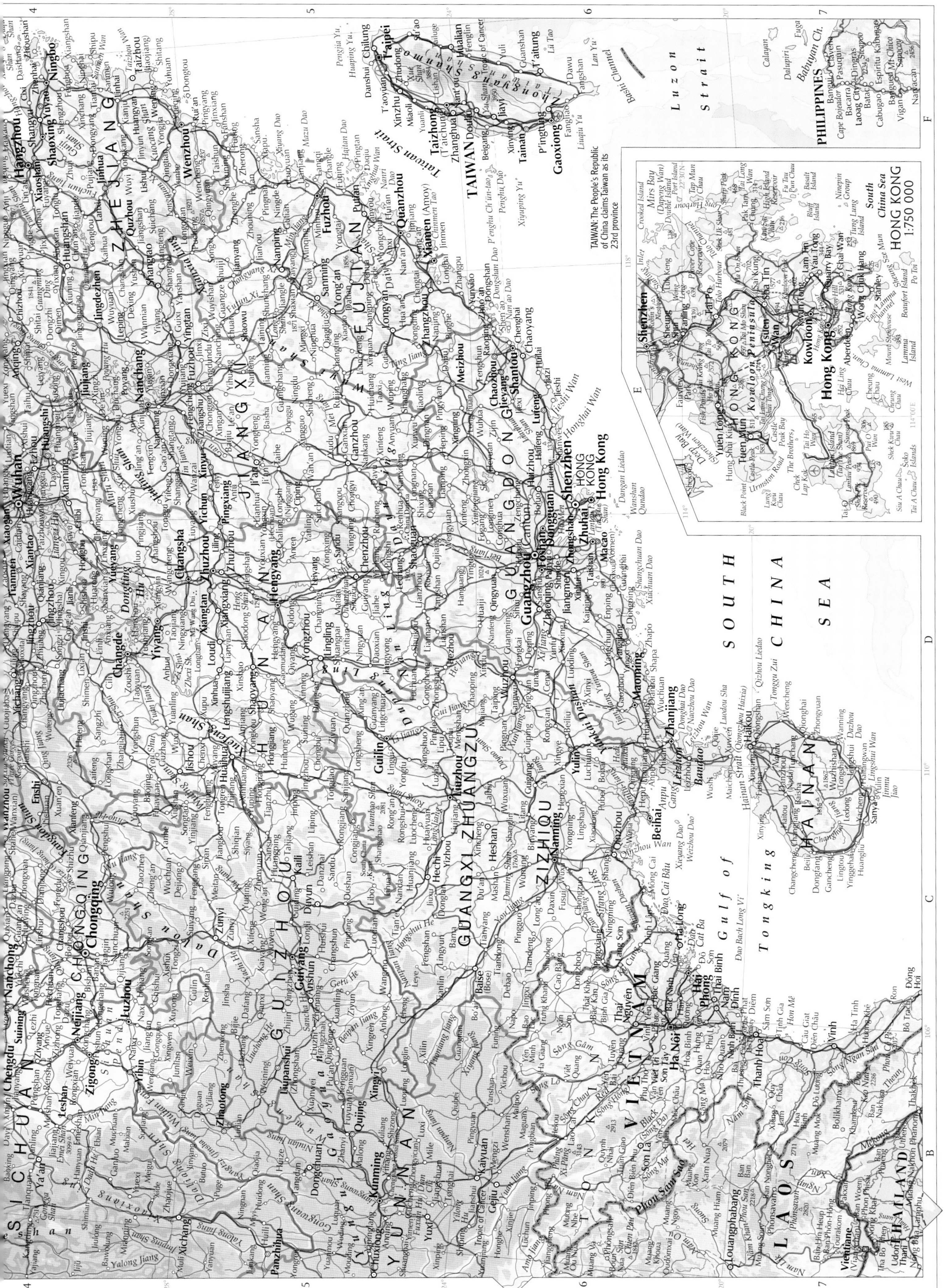


154

135

MILES | KM
0 100 200 300 | 0 100 200 300 400 500

1:7 500 000

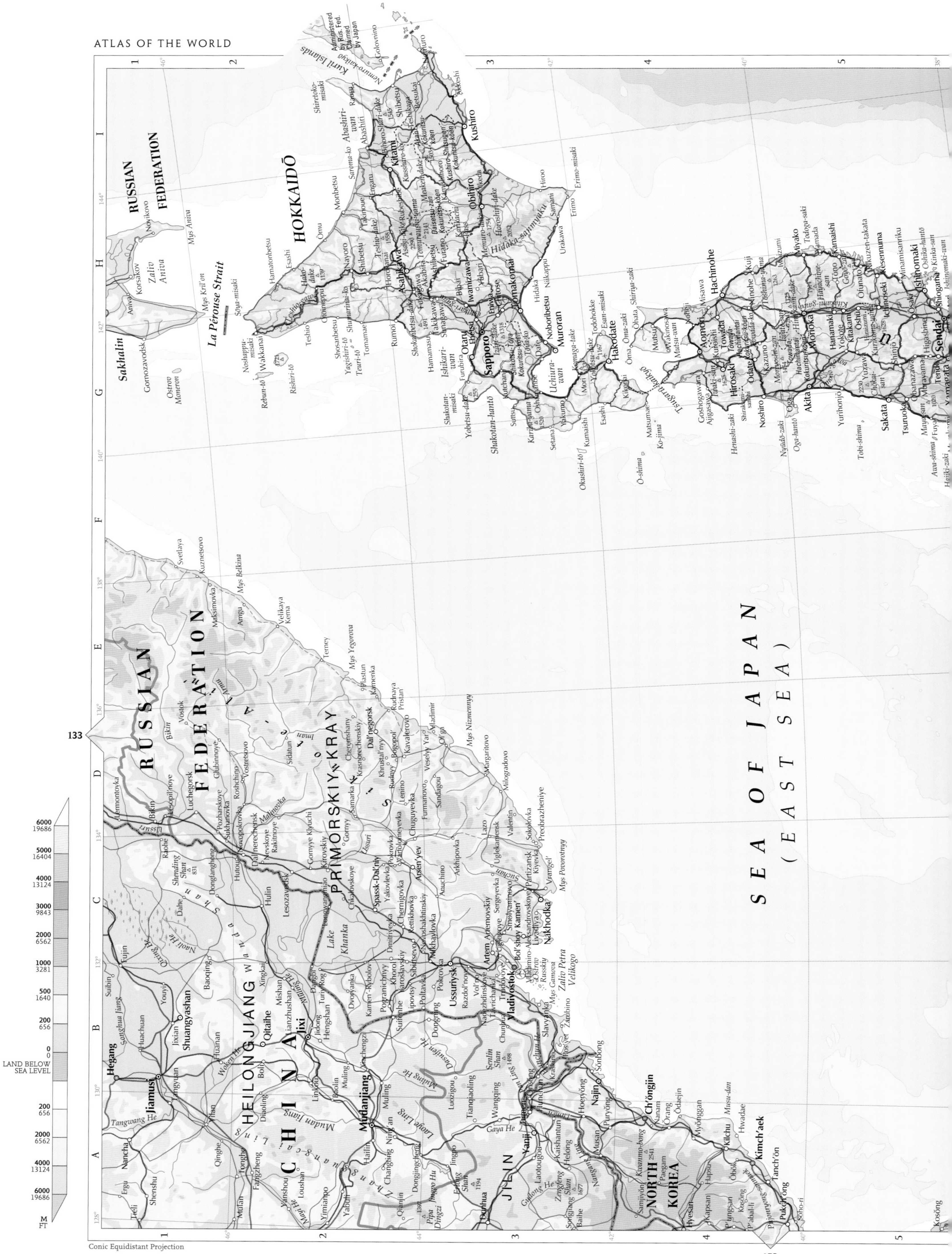


Conic Equidistant Projection

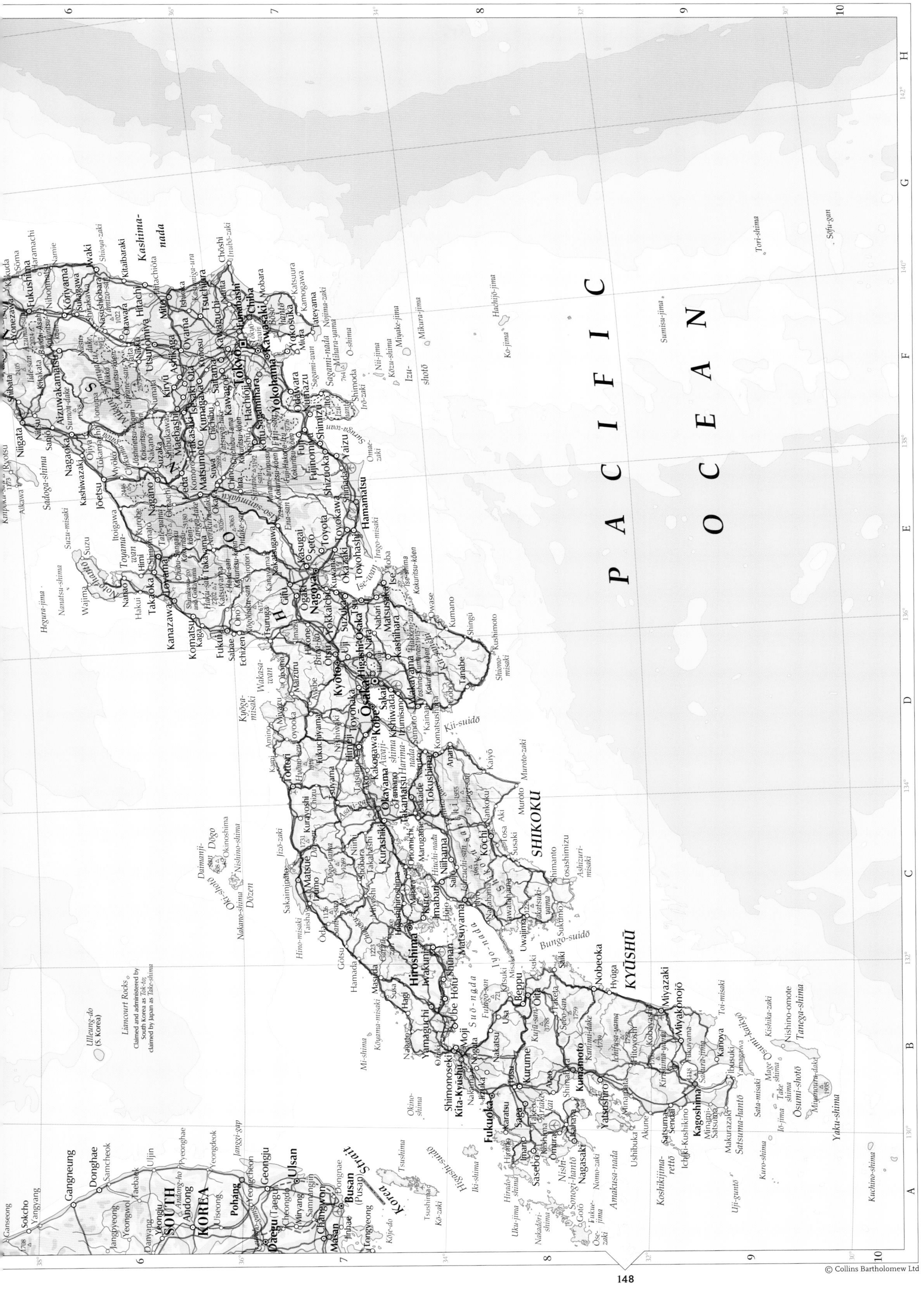
PACIFIC
OCEAN
SHIKOKU
KYŪSHŪ
SOUTH
KOREA
Tōkyō
Yokohama
Nagoya
Ōsaka
Kyōto
Kōbe
Hiroshima
Fukuoka
Kita-Kyūshū
Kagoshima
Nagasaki
Niigata
Nagano
Shizuoka
Hamamatsu
Busan
Daegu
Ulsan
Korea Strait
Hachijō-jima
Tori-shima
Sōfu-gan
Liancourt Rocks
Claimed and administered by South Korea as Tok-to; claimed by Japan as Take-shima

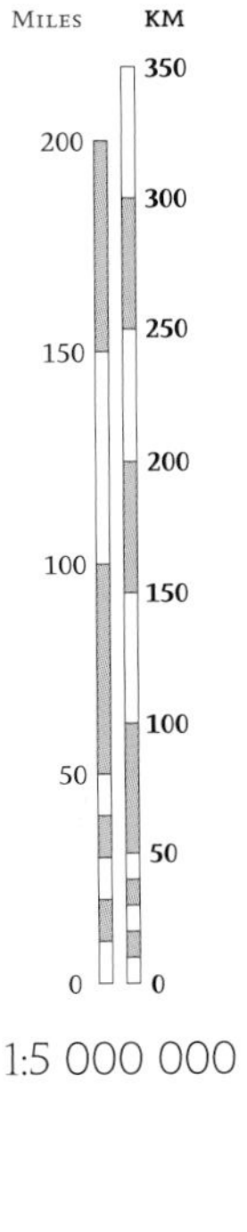
MILES
KM
1:5 000 000

148

# CHINA NORTHEAST, NORTH KOREA AND SOUTH KOREA

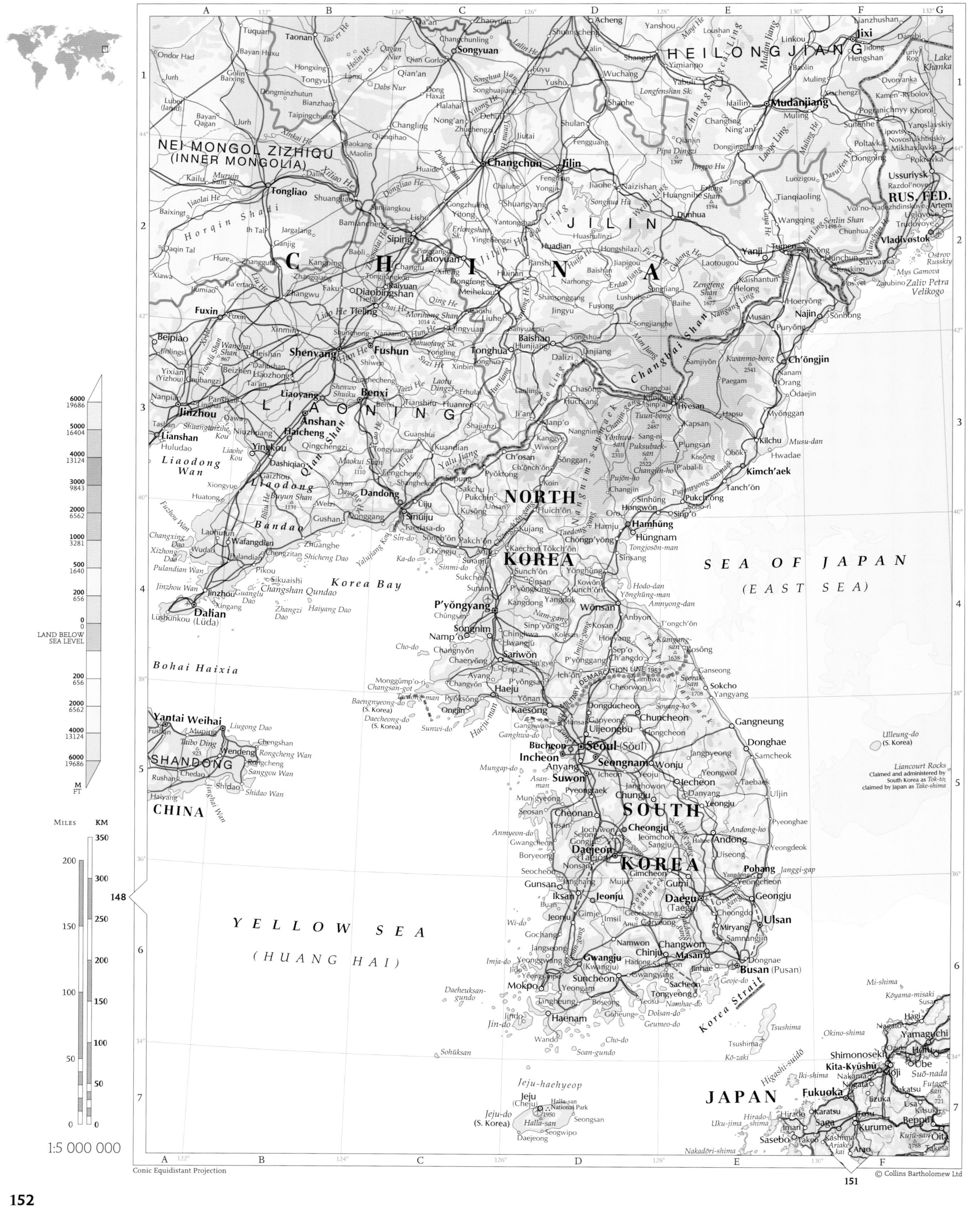


1:5 000 000

Conic Equidistant Projection

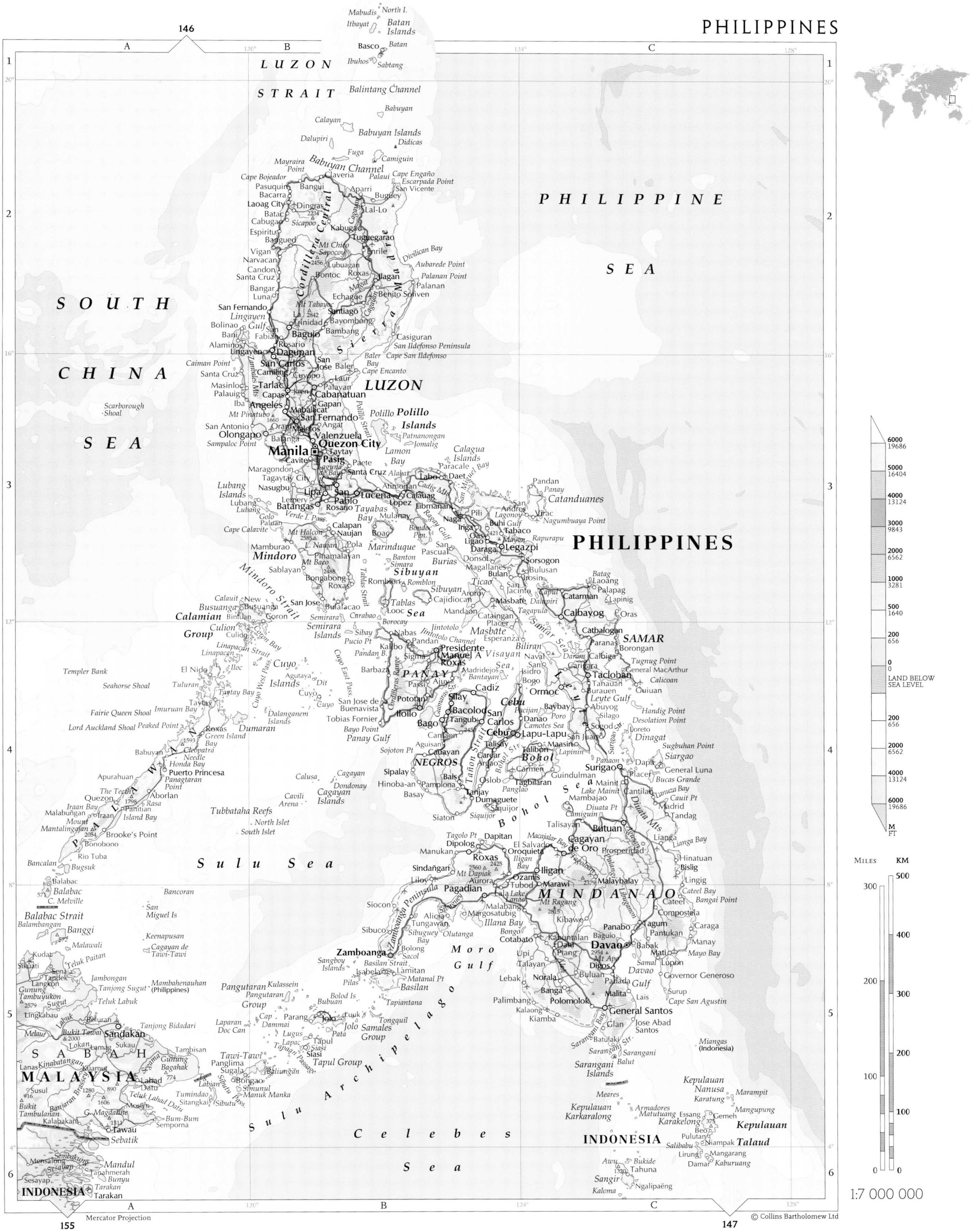
146
155
147
A
B
C
1
2
3
4
5
6
LUZON STRAIT
Batan Islands
Basco
Balintang Channel
Babuyan Islands
Babuyan Channel
Cape Bojeador
Cape Engaño
Laoag City
Aparri
Tuguegarao
Vigan
Cordillera Central
Sierra Madre
Divilican Bay
San Fernando
Lingayen Gulf
Baguio
Dagupan
SOUTH CHINA SEA
Scarborough Shoal
PHILIPPINE SEA
LUZON
Polillo Islands
Tarlac
Angeles
Cabanatuan
San Fernando
Olongapo
Valenzuela
Quezon City
Manila
Pasig
Lamon Bay
Lucena
Batangas
Calagua Islands
San Miguel Bay
Catanduanes
Naga
Iriga
Legazpi
Sorsogon
PHILIPPINES
Lubang Islands
Mindoro
Mindoro Strait
Calapan
Marinduque
Sibuyan Sea
Masbate
Ticao
Burias
Tablas
Busuanga
Calamian Group
Coron
Cuyo Islands
Samar Sea
SAMAR
Calbayog
Catbalogan
Tacloban
Leyte Gulf
Ormoc
Panay Gulf
PANAY
Roxas
Iloilo
Bacolod
NEGROS
Cebu
Lapu-Lapu
Bohol
Bohol Sea
Camotes Sea
Dinagat
Siargao
Surigao
Butuan
Dumaguete
Siquijor
Tubbataha Reefs
Sulu Sea
PALAWAN
Puerto Princesa
Honda Bay
Brooke's Point
Balabac Strait
Balabac
Dipolog
Cagayan de Oro
Iligan
Ozamis
Pagadian
Zamboanga
Zamboanga Peninsula
MINDANAO
Malaybalay
Davao
Davao Gulf
Moro Gulf
Cotabato
Illana Bay
General Santos
Mati
Cape San Agustin
Sarangani Islands
Basilan
Basilan Strait
Jolo
Sulu Archipelago
Tawi-Tawi
Celebes Sea
SABAH
MALAYSIA
Sandakan
Tawau
INDONESIA
Tarakan
Kepulauan Talaud
Kepulauan Nanusa
Kepulauan Karkaralong
Miangas (Indonesia)
Sangir
Mercator Projection
1:7 000 000
MILES
KM
© Collins Bartholomew Ltd

# THAILAND, CAMBODIA AND PENINSULAR MALAYSIA

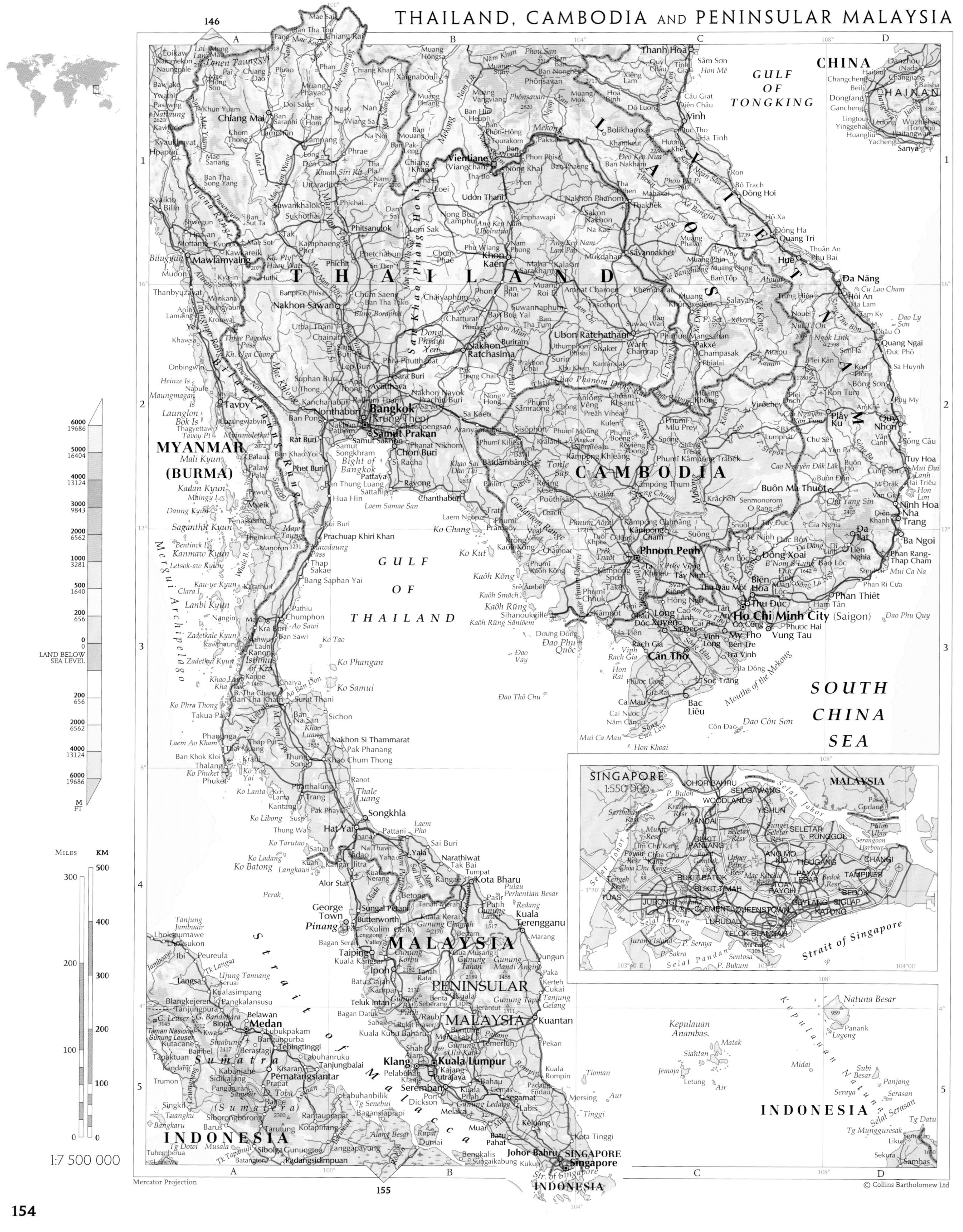


© Collins Bartholomew Ltd

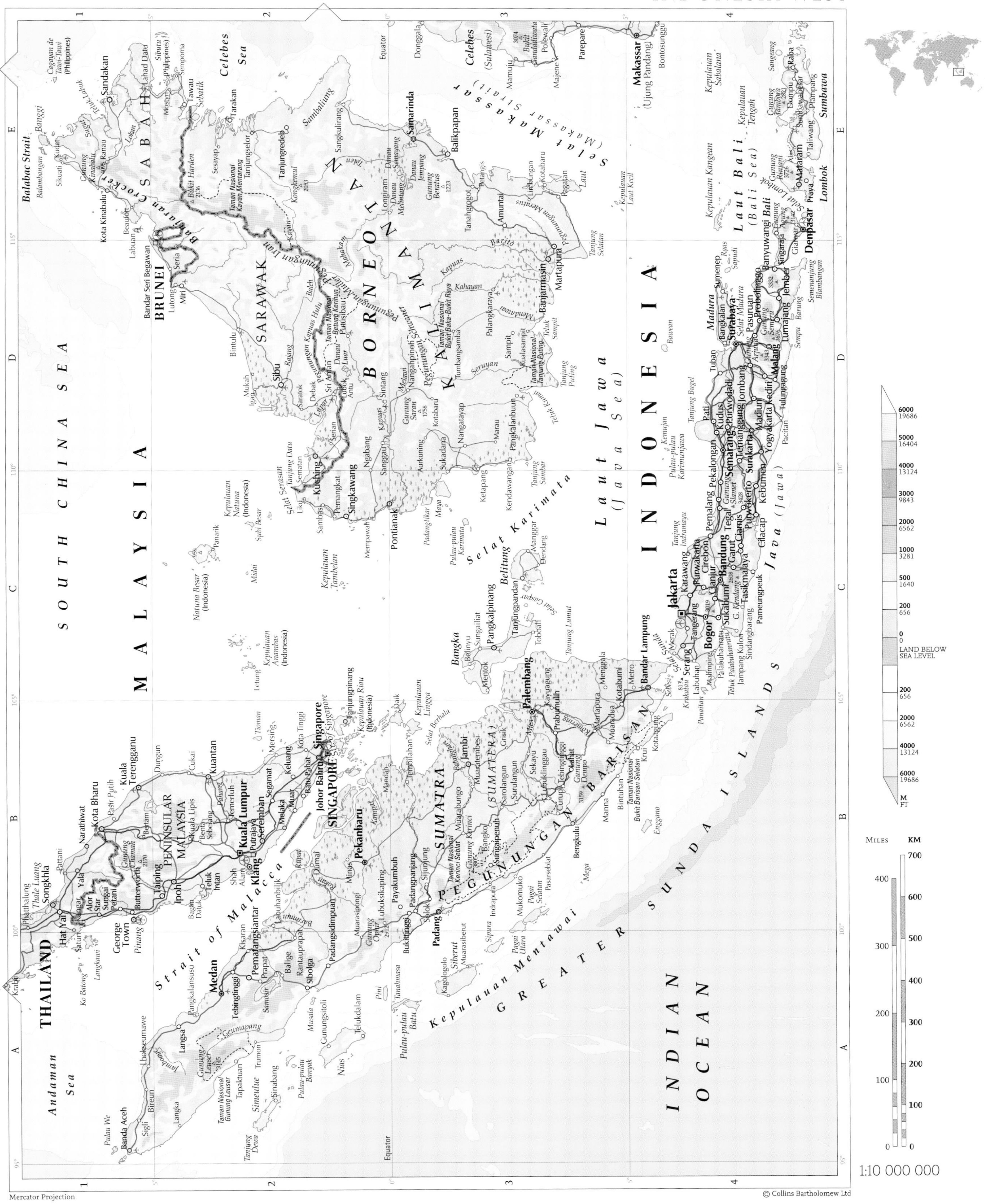


Mercator Projection

A
B
C
D
E
1
2
3
4
5
6
7
NORTH AMERICA
Baffin Bay
Greenland
Arctic Circle
Denmark Strait
Greenland Sea
Jan Mayen
(Norway)
Nordaustlandet
Spitsbergen
Svalbard
(Norway)
Longyearbyen
Zemlya Frantsa-Iosifa
Ostrov Severnyy
BARENTS SEA
Bjørnøya
(Norway)
North Cape
ICELAND
Reykjavík
NORWEGIAN SEA
Faroe Islands
(Denmark)
Tórshavn
Shetland Islands
Orkney Islands
Outer Hebrides
Rockall
NORWAY
SWEDEN
Gulf of Bothnia
Trondheim
Bergen
Oslo
Stockholm
Vänern
Vättern
Skagerrak
Kattegat
Gothenburg
Aalborg
DENMARK
Copenhagen
Malmö
Odense
Bornholm
NORTH SEA
SCOTLAND
Glasgow
Edinburgh
British Isles
NORTHERN IRELAND
Belfast
UNITED KINGDOM
Dublin
IRELAND
Manchester
Leeds
Liverpool
Birmingham
WALES
ENGLAND
Cardiff
London
English Channel
Channel Islands
NETHERLANDS
Amsterdam
The Hague
Rotterdam
Essen
Hamburg
Hannover
Berlin
GERMANY
Düsseldorf
Cologne
Leipzig
Brussels
Lille
BELGIUM
Rhine
LUXEMBOURG
Luxembourg
Frankfurt
Nuremberg
Mannheim
Stuttgart
Strasbourg
Munich
Seine
Paris
Brest
Rennes
Orléans
Loire
Dijon
Zürich
LIECHTENSTEIN
Bern
Innsbruck
SWITZERLAND
Nantes
FRANCE
Geneva
Mont Blanc
4810
Lyon
Milan
Turin
Genoa
ALPS
Bay of Biscay
Bordeaux
Rhône
MONACO
Nice
Toulouse
Marseille
ATLANTIC OCEAN
A Coruña
Bilbao
Pyrenees
Andorra la Vella
ANDORRA
Ebro
Corsica
Oporto
Salamanca
Zaragoza
Barcelona
PORTUGAL
Madrid
SPAIN
Tagus
Valencia
Balearic Islands
Minorca
Majorca
Ibiza
Sardinia
Lisbon
Córdoba
Seville
Cartagena
Cádiz
Málaga
Gibraltar (U.K.)
Ceuta (Spain)
Melilla (Spain)
MED
AF
Flores
Azores
(Portugal)
São Jorge
Terceira
Ponta do Pico
Ponta Delgada
São Miguel
Santa Maria
Arquipélago dos Açores
Madeira
(Portugal)
Funchal
Ilha de Porto Santo

Orthographic Projection

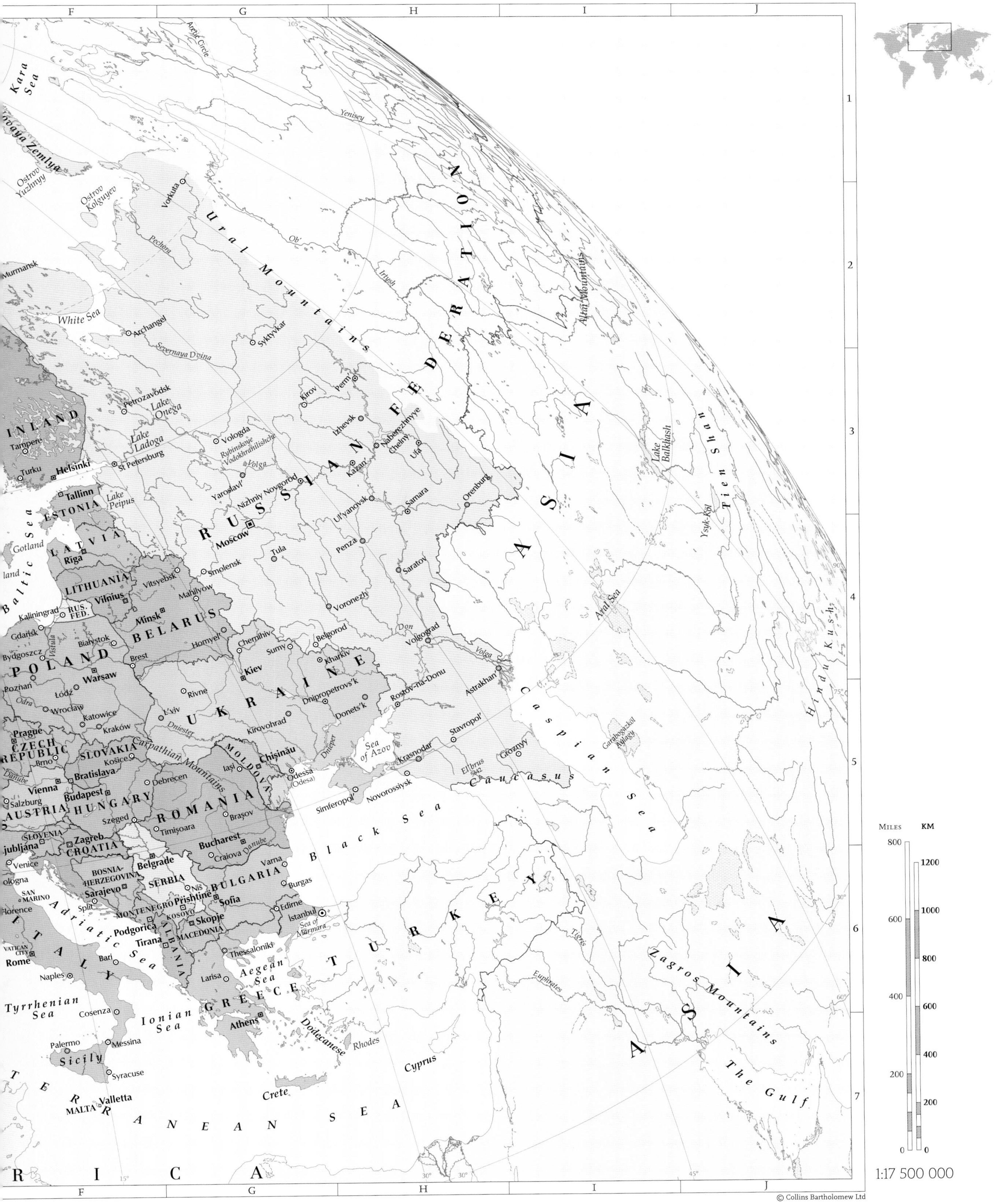
F
G
H
I
J
1
2
3
4
5
6
7
Kara Sea
Novaya Zemlya
Ostrov Yuzhnyy
Ostrov Kolguyev
Arctic Circle
Yenisey
Vorkuta
Pechora
Ob'
Ural Mountains
Irtysh
Murmansk
White Sea
Archangel
Syktyvkar
Severnaya Dvina
RUSSIAN FEDERATION
Altai Mountains
Petrozavodsk
Lake Onega
FINLAND
Tampere
Turku
Helsinki
Lake Ladoga
St Petersburg
Vologda
Rybinskoye Vodokhranilishche
Volga
Kirov
Perm
Izhevsk
Naberezhnyye Chelny
Ufa
Kazan'
Yaroslavl'
Nizhniy Novgorod
Ul'yanovsk
Samara
Orenburg
Lake Balkhash
Tien Shan
Ysyk-Köl
Tallinn
ESTONIA
Lake Peipus
Baltic Sea
Gotland
LATVIA
Riga
Moscow
Tula
Penza
Saratov
LITHUANIA
Vilnius
Vitsyebsk
Smolensk
Mahilyow
Kaliningrad
RUS. FED.
Minsk
BELARUS
Voronezh
Aral Sea
Gdańsk
Vistula
Białystok
Homyel'
Chernihiv
Sumy
Belgorod
Kharkiv
Don
Volgograd
Volga
Bydgoszcz
POLAND
Brest
Warsaw
Kiev
UKRAINE
Poznań
Łódź
Rivne
Dnipropetrovs'k
Rostov-na-Donu
Astrakhan'
Odra
Wrocław
Katowice
Kraków
L'viv
Donets'k
Kirovohrad
Caspian Sea
Hindu Kush
Prague
CZECH REPUBLIC
Brno
Dniester
Carpathian Mountains
SLOVAKIA
Košice
MOLDOVA
Chişinău
Dnieper
Sea of Azov
Krasnodar
Stavropol'
Grozny
Elbrus 5642
Caucasus
Garabogazköl Aylagy
Danube
Vienna
Bratislava
Debrecen
Iaşi
Odesa (Odessa)
Budapest
Simferopol'
Novorossiysk
Salzburg
AUSTRIA
HUNGARY
ROMANIA
Braşov
Szeged
Timişoara
Black Sea
SLOVENIA
Ljubljana
Zagreb
CROATIA
Bucharest
Craiova
Danube
Venice
Belgrade
Varna
Bologna
BOSNIA-HERZEGOVINA
SERBIA
Niš
BULGARIA
Burgas
SAN MARINO
Sarajevo
Prishtinë
Sofia
Florence
Split
MONTENEGRO
KOSOVO
Skopje
Edirne
İstanbul
Adriatic Sea
Podgorica
MACEDONIA
Sea of Marmara
TURKEY
ITALY
VATICAN CITY
Tirana
ALBANIA
Thessaloniki
Tigris
Rome
Bari
Aegean Sea
Zagros Mountains
Naples
Larisa
Euphrates
GREECE
Tyrrhenian Sea
Cosenza
Ionian Sea
Athens
Dodecanese
Rhodes
ASIA
Palermo
Messina
Sicily
Syracuse
Cyprus
The Gulf
MALTA
Valletta
Crete
MEDITERRANEAN SEA
AFRICA
Miles
KM
800
600
400
200
0
1200
1000
800
600
400
200
0
1:17 500 000

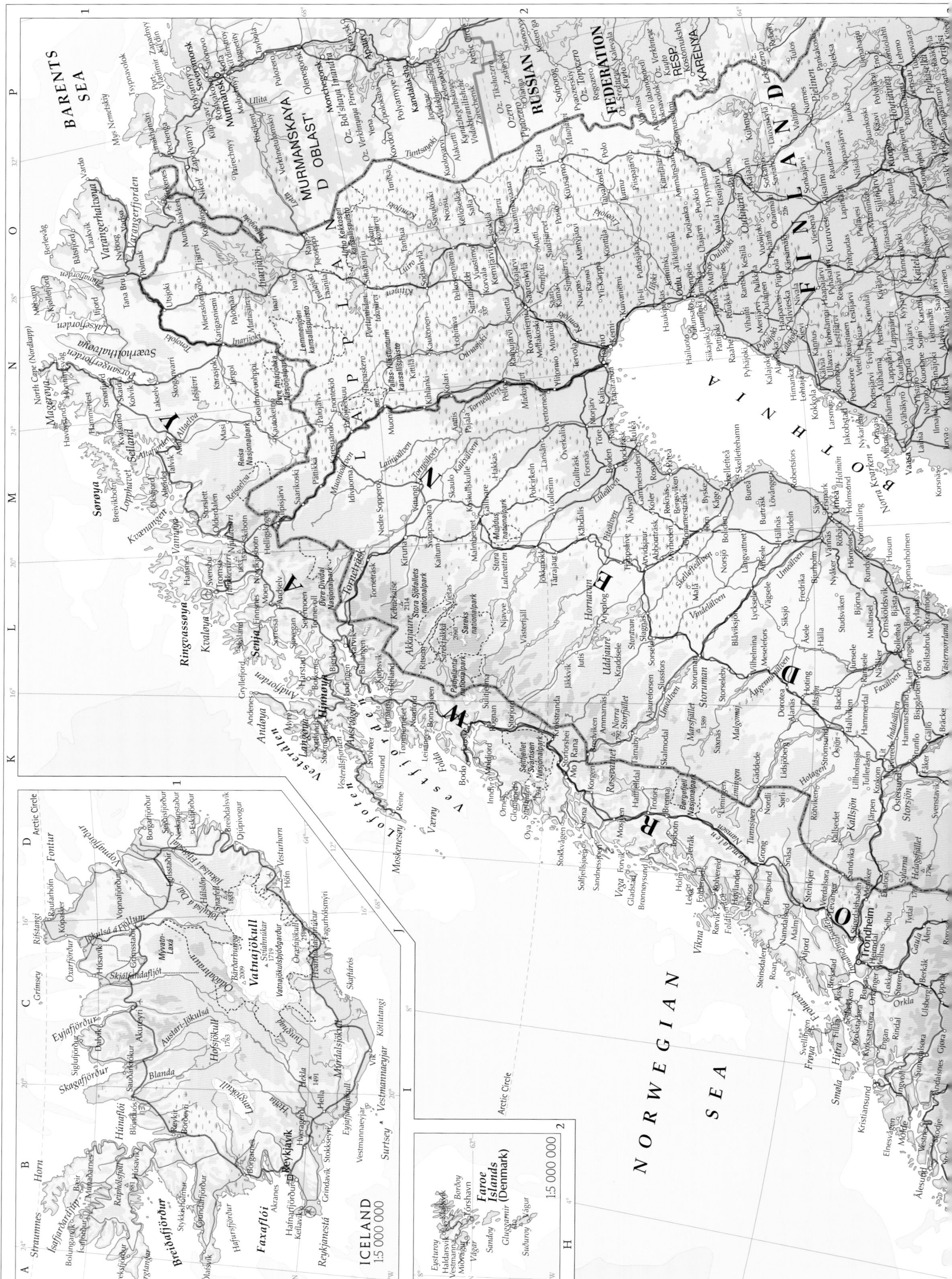


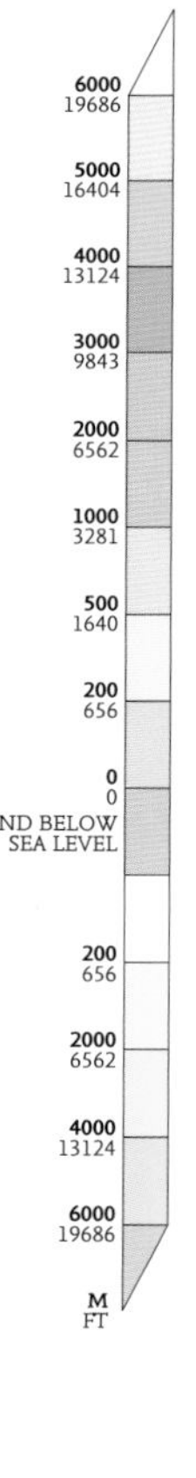


Conic Equidistant Projection

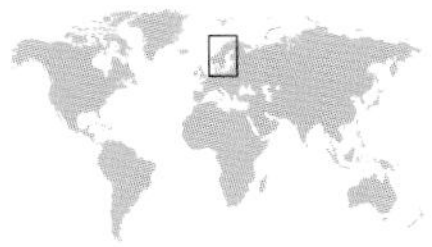

172
169
168
GULF OF FINLAND
Gulf of Riga
BALTIC SEA
NORTH SEA
SKAGERRAK
Kattegat
ESTONIA
LATVIA
LITHUANIA
BELARUS
RUSSIAN FEDERATION
KALININGRAD OBL.
POLAND
GERMANY
DENMARK
SWEDEN
Gotland
Öland
Bornholm (Denmark)
Åland Islands (Finland)
Helsinki (Helsingfors)
Tallinn
Riga
Vilnius
Minsk
Stockholm
Oslo
Copenhagen
Gothenburg (Göteborg)
Hamburg
Kaunas
Gdańsk
Bergen
Stavanger
North Frisian Islands
MILES
KM

1:5 000 000

Conic Equidistant Projection

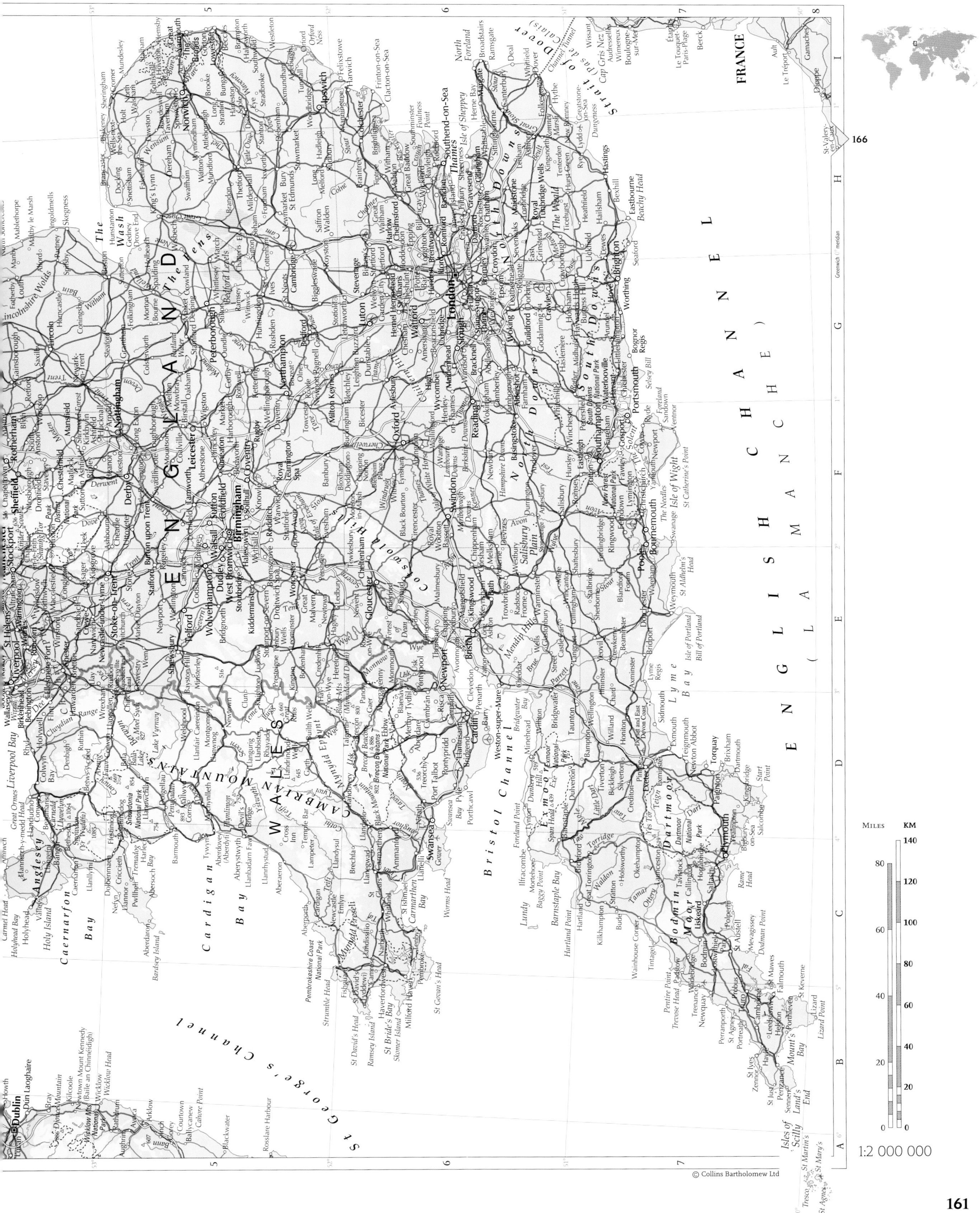
ENGLAND
WALES
FRANCE
ENGLISH CHANNEL
(LA MANCHE)
Bristol Channel
St George's Channel
Cardigan Bay
Strait of Dover (Pas de Calais)
CAMBRIAN MOUNTAINS
Cotswold Hills
North Downs
South Downs
The Wash
The Fens
Lyme Bay
Dartmoor
Exmoor
Bodmin Moor
Salisbury Plain
Isle of Wight
Anglesey
Isles of Scilly
London
Birmingham
Manchester
Liverpool
Sheffield
Nottingham
Leicester
Coventry
Bristol
Cardiff
Swansea
Newport
Plymouth
Exeter
Southampton
Portsmouth
Brighton
Bournemouth
Norwich
Ipswich
Cambridge
Oxford
Reading
Northampton
Peterborough
Lincoln
Derby
Stoke-on-Trent
Wolverhampton
Gloucester
Dublin
1:2 000 000
MILES
KM
166

# SCOTLAND

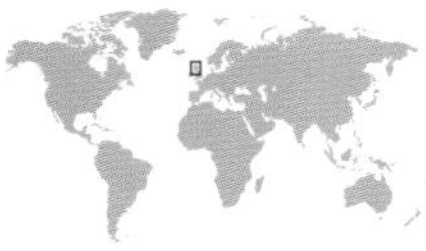

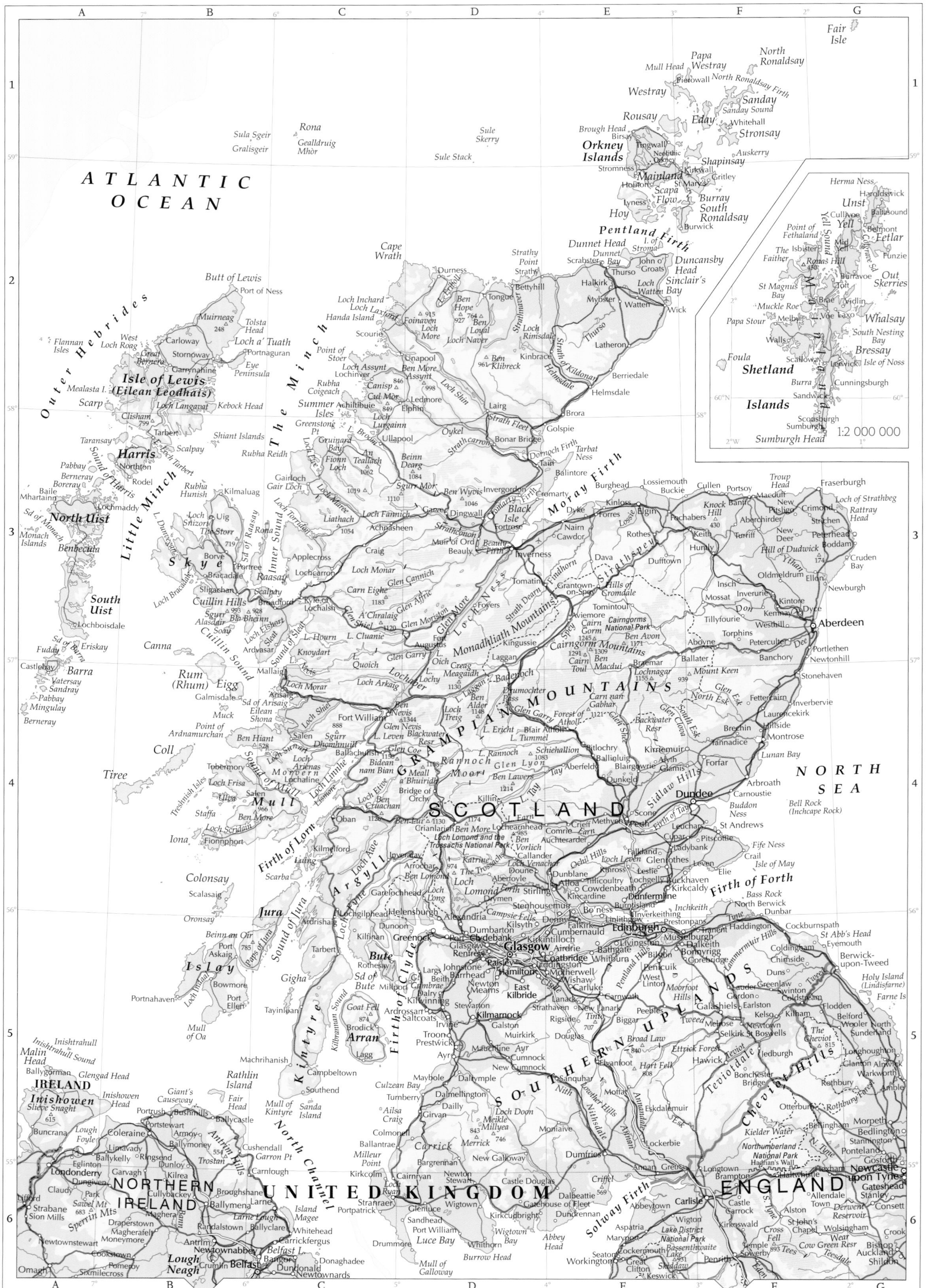


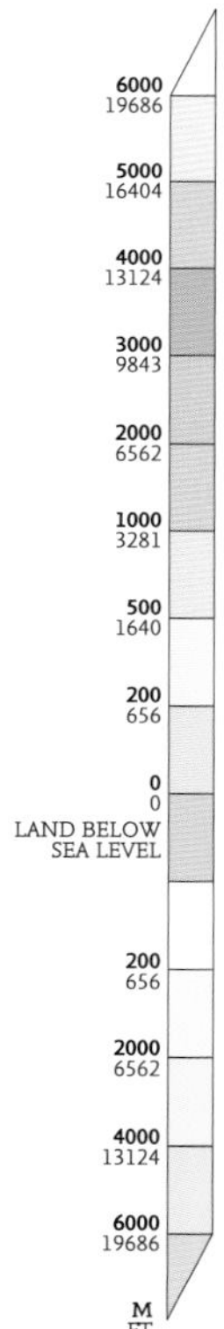


Conic Equidistant Projection


163
160

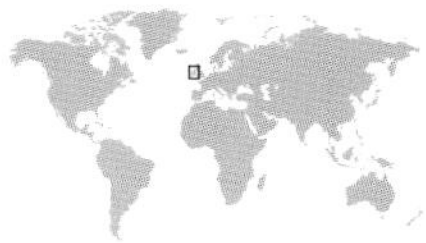

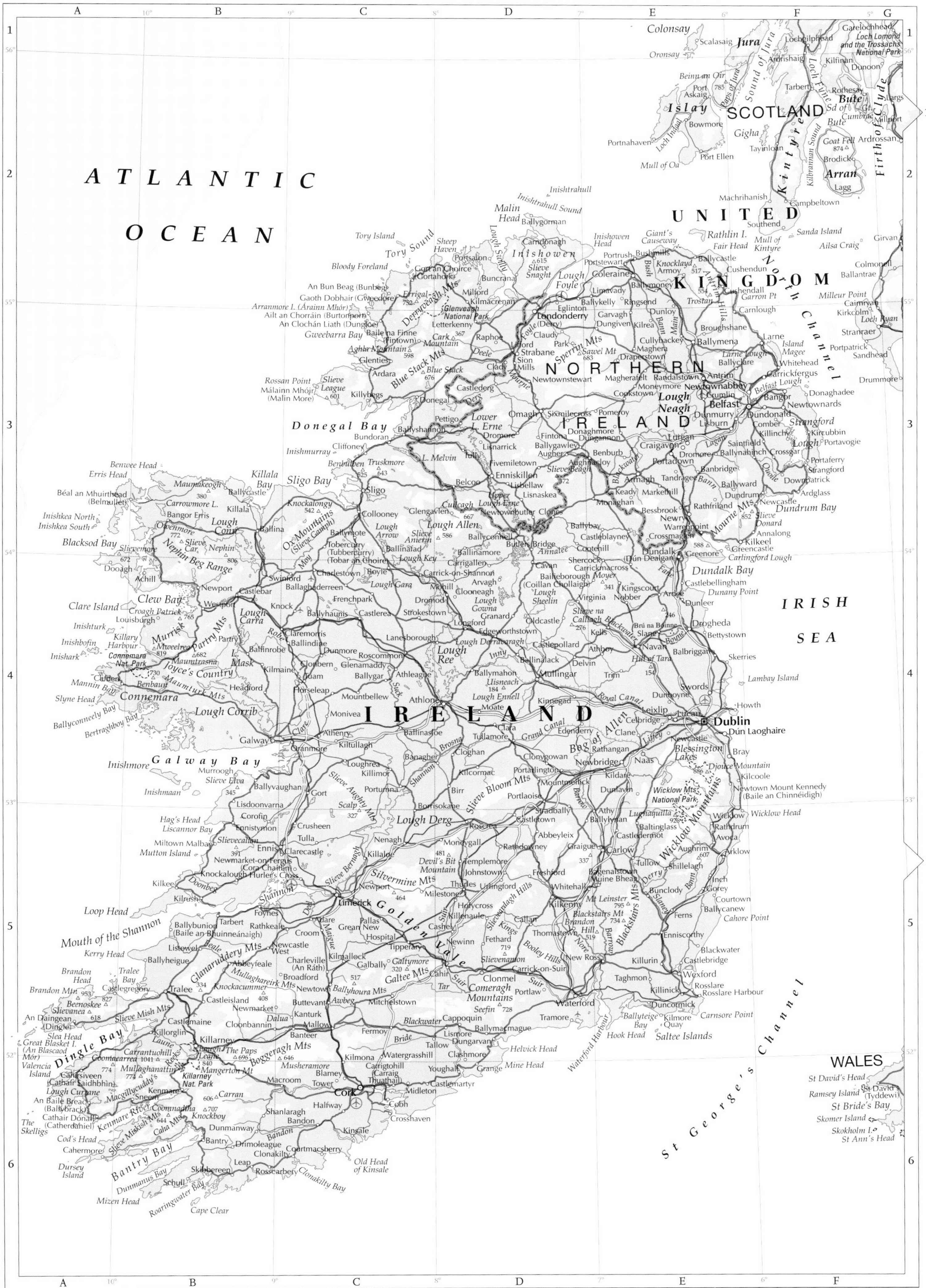


Conic Equidistant Projection

Conic Equidistant Projection

166

159

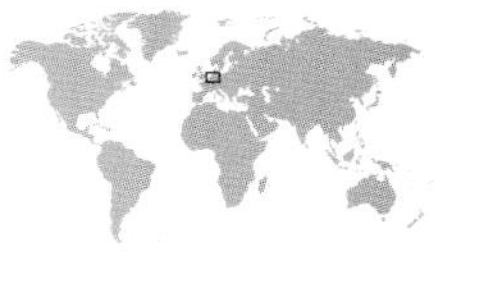

168

168

1:2 000 000

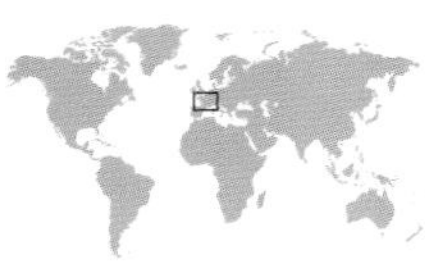

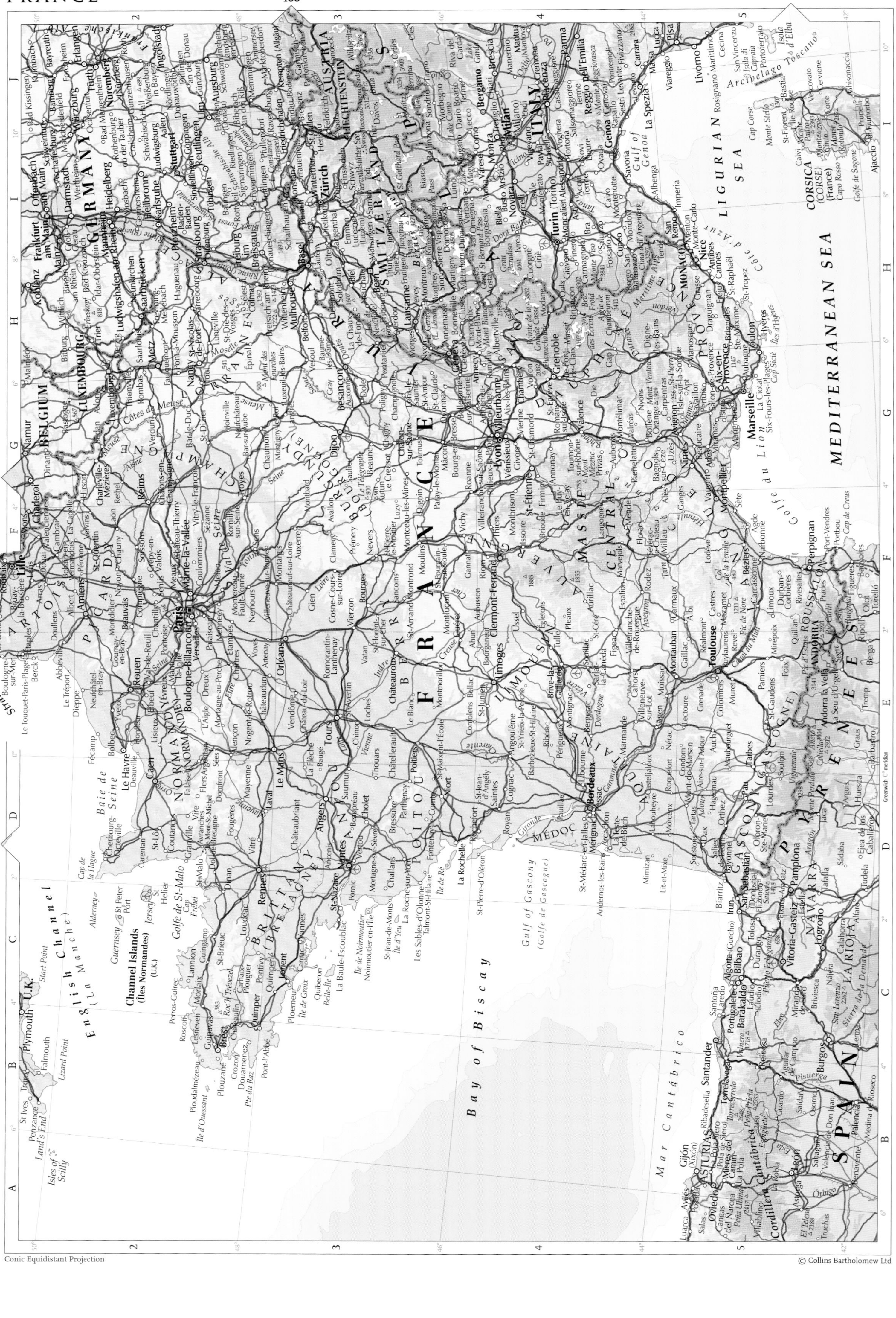


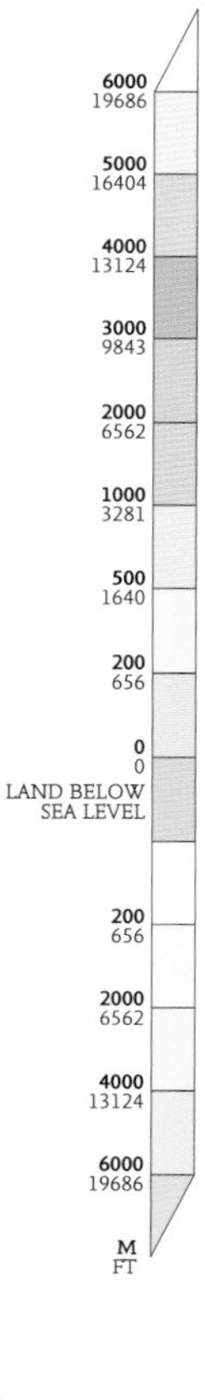


Conic Equidistant Projection

170

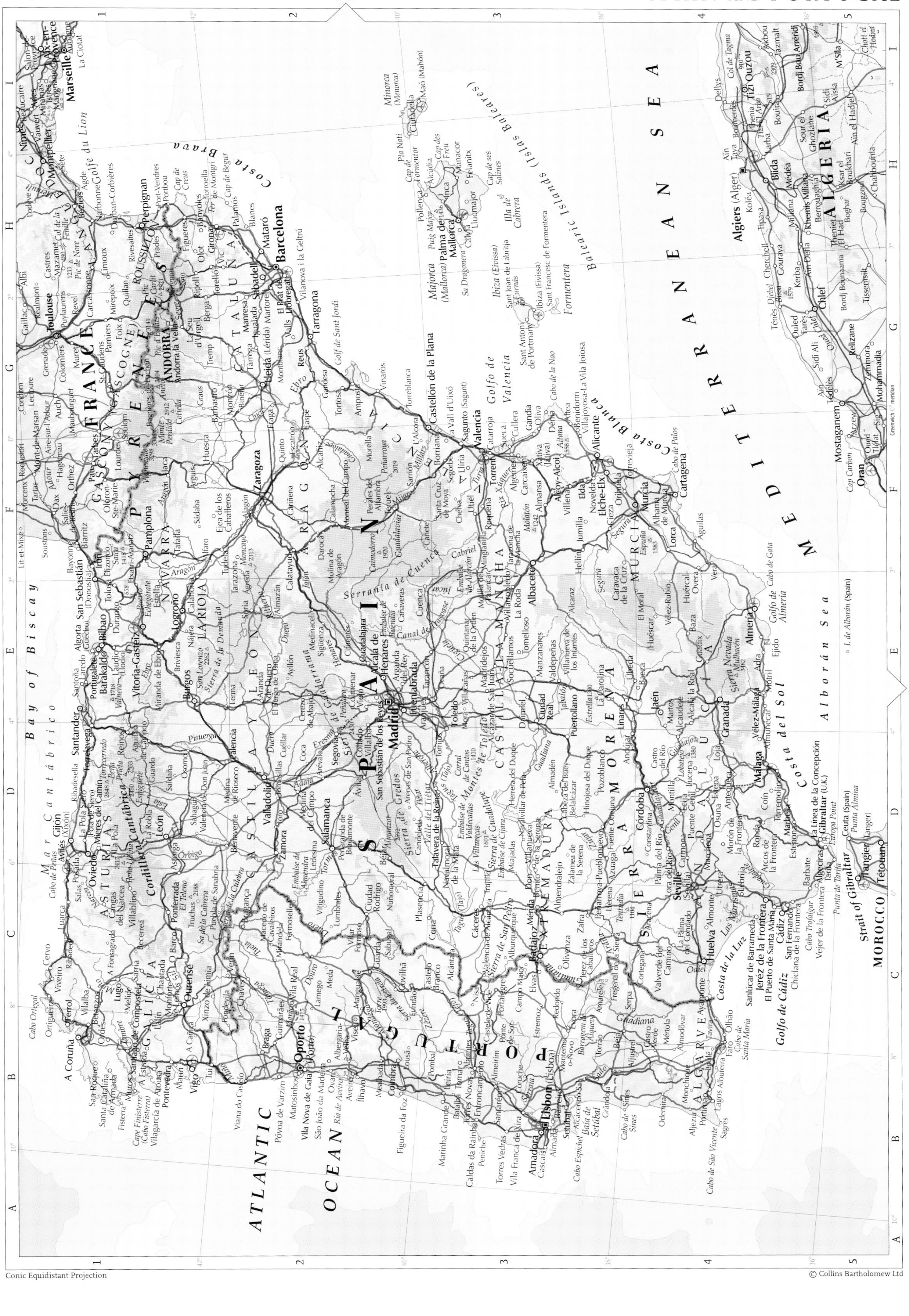


176

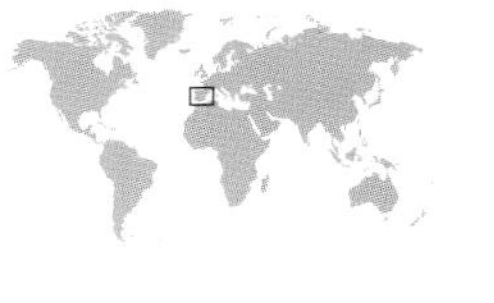

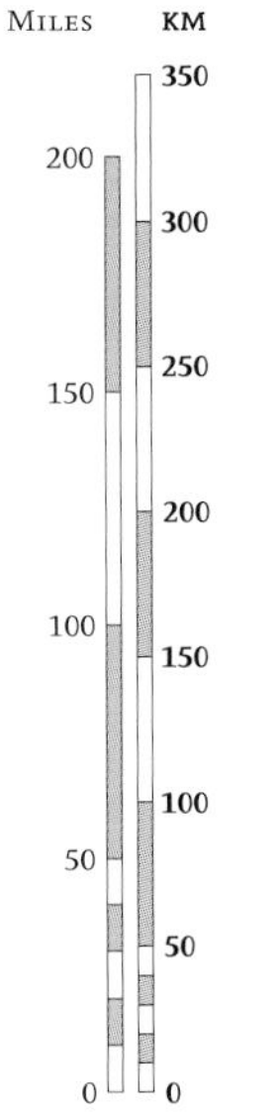


1:5 000 000

Conic Equidistant Projection

159
NORWAY
SKAGERRAK
NORTH SEA
SWEDEN
DENMARK
Kattegat
BALTIC
NETHERLANDS
BELGIUM
LUXEMBOURG
GERMANY
POLAND
CZECH REPUBLIC
AUSTRIA
SWITZERLAND
LIECHTENSTEIN
FRANCE
ITALY
SLOVENIA
ALPS
Copenhagen
Hamburg
Berlin
Amsterdam
Brussels
Prague
Vienna
Munich
Zürich
166
170
LAND BELOW SEA LEVEL
M
FT
Conic Equidistant Projection

159
171
172
173
ESTONIA
LATVIA
LITHUANIA
RUS. FED.
KALININGRAD OBL.
BELARUS
RUSSIAN FEDERATION
PSKOV. OBL.
NOVGOROD. OBL.
TVERSKAYA OBL.
SMOLENSK. OBL.
BRYANSK. OBL.
UKRAINE
MOLDOVA
ROMANIA
HUNGARY
SLOVAKIA
Gulf of Riga
Gulf of Gdańsk
Gotland
Saaremaa (Estonia)
Black Sea
Riga
Tallinn
Tartu
Pärnu
Vilnius
Kaunas
Klaipėda
Šiauliai
Panevėžys
Daugavpils
Liepāja
Kaliningrad
Gdańsk
Gdynia
Olsztyn
Białystok
Warsaw (Warszawa)
Łódź
Lublin
Kraków
Katowice
Rzeszów
Hrodna (Grodno)
Brest
Pinsk
Baranavichy
Minsk
Barysaw
Mahilyow
Babruysk
Homyel'
Vitsyebsk
Polatsk
Orsha
Smolensk
Pskov
Velikiye Luki
Mazyr
Kovel'
Rivne
Lutsk
L'viv (Lvov)
Ternopil'
Khmel'nyts'kyy
Vinnytsya
Zhytomyr
Kiev (Kyiv)
Chernihiv
Bila Tserkva
Uman'
Ivano-Frankivs'k
Chernivtsi
Uzhhorod
Košice
Miskolc
Debrecen
Budapest
Szeged
Cluj-Napoca
Oradea
Satu Mare
Baia Mare
Suceava
Iaşi
Chişinău
Tiraspol
Odessa (Odesa)
Bacău
Târgu Mureş
Carpathian Mountains
Tatry
Alföld
Dnieper (Dnipro)
Dniester (Nistru)
Pripet (Prypyats')
Pripet Marshes
Carpathian Wooden Churches
Residence of Bukovinian and Dalmatian Metropolitans
Gotska Sandön
Fårö
Fårösund
Slite
Ljugarn
Kuressaare
Ventspils
Jūrmala
Jelgava
Sopot
Elbląg
Toruń
Płock
Włocławek
Radom
Kielce
Częstochowa
Tarnów
Chełm
Zamość
Slutsk
Salihorsk
Lida
Maladzyechna
Rechytsa
Korosten'
Berdychiv
Kam"yanets'-Podil's'kyy
Mohyliv-Podil's'kyy
Bălţi
Tighina
Nyíregyháza
Kecskemét
Székesfehérvár
Dunaújváros
Prešov
Poprad
Nizina Mazowiecka
Wyżyna Lubelska
Puszcza Augustowska
Valdayskaya Vozvyshennost'

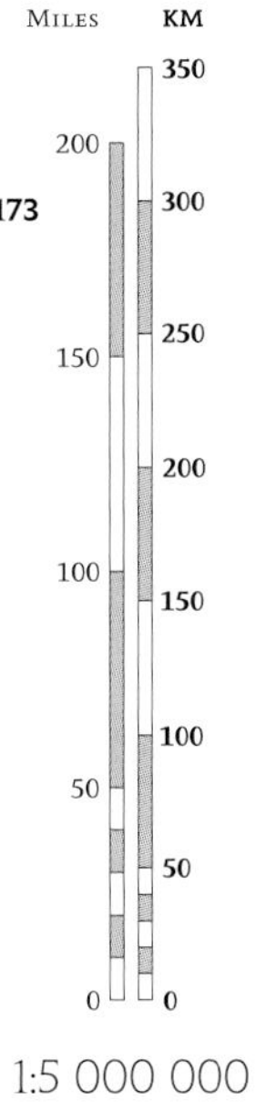
MILES
KM
350
300
250
200
150
100
50
0
200
150
100
50
0
1:5 000 000

168
167
176
SWITZERLAND
AUSTRIA
SLOVENIA
CROATIA
FRANCE
PROVENCE
MONACO
SAN MARINO
VATICAN CITY
ITALY
CORSICA
(CORSE)
(France)
SARDINIA
(SARDEGNA)
(Italy)
SICILY
(SICILIA)
MALTA
ALGERIA
TUNISIA
MEDITERRANEAN
TYRRHENIAN SEA
ADRIATIC SEA
Ligurian Sea
Gulf of Genoa
Gulf of Venice
Strait of Bonifacio
Sicilian Channel
Malta Channel
Milan (Milano)
Turin (Torino)
Genoa (Genova)
Venice (Venezia)
Florence (Firenze)
Rome (Roma)
Naples (Napoli)
Bologna
Palermo
Catania
Messina
Bari
Tunis
Cagliari
Ljubljana
Zagreb
Split
Pescara
Ancona
Taranto
Reggio di Calabria
Syracuse (Siracusa)
Nice
Grenoble
Innsbruck
LIECHTENSTEIN
6000
19686
5000
16404
4000
13124
3000
9843
2000
6562
1000
3281
500
1640
200
656
0
0
LAND BELOW SEA LEVEL
200
656
2000
6562
4000
13124
6000
19686
M
FT
Conic Equidistant Projection

169
173
136
HUNGARY
ROMANIA
CARPATHIAN MTS
Transylvanian Alps (Carpații Meridionali)
MOLDOVA
UKRAINE
SERBIA
VOJVODINA
KOSOVO
MONTENEGRO
BULGARIA
Balkan Mountains (Stara Planina)
Rhodope Mountains
MACEDONIA (F.Y.R.O.M.)
ALBANIA
GREECE
TURKEY
BLACK SEA
AEGEAN SEA
Sea of Marmara (Marmara Denizi)
Ionian Islands (Ionioi Nisoi)
Strait of Otranto
Cyclades (Kyklades)
Dodecanese (Dodekanisa)
Kritiko Pelagos
Myrtoo Pelagos
Thrakiko Pelagos
Crete (Kriti)
Bucharest (București)
Belgrade (Beograd)
Sofia (Sofiya)
Athens (Athina)
Istanbul
Skopje
Tirana (Tiranë)
Thessaloniki
Odessa (Odesa)
Sarajevo
Podgorica
Prishtinë (Priština)
İzmir
Bursa
Constanța
Varna
Iraklion
Rhodes (Rodos)
Lesbos (Lesvos)
Chios
Corfu (Kerkyra)
MILES
KM
1:5 000 000
© Collins Bartholomew Ltd

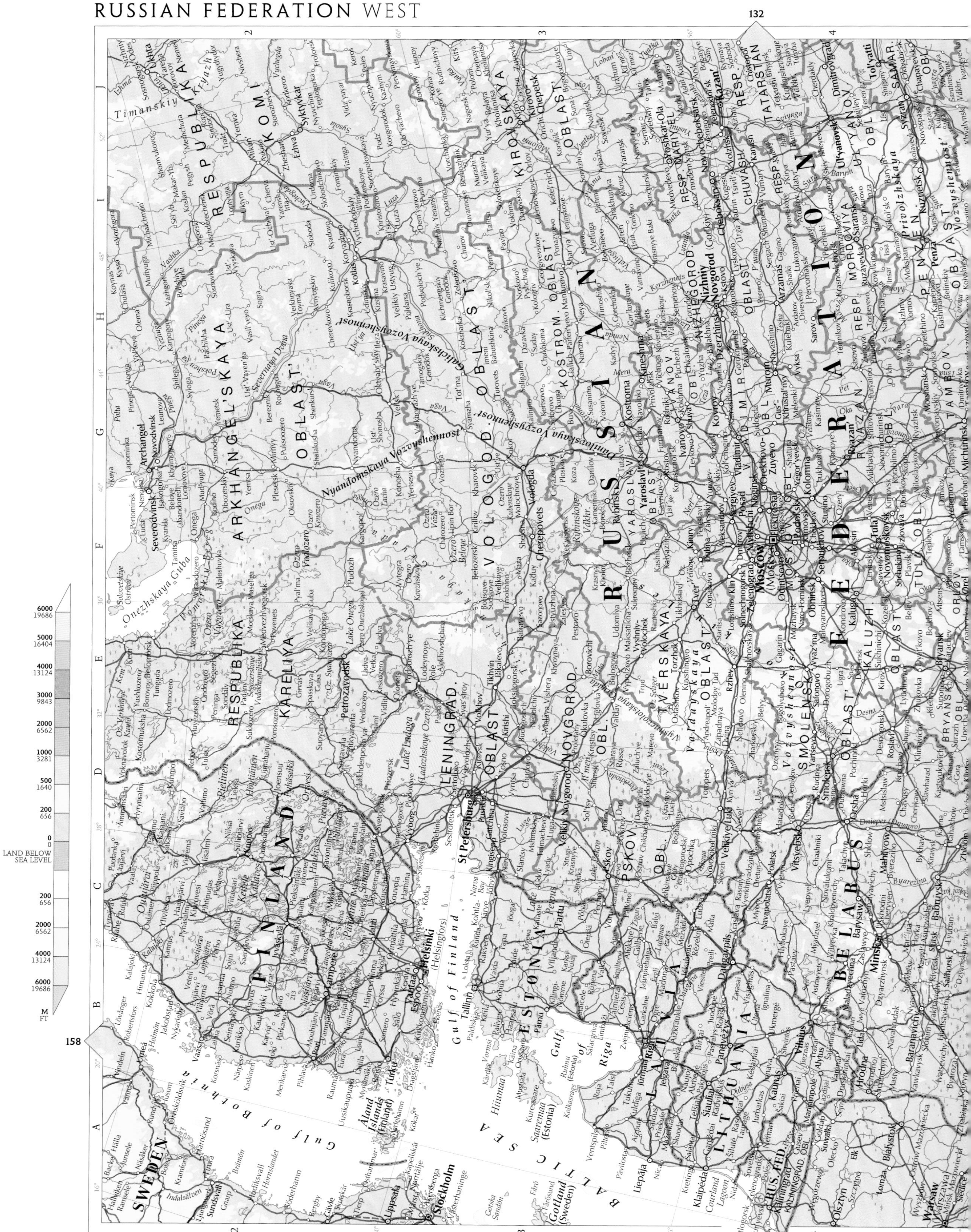


Conic Equidistant Projection

138

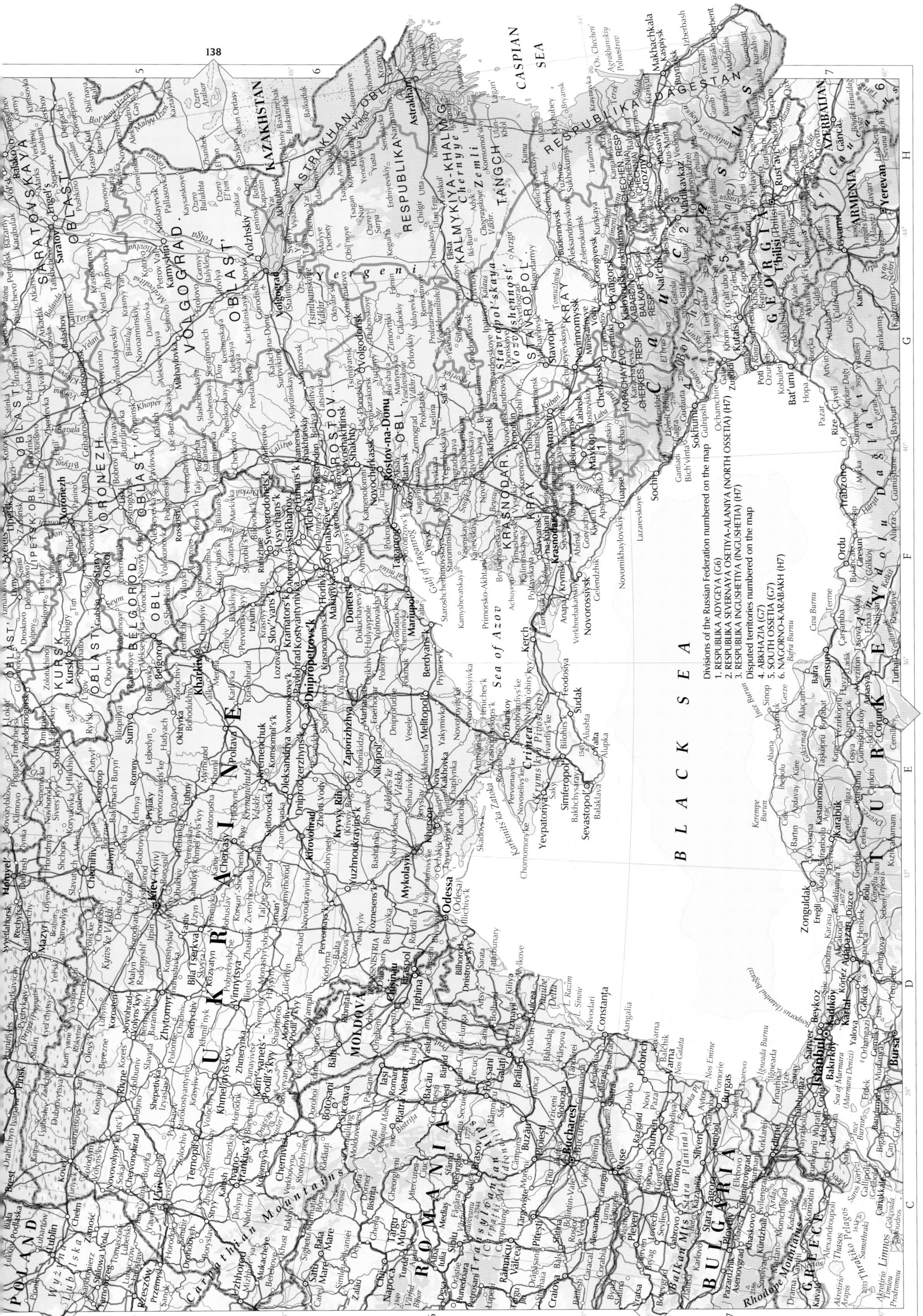


136

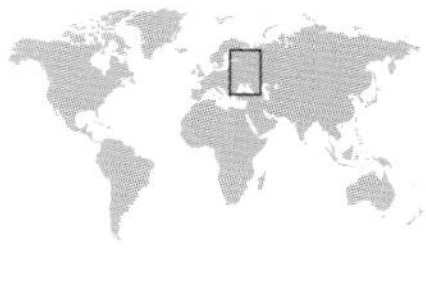

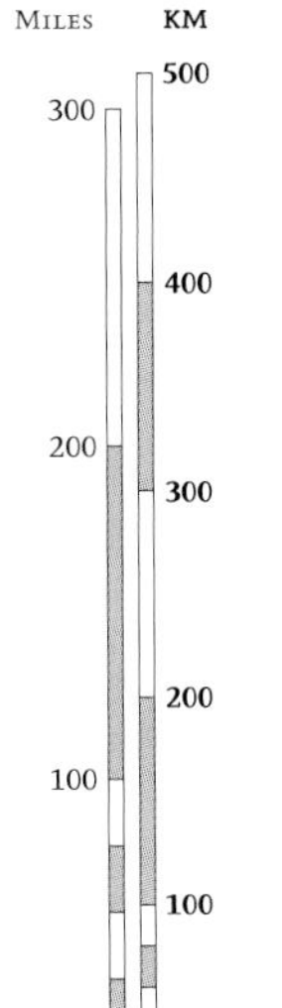


1:7 000 000

168 171

Orthographic Projection

F
G
H
I
J
1
2
3
4
5
6
7
E U R O P E
Adriatic Sea
Ionian Sea
Sicily
Black Sea
Volga
Caspian Sea
Aral Sea
A S I A
M E D I T E R R A N E A N S E A
Crete
Cyprus
Mişrātah
Al Baydā'
Gulf of Sirte
Benghazi
Alexandria
Port Said
Shubrā al Khaymah
Qattara Depression
Giza
Cairo
Suez
Gulf of Suez
Gulf of Aqaba
Al Minyā
Asyūţ
Qinā
Luxor
Aswān
Lake Nasser
L I B Y A
Libyan Desert
E G Y P T
Nile
S A H A R A
Tibesti
Emi Koussi
3415
Dasht-e Kavīr
Zagros Mountains
The Gulf
Gulf of Oman
H I M A L A Y A
Red Sea
Nubian Desert
Port Sudan
Baiyuda Desert
Atbara
Rub' al Khālī
C H A D
Abéché
Lake Chad
Ndjamena
Maiduguri
Maroua
Sarh
Moundou
Ngaoundéré
Omdurman
Khartoum
Wad Medani
Marra Plateau
S U D A N
El Obeid
Blue Nile
ERITREA
Asmara
Gedaref
Ras Dejen
4533
Mek'ele
Lake Tana
Bahir Dar
Tropic of Cancer
A R A B I A N S E A
DJIBOUTI
Djibouti
Gulf of Aden
Socotra
CENTRAL AFRICAN REPUBLIC
Bossangoa
Bouar
Bangui
Ubangi
Wau
Sobat
SOUTH SUDAN
White Nile
Juba
Addis Ababa
Dirē Dawa
Hargeysa
E T H I O P I A
S O M A L I A
Lake Turkana
Congo
C O N G O
Mbandaka
Kisangani
Lake Albert
UGANDA
Kampala
Kisumu
K E N Y A
Mount Kenya
5199
Webi Shabeelle
Mogadishu
I N D I A N O C E A N
Franceville
DEMOCRATIC REPUBLIC OF THE CONGO
Lac Mai-Ndombe
Lomami
Lake Edward
Lake Victoria
Nakuru
Lac Kivu
RWANDA
Kigali
Bukavu
BURUNDI
Bujumbura
Nairobi
Kismaayo
Brazzaville
Kinshasa
Matadi
Kikwit
Mwanza
Kilimanjaro
Arusha
5892
Kigoma
Kananga
Mbuji-Mayi
Kalemie
Tabora
T A N Z A N I A
Tanga
Mombasa
Maldives
Luanda
Cuango
Lake Tanganyika
Dodoma
Pemba Island
Zanzibar
Zanzibar Island
Dar es Salaam
Mafia Island
Kamina
Chaîne des Mitumba
Lake Rukwa
Mbeya
Iringa
Rufiji
Lake Mweru
Victoria
Mahé
Equator
A N G O L A
Likasi
Kasama
S E Y C H E L L E S
Lobito
Benguela
Huambo
Solwezi
Lubumbashi
Aldabra Islands (Seychelles)
Coëtivy
Chingola
Ndola
Rovuma
Lake Nyasa
Farquhar Group (Seychelles)
Lubango
Z A M B I A
Chipata
Ngazidja
COMOROS
Moroni
Kabwe
Lilongwe
MALAWI
Pemba
Îles Glorieuses (France)
Tanjona Bobaomby
Mongu
Lusaka
Zambezi
Mayotte (France)
Antsirañana
Agalega Islands (Mauritius)
Chagos Archipelago
Cunene
Cubango
Kafue
Lake Kariba
Blantyre
Nacala
Victoria Falls
Livingstone
Tete
Nampula
M O Z A M B I Q U E
Mozambique Channel
N a m i b D e s e r t
Etosha Pan
Okavango
Harare
Chitungwiza
Mahajanga
Z I M B A B W E
Mutare
Quelimane
M A D A G A S C A R
NAMIBIA
Okavango Delta
Gweru
Île Tromelin (France)
Makgadikgadi
Bulawayo
Cargados Carajos Islands (Mauritius)
Francistown
Beira
Toamasina
Windhoek
B O T S W A N A
Antananarivo
Limpopo
Bassas da India (France)
Île Europa (France)
Kalahari Desert
Gaborone
Fianarantsoa
MAURITIUS
Port Louis
Pretoria
Drakensberg
Inhambane
Toliara
St Denis
Réunion (France)
Johannesburg
Xai-Xai
Soweto
Maputo
Rodrigues Island (Mauritius)
Vereeniging
Mbabane
SWAZILAND
Orange
Kimberley
Tanjona Vohimena
Bloemfontein
Maseru
LESOTHO
Durban
REPUBLIC OF SOUTH AFRICA
Orange
Great Karoo
Little Karoo
Cape Town
Khayelitsha
East London
Cape of Good Hope
Cape Agulhas
Port Elizabeth
Tropic of Capricorn
15°
30°
45°
60°
75°
90°
Miles
KM
1000
750
500
250
0
1500
1250
1000
750
500
250
0
1:28 000 000

167

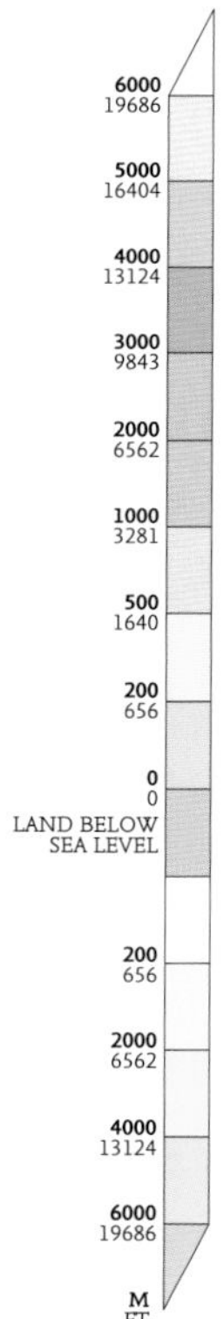


Lambert Azimuthal Equal Area Projection

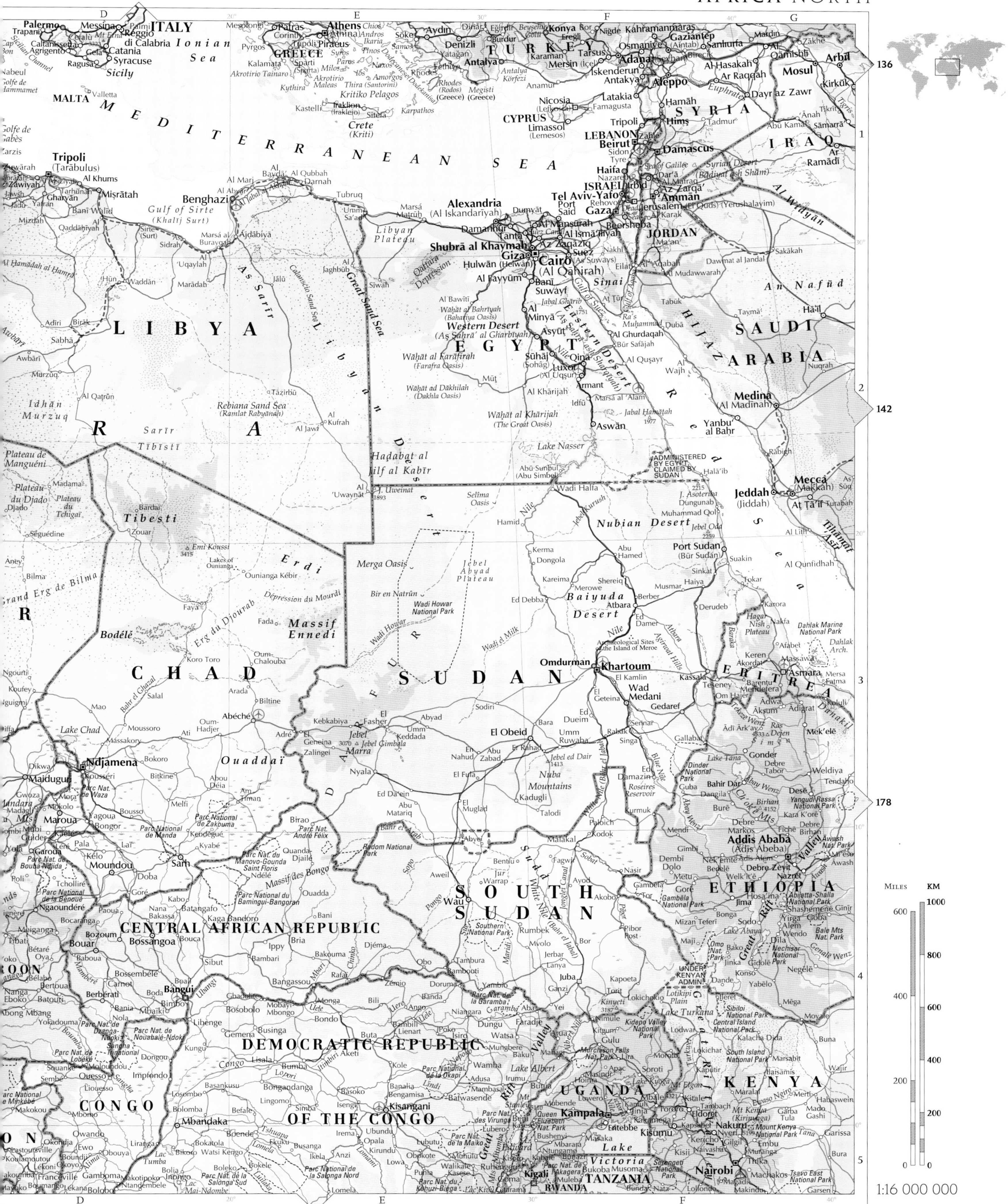
171
136
142
178
178
MEDITERRANEAN SEA
Ionian Sea
Red Sea
ITALY
MALTA
GREECE
TURKEY
CYPRUS
SYRIA
LEBANON
ISRAEL
JORDAN
IRAQ
SAUDI ARABIA
LIBYA
EGYPT
SUDAN
SOUTH SUDAN
CHAD
ERITREA
ETHIOPIA
KENYA
UGANDA
RWANDA
TANZANIA
CENTRAL AFRICAN REPUBLIC
DEMOCRATIC REPUBLIC OF THE CONGO
CONGO
Palermo
Messina
Catania
Syracuse
Sicily
Valletta
Athens
Crete
Konya
Adana
Aleppo
Mosul
Nicosia
Beirut
Damascus
Tel Aviv-Yafo
Jerusalem
'Amman
Gaza
Tripoli (Tarābulus)
Benghazi
Gulf of Sirte
Alexandria (Al Iskandarīyah)
Cairo (Al Qāhirah)
Giza
Suez
Sinai
Luxor
Aswān
Lake Nasser
Western Desert
Great Sand Sea
Libyan Desert
Tibesti
Emi Koussi
Medina (Al Madīnah)
Jeddah (Jiddah)
Mecca (Makkah)
Port Sudan
Nubian Desert
Omdurman
Khartoum
Kassala
Asmara
Massif Ennedi
Ouaddai
Abéché
Lake Chad
Ndjamena
Maiduguri
El Obeid
Nuba Mountains
Juba
Wau
Addis Ababa (Adis Abeba)
Lake Tana
Lake Turkana
Bangui
Kisangani
Mbandaka
Kampala
Lake Victoria
Kigali
Nairobi
1:16 000 000
MILES
KM
0
200
400
600
800
1000

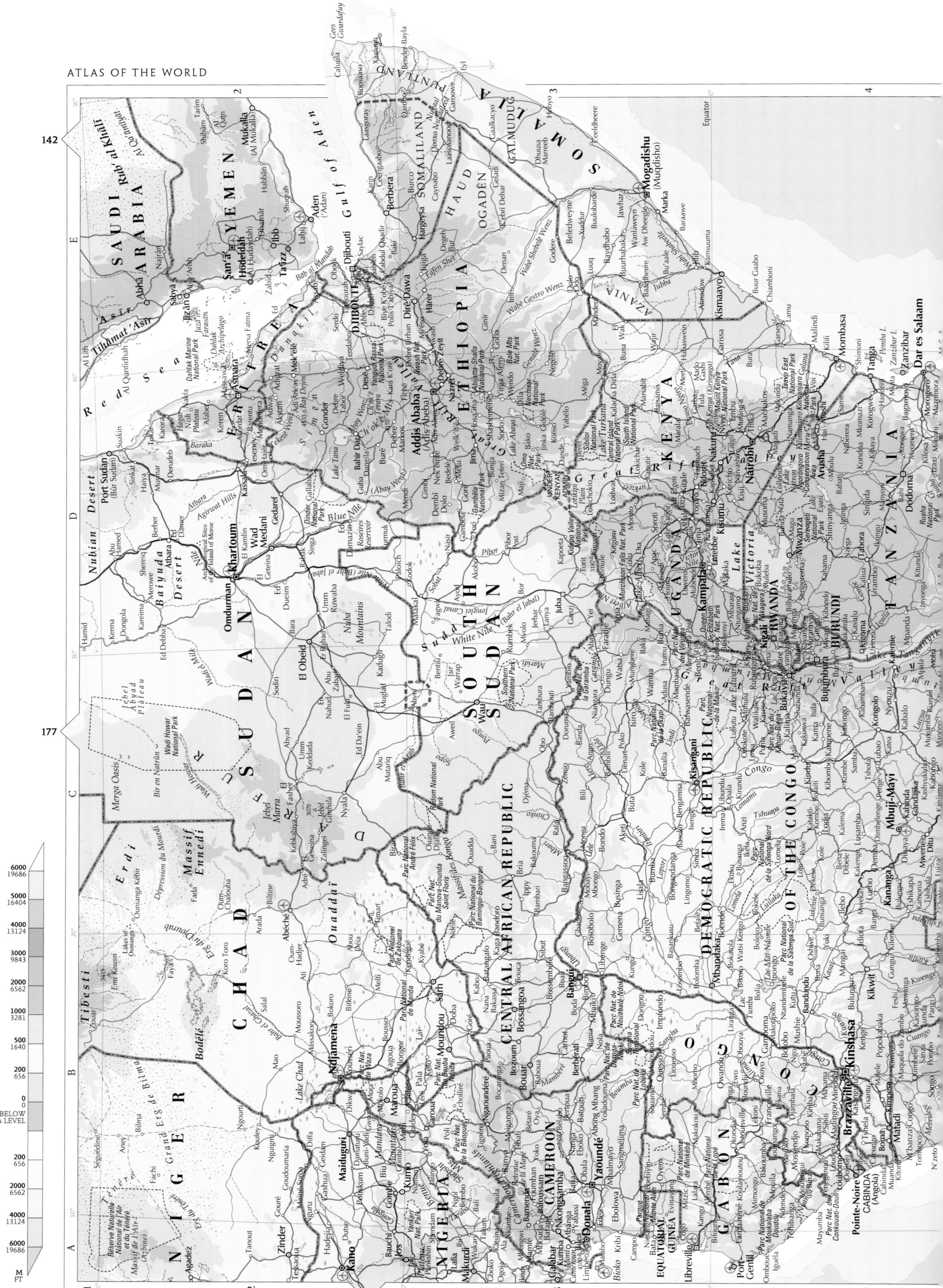


Lambert Azimuthal Equal Area Projection

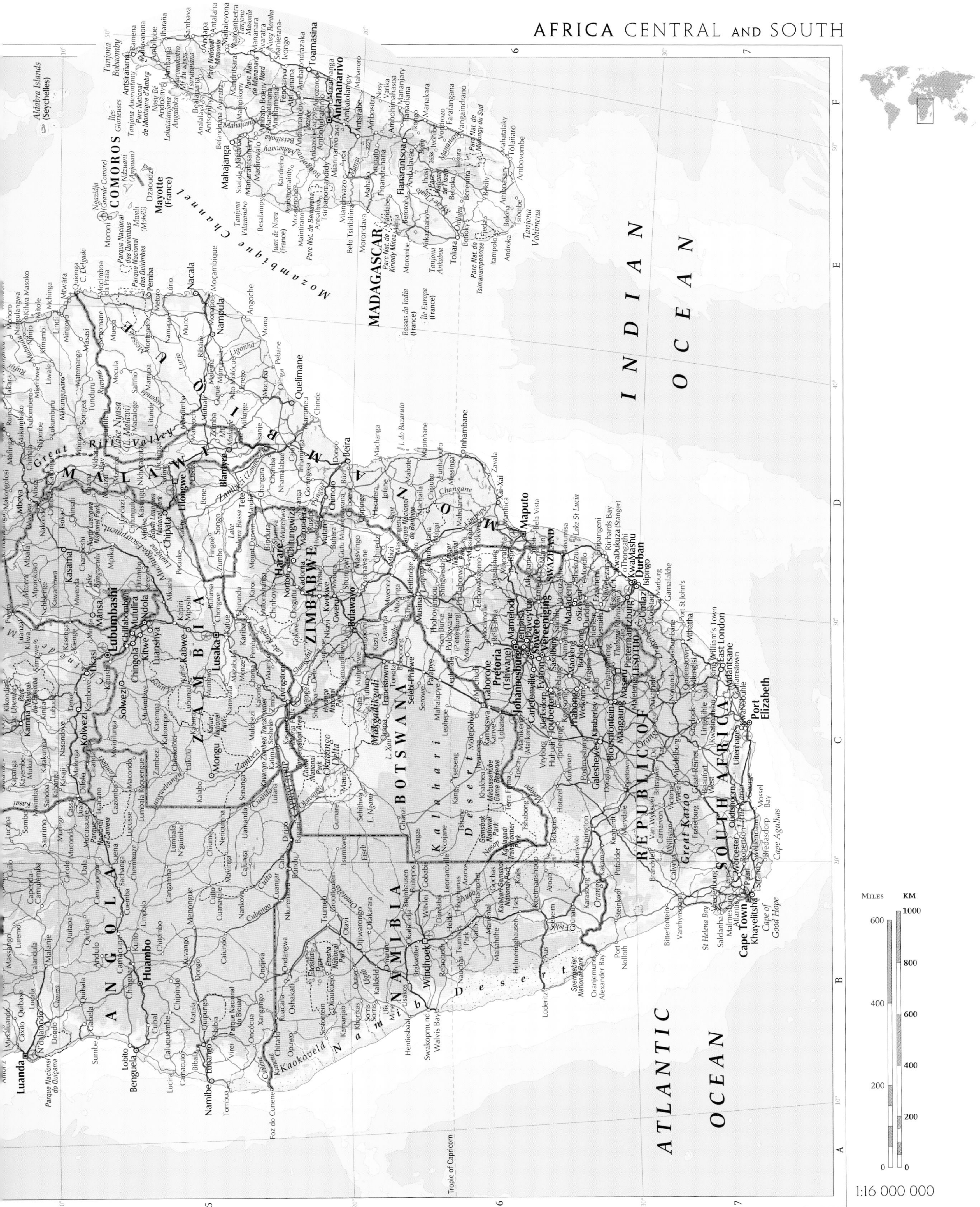
ANGOLA
ZAMBIA
MALAWI
MOZAMBIQUE
ZIMBABWE
BOTSWANA
NAMIBIA
REPUBLIC OF SOUTH AFRICA
LESOTHO
SWAZILAND
MADAGASCAR
COMOROS
Mayotte (France)
Mozambique Channel
Kalahari Desert
Namib Desert
INDIAN OCEAN
ATLANTIC OCEAN
Tropic of Capricorn
Luanda
Lusaka
Harare
Lilongwe
Maputo
Gaborone
Windhoek
Pretoria (Tshwane)
Johannesburg
Cape Town
Durban
Antananarivo
MILES
KM
1:16 000 000

179

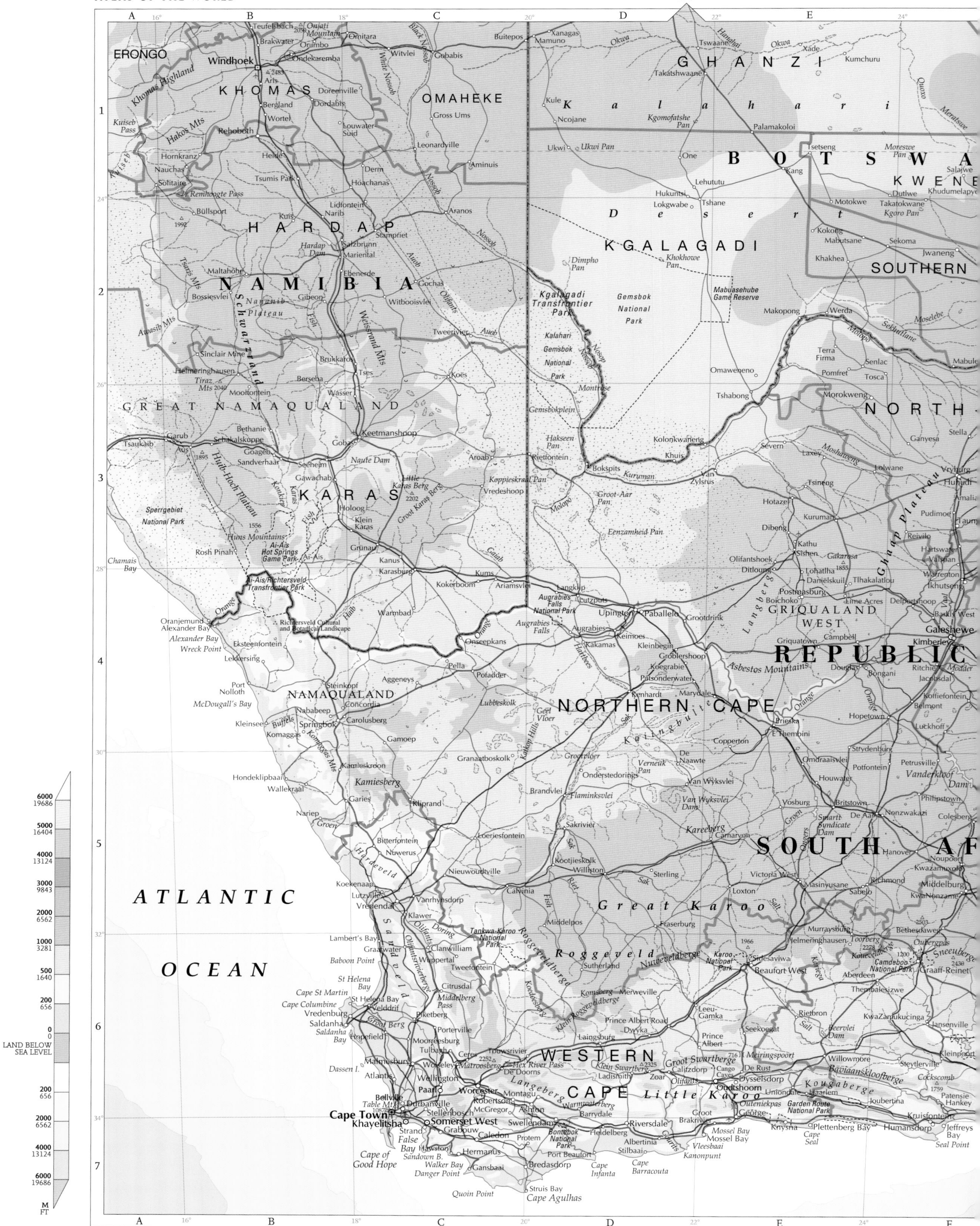


Lambert Azimuthal Equal Area Projection

179

ZIMBABWE
MOZAMBIQUE
GAZA
INHAMBANE
MAPUTO
Maputo
SWAZILAND
LESOTHO
LIMPOPO
MPUMALANGA
GAUTENG
KWAZULU-NATAL
FREE STATE
EASTERN CAPE
CENTRAL
KGATLENG
SOUTH-EAST
GRIQUALAND EAST
INDIAN OCEAN
Pretoria (Tshwane)
Johannesburg
Soweto
Vereeniging
Bloemfontein
Mangaung
Maseru
Pietermaritzburg
Durban
East London
Port Elizabeth
Gaborone
Richards Bay
Tropic of Capricorn
Drakensberg
Limpopo
1:5 000 000
Miles
KM

Administrative divisions abbreviated on the map:

| U.S.A. | | CANADA | |
|---|---|---|---|
| CONN. | CONNECTICUT | P.E.I. | PRINCE EDWARD ISLAND |
| DEL. | DELAWARE | | |
| MD | MARYLAND | | |
| MASS. | MASSACHUSETTS | | |
| N.H. | NEW HAMPSHIRE | | |
| N.J. | NEW JERSEY | | |
| R.I. | RHODE ISLAND | | |
| VER. | VERMONT | | |

Orthographic Projection

F
G
H
I
J
1
2
3
4
5
6
7
EUROPE
AFRICA
ATLANTIC OCEAN
SOUTH AMERICA
Arctic Circle
Station Nord
Greenland Sea
Daneborg
Kong Wilhelm Land
Knud Rasmussen Land
Nares Strait
Ellesmere Island
Amund Ringnes I.
Dundas
Nuussuaq
Greenland (Kalaallit Nunaat) (Denmark)
Kong Christian IX Land
Denmark Strait
Iceland
Devon Island
Lancaster Sd
Baffin Bay
Somerset Island
Prince of Wales I.
Clyde River
Ilulissat
Ammassalik
Kong Frederik VI Kyst
Gulf of Boothia
Boothia Pen.
King William Island
Baffin Island
Davis Strait
Melville Peninsula
Prince Charles I.
Foxe Basin
Cape Mercy
Cumberland Sd
Nuuk (Godthåb)
Nanortalik
Repulse Bay
Iqaluit
Labrador Sea
Southampton Island
Cape Dorset
Resolution I.
Coral Harbour
Hudson Strait
Coats I.
Mansel I.
Péninsule d'Ungava
Ungava Bay
NEWFOUNDLAND AND LABRADOR
Nain
Madeira
Arviat
HUDSON BAY
Labrador
Azores
Smallwood Reservoir
Canary Islands
Belcher Islands
Gander
MANITOBA
Caniapiscau
St John's
Thompson
James Bay
Chisasibi
Newfoundland
Cape Race
QUEBEC
Île d'Anticosti
Sept-Îles
Gulf of St Lawrence
Cabot Str.
St Pierre and Miquelon (France)
Lake Winnipeg
ONTARIO
Moosonee
St Lawrence
Cape Breton I.
Tropic of Cancer
Lake Nipigon
Rouyn-Noranda
Chicoutimi
NEW BRUNSWICK
Charlottetown
P.E.I.
NOVA SCOTIA
Sable Island
Halifax
Winnipeg
Timmins
Quebec
Fredericton
Thunder Bay
Lake Superior
Sault Ste Marie
North Bay
Montréal
MAINE
Cape Sable
Augusta
Grand Forks
MINNESOTA
MICHIGAN
Ottawa
Montpelier
VT.
N.H.
Concord
Boston
Duluth
L. Huron
Toronto
Lake Ontario
NEW YORK
MASS.
Providence
Cape Cod
Minneapolis
St Paul
WISCONSIN
L. Michigan
Buffalo
Albany
Hartford
CONN.
R.I.
Rochester
Sioux Falls
Milwaukee
Lansing
Detroit
L. Erie
Erie
PENNSYLVANIA
New York
Trenton
Philadelphia
IOWA
Chicago
Cleveland
Pittsburgh
Des Moines
ILLINOIS
Columbus
OHIO
Baltimore
MD.
DEL.
Washington D.C.
Omaha
Lincoln
Indianapolis
INDIANA
WEST VIRGINIA
Charleston
Richmond
Kansas City
MISSOURI
St Louis
Cincinnati
VIRGINIA
KENTUCKY
Raleigh
Cape Hatteras
Springfield
Knoxville
Charlotte
N. CAROLINA
Bermuda (U.K.)
Nashville
TENNESSEE
Oklahoma City
ARKANSAS
Memphis
Atlanta
Columbia
S.CAROLINA
OKLAHOMA
Little Rock
Mississippi
MISS.
Montgomery
Savannah
Fort Worth
Dallas
ALABAMA
GEORGIA
Shreveport
Jackson
Tallahassee
Jacksonville
Equator
Cape Canaveral
Austin
Baton Rouge
LOUISIANA
Mobile
New Orleans
Orlando
San Antonio
Houston
Tampa
FLORIDA
THE BAHAMAS
Nassau
Corpus Christi
GULF OF MEXICO
Miami
Straits of Florida
Turks and Caicos Is (U.K.)
DOMINICAN REPUBLIC
Virgin Is (U.K.)
Anguilla (U.K.)
ANTIGUA AND BARBUDA
Montserrat (U.K.)
Guadeloupe (France)
DOMINICA
Martinique (France)
ST LUCIA
BARBADOS
ST VINCENT AND THE GRENADINES
Matamoros
Santa Clara
Holguín
Havana
CUBA
Hispaniola
San Juan
Virgin Is (U.S.A.)
ST KITTS AND NEVIS
Ciudad Victoria
Santiago
HAITI
Santo Domingo
Puerto Rico (U.S.A.)
Port-au-Prince
Greater Antilles
Lesser Antilles
Tampico
Yucatan Channel
Mérida
Cayman Is (U.K.)
Montego Bay
JAMAICA
Kingston
Mexico City
Bahía de Campeche
Yucatán
CARIBBEAN SEA
GRENADA
TRINIDAD AND TOBAGO
Veracruz
Villahermosa
Puebla
BELIZE
Belmopan
Aruba (Neth.)
Curaçao (Neth.)
Port of Spain
Oaxaca
Sari Pedro Sula
Acapulco
Gulf of Tehuantepec
GUATEMALA
Guatemala City
HONDURAS
Tegucigalpa
San Salvador
EL SALVADOR
NICARAGUA
Lake Nicaragua
Managua
Colón
Panama City
COSTA RICA
San José
PANAMA
Gulf of Panama
Amazon (Amazonas)
Cape Verde
Miles
KM
1200
800
400
0
2000
1600
1200
800
400
0
1:32 000 000

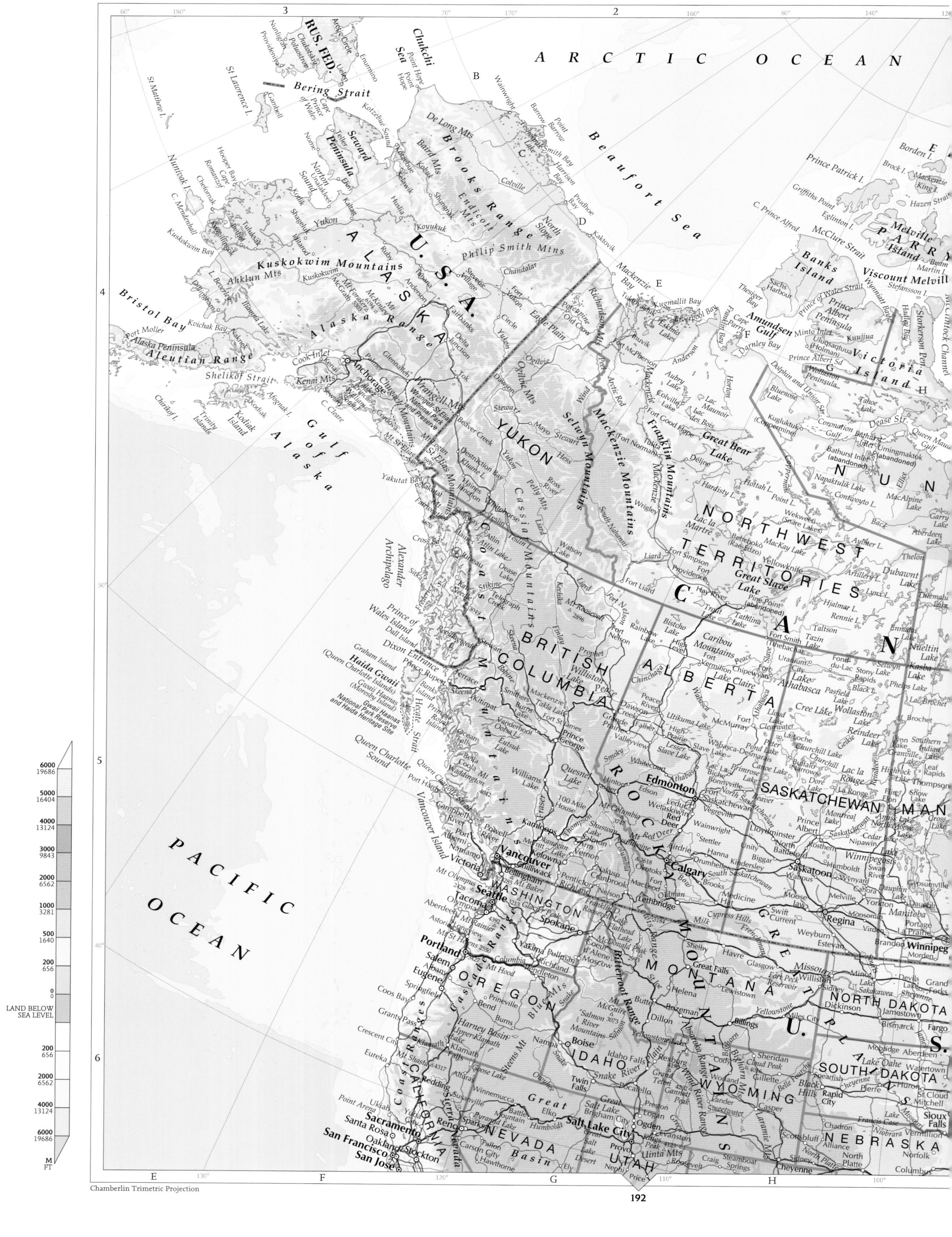


Chamberlin Trimetric Projection

192

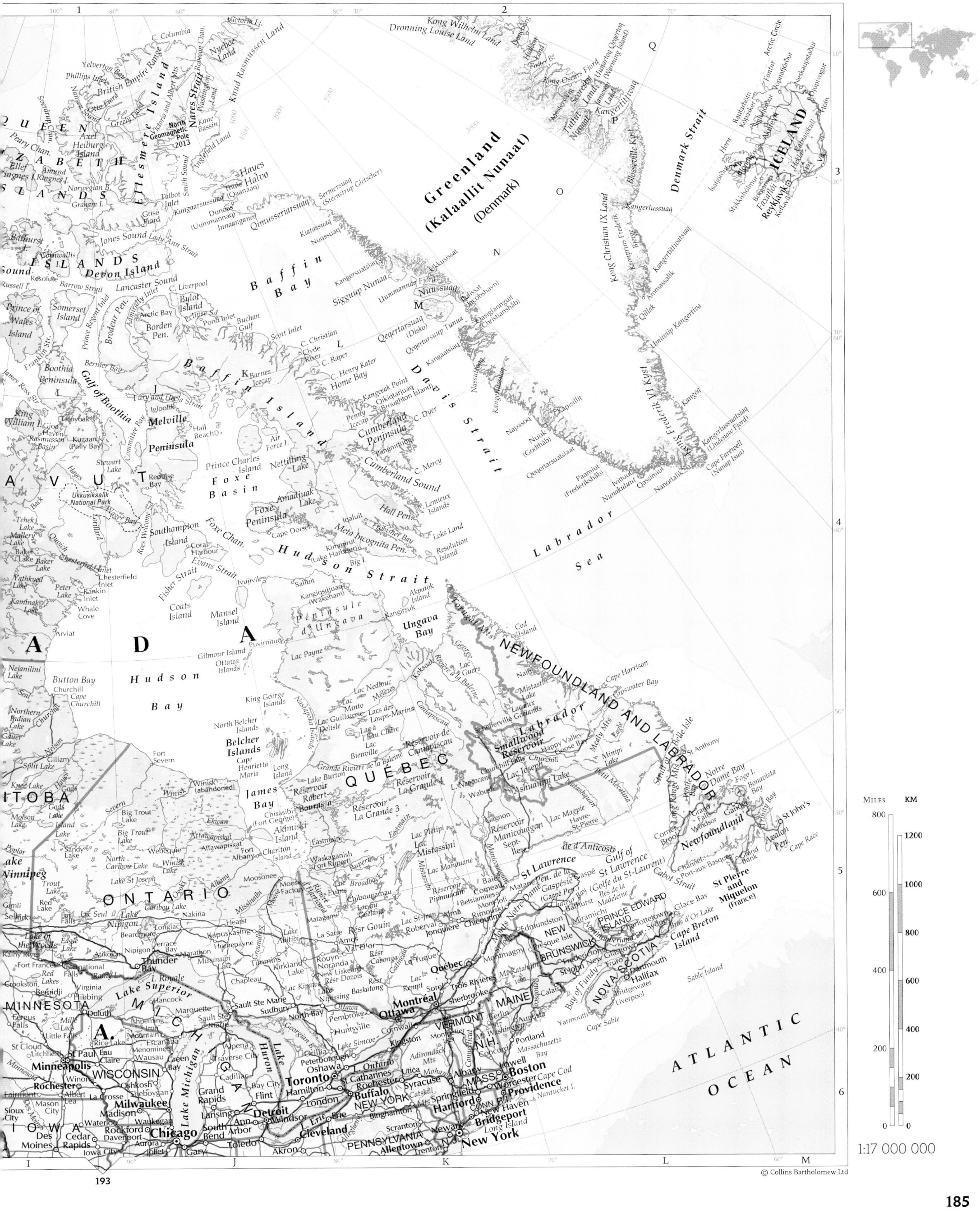


© Collins Bartholomew Ltd

184

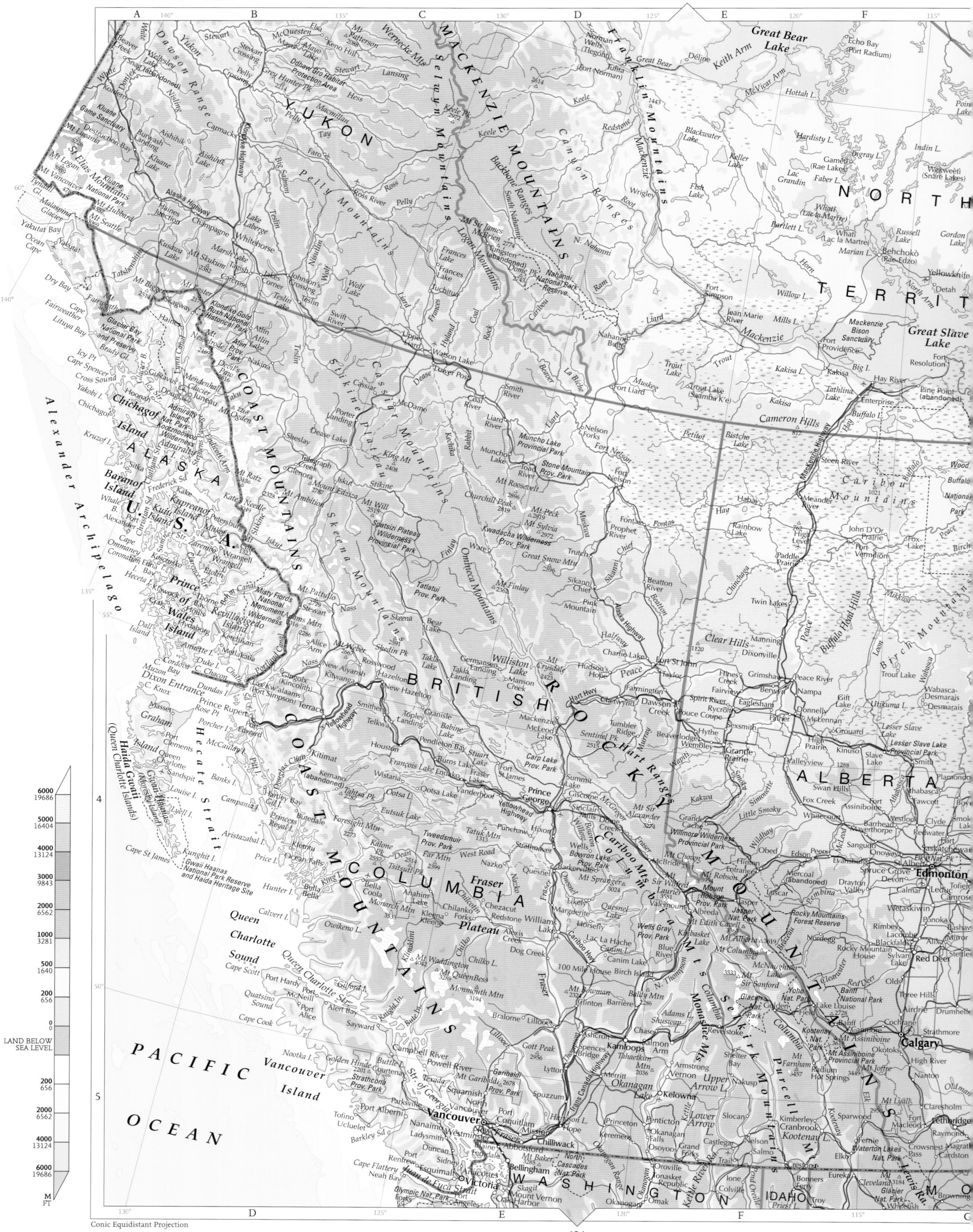


Conic Equidistant Projection

194

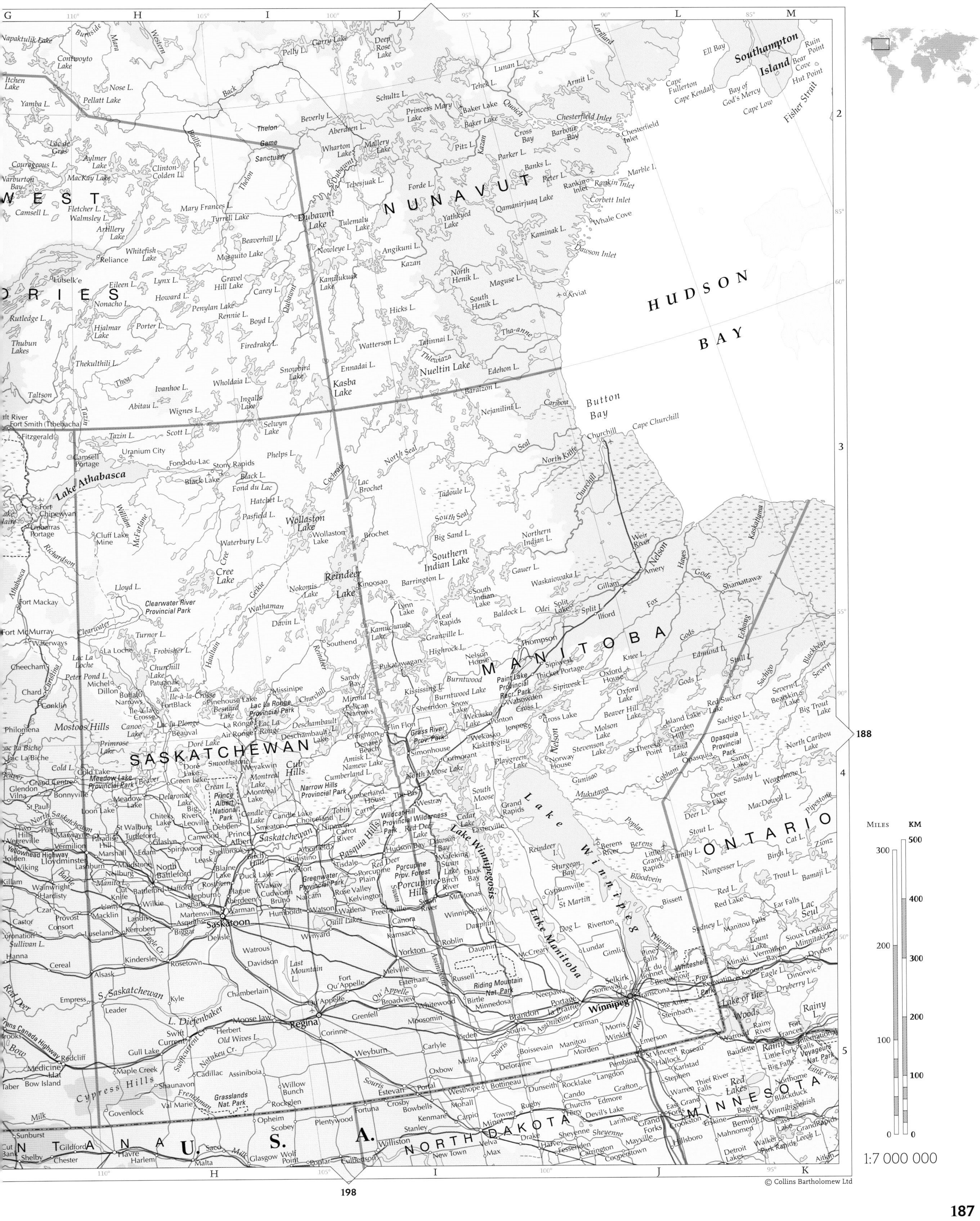
185
188
198
1:7 000 000
MILES
KM
NUNAVUT
MANITOBA
SASKATCHEWAN
ONTARIO
MINNESOTA
NORTH DAKOTA
U. S. A.
HUDSON BAY
Southampton Island
Lake Winnipeg
Lake Winnipegosis
Lake Manitoba
Lake Athabasca
Reindeer Lake
Wollaston Lake
Southern Indian Lake
Nueltin Lake
Kasba Lake
Dubawnt Lake
Baker Lake
Chesterfield Inlet
Rankin Inlet
Arviat
Churchill
Cape Churchill
Button Bay
Thompson
Flin Flon
The Pas
Prince Albert
Saskatoon
Regina
Moose Jaw
Yorkton
Brandon
Winnipeg
Portage la Prairie
Dauphin
Swift Current
North Battleford
Lloydminster
Kenora
Fort McMurray
Uranium City
Fort Chipewyan
Grasslands Nat. Park
Riding Mountain Nat. Park
Prince Albert National Park
Thelon Game Sanctuary
Lake of the Woods
Cypress Hills
Porcupine Hills
Pasquia Hills
Trans Canada Highway
Yellowhead Highway

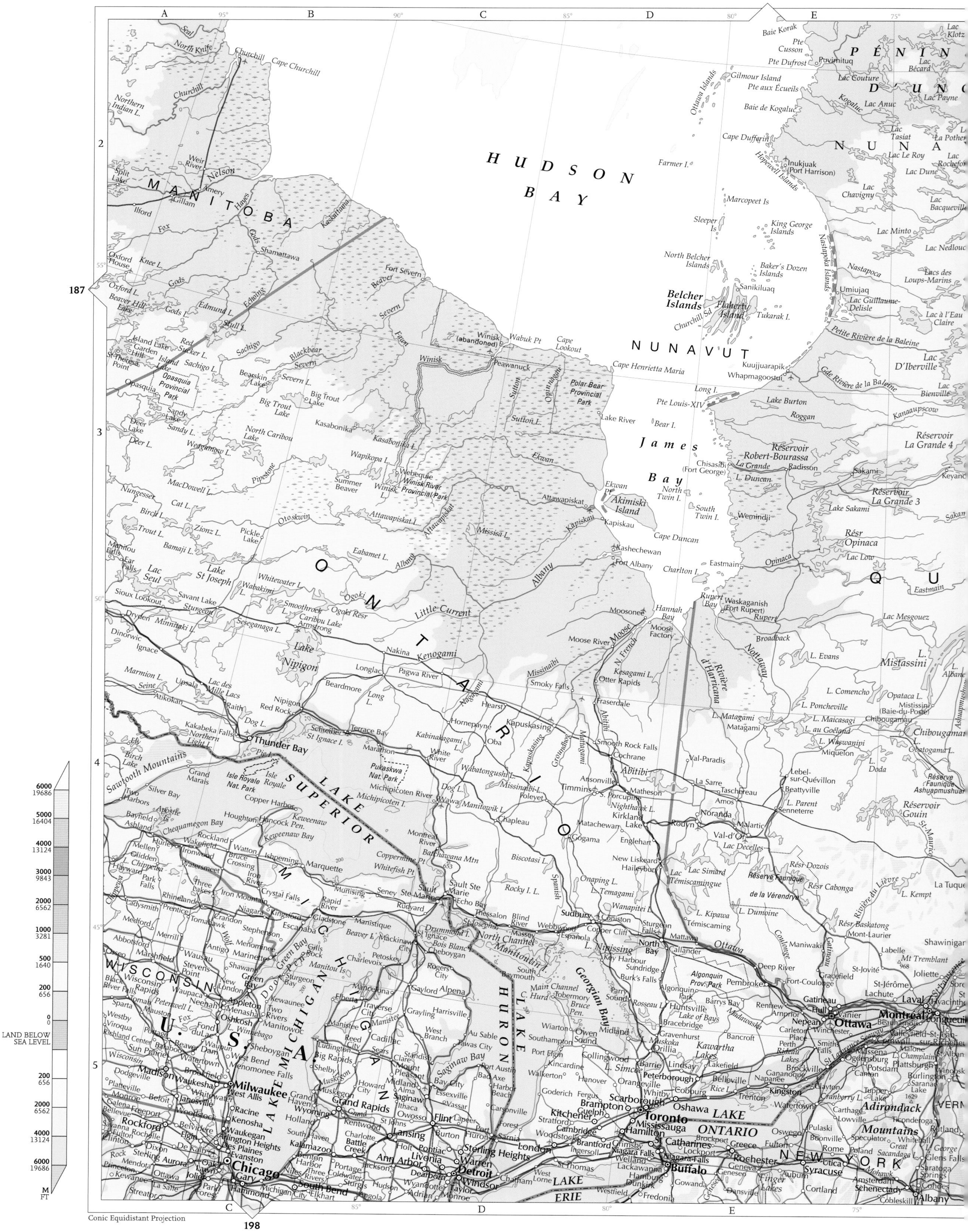
185
187
198
A
B
C
D
E
95°
90°
85°
80°
75°
2
3
4
5
HUDSON BAY
MANITOBA
ONTARIO
NUNAVUT
James Bay
LAKE SUPERIOR
LAKE MICHIGAN
LAKE HURON
Georgian Bay
LAKE ONTARIO
LAKE ERIE
U. S. A.
WISCONSIN
MICHIGAN
NEW YORK
PÉNINSULE D'UNGAVA
Churchill
Cape Churchill
Northern Indian L.
Split Lake
Gillam
Ilford
Fox
Nelson
Hayes
Gods
Shamattawa
Oxford House
Knee L.
Oxford L.
Beaver Hill Lake
Gods L.
Edmund L.
Stull L.
Island Lake
Garden Hill
St Theresa Point
Red Sucker L.
Sachigo L.
Opasquia Provincial Park
Sandy Lake
Sandy L.
Deer Lake
Deer L.
Fort Severn
Severn
Beaver
Winisk (abandoned)
Wabuk Pt
Cape Lookout
Peawanuck
Polar Bear Provincial Park
Sutton L.
Lake River
Cape Henrietta Maria
Big Trout Lake
Kasabonika
Kasabonika L.
North Caribou Lake
Wapikopa L.
Webequie
Winisk River Provincial Park
Summer Beaver
Attawapiskat
Attawapiskat L.
Ekwan Pt
Akimiski Island
Kapiskau
Cape Duncan
Kashechewan
Fort Albany
Albany
Pickle Lake
Eabamet L.
Missisa L.
Lac Seul
Lake St Joseph
Sioux Lookout
Savant Lake
Dryden
Ignace
Ogoki Resr
Armstrong
Lake Nipigon
Little Current
Kenogami
Nakina
Longlac
Moosonee
Moose Factory
Moose River
Hannah Bay
Smoky Falls
Otter Rapids
Fraserdale
Hearst
Kapuskasing
Hornepayne
Oba
Cochrane
Smooth Rock Falls
Timmins
Matheson
Kirkland Lake
Thunder Bay
Nipigon
Red Rock
Schreiber
Terrace Bay
Marathon
Pukaskwa Nat. Park
Isle Royale Nat. Park
Wawa
Chapleau
Sault Ste Marie
Sudbury
North Bay
Mattawa
Algonquin Prov. Park
Pembroke
Ottawa
Montreal
Gatineau
Kingston
Toronto
Mississauga
Hamilton
Oshawa
Peterborough
Barrie
Orillia
Owen Sound
Kitchener
Guelph
Brampton
Scarborough
London
Windsor
Detroit
Sterling Heights
Flint
Lansing
Grand Rapids
Ann Arbor
Toledo
St Catharines
Niagara Falls
Buffalo
Rochester
Syracuse
Albany
Schenectady
Utica
Adirondack Mountains
Milwaukee
Chicago
Gary
Madison
Rockford
Green Bay
Appleton
Oshkosh
South Bend
Kalamazoo
Saginaw
Bay City
Traverse City
Marquette
Houghton
Escanaba
Manitoulin I.
North Channel
Lake Nipissing
Rouyn
Val-d'Or
Amos
Noranda
Matagami
Chibougamau
Lac Mistassini
Waskaganish (Fort Rupert)
Eastmain
Wemindji
Chisasibi (Fort George)
Radisson
Réservoir Robert-Bourassa
Réservoir La Grande 3
Réservoir La Grande 4
Résr Opinaca
Whapmagoostui
Kuujjuarapik
Umiujaq
Inukjuak (Port Harrison)
Puvirnituq
Belcher Islands
Sanikiluaq
Flaherty Island
Ottawa Islands
Sleeper Is
King George Islands
Baker's Dozen Islands
Long I.
Bear I.
Charlton I.
Réserve Faunique de la Vérendrye
Mont-Laurier
Maniwaki
Mt Tremblant 968
St-Jérôme
Laval
Lake Champlain
Plattsburgh
Burlington
Conic Equidistant Projection
6000 19686
5000 16404
4000 13124
3000 9843
2000 6562
1000 3281
500 1640
200 656
0 0
LAND BELOW SEA LEVEL
200 656
2000 6562
4000 13124
6000 19686
M FT

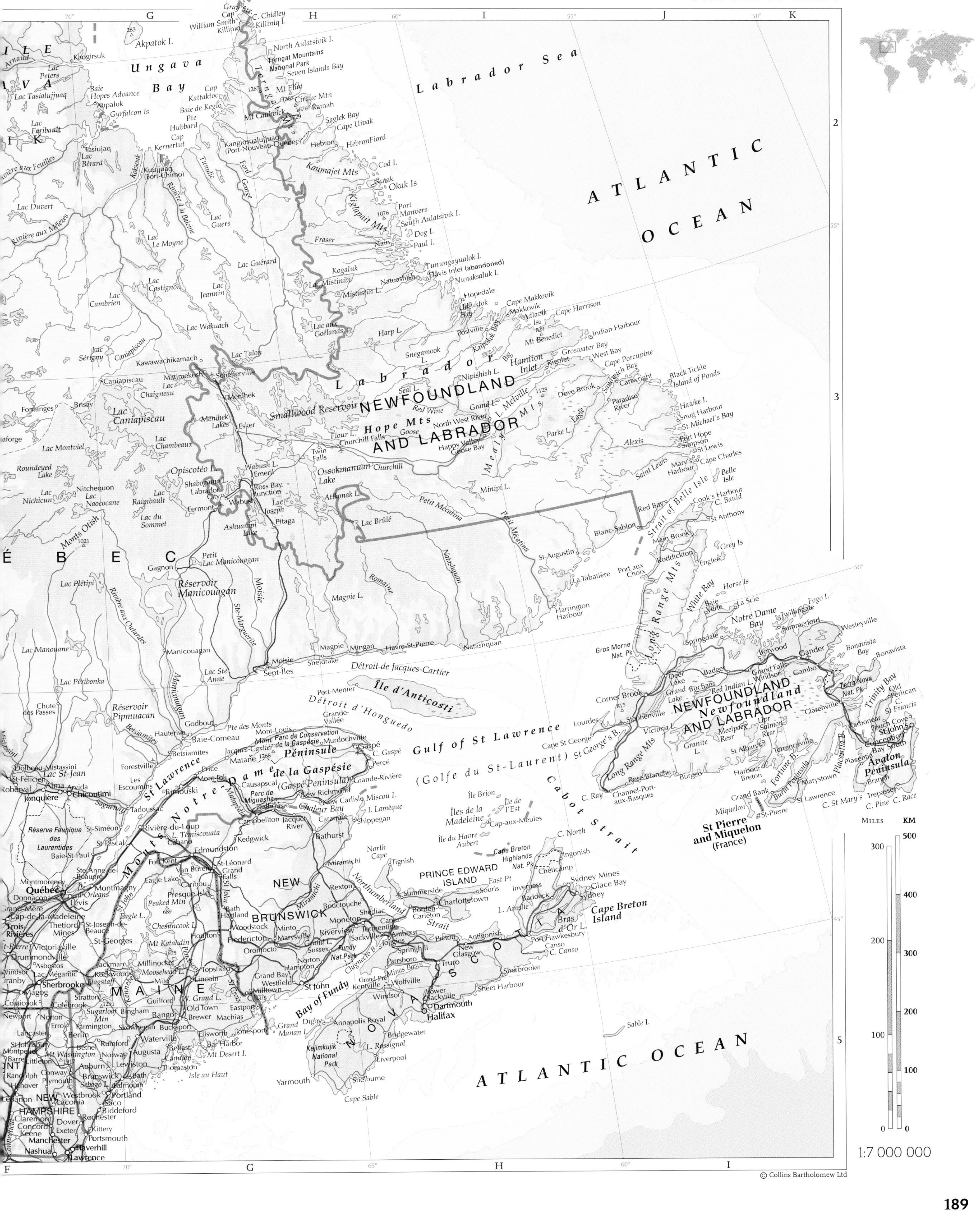
Labrador Sea
ATLANTIC OCEAN
Ungava Bay
Torngat Mountains National Park
Kangiqsualujjuaq (Port-Nouveau-Québec)
Kuujjuaq (Fort-Chimo)
Kaumajet Mts
Okak Is
Kiglapait Mts
Nain
Hopedale
Makkovik
Cape Harrison
Postville
Indian Harbour
Labrador
NEWFOUNDLAND AND LABRADOR
Smallwood Reservoir
Hope Mts
Churchill Falls
Happy Valley-Goose Bay
North West River
Lake Melville
Mealy Mts
Hamilton Inlet
Rigolet
Cartwright
Paradise River
Black Tickle
Island of Ponds
Mary's Harbour
Belle Isle
Strait of Belle Isle
Red Bay
Blanc-Sablon
St Anthony
Schefferville
Lac Caniapiscau
Wabush
Labrador City
Fermont
Ossokmanuan Lake
Atikonak L.
Petit Mécatina
Réservoir Manicouagan
Gagnon
Sept-Îles
Havre-St-Pierre
Natashquan
Détroit de Jacques-Cartier
Île d'Anticosti
Détroit d'Honguedo
Gulf of St Lawrence
(Golfe du St-Laurent)
Cabot Strait
Péninsule de la Gaspésie (Gaspé Peninsula)
Gaspé
Chaleur Bay
Îles de la Madeleine
Long Range Mts
White Bay
Notre Dame Bay
Gros Morne Nat. Pk
Corner Brook
Stephenville
Deer Lake
Grand Falls-Windsor
Gander
Terra Nova Nat. Pk
Bonavista Bay
Trinity Bay
Clarenville
St John's
Avalon Peninsula
Placentia Bay
Fortune B.
Burin Peninsula
Channel-Port-aux-Basques
C. Ray
C. Race
St Pierre and Miquelon (France)
Cape Breton Island
Cape Breton Highlands Nat. Pk
Sydney
PRINCE EDWARD ISLAND
Charlottetown
Northumberland Strait
NEW BRUNSWICK
Fredericton
Moncton
Saint John
Bay of Fundy
NOVA SCOTIA
Halifax
Dartmouth
Kejimkujik National Park
Yarmouth
Cape Sable
Sable I.
MAINE
Bangor
Augusta
Portland
NEW HAMPSHIRE
Manchester
Concord
Québec
Trois-Rivières
Sherbrooke
Chicoutimi
Jonquière
Lac St-Jean
St Lawrence
Monts Notre-Dame
QUÉBEC
MILES
KM
1:7 000 000

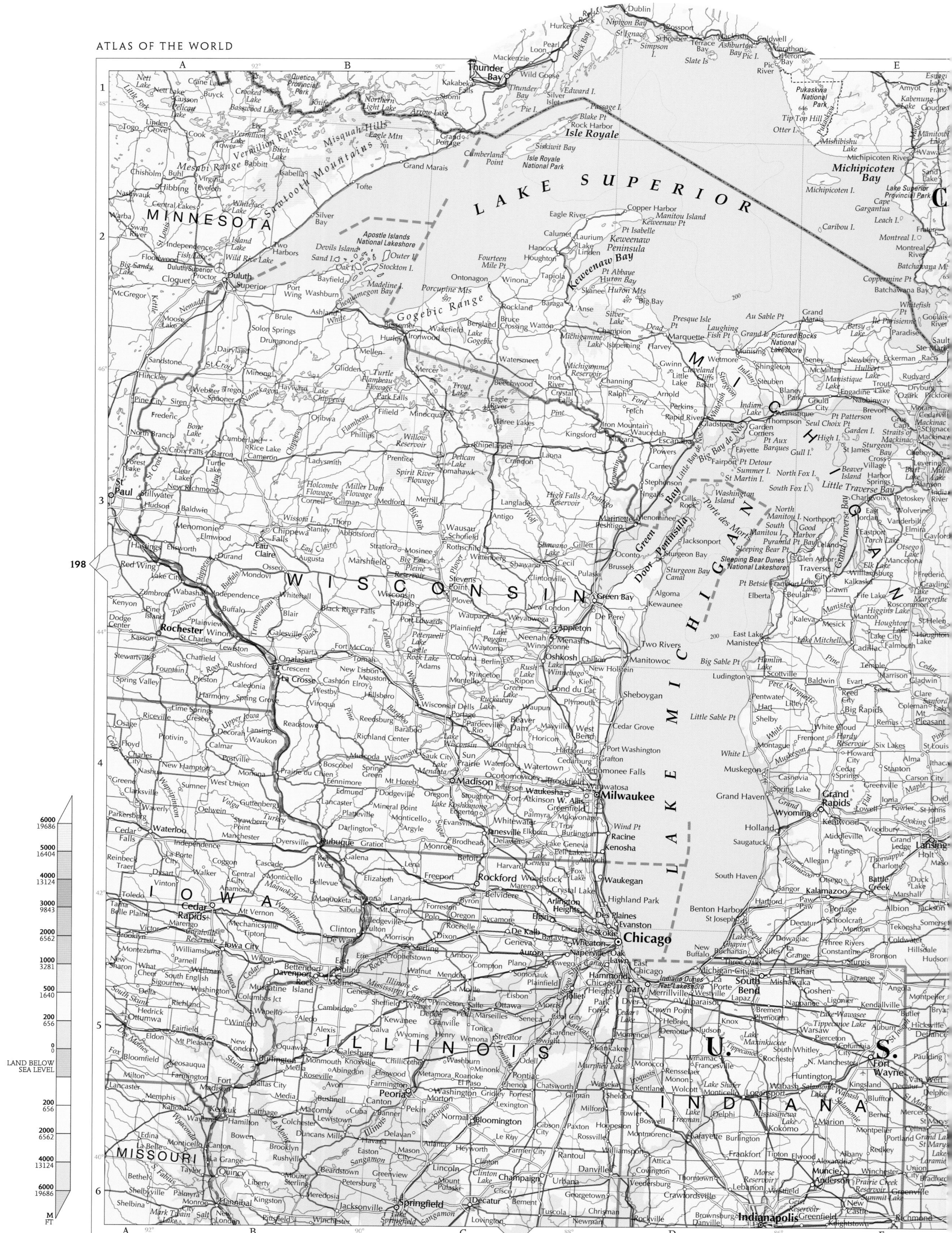


Conic Equidistant Projection

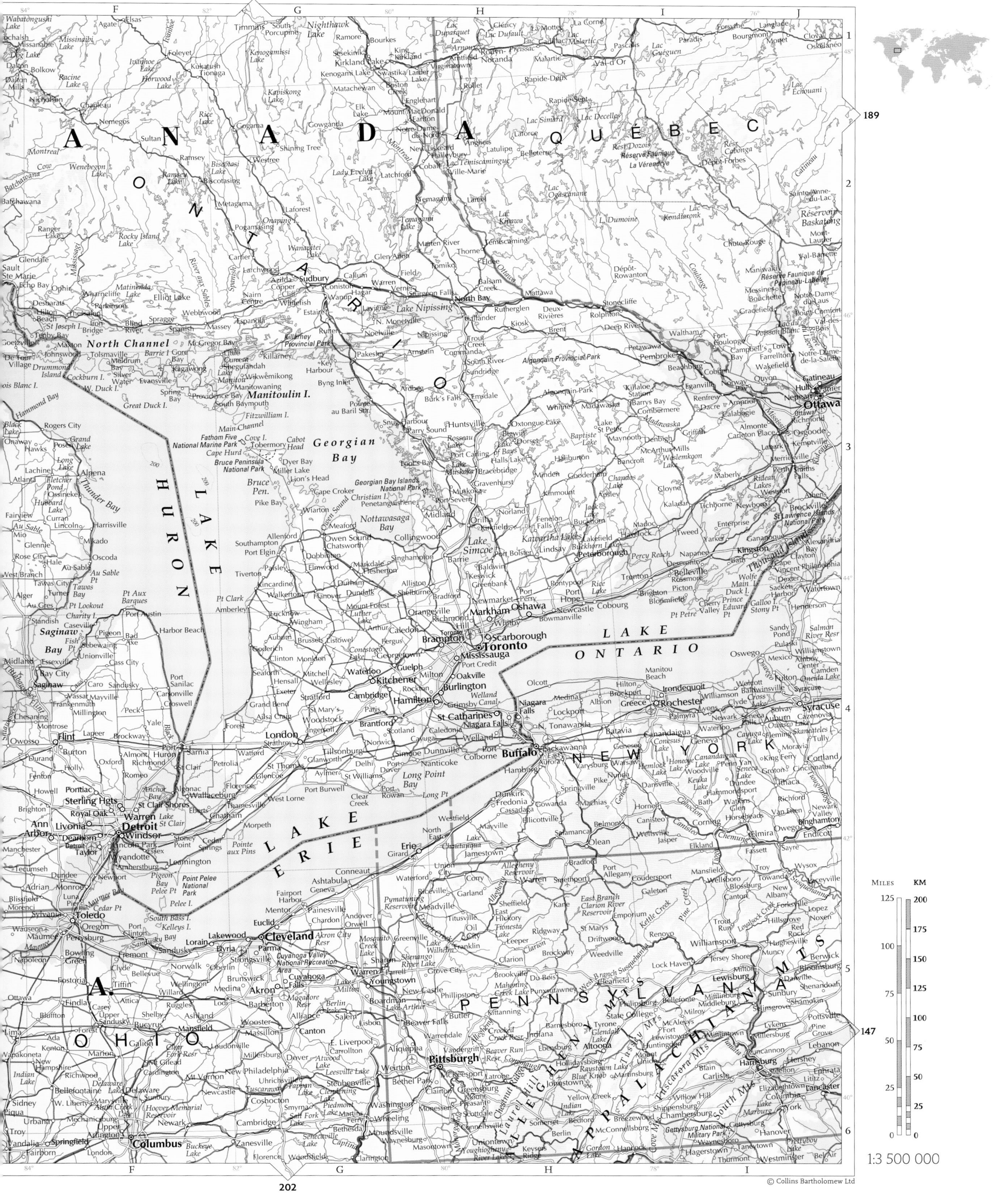
188
189
147
202
C A N A D A
O N T A R I O
Q U É B E C
LAKE HURON
LAKE ONTARIO
LAKE ERIE
Georgian Bay
North Channel
Manitoulin I.
Lake Nipissing
NEW YORK
PENNSYLVANIA
OHIO
U.S.A.
ALLEGHENY MTS
APPALACHIAN MTS
Toronto
Ottawa
Detroit
Windsor
Cleveland
Buffalo
Pittsburgh
Rochester
Syracuse
Hamilton
London
Sudbury
North Bay
Kingston
Toledo
Columbus
Akron
Erie
Algonquin Provincial Park
Miles
KM
1:3 500 000
© Collins Bartholomew Ltd

184

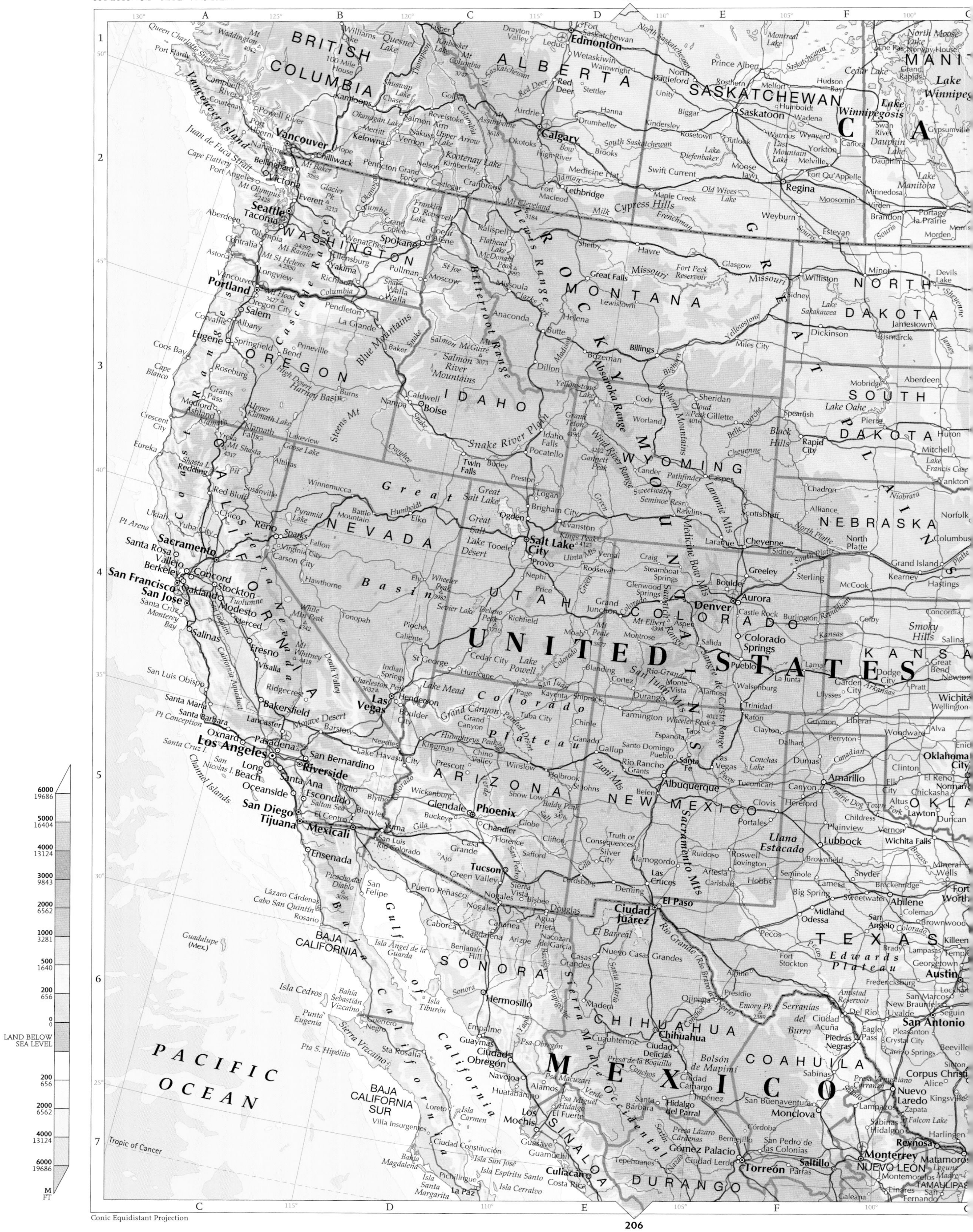
6000
19686
5000
16404
4000
13124
3000
9843
2000
6562
1000
3281
500
1640
200
656
0
0
LAND BELOW SEA LEVEL
200
656
2000
6562
4000
13124
6000
19686
M
FT
BRITISH COLUMBIA
ALBERTA
SASKATCHEWAN
MANI
CA
UNITED STATES
WASHINGTON
OREGON
IDAHO
MONTANA
WYOMING
NORTH DAKOTA
SOUTH DAKOTA
NEBRASKA
KANSA
NEVADA
UTAH
COLORADO
CALIFORNIA
ARIZONA
NEW MEXICO
OKLA
TEXAS
MEXICO
BAJA CALIFORNIA
BAJA CALIFORNIA SUR
SONORA
CHIHUAHUA
COAHUILA
SINALOA
DURANGO
NUEVO LEÓN
PACIFIC OCEAN
ROCKY MOUNTAINS
GREAT PLAINS
Great Basin
Colorado Plateau
Gulf of California
Sierra Nevada
Cascade Range
Coast Ranges
Snake River Plain
Sierra Madre Occidental
Llano Estacado
Edwards Plateau
Vancouver Island
Queen Charlotte Strait
Juan de Fuca Strait
Channel Islands
Tropic of Cancer
Vancouver
Victoria
Seattle
Tacoma
Spokane
Portland
Salem
Eugene
Boise
Calgary
Edmonton
Regina
Saskatoon
Winnipegosis
Helena
Billings
Great Falls
Salt Lake City
Denver
Colorado Springs
Cheyenne
Sacramento
San Francisco
Oakland
San Jose
Fresno
Bakersfield
Los Angeles
Long Beach
Riverside
San Bernardino
San Diego
Tijuana
Mexicali
Las Vegas
Reno
Phoenix
Tucson
Albuquerque
Santa Fe
El Paso
Ciudad Juárez
Lubbock
Amarillo
Abilene
Austin
San Antonio
Hermosillo
Chihuahua
Culiacán
Torreón
Monterrey
Saltillo
Nuevo Laredo
Reynosa
Matamoros
Oklahoma City
Wichita
Conic Equidistant Projection

206

185
CANADA
ONTARIO
QUÉBEC
NEW BRUNSWICK
MAINE
VERMONT
NEW HAMPSHIRE
MASS.
CONN.
RHODE ISLAND
NEW YORK
PENNSYLVANIA
NEW JERSEY
MARYLAND
DEL.
WEST VIRGINIA
VIRGINIA
NORTH CAROLINA
SOUTH CAROLINA
GEORGIA
FLORIDA
ALABAMA
MISSISSIPPI
TENNESSEE
KENTUCKY
OHIO
INDIANA
ILLINOIS
MICHIGAN
WISCONSIN
MINNESOTA
IOWA
MISSOURI
ARKANSAS
LOUISIANA
OF AMERICA
James Bay
Lake Superior
Lake Michigan
Lake Huron
Lake Erie
Lake Ontario
Lake Nipigon
Georgian Bay
St Lawrence
Appalachian Mountains
Blue Ridge
Cumberland Plateau
Ozark Plateau
COASTAL PLAIN
ATLANTIC OCEAN
GULF OF MEXICO
THE BAHAMAS
Straits of Florida
Florida Keys
Tropic of Cancer
Toronto
Ottawa
Montréal
Québec
Boston
Providence
Hartford
New York
Philadelphia
Baltimore
Washington D.C.
Richmond
Virginia Beach
Pittsburgh
Buffalo
Cleveland
Detroit
Columbus
Cincinnati
Indianapolis
Chicago
Milwaukee
Minneapolis
St Paul
Des Moines
St Louis
Kansas City
Louisville
Nashville
Memphis
Charlotte
Atlanta
Birmingham
Jacksonville
Orlando
Tampa
Miami
New Orleans
Houston
Dallas
Nassau
205
MILES
KM
500
400
300
200
100
0
800
700
600
500
400
300
200
100
0
1:12 000 000

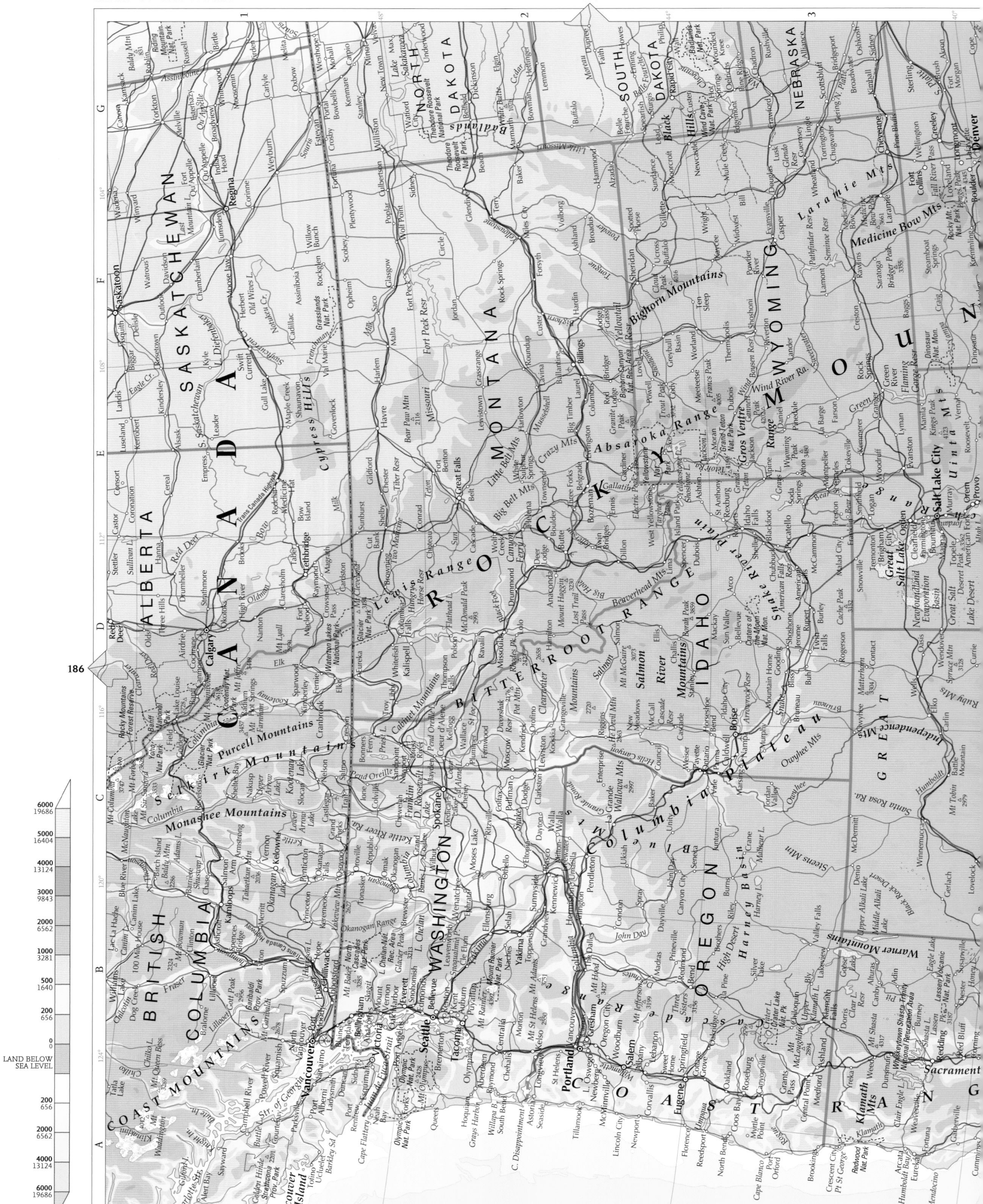


Conic Equidistant Projection

199
206
COLORADO
UTAH
NEVADA
CALIFORNIA
NEW MEXICO
ARIZONA
TEXAS
MEXICO
SONORA
CHIHUAHUA
BAJA CALIFORNIA
PACIFIC OCEAN
Gulf of California
COLORADO PLATEAU
GREAT BASIN
SIERRA NEVADA
San Francisco
Sacramento
Los Angeles
San Diego
Las Vegas
Phoenix
Tucson
Albuquerque
El Paso
Ciudad Juárez
Chihuahua
Hermosillo
Tijuana
Mexicali
MILES
KM
1:7 000 000

194

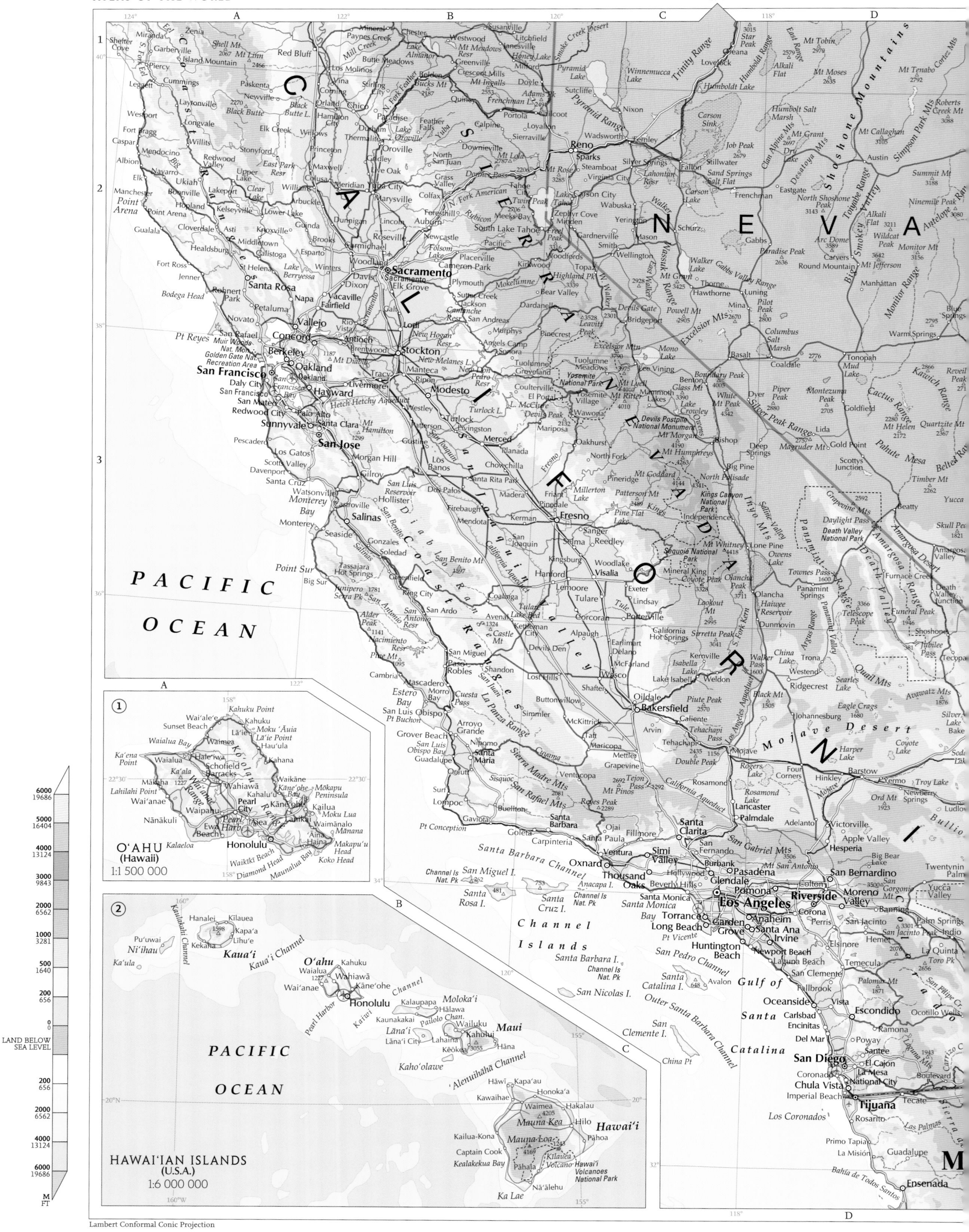


Lambert Conformal Conic Projection

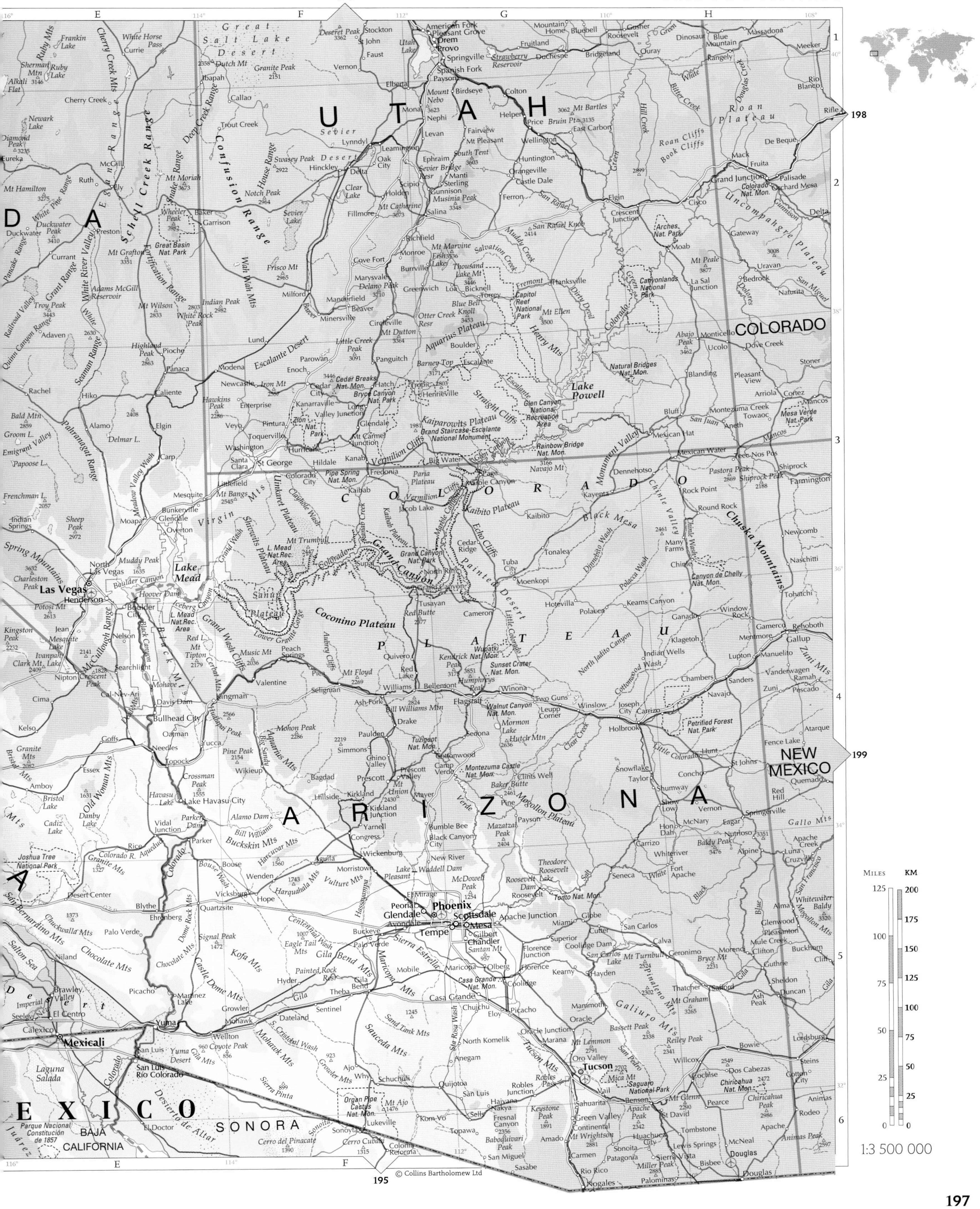
194
198
199
195
UTAH
COLORADO
NEW MEXICO
ARIZONA
MEXICO
SONORA
BAJA CALIFORNIA
COLORADO PLATEAU
Great Salt Lake Desert
Sevier Desert
Escalante Desert
Coconino Plateau
Grand Canyon
Lake Mead
Lake Powell
Las Vegas
Phoenix
Tucson
Mexicali
Provo
Orem
Grand Junction
Flagstaff
Yuma
Glendale
Scottsdale
Mesa
Tempe
Chandler
Henderson
Farmington
Gallup
Kingman
Prescott
Sedona
Nogales
Douglas
Moab
St George
Mogollon Plateau
Painted Desert
Black Mesa
Chuska Mountains
Monument Valley
Kaibab Plateau
Sonoran
Desierto de Altar
Great Basin Nat. Park
Canyonlands National Park
Capitol Reef National Park
Arches Nat. Park
Bryce Canyon Nat. Park
Zion Nat. Park
Grand Canyon Nat. Park
Petrified Forest Nat. Park
Mesa Verde Nat. Park
Saguaro National Park
Organ Pipe Cactus Nat. Mon.
Glen Canyon National Recreation Area
Grand Staircase-Escalante National Monument
Parque Nacional Constitución de 1857
Miles
KM
1:3 500 000
© Collins Bartholomew Ltd

200

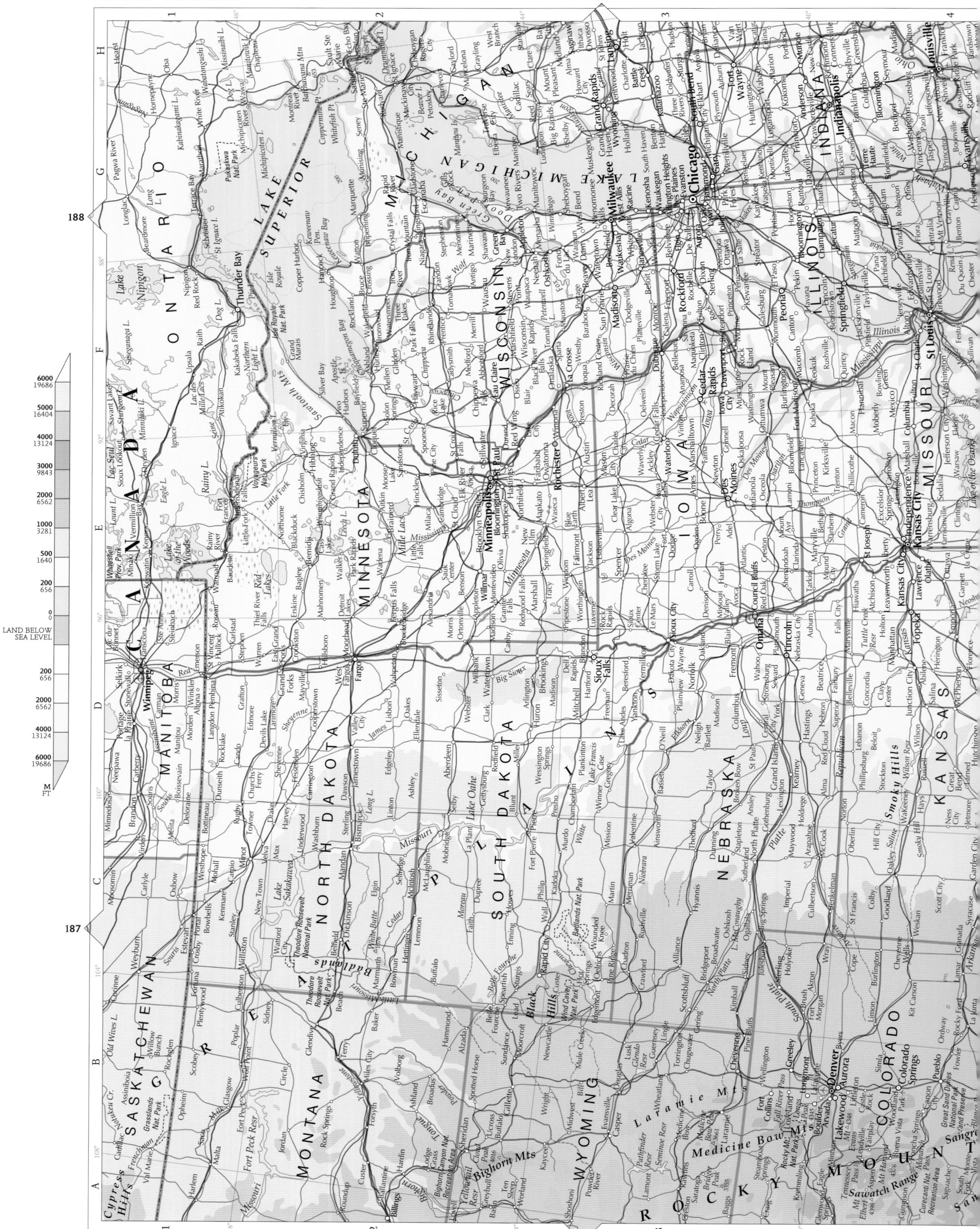


188
187

Lambert Conformal Conic Projection

194

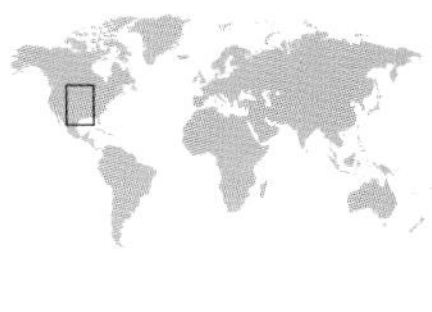

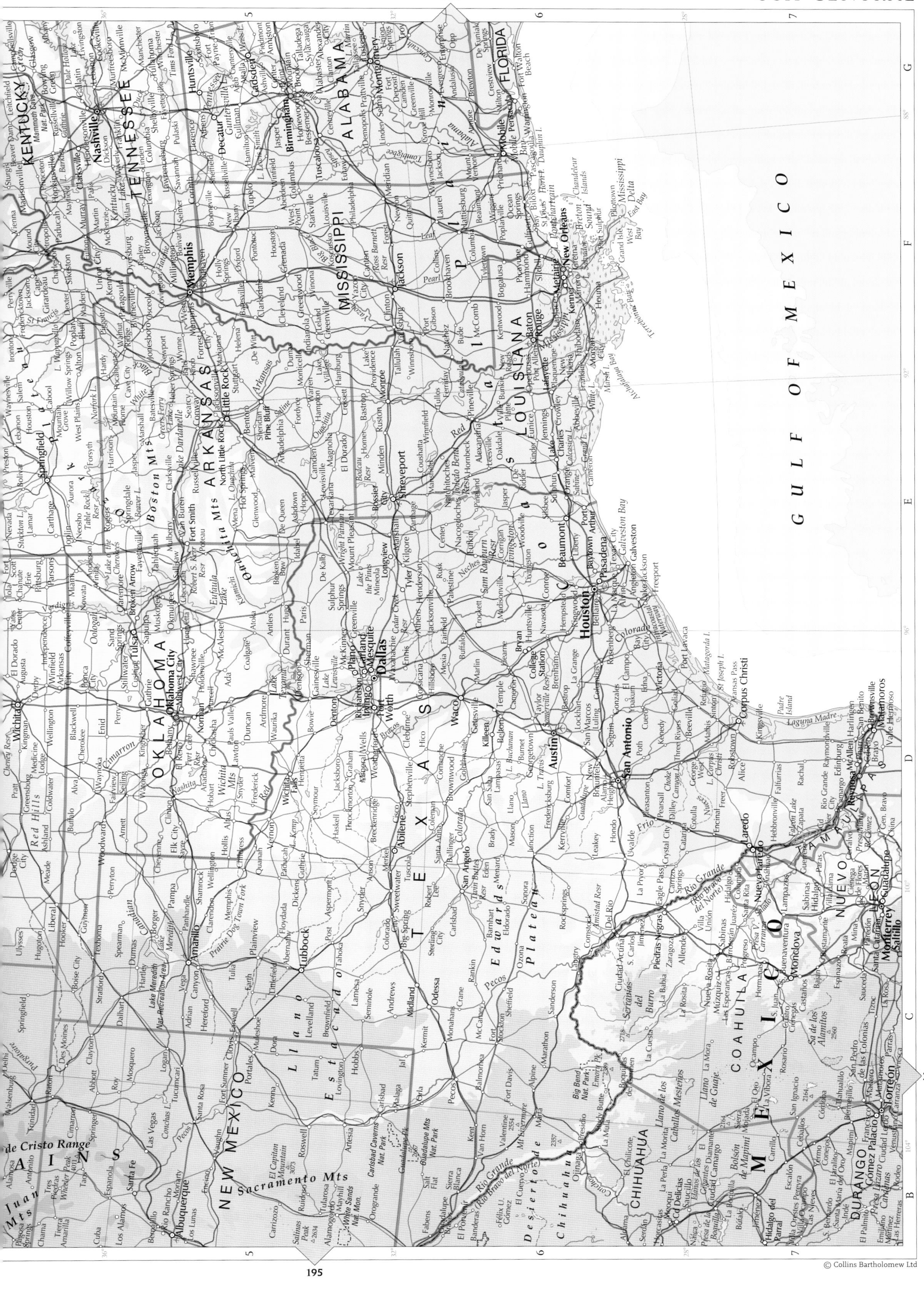

201
195
206
GULF OF MEXICO
TEXAS
OKLAHOMA
ARKANSAS
LOUISIANA
MISSISSIPPI
ALABAMA
TENNESSEE
KENTUCKY
FLORIDA
NEW MEXICO
MEXICO
COAHUILA
NUEVO LEON
TAMAULIPAS
CHIHUAHUA
DURANGO
Dallas
Houston
San Antonio
Austin
Oklahoma City
Memphis
New Orleans
Nashville
Birmingham
Monterrey
Sacramento Mts
Llano Estacado
Edwards Plateau
Ouachita Mts
Boston Mts
Miles
KM
1:7 000 000

189

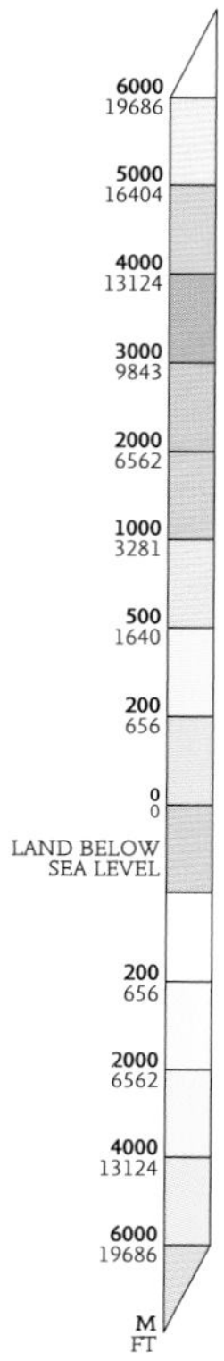

188

Lambert Conformal Conic Projection

198

ATLANTIC
OCEAN
GULF
OF
MEXICO
THE BAHAMAS
TENNESSEE
NORTH CAROLINA
SOUTH CAROLINA
GEORGIA
ALABAMA
MISSISSIPPI
FLORIDA
ARKANSAS
Virginia Beach
Nashville
Memphis
Knoxville
Chattanooga
Atlanta
Birmingham
Montgomery
Charlotte
Greensboro
Raleigh
Durham
Columbia
Charleston
Savannah
Jacksonville
Tallahassee
Orlando
Tampa
St Petersburg
Miami
Fort Lauderdale
West Palm Beach
New Orleans
Mobile
Jackson
Pensacola
Macon
Columbus
Augusta
Nassau
Andros
Great Abaco
Grand Bahama
Eleuthera
Cat Island
Long Island
Great Exuma
Straits of Florida
Tropic of Cancer
Cape Hatteras
Cape Canaveral
MILES
KM
1:7 000 000
205



199

191

190

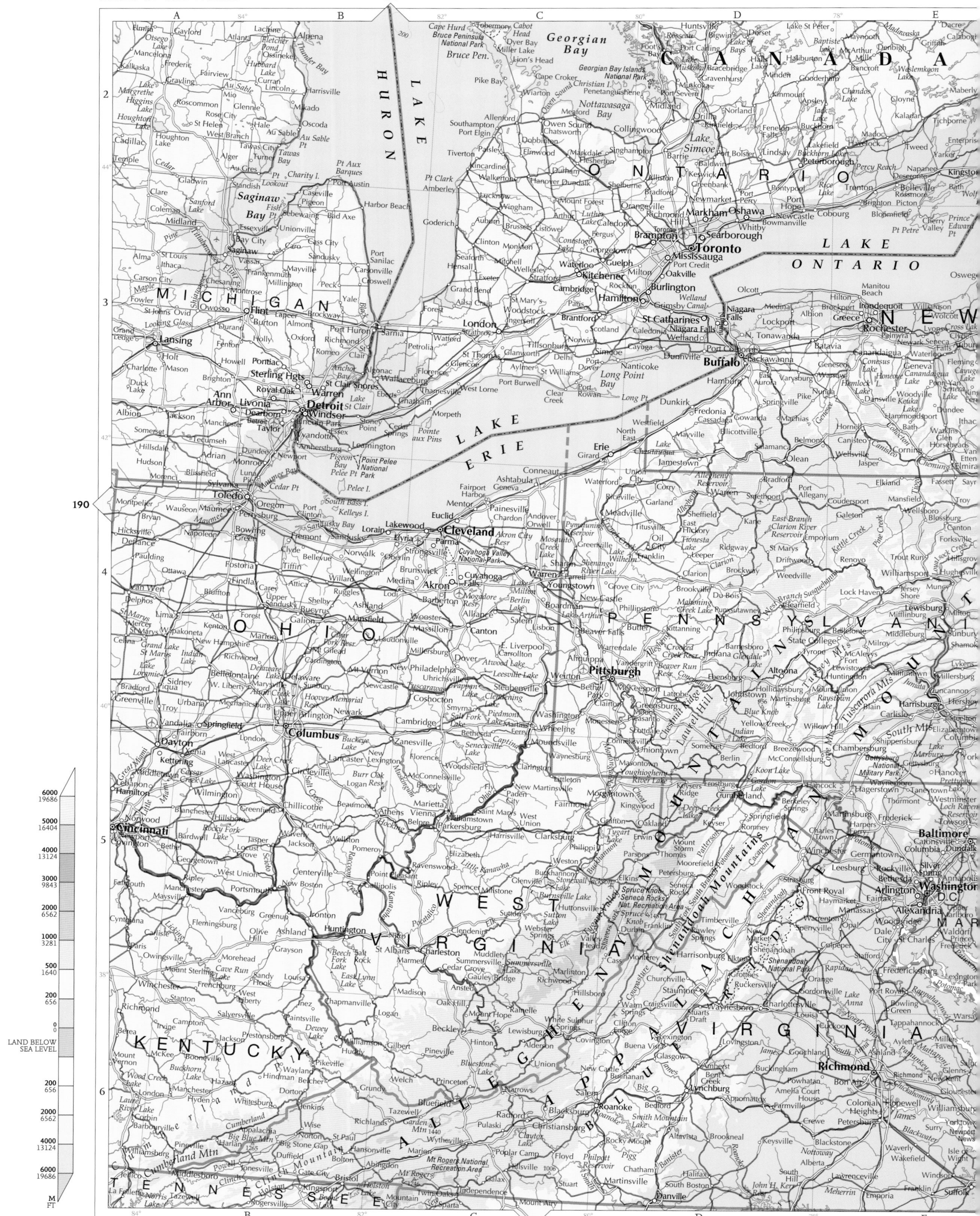


Lambert Conformal Conic Projection

200

189
QUEBEC
NEW YORK
VERMONT
NEW HAMPSHIRE
MAINE
MASSACHUSETTS
CONNECTICUT
RHODE ISLAND
NEW JERSEY
DELAWARE
CANADA
NEW BRUNSWICK
Lake Champlain
Adirondack Mountains
Catskill Mountains
White Mountains
Green Mountains
Boston
Providence
Hartford
Springfield
Worcester
Albany
Syracuse
Utica
Binghamton
Scranton
Allentown
Philadelphia
New York
Newark
Bridgeport
New Haven
Portland
Manchester
Concord
Burlington
Augusta
Bangor
Virginia Beach
Norfolk
Newport News
Portsmouth
Chesapeake
Hampton
Massachusetts Bay
Cape Cod
Cape Cod Bay
Nantucket Sound
Martha's Vineyard
Nantucket Island
Block Island Sound
Long Island Sound
Long Island
Delaware Bay
Chesapeake Bay
ATLANTIC OCEAN
1:3 500 000

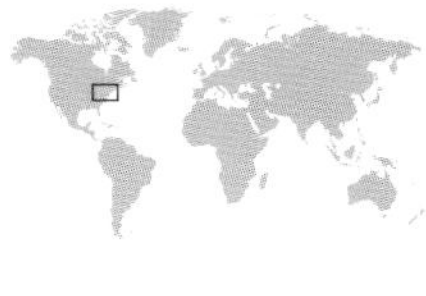

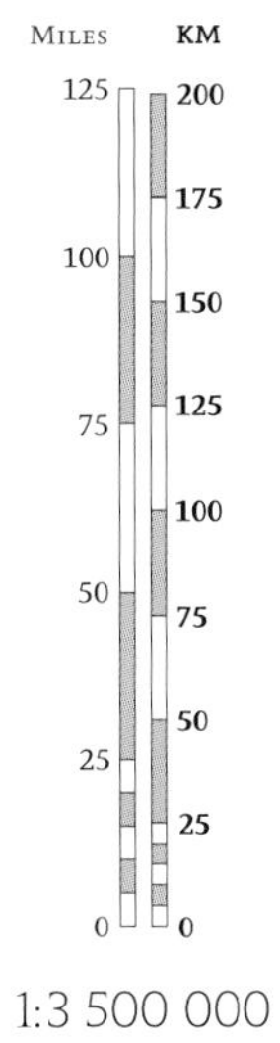
MILES
KM
1:3 500 000

192

A
B
C
D
E
F
G
ARIZONA
NEW MEXICO
OKLAHOMA
ARKANSAS
MISSISSIPPI
TENNESSEE
TEXAS
LOUISIANA
U. S.
MEXICO
GUATEMALA
BELIZE
EL SALVADOR
GULF OF MEXICO
PACIFIC OCEAN
Gulf of California
Baja California
SIERRA MADRE OCCIDENTAL
Sierra Madre Oriental
Sierra Madre del Sur
Llano Estacado
Edwards Plateau
Bolsón de Mapimí
Bahía de Campeche
Gulf of Tehuantepec
Golfo de Fonseca
Yucatán
Tropic of Cancer
Tijuana
Mexicali
Ensenada
Phoenix
Tucson
Albuquerque
Santa Fe
El Paso
Ciudad Juárez
Amarillo
Lubbock
Oklahoma City
Tulsa
Dallas
Fort Worth
Austin
San Antonio
Houston
Galveston
Corpus Christi
Memphis
Nashville
New Orleans
Baton Rouge
Jackson
Shreveport
Little Rock
Hermosillo
Chihuahua
Ciudad Obregón
Los Mochis
Culiacán
La Paz
Mazatlán
Durango
Torreón
Gómez Palacio
Saltillo
Monterrey
Nuevo Laredo
Reynosa
Matamoros
Ciudad Victoria
Tampico
Zacatecas
San Luis Potosí
Aguascalientes
Tepic
Guadalajara
León
Querétaro
Morelia
Mexico City
Toluca
Puebla
Cuernavaca
Acapulco
Oaxaca
Veracruz
Xalapa (Jalapa)
Orizaba
Córdoba
Coatzacoalcos
Villahermosa
Tuxtla Gutiérrez
Campeche
Mérida
Chetumal
Belmopan
Guatemala City
San Salvador
Tegucigalpa
Managua
Islas Revillagigedo (Mex.)
Île Clipperton (France)
Isla de Coco (Costa Rica)
6000 19686
5000 16404
4000 13124
3000 9843
2000 6562
1000 3281
500 1640
200 656
0 0
LAND BELOW SEA LEVEL
200 656
2000 6562
4000 13124
6000 19686
M FT
Lambert Azimuthal Equal Area Projection

193
210
211
ATLANTIC OCEAN
CARIBBEAN SEA
THE BAHAMAS
GREATER ANTILLES
Lesser Antilles
LEEWARD ISLANDS
WINDWARD ISLANDS
HISPANIOLA
Tropic of Cancer
Bermuda (U.K.)
Hamilton
NORTH CAROLINA
SOUTH CAROLINA
GEORGIA
FLORIDA
Charlotte
Raleigh
Durham
Atlanta
Savannah
Charleston
Jacksonville
Orlando
Tampa
Miami
Fort Lauderdale
Key West
Straits of Florida
Great Bahama Bank
Nassau
Andros
Eleuthera
Havana (La Habana)
CUBA
Santa Clara
Cienfuegos
Camagüey
Holguín
Santiago de Cuba
Guantánamo
Isla de la Juventud
Cayman Islands (U.K.)
George Town
Grand Cayman
JAMAICA
Kingston
Montego Bay
Turks and Caicos Islands (U.K.)
Grand Turk (Cockburn Town)
HAITI
Port-au-Prince
Cap-Haïtien
DOMINICAN REPUBLIC
Santo Domingo
Santiago
Pico Duarte 3175
Mona Passage
Windward Pass.
Jamaica Channel
San Juan
Puerto Rico (U.S.A.)
Ponce
Virgin Is (U.S.A.)
Virgin Is (U.K.)
Anguilla (U.K.)
St-Martin (Fr.)
St Maarten (Neth.)
St-Barthélemy (Fr.)
ANTIGUA AND BARBUDA
St John's
ST KITTS AND NEVIS
Basseterre
Montserrat (U.K.)
Guadeloupe (Fr.)
Pointe-à-Pitre
Basse-Terre
DOMINICA
Roseau
Martinique (Fr.)
Fort-de-France
ST LUCIA
Castries
ST VINCENT & THE GRENADINES
Kingstown
BARBADOS
Bridgetown
GRENADA
St George's
TRINIDAD AND TOBAGO
Port of Spain
Aruba (Neth.)
Oranjestad
Curaçao (Neth.)
Willemstad
Bonaire (Neth.)
Islas Los Roques (Ven.)
I. de Margarita
Caracas
Maracaibo
Barquisimeto
Valencia
Maracay
Barcelona
Cumaná
Maturín
Ciudad Guayana
Ciudad Bolívar
VENEZUELA
La Gran Sabana
Pakaraima Mts
BRAZIL
Orinoco
COLOMBIA
Bogotá
Medellín
Cali
Barranquilla
Cartagena
Santa Marta
Cúcuta
Bucaramanga
Villavicencio
Neiva
Pasto
Popayán
Tumaco
Florencia
Cordillera Oriental
Cordillera Central
Cordillera Occidental
Cordillera de Mérida
Sierra Nevada de Santa Marta
Península de la Guajira
G. de Venezuela
PANAMA
Panama City
Colón
Gulf of Panama
Golfo del Darién
COSTA RICA
San José
Puerto Limón
NICARAGUA
Managua
MOSQUITIA
Islas del Cisne (Swan Islands) (Hond.)
Isla de Providencia (Colombia)
Isla de San Andrés (Colombia)
Isla de Malpelo (Colombia)
MILES
KM
1:14 000 000

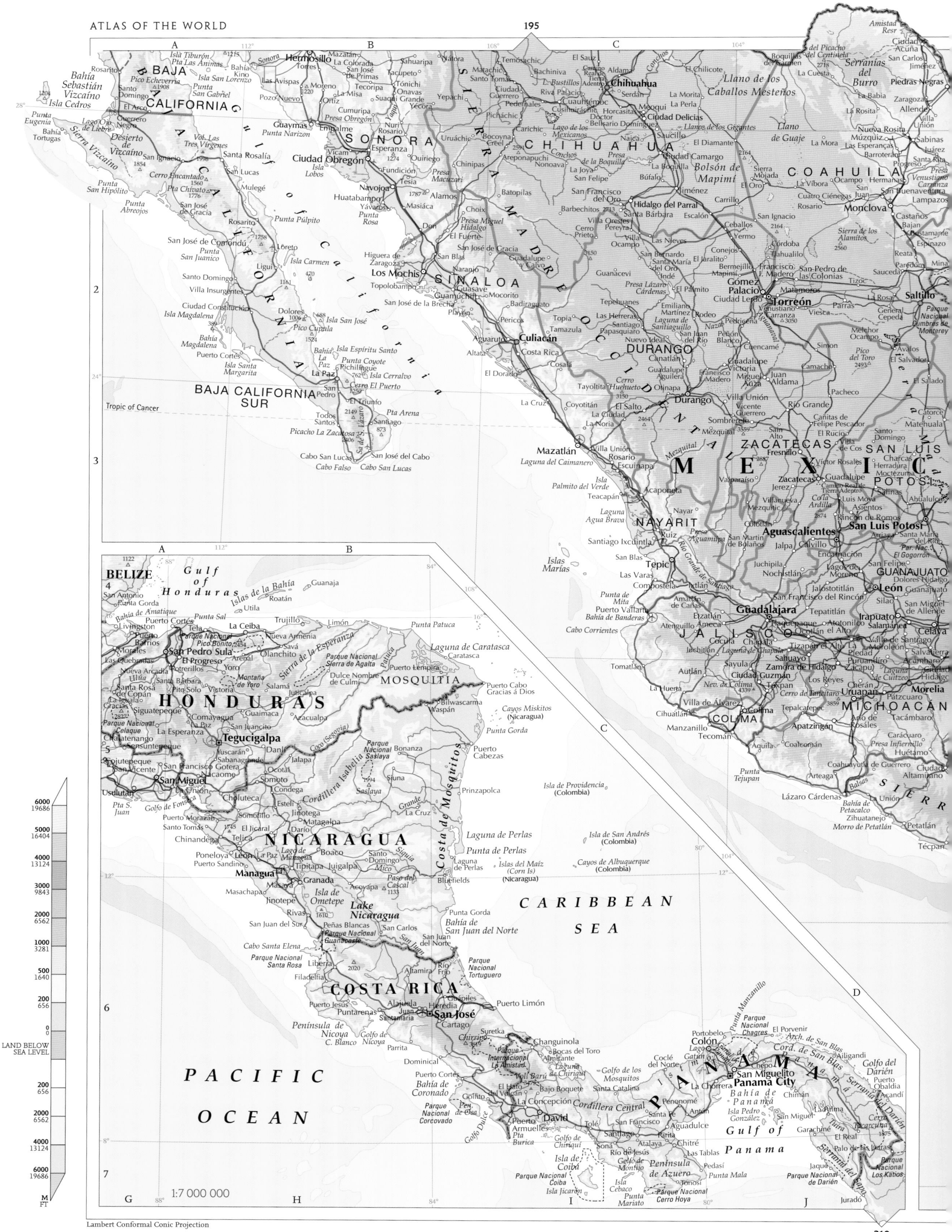


Lambert Conformal Conic Projection

199
205
E
F
G
H
1
2
3
4
5
6
U. S. A.
TEXAS
San Antonio
Corpus Christi
Laredo
Nuevo Laredo
McAllen
Brownsville
Matamoros
Reynosa
Monterrey
Guadalupe
TAMAULIPAS
Ciudad Victoria
Ciudad Madero
Tampico
Ciudad Mante
Ciudad de Valles
Querétaro
HIDALGO
Pachuca
Poza Rica
Tuxpan
Xalapa (Jalapa)
Veracruz
Toluca
Mexico City
Puebla
Tlalnepantla
Cuernavaca
Córdoba
Orizaba
MORELOS
PUEBLA
GUERRERO
Chilpancingo
Acapulco
Oaxaca
OAXACA
Coatzacoalcos
Minatitlán
TABASCO
Villahermosa
CHIAPAS
Tuxtla Gutiérrez
Tapachula
Ciudad del Carmen
Campeche
CAMPECHE
Mérida
YUCATÁN
QUINTANA ROO
Cancún
Chetumal
BELIZE
Belmopan
GUATEMALA
Guatemala City
Quetzaltenango
EL SALVADOR
San Salvador
Santa Ana
San Miguel
HONDURAS
San Pedro Sula
G U L F   O F   M E X I C O
Bahía de Campeche
Gulf of Tehuantepec
Tropic of Cancer
Arrecife Alacrán
Laguna Madre
Padre Island
P A C I F I C
O C E A N
Sierra Madre del Sur
Sierra Madre
MILES
KM
1:7 000 000

Orthographic Projection

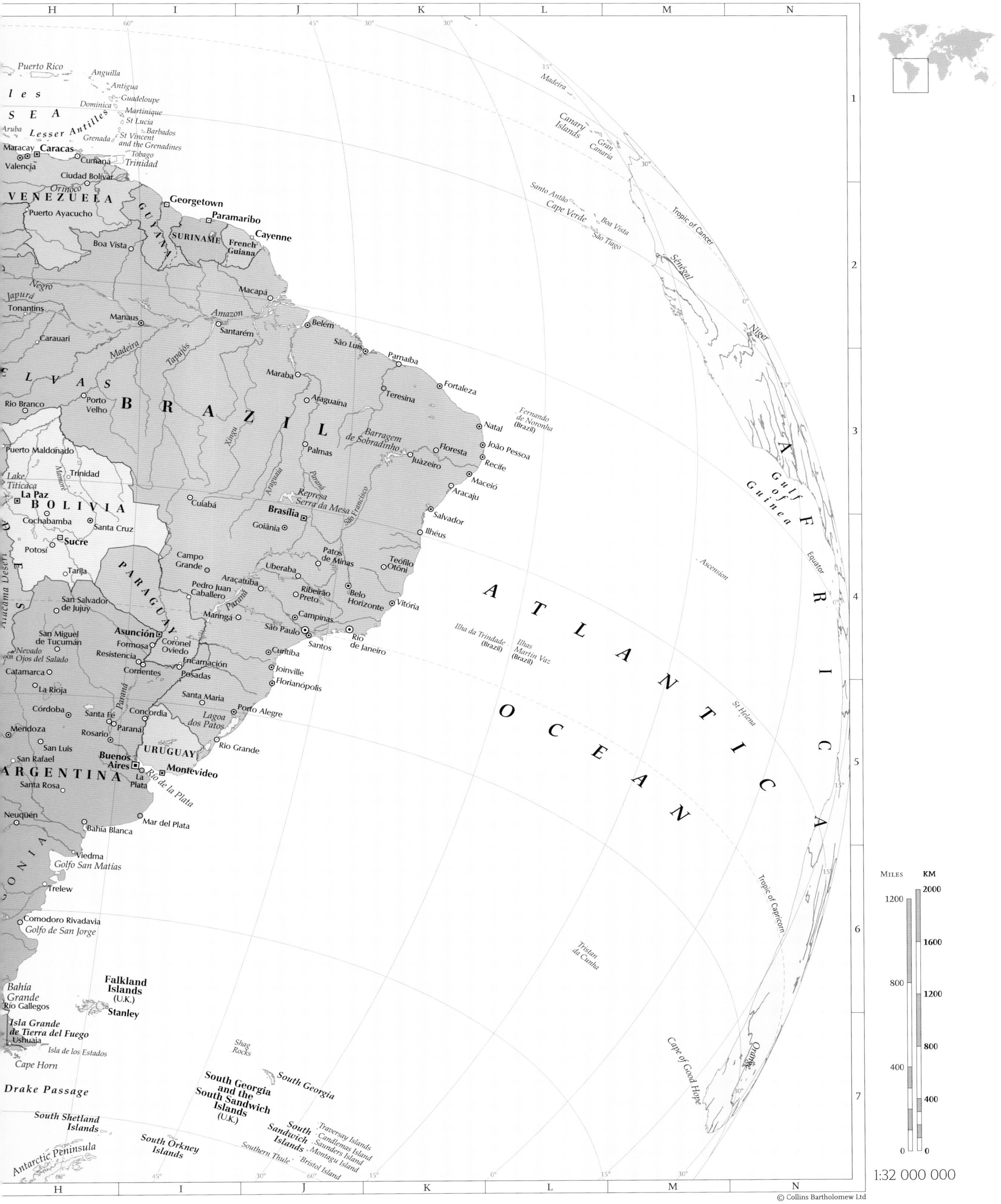
H
I
J
K
L
M
N
1
2
3
4
5
6
7
Puerto Rico
Anguilla
Antigua
Guadeloupe
Dominica
Martinique
St Lucia
Barbados
St Vincent and the Grenadines
Grenada
Tobago
Trinidad
Lesser Antilles
Aruba
Maracay
Caracas
Valencia
Cumaná
Ciudad Bolívar
Orinoco
VENEZUELA
GUYANA
Georgetown
Paramaribo
SURINAME
Cayenne
French Guiana
Puerto Ayacucho
Boa Vista
Negro
Japurá
Tonantins
Macapá
Manaus
Amazon
Santarém
Belém
São Luís
Parnaíba
Carauari
Madeira
Tapajós
Marabá
Fortaleza
Teresina
Araguaína
Rio Branco
Porto Velho
BRAZIL
Fernando de Noronha (Brazil)
Natal
João Pessoa
Recife
Floresta
Juàzeiro
Barragem de Sobradinho
Palmas
Xingu
Puerto Maldonado
Trinidad
Mamoré
Lake Titicaca
La Paz
BOLIVIA
Cochabamba
Santa Cruz
Sucre
Potosí
Tarija
Cuiabá
Araguaia
Paraná
Represa Serra da Mesa
São Francisco
Brasília
Goiânia
Maceió
Aracaju
Salvador
Ilhéus
Campo Grande
Patos de Minas
Teófilo Otôni
Uberaba
Araçatuba
Ribeirão Preto
Belo Horizonte
Vitória
PARAGUAY
Pedro Juan Caballero
Maringá
Campinas
São Paulo
Santos
Rio de Janeiro
San Salvador de Jujuy
San Miguel de Tucumán
Asunción
Formosa
Coronel Oviedo
Resistencia
Nevado Ojos del Salado
Corrientes
Encarnación
Posadas
Curitiba
Joinville
Florianópolis
Catamarca
La Rioja
Córdoba
Santa Fé
Paraná
Concordia
Santa Maria
Porto Alegre
Lagoa dos Patos
Mendoza
Rosario
San Luis
San Rafael
URUGUAY
Rio Grande
Buenos Aires
La Plata
Montevideo
Río de la Plata
ARGENTINA
Santa Rosa
Neuquén
Bahía Blanca
Mar del Plata
Viedma
Golfo San Matías
Trelew
Comodoro Rivadavia
Golfo de San Jorge
Bahía Grande
Río Gallegos
Falkland Islands (U.K.)
Stanley
Isla Grande de Tierra del Fuego
Ushuaia
Isla de los Estados
Cape Horn
Drake Passage
South Shetland Islands
Antarctic Peninsula
South Orkney Islands
Shag Rocks
South Georgia
South Georgia and the South Sandwich Islands (U.K.)
South Sandwich Islands
Traversay Islands
Candlemas Island
Saunders Island
Montagu Island
Bristol Island
Southern Thule
Madeira
Canary Islands
Gran Canaria
Santo Antão
Cape Verde
Boa Vista
São Tiago
Tropic of Cancer
Sénégal
Niger
AFRICA
Gulf of Guinea
Equator
Ascension
ATLANTIC OCEAN
Ilha da Trindade (Brazil)
Ilhas Martin Vaz (Brazil)
St Helena
Tropic of Capricorn
Tristan da Cunha
Cape of Good Hope
Orange
Miles
KM
1200
800
400
0
2000
1600
1200
800
400
0
1:32 000 000

205

Lambert Azimuthal Equal Area Projection

ATLANTIC
OCEAN
TRINIDAD AND TOBAGO
GUYANA
SURINAME
French Guiana
BRAZIL
PARAGUAY
Georgetown
New Amsterdam
Anna Regina
Bartica
Linden
Ituni
Mahdia
Paramaribo
Nieuw Amsterdam
Nieuw Nickerie
Apoera
Albina
St Laurent
Sinnamary
Kourou
Cayenne
Pointe Béhague
Cabo Orange
Cabo Caciporé
Oiapoque
Parque Nacional de Cabo Orange
Professor van Blommestein Meer
Juliana Top
CLAIMED BY SURINAME
Serra Tumucumaque
Parque Indígena do Tumucumaque
Parque Nacional Montanhas do Tumucumaque
Calçoene
Ilha de Maracá
Amapá
Serra do Navio
Macapá
Porto Santana
Mazagão
Mouths of the Amazon
Cabo Maguarinho
Baía de Marajó
Ilha de Marajó
Ilha Queimada
Afuá
Chaves
Salinópolis
Bragança
Capanema
Belém
Castanhal
Viseu
Cândido Mendes
Breves
Abaetetuba
Cametá
Mocajuba
Acará
Irituia
Portel
Represa de Balbina
Oriximiná
Óbidos
Monte Alegre
Almeirim
Boca do Jari
Faro
Alenquer
Santarém
Amazon (Amazonas)
Xingu
Parintins
Urucará
Urucurituba
Barreirinha
Boim
Maués
Brasília Legal
Aveiro
Pacoval
Altamira
Itacoatiara
Parque Nacional da Amazônia
Canumã
Borba
Itaituba
Tapajós
Iriri
Tucuruí
Represa de Tucuruí
Jacundá
Capim
Gurupi
Cururupu
Pinheiro
Baía de São Marcos
São Luís
Barreirinhas
Parque Nacional dos Lençóis Maranhenses
Parnaíba
Camocim
Itapipoca
Caucaia
Fortaleza
Viana
Itapecuru Mirim
Bacabal
Coroatá
Codó
Pedreiras
Caxias
Timon
Teresina
Campo Maior
Piripiri
Sobral
Santa Quitéria
Canindé
Tianguá
Serra da Ibiapaba
Quixadá
Aracati
Areia Branca
Macau
Ponta do Calcanhar
Touros
Cabo de São Roque
Mossoró
Natal
Canguaretama
Guarabira
João Pessoa
Cabedelo
Campina Grande
Goiana
Olinda
Recife
Jaboatão dos Guararapes
Caruaru
Garanhuns
Maceió
Rio Largo
Arapiraca
Aracaju
São Cristóvão
Estância
Serra do Tiracambu
Imperatriz
Marabá
Itupiranga
Araguatins
Tocantinópolis
Grajaú
Barra do Corda
Porto Franco
Carolina
Araguaína
Balsas
Floriano
Oeiras
Picos
Crato
Juazeiro do Norte
Salgueiro
Ouricuri
Paulistana
Petrolina
Juazeiro
Paulo Afonso
Serra dos Dois Irmãos
Barragem de Sobradinho
Chapada Diamantina
Jacobina
Senhor do Bonfim
Euclides da Cunha
Feira de Santana
Alagoinhas
Salvador
Cabo Sto António
Ilha de Tinharé
Ilha Boipeba
Jequié
Ilhéus
Itabuna
Una
Belmonte
Santa Cruz Cabrália
Porto Seguro
Vitória da Conquista
Serra Geral de Goiás
Barreiras
Bom Jesus da Lapa
Guanambi
Brumado
Palmas
Porto Nacional
Dianópolis
Gurupi
Serra dos Xavantes
Ilha do Bananal
Conceição do Araguaia
São Félix
Parque Nacional do Araguaia
Porangatu
Uruaçu
Niquelândia
Brasília
Formosa
Anápolis
Goiânia
Januária
Montes Claros
Serra do Espinhaço
Janaúba
Paracatu
João Pinheiro
Teófilo Otoni
Governador Valadares
Patos de Minas
Uberlândia
Uberaba
Araguari
Ipatinga
Linhares
Colatina
Vitória
Vila Velha
Cachoeiro de Itapemirim
Belo Horizonte
Divinópolis
Juiz de Fora
Barbacena
Campos
Macaé
Cabo Frio
Nova Friburgo
Petrópolis
Volta Redonda
Nova Iguaçu
Niterói
Rio de Janeiro
Taubaté
São José dos Campos
Jacareí
São Paulo
Santo André
Santos
Ilha do São Sebastião
Campinas
Piracicaba
Limeira
São Carlos
Araraquara
Ribeirão Preto
Franca
Barretos
Bauru
Marília
Presidente Prudente
Araçatuba
São José do Rio Preto
Londrina
Maringá
Apucarana
Umuarama
Cascavel
Campo Grande
Dourados
Corumbá
Cuiabá
Cáceres
Rondonópolis
Barra do Garças
Rio Verde
Jataí
Itumbiara
Campo Mourão
Tropic of Capricorn
Equator
Serra do Cachimbo
Serra Formosa
Serra do Roncador
Serra dos Caiabis
Parque Indígena do Xingu
Parque Indígena Aripuanã
Parque Nacional do Juruena
Parque Nacional do Pantanal Matogrossense
Parque Nacional das Emas
Parque Nacional da Chapada dos Veadeiros
Represa Ilha Solteira
Represa Porto Primavera
Pedro Juan Caballero
Concepción
Puerto Casado
Puerto Pinasco
Salto del Guairá
Guaíra
G
H
I
J
K
L
1
2
3
4
5
6
7
8
1:15 000 000

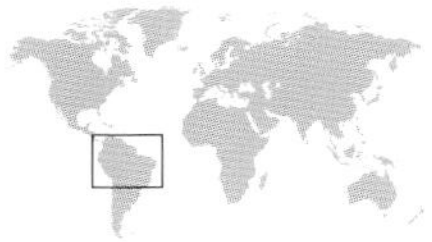

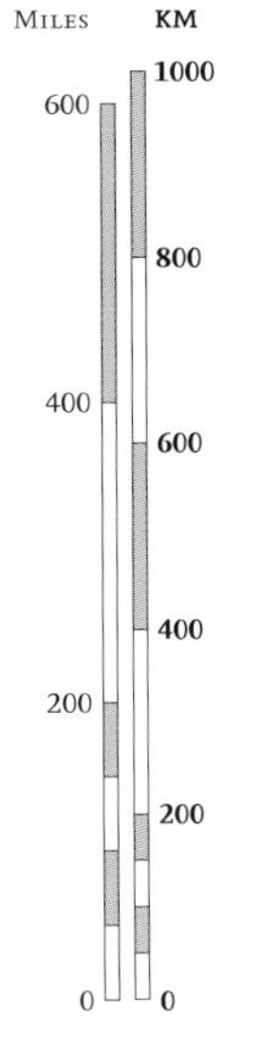
MILES
KM
600
400
200
0
1000
800
600
400
200
0

212

211

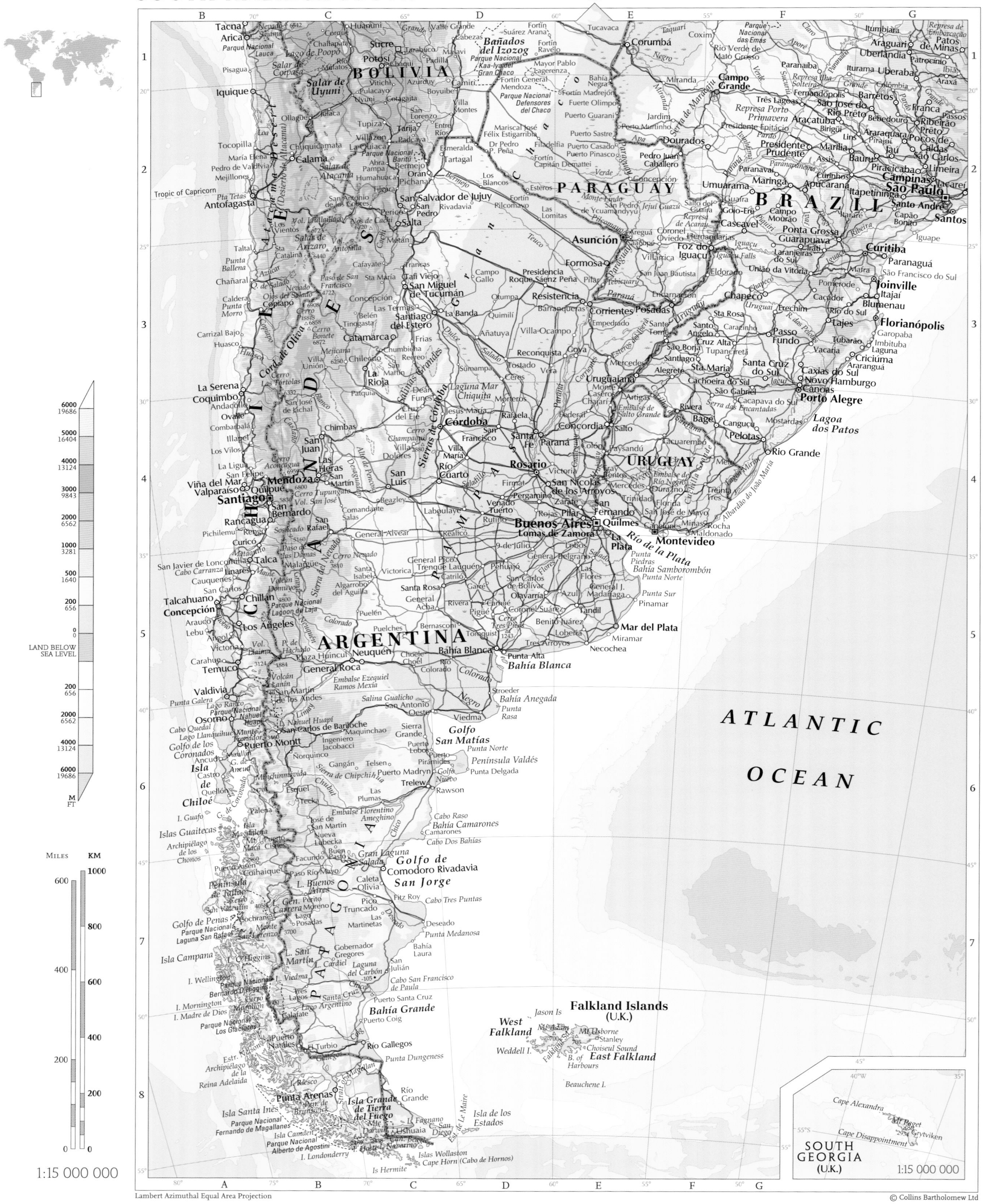
BOLIVIA
PARAGUAY
BRAZIL
URUGUAY
ARGENTINA
CHILE
ANDES
PATAGONIA
PAMPAS
Gran Chaco
Atacama Desert (Desierto de Atacama)
ATLANTIC OCEAN
Falkland Islands (U.K.)
West Falkland
East Falkland
Stanley
SOUTH GEORGIA (U.K.)
Grytviken
Sucre
La Paz
Potosí
Salar de Uyuni
Iquique
Antofagasta
Calama
Tropic of Capricorn
Asunción
São Paulo
Santos
Curitiba
Florianópolis
Porto Alegre
Lagoa dos Patos
Córdoba
Rosario
Santa Fe
Buenos Aires
Montevideo
Río de la Plata
Mar del Plata
Bahía Blanca
Mendoza
Santiago
Valparaíso
Concepción
Temuco
Valdivia
Puerto Montt
Isla de Chiloé
Golfo San Matías
Península Valdés
Golfo de San Jorge
Comodoro Rivadavia
Bahía Grande
Río Gallegos
Punta Arenas
Strait of Magellan
Isla Grande de Tierra del Fuego
Ushuaia
Isla de los Estados
Cape Horn (Cabo de Hornos)
LAND BELOW SEA LEVEL
Miles
KM
1:15 000 000

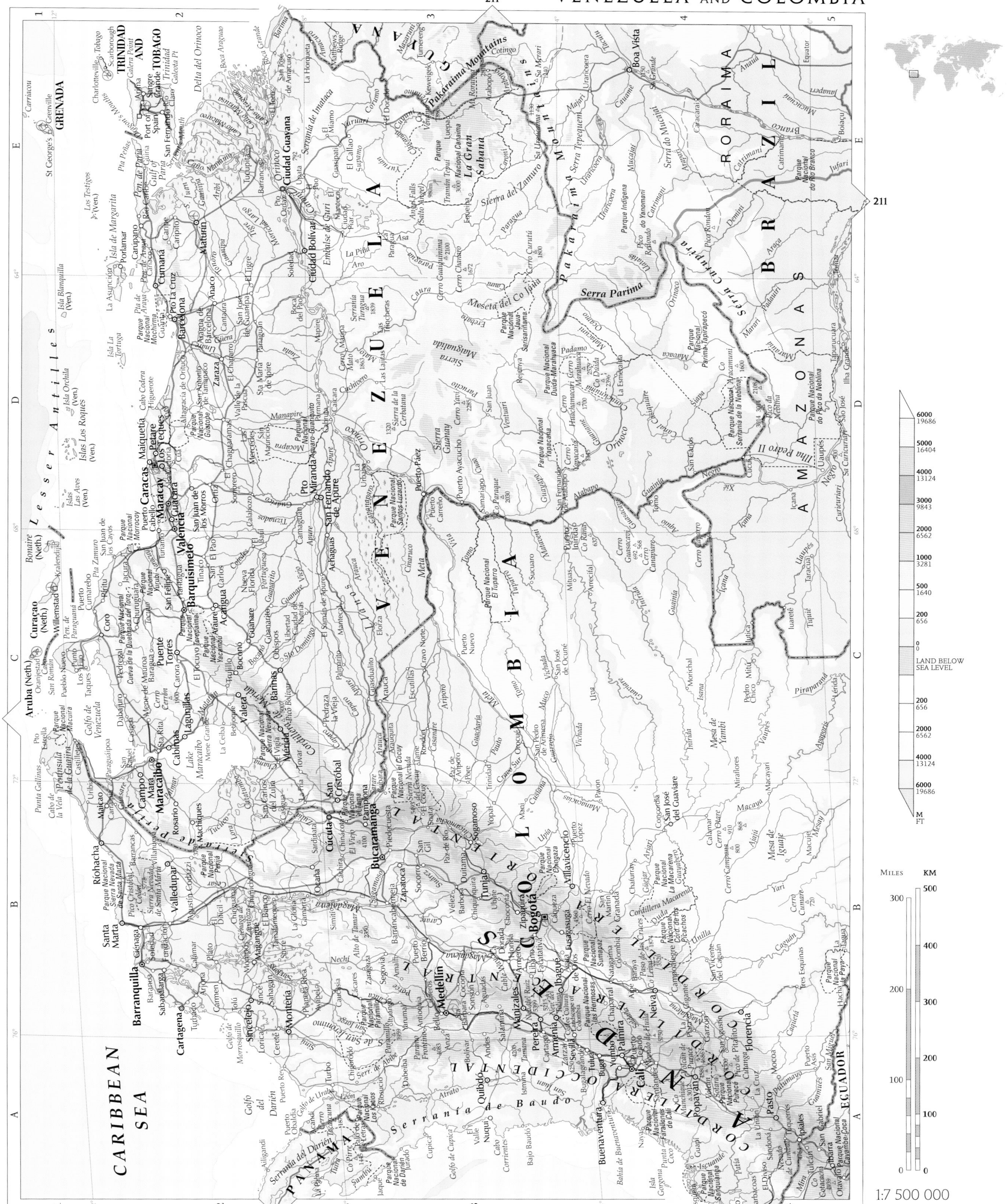
211
205
206
211
VENEZUELA
COLOMBIA
BRAZIL
GUYANA
PANAMA
ECUADOR
CARIBBEAN SEA
Lesser Antilles
TRINIDAD AND TOBAGO
GRENADA
RORAIMA
AMAZONAS
Pakaraima Mountains
Serra Parima
Caracas
Bogotá
Maracaibo
Barranquilla
Medellín
Cali
Ciudad Guayana
Ciudad Bolívar
Boa Vista
Valencia
Barquisimeto
Cartagena
Cúcuta
Bucaramanga
Villavicencio
Puerto Páez
Buenaventura
Pasto
Tumaco
Lambert Azimuthal Equal Area Projection
© Collins Bartholomew Ltd
M
FT
6000
19686
5000
16404
4000
13124
3000
9843
2000
6562
1000
3281
500
1640
200
656
0
0
LAND BELOW SEA LEVEL
200
656
2000
6562
4000
13124
6000
19686
MILES
KM
300
500
400
200
300
200
100
100
0
0
1:7 500 000

# BRAZIL SOUTHEAST

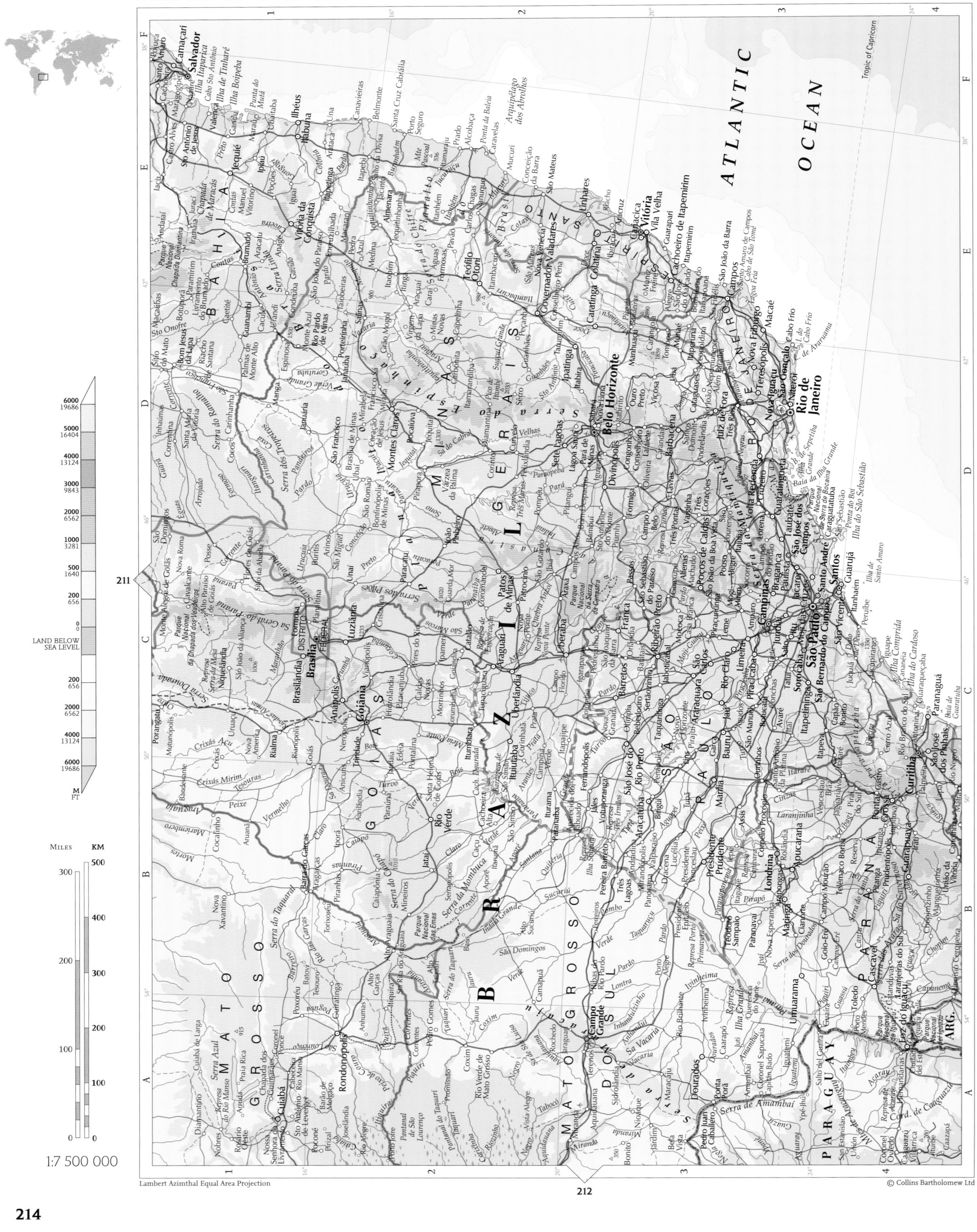


Lambert Azimuthal Equal Area Projection

© Collins Bartholomew Ltd

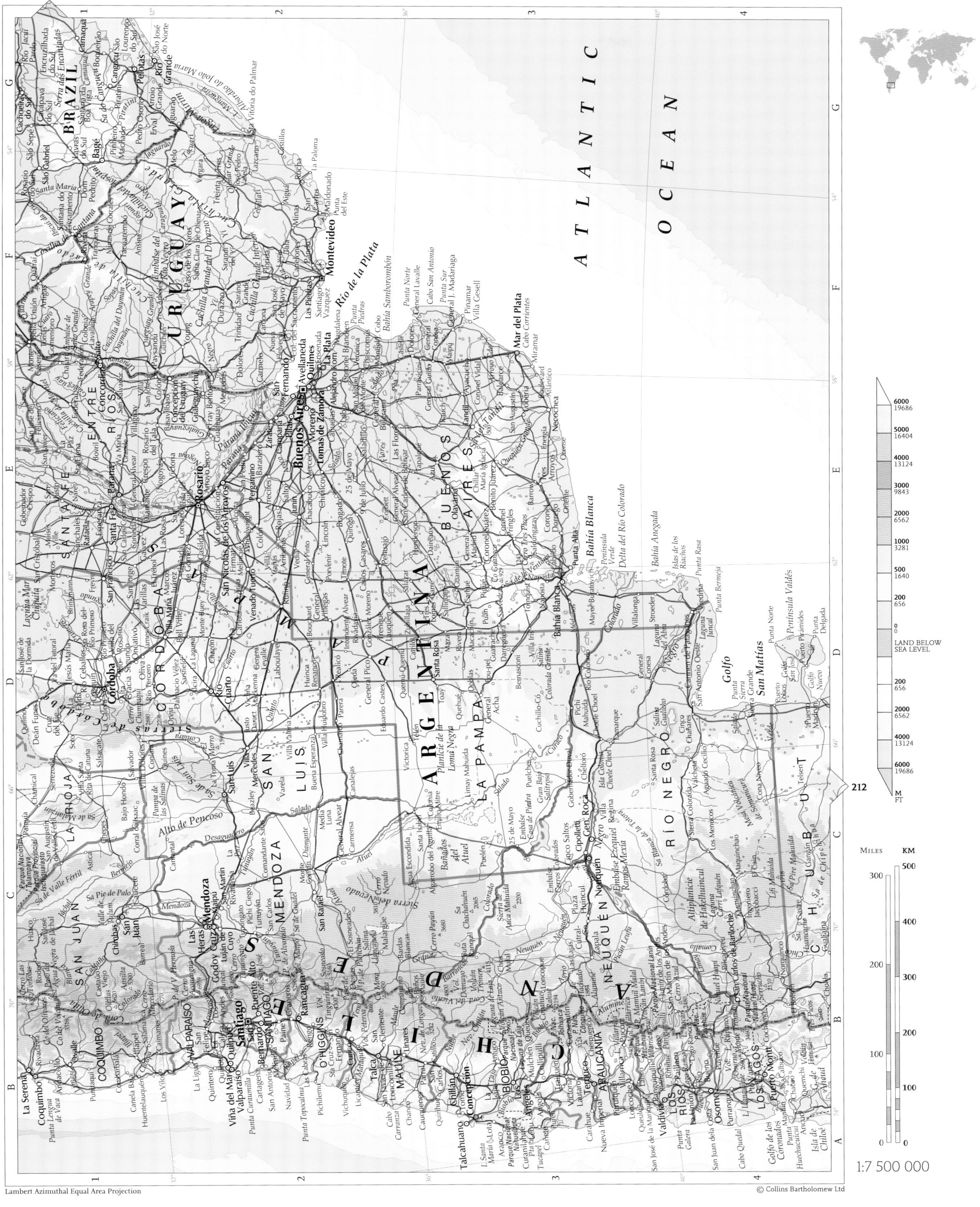


Lambert Azimuthal Equal Area Projection

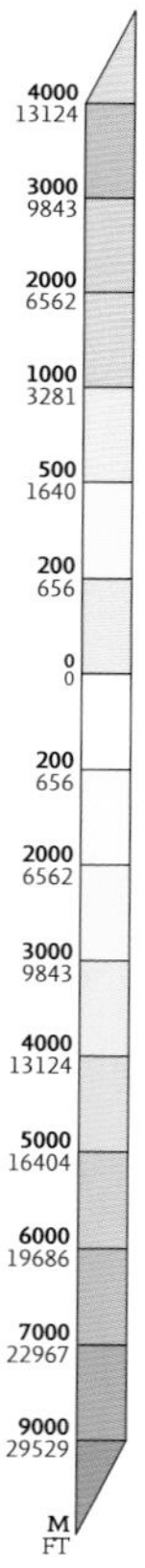

Lambert Azimuthal Equal Area Projection

Point Barrow
Mackenzie
Hudson Bay
James Bay
Newfoundland
St John's
Cape Race
Sable Island
Cape Sable
St Lawrence
Gulf of Alaska
Kodiak Island
Alexander Archipelago
Haida Gwaii (Queen Charlotte Islands)
Vancouver Island
Vancouver
Columbia
Tufts Abyssal Plain
New York
New England Seamounts
Missouri
Cape Hatteras
Bermuda Rise
Hatteras Abyssal Plain
Sargasso Sea
MID - ATLANTIC RIDGE
Tropic of Cancer
Nares Deep
NORTH AMERICA
Colorado
Mississippi
Cape Mendocino
San Francisco
Los Angeles
Rio Grande
New Orleans
The Bahamas
Gulf of Mexico
Straits of Florida
Greater Antilles
Cuba
Milwaukee Deep
NORTHEAST PACIFIC BASIN
Guadalupe
Gulf of California
Sigsbee Deep
Yucatan Channel
Cayman Trench
Jamaica
Hispaniola
Mexico City
Islas Revillagigedo
Isla Clarión
Isla Socorro
CARIBBEAN SEA
Venezuelan Basin
Lesser Antilles
Demerara Abyssal Plain
GUIANA BASIN
O'ahu
Maui
Hawai'i
Middle America Trench
Guatemala Basin
Colombian Basin
Caracas
Panama City
Orinoco
Île Clipperton
East Pacific Rise
EAST PACIFIC RISE
Amazon Cone
Isla de Coco
Cocos Ridge
Isla de Malpelo
Bogotá
Ceara Abyssal Plain
Equator
Tabuaeran
Kiritimati
Colon Ridge
Galapagos Islands
Quito
Gallego Rise
Malden Island
Amazon
Starbuck Island
Penrhyn Basin
Penrhyn
Vostok Island
Flint Island
Caroline Island (Millennium Island)
Nuku Hiva
Marquesas Islands
Hiva Oa
Galapagos Rise
Îles du Désappointement
Îles du Roi-Georges
Îles Palliser
Tuamotu Islands
Manuae
Raiatea
Tahiti
Society Islands
Anaa
Raroia
Hao
Hervey Islands
Rarotonga
Mangaia
Hereheretue
Îles Maria
Îles du Duc de Gloucester
Tubuai
Raivavae
Tubuai Islands
Rapa
Moruroa
Groupe Actéon
Îles Gambier
Henderson Island
Pitcairn Island
Ducie Island
Tiki Basin
Peru Basin
Lima
SOUTH AMERICA
Nazca Ridge
Peru-Chile Trench
Isla Sala y Gómez
Easter Island
Isla San Félix
San Ambrosio
Chile Basin
Roggeveen Basin
Juan Fernández Islands
Santiago
Buenos Aires
Paraná
Rio de Janeiro
Tropic of Capricorn
Santos Plateau
Chile Rise
PACIFIC - ANTARCTIC RIDGE
Mornington Abyssal Plain
Argentine Rise
Argentine Basin
Southeast Pacific Basin
Amundsen Abyssal Plain
Amundsen Ridges
Amundsen Sea
Peter I Island
Antarctic Circle
South Shetland Islands
Cape Horn
Drake Passage
Scotia Sea
Scotia Ridge
Falkland Islands
Falkland Plateau
Antarctic Peninsula

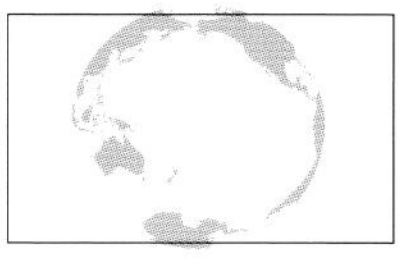

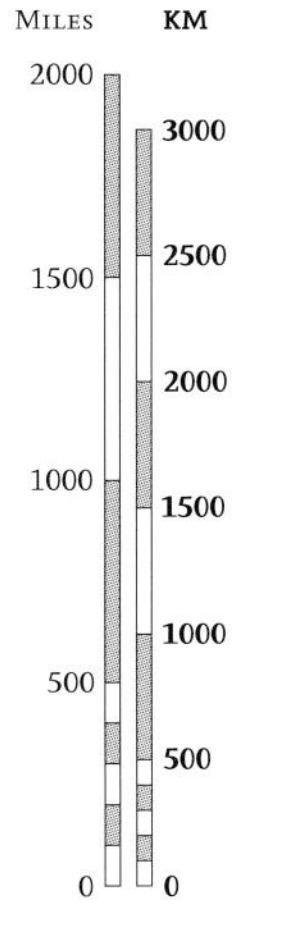
MILES
KM

1:58 000 000

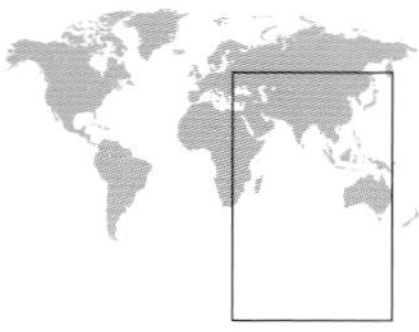

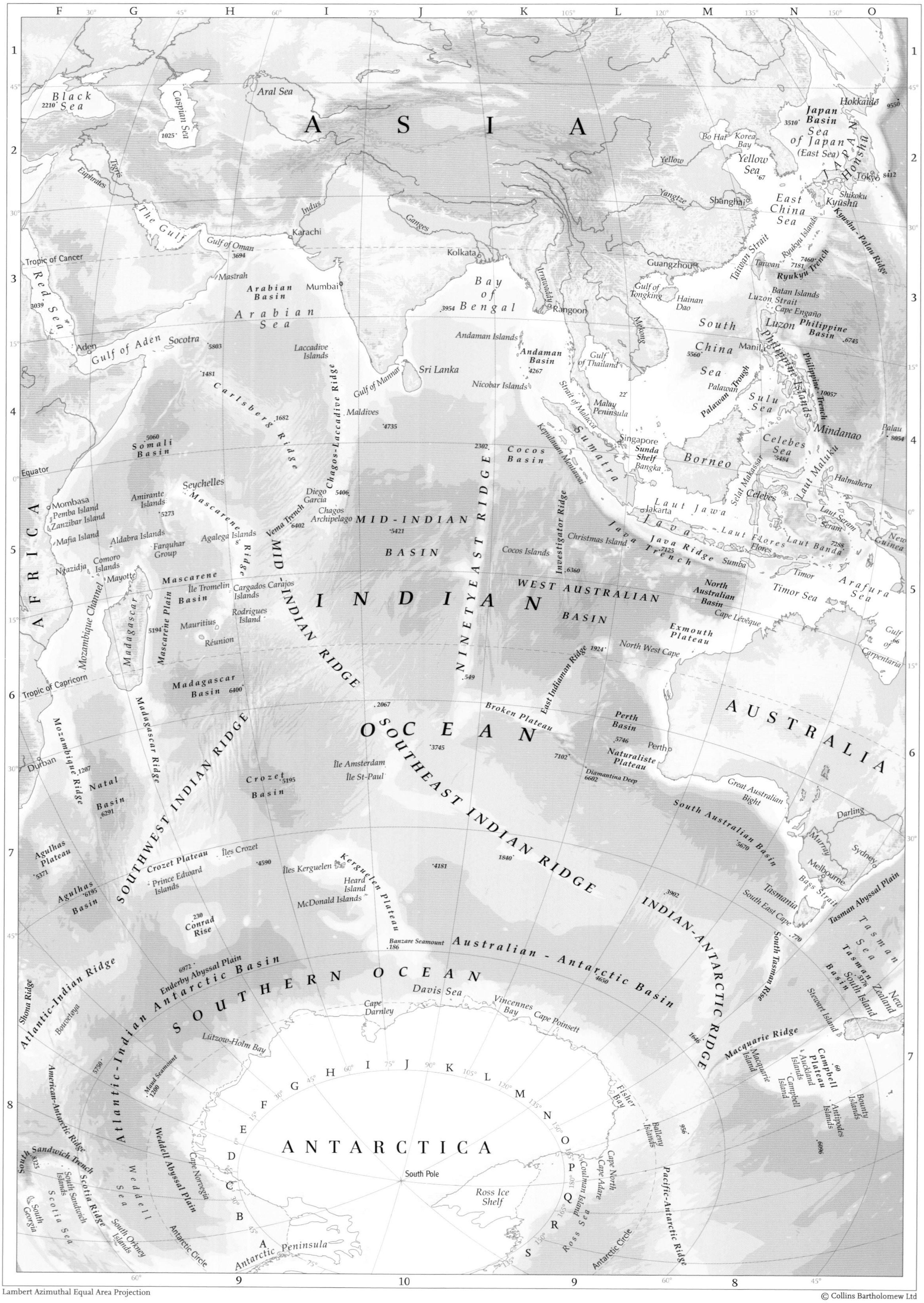
F
G
H
I
J
K
L
M
N
O
30°
45°
60°
75°
90°
105°
120°
135°
150°
1
2
3
4
5
6
7
8
9
10
Black Sea
2210
Caspian Sea
1025
Aral Sea
ASIA
Euphrates
Tigris
The Gulf
Gulf of Oman
3694
Indus
Karachi
Ganges
Kolkata
Tropic of Cancer
Red Sea
3039
Masīrah
Arabian Basin
Mumbai
Arabian Sea
Bay of Bengal
3954
Irrawaddy
Rangoon
Aden
Gulf of Aden
Socotra
5803
Laccadive Islands
Andaman Islands
Andaman Basin
4267
Gulf of Mannar
Sri Lanka
Nicobar Islands
1481
Carlsberg Ridge
1682
Chagos-Laccadive Ridge
Maldives
4735
Somali Basin
5060
Equator
Seychelles
Amirante Islands
5273
Mascarene Ridge
Mombasa
Pemba Island
Zanzibar Island
Mafia Island
Aldabra Islands
Farquhar Group
Agalega Islands
Vema Trench
6402
Diego Garcia
5406
Chagos Archipelago
MID-INDIAN BASIN
5421
2302
Cocos Basin
NINETYEAST RIDGE
Investigator Ridge
Cocos Islands
Christmas Island
6360
Java Trench
7125
Java Ridge
Ngazidja
Comoro Islands
Mayotte
Mascarene Basin
Île Tromelin
Cargados Carajos Islands
Rodrigues Island
Mauritius
Réunion
Mascarene Plain
5194
Mozambique Channel
Madagascar
AFRICA
MID-INDIAN RIDGE
INDIAN
WEST AUSTRALIAN BASIN
Tropic of Capricorn
Madagascar Basin
6400
Madagascar Ridge
549
2067
Broken Plateau
East Indiaman Ridge
1924
Perth Basin
5746
Perth
Naturaliste Plateau
7102
Diamantina Deep
6602
OCEAN
3745
SOUTHEAST INDIAN RIDGE
Île Amsterdam
Île St-Paul
Mozambique Ridge
1207
Durban
Natal Basin
6291
SOUTHWEST INDIAN RIDGE
Crozet Basin
5195
Agulhas Plateau
5371
Agulhas Basin
6195
Crozet Plateau
Îles Crozet
4590
Prince Edward Islands
Îles Kerguelen
Kerguelen Plateau
Heard Island
McDonald Islands
4181
1840
230
Conrad Rise
Banzare Seamount
186
Australian - Antarctic Basin
4650
3902
INDIAN-ANTARCTIC RIDGE
Atlantic-Indian Ridge
Shona Ridge
Bouvetøya
6972
Enderby Abyssal Plain
Atlantic-Indian Antarctic Basin
SOUTHERN OCEAN
Davis Sea
Cape Darnley
Vincennes Bay
Cape Poinsett
Lützow-Holm Bay
5750
Maud Seamount
1200
American-Antarctic Ridge
Weddell Abyssal Plain
Weddell Sea
Cape Norvegia
ANTARCTICA
South Pole
Ross Ice Shelf
Ross Sea
South Sandwich Trench
8325
South Sandwich Islands
Scotia Ridge
Scotia Sea
South Georgia
South Orkney Islands
Antarctic Circle
Antarctic Peninsula
Fisher Bay
Balleny Islands
956
Cape North
Cape Adare
Coulman Island
Pacific-Antarctic Ridge
1646
Hokkaidō
9550
Japan Basin
3510
Sea of Japan (East Sea)
JAPAN
Honshū
Tōkyō
8412
Bo Hai
Korea Bay
Yellow
Yellow Sea
67
Yangtze
Shanghai
East China Sea
Shikoku
Kyūshū
Kyushu-Palau Ridge
Ryukyu Islands
Ryukyu Trench
7460
7181
Taiwan
Taiwan Strait
Guangzhou
Gulf of Tongking
Hainan Dao
Mekong
Batan Islands
Luzon Strait
Cape Engaño
Luzon
Philippine Basin
6745
South China Sea
5560
Manila
Philippine Islands
Philippine Trench
10057
Gulf of Thailand
22
Malay Peninsula
Strait of Malacca
Palawan
Palawan Trough
Sulu Sea
Mindanao
Palau
8054
Kepulauan Mentawai
Sumatra
Singapore
Sunda Shelf
Bangka
Borneo
Celebes Sea
5484
Selat Makassar
Celebes
Laut Maluku
Halmahera
Laut Jawa
Jakarta
Java
Laut Flores
Flores
Laut Seram
Seram
Laut Banda
7288
New Guinea
Sumba
Timor
Timor Sea
Arafura Sea
North Australian Basin
Cape Lévêque
Exmouth Plateau
North West Cape
Gulf of Carpentaria
66
AUSTRALIA
Great Australian Bight
South Australian Basin
5670
Darling
Murray
Sydney
Melbourne
Bass Strait
Tasmania
South East Cape
770
Tasman Abyssal Plain
Tasman Sea
Tasman Basin
5976
South Tasman Rise
South Island
New Zealand
Stewart Island
Macquarie Ridge
Macquarie Island
Campbell Plateau
60
Auckland Islands
Campbell Island
Antipodes Islands
Bounty Islands
6096
A
B
C
D
E
P
Q
R
S
Lambert Azimuthal Equal Area Projection

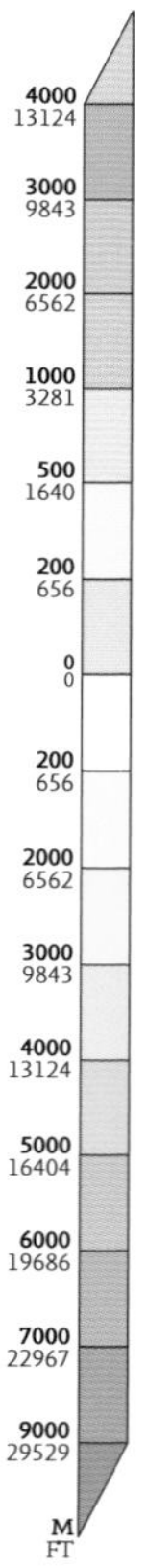
4000
13124
3000
9843
2000
6562
1000
3281
500
1640
200
656
0
0
200
656
2000
6562
3000
9843
4000
13124
5000
16404
6000
19686
7000
22967
9000
29529
M
FT

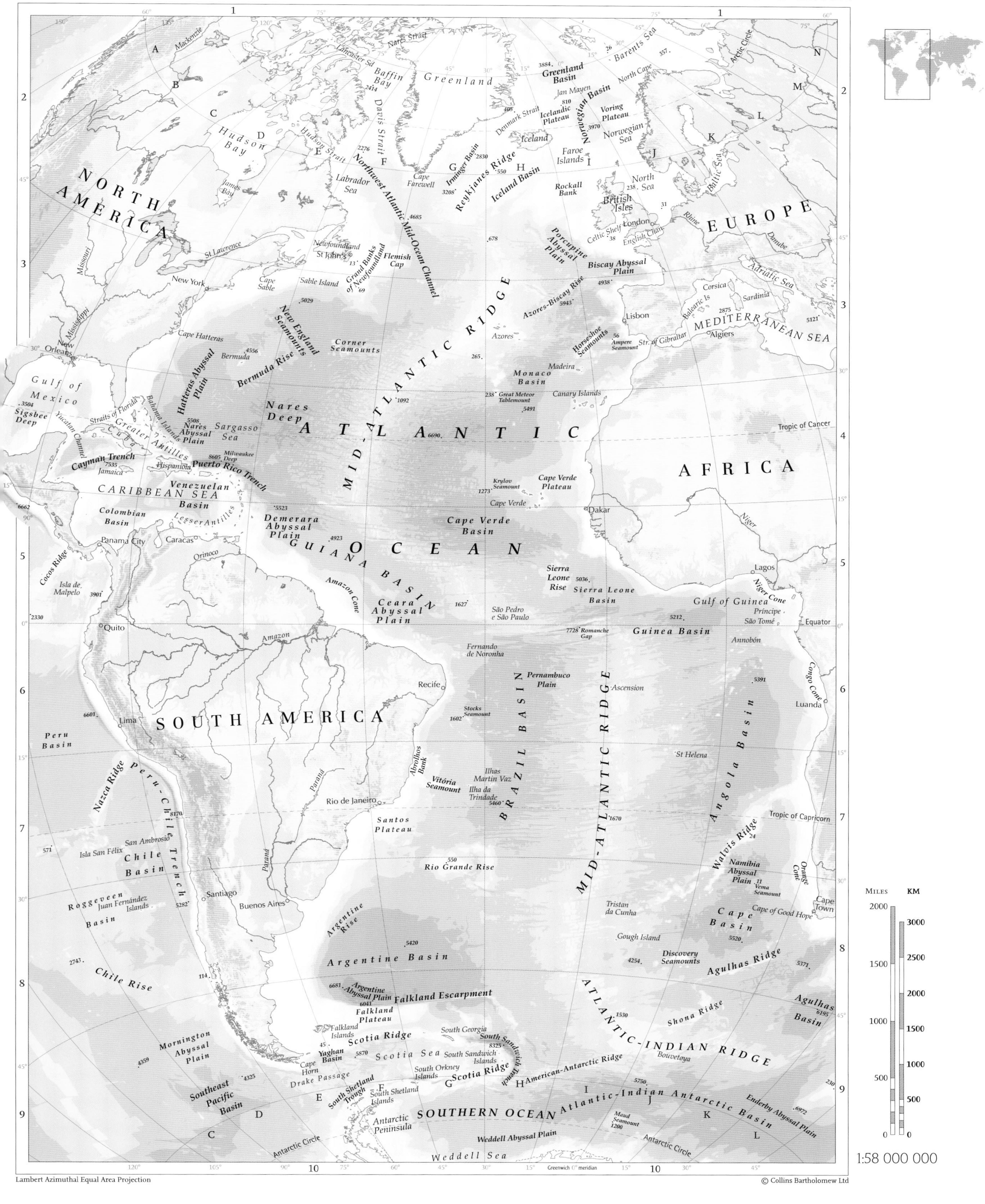


Lambert Azimuthal Equal Area Projection

# ARCTIC OCEAN

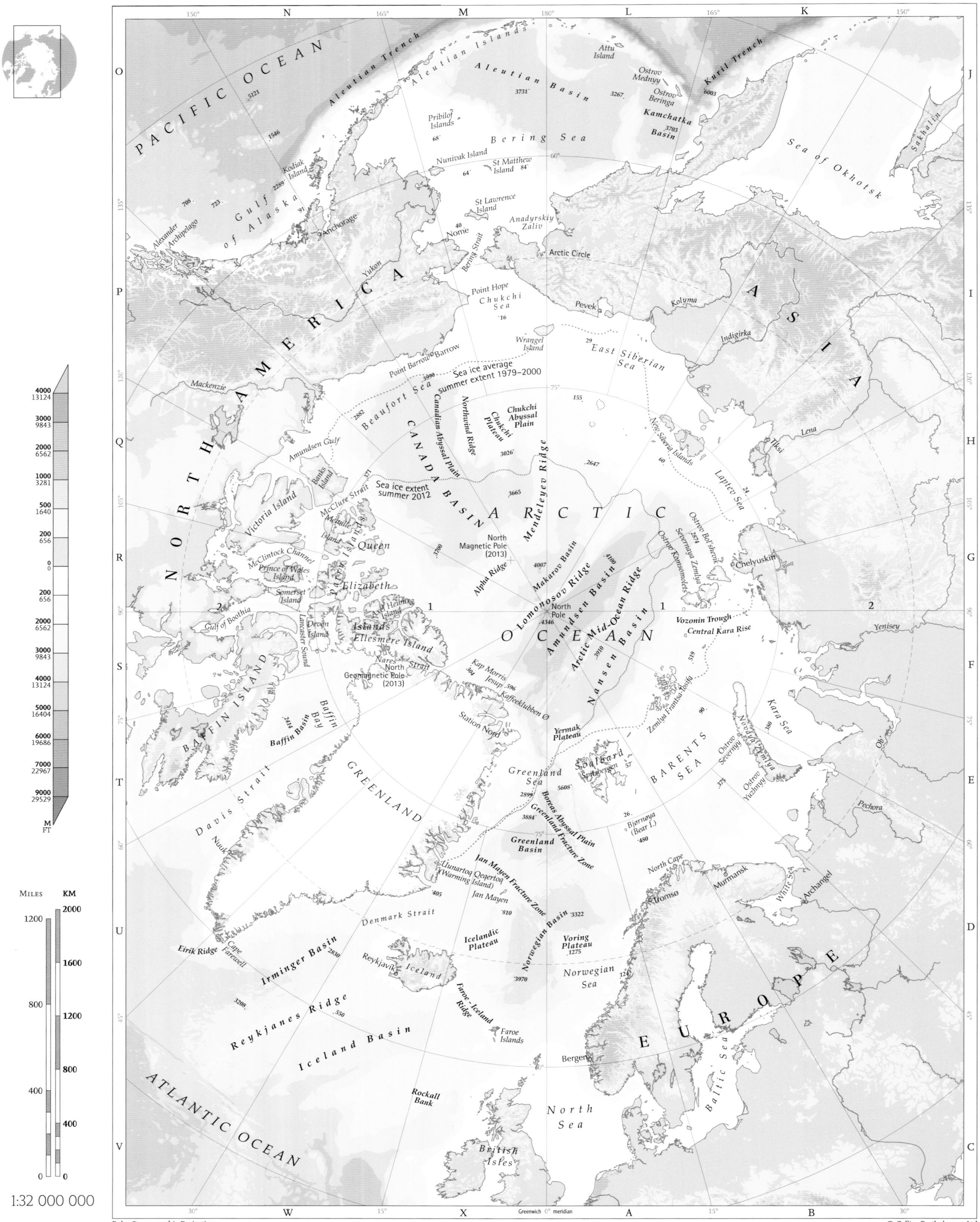


Polar Stereographic Projection

The index includes all names shown on the reference maps in the atlas. Each entry includes the country or geographical area in which the feature is located, a page number and an alphanumeric reference. Additional entry details and aspects of the index are explained below.

## REFERENCING

Names are referenced by page number and by grid reference. The grid reference relates to the alphanumeric values which appear in the margin of each map. These reflect the graticule on the map – the letter relates to longitude divisions, the number to latitude divisions.

Names are generally referenced to the largest scale map page on which they appear. For large geographical features, including countries, the reference is to the largest scale map on which the feature appears in its entirety, or on which the majority of it appears.

Rivers are referenced to their lowest downstream point – either their mouth or their confluence with another river. The river name will generally be positioned as close to this point as possible.

Entries relating to names appearing on insets are indicated by a small box symbol: □ followed by a grid reference if the inset has its own alphanumeric values.

## ALTERNATIVE NAMES

Alternative names appear as cross-references and refer the user to the index entry for the form of the name used on the map.

For rivers with multiple names – for example those which flow through several countries – all alternative name forms are included within the main index entries, with details of the countries in which each form applies.

## ADMINISTRATIVE QUALIFIERS

Administrative divisions are included in an entry to differentiate duplicate names – entries of exactly the same name and feature type within the one country – where these division names are shown on the maps. In such cases, duplicate names are alphabetized in the order of the administrative division names.

Additional qualifiers are included for names within selected geographical areas, to indicate more clearly their location.

## DESCRIPTORS

Entries, other than those for towns and cities, include a descriptor indicating the type of geographical feature. Descriptors are not included where the type of feature is implicit in the name itself, unless there is a town or city of exactly the same name.

## NAME FORMS AND ALPHABETICAL ORDER

Name forms are as they appear on the maps, with additional alternative forms included as cross-references. Names appear in full in the index, although they may appear in abbreviated form on the maps.

The German character ß is alphabetized as 'ss'. Names beginning with Mac or Mc are alphabetized exactly as they appear. The terms Saint, Sainte, etc, are abbreviated to St, Ste, etc, but alphabetized as if in the full form.

## NUMERICAL ENTRIES

Entries beginning with numerals appear at the beginning of the index, in numerical order. Elsewhere, numerals are alphabetized before 'a'.

## PERMUTED TERMS

Names beginning with generic, geographical terms are permuted – the descriptive term is placed after, and the index alphabetized by, the main part of the name. For example, Lake Superior is indexed as Superior, Lake; Mount Everest as Everest, Mount. This policy is applied to all languages. Permuting has not been applied to names of towns, cities or administrative divisions beginning with such geographical terms. These remain in their full form, for example, Lake Isabella, USA.

## INDEX ABBREVIATIONS

| | |
|---|---|
| **admin. dist.** | administrative district |
| **admin. div.** | administrative division |
| **admin. reg.** | administrative region |
| **Afgh.** | Afghanistan |
| **AK** | Alaska |
| **AL** | Alabama |
| **Alg.** | Algeria |
| **Alta** | Alberta |
| **AR** | Arkansas |
| **Arg.** | Argentina |
| **aut. comm.** | autonomous community |
| **aut. reg.** | autonomous region |
| **aut. rep.** | autonomous republic |
| **AZ** | Arizona |
| **Azer.** | Azerbaijan |
| **b.** | bay |
| **Bangl.** | Bangladesh |
| **B.C.** | British Columbia |
| **Bol.** | Bolivia |
| **Bos.-Herz.** | Bosnia-Herzegovina |
| **Bulg.** | Bulgaria |
| **Burkina** | Burkina Faso |
| **c.** | cape |
| **CA** | California |
| **Cent. Afr. Rep.** | Central African Republic |
| **CO** | Colorado |
| **Col.** | Colombia |
| **CT** | Connecticut |
| **Czech Rep.** | Czech Republic |
| **DC** | District of Columbia |
| **DE** | Delaware |
| **Dem. Rep. Congo** | Democratic Republic of the Congo |
| **depr.** | depression |
| **des.** | desert |
| **Dom. Rep.** | Dominican Republic |
| **Equat. Guinea** | Equatorial Guinea |
| **esc.** | escarpment |
| **est.** | estuary |
| **Eth.** | Ethiopia |
| **Fin.** | Finland |
| **FL** | Florida |
| **for.** | forest |
| **Fr. Guiana** | French Guiana |
| **Fr. Polynesia** | French Polynesia |
| **g.** | gulf |
| **GA** | Georgia |
| **Guat.** | Guatemala |
| **h.** | hill |
| **hd** | headland |
| **HI** | Hawaii |
| **Hond.** | Honduras |
| **i.** | island |
| **IA** | Iowa |
| **ID** | Idaho |
| **IL** | Illinois |
| **IN** | Indiana |
| **Indon.** | Indonesia |
| **is** | islands |
| **Kazakh.** | Kazakhstan |
| **KS** | Kansas |
| **KY** | Kentucky |
| **Kyrg.** | Kyrgyzstan |
| **l.** | lake |
| **LA** | Louisiana |
| **lag.** | lagoon |
| **Lith.** | Lithuania |
| **Lux.** | Luxembourg |
| **MA** | Massachusetts |
| **Madag.** | Madagascar |
| **Man.** | Manitoba |
| **MD** | Maryland |
| **ME** | Maine |
| **Mex.** | Mexico |
| **MI** | Michigan |
| **MN** | Minnesota |
| **MO** | Missouri |
| **Mont.** | Montenegro |
| **Moz.** | Mozambique |
| **MS** | Mississippi |
| **MT** | Montana |
| **mt.** | mountain |
| **mts** | mountains |
| **N.** | North, Northern |
| **nat. park** | national park |
| **N.B.** | New Brunswick |
| **NC** | North Carolina |
| **ND** | North Dakota |
| **NE** | Nebraska |
| **Neth.** | Netherlands |
| **Nfld.** | Newfoundland |
| **NH** | New Hampshire |
| **NJ** | New Jersey |
| **NM** | New Mexico |
| **N.S.** | Nova Scotia |
| **N.S.W.** | New South Wales |
| **N.W.T.** | Northwest Territories |
| **N.Z.** | New Zealand |
| **NV** | Nevada |
| **NY** | New York |
| **OH** | Ohio |
| **OK** | Oklahoma |
| **Ont.** | Ontario |
| **OR** | Oregon |
| **PA** | Pennsylvania |
| **Pak.** | Pakistan |
| **Para.** | Paraguay |
| **P.E.I.** | Prince Edward Island |
| **pen.** | peninsula |
| **Phil.** | Philippines |
| **plat.** | plateau |
| **P.N.G.** | Papua New Guinea |
| **Port.** | Portugal |
| **prov.** | province |
| **pt** | point |
| **Qld** | Queensland |
| **Que.** | Québec |
| **r.** | river |
| **reg.** | region |
| **res.** | reserve |
| **resr** | reservoir |
| **RI** | Rhode Island |
| **r. mouth** | river mouth |
| **Rus. Fed.** | Russian Federation |
| **S.** | South |
| **S.A.** | South Australia |
| **S. Africa** | Republic of South Africa |
| **salt l.** | salt lake |
| **Sask.** | Saskatchewan |
| **SC** | South Carolina |
| **SD** | South Dakota |
| **sea chan.** | sea channel |
| **Sing.** | Singapore |
| **Switz.** | Switzerland |
| **Tajik.** | Tajikistan |
| **Tanz.** | Tanzania |
| **Tas.** | Tasmania |
| **terr.** | territory |
| **Thai.** | Thailand |
| **TN** | Tennessee |
| **Trin. and Tob.** | Trinidad and Tobago |
| **Turkm.** | Turkmenistan |
| **TX** | Texas |
| **U.A.E.** | United Arab Emirates |
| **U.K.** | United Kingdom |
| **Ukr.** | Ukraine |
| **U.S.A.** | United States of America |
| **UT** | Utah |
| **Uzbek.** | Uzbekistan |
| **VA** | Virginia |
| **Venez.** | Venezuela |
| **Vic.** | Victoria |
| **vol.** | volcano |
| **vol. crater** | volcanic crater |
| **VT** | Vermont |
| **W.** | Western |
| **WA** | Washington |
| **W.A.** | Western Australia |
| **WI** | Wisconsin |
| **WV** | West Virginia |
| **WY** | Wyoming |
| **Y.T.** | Yukon |

## 1


215 E2 9 de Julio Arg.
215 E2 25 de Mayo Arg.
215 C3 25 de Mayo Arg.
186 E4 100 Mile House Canada


## A


159 J5 Aabenraa Denmark
164 E4 Aachen Germany
159 J4 Aalborg Denmark
159 J4 Aalborg Bugt b. Denmark
168 E6 Aalen Germany
164 C4 Aalst Belgium
159 J4 Aars Denmark
164 C4 Aarschot Belgium
148 A3 Aba China
178 D3 Aba Dem. Rep. Congo
176 C4 Aba Nigeria
140 B5 Abā ad Dūd Saudi Arabia
140 C4 Ābādān Iran
138 D5 Abadan Turkm.
140 D4 Ābādeh Iran
140 D4 Ābādeh Ţashk Iran
176 B1 Abadla Alg.
214 D2 Abaeté r. Brazil
211 I4 Abaetetuba Brazil
216 G6 Abaiang atoll Kiribati
195 E4 Abajo Peak U.S.A.
176 C4 Abakaliki Nigeria
146 B1 Abakan Rus. Fed.
146 A1 Abakanskiy Khrebet mts Rus. Fed.
173 E7 Abana Turkey
210 D6 Abancay Peru
140 D4 Abarkūh Iran
140 D4 Abarkūh, Kavīr-e des. Iran
150 I2 Abashiri Japan
150 I2 Abashiri-wan b. Japan
124 E3 Abau P.N.G.
139 H2 Abay Kazakh.
178 D3 Abaya, Lake Eth.
Ābaya Hāyk' l. Eth. see Abaya, Lake
177 F3 Ābay Wenz r. Eth. alt. Azraq, Bahr el Sudan, conv. Blue Nile
132 K4 Abaza Rus. Fed.
141 E3 'Abbāsābād Iran
170 C4 Abbasanta Sardinia Italy
190 C2 Abbaye, Point U.S.A.
178 E2 Abbe, Lake Eth.
166 E1 Abbeville France
199 E6 Abbeville LA U.S.A.
201 D5 Abbeville SC U.S.A.
163 B5 Abbeyfeale Ireland
162 E6 Abbey Head U.K.
163 D5 Abbeyleix Ireland
160 D3 Abbeytown U.K.
158 L2 Abborrträsk Sweden
129 B3 Abbot Ice Shelf ice feature Antarctica
186 E5 Abbotsford Canada
190 B3 Abbotsford U.S.A.
195 F4 Abbott U.S.A.
144 C2 Abbottabad Pak.
137 H3 'Abd al 'Azīz, Jabal h. Syria
137 K5 Ābdānān Iran
138 C1 Abdulino Rus. Fed.
177 E3 Abéché Chad
128 D4 Abel Tasman National Park N.Z.
176 B4 Abengourou Côte d'Ivoire
Åbenrå Denmark see Aabenraa
165 J6 Abensberg Germany
176 C4 Abeokuta Nigeria
161 C5 Aberaeron U.K.
162 F3 Aberchirder U.K.
127 H5 Abercrombie r. Australia
161 D6 Aberdare U.K.
161 C5 Aberdaron U.K.
127 I4 Aberdeen Australia
187 H4 Aberdeen Canada
149 □ Aberdeen Hong Kong China
180 F6 Aberdeen S. Africa
162 F3 Aberdeen U.K.
203 E5 Aberdeen MD U.S.A.
199 F5 Aberdeen MS U.S.A.
198 D2 Aberdeen SD U.S.A.
194 B2 Aberdeen WA U.S.A.
187 I2 Aberdeen Lake Canada
161 C5 Aberdovey U.K.
Aberdyfi U.K. see Aberdovey
162 E4 Aberfeldy U.K.
160 F4 Aberford U.K.
162 D4 Aberfoyle U.K.
161 D6 Abergavenny U.K.
199 C5 Abernathy U.S.A.
161 C5 Aberporth U.K.
161 C5 Abersoch U.K.
161 C5 Aberystwyth U.K.
142 B6 Abhā Saudi Arabia
140 C2 Abhar Iran
140 C2 Abhar Rūd r. Iran
Ab-i Bazuft r. Iran see Bāzoft, Āb-e
213 A2 Abibe, Serranía de mts Col.
176 B4 Abidjan Côte d'Ivoire
Ab-i-Istada l. Afgh. see Istādah-ye Muqur, Āb-e
178 D3 Abijatta-Shalla National Park Eth.
140 E3 Ab-i-Kavīr salt flat Iran
198 D4 Abilene KS U.S.A.
199 D5 Abilene TX U.S.A.
161 F6 Abingdon U.K.
190 B5 Abingdon IL U.S.A.
202 C6 Abingdon VA U.S.A.
173 F6 Abinsk Rus. Fed.
Ab-i-Safed r. Afgh. see Sīāh, Daryā-ye
Abiseo, Parque Nacional nat. park Peru see Río Abiseo, Parque Nacional
187 H2 Abitau Lake Canada
188 D4 Abitibi r. Canada
188 E4 Abitibi, Lake Canada
173 G7 Abkhazia aut. rep. Georgia
144 C3 Abohar India
176 B4 Aboisso Côte d'Ivoire
176 C4 Abomey Benin
177 D4 Abong Mbang Cameroon
153 A4 Aborlan Phil.
177 D3 Abou Déia Chad
137 J1 Abovyan Armenia
162 F3 Aboyne U.K.
142 C4 Abqaiq Saudi Arabia
Abra, Lago del l. Arg. see Abra, Laguna del
215 D4 Abra, Laguna del l. Arg.
167 B3 Abrantes Port.
212 C2 Abra Pampa Arg.
206 A2 Abreojos, Punta pt Mex.
214 E2 Abrolhos, Arquipélago dos is Brazil
219 G7 Abrolhos Bank sea feature S. Atlantic Ocean
194 E2 Absaroka Range mts U.S.A.
165 H6 Abtsgmünd Germany
140 D5 Abū al Abyaḑ i. U.A.E.
140 C5 Abū 'Alī i. Saudi Arabia
Abu al Jirab i. U.A.E. see Abū al Abyaḑ
142 B6 Abū 'Arīsh Saudi Arabia
142 D5 Abu Dhabi U.A.E.
177 F3 Abu Hamed Sudan
176 C4 Abuja Nigeria
137 H4 Abū Kamāl Syria
177 E3 Abu Matariq Sudan
136 B6 Abū Mīnā tourist site Egypt
140 D5 Abū Mūsá, Jazīreh-ye i. U.A.E.
210 E6 Abunā r. Bol.
210 E5 Abunā Brazil
142 A7 Ābune Yosēf mt. Eth.
136 C6 Abū Qīr, Khalīj b. Egypt
135 F4 Abu Road India
Abu Simbel Egypt see Abū Sunbul
137 J6 Abū Şukhayr Iraq
177 F2 Abū Sunbul Egypt
128 C5 Abut Head N.Z.
153 C4 Abuyog Phil.
177 E3 Abu Zabad Sudan
Abū Ẓaby U.A.E. see Abu Dhabi
137 L6 Abūzam Iran
177 E3 Abyad Sudan
177 E4 Abyei Sudan
140 C2 Ābyek Iran
138 D1 Abzakovo Rus. Fed.
138 D2 Abzanovo Rus. Fed.
203 I2 Acadia National Park U.S.A.
206 D3 Acambaro Mex.
207 G3 Acancéh Mex.
213 A2 Acandí Col.
167 B1 A Cañiza Spain
206 C3 Acaponeta Mex.
207 E4 Acapulco Mex.
211 I4 Acará Brazil
211 J4 Acaraú r. Brazil
214 A4 Acaray r. Para.
212 E3 Acaray, Represa de resr Para.
213 C2 Acarigua Venez.
207 E4 Acatlán Mex.
207 E4 Acatzingo Mex.
207 F4 Acayucán Mex.
176 B4 Accra Ghana
160 E4 Accrington U.K.
213 C3 Achaguas Venez.
144 D5 Achalpur India
143 B2 Achampet India
133 S3 Achayvayam Rus. Fed.
152 D1 Acheng China
164 A4 Achicourt France
163 B4 Achill Ireland
163 A4 Achill Island Ireland
162 C2 Achiltibuie U.K.
165 H1 Achim Germany
146 B1 Achinsk Rus. Fed.
162 C3 Achnasheen U.K.
162 C3 A'Chralaig mt. U.K.
173 F6 Achuyevo Rus. Fed.
136 B3 Acıgöl l. Turkey
136 B3 Acıpayam Turkey
170 F6 Acireale Sicily Italy
198 E3 Ackley U.S.A.
205 J4 Acklins Island Bahamas
161 I5 Acle U.K.
215 B2 Aconcagua r. Chile
215 B2 Aconcagua, Cerro mt. Arg.
211 K5 Acopiara Brazil
156 A6 Açores, Arquipélago dos is N. Atlantic Ocean
167 B1 A Coruña Spain
206 H6 Acoyapa Nicaragua
170 C2 Acqui Terme Italy
126 A4 Acraman, Lake salt flat Australia
Acre Israel see 'Akko
170 G5 Acri Italy
168 I7 Ács Hungary
123 J6 Actéon, Groupe is Fr. Polynesia
202 B4 Ada OH U.S.A.
199 D5 Ada OK U.S.A.
167 D2 Adaja r. Spain
212 E8 Adam, Mount h. Falkland Is
138 D2 Adamovka Rus. Fed.
203 G3 Adams MA U.S.A.
190 C4 Adams WI U.S.A.
194 B2 Adams, Mount U.S.A.
143 B4 Adam's Bridge sea feature India/Sri Lanka
186 F4 Adams Lake Canada
197 E2 Adams McGill Reservoir U.S.A.
186 C3 Adams Mountain U.S.A.
143 C5 Adam's Peak Sri Lanka
196 B2 Adams Peak U.S.A.
'Adan Yemen see Aden
136 E3 Adana Turkey
136 C1 Adapazarı Turkey
163 C5 Adare Ireland
129 B6 Adare, Cape c. Antarctica
197 E2 Adaven U.S.A.
137 J5 Ad Daghghārah Iraq
142 C5 Ad Dahnā' des. Saudi Arabia
Ad Dammām Saudi Arabia see Dammam
140 B5 Ad Dawādimī Saudi Arabia
Ad Dawḩah Qatar see Doha
137 I4 Ad Dawr Iraq
137 K6 Ad Dayr Iraq
140 B5 Ad Dibdibah plain Saudi Arabia
140 B6 Ad Dilam Saudi Arabia
142 C5 Ad Dir'īyah Saudi Arabia
178 D3 Addis Ababa Eth.
203 J2 Addison U.S.A.
137 J6 Ad Dīwānīyah Iraq
161 G6 Addlestone U.K.
181 F6 Addo Elephant National Park S. Africa
137 I6 Ad Duwayd well Saudi Arabia
201 D6 Adel GA U.S.A.
198 E3 Adel IA U.S.A.
126 C5 Adelaide Australia
201 E7 Adelaide Bahamas
181 G6 Adelaide S. Africa
129 B2 Adelaide Island i. Antarctica
124 D3 Adelaide River Australia
196 D4 Adelanto U.S.A.
129 C6 Adélie Land reg. Antarctica
129 C7 Adélie Land reg. Antarctica
127 H5 Adelong Australia
139 G4 Adelunga Uzbek.
142 C7 Aden Yemen
142 C7 Aden, Gulf of Somalia/Yemen
164 E4 Adenau Germany
165 I1 Adendorf Germany
140 D5 Adh Dhayd U.A.E.
147 F7 Adi i. Indon.
178 D2 Ādī Ārk'ay Eth.
178 D2 Ādīgrat Eth.
144 D6 Adilabad India
137 I2 Adilcevaz Turkey
194 B3 Adin U.S.A.
177 D2 Adīrī Libya
203 F2 Adirondack Mountains U.S.A.
Ādīs Ābeba Eth. see Addis Ababa
178 D3 Ādīs Alem Eth.
136 G3 Adıyaman Turkey
169 M7 Adjud Romania
207 E3 Adjuntas, Presa de las resr Mex.
189 I3 Adlavik Islands Canada
124 C3 Admiralty Gulf Australia
185 J2 Admiralty Inlet Canada
186 C3 Admiralty Island U.S.A.
186 C3 Admiralty Island National Monument-Kootznoowoo Wilderness nat. park U.S.A.
124 E2 Admiralty Islands P.N.G.
143 B3 Adoni India
165 K4 Adorf Germany
165 G3 Adorf (Diemelsee) Germany
166 D5 Adour r. France
167 E4 Adra Spain
170 F6 Adrano Sicily Italy
176 B2 Adrar Alg.
176 A2 Adrar mts Alg.
176 A2 Adrar, Ḑhar hills Mauritania
139 G4 Adrasmon Tajik.
177 E3 Adré Chad
191 E5 Adrian MI U.S.A.
199 C5 Adrian TX U.S.A.
170 E2 Adriatic Sea Europe
143 B4 Adur India
178 C3 Adusa Dem. Rep. Congo
178 D2 Ādwa Eth.
133 O3 Adycha r. Rus. Fed.
173 F6 Adygeya, Respublika aut. rep. Rus. Fed.
173 F6 Adygeysk Rus. Fed.
173 H6 Adyk Rus. Fed.
176 B4 Adzopé Côte d'Ivoire
171 K5 Aegean Sea Greece/Turkey
165 H2 Aerzen Germany
167 B1 A Estrada Spain
178 D2 Afabet Eritrea
137 J3 Āfān Iran
141 F3 Afghanistan country Asia
158 J3 Åfjord Norway
178 E3 Afmadow Somalia
184 C4 Afognak Island U.S.A.
167 C1 A Fonsagrada Spain
174 Africa
136 F3 'Afrīn, Nahr r. Syria/Turkey
136 F2 Afşin Turkey
164 D2 Afsluitdijk barrage Neth.
194 E3 Afton U.S.A.
211 H4 Afuá Brazil
136 E5 'Afula Israel
136 C2 Afyon Turkey
165 K4 Aga Germany
176 C3 Agadez Niger
176 B1 Agadir Morocco
175 I5 Agalega Islands Mauritius
138 D1 Agapovka Rus. Fed.
145 G5 Agartala India
144 C6 Agashi India
191 F2 Agate Canada
171 L6 Agathonisi i. Greece
176 B4 Agboville Côte d'Ivoire
137 K1 Ağcabädi Azer.
137 K2 Ağdam (abandoned) Azer.
166 F5 Agde France
166 E4 Agen France
180 C4 Aggeneys S. Africa
164 F4 Agger r. Germany
144 D1 Aghil Dawan China
163 C3 Aghla Mountain h. Ireland
171 K7 Agia Varvara Greece
136 G2 Ağın Turkey
171 J6 Agios Dimitrios Greece
171 K5 Agios Efstratios i. Greece
171 L5 Agios Fokas, Akrotirio pt Greece
171 J5 Agios Konstantinos Greece
171 K7 Agios Nikolaos Greece
171 J4 Agiou Orous, Kolpos b. Greece
177 F3 Agirwat Hills Sudan
181 F3 Agisanang S. Africa
176 B4 Agnibilékrou Côte d'Ivoire
171 K2 Agnita Romania
148 A2 Agong China
144 D4 Agra India
173 H7 Agrakhanskiy Poluostrov pen. Rus. Fed.
167 F2 Ágreda Spain
137 I2 Ağrı Turkey
171 J7 Agria Gramvousa i. Greece
170 E6 Agrigento Sicily Italy
171 I5 Agrinio Greece
215 B3 Agrio r. Arg.
170 F4 Agropoli Italy
137 J1 Ağstafa Azer.
137 L1 Ağsu Azer.
207 G5 Agua, Volcán de vol. Guat.
206 C3 Agua Brava, Laguna lag. Mex.
207 G4 Aguada Mex.
213 B3 Aguadas Col.
213 B3 Agua de Dios Col.
205 K5 Aguadilla Puerto Rico
215 D4 Aguado Cecilio Arg.
206 I6 Aguadulce Panama
215 C3 Agua Escondida Arg.
206 C3 Aguamilpa, Presa l. Mex.
204 D4 Aguanaval r. Mex.
215 C1 Agua Negra, Paso del pass Arg./Chile
214 B3 Aguapeí r. Brazil
204 C2 Agua Prieta Mex.
214 A3 Aguaray Guazú r. Para.
213 D2 Aguaro-Guariquito, Parque Nacional nat. park Venez.
206 C2 Aguaruto Mex.
206 D3 Aguascalientes Mex.
206 D3 Aguascalientes state Mex.
214 E2 Águas Formosas Brazil
214 C3 Agudos Brazil
197 F5 Aguila U.S.A.
167 D1 Aguilar de Campoo Spain
167 F4 Águilas Spain
153 B4 Aguisan Phil.
180 D7 Agulhas, Cape S. Africa
219 K9 Agulhas Basin sea feature Southern Ocean
214 D3 Agulhas Negras mt. Brazil
218 F7 Agulhas Plateau sea feature Southern Ocean
219 J8 Agulhas Ridge sea feature S. Atlantic Ocean
155 E4 Agung, Gunung vol. Indon.
153 C4 Agusan r. Phil.
213 B2 Agustín Codazzi Col.
153 B4 Agutaya Phil.
176 C2 Ahaggar plat. Alg.
176 C2 Ahaggar, Parc National de l' nat. park Alg.
176 C2 Ahaggar, Tassili oua-n- plat. Alg.
140 B2 Ahar Iran
128 C5 Ahaura N.Z.
164 F2 Ahaus Germany
128 F3 Ahimanawa Range mts N.Z.
128 D1 Ahipara N.Z.
128 D1 Ahipara Bay N.Z.
184 B4 Ahklun Mountains U.S.A.
137 I2 Ahlat Turkey
165 F3 Ahlen Germany
144 C5 Ahmadabad India
143 A2 Ahmadnagar India
144 B3 Ahmadpur East Pak.
144 B4 Ahmad Tar Pak.
Ahmedabad India see Ahmadabad
Ahmednagar India see Ahmadnagar
165 I4 Ahorn Germany
140 C4 Ahram Iran
165 I1 Ahrensburg Germany
137 I2 Ahta Dağı mt. Turkey
158 N3 Ähtäri Fin.
159 N4 Ahtme Estonia
137 L6 Āhū Iran
207 G5 Ahuachapán El Salvador
206 D3 Ahualulco Mex.
166 F3 Ahun France
128 B6 Ahuriri r. N.Z.
140 C4 Ahvāz Iran
144 C5 Ahwa India
180 B3 Ai-Ais Namibia
180 B3 Ai-Ais Hot Springs Game Park Namibia
180 B4 Ai-Ais/Richtersveld Transfrontier Park Namibia/S. Africa
148 D1 Aibag He r. China
141 H2 Aībak Afgh.
Aidin Turkm. see Aýdyň
196 □1 'Aiea U.S.A.
Aiea U.S.A. see 'Aiea
136 E4 Aigialousa Cyprus
171 J6 Aigina i. Greece
171 J5 Aigio Greece
166 H4 Aigle de Chambeyron mt. France
215 F2 Aiguá Uruguay
152 C3 Ai He r. China
151 F5 Aikawa Japan
201 D5 Aiken U.S.A.
206 J6 Ailigandi Panama
Ailinglapalap atoll Marshall Is see Ailinglaplap
216 G6 Ailinglaplap atoll Marshall Is
164 A5 Ailly-sur-Noye France
191 G4 Ailsa Craig Canada
162 C5 Ailsa Craig i. U.K.
163 C3 Ailt an Chorráin Ireland
214 E2 Aimorés, Serra dos hills Brazil
196 □1 'Āina Haina U.S.A.
176 C1 Aïn Beïda Alg.
176 B2 'Aïn Ben Tili Mauritania
167 H4 Aïn Defla Alg.
167 H5 Aïn el Hadjel Alg.
176 B1 Aïn Sefra Alg.
189 H4 Ainslie, Lake Canada
198 D3 Ainsworth U.S.A.
Aintab Turkey see Gaziantep
167 H4 Aïn Taya Alg.
167 G5 Aïn Tédélès Alg.
213 B4 Aipe Col.
154 C5 Air i. Indon.
176 C3 Aïr, Massif de l' mts Niger
186 G4 Airdrie Canada
162 E5 Airdrie U.K.
164 D6 Aire r. France
166 D5 Aire-sur-l'Adour France
176 C3 Aïr et du Ténéré, Réserve Naturelle Nationale de l' nature res. Niger
185 K3 Air Force Island Canada
148 D1 Airgin Sum China
187 H3 Air Ronge Canada
148 F2 Ai Shan h. China
186 B2 Aishihik Canada
186 B2 Aishihik Lake Canada
166 G2 Aisne r. France
167 F3 Aitana mt. Spain
124 E2 Aitape P.N.G.
198 E2 Aitkin U.S.A.
138 C1 Aitovo Rus. Fed.
123 I5 Aitutaki i. Pacific Ocean
169 K7 Aiud Romania
166 G5 Aix-en-Provence France
166 G4 Aix-les-Bains France
145 F5 Aiyar Reservoir India
145 H5 Aizawl India
159 N4 Aizkraukle Latvia
159 M4 Aizpute Latvia
151 F6 Aizuwakamatsu Japan
170 C4 Ajaccio Corsica France
213 B4 Ajajú r. Col.
207 E4 Ajalpán Mex.
143 A1 Ajanta India
158 K2 Ajaureforsen Sweden
128 D5 Ajax, Mount N.Z.
177 E1 Ajdābiyā Libya
150 G4 Ajigasawa Japan
176 C2 Ajjer, Tassili n' plat. Alg.
136 E5 'Ajlūn Jordan
140 D5 'Ajman U.A.E.
144 C4 Ajmer India
197 F5 Ajo U.S.A.
197 F5 Ajo, Mount U.S.A.
153 B4 Ajuy Phil.
150 H3 Akabira Japan
139 H2 Akadyr Kazakh.
178 D4 Akagera, Parc National de l' Rwanda
143 B2 Akalkot India
150 I3 Akan Kokuritsu-kōen nat. park Japan
136 D4 Akanthou Cyprus
128 D5 Akaroa N.Z.
128 D5 Akaroa Harbour N.Z.
145 H4 Akas reg. India
139 H3 Akbakay Kazakh.
139 I3 Akbalyk Kazakh.
141 H3 Akbar Khēl Afgh.
145 E4 Akbarpur India
138 E3 Akbasty Kazakh.
139 H2 Akbaur Kazakh.
139 G2 Akbeyit Kazakh.
167 I4 Akbou Alg.
139 I2 Akbulak Vostochnyy Kazakhstan Kazakh.
139 K2 Akbulak Vostochnyy Kazakhstan Kazakh.
138 B2 Akbulak Kazakh.
138 C2 Akbulak Rus. Fed.
136 F2 Akçadağ Turkey
137 G3 Akçakale Turkey
136 C1 Akçakoca Turkey
136 D3 Akçali Dağ mt. Turkey
136 C3 Akdağ mt. Turkey
136 C3 Ak Dağı mt. Turkey
137 H2 Ak Dağı mts Turkey
136 E2 Akdağmadeni Turkey
138 D4 Akdepe Turkm.
159 L4 Åkersberga Sweden
164 C2 Akersloot Neth.
138 E3 Akespe Kazakh.
178 C3 Aketi Dem. Rep. Congo
138 C4 Akgyr Erezi hills Turkm.
137 I1 Akhalkalaki Georgia
173 G7 Akhaltsikhe Georgia
145 G5 Akhaura Bangl.
177 E1 Akhḑar, Al Jabal al mts Libya
142 E5 Akhḑar, Jabal mts Oman
136 A2 Akhisar Turkey
136 F3 Akhtarīn Syria
173 H5 Akhtubinsk Rus. Fed.
138 D1 Akhunovo Rus. Fed.
137 I1 Akhuryan Armenia
151 C8 Aki Japan
188 D3 Akimiski Island Canada
136 E3 Akıncı Burun pt Turkey
136 G1 Akıncılar Turkey
150 G5 Akita Japan
176 A3 Akjoujt Mauritania
138 E2 Akkabak Kazakh.
158 L2 Akkajaure l. Sweden
Akkala Uzbek. see Oqqal'a
138 E2 Akkarga Kazakh.
139 G3 Akkense Kazakh.
138 D2 Akkermanovka Rus. Fed.
150 I3 Akkeshi Japan
138 B3 Akkistau Kazakh.
136 E5 'Akko Israel
139 G2 Akkol' Akmolinskaya Oblast' Kazakh.
139 H3 Akkol' Almatinskaya Oblast' Kazakh.
138 B3 Akkol' Atyrauskaya Oblast' Kazakh.
139 G4 Akkol' Zhambylskaya Oblast' Kazakh.
139 G4 Akkol', Ozero salt l. Kazakh.
139 I2 Akku Kazakh.
138 F3 Akkum Kazakh.
136 F1 Akkuş Turkey
Akkyr, Gory hills Turkm. see Akgyr Erezi
144 D4 Aklera India
159 M4 Akmeņrags pt Latvia
144 D1 Akmeqit China
Akmola Kazakh. see Astana
139 G2 Akmolinskaya Oblast' admin. div. Kazakh.
139 I4 Ak-Moyun Kyrg.
151 D7 Akō Japan
177 F4 Akobo South Sudan
144 D5 Akola India
139 I4 Akongkür China
178 D2 Akordat Eritrea
136 D3 Akören Turkey
144 D5 Akot India
139 H2 Akoy Kazakh.
189 G1 Akpatok Island Canada
139 I4 Akqi China
158 B2 Akranes Iceland
159 I4 Åkrehamn Norway
194 G3 Akron CO U.S.A.
202 C4 Akron OH U.S.A.
202 C4 Akron City Reservoir U.S.A.
144 D2 Aksai Chin terr. Asia
136 E2 Aksaray Turkey
139 H4 Ak-Say r. Kyrg.
173 F6 Aksay Rus. Fed.
144 D2 Aksayqin Hu l. China
136 C2 Akşehir Turkey
136 C2 Akşehir Gölü l. Turkey
136 C3 Akseki Turkey
138 C1 Aksenovo Rus. Fed.
140 D4 Aks-e Rostam r. Iran
138 C2 Akshatau Kazakh.
139 H3 Akshatau Kazakh.
139 I4 Akshi Kazakh.
138 E2 Akshiganak Kazakh.
138 B4 Akshukyr Kazakh.
138 C3 Akshymyrau Kazakh.
139 J4 Aksu Xinjiang China
139 J4 Aksu Xinjiang China
139 I3 Aksu Almatinskaya Oblast' Kazakh.
139 I1 Aksu Pavlodarskaya Oblast' Kazakh.
139 G1 Aksu Severnyy Kazakhstan Kazakh.
139 G4 Aksu Yuzhnyy Kazakhstan Kazakh.
138 C2 Aksu Zapadnyy Kazakhstan Kazakh.
139 I3 Aksu r. Kazakh.
136 C3 Aksu r. Turkey
138 F2 Aksuat Kustanayskaya Oblast' Kazakh.
139 J3 Aksuat Vostochnyy Kazakhstan Kazakh.
139 H2 Aksu-Ayuly Kazakh.
139 J4 Aksu He r. China
178 D2 Āksum Eth.
139 F3 Aksumbe Kazakh.
139 H3 Aksuyek Kazakh.
145 F1 Aktag mt. China
138 F2 Aktas Kazakh.
137 J2 Aktas Dağı mt. Turkey
137 I1 Aktaş Gölü l. Georgia
Aktash Uzbek. see Oqtosh
139 G3 Aktau Karagandinskaya Oblast' Kazakh.
139 H2 Aktau Karagandinskaya Oblast' Kazakh.
138 B4 Aktau Mangistauskaya Oblast' Kazakh.
139 I5 Akto China
138 D2 Aktobe Kazakh.
139 H2 Aktogay Karagandinskaya Oblast' Kazakh.
139 H1 Aktogay Pavlodarskaya Oblast' Kazakh.
139 I3 Aktogay Vostochnyy Kazakhstan Kazakh.
169 N4 Aktsyabrski Belarus
139 F2 Aktuma (abandoned) Kazakh.
138 D3 Aktumsyk Kazakh.
138 D3 Aktumsyk, Mys pt Uzbek.
139 H4 Ak-Tüz Kyrg.
138 D2 Aktyubinskaya Oblast' admin. div. Kazakh.
151 B8 Akune Japan
176 C4 Akure Nigeria
158 C2 Akureyri Iceland
145 G1 Akxokesay China
Akyab Myanmar see Sittwe
139 H3 Akzhal Karagandinskaya Oblast' Kazakh.
139 J2 Akzhal Vostochnyy Kazakhstan Kazakh.
138 D2 Akzhar Aktyubinskaya Oblast' Kazakh.
138 F3 Akzhar Kzyl-Ordinskaya Oblast' Kazakh.
139 J3 Akzhar Vostochnyy Kazakhstan Kazakh.
139 G4 Akzhar Zhambylskaya Oblast' Kazakh.
139 F3 Akzhaykyn, Ozero salt l. Kazakh.
136 G3 Akziyaret Turkey
159 J3 Ål Norway
140 C5 Al 'Abā Saudi Arabia
201 C6 Alabama r. U.S.A.
201 C5 Alabama state U.S.A.
201 C5 Alabaster U.S.A.
153 B3 Alabat i. Phil.
137 J7 Al 'Abţīyah well Iraq
139 G4 Ala-Buka Kyrg.
177 E1 Al Abyār Libya
136 E1 Alaca Turkey
136 F2 Alacahan Turkey
136 E1 Alaçam Turkey
136 B2 Alaçam Dağları mts Turkey
207 G3 Alacrán, Arrecife rf Mex.
137 I2 Ala Dag mt. Turkey
137 I2 Ala Dağlar mts Turkey
136 E3 Ala Dağları mts Turkey
173 H7 Alagir Rus. Fed.
211 K6 Alagoinhas Brazil
167 F2 Alagón Spain
153 C5 Alah r. Phil.
158 M3 Alahärmä Fin.
137 K7 Al Aḩmadī Kuwait
140 D5 Al Ain, Cultural Sites of tourist site U.A.E.
139 G5 Alai Range mts Asia
158 M3 Alajärvi Fin.
206 H6 Alajuela Costa Rica
137 K2 Alajujeh Iran
144 D3 Alaknanda r. India
139 J3 Alakol', Ozero salt l. Kazakh.
158 O2 Alakurtti Rus. Fed.
136 B6 Al 'Alamayn Egypt
210 F4 Alalaú r. Brazil
137 I3 Al 'Amādīyah Iraq
140 B5 Al 'Amār Saudi Arabia
137 K6 Al 'Amārah Iraq
Alamdo China see Alando
137 J7 Al Amghar waterhole Iraq
153 A2 Alaminos Phil.
136 B6 Al 'Āmirīyah Egypt
206 D2 Alamítos, Sierra de los mt. Mex.
197 E3 Alamo U.S.A.
197 F4 Alamo Dam U.S.A.
195 F5 Alamogordo U.S.A.
199 D6 Alamo Heights U.S.A.
195 E6 Alamos Sonora Mex.
206 B2 Alamos Sonora Mex.
195 F4 Alamosa U.S.A.
143 B3 Alampur India
158 K2 Alanäs Sweden
Åland is Fin. see Åland Islands
165 J1 Aland r. Germany
143 B2 Aland India
140 B2 Aland r. Iran
159 L3 Åland Islands Fin.
145 H3 Alando China
154 B5 Alang Besar i. Indon.
Alaniya aut. rep. Rus. Fed. see Severnaya Osetiya-Alaniya, Respublika
190 E3 Alanson U.S.A.
136 D3 Alanya Turkey
140 D4 'Alā' od Dīn Iran
136 C1 Alaplı Turkey
143 B4 Alappuzha India
136 E7 Al 'Aqabah Jordan
141 F3 'Alāqahdārī Gulistān Afgh.
140 C6 Al 'Āqūlah well Saudi Arabia
167 E3 Alarcón, Embalse de resr Spain
136 D6 Al 'Arīsh Egypt
142 C4 Al Arţāwīyah Saudi Arabia
155 E4 Alas Indon.
136 B2 Alaşehir Turkey
137 I6 Al 'Āshūrīyah well Iraq
184 D3 Alaska state U.S.A.
184 D4 Alaska, Gulf of U.S.A.
186 E3 Alaska Highway Canada/U.S.A.
184 B4 Alaska Peninsula U.S.A.
184 D3 Alaska Range mts U.S.A.
137 L2 Älät Azer.
Alat Uzbek. see Olot
137 I6 Al 'Athāmīn hills Iraq
172 H4 Alatyr' Rus. Fed.
172 H4 Alatyr' r. Rus. Fed.
210 C4 Alausí Ecuador
137 J1 Alaverdi Armenia
158 N2 Alavieska Fin.
158 M3 Alavus Fin.
126 D5 Alawoona Australia
137 K1 Alazani r. Azer./Georgia
137 J5 Al 'Azīzīyah Iraq
177 D1 Al 'Azīzīyah Libya
170 C2 Alba Italy
136 F3 Al Bāb Syria
167 F3 Albacete Spain
126 D5 Albacutya, Lake dry lake Australia
137 J6 Al Bādiyah al Janūbīyah des. Iraq
171 J1 Alba Iulia Romania
188 F3 Albanel, Lac Canada
171 I4 Albania country Europe
124 B5 Albany Australia
188 C3 Albany r. Canada
201 C6 Albany GA U.S.A.
190 E5 Albany IN U.S.A.
200 C4 Albany KY U.S.A.
203 G3 Albany NY U.S.A.
194 B2 Albany OR U.S.A.
127 H1 Albany Downs Australia
140 B5 Al Barrah Saudi Arabia
Al Başrah Iraq see Basra
137 J6 Al Baţḩa' marsh Iraq
124 E3 Albatross Bay Australia
127 F8 Albatross Island Australia
Al Bawiti Egypt see Al Bawīţī
177 E2 Al Bawīţī Egypt
177 E1 Al Bayḑā' Libya
210 □ Albemarle, Punta pt Galapagos Is Ecuador
201 E5 Albemarle Sound sea chan. U.S.A.
170 C2 Albenga Italy
167 D3 Alberche r. Spain
124 D4 Alberga watercourse Australia
167 B2 Albergaria-a-Velha Port.
127 G4 Albert Australia
166 F2 Albert France
126 C5 Albert, Lake Australia
178 D3 Albert, Lake Dem. Rep. Congo/Uganda
186 F4 Alberta prov. Canada
202 E6 Alberta U.S.A.
186 F4 Alberta, Mount Canada
180 D7 Albertinia S. Africa
164 D4 Albert Kanaal canal Belgium
198 E3 Albert Lea U.S.A.
178 D3 Albert Nile r. South Sudan/Uganda
212 B8 Alberto de Agostini, Parque Nacional nat. park Chile
181 H3 Alberton S. Africa
166 H4 Albertville France
164 E6 Albestroff France
166 F5 Albi France
211 H2 Albina Suriname
196 A2 Albion CA U.S.A.
203 I2 Albion ME U.S.A.
190 E4 Albion MI U.S.A.
202 D3 Albion NY U.S.A.
167 E5 Alborán, Isla de i. Spain
167 D4 Alboran Sea Europe
Ålborg Denmark see Aalborg
Ålborg Bugt b. Denmark see Aalborg Bugt
Alborz, Reshteh-ye mts Iran see Elburz Mountains
186 F4 Albreda Canada
Al Budayyi Bahrain see Al Budayyi'
140 C5 Al Budayyi' Bahrain
167 B4 Albufeira Port.
195 F5 Albuquerque U.S.A.
206 I5 Albuquerque, Cayos de is Col.
142 E5 Al Buraymī Oman
167 C3 Alburquerque Spain
127 G6 Albury Australia
137 H4 Al Buşayrah Syria
136 G7 Al Busayţā' plain Saudi Arabia
137 K6 Al Buşayyah Iraq
140 B4 Al Bushūk well Saudi Arabia
167 B3 Alcácer do Sal Port.
167 E2 Alcalá de Henares Spain
167 E4 Alcalá la Real Spain
170 E6 Alcamo Sicily Italy
167 F2 Alcañiz Spain
167 C3 Alcántara Spain
167 E3 Alcaraz Spain
167 D4 Alcaudete Spain
167 E3 Alcázar de San Juan Spain
173 F5 Alchevs'k Ukr.
215 D2 Alcira Arg.
214 E2 Alcobaça Brazil
215 E2 Alcorta Arg.
Alcoy Spain see Alcoy-Alcoi
167 F3 Alcoy-Alcoi Spain
167 H3 Alcúdia Spain
179 E4 Aldabra Islands Seychelles
206 C1 Aldama Chihuahua Mex.
207 E3 Aldama Tamaulipas Mex.
133 N4 Aldan Rus. Fed.
133 O3 Aldan r. Rus. Fed.
164 D1 Aldeboarn Neth.
161 I5 Aldeburgh U.K.
166 D2 Alderney i. U.K.
196 B4 Alder Peak U.S.A.
161 G6 Aldershot U.K.
202 C6 Alderson U.S.A.
140 D6 Al Dhafrah reg. U.A.E.
160 D3 Aldingham U.K.
161 F5 Aldridge U.K.
190 B5 Aledo U.S.A.
176 A3 Aleg Mauritania
214 E3 Alegre Brazil
212 E3 Alegrete Brazil
215 E2 Alejandro Korn Arg.
172 E2 Alekhovshchina Rus. Fed.
138 B4 Aleksandra Bekovicha-Cherkasskogo, Zaliv b. Kazakh.
172 F3 Aleksandrov Rus. Fed.
173 I5 Aleksandrov Gay Rus. Fed.
138 C1 Aleksandrovka Orenburgskaya Oblast' Rus. Fed.
138 D1 Aleksandrovka Respublika Bashkortostan Rus. Fed.
173 H6 Aleksandrovskoye Rus. Fed.
133 P4 Aleksandrovsk-Sakhalinskiy Rus. Fed.
132 F1 Aleksandry, Zemlya i. Rus. Fed.
139 G1 Alekseyevka Kokshetauskaya Oblast' Kazakh.
173 F5 Alekseyevka Belgorodskaya Oblast' Rus. Fed.
173 F5 Alekseyevka Belgorodskaya Oblast' Rus. Fed.
173 G5 Alekseyevskaya Rus. Fed.
172 F4 Aleksin Rus. Fed.
171 I3 Aleksinac Serbia
178 B4 Alèmbé Gabon
136 E1 Alembeyli Turkey
214 D3 Além Paraíba Brazil
158 J3 Ålen Norway
166 E2 Alençon France
211 H4 Alenquer Brazil
196 □2 'Alenuihāhā Channel U.S.A.
136 F3 Aleppo Syria
185 M1 Alert Canada
210 D6 Alerta Peru
186 D4 Alert Bay Canada
166 G4 Alès France
169 K7 Aleşd Romania
170 C2 Alessandria Italy
158 I3 Ålesund Norway
216 G2 Aleutian Basin sea feature Bering Sea
182 C2 Aleutian Islands U.S.A.
184 C4 Aleutian Range mts U.S.A.
216 H2 Aleutian Trench sea feature N. Pacific Ocean
133 Q4 Alevina, Mys c. Rus. Fed.
203 J2 Alexander U.S.A.
186 B3 Alexander Archipelago is U.S.A.
180 B4 Alexander Bay b. Namibia/S. Africa
180 B4 Alexander Bay S. Africa
201 C5 Alexander City U.S.A.
129 B3 Alexander Island i. Antarctica
127 F6 Alexandra Australia
128 B6 Alexandra N.Z.
212 □ Alexandra, Cape Atlantic Ocean
171 J4 Alexandreia Greece
203 F2 Alexandria Canada
177 E1 Alexandria Egypt
171 K3 Alexandria Romania
181 G6 Alexandria S. Africa
162 D5 Alexandria U.K.
190 E5 Alexandria IN U.S.A.
199 E6 Alexandria LA U.S.A.
198 E2 Alexandria MN U.S.A.
202 E5 Alexandria VA U.S.A.
203 F2 Alexandria Bay U.S.A.
126 C5 Alexandrina, Lake Australia
171 K4 Alexandroupoli Greece
189 I3 Alexis r. Canada
190 B5 Alexis U.S.A.
186 E4 Alexis Creek Canada
139 J1 Aley r. Rus. Fed.
139 J1 Aleysk Rus. Fed.
164 F4 Alf Germany
167 F1 Alfaro Spain
137 K7 Al Farwānīyah Kuwait
137 I4 Al Fatḩah Iraq
137 L7 Al Fāw Iraq
177 F2 Al Fayyūm Egypt
165 H3 Alfeld (Leine) Germany
214 D3 Alfenas Brazil
137 L7 Al Finţās Kuwait
169 J7 Alföld plain Hungary
161 H4 Alford U.K.
203 F2 Alfred Canada
203 H3 Alfred U.S.A.
137 L7 Al Fuḩayḩīl Kuwait
Al Fujayrah U.A.E. see Fujairah

137 J6 **Al Furāt** r. Iraq/Syria
alt. **Fırat (Turkey)**
conv. **Euphrates**
138 D2 **Alga** Kazakh.
138 C2 **Algabas** Kazakh.
159 I4 **Ålgård** Norway
215 C3 **Algarrobo del Aguilla** Arg.
167 B4 **Algarve** reg. Port.
172 G4 **Algasovo** Rus. Fed.
167 D4 **Algeciras** Spain
167 F3 **Algemesí** Spain
**Alger** Alg. see **Algiers**
191 E3 **Alger** U.S.A.
176 B2 **Algeria** country Africa
165 H2 **Algermissen** Germany
137 J6 **Al Ghammās** Iraq
140 B5 **Al Ghāṭ** Saudi Arabia
142 D6 **Al Ghayḍah** Yemen
170 C4 **Alghero** Sardinia Italy
177 F2 **Al Ghurdaqah** Egypt
142 C4 **Al Ghwaybiyah** Saudi Arabia
176 C1 **Algiers** Alg.
181 F6 **Algoa Bay** S. Africa
190 D3 **Algoma** U.S.A.
198 E3 **Algona** U.S.A.
191 F4 **Algonac** U.S.A.
191 H3 **Algonquin Park** Canada
191 H3 **Algonquin Provincial Park** Canada
167 E1 **Algorta** Spain
137 I7 **Al Habakah** well Saudi Arabia
137 I5 **Al Ḩabbānīyah** Iraq
140 B4 **Al Ḩadaqah** well Saudi Arabia
140 C5 **Al Ḩadd** Bahrain
140 A4 **Al Hadhālīl** plat. Saudi Arabia
137 I4 **Al Ḩadīthah** Iraq
140 A3 **Al Ḩaḍr** Iraq
136 F4 **Al Ḩaffah** Syria
140 B5 **Al Ḩā'ir** Saudi Arabia
141 E6 **Al Hajar** Oman
140 E5 **Al Ḩajar al Gharbī** mts Oman
137 G6 **Al Ḩamād** plain Jordan/Saudi Arabia
167 F4 **Alhama de Murcia** Spain
136 B6 **Al Ḩammām** Egypt
137 I6 **Al Hammām** well Iraq
137 J7 **Al Haniyah** esc. Iraq
140 B6 **Al Hariq** Saudi Arabia
137 G6 **Al Ḩarrah** reg. Saudi Arabia
137 H3 **Al Ḩasakah** Syria
137 J5 **Al Hāshimīyah** Iraq
137 K5 **Al Ḩayy** Iraq
136 F6 **Al Hazīm** Jordan
137 J5 **Al Ḩillah** Iraq
140 B6 **Al Ḩillah** Saudi Arabia
140 B6 **Al Ḩilwah** Saudi Arabia
140 C5 **Al Ḩinnāh** Saudi Arabia
176 B1 **Al Hoceima** Morocco
**Al Ḩudaydah** Yemen see **Hodeidah**
142 C4 **Al Hufūf** Saudi Arabia
140 D6 **Al Ḩumrah** reg. U.A.E.
140 C5 **Al Ḩunayy** Saudi Arabia
140 B6 **Al Huwwah** Saudi Arabia
140 D2 **'Alīābād** Iran
141 E3 **'Alīābād** Iran
141 F4 **'Alīābād** Iran
137 K3 **'Alīābād** Iran
137 K4 **'Alīābād** Iran
171 L5 **Aliağa** Turkey
171 J4 **Aliakmonas** r. Greece
137 K5 **'Alī al Gharbī** Iraq
143 A2 **Alibag** India
144 B4 **Ali Bandar** Pak.
167 F3 **Alicante** Spain
181 G6 **Alice** S. Africa
199 D7 **Alice** U.S.A.
186 D3 **Alice Arm** Canada
124 D4 **Alice Springs** Australia
201 E7 **Alice Town** Bahamas
139 H5 **Alichur** Tajik.
139 H5 **Alichur** r. Tajik.
153 B5 **Alicia** Phil.
144 D4 **Aligarh** India
140 C3 **Alīgūdarz** Iran
146 E1 **Alihe** China
178 B4 **Alima** r. Congo
159 K4 **Alingsås** Sweden
136 B2 **Aliova** r. Turkey
144 B3 **Alipur** Pak.
145 G4 **Alipur Duar** India
202 C4 **Aliquippa** U.S.A.
178 E2 **Ali Sabieh** Djibouti
136 F6 **Al 'Īsāwīyah** Saudi Arabia
137 J2 **'Alī Shāh** Iran
**Al Iskandarīyah** Egypt see **Alexandria**
137 J5 **Al Iskandarīyah** Iraq
177 F1 **Al Ismā'īlīyah** Egypt
171 K5 **Aliveri** Greece
181 G5 **Aliwal North** S. Africa
186 G4 **Alix** Canada
136 F6 **Al Jafr** Jordan
140 C5 **Al Jāfūrah** des. Saudi Arabia
177 E2 **Al Jaghbūb** Libya
137 K7 **Al Jahrah** Kuwait
140 C6 **Al Jawb** reg. Saudi Arabia
177 E2 **Al Jawf** Libya
177 D1 **Al Jawsh** Libya
137 G3 **Al Jazā'ir** reg. Iraq/Syria
167 B4 **Aljezur** Port.
140 C5 **Al Jībān** reg. Saudi Arabia
137 I6 **Al Jil** well Iraq
140 B5 **Al Jilh** esc. Saudi Arabia
140 C5 **Al Jishshah** Saudi Arabia
**Al Jīzah** Egypt see **Giza**
136 E6 **Al Jīzah** Jordan
142 C4 **Al Jubayl** Saudi Arabia
140 B5 **Al Jubaylah** Saudi Arabia
140 C5 **Al Jumaylīyah** Qatar
140 C5 **Al Jurayd** i. Saudi Arabia
140 B5 **Al Jurayfah** Saudi Arabia
167 B4 **Aljustrel** Port.
136 E6 **Al Karak** Jordan
139 G1 **Alkaterek** Kazakh.
137 J5 **Al Kāẓimīyah** Iraq
142 E5 **Al Khābūrah** Oman
137 J5 **Al Khāliş** Iraq
177 F2 **Al Khārijah** Egypt
142 E4 **Al Khaşab** Oman
140 A6 **Al Khāşirah** Saudi Arabia
140 D6 **Al Khatam** reg. U.A.E.
140 C5 **Al Khawr** Qatar
140 C5 **Al Khīşah** well Saudi Arabia
140 C5 **Al Khobar** Saudi Arabia
140 B5 **Al Khuff** reg. Saudi Arabia
177 D1 **Al Khums** Libya
137 J5 **Al Kifl** Iraq
140 C5 **Al Kir'ānah** Qatar
164 C2 **Alkmaar** Neth.
137 J5 **Al Kūfah** Iraq
177 E2 **Al Kufrah** Libya
137 K5 **Al Kumayt** Iraq
137 J5 **Al Kūt** Iraq
**Al Kuwayt** Kuwait see **Kuwait**
137 H7 **Al Labbah** plain Saudi Arabia
**Al Lādhiqīyah** Syria see **Latakia**
203 I1 **Allagash** U.S.A.
203 I1 **Allagash** r. U.S.A.
203 I1 **Allagash Lake** U.S.A.
145 E4 **Allahabad** India
136 F5 **Al Lajā** lava field Syria
133 O3 **Allakh-Yun'** Rus. Fed.
181 G3 **Allanridge** S. Africa
181 H1 **Alldays** S. Africa
190 E4 **Allegan** U.S.A.
202 D4 **Allegheny** r. U.S.A.
202 C6 **Allegheny Mountains** U.S.A.
202 D4 **Allegheny Reservoir** U.S.A.
163 C3 **Allen, Lough** l. Ireland
201 D5 **Allendale** U.S.A.
160 E3 **Allendale Town** U.K.
206 D1 **Allende** Coahuila Mex.
207 D2 **Allende** Nuevo León Mex.
165 G4 **Allendorf (Lumda)** Germany
191 G3 **Allenford** Canada
203 F4 **Allentown** U.S.A.
**Alleppey** India see **Alappuzha**
165 I2 **Aller** r. Germany
198 C3 **Alliance** NE U.S.A.
202 C4 **Alliance** OH U.S.A.
137 I6 **Al Līfīyah** well Iraq
159 K5 **Allinge-Sandvig** Denmark
191 H3 **Alliston** Canada
142 B5 **Al Līth** Saudi Arabia
162 E4 **Alloa** U.K.
127 J2 **Allora** Australia
143 C3 **Allur** India
143 C3 **Alluru Kottapatnam** India
137 I6 **Al Lussuf** well Iraq
189 F4 **Alma** Canada
190 E4 **Alma** MI U.S.A.
198 D3 **Alma** NE U.S.A.
197 H5 **Alma** NM U.S.A.
137 I6 **Al Ma'ānīyah** Iraq
**Alma-Ata** Kazakh. see **Almaty**
167 B3 **Almada** Port.
137 J7 **Al Ma'danīyāt** well Iraq
167 D3 **Almadén** Spain
137 K6 **Al Madīnah** Iraq
**Al Madīnah** Saudi Arabia see **Medina**
136 F5 **Al Mafraq** Jordan
137 J5 **Al Maḩmūdīyah** Iraq
140 B5 **Al Majma'ah** Saudi Arabia
137 K1 **Almalı** Azer.
140 C5 **Al Malsūnīyah** reg. Saudi Arabia
**Almalyk** Uzbek. see **Olmaliq**
**Al Manāmah** Bahrain see **Manama**
196 B1 **Almanor, Lake** U.S.A.
167 F3 **Almansa** Spain
177 F1 **Al Manşūrah** Egypt
167 D2 **Almanzor** mt. Spain
137 K6 **Al Ma'qil** Iraq
140 D6 **Al Mariyyah** U.A.E.
177 E1 **Al Marj** Libya
214 C1 **Almas, Rio das** r. Brazil
139 H3 **Almatinskaya Oblast'** admin. div. Kazakh.
139 I4 **Almaty** Kazakh.
**Al Mawşil** Iraq see **Mosul**
137 H4 **Al Mayādīn** Syria
140 B5 **Al Mazāḩimīyah** Saudi Arabia
167 E2 **Almazán** Spain
133 M3 **Almaznyy** Rus. Fed.
211 H4 **Almeirim** Brazil
167 B3 **Almeirim** Port.
164 E2 **Almelo** Neth.
214 E2 **Almenara** Brazil
167 C2 **Almendra, Embalse de** resr Spain
167 C3 **Almendralejo** Spain
164 D2 **Almere** Neth.
167 E4 **Almería** Spain
167 E4 **Almería, Golfo de** b. Spain
132 G4 **Al'met'yevsk** Rus. Fed.
159 K4 **Älmhult** Sweden
140 B5 **Al Midhnab** Saudi Arabia
167 D5 **Almina, Punta** pt Morocco
177 F2 **Al Minyā** Egypt
206 I6 **Almirante** Panama
142 C4 **Al Mish'āb** Saudi Arabia
136 F5 **Al Mismīyah** Syria
167 B4 **Almodôvar** Port.
191 F4 **Almont** U.S.A.
191 I3 **Almonte** Canada
167 C4 **Almonte** Spain
142 C4 **Al Mubarrez** Saudi Arabia
136 E7 **Al Mudawwarah** Jordan
**Al Muharraq** Bahrain see **Al Muḩarraq**
140 C5 **Al Muḩarraq** Bahrain
**Al Mukallā** Yemen see **Mukalla**
**Al Mukhā** Yemen see **Mocha**
167 E4 **Almuñécar** Spain
137 J5 **Al Muqdādīyah** Iraq
140 B5 **Al Murabba** Saudi Arabia
136 F1 **Almus** Turkey
140 B4 **Al Musannāh** ridge Saudi Arabia
137 J5 **Al Musayyib** Iraq
171 K7 **Almyrou, Ormos** b. Greece
**Alna Haina** U.S.A. see **'Āina Haina**
160 F2 **Alnwick** U.K.
125 J3 **Alofi** Niue
145 H5 **Alon** Myanmar
145 H3 **Along** India
171 J5 **Alonnisos** i. Greece
147 E7 **Alor** i. Indon.
147 E7 **Alor, Kepulauan** is Indon.
155 B1 **Alor Star** Malaysia
**Alost** Belgium see **Aalst**
144 C5 **Alot** India
158 O2 **Alozero (abandoned)** Rus. Fed.
196 C4 **Alpaugh** U.S.A.
164 E3 **Alpen** Germany
191 F3 **Alpena** U.S.A.
220 P1 **Alpha Ridge** sea feature Arctic Ocean
197 H5 **Alpine** AZ U.S.A.
199 C6 **Alpine** TX U.S.A.
194 E3 **Alpine** WY U.S.A.
174 F4 **Alpine National Park** Australia
170 C1 **Alps** mts Europe
142 C6 **Al Qa'āmīyāt** reg. Saudi Arabia
177 D1 **Al Qaddāḩīyah** Libya
136 F4 **Al Qadmūs** Syria
**Al Qāhirah** Egypt see **Cairo**
140 B5 **Al Qā'īyah** well Saudi Arabia
137 H3 **Al Qāmishlī** Syria
136 D6 **Al Qanţarah** Egypt
140 B5 **Al Qar'ah** well Saudi Arabia
136 F4 **Al Qaryatayn** Syria
140 B5 **Al Qaşab** Saudi Arabia
142 C6 **Al Qaţn** Yemen
136 F6 **Al Qaţrānah** Jordan
177 D2 **Al Qaţrūn** Libya
140 B4 **Al Qayşūmah** Saudi Arabia
177 E1 **Al Qubbah** Libya
167 C3 **Alqueva, Barragem de** resr Port.
136 E5 **Al Qunayţirah (abandoned)** Syria
142 B6 **Al Qunfidhah** Saudi Arabia
140 A5 **Al Qurayn** Saudi Arabia
137 K6 **Al Qurnah** Iraq
177 F2 **Al Quşayr** Egypt
137 J6 **Al Qusayr** Iraq
140 B6 **Al Qūşūrīyah** Saudi Arabia
136 F5 **Al Quţayfah** Syria
140 A5 **Al Quwārah** Saudi Arabia
140 B6 **Al Quwayi'** Saudi Arabia
140 B5 **Al Quwayīyah** Saudi Arabia
136 E7 **Al Quwayrah** Jordan
166 H2 **Alsace** reg. France
161 E4 **Alsager** U.K.
137 I6 **Al Samīt** well Iraq
187 H4 **Alsask** Canada
165 H4 **Alsfeld** Germany
165 J3 **Alsleben (Saale)** Germany
160 E3 **Alston** U.K.
127 J2 **Alstonville** Australia
159 M4 **Alsunga** Latvia
158 M1 **Alta** Norway
128 B6 **Alta, Mount** N.Z.
158 M1 **Altaelva** r. Norway
158 M1 **Altafjorden** sea chan. Norway
215 D1 **Alta Gracia** Arg.
213 D2 **Altagracía de Orituco** Venez.
135 G2 **Altai Mountains** China/Mongolia
201 D6 **Altamaha** r. U.S.A.
211 H4 **Altamira** Brazil
206 H6 **Altamira** Costa Rica
170 G4 **Altamura** Italy
148 C2 **Altan Xiret** China
206 C2 **Altata** Mex.
202 D6 **Altavista** U.S.A.
135 G2 **Altay** China
146 B2 **Altay** Mongolia
139 K2 **Altay, Respublika** aut. rep. Rus. Fed.
139 J1 **Altayskiy Kray** admin. div. Rus. Fed.
139 K2 **Altayskoye** Rus. Fed.
167 F3 **Altea** Spain
158 M1 **Alteidet** Norway
164 E4 **Altenahr** Germany
164 F2 **Altenberge** Germany
165 K4 **Altenburg** Germany
164 F4 **Altenkirchen (Westerwald)** Germany
145 H1 **Altenqoke** China
165 L1 **Altentreptow** Germany
137 L1 **Altıağaç** Azer.
137 J4 **Altin Köprü** Iraq
171 L5 **Altınoluk** Turkey
136 C2 **Altıntaş** Turkey
210 E7 **Altiplano** plain Bol.
165 J2 **Altmark** reg. Germany
165 I5 **Altmühl** r. Germany
214 B2 **Alto Araguaia** Brazil
214 B2 **Alto Garças** Brazil
210 E6 **Alto Madidi, Parque Nacional** nat. park Bolivia/Chile
179 D5 **Alto Molócuè** Moz.
200 B4 **Alton** IL U.S.A.
199 F4 **Alton** MO U.S.A.
203 H3 **Alton** NH U.S.A.
198 D1 **Altona** Canada
202 D4 **Altoona** U.S.A.
214 C1 **Alto Paraíso de Goiás** Brazil
214 B2 **Alto Sucuriú** Brazil
214 B2 **Alto Taquarí** Brazil
168 F6 **Altötting** Germany
161 E4 **Altrincham** U.K.
165 K1 **Alt Schwerin** Germany
207 G4 **Altun Ha** tourist site Belize
146 A3 **Altun Shan** mts China
194 B3 **Alturas** U.S.A.
199 D5 **Altus** U.S.A.
138 E3 **Altynasar** tourist site Kazakh.
136 G1 **Alucra** Turkey
159 N4 **Alūksne** Latvia
137 L5 **Alūm** Iran
202 B4 **Alum Creek Lake** U.S.A.
215 B3 **Aluminé** r. Arg.
215 B3 **Aluminé, Lago** l. Arg.
173 E6 **Alupka** Ukr.
177 D1 **Al 'Uqaylah** Libya
140 C5 **Al 'Uqayr** Saudi Arabia
**Al Uqşur** Egypt see **Luxor**
173 E6 **Alushta** Ukr.
137 J4 **'Ālūt** Iran
143 B4 **Aluva** India
177 E2 **Al 'Uwaynāt** Libya
137 I6 **Al 'Uwayqīlah** Saudi Arabia
140 A5 **Al 'Uyūn** Saudi Arabia
137 K6 **Al 'Uzayr** Iraq
199 D4 **Alva** U.S.A.
137 L4 **Alvand, Kūh-e** mt. Iran
207 F4 **Alvarado** Mex.
215 C2 **Alvarado, Paso de** pass Chile
210 F4 **Alvarães** Brazil
159 J3 **Alvdal** Norway
159 K3 **Älvdalen** Sweden
159 K4 **Alvesta** Sweden
159 I3 **Ålvik** Norway
159 L3 **Alvik** Sweden
199 E6 **Alvin** U.S.A.
158 M2 **Älvsbyn** Sweden
137 K7 **Al Wafrah** Kuwait
134 B4 **Al Wajh** Saudi Arabia
140 C5 **Al Wakrah** Qatar
140 C5 **Al Wannān** Saudi Arabia
144 D4 **Alwar** India
140 B5 **Al Warī'ah** Saudi Arabia
137 H5 **Al Widyān** plat. Iraq/Saudi Arabia
140 B4 **Al Wusayţ** well Saudi Arabia
124 D3 **Alyangula** Australia
162 E4 **Alyth** U.K.
159 N5 **Alytus** Lith.
194 F2 **Alzada** U.S.A.
164 E5 **Alzette** r. Lux.
165 G5 **Alzey** Germany
213 E3 **Amacuro** r. Guyana/Venez.
124 D4 **Amadeus, Lake** salt flat Australia
185 K3 **Amadjuak Lake** Canada
197 G6 **Amado** U.S.A.
167 B3 **Amadora** Port.
151 A8 **Amakusa-nada** b. Japan
159 K4 **Åmål** Sweden
143 C2 **Amalapuram** India
146 D1 **Amalat** r. Rus. Fed.
213 B3 **Amalfi** Col.
180 F3 **Amalia** S. Africa
171 I6 **Amaliada** Greece
144 C5 **Amalner** India
147 F7 **Amamapare** Indon.
214 A3 **Amambaí** Brazil
214 A3 **Amambaí** r. Brazil
214 A3 **Amambaí, Serra de** hills Brazil/Para.
146 E4 **Amami-Ō-shima** i. Japan
146 E4 **Amami-shotō** is Japan
138 D2 **Amangel'dy** Kazakh.
138 F2 **Amankel'dy** Kazakh.
139 J4 **Amankol** China
138 E3 **Amanotkel'** Kazakh.
170 G5 **Amantea** Italy
211 H3 **Amapá** Brazil
167 C3 **Amareleja** Port.
196 D3 **Amargosa Desert** U.S.A.
196 D3 **Amargosa Range** mts U.S.A.
196 D3 **Amargosa Valley** U.S.A.
199 C5 **Amarillo** U.S.A.
170 F3 **Amaro, Monte** mt. Italy
144 E4 **Amarpatan** India
136 E1 **Amasya** Turkey
207 F4 **Amatán** Mex.
206 G5 **Amatique, Bahía de** b. Guat.
206 C3 **Amatlán de Cañas** Mex.
164 D4 **Amay** Belgium
211 H4 **Amazon** r. S. America
alt. **Amazonas**
211 I3 **Amazon, Mouths of the** Brazil
213 D4 **Amazonas** state Brazil
211 H4 **Amazonas** r. S. America
conv. **Amazon**
219 F5 **Amazon Cone** sea feature S. Atlantic Ocean
211 G4 **Amazònia, Parque Nacional** nat. park Brazil
144 C6 **Ambad** India
143 B2 **Ambajogai** India
144 D3 **Ambala** India
143 C5 **Ambalangoda** Sri Lanka
179 E6 **Ambalavao** Madag.
179 E5 **Ambanja** Madag.
141 E4 **Ambar** Iran
143 B4 **Ambasamudram** India
210 C4 **Ambato** Ecuador
179 E5 **Ambato Boeny** Madag.
179 E6 **Ambato Finandrahana** Madag.
179 E5 **Ambatolampy** Madag.
179 E5 **Ambatomainty** Madag.
179 E5 **Ambatondrazaka** Madag.
165 J5 **Amberg** Germany
207 H4 **Ambergris Caye** i. Belize
166 G4 **Ambérieu-en-Bugey** France
191 G3 **Amberley** Canada
145 E5 **Ambikapur** India
179 E5 **Ambilobe** Madag.
186 C3 **Ambition, Mount** Canada
160 F2 **Amble** U.K.
160 E3 **Ambleside** U.K.
164 D4 **Amblève** r. Belgium
179 E6 **Amboasary** Madag.
179 E5 **Ambohidratrimo** Madag.
179 E6 **Ambohimahasoa** Madag.
147 E7 **Ambon** Indon.
147 E7 **Ambon** i. Indon.
179 E6 **Ambositra** Madag.
179 E6 **Ambovombe** Madag.
197 E4 **Amboy** CA U.S.A.
190 C5 **Amboy** IL U.S.A.
203 F3 **Amboy Center** U.S.A.
179 B4 **Ambriz** Angola
125 G3 **Ambrym** i. Vanuatu
143 B3 **Ambur** India
**Amdo** China see **Lharigarbo**
206 C3 **Ameca** Mex.
164 D1 **Ameland** i. Neth.
202 E6 **Amelia Court House** U.S.A.
203 G4 **Amenia** U.S.A.
196 B2 **American, North Fork** r. U.S.A.
219 H9 **American-Antarctic Ridge** sea feature S. Atlantic Ocean
194 D3 **American Falls** U.S.A.
194 D3 **American Falls Reservoir** U.S.A.
197 G1 **American Fork** U.S.A.
123 H4 **American Samoa** Pacific Ocean
201 C5 **Americus** U.S.A.
164 D2 **Amersfoort** Neth.
181 H3 **Amersfoort** S. Africa
161 G6 **Amersham** U.K.
187 K3 **Amery** Canada
129 D5 **Amery Ice Shelf** ice feature Antarctica
198 E3 **Ames** U.S.A.
161 F6 **Amesbury** U.K.
203 H3 **Amesbury** U.S.A.
145 E4 **Amethi** India
171 J5 **Amfissa** Greece
133 O3 **Amga** Rus. Fed.
146 F2 **Amgu** Rus. Fed.
176 C2 **Amguid** Alg.
146 F1 **Amgun'** r. Rus. Fed.
189 H4 **Amherst** Canada
203 G3 **Amherst** MA U.S.A.
203 I2 **Amherst** ME U.S.A.
202 D6 **Amherst** VA U.S.A.
191 F4 **Amherstburg** Canada
170 D3 **Amiata, Monte** mt. Italy
166 F2 **Amiens** France
137 H5 **'Amīj, Wādī** watercourse Iraq
143 A4 **Amindivi Islands** India
151 D7 **Amino** Japan
180 C1 **Aminuis** Namibia
140 B3 **Amīrābād** Iran
219 M6 **Amirante Islands** Seychelles
218 H5 **Amirante Trench** sea feature Indian Ocean
141 F4 **Amir Chah** Pak.
187 I4 **Amisk Lake** Canada
199 C6 **Amistad Reservoir** Mex./U.S.A.
127 J1 **Amity Point** Australia
144 D5 **Amla** India
159 J4 **Åmli** Norway
161 C4 **Amlwch** U.K.
136 E6 **'Ammān** Jordan
161 D6 **Ammanford** U.K.
158 O2 **Ämmänsaari** Fin.
158 L2 **Ammarnäs** Sweden
185 O3 **Ammassalik** Greenland
165 F1 **Ammerland** reg. Germany
165 I3 **Ammern** Germany
168 E7 **Ammersee** l. Germany
**Ammochostos** Cyprus see **Famagusta**
154 C2 **Amnat Charoen** Thai.
152 D4 **Amnyong-dan** hd N. Korea
144 C5 **Amod** India
149 B6 **Amo Jiang** r. China
140 D2 **Āmol** Iran
165 H5 **Amorbach** Germany
171 K6 **Amorgos** i. Greece
188 E4 **Amos** Canada
**Amoy** China see **Xiamen**
143 C5 **Ampara** India
214 C3 **Amparo** Brazil
168 E6 **Amper** r. Germany
219 I3 **Ampere Seamount** sea feature N. Atlantic Ocean
167 G2 **Amposta** Spain
136 F6 **'Amrah, Qaşr** tourist site Jordan
144 D5 **Amravati** India
144 B5 **Amreli** India
144 B4 **Amri** Pak.
136 E4 **'Amrīt** Syria
144 C3 **Amritsar** India
144 D3 **Amroha** India
158 L2 **Åmsele** Sweden
164 C2 **Amstelveen** Neth.
164 C2 **Amsterdam** Neth. (City Plan **107**)
181 I3 **Amsterdam** S. Africa
203 F3 **Amsterdam** U.S.A.
218 J7 **Amsterdam, Île** i. Indian Ocean
168 G6 **Amstetten** Austria
177 E3 **Am Timan** Chad
138 D3 **Amudar'ya** r. Turkm./Uzbek.
185 I2 **Amund Ringnes Island** Canada
129 D6 **Amundsen, Mount** mt. Antarctica
217 K10 **Amundsen Abyssal Plain** sea feature Southern Ocean
220 B1 **Amundsen Basin** sea feature Arctic Ocean
129 E4 **Amundsen Bay** b. Antarctica
184 F2 **Amundsen Gulf** Canada
217 K10 **Amundsen Ridges** sea feature Southern Ocean
129 C4 **Amundsen-Scott** research stn Antarctica
217 L10 **Amundsen Sea** Antarctica
155 E3 **Amuntai** Indon.
146 E2 **Amur** r. China/Rus. Fed.
alt. **Heilong Jiang**
133 O4 **Amursk** Rus. Fed.
173 F6 **Amvrosiyivka** Ukr.
190 E1 **Amyot** Canada
145 H6 **An** Myanmar
217 J7 **Anaa** atoll Fr. Polynesia
147 E7 **Anabanua** Indon.
133 M2 **Anabar** r. Rus. Fed.
133 M2 **Anabarskiy Zaliv** b. Rus. Fed.
126 D4 **Ana Branch** r. Australia
196 C4 **Anacapa Island** U.S.A.
213 D2 **Anaco** Venez.
194 D2 **Anaconda** U.S.A.
194 B1 **Anacortes** U.S.A.
199 D5 **Anadarko** U.S.A.
136 D2 **Anadolu** reg. Turkey
136 F1 **Anadolu Dağları** mts Turkey
133 S3 **Anadyr'** Rus. Fed.
133 S3 **Anadyr'** r. Rus. Fed.
133 T3 **Anadyrskiy Zaliv** b. Rus. Fed.
171 K6 **Anafi** i. Greece
214 E1 **Anagé** Brazil
137 H4 **'Ānah** Iraq
196 D5 **Anaheim** U.S.A.
186 D4 **Anahim Lake** Canada
207 D2 **Anáhuac** Mex.
143 B4 **Anaimalai Hills** India
143 B4 **Anai Mudi** India
143 C2 **Anakapalle** India
179 E5 **Analalava** Madag.
210 F4 **Anamã** Brazil
155 C2 **Anambas, Kepulauan** is Indon.
190 B4 **Anamosa** U.S.A.
136 D3 **Anamur** Turkey
136 D3 **Anamur Burnu** pt Turkey
151 D8 **Anan** Japan
144 C5 **Anand** India
145 F5 **Anandapur** India
145 F5 **Anandpur** r. India
139 I4 **Anan'ev** Kyrg.
143 B3 **Anantapur** India
144 C2 **Anantnag** India
144 D4 **Anant Peth** India
173 D6 **Anan'yiv** Ukr.
173 F6 **Anapa** Rus. Fed.
214 C2 **Anápolis** Brazil
140 D4 **Anār** Iran
140 D3 **Anārak** Iran
140 C3 **Anarbar** r. Iran
141 F3 **Anār Darah** Afgh.
**Anatolia** reg. Turkey see **Anadolu**
125 G4 **Anatom** i. Vanuatu
212 D3 **Añatuya** Arg.
213 E4 **Anauá** r. Brazil
163 A6 **An Baile Breac** Ireland
140 C2 **Anbūh** Iran
163 C2 **An Bun Beag** Ireland
152 D4 **Anbyon** N. Korea
166 D3 **Ancenis** France
**Anchang** China see **Anxian**
184 D3 **Anchorage** U.S.A.
191 F4 **Anchor Bay** U.S.A.
143 B4 **Anchuthengu** India
141 F2 **Ancient Merv** tourist site Turkm.
163 C3 **An Clochán Liath** Ireland
170 E3 **Ancona** Italy
212 B6 **Ancud** Chile
215 B4 **Ancud, Golfo de** g. Chile
215 B1 **Andacollo** Chile
163 A5 **An Daingean** Ireland
145 F5 **Andal** India
158 I3 **Åndalsnes** Norway
167 D4 **Andalucía** aut. comm. Spain
199 G6 **Andalusia** U.S.A.
135 H6 **Andaman and Nicobar Islands** union terr. India
218 K4 **Andaman Basin** sea feature Indian Ocean
135 H5 **Andaman Islands** India
135 H5 **Andaman Sea** Asia
126 B3 **Andamooka** Australia
179 E5 **Andapa** Madag.
214 E1 **Andaraí** Brazil
158 L1 **Andenes** Norway
164 D4 **Andenne** Belgium
164 C4 **Anderlecht** Belgium
166 D4 **Andernos-les-Bains** France
184 F3 **Anderson** r. Canada
184 D3 **Anderson** AK U.S.A.
190 E5 **Anderson** IN U.S.A.
199 E4 **Anderson** MO U.S.A.
201 D5 **Anderson** SC U.S.A.
127 G8 **Anderson Bay** Australia
210 C5 **Andes** mts S. America
158 L1 **Andfjorden** sea chan. Norway
143 B2 **Andhra Pradesh** state India
139 H4 **Andijon** Uzbek.
179 E5 **Andilamena** Madag.
179 E5 **Andilanatoby** Madag.
140 C3 **Andīmeshk** Iran
136 F3 **Andırın** Turkey
173 H7 **Andiyskoye Koysu** r. Rus. Fed.
**Andizhan** Uzbek. see **Andijon**
141 G2 **Andkhōy** Afgh.
141 G2 **Andkhvoy** r. Afgh.
179 E5 **Andoany** Madag.
210 C4 **Andoas** Peru
143 B2 **Andol** India
152 E5 **Andong** S. Korea
152 E5 **Andong-ho** l. S. Korea
167 G1 **Andorra** country Europe
167 G1 **Andorra la Vella** Andorra
161 F6 **Andover** U.K.
203 H2 **Andover** ME U.S.A.
202 C4 **Andover** OH U.S.A.
158 K1 **Andøya** i. Norway
214 B3 **Andradina** Brazil
216 H2 **Andreanof Islands** U.S.A.
172 E3 **Andreapol'** Rus. Fed.
160 C3 **Andreas** U.K.
178 C3 **André Félix, Parc National** nat. park Cent. Afr. Rep.
214 D3 **Andrelândia** Brazil
199 C5 **Andrews** U.S.A.
138 B1 **Andreyevka** Rus. Fed.
170 G4 **Andria** Italy
179 E6 **Androka** Madag.
201 E7 **Andros** i. Bahamas
171 K6 **Andros** i. Greece
203 H2 **Androscoggin** r. U.S.A.
201 E7 **Andros Town** Bahamas
143 A4 **Andrott** i. India
173 D5 **Andrushivka** Ukr.
158 L1 **Andselv** Norway
167 D3 **Andújar** Spain
179 B5 **Andulo** Angola
176 C3 **Anéfis** Mali
205 L5 **Anegada** i. Virgin Is (U.K.)
215 D4 **Anegada, Bahía** b. Arg.
197 F5 **Anegam** U.S.A.
176 C4 **Aného** Togo
197 H3 **Aneth** U.S.A.
167 G1 **Aneto** mt. Spain
177 D3 **Aney** Niger
149 E5 **Anfu** China
179 E5 **Angadoka, Lohatanjona** hd Madag.
146 B1 **Angara** r. Rus. Fed.
146 C1 **Angarsk** Rus. Fed.
153 B3 **Angat** Phil.
159 K3 **Ånge** Sweden
**Angel, Salto** waterfall Venez. see **Angel Falls**
204 B3 **Ángel de la Guarda, Isla** i. Mex.
153 B3 **Angeles** Phil.
213 E3 **Angel Falls** Venez.
159 K4 **Ängelholm** Sweden
196 B2 **Angels Camp** U.S.A.
158 L3 **Ångermanälven** r. Sweden
166 D3 **Angers** France
187 J2 **Angikuni Lake** Canada
154 B2 **Angkor** tourist site Cambodia
161 C4 **Anglesey** i. U.K.
199 E6 **Angleton** U.S.A.
191 H2 **Angliers** Canada
154 □ **Ang Mo Kio** Sing.
178 C3 **Ango** Dem. Rep. Congo
179 D5 **Angoche** Moz.
141 E5 **Angohrān** Iran
215 B3 **Angol** Chile
179 B5 **Angola** country Africa
190 E5 **Angola** U.S.A.
219 I7 **Angola Basin** sea feature S. Atlantic Ocean
166 E4 **Angoulême** France
139 G4 **Angren** Uzbek.
154 B2 **Ang Thong** Thai.
205 L5 **Anguilla** terr. Caribbean Sea
143 D1 **Angul** India
148 E1 **Anguli Nur** l. China
148 E2 **Anguo** China
214 A3 **Anhanduí** r. Brazil
159 J4 **Anholt** i. Denmark
149 D4 **Anhua** China
148 E3 **Anhui** prov. China
214 A2 **Anhumas** Brazil
214 C2 **Anicuns** Brazil
138 E2 **Anikhovka** Rus. Fed.
172 G3 **Anikovo** Rus. Fed.
197 H6 **Animas** U.S.A.
197 H6 **Animas Peak** U.S.A.
154 A2 **Anin** Myanmar
150 H1 **Aniva** Rus. Fed.
150 H1 **Aniva, Mys** c. Rus. Fed.
146 G2 **Aniva, Zaliv** b. Rus. Fed.
125 G3 **Aniwa** i. Vanuatu
164 B5 **Anizy-le-Château** France
159 N3 **Anjalankoski** Fin.
149 F4 **Anji** China
144 D5 **Anji** India
149 D5 **Anjiang** China
141 E3 **Anjoman** Iran
166 D3 **Anjou** reg. France
**Anjouan** i. Comoros see **Ndzuani**
179 E5 **Anjozorobe** Madag.
152 C4 **Anjŭ** N. Korea
179 E6 **Ankaboa, Tanjona** pt Madag.
148 C3 **Ankang** China
136 D2 **Ankara** Turkey
179 E6 **Ankazoabo** Madag.
179 E5 **Ankazobe** Madag.
154 D2 **An Khê** Vietnam
144 C5 **Ankleshwar** India
154 C3 **An Lôc** Vietnam
149 B5 **Anlong** China
154 C2 **Ânlóng Vêng** Cambodia
148 D4 **Anlu** China
152 D5 **Anmyeon-do** i. S. Korea
203 H3 **Ann, Cape** U.S.A.
173 G5 **Anna** Rus. Fed.
202 E5 **Anna, Lake** U.S.A.
176 C1 **Annaba** Alg.
165 L4 **Annaberg-Buchholtz** Germany
136 F4 **An Nabk** Syria
142 B4 **An Nafūd** des. Saudi Arabia
137 J5 **An Nahrawān al Qadīm** canal Iraq
137 J6 **An Najaf** Iraq
163 D3 **Annalee** r. Ireland
163 F3 **Annalong** U.K.
162 E6 **Annan** U.K.
162 E6 **Annan** r. U.K.
162 E5 **Annandale** val. U.K.
202 E5 **Annapolis** U.S.A.
189 G5 **Annapolis Royal** Canada
145 E3 **Annapurna I** mt. Nepal
140 C5 **An Naqīrah** well Saudi Arabia
191 F4 **Ann Arbor** U.S.A.
211 G2 **Anna Regina** Guyana
137 K6 **An Nāşirīyah** Iraq
166 H4 **Annecy** France
166 H3 **Annemasse** France
164 E1 **Annen** Neth.
186 C4 **Annette Island** U.S.A.
136 F5 **An Nimārah** Syria
149 B5 **Anning** China
201 C5 **Anniston** U.S.A.
174 E4 **Annobón** i. Equat. Guinea
166 G4 **Annonay** France
142 C4 **An Nu'ayrīyah** Saudi Arabia
137 J5 **An Nu'mānīyah** Iraq
198 E2 **Anoka** U.S.A.
179 E5 **Anorontany, Tanjona** hd Madag.
144 C1 **Ānoshāh Pass** Afgh.
149 D6 **Anpu** China
149 C6 **Anpu Gang** b. China
149 E4 **Anqing** China
148 F2 **Anqiu** China
**An Ráth** Ireland see **Charleville**
149 D5 **Anren** China
164 D4 **Ans** Belgium
148 C2 **Ansai** China
165 I5 **Ansbach** Germany
127 G7 **Anser Group** is Australia
152 B3 **Anshan** China
149 B5 **Anshun** China
215 C1 **Ansilta** mt. Arg.
215 F1 **Ansina** Uruguay
198 D3 **Ansley** U.S.A.
199 D5 **Anson** U.S.A.
176 C3 **Ansongo** Mali
188 D4 **Ansonville** Canada
202 C5 **Ansted** U.S.A.
144 D4 **Anta** India
210 D6 **Antabamba** Peru
136 F3 **Antakya** Turkey
179 F5 **Antalaha** Madag.
136 C3 **Antalya** Turkey
136 C3 **Antalya Körfezi** g. Turkey
179 E5 **Antananarivo** Madag.
129 **Antarctica**
129 B2 **Antarctic Peninsula** pen. Antarctica
162 C3 **An Teallach** mt. U.K.
196 D2 **Antelope Range** mts U.S.A.
167 D4 **Antequera** Spain
195 F5 **Anthony** U.S.A.
176 B2 **Anti-Atlas** mts Morocco
166 H5 **Antibes** France
189 H4 **Anticosti, Île d'** i. Canada
190 C3 **Antigo** U.S.A.
189 H4 **Antigonish** Canada
205 L5 **Antigua** i. Antigua and Barbuda
**Antigua** Guat. see **Antigua Guatemala**
205 L5 **Antigua and Barbuda** country Caribbean Sea
207 G5 **Antigua Guatemala** Guat.
207 E3 **Antiguo-Morelos** Mex.
171 J7 **Antikythira** i. Greece
171 J7 **Antikythiro, Steno** sea chan. Greece
**Antioch** Turkey see **Antakya**
196 B3 **Antioch** CA U.S.A.
190 C4 **Antioch** IL U.S.A.
213 B3 **Antioquia** Col.
123 G7 **Antipodes Islands** N.Z.
171 K5 **Antipsara** i. Greece
199 E5 **Antlers** U.S.A.
212 B2 **Antofagasta** Chile
212 C3 **Antofalla, Volcán** vol. Arg.
164 B4 **Antoing** Belgium
206 I6 **Antón** Panama
214 C4 **Antonina** Brazil
214 E1 **Antônio** r. Brazil
195 F4 **Antonito** U.S.A.
163 E3 **Antrim** U.K.
163 E2 **Antrim Hills** U.K.
179 E5 **Antsalova** Madag.
179 E5 **Antsirabe** Madag.
179 E5 **Antsirañana** Madag.
179 E5 **Antsohihy** Madag.
158 M2 **Anttis** Sweden
159 N3 **Anttola** Fin.
215 B3 **Antuco** Chile
215 B3 **Antuco, Volcán** vol. Chile
164 C3 **Antwerp** Belgium
203 F2 **Antwerp** U.S.A.
188 E2 **Anuc, Lac** l. Canada
150 C3 **Anuchino** Rus. Fed.
152 D6 **Anui** S. Korea
144 C3 **Anupgarh** India
143 C4 **Anuradhapura** Sri Lanka
140 D5 **Anveh** Iran
129 B2 **Anvers Island** i. Antarctica
149 F5 **Anxi** China
148 B4 **Anxian** China
149 D4 **Anxiang** China
148 E2 **Anxin** China
126 A4 **Anxious Bay** Australia
148 E2 **Anyang** China
152 D5 **Anyang** S. Korea
171 K6 **Anydros** i. Greece
146 B3 **A'nyêmaqên Shan** mts China
149 E4 **Anyi** China
149 E5 **Anyuan** China
149 B4 **Anyue** China
133 R3 **Anyuysk** Rus. Fed.
213 B3 **Anzá** Col.
148 D2 **Anze** China
146 A1 **Anzhero-Sudzhensk** Rus. Fed.
178 C4 **Anzi** Dem. Rep. Congo
170 E4 **Anzio** Italy
125 G3 **Aoba** i. Vanuatu
154 A3 **Ao Kham, Laem** pt Thai.
**Aomen** China see **Macao**
150 G4 **Aomori** Japan
144 D3 **Aonla** India
128 C5 **Aoraki** N.Z.
128 C5 **Aoraki** mt. N.Z.
128 C5 **Aoraki/Mount Cook National Park** N.Z.
154 C2 **Aôral, Phnum** mt. Cambodia
128 D4 **Aorere** r. N.Z.
170 B2 **Aosta** Italy
176 B2 **Aoukâr** reg. Mali/Mauritania
211 G8 **Apa** r. Brazil
178 D3 **Apac** Uganda
197 H6 **Apache** U.S.A.
197 H5 **Apache Creek** U.S.A.
197 G5 **Apache Junction** U.S.A.
197 G6 **Apache Peak** U.S.A.
201 C6 **Apalachee Bay** U.S.A.
201 C6 **Apalachicola** U.S.A.
207 E4 **Apan** Mex.
213 C4 **Apaporis** r. Col.
137 J1 **Aparan** Armenia
214 B3 **Aparecida do Tabuado** Brazil
153 B2 **Aparri** Phil.
158 P2 **Apatity** Rus. Fed.
206 D4 **Apatzingán** Mex.
159 N4 **Ape** Latvia
164 D2 **Apeldoorn** Neth.
165 H2 **Apelern** Germany
165 H1 **Apensen** Germany
144 E3 **Api** mt. Nepal
125 I3 **Apia** Samoa
128 E3 **Apiti** N.Z.
153 C5 **Apo, Mount** vol. Phil.
211 G2 **Apoera** Suriname
165 J3 **Apolda** Germany
126 E7 **Apollo Bay** Australia
210 E6 **Apolo** Bol.
201 D6 **Apopka, Lake** U.S.A.
214 B2 **Aporé** Brazil
214 B2 **Aporé** r. Brazil
200 B2 **Apostle Islands** U.S.A.
190 B2 **Apostle Islands National Lakeshore** nature res. U.S.A.
136 E4 **Apostolos Andreas, Cape** Cyprus
202 B6 **Appalachia** U.S.A.
202 C6 **Appalachian Mountains** U.S.A.
170 E3 **Appennino Abruzzese** mts Italy
170 D2 **Appennino Tosco-Emiliano** mts Italy
170 E3 **Appennino Umbro-Marchigiano** mts Italy
127 I5 **Appin** Australia
164 E1 **Appingedam** Neth.
162 C3 **Applecross** U.K.
198 D2 **Appleton** MN U.S.A.
190 C3 **Appleton** WI U.S.A.

196 D4 Apple Valley U.S.A.
202 D6 Appomattox U.S.A.
170 E4 Aprilia Italy
173 F6 Apsheronsk Rus. Fed.
126 D6 Apsley Australia
191 H3 Apsley Canada
166 G5 Apt France
214 B3 Apucarana Brazil
153 A4 Apurahuan Phil.
213 D3 Apure r. Venez.
210 D6 Apurímac r. Peru
177 F2 Aqaba, Gulf of Asia
137 I6 'Aqabah, Birkat al well Iraq
139 I4 Aqal China
140 D2 Aqbana Iran
141 G2 Āqchah Afgh.
140 B2 Aq Chai r. Iran
140 D3 'Aqdā Iran
140 B2 Aqdoghmish r. Iran
137 J3 Āq Kān Dāgh, Kūh-e mt. Iran
138 C5 Āq Qal'eh Iran
137 I3 'Aqrah Iraq
141 G3 Aqrobāţ, Kowtal-e Afgh.
197 F4 Aquarius Mountains U.S.A.
197 G3 Aquarius Plateau U.S.A.
170 G4 Aquaviva delle Fonti Italy
214 A3 Aquidauana Brazil
214 A2 Aquidauana r. Brazil
206 D4 Aquila Mex.
213 D4 Aquio r. Col.
207 E3 Aquismón Mex.
166 D4 Aquitaine reg. France
145 F4 Ara India
141 G4 'Arab Afgh.
201 C5 Arab U.S.A.
177 E3 Arab, Bahr el watercourse South Sudan
136 B6 'Arab, Khalīj al b. Egypt
141 E3 'Arabābād Iran
218 I4 Arabian Basin sea feature Indian Ocean
Arabian Gulf g. Asia see The Gulf
142 B4 Arabian Peninsula Saudi Arabia
134 E5 Arabian Sea Indian Ocean
213 E3 Arabopó Venez.
213 E3 Arabopó r. Venez.
136 D1 Araç Turkey
213 E4 Araça r. Brazil
211 K6 Aracaju Brazil
213 D4 Aracamuni, Cerro h. Venez.
214 A4 Aracanguy, Montes de hills Para.
211 K4 Aracati Brazil
214 E1 Aracatu Brazil
214 B3 Araçatuba Brazil
167 C4 Aracena Spain
214 E2 Aracruz Brazil
214 D2 Araçuaí Brazil
214 D2 Araçuaí r. Brazil
171 I1 Arad Romania
177 E3 Arada Chad
124 D2 Arafura Sea Australia/Indon.
216 D6 Arafura Shelf sea feature Australia/Indon.
214 B1 Aragarças Brazil
137 I1 Aragats Armenia
137 J1 Aragats Lerr mt. Armenia
167 F2 Aragón aut. comm. Spain
167 F1 Aragón r. Spain
211 I5 Araguacema Brazil
213 D2 Aragua de Barcelona Venez.
211 I5 Araguaia r. Brazil
211 H6 Araguaia, Parque Indígena nat. park Brazil
211 H6 Araguaia, Parque Nacional do nat. park Brazil
211 I5 Araguaína Brazil
213 E2 Araguao, Boca r. mouth Venez.
213 E2 Araguao, Caño r. Venez.
214 C2 Araguari Brazil
214 C2 Araguari r. Brazil
211 I5 Araguatins Brazil
173 H7 Aragvi r. Georgia
Árainn Mhór i. Ireland see Arranmore Island
211 J4 Araioses Brazil
176 C2 Arak Alg.
140 C3 Arāk Iran
145 H5 Arakan Yoma mts Myanmar
143 B3 Arakkonam India
139 J4 Aral China
137 J2 Aralık Turkey
138 D3 Aral Sea salt l. Kazakh./Uzbek.
138 E3 Aral'sk Kazakh.
Aral'skoye More salt l. Kazakh./Uzbek. see Aral Sea
138 B2 Aralsor, Ozero l. Kazakh.
138 C2 Aralsor, Ozero salt l. Kazakh.
140 B5 Aramah plat. Saudi Arabia
207 E2 Aramberri Mex.
144 D6 Aran r. India
167 E2 Aranda de Duero Spain
137 K4 Arandān Iran
171 I2 Aranđelovac Serbia
143 B3 Arani India
163 B4 Aran Islands Ireland
167 E2 Aranjuez Spain
179 B6 Aranos Namibia
199 D7 Aransas Pass U.S.A.
214 B2 Arantes r. Brazil
125 H1 Aranuka atoll Kiribati
154 B2 Aranyaprathet Thai.
151 B8 Arao Japan
176 B3 Araouane Mali
198 D3 Arapahoe U.S.A.
213 E4 Arapari r. Brazil
215 F1 Arapey Grande r. Uruguay
136 G2 Arapgir Turkey
211 K5 Arapiraca Brazil
171 K4 Arapis, Akrotirio pt Greece
214 B3 Arapongas Brazil
145 F4 A Rapti Doon r. Nepal
142 B3 'Ar'ar Saudi Arabia
137 I6 'Ar'ar, Wādī watercourse Iraq/Saudi Arabia
212 G3 Araranguá Brazil
214 C3 Araraquara Brazil
211 H5 Araras Brazil
214 B4 Araras, Serra das mts Brazil
137 J2 Ararat Armenia
126 E6 Ararat Australia
137 J2 Ararat, Mount Turkey
145 F4 Araria India
214 D3 Araruama, Lago de lag. Brazil
137 I2 Aras Turkey
137 I1 Aras Nehri r. Turkey alt. Araks (Armenia/Turkey), alt. Araz (Azerbaijan/Iran)
214 E1 Arataca Brazil
213 C3 Arauca Col.
213 C3 Arauca r. Venez.
215 B3 Araucanía admin. reg. Chile
215 B3 Arauco Chile
213 C3 Arauquita Col.
213 C2 Araure Venez.
144 C4 Aravalli Range mts India
159 N4 Aravete Estonia
125 F2 Arawa P.N.G.
214 C2 Araxá Brazil
213 D2 Araya, Península de pen. Venez.
213 D2 Araya, Punta de pt Venez.
136 C2 Arayıt Dağı mt. Turkey
137 L2 Araz r. Azer./Iran alt. Araks (Armenia/Turkey), alt. Aras Nehri (Turkey)
137 J4 Arbat Iraq
172 I3 Arbazh Rus. Fed.
137 J3 Arbīl Iraq
159 K4 Arboga Sweden
187 I4 Arborfield Canada
162 F4 Arbroath U.K.
196 A2 Arbuckle U.S.A.
141 F4 Arbū-ye Shamālī, Dasht-e des. Afgh.
166 D4 Arcachon France
201 D7 Arcadia U.S.A.
194 A3 Arcata U.S.A.
196 D2 Arc Dome mt. U.S.A.
207 D4 Arcelia Mex.
172 G1 Archangel Rus. Fed.
124 E3 Archer r. Australia
197 H2 Arches National Park U.S.A.
Archman Turkm. see Arçman
137 L2 Ărçivan Azer.
126 A2 Arckaringa watercourse Australia
138 D5 Arçman Turkm.
194 D3 Arco U.S.A.
167 D4 Arcos de la Frontera Spain
185 J2 Arctic Bay Canada
220 B1 Arctic Mid-Ocean Ridge sea feature Arctic Ocean
220 Arctic Ocean
184 E3 Arctic Red r. Canada
129 E2 Arctowski research stn Antarctica
140 C2 Ardabīl Iran
137 I1 Ardahan Turkey
140 C4 Ardakān Fārs Iran
140 D3 Ardakān Yazd Iran
140 C4 Ardal Iran
159 I3 Årdalstangen Norway
163 C3 Ardara Ireland
171 K4 Ardas r. Bulg.
172 G4 Ardatov Nizhegorodskaya Oblast' Rus. Fed.
172 H4 Ardatov Respublika Mordoviya Rus. Fed.
191 G3 Ardbeg Canada
163 E4 Ardee Ireland
126 B4 Arden, Mount h. Australia
164 D5 Ardennes dept Belgium
164 C5 Ardennes, Canal des France
140 D3 Ardestān Iran
163 F3 Ardglass U.K.
167 C3 Ardila r. Port.
127 G5 Ardlethan Australia
199 D5 Ardmore U.S.A.
162 B4 Ardnamurchan, Point of U.K.
162 C4 Ardrishaig U.K.
126 B5 Ardrossan Australia
162 D5 Ardrossan U.K.
162 C3 Ardvasar U.K.
215 E2 Areco r. Arg.
212 E3 Areguá Para.
211 K4 Areia Branca Brazil
164 E4 Aremberg h. Germany
153 B4 Arena rf Phil.
196 A2 Arena, Point U.S.A.
206 B3 Arena, Punta pt Mex.
206 H5 Arenal Hond.
167 D2 Arenas de San Pedro Spain
159 J4 Arendal Norway
165 J2 Arendsee (Altmark) Germany
161 D5 Arenig Fawr h. U.K.
171 J6 Areopoli Greece
206 C2 Areponapuchi Mex.
210 D7 Arequipa Peru
211 H4 Arere Brazil
167 D2 Arévalo Spain
170 D3 Arezzo Italy
136 G6 'Arfajah well Saudi Arabia
148 D1 Argalant Mongolia
167 E2 Arganda del Rey Spain
153 B4 Argao Phil.
170 D2 Argenta Italy
166 D2 Argentan France
170 D3 Argentario, Monte h. Italy
170 B2 Argentera, Cima dell' mt. Italy
164 F5 Argenthal Germany
212 C5 Argentina country S. America
129 C4 Argentina Range mts Antarctica
219 F9 Argentine Abyssal Plain sea feature S. Atlantic Ocean
219 G8 Argentine Basin sea feature S. Atlantic Ocean
219 F8 Argentine Rise sea feature S. Atlantic Ocean
212 B8 Argentino, Lago l. Arg.
171 K2 Argeş r. Romania
141 G4 Arghandāb Rōd r. Afgh.
136 C2 Argıthanı Turkey
171 J6 Argolikos Kolpos b. Greece
171 J6 Argos Greece
171 I5 Argostoli Greece
167 F1 Arguis Spain
146 E1 Argun' r. China/Rus. Fed.
173 H7 Argun Rus. Fed.
129 D5 Argus, Dome ice feature Antarctica
196 D4 Argus Range mts U.S.A.
190 C4 Argyle U.S.A.
124 C3 Argyle, Lake Australia
162 C4 Argyll reg. U.K.
159 J4 Århus Denmark
128 E3 Aria N.Z.
127 G5 Ariah Park Australia
151 B8 Ariake-kai b. Japan
179 B6 Ariamsvlei Namibia
170 F4 Ariano Irpino Italy
213 B4 Ariari r. Col.
215 D2 Arias Arg.
135 F6 Ari Atholhu Maldives
213 E2 Aribí r. Venez.
176 B3 Aribinda Burkina Faso
212 B1 Arica Chile
162 C4 Arienas, Loch l. U.K.
136 F4 Arīḩā Syria
194 G4 Arikaree r. U.S.A.
213 E2 Arima Trin. and Tob.
214 C1 Arinos Brazil
211 G6 Arinos r. Brazil
206 D4 Ario de Rosáles Mex.
213 C3 Ariporo r. Col.
210 F5 Aripuanã Brazil
210 F5 Aripuanã r. Brazil
210 G6 Aripuanã, Parque Indígena nat. park Brazil
210 F5 Ariquemes Brazil
214 B2 Ariranhá r. Brazil
180 B1 Aris Namibia
162 C4 Arisaig U.K.
162 C4 Arisaig, Sound of sea chan. U.K.
186 D4 Aristazabal Island Canada
212 C2 Arizaro, Salar de salt flat Arg.
197 G4 Arizona state U.S.A.
192 D5 Arizpe Mex.
140 B5 'Arjah Saudi Arabia
158 L2 Arjeplog Sweden
213 B2 Arjona Col.
155 D4 Arjuna, Gunung vol. Indon.
173 G5 Arkadak Rus. Fed.
199 E5 Arkadelphia U.S.A.
162 C4 Arkaig, Loch l. U.K.
139 F2 Arkalyk Kazakh.
199 F5 Arkansas r. U.S.A.
199 E5 Arkansas state U.S.A.
199 D4 Arkansas City U.S.A.
145 G1 Arka Tag mts China
172 G2 Arkhangel'skaya Oblast' admin. div. Rus. Fed.
172 F4 Arkhangel'skoye Rus. Fed.
150 C3 Arkhipovka Rus. Fed.
163 E5 Arklow Ireland
171 L6 Arkoi i. Greece
168 F3 Arkona, Kap c. Germany
132 J2 Arkticheskogo Instituta, Ostrova is Rus. Fed.
203 F3 Arkville U.S.A.
166 G5 Arles France
181 G4 Arlington S. Africa
194 B2 Arlington OR U.S.A.
198 D2 Arlington SD U.S.A.
202 E5 Arlington VA U.S.A.
190 D4 Arlington Heights U.S.A.
176 C3 Arlit Niger
164 D5 Arlon Belgium
153 C5 Armadores i. Indon.
163 E3 Armagh U.K.
177 F2 Armant Egypt
137 J1 Armavir Armenia
173 G6 Armavir Rus. Fed.
137 J1 Armenia country Asia
213 B3 Armenia Col.
213 B3 Armero Col.
127 I3 Armidale Australia
187 K2 Armit Lake Canada
144 E5 Armori India
163 E2 Armoy U.K.
186 F4 Armstrong B.C. Canada
188 C3 Armstrong Ont. Canada
150 E1 Armu r. Rus. Fed.
143 B2 Armur India
173 E6 Armyans'k Ukr.
Arnaoutis, Cape c. Cyprus see Arnauti, Cape
189 F1 Arnaud r. Canada
136 D4 Arnauti, Cape Cyprus
159 J3 Årnes Norway
199 D4 Arnett U.S.A.
164 D3 Arnhem Neth.
124 D3 Arnhem, Cape Australia
124 D3 Arnhem Bay Australia
124 D3 Arnhem Land reg. Australia
170 D3 Arno r. Italy
126 B4 Arno Bay Australia
161 F4 Arnold U.K.
190 D2 Arnold U.S.A.
191 H1 Arnoux, Lac l. Canada
191 I3 Arnprior Canada
165 G3 Arnsberg Germany
165 I4 Arnstadt Germany
191 H3 Arnstein Canada
165 H5 Arnstein Germany
191 H1 Arntfield Canada
213 E3 Aro r. Venez.
179 B6 Aroab Namibia
165 H3 Arolsen Germany
170 C2 Arona Italy
203 J1 Aroostook Canada
203 I1 Aroostook r. Canada/U.S.A.
125 H2 Arorae i. Kiribati
153 B3 Aroroy Phil.
173 G7 Arpa r. Armenia/Turkey
137 I1 Arpaçay Turkey
141 G5 Arra r. Pak.
137 I5 Ar Raḩḩālīyah Iraq
137 I5 Ar Ramādī Iraq
136 E7 Ar Ramlah Jordan
162 C5 Arran i. U.K.
163 C3 Arranmore Island Ireland
137 G4 Ar Raqqah Syria
166 F1 Arras France
140 A5 Ar Rass Saudi Arabia
136 F4 Ar Rastān Syria
137 I7 Ar Rawḑ well Saudi Arabia
140 C5 Ar Rayyān Qatar
213 C4 Arrecifal Col.
215 E2 Arrecifes Arg.
207 F4 Arriagá Chiapas Mex.
206 D3 Arriaga San Luis Potosí Mex.
215 E2 Arribeños Arg.
137 K6 Ar Rifā'ī Iraq
137 J6 Ar Rihāb salt flat Iraq
142 D5 Ar Rimāl reg. Saudi Arabia
197 H3 Arriola U.S.A.
Ar Riyāḑ Saudi Arabia see Riyadh
162 D4 Arrochar U.K.
215 G2 Arroio Grande Brazil
214 D1 Arrojado r. Brazil
163 C3 Arrow, Lough l. Ireland
190 B1 Arrow Lake Canada
194 D3 Arrowrock Reservoir U.S.A.
128 C5 Arrowsmith, Mount N.Z.
196 B4 Arroyo Grande U.S.A.
215 E2 Arroyo Seco Arg.
207 E3 Arroyo Seco Mex.
140 B5 Ar Rubay'iyah Saudi Arabia
214 A1 Arruda Brazil
137 J6 Ar Rumaythah Iraq
136 G4 Ar Ruşāfah Syria
141 E6 Ar Rustāq Oman
137 H5 Ar Ruţbah Iraq
140 B6 Ar Ruwayḑah Saudi Arabia
Års Denmark see Aars
140 B2 Ars Iran
140 D4 Arsenajān Iran
150 C2 Arsen'yev Rus. Fed.
139 H2 Arshaly Akmolinskaya Oblast' Kazakh.
139 J2 Arshaly Vostochnyy Kazakhstan Kazakh.
143 B3 Arsikere India
172 I3 Arsk Rus. Fed.
136 E3 Arslanköy Turkey
178 E2 Arta Djibouti
171 I5 Arta Greece
137 J2 Artashat Armenia
206 D4 Arteaga Mex.
150 C3 Artem Rus. Fed.
205 H4 Artemisa Cuba
173 F5 Artemivs'k Ukr.
150 C3 Artemovskiy Rus. Fed.
166 E2 Artenay France
195 F5 Artesia U.S.A.
191 G4 Arthur Canada
126 B3 Arthur, Lake salt flat Australia
202 C4 Arthur, Lake U.S.A.
127 G8 Arthur Lake Australia
124 F4 Arthur Point Australia
128 C5 Arthur's Pass N.Z.
128 C5 Arthur's Pass National Park N.Z.
201 F7 Arthur's Town Bahamas
129 E2 Artigas research stn Antarctica
215 F1 Artigas Uruguay
137 I1 Art'ik Armenia
187 H2 Artillery Lake Canada
181 G2 Artisia Botswana
166 F1 Artois reg. France
164 A4 Artois, Collines d' hills France
137 I2 Artos Dağı mt. Turkey
136 F1 Artova Turkey
173 D6 Artsyz Ukr.
129 B2 Arturo Prat research stn Antarctica
139 I5 Artux China
137 H1 Artvin Turkey
147 F7 Aru, Kepulauan is Indon.
178 D3 Arua Uganda
214 B1 Aruanã Brazil
213 C1 Aruba terr. Caribbean Sea
210 F4 Arumã Brazil
145 F4 Arun r. Nepal
145 H3 Arunachal Pradesh state India
161 G7 Arundel U.K.
178 D4 Arusha Tanz.
198 B4 Arvada U.S.A.
163 D4 Arvagh Ireland
146 C2 Arvayheer Mongolia
144 D5 Arvi India
187 K2 Arviat Canada
189 F4 Arvida Canada
158 L2 Arvidsjaur Sweden
159 K4 Arvika Sweden
196 C4 Arvin U.S.A.
140 B6 Arwā' Saudi Arabia
139 G1 Arykbalyk Kazakh.
139 G4 Arys Kazakh.
139 G4 Arys' r. Kazakh.
138 F3 Arys, Ozero salt l. Kazakh.
172 G4 Arzamas Rus. Fed.
165 K4 Arzberg Germany
167 F5 Arzew Alg.
173 H6 Arzgir Rus. Fed.
165 K4 Aš Czech Rep.
213 E3 Asa r. Venez.
176 C4 Asaba Nigeria
136 G3 Asad, Buḩayrat al resr Syria
141 H3 Asadābād Afgh.
140 C3 Asadābād Iran
140 D4 Asadābād Iran
141 E3 Asadābād Iran
154 A5 Asahan r. Indon.
150 H3 Asahi-dake vol. Japan
151 C7 Asahi-gawa r. Japan
150 H3 Asahikawa Japan
139 H4 Asaka Uzbek.
140 C2 Asālem Iran
152 D5 Asan-man b. S. Korea
145 F5 Asansol India
164 F4 Asbach Germany
189 F4 Asbestos Canada
180 E4 Asbestos Mountains S. Africa
203 F4 Asbury Park U.S.A.
170 F4 Ascea Italy
210 F7 Ascensión Bol.
175 C5 Ascension i. S. Atlantic Ocean
207 H4 Ascensión, Bahía de la b. Mex.
165 H5 Aschaffenburg Germany
164 F3 Ascheberg Germany
165 J3 Aschersleben Germany
170 E3 Ascoli Piceno Italy
159 K4 Åseda Sweden
158 L2 Åsele Sweden
171 K3 Asenovgrad Bulg.
138 D5 Aşgabat Turkm.
140 B5 Asharat Saudi Arabia
124 B4 Ashburton watercourse Australia
128 C5 Ashburton N.Z.
190 D1 Ashburton Bay Canada
139 F3 Ashchikol', Ozero salt l. Kazakh.
139 G4 Ashchysay Kazakh.
186 E4 Ashcroft Canada
136 E6 Ashdod Israel
199 E5 Ashdown U.S.A.
201 E5 Asheboro U.S.A.
201 D5 Asheville U.S.A.
127 I2 Ashford Australia
161 H6 Ashford U.K.
197 F4 Ash Fork U.S.A.
Ashgabat Turkm. see Aşgabat
150 H3 Ashibetsu Japan
151 F6 Ashikaga Japan
160 F2 Ashington U.K.
172 I3 Ashit r. Rus. Fed.
151 C8 Ashizuri-misaki pt Japan
140 D4 Ashkazar Iran
199 D4 Ashland KS U.S.A.
202 B5 Ashland KY U.S.A.
203 I1 Ashland ME U.S.A.
194 F2 Ashland MT U.S.A.
203 H3 Ashland NH U.S.A.
202 B4 Ashland OH U.S.A.
194 B3 Ashland OR U.S.A.
202 E6 Ashland VA U.S.A.
190 B2 Ashland WI U.S.A.
127 H2 Ashley Australia
198 D2 Ashley U.S.A.
124 C3 Ashmore and Cartier Islands terr. Australia
172 C4 Ashmyany Belarus
197 H5 Ash Peak U.S.A.
136 E6 Ashqelon Israel
137 I6 Ash Shabakah Iraq
137 H3 Ash Shaddādah Syria
137 J6 Ash Shanāfīyah Iraq
137 H7 Ash Shaqīq well Saudi Arabia
140 B5 Ash Sha'rā' Saudi Arabia
136 E6 Ash Sharāh reg. Jordan
142 E4 Ash Shāriqah U.A.E.
137 I4 Ash Sharqāţ Iraq
137 K6 Ash Shaţrah Iraq
136 D7 Ash Shaţţ Egypt
136 E6 Ash Shawbak Jordan
142 C7 Ash Shiḩr Yemen
140 E5 Ash Şhināş Oman
140 B4 Ash Shu'bah Saudi Arabia
140 B5 Ash Shumlūl Saudi Arabia
202 C4 Ashtabula U.S.A.
137 J1 Ashtarak Armenia
143 A2 Ashti Maharashtra India
144 D5 Ashti Maharashtra India
140 C3 Ashtiān Iran
180 D6 Ashton S. Africa
194 E2 Ashton U.S.A.
160 E4 Ashton-under-Lyne U.K.
185 L4 Ashuanipi Lake Canada
188 F4 Ashuapmushuan r. Canada
188 F4 Ashuapmushuan, Réserve Faunique nature res. Canada
201 C5 Ashville U.S.A.
136 F4 'Āşī, Nahr al r. Asia
130 Asia
206 D3 Asientos Mex.
143 B2 Asifabad India
143 D2 Asika India
170 C4 Asinara, Golfo dell' b. Sardinia Italy
132 J4 Asino Rus. Fed.
172 D4 Asipovichy Belarus
142 B5 'Asīr reg. Saudi Arabia
137 H2 Aşkale Turkey
138 D1 Askarovo Rus. Fed.
159 J4 Asker Norway
159 K4 Askersund Sweden
159 J4 Askim Norway
137 I3 Askī Mawşil Iraq
146 B1 Askiz Rus. Fed.
137 K2 Aşlāndūz Iran
178 D2 Asmara Eritrea
159 K4 Åsnen l. Sweden
144 C4 Asop India
137 L3 Aspar Iran
139 H4 Aspara Kazakh.
160 D3 Aspatria U.K.
195 F4 Aspen U.S.A.
165 H6 Asperg Germany
199 C5 Aspermont U.S.A.
128 B6 Aspiring, Mount N.Z.
187 H4 Asquith Canada
139 G4 Assa Kazakh.
136 F4 As Sa'an Syria
178 E2 Assab Eritrea
140 C5 As Sabsab well Saudi Arabia
136 C7 Aş Şaff Egypt
136 E6 Aş Şāfī Jordan
136 F3 As Safīrah Syria
Aş Şaḩrā' al Gharbīyah des. Egypt see Western Desert
Aş Şaḩrā' ash Sharqīyah des. Egypt see Eastern Desert
140 C5 As Saji well Saudi Arabia
138 D4 Assake-Audan, Vpadina depr. Uzbek.
140 B5 As Salamiyah Saudi Arabia
136 D6 Aş Şāliḩīyah Egypt
137 H4 Aş Şāliḩīyah Syria
137 J6 As Salmān Iraq
136 E5 As Salţ Jordan
145 H4 Assam state India
137 J6 As Samāwah Iraq
136 F5 Aş Şanamayn Syria
177 E2 As Sarīr reg. Libya
203 F5 Assateague Island U.S.A.
203 F6 Assateague Island National Seashore nature res. U.S.A.
164 E1 Assen Neth.
164 B3 Assenede Belgium
164 D4 Assesse Belgium
145 F5 Assia Hills India
177 D1 As Sidrah Libya
187 H5 Assiniboia Canada
187 J5 Assiniboine r. Canada
186 F4 Assiniboine, Mount Canada
214 B3 Assis Brazil
170 E3 Assisi Italy
165 G4 Aßlar Germany
137 K7 Aş Şubayḩīyah Kuwait
140 B4 Aş Şufayrī well Saudi Arabia
137 G4 As Sukhnah Syria
137 J4 As Sulaymānīyah Iraq
142 C5 As Sulayyil Saudi Arabia
140 C5 Aş Şulb reg. Saudi Arabia
140 B5 Aş Şummān plat. Saudi Arabia
142 B5 As Sūq Saudi Arabia
137 H4 Aş Şuwar Syria
136 F5 As Suwaydā' Syria
141 E6 As Suwayq Oman
137 J5 Aş Şuwayrah Iraq
As Suways Egypt see Suez
162 C2 Assynt, Loch l. U.K.
171 L7 Astakida i. Greece
134 F1 Astana Kazakh.
137 L3 Astaneh Iran
137 L2 Āstārā Azer.
170 C2 Asti Italy
196 A2 Asti U.S.A.
215 C1 Astica Arg.
141 F5 Astola Island Pak.
144 C2 Astor Pak.
144 C2 Astor r. Pak.
167 C1 Astorga Spain
194 B2 Astoria U.S.A.
159 K4 Åstorp Sweden
134 C2 Astrakhan' Rus. Fed.
173 H6 Astrakhanskaya Oblast' admin. div. Rus. Fed.
172 C4 Astravyets Belarus
129 D3 Astrid Ridge sea feature Southern Ocean
167 C1 Asturias aut. comm. Spain
171 L6 Astypalaia i. Greece
139 J2 Asubulak Kazakh.
212 E3 Asunción Para.
177 F2 Aswān Egypt
140 A5 Asyāḩ, Safrā' al esc. Saudi Arabia
177 F2 Asyūţ Egypt
125 I4 Ata i. Tonga
213 D4 Atabapo r. Col./Venez.
139 G4 Atabay Kazakh.
Atacama, Desierto de des. Chile see Atacama Desert
212 C2 Atacama, Salar de salt flat Chile
212 C2 Atacama Desert Chile
125 I2 Atafu atoll Tokelau
139 G4 Atakent Kazakh.
176 C4 Atakpamé Togo
171 J5 Atalanti Greece
206 I7 Atalaya Panama
210 D6 Atalaya Peru
138 F5 Atamyrat Turkm.
139 G1 Atansor, Ozero salt l. Kazakh.
176 A2 Atâr Mauritania
154 A1 Ataran r. Myanmar
197 H4 Atarque U.S.A.
196 B4 Atascadero U.S.A.
139 G2 Atasu Kazakh.
147 E7 Ataúro, Ilha de i. East Timor
171 L6 Atavyros mt. Greece
138 D4 Ataýap Turkm.
177 F3 Atbara Sudan
177 F3 Atbara r. Sudan
139 G2 Atbasar Kazakh.
139 H4 At-Bashy Kyrg.
199 F6 Atchafalaya Bay U.S.A.
198 E4 Atchison U.S.A.
206 C3 Atenguillo Mex.
170 E3 Aterno r. Italy
170 F3 Atessa Italy
164 B4 Ath Belgium
186 G4 Athabasca Canada
184 G4 Athabasca r. U.S.A.
187 G3 Athabasca, Lake Canada
137 I6 'Athāmīn, Birkat al well Iraq
163 E4 Athboy Ireland
163 C4 Athenry Ireland
191 J3 Athens Canada
171 J6 Athens Greece (City Plan 107)
201 C5 Athens AL U.S.A.
201 D5 Athens GA U.S.A.
202 B5 Athens OH U.S.A.
201 C5 Athens TN U.S.A.
199 E5 Athens TX U.S.A.
161 F5 Atherstone U.K.
164 A5 Athies France
Athina Greece see Athens
163 C4 Athleague Ireland
163 D4 Athlone Ireland
143 A2 Athni India
128 B6 Athol N.Z.
203 G3 Athol U.S.A.
162 E4 Atholl, Forest of reg. U.K.
171 K4 Athos mt. Greece
136 E7 Ath Thamad Egypt
163 E5 Athy Ireland
177 D3 Ati Chad
210 D7 Atico Peru
188 B4 Atikokan Canada
189 H3 Atikonak Lake Canada
153 B3 Atimonan Phil.
143 B4 Atirampattinam India
207 G5 Atitlán Guat.
207 G5 Átitlán, Volcán vol. Guat.
140 B5 'Atk, Wādī al watercourse Saudi Arabia
133 Q3 Atka Rus. Fed.
173 H5 Atkarsk Rus. Fed.
207 E4 Atlacomulco Mex.
201 C5 Atlanta GA U.S.A.
190 C5 Atlanta IL U.S.A.
191 E3 Atlanta MI U.S.A.
136 D2 Atlantı Turkey
198 E3 Atlantic U.S.A.
203 F5 Atlantic City U.S.A.
218 D9 Atlantic-Indian-Antarctic Basin sea feature S. Atlantic Ocean
218 D8 Atlantic-Indian Ridge sea feature Southern Ocean
219 Atlantic Ocean
180 C6 Atlantis S. Africa
173 B1 Atlas Mountains Africa
176 C1 Atlas Saharien mts Alg.
186 C3 Atlin Canada
186 C3 Atlin Lake Canada
186 C3 Atlin Provincial Park Canada
136 E5 'Atlit Israel
207 E4 Atlixco Mex.
143 B3 Atmakur Andhra Pradesh India
143 B3 Atmakur India
199 G6 Atmore U.S.A.
199 D5 Atoka U.S.A.
206 D3 Atotonilco el Alto Mex.
154 C1 Atouat mt. Laos
207 D4 Atoyac de Álvarez Mex.
145 G4 Atrai r. India
140 E2 Atrak, Rūd-e r. Iran/Turkm. alt. Atrek, alt. Etrek
213 A3 Atrato r. Col.
140 D2 Atrek r. Iran/Turkm. alt. Atrak, Rūd-e, alt. Etrek
203 F5 Atsion U.S.A.
136 E6 Aţ Ţafīlah Jordan
142 B5 Aţ Ţā'if Saudi Arabia
201 C5 Attalla U.S.A.
154 C2 Attapu Laos
188 D3 Attawapiskat Canada
188 C3 Attawapiskat r. Canada
188 C3 Attawapiskat Lake Canada
137 G7 Aţ Ţawīl mts Saudi Arabia
140 A4 At Taysīyah plat. Saudi Arabia
165 F3 Attendorn Germany
168 F7 Attersee l. Austria
190 D5 Attica IN U.S.A.
202 B4 Attica OH U.S.A.
164 C5 Attigny France
203 H3 Attleboro U.S.A.
161 I5 Attleborough U.K.
136 F7 Aţ Ţubayq reg. Saudi Arabia
216 G2 Attu Island U.S.A.
140 B5 Aţ Ţulayḩī well Saudi Arabia
177 F2 Aţ Ţūr Egypt
143 B4 Attur India
215 C2 Atuel r. Arg.
215 C3 Atuel, Bañados del marsh Arg.
159 K4 Åtvidaberg Sweden
202 C4 Atwood Lake U.S.A.
138 B3 Atyrau Kazakh.
138 B3 Atyrauskaya Oblast' admin. div. Kazakh.
165 I5 Aub Germany
166 G5 Aubagne France
164 D5 Aubange Belgium
153 B2 Aubarede Point Phil.
166 G4 Aubenas France
164 D5 Auboué France
197 F4 Aubrey Cliffs mts U.S.A.
184 F3 Aubry Lake Canada
126 C5 Auburn Australia
191 G4 Auburn Canada
201 C5 Auburn AL U.S.A.
196 B2 Auburn CA U.S.A.
190 E5 Auburn IN U.S.A.
203 H2 Auburn ME U.S.A.
198 E3 Auburn NE U.S.A.
202 E3 Auburn NY U.S.A.
194 B2 Auburn WA U.S.A.
166 F4 Aubusson France
215 C3 Auca Mahuida, Sierra de mt. Arg.
166 E5 Auch France
162 E4 Auchterarder U.K.
128 E2 Auckland N.Z. (City Plan 102)
125 G7 Auckland Islands N.Z.
203 H2 Audet Canada
161 I7 Audresselles France
164 A4 Audruicq France
165 K4 Aue Germany
165 K4 Auerbach Germany
165 J5 Auerbach in der Oberpfalz Germany
165 K4 Auersberg mt. Germany
139 J2 Auezov Kazakh.
163 D3 Augher U.K.
163 E3 Aughnacloy U.K.
163 E5 Aughrim Ireland
180 D4 Augrabies S. Africa
180 D4 Augrabies Falls S. Africa
180 D4 Augrabies Falls National Park S. Africa
191 F3 Au Gres U.S.A.
168 E6 Augsburg Germany
170 F6 Augusta Sicily Italy
201 D5 Augusta GA U.S.A.
199 D4 Augusta KS U.S.A.
203 I2 Augusta ME U.S.A.
190 B3 Augusta WI U.S.A.
169 K4 Augustowska, Puszcza for. Poland
124 B4 Augustus, Mount Australia
138 F1 Auliyekol' Kazakh.
164 B4 Aulnoye-Aymeries France
161 I7 Ault France
Auminzatau, Gory hill Uzbek. see Ovminzatov tog'lari
179 B6 Auob watercourse Namibia
189 G2 Aupaluk Canada
154 C5 Aur i. Malaysia
159 M3 Aura Fin.
144 D4 Auraiya India
144 C6 Aurangabad India
164 F1 Aurich Germany
214 B2 Aurilândia Brazil
166 F4 Aurillac France
155 D3 Aurkuning Indon.
153 B5 Aurora Phil.
194 F4 Aurora CO U.S.A.
190 C5 Aurora IL U.S.A.
203 I2 Aurora ME U.S.A.
199 E4 Aurora MO U.S.A.
179 B6 Aus Namibia
191 F3 Au Sable U.S.A.
191 E3 Au Sable r. U.S.A.
203 G2 Ausable r. U.S.A.
203 G2 Au Sable Forks U.S.A.
Ausable Forks U.S.A. see Au Sable Forks
190 D2 Au Sable Point MI U.S.A.
191 F3 Au Sable Point MI U.S.A.
162 F1 Auskerry i. U.K.
158 C2 Austari-Jökulsá r. Iceland
198 E3 Austin MN U.S.A.
196 D2 Austin NV U.S.A.
199 D6 Austin TX U.S.A.
Australes, Îles is Fr. Polynesia see Tubuai Islands
124 C4 Australia country Oceania
219 P9 Australian-Antarctic Basin sea feature Southern Ocean
129 B7 Australian Antarctic Territory reg. Antarctica
127 H5 Australian Capital Territory admin. div. Australia
127 G9 Australian Convict Sites tourist site Australia
168 F7 Austria country Europe
158 K1 Austvågøy i. Norway
206 C4 Autlán Mex.
158 N2 Autti Fin.
166 G3 Autun France
166 F4 Auvergne reg. France
166 F3 Auxerre France
164 A4 Auxi-le-Château France
166 G3 Auxonne France
203 F3 Ava U.S.A.
166 F3 Avallon France
196 C5 Avalon U.S.A.
189 J4 Avalon Peninsula Canada
206 D2 Ávalos Mex.
140 B2 Avān Iran
136 E2 Avanos Turkey
214 C3 Avaré Brazil
137 K2 Āvārsin Iran
196 D4 Avawatz Mountains U.S.A.
141 F3 Āvāz Iran
211 G4 Aveiro Brazil
167 B2 Aveiro Port.
167 B2 Aveiro, Ria de est. Port.
137 L4 Āvej Iran
215 E2 Avellaneda Arg.
170 F4 Avellino Italy
196 B3 Avenal U.S.A.
126 F6 Avenel Australia
170 F4 Aversa Italy
164 B4 Avesnes-sur-Helpe France
159 L3 Avesta Sweden
166 F4 Aveyron r. France
170 E3 Avezzano Italy
162 E3 Aviemore U.K.
170 F4 Avigliano Italy
166 G5 Avignon France
167 D2 Ávila Spain
167 D1 Avilés Spain
164 A4 Avion France
143 C5 Avissawella Sri Lanka
172 H2 Avnyugskiy Rus. Fed.
127 G8 Avoca Tas. Australia
126 E6 Avoca Vic. Australia
126 E6 Avoca r. Australia
163 E5 Avoca Ireland
198 E3 Avoca U.S.A.
170 F6 Avola Sicily Italy
161 E6 Avon r. England U.K.
161 F5 Avon r. England U.K.
161 F7 Avon r. England U.K.
190 B5 Avon U.S.A.
197 F5 Avondale U.S.A.
161 E6 Avonmouth U.K.
201 D7 Avon Park U.S.A.
166 D2 Avranches France
164 A5 Avre r. France
125 G2 Avuavu Solomon Is
151 D7 Awaji-shima i. Japan
128 E3 Awakino N.Z.
Awālī Bahrain see 'Awālī
140 C5 'Awālī Bahrain
128 D1 Awanui N.Z.
128 B6 Awarua Point N.Z.
178 E3 Āwash Eth.
178 D3 Āwash r. Eth.
150 F5 Awa-shima i. Japan
178 D3 Āwash National Park Eth.
180 A2 Awasib Mountains Namibia
139 J4 Awat China
128 D4 Awatere r. N.Z.
177 D2 Awbārī Libya
176 D2 Awbārī, Idhān des. Libya
163 C5 Awbeg r. Ireland
137 K6 'Awdah, Hawr al imp. l. Iraq
178 E3 Aw Dheegle Somalia
162 C4 Awe, Loch l. U.K.
177 E4 Aweil South Sudan
176 C4 Awka Nigeria
153 C6 Awu vol. Indon.
126 F6 Axedale Australia
185 I2 Axel Heiberg Island Canada
176 B4 Axim Ghana
161 E7 Axminster U.K.
164 C5 Ay France
139 J3 Ay Kazakh.
151 D7 Ayabe Japan
215 E3 Ayacucho Arg.
210 D6 Ayacucho Peru
139 J3 Ayagoz Kazakh.
139 I3 Ayagoz watercourse Kazakh.

Ayakkuduk Uzbek. see Oyoqquduq
146 A3 Ayakkum Hu salt l. China
167 C4 Ayamonte Spain
146 F1 Ayan Rus. Fed.
173 E7 Ayancık Turkey
152 C4 Ayang N. Korea
133 R3 Ayanka Rus. Fed.
213 B2 Ayapel Col.
136 D1 Ayaş Turkey
210 D6 Ayaviri Peru
139 G1 Aydabol Kazakh.
173 F5 Aydar r. Ukr.
139 F4 Aydarko'l ko'li l. Uzbek.
Aydarkul', Ozero l. Uzbek. see Aydarko'l ko'li
138 F3 Aydarly Kazakh.
136 A3 Aydın Turkey
136 A2 Aydın Dağları mts Turkey
138 C5 Aýdyň Turkm.
138 D2 Aydyrlinskiy Rus. Fed.
154 □ Ayer Chawan, Pulau i. Sing.
154 □ Ayer Merbau, Pulau i. Sing.
Ayers Rock h. Australia see Uluṟu
139 J2 Aygyrzhal Kazakh.
138 E2 Ayke, Ozero l. Kazakh.
133 M3 Aykhal Rus. Fed.
172 I2 Aykino Rus. Fed.
139 J4 Aykol China
128 D5 Aylesbury N.Z.
161 G6 Aylesbury U.K.
202 E6 Aylett U.S.A.
167 E2 Ayllón Spain
191 G4 Aylmer Canada
187 H2 Aylmer Lake Canada
139 I3 Aynabulak Kazakh.
140 C4 'Ayn al 'Abd well Saudi Arabia
139 G5 Ayní Tajik.
136 G3 'Ayn 'Īsá Syria
177 F4 Ayod South Sudan
133 R3 Ayon, Ostrov i. Rus. Fed.
176 B3 'Ayoûn el 'Atroûs Mauritania
124 E3 Ayr Australia
162 D5 Ayr U.K.
162 D5 Ayr r. U.K.
136 D3 Ayrancı Turkey
160 C3 Ayre, Point of Isle of Man
139 G3 Ayshyrak Kazakh.
138 E3 Ayteke Bi Kazakh.
171 L3 Aytos Bulg.
154 D2 A Yun Pa Vietnam
154 B2 Ayutthaya Thai.
171 L5 Ayvacık Turkey
136 F2 Ayvalı Turkey
171 L5 Ayvalık Turkey
206 H5 Azacualpa Hond.
144 C2 Azad Kashmir admin. div. Pak.
145 E4 Azamgarh India
178 E3 Azania reg. Somalia
176 B3 Azaouâd reg. Mali
176 C3 Azaouagh, Vallée de watercourse Mali/Niger
139 G3 Azat, Gory h. Kazakh.
Azbine mts Niger see Aïr, Massif de l'
136 D1 Azdavay Turkey
137 K1 Azerbaijan country Asia
140 B2 Āzghān Iran
138 E3 Azhar Kazakh.
139 G2 Azhibeksor, Ozero salt l. Kazakh.
191 G2 Azilda Canada
203 H2 Aziscohos Lake U.S.A.
210 C4 Azogues Ecuador
132 F3 Azopol'ye Rus. Fed.
156 A6 Azores terr. N. Atlantic Ocean
219 H3 Azores-Biscay Rise sea feature N. Atlantic Ocean
173 F6 Azov Rus. Fed.
173 F6 Azov, Sea of Rus. Fed./Ukr.
177 F3 Azraq, Bahr el r. Eth./Sudan alt. Ābay Wenz conv. Blue Nile
136 F6 Azraq, Qaşr al Jordan
176 B1 Azrou Morocco
195 F4 Aztec U.S.A.
167 D3 Azuaga Spain
212 B3 Azúcar r. Chile
206 I7 Azuero, Península de pen. Panama
215 E3 Azul Arg.
207 G4 Azul r. Mex.
Azúl r. Mex. see Azul
215 B4 Azul, Cerro mt. Arg.
210 C5 Azul, Cordillera mts Peru
214 A1 Azul, Serra hills Brazil
151 G6 Azuma-san vol. Japan
166 H5 Azur, Côte d' coastal area France
210 F8 Azurduy Bol.
140 C5 Az Za'āyin Qatar
170 B6 Azzaba Alg.
136 F5 Az Zabadānī Syria
137 I6 Az Zafīrī reg. Iraq
Az Zahrān Saudi Arabia see Dhahran
177 F1 Az Zaqāzīq Egypt
136 F5 Az Zarqā' Jordan
177 D1 Az Zāwiyah Libya
140 B5 Az Zilfī Saudi Arabia
137 K6 Az Zubayr Iraq


## B


154 D2 Ba, Sông r. Vietnam
136 E5 Baabda Lebanon
136 F4 Ba'albek Lebanon
127 H3 Baan Baa Australia
178 E3 Baardheere Somalia
141 H3 Bābā, Kōh-e mts Afgh.
171 L5 Baba Burnu pt Turkey
137 L1 Babadağ mt. Azer.
171 M2 Babadag Romania
Babadaykhan Turkm. see Badabaýhan
Babadaykhan Turkm. see Badabaýhan
138 D5 Babadurmaz Turkm.
173 C7 Babaeski Turkey
210 C4 Babahoyo Ecuador
143 B1 Babai India
145 E3 Babai r. Nepal
148 B1 Babai Gaxun China
137 K2 Bābājān Iran
153 C5 Babak Phil.
178 E2 Bāb al Mandab str. Africa/Asia
147 E7 Babar i. Indon.
139 H4 Babash-Ata, Khrebet mt. Kyrg.
178 D4 Babati Tanz.
172 E3 Babayevo Rus. Fed.
173 H7 Babayurt Rus. Fed.
190 B2 Babbitt U.S.A.
127 H7 Babel Island Australia
184 F4 Babine r. Canada
186 D4 Babine Lake Canada
147 F7 Babo Indon.
140 D2 Bābol Iran
138 C5 Bābol Sar Iran
180 C6 Baboon Point S. Africa
197 G6 Baboquivari Peak U.S.A.
178 B3 Baboua Cent. Afr. Rep.
172 D4 Babruysk Belarus
144 B4 Babuhri India
144 C2 Babusar Pass Pak.
172 G3 Babushkina, imeni Rus. Fed.
153 A4 Babuyan Phil.
153 B2 Babuyan i. Phil.
149 F7 Babuyan Channel Phil.
153 B2 Babuyan Islands Phil.
137 J5 Babylon tourist site Iraq
211 J4 Bacabal Brazil
136 C1 Bacakliyayla Tepesi mt. Turkey
207 G4 Bacalar Mex.
147 E7 Bacan i. Indon.
153 B2 Bacarra Phil.
169 M7 Bacău Romania
126 F6 Bacchus Marsh Australia
149 C6 Băc Giang Vietnam
206 C1 Bachiniva Mex.
149 C6 Bach Long Vi, Đao i. Vietnam
139 I5 Bachu China
139 I5 Bachu Liuchang China
187 I1 Back r. Canada
149 B6 Băc Kan Vietnam
171 H2 Bačka Palanka Serbia
186 D2 Backbone Ranges mts Canada
158 L3 Backe Sweden
126 B5 Backstairs Passage sea chan. Australia
162 E4 Backwater Reservoir U.K.
Bac Lac Vietnam see Bao Lac
154 C3 Bac Liêu Vietnam
149 C6 Băc Ninh Vietnam
153 B3 Baco, Mount Phil.
153 B4 Bacolod Phil.
Băc Quang Vietnam see Viêt Quang
188 F2 Bacqueville, Lac l. Canada
138 E5 Badabaýhan Ahal Turkm.
138 E5 Badabaýhan Ahal Turkm.
165 K6 Bad Abbach Germany
148 A1 Badain Jaran Shamo des. China
210 F4 Badajós, Lago l. Brazil
167 C3 Badajoz Spain
143 A3 Badami India
138 D2 Badamsha Kazakh.
137 H6 Badanah Saudi Arabia
145 H4 Badarpur India
191 F4 Bad Axe U.S.A.
165 G1 Bad Bederkesa Germany
165 F5 Bad Bergzabern Germany
165 G3 Bad Berleburg Germany
165 I1 Bad Bevensen Germany
165 J4 Bad Blankenburg Germany
165 G4 Bad Camberg Germany
189 H4 Baddeck Canada
141 G4 Baddo r. Pak.
165 H3 Bad Driburg Germany
165 K3 Bad Düben Germany
165 G5 Bad Dürkheim Germany
165 K3 Bad Dürrenberg Germany
136 C3 Bademli Geçidi pass Turkey
165 F4 Bad Ems Germany
168 H6 Baden Austria
168 D7 Baden Switz.
168 D6 Baden-Baden Germany
162 D4 Badenoch reg. U.K.
165 G5 Baden-Württemberg land Germany
165 G2 Bad Essen Germany
189 I4 Badger Canada
165 I3 Bad Grund (Harz) Germany
165 I3 Bad Harzburg Germany
165 H4 Bad Hersfeld Germany
168 F7 Bad Hofgastein Austria
165 G4 Bad Homburg vor der Höhe Germany
170 D2 Badia Polesine Italy
144 B4 Badin Pak.
206 C2 Badiraguato Mex.
168 F7 Bad Ischl Austria
Bādiyat ash Shām des. Asia see Syrian Desert
165 I4 Bad Kissingen Germany
165 J3 Bad Kösen Germany
165 F5 Bad Kreuznach Germany
165 G4 Bad Laasphe Germany
198 C2 Badlands reg. U.S.A.
198 C3 Badlands National Park U.S.A.
165 I3 Bad Langensalza Germany
165 I3 Bad Lauterberg im Harz Germany
165 G3 Bad Lippspringe Germany
165 F4 Bad Marienberg (Westerwald) Germany
165 H5 Bad Mergentheim Germany
165 G4 Bad Nauheim Germany
164 F4 Bad Neuenahr-Ahrweiler Germany
165 I4 Bad Neustadt an der Saale Germany
165 I1 Bad Oldesloe Germany
148 D4 Badong China
154 C3 Ba Đông Vietnam
165 H3 Bad Pyrmont Germany
137 J5 Badrah Iraq
168 F7 Bad Reichenhall Germany
165 I3 Bad Sachsa Germany
165 I2 Bad Salzdetfurth Germany
165 G2 Bad Salzuflen Germany
165 I4 Bad Salzungen Germany
165 G4 Bad Schwalbach Germany
168 E4 Bad Schwartau Germany
168 E4 Bad Segeberg Germany
165 F5 Bad Sobernheim Germany
124 E3 Badu Island Australia
143 C5 Badulla Sri Lanka
165 G4 Bad Vilbel Germany
165 J2 Bad Wilsnack Germany
165 I5 Bad Windsheim Germany
165 G1 Bad Zwischenahn Germany
158 B1 Bæir Iceland
152 C5 Baengnyeong-do i. S. Korea
127 I4 Baerami Australia
164 E4 Baesweiler Germany
167 E4 Baeza Spain
176 D4 Bafang Cameroon
176 A3 Bafatá Guinea-Bissau
220 T2 Baffin Basin sea feature Arctic Ocean
185 L2 Baffin Bay sea Canada/Greenland
185 K2 Baffin Island Canada
176 D4 Bafia Cameroon
176 A3 Bafing, Réserve du nature res. Mali
176 A3 Bafoulabé Mali
176 D4 Bafoussam Cameroon
140 D4 Bāfq Iran
136 E1 Bafra Turkey
173 E7 Bafra Burnu pt Turkey
140 E4 Bāft Iran
178 C3 Bafwasende Dem. Rep. Congo
145 F4 Bagaha India
153 A5 Bagahak, Gunung h. Sabah Malaysia
143 A2 Bagalkot India
178 D4 Bagamoyo Tanz.
155 B2 Bagan Datuk Malaysia
179 C5 Bagani Namibia
154 B4 Bagan Serai Malaysia
154 B5 Bagansiapiapi Indon.
197 F4 Bagdad U.S.A.
215 F1 Bagé Brazil
163 E5 Bagenalstown Ireland
145 G5 Bagerhat Bangl.
144 D3 Bageshwar India
194 F3 Baggs U.S.A.
161 C6 Baggy Point U.K.
144 C5 Bagh India
140 D4 Bāgh, Chāh-e well Iran
141 F2 Bagh Baghū Iran
137 J5 Baghdād Iraq
141 E4 Bāgh-e Bābū'īyeh Iran
140 C4 Bāgh-e Malek Iran
141 H2 Baghlān Afgh.
141 G3 Baghrān Afgh.
198 E2 Bagley U.S.A.
145 E3 Baglung Nepal
167 G1 Bagnères-de-Luchon France
166 G4 Bagnols-sur-Cèze France
145 F4 Bagnuiti r. Nepal
148 C2 Bag Nur l. China
153 B4 Bago Phil.
169 J3 Bagrationovsk Rus. Fed.
153 B2 Baguio Phil.
153 C5 Baguio Phil.
144 D3 Bahadurgarh India
141 F5 Bāhā Kālāt Iran
205 I3 Bahamas, The country Caribbean Sea
145 G4 Baharampur India
Bahariya Oasis oasis Egypt see Bahrīyah, Wāḥāt al
138 D5 Baharly Turkm.
155 B2 Bahau Malaysia
144 C3 Bahawalnagar Pak.
144 B3 Bahawalpur Pak.
136 F3 Bahçe Turkey
148 C4 Ba He r. China
144 D3 Baheri India
178 D4 Bahi Tanz.
214 E1 Bahia state Brazil
206 H4 Bahía, Islas de la is Hond.
215 D3 Bahía Blanca Arg.
206 B1 Bahía Kino Mex.
212 C7 Bahía Laura Arg.
212 E2 Bahía Negra Para.
206 A2 Bahía Tortugas Mex.
178 D2 Bahir Dar Eth.
142 E5 Bahlā Oman
140 C4 Bahman Yārī-ye Gharbī Iran
145 E4 Bahraich India
140 C5 Bahrain country Asia
140 C5 Bahrain, Gulf of Asia
137 L3 Bahrāmābād Iran
137 L3 Bahrām Beyg Iran
140 E4 Bahrāmjerd Iran
177 E2 Bahrīyah, Wāḥāt al oasis Egypt
210 E6 Bahuaja-Sonene, Parque Nacional nat. park Peru
169 K7 Baia Mare Romania
140 D3 Baiazeh Iran
146 E2 Baicheng Jilin China
139 J4 Baicheng Xinjiang China
189 G4 Baie-Comeau Canada
Baie du Poste Canada see Mistissini
189 F4 Baie-St-Paul Canada
189 I4 Baie Verte Canada
148 E2 Baigou He r. China
144 E5 Baihar India
152 E2 Baihe Jilin China
148 D3 Baihe Shaanxi China
148 E1 Bai He r. China
146 C1 Baikal, Lake Rus. Fed.
Baile an Bhuinneánaigh Ireland see Ballybunion
Baile an Chinnéidigh Ireland see Newtown Mount Kennedy
162 A3 Baile Mhartainn U.K.
163 C3 Baile na Finne Ireland
171 J2 Băileşti Romania
171 J2 Băileştilor, Câmpia plain Romania
163 E4 Bailieborough Ireland
148 D1 Bailingmiao China
164 A4 Bailleul France
187 H2 Baillie r. Canada
148 B3 Bailong Jiang r. China
146 C3 Baima China
148 E4 Baima Jian mt. China
161 G4 Bain r. U.K.
201 C6 Bainbridge GA U.S.A.
203 F3 Bainbridge NY U.S.A.
Baingoin China see Porong
136 F6 Bā'ir Jordan
136 F6 Bā'ir, Wādī watercourse Jordan
145 E2 Bairab Co l. China
145 F4 Bairagnia India
184 C3 Baird Mountains U.S.A.
123 G3 Bairiki Kiribati
148 F1 Bairin Qiao China
127 G6 Bairnsdale Australia
153 B4 Bais Phil.
149 C6 Baise China
149 C7 Baisha Hainan China
149 E5 Baisha Jiangxi China
148 C4 Baisha Sichuan China
152 D2 Baishan China
152 D3 Baishan China
148 B3 Baishui Jiang r. China
149 B7 Bai Thường Vietnam
152 A2 Baixingt China
148 B2 Baiyin China
177 F3 Baiyuda Desert Sudan
171 H1 Baja Hungary
206 A2 Baja California pen. Mex.
192 C6 Baja California state Mex.
206 A2 Baja California Sur state Mex.
137 L3 Bājalān Iran
206 D2 Bajan Mex.
144 E3 Bajang Nepal
145 G5 Baj Baj India
141 E2 Bājgīrān Iran
213 A3 Bajo Baudó Col.
206 I6 Bajo Boquete Panama
215 D1 Bajo Hondo Arg.
139 I3 Bakanas Kazakh.
139 I3 Bakanas watercourse Kazakh.
176 A3 Bakel Senegal
196 D4 Baker CA U.S.A.
194 F2 Baker MT U.S.A.
197 E2 Baker NV U.S.A.
194 C2 Baker OR U.S.A.
194 B1 Baker, Mount vol. U.S.A.
197 G4 Baker Butte mt. U.S.A.
125 I1 Baker Island terr. Pacific Ocean
186 C3 Baker Island U.S.A.
187 J2 Baker Lake Canada
187 J2 Baker Lake l. Canada
188 E2 Baker's Dozen Islands Canada
196 C4 Bakersfield U.S.A.
154 C2 Bâ Kêv Cambodia
Bakhardok Turkm. see Bokurdak
141 F3 Bākharz, Kūhhā-ye mts Iran
144 B4 Bakhasar India
173 E6 Bakhchysaray Ukr.
Bakherden Turkm. see Baharly
173 E5 Bakhmach Ukr.
140 D4 Bakhtegan, Daryācheh-ye l. Iran
Bakı Azer. see Baku
178 E2 Baki Somalia
136 B1 Bakırköy Turkey
178 D3 Bako Eth.
178 C3 Bakouma Cent. Afr. Rep.
178 B4 Bakoumba Gabon
173 G7 Baksan Rus. Fed.
139 J3 Bakty Kazakh.
137 L1 Baku Azer.
178 D3 Baku Dem. Rep. Congo
136 D2 Balâ Turkey
161 D5 Bala U.K.
210 E6 Bala, Cerros de mts Bol.
153 A4 Balabac Phil.
153 A5 Balabac i. Phil.
155 E1 Balabac Strait Malaysia/Phil.
137 J4 Balad Iraq
140 C2 Baladeh Iran
140 C2 Baladeh Iran
140 C4 Bālā Deh Iran
Balagar Gaole China see Bayan Ul
144 E5 Balaghat India
143 A2 Balaghat Range hills India
141 E4 Bālā Ḩowz Iran
137 K1 Balakän Azer.
172 G3 Balakhna Rus. Fed.
126 C5 Balaklava Australia
173 E6 Balaklava Ukr.
173 F5 Balakliya Ukr.
173 H4 Balakovo Rus. Fed.
161 D5 Bala Lake U.K.
155 E1 Balambangan i. Sabah Malaysia
141 F3 Bālā Murghāb Afgh.
144 B4 Balan India
173 H5 Balanda r. Rus. Fed.
136 B3 Balan Dağı h. Turkey
153 B3 Balanga Phil.
143 C1 Balangir India
143 C5 Balangoda Sri Lanka
138 B2 Balashi Rus. Fed.
173 G5 Balashov Rus. Fed.
144 C5 Balasinor India
168 H7 Balaton, Lake Hungary
168 H7 Balatonboglár Hungary
168 H7 Balatonfüred Hungary
141 G2 Bālbālak r. Afgh.
211 G4 Balbina, Represa de resr Brazil
163 E4 Balbriggan Ireland
126 C3 Balcanoona Australia
215 E3 Balcarce Arg.
171 M3 Balchik Bulg.
128 B7 Balclutha N.Z.
199 F5 Bald Knob U.S.A.
197 E3 Bald Mountain U.S.A.
187 J3 Baldock Lake Canada
191 H3 Baldwin Canada
201 D6 Baldwin FL U.S.A.
190 E4 Baldwin MI U.S.A.
190 A3 Baldwin WI U.S.A.
203 E3 Baldwinsville U.S.A.
197 H5 Baldy Peak U.S.A.
Baleares, Islas is Spain see Balearic Islands
167 H3 Balearic Islands is Spain
155 D2 Baleh r. Sarawak Malaysia
214 E2 Baleia, Ponta da pt Brazil
188 F3 Baleine, Grande Rivière de la r. Canada
188 E2 Baleine, Petite Rivière de la r. Canada
189 G2 Baleine, Rivière à la r. Canada
178 D3 Bale Mountains National Park Eth.
153 B3 Baler Phil.
153 B3 Baler Bay Phil.
145 F5 Baleshwar India
159 I3 Balestrand Norway
170 C4 Balestrieri, Punta mt. Italy
128 B6 Balfour N.Z.
155 E4 Bali i. Indon.
176 D4 Bali Nigeria
155 E4 Bali, Laut sea Indon.
Balieborough Ireland see Bailieborough
155 A2 Balige Indon.
143 C1 Baliguda India
148 F1 Balihan China
136 A2 Balıkesir Turkey
155 E3 Balikpapan Indon.
143 C2 Balimila Reservoir India
124 E2 Balimo P.N.G.
168 D6 Balingen Germany
153 B2 Balintang Channel Phil.
162 E3 Balintore U.K.
Bali Sea sea Indon. see Bali, Laut
153 B5 Baliungan i. Phil.
139 G5 Baljuvon Tajik.
164 D2 Balk Neth.
138 C5 Balkanabat Turkm.
171 J3 Balkan Mountains Bulg./Serbia
139 H3 Balkash Kazakh.
139 G1 Balkashino Kazakh.
139 H3 Balkhash, Lake Kazakh.
138 A3 Balkuduk Kazakh.
162 C4 Ballachulish U.K.
124 C5 Balladonia Australia
127 H3 Balladoran Australia
163 C4 Ballaghaderreen Ireland
126 F6 Ballan Australia
158 L1 Ballangen Norway
194 E2 Ballantine U.S.A.
162 D5 Ballantrae U.K.
126 E6 Ballarat Australia
124 C4 Ballard, Lake salt flat Australia
144 D6 Ballarpur India
162 E3 Ballater U.K.
176 B3 Ballé Mali
212 B3 Ballena, Punta pt Chile
129 B6 Balleny Islands is Antarctica
145 F4 Ballia India
127 J2 Ballina Australia
163 B3 Ballina Ireland
163 C3 Ballinafad Ireland
163 D4 Ballinalack Ireland
163 D3 Ballinamore Ireland
163 C4 Ballinasloe Ireland
163 C4 Ballindine Ireland
199 D6 Ballinger U.S.A.
162 E4 Ballinluig U.K.
163 B4 Ballinrobe Ireland
203 G3 Ballston Spa U.S.A.
163 E3 Ballybay Ireland
Ballybrack Ireland see An Baile Breac
163 B5 Ballybunion Ireland
163 E5 Ballycanew Ireland
163 B3 Ballycastle Ireland
163 E2 Ballycastle U.K.
163 F3 Ballyclare U.K.
163 A4 Ballyconneely Bay Ireland
163 D3 Ballyconnell Ireland
163 C4 Ballygar Ireland
163 D3 Ballygawley U.K.
163 D2 Ballygorman Ireland
163 C4 Ballyhaunis Ireland
163 B5 Ballyheigue Ireland
163 C5 Ballyhoura Mountains hills Ireland
163 D2 Ballykelly U.K.
163 D5 Ballylynan Ireland
163 D5 Ballymacmague Ireland
163 D4 Ballymahon Ireland
163 E3 Ballymena U.K.
163 E2 Ballymoney U.K.
163 C3 Ballymote Ireland
163 F3 Ballynahinch U.K.
163 C3 Ballyshannon Ireland
163 E5 Ballyteige Bay Ireland
163 B4 Ballyvaughan Ireland
163 E3 Ballyward U.K.
126 D6 Balmoral Australia
199 C6 Balmorhea U.S.A.
141 G4 Balochistan prov. Pak.
Balochistān reg. Pak. see Balochistan
134 E4 Balochistan reg. Pak.
144 E5 Balod India
143 C1 Baloda Bazar India
127 H2 Balonne r. Australia
144 C4 Balotra India
139 I3 Balpyk Bi Kazakh.
145 E4 Balrampur India
126 E5 Balranald Australia
171 K2 Balş Romania
191 H2 Balsam Creek Canada
211 I5 Balsas Brazil
207 E4 Balsas Mex.
206 D4 Balsas r. Mex.
173 D6 Balta Ukr.
172 I3 Baltasi Rus. Fed.
162 □ Baltasound U.K.
173 C6 Bălţi Moldova
159 L5 Baltic Sea g. Europe
136 C6 Balţīm Egypt
181 H1 Baltimore S. Africa
202 E5 Baltimore U.S.A.
163 E5 Baltinglass Ireland
144 C2 Baltistan reg. Pak.
169 I3 Baltiysk Rus. Fed.
144 D2 Baltoro Glacier Pak.
141 E4 Baluch Ab well Iran
145 G4 Balurghat India
153 C5 Balut i. Phil.
165 F3 Balve Germany
159 N4 Balvi Latvia
171 L5 Balya Turkey
139 I4 Balykchy Kyrg.
138 B3 Balykshi Kazakh.
141 E2 Bām Iran
141 E4 Bam Iran
149 C5 Bama China
124 E3 Bamaga Australia
188 B3 Bamaji Lake Canada
176 B3 Bamako Mali
176 B3 Bamba Mali
153 B2 Bambang Phil.
178 C3 Bambari Cent. Afr. Rep.
154 A5 Bambel Indon.
165 I5 Bamberg Germany
201 D5 Bamberg U.S.A.
178 C3 Bambili Dem. Rep. Congo
181 G5 Bamboesberg mts S. Africa
178 C3 Bambouti Cent. Afr. Rep.
214 D3 Bambuí Brazil
137 L6 Bāmdezh Iran
176 D4 Bamenda Cameroon
Bami Turkm. see Bamy
152 C2 Bamiancheng China
178 C3 Bamingui-Bangoran, Parc National du nat. park Cent. Afr. Rep.
141 F5 Bamposht reg. Iran
161 D7 Bampton U.K.
141 F5 Bampūr Iran
141 E5 Bampūr watercourse Iran
141 F3 Bamrūd Iran
138 D5 Bamy Turkm.
141 G3 Bāmyān Afgh.
125 G2 Banaba i. Kiribati
211 K5 Banabuiu, Açude resr Brazil
163 D4 Banagher Ireland
178 C3 Banalia Dem. Rep. Congo
181 J1 Banamana, Lagoa l. Moz.
176 B3 Banamba Mali
149 C4 Banan China
211 H6 Bananal, Ilha do i. Brazil
143 D2 Banapur India
144 D4 Banas r. India
136 B2 Banaz Turkey
154 B1 Ban Ban Laos
Banbar China see Domartang
163 E3 Banbridge U.K.
154 B2 Ban Bua Yai Thai.
161 F5 Banbury U.K.
153 A4 Bancalan i. Phil.
126 D3 Bancannia Lake salt flat Australia
176 A2 Banc d'Arguin, Parc National du nat. park Mauritania
162 F3 Banchory U.K.
153 A5 Bancoran i. Phil.
191 I3 Bancroft Canada
178 C3 Banda Dem. Rep. Congo
144 E4 Banda India
147 E7 Banda, Kepulauan is Indon.
147 F7 Banda, Laut sea Indon.
155 A1 Banda Aceh Indon.
127 J3 Banda Banda, Mount Australia
144 B2 Banda Daud Shah Pak.
154 A5 Bandahara, Gunung mt. Indon.
151 F6 Bandai-Asahi Kokuritsu-kōen nat. park Japan
141 F4 Bandān Iran
141 F4 Bandān Kūh mts Iran
145 H5 Bandarban Bangl.
140 E5 Bandar-e 'Abbās Iran
140 C2 Bandar-e Anzalī Iran
140 D5 Bandar-e Chārak Iran
140 C4 Bandar-e Deylam Iran
140 C4 Bandar-e Emām Khomeynī Iran
140 D5 Bandar-e Lengeh Iran
140 D5 Bandar-e Maqām Iran
140 C4 Bandar-e Ma'shur Iran
140 D5 Bandar-e Moghūyeh Iran
140 C4 Bandar-e Rīg Iran
140 D2 Bandar-e Torkaman Iran
155 C4 Bandar Lampung Indon.
144 D3 Bandarpunch mt. India
155 D1 Bandar Seri Begawan Brunei
Banda Sea sea Indon. see Banda, Laut
141 G3 Band-e Amīr, Daryā-ye r. Afgh.
141 F3 Band-e Bābā, Silsilah-ye Kōh-e mts Afgh.
141 F5 Band-e Bamposht, Kūh-e mts Iran
214 B1 Bandeirante Brazil
214 E3 Bandeiras, Pico de mt. Brazil
181 H1 Bandelierkop S. Africa
206 C3 Banderas, Bahía de b. Mex.
140 D3 Band-e Sar Qom Iran
144 C4 Bandi r. Rajasthan India
144 C4 Bandi r. Rajasthan India
144 E6 Bandia r. India
176 B3 Bandiagara Mali
Band-i-Amir r. Afgh. see Band-e Amīr, Daryā-ye
Band-i-Baba mts Afgh. see Band-e Bābā, Silsilah-ye Kōh-e
141 E5 Bandīnī Iran
136 A1 Bandırma Turkey
Band-i-Turkestan mts Afgh. see Turkistān, Silsilah-ye Band-e
163 C6 Bandon Ireland
163 C6 Bandon r. Ireland
154 A3 Ban Don, Ao b. Thai.
137 L2 Bändovan Burnu pt Azer.
137 L6 Band Qīr Iran
178 B4 Bandundu Dem. Rep. Congo
155 C4 Bandung Indon.
140 B3 Bāneh Iran
205 I4 Banes Cuba
186 F4 Banff Canada
162 F3 Banff U.K.
186 F4 Banff National Park Canada
176 B3 Banfora Burkina Faso
178 C4 Banga Dem. Rep. Congo
153 C5 Banga Phil.
153 C5 Bangai Point Phil.
143 B3 Bangalore India
144 D4 Banganga r. India
145 G5 Bangaon India
153 B2 Bangar Phil.
178 C3 Bangassou Cent. Afr. Rep.
145 E2 Bangdag Co salt l. China
154 C1 Bangfai, Xé r. Laos
124 C2 Banggai Indon.
147 E7 Banggai, Kepulauan is Indon.
155 E1 Banggi i. Sabah Malaysia
154 C1 Banghiang, Xé r. Laos
155 C3 Bangka i. Indon.
155 D4 Bangkalan Indon.
154 A5 Bangkaru i. Indon.
155 B3 Bangko Indon.
154 B2 Bangkok Thai. (City Plan 103)
154 B2 Bangkok, Bight of b. Thai.
145 G5 Bangladesh country Asia
154 D3 Ba Ngoi Vietnam
176 B4 Bangolo Côte d'Ivoire
144 D2 Bangong Co salt l. China/India
163 F3 Bangor Northern Ireland U.K.
161 C4 Bangor Wales U.K.
203 I2 Bangor ME U.S.A.
190 D4 Bangor MI U.S.A.
203 F4 Bangor PA U.S.A.
163 B3 Bangor Erris Ireland
197 F3 Bangs, Mount U.S.A.
154 A3 Bang Saphan Yai Thai.
158 J2 Bangsund Norway
153 B2 Bangued Phil.
178 B3 Bangui Cent. Afr. Rep.
153 B2 Bangui Phil.
154 A5 Bangunpurba Indon.
179 C5 Bangweulu, Lake Zambia
136 C6 Banhā Egypt
179 D6 Banhine, Parque Nacional de nat. park Moz.
154 B1 Ban Hin Heup Laos
178 C3 Bani Cent. Afr. Rep.
153 A2 Bani Phil.
178 B3 Bania Cent. Afr. Rep.
140 D5 Banī Forūr, Jazīreh-ye i. Iran
144 C2 Banihal Pass and Tunnel India
202 D6 Banister r. U.S.A.
177 F2 Banī Suwayf Egypt
177 D1 Banī Walīd Libya
140 C5 Banī Wuṭayfān well Saudi Arabia
136 E4 Bāniyās Syria
136 E5 Bāniyās Syria
170 G2 Banja Luka Bos.-Herz.
144 D3 Banjar India
155 D3 Banjarmasin Indon.
176 A3 Banjul Gambia
137 L2 Bankä Azer.
145 F4 Banka India
143 A3 Bankapur India
176 B3 Bankass Mali
154 A2 Ban Khao Yoi Thai.
154 A3 Ban Khok Kloi Thai.
145 F5 Banki India
184 E4 Banks Island B.C. Canada
184 F2 Banks Island N.W.T. Canada
125 G3 Banks Islands Vanuatu
187 K2 Banks Lake Canada
194 C2 Banks Lake U.S.A.
128 D5 Banks Peninsula N.Z.
127 H8 Banks Strait Australia
145 F5 Bankura India
154 B1 Ban Mouang Laos
163 E5 Bann r. Ireland
163 E3 Bann r. U.K.
154 C1 Ban Nakham Laos
154 A3 Ban Na San Thai.
190 C5 Banner U.S.A.
201 E7 Bannerman Town Bahamas
196 D5 Banning U.S.A.
154 C1 Ban Nonghèt Laos
215 B3 Baños Maule Chile
154 B1 Ban Pak-Leng Laos
154 C1 Ban Phaeng Thai.
154 B1 Ban Phai Thai.
Ban Phon Laos see Xékong
154 B1 Ban Phôn-Hông Laos
154 A2 Banphot Phisai Thai.
154 A2 Ban Pong Thai.
154 A3 Ban Sawi Thai.
145 E4 Bansi India
169 I6 Banská Bystrica Slovakia
141 F5 Bānsont Iran
154 A1 Ban Sut Ta Thai.
154 C2 Ban Suwan Wari Thai.
143 B2 Banswada India
144 C5 Banswara India
153 B4 Bantayan i. Phil.
163 C5 Banteer Ireland
154 A3 Ban Tha Chang Thai.
154 A3 Ban Tha Kham Thai.
154 A1 Ban Tha Song Yang Thai.
154 B2 Ban Tha Tako Thai.
154 A1 Ban Tha Ton Thai.
154 B2 Ban Tha Tum Thai.
154 A2 Ban Thung Luang Thai.
153 B3 Banton i. Phil.
154 C1 Ban Tôp Laos
163 B6 Bantry Ireland
163 B6 Bantry Bay Ireland
143 A3 Bantval India
154 B1 Ban Woen Laos
155 A2 Banyak, Pulau-pulau is Indon.
176 D4 Banyo Cameroon
167 H1 Banyoles Spain
155 D4 Banyuwangi Indon.
218 J8 Banzare Seamount sea feature Indian Ocean
165 J1 Banzkow Germany
148 B3 Bao'an China
148 E1 Baochang China
148 E2 Baoding China
148 D3 Baofeng China
148 C3 Baoji China
149 C4 Baojing China
148 D4 Baokang Hubei China
152 B1 Baokang Nei Mongol China
149 B6 Bao Lac Vietnam
152 B2 Baoli China
152 E1 Baolin China
154 C3 Bao Lôc Vietnam
150 C1 Baoqing China
146 B4 Baoshan China
148 D1 Baotou China
149 B4 Baoxing China
148 F3 Baoying China
144 C4 Bap India
143 C3 Bapatla India
164 A4 Bapaume France
191 H3 Baptiste Lake Canada
145 H2 Baqên China
145 H3 Baqên China
149 E5 Baqiu China
137 J5 Ba'qūbah Iraq
Baquerizo Moreno Ecuador see Puerto Baquerizo Moreno
171 H3 Bar Montenegro
177 F3 Bara Sudan
178 E3 Baraawe Somalia
145 F4 Barabar Hills India
190 C4 Baraboo U.S.A.
190 B4 Baraboo r. U.S.A.
205 J4 Baracoa Cuba
215 E2 Baradero Arg.
127 H3 Baradine Australia
127 H3 Baradine r. Australia
190 C2 Baraga U.S.A.
213 C2 Baragua Venez.
205 J5 Barahona Dom. Rep.
145 H4 Barail Range mts India
145 H4 Barak r. India
177 F3 Baraka watercourse Eritrea/Sudan
167 E1 Barakaldo Spain
141 H3 Barakī Barak Afgh.
143 D1 Barakot India
144 D2 Bara Lacha La India
187 J3 Baralzon Lake Canada
143 A2 Baramati India
144 D4 Baran India
144 B4 Baran r. Pak.
141 F3 Bārān, Kūh-e mts Iran
172 C4 Baranavichy Belarus
133 R3 Baranikha Rus. Fed.
173 C5 Baranivka Ukr.
213 B2 Baranoa Col.
186 B3 Baranof Island U.S.A.
138 A1 Baranovka Rus. Fed.
214 A2 Barão de Melgaço Brazil
176 B3 Baraouéli Mali
164 D4 Baraque de Fraiture h. Belgium
147 E7 Barat Daya, Kepulauan is Indon.
126 C4 Baratta (abandoned) Australia
144 D3 Baraut India
213 B4 Baraya Col.
214 D3 Barbacena Brazil
213 A4 Barbacoas Col.
205 M6 Barbados country Caribbean Sea
167 G1 Barbastro Spain
167 D4 Barbate Spain
153 B4 Barbaza Phil.
206 C2 Barbechitos Mex.
Barber's Point U.S.A. see Kalaeloa
181 I2 Barberton S. Africa
202 C4 Barberton U.S.A.
166 D4 Barbezieux-St-Hilaire France
213 B3 Barbosa Col.
187 K2 Barbour Bay Canada
202 B6 Barbourville U.S.A.
205 L5 Barbuda i. Antigua and Barbuda
165 J3 Barby (Elbe) Germany
124 E4 Barcaldine Australia
167 H2 Barcelona Spain (City Plan 112)
213 D2 Barcelona Venez.
210 F4 Barcelos Brazil
165 I4 Barchfeld Germany
176 B4 Barclayville Liberia
170 G2 Barcs Hungary
137 K1 Bärdä Azer.
177 D2 Bardaï Chad
158 C2 Bárðarbunga mt. Iceland
215 C2 Bardas Blancas Arg.
136 D6 Bardawīl, Sabkhat al lag. Egypt
145 F5 Barddhaman India
169 J6 Bardejov Slovakia
Bar Đôn Vietnam see Buôn Đôn
161 C5 Bardsey Island U.K.
140 E4 Bardsīr Iran
200 C4 Bardstown U.S.A.
202 B5 Bardwell U.S.A.
144 D3 Bareilly India
132 C2 Barentsburg Svalbard
132 D2 Barentsøya i. Svalbard
132 F2 Barents Sea Arctic Ocean
178 D2 Barentu Eritrea
144 E3 Barga China
143 C1 Bargarh India
144 D5 Bargi India
162 D5 Bargrennan U.K.
165 I1 Bargteheide Germany
145 G5 Barguna Bangl.
203 I2 Bar Harbor U.S.A.
170 G4 Bari Italy
154 C3 Ba Ria Vietnam
144 C3 Bari Doab lowland Pak.
145 E3 Barikot Nepal
213 E2 Barima r. Venez.
213 C2 Barinas Venez.
145 G5 Barisal Bangl.
155 B3 Barisan, Pegunungan mts Indon.
155 D3 Barito r. Indon.
210 F8 Baritú, Parque Nacional nat. park Arg.
141 E6 Barkā Oman
148 B4 Barkam China
140 C4 Barkan, Ra's-e pt Iran
159 N4 Barkava Latvia
186 E4 Barkerville Canada
200 C4 Barkley, Lake U.S.A.
186 D5 Barkley Sound inlet Canada
181 G5 Barkly East S. Africa
124 D3 Barkly Tableland reg. Australia
180 F4 Barkly West S. Africa
146 B2 Barkol China
144 D3 Barkot India

169 M7 **Bârlad** Romania
166 G2 **Bar-le-Duc** France
124 B4 **Barlee, Lake** *salt flat* Australia
170 G4 **Barletta** Italy
127 G5 **Barmedman** Australia
144 B4 **Barmer** India
126 D5 **Barmera** Australia
161 C5 **Barmouth** U.K.
144 C3 **Barnala** India
160 F3 **Barnard Castle** U.K.
127 F3 **Barnato** Australia
132 J4 **Barnaul** Rus. Fed.
203 F5 **Barnegat** U.S.A.
203 F5 **Barnegat Bay** U.S.A.
202 D4 **Barnesboro** U.S.A.
185 K2 **Barnes Icecap** Canada
164 D2 **Barneveld** Neth.
126 F4 **Barneys Lake** *imp. l.* Australia
197 G3 **Barney Top** *mt.* U.S.A.
199 C6 **Barnhart** U.S.A.
160 F4 **Barnsley** U.K.
161 C6 **Barnstaple** U.K.
161 C6 **Barnstaple Bay** U.K.
165 G2 **Barnstorf** Germany
201 D5 **Barnwell** U.S.A.
**Baroda** India *see* **Vadodara**
144 C1 **Barowghīl, Kowtal-e** Afgh.
145 H4 **Barpathar** India
145 G4 **Barpeta** India
190 D3 **Barques, Point Aux** *MI* U.S.A.
191 F3 **Barques, Point Aux** *MI* U.S.A.
213 C2 **Barquisimeto** Venez.
211 J6 **Barra** Brazil
162 A4 **Barra** *i.* U.K.
162 A3 **Barra, Sound of** *sea chan.* U.K.
127 I3 **Barraba** Australia
180 D7 **Barracouta, Cape** S. Africa
211 G6 **Barra do Bugres** Brazil
211 I5 **Barra do Corda** Brazil
214 B1 **Barra do Garças** Brazil
211 G5 **Barra do São Manuel** Brazil
210 C6 **Barranca** Peru
210 C4 **Barranca** Peru
213 B3 **Barrancabermeja** Col.
215 B3 **Barrancas** *r.* Arg.
213 B2 **Barrancas** Col.
213 E2 **Barrancas** Venez.
212 E3 **Barranqueras** Arg.
213 B2 **Barranquilla** Col.
203 G2 **Barre** U.S.A.
215 C1 **Barreal** Arg.
211 J6 **Barreiras** Brazil
211 G4 **Barreirinha** Brazil
211 J4 **Barreirinhas** Brazil
214 B1 **Barreiro** *r.* Brazil
167 B3 **Barreiro** Port.
211 K5 **Barreiros** Brazil
214 C3 **Barretos** Brazil
186 G4 **Barrhead** Canada
162 D5 **Barrhead** U.K.
191 H3 **Barrie** Canada
191 F3 **Barrie Island** Canada
186 E4 **Barrière** Canada
126 D3 **Barrier Range** *hills* Australia
207 H4 **Barrier Reef** Belize
127 I4 **Barrington, Mount** Australia
187 I3 **Barrington Lake** Canada
127 F2 **Barringun** Australia
190 B3 **Barron** U.S.A.
206 D2 **Barroterán** Mex.
215 E3 **Barrow** Arg.
163 E5 **Barrow** *r.* Ireland
184 C2 **Barrow** U.S.A.
184 C2 **Barrow, Point** U.S.A.
124 D4 **Barrow Creek** Australia
160 D3 **Barrow-in-Furness** U.K.
124 B4 **Barrow Island** Australia
185 I2 **Barrow Strait** Canada
161 D6 **Barry** U.K.
180 D6 **Barrydale** S. Africa
191 I3 **Barrys Bay** Canada
138 D3 **Barsakel'mes, Poluostrov** *pen.* Kazakh.
144 C3 **Barsalpur** India
139 I2 **Barshatas** Kazakh.
143 A2 **Barsi** India
165 H2 **Barsinghausen** Germany
144 D5 **Barsi Takli** India
196 D4 **Barstow** U.S.A.
166 G2 **Bar-sur-Aube** France
168 F3 **Barth** Germany
211 G2 **Bartica** Guyana
136 D1 **Bartın** Turkey
124 E3 **Bartle Frere, Mount** Australia
197 G2 **Bartles, Mount** U.S.A.
193 G4 **Bartlesville** U.S.A.
198 D3 **Bartlett** *NE* U.S.A.
203 H2 **Bartlett** *NH* U.S.A.
186 F2 **Bartlett Lake** Canada
203 G2 **Barton** U.S.A.
160 G4 **Barton-upon-Humber** U.K.
169 J3 **Bartoszyce** Poland
206 I6 **Barú, Volcán** *vol.* Panama
155 B2 **Barumun** *r.* Indon.
155 D4 **Barung** *i.* Indon.
154 A5 **Barus** Indon.
**Baruunsuu** Mongolia *see* **Tsogttsetsiy**
146 D2 **Baruun-Urt** Mongolia
144 D5 **Barwah** India
144 C3 **Barwala** India
144 C5 **Barwani** India
127 H2 **Barwon** *r.* Australia
172 D4 **Barysaw** Belarus
172 H4 **Barysh** Rus. Fed.
172 H4 **Barysh** *r.* Rus. Fed.
140 C3 **Barzūk** Iran
140 D5 **Bāsa'īdū** Iran
154 C3 **Basăk, Tônlé** *r.* Cambodia
196 C2 **Basalt** U.S.A.
149 □ **Basalt Island** *Hong Kong* China
178 B3 **Basankusu** Dem. Rep. Congo
143 B2 **Basar** India
171 M2 **Basarabi** Romania
215 E2 **Basavilbaso** Arg.
153 B4 **Basay** Phil.
153 B1 **Basco** Phil.
168 C7 **Basel** Switz.
141 E5 **Bashākerd, Kūhhā-ye** *mts* Iran
186 G4 **Bashaw** Canada
149 F6 **Bashi Channel** Phil./Taiwan
172 G4 **Bashmakovo** Rus. Fed.
140 C4 **Bāsht** Iran
173 E6 **Bashtanka** Ukr.
144 D4 **Basi** India
143 D1 **Basia** India
153 B5 **Basilan** *i.* Phil.
153 B5 **Basilan Strait** Phil.
161 H6 **Basildon** U.K.
194 E2 **Basin** U.S.A.
161 F6 **Basingstoke** U.K.
137 J4 **Bāsīra** *r.* Iraq
145 G5 **Basirhat** India
203 J2 **Baskahegan Lake** U.S.A.
137 J2 **Başkale** Turkey
191 J2 **Baskatong, Réservoir** *resr* Canada
173 H5 **Baskunchak, Ozero** *l.* Rus. Fed.
**Basle** Switz. *see* **Basel**
144 D5 **Basoda** India
178 C3 **Basoko** Dem. Rep. Congo
141 G5 **Basol** *r.* Pak.
137 K6 **Basra** Iraq
170 D2 **Bassano del Grappa** Italy
176 C4 **Bassar** Togo
176 A3 **Bassari Country** *tourist site* Senegal
179 D6 **Bassas da India** *rf* Indian Ocean
147 B5 **Bassein** Myanmar
160 D3 **Bassenthwaite Lake** U.K.
176 A3 **Basse Santa Su** Gambia
205 L5 **Basse-Terre** Guadeloupe
205 L5 **Basseterre** St Kitts and Nevis
198 D3 **Bassett** U.S.A.
197 G5 **Bassett Peak** U.S.A.
203 I2 **Bass Harbor** U.S.A.
176 B3 **Bassikounou** Mauritania
176 C4 **Bassila** Benin
162 F4 **Bass Rock** *i.* U.K.
124 E5 **Bass Strait** Australia
165 G2 **Bassum** Germany
190 B1 **Basswood Lake** U.S.A.
159 K4 **Båstad** Sweden
140 D5 **Bastak** Iran
140 B2 **Bāstānābād** Iran
165 I4 **Bastheim** Germany
145 E4 **Basti** India
170 C3 **Bastia** *Corsica* France
164 D4 **Bastogne** Belgium
199 F5 **Bastrop** *LA* U.S.A.
199 D6 **Bastrop** *TX* U.S.A.
176 C4 **Bata** Equat. Guinea
205 H4 **Batabanó, Golfo de** *b.* Cuba
153 B2 **Batac** Phil.
153 C3 **Batag** *i.* Phil.
133 O3 **Batagay** Rus. Fed.
144 B2 **Batai Pass** Pak.
144 C3 **Batala** India
167 B3 **Batalha** Port.
154 C5 **Batam** *i.* Indon.
133 N3 **Batamay** Rus. Fed.
153 B1 **Batan** *i.* Phil.
178 B3 **Batangafo** Cent. Afr. Rep.
153 B3 **Batangas** Phil.
155 B3 **Batanghari** *r.* Indon.
154 A5 **Batangtoru** Indon.
153 B1 **Batan Islands** Phil.
214 C3 **Batatais** Brazil
190 C5 **Batavia** *IL* U.S.A.
202 D3 **Batavia** *NY* U.S.A.
173 F6 **Bataysk** Rus. Fed.
191 E2 **Batchawana** Canada
191 E2 **Batchawana** *r.* Canada
190 E2 **Batchawana Bay** Canada
188 D4 **Batchawana Mountain** *h.* Canada
124 D3 **Batchelor** Australia
154 B2 **Bătdâmbâng** Cambodia
127 I5 **Batemans Bay** Australia
127 I5 **Batemans Bay** *b.* Australia
199 F5 **Batesville** *AR* U.S.A.
199 F5 **Batesville** *MS* U.S.A.
172 D3 **Batetskiy** Rus. Fed.
189 G4 **Bath** *N.B.* Canada
191 I3 **Bath** *Ont.* Canada
161 E6 **Bath** U.K.
203 I3 **Bath** *ME* U.S.A.
202 E3 **Bath** *NY* U.S.A.
162 E5 **Bathgate** U.K.
144 C3 **Bathinda** India
127 H4 **Bathurst** Australia
189 G4 **Bathurst** Canada
181 G6 **Bathurst** S. Africa
127 H5 **Bathurst, Lake** Australia
184 H3 **Bathurst Inlet** *inlet* Canada
184 H3 **Bathurst Inlet (abandoned)** Canada
124 D3 **Bathurst Island** Australia
185 I2 **Bathurst Island** Canada
137 K7 **Bāţin, Wādī al** *watercourse* Asia
139 G4 **Batken** *admin. div.* Kyrg.
140 D3 **Bāţlāq-e Gavkhūnī** *marsh* Iran
160 F4 **Batley** U.K.
127 H5 **Batlow** Australia
137 H3 **Batman** Turkey
176 C1 **Batna** Alg.
154 □ **Batok, Bukit** *h.* Sing.
154 A4 **Batong, Ko** *i.* Thai.
199 F6 **Baton Rouge** U.S.A.
206 C2 **Batopilas** Mex.
177 D4 **Batouri** Cameroon
214 B1 **Batovi** Brazil
136 E4 **Batroûn** Lebanon
158 O1 **Båtsfjord** Norway
143 C5 **Batticaloa** Sri Lanka
170 F4 **Battipaglia** Italy
187 G4 **Battle** *r.* Canada
190 E4 **Battle Creek** U.S.A.
187 H4 **Battleford** Canada
194 C3 **Battle Mountain** U.S.A.
144 C1 **Battura Glacier** Pak.
155 A3 **Batu, Pulau-pulau** *is* Indon.
154 B4 **Batu Gajah** Malaysia
153 C5 **Batulaki** Phil.
137 H1 **Bat'umi** Georgia
155 B2 **Batu Pahat** Malaysia
154 B4 **Batu Putih, Gunung** *mt.* Malaysia
147 E7 **Baubau** Indon.
176 C3 **Bauchi** Nigeria
198 E1 **Baudette** U.S.A.
213 A3 **Baudo, Serranía de** *mts* Col.
166 D3 **Baugé** France
165 H5 **Bauland** *reg.* Germany
189 J3 **Bauld, Cape** Canada
166 H3 **Baume-les-Dames** France
214 C3 **Bauru** Brazil
214 B2 **Baús** Brazil
164 E4 **Bausendorf** Germany
159 N4 **Bauska** Latvia
138 B3 **Bautino** Kazakh.
168 G5 **Bautzen** Germany
139 G4 **Bauyrzhan Momyshuly** Kazakh.
180 E6 **Baviaanskloofberge** *mts* S. Africa
192 E6 **Bavispe** *r.* Mex.
127 G6 **Baw Baw National Park** Australia
161 I5 **Bawdeswell** U.K.
155 D4 **Bawean** *i.* Indon.
164 F2 **Bawinkel** Germany
176 B3 **Bawku** Ghana
154 A1 **Bawlake** Myanmar
149 A4 **Bawolung** China
148 B3 **Baxi** China
201 D6 **Baxley** U.S.A.
153 B3 **Bay, Laguna de** *lag.* Phil.
205 I4 **Bayamo** Cuba
144 D4 **Bayana** India
139 H2 **Bayanauyl** Kazakh.
148 B1 **Bayandalay** Mongolia
146 B3 **Bayan Har Shan** *mts* China
146 C2 **Bayanhongor** Mongolia
148 B2 **Bayan Hot** China
152 A1 **Bayan Huxu** China
148 C1 **Bayannur** China
148 B1 **Bayan Nurun** China
148 C1 **Bayan Obo** China
148 C1 **Bayan-Ovoo** Mongolia
152 A1 **Bayan Qagan** China
148 D1 **Bayan Shutu** China
146 D2 **Bayan Ul** China
146 D2 **Bayan-Uul** Mongolia
140 D4 **Bayāẕ** Iran
153 C4 **Baybay** Phil.
137 H1 **Bayburt** Turkey
191 F4 **Bay City** *MI* U.S.A.
199 D6 **Bay City** *TX* U.S.A.
132 H3 **Baydaratskaya Guba** Rus. Fed.
178 E3 **Baydhabo** Somalia
165 K5 **Bayerischer Wald** *mts* Germany
165 I5 **Bayern** *land* Germany
139 J1 **Bayevo** Rus. Fed.
190 B2 **Bayfield** U.S.A.
138 F3 **Baygekum** Kazakh.
138 E1 **Baygora** Kazakh.
171 L5 **Bayındır** Turkey
137 I4 **Bayjī** Iraq
**Baykal, Ozero** *l.* Rus. Fed. *see* **Baikal, Lake**
146 C1 **Baykal'skiy Khrebet** *mts* Rus. Fed.
137 H2 **Baykan** Turkey
138 F3 **Baykonur** Kazakh.
138 E3 **Baykonyr** Kazakh.
138 E3 **Baykozha** Kazakh.
139 H5 **Baykurt** China
138 D1 **Baymak** Rus. Fed.
140 D6 **Baynūna'h** *reg.* U.A.E.
153 B2 **Bayombong** Phil.
166 D5 **Bayonne** France
153 B4 **Bayo Point** Phil.
138 E5 **Baýramaly** Turkm.
171 L5 **Bayramiç** Turkey
165 J5 **Bayreuth** Germany
199 F6 **Bay St Louis** U.S.A.
138 C3 **Bayshonas** Kazakh.
203 G4 **Bay Shore** U.S.A.
161 E5 **Bayston Hill** U.K.
**Baysun** Uzbek. *see* **Boysun**
139 F5 **Baysuntau, Gory** *mts* Uzbek.
199 E6 **Baytown** U.S.A.
128 F3 **Bay View** N.Z.
139 G4 **Bayyrkum** Kazakh.
139 G4 **Bayzhansay** Kazakh.
167 E4 **Baza** Spain
139 H5 **Bāzā'ī Gonbad** Afgh.
139 J3 **Bazar** *watercourse* Kazakh.
141 H3 **Bāzārak** Afgh.
**Bazardyuzi, Gora** *mt.* Azer./Rus. Fed. *see* **Bazardyuzyu, Gora**
137 K1 **Bazardyuzyu, Gora** *mt.* Azer./Rus. Fed.
141 G3 **Bāzār-e Mālistān** Afgh.
140 C2 **Bāzār-e Māsāl** Iran
137 J2 **Bāzargān** Iran
173 H4 **Bazarnyy Karabulak** Rus. Fed.
138 B2 **Bazarsholan** Kazakh.
138 B2 **Bazartobe** Kazakh.
179 D6 **Bazaruto, Ilha do** *i.* Moz.
141 G5 **Bazdar** Pak.
148 C4 **Bazhong** China
148 E2 **Bazhou** China
141 F5 **Bazmān** Iran
141 F4 **Bazmān, Kūh-e** *mt.* Iran
140 C3 **Bāzoft, Āb-e** *r.* Iran
136 E4 **Bcharré** Lebanon
**Be** *r.* Vietnam *see* **Be, Sông**
179 E5 **Bé, Nosy** *i.* Madag.
154 C3 **Be, Sông** *r.* Vietnam
198 C2 **Beach** U.S.A.
191 I3 **Beachburg** Canada
203 F5 **Beach Haven** U.S.A.
126 D6 **Beachport** Australia
203 F5 **Beachwood** U.S.A.
161 H7 **Beachy Head** U.K.
203 G4 **Beacon** U.S.A.
181 G6 **Beacon Bay** S. Africa
149 □ **Beacon Hill** *Hong Kong* China
161 G6 **Beaconsfield** U.K.
212 C8 **Beagle, Canal** *sea chan.* Arg.
124 C3 **Beagle Gulf** Australia
179 E5 **Bealanana** Madag.
163 B3 **Béal an Mhuirthead** Ireland
161 E7 **Beaminster** U.K.
194 E3 **Bear** *r.* U.S.A.
187 M2 **Bear Cove** *b.* Canada
188 C4 **Beardmore** Canada
**Beardmore Res.** Australia *see* **Kajarabie, Lake**
190 B5 **Beardstown** U.S.A.
188 D3 **Bear Island** Canada
186 D3 **Bear Lake** Canada
194 E3 **Bear Lake** *l.* U.S.A.
144 D4 **Bearma** *r.* India
194 E1 **Bear Paw Mountain** U.S.A.
188 B3 **Bearskin Lake** Canada
196 B2 **Bear Valley** U.S.A.
144 C3 **Beas** *r.* India
144 C3 **Beas Dam** India
205 J5 **Beata, Cabo** *c.* Dom. Rep.
205 J5 **Beata, Isla** *i.* Dom. Rep.
198 D3 **Beatrice** U.S.A.
186 E3 **Beatton** *r.* Canada
186 E3 **Beatton River** Canada
196 D3 **Beatty** U.S.A.
188 E4 **Beattyville** Canada
166 G5 **Beaucaire** France
212 E8 **Beauchene Island** Falkland Is
126 E6 **Beaufort** Australia
155 E1 **Beaufort** *Sabah* Malaysia
201 D5 **Beaufort** U.S.A.
184 D2 **Beaufort Sea** Canada/U.S.A.
180 E6 **Beaufort West** S. Africa
188 F4 **Beauharnois** Canada
162 D3 **Beauly** U.K.
162 D3 **Beauly Firth** *est.* U.K.
161 C4 **Beaumaris** U.K.
164 C4 **Beaumont** Belgium
128 B6 **Beaumont** N.Z.
199 F6 **Beaumont** *MS* U.S.A.
202 B5 **Beaumont** *OH* U.S.A.
199 E6 **Beaumont** *TX* U.S.A.
166 G3 **Beaune** France
166 D3 **Beaupréau** France
164 A4 **Beauquesne** France
164 C4 **Beauraing** Belgium
187 J4 **Beauséjour** Canada
166 F2 **Beauvais** France
187 H3 **Beauval** Canada
164 A4 **Beauval** France
184 H4 **Beaver** *r. Alta* Canada
186 D2 **Beaver** *r. B.C./Y.T.* Canada
188 C2 **Beaver** *r. Ont.* Canada
197 F2 **Beaver** U.S.A.
197 F2 **Beaver** *r.* U.S.A.
186 A2 **Beaver Creek** Canada
200 C4 **Beaver Dam** *KY* U.S.A.
190 C4 **Beaver Dam** *WI* U.S.A.
202 C4 **Beaver Falls** U.S.A.
194 D2 **Beaverhead Mountains** U.S.A.
187 J4 **Beaver Hill Lake** Canada
187 I2 **Beaverhill Lake** Canada
190 E3 **Beaver Island** U.S.A.
199 E4 **Beaver Lake** *resr* U.S.A.
186 F3 **Beaverlodge** Canada
202 D4 **Beaver Run Reservoir** U.S.A.
144 C4 **Beawar** India
215 C2 **Beazley** Arg.
214 C3 **Bebedouro** Brazil
161 D4 **Bebington** U.K.
165 H4 **Bebra** Germany
188 F1 **Bécard, Lac** *l.* Canada
161 I5 **Beccles** U.K.
171 I2 **Bečej** Serbia
167 C1 **Becerreá** Spain
176 B1 **Béchar** Alg.
165 I5 **Bechhofen** Germany
202 C6 **Beckley** U.S.A.
165 G3 **Beckum** Germany
165 K4 **Bečov nad Teplou** Czech Rep.
160 F3 **Bedale** U.K.
164 E4 **Bedburg** Germany
203 I2 **Beddington** U.S.A.
178 D3 **Bedelē** Eth.
139 I4 **Bedel Pass** China/Kyrg.
203 G2 **Bedford** Canada
181 I4 **Bedford** S. Africa
161 G5 **Bedford** U.K.
200 C4 **Bedford** *IN* U.S.A.
203 H3 **Bedford** *MA* U.S.A.
202 D4 **Bedford** *PA* U.S.A.
202 D6 **Bedford** *VA* U.S.A.
161 G5 **Bedford Level (North Level)** *lowland* U.K.
127 G4 **Bedgerebong** Australia
160 F2 **Bedlington** U.K.
154 □ **Bedok** Sing.
154 □ **Bedok Reservoir** Sing.
197 H2 **Bedrock** U.S.A.
164 E1 **Bedum** Neth.
161 F5 **Bedworth** U.K.
202 B5 **Beech Fork Lake** U.S.A.
190 C2 **Beechwood** U.S.A.
127 G6 **Beechworth** Australia
127 I5 **Beecroft Peninsula** Australia
165 K2 **Beelitz** Germany
127 J1 **Beenleigh** Australia
163 A5 **Beenoskee** *h.* Ireland
164 B3 **Beernem** Belgium
136 E6 **Be'ér Sheva'** Israel
180 E6 **Beervlei Dam** S. Africa
127 J1 **Beerwah** Australia
165 K2 **Beetzsee** *l.* Germany
199 D6 **Beeville** U.S.A.
178 C3 **Befale** Dem. Rep. Congo
179 E5 **Befandriana Avaratra** Madag.
127 H6 **Bega** Australia
144 B3 **Begari** *r.* Pak.
167 H2 **Begur, Cap de** *c.* Spain
145 F4 **Begusarai** India
140 D4 **Behābād** Iran
141 E3 **Behābād** Iran
211 H3 **Béhague, Pointe** *pt* Fr. Guiana
140 C4 **Behbehān** Iran
186 F2 **Behchokò** Canada
186 C3 **Behm Canal** *sea chan.* U.S.A.
129 B3 **Behrendt Mountains** *mts* Antarctica
140 D4 **Behrūsī** Iran
140 D2 **Behshahr** Iran
146 E2 **Bei'an** China
149 C4 **Beibei** China
148 B4 **Beichuan** China
149 F6 **Beigang** Taiwan
149 C6 **Beihai** China
149 D6 **Bei Jiang** *r.* China
148 E2 **Beijing** China (City Plan **103**)
148 E1 **Beijing** *mun.* China
164 E2 **Beilen** Neth.
149 C7 **Beili** China
149 D6 **Beiliu** China
165 J5 **Beilngries** Germany
162 C5 **Beinn an Oir** *h.* U.K.
162 D3 **Beinn Dearg** *mt.* U.K.
149 C5 **Beipan Jiang** *r.* China
152 A3 **Beipiao** China
179 D5 **Beira** Moz.
148 E3 **Beiru He** *r.* China
136 E5 **Beirut** Lebanon
148 D2 **Beitai Ding** *mt.* China
179 C6 **Beitbridge** Zimbabwe
162 D5 **Beith** U.K.
169 K7 **Beiuş** Romania
152 A3 **Beizhen** China
167 C3 **Beja** Port.
176 C1 **Béja** Tunisia
176 C1 **Bejaïa** Alg.
167 D2 **Béjar** Spain
141 E3 **Bejestān** Iran
144 B3 **Beji** *r.* Pak.
138 E3 **Bekbauly** Kazakh.
138 C3 **Bekbike** Kazakh.
**Bekdash** Turkm. *see* **Garabogaz**
169 J7 **Békés** Hungary
169 J7 **Békéscsaba** Hungary
179 E6 **Bekily** Madag.
176 B4 **Bekwai** Ghana
145 E4 **Bela** India
141 G5 **Bela** Pak.
144 B3 **Belab** *r.* Pak.
181 H2 **Bela-Bela** S. Africa
177 D4 **Bélabo** Cameroon
171 I2 **Bela Crkva** Serbia
139 J2 **Bel'agash** Kazakh.
203 E5 **Bel Air** U.S.A.
167 D3 **Belalcázar** Spain
165 K5 **Bělá nad Radbuzou** Czech Rep.
**Belaraboon** Australia *see* **Paddington**
169 M4 **Belarus** *country* Europe
214 A3 **Bela Vista** Brazil
179 D6 **Bela Vista** Moz.
154 A5 **Belawan** Indon.
133 S3 **Belaya** *r.* Rus. Fed.
173 G6 **Belaya Glina** Rus. Fed.
173 G5 **Belaya Kalitva** Rus. Fed.
172 I3 **Belaya Kholunitsa** Rus. Fed.
169 I5 **Bełchatów** Poland
202 B6 **Belcher** U.S.A.
185 J4 **Belcher Islands** Canada
141 G3 **Bēlchirāgh** Afgh.
136 F2 **Belcik** Turkey
163 D3 **Belcoo** U.K.
191 I1 **Belcourt** Canada
196 B1 **Belden** U.S.A.
178 E3 **Beledweyne** Somalia
138 C5 **Belek** Turkm.
211 I4 **Belém** Brazil
212 C3 **Belén** Arg.
136 F3 **Belen** Turkey
195 F5 **Belen** U.S.A.
125 G3 **Belep, Îles** *is* New Caledonia
138 D3 **Beleuli** *tourist site* Uzbek.
172 F4 **Belev** Rus. Fed.
128 D5 **Belfast** N.Z.
163 F3 **Belfast** U.K.
203 I2 **Belfast** U.S.A.
163 F3 **Belfast Lough** *inlet* U.K.
198 C2 **Belfield** U.S.A.
160 F2 **Belford** U.K.
166 H3 **Belfort** France
143 A3 **Belgaum** India
165 L3 **Belgern** Germany
164 C4 **Belgium** *country* Europe
173 F5 **Belgorod** Rus. Fed.
173 F5 **Belgorodskaya Oblast'** *admin. div.* Rus. Fed.
171 I2 **Belgrade** Serbia
194 E2 **Belgrade** U.S.A.
129 C3 **Belgrano II** *research stn* Antarctica
170 E6 **Belice** *r. Sicily* Italy
172 G4 **Belinskiy** Rus. Fed.
155 C3 **Belinyu** Indon.
155 C3 **Belitung** *i.* Indon.
207 G4 **Belize** Belize
207 G4 **Belize** *country* Central America
150 E2 **Belkina, Mys** *pt* Rus. Fed.
133 O2 **Bel'kovskiy, Ostrov** *i.* Rus. Fed.
127 I1 **Bell** Australia
127 H4 **Bell** *r.* Australia
186 D4 **Bella Bella** Canada
166 E3 **Bellac** France
186 D4 **Bella Coola** Canada
199 E6 **Bellaire** U.S.A.
143 B3 **Bellary** India
127 H2 **Bellata** Australia
215 F1 **Bella Unión** Uruguay
127 J3 **Bellbrook** Australia
202 B4 **Bellefontaine** U.S.A.
202 E4 **Bellefonte** U.S.A.
198 C2 **Belle Fourche** U.S.A.
198 C2 **Belle Fourche** *r.* U.S.A.
166 G3 **Bellegarde-sur-Valserine** France
201 D7 **Belle Glade** U.S.A.
166 C3 **Belle-Île** *i.* France
189 J3 **Belle Isle** *i.* Canada
189 I3 **Belle Isle, Strait of** Canada
197 G4 **Bellemont** U.S.A.
190 A5 **Belle Plaine** U.S.A.
191 H2 **Belleterre** Canada
191 I3 **Belleville** Canada
198 D4 **Belleville** U.S.A.
190 B4 **Bellevue** *IA* U.S.A.
194 D3 **Bellevue** *ID* U.S.A.
202 B4 **Bellevue** *OH* U.S.A.
194 B2 **Bellevue** *WA* U.S.A.
127 J3 **Bellingen** Australia
160 E2 **Bellingham** U.K.
194 B1 **Bellingham** U.S.A.
129 E2 **Bellingshausen** *research stn* Antarctica
129 B3 **Bellingshausen Sea** *sea* Antarctica
168 D7 **Bellinzona** Switz.
213 B3 **Bello** Col.
203 G3 **Bellows Falls** U.S.A.
144 B3 **Bellpat** Pak.
162 F4 **Bell Rock** *i.* U.K.
203 F5 **Belltown** U.S.A.
170 E1 **Belluno** Italy
215 D2 **Bell Ville** Arg.
180 C6 **Bellville** S. Africa
165 G2 **Belm** Germany
180 F4 **Belmont** S. Africa
162 □ **Belmont** U.K.
202 D3 **Belmont** U.S.A.
214 E1 **Belmonte** Brazil
207 G4 **Belmopan** Belize
127 J2 **Belmore, Mount** *h.* Australia
**Belmullet** Ireland *see* **Béal an Mhuirthead**
164 B4 **Belœil** Belgium
203 G2 **Belœil** Canada
146 E1 **Belogorsk** Rus. Fed.
179 E6 **Beloha** Madag.
214 D2 **Belo Horizonte** Brazil
198 D4 **Beloit** *KS* U.S.A.
190 C4 **Beloit** *WI* U.S.A.
139 K2 **Belokurikha** Rus. Fed.
172 E1 **Belomorsk** Rus. Fed.
145 G5 **Belonia** India
173 F6 **Belorechensk** Rus. Fed.
136 F3 **Belören** Turkey
138 D1 **Beloretsk** Rus. Fed.
**Belorussia** *country* Europe *see* **Belarus**
179 E5 **Belo Tsiribihina** Madag.
139 J2 **Belousovka** Kazakh.
172 F2 **Beloye, Ozero** *l.* Rus. Fed.
172 F1 **Beloye (abandoned)** Rus. Fed.
**Beloye More** *sea* Rus. Fed. *see* **White Sea**
172 F2 **Belozersk** Rus. Fed.
202 C5 **Belpre** U.S.A.
194 E2 **Belt** U.S.A.
126 C3 **Beltana** Australia
126 B2 **Belt Bay** *salt flat* Australia
196 D3 **Belted Range** *mts* U.S.A.
199 D6 **Belton** U.S.A.
143 A3 **Belur** India
153 A5 **Beluran** *Sabah* Malaysia
190 C4 **Belvidere** U.S.A.
138 D2 **Belyayevka** Rus. Fed.
172 H3 **Belyshevo** Rus. Fed.
172 E4 **Belyy** Rus. Fed.
132 I2 **Belyy, Ostrov** *i.* Rus. Fed.
165 K2 **Belzig** Germany
179 E5 **Bemaraha, Parc National de** Madag.
190 C6 **Bement** U.S.A.
198 E2 **Bemidji** U.S.A.
178 C4 **Bena Dibele** Dem. Rep. Congo
162 D4 **Ben Alder** *mt.* U.K.
127 F6 **Benalla** Australia
170 D6 **Ben Arous** Tunisia
167 D1 **Benavente** Spain
162 E3 **Ben Avon** *mt.* U.K.
163 B4 **Benbaun** *h.* Ireland
162 A3 **Benbecula** *i.* U.K.
163 C3 **Benbulben** *h.* Ireland
163 E3 **Benburb** U.K.
162 C4 **Ben Cruachan** *mt.* U.K.
194 B2 **Bend** U.S.A.
181 G5 **Bendearg** *mt.* S. Africa
127 I3 **Bendemeer** Australia
178 E3 **Bender-Bayla** Somalia
126 F6 **Bendigo** Australia
127 H6 **Bendoc** Australia
179 D5 **Bene** Moz.
189 I3 **Benedict, Mount** *h.* Canada
203 I2 **Benedicta** U.S.A.
179 E6 **Benenitra** Madag.
168 G6 **Benešov** Czech Rep.
164 E6 **Bénestroff** France
170 F4 **Benevento** Italy
135 G5 **Bengal, Bay of** *sea* Asia
178 C3 **Bengamisa** Dem. Rep. Congo
148 E3 **Bengbu** China
177 E1 **Benghazi** Libya
148 F3 **Beng He** *r.* China
154 B5 **Bengkalis** Indon.
155 B3 **Bengkulu** Indon.
159 K4 **Bengtsfors** Sweden
179 B5 **Benguela** Angola
162 B4 **Ben Hiant** *h.* U.K.
162 D2 **Ben Hope** *h.* U.K.
210 E6 **Beni** *r.* Bol.
178 C3 **Beni** Dem. Rep. Congo
176 B1 **Beni Abbès** Alg.
167 F3 **Benidorm** Spain
176 B1 **Beni Mellal** Morocco
176 C4 **Benin** *country* Africa
176 C4 **Benin, Bight of** *g.* Africa
176 C4 **Benin City** Nigeria
176 B1 **Beni Saf** Alg.
215 E3 **Benito Juárez** Arg.
153 B2 **Benito Soliven** Phil.
210 E4 **Benjamim Constant** Brazil
204 B2 **Benjamín Hill** Mex.
124 D2 **Benjina** Indon.
198 C3 **Benkelman** U.S.A.
162 D2 **Ben Klibreck** *h.* U.K.
162 D4 **Ben Lawers** *mt.* U.K.
127 I3 **Ben Lomond** *mt.* Australia
162 D4 **Ben Lomond** *h.* U.K.
127 G8 **Ben Lomond National Park** Australia
162 D2 **Ben Loyal** *h.* U.K.
162 D4 **Ben Lui** *mt.* U.K.
162 E3 **Ben Macdui** *mt.* U.K.
162 B4 **Ben More** *h. Scotland* U.K.
162 D4 **Ben More** *mt. Scotland* U.K.
128 C6 **Benmore, Lake** N.Z.
162 D2 **Ben More Assynt** *h.* U.K.
133 P2 **Bennetta, Ostrov** *i.* Rus. Fed.
162 C4 **Ben Nevis** *mt.* U.K.
203 G3 **Bennington** U.S.A.
181 H3 **Benoni** S. Africa
177 D4 **Bénoué, Parc National de la** *nat. park* Cameroon
165 G5 **Bensheim** Germany
197 G6 **Benson** *AZ* U.S.A.
198 E2 **Benson** *MN* U.S.A.
141 E5 **Bent** Iran
155 B2 **Benta Seberang** Malaysia
202 D6 **Bent Creek** U.S.A.
147 E7 **Benteng** Indon.
124 D3 **Bentinck Island** Australia
154 A3 **Bentinck Island** Myanmar
178 C3 **Bentiu** South Sudan
160 F4 **Bentley** U.K.
203 J2 **Benton** Canada
199 E5 **Benton** *AR* U.S.A.
196 C3 **Benton** *CA* U.S.A.
200 B4 **Benton** *IL* U.S.A.
190 D4 **Benton Harbor** U.S.A.
154 C3 **Bên Tre** Vietnam
154 B5 **Bentung** Malaysia
176 D4 **Benue** *r.* Nigeria
162 D4 **Ben Vorlich** *h.* U.K.
163 B3 **Benwee Head** Ireland
162 D3 **Ben Wyvis** *mt.* U.K.
152 B3 **Benxi** *Liaoning* China
152 C3 **Benxi** *Liaoning* China
153 C5 **Beo** Indon.
**Beograd** Serbia *see* **Belgrade**
144 E5 **Beohari** India
176 B4 **Béoumi** Côte d'Ivoire
151 B8 **Beppu** Japan
125 H3 **Beqa** *i.* Fiji
144 C4 **Berach** *r.* India
171 H3 **Berane** Montenegro
189 G2 **Bérard, Lac** *l.* Canada
144 D5 **Berasia** India
154 A5 **Berastagi** Indon.
171 H4 **Berat** Albania
155 E3 **Beratus, Gunung** *mt.* Indon.
147 F7 **Berau, Teluk** *b.* Indon.
177 F3 **Berber** Sudan
178 E2 **Berbera** Somalia
178 B3 **Berbérati** Cent. Afr. Rep.
166 E1 **Berck** France
137 J1 **Berd** Armenia
133 N3 **Berdigestyakh** Rus. Fed.
146 A1 **Berdsk** Rus. Fed.
173 F6 **Berdyans'k** Ukr.
173 D5 **Berdychiv** Ukr.
202 A6 **Berea** U.S.A.
173 B5 **Berehove** Ukr.
124 E2 **Bereina** P.N.G.
138 C5 **Bereket** Turkm.
139 K2 **Berel'** Kazakh.
187 J4 **Berens** *r.* Canada
187 J4 **Berens River** Canada
198 D3 **Beresford** U.S.A.
173 C5 **Berezhany** Ukr.
173 D6 **Berezivka** Ukr.
173 C5 **Berezne** Ukr.
172 G2 **Bereznik** Rus. Fed.
138 D1 **Berezovka** Rus. Fed.
132 H3 **Berezovo** Rus. Fed.
165 J3 **Berga** Germany
167 G1 **Berga** Spain
171 L5 **Bergama** Turkey
170 C2 **Bergamo** Italy
159 L3 **Bergby** Sweden
168 F3 **Bergen** *Mecklenburg-Vorpommern* Germany
165 H2 **Bergen** *Niedersachsen* Germany
159 I3 **Bergen** Norway
164 C3 **Bergen op Zoom** Neth.
166 E4 **Bergerac** France
164 C6 **Bergères-lès-Vertus** France
164 E4 **Bergheim (Erft)** Germany
164 F4 **Bergisches Land** *reg.* Germany
164 F4 **Bergisch Gladbach** Germany
180 B1 **Bergland** Namibia
190 C2 **Bergland** U.S.A.
159 L3 **Bergsjö** Sweden
158 M2 **Bergsviken** Sweden
165 I5 **Bergtheim** Germany
164 A4 **Bergues** France
**Bergum** Neth. *see* **Burgum**
181 H4 **Bergville** S. Africa
155 B3 **Berhala, Selat** *sea chan.* Indon.
133 R4 **Beringa, Ostrov** *i.* Rus. Fed.
164 D3 **Beringen** Belgium
133 S3 **Beringovskiy** Rus. Fed.
133 S4 **Bering Sea** Pacific Ocean
184 B3 **Bering Strait** Rus. Fed./U.S.A.
158 J3 **Berkåk** Norway
164 E2 **Berkel** *r.* Neth.
196 A3 **Berkeley** U.S.A.
202 D5 **Berkeley Springs** U.S.A.
164 D2 **Berkhout** Neth.
129 C3 **Berkner Island** *i.* Antarctica
171 J3 **Berkovitsa** Bulg.
161 F6 **Berkshire Downs** *hills* U.K.
164 C3 **Berlare** Belgium
158 O1 **Berlevåg** Norway
165 L2 **Berlin** Germany (City Plan **107**)
203 F5 **Berlin** *MD* U.S.A.
203 H2 **Berlin** *NH* U.S.A.
202 D5 **Berlin** *PA* U.S.A.
190 C4 **Berlin** *WI* U.S.A.
185 J2 **Berlinguet Inlet** Canada
202 C4 **Berlin Lake** U.S.A.
127 I6 **Bermagui** Australia
215 D4 **Bermeja, Punta** *pt* Arg.
206 D2 **Bermejíllo** Mex.
215 C1 **Bermejo** *r.* Arg.
212 D2 **Bermejo** *r.* Arg./Bol.
210 F8 **Bermejo** Bol.
205 M2 **Bermuda** *terr.* Atlantic Ocean
219 E4 **Bermuda Rise** *sea feature* N. Atlantic Ocean
168 C7 **Bern** Switz.
195 F5 **Bernalillo** U.S.A.
212 A7 **Bernardo O'Higgins, Parque Nacional** *nat. park* Chile
215 D3 **Bernasconi** Arg.
165 J3 **Bernburg (Saale)** Germany
165 G1 **Berne** Germany
190 E5 **Berne** U.S.A.
168 C7 **Berner Alpen** *mts* Switz.
162 A3 **Berneray** *i. Scotland* U.K.
162 A4 **Berneray** *i. Scotland* U.K.
185 J2 **Bernier Bay** Canada
124 B4 **Bernier Island** Australia
168 E7 **Bernina Pass** Switz.
164 F5 **Bernkastel-Kues** Germany
179 E6 **Beroroha** Madag.
168 G6 **Beroun** Czech Rep.
168 F5 **Berounka** *r.* Czech Rep.
126 D5 **Berri** Australia
162 E2 **Berriedale** U.K.
127 F5 **Berrigan** Australia
127 I5 **Berrima** Australia
167 H4 **Berrouaghia** Alg.
127 I5 **Berry** Australia
166 E3 **Berry** *reg.* France
196 A2 **Berryessa, Lake** U.S.A.
201 E7 **Berry Islands** Bahamas
180 B3 **Berseba** Namibia
165 F2 **Bersenbrück** Germany
173 D5 **Bershad'** Ukr.
138 E1 **Bersuat** Rus. Fed.
155 B1 **Bertam** Malaysia
211 J5 **Bertolinía** Brazil
177 D4 **Bertoua** Cameroon
163 B4 **Bertraghboy Bay** Ireland
125 H2 **Beru** *atoll* Kiribati
**Beruni** Uzbek. *see* **Beruniy**
138 E4 **Beruniy** Uzbek.
210 F4 **Beruri** Brazil
126 F7 **Berwick** Australia
203 E4 **Berwick** U.S.A.
160 E2 **Berwick-upon-Tweed** U.K.
186 F3 **Berwyn** Canada
161 D5 **Berwyn** *hills* U.K.
173 E6 **Beryslav** Ukr.
179 E5 **Besalampy** Madag.
166 H3 **Besançon** France
138 C3 **Besbay** Kazakh.
139 G4 **Beshariq** Uzbek.
**Besharyk** Uzbek. *see* **Beshariq**
**Beshir** Turkm. *see* **Beşir**
138 F5 **Beshkent** Uzbek.
140 D4 **Beshneh** Iran
138 F5 **Beşir** Turkm.
137 H3 **Beşiri** Turkey
173 H7 **Beslan** Rus. Fed.
187 H3 **Besnard Lake** Canada
136 F3 **Besni** Turkey
139 H2 **Besoba** Kazakh.
163 E3 **Bessbrook** U.K.
201 C5 **Bessemer** *AL* U.S.A.
190 B2 **Bessemer** *MI* U.S.A.
138 C3 **Besshoky, Gora** *h.* Kazakh.
138 C2 **Bestamak** *Aktyubinskaya Oblast'* Kazakh.
139 I2 **Bestamak** *Vostochnyy Kazakhstan* Kazakh.
139 H1 **Bestobe** Kazakh.
179 E6 **Betanty** Madag.
167 B1 **Betanzos** Spain
177 D4 **Bétaré Oya** Cameroon
181 H3 **Bethal** S. Africa
180 B3 **Bethanie** Namibia
198 E3 **Bethany** *MO* U.S.A.
199 D5 **Bethany** *OK* U.S.A.
184 B3 **Bethel** *AK* U.S.A.
203 H2 **Bethel** *ME* U.S.A.
190 A6 **Bethel** *MO* U.S.A.
202 A5 **Bethel** *OH* U.S.A.
202 D4 **Bethel Park** U.S.A.
161 C4 **Bethesda** U.K.
202 E5 **Bethesda** *MD* U.S.A.
202 C4 **Bethesda** *OH* U.S.A.
180 F5 **Bethesdaweg** S. Africa
181 H4 **Bethlehem** S. Africa
203 F4 **Bethlehem** U.S.A.
136 E6 **Bethlehem** West Bank
181 F5 **Bethulie** S. Africa
164 A4 **Béthune** France
213 C2 **Betijoque** Venez.
179 E6 **Betioky** Madag.
154 B4 **Betong** Thai.
139 G3 **Betpak-Dala** Kazakh.
139 G3 **Betpakdala** *plain* Kazakh.
179 E6 **Betroka** Madag.
136 E5 **Bet She'an** Israel
189 G4 **Betsiamites** Canada
189 G4 **Betsiamites** *r.* Canada
179 E5 **Betsiboka** *r.* Madag.
190 D3 **Betsie, Point** U.S.A.
150 I3 **Betsukai** Japan
190 E2 **Betsy Lake** U.S.A.
190 B5 **Bettendorf** U.S.A.
145 F4 **Bettiah** India
162 D2 **Bettyhill** U.K.
163 E4 **Bettystown** Ireland
144 D5 **Betul** India
155 D2 **Betung Kerihun, Taman Nasional** *nat. park* Indon./Malaysia
164 D3 **Betuwe** *reg.* Neth.
144 D4 **Betwa** *r.* India
161 D4 **Betws-y-coed** U.K.
165 F4 **Betzdorf** Germany
126 E5 **Beulah** Australia
190 D3 **Beulah** U.S.A.
161 H6 **Beult** *r.* U.K.
160 G4 **Beverley** U.K.
184 C4 **Beverley, Lake** U.S.A.
203 H3 **Beverly** *MA* U.S.A.
202 C5 **Beverly** *OH* U.S.A.
196 C4 **Beverly Hills** U.S.A.
187 I2 **Beverly Lake** Canada
165 G1 **Beverstedt** Germany

165 H3 **Beverungen** Germany
164 C2 **Beverwijk** Neth.
164 F5 **Bexbach** Germany
161 H7 **Bexhill** U.K.
140 B3 **Beyānlū** Iran
136 C3 **Bey Dağları** *mts* Turkey
136 B1 **Beykoz** Turkey
176 B4 **Beyla** Guinea
137 K2 **Beyläqan** Azer.
138 C3 **Beyneu** Kazakh.
136 C1 **Beypazarı** Turkey
136 F2 **Beypınarı** Turkey
143 A4 **Beypore** India
**Beyrouth** Lebanon *see* **Beirut**
136 C3 **Beyşehir** Turkey
136 C3 **Beyşehir Gölü** *l.* Turkey
173 F6 **Beysug** *r.* Rus. Fed.
137 I3 **Beytüşşebap** Turkey
140 E3 **Bezameh** Iran
172 I3 **Bezbozhnik** Rus. Fed.
172 D3 **Bezhanitsy** Rus. Fed.
172 F3 **Bezhetsk** Rus. Fed.
166 F5 **Béziers** France
144 B4 **Bhabhar** India
145 E4 **Bhabhua** India
144 B5 **Bhadar** *r.* India
**Bhadgaon** Nepal *see* **Bhaktapur**
145 E4 **Bhadohi** India
144 C3 **Bhadra** India
143 C2 **Bhadrachalam** India
145 F5 **Bhadrak** India
143 A3 **Bhadra Reservoir** India
143 A3 **Bhadravati** India
144 A3 **Bhag** Pak.
144 D2 **Bhaga** *r.* India
145 F4 **Bhagalpur** India
145 G5 **Bhagirathi** *r.* India
144 D5 **Bhainsdehi** India
145 G4 **Bhairab Bazar** Bangl.
145 E4 **Bhairawa** Nepal
145 F4 **Bhaktapur** Nepal
143 B2 **Bhalki** India
146 B4 **Bhamo** Myanmar
143 C2 **Bhamragarh** India
144 C2 **Bhandal** India
144 D4 **Bhander** India
145 F6 **Bhanjanagar** India
144 C4 **Bhanpura** India
144 D5 **Bhanrer Range** *hills* India
129 D5 **Bharati** *research stn* Antarctica
144 D4 **Bharatpur** India
145 H4 **Bhareli** *r.* India
141 F5 **Bhari** *r.* Pak.
144 C5 **Bharuch** India
143 C1 **Bhatapara** India
143 A3 **Bhatkal** India
145 G5 **Bhatpara** India
143 B4 **Bhavani** India
143 B4 **Bhavani** *r.* India
144 C5 **Bhavnagar** India
144 C3 **Bhawana** Pak.
143 C2 **Bhawanipatna** India
181 I3 **Bhekuzulu** S. Africa
145 E3 **Bheri** *r.* Nepal
145 E5 **Bhilai** India
144 C4 **Bhilwara** India
143 B2 **Bhima** *r.* India
143 C2 **Bhimavaram** India
144 D4 **Bhind** India
144 C4 **Bhindar** India
145 E4 **Bhinga** India
144 C4 **Bhinmal** India
181 G6 **Bhisho** S. Africa
144 D3 **Bhiwani** India
145 F4 **Bhojpur** Nepal
143 B2 **Bhongir** India
181 H5 **Bhongweni** S. Africa
144 D5 **Bhopal** India
143 C2 **Bhopalpatnam** India
143 A2 **Bhor** India
145 F5 **Bhuban** India
145 F5 **Bhubaneshwar** India
144 B5 **Bhuj** India
144 C5 **Bhusawal** India
145 G4 **Bhutan** *country* Asia
144 B4 **Bhuttewala** India
140 E5 **Bīabān** *mts* Iran
144 C2 **Biafo Glacier** Pak.
147 F7 **Biak** Indon.
147 F7 **Biak** *i.* Indon.
169 K4 **Biała Podlaska** Poland
168 G4 **Białogard** Poland
169 K4 **Białystok** Poland
176 B4 **Biankouma** Côte d'Ivoire
152 B1 **Bianzhao** China
144 D5 **Biaora** India
140 D2 **Bīārjomand** Iran
166 D5 **Biarritz** France
140 B5 **Bi'ār Tabrāk** *well* Saudi Arabia
168 D7 **Biasca** Switz.
150 G3 **Bibai** Japan
179 B5 **Bibala** Angola
127 H6 **Bibbenluke** Australia
170 D3 **Bibbiena** Italy
168 D6 **Biberach an der Riß** Germany
145 G4 **Bibiyana** *r.* Bangl.
165 G5 **Biblis** Germany
136 C2 **Biçer** Turkey
161 F6 **Bicester** U.K.
127 H8 **Bicheno** Australia
173 G7 **Bich'vinta** Georgia
124 D3 **Bickerton Island** Australia
161 D7 **Bickleigh** U.K.
197 G2 **Bicknell** U.S.A.
179 B5 **Bicuari, Parque Nacional do** *nat. park* Angola
143 A2 **Bid** India
176 C4 **Bida** Nigeria
153 A5 **Bidadari, Tanjung** *pt Sabah* Malaysia
140 D4 **Bida Khabit** Iran
143 B2 **Bidar** India
141 E6 **Bidbid** Oman
203 H3 **Biddeford** U.S.A.
164 D2 **Biddinghuizen** Neth.
162 C4 **Bidean nam Bian** *mt.* U.K.
161 C6 **Bideford** U.K.
**Bideford Bay** *b.* U.K. *see* **Barnstaple Bay**
169 K4 **Biebrza** *r.* Poland
165 G4 **Biedenkopf** Germany
168 C7 **Biel** Switz.
168 H5 **Bielawa** Poland
165 G2 **Bielefeld** Germany
170 C2 **Biella** Italy
169 I6 **Bielsko-Biała** Poland
169 K4 **Bielsk Podlaski** Poland
165 I1 **Bienenbüttel** Germany
154 C3 **Biên Hoa** Vietnam
188 F2 **Bienville, Lac** *l.* Canada
181 F3 **Biesiesvlei** S. Africa
165 H6 **Bietigheim-Bissingen** Germany
164 D5 **Bièvre** Belgium
178 B4 **Bifoun** Gabon
189 I3 **Big** *r.* Canada
196 A2 **Big** *r.* U.S.A.
173 C7 **Biga** Turkey
136 B2 **Bigadiç** Turkey
171 L5 **Biga Yarımadası** *pen.* Turkey
190 D2 **Big Bay** U.S.A.
190 D3 **Big Bay de Noc** U.S.A.
196 D4 **Big Bear Lake** U.S.A.
194 E2 **Big Belt Mountains** U.S.A.
181 I3 **Big Bend** Swaziland
199 C6 **Big Bend National Park** U.S.A.
199 F5 **Big Black** *r.* U.S.A.
161 D7 **Bigbury-on-Sea** U.K.
201 D7 **Big Cypress National Preserve** U.S.A.
190 C3 **Big Eau Pleine Reservoir** U.S.A.
187 K5 **Big Falls** U.S.A.
187 H4 **Biggar** Canada
162 E5 **Biggar** U.K.
186 B3 **Bigger, Mount** Canada
161 G5 **Biggleswade** U.K.
194 D2 **Big Hole** *r.* U.S.A.
194 F2 **Bighorn** *r.* U.S.A.
194 E2 **Bighorn Canyon National Recreation Area** *park* U.S.A.
194 F2 **Bighorn Mountains** U.S.A.
185 K3 **Big Island** *Nunavut* Canada
186 F2 **Big Island** *N.W.T.* Canada
203 J2 **Big Lake** U.S.A.
176 A3 **Bignona** Senegal
202 D6 **Big Otter** *r.* U.S.A.
196 C3 **Big Pine** U.S.A.
190 E4 **Big Rapids** U.S.A.
190 C3 **Big Rib** *r.* U.S.A.
187 H4 **Big River** Canada
190 D3 **Big Sable Point** U.S.A.
186 C2 **Big Salmon** *r.* Canada
187 J3 **Big Sand Lake** Canada
197 F4 **Big Sandy** *watercourse* U.S.A.
198 D2 **Big Sioux** *r.* U.S.A.
196 D2 **Big Smokey Valley** U.S.A.
199 C5 **Big Spring** U.S.A.
198 C3 **Big Springs** U.S.A.
202 B6 **Big Stone Gap** U.S.A.
196 B3 **Big Sur** U.S.A.
194 E2 **Big Timber** U.S.A.
188 C3 **Big Trout Lake** Canada
188 C3 **Big Trout Lake** *l.* Canada
197 G3 **Big Water** U.S.A.
191 H3 **Bigwin** Canada
170 F2 **Bihać** Bos.-Herz.
145 F4 **Bihar** *state* India
145 F4 **Bihar Sharif** India
169 K7 **Bihor, Vârful** *mt.* Romania
150 I3 **Bihoro** Japan
138 C3 **Biikzhal** Kazakh.
176 A3 **Bijagós, Arquipélago dos** *is* Guinea-Bissau
144 C4 **Bijainagar** India
143 A2 **Bijapur** India
143 C2 **Bijapur** India
140 B3 **Bījār** Iran
171 H2 **Bijeljina** Bos.-Herz.
171 H3 **Bijelo Polje** Montenegro
149 B5 **Bijie** China
145 G4 **Bijni** India
144 D3 **Bijnor** India
144 B3 **Bijnot** Pak.
140 C5 **Bijrān, Khashm** *h.* Saudi Arabia
144 C3 **Bikaner** India
146 F2 **Bikin** Rus. Fed.
150 D1 **Bikin** *r.* Rus. Fed.
216 G5 **Bikini** *atoll* Marshall Is
178 B4 **Bikoro** Dem. Rep. Congo
148 B3 **Bikou** China
144 C4 **Bilara** India
143 C1 **Bilaspur** India
137 L2 **Biläsuvar** Azer.
173 D5 **Bila Tserkva** Ukr.
154 A2 **Bilauktaung Range** *mts* Myanmar/Thai.
167 E1 **Bilbao** Spain
136 C6 **Bilbays** Egypt
171 H3 **Bileća** Bos.-Herz.
136 B1 **Bilecik** Turkey
169 K5 **Biłgoraj** Poland
178 D4 **Bilharamulo** Tanz.
173 D6 **Bilhorod-Dnistrovs'kyy** Ukr.
178 C3 **Bili** Dem. Rep. Congo
133 R3 **Bilibino** Rus. Fed.
153 C4 **Biliran** *i.* Phil.
152 B4 **Biliu He** *r.* China
194 F3 **Bill** U.S.A.
161 H6 **Billericay** U.K.
219 J2 **Billingford** U.K.
160 F3 **Billingham** U.K.
194 E2 **Billings** U.S.A.
161 E7 **Bill of Portland** *hd* U.K.
197 F4 **Bill Williams** *r.* U.S.A.
197 F4 **Bill Williams Mountain** U.S.A.
177 D3 **Bilma** Niger
177 D3 **Bilma, Grand Erg de** *des.* Niger
124 F4 **Biloela** Australia
173 E6 **Bilohirs'k** Ukr.
169 M5 **Bilohir"ya** Ukr.
143 B2 **Biloli** India
173 F5 **Biloluts'k** Ukr.
173 E5 **Bilopillya** Ukr.
173 F5 **Bilovods'k** Ukr.
201 B6 **Biloxi** U.S.A.
124 D4 **Bilpa Morea Claypan** *salt flat* Australia
162 E5 **Bilston** U.K.
177 E3 **Biltine** Chad
154 A1 **Bilugyun Island** Myanmar
206 I5 **Bilwascarma** Nicaragua
172 I4 **Bilyarsk** Rus. Fed.
173 D6 **Bilyayivka** Ukr.
164 D4 **Bilzen** Belgium
127 H5 **Bimberi, Mount** Australia
178 B3 **Bimbo** C.A.R.
201 E7 **Bimini Islands** Bahamas
137 L3 **Bināb** Iran
144 D4 **Bina-Etawa** India
147 E7 **Binaija, Gunung** *mt.* Indon.
136 F2 **Binboğa Daği** *mt.* Turkey
127 G1 **Bindebango** Australia
144 E4 **Bindki** India
127 H1 **Bindle** Australia
179 B4 **Bindu** Dem. Rep. Congo
179 D5 **Bindura** Zimbabwe
167 G2 **Binéfar** Spain
127 I2 **Bingara** *N.S.W.* Australia
127 F2 **Bingara** *Qld* Australia
148 B2 **Bingcaowan** China
165 F5 **Bingen am Rhein** Germany
176 B4 **Bingerville** Côte d'Ivoire
203 I2 **Bingham** U.S.A.
203 F3 **Binghamton** U.S.A.
137 H2 **Bingöl** Turkey
137 H2 **Bingol Dağı** *mt.* Turkey
149 C6 **Binh Gia** Vietnam
**Binh Sơn** Vietnam *see* **Châu Ô**
145 H4 **Bini** India
143 C1 **Binika** India
154 A5 **Binjai** Indon.
140 D5 **Bin Mürkhan** *well* U.A.E.
127 H3 **Binnaway** Australia
154 C5 **Bintan** *i.* Indon.
153 B3 **Bintuan** Phil.
155 B3 **Bintuhan** Indon.
155 D2 **Bintulu** *Sarawak* Malaysia
148 C3 **Binxian** China
127 G5 **Binya** Australia
149 C6 **Binyang** China
148 F2 **Binzhou** China
215 B3 **Biobío** *admin. reg.* Chile
215 B3 **Biobío** *r.* Chile
170 F3 **Biograd na Moru** Croatia
176 C4 **Bioko** *i.* Equat. Guinea
170 G3 **Biokovo** *mts* Croatia
177 D2 **Birāk** Libya
137 H5 **Bi'r al Mulūsi** Iraq
178 C2 **Birao** Cent. Afr. Rep.
136 D6 **Bi'r ar Rummānah** Egypt
138 E4 **Birata** Turkm.
145 F4 **Biratnagar** Nepal
137 G3 **Bi'r Buṭaymān** Syria
186 G3 **Birch** *r.* Canada
187 H4 **Birch Hills** Canada
126 E5 **Birchip** Australia
186 F4 **Birch Island** Canada
188 B3 **Birch Lake** Canada
190 B2 **Birch Lake** U.S.A.
186 G3 **Birch Mountains** Canada
187 I4 **Birch River** Canada
**Birdaard** Neth. *see* **Burdaard**
129 C1 **Bird Island** *i.* S. Georgia
197 G2 **Birdseye** U.S.A.
124 D4 **Birdsville** Australia
136 F3 **Birecik** Turkey
177 E3 **Bir en Natrûn** *well* Sudan
155 A1 **Bireun** Indon.
141 F5 **Bīrg, Kūh-e** *mts* Iran
140 B6 **Bi'r Ghawdah** *well* Saudi Arabia
214 B3 **Birigüi** Brazil
141 E3 **Bīrjand** Iran
137 J6 **Birkát Hamad** *well* Iraq
164 F5 **Birkenfeld** Germany
161 D4 **Birkenhead** U.K.
137 J3 **Bīrkim** Iraq
170 F7 **Birkirkara** Malta
139 H3 **Birlik** Kazakh.
139 H4 **Birlik** Kazakh.
161 F5 **Birmingham** U.K.
201 C5 **Birmingham** U.S.A.
176 A2 **Bîr Mogreïn** Mauritania
136 B6 **Bi'r Nāḩid** *oasis* Egypt
176 C3 **Birnin-Kebbi** Nigeria
176 C3 **Birnin Konni** Niger
146 F2 **Birobidzhan** Rus. Fed.
163 D4 **Birr** Ireland
127 G2 **Birrie** *r.* Australia
137 I5 **Bi'r Sābil** Iraq
162 E1 **Birsay** U.K.
138 D2 **Birshogyr** Kazakh.
161 F5 **Birstall** U.K.
165 H4 **Birstein** Germany
136 E7 **Bi'r Tābah** Egypt
187 I4 **Birtle** Canada
145 H3 **Biru** China
143 A3 **Birur** India
159 N4 **Biržai** Lith.
197 H6 **Bisbee** U.S.A.
166 B4 **Biscay, Bay of** *sea* France/Spain
219 I3 **Biscay Abyssal Plain** *sea feature* N. Atlantic Ocean
201 D7 **Biscayne National Park** U.S.A.
168 F7 **Bischofshofen** Austria
129 B2 **Biscoe Islands** *is* Antarctica
191 F2 **Biscotasi Lake** Canada
191 F2 **Biscotasing** Canada
149 C4 **Bishan** China
137 L5 **Bīsheh** Iran
139 H4 **Bishkek** Kyrg.
145 F5 **Bishnupur** India
196 C3 **Bishop** U.S.A.
160 F3 **Bishop Auckland** U.K.
161 H6 **Bishop's Stortford** U.K.
137 G4 **Bishrī, Jabal** *hills* Syria
146 E1 **Bishui** China
176 C1 **Biskra** Alg.
153 C4 **Bislig** Phil.
198 C2 **Bismarck** U.S.A.
124 E2 **Bismarck Archipelago** *is* P.N.G.
124 E2 **Bismarck Range** *mts* P.N.G.
124 E2 **Bismarck Sea** P.N.G.
165 J2 **Bismark (Altmark)** Germany
137 H3 **Bismil** Turkey
159 J3 **Bismo** Norway
137 K4 **Bīsotūn** Iran
158 L3 **Bispgården** Sweden
165 I1 **Bispingen** Germany
167 G4 **Bissa, Djebel** *mt.* Alg.
143 C2 **Bissamcuttak** India
176 A3 **Bissau** Guinea-Bissau
176 D4 **Bissaula** Nigeria
187 J4 **Bissett** Canada
186 F3 **Bistcho Lake** Canada
169 L7 **Bistrița** Romania
169 M7 **Bistrița** *r.* Romania
164 E5 **Bitburg** Germany
164 F5 **Bitche** France
138 B2 **Bitik** Kazakh.
177 D3 **Bitkine** Chad
137 I2 **Bitlis** Turkey
171 I4 **Bitola** Macedonia
170 G4 **Bitonto** Italy
140 B6 **Bitrān, Jabal** *h.* Saudi Arabia
197 H2 **Bitter Creek** *r.* U.S.A.
165 K3 **Bitterfeld** Germany
180 C5 **Bitterfontein** S. Africa
136 D6 **Bitter Lakes** Egypt
194 D2 **Bitterroot Range** *mts* U.S.A.
165 J2 **Bittkau** Germany
173 G5 **Bityug** *r.* Rus. Fed.
177 D3 **Biu** Nigeria
151 D7 **Biwa-ko** *l.* Japan
139 K1 **Biya** *r.* Rus. Fed.
148 D3 **Biyang** China
178 E2 **Bīye K'obē Polīs T'abīya** Eth.
139 K1 **Biysk** Rus. Fed.
181 H5 **Bizana** S. Africa
176 C1 **Bizerte** Tunisia
141 E5 **Bīzhanābād** Iran
158 A2 **Bjargtangar** *hd* Iceland
158 L3 **Bjästa** Sweden
170 G2 **Bjelovar** Croatia
158 L1 **Bjerkvik** Norway
159 J4 **Bjerringbro** Denmark
159 L3 **Björklinge** Sweden
159 J3 **Bjorli** Norway
158 L3 **Björna** Sweden
132 C2 **Bjørnøya** *i.* Svalbard
158 L3 **Bjurholm** Sweden
176 B3 **Bla** Mali
162 B3 **Bla Bheinn** *h.* U.K.
199 F5 **Black** *r. AR* U.S.A.
197 H5 **Black** *r. AZ* U.S.A.
191 F4 **Black** *r. MI* U.S.A.
190 B3 **Black** *r. WI* U.S.A.
149 B6 **Black** *r.* Vietnam
124 E4 **Blackall** Australia
190 C1 **Black Bay** Canada
188 B3 **Blackbear** *r.* Canada
161 F6 **Black Bourton** U.K.
160 E4 **Blackburn** U.K.
127 J1 **Blackbutt** Australia
196 A2 **Black Butte** *mt.* U.S.A.
196 A2 **Black Butte Lake** U.S.A.
197 E4 **Black Canyon** *gorge* U.S.A.
197 F4 **Black Canyon City** U.S.A.
198 E2 **Blackduck** U.S.A.
186 G4 **Blackfalds** Canada
194 D3 **Blackfoot** U.S.A.
194 D2 **Black Foot** *r.* U.S.A.
168 D6 **Black Forest** *mts* Germany
198 C2 **Black Hills** U.S.A.
162 D3 **Black Isle** *pen.* U.K.
187 H3 **Black Lake** Canada
187 H3 **Black Lake** *l.* Canada
191 E3 **Black Lake** *l.* U.S.A.
197 G3 **Black Mesa** *ridge* U.S.A.
161 D6 **Black Mountain** *hills* U.K.
196 D4 **Black Mountain** U.S.A.
161 D6 **Black Mountains** *hills* U.K.
197 E4 **Black Mountains** U.S.A.
180 C1 **Black Nossob** *watercourse* Namibia
149 □ **Black Point** *Hong Kong* China
160 D4 **Blackpool** U.K.
190 B3 **Black River Falls** U.S.A.
194 C3 **Black Rock Desert** U.S.A.
202 C6 **Blacksburg** U.S.A.
173 E7 **Black Sea** Asia/Europe
163 A3 **Blacksod Bay** Ireland
163 E5 **Blackstairs Mountain** *h.* Ireland
163 E5 **Blackstairs Mountains** *hills* Ireland
202 E6 **Blackstone** U.S.A.
127 I3 **Black Sugarloaf** *mt.* Australia
189 I3 **Black Tickle** Canada
176 B4 **Black Volta** *r.* Africa
163 E5 **Blackwater** Ireland
163 D5 **Blackwater** *r.* Ireland
163 E4 **Blackwater** *r.* Ireland
163 E3 **Blackwater** *r.* Ireland/U.K.
161 H6 **Blackwater** *r.* U.K.
202 E6 **Blackwater** *r.* U.S.A.
186 E2 **Blackwater Lake** Canada
162 D4 **Blackwater Reservoir** U.K.
199 D4 **Blackwell** U.S.A.
124 B5 **Blackwood** *r.* Australia
161 D6 **Blaenavon** U.K.
173 G6 **Blagodarnyy** Rus. Fed.
171 J3 **Blagoevgrad** Bulg.
139 I1 **Blagoveshchenka** Rus. Fed.
146 E1 **Blagoveshchensk** Rus. Fed.
202 E4 **Blain** U.S.A.
194 B1 **Blaine** U.S.A.
187 H4 **Blaine Lake** Canada
198 D3 **Blair** *NE* U.S.A.
190 B3 **Blair** *WI* U.S.A.
162 E4 **Blair Atholl** U.K.
162 E4 **Blairgowrie** U.K.
201 C6 **Blakely** U.S.A.
161 I5 **Blakeney** U.K.
190 C1 **Blake Point** U.S.A.
155 D4 **Blambangan, Semenanjung** *pen.* Indon.
166 H4 **Blanc, Mont** *mt.* France/Italy
215 E3 **Blanca, Bahía** *b.* Arg.
215 C3 **Blanca de la Totora, Sierra** *hills* Arg.
195 F4 **Blanca Peak** U.S.A.
126 C2 **Blanche, Lake** *salt flat* Australia
202 B5 **Blanchester** U.S.A.
126 C5 **Blanchetown** Australia
215 C1 **Blanco** *r.* Arg.
210 F6 **Blanco** *r.* Bol.
206 H6 **Blanco, Cabo** *c.* Costa Rica
194 A3 **Blanco, Cape** U.S.A.
189 I3 **Blanc-Sablon** Canada
127 G4 **Bland** *r.* Australia
158 B2 **Blanda** *r.* Iceland
161 E7 **Blandford Forum** U.K.
197 H3 **Blanding** U.S.A.
167 H2 **Blanes** Spain
190 E2 **Blaney Park** U.S.A.
154 □ **Blangah, Telok** Sing.
154 A5 **Blangkejeren** Indon.
164 B3 **Blankenberge** Belgium
164 E4 **Blankenheim** Germany
213 D2 **Blanquilla, Isla** *i.* Venez.
168 H6 **Blansko** Czech Rep.
179 D5 **Blantyre** Malawi
163 C6 **Blarney** Ireland
165 H5 **Blaufelden** Germany
158 L2 **Blåviksjön** Sweden
127 H4 **Blayney** Australia
165 I1 **Bleckede** Germany
128 D4 **Blenheim** N.Z.
161 F6 **Blenheim Palace** *tourist site* U.K.
164 E3 **Blerick** Neth.
163 E4 **Blessington Lakes** Ireland
161 G5 **Bletchley** U.K.
176 C1 **Blida** Alg.
164 F5 **Blies** *r.* Germany
125 H3 **Bligh Water** *b.* Fiji
191 F2 **Blind River** Canada
126 C3 **Blinman** Australia
194 D3 **Bliss** U.S.A.
191 F5 **Blissfield** U.S.A.
203 H4 **Block Island** U.S.A.
203 H4 **Block Island Sound** *sea chan.* U.S.A.
181 G4 **Bloemfontein** S. Africa
181 F3 **Bloemhof** S. Africa
181 F3 **Bloemhof Dam** S. Africa
165 H3 **Blomberg** Germany
158 B2 **Blönduós** Iceland
203 E5 **Bloodsworth Island** U.S.A.
187 J4 **Bloodvein** *r.* Canada
163 C2 **Bloody Foreland** *pt* Ireland
191 I4 **Bloomfield** Canada
190 A5 **Bloomfield** *IA* U.S.A.
200 C4 **Bloomfield** *IN* U.S.A.
195 E4 **Bloomfield** *NM* U.S.A.
190 C5 **Bloomington** *IL* U.S.A.
200 C4 **Bloomington** *IN* U.S.A.
198 E2 **Bloomington** *MN* U.S.A.
203 E4 **Bloomsburg** U.S.A.
202 E4 **Blossburg** U.S.A.
185 P3 **Blosseville Kyst** *coastal area* Greenland
181 H1 **Blouberg** S. Africa
161 F5 **Bloxham** U.K.
197 H5 **Blue** *watercourse* U.S.A.
197 G1 **Bluebell** U.S.A.
197 G2 **Blue Bell Knoll** *mt.* U.S.A.
198 E3 **Blue Earth** U.S.A.
202 C6 **Bluefield** U.S.A.
206 I5 **Bluefields** Nicaragua
203 I2 **Blue Hill** U.S.A.
191 H5 **Blue Knob** *h.* U.S.A.
145 H5 **Blue Mountain** *mt.* India
197 H1 **Blue Mountain** U.S.A.
203 F3 **Blue Mountain Lake** U.S.A.
181 G4 **Blue Mountain Pass** Lesotho
127 I4 **Blue Mountains** Australia
194 C2 **Blue Mountains** U.S.A.
127 I4 **Blue Mountains National Park** Australia
177 F3 **Blue Nile** *r.* Sudan
*alt.* **Ābay Wenz (Ethiopia),**
*alt.* **Azraq, Bahr el (Eth./Sudan)**
184 G3 **Bluenose Lake** Canada
201 C5 **Blue Ridge** U.S.A.
202 D6 **Blue Ridge** *mts* U.S.A.
186 F4 **Blue River** Canada
196 D2 **Blue Springs** U.S.A.
163 C3 **Blue Stack** *h.* Ireland
163 C3 **Blue Stack Mountains** *hills* Ireland
202 C6 **Bluestone Lake** U.S.A.
128 B7 **Bluff** N.Z.
197 H3 **Bluff** U.S.A.
149 □ **Bluff Island** *Hong Kong* China
190 E5 **Bluffton** *IN* U.S.A.
202 B4 **Bluffton** *OH* U.S.A.
212 G3 **Blumenau** Brazil
198 C2 **Blunt** U.S.A.
194 B3 **Bly** U.S.A.
126 C4 **Blyth** Australia
160 F2 **Blyth** *England* U.K.
161 F4 **Blyth** *England* U.K.
197 E5 **Blythe** U.S.A.
199 F5 **Blytheville** U.S.A.
159 J4 **Bø** Norway
176 A4 **Bo** Sierra Leone
153 B3 **Boac** Phil.
206 H5 **Boaco** Nicaragua
211 J5 **Boa Esperança, Açude** *resr* Brazil
148 D3 **Bo'ai** China
149 C6 **Bo'ai** China
178 B3 **Boali** Cent. Afr. Rep.
181 J3 **Boane** Moz.
202 C4 **Boardman** U.S.A.
181 F1 **Boatlaname** Botswana
127 G1 **Boatman** Australia
211 K5 **Boa Viagem** Brazil
213 E4 **Boa Vista** Brazil
176 □ **Boa Vista** *i.* Cape Verde
127 G4 **Bobadah** Australia
149 D6 **Bobai** China
179 E5 **Bobaomby, Tanjona** *c.* Madag.
143 C2 **Bobbili** India
176 B3 **Bobo-Dioulasso** Burkina Faso
179 C6 **Bobonong** Botswana
139 G4 **Boboyob, Gora** *mt.* Uzbek.
173 G5 **Bobrov** Rus. Fed.
173 D5 **Bobrovytsya** Ukr.
173 E5 **Bobrynets'** Ukr.
179 E6 **Boby** *mt.* Madag.
213 D2 **Boca del Pao** Venez.
205 L7 **Boca de Macareo** Venez.
210 E5 **Boca do Acre** Brazil
211 H4 **Boca do Jari** Brazil
213 E2 **Boca Grande** *r. mouth* Venez.
214 D2 **Bocaiúva** Brazil
213 C2 **Bocanó** *r.* Venez.
178 B3 **Bocaranga** Cent. Afr. Rep.
201 D7 **Boca Raton** U.S.A.
206 I6 **Bocas del Toro** Panama
169 J6 **Bochnia** Poland
164 E3 **Bocholt** Germany
164 F3 **Bochum** Germany
**Bochum** S. Africa *see* **Senwabarwana**
165 I2 **Bockenem** Germany
213 C2 **Boconó** Venez.
206 C2 **Bocoyna** Mex.
178 B3 **Boda** Cent. Afr. Rep.
127 I6 **Bodalla** Australia
146 D1 **Bodaybo** Rus. Fed.
199 E5 **Bodcau Reservoir** U.S.A.
162 G3 **Boddam** U.K.
165 J3 **Bode** *r.* Germany
196 A2 **Bodega Head** U.S.A.
177 D3 **Bodélé** *reg.* Chad
158 M2 **Boden** Sweden
161 E5 **Bodenham** U.K.
**Bodensee** *l.* Germany/Switz. *see* **Constance, Lake**
165 I2 **Bodenteich** Germany
165 H3 **Bodenwerder** Germany
143 B2 **Bodhan** India
145 F4 **Bodh Gaya** India
143 B4 **Bodinayakkanur** India
161 C7 **Bodmin** U.K.
161 C7 **Bodmin Moor** *moorland* U.K.
158 K2 **Bodø** Norway
171 L6 **Bodrum** Turkey
171 L6 **Bodrum-Milas** *airport* Turkey
164 C3 **Boechout** Belgium
178 C4 **Boende** Dem. Rep. Congo
176 A3 **Boffa** Guinea
199 F6 **Bogalusa** U.S.A.
127 G3 **Bogan** *r.* Australia
176 B3 **Bogandé** Burkina Faso
127 G4 **Bogan Gate** Australia
172 I3 **Bogatyye Saby** Rus. Fed.
136 E2 **Boğazlıyan** Turkey
145 F3 **Bogcang Zangbo** *r.* China
138 C1 **Bogdanovka** Rus. Fed.
146 A2 **Bogda Shan** *mts* China
138 E3 **Bogen** Kazakh.
139 H1 **Bogenbay** Kazakh.
127 I2 **Boggabilla** Australia
127 I3 **Boggabri** Australia
163 B5 **Boggeragh Mountains** *hills* Ireland
167 H5 **Boghar** Alg.
161 G7 **Bognor Regis** U.K.
153 C4 **Bogo** Phil.
139 G1 **Bogodukhovka** Kazakh.
163 D4 **Bog of Allen** *reg.* Ireland
172 E4 **Bogolyubovo** Rus. Fed.
127 G6 **Bogong, Mount** Australia
150 D2 **Bogopol'** Rus. Fed.
155 C4 **Bogor** Indon.
172 G3 **Bogorodsk** Rus. Fed.
172 I3 **Bogorodskoye** Rus. Fed.
213 B3 **Bogotá** Col.
146 A1 **Bogotol** Rus. Fed.
145 G4 **Bogra** Bangl.
145 H3 **Bogu** India
133 K4 **Boguchany** Rus. Fed.
173 G5 **Boguchar** Rus. Fed.
176 A3 **Bogué** Mauritania
148 F2 **Bo Hai** *g.* China
152 A4 **Bohai Haixia** *sea chan.* China
166 F2 **Bohain-en-Vermandois** France
148 E2 **Bohai Wan** *b.* China
165 K3 **Böhlen** Germany
181 H4 **Bohlokong** S. Africa
165 K5 **Böhmer Wald** *mts* Germany
165 G2 **Bohmte** Germany
173 E5 **Bohodukhiv** Ukr.
153 C4 **Bohol** *i.* Phil.
153 C4 **Bohol Sea** Phil.
153 B4 **Bohol Strait** Phil.
135 G2 **Bohu** China
173 D5 **Bohuslav** Ukr.
214 D4 **Boi, Ponta do** *pt* Brazil
203 F4 **Boiceville** U.S.A.
180 E4 **Boichoko** S. Africa
181 G3 **Boikhutso** S. Africa
211 G4 **Boim** Brazil
145 H5 **Boinu** *r.* Myanmar
214 E1 **Boipeba, Ilha** *i.* Brazil
214 C2 **Bois** *r.* Brazil
184 F3 **Bois, Lac des** *l.* Canada
191 E3 **Bois Blanc Island** U.S.A.
194 C3 **Boise** U.S.A.
199 C4 **Boise City** U.S.A.
187 I5 **Boissevain** Canada
181 F3 **Boitumelong** S. Africa
165 I1 **Boizenburg** Germany
153 B2 **Bojeador, Cape** Phil.
140 E2 **Bojnūrd** Iran
145 H4 **Bokajan** India
138 E4 **Bo'kantov tog'lari** *hills* Uzbek.
145 F5 **Bokaro** India
178 B4 **Bokatola** Dem. Rep. Congo
176 A3 **Boké** Guinea
139 J2 **Boke** Kazakh.
178 C4 **Bokele** Dem. Rep. Congo
127 G2 **Bokhara** *r.* Australia
159 I4 **Boknafjorden** *sea chan.* Norway
139 I4 **Bökönbaev** Kyrg.
177 D3 **Bokoro** Chad
173 G5 **Bokovskaya** Rus. Fed.
172 E3 **Boksitogorsk** Rus. Fed.
180 D3 **Bokspits** Botswana
138 D5 **Bokurdak** Turkm.
178 C4 **Bolaiti** Dem. Rep. Congo
176 A3 **Bolama** Guinea-Bissau
144 A3 **Bolan** *r.* Pak.
**Bolangir** India *see* **Balangir**
144 A3 **Bolan Pass** Pak.
166 E2 **Bolbec** France
140 C4 **Boldājī** Iran
165 L1 **Boldekow** Germany
138 D4 **Boldumsaz** Turkm.
139 J3 **Bole** China
176 B4 **Bole** Ghana
178 B4 **Boleko** Dem. Rep. Congo
176 B3 **Bolgatanga** Ghana
173 D6 **Bolhrad** Ukr.
150 B2 **Boli** China
178 B4 **Bolia** Dem. Rep. Congo
158 M2 **Boliden** Sweden
155 C1 **Bolikhamxai** Laos
153 A2 **Bolinao** Phil.
171 K2 **Bolintin-Vale** Romania
213 A3 **Bolívar** Col.
210 C5 **Bolívar** Peru
199 E4 **Bolivar** *MO* U.S.A.
201 B5 **Bolivar** *TN* U.S.A.
213 C2 **Bolívar, Pico** *mt.* Venez.
210 E7 **Bolivia** *country* S. America
136 E3 **Bolkar Dağları** *mts* Turkey
172 F4 **Bolkhov** Rus. Fed.
191 F1 **Bolkow** Canada
166 G4 **Bollène** France
159 L3 **Bollnäs** Sweden
127 G2 **Bollon** Australia
158 L3 **Bollstabruk** Sweden
159 K4 **Bolmen** *l.* Sweden
173 H7 **Bolnisi** Georgia
178 B4 **Bolobo** Dem. Rep. Congo
153 B5 **Bolod Islands** Phil.
170 D2 **Bologna** Italy
169 O2 **Bologovo** Rus. Fed.
172 E3 **Bologoye** Rus. Fed.
181 F4 **Bolokanang** S. Africa
178 B3 **Bolomba** Dem. Rep. Congo
207 G3 **Bolonchén de Rejón** Mex.
153 B5 **Bolong** Phil.
132 J4 **Bolotnoye** Rus. Fed.
145 F5 **Bolpur** India
170 D3 **Bolsena, Lago di** *l.* Italy
169 J3 **Bol'shakovo** Rus. Fed.
138 B1 **Bol'shaya Chernigovka** Rus. Fed.
**Bol'shaya Churakova** Kazakh. *see* **Bol'shaya Churakovka**
138 F1 **Bol'shaya Churakovka** Kazakh.
138 B1 **Bol'shaya Glushitsa** Rus. Fed.
158 P2 **Bol'shaya Imandra, Ozero** *l.* Rus. Fed.
138 B1 **Bol'shaya Kinel'** *r.* Rus. Fed.
173 G6 **Bol'shaya Martynovka** Rus. Fed.
139 I2 **Bol'shaya Vladimirovka** Kazakh.
139 H1 **Bol'shegrivskoye** Rus. Fed.
133 L2 **Bol'shevik, Ostrov** *i.* Rus. Fed.
138 D3 **Bol'shiye Barsuki, Peski** *des.* Kazakh.
172 H2 **Bol'shiye Chirki** Rus. Fed.
138 B3 **Bol'shiye Peshnyye, Ostrova** *is* Kazakh.
138 D2 **Bol'shoy Ik** *r.* Rus. Fed.
138 B2 **Bol'shoy Irgiz** *r.* Rus. Fed.
150 C3 **Bol'shoy Kamen'** Rus. Fed.
**Bol'shoy Kavkaz** *mts* Asia/Europe *see* **Caucasus**
173 I5 **Bol'shoy Uzen'** *r.* Rus. Fed.
164 D1 **Bolsward** Neth.
160 E4 **Bolton** U.K.
202 B6 **Bolton** U.S.A.
136 C1 **Bolu** Turkey
158 B1 **Bolungarvík** Iceland
149 E6 **Boluo** China
136 C2 **Bolvadin** Turkey
170 D1 **Bolzano** Italy
178 B4 **Boma** Dem. Rep. Congo
127 I5 **Bomaderry** Australia
127 H6 **Bombala** Australia
**Bombay** India *see* **Mumbai**
147 F7 **Bomberai, Semenanjung** *pen.* Indon.
210 E5 **Bom Comércio** Brazil
214 D2 **Bom Despacho** Brazil
145 H4 **Bomdila** India
145 H3 **Bomi** China
214 D1 **Bom Jesus da Lapa** Brazil
214 E3 **Bom Jesus do Itabapoana** Brazil
159 I4 **Bømlo** *i.* Norway
177 D1 **Bon, Cap** *c.* Tunisia
140 B2 **Bonāb** Iran
202 E6 **Bon Air** U.S.A.
205 K6 **Bonaire** *municipality* West Indies
206 H5 **Bonanza** Nicaragua
124 C3 **Bonaparte Archipelago** *is* Australia
162 D3 **Bonar Bridge** U.K.
189 J4 **Bonavista** Canada
189 J4 **Bonavista Bay** Canada
126 A3 **Bon Bon** Australia
162 F5 **Bonchester Bridge** U.K.
178 C3 **Bondo** Dem. Rep. Congo
153 B3 **Bondoc Peninsula** Phil.
176 B4 **Bondoukou** Côte d'Ivoire
147 E7 **Bone, Teluk** *b.* Indon.
190 A3 **Bone Lake** U.S.A.
165 F3 **Bönen** Germany
147 E7 **Bonerate, Kepulauan** *is* Indon.
162 E4 **Bo'ness** U.K.
214 D2 **Bonfinópolis de Minas** Brazil
178 D3 **Bonga** Eth.
153 B3 **Bongabong** Phil.
145 G4 **Bongaigaon** India
178 C3 **Bongandanga** Dem. Rep. Congo
180 H3 **Bongani** S. Africa
153 A5 **Bongao** Phil.
145 G3 **Bong Co** *l.* China
153 C5 **Bongo** *i.* Phil.
178 C3 **Bongo, Massif des** *mts* Cent. Afr. Rep.
179 E5 **Bongolava** *mts* Madag.
177 D3 **Bongor** Chad
176 B4 **Bongouanou** Côte d'Ivoire
154 D2 **Bông Sơn** Vietnam
164 C3 **Bonheiden** Belgium
170 C4 **Bonifacio** *Corsica* France
170 C4 **Bonifacio, Strait of** France/Italy
146 G4 **Bonin Islands** Japan
214 A3 **Bonito** Brazil
164 F4 **Bonn** Germany
158 K2 **Bonnåsjøen** Norway
194 C1 **Bonners Ferry** U.S.A.
166 H3 **Bonneville** France
126 D6 **Bonney, Lake** Australia
124 B5 **Bonnie Rock** Australia
162 E5 **Bonnyrigg** U.K.
187 G4 **Bonnyville** Canada
153 A4 **Bonobono** Phil.
**Bonom Mhai** *mt.* Vietnam *see* **S'Lung, B'Nom**
170 C4 **Bonorva** *Sardinia* Italy
127 I2 **Bonshaw** Australia
180 D7 **Bontebok National Park** S. Africa
176 A4 **Bonthe** Sierra Leone
153 B2 **Bontoc** Phil.
155 E4 **Bontosunggu** Indon.
181 F6 **Bontrug** S. Africa
181 G1 **Bonwapitse** Botswana
197 H2 **Book Cliffs** *ridge* U.S.A.
126 E4 **Boolaboolka Lake** *imp. l.* Australia
126 C4 **Booleroo Centre** Australia
163 D5 **Booley Hills** Ireland
126 F4 **Booligal** Australia
127 H2 **Boomi** Australia
127 J1 **Boonah** Australia
198 E3 **Boone** *IA* U.S.A.
201 D4 **Boone** *NC* U.S.A.
202 B6 **Boone Lake** U.S.A.
202 B6 **Booneville** *KY* U.S.A.
199 F5 **Booneville** *MS* U.S.A.
196 A2 **Boonville** *CA* U.S.A.
200 C4 **Boonville** *IN* U.S.A.
198 E4 **Boonville** *MO* U.S.A.
203 F3 **Boonville** *NY* U.S.A.
126 F5 **Booroorban** Australia
127 H5 **Boorowa** Australia
126 E6 **Boort** Australia
178 E2 **Boosaaso** Somalia
203 I3 **Boothbay Harbor** U.S.A.
185 I2 **Boothia, Gulf of** Canada
185 I2 **Boothia Peninsula** Canada
161 E4 **Bootle** U.K.
176 A4 **Bopolu** Liberia
164 F4 **Boppard** Germany
215 G1 **Boqueirão** Brazil
206 C2 **Boquilla, Presa de la** *resr* Mex.
206 D1 **Boquillas del Carmen** Mex.
165 K5 **Bor** Czech Rep.
171 J2 **Bor** Serbia
177 F4 **Bor** South Sudan
136 E3 **Bor** Turkey
179 F5 **Boraha, Nosy** *i.* Madag.
194 D2 **Borah Peak** U.S.A.
139 K2 **Boran** Kazakh.
138 C3 **Borankul** Kazakh.
154 B2 **Boraphet, Bung** *l.* Thai.
159 K4 **Borås** Sweden
140 C4 **Borāzjān** Iran
211 G4 **Borba** Brazil
211 K5 **Borborema, Planalto da** *plat.* Brazil
165 G3 **Borchen** Germany
137 H1 **Borçka** Turkey
126 B5 **Borda, Cape** Australia
136 B3 **Bor Dağı** *mt.* Turkey
166 D4 **Bordeaux** France
**Borden** Canada *see* **Borden-Carleton**
189 H4 **Borden-Carleton** Canada
184 G2 **Borden Island** Canada
185 J2 **Borden Peninsula** Canada
126 D6 **Bordertown** Australia
158 B2 **Borðeyri** Iceland
167 I4 **Bordj Bou Arréridj** Alg.
167 G5 **Bordj Bounaama** Alg.
176 C2 **Bordj Omer Driss** Alg.
158 □ **Borðoy** *i.* Faroe Is
139 H4 **Bordu** Kyrg.
162 A3 **Boreray** *i.* U.K.
158 D2 **Borgarfjörður** Iceland
158 B2 **Borgarnes** Iceland
158 K2 **Børgefjell Nasjonalpark** *nat. park* Norway
199 C5 **Borger** U.S.A.
159 L4 **Borgholm** Sweden
170 B2 **Borgo San Dalmazzo** Italy
170 D3 **Borgo San Lorenzo** Italy
170 C2 **Borgosesia** Italy
138 C2 **Borili** Kazakh.
164 B4 **Borinage** *reg.* Belgium
173 G5 **Borisoglebsk** Rus. Fed.
173 F5 **Borisovka** Rus. Fed.
172 F3 **Borisovo-Sudskoye** Rus. Fed.
173 G7 **Borjomi** Georgia
164 E3 **Borken** Germany
158 L1 **Borkenes** Norway
164 E1 **Borkum** Germany
164 E1 **Borkum** *i.* Germany
159 K3 **Borlänge** Sweden
136 B2 **Borlu** Turkey
165 K3 **Borna** Germany
164 D1 **Borndiep** *sea chan.* Neth.
164 E2 **Borne** Neth.
155 D2 **Borneo** *i.* Asia
159 K5 **Bornholm** *i.* Denmark
171 L5 **Bornova** Turkey
153 B4 **Borocay** *i.* Phil.
132 J3 **Borodino** Rus. Fed.
159 O3 **Borodinskoye** Rus. Fed.
173 D5 **Borodyanka** Ukr.
133 O3 **Borogontsy** Rus. Fed.
139 J3 **Borohoro Shan** *mts* China
172 F3 **Borok** Rus. Fed.
176 B3 **Boromo** Burkina Faso
153 C4 **Borongan** Phil.
160 F3 **Boroughbridge** U.K.

172 E3 **Borovichi** Rus. Fed.
139 K1 **Borovlyanka** Rus. Fed.
172 I3 **Borovoy** *Kirovskaya Oblast'* Rus. Fed.
172 E1 **Borovoy** *Respublika Kareliya* Rus. Fed.
172 J2 **Borovoy** *Respublika Komi* Rus. Fed.
138 F1 **Borovskoy** Kazakh.
167 F3 **Borriana** Spain
163 C5 **Borrisokane** Ireland
124 D3 **Borroloola** Australia
158 J3 **Børsa** Norway
169 L7 **Borşa** Romania
138 D4 **Borsakelmas sho'rxogi** *salt marsh* Uzbek.
173 C5 **Borshchiv** Ukr.
146 C2 **Borshchovochnyy Khrebet** *mts* Rus. Fed.
139 J3 **Bortala He** *r.* China
140 C4 **Borūjen** Iran
140 C3 **Borūjerd** Iran
162 B3 **Borve** U.K.
152 D5 **Boryeong** S. Korea
173 B5 **Boryslav** Ukr.
173 D5 **Boryspil'** Ukr.
173 E5 **Borzna** Ukr.
146 D1 **Borzya** Rus. Fed.
139 H3 **Bosaga** Kazakh.
170 G2 **Bosanska Dubica** Bos.-Herz.
170 G2 **Bosanska Gradiška** Bos.-Herz.
170 G2 **Bosanska Krupa** Bos.-Herz.
170 G2 **Bosanski Novi** Bos.-Herz.
170 G2 **Bosansko Grahovo** Bos.-Herz.
190 B4 **Boscobel** U.S.A.
**Bose** China *see* **Baise**
152 D6 **Boseong** S. Korea
181 F4 **Boshof** S. Africa
138 E1 **Boskol'** Kazakh.
170 G2 **Bosnia-Herzegovina** *country* Europe
178 B3 **Bosobolo** Dem. Rep. Congo
151 G7 **Bōsō-hantō** *pen.* Japan
136 B1 **Bosporus** *str.* Turkey
178 B3 **Bossangoa** Cent. Afr. Rep.
178 B3 **Bossembélé** Cent. Afr. Rep.
199 E5 **Bossier City** U.S.A.
180 B2 **Bossiesvlei** Namibia
137 K6 **Bostān** Iran
138 B2 **Bostandyk** Kazakh.
146 A2 **Bosten Hu** *l.* China
161 G5 **Boston** U.K.
203 H3 **Boston** U.S.A.
126 A5 **Boston Bay** Australia
191 H1 **Boston Creek** Canada
203 H3 **Boston-Logan** *airport* U.S.A.
199 E5 **Boston Mountains** U.S.A.
160 F4 **Boston Spa** U.K.
190 D5 **Boswell** U.S.A.
144 B5 **Botad** India
139 H2 **Botakara** Kazakh.
127 I4 **Botany Bay** Australia
158 L3 **Boteå** Sweden
171 K3 **Botev** *mt.* Bulg.
171 J3 **Botevgrad** Bulg.
181 G3 **Bothaville** S. Africa
158 L3 **Bothnia, Gulf of** Fin./Sweden
158 M2 **Bothnian Bay** *g.* Fin./Sweden
127 G9 **Bothwell** Australia
173 H5 **Botkul', Ozero** *l.* Kazakh./Rus. Fed.
169 M7 **Botoşani** Romania
148 E2 **Botou** China
154 C1 **Bô Trach** Vietnam
181 G4 **Botshabelo** S. Africa
179 C6 **Botswana** *country* Africa
170 G5 **Botte Donato, Monte** *mt.* Italy
160 G4 **Bottesford** U.K.
198 C1 **Bottineau** U.S.A.
164 E3 **Bottrop** Germany
214 C3 **Botucatu** Brazil
214 D1 **Botuporã** Brazil
189 J4 **Botwood** Canada
176 B4 **Bouaflé** Côte d'Ivoire
176 B4 **Bouaké** Côte d'Ivoire
178 B3 **Bouar** Cent. Afr. Rep.
176 B1 **Bou Arfa** Morocco
177 D4 **Bouba Ndjida, Parc National de** *nat. park* Cameroon
178 B3 **Bouca** Cent. Afr. Rep.
164 B4 **Bouchain** France
203 G2 **Boucherville** Canada
191 J2 **Bouchette** Canada
176 B3 **Boucle du Baoulé, Parc National de la** *nat. park* Mali
189 H4 **Bouctouche** Canada
125 F2 **Bougainville Island** P.N.G.
176 B3 **Bougouni** Mali
164 D5 **Bouillon** Belgium
167 H4 **Bouira** Alg.
176 A2 **Boujdour** W. Sahara
194 F3 **Boulder** *CO* U.S.A.
194 D2 **Boulder** *MT* U.S.A.
197 G3 **Boulder** *UT* U.S.A.
197 E3 **Boulder Canyon** *gorge* U.S.A.
197 E4 **Boulder City** U.S.A.
196 D5 **Boulevard** U.S.A.
215 E3 **Boulevard Atlántico** Arg.
124 D4 **Boulia** Australia
166 F2 **Boulogne-Billancourt** France
166 E1 **Boulogne-sur-Mer** France
176 B3 **Boulsa** Burkina Faso
178 B4 **Boumango** Gabon
177 D4 **Boumba** *r.* Cameroon
167 H4 **Boumerdès** Alg.
176 B4 **Bouna** Côte d'Ivoire
203 H2 **Boundary Mountains** U.S.A.
196 C3 **Boundary Peak** U.S.A.
176 B4 **Boundiali** Côte d'Ivoire
178 B4 **Boundji** Congo
**Boung** *r.* Vietnam *see* **Thu Bôn, Sông**
149 A6 **Boun Nua** Laos
194 E3 **Bountiful** U.S.A.
125 H6 **Bounty Islands** N.Z.
216 G9 **Bounty Trough** *sea feature* S. Pacific Ocean
176 B3 **Bourem** Mali
166 E4 **Bourganeuf** France
166 G3 **Bourg-en-Bresse** France
166 F3 **Bourges** France
203 F2 **Bourget** Canada
191 J1 **Bourgmont** Canada
**Bourgogne** *reg.* France *see* **Burgundy**
127 F3 **Bourke** Australia
191 G1 **Bourkes** Canada
161 G5 **Bourne** U.K.
161 F7 **Bournemouth** U.K.
164 F2 **Bourtanger Moor** *reg.* Germany
176 C1 **Bou Saâda** Alg.
170 C6 **Bou Salem** Tunisia
197 E5 **Bouse** U.S.A.
197 E5 **Bouse Wash** *watercourse* U.S.A.
177 D3 **Bousso** Chad
164 B4 **Boussu** Belgium
176 A3 **Boutilimit** Mauritania
219 J9 **Bouvetøya** *terr.* Atlantic Ocean
164 C5 **Bouy** France
165 H3 **Bovenden** Germany
**Boven Kapuas, Pegunungan** *mts* Malaysia *see* **Kapuas Hulu, Pegunungan**
215 E1 **Bovril** Arg.
187 G4 **Bow** *r.* Canada
198 C1 **Bowbells** U.S.A.
124 E4 **Bowen** Australia
190 B5 **Bowen** U.S.A.
127 H6 **Bowen, Mount** Australia
127 I1 **Bowenville** Australia
216 G2 **Bowers Ridge** *sea feature* Bering Sea
197 H5 **Bowie** *AZ* U.S.A.
199 D5 **Bowie** *TX* U.S.A.
187 G5 **Bow Island** Canada
200 C4 **Bowling Green** *KY* U.S.A.
198 F4 **Bowling Green** *MO* U.S.A.
202 B4 **Bowling Green** *OH* U.S.A.
202 E5 **Bowling Green** *VA* U.S.A.
198 C2 **Bowman** U.S.A.
186 E4 **Bowman, Mount** Canada
129 D6 **Bowman Island** *i.* Antarctica
191 H4 **Bowmanville** Canada
162 B5 **Bowmore** U.K.
127 I5 **Bowral** Australia
127 J3 **Bowraville** Australia
186 E4 **Bowron** *r.* Canada
186 E4 **Bowron Lake Provincial Park** Canada
165 H5 **Boxberg** Germany
148 F2 **Boxing** China
164 D3 **Boxtel** Neth.
136 E1 **Boyabat** Turkey
171 J3 **Boyana** *tourist site* Bulg.
127 J3 **Boyd** *r.* Australia
187 I2 **Boyd Lake** Canada
186 G4 **Boyle** Canada
163 C4 **Boyle** Ireland
163 E4 **Boyne** *r.* Ireland
201 D7 **Boynton Beach** U.S.A.
194 E3 **Boysen Reservoir** U.S.A.
139 F5 **Boysun** Uzbek.
210 F8 **Boyuibe** Bol.
137 J1 **Böyük Hinaldağ** *mt.* Azer.
138 B3 **Bozashchy, Poluostrov** *pen.* Kazakh.
171 L5 **Bozcaada** *i.* Turkey
171 L5 **Bozdağ** *mt.* Turkey
136 A2 **Boz Dağları** *mts* Turkey
136 B3 **Bozdoğan** Turkey
161 G5 **Bozeat** U.K.
194 E2 **Bozeman** U.S.A.
148 E3 **Bozhou** China
136 D3 **Bozkır** Turkey
178 B3 **Bozoum** Cent. Afr. Rep.
136 G3 **Bozova** Turkey
140 B2 **Bozqūsh, Kūh-e** *mts* Iran
139 H2 **Bozshakol' (abandoned)** Kazakh.
139 F2 **Boztumsyk** Kazakh.
136 C2 **Bozüyük** Turkey
139 J2 **Bozymbay** Kazakh.
170 B2 **Bra** Italy
170 G3 **Brač** *i.* Croatia
162 B3 **Bracadale** U.K.
162 B3 **Bracadale, Loch** *b.* U.K.
170 E3 **Bracciano, Lago di** *l.* Italy
191 H3 **Bracebridge** Canada
158 K3 **Bräcke** Sweden
165 H5 **Brackenheim** Germany
161 G6 **Bracknell** U.K.
170 G4 **Bradano** *r.* Italy
201 D7 **Bradenton** U.S.A.
205 L5 **Brades** Montserrat
191 H3 **Bradford** Canada
160 F4 **Bradford** U.K.
202 A4 **Bradford** *OH* U.S.A.
202 D4 **Bradford** *PA* U.S.A.
203 G3 **Bradford** *VT* U.S.A.
199 D6 **Brady** U.S.A.
186 B3 **Brady Glacier** U.S.A.
162 □ **Brae** U.K.
126 C4 **Braemar** Australia
162 E3 **Braemar** U.K.
167 B2 **Braga** Port.
215 E2 **Bragado** Arg.
211 I4 **Bragança** Brazil
167 C2 **Bragança** Port.
214 C3 **Bragança Paulista** Brazil
173 D5 **Brahin** Belarus
165 I1 **Brahlstorf** Germany
145 G5 **Brahmanbaria** Bangl.
143 D1 **Brahmani** *r.* India
143 D2 **Brahmapur** India
145 G4 **Brahmaputra** *r.* Asia *alt.* **Dihang (India),** *alt.* **Yarlung Zangbo (China)**
171 L2 **Brăila** Romania
164 B5 **Braine** France
164 C4 **Braine-le-Comte** Belgium
198 E2 **Brainerd** U.S.A.
161 H6 **Braintree** U.K.
181 H1 **Brak** *r.* S. Africa
164 B4 **Brakel** Belgium
165 H3 **Brakel** Germany
165 G1 **Brake (Unterweser)** Germany
179 B6 **Brakwater** Namibia
186 E4 **Bralorne** Canada
159 J5 **Bramming** Denmark
159 L3 **Brämön** *i.* Sweden
191 H4 **Brampton** Canada
160 E3 **Brampton** *England* U.K.
161 I5 **Brampton** *England* U.K.
165 G2 **Bramsche** Germany
161 H5 **Brancaster** U.K.
189 J4 **Branch** Canada
213 E4 **Branco** *r.* Brazil
159 J3 **Brandbu** Norway
159 J5 **Brande** Denmark
165 K2 **Brandenburg** Germany
165 K2 **Brandenburg** *land* Germany
181 G4 **Brandfort** S. Africa
165 L3 **Brandis** Germany
187 J5 **Brandon** Canada
161 H5 **Brandon** U.K.
198 D3 **Brandon** *SD* U.S.A.
203 G3 **Brandon** *VT* U.S.A.
163 A5 **Brandon Head** Ireland
163 E5 **Brandon Hill** Ireland
163 A5 **Brandon Mountain** *h.* Ireland
180 D5 **Brandvlei** S. Africa
201 D6 **Branford** U.S.A.
169 I3 **Braniewo** Poland
129 B2 **Bransfield Strait** *str.* Antarctica
191 G4 **Brantford** Canada
126 D6 **Branxholme** Australia
189 H4 **Bras d'Or Lake** Canada
214 E2 **Brasil, Planalto do** *plat.* Brazil
214 C1 **Brasilândia** Brazil
210 E6 **Brasileia** Brazil
214 C1 **Brasília** Brazil
214 D2 **Brasília de Minas** Brazil
211 G4 **Brasília Legal** Brazil
169 M3 **Braslaw** Belarus
171 K2 **Braşov** Romania
153 A5 **Brassey, Banjaran** *mts* Sabah Malaysia
203 I2 **Brassua Lake** U.S.A.
168 H6 **Bratislava** Slovakia
146 C1 **Bratsk** Rus. Fed.
146 C1 **Bratskoye Vodokhranilishche** *resr* Rus. Fed.
203 G3 **Brattleboro** U.S.A.
168 F6 **Braunau am Inn** Austria
165 G4 **Braunfels** Germany
165 I3 **Braunlage** Germany
165 J3 **Braunsbedra** Germany
165 I2 **Braunschweig** Germany
176 □ **Brava** *i.* Cape Verde
159 L4 **Bråviken** *inlet* Sweden
207 E2 **Bravo del Norte, Río** *r.* Mex./U.S.A. *alt.* **Rio Grande**
197 E5 **Brawley** U.S.A.
163 E4 **Bray** Ireland
186 F4 **Brazeau** *r.* Canada
211 H6 **Brazil** *country* S. America
219 H7 **Brazil Basin** *sea feature* S. Atlantic Ocean
199 D5 **Brazos** *r.* U.S.A.
178 B4 **Brazzaville** Congo
171 H2 **Brčko** Bos.-Herz.
128 A6 **Breaksea Sound** *inlet* N.Z.
128 E1 **Bream Bay** N.Z.
128 E1 **Bream Head** N.Z.
161 C6 **Brechfa** U.K.
162 F4 **Brechin** U.K.
164 C3 **Brecht** Belgium
198 D2 **Breckenridge** *MN* U.S.A.
199 D5 **Breckenridge** *TX* U.S.A.
168 H6 **Břeclav** Czech Rep.
161 D6 **Brecon** U.K.
161 D6 **Brecon Beacons** *reg.* U.K.
161 D6 **Brecon Beacons National Park** U.K.
164 C3 **Breda** Neth.
180 D7 **Bredasdorp** S. Africa
127 H5 **Bredbo** Australia
165 K2 **Breddin** Germany
164 E3 **Bredevoort** Neth.
158 K2 **Bredviken** Norway
138 E1 **Bredy** Rus. Fed.
164 D3 **Bree** Belgium
202 D5 **Breezewood** U.S.A.
168 D7 **Bregenz** Austria
158 A2 **Breiðafjörður** *b.* Iceland
158 D2 **Breiðdalsvík** Iceland
165 G4 **Breidenbach** Germany
168 C6 **Breisach am Rhein** Germany
165 I1 **Breitenfelde** Germany
165 I5 **Breitengüßbach** Germany
158 M1 **Breivikbotn** Norway
211 I6 **Brejinho de Nazaré** Brazil
158 J3 **Brekstad** Norway
165 G1 **Bremen** Germany
201 C5 **Bremen** *GA* U.S.A.
190 D5 **Bremen** *IN* U.S.A.
165 G1 **Bremerhaven** Germany
194 B2 **Bremerton** U.S.A.
165 H1 **Bremervörde** Germany
164 F4 **Bremm** Germany
199 D6 **Brenham** U.S.A.
158 K2 **Brenna** Norway
168 E7 **Brenner Pass** Austria/Italy
191 H2 **Brent** Canada
170 D2 **Brenta** *r.* Italy
161 H6 **Brentwood** U.K.
196 B3 **Brentwood** *CA* U.S.A.
203 G4 **Brentwood** *NY* U.S.A.
170 D2 **Brescia** Italy
170 D1 **Bressanone** Italy
162 □ **Bressay** *i.* U.K.
166 D3 **Bressuire** France
173 B4 **Brest** Belarus
166 B2 **Brest** France
**Bretagne** *reg.* France *see* **Brittany**
164 A5 **Breteuil** France
199 F6 **Breton Sound** *b.* U.S.A.
128 E1 **Brett, Cape** N.Z.
165 G5 **Bretten** Germany
161 E4 **Bretton** U.K.
201 D5 **Brevard** U.S.A.
211 H4 **Breves** Brazil
190 E2 **Brevort** U.S.A.
127 G2 **Brewarrina** Australia
203 I2 **Brewer** U.S.A.
194 C1 **Brewster** U.S.A.
199 G6 **Brewton** U.S.A.
181 H3 **Breyten** S. Africa
169 I6 **Brezno** Slovakia
170 G2 **Brezovo Polje** *plain* Croatia
178 C3 **Bria** Cent. Afr. Rep.
166 H4 **Briançon** France
127 G5 **Bribbaree** Australia
127 J1 **Bribie Island** Australia
173 C5 **Briceni** Moldova
166 H4 **Bric Froid** *mt.* France/Italy
163 C5 **Bride** *r.* Ireland
197 G1 **Bridgeland** U.S.A.
161 D6 **Bridgend** U.K.
162 D4 **Bridge of Orchy** U.K.
196 C2 **Bridgeport** *CA* U.S.A.
203 G4 **Bridgeport** *CT* U.S.A.
198 C3 **Bridgeport** *NE* U.S.A.
194 E2 **Bridger** U.S.A.
194 F3 **Bridger Peak** U.S.A.
203 F5 **Bridgeton** U.S.A.
205 M6 **Bridgetown** Barbados
127 G9 **Bridgewater** Australia
189 H5 **Bridgewater** Canada
203 J1 **Bridgewater** U.S.A.
126 D7 **Bridgewater, Cape** Australia
161 E5 **Bridgnorth** U.K.
203 H2 **Bridgton** U.S.A.
161 D6 **Bridgwater** U.K.
161 D6 **Bridgwater Bay** U.K.
160 G3 **Bridlington** U.K.
160 G3 **Bridlington Bay** U.K.
127 G8 **Bridport** Australia
161 E7 **Bridport** U.K.
168 C7 **Brig** Switz.
160 G4 **Brigg** U.K.
194 D3 **Brigham City** U.S.A.
127 G6 **Bright** Australia
161 I6 **Brightlingsea** U.K.
191 I3 **Brighton** Canada
128 C6 **Brighton** N.Z.
161 G7 **Brighton** U.K.
191 F4 **Brighton** U.S.A.
166 H5 **Brignoles** France
176 A3 **Brikama** Gambia
165 G3 **Brilon** Germany
170 G4 **Brindisi** Italy
215 D1 **Brinkmann** Arg.
126 C4 **Brinkworth** Australia
189 H4 **Brion, Île** *i.* Canada
166 F4 **Brioude** France
189 F3 **Brisay** Canada
127 J1 **Brisbane** Australia
203 J1 **Bristol** Canada
161 E6 **Bristol** U.K.
203 G4 **Bristol** *CT* U.S.A.
203 F4 **Bristol** *PA* U.S.A.
202 B6 **Bristol** *TN* U.S.A.
184 B4 **Bristol Bay** U.S.A.
161 C6 **Bristol Channel** *est.* U.K.
209 G7 **Bristol Island** S. Sandwich Is
197 E4 **Bristol Lake** U.S.A.
197 E4 **Bristol Mountains** U.S.A.
129 D3 **British Antarctic Territory** *reg.* Antarctica
186 D3 **British Columbia** *prov.* Canada
185 J1 **British Empire Range** *mts* Canada
130 C7 **British Indian Ocean Territory** *terr.* Indian Ocean
219 I2 **British Isles** *is* Europe
181 G2 **Brits** S. Africa
180 E5 **Britstown** S. Africa
166 C2 **Brittany** *reg.* France
166 E4 **Brive-la-Gaillarde** France
167 E1 **Briviesca** Spain
161 D7 **Brixham** U.K.
**Brlik** Kazakh. *see* **Birlik**
168 H6 **Brno** Czech Rep.
201 D5 **Broad** *r.* U.S.A.
203 F3 **Broadalbin** U.S.A.
188 E3 **Broadback** *r.* Canada
126 F6 **Broadford** Australia
163 C5 **Broadford** Ireland
162 C3 **Broadford** U.K.
162 E5 **Broad Law** *h.* U.K.
161 I6 **Broadstairs** U.K.
194 F2 **Broadus** U.S.A.
187 I4 **Broadview** Canada
127 J2 **Broadwater** Australia
198 C3 **Broadwater** U.S.A.
128 D1 **Broadwood** N.Z.
159 M4 **Brocēni** Latvia
187 I3 **Brochet** Canada
187 I3 **Brochet, Lac** *l.* Canada
165 I3 **Brocken** *mt.* Germany
184 G2 **Brock Island** Canada
202 E3 **Brockport** U.S.A.
203 H3 **Brockton** U.S.A.
191 J3 **Brockville** Canada
191 F4 **Brockway** *MI* U.S.A.
202 D4 **Brockway** *PA* U.S.A.
185 J2 **Brodeur Peninsula** Canada
190 C4 **Brodhead** U.S.A.
162 C5 **Brodick** U.K.
169 I4 **Brodnica** Poland
173 C5 **Brody** Ukr.
199 E4 **Broken Arrow** U.S.A.
127 I4 **Broken Bay** Australia
198 D3 **Broken Bow** *NE* U.S.A.
199 E5 **Broken Bow** *OK* U.S.A.
126 D3 **Broken Hill** Australia
218 K7 **Broken Plateau** *sea feature* Indian Ocean
165 I2 **Brome** Germany
161 G6 **Bromley** U.K.
161 E5 **Bromsgrove** U.K.
159 J4 **Brønderslev** Denmark
181 H2 **Bronkhorstspruit** S. Africa
158 K2 **Brønnøysund** Norway
190 E5 **Bronson** U.S.A.
161 I5 **Brooke** U.K.
153 A4 **Brooke's Point** Phil.
190 C4 **Brookfield** U.S.A.
199 F6 **Brookhaven** U.S.A.
194 A3 **Brookings** *OR* U.S.A.
198 D2 **Brookings** *SD* U.S.A.
203 H3 **Brookline** U.S.A.
190 A5 **Brooklyn** *IA* U.S.A.
190 B5 **Brooklyn** *IL* U.S.A.
198 E2 **Brooklyn Center** U.S.A.
202 D6 **Brookneal** U.S.A.
187 G4 **Brooks** Canada
196 A2 **Brooks** *CA* U.S.A.
203 I2 **Brooks** *ME* U.S.A.
129 C3 **Brooks, Cape** *c.* Antarctica
184 D3 **Brooks Range** *mts* U.S.A.
201 D6 **Brooksville** U.S.A.
202 D4 **Brookville** U.S.A.
162 C3 **Broom, Loch** *inlet* U.K.
124 C3 **Broome** Australia
162 E2 **Brora** U.K.
159 K5 **Brösarp** Sweden
163 D4 **Brosna** *r.* Ireland
194 B3 **Brothers** U.S.A.
149 □ **Brothers, The** *is Hong Kong* China
160 E3 **Brough** U.K.
162 E1 **Brough Head** U.K.
163 E3 **Broughshane** U.K.
126 C4 **Broughton** *r.* Australia
**Broughton Island** Canada *see* **Qikiqtarjuaq**
127 J4 **Broughton Islands** Australia
169 O5 **Brovary** Ukr.
159 J4 **Brovst** Denmark
126 C4 **Brown, Mount** *h.* Australia
199 C5 **Brownfield** U.S.A.
194 D1 **Browning** U.S.A.
190 D6 **Brownsburg** U.S.A.
203 F5 **Browns Mills** U.S.A.
201 B5 **Brownsville** *TN* U.S.A.
199 D7 **Brownsville** *TX* U.S.A.
203 I2 **Brownville** U.S.A.
203 I2 **Brownville Junction** U.S.A.
199 D6 **Brownwood** U.S.A.
169 N4 **Brozha** Belarus
166 F1 **Bruay-la-Bussière** France
190 C2 **Bruce Crossing** U.S.A.
188 D4 **Bruce Peninsula** Canada
191 G3 **Bruce Peninsula National Park** Canada
165 G5 **Bruchsal** Germany
165 K2 **Brück** Germany
168 G7 **Bruck an der Mur** Austria
161 E6 **Brue** *r.* U.K.
**Bruges** Belgium *see* **Brugge**
164 B3 **Brugge** Belgium
165 G5 **Brühl** Germany
164 E4 **Brühl** Germany
145 I3 **Bruini** India
197 G2 **Bruin Point** *mt.* U.S.A.
180 C2 **Brukkaros** Namibia
190 B2 **Brule** U.S.A.
189 H3 **Brûlé, Lac** *l.* Canada
164 C5 **Brûly** Belgium
214 E1 **Brumado** Brazil
159 J3 **Brumunddal** Norway
163 E4 **Brú Na Bóinne** *tourist site* Ireland
165 J2 **Brunau** Germany
194 D3 **Bruneau** U.S.A.
194 D3 **Bruneau** *r.* U.S.A.
155 D2 **Brunei** *country* Asia
158 K3 **Brunflo** Sweden
170 D1 **Brunico** Italy
128 C5 **Brunner, Lake** N.Z.
187 H4 **Bruno** Canada
168 D4 **Brunsbüttel** Germany
201 D6 **Brunswick** *GA* U.S.A.
203 I3 **Brunswick** *ME* U.S.A.
202 C4 **Brunswick** *OH* U.S.A.
212 B8 **Brunswick, Península de** *pen.* Chile
**Brunswick Head** Australia *see* **Brunswick Heads**
127 J2 **Brunswick Heads** Australia
168 H6 **Bruntál** Czech Rep.
129 C3 **Brunt Ice Shelf** *ice feature* Antarctica
181 I4 **Bruntville** S. Africa
127 G9 **Bruny Island** Australia
194 G3 **Brush** U.S.A.
164 C4 **Brussels** Belgium (City Plan **107**)
191 G4 **Brussels** Canada
190 D3 **Brussels** U.S.A.
169 N5 **Brusyliv** Ukr.
127 G6 **Bruthen** Australia
**Bruxelles** Belgium *see* **Brussels**
202 A4 **Bryan** *OH* U.S.A.
199 D6 **Bryan** *TX* U.S.A.
126 C4 **Bryan, Mount** *h.* Australia
172 E4 **Bryansk** Rus. Fed.
173 H6 **Bryansk** Rus. Fed.
172 E4 **Bryanskaya Oblast'** *admin. div.* Rus. Fed.
197 F3 **Bryce Canyon National Park** U.S.A.
197 H5 **Bryce Mountain** U.S.A.
159 I4 **Bryne** Norway
173 F6 **Bryukhovetskaya** Rus. Fed.
168 H5 **Brzeg** Poland
178 E3 **Bu'aale** Somalia
125 F2 **Buala** Solomon Is
152 D6 **Buan** S. Korea
176 A3 **Buba** Guinea-Bissau
137 L7 **Būbiyān, Jazīrat** Kuwait
153 B5 **Bubuan** *i.* Phil.
136 C3 **Bucak** Turkey
213 B3 **Bucaramanga** Col.
153 C4 **Bucas Grande** *i.* Phil.
127 H6 **Buchan** Australia
176 A4 **Buchanan** Liberia
190 D5 **Buchanan** *MI* U.S.A.
202 D6 **Buchanan** *VA* U.S.A.
199 D6 **Buchanan, Lake** U.S.A.
185 K2 **Buchan Gulf** Canada
189 I4 **Buchans** Canada
171 L2 **Bucharest** Romania
165 I1 **Büchen** Germany
165 H5 **Buchen (Odenwald)** Germany
152 D5 **Bucheon** S. Korea
165 K1 **Buchholz** Germany
165 H1 **Bucholz in der Nordheide** Germany
196 B4 **Buchon, Point** U.S.A.
169 L7 **Bucin, Pasul** *pass* Romania
127 F3 **Buckambool Mountain** *h.* Australia
165 H2 **Bückeburg** Germany
165 H2 **Bücken** Germany
197 F5 **Buckeye** U.S.A.
202 B5 **Buckeye Lake** U.S.A.
202 C5 **Buckhannon** U.S.A.
202 C5 **Buckhannon** *r.* U.S.A.
162 E4 **Buckhaven** U.K.
191 H3 **Buckhorn** Canada
197 H5 **Buckhorn** U.S.A.
191 H3 **Buckhorn Lake** Canada
202 B6 **Buckhorn Lake** U.S.A.
162 F3 **Buckie** U.K.
191 J3 **Buckingham** Canada
161 G5 **Buckingham** U.K.
202 D6 **Buckingham** U.S.A.
124 D3 **Buckingham Bay** Australia
124 E4 **Buckland Tableland** *reg.* Australia
126 B4 **Buckleboo** Australia
129 B6 **Buckle Island** *i.* Antarctica
197 F4 **Buckskin Mountains** U.S.A.
196 B2 **Bucks Mountain** U.S.A.
203 I2 **Bucksport** U.S.A.
165 K2 **Bückwitz** Germany
**Bucureşti** Romania *see* **Bucharest**
202 B4 **Bucyrus** U.S.A.
169 O4 **Buda-Kashalyova** Belarus
169 I7 **Budapest** Hungary
144 D3 **Budaun** India
126 F3 **Budda** Australia
162 F4 **Buddon Ness** *pt* U.K.
170 C4 **Buddusò** *Sardinia* Italy
161 C7 **Bude** U.K.
199 F6 **Bude** U.S.A.
173 H6 **Budennovsk** Rus. Fed.
127 J1 **Buderim** Australia
165 H4 **Büdingen** Germany
144 D5 **Budni** India
172 E3 **Budogoshch'** Rus. Fed.
145 H2 **Budongquan** China
170 C4 **Budoni** *Sardinia* Italy
140 C6 **Budū, Ḩadabat al** *plain* Saudi Arabia
140 C6 **Budū', Sabkhat al** *salt pan* Saudi Arabia
176 C4 **Buea** Cameroon
196 B4 **Buellton** U.S.A.
215 D2 **Buena Esperanza** Arg.
213 A4 **Buenaventura** Col.
204 C3 **Buenaventura** Mex.
213 A4 **Buenaventura, Bahía de** *b.* Col.
195 F4 **Buena Vista** *CO* U.S.A.
202 D6 **Buena Vista** *VA* U.S.A.
167 E2 **Buendía, Embalse de** *resr* Spain
215 B4 **Bueno** *r.* Chile
215 E2 **Buenos Aires** Arg. (City Plan **116**)
215 E3 **Buenos Aires** *prov.* Arg.
212 B7 **Buenos Aires, Lago** *l.* Arg./Chile
212 C7 **Buen Pasto** Arg.
206 C2 **Búfalo** Mex.
186 G3 **Buffalo** *r.* Canada
202 D3 **Buffalo** *NY* U.S.A.
199 D4 **Buffalo** *OK* U.S.A.
198 C2 **Buffalo** *SD* U.S.A.
199 D6 **Buffalo** *TX* U.S.A.
190 B3 **Buffalo** *WI* U.S.A.
194 F2 **Buffalo** *WY* U.S.A.
190 B3 **Buffalo** *r.* U.S.A.
127 G6 **Buffalo, Mount** *h.* Australia
186 F3 **Buffalo Head Hills** Canada
186 F2 **Buffalo Lake** Canada
187 H3 **Buffalo Narrows** Canada
180 B4 **Buffels** *watercourse* S. Africa
181 G1 **Buffels Drift** S. Africa
201 D5 **Buford** U.S.A.
171 K2 **Buftea** Romania
169 J4 **Bug** *r.* Poland
213 A4 **Buga** Col.
213 A3 **Bugalagrande** Col.
127 H3 **Bugaldie** Australia
**Bugdayli** Turkm. *see* **Bugdaýly**
138 C5 **Bugdaýly** Turkm.
155 D4 **Bugel, Tanjung** *pt* Indon.
164 C3 **Buggenhout** Belgium
170 G2 **Bugojno** Bos.-Herz.
153 A4 **Bugsuk** *i.* Phil.
153 B2 **Buguey** Phil.
138 C1 **Buguruslan** Rus. Fed.
179 D5 **Buhera** Zimbabwe
153 B3 **Buhi** Phil.
194 D3 **Buhl** *ID* U.S.A.
190 A2 **Buhl** *MN* U.S.A.
137 I3 **Bühtan** *r.* Turkey
169 M7 **Buhuşi** Romania
161 D5 **Builth Wells** U.K.
168 E7 **Buin, Piz** *mt.* Austria/Switz.
176 B4 **Bui National Park** Ghana
172 I4 **Buinsk** Rus. Fed.
137 K4 **Bu'in Soflā** Iran
146 D2 **Buir Nur** *l.* Mongolia
179 B6 **Buitepos** Namibia
171 I3 **Bujanovac** Serbia
178 C4 **Bujumbura** Burundi
146 D1 **Bukachacha** Rus. Fed.
145 G1 **Bukadaban Feng** *mt.* China
125 F2 **Buka Island** P.N.G.
140 B2 **Būkān** Iran
140 D4 **Būkand** Iran
139 J1 **Bukanskoye** Rus. Fed.
**Bukantau, Gory** *hill* Uzbek. *see* **Bo'kantov tog'lari**
178 C4 **Bukavu** Dem. Rep. Congo
**Bukhara** Uzbek. *see* **Buxoro**
153 C6 **Bukide** *i.* Indon.
155 D3 **Bukit Baka-Bukit Raya, Taman Nasional** *nat. park* Indon.
155 B4 **Bukit Barisan Selatan, Taman Nasional** Indon.
154 B5 **Bukit Fraser** Malaysia
155 B3 **Bukittinggi** Indon.
178 D4 **Bukoba** Tanz.
169 L6 **Bukovinian and Dalmatian Metropolitans, Residence of** *tourist site* Ukraine
139 K2 **Buktyrma, Vodokhranilishche** *resr* Kazakh.
154 □ **Bukum, Pulau** *i.* Sing.
147 F7 **Bula** Indon.
172 I4 **Bula** *r.* Rus. Fed.
168 D7 **Bülach** Switz.
127 J4 **Bulahdelah** Australia
**Bulahdelal** Australia *see* **Bulahdelah**
153 B3 **Bulalacao** Phil.
153 B3 **Bulan** Phil.
136 G1 **Bulancak** Turkey
144 D3 **Bulandshahr** India
137 I2 **Bulanık** Turkey
179 C6 **Bulawayo** Zimbabwe
139 G1 **Bulayevo** Kazakh.
136 F3 **Bulbul** Syria
136 B2 **Buldan** Turkey
144 D5 **Buldhana** India
181 I2 **Bulembu** Swaziland
146 C2 **Bulgan** Mongolia
148 B1 **Bulgan** Mongolia
171 K3 **Bulgaria** *country* Europe
126 E1 **Bullawarra, Lake** *salt flat* Australia
126 D3 **Bullea, Lake** *salt flat* Australia
128 D4 **Buller** *r.* N.Z.
127 G6 **Buller, Mount** Australia
197 E4 **Bullhead City** U.S.A.
196 D4 **Bullion Mountains** U.S.A.
126 E2 **Bulloo** *watercourse* Australia
126 E2 **Bulloo Downs** Australia
126 E2 **Bulloo Lake** *salt flat* Australia
180 B2 **Büllsport** Namibia
154 □ **Buloh, Pulau** *i.* Sing.
126 E6 **Buloke, Lake** *dry lake* Australia
181 G4 **Bultfontein** S. Africa
153 C5 **Buluan** Phil.
173 H5 **Bulukhta, Ozero** *l.* Rus. Fed.
124 C2 **Bulukumba** Indon.
133 N2 **Bulun** Rus. Fed.
178 B4 **Bulungu** Dem. Rep. Congo
178 C4 **Bulungu** Dem. Rep. Congo
139 F5 **Bulung'ur** Uzbek.
**Bulungur** Uzbek. *see* **Bulung'ur**
153 C3 **Bulusan** Phil.
178 C3 **Bumba** Dem. Rep. Congo
148 B1 **Bumbat** China
197 F4 **Bumble Bee** U.S.A.
153 A5 **Bum-Bum** *i.* Malaysia
178 B4 **Buna** Dem. Rep. Congo
178 D3 **Buna** Kenya
178 D4 **Bunazi** Tanz.
**Bunbeg** Ireland *see* **An Bun Beag**
124 B5 **Bunbury** Australia
163 E5 **Bunclody** Ireland
163 D2 **Buncrana** Ireland
178 D4 **Bunda** Tanz.
124 F4 **Bundaberg** Australia
127 G2 **Bundaleer** Australia
127 I3 **Bundarra** Australia
144 C4 **Bundi** India
127 J2 **Bundjalung National Park** Australia
163 C3 **Bundoran** Ireland
145 F5 **Bundu** India
161 I5 **Bungay** U.K.
127 H5 **Bungendore** Australia
151 C8 **Bungo-suidō** *sea chan.* Japan
178 D3 **Bunia** Dem. Rep. Congo
178 C4 **Bunianga** Dem. Rep. Congo
126 E6 **Buninyong** Australia
176 D3 **Buni-Yadi** Nigeria
144 C2 **Bunji** Pak.
197 E3 **Bunkerville** U.S.A.
199 E6 **Bunkie** U.S.A.
201 D6 **Bunnell** U.S.A.
136 E2 **Bünyan** Turkey
153 A6 **Bunyu** *i.* Indon.
154 C2 **Buôn Đôn** Vietnam
154 D2 **Buôn Hô** Vietnam
154 D2 **Buôn Ma Thuôt** Vietnam
**Buôn Mê Thuôt** Vietnam *see* **Buôn Ma Thuôt**
133 O2 **Buor-Khaya, Guba** *b.* Rus. Fed.
178 D4 **Bura** Kenya
**Burang** China *see* **Jirang**
214 E2 **Buranhaém** *r.* Brazil
138 C2 **Burannoye** Rus. Fed.
**Burao** Somalia *see* **Burco**
153 C4 **Burauen** Phil.
142 B4 **Buraydah** Saudi Arabia
165 G4 **Burbach** Germany
196 C4 **Burbank** U.S.A.
127 G4 **Burcher** Australia
178 E3 **Burco** Somalia
164 D1 **Burdaard** Neth.
138 F5 **Burdalyk** Turkm.
136 C3 **Burdur** Turkey
178 D2 **Burē** Eth.
161 I5 **Bure** *r.* U.K.
158 M2 **Bureå** Sweden
146 F1 **Bureinskiy Khrebet** *mts* Rus. Fed.
144 C3 **Burewala** Pak.
**Bûr Fu'ad** Egypt *see* **Port Fuad**
171 L3 **Burgas** Bulg.
201 E5 **Burgaw** U.S.A.
165 J2 **Burg bei Magdeburg** Germany
165 I5 **Burgbernheim** Germany
165 I2 **Burgdorf** Germany
189 I4 **Burgeo** Canada
181 G5 **Burgersdorp** S. Africa
181 I2 **Burgersfort** S. Africa
161 G7 **Burgess Hill** U.K.
165 H4 **Burghaun** Germany
168 F6 **Burghausen** Germany
162 E3 **Burghead** U.K.
164 B3 **Burgh-Haamstede** Neth.
170 F6 **Burgio, Serra di** *h. Sicily* Italy
165 K5 **Burglengenfeld** Germany
167 E1 **Burgos** Spain
165 K4 **Burgstädt** Germany
159 L4 **Burgsvik** Sweden
164 E1 **Burgum** Neth.
166 G3 **Burgundy** *reg.* France
146 B3 **Burhan Budai Shan** *mts* China
171 L5 **Burhaniye** Turkey
144 D5 **Burhanpur** India
145 E5 **Burhar-Dhanpuri** India
145 H4 **Burhi Dihing** *r.* India
145 F4 **Burhi Gandak** *r.* India
153 B3 **Burias** *i.* Phil.
138 D2 **Buribay** Rus. Fed.
206 I6 **Burica, Punta** *pt* Costa Rica
145 E4 **Buri Gandak** *r.* Nepal
138 E1 **Burili** Kazakh.
189 I4 **Burin Peninsula** Canada
154 B2 **Buriram** Thai.
211 J5 **Buriti Bravo** Brazil
214 C1 **Buritis** Brazil
141 G4 **Burj Aziz Khan** Pak.
124 D3 **Burketown** Australia
176 B3 **Burkina Faso** *country* Africa
139 I2 **Burkitty** Kazakh.
191 H3 **Burk's Falls** Canada
139 I1 **Burla** Rus. Fed.
139 I1 **Burla** *r.* Rus. Fed.
194 D3 **Burley** U.S.A.
191 H4 **Burlington** Canada
198 C4 **Burlington** *CO* U.S.A.
190 B5 **Burlington** *IA* U.S.A.
190 D5 **Burlington** *IN* U.S.A.
203 I2 **Burlington** *ME* U.S.A.
203 G2 **Burlington** *VT* U.S.A.
190 C4 **Burlington** *WI* U.S.A.
138 D1 **Burly** Rus. Fed.
**Burma** *country* Asia *see* **Myanmar**
199 D6 **Burnet** U.S.A.
194 B3 **Burney** U.S.A.
203 I2 **Burnham** U.S.A.
127 F8 **Burnie** Australia
160 G3 **Burniston** U.K.
160 E4 **Burnley** U.K.
194 C3 **Burns** U.S.A.
187 H1 **Burnside** *r.* Canada
184 F4 **Burns Lake** Canada
202 C5 **Burnsville Lake** U.S.A.
162 E4 **Burntisland** U.K.
187 J3 **Burntwood** *r.* Canada
187 I3 **Burntwood Lake** Canada
126 E5 **Buronga** Australia
138 E4 **Burovoy** Uzbek.
132 J5 **Burqin** China
136 G5 **Burqu'** Jordan
126 C4 **Burra** Australia
162 □ **Burra** *i.* U.K.
162 □ **Burravoe** U.K.
162 F2 **Burray** *i.* U.K.
171 I4 **Burrel** Albania
127 H4 **Burrendong, Lake** Australia
127 H3 **Burren Junction** Australia
127 I5 **Burrewarra Point** Australia
127 H5 **Burrinjuck** Australia
127 H5 **Burrinjuck Reservoir** Australia
206 D1 **Burro, Serranías del** *mts* Mex.
202 B5 **Burr Oak Reservoir** U.S.A.
162 D6 **Burrow Head** U.K.
197 G2 **Burrville** U.S.A.
136 B1 **Bursa** Turkey
177 F2 **Būr Safājah** Egypt
**Būr Sa'īd** Egypt *see* **Port Said**
165 G5 **Bürstadt** Germany
**Būr Sudan** Sudan *see* **Port Sudan**
126 D4 **Burta** Australia
190 E3 **Burt Lake** U.S.A.
191 F4 **Burton** U.S.A.
188 E3 **Burton, Lac** *l.* Canada
**Burtonport** Ireland *see* **Ailt an Chorráin**
161 F5 **Burton upon Trent** U.K.
158 M2 **Burträsk** Sweden
203 J1 **Burtts Corner** Canada
126 E4 **Burtundy** Australia
147 E7 **Buru** *i.* Indon.
136 C6 **Burullus, Buḩayrat al** *lag.* Egypt
178 D4 **Burundi** *country* Africa
178 C4 **Bururi** Burundi
186 B2 **Burwash Landing** Canada
162 F2 **Burwick** U.K.
139 H3 **Burylbaytal** Kazakh.
173 E5 **Buryn'** Ukr.
138 B3 **Burynshyk** Kazakh.
161 H5 **Bury St Edmunds** U.K.
144 C2 **Burzil Pass** Pak.
170 E6 **Busambra, Rocca** *mt. Sicily* Italy
152 E6 **Busan** S. Korea
178 C4 **Busanga** Dem. Rep. Congo
163 E2 **Bush** *r.* U.K.
140 C4 **Būshehr** Iran
145 E2 **Bushêngcaka** China
178 D4 **Bushenyi** Uganda
163 E2 **Bushmills** U.K.
190 B5 **Bushnell** U.S.A.
154 □ **Busing, Pulau** *i.* Sing.
178 C3 **Businga** Dem. Rep. Congo
136 F5 **Buşrá ash Shām** Syria
124 B5 **Busselton** Australia
164 D2 **Bussum** Neth.
206 D2 **Bustamante** Mex.
206 C1 **Bustillos, Lago** Mex.
170 C2 **Busto Arsizio** Italy
153 A3 **Busuanga** *i.* Phil.
178 C3 **Buta** Dem. Rep. Congo
215 C3 **Buta Ranquil** Arg.
178 C4 **Butare** Rwanda
216 G6 **Butaritari** *atoll* Kiribati
126 B4 **Bute** Australia
162 C5 **Bute** *i.* U.K.
162 C5 **Bute, Sound of** *sea chan.* U.K.
186 D4 **Butedale** Canada
186 D4 **Bute Inlet** Canada
181 H4 **Butha-Buthe** Lesotho
165 G1 **Butjadingen** *reg.* Germany
190 E5 **Butler** *IN* U.S.A.
202 D4 **Butler** *PA* U.S.A.
163 D3 **Butlers Bridge** Ireland
147 E7 **Buton** *i.* Indon.
165 K1 **Bütow** Germany
194 D2 **Butte** U.S.A.
165 J3 **Buttelstedt** Germany

196 B1 Butte Meadows U.S.A.
155 B1 Butterworth Malaysia
Butterworth S. Africa see Gcuwa
163 C5 Buttevant Ireland
186 D5 Buttle Lake Canada
162 B2 Butt of Lewis hd U.K.
185 I4 Button Bay Canada
196 C4 Buttonwillow U.S.A.
153 C4 Butuan Phil.
149 B5 Butuo China
173 G5 Buturlinovka Rus. Fed.
145 E4 Butwal Nepal
165 G4 Butzbach Germany
178 E3 Buulobarde Somalia
178 E4 Buur Gaabo Somalia
178 E3 Buurhabaka Somalia
145 F4 Buxar India
138 F5 Buxoro Uzbek.
165 H1 Buxtehude Germany
161 F4 Buxton U.K.
172 G3 Buy Rus. Fed.
190 A1 Buyck U.S.A.
173 H7 Buynaksk Rus. Fed.
141 G2 Buynī Qarah Afgh.
136 A3 Büyükmenderes r. Turkey
152 B3 Buyun Shan mt. China
164 C5 Buzancy France
171 L2 Buzău Romania
179 D5 Búzi Moz.
138 C1 Buzuluk Rus. Fed.
173 G5 Buzuluk r. Rus. Fed.
138 F2 Buzylyk Kazakh.
203 H4 Buzzards Bay U.S.A.
171 K3 Byala Bulg.
171 J3 Byala Slatina Bulg.
169 N4 Byalynichy Belarus
184 H2 Byam Martin Island Canada
172 D4 Byarezina r. Belarus
172 C4 Byaroza Belarus
136 E4 Byblos tourist site Lebanon
168 I4 Bydgoszcz Poland
172 D4 Byerazino Belarus
194 F4 Byers U.S.A.
169 N3 Byeshankovichy Belarus
159 I4 Bygland Norway
172 D4 Bykhaw Belarus
159 I4 Bykle Norway
139 H2 Bylkyldak Kazakh.
185 K2 Bylot Island Canada
191 G3 Byng Inlet Canada
159 I3 Byrkjelo Norway
127 G3 Byrock Australia
190 C4 Byron IL U.S.A.
203 H2 Byron ME U.S.A.
127 J2 Byron, Cape Australia
127 J2 Byron Bay Australia
133 L2 Byrranga, Gory mts Rus. Fed.
158 M2 Byske Sweden
139 K1 Bystryy Istok Rus. Fed.
133 O3 Bytantay r. Rus. Fed.
169 I5 Bytom Poland
168 H3 Bytów Poland

## C

212 E3 Caacupé Para.
214 A4 Caaguazú Para.
214 A4 Caaguazú, Cordillera de hills Para.
214 A3 Caarapó Brazil
214 A4 Caazapá Para.
210 C6 Caballas Peru
210 D4 Caballococha Peru
206 D1 Caballos Mesteños, Llano de los plain Mex.
153 B3 Cabanatuan Phil.
189 G4 Cabano Canada
178 E2 Cabdul Qaadir Somalia
214 A1 Cabeceira Rio Manso Brazil
211 L5 Cabedelo Brazil
167 D3 Cabeza del Buey Spain
210 F7 Cabezas Bol.
215 E3 Cabildo Arg.
213 C2 Cabimas Venez.
178 B4 Cabinda Angola
178 B4 Cabinda prov. Angola
194 C1 Cabinet Mountains U.S.A.
213 B3 Cable Way pass Col.
214 D3 Cabo Frio Brazil
214 E3 Cabo Frio, Ilha do i. Brazil
188 E4 Cabonga, Réservoir resr Canada
199 E4 Cabool U.S.A.
127 J1 Caboolture Australia
211 H3 Cabo Orange, Parque Nacional de nat. park Brazil
210 C4 Cabo Pantoja Peru
179 D5 Cabora Bassa, Lake resr Moz.
204 B2 Caborca Mex.
206 B3 Cabo San Lucas Mex.
191 G3 Cabot Head Canada
189 I4 Cabot Strait Canada
214 D2 Cabral, Serra do mts Brazil
137 K2 Cäbrayıl Azer.
167 H3 Cabrera, Illa de i. Spain
167 C1 Cabrera, Sierra de la mts Spain
167 F3 Cabriel r. Spain
213 D3 Cabruta Venez.
153 B2 Cabugao Phil.
212 F3 Caçador Brazil
207 E4 Cacahuatepec Mex.
171 I3 Čačak Serbia
215 G1 Caçapava do Sul Brazil
202 D5 Cacapon r. U.S.A.
213 B3 Cácares Col.
170 C4 Caccia, Capo c. Sardinia Italy
141 F2 Çäçe Turkm.
211 G7 Cáceres Brazil
167 C3 Cáceres Spain
194 D3 Cache Peak U.S.A.
176 A3 Cacheu Guinea-Bissau
212 C3 Cachi r. Arg.
212 C2 Cachi, Nevados de mts Arg.
211 H5 Cachimbo, Serra do hills Brazil
213 B3 Cáchira Col.
214 E1 Cachoeira Brazil
214 B2 Cachoeira Alta Brazil
215 G1 Cachoeira do Sul Brazil
214 E3 Cachoeiro de Itapemirim Brazil
176 A3 Cacine Guinea-Bissau
211 H3 Caciporé, Cabo c. Brazil
179 B5 Cacolo Angola
178 B4 Cacongo Angola
196 D3 Cactus Range mts U.S.A.
214 B2 Caçu Brazil
214 D1 Caculé Brazil
169 I6 Čadca Slovakia
165 H1 Cadenberge Germany
207 D2 Cadereyta Mex.
126 A2 Cadibarrawirracanna, Lake salt flat Australia
153 B3 Cadig Mountains Phil.
191 H1 Cadillac Que. Canada
187 H5 Cadillac Sask. Canada
190 E3 Cadillac U.S.A.
153 B4 Cadiz Phil.
167 C4 Cádiz Spain
167 C4 Cádiz, Golfo de g. Spain
197 E4 Cadiz Lake U.S.A.
166 D2 Caen France
161 C4 Caernarfon U.K.
161 C4 Caernarfon Bay U.K.
161 D6 Caerphilly U.K.
202 B5 Caesar Creek Lake U.S.A.
136 E5 Caesarea tourist site Israel
214 D1 Caetité Brazil
212 C3 Cafayate Arg.
153 B4 Cagayan i. Phil.
153 B2 Cagayan r. Phil.
153 C4 Cagayan de Oro Phil.
153 A5 Cagayan de Tawi-Tawi i. Phil.
153 B4 Cagayan Islands Phil.
170 E3 Cagli Italy
170 C5 Cagliari Sardinia Italy
170 C5 Cagliari, Golfo di b. Sardinia Italy
213 B4 Caguán r. Col.
138 C4 Çagyl Turkm.
138 D4 Çagyllyşor Çöketligi depr. Turkm.
201 C5 Cahaba r. U.S.A.
163 B6 Caha Mountains hills Ireland
163 A6 Cahermore Ireland
163 D5 Cahir Ireland
163 A6 Cahirsiveen Ireland
Cahora Bassa, Lago de resr Moz. see Cabora Bassa, Lake
163 E5 Cahore Point Ireland
166 E4 Cahors France
210 C5 Cahuapanas Peru
210 D4 Cahuinarí, Parque Nacional nat. park Col.
173 D6 Cahul Moldova
179 D5 Caia Moz.
211 G6 Caiabis, Serra dos hills Brazil
179 C5 Caianda Angola
214 B2 Caiapó r. Brazil
214 B2 Caiapó, Serra do mts Brazil
214 B2 Caiapônia Brazil
205 I4 Caibarién Cuba
149 C6 Cai Bâu, Đao i. Vietnam
154 C3 Cai Be Vietnam
213 D3 Caicara Venez.
205 J4 Caicos Islands Turks and Caicos Is
149 E4 Caidian China
206 C3 Caimanero, Laguna del lag. Mex.
215 B1 Caimanes Chile
153 A3 Caiman Point Phil.
167 F2 Caimodorro mt. Spain
154 C3 Cai Nước Vietnam
162 E3 Cairn Gorm mt. U.K.
162 E3 Cairngorm Mountains U.K.
162 D4 Cairngorms National Park U.K.
162 C6 Cairnryan U.K.
124 E3 Cairns Australia
162 E3 Cairn Toul mt. U.K.
177 F1 Cairo Egypt (City Plan 112)
201 C6 Cairo U.S.A.
170 C2 Cairo Montenotte Italy
179 B5 Caiundo Angola
127 F2 Caiwarro (abandoned) Australia
210 C5 Cajamarca Peru
153 B3 Cajidiocan Phil.
170 G1 Čakovec Croatia
136 B2 Çal Turkey
181 G5 Cala S. Africa
176 C4 Calabar Nigeria
191 I3 Calabogie Canada
213 D2 Calabozo Venez.
171 J3 Calafat Romania
212 B8 Calafate Arg.
153 B3 Calagua Islands Phil.
167 F1 Calahorra Spain
179 B5 Calai Angola
166 E1 Calais France
203 J2 Calais U.S.A.
Calais, Pas de str. France/U.K. see Dover, Strait of
207 G4 Calakmul tourist site Mex.
210 F5 Calama Brazil
212 C2 Calama Chile
213 B2 Calamar Col.
213 B4 Calamar Col.
153 A4 Calamian Group is Phil.
167 F2 Calamocha Spain
179 B4 Calandula Angola
153 B3 Calapan Phil.
171 L2 Călărași Romania
167 F2 Calatayud Spain
153 B3 Calauag Phil.
153 A3 Calauit i. Phil.
153 B3 Calavite, Cape Phil.
153 B2 Calayan i. Phil.
153 C3 Calbayog Phil.
165 J3 Calbe (Saale) Germany
153 C4 Calbiga Phil.
215 B4 Calbuco Chile
211 K5 Calcanhar, Ponta do pt Brazil
199 E6 Calcasieu Lake U.S.A.
211 H3 Calçoene Brazil
Calcutta India see Kolkata
167 B3 Caldas da Rainha Port.
214 C2 Caldas Novas Brazil
165 H3 Calden Germany
212 B3 Caldera Chile
137 I2 Çaldıran Turkey
194 C3 Caldwell U.S.A.
202 D3 Caledon Canada
181 G5 Caledon r. Lesotho/S. Africa
180 C7 Caledon S. Africa
191 H4 Caledonia Canada
190 B4 Caledonia U.S.A.
212 C7 Caleta Olivia Arg.
197 E5 Calexico U.S.A.
160 C3 Calf of Man i. U.K.
186 G4 Calgary Canada
201 C5 Calhoun U.S.A.
213 A4 Cali Col.
153 C4 Calicoan i. Phil.
Calicut India see Kozhikode
196 C4 Caliente CA U.S.A.
197 E3 Caliente NV U.S.A.
196 B3 California state U.S.A.
California, Golfo de g. Mex. see California, Gulf of
206 B2 California, Gulf of Mex.
196 B3 California Aqueduct canal U.S.A.
196 C4 California Hot Springs U.S.A.
137 L2 Cälilabad Azer.
195 D5 Calipatria U.S.A.
196 A2 Calistoga U.S.A.
180 D6 Calitzdorp S. Africa
207 G3 Calkiní Mex.
126 D2 Callabonna, Lake salt flat Australia
196 D2 Callaghan, Mount U.S.A.
201 D6 Callahan U.S.A.
163 D5 Callan Ireland
191 H2 Callander Canada
162 D4 Callander U.K.
210 C6 Callao Peru
197 F2 Callao U.S.A.
207 E3 Calles Mex.
203 F4 Callicoon U.S.A.
161 C7 Callington U.K.
191 G2 Callum Canada
186 G4 Calmar Canada
190 B4 Calmar U.S.A.
197 E4 Cal-Nev-Ari U.S.A.
201 D7 Caloosahatchee r. U.S.A.
207 G3 Calotmul Mex.
127 J1 Caloundra Australia
196 B2 Calpine U.S.A.
207 E4 Calpulálpan Mex.
170 F6 Caltanissetta Sicily Italy
190 C2 Calumet U.S.A.
179 B5 Calunga Angola
179 B5 Caluquembe Angola
153 B4 Calusa i. Phil.
178 F2 Caluula Somalia
197 G5 Calva U.S.A.
186 D4 Calvert Island Canada
170 C3 Calvi Corsica France
167 H3 Calvià Spain
206 D3 Calvillo Mex.
180 C5 Calvinia S. Africa
170 F4 Calvo, Monte mt. Italy
161 H5 Cam r. U.K.
214 E1 Camaçari Brazil
196 B2 Camache Reservoir U.S.A.
206 D2 Camacho Mex.
179 B5 Camacuio Angola
179 B5 Camacupa Angola
213 D2 Camaguán Venez.
205 I4 Camagüey Cuba
205 I4 Camagüey, Archipiélago de is Cuba
Çamalan Turkey see Gülek
210 D7 Camana Peru
179 C5 Camanongue Angola
214 B2 Camapuã Brazil
215 G1 Camaquã Brazil
215 G1 Camaquã r. Brazil
136 E3 Çamardı Turkey
207 E2 Camargo Mex.
212 C6 Camarones Arg.
212 C6 Camarones, Bahía b. Arg.
194 B2 Camas U.S.A.
154 C3 Ca Mau Vietnam
154 C3 Ca Mau, Mui c. Vietnam
161 G6 Camberley U.K.
154 C2 Cambodia country Asia
161 B7 Camborne U.K.
166 F1 Cambrai France
196 B4 Cambria U.S.A.
161 D5 Cambrian Mountains hills U.K.
191 G4 Cambridge Canada
128 E2 Cambridge N.Z.
161 H5 Cambridge U.K.
190 B5 Cambridge IL U.S.A.
203 H3 Cambridge MA U.S.A.
203 E5 Cambridge MD U.S.A.
198 E2 Cambridge MN U.S.A.
203 G3 Cambridge NY U.S.A.
202 C4 Cambridge OH U.S.A.
189 G2 Cambrien, Lac l. Canada
127 I5 Camden Australia
201 C5 Camden AL U.S.A.
199 E5 Camden AR U.S.A.
203 I2 Camden ME U.S.A.
203 F5 Camden NJ U.S.A.
203 F3 Camden NY U.S.A.
201 D5 Camden SC U.S.A.
212 B8 Camden, Isla i. Chile
179 C5 Cameia, Parque Nacional da nat. park Angola
197 G4 Cameron AZ U.S.A.
199 E6 Cameron LA U.S.A.
198 E4 Cameron MO U.S.A.
199 D6 Cameron TX U.S.A.
190 B3 Cameron WI U.S.A.
186 F3 Cameron Hills Canada
196 B2 Cameron Park U.S.A.
176 D4 Cameroon country Africa
176 D4 Cameroon Highlands mts Cameroon/Nigeria
176 C4 Cameroun, Mont vol. Cameroon
211 I4 Cametá Brazil
153 B2 Camiguin i. Phil.
153 C4 Camiguin i. Phil.
153 B3 Camiling Phil.
201 C6 Camilla U.S.A.
195 F6 Camino Real de Tierra Adentro tourist site Mexico/U.S.A.
210 F8 Camiri Bol.
211 J4 Camocim Brazil
124 D3 Camooweal Australia
153 C4 Camotes Sea g. Phil.
215 E2 Campana Arg.
213 B4 Campana, Cerro h. Col.
212 A7 Campana, Isla i. Chile
215 B2 Campanario mt. Arg./Chile
186 D4 Campania Island Canada
180 E4 Campbell S. Africa
128 E4 Campbell, Cape N.Z.
123 F7 Campbell Island N.Z.
216 G9 Campbell Plateau sea feature S. Pacific Ocean
186 D4 Campbell River Canada
191 I3 Campbell's Bay Canada
200 C4 Campbellsville U.S.A.
189 G4 Campbellton Canada
127 G8 Campbell Town Australia
162 C5 Campbeltown U.K.
207 G4 Campeche Mex.
207 G4 Campeche state Mex.
207 F4 Campeche, Bahía de g. Mex.
126 E7 Camperdown Australia
171 K2 Câmpina Romania
211 K5 Campina Grande Brazil
214 C3 Campinas Brazil
214 C2 Campina Verde Brazil
176 C4 Campo Cameroon
213 B4 Campoalegre Col.
170 F4 Campobasso Italy
214 D3 Campo Belo Brazil
211 H6 Campo de Diauarum Brazil
214 C2 Campo Florido Brazil
212 D3 Campo Gallo Arg.
214 A3 Campo Grande Brazil
211 J4 Campo Maior Brazil
167 C3 Campo Maior Port.
213 C2 Campo Mara Venez.
214 B4 Campo Mourão Brazil
214 E3 Campos Brazil
214 C2 Campos Altos Brazil
214 D3 Campos do Jordão Brazil
162 D4 Campsie Fells hills U.K.
202 B6 Campton KY U.S.A.
203 H3 Campton NH U.S.A.
171 K2 Câmpulung Romania
169 L7 Câmpulung Moldovenesc Romania
197 G4 Camp Verde U.S.A.
Cam Ranh Vietnam see Ba Ngoi
186 G4 Camrose Canada
161 B6 Camrose U.K.
187 G2 Camsell Lake Canada
187 H3 Camsell Portage Canada
173 C7 Çan Turkey
154 D3 Ca Na, Mui hd Vietnam
203 G3 Canaan U.S.A.
184 G3 Canada country N. America
220 O1 Canada Basin sea feature Arctic Ocean
215 E2 Cañada de Gómez Arg.
203 H2 Canada Falls Lake U.S.A.
199 C5 Canadian r. U.S.A.
213 E3 Canaima, Parque Nacional nat. park Venez.
203 F3 Canajoharie U.S.A.
173 C7 Çanakkale Turkey
Çanakkale Boğazı str. Turkey see Dardanelles
215 C2 Canalejas Arg.
202 E3 Canandaigua U.S.A.
202 E3 Canandaigua Lake U.S.A.
204 B2 Cananea Mex.
214 C4 Cananéia Brazil
213 C4 Canapiare, Cerro h. Col.
210 C4 Cañar Ecuador
Canarias, Islas terr. N. Atlantic Ocean see Canary Islands
176 A2 Canary Islands terr. N. Atlantic Ocean
203 F3 Canastota U.S.A.
214 C2 Canastra, Serra da mts Brazil
206 C2 Canatlán Mex.
201 D6 Canaveral, Cape U.S.A.
167 E2 Cañaveras Spain
214 E1 Canavieiras Brazil
127 G3 Canbelego Australia
127 H5 Canberra Australia
194 B3 Canby CA U.S.A.
198 D2 Canby MN U.S.A.
207 H3 Cancún Mex.
207 G4 Candelaria Campeche Mex.
195 F6 Candelaria Chihuahua Mex.
207 E5 Candelaria Loxicha Mex.
167 D2 Candeleda Spain
127 H6 Candelo Australia
211 I4 Cândido Mendes Brazil
136 D1 Çandır Turkey
187 H4 Candle Lake Canada
187 H4 Candle Lake l. Canada
209 G7 Candlemas Island S. Sandwich Is
203 G4 Candlewood, Lake U.S.A.
198 D1 Cando U.S.A.
153 B2 Candon Phil.
215 B1 Canela Baja Chile
215 F2 Canelones Uruguay
215 B3 Cañete Chile
167 F2 Cañete Spain
210 D6 Cangallo Peru
179 B5 Cangamba Angola
167 C1 Cangas del Narcea Spain
180 E6 Cango Caves S. Africa
211 K5 Canguaretama Brazil
215 G1 Canguçu Brazil
215 G1 Canguçu, Serra do hills Brazil
149 D6 Cangwu China
148 E2 Cangzhou China
189 G3 Caniapiscau Canada
189 G2 Caniapiscau r. Canada
189 G3 Caniapiscau, Lac Canada
185 K4 Caniapiscau, Réservoir de l. Canada
170 E6 Canicattì Sicily Italy
186 E4 Canim Lake Canada
186 E4 Canim Lake l. Canada
211 K4 Canindé Brazil
211 J5 Canindé r. Brazil
162 C2 Canisp h. U.K.
202 E3 Canisteo U.S.A.
202 E3 Canisteo r. U.S.A.
206 D3 Cañitas de Felipe Pescador Mex.
136 D1 Çankırı Turkey
153 B4 Canlaon Phil.
186 F4 Canmore Canada
162 B3 Canna i. U.K.
Cannanore India see Kannur
143 A4 Cannanore Islands India
166 H5 Cannes France
161 E5 Cannock U.K.
127 H6 Cann River Australia
212 F3 Canoas Brazil
187 H3 Canoe Lake Canada
214 B4 Canoinhas Brazil
195 F4 Canon City U.S.A.
126 D4 Canopus Australia
187 I4 Canora Canada
127 H4 Canowindra Australia
189 H4 Canso, Cape Canada
167 D1 Cantábrica, Cordillera mts Spain
166 B4 Cantábrico, Mar sea France/Spain
215 C2 Cantantal Arg.
213 D2 Cantaura Venez.
203 J2 Canterbury Canada
161 I6 Canterbury U.K.
128 C6 Canterbury Bight b. N.Z.
128 C5 Canterbury Plains N.Z.
154 C3 Cân Thơ Vietnam
153 C4 Cantilan Phil.
211 J5 Canto do Buriti Brazil
Canton China see Guangzhou
190 B5 Canton IL U.S.A.
203 H2 Canton ME U.S.A.
190 B5 Canton MO U.S.A.
199 F5 Canton MS U.S.A.
203 F2 Canton NY U.S.A.
202 C4 Canton OH U.S.A.
202 E4 Canton PA U.S.A.
214 B4 Cantu r. Brazil
214 B4 Cantu, Serra do hills Brazil
215 E2 Cañuelas Arg.
211 G4 Canumã Brazil
127 J2 Canungra Australia
210 F5 Canutama Brazil
128 D4 Canvastown N.Z.
161 H6 Canvey Island U.K.
187 H4 Canwood Canada
199 C5 Canyon U.S.A.
194 C2 Canyon City U.S.A.
197 H3 Canyon de Chelly National Monument nat. park U.S.A.
194 D2 Canyon Ferry Lake U.S.A.
197 H2 Canyonlands National Park U.S.A.
186 D2 Canyon Ranges mts Canada
194 B3 Canyonville U.S.A.
149 C6 Cao Băng Vietnam
152 C3 Cao He r. China
154 C3 Cao Lãnh Vietnam
Cao Nguyên Đắc Lắc plat. Vietnam see Đắk Lắk, Cao Nguyên
152 C2 Caoshi China
148 E3 Caoxian China
153 B5 Cap i. Phil.
213 D3 Capanaparo r. Venez.
211 I4 Capanema Brazil
214 B4 Capanema r. Brazil
214 C4 Capão Bonito Brazil
213 C3 Caparo r. Venez.
213 C4 Caparro, Cerro h. Brazil
153 B3 Capas Phil.
189 H4 Cap-aux-Meules Canada
189 F4 Cap-de-la-Madeleine Canada
127 H8 Cape Barren Island Australia
219 J8 Cape Basin sea feature S. Atlantic Ocean
189 H4 Cape Breton Highlands National Park Canada
189 H4 Cape Breton Island Canada
189 I3 Cape Charles Canada
203 E6 Cape Charles U.S.A.
176 B4 Cape Coast Ghana
203 H4 Cape Cod Bay U.S.A.
203 I4 Cape Cod National Seashore nature res. U.S.A.
201 D7 Cape Coral U.S.A.
191 G3 Cape Croker Canada
185 K3 Cape Dorset Canada
201 E5 Cape Fear r. U.S.A.
199 F4 Cape Girardeau U.S.A.
214 D2 Capelinha Brazil
164 C3 Capelle aan den IJssel Neth.
203 F5 Cape May U.S.A.
203 F5 Cape May Court House U.S.A.
203 F5 Cape May Point U.S.A.
179 B4 Capenda-Camulemba Angola
189 I4 Cape St George Canada
189 H4 Cape Tormentine Canada
180 C6 Cape Town S. Africa (City Plan 112)
176 □ Cape Verde country N. Atlantic Ocean
219 G5 Cape Verde Basin sea feature N. Atlantic Ocean
219 G4 Cape Verde Plateau sea feature N. Atlantic Ocean
203 E2 Cape Vincent U.S.A.
124 E3 Cape York Peninsula Australia
205 J5 Cap-Haïtien Haiti
211 I4 Capim r. Brazil
214 A3 Capitán Bado Para.
147 G5 Capitol Hill N. Mariana Is
197 G2 Capitol Reef National Park U.S.A.
214 B3 Capivara, Represa resr Brazil
170 G3 Čapljina Bos.-Herz.
170 F5 Capo d'Orlando Sicily Italy
163 D5 Cappoquin Ireland
170 C3 Capraia, Isola di i. Italy
170 F4 Capri, Isola di i. Italy
124 F4 Capricorn Channel Australia
179 C5 Caprivi Strip reg. Namibia
196 □2 Captain Cook U.S.A.
127 H5 Captain's Flat Australia
202 C5 Captina r. U.S.A.
153 C3 Capul i. Phil.
210 C3 Caquetá r. Col.
213 B3 Cáqueza Col.
153 B3 Carabao i. Phil.
171 K2 Caracal Romania
213 E4 Caracarai Brazil
213 D2 Caracas Venez. (City Plan 116)
211 J5 Caracol Brazil
206 D4 Carácuaro Mex.
153 C5 Caraga Phil.
215 F2 Caraguatá r. Uruguay
214 D3 Caraguatatuba Brazil
215 B3 Carahue Chile
214 E2 Caraí Brazil
210 C6 Caral-Supe tourist site Peru
214 D3 Carandaí Brazil
214 D3 Carangola Brazil
171 J2 Caransebeș Romania
126 B4 Carappee Hill Australia
189 H4 Caraquet Canada
213 B3 Carare r. Col.
206 I5 Caratasca Hond.
206 I5 Caratasca, Laguna de lag. Hond.
214 D2 Caratinga Brazil
210 E4 Carauari Brazil
167 F3 Caravaca de la Cruz Spain
214 E2 Caravelas Brazil
212 F3 Carazinho Brazil
198 D1 Carberry Canada
167 F5 Carbon, Cap hd Alg.
212 C7 Carbón, Laguna del l. Argentina
170 C5 Carbonara, Capo c. Sardinia Italy
200 B4 Carbondale IL U.S.A.
203 F4 Carbondale PA U.S.A.
189 J4 Carbonear Canada
170 C5 Carbonia Sardinia Italy
214 D2 Carbonita Brazil
167 F3 Carcaixent Spain
153 B4 Carcar Phil.
215 E2 Carcaraña r. Arg.
166 F5 Carcassonne France
186 C2 Carcross Canada
143 B4 Cardamom Hills India
154 B2 Cardamom Range mts Cambodia
Cardamon Hills India see Cardamom Hills
207 E3 Cárdenas Mex.
207 F4 Cárdenas Mex.
126 E2 Cardenyabba watercourse Australia
212 B7 Cardiel, Lago l. Arg.
161 D6 Cardiff U.K.
161 C5 Cardigan U.K.
161 C5 Cardigan Bay U.K.
203 F2 Cardinal Canada
202 B4 Cardington U.S.A.
215 F2 Cardona Uruguay
214 C4 Cardoso, Ilha do i. Brazil
128 B6 Cardrona N.Z.
186 G5 Cardston Canada
169 K7 Carei Romania
166 D2 Carentan France
202 B4 Carey U.S.A.
124 C4 Carey, Lake salt flat Australia
187 I2 Carey Lake Canada
218 H6 Cargados Carajos Islands Mauritius
166 C2 Carhaix-Plouguer France
215 D3 Carhué Arg.
214 E3 Cariacica Brazil
213 E2 Cariaco Venez.
205 I5 Caribbean Sea Atlantic Ocean
186 E4 Cariboo Mountains Canada
187 J3 Caribou r. Man. Canada
186 D2 Caribou r. N.W.T. Canada
203 J1 Caribou U.S.A.
190 E2 Caribou Island Canada
185 J4 Caribou Lake Canada
186 F3 Caribou Mountains Canada
206 C2 Carichic Mex.
153 C4 Carigara Phil.
164 D5 Carignan France
127 G3 Carinda Australia
167 F2 Cariñena Spain
214 D1 Carinhanha Brazil
214 D1 Carinhanha r. Brazil
213 E2 Caripe Venez.
213 E2 Caripito Venez.
163 D3 Cark Mountain h. Ireland
191 I3 Carleton Place Canada
181 G3 Carletonville S. Africa
194 C3 Carlin U.S.A.
163 E3 Carlingford Lough inlet Ireland/U.K.
160 E3 Carlisle U.K.
202 A5 Carlisle KY U.S.A.
202 E4 Carlisle PA U.S.A.
166 E5 Carlit, Pic mt. France
215 E2 Carlos Casares Arg.
214 E2 Carlos Chagas Brazil
163 E5 Carlow Ireland
162 B2 Carloway U.K.
196 D5 Carlsbad CA U.S.A.
195 F5 Carlsbad NM U.S.A.
199 C6 Carlsbad TX U.S.A.
195 F5 Carlsbad Caverns National Park U.S.A.
218 H4 Carlsberg Ridge sea feature Indian Ocean
162 E5 Carluke U.K.
187 I5 Carlyle Canada
186 B2 Carmacks Canada
170 B2 Carmagnola Italy
187 J5 Carman Canada
161 C6 Carmarthen U.K.
161 C6 Carmarthen Bay U.K.
166 F4 Carmaux France
203 I2 Carmel U.S.A.
161 C4 Carmel Head U.K.
207 G4 Carmelita Guat.
215 E2 Carmelo Uruguay
213 B2 Carmen Col.
153 C4 Carmen Phil.
197 G6 Carmen U.S.A.
206 B2 Carmen, Isla i. Mex.
207 G4 Carmen, Isla del i. Mex.
215 D4 Carmen de Patagones Arg.
215 C2 Carmensa Arg.
200 B4 Carmi U.S.A.
196 B2 Carmichael U.S.A.
167 D4 Carmona Spain
166 C3 Carnac France
180 E5 Carnarvon S. Africa
163 D2 Carndonagh Ireland
161 D4 Carnedd Llywelyn mt. U.K.
124 C4 Carnegie, Lake salt flat Australia
217 N6 Carnegie Ridge sea feature S. Pacific Ocean
162 C3 Carn Eige mt. U.K.
190 D3 Carney U.S.A.
129 B4 Carney Island i. Antarctica
160 E3 Carnforth U.K.
163 F3 Carnlough U.K.
162 E4 Carn nan Gabhar mt. U.K.
178 B3 Carnot Cent. Afr. Rep.
126 A5 Carnot, Cape Australia
162 F4 Carnoustie U.K.
163 E5 Carnsore Point Ireland
162 E5 Carnwath U.K.
191 F4 Caro U.S.A.
201 D7 Carol City U.S.A.
211 I5 Carolina Brazil
181 I3 Carolina S. Africa
123 I5 Caroline Island atoll Kiribati
122 D2 Caroline Islands N. Pacific Ocean
128 A6 Caroline Peak N.Z.
180 B4 Carolusberg S. Africa
213 E2 Caroní r. Venez.
213 C2 Carora Venez.
197 E3 Carp U.S.A.
169 L6 Carpathian Mountains Romania/Ukr.
169 K6 Carpathian Primeval Beech Forests tourist site Slovakia/Ukr.
169 J6 Carpathian Wooden Churches tourist site Slovakia
Carpații Meridionali mts Romania see Transylvanian Alps
124 D3 Carpentaria, Gulf of Australia
166 G4 Carpentras France
170 D2 Carpi Italy
211 K5 Carpina Brazil
196 C4 Carpinteria U.S.A.
187 I5 Carpio U.S.A.
186 E4 Carp Lake Provincial Park Canada
163 B4 Carra, Lough l. Ireland
203 H2 Carrabassett U.S.A.
201 C6 Carrabelle U.S.A.
Carraig Thuathail Ireland see Carrigtohill
213 B2 Carraipía Col.
163 B6 Carran h. Ireland
163 B6 Carrantuohill mt. Ireland
215 B2 Carranza, Cabo c. Chile
213 E3 Carrao r. Venez.
170 D2 Carrara Italy
127 F5 Carrathool Australia
215 C3 Carrero, Cerro mt. Arg.
213 E1 Carriacou i. Grenada
162 D5 Carrick reg. U.K.
163 F3 Carrickfergus U.K.
163 E4 Carrickmacross Ireland
163 C4 Carrick-on-Shannon Ireland
163 D5 Carrick-on-Suir Ireland
126 C4 Carrieton Australia
163 D4 Carrigallen Ireland
163 C6 Carrigtohill Ireland
Carri Lafquén, Lago l. Arg. see Carri Lafquén, Laguna
215 C4 Carri Lafquén, Laguna l. Arg.
206 D2 Carrillo Mex.
198 D2 Carrington U.S.A.
212 B3 Carrizal Bajo Chile
197 G4 Carrizo AZ U.S.A.
197 H4 Carrizo AZ U.S.A.
196 D5 Carrizo Creek watercourse U.S.A.
199 D6 Carrizo Springs U.S.A.
195 F5 Carrizozo U.S.A.
198 E3 Carroll U.S.A.
201 C5 Carrollton GA U.S.A.
200 C4 Carrollton KY U.S.A.
198 E4 Carrollton MO U.S.A.
202 C4 Carrollton OH U.S.A.
187 I4 Carrot r. Canada
187 I4 Carrot River Canada
163 B3 Carrowmore Lake Ireland
203 F2 Carry Falls Reservoir U.S.A.
136 F1 Çarşamba Turkey
190 E4 Carson City MI U.S.A.
196 C2 Carson City NV U.S.A.
196 C2 Carson Lake U.S.A.
196 C2 Carson Sink l. U.S.A.
191 F4 Carsonville U.S.A.
215 B2 Cartagena Chile
213 B2 Cartagena Col.
167 F4 Cartagena Spain
213 B3 Cartago Col.
206 I6 Cartago Costa Rica
201 C5 Cartersville U.S.A.
190 B5 Carthage IL U.S.A.
199 E4 Carthage MO U.S.A.
203 F2 Carthage NY U.S.A.
199 E5 Carthage TX U.S.A.
191 G2 Cartier Canada
160 E3 Cartmel U.K.
189 I3 Cartwright Canada
211 K5 Caruarú Brazil
213 E2 Carúpano Venez.
196 D2 Carvers U.S.A.
164 A4 Carvin France
201 E5 Cary U.S.A.
126 E2 Caryapundy Swamp Australia
176 B1 Casablanca Morocco
214 C3 Casa Branca Brazil
195 E6 Casa de Janos Mex.
215 C3 Casa de Piedra, Embalse resr Arg.
197 G5 Casa Grande U.S.A.
197 G5 Casa Grande National Monument nat. park U.S.A.
170 C2 Casale Monferrato Italy
170 D2 Casalmaggiore Italy
213 C3 Casanare r. Col.
171 H4 Casarano Italy
192 E5 Casas Grandes Mex.
128 B6 Cascade r. N.Z.
190 B4 Cascade IA U.S.A.
194 C2 Cascade ID U.S.A.
194 E2 Cascade MT U.S.A.
128 B6 Cascade Point N.Z.
194 B3 Cascade Range mts U.S.A.
194 D2 Cascade Reservoir U.S.A.
167 B3 Cascais Port.
206 H6 Cascal, Paso del pass Nicaragua
214 B4 Cascavel Brazil
203 I3 Casco Bay U.S.A.
170 F4 Caserta Italy
191 F4 Caseville U.S.A.
129 D6 Casey research stn Antarctica
129 E4 Casey Bay b. Antarctica
Caseyr, Raas c. Somalia see Gwardafuy, Gees
163 D5 Cashel Ireland
127 H1 Cashmere Australia
190 B4 Cashton U.S.A.
213 C2 Casigua Venez.
213 B2 Casigua Venez.
153 B2 Casiguran Phil.
215 E2 Casilda Arg.
127 J2 Casino Australia
213 D4 Casiquiare, Canal r. Venez.
210 C5 Casma Peru
190 E4 Casnovia U.S.A.
196 A2 Caspar U.S.A.
167 F2 Caspe Spain
194 F3 Casper U.S.A.
138 B3 Caspian Lowland Kazakh./Rus. Fed.
132 C2 Caspian Sea l. Asia/Europe
202 D5 Cass U.S.A.
191 F4 Cass r. U.S.A.
202 D3 Cassadaga U.S.A.
179 C5 Cassai Angola
191 F4 Cass City U.S.A.
164 A4 Cassel France
203 F2 Casselman Canada
186 D3 Cassiar Canada
186 C3 Cassiar Mountains Canada
127 H4 Cassilis Australia
170 E4 Cassino Italy
198 E2 Cass Lake U.S.A.
211 I4 Castanhal Brazil
215 C1 Castaño r. Arg.
206 D2 Castaños Mex.
215 C1 Castaño Viejo Arg.
170 D2 Castelfranco Veneto Italy
166 E4 Casteljaloux France
170 F4 Castellammare di Stabia Italy
215 F3 Castelli Arg.
167 F3 Castellón de la Plana Spain
167 C3 Castelo Branco Port.
167 C3 Castelo de Vide Port.
170 C4 Castelsardo Sardinia Italy
170 E6 Casteltermini Sicily Italy
170 E6 Castelvetrano Sicily Italy
126 D6 Casterton Australia
189 G2 Castignon, Lac l. Canada
167 E3 Castilla-La Mancha aut. comm. Spain
167 D2 Castilla y León aut. comm. Spain
213 C2 Castilletes Col.
215 G2 Castillos Uruguay
163 B4 Castlebar Ireland
162 A4 Castlebay U.K.
163 E4 Castlebellingham Ireland
163 E3 Castleblayney Ireland
163 E5 Castlebridge Ireland
160 E3 Castle Carrock U.K.
161 E6 Castle Cary U.K.
197 G2 Castle Dale U.S.A.
163 D3 Castlederg U.K.
163 E5 Castledermot Ireland
197 E5 Castle Dome Mountains U.S.A.
161 F5 Castle Donington U.K.
162 E6 Castle Douglas U.K.
160 F4 Castleford U.K.
186 F5 Castlegar Canada
163 A5 Castlegregory Ireland
163 B5 Castleisland Ireland
126 F6 Castlemaine Australia
163 B5 Castlemaine Ireland
163 C6 Castlemartyr Ireland
196 B4 Castle Mountain U.S.A.
149 □ Castle Peak h. Hong Kong China
149 □ Castle Peak Bay Hong Kong China
128 F4 Castlepoint N.Z.
163 D4 Castlepollard Ireland
163 C4 Castlerea Ireland
127 H3 Castlereagh r. Australia
195 F4 Castle Rock U.S.A.
190 B4 Castle Rock Lake U.S.A.
163 D5 Castletown Ireland
160 C3 Castletown Isle of Man
187 G4 Castor Canada
166 F5 Castres France
164 C2 Castricum Neth.
205 L6 Castries St Lucia
214 C4 Castro Brazil
212 B6 Castro Chile
167 D4 Castro del Río Spain
167 B4 Castro Verde Port.
170 G5 Castrovillari Italy
196 B3 Castroville U.S.A.
128 A6 Caswell Sound inlet N.Z.
137 H2 Çat Turkey
210 B5 Catacaos Peru
214 D3 Cataguases Brazil
199 E6 Catahoula Lake U.S.A.
153 B3 Cataingan Phil.
137 I3 Çatak Turkey
214 C2 Catalão Brazil

136 D3 Çatalhöyük, Neolithic Site of tourist site Turkey
167 G2 Cataluña aut. comm. Spain
212 C3 Catamarca Arg.
153 C3 Catanduanes i. Phil.
214 B4 Catanduvas Brazil
170 F6 Catania Sicily Italy
170 G5 Catanzaro Italy
199 D6 Catarina U.S.A.
153 C3 Catarman Phil.
167 F3 Catarroja Spain
126 A5 Catastrophe, Cape Australia
213 B2 Catatumbo r. Venez.
149 C6 Cat Ba, Đao i. Vietnam
153 C4 Catbalogan Phil.
201 E7 Cat Cays is Bahamas
153 C5 Cateel Phil.
153 C5 Cateel Bay Phil.
181 J3 Catembe Moz.
163 A6 Cathair Dónall Ireland
Cathair Saidhbhín Ireland see Cahirsiveen
127 H6 Cathcart Australia
181 G6 Cathcart S. Africa
181 H4 Cathedral Peak S. Africa
Catherdaniel Ireland see Cathair Dónall
197 F2 Catherine, Mount U.S.A.
215 B3 Catillo Chile
201 E7 Cat Island Bahamas
188 B3 Cat Lake Canada
207 H3 Catoche, Cabo Mex.
125 F4 Cato Island and Bank rf Australia
202 E5 Catonsville U.S.A.
206 D3 Catorce Mex.
215 D3 Catriló Arg.
213 E4 Catrimani Brazil
213 E4 Catrimani r. Brazil
164 A4 Cats, Mont des h. France
203 G3 Catskill U.S.A.
203 F4 Catskill Mountains U.S.A.
181 J3 Catuane Moz.
213 E4 Cauamé r. Brazil
153 B4 Cauayan Phil.
189 H2 Caubvick, Mount Canada
213 B3 Cauca r. Col.
211 K4 Caucaia Brazil
213 B3 Caucasia Col.
173 G7 Caucasus mts Asia/Europe
215 C1 Caucete Arg.
203 I1 Caucomgomoc Lake U.S.A.
164 B4 Caudry France
154 C1 Câu Giat Vietnam
153 C4 Cauit Point Phil.
215 B2 Cauquenes Chile
213 D3 Caura r. Venez.
189 G4 Causapscal Canada
169 N7 Căușeni Moldova
166 G5 Cavaillon France
214 C1 Cavalcante Brazil
176 B4 Cavally r. Côte d'Ivoire
163 D4 Cavan Ireland
199 F4 Cave City U.S.A.
214 E1 Caveira r. Brazil
126 E6 Cavendish Australia
214 B4 Cavernoso, Serra do mts Brazil
202 B5 Cave Run Lake U.S.A.
153 B4 Cavili rf Phil.
153 B3 Cavite Phil.
162 E3 Cawdor U.K.
126 D4 Cawndilla Lake imp. l. Australia
161 I5 Cawston U.K.
211 J4 Caxias Brazil
212 F3 Caxias do Sul Brazil
179 B4 Caxito Angola
136 C2 Çay Turkey
201 D5 Cayce U.S.A.
136 D1 Çaycuma Turkey
137 H1 Çayeli Turkey
211 H3 Cayenne Fr. Guiana
136 E3 Çayhan Turkey
136 C1 Çayırhan Turkey
205 I5 Cayman Brac i. Cayman Is
205 H5 Cayman Islands terr. Caribbean Sea
219 D4 Cayman Trench sea feature Caribbean Sea
178 E3 Caynabo Somalia
191 H4 Cayuga Canada
202 E3 Cayuga Lake U.S.A.
203 F3 Cazenovia U.S.A.
179 C5 Cazombo Angola
219 G6 Ceara Abyssal Plain sea feature S. Atlantic Ocean
206 I7 Cebaco, Isla i. Panama
206 C2 Ceballos Mex.
215 F2 Cebollatí r. Uruguay
153 B4 Cebu Phil.
153 B4 Cebu i. Phil.
190 C3 Cecil U.S.A.
127 I1 Cecil Plains Australia
170 D3 Cecina Italy
190 A4 Cedar r. IA U.S.A.
198 C2 Cedar r. ND U.S.A.
197 D4 Cedar Breaks National Monument nat. park U.S.A.
190 D4 Cedarburg U.S.A.
197 F3 Cedar City U.S.A.
199 D5 Cedar Creek Reservoir U.S.A.
190 A4 Cedar Falls U.S.A.
190 D4 Cedar Grove WI U.S.A.
202 C5 Cedar Grove WV U.S.A.
203 F6 Cedar Island U.S.A.
187 I4 Cedar Lake Canada
190 D5 Cedar Lake U.S.A.
202 B4 Cedar Point U.S.A.
190 B5 Cedar Rapids U.S.A.
197 G3 Cedar Ridge U.S.A.
203 F5 Cedar Run U.S.A.
191 F4 Cedar Springs Canada
190 E4 Cedar Springs U.S.A.
201 C5 Cedartown U.S.A.
181 H5 Cedarville S. Africa
190 E3 Cedarville U.S.A.
206 A1 Cedros, Isla i. Mex.
124 D5 Ceduna Australia
178 E3 Ceeldheere Somalia
178 E2 Ceerigaabo Somalia
170 F5 Cefalù Sicily Italy
169 I7 Cegléd Hungary
149 B5 Ceheng China
136 E1 Çekerek Turkey
206 G5 Celaque, Parque Nacional nat. park Hond.
206 D3 Celaya Mex.
163 E4 Celbridge Ireland
155 E3 Celebes i. Indon.
147 E6 Celebes Sea Indon./Phil.
202 A4 Celina U.S.A.
170 F1 Celje Slovenia
165 I2 Celle Germany
219 I2 Celtic Shelf sea feature N. Atlantic Ocean
136 E1 Cemilbey Turkey
136 G2 Çemişgezek Turkey
147 F7 Cenderawasih, Teluk b. Indon.
181 H6 Centane S. Africa
197 F5 Centennial Wash watercourse U.S.A.
199 E6 Center U.S.A.
203 G4 Centereach U.S.A.
201 C5 Center Point U.S.A.
202 B5 Centerville OH U.S.A.
Centerville U.S.A. see Centreville
181 G1 Central admin. dist. Botswana
213 A4 Central, Cordillera mts Col.
206 I6 Central, Cordillera mts Panama
210 C5 Central, Cordillera mts Peru
153 B2 Central, Cordillera mts Phil.
177 D4 Central African Republic country Africa
141 G4 Central Brahui Range mts Pak.
190 B4 Central City IA U.S.A.
198 D3 Central City NE U.S.A.
200 B4 Centralia IL U.S.A.
194 B2 Centralia WA U.S.A.
178 D2 Central Island National Park Kenya
190 A2 Central Lakes U.S.A.
141 G5 Central Makran Range mts Pak.
216 G5 Central Pacific Basin sea feature Pacific Ocean
194 B3 Central Point U.S.A.
124 E2 Central Range mts P.N.G.
132 E4 Central Russian Upland hills Rus. Fed.
133 L3 Central Siberian Plateau Rus. Fed.
201 C5 Centreville U.S.A.
149 D6 Cenxi China
171 I5 Cephalonia i. Greece
Ceram Sea sea Indon. see Seram, Laut
213 D3 Cerbatana, Sierra de la mt. Venez.
197 E4 Cerbat Mountains U.S.A.
187 G4 Cereal Canada
212 D3 Ceres Arg.
180 C6 Ceres S. Africa
213 B2 Cereté Col.
167 E2 Cerezo de Abajo Spain
170 F4 Cerignola Italy
136 D2 Çerikli Turkey
136 D1 Çerkeş Turkey
136 G3 Çermelik Deresi r. Syria
137 G2 Çermik Turkey
171 M2 Cernavodă Romania
207 E2 Cerralvo Mex.
206 B2 Cerralvo, Isla i. Mex.
171 H4 Cërrik Albania
207 D3 Cerritos Mex.
214 C4 Cerro Azul Brazil
207 E3 Cerro Azul Mex.
210 C6 Cerro de Pasco Peru
206 I7 Cerro Hoya, Parque Nacional nat. park Panama
213 D3 Cerro Jáua, Meseta del plat. Venez.
213 C2 Cerrón, Cerro mt. Venez.
206 C2 Cerro Prieto Mex.
215 C3 Cerros Colorados, Embalse resr Arg.
210 B4 Cerros de Amotape, Parque Nacional nat. park Peru
170 F4 Cervati, Monte mt. Italy
170 C3 Cervione Corsica France
167 C1 Cervo Spain
213 B2 Cesar r. Col.
170 E2 Cesena Italy
159 N4 Cēsis Latvia
168 G6 České Budějovice Czech Rep.
168 G6 Český Krumlov Czech Rep.
165 K5 Český les mts Czech Rep./Germany
171 L5 Çeşme Turkey
127 I4 Cessnock Australia
171 H3 Cetinje Montenegro
170 F5 Cetraro Italy
167 D5 Ceuta Spain
125 H4 Ceva-i-Ra rf Fiji
166 F4 Cévennes mts France
136 E3 Ceyhan Turkey
136 E3 Ceyhan r. Turkey
137 H3 Ceylanpınar Turkey
Chaacha Turkm. see Çäçe
164 A5 Chaalis, Abbaye de tourist site France
141 F5 Chābahār Iran
145 F3 Chabyêr Caka salt l. China
215 E2 Chacabuco Arg.
215 B4 Chacao Chile
215 C3 Chachahuén, Sierra mts Arg.
210 C5 Chachapoyas Peru
172 D4 Chachersk Belarus
154 B2 Chachoengsao Thai.
144 B4 Chachro Pak.
195 F4 Chaco Culture National Historical Park nat. park U.S.A.
186 C4 Chacon, Cape U.S.A.
177 D3 Chad country Africa
177 D3 Chad, Lake Africa
135 H1 Chadan Rus. Fed.
181 G1 Chadibe Botswana
Chadileo r. Arg. see Salado
198 C3 Chadron U.S.A.
154 A1 Chae Hom Thai.
139 H4 Chaek Kyrg.
152 C4 Chaeryŏng N. Korea
213 B4 Chafurray Col.
141 G4 Chagai Pak.
141 F4 Chagai Hills Afgh./Pak.
138 F3 Chagan Kazakh.
145 F2 Chagdo Kangri mt. China
141 G3 Chaghcharān Afgh.
139 G1 Chaglinka r. Kazakh.
166 G3 Chagny France
131 C7 Chagos Archipelago is British Indian Ocean Terr.
218 I5 Chagos-Laccadive Ridge sea feature Indian Ocean
218 I5 Chagos Trench sea feature Indian Ocean
172 I4 Chagra r. Rus. Fed.
206 J6 Chagres, Parque Nacional nat. park Panama
213 D2 Chaguaramas Venez.
Chagyl Turkm. see Çagyl
138 C4 Chagyllyshor, Vpadina depr. Turkm.
145 G3 Cha'gyüngoinba China
141 E3 Chāh Ākhvor Iran
141 F4 Chahār Burjak Afgh.
140 C4 Chahār Rūstā'ī Iran
141 E3 Chahār Takāb Iran
137 K3 Chahār Ţāq Iran
140 D3 Chāh Badam Iran
141 H2 Chāh-e Āb Afgh.
141 E3 Chāh-e Khoshāb Iran
140 D3 Chāh-e Nūklok Iran
140 D4 Chāh-e Rāh Iran
140 D3 Chāh-e Shūr Iran
140 D4 Chāh Ḩaqq Iran
Chah-i-Ab Afgh. see Chāh-e Āb
Chah-i-Shurkh Iraq see Chiyā Surkh
141 E5 Chāh Lak Iran
141 F4 Chah Sandan Pak.
145 F5 Chaibasa India
189 G3 Chaigneau, Lac l. Canada
152 C2 Chai He r. China
154 B2 Chainat Thai.
154 B2 Chai Si r. Thai.
149 □ Chai Wan Hong Kong China
154 A3 Chaiya Thai.
154 B2 Chaiyaphum Thai.
215 F1 Chajarí Arg.
144 B3 Chakar r. Pak.
145 H5 Chakaria Bangl.
141 F4 Chakhānsūr Afgh.
145 E4 Chakia India
141 G5 Chakku Pak.
210 D7 Chala Peru
206 G5 Chalatenango El Salvador
189 G4 Chaleur Bay inlet Canada
149 D5 Chaling China
144 C5 Chalisgaon India
171 J5 Chalkida Greece
128 A7 Chalky Inlet N.Z.
166 D3 Challans France
210 E7 Challapata Bol.
216 E5 Challenger Deep sea feature N. Pacific Ocean
194 D2 Challis U.S.A.
166 G2 Châlons-en-Champagne France
166 G3 Chalon-sur-Saône France
152 C2 Chaluhe China
140 C2 Chālūs Iran
165 K5 Cham Germany
154 D2 Cham, Cu Lao i. Vietnam
195 F4 Chama U.S.A.
213 C2 Chama r. Venez.
179 D5 Chama Zambia
155 B1 Chamah, Gunung mt. Malaysia
215 D2 Chamaico Arg.
180 A3 Chamais Bay Namibia
141 G4 Chaman Pak.
144 D4 Chambal r. India
189 G3 Chambeaux, Lac l. Canada
187 H4 Chamberlain Canada
198 D3 Chamberlain U.S.A.
203 I1 Chamberlain Lake U.S.A.
197 H4 Chambers U.S.A.
202 E5 Chambersburg U.S.A.
166 G4 Chambéry France
179 D5 Chambeshi Zambia
170 C7 Chambi, Jebel mt. Tunisia
166 G4 Chamechaude mt. France
140 C3 Cham-e Ḩannā Iran
140 C3 Chameshk Iran
215 C1 Chamical Arg.
145 F4 Chamlang mt. Nepal
154 B3 Châmnar Cambodia
166 H4 Chamonix-Mont-Blanc France
143 C1 Champa India
186 B2 Champagne Canada
166 G2 Champagne France
181 H4 Champagne Castle mt. S. Africa
166 G3 Champagnole France
190 C5 Champaign U.S.A.
215 D1 Champaqui, Cerro mt. Arg.
154 C2 Champasak Laos
145 H5 Champhai India
190 D2 Champion U.S.A.
203 G2 Champlain U.S.A.
203 G2 Champlain, Lake Canada/U.S.A.
207 G4 Champotón Mex.
143 B4 Chamrajnagar India
172 H4 Chamzinka Rus. Fed.
154 B4 Chana Thai.
212 B3 Chañaral Chile
213 E3 Chanaro, Cerro mt. Venez.
215 B2 Chanco Chile
184 D3 Chandalar r. U.S.A.
143 C1 Chandarpur India
144 D3 Chandausi India
199 F6 Chandeleur Islands U.S.A.
144 E5 Chandia India
144 D3 Chandigarh India
197 G5 Chandler U.S.A.
191 I3 Chandos Lake Canada
145 G5 Chandpur Bangl.
144 D3 Chandpur India
145 H5 Chandraghona Bangl.
144 D6 Chandrapur India
144 D5 Chandur India
154 B2 Chang, Ko i. Thai.
179 D6 Changane r. Moz.
179 D5 Changara Moz.
152 E3 Changbai China
152 D3 Changbai Shan mts China/N. Korea
149 C7 Changcheng China
152 C2 Changchun China
152 C1 Changchunling China
148 F2 Changdao China
149 D4 Changde China
152 D4 Ch'angdo N. Korea
148 E3 Changfeng China
154 D1 Changhua Jiang r. China
154 □ Changi Sing.
149 C7 Changjiang China
149 E4 Chang Jiang r. China alt. Jinsha Jiang, alt. Tongtian He, alt. Zhi Qu, conv. Yangtze, long Yangtze Kiang
148 F4 Changjiang Kou China
152 D3 Changjin N. Korea
152 D3 Changjin-gang r. N. Korea
152 D3 Changjin-ho resr N. Korea
149 F5 Changle China
148 F2 Changli China
152 B1 Changling China
145 F3 Changna China
149 D5 Changning China
152 C4 Changnyŏn N. Korea
148 E1 Changping China
152 C4 Changsan-got pt N. Korea
149 D4 Changsha China
149 F4 Changshan China
152 B4 Changshan Qundao is China
149 C4 Changshou China
149 D4 Changshou China
148 F4 Changshu China
149 C5 Changshun China
149 E5 Changtai China
149 E5 Changting Fujian China
152 E1 Changting Heilong. China
152 C2 Changtu China
206 I6 Changuinola Panama
152 E6 Changwon S. Korea
148 C3 Changwu China
152 A4 Changxing Dao i. China
149 D4 Changyang China
148 F2 Changyi China
152 C4 Changyŏn N. Korea
148 E3 Changyuan China
148 D2 Changzhi China
148 F4 Changzhou China
171 K7 Chania Greece
148 B3 Chankou China
143 B3 Channapatna India
166 C2 Channel Islands English Chan.
196 C5 Channel Islands U.S.A.
196 B5 Channel Islands National Park U.S.A.
189 I4 Channel-Port-aux-Basques Canada
161 I6 Channel Tunnel France/U.K.
190 C2 Channing U.S.A.
167 C1 Chantada Spain
154 B2 Chanthaburi Thai.
166 F2 Chantilly France
199 E4 Chanute U.S.A.
132 I4 Chany, Ozero salt l. Rus. Fed.
148 E2 Chaobai Xinhe r. China
148 E4 Chaohu China
148 E4 Chao Hu l. China
154 B2 Chao Phraya r. Thai.
145 H2 Chaowula Shan mt. China
149 E6 Chaoyang Guangdong China
148 F1 Chaoyang Liaoning China
149 E6 Chaozhou China
214 E1 Chapada Diamantina, Parque Nacional nat. park Brazil
214 A1 Chapada dos Guimarães Brazil
214 C1 Chapada dos Veadeiros, Parque Nacional da nat. park Brazil
206 D3 Chapala Mex.
206 D3 Chapala, Laguna de l. Mex.
141 G3 Chāpārī, Kōtal-e Afgh.
213 B4 Chaparral Col.
138 B2 Chapayevo Kazakh.
172 I4 Chapayevsk Rus. Fed.
212 F3 Chapecó Brazil
212 F3 Chapecó r. Brazil
161 F4 Chapel-en-le-Frith U.K.
201 E5 Chapel Hill U.S.A.
164 C4 Chapelle-lez-Herlaimont Belgium
161 F4 Chapeltown U.K.
190 D5 Chapin, Lake U.S.A.
191 F2 Chapleau Canada
172 F4 Chaplygin Rus. Fed.
173 E6 Chaplynka Ukr.
202 B6 Chapmanville U.S.A.
127 G8 Chappell Islands Australia
210 E7 Chaqui Bol.
144 D2 Char India
206 D3 Charcas Mex.
145 H3 Char Chu r. China
129 B3 Charcot Island i. Antarctica
187 G3 Chard Canada
161 E7 Chard U.K.
137 K5 Chardāvol Iran
202 C4 Chardon U.S.A.
166 E3 Charente r. France
140 D4 Charg Iran
141 H3 Chārīkār Afgh.
198 E3 Chariton r. U.S.A.
191 F3 Charity Island U.S.A.
140 C4 Charkas Iran
132 G3 Charkayuvom Rus. Fed.
144 D4 Charkhari India
164 C4 Charleroi Belgium
193 K4 Charles, Cape U.S.A.
190 A4 Charles City U.S.A.
128 C4 Charleston N.Z.
200 B4 Charleston IL U.S.A.
203 I2 Charleston ME U.S.A.
199 F4 Charleston MO U.S.A.
201 E5 Charleston SC U.S.A.
202 C5 Charleston WV U.S.A.
197 E3 Charleston Peak U.S.A.
163 C4 Charlestown Ireland
203 G3 Charlestown NH U.S.A.
203 H4 Charlestown RI U.S.A.
202 E5 Charles Town U.S.A.
124 E4 Charleville Australia
163 C5 Charleville Ireland
166 G2 Charleville-Mézières France
190 E3 Charlevoix U.S.A.
129 C5 Charlie, Dome ice feature Antarctica
186 E3 Charlie Lake Canada
190 E4 Charlotte MI U.S.A.
201 D5 Charlotte NC U.S.A.
201 D7 Charlotte Harbor b. U.S.A.
202 D5 Charlottesville U.S.A.
189 H4 Charlottetown Canada
213 E2 Charlotteville Trin. and Tob.
126 E6 Charlton Australia
188 E3 Charlton Island Canada
172 F2 Charozero Rus. Fed.
144 B2 Charsadda Pak.
124 E4 Charters Towers Australia
166 E2 Chartres France
Charvakskoye Vdkhr. resr Kazakh./Uzbek. see Chorvoq suv ombori
139 J1 Charysh r. Rus. Fed.
139 J2 Charyshskoye Rus. Fed.
215 E2 Chascomús Arg.
186 F4 Chase Canada
138 E5 Chashkent Turkm.
140 E3 Chashmeh Nūrī Iran
140 D3 Chashmeh-ye Palasi Iran
172 D4 Chashniki Belarus
128 B7 Chaslands Mistake c. N.Z.
152 D3 Chasŏng N. Korea
140 D3 Chastab, Kūh-e mts Iran
166 D3 Châteaubriant France
166 E3 Château-du-Loir France
166 E2 Châteaudun France
203 F2 Chateaugay U.S.A.
203 G2 Châteauguay Canada
166 B2 Châteaulin France
166 F3 Châteauneuf-sur-Loire France
166 E3 Châteauroux France
164 E6 Château-Salins France
166 F2 Château-Thierry France
164 C4 Châtelet Belgium
166 E3 Châtellerault France
190 A4 Chatfield U.S.A.
191 F4 Chatham Canada
161 H6 Chatham U.K.
203 H4 Chatham MA U.S.A.
203 G3 Chatham NY U.S.A.
202 D6 Chatham VA U.S.A.
125 I6 Chatham Islands N.Z.
216 H8 Chatham Rise sea feature S. Pacific Ocean
186 C4 Chatham Sound sea chan. Canada
186 C3 Chatham Strait U.S.A.
139 G4 Chatkal r. Kyrg.
139 G4 Chatkal Range mts Kyrg.
145 F4 Chatra India
191 G3 Chatsworth Canada
190 C5 Chatsworth U.S.A.
201 C5 Chattanooga U.S.A.
161 H5 Chatteris U.K.
154 B2 Chatturat Thai.
139 H4 Chatyr-Köl l. Kyrg.
139 I4 Chatyr-Tash Kyrg.
154 C3 Châu Đôc Vietnam
144 B4 Chauhtan India
145 H5 Chauk Myanmar
144 E4 Chauka r. India
144 D3 Chaukhamba mts India
166 G2 Chaumont France
154 A2 Chaungwabyin Myanmar
133 R3 Chaunskaya Guba b. Rus. Fed.
166 F2 Chauny France
154 D2 Châu Ô Vietnam
145 F4 Chauparan India
202 D3 Chautauqua, Lake U.S.A.
139 H4 Chauvay Kyrg.
143 C4 Chavakachcheri Sri Lanka
140 B3 Chavār Iran
211 I4 Chaves Brazil
167 C2 Chaves Port.
188 E2 Chavigny, Lac l. Canada
172 D4 Chavusy Belarus
144 A3 Chawal r. Pak.
Chây r. Vietnam see Chay, Sông
149 B6 Chay, Sông r. Vietnam
215 D2 Chazón Arg.
203 G2 Chazy U.S.A.
161 F5 Cheadle U.K.
202 D5 Cheat r. U.S.A.
168 F5 Cheb Czech Rep.
170 D7 Chebba Tunisia
172 H3 Cheboksary Rus. Fed.
190 E3 Cheboygan U.S.A.
173 H7 Chechen', Ostrov i. Rus. Fed.
Chechenia aut. rep. Rus. Fed. see Chechenskaya Respublika
173 H7 Chechenskaya Respublika aut. rep. Rus. Fed.
Chechnia aut. rep. Rus. Fed. see Chechenskaya Respublika
199 E5 Checotah U.S.A.
152 A5 Chedao China
161 E6 Cheddar U.K.
187 G3 Cheecham Canada
176 B1 Chefchaouene Morocco
184 B3 Chefornak U.S.A.
181 J1 Chefu Moz.
176 B2 Chegga Mauritania
179 D5 Chegutu Zimbabwe
194 B2 Chehalis U.S.A.
141 H3 Chehardar Pass Afgh.
137 K5 Chehariz tourist site Iraq
140 E4 Chehel Pāyeh Iran
Cheju S. Korea see Jeju
146 E3 Cheju do S. Korea
152 D7 Cheju-do i. S. Korea
172 F4 Chekhov Rus. Fed.
194 B2 Chelan, Lake U.S.A.
Cheleken Turkm. see Hazar
215 C3 Chelforó Arg.
138 B2 Chelkar Kazakh.
169 K5 Chełm Poland
161 H6 Chelmer r. U.K.
169 I4 Chełmno Poland
161 H6 Chelmsford U.K.
203 H3 Chelmsford U.S.A.
161 E6 Cheltenham U.K.
167 F3 Chelva Spain
132 H4 Chelyabinsk Rus. Fed.
179 D5 Chemba Moz.
144 D2 Chêm Co l. China
165 K4 Chemnitz Germany
202 E3 Chemung r. U.S.A.
141 H4 Chenab r. India/Pak.
176 B2 Chenachane Alg.
203 F3 Chenango r. U.S.A.
194 C2 Cheney U.S.A.
199 D4 Cheney Reservoir U.S.A.
143 C3 Chengalpattu India
148 E2 Cheng'an China
149 D5 Chengbu China
148 E1 Chengde China
149 B4 Chengdu China
148 C3 Chenggu China
149 B5 Chengguan China
149 E6 Chenghai China
149 B5 Chengjiang Fossil Site tourist site China
148 C4 Chengkou China
147 D5 Chengmai China
152 B5 Chengshan China
152 B4 Chengzitan China
148 F3 Cheniu Shan i. China
143 C3 Chennai India
190 C5 Chenoa U.S.A.
149 D5 Chenxi China
149 D5 Chenzhou China
152 D5 Cheonan S. Korea
152 E6 Cheongdo S. Korea
152 D5 Cheongju S. Korea
Cheo Reo Vietnam see A Yun Pa
152 D4 Cheorwon S. Korea
210 C5 Chepén Peru
215 C1 Chepes Arg.
206 J6 Chepo Panama
161 E6 Chepstow U.K.
172 I3 Cheptsa r. Rus. Fed.
137 K5 Cheqād Kabūd Iran
190 B2 Chequamegon Bay U.S.A.
166 F3 Cher r. France
206 D4 Cherán Mex.
201 E5 Cheraw U.S.A.
166 D2 Cherbourg-Octeville France
167 H4 Cherchell Alg.
172 I4 Cherdakly Rus. Fed.
146 C1 Cheremkhovo Rus. Fed.
139 J1 Cheremnoye Rus. Fed.
150 D2 Cheremshany Rus. Fed.
172 F3 Cherepovets Rus. Fed.
172 H2 Cherevkovo Rus. Fed.
170 B7 Chéria Alg.
173 E5 Cherkasy Ukr.
173 G6 Cherkessk Rus. Fed.
143 C2 Cherla India
139 H1 Cherlak Rus. Fed.
139 H1 Cherlakskoye Rus. Fed.
179 C5 Chermenze Angola
172 I3 Chernaya Kholunitsa Rus. Fed.
150 C2 Chernigovka Rus. Fed.
173 D5 Chernihiv Ukr.
173 F6 Cherninivka Ukr.
173 C5 Chernivtsi Ukr.
146 B1 Chernogorsk Rus. Fed.
139 I1 Chernoretsk Kazakh.
172 H3 Chernovskoye Rus. Fed.
173 D5 Chernyakhiv Ukr.
169 J3 Chernyakhovsk Rus. Fed.
173 F5 Chernyanka Rus. Fed.
133 M3 Chernyshevskiy Rus. Fed.
173 H6 Chernyye Zemli reg. Rus. Fed.
138 C2 Chernyy Otrog Rus. Fed.
173 H5 Chernyy Yar Rus. Fed.
198 E3 Cherokee IA U.S.A.
199 D4 Cherokee OK U.S.A.
199 E4 Cherokees, Lake o' the U.S.A.
201 E7 Cherokee Sound Bahamas
215 B3 Cherquenco Chile
145 G4 Cherrapunji India
197 E2 Cherry Creek U.S.A.
197 E1 Cherry Creek Mountains U.S.A.
203 J2 Cherryfield U.S.A.
125 G3 Cherry Island Solomon Is
191 I4 Cherry Valley Canada
203 F3 Cherry Valley U.S.A.
133 P3 Cherskogo, Khrebet mts Rus. Fed.
173 G5 Chertkovo Rus. Fed.
172 I2 Cherva Rus. Fed.
171 K3 Cherven Bryag Bulg.
173 C5 Chervonohrad Ukr.
173 E5 Chervonozavods'ke Ukr.
172 D4 Chervyen' Belarus
161 F6 Cherwell r. U.K.
172 D4 Cherykaw Belarus
191 E4 Chesaning U.S.A.
203 E6 Chesapeake U.S.A.
203 E5 Chesapeake Bay U.S.A.
161 G6 Chesham U.K.
203 G3 Cheshire U.S.A.
161 E4 Cheshire Plain U.K.
138 E5 Cheshme Vtoroy Turkm.
132 F3 Cheshskaya Guba b. Rus. Fed.
139 H5 Cheshtebe Tajik.
161 G6 Cheshunt U.K.
138 E1 Chesma Rus. Fed.
161 E4 Chester U.K.
196 B1 Chester CA U.S.A.
200 B4 Chester IL U.S.A.
194 E1 Chester MT U.S.A.
203 F5 Chester PA U.S.A.
201 D5 Chester SC U.S.A.
203 E5 Chester r. U.S.A.
161 F4 Chesterfield U.K.
125 F3 Chesterfield, Îles is New Caledonia
187 K2 Chesterfield Inlet Canada
187 K2 Chesterfield Inlet inlet Canada
160 F3 Chester-le-Street U.K.
203 E5 Chestertown MD U.S.A.
203 G3 Chestertown NY U.S.A.
203 F2 Chesterville Canada
202 D4 Chestnut Ridge U.S.A.
203 I1 Chesuncook U.S.A.
203 I1 Chesuncook Lake U.S.A.
170 B6 Chetaïbi Alg.
189 H4 Chéticamp Canada
143 A4 Chetlat i. India
207 G4 Chetumal Mex.
186 E3 Chetwynd Canada
149 □ Cheung Chau Hong Kong China
149 □ Cheung Chau i. Hong Kong China
128 D5 Cheviot N.Z.
160 E2 Cheviot Hills U.K.
194 C1 Chewelah U.S.A.
199 D5 Cheyenne OK U.S.A.
194 F3 Cheyenne WY U.S.A.
198 C3 Cheyenne r. U.S.A.
198 C4 Cheyenne Wells U.S.A.
186 E4 Chezacut Canada
144 C4 Chhapar India
145 F4 Chhapra India
144 D4 Chhatarpur India
144 B3 Chhatr Pak.
145 E5 Chhattisgarh state India
144 D5 Chhindwara India
144 C5 Chhota Udepur India
144 C4 Chhoti Sadri India
145 G4 Chhukha Bhutan
154 C2 Chi, Lam r. Thai.
178 E4 Chiamboni Kenya
154 A1 Chiang Dao Thai.
154 B1 Chiang Kham Thai.
154 B1 Chiang Khan Thai.
154 A1 Chiang Mai Thai.
154 A1 Chiang Rai Thai.
207 F4 Chiapas state Mex.
170 C2 Chiari Italy
207 E4 Chiautla Mex.
151 G7 Chiba Japan
149 D4 Chibi China
179 B5 Chibia Angola
179 D6 Chiboma Moz.
188 F4 Chibougamau Canada
188 F4 Chibougamau, Lac l. Canada
181 J2 Chibuto Moz.
145 G2 Chibuzhang Co l. China
Chibuzhang Hu l. China see Chibuzhang Co
190 D5 Chicago U.S.A. (City Plan 113)
190 D5 Chicago Heights U.S.A.
190 C5 Chicago Ship Canal U.S.A.
213 B3 Chicamocha r. Col.
213 E3 Chicanán r. Venez.
186 B3 Chichagof U.S.A.
186 B3 Chichagof Island U.S.A.
148 E1 Chicheng China
207 G3 Chichén Itzá tourist site Mex.
161 G7 Chichester U.K.
124 B4 Chichester Range mts Australia
151 F7 Chichibu Japan
151 F7 Chichibu-Tama Kokuritsu-kōen nat. park Japan
202 E6 Chickahominy r. U.S.A.
201 C5 Chickamauga Lake U.S.A.
199 D5 Chickasha U.S.A.
167 C4 Chiclana de la Frontera Spain
210 C5 Chiclayo Peru
212 C6 Chico r. Chubut Arg.
215 B4 Chico r. Chubut/Río Negro Arg.
212 C7 Chico r. Arg.
196 B2 Chico U.S.A.
181 K2 Chicomo Moz.
207 F5 Chicomucelo Mex.
203 G3 Chicopee U.S.A.
153 B2 Chico Sapocoy, Mount Phil.
189 F4 Chicoutimi Canada
181 I1 Chicualacuala Moz.
143 B4 Chidambaram India
181 K2 Chidenguele Moz.
189 H1 Chidley, Cape Canada
181 K2 Chiducuane Moz.
201 D6 Chiefland U.S.A.
168 F7 Chiemsee l. Germany
164 D5 Chiers r. France
170 F3 Chieti Italy
207 E4 Chietla Mex.
148 F1 Chifeng China
214 E2 Chifre, Serra do mts Brazil
189 G4 Chignecto Bay Canada
213 A3 Chigorodó Col.
179 D6 Chigubo Moz.
145 G3 Chigu Co l. China
141 G3 Chihil Abdālān, Kōh-e mts Afgh.
206 C1 Chihuahua Mex.
206 C1 Chihuahua state Mex.
195 F6 Chihuahua, Desierto de des. Mex./U.S.A.
149 D6 Chikan China
172 D3 Chikhachevo Rus. Fed.
144 D5 Chikhali Kalan Parasia India
144 D5 Chikhli India
143 B3 Chikkaballapur India
143 A3 Chikmagalur India
151 F6 Chikuma-gawa r. Japan
186 E4 Chilanko Forks Canada
207 E4 Chilapa Mex.
135 F3 Chilas Pak.
143 B5 Chilaw Sri Lanka
196 B2 Chilcoot U.S.A.
186 E4 Chilcotin r. Canada
199 C5 Childress U.S.A.
212 B5 Chile country S. America
217 N8 Chile Basin sea feature S. Pacific Ocean
212 C3 Chilecito Arg.
217 N8 Chile Rise sea feature S. Pacific Ocean
173 H6 Chilgir Rus. Fed.
145 F6 Chilika Lake India
179 C5 Chililabombwe Zambia
186 E4 Chilko r. Canada
186 E4 Chilko Lake Canada
Chilkoot U.S.A. see Chilcoot
215 B3 Chillán Chile
215 B3 Chillán, Nevado mts Chile
215 E3 Chillar Arg.
190 C5 Chillicothe IL U.S.A.
198 E4 Chillicothe MO U.S.A.
202 B5 Chillicothe OH U.S.A.
144 C1 Chillinji Pak.
186 E5 Chilliwack Canada
Chil'mamedkum, Peski des. Turkm. see Çilmämmetgum
212 B6 Chiloé, Isla de i. Chile
194 B3 Chiloquin U.S.A.
207 E4 Chilpancingo Mex.
127 G6 Chiltern Australia
161 G6 Chiltern Hills U.K.
190 C3 Chilton U.S.A.
149 F5 Chilung Taiwan
Chilung Pass India see Pensi La
179 D4 Chimala Tanz.
206 J6 Chimán Panama
164 C4 Chimay Belgium
164 C4 Chimay, Bois de for. Belgium
215 C1 Chimbas Arg.
Chimbay Uzbek. see Chimboy
210 C4 Chimborazo mt. Ecuador
210 C5 Chimbote Peru
138 D4 Chimboy Uzbek.
213 B2 Chimichaguá Col.
179 D5 Chimoio Moz.
146 B3 China country Asia
207 E2 China Mex.
213 B3 Chinácota Col.
149 D5 China Danxia tourist site China
207 G4 Chinajá Guat.
196 D4 China Lake CA U.S.A.
203 I2 China Lake ME U.S.A.
206 H5 Chinandega Nicaragua
196 C5 China Point U.S.A.
Chinaz Uzbek. see Chinoz
210 C6 Chincha Alta Peru
186 F3 Chinchaga r. Canada
204 G5 Chinchorro, Banco sea feature Mex.
203 F6 Chincoteague Bay U.S.A.
179 D5 Chinde Moz.
146 B3 Chindu China
145 H5 Chindwin r. Myanmar
144 C2 Chineni India
213 B3 Chingaza, Parque Nacional nat. park Col.
152 C4 Chinghwa N. Korea
179 C5 Chingola Zambia
179 B5 Chinguar Angola
179 D5 Chinhoyi Zimbabwe
144 C3 Chiniot Pak.
206 B2 Chinipas Mex.
154 C2 Chinit, Stœng r. Cambodia
152 E6 Chinju S. Korea
178 C3 Chinko r. Cent. Afr. Rep.
197 H3 Chinle U.S.A.
197 H3 Chinle Valley U.S.A.
197 H3 Chinle Wash watercourse U.S.A.
149 F5 Chinmen Tao i. Taiwan
143 B2 Chinnur India
151 F7 Chino Japan
166 E3 Chinon France
216 H3 Chinook Trough sea feature N. Pacific Ocean
197 F4 Chino Valley U.S.A.
139 G4 Chinoz Uzbek.
179 D5 Chinsali Zambia
143 B3 Chintamani India
170 E2 Chioggia Italy
171 L5 Chios Greece
171 K5 Chios i. Greece
179 D5 Chipata Zambia
215 C4 Chipchihua, Sierra de mts Arg.
179 B5 Chipindo Angola
179 D6 Chipinge Zimbabwe
143 A2 Chiplun India
161 E6 Chippenham U.K.
190 B3 Chippewa r. U.S.A.
190 B3 Chippewa, Lake U.S.A.
190 B3 Chippewa Falls U.S.A.
161 F6 Chipping Norton U.K.
161 E6 Chipping Sodbury U.K.
203 J2 Chiputneticook Lakes U.S.A.
Chiquibul, Parque Nacional nat. park Belize see Chiquibul National Park
207 G4 Chiquibul National Park Belize
207 G5 Chiquimula Guat.
213 B3 Chiquinquira Col.
173 G5 Chir r. Rus. Fed.
143 C3 Chirada India
143 A4 Chirakkal India
143 C3 Chirala India
141 G3 Chīras Afgh.
144 C3 Chirawa India
Chirchik Uzbek. see Chirchiq
139 G4 Chirchiq Uzbek.
179 D6 Chiredzi Zimbabwe
197 H5 Chiricahua National Monument nat. park U.S.A.
197 H6 Chiricahua Peak U.S.A.
213 B2 Chiriguaná Col.
184 C4 Chirikof Island U.S.A.
206 I6 Chiriquí, Golfo de b. Panama
206 I6 Chiriquí, Laguna de b. Panama
161 D5 Chirk U.K.
162 F5 Chirnside U.K.
171 K3 Chirpan Bulg.
206 I6 Chirripó mt. Costa Rica
179 C5 Chirundu Zambia
188 E3 Chisasibi Canada
207 G5 Chisec Guat.
190 A2 Chisholm U.S.A.
141 F3 Chisht-e Sharīf Afgh.
144 C3 Chishtian Pak.
149 B4 Chishui China

173 D6 Chişinău Moldova
169 J7 Chişineu-Criş Romania
172 I4 Chistopol' Rus. Fed.
146 D1 Chita Rus. Fed.
179 B5 Chitado Angola
179 D5 Chitambo Zambia
178 C4 Chitato Angola
187 H4 Chitek Lake Canada
179 B5 Chitembo Angola
179 D4 Chitipa Malawi
179 C5 Chitokoloki Zambia
150 G3 Chitose Japan
143 B3 Chitradurga India
144 B2 Chitral Pak.
144 B2 Chitral *r.* Pak.
206 I7 Chitré Panama
145 G5 Chittagong Bangl.
145 F5 Chittaranjan India
144 C4 Chittaurgarh India
143 B3 Chittoor India
143 B4 Chittur India
179 D5 Chitungulu Zambia
179 D5 Chitungwiza Zimbabwe
179 C5 Chiume Angola
206 A2 Chívato, Punta *pt* Mex.
179 D5 Chivhu Zimbabwe
215 E2 Chivilcoy Arg.
149 D6 Chixixu China
137 J4 Chiyā Surkh Iraq
149 E4 Chizhou China
151 D7 Chizu Japan
139 G1 Chkalovo Kazakh.
172 G3 Chkalovsk Rus. Fed.
150 C2 Chkalovskoye Rus. Fed.
176 C1 Chlef Alg.
167 G4 Chlef, Oued *r.* Alg.
154 □ Choa Chu Kang Sing.
154 □ Choa Chu Kang *h.* Sing.
154 C2 Chŏâm Khsant Cambodia
215 B1 Choapa *r.* Chile
179 C5 Chobe National Park Botswana
197 E5 Chocolate Mountains U.S.A.
213 B3 Chocontá Col.
152 C4 Cho-do *i.* N. Korea
152 D6 Cho-do *i.* S. Korea
165 K4 Chodov Czech Rep.
215 D3 Choele Choel Arg.
144 C2 Chogo Lungma Glacier Pak.
173 H6 Chograyskoye Vodokhranilishche *resr* Rus. Fed.
187 I4 Choiceland Canada
125 F2 Choiseul *i.* Solomon Is
212 E8 Choiseul Sound *sea chan.* Falkland Is
206 B2 Choix Mex.
168 H4 Chojnice Poland
150 G5 Chōkai-san *vol.* Japan
178 D2 Ch'ok'ē Eth.
199 D6 Choke Canyon Lake U.S.A.
178 D2 Ch'ok'ē Terara *mt.* Eth.
145 F3 Choksum China
133 P2 Chokurdakh Rus. Fed.
179 D6 Chókwè Moz.
166 D3 Cholet France
215 B4 Cholila Arg.
139 H4 Cholpon Kyrg.
139 I4 Cholpon-Ata Kyrg.
206 H5 Choluteca Hond.
179 C5 Choma Zambia
145 G4 Chomo Lhari *mt.* Bhutan
154 A1 Chom Thong Thai.
168 F5 Chomutov Czech Rep.
133 L3 Chona *r.* Rus. Fed.
154 B2 Chon Buri Thai.
152 D3 Ch'ŏnch'ŏn N. Korea
210 B4 Chone Ecuador
152 C4 Ch'ŏngch'ŏn-gang *r.* N. Korea
152 E3 Ch'ŏngjin N. Korea
152 C4 Chŏngju N. Korea
Ch'ŏngju S. Korea *see* Cheongju
154 B2 Chŏng Kal Cambodia
152 D4 Chŏngp'yŏng N. Korea
149 C4 Chongqing China
149 C4 Chongqing *mun.* China
149 E5 Chongren China
181 J2 Chonguene Moz.
179 C5 Chongwe Zambia
149 D4 Chongyang China
149 F5 Chongyang Xi *r.* China
149 E5 Chongyi China
149 C6 Chongzuo China
212 B7 Chonos, Archipiélago de los *is* Chile
145 F3 Cho Oyu *mt.* China
Chơ Phước Hai Vietnam *see* Phước Hai
214 B4 Chopim *r.* Brazil
214 B4 Chopimzinho Brazil
203 F5 Choptank *r.* U.S.A.
144 B4 Chor Pak.
171 K7 Chora Sfakion Greece
160 E4 Chorley U.K.
173 D5 Chornobyl' Ukr.
173 E6 Chornomors'ke Ukr.
173 C5 Chortkiv Ukr.
139 G4 Chorvoq suv ombori *resr* Kazakh./Uzbek.
152 C3 Ch'osan N. Korea
151 G7 Chōshi Japan
215 B3 Chos Malal Arg.
168 G4 Choszczno Poland
210 C5 Chota Peru
194 D2 Choteau U.S.A.
144 B3 Choti Pak.
176 A2 Choûm Mauritania
196 B3 Chowchilla U.S.A.
186 F4 Chown, Mount Canada
139 K2 Choya Rus. Fed.
146 D2 Choybalsan Mongolia
146 C2 Choyr Mongolia
168 H6 Chřiby *hills* Czech Rep.
190 D6 Chrisman U.S.A.
181 I3 Chrissiesmeer S. Africa
128 D5 Christchurch N.Z.
161 F7 Christchurch U.K.
185 L2 Christian, Cape Canada
181 F3 Christiana S. Africa
191 G3 Christian Island Canada
202 C6 Christiansburg U.S.A.
Christianshåb Greenland *see* Qasigiannguit
186 C3 Christian Sound *sea chan.* U.S.A.
187 G3 Christina *r.* Canada
147 C8 Christmas Island *terr.* Indian Ocean
168 G6 Chrudim Czech Rep.
145 G5 Chuadanga Bangl.
181 J2 Chuali, Lago *l.* Moz.
148 C1 Chuanjing China
148 F4 Chuansha China
194 D3 Chubbuck U.S.A.
151 E6 Chūbu-Sangaku Kokuritsu-kōen *nat. park* Japan
215 C4 Chubut *prov.* Arg.
212 C6 Chubut *r.* Arg.
197 E5 Chuckwalla Mountains U.S.A.
173 D5 Chudniv Ukr.
172 D3 Chudovo Rus. Fed.
184 C4 Chugach Mountains U.S.A.
151 C7 Chūgoku-sanchi *mts* Japan
150 C2 Chuguyevka Rus. Fed.
194 F3 Chugwater U.S.A.
173 F5 Chuhuyiv Ukr.
197 G5 Chuichu U.S.A.
146 F1 Chukchagirskoye, Ozero *l.* Rus. Fed.
220 M1 Chukchi Plateau *sea feature* Arctic Ocean
133 U3 Chukchi Sea Rus. Fed./U.S.A.
172 G3 Chukhloma Rus. Fed.
133 T3 Chukotskiy Poluostrov *pen.* Rus. Fed.
172 H1 Chulasa Rus. Fed.
196 D5 Chula Vista U.S.A.
132 J4 Chulym Rus. Fed.
145 G4 Chumbi China
212 C3 Chumbicha Arg.
139 K2 Chumek Kazakh.
146 F1 Chumikan Rus. Fed.
154 B1 Chum Phae Thai.
154 A3 Chumphon Thai.
154 B2 Chum Saeng Thai.
133 K4 Chuna *r.* Rus. Fed.
149 F4 Chun'an China
152 D5 Chuncheon S. Korea
141 H3 Chūnghar, Kūh-e *h.* Afgh.
152 D5 Chungju S. Korea
Chungking China *see* Chongqing
152 C4 Chŭngsan N. Korea
Chungur, Koh-i- *hill* Afgh. *see* Chūnghar, Kūh-e
152 F2 Chunhua China
207 G4 Chunhuhux Mex.
133 L3 Chunya *r.* Rus. Fed.
137 K3 Chūplū Iran
210 D7 Chuquibamba Peru
212 C2 Chuquicamata Chile
168 D7 Chur Switz.
133 O3 Churapcha Rus. Fed.
187 K3 Churchill Canada
187 J3 Churchill *r. Man./Sask.* Canada
189 H3 Churchill *r. Nfld* Canada
187 K3 Churchill, Cape Canada
189 H3 Churchill Falls Canada
187 H3 Churchill Lake Canada
186 D3 Churchill Peak Canada
188 E2 Churchill Sound *sea chan.* Canada
198 D1 Churchs Ferry U.S.A.
202 D5 Churchville U.S.A.
145 F4 Churia Ghati Hills Nepal
172 H3 Churov Rus. Fed.
144 C3 Churu India
Churubay Nura Kazakh. *see* Abay
213 C2 Churuguara Venez.
154 D2 Chư Sê Vietnam
144 D2 Chushul India
197 H3 Chuska Mountains U.S.A.
139 G4 Chust Uzbek.
189 F4 Chute-des-Passes Canada
191 I2 Chute-Rouge Canada
191 J2 Chute-St-Philippe Canada
123 E2 Chuuk *is* Micronesia
172 H4 Chuvashskaya Respublika *aut. rep.* Rus. Fed.
149 A5 Chuxiong China
148 F3 Chuzhou China
148 F3 Chuzhou China
137 J4 Chwārtā Iraq
173 D6 Ciadîr-Lunga Moldova
155 C4 Ciamis Indon.
155 C4 Cianjur Indon.
214 B3 Cianorte Brazil
195 E6 Cibuta Mex.
170 F2 Čićarija *mts* Croatia
136 E2 Çiçekdağı Turkey
173 E7 Cide Turkey
169 J4 Ciechanów Poland
205 I4 Ciego de Ávila Cuba
213 B2 Ciénaga Col.
207 D2 Ciénega de Flores Mex.
205 H4 Cienfuegos Cuba
167 F3 Cieza Spain
167 E2 Cifuentes Spain
137 L2 Çigil Adası *i.* Azer.
167 E3 Cigüela *r.* Spain
136 D2 Cihanbeyli Turkey
206 C4 Cihuatlán Mex.
167 D3 Cíjara, Embalse de *resr* Spain
155 C4 Cilacap Indon.
137 I1 Çıldır Turkey
137 I1 Çıldır Gölü *l.* Turkey
149 D4 Cili China
138 C4 Çilmämmetgum *des.* Turkm.
137 J3 Cilo Dağı *mt.* Turkey
137 M1 Çilov Adası *i.* Azer.
197 E4 Cima U.S.A.
195 F4 Cimarron U.S.A.
199 D4 Cimarron *r.* U.S.A.
173 D6 Cimişlia Moldova
170 D2 Cimone, Monte *mt.* Italy
137 H3 Çınar Turkey
213 C3 Cinaruco *r.* Venez.
167 G2 Cinca *r.* Spain
202 A5 Cincinnati U.S.A.
203 F3 Cincinnatus U.S.A.
215 D4 Cinco Chañares Arg.
215 C3 Cinco Saltos Arg.
161 E6 Cinderford U.K.
136 B3 Çine Turkey
164 D4 Ciney Belgium
207 F4 Cintalapa Mex.
166 I5 Cinto, Monte *mt.* France
214 B3 Cinzas *r.* Brazil
149 E5 Ciping China
215 C3 Cipolletti Arg.
184 D3 Circle *AK* U.S.A.
194 F2 Circle *MT* U.S.A.
202 B5 Circleville *OH* U.S.A.
197 F2 Circleville *UT* U.S.A.
155 C4 Cirebon Indon.
161 F6 Cirencester U.K.
170 B2 Ciriè Italy
170 G5 Cirò Marina Italy
189 H2 Cirque Mountain Canada
190 C6 Cisco *IL* U.S.A.
199 D5 Cisco *TX* U.S.A.
197 H2 Cisco *UT* U.S.A.
205 H5 Cisne, Islas del Hond.
213 B3 Cisneros Col.
201 E7 Cistern Point Bahamas
170 G3 Čitluk Bos.-Herz.
180 C6 Citrusdal S. Africa
170 E3 Città di Castello Italy
171 K2 Ciucaş, Vârful *mt.* Romania
206 D1 Ciudad Acuña Mex.
206 D4 Ciudad Altamirano Mex.
213 E3 Ciudad Bolívar Venez.
206 C2 Ciudad Camargo Mex.
206 B2 Ciudad Constitución Mex.
207 G5 Ciudad Cuauhtémoc Mex.
207 G4 Ciudad del Carmen Mex.
214 A4 Ciudad del Este Para.
206 C1 Ciudad Delicias Mex.
207 E3 Ciudad del Maíz Mex.
213 C2 Ciudad de Nutrias Venez.
207 E3 Ciudad de Valles Mex.
213 E2 Ciudad Guayana Venez.
206 C1 Ciudad Guerrero Mex.
206 D4 Ciudad Guzmán Mex.
206 D4 Ciudad Hidalgo Mex.
207 F4 Ciudad Ixtepec Mex.
204 C2 Ciudad Juárez Mex.
206 D2 Ciudad Lerdo Mex.
207 E3 Ciudad Madero Mex.
207 E3 Ciudad Mante Mex.
207 E4 Ciudad Mendoza Mex.
207 E2 Ciudad Mier Mex.
206 B2 Ciudad Obregón Mex.
213 E3 Ciudad Piar Venez.
167 E3 Ciudad Real Spain
207 E2 Ciudad Río Bravo Mex.
167 C2 Ciudad Rodrigo Spain
207 E3 Ciudad Victoria Mex.
167 H2 Ciutadella Spain
136 F1 Cıva Burnu *pt* Turkey
136 B2 Cıvan Dağ *mt.* Turkey
170 E1 Cividale del Friuli Italy
170 E3 Civita Castellana Italy
170 E3 Civitanova Marche Italy
170 D3 Civitavecchia Italy
136 B2 Çivril Turkey
149 F4 Cixi China
148 E2 Cixian China
137 I3 Cizre Turkey
161 I6 Clacton-on-Sea U.K.
163 D3 Clady U.K.
187 G3 Claire, Lake Canada
194 B3 Clair Engle Lake *resr* U.S.A.
202 D4 Clairton U.S.A.
166 F3 Clamecy France
196 D2 Clan Alpine Mountains U.S.A.
163 E4 Clane Ireland
201 C5 Clanton U.S.A.
180 C6 Clanwilliam S. Africa
163 D4 Clara Ireland
154 A3 Clara Island Myanmar
126 E4 Clare *N.S.W.* Australia
126 C4 Clare *S.A.* Australia
163 C4 Clare *r.* Ireland
190 E4 Clare U.S.A.
163 C5 Clarecastle Ireland
163 A4 Clare Island Ireland
203 G3 Claremont U.S.A.
199 E4 Claremore U.S.A.
163 C4 Claremorris Ireland
127 J2 Clarence *r.* Australia
128 D5 Clarence N.Z.
201 F7 Clarence Town Bahamas
199 C5 Clarendon U.S.A.
189 J4 Clarenville Canada
186 G5 Claresholm Canada
198 E3 Clarinda U.S.A.
202 C5 Clarington U.S.A.
202 D4 Clarion U.S.A.
202 D4 Clarion *r.* U.S.A.
217 L4 Clarión, Isla *i.* Mex.
198 D2 Clark U.S.A.
181 H5 Clarkebury S. Africa
127 H8 Clarke Island Australia
201 D5 Clark Hill Reservoir U.S.A.
197 E4 Clark Mountain U.S.A.
191 G3 Clark Point Canada
202 C5 Clarksburg U.S.A.
199 F5 Clarksdale U.S.A.
192 D2 Clarks Fork *r.* U.S.A.
203 F4 Clarks Summit U.S.A.
194 C2 Clarkston U.S.A.
199 E5 Clarksville *AR* U.S.A.
190 A4 Clarksville *IA* U.S.A.
201 C4 Clarksville *TN* U.S.A.
214 B1 Claro *r. Goiás* Brazil
214 B2 Claro *r. Goiás* Brazil
163 D5 Clashmore Ireland
163 D3 Claudy U.K.
153 B2 Claveria Phil.
164 D4 Clavier Belgium
203 G2 Clayburg U.S.A.
198 D4 Clay Center U.S.A.
197 F3 Clayhole Wash *watercourse* U.S.A.
201 D5 Clayton *GA* U.S.A.
195 G4 Clayton *NM* U.S.A.
203 E2 Clayton *NY* U.S.A.
203 I1 Clayton Lake U.S.A.
202 C6 Claytor Lake U.S.A.
163 B6 Clear, Cape Ireland
191 G4 Clear Creek Canada
197 G4 Clear Creek *r.* U.S.A.
184 D4 Cleare, Cape U.S.A.
202 D4 Clearfield *PA* U.S.A.
194 E3 Clearfield *UT* U.S.A.
202 B4 Clear Fork Reservoir U.S.A.
186 F3 Clear Hills Canada
198 E3 Clear Lake *IA* U.S.A.
190 A3 Clear Lake *WI* U.S.A.
196 A2 Clear Lake *l. CA* U.S.A.
197 F2 Clear Lake *l. UT* U.S.A.
194 B3 Clear Lake Reservoir U.S.A.
186 F4 Clearwater *r. Alta* Canada
187 H3 Clearwater *r. Sask.* Canada
201 D7 Clearwater U.S.A.
149 □ Clear Water Bay *Hong Kong* China
194 D2 Clearwater Mountains U.S.A.
187 H3 Clearwater River Provincial Park Canada
199 D5 Cleburne U.S.A.
194 B2 Cle Elum U.S.A.
160 G4 Cleethorpes U.K.
154 □ Clementi Sing.
202 C5 Clendenin U.S.A.
202 C4 Clendening Lake U.S.A.
153 A4 Cleopatra Needle *mt.* Phil.
191 H1 Cléricy Canada
124 E4 Clermont Australia
164 A5 Clermont France
201 D6 Clermont U.S.A.
164 D5 Clermont-en-Argonne France
166 F4 Clermont-Ferrand France
164 E4 Clervaux Lux.
170 D1 Cles Italy
126 B4 Cleve Australia
161 E6 Clevedon U.K.
199 F5 Cleveland *MS* U.S.A.
202 C4 Cleveland *OH* U.S.A.
201 C5 Cleveland *TN* U.S.A.
194 D1 Cleveland, Mount U.S.A.
190 D2 Cleveland Cliffs Basin *l.* U.S.A.
160 F3 Cleveland Hills U.K.
160 D4 Cleveleys U.K.
163 B4 Clew Bay Ireland
201 D7 Clewiston U.S.A.
163 A4 Clifden Ireland
197 H5 Cliff U.S.A.
163 C3 Cliffoney Ireland
128 E4 Clifford Bay N.Z.
127 I1 Clifton Australia
197 H5 Clifton U.S.A.
202 D6 Clifton Forge U.S.A.
202 B6 Clinch *r.* U.S.A.
202 B6 Clinch Mountain *mts* U.S.A.
186 E4 Clinton *B.C.* Canada
191 G4 Clinton *Ont.* Canada
203 G4 Clinton *CT* U.S.A.
190 B5 Clinton *IA* U.S.A.
190 C5 Clinton *IL* U.S.A.
203 H3 Clinton *MA* U.S.A.
203 I2 Clinton *ME* U.S.A.
198 E4 Clinton *MO* U.S.A.
199 F5 Clinton *MS* U.S.A.
201 E5 Clinton *NC* U.S.A.
199 D5 Clinton *OK* U.S.A.
187 H2 Clinton-Colden Lake Canada
190 C5 Clinton Lake U.S.A.
190 C3 Clintonville U.S.A.
197 G4 Clints Well U.S.A.
204 C6 Clipperton, Île *terr.* Pacific Ocean
162 B3 Clisham *h.* U.K.
160 E4 Clitheroe U.K.
181 G4 Clocolan S. Africa
163 D4 Cloghan Ireland
163 C6 Clonakilty Ireland
163 C6 Clonakilty Bay Ireland
163 C4 Clonbern Ireland
124 E4 Cloncurry Australia
163 D3 Clones Ireland
163 D5 Clonmel Ireland
163 D4 Clonygowan Ireland
163 B5 Cloonbannin Ireland
163 D4 Clooneagh Ireland
165 G2 Cloppenburg Germany
190 A2 Cloquet U.S.A.
194 F2 Cloud Peak U.S.A.
128 E4 Cloudy Bay N.Z.
149 □ Cloudy Hill *Hong Kong* China
191 J1 Clova Canada
196 A2 Cloverdale U.S.A.
199 C5 Clovis U.S.A.
191 I3 Cloyne Canada
162 C3 Cluanie, Loch *l.* U.K.
187 H3 Cluff Lake Mine Canada
169 K7 Cluj-Napoca Romania
161 D5 Clun U.K.
126 E6 Clunes Australia
166 H3 Cluses France
161 D4 Clwydian Range *hills* U.K.
186 G4 Clyde Canada
162 D5 Clyde *r.* U.K.
202 E3 Clyde *NY* U.S.A.
202 B4 Clyde *OH* U.S.A.
162 D5 Clyde, Firth of *est.* U.K.
162 D5 Clydebank U.K.
185 L2 Clyde River Canada
195 C5 Coachella U.S.A.
206 D4 Coahuayutla de Guerrero Mex.
206 D2 Coahuila *state* Mex.
186 D2 Coal *r.* Canada
190 C5 Coal City U.S.A.
206 D4 Coalcomán Mex.
196 D3 Coaldale U.S.A.
199 D5 Coalgate U.S.A.
196 B3 Coalinga U.S.A.
186 D3 Coal River Canada
161 F5 Coalville U.K.
210 F4 Coari Brazil
210 F5 Coari *r.* Brazil
193 I5 Coastal Plain U.S.A.
186 D4 Coast Mountains Canada
194 B2 Coast Ranges *mts* U.S.A.
162 E5 Coatbridge U.K.
207 G5 Coatepeque Guat.
203 F5 Coatesville U.S.A.
189 F4 Coaticook Canada
185 J3 Coats Island Canada
129 C3 Coats Land *reg.* Antarctica
207 F4 Coatzacoalcos Mex.
191 H2 Cobalt Canada
207 G5 Cobán Guat.
127 F3 Cobar Australia
127 H6 Cobargo Australia
127 H6 Cobberas, Mount Australia
126 E7 Cobden Australia
191 I3 Cobden Canada
163 C6 Cobh Ireland
Cóbh Ireland *see* Cobh
187 J4 Cobham *r.* Canada
210 E6 Cobija Bol.
203 F3 Cobleskill U.S.A.
191 H4 Cobourg Canada
124 D3 Cobourg Peninsula Australia
127 F5 Cobram Australia
165 I4 Coburg Germany
210 C4 Coca Ecuador
167 D2 Coca Spain
214 B1 Cocalinho Brazil
210 E7 Cochabamba Bol.
215 B4 Cochamó Chile
164 F4 Cochem Germany
Cochin India *see* Kochi
197 H5 Cochise U.S.A.
186 G4 Cochrane *Alta* Canada
188 D4 Cochrane *Ont.* Canada
187 I3 Cochrane *r.* Canada
212 B7 Cochrane Chile
126 D4 Cockburn Australia
191 F3 Cockburn Island Canada
162 F5 Cockburnspath U.K.
201 F7 Cockburn Town Bahamas
Cockburn Town Turks and Caicos Is *see* Grand Turk
160 D3 Cockermouth U.K.
180 F6 Cockscomb *mt.* S. Africa
206 I6 Coclé del Norte Panama
206 H5 Coco *r.* Hond./Nicaragua
204 G7 Coco, Isla de *i.* Col.
213 A4 Coco, Punta *pt* Col.
197 F4 Coconino Plateau U.S.A.
127 G5 Cocopara National Park Australia
127 G4 Cocoparra Range *hills* Australia
213 B3 Cocorná Col.
214 D1 Cocos Brazil
218 K4 Cocos Basin *sea feature* Indian Ocean
147 B8 Cocos Islands *terr.* Indian Ocean
217 N5 Cocos Ridge *sea feature* N. Pacific Ocean
206 D3 Cocula Mex.
213 B3 Cocuy, Sierra Nevada del *mt.* Col.
203 H4 Cod, Cape U.S.A.
210 F4 Codajás Brazil
213 D2 Codera, Cabo *c.* Venez.
128 A7 Codfish Island N.Z.
170 E2 Codigoro Italy
189 H2 Cod Island Canada
171 K2 Codlea Romania
211 J4 Codó Brazil
161 E5 Codsall U.K.
163 A6 Cod's Head Ireland
194 E2 Cody U.S.A.
124 E3 Coen Australia
164 F3 Coesfeld Germany
175 I5 Coëtivy *i.* Seychelles
194 C2 Coeur d'Alene U.S.A.
194 C2 Coeur d'Alene Lake U.S.A.
164 E2 Coevorden Neth.
181 H5 Coffee Bay S. Africa
213 B3 Coffee Cultural Landscape of Colombia *tourist site* Colombia
199 E4 Coffeyville U.S.A.
126 A5 Coffin Bay Australia
126 A5 Coffin Bay Australia
127 J3 Coffs Harbour Australia
181 G6 Cofimvaba S. Africa
190 B4 Coggon U.S.A.
166 D4 Cognac France
176 C4 Cogo Equat. Guinea
202 E3 Cohocton *r.* U.S.A.
203 G3 Cohoes U.S.A.
126 F5 Cohuna Australia
206 I7 Coiba, Isla de *i.* Panama
206 I7 Coiba, Parque Nacional *nat. park* Panama
212 C8 Coig *r.* Arg.
162 C2 Coigeach, Rubha *pt* U.K.
212 B7 Coihaique Chile
143 B4 Coimbatore India
167 B2 Coimbra Port.
167 D4 Coín Spain
210 E7 Coipasa, Salar de *salt flat* Bol.
213 C2 Cojedes *r.* Venez.
206 G5 Cojutepeque El Salvador
194 E3 Cokeville U.S.A.
126 E7 Colac Australia
214 E2 Colatina Brazil
165 J2 Colbitz Germany
198 C4 Colby U.S.A.
210 D7 Colca *r.* Peru
161 H6 Colchester U.K.
190 B5 Colchester U.S.A.
162 F5 Coldingham U.K.
165 K3 Colditz Germany
187 G4 Cold Lake Canada
187 G4 Cold Lake *l.* Canada
162 F5 Coldstream U.K.
199 D4 Coldwater *KS* U.S.A.
190 E5 Coldwater *MI* U.S.A.
190 D1 Coldwell Canada
203 H2 Colebrook U.S.A.
190 E4 Coleman *MI* U.S.A.
199 D6 Coleman *TX* U.S.A.
181 H4 Colenso S. Africa
126 D6 Coleraine Australia
163 E2 Coleraine U.K.
128 C5 Coleridge, Lake N.Z.
127 H9 Coles Bay Australia
180 F5 Colesberg S. Africa
196 B2 Colfax *CA* U.S.A.
194 C2 Colfax *WA* U.S.A.
162 □ Colgrave Sound *str.* U.K.
181 G3 Coligny S. Africa
206 D4 Colima Mex.
206 D4 Colima *state* Mex.
206 D4 Colima, Nevado de *vol.* Mex.
162 B4 Coll *i.* U.K.
167 E2 Collado Villalba Spain
127 H2 Collarenebri Australia
201 C5 College Park U.S.A.
199 D6 College Station U.S.A.
127 G2 Collerina Australia
127 H3 Collie Australia
124 C3 Collier Bay Australia
191 G3 Collingwood Canada
128 D4 Collingwood N.Z.
199 F6 Collins U.S.A.
200 B4 Collinsville U.S.A.
215 B3 Collipulli Chile
163 C3 Collooney Ireland
166 H2 Colmar France
167 E2 Colmenar Viejo Spain
162 D5 Colmonell U.K.
161 H6 Colne *r.* U.K.
127 I4 Colo *r.* Australia
164 F4 Cologne Germany
190 C3 Coloma U.S.A.
214 C3 Colômbia Brazil
207 E2 Colombia Mex.
213 B3 Colombia *country* S. America
219 D5 Colombian Basin *sea feature* S. Atlantic Ocean
143 B5 Colombo Sri Lanka
166 E5 Colomiers France
215 E2 Colón Arg.
215 E2 Colón Arg.
205 H4 Colón Cuba
206 J6 Colón Panama
195 C6 Colonet, Cabo *c.* Mex.
214 E1 Colônia *r.* Brazil
215 D3 Colonia Choele Choel, Isla *i.* Arg.
215 F2 Colonia del Sacramento Uruguay
215 C3 Colonia Emilio Mitre Arg.
215 F1 Colonia Lavalleja Uruguay
202 E6 Colonial Heights U.S.A.
197 F6 Colonia Reforma Mex.
170 G5 Colonna, Capo *c.* Italy
217 M5 Colon Ridge *sea feature* Pacific Ocean
162 B4 Colonsay *i.* U.K.
215 D3 Colorada Grande, Salina *salt pan* Arg.
215 D3 Colorado *r. La Pampa/Río Negro* Arg.
215 C1 Colorado *r. San Juan* Arg.
197 E5 Colorado *r.* Mex./U.S.A.
199 D6 Colorado *r.* U.S.A.
195 F4 Colorado *state* U.S.A.
215 D3 Colorado, Delta del Río Arg.
197 F3 Colorado City *AZ* U.S.A.
199 C5 Colorado City *TX* U.S.A.
196 D5 Colorado Desert U.S.A.
197 H2 Colorado National Monument *nat. park* U.S.A.
197 G3 Colorado Plateau U.S.A.
197 E4 Colorado River Aqueduct *canal* U.S.A.
195 F4 Colorado Springs U.S.A.
206 D3 Colotlán Mex.
165 L1 Cölpin Germany
161 G5 Colsterworth U.K.
161 I5 Coltishall U.K.
196 D4 Colton *CA* U.S.A.
203 F2 Colton *NY* U.S.A.
197 G2 Colton *UT* U.S.A.
194 B2 Columbia *r.* Canada/U.S.A.
202 E5 Columbia *MD* U.S.A.
198 E4 Columbia *MO* U.S.A.
199 F6 Columbia *MS* U.S.A.
202 E4 Columbia *PA* U.S.A.
201 D5 Columbia *SC* U.S.A.
201 C5 Columbia *TN* U.S.A.
185 K1 Columbia, Cape Canada
202 E5 Columbia, District of *admin. dist.* U.S.A.
186 F4 Columbia, Mount Canada
190 E5 Columbia City U.S.A.
203 J2 Columbia Falls *ME* U.S.A.
194 D1 Columbia Falls *MT* U.S.A.
186 F4 Columbia Mountains Canada
194 C2 Columbia Plateau U.S.A.
180 B6 Columbine, Cape S. Africa
201 C5 Columbus *GA* U.S.A.
200 C4 Columbus *IN* U.S.A.
199 F5 Columbus *MS* U.S.A.
194 E2 Columbus *MT* U.S.A.
198 D3 Columbus *NE* U.S.A.
195 F6 Columbus *NM* U.S.A.
202 B5 Columbus *OH* U.S.A.
199 D6 Columbus *TX* U.S.A.
190 C4 Columbus *WI* U.S.A.
190 B5 Columbus Junction U.S.A.
201 F7 Columbus Point Bahamas
196 D2 Columbus Salt Marsh U.S.A.
196 A2 Colusa U.S.A.
128 E2 Colville N.Z.
194 C1 Colville U.S.A.
184 C3 Colville *r.* U.S.A.
128 E2 Colville Channel N.Z.
184 F3 Colville Lake Canada
161 D4 Colwyn Bay U.K.
170 E2 Comacchio Italy
170 E2 Comacchio, Valli di *lag.* Italy
145 G3 Comai China
215 B4 Comallo *r.* Arg.
199 D6 Comanche U.S.A.
129 E2 Comandante Ferraz *research stn* Antarctica
215 C2 Comandante Salas Arg.
169 M7 Comăneşti Romania
206 H5 Comayagua Hond.
215 B1 Combarbalá Chile
163 F3 Comber U.K.
191 I3 Combermere Canada
145 H6 Combermere Bay Myanmar
164 A4 Combles France
181 J1 Combomune Moz.
127 J3 Comboyne Australia
188 E3 Comencho, Lac *l.* Canada
163 D5 Comeragh Mountains *hills* Ireland
199 D6 Comfort U.S.A.
145 G5 Comilla Bangl.
164 A4 Comines Belgium
170 C4 Comino, Capo *c. Sardinia* Italy
207 F4 Comitán de Domínguez Mex.
203 G4 Commack U.S.A.
191 H3 Commanda Canada
185 J3 Committee Bay Canada
129 B6 Commonwealth Bay *b.* Antarctica
170 C2 Como Italy
170 C2 Como, Lake Italy
145 G3 Como Chamling *l.* China
212 C7 Comodoro Rivadavia Arg.
176 B4 Comoé, Parc National de la *nat. park* Côte d'Ivoire
143 B4 Comorin, Cape India
179 E5 Comoros *country* Africa
166 F2 Compiègne France
206 C3 Compostela Mex.
153 C5 Compostela Phil.
214 C4 Comprida, Ilha *i.* Brazil
190 C5 Compton U.S.A.
173 D6 Comrat Moldova
162 E4 Comrie U.K.
199 C6 Comstock U.S.A.
154 C1 Con, Sông *r.* Vietnam
145 H4 Cona China
176 A4 Conakry Guinea
215 C4 Cona Niyeo Arg.
127 G8 Conara Junction Australia
214 C2 Conceição *r.* Brazil
214 E2 Conceição da Barra Brazil
211 I5 Conceição do Araguaia Brazil
212 C3 Concepción Arg.
210 F7 Concepción Bol.
215 B3 Concepción Chile
Concepción Panama *see* La Concepción
212 E2 Concepción Para.
215 E2 Concepción del Uruguay Arg.
196 B4 Conception, Point U.S.A.
189 J4 Conception Bay South Canada
201 F7 Conception Island Bahamas
214 C3 Conchas Brazil
195 F5 Conchas Lake U.S.A.
197 H4 Concho U.S.A.
206 C2 Conchos *r. Chihuahua* Mex.
207 E2 Conchos *r. Tamaulipas* Mex.
196 A3 Concord *CA* U.S.A.
201 D5 Concord *NC* U.S.A.
203 H3 Concord *NH* U.S.A.
129 C6 Concordia *research stn* Antarctica
215 F1 Concordia Arg.
213 B4 Concordia Col.
180 B4 Concordia S. Africa
198 D4 Concordia U.S.A.
139 H5 Concord Peak Afgh.
127 I1 Condamine Australia
154 C3 Côn Đao Vietnam
206 H5 Condega Nicaragua
214 E1 Condeúba Brazil
127 G4 Condobolin Australia
166 E5 Condom France
194 B2 Condon U.S.A.
164 D4 Condroz *reg.* Belgium
201 C6 Conecuh *r.* U.S.A.
170 E2 Conegliano Italy
206 D2 Conejos Mex.
202 D4 Conemaugh *r.* U.S.A.
191 G4 Conestogo Lake Canada
202 E3 Conesus Lake U.S.A.
Coney Island *i.* Sing. *see* Serangoon, Pulau
203 G4 Coney Island U.S.A.
124 F3 Conflict Group *is* P.N.G.
166 E3 Confolens France
197 F2 Confusion Range *mts* U.S.A.
145 F3 Congdü China
149 D6 Conghua China
149 C5 Congjiang China
161 E4 Congleton U.K.
178 B4 Congo *country* Africa
178 B3 Congo *r.* Africa
178 C4 Congo, Democratic Republic of the *country* Africa
219 J6 Congo Cone *sea feature* S. Atlantic Ocean
214 D3 Congonhas Brazil
197 F4 Congress U.S.A.
215 B3 Conguillo, Parque Nacional *nat. park* Chile
161 G4 Coningsby U.K.
188 D4 Coniston Canada
160 D3 Coniston U.K.
187 G3 Conklin Canada
122 B4 Conkouati-Douli, Parc National de *nat. park* Congo
215 D2 Conlara Arg.
215 D2 Conlara *r.* Arg.
163 B3 Conn, Lough *l.* Ireland
202 C4 Conneaut U.S.A.
200 F3 Connecticut *r.* U.S.A.
203 G4 Connecticut *state* U.S.A.
202 D4 Connellsville U.S.A.
163 B4 Connemara *reg.* Ireland
203 I1 Conners Canada
200 C4 Connersville U.S.A.
126 F4 Conoble Australia
Co Nôi Vietnam *see* Yên Châu
203 E5 Conowingo U.S.A.
194 E1 Conrad U.S.A.
219 L9 Conrad Rise *sea feature* Southern Ocean
199 E6 Conroe U.S.A.
214 D3 Conselheiro Lafaiete Brazil
214 E2 Conselheiro Pena Brazil
160 F3 Consett U.K.
154 C3 Côn Sơn, Đao *i.* Vietnam
187 G4 Consort Canada
168 D7 Constance, Lake Germany/Switz.
210 F5 Constância dos Baetas Brazil
171 M2 Constanţa Romania
167 D4 Constantina Spain
176 C1 Constantine Alg.
190 E5 Constantine U.S.A.
197 E6 Constitución de 1857, Parque Nacional *nat. park* Mex.
194 D3 Contact U.S.A.
210 C5 Contamana Peru
214 E1 Contas *r.* Brazil
197 G6 Continental U.S.A.
203 H3 Contoocook *r.* U.S.A.
187 G1 Contwoyto Lake Canada
199 E5 Conway *AR* U.S.A.
203 H3 Conway *NH* U.S.A.
201 E5 Conway *SC* U.S.A.
126 A2 Conway, Lake *salt flat* Australia
161 D4 Conwy U.K.
161 D4 Conwy *r.* U.K.
124 D4 Coober Pedy Australia
190 A2 Cook U.S.A.
186 D4 Cook, Cape Canada
125 G3 Cook, Grand Récif de *rf* New Caledonia
Cook, Mount *mt.* N.Z. *see* Aoraki
201 C4 Cookeville U.S.A.
181 F6 Cookhouse S. Africa
184 C3 Cook Inlet *sea chan.* U.S.A.
123 I5 Cook Islands Pacific Ocean
203 F3 Cooksburg U.S.A.
189 I3 Cook's Harbour Canada
163 E3 Cookstown U.K.
128 E4 Cook Strait N.Z.
124 E3 Cooktown Australia
127 G3 Coolabah Australia
127 H3 Coolah Australia
127 G5 Coolamon Australia
127 J2 Coolangatta Australia
124 C5 Coolgardie Australia
197 G5 Coolidge U.S.A.
197 G5 Coolidge Dam U.S.A.
127 H6 Cooma Australia
163 A6 Coomacarrea *h.* Ireland
126 D4 Coombah Australia
163 B6 Coomnadiha *h.* Ireland
126 C5 Coonalpyn Australia
127 H3 Coonamble Australia
126 D6 Coonawarra Australia
126 A3 Coondambo Australia
127 F1 Coongoola Australia
126 C2 Cooper Creek *watercourse* Australia
127 J3 Coopernook Australia
203 I2 Coopers Mills U.S.A.
201 E7 Cooper's Town Bahamas
198 D2 Cooperstown *ND* U.S.A.
203 F3 Cooperstown *NY* U.S.A.
194 A3 Coos Bay U.S.A.
127 H5 Cootamundra Australia
163 D3 Cootehill Ireland
215 B3 Copahue, Volcán *vol.* Chile
207 F4 Copainalá Mex.
207 E4 Copala Mex.
207 E4 Copalillo Mex.
207 G5 Copán *tourist site* Hond.
194 G4 Cope U.S.A.
159 K5 Copenhagen Denmark
127 I2 Copeton Reservoir Australia
154 C1 Cô Pi, Phou *mt.* Laos/Vietnam
212 B3 Copiapó Chile
212 B3 Copiapo *r.* Chile
126 C3 Copley Australia
170 D2 Copparo Italy
191 G2 Copper Cliff Canada
190 D2 Copper Harbor U.S.A.
Coppermine Canada *see* Kugluktuk
184 G3 Coppermine *r.* Canada
190 E2 Coppermine Point Canada
180 E4 Copperton S. Africa
145 F3 Coqên China
215 B1 Coquimbo Chile
215 B1 Coquimbo *admin. reg.* Chile
171 K3 Corabia Romania
214 D2 Coração de Jesus Brazil
210 D7 Coracora Peru
127 J2 Coraki Australia
124 B4 Coral Bay Australia
201 D7 Coral Gables U.S.A.
185 J3 Coral Harbour Canada
125 F3 Coral Sea Coral Sea Is Terr.
216 F6 Coral Sea Basin S. Pacific Ocean
124 F3 Coral Sea Islands Territory *terr.* Pacific Ocean
190 B5 Coralville Reservoir U.S.A.
126 E7 Corangamite, Lake Australia
211 G3 Corantijn *r.* Suriname
137 L1 Corat Azer.
164 B5 Corbeny France
215 E2 Corbett Arg.
187 K2 Corbett Inlet Canada
164 A5 Corbie France
202 A6 Corbin U.S.A.
161 G5 Corby U.K.
196 C3 Corcoran U.S.A.
212 B6 Corcovado, Golfo de *sea chan.* Chile
206 I6 Corcovado, Parque Nacional *nat. park* Costa Rica
201 D6 Cordele U.S.A.
213 B4 Cordillera de los Picachos, Parque Nacional *nat. park* Col.
153 B4 Cordilleras Range *mts* Phil.
215 C4 Córdoba Arg.
215 D1 Córdoba Arg.
215 D2 Córdoba *prov.* Arg.
206 D2 Córdoba Mex.
207 E4 Córdoba Mex.
167 D4 Córdoba Spain
215 D2 Córdoba, Sierras de *mts* Arg.
184 D3 Cordova U.S.A.
186 C4 Cordova Bay U.S.A.
203 J2 Corea U.S.A.
171 H5 Corfu *i.* Greece

167 C3 Coria Spain
127 I4 Coricudgy mt. Australia
170 G5 Corigliano Calabro Italy
127 F8 Corinna Australia
203 I2 Corinna U.S.A.
187 I4 Corinne Canada
171 J6 Corinth Greece
199 F5 Corinth MS U.S.A.
203 G3 Corinth NY U.S.A.
171 J5 Corinth, Gulf of sea chan. Greece
214 D2 Corinto Brazil
211 G7 Corixa Grande r. Bol./Brazil
214 A2 Corixinha r. Brazil
163 C6 Cork Ireland
170 E6 Corleone Sicily Italy
136 A1 Çorlu Turkey
187 I4 Cormorant Canada
181 H3 Cornelia S. Africa
214 B3 Cornélio Procópio Brazil
190 B3 Cornell U.S.A.
189 I4 Corner Brook Canada
127 G7 Corner Inlet b. Australia
219 F3 Corner Seamounts sea feature N. Atlantic Ocean
164 C5 Cornillet, Mont h. France
196 A2 Corning CA U.S.A.
202 E3 Corning NY U.S.A.
Corn Islands is Nicaragua see Maíz, Islas del
170 E3 Corno Grande mt. Italy
188 F4 Cornwall Canada
185 I2 Cornwallis Island Canada
126 B5 Corny Point Australia
213 C2 Coro Venez.
211 J4 Coroatá Brazil
210 E7 Corocoro Bol.
163 B5 Corofin Ireland
210 E7 Coroico Bol.
214 C2 Coromandel Brazil
135 G5 Coromandel Coast India
128 E2 Coromandel Peninsula N.Z.
128 E2 Coromandel Range hills N.Z.
153 B3 Coron Phil.
126 D3 Corona Australia
196 D5 Corona U.S.A.
196 D5 Coronado U.S.A.
206 I6 Coronado, Bahía de b. Costa Rica
215 B4 Coronados, Golfo de los b. Chile
187 G4 Coronation Canada
184 G3 Coronation Gulf Canada
129 C2 Coronation Island i. S. Atlantic Ocean
186 C3 Coronation Island U.S.A.
153 B4 Coron Bay Phil.
215 E1 Coronda Arg.
215 E2 Coronel Brandsen Arg.
215 E3 Coronel Dorrego Arg.
212 E3 Coronel Oviedo Para.
214 A1 Coronel Ponce Brazil
215 E3 Coronel Pringles Arg.
214 A3 Coronel Sapucaia Brazil
215 E3 Coronel Suárez Arg.
215 F3 Coronel Vidal Arg.
210 D7 Coropuna, Nudo mt. Peru
171 I4 Çorovodë Albania
127 G5 Corowa Australia
207 G4 Corozal Belize
199 D7 Corpus Christi U.S.A.
199 D6 Corpus Christi, Lake U.S.A.
210 E7 Corque Bol.
167 D3 Corral de Cantos mt. Spain
215 C1 Corral de Isaac Arg.
211 I6 Corrente Brazil
214 D1 Corrente r. Bahia Brazil
214 B2 Corrente r. Goiás Brazil
214 C1 Corrente r. Goiás Brazil
214 A2 Correntes Brazil
214 A2 Correntes r. Brazil
214 D1 Correntina Brazil
163 B4 Corrib, Lough l. Ireland
212 E3 Corrientes Arg.
212 E3 Corrientes r. Arg.
215 F3 Corrientes, Cabo c. Arg.
213 A3 Corrientes, Cabo c. Col.
206 C3 Corrientes, Cabo Mex.
199 E6 Corrigan U.S.A.
161 D5 Corris U.K.
202 D4 Corry U.S.A.
127 G6 Corryong Australia
Corse i. France see Corsica
170 C3 Corse, Cap c. Corsica France
161 E6 Corsham U.K.
166 I5 Corsica i. France
199 D5 Corsicana U.S.A.
170 C3 Corte Corsica France
167 C4 Cortegana Spain
197 H3 Cortez U.S.A.
196 D1 Cortez Mountains U.S.A.
170 E1 Cortina d'Ampezzo Italy
203 E3 Cortland U.S.A.
161 I5 Corton U.K.
170 D3 Cortona Italy
167 B3 Coruche Port.
137 H1 Çoruh r. Turkey
136 E1 Çorum Turkey
211 G7 Corumbá Brazil
214 C2 Corumbá r. Brazil
214 C2 Corumbaíba Brazil
213 E3 Corumo r. Venez.
194 B2 Corvallis U.S.A.
161 D5 Corwen U.K.
206 C2 Cosalá Mex.
170 G5 Cosenza Italy
202 C4 Coshocton U.S.A.
166 F3 Cosne-Cours-sur-Loire France
215 D1 Cosquín Arg.
167 F3 Costa Blanca coastal area Spain
167 H2 Costa Brava coastal area France/Spain
167 C4 Costa de la Luz coastal area Spain
167 D4 Costa del Sol coastal area Spain
206 H6 Costa Rica country Central America
206 C2 Costa Rica Mex.
171 K2 Costești Romania
203 I2 Costigan U.S.A.
165 K3 Coswig Germany
153 C5 Cotabato Phil.
213 A4 Cotacachi, Cerro mt. Ecuador
210 E8 Cotagaita Bol.
214 E2 Cotaxé r. Brazil
186 C3 Cote, Mount U.S.A.
176 B4 Côte d'Ivoire country Africa
161 D5 Cothi r. U.K.
167 G1 Cotiella mt. Spain
213 E3 Cotingo r. Brazil
176 C4 Cotonou Benin
210 C4 Cotopaxi, Volcán vol. Ecuador
161 E6 Cotswold Hills U.K.
194 B3 Cottage Grove U.S.A.
168 G5 Cottbus Germany
143 B3 Cotteliar r. India
161 H5 Cottenham U.K.
197 H5 Cotton City U.S.A.
197 F4 Cottonwood U.S.A.
197 G4 Cottonwood Wash watercourse U.S.A.
199 D6 Cotulla U.S.A.
202 D4 Coudersport U.S.A.
126 B6 Couedic, Cape du Australia
129 B5 Coulman Island i. Antarctica
166 F2 Coulommiers France
191 I2 Coulonge r. Canada
196 B3 Coulterville U.S.A.
194 C2 Council U.S.A.
198 E3 Council Bluffs U.S.A.
126 F7 Councillor Island Australia
187 G2 Courageous Lake Canada
159 M5 Courland Lagoon b. Lith./Rus. Fed.
186 E5 Courtenay Canada
163 C6 Courtmacsherry Ireland
163 E5 Courtown Ireland
199 E5 Coushatta U.S.A.
166 D2 Coutances France
188 E2 Couture, Lac l. Canada
164 C4 Couvin Belgium
197 F2 Cove Fort U.S.A.
191 G3 Cove Island Canada
202 E5 Cove Mountains hills U.S.A.
161 F5 Coventry U.K.
203 E5 Cove Point U.S.A.
167 C2 Covilhã Port.
201 D5 Covington GA U.S.A.
190 D5 Covington IN U.S.A.
202 A5 Covington KY U.S.A.
201 B5 Covington TN U.S.A.
202 D6 Covington VA U.S.A.
191 F2 Cow r. Canada
127 G4 Cowal, Lake dry lake Australia
124 C5 Cowan, Lake salt flat Australia
203 G2 Cowansville Canada
162 E4 Cowdenbeath U.K.
126 B4 Cowell Australia
126 F7 Cowes Australia
161 F7 Cowes U.K.
160 E3 Cow Green Reservoir U.K.
202 D5 Cowpasture r. U.S.A.
127 H4 Cowra Australia
214 D1 Coxá r. Brazil
215 F1 Coxilha de Santana hills Brazil/Uruguay
214 A2 Coxim Brazil
214 A2 Coxim r. Brazil
203 G3 Coxsackie U.S.A.
145 H5 Cox's Bazar Bangl.
206 B2 Coyote, Punta pt Mex.
196 D4 Coyote Lake U.S.A.
197 E5 Coyote Peak h. AZ U.S.A.
196 C3 Coyote Peak CA U.S.A.
206 C3 Coyotitán Mex.
207 D4 Coyuca de Benítez Mex.
145 F2 Cozhê China
145 F3 Cozhê China
171 K2 Cozia, Vârful mt. Romania
207 H3 Cozumel Mex.
207 H3 Cozumel, Isla de i. Mex.
127 H4 Craboon Australia
127 G8 Cradle Mountain Australia
127 G8 Cradle Mountain Lake St Clair National Park Australia
126 C3 Cradock Australia
181 F6 Cradock S. Africa
162 C3 Craig U.K.
186 C3 Craig AK U.S.A.
194 F3 Craig CO U.S.A.
163 E3 Craigavon U.K.
126 F6 Craigieburn Australia
202 D5 Craigsville U.S.A.
162 F4 Crail U.K.
165 I5 Crailsheim Germany
171 J2 Craiova Romania
160 F2 Cramlington U.K.
203 F2 Cranberry Lake U.S.A.
203 F2 Cranberry Lake l. U.S.A.
126 F7 Cranbourne Australia
186 F5 Cranbrook Canada
190 C3 Crandon U.S.A.
194 C3 Crane OR U.S.A.
199 C6 Crane TX U.S.A.
190 A1 Crane Lake U.S.A.
203 H4 Cranston U.S.A.
129 B5 Crary Ice Rise ice feature Antarctica
129 B4 Crary Mountains mts Antarctica
194 B3 Crater Lake U.S.A.
194 B3 Crater Lake National Park U.S.A.
194 D3 Craters of the Moon National Monument nat. park U.S.A.
211 J5 Crateús Brazil
211 K5 Crato Brazil
213 C3 Cravo Norte Col.
213 C3 Cravo Sur r. Col.
198 C3 Crawford U.S.A.
190 D5 Crawfordsville U.S.A.
201 C6 Crawfordville U.S.A.
161 G6 Crawley U.K.
194 E2 Crazy Mountains U.S.A.
162 D4 Creag Meagaidh mt. U.K.
187 H4 Crean Lake Canada
161 E5 Credenhill U.K.
161 D7 Crediton U.K.
187 H3 Cree r. Canada
206 C2 Creel Mex.
187 H3 Cree Lake Canada
187 I4 Creighton Canada
164 A5 Creil France
164 D2 Creil Neth.
165 I2 Cremlingen Germany
170 D2 Cremona Italy
166 F2 Crépy-en-Valois France
170 F2 Cres i. Croatia
194 A3 Crescent City U.S.A.
149 □ Crescent Island Hong Kong China
197 H2 Crescent Junction U.S.A.
196 B1 Crescent Mills U.S.A.
197 E4 Crescent Peak U.S.A.
190 A4 Cresco U.S.A.
215 E2 Crespo Arg.
126 E7 Cressy Australia
186 F5 Creston Canada
198 E3 Creston IA U.S.A.
194 F3 Creston WY U.S.A.
201 C6 Crestview U.S.A.
203 F5 Crestwood Village U.S.A.
126 E6 Creswick Australia
171 K7 Crete i. Greece
167 H1 Creus, Cap de c. Spain
166 E3 Creuse r. France
165 J5 Creußen Germany
164 E5 Creutzwald France
165 I3 Creuzburg Germany
161 E4 Crewe U.K.
202 D6 Crewe U.S.A.
161 E7 Crewkerne U.K.
162 D4 Crianlarich U.K.
161 C5 Criccieth U.K.
212 G3 Criciúma Brazil
162 E4 Crieff U.K.
162 E6 Criffel h. U.K.
Criffell hill U.K. see Criffel
170 F2 Crikvenica Croatia
173 E6 Crimea pen. Ukr.
165 K4 Crimmitschau Germany
162 G3 Crimond U.K.
203 F6 Crisfield U.S.A.
214 C2 Cristalina Brazil
213 B2 Cristóbal Colón, Pico mt. Col.
214 C1 Crixás Brazil
214 C1 Crixás Açu r. Brazil
214 B1 Crixás Mirim r. Brazil
171 H3 Crna Gora aut. rep. Europe
170 F2 Črnomelj Slovenia
163 B4 Croagh Patrick h. Ireland
127 H6 Croajingolong National Park Australia
170 F2 Croatia country Europe
155 E2 Crocker, Banjaran mts Malaysia
199 E6 Crockett U.S.A.
203 F3 Croghan U.S.A.
164 A4 Croisilles France
124 D3 Croker Island Australia
162 D3 Cromarty U.K.
162 D3 Cromarty Firth est. U.K.
162 E3 Cromdale, Hills of U.K.
161 I5 Cromer U.K.
128 B6 Cromwell N.Z.
160 F3 Crook U.K.
202 D4 Crooked Creek Reservoir U.S.A.
205 J4 Crooked Island Bahamas
149 □ Crooked Island Hong Kong China
205 J4 Crooked Island Passage Bahamas
190 B1 Crooked Lake Canada/U.S.A.
198 D2 Crookston U.S.A.
127 H5 Crookwell Australia
163 C5 Croom Ireland
127 I2 Croppa Creek Australia
160 D4 Crosby U.K.
187 I5 Crosby U.S.A.
187 K2 Cross Bay Canada
201 D6 Cross City U.S.A.
203 J1 Cross Creek Canada
199 E5 Crossett U.S.A.
160 E3 Cross Fell h. U.K.
163 F3 Crossgar U.K.
163 C6 Crosshaven Ireland
161 C5 Cross Inn U.K.
187 J4 Cross Lake Canada
187 J4 Cross Lake l. Canada
202 E3 Cross Lake l. U.S.A.
128 D5 Crossley, Mount N.Z.
163 E3 Crossmaglen U.K.
197 E4 Crossman Peak U.S.A.
186 B3 Cross Sound sea chan. U.S.A.
190 E3 Cross Village U.S.A.
201 C5 Crossville U.S.A.
191 F4 Croswell U.S.A.
170 G5 Crotone Italy
161 H6 Crouch r. U.K.
127 G3 Crowal watercourse Australia
161 H6 Crowborough U.K.
127 F4 Crowl watercourse Australia
161 G5 Crowland U.K.
199 E6 Crowley U.S.A.
196 C3 Crowley, Lake U.S.A.
190 D5 Crown Point IN U.S.A.
203 G3 Crown Point NY U.S.A.
127 J1 Crows Nest Australia
186 G5 Crowsnest Pass Canada
161 G6 Croydon U.K.
218 H8 Crozet, Îles is Indian Ocean
219 N8 Crozet Basin sea feature Indian Ocean
218 G7 Crozet Plateau sea feature Indian Ocean
184 G2 Crozier Channel Canada
166 B2 Crozon France
213 B4 Cruces, Paso de las mt. Col.
162 G3 Cruden Bay U.K.
207 E2 Cruillas Mex.
163 E3 Crumlin U.K.
163 C5 Crusheen Ireland
205 I5 Cruz, Cabo c. Cuba
212 F3 Cruz Alta Brazil
215 D1 Cruz del Eje Arg.
214 D3 Cruzeiro Brazil
210 D5 Cruzeiro do Sul Brazil
197 H5 Cruzville U.S.A.
186 E3 Crysdale, Mount Canada
126 C4 Crystal Brook Australia
199 D6 Crystal City U.S.A.
190 C2 Crystal Falls U.S.A.
190 C4 Crystal Lake U.S.A.
169 J7 Csongrád Hungary
137 J5 Ctesiphon tourist site Iraq
213 D2 Cúa Venez.
Cửa Lớn r. Vietnam see Cửa Lớn, Sông
154 C3 Cửa Lớn, Sông r. Vietnam
179 C5 Cuando r. Angola/Zambia
179 B5 Cuangar Angola
178 B4 Cuango r. Angola/Dem. Rep. Congo
179 B4 Cuanza r. Angola
213 D3 Cuao r. Venez.
215 F1 Cuaro r. Uruguay
215 D2 Cuarto r. Arg.
206 D2 Cuatro Ciénegas Mex.
206 C1 Cuauhtémoc Mex.
207 E4 Cuautla Mex.
205 I4 Cuba country Caribbean Sea
190 B5 Cuba IL U.S.A.
195 F4 Cuba NM U.S.A.
197 F6 Cubabi, Cerro mt. Mex.
179 B5 Cubal Angola
179 B5 Cubango r. Angola/Namibia
213 B3 Cubara Col.
187 I4 Cub Hills Canada
136 D1 Çubuk Turkey
215 F1 Cuchilla Grande hills Uruguay
215 F1 Cuchilla Grande Inferior hills Uruguay
215 D3 Cuchillo-Có Arg.
213 D3 Cuchivero r. Venez.
202 E6 Cuckoo U.S.A.
213 D4 Cucuí Brazil
213 B3 Cúcuta Col.
143 B4 Cuddalore India
Cuddapah India see Kadapa
187 H4 Cudworth Canada
167 D2 Cuéllar Spain
179 B5 Cuemba Angola
210 C4 Cuenca Ecuador
167 E2 Cuenca Spain
167 E2 Cuenca, Serranía de mts Spain
206 D2 Cuencamé Mex.
207 E4 Cuernavaca Mex.
199 D6 Cuero U.S.A.
196 B4 Cuesta Pass U.S.A.
207 E3 Cuetzalán Mex.
213 C2 Cueva de la Quebrada del Toro, Parque Nacional nat. park Venez.
171 J2 Cugir Romania
211 G5 Cuiabá Brazil
214 A1 Cuiabá Brazil
214 A2 Cuiabá r. Brazil
214 A1 Cuiabá de Larga Brazil
207 E4 Cuicatlan Mex.
164 D3 Cuijk Neth.
207 G5 Cuilapa Guat.
163 D3 Cuilcagh h. Ireland/U.K.
162 B3 Cuillin Hills U.K.
162 B3 Cuillin Sound sea chan. U.K.
179 B4 Cuilo Angola
214 E2 Cuité r. Brazil
179 B5 Cuito r. Angola
179 B5 Cuito Cuanavale Angola
206 D4 Cuitzeo, Laguna de l. Mex.
155 B2 Cukai Malaysia
137 I3 Çukurca Turkey
194 F1 Culbertson MT U.S.A.
198 C3 Culbertson NE U.S.A.
127 G5 Culcairn Australia
167 C2 Culebra, Sierra de la mts Spain
137 J2 Culfa Azer.
127 G2 Culgoa r. Australia
206 C2 Culiacán Mex.
153 A4 Culion Phil.
153 A4 Culion i. Phil.
162 F3 Cullen U.K.
167 F3 Cullera Spain
162 □ Cullivoe U.K.
201 C5 Cullman U.S.A.
137 H2 Çullu Turkey
163 E3 Cullybackey U.K.
162 C2 Cul Mòr h. U.K.
Cul Mor hill U.K. see Cul Mòr
202 D5 Culpeper U.S.A.
211 H6 Culuene r. Brazil
128 D5 Culverden N.Z.
162 D5 Culzean Bay U.K.
213 D2 Cumaná Venez.
213 B4 Cumare, Cerro h. Col.
213 A4 Cumbal, Nevado de vol. Col.
202 D5 Cumberland MD U.S.A.
190 A3 Cumberland WI U.S.A.
200 C4 Cumberland r. U.S.A.
187 I4 Cumberland House Canada
187 I4 Cumberland Lake Canada
202 B6 Cumberland Mountains U.S.A.
185 L3 Cumberland Peninsula Canada
200 C4 Cumberland Plateau U.S.A.
190 C2 Cumberland Point U.S.A.
185 L3 Cumberland Sound sea chan. Canada
162 E5 Cumbernauld U.K.
206 D2 Cumbres de Monterey, Parque Nacional nat. park Mex.
165 J1 Cumlosen Germany
196 A2 Cummings U.S.A.
126 A5 Cummins Australia
127 H4 Cumnock Australia
162 D5 Cumnock U.K.
136 D3 Çumra Turkey
206 B1 Cumuripa Mex.
207 F4 Cunduacán Mex.
207 G5 Cunén Guat.
179 B5 Cunene r. Angola/Namibia alt. Kunene
170 B2 Cuneo Italy
126 A4 Cungena Australia
154 D2 Cung Sơn Vietnam
137 G2 Çüngüş Turkey
127 F2 Cunnamulla Australia
162 □ Cunningsburgh U.K.
213 D4 Cunucunuma r. Venez.
170 B2 Cuorgnè Italy
162 E4 Cupar U.K.
213 A3 Cupica Col.
213 A3 Cupica, Golfo de b. Col.
206 B2 Cupula, Pico mt. Mex.
211 K5 Curaçá Brazil
205 K6 Curaçao terr. West Indies
215 B3 Curacautín Chile
215 D3 Curacó r. Arg.
215 B3 Curanilahue Chile
210 D4 Curaray r. Ecuador
215 B2 Curaumilla, Punta pt Chile
126 B3 Curdlawidny Lagoon salt flat Australia
195 F4 Curecanti National Recreation Area park U.S.A.
215 B2 Curicó Chile
213 D5 Curicuriari, Serra h. Brazil
213 D5 Curieuriari r. Brazil
214 C4 Curitiba Brazil
126 C3 Curnamona Australia
127 I3 Currabubula Australia
211 K5 Currais Novos Brazil
176 □ Curral Velho Cape Verde
191 F3 Curran U.S.A.
163 A6 Currane, Lough l. Ireland
197 E2 Currant U.S.A.
126 F3 Curranyalpa Australia
201 E7 Current Bahamas
127 E7 Currie Australia
197 E1 Currie U.S.A.
127 I5 Currockbilly, Mount Australia
127 G7 Curtis Group is Australia
124 F4 Curtis Island Australia
211 H5 Curuá r. Brazil
211 I4 Curuçá Brazil
155 B3 Curup Indon.
213 D4 Curupira, Serra mts Brazil/Venez.
211 J4 Cururupu Brazil
213 E3 Curutú, Cerro mt. Venez.
214 D2 Curvelo Brazil
210 D6 Cusco Peru
163 E2 Cushendall U.K.
163 E2 Cushendun U.K.
199 D4 Cushing U.S.A.
213 C3 Cusiana r. Col.
206 C1 Cusihuiráchic Mex.
201 C5 Cusseta U.S.A.
190 A1 Cusson U.S.A.
188 E1 Cusson, Pointe pt Canada
194 F2 Custer MT U.S.A.
198 C3 Custer SD U.S.A.
213 A4 Cutanga, Pico de mt. Col.
194 D1 Cut Bank U.S.A.
201 C6 Cuthbert U.S.A.
187 H4 Cut Knife Canada
203 J2 Cutler U.S.A.
201 D7 Cutler Ridge U.S.A.
215 C3 Cutral-Co Arg.
145 F5 Cuttack India
197 G5 Cutter U.S.A.
165 G1 Cuxhaven Germany
202 C4 Cuyahoga Falls U.S.A.
202 C4 Cuyahoga Valley National Park U.S.A.
196 C4 Cuyama r. U.S.A.
153 B3 Cuyapo Phil.
153 B4 Cuyo Phil.
153 B4 Cuyo i. Phil.
153 B4 Cuyo East Passage Phil.
153 B4 Cuyo Islands Phil.
153 B4 Cuyo West Passage Phil.
213 E3 Cuyuni r. Guyana
Cuzco Peru see Cusco
161 D6 Cwmbrân U.K.
Cwmbran U.K. see Cwmbrân
178 C4 Cyangugu Rwanda
171 K6 Cyclades is Greece
127 G9 Cygnet Australia
202 A5 Cynthiana U.S.A.
187 G5 Cypress Hills Canada
136 D4 Cyprus country Asia
187 G4 Czar Canada
168 G6 Czech Republic country Europe
168 H4 Czersk Poland
169 I5 Częstochowa Poland


## D


Đa, Sông r. Vietnam see Black
152 C1 Da'an China
213 C2 Dabajuro Venez.
176 B4 Dabakala Côte d'Ivoire
148 F1 Daban China
148 A2 Daban Shan mts China
148 C3 Daba Shan mts China
213 A3 Dabeiba Col.
165 J1 Dabel Germany
144 C5 Dabhoi India
143 A2 Dabhol India
148 E4 Dabie Shan mts China
144 D4 Daboh India
176 A3 Dabola Guinea
176 B4 Daboya Ghana
148 C2 Dabqig China
144 D4 Dabra India
169 I5 Dąbrowa Górnicza Poland
152 B1 Dabs Nur l. China
149 E5 Dabu China
Dacca Bangl. see Dhaka
168 E6 Dachau Germany
148 A2 Dachechang China
148 F1 Dachengzi China
143 B2 Dachepalle India
191 I3 Dacre Canada
136 D1 Daday Turkey
201 D6 Dade City U.S.A.
144 C5 Dadra India
144 C5 Dadra and Nagar Haveli union terr. India
144 A4 Dadu Pak.
149 B4 Dadu He r. China
Đa Dung r. Vietnam see Dâng, Đa
152 C5 Daecheong-do i. S. Korea
152 E6 Daegu S. Korea
152 C6 Daeheuksan-gundo is S. Korea
152 D5 Daejeon S. Korea
152 D7 Daejeong S. Korea
153 B3 Daet Phil.
149 B5 Dafang China
148 F3 Dafeng China
145 H4 Dafla Hills India
176 A3 Dagana Senegal
173 H7 Dagestan, Respublika aut. rep. Rus. Fed.
Dağlıq Qarabağ terr. Azer. see Nagorno-Karabakh
149 B5 Daguan China
148 F2 Dagu He r. China
149 □ D'Aguilar Peak h. Hong Kong China
153 B2 Dagupan Phil.
145 H1 Dagur China
145 G3 Dagzê China
145 F3 Dagzê Co salt l. China
144 C6 Dahanu India
150 C1 Dahe China
148 D1 Dahei He r. China
152 C2 Dahei Shan mts China
146 D2 Da Hinggan Ling mts China
178 E2 Dahlak Archipelago is Eritrea
178 E2 Dahlak Marine National Park Eritrea
164 E4 Dahlem Germany
165 I1 Dahlenburg Germany
170 C7 Dahmani Tunisia
165 F5 Dahn Germany
144 C5 Dahod India
144 D2 Dahongliutan China
165 I2 Dähre Germany
137 I3 Dahūk Iraq
152 C3 Dahuofang Shuiku resr China
152 B3 Dahushan China
148 D1 Dai Hai l. China
155 B3 Daik Indon.
154 D2 Đai Lanh, Mui pt Vietnam
162 D5 Dailly U.K.
151 C6 Daimanji-san h. Japan
167 E3 Daimiel Spain
215 E3 Daireaux Arg.
190 A2 Dairyland U.S.A.
151 C7 Dai-sen vol. Japan
150 H3 Daisetsu-zan National Park Japan
149 G4 Daishan China
149 F5 Daiyun Shan mts China
124 D4 Dajarra Australia
148 A4 Dajin Chuan r. China
148 B2 Dajing China
145 H1 Da Juh China
176 A3 Dakar Senegal
145 G3 Dakelangsi China
177 E2 Dākhilah, Wāḥāt ad oasis Egypt
145 G5 Dakhin Shahbazpur Island Bangl.
176 A2 Dakhla W. Sahara
Dakhla Oasis oasis Egypt see Dākhilah, Wāḥāt ad
Dak Kon Vietnam see Plei Kân
154 D2 Đắk Lắk, Cao Nguyên plat. Vietnam
172 D4 Dakol'ka r. Belarus
198 D3 Dakota City U.S.A.
Đakovica Serbia see Gjakovë
171 H2 Đakovo Croatia
179 C5 Dala Angola
176 A3 Dalaba Guinea
148 A1 Dalain Hob China
148 E1 Dalai Nur l. China
137 K4 Dālā Khānī, Kūh-e mt. Iraq
140 C4 Dalaki, Rūd-e r. Iran
148 D1 Dalamamiao China
136 B3 Dalaman Turkey
136 B3 Dalaman r. Turkey
146 C2 Dalandzadgad Mongolia
153 B4 Dalanganem Islands Phil.
154 D3 Đa Lat Vietnam
Dalay Mongolia see Bayandalay
141 G4 Dalbandin Pak.
162 E6 Dalbeattie U.K.
127 I1 Dalby Australia
160 C3 Dalby U.K.
159 I3 Dale Norway
159 I3 Dale Norway
202 E5 Dale City U.S.A.
199 G4 Dale Hollow Lake U.S.A.
164 E2 Dalen Neth.
145 H6 Dalet Myanmar
145 H5 Daletme Myanmar
159 K3 Dalfors Sweden
141 E5 Dalgān Iran
127 H6 Dalgety Australia
199 C4 Dalhart U.S.A.
189 G4 Dalhousie Canada
148 D3 Dali Shaanxi China
146 C4 Dali Yunnan China
152 A4 Dalian China
149 B4 Daliang Shan mts China
152 B2 Dalin China
148 F1 Daling He r. China
152 D3 Dalizi China
162 E5 Dalkeith U.K.
145 F4 Dalkola India
203 F4 Dallas PA U.S.A.
199 D5 Dallas TX U.S.A.
190 B5 Dallas City U.S.A.
186 C4 Dall Island U.S.A.
140 D5 Dalmā i. U.A.E.
215 D2 Dalmacio Vélez Sarsfield Arg.
170 G3 Dalmatia reg. Croatia
144 E4 Dalmau India
162 D5 Dalmellington U.K.
150 D2 Dal'negorsk Rus. Fed.
150 C2 Dal'nerechensk Rus. Fed.
176 B4 Daloa Côte d'Ivoire
149 C5 Dalou Shan mts China
140 B5 Dalqān well Saudi Arabia
162 D5 Dalry U.K.
162 D5 Dalrymple U.K.
124 E4 Dalrymple, Lake Australia
124 E4 Dalrymple, Mount Australia
145 F4 Daltenganj India
191 E1 Dalton Canada
181 I4 Dalton S. Africa
201 C5 Dalton GA U.S.A.
203 G3 Dalton MA U.S.A.
160 D3 Dalton-in-Furness U.K.
191 E1 Dalton Mills Canada
163 C5 Dalua r. Ireland
153 B2 Dalupiri i. Phil.
153 C3 Dalupiri i. Phil.
158 C2 Dalvík Iceland
124 D3 Daly r. Australia
196 A3 Daly City U.S.A.
124 D3 Daly Waters Australia
144 C5 Daman India
144 C5 Daman and Diu union terr. India
177 F1 Damanhūr Egypt
140 C3 Damaq Iran
148 E1 Damaqun Shan mts China
153 C6 Damar Indon.
147 E7 Damar i. Indon.
215 B2 Damas, Paso de las pass Arg./Chile
136 F5 Damascus Syria
176 D3 Damaturu Nigeria
140 D3 Damāvand Iran
140 D3 Damāvand, Qolleh-ye mt. Iran
143 C5 Dambulla Sri Lanka
138 F2 Damdy Kazakh.
140 D2 Dāmghān Iran
Damietta Egypt see Dumyāṭ
148 E2 Daming China
149 C6 Daming Shan mt. China
145 H2 Damjong China
153 B5 Dammai i. Phil.
142 D4 Dammam Saudi Arabia
164 B3 Damme Belgium
165 G2 Damme Germany
144 D5 Damoh India
176 B4 Damongo Ghana
136 E5 Damour Lebanon
124 E2 Dampier Strait P.N.G.
147 F7 Dampir, Selat sea chan. Indon.
145 E3 Damqoq Zangbo r. China
145 H2 Dam Qu r. China
154 C3 Dâmrei, Chuŏr Phnum mts Cambodia
145 H3 Damroh India
164 E1 Damwâld Neth.
178 E2 Danakil des. Eritrea
176 B4 Danané Côte d'Ivoire
154 D1 Đa Năng Vietnam
153 C4 Danao Phil.
148 A4 Danba China
203 G4 Danbury CT U.S.A.
203 H3 Danbury NH U.S.A.
203 G3 Danby U.S.A.
197 E4 Danby Lake U.S.A.
148 E3 Dancheng China
178 D3 Dande Eth.
143 A3 Dandeli India
126 F6 Dandenong Australia
152 C3 Dandong China
161 E4 Dane r. U.K.
185 P2 Daneborg Greenland
203 J2 Danforth U.S.A.
154 C3 Dâng, Đa r. Vietnam
149 E6 Dangan Liedao is China
145 G3 Dangbe La pass China
150 B2 Dangbi Rus. Fed.
148 B3 Dangchang China
Danger Islands atoll Cook Is see Pukapuka
180 C7 Danger Point S. Africa
178 D2 Dangila Eth.
145 G3 Dangqên China
207 G4 Dangriga Belize
148 E3 Dangshan China
148 F4 Dangtu China
149 D4 Dangyang China
194 E3 Daniel U.S.A.
180 E4 Daniëlskuil S. Africa
172 G3 Danilov Rus. Fed.
139 G1 Danilovka Kazakh.
173 H5 Danilovka Rus. Fed.
172 G3 Danilovskaya Vozvyshennost' hills Rus. Fed.
148 D2 Daning China
148 D3 Danjiangkou China
148 D3 Danjiangkou Shuiku resr China
140 E6 Ḑank Oman
144 D2 Dankhar India
172 F4 Dankov Rus. Fed.
139 I4 Dan'kova, Pik mt. Kyrg.
206 H5 Danlí Hond.
149 B4 Danling China
203 G2 Dannemora U.S.A.
165 J1 Dannenberg (Elbe) Germany
165 L1 Dannenwalde Germany
128 F4 Dannevirke N.Z.
181 I4 Dannhauser S. Africa
154 B1 Dan Sai Thai.
149 F5 Danshui Taiwan
202 E3 Dansville U.S.A.
144 C4 Danta India
143 C2 Dantewada India
171 L3 Danube r. Europe alt. Donau (Austria/Germany), alt. Duna (Hungary), alt. Dunaj (Slovakia), alt. Dunărea (Romania), alt. Dunav (Serbia)
171 M2 Danube Delta Romania
190 D5 Danville IL U.S.A.
190 D6 Danville IN U.S.A.
200 C4 Danville KY U.S.A.
191 I5 Danville PA U.S.A.
202 D6 Danville VA U.S.A.
148 F4 Danyang China
152 E5 Danyang S. Korea
149 C5 Danzhai China
149 C7 Danzhou China
176 B4 Daoukro Côte d'Ivoire
149 D5 Daoxian China
149 C4 Daozhen China
153 C4 Dapa Phil.
176 C3 Dapaong Togo
Dapeng Wan b. Hong Kong China see Port Shelter
Dapeng Wan b. China see Mirs Bay
145 I4 Dapha Bum mt. India
136 D6 Daphnae tourist site Egypt
153 B4 Dapiak, Mount Phil.
153 B4 Dapitan Phil.
135 H3 Da Qaidam China
146 E2 Daqing China
148 D1 Daqing Shan mts China
152 A2 Daqin Tal China
149 F5 Daqiu China
140 D3 Daqq-e Dombūn Iran
137 J4 Dāqūq Iraq
149 G4 Daqu Shan i. China
136 F5 Dar'ā Syria
140 D4 Dārāb Iran
153 B3 Daraga Phil.
169 N4 Darahanava Belarus
140 D4 Dārākūyeh Iran
153 C4 Daram i. Phil.
140 D3 Darang, Kūh-e h. Iran
Đa Răng, Sông r. Vietnam see Ba, Sông
133 M4 Darasun Rus. Fed.
139 H3 Darat Kazakh.
139 H5 Daraut-Korgon Kyrg.
172 G3 Daravka Rus. Fed.
140 E4 Darband Iran
139 F5 Darband Uzbek.
145 F4 Darbhanga India
196 C2 Dardanelle U.S.A.
199 E5 Dardanelle, Lake U.S.A.
171 L4 Dardanelles str. Turkey
165 I3 Dardesheim Germany
136 F2 Darende Turkey
178 D4 Dar es Salaam Tanz.
170 D2 Darfo Boario Terme Italy
177 E3 Darfur reg. Sudan
144 B2 Dargai Pak.
128 D1 Dargaville N.Z.
127 G6 Dargo Australia
146 C2 Darhan Mongolia
148 D1 Darhan Ul China
201 D6 Darien U.S.A.
213 A2 Darién, Golfo del g. Col.
206 J7 Darién, Parque Nacional de nat. park Panama
206 J6 Darién, Serranía del mts Panama
138 B2 Dar'inskoye Kazakh.
206 H5 Darío Nicaragua
139 H2 Dariya Kazakh.
Darjeeling India see Darjiling
145 G4 Darjiling India
126 B4 Darke Peak Australia
140 C4 Darkhazīneh Iran
126 E4 Darling r. Australia
127 H1 Darling Downs hills Australia
124 B5 Darling Range hills Australia
160 F3 Darlington U.K.
190 B4 Darlington U.S.A.
127 G5 Darlington Point Australia
168 H3 Darłowo Poland
140 B5 Darmā Saudi Arabia
144 E3 Darma Pass China/India
143 B2 Darmaraopet India
140 E4 Dar Mazār Iran
165 G5 Darmstadt Germany
144 C5 Darna r. India
177 E1 Darnah Libya
181 I4 Darnall S. Africa
126 E4 Darnick Australia
129 E5 Darnley, Cape c. Antarctica
184 F3 Darnley Bay Canada
167 F2 Daroca Spain
172 H3 Darovskoy Rus. Fed.
215 D3 Darregueira Arg.
140 E3 Darreh Bīd Iran
141 E2 Darreh Gaz Iran
143 B3 Darsi India
161 D7 Dart r. U.K.
Darta Turkm. see Tarta
161 H6 Dartford U.K.
126 D6 Dartmoor Australia
161 C7 Dartmoor hills U.K.
161 D7 Dartmoor National Park U.K.
189 H5 Dartmouth Canada
161 D7 Dartmouth U.K.
160 F4 Darton U.K.
124 E2 Daru P.N.G.
176 A4 Daru Sierra Leone
145 G3 Darum Tso l. China
170 G2 Daruvar Croatia
Darvaza Turkm. see Içoguz
140 C4 Darvīshī Iran
141 G4 Darwāzahgêy Afgh.
160 E4 Darwen U.K.
124 D3 Darwin Australia
210 □ Darwin, Isla i. Galapagos Is Ecuador
212 C8 Darwin, Monte mt. Chile
144 B3 Darya Khan Pak.
138 F3 Dar'yalyktakyr, Ravnina plain Kazakh.
141 G3 Darz Āb Afgh.
141 E4 Dārzīn Iran
140 D5 Dās i. U.A.E.
152 B3 Dashiqiao China
Dashoguz Turkm. see Daşoguz
140 E2 Dasht Iran
141 F5 Dasht r. Pak.
140 C4 Dasht-e Palang r. Iran
141 F5 Dashtiari Iran
139 G5 Dashtiobburdon Tajik.
139 G4 Dashtobod Uzbek.
148 C2 Dashuikeng China
148 B2 Dashuitou China
144 C2 Daska Pak.
137 K1 Daşkäsän Azer.
141 F2 Daşköpri Turkm.
138 D4 Daşoguz Turkm.
144 C1 Daspar mt. Pak.

165 H3 Dassel Germany
180 C6 Dassen Island S. Africa
137 K2 Dastakert Armenia
140 E3 Dastgerdān Iran
152 F2 Dasuifen He r. China
171 L6 Datça Turkey
150 G3 Date Japan
197 F5 Dateland U.S.A.
144 D4 Datia India
149 E5 Datian China
148 A2 Datong Qinghai China
148 D1 Datong Shanxi China
148 B2 Datong He r. China
148 A2 Datong Shan mts China
155 C2 Datu, Tanjung c. Indon./Malaysia
153 C5 Datu Piang Phil.
172 C3 Daugava r. Belarus/Latvia alt. Zakhodnyaya Dzvina, alt. Zapadnaya Dvina, conv. Western Dvina
159 N5 Daugavpils Latvia
144 C6 Daulatabad India
164 E4 Daun Germany
143 A2 Daund India
154 A2 Daung Kyun i. Myanmar
187 I4 Dauphin Canada
166 G4 Dauphiné reg. France
199 F6 Dauphin Island U.S.A.
187 J4 Dauphin Lake Canada
144 D4 Dausa India
162 E3 Dava U.K.
143 A3 Davangere India
153 C5 Davao Phil.
153 C5 Davao Gulf Phil.
140 E4 Dāvarān Iran
141 F5 Dāvar Panāh Iran
181 H3 Davel S. Africa
196 A3 Davenport CA U.S.A.
190 B5 Davenport IA U.S.A.
161 F5 Daventry U.K.
181 H3 Daveyton S. Africa
206 I6 David Panama
187 H4 Davidson Canada
187 I3 Davin Lake Canada
129 D5 Davis research stn Antarctica
196 B2 Davis U.S.A.
197 E4 Davis Dam U.S.A.
189 H2 Davis Inlet (abandoned) Canada
129 E6 Davis Sea sea Antarctica
185 M3 Davis Strait Canada/Greenland
168 D7 Davos Switz.
152 B3 Dawa China
148 A1 Dawan China
145 F3 Dawaxung China
148 B4 Dawê China
148 E3 Dawen He r. China
142 A4 Dawmat al Jandal Saudi Arabia
154 A1 Dawna Range mts Myanmar/Thai.
142 D6 Dawqah Oman
184 E3 Dawson Canada
201 C6 Dawson GA U.S.A.
198 D2 Dawson ND U.S.A.
187 I4 Dawson Bay Canada
186 E3 Dawson Creek Canada
187 K2 Dawson Inlet Canada
186 B2 Dawson Range mts Canada
148 E4 Dawu Hubei China
146 C3 Dawu Sichuan China
149 F6 Dawu Taiwan
166 D5 Dax France
149 C6 Daxin China
148 E2 Daxing China
149 A4 Da Xueshan mts China
145 H4 Dayang r. India
152 B4 Dayang He r. China
149 D6 Dayao Shan mts China
149 E4 Daye China
149 B4 Dayi China
126 F6 Daylesford Australia
196 D3 Daylight Pass U.S.A.
215 F1 Daymán r. Uruguay
215 F1 Daymán, Cuchilla del hills Uruguay
137 H4 Dayr az Zawr Syria
202 A5 Dayton OH U.S.A.
201 C5 Dayton TN U.S.A.
194 C2 Dayton WA U.S.A.
201 D6 Daytona Beach U.S.A.
149 E5 Dayu China
149 D5 Dayu Ling mts China
194 C2 Dayville U.S.A.
140 C5 Dayyer Iran
148 C4 Dazhou China
149 D7 Dazhou Dao i. China
149 C4 Dazhu China
149 B4 Dazu China
186 B2 Ddhaw Gro Habitat Protection Area nature res. Canada
180 F5 De Aar S. Africa
203 H2 Dead r. ME U.S.A.
190 D2 Dead r. MI U.S.A.
201 F7 Deadman's Cay Bahamas
197 E4 Dead Mountains U.S.A.
136 E6 Dead Sea salt l. Asia
161 I6 Deal U.K.
181 F4 Dealesville S. Africa
186 D4 Dean r. Canada
149 E4 De'an China
161 E6 Dean, Forest of U.K.
215 D1 Deán Funes Arg.
191 F4 Dearborn U.S.A.
141 G4 Dê Arghistān Rōd r. Afgh.
186 D3 Dease r. Canada
186 C3 Dease Lake Canada
184 H3 Dease Strait Canada
196 D3 Death Valley depr. U.S.A.
196 D3 Death Valley Junction U.S.A.
196 D3 Death Valley National Park U.S.A.
166 E2 Deauville France
155 D2 Debak Sarawak Malaysia
149 C6 Debao China
171 I4 Debar Macedonia
187 H4 Debden Canada
161 I5 Debenham U.K.
197 H2 De Beque U.S.A.
164 C3 De Biesbosch, Nationaal Park nat. park Neth.
203 I2 Deblois U.S.A.
178 D3 Debre Birhan Eth.
169 J7 Debrecen Hungary
178 D2 Debre Markos Eth.
178 D2 Debre Tabor Eth.
178 D3 Debre Zeyit Eth.
171 I3 Deçan Kosovo
201 C5 Decatur AL U.S.A.
201 C5 Decatur GA U.S.A.
190 C6 Decatur IL U.S.A.
190 E5 Decatur IN U.S.A.
190 E4 Decatur MI U.S.A.
143 B2 Deccan plat. India
191 H2 Decelles, Lac resr Canada
127 J1 Deception Bay Australia
168 G5 Děčín Czech Rep.
190 B4 Decorah U.S.A.
161 F6 Deddington U.K.
165 I2 Dedeleben Germany
165 I2 Dedelstorf Germany
164 E2 Dedemsvaart Neth.
214 C4 Dedo de Deus mt. Brazil
180 C6 De Doorns S. Africa
137 K1 Dedoplists'q'aro Georgia
176 B3 Dédougou Burkina Faso
172 D3 Dedovichi Rus. Fed.
179 D5 Dedza Malawi
161 D4 Dee est. U.K.
161 E4 Dee r. England/Wales U.K.
162 F3 Dee r. Scotland U.K.
163 C5 Deel r. Ireland
163 D3 Deele r. Ireland
149 □ Deep Bay Hong Kong China
202 D5 Deep Creek Lake U.S.A.
197 F2 Deep Creek Range mts U.S.A.
191 I2 Deep River Canada
203 G4 Deep River U.S.A.
187 J1 Deep Rose Lake Canada
196 D3 Deep Springs U.S.A.
127 I2 Deepwater Australia
202 B5 Deer Creek Lake U.S.A.
203 J2 Deer Island Canada
203 I2 Deer Island U.S.A.
203 I2 Deer Isle U.S.A.
189 I4 Deer Lake Nfld Canada
188 B3 Deer Lake Ont. Canada
188 B3 Deer Lake l. Canada
194 D2 Deer Lodge U.S.A.
212 D2 Defensores del Chaco, Parque Nacional nat. park Para.
202 A4 Defiance U.S.A.
201 C6 De Funiak Springs U.S.A.
146 B3 Dêgê China
178 E3 Degeh Bur Eth.
165 K6 Deggendorf Germany
144 C3 Degh r. Pak.
164 C2 De Goorn Neth.
164 B3 De Haan Belgium
140 D4 Dehaj Iran
141 F4 Dehak Iran
141 F5 Dehak Iran
140 C3 Dehaq Iran
140 C4 Deh-Dasht Iran
140 E4 Deh-e Sard Iran
141 F4 Deh-e Shū Afgh.
140 C2 Dehgāh Iran
140 B3 Deh Golān Iran
143 B5 Dehiwala-Mount Lavinia Sri Lanka
140 D5 Dehkūyeh Iran
140 B3 Dehlorān Iran
139 F5 Dehqonobod Uzbek.
144 D3 Dehra Dun India
145 F4 Dehri India
141 E4 Deh Salm Iran
137 J4 Deh Sheykh Iran
149 F5 Dehua China
152 C1 Dehui China
164 B4 Deinze Belgium
169 K7 Dej Romania
149 C4 Dejiang China
190 C5 De Kalb IL U.S.A.
199 E5 De Kalb TX U.S.A.
203 F2 De Kalb Junction U.S.A.
142 A6 Dekemhare Eritrea
178 C4 Dekese Dem. Rep. Congo
Dekhkanabad Uzbek. see Dehqonobod
164 C1 De Koog Neth.
164 C2 De Kooy Neth.
197 E3 Delamar Lake U.S.A.
196 C4 Delano U.S.A.
197 F2 Delano Peak U.S.A.
123 G2 Delap-Uliga-Djarrit Marshall Is
181 F3 Delareyville S. Africa
187 H4 Delaronde Lake Canada
190 C5 Delavan IL U.S.A.
190 C4 Delavan WI U.S.A.
202 B4 Delaware U.S.A.
203 F4 Delaware r. U.S.A.
203 F5 Delaware state U.S.A.
203 F5 Delaware Bay U.S.A.
202 B4 Delaware Lake U.S.A.
203 F4 Delaware Water Gap National Recreational Area park U.S.A.
165 G3 Delbrück Germany
127 H6 Delegate Australia
168 C7 Delémont Switz.
164 C2 Delft Neth.
143 B4 Delft Island Sri Lanka
164 E1 Delfzijl Neth.
179 E5 Delgado, Cabo c. Moz.
146 C2 Delgerhaan Mongolia
191 G4 Delhi Canada
146 B3 Delhi China
144 D3 Delhi India (City Plan 106)
195 F4 Delhi CO U.S.A.
203 F3 Delhi NY U.S.A.
137 I2 Deli r. Turkey
136 E2 Delice Turkey
136 E1 Delice r. Turkey
140 C3 Delījān Iran
186 E1 Déline Canada
187 H4 Delisle Canada
165 K3 Delitzsch Germany
165 H3 Delligsen Germany
198 D3 Dell Rapids U.S.A.
167 H4 Dellys Alg.
196 D5 Del Mar U.S.A.
165 G1 Delmenhorst Germany
133 Q2 De-Longa, Ostrova is Rus. Fed.
184 B3 De Long Mountains U.S.A.
187 I5 Deloraine Canada
171 J5 Delphi tourist site Greece
190 D5 Delphi U.S.A.
202 A4 Delphos U.S.A.
180 F4 Delportshoop S. Africa
201 D7 Delray Beach U.S.A.
195 E6 Del Río Mex.
199 C6 Del Rio U.S.A.
159 L3 Delsbo Sweden
197 H2 Delta CO U.S.A.
190 A5 Delta IA U.S.A.
197 F2 Delta UT U.S.A.
184 D3 Delta Junction U.S.A.
203 F3 Delta Reservoir U.S.A.
201 D6 Deltona U.S.A.
127 I2 Delungra Australia
163 D4 Delvin Ireland
171 I5 Delvinë Albania
138 C1 Dema r. Rus. Fed.
167 E1 Demanda, Sierra de la mts Spain
178 C4 Demba Dem. Rep. Congo
178 D3 Dembī Dolo Eth.
219 F5 Demerara Abyssal Plain sea feature S. Atlantic Ocean
172 D4 Demidov Rus. Fed.
195 F5 Deming U.S.A.
213 E4 Demini r. Brazil
136 B2 Demirci Turkey
171 L4 Demirköy Turkey
168 F4 Demmin Germany
201 C5 Demopolis U.S.A.
190 D5 Demotte U.S.A.
155 B3 Dempo, Gunung vol. Indon.
144 D2 Dêmqog China/India
141 G3 Dê Mūsá Qal'ah Rōd r. Afgh.
172 H2 Dem'yanovo Rus. Fed.
169 P2 Demyansk Rus. Fed.
180 D5 De Naawte S. Africa
178 E3 Denan Eth.
187 I4 Denare Beach Canada
Denau Uzbek. see Denov
191 I3 Denbigh Canada
161 D4 Denbigh U.K.
164 C1 Den Burg Neth.
154 B1 Den Chai Thai.
155 C3 Dendang Indon.
164 C3 Dendermonde Belgium
Dendron S. Africa see Mogwadi
148 D3 Dengfeng China
148 C1 Dengkou China
145 H3 Dêngqên China
148 D3 Dengzhou China
Den Haag Neth. see The Hague
124 B4 Denham Australia
164 E2 Den Ham Neth.
164 C2 Den Helder Neth.
167 G3 Dénia Spain
126 F5 Deniliquin Australia
194 C3 Denio U.S.A.
198 E3 Denison IA U.S.A.
199 D5 Denison TX U.S.A.
138 E1 Denisovka Kazakh.
136 B3 Denizli Turkey
127 I4 Denman Australia
129 D6 Denman Glacier glacier Antarctica
124 B5 Denmark Australia
159 J4 Denmark country Europe
185 P3 Denmark Strait Greenland/Iceland
197 H3 Dennehotso U.S.A.
203 H4 Dennis Port U.S.A.
162 E4 Denny U.K.
203 J2 Dennysville U.S.A.
139 F5 Denov Uzbek.
155 E4 Denpasar Indon.
203 F5 Denton MD U.S.A.
199 D5 Denton TX U.S.A.
124 B5 D'Entrecasteaux, Point Australia
125 G3 D'Entrecasteaux, Récifs rf New Caledonia
124 F2 D'Entrecasteaux Islands P.N.G.
194 F4 Denver U.S.A.
145 F4 Deo India
144 D3 Deoband India
143 D1 Deogarh India
145 E5 Deogarh mt. India
145 F4 Deoghar India
144 D5 Deori India
145 E4 Deoria India
144 C2 Deosai, Plains of Pak.
145 E5 Deosil India
164 A3 De Panne Belgium
164 D3 De Peel reg. Neth.
190 C3 De Pere U.S.A.
203 F3 Deposit U.S.A.
191 I2 Dépôt-Forbes Canada
191 I2 Dépôt-Rowanton Canada
190 C5 Depue U.S.A.
133 O3 Deputatskiy Rus. Fed.
145 G3 Dêqên China
146 B4 Dêqên China
149 D6 Deqing Guangdong China
149 F4 Deqing Zhejiang China
199 E5 De Queen U.S.A.
144 B3 Dera Bugti Pak.
144 B3 Dera Ghazi Khan Pak.
144 B3 Dera Ismail Khan Pak.
141 H4 Derakht-e Yaḩyá Ghar Afgh.
144 B3 Derawar Fort Pak.
173 I7 Derbent Rus. Fed.
Derbent Uzbek. see Darband
127 G8 Derby Tas. Australia
124 C3 Derby W.A. Australia
161 F5 Derby U.K.
203 G4 Derby CT U.S.A.
199 D4 Derby KS U.S.A.
161 H5 Dereham U.K.
163 D3 Derg r. Ireland/U.K.
163 C5 Derg, Lough l. Ireland
173 I5 Dergachi Rus. Fed.
173 F5 Derhachi Ukr.
199 E6 De Ridder U.S.A.
137 H3 Derik Turkey
136 E2 Derinkuyu Turkey
173 F5 Derkul r. Rus. Fed./Ukr.
180 C1 Derm Namibia
163 D4 Derravaragh, Lough l. Ireland
163 E5 Derry r. Ireland
Derry U.K. see Londonderry
203 H3 Derry U.S.A.
163 C3 Derryveagh Mountains hills Ireland
148 A1 Derstei China
144 D2 Dêrub China
177 F3 Derudeb Sudan
180 E6 De Rust S. Africa
170 G2 Derventa Bos.-Herz.
127 G9 Derwent r. Australia
161 F4 Derwent r. U.K.
160 G4 Derwent r. U.K.
162 G6 Derwent Reservoir U.K.
160 D3 Derwent Water l. U.K.
138 C1 Derzhavino Rus. Fed.
138 F2 Derzhavinsk Kazakh.
215 C2 Desaguadero r. Arg.
210 E7 Desaguadero r. Bol.
123 J5 Désappointement, Îles du is Fr. Polynesia
196 D2 Desatoya Mountains U.S.A.
191 F2 Desbarats Canada
187 I4 Deschambault Lake Canada
187 I3 Deschambault Lake l. Canada
194 B2 Deschutes r. U.S.A.
178 D2 Desē Eth.
212 C7 Deseado Arg.
212 C7 Deseado r. Arg.
197 F1 Deseret Peak U.S.A.
191 I3 Deseronto Canada
144 B3 Desert Canal Pak.
197 E5 Desert Center U.S.A.
186 G3 Desmarais Canada
198 E3 Des Moines IA U.S.A.
195 G4 Des Moines NM U.S.A.
190 A5 Des Moines r. U.S.A.
172 E5 Desna r. Rus. Fed.
173 D5 Desna Ukr.
172 E4 Desnogorsk Rus. Fed.
153 C4 Desolation Point Phil.
190 D4 Des Plaines U.S.A.
165 K3 Dessau Germany
164 B3 Destelbergen Belgium
191 H1 Destor Canada
126 B5 D'Estrees Bay Australia
186 B2 Destruction Bay Canada
208 F4 Desventuradas, Islas is Chile
171 I2 Deta Romania
186 G2 Detah Canada
179 C5 Dete Zimbabwe
165 G3 Detmold Germany
190 D3 Detour, Point U.S.A.
191 F3 De Tour Village U.S.A.
191 F4 Detroit U.S.A.
198 E2 Detroit Lakes U.S.A.
127 H5 Deua National Park Australia
165 K3 Deuben Germany
164 D3 Deurne Neth.
170 F1 Deutschlandsberg Austria
165 K3 Deutzen Germany
191 H2 Deux-Rivières Canada
171 J2 Deva Romania
143 B2 Devarkonda India
136 E2 Develi Turkey
164 E2 Deventer Neth.
168 H6 Devét skal h. Czech Rep.
144 B4 Devikot India
163 D5 Devil's Bit Mountain h. Ireland
161 D5 Devil's Bridge U.K.
196 C4 Devils Den U.S.A.
196 C2 Devils Gate pass U.S.A.
190 B2 Devils Island U.S.A.
198 D1 Devils Lake U.S.A.
196 C3 Devils Peak U.S.A.
201 F7 Devil's Point Bahamas
196 C3 Devils Postpile National Monument nat. park U.S.A.
161 F6 Devizes U.K.
144 C4 Devli India
171 L3 Devnya Bulg.
186 G4 Devon Canada
161 G5 Devon r. U.K.
185 I2 Devon Island Canada
127 G8 Devonport Australia
136 C1 Devrek Turkey
136 D1 Devrekâni Turkey
136 E1 Devrez r. Turkey
143 A2 Devrukh India
155 A2 Dewa, Tanjung pt Indon.
144 D5 Dewas India
164 E2 De Weerribben, Nationaal Park nat. park Neth.
181 G4 Dewetsdorp S. Africa
202 B6 Dewey Lake U.S.A.
199 F5 De Witt AR U.S.A.
190 B5 De Witt IA U.S.A.
160 F4 Dewsbury U.K.
149 E4 Dexing China
203 I2 Dexter ME U.S.A.
199 F4 Dexter MO U.S.A.
203 E2 Dexter NY U.S.A.
148 B4 Deyang China
140 E3 Deyhūk Iran
137 L3 Deylaman Iran
141 E3 Deym Iran
124 D2 Deyong, Tanjung pt Indon.
137 L6 Dez r. Iran
137 L5 Dez, Sadd-e resr Iran
140 C3 Dezfūl Iran
148 E2 Dezhou China
140 B5 Dhahlān, Jabal h. Saudi Arabia
142 D4 Dhahran Saudi Arabia
145 G5 Dhaka Bangl.
145 G5 Dhaleswari r. Bangl.
145 H4 Dhaleswari r. India
142 B7 Dhamār Yemen
145 F5 Dhamara India
144 C5 Dhamnod India
143 C1 Dhamtari India
144 B3 Dhana Sar Pak.
145 F5 Dhanbad India
144 C5 Dhandhuka India
145 E3 Dhang Range mts Nepal
144 C5 Dhar India
144 D2 Dharamsala India
145 F4 Dharan Nepal
143 B4 Dharapuram India
144 B5 Dhari India
143 B3 Dharmapuri India
143 B3 Dharmavaram India
143 A3 Dharwad India
144 D4 Dhasan r. India
145 E3 Dhaulagiri I mt. Nepal
Dhaulpur India see Dholpur
Dhebar Lake l. India see Jaisamand Lake
145 H4 Dhekiajuli India
136 E6 Dhībān Jordan
145 H4 Dhing India
144 D4 Dholpur India
143 B3 Dhone India
144 B5 Dhoraji India
144 B5 Dhrangadhra India
144 C5 Dhule India
145 F4 Dhulian India
145 F4 Dhunche Nepal
144 D4 Dhund r. India
178 E3 Dhuusa Marreeb Somalia
171 K7 Dia i. Greece
196 B3 Diablo, Mount U.S.A.
204 A2 Diablo, Picacho del mt. Mex.
196 B3 Diablo Range mts U.S.A.
215 E2 Diamante Arg.
215 C2 Diamante r. Arg.
124 D4 Diamantina watercourse Australia
214 D2 Diamantina Brazil
211 J6 Diamantina, Chapada plat. Brazil
218 K7 Diamantina Deep sea feature Indian Ocean
214 A1 Diamantino Brazil
196 □1 Diamond Head U.S.A.
197 E2 Diamond Peak U.S.A.
149 D6 Dianbai China
149 B5 Dian Chi l. China
149 C4 Dianjiang China
211 I6 Dianópolis Brazil
176 B4 Dianra Côte d'Ivoire
152 B2 Diaobingshan China
150 B2 Diaoling China
176 C3 Diapaga Burkina Faso
141 E6 Ḍibab Oman
145 H4 Dibang r. India
178 C4 Dibaya Dem. Rep. Congo
180 E3 Dibeng S. Africa
181 G1 Dibete Botswana
145 H4 Dibrugarh India
199 C5 Dickens U.S.A.
203 I1 Dickey U.S.A.
198 C2 Dickinson U.S.A.
201 C4 Dickson U.S.A.
203 F4 Dickson City U.S.A.
137 H3 Dicle r. Turkey alt. Dijlah, Nahr (Iraq/Syria), conv. Tigris
153 B2 Didicas i. Phil.
144 C4 Didwana India
171 L4 Didymoteicho Greece
166 G4 Die France
164 F4 Dieblich Germany
176 B3 Diébougou Burkina Faso
165 G5 Dieburg Germany
187 H4 Diefenbaker, Lake Canada
218 I5 Diego Garcia atoll British Indian Ocean Terr.
164 E5 Diekirch Lux.
176 B3 Diéma Mali
165 H3 Diemel r. Germany
149 B6 Điên Biên Phu Vietnam
154 C1 Diên Châu Vietnam
154 D2 Diên Khanh Vietnam
165 G2 Diepholz Germany
166 E2 Dieppe France
164 D3 Diessen Neth.
164 D4 Diest Belgium
168 D7 Dietikon Switz.
165 G4 Diez Germany
177 D3 Diffa Niger
143 D2 Digapahandi India
189 G5 Digby Canada
145 F5 Digha India
166 H4 Digne-les-Bains France
166 F3 Digoin France
153 C5 Digos Phil.
144 D5 Digras India
144 B4 Digri Pak.
147 F7 Digul r. Indon.
176 B4 Digya National Park Ghana
145 G4 Dihang r. Asia alt. Yarlung Zangbo (China), conv. Brahmaputra
138 E3 Diirmentobe Kazakh.
137 J5 Dijlah, Nahr r. Iraq/Syria alt. Dicle (Turkey), conv. Tigris
166 G3 Dijon France
178 E2 Dikhil Djibouti
171 L5 Dikili Turkey
164 A3 Diksmuide Belgium
132 J2 Dikson Rus. Fed.
177 D3 Dikwa Nigeria
178 D3 Dīla Eth.
141 F3 Dilārām Afgh.
141 E4 Dilaram Iran
124 C2 Dili East Timor
137 J1 Dilijan Armenia
154 D3 Di Linh Vietnam
165 G4 Dillenburg Germany
199 D6 Dilley U.S.A.
168 E6 Dillingen an der Donau Germany
164 E5 Dillingen (Saar) Germany
184 C4 Dillingham U.S.A.
187 H3 Dillon Canada
194 D2 Dillon MT U.S.A.
201 E5 Dillon SC U.S.A.
179 C5 Dilolo Dem. Rep. Congo
164 D3 Dilsen Belgium
137 J5 Diltāwa Iraq
145 H4 Dimapur India
Dimashq Syria see Damascus
178 C4 Dimbelenge Dem. Rep. Congo
176 B4 Dimbokro Côte d'Ivoire
126 E6 Dimboola Australia
171 K3 Dimitrovgrad Bulg.
172 I4 Dimitrovgrad Rus. Fed.
136 E6 Dimona Israel
180 D2 Dimpho Pan salt pan Botswana
153 C4 Dinagat i. Phil.
145 G4 Dinajpur Bangl.
166 C2 Dinan France
144 C2 Dinanagar India
164 C4 Dinant Belgium
145 F4 Dinapur India
136 C2 Dinar Turkey
140 C4 Dīnār, Kūh-e mt. Iran
Dinara Planina mts Croatia see Dinaric Alps
170 G2 Dinaric Alps mts Croatia
177 F3 Dinder National Park Sudan
143 B4 Dindigul India
181 J1 Dindiza Moz.
144 E5 Dindori India
136 D3 Dinek Turkey
148 C2 Dingbian China
178 B4 Dinge Angola
165 I3 Dingelstädt Germany
145 F3 Dinggyê China
145 F4 Dingla Nepal
Dingle Ireland see An Daingean
163 A5 Dingle Bay Ireland
149 E5 Dingnan China
153 B2 Dingras Phil.
148 E3 Dingtao China
176 A3 Dinguiraye Guinea
162 D3 Dingwall U.K.
148 B3 Dingxi China
148 E2 Dingxing China
148 E3 Dingyuan China
148 E2 Dingzhou China
148 F2 Dingzi Gang b. China
149 C6 Dinh Lâp Vietnam
165 I5 Dinkelsbühl Germany
197 G3 Dinnebito Wash watercourse U.S.A.
181 G1 Dinokwe Botswana
187 K5 Dinorwic U.S.A.
197 H1 Dinosaur U.S.A.
194 E3 Dinosaur National Monument nat. park U.S.A.
164 E3 Dinslaken Germany
176 B3 Dioïla Mali
214 B4 Dionísio Cerqueira Brazil
176 A3 Diourbel Senegal
144 E3 Dipayal Nepal
145 H4 Diphu India
144 B4 Diplo Pak.
153 B4 Dipolog Phil.
128 B6 Dipton N.Z.
136 F2 Dirckli Turkey
176 B3 Diré Mali
124 E3 Direction, Cape Australia
178 E3 Dirē Dawa Eth.
179 C5 Dirico Angola
176 D1 Dirj Libya
124 B4 Dirk Hartog Island Australia
127 H2 Dirranbandi Australia
137 L6 Dīrsīyeh Iran
197 G2 Dirty Devil r. U.S.A.
144 C4 Disa India
194 A2 Disappointment, Cape U.S.A.
124 C4 Disappointment, Lake salt flat Australia
127 H6 Disaster Bay Australia
126 D7 Discovery Bay Australia
149 □ Discovery Bay Hong Kong China
219 J8 Discovery Seamounts sea feature S. Atlantic Ocean
Disko i. Greenland see Qeqertarsuaq
203 E6 Dismal Swamp U.S.A.
145 G4 Dispur India
161 I5 Diss U.K.
214 C1 Distrito Federal admin. dist. Brazil
136 C6 Disūq Egypt
153 B4 Dit i. Phil.
180 E4 Ditloung S. Africa
170 F6 Dittaino r. Sicily Italy
153 C4 Diuata Mountains Phil.
153 C4 Diuata Point Phil.
140 B3 Dīvān Darreh Iran
172 G4 Diveyevo Rus. Fed.
153 B2 Divilican Bay Phil.
214 D3 Divinópolis Brazil
173 G6 Divnoye Rus. Fed.
176 B4 Divo Côte d'Ivoire
136 G2 Divriği Turkey
141 G5 Diwana Pak.
203 H2 Dixfield U.S.A.
203 I2 Dixmont U.S.A.
196 B2 Dixon CA U.S.A.
190 C5 Dixon IL U.S.A.
186 C4 Dixon Entrance sea chan. Canada/U.S.A.
201 F7 Dixon's Bahamas
186 F3 Dixonville Canada
203 H2 Dixville Canada
137 I2 Diyadin Turkey
137 J5 Diyālá, Nahr r. Iraq
137 H3 Diyarbakır Turkey
144 B4 Diyodar India
140 D3 Diz Chah Iran
177 D2 Djado Niger
177 D2 Djado, Plateau du Niger
178 B4 Djambala Congo
176 C2 Djanet Alg.
176 C1 Djelfa Alg.
178 C3 Djéma Cent. Afr. Rep.
176 B3 Djenné Mali
176 B3 Djibo Burkina Faso
178 E2 Djibouti country Africa
178 E2 Djibouti Djibouti
163 E4 Djouce Mountain h. Ireland
176 C4 Djougou Benin
177 D3 Djourab, Erg du des. Chad
158 D2 Djúpivogur Iceland
159 K3 Djurås Sweden
137 J1 Dmanisi Georgia
133 P2 Dmitriya Lapteva, Proliv sea chan. Rus. Fed.
150 C2 Dmitriyevka Primorskiy Kray Rus. Fed.
139 K1 Dmitriyevka Respublika Altay Rus. Fed.
172 G4 Dmitriyevka Tambovskaya Oblast' Rus. Fed.
173 E4 Dmitriyev-L'govskiy Rus. Fed.
172 F3 Dmitrov Rus. Fed.
173 E6 Dnepr r. Rus. Fed. alt. Dnipro (Ukraine), alt. Dnyapro (Belarus), conv. Dnieper
169 O6 Dnieper r. Europe alt. Dnepr (Rus. Fed.), alt. Dnipro (Ukraine), alt. Dnyapro (Belarus)
169 M6 Dniester r. Europe alt. Dnister (Ukraine), alt. Nistru (Moldova)
169 O6 Dnipro r. Ukr. alt. Dnepr (Rus. Fed.), alt. Dnyapro (Belarus), conv. Dnieper
173 E5 Dniprodzerzhyns'k Ukr.
173 E5 Dnipropetrovs'k Ukr.
173 E6 Dniprorudne Ukr.
169 M6 Dnister r. Ukr. alt. Nistru (Moldova), conv. Dniester
172 D3 Dno Rus. Fed.
169 O4 Dnyapro r. Belarus alt. Dnepr (Rus. Fed.), alt. Dnipro (Ukraine), conv. Dnieper
177 D4 Doba Chad
191 G3 Dobbinton Canada
159 M4 Dobele Latvia
165 L3 Döbeln Germany
147 F7 Doberai, Jazirah pen. Indon.
215 D3 Doblas Arg.
147 F7 Dobo Indon.
171 H2 Doboj Bos.-Herz.
165 J4 Döbraberg h. Germany
171 L3 Dobrich Bulg.
173 G4 Dobrinka Rus. Fed.
171 M2 Dobruja reg. Romania
173 D4 Dobrush Belarus
139 J4 Dobyn Kazakh.
153 A5 Doc Can rf Phil.
214 E2 Doce r. Brazil
161 H5 Docking U.K.
207 D3 Doctor Arroyo Mex.
206 C1 Doctor Belisario Domínguez Mex.
212 D2 Doctor Pedro P. Peña Para.
143 B3 Dod Ballapur India
171 L6 Dodecanese is Greece
Dodekanisa is Greece see Dodecanese
194 C2 Dodge U.S.A.
190 A3 Dodge Center U.S.A.
199 C4 Dodge City U.S.A.
127 G9 Dodges Ferry Australia
190 B4 Dodgeville U.S.A.
161 C7 Dodman Point U.K.
178 D4 Dodoma Tanz.
164 E3 Doetinchem Neth.
147 E7 Dofa Indon.
145 G2 Dogai Coring salt l. China
145 G2 Dogaicoring Qangco salt l. China
136 F2 Doğanşehir Turkey
186 E4 Dog Creek Canada
145 G3 Dogên Co l. China
189 H2 Dog Island Canada
187 J4 Dog Lake Canada
191 E1 Dog Lake Canada
151 C6 Dōgo i. Japan
139 F5 D'og'ob Uzbek.
176 C3 Dogondoutchi Niger
151 C7 Dōgo-yama mt. Japan
137 J2 Doğubeyazıt Turkey
145 F3 Dogxung Zangbo r. China
145 G3 Do'gyaling China
140 C5 Doha Qatar
145 H5 Dohazari Bangl.
145 G3 Doilungdêqên China
154 A1 Doi Saket Thai.
211 J5 Dois Irmãos, Serra dos hills Brazil
171 J4 Dojran, Lake Greece/Macedonia
137 J4 Dokan, Sadd Iraq
159 J3 Dokka Norway
164 E1 Dokkum Neth.
144 B4 Dokri Pak.
169 M3 Dokshytsy Belarus
173 F6 Dokuchayevs'k Ukr.
189 F4 Dolbeau-Mistassini Canada
161 C5 Dolbenmaen U.K.
166 D2 Dol-de-Bretagne France
166 G3 Dole France
161 D5 Dolgellau U.K.
165 L1 Dolgen Germany
203 F3 Dolgeville U.S.A.
173 F4 Dolgorukovo Rus. Fed.
173 F4 Dolgoye Rus. Fed.
170 C5 Dolianova Sardinia Italy
146 G2 Dolinsk Rus. Fed.
Dolisie Congo see Loubomo
165 J6 Dollnstein Germany
139 G1 Dolmatovo Kazakh.
147 F7 Dolok, Pulau i. Indon.
170 D1 Dolomites mts Italy
Dolonnur China see Duolun
178 E3 Dolo Odo Eth.
215 F3 Dolores Arg.
207 G4 Dolores Guat.
206 B2 Dolores Mex.
215 E2 Dolores Uruguay
197 H2 Dolores r. U.S.A.
206 D3 Dolores Hidalgo Mex.
184 G3 Dolphin and Union Strait Canada
152 D6 Dolsan-do i. S. Korea
149 B7 Đô Lương Vietnam
173 B5 Dolyna Ukr.
136 B2 Domaniç Turkey
144 E2 Domar China
145 H3 Domartang China
168 F6 Domažlice Czech Rep.
145 H2 Domba China
140 B3 Dom Bākh Iran
138 D2 Dombarovskiy Rus. Fed.
159 J3 Dombås Norway
168 I7 Dombóvár Hungary
Dome Circe ice feature Antarctica see Charlie, Dome
186 E4 Dome Creek Canada
129 D4 Dome Fuji research stn Antarctica
186 D2 Dome Peak Canada
197 E5 Dome Rock Mountains U.S.A.
166 D2 Domfront France
205 L5 Dominica country Caribbean Sea
206 I6 Dominical Costa Rica
205 J5 Dominican Republic country Caribbean Sea
165 J1 Dömitz Germany
154 C2 Dom Noi, Lam r. Thai.
170 C1 Domodossola Italy
171 J5 Domokos Greece
215 F1 Dom Pedrito Brazil
155 E4 Dompu Indon.
215 B3 Domuyo, Volcán vol. Arg.
127 I2 Domville, Mount h. Australia
143 B2 Don r. India
206 B2 Don Mex.
173 G5 Don r. Rus. Fed.
162 F3 Don r. U.K.
154 C2 Don, Xé r. Laos
163 F3 Donaghadee U.K.
163 E3 Donaghmore U.K.
126 E6 Donald Australia
168 G6 Donau r. Austria/Germany alt. Duna (Hungary), alt. Dunaj (Slovakia), alt. Dunărea (Romania), alt. Dunav (Serbia), conv. Danube
168 D7 Donaueschingen Germany
168 E6 Donauwörth Germany
167 D3 Don Benito Spain
160 F4 Doncaster U.K.
179 B4 Dondo Angola
179 D5 Dondo Moz.
153 B4 Dondonay i. Phil.
143 C5 Dondra Head Sri Lanka
163 C3 Donegal Ireland
163 C3 Donegal Bay Ireland
139 J2 Donenbay Kazakh.
173 F6 Donets'k Ukr.
173 F5 Donets'kyy Kryazh hills Rus. Fed./Ukr.
149 D5 Dong'an China
124 B4 Dongara Australia
144 E5 Dongargarh India
146 E2 Dongbei reg. China
149 B5 Dongchuan China
145 F2 Dongco China
152 D5 Dongducheon S. Korea
149 C7 Dongfang China
150 C1 Dongfanghong China
152 C2 Dongfeng China
155 E3 Donggala Indon.
148 F3 Donggang China
152 C4 Donggang China
Donggar China see Doilungdêqên
149 E5 Donggu China
149 D6 Dongguan China
154 C1 Đông Ha Vietnam
152 E5 Donghae S. Korea
148 F3 Donghai China
149 D6 Donghai Dao i. China
152 C1 Dong Haxat China
148 C3 Dong He r. China
154 C1 Đông Hơi Vietnam
148 B2 Donghu China
152 E1 Dongjingcheng China
145 H3 Dongjug Xizang China
145 H3 Dongjug Xizang China
149 D5 Dongkou China
145 G4 Dongkya La pass India
149 C5 Donglan China
148 A2 Dongle China
152 C2 Dongliao He r. China
152 B1 Dongminzhutun China
152 E6 Dongnae S. Korea
152 F2 Dongning China
179 B5 Dongo Angola
177 F3 Dongola Sudan
178 B3 Dongou Congo
154 B2 Dong Phraya Yen esc. Thai.
149 D6 Dongping Guangdong China
Dongping China see Zhoucheng
145 G3 Dongqiao China
149 E6 Dongshan China
149 E6 Dongshan Dao i. China
148 D2 Dongsheng China
148 F3 Dongtai China
148 F3 Dongtai He r. China
149 D4 Dongting Hu l. China
149 F5 Dongtou China
148 B3 Dongxiang China
149 E4 Dongxiang China
154 C3 Đông Xoai Vietnam
149 F4 Dongyang China
148 F2 Dongying China
149 E4 Dongzhi China
186 B2 Donjek r. Canada
164 E1 Donkerbroek Neth.
145 G5 Donmanick Islands Bangl.
189 F4 Donnacona Canada

186 F3 Donnelly Canada
128 D1 Donnellys Crossing N.Z.
196 B2 Donner Pass U.S.A.
Donostia Spain see San Sebastián
171 K6 Donousa i. Greece
172 F4 Donskoy Rus. Fed.
173 G6 Donskoye Rus. Fed.
153 B3 Donsol Phil.
138 D3 Donyztau, Sor dry lake Kazakh.
163 A4 Dooagh Ireland
162 D5 Doon, Loch l. U.K.
163 B5 Doonbeg r. Ireland
164 D2 Doorn Neth.
190 D3 Door Peninsula U.S.A.
164 D3 Doorwerth Neth.
199 C5 Dora U.S.A.
170 C2 Dora Baltea r. Italy
140 C5 Do Rāhak Iran
141 G4 Dōray r. Afgh.
161 E7 Dorchester U.K.
179 B6 Dordabis Namibia
166 E4 Dordogne r. France
164 C3 Dordrecht Neth.
181 G5 Dordrecht S. Africa
180 C1 Doreenville Namibia
187 H4 Doré Lake Canada
187 H4 Doré Lake l. Canada
170 C4 Dorgali Sardinia Italy
145 H2 Dorgê Co l. China
176 B3 Dori Burkina Faso
180 C5 Doring r. S. Africa
161 G6 Dorking U.K.
164 E3 Dormagen Germany
164 B5 Dormans France
162 D3 Dornoch Firth est. U.K.
148 C1 Dornogovĭ prov. Mongolia
164 F1 Dornum Germany
172 E4 Dorogobuzh Rus. Fed.
141 F3 Doroḩ Iran
169 M7 Dorohoi Romania
146 B2 Döröö Nuur salt l. Mongolia
158 L2 Dorotea Sweden
124 B4 Dorre Island Australia
127 J3 Dorrigo Australia
194 B3 Dorris U.S.A.
191 H3 Dorset Canada
161 D7 Dorset and East Devon Coast tourist site U.K.
164 F3 Dortmund Germany
202 B6 Dorton U.S.A.
136 F3 Dörtyol Turkey
140 C3 Dorūd Iran
165 G1 Dorum Germany
178 C3 Doruma Dem. Rep. Congo
140 E3 Dorūneh Iran
165 H2 Dörverden Germany
141 E4 Do Sārī Iran
212 C6 Dos Bahías, Cabo c. Arg.
197 H5 Dos Cabezas U.S.A.
210 C5 Dos de Mayo Peru
149 C6 Đô Sơn Vietnam
Đo Son Vietnam see Đô Sơn
196 B3 Dos Palos U.S.A.
165 K2 Dosse r. Germany
176 C3 Dosso Niger
138 C3 Dossor Kazakh.
139 G4 Do'stlik Uzbek.
139 J3 Dostyk Kazakh.
201 C6 Dothan U.S.A.
166 F1 Douai France
176 C4 Douala Cameroon
166 B2 Douarnenez France
149 □ Double Island Hong Kong China
196 C4 Double Peak U.S.A.
166 H3 Doubs r. France
128 A6 Doubtful Sound inlet N.Z.
128 D1 Doubtless Bay N.Z.
176 B3 Douentza Mali
160 C3 Douglas Isle of Man
180 E4 Douglas S. Africa
162 E5 Douglas U.K.
186 C3 Douglas AK U.S.A.
197 H6 Douglas AZ U.S.A.
201 D6 Douglas GA U.S.A.
194 F3 Douglas WY U.S.A.
127 H8 Douglas Apsley National Park Australia
186 D4 Douglas Channel Canada
197 H2 Douglas Creek r. U.S.A.
149 F6 Douliu Taiwan
166 F1 Doullens France
162 D4 Doune U.K.
214 C2 Dourada, Cachoeira waterfall Brazil
214 B2 Dourada, Serra hills Brazil
214 C1 Dourada, Serra mts Brazil
214 A3 Dourados Brazil
214 A3 Dourados r. Brazil
214 B3 Dourados, Serra dos hills Brazil
167 C2 Douro r. Port. alt. Duero (Spain)
164 D5 Douzy France
161 F4 Dove r. England U.K.
161 I5 Dove r. England U.K.
189 I3 Dove Brook Canada
197 H3 Dove Creek U.S.A.
127 G9 Dover Australia
161 I6 Dover U.K.
203 F5 Dover DE U.S.A.
203 H3 Dover NH U.S.A.
203 F4 Dover NJ U.S.A.
202 C4 Dover OH U.S.A.
161 I7 Dover, Strait of France/U.K.
203 I2 Dover-Foxcroft U.S.A.
161 D5 Dovey r. U.K.
140 B3 Doveyrich r. Iran/Iraq
190 D5 Dowagiac U.S.A.
140 D4 Dow Chāhī Iran
141 E2 Dowghā'ī Iran
154 A5 Dowi, Tanjung pt Indon.
141 F3 Dowlatābād Afgh.
141 G2 Dowlātābād Afgh.
141 G2 Dowlatābād Afgh.
140 D4 Dowlatābād Iran
140 D4 Dowlatābād Iran
140 E4 Dowlatābād Iran
141 F2 Dowlatābād Iran
141 G3 Dowlat Yār Afgh.
196 B2 Downieville U.S.A.
163 F3 Downpatrick U.K.
203 F3 Downsville U.S.A.
137 K4 Dow Sar Iran
141 H3 Dowshī Afgh.
196 B1 Doyle U.S.A.
203 F4 Doylestown U.S.A.
151 C6 Dōzen is Japan
191 I2 Dozois, Réservoir resr Canada
176 B2 Drâa, Hamada du plat. Alg.
214 B3 Dracena Brazil
164 E1 Drachten Neth.
171 K2 Drăgănești-Olt Romania
171 K2 Drăgășani Romania
213 E2 Dragon's Mouths str. Trin. and Tob./Venez.
159 M3 Dragsfjärd Fin.
166 H5 Draguignan France
173 C4 Drahichyn Belarus
127 J2 Drake Australia
197 F4 Drake AZ U.S.A.
187 I5 Drake ND U.S.A.
181 H5 Drakensberg mts Lesotho/S. Africa
181 I2 Drakensberg mts S. Africa
219 E9 Drake Passage sea chan. S. Atlantic Ocean
171 K4 Drama Greece
159 J4 Drammen Norway
159 J4 Drangedal Norway
141 G5 Drangjuk h. Pak.
165 H3 Dransfeld Germany
163 E3 Draperstown U.K.
144 C2 Dras India
168 F7 Drau r. Austria
186 G4 Drayton Valley Canada
170 B6 Dréan Alg.
165 H4 Dreistelzberge h. Germany
168 F5 Dresden Germany
172 D4 Dretun' Belarus
166 E2 Dreux France
159 K3 Drevsjø Norway
160 G3 Driffield U.K.
202 D4 Driftwood U.S.A.
163 B6 Drimoleague Ireland
170 G3 Drniš Croatia
165 H1 Drochtersen Germany
163 E4 Drogheda Ireland
173 B5 Drohobych Ukr.
161 E5 Droitwich Spa U.K.
145 G4 Drokung India
165 I2 Drömling reg. Germany
163 D4 Dromod Ireland
163 D3 Dromore Northern Ireland U.K.
163 E3 Dromore Northern Ireland U.K.
161 F4 Dronfield U.K.
185 P2 Dronning Louise Land reg. Greenland
164 D2 Dronten Neth.
144 B2 Drosh Pak.
173 F4 Droskovo Rus. Fed.
127 F7 Drouin Australia
186 G4 Drumheller Canada
194 D2 Drummond MT U.S.A.
190 B2 Drummond WI U.S.A.
191 F3 Drummond Island U.S.A.
189 F4 Drummondville Canada
162 D6 Drummore U.K.
162 D4 Drumochter, Pass of U.K.
159 N5 Druskininkai Lith.
133 P3 Druzhina Rus. Fed.
171 K3 Dryanovo Bulg.
186 B3 Dry Bay U.S.A.
187 K5 Dryberry Lake Canada
190 E2 Dryburg U.S.A.
188 B4 Dryden Canada
196 D2 Dry Lake U.S.A.
162 D4 Drymen U.K.
124 C3 Drysdale r. Australia
140 C3 Dūāb r. Iran
149 C6 Du'an China
203 F2 Duane U.S.A.
145 G4 Duars reg. India
205 J5 Duarte, Pico mt. Dom. Rep.
134 B4 Ḑubā Saudi Arabia
142 E4 Dubai U.A.E.
169 N7 Dubăsari Moldova
187 I2 Dubawnt r. Canada
187 I2 Dubawnt Lake Canada
Dubayy U.A.E. see Dubai
134 B4 Dubbagh, Jabal ad mt. Saudi Arabia
127 H4 Dubbo Australia
190 D1 Dublin Canada
163 E4 Dublin Ireland
201 D5 Dublin U.S.A.
172 F3 Dubna Rus. Fed.
173 C5 Dubno Ukr.
194 D2 Dubois ID U.S.A.
194 E3 Dubois WY U.S.A.
202 D4 Du Bois U.S.A.
173 H5 Dubovka Rus. Fed.
173 G6 Dubovskoye Rus. Fed.
176 A4 Dubréka Guinea
171 H3 Dubrovnik Croatia
173 C5 Dubrovytsya Ukr.
172 D4 Dubrowna Belarus
190 B4 Dubuque U.S.A.
159 M5 Dubysa r. Lith.
154 C3 Đưc Bôn Vietnam
123 J6 Duc de Gloucester, Îles du is Fr. Polynesia
149 E4 Duchang China
197 G1 Duchesne U.S.A.
123 J7 Ducie Island atoll Pitcairn Is
201 C5 Duck r. U.S.A.
187 I4 Duck Bay Canada
187 H4 Duck Lake Canada
190 E4 Duck Lake U.S.A.
197 E2 Duckwater U.S.A.
197 E2 Duckwater Peak U.S.A.
154 C3 Đức Linh Vietnam
Đức Pho Vietnam see Đức Phô
154 D2 Đức Phô Vietnam
154 C1 Duc Tho Vietnam
Đưc Trong Vietnam see Liên Nghia
213 B4 Duda r. Col.
164 E5 Dudelange Lux.
165 I3 Duderstadt Germany
145 E4 Dudhi India
145 G4 Dudhnai India
132 J3 Dudinka Rus. Fed.
161 E5 Dudley U.K.
144 D6 Dudna r. India
162 F3 Dudwick, Hill of U.K.
176 B4 Duékoué Côte d'Ivoire
167 C2 Duero r. Spain alt. Douro (Portugal)
191 H1 Dufault, Lac l. Canada
164 C3 Duffel Belgium
188 E2 Dufferin, Cape Canada
202 B6 Duffield U.S.A.
125 G2 Duff Islands Solomon Is
162 E3 Dufftown U.K.
170 B2 Dufourspitze mt. Italy/Switz.
188 E1 Dufrost, Pointe pt Canada
170 F3 Dugi Otok i. Croatia
148 D3 Du He r. China
213 D4 Duida, Cerro mt. Venez.
210 E3 Duida-Marahuaca, Parque Nacional Venez.
164 E3 Duisburg Germany
213 B3 Duitama Col.
148 B4 Dujiangyan China
181 G5 Dukathole S. Africa
186 C4 Duke Island U.S.A.
140 C5 Dukhān Qatar
169 P3 Dukhovshchina Rus. Fed.
144 B3 Duki Pak.
159 N5 Dūkštas Lith.
141 E4 Dūlab Iran
146 B3 Dulan China
212 D3 Dulce r. Arg.
206 I6 Dulce, Golfo b. Costa Rica
206 H5 Dulce Nombre de Culmí Hond.
145 E2 Dulishi Hu salt l. China
181 I2 Dullstroom S. Africa
164 F3 Dülmen Germany
171 L3 Dulovo Bulg.
190 A2 Duluth U.S.A.
190 A2 Duluth/Superior airport U.S.A.
161 D6 Dulverton U.K.
136 F5 Dūmā Syria
153 B4 Dumaguete Phil.
155 B2 Dumai Indon.
153 B4 Dumaran i. Phil.
199 F5 Dumas AR U.S.A.
199 C5 Dumas TX U.S.A.
136 F5 Ḑumayr Syria
162 D5 Dumbarton U.K.
181 I3 Dumbe S. Africa
169 I6 Ďumbier mt. Slovakia
144 D2 Dumchele India
145 G5 Dum-Dum India
145 H4 Dum Duma India
162 E5 Dumfries U.K.
145 F4 Dumka India
165 G2 Dümmer l. Germany
188 E4 Dumoine, Lac Canada
129 C6 Dumont d'Urville research stn Antarctica
129 C6 Dumont d'Urville Sea sea Antarctica
164 E4 Dümpelfeld Germany
177 F1 Dumyāṭ Egypt
165 I3 Dün ridge Germany
171 H1 Duna r. Hungary alt. Donau (Austria/Germany), alt. Dunaj (Slovakia), alt. Dunărea (Romania), alt. Dunav (Serbia), conv. Danube
171 L3 Dunaj r. Slovakia alt. Donau (Austria/Germany), alt. Duna (Hungary), alt. Dunărea (Romania), alt. Dunav (Serbia), conv. Danube
168 H7 Dunajská Streda Slovakia
169 I7 Dunakeszi Hungary
127 G9 Dunalley Australia
163 E4 Dunany Point Ireland
171 L3 Dunărea r. Romania alt. Donau (Austria/Germany), alt. Duna (Hungary), alt. Dunaj (Slovakia), alt. Dunav (Serbia), conv. Danube
169 I7 Dunaújváros Hungary
171 L3 Dunav r. alt. Donau (Austria/Germany), alt. Duna (Hungary), alt. Dunaj (Slovakia), alt. Dunărea (Romania), conv. Danube
173 C5 Dunayivtsi Ukr.
128 C6 Dunback N.Z.
162 F4 Dunbar U.K.
162 E4 Dunblane U.K.
163 E4 Dunboyne Ireland
186 E5 Duncan Canada
197 H5 Duncan AZ U.S.A.
199 D5 Duncan OK U.S.A.
188 D3 Duncan, Cape Canada
188 E3 Duncan, Lac l. Canada
202 E4 Duncannon U.S.A.
162 E2 Duncansby Head U.K.
190 B5 Duncans Mills U.S.A.
163 E5 Duncormick Ireland
159 M4 Dundaga Latvia
191 G3 Dundalk Canada
163 E3 Dundalk Ireland
202 E5 Dundalk U.S.A.
163 E4 Dundalk Bay Ireland
185 L2 Dundas Greenland
186 C4 Dundas Island Canada
Dún Dealgan Ireland see Dundalk
181 I4 Dundee S. Africa
162 F4 Dundee U.K.
191 F5 Dundee MI U.S.A.
202 E3 Dundee NY U.S.A.
163 F3 Dundonald U.K.
127 F1 Dundoo Australia
162 E6 Dundrennan U.K.
163 F3 Dundrum U.K.
163 F3 Dundrum Bay U.K.
145 E4 Dundwa Range mts India/Nepal
188 F2 Dune, Lac l. Canada
128 C6 Dunedin N.Z.
201 D6 Dunedin U.S.A.
127 H4 Dunedoo Australia
162 E4 Dunfermline U.K.
163 E3 Dungannon U.K.
144 C5 Dungarpur India
163 D5 Dungarvan Ireland
161 H7 Dungeness hd U.K.
212 C8 Dungeness, Punta pt Arg.
164 F4 Düngenheim Germany
163 E3 Dungiven U.K.
Dungloe Ireland see An Clochán Liath
127 I4 Dungog Australia
178 C3 Dungu Dem. Rep. Congo
155 B2 Dungun Malaysia
177 F2 Dungunab Sudan
152 E2 Dunhua China
146 B2 Dunhuang China
126 E6 Dunkeld Australia
162 E4 Dunkeld U.K.
Dunkerque France see Dunkirk
161 D6 Dunkery Hill U.K.
166 F1 Dunkirk France
202 D3 Dunkirk U.S.A.
176 B4 Dunkwa Ghana
163 E4 Dún Laoghaire Ireland
163 E4 Dunlavin Ireland
163 E4 Dunleer Ireland
163 E2 Dunloy U.K.
163 B6 Dunmanus Bay Ireland
163 B6 Dunmanway Ireland
163 C4 Dunmore Ireland
201 E7 Dunmore Town Bahamas
196 D3 Dunmovin U.S.A.
163 F3 Dunmurry U.K.
201 E5 Dunn U.S.A.
162 E2 Dunnet Bay U.K.
162 E2 Dunnet Head U.K.
196 B2 Dunnigan U.S.A.
198 C3 Dunning U.S.A.
191 H4 Dunnville Canada
126 E6 Dunolly Australia
162 D5 Dunoon U.K.
162 F5 Duns U.K.
198 C1 Dunseith U.S.A.
194 B3 Dunsmuir U.S.A.
161 G6 Dunstable U.K.
128 B6 Dunstan Mountains N.Z.
164 D5 Dun-sur-Meuse France
128 C6 Duntroon N.Z.
162 B3 Dunvegan, Loch b. U.K.
144 B3 Dunyapur Pak.
148 E1 Duolun China
154 C3 Dương Đông Vietnam
149 D5 Dupang Ling mts China
191 H1 Duparquet, Lac l. Canada
171 J3 Dupnitsa Bulg.
198 C2 Dupree U.S.A.
200 B4 Du Quoin U.S.A.
124 C3 Durack r. Australia
136 E1 Durağan Turkey
166 G5 Durance r. France
191 F4 Durand MI U.S.A.
190 B3 Durand WI U.S.A.
206 C2 Durango Mex.
206 C2 Durango state Mex.
167 E1 Durango Spain
195 F4 Durango U.S.A.
199 D5 Durant U.S.A.
215 F2 Durazno Uruguay
215 F1 Durazno, Cuchilla Grande del hills Uruguay
181 I4 Durban S. Africa
166 F5 Durban-Corbières France
180 C6 Durbanville S. Africa
202 D5 Durbin U.S.A.
164 D4 Durbuy Belgium
164 E4 Düren Germany
144 E5 Durg India
145 F5 Durgapur India
191 G3 Durham Canada
160 F3 Durham U.K.
196 B2 Durham CA U.S.A.
201 E4 Durham NC U.S.A.
203 H3 Durham NH U.S.A.
173 D6 Durlești Moldova
165 G6 Durmersheim Germany
171 H3 Durmitor mt. Montenegro
162 D2 Durness U.K.
171 H4 Durrës Albania
161 F6 Durrington U.K.
163 A6 Dursey Island Ireland
136 B2 Dursunbey Turkey
136 F5 Durūz, Jabal ad mt. Syria
124 D2 D'Urville, Tanjung pt Indon.
128 D4 D'Urville Island N.Z.
138 D5 Duşak Turkm.
141 G4 Dushai Pak.
Dushak Turkm. see Duşak
149 C5 Dushan China
139 G5 Dushanbe Tajik.
173 H7 Dusheti Georgia
128 A6 Dusky Sound inlet N.Z.
164 E3 Düsseldorf Germany
Dustlik Uzbek. see Do'stlik
197 F1 Dutch Mountain U.S.A.
180 E1 Dutlwe Botswana
176 C3 Dutse Nigeria
126 B3 Dutton, Lake salt flat Australia
197 F2 Dutton, Mount U.S.A.
181 H6 Dutywa S. Africa
172 H3 Duvannoye Rus. Fed.
189 F2 Duvert, Lac l. Canada
140 C5 Duweihin, Khor b. Saudi Arabia/U.A.E.
149 C5 Duyun China
141 F5 Duzab Pak.
136 C1 Düzce Turkey
173 F5 Dvorichna Ukr.
150 B2 Dvoryanka Rus. Fed.
144 B5 Dwarka India
181 G2 Dwarsberg S. Africa
190 C5 Dwight U.S.A.
164 E2 Dwingelderveld, Nationaal Park nat. park Neth.
194 C2 Dworshak Reservoir U.S.A.
180 D6 Dwyka S. Africa
Dyanev Turkm. see Galkynyş
172 E4 Dyat'kovo Rus. Fed.
162 F3 Dyce U.K.
190 D5 Dyer IN U.S.A.
196 C3 Dyer NV U.S.A.
185 L3 Dyer, Cape Canada
191 G3 Dyer Bay Canada
201 B4 Dyersburg U.S.A.
190 B4 Dyersville U.S.A.
162 E3 Dyke U.K.
Dykh Tau mt. Georgia/Rus. Fed. see Gistola, Gora
165 K5 Dyleň h. Czech Rep.
169 I4 Dylewska Góra h. Poland
126 F2 Dynevor Downs Australia
181 H5 Dyoki S. Africa
190 A4 Dysart U.S.A.
180 E6 Dysselsdorp S. Africa
146 D2 Dzamīn Üüd Mongolia
177 D4 Dzanga-Ndoki, Parc National de nat. park Central African Republic
179 E5 Dzaoudzi Africa
172 G3 Dzerzhinsk Rus. Fed.
169 M5 Dzerzhyns'k Ukr.
146 E1 Dzhagdy, Khrebet mts Rus. Fed.
Dzhalal-Abad Kyrg. see Jalal-Abad
Dzhanga Turkm. see Jaňňa
Dzhangel'dy Uzbek. see Jongeldi
173 E6 Dzhankoy Ukr.
Dzharkurgan Uzbek. see Jarqo'rgo'n
Dzhebel Turkm. see Jebel
Dzhigirbent Turkm. see Jigerbent
Dzhizak Uzbek. see Jizzax
146 F1 Dzhugdzhur, Khrebet mts Rus. Fed.
Dzhuma Uzbek. see Juma
139 I2 Dzhusaly Kazakh.
169 J4 Działdowo Poland
207 G4 Dzibalchén Mex.
207 G3 Dzilam de Bravo Mex.
Dzungaria Basin basin China see Junggar Pendi
139 J3 Dzungarian Gate pass China/Kazakh.
146 C2 Dzuunmod Mongolia
172 C4 Dzyaniskavichy Belarus
172 C4 Dzyarzhynsk Belarus
169 M4 Dzyatlavichy Belarus


# E


188 C3 Eabamet Lake Canada
197 H4 Eagar U.S.A.
189 I3 Eagle r. Canada
195 F4 Eagle U.S.A.
203 F3 Eagle Bay U.S.A.
196 D4 Eagle Crags mt. U.S.A.
187 H4 Eagle Creek r. Canada
187 K5 Eagle Lake l. Canada
203 I1 Eagle Lake U.S.A.
194 B3 Eagle Lake l. CA U.S.A.
203 I1 Eagle Lake l. U.S.A.
190 B2 Eagle Mountain h. U.S.A.
199 C6 Eagle Pass U.S.A.
184 D3 Eagle Plain Canada
190 C2 Eagle River MI U.S.A.
190 C3 Eagle River WI U.S.A.
186 F3 Eaglesham Canada
197 F5 Eagle Tail Mountains U.S.A.
188 B3 Ear Falls Canada
196 C4 Earlimart U.S.A.
162 F5 Earlston U.K.
191 H2 Earlton Canada
162 E4 Earn r. U.K.
162 D4 Earn, Loch l. U.K.
199 C5 Earth U.S.A.
160 H4 Easington U.K.
201 D5 Easley U.S.A.
129 D5 East Antarctica reg. Antarctica
203 F4 East Ararat U.S.A.
202 D3 East Aurora U.S.A.
199 F6 East Bay U.S.A.
203 G2 East Berkshire U.S.A.
161 H7 Eastbourne U.K.
202 D4 East Branch Clarion River Reservoir U.S.A.
203 H4 East Brooklyn U.S.A.
128 G2 East Cape N.Z.
197 G2 East Carbon City U.S.A.
216 E5 East Caroline Basin sea feature N. Pacific Ocean
190 D5 East Chicago U.S.A.
146 E3 East China Sea Asia
128 E2 East Coast Bays N.Z.
203 G2 East Corinth U.S.A.
East Dereham U.K. see Dereham
208 C5 Easter Island S. Pacific Ocean
181 G5 Eastern Cape prov. S. Africa
177 F2 Eastern Desert Egypt
143 C2 Eastern Ghats mts India
144 B4 Eastern Nara canal Pak.
Eastern Transvaal prov. S. Africa see Mpumalanga
187 J4 Easterville Canada
212 E8 East Falkland i. Falkland Is
203 H4 East Falmouth U.S.A.
196 D2 Eastgate U.S.A.
198 D2 East Grand Forks U.S.A.
161 G6 East Grinstead U.K.
203 G3 Easthampton U.S.A.
203 G4 East Hampton U.S.A.
202 D4 East Hickory U.S.A.
218 K6 East Indiaman Ridge sea feature Indian Ocean
203 G3 East Jamaica U.S.A.
190 E3 East Jordan U.S.A.
162 D5 East Kilbride U.K.
190 D3 East Lake U.S.A.
149 □ East Lamma Channel Hong Kong China
161 F7 Eastleigh U.K.
202 C4 East Liverpool U.S.A.
162 B3 East Loch Tarbert inlet U.K.
181 G6 East London S. Africa
202 B5 East Lynn Lake U.S.A.
188 E3 Eastmain Canada
188 F3 Eastmain r. Canada
203 G2 Eastman Canada
201 D5 Eastman U.S.A.
216 F5 East Mariana Basin sea feature Pacific Ocean
203 I2 East Millinocket U.S.A.
190 B5 East Moline U.S.A.
190 C5 Easton IL U.S.A.
203 E5 Easton MD U.S.A.
203 F4 Easton PA U.S.A.
217 L8 East Pacific Ridge sea feature S. Pacific Ocean
217 L4 East Pacific Rise sea feature N. Pacific Ocean
196 A2 East Park Reservoir U.S.A.
189 H4 East Point pt Canada
201 C5 East Point U.S.A.
203 J2 Eastport ME U.S.A.
190 E3 Eastport MI U.S.A.
196 D1 East Range mts U.S.A.
200 B4 East St Louis U.S.A.
East Sea sea Pacific Ocean see Japan, Sea of
133 Q2 East Siberian Sea Rus. Fed.
127 H7 East Sister Island Australia
147 E7 East Timor country Asia
145 F4 East Tons r. India
127 F3 East Toorale Australia
190 C4 East Troy U.S.A.
203 F6 Eastville U.S.A.
196 C2 East Walker r. U.S.A.
203 G3 East Wallingford U.S.A.
201 D5 Eatonton U.S.A.
190 B3 Eau Claire U.S.A.
190 B3 Eau Claire r. U.S.A.
188 F2 Eau Claire, Lac à l' l. Canada
147 G6 Eauripik atoll Micronesia
216 E5 Eauripik Rise-New Guinea Rise sea feature N. Pacific Ocean
207 E3 Ebano Mex.
161 D6 Ebbw Vale U.K.
176 D4 Ebebiyin Equat. Guinea
180 B2 Ebenerde Namibia
202 D4 Ebensburg U.S.A.
136 C2 Eber Gölü l. Turkey
165 I3 Ebergötzen Germany
168 F4 Eberswalde-Finow Germany
191 F4 Eberts Canada
150 G3 Ebetsu Japan
149 B4 Ebian China
139 J3 Ebinur Hu salt l. China
170 F4 Eboli Italy
176 D4 Ebolowa Cameroon
137 J3 Ebrāhim Ḩeṣār Iran
167 G2 Ebro r. Spain
165 I1 Ebstorf Germany
171 L4 Eceabat Turkey
153 B2 Echague Phil.
167 E1 Echegárate, Puerto pass Spain
206 A1 Echeverria, Pico mt. Mex.
151 E7 Echizen Japan
127 G9 Echo, Lake Australia
186 F1 Echo Bay N.W.T. Canada
191 E2 Echo Bay Ont. Canada
197 G3 Echo Cliffs U.S.A.
188 B3 Echoing r. Canada
191 J2 Échouani, Lac l. Canada
164 D3 Echt Neth.
164 E5 Echternach Lux.
126 F6 Echuca Australia
165 G4 Echzell Germany
167 D4 Écija Spain
165 J5 Eckental Germany
190 E2 Eckerman U.S.A.
168 D3 Eckernförde Germany
185 K2 Eclipse Sound sea chan. Canada
166 H4 Écrins, Massif des mts France
210 C4 Ecuador country S. America
188 E2 Écueils, Pointe aux pt Canada
178 E2 Ed Eritrea
159 J4 Ed Sweden
187 H4 Edam Canada
164 D2 Edam Neth.
162 F1 Eday i. U.K.
177 E3 Ed Da'ein Sudan
177 F3 Ed Damazin Sudan
177 F3 Ed Damer Sudan
177 F3 Ed Debba Sudan
177 F3 Ed Dueim Sudan
127 H8 Eddystone Point Australia
164 D2 Ede Neth.
176 D4 Edéa Cameroon
187 J2 Edehon Lake Canada
214 C2 Edéia Brazil
127 H6 Eden Australia
160 E3 Eden r. U.K.
199 D6 Eden U.S.A.
181 F4 Edenburg S. Africa
128 B7 Edendale N.Z.
163 D4 Edenderry Ireland
126 D6 Edenhope Australia
201 E4 Edenton U.S.A.
181 G3 Edenville S. Africa
171 J4 Edessa Greece
165 F1 Edewecht Germany
203 H4 Edgartown U.S.A.
198 D2 Edgeley U.S.A.
198 C3 Edgemont U.S.A.
190 C4 Edgerton U.S.A.
163 D4 Edgeworthstown Ireland
139 K2 Edigan Rus. Fed.
190 A5 Edina U.S.A.
199 D7 Edinburg U.S.A.
162 E5 Edinburgh U.K.
169 M6 Edineț Moldova
173 C7 Edirne Turkey
186 F4 Edith Cavell, Mount Canada
194 B2 Edmonds U.S.A.
186 G4 Edmonton Canada
187 J5 Edmore U.S.A.
190 B4 Edmund U.S.A.
187 K4 Edmund Lake Canada
189 G4 Edmundston Canada
199 D6 Edna U.S.A.
186 C3 Edna Bay U.S.A.
171 L5 Edremit Turkey
159 K3 Edsbyn Sweden
186 F4 Edson Canada
215 D2 Eduardo Castex Arg.
126 F5 Edward r. Australia
178 C4 Edward, Lake Dem. Rep. Congo/Uganda
190 C1 Edward Island Canada
203 F2 Edwards U.S.A.
126 A2 Edward's Creek Australia
199 C6 Edwards Plateau U.S.A.
200 B4 Edwardsville U.S.A.
129 B5 Edward VII Peninsula pen. Antarctica
186 C3 Edziza, Mount Canada
164 B3 Eeklo Belgium
196 A1 Eel r. U.S.A.
196 A2 Eel, South Fork r. U.S.A.
164 E1 Eemshaven pt Neth.
164 E1 Eenrum Neth.
180 D3 Eenzamheid Pan salt pan S. Africa
125 G3 Éfaté i. Vanuatu
Efes tourist site Turkey see Ephesus
200 B4 Effingham U.S.A.
136 D1 Eflâni Turkey
197 E2 Egan Range mts U.S.A.
191 I3 Eganville Canada
169 J7 Eger Hungary
159 I4 Egersund Norway
165 G3 Eggegebirge hills Germany
165 J5 Eggolsheim Germany
164 C4 Eghezée Belgium
158 D2 Egilsstaðir Iceland
136 C3 Eğirdir Turkey
136 C3 Eğirdir Gölü l. Turkey
166 F4 Égletons France
163 D2 Eglinton U.K.
184 F2 Eglinton Island Canada
164 C2 Egmond aan Zee Neth.
128 D3 Egmont, Cape N.Z.
Egmont, Mount vol. N.Z. see Taranaki, Mount
128 E3 Egmont National Park N.Z.
136 B2 Eğrigöz Dağı mts Turkey
160 G3 Egton U.K.
214 D1 Éguas r. Brazil
133 U3 Egvekinot Rus. Fed.
177 E2 Egypt country Africa
148 A2 Ehen Hudag China
168 D6 Ehingen (Donau) Germany
165 I2 Ehra-Lessien Germany
197 E5 Ehrenberg U.S.A.
165 I5 Eibelstadt Germany
164 E2 Eibergen Neth.
165 H4 Eichenzell Germany
165 J6 Eichstätt Germany
159 I3 Eidfjord Norway
159 J3 Eidsvoll Norway
164 E4 Eifel hills Germany
162 B4 Eigg i. U.K.
143 A4 Eight Degree Channel India/Maldives
124 C3 Eighty Mile Beach Australia
136 E7 Eilat Israel
127 F6 Eildon Australia
127 F6 Eildon, Lake Australia
187 H2 Eileen Lake Canada
165 K3 Eilenburg Germany
165 I2 Eimke Germany
165 H3 Einbeck Germany
164 D3 Eindhoven Neth.
168 D7 Einsiedeln Switz.
219 G2 Eirik Ridge sea feature N. Atlantic Ocean
210 E5 Eirunepé Brazil
165 H3 Eisberg h. Germany
179 C5 Eiseb watercourse Namibia
165 I4 Eisenach Germany
165 J4 Eisenberg Germany
168 G4 Eisenhüttenstadt Germany
168 H7 Eisenstadt Austria
165 I4 Eisfeld Germany
162 C3 Eishort, Loch inlet U.K.
165 J3 Eisleben Lutherstadt Germany
165 H4 Eiterfeld Germany
Eivissa Spain see Ibiza
Eivissa i. Spain see Ibiza
167 F1 Ejea de los Caballeros Spain
179 E6 Ejeda Madag.
207 E4 Ejutla Mex.
159 M4 Ekenäs Fin.
138 C5 Ekerem Turkm.
164 C3 Ekeren Belgium
128 E4 Eketahuna N.Z.
133 L3 Ekonda Rus. Fed.
159 K3 Ekshärad Sweden
159 K4 Eksjö Sweden
180 B4 Eksteenfontein S. Africa
178 C4 Ekuku Dem. Rep. Congo
188 D3 Ekwan r. Canada
188 D3 Ekwan Point Canada
171 J6 Elafonisou, Steno sea chan. Greece
181 H2 Elands r. S. Africa
181 H2 Elandsdoorn S. Africa
170 B7 El Aouinet Alg.
167 H4 El Arba, Tizi h. Alg.
206 A1 El Arco Mex.
171 J5 Elassona Greece
137 G2 Elazığ Turkey
170 D3 Elba, Isola d' i. Italy
146 F1 El'ban Rus. Fed.
213 B2 El Banco Col.
192 E5 El Barreal salt l. Mex.
171 I4 Elbasan Albania
136 E2 Elbaşı Turkey
213 C2 El Baúl Venez.
176 C1 El Bayadh Alg.
165 I1 Elbe r. Germany alt. Labe (Czech Rep.)
195 F4 Elbert, Mount U.S.A.
190 D3 Elberta MI U.S.A.
197 G2 Elberta UT U.S.A.
201 D5 Elberton U.S.A.
166 E2 Elbeuf France
136 F2 Elbistan Turkey
169 I3 Elbląg Poland
215 B4 El Bolsón Arg.
201 E7 Elbow Cay i. Bahamas
173 G7 El'brus mt. Rus. Fed.
164 D2 Elburg Neth.
167 E2 El Burgo de Osma Spain
140 C2 Elburz Mountains Iran
215 C4 El Cain Arg.
196 D5 El Cajon U.S.A.
213 E3 El Callao Venez.
199 D6 El Campo U.S.A.
195 F5 El Capitan Mountain U.S.A.
197 E5 El Centro U.S.A.
210 F7 El Cerro Bol.
213 D2 El Chaparro Venez.
Elche Spain see Elche-Elx
167 F3 Elche-Elx Spain
207 F4 El Chichónal vol. Mex.
206 C1 El Chilicote Mex.
124 D3 Elcho Island Australia
213 B3 El Cocuy Col.
213 B3 El Cocuy, Parque Nacional nat. park Col.
207 H3 El Cuyo Mex.
167 F3 Elda Spain
165 J1 Elde r. Germany
191 H2 Eldee Canada
126 D3 Elder, Lake Australia
206 D2 El Diamante Mex.
213 B2 El Difícil Col.
133 O3 El'dikan Rus. Fed.
213 A4 El Diviso Col.
197 E6 El Doctor Mex.
190 A5 Eldon IA U.S.A.
198 E4 Eldon MO U.S.A.
212 F3 Eldorado Arg.
206 C2 El Dorado Mex.
199 E5 El Dorado AR U.S.A.
199 D4 El Dorado KS U.S.A.
199 C6 Eldorado U.S.A.
213 E3 El Dorado Venez.
178 D3 Eldoret Kenya
194 E2 Electric Peak U.S.A.
176 B2 El Eglab plat. Alg.
167 E4 El Ejido Spain
172 F4 Elektrostal' Rus. Fed.
210 D4 El Encanto Col.
165 I3 Elend Germany
143 A2 Elephanta Caves tourist site India
195 F5 Elephant Butte Reservoir U.S.A.
129 B2 Elephant Island i. Antarctica
145 H5 Elephant Point Bangl.
137 I2 Eleşkirt Turkey
207 G5 El Estor Guat.
176 C1 El Eulma Alg.
201 E7 Eleuthera i. Bahamas
170 C6 El Fahs Tunisia
177 E3 El Fasher Sudan
165 H4 Elfershausen Germany
206 B2 El Fuerte Mex.
178 C2 El Fula Sudan
177 E3 El Geneina Sudan
177 F3 El Geteina Sudan
162 E3 Elgin U.K.
190 C4 Elgin IL U.S.A.
198 C2 Elgin ND U.S.A.
197 E3 Elgin NV U.S.A.
197 G2 Elgin UT U.S.A.
133 P3 El'ginskiy Rus. Fed.
206 D3 El Gogorrón, Parque Nacional nat. park Mex.
176 C1 El Goléa Alg.
177 F4 Elgon, Mount Uganda
170 B6 El Hadjar Alg.
206 I6 El Hato del Volcán Panama
176 A2 El Hierro i. Canary Is
207 E3 El Higo Mex.
176 C2 El Homr Alg.
162 F4 Elie U.K.
128 C5 Elie de Beaumont mt. N.Z.
184 B3 Elim U.S.A.
189 H2 Eliot, Mount Canada
173 H6 Elista Rus. Fed.
190 B4 Elizabeth IL U.S.A.
203 F4 Elizabeth NJ U.S.A.
202 C5 Elizabeth WV U.S.A.
201 E4 Elizabeth City U.S.A.
203 H4 Elizabeth Islands U.S.A.
201 D4 Elizabethton U.S.A.
200 C4 Elizabethtown KY U.S.A.
201 E5 Elizabethtown NC U.S.A.
203 G2 Elizabethtown NY U.S.A.
202 E4 Elizabethtown PA U.S.A.
167 F1 Elizondo Spain
176 B1 El Jadida Morocco
206 C2 El Jaralito Mex.
170 D7 El Jem Tunisia
206 H5 El Jicaral Nicaragua
186 G4 Elk r. Canada
169 K4 Ełk Poland
196 A2 Elk U.S.A.
202 C5 Elk r. U.S.A.
170 C6 El Kala Alg.
177 F3 El Kamlin Sudan
199 D5 Elk City U.S.A.
196 A2 Elk Creek U.S.A.
196 B2 Elk Grove U.S.A.
190 E5 Elkhart U.S.A.
176 B2 El Khnâchîch esc. Mali

190 C4 **Elkhorn** U.S.A.
198 D3 **Elkhorn** *r.* U.S.A.
171 L3 **Elkhovo** Bulg.
202 D5 **Elkins** U.S.A.
186 G4 **Elk Island National Park** Canada
191 G2 **Elk Lake** Canada
190 E3 **Elk Lake** *l.* U.S.A.
202 E4 **Elkland** U.S.A.
186 F5 **Elko** Canada
194 D3 **Elko** U.S.A.
187 G4 **Elk Point** Canada
198 E2 **Elk River** U.S.A.
203 F5 **Elkton** *MD* U.S.A.
202 D5 **Elkton** *VA* U.S.A.
187 L2 **Ell Bay** Canada
185 H2 **Ellef Ringnes Island** Canada
197 G2 **Ellen, Mount** U.S.A.
144 C3 **Ellenabad** India
198 D2 **Ellendale** U.S.A.
194 B2 **Ellensburg** U.S.A.
203 F4 **Ellenville** U.S.A.
127 H6 **Ellery, Mount** Australia
128 D5 **Ellesmere, Lake** N.Z.
185 J2 **Ellesmere Island** Canada
161 E4 **Ellesmere Port** U.K.
184 H3 **Ellice** *r.* Canada
202 D3 **Ellicottville** U.S.A.
207 E3 **El Limón** Mex.
165 I5 **Ellingen** Germany
181 G5 **Elliot** S. Africa
181 H5 **Elliotdale** S. Africa
191 F2 **Elliot Lake** Canada
194 D2 **Ellis** U.S.A.
**Ellisras** S. Africa *see* **Lephalale**
126 A4 **Elliston** Australia
162 F3 **Ellon** U.K.
144 C5 **Ellora Caves** *tourist site* India
203 I2 **Ellsworth** *ME* U.S.A.
190 A3 **Ellsworth** *WI* U.S.A.
129 B3 **Ellsworth Land** *reg.* Antarctica
129 B3 **Ellsworth Mountains** *mts* Antarctica
165 I6 **Ellwangen (Jagst)** Germany
136 B3 **Elmalı** Turkey
196 D6 **El Maneadero** Mex.
213 E3 **El Manteco** Venez.
176 C1 **El Meghaïer** Alg.
213 E3 **El Miamo** Venez.
**El Mīna** Lebanon *see* **El Mîna**
136 E4 **El Mîna** Lebanon
190 E3 **Elmira** *MI* U.S.A.
202 E3 **Elmira** *NY* U.S.A.
197 F5 **El Mirage** U.S.A.
167 E4 **El Moral** Spain
126 F6 **Elmore** Australia
215 D2 **El Morro** *mt.* Arg.
176 B2 **El Mreyyé** *reg.* Mauritania
165 H1 **Elmshorn** Germany
177 E3 **El Muglad** Sudan
191 G3 **Elmwood** Canada
190 C5 **Elmwood** *IL* U.S.A.
190 A3 **Elmwood** *WI* U.S.A.
158 I3 **Elnesvågen** Norway
213 B3 **El Nevado, Cerro** *mt.* Col.
153 A4 **El Nido** Phil.
177 F3 **El Obeid** Sudan
206 D2 **El Oro** Mex.
213 C3 **Elorza** Venez.
176 C1 **El Oued** Alg.
197 G5 **Eloy** U.S.A.
206 C2 **El Palmito** Mex.
213 E2 **El Pao** Venez.
213 C2 **El Pao** Venez.
190 C5 **El Paso** *IL* U.S.A.
195 F6 **El Paso** *TX* U.S.A.
162 C2 **Elphin** U.K.
196 C3 **El Portal** U.S.A.
**El Porvenír** Panama *see* **El Porvenir**
206 J6 **El Porvenir** Panama
167 H2 **El Prat de Llobregat** Spain
**El Progreso** Guat. *see* **Guastatoya**
207 H5 **El Progreso** Hond.
206 B2 **El Puerto, Cerro** *mt.* Mex.
167 C4 **El Puerto de Santa María** Spain
**El Quds** Israel/West Bank *see* **Jerusalem**
206 J6 **El Real** Panama
199 D5 **El Reno** U.S.A.
207 D3 **El Retorno** Mex.
190 B4 **Elroy** U.S.A.
206 D3 **El Rucio** Mex.
186 B2 **Elsa** Canada
206 D2 **El Salado** Mex.
206 C3 **El Salto** Mex.
207 G5 **El Salvador** *country* Central America
206 D2 **El Salvador** Mex.
153 C4 **El Salvador** Phil.
213 C3 **El Samán de Apure** Venez.
191 F1 **Elsas** Canada
206 C1 **El Sauz** Mex.
165 G2 **Else** *r.* Germany
**Elsen Nur** *l.* China *see* **Dorgê Co**
196 D5 **Elsinore** U.S.A.
213 D2 **El Sombrero** Venez.
215 C2 **El Sosneado** Arg.
207 E3 **El Tajín** *tourist site* Mex.
213 B3 **El Tama, Parque Nacional** *nat. park* Venez.
170 C6 **El Tarf** Alg.
167 C1 **El Teleno** *mt.* Spain
207 E4 **El Tepozteco, Parque Nacional** *nat. park* Mex.
213 D2 **El Tigre** Venez.
207 G4 **El Tigre, Parque Nacional** *nat. park* Guat.
165 I5 **Eltmann** Germany
213 C2 **El Tocuyo** Venez.
173 H5 **El'ton** Rus. Fed.
173 H5 **El'ton, Ozero** *l.* Rus. Fed.
194 C2 **Eltopia** U.S.A.
213 E2 **El Toro** Venez.
215 E2 **El Trébol** Arg.
206 B3 **El Triunfo** Mex.
213 C3 **El Tuparro, Parque Nacional** *nat. park* Col.
212 B8 **El Turbio** Chile
143 C2 **Eluru** India
159 N4 **Elva** Estonia
213 A3 **El Valle** Col.
162 E5 **Elvanfoot** U.K.
167 C3 **Elvas** Port.
159 J3 **Elverum** Norway
213 B3 **El Viejo** *mt.* Col.
213 C2 **El Vigía** Venez.
210 D5 **Elvira** Brazil
178 E3 **El Wak** Kenya
190 E5 **Elwood** U.S.A.
165 I3 **Elxleben** Germany
161 H5 **Ely** U.K.
190 B2 **Ely** *MN* U.S.A.
197 E2 **Ely** *NV* U.S.A.
202 B4 **Elyria** U.S.A.
165 G4 **Elz** Germany
165 H2 **Elze** Germany
125 G3 **Émaé** *i.* Vanuatu
181 I2 **eMakhazeni** S. Africa
181 H2 **eMalahleni** S. Africa
140 D2 **Emāmrūd** Iran
137 K5 **Emāmzādeh Naşrod Dīn** Iran
159 L4 **Emån** *r.* Sweden
181 I5 **eManzimtoti** S. Africa
214 B2 **Emas, Parque Nacional das** *nat. park* Brazil
139 J3 **Emazar** Kazakh.
138 D2 **Emba** Kazakh.
181 H3 **Embalenhle** S. Africa
187 G3 **Embarras Portage** Canada
214 C2 **Emborcação, Represa de** *resr* Brazil
203 F2 **Embrun** Canada
178 D4 **Embu** Kenya
164 F1 **Emden** Germany
149 B4 **Emeishan** China
149 B4 **Emei Shan** *mt.* China
124 E4 **Emerald** *Qld* Australia
126 F6 **Emerald** *Vic.* Australia
189 G3 **Emeril** Canada
187 J5 **Emerson** Canada
136 B2 **Emet** Turkey
181 I2 **eMgwenya** S. Africa
181 I2 **Emgwenya** S. Africa
197 E3 **Emigrant Valley** U.S.A.
**eMijindini** S. Africa *see* **eMjindini**
177 D3 **Emi Koussi** *mt.* Chad
206 C2 **Emiliano Martínez** Mex.
207 G4 **Emiliano Zapata** Mex.
139 J3 **Emin** China
171 L3 **Emine, Nos** *pt* Bulg.
139 J3 **Emin He** *r.* China
171 L3 **Eminska Planina** *hills* Bulg.
136 C2 **Emirdağ** Turkey
136 C2 **Emir Dağı** *mt.* Turkey
127 G8 **Emita** Australia
181 I2 **eMjindini** S. Africa
181 I3 **eMkhondo** S. Africa
159 K4 **Emmaboda** Sweden
159 M4 **Emmaste** Estonia
127 I2 **Emmaville** Australia
164 D2 **Emmeloord** Neth.
164 F4 **Emmelshausen** Germany
164 E2 **Emmen** Neth.
168 D7 **Emmen** Switz.
164 E3 **Emmerich** Germany
143 B3 **Emmiganuru** India
181 I3 **eMondlo** S. Africa
199 C6 **Emory Peak** U.S.A.
206 B2 **Empalme** Mex.
181 I4 **Empangeni** S. Africa
212 E3 **Empedrado** Arg.
216 G2 **Emperor Seamount Chain** *sea feature* N. Pacific Ocean
216 G2 **Emperor Trough** *sea feature* N. Pacific Ocean
170 D3 **Empoli** Italy
198 D4 **Emporia** *KS* U.S.A.
202 E6 **Emporia** *VA* U.S.A.
202 D4 **Emporium** U.S.A.
187 G4 **Empress** Canada
164 F2 **Ems** *r.* Germany
191 H3 **Emsdale** Canada
164 F2 **Emsdetten** Germany
164 F1 **Ems-Jade-Kanal** *canal* Germany
164 F2 **Emsland** *reg.* Germany
181 H3 **eMzinoni** S. Africa
158 K3 **Enafors** Sweden
147 F7 **Enarotali** Indon.
151 E7 **Ena-san** *mt.* Japan
215 G1 **Encantadas, Serra das** *hills* Brazil
206 A2 **Encantado, Cerro** *mt.* Mex.
153 B3 **Encanto, Cape** Phil.
206 D3 **Encarnación** Mex.
212 E3 **Encarnación** Para.
199 D6 **Encinal** U.S.A.
196 D5 **Encinitas** U.S.A.
195 F5 **Encino** U.S.A.
126 C5 **Encounter Bay** Australia
214 E1 **Encruzilhada** Brazil
215 G1 **Encruzilhada do Sul** Brazil
186 D4 **Endako** Canada
147 E7 **Ende** Indon.
124 E3 **Endeavour Strait** Australia
**Endeh** Indon. *see* **Ende**
219 L9 **Enderby Abyssal Plain** *sea feature* Southern Ocean
129 E4 **Enderby Land** *reg.* Antarctica
203 E3 **Endicott** U.S.A.
186 C3 **Endicott Arm** *est.* U.S.A.
184 C3 **Endicott Mountains** U.S.A.
138 D2 **Energetik** Rus. Fed.
215 E3 **Energía** Arg.
173 E6 **Enerhodar** Ukr.
216 G6 **Enewetak** *atoll* Marshall Is
170 D6 **Enfidaville** Tunisia
203 G3 **Enfield** U.S.A.
190 E2 **Engadine** U.S.A.
158 J3 **Engan** Norway
153 B2 **Engaño, Cape** Phil.
150 H2 **Engaru** Japan
201 F5 **Engelhard** U.S.A.
173 H5 **Engel's** Rus. Fed.
164 C1 **Engelschmangat** *sea chan.* Neth.
126 A2 **Engenina** *watercourse* Australia
155 B4 **Enggano** *i.* Indon.
164 C4 **Enghien** Belgium
161 E5 **England** *admin. div.* U.K.
189 I3 **Englee** Canada
191 H2 **Englehart** Canada
193 H1 **English** *r.* Canada
161 D7 **English Channel** France/U.K.
173 G7 **Enguri** *r.* Georgia
181 I4 **Enhlalakahle** S. Africa
199 D4 **Enid** U.S.A.
150 G3 **Eniwa** Japan
164 D2 **Enkhuizen** Neth.
159 L4 **Enköping** Sweden
170 F6 **Enna** *Sicily* Italy
187 I2 **Ennadai Lake** Canada
177 E3 **En Nahud** Sudan
177 E3 **Ennedi, Massif** *mts* Chad
163 D4 **Ennell, Lough** *l.* Ireland
127 F2 **Enngonia** Australia
198 C2 **Enning** U.S.A.
163 C5 **Ennis** Ireland
194 E2 **Ennis** *MT* U.S.A.
199 D5 **Ennis** *TX* U.S.A.
163 E5 **Enniscorthy** Ireland
163 D3 **Enniskillen** U.K.
163 B5 **Ennistymon** Ireland
168 G7 **Enns** *r.* Austria
158 O3 **Eno** Fin.
197 F3 **Enoch** U.S.A.
158 M1 **Enontekiö** Fin.
149 D6 **Enping** China
153 B2 **Enrile** Phil.
164 D2 **Ens** Neth.
127 G6 **Ensay** Australia
164 E2 **Enschede** Neth.
165 G3 **Ense** Germany
215 F2 **Ensenada** Arg.
204 A2 **Ensenada** Mex.
149 C4 **Enshi** China
186 F2 **Enterprise** *N.W.T.* Canada
191 I3 **Enterprise** *Ont.* Canada
201 C6 **Enterprise** *AL* U.S.A.
194 C2 **Enterprise** *OR* U.S.A.
197 F3 **Enterprise** *UT* U.S.A.
186 F4 **Entrance** Canada
215 E2 **Entre Ríos** *prov.* Arg.
210 F8 **Entre Ríos** Bol.
167 B3 **Entroncamento** Port.
176 C4 **Enugu** Nigeria
133 U3 **Enurmino** Rus. Fed.
210 D5 **Envira** Brazil
210 D5 **Envira** *r.* Brazil
128 C5 **Enys, Mount** N.Z.
164 D2 **Epe** Neth.
164 B5 **Épernay** France
171 L6 **Ephesus** *tourist site* Turkey
197 G2 **Ephraim** U.S.A.
203 E4 **Ephrata** *PA* U.S.A.
194 C2 **Ephrata** *WA* U.S.A.
125 G3 **Épi** *i.* Vanuatu
166 H2 **Épinal** France
136 D4 **Episkopi** Cyprus
170 E4 **Epomeo, Monte** *vol.* Italy
161 H6 **Epping** U.K.
165 G4 **Eppstein** Germany
161 D5 **Eppynt, Mynydd** *hills* U.K.
161 G6 **Epsom** U.K.
215 D3 **Epu-pel** Arg.
140 D4 **Eqlīd** Iran
176 C4 **Equatorial Guinea** *country* Africa
213 E3 **Equeipa** Venez.
153 A4 **Eran Bay** Phil.
136 F1 **Erbaa** Turkey
165 K5 **Erbendorf** Germany
164 F5 **Erbeskopf** *h.* Germany
137 I2 **Erçek** Turkey
137 I2 **Erciş** Turkey
136 E2 **Erciyes Dağı** *mt.* Turkey
169 I7 **Érd** Hungary
145 H2 **Erdaogou Bingzhan** China
152 D2 **Erdao Jiang** *r.* China
136 A1 **Erdek** Turkey
136 E3 **Erdemli** Turkey
**Erdenetsogt** Mongolia *see* **Bayan-Ovoo**
177 E3 **Erdi** *reg.* Chad
173 H6 **Erdniyevskiy** Rus. Fed.
214 B4 **Eré, Campos** *hills* Brazil
213 D3 **Erebato** *r.* Venez.
129 B5 **Erebus, Mount** *vol.* Antarctica
137 J6 **Erech** *tourist site* Iraq
212 F3 **Erechim** Brazil
146 D2 **Ereentsav** Mongolia
136 E3 **Ereğli** Turkey
136 C1 **Ereğli** Turkey
170 F6 **Erei, Monti** *mts Sicily* Italy
**Eréndira** Mex. *see* **Carácuaro**
148 D1 **Erenhot** China
140 E3 **Eresk** Iran
167 D2 **Eresma** *r.* Spain
171 J5 **Eretria** Greece
165 J4 **Erfurt** Germany
137 G2 **Ergani** Turkey
176 B2 **'Erg Chech** *des.* Alg./Mali
**Ergel** Mongolia *see* **Hatanbulag**
171 L4 **Ergene** *r.* Turkey
159 N4 **Ērgļi** Latvia
150 A1 **Ergu** China
152 C3 **Erhulai** China
162 D2 **Eriboll, Loch** *inlet* U.K.
162 D4 **Ericht, Loch** *l.* U.K.
190 B5 **Erie** *IL* U.S.A.
199 E4 **Erie** *KS* U.S.A.
202 C3 **Erie** *PA* U.S.A.
191 G4 **Erie, Lake** Canada/U.S.A.
150 H3 **Erimo** Japan
150 H4 **Erimo-misaki** *c.* Japan
162 A3 **Eriskay** *i.* U.K.
178 D2 **Eritrea** *country* Africa
139 H5 **Erkech-Tam** Kyrg.
136 E2 **Erkilet** Turkey
165 J5 **Erlangen** Germany
124 D4 **Erldunda** Australia
152 E2 **Erlong Shan** *mt.* China
152 C2 **Erlongshan Shuiku** *resr* China
164 D2 **Ermelo** Neth.
181 H3 **Ermelo** S. Africa
136 D3 **Ermenek** Turkey
171 K6 **Ermoupoli** Greece
143 B4 **Ernakulam** India
143 B4 **Erode** India
180 A1 **Erongo** *admin. reg.* Namibia
164 D3 **Erp** Neth.
176 B1 **Er Rachidia** Morocco
177 F3 **Er Rahad** Sudan
179 D5 **Errego** Moz.
170 D7 **Er Remla** Tunisia
163 C2 **Errigal** *h.* Ireland
163 A3 **Erris Head** Ireland
203 H2 **Errol** U.S.A.
125 G3 **Erromango** *i.* Vanuatu
171 I4 **Ersekë** Albania
198 D2 **Erskine** U.S.A.
158 M3 **Ersmark** Sweden
173 G5 **Ertil'** Rus. Fed.
126 C3 **Erudina** Australia
137 I3 **Eruh** Turkey
215 G2 **Erval** Brazil
202 D5 **Erwin** U.S.A.
165 G3 **Erwitte** Germany
165 J2 **Erxleben** *Sachsen-Anhalt* Germany
165 J2 **Erxleben** *Sachsen-Anhalt* Germany
165 K4 **Erzgebirge** *mts* Czech Rep./Germany
136 F3 **Erzin** Turkey
137 G2 **Erzincan** Turkey
137 H2 **Erzurum** Turkey
150 G4 **Esan-misaki** *pt* Japan
150 G4 **Esashi** Japan
150 H2 **Esashi** Japan
159 J5 **Esbjerg** Denmark
197 G3 **Escalante** U.S.A.
197 G3 **Escalante** *r.* U.S.A.
197 F3 **Escalante Desert** U.S.A.
206 C2 **Escalón** Mex.
190 D3 **Escanaba** U.S.A.
207 G4 **Escárcega** Mex.
153 B2 **Escarpada Point** Phil.
167 F2 **Escatrón** Spain
164 B4 **Escaut** *r.* Belgium
164 D3 **Esch** Neth.
164 E2 **Esche** Germany
165 I2 **Eschede** Germany
164 D5 **Esch-sur-Alzette** Lux.
165 I3 **Eschwege** Germany
164 E4 **Eschweiler** Germany
196 D5 **Escondido** U.S.A.
206 C3 **Escuinapa** Mex.
207 G5 **Escuintla** Guat.
207 F5 **Escuintla** Mex.
213 C3 **Escutillas** Col.
136 B3 **Eşen** Turkey
138 C5 **Esenguly** Turkm.
164 F1 **Esens** Germany
140 C3 **Eşfahān** Iran
140 D4 **Esfandārān** Iran
140 E2 **Esfarayen, Reshteh-ye** *mts* Iran
140 C4 **Esfarjān** Iran
140 D5 **Eshkanān** Iran
181 I4 **Eshowe** S. Africa
141 E3 **'Eshqābād** Iran
140 C3 **Eshtehārd** Iran
179 C6 **Esigodini** Zimbabwe
181 J4 **eSikhaleni** S. Africa
**Esikhawini** S. Africa *see* **eSikhaleni**
127 J1 **Esk** Australia
127 G8 **Esk** *r.* Australia
160 D2 **Esk** *r.* U.K.
162 E5 **Eskdalemuir** U.K.
189 G3 **Esker** Canada
158 D2 **Eskifjörður** Iceland
136 B2 **Eski Gediz** Turkey
159 L4 **Eskilstuna** Sweden
184 E3 **Eskimo Lakes** Canada
139 H4 **Eski-Nookat** Kyrg.
136 D1 **Eskipazar** Turkey
136 C2 **Eskişehir** Turkey
167 D1 **Esla** *r.* Spain
140 B3 **Eslāmābād-e Gharb** Iran
141 F3 **Eslām Qal'eh** Afgh.
136 B3 **Esler Dağı** *mt.* Turkey
165 G3 **Eslohe (Sauerland)** Germany
159 K5 **Eslöv** Sweden
136 B2 **Eşme** Turkey
210 C3 **Esmeraldas** Ecuador
190 E1 **Esnagi Lake** Canada
164 B4 **Esnes** France
141 F5 **Espakeh** Iran
166 F4 **Espalion** France
191 G2 **Espanola** Canada
195 F4 **Espanola** U.S.A.
210 □ **Española, Isla** *i. Galapagos Is* Ecuador
196 A2 **Esparto** U.S.A.
165 G2 **Espelkamp** Germany
124 C5 **Esperance** Australia
129 E2 **Esperanza** *research stn* Antarctica
215 E1 **Esperanza** Arg.
206 B2 **Esperanza** Mex.
153 C4 **Esperanza** Phil.
206 H5 **Esperanza, Sierra de la** *mts* Hond.
167 B3 **Espichel, Cabo** *c.* Port.
167 D1 **Espigüete** *mt.* Spain
206 D2 **Espinazo** Mex.
214 D2 **Espinhaço, Serra do** *mts* Brazil
214 D1 **Espinosa** Brazil
214 E2 **Espírito Santo** *state* Brazil
153 B2 **Espiritu** Phil.
125 G3 **Espiritu Santo** *i.* Vanuatu
207 H4 **Espíritu Santo, Bahía del** *b.* Mex.
206 B2 **Espíritu Santo, Isla** *i.* Mex.
159 N3 **Espoo** Fin.
167 F4 **Espuña** *mt.* Spain
212 B6 **Esquel** Arg.
186 E5 **Esquimalt** Canada
153 C5 **Essang** Indon.
176 B1 **Essaouira** Morocco
164 C3 **Essen** Belgium
164 F3 **Essen** Germany
165 F2 **Essen (Oldenburg)** Germany
211 G3 **Essequibo** *r.* Guyana
191 F4 **Essex** Canada
197 E4 **Essex** U.S.A.
203 G2 **Essex Junction** U.S.A.
191 F4 **Essexville** U.S.A.
176 A2 **Es-Smara** W. Sahara
133 Q4 **Esso** Rus. Fed.
189 H4 **Est, Île de l'** *i.* Canada
203 I1 **Est, Lac de l'** *l.* Canada
129 B2 **Estación Marítima Antártica** *research stn* Antarctica
212 D8 **Estados, Isla de los** *i.* Arg.
140 D4 **Eşţahbān** Iran
191 G2 **Estaire** Canada
211 K6 **Estância** Brazil
167 G1 **Estats, Pic d'** *mt.* France/Spain
181 H4 **Estcourt** S. Africa
165 H1 **Este** *r.* Germany
206 H5 **Estelí** Nicaragua
167 E1 **Estella** Spain
167 D4 **Estepa** Spain
167 D4 **Estepona** Spain
187 I4 **Esterhazy** Canada
196 B4 **Estero Bay** U.S.A.
212 D2 **Esteros** Para.
187 I5 **Estevan** Canada
198 E3 **Estherville** U.S.A.
201 D5 **Estill** U.S.A.
159 N4 **Estonia** *country* Europe
164 A5 **Estrées-St-Denis** France
167 C2 **Estrela, Serra da** *mts* Port.
167 E3 **Estrella** *mt.* Spain
197 F5 **Estrella, Sierra** *mts* U.S.A.
167 C3 **Estremoz** Port.
211 I5 **Estrondo, Serra** *hills* Brazil
137 L4 **Estūh** Iran
126 C2 **Etadunna** Australia
144 D4 **Etah** India
164 D5 **Étain** France
166 F2 **Étampes** France
166 E1 **Étaples** France
144 D4 **Etawah** India
181 I3 **Ethandakukhanya** S. Africa
180 E4 **E'Thembini** S. Africa
178 D3 **Ethiopia** *country* Africa
136 D2 **Etimesgut** Turkey
162 C4 **Etive, Loch** *inlet* U.K.
170 F6 **Etna, Mount** *vol. Sicily* Italy
159 I4 **Etne** Norway
186 C3 **Etolin Island** U.S.A.
179 B5 **Etosha National Park** Namibia
179 B5 **Etosha Pan** *salt pan* Namibia
138 C5 **Etrek** Turkm.
171 K3 **Etropole** Bulg.
143 B4 **Ettaiyapuram** India
164 E5 **Ettelbruck** Lux.
164 C3 **Etten-Leur** Neth.
165 G6 **Ettlingen** Germany
162 E5 **Ettrick Forest** *reg.* U.K.
**Etxarri** Spain *see* **Etxarri-Aranatz**
167 E1 **Etxarri-Aranatz** Spain
206 C3 **Etzatlán** Mex.
127 G4 **Euabalong** Australia
124 C5 **Eucla** Australia
202 C4 **Euclid** U.S.A.
211 K6 **Euclides da Cunha** Brazil
127 H6 **Eucumbene, Lake** Australia
126 C5 **Eudunda** Australia
201 C6 **Eufaula** U.S.A.
199 E5 **Eufaula Lake** *resr* U.S.A.
194 B2 **Eugene** U.S.A.
206 A2 **Eugenia, Punta** *pt* Mex.
127 H4 **Eugowra** Australia
127 F2 **Eulo** Australia
127 H3 **Eumungerie** Australia
199 E6 **Eunice** U.S.A.
164 E4 **Eupen** Belgium
137 J6 **Euphrates** *r.* Asia *alt.* **Al Furāt (Iraq/Syria)**, *alt.* **Fırat (Turkey)**
159 M3 **Eura** Fin.
166 E2 **Eure** *r.* France
194 A3 **Eureka** *CA* U.S.A.
194 D1 **Eureka** *MT* U.S.A.
197 E2 **Eureka** *NV* U.S.A.
126 D3 **Eurinilla** *watercourse* Australia
126 D3 **Euriowie** Australia
127 F6 **Euroa** Australia
179 E6 **Europa, Île** *i.* Indian Ocean
167 D4 **Europa Point** Gibraltar
156 **Europe**
164 E4 **Euskirchen** Germany
126 E5 **Euston** Australia
201 C5 **Eutaw** U.S.A.
186 D4 **Eutsuk Lake** Canada
165 K3 **Eutzsch** Germany
181 H3 **Evander** S. Africa
188 E3 **Evans, Lac** *l.* Canada
195 F4 **Evans, Mount** U.S.A.
186 F4 **Evansburg** Canada
127 J2 **Evans Head** Australia
185 J3 **Evans Strait** Canada
190 D4 **Evanston** *IL* U.S.A.
194 E3 **Evanston** *WY* U.S.A.
191 F3 **Evansville** Canada
200 C4 **Evansville** *IN* U.S.A.
190 C4 **Evansville** *WI* U.S.A.
194 F3 **Evansville** *WY* U.S.A.
190 E4 **Evart** U.S.A.
181 G3 **Evaton** S. Africa
140 D5 **Evaz** Iran
190 A2 **Eveleth** U.S.A.
133 Q3 **Evensk** Rus. Fed.
126 A3 **Everard, Lake** *salt flat* Australia
124 D4 **Everard Range** *hills* Australia
164 D3 **Everdingen** Neth.
145 F4 **Everest, Mount** China
203 J1 **Everett** Canada
194 B1 **Everett** U.S.A.
164 B3 **Evergem** Belgium
201 D7 **Everglades** *swamp* U.S.A.
201 D7 **Everglades National Park** U.S.A.
199 G6 **Evergreen** U.S.A.
161 F5 **Evesham** U.K.
161 F5 **Evesham, Vale of** *val.* U.K.
158 M3 **Evijärvi** Fin.
176 D4 **Evinayong** Equat. Guinea
159 I4 **Evje** Norway
167 C3 **Évora** Port.
146 F1 **Evoron, Ozero** *l.* Rus. Fed.
137 J2 **Evowghlī** Iran
166 E2 **Évreux** France
171 J6 **Evrotas** *r.* Greece
136 D4 **Evrychou** Cyprus
171 K5 **Evvoia** *i.* Greece
196 □1 **'Ewa Beach** U.S.A.
178 D3 **Ewaso Ngiro** *r.* Kenya
162 C3 **Ewe, Loch** *b.* U.K.
178 B4 **Ewo** Congo
210 E6 **Exaltación** Bol.
181 G4 **Excelsior** S. Africa
196 C2 **Excelsior Mountain** U.S.A.
196 C2 **Excelsior Mountains** U.S.A.
198 E4 **Excelsior Springs** U.S.A.
161 D6 **Exe** *r.* U.K.
129 B4 **Executive Committee Range** *mts* Antarctica
127 I5 **Exeter** Australia
191 G4 **Exeter** Canada
161 D7 **Exeter** U.K.
196 C3 **Exeter** *CA* U.S.A.
203 H3 **Exeter** *NH* U.S.A.
164 E2 **Exloo** Neth.
161 D7 **Exminster** U.K.
161 D6 **Exmoor** *hills* U.K.
161 D6 **Exmoor National Park** U.K.
203 F6 **Exmore** U.S.A.
161 D7 **Exmouth** U.K.
127 H3 **Exmouth, Mount** Australia
124 B4 **Exmouth Gulf** Australia
218 L6 **Exmouth Plateau** *sea feature* Indian Ocean
167 D3 **Extremadura** *aut. comm.* Spain
201 E7 **Exuma Sound** *sea chan.* Bahamas
178 D4 **Eyasi, Lake** *salt l.* Tanz.
161 I5 **Eye** U.K.
162 F5 **Eyemouth** U.K.
162 B2 **Eye Peninsula** U.K.
158 C3 **Eyjafjallajökull** *ice cap* Iceland
158 C1 **Eyjafjörður** *inlet* Iceland
178 E3 **Eyl** Somalia
161 F6 **Eynsham** U.K.
128 B6 **Eyre Mountains** N.Z.
126 B2 **Eyre (North), Lake** *salt flat* Australia
126 A4 **Eyre Peninsula** Australia
126 B2 **Eyre (South), Lake** *salt flat* Australia
165 H2 **Eystrup** Germany
158 □ **Eysturoy** *i.* Faroe Is
181 I4 **Ezakheni** S. Africa
181 H3 **Ezenzeleni** S. Africa
215 C3 **Ezequiel Ramos Mexía, Embalse** *resr* Arg.
149 E4 **Ezhou** China
172 I2 **Ezhva** Rus. Fed.
171 L5 **Ezine** Turkey
136 F1 **Ezinepazar** Turkey


# F


159 J5 **Faaborg** Denmark
199 B6 **Fabens** U.S.A.
154 □ **Faber, Mount** *h.* Sing.
186 F2 **Faber Lake** Canada
**Fåborg** Denmark *see* **Faaborg**
170 E3 **Fabriano** Italy
213 B3 **Facatativá** Col.
164 B4 **Faches-Thumesnil** France
176 D3 **Fachi** Niger
203 F4 **Factoryville** U.S.A.
212 B7 **Facundo** Arg.
177 E3 **Fada** Chad
176 C3 **Fada-N'Gourma** Burkina Faso
137 H4 **Fadghāmī** Syria
170 D2 **Faenza** Italy
**Faeroes** *terr.* Atlantic Ocean *see* **Faroe Islands**
147 F7 **Fafanlap** Indon.
178 E3 **Fafen Shet'** *watercourse* Eth.
171 K2 **Făgăraş** Romania
159 J3 **Fagernes** Norway
159 K4 **Fagersta** Sweden
212 C8 **Fagnano, Lago** *l.* Arg./Chile
164 C4 **Fagne** *reg.* Belgium
176 B3 **Faguibine, Lac** *l.* Mali
158 C3 **Fagurhólsmýri** Iceland
177 F4 **Fagwir** South Sudan
140 C4 **Fahlīān, Rūdkhāneh-ye** *watercourse* Iran
141 E4 **Fahraj** Iran
136 D6 **Fā'id** Egypt
184 D3 **Fairbanks** U.S.A.
202 B5 **Fairborn** U.S.A.
198 D3 **Fairbury** U.S.A.
202 E5 **Fairfax** U.S.A.
196 A2 **Fairfield** *CA* U.S.A.
190 B5 **Fairfield** *IA* U.S.A.
200 C4 **Fairfield** *OH* U.S.A.
199 D6 **Fairfield** *TX* U.S.A.
203 G3 **Fair Haven** U.S.A.
163 E2 **Fair Head** U.K.
153 A4 **Fairie Queen Shoal** *sea feature* Phil.
162 G1 **Fair Isle** *i.* U.K.
128 C7 **Fairlie** N.Z.
198 E3 **Fairmont** *MN* U.S.A.
202 C5 **Fairmont** *WV* U.S.A.
195 F4 **Fairplay** U.S.A.
190 D3 **Fairport** U.S.A.
202 C4 **Fairport Harbor** U.S.A.
186 F3 **Fairview** Canada
191 E3 **Fairview** *MI* U.S.A.
199 D4 **Fairview** *OK* U.S.A.
197 G2 **Fairview** *UT* U.S.A.
149 □ **Fairview Park** *Hong Kong* China
186 B3 **Fairweather, Cape** U.S.A.
186 B3 **Fairweather, Mount** Canada/U.S.A.
147 G6 **Fais** *i.* Micronesia
144 C3 **Faisalabad** Pak.
164 C5 **Faissault** France
198 C2 **Faith** U.S.A.
141 H2 **Faīẓābād** Afgh.
145 E4 **Faizabad** India
125 I2 **Fakaofo** *atoll* Tokelau
161 H5 **Fakenham** U.K.
158 K3 **Fåker** Sweden
147 F7 **Fakfak** Indon.
140 D4 **Fakhrābād** Iran
152 B2 **Faku** China
161 C7 **Fal** *r.* U.K.
176 A4 **Falaba** Sierra Leone
166 D2 **Falaise** France
145 G4 **Falakata** India
145 H5 **Falam** Myanmar
199 D7 **Falcon Lake** Mex./U.S.A.
199 D7 **Falfurrias** U.S.A.
186 F3 **Falher** Canada
165 L3 **Falkenberg** Germany
159 K4 **Falkenberg** Sweden
165 K1 **Falkenhagen** Germany
165 K3 **Falkenhain** Germany
165 L2 **Falkensee** Germany
165 K5 **Falkenstein** Germany
162 E5 **Falkirk** U.K.
162 E4 **Falkland** U.K.
219 F9 **Falkland Escarpment** *sea feature* S. Atlantic Ocean
212 E8 **Falkland Islands** *terr.* Atlantic Ocean
219 F9 **Falkland Plateau** *sea feature* S. Atlantic Ocean
212 D8 **Falkland Sound** *sea chan.* Falkland Is
159 K4 **Falköping** Sweden
196 D5 **Fallbrook** U.S.A.
165 H2 **Fallingbostel** Germany
196 C2 **Fallon** U.S.A.
203 H4 **Fall River** U.S.A.
194 F3 **Fall River Pass** U.S.A.
198 E3 **Falls City** U.S.A.
161 B7 **Falmouth** U.K.
202 A5 **Falmouth** *KY* U.S.A.
203 H3 **Falmouth** *ME* U.S.A.
190 E3 **Falmouth** *MI* U.S.A.
180 C7 **False Bay** S. Africa
206 B3 **Falso, Cabo** *c.* Mex.
159 J5 **Falster** *i.* Denmark
169 M7 **Fălticeni** Romania
159 K3 **Falun** Sweden
136 D4 **Famagusta** Cyprus
164 E5 **Fameck** France
140 C3 **Famenin** Iran
164 D4 **Famenne** *val.* Belgium
187 J4 **Family Lake** Canada
148 F4 **Fanchang** China
163 E4 **Fane** *r.* Ireland
154 A1 **Fang** Thai.
148 D3 **Fangcheng** China
149 C4 **Fangdou Shan** *mts* China
149 F6 **Fangliao** Taiwan
148 E2 **Fangshan** *Beijing* China
148 D2 **Fangshan** *Shanxi* China
149 F6 **Fangshan** Taiwan
148 D3 **Fangxian** China
150 A2 **Fangzheng** China
149 □ **Fanling** *Hong Kong* China
162 C3 **Fannich, Loch** *l.* U.K.
141 E5 **Fannūj** Iran
170 E3 **Fano** Italy
149 F5 **Fanshan** China
148 D2 **Fanshi** China
**Fan Si Pan** *mt.* Vietnam *see* **Phăng Xi Păng**
178 C3 **Faradje** Dem. Rep. Congo
179 E6 **Farafangana** Madag.
177 E2 **Farāfirah, Wāḥāt al** *oasis* Egypt
**Farafra Oasis** *oasis* Egypt *see* **Farāfirah, Wāḥāt al**
141 F3 **Farāh** Afgh.
141 F4 **Farāh Rōd** *watercourse* Afgh.
213 A4 **Farallones de Cali, Parque Nacional** *nat. park* Col.
176 A3 **Faranah** Guinea
138 E5 **Farap** Turkm.
142 B6 **Farasān, Jazā'ir** *is* Saudi Arabia
147 G6 **Faraulep** *atoll* Micronesia
161 F7 **Fareham** U.K.
185 N4 **Farewell, Cape** Greenland
128 D4 **Farewell, Cape** N.Z.
128 D4 **Farewell Spit** N.Z.
159 K4 **Färgelanda** Sweden
198 D2 **Fargo** U.S.A.
139 G4 **Farg'ona** Uzbek.
198 E2 **Faribault** U.S.A.
189 F2 **Faribault, Lac** *l.* Canada
144 D3 **Faridabad** India
144 C3 **Faridkot** India
145 G5 **Faridpur** Bangl.
176 A3 **Farim** Guinea-Bissau
141 E3 **Farīmān** Iran
159 L4 **Färjestaden** Sweden
139 G5 **Farkhor** Tajik.
137 L4 **Farmahīn** Iran
190 C5 **Farmer City** U.S.A.
188 D2 **Farmer Island** Canada
186 E3 **Farmington** Canada
190 B5 **Farmington** *IA* U.S.A.
190 B5 **Farmington** *IL* U.S.A.
203 H2 **Farmington** *ME* U.S.A.
203 H3 **Farmington** *NH* U.S.A.
197 H3 **Farmington** *NM* U.S.A.
194 E3 **Farmington** *UT* U.S.A.
186 D4 **Far Mountain** Canada
202 D6 **Farmville** U.S.A.
161 G6 **Farnborough** U.K.
160 F2 **Farne Islands** U.K.
161 G6 **Farnham** U.K.
186 F4 **Farnham, Mount** Canada
211 G4 **Faro** Brazil
186 C2 **Faro** Canada
167 C4 **Faro** Port.
159 L4 **Fårö** *i.* Sweden
158 □2 **Faroe Islands** *terr.* N. Atlantic Ocean
159 L4 **Fårösund** Sweden
175 I5 **Farquhar Group** *is* Seychelles
**Farquhar Islands** Seychelles *see* **Farquhar Group**
140 D4 **Farrāshband** Iran
202 C4 **Farrell** U.S.A.
191 J3 **Farrellton** Canada
141 E3 **Farrokhī** Iran
140 D3 **Farsakh** Iran
171 J5 **Farsala** Greece
194 E3 **Farson** U.S.A.
159 I4 **Farsund** Norway
138 D5 **Fārūj** Iran
**Farvel, Kap** *c.* Greenland *see* **Farewell, Cape**
199 C5 **Farwell** U.S.A.
140 E5 **Fāryāb** Iran
140 D4 **Fasā** Iran
170 G4 **Fasano** Italy
165 I2 **Faßberg** Germany
202 E4 **Fassett** U.S.A.
173 D5 **Fastiv** Ukr.
144 D4 **Fatehgarh** India
144 C4 **Fatehpur** *Rajasthan* India
144 E4 **Fatehpur** *Uttar Pradesh* India
144 D4 **Fatehpur Sikri** India
140 D4 **Fatḥābād** Iran
191 G3 **Fathom Five National Marine Park** Canada
176 A3 **Fatick** Senegal
166 H2 **Faulquemont** France
181 F4 **Fauresmith** S. Africa
158 K2 **Fauske** Norway
197 F1 **Faust** U.S.A.
170 E6 **Favignana, Isola** *i. Sicily* Italy
186 G4 **Fawcett** Canada
161 F7 **Fawley** U.K.
188 C3 **Fawn** *r.* Canada
158 B2 **Faxaflói** *b.* Iceland
158 L3 **Faxälven** *r.* Sweden
177 D3 **Faya** Chad
190 D3 **Fayette** U.S.A.
199 E4 **Fayetteville** *AR* U.S.A.
201 E5 **Fayetteville** *NC* U.S.A.
201 C5 **Fayetteville** *TN* U.S.A.
137 L7 **Faylakah** *i.* Kuwait
176 C4 **Fazao Malfakassa, Parc National de** *nat. park* Togo
144 C3 **Fazilka** India
140 C5 **Fazrān, Jabal** *h.* Saudi Arabia
176 A2 **Fdérik** Mauritania
163 B5 **Feale** *r.* Ireland
201 E5 **Fear, Cape** U.S.A.
196 B2 **Feather, North Fork** *r.* U.S.A.
196 B2 **Feather Falls** U.S.A.
128 E4 **Featherston** N.Z.
127 G6 **Feathertop, Mount** Australia
166 E2 **Fécamp** France
215 F1 **Federación** Arg.
212 E4 **Federal** Arg.
138 E1 **Fedorovka** *Kustanayskaya Oblast'* Kazakh.
139 I1 **Fedorovka** *Pavlodarskaya Oblast'* Kazakh.
138 B2 **Fedorovka** *Zapadnyy Kazakhstan* Kazakh.
138 C1 **Fedorovka** Rus. Fed.
168 E3 **Fehmarn** *i.* Germany
165 K2 **Fehrbellin** Germany
214 E3 **Feia, Lagoa** *lag.* Brazil
148 E4 **Feidong** China
148 F3 **Feihuanghe Kou** *r. mouth* China
210 D5 **Feijó** Brazil
128 E4 **Feilding** N.Z.
211 K6 **Feira de Santana** Brazil
148 E4 **Feixi** China
136 E3 **Feke** Turkey
167 H3 **Felanitx** Spain
140 C3 **Felāvarjān** Iran
190 D3 **Felch** U.S.A.
165 L1 **Feldberg** Germany
168 D7 **Feldberg** *mt.* Germany
168 D7 **Feldkirch** Austria
168 G7 **Feldkirchen in Kärnten** Austria
215 E1 **Feliciano** *r.* Arg.
207 G4 **Felipe C. Puerto** Mex.
214 D2 **Felixlândia** Brazil
161 I6 **Felixstowe** U.K.
170 D1 **Feltre** Italy
159 J3 **Femunden** *l.* Norway
159 K3 **Femundsmarka Nasjonalpark** *nat. park* Norway
170 D3 **Fenaio, Punta del** *pt* Italy
197 H4 **Fence Lake** U.S.A.
191 H3 **Fenelon Falls** Canada
171 K4 **Fengari** *mt.* Greece
149 E4 **Fengcheng** *Jiangxi* China
152 C3 **Fengcheng** *Liaoning* China
149 C4 **Fengdu** China
149 C5 **Fenggang** China
152 D1 **Fengguang** China
149 F4 **Fenghua** China
149 C5 **Fenghuang** China
148 C4 **Fengjie** China
149 D6 **Fengkai** China
149 F6 **Fenglin** Taiwan
152 D2 **Fengman** China
148 F2 **Fengnan** China
148 E1 **Fengning** China
148 E3 **Fengqiu** China
149 C5 **Fengshan** China
149 E6 **Fengshun** China
148 E3 **Fengtai** China
149 E4 **Fengxin** China
148 E3 **Fengyang** China
148 D1 **Fengzhen** China
148 D2 **Fen He** *r.* China
145 G5 **Feni** Bangl.
125 F2 **Feni Islands** P.N.G.
166 F5 **Fenille, Col de la** *pass* France
190 B4 **Fennimore** U.S.A.
179 E5 **Fenoarivo Atsinanana** Madag.
191 F4 **Fenton** U.S.A.
148 D2 **Fenxi** China
148 D2 **Fenyang** China
149 E5 **Fenyi** China

173 E6 **Feodosiya** Ukr.
170 B6 **Fer, Cap de** *c.* Alg.
141 E3 **Ferdows** Iran
**Fergana** Uzbek. *see* **Farg'ona**
139 H4 **Fergana Too Tizmegi** *mts* Kyrg.
191 G4 **Fergus** Canada
198 D2 **Fergus Falls** U.S.A.
124 F2 **Fergusson Island** P.N.G.
170 C7 **Fériana** Tunisia
171 I3 **Ferizaj** Kosovo
176 B4 **Ferkessédougou** Côte d'Ivoire
170 E3 **Fermo** Italy
189 G3 **Fermont** Canada
167 C2 **Fermoselle** Spain
163 C5 **Fermoy** Ireland
210 □ **Fernandina, Isla** *i. Galapagos Is* Ecuador
201 D6 **Fernandina Beach** U.S.A.
212 B8 **Fernando de Magallanes, Parque Nacional** *nat. park* Chile
219 G6 **Fernando de Noronha** *i.* Brazil
214 B3 **Fernandópolis** Brazil
194 B1 **Ferndale** U.S.A.
161 F7 **Ferndown** U.K.
186 F5 **Fernie** Canada
127 G2 **Fernlee** Australia
196 C2 **Fernley** U.S.A.
203 F4 **Fernridge** U.S.A.
163 E5 **Ferns** Ireland
194 C2 **Fernwood** U.S.A.
170 D2 **Ferrara** Italy
214 B3 **Ferreiros** Brazil
199 F6 **Ferriday** U.S.A.
170 C4 **Ferro, Capo** *c. Sardinia* Italy
167 B1 **Ferrol** Spain
197 G2 **Ferron** U.S.A.
138 D1 **Fershampenuaz** Rus. Fed.
164 D1 **Ferwerd** Neth.
**Ferwert** Neth. *see* **Ferwerd**
176 B1 **Fès** Morocco
178 B4 **Feshi** Dem. Rep. Congo
187 J5 **Fessenden** U.S.A.
198 F4 **Festus** U.S.A.
162 □ **Fethaland, Point of** U.K.
163 D5 **Fethard** Ireland
136 B3 **Fethiye** Turkey
138 C4 **Fetisovo** Kazakh.
162 □ **Fetlar** *i.* U.K.
162 F4 **Fettercairn** U.K.
165 J5 **Feucht** Germany
165 I5 **Feuchtwangen** Germany
189 F2 **Feuilles, Rivière aux** *r.* Canada
136 F3 **Fevzipaşa** Turkey
141 E3 **Feyẕābād** Iran
161 D5 **Ffestiniog** U.K.
179 E6 **Fianarantsoa** Madag.
178 D3 **Fichē** Eth.
165 K4 **Fichtelgebirge** *hills* Germany
181 G4 **Ficksburg** S. Africa
186 F4 **Field** *B.C.* Canada
191 G2 **Field** *Ont.* Canada
171 H4 **Fier** Albania
190 E3 **Fife Lake** U.S.A.
162 F4 **Fife Ness** *pt* U.K.
127 G4 **Fifield** Australia
190 B3 **Fifield** U.S.A.
166 F4 **Figeac** France
167 B2 **Figueira da Foz** Port.
167 H1 **Figueres** Spain
176 B1 **Figuig** Morocco
125 H3 **Fiji** *country* Pacific Ocean
206 H6 **Filadelfia** Costa Rica
212 D2 **Filadelfia** Para.
129 C3 **Filchner Ice Shelf** *ice feature* Antarctica
160 G3 **Filey** U.K.
171 I5 **Filippiada** Greece
159 K4 **Filipstad** Sweden
158 J3 **Fillan** Norway
196 C4 **Fillmore** *CA* U.S.A.
197 F2 **Fillmore** *UT* U.S.A.
129 D3 **Fimbul Ice Shelf** *ice feature* Antarctica
203 F2 **Finch** Canada
162 E3 **Findhorn** *r.* U.K.
137 H3 **Fındık** Turkey
202 B4 **Findlay** U.S.A.
127 H8 **Fingal** Australia
188 E5 **Finger Lakes** U.S.A.
179 D5 **Fingoè** Moz.
136 C3 **Finike** Turkey
136 C3 **Finike Körfezi** *b.* Turkey
167 B1 **Finisterre, Cape** Spain
172 S5 **Finland** *country* Europe
159 M4 **Finland, Gulf of** Europe
186 D3 **Finlay** *r.* Canada
186 D3 **Finlay, Mount** Canada
127 F5 **Finley** Australia
165 J3 **Finne** *ridge* Germany
126 A4 **Finniss, Cape** Australia
158 L1 **Finnsnes** Norway
159 K4 **Finspång** Sweden
163 D3 **Fintona** U.K.
**Fintown** Ireland *see* **Baile na Finne**
162 C3 **Fionn Loch** *l.* U.K.
162 B4 **Fionnphort** U.K.
128 A6 **Fiordland National Park** N.Z.
137 J6 **Fırat** *r* Turkey
*alt.* **Al Furāt (Iraq/Syria)**
*conv.* **Euphrates**
196 B3 **Firebaugh** U.S.A.
187 I2 **Firedrake Lake** Canada
203 G4 **Fire Island National Seashore** *nature res.* U.S.A.
**Firenze** Italy *see* **Florence**
137 J6 **Firk, Sha'īb** *watercourse* Iraq
215 E2 **Firmat** Arg.
166 G4 **Firminy** France
165 I6 **Firngrund** *reg.* Germany
169 P2 **Firovo** Rus. Fed.
144 B3 **Firoz** Pak.
144 D4 **Firozabad** India
141 G3 **Firozkoh** *reg.* Afgh.
144 C3 **Firozpur** India
203 H2 **First Connecticut Lake** U.S.A.
140 D4 **Fīrūzābād** Iran
164 F5 **Fischbach** Germany
179 B6 **Fish** *watercourse* Namibia
180 D5 **Fish** *r.* S. Africa
129 B6 **Fisher Bay** *b.* Antarctica
203 F6 **Fisherman Island** U.S.A.
203 H4 **Fishers Island** U.S.A.
187 M2 **Fisher Strait** Canada
161 C6 **Fishguard** U.K.
186 E2 **Fish Lake** Canada
190 A2 **Fish Lake** *MN* U.S.A.
197 G2 **Fish Lake** *UT* U.S.A.
191 F4 **Fish Point** U.S.A.
129 C3 **Fiske, Cape** *c.* Antarctica
164 B5 **Fismes** France
167 B1 **Fisterra** Spain
**Fisterra, Cabo** *c.* Spain *see* **Finisterre, Cape**
203 H3 **Fitchburg** U.S.A.
187 G3 **Fitzgerald** Canada
201 D6 **Fitzgerald** U.S.A.
126 B4 **Fitzgerald Bay** Australia
212 C7 **Fitz Roy** Arg.
124 C3 **Fitzroy Crossing** Australia
191 G3 **Fitzwilliam Island** Canada
163 D3 **Fivemiletown** U.K.
170 D2 **Fivizzano** Italy
178 C4 **Fizi** Dem. Rep. Congo
159 J3 **Flå** Norway
181 H5 **Flagstaff** S. Africa
197 G4 **Flagstaff** U.S.A.
203 H2 **Flagstaff Lake** U.S.A.
188 E2 **Flaherty Island** Canada
190 B3 **Flambeau** *r.* U.S.A.
160 G3 **Flamborough Head** U.K.
165 K2 **Fläming** *hills* Germany
194 E3 **Flaming Gorge Reservoir** U.S.A.
180 D5 **Flaminksvlei** *salt pan* S. Africa
164 A3 **Flanders** *reg.* Europe
164 A4 **Flandre** *reg.* France
162 A2 **Flannan Isles** U.K.
158 K2 **Flåsjön** *l.* Sweden
190 E4 **Flat** *r.* U.S.A.
194 D2 **Flathead Lake** U.S.A.
128 E4 **Flat Point** N.Z.
124 E3 **Flattery, Cape** Australia
194 A1 **Flattery, Cape** U.S.A.
165 J2 **Fleetmark** Germany
160 D4 **Fleetwood** U.K.
203 F4 **Fleetwood** U.S.A.
159 I4 **Flekkefjord** Norway
202 E3 **Fleming** U.S.A.
202 B5 **Flemingsburg** U.S.A.
219 G2 **Flemish Cap** *sea feature* N. Atlantic Ocean
159 L4 **Flen** Sweden
168 D3 **Flensburg** Germany
166 D2 **Flers** France
191 G3 **Flesherton** Canada
187 H2 **Fletcher Lake** Canada
191 F3 **Fletcher Pond** *l.* U.S.A.
124 E3 **Flinders** *r.* Australia
124 B5 **Flinders Bay** Australia
126 B5 **Flinders Chase National Park** Australia
126 A4 **Flinders Island** *S.A.* Australia
127 H7 **Flinders Island** *Tas.* Australia
126 C3 **Flinders Ranges** *mts* Australia
126 C3 **Flinders Ranges National Park** Australia
187 I4 **Flin Flon** Canada
161 D4 **Flint** U.K.
191 F4 **Flint** U.S.A.
201 C6 **Flint** *r. GA* U.S.A.
191 F4 **Flint** *r. MI* U.S.A.
217 I5 **Flint Island** Kiribati
127 H1 **Flinton** Australia
159 K3 **Flisa** Norway
160 E2 **Flodden** U.K.
165 L4 **Flöha** Germany
165 L4 **Flöha** *r.* Germany
129 B4 **Flood Range** *mts* Antarctica
190 A2 **Floodwood** U.S.A.
200 B4 **Flora** U.S.A.
166 F4 **Florac** France
164 E5 **Florange** France
210 □ **Floreana, Isla** *i. Galapagos Is* Ecuador
191 F4 **Florence** Canada
170 D3 **Florence** Italy
201 C5 **Florence** *AL* U.S.A.
197 G5 **Florence** *AZ* U.S.A.
198 D4 **Florence** *KS* U.S.A.
202 C5 **Florence** *OH* U.S.A.
194 A3 **Florence** *OR* U.S.A.
201 E5 **Florence** *SC* U.S.A.
197 G5 **Florence Junction** U.S.A.
203 J1 **Florenceville** Canada
213 B4 **Florencia** Col.
164 C4 **Florennes** Belgium
212 C6 **Florentino Ameghino, Embalse** *resr* Arg.
215 E2 **Flores** *r.* Arg.
156 A6 **Flores** *i.* Azores
207 G4 **Flores** Guat.
147 E7 **Flores** *i.* Indon.
147 D7 **Flores, Laut** *sea* Indon.
214 C1 **Flores de Goiás** Brazil
**Flores Sea** *sea* Indon. *see* **Flores, Laut**
211 K5 **Floresta** Brazil
211 J5 **Floriano** Brazil
212 G3 **Florianópolis** Brazil
215 F2 **Florida** Uruguay
201 D6 **Florida** *state* U.S.A.
205 H4 **Florida, Straits of** Bahamas/U.S.A.
201 D7 **Florida Bay** U.S.A.
201 D7 **Florida City** U.S.A.
125 G2 **Florida Islands** Solomon Is
193 J7 **Florida Keys** *is* U.S.A.
171 I4 **Florina** Greece
159 I3 **Florø** Norway
189 H3 **Flour Lake** Canada
190 A4 **Floyd** *IA* U.S.A.
202 C6 **Floyd** *VA* U.S.A.
197 F4 **Floyd, Mount** U.S.A.
199 C5 **Floydada** U.S.A.
164 D2 **Fluessen** *l.* Neth.
124 E2 **Fly** *r.* P.N.G.
202 C5 **Fly** U.S.A.
171 H3 **Foča** Bos.-Herz.
162 E3 **Fochabers** U.K.
181 G3 **Fochville** S. Africa
171 L2 **Focşani** Romania
149 D6 **Fogang** China
170 F4 **Foggia** Italy
176 □ **Fogo** *i.* Cape Verde
189 J4 **Fogo Island** Canada
162 D2 **Foinaven** *h.* U.K.
166 E5 **Foix** France
158 K2 **Folda** *sea chan.* Norway
158 K2 **Foldereid** Norway
158 J2 **Foldfjorden** *sea chan.* Norway
171 K6 **Folegandros** *i.* Greece
191 F1 **Foleyet** Canada
170 E3 **Foligno** Italy
161 I6 **Folkestone** U.K.
161 G5 **Folkingham** U.K.
201 D6 **Folkston** U.S.A.
159 J3 **Folldal** Norway
170 D3 **Follonica** Italy
196 B2 **Folsom Lake** U.S.A.
173 G6 **Fomin** Rus. Fed.
172 I2 **Fominskiy** Rus. Fed.
187 H3 **Fond-du-Lac** Canada
187 I3 **Fond du Lac** *r.* Canada
190 C4 **Fond du Lac** U.S.A.
167 B2 **Fondevila** Spain
170 E4 **Fondi** Italy
125 H2 **Fongafale** *i.* Tuvalu
170 C4 **Fonni** *Sardinia* Italy
206 H5 **Fonseca, Golfo do** *b.* Central America
189 F3 **Fontanges** Canada
186 E3 **Fontas** Canada
186 E3 **Fontas** *r.* Canada
210 E4 **Fonte Boa** Brazil
166 D3 **Fontenay-le-Comte** France
158 D1 **Fontur** *pt* Iceland
191 H3 **Foot's Bay** Canada
148 C3 **Foping** China
127 H4 **Forbes** Australia
194 C1 **Forbes, Mount** Canada
165 J5 **Forchheim** Germany
189 G2 **Ford** *r.* Canada
190 D2 **Ford** *r.* U.S.A.
159 I3 **Førde** Norway
187 J2 **Forde Lake** Canada
161 H5 **Fordham** U.K.
161 F7 **Fordingbridge** U.K.
129 B4 **Ford Range** *mts* Antarctica
127 F2 **Fords Bridge** Australia
199 E5 **Fordyce** U.S.A.
176 A4 **Forécariah** Guinea
161 F7 **Foreland** *hd* U.K.
161 D6 **Foreland Point** U.K.
186 D4 **Foresight Mountain** Canada
191 G4 **Forest** Canada
199 F5 **Forest** *MS* U.S.A.
202 B4 **Forest** *OH* U.S.A.
203 G3 **Forest Dale** U.S.A.
127 G5 **Forest Hill** Australia
196 B2 **Foresthill** U.S.A.
127 H9 **Forestier, Cape** Australia
127 H9 **Forestier Peninsula** Australia
190 A3 **Forest Lake** U.S.A.
201 C5 **Forest Park** U.S.A.
189 G4 **Forestville** Canada
162 F4 **Forfar** U.K.
194 A2 **Forks** U.S.A.
202 E4 **Forksville** U.S.A.
170 E2 **Forlì** Italy
160 D4 **Formby** U.K.
167 G3 **Formentera** *i.* Spain
167 H3 **Formentor, Cap de** *c.* Spain
214 D3 **Formiga** Brazil
212 E3 **Formosa** Arg.
214 C1 **Formosa** Brazil
211 G6 **Formosa, Serra** *hills* Brazil
214 D1 **Formoso** *r.* Brazil
162 E3 **Forres** U.K.
126 E7 **Forrest** Australia
190 C5 **Forrest** U.S.A.
199 F5 **Forrest City** U.S.A.
190 C4 **Forreston** U.S.A.
158 L3 **Fors** Sweden
124 E3 **Forsayth** Australia
158 M2 **Forsnäs** Sweden
159 M3 **Forssa** Fin.
127 J4 **Forster** Australia
199 E4 **Forsyth** *MO* U.S.A.
194 F2 **Forsyth** *MT* U.S.A.
191 I1 **Forsythe** Canada
144 C3 **Fort Abbas** Pak.
188 D3 **Fort Albany** Canada
211 K4 **Fortaleza** Brazil
197 H5 **Fort Apache** U.S.A.
186 G4 **Fort Assiniboine** Canada
190 C4 **Fort Atkinson** U.S.A.
162 D3 **Fort Augustus** U.K.
181 G6 **Fort Beaufort** S. Africa
194 E2 **Fort Benton** U.S.A.
187 H3 **Fort Black** Canada
196 A2 **Fort Bragg** U.S.A.
**Fort-Chimo** Canada *see* **Kuujjuaq**
187 G3 **Fort Chipewyan** Canada
199 D5 **Fort Cobb Reservoir** U.S.A.
194 F3 **Fort Collins** U.S.A.
191 I3 **Fort-Coulonge** Canada
203 F2 **Fort Covington** U.S.A.
199 C6 **Fort Davis** U.S.A.
205 L6 **Fort-de-France** Martinique
201 C5 **Fort Deposit** U.S.A.
198 E3 **Fort Dodge** U.S.A.
198 E1 **Fort Frances** U.S.A.
**Fort George** Canada *see* **Chisasibi**
184 F3 **Fort Good Hope** Canada
162 D4 **Forth** *r.* U.K.
162 F4 **Forth, Firth of** *est.* U.K.
197 E2 **Fortification Range** *mts* U.S.A.
212 D2 **Fortín Capitán Demattei** Para.
212 D2 **Fortín General Mendoza** Para.
212 E2 **Fortín Madrejón** Para.
212 D2 **Fortín Pilcomayo** Arg.
210 F7 **Fortín Ravelo** Bol.
210 F7 **Fortín Suárez Arana** Bol.
203 I1 **Fort Kent** U.S.A.
201 D7 **Fort Lauderdale** U.S.A.
186 E2 **Fort Liard** Canada
187 G3 **Fort Mackay** Canada
186 G5 **Fort Macleod** Canada
190 B5 **Fort Madison** U.S.A.
190 B3 **Fort McCoy** U.S.A.
187 G3 **Fort McMurray** Canada
184 E3 **Fort McPherson** Canada
194 G3 **Fort Morgan** U.S.A.
201 D7 **Fort Myers** U.S.A.
186 E3 **Fort Nelson** Canada
186 E3 **Fort Nelson** *r.* Canada
**Fort Norman** Canada *see* **Tulita**
201 C5 **Fort Payne** U.S.A.
194 F1 **Fort Peck** U.S.A.
194 F2 **Fort Peck Reservoir** U.S.A.
201 D7 **Fort Pierce** U.S.A.
198 C2 **Fort Pierre** U.S.A.
186 F2 **Fort Providence** Canada
187 I4 **Fort Qu'Appelle** Canada
186 G2 **Fort Resolution** Canada
128 B7 **Fortrose** N.Z.
162 D3 **Fortrose** U.K.
196 A2 **Fort Ross** U.S.A.
**Fort Rupert** Canada *see* **Waskaganish**
186 E4 **Fort St James** Canada
186 E3 **Fort St John** Canada
186 G4 **Fort Saskatchewan** Canada
199 E4 **Fort Scott** U.S.A.
188 C2 **Fort Severn** Canada
138 B3 **Fort-Shevchenko** Kazakh.
186 E2 **Fort Simpson** Canada
187 G2 **Fort Smith** Canada
199 E5 **Fort Smith** U.S.A.
199 C6 **Fort Stockton** U.S.A.
195 F5 **Fort Sumner** U.S.A.
194 A3 **Fortuna** *CA* U.S.A.
198 C1 **Fortuna** *ND* U.S.A.
189 I4 **Fortune Bay** Canada
186 F3 **Fort Vermilion** Canada
201 C6 **Fort Walton Beach** U.S.A.
190 E5 **Fort Wayne** U.S.A.
162 C4 **Fort William** U.K.
199 D5 **Fort Worth** U.S.A.
184 D3 **Fort Yukon** U.S.A.
140 D5 **Forūr, Jazīreh-ye** *i.* Iran
158 K2 **Forvik** Norway
149 D6 **Foshan** China
170 B2 **Fossano** Italy
127 G7 **Foster** Australia
186 B3 **Foster, Mount** Canada/U.S.A.
185 P2 **Foster Bugt** *b.* Greenland
202 B4 **Fostoria** U.S.A.
161 G4 **Fotherby** U.K.
166 D2 **Fougères** France
162 □ **Foula** *i.* U.K.
161 H6 **Foulness Point** U.K.
143 C4 **Foul Point** Sri Lanka
128 C4 **Foulwind, Cape** N.Z.
176 D4 **Foumban** Cameroon
129 C4 **Foundation Ice Stream** *glacier* Antarctica
176 A3 **Foundiougne** Senegal
190 A4 **Fountain** U.S.A.
160 F3 **Fountains Abbey and Studley Royal Water Garden** *tourist site* U.K.
166 G2 **Fourches, Mont des** *h.* France
196 D4 **Four Corners** U.S.A.
181 H4 **Fouriesburg** S. Africa
164 C4 **Fourmies** France
171 L6 **Fournoi** *i.* Greece
190 C2 **Fourteen Mile Point** U.S.A.
176 A3 **Fouta Djallon** *reg.* Guinea
128 A7 **Foveaux Strait** N.Z.
201 E7 **Fowl Cay** *i.* Bahamas
195 F4 **Fowler** *CO* U.S.A.
190 D5 **Fowler** *IN* U.S.A.
190 E4 **Fowler** *MI* U.S.A.
129 B3 **Fowler Ice Rise** *ice feature* Antarctica
124 D5 **Fowlers Bay** Australia
137 L3 **Fowman** Iran
187 K3 **Fox** *r.* Canada
190 C4 **Fox** *r.* U.S.A.
186 F4 **Fox Creek** Canada
160 C3 **Foxdale** U.K.
185 J3 **Foxe Basin** *g.* Canada
185 J3 **Foxe Channel** Canada
185 K3 **Foxe Peninsula** Canada
128 C5 **Fox Glacier** N.Z.
186 G3 **Fox Lake** Canada
190 C4 **Fox Lake** U.S.A.
128 E4 **Foxton** N.Z.
162 D3 **Foyers** U.K.
163 D3 **Foyle** *r.* Ireland/U.K.
163 D2 **Foyle, Lough** *b.* Ireland/U.K.
163 B5 **Foynes** Ireland
179 B5 **Foz do Cunene** Angola
214 A4 **Foz do Iguaçu** Brazil
167 G2 **Fraga** Spain
214 C3 **Franca** Brazil
125 G3 **Français, Récif des** *rf* New Caledonia
166 F3 **France** *country* Europe
126 D6 **Frances** Australia
186 D2 **Frances** *r.* Canada
186 D2 **Frances Lake** Canada
186 D2 **Frances Lake** *l.* Canada
190 D5 **Francesville** U.S.A.
178 B4 **Franceville** Gabon
203 H2 **Francis, Lake** U.S.A.
198 D3 **Francis Case, Lake** U.S.A.
206 D2 **Francisco I. Madero** Mex.
206 C2 **Francisco I. Madero** Mex.
214 D2 **Francisco Sá** Brazil
179 C6 **Francistown** Botswana
186 D4 **François Lake** Canada
194 E3 **Francs Peak** U.S.A.
164 D1 **Franeker** Neth.
165 L4 **Frankenberg** Germany
165 G3 **Frankenberg (Eder)** Germany
191 F4 **Frankenmuth** U.S.A.
165 G5 **Frankenthal (Pfalz)** Germany
165 J4 **Frankenwald** *mts* Germany
181 H3 **Frankfort** S. Africa
190 D5 **Frankfort** *IN* U.S.A.
200 C4 **Frankfort** *KY* U.S.A.
190 D3 **Frankfort** *MI* U.S.A.
165 G4 **Frankfurt am Main** Germany
168 G4 **Frankfurt an der Oder** Germany
197 E1 **Frankin Lake** U.S.A.
165 J5 **Fränkische Alb** *hills* Germany
165 J5 **Fränkische Schweiz** *reg.* Germany
194 E3 **Franklin** *ID* U.S.A.
200 C4 **Franklin** *IN* U.S.A.
199 F6 **Franklin** *LA* U.S.A.
203 H3 **Franklin** *MA* U.S.A.
201 D5 **Franklin** *NC* U.S.A.
203 H3 **Franklin** *NH* U.S.A.
203 F4 **Franklin** *NJ* U.S.A.
202 D4 **Franklin** *PA* U.S.A.
201 C5 **Franklin** *TN* U.S.A.
202 E6 **Franklin** *VA* U.S.A.
202 D5 **Franklin** *WV* U.S.A.
184 F3 **Franklin Bay** Canada
194 C1 **Franklin D. Roosevelt Lake** *resr* U.S.A.
127 F9 **Franklin-Gordon National Park** Australia
126 B4 **Franklin Harbor** *b.* Australia
**Franklin Harbour** *b.* Australia *see* **Franklin Harbor**
186 E2 **Franklin Mountains** Canada
128 A6 **Franklin Mountains** N.Z.
127 G8 **Franklin Sound** *sea chan.* Australia
185 I2 **Franklin Strait** Canada
126 F7 **Frankston** Australia
159 L3 **Fränsta** Sweden
132 G2 **Frantsa-Iosifa, Zemlya** *is* Rus. Fed.
190 E1 **Franz** Canada
128 C5 **Franz Josef Glacier** N.Z.
170 C5 **Frasca, Capo della** *c. Sardinia* Italy
170 E4 **Frascati** Italy
186 E4 **Fraser** *r. B.C.* Canada
189 H2 **Fraser** *r. Nfld* Canada
180 D5 **Fraserburg** S. Africa
162 F3 **Fraserburgh** U.K.
188 D4 **Fraserdale** Canada
125 F4 **Fraser Island** Australia
186 E4 **Fraser Lake** Canada
186 E4 **Fraser Plateau** Canada
128 F3 **Frasertown** N.Z.
190 E2 **Frater** Canada
168 D7 **Frauenfeld** Switz.
215 E2 **Fray Bentos** Uruguay
164 E4 **Frechen** Germany
160 E4 **Freckleton** U.K.
190 E3 **Frederic** *MI* U.S.A.
190 A3 **Frederic** *WI* U.S.A.
159 J5 **Fredericia** Denmark
202 E5 **Frederick** *MD* U.S.A.
199 D5 **Frederick** *OK* U.S.A.
199 D6 **Fredericksburg** *TX* U.S.A.
202 E5 **Fredericksburg** *VA* U.S.A.
186 C3 **Frederick Sound** *sea chan.* U.S.A.
199 F4 **Fredericktown** U.S.A.
189 G4 **Fredericton** Canada
**Frederikshåb** Greenland *see* **Paamiut**
159 J4 **Frederikshavn** Denmark
159 K5 **Frederiksværk** Denmark
197 F3 **Fredonia** *AZ* U.S.A.
202 D3 **Fredonia** *NY* U.S.A.
158 L2 **Fredrika** Sweden
159 J4 **Fredrikstad** Norway
203 F4 **Freehold** U.S.A.
203 F4 **Freeland** U.S.A.
126 C3 **Freeling Heights** *h.* Australia
196 C2 **Freel Peak** U.S.A.
198 D3 **Freeman** U.S.A.
190 D5 **Freeman, Lake** U.S.A.
190 C4 **Freeport** *IL* U.S.A.
203 H3 **Freeport** *ME* U.S.A.
203 G4 **Freeport** *NY* U.S.A.
199 E6 **Freeport** *TX* U.S.A.
201 E7 **Freeport City** Bahamas
199 D7 **Freer** U.S.A.
181 G4 **Free State** *prov.* S. Africa
176 A4 **Freetown** Sierra Leone
167 C3 **Fregenal de la Sierra** Spain
166 C2 **Fréhel, Cap** *c.* France
129 E2 **Frei** *research stn* Antarctica
168 C6 **Freiburg im Breisgau** Germany
164 F5 **Freisen** Germany
168 E6 **Freising** Germany
168 G6 **Freistadt** Austria
166 H5 **Fréjus** France
124 B5 **Fremantle** Australia
190 E4 **Fremont** *MI* U.S.A.
198 D3 **Fremont** *NE* U.S.A.
202 B4 **Fremont** *OH* U.S.A.
197 G2 **Fremont** *r.* U.S.A.
202 B6 **Frenchburg** U.S.A.
202 C4 **French Creek** *r.* U.S.A.
211 H3 **French Guiana** *terr.* S. America
126 F7 **French Island** Australia
187 H5 **Frenchman** *r.* Canada/U.S.A.
196 C2 **Frenchman** U.S.A.
196 B2 **Frenchman Lake** U.S.A.
197 E3 **Frenchman Lake** U.S.A.
127 F9 **Frenchman's Cap** *mt.* Australia
163 C4 **Frenchpark** Ireland
128 D4 **French Pass** N.Z.
123 I5 **French Polynesia** *terr.* Pacific Ocean
121 **French Southern and Antarctic Lands** *terr.* Indian Ocean
203 I1 **Frenchville** U.S.A.
164 F2 **Freren** Germany
163 D5 **Freshford** Ireland
197 G6 **Fresnal Canyon** U.S.A.
206 D3 **Fresnillo** Mex.
196 C3 **Fresno** U.S.A.
196 C3 **Fresno** *r.* U.S.A.
167 H3 **Freu, Cap des** *c.* Spain
165 F4 **Freudenberg** Germany
168 D6 **Freudenstadt** Germany
164 A4 **Frévent** France
127 H9 **Freycinet National Park** Australia
127 H9 **Freycinet Peninsula** Australia
165 K1 **Freyenstein** Germany
166 H2 **Freyming-Merlebach** France
215 D1 **Freyre** Arg.
176 A3 **Fria** Guinea
196 C3 **Friant** U.S.A.
212 C3 **Frias** Arg.
168 C7 **Fribourg** Switz.
165 F1 **Friedeburg** Germany
165 L1 **Friedland** Germany
168 D7 **Friedrichshafen** Germany
203 I3 **Friendship** U.S.A.
165 K2 **Friesack** Germany
164 D1 **Friese Wad** *tidal flat* Neth.
165 F1 **Friesoythe** Germany
161 I6 **Frinton-on-Sea** U.K.
199 D6 **Frio** *r.* U.S.A.
162 B4 **Frisa, Loch** *l.* U.K.
197 F2 **Frisco Mountain** U.S.A.
165 H3 **Fritzlar** Germany
185 L3 **Frobisher Bay** Canada
187 H3 **Frobisher Lake** Canada
158 J3 **Frohavet** *b.* Norway
165 K3 **Frohburg** Germany
164 A5 **Froissy** France
173 G5 **Frolovo** Rus. Fed.
172 J2 **Frolovsk** Rus. Fed.
126 C2 **Frome** *watercourse* Australia
161 E6 **Frome** U.K.
126 C3 **Frome, Lake** *salt flat* Australia
126 C3 **Frome Downs** Australia
165 F3 **Fröndenberg** Germany
207 F4 **Frontera** Mex.
207 F4 **Frontera, Punta** *pt* Mex.
202 D5 **Front Royal** U.S.A.
170 E4 **Frosinone** Italy
202 D5 **Frostburg** U.S.A.
129 C6 **Frost Glacier** *glacier* Antarctica
158 J3 **Frøya** *i.* Norway
164 A4 **Fruges** France
197 H2 **Fruita** U.S.A.
197 G1 **Fruitland** U.S.A.
139 G4 **Frunze** Kyrg.
**Frunze** Kyrg. *see* **Bishkek**
168 C7 **Frutigen** Switz.
169 I6 **Frýdek-Místek** Czech Rep.
203 H2 **Fryeburg** U.S.A.
149 F5 **Fu'an** China
149 D5 **Fuchuan** China
149 F4 **Fuchun Jiang** *r.* China
162 A3 **Fuday** *i.* U.K.
149 E5 **Fude** China
149 F5 **Fuding** China
167 E2 **Fuenlabrada** Spain
167 D3 **Fuente Obejuna** Spain
152 D2 **Fu'er He** *r.* China
212 E2 **Fuerte Olimpo** Para.
176 A2 **Fuerteventura** *i.* Canary Is
153 B2 **Fuga** *i.* Phil.
148 E3 **Fugou** China
148 D2 **Fugu** China
137 I4 **Fuḩaymī** Iraq
142 E4 **Fujairah** U.A.E.
151 F7 **Fuji** Japan
149 E5 **Fujian** *prov.* China
148 C4 **Fu Jiang** *r.* China
151 F7 **Fuji-Hakone-Izu Kokuritsu-kōen** *nat. park* Japan
150 B1 **Fujin** China
151 F7 **Fujinomiya** Japan
151 F7 **Fuji-san** *vol.* Japan
150 H3 **Fukagawa** Japan
151 D7 **Fukuchiyama** Japan
151 A8 **Fukue-jima** *i.* Japan
151 E6 **Fukui** Japan
151 B8 **Fukuoka** Japan
151 G6 **Fukushima** Japan
151 B9 **Fukuyama** Japan
140 D2 **Fūlād Maḩalleh** Iran
165 H4 **Fulda** Germany
165 H3 **Fulda** *r.* Germany
161 G6 **Fulham** U.K.
148 E3 **Fuli** China
149 C4 **Fuling** China
187 L2 **Fullerton, Cape** Canada
190 B5 **Fulton** *IL* U.S.A.
200 B4 **Fulton** *KY* U.S.A.
198 F4 **Fulton** *MO* U.S.A.
203 E3 **Fulton** *NY* U.S.A.
181 J2 **Fumane** Moz.
164 C5 **Fumay** France
151 F7 **Funabashi** Japan
125 H2 **Funafuti** *atoll* Tuvalu
176 A1 **Funchal** Madeira
213 B2 **Fundación** Col.
167 C2 **Fundão** Port.
206 B2 **Fundición** Mex.
189 G5 **Fundy, Bay of** *g.* Canada
189 G4 **Fundy National Park** Canada
196 D3 **Funeral Peak** U.S.A.
**Fung Wong Shan** *h. Hong Kong* China *see* **Lantau Peak**
179 D6 **Funhalouro** Moz.
148 F3 **Funing** *Jiangsu* China
149 B6 **Funing** *Yunnan* China
148 D3 **Funiu Shan** *mts* China
176 C3 **Funtua** Nigeria
162 □ **Funzie** U.K.
149 F5 **Fuqing** China
150 H3 **Furano** Japan
140 E5 **Fürgun, Kūh-e** *mt.* Iran
172 G3 **Furmanov** Rus. Fed.
150 D3 **Furmanovo** Rus. Fed.
196 D3 **Furnace Creek** U.S.A.
167 G3 **Furnás** *h.* Spain
214 C3 **Furnas, Represa** *resr* Brazil
124 E6 **Furneaux Group** *is* Australia
165 F2 **Fürstenau** Germany
165 L1 **Fürstenberg** Germany
168 G4 **Fürstenwalde** Germany
165 I5 **Fürth** Germany
165 K5 **Furth im Wald** Germany
150 G3 **Furubira** Japan
185 J3 **Fury and Hecla Strait** Canada
213 B3 **Fusagasugá** Col.
149 C7 **Fushan** *Hainan* China
152 A5 **Fushan** *Shandong* China
152 B3 **Fushun** *Liaoning* China
149 B4 **Fushun** *Sichuan* China
152 D2 **Fusong** China
149 C6 **Fusui** China
151 B8 **Futago-san** *vol.* Japan
125 H3 **Futuna** *i.* Vanuatu
149 E5 **Futun Xi** *r.* China
148 C3 **Fuxian** China
149 B5 **Fuxian Hu** *l.* China
152 A2 **Fuxin** *Liaoning* China
152 A2 **Fuxin** *Liaoning* China
150 F5 **Fuya** Japan
148 E3 **Fuyang** *Anhui* China
149 F4 **Fuyang** *Zhejiang* China
148 E2 **Fuyang He** *r.* China
146 E2 **Fuyu** *Heilong.* China
152 D1 **Fuyu** *Jilin* China
149 B5 **Fuyuan** China
149 F5 **Fuzhou** China
149 E5 **Fuzhou** China
152 A4 **Fuzhou Wan** *b.* China
137 K2 **Füzuli** Azer.
159 J5 **Fyn** *i.* Denmark
162 C5 **Fyne, Loch** *inlet* U.K.
**F.Y.R.O.M. (Former Yugoslav Republic of Macedonia)** *country* Europe *see* **Macedonia**

## G

170 C6 **Gaâfour** Tunisia
178 E3 **Gaalkacyo** Somalia
138 E5 **Gabakly** Turkm.
181 F2 **Gabane** Botswana
196 D2 **Gabbs** U.S.A.
196 C2 **Gabbs Valley Range** *mts* U.S.A.
179 B5 **Gabela** Angola
176 D1 **Gabès** Tunisia
177 D1 **Gabès, Golfe de** *g.* Tunisia
139 H2 **Gabiden Mustafin** Kazakh.
127 H6 **Gabo Island** Australia
178 B4 **Gabon** *country* Africa
179 C6 **Gaborone** Botswana
141 E5 **Gābrīk** Iran
141 E5 **Gābrīk** *watercourse* Iran
171 K3 **Gabrovo** Bulg.
176 A3 **Gabú** Guinea-Bissau
140 C2 **Gach Sār** Iran
140 C4 **Gachsārān** Iran
143 A3 **Gadag** India
144 E5 **Gadchiroli** India
158 K2 **Gäddede** Sweden
165 J1 **Gadebusch** Germany
144 B5 **Gadhra** India
144 B4 **Gadra** Pak.
201 C5 **Gadsden** U.S.A.
143 B2 **Gadwal** India
138 E5 **Gadyn** Turkm.
**Gæi'dnuvuop'pi** Norway *see* **Geaidnovuohppi**
161 D6 **Gaer** U.K.
171 K2 **Găeşti** Romania
170 E4 **Gaeta** Italy
170 E4 **Gaeta, Golfo di** *g.* Italy
216 E5 **Gaferut** *i.* Micronesia
201 D5 **Gaffney** U.S.A.
176 C1 **Gafsa** Tunisia
172 E4 **Gagarin** Rus. Fed.
139 G4 **Gagarin** Uzbek.
172 H4 **Gagino** Rus. Fed.
176 B4 **Gagnoa** Côte d'Ivoire
189 G3 **Gagnon** Canada
173 G7 **Gagra** Georgia
137 K4 **Gahvāreh** Iran
180 C3 **Gaiab** *watercourse* Namibia
145 G4 **Gaibandha** Bangl.
171 K7 **Gaïdouronisi** *i.* Greece
165 H6 **Gaildorf** Germany
166 E5 **Gaillac** France
201 D6 **Gainesville** *FL* U.S.A.
201 D5 **Gainesville** *GA* U.S.A.
199 D5 **Gainesville** *TX* U.S.A.
161 G4 **Gainsborough** U.K.
126 A3 **Gairdner, Lake** *salt flat* Australia
162 C3 **Gairloch** U.K.
162 C3 **Gair Loch** *b.* U.K.
152 B3 **Gaizhou** China
143 C2 **Gajapatinagaram** India
141 G5 **Gajar** Pak.
180 E3 **Gakarosa** *mt.* S. Africa
144 C1 **Gakuch** Pak.
145 G3 **Gala** China
**Galaasiya** Uzbek. *see* **Galaosiyo**
178 D4 **Galana** *r.* Kenya
138 F5 **Galaosiyo** Uzbek.
210 □ **Galápagos, Parque Nacional** *nat. park* Ecuador
217 N6 **Galapagos Islands** Pacific Ocean
217 M6 **Galapagos Rise** *sea feature* Pacific Ocean
162 F5 **Galashiels** U.K.
171 L3 **Galata, Nos** *pt* Bulg.
171 M2 **Galaţi** Romania
171 H4 **Galatina** Italy
202 C6 **Galax** U.S.A.
141 F3 **Galaýmor** Turkm.
163 C5 **Galbally** Ireland
159 J3 **Galdhøpiggen** *mt.* Norway
207 D2 **Galeana** Mex.
140 D5 **Galeh Dār** Iran
190 B4 **Galena** U.S.A.
213 E2 **Galeota Point** Trin. and Tob.
215 B4 **Galera, Punta** *pt* Chile
207 E5 **Galera, Punta** *pt* Mex.
213 E2 **Galera Point** Trin. and Tob.
190 B5 **Galesburg** U.S.A.
180 F4 **Galeshewe** S. Africa
190 B3 **Galesville** U.S.A.
202 E4 **Galeton** U.S.A.
173 G7 **Gali** Georgia
172 G3 **Galich** Rus. Fed.
172 G2 **Galichskaya Vozvyshennost'** *hills* Rus. Fed.
167 C1 **Galicia** *aut. comm.* Spain
136 E5 **Galilee, Sea of** Israel
202 B4 **Galion** U.S.A.
170 C6 **Galite, Canal de la** *sea chan.* Tunisia
197 G5 **Galiuro Mountains** U.S.A.
138 E5 **Galkynyş** Turkm.
177 F3 **Gallabat** Sudan
139 F4 **G'allaorol** Uzbek.
201 C4 **Gallatin** U.S.A.
194 E2 **Gallatin** *r.* U.S.A.
143 C5 **Galle** Sri Lanka
217 L6 **Gallego Rise** *sea feature* Pacific Ocean
212 B8 **Gallegos** *r.* Arg.
213 C1 **Gallinas, Punta** *pt* Col.
171 L4 **Gallipoli** Turkey
202 B5 **Gallipolis** U.S.A.
158 M2 **Gällivare** Sweden
158 K3 **Gällö** Sweden
203 E3 **Gallo Island** U.S.A.
197 H4 **Gallo Mountains** U.S.A.
197 H4 **Gallup** U.S.A.
**Gallyaaral** Uzbek. *see* **G'allaorol**
162 B4 **Galmisdale** U.K.
178 E3 **Galmudug** *reg.* Somalia
127 H5 **Galong** Australia
143 C4 **Galoya** Sri Lanka
143 C5 **Gal Oya** *r.* Sri Lanka
162 D5 **Galston** U.K.
196 B2 **Galt** U.S.A.
176 A2 **Galtat-Zemmour** W. Sahara
163 C5 **Galtee Mountains** *hills* Ireland
163 C5 **Galtymore** *h.* Ireland
141 E3 **Galūgāh-e Āsīyeh** Iran
190 B5 **Galva** U.S.A.
199 E6 **Galveston** U.S.A.
199 E6 **Galveston Bay** U.S.A.
215 E2 **Galvez** Arg.
145 E3 **Galwa** Nepal
163 B4 **Galway** Ireland
163 B4 **Galway Bay** Ireland
**Gâm** *r.* Vietnam *see* **Gâm, Sông**
149 B6 **Gâm, Sông** *r.* Vietnam
161 I8 **Gamaches** France
181 I5 **Gamalakhe** S. Africa
213 B2 **Gamarra** Col.
145 G3 **Gamba** China
178 D3 **Gambēla** Eth.
178 D3 **Gambēla National Park** Eth.
184 A3 **Gambell** U.S.A.
144 D4 **Gambhir** *r.* India
176 A3 **Gambia** *r.* Gambia
176 A3 **Gambia, The** *country* Africa
123 J6 **Gambier, Îles** *is* Fr. Polynesia
126 B5 **Gambier Islands** Australia
189 J4 **Gambo** Canada
178 B4 **Gamboma** Congo
197 H4 **Gamerco** U.S.A.
186 F2 **Gamêtî** Canada
159 L4 **Gamleby** Sweden
158 M2 **Gammelstaden** Sweden
126 C3 **Gammon Ranges National Park** Australia
180 C4 **Gamoep** S. Africa
150 B3 **Gamova, Mys** *pt* Rus. Fed.
143 C5 **Gampola** Sri Lanka
141 F4 **Gamshadzai Kūh** *mts* Iran
171 J3 **Gamzigrad-Romuliana** *tourist site*
148 A3 **Gana** China
197 H4 **Ganado** U.S.A.
181 H3 **Ga-Nala** S. Africa
191 I3 **Gananoque** Canada
137 K1 **Gäncä** Azer.
149 C7 **Gancheng** China
155 E3 **Gandadiwata, Bukit** *mt.* Indon.
145 G3 **Gandaingoin** China
178 C4 **Gandajika** Dem. Rep. Congo
145 E4 **Gandak Barrage** *dam* Nepal
**Gandak Dam** Nepal *see* **Gandak Barrage**
144 B3 **Gandari Mountain** Pak.
144 A3 **Gandava** Pak.
189 J4 **Gander** Canada
165 G1 **Ganderkesee** Germany
167 G2 **Gandesa** Spain
144 C5 **Gandevi** India
144 B5 **Gandhidham** India
144 C5 **Gandhinagar** India
144 C4 **Gandhi Sagar** *resr* India
144 C4 **Gandhi Sagar Dam** India
167 F3 **Gandia** Spain
**Gand-i-Zureh** *plain* Afgh. *see* **Zirah, Gōd-e**
214 E1 **Gandu** Brazil
144 E4 **Ganga** *r.* Bangl./India
*alt.* **Padma,**
*conv.* **Ganges**
143 C5 **Ganga** *r.* Sri Lanka
215 C4 **Gangán** Arg.
144 C3 **Ganganagar** India
144 D4 **Gangapur** India
145 H5 **Gangaw** Myanmar
143 B3 **Gangawati** India
148 A2 **Gangca** China
144 E3 **Gangdisê Shan** *mts* China
144 E4 **Ganges** *r.* Bangl./India
*alt.* **Ganga,**
*alt.* **Padma**
166 F5 **Ganges** France
145 G5 **Ganges, Mouths of the** Bangl./India
218 J3 **Ganges Cone** *sea feature* Indian Ocean
152 D5 **Ganghwa** S. Korea
152 D5 **Ganghwa-do** *i.* S. Korea
152 E5 **Gangneung** S. Korea
144 D3 **Gangoh** India
144 D3 **Gangotri Group** *mts* India
145 G4 **Gangtok** India
148 B3 **Gangu** China
143 D2 **Ganjam** India
140 C4 **Ganjgūn** Iran

149 E4 **Gan Jiang** *r.* China
152 B2 **Ganjig** China
149 B4 **Ganluo** China
127 G5 **Ganmain** Australia
166 F3 **Gannat** France
194 E3 **Gannett Peak** U.S.A.
144 C5 **Ganora** India
148 C2 **Ganquan** China
180 C7 **Gansbaai** S. Africa
152 E4 **Ganseong** S. Korea
148 B3 **Gansu** *prov.* China
148 B2 **Gantang** China
126 B6 **Gantheaume, Cape** Australia
173 G7 **Gantiadi** Georgia
149 E5 **Ganxian** China
180 F3 **Ganyesa** S. Africa
148 F3 **Ganyu** China
138 B3 **Ganyushkino** Kazakh.
149 E5 **Ganzhou** China
177 F4 **Ganzi** South Sudan
176 B3 **Gao** Mali
149 E4 **Gao’an** China
148 E2 **Gaocheng** China
148 F4 **Gaochun** China
148 B2 **Gaolan** China
148 F2 **Gaomi** China
149 D5 **Gaomudang** China
148 D3 **Gaoping** China
148 A2 **Gaotai** China
148 E2 **Gaotang** China
163 C2 **Gaoth Dobhair** Ireland
148 C2 **Gaotouyao** China
176 B3 **Gaoua** Burkina Faso
176 A3 **Gaoual** Guinea
**Gaoxian** China *see* **Wenjiang**
149 F6 **Gaoxiong** Taiwan
148 E2 **Gaoyang** China
148 E2 **Gaoyi** China
148 F3 **Gaoyou** China
148 F3 **Gaoyou Hu** *l.* China
149 D6 **Gaozhou** China
166 H4 **Gap** France
153 B3 **Gapan** Phil.
152 D5 **Gapyeong** S. Korea
144 E2 **Gar** China
163 C4 **Gara, Lough** *l.* Ireland
**Garabekevyul** Turkm. *see* **Garabekewül**
138 F5 **Garabekewül** Turkm.
141 F2 **Garabil Belentligi** *hills* Turkm.
138 C4 **Garabogaz** Turkm.
138 C4 **Garabogazköl** Turkm.
138 C4 **Garabogazköl Aýlagy** *b.* Turkm.
206 J6 **Garachiné** Panama
141 F4 **Garāgheh** Iran
138 D5 **Garagum** *des.* Turkm.
**Garagum** *des.* Turkm. *see* **Karakum Desert**
138 E5 **Garagum Kanaly** *canal* Turkm.
127 H2 **Garah** Australia
138 F5 **Garamätnyýaz** Turkm.
178 C3 **Garamba** *r.* Dem. Rep. Congo
178 C3 **Garamba, Parc National de la** *nat. park* Dem. Rep. Congo
211 K5 **Garanhuns** Brazil
181 G2 **Ga-Rankuwa** S. Africa
178 D3 **Garba Tula** Kenya
196 A1 **Garberville** U.S.A.
165 H2 **Garbsen** Germany
214 C3 **Garça** Brazil
214 B1 **Garças, Rio das** *r.* Brazil
145 G2 **Garco** China
170 D2 **Garda, Lake** Italy
137 J1 **Gardabani** Georgia
170 B6 **Garde, Cap de** *c.* Alg.
165 J2 **Gardelegen** Germany
198 C4 **Garden City** U.S.A.
190 D3 **Garden Corners** U.S.A.
196 C5 **Garden Grove** U.S.A.
187 K4 **Garden Hill** Canada
190 E3 **Garden Island** U.S.A.
180 E6 **Garden Route National Park** *nat. park* S. Africa
141 H3 **Gardēz** Afgh.
**Gardez** Afgh. *see* **Gardēz**
203 I2 **Gardiner** *ME* U.S.A.
194 E2 **Gardiner** *MT* U.S.A.
203 G4 **Gardiners Island** U.S.A.
190 C5 **Gardner** U.S.A.
203 J2 **Gardner Lake** U.S.A.
123 H2 **Gardner Pinnacles** *is* U.S.A.
196 C2 **Gardnerville** U.S.A.
162 D4 **Garelochhead** U.K.
190 E2 **Gargantua, Cape** Canada
137 L6 **Gargar** Iran
159 M5 **Gargždai** Lith.
144 D5 **Garhakota** India
144 A3 **Garhi Khairo** Pak.
144 D4 **Garhi Malehra** India
186 E5 **Garibaldi, Mount** Canada
186 E5 **Garibaldi Provincial Park** Canada
181 F5 **Gariep Dam** *resr* S. Africa
180 B5 **Garies** S. Africa
170 E4 **Garigliano** *r.* Italy
178 D4 **Garissa** Kenya
159 N4 **Garkalne** Latvia
202 D4 **Garland** *PA* U.S.A.
199 D5 **Garland** *TX* U.S.A.
140 C2 **Garmī** Iran
168 E7 **Garmisch-Partenkirchen** Germany
**Garmo, Qullai** *mt.* Tajik. *see* **Ismoili Somoní, Qullai**
140 D3 **Garmsār** Iran
141 F4 **Garmsel** *reg.* Afgh.
198 E4 **Garnett** U.S.A.
126 E4 **Garnpung Lake** *imp. l.* Australia
145 G4 **Garo Hills** India
166 D4 **Garonne** *r.* France
178 E3 **Garoowe** Somalia
212 G3 **Garopaba** Brazil
177 D4 **Garoua** Cameroon
215 D3 **Garré** Arg.
197 E2 **Garrison** U.S.A.
163 F2 **Garron Point** U.K.
141 G4 **Garruk** Pak.
162 D4 **Garry, Loch** *l.* U.K.
187 I1 **Garry Lake** Canada
162 B2 **Garrynahine** U.K.
178 E4 **Garsen** Kenya
138 C4 **Garşy** Turkm.
161 D5 **Garth** U.K.
165 J1 **Gartow** Germany
180 B3 **Garub** Namibia
155 C4 **Garut** Indon.
163 E3 **Garvagh** U.K.
162 D3 **Garve** U.K.
190 D5 **Gary** U.S.A.
144 E3 **Garyarsa** China
151 C7 **Garyū-zan** *mt.* Japan
144 D2 **Gar Zangbo** *r.* China
146 B3 **Garzê** China
213 B4 **Garzón** Col.
**Gascogne, Golfe de** *g.* France/Spain *see* **Gascony, Gulf of**
198 E4 **Gasconade** *r.* U.S.A.
166 D5 **Gascony** *reg.* France
166 C4 **Gascony, Gulf of** France/Spain
124 B4 **Gascoyne** *r.* Australia
144 D2 **Gasherbrum I** *mt.* China/Pakistan
176 D3 **Gashua** Nigeria
141 E3 **Gask** Iran
155 C3 **Gaspar, Selat** *sea chan.* Indon.
189 H4 **Gaspé** Canada
189 H4 **Gaspé, Cap** *c.* Canada
189 G4 **Gaspésie, Parc de Conservation de la** *nature res.* Canada
189 G4 **Gaspésie, Péninsule de la** *pen.* Canada
164 E2 **Gasselte** Neth.
201 D5 **Gastonia** U.S.A.
215 C4 **Gastre** Arg.
167 E4 **Gata, Cabo de** *c.* Spain
136 D4 **Gata, Cape** Cyprus
172 D3 **Gatchina** Rus. Fed.
202 B6 **Gate City** U.S.A.
162 D6 **Gatehouse of Fleet** U.K.
160 F3 **Gateshead** U.K.
199 D6 **Gatesville** U.S.A.
197 H2 **Gateway** U.S.A.
203 F4 **Gateway National Recreational Area** *park* U.S.A.
191 J3 **Gatineau** Canada
191 J2 **Gatineau** *r.* Canada
127 J1 **Gatton** Australia
206 I6 **Gatún, Lago** *l.* Panama
137 L5 **Gatvand** Iran
125 H3 **Gau** *i.* Fiji
187 J3 **Gauer Lake** Canada
158 J3 **Gaula** *r.* Norway
202 C5 **Gauley Bridge** U.S.A.
164 D5 **Gaume** *reg.* Belgium
145 F4 **Gauri Sankar** *mt.* China
181 G3 **Gauteng** *prov.* S. Africa
137 J1 **Gavarr** Armenia
141 F5 **Gavāter** Iran
141 H3 **Gāv Band** Afgh.
140 D5 **Gāvbandī** Iran
140 D5 **Gāvbūs, Kūh-e** *mts* Iran
171 K7 **Gavdos** *i.* Greece
140 B3 **Gāveh Rūd** *r.* Iran
214 E1 **Gavião** *r.* Brazil
137 K4 **Gavīleh** Iran
196 B4 **Gaviota** U.S.A.
141 G3 **Gāv Jān** Afgh.
159 L3 **Gävle** Sweden
172 F3 **Gavrilov-Yam** Rus. Fed.
180 B3 **Gawachab** Namibia
126 C5 **Gawler** Australia
126 A4 **Gawler Ranges** *hills* Australia
148 A1 **Gaxun Nur** *salt l.* China
138 D2 **Gay** Rus. Fed.
145 F4 **Gaya** India
176 C3 **Gaya** Niger
152 E2 **Gaya He** *r.* China
190 E3 **Gaylord** U.S.A.
136 E6 **Gaza** *terr.* Asia
136 E6 **Gaza** Gaza
181 J1 **Gaza** *prov.* Moz.
**Gaz-Achak** Turkm. *see* **Gazojak**
139 G4 **G‘azalkent** Uzbek.
**Gazandzhyk** Turkm. *see* **Bereket**
141 H3 **Gaz Darreh, Band-e** Afgh.
**Gazgan** Uzbek. *see* **G‘ozg‘on**
136 F3 **Gaziantep** Turkey
141 F3 **Gazīk** Iran
136 D3 **Gazipaşa** Turkey
138 E4 **Gazli** Uzbek.
141 E5 **Gaz Māhū** Iran
138 E4 **Gazojak** Turkm.
178 C3 **Gbadolite** Dem. Rep. Congo
176 A4 **Gbangbatok** Sierra Leone
176 B4 **Gbarnga** Liberia
176 C4 **Gboko** Nigeria
181 H6 **Gcuwa** S. Africa
169 I3 **Gdańsk** Poland
169 I3 **Gdańsk, Gulf of** Poland/Rus. Fed.
172 C3 **Gdov** Rus. Fed.
169 I3 **Gdynia** Poland
158 M1 **Geaidnovuohppi** Norway
162 C1 **Gealldruig Mhòr** *i.* U.K.
165 I3 **Gebesee** Germany
177 F3 **Gedaref** Sudan
165 H4 **Gedern** Germany
164 C5 **Gedinne** Belgium
136 A2 **Gediz** *r.* Turkey
161 H5 **Gedney Drove End** U.K.
159 J5 **Gedser** Denmark
164 D3 **Geel** Belgium
126 F7 **Geelong** Australia
180 D4 **Geel Vloer** *salt pan* S. Africa
164 F2 **Geeste** Germany
165 I1 **Geesthacht** Germany
127 G9 **Geeveston** Australia
176 D3 **Geidam** Nigeria
165 H5 **Geiersberg** *h.* Germany
187 I3 **Geikie** *r.* Canada
164 E4 **Geilenkirchen** Germany
159 J3 **Geilo** Norway
159 I3 **Geiranger** Norway
190 E6 **Geist Reservoir** U.S.A.
165 K3 **Geithain** Germany
149 B6 **Gejiu** China
170 F6 **Gela** *Sicily* Italy
178 E3 **Geladī** Eth.
154 B4 **Gelang, Tanjung** *pt* Malaysia
164 E3 **Geldern** Germany
173 F6 **Gelendzhik** Rus. Fed.
169 K3 **Gelgaudiškis** Lith.
**Gelibolu** Turkey *see* **Gallipoli**
136 C2 **Gelincik Dağı** *mt.* Turkey
140 E3 **Gelmord** Iran
165 H4 **Gelnhausen** Germany
164 F3 **Gelsenkirchen** Germany
154 B5 **Gemas** Malaysia
153 C5 **Gemeh** Indon.
178 B3 **Gemena** Dem. Rep. Congo
136 F2 **Gemerek** Turkey
136 B1 **Gemlik** Turkey
170 E1 **Gemona del Friuli** Italy
179 C6 **Gemsbok National Park** Botswana
180 D3 **Gemsbokplein** *well* S. Africa
178 E3 **Genalē Wenz** *r.* Eth.
164 C4 **Genappe** Belgium
140 C4 **Genāveh** Iran
215 D3 **General Acha** Arg.
215 E3 **General Alvear** *Buenos Aires* Arg.
215 E1 **General Alvear** *Entre Ríos* Arg.
215 C2 **General Alvear** *Mendoza* Arg.
215 E2 **General Belgrano** Arg.
207 E2 **General Bravo** Mex.
212 B7 **General Carrera, Lago** *l.* Chile
206 D2 **General Cepeda** Mex.
215 F3 **General Conesa** *Buenos Aires* Arg.
215 D4 **General Conesa** *Río Negro* Arg.
215 F3 **General Guido** Arg.
215 F3 **General Juan Madariaga** Arg.
215 E3 **General La Madrid** Arg.
215 F3 **General Lavalle** Arg.
215 D2 **General Levalle** Arg.
153 C4 **General Luna** Phil.
153 C4 **General MacArthur** Phil.
215 D2 **General Pico** Arg.
215 E2 **General Pinto** Arg.
215 C3 **General Roca** Arg.
153 C5 **General Santos** Phil.
207 E2 **General Terán** Mex.
215 D2 **General Villegas** Arg.
202 D3 **Genesee** *r.* U.S.A.
190 B5 **Geneseo** *IL* U.S.A.
202 E3 **Geneseo** *NY* U.S.A.
181 G3 **Geneva** S. Africa
168 C7 **Geneva** Switz.
190 C5 **Geneva** *IL* U.S.A.
198 D3 **Geneva** *NE* U.S.A.
202 E3 **Geneva** *NY* U.S.A.
202 C4 **Geneva** *OH* U.S.A.
166 H3 **Geneva, Lake** France/Switz.
190 C4 **Geneva, Lake** U.S.A.
**Genève** Switz. *see* **Geneva**
149 F4 **Genglou** China
167 D4 **Genil** *r.* Spain
164 D4 **Genk** Belgium
164 D3 **Gennep** Neth.
127 H6 **Genoa** Australia
170 C2 **Genoa** Italy
170 C2 **Genoa, Gulf of** Italy
**Genova** Italy *see* **Genoa**
**Gent** Belgium *see* **Ghent**
165 K2 **Genthin** Germany
152 D6 **Geochang** S. Korea
124 B5 **Geographe Bay** Australia
152 E6 **Geoje-do** *i.* S. Korea
152 E6 **Geongju** S. Korea
132 F2 **Georga, Zemlya** *i.* Rus. Fed.
189 G2 **George** *r.* Canada
180 E6 **George** S. Africa
127 H5 **George, Lake** *N.S.W.* Australia
126 C6 **George, Lake** *S.A.* Australia
201 D6 **George, Lake** *FL* U.S.A.
203 G3 **George, Lake** *NY* U.S.A.
128 A6 **George Sound** *inlet* N.Z.
126 C4 **Georgetown** Australia
127 G8 **George Town** Australia
201 F7 **George Town** Bahamas
191 H4 **Georgetown** Canada
211 G2 **Georgetown** Guyana
155 B1 **George Town** Malaysia
203 F5 **Georgetown** *DE* U.S.A.
190 D6 **Georgetown** *IL* U.S.A.
200 C4 **Georgetown** *KY* U.S.A.
202 B5 **Georgetown** *OH* U.S.A.
201 E5 **Georgetown** *SC* U.S.A.
199 D6 **Georgetown** *TX* U.S.A.
129 C6 **George V Land** *reg.* Antarctica
199 D6 **George West** U.S.A.
173 G7 **Georgia** *country* Asia
201 D5 **Georgia** *state* U.S.A.
186 E5 **Georgia, Strait of** Canada
191 G3 **Georgian Bay** Canada
191 H3 **Georgian Bay Islands National Park** Canada
124 D4 **Georgina** *watercourse* Australia
139 J2 **Georgiyevka** *Vostochnyy Kazakhstan* Kazakh.
139 G4 **Georgiyevka** *Yuzhnyy Kazakhstan* Kazakh.
173 G6 **Georgiyevsk** Rus. Fed.
172 H3 **Georgiyevskoye** Rus. Fed.
165 K4 **Gera** Germany
164 B4 **Geraardsbergen** Belgium
211 I6 **Geral de Goiás, Serra** *hills* Brazil
128 C6 **Geraldine** N.Z.
214 C1 **Geral do Paraná, Serra** *hills* Brazil
124 B4 **Geraldton** Australia
140 D5 **Gerāsh** Iran
137 H3 **Gercüş** Turkey
136 D1 **Gerede** Turkey
136 D1 **Gerede** *r.* Turkey
154 B4 **Gerik** Malaysia
141 E3 **Gerīmenj** Iran
198 C3 **Gering** U.S.A.
194 C3 **Gerlach** U.S.A.
168 C3 **German Bight** *g.* Denmark/Ger.
186 E3 **Germansen Landing** Canada
202 E5 **Germantown** U.S.A.
168 E5 **Germany** *country* Europe
165 G5 **Germersheim** Germany
181 H3 **Germiston** S. Africa
165 G5 **Gernsheim** Germany
164 E4 **Gerolstein** Germany
165 I5 **Gerolzhofen** Germany
197 G5 **Geronimo** U.S.A.
127 I5 **Gerringong** Australia
165 H4 **Gersfeld (Rhön)** Germany
165 I4 **Gerstungen** Germany
165 J2 **Gerwisch** Germany
145 F2 **Gêrzê** China
173 E7 **Gerze** Turkey
164 F3 **Gescher** Germany
178 E3 **Gestro Wenz, Wabē** *r.* Eth.
164 D4 **Gete** *r.* Belgium
202 E5 **Gettysburg** *PA* U.S.A.
198 D2 **Gettysburg** *SD* U.S.A.
202 E5 **Gettysburg National Military Park** *nat. park* U.S.A.
149 C5 **Getu He** *r.* China
129 B4 **Getz Ice Shelf** *ice feature* Antarctica
155 A2 **Geumapang** *r.* Indon.
152 D6 **Geumeo-do** *i.* S. Korea
152 D5 **Geum-gang** *r.* S. Korea
152 E6 **Geumho-gang** *r.* S. Korea
127 H4 **Geurie** Australia
137 I2 **Gevaş** Turkey
171 J4 **Gevgelija** Macedonia
141 G4 **Gêwārām Band** Afgh.
154 □ **Geylang** Sing.
181 F3 **Geysdorp** S. Africa
136 C1 **Geyve** Turkey
180 F2 **Ghaap Plateau** S. Africa
137 I5 **Ghadaf, Wādī al** *watercourse* Iraq
176 C1 **Ghadāmis** Libya
140 D2 **Gha’em Shahr** Iran
139 G4 **Ghafurov** Tajik.
144 E4 **Ghaghara** *r.* India
145 F5 **Ghaghra** India
176 B4 **Ghana** *country* Africa
140 D5 **Ghanādah, Rās** *pt* U.A.E.
144 C4 **Ghanliala** India
179 C6 **Ghanzi** Botswana
180 E1 **Ghanzi** *admin. dist.* Botswana
140 C5 **Ghār, Ras al** *pt* Saudi Arabia
136 E6 **Gharandal** Jordan
176 C1 **Ghardaïa** Alg.
177 F2 **Ghārib, Jabal** *mt.* Egypt
139 G5 **Gharm** Tajik.
177 D1 **Gharyān** Libya
136 F5 **Gharz, Wādī al** *watercourse* Syria
176 D2 **Ghāt** Libya
144 B3 **Ghauspur** Pak.
177 D3 **Ghazal, Bahr el** *watercourse* Chad
176 B1 **Ghazaouet** Alg.
144 D3 **Ghaziabad** India
145 E4 **Ghazipur** India
144 A3 **Ghazluna** Pak.
141 H3 **Ghaznī** Afgh.
141 H3 **Ghaznī Rōd** *r.* Afgh.
164 B3 **Ghent** Belgium
169 L7 **Gheorgheni** Romania
169 K7 **Gherla** Romania
170 C3 **Ghisonaccia** *Corsica* France
144 C1 **Ghizar** Pak.
143 A2 **Ghod** *r.* India
145 G4 **Ghoraghat** Bangl.
141 H3 **Ghōr Band, Daryā-ye** *r.* Afgh.
144 B4 **Ghotaru** India
144 B4 **Ghotki** Pak.
**Ghuari** *r.* India *see* **Ghugri**
139 H5 **Ghŭdara** Tajik.
145 F4 **Ghugri** *r.* India
144 D6 **Ghugus** India
144 B4 **Ghulam Muhammad Barrage** Pak.
140 D4 **Ghūrī** Iran
141 F3 **Ghūrīān** Afgh.
164 A3 **Ghyvelde** France
**Gia Đinh** Vietnam *see* **Thu Đuc**
173 G6 **Giaginskaya** Rus. Fed.
154 C2 **Gia Nghia** Vietnam
171 J4 **Giannitsa** Greece
181 H4 **Giant’s Castle** *mt.* S. Africa
163 E2 **Giant’s Causeway** *lava field* U.K.
155 E4 **Gianyar** Indon.
154 C3 **Gia Rai** Vietnam
170 F6 **Giarre** *Sicily* Italy
170 B2 **Giaveno** Italy
180 B2 **Gibeon** Namibia
167 D4 **Gibraltar** Europe
167 C5 **Gibraltar, Strait of** Morocco/Spain
190 C5 **Gibson City** U.S.A.
124 C4 **Gibson Desert** Australia
146 B2 **Gichgeniyn Nuruu** *mts* Mongolia
143 B3 **Giddalur** India
178 D3 **Gīdolē** Eth.
166 F3 **Gien** France
165 G4 **Gießen** Germany
165 I2 **Gifhorn** Germany
186 F3 **Gift Lake** Canada
151 E7 **Gifu** Japan
213 B4 **Gigante** Col.
162 C5 **Gigha** *i.* U.K.
138 F4 **G‘ijduvon** Uzbek.
167 D1 **Gijón** Spain
197 F5 **Gila** *r.* U.S.A.
197 F5 **Gila Bend** U.S.A.
197 F5 **Gila Bend Mountains** U.S.A.
197 E5 **Gila Mountains** U.S.A.
137 J4 **Gīlān-e Gharb** Iran
137 L1 **Gilāzi** Azer.
124 E3 **Gilbert** *r.* Australia
197 G5 **Gilbert** *AZ* U.S.A.
202 C6 **Gilbert** *WV* U.S.A.
125 H2 **Gilbert Islands** Kiribati
216 G6 **Gilbert Ridge** *sea feature* Pacific Ocean
211 I5 **Gilbués** Brazil
140 E3 **Gil Chashmeh** Iran
194 E1 **Gildford** U.S.A.
186 D4 **Gilford Island** Canada
127 I2 **Gilgai** Australia
127 H3 **Gilgandra** Australia
178 D4 **Gilgil** Kenya
127 H2 **Gil Gil Creek** *r.* Australia
144 C2 **Gilgit** Pak.
144 C2 **Gilgit** *r.* Pak.
144 C1 **Gilgit-Baltistan** *admin. div.* Pak.
127 G4 **Gilgunnia** Australia
186 D4 **Gil Island** Canada
187 K3 **Gillam** Canada
126 B4 **Gilles, Lake** *salt flat* Australia
190 C3 **Gillett** U.S.A.
194 F2 **Gillette** U.S.A.
161 E6 **Gillingham** *England* U.K.
161 H6 **Gillingham** *England* U.K.
160 F3 **Gilling West** U.K.
190 D3 **Gills Rock** U.S.A.
190 D5 **Gilman** *IL* U.S.A.
190 B3 **Gilman** *WI* U.S.A.
188 E2 **Gilmour Island** Canada
196 B3 **Gilroy** U.S.A.
203 G3 **Gilsum** U.S.A.
177 E3 **Gimbala, Jebel** *mt.* Sudan
178 D3 **Gīmbī** Eth.
152 E5 **Gimcheon** S. Korea
152 D4 **Gimhwa** S. Korea
152 D6 **Gimje** S. Korea
187 J4 **Gimli** Canada
210 E6 **Ginebra, Laguna** *l.* Bol.
143 C5 **Gin Ganga** *r.* Sri Lanka
143 B3 **Gingee** India
186 D3 **Gingolx** Canada
178 E3 **Gīnīr** Eth.
170 G4 **Ginosa** Italy
170 G4 **Gioia del Colle** Italy
127 G6 **Gippsland** *reg.* Australia
144 B4 **Girab** India
141 E5 **Gīrān** Iran
141 E4 **Gīrān Rīg** *mt.* Iran
202 C3 **Girard** U.S.A.
144 B3 **Girdao** Pak.
141 G5 **Girdar Dhor** *r.* Pak.
141 F4 **Gīrdī** Iran
136 G1 **Giresun** Turkey
144 B5 **Gir Forest** India
145 F4 **Giridih** India
127 G3 **Girilambone** Australia
141 G4 **Girishk** Afgh.
144 C5 **Girna** *r.* India
167 H2 **Girona** Spain
166 D4 **Gironde** *est.* France
127 G4 **Girral** Australia
162 D5 **Girvan** U.K.
172 E2 **Girvas** Rus. Fed.
144 E4 **Girwan** India
128 G3 **Gisborne** N.Z.
186 E4 **Giscome** Canada
159 K4 **Gislaved** Sweden
139 F5 **Gissar Range** *mts* Tajik./Uzbek.
173 G7 **Gistola, Gora** *mt.* Georgia/Rus. Fed.
178 C4 **Gitarama** Rwanda
140 D3 **Gītcheh, Kūh-e** *hills* Iran
178 C4 **Gitega** Burundi
170 E3 **Giulianova** Italy
171 K3 **Giurgiu** Romania
171 K2 **Giuvala, Pasul** *pass* Romania
164 C4 **Givet** France
166 G4 **Givors** France
164 C6 **Givry-en-Argonne** France
181 I1 **Giyani** S. Africa
177 F2 **Giza** Egypt
141 G3 **Gīzāb** Afgh.
137 K4 **Gīzeh Rūd** *r.* Iran
**Gizhduvan** Uzbek. *see* **G‘ijduvon**
133 R3 **Gizhiga** Rus. Fed.
171 I3 **Gjakovë** Kosovo
171 I3 **Gjilan** Kosovo
171 I4 **Gjirokastër** Albania
185 I3 **Gjoa Haven** Canada
158 J3 **Gjøra** Norway
159 J3 **Gjøvik** Norway
171 M6 **Gkinas, Akrotirio** *pt* Greece
189 I4 **Glace Bay** Canada
186 B3 **Glacier Bay** U.S.A.
186 B3 **Glacier Bay National Park and Preserve** U.S.A.
186 F4 **Glacier National Park** Canada
194 D1 **Glacier National Park** U.S.A.
194 B1 **Glacier Peak** *vol.* U.S.A.
158 J2 **Gladstad** Norway
124 F4 **Gladstone** *Qld* Australia
126 C4 **Gladstone** *S.A.* Australia
127 H8 **Gladstone** *Tas.* Australia
190 D3 **Gladstone** U.S.A.
190 E4 **Gladwin** U.S.A.
162 E4 **Glamis** U.K.
164 F5 **Glan** *r.* Germany
153 C5 **Glan** Phil.
163 B5 **Glanaruddery Mountains** *hills* Ireland
165 G2 **Glandorf** Germany
160 F2 **Glanton** U.K.
191 G4 **Glanworth** Canada
162 D5 **Glasgow** U.K.
200 C4 **Glasgow** *KY* U.S.A.
194 F1 **Glasgow** *MT* U.S.A.
202 D6 **Glasgow** *VA* U.S.A.
187 H4 **Glaslyn** Canada
196 C3 **Glass Mountain** U.S.A.
161 E6 **Glastonbury** U.K.
165 K4 **Glauchau** Germany
132 G4 **Glazov** Rus. Fed.
173 F4 **Glazunovka** Rus. Fed.
169 O3 **Glazunovo** Rus. Fed.
203 H2 **Glen** U.S.A.
162 C3 **Glen Affric** *val.* U.K.
191 G2 **Glen Afton** Canada
128 E2 **Glen Afton** N.Z.
181 H1 **Glen Alpine Dam** S. Africa
163 C4 **Glenamaddy** Ireland
190 E3 **Glen Arbor** U.S.A.
128 C6 **Glenavy** N.Z.
162 C3 **Glen Cannich** *val.* U.K.
195 E4 **Glen Canyon** *gorge* U.S.A.
197 G3 **Glen Canyon National Recreation Area** *park* U.S.A.
162 E4 **Glen Clova** *val.* U.K.
126 D6 **Glencoe** Australia
191 G4 **Glencoe** Canada
181 I4 **Glencoe** S. Africa
162 C4 **Glen Coe** *val.* U.K.
191 E2 **Glendale** Canada
197 F5 **Glendale** *AZ* U.S.A.
196 C4 **Glendale** *CA* U.S.A.
197 E3 **Glendale** *NV* U.S.A.
197 F3 **Glendale** *UT* U.S.A.
202 D4 **Glendale Lake** U.S.A.
127 I4 **Glen Davis** Australia
194 F2 **Glendive** U.S.A.
187 G4 **Glendon** Canada
194 F3 **Glendo Reservoir** U.S.A.
126 D6 **Glenelg** *r.* Australia
162 F4 **Glen Esk** *val.* U.K.
162 A5 **Glengad Head** Ireland
162 C3 **Glen Garry** *val. Scotland* U.K.
162 D4 **Glen Garry** *val. Scotland* U.K.
163 D3 **Glengavlen** Ireland
127 I2 **Glen Innes** Australia
162 D6 **Glenluce** U.K.
162 D4 **Glen Lyon** *val.* U.K.
162 D3 **Glen More** *val.* U.K.
127 H1 **Glenmorgan** Australia
162 D3 **Glen Moriston** *val.* U.K.
197 G6 **Glenn, Mount** U.S.A.
184 D3 **Glennallen** U.S.A.
162 C4 **Glen Nevis** *val.* U.K.
191 F3 **Glennie** U.S.A.
202 E6 **Glenns** U.S.A.
186 C3 **Glenora** Canada
203 F2 **Glen Robertson** Canada
162 E4 **Glenrothes** U.K.
203 G3 **Glens Falls** U.S.A.
162 E4 **Glen Shee** *val.* U.K.
162 C3 **Glen Shiel** *val.* U.K.
163 C3 **Glenties** Ireland
163 D2 **Glenveagh National Park** Ireland
202 C5 **Glenville** U.S.A.
199 E5 **Glenwood** *AR* U.S.A.
197 H5 **Glenwood** *NM* U.S.A.
195 F4 **Glenwood Springs** U.S.A.
190 B2 **Glidden** U.S.A.
165 I1 **Glinde** Germany
169 I5 **Gliwice** Poland
197 G5 **Globe** U.S.A.
168 H5 **Głogów** Poland
158 K2 **Glomfjord** Norway
159 J4 **Glomma** *r.* Norway
179 E5 **Glorieuses, Îles** *is* Indian Ocean
127 I3 **Gloucester** Australia
161 E6 **Gloucester** U.K.
203 H3 **Gloucester** *MA* U.S.A.
202 E6 **Gloucester** *VA* U.S.A.
203 F3 **Gloversville** U.S.A.
165 K2 **Glöwen** Germany
150 D1 **Glubinnoye** Rus. Fed.
173 G6 **Glubokiy** Rus. Fed.
139 J2 **Glubokoye** Kazakh.
165 H1 **Glückstadt** Germany
158 □ **Gluggarnir** *h.* Faroe Is
160 F4 **Glusburn** U.K.
173 H5 **Gmelinka** Rus. Fed.
168 G6 **Gmünd** Austria
168 F7 **Gmunden** Austria
159 L3 **Gnarp** Sweden
165 H1 **Gnarrenburg** Germany
168 H4 **Gniezno** Poland
143 A3 **Goa** India
143 A3 **Goa** *state* India
180 B3 **Goageb** Namibia
127 I6 **Goalen Head** Australia
145 G4 **Goalpara** India
162 C5 **Goat Fell** *h.* U.K.
178 E3 **Goba** Eth.
179 B6 **Gobabis** Namibia
180 C3 **Gobas** Namibia
215 E1 **Gobernador Crespo** Arg.
215 C3 **Gobernador Duval** Arg.
212 B7 **Gobernador Gregores** Arg.
146 C2 **Gobi Desert** Mongolia
151 D8 **Gobō** Japan
137 L1 **Gobustan Rock Art** *tourist site* Azer.
164 E3 **Goch** Germany
152 D6 **Gochang** S. Korea
179 B6 **Gochas** Namibia
154 C3 **Go Công** Vietnam
161 G6 **Godalming** U.K.
143 C2 **Godavari** *r.* India
143 C2 **Godavari, Mouths of the** India
189 G4 **Godbout** Canada
196 C3 **Goddard, Mount** U.S.A.
178 E3 **Godere** Eth.
191 G4 **Goderich** Canada
144 C5 **Godhra** India
215 C2 **Godoy Cruz** Arg.
187 K3 **Gods** *r.* Canada
187 K4 **Gods Lake** Canada
187 L2 **God’s Mercy, Bay of** Canada
**Godthåb** Greenland *see* **Nuuk**
**Godwin-Austen, Mount** *mt.* China/Pakistan *see* **K2**
164 B3 **Goedereede** Neth.
188 E4 **Goéland, Lac au** *l.* Canada
189 H2 **Goélands, Lac aux** *l.* Canada
164 B3 **Goes** Neth.
191 E2 **Goetzville** U.S.A.
197 E4 **Goffs** U.S.A.
191 G2 **Gogama** Canada
190 C2 **Gogebic, Lake** U.S.A.
190 C2 **Gogebic Range** *hills* U.S.A.
144 D4 **Gohad** India
152 D6 **Goheung** S. Korea
211 L5 **Goiana** Brazil
214 C2 **Goiandira** Brazil
214 C2 **Goiânia** Brazil
214 B1 **Goiás** Brazil
214 B2 **Goiás** *state* Brazil
214 B4 **Goio-Erê** Brazil
144 C3 **Gojra** Pak.
143 A2 **Gokak** India
173 C7 **Gökçeada** *i.* Turkey
136 B2 **Gökçedağ** Turkey
145 G3 **Gokhar La** *pass* China
136 E1 **Gökirmak** *r.* Turkey
138 D4 **Goklenkuy, Solonchak** *salt l.* Turkm.
141 F5 **Gokprosh Hills** Pak.
136 F2 **Göksun** Turkey
136 E3 **Göksu Nehri** *r.* Turkey
179 C5 **Gokwe** Zimbabwe
159 J3 **Gol** Norway
144 E3 **Gola** India
145 H4 **Golaghat** India
141 E4 **Golbāf** Iran
136 F3 **Gölbaşı** Turkey
136 B1 **Gölcük** Turkey
169 K3 **Gołdap** Poland
165 K1 **Goldberg** Germany
127 J2 **Gold Coast** Australia
176 B4 **Gold Coast** *coastal area* Ghana
186 F4 **Golden** Canada
128 D4 **Golden Bay** N.Z.
165 I3 **Goldene Aue** *reg.* Germany
196 A3 **Golden Gate National Recreation Area** *park* U.S.A.
186 D5 **Golden Hinde** *mt.* Canada
165 G2 **Goldenstedt** Germany
163 C5 **Golden Vale** *lowland* Ireland
196 D3 **Goldfield** U.S.A.
196 D3 **Gold Point** U.S.A.
201 E5 **Goldsboro** U.S.A.
199 D6 **Goldthwaite** U.S.A.
137 I1 **Göle** Turkey
196 C4 **Goleta** U.S.A.
206 I6 **Golfito** Costa Rica
199 D6 **Goliad** U.S.A.
152 A1 **Golin Baixing** China
136 F1 **Gölköy** Turkey
165 K2 **Golm** Germany
137 J3 **Golmānkhāneh** Iran
146 B3 **Golmud** China
145 H1 **Golmud He** *r.* China
153 B3 **Golo** *i.* Phil.
150 I3 **Golovnino** Rus. Fed.
140 C3 **Golpāyegān** Iran
136 C1 **Gölpazarı** Turkey
162 E3 **Golspie** U.K.
139 H1 **Golubovka** Kazakh.
171 K4 **Golyama Syutkya** *mt.* Bulg.
171 K4 **Golyam Persenk** *mt.* Bulg.
165 K2 **Golzow** Germany
178 C4 **Goma** Dem. Rep. Congo
145 G3 **Gomang Co** *salt l.* China
144 E4 **Gomati** *r.* India
154 □ **Gombak, Bukit** *h.* Sing.
176 D3 **Gombe** Nigeria
178 D4 **Gombe** *r.* Tanz.
177 D3 **Gombi** Nigeria
206 D2 **Gómez Palacio** Mex.
140 D2 **Gomīshān** Iran
165 J2 **Gommern** Germany
145 F2 **Gomo Co** *salt l.* China
141 E2 **Gonābād** Iran
205 J5 **Gonaïves** Haiti
181 I1 **Gonarezhou National Park** Zimbabwe
205 J5 **Gonâve, Île de la** *i.* Haiti
140 D2 **Gonbad-e Kāvūs** Iran
145 E4 **Gonda** India
144 B5 **Gondal** India
178 D2 **Gonder** Eth.
144 E5 **Gondia** India
136 A1 **Gönen** Turkey
149 D4 **Gong’an** China
**Gongbalou** China *see* **Gamba**
149 D5 **Gongcheng** China
149 A4 **Gongga Shan** *mt.* China
148 A2 **Gonghe** China
148 E1 **Gonghui** China
152 D5 **Gongju** S. Korea
139 J4 **Gongliu** China
214 E1 **Gongogi** *r.* Brazil
176 D3 **Gongola** *r.* Nigeria
127 G3 **Gongolgon** Australia
149 B4 **Gongquan** China
149 B5 **Gongwang Shan** *mts* China
**Gongxian** China *see* **Gongquan**
148 D3 **Gongyi** China
152 C2 **Gongzhuling** China
181 H6 **Gonubie** S. Africa
207 E3 **Gonzáles** Mex.
196 B3 **Gonzales** *CA* U.S.A.
199 D6 **Gonzales** *TX* U.S.A.
215 D2 **González Moreno** Arg.
202 E6 **Goochland** U.S.A.
129 C6 **Goodenough, Cape** *c.* Antarctica
124 F2 **Goodenough Island** P.N.G.
191 H3 **Gooderham** Canada
190 E3 **Good Harbor Bay** U.S.A.
180 C7 **Good Hope, Cape of** S. Africa
194 D3 **Gooding** U.S.A.
198 C4 **Goodland** U.S.A.
127 G2 **Goodooga** Australia
160 G4 **Goole** U.K.
127 F5 **Goolgowi** Australia
127 H4 **Goolma** Australia
127 H4 **Gooloogong** Australia
126 C5 **Goolwa** Australia
127 F2 **Goombalie** Australia
127 I2 **Goondiwindi** Australia
189 H3 **Goose** *r.* Canada
194 B3 **Goose Lake** U.S.A.
143 B3 **Gooty** India
168 D6 **Göppingen** Germany
145 E4 **Gorakhpur** India
171 H3 **Goražde** Bos.-Herz.
172 G3 **Gorchukha** Rus. Fed.
206 I5 **Gorda, Punta** *pt* Nicaragua
201 E7 **Gorda Cay** *i.* Bahamas
136 B2 **Gördes** Turkey
169 O4 **Gordeyevka** Rus. Fed.
127 F9 **Gordon** *r.* Australia
162 F5 **Gordon** U.K.
127 G9 **Gordon, Lake** Australia
186 G2 **Gordon Lake** Canada
202 D5 **Gordon Lake** U.S.A.
202 D5 **Gordonsville** U.S.A.
177 D4 **Goré** Chad
178 D3 **Gorē** Eth.
128 B7 **Gore** N.Z.
191 F3 **Gore Bay** Canada
162 E5 **Gorebridge** U.K.
136 E2 **Göreme Milli Parkı** *nat. park* Turkey
163 E5 **Gorey** Ireland
141 E4 **Gorg** Iran
140 D2 **Gorgān** Iran
213 A4 **Gorgona, Isla** *i.* Col.
203 H2 **Gorham** U.S.A.
173 H7 **Gori** Georgia
164 C3 **Gorinchem** Neth.
137 K2 **Goris** Armenia
170 E2 **Gorizia** Italy
**Gor’kiy** Rus. Fed. *see* **Nizhniy Novgorod**
172 G3 **Gor’kovskoye Vodokhranilishche** *resr* Rus. Fed.
139 J1 **Gor’koye, Ozero** *salt l.* Rus. Fed.
169 J6 **Gorlice** Poland
168 G5 **Görlitz** Germany
144 D4 **Gormi** India
171 K3 **Gorna Oryakhovitsa** Bulg.
171 I2 **Gornji Milanovac** Serbia
170 G3 **Gornji Vakuf** Bos.-Herz.
139 K2 **Gorno-Altaysk** Rus. Fed.
150 G1 **Gornozavodsk** Rus. Fed.
139 J2 **Gornyak** Rus. Fed.
150 C2 **Gornyy** *Primorskiy Kray* Rus. Fed.
173 I5 **Gornyy** *Saratovskaya Oblast’* Rus. Fed.
173 H5 **Gornyy Balykley** Rus. Fed.
150 C2 **Gornyye Klyuchi** Rus. Fed.
172 G3 **Gorodets** Rus. Fed.
173 H5 **Gorodishche** Rus. Fed.
173 G6 **Gorodovikovsk** Rus. Fed.
124 E2 **Goroka** P.N.G.
126 D6 **Goroke** Australia
172 G3 **Gorokhovets** Rus. Fed.
176 B3 **Gorom Gorom** Burkina Faso
179 D5 **Gorongosa** Moz.
147 E6 **Gorontalo** Indon.
173 F5 **Gorshechnoye** Rus. Fed.
163 C4 **Gort** Ireland
**Gortahork** Ireland *see* **Gort an Choirce**
163 C2 **Gort an Choirce** Ireland
214 D1 **Gorutuba** *r.* Brazil
141 E4 **Gorveh** Iran
173 F6 **Goryachiy Klyuch** Rus. Fed.
152 E6 **Goryeong** S. Korea
165 K2 **Görzke** Germany
168 G4 **Gorzów Wielkopolski** Poland
127 I4 **Gosford** Australia
160 F2 **Gosforth** U.K.
190 E5 **Goshen** *IN* U.S.A.
203 F4 **Goshen** *NY* U.S.A.
150 G4 **Goshogawara** Japan
141 F5 **Gosht-e ‘Olyā** Iran
165 I3 **Goslar** Germany
138 C4 **Goşoba** Turkm.
170 F2 **Gospić** Croatia
161 F7 **Gosport** U.K.
171 I4 **Gostivar** Macedonia
**Göteborg** Sweden *see* **Gothenburg**
159 K4 **Götene** Sweden
165 I4 **Gotha** Germany
159 J4 **Gothenburg** Sweden
198 C3 **Gothenburg** U.S.A.
159 L4 **Gotland** *i.* Sweden
151 A8 **Gotō** Japan
171 J4 **Gotse Delchev** Bulg.
159 L4 **Gotska Sandön** *i.* Sweden
151 C7 **Gōtsu** Japan
165 H3 **Göttingen** Germany
186 E4 **Gott Peak** Canada
138 C5 **Goturdepe** Turkm.
152 A3 **Goubangzi** China
164 C2 **Gouda** Neth.
176 A3 **Goudiri** Senegal
176 D3 **Goudoumaria** Niger
190 E1 **Goudreau** Canada
219 I8 **Gough Island** S. Atlantic Ocean
188 F4 **Gouin, Réservoir** *resr* Canada
190 E2 **Goulais River** Canada
127 H5 **Goulburn** Australia
127 I4 **Goulburn** *r. N.S.W.* Australia
126 F6 **Goulburn** *r. Vic.* Australia
124 D3 **Goulburn Islands** Australia
190 E2 **Gould City** U.S.A.
176 B3 **Goundam** Mali
167 G4 **Gouraya** Alg.
176 D3 **Gouré** Niger
180 D7 **Gourits** *r.* S. Africa
176 B3 **Gourma-Rharous** Mali
166 E2 **Gournay-en-Bray** France
127 H6 **Gourock Range** *mts* Australia
164 A5 **Goussainville** France
203 F2 **Gouverneur** U.S.A.
187 H5 **Govenlock** Canada
214 E2 **Governador Valadares** Brazil
153 C5 **Governor Generoso** Phil.
201 E7 **Governor’s Harbour** Bahamas
146 B2 **Govĭ Altayn Nuruu** *mts* Mongolia
145 E4 **Govind Ballash Pant Sagar** *resr* India
144 D3 **Govind Sagar** *resr* India
**Govurdak** Turkm. *see* **Magdanly**
202 D3 **Gowanda** U.S.A.
140 D4 **Gowd-e Aḥmar** Iran
161 C6 **Gower** *pen.* U.K.
191 G2 **Gowganda** Canada
163 D4 **Gowna, Lough** *l.* Ireland
212 E3 **Goya** Arg.
137 K1 **Göyçay** Azer.
138 C4 **Goýmatdag** *hills* Turkm.
137 H2 **Göynük** Turkey
150 G5 **Goyō-zan** *mt.* Japan
137 L2 **Göytäpä** Azer.
141 F3 **Gožareh** Afgh.
**Gōzareh** Afgh. *see* **Gožareh**
136 G2 **Gözene** Turkey
138 F4 **G‘ozg‘on** Uzbek.

144 E2 Gozha Co salt l. China
170 F6 Gozo i. Malta
180 F6 Graaff-Reinet S. Africa
Graaf-Reinet S. Africa see Graaff-Reinet
180 C6 Graafwater S. Africa
165 I4 Grabfeld plain Germany
176 B4 Grabo Côte d'Ivoire
180 C7 Grabouw S. Africa
165 J1 Grabow Germany
170 F2 Gračac Croatia
191 I2 Gracefield Canada
138 C1 Grachevka Rus. Fed.
139 I2 Grachi (abandoned) Kazakh.
206 G5 Gracias Hond.
165 K3 Gräfenhainichen Germany
165 J5 Grafenwöhr Germany
127 J2 Grafton Australia
198 D1 Grafton ND U.S.A.
190 D4 Grafton WI U.S.A.
202 C5 Grafton WV U.S.A.
197 E2 Grafton, Mount U.S.A.
199 D5 Graham U.S.A.
197 H5 Graham, Mount U.S.A.
Graham Bell Island i. Rus. Fed. see Greem-Bell, Ostrov
186 C4 Graham Island B.C. Canada
185 I2 Graham Island Nunavut Canada
203 I2 Graham Lake U.S.A.
181 G6 Grahamstown S. Africa
163 E5 Graigue Ireland
176 A4 Grain Coast Liberia
211 I5 Grajaú Brazil
162 B1 Gralisgeir i. U.K.
171 I4 Grammos mt. Greece
162 D4 Grampian Mountains U.K.
126 E6 Grampians National Park Australia
180 C5 Granaatboskolk S. Africa
213 B4 Granada Col.
206 H6 Granada Nicaragua
167 E4 Granada Spain
198 C4 Granada U.S.A.
163 D4 Granard Ireland
188 F4 Granby Canada
176 A2 Gran Canaria i. Canary Is
212 D3 Gran Chaco reg. Arg./Para.
190 D4 Grand U.S.A.
198 E3 Grand r. U.S.A.
201 E7 Grand Bahama i. Bahamas
189 I4 Grand Bank Canada
219 F3 Grand Banks of Newfoundland sea feature N. Atlantic Ocean
176 B4 Grand-Bassam Côte d'Ivoire
Grand Bay Canada see Grand Bay-Westfield
189 G4 Grand Bay-Westfield Canada
191 G4 Grand Bend Canada
Grand Canal canal China see Jinghang Yunhe
163 D4 Grand Canal Ireland
197 F3 Grand Canyon U.S.A.
197 F3 Grand Canyon gorge U.S.A.
197 F3 Grand Canyon National Park U.S.A.
205 H5 Grand Cayman i. Cayman Is
187 G4 Grand Centre Canada
194 C2 Grand Coulee U.S.A.
215 C3 Grande r. Arg.
210 F7 Grande r. Bol.
211 I6 Grande r. Bahia Brazil
214 B2 Grande r. São Paulo Brazil
215 F3 Grande, Arroyo r. Arg.
212 C8 Grande, Bahía b. Arg.
214 D3 Grande, Ilha i. Brazil
213 E4 Grande, Serra mt. Brazil
186 F4 Grande Cache Canada
166 H4 Grande Casse, Pointe de la mt. France
Grande Comore i. Comoros see Ngazidja
186 F3 Grande Prairie Canada
176 B1 Grand Erg Occidental des. Alg.
176 C2 Grand Erg Oriental des. Alg.
189 H4 Grande-Rivière Canada
194 C2 Grande Ronde r. U.S.A.
212 C4 Grandes, Salinas salt flat Arg.
125 G4 Grande Terre i. S. Pacific Ocean
189 G4 Grande-Vallée Canada
189 G4 Grand Falls Canada
189 I4 Grand Falls-Windsor Canada
186 F5 Grand Forks Canada
198 D2 Grand Forks U.S.A.
203 F3 Grand Gorge U.S.A.
203 J2 Grand Harbour Canada
190 D4 Grand Haven U.S.A.
186 F2 Grandin, Lac l. Canada
198 D3 Grand Island U.S.A.
190 D2 Grand Island i. U.S.A.
199 F6 Grand Isle LA U.S.A.
203 I1 Grand Isle ME U.S.A.
197 H2 Grand Junction U.S.A.
176 B4 Grand-Lahou Côte d'Ivoire
189 H3 Grand Lake Nfld Canada
189 I4 Grand Lake Nfld Canada
199 E6 Grand Lake LA U.S.A.
203 J2 Grand Lake ME U.S.A.
191 F3 Grand Lake MI U.S.A.
203 I1 Grand Lake Matagamon U.S.A.
202 A4 Grand Lake St Marys U.S.A.
203 I1 Grand Lake Seboeis U.S.A.
203 J2 Grand Lake Stream U.S.A.
190 E4 Grand Ledge U.S.A.
189 G5 Grand Manan Island Canada
190 E2 Grand Marais MI U.S.A.
190 B2 Grand Marais MN U.S.A.
189 F4 Grand-Mère Canada
167 B3 Grândola Port.
125 G3 Grand Passage New Caledonia
190 C2 Grand Portage U.S.A.
189 H4 Grand-Pré tourist site Canada
187 J4 Grand Rapids Canada
190 E4 Grand Rapids MI U.S.A.
198 E2 Grand Rapids MN U.S.A.
197 G3 Grand Staircase-Escalante National Monument nat. park U.S.A.
194 E3 Grand Teton mt. U.S.A.
194 E3 Grand Teton National Park U.S.A.
190 E3 Grand Traverse Bay U.S.A.
205 J4 Grand Turk Turks and Caicos Is
194 C2 Grandview U.S.A.
197 F3 Grand Wash watercourse U.S.A.
197 E4 Grand Wash Cliffs mts U.S.A.
215 B2 Graneros Chile
163 D6 Grange Ireland
194 E3 Granger U.S.A.
159 K3 Grängesberg Sweden
194 C2 Grangeville U.S.A.
186 D3 Granisle Canada
198 E2 Granite Falls U.S.A.
189 I4 Granite Lake Canada
197 E4 Granite Mountains U.S.A.
194 E2 Granite Peak MT U.S.A.
197 F1 Granite Peak UT U.S.A.
139 H4 Granitogorsk Kazakh.
170 E6 Granitola, Capo c. Sicily Italy
212 C6 Gran Laguna Salada l. Arg.
159 K4 Gränna Sweden
170 B2 Gran Paradiso mt. Italy
168 E7 Gran Pilastro mt. Austria/Italy
165 K3 Granschütz Germany
165 L1 Gransee Germany
196 C2 Grant, Mount NV U.S.A.
196 D2 Grant, Mount NV U.S.A.
161 G5 Grantham U.K.
129 A4 Grant Island i. Antarctica
162 E3 Grantown-on-Spey U.K.
197 E2 Grant Range mts U.S.A.
195 F5 Grants U.S.A.
194 B3 Grants Pass U.S.A.
166 D2 Granville France
190 C5 Granville IL U.S.A.
203 G3 Granville NY U.S.A.
187 I3 Granville Lake Canada
214 D2 Grão Mogol Brazil
196 C4 Grapevine U.S.A.
196 D3 Grapevine Mountains U.S.A.
203 G3 Graphite U.S.A.
187 G2 Gras, Lac de l. Canada
181 I2 Graskop S. Africa
203 F2 Grass r. U.S.A.
166 H5 Grasse France
160 F3 Grassington U.K.
187 H5 Grasslands National Park Canada
194 E2 Grassrange U.S.A.
187 I4 Grass River Provincial Park Canada
196 B2 Grass Valley U.S.A.
127 F8 Grassy Australia
201 E7 Grassy Creek r. Bahamas
159 K4 Grästorp Sweden
190 B4 Gratiot U.S.A.
167 G1 Graus Spain
187 I2 Gravel Hill Lake Canada
164 A4 Gravelines France
181 I1 Gravelotte S. Africa
191 H3 Gravenhurst Canada
127 I2 Gravesend Australia
161 H6 Gravesend U.K.
170 G4 Gravina in Puglia Italy
190 E3 Grawn U.S.A.
166 G3 Gray France
203 H3 Gray U.S.A.
190 E3 Grayling U.S.A.
161 H6 Grays U.K.
194 A2 Grays Harbor inlet U.S.A.
194 E3 Grays Lake U.S.A.
202 B5 Grayson U.S.A.
189 H1 Gray Strait Canada
200 B4 Grayville U.S.A.
168 G7 Graz Austria
201 E7 Great Abaco i. Bahamas
124 C5 Great Australian Bight g. Australia
161 H6 Great Baddow U.K.
205 I3 Great Bahama Bank sea feature Bahamas
128 E2 Great Barrier Island N.Z.
124 E3 Great Barrier Reef Australia
203 G3 Great Barrington U.S.A.
194 C3 Great Basin U.S.A.
197 E2 Great Basin National Park U.S.A.
203 F5 Great Bay U.S.A.
186 E1 Great Bear r. Canada
186 E1 Great Bear Lake Canada
159 J5 Great Belt sea chan. Denmark
198 D4 Great Bend U.S.A.
162 B2 Great Bernera i. U.K.
163 A5 Great Blasket Island Ireland
160 D3 Great Clifton U.K.
162 D5 Great Cumbrae i. U.K.
124 E5 Great Dividing Range mts Australia
191 F3 Great Duck Island Canada
203 F5 Great Egg Harbor Inlet U.S.A.
205 H4 Greater Antilles is Caribbean Sea
155 A3 Greater Sunda Islands is Indon.
205 I4 Great Exuma i. Bahamas
194 E2 Great Falls U.S.A.
181 G6 Great Fish r. S. Africa
181 G6 Great Fish Point S. Africa
145 F4 Great Gandak r. India
201 E7 Great Guana Cay i. Bahamas
201 E7 Great Harbour Cay i. Bahamas
205 J4 Great Inagua i. Bahamas
180 D5 Great Karoo plat. S. Africa
181 H6 Great Kei r. S. Africa
127 G8 Great Lake Australia
181 I1 Great Limpopo Transfrontier Park nat. park Africa
161 E5 Great Malvern U.K.
219 H4 Great Meteor Tablemount sea feature N. Atlantic Ocean
202 A5 Great Miami r. U.S.A.
180 B3 Great Namaqualand reg. Namibia
Great Oasis, The oasis Egypt see Khārijah, Wāḥāt al
161 D4 Great Ormes Head U.K.
161 H5 Great Ouse r. U.K.
127 H9 Great Oyster Bay Australia
203 G4 Great Peconic Bay U.S.A.
192 F2 Great Plains plain Can./U.S.A.
203 H4 Great Point U.S.A.
161 D5 Great Rhos h. U.K.
178 D3 Great Rift Valley Africa
178 D3 Great Rift Valley Eth.
178 D4 Great Ruaha r. Tanz.
203 F3 Great Sacandaga Lake U.S.A.
170 B2 Great St Bernard Pass Italy/Switz.
201 E7 Great Sale Cay i. Bahamas
194 D3 Great Salt Lake U.S.A.
194 D3 Great Salt Lake Desert U.S.A.
195 F4 Great Sand Dunes National Park and Preserve nat. park U.S.A.
177 E2 Great Sand Sea des. Egypt/Libya
124 C4 Great Sandy Desert Australia
125 H3 Great Sea Reef Fiji
184 G3 Great Slave Lake Canada
201 D5 Great Smoky Mountains U.S.A.
201 D5 Great Smoky Mountains National Park U.S.A.
186 E3 Great Snow Mountain Canada
203 G4 Great South Bay U.S.A.
161 H7 Greatstone-on-Sea U.K.
161 I6 Great Stour r. U.K.
161 C7 Great Torrington U.K.
124 C4 Great Victoria Desert Australia
129 E2 Great Wall research stn Antarctica
148 F1 Great Wall tourist site China
161 H6 Great Waltham U.K.
203 J2 Great Wass Island U.S.A.
127 G8 Great Western Tiers mts Australia
160 F3 Great Whernside h. U.K.
161 I5 Great Yarmouth U.K.
170 E4 Greco, Monte mt. Italy
167 D2 Gredos, Sierra de mts Spain
171 I5 Greece country Europe
194 F3 Greeley U.S.A.
185 J1 Greely Fiord inlet Canada
132 H1 Greem-Bell, Ostrov i. Rus. Fed.
200 C4 Green r. KY U.S.A.
197 H2 Green r. UT/WY U.S.A.
191 H3 Greenbank Canada
190 C3 Green Bay U.S.A.
190 D3 Green Bay b. U.S.A.
127 I6 Green Cape Australia
163 E3 Greencastle U.K.
200 C4 Greencastle U.S.A.
201 E7 Green Cay i. Bahamas
201 D6 Green Cove Springs U.S.A.
190 A4 Greene IA U.S.A.
203 F3 Greene NY U.S.A.
201 D4 Greeneville U.S.A.
196 B3 Greenfield CA U.S.A.
190 E6 Greenfield IN U.S.A.
203 G3 Greenfield MA U.S.A.
202 B5 Greenfield OH U.S.A.
190 C4 Greenfield WI U.S.A.
153 A4 Green Island Bay Phil.
187 H4 Green Lake Canada
190 C4 Green Lake l. U.S.A.
185 N2 Greenland terr. N. America
220 X2 Greenland Basin sea feature Arctic Ocean
220 X1 Greenland Sea Greenland/Svalbard
162 F5 Greenlaw U.K.
126 A5 Greenly Island Australia
203 G2 Green Mountains U.S.A.
162 D5 Greenock U.K.
163 E3 Greenore Ireland
203 G4 Greenport U.S.A.
195 E4 Green River UT U.S.A.
194 E3 Green River WY U.S.A.
201 E4 Greensboro U.S.A.
200 C4 Greensburg IN U.S.A.
199 D4 Greensburg KS U.S.A.
202 D4 Greensburg PA U.S.A.
162 C3 Greenstone Point U.K.
193 K5 Green Swamp U.S.A.
202 B5 Greenup U.S.A.
203 F2 Green Valley Canada
197 G6 Green Valley U.S.A.
190 C5 Greenview U.S.A.
176 B4 Greenville Liberia
201 C6 Greenville AL U.S.A.
196 B1 Greenville CA U.S.A.
201 D6 Greenville FL U.S.A.
203 I2 Greenville ME U.S.A.
190 E4 Greenville MI U.S.A.
199 F5 Greenville MS U.S.A.
201 E5 Greenville NC U.S.A.
203 H3 Greenville NH U.S.A.
202 A4 Greenville OH U.S.A.
202 C4 Greenville PA U.S.A.
201 D5 Greenville SC U.S.A.
199 D5 Greenville TX U.S.A.
187 I4 Greenwater Provincial Park Canada
127 I5 Greenwell Point Australia
161 H6 Greenwich U.K.
203 G4 Greenwich CT U.S.A.
203 G3 Greenwich NY U.S.A.
197 G2 Greenwich UT U.S.A.
199 F5 Greenwood MS U.S.A.
201 D5 Greenwood SC U.S.A.
199 E5 Greers Ferry Lake U.S.A.
198 D3 Gregory U.S.A.
124 C4 Gregory, Lake salt flat Australia
126 C2 Gregory, Lake salt flat Australia
124 E3 Gregory Range hills Australia
168 F3 Greifswald Germany
165 K4 Greiz Germany
136 E4 Greko, Cape Cyprus
159 J4 Grenaa Denmark
213 E1 Grenada country Caribbean Sea
199 F5 Grenada U.S.A.
166 E5 Grenade France
159 J4 Grenen spit Denmark
127 H4 Grenfell Australia
187 I4 Grenfell Canada
166 G4 Grenoble France
213 E1 Grenville Grenada
124 E3 Grenville, Cape Australia
194 B2 Gresham U.S.A.
160 F3 Greta r. U.K.
162 E6 Gretna U.K.
199 F6 Gretna U.S.A.
165 I3 Greußen Germany
164 B3 Grevelingen sea chan. Neth.
164 F2 Greven Germany
171 I4 Grevena Greece
164 D3 Grevenbicht Neth.
164 E3 Grevenbroich Germany
164 E5 Grevenmacher Lux.
168 E4 Grevesmühlen Germany
128 C5 Grey r. N.Z.
194 E2 Greybull U.S.A.
186 B2 Grey Hunter Peak Canada
189 I3 Grey Islands Canada
128 C5 Greymouth N.Z.
126 E2 Grey Range hills Australia
181 I4 Greytown S. Africa
164 C4 Grez-Doiceau Belgium
173 G5 Gribanovskiy Rus. Fed.
196 B2 Gridley CA U.S.A.
190 C5 Gridley IL U.S.A.
201 C5 Griffin U.S.A.
127 G5 Griffith Australia
191 I3 Griffith Canada
184 F2 Griffiths Point Canada
127 F8 Grim, Cape Australia
165 K3 Grimma Germany
168 F3 Grimmen Germany
191 H4 Grimsby Canada
160 G4 Grimsby U.K.
158 C1 Grímsey i. Iceland
186 F3 Grimshaw Canada
158 C2 Grímsstaðir Iceland
159 J4 Grimstad Norway
158 B3 Grindavík Iceland
159 J5 Grindsted Denmark
171 M2 Grindul Chitue spit Romania
198 E3 Grinnell U.S.A.
181 H5 Griqualand East reg. S. Africa
180 E4 Griqualand West reg. S. Africa
180 E4 Griquatown S. Africa
185 J2 Grise Fiord Canada
155 B3 Grisik Indon.
161 I7 Gris Nez, Cap c. France
162 F2 Gritley U.K.
170 G2 Grmeč mts Bos.-Herz.
164 C3 Grobbendonk Belgium
181 H2 Groblersdal S. Africa
180 E4 Groblershoop S. Africa
Grodekovo Rus. Fed. see Pogranichnyy
Grodno Belarus see Hrodna
180 B5 Groen watercourse N. Cape S. Africa
180 E5 Groen watercourse N. Cape S. Africa
166 C3 Groix, Île de i. France
170 D6 Grombalia Tunisia
164 F2 Gronau (Westfalen) Germany
158 K2 Grong Norway
164 E1 Groningen Neth.
164 E1 Groninger Wad tidal flat Neth.
197 E3 Groom Lake U.S.A.
180 D3 Groot-Aar Pan salt pan S. Africa
180 C6 Groot Berg r. S. Africa
180 E7 Groot Brakrivier S. Africa
181 H3 Grootdraaidam dam S. Africa
180 D4 Grootdrink S. Africa
124 D3 Groote Eylandt i. Australia
179 B5 Grootfontein Namibia
180 C3 Groot Karas Berg plat. Namibia
181 I1 Groot Letaba r. S. Africa
181 G2 Groot Marico S. Africa
180 D6 Groot Swartberge mts S. Africa
180 D5 Grootvloer salt pan S. Africa
181 G6 Groot Winterberg mt. S. Africa
190 E3 Gros Cap U.S.A.
189 I4 Gros Morne National Park Canada
165 G2 Große Aue r. Germany
165 I3 Großengottern Germany
165 G2 Großenkneten Germany
165 H4 Großenlüder Germany
165 I4 Großer Beerberg h. Germany
165 L5 Großer Gleichberg h. Germany
168 G7 Grosser Speikkogel mt. Austria
170 D3 Grosseto Italy
165 G5 Groß-Gerau Germany
170 E1 Großglockner mt. Austria
165 I2 Groß Oesingen Germany
165 J3 Großrudestedt Germany
165 L2 Groß Schönebeck Germany
180 C1 Gross Ums Namibia
194 E3 Gros Ventre Range mts U.S.A.
189 I3 Groswater Bay Canada
203 E3 Groton U.S.A.
202 D5 Grottoes U.S.A.
164 D1 Grou Neth.
186 F4 Grouard Canada
188 D4 Groundhog r. Canada
Grouw Neth. see Grou
202 C4 Grove City U.S.A.
201 C6 Grove Hill U.S.A.
196 B3 Groveland U.S.A.
129 D5 Grove Mountains mts Antarctica
196 B4 Grover Beach U.S.A.
203 H2 Groveton U.S.A.
197 F5 Growler U.S.A.
197 F5 Growler Mountains U.S.A.
173 H7 Groznyy Rus. Fed.
169 I4 Grudziądz Poland
162 C3 Gruinard Bay U.K.
179 B6 Grünau Namibia
158 B2 Grundarfjörður Iceland
202 B6 Grundy U.S.A.
165 G5 Grünstadt Germany
173 F4 Gryazi Rus. Fed.
172 G3 Gryazovets Rus. Fed.
168 G4 Gryfice Poland
168 G4 Gryfino Poland
168 G5 Gryfów Śląski Poland
158 L1 Gryllefjord Norway
212 □ Grytviken Atlantic Ocean
143 D1 Gua India
205 I4 Guacanayabo, Golfo de b. Cuba
213 D2 Guacara Venez.
213 C3 Guacharía r. Col.
167 D4 Guadajoz r. Spain
206 D3 Guadalajara Mex.
167 E2 Guadalajara Spain
167 F2 Guadalaviar r. Spain
125 G2 Guadalcanal i. Solomon Is
167 C4 Guadalete r. Spain
167 F2 Guadalope r. Spain
167 D4 Guadalquivir r. Spain
207 D2 Guadalupe Nuevo León Mex.
206 D3 Guadalupe Zacatecas Mex.
192 C6 Guadalupe i. Mex.
196 B4 Guadalupe U.S.A.
199 D6 Guadalupe r. U.S.A.
167 D3 Guadalupe, Sierra de mts Spain
206 C2 Guadalupe Aguilera Mex.
199 B6 Guadalupe Mountains National Park U.S.A.
199 B6 Guadalupe Peak U.S.A.
206 C2 Guadalupe Victoria Mex.
206 C2 Guadalupe y Calvo Mex.
167 D2 Guadarrama, Sierra de mts Spain
215 C2 Guadel, Sierra de mts Arg.
205 L5 Guadeloupe terr. Caribbean Sea
167 C4 Guadiana r. Port./Spain
167 E4 Guadix Spain
212 B6 Guafo, Isla i. Chile
206 H5 Guaimaca Hond.
213 D4 Guainía r. Col./Venez.
213 E3 Guaiquinima, Cerro mt. Venez.
214 A4 Guaíra Brazil
212 B6 Guaitecas, Islas is Chile
Guaizihu China see Ongt Gol
206 D2 Guaje, Llano de plain Mex.
213 C1 Guajira, Península de la pen. Col.
210 C4 Gualaceo Ecuador
196 A2 Gualala U.S.A.
215 E2 Gualeguay Arg.
215 E2 Gualeguay r. Arg.
215 E2 Gualeguaychu Arg.
215 D4 Gualicho, Salina salt flat Arg.
215 B4 Gualjaina Arg.
147 G5 Guam terr. Pacific Ocean
215 D3 Guamini Arg.
206 B2 Guamúchil Mex.
213 A4 Guamués r. Col.
154 B4 Gua Musang Malaysia
206 H6 Guanacaste, Parque Nacional nat. park Costa Rica
206 C2 Guanacevi Mex.
215 D3 Guanaco, Cerro h. Arg.
206 H4 Guanaja Hond.
206 D3 Guanajuato Mex.
206 D3 Guanajuato state Mex.
214 D1 Guanambi Brazil
213 D4 Guaname r. Venez.
213 C2 Guanare Venez.
213 C2 Guanare Viejo r. Venez.
213 C2 Guanarito Venez.
213 C2 Guanarito r. Venez.
213 D3 Guanay, Sierra mts Venez.
148 D2 Guandi Shan mt. China
205 H4 Guane Cuba
149 C4 Guang'an China
149 E5 Guangchang China
149 D6 Guangdong prov. China
149 F4 Guangfeng China
149 D6 Guanghai China
148 B4 Guanghan China
148 B3 Guanghe China
148 E2 Guangling China
152 B4 Guanglu Dao i. China
149 F4 Guangming Ding mt. China
149 B5 Guangnan China
149 D6 Guangning China
148 F2 Guangrao China
148 E4 Guangshan China
148 D4 Guangshui China
149 C6 Guangxi Zhuangzu Zizhiqu aut. reg. China
148 B3 Guangyuan China
149 E5 Guangze China
149 D6 Guangzhou China
214 D2 Guanhães Brazil
214 D2 Guanhães r. Brazil
213 E2 Guanipa r. Venez.
149 B5 Guanling China
148 C4 Guanmian Shan mts China
148 D3 Guanpo China
149 F6 Guanshan Taiwan
152 C3 Guanshui China
213 D2 Guanta Venez.
205 I4 Guantánamo Cuba
148 E1 Guanting Shuiku resr China
149 D5 Guanyang China
148 A4 Guanyinqiao China
148 F3 Guanyun China
213 A4 Guapí Col.
206 I6 Guápiles Costa Rica
210 F6 Guaporé r. Bol./Brazil
210 E7 Guaqui Bol.
214 D1 Guará r. Brazil
211 K5 Guarabira Brazil
214 E3 Guarapari Brazil
214 B4 Guarapuava Brazil
214 C4 Guaraqueçaba Brazil
214 D3 Guaratinguetá Brazil
214 C4 Guaratuba, Baía de b. Brazil
167 C2 Guarda Port.
214 C2 Guarda Mor Brazil
167 D1 Guardo Spain
213 D2 Guárico r. Venez.
213 C3 Guarrojo r. Col.
214 C4 Guarujá Brazil
213 D4 Guasacavi r. Col.
213 C4 Guasacavi, Cerro h. Col.
213 B2 Guasare r. Venez.
206 B2 Guasave Mex.
213 C3 Guasdualito Venez.
213 E3 Guasipati Venez.
214 B4 Guassú r. Brazil
207 G5 Guastatoya Guat.
207 G5 Guatemala country Central America
217 M5 Guatemala Basin sea feature Pacific Ocean
207 G5 Guatemala City Guat.
213 D2 Guatope, Parque Nacional nat. park Venez.
215 D3 Guatrache Arg.
213 C4 Guaviare r. Col.
214 C3 Guaxupé Brazil
213 B4 Guayabero r. Col.
213 D3 Guayapo r. Venez.
210 C4 Guayaquil Ecuador
210 B4 Guayaquil, Golfo de g. Ecuador
210 E6 Guayaramerín Bol.
206 B2 Guaymas Mex.
207 G5 Guazacapán Guat.
146 B2 Guazhou China
178 D2 Guba Eth.
138 D4 Gubadag Turkm.
143 B3 Gubbi India
170 E3 Gubbio Italy
173 F5 Gubkin Rus. Fed.
148 D3 Gucheng China
149 B5 Gucheng China
173 G7 Gudauta Georgia
159 J3 Gudbrandsdalen val. Norway
173 H7 Gudermes Rus. Fed.
143 C2 Gudivada India
143 B3 Gudiyattam India
152 E2 Gudong He r. China
141 G5 Gudri r. Pak.
136 D1 Güdül Turkey
143 B3 Gudur Andhra Pradesh India
143 B3 Gudur Andhra Pradesh India
159 I3 Gudvangen Norway
Guecho Spain see Algorta
176 A4 Guéckédou Guinea
191 I1 Guéguen, Lac l. Canada
213 B4 Güejar r. Col.
176 C1 Guelma Alg.
176 A2 Guelmim Morocco
191 G4 Guelph Canada
207 E3 Guémez Mex.
164 E5 Guénange France
213 D2 Güera r. Venez.
189 G2 Guérard, Lac l. Canada
166 E3 Guéret France
166 C2 Guernsey i. U.K.
194 F3 Guernsey U.S.A.
207 E2 Guerrero Mex.
207 D4 Guerrero state Mex.
206 A2 Guerrero Negro Mex.
185 L4 Guers, Lac l. Canada
140 D3 Gūgerd, Kūh-e mts Iran
219 F5 Guiana Basin sea feature N. Atlantic Ocean
126 C6 Guichen Bay Australia
Guichi China see Chizhou
215 F2 Guichón Uruguay
148 A3 Guide China
177 D4 Guider Cameroon
149 C5 Guiding China
170 E4 Guidonia-Montecelio Italy
149 C6 Guigang China
176 B4 Guiglo Côte d'Ivoire
164 B5 Guignicourt France
181 J2 Guija Moz.
149 D6 Gui Jiang r. China
149 F4 Guiji Shan mts China
161 G6 Guildford U.K.
203 I2 Guilford U.S.A.
149 D5 Guilin China
188 E2 Guillaume-Delisle, Lac l. Canada
167 B2 Guimarães Port.
153 B4 Guimaras Strait Phil.
148 E3 Guimeng Ding mt. China
196 A2 Guinda U.S.A.
153 C4 Guindulman Phil.
176 A3 Guinea country Africa
176 B4 Guinea, Gulf of Africa
219 I5 Guinea Basin sea feature N. Atlantic Ocean
176 A3 Guinea-Bissau country Africa
205 H4 Güines Cuba
166 C2 Guingamp France
166 B2 Guipavas France
149 D6 Guiping China
214 B2 Guiratinga Brazil
213 E2 Güiria Venez.
164 B5 Guiscard France
164 B5 Guise France
153 C4 Guiuan Phil.
149 E4 Guixi China
149 C5 Guiyang Guizhou China
149 D5 Guiyang Hunan China
149 C5 Guizhou prov. China
144 B5 Gujarat state India
144 C2 Gujar Khan Pak.
144 C2 Gujranwala Pak.
144 C2 Gujrat Pak.
173 F5 Gukovo Rus. Fed.
137 J3 Gūk Tappeh Iran
144 D2 Gulabgarh India
Gulabie Uzbek. see Taxiatosh
148 B2 Gulang China
127 H3 Gulargambone Australia
143 B2 Gulbarga India
159 N4 Gulbene Latvia
139 H4 Gülchö Kyrg.
136 E3 Gülek Turkey
142 D4 Gulf, The Asia
Gulf of Martaban g. Myanmar see Mottama, Gulf of
199 F6 Gulfport U.S.A.
127 H4 Gulgong Australia
146 E1 Gulian China
149 B5 Gulin China
141 G4 Gulistan Pak.
Gulistan Uzbek. see Guliston
139 G4 Guliston Uzbek.
165 J1 Gülitz Germany
190 E3 Gull Island U.S.A.
187 H4 Gull Lake Canada
158 M2 Gullträsk Sweden
136 D3 Gülnar Turkey
141 F3 Gulrān Afgh.
173 G7 Gulripshi Georgia
136 E2 Gülşehir Turkey
139 H3 Gul'shat Kazakh.
178 D3 Gulu Uganda
144 B3 Gumal r. Pak.
179 C5 Gumare Botswana
138 C5 Gumdag Turkm.
152 E5 Gumi S. Korea
145 F5 Gumia India
143 D1 Gumla India
164 F3 Gummersbach Germany
136 E1 Gümüşhacıköy Turkey
137 G1 Gümüşhane Turkey
144 D4 Guna India
127 F5 Gunbar Australia
127 F3 Gundabooka National Park nat. park Aust.
127 H5 Gundagai Australia
165 H5 Gundelsheim Germany
136 D3 Gündoğmuş Turkey
136 B2 Güney Turkey
178 B4 Gungu Dem. Rep. Congo
173 H7 Gunib Rus. Fed.
187 J4 Gunisao r. Canada
127 I3 Gunnedah Australia
129 E4 Gunnerus Ridge sea feature Southern Ocean
127 H5 Gunning Australia
195 F4 Gunnison CO U.S.A.
197 G2 Gunnison UT U.S.A.
195 E4 Gunnison r. U.S.A.
152 D6 Gunsan S. Korea
139 G5 Gunt r. Tajik.
143 B3 Guntakal India
165 I3 Güntersberge Germany
201 C5 Guntersville U.S.A.
201 C5 Guntersville Lake U.S.A.
143 C2 Guntur India
155 A2 Gunung Leuser, Taman Nasional Indon.
155 A2 Gunungsitoli Indon.
154 A5 Gunungtua Indon.
143 C2 Gunupur India
168 E6 Günzburg Germany
165 I5 Gunzenhausen Germany
149 D4 Guojiaba China
148 E1 Guojiatun China
148 E3 Guoyang China
148 A2 Gurban Hudag China
148 D1 Gurban Obo China
138 D4 Gurbansoltan Eje Turkm.
141 F5 Gurdim Iran
136 B2 Güre Turkey
144 D3 Gurgaon India
211 J5 Gurgueia r. Brazil
144 B4 Gurha India
213 E3 Guri, Embalse de resr Venez.
214 C2 Gurinhatã Brazil
173 H7 Gurjaani Georgia
141 E4 Gur Khar Iran
138 E4 Gurlan Uzbek.
Gurlen Uzbek. see Gurlan
137 I2 Gürpınar Turkey
145 G3 Guru China
179 D5 Gurué Moz.
136 F2 Gürün Turkey
211 I4 Gurupi r. Brazil
144 C4 Guru Sikhar mt. India
148 A1 Gurvantes Mongolia
172 B4 Gur'yevsk Rus. Fed.
176 C3 Gusau Nigeria
165 J2 Güsen Germany
172 B4 Gusev Rus. Fed.
141 F3 Guşgy r. Turkm.
152 B4 Gushan China
197 H1 Gusher U.S.A.
148 E3 Gushi China
133 L2 Gusikha Rus. Fed.
172 D4 Gusino Rus. Fed.
133 L4 Gusinoozersk Rus. Fed.
145 F5 Guskara India
172 G4 Gus'-Khrustal'nyy Rus. Fed.
170 C5 Guspini Sardinia Italy
186 B3 Gustavus U.S.A.
165 J3 Güsten Germany
196 B3 Gustine U.S.A.
165 K1 Güstrow Germany
145 H3 Gutang China
165 L2 Güterfelde Germany
165 G3 Gütersloh Germany
197 H5 Guthrie AZ U.S.A.
200 C4 Guthrie KY U.S.A.
199 D5 Guthrie OK U.S.A.
199 C5 Guthrie TX U.S.A.
149 E5 Gutian Fujian China
149 F5 Gutian Fujian China
164 E5 Gutland reg. Germany/Lux.
145 F3 Gutsuo China
190 B4 Guttenberg U.S.A.
179 D5 Gutu Mupandawana Zimbabwe
145 G4 Guwahati India
137 I3 Guwēr Iraq
138 C4 Guwlumaýak Turkm.
165 H3 Guxhagen Germany
211 G2 Guyana country S. America
148 D1 Guyang China
199 C4 Guymon U.S.A.
140 D4 Gūyom Iran
127 I3 Guyra Australia
148 E1 Guyuan Hebei China
148 C3 Guyuan Ningxia China
Guzar Uzbek. see G'uzor
149 C4 Guzhang China
148 E3 Guzhen China
138 F5 G'uzor Uzbek.
169 J3 Gvardeysk Rus. Fed.
127 H3 Gwabegar Australia
141 F5 Gwadar Pak.
141 F5 Gwadar West Bay Pak.
186 C4 Gwaii Haanas Canada
184 E4 Gwaii Haanas National Park Reserve and Haida Heritage Site Canada
144 D4 Gwalior India
179 C6 Gwanda Zimbabwe
152 D5 Gwangcheon S. Korea
152 D6 Gwangju S. Korea
152 D6 Gwangyang S. Korea
178 F2 Gwardafuy, Gees c. Somalia
141 G4 Gwash Pak.
141 F5 Gwatar Bay Pak.
163 C3 Gweebarra Bay Ireland
Gweedore Ireland see Gaoth Dobhair
179 C5 Gweru Zimbabwe
190 D2 Gwinn U.S.A.
177 D3 Gwoza Nigeria
127 H2 Gwydir r. Australia
145 H3 Gyaca China
148 B3 Gyagartang China
145 F2 Gyangnyi Caka salt l. China
145 F3 Gyangrang China
145 G3 Gyangzê China
145 G3 Gyaring Co l. China
146 B3 Gyaring Hu l. China
171 K6 Gyaros i. Greece
145 H3 Gyarubtang China
132 I2 Gydan Peninsula Rus. Fed.
Gydanskiy Poluostrov pen. Rus. Fed. see Gydan Peninsula
145 H3 Gyimda China
145 F3 Gyirong Xizang China
145 F3 Gyirong Xizang China
145 H2 Gyiza China
125 F4 Gympie Australia
169 I7 Gyöngyös Hungary
168 H7 Győr Hungary
187 J4 Gypsumville Canada
189 G2 Gyrfalcon Islands Canada
171 J6 Gytheio Greece
169 J7 Gyula Hungary
137 I1 Gyumri Armenia
Gyzylarbat Turkm. see Serdar
138 F5 Gyzylaýak Turkm.
Gyzyletrek Turkm. see Etrek


## H


158 N3 Haapajärvi Fin.
158 N2 Haapavesi Fin.
159 M4 Haapsalu Estonia
164 C2 Haarlem Neth.
180 E6 Haarlem S. Africa
165 G3 Haarstrang ridge Germany
128 B5 Haast N.Z.
141 G5 Hab r. Pak.
143 C4 Habarane Sri Lanka
178 D3 Habaswein Kenya
186 F3 Habay Canada
142 C7 Ḥabbān Yemen
137 I5 Ḥabbānīyah, Hawr al l. Iraq
141 G5 Hab Chauki Pak.
145 G4 Habiganj Bangl.
148 E1 Habirag China
145 G5 Habra India
213 B5 Hacha Col.
215 B3 Hachado, Paso de pass Arg./Chile
151 F8 Hachijō-jima i. Japan
150 G4 Hachinohe Japan
151 F7 Hachiōji Japan
136 E2 Hacıbektaş Turkey
137 H2 Hacıömer Turkey
137 L1 Hacıqabul Azer.
126 C3 Hack, Mount Australia
179 D6 Hacufera Moz.
143 A3 Hadagalli India
142 E5 Ḥadd, Ra's al pt Oman
162 F5 Haddington U.K.
176 D3 Hadejia Nigeria
136 E5 Ḥadera Israel
159 J5 Haderslev Denmark
136 D3 Hadım Turkey
161 H5 Hadleigh U.K.
184 H2 Hadley Bay Canada
152 D6 Hadong S. Korea
136 F6 Ḥadraj, Wādī watercourse Saudi Arabia
142 C6 Ḥaḍramawt reg. Yemen
160 E3 Hadrian's Wall tourist site U.K.
159 J4 Hadsund Denmark
173 E5 Hadyach Ukr.
215 F1 Haedo, Cuchilla de hills Uruguay
152 C4 Haeju N. Korea
152 C5 Haeju-man b. N. Korea
152 D6 Haenam S. Korea
181 H1 Haenertsburg S. Africa
152 B2 Ha'ertao China
140 B4 Ḥafar al Bāţin Saudi Arabia
187 H4 Hafford Canada
136 F2 Hafik Turkey
140 B5 Hafirat Nasah Saudi Arabia
144 C2 Hafizabad Pak.
145 H4 Haflong India
158 B2 Hafnarfjörður Iceland
140 C4 Haft Gel Iran
158 B2 Hafursfjörður b. Iceland
191 G2 Hagar Canada
143 B3 Hagari r. India
178 D2 Hagar Nish Plateau Eritrea
147 G5 Hagåtña Guam
164 C4 Hageland reg. Belgium
164 F3 Hagen Germany
165 J1 Hagenow Germany
202 E5 Hagerstown U.S.A.
166 D5 Hagetmau France
159 K3 Hagfors Sweden
194 D2 Haggin, Mount U.S.A.
151 B7 Hagi Japan
149 B6 Ha Giang Vietnam
161 E5 Hagley U.K.
163 B5 Hag's Head Ireland
187 H4 Hague Canada
166 D2 Hague, Cap de la c. France
166 H2 Haguenau France
146 G4 Hahajima-rettō is Japan
152 E5 Hahoe tourist site South Korea
178 D4 Hai Tanz.
148 F3 Hai'an China
180 B4 Haib watercourse Namibia
152 B3 Haicheng China
186 C4 Haida Gwaii Canada
165 J5 Haidenaab r. Germany
149 C6 Hai Dương Vietnam
136 E5 Haifa Israel

136 E5 **Haifa, Bay of** Israel
149 E6 **Haifeng** China
165 G4 **Haiger** Germany
148 E2 **Hai He** *r.* China
149 D6 **Haikou** China
142 B4 **Ḥā'il** Saudi Arabia
191 H2 **Haileybury** Canada
152 E1 **Hailin** China
161 H7 **Hailsham** U.K.
158 N2 **Hailuoto** Fin.
148 F4 **Haimen** China
149 C7 **Hainan** *prov.* China
147 D5 **Hainan Dao** *i.* China
149 C6 **Hainan Strait** China
186 B3 **Haines** U.S.A.
186 B2 **Haines Junction** Canada
165 I3 **Hainich** *ridge* Germany
165 L4 **Hainichen** Germany
165 I3 **Hainleite** *ridge* Germany
149 C6 **Hai Phong** Vietnam
148 A2 **Hairag** China
149 F5 **Haitan Dao** *i.* China
149 C7 **Haitangwan** China
205 J5 **Haiti** *country* Caribbean Sea
149 C7 **Haitou** China
154 D2 **Hai Triều** Vietnam
197 G5 **Haivana Nakya** U.S.A.
196 D3 **Haiwee Reservoir** U.S.A.
148 E2 **Haixing** China
177 F3 **Haiya** Sudan
148 A2 **Haiyan** *Qinghai* China
149 F4 **Haiyan** *Zhejiang* China
152 A5 **Haiyang** China
152 B4 **Haiyang Dao** *i.* China
148 B2 **Haiyuan** China
148 F3 **Haizhou Wan** *b.* China
169 J7 **Hajdúböszörmény** Hungary
170 C7 **Hajeb El Ayoun** Tunisia
142 D7 **Hajhir** *mt.* Yemen
140 D3 **Haji Abdulla, Chāh** *well* Iran
150 F5 **Hajiki-zaki** *pt* Japan
145 F4 **Hajipur** India
140 D3 **Ḥājj 'Alī Qolī, Kavīr-e** *salt l.* Iran
140 D4 **Ḥājjīābād** Iran
140 D4 **Ḥājjīābād** Iran
145 H5 **Haka** Myanmar
196 □2 **Hakalau** U.S.A.
215 C4 **Hakelhuincul, Altiplanicie de** *plat.* Arg.
137 I3 **Hakkâri** Turkey
158 M2 **Hakkas** Sweden
151 D7 **Hakken-zan** *mt.* Japan
150 H2 **Hako-dake** *mt.* Japan
150 G4 **Hakodate** Japan
180 B1 **Hakos Mountains** Namibia
144 C3 **Hakra Right Distributary** *watercourse* Pak.
180 D3 **Hakseen Pan** *salt pan* S. Africa
151 E6 **Hakui** Japan
151 E6 **Haku-san** *vol.* Japan
151 E6 **Haku-san Kokuritsu-kōen** *nat. park* Japan
144 B4 **Hala** Pak.
**Ḥalab** Syria *see* **Aleppo**
140 B6 **Halabān** Saudi Arabia
137 J4 **Ḥalabja** Iraq
138 F5 **Halaç** Turkm.
152 C1 **Halahai** China
177 F2 **Ḥalā'ib** Sudan
154 D2 **Ha Lam** Vietnam
142 E6 **Ḥalāniyāt, Juzur al** *is* Oman
**Halawa** U.S.A. *see* **Hālawa**
196 □2 **Hālawa** U.S.A.
136 F4 **Halba** Lebanon
**Halban** Mongolia *see* **Tsetserleg**
165 J3 **Halberstadt** Germany
153 B3 **Halcon, Mount** Phil.
158 □ **Haldarsvik** Faroe Is
159 J4 **Halden** Norway
165 J2 **Haldensleben** Germany
145 G5 **Haldi** *r.* India
145 G5 **Haldia** India
145 G4 **Haldibari** India
144 D3 **Haldwani** India
191 F3 **Hale** U.S.A.
140 D5 **Hāleh** Iran
**Haleiwa** U.S.A. *see* **Hale'iwa**
196 □1 **Hale'iwa** U.S.A.
161 E5 **Halesowen** U.K.
161 I5 **Halesworth** U.K.
140 C4 **Haleyleh** Iran
136 F3 **Halfeti** Turkey
128 B7 **Halfmoon Bay** N.Z.
186 E3 **Halfway** *r.* Canada
163 C6 **Halfway** Ireland
164 C2 **Halfweg** Neth.
145 E4 **Halia** India
137 G4 **Ḥalībīyah** Syria
191 H3 **Haliburton** Canada
189 H5 **Halifax** Canada
160 F4 **Halifax** U.K.
202 D6 **Halifax** U.S.A.
148 C1 **Haliut** China
162 E2 **Halkirk** U.K.
158 L3 **Hälla** Sweden
152 D7 **Halla-san** *mt.* S. Korea
152 D7 **Halla-san National Park** *nat. park* S. Korea
126 A5 **Hall Bay** Australia
185 J3 **Hall Beach** Canada
164 C4 **Halle** Belgium
164 E3 **Halle** Neth.
159 K4 **Hällefors** Sweden
168 F7 **Hallein** Austria
165 J3 **Halle-Neustadt** Germany
165 J3 **Halle (Saale)** Germany
129 C3 **Halley** *research stn* Antarctica
122 E2 **Hall Islands** Micronesia
158 L2 **Hällnäs** Sweden
198 D1 **Hallock** U.S.A.
185 L3 **Hall Peninsula** Canada
159 K4 **Hallsberg** Sweden
124 C3 **Halls Creek** Australia
191 H3 **Halls Lake** Canada
164 B4 **Halluin** France
158 K3 **Hallviken** Sweden
147 E6 **Halmahera** *i.* Indon.
159 K4 **Halmstad** Sweden
144 C5 **Halol** India
149 C6 **Ha Long** Vietnam
159 J4 **Hals** Denmark
159 L3 **Hälsingland, Decorated Farmhouses of** *tourist site* Sweden
158 D2 **Hálslón** *resr* Iceland
158 N3 **Halsua** Fin.
164 F3 **Haltern** Germany
160 E3 **Haltwhistle** U.K.
140 D5 **Ḥālūl** *i.* Qatar
164 F3 **Halver** Germany
164 B5 **Ham** France
151 C7 **Hamada** Japan
140 C3 **Hamadān** Iran
136 F4 **Ḥamāh** Syria
150 G3 **Hamamasu** Japan
151 E7 **Hamamatsu** Japan
159 J3 **Hamar** Norway
158 K1 **Hamarøy** Norway
177 F2 **Ḥamāṭah, Jabal** *mt.* Egypt
150 H2 **Hamatonbetsu** Japan
143 C5 **Hambantota** Sri Lanka
165 G1 **Hambergen** Germany
160 F3 **Hambleton Hills** U.K.
165 H1 **Hamburg** Germany
181 G6 **Hamburg** S. Africa
199 F5 **Hamburg** *AR* U.S.A.
202 D3 **Hamburg** *NY* U.S.A.
203 F4 **Hamburg** *PA* U.S.A.
165 G1 **Hamburgisches Wattenmeer, Nationalpark** *nat. park* Germany
203 G4 **Hamden** U.S.A.
159 N3 **Hämeenlinna** Fin.
165 H2 **Hameln** Germany
124 B4 **Hamersley Range** *mts* Australia
152 D4 **Hamhŭng** N. Korea
146 B2 **Hami** China
140 C4 **Ḥamīd** Iran
177 F2 **Hamid** Sudan
126 E6 **Hamilton** Australia
205 L2 **Hamilton** Bermuda
191 H4 **Hamilton** Canada
128 E2 **Hamilton** N.Z.
162 D5 **Hamilton** U.K.
201 C5 **Hamilton** *AL* U.S.A.
190 B5 **Hamilton** *IL* U.S.A.
194 D2 **Hamilton** *MT* U.S.A.
203 F3 **Hamilton** *NY* U.S.A.
202 A5 **Hamilton** *OH* U.S.A.
196 B3 **Hamilton, Mount** *CA* U.S.A.
197 E2 **Hamilton, Mount** *NV* U.S.A.
196 A2 **Hamilton City** U.S.A.
159 N3 **Hamina** Fin.
137 H6 **Ḥāmir, Wādī al** *watercourse* Saudi Arabia
144 D3 **Hamirpur** India
152 D4 **Hamju** N. Korea
126 C5 **Hamley Bridge** Australia
190 D3 **Hamlin Lake** U.S.A.
165 F3 **Hamm** Germany
137 I3 **Ḥammām al 'Alīl** Iraq
170 D6 **Hammamet** Tunisia
177 D1 **Hammamet, Golfe de** *g.* Tunisia
137 K6 **Ḥammār, Hawr al** *imp. l.* Iraq
158 L3 **Hammarstrand** Sweden
165 H4 **Hammelburg** Germany
158 K3 **Hammerdal** Sweden
158 M1 **Hammerfest** Norway
164 E3 **Hamminkeln** Germany
126 C4 **Hammond** Australia
190 D5 **Hammond** *IN* U.S.A.
199 F6 **Hammond** *LA* U.S.A.
194 F2 **Hammond** *MT* U.S.A.
191 E3 **Hammond Bay** U.S.A.
202 E3 **Hammondsport** U.S.A.
203 F5 **Hammonton** U.S.A.
164 D4 **Hamoir** Belgium
128 C6 **Hampden** N.Z.
143 B3 **Hampi** India
161 F6 **Hampshire Downs** *hills* U.K.
189 G4 **Hampton** Canada
199 E5 **Hampton** *AR* U.S.A.
203 H3 **Hampton** *NH* U.S.A.
203 E6 **Hampton** *VA* U.S.A.
177 D2 **Ḥamrā', Al Ḥamādah al** *plat.* Libya
137 J4 **Ḥamrīn, Jabal** *hills* Iraq
154 C3 **Ham Tân** Vietnam
144 D2 **Hamta Pass** India
141 F4 **Hāmūn Şāberī, Daryācheh-ye** *marsh* Afgh./Iran
137 I2 **Hamur** Turkey
139 G4 **Hamza** Uzbek.
164 D4 **Han, Grotte de** *tourist site* Belgium
196 □2 **Hāna** U.S.A.
**Hana** U.S.A. *see* **Hāna**
180 E1 **Hanahai** *watercourse* Botswana/Namibia
196 □2 **Hanalei** U.S.A.
150 G5 **Hanamaki** Japan
165 G4 **Hanau** Germany
146 C2 **Hanbogd** Mongolia
148 D3 **Hancheng** China
202 D5 **Hancock** *MD* U.S.A.
190 C2 **Hancock** *MI* U.S.A.
203 F4 **Hancock** *NY* U.S.A.
162 C2 **Handa Island** U.K.
148 E2 **Handan** China
178 D4 **Handeni** Tanz.
153 C4 **Handig Point** Phil.
196 C3 **Hanford** U.S.A.
143 A3 **Hangal** India
152 D5 **Han-gang** *r.* S. Korea
146 B2 **Hangayn Nuruu** *mts* Mongolia
144 B2 **Hangu** Pak.
149 D5 **Hanguang** China
149 F4 **Hangzhou** China
149 F4 **Hangzhou Wan** *b.* China
137 H2 **Hani** Turkey
140 C5 **Ḥanīdh** Saudi Arabia
**Hanjiang** China *see* **Yangzhou**
148 B2 **Hanjiaoshui** China
165 I2 **Hankensbüttel** Germany
180 F6 **Hankey** S. Africa
159 M4 **Hanko** Fin.
197 G2 **Hanksville** U.S.A.
144 D2 **Hanle** India
128 D5 **Hanmer Springs** N.Z.
187 G4 **Hanna** Canada
188 D3 **Hannah Bay** Canada
190 B6 **Hannibal** U.S.A.
165 H2 **Hannover** Germany
165 H3 **Hannoversch Münden** Germany
164 D4 **Hannut** Belgium
159 K5 **Hanöbukten** *b.* Sweden
149 B6 **Ha Nôi** Vietnam
191 G3 **Hanover** Canada
180 F5 **Hanover** S. Africa
203 G3 **Hanover** *NH* U.S.A.
202 E5 **Hanover** *PA* U.S.A.
129 E5 **Hansen Mountains** *mts* Antarctica
149 D4 **Hanshou** China
148 E4 **Han Shui** *r.* China
144 D3 **Hansi** India
158 L1 **Hansnes** Norway
126 B3 **Hanson, Lake** *salt flat* Australia
202 B6 **Hansonville** U.S.A.
159 J4 **Hanstholm** Denmark
164 E6 **Han-sur-Nied** France
172 C4 **Hantsavichy** Belarus
144 C3 **Hanumangarh** India
127 G5 **Hanwood** Australia
148 C3 **Hanyin** China
149 B4 **Hanyuan** China
141 F5 **Hanzaram** Iran
148 C3 **Hanzhong** China
123 J6 **Hao** *atoll* Fr. Polynesia
145 G5 **Haora** India
158 N2 **Haparanda** Sweden
145 H4 **Hapoli** India
189 H3 **Happy Valley-Goose Bay** Canada
152 E3 **Hapsu** N. Korea
144 D3 **Hapur** India
143 C5 **Haputale** Sri Lanka
140 C5 **Ḥaraḍ** *well* Saudi Arabia
140 C5 **Ḥaraḍh** Saudi Arabia
172 D4 **Haradok** Belarus
151 G6 **Haramachi** Japan
144 C2 **Haramukh** *mt.* India
144 C3 **Harappa Road** Pak.
179 D5 **Harare** Zimbabwe
142 E6 **Ḥarāsīs, Jiddat al** *des.* Oman
146 C2 **Har-Ayrag** Mongolia
176 A4 **Harbel** Liberia
146 E2 **Harbin** China
191 F4 **Harbor Beach** U.S.A.
190 E3 **Harbor Springs** U.S.A.
189 I4 **Harbour Breton** Canada
212 E8 **Harbours, Bay of** Falkland Is
197 F5 **Harcuvar Mountains** U.S.A.
144 D5 **Harda** India
159 I4 **Hardangerfjorden** *sea chan.* Norway
159 I3 **Hardangervidda** *plat.* Norway
159 I3 **Hardangervidda Nasjonalpark** *nat. park* Norway
180 B2 **Hardap** *admin. reg.* Namibia
180 B2 **Hardap Dam** Namibia
155 E2 **Harden, Bukit** *mt.* Indon.
164 E2 **Hardenberg** Neth.
164 D2 **Harderwijk** Neth.
180 C5 **Hardeveld** *mts* S. Africa
165 H5 **Hardheim** Germany
194 F2 **Hardin** U.S.A.
181 H5 **Harding** S. Africa
187 G4 **Hardisty** Canada
186 F2 **Hardisty Lake** Canada
144 E4 **Hardoi** India
203 G2 **Hardwick** U.S.A.
126 B5 **Hardwicke Bay** Australia
199 F4 **Hardy** U.S.A.
**Hardy, Mt** *mt.* N.Z. *see* **Rangipoua**
190 E4 **Hardy Reservoir** U.S.A.
164 B4 **Harelbeke** Belgium
164 E1 **Haren** Neth.
164 F2 **Haren (Ems)** Germany
178 E3 **Hārer** Eth.
203 F4 **Harford** U.S.A.
178 E3 **Hargeysa** Somalia
169 L7 **Harghita-Mădăraş, Vârful** *mt.* Romania
137 H2 **Harhal Dağları** *mts* Turkey
148 C2 **Harhatan** China
146 B3 **Har Hu** *l.* China
176 B2 **Ḥaricha, Ḥamâda El** *des.* Mali
144 D3 **Haridwar** India
143 A3 **Harihar** India
128 C5 **Harihari** N.Z.
151 D7 **Harima-nada** *b.* Japan
145 G5 **Haringhat** *r.* Bangl.
164 C3 **Haringvliet** *est.* Neth.
141 G3 **Harī Rōd** *r.* Afgh./Iran
159 M3 **Harjavalta** Fin.
198 E3 **Harlan** *IA* U.S.A.
202 B6 **Harlan** *KY* U.S.A.
161 C5 **Harlech** U.K.
194 E1 **Harlem** U.S.A.
161 I5 **Harleston** U.K.
164 D1 **Harlingen** Neth.
199 D7 **Harlingen** U.S.A.
161 H6 **Harlow** U.K.
194 E2 **Harlowton** U.S.A.
164 B5 **Harly** France
203 I2 **Harmony** *ME* U.S.A.
190 A4 **Harmony** *MN* U.S.A.
165 I1 **Harmsdorf** Germany
144 A3 **Harnai** Pak.
164 A4 **Harnes** France
194 B3 **Harney Basin** U.S.A.
194 C3 **Harney Lake** U.S.A.
159 L3 **Härnösand** Sweden
146 E2 **Har Nur** China
146 B2 **Har Nuur** *l.* Mongolia
162 □ **Haroldswick** U.K.
176 B4 **Harper** Liberia
196 D4 **Harper Lake** U.S.A.
202 E5 **Harpers Ferry** U.S.A.
189 H2 **Harp Lake** Canada
165 G2 **Harpstedt** Germany
137 G2 **Harput** Turkey
197 F5 **Harquahala Mountains** U.S.A.
137 G3 **Harran** Turkey
188 E3 **Harricana, Rivière d'** *r.* Canada
201 C5 **Harriman** U.S.A.
203 G3 **Harriman Reservoir** U.S.A.
127 J3 **Harrington** Australia
203 F5 **Harrington** U.S.A.
189 I3 **Harrington Harbour** Canada
162 B3 **Harris** *reg.* U.K.
126 A3 **Harris, Lake** *salt flat* Australia
162 A3 **Harris, Sound of** *sea chan.* U.K.
200 B4 **Harrisburg** *IL* U.S.A.
202 E4 **Harrisburg** *PA* U.S.A.
181 H4 **Harrismith** S. Africa
199 E4 **Harrison** *AR* U.S.A.
190 E3 **Harrison** *MI* U.S.A.
189 I3 **Harrison, Cape** Canada
184 C2 **Harrison Bay** U.S.A.
202 D5 **Harrisonburg** U.S.A.
186 E5 **Harrison Lake** Canada
198 E4 **Harrisonville** U.S.A.
191 F3 **Harrisville** *MI* U.S.A.
203 F2 **Harrisville** *NY* U.S.A.
202 C5 **Harrisville** *WV* U.S.A.
160 F4 **Harrogate** U.K.
165 H1 **Harsefeld** Germany
140 B3 **Harsīn** Iran
136 G1 **Harşit** *r.* Turkey
171 L2 **Hârşova** Romania
158 L1 **Harstad** Norway
165 H2 **Harsum** Germany
190 D4 **Hart** U.S.A.
126 B3 **Hart, Lake** *salt flat* Australia
180 D4 **Hartbees** *watercourse* S. Africa
168 G7 **Hartberg** Austria
159 I3 **Harteigan** *mt.* Norway
162 E5 **Hart Fell** *h.* U.K.
203 G4 **Hartford** *CT* U.S.A.
190 D4 **Hartford** *MI* U.S.A.
198 D3 **Hartford** *SD* U.S.A.
190 C4 **Hartford** *WI* U.S.A.
186 E3 **Hart Highway** Canada
189 G4 **Hartland** Canada
161 C7 **Hartland** U.K.
203 I2 **Hartland** U.S.A.
161 C6 **Hartland Point** U.K.
160 F3 **Hartlepool** U.K.
199 C5 **Hartley** U.S.A.
186 D4 **Hartley Bay** Canada
159 N3 **Hartola** Fin.
186 E4 **Hart Ranges** *mts* Canada
168 E6 **Härtsfeld** *hills* Germany
180 F3 **Hartswater** S. Africa
201 D5 **Hartwell Reservoir** U.S.A.
146 B2 **Har Us Nuur** *l.* Mongolia
141 F3 **Hārūt** *r.* Afgh.
141 F3 **Hārūt Rūd** *watercourse* Afgh.
190 C4 **Harvard** U.S.A.
195 F4 **Harvard, Mount** U.S.A.
203 J2 **Harvey** Canada
190 D2 **Harvey** *MI* U.S.A.
198 C2 **Harvey** *ND* U.S.A.
161 I6 **Harwich** U.K.
127 J2 **Harwood** Australia
144 C3 **Haryana** *state* India
165 I3 **Harz** *hills* Germany
136 E6 **Ḥasā, Qal'at al** *tourist site* Jordan
136 F6 **Ḥaşāh, Wādī al** *watercourse* Jordan
139 I5 **Hasalbag** China
136 E2 **Hasan Dağı** *mts* Turkey
137 H3 **Hasankeyf** Turkey
140 E5 **Ḥasan Langī** Iran
143 B2 **Hasanparti** India
140 B2 **Ḥasan Sālārān** Iran
138 D5 **Hasardag** *mt.* Turkm.
136 E5 **Hasbani** *r.* Lebanon
136 E2 **Hasbek** Turkey
143 C1 **Hasdo** *r.* India
165 F2 **Hase** *r.* Germany
164 F2 **Haselünne** Germany
165 I4 **Hasenkopf** *h.* Germany
140 C3 **Hashtgerd** Iran
140 C2 **Hashtpar** Iran
140 B2 **Hashtrud** Iran
140 E3 **Hasht Tekkeh, Gowd-e** *waterhole* Iran
199 D5 **Haskell** U.S.A.
161 G6 **Haslemere** U.K.
169 L7 **Hăşmaşul Mare** *mt.* Romania
143 B3 **Hassan** India
137 J4 **Hassan** Iraq
144 C2 **Hassan Abdal** Pak.
197 F5 **Hassayampa** *watercourse* U.S.A.
165 I4 **Haßberge** *hills* Germany
164 D4 **Hasselt** Belgium
164 E2 **Hasselt** Neth.
176 C1 **Hassi Messaoud** Alg.
159 K4 **Hässleholm** Sweden
126 F7 **Hastings** Australia
127 J3 **Hastings** *r.* Australia
128 F3 **Hastings** N.Z.
161 H7 **Hastings** U.K.
190 E4 **Hastings** *MI* U.S.A.
190 A3 **Hastings** *MN* U.S.A.
198 D3 **Hastings** *NE* U.S.A.
148 C1 **Hatanbulag** Mongolia
197 F3 **Hatch** U.S.A.
187 I3 **Hatchet Lake** Canada
201 B5 **Hatchie** *r.* U.S.A.
126 E4 **Hatfield** Australia
160 G4 **Hatfield** U.K.
146 C1 **Hatgal** Mongolia
144 D4 **Hathras** India
145 F4 **Hatia** Nepal
154 C3 **Ha Tiên** Vietnam
154 C1 **Ha Tinh** Vietnam
137 I4 **Hatra** Iraq
126 E5 **Hattah** Australia
126 E5 **Hattah-Kulkyne National Park** Australia
201 F5 **Hatteras, Cape** U.S.A.
219 E4 **Hatteras Abyssal Plain** *sea feature* S. Atlantic Ocean
158 K2 **Hattfjelldal** Norway
143 C2 **Hatti** *r.* India
201 B6 **Hattiesburg** U.S.A.
164 F3 **Hattingen** Germany
154 B4 **Hat Yai** Thai.
154 C3 **Hâu, Sông** *r.* Vietnam
178 E3 **Haud** *reg.* Eth.
159 I4 **Hauge** Norway
159 I4 **Haugesund** Norway
**Hâu Giang, Sông** *r.* Vietnam *see* **Hâu, Sông**
128 E3 **Hauhungaroa** *mt.* N.Z.
159 I4 **Haukeligrend** Norway
158 N2 **Haukipudas** Fin.
159 O3 **Haukivesi** *l.* Fin.
187 H3 **Haultain** *r.* Canada
128 E2 **Hauraki Gulf** N.Z.
128 A7 **Hauroko, Lake** N.Z.
203 I3 **Haut, Isle au** *i.* U.S.A.
176 B1 **Haut Atlas** *mts* Morocco
189 G4 **Hauterive** Canada
176 B1 **Hauts Plateaux** Alg.
**Hauula** U.S.A. *see* **Hau'ula**
196 □1 **Hau'ula** U.S.A.
205 H4 **Havana** Cuba
190 B5 **Havana** U.S.A.
161 G7 **Havant** U.K.
197 E4 **Havasu, Lake** U.S.A.
165 K2 **Havel** *r.* Germany
164 D4 **Havelange** Belgium
165 K2 **Havelberg** Germany
165 K2 **Havelländisches Luch** *marsh* Germany
191 I3 **Havelock** Canada
201 E5 **Havelock** U.S.A.
128 F3 **Havelock North** N.Z.
161 C6 **Haverfordwest** U.K.
203 H3 **Haverhill** U.S.A.
143 A3 **Haveri** India
164 D4 **Haversin** Belgium
164 F3 **Havixbeck** Germany
168 G6 **Havlíčkův Brod** Czech Rep.
158 N1 **Havøysund** Norway
171 L5 **Havran** Turkey
194 E1 **Havre** U.S.A.
189 H4 **Havre Aubert, Île du** *i.* Canada
203 E5 **Havre de Grace** U.S.A.
189 H3 **Havre-St-Pierre** Canada
171 L4 **Havsa** Turkey
136 E1 **Havza** Turkey
196 □2 **Hawai'i** *i.* U.S.A.
196 □1 **Hawai'ian Islands** N. Pacific Ocean
216 H4 **Hawaiian Ridge** *sea feature* N. Pacific Ocean
**Hawaii Volcanoes National Park** U.S.A. *see* **Hawai'i Volcanoes National Park**
196 □2 **Hawai'i Volcanoes National Park** U.S.A.
137 K7 **Ḥawallī** Kuwait
161 D4 **Hawarden** U.K.
128 B6 **Hawea, Lake** N.Z.
128 E3 **Hawera** N.Z.
160 E3 **Hawes** U.K.
196 □2 **Hāwī** U.S.A.
**Hawi** U.S.A. *see* **Hāwī**
162 F5 **Hawick** U.K.
137 K6 **Ḥawīzah, Hawr al** *imp. l.* Iraq
128 B6 **Hawkdun Range** *mts* N.Z.
128 F3 **Hawke Bay** N.Z.
189 I3 **Hawke Island** Canada
126 C3 **Hawker** Australia
126 D2 **Hawkers Gate** Australia
203 F2 **Hawkesbury** Canada
197 F3 **Hawkins Peak** U.S.A.
191 F3 **Hawks** U.S.A.
203 J2 **Hawkshaw** Canada
203 F4 **Hawley** U.S.A.
137 I5 **Ḥawrān, Wādī** *watercourse* Iraq
140 B6 **Ḥawshah, Jibāl al** *mts* Saudi Arabia
180 C7 **Hawston** S. Africa
196 C2 **Hawthorne** U.S.A.
160 F3 **Haxby** U.K.
126 F5 **Hay** Australia
186 F2 **Hay** *r.* Canada
190 B3 **Hay** *r.* U.S.A.
**Haya** China *see* **Yagan**
150 G5 **Hayachine-san** *mt.* Japan
197 G5 **Hayden** *AZ* U.S.A.
194 C2 **Hayden** *ID* U.S.A.
187 K3 **Hayes** *r. Man.* Canada
185 I3 **Hayes** *r. Nunavut* Canada
185 L2 **Hayes Halvø** *pen.* Greenland
161 B7 **Hayle** U.K.
142 E6 **Haymā'** Oman
136 D2 **Haymana** Turkey
202 E5 **Haymarket** U.S.A.
203 I2 **Haynesville** U.S.A.
161 D5 **Hay-on-Wye** U.K.
173 C7 **Hayrabolu** Turkey
186 F2 **Hay River** Canada
198 D4 **Hays** U.S.A.
173 D5 **Haysyn** Ukr.
196 A3 **Hayward** *CA* U.S.A.
190 B2 **Hayward** *WI* U.S.A.
161 G7 **Haywards Heath** U.K.
138 C5 **Hazar** Turkm.
141 G3 **Hazārah Jāt** *reg.* Afgh.
202 B6 **Hazard** U.S.A.
145 F5 **Hazaribagh** India
145 E5 **Hazaribagh Range** *mts* India
164 A4 **Hazebrouck** France
186 D3 **Hazelton** Canada
184 G2 **Hazen Strait** Canada
164 C2 **Hazerswoude-Rijndijk** Neth.
203 F4 **Hazleton** U.S.A.
138 E4 **Hazorasp** Uzbek.
141 G2 **Ḥaẓrat-e Sulṭān** Afgh.
137 H2 **Hazro** Turkey
215 D2 **H. Bouchard** Arg.
163 B4 **Headford** Ireland
196 A2 **Healdsburg** U.S.A.
126 F6 **Healesville** Australia
161 F4 **Heanor** U.K.
218 I8 **Heard Island** Indian Ocean
199 D6 **Hearne** U.S.A.
188 D4 **Hearst** Canada
161 H7 **Heathfield** U.K.
203 E6 **Heathsville** U.S.A.
199 D7 **Hebbronville** U.S.A.
148 E2 **Hebei** *prov.* China
127 G2 **Hebel** Australia
192 D3 **Heber City** U.S.A.
199 E5 **Heber Springs** U.S.A.
**Hebi** China *see* **Shancheng**
189 H2 **Hebron** Canada
190 D5 **Hebron** *IN* U.S.A.
198 D3 **Hebron** *NE* U.S.A.
203 G3 **Hebron** *NY* U.S.A.
136 E6 **Hebron** West Bank
189 H2 **Hebron Fiord** *inlet* Canada
186 C4 **Hecate Strait** Canada
207 G3 **Hecelchakán** Mex.
186 C3 **Heceta Island** U.S.A.
149 C5 **Hechi** China
149 C4 **Hechuan** China
159 K3 **Hede** Sweden
159 K3 **Hedemora** Sweden
194 C2 **He Devil Mountain** U.S.A.
149 D6 **Hedi Shuiku** *resr* China
190 A5 **Hedrick** U.S.A.
164 D2 **Heeg** Neth.
164 F2 **Heek** Germany
164 C4 **Heer** Belgium
164 E2 **Heerde** Neth.
164 D2 **Heerenveen** Neth.
164 C2 **Heerhugowaard** Neth.
164 D4 **Heerlen** Neth.
**Ḥefa** Israel *see* **Haifa**
148 E4 **Hefei** China
149 D4 **Hefeng** China
150 B1 **Hegang** China
151 E6 **Hegura-jima** *i.* Japan
165 J3 **Heidberg** *h.* Germany
168 D3 **Heide** Germany
179 B6 **Heide** Namibia
165 G5 **Heidelberg** Germany
181 H3 **Heidelberg** *Gauteng* S. Africa
180 D7 **Heidelberg** *W. Cape* S. Africa
181 G3 **Heilbron** S. Africa
165 H5 **Heilbronn** Germany
168 E3 **Heiligenhafen** Germany
149 □ **Hei Ling Chau** *i. Hong Kong* China
152 E1 **Heilongjiang** *prov.* China
146 E2 **Heilong Jiang** *r.* China/Rus. Fed. *alt.* **Amur**
165 I5 **Heilsbronn** Germany
158 J3 **Heimdal** Norway
159 N3 **Heinola** Fin.
154 A2 **Heinze Islands** Myanmar
152 B3 **Heishan** China
164 C3 **Heist-op-den-Berg** Belgium
148 E2 **Hejian** China
149 B4 **Hejiang** China
149 D6 **He Jiang** *r.* China
148 D3 **Hejin** China
136 F2 **Hekimhan** Turkey
158 C3 **Hekla** *vol.* Iceland
148 B2 **Hekou** *Gansu* China
149 B6 **Hekou** *Yunnan* China
158 K3 **Helagsfjället** *mt.* Sweden
148 B2 **Helan Shan** *mts* China
165 J3 **Helbra** Germany
145 H4 **Helem** India
196 D3 **Helen, Mount** U.S.A.
199 F5 **Helena** *AR* U.S.A.
194 E2 **Helena** *MT* U.S.A.
162 D4 **Helensburgh** U.K.
136 E6 **Ḥeleẓ** Israel
168 C3 **Helgoland** *i.* Germany
168 D3 **Helgoländer Bucht** *g.* Germany
127 J1 **Helidon** Australia
158 B3 **Hella** Iceland
158 L1 **Helland** Norway
140 C4 **Helleh** *r.* Iran
164 C3 **Hellevoetsluis** Neth.
158 M1 **Helligskogen** Norway
167 F3 **Hellín** Spain
194 C2 **Hells Canyon** *gorge* U.S.A.
141 F4 **Helmand** *r.* Afgh.
141 F4 **Helmand** *reg.* Afgh.
141 F4 **Helmand, Hāmūn** *salt flat* Afgh./Iran
165 J4 **Helmbrechts** Germany
165 I3 **Helme** *r.* Germany
179 B6 **Helmeringhausen** Namibia
164 D3 **Helmond** Neth.
162 E2 **Helmsdale** U.K.
162 E2 **Helmsdale** *r.* U.K.
165 J2 **Helmstedt** Germany
152 E2 **Helong** China
197 G2 **Helper** U.S.A.
159 K4 **Helsingborg** Sweden
**Helsingfors** Fin. *see* **Helsinki**
159 K4 **Helsingør** Denmark
159 N3 **Helsinki** Fin.
161 B7 **Helston** U.K.
160 D3 **Helvellyn** *h.* U.K.
163 D5 **Helvick Head** Ireland
161 G6 **Hemel Hempstead** U.K.
196 D5 **Hemet** U.S.A.
202 E3 **Hemlock Lake** U.S.A.
165 H2 **Hemmingen** Germany
203 G2 **Hemmingford** Canada
165 H1 **Hemmoor** Germany
199 D6 **Hempstead** U.S.A.
161 I5 **Hemsby** U.K.
159 L4 **Hemse** Sweden
148 A3 **Henan** China
148 D3 **Henan** *prov.* China
167 E2 **Henares** *r.* Spain
150 F4 **Henashi-zaki** *pt* Japan
136 C1 **Hendek** Turkey
215 E3 **Henderson** Arg.
200 C4 **Henderson** *KY* U.S.A.
201 E4 **Henderson** *NC* U.S.A.
197 E3 **Henderson** *NV* U.S.A.
203 E3 **Henderson** *NY* U.S.A.
199 E5 **Henderson** *TX* U.S.A.
123 J7 **Henderson Island** Pitcairn Is
201 D5 **Hendersonville** *NC* U.S.A.
201 C4 **Hendersonville** *TN* U.S.A.
140 C4 **Hendījān** Iran
161 G6 **Hendon** U.K.
140 D5 **Hendorābī** *i.* Iran
141 E5 **Hengām** Iran
146 B4 **Hengduan Shan** *mts* China
164 E2 **Hengelo** Neth.
152 F1 **Hengshan** *Heilong.* China
149 D5 **Hengshan** *Hunan* China
148 C2 **Hengshan** *Shaanxi* China
149 D5 **Heng Shan** *mt. Hunan* China
148 D2 **Heng Shan** *mts Shanxi* China
148 E2 **Hengshui** China
149 C6 **Hengxian** China
149 D5 **Hengyang** *Hunan* China
149 D5 **Hengyang** *Hunan* China
173 E6 **Heniches'k** Ukr.
128 C6 **Henley** N.Z.
161 G6 **Henley-on-Thames** U.K.
203 F5 **Henlopen, Cape** U.S.A.
164 F4 **Hennef (Sieg)** Germany
181 G3 **Hennenman** S. Africa
165 L2 **Hennigsdorf Berlin** Germany
203 H3 **Henniker** U.S.A.
199 D5 **Henrietta** U.S.A.
188 D2 **Henrietta Maria, Cape** Canada
197 G3 **Henrieville** U.S.A.
190 C5 **Henry** U.S.A.
129 C3 **Henry Ice Rise** *ice feature* Antarctica
185 L3 **Henry Kater, Cape** Canada
197 G2 **Henry Mountains** U.S.A.
191 G4 **Hensall** Canada
165 H1 **Henstedt-Ulzburg** Germany
179 B6 **Hentiesbaai** Namibia
127 G5 **Henty** Australia
**Henzada** Myanmar *see* **Hinthada**
187 H4 **Hepburn** Canada
149 E5 **Heping** China
149 C6 **Hepu** China
148 D2 **Hequ** China
141 F3 **Herāt** Afgh.
166 F5 **Hérault** *r.* France
187 H4 **Herbert** Canada
165 G4 **Herborn** Germany
165 H4 **Herbstein** Germany
129 C4 **Hercules Dome** *ice feature* Antarctica
164 F3 **Herdecke** Germany
165 F4 **Herdorf** Germany
206 H6 **Heredia** Costa Rica
161 E5 **Hereford** U.K.
199 C5 **Hereford** U.S.A.
123 J6 **Hereheretue** *atoll* Fr. Polynesia
164 C4 **Herent** Belgium
165 G2 **Herford** Germany
165 I4 **Heringen (Werra)** Germany
198 D4 **Herington** U.S.A.
140 B2 **Herīs** Iran
168 D7 **Herisau** Switz.
203 F3 **Herkimer** U.S.A.
165 I3 **Herleshausen** Germany
206 D2 **Hermanas** Mex.
162 □ **Herma Ness** *hd* U.K.
165 I2 **Hermannsburg** Germany
180 C7 **Hermanus** S. Africa
181 H5 **Hermes, Cape** S. Africa
127 G3 **Hermidale** Australia
194 C2 **Hermiston** U.S.A.
212 C9 **Hermite, Islas** *is* Chile
124 E2 **Hermit Islands** P.N.G.
136 E5 **Hermon, Mount** Lebanon/Syria
206 B1 **Hermosillo** Mex.
212 F3 **Hernandarias** Para.
164 F3 **Herne** Germany
161 I6 **Herne Bay** U.K.
159 J4 **Herning** Denmark
190 D1 **Heron Bay** Canada
206 D3 **Herradura** Mex.
167 D3 **Herrera del Duque** Spain
127 G8 **Herrick** Australia
165 I5 **Herrieden** Germany
202 E4 **Hershey** U.S.A.
161 G6 **Hertford** U.K.
181 F4 **Hertzogville** S. Africa
164 D4 **Herve** Belgium
125 F4 **Hervey Bay** Australia
217 I7 **Hervey Islands** Cook Is
165 K2 **Herzberg** *Brandenburg* Germany
165 L3 **Herzberg** *Brandenburg* Germany
164 F2 **Herzlake** Germany
165 I5 **Herzogenaurach** Germany
165 K1 **Herzsprung** Germany
137 L4 **Ḥeşār** Iran
164 C4 **Hesbaye** *reg.* Belgium
164 F1 **Hesel** Germany
149 C6 **Heshan** China
148 C3 **Heshui** China
148 D2 **Heshun** China
196 D4 **Hesperia** U.S.A.
186 C2 **Hess** *r.* Canada
165 I5 **Heßdorf** Germany
165 I5 **Hesselberg** *h.* Germany
165 H4 **Hessen** *land* Germany
165 H3 **Hessisch Lichtenau** Germany
149 B6 **Het** *r.* Laos
196 B3 **Hetch Hetchy Aqueduct** *canal* U.S.A.
164 D3 **Heteren** Neth.
164 D2 **Het Loo, Paleis** *tourist site* Neth.
198 C2 **Hettinger** U.S.A.
160 E3 **Hetton** U.K.
165 J3 **Hettstedt** Germany
160 E3 **Hexham** U.K.
148 F4 **Hexian** China
148 B2 **Hexipu** China
180 C6 **Hex River Pass** S. Africa
148 D3 **Heyang** China
140 B2 **Ḥeydarābād** Iran
141 F4 **Ḥeydarābād** Iran
160 E3 **Heysham** U.K.
149 E6 **Heyuan** China
126 D7 **Heywood** Australia
160 E4 **Heywood** U.K.
190 C5 **Heyworth** U.S.A.
148 E3 **Heze** China
149 B5 **Hezhang** China
148 B3 **Hezheng** China
149 D5 **Hezhou** China
148 B3 **Hezuo** China
201 D7 **Hialeah** U.S.A.
198 E4 **Hiawatha** U.S.A.
190 A2 **Hibbing** U.S.A.
127 F9 **Hibbs, Point** Australia
201 D5 **Hickory** U.S.A.
128 G2 **Hicks Bay** N.Z.
207 G4 **Hicks Cayes** *is* Belize
187 J2 **Hicks Lake** Canada
202 A4 **Hicksville** U.S.A.
199 D5 **Hico** U.S.A.
150 H3 **Hidaka** Japan
150 H3 **Hidaka-sanmyaku** *mts* Japan
207 E2 **Hidalgo** Mex.
207 E3 **Hidalgo** *state* Mex.
206 C2 **Hidalgo del Parral** Mex.
214 C2 **Hidrolândia** Brazil
151 C7 **Higashihiroshima** Japan
150 G5 **Higashine** Japan
151 D7 **Higashi-Ōsaka** Japan
151 A8 **Higashi-suidō** *sea chan.* Japan
203 F3 **Higgins Bay** U.S.A.
190 E3 **Higgins Lake** U.S.A.
194 B3 **High Desert** U.S.A.
190 C3 **High Falls Reservoir** U.S.A.
190 E3 **High Island** U.S.A.
149 □ **High Island Reservoir** *Hong Kong* China
190 D4 **Highland Park** U.S.A.
196 C2 **Highland Peak** *CA* U.S.A.
197 E3 **Highland Peak** *NV* U.S.A.
186 F3 **High Level** Canada
145 F5 **High Level Canal** India
201 E5 **High Point** U.S.A.
186 F3 **High Prairie** Canada
186 G4 **High River** Canada
201 E7 **High Rock** Bahamas
187 I3 **Highrock Lake** Canada
127 F9 **High Rocky Point** Australia
160 E3 **High Seat** *h.* U.K.
203 F4 **Hightstown** U.S.A.
161 G6 **High Wycombe** U.K.
206 B2 **Higuera de Zaragoza** Mex.
213 D2 **Higuerote** Venez.
159 M4 **Hiiumaa** *i.* Estonia
142 A4 **Hijaz** *reg.* Saudi Arabia
197 E3 **Hiko** U.S.A.
151 E7 **Hikone** Japan
128 G2 **Hikurangi** *mt.* N.Z.
197 F3 **Hildale** U.S.A.
165 I4 **Hildburghausen** Germany
165 I4 **Hilders** Germany
165 H2 **Hildesheim** Germany
145 G4 **Hili** Bangl.
198 D4 **Hill City** U.S.A.
197 H2 **Hill Creek** *r.* U.S.A.
164 C2 **Hillegom** Neth.
159 K5 **Hillerød** Denmark
198 D2 **Hillsboro** *ND* U.S.A.
203 H3 **Hillsboro** *NH* U.S.A.
202 B5 **Hillsboro** *OH* U.S.A.
199 D5 **Hillsboro** *TX* U.S.A.
190 B4 **Hillsboro** *WI* U.S.A.
202 C5 **Hillsboro** *WV* U.S.A.
190 E5 **Hillsdale** *MI* U.S.A.
203 G3 **Hillsdale** *NY* U.S.A.
202 E4 **Hillsgrove** U.S.A.
162 F4 **Hillside** U.K.
197 F4 **Hillside** U.S.A.
127 F4 **Hillston** Australia
202 C6 **Hillsville** U.S.A.
127 I5 **Hilltop** Australia
196 □2 **Hilo** U.S.A.
181 I4 **Hilton** S. Africa
202 E3 **Hilton** U.S.A.
191 F2 **Hilton Beach** Canada
201 D5 **Hilton Head Island** U.S.A.
137 G3 **Hilvan** Turkey
164 D2 **Hilversum** Neth.
144 D3 **Himachal Pradesh** *state* India
144 D2 **Himalaya** *mts* Asia
145 F3 **Himalchul** *mt.* Nepal
158 M2 **Himanka** Fin.
171 H4 **Himarë** Albania
144 C5 **Himatnagar** India
151 D7 **Himeji** Japan
150 G5 **Himekami-dake** *mt.* Japan
181 H4 **Himeville** S. Africa
151 E6 **Himi** Japan
136 F4 **Ḥimş** Syria
153 C4 **Hinatuan** Phil.
169 N7 **Hînceşti** Moldova
124 E3 **Hinchinbrook Island** Australia
161 F5 **Hinckley** U.K.
190 A2 **Hinckley** *MN* U.S.A.
197 F2 **Hinckley** *UT* U.S.A.
203 F3 **Hinckley Reservoir** U.S.A.
144 D3 **Hindan** *r.* India
144 D4 **Hindaun** India
160 G3 **Hinderwell** U.K.
160 E4 **Hindley** U.K.
202 B6 **Hindman** U.S.A.
126 D6 **Hindmarsh, Lake** *dry lake* Australia
143 D1 **Hindola** India
141 G3 **Hindu Kush** *mts* Afgh./Pak.
143 B3 **Hindupur** India
186 F3 **Hines Creek** Canada
201 D6 **Hinesville** U.S.A.
144 D5 **Hinganghat** India
141 G5 **Hinglaj** Pak.
141 G5 **Hingol** *r.* Pak.
144 D6 **Hingoli** India
137 H2 **Hınıs** Turkey
196 D4 **Hinkley** U.S.A.
158 K1 **Hinnøya** *i.* Norway
153 B4 **Hinoba-an** Phil.
167 D3 **Hinojosa del Duque** Spain
151 C7 **Hino-misaki** *pt* Japan
203 G3 **Hinsdale** U.S.A.
164 F1 **Hinte** Germany

147 B5 **Hinthada** Myanmar
186 F4 **Hinton** Canada
202 C6 **Hinton** U.S.A.
164 C2 **Hippolytushoef** Neth.
137 J2 **Hirabit Dağ** *mt.* Turkey
151 A8 **Hirado** Japan
151 A8 **Hirado-shima** *i.* Japan
150 G5 **Hiraizumi** *tourist site* Japan
143 C1 **Hirakud Reservoir** India
150 H3 **Hiroo** Japan
150 G4 **Hirosaki** Japan
151 C7 **Hiroshima** Japan
165 J5 **Hirschaid** Germany
165 J4 **Hirschberg** Germany
168 E7 **Hirschberg** *mt.* Germany
166 G2 **Hirson** France
159 J4 **Hirtshals** Denmark
144 C3 **Hisar** India
137 L3 **Hisar** Iran
141 G3 **Ḥiṣār, Kōh-e** *mts* Afgh.
136 D1 **Hisarönü** Turkey
137 J6 **Ḥisb, Sha'īb** *watercourse* Iraq
139 G5 **Hisor** Tajik.
205 J4 **Hispaniola** *i.* Caribbean Sea
145 F4 **Hisua** India
137 I5 **Hīt** Iraq
151 G6 **Hitachi** Japan
151 G6 **Hitachiōta** Japan
151 B8 **Hitoyoshi** Japan
158 J3 **Hitra** *i.* Norway
165 J1 **Hitzacker** Germany
151 C7 **Hiuchi-nada** *b.* Japan
123 J5 **Hiva Oa** *i.* Fr. Polynesia
186 E4 **Hixon** Canada
137 I2 **Hizan** Turkey
159 K4 **Hjälmaren** *l.* Sweden
187 H2 **Hjalmar Lake** Canada
159 J3 **Hjerkinn** Norway
159 K4 **Hjo** Sweden
159 J4 **Hjørring** Denmark
181 I4 **Hlabisa** S. Africa
181 I3 **Hlatikulu** Swaziland
173 E5 **Hlobyne** Ukr.
181 G4 **Hlohlowane** S. Africa
181 H4 **Hlotse** Lesotho
181 J4 **Hluhluwe** S. Africa
173 E5 **Hlukhiv** Ukr.
169 N4 **Hlusha** Belarus
172 C4 **Hlybokaye** Belarus
176 C4 **Ho** Ghana
149 B6 **Hoa Binh** Vietnam
154 C1 **Hoa Binh** Vietnam
179 B6 **Hoachanas** Namibia
**Hoan Lao** Vietnam *see* **Bô Trach**
127 G9 **Hobart** Australia
199 D5 **Hobart** U.S.A.
199 C5 **Hobbs** U.S.A.
201 D7 **Hobe Sound** U.S.A.
148 D1 **Hobor** China
159 J4 **Hobro** Denmark
178 E3 **Hobyo** Somalia
165 H5 **Höchberg** Germany
165 I3 **Hochharz, Nationalpark** *nat. park* Germany
154 C3 **Ho Chi Minh City** Vietnam
168 G7 **Hochschwab** *mt.* Austria
165 G5 **Hockenheim** Germany
202 B5 **Hocking** *r.* U.S.A.
207 G3 **Hoctúm** Mex.
144 D4 **Hodal** India
171 H3? **Hodder** *r.* U.K.
161 G6 **Hoddesdon** U.K.
142 B7 **Hodeidah** Yemen
203 J1 **Hodgdon** U.S.A.
169 J7 **Hódmezővásárhely** Hungary
167 I5 **Hodna, Chott el** *salt l.* Alg.
152 D4 **Hodo-dan** *pt* N. Korea
149 B6 **Ho Dynasty, Citadel of the** *tourist site* Vietnam
**Hoek van Holland** Neth. *see* **Hook of Holland**
164 D4 **Hoensbroek** Neth.
152 E2 **Hoeryŏng** N. Korea
152 D4 **Hoeyang** N. Korea
165 J4 **Hof** Germany
165 I4 **Hofheim in Unterfranken** Germany
181 F5 **Hofmeyr** S. Africa
158 D2 **Höfn** Iceland
159 L3 **Hofors** Sweden
158 C2 **Hofsjökull** *ice cap* Iceland
151 B7 **Hōfu** Japan
159 K4 **Höganäs** Sweden
127 G7 **Hogan Group** *is* Australia
203 F6 **Hog Island** U.S.A.
159 L4 **Högsby** Sweden
159 I3 **Høgste Breakulen** *mt.* Norway
165 H5 **Hohenloher Ebene** *plain* Germany
165 K3 **Hohenmölsen** Germany
165 K3 **Hohennauen** Germany
165 J4 **Hohenwartetalsperre** *resr* Germany
165 H4 **Hohe Rhön** *mts* Germany
168 F7 **Hohe Tauern** *mts* Austria
164 E4 **Hohe Venn** *moorland* Belgium
148 D1 **Hohhot** China
149 ? **Hoh Sai Hu** *l.* China
145 G2 **Hoh Xil Hu** *salt l.* China
145 G2 **Hoh Xil Shan** *mts* China
154 D2 **Hôi An** Vietnam
178 D3 **Hoima** Uganda
**Hôi Xuân** Vietnam *see* **Quan Hoa**
145 H4 **Hojai** India
138 F5 **Hojambaz** Turkm.
151 C8 **Hōjo** Japan
128 D1 **Hokianga Harbour** N.Z.
128 C5 **Hokitika** N.Z.
150 H3 **Hokkaidō** *i.* Japan
159 J4 **Hokksund** Norway
**Hoktemberyan** Armenia *see* **Armavir**
159 J3 **Hol** Norway
143 B3 **Holalkere** India
159 J5 **Holbæk** Denmark
161 H5 **Holbeach** U.K.
197 G4 **Holbrook** U.S.A.
190 B3 **Holcombe Flowage** *resr* U.S.A.
187 G4 **Holden** Canada
197 F2 **Holden** U.S.A.
199 D5 **Holdenville** U.S.A.
198 D3 **Holdrege** U.S.A.
143 B3 **Hole Narsipur** India
205 I4 **Holguín** Cuba
152 B1 **Holin He** *r.* China
159 K3 **Höljes** Sweden
**Holland** *country* Europe *see* **Netherlands**
190 D4 **Holland** U.S.A.
202 D4 **Hollidaysburg** U.S.A.
186 C3 **Hollis** *AK* U.S.A.
199 D5 **Hollis** *OK* U.S.A.
196 B3 **Hollister** U.S.A.
191 F4 **Holly** U.S.A.
199 F5 **Holly Springs** U.S.A.
196 C4 **Hollywood** U.S.A.
201 D7 **Hollywood** U.S.A.
158 K2 **Holm** Norway
**Holman** Canada *see* **Ulukhaktok**
159 J4 **Holmestrand** Norway
158 M3 **Holmön** *i.* Sweden
158 M3 **Holmsund** Sweden
180 B3 **Holoog** Namibia
159 J4 **Holstebro** Denmark
201 D4 **Holston** *r.* U.S.A.
202 C6 **Holston Lake** U.S.A.
161 C7 **Holsworthy** U.K.
161 I5 **Holt** U.K.
190 E4 **Holt** U.S.A.
198 E4 **Holton** U.S.A.
164 D1 **Holwerd** Neth.
163 D5 **Holycross** Ireland
161 C4 **Holyhead** U.K.
161 C4 **Holyhead Bay** U.K.
162 F5 **Holy Island** *England* U.K.
161 C4 **Holy Island** *Wales* U.K.
203 G3 **Holyoke** U.S.A.
161 D4 **Holywell** U.K.
165 K3 **Holzhausen** Germany
168 E7 **Holzkirchen** Germany
165 H3 **Holzminden** Germany
165 H3 **Homberg (Efze)** Germany
176 B3 **Hombori** Mali
164 F5 **Homburg** Germany
185 L3 **Home Bay** Canada
164 D5 **Homécourt** France
199 E5 **Homer** U.S.A.
201 D6 **Homerville** U.S.A.
201 D7 **Homestead** U.S.A.
201 C5 **Homewood** U.S.A.
143 B2 **Homnabad** India
**Homs** Syria *see* **Ḥimṣ**
173 D4 **Homyel'** Belarus
143 A3 **Honavar** India
213 B3 **Honda** Col.
153 A4 **Honda Bay** Phil.
197 H4 **Hon Dah** U.S.A.
180 B5 **Hondeklipbaai** S. Africa
148 C1 **Hondlon Ju** China
207 G4 **Hondo** *r.* Belize/Mex.
199 D6 **Hondo** U.S.A.
164 E1 **Hondsrug** *reg.* Neth.
206 H5 **Honduras** *country* Central America
206 H4 **Honduras, Gulf of** Belize/Hond.
159 J3 **Hønefoss** Norway
203 F4 **Honesdale** U.S.A.
196 B1 **Honey Lake** *salt l.* U.S.A.
203 E3 **Honeyoye Lake** U.S.A.
166 E2 **Honfleur** France
**Hông, Sông** *r.* Vietnam *see* **Red**
148 E4 **Hong'an** China
152 D5 **Hongcheon** S. Korea
**Hông Gai** Vietnam *see* **Ha Long**
149 E6 **Honghai Wan** *b.* China
149 B6 **Honghe** China
148 E3 **Hong He** *r.* China
149 D4 **Honghu** China
149 C5 **Hongjiang** *Hunan* China
149 C5 **Hongjiang** *Hunan* China
149 E6 **Hong Kong** China (City Plan 103)
149 □ **Hong Kong** *aut. reg.* China
149 □ **Hong Kong Island** *Hong Kong* China
148 C2 **Hongliu He** *r.* China
148 B2 **Hongliuyuan** China
154 C3 **Hồng Ngự** Vietnam
148 D4 **Hongshan** China
148 B2 **Hongshansi** China
152 D2 **Hongshilazi** China
149 D6 **Hongshui He** *r.* China
148 D2 **Hongtong** China
189 G4 **Honguedo, Détroit d'** *sea chan.* Canada
152 D3 **Hongwŏn** N. Korea
152 B1 **Hongxing** China
148 B3 **Hongyuan** China
148 F3 **Hongze** China
148 F3 **Hongze Hu** *l.* China
125 F2 **Honiara** Solomon Is
161 D7 **Honiton** U.K.
150 F4 **Honjō** Japan
143 A3 **Honnali** India
158 N1 **Honningsvåg** Norway
**Honokaa** U.S.A. *see* **Honoka'a**
196 □2 **Honoka'a** U.S.A.
196 □1 **Honolulu** U.S.A.
151 D6 **Honshū** *i.* Japan
191 F4? **Hood, Mount** *vol.* U.S.A.
124 B5 **Hood Point** Australia
203 G2 **Hoogeveen** Neth.
164 E1 **Hoogezand-Sappemeer** Neth.
199 C4 **Hooker** U.S.A.
163 E5 **Hook Head** Ireland
164 C3 **Hook of Holland** Neth.
186 B3 **Hoonah** U.S.A.
184 B3 **Hooper Bay** U.S.A.
180 E3 **Hooper Island** U.S.A.
190 D5 **Hoopeston** U.S.A.
181 F3 **Hoopstad** S. Africa
159 K5 **Höör** Sweden
164 D2 **Hoorn** Neth.
**Hoorn Islands** *is* Wallis and Futuna Is *see* **Horn, Îles de**
203 G3 **Hoosick** U.S.A.
197 E3 **Hoover Dam** U.S.A.
202 B4 **Hoover Memorial Reservoir** U.S.A.
137 H1 **Hopa** Turkey
203 F4 **Hop Bottom** U.S.A.
186 E5 **Hope** Canada
128 D5 **Hope** *r.* N.Z.
199 E5 **Hope** *AR* U.S.A.
197 F5 **Hope** *AZ* U.S.A.
126 C2 **Hope, Lake** *salt flat* Australia
184 B3 **Hope, Point** U.S.A.
189 I2 **Hopedale** Canada
181 G5 **Hopefield** S. Africa
207 G4 **Hopelchén** Mex.
189 H3 **Hope Mountains** Canada
132 D2 **Hopen** *i.* Svalbard
128 D4 **Hope Saddle** *pass* N.Z.
189 G2 **Hopes Advance, Baie** *b.* Canada
126 E5 **Hopetoun** Australia
180 F4 **Hopetown** S. Africa
202 E6 **Hopewell** U.S.A.
188 E2 **Hopewell Islands** Canada
124 C4 **Hopkins, Lake** *salt flat* Australia
200 C4 **Hopkinsville** U.S.A.
196 A2 **Hopland** U.S.A.
194 B2 **Hoquiam** U.S.A.
148 A3 **Hor** China
137 K2 **Horadiz** Azer.
137 I1 **Horasan** Turkey
159 K5 **Hörby** Sweden
206 C1 **Horcasitas** Mex.
139 J3 **Horgos** Kos'an China
148 B1 **Hörh Uul** *mts* Mongolia
190 C4 **Horicon** U.S.A.
148 D1 **Horinger** China
216 H7 **Horizon Deep** *sea feature* S. Pacific Ocean
172 D4 **Horki** Belarus
129 B5? **Horlick Mountains** *mts* Antarctica
173 F5 **Horlivka** Ukr.
141 F4 **Hormak** Iran
140 E5 **Hormoz** *i.* Iran
140 E5 **Hormuz, Strait of** Iran/Oman
168 G6 **Horn** Austria
186 F2 **Horn** *r.* Canada
158 B1 **Horn** *c.* Iceland
212 C9 **Horn, Cape** Chile
125 I3 **Horn, Îles de** *is* Wallis and Futuna Is
158 L2 **Hornavan** *l.* Sweden
199 E6 **Hornbeck** U.S.A.
165 I2 **Hornburg** Germany
161 G4 **Horncastle** U.K.
159 L3 **Horndal** Sweden
165 H1 **Horneburg** Germany
158 L3 **Hörnefors** Sweden
202 E3 **Hornell** U.S.A.
188 D4 **Hornepayne** Canada
201 B6 **Horn Island** U.S.A.
180 B1 **Hornkranz** Namibia
215 B4 **Hornopiren, Volcán** *vol.* Chile
**Hornos, Cabo de** *c.* Chile *see* **Horn, Cape**
127 I4 **Hornsby** Australia
160 G4 **Hornsea** U.K.
159 L3 **Hornslandet** *pen.* Sweden
169 L6 **Horodenka** Ukr.
173 D5 **Horodnya** Ukr.
173 C5 **Horodok** Ukr.
173 B5 **Horodok** Ukr.
150 H2 **Horokanai** Japan
169 L5 **Horokhiv** Ukr.
150 H3 **Horoshiri-dake** *mt.* Japan
152 A2 **Horqin Shadi** *reg.* China
161 C7 **Horrabridge** U.K.
145 G3 **Horru** China
186 E4 **Horsefly** Canada
202 E3 **Horseheads** U.S.A.
189 I3 **Horse Islands** Canada
163 C4 **Horseleap** Ireland
159 J5 **Horsens** Denmark
194 C3 **Horseshoe Bend** U.S.A.
219 H3 **Horseshoe Seamounts** *sea feature* N. Atlantic Ocean
126 E6 **Horsham** Australia
161 G6 **Horsham** U.K.
165 K5 **Horšovský Týn** Czech Rep.
165 H4 **Horst** *h.* Germany
164 F2 **Hörstel** Germany
159 J4 **Horten** Norway
184 F3 **Horton** *r.* Canada
191 F1 **Horwood Lake** Canada
169 M5 **Horyn'** *r.* Ukr.
151 D7 **Hōryūji** *tourist site* Japan
178 D3 **Hosa'ina** Eth.
165 H4 **Hösbach** Germany
143 B3 **Hosdurga** India
137 K4 **Ḥoseynābād** Iran
140 C4 **Ḥoseynīyeh** Iran
141 F5 **Hoshab** Pak.
144 D5 **Hoshangabad** India
144 C3 **Hoshiarpur** India
143 B3 **Hospet** India
163 C5 **Hospital** Ireland
215 F1 **Hospital, Cuchilla del** *hills* Uruguay
212 C9 **Hoste, Isla** *i.* Chile
158 K3 **Hotagen** *r.* Sweden
139 J5 **Hotan** China
139 J5 **Hotan He** *watercourse* China
180 E3 **Hotazel** S. Africa
197 G4 **Hotevilla** U.S.A.
127 G6 **Hotham, Mount** Australia
158 L2 **Hoting** Sweden
199 E5 **Hot Springs** *AR* U.S.A.
198 C3 **Hot Springs** *SD* U.S.A.
186 F1 **Hottah Lake** Canada
205 J5 **Hotte, Massif de la** *mts* Haiti
164 D4 **Houffalize** Belgium
154 □ **Hougang** Sing.
190 C2 **Houghton** U.S.A.
190 E3 **Houghton Lake** U.S.A.
190 E3 **Houghton Lake** *l.* U.S.A.
160 F3 **Houghton le Spring** U.K.
203 J1 **Houlton** U.S.A.
148 D3 **Houma** China
199 F6 **Houma** U.S.A.
162 C3 **Hourn, Loch** *inlet* U.K.
203 G3 **Housatonic** U.S.A.
197 F2 **House Range** *mts* U.S.A.
186 D4 **Houston** Canada
199 F4 **Houston** *MO* U.S.A.
199 F5 **Houston** *MS* U.S.A.
199 E6 **Houston** *TX* U.S.A.
124 B4 **Houtman Abrolhos** *is* Australia
162 E2 **Houton** U.K.
180 E5 **Houwater** S. Africa
146 B2 **Hovd** Mongolia
161 G7 **Hove** U.K.
161 I5 **Hoveton** U.K.
140 C4 **Hoveyzeh** Iran
159 K4 **Hovmantorp** Sweden
148 C1 **Hövsgöl** Mongolia
146 C1 **Hövsgöl Nuur** *l.* Mongolia
**Hövüün** Mongolia *see* **Noyon**
177 E3 **Howar, Wadi** *watercourse* Sudan
190 E4 **Howard City** U.S.A.
187 H2 **Howard Lake** Canada
160 G4 **Howden** U.K.
127 H6 **Howe, Cape** Australia
191 F4 **Howell** U.S.A.
198 C2 **Howes** U.S.A.
203 G2 **Howick** Canada
181 I4 **Howick** S. Africa
126 C1 **Howitt, Lake** *salt flat* Australia
127 G6 **Howitt, Mount** Australia
203 I2 **Howland** U.S.A.
125 I1 **Howland Island** *terr.* Pacific Ocean
127 G5 **Howlong** Australia
163 E4 **Howth** Ireland
137 K6 **Ḥowz-e Dūmatu** Iran
140 E4 **Ḥowz-e Panj** Iran
154 C1 **Hồ Xa** Vietnam
165 H3 **Höxter** Germany
162 E2 **Hoy** *i.* U.K.
165 H2 **Hoya** Germany
159 I3 **Høyanger** Norway
168 G5 **Hoyerswerda** Germany
158 K2 **Høylandet** Norway
165 J3 **Hoym** Germany
158 O3 **Höytiäinen** *l.* Fin.
152 B1 **Hozat** Turkey
154 A1 **Hpa-an** Myanmar
154 A1 **Hpapun** Myanmar
168 G5 **Hradec Králové** Czech Rep.
165 L4 **Hradiště** *h.* Czech Rep.
171 H3 **Hrasnica** Bos.-Herz.
137 J1 **Hrazdan** Armenia
173 E5 **Hrebinka** Ukr.
172 B4 **Hrodna** Belarus
135 H4 **Hsipaw** Myanmar
149 E5 **Hua'an** China
213 D4 **Huachamacari, Cerro** *mt.* Venez.
148 C2 **Huachi** China
210 C6 **Huacho** Peru
148 B2 **Huachuan** China
197 G6 **Huachuca City** U.S.A.
215 C1 **Huaco** Arg.
148 D1 **Huade** China
152 D2 **Huadian** China
149 D6 **Huadu** China
154 A2 **Hua Hin** Thai.
148 E1 **Huai'an** China
148 F3 **Huai'an** *Jiangsu* China
148 E3 **Huaibei** China
148 E3 **Huaibin** China
**Huaicheng** China *see* **Chuzhou**
152 C2 **Huaide** China
148 F3 **Huai He** *r.* China
149 D5 **Huaihua** China
149 D6 **Huaiji** China
148 E1 **Huailai** China
148 E3 **Huainan** China
149 E4 **Huaining** China
148 D2 **Huairen** China
148 E3 **Huaiyang** China
148 F3 **Huaiyin** *Jiangsu* China
**Huaiyin** China *see* **Huai'an**
148 E3 **Huaiyuan** *Anhui* China
149 C5 **Huaiyuan** *Guangxi* China
148 B3 **Huajialing** China
207 E4 **Huajuápan de León** Mex.
147 E7 **Huaki** Indon.
197 F4 **Hualapai Peak** U.S.A.
149 F5 **Hualian** Taiwan
210 C5 **Huallaga** *r.* Peru
148 B2 **Hualong** China
179 B5 **Huambo** Angola
150 B1 **Huanan** China
215 C4 **Huancache, Sierra** *mts* Arg.
210 C6 **Huancayo** Peru
148 E2 **Huangbizhuang Shuiku** *resr* China
148 A2 **Huangcheng** China
148 E3 **Huangchuan** China
149 E4 **Huanggang** China
**Huang Hai** *sea* Pacific Ocean *see* **Yellow Sea**
**Huang He** *r.* China *see* **Yellow**
148 F2 **Huanghe Kou** *r. mouth* China
145 H2 **Huanghetan** China
148 E3 **Huanghua** China
148 C3 **Huangling** China
149 C7 **Huangliu** China
149 C4 **Huangmei** China
149 E4 **Huangnihe** China
149 E4 **Huangpi** China
149 C5 **Huangping** China
148 D1 **Huangqi Hai** *l.* China
149 F4 **Huangshan** China
149 E4 **Huangshi** China
148 B2 **Huang Shui** *r.* China
148 C2 **Huangtu Gaoyuan** *plat.* China
149 F4 **Huangyan** China
148 A2 **Huangyuan** China
**Huangzhou** China *see* **Huanggang**
149 C5 **Huanjiang** China
148 C2 **Huan Jiang** *r.* China
152 C3 **Huanren** China
148 F2 **Huantai** China
210 C5 **Huánuco** Peru
210 E7 **Huanuni** Bol.
148 C2 **Huanxian** China
149 G5 **Huaping Yu** *i.* Taiwan
210 C5 **Huaraz** Peru
210 C6 **Huarmey** Peru
149 D4 **Huarong** China
210 C5 **Huascarán, Nevado de** *mt.* Peru
210 C5 **Huascarán, Parque Nacional** *nat. park* Peru
212 B3 **Huasco** Chile
212 B3 **Huasco** *r.* Chile
152 D2 **Huashulinzi** China
206 B2 **Huatabampo** Mex.
148 C3 **Huating** China
152 A3 **Huatong** China
207 E4 **Huatusco** Mex.
207 E3 **Huauchinango** Mex.
207 E4 **Huautla** Mex.
148 E3 **Huaxian** China
149 C4 **Huaying** China
149 C6 **Huayuan** China
149 D6 **Huazhou** China
**Hubballi** India *see* **Hubli**
186 B2 **Hubbard, Mount** Canada/U.S.A.
189 G2 **Hubbard, Pointe** *pt* Canada
191 F3 **Hubbard Lake** U.S.A.
148 D4 **Hubei** *prov.* China
143 A3 **Hubli** India
152 D3 **Huch'ang** N. Korea
164 E3 **Hückelhoven** Germany
161 F4 **Hucknall** U.K.
**Ḥudaydah** Yemen *see* **Hodeidah**
160 F4 **Huddersfield** U.K.
202 B6 **Huddy** U.S.A.
159 L3 **Hudiksvall** Sweden
190 E5 **Hudson** *MI* U.S.A.
203 G3 **Hudson** *NY* U.S.A.
190 A3 **Hudson** *WI* U.S.A.
200 F3 **Hudson** *r.* U.S.A.
187 I4 **Hudson Bay** Canada
185 J4 **Hudson Bay** *sea* Canada
203 G3 **Hudson Falls** U.S.A.
185 P2 **Hudson Land** *reg.* Greenland
129 B3 **Hudson Mountains** *mts* Antarctica
186 E3 **Hudson's Hope** Canada
185 K3 **Hudson Strait** Canada
154 C1 **Huê** Vietnam
215 A4 **Huechucuicui, Punta** *pt* Chile
207 G5 **Huehuetenango** Guat.
206 C2 **Huehueto, Cerro** *mt.* Mex.
207 E4 **Huejotzingo** Mex.
207 E3 **Huejutla** Mex.
167 C4 **Huelva** Spain
215 B1 **Huentelauquén** Chile
215 B4 **Huequi, Volcán** *vol.* Chile
167 F4 **Huércal-Overa** Spain
167 F1 **Huesca** Spain
167 E4 **Huéscar** Spain
206 D4 **Huétamo** Mex.
202 E4 **Hughesville** U.S.A.
145 F5 **Hugli** *r. mouth* India
145 G5 **Hugli-Chinsurah** India
199 E5 **Hugo** U.S.A.
199 C4 **Hugoton** U.S.A.
148 D2 **Huguan** China
180 F3 **Huhudi** S. Africa
149 F5 **Hui'an** China
148 C2 **Hui'anpu** China
128 F3 **Huiarau Range** *mts* N.Z.
180 B3 **Huib-Hoch Plateau** Namibia
149 E5 **Huichang** China
152 D3 **Huich'ŏn** N. Korea
149 E6 **Huidong** *Guangdong* China
149 B5 **Huidong** *Sichuan* China
152 D2 **Huifa He** *r.* China
164 C3 **Huijbergen** Neth.
148 E3 **Huiji He** *r.* China
213 B4 **Huila, Nevado de** *vol.* Col.
149 E6 **Huilai** China
149 B5 **Huili** China
207 F4 **Huimanguillo** Mex.
148 E2 **Huimin** China
**Huinahuaca** Arg. *see* **Humahuaca**
152 D2 **Huinan** China
215 D2 **Huinca Renancó** Arg.
148 B3 **Huining** China
149 C5 **Huishui** China
152 G2 **Huiten Nur** *l.* China
149 C5 **Huitong** China
159 M3 **Huittinen** Fin.
207 E4 **Huitzuco** Mex.
148 C3 **Huixian** *Gansu* China
148 D3 **Huixian** *Henan* China
207 F5 **Huixtla** Mex.
149 B5 **Huize** China
149 E6 **Huizhou** China
**Hujirt** Mongolia *see* **Delgerhaan**
149 E4 **Hukou** China
180 D1 **Hukuntsi** Botswana
190 E2 **Hulbert Lake** U.S.A.
140 B3 **Hulilan** Iran
150 C2 **Hulin** China
191 H2 **Hull** Canada
191 J3 **Hull** ?
159 L4 **Hultsfred** Sweden
152 A3 **Huludao** China
146 D2 **Hulun Buir** China
146 D2 **Hulun Nur** *l.* China
177 F2 **Ḥulwān** Egypt
173 F6 **Hulyaypole** Ukr.
146 E1 **Huma** China
212 C2 **Humahuaca** Arg.
210 F5 **Humaitá** Brazil
180 F7 **Humansdorp** S. Africa
215 F3? **Humayyān, Jabal** *h.* Saudi Arabia
160 H4 **Humber, Mouth of the** U.K.
187 H4 **Humboldt** Canada
194 C3 **Humboldt** *r.* U.S.A.
194 A3 **Humboldt Bay** U.S.A.
196 C1 **Humboldt Lake** U.S.A.
196 D1 **Humboldt Range** *mts* U.S.A.
196 D2 **Humboldt Salt Marsh** U.S.A.
127 F1 **Humeburn** Australia
149 D6 **Hu Men** *sea chan.* China
169 J6 **Humenné** Slovakia
127 G6 **Hume Reservoir** Australia
196 C3 **Humphreys, Mount** U.S.A.
197 G4 **Humphreys Peak** U.S.A.
177 D2 **Hūn** Libya
158 B2 **Húnaflói** *b.* Iceland
149 D5 **Hunan** *prov.* China
152 F2 **Hunchun** China
152 F2 **Hunchun He** *r.* China
165 K3 **Hundeluft** Germany
159 J5 **Hundested** Denmark
171 J2 **Hunedoara** Romania
165 H4 **Hünfeld** Germany
169 I7 **Hungary** *country* Europe
126 F2 **Hungerford** Australia
**Hung Fa Leng** *hill* China *see* **Robin's Nest**
152 D4 **Hŭngnam** N. Korea
194 D1 **Hungry Horse Reservoir** U.S.A.
149 □ **Hung Shui Kiu** *Hong Kong* China
149 D5? **Hưng Yên** Vietnam
152 B3 **Hun He** *r.* China
162 B3 **Hunish, Rubha** *pt* U.K.
152 C3 **Hun Jiang** *r.* China
180 B3 **Huns Mountains** Namibia
164 F5 **Hunsrück** *hills* Germany
161 H5 **Hunstanton** U.K.
143 B3 **Hunsur** India
197 H4 **Hunt** U.S.A.
165 G2 **Hunte** *r.* Germany
127 I4 **Hunter** *r.* Australia
203 F3 **Hunter** U.S.A.
127 F8 **Hunter Island** Australia
186 D4 **Hunter Island** Canada
125 H4 **Hunter Island** New Caledonia
127 F8 **Hunter Islands** Australia
145 H6 **Hunter's Bay** Myanmar
203 F2 **Huntingdon** Canada
161 G5 **Huntingdon** U.K.
202 E4 **Huntingdon** U.S.A.
190 E5 **Huntington** *IN* U.S.A.
197 G2 **Huntington** *UT* U.S.A.
202 B5 **Huntington** *WV* U.S.A.
196 D5 **Huntington Beach** U.S.A.
128 E2 **Huntly** N.Z.
162 F3 **Huntly** U.K.
126 B2 **Hunt Peninsula** Australia
191 H3 **Huntsville** Canada
201 C5 **Huntsville** *AL* U.S.A.
199 E6 **Huntsville** *TX* U.S.A.
136 D6 **Hunū, Kathīb al** *des.* Egypt
148 D2 **Hunyuan** China
144 C1 **Hunza** Pak.
144 C2 **Hunza** *r.* Pak.
139 J3 **Huocheng** China
154 C1 **Hương Khê** Vietnam
**Hương Thuy** Vietnam *see* **Phu Bai**
124 E2 **Huon Peninsula** P.N.G.
127 G9 **Huonville** Australia
148 E3 **Huoqiu** China
148 E4 **Huoshan** China
148 D2 **Huozhou** China
140 E4 **Ḥūr** Iran
136 D6 **Ḥuraydīn, Wādī** *watercourse* Egypt
191 G3 **Hurd, Cape** Canada
152 A2 **Hure** China
148 C1 **Hure Jadgai** China
190 C1 **Hurkett** Canada
163 C5 **Hurler's Cross** Ireland
190 B2 **Hurley** U.S.A.
198 D2 **Huron** U.S.A.
191 F3 **Huron, Lake** Canada/U.S.A.
190 C2 **Huron Bay** U.S.A.
190 D2 **Huron Mountains** *hills* U.S.A.
197 F3 **Hurricane** U.S.A.
161 F6 **Hursley** U.K.
161 H6 **Hurst Green** U.K.
128 D5 **Hurunui** *r.* N.Z.
158 C1 **Húsavík** Iceland
158 B2 **Húsavík** Iceland
169 N7 **Huşi** Romania
159 K4 **Huskvarna** Sweden
184 C3 **Huslia** U.S.A.
159 I4 **Husnes** Norway
145 F4 **Hussainabad** India
168 D3 **Husum** Germany
158 L3 **Husum** Sweden
**Hutag** Mongolia *see* **Hutag-Öndör**
146 C2 **Hutag-Öndör** Mongolia
198 D4 **Hutchinson** U.S.A.
197 G4 **Hutch Mountain** U.S.A.
154 A1 **Huthi** Myanmar
150 C2 **Hutou** China
187 M2 **Hut Point** Canada
202 D5 **Huttonsville** U.S.A.
148 D2 **Hutuo He** *r.* China
**Hüvek** Turkey *see* **Bozova**
148 C3 **Huxian** China
149 F4 **Huzhou** China
148 A2 **Huzhu** China
158 C2 **Hvannadalshnúkur** *vol.* Iceland
170 G3 **Hvar** *i.* Croatia
173 E6 **Hvardiys'ke** Ukr.
158 B2 **Hveragerði** Iceland
159 J5 **Hvide Sande** Denmark
158 B3 **Hvíta** *r.* Iceland
152 E3 **Hwadae** N. Korea
179 C5 **Hwange** Zimbabwe
179 C5 **Hwange National Park** Zimbabwe
152 C4 **Hwangju** N. Korea
179 D5 **Hwedza** Zimbabwe
203 H4 **Hyannis** *MA* U.S.A.
198 C3 **Hyannis** *NE* U.S.A.
146 B2 **Hyargas Nuur** *salt l.* Mongolia
186 C3 **Hydaburg** U.S.A.
128 C6 **Hyde** N.Z.
124 B5 **Hyden** Australia
202 B6 **Hyden** U.S.A.
203 G4 **Hyde Park** U.S.A.
197 F5 **Hyder** U.S.A.
143 B2 **Hyderabad** India
144 B4 **Hyderabad** Pak.
166 H5 **Hyères** France
166 H5 **Hyères, Îles d'** *is* France
152 E3 **Hyesan** N. Korea
186 D2 **Hyland** *r.* Canada
127 J3 **Hyland, Mount** Australia
159 I3 **Hyllestad** Norway
159 K4 **Hyltebruk** Sweden
126 D6 **Hynam** Australia
151 D7 **Hyōno-sen** *mt.* Japan
159 N3 **Hyrynsalmi** Fin.
186 F3 **Hythe** Canada
161 I6 **Hythe** U.K.
151 B8 **Hyūga** Japan
159 N3 **Hyvinkää** Fin.


# I


210 E6 **Iaco** *r.* Brazil
211 J6 **Iaçu** Brazil
179 E6 **Iakora** Madag.
171 L2 **Ialomiţa** *r.* Romania
171 L2 **Ianca** Romania
169 M7 **Iaşi** Romania
153 A3 **Iba** Phil.
176 C4 **Ibadan** Nigeria
213 B3 **Ibagué** Col.
197 F1 **Ibapah** U.S.A.
210 C3 **Ibarra** Ecuador
142 B7 **Ibb** Yemen
165 F2 **Ibbenbüren** Germany
212 E3 **Iberá, Esteros del** *marsh* Arg.
188 F2 **Iberville, Lac d'** *l.* Canada
147 E6 **Ibi** Indon.
176 C4 **Ibi** Nigeria
211 I7 **Ibiá** Brazil
211 J4 **Ibiapaba, Serra da** *hills* Brazil
215 F1 **Ibicuí da Cruz** *r.* Brazil
214 E2 **Ibiraçu** Brazil
167 G3 **Ibiza** Spain
167 G3 **Ibiza** *i.* Spain
170 F6 **Iblei, Monti** *mts* Sicily Italy
140 B5 **Ibn Buşayyiş** *well* Saudi Arabia
211 J6 **Ibotirama** Brazil
142 E5 **Ibrā'** Oman
142 E5 **Ibrī** Oman
153 B1 **Ibuhos** *i.* Phil.
151 B9 **Ibusuki** Japan
210 C6 **Ica** Peru
207 G4 **Icaiché** Mex.
213 D4 **Içana** Brazil
213 D4 **Içana** *r.* Brazil
197 E3 **Iceberg Canyon** *gorge* U.S.A.
**İçel** Turkey *see* **Mersin**
158 □ **Iceland** *country* Europe
219 H2 **Iceland Basin** *sea feature* N. Atlantic Ocean
219 I1 **Icelandic Plateau** *sea feature* N. Atlantic Ocean
143 A2 **Ichalkaranji** India
143 D2 **Ichchapuram** India
152 D5 **Icheon** S. Korea
151 E6 **Ichifusa-yama** *mt.* Japan
151 B9 **Ichiki-Kushikino** Japan
150 G5 **Ichinoseki** Japan
133 Q4 **Ichinskaya Sopka, Vulkan** *vol.* Rus. Fed.
173 E5 **Ichnya** Ukr.
152 D4 **Ich'ŏn** N. Korea
164 B3 **Ichtegem** Belgium
165 I4 **Ichtershausen** Germany
138 D4 **Içoguz** Turkm.
186 B3 **Icy Point** U.S.A.
186 B3 **Icy Strait** U.S.A.
199 E5 **Idabel** U.S.A.
194 D2 **Idaho** *state* U.S.A.
194 D3 **Idaho City** U.S.A.
194 D3 **Idaho Falls** U.S.A.
164 F5 **Idar-Oberstein** Germany
177 F2 **Idfū** Egypt
178 B4 **Idiofa** Dem. Rep. Congo
184 C3 **Iditarod** U.S.A.
158 M1 **Idivuoma** Sweden
136 C6 **Idkū** Egypt
136 F4 **Idlib** Syria
159 K3 **Idre** Sweden
170 F1 **Idrija** Slovenia
165 G4 **Idstein** Germany
**Idutywa** S. Africa *see* **Dutywa**
159 N4 **Iecava** Latvia
214 B3 **Iepê** Brazil
164 A4 **Ieper** Belgium
171 K7 **Ierapetra** Greece
158 N1 **Iešjávri** *l.* Norway
179 D4 **Ifakara** Tanz.
179 E6 **Ifanadiana** Madag.
176 C4 **Ife** Nigeria
158 N1 **Ifjord** Norway
176 C3 **Ifôghas, Adrar des** *hills* Mali
155 D2 **Igan** *Sarawak* Malaysia
214 C3 **Igarapava** Brazil
132 J3 **Igarka** Rus. Fed.
144 C6 **Igatpuri** India
137 J2 **Iğdır** Turkey
159 L3 **Iggesund** Sweden
170 C5 **Iglesias** *Sardinia* Italy
185 J3 **Igloolik** Canada
188 B4 **Ignace** Canada
159 N5 **Ignalina** Lith.
173 C7 **İğneada** Turkey
171 M4 **İğneada Burnu** *pt* Turkey
169 P3 **Igorevskaya** Rus. Fed.
171 I5 **Igoumenitsa** Greece
132 H3 **Igrim** Rus. Fed.
214 B4 **Iguaçu** *r.* Brazil
214 A4 **Iguaçu, Parque Nacional do** *nat. park* Brazil
212 F3 **Iguaçu Falls** Arg./Brazil
214 E1 **Iguaí** Brazil
213 B4 **Iguaje, Mesa de** *hills* Col.
207 E4 **Iguala** Mex.
167 G2 **Igualada** Spain
214 C4 **Iguape** Brazil
214 D3 **Iguarapé** Brazil
214 C3 **Iguatemi** Brazil
214 A3 **Iguatemi** *r.* Brazil
211 K5 **Iguatu** Brazil
214 B4 **Iguazú, Parque Nacional del** *nat. park* Arg.
178 A4 **Iguéla** Gabon
176 B2 **Iguidi, Erg** *des.* Alg./Mauritania
178 D4 **Igunga** Tanz.
179 E5 **Iharaña** Madag.
**Ihbulag** Mongolia *see* **Hanbogd**
179 E6 **Ihosy** Madag.
152 B2 **Ih Tal** China
151 F6 **Iide-san** *mt.* Japan
158 N1 **Iijärvi** Fin.
158 N2 **Iijoki** *r.* Fin.
158 N3 **Iisalmi** Fin.
151 B8 **Iizuka** Japan
176 C4 **Ijebu-Ode** Nigeria
137 J1 **Ijevan** Armenia
164 C2 **IJmuiden** Neth.
164 D2 **IJssel** *r.* Neth.
164 D2 **IJsselmeer** *l.* Neth.
159 M3 **Ikaalinen** Fin.
181 G2 **Ikageleng** S. Africa
181 G3 **Ikageng** S. Africa
171 L6 **Ikaria** *i.* Greece
159 J4 **Ikast** Denmark
150 H3 **Ikeda** Japan
178 C4 **Ikela** Dem. Rep. Congo
171 J3 **Ikhtiman** Bulg.
180 F4 **Ikhutseng** S. Africa
**Iki** *i.* Japan *see* **Iki-shima**
173 H6 **Iki-Burul** Rus. Fed.
151 A8 **Iki-shima** *i.* Japan
176 C4 **Ikom** Nigeria
179 E6 **Ikongo** Madag.
173 H6 **Ikryanoye** Rus. Fed.
152 D6 **Iksan** S. Korea
178 D4 **Ikungu** Tanz.
153 B2 **Ilagan** Phil.
178 D3 **Ilaisamis** Kenya
140 B3 **Īlām** Iran
145 F4 **Ilam** Nepal
176 C4 **Ilaro** Nigeria
169 I4 **Iława** Poland
187 H3 **Île-à-la-Crosse** Canada
187 H3 **Île-à-la-Crosse, Lac** *l.* Canada
178 C4 **Ilebo** Dem. Rep. Congo
138 C2 **Ilek** Kazakh.
138 C1 **Ilek** *r.* Rus. Fed.
178 D3 **Ileret** Kenya
172 G2 **Ileza** Rus. Fed.
187 J3 **Ilford** Canada
161 H6 **Ilford** U.K.
161 C6 **Ilfracombe** U.K.
136 D1 **Ilgaz** Turkey
136 D1 **Ilgaz Dağları** *mts* Turkey
136 C2 **Ilgın** Turkey
213 D5 **Ilha Grande** Brazil
214 D3 **Ilha Grande, Baía da** *b.* Brazil
214 B3 **Ilha Grande, Represa** *resr* Brazil
181 J2 **Ilhas da Inhaca e dos Portugueses** *nature res.* S. Africa
214 B3 **Ilha Solteíra, Represa** *resr* Brazil
167 B2 **Ílhavo** Port.
214 E1 **Ilhéus** Brazil
139 J4 **Ili** *r.* China
139 I3 **Ili** *r.* Kazakh.
184 C4 **Iliamna Lake** U.S.A.
136 G2 **İliç** Turkey
153 C4 **Iligan** Phil.
153 C4 **Iligan Bay** Phil.
138 D2 **Il'inka** Kazakh.
172 H2 **Il'insko-Podomskoye** Rus. Fed.
203 F3 **Ilion** U.S.A.
143 B3 **Ilkal** India
161 F5 **Ilkeston** U.K.
160 F4 **Ilkley** U.K.
153 B5 **Illana Bay** Phil.
215 B1 **Illapel** Chile
215 B1 **Illapel** *r.* Chile
168 E7 **Iller** *r.* Germany
173 D6 **Illichivs'k** Ukr.
210 E7 **Illimani, Nevado de** *mt.* Bol.
190 C5 **Illinois** *r.* U.S.A.
190 C5 **Illinois** *state* U.S.A.
190 B5 **Illinois and Mississippi Canal** U.S.A.
173 D5 **Illintsi** Ukr.
176 C2 **Illizi** Alg.
165 J4 **Ilm** *r.* Germany
158 M3 **Ilmajoki** Fin.
172 D3 **Il'men', Ozero** *l.* Rus. Fed.
165 I4 **Ilmenau** Germany
165 I1 **Ilmenau** *r.* Germany
161 E7 **Ilminster** U.K.
210 D7 **Ilo** Peru
153 B4 **Iloc** *i.* Phil.
153 B4 **Iloilo** Phil.
158 O3 **Ilomantsi** Fin.
176 C4 **Ilorin** Nigeria
173 F6 **Ilovays'k** Ukr.
173 G5 **Ilovlya** Rus. Fed.
173 H5 **Ilovlya** *r.* Rus. Fed.
165 I2 **Ilsede** Germany
127 J2 **Iluka** Australia
185 M3 **Ilulissat** Greenland
151 C7 **Imabari** Japan
137 J6 **Imām al Ḥamzah** Iraq
137 J5 **Imām Ḥamīd** Iraq
136 E3 **İmamoğlu** *admin. dist.* Turkey
137 I5 **Imām Şāḥib** Afgh.
150 D2 **Iman** *r.* Rus. Fed.
151 A8 **Imari** Japan
213 E3 **Imataca, Serranía de** *mts* Venez.
159 O3 **Imatra** Fin.
151 E7 **Imazu** Japan
212 G3 **Imbituba** Brazil
214 B4 **Imbituva** Brazil
**imeni Atabayeva** Turkm. *see* **Māne**
**imeni C. A. Niyazova** Turkm. *see* **S. A. Nyýazow Adyndaky**
178 E3 **Īmī** Eth.
137 L2 **İmişli** Azer.
152 C5 **Imja-do** *i.* S. Korea
152 D4 **Imjin-gang** *r.* N. Korea

170 D2 **Imola** Italy
181 H4 **Impendle** S. Africa
211 I5 **Imperatriz** Brazil
170 C3 **Imperia** Italy
198 C3 **Imperial** U.S.A.
196 D5 **Imperial Beach** U.S.A.
197 E5 **Imperial Valley** plain U.S.A.
178 B3 **Impfondo** Congo
145 H4 **Imphal** India
171 K4 **İmroz** Turkey
152 D6 **Imsil** S. Korea
136 F5 **Imtān** Syria
153 A4 **Imuruan Bay** Phil.
151 E7 **Ina** Japan
210 E6 **Inambari** r. Peru
176 C2 **In Aménas** Alg.
181 I4 **Inanda** S. Africa
128 C4 **Inangahua Junction** N.Z.
147 F7 **Inanwatan** Indon.
158 N1 **Inari** Fin.
158 N1 **Inarijärvi** l. Fin.
158 N1 **Inarijoki** r. Fin./Norway
167 H3 **Inca** Spain
173 C7 **İnce Burnu** pt Turkey
173 E7 **İnce Burun** pt Turkey
136 D3 **İncekum Burnu** pt Turkey
136 E2 **İncesu** Turkey
163 E5 **Inch** Ireland
162 C2 **Inchard, Loch** b. U.K.
**Inchcape Rock** i. U.K. see **Bell Rock**
152 D5 **Incheon** S. Korea
162 E4 **Inchkeith** i. U.K.
181 J2 **Incomati** r. Moz.
162 B5 **Indaal, Loch** b. U.K.
214 D2 **Indaiá** r. Brazil
214 B2 **Indaiá Grande** r. Brazil
158 L3 **Indalsälven** r. Sweden
159 I3 **Indalstø** Norway
206 C2 **Indé** Mex.
196 C3 **Independence** CA U.S.A.
190 B4 **Independence** IA U.S.A.
199 E4 **Independence** KS U.S.A.
190 A2 **Independence** MN U.S.A.
198 E4 **Independence** MO U.S.A.
202 C6 **Independence** VA U.S.A.
190 B3 **Independence** WI U.S.A.
194 C3 **Independence Mountains** U.S.A.
138 B2 **Inder, Ozero** salt l. Kazakh.
138 B2 **Inderbor** Kazakh.
143 B2 **Indi** India
135 F4 **India** country Asia
190 D2 **Indian** r. U.S.A.
202 D4 **Indiana** U.S.A.
190 D5 **Indiana** state U.S.A.
190 D5 **Indiana Dunes National Lakeshore** nature res. U.S.A.
**Indian-Antarctic Basin** sea feature Southern Ocean see **Australian-Antarctic Basin**
218 L8 **Indian-Antarctic Ridge** sea feature Southern Ocean
190 D6 **Indianapolis** U.S.A.
**Indian Desert** des. India/Pak. see **Thar Desert**
189 I3 **Indian Harbour** Canada
203 F3 **Indian Lake** NY U.S.A.
190 D3 **Indian Lake** l. MI U.S.A.
202 B4 **Indian Lake** l. OH U.S.A.
202 D4 **Indian Lake** l. PA U.S.A.
218 **Indian Ocean**
198 E3 **Indianola** IA U.S.A.
199 F5 **Indianola** MS U.S.A.
197 F2 **Indian Peak** U.S.A.
190 E3 **Indian River** U.S.A.
197 E3 **Indian Springs** U.S.A.
197 G4 **Indian Wells** U.S.A.
133 P2 **Indigirka** r. Rus. Fed.
171 I2 **Inđija** Serbia
186 F2 **Indin Lake** Canada
196 D5 **Indio** U.S.A.
125 G3 **Indispensable Reefs** Solomon Is
147 D7 **Indonesia** country Asia
144 C5 **Indore** India
155 C4 **Indramayu, Tanjung** pt Indon.
155 B3 **Indrapura** Indon.
143 C2 **Indravati** r. India
166 E3 **Indre** r. France
144 B4 **Indus** r. China/Pak. alt. **Shiquan He (China)**
144 A5 **Indus, Mouths of the** Pak.
218 I3 **Indus Cone** sea feature Indian Ocean
181 G5 **Indwe** S. Africa
173 E7 **İnebolu** Turkey
136 B1 **İnegöl** Turkey
202 B6 **Inez** U.S.A.
180 D7 **Infanta, Cape** S. Africa
206 D4 **Infiernillo, Presa** resr Mex.
154 B1 **Ing, Nam Mae** r. Thai.
190 D3 **Ingalls** U.S.A.
196 B2 **Ingalls, Mount** U.S.A.
187 I2 **Ingalls Lake** Canada
164 B4 **Ingelmunster** Belgium
215 C4 **Ingeniero Jacobacci** Arg.
191 G4 **Ingersoll** Canada
138 F5 **Ingichka** Uzbek.
160 E3 **Ingleborough** h. U.K.
185 K2 **Inglefield Land** reg. Greenland
160 E3 **Ingleton** U.K.
127 I2 **Inglewood** Qld Australia
126 E6 **Inglewood** Vic. Australia
161 H4 **Ingoldmells** U.K.
168 E6 **Ingolstadt** Germany
189 H4 **Ingonish** Canada
145 G4 **Ingraj Bazar** India
186 F2 **Ingray Lake** Canada
**Ingushetia** aut. rep. Rus. Fed. see **Ingushetiya, Respublika**
173 H7 **Ingushetiya, Respublika** aut. rep. Rus. Fed.
181 J3 **Ingwavuma** S. Africa
181 J2 **Inhaca** Moz.
181 J3 **Inhaca, Península** pen. Moz.
179 D6 **Inhambane** Moz.
181 J1 **Inhambane** prov. Moz.
179 D5 **Inhaminga** Moz.
214 A3 **Inhanduízinho** r. Brazil
214 D1 **Inhaúmas** Brazil
213 C4 **Inírida** r. Col.
163 A4 **Inishark** i. Ireland
163 A4 **Inishbofin** i. Ireland
163 A3 **Inishkea North** i. Ireland
163 A3 **Inishkea South** i. Ireland
163 B4 **Inishmaan** i. Ireland
163 B4 **Inishmore** i. Ireland
163 C3 **Inishmurray** i. Ireland
163 D2 **Inishowen** pen. Ireland
163 E2 **Inishowen Head** Ireland
163 D2 **Inishtrahull** i. Ireland
163 D2 **Inishtrahull Sound** sea chan. Ireland
163 A4 **Inishturk** i. Ireland
138 E5 **Inkylap** Turkm.
128 D5 **Inland Kaikoura Range** mts N.Z.
185 L2 **Innaanganeq** c. Greenland
126 D1 **Innamincka** Australia
158 K2 **Inndyr** Norway
**Inner Mongolia** aut. reg. China see **Nei Mongol Zizhiqu**
162 C3 **Inner Sound** sea chan. U.K.
124 E3 **Innisfail** Australia
168 E7 **Innsbruck** Austria
163 D4 **Inny** r. Ireland
178 B4 **Inongo** Dem. Rep. Congo
168 I4 **Inowrocław** Poland
176 C2 **In Salah** Alg.
172 H4 **Insar** Rus. Fed.
162 F3 **Insch** U.K.
132 H3 **Inta** Rus. Fed.
215 D2 **Intendente Alvear** Arg.
168 C7 **Interlaken** Switz.
198 E1 **International Falls** U.S.A.
151 G7 **Inubō-zaki** pt Japan
188 E2 **Inukjuak** Canada
184 E3 **Inuvik** Canada
162 C4 **Inveraray** U.K.
162 F4 **Inverbervie** U.K.
128 B7 **Invercargill** N.Z.
127 I2 **Inverell** Australia
162 D3 **Invergordon** U.K.
162 E4 **Inverkeithing** U.K.
189 H4 **Inverness** Canada
162 D3 **Inverness** U.K.
201 D6 **Inverness** U.S.A.
162 F3 **Inverurie** U.K.
218 K5 **Investigator Ridge** sea feature Indian Ocean
126 B5 **Investigator Strait** Australia
135 G1 **Inya** Rus. Fed.
195 C5 **Inyokern** U.S.A.
196 C3 **Inyo Mountains** U.S.A.
178 D4 **Inyonga** Tanz.
172 H4 **Inza** Rus. Fed.
138 D1 **Inzer** Rus. Fed.
173 G4 **Inzhavino** Rus. Fed.
171 I5 **Ioannina** Greece
151 B9 **Iō-jima** i. Japan
199 E4 **Iola** U.S.A.
139 K2 **Iolgo, Khrebet** mts Rus. Fed.
162 B4 **Iona** i. U.K.
194 C1 **Ione** U.S.A.
190 E4 **Ionia** U.S.A.
171 H5 **Ionian Islands** Greece
170 G6 **Ionian Sea** Greece/Italy
**Ionoi Nisoi** is Greece see **Ionian Islands**
146 G1 **Iony, Ostrov** i. Rus. Fed.
137 K1 **Iori** r. Georgia
171 K6 **Ios** i. Greece
146 G4 **Iō-tō** i. Japan
158 O2 **Iovskoye Vodokhranilishche** l. Rus. Fed.
190 B5 **Iowa** r. U.S.A.
190 A4 **Iowa** state U.S.A.
190 B5 **Iowa City** U.S.A.
198 E3 **Iowa Falls** U.S.A.
214 C2 **Ipameri** Brazil
210 D5 **Iparía** Peru
214 D2 **Ipatinga** Brazil
173 G6 **Ipatovo** Rus. Fed.
181 F3 **Ipelegeng** S. Africa
213 A4 **Ipiales** Col.
214 E1 **Ipiaú** Brazil
214 B4 **Ipiranga** Brazil
155 B2 **Ipoh** Malaysia
211 K5 **Ipojuca** r. Brazil
214 B2 **Iporá** Brazil
178 C3 **Ippy** Cent. Afr. Rep.
171 L4 **İpsala** Turkey
127 J1 **Ipswich** Australia
161 I5 **Ipswich** U.K.
185 L3 **Iqaluit** Canada
212 B2 **Iquique** Chile
210 D4 **Iquitos** Peru
153 A4 **Iraan** Phil.
141 F5 **Īrafshān** reg. Iran
151 E7 **Irago-misaki** pt Japan
171 K6 **Irakleia** i. Greece
**Irakleio** Greece see **Iraklion**
171 K7 **Iraklion** Greece
214 E1 **Iramaia** Brazil
140 D3 **Iran** country Asia
155 D2 **Iran, Pegunungan** mts Indon.
140 B2 **Īrānshāh** Iran
141 F5 **Īrānshahr** Iran
206 D3 **Irapuato** Mex.
137 I5 **Iraq** country Asia
203 G2 **Irasville** U.S.A.
214 B4 **Irati** Brazil
136 E5 **Irbid** Jordan
132 H4 **Irbit** Rus. Fed.
211 J6 **Irecê** Brazil
163 D4 **Ireland** country Europe
178 C4 **Irema** Dem. Rep. Congo
137 K2 **Īrī Dāgh** mt. Iran
153 B3 **Iriga** Phil.
176 B3 **Irîgui** reg. Mali/Mauritania
179 D4 **Iringa** Tanz.
143 B4 **Irinjalakuda** India
211 H4 **Iriri** r. Brazil
160 B4 **Irish Sea** Ireland
211 I4 **Irituia** Brazil
140 C5 **'Irj** well Saudi Arabia
146 C1 **Irkutsk** Rus. Fed.
136 D2 **Irmak** Turkey
219 G2 **Irminger Basin** sea feature N. Atlantic Ocean
126 B4 **Iron Baron** Australia
191 F2 **Iron Bridge** Canada
202 E3 **Irondequoit** U.S.A.
171 J2 **Iron Gates** gorge Romania/Serbia
126 B4 **Iron Knob** Australia
190 C3 **Iron Mountain** U.S.A.
197 F3 **Iron Mountain** mt. U.S.A.
190 C2 **Iron River** U.S.A.
199 F4 **Ironton** MO U.S.A.
202 B5 **Ironton** OH U.S.A.
190 B2 **Ironwood** U.S.A.
203 F2 **Iroquois** Canada
190 D5 **Iroquois** r. U.S.A.
153 C3 **Irosin** Phil.
151 F7 **Irō-zaki** pt Japan
173 D5 **Irpin'** Ukr.
145 H5 **Irrawaddy** r. China/Myanmar
147 B5 **Irrawaddy, Mouths of the** Myanmar
144 C1 **Irshad Pass** Afgh./Pak.
172 I2 **Irta** Rus. Fed.
160 E3 **Irthing** r. U.K.
132 H3 **Irtysh** r. Kazakh./Rus. Fed.
178 C3 **Irumu** Dem. Rep. Congo
167 F1 **Irun** Spain
162 D5 **Irvine** U.K.
196 D5 **Irvine** CA U.S.A.
202 B6 **Irvine** KY U.S.A.
199 D5 **Irving** U.S.A.
153 B5 **Isabela** Phil.
210 □ **Isabela, Isla** i. Galapagos Is Ecuador
206 H5 **Isabelia, Cordillera** mts Nicaragua
190 B2 **Isabella** U.S.A.
196 C4 **Isabella Lake** U.S.A.
190 D2 **Isabelle, Point** U.S.A.
158 B1 **Ísafjarðardjúp** est. Iceland
158 B1 **Ísafjörður** Iceland
151 B8 **Isahaya** Japan
144 B2 **Isa Khel** Pak.
172 G1 **Isakogorka** Rus. Fed.
179 E6 **Isalo, Massif de l'** mts Madag.
179 E6 **Isalo, Parc National de l'** nat. park Madag.
213 C4 **Isana** r. Col.
162 □ **Isbister** U.K.
170 E4 **Ischia, Isola d'** i. Italy
215 C1 **Ischigualasto, Parque Provincial** nature res. Arg.
213 A4 **Iscuande** r. Col.
151 E7 **Ise** Japan
178 C3 **Isengi** Dem. Rep. Congo
166 H4 **Isère** r. France
165 F3 **Iserlohn** Germany
165 H2 **Isernhagen** Germany
170 F4 **Isernia** Italy
151 F6 **Isesaki** Japan
151 E7 **Ise-shima Kokuritsu-kōen** nat. park Japan
151 E7 **Ise-wan** b. Japan
176 C4 **Iseyin** Nigeria
**Isfahan** Iran see **Eşfahān**
139 G5 **Isfana** Kyrg.
139 G4 **Isfara** Tajik.
137 J5 **Isḩāq** Iraq
172 I4 **Isheyevka** Rus. Fed.
150 G3 **Ishikari-gawa** r. Japan
150 G3 **Ishikari-wan** b. Japan
139 F2 **Ishimskoye** Kazakh.
150 G5 **Ishinomaki** Japan
150 G5 **Ishinomaki-wan** b. Japan
151 G6 **Ishioka** Japan
151 C8 **Ishizuchi-san** mt. Japan
139 G5 **Ishkoshim** Kazakh.
144 C1 **Ishkuman** Pak.
190 D2 **Ishpeming** U.S.A.
139 F5 **Ishtixon** Uzbek.
**Ishtykhan** Uzbek. see **Ishtixon**
145 G4 **Ishurdi** Bangl.
210 E7 **Isiboro Sécure, Parque Nacional** nat. park Bol.
136 B2 **Işıklı** Turkey
136 B2 **Işıklı Barajı** resr Turkey
132 I4 **Isil'kul'** Rus. Fed.
181 J3 **iSimangaliso Wetland Park** nature res. S. Africa
181 I4 **Isipingo** S. Africa
178 C3 **Isiro** Dem. Rep. Congo
141 G2 **Iskabad Canal (disused)** Afgh.
139 G4 **Iskandar** Uzbek.
136 F3 **İskenderun** Turkey
136 E1 **İskilip** Turkey
146 A1 **Iskitim** Rus. Fed.
171 K3 **Iskŭr** r. Bulg.
186 C3 **Iskut** Canada
186 C3 **Iskut** r. Canada
136 F3 **İslahiye** Turkey
144 C2 **Islamabad** Pak.
144 C3 **Islam Barrage** Pak.
144 B4 **Islamgarh** Pak.
144 B4 **Islamkot** Pak.
201 D7 **Islamorada** U.S.A.
153 A4 **Island Bay** Phil.
203 I1 **Island Falls** U.S.A.
126 B3 **Island Lagoon** salt flat Australia
187 K4 **Island Lake** Canada
187 K4 **Island Lake** l. Canada
190 A2 **Island Lake** l. U.S.A.
196 A1 **Island Mountain** U.S.A.
177 F3 **Island of Meroe, Archaeological Sites of the** tourist site Sudan
194 E2 **Island Park** U.S.A.
203 H2 **Island Pond** U.S.A.
128 E1 **Islands, Bay of** N.Z.
162 B5 **Islay** i. U.K.
160 C3 **Isle of Man** terr. Irish Sea
202 E6 **Isle of Wight** U.S.A.
190 C2 **Isle Royale National Park** U.S.A.
137 L1 **İsmayıllı** Azer.
139 G5 **Ismoili Somoní, Qullai** mt. Tajik.
159 M3 **Isojoki** Fin.
179 D5 **Isoka** Zambia
158 N2 **Isokylä** Fin.
170 G5 **Isola di Capo Rizzuto** Italy
136 C3 **Isparta** Turkey
171 L3 **Isperikh** Bulg.
141 F5 **Ispikan** Pak.
137 H1 **İspir** Turkey
136 E5 **Israel** country Asia
172 H4 **Issa** Rus. Fed.
164 E3 **Isselburg** Germany
176 B4 **Issia** Côte d'Ivoire
137 J6 **Issin** tourist site Iraq
166 F4 **Issoire** France
**Issyk-Kul'** salt l. Kyrg. see **Ysyk-Köl**
137 I4 **Iştablāt** tourist site Iraq
141 H3 **Istādah-ye Muqur, Āb-e** l. Afgh.
136 B1 **İstanbul** Turkey (City Plan **106**)
**İstanbul Boğazı** str. Turkey see **Bosporus**
140 C3 **Īstgāh-e Eznā** Iran
171 J5 **Istiaia** Greece
139 H5 **Istik** r. Tajik.
137 L2 **İstisu** Azer.
213 A3 **Istmina** Col.
170 G2 **Istočni Drvar** Bos.-Herz.
201 D7 **Istokpoga, Lake** U.S.A.
**Istra** pen. Croatia see **Istria**
166 G5 **Istres** France
170 E2 **Istria** pen. Croatia
145 G5 **Iswaripur** Bangl.
138 D1 **Isyangulovo** Rus. Fed.
211 K6 **Itabaianinha** Brazil
211 J6 **Itaberaba** Brazil
214 D2 **Itabira** Brazil
214 D3 **Itabirito** Brazil
214 E1 **Itabuna** Brazil
211 G4 **Itacoatiara** Brazil
214 B3 **Itaguajé** Brazil
214 C3 **Itaí** Brazil
214 A4 **Itaimbey** r. Para.
211 G4 **Itaituba** Brazil
212 G3 **Itajaí** Brazil
214 D3 **Itajubá** Brazil
145 F5 **Itaki** India
170 D3 **Italy** country Europe
211 K7 **Itamaraju** Brazil
214 D2 **Itamarandiba** Brazil
214 E2 **Itambacuri** Brazil
214 E2 **Itambacuri** r. Brazil
214 D2 **Itambé, Pico de** mt. Brazil
179 E6 **Itampolo** Madag.
145 H4 **Itanagar** India
214 D1 **Itanguari** r. Brazil
214 C4 **Itanhaém** Brazil
214 E2 **Itanhém** Brazil
214 E2 **Itanhém** r. Brazil
214 E2 **Itaobím** Brazil
214 C2 **Itapajipe** Brazil
214 E1 **Itaparica, Ilha** i. Brazil
214 E1 **Itapebi** Brazil
211 J4 **Itapecuru Mirim** Brazil
214 E3 **Itapemirim** Brazil
214 E3 **Itaperuna** Brazil
214 E1 **Itapetinga** Brazil
214 C3 **Itapetininga** Brazil
214 C3 **Itapeva** Brazil
211 K6 **Itapicuru** r. Bahia Brazil
211 J5 **Itapicuru** r. Brazil
211 K4 **Itapipoca** Brazil
214 C4 **Itararé** Brazil
214 C3 **Itararé** r. Brazil
144 D5 **Itarsi** India
214 B2 **Itarumã** Brazil
153 B1 **Itbayat** i. Phil.
186 G1 **Itchen Lake** Canada
171 J5 **Itea** Greece
139 G1 **Itemgen, Ozero** l. Kazakh.
190 E4 **Ithaca** MI U.S.A.
202 E3 **Ithaca** NY U.S.A.
165 H2 **Ith Hils** ridge Germany
136 F6 **Ithrah** Saudi Arabia
**Itihusa-yama** mt. Japan see **Ichifusa-yama**
178 C3 **Itimbiri** r. Dem. Rep. Congo
214 E2 **Itinga** Brazil
214 A2 **Itiquira** Brazil
214 A2 **Itiquira** r. Brazil
138 C2 **Itmurinkol', Ozero** l. Kazakh.
151 F7 **Itō** Japan
151 E6 **Itoigawa** Japan
170 C4 **Ittiri** Sardinia Italy
214 C3 **Itu** Brazil
213 B3 **Ituango** Col.
210 D5 **Ituí** r. Brazil
214 C2 **Ituiutaba** Brazil
178 C4 **Itula** Dem. Rep. Congo
214 C2 **Itumbiara** Brazil
211 G2 **Ituni** Guyana
211 I5 **Itupiranga** Brazil
214 B2 **Iturama** Brazil
214 A4 **Iturbe** Para.
146 G2 **Iturup, Ostrov** i. Rus. Fed.
210 E5 **Ituxi** r. Brazil
168 D4 **Itzehoe** Germany
213 C4 **Iuaretê** Brazil
133 U3 **Iul'tin** Rus. Fed.
213 C4 **Iutica** Brazil
214 B3 **Ivaí** r. Brazil
158 N1 **Ivalo** Fin.
158 N1 **Ivalojoki** r. Fin.
173 C4 **Ivanava** Belarus
126 F4 **Ivanhoe** Australia
191 F1 **Ivanhoe** r. Canada
187 H2 **Ivanhoe Lake** N.W.T. Canada
191 F1 **Ivanhoe Lake** Ont. Canada
169 N5 **Ivankiv** Ukr.
173 C5 **Ivano-Frankivs'k** Ukr.
138 C1 **Ivanovka** Rus. Fed.
171 K3 **Ivanovo** tourist site Bulg.
172 G3 **Ivanovo** Rus. Fed.
172 G3 **Ivanovskaya Oblast'** admin. div. Rus. Fed.
197 E4 **Ivanpah Lake** U.S.A.
172 I4 **Ivanteyevka** Rus. Fed.
172 C4 **Ivatsevichy** Belarus
171 L4 **Ivaylovgrad** Bulg.
132 H3 **Ivdel'** Rus. Fed.
214 B3 **Ivinheima** Brazil
214 B3 **Ivinheima** r. Brazil
185 N3 **Ivittuut** Greenland
179 E6 **Ivohibe** Madag.
**Ivory Coast** country Africa see **Côte d'Ivoire**
170 B2 **Ivrea** Italy
171 L5 **İvrindi** Turkey
173 H7 **Ivris Ughelt'ekhili** pass Georgia
185 K3 **Ivujivik** Canada
169 M4 **Ivyanyets** Belarus
150 G5 **Iwaizumi** Japan
151 G6 **Iwaki** Japan
150 G4 **Iwaki-san** vol. Japan
151 C7 **Iwakuni** Japan
150 G3 **Iwamizawa** Japan
150 G5 **Iwate-san** vol. Japan
176 C4 **Iwo** Nigeria
**Iwo Jima** i. Japan see **Iō-tō**
172 C4 **Iwye** Belarus
164 C4 **Ixelles** Belgium
207 E3 **Ixmiquilpán** Mex.
181 I5 **Ixopo** S. Africa
206 C3 **Ixtlán** Mex.
207 E4 **Ixtlán** Mex.
161 H5 **Ixworth** U.K.
151 C8 **Iyo** Japan
151 C8 **Iyo-nada** b. Japan
207 G5 **Izabal, Lago de** l. Guat.
140 D4 **Īzad Khvāst** Iran
150 G3 **Izari-dake** mt. Japan
178 D4 **Izazi** Tanz.
173 H7 **Izberbash** Rus. Fed.
169 P3 **Izdeshkovo** Rus. Fed.
164 B4 **Izegem** Belgium
140 C4 **Īzeh** Iran
132 G4 **Izhevsk** Rus. Fed.
132 G3 **Izhma** Rus. Fed.
172 J1 **Izhma** r. Rus. Fed.
173 F4 **Izmalkovo** Rus. Fed.
173 D6 **Izmayil** Ukr.
171 L5 **İzmir** Turkey
171 L5 **İzmir Körfezi** g. Turkey
136 B1 **İznik Gölü** l. Turkey
173 G6 **Izobil'nyy** Rus. Fed.
210 F7 **Izozog, Bañados del** swamp Bol.
151 F7 **Izu-hantō** pen. Japan
151 D7 **Izumisano** Japan
151 C7 **Izumo** Japan
216 E3 **Izu-Ogasawara Trench** sea feature N. Pacific Ocean
151 F7 **Izu-shotō** is Japan
173 C5 **Izyaslav** Ukr.
138 D3 **Izyndy** Kazakh.
173 F5 **Izyum** Ukr.


## J


140 E3 **Jaba** watercourse Iran
177 F3 **Jabal, Bahr el** r. Sudan/Uganda alt. **Abiad, Bahr el,** conv. **White Nile**
140 C6 **Jabal Dab** Saudi Arabia
167 E3 **Jabalón** r. Spain
144 D5 **Jabalpur** India
136 F3 **Jabbūl** Syria
124 D3 **Jabiru** Australia
136 E4 **Jablah** Syria
170 G3 **Jablanica** Bos.-Herz.
211 L5 **Jaboatão dos Guararapes** Brazil
214 C3 **Jaboticabal** Brazil
167 F1 **Jaca** Spain
211 J6 **Jacaré** r. Brazil
211 G5 **Jacareacanga** Brazil
214 C3 **Jacareí** Brazil
215 C1 **Jáchal** r. Arg.
165 K4 **Jáchymov** Czech Rep.
214 E2 **Jacinto** Brazil
210 F5 **Jaciparaná** r. Brazil
190 D1 **Jackfish** Canada
191 H3 **Jack Lake** Canada
203 H2 **Jackman** U.S.A.
199 D5 **Jacksboro** U.S.A.
199 G6 **Jackson** AL U.S.A.
196 B2 **Jackson** CA U.S.A.
202 B6 **Jackson** KY U.S.A.
190 E4 **Jackson** MI U.S.A.
198 E3 **Jackson** MN U.S.A.
199 F4 **Jackson** MO U.S.A.
199 F5 **Jackson** MS U.S.A.
202 B5 **Jackson** OH U.S.A.
201 B5 **Jackson** TN U.S.A.
194 E3 **Jackson** WY U.S.A.
129 B3 **Jackson, Mount** mt. Antarctica
128 B5 **Jackson Head** N.Z.
194 E2 **Jackson Lake** U.S.A.
190 D3 **Jacksonport** U.S.A.
199 E5 **Jacksonville** AR U.S.A.
201 D6 **Jacksonville** FL U.S.A.
190 B6 **Jacksonville** IL U.S.A.
201 E5 **Jacksonville** NC U.S.A.
199 E6 **Jacksonville** TX U.S.A.
201 D6 **Jacksonville Beach** U.S.A.
205 J5 **Jacmel** Haiti
144 B3 **Jacobabad** Pak.
211 J6 **Jacobina** Brazil
197 F3 **Jacob Lake** U.S.A.
180 F4 **Jacobsdal** S. Africa
189 H4 **Jacques-Cartier, Détroit de** sea chan. Canada
189 G4 **Jacques-Cartier, Mont** mt. Canada
189 G4 **Jacquet River** Canada
215 G1 **Jacuí** r. Brazil
211 K6 **Jacuípe** r. Brazil
211 I4 **Jacundá** Brazil
214 C4 **Jacupiranga** Brazil
213 C2 **Jacura** Venez.
143 B2 **Jadcherla** India
141 F5 **Jaddi, Ras** pt Pak.
165 G1 **Jadebusen** b. Germany
170 G2 **Jadovnik** mt. Bos.-Herz.
177 D1 **Jādū** Libya
210 C5 **Jaén** Peru
153 B3 **Jaen** Phil.
167 E4 **Jaén** Spain
140 C3 **Ja'farābād** Iran
126 C6 **Jaffa, Cape** Australia
143 B4 **Jaffna** Sri Lanka
203 G3 **Jaffrey** U.S.A.
144 D3 **Jagadhri** India
143 B3 **Jagalur** India
143 C2 **Jagdalpur** India
181 F4 **Jagersfontein** S. Africa
144 D2 **Jaggang** China
141 E5 **Jagīn** watercourse Iran
144 C3 **Jagraon** India
165 H5 **Jagst** r. Germany
143 B2 **Jagtial** India
215 G2 **Jaguarão** Brazil
215 G2 **Jaguarão** r. Brazil/Uruguay
214 C4 **Jaguariaíva** Brazil
140 B5 **Jahām, 'Irq** des. Saudi Arabia
**Jahanabad** India see **Jehanabad**
137 L3 **Jahān Dāgh** mt. Iran
144 C4 **Jahazpur** India
137 J7 **Jahmah** well Iraq
140 D4 **Jahrom** Iran
148 B3 **Jainca** China
144 C4 **Jaipur** India
144 B4 **Jaisalmer** India
144 C4 **Jaisamand Lake** India
144 E5 **Jaisinghnagar** India
144 D5 **Jaitgarh** h. India
145 E3 **Jajarkot** Nepal
140 E2 **Jajarm** Iran
170 G2 **Jajce** Bos.-Herz.
141 G4 **Jakān** mt. Afgh.
145 G4 **Jakar** Bhutan
155 C4 **Jakarta** Indon. (City Plan **102**)
186 C2 **Jakes Corner** Canada
144 B5 **Jakhau** India
158 L2 **Jäkkvik** Sweden
**Jakobshavn** Greenland see **Ilulissat**
158 M3 **Jakobstad** Fin.
199 C5 **Jal** U.S.A.
141 H3 **Jalālābād** Afgh.
139 H4 **Jalal-Abad** Kyrg.
136 C7 **Jalālah al Baḩrīyah, Jabal** plat. Egypt
137 G6 **Jalāmid, Ḩazm al** ridge Saudi Arabia
144 C3 **Jalandhar** India
207 G5 **Jalapa** Guat.
206 H5 **Jalapa** Nicaragua
159 M3 **Jalasjärvi** Fin.
137 J4 **Jalawlā'** Iraq
145 G4 **Jaldhaka** r. Bangl.
143 B2 **Jaldrug** India
214 B3 **Jales** Brazil
145 F5 **Jaleshwar** India
144 C5 **Jalgaon** Maharashtra India
144 D5 **Jalgaon** Maharashtra India
137 K6 **Jalībah** Iraq
176 D4 **Jalingo** Nigeria
206 C4 **Jalisco** state Mex.
144 C6 **Jalna** India
141 F5 **Jālo** Iran
167 F2 **Jalón** r. Spain
206 D3 **Jalostotitlán** Mex.
206 D3 **Jalpa** Mex.
145 G4 **Jalpaiguri** India
207 E3 **Jalpan** Mex.
177 E2 **Jālū** Libya
141 F3 **Jām** reg. Iran
141 G3 **Jam, Minaret of** tourist site Afgh.
205 I5 **Jamaica** country Caribbean Sea
205 I5 **Jamaica Channel** Haiti/Jamaica
137 K3 **Jamālābād** Iran
140 C3 **Jamālābād** Iran
145 G4 **Jamalpur** Bangl.
145 F4 **Jamalpur** India
211 G5 **Jamanxim** r. Brazil
155 B3 **Jambi** Indon.
144 C4 **Jambo** India
155 A2 **Jamboaye** r. Indon.
153 A5 **Jambongan** i. Sabah Malaysia
154 A4 **Jambuair, Tanjung** pt Indon.
137 J4 **Jambūr** Iraq
143 A1 **Jambusar** India
198 D2 **James** r. ND U.S.A.
202 D6 **James** r. VA U.S.A.
144 B4 **Jamesabad** Pak.
193 J1 **James Bay** Canada
201 E7 **James Cistern** Bahamas
215 D2 **James Craik** Arg.
185 P2 **Jameson Land** reg. Greenland
128 B6 **James Peak** N.Z.
129 B2 **James Ross Island** i. Antarctica
185 I3 **James Ross Strait** Canada
126 C4 **Jamestown** Australia
181 G5 **Jamestown** S. Africa
174 D7 **Jamestown** St Helena
198 D2 **Jamestown** ND U.S.A.
202 D3 **Jamestown** NY U.S.A.
137 L4 **Jamīlābād** Iran
143 A2 **Jamkhandi** India
143 A2 **Jamkhed** India
143 B3 **Jammalamadugu** India
144 C2 **Jammu** India
144 D2 **Jammu and Kashmir** state India
144 B5 **Jamnagar** India
144 D4 **Jamni** r. India
155 C4 **Jampang Kulon** Indon.
144 B3 **Jampur** Pak.
141 F3 **Jām Rūd** r. Iran
159 N3 **Jämsä** Fin.
159 N3 **Jämsänkoski** Fin.
145 F5 **Jamshedpur** India
145 G5 **Jamuna** r. Bangl.
214 D1 **Janaúba** Brazil
214 B2 **Jandaia** Brazil
140 D3 **Jandaq** Iran
144 B2 **Jandola** Pak.
196 B1 **Janesville** CA U.S.A.
190 C4 **Janesville** WI U.S.A.
141 E3 **Jangal** Iran
152 E5 **Janggi-gap** pt S. Korea
152 D6 **Janghang** S. Korea
152 D6 **Jangheung** S. Korea
152 D5 **Janghowon** S. Korea
145 G4 **Jangipur** India
152 E5 **Jangpyeong** S. Korea
152 D6 **Jangseong** S. Korea
139 G4 **Jangy-Bazar** Kyrg.
137 K2 **Jānī Beyglū** Iran
165 L2 **Jänickendorf** Germany
136 E5 **Janīn** West Bank
176 A3 **Janjanbureh** Gambia
156 C2 **Jan Mayen** terr. Arctic Ocean
138 C4 **Jaňňa** Turkm.
137 K5 **Jannah** Iraq
141 F3 **Jannatābād** Iran
180 F6 **Jansenville** S. Africa
214 D1 **Januária** Brazil
140 B4 **Janūbī, Al Fulayj al** watercourse Saudi Arabia
144 C5 **Jaora** India
150 G5 **Japan** country Asia
150 C4 **Japan, Sea of** Pacific Ocean
216 E3 **Japan Basin** sea feature Sea of Japan
216 E3 **Japan Trench** sea feature N. Pacific Ocean
210 E4 **Japurá** r. Brazil
145 H4 **Japvo** India
206 J7 **Jaqué** Panama
136 G3 **Jarābulus** Syria
214 A3 **Jaraguari** Brazil
148 B2 **Jarantai** China
136 E5 **Jarash** Jordan
214 A3 **Jardim** Brazil
205 I4 **Jardines de la Reina, Archipiélago de los** is Cuba
152 B2 **Jargalang** China
**Jargalant** Mongolia see **Matad**
137 J4 **Jarmo** tourist site Iraq
159 L4 **Järna** Sweden
168 H5 **Jarocin** Poland
169 K5 **Jarosław** Poland
158 K3 **Järpen** Sweden
139 F5 **Jarqo'rgo'n** Uzbek.
140 C4 **Jarrāhi** watercourse Iran
210 F6 **Jarú** Brazil
159 N4 **Järvakandi** Estonia
159 N3 **Järvenpää** Fin.
123 I4 **Jarvis Island** terr. Pacific Ocean
144 B5 **Jasdan** India
141 E5 **Jāsk** Iran
138 D4 **Jasliq** Uzbek.
169 J6 **Jasło** Poland
212 D8 **Jason Islands** Falkland Is
129 B2 **Jason Peninsula** pen. Antarctica
186 F4 **Jasper** Canada
201 C5 **Jasper** AL U.S.A.
199 E4 **Jasper** AR U.S.A.
201 D6 **Jasper** FL U.S.A.
200 C4 **Jasper** IN U.S.A.
202 E3 **Jasper** NY U.S.A.
202 B5 **Jasper** OH U.S.A.
199 E6 **Jasper** TX U.S.A.
186 F4 **Jasper National Park** Canada
137 J5 **Jaşşān** Iraq
169 I6 **Jastrzębie-Zdrój** Poland
144 C4 **Jaswantpura** India
169 I7 **Jászberény** Hungary
214 B2 **Jataí** Brazil
211 G4 **Jatapu** r. Brazil
143 A2 **Jath** India
144 B4 **Jati** Pak.
**Játiva** Spain see **Xàtiva**
144 B3 **Jatoi Janubi** Pak.
214 C3 **Jaú** Brazil
210 F4 **Jaú** r. Brazil
210 F4 **Jaú, Parque Nacional do** nat. park Brazil
213 E5 **Jauaperi** r. Brazil
213 D3 **Jaua-Sarisariñama, Parque Nacional** nat. park Venez.
159 M4 **Jaunlutriņi** Latvia
159 N4 **Jaunpiebalga** Latvia
145 E4 **Jaunpur** India
141 F4 **Jauri** Iran
214 A2 **Jauru** Brazil
214 B2 **Jauru** r. Brazil
173 G7 **Java** Georgia
155 C4 **Java** i. Indon.
143 B3 **Javadi Hills** India
218 L5 **Java Ridge** sea feature Indian Ocean
**Javarthushuu** Mongolia see **Bayan-Uul**
**Java Sea** sea Indon. see **Jawa, Laut**
218 K5 **Java Trench** sea feature Indian Ocean
165 J2 **Jävenitz** Germany
**Jawa** i. Indon. see **Java**
155 D3 **Jawa, Laut** sea Indon.
144 C4 **Jawad** India
144 B4 **Jawai** r. India
136 F3 **Jawbān Bayk** Syria
144 C6 **Jawhar** India
178 E3 **Jawhar** Somalia
168 H5 **Jawor** Poland
147 F7 **Jaya, Puncak** mt. Indon.
147 G7 **Jayapura** Indon.
145 F4 **Jaynagar** India
136 F5 **Jayrūd** Syria
141 E5 **Jaz Mūrīān, Hāmūn-e** salt marsh Iran
137 L3 **Jazvān** Iran
190 D5 **J. C. Murphey Lake** U.S.A.
197 E4 **Jean** U.S.A.
186 E2 **Jean Marie River** Canada
189 G2 **Jeannin, Lac** l. Canada
141 E4 **Jebāl Bārez, Kūh-e** mts Iran
176 C4 **Jebba** Nigeria
138 C5 **Jebel** Turkm.
177 E3 **Jebel Abyad Plateau** Sudan
144 C3 **Jech Doab** lowland Pak.
152 E5 **Jecheon** S. Korea
162 F5 **Jedburgh** U.K.
142 A5 **Jeddah** Saudi Arabia
170 C6 **Jedeida** Tunisia
165 J1 **Jeetze** r. Germany
203 F3 **Jefferson** NY U.S.A.
190 C4 **Jefferson** WI U.S.A.
194 D2 **Jefferson** r. U.S.A.
196 D2 **Jefferson, Mount** U.S.A.
194 B2 **Jefferson, Mount** vol. U.S.A.
198 E4 **Jefferson City** U.S.A.
200 C4 **Jeffersonville** U.S.A.
180 F7 **Jeffreys Bay** S. Africa
145 F4 **Jehanabad** India
152 D7 **Jeju** S. Korea
152 D7 **Jeju-haehyeop** sea chan. S. Korea
212 E2 **Jejuí Guazú** r. Para.
159 N4 **Jēkabpils** Latvia
168 G5 **Jelenia Góra** Poland
145 G4 **Jelep La** pass China
159 M4 **Jelgava** Latvia
202 A6 **Jellico** U.S.A.
154 C5 **Jemaja** i. Indon.
155 D4 **Jember** Indon.
139 K3 **Jeminay** Kazakh.
155 E3 **Jempang, Danau** l. Indon.
165 J4 **Jena** Germany
176 C1 **Jendouba** Tunisia
**Jengish Chokusu** mt. China/Kyrg. see **Pobeda Peak**
202 B6 **Jenkins** U.S.A.
196 A2 **Jenner** U.S.A.
199 E6 **Jennings** U.S.A.
187 J4 **Jenpeg** Canada
152 E5 **Jeomchon** S. Korea
152 D6 **Jeonju** S. Korea
126 E6 **Jeparit** Australia
214 E1 **Jequié** Brazil
214 D2 **Jequitaí** Brazil
214 D2 **Jequitaí** r. Brazil
214 E2 **Jequitinhonha** Brazil
214 E2 **Jequitinhonha** r. Brazil
154 B5 **Jerantut** Malaysia
177 F4 **Jerbar** South Sudan
205 J5 **Jérémie** Haiti
206 D3 **Jerez** Mex.
167 C4 **Jerez de la Frontera** Spain
167 C3 **Jerez de los Caballeros** Spain
**Jerggul** Norway see **Jergol**
158 N1 **Jergol** Norway
171 I5 **Jergucat** Albania
136 E6 **Jericho** West Bank
165 K2 **Jerichow** Germany
127 F5 **Jerilderie** Australia
137 J2 **Jermuk** Armenia
194 D3 **Jerome** U.S.A.
166 C2 **Jersey** i. U.K.
203 F4 **Jersey City** U.S.A.
202 E4 **Jersey Shore** U.S.A.
200 B4 **Jerseyville** U.S.A.
211 J5 **Jerumenha** Brazil
136 E6 **Jerusalem** Israel/West Bank (City Plan **106**)
127 I5 **Jervis Bay** Australia
127 I5 **Jervis Bay** b. Australia
127 I5 **Jervis Bay Territory** admin. div. Australia
170 F1 **Jesenice** Slovenia
170 E3 **Jesi** Italy
165 K3 **Jessen** Germany
159 J3 **Jessheim** Norway
145 G5 **Jessore** Bangl.
165 H1 **Jesteburg** Germany
201 D6 **Jesup** U.S.A.
207 F4 **Jesús Carranza** Mex.
215 D1 **Jesús María** Arg.
144 B5 **Jetalsar** India
198 D4 **Jetmore** U.S.A.
144 B5 **Jetpur** India
165 F1 **Jever** Germany
171 H3 **Jezercë, Maja** mt. Albania
145 F4 **Jha Jha** India
144 D3 **Jhajjar** India
144 C4 **Jhajju** India
144 A3 **Jhal** Pak.
145 G5 **Jhalakati** Bangl.
141 G5 **Jhal Jhao** Pak.
144 C3 **Jhang** Pak.
144 D4 **Jhansi** India
145 F5 **Jharia** India
145 F4 **Jharkhand** state India
143 D1 **Jharsuguda** India
144 B3 **Jhatpat** Pak.
144 C2 **Jhelum** Pak.
144 C2 **Jhelum** r. Pak.
145 G5 **Jhenaidah** Bangl.
144 B4 **Jhudo** Pak.
145 F4 **Jhumritilaiya** India
144 C3 **Jhunjhunun** India
148 C3 **Jiachuan** China
148 F4 **Jiading** China
149 D5 **Jiahe** China
149 B4 **Jiajiang** China
148 B3 **Jialing Jiang** r. China
150 B1 **Jiamusi** China
149 E5 **Ji'an** China
149 E5 **Ji'an** China
152 D3 **Ji'an** China
148 F1 **Jianchang** China
149 F4 **Jiande** China
149 B4 **Jiang'an** China
149 A6 **Jiangcheng** China
149 B5 **Jiangchuan** China
**Jiange** China see **Pu'an**
149 C4 **Jiangjin** China
149 C5 **Jiangkou** China
149 E5 **Jiangle** China
148 B3 **Jiangluo** China
149 D6 **Jiangmen** China
149 F4 **Jiangshan** China
148 F3 **Jiangsu** prov. China

149 E5 Jiangxi prov. China
149 E4 Jiangxia China
148 D3 Jiangxian China
148 F3 Jiangyan China
148 F4 Jiangyin China
149 D5 Jiangyong China
148 B4 Jiangyou China
148 F3 Jianhu China
149 D6 Jian Jiang r. China
149 A5 Jiankang China
149 D4 Jianli China
149 E5 Jianning China
149 F5 Jian'ou China
148 F1 Jianping Liaoning China
148 F1 Jianping Liaoning China
148 E2 Jianqiao China
149 C4 Jianshi China
149 B6 Jianshui China
149 F5 Jianyang Fujian China
149 B4 Jianyang Sichuan China
148 D2 Jiaocheng China
152 D2 Jiaohe China
Jiaojiang China see Taizhou
152 A2 Jiaolai He r. Nei Mongol China
148 F2 Jiaolai He r. Shandong China
149 E5 Jiaoling China
148 F3 Jiaonan China
148 F2 Jiaozhou China
148 F2 Jiaozhou Wan b. China
148 D3 Jiaozuo China
152 D2 Jiapigou China
139 I5 Jiashi China
148 D2 Jiaxian China
148 F4 Jiaxing China
149 F6 Jiayi Taiwan
149 D4 Jiayu China
146 B3 Jiayuguan China
149 E6 Jiazi China
206 I7 Jicarón, Isla i. Panama
Jiddah Saudi Arabia see Jeddah
136 D6 Jiddī, Jabal al h. Egypt
152 D6 Jido S. Korea
152 F1 Jidong China
148 B2 Jieheba China
Jiehkkevarri mt. Norway see Jiehkkevárri
158 L1 Jiehkkevárri mt. Norway
149 E6 Jieshi China
149 E6 Jieshi Wan b. China
148 E3 Jieshou China
Iešjávri l. Norway see Iešjávri
149 E6 Jiexi China
148 D2 Jiexiu China
149 E6 Jieyang China
159 N5 Jieznas Lith.
138 E4 Jigerbent Turkm.
148 A3 Jigzhi China
168 G6 Jihlava Czech Rep.
141 F3 Jījah Afgh.
178 E3 Jijiga Eth.
149 A4 Jijü China
177 E2 Jilf al Kabīr, Haḍabat al plat. Egypt
141 H3 Jilgah r. Afgh.
178 E3 Jilib Somalia
152 D2 Jilin China
152 C2 Jilin prov. China
148 A2 Jiling China
152 C2 Jilin Hada Ling mts China
178 D3 Jīma Eth.
206 C2 Jiménez Chihuahua Mex.
206 D1 Jiménez Coahuila Mex.
207 E2 Jiménez Tamaulipas Mex.
148 F2 Jimo China
203 F4 Jim Thorpe U.S.A.
148 E2 Jinan China
148 B2 Jinchang China
148 D3 Jincheng Shanxi China
148 C4 Jincheng Sichuan China
148 B4 Jinchuan China
144 D3 Jind India
127 H6 Jindabyne Australia
127 G5 Jindera Australia
152 D6 Jindo S. Korea
152 D6 Jin-do i. S. Korea
168 G6 Jindřichův Hradec Czech Rep.
149 E4 Jing'an China
148 C2 Jingbian China
148 C3 Jingchuan China
149 F4 Jingde China
149 E4 Jingdezhen China
149 E4 Jinggongqiao China
148 E2 Jinghai China
152 B5 Jinghai Wan b. China
148 F3 Jinghang Yunhe canal China
139 J3 Jinghe China
148 C3 Jing He r. China
147 C4 Jinghong China
148 F3 Jingjiang China
148 D2 Jingle China
148 D4 Jingmen China
148 B3 Jingning China
148 E1 Jingpeng China
152 E2 Jingpo China
152 E2 Jingpo Hu l. China
148 B2 Jingtai China
149 C6 Jingxi China
149 F4 Jingxian China
152 D2 Jingyu China
148 B2 Jingyuan China
149 D4 Jingzhou Hubei China
149 D4 Jingzhou Hubei China
149 C5 Jingzhou Hunan China
152 E6 Jinhae S. Korea
148 F3 Jinhu China
149 F4 Jinhua China
Jining Nei Mongol China see Ulan Qab
148 E3 Jining Shandong China
178 D3 Jinja Uganda
149 F5 Jinjiang China
149 E4 Jin Jiang r. China
178 D3 Jinka Eth.
152 A3 Jinlingsi China
149 F5 Jinmen Taiwan
149 C7 Jinmu Jiao pt China
206 H5 Jinotega Nicaragua
206 H6 Jinotepe Nicaragua
149 C5 Jinping Guizhou China
149 B6 Jinping Yunnan China
149 A5 Jinping Shan mts China
149 C5 Jinsha China
149 B4 Jinsha Jiang r. China
alt. Chang Jiang,
alt. Tongtian He,
alt. Zhi Qu,
conv. Yangtze,
long Yangtze Kiang
148 F1 Jinshan Nei Mongol China
Jinshan China see Zhujing
149 D4 Jinshi China
148 B4 Jintang China
153 B4 Jintotolo i. Phil.
153 B4 Jintotolo Channel Phil.
144 D6 Jintur India
149 E5 Jinxi China
149 E4 Jinxian China
148 E3 Jinxiang Shandong China
149 F5 Jinxiang Zhejiang China
149 B5 Jinyang China
149 F4 Jinyun China
148 E4 Jinzhai China
148 D2 Jinzhong China
152 A3 Jinzhou Liaoning China
152 A4 Jinzhou Liaoning China
152 A4 Jinzhou Wan b. China
210 F6 Ji-Paraná Brazil
210 F5 Ji-Paraná r. Brazil
210 B4 Jipijapa Ecuador
145 H2 Ji Qu r. China
144 E3 Jirang China
139 G5 Jirgatol Tajik.
141 E4 Jīroft Iran
140 C6 Jirwān Saudi Arabia
140 C6 Jirwan well Saudi Arabia
149 C4 Jishou China
136 F4 Jisr ash Shughūr Syria
154 B4 Jitra Malaysia
148 C2 Jiudengkou China
148 B4 Jiuding Shan mt. China
148 C3 Jiufoping China
149 E4 Jiujiang Jiangxi China
149 E4 Jiujiang Jiangxi China
149 E4 Jiuling Shan mts China
149 A4 Jiulong China
152 A2 Jiumiao China
152 C1 Jiutai China
149 C5 Jiuxu China
148 B3 Jiuzhaigou China
141 F5 Jiwani Pak.
149 F4 Jixi Anhui China
152 F1 Jixi Heilong. China
150 B1 Jixian China
148 D3 Jiyuan China
142 B6 Jīzān Saudi Arabia
148 E2 Jizhou China
151 C7 Jizō-zaki pt Japan
139 F4 Jizzax Uzbek.
215 G2 João Maria, Albardão do coastal area Brazil
211 L5 João Pessoa Brazil
214 C2 João Pinheiro Brazil
196 C2 Job Peak U.S.A.
152 D5 Jochiwon S. Korea
165 K4 Jocketa Germany
143 D1 Joda India
144 C4 Jodhpur India
158 O3 Joensuu Fin.
151 F6 Jōetsu Japan
179 D6 Jofane Moz.
186 F4 Joffre, Mount Canada
159 N4 Jõgeva Estonia
189 H4 Joggins Can.
181 G3 Johannesburg S. Africa
196 D4 Johannesburg U.S.A.
144 E5 Johilla r. India
194 C2 John Day U.S.A.
194 B2 John Day r. U.S.A.
186 F3 John D'Or Prairie Canada
203 G4 John F. Kennedy airport U.S.A.
202 D6 John H. Kerr Reservoir U.S.A.
162 E2 John o' Groats U.K.
201 D4 Johnson City U.S.A.
186 C2 Johnson's Crossing Canada
201 D5 Johnston U.S.A.
123 H2 Johnston Atoll terr. N. Pacific Ocean
162 D5 Johnstone U.K.
163 D5 Johnstown Ireland
203 F3 Johnstown NY U.S.A.
202 D4 Johnstown PA U.S.A.
191 F3 Johnswood U.S.A.
154 □ Johor, Selat str. Malaysia/Sing.
155 B2 Johor Bahru Malaysia
159 N4 Jõhvi Estonia
212 G3 Joinville Brazil
166 G2 Joinville France
129 B2 Joinville Island i. Antarctica
158 L2 Jokkmokk Sweden
158 D2 Jökulsá á Dál r. Iceland
158 C1 Jökulsá á Fjöllum r. Iceland
158 D2 Jökulsá í Fljótsdal r. Iceland
140 B2 Jolfa Iran
190 C5 Joliet U.S.A.
188 F4 Joliette Canada
153 B5 Jolo Phil.
153 B5 Jolo i. Phil.
153 B3 Jomalig i. Phil.
155 D4 Jombang Indon.
207 G4 Jonathan Point Belize
159 N5 Jonava Lith.
148 B3 Jonê China
199 F5 Jonesboro AR U.S.A.
203 J2 Jonesboro ME U.S.A.
203 J2 Jonesport U.S.A.
185 J2 Jones Sound sea chan. Canada
202 B6 Jonesville U.S.A.
138 E4 Jongeldi Uzbek.
177 F4 Jonglei Canal South Sudan
143 C1 Jonk r. India
159 K4 Jönköping Sweden
189 F4 Jonquière Canada
207 F4 Jonuta Mex.
199 E4 Joplin U.S.A.
203 E5 Joppatowne U.S.A.
144 D4 Jora India
136 F6 Jordan country Asia
136 E6 Jordan r. Asia
194 F2 Jordan U.S.A.
194 E3 Jordan r. U.S.A.
194 C3 Jordan Valley U.S.A.
214 B4 Jordão r. Brazil
159 K3 Jordet Norway
145 H4 Jorhat India
139 I5 Jor Hu l. China
165 H1 Jork Germany
158 M2 Jörn Sweden
159 N3 Joroinen Fin.
159 I4 Jørpeland Norway
176 C4 Jos Nigeria
153 C5 Jose Abad Santos Phil.
207 E4 José Cardel Mex.
212 B6 José de San Martín Arg.
214 A2 Joselândia Brazil
215 F2 José Pedro Varela Uruguay
189 G3 Joseph, Lac l. Canada
124 C3 Joseph Bonaparte Gulf Australia
197 G4 Joseph City U.S.A.
151 F6 Jōshinetsu-kōgen Kokuritsu-kōen nat. park Japan
197 E5 Joshua Tree National Park U.S.A.
176 C4 Jos Plateau Nigeria
159 I3 Jostedalsbreen Nasjonalpark nat. park Norway
159 J3 Jotunheimen Nasjonalpark nat. park Norway
180 E6 Joubertina S. Africa
181 G3 Jouberton S. Africa
159 N4 Jõuga Estonia
164 D2 Joure Neth.
159 N3 Joutsa Fin.
159 O3 Joutseno Fin.
164 E5 Jouy-aux-Arches France
145 H4 Jowai India
141 G3 Jowand Afgh.
163 B4 Joyce's Country reg. Ireland
206 D2 Juan Aldama Mex.
194 A1 Juan de Fuca Strait U.S.A.
179 E5 Juan de Nova i. Indian Ocean
208 E5 Juan Fernández, Archipiélago is S. Pacific Ocean
158 O3 Juankoski Fin.
206 H6 Juan Santamaria airport Costa Rica
206 D2 Juárez Mex.
211 J5 Juazeiro Brazil
211 K5 Juazeiro do Norte Brazil
177 F4 Juba South Sudan
129 E2 Jubany research stn Antarctica
178 E3 Jubba r. Somalia
196 D4 Jubilee Pass U.S.A.
207 E4 Juchatengo Mex.
206 D3 Juchipila Mex.
207 F4 Juchitán Mex.
206 C3 Juchitlán Mex.
214 E2 Jucuruçu r. Brazil
159 I4 Judaberg Norway
137 H6 Judaidat al Hamir Iraq
137 G4 Judaydah Syria
137 H6 Judayyidat 'Ar'ar well Iraq
168 G7 Judenburg Austria
159 J5 Juelsminde Denmark
148 C2 Juh China
148 F1 Juhua Dao i. China
206 H5 Juigalpa Nicaragua
164 F1 Juist i. Germany
214 D3 Juiz de Fora Brazil
210 E8 Julaca Bol.
198 C3 Julesburg U.S.A.
210 D7 Juliaca Peru
164 C2 Julianadorp Neth.
170 E1 Julian Alps mts Italy/Slovenia
211 G3 Juliana Top mt. Suriname
164 E4 Jülich Germany
139 F5 Juma Uzbek.
210 C5 Jumbilla Peru
167 F3 Jumilla Spain
145 E3 Jumla Nepal
144 B5 Junagadh India
143 C2 Junagarh India
148 F3 Junan China
215 B2 Juncal mt. Chile
Juncal, Lago l. Arg. see Juncal, Laguna
215 D4 Juncal, Laguna l. Arg.
199 D6 Junction TX U.S.A.
195 D4 Junction UT U.S.A.
198 D4 Junction City U.S.A.
214 C3 Jundiaí Brazil
186 C3 Juneau U.S.A.
127 G5 Junee Australia
168 D7 Jungfrau mt. Switz.
135 G2 Junggar Pendi basin China
144 A4 Jungshahi Pak.
202 E4 Juniata r. U.S.A.
215 E2 Junín Arg.
215 B3 Junín de los Andes Arg.
203 J1 Juniper Canada
196 B3 Junipero Serro Peak U.S.A.
149 B4 Junlian China
143 A2 Junnar India
158 L3 Junsele Sweden
194 C3 Juntura U.S.A.
159 N4 Juodupė Lith.
214 C4 Juquiá Brazil
177 E4 Jur r. South Sudan
166 H3 Jura mts France/Switz.
162 C4 Jura i. U.K.
140 B5 Jur'ā, Nafūd al des. Saudi Arabia
162 C5 Jura, Sound of sea chan. U.K.
214 E1 Jurací Brazil
213 A3 Juradó Col.
159 M5 Jurbarkas Lith.
136 E6 Jurf ad Darāwīsh Jordan
165 K1 Jürgenstorf Germany
152 A1 Jurh Nei Mongol China
152 A1 Jurh Nei Mongol China
145 G2 Jurhen Ul mts China
159 M4 Jūrmala Latvia
158 N2 Jurmu Fin.
148 F4 Jurong China
154 □ Jurong Sing.
154 □ Jurong, Selat str. Sing.
210 E4 Juruá r. Brazil
211 G6 Juruena r. Brazil
211 G5 Juruena, Parque Nacional do nat. park Brazil
158 M3 Jurva Fin.
140 E2 Jūshqān Iran
215 D2 Justo Daract Arg.
210 E4 Jutaí r. Brazil
165 L3 Jüterbog Germany
214 A3 Juti Brazil
207 G5 Jutiapa Guat.
206 H5 Juticalpa Hond.
158 L2 Jutis Sweden
158 O3 Juuka Fin.
159 N3 Juva Fin.
205 H4 Juventud, Isla de la i. Cuba
148 F3 Juxian China
148 A1 Juyan China
148 E3 Juye China
141 E3 Jūymand Iran
140 D4 Jūyom Iran
179 C6 Jwaneng Botswana
139 I4 Jyrgalang Kyrg.
159 N3 Jyväskylä Fin.


## K


144 D2 K2 mt. China/Pakistan
210 F7 Kaa-Iya del Gran Chaco, Parque Nacional nat. park Bol.
Kaala mt. U.S.A. see Ka'ala
196 □1 Ka'ala mt. U.S.A.
159 M3 Kaarina Fin.
165 J1 Kaarßen Germany
164 E3 Kaarst Germany
158 O3 Kaavi Fin.
124 C2 Kabaena i. Indon.
Kabakly Turkm. see Gabakly
176 A4 Kabala Sierra Leone
178 C4 Kabale Uganda
178 C4 Kabalo Dem. Rep. Congo
178 C4 Kabambare Dem. Rep. Congo
138 F1 Kaban' Kazakh.
139 J3 Kabanbay Kazakh.
139 J3 Kabanbay Almatinskaya Oblast' Kazakh.
139 F1 Kabanbay Severnyy Kazakhstan Kazakh.
139 G2 Kabanbay Batyr Kazakh.
179 C5 Kabangu Dem. Rep. Congo
154 A5 Kabanjahe Indon.
138 B1 Kabanovka Rus. Fed.
173 G7 Kabardino-Balkarskaya Respublika aut. rep. Rus. Fed.
178 C4 Kabare Dem. Rep. Congo
158 M2 Kåbdalis Sweden
190 E1 Kabenung Lake Canada
188 D4 Kabinakagami Lake Canada
178 C4 Kabinda Dem. Rep. Congo
140 B3 Kabīrkūh mts Iran
144 B3 Kabirwala Pak.
178 B3 Kabo Cent. Afr. Rep.
179 C5 Kabompo Zambia
178 C4 Kabongo Dem. Rep. Congo
176 B3 Kaboré Tambi, Parc National de nat. park Burkina Faso
141 F3 Kabūdeh Iran
141 E2 Kabūd Gonbad Iran
140 C3 Kabūd Rāhang Iran
153 B2 Kabugao Phil.
141 H3 Kābul Afgh.
141 H3 Kābul r. Afgh.
Kabūl r. Afgh. see Kābul
153 C5 Kabuntalan Phil.
153 C6 Kaburuang i. Indon.
179 C5 Kabwe Zambia
138 E2 Kabyrga r. Kazakh.
Kabzn' Kazakh. see Kaban'
141 F4 Kāchā Kūh mts Iran/Pak.
173 H5 Kachalinskaya Rus. Fed.
144 B5 Kachchh, Gulf of India
144 B5 Kachchh, Little Rann of marsh India
144 B4 Kachchh, Rann of marsh India
146 C1 Kachug Rus. Fed.
137 H1 Kaçkar Dağı mt. Turkey
143 B4 Kadaiyanallur India
144 A3 Kadanai r. Afgh./Pak.
154 A2 Kadan Kyun i. Myanmar
143 B3 Kadapa India
125 H3 Kadavu i. Fiji
125 H3 Kadavu Passage Fiji
176 B4 Kade Ghana
144 C5 Kadi India
136 B1 Kadıköy Turkey
126 B4 Kadina Australia
136 D2 Kadınhanı Turkey
176 B3 Kadiolo Mali
143 B3 Kadiri India
136 F3 Kadirli Turkey
143 A4 Kadmat atoll India
152 C4 Ka-do i. N. Korea
198 C3 Kadoka U.S.A.
179 C5 Kadoma Zimbabwe
177 E3 Kadugli Sudan
176 C3 Kaduna Nigeria
176 C3 Kaduna state Nigeria
145 I3 Kadusam mt. China
172 F3 Kaduy Rus. Fed.
172 G3 Kadyy Rus. Fed.
132 G3 Kadzherom Rus. Fed.
Kadzhi-Say Kyrg. see Kajy-Say
152 C4 Kaechon N. Korea
176 A3 Kaédi Mauritania
177 D3 Kaélé Cameroon
196 □1 Ka'ena Point U.S.A.
Kaena Pt U.S.A. see Ka'ena Point
128 D1 Kaeo N.Z.
152 D5 Kaesŏng N. Korea
136 F6 Kāf Saudi Arabia
179 C4 Kafakumba Dem. Rep. Congo
220 W1 Kaffeklubben Ø i. Greenland
176 A3 Kaffrine Senegal
136 C6 Kafr ash Shaykh Egypt
179 C5 Kafue Zambia
179 C5 Kafue r. Zambia
179 C5 Kafue National Park Zambia
151 E6 Kaga Japan
178 B3 Kaga Bandoro Cent. Afr. Rep.
173 G6 Kagal'nitskaya Rus. Fed.
Kagan Uzbek. see Kogon
191 F3 Kagawong Canada
158 M2 Kåge Sweden
137 I1 Kağızman Turkey
155 A3 Kagologolo Indon.
151 B9 Kagoshima Japan
140 C2 Kahak Iran
196 □1 Kahalu'u U.S.A.
178 D4 Kahama Tanz.
196 □1 Kahana U.S.A.
173 D5 Kaharlyk Ukr.
155 D3 Kahayan r. Indon.
178 B4 Kahemba Dem. Rep. Congo
128 A6 Kaherekoau Mountains N.Z.
165 J4 Kahla Germany
141 E5 Kahnūj Iran
190 B5 Kahoka U.S.A.
Kahoolawe i. U.S.A. see Kaho'olawe
196 □2 Kaho'olawe i. U.S.A.
136 F3 Kahramanmaraş Turkey
144 B3 Kahror Pakka Pak.
136 G3 Kâhta Turkey
196 □1 Kahuku U.S.A.
196 □1 Kahuku Point U.S.A.
196 □2 Kahului U.S.A.
128 D4 Kahurangi National Park N.Z.
128 D4 Kahurangi Point N.Z.
144 C2 Kahuta Pak.
178 C4 Kahuzi-Biega, Parc National du nat. park Dem. Rep. Congo
147 F7 Kai, Kepulauan is Indon.
176 C4 Kaiama Nigeria
128 D5 Kaiapoi N.Z.
195 D4 Kaibab U.S.A.
197 F3 Kaibab U.S.A.
197 F3 Kaibab Plateau U.S.A.
147 F7 Kai Besar i. Indon.
197 G3 Kaibito U.S.A.
197 G3 Kaibito Plateau U.S.A.
148 E3 Kaifeng Henan China
148 E3 Kaifeng Henan China
149 F4 Kaihua China
180 D4 Kaiingveld reg. S. Africa
148 C4 Kaijiang China
147 F7 Kai Kecil i. Indon.
149 □ Kai Keung Leng Hong Kong China
128 D5 Kaikoura N.Z.
128 D5 Kaikoura Peninsula N.Z.
176 A4 Kailahun Sierra Leone
145 G4 Kailashahar India
149 C5 Kaili China
152 A2 Kailu China
196 □1 Kailua U.S.A.
196 □2 Kailua-Kona U.S.A.
128 E2 Kaimai Range hills N.Z.
124 D2 Kaimana Indon.
128 E3 Kaimanawa Mountains N.Z.
145 H2 Kaimar China
144 E4 Kaimur Range hills India
159 M4 Käina Estonia
151 D7 Kainan Japan
176 C3 Kainji Lake National Park Nigeria
176 C3 Kainji Reservoir Nigeria
128 E2 Kaipara Harbour N.Z.
197 G3 Kaiparowits Plateau U.S.A.
149 D6 Kaiping China
189 I3 Kaipokok Bay Canada
144 D3 Kairana India
176 D1 Kairouan Tunisia
165 F5 Kaiserslautern Germany
152 E2 Kaishantun China
128 D1 Kaitaia N.Z.
128 B7 Kaitangata N.Z.
128 F3 Kaitawa N.Z.
144 D3 Kaithal India
158 M2 Kaitum Sweden
124 C2 Kaiwatu Indon.
196 □2 Kaiwi Channel U.S.A.
148 C4 Kaixian China
149 C5 Kaiyang China
151 D8 Kaiyō Japan
152 C2 Kaiyuan Liaoning China
149 B6 Kaiyuan Yunnan China
158 N2 Kajaani Fin.
124 E4 Kajabbi Australia
141 G3 Kajakī Suflá Afgh.
154 B5 Kajang Malaysia
144 B3 Kajanpur Pak.
127 H1 Kajarabie, Lake resr Australia
137 K2 K'ajaran Armenia
141 G3 Kajīrān Afgh.
137 K3 Kaju Iran
139 I4 Kajy-Say Kyrg.
138 D5 Kaka Turkm.
188 C4 Kakabeka Falls Canada
180 D4 Kakamas S. Africa
178 D3 Kakamega Kenya
128 C6 Kakanui Mountains N.Z.
176 A4 Kakata Liberia
128 E3 Kakatahi N.Z.
145 H4 Kakching India
151 C7 Kake Japan
186 C3 Kake U.S.A.
178 C4 Kakenge Dem. Rep. Congo
165 J2 Kakerbeck Germany
173 E6 Kakhovka Ukr.
173 E6 Kakhovs'ke Vodoskhovyshche resr Ukr.
140 C4 Kākī Iran
143 C2 Kakinada India
186 F2 Kakisa Canada
186 F2 Kakisa r. Canada
186 F2 Kakisa Lake Canada
151 D7 Kakogawa Japan
178 C4 Kakoswa Dem. Rep. Congo
144 D4 Kakrala India
139 I4 Kakshaal-Too mts China/Kyrg.
184 D2 Kaktovik U.S.A.
151 G6 Kakuda Japan
186 F4 Kakwa r. Canada
144 B3 Kala Pak.
170 D7 Kalaâ Kebira Tunisia
Kalaallit Nunaat terr. N. America see Greenland
144 B2 Kalabagh Pak.
147 E7 Kalabahi Indon.
153 A5 Kalabakan Sabah Malaysia
126 D3 Kalabity Australia
179 C5 Kalabo Zambia
141 G4 Kalābust Afgh.
173 G5 Kalach Rus. Fed.
178 D3 Kalacha Dida Kenya
173 G5 Kalach-na-Donu Rus. Fed.
145 H5 Kaladan r. India/Myanmar
191 I3 Kaladar Canada
196 □2 Ka Lae pt U.S.A.
196 □1 Kalaeloa hd U.S.A.
179 C6 Kalahari Desert Africa
179 B6 Kalahari Gemsbok National Park S. Africa
Kala-I-Mor Turkm. see Galaýmor
158 M2 Kalajoki Fin.
158 M2 Kalajoki r. Fin.
144 C2 Kalam Pak.
181 G1 Kalamare Botswana
171 J4 Kalamaria Greece
171 J6 Kalamata Greece
190 E4 Kalamazoo U.S.A.
190 D4 Kalamazoo r. U.S.A.
171 I5 Kalampaka Greece
126 C1 Kalamurra, Lake salt flat Australia
144 C3 Kalanaur India
173 E6 Kalanchak Ukr.
141 F4 Kalandi Pak.
126 D6 Kalangadoo Australia
177 E2 Kalanshiyū ar Ramlī al Kabīr, Sarīr des. Libya
144 C3 Kalanwali India
153 C5 Kalaong Phil.
143 C4 Kala Oya r. Sri Lanka
141 F5 Kalar watercourse Iran
137 J4 Kalār Iraq
154 B1 Kalasin Thai.
Kalāt Afgh. see Qalāt
141 E5 Kalāt Iran
141 G4 Kalat Pak.
196 □2 Kalaupapa U.S.A.
173 G6 Kalaus r. Rus. Fed.
139 J2 Kalba, Khrebet mts Kazakh.
137 K1 Kälbäcär Azer.
127 J1 Kalbar Australia
124 B4 Kalbarri Australia
165 J2 Kalbe (Milde) Germany
141 E3 Kalbū Iran
Kalburgi India see Gulbarga
138 C2 Kaldygayty r. Kazakh.
136 B3 Kale Turkey
137 G1 Kale Turkey
136 D1 Kalecik Turkey
165 I3 Kalefeld Germany
137 L3 Kaleh Sarai Iran
178 C4 Kalema Dem. Rep. Congo
178 C4 Kalemie Dem. Rep. Congo
140 E2 Kāl-e Shūr r. Iran
190 D3 Kaleva U.S.A.
158 O2 Kalevala Rus. Fed.
145 H5 Kalewa Myanmar
124 C5 Kalgoorlie Australia
170 F2 Kali Croatia
144 E3 Kali r. India/Nepal
171 M3 Kaliakra, Nos pt Bulg.
153 B4 Kalibo Phil.
145 F4 Kali Gandaki r. Nepal
178 C4 Kalima Dem. Rep. Congo
155 D3 Kalimantan reg. Indon.
143 A3 Kalinadi r. India
144 E4 Kali Nadi r. India
172 B4 Kaliningrad Rus. Fed.
172 B4 Kaliningradskaya Oblast' admin. div. Rus. Fed.
172 G3 Kalinino Rus. Fed.
139 G5 Kalininobod Tajik.
173 H5 Kalininsk Rus. Fed.
173 F6 Kalininskaya Rus. Fed.
173 D4 Kalinkavichy Belarus
138 C2 Kalinovka Kazakh.
144 D4 Kali Sindh r. India
194 D1 Kalispell U.S.A.
168 I5 Kalisz Poland
140 E4 Kalituyeh Iran
173 G5 Kalitva r. Rus. Fed.
178 D4 Kaliua Tanz.
158 M2 Kalix Sweden
158 M2 Kalixälven r. Sweden
145 H4 Kalkalighat India
136 B3 Kalkan Turkey
190 E3 Kalkaska U.S.A.
179 B6 Kalkfeld Namibia
181 F4 Kalkfonteindam dam S. Africa
164 E4 Kall Germany
154 □ Kallang Sing.
159 N4 Kallaste Estonia
158 N3 Kallavesi l. Fin.
158 K3 Kallsedet Sweden
158 K3 Kallsjön l. Sweden
138 F3 Kalmakkyrgan watercourse Kazakh.
139 J1 Kalmanka Rus. Fed.
159 L4 Kalmar Sweden
159 L4 Kalmarsund sea chan. Sweden
165 G5 Kalmit h. Germany
173 F6 Kal'mius r. Ukr.
143 C5 Kalmunai Sri Lanka
173 H6 Kalmykiya-Khalm'g-Tangch, Respublika aut. rep. Rus. Fed.
145 G4 Kalni r. Bangl.
169 M5 Kalodnaye Belarus
144 C5 Kalol India
153 C6 Kaloma i. Indon.
179 C5 Kalomo Zambia
186 D4 Kalone Peak Canada
140 B2 Kalow r. Iran
144 D3 Kalpa India
143 A4 Kalpeni atoll India
144 D4 Kalpi India
139 I4 Kalpin China
137 K4 Kal Safīd Iran
184 C3 Kaltag U.S.A.
165 H1 Kaltenkirchen Germany
165 I4 Kaltensundheim Germany
144 C3 Kalu India
172 F4 Kaluga Rus. Fed.
159 J5 Kalundborg Denmark
144 B2 Kalur Kot Pak.
173 C5 Kalush Ukr.
143 B5 Kalutara Sri Lanka
172 E4 Kaluzhskaya Oblast' admin. div. Rus. Fed.
158 M3 Kälviä Fin.
143 A2 Kalyan India
172 F3 Kalyazin Rus. Fed.
171 L6 Kalymnos i. Greece
169 L6 Kalynivka Ukr.
139 J4 Kalzhat Kazakh.
178 C4 Kama Dem. Rep. Congo
150 G5 Kamaishi Japan
144 C3 Kamalia Pak.
136 D2 Kaman Turkey
179 B5 Kamanjab Namibia
143 B2 Kamareddi India
141 F5 Kamarod Pak.
Kamashi Uzbek. see Qamashi
124 C5 Kambalda Australia
143 B4 Kambam India
139 J4 Kambardi China
144 B4 Kamber Pak.
179 C5 Kambove Dem. Rep. Congo
133 R4 Kamchatka r. Rus. Fed.
216 G2 Kamchatka Basin sea feature Bering Sea
133 Q4 Kamchatka Peninsula Rus. Fed.
171 L3 Kamchiya r. Bulg.
138 B2 Kamelik r. Rus. Fed.
165 F3 Kamen Germany
170 E2 Kamenjak, Rt pt Croatia
172 H4 Kamenka Penzenskaya Oblast' Rus. Fed.
150 E2 Kamenka Primorskiy Kray Rus. Fed.
132 J4 Kamen'-na-Obi Rus. Fed.
172 F3 Kamenniki Rus. Fed.
172 D2 Kamennogorsk Rus. Fed.
173 G6 Kamennomostskiy Rus. Fed.
173 G6 Kamenolomni Rus. Fed.
150 C2 Kamen'-Rybolov Rus. Fed.
133 R3 Kamenskoye Rus. Fed.
173 G5 Kamensk-Shakhtinskiy Rus. Fed.
132 H4 Kamensk-Ural'skiy Rus. Fed.
172 G3 Kameshkovo Rus. Fed.
144 D3 Kamet mt. China
151 D7 Kami Japan
180 C5 Kamiesberge mts S. Africa
180 B5 Kamieskroon S. Africa
187 I2 Kamilukuak Lake Canada
179 C4 Kamina Dem. Rep. Congo
187 K2 Kaminak Lake Canada
169 L5 Kamin'-Kashyrs'kyy Ukr.
150 H3 Kamishihoro Japan
145 H4 Kamjong India
145 F4 Kamla r. India
139 K2 Kamlak Rus. Fed.
186 E4 Kamloops Canada
151 G7 Kamogawa Japan
144 C3 Kamoke Pak.
154 C2 Kamon, Xé r. Laos
178 C4 Kamonia Dem. Rep. Congo
178 D3 Kampala Uganda
155 B2 Kampar r. Indon.
154 B4 Kampar Malaysia
164 D2 Kampen Neth.
178 C4 Kampene Dem. Rep. Congo
154 A1 Kamphaeng Phet Thai.
143 B3 Kampli India
154 C3 Kâmpóng Cham Cambodia
154 C2 Kâmpóng Chhnăng Cambodia
154 C2 Kâmpóng Khleăng Cambodia
154 C3 Kâmpóng Spœ Cambodia
154 C2 Kâmpóng Thum Cambodia
154 C3 Kâmpôt Cambodia
Kampuchea country Asia see Cambodia
147 F7 Kamrau, Teluk b. Indon.
187 I4 Kamsack Canada
132 G4 Kamskoye Vodokhranilishche resr Rus. Fed.
178 E3 Kamsuuma Somalia
187 I3 Kamuchawie Lake Canada
178 D3 Kamuli Uganda
173 C5 Kam"yane Ukr.
173 C5 Kam"yanets'-Podil's'kyy Ukr.
173 C5 Kam"yanka-Buz'ka Ukr.
169 K4 Kamyanyets Belarus
140 B3 Kāmyārān Iran
173 F6 Kamyshevatskaya Rus. Fed.
173 H5 Kamyshin Rus. Fed.
138 E3 Kamystybas Kazakh.
138 E3 Kamystybas, Ozero l. Kazakh.
173 I6 Kamyzyak Rus. Fed.
140 E5 Kamzar Oman
188 F3 Kanaaupscow r. Canada
197 F3 Kanab U.S.A.
197 F3 Kanab Creek r. U.S.A.
141 G4 Kanak Pak.
137 J5 Kan'ān Iraq
178 C4 Kananga Dem. Rep. Congo
127 I4 Kanangra-Boyd National Park Australia
138 D1 Kananikol'skoye Rus. Fed.
197 F3 Kanarraville U.S.A.
172 H4 Kanash Rus. Fed.
202 C5 Kanawha r. U.S.A.
151 E7 Kanayama Japan
151 E6 Kanazawa Japan
154 A2 Kanchanaburi Thai.
143 B3 Kanchipuram India
144 A3 Kand mt. Pak.
141 G4 Kandahār Afgh.
158 P2 Kandalaksha Rus. Fed.
154 A5 Kandang Indon.
144 B2 Kandhura Pak.
176 C3 Kandi Benin
141 G4 Kandi Pak.
144 B4 Kandiaro Pak.
136 C1 Kandıra Turkey
127 H4 Kandos Australia
179 E5 Kandreho Madag.
143 B3 Kandukur India
143 C5 Kandy Sri Lanka
138 D2 Kandyagash Kazakh.
202 D4 Kane U.S.A.
185 L2 Kane Bassin b. Canada/Greenland
140 D5 Kaneh watercourse Iran
Kaneohe U.S.A. see Kāne'ohe
196 □1 Kāne'ohe U.S.A.
Kaneohe Bay U.S.A. see Kāne'ohe Bay
196 □1 Kāne'ohe Bay U.S.A.
173 F6 Kanevskaya Rus. Fed.
179 C6 Kang Botswana
145 G5 Kanga r. Bangl.
185 K2 Kangaarsussuaq c. Greenland
185 M3 Kangaatsiaq Greenland
176 B3 Kangaba Mali
136 F2 Kangal Turkey
140 D5 Kangān Iran
141 E5 Kangān Iran
155 B1 Kangar Malaysia
126 B5 Kangaroo Island Australia
158 O3 Kangaslampi Fin.
159 N3 Kangasniemi Fin.
140 B3 Kangāvar Iran
148 E1 Kangbao China
145 G4 Kangchenjunga mt. Nepal
149 A4 Kangding China
152 D4 Kangdong N. Korea
155 E4 Kangean, Kepulauan is Indon.
185 L3 Kangeeak Point Canada
185 N3 Kangeq c. Greenland
185 M3 Kangerlussuaq inlet Greenland
185 O3 Kangerlussuaq inlet Greenland
185 N3 Kangerlussuatsiaq inlet Greenland
185 M2 Kangersuatsiaq Greenland
185 P2 Kangertittivaq sea chan. Greenland
185 O3 Kangertittivatsiaq inlet Greenland
152 D3 Kanggye N. Korea
189 G2 Kangiqsualujjuaq Canada
185 K3 Kangiqsujuaq Canada
189 G1 Kangirsuk Canada
148 B3 Kangle China
145 F3 Kangmar Xizang China
145 G3 Kangmar Xizang China
178 B3 Kango Gabon
152 B2 Kangping China
145 I3 Kangri Karpo La India
144 E3 Kangrinboqê Feng mt. China
145 H4 Kangto mt. China
145 F2 Kangtog China
148 B3 Kangxian China
144 D5 Kanhan r. India
145 E4 Kanhar r. India
178 C4 Kaniama Dem. Rep. Congo
128 C5 Kaniere, Lake N.Z.
143 B3 Kanigiri India
132 F3 Kanin, Poluostrov pen. Rus. Fed.
137 J3 Kānī Ŗash Iraq
173 D5 Kaniv Ukr.
126 D6 Kaniva Australia
159 M3 Kankaanpää Fin.
190 D5 Kankakee U.S.A.
190 C5 Kankakee r. U.S.A.
176 B3 Kankan Guinea
143 C1 Kanker India
143 C4 Kankesanturai Sri Lanka
154 A3 Kanmaw Kyun i. Myanmar
201 D5 Kannapolis U.S.A.
144 D4 Kannauj India
143 B4 Kanniyakumari India
144 D5 Kannod India
158 N3 Kannonkoski Fin.
143 A4 Kannur India
158 M3 Kannus Fin.
176 C3 Kano Nigeria
139 I2 Kanonerka Kazakh.
180 D7 Kanonpunt pt S. Africa
144 C4 Kanor India
151 B9 Kanoya Japan
144 E4 Kanpur India
141 G5 Kanrach reg. Pak.
198 D4 Kansas r. U.S.A.
198 D4 Kansas state U.S.A.
198 E4 Kansas City KS U.S.A.
198 E4 Kansas City MO U.S.A.
146 B1 Kansk Rus. Fed.
139 H5 Kansu China
139 H4 Kant Kyrg.
145 G4 Kantanagar Bangl.
154 A4 Kantang Thai.
154 C2 Kantaralak Thai.
176 C3 Kantchari Burkina Faso
173 F5 Kantemirovka Rus. Fed.
145 F5 Kanthi India
145 F4 Kanti India
144 C3 Kantli r. India
125 I2 Kanton atoll Kiribati
138 D3 Kantubek (abandoned) Uzbek.
163 C5 Kanturk Ireland
180 C3 Kanus Namibia
181 I2 Kanyamazane S. Africa
179 C6 Kanye Botswana
179 B5 Kaokoveld plat. Namibia
176 A3 Kaolack Senegal
179 C5 Kaoma Zambia
196 □2 Kapa'a U.S.A.
Kapaa U.S.A. see Kapa'a
Kapaau U.S.A. see Kapa'au

196 □2 Kapa‘au U.S.A.
139 I3 Kapal Kazakh.
137 K2 Kapan Armenia
179 C4 Kapanga Dem. Rep. Congo
164 C3 Kapellen Belgium
171 J6 Kapello, Akrotirio pt Greece
159 L4 Kapellskär Sweden
136 A1 Kapıdağı Yarımadası pen. Turkey
216 F6 Kapingamarangi atoll Micronesia
216 F5 Kapingamarangi Rise sea feature N. Pacific Ocean
144 B3 Kapip Pak.
179 C5 Kapiri Mposhi Zambia
185 M3 Kapisillit Greenland
188 D3 Kapiskau Canada
188 D3 Kapiskau r. Canada
191 G2 Kapiskong Lake Canada
128 E4 Kapiti Island N.Z.
138 C4 Kaplankyr, Chink esc. Turkm./Uzbek.
154 A3 Kapoe Thai.
177 F4 Kapoeta South Sudan
168 H7 Kaposvár Hungary
141 F5 Kappar Pak.
164 F5 Kappel Germany
168 D3 Kappeln Germany
144 D4 Kapren India
178 D3 Kapsabet Kenya
152 E3 Kapsan N. Korea
139 I4 Kapshagay Kazakh.
139 I4 Kapshagay, Vodokhranilishche resr Kazakh.
155 D2 Kapuas r. Indon.
155 D3 Kapuas r. Indon.
155 D2 Kapuas Hulu, Pegunungan mts Malaysia
126 C5 Kapunda Australia
144 C4 Kapuriya India
144 C3 Kapurthala India
188 D4 Kapuskasing Canada
188 D4 Kapuskasing r. Canada
173 H5 Kapustin Yar Rus. Fed.
127 I3 Kaputar mt. Australia
178 D3 Kaputir Kenya
168 H7 Kapuvár Hungary
172 C4 Kapyl’ Belarus
139 I5 Kaqung China
176 C4 Kara Togo
137 H2 Kara r. Turkey
171 L5 Kara Ada i. Turkey
136 D2 Karaali Turkey
139 I2 Karaauyl Kazakh.
139 H4 Kara-Balta Kyrg.
138 E1 Karabalyk Kazakh.
139 H2 Karabas Kazakh.
138 C2 Karabau Kazakh.
138 C4 Karabaur, Uval hills Uzbek.
Karabil’, Vozvyshennost’ hills Turkm. see Garabil Belentligi
Kara-Bogaz-Gol, Zaliv b. Turkm. see Garabogazköl Aýlagy
Karabogazkel’ Turkm. see Garabogazköl
136 D1 Karabük Turkey
139 I3 Karabulak Almatinskaya Oblast’ Kazakh.
139 K3 Karabulak Vostochnyy Kazakhstan Kazakh.
139 H2 Karabulakskaya (abandoned) Kazakh.
138 E2 Karabutak Kazakh.
136 B1 Karacabey Turkey
137 G3 Karacadağ Turkey
136 D3 Karacadağ mts Turkey
136 B1 Karacaköy Turkey
137 G3 Karacalı Dağ mt. Turkey
136 B3 Karacasu Turkey
136 C3 Karaca Yarımadası pen. Turkey
173 G7 Karachayevo-Cherkesskaya Respublika aut. rep. Rus. Fed.
173 G7 Karachayevsk Rus. Fed.
172 E4 Karachev Rus. Fed.
141 G5 Karachi Pak. (City Plan 106)
137 I2 Karaçoban Turkey
143 A2 Karad India
136 D3 Kara Dağ mt. Turkey
137 I3 Kara Dağ mt. Turkey
139 H4 Kara-Daryya r. Kyrg.
139 G2 Karagandinskaya Oblast’ admin. div. Kazakh.
139 H2 Karagandy Kazakh.
139 H2 Karagayly Kazakh.
133 R4 Karaginskiy Zaliv b. Rus. Fed.
138 B4 Karagiye, Vpadina depr. Kazakh.
136 B2 Karahallı Turkey
136 E2 Karahasanlı Turkey
143 B4 Karaikal India
143 B4 Karaikkudi India
136 E3 Karaisalı Turkey
143 B4 Karaitivu i. Sri Lanka
140 C3 Karaj Iran
140 C3 Karaj r. Iran
Karakalpakiya Uzbek. see Qoraqalpog‘iston
Karakatinskaya, Vpadina depr. Uzbek. see Qoraqata botig‘i
144 E1 Karakax He r. China
137 G3 Karakeçi Turkey
136 D2 Karakeçili Turkey
147 E6 Karakelong i. Indon.
138 F3 Karaketken Kazakh.
137 H2 Karakoçan Turkey
137 C2 Karakol’ Kazakh.
139 H4 Kara-Köl Kyrg.
139 I4 Karakol Kyrg.
139 I4 Karakol Kyrg.
144 D2 Karakoram Pass China/India
135 F3 Karakoram Range mts Asia
178 D2 Kara K’orē Eth.
139 G3 Karakoyyn, Ozero salt l. Kazakh.
139 J2 Karakozha Kazakh.
Karakul’ Uzbek. see Qorako‘l
138 E1 Karakul’skoye Rus. Fed.
139 I3 Karakum Kazakh.
138 C3 Karakum, Peski des. Kazakh.
141 F2 Karakum Desert Turkm.
Karakumskiy Kanal canal Turkm. see Garagum Kanaly
Kara Kumy des. Turkm. see Garagum
137 I1 Karakurt Turkey
159 M4 Karala Estonia
136 D3 Karaman Turkey
136 B3 Karamanlı Turkey
135 G2 Karamay China
144 C1 Karambar Pass Afgh./Pak.
128 D4 Karamea N.Z.
128 C4 Karamea Bight b. N.Z.
138 F2 Karamendy Kazakh.
Karamet-Niyaz Turkm. see Garamätnyýaz
145 F1 Karamiran China
145 F1 Karamiran Shankou pass China
136 B1 Karamürsel Turkey
172 D3 Karamyshevo Rus. Fed.
140 C5 Karān i. Saudi Arabia
144 D5 Karanja India
143 B2 Karanja r. India
145 F5 Karanjia India
144 C3 Karanpura India
139 I1 Karaoba Kazakh.
139 H3 Karaoy (abandoned) Almatinskaya Oblast’ Kazakh.
139 H3 Karaoy (abandoned) Almatinskaya Oblast’ Kazakh.
138 F3 Karaozek Kazakh.
136 D3 Karapınar Turkey
139 I4 Karaqi China
180 B3 Karas admin. reg. Namibia
180 B3 Karas watercourse Namibia
139 I4 Kara-Say Kyrg.
179 B6 Karasburg Namibia
132 I2 Kara Sea Rus. Fed.
139 H2 Karashoky Kazakh.
Kárášjohka Norway see Karasjok
158 N1 Karasjok Norway
139 H2 Karasor Kazakh.
139 H2 Karasor, Ozero salt l. Karagandinskaya Oblast’ Kazakh.
139 H1 Karasor, Ozero salt l. Pavlodarskaya Oblast’ Kazakh.
139 H3 Karasu Karagandinskaya Oblast’ Kazakh.
138 F1 Karasu Kustanayskaya Oblast’ Kazakh.
139 H1 Karasu r. Kazakh.
136 C1 Karasu Turkey
137 I2 Karasu r. Turkey
139 I1 Karasuk Rus. Fed.
139 H4 Kara-Suu Kyrg.
139 K3 Karatal Kazakh.
136 E3 Karataş Turkey
136 E3 Karataş Burun pt Turkey
139 G4 Karatau Kazakh.
139 F3 Karatau, Khrebet mts Kazakh.
144 E2 Karatax Shan mts China
154 A3 Karathuri Myanmar
138 C2 Karatobe Kazakh.
138 D3 Karatobe, Mys pt Kazakh.
138 D2 Karatogay Kazakh.
139 I3 Karatol r. Kazakh.
138 E1 Karatomarskoye Vodokhranilishche resr Kazakh.
138 C3 Karaton Kazakh.
145 G4 Karatoya r. Bangl.
151 A8 Karatsu Japan
153 C5 Karatung i. Indon.
138 F2 Kara-Turgay r. Kazakh.
Karaulbazar Uzbek. see Qorovulbozor
144 D4 Karauli India
137 I1 Karaurgan Turkey
138 C2 Karauylkel’dy Kazakh.
155 C4 Karawang Indon.
139 K3 Kara Yertis r. Kazakh.
139 J4 Karayulgun China
141 F3 Kārayz-e Ilyās Afgh.
139 G2 Karazhal Kazakh.
138 B3 Karazhambas Kazakh.
Karazhar Uzbek. see Qorajar
139 H3 Karazhingil (abandoned) Kazakh.
137 J5 Karbalā’ Iraq
165 G4 Karben Germany
140 C3 Karbūsh, Kūh-e mt. Iran
169 J7 Karcag Hungary
164 F4 Karden Germany
171 I5 Karditsa Greece
159 M4 Kärdla Estonia
181 G4 Karee S. Africa
180 D5 Kareeberge mts S. Africa
177 F3 Kareima Sudan
173 G7 Kareli Georgia
144 D5 Kareli India
172 E2 Kareliya, Respublika aut. rep. Rus. Fed.
146 D1 Karenga r. Rus. Fed.
144 D4 Karera India
158 M1 Karesuando Sweden
141 F5 Kārevāndar Iran
173 H7 Kargalinskaya Rus. Fed.
139 H2 Kargaly Karagandinskaya Oblast’ Kazakh.
139 J2 Kargaly Vostochnyy Kazakhstan Kazakh.
138 D2 Kargaly Kazakh.
137 H2 Kargapazarı Dağları mts Turkey
136 E1 Kargı Turkey
144 D2 Kargil India
172 F2 Kargopol’ Rus. Fed.
140 E5 Kargūshkī Iran
Karholmsbruk Sweden see Karlholmsbruk
179 C5 Kariba Zimbabwe
179 C5 Kariba, Lake resr Zambia/Zimbabwe
150 F3 Kariba-yama vol. Japan
180 E6 Kariega r. S. Africa
158 N1 Karigasniemi Fin.
159 M3 Karijoki Fin.
128 D1 Karikari, Cape N.Z.
140 D3 Karīmābād Iran
155 C3 Karimata, Pulau-pulau is Indon.
155 C3 Karimata, Selat str. Indon.
143 B2 Karimnagar India
155 D4 Karimunjawa, Pulau-pulau is Indon.
178 E2 Karin Somalia
141 F3 Kārīz Afgh.
143 A2 Karjat India
145 F5 Karkai r. India
143 A3 Karkal India
153 C5 Karkaralong, Kepulauan is Indon.
139 H2 Karkaraly Kazakh.
124 E2 Karkar Island P.N.G.
140 C4 Karkheh, Rūdkhāneh-ye r. Iran
173 E6 Karkinits’ka Zatoka g. Ukr.
159 N3 Kärkölä Fin.
159 N4 Karksi-Nuia Estonia
159 L3 Karlholmsbruk Sweden
137 H2 Karlıova Turkey
173 E5 Karlivka Ukr.
Karl-Marx-Stadt Germany see Chemnitz
170 F2 Karlovac Croatia
171 K3 Karlovo Bulg.
168 F5 Karlovy Vary Czech Rep.
165 G6 Karlsbad Germany
159 K4 Karlsborg Sweden
159 K4 Karlshamn Sweden
159 K4 Karlskoga Sweden
159 K4 Karlskrona Sweden
165 G5 Karlsruhe Germany
159 K4 Karlstad Sweden
198 D1 Karlstad U.S.A.
165 H5 Karlstadt Germany
172 D4 Karma Belarus
143 A2 Karmala India
Karmanovka Kazakh. see Kyrkopa
159 I4 Karmøy i. Norway
144 D3 Karnal India
145 E3 Karnali r. Nepal
145 H5 Karnaphuli Reservoir Bangl.
143 A3 Karnataka state India
171 L3 Karnobat Bulg.
141 G5 Karodi Pak.
179 C5 Karoi Zimbabwe
145 G3 Karo La pass China
145 H4 Karong India
179 D4 Karonga Malawi
139 I4 Karool-Döbö Kyrg.
180 E6 Karoo National Park S. Africa
126 C5 Karoonda Australia
144 B3 Karor Pak.
178 D2 Karora Eritrea
165 K1 Karow Germany
171 L7 Karpathos i. Greece
171 L6 Karpathou, Steno sea chan. Greece
171 I5 Karpenisi Greece
172 H1 Karpogory Rus. Fed.
124 B4 Karratha Australia
140 C4 Karrī Iran
137 I1 Kars Turkey
158 N3 Kärsämäki Fin.
159 N4 Kārsava Latvia
Karshi Turkm. see Garşy
Karshi Uzbek. see Qarshi
145 G4 Karsiyang India
132 G3 Karskiye Vorota, Proliv str. Rus. Fed.
Karskoye More sea Rus. Fed. see Kara Sea
165 J1 Karstädt Germany
158 N3 Karstula Fin.
136 B1 Kartal Turkey
138 E1 Kartaly Rus. Fed.
158 N3 Karttula Fin.
141 F3 Karukh Afgh.
140 C4 Kārūn, Kūh-e h. Iran
140 C4 Kārūn, Rūd-e r. Iran
143 B4 Karur India
159 M3 Karvia Fin.
159 M3 Karvianjoki r. Fin.
143 A3 Karwar India
146 D1 Karymskoye Rus. Fed.
138 C4 Karynzharyk, Peski des. Kazakh.
171 K5 Karystos Greece
136 B3 Kaş Turkey
188 C3 Kasabonika Canada
188 C3 Kasabonika Lake Canada
178 B4 Kasaï r. Dem. Rep. Congo
179 C5 Kasaji Dem. Rep. Congo
179 D5 Kasama Zambia
Kasan Uzbek. see Koson
179 C5 Kasane Botswana
178 B4 Kasangulu Dem. Rep. Congo
Kasansay Uzbek. see Kosonsoy
143 A3 Kasaragod India
187 I2 Kasba Lake Canada
176 B1 Kasba Tadla Morocco
137 K4 Kāseh Garān Iran
179 C5 Kasempa Zambia
179 C5 Kasenga Dem. Rep. Congo
178 C4 Kasese Dem. Rep. Congo
178 D3 Kasese Uganda
144 D4 Kasganj India
140 C3 Kāshān Iran
188 D3 Kashechewan Canada
Kashgar China see Kashi
139 I5 Kashi China
151 D7 Kashihara Japan
151 B8 Kashima Japan
151 G6 Kashima-nada b. Japan
172 F3 Kashin Rus. Fed.
144 D3 Kashipur India
151 F6 Kashiwazaki Japan
137 K5 Kashkan r. Iran
139 H3 Kashkanteniz Kazakh.
140 D4 Kashku’iyeh Iran
141 E3 Kāshmar Iran
144 C2 Kashmir reg. Asia
144 C2 Kashmir, Vale of reg. India
144 B3 Kashmore Pak.
141 H3 Kashmund Ghar reg. Afgh.
139 I1 Kashyr Kazakh.
178 C4 Kashyukulu Dem. Rep. Congo
172 G4 Kasimov Rus. Fed.
200 B4 Kaskaskia r. U.S.A.
187 K3 Kaskattama r. Canada
139 I4 Kaskelen Kazakh.
159 M3 Kaskinen Fin.
178 C4 Kasongo Dem. Rep. Congo
178 B4 Kasongo-Lunda Dem. Rep. Congo
171 L7 Kasos i. Greece
171 L7 Kasou, Steno sea chan. Greece
173 H7 K’asp’i Georgia
173 H7 Kaspiysk Rus. Fed.
169 O3 Kasplya Rus. Fed.
177 F3 Kassala Sudan
171 J4 Kassandras, Chersonisos pen. Greece
171 J4 Kassandras, Kolpos b. Greece
165 H3 Kassel Germany
176 C1 Kasserine Tunisia
190 A3 Kasson U.S.A.
136 D1 Kastamonu Turkey
164 F4 Kastellaun Germany
171 J7 Kastellia Greece
164 C3 Kasterlee Belgium
171 I4 Kastoria Greece
172 E4 Kastsyukovichy Belarus
151 E7 Kasugai Japan
178 D4 Kasulu Tanz.
151 G6 Kasumiga-ura l. Japan
173 I7 Kasumkent Rus. Fed.
179 D5 Kasungu Malawi
144 C3 Kasur Pak.
203 I2 Katahdin, Mount U.S.A.
141 G3 Katah Sang Srah Afgh.
144 D2 Kataklik India
178 C4 Katako-Kombe Dem. Rep. Congo
144 D5 Katangi India
124 B5 Katanning Australia
141 H3 Katāwāz Afgh.
178 C4 Katea Dem. Rep. Congo
171 J4 Katerini Greece
186 C3 Kate’s Needle mt. Canada/U.S.A.
179 D5 Katete Zambia
143 C1 Katghora India
146 B4 Katha Myanmar
124 D3 Katherine r. Australia
144 B5 Kathiawar pen. India
143 C4 Kathiraveli Sri Lanka
Kathlehong S. Africa see Katlehong
145 F4 Kathmandu Nepal
180 E3 Kathu S. Africa
144 C2 Kathua India
176 B3 Kati Mali
145 F4 Katihar India
128 E2 Katikati N.Z.
181 G6 Katikati S. Africa
179 C5 Katima Mulilo Namibia
176 B4 Katiola Côte d’Ivoire
180 D4 Katkop Hills S. Africa
181 H3 Katlehong S. Africa
171 I5 Kato Achaïa Greece
144 D5 Katol India
154 □ Katong Sing.
139 K2 Katonkaragay Kazakh.
127 I4 Katoomba Australia
169 I5 Katowice Poland
145 G5 Katoya India
162 D4 Katrine, Loch l. U.K.
159 L4 Katrineholm Sweden
176 C3 Katsina Nigeria
176 C4 Katsina-Ala Nigeria
151 G7 Katsuura Japan
151 E6 Katsuyama Japan
189 G2 Kattaktoc, Cap c. Canada
Kattakurgan Uzbek. see Kattaqo‘rg‘on
138 F5 Kattaqo‘rg‘on Uzbek.
159 J4 Kattegat str. Denmark/Sweden
139 K1 Katun’ r. Rus. Fed.
144 B3 Katuri Pak.
164 C2 Katwijk aan Zee Neth.
165 H5 Katzenbuckel h. Germany
Kauai i. U.S.A. see Kaua‘i
196 □2 Kaua‘i i. U.S.A.
196 □2 Kaua‘i Channel U.S.A.
165 F4 Kaub Germany
165 H3 Kaufungen Germany
159 M3 Kauhajoki Fin.
158 M3 Kauhava Fin.
158 N2 Kaukonen Fin.
196 □2 Ka‘ula i. U.S.A.
196 □2 Kaulakahi Channel U.S.A.
189 H2 Kaumajet Mountains Canada
196 □2 Kaunakakai U.S.A.
159 M5 Kaunas Lith.
159 N4 Kaunata Latvia
138 C4 Kaundy, Vpadina depr. Kazakh.
176 C3 Kaura-Namoda Nigeria
149 □ Kau Sai Chau i. Hong Kong China
158 M3 Kaustinen Fin.
158 M1 Kautokeino Norway
154 A3 Kau-ye Kyun i. Myanmar
171 J4 Kavadarci Macedonia
136 F1 Kavak Turkey
171 K4 Kavala Greece
150 D2 Kavalerovo Rus. Fed.
143 C3 Kavali India
179 C5 Kavango Zambezi Transfrontier Conservation Area nat. park Africa
140 D4 Kavār Iran
143 A4 Kavaratti atoll India
171 M3 Kavarna Bulg.
143 B4 Kaveri r. India
140 E3 Kavīr, Chāh-e well Iran
140 D3 Kavīr, Dasht-e des. Iran
151 F7 Kawagoe Japan
151 F7 Kawaguchi Japan
196 □2 Kawaihae U.S.A.
128 E1 Kawakawa N.Z.
179 C4 Kawambwa Zambia
188 E5 Kawartha Lakes Canada
151 F7 Kawasaki Japan
128 E2 Kawau Island N.Z.
189 G2 Kawawachikamach Canada
128 F3 Kawerau N.Z.
128 E3 Kawhia N.Z.
128 E3 Kawhia Harbour N.Z.
196 D3 Kawich Range mts U.S.A.
154 A1 Kawkareik Myanmar
154 A1 Kawludo Myanmar
140 E6 Kawr, Jabal mt. Oman
154 A3 Kawthaung Myanmar
139 I5 Kaxgar He r. China
139 J4 Kax He r. China
144 D1 Kaxtexi China
176 B3 Kaya Burkina Faso
136 F2 Kayadibi Turkey
155 E2 Kayan r. Indon.
143 B4 Kayankulam India
155 E2 Kayan Mentarang, Taman Nasional nat. park Indon.
178 C4 Kayanza Burundi
194 F3 Kaycee U.S.A.
138 C3 Kaydak, Sor dry lake Kazakh.
179 C4 Kayembe-Mukulu Dem. Rep. Congo
197 G3 Kayenta U.S.A.
176 A3 Kayes Mali
138 F2 Kayga Kazakh.
176 A4 Kayima Sierra Leone
139 H1 Kaymanachikha Kazakh.
139 I2 Kaynar Vostochnyy Kazakhstan Kazakh.
139 H4 Kaynar Zhambylskaya Oblast’ Kazakh.
136 F2 Kaynar Turkey
136 F3 Kaypak Turkey
173 H5 Kaysatskoye Rus. Fed.
136 E2 Kayseri Turkey
143 B4 Kayts Island Sri Lanka
155 B3 Kayuagung Indon.
132 J3 Kayyerkan Rus. Fed.
138 B2 Kayyndy Kazakh.
139 H4 Kayyngdy Kyrg.
133 O2 Kazach’ye Rus. Fed.
Kazakhdar’ya Uzbek. see Qozoqdaryo
138 C4 Kazakhskiy Zaliv b. Kazakh.
138 D3 Kazakhstan country Asia
138 E3 Kazaly Kazakh.
187 J2 Kazan r. Canada
172 I4 Kazan’ Rus. Fed.
136 D3 Kazancı Turkey
172 I4 Kazanka r. Rus. Fed.
171 K3 Kazanlŭk Bulg.
Kazan-rettō is Japan see Volcano Islands
173 G5 Kazanskaya Rus. Fed.
139 H4 Kazarman Kyrg.
138 D2 Kazatskiy Kazakh.
173 H7 Kazbek mt. Georgia/Rus. Fed.
171 L5 Kaz Dağı mts Turkey
140 C4 Kāzerūn Iran
141 F5 Kazhmak r. Pak.
172 I2 Kazhym Rus. Fed.
169 J6 Kazincbarcika Hungary
145 H4 Kaziranga National Park India
173 H7 K’azreti Georgia
138 B2 Kaztalovka Kazakh.
150 G4 Kazuno Japan
139 G4 Kazygurt Kazakh.
132 H3 Kazym-Mys Rus. Fed.
163 E3 Keady U.K.
196 □2 Kealakekua Bay U.S.A.
197 G4 Keams Canyon U.S.A.
198 D3 Kearney U.S.A.
197 G5 Kearny U.S.A.
136 G2 Keban Turkey
136 G2 Keban Barajı resr Turkey
176 A3 Kébémèr Senegal
136 F4 Kebīr, Nahr al r. Lebanon/Syria
177 E3 Kebkabiya Sudan
158 L2 Kebnekaise mt. Sweden
162 B2 Kebock Head U.K.
178 E3 K’ebrī Dehar Eth.
155 C4 Kebumen Indon.
186 D3 Kechika r. Canada
136 C3 Keçiborlu Turkey
169 I7 Kecskemét Hungary
137 H1 Keda Georgia
159 M5 Kėdainiai Lith.
144 D3 Kedar Kantha mt. India
144 D3 Kedarnath Peak India
189 G4 Kedgwick Canada
155 D4 Kediri Indon.
176 A3 Kédougou Senegal
186 D2 Keele r. Canada
186 C2 Keele Peak Canada
195 C4 Keeler U.S.A.
Keeling Is terr. Indian Ocean see Cocos Islands
162 F4 Keen, Mount h. U.K.
153 A5 Keenapusan i. Phil.
203 G3 Keene U.S.A.
127 I3 Keepit, Lake resr Australia
164 C3 Keerbergen Belgium
179 B6 Keetmanshoop Namibia
187 K6 Keewatin Canada
187 K5 Keewatin U.S.A.
Kefallonia i. Greece see Cephalonia
147 E7 Kefamenanu Indon.
158 B2 Keflavík Iceland
143 C5 Kegalla Sri Lanka
139 I4 Kegen Kazakh.
138 D4 Kegeyli Uzbek.
189 G2 Keglo, Baie de b. Canada
173 H6 Kegul’ta Rus. Fed.
159 N4 Kehra Estonia
160 F4 Keighley U.K.
159 N4 Keila Estonia
180 D4 Keimoes S. Africa
158 N3 Keitele Fin.
158 N3 Keitele l. Fin.
126 D6 Keith Australia
162 F3 Keith U.K.
186 E1 Keith Arm b. Canada
189 G5 Kejimkujik National Park Canada
196 □2 Kekaha U.S.A.
169 J7 Kékes mt. Hungary
144 C4 Kekri India
135 F6 Kelaa i. Maldives
148 D2 Kelan China
Kelang Malaysia see Klang
154 B4 Kelantan r. Malaysia
164 E4 Kelberg Germany
139 J3 Kel’demurat Kazakh.
139 G4 Keles Uzbek.
165 J6 Kelheim Germany
170 D6 Kelibia Tunisia
138 F5 Kelif Turkm.
Kelifskiy Uzboy marsh Turkm. see Kelif Uzboýy
138 E5 Kelif Uzboýy marsh Turkm.
165 G4 Kelkheim (Taunus) Germany
137 G1 Kelkit Turkey
136 F1 Kelkit r. Turkey
186 E2 Keller Lake Canada
139 G1 Kellerovka Kazakh.
202 B4 Kelleys Island U.S.A.
194 C2 Kellogg U.S.A.
158 O2 Kelloselkä Fin.
163 E4 Kells Ireland
159 M5 Kelmė Lith.
164 E4 Kelmis Belgium
177 D4 Kélo Chad
186 F5 Kelowna Canada
196 A2 Kelseyville U.S.A.
162 F5 Kelso U.K.
197 E4 Kelso CA U.S.A.
194 B2 Kelso WA U.S.A.
155 B2 Keluang Malaysia
187 I4 Kelvington Canada
172 E1 Kem’ Rus. Fed.
172 E1 Kem’ r. Rus. Fed.
137 G2 Kemah Turkey
136 G2 Kemaliye Turkey
171 L5 Kemalpaşa Turkey
186 D4 Kemano (abandoned) Canada
136 C3 Kemer Turkey
136 B3 Kemer Turkey
136 B3 Kemer Barajı resr Turkey
146 A1 Kemerovo Rus. Fed.
158 N2 Kemi Fin.
158 N2 Kemijärvi Fin.
158 N2 Kemijärvi l. Fin.
158 O2 Kemijoki r. Fin.
139 H4 Kemin Kyrg.
194 E3 Kemmerer U.S.A.
165 J5 Kemnath Germany
162 F3 Kemnay U.K.
199 D5 Kemp, Lake U.S.A.
158 N2 Kempele Fin.
164 C3 Kempen reg. Belgium
164 E3 Kempen Germany
129 D5 Kemp Land pen. Antarctica
129 C3 Kemp Peninsula pen. Antarctica
201 E7 Kemp’s Bay Bahamas
127 J3 Kempsey Australia
188 F4 Kempt, Lac l. Canada
168 E7 Kempten (Allgäu) Germany
127 G9 Kempton Australia
181 H3 Kempton Park S. Africa
191 J3 Kemptville Canada
155 D4 Kemujan i. Indon.
144 E4 Ken r. India
184 C3 Kenai U.S.A.
184 C4 Kenai Mountains U.S.A.
160 E3 Kendal U.K.
127 J3 Kendall Australia
187 L2 Kendall, Cape Canada
190 E5 Kendallville U.S.A.
155 C4 Kendang, Gunung vol. Indon.
147 E7 Kendari Indon.
155 D3 Kendawangan Indon.
177 D3 Kendégué Chad
138 C4 Kendirli-Kiyasan, Plato plat. Kazakh.
145 F5 Kendrapara India
194 C2 Kendrick U.S.A.
197 G4 Kendrick Peak U.S.A.
139 H4 Kendyktas mts Kazakh.
138 C4 Kendyrlisor, Solonchak salt l. Kazakh.
127 H3 Kenebri Australia
199 D6 Kenedy U.S.A.
176 A4 Kenema Sierra Leone
Keneurgench Turkm. see Köneürgenç
178 B4 Kenge Dem. Rep. Congo
138 D4 Keng-Peli Uzbek.
147 B4 Kengtung Myanmar
180 D4 Kenhardt S. Africa
176 A3 Kéniéba Mali
176 B1 Kenitra Morocco
148 F2 Kenli China
163 B6 Kenmare Ireland
198 C1 Kenmare U.S.A.
163 A6 Kenmare River inlet Ireland
164 E5 Kenn Germany
195 G5 Kenna U.S.A.
203 I2 Kennebec r. U.S.A.
203 H3 Kennebunk U.S.A.
203 H3 Kennebunkport U.S.A.
199 F6 Kenner U.S.A.
161 F6 Kennet r. U.K.
199 F4 Kennett U.S.A.
194 C2 Kennewick U.S.A.
Keno Canada see Keno Hill
191 G1 Kenogami Lake Canada
191 G1 Kenogamissi Lake Canada
186 B2 Keno Hill Canada
187 K5 Kenora Canada
190 D4 Kenosha U.S.A.
172 F2 Kenozero, Ozero l. Rus. Fed.
160 E3 Kent r. U.K.
203 G4 Kent CT U.S.A.
199 B6 Kent TX U.S.A.
194 B2 Kent WA U.S.A.
139 G4 Kentau Kazakh.
127 G7 Kent Group is Australia
190 D5 Kentland U.S.A.
202 B4 Kenton U.S.A.
193 J4 Kentucky r. U.S.A.
202 A6 Kentucky state U.S.A.
201 B4 Kentucky Lake U.S.A.
189 H4 Kentville Canada
199 F6 Kentwood LA U.S.A.
190 E4 Kentwood MI U.S.A.
178 D3 Kenya country Africa
178 D3 Kenya, Mount Kenya
190 A3 Kenyon U.S.A.
139 G2 Kenzharyk Kazakh.
196 □2 Kēōkea U.S.A.
Keokea U.S.A. see Kēōkea
190 B5 Keokuk U.S.A.
144 D4 Keoladeo National Park India
Keo Neua, Col de pass Laos/Vietnam see Keo Nưa, Đeo
154 C1 Keo Nưa, Đeo pass Laos/Vietnam
190 B5 Keosauqua U.S.A.
124 F4 Keppel Bay Australia
154 □ Keppel Harbour sea chan. Sing.
136 B2 Kepsut Turkey
141 E4 Kerāh Iran
143 A4 Kerala state India
176 C4 Kéran, Parc National de la nat. park Togo
126 E5 Kerang Australia
159 N3 Kerava Fin.
167 G4 Kerba Alg.
139 G4 Kerben Kyrg.
173 F6 Kerch Ukr.
124 E2 Kerema P.N.G.
186 F5 Keremeos Canada
173 E7 Kerempe Burun pt Turkey
178 D2 Keren Eritrea
140 B3 Kerend Iran
139 G2 Kerey watercourse Kazakh.
139 G2 Kerey, Ozero salt l. Kazakh.
138 D5 Kergeli Turkm.
218 I8 Kerguelen, Îles is Indian Ocean
218 I8 Kerguelen Plateau sea feature Indian Ocean
178 D4 Kericho Kenya
128 D1 Kerikeri N.Z.
159 O3 Kerimäki Fin.
155 B3 Kerinci, Gunung vol. Indon.
155 B3 Kerinci Seblat, Taman Nasional Indon.
139 J5 Keriya He watercourse China
145 E2 Keriya Shankou pass China
164 E3 Kerken Germany
Kerki Turkm. see Atamyrat
Kerkichi Turkm. see Kerkiçi
138 F5 Kerkiçi Turkm.
171 J4 Kerkini, Limni l. Greece
171 H5 Kerkyra Greece
Kerkyra i. Greece see Corfu
177 F3 Kerma Sudan
123 H5 Kermadec Islands S. Pacific Ocean
216 H8 Kermadec Trench sea feature S. Pacific Ocean
140 E4 Kermān Iran
196 B3 Kerman U.S.A.
141 E4 Kermān, Bīābān-e des. Iran
Kermān Desert Iran see Kermān, Bīābān-e
140 B3 Kermānshāh Iran
140 D4 Kermānshāh Iran
199 C6 Kermit U.S.A.
195 C5 Kern r. U.S.A.
196 C4 Kern, South Fork r. U.S.A.
189 G2 Kernertut, Cap c. Canada
196 C4 Kernville U.S.A.
172 J2 Keros Rus. Fed.
171 K6 Keross i. Greece
176 B4 Kérouané Guinea
164 E4 Kerpen Germany
129 B5 Kerr, Cape c. Antarctica
187 H4 Kerrobert Canada
199 D6 Kerrville U.S.A.
163 B5 Kerry Head Ireland
154 B4 Kerteh Malaysia
159 J5 Kerteminde Denmark
Keryneia Cyprus see Kyrenia
172 H3 Kerzhenets r. Rus. Fed.
188 D3 Kesagami Lake Canada
159 O3 Kesälahti Fin.
173 C7 Keşan Turkey
136 G1 Keşap Turkey
150 G5 Kesennuma Japan
144 B5 Keshod India
137 L5 Keshvar Iran
136 D2 Keskin Turkey
172 E2 Keskozero Rus. Fed.
164 E3 Kessel Neth.
181 H4 Kestell S. Africa
158 O2 Kesten’ga Rus. Fed.
158 N2 Kestilä Fin.
191 H3 Keswick Canada
160 D3 Keswick U.K.
168 H7 Keszthely Hungary
132 J4 Ket’ r. Rus. Fed.
176 C4 Keta Ghana
154 □ Ketam, Pulau i. Sing.
155 D3 Ketapang Indon.
186 C3 Ketchikan U.S.A.
164 D2 Ketelmeer l. Neth.
141 G5 Keti Bandar Pak.
139 J4 Ketmen’, Khrebet mts China/Kazakh.
161 G5 Kettering U.K.
202 A5 Kettering U.S.A.
186 F5 Kettle r. Canada
190 A2 Kettle r. U.S.A.
202 E4 Kettle Creek r. U.S.A.
196 C3 Kettleman City U.S.A.
194 C1 Kettle River Range mts U.S.A.
202 E3 Keuka Lake U.S.A.
159 N3 Keuruu Fin.
190 C5 Kewanee U.S.A.
190 D3 Kewaunee U.S.A.
190 C2 Keweenaw Bay U.S.A.
190 C2 Keweenaw Peninsula U.S.A.
190 D2 Keweenaw Point U.S.A.
213 E3 Keweigek Guyana
163 C3 Key, Lough l. Ireland
188 F3 Keyano Canada
191 G3 Key Harbour Canada
139 J4 Keyi China
201 D7 Key Largo U.S.A.
144 D2 Keylong India
161 E6 Keynsham U.K.
202 D5 Keyser U.S.A.
202 D5 Keysers Ridge U.S.A.
197 G6 Keystone Peak U.S.A.
202 D6 Keysville U.S.A.
137 L4 Keytū Iran
201 D7 Key West FL U.S.A.
190 B4 Key West IA U.S.A.
203 H3 Kezar Falls U.S.A.
179 C6 Kezi Zimbabwe
169 J6 Kežmarok Slovakia
180 D2 Kgalagadi admin. dist. Botswana
180 D2 Kgalagadi Transfrontier Park nat. park Botswana/S. Africa
181 G2 Kgatleng admin. dist. Botswana
180 D1 Kgomofatshe Pan salt pan Botswana
180 F2 Kgoro Pan salt pan Botswana
181 G3 Kgotsong S. Africa
146 F2 Khabarovsk Rus. Fed.
139 I1 Khabary Rus. Fed.
137 H4 Khābūr, Nahr al r. Syria
137 I7 Khadd, Wādī al watercourse Saudi Arabia
141 G3 Khadīr Afgh.
141 F3 Khāf Iran
140 B6 Khafs Daghrah Saudi Arabia
144 E4 Khaga India
145 G5 Khagrachari Bangl.
144 B3 Khairgarh Pak.
144 B4 Khairpur Pak.
144 D4 Khajuraho India
179 C6 Khakhea Botswana
Khakīr Afgh. see Khadīr
141 G4 Khāk Rayz Afgh.
141 G4 Khākrīz reg. Afgh.
Khalach Turkm. see Halaç
140 C3 Khalajestan reg. Iran
144 D2 Khalatse India
144 A3 Khalifat mt. Pak.
141 E3 Khalīlābād Iran
Khalkabad Uzbek. see Xalqobod
140 C2 Khalkhāl Iran
143 D2 Khallikot India
172 D4 Khalopyenichy Belarus
146 C1 Khamar-Daban, Khrebet mts Rus. Fed.
144 C5 Khambhat India
144 B5 Khambhat, Gulf of India
144 D5 Khamgaon India
140 D5 Khamīr Iran
154 C1 Khamkeut Laos
140 B5 Khamma well Saudi Arabia
143 C2 Khammam India
133 M3 Khamra Rus. Fed.
140 C3 Khamseh reg. Iran
Khamza Uzbek. see Hamza
154 B1 Khan, Nâm r. Laos
141 H2 Khānābād Afgh.
Khanabad Uzbek. see Xonobod
137 I5 Khān al Baghdādī Iraq
137 J5 Khān al Maḥāwīl Iraq
137 J5 Khān al Mashāhidah Iraq
137 J5 Khān al Muṣallá Iraq
143 A3 Khanapur India
140 B2 Khānaqāh Iran
137 J4 Khānaqīn Iraq
137 J6 Khān ar Raḥbah Iraq
137 J2 Khanasur Pass Iran/Turkey
136 F6 Khān az Zabīb tourist site Jordan
144 C2 Khanbari Pass Pak.
127 H6 Khancoban Australia
144 B2 Khand Pass Afgh./Pak.
139 H5 Khandūd Afgh.
144 D5 Khandwa India
133 O3 Khandyga Rus. Fed.
144 B3 Khanewal Pak.
Khanh Dương Vietnam see M’Đrăk
144 D4 Khaniadhana India
140 D4 Khānī Yek Iran
137 J5 Khān Jadwal Iraq
150 C2 Khanka, Lake China/Rus. Fed.
144 C2 Khanki Weir Pak.
144 D3 Khanna India
138 A2 Khan Ordasy Kazakh.
144 B3 Khanpur Balochistan Pak.
144 B3 Khanpur Punjab Pak.
136 F4 Khān Shaykhūn Syria
139 H3 Khantau Kazakh.
132 K3 Khantayskoye, Ozero l. Rus. Fed.
Khan-Tengri mt. Kyrg. see Khan-Tengri, Pik
139 J4 Khan-Tengri, Pik mt. Kyrg.
132 H3 Khanty-Mansiysk Rus. Fed.
136 E6 Khān Yūnus Gaza
154 A3 Khao Chum Thong Thai.
144 D5 Khapa India
173 H6 Kharabali Rus. Fed.
145 F5 Kharagpur India
140 E2 Kharakī Iran
140 E5 Khārān r. Iran
141 G4 Kharan Pak.
140 D3 Kharānaq Iran
140 D3 Kharānaq, Kūh-e mt. Iran
144 B2 Kharbin Pass Afgh.
144 C6 Khardi India
144 D2 Khardung La pass India
137 K6 Kharfiyah Iraq
140 C4 Kharg Islands Iran
144 C5 Khargon India
144 C4 Khari r. Rajasthan India
144 C4 Khari r. Rajasthan India
144 C2 Kharian Pak.
143 C1 Khariar India
177 F2 Khārijah, Wāḥāt al oasis Egypt
173 F5 Kharkiv Ukr.
171 K4 Kharmanli Bulg.
172 G3 Kharovsk Rus. Fed.
140 C3 Khar Rūd r. Iran
143 C1 Kharsia India
177 F3 Khartoum Sudan
Khasardag, Gora mt. Turkm. see Hasardag
Khasav’yurt Rus. Fed. see Khasavyurt
173 H7 Khasavyurt Rus. Fed.
141 F4 Khāsh Iran
141 F4 Khāsh, Dasht-e Afgh.
141 F4 Khāsh Rōd r. Afgh.
141 F4 Khāsh Rūd Afgh.
173 G7 Khashuri Georgia
145 G4 Khasi Hills India
171 K4 Khaskovo Bulg.
133 L2 Khatanga Rus. Fed.
133 L2 Khatangskiy Zaliv b. Rus. Fed.
Khatmia Pass Egypt see Khutmīyah, Mamarr al

133 S3 **Khatyrka** Rus. Fed.
**Khavast** Uzbek. *see* **Xovos**
144 B5 **Khavda** India
141 H3 **Khāwāk, Kōtal-e** Afgh.
140 E5 **Khawr Fakkan** U.A.E.
154 A2 **Khawsa** Myanmar
181 F5 **Khayamnandi** S. Africa
139 G5 **Khaydarken** Kyrg.
180 C7 **Khayelitsha** S. Africa
**Khazarasp** Uzbek. *see* **Hazorasp**
137 I3 **Khāzir, Nahr al** *r.* Iraq
**Khê Bo** Vietnam *see* **Hoa Binh**
143 A2 **Khed** India
144 C4 **Khedbrahma** India
141 E3 **Khedrī** Iran
144 E3 **Khela** India
167 H4 **Khemis Miliana** Alg.
154 C1 **Khemmarat** Thai.
176 C1 **Khenchela** Alg.
176 B1 **Khenifra** Morocco
140 D4 **Kherāmeh** Iran
**Kherli** India *see* **Pathena**
140 C4 **Khersan** *r.* Iran
173 E6 **Kherson** Ukr.
140 C4 **Khesht** Iran
133 K2 **Kheta** *r.* Rus. Fed.
140 D4 **Kheyrābād** Iran
140 D2 **Khezerābād** Iran
144 D4 **Khilchipur** India
144 B4 **Khipro** Pak.
136 F4 **Khirbat Isrīyah** Syria
141 G3 **Khisrow** Afgh.
144 D2 **Khitai Dawan** Aksai Chin
**Khiva** Uzbek. *see* **Xiva**
140 B2 **Khīyāv** Iran
159 O3 **Khiytola** Rus. Fed.
154 B2 **Khlong, Mae** *r.* Thai.
173 C5 **Khmel'nyts'kyy** Ukr.
173 C5 **Khmil'nyk** Ukr.
154 C3 **Khoai, Hon** *i.* Vietnam
140 B2 **Khodā Āfarīn** Iran
**Khodzhambaz** Turkm. *see* **Hojambaz**
**Khodzheyli** Uzbek. *see* **Xo'jayli**
180 D2 **Khokhowe Pan** *salt pan* Botswana
144 B4 **Khokhropar** Pak.
172 G1 **Kholmogory** Rus. Fed.
146 G2 **Kholmsk** Rus. Fed.
169 P3 **Kholm-Zhirkovskiy** Rus. Fed.
137 L3 **Khoman** Iran
180 B1 **Khomas** *admin. reg.* Namibia
180 A1 **Khomas Highland** *hills* Namibia
140 C3 **Khomeyn** Iran
140 C3 **Khomeynīshahr** Iran
137 L4 **Khondāb** Iran
173 G7 **Khoni** Georgia
140 D5 **Khonj** Iran
154 B1 **Khon Kaen** Thai.
133 P3 **Khonuu** Rus. Fed.
173 G5 **Khoper** *r.* Rus. Fed.
146 F2 **Khor** Rus. Fed.
146 F2 **Khor** *r.* Rus. Fed.
141 H5 **Khora** Pak.
140 D3 **Khorāsān, Chāh-e** *well* Iran
145 F5 **Khordha** India
146 C1 **Khorinsk** Rus. Fed.
179 B6 **Khorixas** Namibia
150 C2 **Khorol** Rus. Fed.
173 E5 **Khorol** Ukr.
137 K2 **Khoroslū Dāgh** *hills* Iran
140 C3 **Khorramābād** Iran
137 L3 **Khorram Darreh** Iran
140 C4 **Khorramshahr** Iran
139 G5 **Khorugh** Tajik.
173 H6 **Khosheutovo** Rus. Fed.
141 E4 **Khoshkrūd** Iran
140 C4 **Khosravī** Iran
140 C4 **Khosrowābād** Iran
137 J4 **Khosrowvī** Iran
141 H3 **Khōst** Afgh.
140 D4 **Khowrjān** Iran
145 H5 **Khreum** Myanmar
145 G4 **Khri** *r.* India
172 H2 **Khristoforovo** Rus. Fed.
133 P2 **Khroma** *r.* Rus. Fed.
138 D2 **Khromtau** Kazakh.
150 D2 **Khrustal'nyy** Rus. Fed.
169 N6 **Khrystynivka** Ukr.
141 G5 **Khudo Range** Pak.
180 F1 **Khudumelapye** Botswana
140 B5 **Khuff** Saudi Arabia
141 F5 **Khūh Lab, Ra's** *pt* Iran
180 D3 **Khuis** Botswana
139 G4 **Khŭjand** Tajik.
154 C2 **Khu Khan** Thai.
141 G3 **Khulm, Daryā-ye** *r.* Afgh.
145 G5 **Khulna** Bangl.
137 I1 **Khulo** Georgia
181 G3 **Khuma** S. Africa
144 C2 **Khunjerab Pass** China/Pakistan
145 F5 **Khunti** India
154 A1 **Khun Yuam** Thai.
141 E3 **Khūr** Iran
144 D4 **Khurai** India
140 D5 **Khūran** *sea chan.* Iran
144 D3 **Khurja** India
141 F3 **Khurmāliq** Afgh.
137 I6 **Khurr, Wādī al** *watercourse* Saudi Arabia
141 E3 **Khūsf** Iran
144 C2 **Khushab** Pak.
137 L3 **Khūshāvar** Iran
141 F3 **Khuspās** Afgh.
173 B5 **Khust** Ukr.
136 D6 **Khutmīyah, Mamarr al** *pass* Egypt
181 G3 **Khutsong** S. Africa
141 G5 **Khuzdar** Pak.
141 G2 **Khvājeh Do Kūh** *h.* Afgh.
141 H2 **Khvājeh Moḩammad, Kūh-e** *mts* Afgh.
172 I4 **Khvalynsk** Rus. Fed.
140 C3 **Khvānsār** Iran
140 D3 **Khvor** Iran
140 E3 **Khvord Nārvan** Iran
140 C4 **Khvormūj** Iran
138 B1 **Khvorostyanka** Rus. Fed.
137 K3 **Khvosh Maqām** Iran
140 B2 **Khvoy** Iran
172 E3 **Khvoynaya** Rus. Fed.
154 A2 **Khwae Noi** *r.* Thai.
141 F4 **Khwājah 'Alī Suflá** Afgh.
144 C2 **Khyber Pakhtunkhwa** *prov.* Pak.
144 B2 **Khyber Pass** Afgh./Pak.
127 I5 **Kiama** Australia
153 C5 **Kiamba** Phil.
178 C4 **Kiambi** Dem. Rep. Congo
199 E5 **Kiamichi** *r.* U.S.A.
158 O2 **Kiantajärvi** *l.* Fin.
140 D2 **Kīāsar** Iran
185 L2 **Kiatassuaq** *i.* Greenland
153 C5 **Kibawe** Phil.
178 D4 **Kibaya** Tanz.
144 D2 **Kibber** India
179 D4 **Kibiti** Tanz.
178 C4 **Kibombo** Dem. Rep. Congo
178 D4 **Kibondo** Tanz.
171 I4 **Kičevo** Macedonia
172 H3 **Kichmengskiy Gorodok** Rus. Fed.
138 C5 **Kiçi Balkan Daglary** *h.* Turkm.
176 C3 **Kidal** Mali
161 E5 **Kidderminster** U.K.
178 D3 **Kidepo Valley National Park** Uganda
176 A3 **Kidira** Senegal
144 D2 **Kidmang** India
128 F3 **Kidnappers, Cape** N.Z.
161 E4 **Kidsgrove** U.K.
168 E3 **Kiel** Germany
190 C4 **Kiel** U.S.A.
168 D3 **Kiel Canal** Germany
169 J5 **Kielce** Poland
160 E2 **Kielder Water** *resr* U.K.
168 E3 **Kieler Bucht** *b.* Germany
179 C5 **Kienge** Dem. Rep. Congo
164 F3 **Kierspe** Germany
173 D5 **Kiev** Ukr.
176 A3 **Kiffa** Mauritania
171 J5 **Kifisia** Greece
137 J4 **Kifrī** Iraq
178 D4 **Kigali** Rwanda
137 H2 **Kiğı** Turkey
189 H2 **Kiglapait Mountains** Canada
178 C4 **Kigoma** Tanz.
158 M2 **Kihlanki** Fin.
159 M3 **Kihniö** Fin.
139 H3 **Kiik** Kazakh.
158 N2 **Kiiminki** Fin.
151 D8 **Kii-sanchi** *mts* Japan
151 D8 **Kii-suidō** *sea chan.* Japan
171 I2 **Kikinda** Serbia
141 F5 **Kikki** Pak.
172 H3 **Kiknur** Rus. Fed.
150 G4 **Kikonai** Japan
179 C4 **Kikondja** Dem. Rep. Congo
124 E2 **Kikori** P.N.G.
124 E2 **Kikori** *r.* P.N.G.
178 B4 **Kikwit** Dem. Rep. Congo
159 L3 **Kilafors** Sweden
143 B4 **Kilakkarai** India
144 D2 **Kilar** India
196 □2 **Kīlauea** U.S.A.
196 □2 **Kīlauea Volcano** U.S.A.
162 C5 **Kilbrannan Sound** *sea chan.* U.K.
152 E3 **Kilchu** N. Korea
163 E4 **Kilcoole** Ireland
163 D4 **Kilcormac** Ireland
127 J1 **Kilcoy** Australia
163 E4 **Kildare** Ireland
158 P1 **Kil'dinstroy** Rus. Fed.
178 B4 **Kilembe** Dem. Rep. Congo
162 C5 **Kilfinan** U.K.
199 E5 **Kilgore** U.S.A.
160 E2 **Kilham** U.K.
178 D4 **Kilifi** Kenya
178 D4 **Kilimanjaro** *vol.* Tanz.
178 D4 **Kilimanjaro National Park** Tanz.
125 F2 **Kilinailau Islands** P.N.G.
179 D4 **Kilindoni** Tanz.
159 N4 **Kilingi-Nõmme** Estonia
143 C4 **Kilinochchi** Sri Lanka
136 F3 **Kilis** Turkey
173 D6 **Kiliya** Ukr.
163 B5 **Kilkee** Ireland
163 F3 **Kilkeel** U.K.
163 D5 **Kilkenny** Ireland
161 C7 **Kilkhampton** U.K.
171 J4 **Kilkis** Greece
163 B3 **Killala** Ireland
163 B3 **Killala Bay** Ireland
163 C5 **Killaloe** Ireland
191 I3 **Killaloe Station** Canada
187 G4 **Killam** Canada
127 J2 **Killarney** Australia
191 G3 **Killarney** Canada
163 B5 **Killarney** Ireland
163 B6 **Killarney National Park** Ireland
191 G2 **Killarney Provincial Park** Canada
163 B4 **Killary Harbour** *b.* Ireland
199 D6 **Killeen** U.S.A.
163 D5 **Killenaule** Ireland
163 C4 **Killimor** Ireland
162 D4 **Killin** U.K.
163 F3 **Killinchy** U.K.
163 E5 **Killinick** Ireland
189 H1 **Killiniq** Canada
189 H1 **Killiniq Island** Canada
163 B5 **Killorglin** Ireland
163 E5 **Killurin** Ireland
163 C3 **Killybegs** Ireland
163 D2 **Kilmacrenan** Ireland
163 B4 **Kilmaine** Ireland
163 C5 **Kilmallock** Ireland
162 B3 **Kilmaluag** U.K.
162 D5 **Kilmarnock** U.K.
162 C4 **Kilmelford** U.K.
172 I3 **Kil'mez'** Rus. Fed.
172 I3 **Kil'mez'** *r.* Rus. Fed.
163 C6 **Kilmona** Ireland
126 F6 **Kilmore** Australia
163 E5 **Kilmore Quay** Ireland
178 D4 **Kilosa** Tanz.
158 M1 **Kilpisjärvi** Fin.
158 P1 **Kilp"yavr** Rus. Fed.
163 E3 **Kilrea** U.K.
163 B5 **Kilrush** Ireland
162 D5 **Kilsyth** U.K.
143 A4 **Kiltan** *atoll* India
163 C4 **Kiltullagh** Ireland
179 C4 **Kilwa** Dem. Rep. Congo
179 D4 **Kilwa Masoko** Tanz.
162 D5 **Kilwinning** U.K.
139 F2 **Kima** Kazakh.
179 D4 **Kimambi** Tanz.
126 B4 **Kimba** Australia
178 B4 **Kimba** Congo
198 C3 **Kimball** U.S.A.
124 F2 **Kimbe** P.N.G.
186 F5 **Kimberley** Canada
180 F4 **Kimberley** S. Africa
124 C3 **Kimberley Plateau** Australia
128 E4 **Kimbolton** N.Z.
152 E3 **Kimch'aek** N. Korea
159 M3 **Kimito** Fin.
152 D3 **Kimjŏngsuk** N. Korea
185 L3 **Kimmirut** Canada
171 K6 **Kimolos** *i.* Greece
172 F4 **Kimovsk** Rus. Fed.
178 B4 **Kimpese** Dem. Rep. Congo
172 F3 **Kimry** Rus. Fed.
178 B4 **Kimvula** Dem. Rep. Congo
155 E1 **Kinabalu, Gunung** *mt. Sabah* Malaysia
153 A5 **Kinabatangan** *r. Sabah* Malaysia
171 L6 **Kinaros** *i.* Greece
186 F4 **Kinbasket Lake** Canada
162 E2 **Kinbrace** U.K.
191 G3 **Kincardine** Canada
162 E4 **Kincardine** U.K.
126 E4 **Kinchega National Park** Australia
**Kincolith** Canada *see* **Gingolx**
179 C4 **Kinda** Dem. Rep. Congo
145 H5 **Kindat** Myanmar
199 E6 **Kinder** U.S.A.
161 F4 **Kinder Scout** *h.* U.K.
187 H4 **Kindersley** Canada
176 A3 **Kindia** Guinea
178 C4 **Kindu** Dem. Rep. Congo
138 B1 **Kinel'** Rus. Fed.
172 G3 **Kineshma** Rus. Fed.
124 F4 **Kingaroy** Australia
196 B3 **King City** U.S.A.
129 C1 **King Edward Point** *research stn* Antarctica
202 E3 **King Ferry** U.S.A.
203 H2 **Kingfield** U.S.A.
199 D5 **Kingfisher** U.S.A.
129 B2 **King George Island** Antarctica
188 E2 **King George Islands** Canada
172 D3 **Kingisepp** Rus. Fed.
127 F8 **King Island** Australia
186 D4 **King Island** Canada
191 H1 **King Kirkland** Canada
126 F6 **Kinglake National Park** Australia
124 C3 **King Leopold Ranges** *hills* Australia
197 E4 **Kingman** *AZ* U.S.A.
199 D4 **Kingman** *KS* U.S.A.
203 I2 **Kingman** *ME* U.S.A.
123 I3 **Kingman Reef** *terr.* N. Pacific Ocean
186 D3 **King Mountain** Canada
126 A3 **Kingoonya** Australia
163 D5 **Kings** *r.* Ireland
196 C3 **Kings** *r.* U.S.A.
161 D7 **Kingsbridge** U.K.
196 C3 **Kingsburg** U.S.A.
203 I2 **Kingsbury** U.S.A.
196 C3 **Kings Canyon National Park** U.S.A.
127 J2 **Kingscliff** Australia
126 B5 **Kingscote** Australia
163 E4 **Kingscourt** Ireland
129 E2 **King Sejong** *research stn* Antarctica
190 C3 **Kingsford** U.S.A.
201 D6 **Kingsland** *GA* U.S.A.
190 E5 **Kingsland** *IN* U.S.A.
161 H5 **King's Lynn** U.K.
125 H2 **Kingsmill Group** *is* Kiribati
161 H6 **Kingsnorth** U.K.
124 C3 **King Sound** *b.* Australia
194 E3 **Kings Peak** U.S.A.
202 B6 **Kingsport** U.S.A.
191 I3 **Kingston** Canada
205 I5 **Kingston** Jamaica
128 B6 **Kingston** N.Z.
190 B6 **Kingston** *IL* U.S.A.
203 F4 **Kingston** *NY* U.S.A.
127 G9 **Kingston**
197 E4 **Kingston Peak** U.S.A.
126 C6 **Kingston South East** Australia
160 G4 **Kingston upon Hull** U.K.
205 L6 **Kingstown** St Vincent
199 D7 **Kingsville** U.S.A.
161 E6 **Kingswood** U.K.
161 D5 **Kington** U.K.
162 D3 **Kingussie** U.K.
185 I3 **King William Island** Canada
181 G6 **King William's Town** S. Africa
199 E6 **Kingwood** *TX* U.S.A.
202 D5 **Kingwood** *WV* U.S.A.
187 I4 **Kinistino** Canada
150 G5 **Kinka-san** *i.* Japan
128 B6 **Kinloch** N.Z.
162 E3 **Kinloss** U.K.
191 H3 **Kinmount** Canada
159 K4 **Kinna** Sweden
163 D4 **Kinnegad** Ireland
**Kinneret, Yam** *l.* Israel *see* **Galilee, Sea of**
143 C4 **Kinniyai** Sri Lanka
158 N3 **Kinnula** Fin.
187 I3 **Kinoosao** Canada
151 F5 **Kinpoku-san** *mt.* Japan
162 E4 **Kinross** U.K.
163 C6 **Kinsale** Ireland
178 B4 **Kinshasa** Dem. Rep. Congo
198 D4 **Kinsley** U.S.A.
201 E5 **Kinston** U.S.A.
159 M5 **Kintai** Lith.
176 B4 **Kintampo** Ghana
162 F3 **Kintore** U.K.
162 C5 **Kintyre** *pen.* U.K.
186 F3 **Kinuso** Canada
177 F4 **Kinyeti** *mt.* South Sudan
138 D2 **Kinzhaly** Kazakh.
165 H4 **Kinzig** *r.* Germany
191 H2 **Kiosk** Canada
188 E4 **Kipawa, Lac** *l.* Canada
203 F6 **Kiptopeke** U.S.A.
179 C5 **Kipushi** Dem. Rep. Congo
125 G3 **Kirakira** Solomon Is
143 C2 **Kirandul** India
172 D4 **Kirawsk** Belarus
165 G2 **Kirchdorf** Germany
165 G5 **Kirchheim-Bolanden** Germany
163 F3 **Kircubbin** U.K.
147 C1 **Kirenga** *r.* Rus. Fed.
146 C1 **Kirensk** Rus. Fed.
139 H4 **Kirghiz Range** *mts* Asia
123 H4 **Kiribati** *country* Pacific Ocean
137 H1 **Kırık** Turkey
136 F3 **Kırıkhan** Turkey
136 D2 **Kırıkkale** Turkey
172 F3 **Kirillov** Rus. Fed.
179 E6 **Kirindi Mitea, Parc National de** Madag.
**Kirinyaga** *mt.* Kenya *see* **Kenya, Mount**
172 E3 **Kirishi** Rus. Fed.
151 B9 **Kirishima-yama** *vol.* Japan
123 I4 **Kiritimati** *atoll* Kiribati
136 A2 **Kırkağaç** Turkey
140 B2 **Kirk Bulāg Dāgi** *mt.* Iran
161 E4 **Kirkby** U.K.
161 F4 **Kirkby in Ashfield** U.K.
160 E3 **Kirkby Lonsdale** U.K.
160 E3 **Kirkby Stephen** U.K.
162 E4 **Kirkcaldy** U.K.
162 C6 **Kirkcolm** U.K.
162 D6 **Kirkcudbright** U.K.
159 K3 **Kirkenær** Norway
158 O1 **Kirkenes** Norway
191 H3 **Kirkfield** Canada
162 D5 **Kirkintilloch** U.K.
159 N3 **Kirkkonummi** Fin.
197 F4 **Kirkland** U.S.A.
197 F4 **Kirkland Junction** U.S.A.
191 G1 **Kirkland Lake** Canada
173 C7 **Kırklareli** Turkey
160 C3 **Kirk Michael** U.K.
160 E3 **Kirkoswald** U.K.
129 C5 **Kirkpatrick, Mount** Antarctica
198 E3 **Kirksville** U.S.A.
137 J4 **Kirkūk** Iraq
162 F2 **Kirkwall** U.K.
181 F6 **Kirkwood** S. Africa
196 B2 **Kirkwood** *CA* U.S.A.
198 F4 **Kirkwood** *MO* U.S.A.
136 C1 **Kırmır** *r.* Turkey
164 F5 **Kirn** Germany
172 E4 **Kirov** *Kaluzhskaya Oblast'* Rus. Fed.
172 I3 **Kirov** *Kirovskaya Oblast'* Rus. Fed.
**Kirovabad** Azer. *see* **Gäncä**
138 C2 **Kirovo** Kazakh.
172 I3 **Kirovo-Chepetsk** Rus. Fed.
173 E5 **Kirovohrad** Ukr.
172 D3 **Kirovsk** *Leningradskaya Oblast'* Rus. Fed.
158 P2 **Kirovsk** *Murmanskaya Oblast'* Rus. Fed.
172 I3 **Kirovskaya Oblast'** *admin. div.* Rus. Fed.
150 C2 **Kirovskiy** Rus. Fed.
138 D5 **Kirpili** Turkm.
162 E4 **Kirriemuir** U.K.
172 J3 **Kirs** Rus. Fed.
172 G4 **Kirsanov** Rus. Fed.
136 E2 **Kırşehir** Turkey
141 G5 **Kirthar Range** *mts* Pak.
165 H4 **Kirtorf** Germany
158 M2 **Kiruna** Sweden
178 C4 **Kirundu** Dem. Rep. Congo
172 H4 **Kirya** Rus. Fed.
151 F6 **Kiryū** Japan
159 K4 **Kisa** Sweden
178 C3 **Kisangani** Dem. Rep. Congo
178 B4 **Kisantu** Dem. Rep. Congo
155 A2 **Kisaran** Indon.
146 A1 **Kiselevsk** Rus. Fed.
140 D5 **Kish** *i.* Iran
145 F4 **Kishanganj** India
144 B4 **Kishangarh** *Rajasthan* India
144 C4 **Kishangarh** *Rajasthan* India
144 C2 **Kishen Ganga** *r.* India/Pak.
176 C4 **Kishi** Nigeria
139 G3 **Kishi Kamkaly** Kazakh.
151 B9 **Kishika-zaki** *pt* Japan
141 H2 **Kishim** Afgh.
141 G2 **Kishindih-ye Bālā** Afgh.
**Kishinev** Moldova *see* **Chişinău**
151 D7 **Kishiwada** Japan
139 H1 **Kishkenekol'** Kazakh.
145 G4 **Kishoreganj** Bangl.
**Kishorganj** Bangl. *see* **Kishoreganj**
144 C2 **Kishtwar** India
**Kisi** Nigeria *see* **Kishi**
178 D4 **Kisii** Kenya
187 J4 **Kiskittogisu Lake** Canada
169 I7 **Kiskunfélegyháza** Hungary
169 I7 **Kiskunhalas** Hungary
173 G7 **Kislovodsk** Rus. Fed.
178 E4 **Kismaayo** Somalia
178 C4 **Kisoro** Uganda
151 E7 **Kiso-sanmyaku** *mts* Japan
176 A4 **Kissidougou** Guinea
201 D6 **Kissimmee** U.S.A.
201 D7 **Kissimmee, Lake** U.S.A.
178 D4 **Kisumu** Kenya
176 B3 **Kita** Mali
**Kitab** Uzbek. *see* **Kitob**
151 G6 **Kitaibaraki** Japan
150 G5 **Kitakami** Japan
150 G5 **Kitakami-gawa** *r.* Japan
151 F6 **Kitakata** Japan
151 B8 **Kita-Kyūshū** Japan
178 D3 **Kitale** Kenya
133 P5 **Kitami** Japan
195 G4 **Kit Carson** U.S.A.
191 G4 **Kitchener** Canada
158 O3 **Kitee** Fin.
178 D3 **Kitgum** Uganda
186 D4 **Kitimat** Canada
158 N2 **Kitinen** *r.* Fin.
139 F5 **Kitob** Uzbek.
178 B4 **Kitona** Dem. Rep. Congo
151 B8 **Kitsuki** Japan
126 C2 **Kittakittaooloo, Lake** *salt flat* Australia
202 D4 **Kittanning** U.S.A.
203 F4 **Kittatinny Mountains** *hills* U.S.A.
203 H3 **Kittery** U.S.A.
158 N2 **Kittilä** Fin.
201 F4 **Kitty Hawk** U.S.A.
178 D4 **Kitunda** Tanz.
186 D3 **Kitwanga** Canada
179 C5 **Kitwe** Zambia
168 F7 **Kitzbüheler Alpen** *mts* Austria
165 I5 **Kitzingen** Germany
165 K3 **Kitzscher** Germany
158 N3 **Kiuruvesi** Fin.
158 N3 **Kivijärvi** Fin.
159 N4 **Kiviõli** Estonia
178 C4 **Kivu, Lac** Dem. Rep. Congo/Rwanda
139 G2 **Kiyakty, Ozero** *salt l.* Kazakh.
139 G2 **Kiyevka** Kazakh.
150 C3 **Kiyevka** Rus. Fed.
171 M4 **Kıyıköy** Turkey
132 G4 **Kizel** Rus. Fed.
172 H2 **Kizema** Rus. Fed.
139 J4 **Kizil** China
136 B3 **Kızılca Dağ** *mt.* Turkey
136 D1 **Kızılcahamam** Turkey
136 G2 **Kızıl Dağı** *mt.* Turkey
136 D1 **Kızılırmak** Turkey
136 D2 **Kızılırmak** *r.* Turkey
136 C3 **Kızılkaya** Turkey
136 D3 **Kızılören** Turkey
138 D1 **Kizil'skoye** Rus. Fed.
137 H3 **Kızıltepe** Turkey
**Kizil"yurt** Rus. Fed. *see* **Kizilyurt**
173 H7 **Kizilyurt** Rus. Fed.
173 H7 **Kizlyar** Rus. Fed.
**Kizylayak** Turkm. *see* **Gyzylaýak**
158 N1 **Kjøllefjord** Norway
158 L1 **Kjøpsvik** Norway
168 G5 **Kladno** Czech Rep.
168 G7 **Klagenfurt** Austria
197 H4 **Klagetoh** U.S.A.
159 M5 **Klaipėda** Lith.
158 □ **Klaksvík** Faroe Is
194 B3 **Klamath** *r.* U.S.A.
194 B3 **Klamath Falls** U.S.A.
194 B3 **Klamath Mountains** U.S.A.
155 B2 **Klang** Malaysia
159 K4 **Klarälven** *r.* Sweden
168 F6 **Klatovy** Czech Rep.
180 C5 **Klawer** S. Africa
186 C3 **Klawock** U.S.A.
164 E2 **Klazienaveen** Neth.
186 E4 **Kleena Kleene** Canada
180 D4 **Kleinbegin** S. Africa
180 C3 **Klein Karas** Namibia
180 F6 **Kleinpoort** S. Africa
180 D6 **Klein Roggeveldberge** *mts* S. Africa
180 B4 **Kleinsee** S. Africa
180 D6 **Klein Swartberg** *mt.* S. Africa
186 D4 **Klemtu** Canada
181 G3 **Klerksdorp** S. Africa
172 E4 **Kletnya** Rus. Fed.
173 G5 **Kletskaya** Rus. Fed.
164 E3 **Kleve** Germany
172 D4 **Klimavichy** Belarus
173 E4 **Klimovo** Rus. Fed.
172 F4 **Klimovsk** Rus. Fed.
172 F3 **Klin** Rus. Fed.
186 D4 **Klinaklini** *r.* Canada
165 H5 **Klingenberg am Main** Germany
165 K4 **Klingenthal** Germany
165 K1 **Klink** Germany
168 F5 **Klínovec** *mt.* Czech Rep.
159 L4 **Klintehamn** Sweden
173 I5 **Klintsovka** Rus. Fed.
172 E4 **Klintsy** Rus. Fed.
180 C5 **Kliprand** S. Africa
170 G2 **Ključ** Bos.-Herz.
168 H5 **Kłodzko** Poland
186 C3 **Klondike Gold Rush National Historical Park** *nat. park* U.S.A.
164 E2 **Kloosterhaar** Neth.
168 H6 **Klosterneuburg** Austria
188 F1 **Klotz, Lac** *l.* Canada
165 J2 **Klötze (Altmark)** Germany
186 A2 **Kluane Game Sanctuary** *nature res.* Canada
186 B2 **Kluane Lake** Canada
186 B2 **Kluane National Park** Canada
168 I5 **Kluczbork** Poland
172 C4 **Klyetsk** Belarus
133 R4 **Klyuchevskaya Sopka, Vulkan** *vol.* Rus. Fed.
139 I1 **Klyuchi** Rus. Fed.
159 K3 **Knåda** Sweden
160 F3 **Knaresborough** U.K.
187 K3 **Knee Lake** Canada
165 I5 **Knetzgau** Germany
190 B1 **Knife Lake** Canada/U.S.A.
186 D4 **Knight Inlet** Canada
161 D5 **Knighton** U.K.
190 E6 **Knightstown** U.S.A.
170 G2 **Knin** Croatia
168 G7 **Knittelfeld** Austria
171 J3 **Knjaževac** Serbia
163 C4 **Knock** Ireland
163 B5 **Knockacummer** *h.* Ireland
163 C3 **Knockalongy** *h.* Ireland
163 B5 **Knockalough** Ireland
163 B6 **Knockboy** *h.* Ireland
162 F3 **Knock Hill** U.K.
163 E2 **Knocklayd** *h.* U.K.
164 B3 **Knokke-Heist** Belgium
165 L1 **Knorrendorf** Germany
171 K7 **Knossos** *tourist site* Greece
161 F5 **Knowle** U.K.
129 B3 **Knowles, Cape** *c.* Antarctica
203 I1 **Knowles Corner** U.S.A.
203 G2 **Knowlton** Canada
190 D5 **Knox** U.S.A.
186 C4 **Knox, Cape** Canada
196 A2 **Knoxville** *CA* U.S.A.
190 B5 **Knoxville** *IL* U.S.A.
201 D4 **Knoxville** *TN* U.S.A.
162 C3 **Knoydart** *mts* U.K.
185 M1 **Knud Rasmussen Land** *reg.* Greenland
180 E7 **Knysna** S. Africa
151 B9 **Kobayashi** Japan
158 O1 **Kobbfoss** Norway
138 C2 **Kobda** Kazakh.
151 D7 **Kōbe** Japan
**København** Denmark *see* **Copenhagen**
176 B3 **Kobenni** Mauritania
164 F4 **Koblenz** Germany
172 I3 **Kobra** Rus. Fed.
147 F7 **Kobroör** *i.* Indon.
172 C4 **Kobryn** Belarus
173 G7 **Kobuleti** Georgia
171 J4 **Kočani** Macedonia
136 B1 **Kocasu** *r.* Turkey
170 F2 **Kočevje** Slovenia
145 G4 **Koch Bihar** India
165 H5 **Kocher** *r.* Germany
143 B4 **Kochi** India
151 C8 **Kōchi** Japan
139 H4 **Kochkor** Kyrg.
172 H4 **Kochkurovo** Rus. Fed.
173 H6 **Kochubey** Rus. Fed.
173 G6 **Kochubeyevskoye** Rus. Fed.
143 B4 **Kodaikanal** India
143 D2 **Kodala** India
184 C4 **Kodiak** U.S.A.
184 C4 **Kodiak Island** U.S.A.
181 G1 **Kodibeleng** Botswana
172 F2 **Kodino** Rus. Fed.
177 F4 **Kodok** South Sudan
173 G7 **K'odori** *r.* Georgia
173 D5 **Kodyma** Ukr.
171 K4 **Kodzhaele** *mt.* Bulg./Greece
180 D6 **Koedoesberg** *mts* S. Africa
180 D4 **Koegrabie** S. Africa
180 C5 **Koekenaap** S. Africa
145 E4 **Koel** *r.* India
164 D3 **Koersel** Belgium
179 B6 **Koës** Namibia
197 F5 **Kofa Mountains** U.S.A.
180 F4 **Koffiefontein** S. Africa
176 B4 **Koforidua** Ghana
151 F7 **Kōfu** Japan
188 E2 **Kogaluc** *r.* Canada
188 E2 **Kogaluc, Baie de** *b.* Canada
189 H2 **Kogaluk** *r.* Canada
139 I3 **Kogaly** Kazakh.
127 I1 **Kogan** Australia
159 K5 **Køge** Denmark
138 F5 **Kogon** Uzbek.
141 G5 **Kohan** Pak.
144 B2 **Kohat** Pak.
159 N4 **Kohila** Estonia
145 H4 **Kohima** India
141 F3 **Kōhistān** Afgh.
144 B3 **Kohlu** Pak.
159 N4 **Kohtla-Järve** Estonia
128 E2 **Kohukohunui** *h.* N.Z.
186 A2 **Koidern** Canada
176 A4 **Koidu-Sefadu** Sierra Leone
143 B3 **Koilkuntla** India
152 D3 **Koin** N. Korea
137 J3 **Koi Sanjaq** Iraq
150 F4 **Ko-jima** *i.* Japan
151 F8 **Ko-jima** *i.* Japan
154 A1 **Kok, Nam Mae** *r.* Thai.
203 I2 **Kokadjo** U.S.A.
138 F2 **Kokalaat** Kazakh.
**Kokand** Uzbek. *see* **Qo'qon**
159 M4 **Kökar** Fin.
138 E3 **Kokaral (abandoned)** Kazakh.
138 E3 **Kokaral Dam** Kazakh.
139 H4 **Kök-Art** Kyrg.
139 H4 **Kök-Aygyr** Kyrg.
141 H2 **Kōkchah, Daryā-ye** *r.* Afgh.
159 M3 **Kokemäenjoki** *r.* Fin.
180 C4 **Kokerboom** Namibia
169 N3 **Kokhanava** Belarus
172 G3 **Kokhma** Rus. Fed.
139 H4 **Kök-Janggak** Kyrg.
143 C4 **Kokkilai** Sri Lanka
158 M3 **Kokkola** Fin.
124 E2 **Kokoda** P.N.G.
196 □1 **Koko Head** U.S.A.
190 D5 **Kokomo** U.S.A.
180 E2 **Kokong** Botswana
181 G3 **Kokosi** S. Africa
139 J2 **Kokpekty** Kazakh.
152 D4 **Koksan** N. Korea
139 G4 **Koksaray** Kazakh.
172 H3 **Koksharka** Rus. Fed.
139 G1 **Kokshetau** Kazakh.
139 G1 **Kokshetauskaya Oblast'** Kazakh.
189 G2 **Koksoak** *r.* Canada
181 H5 **Kokstad** S. Africa
139 I3 **Koksu** *Almatinskaya Oblast'* Kazakh.
139 G4 **Koksu** *Yuzhnyy Kazakhstan* Kazakh.
139 I3 **Koktal** Kazakh.
139 H2 **Koktas** Kazakh.
139 I3 **Kokterek** *Almatinskaya Oblast'* Kazakh.
138 B2 **Kokterek** *Zapadnyy Kazakhstan* Kazakh.
139 I2 **Koktobe** Kazakh.
138 D2 **Koktubek** Kazakh.
139 J3 **Koktuma** Kazakh.
139 I5 **Kokyar** China
139 J2 **Kokzhayyk** Kazakh.
158 P1 **Kola** Rus. Fed.
141 G5 **Kolachi** *r.* Pak.
144 C2 **Kolahoi** *mt.* India
147 E7 **Kolaka** Indon.
154 A4 **Ko Lanta** Thai.
132 E3 **Kola Peninsula** Rus. Fed.
143 B3 **Kolar** *Karnataka* India
144 E6 **Kolar** *Madhya Pradesh* India
144 D4 **Kolaras** India
143 B3 **Kolar Gold Fields** India
158 M2 **Kolari** Fin.
144 C4 **Kolayat** India
172 F3 **Kol'chugino** Rus. Fed.
176 A3 **Kolda** Senegal
159 J5 **Kolding** Denmark
178 C3 **Kole** Dem. Rep. Congo
178 C4 **Kole** Dem. Rep. Congo
167 H4 **Koléa** Alg.
158 M2 **Koler** Sweden
132 F3 **Kolguyev, Ostrov** *i.* Rus. Fed.
145 F5 **Kolhan** *reg.* India
143 A2 **Kolhapur** India
159 M4 **Kõljala** Estonia
159 M4 **Kolkasrags** *pt* Latvia
145 G5 **Kolkata** India
139 G5 **Kolkhozobod** Tajik.
143 B4 **Kollam** India
143 B3 **Kollegal** India
143 C2 **Kolleru Lake** India
143 B4 **Kollidam** *r.* India
164 E1 **Kollum** Neth.
**Köln** Germany *see* **Cologne**
168 G3 **Kołobrzeg** Poland
172 H3 **Kologriv** Rus. Fed.
176 B3 **Kolokani** Mali
125 F2 **Kolombangara** *i.* Solomon Is
172 F4 **Kolomna** Rus. Fed.
173 C5 **Kolomyya** Ukr.
176 B3 **Kolondiéba** Mali
124 C2 **Kolonedale** Indon.
**Kolonkwane** Botswana *see* **Kolonkwaneng**
180 D3 **Kolonkwaneng** Botswana
138 B2 **Kolovertnoye** Kazakh.
132 J4 **Kolpashevo** Rus. Fed.
173 F4 **Kolpny** Rus. Fed.
138 E4 **Ko'lquduq** Uzbek.
**Kol'skiy Poluostrov** *pen.* Rus. Fed. *see* **Kola Peninsula**
138 B1 **Koltubanovskiy** Rus. Fed.
142 B7 **Koluli** Eritrea
139 G2 **Koluton** Kazakh.
143 A2 **Kolvan** India
158 J2 **Kolvereid** Norway
158 N1 **Kolvik** Norway
141 G5 **Kolwa** *reg.* Pak.
179 C5 **Kolwezi** Dem. Rep. Congo
133 Q3 **Kolyma** *r.* Rus. Fed.
133 Q3 **Kolymskaya Nizmennost'** *lowland* Rus. Fed.
133 Q3 **Kolymskoye Nagor'ye** *mts* Rus. Fed.
172 H4 **Kolyshley** Rus. Fed.
171 J3 **Kom** *mt.* Bulg.
150 G3 **Komaga-take** *vol.* Japan
180 B4 **Komaggas** S. Africa
180 B4 **Komaggas Mountains** S. Africa
133 R4 **Komandorskiye Ostrova** *is* Rus. Fed.
168 I7 **Komárno** Slovakia
181 I2 **Komatipoort** S. Africa
151 E6 **Komatsu** Japan
151 D7 **Komatsushima** Japan
178 C4 **Kombe** Dem. Rep. Congo
176 B3 **Kombissiri** Burkina Faso
155 B3 **Komering** *r.* Indon.
181 G6 **Komga** S. Africa
172 I2 **Komi, Respublika** *aut. rep.* Rus. Fed.
173 D6 **Kominternivs'ke** Ukr.
170 G3 **Komiža** Croatia
171 H1 **Komló** Hungary
178 B4 **Komono** Congo
151 F6 **Komoro** Japan
171 K4 **Komotini** Greece
180 D6 **Komsberg** *mts* S. Africa
138 C3 **Komsomol** Kazakh.
138 E5 **Komsomol** Turkm.
133 K1 **Komsomolets, Ostrov** *i.* Rus. Fed.
138 C3 **Komsomolets, Zaliv** *b.* Kazakh.
172 G3 **Komsomol'sk** Rus. Fed.
**Komsomol'sk** Turkm. *see* **Komsomol**
173 E5 **Komsomol's'k** Ukr.
173 H6 **Komsomol'skiy** Rus. Fed.
172 H4 **Komsomol'skiy** Rus. Fed.
146 F1 **Komsomol'sk-na-Amure** Rus. Fed.
**Komsomol'sk-na-Ustyurte** Uzbek. *see* **Kubla Ustyurt**
138 E2 **Komsomol'skoye** Kazakh.
137 I1 **Kömürlü** Turkey
197 F6 **Kom Vo** U.S.A.
172 F3 **Konakovo** Rus. Fed.
145 F6 **Konarka** India
145 F5 **Konar Reservoir** India
141 F3 **Konār̲ Tapah** Afgh.
144 D4 **Konch** India
143 C2 **Kondagaon** India
191 I2 **Kondiaronk, Lac** *l.* Canada
178 D4 **Kondoa** Tanz.
172 E2 **Kondopoga** Rus. Fed.
172 E4 **Kondrovo** Rus. Fed.
**Kondūz** Afgh. *see* **Kunduz**
**Kondūz** *r.* Afgh. *see* **Kunduz, Daryā-ye**
138 D4 **Köneürgenç** Turkm.
154 B3 **Kŏng, Kaôh** *i.* Cambodia
154 C2 **Kông, Tônlé** *r.* Cambodia
154 C2 **Kong, Xé** *r.* Laos
185 O3 **Kong Christian IX Land** *reg.* Greenland
185 N3 **Kong Frederik VI Kyst** *coastal area* Greenland
132 D2 **Kong Karls Land** *is* Svalbard
155 E2 **Kongkemul** *mt.* Indon.
178 C4 **Kongolo** Dem. Rep. Congo
185 P2 **Kong Oscars Fjord** *inlet* Greenland
176 B3 **Kongoussi** Burkina Faso
159 J4 **Kongsberg** Norway
159 K3 **Kongsvinger** Norway
139 H5 **Kongur Shan** *mt.* China
178 D4 **Kongwa** Tanz.
185 P2 **Kong Wilhelm Land** *reg.* Greenland
139 G4 **Konibodom** Tajik.
165 J4 **Königsee** Germany
164 F4 **Königswinter** Germany
168 I4 **Konin** Poland
146 F1 **Konin** *r.* Rus. Fed.
171 G3 **Konjic** Bos.-Herz.
180 B3 **Konkiep** *watercourse* Namibia
176 B3 **Konna** Mali
165 J3 **Könnern** Germany
158 N3 **Konnevesi** Fin.
172 G2 **Konosha** Rus. Fed.
151 F6 **Kōnosu** Japan
173 E5 **Konotop** Ukr.
154 D2 **Kon Plông** Vietnam
178 D3 **Konso** Ethiopia
165 K5 **Konstantinovy Lázně** Czech Rep.
168 D7 **Konstanz** Germany
176 C3 **Kontagora** Nigeria
158 O3 **Kontiolahti** Fin.
158 N2 **Konttila** Fin.
154 C2 **Kon Tum** Vietnam
154 D2 **Kon Tum, Cao Nguyên** *plat.* Vietnam
**Kontum, Plateau du** Vietnam *see* **Kon Tum, Cao Nguyên**
136 D3 **Konya** Turkey
139 H3 **Konyrat** Kazakh.
139 I3 **Konyrolen** Kazakh.
138 C2 **Konystanu** Kazakh.
164 E5 **Konz** Germany
196 □1 **Ko'olau Range** *mts* U.S.A.
**Koolau Range** *mts* U.S.A. *see* **Ko'olau Range**
126 F5 **Koondrook** Australia
202 D5 **Koon Lake** U.S.A.
127 H5 **Koorawatha** Australia
194 C2 **Kooskia** U.S.A.
186 F5 **Kootenay** *r.* Canada/U.S.A.
186 F5 **Kootenay Lake** Canada
186 F4 **Kootenay National Park** Canada
180 D5 **Kootjieskolk** S. Africa
139 I3 **Kopa** Kazakh.
173 H6 **Kopanovka** Rus. Fed.
144 C6 **Kopargaon** India
158 C1 **Kópasker** Iceland
139 I3 **Kopbirlik** Kazakh.
170 E2 **Koper** Slovenia
138 D5 **Kopet Dag** *mts* Iran/Turkm.
145 G4 **Kopili** *r.* India
159 L4 **Köping** Sweden
158 L3 **Köpmanholmen** Sweden
181 F2 **Kopong** Botswana
143 B3 **Koppal** India
159 J3 **Koppang** Norway
159 K4 **Kopparberg** Sweden
181 G3 **Koppies** S. Africa
180 D3 **Koppieskraal Pan** *salt pan* S. Africa
170 G1 **Koprivnica** Croatia
136 C3 **Köprü** *r.* Turkey
140 D4 **Kor, Rūd-e** *watercourse* Iran
172 G4 **Korablino** Rus. Fed.
141 G5 **Korak** Pak.
188 E1 **Korak, Baie** *b.* Canada
143 B2 **Korangal** India
141 G5 **Korangi** Pak.
143 C2 **Koraput** India
143 C1 **Korba** India
170 D6 **Korba** Tunisia
165 G3 **Korbach** Germany
154 B4 **Korbu, Gunung** *mt.* Malaysia
171 I4 **Korçë** Albania
139 J1 **Korchino** Rus. Fed.
170 G3 **Korčula** Croatia
170 G3 **Korčula** *i.* Croatia
170 G3 **Korčulanski Kanal** *sea chan.* Croatia
139 H4 **Korday** Kazakh.
137 L4 **Kord Khvord** Iran
140 D2 **Kord Kūy** Iran
141 F5 **Kords** *reg.* Iran
152 D3 **Korea, North** *country* Asia
152 D5 **Korea, South** *country* Asia
152 B4 **Korea Bay** *g.* China/N. Korea
151 A7 **Korea Strait** Japan/S. Korea
143 A2 **Koregaon** India
173 F6 **Korenovsk** Rus. Fed.
173 C5 **Korets'** Ukr.
136 B1 **Körfez** Turkey
129 C3 **Korff Ice Rise** *ice feature* Antarctica
139 G2 **Korgalzhyn** Kazakh.
138 F2 **Korgasyn** Kazakh.
158 K2 **Korgen** Norway
176 B4 **Korhogo** Côte d'Ivoire
144 B5 **Kori Creek** *inlet* India
168 H7 **Kőris-hegy** *h.* Hungary
140 E3 **Korīt** Iran
171 I3 **Koritnik** *mt.* Albania
151 G6 **Kōriyama** Japan
136 C3 **Korkuteli** Turkey
136 D4 **Kormakitis, Cape** Cyprus
168 H7 **Körmend** Hungary
139 H2 **Korneyevka** *Karagandinskaya Oblast'* Kazakh.
139 G1 **Korneyevka** *Severnyy Kazakhstan* Kazakh.
139 J1 **Kornilovo** Rus. Fed.
176 B4 **Koro** Côte d'Ivoire
125 H3 **Koro** *i.* Fiji
176 B3 **Koro** Mali
173 F5 **Korocha** Rus. Fed.
136 D1 **Köroğlu Dağları** *mts* Turkey
136 D1 **Köroğlu Tepesi** *mt.* Turkey
178 D4 **Korogwe** Tanz.
126 E7 **Koroit** Australia
171 J4 **Koroneia, Limni** *l.* Greece
126 E6 **Korong Vale** Australia
125 H3 **Koro Sea** Fiji
173 D5 **Korosten'** Ukr.
173 D5 **Korostyshiv** Ukr.
177 D3 **Koro Toro** Chad
159 N3 **Korpilahti** Fin.
159 M3 **Korpo** Fin.

138 C3 Korsak Kazakh.
146 G2 Korsakov Rus. Fed.
172 I3 Korshik Rus. Fed.
158 M3 Korsnäs Fin.
159 J5 Korsør Denmark
173 D5 Korsun'-Shevchenkivs'kyy Ukr.
169 J3 Korsze Poland
158 M3 Kortesjärvi Fin.
172 I2 Kortkeros Rus. Fed.
164 B4 Kortrijk Belgium
172 G3 Kortsovo Rus. Fed.
127 F7 Korumburra Australia
176 D4 Korup, Parc National de nat. park Cameroon
158 N2 Korvala Fin.
144 D4 Korwai India
146 H1 Koryakskaya, Sopka vol. Rus. Fed.
133 R3 Koryakskoye Nagor'ye mts Rus. Fed.
172 H2 Koryazhma Rus. Fed.
173 E5 Koryukivka Ukr.
138 C2 Korzhyn Kazakh.
171 L6 Kos i. Greece
138 E2 Kosagal Kazakh.
139 H1 Kosagash Kazakh.
152 D4 Kosan N. Korea
138 F2 Kosay Kazakh.
168 H4 Kościan Poland
199 F5 Kosciusko U.S.A.
186 C3 Kosciusko Island U.S.A.
127 H6 Kosciuszko, Mount Australia
127 H6 Kosciuszko National Park Australia
137 G1 Köse Turkey
136 F1 Köse Dağı mt. Turkey
143 B2 Kosgi India
135 G2 Kosh-Agach Rus. Fed.
138 B2 Koshankol' Kazakh.
139 H4 Kosh-Döbö Kyrg.
151 A9 Koshikijima-rettō is Japan
138 B2 Koshim Kazakh.
138 B2 Koshim r. Kazakh.
141 F3 Koshkak Iran
139 J3 Koshkarkol', Ozero l. Kazakh.
190 C4 Koshkonong, Lake U.S.A.
Koshkupyr Uzbek. see Qo'shko'pir
Koshoba Turkm. see Goşoba
Koshrabad Uzbek. see Qo'shrabot
151 F7 Kōshū Japan
144 D4 Kosi India
144 D3 Kosi r. India
181 J3 Kosi Bay S. Africa
169 J6 Košice Slovakia
143 B3 Kosigi India
145 F4 Kosi Reservoir Nepal
138 D2 Kosistek Kazakh.
139 F2 Koskol' Kazakh.
139 I3 Koskudyk Kazakh.
158 M2 Koskullskulle Sweden
172 I2 Koslan Rus. Fed.
138 F5 Koson Uzbek.
152 E3 Kosŏng N. Korea
152 E4 Kosŏng N. Korea
139 G4 Kosonsoy Uzbek.
171 I3 Kosovo Country Europe
123 F2 Kosrae atoll Micronesia
165 J5 Kösseine h. Germany
138 C3 Kosshagyl Kazakh.
176 B4 Kossou, Lac de l. Côte d'Ivoire
138 E1 Kostanay Kazakh.
138 E1 Kostanayskaya Oblast' admin. div. Kazakh.
171 J3 Kostenets Bulg.
181 G2 Koster S. Africa
171 J3 Kostinbrod Bulg.
132 J3 Kostino Rus. Fed.
172 D1 Kostomuksha Rus. Fed.
173 C5 Kostopil' Ukr.
172 G3 Kostroma Rus. Fed.
172 G3 Kostroma r. Rus. Fed.
172 G3 Kostromskaya Oblast' admin. div. Rus. Fed.
168 G4 Kostrzyn Poland
173 F5 Kostyantynivka Ukr.
168 H3 Koszalin Poland
168 H7 Kőszeg Hungary
143 C1 Kota Chhattisgarh India
144 C4 Kota Rajasthan India
155 B4 Kotaagung Indon.
144 C4 Kota Barrage India
155 D3 Kotabaru Indon.
155 E3 Kotabaru Indon.
155 B1 Kota Bharu Malaysia
155 B3 Kotabumi Indon.
144 C4 Kota Dam India
155 E1 Kota Kinabalu Sabah Malaysia
139 I3 Kotanemel', Gora mt. Kazakh.
143 C2 Kotaparh India
154 B5 Kotapinang Indon.
144 C4 Kotari r. India
155 B2 Kota Tinggi Malaysia
172 I3 Kotel'nich Rus. Fed.
173 G6 Kotel'nikovo Rus. Fed.
133 O2 Kotel'nyy, Ostrov i. Rus. Fed.
144 D3 Kotgarh India
165 J3 Köthen (Anhalt) Germany
144 E4 Kothi India
159 N3 Kotka Fin.
144 C3 Kot Kapura India
172 H2 Kotlas Rus. Fed.
144 C2 Kotli Pak.
184 B3 Kotlik U.S.A.
158 C3 Kötlutangi pt Iceland
159 O4 Kotly Rus. Fed.
170 G2 Kotor Varoš Bos.-Herz.
176 B4 Kotouba Côte d'Ivoire
173 H5 Kotovo Rus. Fed.
173 G4 Kotovsk Rus. Fed.
173 D6 Kotovs'k Ukr.
144 C4 Kotra India
144 E6 Kotri r. India
144 B4 Kotri Pak.
144 A5 Kot Sarae Pak.
143 C2 Kottagudem India
143 B4 Kottarakara India
143 B4 Kottayam India
143 B3 Kotturu India
Koturdepe Turkm. see Goturdepe
133 L2 Kotuy r. Rus. Fed.
138 D2 Kotyrtas Kazakh.
184 B3 Kotzebue U.S.A.
184 B3 Kotzebue Sound sea chan. U.S.A.
165 K5 Kötzting Germany
176 A3 Koubia Guinea
176 B3 Koudougou Burkina Faso
180 E6 Koueveldberge mts S. Africa
177 D3 Koufey Niger
171 L7 Koufonisi i. Greece
180 E6 Kougaberge mts S. Africa
136 D4 Kouklia Cyprus
178 B4 Koulamoutou Gabon
176 B3 Koulikoro Mali
125 G4 Koumac New Caledonia
176 A3 Koundâra Guinea
176 B3 Koupéla Burkina Faso
211 H2 Kourou Fr. Guiana
176 B3 Kouroussa Guinea
177 D3 Kousséri Cameroon
176 B3 Koutiala Mali
159 N3 Kouvola Fin.
158 O2 Kovdor Rus. Fed.
173 C5 Kovel' Ukr.
172 G3 Kovernino Rus. Fed.
143 B4 Kovilpatti India
172 G3 Kovrov Rus. Fed.
172 G4 Kovylkino Rus. Fed.
172 F2 Kovzhskoye, Ozero l. Rus. Fed.
128 C5 Kowhitirangi N.Z.
149 □ Kowloon Peak h. Hong Kong China
149 □ Kowloon Peninsula Hong Kong China
152 D4 Kowŏn N. Korea
139 I5 Koxrap China
139 I5 Koxtag China
151 B7 Kōyama-misaki pt Japan
Koyamutthoor India see Coimbatore
138 F1 Koybagar, Ozero l. Kazakh.
136 B3 Köyceğiz Turkey
172 I2 Koygorodok Rus. Fed.
Koymatdag, Gory hills Turkm. see Goýmatdag
143 A2 Koyna Reservoir India
172 H1 Koynas Rus. Fed.
184 C3 Koyukuk r. U.S.A.
136 F1 Koyulhisar Turkey
172 F3 Koza Rus. Fed.
151 A7 Kō-zaki pt Japan
136 E3 Kozan Turkey
171 I4 Kozani Greece
170 G2 Kozara mts Bos.-Herz.
173 D5 Kozelets' Ukr.
172 E4 Kozel'sk Rus. Fed.
143 A4 Kozhikode India
136 C1 Kozlu Turkey
172 H3 Koz'modem'yansk Rus. Fed.
139 G4 Kozmoldak Kazakh.
171 J4 Kožuf mts Greece/Macedonia
151 F7 Kōzu-shima i. Japan
173 D5 Kozyatyn Ukr.
154 A3 Kra, Isthmus of Thai.
154 A3 Krabi Thai.
154 A3 Kra Buri Thai.
154 C2 Krâchéh Cambodia
158 L2 Kraddsele Sweden
159 J4 Kragerø Norway
164 D2 Kraggenburg Neth.
171 I2 Kragujevac Serbia
165 G5 Kraichgau reg. Germany
155 C4 Krakatau i. Indon.
154 C2 Krâkôr Cambodia
169 I5 Kraków Poland
165 K1 Krakower See l. Germany
154 B2 Krâlănh Cambodia
213 C1 Kralendijk Bonaire
173 F5 Kramators'k Ukr.
158 L3 Kramfors Sweden
164 C3 Krammer est. Neth.
171 J6 Kranidi Greece
170 F1 Kranj Slovenia
154 □ Kranji Reservoir Sing.
181 I4 Kranskop S. Africa
172 H2 Krasavino Rus. Fed.
132 G2 Krasino Rus. Fed.
150 B3 Kraskino Rus. Fed.
159 N5 Krāslava Latvia
165 K4 Kraslice Czech Rep.
169 O4 Krasnapollye Belarus
172 D4 Krasnaya Gora Rus. Fed.
139 H2 Krasnaya Polyana Kazakh.
173 H5 Krasnoarmeysk Rus. Fed.
173 F5 Krasnoarmiys'k Ukr.
172 H2 Krasnoborsk Rus. Fed.
173 F6 Krasnodar Rus. Fed.
173 F6 Krasnodarskiy Kray admin. div. Rus. Fed.
173 F6 Krasnodarskoye Vodokhranilishche resr Rus. Fed.
173 F5 Krasnodon Ukr.
172 D3 Krasnogorodsk Rus. Fed.
173 G6 Krasnogvardeyskoye Rus. Fed.
173 E5 Krasnohrad Ukr.
173 E6 Krasnohvardiys'ke Ukr.
138 C2 Krasnokholm Rus. Fed.
169 Q2 Krasnomayskiy Rus. Fed.
173 E6 Krasnoperekops'k Ukr.
150 D2 Krasnorechenskiy Rus. Fed.
159 O3 Krasnosel'skoye Rus. Fed.
172 G4 Krasnoslobodsk Rus. Fed.
138 D1 Krasnousol'skiy Rus. Fed.
138 C5 Krasnovodsk, Mys pt Turkm.
Krasnovodskiy Zaliv b. Turkm. see Türkmenbaşy Aýlagy
138 C4 Krasnovodskoye Plato plat. Turkm.
146 B1 Krasnoyarsk Rus. Fed.
169 O3 Krasnyy Rus. Fed.
172 H3 Krasnyye Baki Rus. Fed.
173 H6 Krasnyye Barrikady Rus. Fed.
172 F3 Krasnyy Kholm Rus. Fed.
173 H5 Krasnyy Kut Rus. Fed.
172 D3 Krasnyy Luch Rus. Fed.
173 F5 Krasnyy Lyman Ukr.
139 I3 Krasnyy Oktyabr' Kazakh.
139 G1 Krasnyy Yar Kazakh.
173 I6 Krasnyy Yar Astrakhanskaya Oblast' Rus. Fed.
138 B1 Krasnyy Yar Samarskaya Oblast' Rus. Fed.
173 H5 Krasnyy Yar Volgogradskaya Oblast' Rus. Fed.
173 C5 Krasyliv Ukr.
173 H7 Kraynovka Rus. Fed.
164 E3 Krefeld Germany
173 E5 Kremenchuk Ukr.
173 E5 Kremenchuts'ke Vodoskhovyshche resr Ukr.
173 G5 Kremenskaya Rus. Fed.
168 G6 Křemešník h. Czech Rep.
194 F3 Kremmling U.S.A.
168 G6 Krems an der Donau Austria
133 T3 Kresta, Zaliv g. Rus. Fed.
172 E3 Kresttsy Rus. Fed.
159 M5 Kretinga Lith.
164 E4 Kreuzau Germany
165 F4 Kreuztal Germany
169 M3 Kreva Belarus
176 C4 Kribi Cameroon
Kriel S. Africa see Ga-Nala
171 I5 Krikellos Greece
150 H2 Kril'on, Mys c. Rus. Fed.
135 F5 Krishna r. India
135 G5 Krishna, Mouths of the India
143 B3 Krishnagiri India
145 G5 Krishnanagar India
143 B3 Krishnaraja Sagara l. India
159 I4 Kristiansand Norway
159 K4 Kristianstad Sweden
158 I3 Kristiansund Norway
Kristiinankaupunki Fin. see Kristinestad
159 K4 Kristinehamn Sweden
159 M3 Kristinestad Fin.
Kriti i. Greece see Crete
171 K6 Kritiko Pelagos sea Greece
Krivoy Rog Ukr. see Kryvyy Rih
170 G1 Križevci Croatia
170 F2 Krk i. Croatia
158 K3 Krokom Sweden
158 J3 Krokstadøra Norway
158 K2 Krokstranda Norway
173 E5 Krolevets' Ukr.
165 J4 Kronach Germany
154 B3 Krŏng Kaôh Kŏng Cambodia
158 M3 Kronoby Fin.
185 O3 Kronprins Frederik Bjerge nunataks Greenland
154 A2 Kronwa Myanmar
181 G3 Kroonstad S. Africa
173 G6 Kropotkin Rus. Fed.
165 K3 Kropstädt Germany
169 J6 Krosno Poland
168 H5 Krotoszyn Poland
181 I2 Kruger National Park S. Africa
169 N3 Kruhlaye Belarus
155 B4 Krui Indon.
180 F7 Kruisfontein S. Africa
171 H4 Krujë Albania
171 K4 Krumovgrad Bulg.
Krung Thep Thai. see Bangkok
169 N3 Krupki Belarus
171 I3 Kruševac Serbia
165 K4 Krušné hory mts Czech Rep.
186 B3 Kruzof Island U.S.A.
172 D4 Krychaw Belarus
219 H4 Krylov Seamount sea feature N. Atlantic Ocean
173 F6 Krymsk Rus. Fed.
Kryms'kyy Pivostriv pen. Ukr. see Crimea
139 H3 Krypsalo (abandoned) Kazakh.
173 E6 Kryvyy Rih Ukr.
176 B2 Ksabi Alg.
176 C1 Ksar el Boukhari Alg.
176 B1 Ksar el Kebir Morocco
173 F5 Kshenskiy Rus. Fed.
170 D7 Ksour Essaf Tunisia
172 H3 Kstovo Rus. Fed.
140 B5 Kū', Jabal al h. Saudi Arabia
154 A4 Kuah Malaysia
154 B4 Kuala Kangsar Malaysia
154 B4 Kuala Kerai Malaysia
154 B5 Kuala Kubu Baharu Malaysia
155 B2 Kuala Lipis Malaysia
155 B2 Kuala Lumpur Malaysia
154 B4 Kuala Nerang Malaysia
154 B5 Kuala Pilah Malaysia
154 B5 Kuala Rompin Malaysia
155 D3 Kualasampit Indon.
154 A4 Kualasimpang Indon.
155 B1 Kuala Terengganu Malaysia
153 A5 Kuamut Sabah Malaysia
152 C3 Kuandian China
155 B2 Kuantan Malaysia
173 G6 Kuban' r. Rus. Fed.
137 G4 Kubār Syria
137 I5 Kubaysah Iraq
172 F3 Kubenskoye, Ozero l. Rus. Fed.
138 D4 Kubla Ustyurt Uzbek.
172 H4 Kubnya r. Rus. Fed.
171 L3 Kubrat Bulg.
144 C4 Kuchaman India
144 C4 Kuchera India
155 D2 Kuching Sarawak Malaysia
151 A10 Kuchino-shima i. Japan
141 G4 Kuchnay Darwayshān Afgh.
139 I1 Kuchukskoye, Ozero salt l. Rus. Fed.
171 H4 Kuçovë Albania
143 A3 Kudal India
155 E1 Kudat Sabah Malaysia
143 B3 Kudligi India
143 A3 Kudremukh mt. India
155 D4 Kudus Indon.
168 F7 Kufstein Austria
185 J3 Kugaaruk Canada
172 H3 Kugesi Rus. Fed.
184 G3 Kugluktuk Canada
184 E3 Kugmallit Bay Canada
140 E5 Kūh, Ra's-al- pt Iran
140 D3 Kūh, Sīāh mts Iran
141 F5 Kūhak Iran
145 E3 Kuhanbokano mt. China
140 E4 Kūh Baneh Iran
165 K1 Kuhbier Germany
140 B3 Kūhdasht Iran
137 L3 Kūhīn Iran
158 O2 Kuhmo Fin.
159 N3 Kuhmoinen Fin.
140 D3 Kūhpāyeh Iran
165 K3 Kühren Germany
154 A2 Kui Buri Thai.
180 B2 Kuis Namibia
180 A1 Kuiseb Pass Namibia
179 B5 Kuito Angola
186 C3 Kuiu Island U.S.A.
158 N2 Kuivaniemi Fin.
145 F5 Kujang India
152 C4 Kujang N. Korea
150 G4 Kuji Japan
151 B8 Kujū-san vol. Japan
191 F1 Kukatush Canada
171 I3 Kukës Albania
172 I3 Kukmor Rus. Fed.
154 B5 Kukup Malaysia
138 D5 Kükürtli Turkm.
140 D5 Kūl r. Iran
136 B2 Kula Turkey
145 G3 Kula Kangri mt. Bhutan
138 B3 Kulaly, Ostrov i. Kazakh.
139 H4 Kulan Kazakh.
139 H4 Kulanak Kyrg.
141 F5 Kulanch reg. Pak.
138 D3 Kulandy Kazakh.
138 D3 Kulandy, Poluostrov pen. Kazakh.
139 G2 Kulanotpes watercourse Kazakh.
139 I4 Kulansarak China
141 G4 Kulao r. Pak.
133 O2 Kular Rus. Fed.
153 B5 Kulassein i. Phil.
145 H4 Kulaura Bangl.
159 M4 Kuldīga Latvia
Kul'dzhuktau, Gory hill Uzbek. see Quljuqtov tog'lari
180 D1 Kule Botswana
172 G4 Kulebaki Rus. Fed.
154 C2 Kulen Cambodia
138 E1 Kulevchi Rus. Fed.
172 H2 Kulikovo Rus. Fed.
154 B4 Kulim Malaysia
Kulkuduk Uzbek. see Ko'lquduq
126 F3 Kulkyne watercourse Australia
144 D3 Kullu India
165 J4 Kulmbach Germany
139 G5 Kŭlob Tajik.
137 H2 Kulp Turkey
144 D4 Kulpahar India
203 F4 Kulpsville U.S.A.
138 C3 Kul'sary Kazakh.
165 H5 Külsheim Germany
136 D2 Kulu Turkey
136 C3 Kulübe Tepe mt. Turkey
139 I1 Kulunda Rus. Fed.
139 J1 Kulunda r. Rus. Fed.
139 H1 Kulundinskaya Ravnina plain Kazakh./Rus. Fed.
139 I1 Kulundinskoye, Ozero salt l. Rus. Fed.
140 D4 Kūlvand Iran
126 E5 Kulwin Australia
139 H1 Kulykol' Kazakh.
173 H6 Kuma r. Rus. Fed.
151 F6 Kumagaya Japan
155 D3 Kumai, Teluk b. Indon.
150 F3 Kumaishi Japan
138 E2 Kumak Rus. Fed.
138 D2 Kumak r. Rus. Fed.
151 B8 Kumamoto Japan
151 E8 Kumano Japan
171 I3 Kumanovo Macedonia
176 B4 Kumasi Ghana
176 C4 Kumba Cameroon
143 B4 Kumbakonam India
136 C2 Kümbet Turkey
180 E1 Kumchuru Botswana
140 D3 Kumel well Iran
138 C1 Kumertau Rus. Fed.
152 E4 Kŭmgang-san mt. N. Korea
159 K4 Kumla Sweden
165 L2 Kummersdorf-Alexanderdorf Germany
176 D3 Kumo Nigeria
139 F3 Kumola watercourse Kazakh.
154 B1 Kumphawapi Thai.
180 C4 Kums Namibia
143 A3 Kumta India
173 H7 Kumukh Rus. Fed.
141 H3 Kunar Sīnd r. Afgh.
146 G2 Kunashir, Ostrov i. Rus. Fed.
145 E2 Kunchuk Tso salt l. China
159 N4 Kunda Estonia
145 E4 Kunda India
143 A3 Kundapura India
144 B2 Kundar r. Afgh./Pak.
141 H2 Kunduz Afgh.
141 H2 Kunduz, Daryā-ye r. Afgh.
141 H3 Kunduz, Daryā-ye r. Afgh.
139 H2 Kundykol' Kazakh.
179 B5 Kunene r. Angola/Namibia alt. Cunene
Künes China see Xinyuan
139 J4 Künes Chang China
139 J4 Künes He r. China
159 J4 Kungälv Sweden
139 I4 Kungei Alatau mts Kazakh./Kyrg.
186 C4 Kunghit Island Canada
Kungrad Uzbek. see Qo'ng'irot
138 E4 Kungradkol' Uzbek.
159 K4 Kungsbacka Sweden
159 J4 Kungshamn Sweden
178 B3 Kungu Dem. Rep. Congo
144 D6 Kuni r. India
151 B8 Kunimi-dake mt. Japan
145 F5 Kunjabar India
145 G4 Kunlui r. India/Nepal
135 F3 Kunlun Shan mts China
145 H2 Kunlun Shankou pass China
149 B5 Kunming China
144 D4 Kuno r. India
148 F4 Kunshan China
124 C3 Kununurra Australia
144 D4 Kunwari r. India
172 D3 Kun'ya Rus. Fed.
Kunyu Shan hill China see Taibo Ding
165 H5 Künzelsau Germany
165 J3 Künzels-Berg h. Germany
149 F4 Kuocang Shan mts China
159 N3 Kuohijärvi l. Fin.
158 O2 Kuoloyarvi Rus. Fed.
158 N3 Kuopio Fin.
158 M3 Kuortane Fin.
170 2 Kupa r. Croatia/Slovenia
147 E8 Kupang Indon.
159 N5 Kupiškis Lith.
186 C3 Kupreanof Island U.S.A.
173 F5 Kup"yans'k Ukr.
139 J4 Kuqa China
137 L2 Kür r. Azer.
137 J1 Kura r. Azer./Georgia
173 G7 Kura r. Georgia/Rus. Fed.
139 H4 Kuragaty Kazakh.
173 H7 Kurakh Rus. Fed.
138 D2 Kurashasayskiy Kazakh.
151 C7 Kurashiki Japan
145 E5 Kurasia India
151 C7 Kurayoshi Japan
136 B1 Kurban Dağı mt. Turkey
173 E5 Kurchatov Rus. Fed.
141 G3 Kürd, Küh-e mt. Afgh.
137 L1 Kürdämir Azer.
139 H4 Kurday (abandoned) Kazakh.
137 L2 Kür Dili pt Azer.
143 A2 Kurduvadi India
171 K4 Kŭrdzhali Bulg.
151 C7 Kure Japan
136 D1 Küre Turkey
123 G1 Kure Atoll U.S.A.
159 M4 Kuressaare Estonia
132 H4 Kurgan Rus. Fed.
173 G6 Kurganinsk Rus. Fed.
141 H2 Kūrī Afgh.
144 B4 Kuri India
Kuria Muria Islands is Oman see Ḥalāniyāt, Juzur al
145 G4 Kuri Chhu r. Bhutan
158 M3 Kurikka Fin.
150 G5 Kurikoma-yama vol. Japan
216 E2 Kuril Basin sea feature Sea of Okhotsk
146 G2 Kuril Islands Rus. Fed.
138 B2 Kurilovka Rus. Fed.
146 G2 Kuril'sk Japan
Kuril'skiye Ostrova is Rus. Fed. see Kuril Islands
216 E3 Kuril Trench sea feature N. Pacific Ocean
138 B1 Kurmanayevka Rus. Fed.
177 F3 Kurmuk Sudan
143 B3 Kurnool India
136 E6 Kurnub tourist site Israel
151 E6 Kurobe Japan
150 G4 Kuroishi Japan
151 A9 Kuro-shima i. Japan
172 F4 Kurovskoye Rus. Fed.
128 C6 Kurow N.Z.
144 B2 Kurram r. Afgh./Pak.
127 I4 Kurri Kurri Australia
139 J2 Kurshim Kazakh.
173 F5 Kursk Rus. Fed.
173 H6 Kurskaya Rus. Fed.
173 F5 Kurskaya Oblast' admin. div. Rus. Fed.
136 D1 Kurşunlu Turkey
137 H3 Kurtalan Turkey
139 I3 Kurtty r. Kazakh.
136 G2 Kuruçay Turkey
144 D3 Kurukshetra India
180 E3 Kuruman S. Africa
180 D3 Kuruman watercourse S. Africa
151 B8 Kurume Japan
146 D1 Kurumkan Rus. Fed.
143 C5 Kurunegala Sri Lanka
177 F2 Kurush, Jebel hills Sudan
139 J2 Kur'ya Rus. Fed.
138 B4 Kuryk Kazakh.
171 L6 Kuşadası Turkey
171 L6 Kuşadası, Gulf of b. Turkey
186 B2 Kusawa Lake Canada
164 F5 Kusel Germany
136 A1 Kuş Gölü l. Turkey
173 F6 Kushchevskaya Rus. Fed.
151 D8 Kushimoto Japan
150 I3 Kushiro Japan
150 I3 Kushiro-Shitsugen Kokuritsu-kōen nat. park Japan
137 L5 Kūshkak Iran
141 F3 Kushk-e Kuhnah Afgh.
143 B3 Kushtagi India
145 G5 Kushtia Bangl.
148 C2 Kushui He r. China
184 C3 Kuskokwim r. U.S.A.
184 B4 Kuskokwim Bay U.S.A.
184 C3 Kuskokwim Mountains U.S.A.
138 F1 Kusmuryn Kazakh.
152 C4 Kusŏng N. Korea
150 I3 Kussharo-ko l. Japan
165 F1 Küstenkanal canal Germany
140 C4 Kut Iran
154 B3 Kut, Ko i. Thai.
137 L6 Küt 'Abdollāh Iran
154 A5 Kutacane Indon.
136 B2 Kütahya Turkey
173 G7 Kutaisi Georgia
173 H6 Kutan Rus. Fed.
150 G3 Kutchan Japan
137 L5 Kūt-e Gapu tourist site Iran
170 G2 Kutina Croatia
170 G2 Kutjevo Croatia
169 I4 Kutno Poland
178 B4 Kutu Dem. Rep. Congo
145 G5 Kutubdia Island Bangl.
184 G2 Kuujjua r. Canada
189 G2 Kuujjuaq Canada
188 E2 Kuujjuarapik Canada
Kuuli-Mayak Turkm. see Guwlumaýak
158 O2 Kuusamo Fin.
159 N3 Kuusankoski Fin.
138 D2 Kuvandyk Rus. Fed.
179 B5 Kuvango Angola
172 E3 Kuvshinovo Rus. Fed.
137 K7 Kuwait country Asia
137 K7 Kuwait Kuwait
137 K7 Kuwait Jun b. Kuwait
151 E7 Kuwana Japan
172 G1 Kuya Rus. Fed.
132 I4 Kuybyshev Novosibirskaya Oblast' Rus. Fed.
Kuybyshev Samarskaya Oblast' Rus. Fed. see Samara
172 I4 Kuybyshevskoye Vodokhranilishche resr Rus. Fed.
148 D2 Kuye He r. China
139 H3 Kuygan Kazakh.
135 G2 Kuytun China
139 J3 Kuytun He r. China
171 M6 Kuyucak Turkey
138 F2 Kuyukkol', Ozero salt l. Kazakh.
139 K2 Kuyus Rus. Fed.
138 D3 Kuyushe Kazakh.
159 O3 Kuznechnoye Rus. Fed.
172 H4 Kuznetsk Rus. Fed.
150 F1 Kuznetsovo Rus. Fed.
173 C5 Kuznetsovs'k Ukr.
158 M1 Kvænangen sea chan. Norway
158 L1 Kvaløya i. Norway
158 M1 Kvalsund Norway
138 D1 Kvarkeno Rus. Fed.
170 F2 Kvarnerić sea chan. Croatia
184 C4 Kvichak Bay U.S.A.
186 D3 Kwadacha Wilderness Provincial Park Canada
181 I4 KwaDukuza S. Africa
149 □ Kwai Tau Leng h. Hong Kong China
216 G6 Kwajalein atoll Marshall Is
154 A5 Kwala Indon.
181 I4 KwaMashu S. Africa
181 H2 KwaMhlanga S. Africa
Kwangju S. Korea see Gwangju
178 B4 Kwango r. Dem. Rep. Congo
178 D4 Kwangwazi Tanz.
152 E3 Kwanmo-bong mt. N. Korea
181 F6 KwaNobuhle S. Africa
181 F6 KwaNojoli S. Africa
181 G6 Kwanonqubela S. Africa
180 F5 KwaNonzame S. Africa
181 G6 Kwatinidubu S. Africa
181 H3 KwaZamokuhle S. Africa
180 F6 KwaZamukucinga S. Africa
180 F5 Kwazamuxolo S. Africa
181 H3 KwaZanele S. Africa
181 I4 KwaZulu-Natal prov. S. Africa
179 C5 Kwekwe Zimbabwe
180 F1 Kweneng admin. dist. Botswana
178 B4 Kwenge r. Dem. Rep. Congo
181 G5 Kwezi-Naledi S. Africa
169 I4 Kwidzyn Poland
184 B4 Kwigillingok U.S.A.
124 E2 Kwikila P.N.G.
178 B4 Kwilu r. Angola/Dem. Rep. Congo
147 F7 Kwoka mt. Indon.
149 □ Kwun Tong Hong Kong China
177 D4 Kyabé Chad
126 F6 Kyabram Australia
154 A1 Kya-in Seikkyi Myanmar
146 C1 Kyakhta Rus. Fed.
126 E5 Kyalite Australia
126 A4 Kyancutta Australia
172 F1 Kyanda Rus. Fed.
154 A1 Kyaukhnyat Myanmar
145 H6 Kyaukpyu Myanmar
145 H5 Kyauktaw Myanmar
159 M5 Kybartai Lith.
126 D6 Kybybolite Australia
149 C6 Ky Cung, Sông r. Vietnam
148 A2 Kyikug China
Kyiv Ukr. see Kiev
173 D5 Kyivs'ke Vodoskhovyshche resr Ukr.
Kyklades is Greece see Cyclades
187 H4 Kyle Canada
162 C3 Kyle of Lochalsh U.K.
164 E5 Kyll r. Germany
171 J6 Kyllini mt. Greece
158 P2 Kynazhegubskoye Vodokhranilishche l. Rus. Fed.
126 F6 Kyneton Australia
178 D3 Kyoga, Lake Uganda
151 D7 Kyōga-misaki pt Japan
127 J2 Kyogle Australia
154 A1 Kyondo Myanmar
151 D7 Kyōto Japan
171 I6 Kyparissia Greece
171 I6 Kyparissiakos Kolpos b. Greece
171 K5 Kyra Panagia i. Greece
136 D4 Kyrenia Cyprus
139 H4 Kyrgyzstan country Asia
165 K2 Kyritz Germany
138 B2 Kyrkopa Kazakh.
158 J3 Kyrksæterøra Norway
132 G3 Kyrta Rus. Fed.
172 H1 Kyssa Rus. Fed.
133 O3 Kytalyktakh Rus. Fed.
171 J6 Kythira i. Greece
171 K6 Kythnos i. Greece
154 A2 Kyungyaung Myanmar
151 B8 Kyūshū i. Japan
216 E4 Kyushu-Palau Ridge sea feature N. Pacific Ocean
171 J3 Kyustendil Bulg.
127 G5 Kywong Australia
158 N3 Kyyjärvi Fin.
138 C3 Kyzan Kazakh.
146 B1 Kyzyl Rus. Fed.
139 G4 Kyzyl-Adyr Kyrg.
139 H5 Kyzylart Pass Kyrg.
139 H3 Kyzylbelen, Gora h. Kazakh.
139 G2 Kyzyldikan Kazakh.
139 J3 Kyzylkesek Kazakh.
138 C2 Kyzylkoga Kazakh.
138 E2 Kyzylkol', Ozero l. Kazakh.
138 E4 Kyzylkum Desert Uzbek.
139 H4 Kyzyl-Kyya Kyrg.
138 F3 Kyzylorda Kazakh.
138 E3 Kyzylordinskaya Oblast' admin. div. Kazakh.
138 C4 Kyzylsay Kazakh.
139 I4 Kyzyl-Suu Kyrg.
139 H5 Kyzyl-Suu r. Kyrg.
139 H2 Kyzyltas Kazakh.
139 H3 Kyzyltau Kazakh.
138 F2 Kyzyluy Kazakh.
138 B3 Kyzylysor Kazakh.
138 C2 Kyzylzhar Aktyubinskaya Oblast' Kazakh.
139 G2 Kyzylzhar Karagandinskaya Oblast' Kazakh.


## L


164 F4 Laacher See l. Germany
159 N4 Laagri Estonia
206 I6 La Amistad, Parque Internacional nat. park Costa Rica/Panama
207 F5 La Angostura, Presa de resr Mex.
158 N1 Laanila Fin.
206 D3 La Ardilla, Cerro mt. Mex.
178 E3 Laascaanood Somalia
178 E2 Laasgoray Somalia
213 E2 La Asunción Venez.
176 A2 Laâyoune W. Sahara
173 G6 Laba r. Rus. Fed.
206 D1 La Babia Mex.
212 D3 La Banda Arg.
194 E3 La Barge U.S.A.
125 H3 Labasa Fiji
166 C3 La Baule-Escoublac France
176 A3 Labé Guinea
188 F4 Labelle Canada
190 B5 La Belle U.S.A.
186 B2 Laberge, Lake Canada
153 A5 Labian, Tanjung pt Sabah Malaysia
186 E2 La Biche r. Canada
187 G4 La Biche, Lac l. Canada
173 G6 Labinsk Rus. Fed.
154 B5 Labis Malaysia
153 B3 Labo Phil.
206 C2 La Boquilla Mex.
136 F4 Laboué Lebanon
166 D4 Labouheyre France
215 D2 Laboulaye Arg.
189 H3 Labrador reg. Canada
189 G3 Labrador City Canada
185 M3 Labrador Sea Canada/Greenland
210 F5 Lábrea Brazil
155 E1 Labuan Malaysia
155 C4 Labuhan Indon.
155 B2 Labuhanbilik Indon.
154 A5 Labuhanruku Indon.
153 A5 Labuk r. Sabah Malaysia
155 E1 Labuk, Teluk b. Sabah Malaysia
147 E7 Labuna Indon.
126 A3 Labyrinth, Lake salt flat Australia
132 H3 Labytnangi Rus. Fed.
171 H4 Laç Albania
215 D1 La Calera Arg.
215 B2 La Calera Chile
166 F2 La Capelle France
215 B4 Lácar, Lago l. Arg.
215 D2 La Carlota Arg.
167 E3 La Carolina Spain
171 L2 Lăcăuţi, Vârful mt. Romania
203 I1 Lac-Baker Canada
134 F5 Laccadive Islands India
187 J4 Lac du Bonnet Canada
206 H5 La Ceiba Hond.
213 C2 La Ceiba Venez.
126 C6 Lacepede Bay Australia
203 E4 Laceyville U.S.A.
203 H1 Lac-Frontière Canada
172 F2 Lacha, Ozero l. Rus. Fed.
168 C7 La Chaux-de-Fonds tourist site Switz.
165 I2 Lachendorf Germany
191 F3 Lachine U.S.A.
126 F5 Lachlan r. Australia
206 J6 La Chorrera Panama
188 F4 Lachute Canada
137 K2 Laçın Azer.
166 G5 La Ciotat France
206 C3 La Ciudad Mex.
202 D3 Lackawanna U.S.A.
187 G4 Lac La Biche Canada
186 E4 Lac La Hache Canada
Lac la Martre Canada see Whatî
187 H3 Lac La Ronge Provincial Park Canada
189 F4 Lac-Mégantic Canada
203 G2 Lacolle Canada
206 B1 La Colorada Mex.
186 G4 Lacombe Canada
206 I6 La Concepción Panama
207 F4 La Concordia Mex.
170 C5 Laconi Sardinia Italy
203 H3 Laconia U.S.A.
191 I1 La Corne Canada
190 B4 La Crescent U.S.A.
190 B4 La Crosse U.S.A.
213 A4 La Cruz Col.
206 C3 La Cruz Sinaloa Mex.
207 E2 La Cruz Tamaulipas Mex.
206 H5 La Cruz Nicaragua
206 D1 La Cuesta Mex.
198 E4 La Cygne U.S.A.
144 D2 Ladakh Range mts India
154 A4 Ladang, Ko i. Thai.
136 E1 Ladik Turkey
180 D6 Ladismith S. Africa
141 F4 Lādīz Iran
144 C4 Ladnun India
172 D2 Ladoga, Lake Rus. Fed.
213 B3 La Dorada Col.
Ladozhskoye Ozero l. Rus. Fed. see Ladoga, Lake
145 H4 Ladu mt. India
172 E2 Ladva Rus. Fed.
172 E2 Ladva-Vetka Rus. Fed.
185 J2 Lady Ann Strait Canada
162 E4 Ladybank U.K.
181 G4 Ladybrand S. Africa
191 G2 Lady Evelyn Lake Canada
181 G5 Lady Frere S. Africa
181 G5 Lady Grey S. Africa
186 E5 Ladysmith Canada
181 H4 Ladysmith S. Africa
190 B3 Ladysmith U.S.A.
124 E2 Lae P.N.G.
154 B2 Laem Ngop Thai.
159 I3 Lærdalsøyri Norway
210 F8 La Esmeralda Bol.
213 D4 La Esmeralda Venez.
159 J4 Læsø i. Denmark
206 G5 La Esperanza Hond.
215 D1 La Falda Arg.
194 F4 Lafayette CO U.S.A.
190 D5 Lafayette IN U.S.A.
199 E6 Lafayette LA U.S.A.
201 C5 La Fayette U.S.A.
164 B5 La Fère France
164 B5 La-Ferté-Milon France
164 B6 La Ferté-sous-Jouarre France
140 C5 Laffān, Ra's pt Qatar
176 C4 Lafia Nigeria
166 D3 La Flèche France
202 A6 La Follette U.S.A.
191 H2 Laforce Canada
191 G2 Laforest Canada
189 F3 Laforge Canada
213 B2 La Fría Venez.
140 D5 Lāft Iran
170 C6 La Galite i. Tunisia
173 H6 Lagan' Rus. Fed.
132 C4 Lagan Sweden
163 E3 Lagan r. U.K.
211 K6 Lagarto Brazil
165 G3 Lage Germany
159 J4 Lågen r. Norway
162 C5 Lagg U.K.
162 D3 Laggan U.K.
162 D4 Laggan, Loch l. U.K.
176 C1 Laghouat Alg.
145 F2 Lagkor Co salt l. China
213 B2 La Gloria Col.
Lago Agrio Ecuador see Nueva Loja
214 D2 Lagoa Santa Brazil
137 K1 Lagodekhi Georgia
176 A2 La Gomera i. Canary Is
154 D5 Lagong i. Indon.
153 B3 Lagonoy Gulf Phil.
212 B7 Lago Posadas Arg.
215 B4 Lago Ranco Chile
176 C4 Lagos Nigeria
167 B4 Lagos Port.
206 D3 Lagos de Moreno Mex.
188 E3 La Grande r. Canada
194 C2 La Grande U.S.A.
188 E3 La Grande 3, Réservoir resr Canada
188 F3 La Grande 4, Réservoir resr Canada
Lagrange Australia see La Grange
124 C3 La Grange Australia
201 C5 La Grange GA U.S.A.
203 I2 La Grange ME U.S.A.
190 D5 La Grange MI U.S.A.
190 B5 La Grange MO U.S.A.
199 D6 La Grange TX U.S.A.
190 E5 Lagrange U.S.A.
213 E3 La Gran Sabana plat. Venez.
212 G3 Laguna Brazil
196 D5 Laguna Beach U.S.A.
215 B3 Laguna de Laja, Parque Nacional nat. park Chile
206 I5 Laguna de Perlas Nicaragua
196 D5 Laguna Mountains U.S.A.
210 C5 Lagunas Peru
212 A7 Laguna San Rafael, Parque Nacional nat. park Chile
207 E5 Lagunas de Chacahua, Parque Nacional nat. park Mex.
213 C2 Lagunillas Venez.
La Habana Cuba see Havana
155 E1 Lahad Datu Sabah Malaysia
153 A5 Lahad Datu, Teluk b. Sabah Malaysia
196 □2 Lahaina U.S.A.
155 B3 Lahat Indon.
154 A5 Lahewa Indon.
142 B7 Laḥij Yemen
140 C2 Lāhījān Iran
196 □1 Lahilahi Point U.S.A.
165 F4 Lahn r. Germany
164 F4 Lahnstein Germany
159 K4 Laholm Sweden
196 C2 Lahontan Reservoir U.S.A.
144 C3 Lahore Pak.
213 E3 La Horqueta Venez.
144 B3 Lahri Pak.
159 N3 Lahti Fin.
206 C4 La Huerta Mex.
177 D4 Laï Chad
148 F3 Lai'an China
149 C6 Laibin China
127 J1 Laidley Australia
196 □1 Lā'ie U.S.A.
196 □1 Lā'ie Point U.S.A.
149 C4 Laifeng China
166 E2 L'Aigle France
206 G5 La Iguala Hond.
158 M3 Laihia Fin.
145 H4 Laimakuri India
180 D6 Laingsburg S. Africa
158 M2 Lainioälven r. Sweden
162 D2 Lairg U.K.

153 C5 **Lais** Phil.
159 M3 **Laitila** Fin.
170 D1 **Laives** Italy
148 E2 **Laiwu** China
148 F2 **Laiyang** China
148 E2 **Laiyuan** China
148 F2 **Laizhou** China
148 F2 **Laizhou Wan** b. China
215 B3 **Laja** r. Chile
215 B3 **Laja, Laguna de** l. Chile
124 D3 **Lajamanu** Australia
211 K5 **Lajes** Brazil
212 F3 **Lajes** Brazil
206 C2 **La Joya** Mex.
195 G4 **La Junta** U.S.A.
194 E2 **Lake** U.S.A.
198 D3 **Lake Andes** U.S.A.
136 D6 **Lake Bardawil Reserve** nature res. Egypt
126 E6 **Lake Bolac** Australia
127 G4 **Lake Cargelligo** Australia
127 J3 **Lake Cathie** Australia
199 E6 **Lake Charles** U.S.A.
194 B1 **Lake Chelan National Recreation Area** park U.S.A.
201 D6 **Lake City** FL U.S.A.
190 E3 **Lake City** MI U.S.A.
190 A3 **Lake City** MN U.S.A.
201 E5 **Lake City** SC U.S.A.
160 D3 **Lake District National Park** U.K.
126 B2 **Lake Eyre National Park** Australia
191 H3 **Lakefield** Canada
190 C4 **Lake Geneva** U.S.A.
**Lake Harbour** Canada see **Kimmirut**
197 E4 **Lake Havasu City** U.S.A.
196 C4 **Lake Isabella** U.S.A.
199 E6 **Lake Jackson** U.S.A.
201 D6 **Lakeland** U.S.A.
190 C2 **Lake Linden** U.S.A.
186 F4 **Lake Louise** Canada
197 E4 **Lake Mead National Recreation Area** park U.S.A.
199 C5 **Lake Meredith National Recreation Area** park U.S.A.
203 I2 **Lake Moxie** U.S.A.
194 B2 **Lake Oswego** U.S.A.
128 B5 **Lake Paringa** N.Z.
203 G2 **Lake Placid** U.S.A.
196 A2 **Lakeport** U.S.A.
199 F5 **Lake Providence** U.S.A.
188 D3 **Lake River** Canada
191 H3 **Lake St Peter** Canada
127 H6 **Lakes Entrance** Australia
190 E2 **Lake Superior Provincial Park** Canada
127 I5 **Lake Tabourie** Australia
128 C6 **Lake Tekapo** N.Z.
194 B3 **Lakeview** U.S.A.
199 F5 **Lake Village** U.S.A.
194 F4 **Lakewood** CO U.S.A.
203 F4 **Lakewood** NJ U.S.A.
202 C4 **Lakewood** OH U.S.A.
201 D7 **Lake Worth** U.S.A.
172 D2 **Lakhdenpokh'ya** Rus. Fed.
144 E4 **Lakhimpur** India
145 F4 **Lakhisarai** India
144 D5 **Lakhnadon** India
144 B5 **Lakhpat** India
171 J6 **Lakonikos Kolpos** b. Greece
176 B4 **Lakota** Côte d'Ivoire
158 N1 **Laksefjorden** sea chan. Norway
158 N1 **Lakselv** Norway
134 F5 **Lakshadweep** union terr. India
145 G5 **Laksham** Bangl.
143 B2 **Lakshettipet** India
145 G5 **Lakshmikantapur** India
153 B5 **Lala** Phil.
215 D2 **La Laguna** Arg.
215 B3 **La Laja** Chile
178 B3 **Lalara** Gabon
167 F2 **L'Alcora** Spain
165 K1 **Lalendorf** Germany
140 C3 **Lālī** Iran
207 G5 **La Libertad** El Salvador
207 G4 **La Libertad** Guat.
215 B2 **La Ligua** Chile
152 D1 **Lalin** China
167 B1 **Lalín** Spain
167 D4 **La Línea de la Concepción** Spain
152 C1 **Lalin He** r. China
144 D4 **Lalitpur** India
153 B2 **Lal-Lo** Phil.
187 H3 **La Loche** Canada
187 H3 **La Loche, Lac** l. Canada
164 C4 **La Louvière** Belgium
172 H2 **Lal'sk** Rus. Fed.
145 H5 **Lama** Bangl.
213 B4 **La Macarena, Parque Nacional** nat. park Col.
170 C4 **La Maddalena** Sardinia Italy
153 A5 **Lamag** Sabah Malaysia
154 A2 **Lamaing** Myanmar
**La Manche** str. France/U.K. see **English Channel**
198 C4 **Lamar** CO U.S.A.
199 E4 **Lamar** MO U.S.A.
140 D5 **Lamard** Iran
170 C5 **La Marmora, Punta** mt. Sardinia Italy
215 D3 **Lamarque** Arg.
199 E6 **La Marque** U.S.A.
186 F2 **La Martre, Lac** l. Canada
178 B4 **Lambaréné** Gabon
210 C5 **Lambayeque** Peru
163 F4 **Lambay Island** Ireland
129 D5 **Lambert Glacier** glacier Antarctica
180 C6 **Lambert's Bay** S. Africa
144 C3 **Lambi** India
161 F6 **Lambourn Downs** hills U.K.
167 C2 **Lamego** Port.
189 H4 **Lamèque, Île** i. Canada
210 C6 **La Merced** Peru
126 D5 **Lameroo** Australia
196 D5 **La Mesa** U.S.A.
199 C5 **Lamesa** U.S.A.
171 J5 **Lamia** Greece
127 J2 **Lamington National Park** Australia
206 B1 **La Misa** Mex.
196 D5 **La Misión** Mex.
153 B5 **Lamitan** Phil.
149 □ **Lamma Island** Hong Kong China
128 B6 **Lammerlaw Range** mts N.Z.
162 F5 **Lammermuir Hills** U.K.
159 K4 **Lammhult** Sweden
159 N3 **Lammi** Fin.
190 C5 **La Moille** U.S.A.
203 G2 **Lamoille** r. U.S.A.
190 B5 **La Moine** r. U.S.A.
153 B3 **Lamon Bay** Phil.
198 E3 **Lamoni** U.S.A.
194 F3 **Lamont** U.S.A.
206 D2 **La Mora** Mex.
206 C1 **La Morita** Mex.
191 H1 **La Motte** Canada
154 A1 **Lampang** Thai.
154 B1 **Lam Pao, Ang Kep Nam** Thai.
199 D6 **Lampasas** U.S.A.
206 D2 **Lampazos** Mex.
170 E7 **Lampedusa, Isola di** i. Sicily Italy
161 C5 **Lampeter** U.K.
154 A1 **Lamphun** Thai.
172 F4 **Lamskoye** Rus. Fed.
149 □ **Lam Tin** Hong Kong China
178 E4 **Lamu** Kenya
145 H6 **Lamu** Myanmar
154 A1 **Lan, Loi** mt. Myanmar/Thai.
**Lanai** i. U.S.A. see **Lāna'i**
196 □2 **Lāna'i** i. U.S.A.
**Lanai City** U.S.A. see **Lāna'i City**
196 □2 **Lāna'i City** U.S.A.
153 C5 **Lanao, Lake** Phil.
191 I3 **Lanark** Canada
162 E5 **Lanark** U.K.
190 C4 **Lanark** U.S.A.
153 A5 **Lanas** Sabah Malaysia
154 A3 **Lanbi Kyun** i. Myanmar
146 B3 **Lancang Jiang** r. China conv. **Mekong**
203 F2 **Lancaster** Canada
160 E3 **Lancaster** U.K.
196 C4 **Lancaster** CA U.S.A.
190 A5 **Lancaster** MO U.S.A.
203 H2 **Lancaster** NH U.S.A.
202 B5 **Lancaster** OH U.S.A.
203 E4 **Lancaster** PA U.S.A.
201 D5 **Lancaster** SC U.S.A.
190 B4 **Lancaster** WI U.S.A.
160 E4 **Lancaster Canal** U.K.
185 J2 **Lancaster Sound** str. Canada
170 F3 **Lanciano** Italy
215 B3 **Lanco** Chile
148 F2 **Lancun** China
168 F6 **Landau an der Isar** Germany
165 G5 **Landau in der Pfalz** Germany
141 H3 **Landay Sīn** r. Afgh.
168 E7 **Landeck** Austria
194 E3 **Lander** U.S.A.
165 H2 **Landesbergen** Germany
187 H4 **Landis** Canada
168 E6 **Landsberg am Lech** Germany
161 B7 **Land's End** pt U.K.
168 F6 **Landshut** Germany
159 K5 **Landskrona** Sweden
164 F5 **Landstuhl** Germany
165 G1 **Land Wursten** reg. Germany
163 D4 **Lanesborough** Ireland
**La Nga** r. Vietnam see **La Nga, Sông**
154 C3 **La Nga, Sông** r. Vietnam
144 E3 **La'nga Co** l. China
148 C3 **Langao** China
139 H5 **Langar** Afgh.
138 F4 **Langar** Uzbek.
162 B2 **Langavat, Loch** l. U.K.
180 E4 **Langberg** mts S. Africa
198 D1 **Langdon** U.S.A.
180 C6 **Langeberg** mts S. Africa
159 J5 **Langeland** i. Denmark
159 N3 **Längelmäki** Fin.
159 N3 **Längelmävesi** l. Fin.
165 I3 **Langelsheim** Germany
165 G1 **Langen** Germany
165 H2 **Langenhagen** Germany
165 F4 **Langenhahn** Germany
165 F5 **Langenlonsheim** Germany
168 C7 **Langenthal** Switz.
165 J2 **Langenweddingen** Germany
164 F1 **Langeoog** Germany
164 F1 **Langeoog** i. Germany
159 J4 **Langesund** Norway
154 B5 **Langgapayung** Indon.
165 G4 **Langgöns** Germany
187 H4 **Langham** Canada
158 B2 **Langjökull** ice cap Iceland
155 A2 **Langka** Indon.
155 A1 **Langkawi** i. Malaysia
154 A3 **Lang Kha Toek, Khao** mt. Thai.
180 D4 **Langklip** S. Africa
153 A5 **Langkon** Sabah Malaysia
191 J1 **Langlade** Canada
190 C3 **Langlade** U.S.A.
148 B3 **Langmusi** China
166 F4 **Langogne** France
158 K1 **Langøya** i. Norway
145 F3 **Langphu** mt. China
161 E6 **Langport** U.K.
144 D3 **Langqên Zangbo** r. China
149 F5 **Langqi** China
166 G3 **Langres** France
144 D1 **Langru** China
155 A2 **Langsa** Indon.
154 A4 **Langsa, Teluk** b. Indon.
158 L3 **Långsele** Sweden
148 C1 **Langshan** China
148 C1 **Lang Shan** mts China
149 C6 **Lang Sơn** Vietnam
160 G3 **Langtoft** U.K.
199 C6 **Langtry** U.S.A.
166 F5 **Languedoc** reg. France
158 M2 **Långvattnet** Sweden
165 H2 **Langwedel** Germany
148 F4 **Langxi** China
148 C4 **Langzhong** China
191 H2 **Laniel** Canada
187 H4 **Lanigan** Canada
196 □1 **Lanikai** U.S.A.
215 B3 **Lanín, Parque Nacional** nat. park Arg.
215 B3 **Lanín, Volcán** vol. Arg.
148 E3 **Lankao** China
137 L2 **Länkäran** Azer.
166 C2 **Lannion** France
206 C3 **La Noria** Mex.
158 M2 **Lansån** Sweden
190 C2 **L'Anse** U.S.A.
186 C2 **Lansing** r. Canada
190 B4 **Lansing** IA U.S.A.
190 E4 **Lansing** MI U.S.A.
154 A4 **Lanta, Ko** i. Thai.
149 □ **Lantau Island** Hong Kong China
149 □ **Lantau Peak** h. Hong Kong China
153 C4 **Lanuza Bay** Phil.
149 F4 **Lanxi** China
177 F4 **Lanya** South Sudan
149 F6 **Lan Yu** i. Taiwan
176 A2 **Lanzarote** i. Canary Is
148 B2 **Lanzhou** China
152 B1 **Lanzi** China
154 A1 **Lao, Nam Mae** r. Thai.
153 B2 **Laoag City** Phil.
153 C3 **Laoang** Phil.
149 B6 **Lao Cai** Vietnam
139 J3 **Laofengkou** China
148 F1 **Laoha He** r. China
148 D3 **Laohekou** China
152 A4 **Laohutun** China
146 B3 **Laojunmiao** China
152 D3 **Laoling** China
152 D3 **Lao Ling** mts China
146 B3 **Lao Mangnai** China
166 F2 **Laon** France
190 C3 **Laona** U.S.A.
147 C5 **Laos** country Asia
148 F2 **Lao Shan** mt. China
152 E2 **Laotougou** China
152 C3 **Laotu Dingzi** h. China
148 A1 **Laoximiao** China
152 E2 **Laoye Ling** mts China
214 C4 **Lapa** Brazil
153 B5 **Lapac** i. Phil.
176 A2 **La Palma** i. Canary Is
206 J6 **La Palma** Panama
167 C4 **La Palma del Condado** Spain
215 F2 **La Paloma** Uruguay
215 D3 **La Pampa** prov. Arg.
196 B4 **La Panza Range** mts U.S.A.
213 E3 **La Paragua** Venez.
153 A5 **Laparan** i. Phil.
213 B4 **La Paya, Parque Nacional** nat. park Col.
215 E1 **La Paz** Entre Ríos Arg.
215 C2 **La Paz** Mendoza Arg.
210 E7 **La Paz** Bol.
206 H5 **La Paz** Hond.
206 B2 **La Paz** Mex.
206 H5 **La Paz** Nicaragua
190 D5 **Lapaz** U.S.A.
206 B2 **La Paz, Bahía** b. Mex.
210 E4 **La Pedrera** Col.
191 F4 **Lapeer** U.S.A.
206 C1 **La Perla** Mex.
150 G2 **La Pérouse Strait** Japan/Rus. Fed.
207 E3 **La Pesca** Mex.
206 D3 **La Piedad** Mex.
213 E3 **La Piña** r. Venez.
194 B3 **La Pine** U.S.A.
153 C3 **Lapinig** Phil.
153 C4 **Lapinin** i. Phil.
158 N3 **Lapinlahti** Fin.
136 D4 **Lapithos** Cyprus
199 F6 **Laplace** U.S.A.
198 C2 **La Plant** U.S.A.
215 F2 **La Plata** Arg.
213 B4 **La Plata** Col.
210 B4 **La Plata, Isla** i. Ecuador
215 F2 **La Plata, Río de** sea chan. Arg./Uruguay
187 H3 **La Plonge, Lac** l. Canada
167 D1 **La Pola** Spain
167 D1 **La Pola Siero** Spain
172 G1 **Lapominka** Rus. Fed.
190 D5 **La Porte** U.S.A.
190 A4 **La Porte City** U.S.A.
188 F2 **La Potherie, Lac** l. Canada
158 M3 **Lappajärvi** Fin.
158 M3 **Lappajärvi** l. Fin.
159 O3 **Lappeenranta** Fin.
165 K5 **Lappersdorf** Germany
159 M3 **Lappi** Fin.
158 L2 **Lappland** reg. Europe
203 G2 **La Prairie** Canada
199 D6 **La Pryor** U.S.A.
171 L4 **Lâpseki** Turkey
133 M2 **Laptev Sea** Rus. Fed.
**Laptevykh, More** sea Rus. Fed. see **Laptev Sea**
158 M3 **Lapua** Fin.
153 B4 **Lapu-Lapu** Phil.
212 C2 **La Quiaca** Arg.
170 E3 **L'Aquila** Italy
196 D5 **La Quinta** U.S.A.
140 D5 **Lār** Iran
176 B1 **Larache** Morocco
140 E5 **Lārak** i. Iran
194 F3 **Laramie** U.S.A.
194 F3 **Laramie Mountains** U.S.A.
214 B4 **Laranjeiras do Sul** Brazil
214 B3 **Laranjinha** r. Brazil
147 E7 **Larantuka** Indon.
147 F7 **Larat** i. Indon.
167 H4 **Larba** Alg.
159 L4 **Lärbro** Sweden
191 G2 **Larchwood** Canada
191 H1 **Larder Lake** Canada
167 E1 **Laredo** Spain
199 D7 **Laredo** U.S.A.
207 E3 **La Reforma** Mex.
201 D7 **Largo** U.S.A.
162 D5 **Largs** U.K.
140 B2 **Lārī** Iran
170 D6 **L'Ariana** Tunisia
187 J5 **Larimore** U.S.A.
212 C3 **La Rioja** Arg.
215 C1 **La Rioja** prov. Arg.
167 E1 **La Rioja** aut. comm. Spain
171 J5 **Larisa** Greece
140 E5 **Laristan** reg. Iran
144 B4 **Larkana** Pak.
168 C7 **Larmont** mt. France/Switz.
136 D4 **Larnaca** Cyprus
**Larnaka** Cyprus see **Larnaca**
163 F3 **Larne** U.K.
198 D4 **Larned** U.S.A.
162 C6 **Larne Lough** inlet U.K.
167 D1 **La Robla** Spain
164 D4 **La Roche-en-Ardenne** Belgium
166 D3 **La Rochelle** France
166 D3 **La Roche-sur-Yon** France
167 E3 **La Roda** Spain
205 K5 **La Romana** Dom. Rep.
187 H3 **La Ronge** Canada
187 H3 **La Ronge, Lac** l. Canada
206 D2 **La Rosa** Mex.
206 D1 **La Rosita** Mex.
124 D3 **Larrimah** Australia
129 B2 **Larsen Ice Shelf** ice feature Antarctica
158 M3 **Larsmo** Fin.
159 J4 **Larvik** Norway
197 H2 **La Sal Junction** U.S.A.
203 G2 **LaSalle** Canada
190 C5 **La Salle** U.S.A.
206 A1 **Las Ánimas, Punta** pt Mex.
188 E4 **La Sarre** Canada
213 D2 **Las Aves, Islas** is Venez.
206 B1 **Las Avispas** Mex.
215 B2 **Las Cabras** Chile
189 I4 **La Scie** Canada
195 F5 **Las Cruces** U.S.A.
205 J5 **La Selle, Pic** mt. Haiti
215 B1 **La Serena** Chile
206 D2 **Las Esperanças** Mex.
167 G1 **La Seu d'Urgell** Spain
215 E3 **Las Flores** Arg.
141 F5 **Lāshār, Rūd-e** r. Iran
187 H4 **Lashburn** Canada
141 F4 **Lāsh-e Joway** Afgh.
215 C2 **Las Heras** Arg.
213 B4 **Las Hermosas, Parque Nacional** nat. park Col.
206 C2 **Las Herreras** Mex.
146 B4 **Lashio** Myanmar
141 G4 **Lashkar Gāh** Afgh.
215 B3 **Las Lajas** Arg.
213 D3 **Las Lajitas** Venez.
212 D2 **Las Lomitas** Arg.
167 C4 **Las Marismas** marsh Spain
212 C7 **Las Martinetas** Arg.
213 D2 **Las Mercedes** Venez.
206 C2 **Las Nieves** Mex.
**La Société, Archipel de** is Fr. Polynesia see **Society Islands**
196 D5 **Las Palmas** watercourse Mex.
176 A2 **Las Palmas de Gran Canaria** Canary Is
170 C2 **La Spezia** Italy
215 F2 **Las Piedras** Uruguay
212 C6 **Las Plumas** Arg.
206 G5 **Las Quebradas** Guat.
215 E2 **Las Rosas** Arg.
194 B3 **Lassen Peak** vol. U.S.A.
194 B3 **Lassen Volcanic National Park** U.S.A.
206 I7 **Las Tablas** Panama
212 D3 **Las Termas** Arg.
187 H4 **Last Mountain Lake** Canada
215 C1 **Las Tórtolas, Cerro** mt. Chile
178 B4 **Lastoursville** Gabon
170 G3 **Lastovo** i. Croatia
206 A2 **Las Tres Vírgenes, Volcán** vol. Mex.
213 D3 **Las Trincheras** Venez.
165 F2 **Lastrup** Germany
205 I4 **Las Tunas** Cuba
195 F6 **Las Varas** Chihuahua Mex.
206 C3 **Las Varas** Nayarit Mex.
215 D1 **Las Varillas** Arg.
195 F5 **Las Vegas** NM U.S.A.
197 E3 **Las Vegas** NV U.S.A.
167 D3 **Las Villuercas** mt. Spain
189 I3 **La Tabatière** Canada
210 C4 **Latacunga** Ecuador
213 B5 **La Tagua** Col.
136 E4 **Latakia** Syria
191 H2 **Latchford** Canada
145 F5 **Latehar** India
**La Teste** France see **La Teste-de-Buch**
166 D4 **La Teste-de-Buch** France
164 F2 **Lathen** Germany
162 E2 **Latheron** U.K.
170 E4 **Latina** Italy
215 D2 **La Toma** Arg.
213 D2 **La Tortuga, Isla** i. Venez.
127 G8 **Latrobe** Australia
202 D4 **Latrobe** U.S.A.
164 E2 **Lattrop** Neth.
191 H2 **Latulipe** Canada
188 F4 **La Tuque** Canada
143 B2 **Latur** India
159 M4 **Latvia** country Europe
212 C1 **Lauca, Parque Nacional** nat. park Chile
168 F5 **Lauchhammer** Germany
162 F5 **Lauder** U.K.
167 E1 **Laudio** Spain
165 H1 **Lauenbrück** Germany
165 I1 **Lauenburg (Elbe)** Germany
165 J5 **Lauf an der Pegnitz** Germany
166 H3 **Laufen** Switz.
190 D2 **Laughing Fish Point** U.S.A.
159 M4 **Lauka** Estonia
158 O1 **Laukvik** Norway
154 A3 **Laun** Thai.
127 G8 **Launceston** Australia
161 C7 **Launceston** U.K.
163 B5 **Laune** r. Ireland
154 A2 **Launglon Bok Islands** Myanmar
215 B4 **La Unión** Chile
213 A4 **La Unión** Col.
207 H5 **La Unión** El Salvador
206 D4 **La Unión** Mex.
153 B3 **Laur** Phil.
124 E3 **Laura** Qld Australia
126 C4 **Laura** S.A. Australia
213 D3 **La Urbana** Venez.
203 F5 **Laurel** DE U.S.A.
199 F6 **Laurel** MS U.S.A.
194 E2 **Laurel** MT U.S.A.
202 D4 **Laurel Hill** hills U.S.A.
202 A6 **Laurel River Lake** U.S.A.
162 F4 **Laurencekirk** U.K.
189 F4 **Laurentides, Réserve Faunique des** nature res. Canada
170 F4 **Lauria** Italy
127 J3 **Laurieton** Australia
201 E5 **Laurinburg** U.S.A.
190 C2 **Laurium** U.S.A.
168 C7 **Lausanne** Switz.
155 E3 **Laut** i. Indon.
215 B3 **Lautaro** Chile
165 H4 **Lautersbach (Hessen)** Germany
155 E3 **Laut Kecil, Kepulauan** is Indon.
125 H3 **Lautoka** Fiji
158 O3 **Lauvuskylä** Fin.
188 F4 **Laval** Canada
166 D2 **Laval** France
167 F3 **La Vall d'Uixó** Spain
140 D5 **Lāvān** Iran
140 D5 **Lāvān** i. Iran
170 F1 **Lavant** r. Austria/Slovenia
212 B5 **Lavapié, Punta** pt Chile
140 C4 **Lāvar** Iran
207 F4 **La Venta** tourist site Mex.
**La Ventana, Serra de** hills Arg. see **Ventana, Sierra de la**
191 I2 **La Vérendrye, Réserve Faunique** nature res. Canada
126 E7 **Lavers Hill** Australia
124 C4 **Laverton** Australia
206 D2 **La Víbora** Mex.
213 D2 **La Victoria** Venez.
191 G2 **Lavigne** Canada
194 E2 **Lavina** U.S.A.
214 D3 **Lavras** Brazil
215 G1 **Lavras do Sul** Brazil
181 I3 **Lavumisa** Swaziland
144 B2 **Lawa** Pak.
154 B4 **Lawit, Gunung** mt. Malaysia
137 I7 **Lawqah** waterhole Saudi Arabia
176 B3 **Lawra** Ghana
198 E4 **Lawrence** KS U.S.A.
203 H3 **Lawrence** MA U.S.A.
201 C5 **Lawrenceburg** U.S.A.
203 J2 **Lawrence Station** Canada
202 E6 **Lawrenceville** U.S.A.
199 D5 **Lawton** U.S.A.
134 B4 **Lawz, Jabal al** mt. Saudi Arabia
159 K4 **Laxå** Sweden
180 E3 **Laxey** S. Africa
160 C3 **Laxey** U.K.
162 C2 **Laxford, Loch** inlet U.K.
186 C4 **Lax Kw'alaams** Canada
162 □ **Laxo** U.K.
137 J4 **Laylān** Iraq
123 H2 **Laysan Island** U.S.A.
196 A2 **Laytonville** U.S.A.
144 B3 **Layyah** Pak.
206 B3 **La Zacatosa, Picacho** mt. Mex.
171 I2 **Lazarevac** Serbia
173 F7 **Lazarevskoye** Rus. Fed.
195 D6 **Lázaro Cárdenas** Mex.
204 A2 **Lázaro Cárdenas** Mex.
206 D4 **Lázaro Cárdenas** Mex.
206 C2 **Lázaro Cárdenas, Presa** resr Mex.
215 F2 **Lazcano** Uruguay
159 M5 **Lazdijai** Lith.
150 C3 **Lazo** Primorskiy Kray Rus. Fed.
133 O3 **Lazo** Rus. Fed.
154 B2 **Leach** Cambodia
190 E2 **Leach Island** Canada
198 C2 **Lead** U.S.A.
187 H4 **Leader** Canada
127 H4 **Leadville** Australia
195 F4 **Leadville** U.S.A.
199 F6 **Leaf** r. U.S.A.
187 I3 **Leaf Rapids** Canada
199 D6 **Leakey** U.S.A.
191 F4 **Leamington** Canada
197 F2 **Leamington** U.S.A.
161 F5 **Leamington Spa, Royal** U.K.
149 E5 **Le'an** China
163 B5 **Leane, Lough** l. Ireland
163 B6 **Leap** Ireland
187 H4 **Leask** Canada
161 G6 **Leatherhead** U.K.
198 E4 **Leavenworth** KS U.S.A.
194 B2 **Leavenworth** WA U.S.A.
196 C2 **Leavitt Peak** U.S.A.
164 E5 **Lebach** Germany
153 C5 **Lebak** Phil.
136 E5 **Lebanon** country Asia
190 D5 **Lebanon** IN U.S.A.
198 D4 **Lebanon** KS U.S.A.
199 E4 **Lebanon** MO U.S.A.
203 G3 **Lebanon** NH U.S.A.
203 F4 **Lebanon** NJ U.S.A.
202 A5 **Lebanon** OH U.S.A.
194 B2 **Lebanon** OR U.S.A.
203 E4 **Lebanon** PA U.S.A.
201 C4 **Lebanon** TN U.S.A.
138 E4 **Lebap** Turkm.
164 C3 **Lebbeke** Belgium
172 F4 **Lebedyan'** Rus. Fed.
173 E5 **Lebedyn** Ukr.
166 E3 **Le Blanc** France
168 H3 **Lębork** Poland
181 H2 **Lebowakgomo** S. Africa
167 C4 **Lebrija** Spain
168 H3 **Łebsko, Jezioro** lag. Poland
215 B3 **Lebu** Chile
164 B4 **Le Cateau-Cambrésis** France
164 B4 **Le Catelet** France
171 H4 **Lecce** Italy
170 C2 **Lecco** Italy
168 E7 **Lech** r. Austria/Germany
171 I6 **Lechaina** Greece
149 D5 **Lechang** China
164 C5 **Le Chesne** France
168 E7 **Lechtaler Alpen** mts Austria
168 D3 **Leck** Germany
166 G3 **Le Creusot** France
166 E5 **Lectoure** France
154 B5 **Ledang, Gunung** mt. Malaysia
161 E5 **Ledbury** U.K.
167 D2 **Ledesma** Spain
162 D2 **Ledmore** U.K.
172 E1 **Ledmozero** Rus. Fed.
149 C7 **Ledong** China
148 B2 **Ledu** China
186 G4 **Leduc** Canada
203 G3 **Lee** U.S.A.
198 E2 **Leech Lake** U.S.A.
160 F4 **Leeds** U.K.
203 H2 **Leeds Junction** U.S.A.
161 B7 **Leedstown** U.K.
164 E1 **Leek** Neth.
161 E4 **Leek** U.K.
164 D3 **Leende** Neth.
202 D4 **Leeper** U.S.A.
164 F1 **Leer (Ostfriesland)** Germany
201 D6 **Leesburg** FL U.S.A.
202 E5 **Leesburg** VA U.S.A.
165 H2 **Leese** Germany
199 E6 **Leesville** U.S.A.
202 C4 **Leesville Lake** U.S.A.
127 G5 **Leeton** Australia
180 D6 **Leeu-Gamka** S. Africa
164 D1 **Leeuwarden** Neth.
124 B5 **Leeuwin, Cape** Australia
196 C3 **Lee Vining** U.S.A.
205 L5 **Leeward Islands** Caribbean Sea
136 D4 **Lefka** Cyprus
171 I5 **Lefkada** Greece
171 I5 **Lefkada** i. Greece
**Lefkara** Cyprus see **Pano Lefkara**
171 I5 **Lefkimmi** Greece
**Lefkosia** Cyprus see **Nicosia**
153 B3 **Legazpi** Phil.
164 F2 **Legden** Germany
127 G8 **Legges Tor** mt. Australia
196 A2 **Leggett** U.S.A.
170 D2 **Legnago** Italy
168 H5 **Legnica** Poland
144 D2 **Leh** India
166 E2 **Le Havre** France
203 F4 **Lehighton** U.S.A.
158 O3 **Lehmo** Fin.
165 K2 **Lehnin** Germany
165 I2 **Lehre** Germany
165 H2 **Lehrte** Germany
158 M3 **Lehtimäki** Fin.
180 D1 **Lehututu** Botswana
168 G7 **Leibnitz** Austria
161 F5 **Leicester** U.K.
124 D3 **Leichhardt** r. Australia
164 C2 **Leiden** Neth.
126 C3 **Leigh** watercourse Australia
128 E2 **Leigh** N.Z.
160 E4 **Leigh** U.K.
126 C3 **Leigh Creek** Australia
161 G6 **Leighton Buzzard** U.K.
165 G5 **Leimen** Germany
165 H2 **Leine** r. Germany
165 I3 **Leinefelde** Germany
163 E5 **Leinster, Mount** h. Ireland
171 L6 **Leipsoi** i. Greece
165 K3 **Leipzig** Germany
158 K2 **Leiranger** Norway
167 B3 **Leiria** Port.
159 I4 **Leirvik** Norway
149 C5 **Leishan** China
149 D5 **Lei Shui** r. China
165 K3 **Leisnig** Germany
200 C4 **Leitchfield** U.S.A.
213 B4 **Leiva, Cerro** mt. Col.
163 E4 **Leixlip** Ireland
149 D5 **Leiyang** China
149 E4 **Leiyang** China
149 D6 **Leizhou** China
149 C6 **Leizhou Bandao** pen. China
149 D6 **Leizhou Wan** b. China
158 J2 **Leka** Norway
178 B4 **Lékana** Congo
170 C6 **Le Kef** Tunisia
180 B4 **Lekkersing** S. Africa
178 B4 **Lékoni** Gabon
159 K3 **Leksand** Sweden
158 O3 **Leksozero, Ozero** l. Rus. Fed.
190 E3 **Leland** MI U.S.A.
199 F5 **Leland** MS U.S.A.
176 A3 **Lélouma** Guinea
164 D2 **Lelystad** Neth.
212 C9 **Le Maire, Estrecho de** sea chan. Arg.
**Léman, Lac** l. France/Switz. see **Geneva, Lake**
166 E2 **Le Mans** France
198 D3 **Le Mars** U.S.A.
164 F5 **Lemberg** France
165 G2 **Lembruch** Germany
214 C3 **Leme** Brazil
164 E2 **Lemele** Neth.
153 B3 **Lemery** Phil.
**Lemesos** Cyprus see **Limassol**
165 G2 **Lemgo** Germany
159 N3 **Lemi** Fin.
185 L3 **Lemieux Islands** Canada
158 N1 **Lemmenjoen kansallispuisto** nat. park Fin.
164 D2 **Lemmer** Neth.
198 C2 **Lemmon** U.S.A.
197 G5 **Lemmon, Mount** U.S.A.
166 D2 **Le Mont-St-Michel** tourist site France
196 C3 **Lemoore** U.S.A.
189 G2 **Le Moyne, Lac** l. Canada
145 H5 **Lemro** r. Myanmar
170 G4 **Le Murge** hills Italy
159 J4 **Lemvig** Denmark
146 C1 **Lena** r. Rus. Fed.
190 C4 **Lena** U.S.A.
133 N3 **Lena Pillars Nature Park** tourist site Rus. Fed.
145 E2 **Lenchung Tso** salt l. China
211 J4 **Lençóis Maranhenses, Parque Nacional dos** nat. park Brazil
141 F3 **Lengar** Iran
141 E4 **Lengbarūt** Iran
139 G4 **Lenger** Kazakh.
165 F2 **Lengerich** Germany
154 B4 **Lenggong Valley** tourist site Malaysia
148 A2 **Lenglong Ling** mts China
149 D5 **Lengshuijiang** China
215 B1 **Lengua de Vaca, Punta** pt Chile
161 H6 **Lenham** U.K.
159 K4 **Lenhovda** Sweden
139 G5 **Lenin** Tajik.
173 H7 **Lenina, Kanal imeni** canal Rus. Fed.
**Leninabad** Uzbek. see **Qanliko'l**
**Leningrad** Rus. Fed. see **St Petersburg**
139 G5 **Leningrad** Tajik.
173 F6 **Leningradskaya** Rus. Fed.
172 E3 **Leningradskaya Oblast'** admin. div. Rus. Fed.
133 S3 **Leningradskiy** Rus. Fed.
150 D2 **Lenino** Rus. Fed.
139 H5 **Lenin Peak** Tajik.
139 G4 **Leninpol'** Kyrg.
**Leninsk** Kazakh. see **Baykonyr**
173 H5 **Leninsk** Rus. Fed.
172 F4 **Leninskiy** Rus. Fed.
146 A1 **Leninsk-Kuznetskiy** Rus. Fed.
172 H3 **Leninskoye** Rus. Fed.
165 F3 **Lenne** r. Germany
127 J2 **Lennox Head** Australia
201 D5 **Lenoir** U.S.A.
203 G3 **Lenox** U.S.A.
166 F1 **Lens** France
133 M3 **Lensk** Rus. Fed.
173 G7 **Lent'ekhi** Georgia
168 H7 **Lenti** Hungary
170 F6 **Lentini** Sicily Italy
165 J1 **Lenzen** Germany
176 B3 **Léo** Burkina Faso
168 G7 **Leoben** Austria
161 E5 **Leominster** U.K.
203 H3 **Leominster** U.S.A.
213 A3 **León** r. Col.
206 D3 **León** Mex.
206 H5 **León** Nicaragua
167 D1 **León** Spain
179 B6 **Leonardville** Namibia
136 E4 **Leonarisson** Cyprus
127 F7 **Leongatha** Australia
124 C4 **Leonora** Australia
214 D3 **Leopoldina** Brazil
187 H4 **Leoville** Canada
181 G1 **Lephalala** r. S. Africa
181 G1 **Lephalale** S. Africa
179 C6 **Lephepe** Botswana
181 F5 **Lephoi** S. Africa
149 E4 **Leping** China
166 G4 **Le Pont-de-Claix** France
158 N3 **Leppävirta** Fin.
139 I3 **Lepsi** Kazakh.
139 J3 **Lepsi** Kazakh.
139 I3 **Lepsi** r. Kazakh.
166 F4 **Le Puy-en-Velay** France
164 B4 **Le Quesnoy** France
181 G1 **Lerala** Botswana
181 G4 **Leratswana** S. Africa
177 D4 **Léré** Chad
213 C5 **Lérida** Col.
**Lérida** Spain see **Lleida**
137 L2 **Lerik** Azer.
167 E1 **Lerma** Spain
173 G6 **Lermontov** Rus. Fed.
150 D1 **Lermontovka** Rus. Fed.
171 L6 **Leros** i. Greece
190 C5 **Le Roy** U.S.A.
188 E2 **Le Roy, Lac** l. Canada
159 K4 **Lerum** Sweden
162 □ **Lerwick** U.K.
171 K5 **Lesbos** i. Greece
205 J5 **Les Cayes** Haiti
189 G4 **Les Escoumins** Canada
203 I1 **Les Étroits** Canada
149 B4 **Leshan** China
171 I3 **Leskovac** Serbia
162 E4 **Leslie** U.K.
166 B2 **Lesneven** France
172 J3 **Lesnoy** Rus. Fed.
150 D1 **Lesopil'noye** Rus. Fed.
132 K4 **Lesosibirsk** Rus. Fed.
181 H4 **Lesotho** country Africa
150 C2 **Lesozavodsk** Rus. Fed.
166 D3 **Les Sables-d'Olonne** France
164 D4 **Lesse** r. Belgium
205 K6 **Lesser Antilles** is Caribbean Sea
137 I1 **Lesser Caucasus** mts Asia
186 G3 **Lesser Slave Lake** Canada
186 G3 **Lesser Slave Lake Provincial Park** Canada
147 D7 **Lesser Sunda Islands** is Indon.
164 B4 **Lessines** Belgium
158 N3 **Lestijärvi** Fin.
158 N3 **Lestijärvi** l. Fin.
**Lesvos** i. Greece see **Lesbos**
168 H5 **Leszno** Poland
181 I1 **Letaba** S. Africa
161 G6 **Letchworth Garden City** U.K.
166 G3 **Le Télégraphe** h. France
144 D4 **Leteri** India
145 H5 **Letha Range** mts Myanmar
186 G5 **Lethbridge** Canada
210 G3 **Lethem** Guyana
147 E7 **Leti, Kepulauan** is Indon.
210 E4 **Leticia** Col.
148 F2 **Leting** China
181 F2 **Letlhakeng** Botswana
161 I7 **Le Touquet-Paris-Plage** France
166 E1 **Le Tréport** France
181 I1 **Letsitele** S. Africa
154 A3 **Letsok-aw Kyun** i. Myanmar
181 F3 **Letsopa** S. Africa
163 D3 **Letterkenny** Ireland
155 C2 **Letung** Indon.
165 J2 **Letzlingen** Germany
162 F4 **Leuchars** U.K.
172 G1 **Leunovo** Rus. Fed.
197 G4 **Leupp Corner** U.S.A.
164 D2 **Leusden** Neth.
155 A2 **Leuser, Gunung** mt. Indon.
165 I5 **Leutershausen** Germany
164 C4 **Leuven** Belgium
197 G2 **Levan** U.S.A.
158 J3 **Levanger** Norway
170 C2 **Levanto** Italy
170 E5 **Levanzo, Isola di** i. Sicily Italy
173 H7 **Levashi** Rus. Fed.
199 C5 **Levelland** U.S.A.
160 G4 **Leven** England U.K.
162 F4 **Leven** Scotland U.K.
162 C4 **Leven, Loch** inlet U.K.
162 E4 **Leven, Loch** l. U.K.
124 C3 **Lévêque, Cape** Australia
190 E3 **Levering** U.S.A.
164 E3 **Leverkusen** Germany
169 I6 **Levice** Slovakia
128 E4 **Levin** N.Z.
189 F4 **Lévis** Canada
171 L6 **Levitha** i. Greece
203 G4 **Levittown** NY U.S.A.
203 F4 **Levittown** PA U.S.A.
171 K3 **Levski** Bulg.
161 H7 **Lewes** U.K.
203 F5 **Lewes** U.S.A.
162 B2 **Lewis, Isle of** i. U.K.
202 E4 **Lewisburg** PA U.S.A.
202 C6 **Lewisburg** WV U.S.A.
128 D5 **Lewis Pass** N.Z.
194 D1 **Lewis Range** mts U.S.A.
201 C5 **Lewis Smith, Lake** U.S.A.
197 G6 **Lewis Springs** U.S.A.
194 C2 **Lewiston** ID U.S.A.
203 H2 **Lewiston** ME U.S.A.
190 B4 **Lewiston** MN U.S.A.
190 B5 **Lewistown** IL U.S.A.
194 E2 **Lewistown** MT U.S.A.
202 E4 **Lewistown** PA U.S.A.
199 E5 **Lewisville** U.S.A.
199 D5 **Lewisville, Lake** U.S.A.
190 C5 **Lexington** IL U.S.A.
200 C4 **Lexington** KY U.S.A.
198 E4 **Lexington** MO U.S.A.
201 D5 **Lexington** NC U.S.A.
198 D3 **Lexington** NE U.S.A.
201 B5 **Lexington** TN U.S.A.
202 D6 **Lexington** VA U.S.A.
202 E5 **Lexington Park** U.S.A.
181 I1 **Leydsdorp** S. Africa
149 C5 **Leye** China
137 K3 **Leyla Dāgh** mt. Iran
153 C4 **Leyte** i. Phil.
153 C4 **Leyte Gulf** Phil.
171 H4 **Lezhë** Albania
149 B4 **Lezhi** China
173 E5 **L'gov** Rus. Fed.
**Lhari** China see **Si'erdingka**
145 G2 **Lharigarbo** China
145 G3 **Lhasa** China
145 G3 **Lhasa He** r. China
145 F3 **Lhazê** China
145 F3 **Lhazhong** China
155 A1 **Lhokseumawe** Indon.
154 A4 **Lhoksukon** Indon.
145 H3 **Lhorong** China
145 H3 **Lhünzê** China
**Lhünzhub** China see **Poindo**
154 A1 **Li, Mae** r. Thai.
171 J5 **Liakoura** mt. Greece
149 E5 **Liancheng** China
164 A5 **Liancourt** France
151 B6 **Liancourt Rocks** i. N. Pacific Ocean
153 C4 **Lianga** Phil.
153 C4 **Lianga Bay** Phil.
148 D1 **Liangcheng** China
148 C3 **Liangdang** China
148 B3 **Lianghekou** China
149 C4 **Liangping** China
149 B5 **Liangwang Shan** mts China
148 C2 **Liangzhen** China
149 E4 **Liangzi Hu** l. China
149 D5 **Lianhua** China
149 E6 **Lianhua Shan** mts China
149 F5 **Lianjiang** Fujian China
149 D6 **Lianjiang** Guangdong China
149 D5 **Liannan** China
149 E5 **Lianping** China
149 D5 **Lianshan** Guangdong China
152 A3 **Lianshan** Liaoning China
148 F3 **Lianshui** China
149 D5 **Lianyuan** China
148 F3 **Lianyungang** Jiangsu China
148 F3 **Lianyungang** Jiangsu China
149 D5 **Lianzhou** China
152 F1 **Lianzhushan** China
148 E2 **Liaocheng** China
152 B3 **Liaodong Bandao** pen. China
152 A3 **Liaodong Wan** b. China
152 B2 **Liao He** r. China
152 B3 **Liaohe Kou** r. mouth China
152 B3 **Liaoning** prov. China
152 B3 **Liaoyang** China
152 C2 **Liaoyuan** China
152 B3 **Liaozhong** China
171 H5 **Liapades** Greece
186 E2 **Liard** r. Canada
186 D3 **Liard River** Canada

141 G5 Liari Pak.
162 C3 Liathach mt. U.K.
136 F4 Liban, Jebel mts Lebanon
213 B3 Libano Col.
194 D1 Libby U.S.A.
178 B3 Libenge Dem. Rep. Congo
199 C4 Liberal U.S.A.
168 G5 Liberec Czech Rep.
176 B4 Liberia country Africa
206 H6 Liberia Costa Rica
213 C2 Libertad Venez.
213 C2 Libertad Venez.
190 B6 Liberty IL U.S.A.
203 I2 Liberty ME U.S.A.
198 E4 Liberty MO U.S.A.
203 F4 Liberty NY U.S.A.
199 E6 Liberty TX U.S.A.
164 D5 Libin Belgium
153 B3 Libmanan Phil.
149 C5 Libo China
181 H5 Libode S. Africa
154 A4 Libong, Ko i. Thai.
166 D4 Libourne France
178 A3 Libreville Gabon
153 C5 Libuganon r. Phil.
177 D2 Libya country Africa
177 E2 Libyan Desert Egypt/Libya
177 E1 Libyan Plateau Egypt
215 B2 Licantén Chile
170 E6 Licata Sicily Italy
137 H2 Lice Turkey
165 G4 Lich Germany
161 F5 Lichfield U.K.
179 D5 Lichinga Moz.
165 J4 Lichte Germany
165 G3 Lichtenau Germany
181 G3 Lichtenburg S. Africa
165 J4 Lichtenfels Germany
164 E3 Lichtenvoorde Neth.
149 C4 Lichuan Hubei China
149 E5 Lichuan Jiangxi China
202 B5 Licking r. U.S.A.
172 C4 Lida Belarus
196 D3 Lida U.S.A.
180 C2 Lidfontein Namibia
159 K4 Lidköping Sweden
158 K2 Lidsjöberg Sweden
165 H2 Liebenau Germany
165 I2 Liebenburg Germany
165 L2 Liebenwalde Germany
124 D4 Liebig, Mount Australia
166 I3 Liechtenstein country Europe
164 D4 Liège Belgium
158 O3 Lieksa Fin.
169 L2 Lielupe r. Latvia
159 N4 Lielvārde Latvia
158 L3 Lien Sweden
178 C3 Lienart Dem. Rep. Congo
154 D3 Liên Nghia Vietnam
168 F7 Lienz Austria
159 M4 Liepāja Latvia
164 C3 Lier Belgium
164 D3 Lieshout Neth.
164 A4 Liévin France
191 J2 Lièvre, Rivière du r. Canada
168 G7 Liezen Austria
163 E4 Liffey r. Ireland
163 D3 Lifford Ireland
215 C4 Lifi Mahuida mt. Arg.
125 G4 Lifou i. New Caledonia
153 B3 Ligao Phil.
159 N4 Līgatne Latvia
127 G2 Lightning Ridge Australia
179 D5 Ligonha r. Moz.
190 E5 Ligonier U.S.A.
206 B2 Ligui Mex.
166 I5 Ligurian Sea France/Italy
124 F2 Lihir Group is P.N.G.
149 C5 Lihua China
Lihue U.S.A. see Līhu'e
196 □2 Līhu'e U.S.A.
149 D5 Li Jiang r. China
148 F2 Lijin China
154 B1 Lik, Nam r. Laos
179 C5 Likasi Dem. Rep. Congo
186 E4 Likely Canada
172 E3 Likhoslavl' Rus. Fed.
155 C2 Liku Indon.
172 G3 Likurga Rus. Fed.
170 C3 L'Île-Rousse Corsica France
165 G1 Lilienthal Germany
149 D5 Liling China
144 C2 Lilla Pak.
159 K4 Lilla Edet Sweden
164 C3 Lille Belgium
166 F1 Lille France
Lille Bælt sea chan. Denmark see Little Belt
159 J3 Lillehammer Norway
164 A4 Lillers France
159 J4 Lillesand Norway
159 J4 Lillestrøm Norway
190 E4 Lilley U.S.A.
158 K3 Lillholmsjö Sweden
186 E4 Lillooet Canada
186 E4 Lillooet r. Canada
145 H4 Lilong India
179 D5 Lilongwe Malawi
153 B4 Liloy Phil.
126 C4 Lilydale S.A. Australia
127 G8 Lilydale Tas. Australia
210 C6 Lima Peru
(City Plan 116)
194 D2 Lima MT U.S.A.
202 A4 Lima OH U.S.A.
140 E5 Līmah Oman
137 L2 Liman Azer.
173 H6 Liman Rus. Fed.
215 B1 Limarí r. Chile
145 E2 Lima Ringma Tso salt l. China
136 D4 Limassol Cyprus
163 E2 Limavady U.K.
215 C3 Limay r. Arg.
215 C3 Limay Mahuida Arg.
159 N4 Limbaži Latvia
176 C4 Limbe Cameroon
155 E3 Limbungan Indon.
165 G4 Limburg an der Lahn Germany
154 □ Lim Chu Kang Sing.
154 □ Lim Chu Kang h. Sing.
180 E4 Lime Acres S. Africa
214 C3 Limeira Brazil
163 C5 Limerick Ireland
190 A4 Lime Springs U.S.A.
203 J1 Limestone U.S.A.
158 K2 Limingen Norway
158 K2 Limingen l. Norway
203 H3 Limington U.S.A.
158 N2 Liminka Fin.
171 K5 Limnos i. Greece
203 F2 Limoges Canada
166 E4 Limoges France
Limón Costa Rica see Puerto Limón
206 H5 Limón Hond.
195 G4 Limon U.S.A.
136 E3 Limonlu Turkey
166 E4 Limousin reg. France
166 F5 Limoux France
181 J1 Limpopo r. Africa
181 H1 Limpopo prov. S. Africa
181 I1 Limpopo National Park S. Africa
140 A4 Līnah well Saudi Arabia
158 O1 Linakhamari Rus. Fed.
149 F4 Lin'an China
153 A4 Linapacan i. Phil.
153 A4 Linapacan Strait Phil.
215 B2 Linares Chile
207 E2 Linares Mex.
167 E3 Linares Spain
146 C4 Lincang China
148 E2 Lincheng China
Linchuan China see Fuzhou
215 E2 Lincoln Arg.
161 G4 Lincoln U.K.
196 B2 Lincoln CA U.S.A.
190 C5 Lincoln IL U.S.A.
203 I2 Lincoln ME U.S.A.
191 F3 Lincoln MI U.S.A.
198 D3 Lincoln NE U.S.A.
203 H2 Lincoln NH U.S.A.
194 A2 Lincoln City U.S.A.
191 F4 Lincoln Park U.S.A.
161 G4 Lincolnshire Wolds hills U.K.
203 I2 Lincolnville U.S.A.
214 E1 Linda, Serra hills Brazil
165 K2 Lindau Germany
168 D7 Lindau (Bodensee) Germany
165 G4 Linden Germany
211 G2 Linden Guyana
201 C5 Linden AL U.S.A.
201 C5 Linden TN U.S.A.
190 A2 Linden Grove U.S.A.
Lindenow Fjord inlet Greenland see Kangerlussuatsiaq
165 F2 Lindern (Oldenburg) Germany
159 I4 Lindesnes c. Norway
178 C3 Lindi r. Dem. Rep. Congo
179 D4 Lindi Tanz.
Lindisfarne i. U.K. see Holy Island
181 G3 Lindley S. Africa
148 F1 Lindong China
203 J1 Lindsay N.B. Canada
191 H3 Lindsay Ont. Canada
196 C3 Lindsay U.S.A.
123 I3 Line Islands S. Pacific Ocean
148 D2 Linfen China
143 A3 Linganamakki Reservoir India
153 B2 Lingayen Phil.
153 B2 Lingayen Gulf Phil.
148 D3 Lingbao China
148 E3 Lingbi China
149 D5 Lingchuan Guangxi China
148 D3 Lingchuan Shanxi China
181 G6 Lingelethu S. Africa
181 F6 Lingelihle S. Africa
164 F2 Lingen (Ems) Germany
155 B3 Lingga, Kepulauan is Indon.
152 A3 Linghai China
153 C5 Lingig Phil.
153 A5 Lingkabau Sabah Malaysia
194 F3 Lingle U.S.A.
149 D5 Lingling China
178 C3 Lingomo Dem. Rep. Congo
148 E2 Lingqiu China
149 C6 Lingshan China
149 C7 Lingshui China
149 C7 Lingshui Wan b. China
143 B2 Lingsugur India
148 C3 Lingtai China
149 C7 Lingtou China
176 A3 Linguère Senegal
149 D5 Lingui China
148 C2 Lingwu China
148 F1 Lingyuan China
149 C5 Lingyun China
144 D2 Lingzi Tang reg. Aksai Chin
154 C2 Linh, Ngok mt. Vietnam
149 F4 Linhai China
214 E2 Linhares Brazil
Linh Cam Vietnam see Duc Tho
Linhe China see Bayannur
203 H1 Linière Canada
137 I3 Līnik, Chiyā-ē mt. Iraq
152 D3 Linjiang China
159 K4 Linköping Sweden
152 F1 Linkou China
149 D4 Linli China
162 E5 Linlithgow U.K.
148 D2 Linlü Shan mt. China
196 A1 Linn, Mount U.S.A.
162 C4 Linnhe, Loch inlet U.K.
164 E4 Linnich Germany
148 E2 Linqing China
148 F2 Linqu China
148 E3 Linquan China
214 C3 Lins Brazil
148 F3 Linshu China
149 C4 Linshui China
148 B3 Lintan China
148 B3 Lintao China
198 C2 Linton U.S.A.
148 C3 Lintong China
148 F1 Linxi China
148 B3 Linxia China
148 D2 Linxian China
149 D4 Linxiang China
148 E2 Linyi Shandong China
148 F3 Linyi Shandong China
148 D3 Linyi Shanxi China
148 E3 Linying China
168 G6 Linz Austria
148 A2 Linze China
166 F5 Lion, Golfe du g. France
191 G3 Lion's Head Canada
203 F4 Lionville U.S.A.
178 B3 Liouesso Congo
153 B3 Lipa Phil.
170 F5 Lipari Isole Lipari Italy
170 F5 Lipari, Isola i. Isole Lipari Italy
170 F5 Lipari, Isole is Italy
173 F4 Lipetsk Rus. Fed.
173 F4 Lipetskaya Oblast' admin. div. Rus. Fed.
172 F2 Lipin Bor Rus. Fed.
149 C5 Liping China
171 I1 Lipova Romania
150 B2 Lipovtsy Rus. Fed.
165 E3 Lippe r. Germany
165 G3 Lippstadt Germany
144 E3 Lipti Lekh pass Nepal
127 F7 Liptrap, Cape Australia
149 D5 Lipu China
178 D3 Lira Uganda
178 B4 Liranga Congo
153 C6 Lirung Indon.
138 E1 Lisakovsk Kazakh.
178 C3 Lisala Dem. Rep. Congo
163 D3 Lisbellaw U.K.
Lisboa Port. see Lisbon
167 B3 Lisbon Port.
190 C5 Lisbon IL U.S.A.
203 H2 Lisbon ME U.S.A.
198 D2 Lisbon ND U.S.A.
203 H2 Lisbon NH U.S.A.
202 C4 Lisbon OH U.S.A.
163 E3 Lisburn U.K.
163 B5 Liscannor Bay Ireland
163 B4 Lisdoonvarna Ireland
149 F5 Lishan Taiwan
152 C2 Lishu China
148 F4 Lishui Jiangsu China
149 F4 Lishui Zhejiang China
149 D4 Li Shui r. China
123 H2 Lisianski Island U.S.A.
166 E2 Lisieux France
161 C7 Liskeard U.K.
173 F5 Liski Rus. Fed.
164 A5 L'Isle-Adam France
166 G5 L'Isle-sur-la-Sorgue France
127 J2 Lismore Australia
163 D5 Lismore Ireland
162 C4 Lismore i. U.K.
163 D3 Lisnarrick U.K.
163 D3 Lisnaskea U.K.
191 G4 Listowel Canada
163 B5 Listowel Ireland
158 K3 Lit Sweden
149 C6 Litang Guangxi China
146 C3 Litang Sichuan China
211 H3 Litani r. Fr. Guiana/Suriname
Lītāni r. Lebanon see Lîtâni, Nahr el
136 E5 Lîtâni, Nahr el r. Lebanon
196 B1 Litchfield CA U.S.A.
200 B4 Litchfield IL U.S.A.
193 H2 Litchfield MN U.S.A.
166 D4 Lit-et-Mixe France
127 I4 Lithgow Australia
159 M5 Lithuania country Europe
203 E4 Lititz U.S.A.
168 G5 Litoměřice Czech Rep.
201 E7 Little Abaco i. Bahamas
201 E7 Little Bahama Bank sea feature Bahamas
128 E2 Little Barrier i. N.Z.
190 D3 Little Bay de Noc U.S.A.
159 J5 Little Belt sea chan. Denmark
194 E2 Little Belt Mountains U.S.A.
205 H5 Little Cayman i. Cayman Is
197 H4 Little Colorado r. U.S.A.
197 F3 Little Creek Peak U.S.A.
191 G3 Little Current Canada
188 C3 Little Current r. Canada
161 D7 Little Dart r. U.K.
126 D6 Little Desert National Park Australia
203 F5 Little Egg Harbor inlet U.S.A.
201 F7 Little Exuma i. Bahamas
198 E2 Little Falls MN U.S.A.
203 F3 Little Falls NY U.S.A.
197 F3 Littlefield AZ U.S.A.
199 C5 Littlefield TX U.S.A.
198 E1 Little Fork U.S.A.
190 A1 Little Fork r. U.S.A.
145 F4 Little Gandak r. India
187 J4 Little Grand Rapids Canada
161 G7 Littlehampton U.K.
202 C5 Little Kanawha r. U.S.A.
180 C3 Little Karas Berg plat. Namibia
180 D6 Little Karoo plat. S. Africa
190 D2 Little Lake U.S.A.
202 A5 Little Miami r. U.S.A.
162 B3 Little Minch sea chan. U.K.
198 C2 Little Missouri r. U.S.A.
161 H5 Little Ouse r. U.K.
139 H5 Little Pamir mts Afgh.
190 D1 Little Pic r. Canada
199 E5 Little Rock U.S.A.
190 D4 Little Sable Point U.S.A.
201 F7 Little San Salvador i. Bahamas
186 F4 Little Smoky r. Canada
195 F4 Littleton CO U.S.A.
203 H2 Littleton NH U.S.A.
202 C5 Littleton WV U.S.A.
190 E3 Little Traverse Bay U.S.A.
179 D5 Litunde Moz.
186 B3 Lituya Bay U.S.A.
148 C3 Liuba China
149 C5 Liuchong He r. China
152 B5 Liugong Dao i. China
148 F1 Liugu He r. China
152 C2 Liuhe China
152 B2 Liu He r. China
149 D4 Liujiachang China
149 C5 Liujiang China
148 B3 Liujiaxia Shuiku resr China
148 C3 Liupan Shan mts China
149 B5 Liupanshui China
149 F6 Liuqiu Yu i. Taiwan
149 D4 Liuyang China
149 B5 Liuzhi China
149 C5 Liuzhou China
171 J5 Livadeia Greece
150 C3 Livadiya Rus. Fed.
159 N4 Līvāni Latvia
196 B2 Live Oak CA U.S.A.
201 D6 Live Oak FL U.S.A.
124 C3 Liveringa Australia
196 B3 Livermore U.S.A.
199 B6 Livermore, Mount U.S.A.
203 H2 Livermore Falls U.S.A.
127 I4 Liverpool Australia
189 H5 Liverpool Canada
161 E4 Liverpool U.K.
185 K2 Liverpool, Cape Canada
184 E3 Liverpool Bay Canada
161 D4 Liverpool Bay U.K.
127 I3 Liverpool Plains Australia
127 I3 Liverpool Range mts Australia
206 G5 Livingston Guat.
162 E5 Livingston U.K.
196 B3 Livingston CA U.S.A.
194 E2 Livingston MT U.S.A.
201 C4 Livingston TN U.S.A.
199 E6 Livingston TX U.S.A.
199 E6 Livingston, Lake U.S.A.
179 C5 Livingstone Zambia
129 B2 Livingston Island i. Antarctica
170 G3 Livno Bos.-Herz.
173 F4 Livny Rus. Fed.
158 N2 Livojoki r. Fin.
191 F4 Livonia U.S.A.
170 D3 Livorno Italy
214 E1 Livramento do Brumado Brazil
140 E5 Liwā Oman
179 D4 Liwale Tanz.
148 B3 Lixian Gansu China
149 D4 Lixian Hunan China
148 B4 Lixian Sichuan China
148 E3 Lixin China
148 F4 Liyang China
161 B8 Lizard U.K.
161 B8 Lizard Point U.K.
164 B5 Lizy-sur-Ourcq France
170 F1 Ljubljana Slovenia
159 L4 Ljugarn Sweden
159 L3 Ljungan r. Sweden
159 L3 Ljungaverk Sweden
159 K4 Ljungby Sweden
159 L3 Ljusdal Sweden
159 L3 Ljusnan r. Sweden
159 L3 Ljusne Sweden
212 B5 Llaima, Volcán vol. Chile
161 C5 Llanbadarn Fawr U.K.
161 D5 Llanbister U.K.
215 C2 Llancanelo, Salina salt flat Arg.
161 D6 Llandeilo U.K.
161 C6 Llandissilio U.K.
161 D6 Llandovery U.K.
161 D5 Llandrindod Wells U.K.
161 D4 Llandudno U.K.
161 C5 Llandysul U.K.
161 C6 Llanegwad U.K.
161 C6 Llanelli U.K.
161 D5 Llanfair Caereinion U.K.
161 C4 Llangefni U.K.
161 D5 Llangollen U.K.
161 D5 Llangurig U.K.
161 C4 Llanllyfni U.K.
161 C4 Llannerch-y-medd U.K.
161 C5 Llannor U.K.
199 D6 Llano U.S.A.
199 D6 Llano r. U.S.A.
199 C5 Llano Estacado plain U.S.A.
213 C3 Llanos plain Col./Venez.
215 B4 Llanquihue, Lago l. Chile
161 C5 Llanrhystud U.K.
161 D6 Llantrisant U.K.
161 D5 Llanuwchllyn U.K.
161 D5 Llanwnog U.K.
161 D4 Llay U.K.
167 G2 Lleida Spain
167 C3 Llerena Spain
167 F3 Llíria Spain
Llodio Spain see Laudio
184 F4 Lloyd George, Mount Canada
187 H3 Lloyd Lake Canada
187 G4 Lloydminster Canada
167 H3 Llucmajor Spain
212 C2 Llullaillaco, Volcán vol. Chile
Llyn Tegid l. U.K. see Bala Lake
Lô r. China/Vietnam see Lô, Sông
149 B6 Lô, Sông r. China/Vietnam
212 C2 Loa r. Chile
197 G2 Loa U.S.A.
172 I3 Loban' r. Rus. Fed.
167 D4 Lobatejo mt. Spain
179 C6 Lobatse Botswana
165 J3 Löbejün Germany
177 D4 Lobéké, Parc National de nat. park Cameroon
165 K3 Löbenberg h. Germany
215 E3 Loberia Arg.
179 B5 Lobito Angola
215 E2 Lobos Arg.
206 B2 Lobos, Isla i. Mex.
165 K2 Loburg Germany
162 D4 Lochaber reg. U.K.
162 C4 Lochaline U.K.
191 E1 Lochalsh Canada
162 A3 Lochboisdale U.K.
162 C3 Lochcarron U.K.
160 C1 Lochearnhead U.K.
164 E2 Lochem Neth.
166 E3 Loches France
162 E4 Lochgelly U.K.
162 C4 Lochgilphead U.K.
162 C2 Lochinver U.K.
162 E3 Loch Lomond and the Trossachs National Park U.K.
162 A3 Lochmaddy U.K.
162 E4 Lochnagar mt. U.K.
202 E5 Loch Raven Reservoir U.S.A.
162 D4 Lochy, Loch l. U.K.
126 A4 Lock Australia
162 E5 Lockerbie U.K.
127 G5 Lockhart Australia
199 D6 Lockhart U.S.A.
202 E4 Lock Haven U.S.A.
202 D3 Lockport U.S.A.
154 C3 Lôc Ninh Vietnam
202 B5 Locust Grove U.S.A.
136 E6 Lod Israel
126 E5 Loddon r. Australia
166 F5 Lodève France
172 E2 Lodeynoye Pole Rus. Fed.
194 F2 Lodge Grass U.S.A.
144 B3 Lodhran Pak.
170 C2 Lodi Italy
196 B2 Lodi CA U.S.A.
202 B4 Lodi OH U.S.A.
158 K1 Lødingen Norway
178 C4 Lodja Dem. Rep. Congo
178 D3 Lodwar Kenya
169 I5 Łódź Poland
154 B1 Loei Thai.
180 C5 Loeriesfontein S. Africa
158 K1 Lofoten is Norway
173 G5 Log Rus. Fed.
127 J1 Logan r. Australia
195 G5 Logan NM U.S.A.
202 B5 Logan OH U.S.A.
194 E3 Logan UT U.S.A.
202 C6 Logan WV U.S.A.
186 A2 Logan, Mount Canada
186 D2 Logan Mountains Canada
190 D5 Logansport U.S.A.
170 F2 Logatec Slovenia
167 E1 Logroño Spain
180 E4 Lohatlha S. Africa
165 H3 Lohfelden Germany
158 N2 Lohiniva Fin.
145 H4 Lohit r. India
159 M3 Lohjanjärvi l. Fin.
165 G2 Löhne Germany
165 G2 Lohne (Oldenburg) Germany
158 M2 Lohtaja Fin.
154 A1 Loikaw Myanmar
159 M3 Loimaa Fin.
166 E3 Loire r. France
210 C4 Loja Ecuador
167 D4 Loja Spain
155 E1 Lokan r. Sabah Malaysia
158 N2 Lokan tekojärvi resr Fin.
141 H3 Lōkär Afgh.
164 C3 Lokeren Belgium
180 D2 Lokgwabe Botswana
178 D3 Lokichar Kenya
178 D3 Lokichokio Kenya
159 J4 Løkken Denmark
158 J3 Løkken Norway
169 O2 Loknya Rus. Fed.
176 C4 Lokoja Nigeria
176 C4 Lokossa Benin
173 E4 Lokot' Rus. Fed.
159 N4 Loksa Estonia
185 L3 Loks Land i. Canada
145 H4 Loktak Lake India
176 B4 Lola Guinea
196 B2 Lola, Mount U.S.A.
159 J5 Lolland i. Denmark
178 D4 Lollondo Tanz.
194 D2 Lolo U.S.A.
180 E3 Lolwane S. Africa
171 J3 Lom Bulg.
159 J3 Lom Norway
178 C4 Lomami r. Dem. Rep. Congo
215 D3 Loma Negra, Planicie de la plain Arg.
141 G3 Lomar Pass Afgh.
215 E2 Lomas de Zamora Arg.
124 C2 Lomblen i. Indon.
155 E4 Lombok i. Indon.
155 E4 Lombok, Selat sea chan. Indon.
176 C4 Lomé Togo
178 C4 Lomela Dem. Rep. Congo
178 C4 Lomela r. Dem. Rep. Congo
164 A4 Lomme France
164 D3 Lommel Belgium
162 D4 Lomond, Loch l. U.K.
138 F1 Lomonosovka Kazakh.
220 M1 Lomonosov Ridge sea feature Arctic Ocean
172 G1 Lomovoye Rus. Fed.
147 D7 Lompobattang, Gunung mt. Indon.
196 B4 Lompoc U.S.A.
154 B1 Lom Sak Thai.
169 K4 Łomża Poland
154 D2 Lơn, Hon i. Vietnam
144 D6 Lonar India
215 B3 Loncoche Chile
215 B3 Loncopue Arg.
191 G4 London Canada
161 G6 London U.K.
(City Plan 108)
202 A6 London KY U.S.A.
202 B5 London OH U.S.A.
163 D3 Londonderry U.K.
203 G3 Londonderry U.S.A.
124 C3 Londonderry, Cape Australia
212 B9 Londonderry, Isla i. Chile
214 B3 Londrina Brazil
196 C3 Lone Pine U.S.A.
154 A1 Long Thai.
162 D4 Long, Loch inlet U.K.
133 S2 Longa, Proliv sea chan. Rus. Fed.
149 C6 Long'an China
161 E6 Long Ashton U.K.
215 B3 Longaví, Nevado de mt. Chile
201 E5 Long Bay U.S.A.
128 C6 Longbeach N.Z.
196 C5 Long Beach CA U.S.A.
203 G4 Long Beach NY U.S.A.
203 F4 Long Branch U.S.A.
190 A6 Long Branch Lake U.S.A.
149 B4 Longchang China
149 E5 Longchuan China
161 F5 Long Eaton U.K.
152 D1 Longfengshan Shuiku resr China
163 D4 Longford Ireland
149 E5 Longhai China
149 □ Long Harbour Hong Kong China
160 F2 Longhoughton U.K.
155 E3 Longiram Indon.
205 I4 Long Island Bahamas
188 E3 Long Island Canada
124 E2 Long Island P.N.G.
203 G4 Long Island U.S.A.
203 G4 Long Island Sound sea chan. U.S.A.
149 C5 Long Jiang r. China
145 H3 Longju China
148 F2 Longkou China
148 F2 Longkou Gang b. China
188 C4 Longlac Canada
188 C4 Long Lake l. Canada
203 F3 Long Lake U.S.A.
203 I1 Long Lake l. ME U.S.A.
190 E3 Long Lake l. MI U.S.A.
191 F3 Long Lake l. MI U.S.A.
198 C2 Long Lake l. ND U.S.A.
203 F2 Long Lake l. NY U.S.A.
149 C5 Longli China
149 B5 Longlin China
161 H5 Long Melford U.K.
149 E6 Longmen China
148 B3 Longmen Shan mts China
194 F3 Longmont U.S.A.
148 B3 Longnan China
149 E5 Longnan China
170 E1 Longobards in Italy tourist site Italy
191 G4 Long Point Canada
128 B7 Long Point N.Z.
191 G4 Long Point Bay Canada
160 E3 Long Preston U.K.
149 F4 Longquan China
149 F4 Longquan Xi r. China
185 M5 Long Range Mountains Canada
189 I4 Long Range Mountains Canada
124 E4 Longreach Australia
148 B3 Longriba China
149 C4 Longshan China
149 D5 Longsheng China
149 D5 Longshi China
194 F3 Longs Peak U.S.A.
161 I5 Long Stratton U.K.
149 D4 Longtian China
160 E2 Longtown U.K.
188 F4 Longueuil Canada
164 D5 Longuyon France
196 A2 Longvale U.S.A.
197 F3 Long Valley Junction U.S.A.
199 E5 Longview TX U.S.A.
194 B2 Longview WA U.S.A.
150 C2 Longwangmiao Rus. Fed.
148 B3 Longxi China
148 C3 Longxian China
149 E5 Longxi Shan mt. China
154 C3 Long Xuyên Vietnam
149 E5 Longyan China
148 E2 Longyao China
149 C6 Longzhou China
165 F2 Löningen Germany
159 K4 Lönsboda Sweden
126 E6 Lonsdale, Lake Australia
166 G3 Lons-le-Saunier France
214 B3 Lontra r. Brazil
153 B3 Looc Phil.
190 E4 Looking Glass r. U.S.A.
203 F4 Lookout U.S.A.
188 D2 Lookout, Cape Canada
201 E5 Lookout, Cape U.S.A.
127 J1 Lookout, Point Australia
191 F3 Lookout, Point U.S.A.
196 C3 Lookout Mountain U.S.A.
190 C1 Loon Canada
186 F3 Loon r. Canada
187 H4 Loon Lake Canada
203 I1 Loon Lake l. U.S.A.
163 B5 Loop Head Ireland
144 E1 Lop China
146 G1 Lopatina, Gora mt. Rus. Fed.
172 H4 Lopatino Rus. Fed.
154 B2 Lop Buri Thai.
178 B4 Lopé, Parc National de la nat. park Gabon
153 B3 Lopez Phil.
203 E4 Lopez U.S.A.
146 B2 Lop Nur salt flat China
178 C3 Lopori r. Dem. Rep. Congo
158 M1 Lopphavet b. Norway
172 I2 Loptyuga Rus. Fed.
126 A2 Lora watercourse Australia
213 B2 Lora r. Venez.
141 G4 Lora, Hāmūn-i- dry lake Pak.
167 D4 Lora del Río Spain
202 B4 Lorain U.S.A.
144 B3 Loralai Pak.
144 B3 Loralai r. Pak.
202 A4 Loramie, Lake U.S.A.
167 F4 Lorca Spain
165 F4 Lorch Germany
153 A4 Lord Auckland Shoal sea feature Phil.
140 C4 Lordegān Iran
125 F5 Lord Howe Island Pacific Ocean
216 F7 Lord Howe Rise sea feature S. Pacific Ocean
197 H5 Lordsburg U.S.A.
165 F4 Loreley tourist site Germany
214 D3 Lorena Brazil
147 F7 Lorentz r. Indon.
207 E3 Lorenzo del Real Mex.
210 F7 Loreto Bol.
211 I5 Loreto Brazil
206 B2 Loreto Mex.
153 C4 Loreto Phil.
213 B2 Lorica Col.
166 C3 Lorient France
187 K1 Lorillard r. Canada
162 C4 Lorn, Firth of est. U.K.
126 E7 Lorne Australia
145 H3 Loro r. China
166 G2 Lorraine reg. France
165 G5 Lorsch Germany
165 F2 Lorup Germany
144 C4 Losal India
195 F5 Los Alamos U.S.A.
215 B2 Los Andes Chile
215 B3 Los Ángeles Chile
196 C5 Los Angeles U.S.A.
(City Plan 113)
196 C4 Los Angeles Aqueduct canal U.S.A.
196 B3 Los Banos U.S.A.
212 D2 Los Blancos Arg.
196 D5 Los Coronados, Islas is Mex.
196 B3 Los Gatos U.S.A.
206 C1 Los Gigantes, Llanos de plain Mex.
212 B8 Los Glaciares, Parque Nacional nat. park Arg.
164 E5 Losheim Germany
170 F2 Lošinj i. Croatia
213 A3 Los Katios, Parque Nacional nat. park Col.
181 H2 Loskop Dam S. Africa
215 B4 Los Lagos admin. reg. Chile
195 F5 Los Lunas U.S.A.
207 E3 Los Mármoles, Parque Nacional nat. park Mex.
215 C4 Los Menucos Arg.
206 B2 Los Mochis Mex.
196 A1 Los Molinos U.S.A.
178 B3 Losombo Dem. Rep. Congo
206 D4 Los Reyes Mex.
215 B4 Los Ríos admin. reg. Chile
213 D2 Los Roques, Islas is Venez.
164 E2 Losser Neth.
162 E3 Lossie r. U.K.
162 E3 Lossiemouth U.K.
165 K4 Lößnitz Germany
213 C2 Los Taques Venez.
213 D2 Los Teques Venez.
213 E2 Los Testigos is Venez.
196 C4 Lost Hills U.S.A.
194 D2 Lost Trail Pass U.S.A.
161 C7 Lostwithiel U.K.
212 C2 Los Vientos Chile
215 B1 Los Vilos Chile
215 B3 Lota Chile
138 D5 Loţfābād Iran
181 I3 Lothair S. Africa
178 D3 Lotikipi Plain Kenya/South Sudan
178 C4 Loto Dem. Rep. Congo
172 E3 Lotoshino Rus. Fed.
181 G1 Lotsane r. Botswana
158 O1 Lotta r. Fin./Rus. Fed.
165 F2 Lotte Germany
Louang Namtha Laos see Louangnamtha
147 C4 Louangnamtha Laos
147 C5 Louangphabang Laos
Louangphrabang Laos see Louangphabang
178 B4 Loubomo Congo
166 C2 Loudéac France
149 D5 Loudi China
178 B4 Loudima Congo
202 B4 Loudonville U.S.A.
176 A3 Louga Senegal
161 F5 Loughborough U.K.
161 C6 Loughor r. U.K.
163 C4 Loughrea Ireland
161 H6 Loughton U.K.
202 B5 Louisa KY U.S.A.
202 E5 Louisa VA U.S.A.
163 B4 Louisburgh Ireland
186 C4 Louise Island Canada
125 F3 Louisiade Archipelago is P.N.G.
199 E6 Louisiana state U.S.A.
201 D5 Louisville GA U.S.A.
200 C4 Louisville KY U.S.A.
199 F5 Louisville MS U.S.A.
216 H8 Louisville Ridge sea feature S. Pacific Ocean
188 E3 Louis-XIV, Pointe pt Canada
132 E3 Loukhi Rus. Fed.
167 B4 Loulé Port.
187 K4 Lount Lake Canada
168 F5 Louny Czech Rep.
198 D3 Loup r. U.S.A.
188 F2 Loups Marins, Lacs des lakes Canada
189 I4 Lourdes Canada
166 D5 Lourdes France
167 B2 Lousã Port.
152 E1 Loushan China
127 F3 Louth Australia
161 G4 Louth U.K.
171 J5 Loutra Aidipsou Greece
Louvain Belgium see Leuven
180 B1 Louwater-Suid Namibia
181 I3 Louwsburg S. Africa
158 M2 Lövånger Sweden
172 D3 Lovat' r. Rus. Fed.
171 K3 Lovech Bulg.
194 F3 Loveland U.S.A.
194 E2 Lovell U.S.A.
196 C1 Lovelock U.S.A.
164 B3 Lovendegem Belgium
159 N3 Loviisa Fin.
202 D6 Lovingston U.S.A.
190 C6 Lovington IL U.S.A.
199 C5 Lovington NM U.S.A.
191 J3 Low Canada
187 L2 Low, Cape Canada
188 E3 Low, Lac l. Canada
178 C4 Lowa Dem. Rep. Congo
144 B2 Lowarai Pass Pak.
203 H3 Lowell MA U.S.A.
190 E4 Lowell MI U.S.A.
203 G2 Lowell VT U.S.A.
186 F5 Lower Arrow Lake Canada
Lower California pen. Mex. see Baja California
126 D7 Lower Glenelg National Park Australia
197 F4 Lower Granite Gorge U.S.A.
128 E4 Lower Hutt N.Z.
196 A2 Lower Lake U.S.A.
163 D3 Lower Lough Erne l. U.K.
154 □ Lower Peirce Reservoir Sing.
186 D3 Lower Post Canada
189 H5 Lower Sackville Canada
161 I5 Lowestoft U.K.
169 I4 Łowicz Poland
127 F9 Low Rocky Point Australia
162 E5 Lowther Hills U.K.
203 F3 Lowville U.S.A.
141 H3 Lowyah Dakkah Afgh.
165 G1 Loxstedt Germany
126 D5 Loxton Australia
180 E5 Loxton S. Africa
202 E4 Loyalsock Creek r. U.S.A.
196 B2 Loyalton U.S.A.
125 G4 Loyauté, Îles is New Caledonia
173 D5 Loyew Belarus
171 H2 Loznica Serbia
173 F5 Lozova Ukr.
139 I1 Lozovoye Kazakh.
179 C5 Luacano Angola
148 E4 Lu'an China
148 D3 Luanchuan China
179 B4 Luanda Angola
149 B7 Luang, Huai r. Thai.
154 A3 Luang, Khao mt. Thai.
154 B4 Luang, Thale lag. Thai.
179 D5 Luangwa r. Zambia
145 H2 Luanhaizi China
148 F1 Luan He r. China
148 F2 Luannan China
148 E1 Luanping China
179 C5 Luanshya Zambia
148 F2 Luanxian China
179 C4 Luanza Dem. Rep. Congo
155 D2 Luar, Danau l. Indon.
167 C1 Luarca Spain
179 C5 Luau Angola
207 G4 Lubaantum tourist site Belize
169 K5 Lubaczów Poland
159 N4 Lubānas ezers l. Latvia
153 B3 Lubang Phil.
153 B3 Lubang i. Phil.
153 A3 Lubang Islands Phil.
179 B5 Lubango Angola
178 C4 Lubao Dem. Rep. Congo
169 K5 Lubartów Poland
165 G2 Lübbecke Germany
180 C4 Lubbeskolk salt pan S. Africa
199 C5 Lubbock U.S.A.
165 J2 Lübbow Germany
165 I1 Lübeck Germany
152 A1 Lubei China
169 K5 Lubelska, Wyżyna hills Poland
138 C2 Lubenka Kazakh.
178 C4 Lubero Dem. Rep. Congo
168 H5 Lubin Poland
169 K5 Lublin Poland
173 E5 Lubny Ukr.
155 D2 Lubok Antu Sarawak Malaysia
165 J1 Lübstorf Germany
165 J1 Lübtheen Germany
153 B2 Lubuagan Phil.
179 C4 Lubudi Dem. Rep. Congo
155 B3 Lubuklinggau Indon.
154 A5 Lubukpakam Indon.
154 B2 Lubuksikaping Indon.
179 C5 Lubumbashi Dem. Rep. Congo
179 C5 Lubungu Zambia
178 C4 Lubutu Dem. Rep. Congo
165 K1 Lübz Germany
179 B4 Lucala Angola
163 E4 Lucan Ireland
186 A2 Lucania, Mount Canada
179 C4 Lucapa Angola
201 E7 Lucaya Bahamas
170 D3 Lucca Italy
162 D6 Luce Bay U.K.
214 B3 Lucélia Brazil
153 B3 Lucena Phil.
167 D4 Lucena Spain
169 I6 Lučenec Slovakia
170 F4 Lucera Italy
168 D7 Lucerne Switz.
150 D1 Luchegorsk Rus. Fed.
149 D6 Luchuan China
149 B6 Lüchun China
126 D6 Lucindale Australia
179 B5 Lucira Angola
Luckeesarai India see Lakhisarai
165 L2 Luckenwalde Germany
180 F4 Luckhoff S. Africa
191 G4 Lucknow Canada
144 E4 Lucknow India
179 C5 Lucusse Angola
172 F1 Luda Rus. Fed.
164 F3 Lüdenscheid Germany
179 B6 Lüderitz Namibia
165 I1 Lüdersdorf Germany
144 C3 Ludhiana India
149 B5 Ludian China
190 D4 Ludington U.S.A.
161 E5 Ludlow U.K.
196 D4 Ludlow CA U.S.A.
203 I1 Ludlow ME U.S.A.
203 G3 Ludlow VT U.S.A.
171 L3 Ludogorie reg. Bulg.
159 K3 Ludvika Sweden
165 H6 Ludwigsburg Germany
165 L2 Ludwigsfelde Germany
165 G5 Ludwigshafen am Rhein Germany
165 J1 Ludwigslust Germany

159 N4 Ludza Latvia
178 C4 Luebo Dem. Rep. Congo
179 B5 Luena Angola
213 E3 Luepa Venez.
148 C3 Lüeyang China
149 E6 Lufeng China
199 E6 Lufkin U.S.A.
172 D3 Luga Rus. Fed.
172 D3 Luga r. Rus. Fed.
170 C1 Lugano Switz.
165 K4 Lugau Germany
165 H3 Lügde Germany
179 D5 Lugenda r. Moz.
161 D5 Lugg r. U.K.
163 E5 Lugnaquilla h. Ireland
170 D2 Lugo Italy
167 C1 Lugo Spain
171 I2 Lugoj Romania
139 H4 Lugovoy Kazakh.
153 B5 Lugus i. Phil.
173 F5 Luhans'k Ukr.
148 F3 Luhe China
165 I1 Luhe r. Germany
179 D4 Luhombero Tanz.
173 D5 Luhyny Ukr.
179 C5 Luiana Angola
178 C4 Luilaka r. Dem. Rep. Congo
162 C4 Luing i. U.K.
170 C2 Luino Italy
158 N2 Luiro r. Fin.
206 D3 Luis Moya Mex.
178 C4 Luiza Dem. Rep. Congo
215 E2 Lujan r. Arg.
215 C2 Luján de Cuyo Arg.
148 E4 Lujiang China
171 H2 Lukavac Bos.-Herz.
178 C4 Lukenie r. Dem. Rep. Congo
197 F6 Lukeville U.S.A.
172 G3 Lukh r. Rus. Fed.
172 F4 Lukhovitsy Rus. Fed.
171 K3 Lukovit Bulg.
169 K5 Łuków Poland
172 H4 Lukoyanov Rus. Fed.
179 C5 Lukulu Zambia
179 D4 Lukumburu Tanz.
158 M2 Luleå Sweden
158 M2 Luleälven r. Sweden
136 A1 Lüleburgaz Turkey
148 D2 Lüliang China
149 B5 Luliang China
148 D2 Lüliang Shan mts China
199 D6 Luling U.S.A.
148 F2 Lulong China
145 F3 Lumachomo China
155 D4 Lumajang Indon.
145 E2 Lumajangdong Co salt l. China
137 K5 Lūmār Iran
179 C5 Lumbala Kaquengue Angola
179 C5 Lumbala N'guimbo Angola
201 E5 Lumberton U.S.A.
167 C2 Lumbrales Spain
145 H4 Lumding India
158 N2 Lumijoki Fin.
154 C2 Lumphăt Cambodia
128 B6 Lumsden N.Z.
155 C3 Lumut, Tanjung pt Indon.
153 B2 Luna Phil.
197 H5 Luna U.S.A.
162 F4 Lunan Bay U.K.
187 K2 Lunan Lake Canada
191 F5 Luna Pier U.S.A.
144 C5 Lunavada India
144 B4 Lund Pak.
159 K5 Lund Sweden
197 F2 Lund U.S.A.
187 J4 Lundar Canada
179 D5 Lundazi Zambia
161 C6 Lundy i. U.K.
Lundy Island U.K. see Lundy
160 E3 Lune r. U.K.
165 I1 Lüneburg Germany
165 I1 Lüneburger Heide reg. Germany
164 F3 Lünen Germany
166 H2 Lunéville France
179 C5 Lunga r. Zambia
145 E2 Lungdo China
145 E3 Lunggar China
176 A4 Lungi Sierra Leone
149 □ Lung Kwu Chau i. Hong Kong China
145 H5 Lunglei India
179 C5 Lungwebungu r. Zambia
144 C4 Luni India
144 C4 Luni r. India
144 B3 Luni r. Pak.
196 C2 Luning U.S.A.
172 H4 Lunino Rus. Fed.
173 C4 Luninyets Belarus
144 C1 Lunkho mt. Afgh./Pak.
164 F2 Lünne Germany
176 A4 Lunsar Sierra Leone
181 H2 Lunsklip S. Africa
135 G2 Luntai China
149 C5 Luocheng China
148 C3 Luochuan China
149 C5 Luodian China
149 D6 Luoding China
149 D6 Luodou Sha i. China
148 E3 Luohe China
148 D3 Luo He r. Henan China
148 C3 Luo He r. Shaanxi China
148 D3 Luoning China
149 B5 Luoping China
148 E3 Luoshan China
149 E4 Luotian China
Luoto Fin. see Larsmo
148 D3 Luoyang China
149 F5 Luoyuan China
152 F2 Luozigou China
179 C5 Lupane Zimbabwe
155 D2 Lupar r. Sarawak Malaysia
171 J2 Lupeni Romania
179 D5 Lupilichi Moz.
153 C5 Lupon Phil.
197 H4 Lupton U.S.A.
148 B3 Luqu China
148 E2 Luquan Hebei China
149 B5 Luquan Yunnan China
137 J3 Lūrā Shīrīn Iran
179 B4 Luremo Angola
162 C2 Lurgainn, Loch l. U.K.
163 E3 Lurgan U.K.
179 E5 Lúrio Moz.
179 D5 Lurio r. Moz.
154 □ Lurudal Sing.
179 C5 Lusaka Zambia
178 C4 Lusambo Dem. Rep. Congo
124 F2 Lusancay Islands and Reefs P.N.G.
186 F4 Luscar Canada
187 H4 Luseland Canada
148 D3 Lushi China
171 H4 Lushnjë Albania
152 D2 Lushuihe China
152 A4 Lüshunkou China
181 H5 Lusikisiki S. Africa
194 F3 Lusk U.S.A.
141 E4 Lūt, Kavīr-e des. Iran
149 F6 Lü Tao i. Taiwan
191 G4 Luther Lake Canada
161 G6 Luton U.K.
155 D2 Lutong Sarawak Malaysia
187 G2 Łutselk'e Canada
173 C5 Luts'k Ukr.
164 D2 Luttelgeest Neth.
164 E2 Luttenberg Neth.
165 H5 Lützelbach Germany
129 E4 Lützow-Holm Bay b. Antarctica
180 D4 Lutzputs S. Africa
180 C5 Lutzville S. Africa
153 B5 Luuk Phil.
159 N3 Luumäki Fin.
178 E3 Luuq Somalia
198 D3 Luverne U.S.A.
178 C4 Luvua r. Dem. Rep. Congo
181 I1 Luvuvhu r. S. Africa
178 D3 Luwero Uganda
147 E7 Luwuk Indon.
164 E5 Luxembourg country Europe
164 E5 Luxembourg Lux.
166 H3 Luxeuil-les-Bains France
149 B5 Luxi Yunnan China
Luxi China see Wuxi
181 F5 Luxolweni S. Africa
177 F2 Luxor Egypt
148 E3 Luyi China
164 D3 Luyksgestel Neth.
172 H2 Luza Rus. Fed.
172 I2 Luza r. Rus. Fed.
Luzern Switz. see Lucerne
149 C5 Luzhai China
149 B4 Luzhou China
214 C2 Luziânia Brazil
211 J4 Luzilândia Brazil
153 B3 Luzon i. Phil.
153 B1 Luzon Strait Phil.
166 F3 Luzy France
173 C5 L'viv Ukr.
Lvov Ukr. see L'viv
141 G4 Lwarah Rōd r. Afgh.
172 D3 Lyady Rus. Fed.
172 C4 Lyakhavichy Belarus
186 G5 Lyall, Mount Canada
Lyangar Uzbek. see Langar
158 L2 Lycksele Sweden
161 H7 Lydd U.K.
129 C3 Lyddan Island i. Antarctica
Lydenburg S. Africa see Mashishing
161 E6 Lydney U.K.
173 D5 Lyel'chytsy Belarus
196 C3 Lyell, Mount U.S.A.
186 C4 Lyell Island Canada
172 D4 Lyepyel' Belarus
202 E4 Lykens U.S.A.
194 E3 Lyman U.S.A.
161 E7 Lyme Bay U.K.
161 E7 Lyme Regis U.K.
161 F7 Lymington U.K.
202 D6 Lynchburg U.S.A.
203 H2 Lynchville U.S.A.
127 H4 Lyndhurst N.S.W. Australia
126 C3 Lyndhurst S.A. Australia
203 G2 Lyndonville U.S.A.
162 E2 Lyness U.K.
159 I4 Lyngdal Norway
203 H3 Lynn U.S.A.
186 B3 Lynn Canal sea chan. U.S.A.
197 F2 Lynndyl U.S.A.
187 I3 Lynn Lake Canada
161 D6 Lynton U.K.
187 H2 Lynx Lake Canada
166 G4 Lyon France
203 G2 Lyon Mountain U.S.A.
201 D5 Lyons GA U.S.A.
202 E3 Lyons NY U.S.A.
203 F3 Lyons Falls U.S.A.
172 D4 Lyozna Belarus
125 F2 Lyra Reef P.N.G.
159 J4 Lysekil Sweden
172 H3 Lyskovo Rus. Fed.
154 D2 Ly Sơn, Đao i. Vietnam
132 G4 Lys'va Rus. Fed.
173 F5 Lysychans'k Ukr.
160 D4 Lytham St Anne's U.K.
186 E4 Lytton Canada
172 D4 Lyuban' Belarus
173 C5 Lyubeshiv Ukr.
172 E4 Lyudinovo Rus. Fed.
172 H3 Lyunda r. Rus. Fed.


# M


149 B6 Ma, Sông r. Laos/Vietnam
179 C5 Maamba Zambia
Ma'an Jordan see Ma'ān
136 E6 Ma'ān Jordan
158 N3 Maaninka Fin.
158 O2 Maaninkavaara Fin.
148 F4 Ma'anshan China
159 N4 Maardu Estonia
136 F4 Ma'arrat an Nu'mān Syria
164 D2 Maarssen Neth.
164 E3 Maas r. Neth. alt. Meuse (Belgium/France)
164 D3 Maaseik Belgium
153 C4 Maasin Phil.
164 D4 Maasmechelen Belgium
164 D3 Maas-Schwalm-Nette, Naturpark nat. park Neth.
181 H1 Maasstroom S. Africa
164 D4 Maastricht Neth.
127 G9 Maatsuyker Group is Australia
153 B3 Mabalacat Phil.
179 D6 Mabalane Moz.
210 G2 Mabaruma Guyana
191 I3 Maberly Canada
149 B4 Mabian China
161 H4 Mablethorpe U.K.
181 H2 Mabopane S. Africa
179 D6 Mabote Moz.
180 E2 Mabuasehube Game Reserve nature res. Botswana
153 B1 Mabudis i. Phil.
180 F2 Mabule Botswana
180 E2 Mabutsane Botswana
212 B7 Macá, Monte mt. Chile
215 D3 Macachín Arg.
214 E3 Macaé Brazil
153 C4 Macajalar Bay Phil.
127 G6 Macalister r. Australia
179 D5 Macaloge Moz.
184 H3 MacAlpine Lake Canada
181 J1 Macandze Moz.
149 D6 Macao China
211 H3 Macapá Brazil
210 C4 Macará Ecuador
214 E1 Macarani Brazil
213 B4 Macarena, Cordillera mts Col.
213 E2 Macareo, Caño r. Venez.
181 J2 Macarretane Moz.
126 E7 Macarthur Australia
210 C4 Macas Ecuador
Macassar Strait str. Indon. see Makassar, Selat
211 K5 Macau Brazil
211 H6 Macaúba Brazil
214 D1 Macaúbas Brazil
213 B4 Macaya r. Col.
213 B4 Macayari Col.
161 E4 Macclesfield U.K.
124 C4 Macdonald, Lake salt flat Australia
124 D4 Macdonnell Ranges mts Australia
188 B3 MacDowell Lake Canada
162 F3 Macduff U.K.
167 C2 Macedo de Cavaleiros Port.
126 F6 Macedon mt. Australia
171 I4 Macedonia country Europe
171 J4 Macedonia reg. Greece/Macedonia
211 K5 Maceió Brazil
176 B4 Macenta Guinea
170 E3 Macerata Italy
126 B4 Macfarlane, Lake salt flat Australia
163 B6 Macgillycuddy's Reeks mts Ireland
144 A3 Mach Pak.
210 C4 Machachi Ecuador
214 D3 Machado Brazil
179 D6 Machaila Moz.
178 D4 Machakos Kenya
210 C4 Machala Ecuador
146 B3 Machali China
179 D6 Machanga Moz.
181 J2 Machatuine Moz.
164 C5 Machault France
148 E4 Macheng China
143 B2 Macherla India
143 C2 Machhakund Reservoir India
203 J2 Machias ME U.S.A.
202 D3 Machias NY U.S.A.
203 I1 Machias r. U.S.A.
143 C2 Machilipatnam India
213 B2 Machiques Venez.
162 C5 Machrihanish U.K.
210 D6 Machu Picchu tourist site Peru
161 D5 Machynlleth U.K.
181 J2 Macia Moz.
171 M2 Măcin Romania
176 B3 Macina Mali
127 I2 Macintyre r. Australia
127 I2 Macintyre Brook r. Australia
197 H2 Mack U.S.A.
137 G1 Maçka Turkey
124 E4 Mackay Australia
194 D2 Mackay U.S.A.
124 C4 Mackay, Lake salt flat Australia
187 G2 MacKay Lake Canada
186 E3 Mackenzie B.C. Canada
190 C1 Mackenzie Ont. Canada
184 E3 Mackenzie r. Canada
129 E5 Mackenzie Bay b. Antarctica
184 E3 Mackenzie Bay Canada
186 F2 Mackenzie Bison Sanctuary nature res. Canada
184 G2 Mackenzie King Island Canada
186 C2 Mackenzie Mountains Canada
190 E3 Mackinac, Straits of lake channel U.S.A.
190 E3 Mackinac Island U.S.A.
190 C5 Mackinaw r. U.S.A.
190 E3 Mackinaw City U.S.A.
187 H4 Macklin Canada
127 J3 Macksville Australia
127 J2 Maclean Australia
181 H5 Maclear S. Africa
127 J3 Macleay r. Australia
124 B4 MacLeod, Lake dry lake Australia
186 C2 Macmillan r. Canada
190 B5 Macomb U.S.A.
170 C4 Macomer Sardinia Italy
166 G3 Mâcon France
201 D5 Macon GA U.S.A.
198 E4 Macon MO U.S.A.
179 C5 Macondo Angola
127 G3 Macquarie r. N.S.W. Australia
127 G8 Macquarie r. Tas. Australia
127 I4 Macquarie, Lake b. Australia
127 F9 Macquarie Harbour Australia
135 F7 Macquarie Island S. Pacific Ocean
127 G3 Macquarie Marshes Australia
127 H4 Macquarie Mountain Australia
216 F9 Macquarie Ridge sea feature S. Pacific Ocean
154 □ MacRitchie Reservoir Sing.
129 E5 Mac. Robertson Land reg. Antarctica
163 C6 Macroom Ireland
213 C1 Macuira, Parque Nacional nat. park Col.
213 B4 Macuje Col.
124 D4 Macumba watercourse Australia
210 D6 Macusani Peru
207 F4 Macuspana Mex.
206 B2 Macuzari, Presa resr Mex.
203 I2 Macwahoc U.S.A.
136 E6 Mādabā Jordan
181 I3 Madadeni S. Africa
177 D3 Madagali Nigeria
179 E6 Madagascar country Africa
218 H6 Madagascar i. Africa
218 H6 Madagascar Basin sea feature Indian Ocean
218 G7 Madagascar Ridge sea feature Indian Ocean
143 B3 Madakasira India
177 D2 Madama Niger
171 K4 Madan Bulg.
143 B3 Madanapalle India
124 E2 Madang P.N.G.
176 C3 Madaoua Niger
145 G5 Madaripur Bangl.
191 I3 Madawaska Canada
191 I3 Madawaska r. Canada
203 I1 Madawaska U.S.A.
176 A1 Madeira terr. Atlantic Ocean
210 F5 Madeira r. Brazil
219 H3 Madeira, Arquipélago da is Port.
189 H4 Madeleine, Îles de la is Canada
190 B2 Madeline Island U.S.A.
137 G2 Maden Turkey
139 I3 Madeniyet Kazakh.
204 C3 Madera Mex.
196 B3 Madera U.S.A.
143 A3 Madgaon India
145 F4 Madhepura India
143 C2 Madhira India
145 F4 Madhubani India
144 D5 Madhya Pradesh state India
181 F3 Madibogo S. Africa
210 E6 Madidi r. Bol.
126 B2 Madigan Gulf salt flat Australia
143 A3 Madikeri India
181 G2 Madikwe Game Reserve nature res. S. Africa
140 C5 Madīnat ash Shamāl Qatar
178 B4 Madingou Congo
Madini r. Bol. see Madidi
179 E5 Madirovalo Madag.
200 C4 Madison IN U.S.A.
203 I2 Madison ME U.S.A.
198 D2 Madison MN U.S.A.
198 D3 Madison NE U.S.A.
198 D2 Madison SD U.S.A.
190 C4 Madison WI U.S.A.
202 C5 Madison WV U.S.A.
192 D2 Madison r. U.S.A.
200 C4 Madisonville KY U.S.A.
199 E6 Madisonville TX U.S.A.
155 D4 Madiun Indon.
191 I3 Madoc Canada
178 D3 Mado Gashi Kenya
159 N4 Madona Latvia
144 B4 Madpura India
171 L5 Madra Dağı mts Turkey
Madras India see Chennai
194 B2 Madras U.S.A.
207 E2 Madre, Laguna lag. Mex.
199 D7 Madre, Laguna lag. U.S.A.
153 B2 Madre, Sierra mt. Phil.
207 F4 Madre de Chiapas, Sierra mts Mex.
210 D6 Madre de Dios r. Peru
212 A8 Madre de Dios, Isla i. Chile
206 D4 Madre del Sur, Sierra mts Mex.
206 B1 Madre Occidental, Sierra mts Mex.
206 D2 Madre Oriental, Sierra mts Mex.
153 C4 Madrid Phil.
167 E2 Madrid Spain (City Plan 112)
153 B4 Madridejos Phil.
167 E3 Madridejos Spain
143 C2 Madugula India
155 D4 Madura i. Indon.
155 D4 Madura, Selat sea chan. Indon.
143 B4 Madurai India
145 E4 Madwas India
144 C2 Madyan Pak.
173 H7 Madzhalis Rus. Fed.
151 F6 Maebashi Japan
154 A1 Mae Hong Son Thai.
154 A1 Mae Sai Thai.
154 A1 Mae Sariang Thai.
154 A1 Mae Sot Thai.
205 I5 Maestra, Sierra mts Cuba
179 E5 Maevatanana Madag.
125 G3 Maéwo i. Vanuatu
187 I4 Mafeking Canada
181 G4 Mafeteng Lesotho
127 G6 Maffra Australia
179 D4 Mafia Island Tanz.
Mafikeng S. Africa see Mahikeng
179 D4 Mafinga Tanz.
214 C4 Mafra Brazil
181 I5 Magabeni S. Africa
133 Q4 Magadan Rus. Fed.
178 D4 Magadi Kenya
203 J2 Magaguadavic Lake Canada
181 J1 Magaiza Moz.
153 B3 Magallanes Phil.
212 B8 Magallanes, Estrecho de Chile
213 B2 Magangué Col.
136 D3 Mağara Turkey
173 H7 Magas Rus. Fed.
153 B2 Magat r. Phil.
215 F2 Magdalena Arg.
210 F6 Magdalena Bol.
213 B3 Magdalena r. Col.
204 B2 Magdalena Mex.
195 E6 Magdalena r. Mex.
195 F5 Magdalena U.S.A.
206 A2 Magdalena, Bahía b. Mex.
212 B6 Magdalena, Isla i. Chile
206 A2 Magdalena, Isla i. Mex.
153 A5 Magdaline, Gunung mt. Sabah Malaysia
138 F5 Magdanly Turkm.
165 J2 Magdeburg Germany
163 F3 Magee, Island pen. U.K.
216 E4 Magellan Seamounts sea feature N. Pacific Ocean
158 N1 Magerøya i. Norway
151 B9 Mage-shima i. Japan
170 C2 Maggiorasca, Monte mt. Italy
170 C2 Maggiore, Lake Italy
176 A3 Maghama Mauritania
163 E3 Maghera U.K.
163 E3 Magherafelt U.K.
160 E4 Maghull U.K.
194 D3 Magna U.S.A.
170 F6 Magna Grande mt. Sicily Italy
129 E5 Magnet Bay b. Antarctica
124 E3 Magnetic Island Australia
158 P1 Magnetity Rus. Fed.
138 D1 Magnitogorsk Rus. Fed.
199 E5 Magnolia U.S.A.
189 F4 Magog Canada
207 E3 Magozal Mex.
189 H3 Magpie Canada
190 E1 Magpie r. Canada
189 H3 Magpie, Lac l. Canada
186 G5 Magrath Canada
196 D3 Magruder Mountain U.S.A.
176 A3 Magta' Lahjar Mauritania
138 D5 Magtymguly Turkm.
178 D4 Magu Tanz.
149 B6 Maguan China
211 I4 Maguarinho, Cabo c. Brazil
181 J2 Magude Moz.
203 J2 Magundy Canada
187 J2 Maguse Lake Canada
145 H5 Magwe Myanmar
145 H5 Magyichaung Myanmar
140 B2 Mahābād Iran
143 A2 Mahabaleshwar India
145 F4 Mahabharat Range mts Nepal
179 E6 Mahabo Madag.
143 A2 Mahad India
144 D5 Mahadeo Hills India
178 D3 Mahagi Dem. Rep. Congo
179 E5 Mahajamba r. Madag.
144 C3 Mahajan India
179 E5 Mahajanga Madag.
155 D2 Mahakam r. Indon.
179 C6 Mahalapye Botswana
179 E5 Mahalevona Madag.
140 C3 Maḩallāt-e Bālā Iran
144 D3 Maham India
140 E4 Māhān Iran
143 D1 Mahanadi r. India
179 E5 Mahanoro Madag.
144 C6 Maharashtra state India
143 C1 Mahasamund India
154 B1 Maha Sarakham Thai.
179 E6 Mahatalaky Madag.
136 F6 Maḩaţţat Ḑab'ah Jordan
179 E5 Mahavanona Madag.
179 E5 Mahavavy r. Madag.
143 C5 Mahaweli Ganga r. Sri Lanka
154 C1 Mahaxai Laos
143 C2 Mahbubabad India
143 B2 Mahbubnagar India
140 D5 Maḩḑah Oman
211 G2 Mahdia Guyana
170 D7 Mahdia Tunisia
175 I5 Mahé i. Seychelles
143 D2 Mahendragiri mt. India
144 C5 Mahesana India
144 C5 Maheshwar India
144 C5 Mahi r. India
141 E4 Māhī watercourse Iran
128 F3 Mahia Peninsula N.Z.
181 F2 Mahikeng S. Africa
172 D4 Mahilyow Belarus
143 C5 Mahiyangana Sri Lanka
181 I4 Mahlabatini S. Africa
165 J2 Mahlsdorf Germany
Maḩmūd-e 'Erāqī Afgh. see Maḩmūd-e Rāqī
141 H3 Maḩmūd-e Rāqī Afgh.
137 L4 Mahniān Iran
198 D2 Mahnomen U.S.A.
144 D4 Mahoba India
Mahón Spain see Maó
202 D4 Mahoning Creek Lake U.S.A.
145 H5 Mahudaung mts Myanmar
144 B5 Mahuva India
171 L4 Mahya Dağı mt. Turkey
140 C3 Mahyār Iran
145 H4 Maibong India
213 B2 Maicao Col.
188 E4 Maicasagi, Lac l. Canada
149 C6 Maichen China
141 H3 Maīdān Shahr Afgh.
161 G6 Maidenhead U.K.
187 H4 Maidstone Canada
161 H6 Maidstone U.K.
177 D3 Maiduguri Nigeria
213 D3 Maigualida, Sierra mts Venez.
163 C5 Maigue r. Ireland
144 E4 Maihar India
148 C3 Maiji Shan mt. China
144 E5 Maikala Range hills India
178 C4 Maiko, Parc National de la nat. park Dem. Rep. Congo
144 E3 Mailani India
141 G3 Maīmanah Afgh.
165 H5 Main r. Germany
163 E3 Main r. U.K.
189 I3 Main Brook Canada
191 F3 Main Channel lake channel Canada
178 B4 Mai-Ndombe, Lac l. Dem. Rep. Congo
165 J5 Main-Donau-Kanal canal Germany
Maindong China see Coqên
191 I4 Main Duck Island Canada
203 I2 Maine state U.S.A.
176 D3 Maïné-Soroa Niger
154 A2 Maingy Island Myanmar
165 H5 Mainhardt Germany
153 C4 Mainit Phil.
153 C4 Mainit, Lake Phil.
162 E1 Mainland i. Orkney, Scotland U.K.
162 □ Mainland i. Shetland, Scotland U.K.
165 J4 Mainleus Germany
145 E5 Mainpat reg. India
144 D4 Mainpuri India
127 J1 Main Range National Park Australia
179 E5 Maintirano Madag.
165 G4 Mainz Germany
176 □ Maio i. Cape Verde
215 C2 Maipó, Volcán vol. Chile
215 F3 Maipú Arg.
215 C2 Maipú Arg.
213 D2 Maiquetía Venez.
145 G5 Maiskhal Island Bangl.
179 C6 Maitengwe Botswana
127 I4 Maitland N.S.W. Australia
126 B5 Maitland S.A. Australia
129 D3 Maitri research stn Antarctica
206 I5 Maíz, Islas del is Nicaragua
145 G3 Maizhokunggar China
151 D7 Maizuru Japan
143 B2 Majalgaon India
213 E4 Majari r. Brazil
136 E5 Majdel Aanjar tourist site Lebanon
155 E3 Majene Indon.
140 C6 Majhūd well Saudi Arabia
178 D3 Majī Eth.
148 E2 Majia He r. China
149 D6 Majiang China
141 F3 Majnābād Iran
167 H3 Major, Puig mt. Spain
167 H3 Majorca i. Spain
145 H4 Majuli Island India
Majuro atoll Marshall Is see Taongi
181 G4 Majwemasweu S. Africa
178 B4 Makabana Congo
Makaha U.S.A. see Mākaha
196 □1 Mākaha U.S.A.
147 D7 Makale Indon.
145 F4 Makalu mt. China
178 C4 Makamba Burundi
139 J3 Makanshy Kazakh.
Makapuu Hd hd U.S.A. see Makapu'u Head
196 □1 Makapu'u Head U.S.A.
220 M1 Makarov Basin sea feature Arctic Ocean
170 G3 Makarska Croatia
172 I2 Makar-Yb Rus. Fed.
155 E4 Makassar Indon.
155 E3 Makassar, Selat str. Indon.
138 C3 Makat Kazakh.
181 J3 Makatini Flats lowland S. Africa
176 A4 Makeni Sierra Leone
179 C6 Makgadikgadi depr. Botswana
173 H7 Makhachkala Rus. Fed.
181 H1 Makhado S. Africa
138 B3 Makhambet Kazakh.
136 G4 Makhfar al Ḩammām Syria
137 I4 Makhmūr Iraq
139 G1 Makhorovka Kazakh.
178 D4 Makindu Kenya
139 G1 Makinsk Kazakh.
173 F5 Makiyivka Ukr.
Makkah Saudi Arabia see Mecca
189 I2 Makkovik Canada
189 I2 Makkovik, Cape Canada
164 D1 Makkum Neth.
171 I1 Makó Hungary
178 B3 Makokou Gabon
179 D4 Makongolosi Tanz.
180 E2 Makopong Botswana
178 B4 Makotipoko Congo
141 F5 Makran reg. Iran/Pak.
144 C4 Makrana India
141 F5 Makran Coast Range mts Pak.
143 C2 Makri India
171 K6 Makronisos i. Greece
172 E3 Maksatikha Rus. Fed.
150 E1 Maksimovka Rus. Fed.
141 F4 Maksotag Iran
140 B2 Mākū Iran
145 H4 Makum India
179 D4 Makumbako Tanz.
179 D5 Makunguwiro Tanz.
151 B9 Makurazaki Japan
176 C4 Makurdi Nigeria
140 D4 Makūyeh Iran
181 F3 Makwassie S. Africa
158 L2 Malå Sweden
206 I7 Mala, Punta pt Panama
153 C5 Malabang Phil.
143 A3 Malabar Coast India
176 C4 Malabo Equat. Guinea
153 A4 Malabuñgan Phil.
155 A2 Malacca, Strait of Indon./Malaysia
194 D3 Malad City U.S.A.
172 C4 Maladzyechna Belarus
167 D4 Málaga Spain
203 F5 Malaga NJ U.S.A.
195 F5 Malaga NM U.S.A.
163 C3 Málainn Mhóir Ireland
125 G2 Malaita i. Solomon Is
177 F4 Malakal South Sudan
125 G3 Malakula i. Vanuatu
144 C2 Malakwal Pak.
147 E7 Malamala Indon.
141 G5 Malan, Ras pt Pak.
155 D4 Malang Indon.
179 B4 Malanje Angola
215 C1 Malanzán, Sierra de mts Arg.
143 B4 Malappuram India
159 L4 Mälaren l. Sweden
215 C2 Malargüe Arg.
191 H1 Malartic Canada
191 H1 Malartic, Lac l. Canada
186 A3 Malaspina Glacier U.S.A.
136 G2 Malatya Turkey
144 C3 Malaut India
137 K5 Malāvī Iran
153 A5 Malawali i. Sabah Malaysia
179 D5 Malawi country Africa
Malawi, Lake l. Africa see Nyasa, Lake
172 E3 Malaya Vishera Rus. Fed.
153 C4 Malaybalay Phil.
140 C3 Malāyer Iran
131 F6 Malay Peninsula pen. Asia
139 I3 Malaysary Kazakh.
155 C2 Malaysia country Asia
155 B2 Malaysia, Semenanjung Malaysia
137 I2 Malazgirt Turkey
169 I3 Malbork Poland
164 E5 Malborn Germany
165 K1 Malchin Germany
165 K1 Malchiner See l. Germany
145 G4 Maldah India
164 B3 Maldegem Belgium
199 F4 Malden U.S.A.
123 I4 Malden Island Kiribati
130 C6 Maldives country Indian Ocean
161 H6 Maldon U.K.
215 F2 Maldonado Uruguay
130 C6 Male Maldives
171 J6 Maleas, Akrotirio pt Greece
135 F6 Male Atholhu Maldives
181 F4 Malebogo S. Africa
143 B2 Malegaon Maharashtra India
144 C5 Malegaon Maharashtra India
168 H6 Malé Karpaty hills Slovakia
140 C4 Māl-e Khalīfeh Iran
137 K3 Malek Kandī Iran
178 B4 Malele Dem. Rep. Congo
179 D5 Malema Moz.
144 C3 Maler Kotla India
173 H7 Malgobek Rus. Fed.
158 L2 Malgomaj l. Sweden
140 B5 Malham Saudi Arabia
194 C3 Malheur Lake U.S.A.
176 B3 Mali country Africa
178 C4 Mali Dem. Rep. Congo
176 A3 Mali Guinea
148 C3 Malian He r. China
144 E4 Malihabad India
141 F4 Malik Naro mt. Pak.
154 A2 Mali Kyun i. Myanmar
147 E7 Malili Indon.
155 C4 Malimping Indon.
178 E4 Malindi Kenya
163 D2 Malin Head Ireland
Malin More Ireland see Málainn Mhóir
139 G2 Malinovka Kazakh.
150 D2 Malinovka r. Rus. Fed.
139 I2 Malinovoye Ozero Rus. Fed.
149 B6 Malipo China
170 F2 Mali Raginac mt. Croatia
153 C5 Malita Phil.
154 A3 Maliwun Myanmar
144 B5 Maliya India
137 K5 Malkaili Iran
143 C2 Malkangiri India
144 D5 Malkapur India
173 C7 Malkara Turkey
169 M4 Mal'kavichy Belarus
171 L4 Malko Tŭrnovo Bulg.
127 H6 Mallacoota Australia
127 H6 Mallacoota Inlet b. Australia
162 C4 Mallaig U.K.
126 C5 Mallala Australia
126 E5 Mallee Cliffs National Park Australia
187 J2 Mallery Lake Canada
Mallorca i. Spain see Majorca
163 C5 Mallow Ireland
161 D5 Mallwyd U.K.
158 J2 Malm Norway
158 M2 Malmberget Sweden
164 E4 Malmédy Belgium
180 C6 Malmesbury S. Africa
161 E6 Malmesbury U.K.
159 K5 Malmö Sweden
172 I3 Malmyzh Rus. Fed.
125 G3 Malo i. Vanuatu
153 B3 Malolos Phil.
203 F2 Malone U.S.A.
149 B5 Malong China
179 C5 Malonga Dem. Rep. Congo
172 F2 Maloshuyka Rus. Fed.
159 I3 Måløy Norway
172 F4 Maloyaroslavets Rus. Fed.
210 B3 Malpelo, Isla de i. Col.
143 A3 Malprabha r. India
170 F7 Malta country Europe
159 N4 Malta Latvia
194 F1 Malta U.S.A.
170 F6 Malta Channel Italy/Malta
179 B6 Maltahöhe Namibia
161 F4 Maltby U.K.
161 H4 Maltby le Marsh U.K.
160 G3 Malton U.K.
Maluku is Indon. see Moluccas
147 E7 Maluku, Laut sea Indon.
159 K3 Malung Sweden
181 H4 Maluti Mountains Lesotho
125 G2 Malu'u Solomon Is
143 A2 Malvan India
199 E5 Malvern U.S.A.
173 D5 Malyn Ukr.
133 R3 Malyy Anyuy r. Rus. Fed.
Malyy Balkhan, Khrebet h. Turkm. see Kiçi Balkan Daglary
173 H6 Malyye Derbety Rus. Fed.
138 B1 Malyy Irgiz r. Rus. Fed.
Malyy Kavkaz mts Asia see Lesser Caucasus
133 P2 Malyy Lyakhovskiy, Ostrov i. Rus. Fed.
181 H3 Mamafubedu S. Africa
143 C3 Mamallapuram India
153 A5 Mambahenauhan i. Phil.
153 C4 Mambajao Phil.
178 C3 Mambasa Dem. Rep. Congo
178 B3 Mambéré r. Cent. Afr. Rep.
153 B3 Mamburao Phil.
181 H2 Mamelodi S. Africa
176 C4 Mamfe Cameroon
Mamfé Cameroon see Mamfe
139 F1 Mamlyutka Kazakh.
197 G5 Mammoth U.S.A.
200 C4 Mammoth Cave National Park U.S.A.
196 C3 Mammoth Lakes U.S.A.
210 E6 Mamoré r. Bol./Brazil
176 A3 Mamou Guinea
179 E5 Mampikony Madag.
176 B4 Mampong Ghana
215 B3 Mamuil Malal, Paso pass Arg./Chile
155 E3 Mamuju Indon.
180 D1 Mamuno Botswana
138 D2 Mamyt Kazakh.
176 B4 Man Côte d'Ivoire
160 C3 Man, Isle of terr. Irish Sea
213 B3 Manacacias r. Col.
210 F4 Manacapuru Brazil
167 H3 Manacor Spain
147 E6 Manado Indon.
206 H5 Managua Nicaragua
206 H5 Managua, Lago de l. Nicaragua
179 E6 Manakara Madag.
128 D5 Manakau mt. N.Z.
140 C5 Manama Bahrain
124 E2 Manam Island P.N.G.
213 E2 Manamo, Caño r. Venez.
196 □1 Mānana i. U.S.A.
Manana i. U.S.A. see Mānana
179 E6 Mananara r. Madag.
179 E5 Mananara Avaratra Madag.
179 E5 Mananara Nord, Parc National de nat. park Madag.
126 E5 Manangatang Australia
179 E6 Mananjary Madag.
143 B4 Mananthavady India
144 D3 Mana Pass India
213 D2 Manapire r. Venez.
128 A6 Manapouri, Lake N.Z.
179 E5 Manarantsandry Madag.
145 G4 Manas r. Bhutan
146 A2 Manas Hu l. China
145 F3 Manaslu mt. Nepal
145 G4 Manas National Park nature res. Bhutan
202 E5 Manassas U.S.A.
147 E7 Manatuto East Timor
210 F4 Manaus Brazil
136 C3 Manavgat Turkey
128 E4 Manawatu r. N.Z.
153 C5 Manay Phil.
136 F3 Manbij Syria
161 H4 Manby U.K.
190 E3 Mancelona U.S.A.
161 E4 Manchester U.K.
196 A2 Manchester CA U.S.A.
203 G4 Manchester CT U.S.A.
190 B4 Manchester IA U.S.A.
202 B6 Manchester KY U.S.A.
191 E4 Manchester MI U.S.A.
203 H3 Manchester NH U.S.A.
202 B5 Manchester OH U.S.A.
201 C5 Manchester TN U.S.A.
203 G3 Manchester VT U.S.A.
144 A4 Manchhar Lake Pak.
136 F2 Mancılık Turkey
197 H3 Mancos U.S.A.
197 H3 Mancos r. U.S.A.
141 F5 Mand Pak.
140 D4 Mand, Rūd-e r. Iran
177 D4 Manda, Parc National de nat. park Chad
179 E6 Mandabe Madag.
155 B2 Mandah Indon.
154 □ Mandai Sing.
144 C4 Mandal India
159 I4 Mandal Norway
147 G7 Mandala, Puncak mt. Indon.
147 B4 Mandalay Myanmar
146 C2 Mandalgovĭ Mongolia
137 J5 Mandalī Iraq
148 D1 Mandalt China
198 C2 Mandan U.S.A.
153 B3 Mandaon Phil.
177 D3 Mandara Mountains Cameroon/Nigeria
170 C5 Mandas Sardinia Italy
178 E3 Mandera Kenya
197 F2 Manderfield U.S.A.
164 E4 Manderscheid Germany
205 I5 Mandeville Jamaica
128 B6 Mandeville N.Z.
144 B4 Mandha India
176 B3 Mandiana Guinea
154 B4 Mandi Angin, Gunung mt. Malaysia
179 D5 Mandié Moz.
179 D5 Mandimba Moz.
181 I4 Mandini S. Africa
145 F5 Mandira Dam India
144 E5 Mandla India
179 E5 Mandritsara Madag.
144 C4 Mandsaur India
153 A6 Mandul i. Indon.
124 B5 Mandurah Australia
170 G4 Manduria Italy
144 B5 Mandvi Gujarat India
144 C5 Mandvi Gujarat India
143 B3 Mandya India
138 E5 Mäne Turkm.
143 B2 Maner r. India
170 D2 Manerbio Italy
137 K5 Manesht Kūh mt. Iran
169 L5 Manevychi Ukr.

170 F4 Manfredonia Italy
170 G4 Manfredonia, Golfo di g. Italy
214 D1 Manga Brazil
176 B3 Manga Burkina Faso
178 B4 Mangai Dem. Rep. Congo
123 I5 Mangaia i. Cook Is
128 E3 Mangakino N.Z.
143 C2 Mangalagiri India
145 H4 Mangaldai India
171 M3 Mangalia Romania
143 A3 Mangalore India
143 A2 Mangalvedha India
145 G4 Mangan India
143 C2 Mangapet India
153 C6 Mangarang Indon.
181 G4 Mangaung S. Africa
128 E3 Mangaweka N.Z.
145 G4 Mangde Chhu r. Bhutan
163 B6 Mangerton Mountain h. Ireland
155 C3 Manggar Indon.
141 F3 Manghāl Afgh.
138 B4 Mangistau Kazakh.
Mangit Uzbek. see Mang'it
138 E4 Mang'it Uzbek.
179 D5 Mangochi Malawi
147 E7 Mangole i. Indon.
161 E6 Mangotsfield U.K.
148 A3 Mangra China
144 B5 Mangrol India
167 C2 Mangualde Port.
141 G4 Manguchar Pak.
215 G2 Mangueira, Lagoa l. Brazil
214 B4 Mangueirinha Brazil
177 D2 Manguéni, Plateau du Niger
146 E1 Mangui China
153 C5 Mangupung i. Indon.
138 B3 Mangystau, Poluostrov pen. Kazakh.
138 B3 Mangystau, Zaliv b. Kazakh.
138 C3 Mangystauskaya Oblast' admin. div. Kazakh.
198 D4 Manhattan KS U.S.A.
196 D2 Manhattan NV U.S.A.
179 D6 Manhica Moz.
181 J3 Manhoca Moz.
214 D3 Manhuaçu Brazil
214 E2 Manhuaçu r. Brazil
213 B3 Mani Col.
179 E5 Mania r. Madag.
170 E1 Maniago Italy
210 F5 Manicoré Brazil
189 G3 Manicouagan Canada
189 G3 Manicouagan r. Canada
189 G3 Manicouagan, Petit Lac l. Canada
189 G3 Manicouagan, Réservoir resr Canada
140 C5 Manīfah Saudi Arabia
123 I4 Manihiki atoll Cook Is
Manikgarh India see Rajura
144 E4 Manikpur India
153 B3 Manila Phil.
194 E3 Manila U.S.A.
127 H4 Manildra Australia
127 I3 Manilla Australia
145 H4 Manipur state India
171 L5 Manisa Turkey
190 D3 Manistee U.S.A.
190 E3 Manistee r. U.S.A.
190 D3 Manistique U.S.A.
190 E2 Manistique Lake U.S.A.
188 B2 Manitoba prov. Canada
187 J4 Manitoba, Lake Canada
187 H4 Manito Lake Canada
187 J5 Manitou Canada
191 G3 Manitou, Lake Canada
202 E3 Manitou Beach U.S.A.
188 B3 Manitou Falls Canada
190 D2 Manitou Island U.S.A.
200 C2 Manitou Islands U.S.A.
191 F3 Manitoulin Island Canada
191 G3 Manitowaning Canada
190 E1 Manitowik Lake Canada
190 D3 Manitowoc U.S.A.
191 J2 Maniwaki Canada
213 B3 Manizales Col.
179 E6 Manja Madag.
181 J2 Manjacaze Moz.
143 B4 Manjeri India
152 D3 Man Jiang r. China
137 L3 Manjil Iran
143 B2 Manjra r. India
198 E2 Mankato U.S.A.
181 I3 Mankayane Swaziland
176 B4 Mankono Côte d'Ivoire
143 C4 Mankulam Sri Lanka
148 C1 Manlay Mongolia
127 I4 Manly Australia
144 C5 Manmad India
155 B3 Manna Indon.
126 C4 Mannahill Australia
143 B4 Mannar Sri Lanka
143 B4 Mannar, Gulf of India/Sri Lanka
143 B3 Manneru r. India
165 G5 Mannheim Germany
163 A4 Mannin Bay Ireland
186 F3 Manning Canada
201 D5 Manning U.S.A.
161 I6 Manningtree U.K.
170 C4 Mannu, Capo c. Sardinia Italy
126 C5 Mannum Australia
147 F7 Manokwari Indon.
178 C4 Manono Dem. Rep. Congo
154 A3 Manoron Myanmar
166 G5 Manosque France
185 K4 Manouane, Lac l. Canada
178 C3 Manovo-Gounda Saint Floris, Parc National du nat. park Cent. Afr. Rep.
152 D3 Manp'o N. Korea
125 I2 Manra i. Kiribati
167 G2 Manresa Spain
144 C3 Mansa India
179 C5 Mansa Zambia
176 A3 Mansa Konko Gambia
144 C2 Mansehra Pak.
185 K3 Mansel Island Canada
127 G6 Mansfield Australia
161 F4 Mansfield U.K.
199 E5 Mansfield LA U.S.A.
202 B4 Mansfield OH U.S.A.
202 E4 Mansfield PA U.S.A.
186 E3 Manson Creek Canada
137 L6 Manşūrī Iran
136 E3 Mansurlu Turkey
210 B4 Manta Ecuador
210 B4 Manta, Bahía de b. Ecuador
153 A4 Mantalingajan, Mount Phil.
196 B3 Manteca U.S.A.
213 C3 Mantecal Venez.
165 K5 Mantel Germany
201 F5 Manteo U.S.A.
166 E2 Mantes-la-Jolie France
143 B2 Manthani India
197 G2 Manti U.S.A.
214 D3 Mantiqueira, Serra da mts Brazil
190 E3 Manton U.S.A.
Mantova Italy see Mantua
159 N3 Mäntsälä Fin.
159 N3 Mänttä Fin.
170 D2 Mantua Italy
172 H3 Manturovo Rus. Fed.
159 N3 Mäntyharju Fin.
158 N2 Mäntyjärvi Fin.
210 D6 Manu, Parque Nacional nat. park Peru
217 I7 Manuae atoll Fr. Polynesia
Manua Islands American Samoa see Manu'a Islands
123 H4 Manu'a Islands American Samoa
197 H4 Manuelito U.S.A.
215 F2 Manuel J. Cobo Arg.
214 E1 Manuel Vitorino Brazil
211 H5 Manuelzinho Brazil
147 F7 Manui i. Indon.
141 E5 Manūjān Iran
153 B4 Manukan Phil.
128 E2 Manukau N.Z.
128 E2 Manukau Harbour N.Z.
153 A5 Manuk Manka i. Phil.
126 C4 Manunda watercourse Australia
124 E2 Manus Island P.N.G.
143 B3 Manvi India
181 I2 Manyakatana S. Africa
181 F2 Manyana Botswana
197 H3 Many Farms U.S.A.
178 D4 Manyoni Tanz.
167 E3 Manzanares Spain
205 I4 Manzanillo Cuba
206 C4 Manzanillo Mex.
206 J6 Manzanillo, Punta pt Panama
140 C3 Manzarīyeh Iran
146 D2 Manzhouli China
136 D6 Manzilah, Buḩayrat al lag. Egypt
181 I3 Manzini Swaziland
177 D3 Mao Chad
167 I3 Maó Spain
148 C2 Maojiachuan China
147 F7 Maoke, Pegunungan mts Indon.
181 G3 Maokeng S. Africa
152 B3 Maokui Shan mt. China
152 B2 Maolin China
148 B2 Maomao Shan mt. China
149 D6 Maoming China
149 □ Ma On Shan h. Hong Kong China
179 D6 Mapai Moz.
144 E3 Mapam Yumco l. China
124 C2 Mapane Indon.
178 B3 Mapé, Retenue de la resr Cameroon
181 F5 Maphodi S. Africa
206 D2 Mapimí Mex.
206 C2 Mapimí, Bolsón de des. Mex.
179 D6 Mapinhane Moz.
213 D3 Mapire Venez.
198 C1 Maple r. U.S.A.
187 H5 Maple Creek Canada
216 G4 Mapmaker Seamounts sea feature N. Pacific Ocean
181 G4 Mapoteng Lesotho
211 G4 Mapuera r. Brazil
181 J2 Mapulanguene Moz.
181 H1 Mapungubwe National Park S. Africa
179 D6 Maputo Moz.
181 J2 Maputo prov. Moz.
181 J3 Maputo r. Moz.
181 G4 Maputsoe Lesotho
137 H6 Maqar an Na'am well Iraq
148 B3 Maqu China
Maquan He r. China see Damqog Zangbo
178 B4 Maquela do Zombo Angola
215 C4 Maquinchao Arg.
215 C4 Maquinchao r. Arg.
190 B4 Maquoketa U.S.A.
190 B4 Maquoketa r. U.S.A.
141 G5 Mar r. Pak.
214 D3 Mar, Serra do mts Brazil
187 H1 Mara r. Canada
145 E5 Mara India
181 H1 Mara S. Africa
210 E4 Maraã Brazil
211 I5 Marabá Brazil
211 H3 Maracá, Ilha de i. Brazil
213 C2 Maracaibo Venez.
213 C2 Maracaibo, Lake inlet Venez.
214 A3 Maracaju Brazil
214 A3 Maracaju, Serra de hills Brazil
214 E1 Maracás, Chapada de hills Brazil
213 D2 Maracay Venez.
177 D2 Marādah Libya
176 C3 Maradi Niger
140 B2 Marāgheh Iran
214 E1 Maragogipe Brazil
153 B3 Maragondon Phil.
213 D4 Marahuaca, Cerro mt. Venez.
211 I4 Marajó, Baía de est. Brazil
211 I3 Marajó, Ilha de i. Brazil
181 G2 Marakele National Park S. Africa
143 B3 Marakkanam India
178 D3 Maralal Kenya
144 B3 Marala Weir Pak.
137 I1 Maralik Armenia
124 D5 Maralinga Australia
125 G2 Maramasike i. Solomon Is
129 E2 Marambio research stn Antarctica
153 C5 Marampit i. Indon.
137 J4 Marāna Iraq
197 G5 Marana U.S.A.
140 B2 Marand Iran
154 B4 Marang Malaysia
154 A3 Marang Myanmar
214 C1 Maranhão r. Brazil
210 D4 Marañón r. Peru
181 K2 Marão Moz.
167 C2 Marão mt. Port.
213 D4 Marari r. Brazil
128 A6 Mararoa r. N.Z.
190 D1 Marathon Canada
201 D7 Marathon FL U.S.A.
199 C6 Marathon TX U.S.A.
214 E1 Maraú Brazil
155 D3 Marau Indon.
213 C4 Marauiá r. Brazil
140 D2 Marāveh Tappeh Iran
153 C4 Marawi Phil.
167 D4 Marbella Spain
124 B4 Marble Bar Australia
197 G3 Marble Canyon U.S.A.
197 G3 Marble Canyon gorge U.S.A.
181 H2 Marble Hall S. Africa
203 H3 Marblehead U.S.A.
187 K2 Marble Island Canada
181 I5 Marburg S. Africa
202 E5 Marburg, Lake U.S.A.
165 G4 Marburg an der Lahn Germany
168 H7 Marcali Hungary
161 H5 March U.K.
126 C4 Marchant Hill Australia
164 D4 Marche-en-Famenne Belgium
167 D4 Marchena Spain
210 □ Marchena, Isla i. Galapagos Is Ecuador
Mar Chiquita, Lago l. Arg. see Mar Chiquita, Laguna
215 D1 Mar Chiquita, Laguna l. Arg.
168 G6 Marchtrenk Austria
201 D7 Marco U.S.A.
164 B4 Marcoing France
188 E2 Marcopeet Islands Canada
215 D2 Marcos Juárez Arg.
203 G2 Marcy, Mount U.S.A.
144 C2 Mardan Pak.
215 F3 Mar del Plata Arg.
137 H3 Mardin Turkey
125 G4 Maré i. New Caledonia
162 C3 Maree, Loch l. U.K.
190 A5 Marengo IA U.S.A.
190 C4 Marengo IL U.S.A.
170 E6 Marettimo, Isola i. Sicily Italy
172 E3 Marevo Rus. Fed.
199 B6 Marfa U.S.A.
126 B2 Margaret watercourse Australia
124 B5 Margaret River Australia
213 E2 Margarita, Isla de i. Venez.
150 D2 Margaritovo Rus. Fed.
127 G9 Margate Australia
181 I5 Margate S. Africa
161 I6 Margate U.K.
178 C3 Margherita Peak mt. Dem. Rep. Congo/Uganda
Margilan Uzbek. see Marg'ilon
139 G4 Marg'ilon Uzbek.
141 F4 Mārgō, Dasht-e des. Afgh.
Margo, Dasht-i des. Afgh. see Mārgō, Dasht-e
153 B5 Margosatubig Phil.
164 D4 Margraten Neth.
190 E3 Margrethe, Lake U.S.A.
186 E4 Marguerite Canada
129 B2 Marguerite Bay b. Antarctica
145 G3 Margyang China
137 K5 Marhaj Khalīl Iraq
139 H4 Marhamat Uzbek.
137 I3 Marhan Dāgh h. Iraq
173 E6 Marhanets' Ukr.
217 I7 Maria atoll Fr. Polynesia
212 C2 María Elena Chile
215 E3 María Ignacia Arg.
127 H9 Maria Island Australia
124 D3 Maria Island Australia
216 E4 Mariana Ridge sea feature N. Pacific Ocean
216 E5 Mariana Trench sea feature N. Pacific Ocean
145 H4 Mariani India
186 F2 Marian Lake Canada
199 F5 Marianna AR U.S.A.
201 C6 Marianna FL U.S.A.
168 F6 Mariánské Lázně Czech Rep.
206 C3 Marías, Islas is Mex.
206 I7 Mariato, Punta pt Panama
128 D1 Maria van Diemen, Cape N.Z.
170 F1 Maribor Slovenia
197 F5 Maricopa AZ U.S.A.
196 C4 Maricopa CA U.S.A.
197 F5 Maricopa Mountains U.S.A.
178 C3 Maridi watercourse South Sudan
129 B4 Marie Byrd Land reg. Antarctica
205 L5 Marie-Galante i. Guadeloupe
159 L3 Mariehamn Fin.
214 B1 Mariembero r. Brazil
165 L4 Marienberg Germany
164 F1 Marienhafe Germany
179 B6 Mariental Namibia
159 K4 Mariestad Sweden
201 C5 Marietta GA U.S.A.
202 C5 Marietta OH U.S.A.
166 G5 Marignane France
146 G1 Marii, Mys pt Rus. Fed.
146 A1 Mariinsk Rus. Fed.
138 E1 Mariinskiy Rus. Fed.
159 M5 Marijampolė Lith.
214 C3 Marília Brazil
207 D2 Marín Mex.
141 G4 Marin mt. Pak.
167 B1 Marín Spain
170 G5 Marina di Gioiosa Ionica Italy
172 D4 Mar"ina Horka Belarus
153 B3 Marinduque i. Phil.
190 D3 Marinette U.S.A.
214 B3 Maringá Brazil
167 B3 Marinha Grande Port.
200 B4 Marion IL U.S.A.
190 E5 Marion IN U.S.A.
203 J2 Marion ME U.S.A.
202 B4 Marion OH U.S.A.
201 E5 Marion SC U.S.A.
202 C6 Marion VA U.S.A.
201 D5 Marion, Lake U.S.A.
126 B5 Marion Bay Australia
213 D3 Maripa Venez.
196 C3 Mariposa U.S.A.
Mariscal Estigarribia Para. see Mariscal José Félix Estigarribia
212 D2 Mariscal José Félix Estigarribia Para.
166 H4 Maritime Alps mts France/Italy
171 K3 Maritsa r. Bulg.
172 I3 Mari-Turek Rus. Fed.
173 F6 Mariupol' Ukr.
213 E2 Mariusa, Caño r. Venez.
140 B3 Marīvān Iran
172 I3 Mariy El, Respublika aut. rep. Rus. Fed.
178 E3 Marka Somalia
139 K2 Markakol', Ozero l. Kazakh.
137 J2 Mārkān Iran
143 B3 Markapur India
159 K4 Markaryd Sweden
141 H3 Markaz-e Sayyidābād Afgh.
191 G3 Markdale Canada
181 H1 Marken S. Africa
164 D2 Markermeer l. Neth.
161 G5 Market Deeping U.K.
161 E5 Market Drayton U.K.
161 G5 Market Harborough U.K.
163 E3 Markethill U.K.
160 G4 Market Weighton U.K.
133 M3 Markha r. Rus. Fed.
191 H4 Markham Canada
Markhamet Uzbek. see Marhamat
139 I5 Markit China
173 F5 Markivka Ukr.
165 K3 Markkleeberg Germany
165 H2 Marklohe Germany
148 B3 Markog Qu r. China
165 K3 Markranstädt Germany
173 H5 Marks Rus. Fed.
165 H5 Marktheidenfeld Germany
168 E7 Marktoberdorf Germany
165 K4 Marktredwitz Germany
190 B6 Mark Twain Lake U.S.A.
164 F3 Marl Germany
203 H3 Marlborough U.S.A.
161 F6 Marlborough Downs hills U.K.
164 B5 Marle France
199 D6 Marlin U.S.A.
202 C5 Marlinton U.S.A.
127 F6 Marlo Australia
166 E4 Marmande France
136 B1 Marmara, Sea of g. Turkey
Marmara Denizi g. Turkey see Marmara, Sea of
136 B2 Marmara Gölü l. Turkey
136 B3 Marmaris Turkey
198 C2 Marmarth U.S.A.
202 C5 Marmet U.S.A.
188 B4 Marmion Lake Canada
170 D1 Marmolada mt. Italy
166 F2 Marne-la-Vallée France
137 J1 Marneuli Georgia
165 J1 Marnitz Germany
126 B3 Marnoo Australia
179 E5 Maroantsetra Madag.
165 I4 Maroldsweisach Germany
179 E5 Maromokotro mt. Madag.
179 D5 Marondera Zimbabwe
211 H2 Maroni r. Fr. Guiana
127 J1 Maroochydore Australia
123 I6 Marotiri is Fr. Polynesia
177 D3 Maroua Cameroon
179 E5 Marovoay Madag.
137 H4 Marqādah Syria
181 G4 Marquard S. Africa
123 J5 Marquesas Islands Fr. Polynesia
201 D7 Marquesas Keys is U.S.A.
190 D2 Marquette U.S.A.
164 B4 Marquion France
Marquises, Îles is Fr. Polynesia see Marquesas Islands
126 E3 Marra Australia
127 G3 Marra r. Australia
177 E3 Marra, Jebel Sudan
181 J2 Marracuene Moz.
176 B1 Marrakech Morocco
181 K2 Marrangua, Lagoa l. Moz.
127 G5 Marrar Australia
127 F8 Marrawah Australia
126 C2 Marree Australia
199 F6 Marrero U.S.A.
179 D5 Marromeu Moz.
179 D5 Marrupa Moz.
177 F2 Marsá al 'Alam Egypt
177 D1 Marsá al Burayqah Libya
178 D3 Marsabit Kenya
170 E6 Marsala Sicily Italy
177 E1 Marsá Maṭrūḥ Egypt
165 G3 Marsberg Germany
170 E3 Marsciano Italy
127 G4 Marsden Australia
164 C2 Marsdiep sea chan. Neth.
166 G5 Marseille France
190 C5 Marseilles U.S.A.
158 K2 Marsfjället mt. Sweden
187 H4 Marshall Canada
199 E5 Marshall AR U.S.A.
200 C4 Marshall IL U.S.A.
190 E4 Marshall MI U.S.A.
198 E2 Marshall MN U.S.A.
198 E4 Marshall MO U.S.A.
199 E5 Marshall TX U.S.A.
127 G7 Marshall Bay Australia
123 F2 Marshall Islands country N. Pacific Ocean
198 E3 Marshalltown U.S.A.
190 B3 Marshfield U.S.A.
201 E7 Marsh Harbour Bahamas
203 J1 Mars Hill U.S.A.
199 F6 Marsh Island U.S.A.
186 C2 Marsh Lake Canada
137 L3 Marshūn Iran
194 C3 Marsing U.S.A.
159 L4 Märsta Sweden
145 F4 Marsyangdi r. Nepal
Martaban Myanmar see Mottama
155 D3 Martapura Indon.
155 B3 Martapura Indon.
191 H2 Marten River Canada
187 H4 Martensville Canada
207 E2 Marte R. Gómez, Presa resr Mex.
203 H4 Martha's Vineyard i. U.S.A.
168 C7 Martigny Switz.
169 I6 Martin Slovakia
198 C3 Martin SD U.S.A.
201 B4 Martin TN U.S.A.
201 C5 Martin, Lake U.S.A.
207 E3 Martínez Mex.
197 E5 Martinez Lake U.S.A.
205 L6 Martinique terr. Caribbean Sea
129 B2 Martin Peninsula pen. Antarctica
202 D4 Martinsburg PA U.S.A.
202 E5 Martinsburg WV U.S.A.
202 C4 Martins Ferry U.S.A.
202 D6 Martinsville U.S.A.
219 H7 Martin Vaz, Ilhas is S. Atlantic Ocean
138 D2 Martok Kazakh.
128 E4 Marton N.Z.
167 G2 Martorell Spain
167 E4 Martos Spain
137 J1 Martuni Armenia
151 C7 Marugame Japan
128 D5 Maruia r. N.Z.
211 K6 Maruim Brazil
173 G7 Marukhis Ughelt'ekhili pass Georgia/Rus. Fed.
127 H5 Marulan Australia
139 K1 Marushka Rus. Fed.
140 D4 Marvast Iran
166 F4 Marvejols France
197 G2 Marvine, Mount U.S.A.
187 G4 Marwayne Canada
141 F2 Mary Turkm.
125 F4 Maryborough Qld Australia
126 E6 Maryborough Vic. Australia
180 E3 Marydale S. Africa
172 I4 Mar'yevka Rus. Fed.
187 H2 Mary Frances Lake Canada
203 E5 Maryland state U.S.A.
160 D3 Maryport U.K.
189 I3 Mary's Harbour Canada
189 J4 Marystown Canada
197 F2 Marysvale U.S.A.
189 G4 Marysville Canada
196 B2 Marysville CA U.S.A.
198 D4 Marysville KS U.S.A.
202 B4 Marysville OH U.S.A.
198 E3 Maryville MO U.S.A.
201 C5 Maryville TN U.S.A.
165 K2 Marzahna Germany
206 H6 Masachapa Nicaragua
136 E6 Masada tourist site Israel
140 D3 Masāhūn, Kūh-e mt. Iran
178 D4 Masaka Uganda
181 G5 Masakhane S. Africa
137 L2 Masallı Azer.
124 C2 Masamba Indon.
152 E6 Masan S. Korea
203 I1 Masardis U.S.A.
179 D5 Masasi Tanz.
210 F7 Masavi Bol.
206 H6 Masaya Nicaragua
153 B3 Masbate Phil.
153 B3 Masbate i. Phil.
176 C1 Mascara Alg.
218 H6 Mascarene Basin sea feature Indian Ocean
218 H6 Mascarene Plain sea feature Indian Ocean
218 H5 Mascarene Ridge sea feature Indian Ocean
203 G2 Mascouche Canada
181 G4 Maseru Lesotho
181 H4 Mashai Lesotho
149 C6 Mashan China
144 D2 Masherbrum mt. Pak.
141 E2 Mashhad Iran
144 C4 Mashi r. India
140 B3 Mashīrān Iran
181 I2 Mashishing S. Africa
141 F4 Mashkel, Hamun-i- salt flat Pak.
141 F5 Mashkel, Rudi-i r. Pak.
141 F4 Mashki Chah Pak.
141 F5 Māshkīd, Rūdkhāneh-ye r. Iran
158 M1 Masi Norway
206 B2 Masiáca Mex.
181 G5 Masibambane S. Africa
181 G4 Masilo S. Africa
178 D3 Masindi Uganda
153 A3 Masinloc Phil.
180 E5 Masinyusane S. Africa
Masira Island i. Oman see Maşīrah, Jazīrat
142 E5 Maşīrah, Jazīrat i. Oman
142 E6 Maşīrah, Khalīj b. Oman
137 J1 Masis Armenia
140 C4 Masjed-e Soleymān Iran
163 B4 Mask, Lough l. Ireland
136 G3 Maskanah Syria
141 E5 Maskūtān Iran
141 G4 Maslti Pak.
179 E5 Masoala, Parc National Madag.
179 F5 Masoala, Tanjona c. Madag.
190 E4 Mason MI U.S.A.
196 C2 Mason NV U.S.A.
199 D6 Mason TX U.S.A.
128 A7 Mason Bay N.Z.
198 E3 Mason City IA U.S.A.
190 C5 Mason City IL U.S.A.
202 D5 Masontown U.S.A.
Masqat Oman see Muscat
170 D2 Massa Italy
203 G3 Massachusetts state U.S.A.
203 H3 Massachusetts Bay U.S.A.
197 H1 Massadona U.S.A.
170 G4 Massafra Italy
177 D3 Massakory Chad
170 D3 Massa Marittimo Italy
179 D6 Massangena Moz.
179 B4 Massango Angola
178 D2 Massawa Eritrea
203 F2 Massawippi, Lac l. Canada
203 F2 Massena U.S.A.
186 C4 Masset Canada
191 F2 Massey Canada
166 F4 Massif Central mts France
202 C4 Massillon U.S.A.
179 D6 Massinga Moz.
179 D6 Massingir Moz.
181 J1 Massingir, Barragem de resr Moz.
181 J2 Massintonto r. Moz./S. Africa
203 G2 Masson-Angers Canada
137 L1 Maştağa Azer.
139 G5 Mastchoh Tajik.
138 B2 Masteksay Kazakh.
128 E4 Masterton N.Z.
201 E7 Mastic Point Bahamas
144 C1 Mastuj Pak.
141 G4 Mastung Pak.
172 C4 Masty Belarus
151 B7 Masuda Japan
137 L3 Masuleh Iran
179 D6 Masvingo Zimbabwe
136 F4 Maşyāf Syria
191 G2 Matachewan Canada
206 C1 Matachic Mex.
213 D4 Matacuni r. Venez.
146 D2 Matad Mongolia
178 B4 Matadi Dem. Rep. Congo
206 H5 Matagalpa Nicaragua
188 E4 Matagami Canada
188 E4 Matagami, Lac l. Canada
199 D6 Matagorda Island U.S.A.
148 C2 Mataigou China
154 C5 Matak i. Indon.
139 H2 Matak Kazakh.
128 F2 Matakana Island N.Z.
179 B5 Matala Angola
143 C5 Matale Sri Lanka
176 A3 Matam Senegal
206 D2 Matamoros Coahuila Mex.
207 E2 Matamoros Tamaulipas Mex.
153 B5 Matanal Point Phil.
179 D4 Matandu r. Tanz.
189 G4 Matane Canada
144 B2 Matanni Pak.
205 H4 Matanzas Cuba
189 G4 Matapédia r. Canada
215 B2 Mataquito r. Chile
143 C5 Matara Sri Lanka
155 E4 Mataram Indon.
210 D7 Matarani Peru
124 D3 Mataranka Australia
167 H2 Mataró Spain
181 H5 Matatiele S. Africa
128 B7 Mataura N.Z.
128 B7 Mataura r. N.Z.
125 J3 Matā'utu Wallis and Futuna Is
213 C3 Mataveni r. Col.
128 F3 Matawai N.Z.
210 F6 Mategua Bol.
206 D3 Matehuala Mex.
179 D5 Matemanga Tanz.
170 G4 Matera Italy
170 C6 Mateur Tunisia
188 D4 Matheson Canada
199 D6 Mathis U.S.A.
126 F5 Mathoura Australia
144 D4 Mathura India
153 C5 Mati Phil.
145 G4 Matiali India
149 D5 Matian China
144 B4 Matiari Pak.
207 F4 Matías Romero Mex.
189 G3 Matimekosh Canada
191 F2 Matinenda Lake Canada
203 I3 Matinicus Island U.S.A.
145 G5 Matla r. India
181 G2 Matlabas S. Africa
181 G2 Matlabas r. S. Africa
144 B4 Matli Pak.
161 F4 Matlock U.K.
213 D3 Mato r. Venez.
213 D3 Mato, Cerro mt. Venez.
210 G7 Mato Grosso Brazil
214 A1 Mato Grosso state Brazil
214 A1 Mato Grosso, Planalto do plat. Brazil
214 A3 Mato Grosso do Sul state Brazil
181 J2 Matola Moz.
167 B2 Matosinhos Port.
142 E5 Maţraḩ Oman
180 C6 Matroosberg mt. S. Africa
151 C7 Matsue Japan
150 G4 Matsumae Japan
151 E6 Matsumoto Japan
151 E7 Matsusaka Japan
151 C8 Matsuyama Japan
188 D4 Mattagami r. Canada
191 H2 Mattawa Canada
203 I2 Mattawamkeag U.S.A.
170 B2 Matterhorn mt. Italy/Switz.
194 D3 Matterhorn mt. U.S.A.
123 G2 Matthew Island S. Pacific Ocean
213 E3 Matthews Ridge Guyana
205 J4 Matthew Town Bahamas
140 D6 Maţţī, Sabkhat salt pan Saudi Arabia
200 B4 Mattoon U.S.A.
143 C5 Matugama Sri Lanka
125 H3 Matuku i. Fiji
213 E2 Maturín Venez.
153 C5 Matutuang i. Indon.
181 G4 Matwabeng S. Africa
144 E4 Mau India
145 E4 Mau Aimma India
164 B4 Maubeuge France
166 E5 Maubourguet France
162 D5 Mauchline U.K.
219 J10 Maud Seamount sea feature S. Atlantic Ocean
211 G4 Maués Brazil
144 E4 Mauganj India
196 □2 Maui i. U.S.A.
165 G6 Maulbronn Germany
215 B2 Maule admin. reg. Chile
215 B2 Maule r. Chile
215 B4 Maullín Chile
163 B3 Maumakeogh h. Ireland
202 B4 Maumee U.S.A.
202 B4 Maumee r. U.S.A.
191 F5 Maumee Bay U.S.A.
163 B4 Maumtrasna h. Ireland
163 B4 Maumturk Mountains hills Ireland
179 C5 Maun Botswana
196 □2 Mauna Kea vol. U.S.A.
196 □2 Mauna Loa vol. U.S.A.
196 □1 Maunalua Bay U.S.A.
145 E4 Maunath Bhanjan India
181 G1 Maunatlala Botswana
128 E2 Maungaturoto N.Z.
145 H5 Maungdaw Myanmar
154 A2 Maungmagan Islands Myanmar
184 F3 Maunoir, Lac l. Canada
126 B5 Maupertuis Bay Australia
124 D4 Maurice, Lake salt flat Australia
164 D3 Maurik Neth.
176 A3 Mauritania country Africa
175 I6 Mauritius country Indian Ocean
190 B4 Mauston U.S.A.
213 D4 Mavaca r. Venez.
179 C5 Mavinga Angola
181 G5 Mavuya S. Africa
144 D3 Mawana India
178 B4 Mawanga Dem. Rep. Congo
149 D4 Ma Wang Dui tourist site China
154 A3 Mawdaung Pass Myanmar/Thai.
128 G3 Mawhai Point N.Z.
154 A1 Mawlamyaing Myanmar
129 E5 Mawson research stn Antarctica
129 D5 Mawson Escarpment esc. Antarctica
129 B6 Mawson Peninsula pen. Antarctica
154 A3 Maw Taung mt. Myanmar
198 C2 Max U.S.A.
207 G3 Maxcanú Mex.
170 C5 Maxia, Punta mt. Sardinia Italy
190 D5 Maxinkuckee, Lake U.S.A.
158 M3 Maxmo Fin.
191 F2 Maxton U.S.A.
196 A2 Maxwell U.S.A.
162 F4 May, Isle of i. U.K.
155 C3 Maya i. Indon.
146 F1 Maya r. Rus. Fed.
205 J4 Mayaguana i. Bahamas
205 K5 Mayagüez Puerto Rico
176 C3 Mayahi Niger
141 H2 Mayakovskiy, Qullai mt. Tajik.
139 G4 Mayakum Kazakh.
178 B4 Mayama Congo
140 D2 Mayamey Iran
207 G4 Maya Mountains Belize
149 C5 Mayang China
148 B3 Mayanhe China
150 F5 Maya-san mt. Japan
162 D5 Maybole U.K.
137 J4 Maydān Sarāy Iraq
Maydā Shahr Afgh. see Maīdān Shahr
127 G9 Maydena Australia
164 F4 Mayen Germany
166 D2 Mayenne France
166 D2 Mayenne r. France
197 F4 Mayer U.S.A.
186 F4 Mayerthorpe Canada
128 C5 Mayfield N.Z.
200 B4 Mayfield U.S.A.
195 F5 Mayhill U.S.A.
152 E1 Mayi He r. China
139 I3 Maykamys Kazakh.
139 H2 Maykayyn Kazakh.
139 G5 Maykhura Tajik.
173 G6 Maykop Rus. Fed.
139 H4 Mayluu-Suu Kyrg.
138 E3 Maylybas Kazakh.
139 K1 Mayma Rus. Fed.
139 G4 Maymak Kazakh.
Maymyo Myanmar see Pyin-U-Lwin
146 B1 Mayna Rus. Fed.
143 A2 Mayni India
191 I3 Maynooth Canada
186 B2 Mayo Canada
153 C5 Mayo Bay Phil.
178 B4 Mayoko Congo
186 B2 Mayo Lake Canada
153 B3 Mayon vol. Phil.
215 D3 Mayor Buratovich Arg.
128 F2 Mayor Island N.Z.
212 D1 Mayor Pablo Lagerenza Para.
179 E5 Mayotte terr. Africa
153 B2 Mayraira Point Phil.
146 E1 Mayskiy Rus. Fed.
202 B5 Maysville U.S.A.
178 B4 Mayumba Gabon
145 E3 Mayum La pass China
143 B4 Mayuram India
191 F4 Mayville MI U.S.A.
198 D2 Mayville ND U.S.A.
202 D3 Mayville NY U.S.A.
190 C4 Mayville WI U.S.A.
198 C3 Maywood U.S.A.
215 D3 Maza Arg.
172 F3 Maza Rus. Fed.
179 C5 Mazabuka Zambia
211 H4 Mazagão Brazil
166 F5 Mazamet France
144 D1 Mazar China
141 G3 Mazār, Kūh-e mt. Afgh.
170 E6 Mazara del Vallo Sicily Italy
141 G2 Mazār-e Sharīf Afgh.
213 E3 Mazaruni r. Guyana
206 B1 Mazatán Mex.
207 G5 Mazatenango Guat.
206 C3 Mazatlán Mex.
197 G4 Mazatzal Peak U.S.A.
137 J3 Mazdaj Iran
141 F2 Mazdāvand Iran
159 M4 Mažeikiai Lith.
137 G2 Mazgirt Turkey
140 A5 Maẓhūr, 'Irq al des. Saudi Arabia
159 M4 Mazirbe Latvia
178 D4 Mazomora Tanz.
169 J4 Mazowiecka, Nizina lowland Poland
137 L3 Mazr'eh Iran
137 L5 Mazū Iran
149 F5 Mazu Dao i. Taiwan
179 C6 Mazunga Zimbabwe
172 D4 Mazyr Belarus
181 I3 Mbabane Swaziland
176 B4 Mbahiakro Côte d'Ivoire
178 B3 Mbaïki Cent. Afr. Rep.
179 D4 Mbala Zambia
178 D3 Mbale Uganda
176 D4 Mbalmayo Cameroon
178 B4 Mbandaka Dem. Rep. Congo
176 C4 Mbanga Cameroon
178 B4 M'banza Congo Angola
178 D4 Mbarara Uganda
178 C3 Mbari r. Cent. Afr. Rep.
181 J3 Mbaswana S. Africa
176 D4 Mbengwi Cameroon
179 D4 Mbeya Tanz.
181 H6 Mbhashe r. S. Africa
179 D5 Mbinga Tanz.
179 D6 Mbizi Zimbabwe
181 I2 Mbombela S. Africa
178 B3 Mbomo Congo
176 D4 Mbouda Cameroon
176 A3 Mbour Senegal
176 A3 Mbout Mauritania
179 D4 Mbozi Tanz.
178 C4 Mbuji-Mayi Dem. Rep. Congo
179 D4 Mbulu Tanz.
178 D4 Mbuyuni Tanz.
203 J2 McAdam Canada
199 E5 McAlester U.S.A.
202 E4 McAlevys Fort U.S.A.
127 H5 McAlister mt. Australia
199 D7 McAllen U.S.A.
202 B5 McArthur U.S.A.
191 I3 McArthur Mills Canada
186 E4 McBride Canada
194 C2 McCall U.S.A.
199 C6 McCamey U.S.A.
194 D3 McCammon U.S.A.
186 C4 McCauley Island Canada
184 H2 McClintock Channel Canada
196 B3 McClure, Lake U.S.A.
184 F2 McClure Strait Canada
199 F6 McComb U.S.A.
198 C3 McConaughy, Lake U.S.A.
202 E5 McConnellsburg U.S.A.
202 C5 McConnelsville U.S.A.
198 C3 McCook U.S.A.
187 J4 McCreary Canada
197 E4 McCullough Range mts U.S.A.
186 D3 McDame Canada
194 C3 McDermitt U.S.A.
218 I8 McDonald Islands Indian Ocean
194 D2 McDonald Peak U.S.A.
126 C2 McDonnell Creek watercourse Australia
180 B4 McDougall's Bay S. Africa
197 G5 McDowell Peak U.S.A.
196 C4 McFarland U.S.A.
187 H3 McFarlane r. Canada
197 E2 McGill U.S.A.
184 C3 McGrath U.S.A.
186 E4 McGregor r. Canada
180 C6 McGregor S. Africa
190 A2 McGregor U.S.A.
191 G2 McGregor Bay Canada
194 D3 McGuire, Mount U.S.A.
179 D4 Mchinga Tanz.
203 G2 McIndoe Falls U.S.A.
198 C2 McIntosh U.S.A.
125 I2 McKean i. Kiribati
202 A6 McKee U.S.A.
202 D4 McKeesport U.S.A.
203 F3 McKeever U.S.A.
201 B4 McKenzie U.S.A.
184 C3 McKinley, Mount U.S.A.
199 D5 McKinney U.S.A.
196 C4 McKittrick U.S.A.
198 C2 McLaughlin U.S.A.
186 F4 McLennan Canada
186 E3 McLeod r. Canada
186 E4 McLeod Lake Canada
194 B3 McLoughlin, Mount U.S.A.
190 E2 McMillan U.S.A.
194 B2 McMinnville OR U.S.A.
201 C5 McMinnville TN U.S.A.
129 B5 McMurdo research stn Antarctica
197 H4 McNary U.S.A.
186 F4 McNaughton Lake Canada
197 H6 McNeal U.S.A.
198 D4 McPherson U.S.A.
127 J2 McPherson Range mts Australia
186 B2 McQuesten r. Canada
201 D5 McRae U.S.A.
186 E1 McVicar Arm b. Canada
181 G6 Mdantsane S. Africa
170 B6 M'Daourouch Alg.
154 D2 M'Đrăk Vietnam
154 C1 Mê, Hon i. Vietnam
197 E3 Mead, Lake resr U.S.A.
199 C4 Meade U.S.A.
187 H4 Meadow Lake Canada
187 H4 Meadow Lake Provincial Park Canada
197 E3 Meadow Valley Wash r. U.S.A.
202 C4 Meadville U.S.A.
191 G3 Meaford Canada
150 I3 Meaken-dake vol. Japan

162 A2 Mealasta Island U.K.
167 B2 Mealhada Port.
162 D4 Meall a' Bhuiridh mt. U.K.
189 I3 Mealy Mountains Canada
127 H1 Meandarra Australia
186 F3 Meander River Canada
153 C5 Meares i. Indon.
166 F2 Meaux France
178 B4 Mebridege r. Angola
142 A5 Mecca Saudi Arabia
203 H2 Mechanic Falls U.S.A.
202 B4 Mechanicsburg U.S.A.
190 B5 Mechanicsville U.S.A.
164 C3 Mechelen Belgium
164 D4 Mechelen Neth.
176 B1 Mecheria Alg.
164 E4 Mechernich Germany
136 E1 Mecitözü Turkey
164 F4 Meckenheim Germany
168 E3 Mecklenburger Bucht b. Germany
165 J1 Mecklenburgische Seenplatte reg. Germany
165 K1 Mecklenburg-Vorpommern land Germany
179 D5 Mecula Moz.
167 C2 Meda Port.
143 B2 Medak India
155 A2 Medan Indon.
215 D3 Médanos Arg.
212 C7 Medanosa, Punta pt Arg.
143 C4 Medawachchiya Sri Lanka
143 B2 Medchal India
203 J2 Meddybemps Lake U.S.A.
167 H4 Médéa Alg.
165 G3 Medebach Germany
213 B3 Medellín Col.
161 F4 Meden r. U.K.
176 D1 Medenine Tunisia
176 A3 Mederdra Mauritania
194 B3 Medford OR U.S.A.
190 B3 Medford WI U.S.A.
203 F5 Medford Farms U.S.A.
171 M2 Medgidia Romania
190 B5 Media U.S.A.
215 C2 Media Luna Arg.
169 L7 Mediaş Romania
194 C2 Medical Lake U.S.A.
194 F3 Medicine Bow U.S.A.
194 F3 Medicine Bow Mountains U.S.A.
194 F3 Medicine Bow Peak U.S.A.
187 G4 Medicine Hat Canada
199 D4 Medicine Lodge U.S.A.
214 E2 Medina Brazil
142 A5 Medina Saudi Arabia
202 D3 Medina NY U.S.A.
202 C4 Medina OH U.S.A.
167 E2 Medinaceli Spain
167 D2 Medina del Campo Spain
167 D2 Medina de Rioseco Spain
145 F5 Medinipur India
156 F5 Mediterranean Sea Africa/Europe
170 B6 Medjerda, Monts de la mts Alg.
138 D2 Mednogorsk Rus. Fed.
166 D4 Médoc reg. France
172 H3 Medvedevo Rus. Fed.
173 H5 Medveditsa r. Rus. Fed.
170 F2 Medvednica mts Croatia
133 R2 Medvezh'i, Ostrova is Rus. Fed.
146 F2 Medvezh'ya, Gora mt. China/Rus. Fed.
172 E2 Medvezh'yegorsk Rus. Fed.
161 H6 Medway r. U.K.
124 B4 Meekatharra Australia
197 H1 Meeker U.S.A.
196 B2 Meeks Bay U.S.A.
189 I4 Meelpaeg Reservoir Canada
165 K4 Meerane Germany
164 E3 Meerlo Neth.
144 D3 Meerut India
194 E2 Meeteetse U.S.A.
178 D3 Mēga Eth.
155 B3 Mega i. Indon.
145 G4 Meghalaya state India
145 F5 Meghasani mt. India
145 G5 Meghna r. Bangl.
137 K2 Meghri Armenia
136 B3 Megisti i. Greece
158 N1 Mehamn Norway
141 G5 Mehar Pak.
124 B4 Meharry, Mount Australia
137 K4 Mehdīkhān Iran
144 D5 Mehekar India
145 G5 Meherpur Bangl.
202 E6 Meherrin r. U.S.A.
137 K2 Mehrābān Iran
140 D5 Mehrān watercourse Iran
137 K5 Mehrān Iraq
164 E4 Mehren Germany
140 D4 Mehrīz Iran
141 H3 Mehtar Lām Afgh.
214 C2 Meia Ponte r. Brazil
177 D4 Meiganga Cameroon
149 B4 Meigu China
152 C2 Meihekou China
149 E5 Mei Jiang r. China
162 D5 Meikle Millyea h. U.K.
147 B4 Meiktila Myanmar
165 I2 Meine Germany
165 I2 Meinersen Germany
165 I4 Meiningen Germany
180 E6 Meiringspoort pass S. Africa
149 B4 Meishan China
168 F5 Meißen Germany
149 C5 Meitan China
148 C3 Meixian China
149 E5 Meizhou China
144 D4 Mej r. India
215 C2 Mejicana mt. Arg.
212 B2 Mejillones Chile
178 D2 Mek'elē Eth.
176 A3 Mékhé Senegal
144 B3 Mekhtar Pak.
170 C7 Meknassy Tunisia
176 B1 Meknès Morocco
154 C2 Mekong r. Asia
146 B3 Mekong r. China
alt. Lancang Jiang
154 C3 Mekong, Mouths of the Vietnam
155 B2 Melaka Malaysia
216 F6 Melanesia is Oceania
216 F5 Melanesian Basin sea feature Pacific Ocean
153 A5 Melaut r. Malaysia
155 D3 Melawi r. Indon.
126 F6 Melbourne Australia (City Plan 102)
201 D6 Melbourne U.S.A.
162 □ Melby U.K.
207 G4 Melchor de Mencos Guat.
206 D2 Melchor Ocampo Mex.
168 D3 Meldorf Germany
191 F3 Meldrum Bay Canada
147 F6 Melekeok Palau
136 E2 Melendiz Dağı mt. Turkey
172 G4 Melenki Rus. Fed.
138 C1 Meleuz Rus. Fed.
189 F2 Mélèzes, Rivière aux r. Canada
177 D3 Melfi Chad
170 F4 Melfi Italy
187 I4 Melfort Canada
158 J3 Melhus Norway
167 C1 Melide Spain
176 B1 Melilla Spain
215 E2 Melincué Arg.
155 E3 Melintang, Danau l. Indon.
215 B2 Melipilla Chile
164 B3 Meliskerke Neth.
187 I5 Melita Canada
173 E6 Melitopol' Ukr.
168 G6 Melk Austria
181 H1 Melkrivier S. Africa
161 E6 Melksham U.K.
158 N2 Mellakoski Fin.
158 L3 Mellansel Sweden
165 G2 Melle Germany
190 B2 Mellen U.S.A.
159 K4 Mellerud Sweden
165 I4 Mellrichstadt Germany
165 G1 Mellum i. Germany
181 I4 Melmoth S. Africa
215 F2 Melo Uruguay
126 C4 Melrose Australia
162 F5 Melrose U.K.
165 H3 Melsungen Germany
161 G5 Melton Mowbray U.K.
166 F2 Melun France
187 I4 Melville Canada
124 E3 Melville, Cape Australia
153 A5 Melville, Cape Phil.
189 I3 Melville, Lake Canada
124 D3 Melville Island Australia
184 G2 Melville Island Canada
185 J3 Melville Peninsula Canada
163 C3 Melvin, Lough l. Ireland/U.K.
145 E2 Mêmar Co salt l. China
147 F7 Memberamo r. Indon.
181 H3 Memel S. Africa
165 I5 Memmelsdorf Germany
168 E7 Memmingen Germany
164 C5 Mémorial Américain tourist site France
155 C2 Mempawah Indon.
136 C7 Memphis tourist site Egypt
190 A5 Memphis MO U.S.A.
201 B5 Memphis TN U.S.A.
199 C5 Memphis TX U.S.A.
203 G2 Memphrémagog, Lac l. Canada
150 H3 Memuro-dake mt. Japan
173 E5 Mena Ukr.
199 E5 Mena U.S.A.
176 C3 Ménaka Mali
199 D6 Menard U.S.A.
190 C3 Menasha U.S.A.
155 D3 Mendawai r. Indon.
166 F4 Mende France
178 D2 Mendefera Eritrea
137 L3 Mendejīn Iran
220 M1 Mendeleyev Ridge sea feature Arctic Ocean
184 B4 Mendenhall, Cape U.S.A.
186 C3 Mendenhall Glacier U.S.A.
139 F2 Mendesh (abandoned) Kazakh.
207 E2 Méndez Mex.
178 D3 Mendī Eth.
124 E2 Mendi P.N.G.
161 E6 Mendip Hills U.K.
196 A2 Mendocino U.S.A.
194 A3 Mendocino, Cape U.S.A.
190 E4 Mendon U.S.A.
127 H3 Mendooran Australia
196 B3 Mendota CA U.S.A.
190 C5 Mendota IL U.S.A.
190 C4 Mendota, Lake U.S.A.
215 C2 Mendoza Arg.
215 C2 Mendoza prov. Arg.
215 C2 Mendoza r. Arg.
213 C2 Mene de Mauroa Venez.
213 C2 Mene Grande Venez.
171 L5 Menemen Turkey
148 E3 Mengcheng China
136 D1 Mengen Turkey
155 C3 Menggala Indon.
149 D5 Mengshan China
148 F3 Meng Shan mts China
148 E3 Mengyin China
149 B6 Mengzi China
189 G3 Menihek Canada
189 G3 Menihek Lakes Canada
126 E4 Menindee Australia
126 E4 Menindee, Lake Australia
126 C5 Meningie Australia
137 L4 Menjān Iran
133 N3 Menkere Rus. Fed.
166 F2 Mennecy France
190 D3 Menominee U.S.A.
190 D3 Menominee r. U.S.A.
190 C4 Menomonee Falls U.S.A.
190 B3 Menomonie U.S.A.
179 B5 Menongue Angola
Menorca i. Spain see Minorca
153 A6 Mensalong Indon.
154 B5 Mentakab Malaysia
155 A3 Mentawai, Kepulauan is Indon.
165 I3 Menteroda Germany
197 H4 Mentmore U.S.A.
155 C3 Mentok Indon.
166 H5 Menton France
202 C4 Mentor U.S.A.
176 C1 Menzel Bourguiba Tunisia
170 D6 Menzel Temime Tunisia
124 C4 Menzies Australia
129 D5 Menzies, Mount mt. Antarctica
206 C1 Meoqui Mex.
164 E2 Meppel Neth.
164 F2 Meppen Germany
181 J1 Mepuze Moz.
181 G4 Meqheleng S. Africa
172 G3 Mera r. Rus. Fed.
155 C4 Merak Indon.
158 J3 Meråker Norway
198 F4 Meramec r. U.S.A.
170 D1 Merano Italy
213 E3 Merari, Serra mt. Brazil
180 F1 Meratswe r. Botswana
155 E3 Meratus, Pegunungan mts Indon.
147 G7 Merauke Indon.
126 E5 Merbein Australia
196 B3 Merced U.S.A.
215 B1 Mercedario, Cerro mt. Arg.
215 E2 Mercedes Buenos Aires Arg.
212 E3 Mercedes Arg.
Mercedes Arg. see Villa Mercedes
215 E2 Mercedes Uruguay
202 A4 Mercer OH U.S.A.
190 B2 Mercer WI U.S.A.
186 F4 Mercoal (abandoned) Canada
128 E2 Mercury Islands N.Z.
185 L3 Mercy, Cape Canada
164 B4 Mere Belgium
161 E6 Mere U.K.
203 H3 Meredith U.S.A.
199 C5 Meredith, Lake U.S.A.
190 B6 Meredosia U.S.A.
173 F5 Merefa Ukr.
177 E3 Merga Oasis Sudan
138 B2 Mergen Kazakh.
Mergui Myanmar see Myeik
126 D5 Meribah Australia
171 L4 Meriç r. Greece/Turkey
207 G3 Mérida Mex.
167 C3 Mérida Spain
213 C2 Mérida Venez.
213 C2 Mérida, Cordillera de mts Venez.
203 G4 Meriden U.S.A.
196 B2 Meridian CA U.S.A.
199 F5 Meridian MS U.S.A.
166 D4 Mérignac France
158 N2 Merijärvi Fin.
159 M3 Merikarvia Fin.
127 H6 Merimbula Australia
126 D5 Meringur Australia
126 D6 Merino Australia
199 C5 Merkel U.S.A.
139 H4 Merki Kazakh.
154 □ Merlimau, Pulau reg. Sing.
177 F3 Merowe Sudan
124 B5 Merredin Australia
162 D5 Merrick h. U.K.
191 J3 Merrickville Canada
190 C3 Merrill U.S.A.
190 D5 Merrillville U.S.A.
198 C3 Merriman U.S.A.
186 E4 Merritt Canada
201 D6 Merritt Island U.S.A.
127 I4 Merriwa Australia
127 H3 Merrygoen Australia
178 E2 Mersa Fatma Eritrea
164 E5 Mersch Lux.
165 J3 Merseburg (Saale) Germany
161 E4 Mersey est. U.K.
136 E3 Mersin Turkey
155 B2 Mersing Malaysia
159 M4 Mērsrags Latvia
144 C4 Merta India
161 D6 Merthyr Tydfil U.K.
178 D3 Merti Kenya
167 C4 Mértola Port.
138 C3 Mertvyy Kultuk, Sor dry lake Kazakh.
129 C6 Mertz Glacier glacier Antarctica
178 D4 Meru vol. Tanz.
141 F4 Merui Pak.
180 D6 Merweville S. Africa
136 E1 Merzifon Turkey
164 E5 Merzig Germany
129 B3 Merz Peninsula pen. Antarctica
197 G5 Mesa U.S.A.
190 A2 Mesabi Range hills U.S.A.
170 G4 Mesagne Italy
197 H3 Mesa Verde National Park U.S.A.
213 B4 Mesay r. Col.
165 G3 Meschede Germany
158 L2 Meselefors Sweden
188 F3 Mesgouez, Lac l. Canada
Mesgouez Lake Canada see Mesgouez, Lac
172 I2 Meshchura Rus. Fed.
138 E4 Meshekli Uzbek.
141 E2 Meshkān Iran
173 G5 Meshkovskaya Rus. Fed.
190 E3 Mesick U.S.A.
171 J4 Mesimeri Greece
171 I5 Mesolongi Greece
137 I4 Mesopotamia reg. Iraq
197 E3 Mesquite NV U.S.A.
199 D5 Mesquite TX U.S.A.
197 E4 Mesquite Lake U.S.A.
179 D5 Messalo r. Moz.
171 K7 Messaras, Kolpos b. Greece
170 F5 Messina Sicily Italy
Messina S. Africa see Musina
170 F5 Messina, Strait of Italy
Messina, Stretta di str. Italy see Messina, Strait of
191 I2 Messines Canada
171 J6 Messini Greece
171 J6 Messiniakos Kolpos b. Greece
171 K5 Mesta, Akrotirio pt Greece
185 P2 Mesters Vig b. Greenland
165 J1 Mestlin Germany
170 E2 Mestre Italy
136 F1 Mesudiye Turkey
213 C3 Meta r. Col./Venez.
191 G2 Metagama Canada
185 K3 Meta Incognita Peninsula Canada
199 F6 Metairie U.S.A.
190 C5 Metamora U.S.A.
212 C3 Metán Arg.
171 I6 Methoni Greece
203 H3 Methuen U.S.A.
162 E4 Methven U.K.
170 G3 Metković Croatia
186 C3 Metlakatla U.S.A.
179 D5 Metoro Moz.
155 C4 Metro Indon.
200 B4 Metropolis U.S.A.
164 C4 Mettet Belgium
165 F2 Mettingen Germany
196 C4 Mettler U.S.A.
143 B4 Mettur India
178 D3 Metu Eth.
166 H2 Metz France
164 D4 Meuse r. Belgium/France
alt. Maas (Neth.)
166 G2 Meuse, Côtes de ridge France
165 K3 Meuselwitz Germany
161 C7 Mevagissey U.K.
148 B3 Mêwa China
199 D6 Mexia U.S.A.
204 A2 Mexicali Mex.
197 H3 Mexican Hat U.S.A.
206 C1 Mexicanos, Lago de los l. Mex.
197 H3 Mexican Water U.S.A.
206 C3 Mexico country Central America
207 E4 México state Mex.
203 H2 Mexico ME U.S.A.
198 F4 Mexico MO U.S.A.
203 E3 Mexico NY U.S.A.
207 F3 Mexico, Gulf of Mex./U.S.A.
207 E4 Mexico City Mex. (City Plan 116)
140 D3 Meybod Iran
165 K1 Meyenburg Germany
140 C3 Meymeh Iran
140 C3 Meymeh, Rūdkhāneh-ye r. Iran
207 F4 Mezcalapa Mex.
207 F4 Mezcalapa r. Mex.
171 J3 Mezdra Bulg.
132 F3 Mezen' Rus. Fed.
166 G4 Mézenc, Mont mt. France
146 A1 Mezhdurechensk Rus. Fed.
172 I2 Mezhdurechensk Respublika Komi Rus. Fed.
132 G2 Mezhdusharskiy, Ostrov i. Rus. Fed.
172 G3 Mezhozernyy Rus. Fed.
169 J7 Mezőtúr Hungary
206 C3 Mezquital Mex.
206 C3 Mezquital r. Mex.
206 D3 Mezquitic Mex.
159 N4 Mežvidi Latvia
181 I4 Mfolozi r. S. Africa
179 D5 Mfuwe Zambia
143 A2 Mhasvad India
181 I3 Mhlume Swaziland
144 C5 Mhow India
145 H5 Mi r. Myanmar
207 E4 Miahuatlán Mex.
167 D3 Miajadas Spain
197 G5 Miami AZ U.S.A.
201 D7 Miami FL U.S.A.
199 E4 Miami OK U.S.A.
201 D7 Miami Beach U.S.A.
140 C4 Mīān Āb Iran
141 F5 Mianaz Pak.
140 D2 Mīān Darreh Iran
140 B2 Mīāndowāb Iran
179 E5 Miandrivazo Madag.
140 B2 Mīāneh Iran
153 C5 Miangas i. Phil.
141 G5 Miani Hor b. Pak.
141 G3 Mīān Jōy Afgh.
149 B4 Mianning China
144 B2 Mianwali Pak.
148 C3 Mianxian China
148 C3 Mianyang China
149 C4 Mianyang China
148 F2 Miao Dao i. China
148 F2 Miaodao Qundao is China
139 J3 Miao'ergou China
149 F5 Miaoli Taiwan
179 E5 Miarinarivo Madag.
132 H4 Miass Rus. Fed.
197 G5 Mica Mountain U.S.A.
148 C3 Micang Shan mts China
169 J6 Michalovce Slovakia
187 H3 Michel Canada
165 J4 Michelau in Oberfranken Germany
165 H5 Michelstadt Germany
165 L2 Michendorf Germany
190 D2 Michigamme Lake U.S.A.
190 C2 Michigamme Reservoir U.S.A.
190 D2 Michigan state U.S.A.
190 D4 Michigan, Lake U.S.A.
190 D5 Michigan City U.S.A.
190 E2 Michipicoten Bay Canada
190 E2 Michipicoten Island Canada
190 E1 Michipicoten River Canada
206 D4 Michoacán state Mex.
172 G4 Michurinsk Rus. Fed.
206 H5 Mico r. Nicaragua
216 E5 Micronesia is Pacific Ocean
122 F2 Micronesia, Federated States of country Pacific Ocean
155 C2 Midai i. Indon.
219 F4 Mid-Atlantic Ridge sea feature Atlantic Ocean
219 H8 Mid-Atlantic Ridge sea feature Atlantic Ocean
180 C6 Middelberg Pass S. Africa
164 B3 Middelburg Neth.
180 F5 Middelburg Eastern Cape S. Africa
181 H2 Middelburg Mpumalanga S. Africa
159 J5 Middelfart Denmark
164 C3 Middelharnis Neth.
180 D5 Middelpos S. Africa
181 G2 Middelwit S. Africa
194 C3 Middle Alkali Lake U.S.A.
217 M5 Middle America Trench sea feature N. Pacific Ocean
203 H4 Middleboro U.S.A.
202 E4 Middleburg U.S.A.
203 F3 Middleburgh U.S.A.
203 G2 Middlebury U.S.A.
128 C6 Middlemarch N.Z.
202 B6 Middlesboro U.S.A.
160 F3 Middlesbrough U.K.
207 G4 Middlesex Belize
196 A2 Middletown CA U.S.A.
203 G4 Middletown CT U.S.A.
203 F5 Middletown DE U.S.A.
203 F4 Middletown NY U.S.A.
202 A5 Middletown OH U.S.A.
190 E4 Middleville U.S.A.
161 G7 Midhurst U.K.
166 E5 Midi, Canal du France
218 H7 Mid-Indian Basin sea feature Indian Ocean
218 I6 Mid-Indian Ridge sea feature Indian Ocean
191 H3 Midland Canada
191 E4 Midland MI U.S.A.
199 C5 Midland TX U.S.A.
163 C6 Midleton Ireland
123 E6 Midongy du Sud, Parc National de Madag.
216 F4 Mid-Pacific Mountains sea feature N. Pacific Ocean
158 □ Miðvágur Faroe Is
123 H2 Midway Islands terr. N. Pacific Ocean
194 F3 Midwest U.S.A.
199 D5 Midwest City U.S.A.
164 D2 Midwoud Neth.
137 H3 Midyat Turkey
162 □ Mid Yell U.K.
171 J3 Midzhur mt. Bulg./Serbia
159 N3 Miehikkälä Fin.
158 N2 Miekojärvi l. Fin.
169 J5 Mielec Poland
179 D4 Miembwe Tanz.
126 F4 Miena Australia
158 N1 Mieraslompolo Fin.
169 L7 Miercurea-Ciuc Romania
167 D1 Mieres del Camín Spain
178 E3 Mī'ēso Eth.
165 J2 Mieste Germany
203 F4 Mifflinburg U.S.A.
202 E4 Mifflintown U.S.A.
148 C3 Migang Shan mt. China
181 F3 Migdol S. Africa
141 E4 Mighān Iran
145 H3 Miging India
189 G4 Miguasha, Parc de nature res. Canada
207 E4 Miguel Alemán, Presa resr Mex.
206 D2 Miguel Auza Mex.
206 B2 Miguel Hidalgo, Presa resr Mex.
136 C2 Mihalıççık Turkey
151 C7 Mihara Japan
151 F7 Mihara-yama vol. Japan
167 F2 Mijares r. Spain
164 C2 Mijdrecht Neth.
191 F3 Mikado U.S.A.
169 M4 Mikashevichy Belarus
133 R3 Mikhalkino Rus. Fed.
172 F4 Mikhaylov Rus. Fed.
129 E6 Mikhaylov Island i. Antarctica
139 I1 Mikhaylovka Kazakh.
150 C3 Mikhaylovka Primorskiy Kray Rus. Fed.
173 G5 Mikhaylovka Volgogradskaya Oblast' Rus. Fed.
173 G6 Mikhaylovsk Rus. Fed.
139 I2 Mikhaylovskoye Rus. Fed.
145 H4 Mikir Hills India
159 N3 Mikkeli Fin.
159 N3 Mikkelin mlk Fin.
186 G3 Mikkwa r. Canada
178 D4 Mikumi Tanz.
172 I2 Mikun' Rus. Fed.
151 E6 Mikuni-sanmyaku mts Japan
151 F8 Mikura-jima i. Japan
198 E2 Milaca U.S.A.
143 A5 Miladhunmadulu Maldives
170 C2 Milan Italy (City Plan 112)
201 B5 Milan U.S.A.
126 C5 Milang Australia
179 D5 Milange Moz.
Milano Italy see Milan
136 A3 Milas Turkey
170 F5 Milazzo Sicily Italy
198 D2 Milbank U.S.A.
161 H5 Mildenhall U.K.
126 E5 Mildura Australia
149 B5 Mile China
194 F2 Miles City U.S.A.
163 C5 Milestone Ireland
170 F4 Miletto, Monte mt. Italy
163 D2 Milford Ireland
196 B1 Milford CA U.S.A.
203 G4 Milford CT U.S.A.
203 F5 Milford DE U.S.A.
190 C5 Milford IL U.S.A.
203 H3 Milford MA U.S.A.
203 I2 Milford ME U.S.A.
203 H3 Milford NH U.S.A.
203 F3 Milford NY U.S.A.
197 F2 Milford UT U.S.A.
161 B6 Milford Haven U.K.
128 A6 Milford Sound N.Z.
128 A6 Milford Sound inlet N.Z.
167 H4 Miliana Alg.
138 E2 Miliy Kazakh.
184 G5 Milk r. Canada
177 E3 Milk, Wadi el watercourse Sudan
133 Q4 Mil'kovo Rus. Fed.
167 F3 Millárs r. Spain
166 F4 Millau France
196 B1 Mill Creek r. U.S.A.
201 D5 Milledgeville GA U.S.A.
190 C5 Milledgeville IL U.S.A.
198 E2 Mille Lacs lakes U.S.A.
188 B4 Mille Lacs, Lac des l. Canada
126 A2 Miller watercourse Australia
198 D2 Miller U.S.A.
190 B3 Miller Dam Flowage resr U.S.A.
191 G3 Miller Lake Canada
173 G5 Millerovo Rus. Fed.
197 G6 Miller Peak U.S.A.
202 C4 Millersburg OH U.S.A.
202 E4 Millersburg PA U.S.A.
126 B3 Millers Creek Australia
202 E6 Millers Tavern U.S.A.
196 C3 Millerton Lake U.S.A.
162 C5 Millerur Point U.K.
126 D6 Millicent Australia
191 H3 Millington MI U.S.A.
201 B5 Millington TN U.S.A.
203 I2 Millinocket U.S.A.
129 D6 Mill Island i. Antarctica
127 I1 Millmerran Australia
160 D3 Millom U.K.
161 D7 Millport U.K.
203 F5 Millsboro U.S.A.
186 F2 Mills Lake Canada
202 C5 Millstone U.S.A.
189 G4 Milltown Canada
203 F5 Millville U.S.A.
203 J1 Milltown Canada
203 F5 Millville U.S.A.
203 I2 Milo U.S.A.
150 D3 Milogradovo Rus. Fed.
171 K6 Milos i. Greece
172 F4 Miloslavskoye Rus. Fed.
126 D2 Milparinka Australia
202 E4 Milroy U.S.A.
191 H4 Milton Canada
128 B7 Milton N.Z.
201 C6 Milton FL U.S.A.
190 A5 Milton IA U.S.A.
202 E4 Milton PA U.S.A.
203 G2 Milton VT U.S.A.
202 C4 Milton, Lake U.S.A.
194 C2 Milton-Freewater U.S.A.
161 G5 Milton Keynes U.K.
163 B5 Miltown Malbay Ireland
149 D4 Miluo China
190 D4 Milwaukee U.S.A.
219 E4 Milwaukee Deep sea feature Caribbean Sea
139 H2 Milybulak Kazakh.
173 G5 Milyutinskaya Rus. Fed.
166 D4 Mimizan France
178 B4 Mimongo Gabon
206 D2 Mina Mex.
196 C2 Mina U.S.A.
140 E5 Mīnāb Iran
147 E6 Minahasa, Semenanjung pen. Indon.
140 D5 Mīnā' Jabal 'Alī U.A.E.
187 K4 Minaki Canada
151 B8 Minamata Japan
151 E7 Minami-arupusu Kokuritsu-kōen nat. park Japan
150 G5 Minamisanriku Japan
151 B9 Minami-Satsuma Japan
155 B2 Minas Indon.
215 F2 Minas Uruguay
207 G5 Minas, Sierra de las mts Guat.
137 L7 Mīnā' Sa'ūd Kuwait
189 H4 Minas Basin b. Canada
215 F1 Minas de Corrales Uruguay
214 D2 Minas Gerais state Brazil
214 D2 Minas Novas Brazil
207 F4 Minatitlán Mex.
145 H5 Minbu Myanmar
145 H5 Minbya Myanmar
212 B6 Minchinmávida vol. Chile
170 D2 Mincio r. Italy
137 K2 Mincivan Azer.
153 C5 Mindanao i. Phil.
126 D5 Mindarie Australia
176 □ Mindelo Cape Verde
191 H3 Minden Canada
165 G2 Minden Germany
199 E5 Minden LA U.S.A.
196 C2 Minden NV U.S.A.
145 H6 Mindon Myanmar
126 E4 Mindona Lake imp. l. Australia
153 B3 Mindoro i. Phil.
153 A3 Mindoro Strait Phil.
178 B4 Mindouli Congo
138 D1 Mindyak Rus. Fed.
163 D6 Mine Head Ireland
161 D6 Minehead U.K.
214 B2 Mineiros Brazil
199 E5 Mineola U.S.A.
196 B1 Mineral U.S.A.
196 C3 Mineral King U.S.A.
173 G6 Mineral'nyye Vody Rus. Fed.
190 B4 Mineral Point U.S.A.
199 D5 Mineral Wells U.S.A.
197 F2 Minersville U.S.A.
170 G4 Minervino Murge Italy
145 E1 Minfeng China
179 C5 Minga Dem. Rep. Congo
137 K1 Mingäçevir Azer.
137 K1 Mingäçevir Su Anbarı resr Azer.
189 H3 Mingan Canada
148 E1 Ming'antu China
126 D4 Mingary Australia
Mingbulak Uzbek. see Mingbuloq
138 E4 Mingbuloq Uzbek.
148 E3 Minggang China
148 F3 Mingguang China
139 H4 Ming-Kush Kyrg.
167 F3 Minglanilla Spain
179 D5 Mingoyo Tanz.
149 B4 Mingshan China
146 E2 Mingshui China
162 A4 Mingulay i. U.K.
149 E5 Mingxi China
148 B2 Minhe China
149 E5 Minhou China
143 A4 Minicoy atoll India
124 B4 Minilya Australia
189 H3 Minipi Lake Canada
187 I4 Minitonas Canada
149 F5 Min Jiang r. Fujian China
148 B4 Min Jiang r. Sichuan China
178 B3 Minkébé, Parc National de nat. park Gabon
148 A2 Minle China
176 C4 Minna Nigeria
159 K3 Minne Sweden
198 E2 Minneapolis U.S.A.
187 J4 Minnedosa Canada
193 G2 Minnesota r. U.S.A.
198 E2 Minnesota state U.S.A.
126 A4 Minnipa Australia
188 B4 Minnitaki Lake Canada
167 B2 Miño r. Port./Spain
190 C3 Minocqua U.S.A.
190 B2 Minong U.S.A.
190 C5 Minonk U.S.A.
167 I2 Minorca i. Spain
198 C1 Minot U.S.A.
148 B2 Minqin China
149 F5 Minqing China
148 B3 Min Shan mts China
145 H4 Minsin Myanmar
172 C4 Minsk Belarus
169 J4 Mińsk Mazowiecki Poland
161 E5 Minsterley U.K.
144 C1 Mintaka Pass China/Pakistan
143 A3 Mintang China
189 G4 Minto Canada
188 F2 Minto, Lac l. Canada
184 G2 Minto Inlet Canada
195 F4 Minturn U.S.A.
136 C6 Minūf Egypt
146 B1 Minusinsk Rus. Fed.
145 H3 Minutang India
148 B3 Minxian China
126 E6 Minyip Australia
191 E3 Mio U.S.A.
188 E4 Miquelon Canada
189 I4 Miquelon i. N. America
213 A4 Mira r. Col.
141 F4 Mīrābād Afgh.
203 F2 Mirabel Canada
214 D2 Mirabela Brazil
211 I5 Miracema do Tocantins Brazil
211 I5 Mirador, Parque Nacional de nat. park Brazil
207 G4 Mirador-Dos Lagunos-Río Azul, Parque Nacional nat. park Guat.
213 B4 Miraflores Col.
137 H5 Mīrah, Wādī al watercourse Iraq/Saudi Arabia
214 D2 Miralta Brazil
215 F3 Miramar Arg.
207 G4 Miramar, Lago l. Mex.
166 G5 Miramas France
189 G4 Miramichi Canada
171 K7 Mirampellou, Kolpos b. Greece
214 A3 Miranda Brazil
214 A3 Miranda r. Brazil
196 A1 Miranda U.S.A.
167 E1 Miranda de Ebro Spain
167 C2 Mirandela Port.
170 D2 Mirandola Italy
214 B3 Mirandópolis Brazil
144 B2 Miran Shah Pak.
142 D6 Mirbāţ Oman
166 E5 Mirepoix France
155 D2 Miri Sarawak Malaysia
141 F4 Miri mt. Pak.
143 B2 Mirialguda India
215 G2 Mirim, Lagoa l. Brazil
141 F4 Mīrjāveh Iran
129 D6 Mirny research stn Antarctica
172 G2 Mirnyy Arkhangel'skaya Oblast' Rus. Fed.
133 M3 Mirnyy Rus. Fed.
187 I3 Mirond Lake Canada
165 K1 Mirow Germany
144 C2 Mirpur Pak.
144 B4 Mirpur Batoro Pak.
144 B4 Mirpur Khas Pak.
144 A4 Mirpur Sakro Pak.
186 G4 Mirror Canada
149 □ Mirs Bay Hong Kong China
152 E6 Miryang S. Korea
140 D3 Mīrzā, Chāh-e well Iran
145 E4 Mirzapur India
151 C8 Misaki Japan
139 J5 Misalay China
150 G4 Misawa Japan
189 H4 Miscou Island Canada
141 C1 Misgar Pak.
150 B2 Mishan China
140 C5 Mishāsh al Hādī well Saudi Arabia
190 D5 Mishawaka U.S.A.
190 E1 Mishibishu Lake Canada
151 B7 Mi-shima i. Japan
145 H3 Mishmi Hills India
124 F3 Misima Island P.N.G.
206 I5 Miskitos, Cayos is Nicaragua
169 J6 Miskolc Hungary
147 F7 Misoöl i. Indon.
190 B2 Misquah Hills U.S.A.
177 D1 Mişrātah Libya
144 E4 Misrikh India
191 E1 Missanabie Canada
188 D3 Missinaibi r. Canada
191 F1 Missinaibi Lake Canada
187 I3 Missinipe Canada
186 E5 Mission Canada
198 C3 Mission SD U.S.A.
207 E2 Mission TX U.S.A.
188 D3 Missisa Lake Canada
191 F2 Mississagi r. Canada
191 H4 Mississauga Canada
190 E5 Mississinewa Lake U.S.A.
191 I3 Mississippi r. Canada
199 F6 Mississippi r. U.S.A.
199 F5 Mississippi state U.S.A.
199 F6 Mississippi Delta U.S.A.
194 D2 Missoula U.S.A.
198 C2 Missouri r. U.S.A.
190 A6 Missouri state U.S.A.
198 E3 Missouri Valley U.S.A.
185 K4 Mistassibi r. Canada
189 F4 Mistassini r. Canada
188 F3 Mistassini, Lac l. Canada
189 H2 Mistastin Lake Canada
168 H6 Mistelbach Austria
189 H2 Mistinibi, Lac l. Canada
188 F3 Mistissini Canada
186 C3 Misty Fiords National Monument Wilderness nat. park U.S.A.
206 C3 Mita, Punta de pt Mex.
124 E4 Mitchell Australia
127 J2 Mitchell r. N.S.W. Australia
124 E3 Mitchell r. Qld Australia
127 G6 Mitchell r. Vic. Australia
191 G4 Mitchell Canada
198 D3 Mitchell U.S.A.
190 E3 Mitchell, Lake U.S.A.
201 D5 Mitchell, Mount U.S.A.
163 C5 Mitchelstown Ireland
136 C6 Mīt Ghamr Egypt
144 B4 Mithankot Pak.
144 B4 Mithi Pak.
144 B4 Mithrani Canal canal Pak.
171 L5 Mithymna Greece
186 C3 Mitkof Island U.S.A.
151 G6 Mito Japan
179 D4 Mitole Tanz.
128 E4 Mitre mt. N.Z.
125 H3 Mitre Island Solomon Is
171 I3 Mitrovicë Kosovo
127 I5 Mittagong Australia
127 G6 Mitta Mitta Australia
165 G2 Mittellandkanal canal Germany
165 K5 Mitterteich Germany
165 K4 Mittweida Germany
213 C4 Mitú Col.
213 C4 Mituas Col.
179 C5 Mitumba, Chaîne des mts Dem. Rep. Congo
178 C4 Mitumba, Monts mts Dem. Rep. Congo
178 B3 Mitzic Gabon
151 F7 Miura Japan
137 G4 Miyāh, Wādī al watercourse Syria
151 F7 Miyake-jima i. Japan
150 G5 Miyako Japan
151 B9 Miyakonojō Japan
148 B4 Miyaluo China
138 C2 Miyaly Kazakh.
144 B5 Miyani India
151 E6 Miyanoura-dake mt. Japan
151 B9 Miyazaki Japan
151 D7 Miyazu Japan
149 B5 Miyi China
151 C7 Miyoshi Japan
148 E1 Miyun China
148 E1 Miyun Shuiku resr China
141 G3 Mīzān 'Alāqahdārī Afgh.
178 D3 Mīzan Teferī Eth.
177 D1 Mizdah Libya
163 B6 Mizen Head Ireland
173 B5 Mizhhirr"ya Ukr.
148 D2 Mizhi China
145 H5 Mizoram state India
159 K4 Mjölby Sweden
178 D4 Mkata Tanz.
179 D4 Mkomazi Tanz.
179 C5 Mkushi Zambia
168 G5 Mladá Boleslav Czech Rep.
171 I2 Mladenovac Serbia
169 J4 Mława Poland
170 G3 Mljet i. Croatia
181 G5 Mlungisi S. Africa
169 L5 Mlyniv Ukr.
181 F2 Mmabatho S. Africa
181 G1 Mmamabula Botswana
181 F2 Mmathethe Botswana
159 I3 Mo Norway
197 H2 Moab U.S.A.
124 E3 Moa Island Australia
125 I3 Moala i. Fiji
140 D3 Mo'alla Iran
181 J2 Moamba Moz.
126 D2 Moanba, Lake salt flat Australia
197 E3 Moapa U.S.A.
163 D4 Moate Ireland
178 C4 Moba Dem. Rep. Congo
151 G7 Mobara Japan
140 C3 Mobārakeh Iran
140 D4 Mobārakeh Iran
178 C3 Mobayi-Mbongo Dem. Rep. Congo
198 E4 Moberly U.S.A.
201 B6 Mobile AL U.S.A.
197 F5 Mobile AZ U.S.A.
201 B6 Mobile Bay U.S.A.
198 C2 Mobridge U.S.A.
211 I4 Mocajuba Brazil
179 E5 Moçambique Moz.
213 D2 Mocapra r. Venez.
154 C3 Môc Châu Vietnam
142 B7 Mocha Yemen
213 D2 Mochirma, Parque Nacional nat. park Venez.
179 C6 Mochudi Botswana
179 E5 Mocimboa da Praia Moz.
165 J2 Möckern Germany
165 H5 Möckmühl Germany
158 M2 Mockträsk Sweden
213 A4 Mocoa Col.
214 C3 Mococa Brazil
206 C2 Mocorito Mex.
206 C2 Moctezuma Mex.
179 D5 Mocuba Moz.
166 H4 Modane France
144 C5 Modasa India
180 F4 Modder r. S. Africa
170 D2 Modena Italy

197 F3 Modena U.S.A.
196 B3 Modesto U.S.A.
181 H2 Modimolle S. Africa
181 I1 Modjadjiskloof S. Africa
127 G7 Moe Australia
161 D5 Moel Sych h. U.K.
159 J3 Moelv Norway
158 L1 Moen Norway
197 G3 Moenkopi U.S.A.
128 C6 Moeraki Point N.Z.
164 E3 Moers Germany
162 E5 Moffat U.K.
144 C3 Moga India
178 E3 Mogadishu Somalia
202 C4 Mogadore Reservoir U.S.A.
181 H1 Mogalakwena r. S. Africa
181 H2 Moganyaka S. Africa
165 K2 Mögelin Germany
139 F5 Moghiyon Tajik.
214 C3 Mogi-Mirim Brazil
146 D1 Mogocha Rus. Fed.
170 C6 Mogod mts Tunisia
181 F2 Mogoditshane Botswana
146 B4 Mogok Myanmar
197 H5 Mogollon Mountains U.S.A.
197 G4 Mogollon Plateau U.S.A.
181 H1 Mogwadi S. Africa
181 H1 Mogwadi r. S. Africa
181 G2 Mogwase S. Africa
171 H2 Mohács Hungary
128 F3 Mohaka r. N.Z.
181 G5 Mohale's Hoek Lesotho
144 D3 Mohali India
187 I5 Mohall U.S.A.
141 E3 Moḩammad Iran
167 G5 Mohammadia Alg.
144 E3 Mohan r. India/Nepal
197 E4 Mohave, Lake U.S.A.
197 F5 Mohawk U.S.A.
203 F3 Mohawk r. U.S.A.
197 F5 Mohawk Mountains U.S.A.
Mohéli i. Comoros see Mwali
141 H5 Mohenjo Daro tourist site Pak.
163 D4 Mohill Ireland
165 G3 Möhne r. Germany
197 F4 Mohon Peak U.S.A.
179 D4 Mohoro Tanz.
173 C5 Mohyliv-Podil's'kyy Ukr.
159 I4 Moi Norway
181 G1 Moijabana Botswana
181 J2 Moine Moz.
169 M7 Moinești Romania
203 F2 Moira U.S.A.
158 K2 Mo i Rana Norway
145 H4 Moirang India
159 N4 Mõisaküla Estonia
215 E1 Moisés Ville Arg.
189 G3 Moisie Canada
189 G3 Moisie r. Canada
166 E4 Moissac France
196 C4 Mojave U.S.A.
196 D4 Mojave r. U.S.A.
196 D4 Mojave Desert U.S.A.
151 B8 Moji Japan
214 C3 Moji das Cruzes Brazil
214 C3 Moji-Guaçu r. Brazil
145 F4 Mokama India
Mokapu Pen. U.S.A. see Mōkapu Peninsula
196 □1 Mōkapu Peninsula U.S.A.
128 E3 Mokau N.Z.
128 E3 Mokau r. N.Z.
196 B2 Mokelumne r. U.S.A.
140 D4 Mokh, Gowd-e l. Iran
181 H4 Mokhoabong Pass Lesotho
181 H4 Mokhotlong Lesotho
170 D7 Moknine Tunisia
128 E1 Mokohinau Islands N.Z.
177 D3 Mokolo Cameroon
181 G2 Mokolo r. S. Africa
181 H2 Mokopane S. Africa
152 D6 Mokpo S. Korea
172 G4 Moksha r. Rus. Fed.
172 H4 Mokshan Rus. Fed.
196 □1 Moku 'Āuia i. U.S.A.
Mokuauia I. U.S.A. see Moku 'Āuia
196 □1 Moku Lua is U.S.A.
Mokulua Is U.S.A. see Moku Lua
139 I3 Molaly Kazakh.
207 E3 Molango Mex.
167 F3 Molatón mt. Spain
Moldavia country Europe see Moldova
158 I3 Molde Norway
158 K2 Moldjord Norway
173 D6 Moldova country Europe
171 K2 Moldoveanu, Vârful mt. Romania
161 D7 Mole r. U.K.
176 B4 Mole National Park Ghana
179 C6 Molepolole Botswana
159 N5 Molėtai Lith.
170 G4 Molfetta Italy
167 F2 Molina de Aragón Spain
190 B5 Moline U.S.A.
159 K4 Molkom Sweden
137 L4 Mollā Bodāgh Iran
145 H4 Mol Len mt. India
165 L1 Möllenbeck Germany
210 D7 Mollendo Peru
165 I1 Mölln Germany
159 K4 Mölnlycke Sweden
172 F3 Molochnoye Rus. Fed.
158 P1 Molochnyy Rus. Fed.
139 G1 Molodogvardeyskoye Kazakh.
172 E3 Molodoy Tud Rus. Fed.
Molokai i. U.S.A. see Moloka'i
196 □2 Moloka'i i. U.S.A.
172 I3 Moloma r. Rus. Fed.
127 H4 Molong Australia
180 F2 Molopo watercourse Botswana/S. Africa
177 D4 Moloundou Cameroon
187 J4 Molson Lake Canada
147 E7 Moluccas is Indon.
Molucca Sea sea Indon. see Maluku, Laut
179 D5 Moma Moz.
133 P3 Moma r. Rus. Fed.
126 E3 Momba Australia
178 D4 Mombasa Kenya
145 H4 Mombi New India
214 B2 Mombuca, Serra da hills Brazil
173 C7 Momchilgrad Bulg.
190 D5 Momence U.S.A.
213 B2 Mompós Col.
159 K5 Møn i. Denmark
197 G2 Mona U.S.A.
205 K5 Mona, Isla i. Puerto Rico
162 A3 Monach, Sound of sea chan. U.K.
162 A3 Monach Islands U.K.
166 H5 Monaco country Europe
219 H4 Monaco Basin sea feature N. Atlantic Ocean
162 D3 Monadhliath Mountains U.K.
163 E3 Monaghan Ireland
199 C6 Monahans U.S.A.
205 K5 Mona Passage Dom. Rep./Puerto Rico
179 E5 Monapo Moz.
162 C3 Monar, Loch l. U.K.
186 D4 Monarch Mountain Canada
195 F4 Monarch Pass U.S.A.
186 F4 Monashee Mountains Canada
170 D7 Monastir Tunisia
169 O3 Monastyrshchina Rus. Fed.
173 D5 Monastyryshche Ukr.
150 H2 Monbetsu Japan
170 B2 Moncalieri Italy
167 F2 Moncayo mt. Spain
158 P2 Monchegorsk Rus. Fed.
164 E3 Mönchengladbach Germany
167 B4 Monchique Port.
201 E5 Moncks Corner U.S.A.
206 D2 Monclova Mex.
189 H4 Moncton Canada
167 C2 Mondego r. Port.
170 B2 Mondovì Italy
190 B3 Mondovi U.S.A.
170 E4 Mondragone Italy
171 J6 Monemvasia Greece
150 G1 Moneron, Ostrov i. Rus. Fed.
202 D4 Monessen U.S.A.
191 J1 Monet Canada
163 D5 Moneygall Ireland
163 E3 Moneymore U.K.
170 E2 Monfalcone Italy
167 C1 Monforte de Lemos Spain
178 C3 Monga Dem. Rep. Congo
149 C6 Mông Cai Vietnam
152 C4 Monggŭmp'o-ri N. Korea
154 A1 Mong Mau Myanmar
146 B2 Mongolia country Asia
146 A2 Mongolian Altai, Petroglyphic Complexes of the tourist site Mongolia
144 C2 Mongora Pak.
179 C5 Mongu Zambia
203 I3 Monhegan Island U.S.A.
162 E5 Moniaive U.K.
196 D2 Monitor Mountain U.S.A.
196 D2 Monitor Range mts U.S.A.
163 C4 Monivea Ireland
191 G4 Monkton Canada
145 F3 Mon La pass China
161 E6 Monmouth U.K.
190 B5 Monmouth IL U.S.A.
203 H2 Monmouth ME U.S.A.
186 E4 Monmouth Mountain Canada
161 E6 Monnow r. U.K.
176 C3 Mono r. Togo
196 C3 Mono Lake U.S.A.
203 H4 Monomoy Point U.S.A.
190 D5 Monon U.S.A.
190 B4 Monona U.S.A.
202 C5 Monongahela r. U.S.A.
170 G4 Monopoli Italy
167 F2 Monreal del Campo Spain
170 E5 Monreale Sicily Italy
199 E5 Monroe LA U.S.A.
191 F5 Monroe MI U.S.A.
201 D5 Monroe NC U.S.A.
203 F4 Monroe NY U.S.A.
197 F2 Monroe UT U.S.A.
190 C4 Monroe WI U.S.A.
190 B6 Monroe City U.S.A.
201 C6 Monroeville U.S.A.
176 A4 Monrovia Liberia
164 B4 Mons Belgium
164 E4 Monschau Germany
170 D2 Monselice Italy
165 F4 Montabaur Germany
179 E5 Montagne d'Ambre, Parc National de nat. park Madag.
180 D6 Montagu S. Africa
190 D4 Montague U.S.A.
209 G7 Montagu Island S. Sandwich Is
170 F5 Montalto mt. Italy
170 G5 Montalto Uffugo Italy
171 J3 Montana Bulg.
194 E2 Montana state U.S.A.
206 H5 Montaña de Yoro nat. park Hond.
211 H3 Montanhas do Tumucumaque, Parque Nacional nat. park Brazil
166 F3 Montargis France
166 E4 Montauban France
203 G4 Montauk U.S.A.
203 H4 Montauk Point U.S.A.
181 H4 Mont-aux-Sources mt. Lesotho
166 G3 Montbard France
166 H4 Mont Blanc mt. France/Italy
167 G2 Montblanc Spain
166 G4 Montbrison France
166 G3 Montceau-les-Mines France
164 C5 Montcornet France
166 D5 Mont-de-Marsan France
166 F2 Montdidier France
207 E4 Monte Albán tourist site Mex.
211 H4 Monte Alegre Brazil
214 C1 Monte Alegre de Goiás Brazil
176 D4 Monte Alen, Parque Nacional nat. park Equat. Guinea
214 D1 Monte Azul Brazil
188 E4 Montebello Canada
170 F6 Montebello Ionico Italy
170 E2 Montebelluna Italy
215 D2 Monte Buey Arg.
166 H5 Monte-Carlo Monaco
215 F1 Monte Caseros Arg.
Monte Christo S. Africa see Monte Cristo
215 C2 Monte Comán Arg.
205 J5 Monte Cristi Dom. Rep.
181 G1 Monte Cristo S. Africa
170 D3 Montecristo, Isola di i. Italy
205 I5 Montego Bay Jamaica
166 G4 Montélimar France
212 E2 Monte Lindo r. Para.
170 F4 Montella Italy
190 C4 Montello U.S.A.
207 E2 Montemorelos Mex.
167 B3 Montemor-o-Novo Port.
171 H3 Montenegro country Europe
179 D5 Montepuez Moz.
170 D3 Montepulciano Italy
166 F2 Montereau-Fault-Yonne France
196 B3 Monterey CA U.S.A.
202 D5 Monterey VA U.S.A.
196 B3 Monterey Bay U.S.A.
213 B2 Montería Col.
210 F7 Montero Bol.
207 D2 Monterrey Mex.
170 F4 Montesano sulla Marcellana Italy
211 K6 Monte Santo Brazil
214 D2 Montes Claros Brazil
170 F3 Montesilvano Italy
170 D3 Montevarchi Italy
215 F2 Montevideo Uruguay
198 E2 Montevideo U.S.A.
195 F4 Monte Vista U.S.A.
190 A5 Montezuma U.S.A.
197 G4 Montezuma Castle National Monument nat. park U.S.A.
197 H3 Montezuma Creek U.S.A.
196 D3 Montezuma Peak U.S.A.
164 D3 Montfort Neth.
161 D5 Montgomery U.K.
201 C5 Montgomery U.S.A.
168 C7 Monthey Switz.
199 F5 Monticello AR U.S.A.
201 D6 Monticello FL U.S.A.
190 B4 Monticello IA U.S.A.
190 D5 Monticello IN U.S.A.
203 J1 Monticello ME U.S.A.
190 B5 Monticello MO U.S.A.
203 F4 Monticello NY U.S.A.
197 H3 Monticello UT U.S.A.
190 C4 Monticello WI U.S.A.
215 E1 Montiel, Cuchilla de hills Arg.
166 E4 Montignac France
164 C4 Montignies-le-Tilleul Belgium
166 G2 Montigny-le-Roi France
164 E5 Montigny-lès-Metz France
206 I7 Montijo, Golfo de b. Panama
167 D4 Montilla Spain
189 G4 Mont-Joli Canada
191 J2 Mont-Laurier Canada
189 G4 Mont-Louis Canada
166 F3 Montluçon France
189 F4 Montmagny Canada
164 D5 Montmédy France
164 B6 Montmirail France
190 D5 Montmorenci U.S.A.
189 F4 Montmorency Canada
166 E3 Montmorillon France
164 B6 Montmort-Lucy France
124 F4 Monto Australia
194 E3 Montpelier ID U.S.A.
190 E5 Montpelier IN U.S.A.
202 A4 Montpelier OH U.S.A.
203 G2 Montpelier VT U.S.A.
166 F5 Montpellier France
188 F4 Montréal Canada (City Plan 113)
191 F2 Montreal r. Ont. Canada
191 G2 Montreal r. Ont. Canada
Montréal-Dorval Canada see Montréal-Trudeau
190 E2 Montreal Island Canada
187 H4 Montreal Lake Canada
187 H4 Montreal Lake l. Canada
203 F2 Montréal-Mirabel airport Canada
190 E2 Montreal River Canada
203 G2 Montréal-Trudeau airport Canada
168 C7 Montreux Switz.
180 D3 Montrose well S. Africa
162 F4 Montrose U.K.
195 F4 Montrose CO U.S.A.
191 F4 Montrose MI U.S.A.
203 F4 Montrose PA U.S.A.
189 G4 Monts, Pointe des pt Canada
205 L5 Montserrat terr. Caribbean Sea
189 F3 Montviel, Lac l. Canada
197 G3 Monument Valley reg. U.S.A.
146 B4 Monywa Myanmar
170 C2 Monza Italy
179 C5 Monze Zambia
167 G2 Monzón Spain
181 I4 Mooi r. S. Africa
180 B3 Mooifontein Namibia
181 I4 Mooirivier S. Africa
181 G1 Mookane Botswana
181 H2 Mookgophong S. Africa
126 C2 Moolawatana Australia
127 H2 Moomin Creek r. Australia
126 A3 Moonaree Australia
127 I3 Moonbi Range mts Australia
127 I1 Moonie Australia
127 H2 Moonie r. Australia
126 B5 Moonta Australia
194 F2 Moorcroft U.S.A.
124 B4 Moore, Lake salt flat Australia
202 D5 Moorefield U.S.A.
201 E7 Moores Island Bahamas
203 J2 Moores Mills Canada
162 E5 Moorfoot Hills U.K.
198 D2 Moorhead U.S.A.
126 E4 Moornanyah Lake imp. l. Australia
126 D5 Moorook Australia
126 F6 Mooroopna Australia
180 C6 Moorreesburg S. Africa
188 D3 Moose r. Canada
188 D3 Moose Factory Canada
203 I2 Moosehead Lake U.S.A.
187 H4 Moose Jaw Canada
190 A2 Moose Lake U.S.A.
203 H2 Mooselookmeguntic Lake U.S.A.
188 D3 Moose River Canada
187 I4 Moosomin Canada
188 D3 Moosonee Canada
126 E3 Mootwingee Australia
127 E3 Mootwingee National Park Australia
181 H1 Mopane S. Africa
176 B3 Mopti Mali
210 D7 Moquegua Peru
177 D3 Mora Cameroon
167 E3 Mora Spain
159 K3 Mora Sweden
215 B2 Mora, Cerro mt. Arg./Chile
144 A3 Morad r. Pak.
144 D3 Moradabad India
179 E5 Morafenobe Madag.
206 G5 Morales Guat.
143 B2 Moram India
179 E5 Moramanga Madag.
190 E3 Moran MI U.S.A.
194 E3 Moran WY U.S.A.
162 C4 Morar, Loch l. U.K.
144 D2 Morari, Tso l. India
143 B5 Moratuwa Sri Lanka
168 H6 Morava r. Austria/Slovakia
203 E3 Moravia U.S.A.
162 E3 Moray Firth b. U.K.
164 F5 Morbach Germany
170 C1 Morbegno Italy
144 B5 Morbi India
166 D4 Morcenx France
146 E1 Mordaga China
137 J3 Mor Dağı mt. Turkey
187 J5 Morden Canada
126 F7 Mordialloc Australia
172 H4 Mordoviya, Respublika aut. rep. Rus. Fed.
173 G4 Mordovo Rus. Fed.
162 D2 More, Loch l. U.K.
198 C2 Moreau r. U.S.A.
181 H1 Morebeng S. Africa
160 E3 Morecambe U.K.
160 D3 Morecambe Bay U.K.
127 H2 Moree Australia
124 E2 Morehead P.N.G.
202 B5 Morehead U.S.A.
201 E5 Morehead City U.S.A.
144 D4 Morel r. India
206 D4 Morelia Mex.
167 F2 Morella Spain
207 G4 Morelos Mex.
207 E4 Morelos state Mex.
144 D4 Morena India
167 D3 Morena, Sierra mts Spain
197 H5 Morenci AZ U.S.A.
191 E5 Morenci MI U.S.A.
171 K2 Moreni Romania
215 E2 Moreno Arg.
206 B1 Moreno Mex.
196 D5 Moreno Valley U.S.A.
Moresby Island i. Canada see Gwaii Haanas
180 F1 Moreswe Pan salt pan Botswana
127 J1 Moreton Bay Australia
161 F6 Moreton-in-Marsh U.K.
127 J1 Moreton Island Australia
164 A5 Moreuil France
136 D4 Morfou Cyprus
136 D4 Morfou Bay Cyprus
126 C5 Morgan Australia
196 C3 Morgan, Mount U.S.A.
199 F6 Morgan City U.S.A.
196 B3 Morgan Hill U.S.A.
203 F4 Morgantown PA U.S.A.
202 D5 Morgantown WV U.S.A.
181 H3 Morgenzon S. Africa
168 C7 Morges Switz.
141 G3 Morghāb, Daryā-ye r. Afgh.
145 F4 Morhar r. India
150 G3 Mori Japan
197 E2 Moriah, Mount U.S.A.
195 F5 Moriarty U.S.A.
127 F2 Moriarty's Range hills Australia
213 C4 Morichal Col.
213 E2 Morichal Largo r. Venez.
152 C2 Morihong Shan mt. China
181 G4 Morija Lesotho
165 H3 Moringen Germany
172 D3 Morino Rus. Fed.
150 G5 Morioka Japan
127 I4 Morisset Australia
150 G5 Moriyoshi-zan vol. Japan
158 M2 Morjärv Sweden
141 F4 Morjen r. Pak.
172 I3 Morki Rus. Fed.
166 C2 Morlaix France
160 F4 Morley U.K.
197 G4 Mormon Lake U.S.A.
212 A7 Mornington, Isla i. Chile
219 D9 Mornington Abyssal Plain sea feature S. Atlantic Ocean
124 D3 Mornington Island Australia
126 F7 Mornington Peninsula National Park Australia
144 A4 Moro Pak.
124 E2 Morobe P.N.G.
176 B1 Morocco country Africa
190 D5 Morocco U.S.A.
178 D4 Morogoro Tanz.
153 B5 Moro Gulf Phil.
181 G4 Morojaneng S. Africa
180 E3 Morokweng S. Africa
206 D3 Moroleón Mex.
179 E6 Morombe Madag.
205 I4 Morón Cuba
146 C2 Mörön Mongolia
179 E6 Morondava Madag.
167 D4 Morón de la Frontera Spain
148 A1 Moron Gol watercourse China
179 E5 Moroni Comoros
147 E6 Morotai i. Indon.
178 D3 Moroto Uganda
173 G5 Morozovsk Rus. Fed.
191 G4 Morpeth Canada
160 F2 Morpeth U.K.
214 C2 Morrinhos Brazil
187 J5 Morris Canada
190 C5 Morris IL U.S.A.
198 E2 Morris MN U.S.A.
203 F2 Morrisburg Canada
190 C5 Morrison U.S.A.
197 F5 Morristown AZ U.S.A.
203 F4 Morristown NJ U.S.A.
203 F2 Morristown NY U.S.A.
201 D4 Morristown TN U.S.A.
203 F4 Morrisville PA U.S.A.
203 G2 Morrisville VT U.S.A.
212 B3 Morro, Punta pt Chile
196 B4 Morro Bay U.S.A.
213 C2 Morrocoy, Parque Nacional nat. park Venez.
206 D4 Morro de Petatlán hd Mex.
211 H4 Morro Grande h. Brazil
213 B2 Morrosquillo, Golfo de b. Col.
165 H3 Morschen Germany
190 D5 Morse Reservoir U.S.A.
172 G4 Morshansk Rus. Fed.
172 E2 Morskaya Masel'ga Rus. Fed.
170 C7 Morsott Alg.
166 E2 Mortagne-au-Perche France
166 D3 Mortagne-sur-Sèvre France
161 C6 Mortehoe U.K.
215 E1 Morteros Arg.
211 H6 Mortes, Rio das r. Brazil
201 F7 Mortimer's Bahamas
126 E7 Mortlake Australia
123 E2 Mortlock Islands Micronesia
161 G5 Morton U.K.
190 C5 Morton IL U.S.A.
194 B2 Morton WA U.S.A.
127 I5 Morton National Park Australia
127 G5 Morundah Australia
181 G1 Morupule Botswana
127 I5 Moruya Australia
162 C4 Morvern reg. U.K.
127 G7 Morwell Australia
165 H5 Mosbach Germany
161 F4 Mosborough U.K.
172 F4 Moscow Rus. Fed. (City Plan 107)
194 C2 Moscow U.S.A.
164 F4 Mosel r. Germany
180 F2 Moselebe watercourse Botswana
166 H2 Moselle r. France
165 J2 Möser Germany
196 D1 Moses, Mount U.S.A.
194 C2 Moses Lake U.S.A.
128 C6 Mosgiel N.Z.
180 E3 Moshaweng watercourse S. Africa
178 D4 Moshi Tanz.
190 C3 Mosinee U.S.A.
158 K2 Mosjøen Norway
158 K2 Moskenesøy i. Norway
172 F4 Moskovskaya Oblast' admin. div. Rus. Fed.
Moskva Rus. Fed. see Moscow
168 H7 Mosonmagyaróvár Hungary
213 A4 Mosquera Col.
195 F5 Mosquero U.S.A.
205 H5 Mosquitia reg. Hond.
214 E1 Mosquito r. Brazil
202 C4 Mosquito Creek Lake U.S.A.
187 I2 Mosquito Lake Canada
206 I5 Mosquitos, Costa de coastal area Nicaragua
206 I6 Mosquitos, Golfo de los b. Panama
159 J4 Moss Norway
162 F3 Mossat U.K.
128 B6 Mossburn N.Z.
180 E7 Mossel Bay S. Africa
180 E7 Mossel Bay b. S. Africa
178 B4 Mossendjo Congo
126 F4 Mossgiel Australia
124 E3 Mossman Australia
211 K5 Mossoró Brazil
127 I5 Moss Vale Australia
168 F5 Most Czech Rep.
140 D3 Moşţafáābād Iran
176 C1 Mostaganem Alg.
170 G3 Mostar Bos.-Herz.
212 F4 Mostardas Brazil
187 G3 Mostoos Hills Canada
173 G6 Mostovskoy Rus. Fed.
155 E2 Mostyn Sabah Malaysia
137 I3 Mosul Iraq
159 J4 Møsvatnet l. Norway
207 G5 Motagua r. Guat.
159 K4 Motala Sweden
213 C2 Motatán r. Venez.
181 J2 Motaze Moz.
181 H2 Motetema S. Africa
144 D4 Moth India
162 E5 Motherwell U.K.
152 B3 Motian Ling h. China
145 F4 Motihari India
167 F3 Motilla del Palancar Spain
128 F2 Motiti Island N.Z.
180 E2 Motokwe Botswana
207 F5 Motozintla Mex.
167 E4 Motril Spain
171 J2 Motru Romania
154 A1 Mottama Myanmar
147 B5 Mottama, Gulf of Myanmar
207 G3 Motul Mex.
123 I5 Motu One atoll Fr. Polynesia
149 A5 Mouding China
176 A3 Moudjéria Mauritania
171 K5 Moudros Greece
159 M3 Mouhijärvi Fin.
178 B4 Mouila Gabon
178 B3 Moukalaba Doudou, Parc National de nat. park Gabon
126 F5 Moulamein Australia
126 F5 Moulamein Creek r. Australia
178 B4 Moulèngui Binza Gabon
166 F3 Moulins France
Moulmein Myanmar see Mawlamyaing
201 D6 Moultrie U.S.A.
193 K5 Moultrie, Lake U.S.A.
200 B4 Mound City IL U.S.A.
198 E3 Mound City MO U.S.A.
177 D4 Moundou Chad
202 C5 Moundsville U.S.A.
144 C4 Mount Abu India
201 C5 Mountain Brook U.S.A.
202 C6 Mountain City U.S.A.
199 E4 Mountain Grove U.S.A.
199 E4 Mountain Home AR U.S.A.
194 D3 Mountain Home ID U.S.A.
181 F6 Mountain Zebra National Park S. Africa
202 C6 Mount Airy U.S.A.
128 B6 Mount Aspiring National Park N.Z.
186 F4 Mount Assiniboine Provincial Park Canada
181 H5 Mount Ayliff S. Africa
198 E3 Mount Ayr U.S.A.
126 C5 Mount Barker Australia
127 G6 Mount Beauty Australia
163 C4 Mountbellew Ireland
127 G6 Mount Buffalo National Park Australia
203 J1 Mount Carleton Provincial Park Canada
136 E5 Mount Carmel tourist site Israel
197 F3 Mount Carmel Junction U.S.A.
190 C4 Mount Carroll U.S.A.
Mount Cook N.Z. see Aoraki
179 D5 Mount Darwin Zimbabwe
203 I2 Mount Desert Island U.S.A.
126 A1 Mount Dutton Australia
126 A3 Mount Eba Australia
127 G9 Mount Field National Park Australia
181 H5 Mount Fletcher S. Africa
191 G4 Mount Forest Canada
181 H5 Mount Frere S. Africa
126 D6 Mount Gambier Australia
202 B4 Mount Gilead U.S.A.
127 F4 Mount Hope N.S.W. Australia
126 A5 Mount Hope S.A. Australia
202 C6 Mount Hope U.S.A.
190 C4 Mount Horeb U.S.A.
124 D4 Mount Isa Australia
178 D3 Mount Kenya National Park Kenya
203 G4 Mount Kisco U.S.A.
126 C5 Mount Lofty Range mts Australia
191 G2 Mount MacDonald Canada
124 B4 Mount Magnet Australia
126 E4 Mount Manara Australia
196 B1 Mount Meadows Reservoir U.S.A.
163 D4 Mountmellick Ireland
181 G5 Mount Moorosi Lesotho
126 E3 Mount Murchison Australia
190 B5 Mount Pleasant IA U.S.A.
200 C3 Mount Pleasant MI U.S.A.
202 D4 Mount Pleasant PA U.S.A.
201 E5 Mount Pleasant SC U.S.A.
199 E5 Mount Pleasant TX U.S.A.
197 G2 Mount Pleasant UT U.S.A.
190 C5 Mount Pulaski U.S.A.
194 B2 Mount Rainier National Park U.S.A.
186 F4 Mount Robson Provincial Park Canada
202 C6 Mount Rogers National Recreation Area park U.S.A.
161 B7 Mount's Bay U.K.
161 F5 Mountsorrel U.K.
190 B6 Mount Sterling IL U.S.A.
202 B5 Mount Sterling KY U.S.A.
202 D5 Mount Storm U.S.A.
202 E4 Mount Union U.S.A.
201 B6 Mount Vernon AL U.S.A.
190 B5 Mount Vernon IA U.S.A.
200 B4 Mount Vernon IL U.S.A.
202 A6 Mount Vernon KY U.S.A.
202 B4 Mount Vernon OH U.S.A.
194 B1 Mount Vernon WA U.S.A.
126 A4 Mount Wedge Australia
127 H8 Mount William National Park Australia
124 E4 Moura Australia
210 F4 Moura Brazil
177 E3 Mourdi, Dépression du depr. Chad
163 D3 Mourne r. U.K.
163 E3 Mourne Mountains hills U.K.
164 B4 Mouscron Belgium
177 D3 Moussoro Chad
147 E6 Moutong Indon.
164 A5 Mouy France
176 C2 Mouydir, Monts du plat. Alg.
164 D5 Mouzon France
140 C4 Moveyleh Iran
127 I1 Mowbullan, Mount Australia
201 E7 Moxey Town Bahamas
163 C4 Moy r. Ireland
178 D3 Moyale Eth.
176 A4 Moyamba Sierra Leone
143 B4 Moyar r. India
176 B1 Moyen Atlas mts Morocco
181 G5 Moyeni Lesotho
163 E4 Moyer h. Ireland
138 D4 Mo'ynoq Uzbek.
139 I5 Moyu China
139 H3 Moyynkum Kazakh.
139 F3 Moyynkum, Peski des. Karagandinskaya Oblast' Kazakh.
139 G3 Moyynkum, Peski des. Yuzhnyy Kazakhstan Kazakh.
139 H3 Moyynty Kazakh.
179 D6 Mozambique country Africa
179 E5 Mozambique Channel Africa
218 G6 Mozambique Ridge sea feature Indian Ocean
173 H7 Mozdok Rus. Fed.
172 F4 Mozhaysk Rus. Fed.
145 H5 Mozo Myanmar
178 C4 Mpala Dem. Rep. Congo
178 D4 Mpanda Tanz.
179 D5 Mpika Zambia
181 I4 Mpolweni S. Africa
179 D4 Mporokoso Zambia
181 H2 Mpumalanga prov. S. Africa
181 H5 Mqanduli S. Africa
145 H5 Mrauk-U Myanmar
170 G2 Mrkonjić-Grad Bos.-Herz.
176 D1 M'Saken Tunisia
172 D3 Mshinskaya Rus. Fed.
167 I5 M'Sila Alg.
172 E3 Msta r. Rus. Fed.
172 D4 Mstsislaw Belarus
181 H5 Mthatha S. Africa
172 F4 Mtsensk Rus. Fed.
181 J4 Mtubatuba S. Africa
181 I4 Mtunzini S. Africa
179 E5 Mtwara Tanz.
178 B4 Muanda Dem. Rep. Congo
149 B6 Muang Hiam Laos
154 B1 Muang Hôngsa Laos
Muang Khammouan Laos see Thakhèk
154 C2 Muang Không Laos
154 C2 Muang Khôngxédôn Laos
149 B6 Muang Khoua Laos
154 A3 Muang Kirirath r. Thai.
154 C1 Muang Mok Laos
149 B6 Muang Ngoy Laos
154 C1 Muang Nong Laos
149 A6 Muang Ou Nua Laos
Muang Pakxan Laos see Pakxan
154 C1 Muang Phalan Laos
154 B1 Muang Phiang Laos
154 C1 Muang Phin Laos
154 B1 Muang Souy Laos
149 B6 Muang Va Laos
154 B1 Muang Vangviang Laos
Muang Xaignabouri Laos see Xaignabouli
Muang Xay Laos see Oudômxai
149 B6 Muang Xon Laos
155 B2 Muar Malaysia
154 B5 Muar r. Malaysia
155 B3 Muarabungo Indon.
155 B3 Muaradua Indon.
155 A3 Muarasiberut Indon.
155 A2 Muarasipongi Indon.
155 B3 Muaratembesi Indon.
145 E4 Mubarakpur India
Mubarek Uzbek. see Muborak
137 H7 Mubarraz well Saudi Arabia
178 D3 Mubende Uganda
177 D3 Mubi Nigeria
138 F5 Muborak Uzbek.
213 E4 Mucajaí r. Brazil
213 E4 Mucajaí, Serra do mts Brazil
164 F4 Much Germany
179 D5 Muchinga Escarpment Zambia
149 B4 Muchuan China
162 B4 Muck i. U.K.
162 □ Muckle Roe i. U.K.
213 C3 Muco r. Col.
179 C5 Muconda Angola
213 E4 Mucucuaú r. Brazil
136 E2 Mucur Turkey
214 E2 Mucuri Brazil
214 E2 Mucuri r. Brazil
179 C5 Mucussueje Angola
154 B4 Muda r. Malaysia
143 A3 Mudabidri India
152 E1 Mudanjiang China
152 E1 Mudan Jiang r. China
136 B1 Mudanya Turkey
137 K7 Mudayrah Kuwait
202 C5 Muddlety U.S.A.
158 L2 Muddus nationalpark nat. park Sweden
197 G2 Muddy Creek r. U.S.A.
197 E3 Muddy Peak U.S.A.
141 E3 Mūd-e Dahanāb Iran
165 F4 Mudersbach Germany
127 H4 Mudgee Australia
143 A2 Mudhol India
144 C3 Mudki India
196 D3 Mud Lake U.S.A.
154 A1 Mudon Myanmar
136 C1 Mudurnu Turkey
172 F2 Mud'yuga Rus. Fed.
179 D5 Mueda Moz.
207 F4 Muerto, Mar lag. Mex.
172 H1 Muftyuga Rus. Fed.
179 C5 Mufulira Zambia
179 C5 Mufumbwe Zambia
149 E4 Mufu Shan mts China
137 L2 Muğan Düzü lowland Azer.
145 F2 Mugarripug China
145 E4 Mughal Sarai India
140 D3 Mūghār Iran
136 F7 Mughayrā' Saudi Arabia
139 G5 Mughsu r. Tajik.
136 B3 Muğla Turkey
138 D3 Mugodzhary, Gory mts Kazakh.
145 H2 Mug Qu r. China
145 E3 Mugu Karnali r. Nepal
145 H2 Mugxung China
177 F2 Muḩammad, Ra's pt Egypt
144 B4 Muhammad Ashraf Pak.
177 F2 Muhammad Qol Sudan
140 B5 Muḩayriqah Saudi Arabia
165 K3 Mühlanger Germany
165 L3 Mühlberg Germany
165 I3 Mühlhausen (Thüringen) Germany
158 N2 Muhos Fin.
178 C4 Muhulu Dem. Rep. Congo
Mui Dinh hd Vietnam see Ca Na, Mui
Muine Bheag Ireland see Bagenalstown
162 D5 Muirkirk U.K.
162 B2 Muirneag h. U.K.
162 D3 Muir of Ord U.K.
196 A3 Muir Woods National Monument nat. park U.S.A.
179 D5 Muite Moz.
140 D3 Mūjān, Chāh-e well Iran
207 H3 Mujeres, Isla i. Mex.
152 D6 Muju S. Korea
173 B5 Mukacheve Ukr.
155 D2 Mukah Sarawak Malaysia
142 C7 Mukalla Yemen
145 F3 Mükangsar China
154 C1 Mukdahan Thai.
124 B5 Mukinbudin Australia
155 B3 Mukomuko Indon.
138 F5 Mukry Turkm.
144 C3 Muktsar India
187 J4 Mukutawa r. Canada
190 C4 Mukwonago U.S.A.
138 C3 Mukyr Atyrauskaya Oblast' Kazakh.
139 J2 Mukyr Vostochnyy Kazakhstan Kazakh.
144 D5 Mul India
143 A2 Mula r. India
144 A3 Mula r. Pak.
150 A2 Mulan China
153 B3 Mulanay Phil.
179 D5 Mulanje, Mount Malawi
140 B5 Mulayḩ Saudi Arabia
199 E5 Mulberry U.S.A.
215 B3 Mulchén Chile
165 K3 Mulde r. Germany
178 D4 Muleba Tanz.
197 H5 Mule Creek NM U.S.A.
194 F3 Mule Creek WY U.S.A.
206 A2 Mulegé Mex.
199 C5 Muleshoe U.S.A.
167 E4 Mulhacén mt. Spain
164 E3 Mülheim an der Ruhr Germany
166 H3 Mulhouse France
149 A5 Muli China
152 F1 Muling Heilong. China
152 F1 Muling Heilong. China
152 G1 Muling He r. China
162 C4 Mull i. U.K.
162 B4 Mull, Sound of sea chan. U.K.
137 L3 Mulla Ali Iran
163 B6 Mullaghanattin h. Ireland
163 B5 Mullaghareirk Mountains hills Ireland
143 C4 Mullaittivu Sri Lanka
127 H3 Mullaley Australia
127 G3 Mullengudgery Australia
155 D2 Muller, Pegunungan mts Indon.
190 E3 Mullett Lake U.S.A.
124 B4 Mullewa Australia
162 F1 Mull Head U.K.
203 F5 Mullica r. U.S.A.
163 D4 Mullingar Ireland
127 H4 Mullion Creek Australia
162 D6 Mull of Galloway c. U.K.
162 C5 Mull of Kintyre hd U.K.
162 B5 Mull of Oa hd U.K.
179 C5 Mulobezi Zambia
143 A2 Mulshi Lake India
144 D5 Multai India
144 B3 Multan Pak.
159 N3 Multia Fin.
164 A6 Multien reg. France
141 F5 Mūmān Iran
143 A2 Mumbai India (City Plan 106)
127 H4 Mumbil Australia
179 C5 Mumbwa Zambia
Mŭ'minobod Tajik. see Leningrad
173 H6 Mumra Rus. Fed.
154 C2 Mun, Mae Nam r. Thai.
124 C2 Muna i. Indon.
207 G3 Muna Mex.
133 M3 Muna r. Rus. Fed.
158 B1 Munaðarnes Iceland
138 C3 Munayly Kazakh.
138 C4 Munayshy Kazakh.
165 J4 Münchberg Germany
München Germany see Munich
165 G4 Münchhausen Germany
213 A4 Munchique, Cerro mt. Col.
186 D3 Muncho Lake Canada
186 D3 Muncho Lake Provincial Park Canada
152 D4 Munch'ŏn N. Korea
190 E5 Muncie U.S.A.
202 E4 Muncy U.S.A.
143 B5 Mundel Lake Sri Lanka
161 I5 Mundesley U.K.
161 H5 Mundford U.K.
124 C5 Mundrabilla Australia
144 C4 Mundwa India
143 C2 Muneru r. India
127 G2 Mungallala Creek r. Australia
144 D4 Mungaoli India
152 D5 Mungap-do i. S. Korea
178 C3 Mungbere Dem. Rep. Congo
143 C1 Mungeli India
145 F4 Munger India
126 C2 Mungeranie Australia
154 D5 Mungguresak, Tanjung pt Indon.
127 H2 Mungindi Australia
127 E4 Mungo National Park Australia
152 D5 Mun'gyeong S. Korea
168 E6 Munich Germany
211 J4 Munim r. Brazil
190 D2 Munising U.S.A.
214 E3 Muniz Freire Brazil
158 O1 Munkebakken Norway
159 J4 Munkedal Sweden
Munkelva Norway see Munkebakken
159 K4 Munkfors Sweden
165 I4 Münnerstadt Germany
181 H1 Munnik S. Africa
127 H8 Munro, Mount Australia
152 D5 Munsan S. Korea
168 C7 Münsingen Switz.
165 G5 Münster Germany

165 I2 Münster Germany
164 F3 Münster Germany
164 F3 Münsterland reg. Germany
158 O2 Muojärvi l. Fin.
Mương Lam Vietnam see Xiêng Lam
149 B6 Mương Nhe Vietnam
Mương Nhie Vietnam see Mương Nhe
158 M2 Muonio Fin.
158 M2 Muonioälven r. Fin./Sweden
152 A5 Muping China
Muqdisho Somalia see Mogadishu
137 L1 Müqtädır Azer.
141 G3 Muqur Afgh.
137 I2 Muradiye Turkey
154 □ Murai Reservoir Sing.
150 F5 Murakami Japan
212 B7 Murallón, Cerro mt. Chile
178 C4 Muramvya Burundi
Muranga Kenya see Murang'a
178 D4 Murang'a Kenya
172 I3 Murashi Rus. Fed.
137 H2 Murat r. Turkey
136 B2 Murat Dağı mts Turkey
136 A1 Muratlı Turkey
150 G5 Murayama Japan
140 C3 Mürcheh Khvort Iran
126 F6 Murchison Australia
124 B4 Murchison watercourse Australia
178 D3 Murchison Falls National Park Uganda
167 F4 Murcia Spain
167 F4 Murcia aut. comm. Spain
198 C3 Murdo U.S.A.
189 G4 Murdochville Canada
179 D5 Murehwa Zimbabwe
Mureș r. Romania see Mureșul
169 L7 Mureșul r. Romania
166 E5 Muret France
201 E4 Murfreesboro NC U.S.A.
201 C5 Murfreesboro TN U.S.A.
138 E5 Murgap Turkm.
141 F2 Murgap r. Turkm.
141 H3 Murgh, Kōtal-e Afgh.
144 B3 Murgha Kibzai Pak.
139 H5 Murghob Tajik.
139 H5 Murghob r. Tajik.
148 A2 Muri China
145 F5 Muri India
140 E2 Mūrī Iran
214 D3 Muriaé Brazil
141 F3 Mūrīchāq Afgh.
179 C4 Muriege Angola
165 K1 Müritz l. Germany
165 L1 Müritz, Nationalpark nat. park Germany
165 K1 Müritz Seenpark nature res. Germany
158 P1 Murmansk Rus. Fed.
158 O1 Murmanskaya Oblast' admin. div. Rus. Fed.
170 C4 Muro, Capo di c. Corsica France
172 G4 Murom Rus. Fed.
150 G3 Muroran Japan
167 B1 Muros Spain
151 D8 Muroto Japan
151 D8 Muroto-zaki pt Japan
194 C3 Murphy ID U.S.A.
201 D5 Murphy NC U.S.A.
196 B2 Murphys U.S.A.
127 I5 Murramarang National Park Australia
127 G2 Murra Murra Australia
126 D5 Murray r. Australia
186 E3 Murray r. Canada
200 B4 Murray KY U.S.A.
194 E3 Murray UT U.S.A.
124 E2 Murray, Lake P.N.G.
201 D5 Murray, Lake U.S.A.
126 C5 Murray Bridge Australia
180 E5 Murraysburg S. Africa
126 D5 Murrayville Australia
165 H6 Murrhardt Germany
127 H5 Murringo Australia
163 B4 Murrisk reg. Ireland
163 B4 Murroogh Ireland
127 H5 Murrumbateman Australia
126 F5 Murrumbidgee r. Australia
179 D5 Murrupula Moz.
127 I3 Murrurundi Australia
170 G1 Murska Sobota Slovenia
126 D2 Murteree, Lake salt flat Australia
126 E6 Murtoa Australia
143 A2 Murud India
152 A2 Muruin Sum Shuiku resr China
143 C4 Murunkan Sri Lanka
128 F3 Murupara N.Z.
123 J6 Mururoa atoll Fr. Polynesia
144 E5 Murwara India
127 J2 Murwillumbah Australia
138 E5 Murzechirla Turkm.
177 D2 Murzūq Libya
177 D2 Murzuq, Idhān des. Libya
168 G7 Mürzzuschlag Austria
137 H2 Muş Turkey
144 B3 Musakhel Pak.
171 J3 Musala mt. Bulg.
155 A2 Musala i. Indon.
152 E2 Musan N. Korea
140 E5 Musandam Peninsula Oman
Musa Qala, Rūd-i r. Afgh. see Dê Mūsá Qal'ah Rōd
141 G3 Mūsá Qal'ah Afgh.
142 E5 Muscat Oman
190 B5 Muscatine U.S.A.
190 B4 Muscoda U.S.A.
203 I3 Muscongus Bay U.S.A.
124 D4 Musgrave Ranges mts Australia
163 C5 Musheramore h. Ireland
178 B4 Mushie Dem. Rep. Congo
143 B2 Musi r. India
155 B3 Musi r. Indon.
197 F4 Music Mountain U.S.A.
181 I1 Musina S. Africa
197 G2 Musinia Peak U.S.A.
186 E2 Muskeg r. Canada
203 H4 Muskeget Channel U.S.A.
190 D4 Muskegon U.S.A.
190 D4 Muskegon r. U.S.A.
202 C5 Muskingum r. U.S.A.
199 E5 Muskogee U.S.A.
191 H3 Muskoka Canada
191 H3 Muskoka, Lake Canada
186 E3 Muskwa r. Canada
136 F3 Muslimīyah Syria
177 F3 Musmar Sudan
178 D4 Musoma Tanz.
124 E2 Mussau Island P.N.G.
162 E5 Musselburgh U.K.
164 F2 Musselkanaal Neth.
194 E2 Musselshell r. U.S.A.
136 B1 Mustafakemalpaşa Turkey
138 C2 Mustayevo Rus. Fed.
159 M4 Mustjala Estonia
152 E3 Musu-dan pt N. Korea
127 I4 Muswellbrook Australia
177 E2 Mūţ Egypt
136 D3 Mut Turkey
214 E1 Mutá, Ponta do pt Brazil
179 D5 Mutare Zimbabwe
147 E7 Mutis, Gunung mt. Indon.
126 D4 Mutooroo Australia
179 D5 Mutorashanga Zimbabwe
150 G4 Mutsu Japan
150 G4 Mutsu-wan b. Japan
128 B7 Muttonbird Islands N.Z.
163 B5 Mutton Island Ireland
179 D5 Mutuali Moz.
214 C1 Mutunópolis Brazil
143 C4 Mutur Sri Lanka
158 N1 Mutusjärvi r. Fin.
158 N2 Muurola Fin.
148 C2 Mu Us Shadi des. China
179 B4 Muxaluando Angola
172 E2 Muyezerskiy Rus. Fed.
178 D4 Muyinga Burundi
Muynak Uzbek. see Mo'ynoq
148 D4 Muyu China
178 C4 Muyumba Dem. Rep. Congo
144 C2 Muzaffarabad Pak.
144 B3 Muzaffargarh Pak.
144 D3 Muzaffarnagar India
145 F4 Muzaffarpur India
181 J1 Muzamane Moz.
139 J4 Muzat He r. China
141 F5 Mūzīn Iran
186 C4 Muzon, Cape U.S.A.
206 D2 Múzquiz Mex.
144 E2 Muz Shan mt. China
145 F1 Muz Tag mt. China
Muztag mt. China see Muz Tag
139 H5 Muztagata mt. China
177 E4 Mvolo South Sudan
178 D4 Mvomero Tanz.
179 D5 Mvuma Zimbabwe
179 E5 Mwali i. Comoros
179 C4 Mwanza Dem. Rep. Congo
178 D4 Mwanza Tanz.
178 C4 Mwaro Burundi
163 B4 Mweelrea h. Ireland
178 C4 Mweka Dem. Rep. Congo
179 C5 Mwenda Zambia
178 C4 Mwene-Ditu Dem. Rep. Congo
179 D6 Mwenezi Zimbabwe
179 C4 Mweru, Lake Dem. Rep. Congo/Zambia
179 C4 Mwimba Dem. Rep. Congo
179 C5 Mwinilunga Zambia
172 C4 Myadzyel Belarus
145 H5 Myaing Myanmar
144 B4 Myajlar India
127 J4 Myall Lake Australia
146 B2 Myanmar country Asia
162 E2 Mybster U.K.
171 J6 Mycenae tourist site Greece
145 H5 Myebon Myanmar
154 A2 Myeik Myanmar
154 A3 Myeik Kyunzu is Myanmar
147 B4 Myingyan Myanmar
154 A2 Myinmoletkat mt. Myanmar
146 B4 Myitkyina Myanmar
154 A2 Myitta Myanmar
145 H5 Myittha r. Myanmar
173 E6 Mykolayiv Ukr.
171 K6 Mykonos Greece
171 K6 Mykonos i. Greece
132 G3 Myla Rus. Fed.
145 G4 Mymensingh Bangl.
159 M3 Mynämäki Fin.
139 H3 Mynaral Kazakh.
Myohaung Myanmar see Mrauk-U
151 F6 Myōkō. Japan
152 E3 Myŏnggan N. Korea
172 C4 Myory Belarus
158 C3 Mýrdalsjökull ice cap Iceland
158 K1 Myre Norway
158 M2 Myrheden Sweden
173 E5 Myrhorod Ukr.
173 D5 Myronivka Ukr.
201 E5 Myrtle Beach U.S.A.
127 G6 Myrtleford Australia
194 A3 Myrtle Point U.S.A.
171 J6 Myrtoo Pelagos sea Greece
139 G4 Myrzakent Kazakh.
168 G4 Myślibórz Poland
143 B3 Mysore India
133 T3 Mys Shmidta Rus. Fed.
203 F5 Mystic Islands U.S.A.
Mysuru India see Mysore
154 C3 My Tho Vietnam
171 L5 Mytilini Greece
172 F4 Mytishchi Rus. Fed.
158 C2 Mývatn-Laxá nature res. Iceland
181 G5 Mzamomhle S. Africa
165 K5 Mže r. Czech Rep.
179 D5 Mzimba Malawi
179 D5 Mzuzu Malawi


# N


149 B6 Na, Nam r. China/Vietnam
165 J5 Naab r. Germany
196 □2 Nā'ālehu U.S.A.
Naalehu U.S.A. see Nā'ālehu
159 M3 Naantali Fin.
163 E4 Naas Ireland
180 B4 Nababeep S. Africa
143 C2 Nabarangapur India
151 E7 Nabari Japan
153 B4 Nabas Phil.
136 E5 Nabatîyé et Tahta Lebanon
Nabatiyet et Tahta Lebanon see Nabatîyé et Tahta
165 K5 Nabburg Germany
178 D4 Naberera Tanz.
132 G4 Naberezhnyye Chelny Rus. Fed.
177 D1 Nabeul Tunisia
144 D3 Nabha India
127 J4 Nabiac Australia
147 F7 Nabire Indon.
136 E5 Nāblus West Bank
154 A2 Nabule Myanmar
179 E5 Nacala Moz.
206 H5 Nacaome Hond.
194 B2 Naches U.S.A.
144 B4 Nachna India
196 B4 Nacimiento Reservoir U.S.A.
199 E6 Nacogdoches U.S.A.
204 C2 Nacozari de García Mex.
144 C5 Nadiad India
140 D4 Nadīk Iran
176 B1 Nador Morocco
140 D3 Nadūshan Iran
173 C5 Nadvirna Ukr.
132 E3 Nadvoitsy Rus. Fed.
132 I3 Nadym Rus. Fed.
159 J5 Næstved Denmark
171 I5 Nafpaktos Greece
171 J6 Nafplio Greece
137 J5 Naft, Āb r. Iraq
140 C4 Naft-e Sefīd Iran
137 J5 Naft Khāneh Iraq
140 B3 Naft Shahr Iran
140 A5 Nafy Saudi Arabia
145 G2 Nag, Co l. China
153 B3 Naga Phil.
188 D4 Nagagami r. Canada
151 C8 Nagahama Japan
145 H4 Naga Hills India
151 G5 Nagai Japan
145 H4 Nagaland state India
126 F6 Nagambie Australia
151 F6 Nagano Japan
151 F6 Nagaoka Japan
145 H4 Nagaon India
143 B4 Nagapattinam India
144 D2 Nagar India
143 B2 Nagarjuna Sagar Reservoir India
144 B4 Nagar Parkar Pak.
145 G3 Nagarzê China
151 A8 Nagasaki Japan
151 B7 Nagato Japan
144 C4 Nagaur India
143 C2 Nagavali r. India
144 C5 Nagda India
143 B4 Nagercoil India
141 G5 Nagha Kalat Pak.
144 D3 Nagina India
145 E3 Nagma Nepal
137 K2 Nagorno-Karabakh terr. Azer.
172 I3 Nagorsk Rus. Fed.
151 E7 Nagoya Japan
144 D5 Nagpur India
145 H3 Nagqu China
153 C3 Nagumbuaya Point Phil.
132 F1 Nagurskoye Rus. Fed.
170 G1 Nagyatád Hungary
168 H7 Nagykanizsa Hungary
146 E4 Naha Japan
144 D3 Nahan India
141 F5 Nahang r. Iran/Pak.
186 E2 Nahanni Butte Canada
Nahanni National Park Canada see Nahanni National Park Reserve
186 D2 Nahanni National Park Reserve Canada
136 E5 Nahariyya Israel
140 C3 Nahāvand Iran
165 F5 Nahe r. Germany
141 H2 Nahrīn Afgh.
141 H3 Nahrīn reg. Afgh.
215 B3 Nahuelbuta, Parque Nacional nat. park Chile
215 B4 Nahuel Huapí, Lago l. Arg.
215 B4 Nahuel Huapí, Parque Nacional nat. park Arg.
201 D6 Nahunta U.S.A.
206 C2 Naica Mex.
145 H2 Naij Tal China
189 H2 Nain Canada
140 D3 Nā'īn Iran
144 D3 Nainital India
144 E5 Nainpur India
162 E3 Nairn U.K.
191 G2 Nairn Centre Canada
178 D4 Nairobi Kenya
178 D4 Naivasha Kenya
152 D2 Naizishan China
140 B5 Na'jān Saudi Arabia
142 B4 Najd reg. Saudi Arabia
167 E1 Nájera Spain
144 D3 Najibabad India
152 F2 Najin N. Korea
142 B6 Najrān Saudi Arabia
151 A8 Nakadōri-shima i. Japan
154 C1 Na Kae Thai.
151 B8 Nakama Japan
133 L3 Nakanno Rus. Fed.
151 F6 Nakano Japan
151 C6 Nakano-shima i. Japan
141 H3 Naka Pass Afgh.
151 B8 Nakatsu Japan
151 E7 Nakatsugawa Japan
152 E6 Nakdong-gang r. S. Korea
178 D2 Nakfa Eritrea
177 F1 Nakhl Egypt
146 F2 Nakhodka Rus. Fed.
154 B2 Nakhon Nayok Thai.
154 B2 Nakhon Pathom Thai.
154 C1 Nakhon Phanom Thai.
154 B2 Nakhon Ratchasima Thai.
154 B2 Nakhon Sawan Thai.
154 A3 Nakhon Si Thammarat Thai.
144 B5 Nakhtarana India
186 C3 Nakina B.C. Canada
188 C3 Nakina Ont. Canada
184 C4 Naknek U.S.A.
179 D4 Nakonde Zambia
159 J5 Nakskov Denmark
178 D4 Nakuru Kenya
186 F4 Nakusp Canada
141 G5 Nal Pak.
141 G5 Nal r. Pak.
181 J2 Nalázi Moz.
145 G4 Nalbari India
173 G7 Nal'chik Rus. Fed.
143 B2 Naldurg India
143 B2 Nalgonda India
143 B3 Nallamala Hills India
136 C1 Nallıhan Turkey
139 G1 Nalobino Kazakh.
176 D1 Nālūt Libya
181 J2 Namaacha Moz.
181 H3 Namahadi S. Africa
140 C3 Namak, Daryācheh-ye salt flat Iran
141 E3 Namak, Kavīr-e salt flat Iran
141 E4 Namakzar-e Shadad salt flat Iran
178 D4 Namanga Kenya
139 G4 Namangan Uzbek.
179 D5 Namapa Moz.
180 B4 Namaqualand reg. S. Africa
137 J3 Namashīr Iran
124 F2 Namatanai P.N.G.
127 J1 Nambour Australia
127 J3 Nambucca Heads Australia
154 C3 Năm Căn Vietnam
Namch'ŏn N. Korea see P'yŏngsan
146 B3 Nam Co salt l. China
158 K2 Namdalen val. Norway
158 J2 Namdalseid Norway
149 C6 Nam Đinh Vietnam
190 B3 Namekagon r. U.S.A.
152 D4 Nam-gang r. N. Korea
152 E6 Namhae-do i. S. Korea
179 B6 Namib Desert Namibia
179 B5 Namibe Angola
179 B6 Namibia country Africa
219 J8 Namibia Abyssal Plain sea feature S. Atlantic Ocean
151 G6 Namie Japan
145 H3 Namjagbarwa Feng mt. China
147 E7 Namlea Indon.
154 A1 Nammekon Myanmar
127 H3 Namoi r. Australia
186 F3 Nampa Canada
144 E3 Nampa mt. Nepal
194 C3 Nampa U.S.A.
176 B3 Nampala Mali
154 B1 Nam Pat Thai.
154 B1 Nam Phong Thai.
152 C4 Namp'o N. Korea
179 D5 Nampula Moz.
135 H4 Namrup India
145 H4 Namsai India
145 E3 Namsê La pass Nepal
158 J2 Namsen r. Norway
145 G3 Namsi La pass Bhutan
158 J2 Namsos Norway
133 N3 Namtsy Rus. Fed.
146 B4 Namtu Myanmar
164 C4 Namur Belgium
179 C5 Namwala Zambia
152 D6 Namwon S. Korea
154 B1 Nan Thai.
154 B2 Nan, Mae Nam r. Thai.
178 B3 Nana Bakassa Cent. Afr. Rep.
186 E5 Nanaimo Canada
196 □1 Nānākuli U.S.A.
Nanakuli U.S.A. see Nānākuli
152 E3 Nanam N. Korea
149 F5 Nan'an China
180 B2 Nananib Plateau Namibia
151 E6 Nanao Japan
149 E6 Nan'ao Dao i. China
151 E6 Nanatsu-shima i. Japan
148 C4 Nanbu China
150 A1 Nancha China
149 E4 Nanchang Jiangxi China
149 E4 Nanchang Jiangxi China
149 E5 Nancheng China
149 C4 Nanchong China
149 C4 Nanchuan China
166 H2 Nancy France
144 E3 Nanda Devi mt. India
144 E3 Nanda Kot mt. India
149 C5 Nandan China
143 B2 Nanded India
127 I3 Nandewar Range mts Australia
144 C5 Nandgaon India
149 D6 Nandu Jiang r. China
144 C5 Nandurbar India
143 B3 Nandyal India
149 D6 Nanfeng Guangdong China
149 E5 Nanfeng Jiangxi China
145 H3 Nang China
177 D4 Nanga Eboko Cameroon
155 D3 Nangahpinoh Indon.
152 E2 Nangang Ling mts China/N. Korea
144 C2 Nanga Parbat mt. Pak.
155 D3 Nangatayap Indon.
154 A3 Nangin Myanmar
152 D3 Nangnim N. Korea
152 D3 Nangnim-sanmaek mts N. Korea
148 E2 Nangong China
179 D4 Nangulangwa Tanz.
148 A2 Nanhua China
148 F4 Nanhui China
143 B3 Nanjangud India
148 C3 Nanjiang China
149 E5 Nanjing Fujian China
148 F3 Nanjing Jiangsu China
149 E5 Nankang China
Nanking China see Nanjing
151 C8 Nankoku Japan
179 B5 Nankova Angola
148 E2 Nanle China
148 F4 Nanling China
149 D5 Nan Ling mts China
149 C6 Nanliu Jiang r. China
149 C6 Nanning China
154 B1 Na Noi Thai.
185 N3 Nanortalik Greenland
149 C5 Nanpan Jiang r. China
152 A3 Nanpiao China
149 F5 Nanping China
149 F5 Nanri Dao i. China
Nansei-shotō is Japan see Ryukyu Islands
220 B1 Nansen Basin sea feature Arctic Ocean
185 I1 Nansen Sound sea chan. Canada
166 D3 Nantes France
164 A5 Nanteuil-le-Haudouin France
143 C4 Nanthi Kadal Lagoon lag. Sri Lanka
191 G4 Nanticoke Canada
203 F5 Nanticoke r. U.S.A.
186 G4 Nanton Canada
148 F4 Nantong China
149 F6 Nant'ou Taiwan
203 H4 Nantucket U.S.A.
203 H4 Nantucket Island U.S.A.
203 H4 Nantucket Sound g. U.S.A.
161 E4 Nantwich U.K.
125 H2 Nanumanga i. Tuvalu
125 H2 Nanumea atoll Tuvalu
214 E2 Nanuque Brazil
153 C5 Nanusa, Kepulauan is Indon.
149 B4 Nanxi China
149 D4 Nanxian China
149 E5 Nanxiong China
148 D3 Nanyang China
152 C3 Nanzamu China
148 D4 Nanzhang China
148 D3 Nanzhao China
167 G3 Nao, Cabo de la c. Spain
189 F3 Naococane, Lac l. Canada
145 G4 Naogaon Bangl.
150 C1 Naoli He r. China
141 F3 Nāomīd, Dasht-e des. Afgh./Iran
144 C2 Naoshera India
149 D6 Naozhou Dao i. China
196 A2 Napa U.S.A.
203 J1 Napadogan Canada
187 G1 Napaktulik Lake Canada
191 I3 Napanee Canada
144 C4 Napasar India
185 M3 Napasoq Greenland
190 C5 Naperville U.S.A.
128 F3 Napier N.Z.
203 G2 Napierville Canada
170 F4 Naples Italy
201 D7 Naples FL U.S.A.
203 H3 Naples ME U.S.A.
149 B6 Napo China
210 D4 Napo r. Ecuador/Peru
202 A4 Napoleon U.S.A.
Napoli Italy see Naples
215 D3 Naposta Arg.
215 D3 Naposta r. Arg.
190 E5 Nappanee U.S.A.
137 J3 Naqadeh Iran
137 L4 Naqqash Iran
151 D7 Nara Japan
176 B3 Nara Mali
169 M3 Narach Belarus
126 D6 Naracoorte Australia
127 G4 Naradhan Australia
144 C4 Naraina India
206 B2 Naranjo Mex.
207 E3 Naranjos Mex.
143 D2 Narasannapeta India
143 C2 Narasapatnam, Point India
143 C2 Narasapur India
143 C2 Narasaraopet India
145 F5 Narasinghapur India
154 B4 Narathiwat Thai.
143 A2 Narayangaon India
144 E6 Narayanpur India
161 C6 Narberth U.K.
166 F5 Narbonne France
167 C1 Narcea r. Spain
140 D2 Nardin Iran
170 H4 Nardò Italy
215 E1 Nare Arg.
144 B3 Narechi r. Pak.
219 E4 Nares Abyssal Plain sea feature N. Atlantic Ocean
219 E4 Nares Deep sea feature N. Atlantic Ocean
185 L1 Nares Strait Canada/Greenland
169 J4 Narew r. Poland
152 D2 Narhong China
144 A3 Nari r. Pak.
179 B6 Narib Namibia
180 B5 Nariep S. Africa
173 H6 Narimanov Rus. Fed.
136 G3 Narince Turkey
145 H1 Narin Gol watercourse China
151 G7 Narita Japan
206 B2 Narizon, Punta pt Mex.
144 C5 Narmada r. India
137 H1 Narman Turkey
144 D3 Narnaul India
170 E3 Narni Italy
169 N5 Narodychi Ukr.
172 F4 Naro-Fominsk Rus. Fed.
127 I6 Narooma Australia
172 G4 Narovchat Rus. Fed.
173 D5 Narowlya Belarus
159 M3 Närpes Fin.
127 H3 Narrabri Australia
203 H4 Narragansett Bay U.S.A.
127 G2 Narran r. Australia
127 G5 Narrandera Australia
127 G2 Narran Lake Australia
127 H4 Narromine Australia
187 I4 Narrow Hills Provincial Park Canada
202 C6 Narrows U.S.A.
203 F4 Narrowsburg U.S.A.
Narsimhapur India see Narsinghpur
145 G5 Narsingdi Bangl.
144 D5 Narsinghgarh India
144 D5 Narsinghpur India
143 C2 Narsipatnam India
148 E1 Nart China
151 D7 Naruto Japan
159 O4 Narva Estonia
159 N4 Narva Bay Estonia/Rus. Fed.
153 B2 Narvacan Phil.
159 O4 Narva Reservoir resr Estonia/Rus. Fed.
158 L1 Narvik Norway
144 D3 Narwana India
144 D4 Narwar India
132 G3 Nar'yan-Mar Rus. Fed.
139 H4 Naryn Kyrg.
139 H4 Naryn r. Kyrg.
139 K2 Naryn, Khrebet mts Kazakh.
139 J4 Narynkol Kazakh.
158 L3 Näsåker Sweden
Na Scealagae Skelligs is Ireland see The Skelligs
197 H3 Naschitti U.S.A.
128 C6 Naseby N.Z.
144 C5 Nashik India
190 A4 Nashua IA U.S.A.
203 H3 Nashua NH U.S.A.
201 C4 Nashville U.S.A.
136 F5 Naşīb Syria
159 M3 Näsijärvi l. Fin.
177 F4 Nasir South Sudan
177 F2 Nāşir, Buḩayrat resr Egypt
144 B3 Nasirabad Pak.
179 C5 Nasondoye Dem. Rep. Congo
136 C6 Naşr Egypt
141 E3 Naşrābād Iran
137 K5 Naşrīān-e Pā'īn Iran
186 D3 Nass r. Canada
201 E7 Nassau Bahamas
216 H6 Nassau i. Cook Is
159 K4 Nässjö Sweden
185 M3 Nassuttooq inlet Greenland
188 E2 Nastapoca r. Canada
188 E2 Nastapoka Islands Canada
151 F6 Nasu-dake vol. Japan
153 B3 Nasugbu Phil.
151 G6 Nasushiobara Japan
169 O2 Nasva Rus. Fed.
179 C6 Nata Botswana
178 D4 Nata Tanz.
213 B4 Natagaima Col.
211 K5 Natal Brazil
Natal prov. S. Africa see KwaZulu-Natal
218 G7 Natal Basin sea feature Indian Ocean
140 C3 Naţanz Iran
189 H3 Natashquan Canada
189 H3 Natashquan r. Canada
199 F6 Natchez U.S.A.
199 E6 Natchitoches U.S.A.
168 G4 Natecka, Puszcza for. Poland
126 F6 Nathalia Australia
154 B4 Na Thawi Thai.
144 C4 Nathdwara India
167 H2 Nati, Punta pt Spain
126 D6 Natimuk Australia
196 D5 National City U.S.A.
176 C3 Natitingou Benin
211 I6 Natividade Brazil
206 B1 Nátora Mex.
150 G5 Natori Japan
178 D4 Natron, Lake salt l. Tanz.
154 A1 Nattaung mt. Myanmar
189 H2 Natuashish Canada
155 C2 Natuna, Kepulauan is Indon.
155 C2 Natuna Besar i. Indon.
203 F2 Natural Bridge U.S.A.
197 G3 Natural Bridges National Monument nat. park U.S.A.
218 L7 Naturaliste Plateau sea feature Indian Ocean
197 H2 Naturita U.S.A.
190 E2 Naubinway U.S.A.
179 B6 Nauchas Namibia
165 K2 Nauen Germany
203 G4 Naugatuck U.S.A.
153 B3 Naujan Phil.
153 B3 Naujan, Lake Phil.
159 M4 Naujoji Akmenė Lith.
144 C4 Naukh India
144 B4 Naukot Pak.
165 H3 Naumburg (Hessen) Germany
165 J3 Naumburg (Saale) Germany
154 A1 Naungpale Myanmar
136 E6 Na'ūr Jordan
141 G4 Nauroz Kalat Pak.
125 G2 Nauru country Pacific Ocean
144 B4 Naushara Pak.
159 I3 Naustdal Norway
210 D4 Nauta Peru
180 C3 Naute Dam Namibia
207 E3 Nautla Mex.
145 G5 Navadwip India
172 C4 Navahrudak Belarus
197 H4 Navajo U.S.A.
195 F4 Navajo Lake U.S.A.
197 G3 Navajo Mountain U.S.A.
153 C4 Naval Phil.
167 D3 Navalmoral de la Mata Spain
167 D3 Navalvillar de Pela Spain
163 E4 Navan Ireland
172 D4 Navapolatsk Belarus
133 S3 Navarin, Mys c. Rus. Fed.
212 C9 Navarino, Isla i. Chile
167 F1 Navarra aut. comm. Spain
126 E6 Navarre Australia
196 A2 Navarro U.S.A.
172 G4 Navashino Rus. Fed.
199 D6 Navasota U.S.A.
162 D2 Naver, Loch l. U.K.
158 K3 Näverede Sweden
215 B2 Navidad Chile
143 A2 Navi Mumbai India
172 E4 Navlya Rus. Fed.
171 M2 Năvodari Romania
Navoi Uzbek. see Navoiy
138 F4 Navoiy Uzbek.
206 B2 Navojoa Mex.
172 G3 Navoloki Rus. Fed.
144 C5 Navsari India
144 C4 Nawa India
136 F5 Nawá Syria
145 G4 Nawabganj Bangl.
144 B4 Nawabshah Pak.
145 F4 Nawada India
141 G3 Nāwah Afgh.
144 C4 Nawalgarh India
137 J2 Naxçıvan Azer.
149 B4 Naxi China
171 K6 Naxos Greece
171 K6 Naxos i. Greece
Nây, Mui pt Vietnam see Đai Lanh, Mui
213 A4 Naya Col.
143 D1 Nayagarh India
206 C3 Nayar Mex.
206 C3 Nayarit state Mex.
141 E3 Nāy Band Iran
150 H2 Nayoro Japan
135 H5 Nay Pyi Taw Myanmar
143 B3 Nayudupeta India
214 E1 Nazaré Brazil
143 B4 Nazareth India
136 E5 Nazareth Israel
199 B7 Nazas Mex.
206 C2 Nazas r. Mex.
210 D6 Nazca Peru
217 N7 Nazca Ridge sea feature S. Pacific Ocean
Nazerat Israel see Nazareth
137 J2 Nāzīk Iran
137 I2 Nazik Gölü l. Turkey
141 F4 Nāzīl Iran
136 B3 Nazilli Turkey
141 G5 Nazimabad Pak.
137 G2 Nazımiye Turkey
145 H4 Nazira India
186 E4 Nazko Canada
186 E4 Nazko r. Canada
137 J3 Nāzlū r. Iran
173 H7 Nazran' Rus. Fed.
178 D3 Nazrēt Eth.
142 E5 Nazwá Oman
179 C4 Nchelenge Zambia
179 C6 Ncojane Botswana
179 B4 N'dalatando Angola
178 C3 Ndélé Cent. Afr. Rep.
178 B4 Ndendé Gabon
177 D3 Ndjamena Chad
179 C5 Ndola Zambia
181 I4 Ndwedwe S. Africa
179 E5 Ndzuani i. Comoros
127 G1 Neabul Creek r. Australia
163 E3 Neagh, Lough l. U.K.
194 A1 Neah Bay U.S.A.
124 D4 Neale, Lake salt flat Australia
126 B2 Neales watercourse Australia
171 J5 Nea Liosia Greece
171 J6 Neapoli Greece
161 D6 Neath U.K.
161 D6 Neath r. U.K.
127 G1 Nebine Creek r. Australia
Nebitdag Turkm. see Balkanabat
213 D4 Neblina, Pico da mt. Brazil
197 G2 Nebo, Mount U.S.A.
172 E3 Nebolchi Rus. Fed.
198 C3 Nebraska state U.S.A.
198 E3 Nebraska City U.S.A.
170 F6 Nebrodi, Monti mts Sicily Italy
199 E6 Neches r. U.S.A.
213 B3 Nechí r. Col.
178 D3 Nechisar National Park Eth.
165 G5 Neckar r. Germany
165 H5 Neckarsulm Germany
123 H2 Necker Island U.S.A.
215 E3 Necochea Arg.
165 L1 Neddemin Germany
188 F2 Nedlouc, Lac l. Canada
145 G3 Nêdong China
158 M1 Nedre Soppero Sweden
197 E4 Needles U.S.A.
144 C4 Neemuch India
190 C3 Neenah U.S.A.
187 J4 Neepawa Canada
185 J2 Neergaard Lake Canada
164 D3 Neerijnen Neth.
164 D3 Neerpelt Belgium
137 L2 Neftçala Azer.
138 B1 Neftegorsk Rus. Fed.
132 G4 Neftekamsk Rus. Fed.
173 H6 Neftekumsk Rus. Fed.
132 I3 Nefteyugansk Rus. Fed.
161 C5 Nefyn U.K.
170 C6 Nefza Tunisia
178 B4 Negage Angola
178 D3 Negēlē Eth.
214 A3 Negla r. Para.
179 D5 Negomane Moz.
143 B5 Negombo Sri Lanka
171 J4 Negotino Macedonia
210 C5 Negra, Cordillera mts Peru
210 B5 Negra, Punta pt Peru
170 B7 Négrine Alg.
210 B4 Negritos Peru
215 D4 Negro r. Arg.
214 A2 Negro r. Brazil
210 F4 Negro r. S. America
215 F2 Negro r. Uruguay
153 B4 Negros i. Phil.
171 M3 Negru Vodă Romania
137 L4 Nehavand Iran
141 F4 Nehbandān Iran
146 E2 Nehe China
149 B4 Neijiang China
187 H4 Neilburg Canada
148 B1 Nei Mongol Zizhiqu aut. reg. China
165 J3 Neinstedt Germany
168 G5 Neiße r. Germany/Poland
213 B4 Neiva Col.
148 D3 Neixiang China
187 J3 Nejanilini Lake Canada
140 D2 Nekā Iran
178 D3 Nek'emtē Eth.
159 K5 Neksø Denmark
144 D3 Nelang India
172 E3 Nelidovo Rus. Fed.
198 D3 Neligh U.S.A.
133 P3 Nel'kan Rus. Fed.
146 F1 Nel'kan Rus. Fed.
143 B3 Nelligere India
143 B3 Nellore India
186 F5 Nelson Canada
187 K3 Nelson r. Canada
128 D4 Nelson N.Z.
160 E4 Nelson U.K.
197 E4 Nelson U.S.A.
126 D7 Nelson, Cape Australia
212 B8 Nelson, Estrecho str. Chile
127 J4 Nelson Bay Australia
186 E3 Nelson Forks Canada
187 J3 Nelson House Canada
Nelspruit S. Africa see Mbombela
176 B3 Néma Mauritania
172 I3 Nema Rus. Fed.
190 A2 Nemadji r. U.S.A.
172 B4 Neman Rus. Fed.
141 E4 Ne'matābād Iran
172 G3 Nemda r. Rus. Fed.
172 J2 Nemed Rus. Fed.
191 F2 Nemegos Canada
158 O1 Nemetskiy, Mys c. Rus. Fed.
166 F2 Nemours France
137 I2 Nemrut Dağı mt. Turkey
150 I3 Nemuro Japan
150 I3 Nemuro-kaikyō sea chan. Japan
173 D5 Nemyriv Ukr.
163 C5 Nenagh Ireland
125 G3 Nendo i. Solomon Is
161 H5 Nene r. U.K.
146 E2 Nenjiang China
164 E5 Nennig tourist site Germany
172 F1 Nenoksa Rus. Fed.
162 E1 Neolithic Orkney tourist site U.K.
199 E4 Neosho U.S.A.
198 E4 Neosho r. U.S.A.
145 E3 Nepal country Asia
191 J3 Nepean Canada
197 G2 Nephi U.S.A.
163 B3 Nephin h. Ireland
163 B3 Nephin Beg Range hills Ireland
178 C3 Nepoko r. Dem. Rep. Congo
Neptune U.S.A. see Neptune City
203 F4 Neptune City U.S.A.
166 E4 Nérac France
127 J1 Nerang Australia
146 D1 Nerchinsk Rus. Fed.
172 G3 Nerekhta Rus. Fed.
170 G3 Neretva r. Bos.-Herz./Croatia
179 C5 Neriquinha Angola
159 M5 Neris r. Lith.
172 F3 Nerl' r. Rus. Fed.
214 C2 Nerópolis Brazil
146 E1 Neryungri Rus. Fed.
164 D1 Nes Neth.
159 J3 Nes Norway
159 J3 Nesbyen Norway
158 D2 Neskaupstaður Iceland
164 A5 Nesle France
158 K2 Nesna Norway
162 D3 Ness, Loch l. U.K.
198 D4 Ness City U.S.A.
165 I4 Nesse r. Germany
186 C3 Nesselrode, Mount Canada/U.S.A.
171 K4 Nestos r. Greece
136 E5 Netanya Israel
187 M2 Netchek, Cape Canada
164 D2 Netherlands country Europe
Netherlands Antilles Caribbean Sea see Bonaire, Curaçao, Sint Eustatius Sint Maarten
165 G4 Netphen Germany
145 G4 Netrakona Bangl.
144 C5 Netrang India
185 K3 Nettilling Lake Canada
190 A1 Nett Lake U.S.A.
190 A1 Nett Lake l. U.S.A.
165 L1 Neubrandenburg Germany
168 C7 Neuchâtel Switz.
168 C7 Neuchâtel, Lac de l. Switz.
165 I5 Neuendettelsau Germany
164 E2 Neuenhaus Germany
165 H1 Neuenkirchen Germany
165 G2 Neuenkirchen (Oldenburg) Germany
164 D5 Neufchâteau Belgium
166 G2 Neufchâteau France
166 E2 Neufchâtel-en-Bray France
165 F1 Neuharlingersiel Germany
165 H1 Neuhaus (Oste) Germany
165 H4 Neuhof Germany
165 J1 Neu Kaliß Germany
165 H4 Neukirchen Hessen Germany
165 K4 Neukirchen Sachsen Germany
165 J5 Neumarkt in der Oberpfalz Germany
129 D3 Neumayer III research stn Antarctica
168 D3 Neumünster Germany
165 K5 Neunburg vorm Wald Germany
168 H7 Neunkirchen Austria
164 F5 Neunkirchen Germany
215 C3 Neuquén Arg.
215 C3 Neuquén prov. Arg.
215 C3 Neuquén r. Arg.
165 K2 Neuruppin Germany
201 E5 Neuse r. U.S.A.
168 H7 Neusiedler See l. Austria/Hungary

164 E3 Neuss Germany
165 H2 Neustadt am Rübenberge Germany
165 I5 Neustadt an der Aisch Germany
165 K5 Neustadt an der Waldnaab Germany
165 G5 Neustadt an der Weinstraße Germany
165 J4 Neustadt bei Coburg Germany
165 J1 Neustadt-Glewe Germany
164 F4 Neustadt (Wied) Germany
165 L1 Neustrelitz Germany
165 K6 Neutraubling Germany
164 F4 Neuwied Germany
165 H1 Neu Wulmstorf Germany
199 E4 Nevada U.S.A.
196 D2 Nevada *state* U.S.A.
167 E4 Nevada, Sierra *mts* Spain
196 B1 Nevada, Sierra *mts* U.S.A.
215 C2 Nevado, Cerro *mt.* Arg.
215 C3 Nevado, Sierra del *mts* Arg.
207 E4 Nevado de Toluca, Volcán *vol.* Mex.
172 D3 Nevel' Rus. Fed.
166 F3 Nevers France
127 G3 Nevertire Australia
171 H3 Nevesinje Bos.-Herz.
173 G6 Nevinnomyssk Rus. Fed.
162 C3 Nevis, Loch *inlet* U.K.
136 E2 Nevşehir Turkey
150 C2 Nevskoye Rus. Fed.
197 E5 New *r. CA* U.S.A.
202 C6 New *r. WV* U.S.A.
186 D3 New Aiyansh Canada
200 C4 New Albany *IN* U.S.A.
199 F5 New Albany *MS* U.S.A.
203 E4 New Albany *PA* U.S.A.
211 G2 New Amsterdam Guyana
127 G2 New Angledool Australia
203 F5 Newark *DE* U.S.A.
203 F5 Newark *MD* U.S.A.
203 F4 Newark *NJ* U.S.A.
202 E3 Newark *NY* U.S.A.
202 B4 Newark *OH* U.S.A.
197 E2 Newark Lake U.S.A.
203 F4 Newark Liberty *airport* U.S.A.
161 G4 Newark-on-Trent U.K.
203 E3 Newark Valley U.S.A.
203 H4 New Bedford U.S.A.
194 B2 Newberg U.S.A.
203 F3 New Berlin U.S.A.
201 E5 New Bern U.S.A.
190 E2 Newberry *MI* U.S.A.
201 D5 Newberry *SC* U.S.A.
196 D4 Newberry Springs U.S.A.
160 F2 Newbiggin-by-the-Sea U.K.
201 F7 New Bight Bahamas
191 I3 Newboro Canada
203 G3 New Boston *MA* U.S.A.
202 B5 New Boston *OH* U.S.A.
199 D6 New Braunfels U.S.A.
163 E4 Newbridge Ireland
124 E2 New Britain *i.* P.N.G.
203 G4 New Britain U.S.A.
216 F6 New Britain Trench *sea feature* Pacific Ocean
189 G4 New Brunswick *prov.* Canada
203 F4 New Brunswick U.S.A.
190 D5 New Buffalo U.S.A.
162 F3 Newburgh U.K.
203 F4 Newburgh U.S.A.
161 F6 Newbury U.K.
203 H3 Newburyport U.S.A.
153 A3 New Busuanga Phil.
160 E3 Newby Bridge U.K.
125 G4 New Caledonia *terr.* S. Pacific Ocean
216 F7 New Caledonia Trough *sea feature* Tasman Sea
189 G4 New Carlisle Canada
127 I4 Newcastle Australia
191 H4 Newcastle Canada
163 E4 Newcastle Ireland
181 H3 Newcastle S. Africa
163 F3 Newcastle U.K.
196 B2 Newcastle *CA* U.S.A.
190 E6 New Castle *IN* U.S.A.
202 B4 Newcastle *OH* U.S.A.
202 C4 New Castle *PA* U.S.A.
197 F3 Newcastle *UT* U.S.A.
202 C6 New Castle *VA* U.S.A.
194 F3 Newcastle *WY* U.S.A.
161 C5 Newcastle Emlyn U.K.
161 E4 Newcastle-under-Lyme U.K.
160 F3 Newcastle upon Tyne U.K.
163 B5 Newcastle West Ireland
203 F6 New Church U.S.A.
197 H3 Newcomb U.S.A.
162 D5 New Cumnock U.K.
162 F3 New Deer U.K.
144 D3 New Delhi India
203 J1 New Denmark Canada
196 B3 New Don Pedro Reservoir U.S.A.
127 I3 New England Range *mts* Australia
219 F3 New England Seamounts *sea feature* N. Atlantic Ocean
161 E6 Newent U.K.
161 F7 New Forest National Park *nat. park* U.K.
185 M5 Newfoundland *i.* Canada
Newfoundland *prov.* Canada *see* Newfoundland and Labrador
189 I4 Newfoundland and Labrador *prov.* Canada
194 D3 Newfoundland Evaporation Basin *salt l.* U.S.A.
162 D5 New Galloway U.K.
125 F2 New Georgia *i.* Solomon Is
125 F2 New Georgia Islands Solomon Is
125 F2 New Georgia Sound *sea chan.* Solomon Is
189 H4 New Glasgow Canada
124 E2 New Guinea *i.* Asia
202 B4 New Hampshire U.S.A.
203 G3 New Hampshire *state* U.S.A.
190 A4 New Hampton U.S.A.
124 F2 New Hanover *i.* P.N.G.
181 I4 New Hanover S. Africa
203 G4 New Haven U.S.A.
186 D3 New Hazelton Canada
216 G7 New Hebrides Trench *sea feature* Pacific Ocean
196 B2 New Hogan Reservoir U.S.A.
190 C4 New Holstein U.S.A.
199 F6 New Iberia U.S.A.
163 D5 Newinn Ireland
124 F2 New Ireland *i.* P.N.G.
203 F5 New Jersey *state* U.S.A.
202 E6 New Kent U.S.A.
162 E5 New Lanark U.K.
202 B5 New Lexington U.S.A.
190 B4 New Lisbon U.S.A.
191 H2 New Liskeard Canada
203 G4 New London *CT* U.S.A.
190 B5 New London *IA* U.S.A.
190 B6 New London *MO* U.S.A.
190 C3 New London *WI* U.S.A.
124 B4 Newman Australia
190 D6 Newman U.S.A.
191 H3 Newmarket Canada
163 B5 Newmarket Ireland
161 H5 Newmarket U.K.
202 D5 New Market U.S.A.
163 C5 Newmarket-on-Fergus Ireland
202 C5 New Martinsville U.S.A.
194 C2 New Meadows U.S.A.
196 B3 New Melones Lake U.S.A.
195 F5 New Mexico *state* U.S.A.
201 C5 Newnan U.S.A.
127 G9 New Norfolk Australia
199 F6 New Orleans U.S.A.
203 F4 New Paltz U.S.A.
202 C4 New Philadelphia U.S.A.
162 F3 New Pitsligo U.K.
128 E3 New Plymouth N.Z.
163 B4 Newport Ireland
163 C5 Newport Ireland
161 E5 Newport *England* U.K.
161 F7 Newport *England* U.K.
161 D6 Newport *Wales* U.K.
199 F5 Newport *AR* U.S.A.
202 A5 Newport *KY* U.S.A.
203 I2 Newport *ME* U.S.A.
191 F5 Newport *MI* U.S.A.
203 G3 Newport *NH* U.S.A.
194 A2 Newport *OR* U.S.A.
203 H4 Newport *RI* U.S.A.
203 G2 Newport *VT* U.S.A.
194 C1 Newport *WA* U.S.A.
196 D5 Newport Beach U.S.A.
193 K4 Newport News U.S.A.
202 E6 Newport News *airport* U.S.A.
161 G5 Newport Pagnell U.K.
201 E7 New Providence *i.* Bahamas
161 B7 Newquay U.K.
189 G4 New Richmond Canada
190 A3 New Richmond U.S.A.
197 F5 New River U.S.A.
199 F6 New Roads U.S.A.
161 H7 New Romney U.K.
163 E5 New Ross Ireland
163 E3 Newry U.K.
190 A5 New Sharon U.S.A.
133 P2 New Siberia Islands Rus. Fed.
201 D6 New Smyrna Beach U.S.A.
127 G4 New South Wales *state* Australia
144 D3 New Tehri India
149 □ New Territories *reg. Hong Kong* China
160 E4 Newton U.K.
198 E3 Newton *IA* U.S.A.
198 D4 Newton *KS* U.S.A.
203 H3 Newton *MA* U.S.A.
199 F5 Newton *MS* U.S.A.
203 F4 Newton *NJ* U.S.A.
161 D7 Newton Abbot U.K.
162 F3 Newtonhill U.K.
162 D5 Newton Mearns U.K.
162 D6 Newton Stewart U.K.
163 C5 Newtown Ireland
161 E5 Newtown *England* U.K.
161 D5 Newtown *Wales* U.K.
198 C1 New Town U.S.A.
163 F3 Newtownabbey U.K.
163 F3 Newtownards U.K.
163 D3 Newtownbutler U.K.
163 E4 Newtown Mount Kennedy Ireland
162 F5 Newtown St Boswells U.K.
163 D3 Newtownstewart U.K.
198 E2 New Ulm U.S.A.
196 A2 Newville U.S.A.
186 E5 New Westminster Canada
203 G4 New York U.S.A. (City Plan 114)
203 E3 New York *state* U.S.A.
128 New Zealand *country* Oceania
172 G3 Neya Rus. Fed.
141 E4 Ney Bīd Iran
140 D4 Neyrīz Iran
141 E2 Neyshābūr Iran
143 B4 Neyyattinkara India
207 F4 Nezahualcóyotl, Presa *resr* Mex.
155 D2 Ngabang Indon.
178 B4 Ngabé Congo
154 A2 Nga Chong, Khao *mt.* Myanmar/Thai.
153 C6 Ngalipaëng Indon.
179 C6 Ngami, Lake Botswana
145 F3 Ngamring China
145 E3 Ngangla Ringco *salt l.* China
144 E2 Nganglong Kangri *mt.* China
144 E2 Nganglong Kangri *mts* China
145 F3 Ngangzê Co *salt l.* China
154 C1 Ngan Sâu, Sông *r.* Vietnam
Ngan Sau, Sông *r.* Vietnam *see* Ngan Sâu, Sông
149 B6 Ngân Sơn Vietnam
154 A1 Ngao Thai.
177 D4 Ngaoundéré Cameroon
128 E2 Ngaruawahia N.Z.
128 F3 Ngaruroro *r.* N.Z.
128 E3 Ngauruhoe *vol.* N.Z.
179 E5 Ngazidja *i.* Comoros
181 G5 Ngcobo S. Africa
154 B1 Ngiap *r.* Laos
178 B4 Ngo Congo
Ngoc Linh *mt.* Vietnam *see* Linh, Ngok
145 F3 Ngoin, Co *salt l.* China
176 D4 Ngol Bembo Nigeria
145 F2 Ngoqumaima China
146 B3 Ngoring Hu *l.* China
178 D4 Ngorongoro Conservation Area *nature res.* Tanz.
177 D3 Ngourti Niger
181 G6 Ngqamakhwe S. Africa
177 D3 Nguigmi Niger
147 F6 Ngulu *atoll* Micronesia
154 B1 Ngum, Nâm *r.* Laos
176 D3 Nguru Nigeria
Nguyên Binh Vietnam *see* Ngân Sơn
Ngwaketse *admin. dist.* Botswana *see* Southern
181 G3 Ngwathe S. Africa
181 I3 Ngwavuma *r.* Swaziland
181 I4 Ngwelezana S. Africa
179 D5 Nhamalabué Moz.
154 D2 Nha Trang Vietnam
126 D6 Nhill Australia
181 I3 Nhlangano Swaziland
149 B6 Nho Quan Vietnam
124 D3 Nhulunbuy Australia
187 I4 Niacam Canada
176 B3 Niafounké Mali
191 H4 Niagara *r.* Canada/U.S.A.
190 D3 Niagara U.S.A.
191 H4 Niagara Falls Canada
202 D3 Niagara Falls U.S.A.
176 C3 Niamey Niger
153 C5 Niampak Indon.
179 D4 Niangandu Tanz.
178 C3 Niangara Dem. Rep. Congo
155 A2 Nias *i.* Indon.
159 M4 Nīca Latvia
206 H5 Nicaragua *country* Central America
206 H6 Nicaragua, Lake Nicaragua
170 G5 Nicastro Italy
166 H5 Nice France
189 F3 Nichicun, Lac *l.* Canada
145 E4 Nichlaul India
201 E7 Nicholl's Town Bahamas
191 F2 Nicholson Canada
135 H6 Nicobar Islands India
136 D4 Nicosia Cyprus
206 H6 Nicoya, Golfo de *b.* Costa Rica
206 H6 Nicoya, Península de *pen.* Costa Rica
203 J1 Nictau Canada
159 M5 Nida Lith.
160 F4 Nidd *r.* U.K.
165 H4 Nidda Germany
165 H4 Nidder *r.* Germany
169 J4 Nidzica Poland
168 D3 Niebüll Germany
164 E5 Niederanven Lux.
165 H4 Niederaula Germany
168 F7 Niedere Tauern *mts* Austria
165 G2 Niedersachsen *land* Germany
164 E1 Niedersächsisches Wattenmeer, Nationalpark Germany
176 D4 Niefang Equat. Guinea
176 B3 Niellé Côte d'Ivoire
165 H2 Nienburg (Weser) Germany
164 E3 Niers *r.* Germany
165 G5 Nierstein Germany
211 G2 Nieuw Amsterdam Suriname
164 C2 Nieuwe Niedorp Neth.
164 E1 Nieuwe Pekela Neth.
164 C3 Nieuwerkerk aan den IJssel Neth.
211 G2 Nieuw Nickerie Suriname
164 E1 Nieuwolda Neth.
180 C5 Nieuwoudtville S. Africa
164 A3 Nieuwpoort Belgium
164 C3 Nieuw-Vossemeer Neth.
136 E3 Niğde Turkey
176 C3 Niger *country* Africa
176 C4 Niger *r.* Africa
176 C4 Niger, Mouths of the Nigeria
219 J5 Niger Cone *sea feature* S. Atlantic Ocean
176 C4 Nigeria *country* Africa
191 G1 Nighthawk Lake Canada
171 J4 Nigrita Greece
151 G6 Nihonmatsu Japan
151 F6 Niigata Japan
151 C8 Niihama Japan
Niihau *i.* U.S.A. *see* Ni'ihau
196 □2 Ni'ihau *i.* U.S.A.
151 F7 Nii-jima *i.* Japan
150 H3 Niikappu Japan
151 C7 Niimi Japan
151 F6 Niitsu Japan
164 D2 Nijkerk Neth.
164 D3 Nijmegen Neth.
164 E2 Nijverdal Neth.
158 O1 Nikel' Rus. Fed.
176 C4 Nikki Benin
151 F6 Nikkō Japan
151 F6 Nikkō Kokuritsu-kōen *nat. park* Japan
139 F1 Nikolayevka Kazakh.
138 E1 Nikolayevka *Chelyabinskaya Oblast'* Rus. Fed.
172 H4 Nikolayevka *Ul'yanovskaya Oblast'* Rus. Fed.
173 H5 Nikolayevsk Rus. Fed.
172 H4 Nikol'sk Rus. Fed.
172 H3 Nikol'sk Rus. Fed.
133 R4 Nikol'skoye Rus. Fed.
173 E6 Nikopol' Ukr.
137 L3 Nīk Pey Iran
136 F1 Niksar Turkey
141 F5 Nīkshahr Iran
171 H3 Nikšić Montenegro
125 I2 Nikumaroro *atoll* Kiribati
125 H2 Nikunau *i.* Kiribati
144 C2 Nila Pak.
145 F5 Nilagiri India
197 E5 Niland U.S.A.
143 B2 Nilanga India
178 F1 Nile *r.* Africa
190 D5 Niles U.S.A.
143 A3 Nileshwar India
143 B4 Nilgiri Hills India
141 G3 Nīlī Afgh.
139 J4 Nilka China
158 O3 Nilsiä Fin.
207 F4 Niltepec Mex.
Nimach India *see* Neemuch
127 J2 Nimbin Australia
166 G5 Nîmes France
127 H6 Nimmitabel Australia
129 C5 Nimrod Glacier *glacier* Antarctica
177 F4 Nimule South Sudan
137 I3 Nīnawá *tourist site* Iraq
127 H2 Nindigully Australia
143 A4 Nine Degree Channel India
126 E3 Nine Mile Lake *salt flat* Australia
196 D2 Ninemile Peak U.S.A.
149 □ Ninepin Group *is Hong Kong* China
218 J7 Ninetyeast Ridge *sea feature* Indian Ocean
127 G7 Ninety Mile Beach Australia
128 D1 Ninety Mile Beach N.Z.
Nineveh Iraq *see* Nīnawá
203 F3 Nineveh U.S.A.
124 B4 Ningaloo Coast *tourist site* Australia
152 E1 Ning'an China
149 F4 Ningbo China
148 F1 Ningcheng China
149 F5 Ningde China
149 E5 Ningdu China
Ninggang China *see* Longshi
149 F4 Ningguo China
149 F4 Ninghai China
148 E2 Ninghe China
149 E5 Ninghua China
146 B3 Ningjing Shan *mts* China
148 E3 Ningling China
149 C6 Ningming China
149 B5 Ningnan China
148 C3 Ningqiang China
148 C3 Ningshan China
148 D2 Ningwu China
148 B2 Ningxia Huizu Zizhiqu *aut. reg.* China
148 C3 Ningxian China
149 D4 Ningxiang China
148 E3 Ningyang China
149 D5 Ningyuan China
149 C6 Ninh Binh Vietnam
154 D2 Ninh Hoa Vietnam
129 C6 Ninnis Glacier *glacier* Antarctica
150 G4 Ninohe Japan
214 A3 Nioaque Brazil
198 C3 Niobrara *r.* U.S.A.
176 A3 Niokolo Koba, Parc National du *nat. park* Senegal
145 H4 Nioku India
176 B3 Niono Mali
176 B3 Nioro Mali
166 D3 Niort France
143 A2 Nipani India
187 I4 Nipawin Canada
188 C4 Nipigon Canada
188 C4 Nipigon, Lake Canada
190 C1 Nipigon Bay Canada
189 H3 Nipishish Lake Canada
191 H2 Nipissing Canada
191 G2 Nipissing, Lake Canada
196 B4 Nipomo U.S.A.
137 J5 Nippur *tourist site* Iraq
197 E4 Nipton U.S.A.
214 C1 Niquelândia Brazil
140 B2 Nir Iran
143 A2 Nira *r.* India
143 B2 Nirmal India
143 B2 Nirmal Range *hills* India
171 I3 Niš Serbia
167 C3 Nisa Port.
138 D5 Nisa *tourist site* Turkm.
140 B5 Nisah, Wādī *watercourse* Saudi Arabia
170 F6 Niscemi *Sicily* Italy
151 B9 Nishino-omote Japan
151 C6 Nishino-shima *i.* Japan
151 A8 Nishi-Sonogi-hantō *pen.* Japan
151 D7 Nishiwaki Japan
144 D6 Nishtun Yemen
186 B2 Nisling *r.* Canada
164 C3 Nispen Neth.
159 K4 Nissan *r.* Sweden
169 M6 Nistru *r.* Moldova *alt.* Dnister (Ukr.), *conv.* Dniester
169 N7 Nistrului Inferior, Cîmpia *lowland* Moldova
186 C2 Nisutlin *r.* Canada
171 L6 Nisyros *i.* Greece
140 C5 Niţā Saudi Arabia
189 F3 Nitchequon Canada
214 D3 Niterói Brazil
162 E5 Nith *r.* U.K.
162 E5 Nithsdale *val.* U.K.
144 D3 Niti Pass China
168 I6 Nitra Slovakia
202 C5 Nitro U.S.A.
Niuafo'ou *i.* Tonga *see* Niuafo'ou
123 H4 Niuafo'ou *i.* Tonga
125 I3 Niuatoputopu *i.* Tonga
125 J3 Niue *terr.* Pacific Ocean
125 H3 Niulakita *i.* Tuvalu
149 B5 Niulan Jiang *r.* China
125 H2 Niutao *i.* Tuvalu
152 B3 Niuzhuang China
158 N3 Nivala Fin.
164 C4 Nivelles Belgium
172 J2 Nivshera Rus. Fed.
144 C4 Niwai India
196 C2 Nixon U.S.A.
145 E1 Niya He *r.* China
137 L1 Niyazoba Azer.
143 B2 Nizamabad India
143 B2 Nizam Sagar *l.* India
172 H3 Nizhegorodskaya Oblast' *admin. div.* Rus. Fed.
133 R3 Nizhnekolymsk Rus. Fed.
146 B1 Nizhneudinsk Rus. Fed.
132 I3 Nizhnevartovsk Rus. Fed.
133 O2 Nizhneyansk Rus. Fed.
172 G4 Nizhniy Lomov Rus. Fed.
172 G3 Nizhniy Novgorod Rus. Fed.
172 J2 Nizhniy Odes Rus. Fed.
172 H3 Nizhniy Yenansk Rus. Fed.
139 I1 Nizhnyaya Suyetka Rus. Fed.
146 C1 Nizhnyaya Tunguska *r.* Rus. Fed.
173 D5 Nizhyn Ukr.
Nizina *reg.* Poland *see* Mazowiecka, Nizina
136 F3 Nizip Turkey
150 D3 Nizmennyy, Mys *pt* Rus. Fed.
158 M1 Njallavarri *mt.* Norway
158 L2 Njavve Sweden
179 D4 Njinjo Tanz.
179 D4 Njombe Tanz.
159 L3 Njurundabommen Sweden
176 D4 Nkambe Cameroon
181 I4 Nkandla S. Africa
176 B4 Nkawkaw Ghana
179 C5 Nkayi Zimbabwe
179 D5 Nkhata Bay Malawi
179 D5 Nkhotakota Malawi
176 C4 Nkongsamba Cameroon
181 G5 Nkululeko S. Africa
179 B5 Nkurenkuru Namibia
181 G6 Nkwenkwezi S. Africa
145 I4 Noa Dihing *r.* India
145 G5 Noakhali Bangl.
143 D1 Noamundi India
163 E4 Nobber Ireland
151 B8 Nobeoka Japan
150 G3 Noboribetsu Japan
214 A1 Nobres Brazil
126 E1 Noccundra Australia
206 D3 Nochistlán Mex.
126 E1 Nockatunga Australia
210 F6 Noel Kempff Mercado, Parque Nacional *nat. park* Bol.
191 G2 Noelville Canada
204 B2 Nogales Mex.
192 D5 Nogales U.S.A.
151 B8 Nōgata Japan
138 C2 Nogayty Kazakh.
166 E2 Nogent-le-Rotrou France
164 A5 Nogent-sur-Oise France
172 F4 Noginsk Rus. Fed.
151 E7 Nōgōhaku-san *mt.* Japan
215 E2 Nogoyá Arg.
215 E2 Nogoya *r.* Arg.
144 C3 Nohar India
150 G4 Noheji Japan
164 F5 Nohfelden Germany
166 C3 Noirmoutier, Île de *i.* France
166 C3 Noirmoutier-en-l'Île France
164 E5 Noisseville France
151 F7 Nojima-zaki *c.* Japan
144 C4 Nokha India
141 F4 Nok Kundi Pak.
187 I3 Nokomis Lake Canada
178 B3 Nola Cent. Afr. Rep.
172 I3 Nolinsk Rus. Fed.
203 H4 No Mans Land *i.* U.S.A.
184 B3 Nome U.S.A.
148 B1 Nomgon Mongolia
145 I1 Nomhon China
181 G5 Nomonde S. Africa
151 A8 Nomo-zaki *pt* Japan
172 G3 Nomzha Rus. Fed.
187 H2 Nonacho Lake Canada
181 I4 Nondweni S. Africa
152 C1 Nong'an China
154 B1 Nong Bua Lamphu Thai.
154 B2 Nong Hong Thai.
154 B1 Nong Khai Thai.
181 I3 Nongoma S. Africa
126 B4 Nonning Australia
164 E5 Nonnweiler Germany
206 C2 Nonoava Mex.
125 H2 Nonouti *atoll* Kiribati
152 D5 Nonsan S. Korea
154 B2 Nonthaburi Thai.
180 F5 Nonzwakazi S. Africa
127 G2 Noorama Creek *watercourse* Australia
164 B3 Noordbeveland *i.* Neth.
164 E1 Noordbroek-Uiterburen Neth.
164 C2 Noorderhaaks *i.* Neth.
164 D2 Noordoost Polder Neth.
164 C2 Noordwijk Neth.
186 D5 Nootka Island Canada
139 G5 Norak Tajik.
153 C5 Norala Phil.
191 H1 Noranda Canada
159 K3 Norberg Sweden
132 D2 Nordaustlandet *i.* Svalbard
186 F4 Nordegg Canada
164 F1 Norden Germany
132 K2 Nordenshel'da, Arkhipelag *is* Rus. Fed.
164 F1 Norderland *reg.* Germany
164 F1 Norderney Germany
164 F1 Norderney *i.* Germany
165 I1 Norderstedt Germany
159 I3 Nordfjordeid Norway
158 K2 Nordfold Norway
168 C3 Nordfriesische Inseln Germany
165 I3 Nordhausen Germany
165 G1 Nordholz Germany
164 F2 Nordhorn Germany
Nordkapp *c.* Norway *see* North Cape
158 L1 Nordkjosbotn Norway
158 K2 Nordli Norway
168 E6 Nördlingen Germany
158 L3 Nordmaling Sweden
164 B4 Nord-Pas de Calais Mining Basin *tourist site* France
165 F5 Nordpfälzer Bergland *reg.* Germany
164 F3 Nordrhein-Westfalen *land* Germany
163 D5 Nore *r.* Ireland
166 F5 Nore, Pic de *mt.* France
198 D3 Norfolk *NE* U.S.A.
203 F2 Norfolk *NY* U.S.A.
203 E6 Norfolk *VA* U.S.A.
125 G4 Norfolk Island *terr.* Pacific Ocean
216 G7 Norfolk Island Ridge *sea feature* Tasman Sea
199 E4 Norfork Lake U.S.A.
164 E1 Norg Neth.
159 I3 Norheimsund Norway
151 E6 Norikura-dake *vol.* Japan
132 J3 Noril'sk Rus. Fed.
137 J1 Nor Kharberd Armenia
191 H3 Norland Canada
190 C5 Normal U.S.A.
199 D5 Norman U.S.A.
201 D5 Norman, Lake *resr* U.S.A.
124 F2 Normanby Island P.N.G.
Normandes, Îles *is* English Chan. *see* Channel Islands
Normandie *reg.* France *see* Normandy
166 D2 Normandy *reg.* France
124 E3 Normanton Australia
126 C5 Normanville Australia
186 D1 Norman Wells Canada
215 B4 Ñorquinco Arg.
158 M3 Norra Kvarken *str.* Fin./Sweden
158 K2 Norra Storfjället *mts* Sweden
164 A4 Norrent-Fontes France
202 B6 Norris Lake U.S.A.
203 F4 Norristown U.S.A.
159 L4 Norrköping Sweden
159 L4 Norrtälje Sweden
124 C5 Norseman Australia
158 L2 Norsjö Sweden
125 G3 Norsup Vanuatu
215 F3 Norte, Punta *pt Buenos Aires* Arg.
212 D6 Norte, Punta *pt Chubut* Arg.
165 H3 Nörten-Hardenberg Germany
129 B6 North, Cape *c.* Antarctica
189 H4 North, Cape Canada
203 G3 North Adams U.S.A.
160 F3 Northallerton U.K.
182 North America
124 B4 Northampton Australia
161 G5 Northampton U.K.
203 G3 Northampton U.S.A.
202 E5 North Anna *r.* U.S.A.
203 I2 North Anson U.S.A.
186 G2 North Arm *b.* Canada
201 D5 North Augusta U.S.A.
189 H2 North Aulatsivik Island Canada
218 L5 North Australian Basin *sea feature* Indian Ocean
187 H4 North Battleford Canada
191 H2 North Bay Canada
188 E2 North Belcher Islands Canada
194 A3 North Bend U.S.A.
162 F4 North Berwick U.K.
203 H3 North Berwick U.S.A.
127 F3 North Bourke Australia
190 A3 North Branch U.S.A.
189 H4 North Cape Canada
158 N1 North Cape Norway
128 D1 North Cape N.Z.
188 B3 North Caribou Lake Canada
201 D5 North Carolina *state* U.S.A.
194 B1 North Cascades National Park U.S.A.
191 F2 North Channel *lake channel* Canada
163 E2 North Channel U.K.
203 H2 North Conway U.S.A.
198 C2 North Dakota *state* U.S.A.
161 H6 North Downs *hills* U.K.
202 D3 North East U.S.A.
217 I4 Northeast Pacific Basin *sea feature* Pacific Ocean
201 E7 Northeast Providence Channel Bahamas
165 H3 Northeim Germany
201 F7 North End Point Bahamas
Northern *prov.* S. Africa *see* Limpopo
180 D4 Northern Cape *prov.* S. Africa
187 J3 Northern Indian Lake Canada
163 D3 Northern Ireland *prov.* U.K.
188 B4 Northern Light Lake Canada
147 G5 Northern Mariana Islands *terr.* Pacific Ocean
136 F3 Northern Syria, Ancient Villages of *tourist site* Syria
124 D3 Northern Territory *admin. div.* Australia
162 F4 North Esk *r.* U.K.
203 G3 Northfield *MA* U.S.A.
198 E2 Northfield *MN* U.S.A.
203 G2 Northfield *VT* U.S.A.
161 I6 North Foreland *c.* U.K.
196 C3 North Fork U.S.A.
190 E3 North Fox Island U.S.A.
188 D3 North French *r.* Canada
220 T1 North Geomagnetic Pole
160 G3 North Grimston U.K.
203 J2 North Head Canada
128 E2 North Head *hd* N.Z.
187 J2 North Henik Lake Canada
203 G3 North Hudson U.S.A.
128 E3 North Island N.Z.
153 B1 North Island Phil.
153 B4 North Islet *rf* Phil.
197 G4 North Jadito Canyon *gorge* U.S.A.
190 D5 North Judson U.S.A.
187 J3 North Knife *r.* Canada
145 E4 North Koel *r.* India
197 G5 North Komelik U.S.A.
152 D3 North Korea *country* Asia
145 H4 North Lakhimpur India
197 E3 North Las Vegas U.S.A.
199 E5 North Little Rock U.S.A.
179 D5 North Luangwa National Park Zambia
220 O1 North Magnetic Pole
190 E5 North Manchester U.S.A.
190 D3 North Manitou Island U.S.A.
187 I4 North Moose Lake Canada
186 D2 North Nahanni *r.* Canada
187 K5 Northome U.S.A.
North Ossetia *aut. rep.* Rus. Fed. *see* Severnaya Osetiya-Alaniya Respublika
196 C3 North Palisade *mt.* U.S.A.
198 C3 North Platte U.S.A.
198 C3 North Platte *r.* U.S.A.
127 G7 North Point Australia
149 □ North Point *Hong Kong* China
220 A1 North Pole Arctic Ocean
190 E3 Northport U.S.A.
197 F3 North Rim U.S.A.
162 F1 North Ronaldsay *i.* U.K.
162 F1 North Ronaldsay Firth *sea chan.* U.K.
196 B2 North San Juan U.S.A.
187 G4 North Saskatchewan *r.* Canada
161 H1 North Sea Europe
187 I3 North Seal *r.* Canada
160 F2 North Shields U.K.
196 D2 North Shoshone Peak U.S.A.
184 D3 North Slope *plain* U.S.A.
161 H4 North Somercotes U.K.
127 J1 North Stradbroke Island Australia
203 H2 North Stratford U.S.A.
160 F2 North Sunderland U.K.
128 E3 North Taranaki Bight *b.* N.Z.
186 F4 North Thompson *r.* Canada
162 A3 Northton U.K.
202 D3 North Tonawanda U.S.A.
128 A7 North Trap *rf* N.Z.
203 G2 North Troy U.S.A.
188 D3 North Twin Island Canada
160 E2 North Tyne *r.* U.K.
162 A3 North Uist *i.* U.K.
160 E2 Northumberland National Park U.K.
189 H4 Northumberland Strait Canada
186 E5 North Vancouver Canada
203 F3 Northville U.S.A.
161 I5 North Walsham U.K.
180 F3 North West *prov.* S. Africa
219 F1 Northwest Atlantic Mid-Ocean Channel *sea chan.* N. Atlantic Ocean
124 B4 North West Cape Australia
North West Frontier *prov.* Pak. *see* Khyber Pakhtunkhwa
216 F3 Northwest Pacific Basin *sea feature* N. Pacific Ocean
201 E7 Northwest Providence Channel Bahamas
189 I3 North West River Canada
187 G2 Northwest Territories *admin. div.* Canada
161 E4 Northwich U.K.
203 F5 North Wildwood U.S.A.
220 N1 Northwind Ridge *sea feature* Arctic Ocean
203 H2 North Woodstock U.S.A.
160 G3 North York Moors *moorland* U.K.
160 G3 North York Moors National Park U.K.
189 G4 Norton Canada
160 G3 Norton U.K.
198 D4 Norton *KS* U.S.A.
202 B6 Norton *VA* U.S.A.
203 H2 Norton *VT* U.S.A.
179 D5 Norton Zimbabwe
184 B3 Norton Sound *sea chan.* U.S.A.
129 D3 Norvegia, Cape *c.* Antarctica
203 G4 Norwalk *CT* U.S.A.
202 B4 Norwalk *OH* U.S.A.
159 J3 Norway *country* Europe
203 H2 Norway U.S.A.
191 I3 Norway Bay Canada
187 J4 Norway House Canada
219 I1 Norwegian Basin *sea feature* N. Atlantic Ocean
185 I2 Norwegian Bay Canada
157 D3 Norwegian Sea N. Atlantic Ocean
191 G4 Norwich Canada
161 I5 Norwich U.K.
203 G4 Norwich *CT* U.S.A.
203 F3 Norwich *NY* U.S.A.
203 H3 Norwood *MA* U.S.A.
203 F2 Norwood *NY* U.S.A.
202 A5 Norwood *OH* U.S.A.
187 H1 Nose Lake Canada
150 G2 Noshappu-misaki *hd* Japan
150 G4 Noshiro Japan
173 D5 Nosivka Ukr.
172 H3 Noskovo Rus. Fed.
180 D2 Nosop *watercourse* Africa *alt.* Nossob
132 G3 Nosovaya Rus. Fed.
141 E4 Noşratābād Iran
162 □ Noss, Isle of *i.* U.K.
214 A1 Nossa Senhora do Livramento Brazil
159 K4 Nossebro Sweden
180 C2 Nossob *watercourse* Africa *alt.* Nosop
179 E6 Nosy Varika Madag.
197 F2 Notch Peak U.S.A.
168 H4 Noteć *r.* Poland
170 F6 Noto, Golfo di *g. Sicily* Italy
159 J4 Notodden Norway
151 E6 Noto-hantō *pen.* Japan
189 G4 Notre-Dame, Monts *mts* Canada
189 J4 Notre Dame Bay Canada
191 J3 Notre-Dame-de-la-Salette Canada
203 H2 Notre-Dame-des-Bois Canada
191 J2 Notre-Dame-du-Laus Canada
191 H2 Notre-Dame-du-Nord Canada
191 G3 Nottawasaga Bay Canada
188 E3 Nottaway *r.* Canada
161 F5 Nottingham U.K.
202 E6 Nottoway *r.* U.S.A.
164 F3 Nottuln Germany
187 H5 Notukeu Creek *r.* Canada
178 B3 Nouabalé-Ndoki, Parc National de *nat. park* Congo
176 A2 Nouâdhibou Mauritania
176 A3 Nouakchott Mauritania
176 A3 Nouâmghâr Mauritania
154 C2 Nouei Vietnam
125 G4 Nouméa New Caledonia
176 B3 Nouna Burkina Faso
180 F5 Noupoort S. Africa
158 O2 Nousu Fin.
139 G4 Nov Tajik.
214 C1 Nova América Brazil
214 B3 Nova Esperança Brazil
214 D3 Nova Friburgo Brazil
170 G2 Nova Gradiška Croatia
214 C3 Nova Granada Brazil
214 D3 Nova Iguaçu Brazil
173 E6 Nova Kakhovka Ukr.
214 D2 Nova Lima Brazil
172 D4 Novalukoml' Belarus
173 D6 Nova Odesa Ukr.
214 C2 Nova Ponte Brazil
214 C2 Nova Ponte, Represa *resr* Brazil
170 C2 Novara Italy
214 C1 Nova Roma Brazil
189 H5 Nova Scotia *prov.* Canada
196 A2 Novato U.S.A.
214 E2 Nova Venécia Brazil
214 B1 Nova Xavantino Brazil
133 Q2 Novaya Sibir', Ostrov *i.* Rus. Fed.
132 G2 Novaya Zemlya *is* Rus. Fed.
171 L3 Nova Zagora Bulg.
167 F3 Novelda Spain
168 I7 Nové Zámky Slovakia
172 E3 Novgorodskaya Oblast' *admin. div.* Rus. Fed.
173 E5 Novhorod-Sivers'kyy Ukr.
139 J1 Novichikha Rus. Fed.
171 J3 Novi Iskŭr Bulg.
150 H1 Novikovo Rus. Fed.
170 C2 Novi Ligure Italy
171 L3 Novi Pazar Bulg.
171 I3 Novi Pazar Serbia
171 H2 Novi Sad Serbia
173 G6 Novoaleksandrovsk Rus. Fed.
173 G5 Novoanninskiy Rus. Fed.
210 F5 Novo Aripuanã Brazil
173 F6 Novoazovs'k Ukr.
139 G5 Novobod Tajik.
172 H3 Novocheboksarsk Rus. Fed.
173 G6 Novocherkassk Rus. Fed.
139 H2 Novodolinka Kazakh.
172 G1 Novodvinsk Rus. Fed.
212 F3 Novo Hamburgo Brazil
214 C3 Novo Horizonte Brazil
168 G6 Novohradské hory *mts* Czech Rep.
173 C5 Novohrad-Volyns'kyy Ukr.
138 F1 Novoishimskiy Kazakh.
138 D1 Novokaolinovyy Rus. Fed.
173 G6 Novokubansk Rus. Fed.
138 B1 Novokuybyshevsk Rus. Fed.
146 A1 Novokuznetsk Rus. Fed.
129 D3 Novolazarevskaya *research stn* Antarctica
139 H2 Novomarkovka Kazakh.
170 F2 Novo mesto Slovenia
172 F4 Novomichurinsk Rus. Fed.
173 F6 Novomikhaylovskiy Rus. Fed.
172 F4 Novomoskovsk Rus. Fed.
173 E5 Novomoskovs'k Ukr.
173 D5 Novomyrhorod Ukr.
173 G5 Novonikolayevskiy Rus. Fed.
139 G1 Novonikolskoye Kazakh.
173 E6 Novooleksiyivka Ukr.
138 D2 Novoorsk Rus. Fed.
138 F1 Novopokrovka *Kustanayskaya Oblast'* Kazakh.
139 F1 Novopokrovka *Severnyy Kazakhstan* Kazakh.
139 J2 Novopokrovka *Vostochnyy Kazakhstan* Kazakh.
150 D2 Novopokrovka Rus. Fed.
173 G6 Novopokrovskaya Rus. Fed.
173 I5 Novorepnoye Rus. Fed.
173 F6 Novorossiysk Rus. Fed.
133 L2 Novorybnaya Rus. Fed.
169 N2 Novorzhev Rus. Fed.
173 E6 Novoselivs'ke Ukr.
169 N1 Novosel'ye Rus. Fed.
138 C1 Novosergiyevka Rus. Fed.
173 F6 Novoshakhtinsk Rus. Fed.
150 C2 Novoshakhtinskiy Rus. Fed.
132 J4 Novosibirsk Rus. Fed.
Novosibirskiye Ostrova *is* Rus. Fed. *see* New Siberia Islands
172 D3 Novosokol'niki Rus. Fed.
172 H4 Novospasskoye Rus. Fed.
138 D2 Novotroitsk Rus. Fed.
173 E6 Novotroyits'ke Ukr.
173 D5 Novoukrayinka Ukr.
138 D2 Novoural'sk Rus. Fed.
173 I5 Novouzensk Rus. Fed.
139 H1 Novovarshavka Rus. Fed.
173 C5 Novovolyns'k Ukr.
173 F5 Novovoronezh Rus. Fed.
139 J2 Novoyegor'yevskoye Rus. Fed.
173 D4 Novozybkov Rus. Fed.
168 H6 Nový Jičín Czech Rep.
173 F5 Novyy Oskol Rus. Fed.
132 I3 Novyy Port Rus. Fed.
172 I3 Novyy Tor"yal Rus. Fed.
132 I3 Novyy Urengoy Rus. Fed.
146 F1 Novyy Urgal Rus. Fed.
140 D4 Now Iran
199 E4 Nowata U.S.A.
140 C3 Nowbarān Iran
141 E3 Now Deh Iran
137 L3 Nowdī Iran
144 D4 Nowgong India
187 I2 Nowleye Lake Canada
168 G4 Nowogard Poland
127 I5 Nowra Australia
140 C2 Nowshahr Iran
140 C2 Nowshahr Iran
144 C2 Nowshera Pak.
169 J6 Nowy Sącz Poland
169 J6 Nowy Targ Poland
141 G3 Now Zād Afgh.
203 E4 Noxen U.S.A.
154 C1 Noy, Xé *r.* Laos
154 C1 Noy, Xé *r.* Laos

132 I3 Noyabr'sk Rus. Fed.
186 C3 Noyes Island U.S.A.
166 F2 Noyon France
146 C2 Noyon Mongolia
181 F5 Nozizwe S. Africa
181 I4 Nqutu S. Africa
179 D5 Nsanje Malawi
181 H5 Ntabankulu S. Africa
178 B4 Ntandembele Dem. Rep. Congo
181 G3 Ntha S. Africa
171 K5 Ntoro, Kavo pt Greece
178 D4 Ntungamo Uganda
177 F3 Nuba Mountains Sudan
137 J1 Nubarashen Armenia
177 F2 Nubian Desert Sudan
215 B3 Ñuble r. Chile
Nüden Mongolia see Ulaanbadrah
199 D6 Nueces r. U.S.A.
187 J2 Nueltin Lake Canada
206 G5 Nueva Arcadia Hond.
206 H5 Nueva Armenia Hond.
213 C2 Nueva Florida Venez.
205 H4 Nueva Gerona Cuba
215 F2 Nueva Helvecia Uruguay
215 B3 Nueva Imperial Chile
213 A4 Nueva Loja Ecuador
212 B6 Nueva Lubecka Arg.
207 G5 Nueva Ocotepeque Hond.
206 D2 Nueva Rosita Mex.
Nueva San Salvador El Salvador see Santa Tecla
205 I4 Nuevitas Cuba
215 D4 Nuevo, Golfo g. Arg.
204 C2 Nuevo Casas Grandes Mex.
206 C2 Nuevo Ideal Mex.
207 E2 Nuevo Laredo Mex.
207 E2 Nuevo León state Mex.
178 E3 Nugaal watercourse Somalia
178 E3 Nugaaleed, Dooxo val. Somalia
128 B7 Nugget Point N.Z.
125 F2 Nuguria Islands P.N.G.
128 F3 Nuhaka N.Z.
125 H2 Nui atoll Tuvalu
146 B4 Nu Jiang r. China/Myanmar
126 A4 Nukey Bluff h. Australia
140 D3 Nūklok, Chāh-e well Iran
Nuku'alofa Tonga see Nuku'alofa
125 I4 Nuku'alofa Tonga
125 H2 Nukufetau atoll Tuvalu
123 J5 Nuku Hiva i. Fr. Polynesia
125 H2 Nukulaelae atoll Tuvalu
125 F2 Nukumanu Islands P.N.G.
Nukunono i. Pacific Ocean see Nukunonu
125 I2 Nukunonu atoll Pacific Ocean
138 D4 Nukus Uzbek.
124 C4 Nullagine Australia
124 C5 Nullarbor Plain Australia
148 F1 Nulu'erhu Shan mts China
126 F2 Numalla, Lake salt flat Australia
176 D4 Numan Nigeria
151 F6 Numata Japan
151 F7 Numazu Japan
159 J3 Numedal val. Norway
147 F7 Numfoor i. Indon.
127 F6 Numurkah Australia
189 H2 Nunaksaluk Island Canada
185 N3 Nunakuluut i. Greenland
Nunap Isua c. Greenland see Farewell, Cape
188 E2 Nunavik reg. U.S.A.
185 H3 Nunavut admin. div. Canada
202 E3 Nunda U.S.A.
127 I3 Nundle Australia
161 F5 Nuneaton U.K.
188 B3 Nungesser Lake Canada
186 B3 Nunivak Island U.S.A.
144 D2 Nunkun mt. India
133 T3 Nunligran Rus. Fed.
167 C2 Nuñomoral Spain
164 D2 Nunspeet Neth.
170 C4 Nuoro Sardinia Italy
125 G3 Nupani i. Solomon Is
142 B4 Nuqrah Saudi Arabia
213 A3 Nuquí Col.
144 E1 Nur China
139 H2 Nura Kazakh.
139 G2 Nura r. Kazakh.
140 C4 Nūrābād Iran
Nurata Uzbek. see Nurota
Nuratau, Khrebet mts Uzbek. see Nurota tizmasi
165 J5 Nuremberg Germany
141 H3 Nūrestān reg. Afgh.
137 I2 Nurettin Turkey
206 B1 Nuri Mex.
126 C5 Nuriootpa Australia
172 I4 Nurlaty Rus. Fed.
158 O3 Nurmes Fin.
158 M3 Nurmo Fin.
Nürnberg Germany see Nuremberg
138 F4 Nurota Uzbek.
139 F4 Nurota tizmasi mts Uzbek.
127 G3 Nurri, Mount h. Australia
140 D2 Nūr Rūd r. Iran
145 H1 Nur Turu China
137 H3 Nusaybin Turkey
136 F4 Nuşayrīyah, Jabal an mts Syria
140 C3 Nūshābād Iran
141 G4 Nushki Pak.
189 H2 Nutak Canada
197 H5 Nutrioso U.S.A.
144 B3 Nuttal Pak.
220 U2 Nuuk Greenland
158 N2 Nuupas Fin.
185 M2 Nuussuaq Greenland
185 M2 Nuussuaq pen. Greenland
143 C5 Nuwara Eliya Sri Lanka
180 C5 Nuwerus S. Africa
180 D6 Nuweveldberge mts S. Africa
137 J4 Nuzi tourist site Iraq
181 I1 Nwanedi Nature Reserve S. Africa
132 H3 Nyagan' Rus. Fed.
126 E5 Nyah West Australia
145 G3 Nyainqêntanglha Feng mt. China
145 G3 Nyainqêntanglha Shan mts China
145 H2 Nyainrong China
158 L3 Nyåker Sweden
177 E3 Nyala Sudan
Nyalam China see Congdü
179 C5 Nyamandhlovu Zimbabwe
172 G2 Nyandoma Rus. Fed.
172 F2 Nyandomskaya Vozvyshennost' hills Rus. Fed.
178 B4 Nyanga r. Gabon
179 D5 Nyanga Zimbabwe
145 G3 Nyang Qu r. Xizang China
145 H3 Nyang Qu r. Xizang China
144 D3 Nyar r. India
179 D5 Nyasa, Lake Africa
172 C4 Nyasvizh Belarus
159 J5 Nyborg Denmark
158 O1 Nyborg Norway
159 K4 Nybro Sweden
185 M1 Nyeboe Land reg. Greenland
145 G3 Nyêmo China
178 D4 Nyeri Kenya
146 B4 Nyingchi China
169 J7 Nyíregyháza Hungary
158 M3 Nykarleby Fin.
159 J5 Nykøbing Denmark
159 J5 Nykøbing Sjælland Denmark
159 L4 Nyköping Sweden
158 L3 Nyland Sweden
Nylstroom S. Africa see Modimolle
127 G4 Nymagee Australia
127 J2 Nymboida Australia
127 J2 Nymboida r. Australia
159 L4 Nynäshamn Sweden
127 G3 Nyngan Australia
169 K4 Nyoman r. Belarus/Lith.
168 C7 Nyon Switz.
145 F3 Nyonni Ri mt. China
166 G4 Nyons France
132 G3 Nyrob Rus. Fed.
168 H5 Nysa Poland
172 I2 Nyuchpas Rus. Fed.
150 F5 Nyūdō-zaki pt Japan
178 C4 Nyunzu Dem. Rep. Congo
133 M3 Nyurba Rus. Fed.
172 I2 Nyuvchim Rus. Fed.
173 E6 Nyzhn'ohirs'kyy Ukr.
178 D4 Nzega Tanz.
176 B4 Nzérékoré Guinea
178 B4 N'zeto Angola
181 I1 Nzhelele Dam S. Africa


# O


198 C2 Oahe, Lake U.S.A.
Oahu i. U.S.A. see O'ahu
196 □1 O'ahu i. U.S.A.
126 D4 Oakbank Australia
197 F2 Oak City U.S.A.
196 A2 Oakdale U.S.A.
198 D2 Oakes U.S.A.
127 I1 Oakey Australia
161 G5 Oakham U.K.
194 B1 Oak Harbor U.S.A.
202 C6 Oak Hill U.S.A.
196 C3 Oakhurst U.S.A.
190 B2 Oak Island U.S.A.
196 A3 Oakland CA U.S.A.
202 D5 Oakland MD U.S.A.
198 D3 Oakland NE U.S.A.
194 B3 Oakland OR U.S.A.
127 G5 Oaklands Australia
190 D5 Oak Lawn U.S.A.
199 E6 Oakley U.S.A.
124 C4 Oakover r. Australia
194 B3 Oakridge U.S.A.
201 C4 Oak Ridge U.S.A.
126 D4 Oakvale Australia
191 H4 Oakville Canada
128 C6 Oamaru N.Z.
128 D5 Oaro N.Z.
153 B3 Oas Phil.
194 D3 Oasis U.S.A.
129 B6 Oates Land reg. Antarctica
127 G9 Oatlands Australia
197 E4 Oatman U.S.A.
207 E4 Oaxaca Mex.
207 E4 Oaxaca state Mex.
132 H3 Ob' r. Rus. Fed.
139 J2 Oba r. Kazakh.
176 D4 Obala Cameroon
151 D7 Obama Japan
162 C4 Oban U.K.
150 G5 Obanazawa Japan
167 C1 O Barco Spain
188 F4 Obatogamau, Lac Canada
186 F4 Obed Canada
128 B6 Obelisk mt. N.Z.
165 H4 Oberaula Germany
165 I3 Oberdorla Germany
164 E3 Oberhausen Germany
198 C4 Oberlin KS U.S.A.
202 B4 Oberlin OH U.S.A.
165 F5 Obermoschel Germany
127 H4 Oberon Australia
165 K5 Oberpfälzer Wald mts Germany
165 H4 Obersinn Germany
165 H4 Oberthulba Germany
165 G4 Obertshausen Germany
165 H3 Oberwälder Land reg. Germany
147 E7 Obi i. Indon.
211 G4 Óbidos Brazil
139 G5 Obigarm Tajik.
150 H3 Obihiro Japan
173 H6 Obil'noye Rus. Fed.
213 C2 Obispos Venez.
146 F2 Obluch'ye Rus. Fed.
172 F4 Obninsk Rus. Fed.
178 C3 Obo Cent. Afr. Rep.
148 A2 Obo China
178 E2 Obock Djibouti
152 E3 Ŏbŏk N. Korea
178 C4 Obokote Dem. Rep. Congo
178 B4 Obouya Congo
173 F5 Oboyan' Rus. Fed.
172 G2 Obozerskiy Rus. Fed.
145 E4 Obra India
145 E4 Obra Dam India
206 B1 Obregón, Presa resr Mex.
171 I2 Obrenovac Serbia
136 D2 Obruk Turkey
138 B2 Obshchiy Syrt hills Rus. Fed.
132 I2 Obskaya Guba sea chan. Rus. Fed.
176 B4 Obuasi Ghana
173 D5 Obukhiv Ukr.
172 I2 Ob"yachevo Rus. Fed.
201 D6 Ocala U.S.A.
213 D4 Ocamo r. Venez.
206 D2 Ocampo Mex.
213 B2 Ocaña Col.
167 E3 Ocaña Spain
210 E7 Occidental, Cordillera mts Chile
213 A4 Occidental, Cordillera mts Col.
210 C6 Occidental, Cordillera mts Peru
186 B3 Ocean Cape U.S.A.
203 F5 Ocean City MD U.S.A.
203 F5 Ocean City NJ U.S.A.
186 D4 Ocean Falls Canada
196 D5 Oceanside U.S.A.
199 F6 Ocean Springs U.S.A.
173 D6 Ochakiv Ukr.
173 G7 Och'amchire Georgia
162 E4 Ochil Hills U.K.
144 C1 Ochili Pass Afgh.
165 I5 Ochsenfurt Germany
164 F2 Ochtrup Germany
159 L3 Ockelbo Sweden
169 L7 Ocolașul Mare, Vârful mt. Romania
193 J5 Oconee r. U.S.A.
190 C4 Oconomowoc U.S.A.
190 D3 Oconto U.S.A.
207 F4 Ocosingo Mex.
206 H5 Ocotal Nicaragua
196 D5 Ocotillo Wells U.S.A.
206 D3 Ocotlán Mex.
176 B4 Oda Ghana
151 C7 Ōda Japan
158 C2 Ódáðahraun lava field Iceland
152 E3 Ŏdaejin N. Korea
150 G4 Ōdate Japan
151 F7 Odawara Japan
159 I3 Odda Norway
187 J3 Odei r. Canada
190 C5 Odell U.S.A.
167 B4 Odemira Port.
136 A2 Ödemiş Turkey
181 G3 Odendaalsrus S. Africa
159 J5 Odense Denmark
165 G5 Odenwald reg. Germany
165 I3 Oder r. Germany
alt. Odra (Poland)
168 G3 Oderbucht b. Germany
Odesa Ukr. see Odessa
159 K4 Ödeshog Sweden
173 D6 Odessa Ukr.
199 C6 Odessa U.S.A.
139 H1 Odesskoye Rus. Fed.
167 C4 Odiel r. Spain
176 B4 Odienné Côte d'Ivoire
172 F4 Odintsovo Rus. Fed.
143 D1 Odisha state India
154 C3 Ŏdŏngk Cambodia
168 G4 Odra r. Poland
alt. Oder (Germany)
211 J5 Oeiras Brazil
198 C3 Oelrichs U.S.A.
190 B4 Oelwein U.S.A.
165 K4 Oenkerk Neth.
164 D1 Oenkerk Neth.
137 H1 Of Turkey
170 G4 Ofanto r. Italy
165 G4 Offenbach am Main Germany
164 F6 Offenburg Germany
171 L6 Ofidoussa i. Greece
150 G5 Ōfunato Japan
150 F5 Oga Japan
178 E3 Ogadēn reg. Eth.
150 F5 Oga-hantō pen. Japan
151 E7 Ōgaki Japan
198 C3 Ogallala U.S.A.
Ogasawara-shotō is Japan see Bonin Islands
191 H2 Ogascanane, Lac l. Canada
176 C4 Ogbomosho Nigeria
Ogbomoso Nigeria see Ogbomosho
198 E3 Ogden IA U.S.A.
194 E3 Ogden UT U.S.A.
186 C3 Ogden, Mount Canada
203 F2 Ogdensburg U.S.A.
184 E3 Ogilvie r. Canada
184 E3 Ogilvie Mountains Canada
138 C5 Oglanly Turkm.
201 C5 Oglethorpe, Mount U.S.A.
170 D1 Oglio r. Italy
176 C4 Ogoja Nigeria
188 C3 Ogoki r. Canada
188 C3 Ogoki Reservoir Canada
171 J3 Ogosta r. Bulg.
159 N4 Ogre Latvia
170 F2 Ogulin Croatia
Ogurchinskiy, Ostrov i. Turkm. see Ogurjaly Adasy
138 C5 Ogurjaly Adasy i. Turkm.
137 K1 Oğuz Azer.
128 A6 Ohai N.Z.
128 E3 Ohakune N.Z.
150 G4 Ōhata Japan
128 B6 Ohau, Lake N.Z.
215 B2 O'Higgins admin. reg. Chile
212 B7 O'Higgins, Lago l. Chile
129 E2 O'Higgins (Chile) research stn Antarctica
200 C4 Ohio r. U.S.A.
202 B4 Ohio state U.S.A.
165 G4 Ohm r. Germany
165 I4 Ohrdruf Germany
165 K4 Ohře r. Czech Rep.
165 J2 Ohre r. Germany
171 I4 Ohrid Macedonia
171 I4 Ohrid, Lake Albania/Macedonia
181 I2 Ohrigstad S. Africa
165 H5 Öhringen Germany
128 E3 Ohura N.Z.
211 H3 Oiapoque Brazil
162 D3 Oich, Loch l. U.K.
145 H3 Oiga China
164 A4 Oignies France
202 D4 Oil City U.S.A.
196 C4 Oildale U.S.A.
166 F2 Oise r. France
164 B5 Oise à l'Aisne, Canal de l' France
151 B8 Ōita Japan
171 J5 Oiti mt. Greece
196 C4 Ojai U.S.A.
215 D2 Ojeda Arg.
190 B3 Ojibwa U.S.A.
204 D3 Ojinaga Mex.
207 E4 Ojitlán Mex.
151 F6 Ojiya Japan
206 A2 Ojo de Liebre, Lago b. Mex.
212 C3 Ojos del Salado, Nevado mt. Arg.
172 G4 Oka r. Rus. Fed.
179 B6 Okahandja Namibia
128 E3 Okahukura N.Z.
179 B6 Okakarara Namibia
189 H2 Okak Islands Canada
186 F5 Okanagan Falls Canada
186 F4 Okanagan Lake Canada
194 C1 Okanogan r. Canada/U.S.A.
186 F5 Okanogan U.S.A.
194 B1 Okanogan Range mts U.S.A.
178 C3 Okapi, Parc National de la nat. park Dem. Rep. Congo
144 C3 Okara Pak.
Okarem Turkm. see Ekerem
179 B5 Okaukuejo Namibia
179 C5 Okavango r. Botswana/Namibia
179 C5 Okavango Delta swamp Botswana
151 F6 Okaya Japan
151 C7 Okayama Japan
151 E7 Okazaki Japan
201 D7 Okeechobee U.S.A.
201 D7 Okeechobee, Lake U.S.A.
201 D6 Okefenokee Swamp U.S.A.
161 C7 Okehampton U.K.
176 C4 Okene Nigeria
165 I2 Oker r. Germany
144 B5 Okha India
146 G1 Okha Rus. Fed.
145 F4 Okhaldhunga Nepal
144 B5 Okha Rann marsh India
133 P3 Okhota r. Rus. Fed.
133 P4 Okhotsk Rus. Fed.
133 P4 Okhotsk, Sea of Rus. Fed.
Okhotskoye More sea Rus. Fed. see Okhotsk, Sea of
173 E5 Okhtyrka Ukr.
146 E4 Okinawa i. Japan
Okinawa-guntō is Japan see Okinawa-shotō
146 E4 Okinawa-shotō is Japan
151 C6 Okinoshima Japan
151 B7 Okino-shima i. Japan
151 D6 Oki-shotō is Japan
199 D5 Oklahoma state U.S.A.
199 D5 Oklahoma City U.S.A.
199 D5 Okmulgee U.S.A.
178 B4 Okondja Gabon
186 G4 Okotoks Canada
172 E4 Okovskiy Les for. Rus. Fed.
178 B4 Okoyo Congo
138 B3 Okpan, Gora h. Kazakh.
139 J3 Okpety, Gora mt. Kazakh.
158 M1 Øksfjord Norway
172 F2 Oksovskiy Rus. Fed.
139 G5 Oktyabr Tajik.
172 I4 Oktyabr'sk Rus. Fed.
150 D2 Oktyabr'skiy Rus. Fed.
173 G6 Oktyabr'skiy Rus. Fed.
132 G4 Oktyabr'skiy Rus. Fed.
146 H1 Oktyabr'skiy Rus. Fed.
139 F5 Oktyabr'skiy Uzbek.
138 F1 Oktyabr'skoye Kazakh.
138 E1 Oktyabr'skoye Rus. Fed.
138 E1 Oktyabr'skoye Rus. Fed.
132 H3 Oktyabr'skoye Rus. Fed.
133 K2 Oktyabr'skoy Revolyutsii, Ostrov i. Rus. Fed.
Oktyah'sk Turkm. see Saparmyrat Türkmenbaşy
172 E3 Okulovka Rus. Fed.
150 G3 Okushiri-tō i. Japan
180 E1 Okwa watercourse Botswana
158 B2 Ólafsvík Iceland
196 C3 Olancha U.S.A.
196 C3 Olancha Peak U.S.A.
206 H5 Olanchito Hond.
159 L4 Öland i. Sweden
158 O2 Olanga Rus. Fed.
126 D4 Olary Australia
126 D4 Olary watercourse Australia
198 E4 Olathe U.S.A.
215 E3 Olavarría Arg.
168 H5 Oława Poland
197 G5 Olberg U.S.A.
170 C4 Olbia Sardinia Italy
202 D3 Olcott U.S.A.
127 H6 Old Adaminaby Australia
127 J3 Old Bar Australia
143 C2 Old Bastar India
163 D4 Oldcastle Ireland
184 E3 Old Crow Canada
Oldeboorn Neth. see Aldeboarn
165 G1 Oldenburg Germany
168 E3 Oldenburg in Holstein Germany
164 E2 Oldenzaal Neth.
158 M1 Olderdalen Norway
203 F3 Old Forge NY U.S.A.
203 F4 Old Forge PA U.S.A.
160 E4 Oldham U.K.
163 C6 Old Head of Kinsale Ireland
186 G4 Oldman r. Canada
162 F3 Oldmeldrum U.K.
203 H3 Old Orchard Beach U.S.A.
189 J4 Old Perlican Canada
186 G4 Olds Canada
203 I2 Old Town U.S.A.
171 I6 Olduvai Gorge tourist site Tanz.
187 H4 Old Wives Lake Canada
197 E4 Old Woman Mountains U.S.A.
202 D3 Olean U.S.A.
169 K3 Olecko Poland
133 N3 Olekma r. Rus. Fed.
133 N3 Olekminsk Rus. Fed.
173 E5 Oleksandriya Ukr.
172 H1 Olema Rus. Fed.
159 I4 Ølen Norway
158 P1 Olenegorsk Rus. Fed.
133 M3 Olenek Rus. Fed.
133 N2 Olenek r. Rus. Fed.
133 N2 Olenekskiy Zaliv b. Rus. Fed.
172 E3 Olenino Rus. Fed.
138 C2 Olenti r. Kazakh.
139 H1 Olenty r. Kazakh.
173 C5 Olevs'k Ukr.
150 D3 Ol'ga Rus. Fed.
167 C4 Olhão Port.
180 C4 Olifants watercourse Namibia
181 I1 Olifants S. Africa
180 C5 Olifants r. W. Cape S. Africa
180 D6 Olifants r. W. Cape S. Africa
180 E3 Olifantshoek S. Africa
180 C6 Olifantsrivierberge mts S. Africa
215 F2 Olimar Grande r. Uruguay
214 C3 Olímpia Brazil
207 E4 Olinalá Mex.
211 L5 Olinda Brazil
179 D5 Olinga Moz.
181 G2 Oliphants Drift Botswana
215 D2 Oliva Arg.
167 F3 Oliva Spain
212 C3 Oliva, Cordillera de mts Arg./Chile
212 C3 Olivares, Cerro de mt. Chile
202 B5 Olive Hill U.S.A.
214 D3 Oliveira Brazil
167 C3 Olivenza Spain
198 E2 Olivia U.S.A.
148 B1 Olji China
148 C1 Olji China
137 G2 Ol'keyek r. Kazakh.
172 G4 Ol'khi Rus. Fed.
212 C2 Ollagüe Chile
215 B1 Ollita, Cordillera de mts Arg./Chile
215 B1 Ollitas mt. Arg.
139 G4 Olmaliq Uzbek.
210 C5 Olmos Peru
203 G3 Olmstedville U.S.A.
161 G5 Olney U.K.
200 C4 Olney U.S.A.
159 K4 Olofström Sweden
168 H6 Olomouc Czech Rep.
172 E2 Olonets Rus. Fed.
153 B3 Olongapo Phil.
166 D5 Oloron-Ste-Marie France
167 H1 Olot Spain
138 E5 Olot Uzbek.
146 D1 Olovyannaya Rus. Fed.
133 R3 Oloy r. Rus. Fed.
144 C5 Olpad India
165 F3 Olpe Germany
169 J4 Olsztyn Poland
197 G5 Olten Switz.
171 K2 Oltenița Romania
137 H1 Oltu Turkey
153 B5 Olutanga i. Phil.
171 I6 Olympia tourist site Greece
194 B2 Olympia U.S.A.
194 A2 Olympic National Park U.S.A.
136 C4 Olympos tourist site Turkey
136 D4 Olympus, Mount Cyprus
171 J4 Olympus, Mount Greece
194 B2 Olympus, Mount U.S.A.
133 S4 Olyutorskiy, Mys c. Rus. Fed.
133 R4 Olyutorskiy Zaliv b. Rus. Fed.
145 G2 Oma China
150 G4 Ōma Japan
151 E6 Ōmachi Japan
151 F7 Omae-zaki pt Japan
163 D3 Omagh U.K.
198 E3 Omaha U.S.A.
180 C1 Omaheke admin. reg. Namibia
139 C1 Omak U.S.A.
142 E6 Oman country Asia
141 E5 Oman, Gulf of Asia
128 B6 Omarama N.Z.
179 B6 Omaruru Namibia
179 B5 Omatako watercourse Namibia
210 D7 Omate Peru
180 E2 Omaweneno Botswana
150 G4 Ōma-zaki c. Japan
178 A4 Omboué Gabon
170 D3 Ombrone r. Italy
170 D3 Ombu China
181 H5 Omdraaisvlei S. Africa
177 F3 Omdurman Sudan
170 C2 Omegna Italy
127 G6 Omeo Australia
206 H6 Ometepe, Isla de i. Nicaragua
178 D2 Om Hajër Eritrea
140 C4 Omīdīyeh Iran
186 D3 Omineca Mountains Canada
180 C1 Omitara Namibia
186 C3 Ommaney, Cape U.S.A.
164 E2 Ommen Neth.
148 B1 Ömnögovĭ prov. Mongolia
133 R3 Omolon Rus. Fed.
133 O3 Omoloy r. Rus. Fed.
178 D3 Omo National Park Eth.
148 A1 Omon Gol watercourse China
150 G5 Omono-gawa r. Japan
141 E3 'Omrānī Iran
132 I4 Omsk Rus. Fed.
133 Q3 Omsukchan Rus. Fed.
150 H2 Ōmu Japan
171 K2 Omu, Vârful mt. Romania
151 A8 Ōmura Japan
190 B4 Onalaska U.S.A.
203 F6 Onancock U.S.A.
188 D4 Onaping Lake Canada
206 B1 Onavas Mex.
191 E3 Onaway U.S.A.
141 F3 Onay, Kōtal-e Afgh.
154 A2 Onbingwin Myanmar
215 D1 Oncativo Arg.
160 C3 Onchan U.K.
179 B5 Oncócua Angola
179 B5 Ondangwa Namibia
180 B1 Ondekaremba Namibia
180 D5 Onderstedorings S. Africa
179 B5 Ondjiva Angola
176 C4 Ondo Nigeria
146 D2 Öndörhaan Mongolia
152 A1 Ondor Had China
148 B1 Ondor Mod China
148 D1 Ondor Sum China
172 G2 Ondozero Rus. Fed.
180 D1 One Botswana
172 F2 Onega Rus. Fed.
172 F2 Onega r. Rus. Fed.
172 E2 Onega, Lake Rus. Fed.
203 F3 Oneida U.S.A.
203 F3 Oneida Lake U.S.A.
198 D3 O'Neill U.S.A.
146 H2 Onekotan, Ostrov i. Rus. Fed.
203 F3 Oneonta U.S.A.
128 E2 Oneroa N.Z.
169 M7 Onești Romania
172 E1 Onezhskaya Guba g. Rus. Fed.
132 E3 Onezhskoye Ozero Rus. Fed.
Onezhskoye Ozero l. Rus. Fed. see Onega, Lake
143 C1 Ong r. India
178 B4 Onga Gabon
128 F3 Ongaonga N.Z.
180 E4 Ongers watercourse S. Africa
152 C5 Ongjin N. Korea
143 C3 Ongole India
148 B1 Ongt Gol China
139 K2 Onguday Rus. Fed.
173 G7 Oni Georgia
179 E6 Onilahy r. Madag.
176 C4 Onitsha Nigeria
180 B1 Onjati Mountain Namibia
151 E7 Ōno Japan
125 I4 Ono-i-Lau i. Fiji
151 C7 Onomichi Japan
125 H2 Onotoa atoll Kiribati
186 G4 Onoway Canada
180 C4 Onseepkans S. Africa
124 B4 Onslow Australia
201 E5 Onslow Bay U.S.A.
152 F2 Onsŏng N. Korea
164 F1 Onstwedde Neth.
151 E7 Ontake-san vol. Japan
188 B3 Ontario prov. Canada
194 C2 Ontario U.S.A.
191 H4 Ontario, Lake Canada/U.S.A.
190 C2 Ontonagon U.S.A.
125 F2 Ontong Java Atoll Solomon Is
124 D4 Oodnadatta Australia
124 D5 Ooldea Australia
124 D5 Oolambeyan National Park Australia
199 E4 Oologah Lake resr U.S.A.
164 B3 Oostburg Neth.
Oostende Belgium see Ostend
164 D2 Oostendorp Neth.
164 C3 Oosterhout Neth.
164 B3 Oosterschelde est. Neth.
164 E2 Oosterwolde Neth.
164 A4 Oostvleteren Belgium
164 D1 Oost-Vlieland Neth.
186 D4 Ootsa Lake Canada
186 D4 Ootsa Lake l. Canada
202 E5 Opal U.S.A.
178 C4 Opala Dem. Rep. Congo
172 I3 Oparino Rus. Fed.
188 B3 Opasquia Canada
188 B3 Opasquia Provincial Park Canada
188 F3 Opataca, Lac l. Canada
168 H6 Opava Czech Rep.
201 C5 Opelika U.S.A.
199 E6 Opelousas U.S.A.
194 F1 Opheim U.S.A.
191 F2 Ophir Canada
155 B2 Ophir, Gunung vol. Indon.
128 C6 Opihi r. N.Z.
188 E3 Opinaca r. Canada
188 E3 Opinaca, Réservoir resr Canada
188 D3 Opinnagau r. Canada
137 J5 Opis tourist site Iraq
189 G3 Opiscotéo, Lac l. Canada
164 C2 Opmeer Neth.
172 D3 Opochka Rus. Fed.
168 H5 Opole Poland
167 B2 Oporto Port.
128 F3 Opotiki N.Z.
201 C6 Opp U.S.A.
158 J3 Oppdal Norway
128 D3 Opunake N.Z.
179 B5 Opuwo Namibia
138 B3 Opytnoye Kazakh.
138 D4 Oqqal'a Uzbek.
139 H5 Oqsu r. Tajik.
138 F5 Oqtosh Uzbek.
190 B5 Oquawka U.S.A.
203 H2 Oquossoc U.S.A.
138 D2 Or' r. Rus. Fed.
197 G5 Oracle U.S.A.
197 G5 Oracle Junction U.S.A.
169 J7 Oradea Romania
158 C2 Öræfajökull glacier Iceland
144 D4 Orai India
176 B1 Oran Alg.
212 D2 Orán Arg.
154 C2 O Rang Cambodia
152 E3 Ŏrang N. Korea
127 H4 Orange Australia
166 G4 Orange France
180 B4 Orange r. Namibia/S. Africa
203 G3 Orange MA U.S.A.
199 E6 Orange TX U.S.A.
202 D5 Orange VA U.S.A.
211 H3 Orange, Cabo c. Brazil
201 D5 Orangeburg U.S.A.
219 J8 Orange Cone sea feature S. Atlantic Ocean
Orange Free State prov. S. Africa see Free State
191 G3 Orangeville Canada
197 G2 Orangeville U.S.A.
207 G4 Orange Walk Belize
153 B3 Orani Phil.
165 L2 Oranienburg Germany
179 B6 Oranjemund Namibia
213 C1 Oranjestad Aruba
163 C4 Oranmore Ireland
179 C6 Orapa Botswana
153 C3 Oras Phil.
171 J2 Orăștie Romania
158 M3 Oravais Fin.
171 I2 Oravița Romania
144 E1 Orba Co l. China
170 D3 Orbetello Italy
167 D1 Órbigo r. Spain
127 H6 Orbost Australia
129 C2 Orcadas research stn S. Atlantic Ocean
197 H2 Orchard Mesa U.S.A.
213 D2 Orchila, Isla i. Venez.
196 B4 Orcutt U.S.A.
124 C3 Ord r. Australia
124 C3 Ord, Mount h. Australia
195 D4 Orderville U.S.A.
167 B1 Ordes Spain
196 D4 Ord Mountain U.S.A.
Ordos China see Dongsheng
136 F1 Ordu Turkey
137 K2 Ordubad Azer.
195 G4 Ordway U.S.A.
Ordzhonikidze Rus. Fed. see Vladikavkaz
173 E6 Ordzhonikidze Ukr.
196 C1 Oreana U.S.A.
159 K3 Örebro Sweden
190 C4 Oregon IL U.S.A.
202 B4 Oregon OH U.S.A.
190 C4 Oregon WI U.S.A.
194 B3 Oregon state U.S.A.
194 B2 Oregon City U.S.A.
172 F4 Orekhovo-Zuyevo Rus. Fed.
139 K2 Orel' Kazakh.
172 F4 Orel Rus. Fed.
146 F1 Orel', Ozero l. Rus. Fed.
197 G1 Orem U.S.A.
136 A2 Ören Turkey
171 L6 Ören Turkey
138 C2 Orenburg Rus. Fed.
138 C2 Orenburgskaya Oblast' admin. div. Rus. Fed.
215 E3 Orense Arg.
128 A7 Orepuki N.Z.
159 K5 Öresund str. Denmark
128 B7 Oreti r. N.Z.
128 E2 Orewa N.Z.
164 D4 Oreye Belgium
171 J4 Orfanou, Kolpos b. Greece
127 G9 Orford Australia
161 I5 Orford U.K.
161 I5 Orford Ness hd U.K.
197 F5 Organ Pipe Cactus National Monument nat. park U.S.A.
136 B2 Orhaneli Turkey
173 D7 Orhangazi Turkey
169 N7 Orhei Moldova
146 F1 Orichi Rus. Fed.
172 I3 Orichi Rus. Fed.
203 J2 Orient U.S.A.
210 E7 Oriental, Cordillera mts Bol.
213 B3 Oriental, Cordillera mts Col.
210 D6 Oriental, Cordillera mts Peru
215 E3 Oriente Arg.
167 F3 Orihuela Spain
173 E6 Orikhiv Ukr.
191 H3 Orillia Canada
159 N3 Orimattila Fin.
213 E2 Orinoco r. Col./Venez.
213 E2 Orinoco, Delta del Venez.
Orissa state India see Odisha
159 M4 Orissaare Estonia
170 C5 Oristano Sardinia Italy
159 N3 Orivesi Fin.
158 O3 Orivesi l. Fin.
211 G4 Oriximiná Brazil
207 E4 Orizaba Mex.
207 E4 Orizaba, Pico de vol. Mex.
158 J3 Orkanger Norway
159 K4 Örkelljunga Sweden
158 J3 Orkla r. Norway
181 G3 Orkney S. Africa
162 E1 Orkney Islands U.K.
199 C6 Orla U.S.A.
196 A2 Orland U.S.A.
214 C3 Orlândia Brazil
201 D6 Orlando U.S.A.
166 E3 Orléans France
203 I4 Orleans MA U.S.A.
203 G2 Orleans VT U.S.A.
172 I3 Orlov Rus. Fed.
172 F4 Orlovskaya Oblast' admin. div. Rus. Fed.
173 G6 Orlovskiy Rus. Fed.
141 G5 Ormara Pak.
141 G5 Ormara, Ras hd Pak.
153 C4 Ormoc Phil.
201 D6 Ormond Beach U.S.A.
160 E4 Ormskirk U.K.
203 G2 Ormstown Canada
166 D2 Orne r. France
158 K2 Ørnes Norway
158 L3 Örnsköldsvik Sweden
152 D4 Oro N. Korea
213 C3 Orocué Col.
176 B3 Orodara Burkina Faso
194 C2 Orofino U.S.A.
195 F5 Orogrande U.S.A.
189 G4 Oromocto Canada
136 E6 Oron Israel
125 I2 Orona atoll Kiribati
203 I2 Orono U.S.A.
162 B4 Oronsay i. U.K.
153 B4 Oroquieta Phil.
211 K5 Orós, Açude resr Brazil
170 C4 Orosei Sardinia Italy
170 C4 Orosei, Golfo di b. Sardinia Italy
169 J7 Orosháza Hungary
197 G5 Oro Valley U.S.A.
196 B2 Oroville CA U.S.A.
194 C1 Oroville WA U.S.A.
196 B2 Oroville, Lake resr U.S.A.
126 C4 Orroroo Australia
159 K3 Orsa Sweden
172 D4 Orsha Belarus
138 D2 Orsk Rus. Fed.
159 I3 Ørsta Norway
167 C1 Ortegal, Cabo c. Spain
166 D5 Orthez France
167 C1 Ortigueira Spain
206 B1 Ortíz Mex.
213 D2 Ortíz Venez.
170 D1 Ortles mt. Italy
160 E3 Orton U.K.
170 F3 Ortona Italy
198 D2 Ortonville U.S.A.
133 N3 Orulgan, Khrebet mts Rus. Fed.
180 B1 Orumbo Namibia
Orūmīyeh Iran see Urmia
Orūmīyeh, Daryācheh-ye salt l. Iran see Urmia, Lake
210 E7 Oruro Bol.
164 D5 Orval, Abbaye d' tourist site Belgium
170 E3 Orvieto Italy
202 C4 Orwell OH U.S.A.
203 G3 Orwell VT U.S.A.
159 J3 Os Norway
206 I6 Osa, Península de Costa Rica
190 A4 Osage U.S.A.
198 E4 Osage r. U.S.A.
151 D7 Ōsaka Japan
139 H2 Osakarovka Kazakh.
150 G5 Ōsaki Japan
159 K4 Osby Sweden
199 F5 Osceola AR U.S.A.
198 E3 Osceola IA U.S.A.
165 L3 Oschatz Germany
165 J2 Oschersleben (Bode) Germany
170 C4 Oschiri Sardinia Italy
191 F3 Oscoda U.S.A.
172 F4 Osetr r. Rus. Fed.
151 A8 Ōse-zaki pt Japan
191 J3 Osgoode Canada
139 H4 Osh Kyrg.
179 B5 Oshakati Namibia
151 E6 Oshamanbe Japan
191 H4 Oshawa Canada
150 G5 Oshika-hantō pen. Japan
150 F4 Ō-shima i. Japan
151 F7 Ō-shima i. Japan
198 C3 Oshkosh NE U.S.A.
190 C3 Oshkosh WI U.S.A.
140 B2 Oshnovīyeh Iran
176 C4 Oshogbo Nigeria
137 L5 Oshtorān Kūh mt. Iran
137 L5 Oshtorīnān Iran
150 G5 Ōshū Japan
178 B4 Oshwe Dem. Rep. Congo
171 H2 Osijek Croatia
170 E3 Osimo Italy
144 C4 Osiyan India
181 I3 oSizweni S. Africa
170 G2 Osječenica mts Bos.-Herz.
158 K3 Osjön l. Sweden
198 E3 Oskaloosa U.S.A.
159 L4 Oskarshamn Sweden
191 J1 Oskélanéo Canada
173 F5 Oskol r. Rus. Fed.
159 J4 Oslo Norway
153 B4 Oslob Phil.
159 J4 Oslofjorden sea chan. Norway
143 B2 Osmanabad India
136 E1 Osmancık Turkey
136 B1 Osmaneli Turkey
136 F3 Osmaniye Turkey
159 O4 Os'mino Rus. Fed.
165 G2 Osnabrück Germany
171 J3 Osogovska Planina mts Bulg./Macedonia
215 B4 Osorno Chile
167 D1 Osorno Spain
215 B4 Osorno, Volcán vol. Chile
186 F5 Osoyoos Canada
159 I3 Osøyri Norway
124 E3 Osprey Reef Coral Sea Is Terr.
164 D3 Oss Neth.
127 G8 Ossa, Mount Australia
190 B3 Osseo U.S.A.
191 F3 Ossineke U.S.A.
203 H3 Ossipee Lake U.S.A.
165 J3 Oßmannstedt Germany
189 H3 Ossokmanuan Lake Canada
164 D5 Ossuaire, Cimetière d' tourist site France
172 E3 Ostashkov Rus. Fed.
165 F2 Ostbevern Germany
165 H1 Oste r. Germany
164 A3 Ostend Belgium
169 O5 Oster Ukr.
165 J2 Osterburg (Altmark) Germany
159 K4 Österbymo Sweden
159 K3 Österdalälven l. Sweden
159 J3 Østerdalen val. Norway
165 J3 Osterfeld Germany
165 I2 Osterholz-Scharmbeck Germany
165 G1 Osterode am Harz Germany
165 I3 Osterode am Harz Germany
158 K3 Östersund Sweden
165 I3 Osterwieck Germany
164 E1 Ostfriesische Inseln Germany
164 F1 Ostfriesland reg. Germany
159 L3 Östhammar Sweden
168 I6 Ostrava Czech Rep.

169 I4 **Ostróda** Poland
173 F5 **Ostrogozhsk** Rus. Fed.
165 K4 **Ostrov** Czech Rep.
172 D3 **Ostrov** Rus. Fed.
169 J5 **Ostrowiec Świętokrzyski** Poland
169 J4 **Ostrów Mazowiecka** Poland
168 H5 **Ostrów Wielkopolski** Poland
171 K3 **Osŭm** *r.* Bulg.
151 B9 **Ōsumi-kaikyō** *sea chan.* Japan
151 B9 **Ōsumi-shotō** *is* Japan
167 D4 **Osuna** Spain
203 F2 **Oswegatchie** U.S.A.
190 C5 **Oswego** *IL* U.S.A.
202 E3 **Oswego** *NY* U.S.A.
203 E3 **Oswego** *r.* U.S.A.
161 D5 **Oswestry** U.K.
151 F6 **Ōta** Japan
128 C6 **Otago Peninsula** N.Z.
128 E4 **Otaki** N.Z.
158 N2 **Otanmäki** Fin.
139 H4 **Otar** Kazakh.
213 B4 **Otare, Cerro** *h.* Col.
150 G3 **Otaru** Japan
128 B7 **Otatara** N.Z.
210 C3 **Otavalo** Ecuador
179 B5 **Otavi** Namibia
151 G6 **Ōtawara** Japan
139 I4 **Otegen Batyr** Kazakh.
128 C6 **Otematata** N.Z.
159 N4 **Otepää** Estonia
138 C3 **Otes** Kazakh.
194 C2 **Othello** U.S.A.
181 I4 **oThongathi** S. Africa
206 C2 **Otinapa** Mex.
128 C5 **Otira** N.Z.
203 E3 **Otisco Lake** U.S.A.
189 F3 **Otish, Monts** *hills* Canada
179 B6 **Otjiwarongo** Namibia
160 F4 **Otley** U.K.
150 H2 **Otoineppu** Japan
128 E3 **Otorohanga** N.Z.
188 C3 **Otoskwin** *r.* Canada
138 B1 **Otradnyy** Rus. Fed.
171 H4 **Otranto** Italy
171 H4 **Otranto, Strait of** Albania/Italy
190 E4 **Otsego** U.S.A.
190 E3 **Otsego Lake** *MI* U.S.A.
203 F3 **Otsego Lake** *NY* U.S.A.
203 F3 **Otselic** U.S.A.
151 D7 **Ōtsu** Japan
159 J3 **Otta** Norway
191 J3 **Ottawa** Canada
191 H2 **Ottawa** *r.* Canada
190 C5 **Ottawa** *IL* U.S.A.
198 E4 **Ottawa** *KS* U.S.A.
202 A4 **Ottawa** *OH* U.S.A.
188 D2 **Ottawa Islands** Canada
160 E2 **Otterburn** U.K.
197 G2 **Otter Creek Reservoir** U.S.A.
190 D1 **Otter Island** Canada
188 D3 **Otter Rapids** Canada
165 H1 **Ottersberg** Germany
161 C7 **Ottery** *r.* U.K.
164 C4 **Ottignies** Belgium
185 J1 **Otto Fiord** *inlet* Canada
139 H4 **Ottuk** Kyrg.
190 A5 **Ottumwa** U.S.A.
164 F5 **Ottweiler** Germany
176 C4 **Otukpo** Nigeria
212 D3 **Otumpa** Arg.
210 C5 **Otuzco** Peru
126 E7 **Otway, Cape** Australia
149 B6 **Ou, Nâm** *r.* Laos
199 E5 **Ouachita** *r.* U.S.A.
199 E5 **Ouachita, Lake** U.S.A.
199 E5 **Ouachita Mountains** U.S.A.
176 A2 **Ouadâne** Mauritania
178 C3 **Ouadda** Cent. Afr. Rep.
177 E3 **Ouaddaï** *reg.* Chad
176 B3 **Ouagadougou** Burkina Faso
176 B3 **Ouahigouya** Burkina Faso
176 B3 **Oualâta** Mauritania
178 C3 **Ouanda Djallé** Cent. Afr. Rep.
176 B2 **Ouarâne** *reg.* Mauritania
176 C1 **Ouargla** Alg.
176 B1 **Ouarzazate** Morocco
180 F6 **Oubergpas** *pass* S. Africa
164 B4 **Oudenaarde** Belgium
164 F1 **Oude Pekela** Neth.
149 B6 **Oudômxai** Laos
180 E6 **Oudtshoorn** S. Africa
164 C3 **Oud-Turnhout** Belgium
167 F5 **Oued Tlélat** Alg.
176 B1 **Oued Zem** Morocco
170 B6 **Oued Zénati** Alg.
166 B2 **Ouessant, Île d'** *i.* France
178 B3 **Ouesso** Congo
176 C4 **Ouidah** Benin
206 B2 **Ouiriego** Mex.
176 B1 **Oujda** Morocco
158 N2 **Oulainen** Fin.
167 G4 **Ouled Farès** Alg.
158 N2 **Oulu** Fin.
158 N2 **Oulujärvi** *l.* Fin.
158 N2 **Oulujoki** *r.* Fin.
158 N2 **Oulunsalo** Fin.
166 H4 **Oulx** Italy
177 E3 **Oum-Chalouba** Chad
176 B4 **Oumé** Côte d'Ivoire
177 D3 **Oum-Hadjer** Chad
158 N2 **Ounasjoki** *r.* Fin.
161 G5 **Oundle** U.K.
177 E3 **Ounianga, Lakes of** *tourist site* Chad
177 E3 **Ounianga Kébir** Chad
164 D4 **Oupeye** Belgium
164 E5 **Our** *r.* Lux.
168 C6 **Our, Vallée de l'** *val.* Germany/Lux.
171 L5 **Oura, Akrotirio** *pt* Greece
195 F4 **Ouray** *CO* U.S.A.
197 H1 **Ouray** *UT* U.S.A.
167 C1 **Ourense** Spain
211 J5 **Ouricuri** Brazil
214 C3 **Ourinhos** Brazil
214 C1 **Ouro** *r.* Brazil
214 D3 **Ouro Preto** Brazil
164 D4 **Ourthe** *r.* Belgium
160 G4 **Ouse** *r. England* U.K.
161 H7 **Ouse** *r. England* U.K.
189 G3 **Outardes, Rivière aux** *r.* Canada
180 E6 **Outeniekpas** *pass* S. Africa
162 A2 **Outer Hebrides** *is* U.K.
190 B2 **Outer Island** U.S.A.
196 C5 **Outer Santa Barbara Channel** U.S.A.
179 B6 **Outjo** Namibia
184 H4 **Outlook** Canada
158 O3 **Outokumpu** Fin.
162 □ **Out Skerries** *is* U.K.
125 G4 **Ouvéa** *atoll* New Caledonia
149 D5 **Ouyanghai Shuiku** *resr* China
126 E5 **Ouyen** Australia
161 G5 **Ouzel** *r.* U.K.
170 C4 **Ovace, Punta d'** *mt. Corsica* France
137 G2 **Ovacık** Turkey
170 C2 **Ovada** Italy
125 H3 **Ovalau** *i.* Fiji
215 B1 **Ovalle** Chile
167 B2 **Ovar** Port.
215 D2 **Oveja** *mt.* Arg.
127 G6 **Ovens** *r.* Australia
164 F4 **Overath** Germany
158 M2 **Överkalix** Sweden
197 E3 **Overton** U.S.A.
158 M2 **Övertorneå** Sweden
159 L4 **Överum** Sweden
164 C2 **Overveen** Neth.
190 E4 **Ovid** U.S.A.
167 D1 **Oviedo** Spain
138 E4 **Ovminzatov tog'lari** *hills* Uzbek.
158 N1 **Øvre Anárjohka Nasjonalpark** *nat. park* Norway
**Øvre Anarjokka Nasjonalpark** *nat. park* Norway *see* **Øvre Anárjohka Nasjonalpark**
158 L1 **Øvre Dividal Nasjonalpark** *nat. park* Norway
159 J3 **Øvre Rendal** Norway
173 D5 **Ovruch** Ukr.
128 B7 **Owaka** N.Z.
178 B4 **Owando** Congo
151 E7 **Owase** Japan
198 E2 **Owatonna** U.S.A.
141 F3 **Owbī** Afgh.
203 E3 **Owego** U.S.A.
163 B3 **Owenmore** *r.* Ireland
128 D4 **Owen River** N.Z.
196 C3 **Owens** *r.* U.S.A.
200 C4 **Owensboro** U.S.A.
196 D3 **Owens Lake** U.S.A.
191 G3 **Owen Sound** Canada
191 G3 **Owen Sound** *inlet* Canada
124 E2 **Owen Stanley Range** *mts* P.N.G.
176 C4 **Owerri** Nigeria
186 D4 **Owikeno Lake** Canada
202 B5 **Owingsville** U.S.A.
203 I2 **Owls Head** U.S.A.
176 C4 **Owo** Nigeria
191 E4 **Owosso** U.S.A.
137 K4 **Owrāmān, Kūh-e** *mts* Iran/Iraq
194 C3 **Owyhee** U.S.A.
194 C3 **Owyhee** *r.* U.S.A.
194 C3 **Owyhee Mountains** U.S.A.
210 C6 **Oxapampa** Peru
158 C1 **Öxarfjörður** *b.* Iceland
187 I5 **Oxbow** Canada
203 I1 **Oxbow** U.S.A.
159 L4 **Oxelösund** Sweden
128 D5 **Oxford** N.Z.
161 F6 **Oxford** U.K.
191 F4 **Oxford** *MI* U.S.A.
199 F5 **Oxford** *MS* U.S.A.
203 F3 **Oxford** *NY* U.S.A.
203 F5 **Oxford** *PA* U.S.A.
187 J4 **Oxford House** Canada
187 J4 **Oxford Lake** Canada
126 F5 **Oxley** Australia
127 I3 **Oxleys Peak** Australia
163 C3 **Ox Mountains** *hills* Ireland
196 C4 **Oxnard** U.S.A.
191 H3 **Oxtongue Lake** Canada
158 K2 **Øya** Norway
151 F6 **Oyama** Japan
211 H3 **Oyapock** *r.* Brazil/Fr. Guiana
178 B3 **Oyem** Gabon
162 D3 **Oykel** *r.* U.K.
176 C4 **Oyo** Nigeria
166 G3 **Oyonnax** France
138 F4 **Oyoqog'itma botig'i** *depr.* Uzbek.
138 F4 **Oyoqquduq** Uzbek.
139 J3 **Oyshilik** Kazakh.
145 H5 **Oyster Island** Myanmar
139 H4 **Oy-Tal** Kyrg.
165 H1 **Oyten** Germany
145 F1 **Oyyaylak** China
139 G4 **Oyyk** Kazakh.
138 C2 **Oyyl** Kazakh.
138 C2 **Oyyl** *r.* Kazakh.
137 I2 **Özalp** Turkey
153 B4 **Ozamis** Phil.
201 C6 **Ozark** *AL* U.S.A.
190 E2 **Ozark** *MI* U.S.A.
199 E4 **Ozark Plateau** U.S.A.
198 E4 **Ozarks, Lake of the** U.S.A.
140 E3 **Ozbakūh** Iran
146 H1 **Ozernovskiy** Rus. Fed.
138 E1 **Ozernoye** Kazakh.
138 B2 **Ozernoye** Rus. Fed.
138 E2 **Ozernyy** *Orenburgskaya Oblast'* Rus. Fed.
172 E4 **Ozernyy** *Smolenskaya Oblast'* Rus. Fed.
169 K3 **Ozersk** Rus. Fed.
172 F4 **Ozery** Rus. Fed.
139 H4 **Özgön** Kyrg.
170 C4 **Ozieri** *Sardinia* Italy
138 B2 **Ozinki** Rus. Fed.
199 C6 **Ozona** U.S.A.
151 B7 **Ozuki** Japan
173 G7 **Ozurgeti** Georgia


## P


185 N3 **Paamiut** Greenland
**Pa-an** Myanmar *see* **Hpa-an**
180 C6 **Paarl** S. Africa
180 D4 **Paballelo** S. Africa
152 E3 **P'abal-li** N. Korea
162 A3 **Pabbay** *i. Scotland* U.K.
162 A4 **Pabbay** *i. Scotland* U.K.
169 I5 **Pabianice** Poland
145 G4 **Pabna** Bangl.
159 N5 **Pabradė** Lith.
141 G5 **Pab Range** *mts* Pak.
210 F6 **Pacaás Novos, Parque Nacional** *nat. park* Brazil
210 C5 **Pacasmayo** Peru
195 E6 **Pacheco** *Chihuahua* Mex.
206 D2 **Pacheco** *Zacatecas* Mex.
172 H2 **Pachikha** Rus. Fed.
170 F6 **Pachino** *Sicily* Italy
143 B1 **Pachmarhi** India
144 D5 **Pachor** India
207 E3 **Pachuca** Mex.
196 B2 **Pacific** U.S.A.
217 I9 **Pacific-Antarctic Ridge** *sea feature* Pacific Ocean
216 **Pacific Ocean**
153 C4 **Pacijan** *i.* Phil.
155 D4 **Pacitan** Indon.
211 H4 **Pacoval** Brazil
214 D2 **Pacuí** *r.* Brazil
168 H5 **Paczków** Poland
153 C5 **Padada** Phil.
213 D4 **Padamo** *r.* Venez.
155 B3 **Padang** Indon.
154 B5 **Padang Endau** Malaysia
155 B3 **Padangpanjang** Indon.
155 A2 **Padangsidimpuan** Indon.
155 C3 **Padangtikar** *i.* Indon.
172 E2 **Padany** Rus. Fed.
137 L5 **Padatha, Kūh-e** *mt.* Iran
213 D4 **Padauiri** *r.* Brazil
210 F8 **Padcaya** Bol.
127 F4 **Paddington** Australia
186 F3 **Paddle Prairie** Canada
202 C5 **Paden City** U.S.A.
165 G3 **Paderborn** Germany
171 J2 **Padeșu, Vârful** *mt.* Romania
210 F7 **Padilla** Bol.
158 L2 **Padjelanta nationalpark** *nat. park* Sweden
145 G5 **Padma** *r.* Bangl.
*alt.* **Ganga,**
*conv.* **Ganges**
**Padova** Italy *see* **Padua**
199 D7 **Padre Island** U.S.A.
170 C3 **Padro, Monte** *mt. Corsica* France
161 C7 **Padstow** U.K.
169 M3 **Padsvillye** Belarus
126 D6 **Padthaway** Australia
143 C2 **Padua** India
170 D2 **Padua** Italy
200 B4 **Paducah** *KY* U.S.A.
199 C5 **Paducah** *TX* U.S.A.
144 D2 **Padum** India
152 E3 **Paegam** N. Korea
128 E2 **Paeroa** N.Z.
153 B3 **Paete** Phil.
**Pafos** Cyprus *see* **Paphos**
181 I1 **Pafuri** Moz.
170 F2 **Pag** Croatia
170 F2 **Pag** *i.* Croatia
153 B5 **Pagadian** Phil.
155 B3 **Pagai Selatan** *i.* Indon.
155 B3 **Pagai Utara** *i.* Indon.
147 G5 **Pagan** *i.* N. Mariana Is
155 E3 **Pagatan** Indon.
197 G3 **Page** U.S.A.
159 M5 **Pagėgiai** Lith.
212 □ **Paget, Mount** Atlantic Ocean
195 F4 **Pagosa Springs** U.S.A.
145 G4 **Pagri** China
188 C3 **Pagwa River** Canada
**Pahala** U.S.A. *see* **Pāhala**
196 □2 **Pāhala** U.S.A.
155 B2 **Pahang** *r.* Malaysia
145 G4 **Paharpur** *tourist site* Bangl.
144 B2 **Paharpur** Pak.
128 A7 **Pahia Point** N.Z.
**Pahoa** U.S.A. *see* **Pāhoa**
196 □2 **Pāhoa** U.S.A.
201 D7 **Pahokee** U.S.A.
197 E3 **Pahranagat Range** *mts* U.S.A.
144 D4 **Pahuj** *r.* India
196 D3 **Pahute Mesa** *plat.* U.S.A.
154 A1 **Pai** Thai.
159 N4 **Paide** Estonia
161 D7 **Paignton** U.K.
159 N3 **Päijänne** *l.* Fin.
145 F3 **Paikü Co** *l.* China
154 B2 **Pailĭn** Cambodia
215 B4 **Paillaco** Chile
196 □2 **Pailolo Channel** U.S.A.
159 M3 **Paimio** Fin.
215 B2 **Paine** Chile
202 C4 **Painesville** U.S.A.
197 G3 **Painted Desert** U.S.A.
197 F5 **Painted Rock Reservoir** U.S.A.
126 C3 **Painter, Mount** *h.* Australia
187 J3 **Paint Lake Provincial Recreation Park** Canada
202 B6 **Paintsville** U.S.A.
191 G3 **Paisley** Canada
162 D5 **Paisley** U.K.
210 B5 **Paita** Peru
153 A5 **Paitan, Teluk** *b. Sabah* Malaysia
149 D4 **Paizhouwan** China
158 M2 **Pajala** Sweden
211 K5 **Pajeú** *r.* Brazil
154 B4 **Paka** Malaysia
213 E4 **Pakaraima Mountains** Brazil
210 F2 **Pakaraima Mountains** Guyana
152 C4 **Pakch'ŏn** N. Korea
191 G3 **Pakesley** Canada
133 R3 **Pakhachi** Rus. Fed.
138 D2 **Pakhar'** Kazakh.
**Pakhtaabad** Uzbek. *see* **Paxtaobod**
141 G4 **Pakistan** *country* Asia
128 D1 **Pakotai** N.Z.
144 C3 **Pakpattan** Pak.
154 B3 **Pak Phanang** Thai.
154 B4 **Pak Phayun** Thai.
159 M5 **Pakruojis** Lith.
169 I7 **Paks** Hungary
154 B2 **Pak Thong Chai** Thai.
141 H3 **Paktīkā** *prov.* Afgh.
154 B1 **Pakxan** Laos
154 C2 **Pakxé** Laos
177 D4 **Pala** Chad
154 A2 **Pala** Myanmar
155 C4 **Palabuhanratu** Indon.
155 C4 **Palabuhanratu, Teluk** *b.* Indon.
170 G3 **Palagruža** *i.* Croatia
171 J7 **Palaiochora** Greece
166 F2 **Palaiseau** France
143 B4 **Palakkad** India
143 D1 **Pala Laharha** India
180 E1 **Palamakoloi** Botswana
167 H2 **Palamós** Spain
144 C4 **Palana** India
133 Q4 **Palana** Rus. Fed.
153 B2 **Palanan** Phil.
153 B2 **Palanan Point** Phil.
140 B3 **Palangān** Iran
141 F4 **Palangān, Kūh-e** *mts* Iran
155 D3 **Palangkaraya** Indon.
143 B4 **Palani** India
144 C4 **Palanpur** India
141 G5 **Palantak** Pak.
153 C3 **Palapag** Phil.
179 C6 **Palapye** Botswana
143 B3 **Palar** *r.* India
145 G4 **Palasbari** India
133 Q3 **Palatka** Rus. Fed.
147 F6 **Palau** *country* Pacific Ocean
153 B2 **Palaui** *i.* Phil.
153 A3 **Palauig** Phil.
216 D5 **Palau Islands** Palau
154 A2 **Palauk** Myanmar
216 D5 **Palau Trench** *sea feature* N. Pacific Ocean
154 A2 **Palaw** Myanmar
153 A4 **Palawan** *i.* Phil.
216 C5 **Palawan Trough** *sea feature* N. Pacific Ocean
153 B3 **Palayan** Phil.
159 N4 **Paldiski** Estonia
145 H5 **Pale** Myanmar
155 B3 **Palembang** Indon.
212 B6 **Palena** Chile
167 D1 **Palencia** Spain
207 G4 **Palenque** Mex.
170 E5 **Palermo** *Sicily* Italy
199 E6 **Palestine** U.S.A.
145 H5 **Paletwa** Myanmar
**Palghat** India *see* **Palakkad**
144 C4 **Pali** India
123 F2 **Palikir** Micronesia
153 C5 **Palimbang** Phil.
176 C4 **Palimé** Togo
170 F4 **Palinuro, Capo** *c.* Italy
197 H2 **Palisade** U.S.A.
164 D5 **Paliseul** Belgium
144 B5 **Palitana** India
159 M4 **Palivere** Estonia
143 B4 **Palk Bay** Sri Lanka
172 D3 **Palkino** Rus. Fed.
143 C2 **Palkohda** India
143 B3 **Palkonda Range** *mts* India
143 B4 **Palk Strait** India/Sri Lanka
127 I2 **Pallamallawa** Australia
163 C5 **Pallas Grean New** Ireland
173 H5 **Pallasovka** Rus. Fed.
158 M1 **Pallas-Yllästunturin kansallispuisto** *nat. park* Fin.
143 C3 **Pallavaram** India
143 B2 **Palleru** *r.* India
128 E4 **Palliser, Cape** N.Z.
128 E4 **Palliser Bay** N.Z.
144 C3 **Pallu** India
167 D4 **Palma del Río** Spain
167 H3 **Palma de Mallorca** Spain
213 B2 **Palmar** *r.* Venez.
213 C3 **Palmarito** Venez.
211 I6 **Palmas** Brazil
176 B4 **Palmas, Cape** Liberia
214 D1 **Palmas de Monte Alto** Brazil
201 D7 **Palm Bay** U.S.A.
201 D7 **Palm Beach** U.S.A.
196 C4 **Palmdale** U.S.A.
214 B4 **Palmeira** Brazil
211 K5 **Palmeira dos Índios** Brazil
211 J5 **Palmeirais** Brazil
129 E2 **Palmer** *research stn* Antarctica
184 D3 **Palmer** U.S.A.
123 I5 **Palmerston** *atoll* Cook Is
128 C6 **Palmerston** N.Z.
128 E4 **Palmerston North** N.Z.
203 F4 **Palmerton** U.S.A.
201 E7 **Palmetto Point** Bahamas
170 F5 **Palmi** Italy
207 E3 **Palmillas** Mex.
213 A4 **Palmira** Col.
206 C3 **Palmito del Verde, Isla** *i.* Mex.
196 D5 **Palm Springs** U.S.A.
**Palmyra** Syria *see* **Tadmur**
190 B6 **Palmyra** *MO* U.S.A.
202 E3 **Palmyra** *NY* U.S.A.
190 C4 **Palmyra** *WI* U.S.A.
123 I3 **Palmyra Atoll** *terr.* N. Pacific Ocean
145 F5 **Palmyras Point** India
196 A3 **Palo Alto** U.S.A.
213 A3 **Palo de las Letras** Col.
177 F3 **Paloich** South Sudan
158 M1 **Palojärvi** Fin.
158 N1 **Palomaa** Fin.
207 F4 **Palomares** Mex.
196 D5 **Palomar Mountain** U.S.A.
197 G6 **Palominas** U.S.A.
143 C2 **Paloncha** India
147 E7 **Palopo** Indon.
167 F4 **Palos, Cabo de** *c.* Spain
197 F5 **Palo Verde** *AZ* U.S.A.
197 E5 **Palo Verde** *CA* U.S.A.
158 N2 **Paltamo** Fin.
147 D7 **Palu** Indon.
137 G2 **Palu** Turkey
153 B3 **Paluan** Phil.
138 F5 **Pal'vart** Turkm.
144 D3 **Palwal** India
133 S3 **Palyavaam** *r.* Rus. Fed.
148 A4 **Pamai** China
143 B4 **Pamban Channel** India
127 H6 **Pambula** Australia
155 C4 **Pameungpeuk** Indon.
143 B3 **Pamidi** India
166 E5 **Pamiers** France
139 H5 **Pamir** *r.* Afgh./Tajik.
139 H5 **Pamir** *mts* Asia
201 E5 **Pamlico Sound** *sea chan.* U.S.A.
199 C5 **Pampa** U.S.A.
210 F7 **Pampa Grande** Bol.
215 D2 **Pampas** *reg.* Arg.
213 B3 **Pamplona** Col.
153 B4 **Pamplona** Phil.
167 F1 **Pamplona** Spain
165 J1 **Pampow** Germany
136 C1 **Pamukova** Turkey
202 E6 **Pamunkey** *r.* U.S.A.
144 D2 **Pamzal** India
200 B4 **Pana** U.S.A.
207 G3 **Panabá** Mex.
153 C5 **Panabo** Phil.
197 E3 **Panaca** U.S.A.
153 A4 **Panagtaran Point** Phil.
155 C4 **Panaitan** *i.* Indon.
143 A3 **Panaji** India
206 I6 **Panama** *country* Central America
206 J6 **Panamá, Bahía de** *b.* Panama
206 J6 **Panamá, Canal de** Panama
206 J7 **Panama, Gulf of** Panama
206 I6 **Panamá, Istmo de** *isth.* Panama
206 J6 **Panama City** Panama
201 C6 **Panama City** U.S.A.
196 D3 **Panamint Range** *mts* U.S.A.
196 D3 **Panamint Springs** U.S.A.
196 D3 **Panamint Valley** U.S.A.
153 C4 **Panaon** *i.* Phil.
145 G4 **Panar** *r.* India
170 F5 **Panarea, Isola** *i. Isole Lipari* Italy
155 C2 **Panarik** Indon.
153 B4 **Panay** *i.* Phil.
153 C3 **Panay** *i.* Phil.
153 B4 **Panay Gulf** Phil.
197 E2 **Pancake Range** *mts* U.S.A.
171 I2 **Pančevo** Serbia
153 B4 **Pandan** Phil.
153 C3 **Pandan** Phil.
154 □ **Pandan, Selat** *str.* Sing.
153 B4 **Pandan Bay** Phil.
154 □ **Pandan Reservoir** Sing.
144 E5 **Pandaria** India
214 D1 **Pandeiros** *r.* Brazil
143 A2 **Pandharpur** India
144 D5 **Pandhurna** India
215 F2 **Pando** Uruguay
161 E6 **Pandy** U.K.
159 N5 **Panevėžys** Lith.
144 C2 **Pangi Range** *mts* Pak.
155 D3 **Pangkalanbuun** Indon.
155 A2 **Pangkalansusu** Indon.
155 C3 **Pangkalpinang** Indon.
147 E7 **Pangkalsiang, Tanjung** *pt* Indon.
145 G3 **Pangkog Co** *salt l.* China
153 B4 **Panglao** *i.* Phil.
153 A5 **Panglima Sugala** Phil.
185 L3 **Pangnirtung** Canada
132 I3 **Pangody** Rus. Fed.
215 B3 **Panguipulli** Chile
215 B3 **Panguipulli, Lago** *l.* Chile
197 F3 **Panguitch** U.S.A.
154 A5 **Pangururan** Indon.
153 B5 **Pangutaran** *i.* Phil.
153 B5 **Pangutaran Group** *is* Phil.
199 C5 **Panhandle** U.S.A.
178 C4 **Pania-Mwanga** Dem. Rep. Congo
144 B5 **Panikoita** *i.* India
173 G5 **Panino** Rus. Fed.
144 D3 **Panipat** India
153 A4 **Panitian** Phil.
144 B1 **Panj** *r.* Afgh./Tajik.
139 G5 **Panj** Tajik.
141 G3 **Panjāb** Afgh.
139 F5 **Panjakent** Tajik.
154 D5 **Panjang** *i.* Indon.
154 □ **Panjang, Bukit** Sing.
137 K5 **Panjbarār** Iran
141 G5 **Panjgur** Pak.
144 C5 **Panjhra** *r.* India
**Panjin** China *see* **Panshan**
144 B2 **Panjkora** *r.* Pak.
144 B3 **Panjnad** *r.* Pak.
158 O3 **Pankakoski** Fin.
176 C4 **Pankshin** Nigeria
152 F2 **Pan Ling** *mts* China
144 D4 **Panna** *reg.* India
124 B4 **Pannawonica** Australia
136 D4 **Pano Lefkara** Cyprus
214 B3 **Panorama** Brazil
143 B4 **Panruti** India
152 B3 **Panshan** China
152 D2 **Panshi** China
211 G7 **Pantanal Matogrossense, Parque Nacional do** *nat. park* Brazil
170 D6 **Pantelleria** *Sicily* Italy
170 E6 **Pantelleria, Isola di** *i. Sicily* Italy
153 C5 **Pantukan** Phil.
207 E3 **Pánuco** Mex.
207 E3 **Pánuco** *r.* Mex.
143 A2 **Panvel** India
**Panxian** China *see* **Chengguan**
149 D6 **Panyu** China
149 A5 **Panzhihua** China
178 B4 **Panzi** Dem. Rep. Congo
207 G5 **Panzos** Guat.
213 E3 **Pao** *r.* Venez.
170 G5 **Paola** Italy
200 C4 **Paoli** U.S.A.
178 B3 **Paoua** Cent. Afr. Rep.
**Pap** Uzbek. *see* **Pop**
168 H7 **Pápa** Hungary
170 F4 **Papa, Monte del** *mt.* Italy
128 E2 **Papakura** N.Z.
207 E3 **Papantla** Mex.
143 C2 **Paparhahandi** India
128 C5 **Paparoa National Park** N.Z.
128 C5 **Paparoa Range** *mts* N.Z.
162 □ **Papa Stour** *i.* U.K.
128 E2 **Papatoetoe** N.Z.
128 B7 **Papatowai** N.Z.
162 F1 **Papa Westray** *i.* U.K.
164 F1 **Papenburg** Germany
136 D4 **Paphos** Cyprus
192 E6 **Papigochic** *r.* Mex.
191 J2 **Papineau-Labelle, Réserve Faunique de** *nature res.* Canada
197 E3 **Papoose Lake** U.S.A.
165 I6 **Pappenheim** Germany
162 B5 **Paps of Jura** *hills* U.K.
124 E2 **Papua, Gulf of** P.N.G.
124 E2 **Papua New Guinea** *country* Oceania
**Papun** Myanmar *see* **Hpapun**
161 C7 **Par** U.K.
214 D2 **Pará** *r.* Brazil
172 G4 **Para** *r.* Rus. Fed.
211 I4 **Pará, Rio do** *r.* Brazil
124 B4 **Paraburdoo** Australia
153 B3 **Paracale** Phil.
214 C2 **Paracatu** Brazil
214 D2 **Paracatu** *r.* Brazil
147 D5 **Paracel Islands** S. China Sea
126 C3 **Parachilna** Australia
171 I3 **Paraćin** Serbia
214 D2 **Pará de Minas** Brazil
191 I1 **Paradis** Canada
196 B2 **Paradise** *CA* U.S.A.
190 E2 **Paradise** *MI* U.S.A.
187 H4 **Paradise Hill** Canada
196 D2 **Paradise Peak** U.S.A.
189 I3 **Paradise River** Canada
199 F4 **Paragould** U.S.A.
210 F6 **Paragua** *r.* Bol.
213 E3 **Paragua** *r.* Venez.
211 G7 **Paraguai** *r.* Brazil
213 C2 **Paraguáipoa** Venez.
213 C1 **Paraguaná, Península de** *pen.* Venez.
212 E3 **Paraguay** *r.* Arg./Para.
212 E2 **Paraguay** *country* S. America
211 K5 **Paraíba** *r.* Brazil
214 D3 **Paraíba do Sul** *r.* Brazil
207 F4 **Paraíso** Mex.
176 C4 **Parakou** Benin
126 B3 **Parakylia** Australia
143 D2 **Paralakhemundi** India
144 E6 **Paralkot** India
143 B4 **Paramakkudi** India
211 G2 **Paramaribo** Suriname
213 B3 **Paramillo** *mt.* Col.
213 A3 **Paramillo, Parque Nacional** *nat. park* Col.
214 D1 **Paramirim** Brazil
213 A3 **Paramo Frontino** *mt.* Col.
203 F4 **Paramus** U.S.A.
146 H1 **Paramushir, Ostrov** *i.* Rus. Fed.
215 E1 **Paraná** Arg.
211 I6 **Paranã** Brazil
214 C1 **Paraná** *r.* Brazil
214 B4 **Paraná** *state* Brazil
212 E4 **Paraná** *r.* S. America
214 C1 **Paraná, Serra do** *hills* Brazil
214 C4 **Paranaguá** Brazil
214 B2 **Paranaíba** Brazil
214 B2 **Paranaíba** *r.* Brazil
215 E2 **Paraná Ibicuy** *r.* Arg.
214 B3 **Paranapanema** *r.* Brazil
214 C4 **Paranapiacaba, Serra** *mts* Brazil
153 C4 **Paranas** Phil.
214 B3 **Paranavaí** Brazil
153 B5 **Parang** Phil.
143 B4 **Parangipettai** India
171 J2 **Parângul Mare, Vârful** *mt.* Romania
214 D2 **Paraopeba** *r.* Brazil
137 J4 **Pārapāra** Iraq
128 E4 **Paraparaumu** N.Z.
213 D3 **Paraque, Cerro** *mt.* Venez.
207 E2 **Paras** Mex.
144 D5 **Paratwada** India
137 K4 **Parāū, Kūh-e** *mt.* Iraq
214 B2 **Paraúna** Brazil
166 G3 **Paray-le-Monial** France
144 D4 **Parbati** *r.* India
143 B2 **Parbhani** India
139 F1 **Parchevka** Kazakh.
165 J1 **Parchim** Germany
190 C4 **Pardeeville** U.S.A.
145 G2 **Parding** China
214 E1 **Pardo** *r. Bahia/Minas Gerais* Brazil
214 B3 **Pardo** *r. Mato Grosso do Sul* Brazil
214 D1 **Pardo** *r. Minas Gerais* Brazil
214 C3 **Pardo** *r. São Paulo* Brazil
168 G5 **Pardubice** Czech Rep.
144 D2 **Pare Chu** *r.* China
210 F6 **Parecis, Serra dos** *hills* Brazil
206 D2 **Paredón** Mex.
140 B2 **Pareh** Iran
128 D1 **Parengarenga Harbour** N.Z.
188 E4 **Parent, Lac** *l.* Canada
128 C6 **Pareora** N.Z.
155 E3 **Parepare** Indon.
215 D2 **Parera** Arg.
172 G3 **Parfen'yevo** Rus. Fed.
169 O2 **Parfino** Rus. Fed.
171 I5 **Parga** Greece
159 M3 **Pargas** Fin.
213 E2 **Paria, Gulf of** Trin. and Tob./Venez.
213 E2 **Paria, Península de** *pen.* Venez.
213 D2 **Pariaguán** Venez.
197 F3 **Paria Plateau** U.S.A.
159 O3 **Parikkala** Fin.
213 D4 **Parima, Serra** *mts* Brazil
213 D4 **Parima-Tapirapecó, Parque Nacional** *nat. park* Venez.
210 B4 **Pariñas, Punta** *pt* Peru
126 D5 **Paringa** Australia
211 G4 **Parintins** Brazil
191 G4 **Paris** Canada
166 F2 **Paris** France (City Plan **110**)
202 A5 **Paris** *KY* U.S.A.
201 B4 **Paris** *TN* U.S.A.
199 E5 **Paris** *TX* U.S.A.
164 A5 **Paris (Charles de Gaulle)** *airport* France
190 E2 **Parisienne, Île** *i.* Canada
206 I7 **Parita** Panama
140 D4 **Pārīz** Iran
138 E1 **Parizh** Rus. Fed.
163 D3 **Park** U.K.
143 B2 **Parkal** India
159 M3 **Parkano** Fin.
189 I3 **Parke Lake** Canada
139 G4 **Parkent** Uzbek.
197 E4 **Parker** U.S.A.
149 □ **Parker, Mount** *h. Hong Kong* China
197 E4 **Parker Dam** U.S.A.
187 J2 **Parker Lake** Canada
190 A4 **Parkersburg** *IA* U.S.A.
202 C5 **Parkersburg** *WV* U.S.A.
127 H4 **Parkes** Australia
190 B3 **Park Falls** U.S.A.
190 D5 **Park Forest** U.S.A.
191 F2 **Parkinson** Canada
198 E2 **Park Rapids** U.S.A.
186 E5 **Parksville** Canada
203 F4 **Parksville** U.S.A.
143 D2 **Parla Kimedi** India
143 B2 **Parli Vaijnath** India
170 D2 **Parma** Italy
194 C3 **Parma** *ID* U.S.A.
202 C4 **Parma** *OH* U.S.A.
213 D3 **Parmana** Venez.
211 J4 **Parnaíba** Brazil
211 J4 **Parnaíba** *r.* Brazil
128 D5 **Parnassus** N.Z.
**Parnassus, Mount** *mt.* Greece *see* **Liakoura**
126 B5 **Parndana** Australia
190 A5 **Parnell** U.S.A.
171 J6 **Parnonas** *mts* Greece
159 N4 **Pärnu** Estonia
159 N4 **Pärnu-Jaagupi** Estonia
171 K6 **Paroikia** Greece
126 F2 **Paroo** *watercourse* Australia
126 E3 **Paroo-Darling National Park** Australia
**Paropamisus** *mts* Afgh. *see* **Sefīd Kūh, Selseleh-ye**
171 K6 **Paros** *i.* Greece
197 F3 **Parowan** U.S.A.
215 B3 **Parral** Chile
203 F6 **Parramore Island** U.S.A.
206 D2 **Parras** Mex.
215 F3 **Parravicini** Arg.
161 E6 **Parrett** *r.* U.K.
206 H6 **Parrita** Costa Rica
189 H4 **Parrsboro** Canada
184 F2 **Parry, Cape** Canada
184 G2 **Parry Islands** Canada
191 G3 **Parry Sound** Canada
199 E4 **Parsons** *KS* U.S.A.
202 D5 **Parsons** *WV* U.S.A.
165 H4 **Partenstein** Germany
166 D3 **Parthenay** France
150 C3 **Partizansk** Rus. Fed.
161 H4 **Partney** U.K.
163 B4 **Partry** Ireland
163 B4 **Partry Mountains** *hills* Ireland
211 H4 **Paru** *r.* Brazil
213 D3 **Parucito** *r.* Venez.
143 C2 **Parvatipuram** India
144 C4 **Parvatsar** India
144 D4 **Parwan** *r.* India
145 E3 **Paryang** China
181 G3 **Parys** S. Africa
140 D3 **Pās, Chāh** *well* Iran
196 C4 **Pasadena** *CA* U.S.A.
199 E6 **Pasadena** *TX* U.S.A.
210 B4 **Pasado, Cabo** *c.* Ecuador
154 B2 **Pa Sak, Mae Nam** *r.* Thai.
140 D4 **Pasargadae** *tourist site* Iran
155 B3 **Pasarseblat** Indon.
154 A1 **Pasawng** Myanmar
199 F6 **Pascagoula** U.S.A.
191 I1 **Pascalis** Canada
169 M7 **Pașcani** Romania
194 C2 **Pasco** U.S.A.
214 E2 **Pascoal, Monte** *h.* Brazil
**Pascua, Isla de** *i.* S. Pacific Ocean *see* **Easter Island**
**Pas de Calais** *str.* France/U.K. *see* **Dover, Strait of**
168 G4 **Pasewalk** Germany
187 H3 **Pasfield Lake** Canada
141 F3 **Pāsgāh-e Gol Vardeh** Iran
172 E2 **Pasha** Rus. Fed.
153 B3 **Pasig** Phil.
137 H2 **Pasinler** Turkey
154 □ **Pasir Gudang** Malaysia
**Pasir Panjang** Sing. *see* **Lurudal**
155 B1 **Pasir Putih** Malaysia
196 A2 **Paskenta** U.S.A.
141 F5 **Paskūh** Iran
141 F5 **Pasni** Pak.
207 G4 **Paso Caballos** Guat.
215 F2 **Paso de los Toros** Uruguay
212 B7 **Paso Río Mayo** Arg.
196 B4 **Paso Robles** U.S.A.
187 I4 **Pasquia Hills** Canada
203 I2 **Passadumkeag** U.S.A.
190 C1 **Passage Island** U.S.A.
168 F6 **Passau** Germany
153 B4 **Passi** Phil.
212 F3 **Passo Fundo** Brazil
214 C3 **Passos** Brazil
172 C4 **Pastavy** Belarus
210 C4 **Pastaza** *r.* Peru
213 A4 **Pasto** Col.
197 H3 **Pastora Peak** U.S.A.
153 B2 **Pasuquin** Phil.
155 D4 **Pasuruan** Indon.
159 N4 **Pasvalys** Lith.
153 B5 **Pata** *i.* Phil.
212 B7 **Patagonia** *reg.* Arg.
197 G6 **Patagonia** U.S.A.
145 G4 **Patakata** India
144 C5 **Patan** *Gujarat* India
144 D5 **Patan** *Madhya Pradesh* India
145 F4 **Patan** Nepal
126 E5 **Patchewollock** Australia
128 E3 **Patea** N.Z.
128 E3 **Patea** *r.* N.Z.
160 F3 **Pateley Bridge** U.K.
145 G5 **Patenga Point** Bangl.
180 F6 **Patensie** S. Africa
170 F6 **Paternò** *Sicily* Italy
127 I4 **Paterson** Australia
127 G1 **Paterson** *r.* Australia
203 F4 **Paterson** U.S.A.
144 C2 **Pathankot** India
144 D4 **Pathena** India
194 F3 **Pathfinder Reservoir** U.S.A.
154 A3 **Pathiu** Thai.
143 B2 **Pathri** India
154 B2 **Pathum Thani** Thai.
155 D4 **Pati** Indon.
213 A4 **Patía** *r.* Col.
144 D3 **Patiala** India
171 L6 **Patmos** *i.* Greece
145 F4 **Patna** India
143 C1 **Patnagarh** India
153 B3 **Patnanongan** *i.* Phil.
137 I2 **Patnos** Turkey
144 E3 **Paton** India
171 H4 **Patos** Albania
211 K5 **Patos** Brazil
212 F4 **Patos, Lagoa dos** *l.* Brazil
214 C2 **Patos de Minas** Brazil
215 C1 **Patquía** Arg.
171 I5 **Patras** Greece
158 B2 **Patreksfjörður** Iceland
214 C2 **Patrocínio** Brazil
158 O1 **Patsoyoki** *r.* Europe
143 A2 **Pattadakal** *tourist site* India
154 B4 **Pattani** Thai.
154 B4 **Pattani, Mae Nam** *r.* Thai.
154 B2 **Pattaya** Thai.
203 I2 **Patten** U.S.A.
165 H2 **Pattensen** Germany
196 B3 **Patterson** U.S.A.
202 D5 **Patterson** *r.* U.S.A.
186 C2 **Patterson, Mount** Canada
190 E3 **Patterson, Point** U.S.A.
196 C3 **Patterson Mountain** U.S.A.
158 N2 **Pattijoki** Fin.
158 M1 **Pättikkä** Fin.
143 B3 **Pattikonda** India
186 D3 **Pattullo, Mount** Canada
145 G5 **Patuakhali** Bangl.
187 H3 **Patuanak** Canada
206 H5 **Patuca** *r.* Hond.
206 H5 **Patuca, Punta** *pt* Hond.
202 E5 **Patuxent** *r.* U.S.A.
206 D4 **Pátzcuaro** Mex.
166 D5 **Pau** France
166 D4 **Pauillac** France
145 H5 **Pauktaw** Myanmar
197 F4 **Paulden** U.S.A.
202 A4 **Paulding** U.S.A.
189 H2 **Paul Island** Canada
211 J5 **Paulistana** Brazil
211 K5 **Paulo Afonso** Brazil
181 I3 **Paulpietersburg** S. Africa
181 G4 **Paul Roux** S. Africa
203 F2 **Paul Smiths** U.S.A.
199 D5 **Pauls Valley** U.S.A.
213 C3 **Pauto** *r.* Col.
214 E2 **Pavão** Brazil
140 B3 **Pāveh** Iran
170 C2 **Pavia** Italy
159 M4 **Pāvilosta** Latvia
172 H3 **Pavino** Rus. Fed.
171 K3 **Pavlikeni** Bulg.
139 I1 **Pavlodar** Kazakh.
139 H2 **Pavlodarskaya Oblast'** *admin. div.* Kazakh.
139 H1 **Pavlogradka** Rus. Fed.
173 E5 **Pavlohrad** Ukr.
139 H2 **Pavlovka** Kazakh.
172 H4 **Pavlovka** Rus. Fed.
172 G4 **Pavlovo** Rus. Fed.
173 G5 **Pavlovsk** Rus. Fed.
173 F6 **Pavlovskaya** Rus. Fed.
213 B4 **Pavon** Col.
144 E3 **Pawayan** India
190 E4 **Paw Paw** U.S.A.
203 H4 **Pawtucket** U.S.A.
154 A2 **Pawut** Myanmar
139 H4 **Paxtaobod** Uzbek.
190 C5 **Paxton** U.S.A.
155 B3 **Payakumbuh** Indon.
154 □ **Paya Lebar** Sing.
194 C2 **Payette** U.S.A.
132 H3 **Pay-Khoy, Khrebet** *hills* Rus. Fed.
188 F2 **Payne, Lac** *l.* Canada
196 B1 **Paynes Creek** U.S.A.
215 E2 **Paysandú** Uruguay
197 G4 **Payson** *AZ* U.S.A.
197 G1 **Payson** *UT* U.S.A.
215 C3 **Payún, Cerro** *vol.* Arg.
136 D1 **Pazar** Turkey
137 H1 **Pazar** Turkey
136 F3 **Pazarcık** Turkey
171 K3 **Pazardzhik** Bulg.
213 C3 **Paz de Ariporo** Col.

213 B3 Paz de Rio Col.
170 E2 Pazin Croatia
186 G3 Peace r. Canada
186 F3 Peace River Canada
197 F4 Peach Springs U.S.A.
161 F4 Peak District National Park U.K.
126 A2 Peake watercourse Australia
189 G4 Peaked Mountain h. U.S.A.
153 A4 Peaked Point Phil.
127 H4 Peak Hill Australia
197 H2 Peale, Mount U.S.A.
197 H6 Pearce U.S.A.
190 C1 Pearl Canada
199 F6 Pearl r. U.S.A.
123 H1 Pearl and Hermes Atoll U.S.A.
196 □1 Pearl City U.S.A.
196 □1 Pearl Harbor inlet U.S.A.
199 D6 Pearsall U.S.A.
201 D6 Pearson U.S.A.
185 H2 Peary Channel Canada
188 C2 Peawanuck Canada
179 D5 Pebane Moz.
Peć Kosovo see Pejë
214 D2 Peçanha Brazil
158 O1 Pechenga Rus. Fed.
132 G3 Pechora Rus. Fed.
220 D2 Pechora r. Rus. Fed.
172 C3 Pechory Rus. Fed.
191 F4 Peck U.S.A.
186 E3 Peck, Mount Canada
154 C2 Pe Cô, Krông r. Vietnam
199 C6 Pecos U.S.A.
199 C6 Pecos r. U.S.A.
171 H1 Pécs Hungary
206 I7 Pedasí Panama
127 G9 Pedder, Lake Australia
181 G6 Peddie S. Africa
206 C1 Pedernales Mex.
158 M3 Pedersöre Fin.
Pêdo La pass China see Pindu Pass
214 E1 Pedra Azul Brazil
213 C3 Pedraza la Vieja Venez.
213 C2 Pedregal Venez.
214 C3 Pedregulho Brazil
211 J4 Pedreiras Brazil
206 D2 Pedriceña Mex.
143 C4 Pedro, Point Sri Lanka
211 I5 Pedro Afonso Brazil
213 C4 Pedro Chico Col.
212 C2 Pedro de Valdivia Chile
214 A2 Pedro Gomes Brazil
206 J6 Pedro González, Isla i. Panama
211 J4 Pedro II Brazil
213 D4 Pedro II, Ilha reg. Brazil
212 E2 Pedro Juan Caballero Para.
Pedroll Brazil see Pedro II
215 G1 Pedro Osório Brazil
162 E5 Peebles U.K.
201 E5 Pee Dee r. U.S.A.
203 G4 Peekskill U.S.A.
127 I3 Peel r. Australia
184 E3 Peel r. Canada
160 C3 Peel U.K.
164 D3 Peer Belgium
186 F4 Peers Canada
126 E3 Peery Lake salt l. Australia
128 D5 Pegasus Bay N.Z.
165 J5 Pegnitz Germany
165 J5 Pegnitz r. Germany
147 B5 Pegu Myanmar
172 I2 Pegysh Rus. Fed.
215 E2 Pehuajó Arg.
165 I2 Peine Germany
159 N4 Peipus, Lake Estonia/Rus. Fed.
165 J3 Peißen Germany
148 E3 Peitun China
211 I6 Peixe Brazil
214 B1 Peixe r. Goiás Brazil
214 B3 Peixe r. São Paulo Brazil
148 E3 Peixian China
214 A2 Peixo de Couro r. Brazil
171 I3 Pejë Kosovo
181 G4 Peka Lesotho
155 C4 Pekalongan Indon.
154 B5 Pekan Malaysia
155 B2 Pekanbaru Indon.
190 C5 Pekin U.S.A.
Pelabuhan Kelang Malaysia see Pelabuhan Klang
154 B5 Pelabuhan Klang Malaysia
191 F5 Pelee Island Canada
191 F5 Pelee Point Canada
147 E7 Peleng i. Indon.
172 I2 Peles Rus. Fed.
190 A1 Pelican Lake MN U.S.A.
190 C3 Pelican Lake WI U.S.A.
187 I3 Pelican Narrows Canada
158 N2 Pelkosenniemi Fin.
180 C4 Pella S. Africa
187 H1 Pellatt Lake Canada
124 E2 Pelleluhu Islands P.N.G.
190 C4 Pell Lake U.S.A.
158 M2 Pello Fin.
186 B2 Pelly r. Canada
Pelly Bay Canada see Kugaaruk
186 B2 Pelly Crossing Canada
187 I1 Pelly Lake Canada
186 C2 Pelly Mountains Canada
215 G1 Pelotas Brazil
212 F3 Pelotas, Rio das r. Brazil
136 D6 Pelusium tourist site Egypt
203 I2 Pemadumcook Lake U.S.A.
155 C4 Pemalang Indon.
155 C2 Pemangkat Indon.
155 A2 Pematangsiantar Indon.
179 E5 Pemba Moz.
179 C5 Pemba Zambia
178 D4 Pemba Island Tanz.
186 F4 Pembina r. Canada
198 D1 Pembina U.S.A.
191 I3 Pembroke Canada
161 C6 Pembroke U.K.
203 J2 Pembroke U.S.A.
161 B5 Pembrokeshire Coast National Park U.K.
143 A2 Pen India
145 H5 Pen r. Myanmar
167 E2 Peñalara mt. Spain
207 E3 Peñamiller Mex.
207 E3 Peña Nevada, Cerro mt. Mex.
214 B3 Penápolis Brazil
167 D2 Peñaranda de Bracamonte Spain
126 E5 Penarie Australia
167 F2 Peñarroya mt. Spain
167 D3 Peñarroya-Pueblonuevo Spain
161 D6 Penarth U.K.
167 D1 Peñas, Cabo de c. Spain
212 A7 Penas, Golfo de g. Chile
213 E2 Peñas, Punta pt Venez.
206 H6 Peñas Blancas Nicaragua
144 D5 Pench r. India
129 D6 Penck, Cape c. Antarctica
215 C2 Pencoso, Alto de hills Arg.
176 C3 Pendjari, Parc National de la nat. park Benin
160 E4 Pendle Hill U.K.
194 C2 Pendleton U.S.A.
186 D4 Pendleton Bay Canada
194 C1 Pend Oreille r. U.S.A.
194 C2 Pend Oreille Lake U.S.A.
143 C1 Pendra India
191 H3 Penetanguishene Canada
148 C4 Peng'an China
144 D6 Penganga r. India
149 □ Peng Chau i. Hong Kong China
178 C4 Penge Dem. Rep. Congo
181 I2 Penge S. Africa
149 F6 P'enghu Ch'ün-tao is Taiwan
149 F6 Penghu Dao i. Taiwan
149 G5 Pengjia Yu i. Taiwan
154 □ Peng Kang h. Sing.
148 F2 Penglai China
149 B4 Pengshan China
149 C4 Pengshui China
149 B4 Pengxi China
149 E4 Pengze China
181 G5 Penhoek Pass S. Africa
167 B3 Peniche Port.
162 E5 Penicuik U.K.
165 K4 Penig Germany
172 E2 Peninga Rus. Fed.
137 J4 Pēnjwīn Iraq
170 E3 Penne Italy
143 B3 Penner r. India
126 B5 Penneshaw Australia
160 E3 Pennines hills U.K.
181 I5 Pennington S. Africa
203 F5 Pennsville U.S.A.
202 D4 Pennsylvania state U.S.A.
202 E3 Penn Yan U.S.A.
185 L3 Penny Icecap Canada
203 I2 Penobscot r. U.S.A.
203 I2 Penobscot Bay U.S.A.
126 D6 Penola Australia
206 C2 Peñón Blanco Mex.
124 D5 Penong Australia
206 I6 Penonomé Panama
123 I4 Penrhyn atoll Cook Is
217 I6 Penrhyn Basin sea feature Pacific Ocean
160 E3 Penrith U.K.
201 C6 Pensacola U.S.A.
129 C4 Pensacola Mountains mts Antarctica
137 L2 Pensär Azer.
126 E6 Penshurst Australia
144 D2 Pensi La pass India
125 G3 Pentecost Island Vanuatu
186 F5 Penticton Canada
161 B7 Pentire Point U.K.
162 E2 Pentland Firth sea chan. U.K.
162 E5 Pentland Hills U.K.
190 D4 Pentwater U.S.A.
143 B3 Penukonda India
161 D5 Penygadair h. U.K.
160 E3 Pen-y-Ghent h. U.K.
187 H2 Penylan Lake Canada
172 H4 Penza Rus. Fed.
161 B7 Penzance U.K.
172 H4 Penzenskaya Oblast' admin. div. Rus. Fed.
133 R3 Penzhinskaya Guba b. Rus. Fed.
197 F5 Peoria AZ U.S.A.
190 C5 Peoria IL U.S.A.
154 B4 Perai Malaysia
154 A4 Perak i. Malaysia
154 B4 Perak r. Malaysia
167 F2 Perales del Alfambra Spain
143 B4 Perambalur India
189 H4 Percé Canada
203 H2 Percy U.S.A.
124 F4 Percy Isles Australia
191 I3 Percy Reach l. Canada
167 G1 Perdido, Monte mt. Spain
132 H3 Peregrebnoye Rus. Fed.
213 B3 Pereira Col.
214 B3 Pereira Barreto Brazil
172 D3 Perekhoda r. Rus. Fed.
173 G5 Perelazovskiy Rus. Fed.
138 B2 Perelyub Rus. Fed.
190 D4 Pere Marquette r. U.S.A.
138 B2 Peremetnoye Kazakh.
169 L6 Peremyshlyany Ukr.
172 F3 Pereslavl'-Zalesskiy Rus. Fed.
138 C2 Perevolotskiy Rus. Fed.
172 H4 Perevoz Rus. Fed.
173 D5 Pereyaslav-Khmel'nyts'kyy Ukr.
215 E2 Pergamino Arg.
154 B4 Perhentian Besar, Pulau i. Malaysia
158 N3 Perho Fin.
Péribonca, Lac l. Canada see Péribonka, Lac
189 F3 Péribonka, Lac l. Canada
212 C2 Perico Arg.
206 C2 Pericos Mex.
166 E4 Périgueux France
213 B2 Perijá, Parque Nacional nat. park Venez.
213 B2 Perijá, Sierra de mts Venez.
212 B7 Perito Moreno Arg.
190 D3 Perkins U.S.A.
206 I5 Perlas, Laguna de lag. Nicaragua
206 I5 Perlas, Punta de pt Nicaragua
165 J1 Perleberg Germany
132 G4 Perm' Rus. Fed.
172 H3 Permas Rus. Fed.
Pernambuco Abyssal Plain sea feature S. Atlantic Ocean see Pernambuco Plain
219 H6 Pernambuco Plain sea feature S. Atlantic Ocean
126 B3 Pernatty Lagoon salt flat Australia
171 J3 Pernik Bulg.
166 F2 Péronne France
207 E4 Perote Mex.
166 F5 Perpignan France
161 B7 Perranporth U.K.
196 D5 Perris U.S.A.
166 C2 Perros-Guirec France
201 D6 Perry FL U.S.A.
201 D5 Perry GA U.S.A.
198 E3 Perry IA U.S.A.
199 D4 Perry OK U.S.A.
202 B4 Perrysburg U.S.A.
199 C4 Perryton U.S.A.
199 F4 Perryville U.S.A.
140 D4 Persepolis tourist site Iran
161 E5 Pershore U.K.
140 C3 Persian Garden, The tourist site Iran
Persian Gulf g. Asia see The Gulf
137 G2 Pertek Turkey
124 B5 Perth Australia
191 I3 Perth Canada
162 E4 Perth U.K.
203 F4 Perth Amboy U.S.A.
203 J1 Perth-Andover Canada
218 L6 Perth Basin sea feature Indian Ocean
172 F1 Pertominsk Rus. Fed.
166 G5 Pertuis France
159 N3 Pertunmaa Fin.
170 C4 Pertusato, Capo c. Corsica France
210 C5 Peru country S. America
190 C5 Peru U.S.A.
217 M7 Peru Basin sea feature S. Pacific Ocean
217 N6 Peru-Chile Trench sea feature S. Pacific Ocean
170 E3 Perugia Italy
214 C4 Peruíbe Brazil
164 B4 Péruwelz Belgium
172 G4 Pervomaysk Rus. Fed.
173 D5 Pervomays'k Ukr.
172 J2 Pervomayskaya Rus. Fed.
173 E6 Pervomays'ke Ukr.
139 J2 Pervomayskiy Kazakh.
138 C2 Pervomayskiy Orenburgskaya Oblast' Rus. Fed.
172 G4 Pervomayskiy Tambovskaya Oblast' Rus. Fed.
173 F5 Pervomays'kyy Ukr.
133 R3 Pervorechenskiy (abandoned) Rus. Fed.
170 E3 Pesaro Italy
196 A3 Pescadero U.S.A.
197 H4 Pescado U.S.A.
170 F3 Pescara Italy
170 F3 Pescara r. Italy
173 G6 Peschanokopskoye Rus. Fed.
138 B4 Peschanyy, Mys pt Kazakh.
154 □ Pesek, Pulau i. Sing.
144 B2 Peshawar Pak.
171 I4 Peshkopi Albania
171 K3 Peshtera Bulg.
190 D3 Peshtigo U.S.A.
190 C3 Peshtigo r. U.S.A.
139 F1 Peski Kazakh.
138 E5 Peski Turkm.
170 F1 Pesnica Slovenia
166 D4 Pessac France
165 K2 Pessin Germany
172 E3 Pestovo Rus. Fed.
172 G4 Pet r. Rus. Fed.
206 D4 Petacalco, Bahía de b. Mex.
136 E5 Petah Tiqwa Israel
159 N3 Petäjävesi Fin.
171 K5 Petalioi i. Greece
196 A2 Petaluma U.S.A.
164 D5 Pétange Lux.
155 E3 Petangis Indon.
213 D2 Petare Venez.
206 D4 Petatlán Mex.
179 D5 Petauke Zambia
191 I3 Petawawa Canada
207 G4 Petén Itzá, Lago l. Guat.
190 C3 Petenwell Lake U.S.A.
126 C4 Peterborough S.A. Australia
126 E7 Peterborough Vic. Australia
191 H3 Peterborough Canada
161 G5 Peterborough U.K.
162 F3 Peterculter U.K.
162 G3 Peterhead U.K.
129 B3 Peter I Island i. Antarctica
187 K2 Peter Lake Canada
160 F3 Peterlee U.K.
124 C4 Petermann Ranges mts Australia
215 B2 Peteroa, Volcán vol. Chile
187 H3 Peter Pond Lake Canada
189 F2 Peters, Lac l. Canada
165 H4 Petersberg Germany
186 C3 Petersburg AK U.S.A.
190 C6 Petersburg IL U.S.A.
202 E6 Petersburg VA U.S.A.
202 D5 Petersburg WV U.S.A.
161 G6 Petersfield U.K.
165 G2 Petershagen Germany
170 G5 Petilia Policastro Italy
203 J2 Petit Manan Point U.S.A.
189 H3 Petit Mécatina r. Canada
189 I3 Petit Mécatina r. Canada
186 E3 Petitot r. Canada
207 E4 Petlalcingo Mex.
207 G3 Peto Mex.
190 E3 Petoskey U.S.A.
136 E6 Petra tourist site Jordan
146 F2 Petra Velikogo, Zaliv b. Rus. Fed.
191 I4 Petre, Point Canada
171 J4 Petrich Bulg.
197 H4 Petrified Forest National Park U.S.A.
170 G2 Petrinja Croatia
171 J3 Petrokhanski Prokhod pass Bulg.
191 F4 Petrolia Canada
211 J5 Petrolina Brazil
139 J3 Petropavlovka Kazakh.
173 G5 Petropavlovka Rus. Fed.
146 H1 Petropavlovsk-Kamchatskiy Rus. Fed.
139 G1 Petropavlovskoye Kazakh.
171 J2 Petroșani Romania
139 G1 Petrovka Kazakh.
138 B1 Petrovka Rus. Fed.
173 H4 Petrovsk Rus. Fed.
146 C1 Petrovsk-Zabaykal'skiy Rus. Fed.
173 H5 Petrov Val Rus. Fed.
172 E2 Petrozavodsk Rus. Fed.
181 F4 Petrusburg S. Africa
181 H3 Petrus Steyn S. Africa
180 F5 Petrusville S. Africa
164 C2 Petten Neth.
163 D3 Pettigo U.K.
132 H4 Petukhovo Rus. Fed.
154 A4 Peureula Indon.
133 S3 Pevek Rus. Fed.
168 H6 Pezinok Slovakia
165 F5 Pfälzer Wald hills Germany
165 G6 Pforzheim Germany
168 D7 Pfullendorf Germany
165 G5 Pfungstadt Germany
181 H2 Phagameng S. Africa
144 C3 Phagwara India
181 G4 Phahameng Free State S. Africa
Phahameng S. Africa see Phagameng
181 I1 Phalaborwa S. Africa
144 C4 Phalodi India
144 B4 Phalsund India
143 A2 Phaltan India
154 A1 Phan Thai.
154 B2 Phanat Nikhom Thai.
154 B3 Phangan, Ko i. Thai.
154 B1 Phang Hoei, San Khao mts Thai.
154 A3 Phangnga Thai.
149 B6 Phăng Xi Păng mt. Vietnam
154 C2 Phanom Dong Rak, Thiu Khao mts Cambodia/Thai.
Phan Rang Vietnam see Phan Rang-Thap Cham
154 D3 Phan Rang-Thap Cham Vietnam
Phan Ri Vietnam see Phan Ri Cửa
154 D3 Phan Ri Cửa Vietnam
154 D3 Phan Thiêt Vietnam
199 D7 Pharr U.S.A.
149 C6 Phat Diêm Vietnam
154 B4 Phatthalung Thai.
154 A1 Phayao Thai.
145 H4 Phek India
187 I3 Phelps Lake Canada
154 B1 Phen Thai.
201 C5 Phenix City U.S.A.
154 A2 Phet Buri Thai.
154 B1 Phetchabun Thai.
154 C2 Phiafai Laos
154 B1 Phichai Thai.
154 B1 Phichit Thai.
199 F5 Philadelphia MS U.S.A.
203 F2 Philadelphia NY U.S.A.
203 F5 Philadelphia PA U.S.A.
198 C2 Philip U.S.A.
164 C4 Philippeville Belgium
202 C5 Philippi U.S.A.
164 B3 Philippine Neth.
216 D4 Philippine Basin sea feature N. Pacific Ocean
153 Philippines country Asia
153 C2 Philippine Sea Phil.
216 D4 Philippine Trench sea feature N. Pacific Ocean
181 F5 Philippolis S. Africa
165 G5 Philippsburg Germany
202 D4 Philipsburg U.S.A.
164 C3 Philipsdam barrage Neth.
184 D3 Philip Smith Mountains U.S.A.
180 F5 Philipstown S. Africa
126 F7 Phillip Island Australia
203 H2 Phillips ME U.S.A.
190 B3 Phillips WI U.S.A.
198 D4 Phillipsburg KS U.S.A.
203 F4 Phillipsburg NJ U.S.A.
185 I1 Phillips Inlet Canada
202 D4 Phillipston U.S.A.
203 G3 Philmont U.S.A.
187 G3 Philomena Canada
202 C6 Philpott Reservoir U.S.A.
154 B2 Phimae tourist site Thai.
154 C2 Phimun Mangsahan Thai.
181 G3 Phiritona S. Africa
154 B1 Phitsanulok Thai.
154 C3 Phnom Penh Cambodia
Phnum Pénh Cambodia see Phnom Penh
154 B4 Pho, Laem pt Thai.
197 F5 Phoenix U.S.A.
125 I2 Phoenix Islands Pacific Ocean
125 I2 Phoenix Islands Protected Area res. Kiribati
181 G3 Phomolong S. Africa
154 B2 Phon Thai.
147 C4 Phôngsali Laos
149 B6 Phong Thô Vietnam
154 B1 Phon Phisai Thai.
154 B1 Phônsavan Laos
154 B1 Phônsavan mt. Laos
154 B1 Phon Thong Thai.
126 E7 Phoques Bay Australia
154 B1 Phrae Thai.
154 A1 Phrao Thai.
154 B2 Phra Phutthabat Thai.
154 A3 Phra Thong, Ko i. Thai.
154 C1 Phu Bai Vietnam
149 B6 Phuc Yên Vietnam
Phu Hôi Vietnam see Van Gia
154 A4 Phuket Thai.
154 A4 Phuket, Ko i. Thai.
144 C4 Phulera India
145 G5 Phultala Bangl.
149 B6 Phu Ly Vietnam
154 B2 Phumĭ Bâvĭl Cambodia
154 C2 Phumĭ Boêng Cambodia
154 C3 Phumĭ Chhuk Cambodia
154 C2 Phumĭ Kâmpóng Trâbêk Cambodia
154 B3 Phumĭ Kaôh Kŏng Cambodia
154 B2 Phumĭ Kiliěk Cambodia
154 C2 Phumĭ Mlu Prey Cambodia
154 B2 Phumĭ Moŭng Cambodia
154 B2 Phumĭ Prâmaôy Cambodia
154 B2 Phumĭ Sâmraông Cambodia
154 D2 Phu My Vietnam
Phu Nhơn Vietnam see Chư Sê
154 C3 Phước Hai Vietnam
154 C3 Phước Long Vietnam
Phu Quôc Vietnam see Dương Đông
154 B3 Phu Quôc, Đao i. Vietnam
154 D3 Phu Quy, Đao i. Vietnam
181 H4 Phuthaditjhaba S. Africa
Phư Tho Vietnam see Phu Tho
149 B6 Phu Tho Vietnam
154 B1 Phu Wiang Thai.
211 I5 Piaca Brazil
170 C2 Piacenza Italy
127 H3 Pian r. Australia
148 D2 Pianguan China
170 D3 Pianosa, Isola i. Italy
169 M7 Piatra Neamț Romania
211 J5 Piauí r. Brazil
170 E1 Piave r. Italy
177 F4 Pibor r. South Sudan
177 F4 Pibor Post South Sudan
190 D1 Pic r. Canada
197 F4 Pica U.S.A.
197 G5 Picacho AZ U.S.A.
197 E5 Picacho CA U.S.A.
166 F2 Picardy reg. France
201 B6 Picayune U.S.A.
206 C1 Picháchic Mex.
212 D2 Pichanal Arg.
215 C2 Pichi Ciego Arg.
215 B2 Pichilemu Chile
206 B2 Pichilingue Mex.
215 D3 Pichi Mahuida Arg.
144 D4 Pichor India
207 F4 Pichucalco Mex.
190 D1 Pic Island Canada
160 G3 Pickering U.K.
160 G3 Pickering, Vale of val. U.K.
190 E2 Pickford U.S.A.
188 B3 Pickle Lake Canada
156 A6 Pico, Ponta do i. Azores
206 H5 Pico Bonito, Parque Nacional nat. park Hond.
213 D4 Pico da Neblina, Parque Nacional do nat. park Brazil
207 E4 Pico de Orizaba, Parque Nacional nat. park Mex.
211 J5 Picos Brazil
212 C7 Pico Truncado Arg.
190 D1 Pic River Canada
127 I5 Picton Australia
191 I4 Picton Canada
127 G9 Picton, Mount Australia
189 H4 Pictou Canada
190 D2 Pictured Rocks National Lakeshore nature res. U.S.A.
215 C3 Picún Leufú r. Arg.
141 F5 Pidarak Pak.
143 C5 Pidurutalagala mt. Sri Lanka
213 B3 Piedecuesta Col.
215 C1 Pie de Palo, Sierra mts Arg.
201 C5 Piedmont U.S.A.
202 C4 Piedmont Lake U.S.A.
215 F2 Piedras, Punta pt Arg.
210 D6 Piedras, Río de las r. Peru
206 D1 Piedras Negras Coahuila Mex.
207 E4 Piedras Negras Veracruz Mex.
190 C1 Pie Island Canada
158 N3 Pieksämäki Fin.
158 N3 Pielavesi Fin.
158 O3 Pielinen l. Fin.
181 H2 Pienaarsrivier S. Africa
190 E5 Pierceton U.S.A.
196 A2 Piercy U.S.A.
171 J4 Pieria mts Greece
162 F1 Pierowall U.K.
198 C2 Pierre U.S.A.
166 G4 Pierrelatte France
181 I4 Pietermaritzburg S. Africa
Pietersburg S. Africa see Polokwane
170 G5 Pietra Spada, Passo di pass Italy
Piet Retief S. Africa see eMkhondo
169 L7 Pietrosa mt. Romania
191 F4 Pigeon U.S.A.
191 F5 Pigeon Bay Canada
202 D6 Pigg r. U.S.A.
199 F4 Piggott U.S.A.
181 I2 Pigg's Peak Swaziland
215 D3 Pigüé Arg.
207 E3 Piguicas mt. Mex.
144 E4 Pihani India
148 E3 Pi He r. China
159 O3 Pihlajavesi l. Fin.
159 M3 Pihlava Fin.
158 N3 Pihtipudas Fin.
158 N2 Piippola Fin.
158 O2 Piispajärvi Fin.
207 F5 Pijijiapan Mex.
172 E3 Pikalevo Rus. Fed.
202 D3 Pike U.S.A.
191 G3 Pike Bay Canada
122 E2 Pikelot i. Micronesia
192 F4 Pikes Peak U.S.A.
180 C6 Piketberg S. Africa
202 B6 Pikeville U.S.A.
152 B4 Pikou China
215 E3 Pila Arg.
168 H4 Piła Poland
181 G2 Pilanesberg National Park S. Africa
215 E2 Pilar Arg.
212 E3 Pilar Para.
153 B5 Pilas i. Phil.
215 B4 Pilcaniyeu Arg.
212 E2 Pilcomayo r. Bol./Para.
153 B3 Pili Phil.
144 D3 Pilibhit India
127 H9 Pillar, Cape Australia
149 □ Pillar Pt Hong Kong China
127 H3 Pilliga Australia
215 E2 Pillo, Isla del i. Arg.
214 C2 Pilões, Serra dos mts Brazil
196 D2 Pilot Peak U.S.A.
199 F6 Pilottown U.S.A.
159 M4 Piltene Latvia
210 F6 Pimenta Bueno Brazil
144 C5 Pimpalner India
144 D2 Pin r. India
197 F6 Pinacate, Cerro del mt. Mex.
144 D4 Pinahat India
197 G5 Pinaleno Mountains U.S.A.
153 B3 Pinamalayan Phil.
215 F3 Pinamar Arg.
155 B1 Pinang i. Malaysia
136 F2 Pınarbaşı Turkey
205 H4 Pinar del Río Cuba
173 C7 Pinarhisar Turkey
153 B3 Pinatubo, Mount vol. Phil.
169 J5 Pińczów Poland
144 D3 Pindar r. India
211 I4 Pindaré r. Brazil
144 C2 Pindi Gheb Pak.
Pindos mts Greece see Pindus Mountains
145 E3 Pindu Pass China
171 I5 Pindus Mountains Greece
197 G4 Pine U.S.A.
190 E3 Pine r. MI U.S.A.
190 E4 Pine r. MI U.S.A.
190 C3 Pine r. WI U.S.A.
189 J4 Pine, Cape Canada
199 E5 Pine Bluff U.S.A.
194 F3 Pine Bluffs U.S.A.
190 A3 Pine City U.S.A.
124 D3 Pine Creek Australia
202 E4 Pine Creek r. U.S.A.
196 B2 Pinecrest U.S.A.
196 C3 Pinedale CA U.S.A.
194 E3 Pinedale WY U.S.A.
187 J4 Pine Falls Canada
196 C3 Pine Flat Lake U.S.A.
172 G1 Pinega Rus. Fed.
172 G1 Pinega r. Rus. Fed.
203 E4 Pine Grove U.S.A.
201 D6 Pine Hills U.S.A.
187 H3 Pinehouse Lake Canada
190 A3 Pine Island U.S.A.
129 B3 Pine Island Bay b. Antarctica
203 F3 Pine Lake U.S.A.
199 E6 Pineland U.S.A.
196 B4 Pine Mountain U.S.A.
197 F4 Pine Peak U.S.A.
186 G2 Pine Point (abandoned) Canada
196 C3 Pineridge U.S.A.
198 C3 Pine Ridge U.S.A.
170 B2 Pinerolo Italy
199 E5 Pines, Lake o' the U.S.A.
181 I4 Pinetown S. Africa
202 B6 Pineville KY U.S.A.
199 E6 Pineville LA U.S.A.
202 C6 Pineville WV U.S.A.
154 B2 Ping, Mae Nam r. Thai.
148 B2 Ping'an China
149 B6 Pingbian China
148 F3 Ping Dao i. China
148 D2 Pingding China
148 D3 Pingdingshan China
148 F2 Pingdu China
152 C2 Pinggang China
149 C6 Pingguo China
149 E5 Pinghe China
149 D4 Pingjiang China
149 D5 Pingle China
148 C3 Pingli China
148 C3 Pingliang China
148 D2 Pinglu China
148 C2 Pingluo China
149 F5 Pingnan Fujian China
149 D6 Pingnan Guangxi China
148 E3 Pingqiao China
148 F1 Pingquan China
148 E2 Pingshan China
149 D5 Pingshi China
149 F5 Pingtan China
149 C5 Pingtang China
149 F6 P'ingtung Taiwan
148 B3 Pingwu China
149 C6 Pingxiang Guangxi China
149 D5 Pingxiang Jiangxi China
149 F5 Pingyang China
148 D2 Pingyao China
148 E3 Pingyi China
148 E2 Pingyin China
148 E3 Pingyu China
149 B6 Pingyuan China
149 E5 Pingyuan China
149 □ Ping Yuen Ho r. Hong Kong China
Pingzhai China see Liuzhi
211 I4 Pinheiro Brazil
215 G1 Pinheiro Machado Brazil
161 D7 Pinhoe U.K.
155 A2 Pini i. Indon.
186 E3 Pink Mountain Canada
128 D4 Pinnacle mt. N.Z.
126 D5 Pinnaroo Australia
165 H1 Pinneberg Germany
196 C4 Pinos, Mount U.S.A.
207 E4 Pinotepa Nacional Mex.
125 G4 Pins, Île des i. New Caledonia
191 G4 Pins, Pointe aux pt Canada
173 C4 Pinsk Belarus
210 □ Pinta, Isla i. Galapagos Is Ecuador
197 F5 Pinta, Sierra h. U.S.A.
197 F3 Pintura U.S.A.
197 E3 Pioche U.S.A.
179 C4 Piodi Dem. Rep. Congo
132 J1 Pioner, Ostrov i. Rus. Fed.
169 J3 Pionerskiy Rus. Fed.
169 J5 Pionki Poland
128 E3 Piopio N.Z.
210 F4 Piorini, Lago l. Brazil
169 I5 Piotrków Trybunalski Poland
141 F5 Pīp Iran
152 E2 Pipa Dingzi mt. China
144 C4 Pipar India
144 D5 Piparia India
171 K5 Piperi i. Greece
196 D3 Piper Peak U.S.A.
197 F3 Pipe Spring National Monument nat. park U.S.A.
188 B3 Pipestone r. Canada
198 D3 Pipestone U.S.A.
128 E3 Pipiriki N.Z.
144 B2 Piplan Pak.
144 C3 Pipli India
189 F4 Pipmuacan, Réservoir resr Canada
145 E4 Pipra Dam India
139 J4 Piqanlik China
202 A4 Piqua U.S.A.
214 A2 Piquiri r. Mato Grosso do Sul Brazil
214 B4 Piquiri r. Paraná Brazil
214 C2 Piracanjuba Brazil
214 C3 Piracicaba Brazil
214 D2 Piracicaba r. Minas Gerais Brazil
214 C3 Piracicaba r. São Paulo Brazil
214 C3 Piraçununga Brazil
211 J4 Piracuruca Brazil
171 J6 Piraeus Greece
214 C4 Piraí do Sul Brazil
214 C3 Pirajuí Brazil
144 C5 Piram Island India
214 B2 Piranhas Brazil
214 B2 Piranhas r. Goiás Brazil
211 K5 Piranhas r. Brazil
213 C4 Piraparaná r. Col.
214 B3 Pirapó r. Brazil
214 D2 Pirapora Brazil
215 G1 Piratini Brazil
215 G1 Piratini r. Brazil
144 D4 Pirawa India
215 C4 Pire Mahuida, Sierra mts Arg.
214 C2 Pires do Rio Brazil
145 G4 Pirganj Bangl.
211 J4 Piripiri Brazil
213 C2 Píritu Venez.
214 A2 Pirizal Brazil
164 F5 Pirmasens Germany
171 J3 Pirot Serbia
144 C2 Pir Panjal Pass India
144 C2 Pir Panjal Range mts India/Pak.
213 A3 Pirre, Cerro mt. Panama
137 L2 Pirsaat Azer.
137 L1 Pirsaat r. Azer.
141 F4 Pīr Shūrān, Selseleh-ye mts Iran
147 E7 Piru Indon.
170 D3 Pisa Italy
128 B6 Pisa, Mount N.Z.
212 B1 Pisagua Chile
203 F4 Piscataway U.S.A.
210 C6 Pisco Peru
210 C6 Pisco, Bahía de b. Peru
203 F3 Piseco Lake U.S.A.
168 G6 Písek Czech Rep.
139 I5 Pishan China
141 F5 Pīshīn Iran
144 A3 Pishin Pak.
141 G4 Pishin Lora r. Pak.
212 C3 Pissis, Cerro mt. Arg.
207 G3 Pisté Mex.
170 G4 Pisticci Italy
170 D3 Pistoia Italy
167 D1 Pisuerga r. Spain
194 B3 Pit r. U.S.A.
176 A3 Pita Guinea
189 G3 Pitaga Canada
207 G4 Pital Mex.
213 A4 Pitalito Col.
214 B4 Pitanga Brazil
214 D2 Pitangui Brazil
126 E5 Pitarpunga Lake imp. l. Australia
123 J7 Pitcairn Island S. Pacific Ocean
123 J7 Pitcairn Islands terr. Pacific Ocean
158 M2 Piteå Sweden
158 M2 Piteälven r. Sweden
173 H5 Piterka Rus. Fed.
171 K2 Pitești Romania
143 C2 Pithapuram India
195 D6 Pitiquito Mex.
172 D2 Pitkyaranta Rus. Fed.
162 E4 Pitlochry U.K.
207 H5 Pito Solo Hond.
215 B3 Pitrufquén Chile
181 F2 Pitsane Siding Botswana
162 F4 Pitscottie U.K.
186 D4 Pitt Island Canada
125 I6 Pitt Island Pacific Ocean
199 E4 Pittsburg U.S.A.
202 D4 Pittsburgh U.S.A.
190 B6 Pittsfield IL U.S.A.
203 G3 Pittsfield MA U.S.A.
203 I2 Pittsfield ME U.S.A.
203 H3 Pittsfield NH U.S.A.
203 G3 Pittsfield VT U.S.A.
127 I1 Pittsworth Australia
187 J2 Pitz Lake Canada
214 D3 Piumhí Brazil
210 B5 Piura Peru
196 C4 Piute Peak U.S.A.
145 E3 Piuthan Nepal
169 N6 Pivdennyy Buh r. Ukr.
170 F2 Pivka Slovenia
207 G4 Pixoyal Mex.
172 H3 Pizhma Rus. Fed.
172 H3 Pizhma r. Rus. Fed.
148 F3 Pizhou China
189 J4 Placentia Canada
189 J4 Placentia Bay Canada
153 B4 Placer Phil.
153 C4 Placer Phil.
196 B2 Placerville U.S.A.
205 I4 Placetas Cuba
154 B2 Plai Mat, Lam r. Thai.
203 H4 Plainfield CT U.S.A.
190 C5 Plainfield IL U.S.A.
190 C3 Plainfield WI U.S.A.
190 A3 Plainview MN U.S.A.
198 D3 Plainview NE U.S.A.
199 C5 Plainview TX U.S.A.
203 I1 Plaisted U.S.A.
186 G4 Plamondon Canada
155 E4 Plampang Indon.
165 K5 Planá Czech Rep.
196 B3 Planada U.S.A.
214 C1 Planaltina Brazil
215 B2 Planchón, Paso del pass Arg.
213 B2 Planeta Rica Col.
198 D3 Plankinton U.S.A.
190 C5 Plano IL U.S.A.
199 D5 Plano TX U.S.A.
201 D7 Plantation U.S.A.
199 F6 Plaquemine U.S.A.
167 C2 Plasencia Spain
138 E1 Plast Rus. Fed.
203 J1 Plaster Rock Canada
150 E2 Plastun Rus. Fed.
170 E6 Platani r. Sicily Italy
181 H4 Platberg mt. S. Africa
133 U4 Platinum U.S.A.
213 B2 Plato Col.
198 C3 Platte r. U.S.A.
190 B4 Platteville U.S.A.
165 K6 Plattling Germany
203 G2 Plattsburgh U.S.A.
198 E3 Plattsmouth U.S.A.
165 K1 Plau Germany
165 K4 Plauen Germany
165 K1 Plauer See l. Germany
172 F4 Plavsk Rus. Fed.
195 E6 Playa Noriega, Lago l. Mex.
210 B4 Playas Ecuador
187 J4 Playgreen Lake Canada
154 D2 Plây Ku Vietnam
206 B2 Playón Mex.
215 C3 Plaza Huincul Arg.
197 F5 Pleasant, Lake l. U.S.A.
203 I4 Pleasant Bay U.S.A.
197 G1 Pleasant Grove U.S.A.
197 H5 Pleasanton NM U.S.A.
199 D6 Pleasanton TX U.S.A.
128 C6 Pleasant Point N.Z.
197 H3 Pleasant View U.S.A.
203 F5 Pleasantville U.S.A.
200 C4 Pleasure Ridge Park U.S.A.
166 F4 Pleaux France
154 C2 Plei Doch Vietnam
154 C2 Plei Kân Vietnam
165 I5 Pleinfeld Germany
128 F2 Plenty, Bay of g. N.Z.
194 F1 Plentywood U.S.A.
172 G2 Plesetsk Rus. Fed.
189 F3 Plétipi, Lac l. Canada
165 F3 Plettenberg Germany
180 E7 Plettenberg Bay S. Africa
171 K3 Pleven Bulg.
171 H3 Pljevlja Montenegro
169 I4 Płock Poland
170 G3 Pločno mt. Bos.-Herz.
172 D2 Plodovoye Rus. Fed.
166 C3 Ploemeur France
171 L2 Ploiești Romania
169 O2 Ploskosh' Rus. Fed.
172 G3 Ploskoye Rus. Fed.
168 G4 Płoty Poland
166 B2 Ploudalmézeau France
166 B2 Plouzané France
171 K3 Plovdiv Bulg.
190 C3 Plover U.S.A.
190 C3 Plover r. U.S.A.
149 □ Plover Cove Reservoir Hong Kong China
203 G4 Plum Island U.S.A.
194 C2 Plummer U.S.A.
159 M5 Plungė Lith.
169 M3 Plyeshchanitsy Belarus
154 A1 Ply Huey Wati, Khao mt. Myanmar/Thai.
161 C7 Plymouth U.K.
196 B2 Plymouth CA U.S.A.
190 D5 Plymouth IN U.S.A.
203 H4 Plymouth MA U.S.A.
203 H3 Plymouth NH U.S.A.
200 F3 Plymouth PA U.S.A.
190 D4 Plymouth WI U.S.A.
203 H4 Plymouth Bay U.S.A.
161 D5 Plynlimon h. U.K.
168 F6 Plzeň Czech Rep.
176 B3 Pô Burkina Faso
170 D2 Po r. Italy
219 P10 Pobeda Ice Island Antarctica
139 J4 Pobeda Peak China/Kyrg.
199 F4 Pocahontas U.S.A.
202 C5 Pocatalico r. U.S.A.
194 D3 Pocatello U.S.A.
173 C5 Pochayiv Ukr.
172 E4 Pochep Rus. Fed.
172 H4 Pochinki Rus. Fed.
172 E4 Pochinok Rus. Fed.
168 F6 Pocking Germany
160 G4 Pocklington U.K.
214 E1 Poções Brazil
203 F5 Pocomoke City U.S.A.
203 F6 Pocomoke Sound b. U.S.A.
214 A2 Poconé Brazil
203 F4 Pocono Mountains hills U.S.A.
203 F4 Pocono Summit U.S.A.
214 C3 Poços de Caldas Brazil
172 D3 Poddor'ye Rus. Fed.
173 F5 Podgorenskiy Rus. Fed.
171 H3 Podgorica Montenegro
132 J4 Podgornoye Rus. Fed.
143 B3 Podile India
133 K3 Podkamennaya Tunguska r. Rus. Fed.
138 A2 Podlesnoye Rus. Fed.
210 C4 Podocarpus, Parque Nacional nat. park Ecuador

172 F4 **Podol'sk** Rus. Fed.
172 E2 **Podporozh'ye** Rus. Fed.
170 G1 **Podravina** *reg.* Hungary
171 I3 **Podujevë** Kosovo
172 H2 **Podvoloch'ye** Rus. Fed.
172 I2 **Podz'** Rus. Fed.
180 C4 **Pofadder** S. Africa
191 G2 **Pogamasing** Canada
173 E4 **Pogar** Rus. Fed.
170 D3 **Poggibonsi** Italy
171 I4 **Pogradec** Albania
150 B2 **Pogranichnyy** Rus. Fed.
214 A2 **Poguba** *r.* Brazil
152 E5 **Pohang** S. Korea
123 F2 **Pohnpei** *atoll* Micronesia
173 D5 **Pohrebyshche** Ukr.
144 D4 **Pohri** India
171 J3 **Poiana Mare** Romania
178 C4 **Poie** Dem. Rep. Congo
145 G3 **Poindo** China
129 D6 **Poinsett, Cape** *c.* Antarctica
196 A2 **Point Arena** U.S.A.
191 J2 **Point-Comfort** Canada
205 L5 **Pointe-à-Pitre** Guadeloupe
191 G3 **Pointe au Baril Station** Canada
178 B4 **Pointe-Noire** Congo
184 B3 **Point Hope** U.S.A.
126 A4 **Point Kenny** Australia
186 G1 **Point Lake** Canada
127 J3 **Point Lookout** *mt.* Australia
**Point Nepean National Park** *nat. park* Australia *see* **Mornington Peninsula National Park**
191 F5 **Point Pelee National Park** Canada
203 F4 **Point Pleasant** *NJ* U.S.A.
202 B5 **Point Pleasant** *WV* U.S.A.
191 J3 **Poisson Blanc, Lac du** *l.* Canada
166 E3 **Poitiers** France
166 D3 **Poitou** *reg.* France
214 E1 **Pojuca** Brazil
144 B4 **Pokaran** India
127 H2 **Pokataroo** Australia
145 E3 **Pokhara** Nepal
144 A4 **Pokhran Landi** Pak.
138 C1 **Pokhvistnevo** Rus. Fed.
178 C3 **Poko** Dem. Rep. Congo
139 G2 **Pokrovka** Kazakh.
150 B3 **Pokrovka** *Primorskiy Kray* Rus. Fed.
150 C2 **Pokrovka** *Primorskiy Kray* Rus. Fed.
133 N3 **Pokrovsk** Rus. Fed.
173 F6 **Pokrovskoye** Rus. Fed.
172 H2 **Pokshen'ga** *r.* Rus. Fed.
153 B3 **Pola** Phil.
197 G4 **Polacca** U.S.A.
197 G4 **Polacca Wash** *watercourse* U.S.A.
**Pola de Siero** Spain *see* **La Pola Siero**
168 H4 **Poland** *country* Europe
203 F3 **Poland** U.S.A.
188 D3 **Polar Bear Provincial Park** Canada
129 C4 **Polar Plateau** *plat.* Antarctica
136 D2 **Polatlı** Turkey
172 D4 **Polatsk** Belarus
169 M3 **Polatskaya Nizina** *lowland* Belarus
143 C2 **Polavaram** India
158 M2 **Polcirkeln** Sweden
172 H2 **Poldarsa** Rus. Fed.
140 B2 **Pol Dasht** Iran
140 D4 **Pol-e Fāsā** Iran
**Pole-Khatum** Iran *see* **Pol-e Khātūn**
141 F2 **Pol-e Khātūn** Iran
172 B4 **Polessk** Rus. Fed.
155 E3 **Polewali** Indon.
177 D4 **Poli** Cameroon
168 G4 **Police** Poland
170 G4 **Policoro** Italy
166 G3 **Poligny** France
153 B3 **Polillo** *i.* Phil.
153 B3 **Polillo Islands** Phil.
153 B3 **Polillo Strait** Phil.
136 D4 **Polis** Cyprus
173 D5 **Polis'ke** Ukr.
168 H5 **Polkowice** Poland
143 B4 **Pollachi** India
165 H3 **Polle** Germany
167 H3 **Pollença** Spain
170 G5 **Pollino, Monte** *mt.* Italy
158 N1 **Polmak** Norway
158 O2 **Polo** Fin.
190 C5 **Polo** U.S.A.
173 F6 **Polohy** Ukr.
181 H1 **Polokwane** S. Africa
181 H1 **Polokwane** *r.* S. Africa
172 I3 **Polom** Rus. Fed.
153 C5 **Polomolok** Phil.
143 C5 **Polonnaruwa** Sri Lanka
173 C5 **Polonne** Ukr.
161 C7 **Polperro** U.K.
194 D2 **Polson** U.S.A.
172 G1 **Polta** *r.* Rus. Fed.
173 E5 **Poltava** Ukr.
150 B2 **Poltavka** Rus. Fed.
173 F6 **Poltavskaya** Rus. Fed.
159 N4 **Põltsamaa** Estonia
159 N4 **Põlva** Estonia
158 O3 **Polvijärvi** Fin.
133 S3 **Polyarnyy** Rus. Fed.
158 P1 **Polyarnyy** *Murmanskaya Oblast'* Rus. Fed.
158 P2 **Polyarnyye Zori** Rus. Fed.
171 J4 **Polygyros** Greece
171 J4 **Polykastro** Greece
216 H6 **Polynesia** *is* Oceania
159 M3 **Pomarkku** Fin.
214 D3 **Pomba** *r.* Brazil
167 B3 **Pombal** Port.
214 B3 **Pombo** *r.* Brazil
168 G3 **Pomeranian Bay** Poland
212 G3 **Pomerode** Brazil
181 I4 **Pomeroy** S. Africa
163 E3 **Pomeroy** U.K.
202 B5 **Pomeroy** U.S.A.
170 E4 **Pomezia** Italy
180 E2 **Pomfret** S. Africa
124 F2 **Pomio** P.N.G.
196 D4 **Pomona** U.S.A.
171 L3 **Pomorie** Bulg.
**Pomorska, Zatoka** *b.* Poland *see* **Pomeranian Bay**
172 E1 **Pomorskiy Bereg** *coastal area* Rus. Fed.
201 D7 **Pompano Beach** U.S.A.
170 F4 **Pompei** Italy
214 D2 **Pompéu** Brazil
172 H3 **Ponazyrevo** Rus. Fed.
199 D4 **Ponca City** U.S.A.
205 K5 **Ponce** Puerto Rico
195 F4 **Poncha Springs** U.S.A.
188 E3 **Poncheville, Lac** *l.* Canada
**Pondicherry** India *see* **Puducherry**
185 K2 **Pond Inlet** Canada
189 I3 **Ponds, Island of** Canada
206 H5 **Poneloya** Nicaragua
167 C1 **Ponferrada** Spain
128 F4 **Pongaroa** N.Z.
177 E4 **Pongo** *watercourse* South Sudan
181 I3 **Pongola** *r.* S. Africa
181 I3 **Pongolapoort Dam** *l.* S. Africa
169 O3 **Ponizov'ye** Rus. Fed.
143 B3 **Ponnaiyar** *r.* India
143 A4 **Ponnani** India
145 H5 **Ponnyadaung Range** *mts* Myanmar
186 G4 **Ponoka** Canada
138 C1 **Ponomarevka** Rus. Fed.
156 A6 **Ponta Delgada** Azores
176 □ **Ponta do Sol** Cape Verde
214 B4 **Ponta Grossa** Brazil
214 C2 **Pontalina** Brazil
166 H2 **Pont-à-Mousson** France
214 A3 **Ponta Porã** Brazil
166 H3 **Pontarlier** France
199 F6 **Pontchartrain, Lake** U.S.A.
161 D5 **Pontcysyllte Aqueduct and Canal** *tourist site* U.K.
164 C4 **Pont-de-Loup** Belgium
167 B3 **Ponte de Sor** Port.
160 F4 **Pontefract** U.K.
160 F2 **Ponteland** U.K.
211 G7 **Pontes e Lacerda** Brazil
167 B1 **Pontevedra** Spain
190 C5 **Pontiac** *IL* U.S.A.
191 F4 **Pontiac** *MI* U.S.A.
155 C3 **Pontianak** Indon.
166 C2 **Pontivy** France
166 B3 **Pont-l'Abbé** France
166 F2 **Pontoise** France
187 J4 **Ponton** Canada
199 F5 **Pontotoc** U.S.A.
170 C2 **Pontremoli** Italy
164 A5 **Pont-Ste-Maxence** France
127 G9 **Pontville** Australia
191 H3 **Pontypool** Canada
161 D6 **Pontypool** U.K.
161 D6 **Pontypridd** U.K.
170 E4 **Ponza, Isola di** *i.* Italy
170 E4 **Ponziane, Isole** *is* Italy
126 A4 **Poochera** Australia
161 F7 **Poole** U.K.
**Poona** India *see* **Pune**
126 E4 **Pooncarie** Australia
126 F3 **Poopelloe Lake** *salt l.* Australia
210 E7 **Poopó, Lago de** *l.* Bol.
128 E1 **Poor Knights Islands** N.Z.
139 G4 **Pop** Uzbek.
213 A4 **Popayán** Col.
164 A4 **Poperinge** Belgium
133 L2 **Popigay** *r.* Rus. Fed.
126 D4 **Popiltah** Australia
126 D4 **Popilta Lake** *imp. l.* Australia
187 J4 **Poplar** *r.* Canada
194 F1 **Poplar** U.S.A.
199 F4 **Poplar Bluff** U.S.A.
202 C6 **Poplar Camp** U.S.A.
199 F6 **Poplarville** U.S.A.
207 E4 **Popocatépetl, Volcán** *vol.* Mex.
178 B4 **Popokabaka** Dem. Rep. Congo
171 L3 **Popovo** Bulg.
165 I3 **Poppenberg** *h.* Germany
169 J6 **Poprad** Slovakia
141 G5 **Porali** *r.* Pak.
128 F4 **Porangahau** N.Z.
214 C1 **Porangatu** Brazil
144 B5 **Porbandar** India
213 B3 **Porce** *r.* Col.
186 C4 **Porcher Island** Canada
184 E3 **Porcupine** *r.* Canada/U.S.A.
189 I3 **Porcupine, Cape** Canada
219 H2 **Porcupine Abyssal Plain** *sea feature* N. Atlantic Ocean
187 I4 **Porcupine Hills** Canada
190 C2 **Porcupine Mountains** U.S.A.
187 I4 **Porcupine Plain** Canada
187 I4 **Porcupine Provincial Forest** *nature res.* Canada
213 C3 **Pore** Col.
170 E2 **Poreč** Croatia
172 H4 **Poretskoye** Rus. Fed.
159 M3 **Pori** Fin.
128 E4 **Porirua** N.Z.
172 D3 **Porkhov** Rus. Fed.
213 E2 **Porlamar** Venez.
166 C3 **Pornic** France
153 C4 **Poro** *i.* Phil.
146 G2 **Poronaysk** Rus. Fed.
145 G3 **Porong** China
171 J6 **Poros** Greece
172 E2 **Porosozero** Rus. Fed.
**Porsangen** *sea chan.* Norway *see* **Porsangerfjorden**
158 N1 **Porsangerfjorden** *sea chan.* Norway
159 J4 **Porsgrunn** Norway
136 C2 **Porsuk** *r.* Turkey
126 C5 **Port Adelaide** Australia
163 E3 **Portadown** U.K.
163 F3 **Portaferry** U.K.
203 I1 **Portage** *ME* U.S.A.
190 E4 **Portage** *MI* U.S.A.
190 C4 **Portage** *WI* U.S.A.
187 J5 **Portage la Prairie** Canada
198 C1 **Portal** U.S.A.
186 E5 **Port Alberni** Canada
127 G7 **Port Albert** Australia
167 C3 **Portalegre** Port.
199 C5 **Portales** U.S.A.
186 C3 **Port Alexander** U.S.A.
181 G6 **Port Alfred** S. Africa
186 D4 **Port Alice** Canada
202 D4 **Port Allegany** U.S.A.
199 F6 **Port Allen** U.S.A.
194 B1 **Port Angeles** U.S.A.
163 D4 **Portarlington** Ireland
127 G9 **Port Arthur** Australia
199 E6 **Port Arthur** U.S.A.
162 B5 **Port Askaig** U.K.
126 B4 **Port Augusta** Australia
205 J5 **Port-au-Prince** Haiti
191 F3 **Port Austin** U.S.A.
189 I3 **Port aux Choix** Canada
163 F3 **Portavogie** U.K.
180 D7 **Port Beaufort** S. Africa
135 H5 **Port Blair** India
191 H3 **Port Bolster** Canada
167 H1 **Portbou** Spain
191 G4 **Port Burwell** Canada
126 E7 **Port Campbell** Australia
191 H3 **Port Carling** Canada
128 C6 **Port Chalmers** N.Z.
201 D7 **Port Charlotte** U.S.A.
203 G4 **Port Chester** U.S.A.
186 C4 **Port Clements** Canada
202 B4 **Port Clinton** U.S.A.
203 I3 **Port Clyde** U.S.A.
191 H4 **Port Colborne** Canada
186 E5 **Port Coquitlam** Canada
191 H4 **Port Credit** Canada
127 F9 **Port Davey** *b.* Australia
205 J5 **Port-de-Paix** Haiti
154 B5 **Port Dickson** Malaysia
202 C3 **Port Dover** Canada
190 D3 **Porte des Morts** *lake channel* U.S.A.
186 C4 **Port Edward** Canada
181 I5 **Port Edward** S. Africa
190 C3 **Port Edwards** U.S.A.
214 D1 **Porteirinha** Brazil
211 H4 **Portel** Brazil
191 G3 **Port Elgin** Canada
181 F6 **Port Elizabeth** S. Africa
162 B5 **Port Ellen** U.K.
126 C5 **Port Elliot** Australia
160 C3 **Port Erin** U.K.
187 H2 **Porter Lake** Canada
186 C3 **Porter Landing** Canada
180 C6 **Porterville** S. Africa
196 C3 **Porterville** U.S.A.
126 E7 **Port Fairy** Australia
128 E2 **Port Fitzroy** N.Z.
136 D6 **Port Fuad** Egypt
178 A4 **Port-Gentil** Gabon
126 C4 **Port Germein** Australia
199 F6 **Port Gibson** U.S.A.
162 D5 **Port Glasgow** U.K.
176 C4 **Port Harcourt** Nigeria
186 D4 **Port Hardy** Canada
**Port Harrison** Canada *see* **Inukjuak**
189 H4 **Port Hawkesbury** Canada
161 D6 **Porthcawl** U.K.
124 B4 **Port Hedland** Australia
203 G2 **Port Henry** U.S.A.
161 B7 **Porthleven** U.K.
161 C5 **Porthmadog** U.K.
191 H4 **Port Hope** Canada
189 I3 **Port Hope Simpson** Canada
191 F4 **Port Huron** U.S.A.
167 B4 **Portimão** Port.
149 □ **Port Island** *Hong Kong* China
127 I4 **Port Jackson** *inlet* Australia
203 G4 **Port Jefferson** U.S.A.
203 F4 **Port Jervis** U.S.A.
210 G2 **Port Kaituma** Guyana
127 I5 **Port Kembla** Australia
127 H4 **Portland** *N.S.W.* Australia
126 D7 **Portland** *Vic.* Australia
190 E5 **Portland** *IN* U.S.A.
203 H3 **Portland** *ME* U.S.A.
194 B2 **Portland** *OR* U.S.A.
161 E7 **Portland, Isle of** *pen.* U.K.
186 C3 **Portland Canal** *inlet* Canada
128 F3 **Portland Island** N.Z.
163 D4 **Portlaoise** Ireland
199 D6 **Port Lavaca** U.S.A.
163 D5 **Portlaw** Ireland
162 F3 **Portlethen** U.K.
126 A5 **Port Lincoln** Australia
176 A4 **Port Loko** Sierra Leone
126 D7 **Port MacDonnell** Australia
127 J3 **Port Macquarie** Australia
189 H2 **Port Manvers** *inlet* Canada
186 D4 **Port McNeill** Canada
189 H4 **Port-Menier** Canada
184 B4 **Port Moller** *b.* U.S.A.
194 B1 **Port Moody** Canada
124 E2 **Port Moresby** P.N.G.
162 B2 **Portnaguran** U.K.
162 B5 **Portnahaven** U.K.
126 B5 **Port Neill** Australia
201 F7 **Port Nelson** Bahamas
**Port Nis** U.K. *see* **Port of Ness**
180 B4 **Port Nolloth** S. Africa
**Port-Nouveau-Québec** Canada *see* **Kangiqsualujjuaq**
**Porto** Port. *see* **Oporto**
210 E5 **Porto Acre** Brazil
214 B3 **Porto Alegre** *Mato Grosso do Sul* Brazil
212 F4 **Porto Alegre** Brazil
211 G6 **Porto Artur** Brazil
206 J6 **Portobelo** Panama
211 G6 **Porto dos Gaúchos Óbidos** Brazil
211 G7 **Porto Esperidião** Brazil
170 D3 **Portoferraio** Italy
162 B2 **Port of Ness** U.K.
211 I5 **Porto Franco** Brazil
213 E2 **Port of Spain** Trin. and Tob.
170 E2 **Portogruaro** Italy
214 A2 **Porto Jofre** Brazil
196 B2 **Portola** U.S.A.
170 D2 **Portomaggiore** Italy
214 A4 **Porto Mendes** Para.
211 G8 **Porto Murtinho** Brazil
211 I6 **Porto Nacional** Brazil
176 C4 **Porto-Novo** Benin
214 B3 **Porto Primavera, Represa** *resr* Brazil
194 A3 **Port Orford** U.S.A.
211 H4 **Porto Santana** Brazil
214 E2 **Porto Seguro** Brazil
170 E2 **Porto Tolle** Italy
170 C4 **Porto Torres** *Sardinia* Italy
170 C4 **Porto-Vecchio** *Corsica* France
210 F5 **Porto Velho** Brazil
210 B4 **Portoviejo** Ecuador
162 C6 **Portpatrick** U.K.
191 H3 **Port Perry** Canada
126 F7 **Port Phillip Bay** Australia
126 C4 **Port Pirie** Australia
161 B7 **Portreath** U.K.
162 B3 **Portree** U.K.
186 E5 **Port Renfrew** Canada
191 G4 **Port Rowan** Canada
202 E5 **Port Royal** U.S.A.
163 E2 **Portrush** U.K.
177 F1 **Port Said** Egypt
201 C6 **Port St Joe** U.S.A.
181 H5 **Port St Johns** S. Africa
160 C3 **Port St Mary** U.K.
163 D2 **Portsalon** Ireland
191 F4 **Port Sanilac** U.S.A.
191 H3 **Port Severn** Canada
149 □ **Port Shelter** *b. Hong Kong* China
181 I5 **Port Shepstone** S. Africa
**Port Simpson** Canada *see* **Lax Kw'alaams**
161 F7 **Portsmouth** U.K.
203 H3 **Portsmouth** *NH* U.S.A.
202 B5 **Portsmouth** *OH* U.S.A.
203 E6 **Portsmouth** *VA* U.S.A.
162 F3 **Portsoy** U.K.
127 J4 **Port Stephens** *b.* Australia
163 E2 **Portstewart** U.K.
177 F3 **Port Sudan** Sudan
201 B6 **Port Sulphur** U.S.A.
161 D6 **Port Talbot** U.K.
158 N1 **Porttipahdan tekojärvi** *resr* Fin.
167 B3 **Portugal** *country* Europe
167 E1 **Portugalete** Spain
213 C2 **Portuguesa** *r.* Venez.
163 C4 **Portumna** Ireland
166 F5 **Port-Vendres** France
126 B5 **Port Victoria** Australia
125 G3 **Port Vila** Vanuatu
158 P1 **Port-Vladimir** Rus. Fed.
128 E2 **Port Waikato** N.Z.
126 C5 **Port Wakefield** Australia
190 D4 **Port Washington** U.S.A.
162 D6 **Port William** U.K.
190 B2 **Port Wing** U.S.A.
215 D2 **Porvenir** Arg.
159 N3 **Porvoo** Fin.
167 D1 **Posada** Spain
212 E3 **Posadas** Arg.
171 H2 **Posavina** *reg.* Bos.-Herz./Croatia
191 F3 **Posen** U.S.A.
137 K5 **Posht-e Kūh** *mts* Iran
140 C2 **Posht Kūh** *h.* Iran
158 O2 **Posio** Fin.
147 E7 **Poso** Indon.
137 I1 **Posof** Turkey
139 J1 **Pospelikha** Rus. Fed.
214 C1 **Posse** Brazil
129 B5 **Possession Islands** *is* Antarctica
165 J4 **Pößneck** Germany
199 C5 **Post** U.S.A.
**Poste-de-la-Baleine** Canada *see* **Kuujjuarapik**
180 E4 **Postmasburg** S. Africa
189 I3 **Postville** Canada
190 B4 **Postville** U.S.A.
170 G3 **Posušje** Bos.-Herz.
150 B3 **Pos'yet** Rus. Fed.
181 G3 **Potchefstroom** S. Africa
199 E5 **Poteau** U.S.A.
211 K5 **Potengi** *r.* Brazil
170 F4 **Potenza** Italy
128 A7 **Poteriteri, Lake** N.Z.
180 F5 **Potfontein** S. Africa
**Potgietersrus** S. Africa *see* **Mokopane**
199 D6 **Poth** U.S.A.
211 J5 **Poti** *r.* Brazil
173 G7 **Poti** Georgia
143 C2 **Potikal** India
176 D3 **Potiskum** Nigeria
194 D2 **Pot Mountain** U.S.A.
149 □ **Po Toi** *i. Hong Kong* China
202 E5 **Potomac** *r.* U.S.A.
202 D5 **Potomac, South Branch** *r.* U.S.A.
202 D5 **Potomac, South Fork South Branch** *r.* U.S.A.
210 E7 **Potosí** Bol.
198 F4 **Potosi** U.S.A.
197 E4 **Potosi Mountain** U.S.A.
153 B4 **Pototan** Phil.
207 H5 **Potrerillos** Hond.
165 L2 **Potsdam** Germany
203 F2 **Potsdam** U.S.A.
161 E6 **Potterne** U.K.
161 G6 **Potters Bar** U.K.
203 F4 **Pottstown** U.S.A.
203 E4 **Pottsville** U.S.A.
143 C5 **Pottuvil** Sri Lanka
186 E3 **Pouce Coupe** Canada
189 J4 **Pouch Cove** Canada
203 G4 **Poughkeepsie** U.S.A.
203 G3 **Poultney** U.S.A.
160 E4 **Poulton-le-Fylde** U.K.
214 D3 **Pouso Alegre** Brazil
154 B2 **Poŭthĭsăt** Cambodia
169 I6 **Považská Bystrica** Slovakia
172 E2 **Povenets** Rus. Fed.
128 F3 **Poverty Bay** N.Z.
171 H2 **Povlen** *mt.* Serbia
167 B2 **Póvoa de Varzim** Port.
173 G5 **Povorino** Rus. Fed.
150 C3 **Povorotnyy, Mys** *hd* Rus. Fed.
196 D5 **Poway** U.S.A.
194 F2 **Powder** *r.* U.S.A.
194 F3 **Powder River** U.S.A.
194 E2 **Powell** U.S.A.
202 B6 **Powell** *r.* U.S.A.
197 G3 **Powell, Lake** *resr* U.S.A.
196 C2 **Powell Mountain** U.S.A.
201 E7 **Powell Point** Bahamas
186 E5 **Powell River** Canada
190 D3 **Powers** U.S.A.
202 E6 **Powhatan** U.S.A.
214 A1 **Poxoréu** Brazil
149 E4 **Poyang** China
149 E4 **Poyang Hu** *l.* China
154 □ **Poyan Reservoir** Sing.
190 C3 **Poygan, Lake** U.S.A.
136 E3 **Pozantı** Turkey
171 I2 **Požarevac** Serbia
207 E3 **Poza Rica** Mex.
170 G2 **Požega** Croatia
171 I3 **Požega** Serbia
150 D1 **Pozharskoye** Rus. Fed.
168 H4 **Poznań** Poland
167 D3 **Pozoblanco** Spain
206 B1 **Pozo Nuevo** Mex.
170 F4 **Pozzuoli** Italy
155 B3 **Prabumulih** Indon.
168 G6 **Prachatice** Czech Rep.
145 F6 **Prachi** *r.* India
154 B2 **Prachin Buri** Thai.
154 A3 **Prachuap Khiri Khan** Thai.
166 F5 **Prades** France
214 E2 **Prado** Brazil
168 G5 **Prague** Czech Rep.
**Praha** Czech Rep. *see* **Prague**
176 □ **Praia** Cape Verde
181 J2 **Praia do Bilene** Moz.
214 A1 **Praia Rica** Brazil
190 E5 **Prairie Creek Reservoir** U.S.A.
199 C5 **Prairie Dog Town Fork** *r.* U.S.A.
190 B4 **Prairie du Chien** U.S.A.
154 B2 **Prakhon Chai** Thai.
154 B2 **Pran** *r.* Thai.
143 B2 **Pranhita** *r.* India
144 C5 **Prantij** India
155 A2 **Prapat** Indon.
171 L7 **Prasonisi, Akrotirio** *pt* Greece
214 C2 **Prata** Brazil
214 C2 **Prata** *r.* Brazil
170 D3 **Prato** Italy
199 D4 **Pratt** U.S.A.
199 G5 **Prattville** U.S.A.
143 A2 **Pravara** *r.* India
169 J3 **Pravdinsk** Rus. Fed.
155 E4 **Praya** Indon.
**Preăh Vihear** Cambodia *see* **Preăh Vihéar**
154 C2 **Preăh Vihéar** Cambodia
169 P3 **Prechistoye** Rus. Fed.
187 I4 **Preeceville** Canada
172 B4 **Pregolya** *r.* Rus. Fed.
159 N4 **Preiļi** Latvia
191 H1 **Preissac, Lac** *l.* Canada
127 H3 **Premer** Australia
166 F3 **Prémery** France
165 K2 **Premnitz** Germany
190 B3 **Prentice** U.S.A.
168 F4 **Prenzlau** Germany
150 C3 **Preobrazheniye** Rus. Fed.
168 H6 **Přerov** Czech Rep.
203 F2 **Prescott** Canada
197 F4 **Prescott** U.S.A.
197 F4 **Prescott Valley** U.S.A.
161 C6 **Preseli, Mynydd** *hills* U.K.
171 I3 **Preševo** Serbia
198 C3 **Presho** U.S.A.
212 D3 **Presidencia Roque Sáenz Peña** Arg.
211 J5 **Presidente Dutra** Brazil
214 B3 **Presidente Epitácio** Brazil
210 F6 **Presidente Hermes** Brazil
153 B4 **Presidente Manuel A Roxas** Phil.
214 B3 **Presidente Prudente** Brazil
214 B3 **Presidente Venceslau** Brazil
199 B6 **Presidio** U.S.A.
138 F1 **Presnogor'kovka** Kazakh.
139 F1 **Presnovka** Kazakh.
169 J6 **Prešov** Slovakia
171 I4 **Prespa, Lake** Europe
203 J1 **Presque Isle** U.S.A.
190 D2 **Presque Isle Point** U.S.A.
161 D5 **Presteigne** U.K.
160 E4 **Preston** U.K.
194 E3 **Preston** *ID* U.S.A.
190 A4 **Preston** *MN* U.S.A.
199 E4 **Preston** *MO* U.S.A.
197 E2 **Preston** *NV* U.S.A.
162 F5 **Prestonpans** U.K.
202 B6 **Prestonsburg** U.S.A.
162 D5 **Prestwick** U.K.
214 E1 **Preto** *r. Bahia* Brazil
214 C2 **Preto** *r. Minas Gerais* Brazil
181 H2 **Pretoria** S. Africa
202 E5 **Prettyboy Lake** U.S.A.
165 K3 **Pretzsch** Germany
171 I5 **Preveza** Greece
154 C3 **Prey Vêng** Cambodia
138 E3 **Priaral'skiy Karakum** *des.* Kazakh.
133 U4 **Pribilof Islands** U.S.A.
171 H3 **Priboj** Serbia
189 G4 **Price** Canada
197 G2 **Price** U.S.A.
186 D4 **Price Island** Canada
201 B6 **Prichard** U.S.A.
159 M4 **Priekule** Latvia
159 N4 **Priekuļi** Latvia
159 M5 **Prienai** Lith.
180 E4 **Prieska** S. Africa
194 C1 **Priest Lake** U.S.A.
194 C1 **Priest River** U.S.A.
167 D1 **Prieta, Peña** *mt.* Spain
169 I6 **Prievidza** Slovakia
165 K1 **Prignitz** *reg.* Germany
170 G2 **Prijedor** Bos.-Herz.
171 H3 **Prijepolje** Serbia
**Prikaspiyskaya Nizmennost'** *lowland* Kazakh./Rus. Fed. *see* **Caspian Lowland**
171 I4 **Prilep** Macedonia
165 K5 **Přimda** Czech Rep.
215 D1 **Primero** *r.* Arg.
127 G8 **Prime Seal Island** Australia
159 O3 **Primorsk** Rus. Fed.
150 C2 **Primorskiy Kray** *admin. div.* Rus. Fed.
173 F6 **Primorsko-Akhtarsk** Rus. Fed.
196 D5 **Primo Tapia** Mex.
187 H4 **Primrose Lake** Canada
187 H4 **Prince Albert** Canada
180 E6 **Prince Albert** S. Africa
187 H4 **Prince Albert National Park** Canada
184 G2 **Prince Albert Peninsula** Canada
180 D6 **Prince Albert Road** S. Africa
184 G2 **Prince Albert Sound** *sea chan.* Canada
184 F2 **Prince Alfred, Cape** Canada
185 K3 **Prince Charles Island** Canada
129 D5 **Prince Charles Mountains** *mts* Antarctica
189 H4 **Prince Edward Island** *prov.* Canada
218 G8 **Prince Edward Islands** Indian Ocean
191 I4 **Prince Edward Point** Canada
202 E5 **Prince Frederick** U.S.A.
186 E4 **Prince George** Canada
184 B3 **Prince of Wales, Cape** U.S.A.
124 E3 **Prince of Wales Island** Australia
185 I2 **Prince of Wales Island** Canada
186 C3 **Prince of Wales Island** U.S.A.
184 G2 **Prince of Wales Strait** Canada
184 F2 **Prince Patrick Island** Canada
185 I2 **Prince Regent Inlet** *sea chan.* Canada
186 C4 **Prince Rupert** Canada
203 F5 **Princess Anne** U.S.A.
124 E3 **Princess Charlotte Bay** Australia
129 D4 **Princess Elisabeth** *research stn* Antarctica
129 D5 **Princess Elizabeth Land** *reg.* Antarctica
187 J2 **Princess Mary Lake** Canada
186 D4 **Princess Royal Island** Canada
186 E5 **Princeton** Canada
196 A2 **Princeton** *CA* U.S.A.
190 C5 **Princeton** *IL* U.S.A.
200 C4 **Princeton** *IN* U.S.A.
200 C4 **Princeton** *KY* U.S.A.
203 J2 **Princeton** *ME* U.S.A.
198 E3 **Princeton** *MO* U.S.A.
203 F4 **Princeton** *NJ* U.S.A.
190 C4 **Princeton** *WI* U.S.A.
202 C6 **Princeton** *WV* U.S.A.
203 J2 **Prince William** Canada
184 D3 **Prince William Sound** *b.* U.S.A.
176 C4 **Príncipe** *i.* São Tomé and Príncipe
194 B2 **Prineville** U.S.A.
132 C2 **Prins Karls Forland** *i.* Svalbard
206 I5 **Prinzapolca** Nicaragua
172 D2 **Priozersk** Rus. Fed.
169 L5 **Pripet** *r.* Belarus/Ukr. *alt.* **Pryp"yat' (Ukraine),** *alt.* **Prypyats' (Belarus)**
158 O1 **Prirechnyy** Rus. Fed.
171 I3 **Prishtinë** Kosovo
**Priština** Kosovo *see* **Prishtinë**
165 J1 **Pritzier** Germany
165 K1 **Pritzwalk** Germany
166 G4 **Privas** France
170 F2 **Privlaka** Croatia
172 G3 **Privolzhsk** Rus. Fed.
172 H4 **Privolzhskaya Vozvyshennost'** *hills* Rus. Fed.
138 B1 **Privolzh'ye** Rus. Fed.
173 G6 **Priyutnoye** Rus. Fed.
171 I3 **Prizren** Kosovo
155 D4 **Probolinggo** Indon.
165 J4 **Probstzella** Germany
161 C7 **Probus** U.K.
190 A2 **Proctor** *MN* U.S.A.
203 G3 **Proctor** *VT* U.S.A.
211 G3 **Professor van Blommestein Meer** *resr* Suriname
**Progreso** Hond. *see* **El Progreso**
206 D2 **Progreso** *Coahuila* Mex.
207 E3 **Progreso** *Hidalgo* Mex.
207 G3 **Progreso** *Yucatán* Mex.
129 D5 **Progress** *research stn* Antarctica
173 H7 **Prokhladnyy** Rus. Fed.
132 J4 **Prokop'yevsk** Rus. Fed.
171 I3 **Prokuplje** Serbia
172 D3 **Proletariy** Rus. Fed.
173 G6 **Proletarsk** Rus. Fed.
173 G6 **Proletarskoye Vodokhranilishche** *l.* Rus. Fed.
214 A2 **Promissão** Brazil
184 F4 **Prophet** *r.* Canada
186 E3 **Prophet River** Canada
190 C5 **Prophetstown** U.S.A.
124 E4 **Proserpine** Australia
203 F3 **Prospect** U.S.A.
153 C4 **Prosperidad** Phil.
180 D7 **Protem** S. Africa
190 A4 **Protivin** U.S.A.
171 L3 **Provadiya** Bulg.
166 H5 **Provence** *reg.* France
203 H4 **Providence** U.S.A.
128 A7 **Providence, Cape** N.Z.
191 F3 **Providence Bay** Canada
206 I5 **Providencia, Isla de** *i.* Col.
184 A3 **Provideniya** Rus. Fed.
203 H3 **Provincetown** U.S.A.
197 G1 **Provo** U.S.A.
187 G4 **Provost** Canada
214 B4 **Prudentópolis** Brazil
184 D2 **Prudhoe Bay** U.S.A.
164 E4 **Prüm** Germany
164 E4 **Prüm** *r.* Germany
170 C3 **Prunelli-di-Fiumorbo** *Corsica* France
169 J4 **Pruszków** Poland
173 D6 **Prut** *r.* Moldova/Romania
129 E5 **Prydz Bay** *b.* Antarctica
173 E5 **Pryluky** Ukr.
173 F6 **Prymors'k** Ukr.
193 G4 **Pryor** U.S.A.
169 L5 **Pryp"yat'** *r.* Ukr. *alt.* **Prypyats' (Belarus),** *conv.* **Pripet**
169 O5 **Pryp"yat' (abandoned)** Ukr.
169 M4 **Prypyats'** *r.* Belarus *alt.* **Pryp"yat' (Ukraine),** *conv.* **Pripet**
169 K6 **Przemyśl** Poland
**Przheval'sk** Kyrg. *see* **Karakol**
171 K5 **Psara** *i.* Greece
173 G6 **Psebay** Rus. Fed.
173 F6 **Pshish** *r.* Rus. Fed.
172 D3 **Pskov** Rus. Fed.
159 N4 **Pskov, Lake** Estonia/Rus. Fed.
172 D3 **Pskovskaya Oblast'** *admin. div.* Rus. Fed.
171 I4 **Ptolemaïda** Greece
170 F1 **Ptuj** Slovenia
154 B1 **Pua** Thai.
215 D3 **Puán** Arg.
148 B4 **Pu'an** China
149 B5 **Pu'an** China
149 C6 **Pubei** China
210 D5 **Pucallpa** Peru
149 F5 **Pucheng** *Fujian* China
148 C3 **Pucheng** *Shaanxi* China
172 G3 **Puchezh** Rus. Fed.
153 B4 **Pucio Point** Phil.
168 I3 **Puck** Poland
190 C4 **Puckaway Lake** U.S.A.
215 B3 **Pucón** Chile
141 F4 **Pūdah Tal, Shaylah-ye** *watercourse* Afgh.
140 D3 **Pūdanū** Iran
158 N2 **Pudasjärvi** Fin.
180 F3 **Pudimoe** S. Africa
148 F4 **Pudong** China
172 F2 **Pudozh** Rus. Fed.
160 F4 **Pudsey** U.K.
143 B4 **Puducherry** India
143 B4 **Puducherry** *union terr.* India
143 B4 **Pudukkottai** India
207 E4 **Puebla** Mex.
207 E4 **Puebla** *state* Mex.
167 C1 **Puebla de Sanabria** Spain
195 F4 **Pueblo** U.S.A.
213 C2 **Pueblo Nuevo** Venez.
207 F4 **Pueblo Viejo** *tourist site* Mex.
215 D3 **Puelches** Arg.
215 C3 **Puelén** Arg.
215 B2 **Puente Alto** Chile
207 E4 **Puente de Ixtla** Mex.
167 D4 **Puente Genil** Spain
213 C2 **Puente Torres** Venez.
212 B7 **Puerto Aisén** Chile
210 F6 **Puerto Alegre** Bol.
207 E5 **Puerto Ángel** Mex.
207 F5 **Puerto Arista** Mex.
206 I6 **Puerto Armuelles** Panama
213 A4 **Puerto Asís** Col.
213 D3 **Puerto Ayacucho** Venez.
210 □ **Puerto Baquerizo Moreno** *Galapagos Is* Ecuador
206 G5 **Puerto Barrios** Guat.
213 B3 **Puerto Berrío** Col.
213 C2 **Puerto Cabello** Venez.
206 I5 **Puerto Cabezas** Nicaragua
206 I5 **Puerto Cabo Gracias á Dios** Nicaragua
213 D3 **Puerto Carreño** Col.
212 E2 **Puerto Casado** Para.
212 B6 **Puerto Cisnes** Chile
212 C8 **Puerto Coig** Arg.
206 I6 **Puerto Cortés** Costa Rica
207 H5 **Puerto Cortés** Hond.
206 B2 **Puerto Cortés** Mex.
213 C2 **Puerto Cumarebo** Venez.
207 H3 **Puerto de Morelos** Mex.
207 E5 **Puerto Escondido** Mex.
213 C1 **Puerto Estrella** Col.
210 F6 **Puerto Frey** Bol.
212 E2 **Puerto Guarani** Para.
210 E6 **Puerto Heath** Bol.
213 D4 **Puerto Inírida** Col.
211 G7 **Puerto Isabel** Bol.
206 H6 **Puerto Jesús** Costa Rica
207 H3 **Puerto Juáres** Mex.
213 D2 **Puerto La Cruz** Venez.
210 D4 **Puerto Leguizamo** Col.
206 I5 **Puerto Lempira** Hond.
206 I6 **Puerto Limón** Costa Rica
167 D3 **Puertollano** Spain
215 D4 **Puerto Lobos** Arg.
213 B3 **Puerto López** Col.
207 F5 **Puerto Madero** Mex.
215 D4 **Puerto Madryn** Arg.
210 E6 **Puerto Maldonado** Peru
210 B4 **Puerto Máncora** Peru
213 D3 **Puerto Miranda** Venez.
215 B4 **Puerto Montt** Chile
206 H5 **Puerto Morazán** Nicaragua
212 B8 **Puerto Natales** Chile
213 C3 **Puerto Nuevo** Col.
206 J6 **Puerto Obaldia** Panama
213 E2 **Puerto Ordaz** Venez.
213 D3 **Puerto Páez** Venez.
204 B2 **Puerto Peñasco** Mex.
212 E2 **Puerto Pinasco** Para.
215 D4 **Puerto Pirámides** Arg.
205 J5 **Puerto Plata** Dom. Rep.
210 D5 **Puerto Portillo** Peru
153 A4 **Puerto Princesa** Phil.
213 A2 **Puerto Rey** Col.
205 K5 **Puerto Rico** *terr.* Caribbean Sea
219 E4 **Puerto Rico Trench** *sea feature* Caribbean Sea
206 H5 **Puerto Sandino** Nicaragua
207 G5 **Puerto San José** Guat.
212 C8 **Puerto Santa Cruz** Arg.
212 E2 **Puerto Sastre** Para.
213 A4 **Puerto Tejado** Col.
206 C3 **Puerto Vallarta** Mex.
215 B4 **Puerto Varas** Chile
173 I4 **Pugachev** Rus. Fed.
144 C3 **Pugal** India
149 B5 **Puge** China
140 D5 **Pūhāl-e Khamīr, Kūh-e** *mts* Iran
148 C3 **Pu He** *r.* China
167 H1 **Puigmal** *mt.* France/Spain
149 □ **Pui O Wan** *b. Hong Kong* China
149 F4 **Pujiang** China
152 D3 **Pujŏn-ho** *resr* N. Korea
152 E3 **Pujonryong-sanmaek** *mts* N. Korea
128 C6 **Pukaki, Lake** N.Z.
216 H6 **Pukapuka** *atoll* Cook Is
190 E1 **Pukaskwa** *r.* Canada
190 E1 **Pukaskwa National Park** Canada
187 I3 **Pukatawagan** Canada
152 C3 **Pukchin** N. Korea
152 E3 **Pukch'ŏng** N. Korea
128 E2 **Pukekohe** N.Z.
128 D5 **Puketeraki Range** *mts* N.Z.
128 F4 **Puketoi Range** *hills* N.Z.
128 C6 **Pukeuri Junction** N.Z.
169 O3 **Pukhnovo** Rus. Fed.
172 G2 **Puksoozero** Rus. Fed.
152 D3 **Puksubaek-san** *mt.* N. Korea
170 E2 **Pula** Croatia
210 E8 **Pulacayo** Bol.
152 B4 **Pulandian** China
152 A4 **Pulandian Wan** *b.* China
153 C5 **Pulangi** *r.* Phil.
203 E3 **Pulaski** *NY* U.S.A.
201 C5 **Pulaski** *TN* U.S.A.
202 C6 **Pulaski** *VA* U.S.A.
190 C3 **Pulaski** *WI* U.S.A.
169 J5 **Puławy** Poland
141 H3 **Pul-e 'Alam** Afgh.
141 H3 **Pul-e Khumrī** Afgh.
164 E3 **Pulheim** Germany
143 C3 **Pulicat Lake** *inlet* India
143 B3 **Pulivendla** India
143 B4 **Puliyangudi** India
158 N2 **Pulkkila** Fin.
194 C2 **Pullman** U.S.A.
158 P1 **Pulozero** Rus. Fed.
206 B2 **Púlpito, Punta** *pt* Mex.
144 E1 **Pulu** China
137 G2 **Pülümür** Turkey
153 C5 **Pulutan** Indon.
145 G3 **Puma Yumco** *l.* China
210 B4 **Puná, Isla** *i.* Ecuador
145 G4 **Punakha** Bhutan
144 C2 **Punch** India
186 E4 **Punchaw** Canada
145 G3 **Püncogling** China
181 I1 **Punda Maria** S. Africa
144 D3 **Pundri** India
143 A2 **Pune** India
154 □ **Punggol** Sing.
152 E3 **P'ungsan** N. Korea
179 D5 **Púnguè** *r.* Moz.
178 C4 **Punia** Dem. Rep. Congo
215 B1 **Punitaqui** Chile
144 C3 **Punjab** *state* India
144 B3 **Punjab** *prov.* Pak.
144 D2 **Punmah Glacier** Pak.
145 F4 **Punpun** *r.* India
205 K5 **Punta, Cerro de** *mt.* Puerto Rico
215 D3 **Punta Alta** Arg.
212 B8 **Punta Arenas** Chile
215 F2 **Punta del Este** Uru.
215 D4 **Punta Delgada** Arg.
206 G4 **Punta Gorda** Belize
206 I6 **Punta Gorda** Nicaragua
201 D7 **Punta Gorda** U.S.A.
215 D4 **Punta Norte** Arg.
206 H6 **Puntarenas** Costa Rica
134 C6 **Puntland** *reg.* Somalia
213 C2 **Punto Fijo** Venez.
202 D4 **Punxsutawney** U.S.A.
158 N2 **Puokio** Fin.
158 N2 **Puolanka** Fin.
140 E5 **Pūr** Iran
132 I3 **Pur** *r.* Rus. Fed.
213 A4 **Puracé, Parque Nacional** *nat. park* Col.
213 A4 **Puracé, Volcán de** *vol.* Col.
199 D5 **Purcell** U.S.A.
186 F4 **Purcell Mountains** Canada
215 B3 **Purén** Chile
195 G4 **Purgatoire** *r.* U.S.A.
145 F6 **Puri** India
164 C2 **Purmerend** Neth.
143 B2 **Purna** India
144 D5 **Purna** *r. Maharashtra* India
144 D6 **Purna** *r. Maharashtra* India
145 G4 **Purnabhaba** *r.* India
145 F4 **Purnia** India
215 B4 **Purranque** Chile
206 D3 **Puruandíro** Mex.
145 F5 **Puruliya** India
210 F4 **Purus** *r.* Brazil
159 O3 **Puruvesi** *l.* Fin.
155 C4 **Purwakarta** Indon.
155 D4 **Purwodadi** Indon.
155 C4 **Purwokerto** Indon.
152 E2 **Puryŏng** N. Korea
144 D6 **Pus** *r.* India
144 D6 **Pusad** India
**Pusan** S. Korea *see* **Busan**
203 I2 **Pushaw Lake** U.S.A.
144 C4 **Pushkar** India
172 D3 **Pushkin** Rus. Fed.
173 H5 **Pushkino** Rus. Fed.
172 D3 **Pushkinskiye Gory** Rus. Fed.
172 H2 **Pushma** Rus. Fed.
**Pusht-i-Rud** *reg.* Afgh. *see* **Zamīndāwar**
169 N2 **Pustoshka** Rus. Fed.
146 B4 **Putao** Myanmar
149 F5 **Putian** China
155 D3 **Puting, Tanjung** *pt* Indon.
139 K2 **Putintsevo** Kazakh.

207 E4 **Putla** Mex.
141 G4 **Putla Khan** Afgh.
165 K1 **Putlitz** Germany
171 L2 **Putna** r. Romania
203 H4 **Putnam** U.S.A.
203 G3 **Putney** U.S.A.
132 K3 **Putorana, Plato** plat. Rus. Fed.
135 I6 **Putrajaya** Indon.
145 H3 **Putrang La** pass China
180 D4 **Putsonderwater** S. Africa
143 B4 **Puttalam** Sri Lanka
143 B4 **Puttalam Lagoon** Sri Lanka
164 E5 **Puttelange-aux-Lacs** France
164 D2 **Putten** Neth.
164 C3 **Puttershoek** Neth.
168 E3 **Puttgarden** Germany
210 D4 **Putumayo** r. Col.
136 G2 **Pütürge** Turkey
155 D2 **Putusibau** Indon.
172 G4 **Putyatino** Rus. Fed.
173 E5 **Putyvl'** Ukr.
159 O3 **Puumala** Fin.
196 □2 **Pu'uwai** U.S.A.
**Puuwai** U.S.A. see **Pu'uwai**
188 E1 **Puvirnituq** Canada
**Puvurnituq** Canada see **Puvirnituq**
194 B2 **Puyallup** U.S.A.
148 E3 **Puyang** China
215 B4 **Puyehue** Chile
215 B4 **Puyehue, Parque Nacional** nat. park Chile
166 F5 **Puylaurens** France
128 A7 **Puysegur Point** N.Z.
141 F4 **Pūzak, Hāmūn-e** marsh Afgh.
179 C4 **Pweto** Dem. Rep. Congo
161 C5 **Pwllheli** U.K.
172 E2 **Pyal'ma** Rus. Fed.
172 H4 **P'yana** r. Rus. Fed.
158 O2 **Pyaozero, Ozero** l. Rus. Fed.
158 O2 **Pyaozerskiy** Rus. Fed.
132 J2 **Pyasina** r. Rus. Fed.
173 G6 **Pyatigorsk** Rus. Fed.
138 B2 **Pyatimarskoye** Kazakh.
173 E5 **P"yatykhatky** Ukr.
147 B5 **Pyè** Myanmar
128 B7 **Pye, Mount** h. N.Z.
152 E5 **Pyeonghae** S. Korea
152 D5 **Pyeongtaek** S. Korea
173 D4 **Pyetrykaw** Belarus
158 N2 **Pyhäjoki** Fin.
158 N2 **Pyhäjoki** r. Fin.
158 N2 **Pyhäntä** Fin.
158 N3 **Pyhäsalmi** Fin.
158 O3 **Pyhäselkä** l. Fin.
145 H5 **Pyingaing** Myanmar
146 B4 **Pyin-U-Lwin** Myanmar
161 D6 **Pyle** U.K.
132 J3 **Pyl'karamo** Rus. Fed.
171 I6 **Pylos** Greece
202 C4 **Pymatuning Reservoir** U.S.A.
152 C5 **Pyŏksŏng** N. Korea
152 C3 **Pyŏktong** N. Korea
152 D4 **P'yŏnggang** N. Korea
152 D4 **P'yŏngsan** N. Korea
152 C4 **P'yŏngsong** N. Korea
152 C4 **P'yŏngyang** N. Korea
126 F6 **Pyramid Hill** Australia
196 C1 **Pyramid Lake** U.S.A.
190 E3 **Pyramid Point** U.S.A.
196 C2 **Pyramid Range** mts U.S.A.
136 C7 **Pyramids of Giza** tourist site Egypt
166 F5 **Pyrenees** mts France/Spain
171 I6 **Pyrgos** Greece
173 E5 **Pyryatyn** Ukr.
168 G4 **Pyrzyce** Poland
172 H3 **Pyshchug** Rus. Fed.
169 M2 **Pytalovo** Rus. Fed.
171 J5 **Pyxaria** mt. Greece

## Q

136 F4 **Qaa** Lebanon
**Qaanaaq** Greenland see **Thule**
140 D6 **Qābil** Oman
137 I6 **Qabr Bandar** tourist site Iraq
181 H5 **Qacha's Nek** Lesotho
140 D4 **Qāder Ābād** Iran
137 J4 **Qādir Karam** Iraq
137 I4 **Qādisīyah, Sadd** dam Iraq
141 E3 **Qā'en** Iran
148 C2 **Qagan Nur** Nei Mongol China
148 E1 **Qagan Nur** China
148 E1 **Qagan Nur** l. Nei Mongol China
148 E1 **Qagan Nur** resr China
152 C1 **Qagan Nur** salt l. China
148 D1 **Qagan Obo** Mongolia
148 D1 **Qagan Teg** China
139 J3 **Qagan Tungge** China
148 E1 **Qagan Us** China
145 H3 **Qagbasêrag** China
145 E2 **Qagcaka** China
146 B3 **Qaidam Pendi** basin China
**Qaisar, Koh-i-** mt. Afgh. see **Qeyşār, Kūh-e**
137 J3 **Qalā Diza** Iraq
141 G3 **Qal'ah Sang-e Takht** Afgh.
141 F3 **Qal'ah-ye Fārsī** Afgh.
141 F3 **Qal'ah-ye Now** Afgh.
141 G4 **Qal'ah-ye Rashīd** Afgh.
141 F3 **Qal'ah-ye Walī** Afgh.
139 G5 **Qal'aikhum** Tajik.
141 G3 **Qalāt** Afgh.
140 D4 **Qalāt** Iran
137 K6 **Qal'at Şāliḩ** Iraq
137 K6 **Qal'at Sukkar** Iraq
140 B2 **Qal'eh Dāgh** mt. Iran
137 L5 **Qal'eh-ye Now** Iran
137 J7 **Qalīb Bāqūr** well Iraq
136 C6 **Qalyūb** Egypt
187 J2 **Qamanirjuaq Lake** Canada
139 F5 **Qamashi** Uzbek.
181 G5 **Qamata** S. Africa
137 K4 **Qāmchīān** Iran
144 B3 **Qamruddin Karez** Pak.
140 C3 **Qamşar** Iran
140 B2 **Qandarānbāshī, Kūh-e** mt. Iran
138 D4 **Qanliko'l** Uzbek.
139 J4 **Qapqal** China
137 L2 **Qaraçala** Azer.
137 I4 **Qarachōq, Jabal** mts Iraq
137 J4 **Qara Dāgh** mt. Iraq
137 H7 **Qārah** Saudi Arabia
140 A5 **Qa'rah, Jabal al** h. Saudi Arabia
141 H3 **Qarah Bāgh** Afgh.
137 K3 **Qaranqu** r. Iran
178 E3 **Qardho** Somalia
137 K3 **Qar'eh Aqāj** Iran
137 K2 **Qareh Dāgh** mts Iran
137 K3 **Qareh Dāsh, Kūh-e** mt. Iran
140 B2 **Qareh Sū** r. Iran
137 K3 **Qareh Urgān, Kūh-e** mt. Iran
145 H1 **Qarhan** China
139 H5 **Qarokŭl** l. Tajik.
139 J4 **Qarqi** China
141 G2 **Qarqīn** Afgh.
138 F5 **Qarshi** Uzbek.
136 C7 **Qārūn, Birkat** salt l. Egypt
137 J6 **Qaryat al Gharab** Iraq
140 B5 **Qaryat al Ulyā** Saudi Arabia
140 E3 **Qasamī** Iran
141 F3 **Qasa Murg** mts Afgh.
140 C4 **Qash Qā'ī** reg. Iran
185 M3 **Qasigiannguit** Greenland
148 D1 **Qasq** China
137 I5 **Qaşr al Khubbāz** Iraq
137 L7 **Qaşr aş Şabīyah** Kuwait
141 F5 **Qaşr-e Qand** Iran
140 B3 **Qaşr-e Shīrīn** Iran
185 N3 **Qassimiut** Greenland
136 F5 **Qaţanā** Syria
140 C5 **Qatar** country Asia
136 C7 **Qaţrānī, Jabal** esc. Egypt
140 D4 **Qaţrūyeh** Iran
177 E2 **Qattara Depression** Egypt
136 F4 **Qaţţīnah, Buḩayrat** resr Syria
**Qausuittuq** Canada see **Resolute**
137 K1 **Qax** Azer.
139 J4 **Qaxi** China
141 G3 **Qayşār** Afgh.
145 H3 **Qayü** China
137 I4 **Qayyārah** Iraq
137 K2 **Qazangöldağ** mt. Azer.
137 J1 **Qazax** Azer.
144 B4 **Qazi Ahmad** Pak.
140 C2 **Qazvīn** Iran
148 A1 **Qeh** China
185 M3 **Qeqertarsuaq** i. Greenland
185 M3 **Qeqertarsuatsiaat** Greenland
185 M3 **Qeqertarsuup Tunua** b. Greenland
137 K4 **Qeshlāq** Iran
140 B3 **Qeshlāq, Rūdkhāneh-ye** r. Iran
140 E5 **Qeshm** Iran
140 C2 **Qeydār** Iran
140 D4 **Qeyşar, Chāh-e** well Iran
141 G3 **Qeyşār, Kūh-e** mt. Afgh.
140 C2 **Qezel Owzan, Rūdkhāneh-ye** r. Iran
136 E6 **Qezi'ot** Israel
148 F2 **Qian'an** China
152 C1 **Qian'an** China
149 F4 **Qiandao Hu** resr China
139 J4 **Qianfodong** China
152 C1 **Qian Gorlos** China
148 C3 **Qian He** r. China
149 D4 **Qianjiang** Hubei China
149 C4 **Qianjiang** Sichuan China
152 E1 **Qianjin** China
152 B1 **Qianqihao** China
152 B3 **Qian Shan** mts China
148 E2 **Qianshangjie** China
219 R4 **Qiansuo** China
149 C5 **Qianxi** China
148 C3 **Qianxian** China
148 C3 **Qianyang** China
148 D2 **Qiaocun** China
149 B5 **Qiaojia** China
137 J2 **Qīās** Iran
140 B5 **Qibā'** Saudi Arabia
181 G4 **Qibing** S. Africa
149 D5 **Qidong** Hunan China
148 F4 **Qidong** Jiangsu China
145 H2 **Qidukou** China
135 G3 **Qiemo** China
148 E2 **Qihe** China
149 C4 **Qijiang** China
132 K5 **Qijiaojing** China
185 L3 **Qikiqtarjuaq** Canada
141 G4 **Qila Abdullah** Pak.
141 F5 **Qila Ladgasht** Pak.
148 E1 **Qilaotu Shan** mts China
141 F4 **Qila Safed** Pak.
144 B3 **Qila Saifullah** Pak.
146 B3 **Qilian Shan** mts China
185 O3 **Qillak** i. Greenland
145 G1 **Qiman Tag** mts China
149 E4 **Qimen** China
185 L2 **Qimusseriarsuaq** b. Greenland
177 F2 **Qinā** Egypt
148 B3 **Qin'an** China
148 C2 **Qingcheng** China
152 B3 **Qingchengzi** China
148 F2 **Qingdao** China
148 A2 **Qinghai** prov. China
148 A2 **Qinghai Hu** salt l. China
146 B3 **Qinghai Nanshan** mts China
150 A1 **Qinghe** China
152 C2 **Qing He** r. China
152 C3 **Qinghecheng** China
148 D2 **Qingjian** China
149 D4 **Qing Jiang** r. China
149 E5 **Qingliu** China
149 B5 **Qinglong** Guizhou China
148 F1 **Qinglong** Hebei China
148 F2 **Qinglong He** r. China
149 C6 **Qingping** China
148 F4 **Qingpu** China
148 C3 **Qingshui** China
139 J3 **Qingshuihe** China
148 D2 **Qingshuihe** China
149 F4 **Qingtian** China
148 C2 **Qingtongxia** China
148 E2 **Qingxian** China
148 D2 **Qingxu** China
149 E4 **Qingyang** Anhui China
148 C3 **Qingyang** Gansu China
149 D6 **Qingyuan** Guangdong China
152 C2 **Qingyuan** Liaoning China
149 F5 **Qingyuan** Zhejiang China
**Qingzang Gaoyuan** plat. China see **Tibet, Plateau of**
149 C5 **Qingzhen** China
149 D4 **Qingzhou** China
148 F2 **Qingzhou** China
148 D3 **Qin He** r. China
148 F2 **Qinhuangdao** China
148 C3 **Qin Ling** mts China
148 D2 **Qinxian** China
148 D3 **Qinyang** China
148 D2 **Qinyuan** China
149 C6 **Qinzhou** China
149 C6 **Qinzhou Wan** b. China
149 D7 **Qionghai** China
149 B4 **Qionglai** China
148 B4 **Qionglai Shan** mts China
149 D7 **Qiongshan** China
**Qiongzhou Haixia** str. China see **Hainan Strait**
146 E2 **Qiqihar** China
137 L5 **Qīr** Iran
140 D4 **Qīr** Iran
144 E1 **Qira** China
136 E6 **Qiryat Gat** Israel
136 F6 **Qitab ash Shāmah** vol. crater Saudi Arabia
150 B2 **Qitaihe** China
149 B5 **Qiubei** China
148 F2 **Qixia** China
148 E3 **Qixian** Henan China
148 D2 **Qixian** Shanxi China
150 C1 **Qixing He** r. China
149 D5 **Qiyang** China
148 C2 **Qiying** China
149 D7 **Qizhou Liedao** i. China
137 L2 **Qızılağac Körfäzi** b. Azer.
139 H5 **Qizilrabot** Tajik.
140 D3 **Qobād, Chāh-e** well Iran
137 L1 **Qobustan** Azer.
137 L1 **Qobustan Qoruğu** nature res. Azer.
**Qogir Feng** mt. China/Pakistan see **K2**
140 B2 **Qojūr** Iran
140 C3 **Qom** Iran
**Qomolangma Feng** mt. China see **Everest, Mount**
**Qomsheh** Iran see **Shāhreẕā**
140 C3 **Qonāq, Kūh-e** h. Iran
137 L1 **Qonaqkänd** Azer.
145 G3 **Qonggyai** China
138 D4 **Qo'ng'irot** Uzbek.
145 E2 **Qong Muztag** mt. China
139 G4 **Qo'qon** Uzbek.
138 D4 **Qorajar** Uzbek.
138 E5 **Qorako'l** Bukharskaya Oblast' Uzbek.
138 E5 **Qorako'l** Bukharskaya Oblast' Uzbek.
138 D3 **Qoraqalpog'iston** Uzbek.
138 F4 **Qoraqata botig'i** depr. Uzbek.
136 F4 **Qornet es Saouda** mt. Lebanon
138 F5 **Qorovulbozor** Uzbek.
140 B3 **Qorveh** Iran
138 E4 **Qo'shko'pir** Uzbek.
139 F4 **Qo'shrabot** Uzbek.
140 E5 **Qoţbābād** Iran
137 J2 **Qoţūr** Iran
138 D4 **Qozoqdaryo** Uzbek.
203 G3 **Quabbin Reservoir** U.S.A.
196 D4 **Quail Mountains** U.S.A.
165 F2 **Quakenbrück** Germany
203 F4 **Quakertown** U.S.A.
126 E5 **Quambatook** Australia
127 G3 **Quambone** Australia
199 D5 **Quanah** U.S.A.
148 D3 **Quanbao Shan** mt. China
154 D2 **Quang Ngai** Vietnam
154 C1 **Quang Tri** Vietnam
149 C6 **Quang Yên** Vietnam
149 B6 **Quan Hoa** Vietnam
149 E5 **Quannan** China
149 F5 **Quanzhou** Fujian China
149 D5 **Quanzhou** Guangxi China
187 I4 **Qu'Appelle** Canada
187 I4 **Qu'Appelle** r. Canada
215 F1 **Quaraí** Brazil
215 F1 **Quaraí** r. Brazil
149 □ **Quarry Bay** Hong Kong China
170 C5 **Quartu Sant'Elena** Sardinia Italy
196 D3 **Quartzite Mountain** U.S.A.
197 E5 **Quartzsite** U.S.A.
186 D4 **Quatsino Sound** inlet Canada
138 A4 **Quba** Azer.
141 E2 **Qūchān** Iran
127 H5 **Queanbeyan** Australia
189 F4 **Québec** Canada
185 K4 **Québec** prov. Canada
214 C2 **Quebra Anzol** r. Brazil
215 B4 **Quedal, Cabo** c. Chile
165 J3 **Quedlinburg** Germany
186 E4 **Queen Bess, Mount** Canada
186 C4 **Queen Charlotte** Canada
**Queen Charlotte Islands** is Canada see **Haida Gwaii**
186 D4 **Queen Charlotte Sound** sea chan. Canada
186 D4 **Queen Charlotte Strait** Canada
185 H1 **Queen Elizabeth Islands** Canada
178 D3 **Queen Elizabeth National Park** Uganda
129 D6 **Queen Mary Land** reg. Antarctica
184 H3 **Queen Maud Gulf** Canada
129 D3 **Queen Maud Land** reg. Antarctica
129 E3 **Queen Maud Land** reg. Antarctica
129 C4 **Queen Maud Mountains** mts Antarctica
124 E4 **Queensland** state Australia
127 F9 **Queenstown** Australia
128 B6 **Queenstown** N.Z.
181 G5 **Queenstown** S. Africa
154 □ **Queenstown** Sing.
203 E5 **Queenstown** U.S.A.
194 A2 **Queets** U.S.A.
215 F2 **Queguay Grande** r. Uruguay
215 D3 **Quehué** Arg.
211 H4 **Queimada, Ilha** i. Brazil
179 D5 **Quelimane** Moz.
212 B6 **Quellón** Chile
197 H4 **Quemado** U.S.A.
215 B4 **Quemchi** Chile
215 D3 **Quemú-Quemú** Arg.
215 E3 **Quequén Grande** r. Arg.
214 B3 **Querência do Norte** Brazil
207 D3 **Querétaro** Mex.
207 E3 **Querétaro** state Mex.
165 J3 **Querfurt** Germany
148 E3 **Queshan** China
186 E4 **Quesnel** Canada
186 E4 **Quesnel** r. Canada
186 E4 **Quesnel Lake** Canada
190 B1 **Quetico Provincial Park** Canada
144 A3 **Quetta** Pak.
207 G5 **Quetzaltenango** Guat.
215 B3 **Queuco** Chile
215 B3 **Queule** Chile
**Quezaltenango** Guat. see **Quetzaltenango**
153 A4 **Quezon** Phil.
153 B3 **Quezon City** Phil.
148 E3 **Qufu** China
179 B5 **Quibala** Angola
179 B4 **Quibaxe** Angola
213 A3 **Quibdó** Col.
166 C3 **Quiberon** France
179 B4 **Quiçama, Parque Nacional do** nat. park Angola
197 F5 **Quijotoa** U.S.A.
215 D1 **Quilino** Arg.
166 F5 **Quillan** France
187 I4 **Quill Lakes** Canada
215 B2 **Quillota** Chile
215 E2 **Quilmes** Arg.
**Quilon** India see **Kollam**
124 E4 **Quilpie** Australia
215 B2 **Quilpué** Chile
178 B4 **Quimbele** Angola
212 D3 **Quimilí** Arg.
166 B3 **Quimper** France
166 C3 **Quimperlé** France
210 D6 **Quince Mil** Peru
196 B2 **Quincy** CA U.S.A.
201 C6 **Quincy** FL U.S.A.
190 B6 **Quincy** IL U.S.A.
203 H3 **Quincy** MA U.S.A.
215 D2 **Quines** Arg.
**Qui Nhơn** Vietnam see **Quy Nhơn**
197 E3 **Quinn Canyon Range** mts U.S.A.
167 E3 **Quintanar de la Orden** Spain
207 G4 **Quintana Roo** state Mex.
215 B2 **Quintero** Chile
215 D2 **Quinto** r. Arg.
167 F2 **Quinto** Spain
179 E5 **Quionga** Moz.
179 B5 **Quipungo** Angola
207 G5 **Quiriguá** tourist site Guat.
215 B3 **Quirihue** Chile
179 B5 **Quirima** Angola
179 E5 **Quirimbas, Parque Nacional das** nat. park Moz.
127 I3 **Quirindi** Australia
215 E2 **Quiroga** Arg.
179 B5 **Quitapa** Angola
214 B2 **Quitéria** r. Brazil
201 D6 **Quitman** GA U.S.A.
201 B5 **Quitman** MS U.S.A.
210 C4 **Quito** Ecuador
195 D6 **Quitovac** Mex.
197 F4 **Quivero** U.S.A.
211 K4 **Quixadá** Brazil
149 D5 **Qujiang** China
149 C4 **Qu Jiang** r. China
149 D6 **Qujie** China
149 B5 **Qujing** China
137 K7 **Qulbān Layyah** well Iraq
138 E4 **Quljuqtov tog'lari** hills Uzbek.
145 H2 **Qumar He** r. China
145 H2 **Qumarheyan** China
145 H2 **Qumarrabdün** China
181 H5 **Qumbu** S. Africa
145 H3 **Qumdo** China
181 G6 **Qumrha** S. Africa
140 B5 **Qunayfidhah, Nafūd** des. Saudi Arabia
140 B6 **Qunayy** well Saudi Arabia
187 K2 **Quoich** r. Canada
162 C3 **Quoich, Loch** l. U.K.
163 F3 **Quoile** r. U.K.
180 C7 **Quoin Point** S. Africa
180 F1 **Quoxo** r. Botswana
141 E6 **Qurayat** Oman
139 G5 **Qŭrghonteppa** Tajik.
137 J2 **Qūrū Gol** pass Iran
138 A4 **Qusar** Azer.
140 B2 **Qūshchī** Iran
137 K2 **Qūsheh Dāgh** mts Iran
140 C3 **Qūtīābād** Iran
148 B2 **Quwu Shan** mts China
148 C4 **Quxian** China
145 G3 **Qüxü** China
154 C1 **Quy Châu** Vietnam
**Quynh Lưu** Vietnam see **Câu Giat**
149 B6 **Quynh Nhai** Vietnam
154 D2 **Quy Nhơn** Vietnam
191 I3 **Quyon** Canada
148 E2 **Quzhou** Hebei China
149 F4 **Quzhou** Zhejiang China
173 H7 **Q'vareli** Georgia

## R

168 H7 **Raab** r. Austria
158 N2 **Raahe** Fin.
158 O3 **Rääkkylä** Fin.
164 E2 **Raalte** Neth.
158 N2 **Raanujärvi** Fin.
155 D4 **Raas** i. Indon.
162 B3 **Raasay** i. U.K.
162 B3 **Raasay, Sound of** sea chan. U.K.
155 E4 **Raba** Indon.
177 F3 **Rabak** Sudan
144 E2 **Rabang** China
139 G4 **Rabat** Kazakh.
170 F7 **Rabat** Malta
176 B1 **Rabat** Morocco
141 E3 **Rabāt-e Kamah** Iran
141 F4 **Rabāţ Māndêh** r. Afgh.
124 F2 **Rabaul** P.N.G.
186 D3 **Rabbit** r. Canada
142 A5 **Rābigh** Saudi Arabia
145 G5 **Rabnabad Islands** Bangl.
140 E4 **Rābor** Iran
139 H5 **Rabotoqbaytal** Tajik.
**Rabyānah, Ramlat** des. Libya see **Rebiana Sand Sea**
202 B5 **Raccoon Creek** r. U.S.A.
189 J4 **Race, Cape** Canada
203 H3 **Race Point** U.S.A.
136 E5 **Rachaïya** Lebanon
199 D7 **Rachal** U.S.A.
197 E3 **Rachel** U.S.A.
154 C3 **Rach Gia** Vietnam
154 C3 **Rach Gia, Vinh** b. Vietnam
168 I5 **Racibórz** Poland
190 D4 **Racine** U.S.A.
191 F1 **Racine Lake** Canada
190 E2 **Raco** U.S.A.
169 L7 **Rădăuţi** Romania
200 C4 **Radcliff** U.S.A.
202 C6 **Radford** U.S.A.
144 B5 **Radhanpur** India
138 A1 **Radishchevo** Rus. Fed.
188 E3 **Radisson** Canada
186 F4 **Radium Hot Springs** Canada
171 K3 **Radnevo** Bulg.
169 J5 **Radom** Poland
171 J3 **Radomir** Bulg.
177 E4 **Radom National Park** Sudan
169 I5 **Radomsko** Poland
173 D5 **Radomyshl'** Ukr.
171 J4 **Radoviš** Macedonia
161 E6 **Radstock** U.K.
172 C4 **Radun'** Belarus
159 M5 **Radviliškis** Lith.
169 L5 **Radyvyliv** Ukr.
144 E4 **Rae Bareli** India
**Rae-Edzo** Canada see **Behchokò**
**Rae Lakes** Canada see **Gamètì**
128 E3 **Raetihi** N.Z.
215 E1 **Rafaela** Arg.
136 E6 **Rafaḩ** Gaza
178 C3 **Rafaï** Cent. Afr. Rep.
142 B4 **Rafḩā'** Saudi Arabia
140 E4 **Rafsanjān** Iran
153 C5 **Ragang, Mount** vol. Phil.
153 B3 **Ragay Gulf** Phil.
165 K1 **Rägelin** Germany
203 I3 **Ragged Island** U.S.A.
140 B4 **Raghwah** Saudi Arabia
165 K2 **Ragösen** Germany
165 K3 **Raguhn** Germany
170 F6 **Ragusa** Sicily Italy
148 A3 **Ra'gya** China
124 C2 **Raha** Indon.
172 D4 **Rahachow** Belarus
165 G2 **Rahden** Germany
143 A2 **Rahimatpur** India
144 B3 **Rahimyar Khan** Pak.
140 C3 **Rāhjerd** Iran
141 E4 **Raḩmān, Chāh-e** well Iran
171 I3 **Rahovec** Kosovo
215 B3 **Rahue** mt. Chile
143 A2 **Rahuri** India
154 C3 **Rai, Hon** i. Vietnam
217 I7 **Raiatea** i. Fr. Polynesia
143 B2 **Raichur** India
145 G4 **Raiganj** India
143 C1 **Raigarh** India
197 E2 **Railroad Valley** U.S.A.
189 G3 **Raimbault, Lac** l. Canada
126 E5 **Rainbow** Australia
197 G3 **Rainbow Bridge National Monument** nat. park U.S.A.
186 F3 **Rainbow Lake** Canada
202 C6 **Rainelle** U.S.A.
144 B3 **Raini** r. Pak.
194 B2 **Rainier, Mount** vol. U.S.A.
188 B4 **Rainy** r. U.S.A.
185 I5 **Rainy Lake** Canada
187 K5 **Rainy River** Canada
143 C1 **Raipur** Chhattisgarh India
144 C4 **Raipur** Rajasthan India
159 M3 **Raisio** Fin.
164 B4 **Raismes** France
144 D5 **Raitalai** India
217 J7 **Raivavae** i. Fr. Polynesia
143 C2 **Rajahmundry** India
158 O1 **Raja-Jooseppi** Fin.
143 B3 **Rajampet** India
155 D2 **Rajang** r. Sarawak Malaysia
143 B4 **Rajapalayam** India
143 A2 **Rajapur** India
144 C4 **Rajasthan** state India
144 C3 **Rajasthan Canal** India
145 F4 **Rajauli** India
145 G5 **Rajbari** Bangl.
144 C3 **Rajgarh** Rajasthan India
144 D4 **Rajgarh** Rajasthan India
136 F6 **Rājil, Wādī** watercourse Jordan
143 C1 **Rajim** India
144 B5 **Rajkot** India
145 F4 **Rajmahal** India
145 F4 **Rajmahal Hills** India
144 E5 **Raj Nandgaon** India
144 D3 **Rajpura** India
145 G4 **Rajshahi** Bangl.
143 B2 **Rajura** India
145 F3 **Raka** China
123 I4 **Rakahanga** atoll Pacific Ocean
128 C5 **Rakaia** r. N.Z.
144 C1 **Rakaposhi** mt. Pak.
173 C5 **Rakhiv** Ukr.
144 B3 **Rakhni** Pak.
144 B3 **Rakhni** r. Pak.
141 G5 **Rakhshan** r. Pak.
173 E5 **Rakitnoye** Belgorodskaya Oblast' Rus. Fed.
150 D2 **Rakitnoye** Primorskiy Kray Rus. Fed.
184 A7 **Rakiura National Park** nat. park N.Z.
159 N4 **Rakke** Estonia
159 J4 **Rakkestad** Norway
138 C3 **Rakusha** Kazakh.
138 B4 **Rakushechnyy, Mys** pt Kazakh.
159 N4 **Rakvere** Estonia
201 E5 **Raleigh** U.S.A.
123 G2 **Ralik Chain** is Marshall Is
190 D2 **Ralph** U.S.A.
186 E2 **Ram** r. Canada
189 H2 **Ramah** Canada
197 H4 **Ramah** U.S.A.
214 D1 **Ramalho, Serra do** hills Brazil
136 E6 **Rāmallāh** West Bank
143 B3 **Ramanagaram** India
143 B4 **Ramanathapuram** India
216 E3 **Ramapo Deep** sea feature N. Pacific Ocean
143 A3 **Ramas, Cape** India
181 F2 **Ramatlabama** S. Africa
124 E2 **Rambutyo Island** P.N.G.
143 A3 **Ramdurg** India
161 C7 **Rame Head** U.K.
179 E5 **Ramena** Madag.
172 F3 **Rameshki** Rus. Fed.
143 B4 **Rameswaram** India
144 D4 **Ramganga** r. India
145 G5 **Ramgarh** Bangl.
145 F5 **Ramgarh** Bihar India
144 B4 **Ramgarh** Rajasthan India
140 C4 **Rāmhormoz** Iran
136 E6 **Ramla** Israel
136 E7 **Ramm, Jabal** mts Jordan
144 D3 **Ramnagar** India
171 L2 **Râmnicu Sărat** Romania
171 K2 **Râmnicu Vâlcea** Romania
196 D5 **Ramona** U.S.A.
191 G1 **Ramore** Canada
179 C6 **Ramotswa** Botswana
144 D3 **Rampur** India
144 C4 **Rampura** India
145 F4 **Rampur Hat** India
145 H6 **Ramree Island** Myanmar
140 C2 **Rāmsar** Iran
158 L3 **Ramsele** Sweden
191 F2 **Ramsey** Canada
160 C3 **Ramsey** Isle of Man
161 G5 **Ramsey** U.K.
161 B6 **Ramsey Island** U.K.
191 F2 **Ramsey Lake** Canada
161 I6 **Ramsgate** U.K.
140 C4 **Rāmshir** Iran
144 D5 **Ramtek** India
159 N5 **Ramygala** Lith.
213 C4 **Rana, Cerro** h. Col.
145 G5 **Ranaghat** India
144 C5 **Ranapur** India
155 E1 **Ranau** Sabah Malaysia
215 B2 **Rancagua** Chile
145 F5 **Ranchi** India
215 B4 **Ranco, Lago** l. Chile
127 G5 **Rand** Australia
163 E3 **Randalstown** U.K.
170 F6 **Randazzo** Sicily Italy
159 J4 **Randers** Denmark
203 H3 **Randolph** MA U.S.A.
203 G3 **Randolph** VT U.S.A.
159 K3 **Randsjö** Sweden
158 M2 **Råneå** Sweden
128 C6 **Ranfurly** N.Z.
154 B4 **Rangae** Thai.
145 H5 **Rangamati** Bangl.
128 D1 **Rangaunu Bay** N.Z.
203 H2 **Rangeley** U.S.A.
203 H2 **Rangeley Lake** U.S.A.
197 H1 **Rangely** U.S.A.
191 F2 **Ranger Lake** Canada
128 D5 **Rangiora** N.Z.
128 F2 **Rangipoua** mt. N.Z.
123 I5 **Rangiroa** atoll Fr. Polynesia
128 F3 **Rangitaiki** r. N.Z.
128 C5 **Rangitata** r. N.Z.
128 E4 **Rangitikei** r. N.Z.
139 H5 **Rangkŭl** Tajik.
147 B5 **Rangoon** Myanmar
145 G4 **Rangpur** Bangl.
143 A3 **Ranibennur** India
145 F5 **Raniganj** India
143 C1 **Ranijula Peak** India
144 B4 **Ranipur** Pak.
199 C6 **Rankin** U.S.A.
187 K2 **Rankin Inlet** Canada
187 K2 **Rankin Inlet** inlet Canada
127 G4 **Rankin's Springs** Australia
159 N4 **Ranna** Estonia
138 C2 **Ranneye** Rus. Fed.
162 D4 **Rannoch, Loch** U.K.
162 D4 **Rannoch Moor** moorland U.K.
154 A3 **Ranong** Thai.
154 B4 **Ranot** Thai.
172 G4 **Ranova** r. Rus. Fed.
137 L5 **Rānsa** Iran
159 K3 **Ransby** Sweden
147 F7 **Ransiki** Indon.
159 O3 **Rantasalmi** Fin.
155 A2 **Rantauprapat** Indon.
190 C5 **Rantoul** U.S.A.
169 Q2 **Rantsevo** Rus. Fed.
158 N2 **Rantsila** Fin.
158 N2 **Ranua** Fin.
137 J3 **Ŗānya** Iraq
150 C1 **Raohe** China
149 E6 **Raoping** China
125 J4 **Raoul Island** i. N.Z.
123 I6 **Rapa** i. Fr. Polynesia
170 C2 **Rapallo** Italy
**Rapa Nui** i. S. Pacific Ocean see **Easter Island**
144 B5 **Rapar** India
141 E5 **Rapch** watercourse Iran
215 B2 **Rapel** r. Chile
185 L3 **Raper, Cape** Canada
163 D3 **Raphoe** Ireland
202 E5 **Rapidan** r. U.S.A.
126 C5 **Rapid Bay** Australia
198 C2 **Rapid City** U.S.A.
191 H2 **Rapide-Deux** Canada
191 H2 **Rapide-Sept** Canada
190 D3 **Rapid River** U.S.A.
159 N4 **Rapla** Estonia
202 E5 **Rappahannock** r. U.S.A.
145 E4 **Rapti** r. India
144 B5 **Rapur** India
153 C3 **Rapurapu** i. Phil.
203 F2 **Raquette** r. U.S.A.
203 F3 **Raquette Lake** U.S.A.
203 F3 **Raquette Lake** l. U.S.A.
203 F4 **Raritan Bay** U.S.A.
217 J7 **Raroia** atoll Fr. Polynesia
123 I5 **Rarotonga** i. Cook Is
153 A4 **Rasa** i. Phil.
215 D4 **Rasa, Punta** pt Arg.
140 D5 **Ra's al Khaymah** U.A.E.
136 E6 **Ra's an Naqb** Jordan
**Ras Dashen** mt. Eth. see **Ras Dejen**
178 D2 **Ras Dejen** mt. Eth.
159 M5 **Raseiniai** Lith.
136 C6 **Rashīd** Egypt
140 C2 **Rasht** Iran
143 B4 **Rasipuram** India
141 F5 **Rāsk** Iran
141 G4 **Raskoh** mts Pak.
185 I3 **Rasmussen Basin** sea feature Canada
212 C6 **Raso, Cabo** c. Arg.
172 D4 **Rasony** Belarus
145 E4 **Rasra** India
170 D6 **Rass Jebel** Tunisia
172 G4 **Rasskazovo** Rus. Fed.
142 D4 **Ras Tannūrah** Saudi Arabia
165 G1 **Rastede** Germany
165 J1 **Rastow** Germany
140 D5 **Rasūl** watercourse Iran
123 G2 **Ratak Chain** is Marshall Is
159 K3 **Rätan** Sweden
181 H3 **Ratanda** S. Africa
144 C3 **Ratangarh** India
143 C1 **Ratanpur** India
159 K3 **Rätansbyn** Sweden
154 A2 **Rat Buri** Thai.
138 C1 **Ratchino** Rus. Fed.
144 D4 **Rath** India
163 E4 **Rathangan** Ireland
163 D5 **Rathdowney** Ireland
163 E5 **Rathdrum** Ireland
145 H5 **Rathedaung** Myanmar
165 K2 **Rathenow** Germany
163 E3 **Rathfriland** U.K.
163 C5 **Rathkeale** Ireland
163 E2 **Rathlin Island** U.K.
164 E3 **Ratingen** Germany
144 C3 **Ratiya** India
144 C5 **Ratlam** India
143 A2 **Ratnagiri** India
143 C5 **Ratnapura** Sri Lanka
173 C5 **Ratne** Ukr.
144 B4 **Rato Dero** Pak.
195 F4 **Raton** U.S.A.
162 G3 **Rattray Head** U.K.
159 K3 **Rättvik** Sweden
186 C3 **Ratz, Mount** Canada
165 I1 **Ratzeburg** Germany
154 B5 **Raub** Malaysia
215 E3 **Rauch** Arg.
137 K7 **Raudhatain** Kuwait
165 J4 **Rauenstein** Germany
158 D1 **Raufarhöfn** Iceland
128 G2 **Raukumara** mt. N.Z.
128 F3 **Raukumara Range** mts N.Z.
159 M3 **Rauma** Fin.
143 D1 **Raurkela** India
150 I2 **Rausu** Japan
158 O3 **Rautavaara** Fin.
159 O3 **Rautjärvi** Fin.
194 D2 **Ravalli** U.S.A.
137 K4 **Ravānsar** Iran
140 E4 **Rāvar** Iran
139 G5 **Ravat** Kyrg.
164 C3 **Ravels** Belgium
203 G3 **Ravena** U.S.A.
160 D3 **Ravenglass** U.K.
170 E2 **Ravenna** Italy
168 D7 **Ravensburg** Germany
202 C5 **Ravenswood** U.S.A.
144 C3 **Ravi** r. Pak.
**Ravnina** Turkm. see **Rawnina**
138 D4 **Ravshan** Uzbek.
137 H4 **Rāwah** Iraq
123 H4 **Rawaki** i. Kiribati
144 C2 **Rawalpindi** Pak.
137 J3 **Ŗawāndiz** Iraq
144 C3 **Rawatsar** India
168 H5 **Rawicz** Poland
202 D5 **Rawley Springs** U.S.A.
194 F3 **Rawlins** U.S.A.
138 E5 **Rawnina** Turkm.
141 F2 **Rawnina** Turkm.
212 C6 **Rawson** Arg.
145 F4 **Raxaul** India
189 I4 **Ray, Cape** Canada
143 B3 **Rayachoti** India
143 B3 **Rayadurg** India
143 C2 **Rayagada** India
136 F5 **Rayak** Lebanon
146 E2 **Raychikhinsk** Rus. Fed.
196 C4 **Rayes Peak** U.S.A.
138 C1 **Rayevskiy** Rus. Fed.
161 H6 **Rayleigh** U.K.
186 G5 **Raymond** Canada
203 H3 **Raymond** NH U.S.A.
194 B2 **Raymond** WA U.S.A.
127 I4 **Raymond Terrace** Australia
199 D7 **Raymondville** U.S.A.
154 B2 **Rayong** Thai.
202 D4 **Raystown Lake** U.S.A.
166 B2 **Raz, Pointe du** pt France
137 L5 **Rāzān** Iran
140 C3 **Razan** Iran
137 I5 **Razāzah, Buḩayrat ar** l. Iraq
150 B3 **Razdol'noye** Rus. Fed.
140 C3 **Razeh** Iran
171 L3 **Razgrad** Bulg.
171 M2 **Razim, Lacul** lag. Romania
171 J4 **Razlog** Bulg.
**Re, Cu Lao** i. Vietnam see **Ly Sơn, Đao**
166 D3 **Ré, Île de** i. France
161 G6 **Reading** U.K.
203 F4 **Reading** U.S.A.
190 B4 **Readstown** U.S.A.
181 G2 **Reagile** S. Africa
215 D2 **Realicó** Arg.
166 F5 **Réalmont** France
154 B2 **Reăng Kesei** Cambodia
206 D2 **Reata** Mex.
164 B6 **Rebais** France
177 E2 **Rebiana Sand Sea** des. Libya
172 D2 **Reboly** Rus. Fed.
139 J1 **Rebrikha** Rus. Fed.
150 G2 **Rebun-tō** i. Japan
124 C5 **Recherche, Archipelago of the** is Australia
144 C3 **Rechna Doab** lowland Pak.
173 D4 **Rechytsa** Belarus
211 L5 **Recife** Brazil
181 F7 **Recife, Cape** S. Africa
164 F3 **Recklinghausen** Germany
212 E3 **Reconquista** Arg.
212 C3 **Recreo** Arg.
187 J5 **Red** r. Canada/U.S.A.
199 E6 **Red** r. U.S.A.
149 C6 **Red** r. Vietnam
154 B4 **Redang** i. Malaysia
203 F4 **Red Bank** NJ U.S.A.
201 C5 **Red Bank** TN U.S.A.
189 I3 **Red Bay** Canada
196 A1 **Red Bluff** U.S.A.
197 F4 **Red Butte** mt. U.S.A.
160 F3 **Redcar** U.K.
187 G4 **Redcliff** Canada
126 E5 **Red Cliffs** Australia
198 D3 **Red Cloud** U.S.A.
186 G4 **Red Deer** Canada
187 G4 **Red Deer** r. Alta Canada
187 I4 **Red Deer** r. Sask. Canada
187 I4 **Red Deer Lake** Canada
203 F5 **Redden** U.S.A.
181 G4 **Reddersburg** S. Africa
194 B3 **Redding** U.S.A.
161 F5 **Redditch** U.K.
203 F3 **Redfield** NY U.S.A.
198 D2 **Redfield** SD U.S.A.
126 C4 **Redhill** Australia
197 H4 **Red Hill** U.S.A.
199 D4 **Red Hills** U.S.A.
189 I4 **Red Indian Lake** Canada
190 E5 **Redkey** U.S.A.
187 K4 **Red Lake** Canada
187 K4 **Red Lake** l. Canada
197 E4 **Red Lake** U.S.A.
198 E1 **Red Lakes** U.S.A.
194 E2 **Red Lodge** U.S.A.
194 B2 **Redmond** U.S.A.
198 E3 **Red Oak** U.S.A.
167 C3 **Redondo** Port.
213 E4 **Redondo, Pico** h. Brazil
190 C1 **Red Rock** Canada
203 E4 **Red Rock** U.S.A.
134 B4 **Red Sea** Africa/Asia
186 E4 **Redstone** Canada
186 D2 **Redstone** r. Canada
187 K4 **Red Sucker Lake** Canada
164 D1 **Reduzum** Neth.
186 G4 **Redwater** Canada
189 H3 **Red Wine** r. Canada
190 A3 **Red Wing** U.S.A.
196 A3 **Redwood City** U.S.A.
198 E2 **Redwood Falls** U.S.A.
194 B3 **Redwood National Park** U.S.A.
196 A2 **Redwood Valley** U.S.A.
163 D4 **Ree, Lough** l. Ireland
190 E4 **Reed City** U.S.A.
196 C3 **Reedley** U.S.A.
190 C4 **Reedsburg** U.S.A.
194 A3 **Reedsport** U.S.A.
203 E6 **Reedville** U.S.A.
128 C5 **Reefton** N.Z.
164 E3 **Rees** Germany
136 G2 **Refahiye** Turkey
199 D6 **Refugio** U.S.A.
168 F6 **Regen** Germany
165 K5 **Regen** r. Germany
165 K5 **Regensburg** Germany
165 K5 **Regenstauf** Germany
176 C2 **Reggane** Alg.
170 F5 **Reggio di Calabria** Italy
170 D2 **Reggio nell'Emilia** Italy
169 L7 **Reghin** Romania
187 I4 **Regina** Canada
158 O2 **Regozero** Rus. Fed.
165 K4 **Rehau** Germany
165 H2 **Rehburg (Rehburg-Loccum)** Germany
144 D5 **Rehli** India
165 J1 **Rehna** Germany
179 B6 **Rehoboth** Namibia
197 H4 **Rehoboth** U.S.A.
203 F5 **Rehoboth Bay** U.S.A.
203 F5 **Rehoboth Beach** U.S.A.

136 E6 Rehovot Israel
165 K3 Reibitz Germany
165 K4 Reichenbach Germany
165 F6 Reichshoffen France
162 C3 Reidh, Rubha pt U.K.
201 E4 Reidsville U.S.A.
161 G6 Reigate U.K.
197 G5 Reiley Peak U.S.A.
166 G2 Reims France
212 B8 Reina Adelaida, Archipiélago de la is Chile
190 A4 Reinbeck U.S.A.
165 I1 Reinbek Germany
187 I3 Reindeer r. Canada
187 J4 Reindeer Island Canada
187 I3 Reindeer Lake Canada
158 K2 Reine Norway
165 I1 Reinfeld (Holstein) Germany
128 D1 Reinga, Cape N.Z.
167 D1 Reinosa Spain
164 E5 Reinsfeld Germany
158 B2 Reiphólsfjöll h. Iceland
158 M1 Reisaelva r. Norway
158 M1 Reisa Nasjonalpark nat. park Norway
158 N3 Reisjärvi Fin.
181 H3 Reitz S. Africa
180 F3 Reivilo S. Africa
213 D3 Rejunya Venez.
164 F3 Reken Germany
187 H2 Reliance Canada
176 C1 Relizane Alg.
165 H1 Rellingen Germany
164 F4 Remagen Germany
126 C4 Remarkable, Mount h. Australia
141 E5 Remeshk Iran
180 B1 Remhoogte Pass Namibia
168 C6 Remiremont France
Remo Glacier India see Rimo Glacier
173 G6 Remontnoye Rus. Fed.
164 F3 Remscheid Germany
190 E4 Remus U.S.A.
159 J3 Rena Norway
143 B2 Renapur India
200 B4 Rend Lake U.S.A.
125 F2 Rendova i. Solomon Is
168 D3 Rendsburg Germany
191 I3 Renfrew Canada
162 D5 Renfrew U.K.
215 B2 Rengo Chile
148 E4 Renhe China
148 C3 Ren He r. China
149 D5 Renhua China
149 C5 Renhuai China
173 D6 Reni Ukr.
126 D5 Renmark Australia
125 G3 Rennell i. Solomon Is
165 G4 Rennerod Germany
166 D2 Rennes France
129 B6 Rennick Glacier glacier Antarctica
187 H2 Rennie Lake Canada
170 D2 Reno r. Italy
196 C2 Reno U.S.A.
202 E4 Renovo U.S.A.
148 E2 Renqiu China
149 B4 Renshou China
190 D5 Rensselaer IN U.S.A.
203 G3 Rensselaer NY U.S.A.
164 D2 Renswoude Neth.
194 B2 Renton U.S.A.
145 E4 Renukut India
128 D4 Renwick N.Z.
176 B3 Réo Burkina Faso
147 E7 Reo Indon.
138 E5 Repetek Turkm.
154 C2 Repou, Tônle r. Laos
194 C1 Republic U.S.A.
198 D3 Republican r. U.S.A.
185 J3 Repulse Bay Canada
210 D5 Requena Peru
167 F3 Requena Spain
136 F1 Reşadiye Turkey
137 I2 Reşadıye Turkey
214 B4 Reserva Brazil
140 D3 Reshm Iran
212 E3 Resistencia Arg.
171 I2 Reşiţa Romania
185 I2 Resolute Canada
185 L3 Resolution Island Canada
128 A6 Resolution Island N.Z.
207 G5 Retalhuleu Guat.
154 □ Retan Laut, Pulau i. Sing.
161 G4 Retford U.K.
166 G2 Rethel France
165 H2 Rethem (Aller) Germany
171 K7 Rethymno Greece
150 C2 Rettikhovka Rus. Fed.
165 K2 Reuden Germany
175 I6 Réunion terr. Indian Ocean
167 G2 Reus Spain
168 D6 Reutlingen Germany
196 D3 Reveille Peak U.S.A.
166 F5 Revel France
186 F4 Revelstoke Canada
204 B5 Revillagigedo, Islas is Mex.
186 C3 Revillagigedo Island U.S.A.
164 C5 Revin France
136 E6 Revivim Israel
144 E4 Rewa India
144 D3 Rewari India
194 E3 Rexburg U.S.A.
189 H4 Rexton Canada
196 A2 Reyes, Point U.S.A.
136 F3 Reyhanlı Turkey
158 B2 Reykir Iceland
219 G2 Reykjanes Ridge sea feature N. Atlantic Ocean
158 B3 Reykjanestá pt Iceland
158 B2 Reykjavík Iceland
207 E2 Reynosa Mex.
159 N4 Rēzekne Latvia
137 L3 Rezvānshahr Iran
161 D5 Rhayader U.K.
165 G3 Rheda-Wiedenbrück Germany
164 E3 Rhede Germany
164 E3 Rhein r. Germany alt. Rhin (France), conv. Rhine
164 F2 Rheine Germany
164 E4 Rheinisches Schiefergebirge hills Germany
164 F5 Rheinland-Pfalz land Germany
165 K1 Rheinsberg Germany
165 G6 Rheinstetten Germany
166 H2 Rhin r. France alt. Rhein (Germany), conv. Rhine
168 C5 Rhine r. Europe alt. Rhein (Germany), alt. Rhin (France)
203 G4 Rhinebeck U.S.A.
190 C3 Rhinelander U.S.A.
165 K2 Rhinkanal canal Germany
165 K2 Rhinluch marsh Germany
165 K2 Rhinow Germany
170 C2 Rho Italy
203 H4 Rhode Island state U.S.A.
171 M6 Rhodes Greece
171 M6 Rhodes i. Greece
194 D2 Rhodes Peak U.S.A.
171 K4 Rhodope Mountains Bulg./Greece
166 G4 Rhône r. France/Switz.
161 D4 Rhyl U.K.
214 E2 Riacho Brazil
214 D1 Riacho de Santana Brazil
215 D4 Riachos, Islas de los is Arg.
214 C1 Rialma Brazil
214 C1 Rianópolis Brazil
144 C2 Riasi India
155 B2 Riau, Kepulauan is Indon.
167 C1 Ribadeo Spain
167 D1 Ribadesella Spain
214 B3 Ribas do Rio Pardo Brazil
141 F4 Ribat Qila Pak.
179 D5 Ribáuè Moz.
160 E4 Ribble r. U.K.
159 J5 Ribe Denmark
164 A5 Ribécourt-Dreslincourt France
214 C4 Ribeira r. Brazil
214 C3 Ribeirão Preto Brazil
164 B5 Ribemont France
166 E4 Ribérac France
210 E6 Riberalta Bol.
173 D6 Rîbniţa Moldova
168 F3 Ribnitz-Damgarten Germany
168 G6 Říčany Czech Rep.
197 E4 Rice U.S.A.
191 F2 Rice Lake l. Canada
190 B3 Rice Lake U.S.A.
190 A4 Riceville IA U.S.A.
202 D4 Riceville PA U.S.A.
181 J4 Richards Bay S. Africa
187 G3 Richardson r. Canada
199 D5 Richardson U.S.A.
203 H2 Richardson Lakes U.S.A.
184 E3 Richardson Mountains Canada
128 B6 Richardson Mountains N.Z.
197 F2 Richfield U.S.A.
203 F3 Richfield Springs U.S.A.
203 E3 Richford NY U.S.A.
203 G2 Richford VT U.S.A.
190 B5 Richland IA U.S.A.
192 C2 Richland WA U.S.A.
190 B4 Richland Center U.S.A.
202 C6 Richlands U.S.A.
127 I4 Richmond N.S.W. Australia
124 E4 Richmond Qld Australia
191 J3 Richmond Canada
128 D4 Richmond N.Z.
181 I4 Richmond Kwazulu-Natal S. Africa
180 E5 Richmond N. Cape S. Africa
160 F3 Richmond U.K.
190 E6 Richmond IN U.S.A.
202 A6 Richmond KY U.S.A.
203 I2 Richmond ME U.S.A.
191 F4 Richmond MI U.S.A.
202 E6 Richmond VA U.S.A.
203 G2 Richmond VT U.S.A.
128 D4 Richmond, Mount N.Z.
191 H4 Richmond Hill Canada
127 J2 Richmond Range hills Australia
180 B4 Richtersveld Cultural and Botanical Landscape tourist site S. Africa
202 B4 Richwood OH U.S.A.
202 C5 Richwood WV U.S.A.
139 J2 Ridder Kazakh.
191 J3 Rideau r. Canada
191 I3 Rideau Lakes Canada
196 D4 Ridgecrest U.S.A.
202 D4 Ridgway U.S.A.
187 I4 Riding Mountain National Park Canada
168 D6 Riedlingen Germany
164 D4 Riemst Belgium
165 L3 Riesa Germany
212 B8 Riesco, Isla i. Chile
180 D5 Riet watercourse S. Africa
159 M5 Rietavas Lith.
180 E6 Rietbron S. Africa
180 D3 Rietfontein S. Africa
170 E3 Rieti Italy
195 F4 Rifle U.S.A.
158 C1 Rifstangi pt Iceland
145 H3 Riga India
159 N4 Rīga Latvia
159 M4 Riga, Gulf of Estonia/Latvia
141 E4 Rīgān Iran
203 F2 Rigaud Canada
141 G4 Rīgestān reg. Afgh.
194 C2 Riggins U.S.A.
189 I3 Rigolet Canada
162 E5 Rigside U.K.
140 E3 Rīgū Iran
145 E4 Rihand r. India
145 E4 Rihand Dam India
159 N3 Riihimäki Fin.
129 D3 Riiser-Larsen Ice Shelf ice feature Antarctica
129 E3 Riiser-Larsen Sea sea Southern Ocean
195 D5 Riito Mex.
170 F2 Rijeka Croatia
150 G5 Rikuzen-takata Japan
171 J3 Rila mts Bulg.
194 C3 Riley U.S.A.
166 G4 Rillieux-la-Pape France
169 J6 Rimavská Sobota Slovakia
186 G4 Rimbey Canada
170 E2 Rimini Italy
144 D2 Rimo Glacier India
189 G4 Rimouski Canada
165 H5 Rimpar Germany
162 D2 Rimsdale, Loch l. U.K.
145 G3 Rinbung China
206 D3 Rincón de Romos Mex.
144 E4 Rind r. India
158 J3 Rindal Norway
127 G8 Ringarooma Bay Australia
144 C4 Ringas India
145 G2 Ring Co salt l. China
164 E2 Ringe Germany
159 J3 Ringebu Norway
159 J4 Ringkøbing Denmark
163 E2 Ringsend U.K.
159 J5 Ringsted Denmark
Ringvassøy i. Norway see Ringvassøya
158 L1 Ringvassøya i. Norway
161 F7 Ringwood U.K.
215 B3 Riñihue Chile
215 B3 Riñihue, Lago l. Chile
155 E4 Rinjani, Gunung vol. Indon.
145 E3 Rinqin Xubco salt l. China
165 H2 Rinteln Germany
190 C4 Rio U.S.A.
210 C5 Río Abiseo, Parque Nacional nat. park Peru
214 A2 Rio Alegre Brazil
210 C4 Riobamba Ecuador
197 H2 Rio Blanco U.S.A.
210 E6 Rio Branco Brazil
213 E4 Rio Branco, Parque Nacional do nat. park Brazil
214 C4 Rio Branco do Sul Brazil
214 A3 Rio Brilhante Brazil
215 B4 Río Bueno Chile
213 E2 Río Caribe Venez.
215 D1 Río Ceballos Arg.
214 C3 Rio Claro Brazil
213 E2 Rio Claro Trin. and Tob.
215 D3 Río Colorado Arg.
215 D2 Río Cuarto Arg.
214 D3 Rio de Janeiro Brazil (City Plan 116)
214 D3 Rio de Janeiro state Brazil
206 I7 Río de Jesús Panama
212 G3 Rio do Sul Brazil
206 I6 Río Frío Costa Rica
212 C8 Río Gallegos Arg.
212 C8 Río Grande Arg.
215 G2 Rio Grande Brazil
206 D3 Río Grande Mex.
207 E2 Rio Grande r. Mex./U.S.A. alt. Bravo del Norte, Río
199 D7 Rio Grande City U.S.A.
219 G8 Rio Grande Rise sea feature S. Atlantic Ocean
213 B2 Ríohacha Col.
210 C5 Rioja Peru
207 G3 Río Lagartos Mex.
211 K5 Rio Largo Brazil
166 F4 Riom France
214 A1 Rio Manso, Represa do resr Brazil
210 E7 Río Mulatos Bol.
215 C4 Río Negro prov. Arg.
214 C4 Rio Negro Brazil
215 F2 Río Negro, Embalse del resr Uruguay
173 G7 Rioni r. Georgia
215 G1 Río Pardo Brazil
214 D1 Rio Pardo de Minas Brazil
215 D1 Río Primero Arg.
195 F5 Rio Rancho U.S.A.
197 G6 Rio Rico U.S.A.
215 D1 Río Segundo Arg.
213 A3 Ríosucio Col.
215 D2 Río Tercero Arg.
210 C4 Río Tigre Ecuador
153 A4 Rio Tuba Phil.
214 B2 Rio Verde Brazil
207 E3 Río Verde Mex.
207 G4 Río Verde Mex.
214 A2 Rio Verde de Mato Grosso Brazil
196 B2 Rio Vista U.S.A.
214 A2 Riozinho r. Brazil
169 O5 Ripky Ukr.
160 F3 Ripley England U.K.
161 F4 Ripley England U.K.
202 B5 Ripley OH U.S.A.
201 B5 Ripley TN U.S.A.
202 C5 Ripley WV U.S.A.
167 H1 Ripoll Spain
160 F3 Ripon U.K.
196 B3 Ripon CA U.S.A.
190 C4 Ripon WI U.S.A.
161 D6 Risca U.K.
150 G2 Rishiri-tō i. Japan
136 E6 Rishon LeZiyyon Israel
141 F5 Rish Pish Iran
159 J4 Risør Norway
158 J3 Rissa Norway
159 N3 Ristiina Fin.
158 O2 Ristijärvi Fin.
158 O1 Ristikent Rus. Fed.
180 F4 Ritchie S. Africa
129 D3 Ritscher Upland mts Antarctica
158 L2 Ritsem Sweden
196 C3 Ritter, Mount U.S.A.
165 G1 Ritterhude Germany
167 E2 Rituerto r. Spain
194 C2 Ritzville U.S.A.
215 D2 Rivadavia Buenos Aires Arg.
215 C2 Rivadavia Mendoza Arg.
212 D2 Rivadavia Arg.
215 B1 Rivadavia Chile
170 D2 Riva del Garda Italy
206 C1 Riva Palacio Mex.
206 H6 Rivas Nicaragua
141 E3 Rīvash Iran
215 D3 Rivera Arg.
215 F1 Rivera Uruguay
176 B4 River Cess Liberia
203 G4 Riverhead U.S.A.
127 F5 Riverina reg. Australia
180 D7 Riversdale S. Africa
181 H5 Riverside S. Africa
196 D5 Riverside U.S.A.
126 C5 Riverton Australia
187 J4 Riverton Canada
128 B7 Riverton N.Z.
194 E3 Riverton U.S.A.
189 H4 Riverview Canada
166 F5 Rivesaltes France
201 D7 Riviera Beach U.S.A.
203 I1 Rivière-Bleue Canada
189 G4 Rivière-du-Loup Canada
173 C5 Rivne Ukr.
128 D4 Riwaka N.Z.
142 C5 Riyadh Saudi Arabia
140 D3 Riza well Iran
137 H1 Rize Turkey
Rizhao China see Donggang
136 E4 Rizokarpason Cyprus
140 E4 Rīzū'īyeh Iran
159 J4 Rjukan Norway
159 I4 Rjuvbrokkene mt. Norway
176 A3 Rkîz Mauritania
159 J3 Roa Norway
161 G5 Roade U.K.
158 J2 Roan Norway
197 H2 Roan Cliffs ridge U.S.A.
166 G3 Roanne France
201 C5 Roanoke AL U.S.A.
190 C5 Roanoke IL U.S.A.
202 D6 Roanoke VA U.S.A.
200 E4 Roanoke r. U.S.A.
201 E4 Roanoke Rapids U.S.A.
197 H2 Roan Plateau U.S.A.
163 B6 Roaringwater Bay Ireland
206 H4 Roatán Hond.
158 M3 Röbäck Sweden
140 E4 Robāţ Iran
140 E3 Robāţ-e Khān Iran
127 F8 Robbins Island Australia
126 C6 Robe Australia
163 B4 Robe r. Ireland
126 D3 Robe, Mount h. Australia
165 K1 Röbel Germany
188 E3 Robert-Bourassa, Réservoir resr Canada
199 C6 Robert Lee U.S.A.
194 D3 Roberts U.S.A.
127 J2 Roberts, Mount Australia
196 D2 Roberts Creek Mountain U.S.A.
158 M2 Robertsfors Sweden
145 E4 Robertsganj India
199 E5 Robert S. Kerr Reservoir U.S.A.
180 C6 Robertson S. Africa
176 A4 Robertsport Liberia
126 C4 Robertstown Australia
189 F4 Roberval Canada
185 L1 Robeson Channel Canada/Greenland
160 G3 Robin Hood's Bay U.K.
149 □ Robin's Nest h. Hong Kong China
200 C4 Robinson U.S.A.
124 B4 Robinson Ranges hills Australia
126 E5 Robinvale Australia
197 G5 Robles Junction U.S.A.
197 G5 Robles Pass U.S.A.
187 I4 Roblin Canada
186 F4 Robson, Mount Canada
199 D7 Robstown U.S.A.
207 F4 Roca Partida, Punta pt Mex.
215 F2 Rocha Uruguay
160 E4 Rochdale U.K.
214 A2 Rochedo Brazil
164 D4 Rochefort Belgium
166 D4 Rochefort France
188 F2 Rochefort, Lac l. Canada
172 G2 Rochegda Rus. Fed.
190 C5 Rochelle U.S.A.
126 F6 Rochester Australia
161 H6 Rochester U.K.
190 D5 Rochester IN U.S.A.
190 A3 Rochester MN U.S.A.
203 H3 Rochester NH U.S.A.
202 E3 Rochester NY U.S.A.
161 H6 Rochford U.K.
165 K3 Rochlitz Germany
166 C2 Roc'h Trévezel h. France
186 D2 Rock r. Canada
190 B5 Rock r. U.S.A.
156 C4 Rockall i. N. Atlantic Ocean
219 H2 Rockall Bank sea feature N. Atlantic Ocean
129 B4 Rockefeller Plateau plat. Antarctica
190 C4 Rockford U.S.A.
187 H5 Rockglen Canada
124 F4 Rockhampton Australia
190 C1 Rock Harbor U.S.A.
201 D5 Rock Hill U.S.A.
124 B5 Rockingham Australia
201 E5 Rockingham U.S.A.
203 G2 Rock Island Canada
190 B5 Rock Island U.S.A.
147 F6 Rock Islands Southern Lagoon tourist site Palau
198 D1 Rocklake U.S.A.
203 F2 Rockland Canada
203 H3 Rockland MA U.S.A.
203 I2 Rockland ME U.S.A.
190 C2 Rockland MI U.S.A.
126 E6 Rocklands Reservoir Australia
197 H3 Rock Point U.S.A.
203 H3 Rockport U.S.A.
198 D3 Rock Rapids U.S.A.
194 F2 Rock Springs MT U.S.A.
194 E3 Rock Springs WY U.S.A.
199 C6 Rocksprings U.S.A.
202 D3 Rockton Canada
190 D6 Rockville IN U.S.A.
202 E5 Rockville MD U.S.A.
203 I2 Rockwood U.S.A.
195 G4 Rocky Ford U.S.A.
202 B5 Rocky Fork Lake U.S.A.
191 F2 Rocky Island Lake Canada
201 E5 Rocky Mount NC U.S.A.
202 D6 Rocky Mount VA U.S.A.
186 G4 Rocky Mountain House Canada
194 F3 Rocky Mountain National Park U.S.A.
192 D2 Rocky Mountains Canada/U.S.A.
186 F4 Rocky Mountains Forest Reserve nature res. Canada
164 B5 Rocourt-St-Martin France
164 C5 Rocroi France
159 J3 Rodberg Norway
159 J5 Rødbyhavn Denmark
189 I3 Roddickton Canada
162 B3 Rodel U.K.
164 E1 Roden Neth.
165 J4 Rödental Germany
215 C1 Rodeo Arg.
206 C2 Rodeo Mex.
197 H6 Rodeo U.S.A.
166 F4 Rodez France
165 K5 Roding Germany
139 J1 Rodino Rus. Fed.
141 G5 Rodkhan Pak.
172 G3 Rodniki Rus. Fed.
138 D2 Rodnikovka Kazakh.
Rodos Greece see Rhodes
Rodos i. Greece see Rhodes
218 I6 Rodrigues Island Mauritius
124 B4 Roebourne Australia
124 C3 Roebuck Bay Australia
181 H2 Roedtan S. Africa
164 D3 Roermond Neth.
164 B4 Roeselare Belgium
185 J3 Roes Welcome Sound sea chan. Canada
165 J2 Rogätz Germany
199 E4 Rogers U.S.A.
191 F3 Rogers City U.S.A.
196 D4 Rogers Lake U.S.A.
194 D3 Rogerson U.S.A.
202 B6 Rogersville U.S.A.
188 E3 Roggan r. Canada
217 N8 Roggeveen Basin sea feature S. Pacific Ocean
180 D6 Roggeveld plat. S. Africa
180 D6 Roggeveldberge esc. S. Africa
158 K2 Rognan Norway
194 A3 Rogue r. U.S.A.
196 A2 Rohnert Park U.S.A.
168 F6 Rohrbach in Oberösterreich Austria
164 F5 Rohrbach-lès-Bitche France
144 B4 Rohri Sangar Pak.
144 D3 Rohtak India
154 B1 Roi Et Thai.
123 J5 Roi-Georges, Îles du is Fr. Polynesia
164 B5 Roisel France
159 M4 Roja Latvia
215 E2 Rojas Arg.
144 B3 Rojhan Pak.
207 E3 Rojo, Cabo Mex.
155 B2 Rokan r. Indon.
159 N5 Rokiškis Lith.
158 M2 Roknäs Sweden
173 C5 Rokytne Ukr.
214 B3 Rolândia Brazil
198 F4 Rolla U.S.A.
159 J3 Rollag Norway
128 D5 Rolleston N.Z.
191 H2 Rollet Canada
201 F7 Rolleville Bahamas
191 I2 Rolphton Canada
124 E4 Roma Australia
Roma Italy see Rome
181 G4 Roma Lesotho
159 L4 Roma Sweden
201 E5 Romain, Cape U.S.A.
189 H3 Romaine r. Canada
169 M7 Roman Romania
219 H6 Romanche Gap sea feature S. Atlantic Ocean
147 E7 Romang, Pulau i. Indon.
171 K1 Romania country Europe
146 D1 Romanovka Rus. Fed.
173 G5 Romanovka Saratovskaya Oblast' Rus. Fed.
139 J1 Romanovo Rus. Fed.
166 G4 Romans-sur-Isère France
184 B3 Romanzof, Cape U.S.A.
166 H2 Rombas France
153 B3 Romblon Phil.
153 B3 Romblon i. Phil.
Rombo, Ilhéus Secos ou do i. Cape Verde see Secos, Ilhéus
170 E4 Rome Italy (City Plan 112)
201 C5 Rome GA U.S.A.
203 I2 Rome ME U.S.A.
203 F3 Rome NY U.S.A.
191 F4 Romeo U.S.A.
161 H6 Romford U.K.
166 F2 Romilly-sur-Seine France
Romitan Uzbek. see Romiton
138 F5 Romiton Uzbek.
202 D5 Romney U.S.A.
161 H6 Romney Marsh reg. U.K.
173 E5 Romny Ukr.
159 J5 Rømø i. Denmark
166 E3 Romorantin-Lanthenay France
154 B5 Rompin r. Malaysia
161 F7 Romsey U.K.
143 A3 Ron India
154 C1 Ron Vietnam
162 C1 Rona i. Scotland U.K.
162 C3 Rona i. Scotland U.K.
162 □ Ronas Hill U.K.
211 H6 Roncador, Serra do hills Brazil
125 F2 Roncador Reef Solomon Is
167 D4 Ronda Spain
159 J3 Rondane Nasjonalpark nat. park Norway
213 C3 Rondón Col.
213 E4 Rondon, Pico h. Brazil
214 A2 Rondonópolis Brazil
135 F3 Rondu Pak.
149 C5 Rong'an China
149 B4 Rongchang China
152 B5 Rongcheng China
152 B5 Rongcheng Wan b. China
145 G3 Rong Chu r. China
216 G6 Rongelap atoll Marshall Is
149 C5 Rongjiang China
149 C6 Rong Jiang r. China
145 H5 Rongklang Range mts Myanmar
128 E4 Rongotea N.Z.
149 C5 Rongshui China
149 D6 Rongxian Guangxi China
149 B4 Rongxian Sichuan China
159 K5 Rønne Denmark
159 K4 Ronneby Sweden
129 B3 Ronne Entrance str. Antarctica
129 B3 Ronne Ice Shelf ice feature Antarctica
165 H2 Ronnenberg Germany
164 B4 Ronse Belgium
181 G3 Roodepoort S. Africa
164 E1 Roodeschool Neth.
Roordahuizum Neth. see Reduzum
144 D3 Roorkee India
164 C3 Roosendaal Neth.
197 G5 Roosevelt AZ U.S.A.
197 G1 Roosevelt UT U.S.A.
186 D3 Roosevelt, Mount Canada
129 B5 Roosevelt Island i. Antarctica
186 E2 Root r. Canada
190 B4 Root r. U.S.A.
172 J2 Ropcha Rus. Fed.
166 D4 Roquefort France
213 E4 Roraima state Brazil
210 F2 Roraima, Mount Guyana
158 J3 Røros Norway
158 J2 Rørvik Norway
169 O6 Ros' r. Ukr.
210 □ Rosa, Cabo c. Galapagos Is Ecuador
201 D2 Rosa, Lake Bahamas
206 B2 Rosa, Punta pt Mex.
196 C4 Rosamond U.S.A.
196 C4 Rosamond Lake U.S.A.
215 E2 Rosario Arg.
204 A2 Rosario Baja California Mex.
206 D2 Rosario Coahuila Mex.
206 C3 Rosario Sinaloa Mex.
206 B2 Rosario Sonora Mex.
153 B2 Rosario Phil.
153 B3 Rosario Phil.
213 B2 Rosario Venez.
215 E2 Rosario del Tala Arg.
215 F1 Rosário do Sul Brazil
214 A1 Rosário Oeste Brazil
206 A1 Rosarito Baja California Mex.
206 B2 Rosarito Baja California Sur Mex.
170 F5 Rosarno Italy
203 F4 Roscoe U.S.A.
166 C2 Roscoff France
163 C4 Roscommon Ireland
190 E3 Roscommon U.S.A.
163 D5 Roscrea Ireland
196 C2 Rose, Mount U.S.A.
205 L5 Roseau Dominica
187 J5 Roseau U.S.A.
127 F8 Rosebery Australia
189 I4 Rose Blanche Canada
194 B3 Roseburg U.S.A.
191 E3 Rose City U.S.A.
160 G3 Rosedale Abbey U.K.
177 F3 Roseires Reservoir Sudan
123 H4 Rose Island atoll American Samoa
199 E6 Rosenberg U.S.A.
159 I4 Rosendal Norway
181 G4 Rosendal S. Africa
168 F7 Rosenheim Germany
186 C4 Rose Point Canada
170 F3 Roseto degli Abruzzi Italy
187 H4 Rosetown Canada
187 I4 Rose Valley Canada
196 B2 Roseville CA U.S.A.
190 B5 Roseville IL U.S.A.
127 J1 Rosewood Australia
172 D2 Roshchino Leningradskaya Oblast' Rus. Fed.
150 D2 Roshchino Primorskiy Kray Rus. Fed.
180 B3 Rosh Pinah Namibia
141 E3 Roshtkhvār Iran
139 G5 Roshtqal'a Tajik.
170 D3 Rosignano Marittimo Italy
171 K2 Roşiori de Vede Romania
159 K5 Roskilde Denmark
172 E4 Roslavl' Rus. Fed.
158 P1 Roslyakovo Rus. Fed.
127 G9 Ross Australia
186 C2 Ross r. Canada
128 C5 Ross N.Z.
128 E4 Ross, Mount h. N.Z.
170 G5 Rossano Italy
163 C3 Rossan Point Ireland
199 F5 Ross Barnett Reservoir U.S.A.
189 G3 Ross Bay Junction Canada
163 B6 Rosscarbery Ireland
129 A5 Ross Dependency reg. Antarctica
125 F3 Rossel Island P.N.G.
129 B5 Ross Ice Shelf ice feature Antarctica
189 H5 Rossignol, Lake Canada
129 B5 Ross Island i. Antarctica
163 E5 Rosslare Ireland
161 A5 Rosslare Harbour Ireland
165 K3 Roßlau Germany
191 I3 Rossmore Canada
176 A3 Rosso Mauritania
170 C3 Rosso, Capo c. Corsica France
161 E6 Ross-on-Wye U.K.
173 F5 Rossosh' Rus. Fed.
190 D1 Rossport Canada
186 C2 Ross River Canada
129 B5 Ross Sea sea Antarctica
165 I5 Roßtal Germany
158 K2 Røssvatnet l. Norway
190 D5 Rossville U.S.A.
165 L3 Roßwein Germany
186 D3 Rosswood Canada
137 J3 Rōst Iraq
140 D5 Rostāq Iran
187 H4 Rosthern Canada
168 F3 Rostock Germany
172 F3 Rostov Rus. Fed.
173 F6 Rostov-na-Donu Rus. Fed.
173 G6 Rostovskaya Oblast' admin. div. Rus. Fed.
158 M2 Rosvik Sweden
201 C5 Roswell GA U.S.A.
195 F5 Roswell NM U.S.A.
147 G5 Rota i. N. Mariana Is
165 I5 Rot am See Germany
147 E8 Rote i. Indon.
165 H1 Rotenburg (Wümme) Germany
165 J4 Roter Main r. Germany
165 J5 Roth Germany
165 G4 Rothaargebirge hills Germany
160 F2 Rothbury U.K.
160 F2 Rothbury Forest U.K.
165 I5 Rothenburg ob der Tauber Germany
161 G7 Rother r. U.K.
129 E2 Rothera research stn Antarctica
128 D5 Rotherham N.Z.
161 F4 Rotherham U.K.
162 E3 Rothes U.K.
162 C5 Rothesay U.K.
190 C3 Rothschild U.S.A.
161 G5 Rothwell U.K.
127 F4 Roto Australia
128 C5 Rotomanu N.Z.
170 C3 Rotondo, Monte mt. Corsica France
128 D4 Rotoroa, Lake N.Z.
128 F3 Rotorua N.Z.
128 F3 Rotorua, Lake N.Z.
168 F6 Rott r. Germany
165 J5 Röttenbach Germany
165 I5 Rottendorf Germany
168 G7 Rottenmann Austria
164 C3 Rotterdam Neth.
165 I3 Rottleberode Germany
164 E1 Rottumeroog i. Neth.
164 E1 Rottumerplaat i. Neth.
168 D6 Rottweil Germany
125 H3 Rotuma i. Fiji
158 K3 Rötviken Sweden
165 K5 Rötz Germany
166 F1 Roubaix France
166 E2 Rouen France
128 B6 Rough Ridge N.Z.
Roulers Belgium see Roeselare
189 F3 Roundeyed Lake Canada
160 F3 Round Hill U.K.
127 J3 Round Mountain Australia
196 D2 Round Mountain U.S.A.
197 H3 Round Rock U.S.A.
194 E2 Roundup U.S.A.
162 E1 Rousay i. U.K.
203 G2 Rouses Point U.S.A.
166 F5 Roussillon reg. France
181 G5 Rouxville S. Africa
Rouyn Canada see Rouyn-Noranda
191 H1 Rouyn-Noranda Canada
158 N2 Rovaniemi Fin.
173 F5 Roven'ki Rus. Fed.
170 D2 Rovereto Italy
154 C2 Rôviĕng Tbong Cambodia
170 D2 Rovigo Italy
170 E2 Rovinj Croatia
173 H5 Rovnoye Rus. Fed.
127 H2 Rowena Australia
153 A4 Roxas Phil.
153 B2 Roxas Phil.
153 B3 Roxas Phil.
153 B4 Roxas Phil.
201 E4 Roxboro U.S.A.
128 B6 Roxburgh N.Z.
126 B3 Roxby Downs Australia
195 F4 Roy U.S.A.
163 E4 Royal Canal Ireland
145 F4 Royal Chitwan National Park Nepal
190 C1 Royale, Isle i. U.S.A.
181 H4 Royal Natal National Park S. Africa
191 F4 Royal Oak U.S.A.
166 D4 Royan France
164 A5 Roye France
161 G5 Royston U.K.
141 F3 Rōzanak Afgh.
173 D6 Rozdil'na Ukr.
173 E6 Rozdol'ne Ukr.
173 F6 Rozivka Ukr.
140 C3 Rozveh Iran
173 G4 Rtishchevo Rus. Fed.
161 D5 Ruabon U.K.
179 B5 Ruacana Namibia
178 D4 Ruaha National Park Tanz.
128 F3 Ruahine Range mts N.Z.
128 E3 Ruapehu, Mount vol. N.Z.
128 B7 Ruapuke Island N.Z.
128 G2 Ruatoria N.Z.
172 D4 Ruba Belarus
142 C6 Rub' al Khālī des. Saudi Arabia
150 H3 Rubeshibe Japan
196 B2 Rubicon r. U.S.A.
173 F5 Rubizhne Ukr.
139 J2 Rubtsovsk Rus. Fed.
184 C3 Ruby U.S.A.
197 E1 Ruby Lake U.S.A.
197 E1 Ruby Mountains U.S.A.
149 D5 Rucheng China
202 D5 Ruckersville U.S.A.
145 E4 Rudauli India
141 F4 Rūdbār Afgh.
137 L3 Rūdbār Iran
Rūd-i-Shur watercourse Iran see Shūr, Rūd-e
159 J5 Rudkøbing Denmark
146 F2 Rudnaya Pristan' Rus. Fed.
172 J3 Rudnichnyy Rus. Fed.
172 D4 Rudnya Rus. Fed.
138 E1 Rudnyy Kazakh.
150 D2 Rudnyy Rus. Fed.
132 G1 Rudol'fa, Ostrov i. Rus. Fed.
165 J4 Rudolstadt Germany
148 F3 Rudong China
140 C2 Rūdsar Iran
190 E2 Rudyard U.S.A.
179 D4 Rufiji r. Tanz.
215 D2 Rufino Arg.
176 A3 Rufisque Senegal
179 C5 Rufunsa Zambia
148 F3 Rugao China
161 F5 Rugby U.K.
198 C1 Rugby U.S.A.
161 F5 Rugeley U.K.
168 F3 Rügen i. Germany
202 B4 Ruggles U.S.A.
165 I5 Rügland Germany
140 B5 Ruḩayyat al Ḩamr'ā' waterhole Saudi Arabia
178 C4 Ruhengeri Rwanda
159 M4 Ruhnu i. Estonia
164 E4 Ruhr r. Germany
149 F5 Rui'an China
195 F5 Ruidoso U.S.A.
149 E5 Ruijin China
187 M2 Ruin Point Canada
179 D4 Ruipa Tanz.
206 C3 Ruiz Mex.
213 B3 Ruiz, Nevado del vol. Col.
136 F5 Rujaylah, Ḩarrat ar lava field Jordan
159 N4 Rūjiena Latvia
140 C5 Rukbah well Saudi Arabia
145 E3 Rukumkot Nepal
178 D4 Rukwa, Lake Tanz.
140 E5 Rūl Ḑadnah U.A.E.
141 E3 Rūm Iran
162 B4 Rum i. U.K.
171 H2 Ruma Serbia
140 B5 Rumāh Saudi Arabia
177 E4 Rumbek South Sudan
201 F7 Rum Cay i. Bahamas
203 H2 Rumford U.S.A.
166 G4 Rumilly France
124 D3 Rum Jungle Australia
150 G3 Rumoi Japan
148 E3 Runan China
128 C5 Runanga N.Z.
128 F2 Runaway, Cape N.Z.
161 E4 Runcorn U.K.
179 B5 Rundu Namibia
158 L3 Rundvik Sweden
154 B3 Rŭng, Kaôh i. Cambodia
154 B3 Rŭng Sânlŏem, Kaôh i. Cambodia
148 E3 Runhe China
159 O3 Ruokolahti Fin.
146 A3 Ruoqiang China
145 H4 Rupa India
215 B4 Rupanco, Lago l. Chile
126 E6 Rupanyup Australia
155 B2 Rupat i. Indon.
188 E3 Rupert r. Canada
194 D3 Rupert U.S.A.
188 E3 Rupert Bay Canada
179 D5 Rusape Zimbabwe
171 K3 Ruse Bulg.
152 A5 Rushan China
161 G5 Rushden U.K.
190 B4 Rushford U.S.A.
190 C4 Rush Lake U.S.A.
145 H3 Rushon India
139 G5 Rushon Tajik.
190 B5 Rushville IL U.S.A.
198 C3 Rushville NE U.S.A.
126 F6 Rushworth Australia
199 E6 Rusk U.S.A.
201 D7 Ruskin U.S.A.
187 I4 Russell Man. Canada
203 F2 Russell Ont. Canada
128 E1 Russell N.Z.
198 D4 Russell U.S.A.
185 I2 Russell Island Canada
125 F2 Russell Islands Solomon Is
186 F2 Russell Lake Canada
201 C4 Russellville AL U.S.A.
199 E5 Russellville AR U.S.A.
200 C4 Russellville KY U.S.A.
165 G4 Rüsselsheim Germany
132 G3 Russian Federation country Asia/Europe
139 H1 Russkaya-Polyana Rus. Fed.
150 C3 Russkiy, Ostrov i. Rus. Fed.
141 H2 Rustāq Afgh.
137 J1 Rustavi Georgia
181 G2 Rustenburg S. Africa
199 E5 Ruston U.S.A.
147 E7 Ruteng Indon.
197 E2 Ruth U.S.A.
165 G3 Rüthen Germany
191 H2 Rutherglen Canada
161 D4 Ruthin U.K.
172 H3 Rutka r. Rus. Fed.
203 G3 Rutland U.S.A.
161 G5 Rutland Water resr U.K.
187 G2 Rutledge Lake Canada
Rutög China see Dêrub
191 G2 Rutter Canada
158 N2 Ruukki Fin.
140 E5 Rū'us al Jibāl hills Oman
179 D5 Ruvuma r. Moz./Tanz.
136 F5 Ruwayshid, Wādī watercourse Jordan
140 D5 Ruweis U.A.E.
149 D5 Ruyuan China
139 F1 Ruzayevka Kazakh.
172 H4 Ruzayevka Rus. Fed.
148 D3 Ruzhou China
169 I6 Ružomberok Slovakia
178 C4 Rwanda country Africa
140 D2 Ryābād Iran
172 H2 Ryadovo Rus. Fed.
162 C5 Ryan, Loch b. U.K.
172 F4 Ryazan' Rus. Fed.
172 G4 Ryazanskaya Oblast' admin. div. Rus. Fed.
172 G4 Ryazhsk Rus. Fed.

132 E2 **Rybachiy, Poluostrov** *pen.* Rus. Fed.
138 D3 **Rybachiy Poselok** Uzbek.
139 J3 **Rybach'ye** Kazakh.
172 F3 **Rybinsk** Rus. Fed.
172 F3 **Rybinskoye Vodokhranilishche** *resr* Rus. Fed.
172 I4 **Rybnaya Sloboda** Rus. Fed.
169 I5 **Rybnik** Poland
172 F4 **Rybnoye** Rus. Fed.
186 F3 **Rycroft** Canada
159 K4 **Ryd** Sweden
129 B3 **Rydberg Peninsula** *pen.* Antarctica
161 F7 **Ryde** U.K.
161 H7 **Rye** U.K.
160 G3 **Rye** *r.* U.K.
173 E5 **Ryl'sk** Rus. Fed.
127 H4 **Rylstone** Australia
138 B3 **Ryn-Peski** *des.* Kazakh.
151 F5 **Ryōtsu** Japan
146 E4 **Ryukyu Islands** Japan
218 M3 **Ryukyu Trench** *sea feature* N. Pacific Ocean
169 K5 **Rzeszów** Poland
173 G4 **Rzhaksa** Rus. Fed.
172 E3 **Rzhev** Rus. Fed.


## S


140 E3 **Sa'ābād** Iran
140 D4 **Sa'ādatābād** Iran
165 J6 **Saal an der Donau** Germany
165 J3 **Saale** *r.* Germany
165 J4 **Saalfeld** Germany
164 E5 **Saar** *r.* Germany
164 E5 **Saarbrücken** Germany
159 M4 **Saaremaa** *i.* Estonia
158 N2 **Saarenkylä** Fin.
164 E5 **Saargau** *reg.* Germany
158 N3 **Saarijärvi** Fin.
158 N2 **Saari-Kämä** Fin.
158 M1 **Saarikoski** Fin.
164 E5 **Saarland** *land* Germany
164 E5 **Saarlouis** Germany
137 L2 **Saatlı** Azer.
215 D3 **Saavedra** Arg.
136 F5 **Sab' Ābār** Syria
171 H2 **Šabac** Serbia
167 H2 **Sabadell** Spain
151 E7 **Sabae** Japan
155 E1 **Sabah** *state* Malaysia
154 B5 **Sabak** Malaysia
137 K2 **Sabalan, Kūhhā-ye** *mts* Iran
155 E4 **Sabalana, Kepulauan** *is* Indon.
144 D4 **Sabalgarh** India
**Sabamagrande** Hond. *see* **Sabanagrande**
205 H4 **Sabana, Archipiélago de** *is* Cuba
206 H5 **Sabanagrande** Hond.
213 B2 **Sabanalarga** Col.
136 D1 **Şabanözü** Turkey
214 D2 **Sabará** Brazil
143 C2 **Sabari** *r.* India
144 C5 **Sabarmati** *r.* India
170 E4 **Sabaudia** Italy
141 E3 **Sabeh** Iran
180 E5 **Sabelo** S. Africa
177 D2 **Sabhā** Libya
140 B6 **Şabḩā'** Saudi Arabia
144 D3 **Sabi** *r.* India
181 J2 **Sabie** Moz.
181 J2 **Sabie** *r.* Moz./S. Africa
181 I2 **Sabie** S. Africa
206 D2 **Sabinas** Mex.
207 D2 **Sabinas Hidalgo** Mex.
199 E6 **Sabine Lake** U.S.A.
137 L1 **Sabirabad** Azer.
153 B3 **Sablayan** Phil.
185 L5 **Sable, Cape** Canada
201 D7 **Sable, Cape** U.S.A.
185 M5 **Sable Island** Canada
191 F2 **Sables, River aux** *r.* Canada
140 D4 **Sablū'īyeh** Iran
138 A4 **Şabran** Azer.
177 D1 **Şabrātah** Libya
129 C6 **Sabrina Coast** *coastal area* Antarctica
153 B1 **Sabtang** *i.* Phil.
167 C2 **Sabugal** Port.
190 B4 **Sabula** U.S.A.
142 B6 **Şabyā** Saudi Arabia
141 E2 **Sabzevār** Iran
171 M2 **Sacalinul Mare, Insula** *i.* Romania
171 K2 **Săcele** Romania
179 B5 **Sachanga** Angola
152 E6 **Sacheon** S. Korea
152 E6 **Sacheon** S. Korea
188 B3 **Sachigo** *r.* Canada
188 B3 **Sachigo Lake** Canada
144 C5 **Sachin** India
144 D2 **Sach Pass** India
165 K3 **Sachsen** *land* Germany
165 J3 **Sachsen-Anhalt** *land* Germany
165 H6 **Sachsenheim** Germany
184 F2 **Sachs Harbour** Canada
203 E3 **Sackets Harbor** U.S.A.
165 G4 **Sackpfeife** *h.* Germany
189 H4 **Sackville** Canada
203 H3 **Saco** *ME* U.S.A.
194 F1 **Saco** *MT* U.S.A.
153 B5 **Sacol** *i.* Phil.
196 B2 **Sacramento** U.S.A.
196 B2 **Sacramento** *r.* U.S.A.
195 F5 **Sacramento Mountains** U.S.A.
194 B3 **Sacramento Valley** U.S.A.
181 G6 **Sada** S. Africa
167 F1 **Sádaba** Spain
140 C4 **Sa'dābād** Iran
136 F4 **Şadad** Syria
154 B4 **Sadao** Thai.
137 J5 **Saddat al Hindīyah** Iraq
181 I2 **Saddleback** *pass* S. Africa
154 C3 **Sa Đec** Vietnam
145 H3 **Sadêng** China
141 E5 **Sadīj** *watercourse* Iran
144 B3 **Sadiqabad** Pak.
144 C1 **Sad Ishtrāgh** *mt.* Afgh./Pak.
137 K5 **Sa'dīyah, Hawr as** *imp. l.* Iraq
140 D5 **Sa'diyyat** *i.* U.A.E.
140 E2 **Sad Kharv** Iran
167 B3 **Sado** *r.* Port.
151 F6 **Sadoga-shima** *i.* Japan
146 F3 **Sado-shima** *i.* Japan
167 H3 **Sa Dragonera** *i.* Spain
159 J4 **Sæby** Denmark
140 D4 **Safāshahr** Iran
137 K6 **Safayal Maqūf** *well* Iraq
141 H2 **Safayd Khirs, Kōh-e** *mts* Afgh.
159 K4 **Säffle** Sweden
197 H5 **Safford** U.S.A.
161 H5 **Saffron Walden** U.K.
176 B1 **Safi** Morocco
140 C2 **Safīd** *r.* Iran
140 D3 **Safid Ab** Iran
141 F4 **Safidabeh** Iran
137 L5 **Safid Dasht** Iran
136 F4 **Şāfītā** Syria
132 F3 **Safonovo** *Arkhangel'skaya Oblast'* Rus. Fed.
158 P1 **Safonovo** *Murmanskaya Oblast'* Rus. Fed.
172 E4 **Safonovo** *Smolenskaya Oblast'* Rus. Fed.
136 D1 **Safranbolu** Turkey
137 K6 **Safwān** Iraq
145 F3 **Saga** China
151 B8 **Saga** Japan
138 E2 **Saga** *Kostanayskaya Oblast'* Kazakh.
138 F2 **Saga** *Kostanayskaya Oblast'* Kazakh.
151 F7 **Sagamihara** Japan
151 F7 **Sagami-nada** *g.* Japan
151 F7 **Sagami-wan** *b.* Japan
213 B3 **Sagamoso** *r.* Col.
139 I4 **Sagankuduk** China
154 A2 **Saganthit Kyun** *i.* Myanmar
143 A3 **Sagar** *Karnataka* India
143 B2 **Sagar** *Karnataka* India
144 D5 **Sagar** *Madhya Pradesh* India
173 H7 **Sagarejo** Georgia
145 G5 **Sagar Island** India
133 N2 **Sagastyr** Rus. Fed.
140 D3 **Sāghand** Iran
141 F3 **Sāghar** Afgh.
143 B3 **Sagileru** *r.* India
191 F4 **Saginaw** U.S.A.
191 F4 **Saginaw Bay** U.S.A.
189 H2 **Saglek Bay** Canada
170 C3 **Sagone, Golfe de** *b. Corsica* France
167 B4 **Sagres** Port.
145 H5 **Sagu** Myanmar
195 F4 **Saguache** U.S.A.
205 H4 **Sagua la Grande** Cuba
197 G5 **Saguaro National Park** U.S.A.
189 F4 **Saguenay** *r.* Canada
167 F3 **Sagunto** Spain
144 C5 **Sagwara** India
138 C2 **Sagyz** Kazakh.
138 C2 **Sagyz** *r.* Kazakh.
213 B2 **Sahagún** Col.
167 D1 **Sahagún** Spain
137 K3 **Sahand, Kūh-e** *mt.* Iran
176 C2 **Sahara** *des.* Africa
144 D3 **Saharanpur** India
145 F4 **Saharsa** India
144 D3 **Sahaswan** India
140 C6 **Sahbā', Wādī as** *watercourse* Saudi Arabia
137 L1 **Sahil** Azer.
144 C3 **Sahiwal** Pak.
141 E3 **Sahlābād** Iran
137 K4 **Şaḩneh** Iran
137 J6 **Şaḩrā al Ḩijārah** *reg.* Iraq
206 B1 **Sahuaripa** Mex.
197 G6 **Sahuarita** U.S.A.
206 D3 **Sahuayo** Mex.
154 D2 **Sa Huynh** Vietnam
144 C5 **Sahyadriparvat Range** *hills* India
144 E4 **Sai** *r.* India
154 B4 **Sai Buri** Thai.
154 B4 **Sai Buri, Mae Nam** *r.* Thai.
**Saïda** Lebanon *see* **Sidon**
154 B2 **Sai Dao Tai, Khao** *mt.* Thai.
141 F5 **Sa'īdī** Iran
145 G4 **Saidpur** Bangl.
144 C2 **Saidu** Pak.
**Saigon** Vietnam *see* **Ho Chi Minh City**
154 C3 **Sai Gon, Sông** *r.* Vietnam
**Saigon, Sông** *r.* Vietnam *see* **Sai Gon, Sông**
145 H5 **Saiha** India
148 D1 **Saihan Tal** China
148 A1 **Saihan Toroi** China
151 C8 **Saijō** Japan
151 B8 **Saiki** Japan
149 □ **Sai Kung** *Hong Kong* China
159 O3 **Saimaa** *l.* Fin.
136 F2 **Saimbeyli** Turkey
206 D3 **Sain Alto** Mex.
141 F4 **Saindak** Pak.
140 B2 **Sa'īndezh** Iran
162 F5 **St Abb's Head** U.K.
161 B7 **St Agnes** U.K.
161 A8 **St Agnes** *i.* U.K.
189 I4 **St Alban's** Canada
161 G6 **St Albans** U.K.
203 G2 **St Albans** *VT* U.S.A.
202 C5 **St Albans** *WV* U.S.A.
**St Alban's Head** *hd* U.K. *see* **St Aldhelm's Head**
186 G4 **St Albert** Canada
161 E7 **St Aldhelm's Head** U.K.
164 B4 **St-Amand-les-Eaux** France
166 F3 **St-Amand-Montrond** France
166 G3 **St-Amour** France
203 J2 **St Andrews** Canada
162 F4 **St Andrews** U.K.
205 I5 **St Ann's Bay** Jamaica
163 F6 **St Ann's Head** U.K.
189 I3 **St Anthony** Canada
194 E3 **St Anthony** U.S.A.
126 E6 **St Arnaud** Australia
128 D5 **St Arnaud Range** *mts* N.Z.
189 I3 **St-Augustin** Canada
201 D6 **St Augustine** U.S.A.
161 C7 **St Austell** U.K.
166 E3 **St-Avertin** France
164 E5 **St-Avold** France
205 L5 **St-Barthélemy** *terr.* Caribbean Sea
160 D3 **St Bees** U.K.
160 D3 **St Bees Head** U.K.
161 B6 **St Bride's Bay** U.K.
166 C2 **St-Brieuc** France
191 H4 **St Catharines** Canada
201 D6 **St Catherines Island** U.S.A.
161 F7 **St Catherine's Point** U.K.
166 E4 **St-Céré** France
203 G2 **St-Césaire** Canada
166 G4 **St-Chamond** France
194 E3 **St Charles** *ID* U.S.A.
202 E5 **St Charles** *MD* U.S.A.
190 A4 **St Charles** *MN* U.S.A.
198 F4 **St Charles** *MO* U.S.A.
191 F4 **St Clair** U.S.A.
191 F4 **St Clair Shores** U.S.A.
166 G3 **St-Claude** France
161 C6 **St Clears** U.K.
198 E2 **St Cloud** U.S.A.
189 G4 **St Croix** *r.* Canada
190 A2 **St Croix** *r.* U.S.A.
205 L5 **St Croix** *i.* Virgin Is (U.S.A.)
190 A3 **St Croix Falls** U.S.A.
197 G6 **St David** U.S.A.
163 F6 **St David's** U.K.
161 B6 **St David's Head** U.K.
164 A6 **St-Denis** France
166 H2 **St-Dié-des-Vosges** France
166 G2 **St-Dizier** France
187 J5 **Sainte Anne** Canada
189 G3 **Ste-Anne, Lac** *l.* Canada
189 F4 **Ste-Anne-de-Beaupré** Canada
203 I1 **Ste-Anne-de-Madawaska** Canada
191 J2 **Ste-Anne-du-Lac** Canada
203 H1 **Ste-Camille-de-Lellis** Canada
166 G4 **St-Égrève** France
203 H1 **Ste-Justine** Canada
203 I1 **St-Éleuthère** Canada
186 B2 **St Elias Mountains** Canada
189 G3 **Ste-Marguerite** *r.* Canada
166 H5 **Ste-Maxime** France
166 D4 **Saintes** France
203 G2 **Ste-Thérèse** Canada
166 G4 **St-Étienne** France
203 F2 **St Eugene** Canada
203 G2 **St-Eustache** Canada
189 F4 **St-Félicien** Canada
163 F3 **Saintfield** U.K.
170 C3 **St-Florent** *Corsica* France
166 F3 **St-Florent-sur-Cher** France
203 I1 **St Francis** *r.* Canada/U.S.A.
198 C4 **St Francis** *KS* U.S.A.
203 I1 **St Francis** *ME* U.S.A.
199 F4 **St Francis** *r.* U.S.A.
189 J4 **St Francis, Cape** Canada
203 I1 **St Froid Lake** U.S.A.
166 E5 **St-Gaudens** France
203 H2 **St-Gédéon** Canada
127 H2 **St George** Australia
203 J2 **St George** Canada
201 D5 **St George** *SC* U.S.A.
197 F3 **St George** *UT* U.S.A.
125 F2 **St George, Cape** P.N.G.
194 A3 **St George, Point** U.S.A.
201 C6 **St George Island** U.S.A.
189 F4 **St-Georges** Canada
205 L6 **St George's** Grenada
189 I4 **St George's Bay** Canada
161 A6 **St George's Channel** Ireland/U.K.
124 F2 **St George's Channel** P.N.G.
168 D7 **St Gotthard Pass** *pass* Switz.
161 C6 **St Govan's Head** U.K.
190 E3 **St Helen** U.S.A.
174 D6 **St Helena** *i.* Atlantic Ocean
120 **St Helena, Ascension and Tristan da Cunha** *terr.* Atlantic Ocean
180 C6 **St Helena Bay** S. Africa
180 C6 **St Helena Bay** *b.* S. Africa
127 H8 **St Helens** Australia
161 E4 **St Helens** U.K.
194 B2 **St Helens** U.S.A.
194 B2 **St Helens, Mount** *vol.* U.S.A.
127 H8 **St Helens Point** Australia
166 C2 **St Helier** U.K.
164 D4 **St-Hubert** Belgium
188 F4 **St-Hyacinthe** Canada
190 E3 **St Ignace** U.S.A.
190 C1 **St Ignace Island** Canada
161 C6 **St Ishmael** U.K.
161 B7 **St Ives** *England* U.K.
161 G5 **St Ives** *England* U.K.
203 I1 **St-Jacques** Canada
190 E3 **St James** U.S.A.
186 C4 **St James, Cape** Canada
189 F4 **St-Jean, Lac** *l.* Canada
166 D4 **St-Jean-d'Angély** France
166 C3 **St-Jean-de-Monts** France
188 F4 **St-Jean-sur-Richelieu** Canada
188 F4 **St-Jérôme** Canada
194 C2 **St Joe** *r.* U.S.A.
189 G4 **Saint John** Canada
203 J2 **St John** *r.* Canada/U.S.A.
197 F1 **St John** U.S.A.
205 L5 **St John** *i.* Virgin Is (U.S.A.)
205 L5 **St John's** Antigua and Barbuda
189 J4 **St John's** Canada
197 H4 **St Johns** *AZ* U.S.A.
190 E4 **St Johns** *MI* U.S.A.
201 D6 **St Johns** *r.* U.S.A.
203 H2 **St Johnsbury** U.S.A.
160 E3 **St John's Chapel** U.K.
190 D4 **St Joseph** *MI* U.S.A.
198 E4 **St Joseph** *MO* U.S.A.
190 E5 **St Joseph** *r.* U.S.A.
188 B3 **St Joseph, Lake** Canada
189 F4 **St-Joseph-de-Beauce** Canada
191 F2 **St Joseph Island** Canada
199 D7 **St Joseph Island** U.S.A.
188 F4 **St-Jovité** Canada
166 E4 **St-Junien** France
161 B7 **St Just** U.K.
164 A5 **St-Just-en-Chaussée** France
161 B7 **St Keverne** U.K.
205 L5 **St Kitts and Nevis** *country* Caribbean Sea
**St-Laurent, Golfe du** *g.* Canada/U.S.A. *see* **St Lawrence, Gulf of**
211 H2 **St-Laurent-du-Maroni** Fr. Guiana
189 J4 **St Lawrence** Canada
189 G4 **St Lawrence** *inlet* Canada
189 H4 **St Lawrence, Gulf of** Canada/U.S.A.
184 B3 **St Lawrence Island** U.S.A.
191 J3 **St Lawrence Islands National Park** Canada
203 F2 **St Lawrence Seaway** *sea chan.* Canada/U.S.A.
189 G4 **St-Léonard** Canada
189 I3 **St Lewis** Canada
189 I3 **St Lewis** *r.* Canada
166 D2 **St-Lô** France
176 A3 **St-Louis** Senegal
190 E4 **St Louis** *MI* U.S.A.
198 F4 **St Louis** *MO* U.S.A.
190 A2 **St Louis** *r.* U.S.A.
205 L6 **St Lucia** *country* Caribbean Sea
181 J3 **St Lucia, Lake** S. Africa
181 J4 **St Lucia Estuary** S. Africa
162 □ **St Magnus Bay** U.K.
166 D3 **St-Maixent-l'École** France
166 C2 **St-Malo** France
166 C2 **St-Malo, Golfe de** *g.* France
181 G6 **St Marks** S. Africa
205 L5 **St-Martin** *terr.* Caribbean Sea
180 B6 **St Martin, Cape** S. Africa
187 J4 **St Martin, Lake** Canada
190 D3 **St Martin Island** U.S.A.
161 A8 **St Martin's** *i.* U.K.
145 H5 **St Martin's Island** Bangl.
126 C3 **St Mary Peak** Australia
127 H8 **St Marys** Australia
191 G4 **St Mary's** Canada
162 F2 **St Mary's** U.K.
161 A8 **St Mary's** *i.* U.K.
202 A4 **St Marys** *OH* U.S.A.
202 D4 **St Marys** *PA* U.S.A.
202 C5 **St Marys** *WV* U.S.A.
202 A4 **St Marys** *r.* U.S.A.
189 J4 **St Mary's, Cape** Canada
184 A3 **St Matthew Island** U.S.A.
124 E2 **St Matthias Group** *is* P.N.G.
188 F4 **St-Maurice** *r.* Canada
161 B7 **St Mawes** U.K.
166 D4 **St-Médard-en-Jalles** France
189 I3 **St Michael's Bay** Canada
166 C3 **St-Nazaire** France
161 G5 **St Neots** U.K.
166 H2 **St-Nicolas-de-Port** France
166 F1 **St-Omer** France
203 I1 **St-Pamphile** Canada
189 G4 **St-Pascal** Canada
187 G4 **St Paul** Canada
190 A3 **St Paul** *MN* U.S.A.
198 D3 **St Paul** *NE* U.S.A.
202 B6 **St Paul** *VA* U.S.A.
218 J7 **St-Paul, Île** *i.* Indian Ocean
193 H3 **St Peter** U.S.A.
166 C2 **St Peter Port** U.K.
172 D3 **St Petersburg** Rus. Fed. (City Plan **107**)
201 D7 **St Petersburg** U.S.A.
166 G5 **St-Pierre** *mt.* France
189 I4 **St-Pierre** N. America
188 F4 **St-Pierre, Lac** *l.* Canada
185 M5 **St Pierre and Miquelon** *terr.* N. America
166 D4 **St-Pierre-d'Oléron** France
166 F3 **St-Pierre-le-Moûtier** France
164 A4 **St-Pol-sur-Ternoise** France
166 F3 **St-Pourçain-sur-Sioule** France
203 H1 **St-Prosper** Canada
166 F2 **St-Quentin** France
166 H5 **St-Raphaël** France
203 F2 **St Regis** *r.* U.S.A.
203 F2 **St Regis Falls** U.S.A.
203 G2 **St-Rémi** Canada
203 H2 **St-Sébastien** Canada
189 G4 **St-Siméon** Canada
201 D6 **St Simons Island** U.S.A.
203 J2 **St Stephen** Canada
201 E5 **St Stephen** U.S.A.
203 H2 **St-Théophile** Canada
187 K4 **St Theresa Point** Canada
191 G4 **St Thomas** Canada
166 H5 **St-Tropez** France
187 J5 **St Vincent** U.S.A.
127 F9 **St Vincent, Cape** Australia
126 B5 **St Vincent, Gulf** Australia
205 L6 **St Vincent and the Grenadines** *country* Caribbean Sea
164 E4 **St-Vith** Belgium
187 H4 **St Walburg** Canada
191 G4 **St Williams** Canada
166 E4 **St-Yrieix-la-Perche** France
148 C1 **Sain Us** China
167 F1 **Saioa** *mt.* Spain
144 E3 **Saipal** *mt.* Nepal
147 G5 **Saipan** *i.* N. Mariana Is
149 □ **Sai Pok Liu Hoi Hap** *Hong Kong* China
151 F7 **Saitama** Japan
145 H5 **Saitlai** Myanmar
158 N2 **Saittanulkki** *h.* Fin.
210 E7 **Sajama, Nevado** *mt.* Bol.
140 B5 **Sājir** Saudi Arabia
180 D5 **Sak** *watercourse* S. Africa
154 B2 **Sa Kaeo** Thai.
151 D7 **Sakai** Japan
151 C7 **Sakaide** Japan
151 C7 **Sakaiminato** Japan
142 B3 **Sakākah** Saudi Arabia
141 G5 **Saka Kalat** Pak.
198 C2 **Sakakawea, Lake** U.S.A.
188 E3 **Sakami** Canada
188 F3 **Sakami** *r.* Canada
188 E3 **Sakami Lake** Canada
171 L4 **Sakar** *mts* Bulg.
**Sakarya** Turkey *see* **Adapazarı**
136 C1 **Sakarya** *r.* Turkey
150 F5 **Sakata** Japan
152 C3 **Sakchu** N. Korea
139 H2 **Saken Seyfullin** Kazakh.
154 B2 **Sa Keo** *r.* Thai.
176 C4 **Sakété** Benin
146 G2 **Sakhalin** *i.* Rus. Fed.
146 G1 **Sakhalinskiy Zaliv** *b.* Rus. Fed.
144 C3 **Sakhi** India
181 H3 **Sakhile** S. Africa
137 K1 **Şäki** Azer.
159 M5 **Šakiai** Lith.
144 A3 **Sakir** *mt.* Pak.
146 E4 **Sakishima-shotō** *is* Japan
154 C1 **Sakon Nakhon** Thai.
154 □ **Sakra, P.** Sing.
144 B4 **Sakrand** Pak.
180 D5 **Sakrivier** S. Africa
138 E3 **Saksaul'skiy** Kazakh.
151 B9 **Sakura-jima** *vol.* Japan
173 E6 **Saky** Ukr.
159 M3 **Säkylä** Fin.
176 □ **Sal** *i.* Cape Verde
173 G6 **Sal** *r.* Rus. Fed.
206 H5 **Sal, Punta** *pt* Hond.
159 M4 **Sala** Latvia
159 L4 **Sala** Sweden
188 F4 **Salaberry-de-Valleyfield** Canada
159 N4 **Salacgrīva** Latvia
170 F4 **Sala Consilina** Italy
197 E5 **Salada, Laguna** *salt l.* Mex.
215 E2 **Saladillo** Arg.
215 D2 **Saladillo** *r.* Arg.
215 E2 **Salado** *r. Buenos Aires* Arg.
215 C2 **Salado** *r. Mendoza/San Luis* Arg.
215 D4 **Salado** *r. Río Negro* Arg.
215 E1 **Salado** *r. Santa Fé* Arg.
215 C3 **Salado** *r.* Arg.
207 E2 **Salado** *r.* Mex.
212 B3 **Salado, Quebrada de** *r.* Chile
176 B4 **Salaga** Ghana
180 F1 **Salajwe** Botswana
177 D3 **Salal** Chad
142 D6 **Şalālah** Oman
207 G5 **Salamá** Guat.
206 H5 **Salamá** Hond.
215 B1 **Salamanca** Chile
206 D3 **Salamanca** Mex.
167 D2 **Salamanca** Spain
202 D3 **Salamanca** U.S.A.
181 J3 **Salamanga** Moz.
140 B3 **Salāmatābād** Iran
213 B3 **Salamina** Col.
136 F4 **Salamīyah** Syria
190 E5 **Salamonie** *r.* U.S.A.
190 E5 **Salamonie Lake** U.S.A.
145 F5 **Salandi** *r.* India
159 M4 **Salantai** Lith.
148 D1 **Salaqi** China
167 C1 **Salas** Spain
159 N4 **Salaspils** Latvia
154 C2 **Salavan** Laos
138 C1 **Salavat** Rus. Fed.
147 F7 **Salawati** *i.* Indon.
144 B5 **Salaya** India
208 C5 **Sala y Gómez, Isla** *i.* S. Pacific Ocean
215 D3 **Salazar** Arg.
159 N5 **Šalčininkai** Lith.
161 D7 **Salcombe** U.K.
213 B4 **Saldaña** *r.* Col.
167 D1 **Saldaña** Spain
180 B6 **Saldanha** S. Africa
180 B6 **Saldanha Bay** S. Africa
215 E3 **Saldungaray** Arg.
159 M4 **Saldus** Latvia
127 G7 **Sale** Australia
137 K5 **Şāleḩābād** Iran
140 C3 **Şāleḩābād** Iran
132 H3 **Salekhard** Rus. Fed.
143 B4 **Salem** India
203 H3 **Salem** *MA* U.S.A.
199 F4 **Salem** *MO* U.S.A.
200 F4 **Salem** *NJ* U.S.A.
203 G3 **Salem** *NY* U.S.A.
202 C4 **Salem** *OH* U.S.A.
194 B2 **Salem** *OR* U.S.A.
200 D4 **Salem** *VA* U.S.A.
162 C4 **Salen** *Scotland* U.K.
162 C4 **Salen** *Scotland* U.K.
170 F4 **Salerno** Italy
170 F4 **Salerno, Golfo di** *g.* Italy
161 E4 **Salford** U.K.
211 K5 **Salgado** *r.* Brazil
169 I6 **Salgótarján** Hungary
211 K5 **Salgueiro** Brazil
153 C6 **Salibabu** *i.* Indon.
192 E4 **Salida** U.S.A.
166 D5 **Salies-de-Béarn** France
141 F4 **Şāliḩān** Afgh.
136 B2 **Salihli** Turkey
172 C4 **Salihorsk** Belarus
179 D5 **Salima** Malawi
179 D5 **Salimo** Moz.
198 D4 **Salina** *KS* U.S.A.
197 G2 **Salina** *UT* U.S.A.
170 F5 **Salina, Isola** *i. Isole Lipari* Italy
207 F4 **Salina Cruz** Mex.
214 D2 **Salinas** Brazil
210 B4 **Salinas** Ecuador
206 D3 **Salinas** Mex.
196 B3 **Salinas** *r.* U.S.A.
196 B3 **Salinas** *r. CA* U.S.A.
215 C2 **Salinas, Pampa de las** *salt pan* Arg.
195 F5 **Salinas Peak** U.S.A.
199 E5 **Saline** *r. AR* U.S.A.
198 C4 **Saline** *r. KS* U.S.A.
167 H3 **Salines, Cap de ses** *c.* Spain
196 D3 **Saline Valley** *depr.* U.S.A.
211 I4 **Salinópolis** Brazil
210 C6 **Salinosó Lachay, Punta** *pt* Peru
161 F6 **Salisbury** U.K.
203 F5 **Salisbury** *MD* U.S.A.
201 D5 **Salisbury** *NC* U.S.A.
161 E6 **Salisbury Plain** U.K.
211 J6 **Salitre** *r.* Brazil
215 C3 **Salitroso, Gran Bajo** *salt flat* Arg.
136 F5 **Şalkhad** Syria
143 D1 **Salki** *r.* India
158 O2 **Salla** Fin.
215 D3 **Salliqueló** Arg.
199 E5 **Sallisaw** U.S.A.
185 K3 **Salluit** Canada
145 E3 **Sallyana** Nepal
140 B2 **Salmās** Iran
172 D2 **Salmi** Rus. Fed.
186 F5 **Salmo** Canada
194 D2 **Salmon** U.S.A.
194 D2 **Salmon** *r.* U.S.A.
186 F4 **Salmon Arm** Canada
203 F3 **Salmon Reservoir** U.S.A.
194 D2 **Salmon River Mountains** U.S.A.
164 E5 **Salmtal** Germany
159 M3 **Salo** Fin.
145 E4 **Salon** India
166 G5 **Salon-de-Provence** France
178 C4 **Salonga Nord, Parc National de la** *nat. park* Dem. Rep. Congo
178 C4 **Salonga Sud, Parc National de la** *nat. park* Dem. Rep. Congo
169 J7 **Salonta** Romania
176 A3 **Saloum Delta** *tourist site* Senegal
176 □ **Sal Rei** Cape Verde
215 D1 **Salsacate** Arg.
173 G6 **Sal'sk** Rus. Fed.
170 C2 **Salsomaggiore Terme** Italy
180 E5 **Salt** *watercourse* S. Africa
197 G5 **Salt** *r. AZ* U.S.A.
190 B6 **Salt** *r. MO* U.S.A.
212 C2 **Salta** Arg.
160 F4 **Saltaire** U.K.
161 C7 **Saltash** U.K.
162 D5 **Saltcoats** U.K.
202 B5 **Salt Creek** *r.* U.S.A.
163 E5 **Saltee Islands** Ireland
158 K2 **Saltfjellet Svartisen Nasjonalpark** *nat. park* Norway
199 B6 **Salt Flat** U.S.A.
202 C4 **Salt Fork Lake** U.S.A.
206 D2 **Saltillo** Mex.
194 E3 **Salt Lake City** U.S.A.
215 E2 **Salto** Arg.
214 C3 **Salto** Brazil
215 F1 **Salto** Uruguay
214 E2 **Salto da Divisa** Brazil
214 A4 **Salto del Guairá** Para.
212 E4 **Salto Grande, Embalse de** *resr* Uruguay
197 E5 **Salton Sea** *salt l.* U.S.A.
144 C2 **Salt Range** *hills* Pak.
187 G2 **Salt River** Canada
202 B5 **Salt Rock** U.S.A.
201 D5 **Saluda** *SC* U.S.A.
202 E6 **Saluda** *VA* U.S.A.
144 C4 **Salumbar** India
143 C2 **Salur** India
170 B2 **Saluzzo** Italy
215 D1 **Salvador** Arg.
214 E1 **Salvador** Brazil
199 F6 **Salvador, Lake** U.S.A.
206 D3 **Salvatierra** Mex.
197 G2 **Salvation Creek** *r.* U.S.A.
140 C5 **Salwah** Qatar
140 C5 **Salwah, Dawḩat** *b.* Qatar/Saudi Arabia
147 B5 **Salween** *r.* China/Myanmar
137 L2 **Salyan** Azer.
202 B6 **Salyersville** U.S.A.
180 B2 **Salzbrunn** Namibia
168 F7 **Salzburg** Austria
165 I2 **Salzgitter** Germany
165 I1 **Salzhausen** Germany
165 G3 **Salzkotten** Germany
165 J3 **Salzmünde** Germany
165 J2 **Salzwedel** Germany
144 B4 **Sam** India
149 B7 **Sam, Nâm** *r.* Laos/Vietnam
154 B2 **Samae San, Laem** *c.* Thai.
140 B4 **Samāh** *well* Saudi Arabia
210 F7 **Samaipata** Bol.
153 C5 **Samal** *i.* Phil.
153 B5 **Samales Group** *is* Phil.
143 C2 **Samalkot** India
136 E3 **Samandağı** Turkey
150 H3 **Samani** Japan
136 C6 **Samannūd** Egypt
153 C4 **Samar** *i.* Phil.
138 B1 **Samara** Rus. Fed.
138 B1 **Samara** *r.* Rus. Fed.
213 D3 **Samariapo** Venez.
155 E3 **Samarinda** Indon.
139 H2 **Samarka** Kazakh.
150 D2 **Samarka** Rus. Fed.
**Samarkand** Uzbek. *see* **Samarqand**
139 F5 **Samarqand** Uzbek.
139 G5 **Samarqand, Qullai** *mt.* Tajik.
137 I4 **Sāmarrā'** Iraq
153 C4 **Samar Sea** *g.* Phil.
172 I4 **Samarskaya Oblast'** *admin. div.* Rus. Fed.
139 J2 **Samarskoye** Kazakh.
137 L1 **Şamaxı** Azer.
178 C4 **Samba** Dem. Rep. Congo
155 E2 **Sambaliung** *mts* Indon.
143 D1 **Sambalpur** India
155 D3 **Sambar, Tanjung** *pt* Indon.
155 C2 **Sambas** Indon.
179 F5 **Sambava** Madag.
145 G4 **Sambha** India
144 D3 **Sambhal** India
144 C4 **Sambhar Lake** India
173 B5 **Sambir** Ukr.
211 J5 **Sambito** *r.* Brazil
215 F2 **Samborombón, Bahía** *b.* Arg.
164 B4 **Sambre** *r.* Belgium/France
213 A3 **Sambú** *r.* Panama
152 E5 **Samcheok** S. Korea
137 J3 **Samdi Dag** *mt.* Turkey
178 D4 **Same** Tanz.
**Samirum** Iran *see* **Īzad Khvāst**
152 E3 **Samjiyŏn** N. Korea
137 K1 **Şämkir** Azer.
152 E6 **Samnangjin** S. Korea
125 I3 **Samoa** *country* Pacific Ocean
216 H7 **Samoa Basin** *sea feature* Pacific Ocean
170 F2 **Samobor** Croatia
172 G2 **Samoded** Rus. Fed.
171 J3 **Samokov** Bulg.
168 H6 **Šamorín** Slovakia
171 L6 **Samos** *i.* Greece
155 A2 **Samosir** *i.* Indon.
171 K4 **Samothraki** Greece
171 K4 **Samothraki** *i.* Greece
153 B3 **Sampaloc Point** Phil.
155 D3 **Sampit** Indon.
155 D3 **Sampit, Teluk** *b.* Indon.
179 C4 **Sampwe** Dem. Rep. Congo
199 E6 **Sam Rayburn Reservoir** U.S.A.
145 E3 **Samsang** China
149 B6 **Sam Sao, Phou** *mts* Laos/Vietnam
154 C1 **Sâm Sơn** Vietnam
136 F1 **Samsun** Turkey
173 G7 **Samt'redia** Georgia
154 B3 **Samui, Ko** *i.* Thai.
173 I7 **Samur** *r.* Azer./Rus. Fed.
154 B2 **Samut Prakan** Thai.
154 B2 **Samut Sakhon** Thai.
154 B2 **Samut Songkhram** Thai.
145 G3 **Samyai** China
176 B3 **San** Mali
154 B1 **San, Phou** *mt.* Laos
154 C2 **San, Tônlé** *r.* Cambodia
142 B6 **Şan'ā'** Yemen
129 D3 **SANAE IV** *research stn* Antarctica
177 D4 **Sanaga** *r.* Cameroon
213 A4 **San Agustín** Col.
153 C5 **San Agustin, Cape** Phil.
140 B6 **Sanām** Saudi Arabia
217 N7 **San Ambrosio, Isla** *i.* S. Pacific Ocean
140 B3 **Sanandaj** Iran
196 B2 **San Andreas** U.S.A.
153 C3 **San Andres** Phil.
206 I5 **San Andrés, Isla de** *i.* Col.
195 F5 **San Andres Mountains** U.S.A.
207 F4 **San Andrés Tuxtla** Mex.
199 C6 **San Angelo** U.S.A.
206 G4 **San Antonio** Belize
215 B2 **San Antonio** Chile
153 B3 **San Antonio** Phil.
199 D6 **San Antonio** U.S.A.
196 B3 **San Antonio** *r.* U.S.A.
215 F3 **San Antonio, Cabo** *c.* Arg.
205 H4 **San Antonio, Cabo** *c.* Cuba
196 D4 **San Antonio, Mount** U.S.A.
212 C2 **San Antonio de los Cobres** Arg.
213 D2 **San Antonio de Tamanaco** Venez.
215 D4 **San Antonio Oeste** Arg.
196 B4 **San Antonio Reservoir** U.S.A.
196 B3 **San Ardo** U.S.A.
215 E3 **San Augustín** Arg.
215 C1 **San Augustín de Valle Fértil** Arg.
144 D5 **Sanawad** India
207 D3 **San Bartolo** Mex.
170 E3 **San Benedetto del Tronto** Italy
204 B5 **San Benedicto, Isla** *i.* Mex.
199 D7 **San Benito** U.S.A.
196 B3 **San Benito** *r.* U.S.A.
196 B3 **San Benito Mountain** U.S.A.
196 D4 **San Bernardino** U.S.A.
195 C5 **San Bernardino Mountains** U.S.A.
215 B2 **San Bernardo** Chile
206 C2 **San Bernardo** Mex.
151 C7 **Sanbe-san** *vol.* Japan
206 C3 **San Blas** *Nayarit* Mex.
206 B2 **San Blas** *Sinaloa* Mex.
206 J6 **San Blas, Archipiélago de** *is* Panama
201 C6 **San Blas, Cape** U.S.A.
206 J6 **San Blas, Cordillera de** *mts* Panama
210 E6 **San Borja** Bol.
203 H3 **Sanbornville** U.S.A.
206 D2 **San Buenaventura** Mex.
215 C2 **San Carlos** Arg.
215 B3 **San Carlos** Chile
206 D1 **San Carlos** *Coahuila* Mex.
207 E2 **San Carlos** *Tamaulipas* Mex.
206 H6 **San Carlos** Nicaragua
153 B3 **San Carlos** Phil.
153 B4 **San Carlos** Phil.
215 F2 **San Carlos** Uruguay
197 G5 **San Carlos** U.S.A.
213 D4 **San Carlos** Venez.
213 C2 **San Carlos** Venez.
215 E1 **San Carlos Centro** Arg.
215 B4 **San Carlos de Bariloche** Arg.
215 E3 **San Carlos de Bolívar** Arg.
213 C2 **San Carlos del Zulia** Venez.
197 G5 **San Carlos Lake** U.S.A.
148 C2 **Sancha** *Gansu* China
148 D2 **Sancha** *Shanxi* China
149 C5 **Sancha He** *r.* China
139 I5 **Sanchakou** China
144 D5 **Sanchi** India
149 B6 **San Chien Pau** *mt.* Laos
144 B4 **Sanchor** India
148 D2 **Sanchuan He** *r.* China
172 H3 **Sanchursk** Rus. Fed.
207 E3 **San Ciro de Acosta** Mex.
215 B2 **San Clemente** Chile
196 D5 **San Clemente** U.S.A.
196 C5 **San Clemente Island** U.S.A.
166 F3 **Sancoins** France
215 E1 **San Cristóbal** Arg.
125 G3 **San Cristobal** *i.* Solomon Is
213 B3 **San Cristóbal** Venez.
210 □ **San Cristóbal, Isla** *i. Galapagos Is* Ecuador
207 F4 **San Cristóbal de las Casas** Mex.
197 F5 **San Cristobal Wash** *watercourse* U.S.A.
205 I4 **Sancti Spíritus** Cuba
150 D3 **Sandagou** Rus. Fed.
162 C5 **Sanda Island** U.K.
155 E1 **Sandakan** *Sabah* Malaysia
159 I3 **Sandane** Norway
171 J4 **Sandanski** Bulg.
165 K2 **Sandau** Germany
162 F1 **Sanday** *i.* U.K.
162 F1 **Sanday Sound** *sea chan.* U.K.
161 E4 **Sandbach** U.K.
159 J4 **Sandefjord** Norway
129 E4 **Sandercock Nunataks** *nunataks* Antarctica
197 H4 **Sanders** U.S.A.
165 J3 **Sandersleben** Germany
199 C6 **Sanderson** U.S.A.
127 J1 **Sandgate** Australia
162 D6 **Sandhead** U.K.
210 E6 **Sandia** Peru
196 D5 **San Diego** U.S.A.
212 C8 **San Diego, Cabo** *c.* Arg.
136 C2 **Sandıklı** Turkey
144 E4 **Sandila** India
190 B2 **Sand Island** U.S.A.
190 E2 **Sand Lake** Canada
159 I4 **Sandnes** Norway
158 K2 **Sandnessjøen** Norway
179 C4 **Sandoa** Dem. Rep. Congo
169 J5 **Sandomierz** Poland
213 A4 **Sandoná** Col.
170 E2 **San Donà di Piave** Italy
**Sandoway** Myanmar *see* **Thandwè**
161 F7 **Sandown** U.K.
180 C7 **Sandown Bay** S. Africa
158 □ **Sandoy** *i.* Faroe Is
194 C1 **Sandpoint** U.S.A.
162 A4 **Sandray** *i.* U.K.
169 M7 **Şandrul Mare, Vârful** *mt.* Romania
159 K3 **Sandsjö** Sweden
186 C4 **Sandspit** Canada
199 D4 **Sand Springs** U.S.A.
196 C2 **Sand Springs Salt Flat** U.S.A.
190 A2 **Sandstone** U.S.A.
197 F5 **Sand Tank Mountains** U.S.A.
149 C5 **Sandu** *Guizhou* China
149 D5 **Sandu** *Hunan* China
191 F4 **Sandusky** *MI* U.S.A.
202 B4 **Sandusky** *OH* U.S.A.
202 B4 **Sandusky Bay** U.S.A.
180 C5 **Sandveld** *mts* S. Africa
180 B3 **Sandverhaar** Namibia
159 J4 **Sandvika** Norway
158 K3 **Sandvika** Sweden
159 L3 **Sandviken** Sweden
189 I3 **Sandwich Bay** Canada
162 □ **Sandwick** U.K.
145 G5 **Sandwip Channel** Bangl.
203 H2 **Sandy** *r.* U.S.A.
187 I3 **Sandy Bay** Canada
125 F4 **Sandy Cape** Australia
127 F8 **Sandy Cape** Australia
202 B5 **Sandy Hook** U.S.A.
203 F4 **Sandy Hook** *pt* U.S.A.
**Sandykachi** Turkm. *see* **Sandykgaçy**
141 F2 **Sandykgaçy** Turkm.
138 E5 **Sandykly Gumy** *des.* Turkm.
188 B3 **Sandy Lake** Canada
188 B3 **Sandy Lake** *l.* Canada
203 E3 **Sandy Pond** U.S.A.
214 A4 **San Estanislao** Para.
153 B2 **San Fabian** Phil.
215 B2 **San Felipe** Chile
204 B2 **San Felipe** *Baja California* Mex.
206 C2 **San Felipe** *Chihuahua* Mex.
206 D3 **San Felipe** *Guanajuato* Mex.
213 C2 **San Felipe** Venez.
196 D5 **San Felipe Creek** *watercourse* U.S.A.
217 N7 **San Félix, Isla** *i.* S. Pacific Ocean
215 E2 **San Fernando** Arg.
215 B2 **San Fernando** Chile
207 E2 **San Fernando** Mex.
153 B2 **San Fernando** Phil.
153 B3 **San Fernando** Phil.
167 C4 **San Fernando** Spain
213 E2 **San Fernando** Trin. and Tob.
196 C4 **San Fernando** U.S.A.
213 D3 **San Fernando de Apure** Venez.
213 D3 **San Fernando de Atabapo** Venez.
201 D6 **Sanford** *FL* U.S.A.
203 H3 **Sanford** *ME* U.S.A.
201 E5 **Sanford** *NC* U.S.A.
190 E4 **Sanford Lake** U.S.A.
215 D1 **San Francisco** Arg.
206 I6 **San Francisco** Panama
196 A3 **San Francisco** U.S.A. (City Plan **113**)
197 H5 **San Francisco** *r.* U.S.A.
212 C3 **San Francisco, Paso de** *pass* Arg.
196 A3 **San Francisco Bay** *inlet* U.S.A.
206 C2 **San Francisco del Oro** Mex.
206 D3 **San Francisco del Rincón** Mex.
205 J5 **San Francisco de Macorís** Dom. Rep.
212 C7 **San Francisco de Paula, Cabo** *c.* Arg.
207 E3 **San Francisco el Alto** Mex.
206 G5 **San Francisco Gotera** El Salvador
213 A4 **San Gabriel** Ecuador
206 A1 **San Gabriel, Punta** *pt* Mex.
196 C4 **San Gabriel Mountains** U.S.A.
144 C6 **Sangamner** India
190 C6 **Sangamon** *r.* U.S.A.
141 G3 **Sangān** Afgh.
**Sangan, Koh-i-** *mt.* Afgh. *see* **Sangān, Kūh-e**
141 G3 **Sangān, Kūh-e** *mt.* Afgh.
133 N3 **Sangar** Rus. Fed.
143 B2 **Sangareddi** India
170 C5 **San Gavino Monreale** *Sardinia* Italy
210 C4 **Sangay, Parque Nacional** *nat. park* Ecuador

141 E3 Sang Bast Iran
153 B5 Sangboy Islands Phil.
155 E4 Sangeang i. Indon.
148 B1 Sangejing China
196 C3 Sanger U.S.A.
165 J3 Sangerhausen Germany
148 E1 Sanggan He r. China
148 B3 Sanggarmai China
155 D2 Sanggau Indon.
152 B5 Sanggou Wan b. China
178 B3 Sangha r. Congo
144 B4 Sanghar Pak.
144 B3 Sanghar r. Pak.
177 D4 Sangha Trinational nat. park Africa
213 B3 San Gil Col.
170 G5 San Giovanni in Fiore Italy
170 F4 San Giovanni Rotondo Italy
153 C6 Sangir i. Indon.
147 E6 Sangir, Kepulauan is Indon.
152 E5 Sangju S. Korea
154 B2 Sângke, Stœng r. Cambodia
155 E2 Sangkulirang Indon.
143 A2 Sangli India
141 H2 Sanglīch Afgh.
176 D4 Sangmélima Cameroon
144 D3 Sangnam India
145 H3 Sangngagqoiling China
152 E3 Sang-ni N. Korea
179 D6 Sango Zimbabwe
143 A2 Sangole India
196 D4 San Gorgonio Mountain U.S.A.
195 F4 Sangre de Cristo Range mts U.S.A.
213 E2 Sangre Grande Trin. and Tob.
144 C3 Sangrur India
145 F3 Sangsang China
186 G4 Sangudo Canada
211 G6 Sangue r. Brazil
140 E4 Sangū'īyeh Iran
181 J1 Sangutane r. Moz.
139 G5 Sangvor Tajik.
149 D4 Sangzhi China
206 A2 San Hipólito, Punta pt Mex.
136 C7 Sanhūr Egypt
207 G4 San Ignacio Belize
210 E6 San Ignacio Bol.
210 F7 San Ignacio Bol.
206 A2 San Ignacio Baja California Sur Mex.
206 D2 San Ignacio Durango Mex.
188 E2 Sanikiluaq Canada
153 B2 San Ildefonso, Cape Phil.
153 B2 San Ildefonso Peninsula Phil.
153 C4 San Isidro Phil.
153 B3 San Jacinto Phil.
196 D5 San Jacinto U.S.A.
196 D5 San Jacinto Peak U.S.A.
145 F5 Sanjai r. India
215 E1 San Javier Arg.
215 B2 San Javier de Loncomilla Chile
144 B3 Sanjawi Pak.
179 D4 Sanje Tanz.
213 A3 San Jerónimo, Serranía de mts Col.
149 C5 Sanjiang China
152 B2 Sanjiangkou China
151 F6 Sanjō Japan
196 B3 San Joaquin U.S.A.
196 B3 San Joaquin r. U.S.A.
196 B3 San Joaquin Valley U.S.A.
215 E1 San Jorge Arg.
213 B2 San Jorge r. Col.
212 C7 San Jorge, Golfo de g. Arg.
206 H6 San José Costa Rica
153 B3 San Jose Phil.
153 B3 San Jose Phil.
196 B3 San Jose U.S.A.
215 D4 San José, Golfo g. Arg.
206 B2 San José, Isla i. Mex.
215 C2 San José, Volcán vol. Chile
213 E2 San José de Amacuro Venez.
153 B4 San Jose de Buenavista Phil.
210 F7 San José de Chiquitos Bol.
206 B2 San José de Comondú Mex.
215 E1 San José de Feliciano Arg.
206 A2 San José de Gracia Mex.
206 C2 San José de Gracia Mex.
213 D2 San José de Guanipa Venez.
215 C1 San José de Jáchal Arg.
206 B2 San José de la Brecha Mex.
215 D1 San José de la Dormida Arg.
215 B3 San José de la Mariquina Chile
205 H4 San José de las Lajas Cuba
206 B3 San José del Cabo Mex.
213 B4 San José del Guaviare Col.
215 F2 San José de Mayo Uruguay
213 C3 San José de Ocuné Col.
206 B1 San José de Primas Mex.
207 D2 San José de Raíces Mex.
215 C1 San Juan Arg.
215 C1 San Juan prov. Arg.
213 A3 San Juan r. Col.
206 D2 San Juan Mex.
206 H6 San Juan r. Nicaragua/Panama
153 C4 San Juan Phil.
205 K5 San Juan Puerto Rico
196 B4 San Juan r. CA U.S.A.
197 H3 San Juan r. UT U.S.A.
213 D3 San Juan Venez.
213 E2 San Juan r. Venez.
206 G5 San Juan, Punta pt El Salvador
212 E3 San Juan Bautista Para.
207 E4 San Juan Bautista Tuxtepec Mex.
206 H5 San Juancito Hond.
215 B4 San Juan dela Costa Chile
206 I6 San Juan del Norte Nicaragua
206 I6 San Juan del Norte, Bahía de b. Nicaragua
213 C2 San Juan de los Cayos Venez.
213 D2 San Juan de los Morros Venez.
206 C2 San Juan del Río Mex.
207 E3 San Juan del Río Mex.
206 H6 San Juan del Sur Nicaragua
206 A2 San Juanico, Punta pt Mex.
197 F4 San Juan Mountains U.S.A.
144 D1 Sanju He watercourse China
212 C7 San Julián Arg.
215 E1 San Justo Arg.
143 A2 Sankeshwar India
143 D1 Sankh r. India
Sanko India see Sanku
164 F4 Sankt Augustin Germany
168 D7 Sankt Gallen Switz.
168 D7 Sankt Moritz Switz.
Sankt-Peterburg Rus. Fed. see St Petersburg
168 G6 Sankt Pölten Austria
164 F5 Sankt Wendel Germany
144 D2 Sanku India
206 B3 San Lázaro, Sierra de mts Mex.
136 G3 Şanlıurfa Turkey
215 E2 San Lorenzo Arg.
210 F8 San Lorenzo Bol.
210 C3 San Lorenzo Ecuador
195 F6 San Lorenzo Mex.
167 E1 San Lorenzo mt. Spain
206 A1 San Lorenzo, Isla i. Mex.
210 C6 San Lorenzo, Isla i. Peru
212 B7 San Lorenzo, Monte mt. Arg./Chile
167 C4 Sanlúcar de Barrameda Spain
206 A2 San Lucas Mex.
206 B3 San Lucas, Cabo c. Mex.
215 C2 San Luis Arg.
215 C2 San Luis prov. Arg.
207 G4 San Luis Guat.
197 E5 San Luis AZ U.S.A.
197 G5 San Luis AZ U.S.A.
215 C2 San Luis, Sierra de mts Arg.
207 D3 San Luis de la Paz Mex.
196 B4 San Luis Obispo U.S.A.
196 B4 San Luis Obispo Bay U.S.A.
206 D3 San Luis Potosí Mex.
206 D3 San Luis Potosí state Mex.
196 B3 San Luis Reservoir U.S.A.
204 B2 San Luis Río Colorado Mex.
170 E6 San Marco, Capo c. Sicily Italy
207 G5 San Marcos Guat.
207 E4 San Marcos Mex.
199 D6 San Marcos U.S.A.
170 E3 San Marino country Europe
170 E3 San Marino San Marino
129 E2 San Martín research stn Antarctica
212 C3 San Martín Arg.
215 C2 San Martín Arg.
210 F6 San Martín r. Bol.
213 B4 San Martín Col.
212 B7 San Martín, Lago l. Arg./Chile
206 D3 San Martín de Bolaños Mex.
215 B4 San Martín de los Andes Arg.
196 A3 San Mateo U.S.A.
215 D4 San Matías, Golfo g. Arg.
213 D2 San Mauricio Venez.
149 F4 Sanmen China
149 F4 Sanmen Wan b. China
148 D3 Sanmenxia China
210 F6 San Miguel r. Bol.
213 B4 San Miguel r. Col.
206 G5 San Miguel El Salvador
206 J6 San Miguel Panama
197 G6 San Miguel AZ U.S.A.
196 B4 San Miguel CA U.S.A.
197 H2 San Miguel r. U.S.A.
153 B3 San Miguel Bay Phil.
206 D3 San Miguel de Allende Mex.
215 E2 San Miguel del Monte Arg.
212 C3 San Miguel de Tucumán Arg.
196 B4 San Miguel Island U.S.A.
153 A5 San Miguel Islands Phil.
206 J6 San Miguelito Panama
207 E4 San Miguel Sola de Vega Mex.
149 E5 Sanming China
153 B3 San Narciso Phil.
170 F4 Sannicandro Garganico Italy
215 E2 San Nicolás de los Arroyos Arg.
196 C5 San Nicolas Island U.S.A.
181 F3 Sannieshof S. Africa
176 B4 Sanniquellie Liberia
169 K6 Sanok Poland
207 E3 San Pablo Mex.
153 B3 San Pablo Phil.
153 B3 San Pascual Phil.
215 E2 San Pedro Buenos Aires Arg.
212 D2 San Pedro Arg.
207 H4 San Pedro Belize
210 F7 San Pedro Bol.
176 B4 San-Pédro Côte d'Ivoire
206 B3 San Pedro Mex.
197 G5 San Pedro watercourse U.S.A.
167 C3 San Pedro, Sierra de mts Spain
196 C5 San Pedro Channel U.S.A.
213 C3 San Pedro de Arimena Col.
206 D2 San Pedro de las Colonias Mex.
212 E2 San Pedro de Ycuamandyyú Para.
206 G5 San Pedro Sula Hond.
170 C5 San Pietro, Isola di i. Sardinia Italy
162 E5 Sanquhar U.K.
210 C3 Sanquianga, Parque Nacional nat. park Col.
204 A2 San Quintín, Cabo c. Mex.
215 C2 San Rafael Arg.
196 A3 San Rafael U.S.A.
197 G2 San Rafael r. U.S.A.
213 C2 San Rafael Venez.
197 G2 San Rafael Knob mt. U.S.A.
196 C4 San Rafael Mountains U.S.A.
210 F6 San Ramón Bol.
170 B3 San Remo Italy
213 C1 San Román, Cabo c. Venez.
167 B1 San Roque Spain
199 D6 San Saba U.S.A.
215 E1 San Salvador Arg.
205 J4 San Salvador i. Bahamas
207 G5 San Salvador El Salvador
212 C2 San Salvador de Jujuy Arg.
167 F1 San Sebastián Spain
167 E2 San Sebastián de los Reyes Spain
170 E3 Sansepolcro Italy
170 F4 San Severo Italy
149 F5 Sansha China
149 D6 Sanshui China
170 G2 Sanski Most Bos.-Herz.
149 C5 Sansui China
210 E7 Santa Ana Bol.
207 G5 Santa Ana El Salvador
125 G3 Santa Ana i. Solomon Is
196 D5 Santa Ana U.S.A.
199 D6 Santa Anna U.S.A.
213 B3 Santa Bárbara Col.
206 G5 Santa Bárbara Hond.
206 C2 Santa Bárbara Mex.
196 C4 Santa Barbara U.S.A.
196 B4 Santa Barbara Channel U.S.A.
196 C5 Santa Barbara Island U.S.A.
212 C3 Santa Catalina Chile
206 I6 Santa Catalina Panama
196 D5 Santa Catalina, Gulf of U.S.A.
Santa Catalina de Armada Spain see Santa Cataliña de Armada
167 B1 Santa Cataliña de Armada Spain
196 C5 Santa Catalina Island U.S.A.
207 D2 Santa Catarina Mex.
210 E4 Santa Clara Col.
205 I4 Santa Clara Cuba
196 B3 Santa Clara CA U.S.A.
197 F3 Santa Clara UT U.S.A.
215 F2 Santa Clara de Olimar Uruguay
196 C4 Santa Clarita U.S.A.
170 F6 Santa Croce, Capo c. Sicily Italy
212 C8 Santa Cruz r. Arg.
210 F7 Santa Cruz Bol.
215 B2 Santa Cruz Chile
153 B2 Santa Cruz Phil.
153 B3 Santa Cruz Phil.
153 A3 Santa Cruz Phil.
196 A3 Santa Cruz U.S.A.
195 E5 Santa Cruz watercourse U.S.A.
210 □ Santa Cruz, Isla i. Galapagos Is Ecuador
207 G5 Santa Cruz Barillas Guat.
214 E2 Santa Cruz Cabrália Brazil
167 F3 Santa Cruz de Moya Spain
176 A2 Santa Cruz de Tenerife Canary Is
212 F3 Santa Cruz do Sul Brazil
196 C4 Santa Cruz Island U.S.A.
125 G3 Santa Cruz Islands Solomon Is
215 E1 Santa Elena Arg.
210 B4 Santa Elena, Bahía de b. Ecuador
206 H6 Santa Elena, Cabo c. Costa Rica
170 G5 Santa Eufemia, Golfo di g. Italy
215 E1 Santa Fe Arg.
215 E1 Santa Fe prov. Arg.
206 I6 Santa Fe Panama
195 F5 Santa Fe U.S.A.
214 B2 Santa Helena de Goiás Brazil
148 B4 Santai Sichuan China
139 J3 Santai Xinjiang China
212 B8 Santa Inés, Isla i. Chile
215 C3 Santa Isabel Arg.
125 F2 Santa Isabel i. Solomon Is
207 G5 Santa Lucia Guat.
215 F2 Santa Lucia r. Uruguay
195 B4 Santa Lucia Range mts U.S.A.
214 A2 Santa Luisa, Serra de hills Brazil
176 □ Santa Luzia i. Cape Verde
206 B2 Santa Margarita, Isla i. Mex.
212 C3 Santa María Arg.
156 A7 Santa Maria i. Azores
211 G4 Santa Maria Amazonas Brazil
212 F3 Santa Maria Brazil
215 F1 Santa Maria r. Brazil
176 □ Santa Maria Cape Verde
204 C2 Santa María r. Mex.
210 D4 Santa María Peru
196 B4 Santa Maria U.S.A.
181 J3 Santa Maria, Cabo de c. Moz.
167 C4 Santa Maria, Cabo de c. Port.
201 F7 Santa Maria, Cape Bahamas
215 B3 Santa María, Isla i. Chile
211 I5 Santa Maria das Barreiras Brazil
214 D1 Santa Maria da Vitória Brazil
213 D2 Santa María de Ipire Venez.
206 C2 Santa María del Oro Mex.
206 D3 Santa María del Río Mex.
171 H5 Santa Maria di Leuca, Capo c. Italy
125 G3 Santa Maria Island Vanuatu
213 B2 Santa Marta Col.
213 B2 Santa Marta, Sierra Nevada de mts Col.
196 C4 Santa Monica U.S.A.
196 C5 Santa Monica Bay U.S.A.
211 J6 Santana Brazil
214 B2 Santana r. Brazil
215 G1 Santana da Boa Vista Brazil
215 F1 Santana do Livramento Brazil
213 A4 Santander Col.
167 E1 Santander Spain
197 G5 Santan Mountain h. U.S.A.
170 C5 Sant'Antioco Sardinia Italy
170 C5 Sant'Antioco, Isola di i. Sardinia Italy
167 G3 Sant Antoni de Portmany Spain
196 C4 Santa Paula U.S.A.
211 J4 Santa Quitéria Brazil
211 H4 Santarém Brazil
167 B3 Santarém Port.
206 D2 Santa Rita Mex.
213 C2 Santa Rita Venez.
214 B2 Santa Rita do Araguaia Brazil
196 B3 Santa Rita Park U.S.A.
215 D3 Santa Rosa La Pampa Arg.
215 C4 Santa Rosa Río Negro Arg.
212 F3 Santa Rosa Brazil
207 G4 Santa Rosa Mex.
196 A2 Santa Rosa CA U.S.A.
195 F5 Santa Rosa NM U.S.A.
206 H6 Santa Rosa, Parque Nacional nat. park Costa Rica
206 G5 Santa Rosa de Copán Hond.
215 D1 Santa Rosa del Río Primero Arg.
210 D5 Santa Rosa do Purus Brazil
196 B5 Santa Rosa Island U.S.A.
206 A2 Santa Rosalía Mex.
194 C3 Santa Rosa Range mts U.S.A.
197 G5 Santa Rosa Wash watercourse U.S.A.
207 G5 Santa Tecla El Salvador
215 G2 Santa Vitória do Palmar Brazil
196 D5 Santee U.S.A.
201 E5 Santee r. U.S.A.
167 G3 Sant Francesc de Formentera Spain
212 F3 Santiago Brazil
176 □ Santiago i. Cape Verde
215 B2 Santiago Chile
215 B2 Santiago admin. reg. Chile
205 J5 Santiago Dom. Rep.
206 B3 Santiago Mex.
206 I6 Santiago Panama
153 B2 Santiago Phil.
210 □ Santiago, Isla i. Galapagos Is Ecuador
206 C3 Santiago, Río Grande de r. Mex.
207 F4 Santiago Astata Mex.
167 B1 Santiago de Compostela Spain
205 I4 Santiago de Cuba Cuba
212 D3 Santiago del Estero Arg.
206 C3 Santiago Ixcuintla Mex.
206 C2 Santiago Papasquiaro Mex.
215 F2 Santiago Vazquez Uruguay
206 C2 Santiaguillo, Laguna de l. Mex.
187 M2 Santianna Point Canada
167 G3 Sant Joan de Labritja Spain
167 G2 Sant Jordi, Golf de g. Spain
214 E1 Santo Amaro Brazil
214 C4 Santo Amaro, Ilha de i. Brazil
214 E3 Santo Amaro de Campos Brazil
214 C3 Santo André Brazil
212 F3 Santo Angelo Brazil
176 □ Santo Antão i. Cape Verde
214 D2 Santo Antônio r. Brazil
214 E1 Santo Antônio, Cabo c. Brazil
214 B3 Santo Antônio da Platina Brazil
214 E1 Santo Antônio de Jesus Brazil
214 A1 Santo Antônio de Leverger Brazil
210 E4 Santo Antônio do Içá Brazil
214 D3 Santo Antônio do Monte Brazil
211 G7 Santo Corazón Bol.
205 K5 Santo Domingo Dom. Rep.
207 G5 Santo Domingo Guat.
206 A1 Santo Domingo Baja California Mex.
206 B2 Santo Domingo Baja California Sur Mex.
206 D3 Santo Domingo San Luis Potosí Mex.
206 H5 Santo Domingo Nicaragua
213 C2 Santo Domingo r. Venez.
192 E4 Santo Domingo Pueblo U.S.A.
167 E1 Santoña Spain
152 D2 Santong He r. China
214 D1 Santo Onofre r. Brazil
171 K6 Santorini i. Greece
214 C3 Santos Brazil
214 D3 Santos Dumont Brazil
213 D3 Santos Luzardo, Parque Nacional nat. park Venez.
219 F7 Santos Plateau sea feature S. Atlantic Ocean
206 C1 Santo Tomás Mex.
206 H5 Santo Tomás Nicaragua
210 D6 Santo Tomás Peru
212 E3 Santo Tomé Arg.
197 F3 Sanup Plateau U.S.A.
212 B7 San Valentín, Cerro mt. Chile
206 G5 San Vicente El Salvador
153 B2 San Vicente Phil.
210 C6 San Vicente de Cañete Peru
213 B4 San Vicente del Caguán Col.
170 D3 San Vincenzo Italy
170 E5 San Vito, Capo c. Sicily Italy
149 C4 Sanxia Shuiku resr China
149 C7 Sanya China
148 C3 Sanyuan China
152 C2 Sanyuanpu China
141 F2 S. A. Nyýazow Adyndaky Turkm.
178 B4 Sanza Pombo Angola
214 C3 São Bernardo do Campo Brazil
212 E3 São Borja Brazil
214 C3 São Carlos Brazil
211 K6 São Cristóvão Brazil
214 C1 São Domingos Brazil
214 B2 São Domingos r. Brazil
211 H6 São Félix Brazil
211 H5 São Félix Brazil
214 E3 São Fidélis Brazil
176 □ São Filipe Cape Verde
214 D1 São Francisco Brazil
211 K5 São Francisco r. Brazil
212 G3 São Francisco do Sul Brazil
215 F1 São Gabriel Brazil
214 D3 São Gonçalo Brazil
214 D2 São Gotardo Brazil
214 C1 São João da Aliança Brazil
214 E3 São João da Barra Brazil
214 C3 São João da Boa Vista Brazil
167 B2 São João da Madeira Port.
214 D1 São João do Paraíso Brazil
214 D3 São João Nepomuceno Brazil
214 C3 São Joaquim da Barra Brazil
156 A6 São Jorge i. Azores
213 D5 São José Brazil
214 E3 São José do Calçado Brazil
215 G2 São José do Norte Brazil
214 C3 São José do Rio Preto Brazil
214 D3 São José dos Campos Brazil
214 C4 São José dos Pinhais Brazil
214 D3 São Lourenço Brazil
214 A2 São Lourenço r. Brazil
214 A2 São Lourenço, Pantanal de marsh Brazil
215 G1 São Lourenço do Sul Brazil
211 J4 São Luís Brazil
214 C3 São Manuel Brazil
214 C2 São Marcos r. Brazil
211 J4 São Marcos, Baía de b. Brazil
214 E2 São Mateus Brazil
214 E2 São Mateus r. Brazil
156 A6 São Miguel i. Azores
214 C2 São Miguel r. Brazil
166 G3 Saône r. France
176 □ São Nicolau i. Cape Verde
214 C3 São Paulo Brazil (City Plan 116)
214 C3 São Paulo state Brazil
219 H5 São Pedro e São Paulo is N. Atlantic Ocean
211 J5 São Raimundo Nonato Brazil
214 D2 São Romão Brazil
211 K5 São Roque, Cabo de c. Brazil
214 D3 São Sebastião Brazil
214 D3 São Sebastião, Ilha do i. Brazil
214 C3 São Sebastião do Paraíso Brazil
215 G1 São Sepé Brazil
214 B2 São Simão Brazil
214 B2 São Simão, Barragem de resr Brazil
147 E6 Sao-Siu Indon.
São Tiago i. Cape Verde see Santiago
176 C4 São Tomé i. São Tomé and Príncipe
214 E3 São Tomé, Cabo de c. Brazil
176 C4 São Tomé and Príncipe country Africa
214 C3 São Vicente Brazil
176 □ São Vicente i. Cape Verde
167 B4 São Vicente, Cabo de c. Port.
136 C1 Sapanca Turkey
138 D4 Saparmyrat Türkmenbaşy Turkm.
124 C2 Saparua Indon.
136 C2 Şaphane Dağı mt. Turkey
206 J7 Sapo, Serranía del mts Panama
176 B4 Sapo National Park Liberia
150 G3 Sapporo Japan
170 F4 Sapri Italy
155 D4 Sapudi i. Indon.
199 D4 Sapulpa U.S.A.
141 E3 Sāqī Iran
140 B2 Saqqez Iran
137 K3 Sarā Iran
140 B2 Sarāb Iran
137 K5 Sarābe Meymeh Iran
154 B2 Sara Buri Thai.
141 F2 Saragt Turkm.
210 C4 Saraguro Ecuador
171 H3 Sarajevo Bos.-Herz.
141 F2 Sarakhs Iran
138 D2 Saraktash Rus. Fed.
138 C2 Saralzhin Kazakh.
145 H4 Saramati mt. India
139 H2 Saran' Kazakh.
155 D3 Saran, Gunung mt. Indon.
203 G2 Saranac r. U.S.A.
203 F2 Saranac Lake U.S.A.
171 I5 Sarandë Albania
215 F2 Sarandí del Yí Uruguay
215 F2 Sarandí Grande Uruguay
153 C5 Sarangani i. Phil.
153 C5 Sarangani Bay Phil.
153 C5 Sarangani Islands Phil.
153 C5 Sarangani Strait Phil.
172 H4 Saransk Rus. Fed.
154 A1 Saraphi Thai.
132 G4 Sarapul Rus. Fed.
213 C3 Sarare r. Venez.
201 D7 Sarasota U.S.A.
144 B5 Saraswati r. India
173 D6 Sarata Ukr.
194 F3 Saratoga U.S.A.
203 G3 Saratoga Springs U.S.A.
155 D2 Saratok Sarawak Malaysia
173 H5 Saratov Rus. Fed.
173 H5 Saratovskaya Oblast' admin. div. Rus. Fed.
172 I4 Saratovskoye Vodokhranilishche resr Rus. Fed.
171 K5 Saratsina, Akrotirio pt Greece
141 F5 Sarāvān Iran
Saravan Laos see Salavan
154 A2 Sarawa r. Myanmar
155 D2 Sarawak state Malaysia
136 A1 Saray Turkey
136 B3 Sarayköy Turkey
136 D2 Sarayönü Turkey
139 F5 Sarazm tourist site Tajikistan
141 F5 Sarbāz Iran
141 F5 Sarbāz r. Iran
141 E3 Sarbīsheh Iran
170 D2 Sarca r. Italy
137 L3 Sarcham Iran
144 E3 Sarda r. India/Nepal
145 E3 Sarda r. Nepal
144 C3 Sardarshahr India
137 L5 Sardasht Iran
140 B2 Sar Dasht Iran
Sardegna i. Sardinia Italy see Sardinia
213 B2 Sardinata Col.
170 C4 Sardinia i. Sardinia Italy
137 K3 Sardrūd Iran
140 C5 Sareb, Rās as pt U.A.E.
158 L2 Sareks nationalpark nat. park Sweden
158 L2 Sarektjåkkå mt. Sweden
140 B3 Sar-e Pol-e Žahāb Iran
141 G2 Sar-e Pul Afgh.
141 G3 Sar-e Pul Afgh.
139 H5 Sarez, Kŭli l. Tajik.
219 E4 Sargasso Sea Atlantic Ocean
144 C2 Sargodha Pak.
177 D4 Sarh Chad
140 D2 Sārī Iran
171 L7 Saria i. Greece
144 D2 Sarigh Jilganang Kol salt l. Aksai Chin
136 B2 Sarıgöl Turkey
137 I1 Sarıkamış Turkey
136 D3 Sarıkavak Turkey
144 D4 Sarila India
154 □ Sarimbun Reservoir Sing.
124 E4 Sarina Australia
136 E2 Sarıoğlan Turkey
Sar-i-Pul Afgh. see Sar-e Pul
137 I2 Sarısu Turkey
152 C4 Sariwŏn N. Korea
136 C2 Sarıyar Barajı resr Turkey
136 B1 Sarıyer Turkey
136 F2 Sarız Turkey
144 E4 Sarju r. India
139 I3 Sarkand Kazakh.
144 B4 Sarkari Tala India
136 C2 Şarkikaraağaç Turkey
136 F2 Şarkışla Turkey
173 C7 Şarköy Turkey
141 G4 Sarlath Range mts Afgh./Pak.
166 E4 Sarlat-la-Canéda France
138 C5 Şarlawuk Turkm.
147 F7 Sarmi Indon.
159 K3 Särna Sweden
137 K5 Sarneh Iran
170 C1 Sarnen Switz.
191 F4 Sarnia Canada
173 C5 Sarny Ukr.
155 B3 Sarolangun Indon.
150 H2 Saroma-ko l. Japan
171 J6 Saronikos Kolpos g. Greece
173 C7 Saros Körfezi b. Turkey
144 C4 Sarotra India
172 G4 Sarov Rus. Fed.
173 H6 Sarpa, Ozero l. Respublika Kalmykiya-Khalm'g-Tangch Rus. Fed.
173 H5 Sarpa, Ozero l. Volgogradskaya Oblast' Rus. Fed.
159 J4 Sarpsborg Norway
166 H2 Sarrebourg France
164 F5 Sarreguemines France
167 C1 Sarria Spain
167 F2 Sarrión Spain
164 C6 Sarry France
170 C4 Sartène Corsica France
140 C3 Sarud, Rūdkhāneh-ye r. Iran
141 G5 Saruna Pak.
137 L4 Sārūq Iran
137 J2 Şärur Azer.
141 F4 Saru Tara tourist site Afgh.
137 K4 Sarvābād Iran
168 H7 Sárvár Hungary
140 D4 Sarvestān Iran
139 G4 Saryagash Kazakh.
139 G2 Saryarka plain Kazakh.
140 D4 Sar Yazd Iran
138 E3 Sarybasat Kazakh.
139 H4 Sary-Bulak Kyrg.
139 I4 Sary-Jaz r. Kyrg.
139 F2 Sarykamys Karagandinskaya Oblast' Kazakh.
138 C3 Sarykamys Mangistauskaya Oblast' Kazakh.
138 D4 Sarykamyshskoye Ozero salt l. Turkm./Uzbek.
139 G4 Sarykemer Kazakh.
139 H2 Sarykiyak Kazakh.
138 F1 Sarykol' Kazakh.
139 H5 Sarykol Range mts China/Tajik.
139 H3 Sarykomey Kazakh.
139 I3 Saryozek Kazakh.
138 B2 Saryozen r. Kazakh./Rus. Fed.
139 H3 Saryshagan Kazakh.
139 F3 Sarysu watercourse Kazakh.
138 B3 Sarytash Kazakh.
139 H5 Sary-Tash Kyrg.
Sary Yazikskoye Vodokhranilishche resr Turkm. see Saryýazy Suw Howdany
141 F2 Saryýazy Suw Howdany resr Turkm.
139 H3 Saryyesik-Atyrau, Peski des. Kazakh.
139 I4 Saryzhaz Kazakh.
138 B4 Sarzha Kazakh.
197 G6 Sasabe U.S.A.
145 F4 Sasaram India
151 A8 Sasebo Japan
187 H4 Saskatchewan prov. Canada
187 I4 Saskatchewan r. Canada
187 H4 Saskatoon Canada
133 M2 Saskylakh Rus. Fed.
206 H5 Saslaya mt. Nicaragua
206 H5 Saslaya, Parque Nacional nat. park Nicaragua
181 G3 Sasolburg S. Africa
172 G4 Sasovo Rus. Fed.
203 F5 Sassafras U.S.A.
176 B4 Sassandra Côte d'Ivoire
170 C4 Sassari Sardinia Italy
165 G3 Sassenberg Germany
168 F3 Sassnitz Germany
139 J3 Sasykkol', Ozero l. Kazakh.
173 H6 Sasykoli Rus. Fed.
176 A3 Satadougou Mali
151 B9 Sata-misaki c. Japan
144 C5 Satana India
143 A2 Satara India
181 I2 Satara S. Africa
173 G4 Satinka Rus. Fed.
145 G5 Satkhira Bangl.
144 C3 Satluj r. Pak.
143 B2 Satmala Range hills India
144 E4 Satna India
139 F2 Satpayev Kazakh.
144 C5 Satpura Range mts India
151 B9 Satsuma-hantō pen. Japan
151 B9 Satsuma-Sendai Japan
154 B2 Sattahip Thai.
165 I5 Satteldorf Germany
144 D2 Satti India
169 K7 Satu Mare Romania
154 B4 Satun Thai.
215 E1 Sauce Arg.
206 D2 Sauceda Mex.
197 F5 Sauceda Mountains U.S.A.
206 C1 Saucillo Mex.
159 I4 Sauda Norway
139 G4 Saudakent Kazakh.
158 C2 Sauðárkrókur Iceland
142 B4 Saudi Arabia country Asia
165 F3 Sauerland reg. Germany
190 D4 Saugatuck U.S.A.
203 G3 Saugerties U.S.A.
198 E2 Sauk Center U.S.A.
190 C4 Sauk City U.S.A.
166 G3 Saulieu France
191 E2 Sault Sainte Marie Canada
190 E2 Sault Sainte Marie U.S.A.
139 G1 Saumalkol' Kazakh.
147 F7 Saumlakki Indon.
166 D3 Saumur France
209 G7 Saunders Island S. Sandwich Is
145 F4 Saura r. India
138 B3 Saura Kazakh.
179 C4 Saurimo Angola
144 D5 Sausar India
171 I2 Sava r. Europe
206 H5 Savá Hond.
127 F8 Savage River Australia
125 I3 Savai'i i. Samoa
173 G5 Savala r. Rus. Fed.
176 C4 Savalou Benin
190 B4 Savanna U.S.A.
201 D6 Savannah GA U.S.A.
201 B5 Savannah TN U.S.A.
201 D5 Savannah r. U.S.A.
201 E7 Savannah Sound Bahamas
154 C1 Savannakhét Laos
205 I5 Savanna-la-Mar Jamaica
188 B3 Savant Lake Canada
143 A3 Savanur India
158 M3 Sävar Sweden
171 L5 Savaştepe Turkey
176 C4 Savè Benin
179 D6 Save r. Moz.
140 C3 Sāveh Iran
158 O3 Saviaho Fin.
132 F3 Savinskiy Rus. Fed.
170 C2 Savona Italy
159 O3 Savonlinna Fin.
158 O3 Savonranta Fin.
166 H4 Savoy reg. France
137 I1 Şavşat Turkey
159 K4 Sävsjö Sweden
158 O2 Savukoski Fin.
137 H3 Savur Turkey
Savu Sea sea Indon. see Sawu, Laut
144 D4 Sawai Madhopur India
154 A1 Sawankhalok Thai.
195 F4 Sawatch Range mts U.S.A.
162 A6 Sawel Mountain h. U.K.
154 A3 Sawi, Ao b. Thai.
127 J3 Sawtell Australia
190 B2 Sawtooth Mountains hills U.S.A.
147 E7 Sawu, Laut sea Indon.
161 G4 Saxilby U.K.
161 I5 Saxmundham U.K.
158 K2 Saxnäs Sweden
139 I3 Sayak Kazakh.
146 B1 Sayano-Shushenskoye Vodokhranilishche resr Rus. Fed.
138 E5 Saýat Turkm.
Sayat Turkm. see Saýat
207 G4 Sayaxché Guat.
140 D4 Sāyen Iran
142 D6 Sayḩūt Yemen
138 A2 Saykyn Kazakh.
178 E2 Saylac Somalia
Sāylac Somalia see Saylac
146 D2 Saynshand Mongolia
139 J3 Sayram Hu salt l. China
199 D5 Sayre OK U.S.A.
202 E4 Sayre PA U.S.A.
206 D4 Sayula Jalisco Mex.
207 F4 Sayula Veracruz Mex.
186 D4 Sayward Canada
138 B3 Sazdy Kazakh.
144 C2 Sazin Pak.
172 E3 Sazonovo Rus. Fed.
176 B2 Sbaa Alg.
176 C1 Sbeitla Tunisia
160 D3 Scafell Pike h. U.K.
162 B4 Scalasaig U.K.
170 F5 Scalea Italy
162 □ Scalloway U.K.
163 C5 Scalp h. Ireland
162 B3 Scalpay i. Scotland U.K.
162 C3 Scalpay i. Scotland U.K.
127 H8 Scamander Australia
162 E2 Scapa Flow inlet U.K.
162 C4 Scarba i. U.K.
191 H4 Scarborough Canada
213 E2 Scarborough Trin. and Tob.
160 G3 Scarborough U.K.
153 A3 Scarborough Shoal sea feature Phil.
162 A2 Scarp i. U.K.
165 I1 Schaale r. Germany
165 I1 Schaalsee l. Germany
164 C4 Schaerbeek Belgium
168 D7 Schaffhausen Switz.
165 J3 Schafstädt Germany
164 C2 Schagen Neth.
164 C2 Schagerbrug Neth.
180 B3 Schakalskuppe Namibia
141 F4 Schao watercourse Afgh./Iran
168 F6 Schärding Austria
164 B3 Scharendijke Neth.
165 I5 Schebheim Germany
165 H1 Scheeßel Germany
189 G3 Schefferville Canada
Schelde r. Belgium see Scheldt
164 C3 Scheldt r. Belgium
197 E2 Schell Creek Range mts U.S.A.
165 I2 Schellerten Germany
203 G3 Schenectady U.S.A.
165 H1 Schenefeld Germany
164 C2 Schermerhorn Neth.
162 D4 Schiehallion mt. U.K.
165 K6 Schierling Germany
164 E1 Schiermonnikoog Neth.
164 E1 Schiermonnikoog i. Neth.
164 E1 Schiermonnikoog Nationaal Park nat. park Neth.
165 G1 Schiffdorf Germany
165 J1 Schilde r. Germany
164 D4 Schinnen Neth.
170 D2 Schio Italy
165 K3 Schkeuditz Germany
164 E4 Schleiden Germany
165 J4 Schleiz Germany
168 D3 Schleswig Germany
165 H1 Schleswig-Holstein land Germany
165 I4 Schleusingen Germany
165 H4 Schlitz Germany
165 G3 Schloss Holte-Stukenbrock Germany
165 H4 Schlüchtern Germany
165 I5 Schlüsselfeld Germany
165 I4 Schmalkalden, Kurort Germany
165 G3 Schmallenberg Germany
165 K4 Schneeberg Germany
165 J3 Schneidlingen Germany
165 H1 Schneverdingen Germany
203 G3 Schodack Center U.S.A.
190 C3 Schofield U.S.A.
196 □1 Schofield Barracks military base U.S.A.
164 D2 Schokland tourist site Neth.
165 K1 Schönebeck Germany
165 J2 Schönebeck (Elbe) Germany
165 I2 Schöningen Germany
165 H5 Schöntal Germany
203 I2 Schoodic Lake U.S.A.
190 E4 Schoolcraft U.S.A.
164 C3 Schoonhoven Neth.
165 I5 Schopfloch Germany
165 I2 Schöppenstedt Germany
165 F1 Schortens Germany
127 H9 Schouten Island Australia
124 E2 Schouten Islands P.N.G.
190 D1 Schreiber Canada
203 G3 Schroon Lake U.S.A.
197 F5 Schuchuli U.S.A.
163 B6 Schull Ireland
187 J2 Schultz Lake Canada
196 C2 Schurz U.S.A.
164 F2 Schüttorf Germany
203 G3 Schuylerville U.S.A.
165 J5 Schwabach Germany
168 D6 Schwäbische Alb mts Germany
165 H5 Schwäbisch Hall Germany
168 E6 Schwabmünchen Germany
165 G2 Schwaförden Germany
165 H4 Schwalmstadt-Ziegenhain Germany
165 K5 Schwandorf Germany
155 D3 Schwaner, Pegunungan mts Indon.
165 G1 Schwanewede Germany
165 H2 Schwarmstedt Germany
165 L3 Schwarze Elster r. Germany
165 I1 Schwarzenbek Germany
165 K4 Schwarzenberg Germany
164 E4 Schwarzer Mann h. Germany
180 B2 Schwarzrand mts Namibia
Schwarzwald mts Germany see Black Forest
168 E7 Schwaz Austria
168 G4 Schwedt an der Oder Germany
165 G5 Schwegenheim Germany
164 E5 Schweich Germany
165 I4 Schweinfurt Germany
165 L3 Schweinitz Germany
165 K1 Schweinrich Germany
181 F3 Schweizer-Reneke S. Africa
164 F3 Schwelm Germany
168 D6 Schwenningen Germany
165 J1 Schwerin Germany
165 J1 Schweriner See l. Germany
165 G5 Schwetzingen Germany
168 D7 Schwyz Switz.
170 E6 Sciacca Sicily Italy
170 F6 Scicli Italy
161 A8 Scilly, Isles of U.K.
202 B5 Scioto r. U.S.A.
197 F2 Scipio U.S.A.
194 F1 Scobey U.S.A.
161 I5 Scole U.K.
127 I4 Scone Australia
162 E4 Scone U.K.
185 P2 Scoresby Land reg. Greenland
219 G9 Scotia Ridge sea feature S. Atlantic Ocean
219 G9 Scotia Sea S. Atlantic Ocean
191 G4 Scotland Canada
162 D4 Scotland admin. div. U.K.
186 D4 Scott, Cape Canada
129 B5 Scott Base research stn Antarctica
181 I5 Scottburgh S. Africa
198 C4 Scott City U.S.A.
129 B5 Scott Coast coastal area Antarctica
202 D4 Scottdale U.S.A.
185 K2 Scott Inlet Canada
129 A6 Scott Island i. Antarctica
187 H3 Scott Lake Canada
129 E4 Scott Mountains mts Antarctica
198 C3 Scottsbluff U.S.A.
201 C5 Scottsboro U.S.A.
200 C4 Scottsburg U.S.A.
127 G8 Scottsdale Australia
195 E5 Scottsdale U.S.A.
196 A3 Scotts Valley U.S.A.
190 D4 Scottville U.S.A.
196 D3 Scottys Junction U.S.A.
162 C2 Scourie U.K.
162 □ Scousburgh U.K.
162 E2 Scrabster U.K.
203 F4 Scranton U.S.A.
162 B4 Scridain, Loch inlet U.K.
160 G4 Scunthorpe U.K.
161 H7 Seaford U.K.
203 F5 Seaford U.S.A.
191 G4 Seaforth Canada
153 A4 Seahorse Shoal sea feature Phil.
187 J3 Seal r. Canada
180 E7 Seal, Cape S. Africa
126 E5 Sea Lake Australia
203 I3 Seal Island U.S.A.
189 H3 Seal Lake Canada
180 F7 Seal Point S. Africa
197 E3 Seaman Range mts U.S.A.
160 G3 Seamer U.K.
197 E4 Searchlight U.S.A.
199 F5 Searcy U.S.A.
196 D4 Searles Lake U.S.A.
190 E4 Sears U.S.A.
203 I2 Searsport U.S.A.
196 B3 Seaside CA U.S.A.
194 B2 Seaside OR U.S.A.
162 E6 Seaton U.K.
194 B2 Seattle U.S.A.
186 B2 Seattle, Mount Canada/U.S.A.
203 F5 Seaville U.S.A.
203 H3 Sebago Lake U.S.A.
206 A1 Sebastián Vizcaíno, Bahía b. Mex.
203 I2 Sebasticook r. U.S.A.
155 E2 Sebatik i. Indon.

136 C1 **Seben** Turkey
171 J2 **Sebeş** Romania
155 C4 **Sebesi** *i.* Indon.
191 F4 **Sebewaing** U.S.A.
172 D3 **Sebezh** Rus. Fed.
136 E3 **Sebil** Turkey
136 G1 **Şebinkarahisar** Turkey
203 I2 **Seboeis Lake** U.S.A.
203 I2 **Seboomook** U.S.A.
203 I2 **Seboomook Lake** U.S.A.
201 D7 **Sebring** U.S.A.
173 G5 **Sebrovo** Rus. Fed.
210 B5 **Sechura** Peru
210 B5 **Sechura, Bahía de** *b.* Peru
165 H5 **Seckach** Germany
203 H2 **Second Lake** U.S.A.
176 □ **Secos, Ilhéus** *is* Cape Verde
128 A6 **Secretary Island** N.Z.
181 H3 **Secunda** S. Africa
143 B2 **Secunderabad** India
198 E4 **Sedalia** U.S.A.
143 B2 **Sedam** India
126 C5 **Sedan** Australia
166 G2 **Sedan** France
128 E4 **Seddon** N.Z.
128 C4 **Seddonville** N.Z.
141 E3 **Sedeh** Iran
203 I2 **Sedgwick** U.S.A.
176 A3 **Sédhiou** Senegal
168 G6 **Sedlčany** Czech Rep.
136 E6 **Sedom** Israel
197 G4 **Sedona** U.S.A.
170 B6 **Sédrata** Alg.
159 M5 **Šeduva** Lith.
165 I1 **Seedorf** Germany
163 D5 **Seefin** *h.* Ireland
165 J2 **Seehausen** Germany
165 J2 **Seehausen (Altmark)** Germany
179 B6 **Seeheim** Namibia
165 G5 **Seeheim-Jugenheim** Germany
180 E6 **Seekoegat** S. Africa
197 E5 **Seeley** U.S.A.
129 B4 **Seelig, Mount** *mt.* Antarctica
165 H2 **Seelze** Germany
166 E2 **Sées** France
165 I3 **Seesen** Germany
165 I1 **Seevetal** Germany
181 G1 **Sefare** Botswana
171 L5 **Seferihisar** Turkey
141 G3 **Sefīd Kūh** *mts* Afgh.
141 F3 **Sefīd Kūh, Selseleh-ye** *mts* Afgh.
181 G1 **Sefophe** Botswana
159 J3 **Segalstad** Norway
153 A5 **Segama** *r. Sabah* Malaysia
155 B2 **Segamat** Malaysia
165 K2 **Segeletz** Germany
172 E2 **Segezha** Rus. Fed.
139 F3 **Segiz** *salt l.* Kazakh.
139 F3 **Segiz, Ozera** *lakes* Kazakh.
167 F3 **Segorbe** Spain
176 B3 **Ségou** Mali
213 B3 **Segovia** Col.
167 D2 **Segovia** Spain
172 E2 **Segozerskoye Vodokhranilishche** *resr* Rus. Fed.
167 G1 **Segre** *r.* Spain
177 D2 **Séguédine** Niger
176 B4 **Séguéla** Côte d'Ivoire
199 D6 **Seguin** U.S.A.
215 D1 **Segundo** *r.* Arg.
167 F3 **Segura** *r.* Spain
179 C6 **Sehithwa** Botswana
181 H4 **Sehlabathebe National Park** Lesotho
144 D5 **Sehore** India
158 M1 **Seiland** *i.* Norway
199 D4 **Seiling** U.S.A.
158 M3 **Seinäjoki** Fin.
188 B4 **Seine** *r.* Canada
166 E2 **Seine** *r.* France
166 D2 **Seine, Baie de** *b.* France
166 F2 **Seine, Val de** *val.* France
169 K3 **Sejny** Poland
152 D5 **Sejong** South Korea
155 B3 **Sekayu** Indon.
180 E2 **Sekoma** Botswana
176 B4 **Sekondi** Ghana
141 F4 **Sekūheh** Iran
154 D5 **Sekura** Indon.
194 B2 **Selah** U.S.A.
147 F7 **Selaru** *i.* Indon.
155 D3 **Selatan, Tanjung** *pt* Indon.
184 B3 **Selawik** U.S.A.
147 E7 **Selayar, Pulau** *i.* Indon.
165 K4 **Selb** Germany
158 J3 **Selbekken** Norway
158 J3 **Selbu** Norway
160 F4 **Selby** U.K.
198 C2 **Selby** U.S.A.
179 C6 **Selebi-Phikwe** Botswana
146 F1 **Selemdzhinskiy Khrebet** *mts* Rus. Fed.
136 B2 **Selendi** Turkey
146 C1 **Selenga** *r.* Rus. Fed.
166 H2 **Sélestat** France
154 □ **Seletar** Sing.
154 □ **Seletar, Pulau** *i.* Sing.
154 □ **Seletar Reservoir** Sing.
198 C2 **Selfridge** U.S.A.
176 A3 **Sélibabi** Mauritania
165 G4 **Seligenstadt** Germany
172 E3 **Seliger, Ozero** *l.* Rus. Fed.
197 F4 **Seligman** U.S.A.
177 E2 **Selîma Oasis** Sudan
191 I5 **Selinsgrove** U.S.A.
169 P2 **Selishche** Rus. Fed.
173 H6 **Selitrennoye** Rus. Fed.
169 P2 **Selizharovo** Rus. Fed.
159 J4 **Seljord** Norway
165 J3 **Selke** *r.* Germany
187 J4 **Selkirk** Canada
162 F5 **Selkirk** U.K.
186 F4 **Selkirk Mountains** Canada
160 D3 **Sellafield** U.K.
197 G6 **Sells** U.S.A.
164 F3 **Selm** Germany
201 C5 **Selma** *AL* U.S.A.
196 C3 **Selma** *CA* U.S.A.
201 B5 **Selmer** U.S.A.
161 G7 **Selsey Bill** *hd* U.K.
154 C4 **Seluan** *i.* Indon.
210 D5 **Selvas** *reg.* Brazil
187 I3 **Selwyn Lake** Canada
186 C2 **Selwyn Mountains** Canada
124 D4 **Selwyn Range** *hills* Australia
172 I2 **Sël'yb** Rus. Fed.
155 D4 **Semarang** Indon.
155 C2 **Sematan** *Sarawak* Malaysia
155 E3 **Semayang, Danau** *l.* Indon.
153 A6 **Sembakung** *r.* Indon.
154 □ **Sembawang** Sing.
178 B3 **Sembé** Congo
137 J3 **Şemdinli** Turkey
173 E4 **Semenivka** Ukr.
138 C1 **Semenkino** Rus. Fed.
172 H3 **Semenov** Rus. Fed.
155 D4 **Semeru, Gunung** *vol.* Indon.
139 J2 **Semey** Kazakh.
173 G6 **Semikarakorsk** Rus. Fed.
173 F5 **Semiluki** Rus. Fed.
194 F3 **Seminoe Reservoir** U.S.A.
199 C5 **Seminole** U.S.A.
201 C6 **Seminole, Lake** U.S.A.
139 K2 **Seminskiy Khrebet** *mts* Rus. Fed.
139 I2 **Semipalatinskaya Oblast'** Kazakh.
139 F1 **Semipolka** Kazakh.
153 B3 **Semirara** *i.* Phil.
153 B4 **Semirara Islands** Phil.
140 C4 **Semīrom** Iran
139 I2 **Semiyarka** Kazakh.
139 H2 **Semizbuga** Kazakh.
140 D3 **Semnān** Iran
140 D3 **Semnān va Dāmghaān** *reg.* Iran
164 D5 **Semois** *r.* Belgium
164 D5 **Semois, Vallée de la** *val.* Belgium/France
155 E2 **Semporna** *Sabah* Malaysia
155 D4 **Sempu** *i.* Indon.
154 C2 **Sên, Stœng** *r.* Cambodia
153 A5 **Senaja** *Sabah* Malaysia
173 G7 **Senak'i** Georgia
210 E5 **Sena Madureira** Brazil
143 C5 **Senanayake Samudra** *l.* Sri Lanka
179 C5 **Senanga** Zambia
150 G5 **Sendai** Japan
145 H3 **Sêndo** China
154 B5 **Senebui, Tanjung** *pt* Indon.
197 G5 **Seneca** *AZ* U.S.A.
190 C5 **Seneca** *IL* U.S.A.
194 C2 **Seneca** *OR* U.S.A.
202 E3 **Seneca Falls** U.S.A.
202 E3 **Seneca Lake** U.S.A.
202 D5 **Seneca Rocks** U.S.A.
202 C5 **Senecaville Lake** U.S.A.
176 A3 **Senegal** *country* Africa
176 A3 **Sénégal** *r.* Mauritania/Senegal
181 G4 **Senekal** S. Africa
190 E2 **Seney** U.S.A.
168 G5 **Senftenberg** Germany
144 D4 **Sengar** *r.* India
178 D4 **Sengerema** Tanz.
172 I4 **Sengiley** Rus. Fed.
124 C2 **Sengkang** Indon.
211 J6 **Senhor do Bonfim** Brazil
170 E3 **Senigallia** Italy
170 F2 **Senj** Croatia
158 L1 **Senja** *i.* Norway
137 I1 **Şenkaya** Turkey
180 E2 **Senlac** S. Africa
152 F2 **Senlin Shan** *mt.* China
166 F2 **Senlis** France
154 C2 **Senmonorom** Cambodia
161 B7 **Sennen** U.K.
191 I1 **Senneterre** Canada
181 H5 **Senqu** *r.* Lesotho
166 F2 **Sens** France
164 B4 **Sensée** *r.* France
206 G5 **Sensuntepeque** El Salvador
171 I2 **Senta** Serbia
144 D3 **Senthal** India
197 F5 **Sentinel** U.S.A.
186 E3 **Sentinel Peak** Canada
154 □ **Sentosa** *i.* Sing.
181 H1 **Senwabarwana** S. Africa
137 H3 **Şenyurt** Turkey
152 D5 **Seocheon** S. Korea
152 D7 **Seogwipo** S. Korea
152 D5 **Seongnam** S. Korea
152 D7 **Seongsan** S. Korea
144 D5 **Seoni** India
152 E4 **Seorak-san** *mt.* S. Korea
143 C1 **Seorinarayan** India
152 D5 **Seosan** S. Korea
152 D5 **Seoul** S. Korea (City Plan **103**)
128 D4 **Separation Point** N.Z.
137 K4 **Separ Shāhābād** Iran
214 D3 **Sepetiba, Baía de** *b.* Brazil
124 E2 **Sepik** *r.* P.N.G.
152 D4 **Sep'o** N. Korea
189 G3 **Sept-Îles** Canada
196 C3 **Sequoia National Park** U.S.A.
173 G5 **Serafimovich** Rus. Fed.
147 E7 **Seram** *i.* Indon.
147 F7 **Seram, Laut** *sea* Indon.
155 C4 **Serang** Indon.
154 □ **Serangoon, Pulau** *i.* Sing.
154 □ **Serangoon Harbour** *b.* Sing.
154 D5 **Serasan** *i.* Indon.
155 C2 **Serasan, Selat** *sea chan.* Indon.
154 D5 **Seraya** *i.* Indon.
154 □ **Seraya, Pulau** *reg.* Sing.
171 I3 **Serbia** *country* Europe
206 C1 **Serdán** Mex.
138 D5 **Serdar** Turkm.
178 E2 **Serdo** Eth.
173 H4 **Serdoba** *r.* Rus. Fed.
173 H4 **Serdobsk** Rus. Fed.
139 J2 **Serebryansk** Kazakh.
172 D3 **Seredka** Rus. Fed.
136 D2 **Şereflikoçhisar** Turkey
155 B2 **Seremban** Malaysia
178 D4 **Serengeti National Park** Tanz.
179 D5 **Serenje** Zambia
172 H4 **Sergach** Rus. Fed.
139 G2 **Sergeyevka** *Akmolinskaya Oblast'* Kazakh.
139 F1 **Sergeyevka** *Severnyy Kazakhstan* Kazakh.
150 C3 **Sergeyevka** Rus. Fed.
172 F3 **Sergiyev Posad** Rus. Fed.
141 F3 **Serhetabat** Turkm.
155 D2 **Seria** Brunei
155 D2 **Serian** *Sarawak* Malaysia
171 K6 **Serifos** *i.* Greece
189 G2 **Sérigny, Lac** *l.* Canada
136 C3 **Serik** Turkey
139 I5 **Serikbuya** China
126 C3 **Serle, Mount** *h.* Australia
147 E7 **Sermata, Kepulauan** *is* Indon.
185 M2 **Sermersuaq** *glacier* Greenland
172 I3 **Sernur** Rus. Fed.
173 H6 **Seroglazka** Rus. Fed.
132 H4 **Serov** Rus. Fed.
179 C6 **Serowe** Botswana
167 C4 **Serpa** Port.
213 E2 **Serpent's Mouth** *sea chan.* Trin. and Tob./Venez.
172 F4 **Serpukhov** Rus. Fed.
214 C3 **Serra da Canastra, Parque Nacional da** *nat. park* Brazil
214 C1 **Serra da Mesa, Represa** *resr* Brazil
211 H3 **Serra do Navio** Brazil
213 D4 **Serranía de la Neblina, Parque Nacional** *nat. park* Venez.
214 B2 **Serranópolis** Brazil
164 B5 **Serre** *r.* France
171 J4 **Serres** Greece
215 D1 **Serrezuela** Arg.
211 K6 **Serrinha** Brazil
214 D2 **Sêrro** Brazil
215 B4 **Serrucho** *mt.* Arg.
170 C6 **Sers** Tunisia
214 C3 **Sertãozinho** Brazil
172 D2 **Sertolovo** Rus. Fed.
154 A4 **Seruai** Indon.
155 D3 **Seruyan** *r.* Indon.
145 H2 **Sêrwolungwa** China
146 B3 **Sêrxü** China
155 E2 **Sesayap** Indon.
153 A6 **Sesayap** *r.* Indon.
188 B3 **Seseganaga Lake** Canada
191 G1 **Sesekinika** Canada
179 B5 **Sesfontein** Namibia
181 H1 **Seshego** S. Africa
179 C5 **Sesheke** Zambia
170 E4 **Sessa Aurunca** Italy
170 C2 **Sestri Levante** Italy
172 D2 **Sestroretsk** Rus. Fed.
154 C2 **Set, Phou** *mt.* Laos
150 F3 **Setana** Japan
166 F5 **Sète** France
214 D2 **Sete Lagoas** Brazil
158 L1 **Setermoen** Norway
159 I4 **Setesdal** *val.* Norway
145 F4 **Seti** *r.* Nepal
144 E3 **Seti** *r.* Nepal
176 C1 **Sétif** Alg.
151 E7 **Seto** Japan
176 B1 **Settat** Morocco
160 E3 **Settle** U.K.
167 B3 **Setúbal** Port.
167 B3 **Setúbal, Baía de** *b.* Port.
188 B3 **Seul, Lac** *l.* Canada
190 E3 **Seul Choix Point** U.S.A.
137 J1 **Sevan** Armenia
137 J1 **Sevan, Lake** Armenia
**Sevana Lich** *l.* Armenia *see* **Sevan, Lake**
173 E6 **Sevastopol'** Ukr.
189 H2 **Seven Islands Bay** Canada
161 H6 **Sevenoaks** U.K.
166 F4 **Sévérac-le-Château** France
127 I2 **Severn** *r.* Australia
188 B3 **Severn** *r.* Canada
180 E3 **Severn** S. Africa
161 E6 **Severn** *r.* U.K.
172 G2 **Severnaya Dvina** *r.* Rus. Fed.
173 H7 **Severnaya Osetiya-Alaniya, Respublika** *aut. rep.* Rus. Fed.
133 L1 **Severnaya Zemlya** *is* Rus. Fed.
188 B3 **Severn Lake** Canada
132 H3 **Severnyy** Rus. Fed.
132 G2 **Severnyy, Ostrov** *i.* Rus. Fed.
138 D3 **Severnyy Chink Ustyurta** *esc.* Kazakh.
139 G1 **Severnyy Kazakhstan** *admin. div.* Kazakh.
146 D1 **Severo-Baykal'skoye Nagor'ye** *mts* Rus. Fed.
172 F1 **Severodvinsk** Rus. Fed.
133 Q4 **Severo-Kuril'sk** Rus. Fed.
158 P1 **Severomorsk** Rus. Fed.
132 K3 **Severo-Yeniseyskiy** Rus. Fed.
173 F6 **Severskaya** Rus. Fed.
195 D4 **Sevier** *r.* U.S.A.
197 G2 **Sevier Bridge Reservoir** U.S.A.
197 F2 **Sevier Desert** U.S.A.
197 F2 **Sevier Lake** U.S.A.
213 B3 **Sevilla** Col.
**Sevilla** Spain *see* **Seville**
167 D4 **Seville** Spain
171 K3 **Sevlievo** Bulg.
144 C3 **Sewani** India
184 D3 **Seward** *AK* U.S.A.
198 D3 **Seward** *NE* U.S.A.
184 B3 **Seward Peninsula** U.S.A.
186 F3 **Sexsmith** Canada
192 E6 **Sextín** *r.* Mex.
132 I2 **Seyakha** Rus. Fed.
207 G4 **Seybaplaya** Mex.
175 I5 **Seychelles** *country* Indian Ocean
**Seydi** Turkm. *see* **Seýdi**
138 E5 **Seýdi** Turkm.
136 C3 **Seydişehir** Turkey
158 D2 **Seyðisfjörður** Iceland
140 B2 **Seydvān** Iran
**Seyhan** Turkey *see* **Adana**
136 E3 **Seyhan** *r.* Turkey
173 E5 **Seym** *r.* Rus. Fed.
133 Q3 **Seymchan** Rus. Fed.
126 F6 **Seymour** Australia
181 G6 **Seymour** S. Africa
200 C4 **Seymour** *IN* U.S.A.
199 D5 **Seymour** *TX* U.S.A.
166 F2 **Sézanne** France
171 K2 **Sfântu Gheorghe** Romania
176 D1 **Sfax** Tunisia
171 J4 **Sfikias, Limni** *resr* Greece
164 D2 **'s-Graveland** Neth.
**'s-Gravenhage** Neth. *see* **The Hague**
162 C4 **Sgurr Dhomhnuill** *h.* U.K.
**Sgurr Mor** *mt.* U.K. *see* **Sgurr Mòr**
162 C3 **Sgurr Mòr** *mt.* U.K.
148 C3 **Shaanxi** *prov.* China
**Shabeelle, Webi** *r.* Ethiopia/Somalia *see* **Shebelē Wenz, Wabē**
140 B2 **Shabestar** Iran
171 M3 **Shabla, Nos** *pt* Bulg.
189 G3 **Shabogamo Lake** Canada
178 C4 **Shabunda** Dem. Rep. Congo
139 I5 **Shache** China
129 C5 **Shackleton Coast** *coastal area* Antarctica
129 D6 **Shackleton Ice Shelf** *ice feature* Antarctica
129 C3 **Shackleton Range** *mts* Antarctica
140 C4 **Shādegān** Iran
144 A3 **Shadikhak Pass** Pak.
140 D4 **Shādkām** *watercourse* Iran
190 D5 **Shafer, Lake** U.S.A.
129 B5 **Shafer Peak** *mt.* Antarctica
196 C4 **Shafter** U.S.A.
161 E6 **Shaftesbury** U.K.
139 G1 **Shagalalyteniz, Ozero** *l.* Kazakh.
139 G1 **Shagalalyteniz, Ozero** *l.* Kazakh.
139 I2 **Shagan** *Vostochnyy Kazakhstan* Kazakh.
138 D3 **Shagan** *watercourse Aktyubinskaya Oblast'* Kazakh.
139 I2 **Shagan** *watercourse Vostochnyy Kazakhstan* Kazakh.
184 C3 **Shageluk** U.S.A.
138 D4 **Shag'irlik** Uzbek.
128 C6 **Shag Point** N.Z.
219 G9 **Shag Rocks** *is* S. Georgia
138 D3 **Shagyray, Plato** *plat.* Kazakh.
**Shagyrlyk** Uzbek. *see* **Shag'irlik**
143 B2 **Shahabad** *Karnataka* India
144 E4 **Shahabad** *Uttar Pradesh* India
140 E4 **Shāhābād** Iran
144 C5 **Shahada** India
155 B2 **Shah Alam** Malaysia
143 A3 **Shahapur** India
144 A4 **Shah Bandar** Pak.
141 G5 **Shahbaz Kalat** Pak.
145 G5 **Shahbazpur** *sea chan.* Bangl.
141 E4 **Shāhdād** Iran
144 A4 **Shahdad Kot** Pak.
144 E5 **Shahdol** India
149 C4 **Shahe** China
148 E2 **Sha He** *r.* China
137 J3 **Shāhedān** Iraq
141 G3 **Shāh Fōlādī** *mt.* Afgh.
144 B4 **Shahgarh** India
137 J3 **Shāhī, Jazīreh-ye** *pen.* Iran
**Shahi Peninsula** Iran *see* **Shāhī, Jazīreh-ye**
140 E2 **Shāh Jahān, Kūh-e** *mts* Iran
144 D4 **Shahjahanpur** India
141 E4 **Shāh Kūh** *mt.* Iran
140 D3 **Shahmīrzād** Iran
143 B2 **Shahpur** India
144 B3 **Shahpur** Pak.
144 E5 **Shahpura** *Madhya Pradesh* India
144 D4 **Shahpura** *Rajasthan* India
141 G3 **Shahrak** Afgh.
141 F3 **Shāh Rakht** Iran
140 D4 **Shahr-e Bābak** Iran
140 C3 **Shahr-e Kord** Iran
140 C3 **Shāhreẕā** Iran
139 F5 **Shahrisabz** Uzbek.
140 C3 **Shahr Rey** Iran
139 G5 **Shahrtuz** Tajik.
140 C2 **Shāhrūd, Rūdkhāneh-ye** *r.* Iran
140 D3 **Shāhrūd Bustām** *reg.* Iran
141 G4 **Shaikh Husain** *mt.* Pak.
140 C5 **Shaj'ah, Jabal** *h.* Saudi Arabia
152 C3 **Shajianzi** China
137 K3 **Shakar Bolāghī** Iran
181 I4 **Shakaville** S. Africa
139 G5 **Shakhdara** *r.* Tajik.
141 E3 **Shākhen** Iran
172 E3 **Shakhovskaya** Rus. Fed.
**Shakhrisabz** Uzbek. *see* **Shahrisabz**
139 H2 **Shakhtinsk** Kazakh.
138 D2 **Shakhty** Kazakh.
173 G6 **Shakhty** Rus. Fed.
172 H3 **Shakhun'ya** Rus. Fed.
198 E2 **Shakopee** U.S.A.
150 G3 **Shakotan-hantō** *pen.* Japan
150 G3 **Shakotan-misaki** *c.* Japan
172 G2 **Shalakusha** Rus. Fed.
139 I2 **Shalday** Kazakh.
139 G3 **Shalginskiy (abandoned)** Kazakh.
138 D3 **Shalkar** Kazakh.
138 B2 **Shalkar, Ozero** *salt l.* Kazakh.
138 E2 **Shalkar Karashatau** *salt l.* Kazakh.
138 E2 **Shalkarteniz, Solonchak** *salt marsh* Kazakh.
139 I4 **Shalkodesu** Kazakh.
146 B3 **Shaluli Shan** *mts* China
145 I3 **Shaluni** *mt.* India
187 K3 **Shamattawa** Canada
140 E5 **Shamīl** Iran
140 D6 **Shamis** U.A.E.
202 E4 **Shamokin** U.S.A.
199 C5 **Shamrock** U.S.A.
179 D5 **Shamva** Zimbabwe
148 C2 **Shancheng** China
148 E3 **Shancheng** China
141 F4 **Shand** Afgh.
141 F4 **Shāndak** Iran
148 A2 **Shandan** China
137 L3 **Shānderman** Iran
148 E1 **Shandian He** *r.* China
141 E2 **Shāndīz** Iran
196 B4 **Shandon** U.S.A.
152 A5 **Shandong** *prov.* China
148 F2 **Shandong Bandao** *pen.* China
137 J5 **Shandrūkh** Iraq
144 C1 **Shandur Pass** Pak.
179 C5 **Shangani** *r.* Zimbabwe
148 E3 **Shangcai** China
149 C5 **Shangchao** China
148 E4 **Shangcheng** China
145 G3 **Shang Chu** *r.* China
149 D6 **Shangchuan Dao** *i.* China
148 D1 **Shangdu** China
148 E1 **Shangdu** China
149 E5 **Shangdundu** China
149 E4 **Shanggao** China
148 F4 **Shanghai** China (City Plan **103**)
148 F4 **Shanghai** *mun.* China
149 E5 **Shanghang** China
148 E2 **Shanghe** China
152 C3 **Shanghekou** China
148 D3 **Shangjin** China
149 C6 **Shanglin** China
148 C3 **Shangluo** China
148 D3 **Shangnan** China
148 E3 **Shangqiu** China
149 E4 **Shangrao** *Jiangxi* China
149 E4 **Shangrao** *Jiangxi* China
139 J3 **Shangsanshilipu** China
148 E3 **Shangshui** China
149 C6 **Shangsi** China
149 E4 **Shangtang** China
148 D1 **Shangyi** China
149 E5 **Shangyou** China
139 J4 **Shangyou Shuiku** *resr* China
**Shangyou Sk.** *salt flat* China *see* **Shangyou Shuiku**
149 F4 **Shangyu** China
152 D1 **Shangzhi** China
**Shangzhou** China *see* **Shangluo**
152 D1 **Shanhe** China
148 F3 **Shanhou He** *r.* China
163 B6 **Shanlaragh** Ireland
163 C5 **Shannon** *est.* Ireland
163 C4 **Shannon** *r.* Ireland
163 B5 **Shannon, Mouth of the** Ireland
152 D2 **Shansonggang** China
145 G5 **Shantipur** India
149 E6 **Shantou** China
149 E6 **Shanwei** China
148 D2 **Shanxi** *prov.* China
148 E3 **Shanxian** China
148 C3 **Shanyang** China
148 D2 **Shanyin** China
149 D5 **Shaodong** China
149 D5 **Shaoguan** China
149 E5 **Shaowu** China
149 F4 **Shaoxing** China
149 D5 **Shaoyang** *Hunan* China
149 D5 **Shaoyang** *Hunan* China
160 E3 **Shap** U.K.
149 D6 **Shapa** China
162 F1 **Shapinsay** *i.* U.K.
142 C4 **Shaqrā'** Saudi Arabia
137 K6 **Shaqrah, Qaşr** *tourist site* Iraq
139 J2 **Shar** Kazakh.
137 I6 **Sharaf** *well* Iraq
144 B3 **Sharan Jogizai** Pak.
139 I1 **Sharbakty** Kazakh.
139 J1 **Sharchino** Rus. Fed.
139 F4 **Shardara** Kazakh.
139 F4 **Shardara, Step'** *plain* Kazakh.
139 G4 **Shardarinskoye Vodokhranilishche** *resr* Kazakh./Uzbek.
139 F5 **Sharg'un** Uzbek.
**Shargun'** Uzbek. *see* **Sharg'un**
173 D5 **Sharhorod** Ukr.
137 J4 **Shārī, Buḩayrat** *imp. l.* Iraq
150 I3 **Shari-dake** *vol.* Japan
169 M3 **Sharkawshchyna** Belarus
124 B4 **Shark Bay** Australia
**Sharlouk** Turkm. *see* **Şarlawuk**
138 C1 **Sharlyk** Rus. Fed.
203 G4 **Sharon** *CT* U.S.A.
202 C4 **Sharon** *PA* U.S.A.
149 □ **Sharp Peak** *Hong Kong* China
136 E5 **Sharqī, Jabal ash** *mts* Lebanon/Syria
138 D4 **Sharqiy Ustyurt Chink** *esc.* Uzbek.
172 H3 **Shar'ya** Rus. Fed.
139 I4 **Sharyn** Kazakh.
139 I4 **Sharyn** *r.* Kazakh.
179 C6 **Shashe** *r.* Botswana/Zimbabwe
178 D3 **Shashemenē** Eth.
139 H3 **Shashubay** Kazakh.
194 B3 **Shasta, Mount** *vol.* U.S.A.
194 B3 **Shasta Lake** U.S.A.
149 □ **Sha Tin** *Hong Kong* China
172 H4 **Shatki** Rus. Fed.
140 C4 **Shaţţ, Ra's osh** *pt* Iran
137 L7 **Shaţţ al 'Arab** *r.* Iran/Iraq
137 J6 **Shaţţ al Hillah** *r.* Iraq
172 F4 **Shatura** Rus. Fed.
139 G4 **Shauil'dir** Kazakh.
187 H5 **Shaunavon** Canada
202 D5 **Shavers Fork** *r.* U.S.A.
203 F4 **Shawangunk Mountains** *hills* U.S.A.
190 C3 **Shawano** U.S.A.
190 C3 **Shawano Lake** U.S.A.
188 F4 **Shawinigan** Canada
136 F4 **Shawmarīyah, Jabal ash** *mts* Syria
199 D5 **Shawnee** U.S.A.
149 F5 **Sha Xi** *r.* China
149 E5 **Shaxian** China
139 G4 **Shayan** Kazakh.
149 D4 **Shayang** China
141 H3 **Shaybar, Kōtal-e** Afgh.
124 C4 **Shay Gap (abandoned)** Australia
137 K5 **Shaykh Jūwī** Iraq
137 K5 **Shaykh Sa'd** Iraq
139 H5 **Shazud** Tajik.
172 F4 **Shchekino** Rus. Fed.
173 F5 **Shchigry** Rus. Fed.
173 D5 **Shchors** Ukr.
139 G1 **Shchuchinsk** Kazakh.
172 C4 **Shchuchyn** Belarus
139 K2 **Shebalino** Rus. Fed.
173 F5 **Shebekino** Rus. Fed.
178 E3 **Shebelē Wenz, Wabē** *r.* Ethiopia/Somalia
190 D4 **Sheboygan** U.S.A.
176 D4 **Shebshi Mountains** Nigeria
189 H4 **Shediac** Canada
186 D3 **Shedin Peak** Canada
163 D4 **Sheelin, Lough** *l.* Ireland
163 D2 **Sheep Haven** *b.* Ireland
181 I3 **Sheepmoor** S. Africa
197 E3 **Sheep Peak** U.S.A.
161 H6 **Sheerness** U.K.
189 H5 **Sheet Harbour** Canada
127 G8 **Sheffield** Australia
128 D5 **Sheffield** N.Z.
161 F4 **Sheffield** U.K.
201 C5 **Sheffield** *AL* U.S.A.
190 C5 **Sheffield** *IL* U.S.A.
202 D4 **Sheffield** *PA* U.S.A.
199 C6 **Sheffield** *TX* U.S.A.
191 G3 **Sheguiandah** Canada
148 B4 **Shehong** China
**Sheikh, Jebel esh** *mt.* Lebanon/Syria *see* **Hermon, Mount**
144 C3 **Sheikhupura** Pak.
149 □ **Shek Kwu Chau** *i. Hong Kong* China
149 □ **Shek Pik Reservoir** *Hong Kong* China
172 F3 **Sheksna** Rus. Fed.
149 □ **Shek Uk Shan** *mt. Hong Kong* China
133 S2 **Shelagskiy, Mys** *pt* Rus. Fed.
141 F4 **Shēlah, Rōd-e** *watercourse* Afgh./Iran
190 A6 **Shelbina** U.S.A.
189 G5 **Shelburne** *N.S.* Canada
191 G3 **Shelburne** *Ont.* Canada
203 G3 **Shelburne Falls** U.S.A.
190 D4 **Shelby** *MI* U.S.A.
194 E1 **Shelby** *MT* U.S.A.
201 D5 **Shelby** *NC* U.S.A.
202 B4 **Shelby** *OH* U.S.A.
200 C4 **Shelbyville** *IN* U.S.A.
190 A6 **Shelbyville** *MO* U.S.A.
201 C5 **Shelbyville** *TN* U.S.A.
197 H5 **Sheldon** *AZ* U.S.A.
190 D5 **Sheldon** *IL* U.S.A.
203 G2 **Sheldon Springs** U.S.A.
189 H3 **Sheldrake** Canada
133 Q3 **Shelikhova, Zaliv** *g.* Rus. Fed.
184 C4 **Shelikof Strait** U.S.A.
187 H4 **Shellbrook** Canada
194 D3 **Shelley** U.S.A.
127 I5 **Shellharbour** Australia
196 A1 **Shell Mountain** U.S.A.
186 F4 **Shelter Bay** Canada
196 A1 **Shelter Cove** U.S.A.
149 □ **Shelter Island** *Hong Kong* China
203 G4 **Shelter Island** U.S.A.
128 B7 **Shelter Point** N.Z.
139 J2 **Shemonaikha** Kazakh.
198 E3 **Shenandoah** *IA* U.S.A.
203 E4 **Shenandoah** *PA* U.S.A.
202 D5 **Shenandoah** *VA* U.S.A.
202 D5 **Shenandoah** *r.* U.S.A.
202 D5 **Shenandoah Mountains** U.S.A.
202 D5 **Shenandoah National Park** U.S.A.
202 C4 **Shenango River Lake** U.S.A.
149 E6 **Shen'ao** China
138 E2 **Shenbertal** Kazakh.
176 C4 **Shendam** Nigeria
150 C1 **Shending Shan** *h.* China
138 E3 **Shengel'dy** Kazakh.
148 G4 **Shengsi** China
149 F4 **Shengzhou** China
172 G2 **Shenkursk** Rus. Fed.
148 D2 **Shenmu** China
148 D4 **Shennong Ding** *mt.* China
148 D4 **Shennongjia** China
148 E3 **Shenqiu** China
150 A1 **Shenshu** China
152 B3 **Shenwo Shuiku** *resr* China
152 B3 **Shenyang** China
149 E6 **Shenzhen** China
149 □ **Shenzhen He** *r. Hong Kong* China
**Shenzhen Wan** *b. Hong Kong* China *see* **Deep Bay**
173 C5 **Shepetivka** Ukr.
125 G3 **Shepherd Islands** Vanuatu
127 F6 **Shepparton** Australia
161 H6 **Sheppey, Isle of** *i.* U.K.
**Sherabad** Uzbek. *see* **Sherobod**
161 E7 **Sherborne** U.K.
189 H4 **Sherbrooke** *N.S.* Canada
189 F4 **Sherbrooke** *Que.* Canada
203 F3 **Sherburne** U.S.A.
163 E4 **Shercock** Ireland
141 H3 **Sher Dahan Pass** Afgh.
177 F3 **Shereiq** Sudan
144 C4 **Shergarh** India
199 E5 **Sheridan** *AR* U.S.A.
194 F2 **Sheridan** *WY* U.S.A.
126 A4 **Sheringa** Australia
161 I5 **Sheringham** U.K.
199 D5 **Sherman** U.S.A.
203 I2 **Sherman Mills** U.S.A.
197 E1 **Sherman Mountain** U.S.A.
139 F5 **Sherobod** Uzbek.
145 G4 **Sherpur** Bangl.
187 I3 **Sherridon** Canada
164 D3 **'s-Hertogenbosch** Neth.
161 F4 **Sherwood Forest** *reg.* U.K.
186 C3 **Sheslay** Canada
132 A3 **Shetland Islands** *is* U.K.
138 C3 **Shetpe** Kazakh.
149 □ **Sheung Shui** *Hong Kong* China
149 □ **Sheung Sze Mun** *sea chan. Hong Kong* China
143 B4 **Shevaroy Hills** India
138 E3 **Shevchenko, Zaliv** *l.* Kazakh.
141 H2 **Shēwah, Kōl-e** *l.* Afgh.
149 F4 **Shexian** China
148 F3 **Sheyang** China
198 D2 **Sheyenne** U.S.A.
198 D2 **Sheyenne** *r.* U.S.A.
140 D4 **Sheyţūr** Iran
138 B2 **Shezhin II** Kazakh.
162 B3 **Shiant Islands** U.K.
146 H2 **Shiashkotan, Ostrov** *i.* Rus. Fed.
191 E4 **Shiawassee** *r.* U.S.A.
142 C6 **Shibām** Yemen
151 F6 **Shibata** Japan
150 H2 **Shibetsu** Japan
150 I3 **Shibetsu** Japan
136 C6 **Shibīn al Kawm** Egypt
141 G2 **Shibirghān** Afgh.
151 F6 **Shibukawa** Japan
149 E5 **Shicheng** China
152 B4 **Shicheng Dao** *i.* China
203 E4 **Shickshinny** U.S.A.
136 G6 **Shidād al Mismā'** *h.* Saudi Arabia
152 B5 **Shidao** China
152 B5 **Shidao Wan** *b.* China
139 H2 **Shiderty** *r.* Kazakh.
162 C4 **Shiel, Loch** *l.* U.K.
148 B4 **Shifang** China
172 I4 **Shigony** Rus. Fed.
148 D1 **Shiguai** China
135 G2 **Shihezi** China
148 E2 **Shijiazhuang** China
141 F4 **Shikar** *r.* Pak.
141 H3 **Shikārī, Darah-ye** *r.* Afgh.
143 A3 **Shikarpur** India
144 B4 **Shikarpur** Pak.
144 D4 **Shikohabad** India
151 C8 **Shikoku** *i.* Japan
151 C8 **Shikoku-sanchi** *mts* Japan
150 G3 **Shikotsu-Tōya Kokuritsu-kōen** *nat. park* Japan
138 D2 **Shil'da** Rus. Fed.
160 F3 **Shildon** U.K.
172 H1 **Shilega** Rus. Fed.
145 G4 **Shiliguri** India
139 I4 **Shilik** Kazakh.
149 D4 **Shilipu** China
144 D2 **Shilla** *mt.* India
163 E5 **Shillelagh** Ireland
191 G1 **Shillington** Canada
145 G4 **Shillong** India
138 B2 **Shil'naya Balka** Kazakh.
203 F5 **Shiloh** U.S.A.
148 D2 **Shilou** China
172 G4 **Shilovo** Rus. Fed.
151 B8 **Shimabara** Japan
151 F7 **Shimada** Japan
146 E1 **Shimanovsk** Rus. Fed.
151 C8 **Shimanto** Japan
149 D4 **Shimen** China
149 B4 **Shimian** China
151 F7 **Shimizu** Japan
144 D3 **Shimla** India
151 F7 **Shimoda** Japan
143 A3 **Shimoga** India
178 D4 **Shimoni** Kenya
151 B8 **Shimonoseki** Japan
144 C1 **Shimshal** Pak.
172 D3 **Shimsk** Rus. Fed.
162 D2 **Shin, Loch** *l.* U.K.
141 F3 **Shīndand** Afgh.
144 B3 **Shinghar** Pak.
144 C1 **Shinghshal Pass** Pak.
190 D2 **Shingleton** U.S.A.
151 E8 **Shingū** Japan
181 I1 **Shingwedzi** S. Africa
181 I1 **Shingwedzi** *r.* S. Africa
161 E4 **Shining Tor** *h.* U.K.
191 G2 **Shining Tree** Canada
150 G5 **Shinjō** Japan
141 G4 **Shīnkay** Afgh.
151 E6 **Shinminato** Japan
203 I1 **Shin Pond** U.S.A.
178 D4 **Shinyanga** Tanz.
150 G5 **Shiogama** Japan
151 D8 **Shiono-misaki** *c.* Japan
151 G6 **Shioya-zaki** *pt* Japan
149 E4 **Shipai** China
201 E7 **Ship Chan Cay** *i.* Bahamas
149 B6 **Shiping** China
144 D3 **Shipki La** China/India
160 F4 **Shipley** U.K.
189 H4 **Shippegan** Canada
202 E4 **Shippensburg** U.S.A.
197 H3 **Shiprock** U.S.A.
197 H3 **Shiprock Peak** U.S.A.
149 F4 **Shipu** China
139 J1 **Shipunovo** Rus. Fed.
149 C5 **Shiqian** China
148 C3 **Shiquan** China
144 E2 **Shiquan He** *r.* China *conv.* **Indus**
148 C3 **Shiquan Shuiku** *resr* China
137 L2 **Shīrābād** Iran
150 G4 **Shirakami-sanchi** *tourist site* Japan
151 G6 **Shirakawa** Japan
151 E6 **Shirakawa-go and Gokayama** *tourist site* Japan
146 F3 **Shirane-san** *mt.* Japan
151 F6 **Shirane-san** *vol.* Japan
129 E4 **Shirase Glacier** *glacier* Antarctica
140 D4 **Shīrāz** Iran
136 C6 **Shirbīn** Egypt
150 I2 **Shiretoko-misaki** *c.* Japan
138 E3 **Shirikrabat** *tourist site* Kazakh.
139 G4 **Shirin** Uzbek.
141 G4 **Shirinab** *r.* Pak.
150 G4 **Shiriya-zaki** *c.* Japan
138 D3 **Shirkala** *reg.* Kazakh.
203 G4 **Shirley** U.S.A.
203 I2 **Shirley Mills** U.S.A.
151 E7 **Shirotori** Japan
144 C5 **Shirpur** India
141 E2 **Shīrvān** Iran
149 D4 **Shishou** China
149 E4 **Shitai** China
149 F4 **Shitang** China
137 I5 **Shithāthah** Iraq
144 B4 **Shiv** India
**Shivamogga** India *see* **Shimoga**
133 R4 **Shiveluch, Vulkan** *vol.* Rus. Fed.
200 C4 **Shively** U.S.A.
144 D4 **Shivpuri** India
197 F3 **Shivwits Plateau** U.S.A.
149 C6 **Shiwan Dashan** *mts* China
152 B3 **Shiwen** China
149 E5 **Shixing** China
148 D3 **Shiyan** China
139 F3 **Shiyeli** Kazakh.
148 E3 **Shizhong** China
149 C4 **Shizhu** China
149 B5 **Shizong** China
148 C2 **Shizuishan** China
151 F7 **Shizuoka** Japan
142 B1 **Shkhara** *mt.* Georgia/Rus. Fed.
172 D4 **Shklow** Belarus
171 H3 **Shkodër** Albania
132 J1 **Shmidta, Ostrov** *i.* Rus. Fed.
151 C7 **Shōbara** Japan
139 G5 **Shoh** Tajik.
150 G3 **Shokanbetsu-dake** *mt.* Japan
139 H4 **Shokpar** Kazakh.
139 G4 **Sholakkorgan** Kazakh.
138 F2 **Sholaksay** Kazakh.
138 D3 **Shomishkol'** Kazakh.
172 I2 **Shomvukovo** Rus. Fed.
162 C4 **Shona, Eilean** *i.* U.K.
219 J9 **Shona Ridge** *sea feature* S. Atlantic Ocean
139 I4 **Shonzhy** Kazakh.
138 D3 **Shoptykol'** Kazakh.
139 H2 **Shoptykol'** Kazakh.
144 D2 **Shor** India
143 B4 **Shoranur** India
141 G5 **Shorap** Pak.
**Shor Barsa-Kel'mes** *salt marsh* Uzbek. *see* **Borsakelmas sho'rxogi**
139 F5 **Sho'rchi** Uzbek.
137 J3 **Shor Gol** Iran
144 C3 **Shorkot** Pak.
138 C4 **Shorkozakhly, Solonchak** *salt flat* Turkm.
139 G4 **Shornak** Kazakh.
139 G2 **Shortandy** Kazakh.
150 G2 **Shosanbetsu** Japan
196 D4 **Shoshone** *CA* U.S.A.
194 D3 **Shoshone** *ID* U.S.A.
194 E2 **Shoshone** *r.* U.S.A.
194 E2 **Shoshone Lake** U.S.A.
195 C4 **Shoshone Mountains** U.S.A.
181 G1 **Shoshong** Botswana
194 E3 **Shoshoni** U.S.A.
173 E5 **Shostka** Ukr.
140 D3 **Shotoran, Chashmeh-ye** *well* Iran
141 G3 **Shotor Khūn** Afgh.
148 F2 **Shouguang** China
149 F5 **Shouning** China
148 E3 **Shouxian** China
148 D2 **Shouyang** China
148 C3 **Shouyang Shan** *mt.* China
197 G4 **Show Low** U.S.A.
173 D5 **Shpola** Ukr.
199 E5 **Shreveport** U.S.A.
161 E5 **Shrewsbury** U.K.
143 A2 **Shrigonda** India
145 G5 **Shrirampur** India
139 H4 **Shu** Kazakh.
132 H5 **Shu** *r.* Kazakh.
137 K6 **Shu'aiba** Iraq
149 A5 **Shuangbai** China
152 D1 **Shuangcheng** China
148 C4 **Shuanghe** China
152 B2 **Shuangliao** China
149 D5 **Shuangpai** China
152 A3 **Shuangtaizihe Kou** *r. mouth* China
152 C2 **Shuangyang** China
150 B1 **Shuangyashan** China
138 D2 **Shubarkudyk** Kazakh.
138 D2 **Shubarshi** Kazakh.
137 C6 **Shubrā al Khaymah** Egypt
148 E4 **Shucheng** China
139 H5 **Shufu** China
148 F3 **Shu He** *r.* China
149 F5 **Shuiji** China
149 D5 **Shuikou** China
139 H3 **Shu-Ile, Gory** *mts* Kazakh.
148 A2 **Shuiquanzi** China
144 B3 **Shujaabad** Pak.
152 D1 **Shulan** China
139 I5 **Shule** China
148 D1 **Shulinzhao** China
138 D4 **Shumanay** Uzbek.
150 H2 **Shumarinai-ko** *l.* Japan
179 C5 **Shumba** Zimbabwe
171 L3 **Shumen** Bulg.
172 H4 **Shumerlya** Rus. Fed.
169 N3 **Shumilina** Belarus
197 G4 **Shumway** U.S.A.
172 E4 **Shumyachi** Rus. Fed.
139 H3 **Shunak, Gora** *mt.* Kazakh.
151 B7 **Shūnan** Japan
149 E5 **Shunchang** China
152 B3 **Shuncheng** China
149 D6 **Shunde** China
184 C3 **Shungnak** U.S.A.
148 E1 **Shunyi** China
149 C6 **Shuolong** China
148 D2 **Shuozhou** China
142 C7 **Shuqrah** Yemen
140 D4 **Shūr** *r.* Iran
140 D4 **Shūr** *r.* Iran
141 F3 **Shūr** *r.* Iran
140 D4 **Shūr** *watercourse* Iran
140 D5 **Shūr** *watercourse* Iran
141 E3 **Shur** *watercourse* Iran
140 D3 **Shūr, Chāh-e** *well* Iran
141 E4 **Shūr, Rūd-e** *watercourse* Iran
140 C3 **Shūr Āb** Iran

140 D3 **Shūrāb** Iran
140 E3 **Shūrāb** Iran
140 E4 **Shūr Āb** *watercourse* Iran
141 G4 **Shūrawak** *reg.* Afgh.
**Shurchi** Uzbek. *see* **Sho'rchi**
140 D3 **Shureghestan** Iran
141 E4 **Shūr Gaz** Iran
140 D4 **Shūrjestān** Iran
139 G4 **Shūrob** Tajik.
179 D5 **Shurugwi** Zimbabwe
137 J6 **Shuruppak** *tourist site* Iraq
141 F4 **Shūsf** Iran
140 C3 **Shūsh** Iran
140 C3 **Shushtar** Iran
186 F4 **Shuswap Lake** Canada
136 F6 **Shuwaysh, Tall ash** *h.* Jordan
172 G3 **Shuya** Rus. Fed.
148 F3 **Shuyang** China
154 A1 **Shwegun** Myanmar
139 G3 **Shyganak** Kazakh.
139 H3 **Shyganak** Kazakh.
139 H3 **Shygys Konyrat** Kazakh.
139 G4 **Shymkent** Kazakh.
138 C2 **Shyngyrlau** Kazakh.
138 C2 **Shyngyrlau** *r.* Kazakh.
139 I2 **Shyngystau, Khrebet** *mts* Kazakh.
139 J3 **Shynkozha** Kazakh.
144 D2 **Shyok** India
144 D2 **Shyok** *r.* India
173 F5 **Shypuvate** Ukr.
173 E6 **Shyroke** Ukr.
147 F7 **Sia** Indon.
144 D2 **Siachen Glacier** India
141 G2 **Sīāh, Daryā-ye** *r.* Afgh.
141 F5 **Siahan Range** *mts* Pak.
141 F3 **Sīāh Band, Kūh-e** *mts* Afgh.
137 J2 **Sīāh Chashmeh** Iran
141 G3 **Sīāh Kūh** *mts* Afgh.
140 D3 **Sīāh Kūh, Kavīr-e** *salt flat* Iran
141 G4 **Sīāh Sang, Kowtal-e** Afgh.
144 C2 **Sialkot** Pak.
207 H4 **Sian Ka'an, Reserva de la Biósfera** *nature res.* Mex.
154 C5 **Siantan** *i.* Indon.
213 D4 **Siapa** *r.* Venez.
141 F4 **Sīāreh** Iran
153 C4 **Siargao** *i.* Phil.
153 B5 **Siasi** Phil.
153 B5 **Siasi** *i.* Phil.
153 B4 **Siaton** Phil.
159 M5 **Šiauliai** Lith.
141 F5 **Sīb** Iran
140 C3 **Sībak** Iran
181 I1 **Sibasa** S. Africa
153 B4 **Sibay** *i.* Phil.
138 D1 **Sibay** Rus. Fed.
181 J3 **Sibayi, Lake** S. Africa
129 B5 **Sibbald, Cape** *c.* Antarctica
170 F3 **Šibenik** Croatia
133 M3 **Siberia** *reg.* Rus. Fed.
155 A3 **Siberut** *i.* Indon.
144 A3 **Sibi** Pak.
178 D3 **Sibiloi National Park** Kenya
**Sibir'** *reg.* Rus. Fed. *see* **Siberia**
150 C2 **Sibirtsevo** Rus. Fed.
178 B4 **Sibiti** Congo
171 K2 **Sibiu** Romania
155 A2 **Sibolga** Indon.
154 A5 **Siborongborong** Indon.
155 D2 **Sibu** *Sarawak* Malaysia
153 B5 **Sibuco** Phil.
153 B5 **Sibuguey** *r.* Phil.
153 B5 **Sibuguey Bay** Phil.
178 B3 **Sibut** Cent. Afr. Rep.
153 A5 **Sibutu** *i.* Phil.
153 A5 **Sibutu Passage** Phil.
153 B3 **Sibuyan** *i.* Phil.
153 B3 **Sibuyan Sea** Phil.
153 B2 **Sicapoo** *mt.* Phil.
154 A3 **Sichon** Thai.
149 B4 **Sichuan** *prov.* China
148 B4 **Sichuan Giant Panda Sanctuaries** *tourist site* China
149 B4 **Sichuan Pendi** *basin* China
166 G5 **Sicié, Cap** *c.* France
**Sicilia** *i.* Italy *see* **Sicily**
170 E6 **Sicilian Channel** Italy/Tunisia
170 E6 **Sicily** *i.* Italy
210 D6 **Sicuani** Peru
143 B2 **Siddipet** India
171 L7 **Sideros, Akrotirio** *pt* Greece
180 E6 **Sidesaviwa** S. Africa
144 C5 **Sidhpur** India
167 H5 **Sidi Aïssa** Alg.
167 G4 **Sidi Ali** Alg.
176 B1 **Sidi Bel Abbès** Alg.
170 C7 **Sidi Bouzid** Tunisia
170 D7 **Sidi El Hani, Sebkhet de** *salt pan* Tunisia
176 A2 **Sidi Ifni** Morocco
176 B1 **Sidi Kacem** Morocco
154 A5 **Sidikalang** Indon.
162 E4 **Sidlaw Hills** U.K.
129 B4 **Sidley, Mount** *mt.* Antarctica
161 D7 **Sidmouth** U.K.
186 E5 **Sidney** Canada
194 F2 **Sidney** *MT* U.S.A.
198 C3 **Sidney** *NE* U.S.A.
203 F3 **Sidney** *NY* U.S.A.
202 A4 **Sidney** *OH* U.S.A.
201 D5 **Sidney Lanier, Lake** U.S.A.
145 H5 **Sidoktaya** Myanmar
136 E5 **Sidon** Lebanon
172 G3 **Sidorovo** Rus. Fed.
214 A3 **Sidrolândia** Brazil
181 I3 **Sidvokodvo** Swaziland
**Sidzhak** Uzbek. *see* **Sijjaq**
166 F5 **Sié, Col de** *pass* France
169 K4 **Siedlce** Poland
165 G4 **Siegen** Germany
154 B2 **Siĕmréab** Cambodia
170 D3 **Siena** Italy
169 I5 **Sieradz** Poland
145 H3 **Si'erdingka** China
215 D4 **Sierra, Punta** *pt* Arg.
199 B6 **Sierra Blanca** U.S.A.
215 C4 **Sierra Colorada** Arg.
206 H5 **Sierra de Agalta, Parque Nacional** *nat. park* Hond.
215 D4 **Sierra Grande** Arg.
176 A4 **Sierra Leone** *country* Africa
219 H5 **Sierra Leone Basin** *sea feature* N. Atlantic Ocean
219 H5 **Sierra Leone Rise** *sea feature* N. Atlantic Ocean
196 C4 **Sierra Madre Mountains** U.S.A.
206 D2 **Sierra Mojada** Mex.
213 C2 **Sierra Nevada, Parque Nacional** *nat. park* Venez.
213 B2 **Sierra Nevada de Santa Marta, Parque Nacional** *nat. park* Col.
196 B2 **Sierraville** U.S.A.
197 G6 **Sierra Vista** U.S.A.
168 C7 **Sierre** Switz.
158 N3 **Sievi** Fin.
149 C6 **Sifang Ling** *mts* China
171 K6 **Sifnos** *i.* Greece
167 F5 **Sig** Alg.
185 M2 **Sigguup Nunaa** *pen.* Greenland
169 K7 **Sighetu Marmației** Romania
169 L7 **Sighișoara** Romania
143 C5 **Sigiriya** Sri Lanka
154 □ **Siglap** Sing.
155 A1 **Sigli** Indon.
158 C1 **Siglufjörður** Iceland
153 B4 **Sigma** Phil.
168 D6 **Sigmaringen** Germany
164 E4 **Signal de Botrange** *h.* Belgium
197 E5 **Signal Peak** U.S.A.
164 C5 **Signy-l'Abbaye** France
190 A5 **Sigourney** U.S.A.
219 C4 **Sigsbee Deep** *sea feature* G. of Mexico
207 H5 **Siguatepeque** Hond.
167 E2 **Sigüenza** Spain
176 B3 **Siguiri** Guinea
159 N4 **Sigulda** Latvia
154 B3 **Sihanoukville** Cambodia
148 F3 **Sihong** China
144 E5 **Sihora** India
149 D6 **Sihui** China
158 N2 **Siikajoki** Fin.
158 N3 **Siilinjärvi** Fin.
137 H3 **Siirt** Turkey
139 G4 **Sijjaq** Uzbek.
155 B3 **Sijunjung** Indon.
186 E3 **Sikanni Chief** Canada
186 E3 **Sikanni Chief** *r.* Canada
144 C4 **Sikar** India
141 H3 **Sīkaram** *mt.* Afgh.
176 B3 **Sikasso** Mali
139 K3 **Sikeshu** China
199 F4 **Sikeston** U.S.A.
146 F2 **Sikhote-Alin'** *mts* Rus. Fed.
171 K6 **Sikinos** *i.* Greece
144 B5 **Sikka** India
145 G4 **Sikkim** *state* India
158 L2 **Siksjö** Sweden
152 B4 **Sikuaishi** China
155 E1 **Sikuati** *Sabah* Malaysia
167 C1 **Sil** *r.* Spain
153 C4 **Silago** Phil.
159 M5 **Šilalė** Lith.
206 D3 **Silao** Mex.
153 B4 **Silay** Phil.
165 H1 **Silberberg** *h.* Germany
145 H4 **Silchar** India
136 B1 **Şile** Turkey
143 C2 **Sileru** *r.* India
139 H2 **Silety** Kazakh.
139 H1 **Silety** *r.* Kazakh.
139 H1 **Siletyteniz, Ozero** *salt l.* Kazakh.
170 C6 **Siliana** Tunisia
136 D3 **Silifke** Turkey
145 G3 **Siling Co** *salt l.* China
171 L2 **Silistra** Bulg.
136 B1 **Silivri** Turkey
159 K3 **Siljan** *l.* Sweden
159 J4 **Silkeborg** Denmark
159 N4 **Sillamäe** Estonia
144 C5 **Sillod** India
181 I3 **Silobela** S. Africa
145 G3 **Silong** China
199 E6 **Silsbee** U.S.A.
158 N2 **Siltaharju** Fin.
141 F5 **Sīlūp** *r.* Iran
159 M5 **Šilutė** Lith.
137 H2 **Silvan** Turkey
144 C5 **Silvassa** India
190 B2 **Silver Bay** U.S.A.
195 E5 **Silver City** U.S.A.
190 C1 **Silver Islet** Canada
194 B3 **Silver Lake** U.S.A.
196 D4 **Silver Lake** *l. CA* U.S.A.
190 D2 **Silver Lake** *l. MI* U.S.A.
163 C5 **Silvermine Mountains** *hills* Ireland
196 D3 **Silver Peak Range** *mts* U.S.A.
202 E5 **Silver Spring** U.S.A.
196 C2 **Silver Springs** U.S.A.
126 D3 **Silverton** Australia
161 D7 **Silverton** U.K.
191 F3 **Silver Water** Canada
207 G4 **Silvituc** Mex.
153 B3 **Simara** *i.* Phil.
191 H2 **Simard, Lac** *l.* Canada
137 K5 **Şīmareh, Rūdkhāneh-ye** *r.* Iran
145 F4 **Simaria** India
136 B2 **Simav** Turkey
136 B2 **Simav Dağları** *mts* Turkey
178 C3 **Simba** Dem. Rep. Congo
191 G4 **Simcoe** Canada
191 H3 **Simcoe, Lake** Canada
143 D1 **Simdega** India
178 D2 **Simēn** *mts* Eth.
**Simēn Mountains** Eth. *see* **Simēn**
155 A2 **Simeulue** *i.* Indon.
**Simeuluë** *i.* Indon. *see* **Simeulue**
173 E6 **Simferopol'** Ukr.
145 E3 **Simikot** Nepal
213 B3 **Simití** Col.
196 C4 **Simi Valley** U.S.A.
195 F4 **Simla** U.S.A.
169 K7 **Şimleu Silvaniei** Romania
164 E4 **Simmerath** Germany
164 F5 **Simmern (Hunsrück)** Germany
196 C4 **Simmler** U.S.A.
197 F4 **Simmons** U.S.A.
201 F7 **Simm's** Bahamas
158 N2 **Simojärvi** *l.* Fin.
206 D2 **Simon** Mex.
186 F4 **Simonette** *r.* Canada
187 I4 **Simonhouse** Canada
168 D7 **Simplon Pass** Switz.
124 D4 **Simpson Desert** Australia
190 D1 **Simpson Island** Canada
196 D2 **Simpson Park Mountains** U.S.A.
159 K5 **Simrishamn** Sweden
153 A5 **Simunul** *i.* Phil.
146 H2 **Simushir, Ostrov** *i.* Rus. Fed.
143 A2 **Sina** *r.* India
177 F2 **Sīnā', Shibh Jazīrat** *pen.* Egypt
155 A2 **Sinabang** Indon.
154 A5 **Sinabung** *vol.* Indon.
164 C5 **Sinai, Mont** *h.* France
206 B2 **Sinaloa** *state* Mex.
170 D3 **Sinalunga** Italy
149 C5 **Sinan** China
152 C4 **Sinanju** N. Korea
145 H5 **Sinbyugyun** Myanmar
136 F2 **Sincan** Turkey
213 B2 **Sincé** Col.
213 B2 **Sincelejo** Col.
201 D5 **Sinclair, Lake** U.S.A.
186 E4 **Sinclair Mills** Canada
180 B2 **Sinclair Mine** Namibia
162 E2 **Sinclair's Bay** U.K.
144 D4 **Sind** *r.* India
153 B4 **Sindañgan** Phil.
155 C4 **Sindangbarang** Indon.
144 B4 **Sindari** India
168 D6 **Sindelfingen** Germany
143 B2 **Sindgi** India
144 B4 **Sindh** *prov.* Pak.
143 B3 **Sindhnur** India
136 B2 **Sındırgı** Turkey
144 D6 **Sindkhed** India
144 C5 **Sindkheda** India
152 C4 **Sin-do** *i.* China
172 I2 **Sindor** Rus. Fed.
145 F5 **Sindri** India
144 B3 **Sind Sagar Doab** *lowland* Pak.
172 I3 **Sinegor'ye** Rus. Fed.
171 L4 **Sinekçi** Turkey
167 B4 **Sines** Port.
167 B4 **Sines, Cabo de** *c.* Port.
158 N2 **Sinettä** Fin.
176 B4 **Sinfra** Côte d'Ivoire
177 F3 **Singa** Sudan
144 E3 **Singahi** India
144 D2 **Singa Pass** India
154 □ **Singapore** *country* Asia
154 B5 **Singapore** Sing. (City Plan 103)
154 □ **Singapore, Strait of** Indon./Sing.
155 E4 **Singaraja** Indon.
154 B2 **Sing Buri** Thai.
191 G3 **Singhampton** Canada
178 D4 **Singida** Tanz.
155 C2 **Singkawang** Indon.
154 A5 **Singkil** Indon.
127 I4 **Singleton** Australia
152 D4 **Sin'gye** N. Korea
143 C5 **Sinharaja Forest Reserve** *nature res.* Sri Lanka
152 D3 **Sinhŭng** N. Korea
170 C4 **Siniscola** *Sardinia* Italy
138 E2 **Siniy-Shikhan** Rus. Fed.
170 G3 **Sinj** Croatia
124 C2 **Sinjai** Indon.
137 H3 **Sinjār** Iraq
137 H3 **Sinjār, Jabal** *mt.* Iraq
137 J3 **Sīnji** Iran
177 F3 **Sinkat** Sudan
**Sinkiang** *aut. reg.* China *see* **Xinjiang Uygur Zizhiqu**
152 C4 **Sinmi-do** *i.* N. Korea
165 G4 **Sinn** Germany
211 H2 **Sinnamary** Fr. Guiana
171 M2 **Sinoie, Lacul** *lag.* Romania
173 E7 **Sinop** Turkey
**Sinp'a** N. Korea *see* **Kimjŏngsuk**
152 E3 **Sinp'o** N. Korea
152 D4 **Sinp'yŏng** N. Korea
152 D4 **Sinsang** N. Korea
165 G5 **Sinsheim** Germany
155 D2 **Sintang** Indon.
205 L5 **Sint Eustatius** *municipality* West Indies
164 B3 **Sint-Laureins** Belgium
205 L5 **Sint Maarten** *terr.* West Indies
164 C3 **Sint-Niklaas** Belgium
199 D6 **Sinton** U.S.A.
164 D4 **Sint-Truiden** Belgium
213 A2 **Sinú** *r.* Col.
152 C3 **Sinŭiju** N. Korea
164 F4 **Sinzig** Germany
153 B5 **Siocon** Phil.
168 I7 **Siófok** Hungary
168 C7 **Sion** Switz.
163 D3 **Sion Mills** U.K.
198 D3 **Sioux Center** U.S.A.
198 D3 **Sioux City** U.S.A.
198 D3 **Sioux Falls** U.S.A.
188 B3 **Sioux Lookout** Canada
207 G5 **Sipacate** Guat.
153 B4 **Sipalay** Phil.
152 C2 **Siping** China
187 J3 **Sipiwesk** Canada
187 J3 **Sipiwesk Lake** Canada
144 C5 **Sipra** *r.* India
201 C5 **Sipsey** *r.* U.S.A.
155 A3 **Sipura** *i.* Indon.
206 H5 **Siquia** *r.* Nicaragua
153 B4 **Siquijor** Phil.
153 B4 **Siquijor** *i.* Phil.
144 B5 **Sir** *r.* Pak.
143 B3 **Sira** India
159 I4 **Sira** *r.* Norway
140 D5 **Şīr Abū Nu'āyr** *i.* U.A.E.
154 B2 **Si Racha** Thai.
**Siracusa** *Sicily* Italy *see* **Syracuse**
186 E4 **Sir Alexander, Mount** Canada
137 G1 **Şiran** Turkey
141 G5 **Siranda Lake** Pak.
140 D5 **Şīr Banī Yās** *i.* U.A.E.
137 L3 **Sīrdān** Iran
139 G4 **Sirdaryo** Uzbek.
124 D3 **Sir Edward Pellew Group** *is* Australia
190 A3 **Siren** U.S.A.
140 E5 **Sīrīk** Iran
154 B1 **Siri Kit, Khuan** Thai.
140 D4 **Siriz** Iran
186 D2 **Sir James MacBrien, Mount** Canada
140 D4 **Sīrjān** Iran
140 D4 **Sīrjān** *salt flat* Iran
126 B5 **Sir Joseph Banks Group** *is* Australia
144 E4 **Sirmour** India
137 I3 **Şırnak** Turkey
143 C2 **Sironcha** India
144 D4 **Sironj** India
143 B2 **Sirpur** India
196 C4 **Sirretta Peak** U.S.A.
140 D5 **Sīrrī, Jazīreh-ye** *i.* Iran
144 C3 **Sirsa** *Haryana* India
145 E4 **Sirsa** *Uttar Pradesh* India
186 F4 **Sir Sandford, Mount** Canada
143 A3 **Sirsi** *Karnataka* India
144 D3 **Sirsi** *Uttar Pradesh* India
143 B2 **Sirsilla** India
177 D1 **Sirte** Libya
177 D1 **Sirte, Gulf of** Libya
143 A2 **Sirur** India
137 L2 **Şirvan** Azer.
137 I2 **Şirvan** Turkey
159 N5 **Širvintos** Lith.
137 J4 **Sīrwān** *r.* Iraq
186 F4 **Sir Wilfrid Laurier, Mount** Canada
170 G2 **Sisak** Croatia
154 C2 **Sisaket** Thai.
207 G3 **Sisal** Mex.
180 E3 **Sishen** S. Africa
148 C2 **Sishilisu** China
137 K2 **Sisian** Armenia
190 C2 **Siskiwit Bay** U.S.A.
154 B2 **Sisŏphŏn** Cambodia
196 B4 **Sisquoc** *r.* U.S.A.
198 D2 **Sisseton** U.S.A.
203 J1 **Sisson Branch Reservoir** Canada
141 F4 **Sīstān** *reg.* Iran
127 F8 **Sisters Beach** Australia
141 E5 **Sīt** Iran
144 C5 **Sitamau** India
153 A5 **Sitangkai** Phil.
144 E4 **Sitapur** India
171 L7 **Siteia** Greece
181 I3 **Siteki** Swaziland
171 J4 **Sithonias, Chersonisos** *pen.* Greece
214 C1 **Sítio da Abadia** Brazil
214 D1 **Sítio do Mato** Brazil
186 B3 **Sitka** U.S.A.
144 B3 **Sitpur** Pak.
164 D4 **Sittard** Neth.
145 H4 **Sittaung** Myanmar
165 H1 **Sittensen** Germany
161 H6 **Sittingbourne** U.K.
145 H5 **Sittwe** Myanmar
149 □ **Siu A Chau** *i. Hong Kong* China
206 H5 **Siuna** Nicaragua
145 F5 **Siuri** India
143 B4 **Sivaganga** India
143 B4 **Sivakasi** India
140 D4 **Sivand** Iran
136 F2 **Sivas** Turkey
145 H4 **Sivasagar** India
136 B2 **Sivaslı** Turkey
137 G3 **Siverek** Turkey
137 G2 **Sivrice** Turkey
136 C2 **Sivrihisar** Turkey
181 H3 **Sivukile** S. Africa
177 E2 **Sīwah** Egypt
144 D3 **Siwalik Range** *mts* India/Nepal
145 F4 **Siwan** India
144 C4 **Siwana** India
166 G5 **Six-Fours-les-Plages** France
148 E3 **Sixian** China
190 E4 **Six Lakes** U.S.A.
163 D3 **Sixmilecross** U.K.
181 H2 **Siyabuswa** S. Africa
148 F3 **Siyang** China
149 C5 **Siyang** China
138 A4 **Siyäzän** Azer.
148 C1 **Siyitang** China
140 D3 **Sīyunī** Iran
**Sjælland** *i.* Denmark *see* **Zealand**
171 I3 **Sjenica** Serbia
159 K5 **Sjöbo** Sweden
158 L1 **Sjøvegan** Norway
173 E6 **Skadovs'k** Ukr.
158 C3 **Skaftárós** *r. mouth* Iceland
158 C1 **Skagafjörður** *inlet* Iceland
159 J4 **Skagen** Denmark
159 J4 **Skagerrak** *str.* Denmark/Norway
194 B1 **Skagit** *r.* Canada/U.S.A.
186 B3 **Skagway** U.S.A.
158 N1 **Skaidi** Norway
158 L1 **Skaland** Norway
158 K2 **Skalmodal** Sweden
159 J4 **Skanderborg** Denmark
203 E3 **Skaneateles Lake** U.S.A.
190 C2 **Skanee** U.S.A.
171 K5 **Skantzoura** *i.* Greece
159 K4 **Skara** Sweden
159 M4 **Skärgårdshavets nationalpark** *nat. park* Fin.
159 J3 **Skarnes** Norway
169 J5 **Skarżysko-Kamienna** Poland
158 M2 **Skaulo** Sweden
169 I6 **Skawina** Poland
186 D3 **Skeena** *r.* Canada
186 D3 **Skeena Mountains** Canada
161 H4 **Skegness** U.K.
158 M2 **Skellefteå** Sweden
158 M2 **Skellefteälven** *r.* Sweden
158 M2 **Skelleftehamn** Sweden
160 E4 **Skelmersdale** U.K.
163 E4 **Skerries** Ireland
159 J4 **Ski** Norway
171 J5 **Skiathos** *i.* Greece
163 B6 **Skibbereen** Ireland
158 M1 **Skibotn** Norway
160 D3 **Skiddaw** *h.* U.K.
159 J4 **Skien** Norway
169 J5 **Skierniewice** Poland
176 C1 **Skikda** Alg.
160 G4 **Skipsea** U.K.
126 E6 **Skipton** Australia
160 E4 **Skipton** U.K.
160 G4 **Skirlaugh** U.K.
159 J4 **Skive** Denmark
158 C2 **Skjálfandafljót** *r.* Iceland
159 J5 **Skjern** Denmark
159 I3 **Skjolden** Norway
139 H5 **Skobeleva, Pik** *mt.* Kyrg.
158 I3 **Skodje** Norway
**Skoganvarre** Norway *see* **Skoganvarri**
158 N1 **Skoganvarri** Norway
163 F6 **Skokholm Island** U.K.
190 D4 **Skokie** U.S.A.
138 E2 **Skol'** Kazakh.
161 B6 **Skomer Island** U.K.
171 J5 **Skopelos** *i.* Greece
172 F4 **Skopin** Rus. Fed.
171 I4 **Skopje** Macedonia
173 F5 **Skorodnoye** Rus. Fed.
159 K4 **Skövde** Sweden
203 I2 **Skowhegan** U.S.A.
159 M4 **Skrunda** Latvia
186 B2 **Skukum, Mount** Canada
181 I2 **Skukuza** S. Africa
196 D3 **Skull Peak** U.S.A.
190 B5 **Skunk** *r.* U.S.A.
159 M4 **Skuodas** Lith.
159 K5 **Skurup** Sweden
159 L3 **Skutskär** Sweden
173 D5 **Skvyra** Ukr.
162 B3 **Skye** *i.* U.K.
171 K5 **Skyros** Greece
171 K5 **Skyros** *i.* Greece
159 J5 **Slagelse** Denmark
158 L2 **Slagnäs** Sweden
155 C4 **Slamet, Gunung** *vol.* Indon.
163 E4 **Slane** Ireland
163 E5 **Slaney** *r.* Ireland
172 D3 **Slantsy** Rus. Fed.
173 G5 **Slashchevskaya** Rus. Fed.
190 D1 **Slate Islands** Canada
170 G2 **Slatina** Croatia
171 K2 **Slatina** Romania
187 G2 **Slave** *r.* Canada
176 C4 **Slave Coast** Africa
186 G3 **Slave Lake** Canada
139 I1 **Slavgorod** Rus. Fed.
169 N2 **Slavkovichi** Rus. Fed.
**Slavonia** *reg.* Croatia *see* **Slavonija**
171 H2 **Slavonija** *reg.* Croatia
171 H2 **Slavonski Brod** Croatia
173 C5 **Slavuta** Ukr.
173 D5 **Slavutych** Ukr.
150 B3 **Slavyanka** Rus. Fed.
173 F6 **Slavyansk-na-Kubani** Rus. Fed.
172 D4 **Slawharad** Belarus
168 H3 **Sławno** Poland
161 G4 **Sleaford** U.K.
126 A5 **Sleaford Bay** Australia
163 A5 **Slea Head** Ireland
162 C3 **Sleat** *pen.* U.K.
162 C3 **Sleat, Sound of** *sea chan.* U.K.
188 E2 **Sleeper Islands** Canada
190 D3 **Sleeping Bear Dunes National Lakeshore** *nature res.* U.S.A.
190 D3 **Sleeping Bear Point** U.S.A.
173 H7 **Sleptsovskaya** Rus. Fed.
129 C3 **Slessor Glacier** *glacier* Antarctica
199 F6 **Slidell** U.S.A.
163 A5 **Slievanea** *h.* Ireland
163 D3 **Slieve Anierin** *h.* Ireland
163 D5 **Slieveardagh Hills** Ireland
163 C4 **Slieve Aughty Mountains** *hills* Ireland
163 D3 **Slieve Beagh** *h.* Ireland/U.K.
163 C5 **Slieve Bernagh** *hills* Ireland
163 D4 **Slieve Bloom Mountains** *hills* Ireland
163 B5 **Slievecallan** *h.* Ireland
163 B3 **Slieve Car** *h.* Ireland
163 F3 **Slieve Donard** *h.* U.K.
163 B4 **Slieve Elva** *h.* Ireland
**Slieve Gamph** *hills* Ireland *see* **Ox Mountains**
163 C3 **Slieve League** *h.* Ireland
163 B5 **Slieve Mish Mountains** *hills* Ireland
163 B5 **Slieve Miskish Mountains** *hills* Ireland
163 A3 **Slievemore** *h.* Ireland
163 D4 **Slieve na Calliagh** *h.* Ireland
163 D5 **Slievenamon** *h.* Ireland
163 D2 **Slieve Snaght** *h.* Ireland
162 B3 **Sligachan** U.K.
163 C3 **Sligo** Ireland
163 C3 **Sligo Bay** Ireland
159 L4 **Slite** Sweden
171 L3 **Sliven** Bulg.
172 H2 **Sloboda** Rus. Fed.
172 I2 **Slobodchikovo** Rus. Fed.
171 L2 **Slobozia** Romania
186 F5 **Slocan** Canada
164 E1 **Slochteren** Neth.
172 C4 **Slonim** Belarus
164 C2 **Slootdorp** Neth.
164 D2 **Sloten** Neth.
164 D2 **Slotermeer** *l.* Neth.
161 G6 **Slough** U.K.
169 I6 **Slovakia** *country* Europe
170 F1 **Slovenia** *country* Europe
170 F1 **Slovenj Gradec** Slovenia
173 F5 **Slov"yans'k** Ukr.
154 C3 **S'Lung, B'Nom** *mt.* Vietnam
168 H3 **Słupsk** Poland
158 L2 **Slussfors** Sweden
172 C4 **Slutsk** Belarus
163 A4 **Slyne Head** Ireland
133 L4 **Slyudyanka** Rus. Fed.
154 B3 **Smăch, Kaôh** *i.* Cambodia
203 I3 **Small Point** U.S.A.
189 H3 **Smallwood Reservoir** Canada
172 D4 **Smalyavichy** Belarus
169 M3 **Smarhon'** Belarus
180 E5 **Smartt Syndicate Dam** *resr* S. Africa
187 I4 **Smeaton** Canada
171 I2 **Smederevo** Serbia
171 I2 **Smederevska Palanka** Serbia
202 D4 **Smethport** U.S.A.
173 D5 **Smila** Ukr.
164 E2 **Smilde** Neth.
159 N4 **Smiltene** Latvia
139 G1 **Smirnovo** Kazakh.
186 G3 **Smith** Canada
196 C2 **Smith** U.S.A.
202 C6 **Smith** *r.* U.S.A.
184 C2 **Smith Bay** U.S.A.
186 D4 **Smithers** Canada
181 G5 **Smithfield** S. Africa
201 E5 **Smithfield** *NC* U.S.A.
194 E3 **Smithfield** *UT* U.S.A.
203 E5 **Smith Island** *MD* U.S.A.
203 F6 **Smith Island** *VA* U.S.A.
202 D6 **Smith Mountain Lake** U.S.A.
186 D3 **Smith River** Canada
191 I3 **Smiths Falls** Canada
185 K2 **Smith Sound** *sea chan.* Canada/Greenland
127 F8 **Smithton** Australia
196 C1 **Smoke Creek Desert** U.S.A.
186 F4 **Smoky** *r.* Canada
127 J3 **Smoky Cape** Australia
188 D3 **Smoky Falls** Canada
198 C4 **Smoky Hill** *r.* U.S.A.
198 D4 **Smoky Hills** U.S.A.
186 G4 **Smoky Lake** Canada
158 I3 **Smøla** *i.* Norway
138 B2 **Smolenka** Rus. Fed.
172 E4 **Smolensk** Rus. Fed.
172 E4 **Smolenskaya Oblast'** *admin. div.* Rus. Fed.
139 K1 **Smolenskoye** Rus. Fed.
171 K4 **Smolyan** Bulg.
150 C3 **Smolyaninovo** Rus. Fed.
188 D4 **Smooth Rock Falls** Canada
188 C3 **Smoothrock Lake** Canada
187 H4 **Smoothstone Lake** Canada
158 N1 **Smørfjord** Norway
203 F5 **Smyrna** *DE* U.S.A.
201 C5 **Smyrna** *GA* U.S.A.
202 C4 **Smyrna** *OH* U.S.A.
203 I1 **Smyrna Mills** U.S.A.
158 D2 **Snæfell** *mt.* Iceland
160 C3 **Snaefell** *h.* U.K.
186 A2 **Snag (abandoned)** Canada
194 D3 **Snake** *r.* U.S.A.
197 E2 **Snake Range** *mts* U.S.A.
194 D3 **Snake River Plain** U.S.A.
**Snare Lakes** Canada *see* **Wekweètì**
125 G6 **Snares Islands** N.Z.
158 K2 **Snåsa** Norway
164 D1 **Sneek** Neth.
163 B6 **Sneem** Ireland
180 F6 **Sneeuberge** *mts* S. Africa
189 H3 **Snegamook Lake** Canada
161 H5 **Snettisham** U.K.
132 J3 **Snezhnogorsk** Rus. Fed.
170 F2 **Snežnik** *mt.* Slovenia
169 J4 **Śniardwy, Jezioro** *l.* Poland
173 E6 **Snihurivka** Ukr.
162 B3 **Snizort, Loch** *b.* U.K.
194 B2 **Snohomish** U.S.A.
194 B2 **Snoqualmie Pass** U.S.A.
158 K2 **Snøtinden** *mt.* Norway
187 I2 **Snowbird Lake** Canada
161 C4 **Snowdon** *mt.* U.K.
161 D5 **Snowdonia National Park** U.K.
197 G4 **Snowflake** U.S.A.
203 F5 **Snow Hill** *MD* U.S.A.
201 E5 **Snow Hill** *NC* U.S.A.
187 I4 **Snow Lake** Canada
126 C4 **Snowtown** Australia
194 D3 **Snowville** U.S.A.
127 H6 **Snowy** *r.* Australia
127 H6 **Snowy Mountains** Australia
127 G9 **Snug** Australia
189 I3 **Snug Harbour** *Nfld* Canada
191 G3 **Snug Harbour** *Ont.* Canada
154 C2 **Snuŏl** Cambodia
199 D5 **Snyder** *OK* U.S.A.
199 C5 **Snyder** *TX* U.S.A.
179 E5 **Soalala** Madag.
144 B2 **Soan** *r.* Pak.
152 D6 **Soan-gundo** *is* S. Korea
179 E5 **Soanierana-Ivongo** Madag.
213 B3 **Soata** Col.
162 B3 **Soay** *i.* U.K.
152 D6 **Sobaek-sanmaek** *mts* S. Korea
177 F4 **Sobat** *r.* South Sudan
147 G7 **Sobger** *r.* Indon.
151 B8 **Sobo-san** *mt.* Japan
211 J6 **Sobradinho, Barragem de** *resr* Brazil
211 J4 **Sobral** Brazil
173 F7 **Sochi** Rus. Fed.
123 I5 **Society Islands** Fr. Polynesia
214 C3 **Socorro** Brazil
213 B3 **Socorro** Col.
195 F5 **Socorro** U.S.A.
204 B5 **Socorro, Isla** *i.* Mex.
142 D7 **Socotra** *i.* Yemen
154 C3 **Soc Trăng** Vietnam
167 E3 **Socuéllamos** Spain
196 D4 **Soda Lake** U.S.A.
158 N2 **Sodankylä** Fin.
144 D2 **Soda Plains** Aksai Chin
194 E3 **Soda Springs** U.S.A.
159 L3 **Söderhamn** Sweden
159 L4 **Söderköping** Sweden
159 L4 **Södertälje** Sweden
177 E3 **Sodiri** Sudan
178 D3 **Sodo** Eth.
159 L3 **Södra Kvarken** *str.* Fin./Sweden
164 D3 **Soerendonk** Neth.
165 G3 **Soest** Germany
164 D2 **Soest** Neth.
127 H4 **Sofala** Australia
171 J3 **Sofia** Bulg.
**Sofiya** Bulg. *see* **Sofia**
158 O2 **Sofporog** Rus. Fed.
171 L6 **Sofrana** *i.* Greece
151 G10 **Sōfu-gan** *i.* Japan
145 H3 **Sog** China
213 B3 **Sogamoso** Col.
137 G1 **Soğanlı Dağları** *mts* Turkey
164 F2 **Sögel** Germany
159 I4 **Søgne** Norway
159 I3 **Sognefjorden** *inlet* Norway
153 C4 **Sogod** Phil.
172 H2 **Sogra** Rus. Fed.
148 A3 **Sogruma** China
136 C1 **Söğüt** Turkey
**Sohâg** Egypt *see* **Sūhāj**
144 D5 **Sohagpur** India
161 H5 **Soham** U.K.
125 F2 **Sohano** P.N.G.
143 C1 **Sohela** India
144 D3 **Sohna** India
152 E3 **Sŏho-ri** N. Korea
152 C6 **Sohŭksan** S. Korea
164 C4 **Soignes, Forêt de** *for.* Belgium
164 C4 **Soignies** Belgium
158 N3 **Soini** Fin.
166 F2 **Soissons** France
144 C4 **Sojat** India
153 B4 **Sojoton Point** Phil.
173 C5 **Sokal'** Ukr.
152 E4 **Sokcho** S. Korea
171 L6 **Söke** Turkey
173 G7 **Sokhumi** Georgia
176 C4 **Sokodé** Togo
149 □ **Soko Islands** *Hong Kong* China
172 G3 **Sokol** Rus. Fed.
169 K4 **Sokółka** Poland
176 B3 **Sokolo** Mali
165 K4 **Sokolov** Czech Rep.
150 C3 **Sokolovka** Rus. Fed.
169 K4 **Sokołow Podlaski** Poland
176 C3 **Sokoto** Nigeria
176 C3 **Sokoto** *r.* Nigeria
173 C5 **Sokyryany** Ukr.
144 D3 **Solan** India
128 A7 **Solander Island** N.Z.
143 A2 **Solapur** India
213 B2 **Soledad** Col.
196 B3 **Soledad** U.S.A.
213 E2 **Soledad** Venez.
207 E4 **Soledad de Doblado** Mex.
173 G6 **Solenoye** Rus. Fed.
158 K2 **Solfjellsjøen** Norway
137 H2 **Solhan** Turkey
172 G3 **Soligalich** Rus. Fed.
161 F5 **Solihull** U.K.
132 G4 **Solikamsk** Rus. Fed.
138 C2 **Sol'-Iletsk** Rus. Fed.
207 H4 **Solimón, Punta** *pt* Mex.
164 F3 **Solingen** Germany
180 A1 **Solitaire** Namibia
137 L1 **Şollar** Azer.
158 L3 **Sollefteå** Sweden
165 K3 **Söllichau** Germany
165 H3 **Solling** *hills* Germany
165 I3 **Sollstedt** Germany
165 G4 **Solms** Germany
172 F3 **Solnechnogorsk** Rus. Fed.
155 B3 **Solok** Indon.
207 G5 **Sololá** Guat.
125 G2 **Solomon Islands** *country* Pacific Ocean
124 F2 **Solomon Sea** P.N.G./Solomon Is
139 K2 **Soloneshnoye** Rus. Fed.
190 B2 **Solon Springs** U.S.A.
147 E7 **Solor, Kepulauan** *is* Indon.
168 C7 **Solothurn** Switz.
172 E1 **Solovetskiye Ostrova** *is* Rus. Fed.
172 H3 **Solovetskoye** Rus. Fed.
170 G3 **Šolta** *i.* Croatia
141 E2 **Solţānābād** Iran
141 E3 **Solţānābād** Iran
165 H2 **Soltau** Germany
172 D3 **Sol'tsy** Rus. Fed.
203 E3 **Solvay** U.S.A.
159 K4 **Sölvesborg** Sweden
162 E6 **Solway Firth** *est.* U.K.
179 C5 **Solwezi** Zambia
151 G6 **Sōma** Japan
136 A2 **Soma** Turkey
164 B4 **Somain** France
178 E3 **Somalia** *country* Africa
218 H5 **Somali Basin** *sea feature* Indian Ocean
178 E3 **Somaliland** *terr.* Somalia
179 C4 **Sombo** Angola
171 H2 **Sombor** Serbia
206 D3 **Sombrerete** Mex.
144 C4 **Somdari** India
203 I2 **Somerest Junction** U.S.A.
159 M3 **Somero** Fin.
200 C4 **Somerset** *KY* U.S.A.
190 E4 **Somerset** *MI* U.S.A.
202 D5 **Somerset** *PA* U.S.A.
181 F6 **Somerset East** S. Africa
185 I2 **Somerset Island** Canada
203 G3 **Somerset Reservoir** U.S.A.
180 C7 **Somerset West** S. Africa
203 H3 **Somersworth** U.S.A.
199 D6 **Somerville Reservoir** U.S.A.
140 B3 **Someydeh** Iran
159 K4 **Sommen** *l.* Sweden
165 J3 **Sömmerda** Germany
189 G3 **Sommet, Lac du** *l.* Canada
144 B5 **Somnath** India
190 C5 **Somonauk** U.S.A.
206 H5 **Somotillo** Nicaragua
206 H5 **Somoto** Nicaragua
215 C4 **Somuncurá, Mesa Volcánica de** *plat.* Arg.
145 F4 **Son** *r.* India
206 I7 **Soná** Panama
139 G2 **Sonaly** *Karagandinskaya Oblast'* Kazakh.
139 G2 **Sonaly** *Karagandinskaya Oblast'* Kazakh.
145 F5 **Sonamukhi** India
145 G5 **Sonamura** India
143 C1 **Sonapur** India
144 D4 **Sonar** *r.* India
145 H4 **Sonari** India
152 F2 **Sŏnbong** N. Korea
152 C4 **Sŏnch'ŏn** N. Korea
172 E2 **Sondaly** Rus. Fed.
159 J5 **Sønderborg** Denmark
165 I3 **Sondershausen** Germany
170 C1 **Sondrio** Italy
143 B2 **Sonepet** India
144 B5 **Songadh** India
148 E4 **Songbu** China
154 D2 **Sông Câu** Vietnam
**Sông Cau** Vietnam *see* **Sông Câu**
179 D5 **Songea** Tanz.
152 D3 **Sŏnggan** N. Korea
152 D2 **Songhua Hu** *resr* China
152 C1 **Songhuajiang** China
150 B1 **Songhua Jiang** *r.* China
152 C1 **Songhua Jiang** *r.* China
152 E2 **Songjiang** *Jilin* China
148 F4 **Songjiang** *Shanghai* China
152 D2 **Songjianghe** China
149 C4 **Songkan** China
154 B4 **Songkhla** Thai.
139 H4 **Songköl** *l.* Kyrg.
148 F1 **Song Ling** *mts* China
152 C4 **Songnim** N. Korea
178 B4 **Songo** Angola
179 D5 **Songo** Moz.
148 B3 **Songpan** China
145 G4 **Songsak** India
148 D3 **Song Shan** *mt.* China
152 D3 **Songshu** China
149 C4 **Songtao** China
149 F5 **Songxi** China
148 D3 **Songxian** China
152 C1 **Songyuan** China
149 D4 **Songzi** China
154 D2 **Sơn Ha** Vietnam
154 D3 **Sơn Hai** Vietnam
144 D3 **Sonipat** India
158 N3 **Sonkajärvi** Fin.
149 B6 **Sơn La** Vietnam
141 G5 **Sonmiani** Pak.
141 G5 **Sonmiani Bay** Pak.
165 J4 **Sonneberg** Germany
214 D2 **Sono** *r. Minas Gerais* Brazil
211 I6 **Sono** *r.* Brazil
197 F6 **Sonoita** Mex.
197 F6 **Sonoita** *watercourse* Mex.
197 G6 **Sonoita** U.S.A.
206 B1 **Sonora** *r.* Mex.
206 B2 **Sonora** *state* Mex.
196 B3 **Sonora** *CA* U.S.A.
199 C6 **Sonora** *TX* U.S.A.
140 B3 **Sonqor** Iran
213 B3 **Sonsón** Col.
207 G5 **Sonsonate** El Salvador
149 B6 **Sơn Tây** Vietnam
181 H5 **Sonwabile** S. Africa
215 F1 **Sopas** *r.* Uruguay
177 E4 **Sopo** *watercourse* South Sudan
171 K3 **Sopot** Bulg.
169 I3 **Sopot** Poland
168 H7 **Sopron** Hungary
139 H4 **Sopu-Korgon** Kyrg.
170 E4 **Sora** Italy
143 D2 **Sorada** India
159 L3 **Söråker** Sweden
188 F4 **Sorel** Canada
127 G9 **Sorell** Australia
127 G9 **Sorell Lake** Australia
136 E2 **Sorgun** Turkey
167 E2 **Soria** Spain
132 C2 **Sørkappøya** *i.* Svalbard
140 D3 **Sorkh, Daqq-e** *salt flat* Iran
**Sorkh, Kavīr-e Daqq-e** *salt flat* Iran *see* **Sorkh, Daqq-e**
140 D3 **Sorkh, Kūh-e** *mts* Iran
140 D3 **Sorkheh** Iran
158 K2 **Sørli** Norway
159 J5 **Sorø** Denmark
145 F5 **Soro** India
173 D5 **Soroca** Moldova
214 C3 **Sorocaba** Brazil
138 C1 **Sorochinsk** Rus. Fed.
139 K1 **Sorokino** Rus. Fed.
147 G6 **Sorol** *atoll* Micronesia
147 F7 **Sorong** Indon.
178 D3 **Soroti** Uganda
158 M1 **Sørøya** *i.* Norway
167 B3 **Sorraia** *r.* Port.
158 L1 **Sørreisa** Norway
126 F7 **Sorrento** Australia
170 F4 **Sorrento** Italy
179 B6 **Sorris Sorris** Namibia
158 L2 **Sorsele** Sweden
153 C3 **Sorsogon** Phil.
172 D2 **Sortavala** Rus. Fed.
158 K1 **Sortland** Norway
172 I2 **Sortopolovskaya** Rus. Fed.
172 I3 **Sorvizhi** Rus. Fed.
181 H2 **Soshanguve** S. Africa
173 F4 **Sosna** *r.* Rus. Fed.
215 C2 **Sosneado** *mt.* Arg.
172 J2 **Sosnogorsk** Rus. Fed.
139 I2 **Sosnovka** Kazakh.
172 H2 **Sosnovka** *Arkhangel'skaya Oblast'* Rus. Fed.

132 F3 Sosnovka Murmanskaya Oblast' Rus. Fed.
172 G4 Sosnovka Tambovskaya Oblast' Rus. Fed.
158 P2 Sosnovyy Rus. Fed.
159 O4 Sosnovyy Bor Rus. Fed.
169 I5 Sosnowiec Poland
173 F6 Sosyka r. Rus. Fed.
213 A4 Sotara, Volcán vol. Col.
158 O2 Sotkamo Fin.
215 D1 Soto Arg.
207 E3 Soto la Marina Mex.
207 G3 Sotuta Mex.
178 B3 Souanké Congo
176 B4 Soubré Côte d'Ivoire
203 F4 Souderton U.S.A.
171 L4 Soufli Greece
166 E4 Souillac France
164 D5 Souilly France
176 C1 Souk Ahras Alg.
Sŏul S. Korea see Seoul
166 D5 Soulom France
Soûr Lebanon see Tyre
167 H4 Sour el Ghozlane Alg.
187 I5 Souris Man. Canada
189 H4 Souris P.E.I. Canada
187 I5 Souris r. Canada/U.S.A.
211 K5 Sousa Brazil
176 D1 Sousse Tunisia
166 D5 Soustons France
180 E4 South Africa, Republic of country Africa
208 South America
191 G3 Southampton Canada
161 F7 Southampton U.K.
203 G4 Southampton U.S.A.
187 L2 Southampton Island Canada
202 E6 South Anna r. U.S.A.
161 F4 South Anston U.K.
189 H2 South Aulatsivik Island Canada
124 D5 South Australia state Australia
218 L7 South Australian Basin sea feature Indian Ocean
199 F5 Southaven U.S.A.
195 F5 South Baldy mt. U.S.A.
160 F3 South Bank U.K.
202 B4 South Bass Island U.S.A.
191 F3 South Baymouth Canada
190 D5 South Bend IN U.S.A.
194 B2 South Bend WA U.S.A.
201 E7 South Bight sea chan. Bahamas
202 D6 South Boston U.S.A.
128 D5 Southbridge N.Z.
203 G3 Southbridge U.S.A.
South Cape pt U.S.A. see Ka Lae
201 D5 South Carolina state U.S.A.
203 I2 South China U.S.A.
155 C1 South China Sea Pacific Ocean
198 C2 South Dakota state U.S.A.
203 G3 South Deerfield U.S.A.
161 G7 South Downs hills U.K.
161 G7 South Downs National Park nat. park U.K.
181 F2 South-East admin. dist. Botswana
127 G9 South East Cape Australia
127 H6 South East Forests National Park Australia
218 J7 Southeast Indian Ridge sea feature Indian Ocean
217 L10 Southeast Pacific Basin sea feature S. Pacific Ocean
187 I3 Southend Canada
162 C5 Southend U.K.
161 H6 Southend-on-Sea U.K.
190 A5 South English U.S.A.
180 E2 Southern admin. dist. Botswana
128 C5 Southern Alps mts N.Z.
124 B5 Southern Cross Australia
187 J3 Southern Indian Lake Canada
177 E4 Southern National Park South Sudan
216 E10 Southern Ocean World
201 E5 Southern Pines U.S.A.
209 G7 Southern Thule S. Sandwich Is
162 D5 Southern Uplands hills U.K.
162 F4 South Esk r. U.K.
190 B6 South Fabius r. U.S.A.
216 G7 South Fiji Basin sea feature S. Pacific Ocean
195 F4 South Fork U.S.A.
South Fork South Branch r. U.S.A. see Potomac, South Fork South Branch
190 E3 South Fox Island U.S.A.
129 C5 South Geomagnetic Pole Antarctica
212 □ South Georgia terr. S. Atlantic Ocean
209 G7 South Georgia and the South Sandwich Islands terr. Atlantic Ocean
162 A3 South Harris pen. U.K.
145 G5 South Hatia Island Bangl.
190 D4 South Haven U.S.A.
187 J2 South Henik Lake Canada
203 G2 South Hero U.S.A.
202 D6 South Hill U.S.A.
216 E3 South Honshu Ridge sea feature N. Pacific Ocean
187 J3 South Indian Lake Canada
203 G4 Southington U.S.A.
128 C6 South Island N.Z.
178 D3 South Island National Park Kenya
153 A4 South Islet rf Phil.
143 D1 South Koel r. India
152 D5 South Korea country Asia
196 B2 South Lake Tahoe U.S.A.
179 D5 South Luangwa National Park Zambia
129 C6 South Magnetic Pole Antarctica
190 D3 South Manitou Island U.S.A.
201 D7 South Miami U.S.A.
161 H6 Southminster U.K.
187 I4 South Moose Lake Canada
202 E5 South Mountains hills U.S.A.
184 F3 South Nahanni r. Can.
162 □ South Nesting Bay U.K.
219 G10 South Orkney Islands S. Atlantic Ocean
173 G7 South Ossetia terr. Georgia
125 H5 South Pacific Ocean
203 H2 South Paris U.S.A.
194 G3 South Platte r. U.S.A.
129 C4 South Pole Antarctica
191 G1 South Porcupine Canada
127 J1 Southport Australia
160 D4 Southport U.K.
203 H3 South Portland U.S.A.
191 H3 South River Canada
162 F2 South Ronaldsay i. U.K.
203 G3 South Royalton U.S.A.
181 I5 South Sand Bluff pt S. Africa
219 H9 South Sandwich Islands S. Atlantic Ocean
219 H9 South Sandwich Trench sea feature S. Atlantic Ocean
187 H4 South Saskatchewan r. Canada
187 J3 South Seal r. Canada
129 B2 South Shetland Islands is Antarctica
219 E10 South Shetland Trough sea feature S. Atlantic Ocean
160 F2 South Shields U.K.
190 A5 South Skunk r. U.S.A.
216 F6 South Solomon Trench sea feature Pacific Ocean
177 E4 South Sudan country Africa
128 E3 South Taranaki Bight b. N.Z.
218 N8 South Tasman Rise sea feature Southern Ocean
197 G2 South Tent mt. U.S.A.
145 E4 South Tons r. India
188 E3 South Twin Island Canada
160 E3 South Tyne r. U.K.
162 A3 South Uist i. U.K.
127 G9 South West Cape Australia
128 A7 South West Cape N.Z.
218 G7 Southwest Indian Ridge sea feature Indian Ocean
189 G4 Southwest Miramichi r. Canada
127 G9 South West National Park Australia
217 I8 Southwest Pacific Basin sea feature S. Pacific Ocean
South-West Peru Ridge sea feature S. Pacific Ocean see Nazca Ridge
127 J3 South West Rocks Australia
190 E5 South Whitley U.S.A.
203 H3 South Windham U.S.A.
161 I5 Southwold U.K.
181 H1 Soutpansberg mts S. Africa
170 G5 Soverato Italy
172 B4 Sovetsk Kaliningradskaya Oblast' Rus. Fed.
172 I3 Sovetsk Kirovskaya Oblast' Rus. Fed.
146 G2 Sovetskaya Gavan' Rus. Fed.
132 H3 Sovetskiy Rus. Fed.
172 D2 Sovetskiy Leningradskaya Oblast' Rus. Fed.
172 I3 Sovetskiy Respublika Mariy El Rus. Fed.
181 G3 Soweto S. Africa
139 G5 So'x Tajik.
207 F4 Soyaló Mex.
150 G2 Sōya-misaki c. Japan
152 D4 Soyang-ho l. S. Korea
139 G3 Sozak Kazakh.
169 O4 Sozh r. Belarus
171 L3 Sozopol Bulg.
164 D4 Spa Belgium
167 D2 Spain country Europe
161 G5 Spalding U.K.
161 D6 Span Head h. U.K.
191 F2 Spanish Canada
191 G2 Spanish r. Canada
197 G1 Spanish Fork U.S.A.
205 I5 Spanish Town Jamaica
196 C2 Sparks U.S.A.
Sparta Greece see Sparti
202 C6 Sparta NC U.S.A.
190 B4 Sparta WI U.S.A.
201 D5 Spartanburg U.S.A.
171 J6 Sparti Greece
170 G6 Spartivento, Capo c. Italy
186 G5 Sparwood Canada
172 E4 Spas-Demensk Rus. Fed.
172 E2 Spasskaya Guba Rus. Fed.
146 F2 Spassk-Dal'niy Rus. Fed.
171 J7 Spatha, Akrotirio pt Greece
186 D3 Spatsizi Plateau Wilderness Provincial Park Canada
198 C2 Spearfish U.S.A.
199 C4 Spearman U.S.A.
203 F3 Speculator U.S.A.
198 E3 Spencer IA U.S.A.
194 D2 Spencer ID U.S.A.
202 C5 Spencer WV U.S.A.
126 B5 Spencer, Cape Australia
186 B3 Spencer, Cape U.S.A.
126 B5 Spencer Gulf est. Australia
186 E4 Spences Bridge Canada
160 F3 Spennymoor U.K.
180 A3 Sperrgebiet National Park nat. park Namibia
163 D3 Sperrin Mountains hills U.K.
202 D5 Sperryville U.S.A.
165 H5 Spessart reg. Germany
171 J6 Spetses i. Greece
162 E3 Spey r. U.K.
165 G5 Speyer Germany
141 G4 Spezand Pak.
165 F1 Spiekeroog i. Germany
168 C7 Spiez Switz.
164 E1 Spijk Neth.
164 C3 Spijkenisse Neth.
170 E1 Spilimbergo Italy
161 H4 Spilsby U.K.
141 G4 Spīn Bōldak Afgh.
144 B3 Spintangi Pak.
186 F3 Spirit River Canada
190 C3 Spirit River Flowage resr U.S.A.
187 H4 Spiritwood Canada
141 G3 Spirsang Pass Afgh.
169 J6 Spišská Nová Ves Slovakia
137 J1 Spitak Armenia
144 D3 Spiti r. India
132 C2 Spitsbergen i. Svalbard
168 F7 Spittal an der Drau Austria
170 G3 Split Croatia
187 J3 Split Lake Canada
187 J3 Split Lake l. Canada
194 C2 Spokane U.S.A.
170 E3 Spoleto Italy
Spong Cambodia see Spóng
154 C2 Spóng Cambodia
190 B3 Spooner U.S.A.
165 J1 Spornitz Germany
194 F2 Spotted Horse U.S.A.
191 F2 Spragge Canada
186 E4 Spranger, Mount Canada
147 D6 Spratly Islands S. China Sea
194 C2 Spray U.S.A.
168 G5 Spree r. Germany
164 D4 Sprimont Belgium
191 F3 Spring Bay Canada
180 B4 Springbok S. Africa
189 I4 Springdale Canada
199 E4 Springdale U.S.A.
165 H2 Springe Germany
195 F4 Springer U.S.A.
197 H4 Springerville U.S.A.
199 C4 Springfield CO U.S.A.
190 C6 Springfield IL U.S.A.
203 G3 Springfield MA U.S.A.
203 I2 Springfield ME U.S.A.
198 E2 Springfield MN U.S.A.
199 E4 Springfield MO U.S.A.
202 B5 Springfield OH U.S.A.
199 C4 Springfield OR U.S.A.
203 G3 Springfield VT U.S.A.
202 D5 Springfield WV U.S.A.
190 C6 Springfield, Lake U.S.A.
181 F5 Springfontein S. Africa
190 B4 Spring Green U.S.A.
190 B4 Spring Grove U.S.A.
189 H4 Springhill Canada
201 D6 Spring Hill U.S.A.
190 D4 Spring Lake U.S.A.
197 E3 Spring Mountains U.S.A.
128 D5 Springs Junction N.Z.
190 A4 Spring Valley U.S.A.
202 D3 Springville NY U.S.A.
197 G1 Springville UT U.S.A.
161 I5 Sprowston U.K.
186 G4 Spruce Grove Canada
202 D5 Spruce Knob-Seneca Rocks National Recreation Area park U.S.A.
194 D3 Spruce Mountain U.S.A.
160 H4 Spurn Head U.K.
186 E5 Spuzzum Canada
186 E5 Squamish Canada
203 H3 Squam Lake U.S.A.
203 I1 Squapan Lake U.S.A.
203 I1 Square Lake U.S.A.
170 G5 Squillace, Golfo di g. Italy
171 I3 Srbija aut. rep. Europe
154 B3 Srê Âmběl Cambodia
171 H2 Srebrenica Bos.-Herz.
171 L3 Sredets Bulg.
133 Q4 Sredinnyy Khrebet mts Rus. Fed.
171 J3 Sredna Gora mts Bulg.
133 Q3 Srednekolymsk Rus. Fed.
Sredne-Russkaya Vozvyshennost' hills Rus. Fed. see Central Russian Upland
Sredne-Sibirskoye Ploskogor'ye plat. Rus. Fed. see Central Siberian Plateau
158 O2 Sredneye Kuyto, Ozero l. Rus. Fed.
154 C2 Srêpok, Tônlé r. Cambodia
146 D1 Sretensk Rus. Fed.
155 D2 Sri Aman Sarawak Malaysia
143 C3 Sriharikota Island India
143 B5 Sri Jayewardenepura Kotte Sri Lanka
143 D2 Srikakulam India
143 B3 Sri Kalahasti India
144 D3 Srikanta mt. India
218 C5 Sri Lanka country Asia
144 C2 Srinagar India
144 D3 Srinagar India
Sri Pada mt. Sri Lanka see Adam's Peak
143 B4 Srirangam India
154 B1 Sri Thep tourist site Thai.
143 B4 Srivaikuntam India
143 A2 Srivardhan India
143 B4 Srivilliputtur India
139 K1 Srostki Rus. Fed.
143 C2 Srungavarapukota India
165 H1 Stade Germany
164 B4 Staden Belgium
164 E2 Stadskanaal Neth.
165 H4 Stadtallendorf Germany
165 H2 Stadthagen Germany
165 J4 Stadtilm Germany
164 E3 Stadtlohn Germany
165 H3 Stadtoldendorf Germany
165 J4 Stadtroda Germany
162 B4 Staffa i. U.K.
165 J4 Staffelberg h. Germany
165 I4 Staffelstein Germany
161 E5 Stafford U.K.
202 E5 Stafford U.S.A.
159 N4 Staicele Latvia
161 G6 Staines-upon-Thames U.K.
173 F5 Stakhanov Ukr.
161 E7 Stalbridge U.K.
161 I5 Stalham U.K.
Stalingrad Rus. Fed. see Volgograd
169 K5 Stalowa Wola Poland
171 K3 Stamboliyski Bulg.
161 G5 Stamford U.K.
203 G4 Stamford CT U.S.A.
203 F3 Stamford NY U.S.A.
179 B6 Stampriet Namibia
158 K1 Stamsund Norway
198 E3 Stanberry U.S.A.
164 C3 Standdaarbuiten Neth.
181 H3 Standerton S. Africa
191 F4 Standish U.S.A.
200 C4 Stanford U.S.A.
Stanger S. Africa see KwaDukuza
201 E7 Staniard Creek Bahamas
165 L5 Staňkov Czech Rep.
127 F8 Stanley Australia
203 J1 Stanley Canada
149 □ Stanley Hong Kong China
212 E8 Stanley Falkland Is
160 F3 Stanley U.K.
194 D2 Stanley ID U.S.A.
198 C1 Stanley ND U.S.A.
190 B3 Stanley WI U.S.A.
127 F8 Stanley, Mount h. Australia
143 B4 Stanley Reservoir India
160 F2 Stannington U.K.
146 D1 Stanovoye Nagor'ye mts Rus. Fed.
146 E1 Stanovoy Khrebet mts Rus. Fed.
127 I2 Stanthorpe Australia
161 H5 Stanton U.K.
202 B6 Stanton KY U.S.A.
190 E4 Stanton MI U.S.A.
198 C3 Stapleton U.S.A.
169 J5 Starachowice Poland
Stara Planina mts Bulg./Serbia see Balkan Mountains
172 H4 Staraya Kulatka Rus. Fed.
173 H5 Staraya Poltavka Rus. Fed.
172 D3 Staraya Russa Rus. Fed.
169 O2 Staraya Toropa Rus. Fed.
172 I4 Staraya Tumba Rus. Fed.
171 K3 Stara Zagora Bulg.
123 I4 Starbuck Island Kiribati
168 G4 Stargard Szczeciński Poland
172 E3 Staritsa Rus. Fed.
201 D6 Starke U.S.A.
199 F5 Starkville U.S.A.
168 E7 Starnberger See l. Germany
139 J2 Staroaleyskoye Rus. Fed.
173 F5 Starobil's'k Ukr.
169 P4 Starodub Rus. Fed.
169 I4 Starogard Gdański Poland
173 C5 Starokostyantyniv Ukr.
173 F6 Starominskaya Rus. Fed.
173 F6 Staroshcherbinovskaya Rus. Fed.
138 D1 Starosubkhangulovo Rus. Fed.
196 C1 Star Peak U.S.A.
161 D7 Start Point U.K.
169 N4 Staryya Darohi Belarus
138 D2 Staryy Karabutak Kazakh.
133 L2 Staryy Kayak Rus. Fed.
173 F5 Staryy Oskol Rus. Fed.
165 J3 Staßfurt Germany
202 E4 State College U.S.A.
201 D5 Statesboro U.S.A.
201 D5 Statesville U.S.A.
220 W1 Station Nord Greenland
165 L3 Stauchitz Germany
165 G4 Staufenberg Germany
202 D5 Staunton U.S.A.
159 I4 Stavanger Norway
161 F4 Staveley U.K.
165 K1 Stavenhagen, Reuterstadt Germany
173 G6 Stavropol' Rus. Fed.
138 F1 Stavropolka Kazakh.
173 G6 Stavropol'skaya Vozvyshennost' hills Rus. Fed.
173 G6 Stavropol'skiy Kray admin. div. Rus. Fed.
126 E6 Stawell Australia
181 H4 Steadville S. Africa
196 C2 Steamboat U.S.A.
194 F3 Steamboat Springs U.S.A.
202 E4 Steelton U.S.A.
164 E2 Steenderen Neth.
181 I2 Steenkampsberge mts S. Africa
186 F3 Steen River Canada
194 C3 Steens Mountain U.S.A.
Steenstrup Gletscher glacier Greenland see Sermersuaq
164 A4 Steenvoorde France
164 E2 Steenwijk Neth.
184 H2 Stefansson Island Canada
165 I5 Steigerwald mts Germany
165 J5 Stein Germany
165 J4 Steinach Germany
187 J5 Steinbach Canada
165 G2 Steinfeld (Oldenburg) Germany
164 F2 Steinfurt Germany
179 B6 Steinhausen Namibia
165 H3 Steinheim Germany
165 H2 Steinhuder Meer l. Germany
158 J2 Steinkjer Norway
180 B4 Steinkopf S. Africa
197 H5 Steins U.S.A.
158 J2 Steinsdalen Norway
180 F3 Stella S. Africa
201 F7 Stella Maris Bahamas
180 C6 Stellenbosch S. Africa
170 C3 Stello, Monte mt. Corsica France
164 D5 Stenay France
165 J2 Stendal Germany
149 □ Stenhouse, Mount h. Hong Kong China
162 E4 Stenhousemuir U.K.
159 J4 Stenungsund Sweden
Stepanakert Azer. see Xankändi
173 H7 Step'anavan Armenia
187 J5 Stephen U.S.A.
126 D4 Stephens watercourse Australia
128 D4 Stephens, Cape N.Z.
126 D3 Stephens Creek Australia
190 D3 Stephenson U.S.A.
186 C3 Stephens Passage U.S.A.
189 I4 Stephenville Canada
199 D5 Stephenville U.S.A.
139 G1 Stepnogorsk Kazakh.
139 H4 Stepnoy Kyrg.
138 E1 Stepnoye Chelyabinskaya Oblast' Rus. Fed.
173 H5 Stepnoye Saratovskaya Oblast' Rus. Fed.
139 G1 Stepnyak Kazakh.
181 H4 Sterkfontein Dam resr S. Africa
181 G5 Sterkstroom S. Africa
138 C1 Sterlibashevo Rus. Fed.
180 D5 Sterling S. Africa
194 G3 Sterling CO U.S.A.
190 C5 Sterling IL U.S.A.
198 C2 Sterling ND U.S.A.
197 G2 Sterling UT U.S.A.
199 C6 Sterling City U.S.A.
191 F4 Sterling Heights U.S.A.
138 C1 Sterlitamak Rus. Fed.
165 J1 Sternberg Germany
186 G4 Stettler Canada
190 D2 Steuben U.S.A.
202 C4 Steubenville U.S.A.
161 G6 Stevenage U.K.
187 J4 Stevenson Lake Canada
190 C3 Stevens Point U.S.A.
184 D3 Stevens Village U.S.A.
186 D3 Stewart Canada
186 B2 Stewart r. Canada
186 B2 Stewart Crossing Canada
128 A7 Stewart Island N.Z.
125 G2 Stewart Islands Solomon Is
185 J3 Stewart Lake Canada
162 D5 Stewarton U.K.
190 A4 Stewartville U.S.A.
181 F5 Steynsburg S. Africa
168 G6 Steyr Austria
180 F6 Steytlerville S. Africa
164 D1 Stiens Neth.
186 C3 Stikine r. Canada/U.S.A.
186 C3 Stikine Plateau Canada
180 D7 Stilbaai S. Africa
190 A3 Stillwater MN U.S.A.
196 C2 Stillwater NV U.S.A.
199 D4 Stillwater OK U.S.A.
195 C4 Stillwater Range mts U.S.A.
161 G5 Stilton U.K.
171 J4 Štip Macedonia
126 C5 Stirling Australia
162 E4 Stirling U.K.
196 B2 Stirling City U.S.A.
126 B4 Stirling North Australia
158 J3 Stjørdalshalsen Norway
168 H6 Stockerau Austria
165 J4 Stockheim Germany
159 L4 Stockholm Sweden
203 I1 Stockholm U.S.A.
161 E4 Stockport U.K.
219 G6 Stocks Seamount sea feature S. Atlantic Ocean
196 B3 Stockton CA U.S.A.
198 D4 Stockton KS U.S.A.
197 F1 Stockton UT U.S.A.
190 B2 Stockton Island U.S.A.
199 E4 Stockton Lake U.S.A.
160 F3 Stockton-on-Tees U.K.
203 I2 Stockton Springs U.S.A.
159 L3 Stöde Sweden
154 C2 Stœng Trêng Cambodia
162 C2 Stoer, Point of U.K.
161 E4 Stoke-on-Trent U.K.
160 F3 Stokesley U.K.
127 E8 Stokes Point Australia
158 B3 Stokkseyri Iceland
158 K2 Stokkvågen Norway
158 K1 Stokmarknes Norway
171 G3 Stolac Bos.-Herz.
164 E4 Stolberg (Rheinland) Germany
139 K2 Stolboukha (abandoned) Kazakh.
173 C5 Stolin Belarus
165 K4 Stollberg Germany
165 H2 Stolzenau Germany
161 E5 Stone U.K.
191 I2 Stonecliffe Canada
203 F5 Stone Harbor U.S.A.
162 F4 Stonehaven U.K.
161 F6 Stonehenge tourist site U.K.
186 E3 Stone Mountain Provincial Park Canada
197 H3 Stoner U.S.A.
203 F4 Stone Ridge U.S.A.
187 J4 Stonewall Canada
202 C5 Stonewall Jackson Lake U.S.A.
191 F4 Stoney Point Canada
203 I2 Stonington U.S.A.
196 A2 Stonyford U.S.A.
203 E3 Stony Point U.S.A.
187 H3 Stony Rapids Canada
158 L2 Stora Lulevatten l. Sweden
158 L2 Stora Sjöfallets nationalpark nat. park Sweden
158 L2 Storavan l. Sweden
Store Bælt sea chan. Denmark see Great Belt
158 J3 Støren Norway
158 K2 Storforshei Norway
158 K2 Storjord Norway
184 H2 Storkerson Peninsula Canada
127 G9 Storm Bay Australia
181 G5 Stormberg S. Africa
181 G5 Stormberge mts S. Africa
198 E3 Storm Lake U.S.A.
162 B2 Stornoway U.K.
172 J2 Storozhevsk Rus. Fed.
173 C5 Storozhynets' Ukr.
203 G4 Storrs U.S.A.
158 L2 Storseleby Sweden
158 K3 Storsjön l. Sweden
159 J3 Storskrymten mt. Norway
158 M1 Storslett Norway
164 D1 Stortemelk sea chan. Neth.
158 L2 Storuman Sweden
158 L2 Storuman l. Sweden
159 L3 Storvik Sweden
159 J4 Storvorde Denmark
159 L4 Storvreta Sweden
161 G5 Stotfold U.K.
190 C4 Stoughton U.S.A.
161 E7 Stour r. England U.K.
161 F5 Stour r. England U.K.
161 H6 Stour r. England U.K.
161 I6 Stour r. England U.K.
161 E5 Stourbridge U.K.
161 E5 Stourport-on-Severn U.K.
187 K4 Stout Lake Canada
172 C4 Stowbtsy Belarus
203 F4 Stowe U.S.A.
161 H5 Stowmarket U.K.
163 D3 Strabane U.K.
163 D4 Stradbally Ireland
161 I5 Stradbroke U.K.
170 C2 Stradella Italy
127 F9 Strahan Australia
197 G3 Straight Cliffs ridge U.S.A.
168 F6 Strakonice Czech Rep.
168 F3 Stralsund Germany
180 C7 Strand S. Africa
158 I3 Stranda Norway
201 E7 Strangers Cay i. Bahamas
163 F3 Strangford U.K.
163 F3 Strangford Lough inlet U.K.
162 C6 Stranraer U.K.
166 H2 Strasbourg France
202 D5 Strasburg U.S.A.
127 G6 Stratford Australia
191 G4 Stratford Canada
128 E3 Stratford N.Z.
199 C4 Stratford TX U.S.A.
190 B3 Stratford WI U.S.A.
161 F5 Stratford-upon-Avon U.K.
126 C5 Strathalbyn Australia
162 D5 Strathaven U.K.
162 G3 Strathbeg, Loch of l. U.K.
162 D3 Strathcarron val. U.K.
186 D5 Strathcona Provincial Park Canada
162 D3 Strathconon val. U.K.
162 D3 Strath Dearn val. U.K.
162 D2 Strath Fleet val. U.K.
186 G4 Strathmore Canada
186 E4 Strathnaver Canada
162 D2 Strathnaver val. U.K.
162 E2 Strath of Kildonan val. U.K.
191 G4 Strathroy Canada
162 E3 Strathspey val. U.K.
162 E2 Strathy U.K.
162 D2 Strathy Point U.K.
161 C7 Stratton U.K.
203 H2 Stratton U.S.A.
165 K6 Straubing Germany
158 B1 Straumnes pt Iceland
190 B4 Strawberry Point U.S.A.
197 G1 Strawberry Reservoir U.S.A.
124 D5 Streaky Bay Australia
124 D5 Streaky Bay b. Australia
190 C5 Streator U.S.A.
161 E6 Street U.K.
171 J2 Strehaia Romania
165 L3 Strehla Germany
133 Q3 Strelka Rus. Fed.
159 N4 Strenči Latvia
165 K5 Stříbro Czech Rep.
162 F3 Strichen U.K.
215 D4 Stroeder Arg.
163 C4 Strokestown Ireland
162 E2 Stroma, Island of U.K.
170 F5 Stromboli, Isola i. Isole Lipari Italy
162 E2 Stromness U.K.
198 D3 Stromsburg U.S.A.
159 J4 Strömstad Sweden
158 K3 Strömsund Sweden
202 C4 Strongsville U.S.A.
162 F1 Stronsay i. U.K.
127 I4 Stroud Australia
161 E6 Stroud U.K.
127 I4 Stroud Road Australia
203 F4 Stroudsburg U.S.A.
159 J4 Struer Denmark
171 I4 Struga Macedonia
172 D3 Strugi-Krasnyye Rus. Fed.
180 D7 Struis Bay S. Africa
165 I5 Strullendorf Germany
171 J4 Struma r. Bulg.
161 B5 Strumble Head U.K.
171 J4 Strumica Macedonia
171 K3 Stryama r. Bulg.
180 E4 Strydenburg S. Africa
171 J4 Strymonas r. Greece
159 I3 Stryn Norway
173 B5 Stryy Ukr.
126 D2 Strzelecki Creek watercourse Australia
126 D2 Strzelecki Desert des. Austr.
127 H8 Strzelecki Peak h. Australia
201 D7 Stuart FL U.S.A.
202 C6 Stuart VA U.S.A.
186 E4 Stuart Lake Canada
202 D5 Stuarts Draft U.S.A.
127 H4 Stuart Town Australia
128 C6 Studholme Junction N.Z.
158 L3 Studsviken Sweden
199 C6 Study Butte U.S.A.
187 K4 Stull Lake Canada
172 F4 Stupino Rus. Fed.
129 B6 Sturge Island i. Antarctica
190 D2 Sturgeon r. U.S.A.
187 J4 Sturgeon Bay b. Canada
190 D3 Sturgeon Bay U.S.A.
190 E3 Sturgeon Bay b. U.S.A.
190 D3 Sturgeon Bay Canal lake channel U.S.A.
191 H2 Sturgeon Falls Canada
188 B3 Sturgeon Lake Canada
200 C4 Sturgis KY U.S.A.
190 E5 Sturgis MI U.S.A.
198 C2 Sturgis SD U.S.A.
126 D2 Sturt, Mount h. Australia
126 B5 Sturt Bay Australia
124 C3 Sturt Creek watercourse Australia
126 D2 Sturt National Park Australia
126 D2 Sturt Stony Desert Australia
181 G6 Stutterheim S. Africa
168 D6 Stuttgart Germany
199 F5 Stuttgart U.S.A.
158 B2 Stykkishólmur Iceland
169 L5 Styr r. Ukr.
214 D2 Suaçuí Grande r. Brazil
177 F3 Suakin Sudan
149 F5 Su'ao Taiwan
206 B1 Suaqui Grande Mex.
213 B3 Suárez r. Col.
169 L3 Subačius Lith.
145 H4 Subansiri r. India
145 F5 Subarnarekha r. India
137 G6 Şubayḩah Saudi Arabia
155 C2 Subi Besar i. Indon.
148 A1 Sub Nur l. China
171 H1 Subotica Serbia
169 M7 Suceava Romania
150 C3 Suchan r. Rus. Fed.
163 C4 Suck r. Ireland
165 J1 Suckow Germany
210 E7 Sucre Bol.
213 B2 Sucre Col.
213 C3 Sucuaro Col.
214 B2 Sucuriú r. Brazil
125 G4 Sud, Grand Récif du rf New Caledonia
173 E6 Sudak Ukr.
177 E3 Sudan country Africa
172 G3 Suday Rus. Fed.
137 J6 Sudayr, Sha'īb watercourse Iraq
191 G2 Sudbury Canada
161 H5 Sudbury U.K.
177 E4 Sudd swamp South Sudan
165 J1 Sude r. Germany
168 H5 Sudety mts Czech Rep./Poland
203 F5 Sudlersville U.S.A.
172 G4 Sudogda Rus. Fed.
136 D7 Sudr Egypt
158 □ Suðuroy i. Faroe Is
177 E4 Sue watercourse South Sudan
167 F3 Sueca Spain
177 F2 Suez Egypt
202 E6 Suffolk U.S.A.
140 B2 Sūfiān Iran
190 C4 Sugar r. U.S.A.
203 H2 Sugarloaf Mountain U.S.A.
127 J4 Sugarloaf Point Australia
153 C4 Sugbuhan Point Phil.
139 I5 Sugun China
155 E1 Sugut r. Sabah Malaysia
153 A5 Sugut, Tanjung pt Sabah Malaysia
148 B2 Suhait China
177 F2 Sūhāj Egypt
142 E5 Şuḩār Oman
146 C1 Sühbaatar Mongolia
165 I4 Suhl Germany
165 I2 Suhlendorf Germany
136 C2 Şuhut Turkey
144 B3 Sui Pak.
150 B1 Suibin China
149 F4 Suichang China
149 E5 Suichuan China
148 D2 Suide China
152 F1 Suifenhe China
144 B4 Suigam India
146 E2 Suihua China
149 B4 Suijiang China
149 D5 Suining Hunan China
148 E3 Suining Jiangsu China
149 B4 Suining Sichuan China
148 E3 Suiping China
164 C5 Suippes France
163 D5 Suir r. Ireland
148 E3 Suixi China
148 E3 Suixian China
149 C5 Suiyang Guizhou China
148 E3 Suiyang Henan China
148 F1 Suizhong China
148 D4 Suizhou China
148 C1 Suj China
144 C4 Sujangarh India
144 B4 Sujawal Pak.
155 C4 Sukabumi Indon.
155 C3 Sukadana Indon.
151 G6 Sukagawa Japan
153 A5 Sukau Sabah Malaysia
152 C4 Sukchŏn N. Korea
150 C1 Sukhanovka Rus. Fed.
172 E4 Sukhinichi Rus. Fed.
172 H2 Sukhona r. Rus. Fed.
154 A1 Sukhothai Thai.
172 E2 Sukkozero Rus. Fed.
144 B4 Sukkur Pak.
143 C2 Sukma India
144 C4 Sukri r. India
172 F3 Sukromny Rus. Fed.
151 C8 Sukumo Japan
159 I3 Sula i. Norway
147 E7 Sula, Kepulauan is Indon.
144 B3 Sulaiman Range mts Pak.
173 H7 Sulak r. Rus. Fed.
140 C4 Sūlār Iran
162 B1 Sula Sgeir i. U.K.
Sulawesi i. Indon. see Celebes
137 J4 Sulaymān Beg Iraq
140 C2 Suledeh Iran
162 D1 Sule Skerry i. U.K.
162 D1 Sule Stack i. U.K.
136 F3 Süleymanlı Turkey
176 A4 Sulima Sierra Leone
165 G2 Sulingen Germany
158 L2 Sulitjelma Norway
159 O3 Sulkava Fin.
141 F4 Sūlkī-ye Sangān Iran
210 B4 Sullana Peru
198 F4 Sullivan U.S.A.
187 G4 Sullivan Lake Canada
203 I1 Sully Canada
170 E3 Sulmona Italy
199 E6 Sulphur U.S.A.
199 E5 Sulphur Springs U.S.A.
191 F2 Sultan Canada
141 F4 Sultan, Koh-i- mts Pak.
136 C2 Sultan Dağları mts Turkey
136 D2 Sultanhanı Turkey
145 E4 Sultanpur India
153 B5 Sulu Archipelago is Phil.
139 H5 Suluke China
139 G5 Sülüktü Kyrg.
136 F2 Sulusaray Turkey
153 A4 Sulu Sea Phil.
138 F3 Sulutobe Kazakh.
165 J5 Sulzbach-Rosenberg Germany
129 B5 Sulzberger Bay b. Antarctica
141 E6 Sumāil Oman
212 D3 Sumampa Arg.
213 B4 Sumapaz, Parque Nacional nat. park Col.
137 J5 Sūmār Iran
Sumatera i. Indon. see Sumatra
155 B3 Sumatra i. Indon.
168 F6 Šumava mts Czech Rep.
147 E7 Sumba i. Indon.
147 D7 Sumba, Selat sea chan. Indon.
138 C5 Sumbar r. Turkm.
155 E4 Sumbawa i. Indon.
155 E4 Sumbawabesar Indon.
179 D4 Sumbawanga Tanz.
179 B5 Sumbe Angola
162 □ Sumburgh U.K.
162 □ Sumburgh Head U.K.
144 D2 Sumdo Aksai Chin
137 L3 Sume'eh Sarā Iran
155 D4 Sumenep Indon.
151 F9 Sumisu-jima i. Japan
137 I3 Summēl Iraq
188 C3 Summer Beaver Canada
189 J4 Summerford Canada
190 D3 Summer Island U.S.A.
162 C2 Summer Isles U.K.
189 H4 Summerside Canada
202 C5 Summersville U.S.A.
202 C5 Summersville Lake U.S.A.
186 E4 Summit Lake Canada
190 E5 Summit Lake l. U.S.A.
196 D2 Summit Mountain U.S.A.
144 D2 Sumnal China/India
128 D5 Sumner N.Z.
190 A4 Sumner U.S.A.
128 D5 Sumner, Lake N.Z.
186 C3 Sumner Strait U.S.A.
151 F6 Sumon-dake mt. Japan
151 D7 Sumoto Japan
168 H6 Šumperk Czech Rep.
138 A4 Sumqayıt Azer.
137 L1 Sumqayıtçay r. Azer.
144 B4 Sumrahu Pak.
201 D5 Sumter U.S.A.
173 E5 Sumy Ukr.
194 D2 Sun r. U.S.A.
172 I3 Suna Rus. Fed.
150 G3 Sunagawa Japan
145 G4 Sunamganj Bangl.
152 C4 Sunan N. Korea
162 C4 Sunart, Loch inlet U.K.
140 D6 Şunaynah Oman
137 J4 Sunbula Kūh mts Iran
194 E1 Sunburst U.S.A.
126 F6 Sunbury Australia
202 B4 Sunbury OH U.S.A.
202 E4 Sunbury PA U.S.A.
215 E1 Sunchales Arg.
152 D6 Suncheon S. Korea
152 C4 Sunch'ŏn N. Korea
181 G2 Sun City S. Africa
203 H3 Suncook U.S.A.
155 C4 Sunda, Selat str. Indon.
194 F2 Sundance U.S.A.
145 G5 Sundarbans coastal area Bangl./India
145 G5 Sundarbans National Park Bangl./India
143 D1 Sundargarh India
144 D3 Sundarnagar India
218 L4 Sunda Shelf sea feature Indian Ocean
160 F3 Sunderland U.K.
165 G3 Sundern (Sauerland) Germany
136 C2 Sündiken Dağları mts Turkey
191 H3 Sundridge Canada
159 L3 Sundsvall Sweden
132 C3 Sundsvall commune Sweden
Sundukli, Peski des. Turkm. see Sandykly Gumy
181 I4 Sundumbili S. Africa
144 D4 Sunel India
154 B5 Sungaikabung Indon.
155 C3 Sungailiat Indon.
155 B3 Sungaipenuh Indon.
155 B1 Sungai Petani Malaysia
Sungei Petani Malaysia see Sungai Petani
154 □ Sungei Seletar Reservoir Sing.
136 E1 Sungurlu Turkey
139 H3 Sunkar, Gora mt. Kazakh.
145 F4 Sun Kosi r. Nepal
159 I3 Sunndal Norway
158 J3 Sunndalsøra Norway
159 K4 Sunne Sweden
194 C2 Sunnyside U.S.A.
196 A3 Sunnyvale U.S.A.
190 C4 Sun Prairie U.S.A.
196 □1 Sunset Beach U.S.A.
197 G4 Sunset Crater National Monument nat. park U.S.A.
133 M3 Suntar Rus. Fed.
141 F5 Suntsar Pak.
194 D3 Sun Valley U.S.A.
152 C5 Sunwi-do i. N. Korea
176 B4 Sunyani Ghana
158 O2 Suolijärvet l. Fin.
190 C1 Suomi Canada
158 O2 Suomussalmi Fin.
151 B8 Suō-nada b. Japan
Suonan China see Dongxiang
158 N3 Suonenjoki Fin.
154 C3 Suŏng Cambodia
149 B7 Suong r. Laos
172 E2 Suoyarvi Rus. Fed.
143 A3 Supa India
197 F3 Supai U.S.A.
213 E3 Supamo r. Venez.
145 F4 Supaul India
197 G5 Superior AZ U.S.A.
198 D3 Superior NE U.S.A.
190 A2 Superior WI U.S.A.
207 F4 Superior, Laguna lag. Mex.
190 C2 Superior, Lake Canada/U.S.A.
154 B2 Suphan Buri Thai.
137 I2 Süphan Dağı mt. Turkey
172 E4 Suponevo Rus. Fed.

152 C3 Supung N. Korea
137 K6 Sūq ash Shuyūkh Iraq
148 F3 Suqian China
Suquţrá i. Yemen see Socotra
142 E5 Şūr Oman
196 B3 Sur, Point U.S.A.
215 F3 Sur, Punta pt Arg.
172 H4 Sura Rus. Fed.
172 H4 Sura r. Rus. Fed.
137 L1 Şuraabad Azer.
141 G4 Surab Pak.
155 D4 Surabaya Indon.
141 E5 Sūrak Iran
155 D4 Surakarta Indon.
127 H1 Surat Australia
144 C5 Surat India
144 C3 Suratgarh India
154 A3 Surat Thani Thai.
172 E4 Surazh Rus. Fed.
137 J4 Sūrdāsh Iraq
171 J3 Surdulica Serbia
164 E5 Sûre r. Lux.
144 B5 Surendranagar India
206 I6 Suretka Costa Rica
196 B4 Surf U.S.A.
132 I3 Surgut Rus. Fed.
143 B2 Suriapet India
153 C4 Surigao Phil.
153 C4 Surigao Strait Phil.
154 B2 Surin Thai.
211 G3 Suriname country S. America
139 F5 Surkhandar'ya r. Uzbek.
145 E3 Surkhet Nepal
139 G5 Surkhob r. Tajik.
140 D4 Sūrmaq Iran
137 H1 Sürmene Turkey
173 G5 Surovikino Rus. Fed.
140 A6 Surrah, Nafūd as des. Saudi Arabia
202 E6 Surry U.S.A.
172 H4 Sursk Rus. Fed.
Surt Libya see Sirte
Surt, Khalīj g. Libya see Sirte, Gulf of
158 B3 Surtsey i. Iceland
141 E5 Sūrū Iran
141 H3 Surūbay Afgh.
136 G3 Suruç Turkey
151 F7 Suruga-wan b. Japan
155 B3 Surulangun Indon.
153 C5 Surup Phil.
164 F2 Surwold Germany
137 K2 Suşa Azer.
151 B7 Susa Japan
151 C8 Susaki Japan
140 C4 Sūsangerd Iran
172 G3 Susanino Rus. Fed.
196 B1 Susanville U.S.A.
136 G1 Suşehri Turkey
154 A4 Suso Thai.
149 E4 Susong China
203 E4 Susquehanna r. U.S.A.
202 D4 Susquehanna, West Branch r. U.S.A.
189 G4 Sussex Canada
203 F4 Sussex U.S.A.
153 A5 Susul Sabah Malaysia
133 P3 Susuman Rus. Fed.
136 B2 Susurluk Turkey
144 D2 Sutak India
196 C2 Sutcliffe U.S.A.
180 D6 Sutherland S. Africa
198 C3 Sutherland U.S.A.
Sutlej r. Pak. see Satluj
196 B2 Sutter Creek U.S.A.
161 G5 Sutterton U.K.
203 G2 Sutton Canada
188 D3 Sutton r. Canada
161 H5 Sutton U.K.
202 C5 Sutton U.S.A.
161 F5 Sutton Coldfield U.K.
161 F4 Sutton in Ashfield U.K.
188 D3 Sutton Lake Canada
202 C5 Sutton Lake U.S.A.
150 G3 Suttsu Japan
139 H4 Suusamyr Kyrg.
125 H3 Suva Fiji
172 F4 Suvorov Rus. Fed.
151 F6 Suwa Japan
169 K3 Suwałki Poland
154 B2 Suwannaphum Thai.
201 D6 Suwannee r. U.S.A.
123 I4 Suwarrow atoll Cook Is
137 J5 Suwayqīyah, Hawr as imp. l. Iraq
137 H6 Suwayr well Saudi Arabia
177 F2 Suways, Khalīj as Egypt
177 F1 Suways, Qanāt as Egypt
152 D5 Suwon S. Korea
138 C4 Suz, Mys pt Kazakh.
151 F6 Suzaka Japan
172 G3 Suzdal' Rus. Fed.
148 E3 Suzhou Anhui China
148 F4 Suzhou Jiangsu China
152 C3 Suzi He r. China
151 E6 Suzu Japan
151 E6 Suzuka Japan
151 E6 Suzu-misaki pt Japan
158 N1 Sværholthalvøya pen. Norway
132 C2 Svalbard terr. Arctic Ocean
173 F5 Svatove Ukr.
154 C3 Svay Riĕng Cambodia
159 K3 Sveg Sweden
159 N4 Sveķi Latvia
159 I3 Svelgen Norway
158 J3 Svellingen Norway
159 N5 Švenčionėliai Lith.
159 N5 Švenčionys Lith.
159 J5 Svendborg Denmark
158 L1 Svensbu Norway
Svensby Norway see Svensbu
158 K3 Svenstavik Sweden
Sverdlovsk Rus. Fed. see Yekaterinburg
173 F5 Sverdlovs'k Ukr.
185 I1 Sverdrup Channel Canada
171 I4 Sveti Nikole Macedonia
146 F2 Svetlaya Rus. Fed.
172 B4 Svetlogorsk Kaliningradskaya Oblast' Rus. Fed.
132 J3 Svetlogorsk Rus. Fed.
173 G6 Svetlograd Rus. Fed.
172 B4 Svetlyy Kaliningradskaya Oblast' Rus. Fed.
138 E2 Svetlyy Orenburgskaya Oblast' Rus. Fed.
173 H5 Svetlyy Yar Rus. Fed.
172 D2 Svetogorsk Rus. Fed.
158 C2 Svíahnúkar vol. Iceland
171 L4 Svilengrad Bulg.
171 J2 Svinecea Mare, Vârful mt. Romania
172 C4 Svir Belarus
172 E2 Svir' r. Rus. Fed.
171 K3 Svishtov Bulg.
168 H6 Svitava r. Czech Rep.
168 H6 Svitavy Czech Rep.
173 E5 Svitlovods'k Ukr.
172 I4 Sviyaga r. Rus. Fed.
146 E1 Svobodnyy Rus. Fed.
158 K1 Svolvær Norway
171 J3 Svrljiške Planine mts Serbia
173 D4 Svyetlahorsk Belarus
161 F5 Swadlincote U.K.
161 H5 Swaffham U.K.
124 F4 Swain Reefs Australia
201 D5 Swainsboro U.S.A.
123 H4 Swains Island atoll American Samoa
179 B6 Swakopmund Namibia
160 F3 Swale r. U.K.
125 G3 Swallow Islands Solomon Is
187 I4 Swan r. Canada
161 F7 Swanage U.K.
126 E5 Swan Hill Australia
186 F4 Swan Hills Canada
Swan Islands is Hond. see Cisne, Islas del
187 I4 Swan Lake Canada
161 H6 Swanley U.K.
126 C5 Swan Reach Australia
187 I4 Swan River Canada
127 I4 Swansea N.S.W. Australia
127 H9 Swansea Tas. Australia
161 D6 Swansea U.K.
161 D6 Swansea Bay U.K.
203 I2 Swans Island U.S.A.
203 G2 Swanton U.S.A.
181 G2 Swartruggens S. Africa
197 F2 Swasey Peak U.S.A.
191 G1 Swastika Canada
144 B2 Swat r. Pak.
Swatow China see Shantou
181 I3 Swaziland country Africa
159 K3 Sweden country Europe
194 B2 Sweet Home U.S.A.
201 C5 Sweetwater TN U.S.A.
199 C5 Sweetwater TX U.S.A.
194 E3 Sweetwater r. U.S.A.
180 D7 Swellendam S. Africa
168 H5 Świdnica Poland
168 G4 Świdwin Poland
168 G4 Świebodzin Poland
169 I4 Świecie Poland
203 H2 Swift r. U.S.A.
187 H4 Swift Current Canada
187 H5 Swiftcurrent Creek r. Canada
186 C2 Swift River Canada
163 D2 Swilly, Lough inlet Ireland
161 F6 Swindon U.K.
163 C4 Swinford Ireland
168 G4 Świnoujście Poland
162 F5 Swinton U.K.
166 I3 Swiss Tectonic Area Sardona tourist site Switz.
166 H3 Switzerland country Europe
163 E4 Swords Ireland
172 E2 Syamozero, Ozero l. Rus. Fed.
172 G2 Syamzha Rus. Fed.
169 N3 Syanno Belarus
172 E2 Syas'stroy Rus. Fed.
172 H3 Syava Rus. Fed.
190 C5 Sycamore U.S.A.
127 I4 Sydney Australia (City Plan 102)
189 H4 Sydney Canada
187 K4 Sydney Lake Canada
189 H4 Sydney Mines Canada
173 F5 Syeverodonets'k Ukr.
165 G2 Syke Germany
172 I2 Syktyvkar Rus. Fed.
201 C5 Sylacauga U.S.A.
158 K3 Sylarna mt. Norway/Sweden
145 G4 Sylhet Bangl.
172 J2 Syloga Rus. Fed.
168 D3 Sylt i. Germany
201 D5 Sylvania GA U.S.A.
202 B4 Sylvania OH U.S.A.
186 G4 Sylvan Lake Canada
201 D6 Sylvester U.S.A.
186 E3 Sylvia, Mount Canada
171 L6 Symi i. Greece
173 E5 Synel'nykove Ukr.
138 C4 Syngyrli, Mys pt Kazakh.
139 J2 Syntas Kazakh.
129 E4 Syowa research stn Antarctica
170 F6 Syracuse Sicily Italy
198 C4 Syracuse KS U.S.A.
203 E3 Syracuse NY U.S.A.
139 F4 Syrdar'ya r. Kazakh.
Syrdar'ya Uzbek. see Sirdaryo
136 G4 Syria country Asia
137 G5 Syrian Desert Asia
171 L6 Syrna i. Greece
171 K6 Syros i. Greece
159 N3 Sysmä Fin.
172 I2 Sysola r. Rus. Fed.
172 I4 Syzran' Rus. Fed.
168 G4 Szczecin Poland
168 H4 Szczecinek Poland
169 J4 Szczytno Poland
169 I7 Szeged Hungary
169 I7 Székesfehérvár Hungary
169 I7 Szekszárd Hungary
169 J7 Szentes Hungary
168 H7 Szentgotthárd Hungary
170 G1 Szigetvár Hungary
169 I7 Szolnok Hungary
168 H7 Szombathely Hungary


## T


153 B3 Taal, Lake Phil.
153 B3 Tabaco Phil.
136 G4 Ţabaqah Syria
124 F2 Tabar Islands P.N.G.
136 E4 Tabarja Lebanon
170 C6 Tabarka Tunisia
140 E3 Ţabas Iran
207 F4 Tabasco state Mex.
141 E4 Tabāsīn Iran
140 C4 Tābask, Kūh-e mt. Iran
210 E4 Tabatinga Col.
153 B2 Tabayoc, Mount Phil.
127 F5 Tabbita Australia
176 B2 Tabelbala Alg.
187 G5 Taber Canada
125 H2 Tabiteuea atoll Kiribati
159 N4 Tabivere Estonia
153 B3 Tablas i. Phil.
153 B3 Tablas Strait Phil.
128 F3 Table Cape N.Z.
180 C6 Table Mountain h. S. Africa
199 E4 Table Rock Reservoir U.S.A.
214 A2 Tabocó r. Brazil
168 G6 Tábor Czech Rep.
178 D4 Tabora Tanz.
139 G4 Taboshar Tajik.
176 B4 Tabou Côte d'Ivoire
140 B2 Tabrīz Iran
123 I3 Tabuaeran atoll Kiribati
148 D1 Tabu He r. China
136 F5 Tabūk Saudi Arabia
127 J2 Tabulam Australia
139 I1 Tabuny Rus. Fed.
125 G3 Tabwemasana, Mount Vanuatu
159 L4 Täby Sweden
206 D4 Tacámbaro Mex.
207 F5 Tacaná, Volcán de vol. Mex.
206 J6 Tacarcuna, Cerro mt. Panama
139 J3 Tacheng China
168 F6 Tachov Czech Rep.
153 C4 Tacloban Phil.
210 D7 Tacna Peru
194 B2 Tacoma U.S.A.
215 F1 Tacuarembó Uruguay
215 G2 Tacuarí r. Uruguay
206 B1 Tacupeto Mex.
213 E4 Tacutu r. Brazil
160 F4 Tadcaster U.K.
176 C2 Tademaït, Plateau du Alg.
125 G4 Tadin New Caledonia
178 E2 Tadjourah Djibouti
136 G4 Tadmur Syria
187 J3 Tadoule Lake Canada
189 G4 Tadoussac Canada
152 E5 Taebaek S. Korea
152 E5 Taebaek-sanmaek mts N. Korea/S. Korea
152 C4 Taedasa-do N. Korea
152 C4 Taedong-gang r. N. Korea
152 C5 Taedong-man b. N. Korea
Taegu S. Korea see Daegu
Taejŏn S. Korea see Daejeon
161 C6 Taf r. U.K.
125 I3 Tafahi i. Tonga
167 F1 Tafalla Spain
176 B4 Tafiré Côte d'Ivoire
212 C3 Tafí Viejo Arg.
140 C3 Tafresh Iran
140 D4 Taft Iran
196 C4 Taft U.S.A.
141 F4 Taftān, Kūh-e mt. Iran
173 F6 Taganrog Rus. Fed.
173 F6 Taganrog, Gulf of Rus. Fed./Ukr.
153 C3 Tagapula i. Phil.
153 B3 Tagaytay City Phil.
153 B4 Tagbilaran Phil.
145 E2 Tagchagpu Ri mt. China
163 E5 Taghmon Ireland
186 C2 Tagish Canada
170 E1 Tagliamento r. Italy
167 I4 Tagma, Col de pass Alg.
153 C4 Tagoloan r. Phil.
153 B4 Tagolo Point Phil.
138 D4 Tagta Turkm.
141 F3 Tagtabazar Turkm.
125 F3 Tagula Island P.N.G.
153 C5 Tagum Phil.
167 B3 Tagus r. Port./Spain alt. Tajo (Spain), alt. Tejo (Portugal)
186 F4 Tahaetkun Mountain Canada
154 B4 Tahan, Gunung mt. Malaysia
176 C2 Tahat, Mont mt. Alg.
146 E1 Tahe China
128 E1 Taheke N.Z.
123 I5 Tahiti i. Fr. Polynesia
141 F4 Tahlab, Dasht-i- plain Pak.
199 E5 Tahlequah U.S.A.
196 B2 Tahoe, Lake U.S.A.
196 B2 Tahoe City U.S.A.
184 H3 Tahoe Lake Canada
199 C5 Tahoka U.S.A.
176 C3 Tahoua Niger
186 D4 Tahtsa Peak Canada
153 C6 Tahuna Indon.
176 B4 Taï, Parc National de nat. park Côte d'Ivoire
149 □ Tai A Chau Hong Kong China
152 B3 Tai'an China
148 E2 Tai'an China
148 C3 Taibai Shan mt. China
152 A5 Taibo Ding h. China
T'aichung Taiwan see Taizhong
128 C6 Taieri r. N.Z.
148 D2 Taigu China
148 D2 Taihang Shan mts China
128 E3 Taihape N.Z.
148 E3 Taihe Anhui China
149 E5 Taihe Jiangxi China
149 E4 Taihu China
146 E3 Tai Hu l. China
149 C5 Taijiang China
148 E3 Taikang China
Tai Lam Chung Res. China see
149 □ Tai Lam Chung Shui Tong
Tai Lam Chung Shui Tong resr Hong Kong China
126 C5 Tailem Bend Australia
Tai Long Bay China see Tai Long Wan
149 □ Tai Long Wan b. Hong Kong China
149 F5 Tailuge Taiwan
141 F3 Taimani reg. Afgh.
149 □ Tai Mo Shan h. Hong Kong China
149 F6 Tainan Taiwan
171 J6 Tainaro, Akrotirio pt Greece
149 E5 Taining China
149 □ Tai O Hong Kong China
214 D1 Taiobeiras Brazil
149 F5 T'aipei Taiwan
149 D6 Taiping China
155 B2 Taiping Malaysia
152 B1 Taipingchuan China
148 A2 Taipingpu China
149 □ Tai Po Hong Kong China
149 □ Tai Po Hoi b. Hong Kong China see Tolo Harbour
151 C7 Taisha Japan
149 D6 Taishan China
149 F5 Taishun China
Tai Siu Mo To is Hong Kong China see Brothers, The
164 C5 Taissy France
212 B7 Taitao, Península de pen. Chile
128 D5 Taitu N.Z.
149 F6 T'aitung Taiwan
158 O2 Taivalkoski Fin.
158 N1 Taivaskero h. Fin.
149 F6 Taiwan country Asia
Taiwan Shan mts Taiwan see Zhongyang Shanmo
149 F5 Taiwan Strait China/Taiwan
148 F3 Taixing China
139 G1 Taiynsha Kazakh.
148 D2 Taiyuan China
149 E5 Taiyue Shan mts China
149 F5 Taizhong Taiwan
148 F3 Taizhou Jiangsu China
149 F4 Taizhou Zhejiang China
149 F4 Taizhou Wan b. China
152 C3 Taizi He r. China
142 B7 Ta'izz Yemen
170 C7 Tajerouine Tunisia
139 G5 Tajikistan country Asia
144 B4 Tajjal Pak.
144 D4 Taj Mahal tourist site India
167 C3 Tajo r. Spain alt. Tejo (Portugal), conv. Tagus
207 G5 Tajumulco, Volcán de vol. Guat.
154 A1 Tak Thai.
140 B2 Takāb Iran
151 C7 Takahashi Japan
128 D4 Takaka N.Z.
144 D5 Takal India
151 D7 Takamatsu Japan
151 E6 Takaoka Japan
128 F4 Takapau N.Z.
128 E2 Takapuna N.Z.
151 F6 Takasaki Japan
180 F2 Takatokwane Botswana
180 D1 Takatshwaane Botswana
151 C8 Takatsuki-yama mt. Japan
151 E6 Takayama Japan
154 B4 Tak Bai Thai.
139 G4 Takelī Tajik.
151 B8 Takeo Japan
151 B9 Take-shima i. Japan
Take-shima i. N. Pacific Ocean see Liancourt Rocks
140 C2 Takestān Iran
151 B8 Taketa Japan
154 C3 Takêv Cambodia
137 J7 Takhādīd well Iraq
154 C3 Ta Khmau Cambodia
139 F4 Takhtabrod Kazakh.
141 G4 Takhtah Pul Afgh.
Takhtakupyr Uzbek. see Taxtako'pir
137 L5 Takht Apān, Kūh-e mt. Iran
140 C2 Takht-e Soleymān mt. Iran
137 K3 Takht-e Soleymān tourist site Iran
144 B2 Takht-i-Bahi tourist site Pak.
144 B3 Takht-i-Sulaiman mt. Pak.
Takht-i-Suleiman mt. Iran see Takht-e Soleymān
150 G3 Takikawa Japan
150 H2 Takinoue Japan
128 A6 Takitimu Mountains N.Z.
186 D3 Takla Lake Canada
186 D3 Takla Landing Canada
135 G3 Taklimakan Desert China
Taklimakan Shamo des. China see Taklimakan Desert
139 G5 Takob Tajik.
145 H3 Takpa Shiri mt. China
186 C3 Taku r. Canada
154 A4 Takua Pa Thai.
176 C4 Takum Nigeria
125 F2 Takuu Islands atoll P.N.G.
215 F2 Tala Uruguay
141 F4 Talab r. Iran/Pak.
172 D4 Talachyn Belarus
143 B4 Talaimannar Sri Lanka
144 D5 Talaja India
215 C1 Talampaya, Parque Nacional nat. park Arg.
145 H4 Talap India
210 B4 Talara Peru
Talar-i-Band mts Pak. see Makran Coast Range
139 G4 Talas r. Kazakh./Kyrg.
139 H4 Talas Kyrg.
139 G4 Talas Ala-Too mts Kyrg.
147 E6 Talaud, Kepulauan is Indon.
167 D3 Talavera de la Reina Spain
133 Q3 Talaya Rus. Fed.
153 C5 Talayan Phil.
185 K2 Talbot Inlet Canada
127 H4 Talbragar r. Australia
215 B2 Talca Chile
215 B3 Talcahuano Chile
143 D1 Talcher India
138 D4 Taldyk Uzbek.
139 I3 Taldykorgan Kazakh.
139 I3 Taldykorganskaya Oblast' Kazakh.
139 G2 Taldysay Kazakh.
139 I4 Taldy-Suu Kyrg.
137 L5 Taleh Zang Iran
140 C2 Tālesh Iran
139 I4 Talgar Kazakh.
126 D6 Talgarth U.K.
176 B1 Talia Australia
147 E7 Taliabu i. Indon.
153 C4 Talibon Phil.
143 B2 Talikota India
137 I1 T'alin Armenia
143 A3 Taliparamba India
153 B4 Talisay Phil.
153 C4 Talisayan Phil.
137 L2 Taliş Dağları mts Azer./Iran
172 H3 Talitsa Rus. Fed.
155 E4 Taliwang Indon.
201 C5 Talladega U.S.A.
137 I3 Tall 'Afar Iraq
201 C6 Tallahassee U.S.A.
127 G6 Tallangatta Australia
201 C5 Tallassee U.S.A.
137 H3 Tall Baydar Syria
138 F5 Tallimarjon Uzbek.
159 N4 Tallinn Estonia
136 F4 Tall Kalakh Syria
137 I3 Tall Kayf Iraq
137 I3 Tall Küjik Syria
163 C5 Tallow Ireland
199 F5 Tallulah U.S.A.
137 I3 Tall 'Uwaynāt Iraq
166 D3 Talmont-St-Hilaire France
173 D5 Tal'ne Ukr.
177 F3 Talodi Sudan
189 G2 Talon, Lac l. Canada
141 H2 Tāloqān Afgh.
138 B2 Talovaya Kazakh.
173 G5 Talovaya Rus. Fed.
185 I3 Taloyoak Canada
144 C2 Tal Pass Pak.
159 M4 Talsi Latvia
141 F4 Tal Sīyāh Iran
212 B3 Taltal Chile
187 G2 Taltson r. Canada
140 B3 Talvār, Rūdkhāneh-ye r. Iran
158 M1 Talvik Norway
127 H2 Talwood Australia
127 F3 Talyawalka r. Australia
172 G3 Taly Rus. Fed.
126 E4 Talyawalka r. Australia
190 A4 Tama U.S.A.
213 B2 Tamalameque Col.
176 B4 Tamale Ghana
213 A3 Tamana mt. Col.
125 H2 Tamana i. Kiribati
151 B8 Tamano Japan
176 C2 Tamanrasset Alg.
145 H4 Tamanthi Myanmar
203 F4 Tamaqua U.S.A.
161 C7 Tamar r. U.K.
213 B3 Tamar, Alto de mt. Col.
181 G1 Tamasane Botswana
207 E3 Tamaulipas state Mex.
206 C2 Tamazula Mex.
207 E4 Tamazulápam Mex.
207 E3 Tamazunchale Mex.
178 D3 Tambach Kenya
176 A3 Tambacounda Senegal
145 F4 Tamba Kosi r. Nepal
155 C2 Tambelan, Kepulauan is Indon.
153 A5 Tambisan Sabah Malaysia
127 G6 Tambo r. Australia
155 E4 Tambora, Gunung vol. Indon.
127 G6 Tamboritha mt. Australia
172 G4 Tambov Rus. Fed.
172 G4 Tambovskaya Oblast' admin. div. Rus. Fed.
167 B1 Tambre r. Spain
153 A5 Tambulanan, Bukit h. Sabah Malaysia
177 E4 Tambura South Sudan
153 A5 Tambuyukon, Gunung mt. Sabah Malaysia
176 A3 Tâmchekket Mauritania
138 D2 Tamdy Kazakh.
Tamdybulak Uzbek. see Tomdibuloq
213 C3 Tame Col.
167 C2 Tâmega r. Port.
145 H4 Tamenglong India
170 B7 Tamerza Tunisia
145 D5 Tamia India
207 E3 Tamiahua Mex.
207 E3 Tamiahua, Laguna de lag. Mex.
154 A4 Tamiang, Ujung pt Indon.
143 B4 Tamil Nadu state India
172 F1 Tamitsa Rus. Fed.
136 C7 Ţāmīyah Egypt
138 E2 Tamkamys Kazakh.
145 F4 Tamkuhi India
154 D2 Tam Ky Vietnam
201 D7 Tampa U.S.A.
201 D7 Tampa Bay U.S.A.
159 M3 Tampere Fin.
207 E3 Tampico Mex.
154 □ Tampines Sing.
148 B1 Tamsag Bulag China
146 D2 Tamsagbulag Mongolia
168 F7 Tamsweg Austria
145 H4 Tamu Myanmar
207 E3 Tamuín Mex.
145 E3 Tamur r. Nepal
127 I3 Tamworth Australia
161 F5 Tamworth U.K.
139 I2 Tan Kazakh.
178 E4 Tana r. Kenya
158 O1 Tana r. Fin./Norway
151 D8 Tanabe Japan
158 O1 Tana Bru Norway
158 O1 Tanafjorden inlet Norway
155 C4 Tanah, Tanjung pt Indon.
178 D2 T'ana Hāyk' Eth.
155 E3 Tanahgrogot Indon.
147 E7 Tanahjampea i. Indon.
155 A3 Tanahmasa i. Indon.
155 A6 Tanahmerah Indon.
154 A5 Tanah Merah Malaysia
154 B4 Tanah Rata Malaysia
124 D3 Tanami Desert Australia
154 C3 Tân An Vietnam
184 C3 Tanana U.S.A.
170 C2 Tanaro r. Italy
153 C4 Tanauan Phil.
148 E1 Tancheng China
152 E3 Tanch'ŏn N. Korea
206 D4 Tancítaro, Cerro de mt. Mex.
176 B4 Tanda Côte d'Ivoire
145 E4 Tanda India
153 C4 Tandag Phil.
171 L2 Ţăndărei Romania
153 A5 Tandek Sabah Malaysia
144 D2 Tandi India
215 E3 Tandil Arg.
215 E3 Tandil, Sierra del hills Arg.
144 B4 Tando Adam Pak.
144 B4 Tando Bago Pak.
126 E4 Tandou Lake imp. l. Australia
163 E3 Tandragee U.K.
143 B2 Tandur India
128 F3 Taneatua N.Z.
151 B9 Tanega-shima i. Japan
154 A1 Tanen Taunggyi mts Thai.
202 E5 Taneytown U.S.A.
176 B2 Tanezrouft reg. Alg./Mali
178 D4 Tanga Tanz.
128 E2 Tangaehe N.Z.
145 G4 Tangail Bangl.
125 F2 Tanga Islands P.N.G.
143 C5 Tangalla Sri Lanka
178 C4 Tanganyika, Lake Africa
143 B4 Tangasseri India
148 D3 Tangdan China
140 D4 Tang-e Kalleh Iran
138 C5 Tangeli Iran
Tanger Morocco see Tangier
155 C4 Tangerang Indon.
165 J2 Tangerhütte Germany
165 J2 Tangermünde Germany
140 E4 Tang-e Sarkheh Iran
145 G2 Tanggor China
148 B3 Tanggulashan China
145 H2 Tanggula Shan mts China
145 G2 Tanggula Shankou pass China
148 D3 Tanghe China
144 B2 Tangi Pak.
176 B1 Tangier Morocco
203 E6 Tangier Island U.S.A.
145 G4 Tangla India
154 □ Tanglin Sing.
145 H3 Tangmai China
140 D2 Tangrāh Iran
145 F3 Tangra Yumco salt l. China
148 F2 Tangshan China
153 B4 Tangub Phil.
176 C3 Tanguiéta Benin
150 A1 Tangwang He r. China
148 E3 Tangyin China
150 A1 Tangyuan China
148 F3 Tanhua Fin.
158 N2 Tanhua Fin.
154 C2 Tani Cambodia
145 H3 Taniantaweng Shan mts China
147 F7 Tanimbar, Kepulauan is Indon.
153 B4 Tanjay Phil.
154 A5 Tanjungbalai Indon.
Tanjungkarang-Telukbetung Indon. see Bandar Lampung
155 C3 Tanjungpandan Indon.
155 B2 Tanjungpinang Indon.
154 A5 Tanjungpura Indon.
155 E2 Tanjungredeb Indon.
155 E2 Tanjungselor Indon.
144 B2 Tank Pak.
144 D2 Tanktse India
Tankuhi India see Tamkuhi
180 C6 Tankwa-Karoo National Park S. Africa
125 G3 Tanna i. Vanuatu
162 F4 Tannadice U.K.
159 K3 Tännäs Sweden
146 B1 Tannu-Ola, Khrebet mts Rus. Fed.
153 B4 Tañon Strait Phil.
144 B4 Tanot India
176 C3 Tanout Niger
145 G4 Tansen Nepal
139 J3 Tansyk Kazakh.
177 F1 Ţanţā Egypt
176 A2 Tan-Tan Morocco
126 D6 Tantanoola Australia
207 E3 Tantoyuca Mex.
143 C2 Tanuku India
159 J4 Tanumshede Sweden
126 C5 Tanunda Australia
178 D4 Tanzania country Africa
153 A5 Tao, Ko i. Thai.
152 B1 Tao'er He r. China
148 B3 Tao He r. China
149 D4 Taojiang China
152 B1 Taonan China
216 G6 Taongi atoll Marshall Is
170 F6 Taormina Sicily Italy
195 F4 Taos U.S.A.
176 B2 Taoudenni Mali
176 B1 Taourirt Morocco
149 E5 Taoxi China
149 D4 Taoyuan China
149 F5 T'aoyüan Taiwan
159 N4 Tapa Estonia
207 F5 Tapachula Mex.
211 G4 Tapajós r. Brazil
155 A2 Tapaktuan Indon.
215 E3 Tapalqué Arg.
207 F4 Tapanatepec Mex.
155 A3 Tapanuli, Teluk b. Indon.
210 F5 Tapauá Brazil
210 E5 Tapauá r. Brazil
176 B4 Tapeta Liberia
154 A3 Ta Pi, Mae Nam r. Thai.
153 B5 Tapiantana i. Phil.
190 C2 Tapiola U.S.A.
154 B4 Tapis, Gunung mt. Malaysia
145 F4 Taplejung Nepal
149 □ Tap Mun Chau i. Hong Kong China
202 E6 Tappahannock U.S.A.
202 C4 Tappan Lake U.S.A.
140 C3 Tappeh, Kūh-e h. Iran
144 C5 Tapti r. India
128 D4 Tapuaenuku mt. N.Z.
153 B5 Tapul Phil.
153 B5 Tapul Group is Phil.
213 D5 Tapurucuara Brazil
137 J4 Ţaqţaq Iraq
214 B1 Taquaral, Serra do hills Brazil
Taquari Brazil see Alto Taquarí
211 G7 Taquari r. Brazil
214 A2 Taquari, Pantanal do marsh Brazil
214 A2 Taquari, Serra do hills Brazil
214 C3 Taquaritinga Brazil
214 A2 Taquaruçu r. Brazil
163 D5 Tar r. Ireland
127 I1 Tara Australia
163 E4 Tara, Hill of Ireland
176 D4 Taraba r. Nigeria
210 F7 Tarabuco Bol.
Tarābulus Libya see Tripoli
213 C4 Taracua Brazil
144 E4 Tarahuwan India
145 G4 Tarai reg. India
155 E2 Tarakan Indon.
155 A6 Tarakan i. Indon.
136 C1 Taraklı Turkey
127 H5 Taralga Australia
169 I3 Taran, Mys pt Rus. Fed.
127 H4 Tarana Australia
144 D5 Tarana India
144 D4 Taranagar India
128 E3 Taranaki, Mount vol. N.Z.
167 E2 Tarancón Spain
162 A3 Taransay i. U.K.
170 G4 Taranto Italy
170 G4 Taranto, Golfo di g. Italy
210 C5 Tarapoto Peru
128 F4 Tararua Range mts N.Z.
169 O6 Tarashcha Ukr.
210 D5 Tarauacá Brazil
210 E5 Tarauacá r. Brazil
123 G3 Tarawa atoll Kiribati
128 F3 Tarawera N.Z.
128 F3 Tarawera, Mount vol. N.Z.
139 G4 Taraz Kazakh.
167 F2 Tarazona Spain
167 F3 Tarazona de la Mancha Spain
139 J3 Tarbagatay Kazakh.
139 J3 Tarbagatay, Khrebet mts Kazakh.
162 E3 Tarbat Ness pt U.K.
144 C2 Tarbela Dam Pak.
163 B5 Tarbert Ireland
162 B3 Tarbert Scotland U.K.
162 C5 Tarbert Scotland U.K.
166 E5 Tarbes France
201 E5 Tarboro U.S.A.
126 A3 Tarcoola Australia
127 G3 Tarcoon Australia
127 I3 Tarcutta Australia
146 F2 Tardoki-Yangi, Gora mt. Rus. Fed.
127 J3 Taree Australia
126 E3 Tarella Australia
132 K2 Tareya Rus. Fed.
140 C6 Ţarfā', Baţn aţ depr. Saudi Arabia
194 E2 Targhee Pass U.S.A.
171 K2 Târgovişte Romania
171 J2 Târgu Jiu Romania
169 L7 Târgu Mureş Romania
169 M7 Târgu Neamţ Romania
169 M7 Târgu Secuiesc Romania
140 B3 Tarhān Iran
177 D1 Tarhūnah Libya
148 C2 Tarian Gol China
140 D5 Tarif U.A.E.
167 D4 Tarifa Spain
167 D4 Tarifa, Punta de pt Spain
210 F8 Tarija Bol.
147 F7 Tariku r. Indon.
142 C6 Tarīm Yemen
135 G3 Tarim Basin China
139 J4 Tarim He r. China
Tarim Pendi basin China see Tarim Basin
141 G3 Tarīn Kōţ Afgh.
147 F7 Taritatu r. Indon.
137 J4 Tarjil Iraq
181 F6 Tarka r. S. Africa
181 G6 Tarkastad S. Africa
198 E3 Tarkio U.S.A.
132 I3 Tarko-Sale Rus. Fed.
176 B4 Tarkwa Ghana
153 B3 Tarlac Phil.
146 B3 Tarlag China
165 H1 Tarmstedt Germany
166 F4 Tarn r. France
158 K2 Tärnaby Sweden
141 G3 Tarnak Rōd r. Afgh.
169 L7 Târnăveni Romania
169 J5 Tarnobrzeg Poland
172 G2 Tarnogskiy Gorodok Rus. Fed.
169 J5 Tarnów Poland
145 E3 Taro Co salt l. China
140 D4 Ţārom Iran
176 B1 Taroudannt Morocco
126 D6 Tarpeena Australia
201 E7 Tarpum Bay Bahamas
140 C3 Ţarq Iran
146 E2 Tarqi China
170 D3 Tarquinia Italy
176 □ Tarrafal Cape Verde
167 G2 Tarragona Spain
158 L2 Tårrajaur Sweden
127 G9 Tarraleah Australia
127 G4 Tarran Hills Australia
128 B6 Tarras N.Z.
167 G2 Tàrrega Spain
136 E3 Tarsus Turkey
138 C4 Tarta Turkm.
212 D2 Tartagal Arg.
137 K1 Tärtär Azer.
137 K1 Tärtär r. Azer.
166 D5 Tartas France
159 N4 Tartu Estonia
136 E4 Ţarţūs Syria
214 E2 Tarumirim Brazil
173 H6 Tarumovka Rus. Fed.
154 A4 Tarutao, Ko i. Thai.
154 A5 Tarutung Indon.
170 E1 Tarvisio Italy
140 E4 Tarz Iran
139 H3 Tasaral Kazakh.
138 F3 Tasbuget Kazakh.
188 E4 Taschereau Canada
143 A2 Tasgaon India
152 A3 Tashan China
Tashigang Bhutan see Trashigang
144 C1 Tashikuzuke Shan mts China
137 J1 Tashir Armenia
140 D4 Tashk, Daryācheh-ye l. Iran
Tashkepri Turkm. see Daşköpri
139 H4 Tash-Kömür Kyrg.
138 C2 Tashla Rus. Fed.
189 F2 Tasialujjuaq, Lac l. Canada
188 F2 Tasiat, Lac l. Canada
155 C4 Tasikmalaya Indon.
189 G2 Tasiujaq Canada
138 B2 Taskala Kazakh.
139 J3 Taskesken Kazakh.
136 E1 Taşköprü Turkey
137 I2 Taşlıçay Turkey
216 F8 Tasman Abyssal Plain sea feature Australia
218 O7 Tasman Basin sea feature Tasman Sea
128 D4 Tasman Bay N.Z.
127 G9 Tasman Head Australia
127 F9 Tasmania state Australia
128 D4 Tasman Mountains N.Z.
127 H9 Tasman Peninsula Australia
125 F5 Tasman Sea Pacific Ocean
136 F1 Taşova Turkey
196 B3 Tassajara Hot Springs U.S.A.
176 C2 Tassili n'Ajjer, Parc National de nat. park Alg.
139 G3 Tasty Kazakh.
138 F2 Tasty-Taldy Kazakh.
137 J2 Tasūj Iran
133 M3 Tas-Yuryakh Rus. Fed.
169 I7 Tatabánya Hungary
147 E7 Tatamailau, Foho mt. East Timor
173 D6 Tatarbunary Ukr.
132 I4 Tatarsk Rus. Fed.
138 C2 Tatarskaya Kargala Rus. Fed.
146 G1 Tatarskiy Proliv str. Rus. Fed.
172 I4 Tatarstan, Respublika aut. rep. Rus. Fed.
140 B2 Tatavi r. Iran
151 F7 Tateyama Japan
151 E6 Tate-yama vol. Japan
186 F2 Tathlina Lake Canada
142 B5 Tathlith, Wādī watercourse Saudi Arabia
127 H6 Tathra Australia
187 J2 Tatinnai Lake Canada
173 H5 Tatishchevo Rus. Fed.
194 A1 Tatla Lake Canada
186 D3 Tatlatui Provincial Park Canada
Tat Mailau, Gunung mt. East Timor see Tatamailau, Foho
127 G6 Tatong Australia
Tatra Mountains reg. Poland see Tatry
169 I6 Tatry reg. Poland
186 B3 Tatshenshini r. Canada
173 G5 Tatsinskaya Rus. Fed.
151 D7 Tatsuno Japan
139 H4 Tatty Kazakh.
214 C3 Tatuí Brazil
186 E4 Tatuk Mountain Canada
199 C5 Tatum U.S.A.
126 F6 Tatura Australia
137 I2 Tatvan Turkey
159 I4 Tau Norway
211 J5 Tauá Brazil
214 D3 Taubaté Brazil
165 H5 Tauber r. Germany
165 H5 Tauberbischofsheim Germany
165 K3 Taucha Germany
165 H4 Taufstein h. Germany
139 H3 Taukum, Peski des. Kazakh.
180 F3 Taung S. Africa
147 B4 Taunggyi Myanmar
147 B5 Taung-ngu Myanmar
154 A2 Taungnyo Range mts Myanmar
161 D6 Taunton U.K.
203 H4 Taunton U.S.A.
165 F4 Taunus hills Germany
128 F3 Taupo N.Z.
128 E3 Taupo, Lake N.Z.
159 M5 Tauragė Lith.
128 F2 Tauranga N.Z.
170 G5 Taurianova Italy
128 D1 Tauroa Point N.Z.
136 D3 Taurus Mountains Turkey
138 B3 Taushyk Kazakh.
Tauu Islands P.N.G. see Takuu Islands
136 B3 Tavas Turkey
161 I5 Taverham U.K.

167 C4 Tavira Port.
161 C7 Tavistock U.K.
154 A2 Tavoy Myanmar
154 A2 Tavoy Point Myanmar
150 B3 Tavrichanka Rus. Fed.
136 B2 Tavşanlı Turkey
161 C6 Taw r. U.K.
153 A5 Tawai, Bukit mt. Sabah Malaysia
139 J5 Tawakkul China
191 F3 Tawas Bay U.S.A.
191 F3 Tawas City U.S.A.
155 E2 Tawau Sabah Malaysia
161 D6 Tawe r. U.K.
144 C2 Tawi r. India
153 A5 Tawi-Tawi i. Phil.
207 E4 Taxco Mex.
138 D4 Taxiatosh Uzbek.
144 C2 Taxila tourist site Pak.
139 H5 Taxkorgan China
138 E4 Taxtako'pir Uzbek.
186 C2 Tay r. Canada
162 E4 Tay r. U.K.
162 E4 Tay, Firth of est. U.K.
162 D4 Tay, Loch l. U.K.
153 B3 Tayabas Bay Phil.
141 F3 Tāybād Iran
158 P1 Taybola Rus. Fed.
162 C5 Tayinloan U.K.
186 E3 Taylor Canada
197 G4 Taylor AZ U.S.A.
191 F4 Taylor MI U.S.A.
190 B6 Taylor MO U.S.A.
198 D3 Taylor NE U.S.A.
199 D6 Taylor TX U.S.A.
203 E5 Taylors Island U.S.A.
200 B4 Taylorville U.S.A.
142 A4 Taymā' Saudi Arabia
133 K3 Taymura r. Rus. Fed.
133 L2 Taymyr, Ozero l. Rus. Fed.
Taymyr, Poluostrov pen. Rus. Fed. see Taymyr Peninsula
133 K2 Taymyr Peninsula Rus. Fed.
139 G1 Tayncha Kazakh.
154 C3 Tây Ninh Vietnam
206 C2 Tayoltita Mex.
138 B2 Taypak Kazakh.
138 C2 Taysoygan, Peski des. Kazakh.
153 A4 Taytay Phil.
153 B3 Taytay Phil.
153 A4 Taytay Bay Phil.
133 J2 Taz r. Rus. Fed.
176 B1 Taza Morocco
137 J4 Tāza Khurmātū Iraq
137 K2 Tazeh Kand Azer.
202 B6 Tazewell TN U.S.A.
202 C6 Tazewell VA U.S.A.
187 H2 Tazin r. Canada
187 H3 Tazin Lake Canada
177 E2 Tāzirbū Libya
167 I4 Tazmalt Alg.
132 I3 Tazovskaya Guba sea chan. Rus. Fed.
Tbilisi Georgia see T'bilisi
173 H7 T'bilisi Georgia
173 G6 Tbilisskaya Rus. Fed.
178 B4 Tchibanga Gabon
177 D2 Tchigaï, Plateau du Niger
177 D4 Tcholliré Cameroon
169 I3 Tczew Poland
206 C3 Teacapán Mex.
128 A6 Te Anau N.Z.
128 A6 Te Anau, Lake N.Z.
207 F4 Teapa Mex.
128 G2 Te Araroa N.Z.
128 E2 Te Aroha N.Z.
128 E3 Te Awamutu N.Z.
160 E3 Tebay U.K.
187 J2 Tebesjuak Lake Canada
176 C1 Tébessa Alg.
170 B7 Tébessa, Monts de mts Alg.
212 E3 Tebicuary r. Para.
155 A2 Tebingtinggi Indon.
155 B3 Tebingtinggi Indon.
170 C6 Tébourba Tunisia
170 C6 Téboursouk Tunisia
173 H7 T'ebulos Mta Georgia/Rus. Fed.
176 B4 Techiman Ghana
212 B6 Tecka Arg.
164 F2 Tecklenburger Land reg. Germany
207 E3 Tecolutla Mex.
206 D4 Tecomán Mex.
196 D4 Tecopa U.S.A.
206 B1 Tecoripa Mex.
206 D4 Técpan Mex.
169 M7 Tecuci Romania
191 F5 Tecumseh U.S.A.
Tedzhen Turkm. see Tejen
Tedzhen r. Turkm. see Tejen
141 F2 Tedzhenstroy Turkm.
197 H3 Teec Nos Pos U.S.A.
135 H1 Teeli Rus. Fed.
160 F3 Tees r. U.K.
160 E3 Teesdale val. U.K.
210 E4 Tefé r. Brazil
136 B3 Tefenni Turkey
155 C4 Tegal Indon.
165 L2 Tegel airport Germany
206 H5 Tegucigalpa Hond.
176 C3 Teguidda-n-Tessoumt Niger
196 C4 Tehachapi U.S.A.
195 C5 Tehachapi Mountains U.S.A.
196 C4 Tehachapi Pass U.S.A.
187 J2 Tehek Lake Canada
Teheran Iran see Tehrān
176 B4 Téhini Côte d'Ivoire
140 C3 Tehrān Iran
(City Plan 106)
207 E4 Tehuacán Mex.
207 F5 Tehuantepec, Gulf of Mex.
207 F4 Tehuantepec, Istmo de isth. Mex.
217 M5 Tehuantepec Ridge sea feature N. Pacific Ocean
207 E4 Tehuitzingo Mex.
161 C5 Teifi r. U.K.
161 D7 Teign r. U.K.
161 D7 Teignmouth U.K.
138 E5 Tejen Turkm.
141 F2 Tejen r. Turkm.
167 B3 Tejo r. Port.
alt. Tajo (Spain),
conv. Tagus
196 C4 Tejon Pass U.S.A.
206 D4 Tejupan, Punta pt Mex.
128 D1 Te Kao N.Z.
128 C5 Tekapo, Lake N.Z.
145 F4 Tekari India
207 G3 Tekax Mex.
139 H1 Teke, Ozero salt l. Kazakh.
138 E2 Tekeli Aktyubinskaya Oblast' Kazakh.
139 I3 Tekeli Almatinskaya Oblast' Kazakh.
136 E5 Tekes China
139 J4 Tekes Kazakh.
139 J3 Tekes He r. China
178 D2 Tekezē Wenz r. Eritrea/Eth.
144 E1 Tekiliktag mt. China
136 A1 Tekirdağ Turkey
143 D2 Tekkali India
137 H2 Tekman Turkey
145 H5 Teknaf Bangl.
190 E4 Tekonsha U.S.A.
128 E3 Te Kuiti N.Z.
143 C1 Tel r. India
206 H5 Tela Hond.
173 H7 Telavi Georgia
136 E5 Tel Aviv-Yafo Israel
168 G6 Telč Czech Rep.
207 G3 Telchac Puerto Mex.
186 C3 Telegraph Creek Canada
214 B4 Telêmaco Borba Brazil
215 D3 Telén Arg.
155 E2 Telen r. Indon.
171 K2 Teleorman r. Romania
196 D3 Telescope Peak U.S.A.
211 G5 Teles Pires r. Brazil
161 E5 Telford U.K.
165 F3 Telgte Germany
136 E5 Tel Hazor tourist site Israel
206 H5 Telica Nicaragua
176 A3 Télimélé Guinea
186 D4 Telkwa Canada
184 B3 Teller U.S.A.
164 D4 Tellin Belgium
137 K6 Telloh Iraq
207 E4 Teloloapán Mex.
215 C4 Telsen Arg.
159 M5 Telšiai Lith.
165 L2 Teltow Germany
Teluk Anson Malaysia see Teluk Intan
155 A2 Telukdalam Indon.
155 B2 Teluk Intan Malaysia
191 H2 Temagami Canada
191 G2 Temagami Lake Canada
155 D4 Temanggung Indon.
207 G3 Temax Mex.
181 H2 Temba S. Africa
133 K3 Tembenchi r. Rus. Fed.
155 B3 Tembilahan Indon.
181 H3 Tembisa S. Africa
178 B4 Tembo Aluma Angola
161 E5 Teme r. U.K.
196 D5 Temecula U.S.A.
136 D2 Temelli Turkey
155 B2 Temerluh Malaysia
137 L5 Temileh Iran
138 D2 Temir Kazakh.
139 G4 Temir Kazakh.
139 H2 Temirlan Kazakh.
139 H2 Temirtau Kazakh.
191 H2 Témiscaming Canada
Témiscaming Canada see Témiscaming
191 H2 Témiscamingue, Lac l. Canada
189 G4 Témiscouata, Lac l. Canada
127 F8 Temma Australia
158 N2 Temmes Fin.
172 G4 Temnikov Rus. Fed.
125 G5 Temora Australia
206 C1 Temósachic Mex.
197 G5 Tempe U.S.A.
165 L2 Tempelhof airport Germany
170 C4 Tempio Pausania Sardinia Italy
190 E3 Temple MI U.S.A.
199 D6 Temple TX U.S.A.
161 C5 Temple Bar U.K.
163 D5 Templemore Ireland
153 A4 Templer Bank sea feature Phil.
160 E3 Temple Sowerby U.K.
165 L1 Templin Germany
207 E3 Tempoal Mex.
173 F6 Temryuk Rus. Fed.
215 B3 Temuco Chile
128 C6 Temuka N.Z.
210 C4 Tena Ecuador
196 D1 Tenabo, Mount U.S.A.
143 C2 Tenali India
207 E4 Tenancingo Mex.
154 A2 Tenasserim Myanmar
154 A2 Tenasserim r. Myanmar
161 E5 Tenbury Wells U.K.
161 C6 Tenby U.K.
191 F2 Tenby Bay Canada
178 E2 Tendaho Eth.
166 H4 Tende France
135 H6 Ten Degree Channel India
150 G5 Tendō Japan
137 I2 Tendürek Dağı mt. Turkey
176 B3 Ténenkou Mali
176 D3 Ténéré reg. Niger
176 D3 Ténéré, Erg du des. Niger
176 D2 Ténéré du Tafassâsset des. Niger
176 A2 Tenerife i. Canary Is
167 G4 Ténès Alg.
155 E4 Tengah, Kepulauan is Indon.
138 C4 Tenge Kazakh.
154 □ Tengeh Reservoir Sing.
148 B2 Tengger Shamo des. China
154 B4 Tenggul i. Malaysia
139 G2 Tengiz, Ozero salt l. Kazakh.
176 B3 Tengréla Côte d'Ivoire
149 D6 Tengxian China
148 E3 Tengzhou China
138 F1 Teniz, Ozero l. Kazakh.
179 C5 Tenke Dem. Rep. Congo
133 P2 Tenkeli Rus. Fed.
176 B3 Tenkodogo Burkina Faso
124 D3 Tennant Creek Australia
201 C5 Tennessee r. U.S.A.
202 B6 Tennessee state U.S.A.
195 F4 Tennessee Pass U.S.A.
158 L1 Tennevoll Norway
215 B2 Teno r. Chile
158 O1 Tenojoki r. Fin./Norway
207 G4 Tenosique Mex.
194 F2 Ten Sleep U.S.A.
124 C2 Tenteno Indon.
161 H6 Tenterden U.K.
127 J2 Tenterfield Australia
201 D7 Ten Thousand Islands U.S.A.
167 C3 Tentudia mt. Spain
213 B3 Teodoro Sampaio Brazil
214 E2 Teófilo Otoni Brazil
207 F4 Teopisca Mex.
207 E4 Teotihuacán tourist site Mex.
195 E6 Tepache Mex.
128 D1 Te Paki N.Z.
206 D4 Tepalcatepec Mex.
206 D3 Tepatitlán Mex.
137 H3 Tepe Turkey
137 I3 Tepe Gawra tourist site Iraq
206 C2 Tepehuanes Mex.
207 E4 Tepeji Mex.
171 I4 Tepelenë Albania
207 E4 Tepelmeme de Morelos Mex.
165 K5 Tepelská vrchovina hills Czech Rep.
213 E4 Tepequem, Serra mts Brazil
206 C3 Tepic Mex.
128 C5 Te Pirita N.Z.
168 F5 Teplice Czech Rep.
173 G5 Teplogorka Rus. Fed.
172 F4 Teploye Rus. Fed.
128 F2 Te Puke N.Z.
207 F4 Tequisistlán Mex.
207 E3 Tequisquiapán Mex.
167 H1 Ter r. Spain
123 I3 Teraina i. Kiribati
144 D2 Teram Kangri mt. China
170 E3 Teramo Italy
126 E7 Terang Australia
164 F2 Ter Apel Neth.
173 F4 Terbuny Rus. Fed.
137 H2 Tercan Turkey
156 A6 Terceira i. Azores
169 L6 Terebovlya Ukr.
173 H7 Terek Rus. Fed.
173 H7 Terek r. Rus. Fed.
139 G2 Terekty Karagandinskaya Oblast' Kazakh.
139 K2 Terekty Vostochnyy Kazakhstan Kazakh.
172 I4 Teren'ga Rus. Fed.
214 A3 Terenos Brazil
138 F3 Terenozek Kazakh.
138 D2 Terensay Rus. Fed.
213 C2 Terepaima, Parque Nacional nat. park Venez.
172 H4 Tereshka r. Rus. Fed.
211 J5 Teresina Brazil
214 D3 Teresópolis Brazil
164 B5 Tergnier France
139 F2 Terisakkan r. Kazakh.
136 F1 Terme Turkey
Termez Uzbek. see Termiz
170 E6 Termini Imerese Sicily Italy
207 G4 Términos, Laguna de lag. Mex.
139 F5 Termiz Uzbek.
170 F4 Termoli Italy
161 F5 Tern r. U.K.
147 E6 Ternate Indon.
164 B3 Terneuzen Neth.
150 E2 Terney Rus. Fed.
170 E3 Terni Italy
173 C5 Ternopil' Ukr.
126 C4 Terowie Australia
146 G2 Terpeniya, Mys c. Rus. Fed.
146 G2 Terpeniya, Zaliv g. Rus. Fed.
186 D4 Terrace Canada
190 D1 Terrace Bay Canada
180 E2 Terra Firma S. Africa
158 K2 Terråk Norway
170 C5 Terralba Sardinia Italy
189 J4 Terra Nova National Park Canada
199 F6 Terrebonne Bay U.S.A.
200 C4 Terre Haute U.S.A.
189 J4 Terrenceville Canada
194 F2 Terry U.S.A.
173 G5 Tersa r. Rus. Fed.
164 D1 Terschelling i. Neth.
139 I4 Terskey Ala-Too mts Kyrg.
170 C5 Tertenia Sardinia Italy
167 F2 Teruel Spain
158 N2 Tervola Fin.
170 G2 Tešanj Bos.-Herz.
178 D2 Teseney Eritrea
172 G4 Tesha r. Rus. Fed.
184 C2 Teshekpuk Lake U.S.A.
150 I3 Teshikaga Japan
150 G2 Teshio Japan
150 H3 Teshio-dake mt. Japan
150 G2 Teshio-gawa r. Japan
206 B2 Tesia Mex.
186 C2 Teslin Canada
186 C2 Teslin r. Canada
186 C2 Teslin Lake Canada
214 B1 Tesouras r. Brazil
214 B2 Tesouro Brazil
176 C3 Tessaoua Niger
161 F6 Test r. U.K.
170 C6 Testour Tunisia
212 B2 Tetas, Punta pt Chile
179 D5 Tete Moz.
128 F3 Te Teko N.Z.
169 O5 Teteriv r. Ukr.
165 K1 Teterow Germany
169 N6 Tetiyiv Ukr.
160 G4 Tetney U.K.
194 E2 Teton r. U.S.A.
194 E3 Teton Range mts U.S.A.
176 B1 Tétouan Morocco
171 I3 Tetovo Macedonia
172 I4 Tetyushi Rus. Fed.
212 D2 Teuco r. Arg.
180 B1 Teufelsbach Namibia
165 G1 Teufelsmoor reg. Germany
128 F3 Te Urewera National Park N.Z.
150 G3 Teuri-tō i. Japan
165 G2 Teutoburger Wald hills Germany
159 M3 Teuva Fin.
Tevere r. Italy see Tiber
Teverya Israel see Tiberias
162 F5 Teviot r. U.K.
162 F5 Teviotdale val. U.K.
128 A7 Te Waewae Bay N.Z.
181 G1 Tewane Botswana
125 F4 Tewantin Australia
128 E4 Te Wharau N.Z.
161 E6 Tewkesbury U.K.
148 B3 Têwo China
186 E4 Texada Island Canada
199 E5 Texarkana U.S.A.
127 I2 Texas Australia
199 D6 Texas state U.S.A.
199 E6 Texas City U.S.A.
207 E4 Texcoco Mex.
164 C1 Texel i. Neth.
199 C4 Texhoma U.S.A.
199 D5 Texoma, Lake U.S.A.
181 G4 Teyateyaneng Lesotho
172 G3 Teykovo Rus. Fed.
141 G3 Teyvareh Afgh.
172 G3 Teza r. Rus. Fed.
207 E3 Teziutlán Mex.
145 H4 Tezpur India
145 H4 Tezu India
187 J2 Tha-anne r. Canada
181 H4 Thabana-Ntlenyana mt. Lesotho
181 G4 Thaba Nchu S. Africa
181 G4 Thaba Putsoa mt. Lesotho
181 H4 Thaba-Tseka Lesotho
181 G2 Thabazimbi S. Africa
154 B1 Tha Bo Laos
181 G3 Thabong S. Africa
137 K6 Thādiq Saudi Arabia
154 A2 Thagyettaw Myanmar
149 C6 Thai Binh Vietnam
154 A1 Thailand country Asia
154 B3 Thailand, Gulf of Asia
154 A3 Thai Muang Thai.
149 B6 Thai Nguyên Vietnam
140 C5 Thaj Saudi Arabia
154 C1 Thakhèk Laos
145 F4 Thakurtola India
165 I4 Thal Germany
144 B2 Thal Pak.
170 D7 Thala Tunisia
154 A3 Thalang Thai.
143 A4 Thalassery India
144 B3 Thal Desert Pak.
165 J3 Thale (Harz) Germany
154 B1 Tha Li Thai.
127 H2 Thallon Australia
141 G4 Thalo Pak.
181 F2 Thamaga Botswana
140 B5 Thāmām, 'Irq ath des. Saudi Arabia
142 B7 Thamar, Jabal mt. Yemen
142 D6 Thamarīt Oman
161 G5 Thame r. U.K.
128 E2 Thames N.Z.
161 H6 Thames est. U.K.
161 G6 Thames r. U.K.
191 G4 Thamesville Canada
144 B5 Thān India
154 A2 Thanbyuzayat Myanmar
144 C5 Thandla India
147 B5 Thandwè Myanmar
143 A2 Thane India
Thăng Binh Vietnam see Ha Lam
154 C1 Thanh Hoa Vietnam
143 B4 Thanjavur India
154 B1 Tha Pla Thai.
154 A3 Thap Put Thai.
154 A3 Thap Sakae Thai.
144 B4 Tharad India
144 B4 Thar Desert India/Pak.
126 E1 Thargomindah Australia
137 I4 Tharthār, Buḩayrat ath l. Iraq
137 I4 Tharthār, Wādī ath r. Iraq
171 K4 Thasos i. Greece
197 H5 Thatcher U.S.A.
149 C6 Thât Khê Vietnam
147 B5 Thaton Myanmar
144 A4 Thatta Pak.
145 H5 Thaungdut Myanmar
154 A1 Thaungyin r. Myanmar/Thai.
154 C1 Tha Uthen Thai.
147 B5 Thayetmyo Myanmar
128 F2 The Aldermen Islands N.Z.
197 F5 Theba U.S.A.
205 I3 The Bahamas country Caribbean Sea
201 E7 The Bluff Bahamas
160 E2 The Cheviot h. U.K.
126 C5 The Coorong inlet Australia
194 B2 The Dalles U.S.A.
198 C3 Thedford U.S.A.
162 □ The Faither stack U.K.
161 G5 The Fens reg. U.K.
203 I2 The Forks U.S.A.
176 A3 The Gambia country Africa
126 E6 The Grampians mts Australia
142 D4 The Gulf Asia
164 C2 The Hague Neth.
128 C6 The Hunters Hills N.Z.
154 A3 Theinkun Myanmar
128 A6 The Key N.Z.
187 H2 Thekulthili Lake Canada
187 I2 Thelon r. Canada
187 I2 Thelon Game Sanctuary nature res. Canada
165 I4 Themar Germany
180 F6 Thembalesizwe S. Africa
181 H3 Thembalihle S. Africa
162 C2 The Minch sea chan. U.K.
161 F7 The Needles stack U.K.
167 H4 Thenia Alg.
167 H5 Theniet El Had Alg.
210 F5 Theodore Roosevelt r. Brazil
197 G5 Theodore Roosevelt Dam U.S.A.
197 G5 Theodore Roosevelt Lake U.S.A.
198 C2 Theodore Roosevelt National Park U.S.A.
163 B5 The Paps h. Ireland
187 I4 The Pas Canada
127 H6 The Pilot mt. Australia
164 A5 Thérain r. France
203 F2 Theresa U.S.A.
171 J4 Thermaïkos Kolpos g. Greece
196 B2 Thermalito U.S.A.
194 E3 Thermopolis U.S.A.
127 G5 The Rock Australia
164 A4 Thérouanne France
126 E3 The Salt Lake salt l. Australia
184 F2 Thesiger Bay Canada
163 A6 The Skelligs is Ireland
161 F7 The Solent str. U.K.
191 F2 Thessalon Canada
171 J4 Thessaloniki Greece
162 B3 The Storr h. U.K.
161 H5 Thet r. U.K.
153 A4 The Teeth mt. Phil.
161 H5 Thetford U.K.
189 F4 Thetford Mines Canada
162 D4 The Trossachs hills U.K.
126 A2 The Twins Australia
154 C1 Theun r. Laos
181 G4 Theunissen S. Africa
161 H5 The Wash b. U.K.
161 H6 The Weald reg. U.K.
199 F6 Thibodaux U.S.A.
187 J3 Thicket Portage Canada
198 D1 Thief River Falls U.S.A.
129 C4 Thiel Mountains mts Antarctica
166 F4 Thiers France
176 A3 Thiès Senegal
178 D4 Thika Kenya
Thiladhunmathee Atoll Maldives see Thiladhunmathi
143 A5 Thiladhunmathi Maldives
145 G4 Thimphu Bhutan
164 E5 Thionville France
Thira i. Greece see Santorini
171 K6 Thirasia i. Greece
160 F3 Thirsk U.K.
143 B4 Thiruvananthapuram India
159 J4 Thisted Denmark
126 B5 Thistle Island Australia
171 J5 Thiva Greece
187 J2 Thlewiaza r. Canada
187 H2 Thoa r. Canada
154 B3 Thô Chu, Đao i. Vietnam
181 I1 Thohoyandou S. Africa
164 C3 Tholen Neth.
164 F5 Tholey Germany
202 D5 Thomas U.S.A.
201 C5 Thomaston GA U.S.A.
203 I2 Thomaston ME U.S.A.
203 J2 Thomaston Corner Canada
163 D5 Thomastown Ireland
201 D6 Thomasville U.S.A.
164 E4 Thommen Belgium
187 J3 Thompson Canada
186 E4 Thompson r. Canada
190 D3 Thompson MI U.S.A.
203 F4 Thompson PA U.S.A.
198 E3 Thompson r. U.S.A.
194 D2 Thompson Falls U.S.A.
201 D5 Thomson U.S.A.
Thôn Cư Lai Vietnam see Thuân An
168 C7 Thonon-les-Bains France
Thôn Sơn Hai Vietnam see Sơn Hai
Thoothukudi India see Tuticorin
195 E5 Thoreau U.S.A.
127 F2 Thorlindah, Lake salt flat Australia
164 D3 Thorn Neth.
160 F3 Thornaby-on-Tees U.K.
190 E4 Thornapple r. U.S.A.
161 E6 Thornbury U.K.
191 H2 Thorne Canada
160 G4 Thorne U.K.
196 C2 Thorne U.S.A.
186 C3 Thorne Bay U.S.A.
190 D5 Thorntown U.S.A.
190 B3 Thorp U.S.A.
129 D4 Thorshavnheiane reg. Antarctica
181 G4 Thota-ea-Moli Lesotho
166 D3 Thouars France
203 E2 Thousand Islands Canada
197 G2 Thousand Lake Mountain U.S.A.
196 C4 Thousand Oaks U.S.A.
171 L4 Thrace reg. Europe
171 K4 Thrakiko Pelagos sea Greece
194 E2 Three Forks U.S.A.
Three Gorges Dam Project resr China see Sanxia Shuiku
186 G4 Three Hills Canada
127 F8 Three Hummock Island Australia
128 D1 Three Kings Islands N.Z.
190 C3 Three Lakes U.S.A.
190 D5 Three Oaks U.S.A.
154 A2 Three Pagodas Pass Myanmar/Thai.
176 B4 Three Points, Cape Ghana
190 E5 Three Rivers MI U.S.A.
199 D6 Three Rivers TX U.S.A.
194 B2 Three Sisters mt. U.S.A.
143 B4 Thrissur India
199 D5 Throckmorton U.S.A.
Thu, Cu Lao i. Vietnam see Phu Quy, Đao
154 C1 Thuân An Vietnam
154 C1 Thu Bồn, Sông r. Vietnam
187 G2 Thubun Lakes Canada
154 C3 Thu Dâu Một Vietnam
154 C3 Thu Đuc Vietnam
164 C4 Thuin Belgium
185 L2 Thule Greenland
179 C6 Thuli Zimbabwe
168 C7 Thun Switz.
190 C1 Thunder Bay Canada
190 C1 Thunder Bay b. Canada
191 F3 Thunder Bay b. U.S.A.
165 H5 Thüngen Germany
154 A3 Thung Song Thai.
154 B1 Thung Wa Thai.
165 I4 Thüringen land Germany
165 J3 Thüringer Becken reg. Germany
165 I4 Thüringer Wald mts Germany
163 D5 Thurles Ireland
202 E5 Thurmont U.S.A.
168 F7 Thurn, Pass Austria
203 F2 Thurso Canada
162 E2 Thurso U.K.
162 E2 Thurso r. U.K.
129 A3 Thurston Island i. Antarctica
165 H2 Thüster Berg h. Germany
160 E3 Thwaite U.K.
159 J4 Thyborøn Denmark
148 A1 Tiancang China
148 E2 Tianchang China
149 C6 Tiandeng China
149 C6 Tiandong China
149 C5 Tian'e China
211 J4 Tianguá Brazil
148 E2 Tianjin China
148 E2 Tianjin mun. China
148 A2 Tianjun China
149 C5 Tianlin China
149 D4 Tianmen China
149 F4 Tianmu Shan mts China
152 E2 Tianqiaoling China
149 B4 Tianquan China
152 C3 Tianshifu China
148 B3 Tianshui China
144 D2 Tianshuihai Aksai Chin
144 F4 Tiantai China
148 E1 Tiantaiyong China
149 C6 Tianyang China
148 B2 Tianzhu Gansu China
149 C5 Tianzhu Guizhou China
176 C1 Tiaret Alg.
176 B4 Tiassalé Côte d'Ivoire
214 B4 Tibagi r. Brazil
137 I5 Tibal, Wādī watercourse Iraq
177 D4 Tibati Cameroon
170 E3 Tiber r. Italy
136 E5 Tiberias Israel
Tiberias, Lake l. Israel see Galilee, Sea of
194 E1 Tiber Reservoir U.S.A.
177 D2 Tibesti mts Chad
Tibet aut. reg. China see Xizang Zizhiqu
135 G3 Tibet, Plateau of China
177 D2 Tibīsti, Sarīr des. Libya
126 E2 Tibooburra Australia
145 E3 Tibrikot Nepal
159 K4 Tibro Sweden
206 A1 Tiburón, Isla i. Mex.
153 B3 Ticao i. Phil.
161 H6 Ticehurst U.K.
191 I3 Tichborne Canada
176 B3 Tîchît Mauritania
176 A2 Tichla W. Sahara
168 D7 Ticino r. Switz.
203 G3 Ticonderoga U.S.A.
207 G3 Ticul Mex.
159 K4 Tidaholm Sweden
145 H5 Tiddim Myanmar
176 C2 Tidikelt, Plaine du plain Alg.
176 A3 Tidjikja Mauritania
139 K3 Tiechanggou China
Tiefa China see Diaobingshan
164 D3 Tiel Neth.
150 A1 Tieli China
152 B2 Tieling China
144 D2 Tielongtan Aksai Chin
164 B4 Tielt Belgium
176 B4 Tiémé Côte d'Ivoire
164 C4 Tienen Belgium
135 F2 Tien Shan mts China/Kyrg.
Tientsin China see Tianjin
159 L3 Tierp Sweden
195 F4 Tierra Amarilla U.S.A.
207 E4 Tierra Blanca Mex.
207 E4 Tierra Colorada Mex.
212 C8 Tierra del Fuego, Isla Grande de i. Arg./Chile
167 D2 Tiétar r. Spain
167 D2 Tiétar, Valle del val. Spain
214 C3 Tietê Brazil
214 B3 Tietê r. Brazil
202 B4 Tiffin U.S.A.
Tiflis Georgia see T'bilisi
201 D6 Tifton U.S.A.
138 B3 Tigen Kazakh.
171 K3 Tigheciului, Dealurile hills Moldova
173 D6 Tighina Moldova
139 J2 Tigiretskiy Khrebet mts Kazakh./Rus. Fed.
145 F5 Tigiria India
177 D4 Tignère Cameroon
189 H4 Tignish Canada
210 C4 Tigre r. Ecuador/Peru
213 E2 Tigre r. Venez.
137 K5 Tigris r. Asia
alt. Dicle (Turkey),
alt. Dijlah, Nahr (Iraq/Syria)
136 D7 Tīh, Jabal at plat. Egypt
137 I7 Tihāmat 'Asīr reg. Saudi Arabia
204 A2 Tijuana Mex.
214 C2 Tijuco r. Brazil
207 G4 Tikal tourist site Guat.
207 G4 Tikal, Parque Nacional nat. park Guat.
144 D4 Tikamgarh India
173 G6 Tikhoretsk Rus. Fed.
172 E3 Tikhvin Rus. Fed.
172 E3 Tikhvinskaya Gryada ridge Rus. Fed.
217 K7 Tiki Basin sea feature Pacific Ocean
128 F3 Tikokino N.Z.
125 G3 Tikopia i. Solomon Is
137 I4 Tikrīt Iraq
158 P2 Tikshozero, Ozero l. Rus. Fed.
133 N2 Tiksi Rus. Fed.
145 E3 Tila r. Nepal
145 F4 Tilaiya Reservoir India
140 D2 Tīlavar Iran
127 F1 Tilbooroo Australia
164 D3 Tilburg Neth.
161 H6 Tilbury U.K.
212 C2 Tilcara Arg.
126 D2 Tilcha (abandoned) Australia
139 G2 Tilekey Kazakh.
145 H5 Tilin Myanmar
176 C3 Tillabéri Niger
194 B2 Tillamook U.S.A.
154 A4 Tillanchong Island India
162 E4 Tillicoultry U.K.
191 G4 Tillsonburg Canada
162 F3 Tillyfourie U.K.
171 L6 Tilos i. Greece
126 E3 Tilpa Australia
173 F5 Tim Rus. Fed.
154 □ Timah, Bukit Sing.
172 J1 Timanskiy Kryazh ridge Rus. Fed.
137 I2 Timar Turkey
128 C6 Timaru N.Z.
173 F6 Timashevsk Rus. Fed.
176 B3 Timbedgha Mauritania
124 D3 Timber Creek Australia
196 D3 Timber Mountain U.S.A.
202 D5 Timberville U.S.A.
126 E7 Timboon Australia
176 B3 Timbuktu Mali
176 B3 Timétrine reg. Mali
176 C2 Timimoun Alg.
173 C7 Timiou Prodromou, Akrotirio pt Greece
139 F1 Timiryazev Kazakh.
138 F1 Timiryazevo Kazakh.
171 I2 Timișoara Romania
191 G1 Timmins Canada
172 F3 Timokhino Rus. Fed.
211 J5 Timon Brazil
147 E7 Timor i. Indon.
Timor-Leste country Asia see East Timor
124 C3 Timor Sea Australia/Indon.
173 H3 Timoshino Rus. Fed.
215 D2 Timote Arg.
159 L3 Timrå Sweden
201 C5 Tims Ford Lake U.S.A.
145 D5 Timurni Muafi India
213 C2 Tinaco Venez.
143 B3 Tindivanam India
176 B2 Tindouf Alg.
154 C5 Tinggi i. Malaysia
127 I2 Tingha Australia
149 E5 Ting Jiang r. China
145 F3 Tingri China
159 K4 Tingsryd Sweden
215 B2 Tinguiririca, Volcán vol. Chile
158 J3 Tingvoll Norway
162 E1 Tingwall U.K.
214 E1 Tinharé, Ilha de i. Brazil
154 C1 Tinh Gia Vietnam
147 G5 Tinian i. N. Mariana Is
212 C3 Tinogasta Arg.
171 K6 Tinos i. Greece
164 B5 Tinqueux France
176 C2 Tinrhert, Hamada de Alg.
145 H4 Tinsukia India
161 C7 Tintagel U.K.
126 D5 Tintinara Australia
162 E5 Tinto h. U.K.
202 E4 Tioga r. U.S.A.
155 B2 Tioman i. Malaysia
154 C2 Ti On, Nui mt. Vietnam
191 F1 Tionaga Canada
202 D4 Tionesta Lake U.S.A.
203 E3 Tioughnioga r. U.S.A.
167 H3 Tipasa Alg.
206 H5 Tipitapa Nicaragua
190 D5 Tippecanoe r. U.S.A.
190 E5 Tippecanoe Lake U.S.A.
163 C5 Tipperary Ireland
145 F4 Tiptala Bhanjyang pass Nepal
190 B5 Tipton IA U.S.A.
190 D5 Tipton IN U.S.A.
197 E4 Tipton, Mount U.S.A.
190 E1 Tip Top Hill Canada
161 H6 Tiptree U.K.
213 C4 Tiquié r. Brazil
207 G5 Tiquisate Guat.
211 I4 Tiracambu, Serra do hills Brazil
171 H4 Tirana Albania
Tiranë Albania see Tirana
170 D1 Tirano Italy
173 D6 Tiraspol Moldova
144 B5 Tira Sujanpur India
180 B3 Tiraz Mountains Namibia
136 A2 Tire Turkey
162 B4 Tiree i. U.K.
141 H3 Tīreh, Kowtal-e Afgh.
144 B1 Tirich Mir mt. Pak.
143 B2 Tirna r. India
143 A3 Tirthahalli India
145 F5 Tirtol India
143 B4 Tiruchchendur India
143 B4 Tiruchchirappalli India
143 B4 Tiruchengodu India
143 B4 Tirunelveli India
143 B3 Tirupati India
143 B3 Tiruppattur India
143 B4 Tiruppur India
143 B3 Tiruttturaippundi India
143 B3 Tiruvannamalai India
143 B4 Tisaiyanvilai India
187 I4 Tisdale Canada
143 C5 Tissamaharama Sri Lanka
167 G5 Tissemsilt Alg.
145 G4 Tista r. India
129 C4 Titan Dome ice feature Antarctica
133 N2 Tit-Ary Rus. Fed.
210 E7 Titicaca, Lago Bol./Peru
143 C1 Titlagarh India
191 E4 Tittabawassee r. U.S.A.
171 K2 Titu Romania
201 D6 Titusville FL U.S.A.
202 D4 Titusville PA U.S.A.
191 G3 Tiverton Canada
161 D7 Tiverton U.K.
170 E4 Tivoli Italy
207 G3 Tixkokob Mex.
207 E4 Tixtla Mex.
206 D3 Tizapán el Alto Mex.
207 G3 Tizimín Mex.
167 I4 Tizi Ouzou Alg.
213 D2 Tiznados r. Venez.
139 I5 Tiznap He r. China
176 B2 Tiznit Morocco
206 C2 Tizoc Mex.
181 I2 Tjaneni Swaziland
158 L2 Tjappsåive Sweden
164 D2 Tjeukemeer l. Neth.
159 I4 Tjorhom Norway
207 E4 Tlacolula Mex.
207 E4 Tlacotalpán Mex.
206 D2 Tlahualilo Mex.
207 E4 Tlalnepantla Mex.
207 E4 Tlapa Mex.
206 D3 Tlaquepaque Mex.
207 E4 Tlaxcala Mex.
207 E4 Tlaxcala state Mex.
207 E4 Tlaxiaco Mex.
176 B1 Tlemcen Alg.
181 F3 Tlhakalatlou S. Africa
181 H4 Tlholong S. Africa
181 F2 Tlokweng Botswana
154 C3 Tnaôt, Prêk l. Cambodia
186 D3 Toad River Canada
179 E5 Toamasina Madag.
154 □ Toa Payoh Sing.
215 D3 Toay Arg.
151 E7 Toba Japan
154 A5 Toba, Danau l. Indon.
144 A3 Toba and Kakar Ranges mts Pak.
210 F1 Tobago i. Trin. and Tob.
Tobar an Choire Ireland see Tobercurry
147 E6 Tobelo Indon.
163 C3 Tobercurry Ireland
191 G3 Tobermory Canada
162 B4 Tobermory U.K.
153 B4 Tobias Fornier Phil.
196 D1 Tobin, Mount U.S.A.
187 I4 Tobin Lake Canada
203 J1 Tobique r. Canada
150 F5 Tobi-shima i. Japan
155 C3 Toboali Indon.
Tô Bong Vietnam see Hai Triều
138 E1 Tobyl Kazakh.
132 H4 Tobyl r. Kazakh./Rus. Fed.
211 I5 Tocantinópolis Brazil
211 I4 Tocantins r. Brazil
214 C1 Tocantinzinha r. Brazil
201 D5 Toccoa U.S.A.
144 B2 Tochi r. Pak.
159 J4 Töcksfors Sweden
212 B2 Tocopilla Chile
127 F5 Tocumwal Australia
213 C2 Tocuyo r. Venez.
170 E3 Todi Italy
168 D7 Todi mt. Switz.
139 J3 Todog China
150 H5 Todoga-saki pt Japan
150 G4 Todohokke Japan
210 E7 Todos Santos Bol.
206 B3 Todos Santos Mex.
206 B3 Todos Santos, Bahía de b. Mex.
186 G4 Tofield Canada
186 D5 Tofino Canada
162 □ Toft U.K.
190 B2 Tofte U.S.A.
125 I3 Tofua i. Tonga
147 E7 Togian, Kepulauan is Indon.
176 C4 Togo country Africa
190 A2 Togo U.S.A.
148 D1 Togrog Ul China
148 D1 Togtoh China
145 H2 Togton He r. China
138 E3 Togyz Kazakh.
197 H4 Tohatchi U.S.A.
158 N3 Toholampi Fin.
148 B1 Tohom China
145 G3 Toiba China
158 M3 Toijala Fin.
151 B9 Toi-misaki pt Japan
158 N3 Toivakka Fin.
196 D2 Toiyabe Range mts U.S.A.
139 G5 Tojikobod Tajik.
138 C1 Tok r. Rus. Fed.
184 D3 Tok U.S.A.
151 F6 Tōkamachi Japan
128 B7 Tokanui N.Z.
177 F3 Tokar Sudan
146 E4 Tokara-rettō is Japan
136 F1 Tokat Turkey
152 D4 Tŏkch'ŏn N. Korea
125 I2 Tokelau terr. Pacific Ocean
173 E6 Tokmak Ukr.
139 H4 Tokmok Kyrg.
128 G3 Tokomaru Bay N.Z.
128 E3 Tokoroa N.Z.
181 H3 Tokoza S. Africa
132 J5 Toksun China
Tok-tō i. N. Pacific Ocean see Liancourt Rocks
139 H4 Toktogul Kyrg.
139 H4 Toktogul Suu Saktagychy resr Kyrg.
139 J3 Tokty Kazakh.
151 D7 Tokushima Japan
151 F7 Tōkyō Japan
(City Plan 104)
151 F7 Tōkyō-wan b. Japan
128 G3 Tolaga Bay N.Z.
179 E6 Tôlañaro Madag.
138 C1 Tolbazy Rus. Fed.
206 I6 Tolé Panama

207 E3 **Toleant** *tourist site* Mex.
139 H4 **Tole Bi** Kazakh.
214 B4 **Toledo** Brazil
167 D3 **Toledo** Spain
190 A5 **Toledo** *IA* U.S.A.
202 B4 **Toledo** *OH* U.S.A.
167 D3 **Toledo, Montes de** *mts* Spain
199 E6 **Toledo Bend Reservoir** U.S.A.
215 B3 **Tolhuaca, Parque Nacional** *nat. park* Chile
139 J3 **Toli** China
179 E6 **Toliara** Madag.
213 B3 **Tolima, Nevado del** *vol.* Col.
147 E6 **Tolitoli** Indon.
132 J3 **Tol'ka** Rus. Fed.
165 L1 **Tollensesee** *l.* Germany
172 D3 **Tolmachevo** Rus. Fed.
170 E1 **Tolmezzo** Italy
149 □ **Tolo Channel** *Hong Kong* China
149 □ **Tolo Harbour** *b. Hong Kong* China
167 E1 **Tolosa** Spain
191 F3 **Tolsmaville** Canada
162 B2 **Tolsta Head** U.K.
213 B2 **Tolú** Col.
207 E4 **Toluca** Mex.
172 I4 **Tol'yatti** Rus. Fed.
138 E2 **Tolybay** Kazakh.
138 E2 **Tolybay** Kazakh.
190 B4 **Tomah** U.S.A.
190 C3 **Tomahawk** U.S.A.
150 G3 **Tomakomai** Japan
150 G2 **Tomamae** Japan
125 H3 **Tomanivi** *mt.* Fiji
213 E5 **Tomar** Brazil
167 B3 **Tomar** Port.
136 E2 **Tomarza** Turkey
215 F1 **Tomás Gomensoro** Uruguay
169 K5 **Tomaszów Lubelski** Poland
169 J5 **Tomaszów Mazowiecki** Poland
162 E3 **Tomatin** U.K.
206 C4 **Tomatlán** Mex.
201 B6 **Tombigbee** *r.* U.S.A.
178 B4 **Tomboco** Angola
214 D3 **Tombos** Brazil
**Tombouctou** Mali *see* **Timbuktu**
197 G6 **Tombstone** U.S.A.
179 B5 **Tombua** Angola
181 H1 **Tom Burke** S. Africa
138 F4 **Tomdibuloq** Uzbek.
215 B3 **Tomé** Chile
181 K1 **Tome** Moz.
159 K5 **Tomelilla** Sweden
167 E3 **Tomelloso** Spain
139 F4 **Tomenaryk** Kazakh.
139 H2 **Tomengi Kayrakty** Kazakh.
191 H2 **Tomiko** Canada
127 H4 **Tomingley** Australia
147 E7 **Tomini, Teluk** *g.* Indon.
176 B3 **Tominian** Mali
162 E3 **Tomintoul** U.K.
170 G3 **Tomislavgrad** Bos.-Herz.
158 K2 **Tømmerneset** Norway
133 N4 **Tommot** Rus. Fed.
213 D4 **Tomo** Col.
213 C3 **Tomo** *r.* Col.
148 D1 **Tomortei** China
133 O3 **Tompo** Rus. Fed.
124 B4 **Tom Price** Australia
146 A1 **Tomsk** Rus. Fed.
159 K4 **Tomtabacken** *h.* Sweden
133 P3 **Tomtor** Rus. Fed.
150 H3 **Tomuraushi-yama** *mt.* Japan
173 G6 **Tomuzlovka** *r.* Rus. Fed.
207 F4 **Tonalá** Mex.
197 G3 **Tonalea** U.S.A.
210 E4 **Tonantins** Brazil
194 C1 **Tonasket** U.S.A.
140 D5 **Tonb-e Bozorg, Jazīreh-ye** *i.* Iran
161 H6 **Tonbridge** U.K.
147 E6 **Tondano** Indon.
159 J5 **Tønder** Denmark
161 E6 **Tone** *r.* U.K.
125 I4 **Tonga** *country* Pacific Ocean
126 F6 **Tongala** Australia
149 F5 **Tong'an** China
128 E3 **Tongariro National Park** N.Z.
125 I4 **Tongatapu Group** *is* Tonga
216 H7 **Tonga Trench** *sea feature* S. Pacific Ocean
148 D3 **Tongbai** China
148 D3 **Tongbai Shan** *mts* China
148 E4 **Tongcheng** *Anhui* China
149 D4 **Tongcheng** *Hubei* China
152 D4 **T'ongch'ŏn** N. Korea
148 C3 **Tongchuan** China
149 C5 **Tongdao** China
148 A3 **Tongde** China
164 D4 **Tongeren** Belgium
149 E4 **Tonggu** China
149 D7 **Tonggu Zui** *pt* China
149 B5 **Tonghai** China
150 A2 **Tonghe** China
152 C3 **Tonghua** *Jilin* China
152 C3 **Tonghua** *Jilin* China
148 C4 **Tongjiang** China
152 B2 **Tongjiangkou** China
152 D4 **Tongjosŏn-man** *b.* N. Korea
149 C6 **Tongking, Gulf of** China/Vietnam
149 C4 **Tongliang** China
152 B2 **Tongliao** China
148 E4 **Tongling** China
149 F4 **Tonglu** China
149 B4 **Tongnan** China
126 E3 **Tongo** Australia
126 E3 **Tongo Lake** *salt flat* Australia
153 B5 **Tongquil** *i.* Phil.
149 C5 **Tongren** *Guizhou* China
148 A3 **Tongren** *Qinghai* China
149 E4 **Tongshan** *Hubei* China
**Tongshan** China *see* **Xuzhou**
**Tongshi** China *see* **Wuzhishan**
162 D2 **Tongue** U.K.
194 F2 **Tongue** *r.* U.S.A.
201 E7 **Tongue of the Ocean** *sea chan.* Bahamas
148 B3 **Tongwei** China
148 B2 **Tongxin** China
148 E4 **Tongyang** China
152 E6 **Tongyeong** S. Korea
152 B1 **Tongyu** China
152 B1 **Tongyuanpu** China
148 E2 **Tongzhou** *Beijing* China
148 F3 **Tongzhou** *Jiangsu* China
149 C4 **Tongzi** China
190 C5 **Tonica** U.S.A.
206 B1 **Tónichi** Mex.
144 C4 **Tonk** India
140 C2 **Tonkābon** Iran
149 B6 **Tonkin** *reg.* Vietnam
172 H3 **Tonkino** Rus. Fed.
**Tônlé Sab** *l.* Cambodia *see* **Tonle Sap**
154 B2 **Tonle Sap** *l.* Cambodia
150 G5 **Tōno** Japan
197 D2 **Tonopah** U.S.A.
213 E2 **Tonoro** *r.* Venez.
206 I7 **Tonosí** Panama
179 C6 **Tonota** Botswana
144 D3 **Tons** *r.* India
159 J4 **Tønsberg** Norway
159 I4 **Tonstad** Norway
197 G5 **Tonto National Monument** *nat. park* U.S.A.
145 H5 **Tonzang** Myanmar
127 H2 **Toobeah** Australia
194 D3 **Tooele** U.S.A.
127 J1 **Toogoolawah** Australia
126 E5 **Tooleybuc** Australia
126 A4 **Tooligie** Australia
127 H6 **Tooma** *r.* Australia
127 G7 **Toora** Australia
127 H3 **Tooraweenah** Australia
180 F6 **Toorberg** *mt.* S. Africa
127 I1 **Toowoomba** Australia
197 G6 **Topawa** U.S.A.
196 C2 **Topaz** U.S.A.
139 J1 **Topchikha** Rus. Fed.
198 E4 **Topeka** U.S.A.
206 C2 **Topia** Mex.
186 D4 **Topley Landing** Canada
165 K2 **Töplitz** Germany
215 B2 **Topocalma, Punta** *pt* Chile
197 E4 **Topock** U.S.A.
168 I6 **Topoľčany** Slovakia
138 B3 **Topoli** Kazakh.
206 B2 **Topolobampo** Mex.
171 L3 **Topolovgrad** Bulg.
158 P2 **Topozero, Ozero** *l.* Rus. Fed.
194 B2 **Toppenish** U.S.A.
203 J2 **Topsfield** U.S.A.
197 F3 **Toquerville** U.S.A.
171 L5 **Torbalı** Turkey
141 E3 **Torbat-e Ḩeydarīyeh** Iran
141 F3 **Torbat-e Jām** Iran
172 G4 **Torbeyevo** Rus. Fed.
190 E3 **Torch Lake** U.S.A.
167 D2 **Tordesillas** Spain
158 M2 **Töre** Sweden
167 H1 **Torelló** Spain
164 D2 **Torenberg** *h.* Neth.
165 K3 **Torgau** Germany
139 H2 **Torgay** *Akmolinskaya Oblast'* Kazakh.
138 E2 **Torgay** *Kostanayskaya Oblast'* Kazakh.
173 H5 **Torgun** *r.* Rus. Fed.
164 B3 **Torhout** Belgium
178 D3 **Torī** Eth.
**Torino** Italy *see* **Turin**
151 G9 **Tori-shima** *i.* Japan
177 F4 **Torit** South Sudan
**Torixoreu** Brazil *see* **Torixoréu**
214 B2 **Torixoréu** Brazil
137 K3 **Torkamān** Iran
172 G3 **Tor'kovskoye Vodokhranilishche** *resr* Rus. Fed.
167 D2 **Tormes** *r.* Spain
158 M2 **Torneälven** *r.* Fin./Sweden
158 L1 **Torneträsk** Sweden
158 L1 **Torneträsk** *l.* Sweden
189 H2 **Torngat Mountains** Canada
189 H2 **Torngat Mountains National Park** *nat. park* Can.
158 N2 **Tornio** Fin.
215 D3 **Tornquist** Arg.
167 D2 **Toro** Spain
206 D2 **Toro, Pico del** *mt.* Mex.
146 F1 **Torom** *r.* Rus. Fed.
127 I4 **Toronto** Australia
191 H4 **Toronto** Canada (City Plan **113**)
196 D5 **Toro Peak** U.S.A.
172 D3 **Toropets** Rus. Fed.
178 D3 **Tororo** Uganda
**Toros Dağları** *mts* Turkey *see* **Taurus Mountains**
162 F3 **Torphins** U.K.
161 D7 **Torquay** U.K.
196 C5 **Torrance** U.S.A.
167 B3 **Torrão** Port.
167 C2 **Torre** *mt.* Port.
167 G2 **Torreblanca** Spain
167 D1 **Torrecerredo** *mt.* Spain
170 F4 **Torre del Greco** Italy
167 D1 **Torrelavega** Spain
167 D4 **Torremolinos** Spain
126 B3 **Torrens, Lake** *imp. l.* Australia
167 F3 **Torrent** Spain
206 D2 **Torreón** Mex.
206 B1 **Torres** Mex.
125 G3 **Torres Islands** Vanuatu
167 B3 **Torres Novas** Port.
124 E2 **Torres Strait** Australia
167 B3 **Torres Vedras** Port.
167 F4 **Torrevieja** Spain
197 G2 **Torrey** U.S.A.
161 C7 **Torridge** *r.* U.K.
162 C3 **Torridon, Loch** *b.* U.K.
167 D3 **Torrijos** Spain
127 I2 **Torrington** Australia
203 G4 **Torrington** *CT* U.S.A.
194 F3 **Torrington** *WY* U.S.A.
167 H1 **Torroella de Montgrí** Spain
159 K3 **Torsby** Sweden
158 □ **Tórshavn** Faroe Is
139 G4 **Tortkol'** Kazakh.
138 E4 **To'rtko'l** Uzbek.
139 H2 **Tortkuduk** Kazakh.
170 C5 **Tortolì** *Sardinia* Italy
170 C2 **Tortona** Italy
167 G2 **Tortosa** Spain
206 I6 **Tortuguero, Parque Nacional** *nat. park* Costa Rica
137 H1 **Tortum** Turkey
139 I4 **Toru-Aygyr** Kyrg.
140 D3 **Ţorūd** Iran
137 G1 **Torul** Turkey
169 I4 **Toruń** Poland
162 B3 **Tory Island** Ireland
163 C2 **Tory Sound** *sea chan.* Ireland
172 E3 **Torzhok** Rus. Fed.
151 C8 **Tosa** Japan
151 C8 **Tosashimizu** Japan
158 K2 **Tosbotn** Norway
180 E2 **Tosca** S. Africa
170 C3 **Toscano, Arcipelago** *is* Italy
150 G4 **Tōshima-yama** *mt.* Japan
139 G4 **Toshkent** Uzbek.
172 D3 **Tosno** Rus. Fed.
212 D3 **Tostado** Arg.
165 H1 **Tostedt** Germany
151 B8 **Tosu** Japan
136 E1 **Tosya** Turkey
172 G3 **Tot'ma** Rus. Fed.
207 E4 **Totolapan** Mex.
172 G3 **Totskoye** Rus. Fed.
161 F7 **Totton** U.K.
151 D7 **Tottori** Japan
176 B4 **Touba** Côte d'Ivoire
176 A3 **Touba** Senegal
176 B1 **Toubkal, Jebel** *mt.* Morocco
148 B2 **Toudaohu** China
176 B3 **Tougan** Burkina Faso
176 C1 **Touggourt** Alg.
176 A3 **Tougué** Guinea
166 G2 **Toul** France
166 G5 **Toulon** France
166 E5 **Toulouse** France
176 B4 **Toumodi** Côte d'Ivoire
176 B2 **Tounassine, Hamada** *des.* Alg.
**Toungoo** Myanmar *see* **Taung-ngu**
149 D5 **Toupai** China
154 B1 **Tourakom** Laos
164 B4 **Tourcoing** France
164 B4 **Tournai** Belgium
166 G4 **Tournon-sur-Rhône** France
166 G3 **Tournus** France
211 K5 **Touros** Brazil
166 E3 **Tours** France
180 D6 **Touwsrivier** S. Africa
165 K4 **Toužim** Czech Rep.
213 C2 **Tovar** Venez.
161 F5 **Tove** *r.* U.K.
137 J1 **Tovuz** Azer.
150 G4 **Towada** Japan
150 G5 **Towada-Hachimantai Kokuritsu-kōen** *nat. park* Japan
150 G4 **Towada-ko** *l.* Japan
128 E1 **Towai** N.Z.
203 E4 **Towanda** U.S.A.
197 H3 **Towaoc** U.S.A.
161 G5 **Towcester** U.K.
163 C6 **Tower** Ireland
190 A2 **Tower** U.S.A.
187 I5 **Towner** U.S.A.
196 D3 **Townes Pass** U.S.A.
194 E2 **Townsend** U.S.A.
127 H6 **Townsend, Mount** Australia
124 E3 **Townsville** Australia
147 E7 **Towori, Teluk** *b.* Indon.
202 E5 **Towson** U.S.A.
139 I4 **Toxkan He** *r.* China
150 G3 **Tōya-ko** *l.* Japan
151 E6 **Toyama** Japan
151 E6 **Toyama-wan** *b.* Japan
151 E7 **Toyohashi** Japan
151 E7 **Toyokawa** Japan
151 D7 **Toyonaka** Japan
151 D7 **Toyooka** Japan
151 E7 **Toyota** Japan
139 G4 **To'ytepa** Uzbek.
**Toytepa** Uzbek. *see* **To'ytepa**
176 C1 **Tozeur** Tunisia
173 G7 **T'q'ibuli** Georgia
173 G7 **T'q'varcheli** Georgia
164 F5 **Traben** Germany
**Trâblous** Lebanon *see* **Tripoli**
171 J4 **Trabotivište** Macedonia
137 G1 **Trabzon** Turkey
203 J2 **Tracy** Canada
196 B3 **Tracy** *CA* U.S.A.
198 E2 **Tracy** *MN* U.S.A.
190 A4 **Traer** U.S.A.
167 C4 **Trafalgar, Cabo** *c.* Spain
215 B3 **Traiguén** Chile
186 F5 **Trail** Canada
159 N5 **Trakai** Lith.
172 I2 **Trakt** Rus. Fed.
163 B5 **Tralee** Ireland
163 B5 **Tralee Bay** Ireland
213 E3 **Tramán Tepuí** *mt.* Venez.
163 D5 **Tramore** Ireland
159 K4 **Tranås** Sweden
212 C3 **Trancas** Arg.
159 K4 **Tranemo** Sweden
162 F5 **Tranent** U.K.
154 A4 **Trang** Thai.
147 F7 **Trangan** *i.* Indon.
127 G4 **Trangie** Australia
215 F1 **Tranqueras** Uruguay
129 B5 **Transantarctic Mountains** *mts* Antarctica
187 G4 **Trans Canada Highway** Canada
187 J5 **Transcona** Canada
169 N7 **Transnistria** *terr.* Moldova
171 J2 **Transylvanian Alps** *mts* Romania
170 E5 **Trapani** *Sicily* Italy
127 G7 **Traralgon** Australia
145 G4 **Trashigang** Bhutan
170 E3 **Trasimeno, Lago** *l.* Italy
167 E3 **Trasvase, Canal de** Spain
154 B2 **Trat** Thai.
144 B3 **Tratani** *r.* Pak.
168 F7 **Traunsee** *l.* Austria
168 F7 **Traunstein** Germany
126 E4 **Travellers Lake** *imp. l.* Australia
128 D5 **Travers, Mount** N.Z.
209 G7 **Traversay Islands** S. Sandwich Is
190 E3 **Traverse City** U.S.A.
154 C3 **Tra Vinh** Vietnam
199 D6 **Travis, Lake** U.S.A.
170 G2 **Travnik** Bos.-Herz.
170 F1 **Trbovlje** Slovenia
125 F2 **Treasury Islands** Solomon Is
165 L2 **Trebbin** Germany
168 G6 **Třebíč** Czech Rep.
171 H3 **Trebinje** Bos.-Herz.
169 J6 **Trebišov** Slovakia
170 F2 **Trebnje** Slovenia
165 G5 **Trebur** Germany
165 I3 **Treffurt** Germany
190 B3 **Trego** U.S.A.
162 D4 **Treig, Loch** *l.* U.K.
215 F2 **Treinta y Tres** Uruguay
212 C6 **Trelew** Arg.
159 K5 **Trelleborg** Sweden
164 C4 **Trélon** France
161 C5 **Tremadog Bay** U.K.
188 F4 **Tremblant, Mont** *h.* Canada
170 F3 **Tremiti, Isole** *is* Italy
194 D3 **Tremonton** U.S.A.
167 G1 **Tremp** Spain
190 B3 **Trempealeau** *r.* U.S.A.
161 B7 **Trenance** U.K.
168 I6 **Trenčín** Slovakia
165 H3 **Trendelburg** Germany
215 D2 **Trenque Lauquén** Arg.
160 G4 **Trent** *r.* U.K.
170 D1 **Trento** Italy
191 I3 **Trenton** Canada
190 A5 **Trenton** *MO* U.S.A.
203 F4 **Trenton** *NJ* U.S.A.
161 D6 **Treorchy** U.K.
189 J4 **Trepassey** Canada
215 F2 **Tres Arboles** Uruguay
215 E3 **Tres Arroyos** Arg.
161 A8 **Tresco** *i.* U.K.
214 D3 **Três Corações** Brazil
213 B4 **Tres Esquinas** Col.
162 B4 **Treshnish Isles** U.K.
214 B3 **Três Irmãos, Represa** *resr* Brazil
214 B3 **Três Lagoas** Brazil
212 B7 **Tres Lagos** Arg.
215 D3 **Tres Lomas** Arg.
214 D2 **Três Marias, Represa** *resr* Brazil
215 B4 **Tres Picos** *mt.* Arg.
207 F5 **Tres Picos** Mex.
215 E3 **Tres Picos, Cerro** *mt.* Arg.
195 F4 **Tres Piedras** U.S.A.
214 D3 **Três Pontas** Brazil
212 C7 **Tres Puntas, Cabo** *c.* Arg.
214 D3 **Três Rios** Brazil
207 E4 **Tres Valles** Mex.
207 F4 **Tres Zapotes** *tourist site* Mex.
159 J3 **Tretten** Norway
165 I6 **Treuchtlingen** Germany
165 K2 **Treuenbrietzen** Germany
159 J4 **Treungen** Norway
170 C2 **Treviglio** Italy
170 E2 **Treviso** Italy
161 B7 **Trevose Head** U.K.
127 G9 **Triabunna** Australia
171 L6 **Tria Nisia** *i.* Greece
171 M6 **Trianta** Greece
144 B2 **Tribal Areas** *admin. div.* Pak.
171 H5 **Tricase** Italy
**Trichur** India *see* **Thrissur**
164 A5 **Tricot** France
127 F4 **Trida** Australia
164 E5 **Trier** Germany
170 E2 **Trieste** Italy
170 E1 **Triglav** *mt.* Slovenia
171 I5 **Trikala** Greece
136 D4 **Trikomon** Cyprus
147 F7 **Trikora, Puncak** *mt.* Indon.
163 E4 **Trim** Ireland
143 C4 **Trincomalee** Sri Lanka
214 C2 **Trindade** Brazil
219 H7 **Trindade, Ilha da** *i.* S. Atlantic Ocean
210 F6 **Trinidad** Bol.
213 C3 **Trinidad** Col.
205 I4 **Trinidad** Cuba
210 F1 **Trinidad** *i.* Trin. and Tob.
215 F2 **Trinidad** Uruguay
195 F4 **Trinidad** U.S.A.
213 E2 **Trinidad and Tobago** *country* Caribbean Sea
189 J4 **Trinity Bay** Canada
184 C4 **Trinity Islands** U.S.A.
196 C1 **Trinity Range** *mts* U.S.A.
201 C5 **Trion** U.S.A.
165 J1 **Tripkau** Germany
171 J6 **Tripoli** Greece
136 E4 **Tripoli** Lebanon
177 D1 **Tripoli** Libya
143 B4 **Tripunittura** India
145 G5 **Tripura** *state* India
219 I8 **Tristan da Cunha** *i.* S. Atlantic Ocean
144 D3 **Trisul** *mt.* India
145 F4 **Trisul Dam** Nepal
165 I1 **Trittau** Germany
164 E5 **Trittenheim** Germany
**Trivandrum** India *see* **Thiruvananthapuram**
170 F4 **Trivento** Italy
168 H6 **Trnava** Slovakia
124 F2 **Trobriand Islands** P.N.G.
158 K2 **Trofors** Norway
170 G3 **Trogir** Croatia
170 F4 **Troia** Italy
164 F4 **Troisdorf** Germany
164 D4 **Trois-Ponts** Belgium
189 F4 **Trois-Rivières** Canada
138 E1 **Troitsk** Rus. Fed.
139 K1 **Troitskoye** *Altayskiy Kray* Rus. Fed.
138 C1 **Troitskoye** *Orenburgskaya Oblast'* Rus. Fed.
138 D1 **Troitskoye** *Respublika Bashkortostan* Rus. Fed.
173 H6 **Troitskoye** *Respublika Kalmykiya - Khalm'g-Tangch* Rus. Fed.
129 D3 **Troll** *research stn* Antarctica
159 K4 **Trollhättan** Sweden
211 G3 **Trombetas** *r.* Brazil
175 I6 **Tromelin, Île** *i.* Indian Ocean
215 B3 **Tromen, Volcán** *vol.* Arg.
181 F5 **Trompsburg** S. Africa
158 L1 **Tromsø** Norway
196 D4 **Trona** U.S.A.
215 B4 **Tronador, Monte** *mt.* Arg.
158 J3 **Trondheim** Norway
158 J3 **Trondheimsfjorden** *sea chan.* Norway
145 G4 **Trongsa Chhu** *r.* Bhutan
136 D4 **Troödos** Cyprus
162 D5 **Troon** U.K.
214 D1 **Tropeiros, Serra dos** *hills* Brazil
197 F3 **Tropic** U.S.A.
163 E2 **Trostan** *h.* U.K.
162 F3 **Troup Head** U.K.
186 E2 **Trout** *r.* Canada
191 H3 **Trout Creek** Canada
197 F2 **Trout Creek** U.S.A.
186 G3 **Trout Lake** *Alta* Canada
186 E2 **Trout Lake** Canada
186 E2 **Trout Lake** *l. N.W.T.* Canada
188 B3 **Trout Lake** *l. Ont.* Canada
190 E2 **Trout Lake** U.S.A.
190 C2 **Trout Lake** *l.* U.S.A.
194 E2 **Trout Peak** U.S.A.
202 E4 **Trout Run** U.S.A.
161 E6 **Trowbridge** U.K.
127 F8 **Trowutta** Australia
171 L5 **Troy** *tourist site* Turkey
201 C6 **Troy** *AL* U.S.A.
194 D2 **Troy** *MT* U.S.A.
203 G3 **Troy** *NH* U.S.A.
203 G3 **Troy** *NY* U.S.A.
202 A4 **Troy** *OH* U.S.A.
202 E4 **Troy** *PA* U.S.A.
171 K3 **Troyan** Bulg.
166 G2 **Troyes** France
196 D4 **Troy Lake** U.S.A.
197 E2 **Troy Peak** U.S.A.
171 I3 **Trstenik** Serbia
173 E4 **Trubchevsk** Rus. Fed.
167 C1 **Truchas** Spain
172 E3 **Trud** Rus. Fed.
150 C3 **Trudovoye** Rus. Fed.
206 H5 **Trujillo** Hond.
210 C5 **Trujillo** Peru
167 D3 **Trujillo** Spain
213 C2 **Trujillo** Venez.
164 F5 **Trulben** Germany
203 G4 **Trumbull** U.S.A.
197 F3 **Trumbull, Mount** U.S.A.
155 A2 **Trumon** Indon.
127 G4 **Trundle** Australia
154 C2 **Trưng Hiệp** Vietnam
149 C6 **Trưng Khanh** China
189 H4 **Truro** Canada
161 B7 **Truro** U.K.
163 C3 **Truskmore** *h.* Ireland
186 E3 **Trutch** Canada
195 F5 **Truth or Consequences** U.S.A.
168 G5 **Trutnov** Czech Rep.
**Truva** *tourist site* Turkey *see* **Troy**
171 K7 **Trypiti, Akrotirio** *pt* Greece
159 K3 **Trysil** Norway
168 G3 **Trzebiatów** Poland
146 A2 **Tsagaannuur** Mongolia
173 H6 **Tsagan Aman** Rus. Fed.
173 H6 **Tsagan Nur** Rus. Fed.
173 G7 **Tsageri** Georgia
137 J1 **Ts'alk'a** Georgia
179 E5 **Tsaratanana, Massif du** *mts* Madag.
171 L3 **Tsarevo** Bulg.
180 B2 **Tsaris Mountains** Namibia
173 H5 **Tsatsa** Rus. Fed.
180 A3 **Tsaukaib** Namibia
178 D4 **Tsavo East National Park** Kenya
173 G6 **Tsentral'nyy** Rus. Fed. 
179 B6 **Tses** Namibia
179 C6 **Tsetseng** Botswana
146 B2 **Tsetserleg** Mongolia
146 C2 **Tsetserleg** Mongolia
179 C6 **Tshabong** Botswana
179 C6 **Tshane** Botswana
178 B4 **Tshela** Dem. Rep. Congo
178 C4 **Tshibala** Dem. Rep. Congo
178 C4 **Tshikapa** Dem. Rep. Congo
178 C4 **Tshikapa** *r.* Dem. Rep. Congo
181 G3 **Tshing** S. Africa
181 I1 **Tshipise** S. Africa
179 C4 **Tshitanzu** Dem. Rep. Congo
178 C4 **Tshofa** Dem. Rep. Congo
181 I2 **Tshokwane** S. Africa
178 C4 **Tshuapa** *r.* Dem. Rep. Congo
**Tshwane** S. Africa *see* **Pretoria**
173 G6 **Tsimlyansk** Rus. Fed.
173 G6 **Tsimlyanskoye Vodokhranilishche** *resr* Rus. Fed.
179 E6 **Tsimmanampesotse, Parc National de** Madag.
180 E3 **Tsineng** S. Africa
**Tsing Shan Wan** *b.* China *see* **Castle Peak Bay**
**Tsing Shui Wan** *b.* China *see* **Clear Water Bay**
**Tsingtao** China *see* **Qingdao**
149 □ **Tsing Yi** *i. Hong Kong* China
179 E6 **Tsiombe** Madag.
179 E5 **Tsiroanomandidy** Madag.
186 D4 **Tsitsutl Peak** Canada
172 H4 **Tsivil'sk** Rus. Fed.
137 H1 **Tskhinvali** Georgia
172 G4 **Tsna** *r.* Rus. Fed.
149 D5 **Tsogttsetsiy** Mongolia
148 B1 **Tsokar Chumo** *l.* India
144 D2 **Tsokr Chumo** *l.* India *see* **Tsokar Chumo**
181 H5 **Tsolo** S. Africa
181 G6 **Tsomo** S. Africa
**Tso Morari Lake** India *see* **Morari, Tso**
173 G7 **Ts'q'alt'ubo** Georgia
151 E7 **Tsu** Japan
151 G6 **Tsuchiura** Japan
149 □ **Tsuen Wan** *Hong Kong* China
150 G4 **Tsugarū-kaikyō** *str.* Japan
179 B5 **Tsumeb** Namibia
179 B6 **Tsumis Park** Namibia
179 C5 **Tsumkwe** Namibia
145 G4 **Tsunthang** India
151 C8 **Tsuruga** Japan
151 D8 **Tsurugi-san** *mt.* Japan
150 F5 **Tsuruoka** Japan
151 A7 **Tsushima** Japan
151 A7 **Tsushima** *is* Japan
151 D7 **Tsuyama** Japan
180 D1 **Tswaane** Botswana
181 G3 **Tswaraganang** S. Africa
181 F3 **Tswelelang** S. Africa
169 L4 **Tsyelyakhany** Belarus
158 P1 **Tsypnavolok** Rus. Fed.
173 E6 **Tsyurupyns'k** Ukr.
147 F7 **Tual** Indon.
163 C4 **Tuam** Ireland
128 D4 **Tuamarina** N.Z.
**Tuamotu, Archipel des** *is* Fr. Polynesia *see* **Tuamotu Islands**
123 J5 **Tuamotu Islands** Fr. Polynesia
149 B6 **Tuân Giao** Vietnam
154 A5 **Tuangku** *i.* Indon.
173 F6 **Tuapse** Rus. Fed.
154 □ **Tuas** Sing.
128 A7 **Tuatapere** N.Z.
162 B2 **Tuath, Loch a'** *b.* U.K.
197 G3 **Tuba City** U.S.A.
155 D4 **Tuban** Indon.
212 G3 **Tubarão** Brazil
153 A4 **Tubbataha Reefs** Phil.
**Tubbercurry** Ireland *see* **Tobercurry**
168 D6 **Tübingen** Germany
176 A4 **Tubmanburg** Liberia
153 B4 **Tubod** Phil.
177 E1 **Tubruq** Libya
217 J7 **Tubuai** *i.* Fr. Polynesia
123 I6 **Tubuai Islands** Fr. Polynesia
211 K6 **Tucano** Brazil
215 B3 **Tucapel, Punta** *pt* Chile
211 G7 **Tucavaca** Bol.
165 K1 **Tüchen** Germany
165 K2 **Tuchheim** Germany
186 D2 **Tuchitua** Canada
203 F5 **Tuckerton** U.S.A.
197 G5 **Tucson** U.S.A.
197 G5 **Tucson Mountains** U.S.A.
213 B2 **Tucuco** *r.* Venez.
195 G5 **Tucumcari** U.S.A.
213 E2 **Tucupita** Venez.
211 I4 **Tucuruí** Brazil
211 I4 **Tucuruí, Represa de** *resr* Brazil
137 L5 **Tū Dār** Iran
167 F1 **Tudela** Spain
167 B2 **Tuela** *r.* Port.
149 □ **Tuen Mun** *Hong Kong* China
145 H4 **Tuensang** India
140 C5 **Ţufayḩ** Saudi Arabia
217 J2 **Tufts Abyssal Plain** *sea feature* N. Pacific Ocean
153 C4 **Tugnug Point** Phil.
153 B2 **Tuguegarao** Phil.
133 O4 **Tugur** Rus. Fed.
139 K3 **Tugyl** Kazakh.
148 F2 **Tuhai He** *r.* China
145 A5 **Tuhemberua** Indon.
167 B1 **Tui** Spain
206 J6 **Tuira** *r.* Panama
138 D1 **Tukan** Rus. Fed.
147 E7 **Tukangbesi, Kepulauan** *is* Indon.
188 E2 **Tukarak Island** Canada
139 H5 **Tŭkhtamish** Tajik.
128 F3 **Tukituki** *r.* N.Z.
184 E3 **Tuktoyaktuk** Canada
159 M4 **Tukums** Latvia
141 G3 **Tukzār** Afgh.
207 E3 **Tula** Mex.
172 F4 **Tula** Rus. Fed.
145 H1 **Tulagt Ar Gol** *r.* China
207 E3 **Tulancingo** Mex.
196 C3 **Tulare** U.S.A.
196 C4 **Tulare Lake Bed** U.S.A.
195 F5 **Tularosa** U.S.A.
143 C2 **Tulasi** *mt.* India
180 C6 **Tulbagh** S. Africa
210 C3 **Tulcán** Ecuador
171 M2 **Tulcea** Romania
173 D5 **Tul'chyn** Ukr.
196 C3 **Tule** *r.* U.S.A.
140 D3 **Tuleh** Iran
145 G4 **Tule La** *pass* Bhutan
**Tule-la Pass** Bhutan *see* **Tule La**
187 I2 **Tulemalu Lake** Canada
199 C5 **Tulia** U.S.A.
186 D2 **Tulita** Canada
136 E5 **Ţulkarm** West Bank
163 C5 **Tulla** Ireland
127 F8 **Tullah** Australia
201 C5 **Tullahoma** U.S.A.
127 G4 **Tullamore** Australia
163 D4 **Tullamore** Ireland
166 E4 **Tulle** France
159 K3 **Tulleråsen** Sweden
127 G4 **Tullibigeal** Australia
199 E6 **Tullos** U.S.A.
163 E5 **Tullow** Ireland
124 E3 **Tully** Australia
163 D3 **Tully** U.K.
203 E3 **Tully** U.S.A.
172 D2 **Tulos** Rus. Fed.
199 D4 **Tulsa** U.S.A.
172 F4 **Tul'skaya Oblast'** *admin. div.* Rus. Fed.
213 A3 **Tuluá** Col.
184 B3 **Tuluksak** U.S.A.
207 H3 **Tulum** *tourist site* Mex.
215 C1 **Tulum, Valle de** *val.* Arg.
146 C1 **Tulun** Rus. Fed.
155 D4 **Tulungagung** Indon.
145 H4 **Tulung La** *pass* China
153 A4 **Tuluran** *i.* Phil.
213 A4 **Tumaco** Col.
181 G3 **Tumahole** S. Africa
173 I6 **Tumak** Rus. Fed.
**Tumakuru** India *see* **Tumkur**
159 L4 **Tumba** Sweden
178 B4 **Tumba, Lac** *l.* Dem. Rep. Congo
155 D3 **Tumbangsamba** Indon.
210 B4 **Tumbes** Peru
186 E3 **Tumbler Ridge** Canada
126 B5 **Tumby Bay** Australia
148 B2 **Tumen** China
152 E2 **Tumen** China
152 E2 **Tumen** *r.* China/N. Korea
210 F2 **Tumereng** Guyana
143 A5 **Tumindao** *i.* Phil.
143 B3 **Tumkur** India
145 G3 **Tum La** *pass* China
162 E4 **Tummel, Loch** *l.* U.K.
146 G2 **Tumnin** *r.* Rus. Fed.
141 F5 **Tump** Pak.
154 B4 **Tumpat** Malaysia
176 B3 **Tumu** Ghana
211 G3 **Tumucumaque, Parque Indígena do** *nat. park* Brazil
211 G3 **Tumucumaque, Serra** *hills* Brazil
127 H5 **Tumut** Australia
127 H5 **Tumut** *r.* Australia
139 J4 **Tumxuk** China
161 H6 **Tunbridge Wells, Royal** U.K.
137 G2 **Tunceli** Turkey
149 D7 **Tunchang** China
127 J4 **Tuncurry** Australia
141 F3 **Tundī** *imp. l.* Afgh.
144 D4 **Tundla** India
179 D5 **Tunduru** Tanz.
171 L3 **Tundzha** *r.* Bulg.
143 B3 **Tungabhadra** *r.* India
143 A3 **Tungabhadra Reservoir** India
145 H3 **Tunga La** China/India
153 B5 **Tungawan** Phil.
149 □ **Tung Chung Wan** *b. Hong Kong* China
158 C2 **Tungnaá** *r.* Iceland
**Tung Pok Liu Hoi Hap** China *see* **East Lamma Channel**
186 D2 **Tungsten (abandoned)** Canada
172 E1 **Tunguda** Rus. Fed.
149 □ **Tung Wan** *b. Hong Kong* China
143 C2 **Tuni** India
176 D1 **Tunis** Tunisia
170 D6 **Tunis, Golfe de** *g.* Tunisia
176 C1 **Tunisia** *country* Africa
213 B3 **Tunja** Col.
148 D2 **Tunliu** China
158 K2 **Tunnsjøen** *l.* Norway
162 □ **Tunstall** U.K.
161 I5 **Tuntsa** Fin.
158 O2 **Tuntsayoki** *r.* Fin./Rus. Fed.
189 G2 **Tunulic** *r.* Canada
189 H2 **Tunungayualok Island** Canada
215 C2 **Tunuyán** Arg.
215 C2 **Tunuyán** *r.* Arg.
148 E3 **Tuo He** *r.* China
148 F2 **Tuoji Dao** *i.* China
154 C3 **Tuŏl Khpos** Cambodia
196 B3 **Tuolumne** U.S.A.
196 C3 **Tuolumne** *r.* U.S.A.
192 B4 **Tuolumne Meadows** U.S.A.
196 C3 **Tuoniang Jiang** *r.* China
**Tuotuo He** *r.* China *see* **Togton He**
139 I4 **Tüp** Kyrg.
214 B3 **Tupã** Brazil
214 C2 **Tupaciguara** Brazil
137 K3 **Tūp Āghāj** Iran
212 F3 **Tupanciretã** Brazil
213 C3 **Tuparro** *r.* Col.
199 F5 **Tupelo** U.S.A.
210 E8 **Tupiza** Bol.
138 B3 **Tupkaragan, Mys** *pt* Kazakh.
203 F2 **Tupper Lake** U.S.A.
203 F2 **Tupper Lake** *l.* U.S.A.
215 C2 **Tupungato** Arg.
215 C2 **Tupungato, Cerro** *mt.* Arg./Chile
137 J7 **Tuqayyid** *well* Iraq
152 A1 **Tuquan** China
213 A4 **Túquerres** Col.
145 G4 **Tura** India
133 L3 **Tura** Rus. Fed.
142 B5 **Turabah** Saudi Arabia
213 D3 **Turagua, Serranía** *mt.* Venez.
128 E4 **Turakina** N.Z.
140 E3 **Turan** Iran
146 F1 **Turana, Khrebet** *mts* Rus. Fed.
128 E3 **Turangi** N.Z.
140 E2 **Turan Lowland** Asia
139 G4 **Turar Ryskulov** Kazakh.
**Ţurayf** Saudi Arabia *see* **Ţurayf**
136 G6 **Ţurayf** Saudi Arabia
140 C5 **Ţurayf** *well* Saudi Arabia
**Ţurayf** *well* Saudi Arabia *see* **Ţurayf**
159 N4 **Turba** Estonia
213 B2 **Turbaco** Col.
141 F5 **Turbat** Pak.
213 B2 **Turbo** Col.
169 K7 **Turda** Romania
140 C3 **Tūreh** Iran
**Turfan** China *see* **Turpan**
138 E3 **Turgay** *r.* Kazakh.
138 E2 **Turgayskaya Dolina** *val.* Kazakh.
138 F2 **Turgayskaya Oblast'** Kazakh.
138 E2 **Turgayskaya Stolovaya Strana** *reg.* Kazakh.
171 L3 **Tŭrgovishte** Bulg.
136 C2 **Turgut** Turkey
136 A2 **Turgutlu** Turkey
136 F1 **Turhal** Turkey
159 N4 **Türi** Estonia
167 F3 **Turia** *r.* Spain
213 D2 **Turiamo** Venez.
170 B2 **Turin** Italy
150 B2 **Turiy Rog** Rus. Fed.
173 C5 **Turiys'k** Ukr.
178 D3 **Turkana, Lake** *salt l.* Eth./Kenya
171 L4 **Türkeli Adası** *i.* Turkey
139 G5 **Turkestan Range** *mts* Asia
136 E2 **Turkey** *country* Asia
190 B4 **Turkey** *r.* U.S.A.
173 G5 **Turki** Rus. Fed.
139 G4 **Turkistan** Kazakh.
141 F3 **Turkistān, Silsilah-ye Band-e** *mts* Afgh.
138 E5 **Türkmenabat** Turkm.
**Türkmenabat** Turkm. *see* **Türkmenabat**
138 C5 **Türkmen Aýlagy** *b.* Turkm.
**Türkmenbashi** Turkm. *see* **Türkmenbaşy**
138 C4 **Türkmenbaşy** Turkm.
138 C5 **Türkmenbaşy Aýlagy** *b.* Turkm.
136 C2 **Türkmen Dağı** *mt.* Turkey
138 E5 **Türkmengala** Turkm.
**Türkmengala** Turkm. *see* **Türkmengala**
138 C5 **Turkmenistan** *country* Asia
**Turkmenskiy Zaliv** *b.* Turkm. *see* **Türkmen Aýlagy**
136 F3 **Türkoğlu** Turkey
205 J4 **Turks and Caicos Islands** *terr.* Caribbean Sea
205 J4 **Turks Islands** Turks and Caicos Is
159 M3 **Turku** Fin.
178 D3 **Turkwel** *watercourse* Kenya
196 B3 **Turlock** U.S.A.
196 B3 **Turlock Lake** U.S.A.
128 F4 **Turnagain, Cape** N.Z.
162 D5 **Turnberry** U.K.
197 G5 **Turnbull, Mount** U.S.A.
207 H4 **Turneffe Islands** *atoll* Belize
191 F3 **Turner** U.S.A.
164 C3 **Turnhout** Belgium
187 H3 **Turnor Lake** Canada
171 K3 **Turnu Măgurele** Romania
127 H4 **Turon** *r.* Australia
172 G3 **Turovets** Rus. Fed.
146 A2 **Turpan** China
146 A2 **Turpan Pendi** *depr.* China
205 I4 **Turquino, Pico** *mt.* Cuba
162 F3 **Turriff** U.K.
137 J5 **Turšāq** Iraq
**Turtkul'** Uzbek. *see* **To'rtko'l**
190 B2 **Turtle Flambeau Flowage** *resr* U.S.A.
187 H4 **Turtleford** Canada
190 A3 **Turtle Lake** U.S.A.
139 H4 **Turugart Pass** China/Kyrg.
214 B2 **Turvo** *r. Goiás* Brazil
214 C3 **Turvo** *r. São Paulo* Brazil
138 D3 **Turysh** Kazakh.
197 F4 **Tusayan** U.S.A.
201 C5 **Tuscaloosa** U.S.A.
202 C4 **Tuscarawas** *r.* U.S.A.
202 E4 **Tuscarora Mountains** *hills* U.S.A.
190 C6 **Tuscola** *IL* U.S.A.
199 D5 **Tuscola** *TX* U.S.A.
140 E3 **Tusharīk** Iran
201 C5 **Tuskegee** U.S.A.
202 D4 **Tussey Mountains** *hills* U.S.A.
137 I2 **Tutak** Turkey
172 F3 **Tutayev** Rus. Fed.
143 B4 **Tuticorin** India
198 D4 **Tuttle Creek Reservoir** U.S.A.
168 D7 **Tuttlingen** Germany
185 P2 **Tuttut Nunaat** *reg.* Greenland
125 I3 **Tutuila** *i.* Pacific Ocean
179 C6 **Tutume** Botswana
207 E4 **Tutupec** Mex.
152 D3 **Tuun-bong** *mt.* N. Korea
158 O3 **Tuupovaara** Fin.
158 O3 **Tuusniemi** Fin.
125 H2 **Tuvalu** *country* Pacific Ocean
140 B5 **Ţuwayq, Jabal** *hills* Saudi Arabia
206 D4 **Tuxpan** *Jalisco* Mex.
207 E3 **Tuxpan** *Veracruz* Mex.
207 F4 **Tuxtla Gutiérrez** Mex.
213 D2 **Tuy** *r.* Venez.
**Tuy Đức** Vietnam *see* **Tuy Đưc**
154 C2 **Tuy Đưc** Vietnam
149 B6 **Tuyên Quang** Vietnam
154 D2 **Tuy Hoa** Vietnam
140 C3 **Tūysarkān** Iran
139 I4 **Tuyyk** Kazakh.
136 D2 **Tuz, Lake** *salt l.* Turkey
**Tuz Gölü** *salt l.* Turkey *see* **Tuz, Lake**
197 F4 **Tuzigoot National Monument** *nat. park* U.S.A.
137 J4 **Tuz Khurmātū** Iraq
171 H2 **Tuzla** Bos.-Herz.
137 H2 **Tuzla** *r.* Turkey
173 F6 **Tuzlov** *r.* Rus. Fed.
159 J4 **Tvedestrand** Norway
172 E3 **Tver'** Rus. Fed.
172 E3 **Tverskaya Oblast'** *admin. div.* Rus. Fed.
191 I3 **Tweed** Canada
162 F5 **Tweed** *r.* U.K.
127 J2 **Tweed Heads** Australia
186 D4 **Tweedsmuir Provincial Park** Canada
180 C6 **Tweefontein** S. Africa
180 C2 **Twee Rivier** Namibia
164 E2 **Twente** *reg.* Neth.
196 D4 **Twentynine Palms** U.S.A.
189 J4 **Twillingate** Canada
194 D2 **Twin Bridges** U.S.A.
190 C6 **Twin Buttes Reservoir** U.S.A.
189 H3 **Twin Falls** Canada
194 D3 **Twin Falls** U.S.A.
186 F3 **Twin Lakes** Canada
203 H2 **Twin Mountain** U.S.A.
202 C6 **Twin Oaks** U.S.A.

196 B2 **Twin Peak** U.S.A.
165 G2 **Twistringen** Germany
128 C6 **Twizel** N.Z.
127 H6 **Twofold Bay** Australia
197 G4 **Two Guns** U.S.A.
190 B2 **Two Harbors** U.S.A.
187 G4 **Two Hills** Canada
194 D1 **Two Medicine** *r.* U.S.A.
190 D3 **Two Rivers** U.S.A.
145 H5 **Tyao** *r.* India/Myanmar
158 J3 **Tydal** Norway
**Tyddewi** U.K. *see* **St David's**
202 D5 **Tygart Lake** U.S.A.
202 D5 **Tygart Valley** U.S.A.
146 E1 **Tygda** Rus. Fed.
199 E5 **Tyler** U.S.A.
199 F6 **Tylertown** U.S.A.
146 E1 **Tynda** Rus. Fed.
186 A2 **Tyndall Glacier** U.S.A.
162 F4 **Tyne** *r.* U.K.
160 F2 **Tynemouth** U.K.
159 J3 **Tynset** Norway
136 E5 **Tyre** Lebanon
129 B3 **Tyree, Mount** *mt.* Antarctica
158 N2 **Tyrnävä** Fin.
171 J5 **Tyrnavos** Greece
202 D4 **Tyrone** U.S.A.
126 E5 **Tyrrell** *r.* Australia
126 E5 **Tyrrell, Lake** *dry lake* Australia
187 H2 **Tyrrell Lake** Canada
170 D4 **Tyrrhenian Sea** France/Italy
133 P3 **Tyubelyakh** Rus. Fed.
132 I4 **Tyukalinsk** Rus. Fed.
138 B3 **Tyuleni, Ostrova** *is* Kazakh.
138 D1 **Tyul'gan** Rus. Fed.
132 H4 **Tyumen'** Rus. Fed.
139 J1 **Tyumentsevo** Rus. Fed.
133 M3 **Tyung** *r.* Rus. Fed.
138 F1 **Tyuntyugur** Kazakh.
162 C6 **Tywi** *r.* U.K.
161 C5 **Tywyn** U.K.
181 I1 **Tzaneen** S. Africa
171 K6 **Tzia** *i.* Greece


## U


179 C5 **Uamanda** Angola
213 E4 **Uatatás** *r.* Brazil
211 K5 **Uauá** Brazil
213 D5 **Uaupés** Brazil
213 C4 **Uaupés** *r.* Brazil
207 G4 **Uaxactún** Guat.
140 B4 **U'aywij** *well* Saudi Arabia
137 I7 **U'aywij, Wādī al** *watercourse* Saudi Arabia
214 D3 **Ubá** Brazil
138 F1 **Ubagan** *r.* Kazakh.
214 D2 **Ubaí** Brazil
214 E1 **Ubaitaba** Brazil
178 B3 **Ubangi** *r.* Cent. Afr. Rep./Dem. Rep. Congo
213 B3 **Ubate** Col.
137 I5 **Ubayyiḍ, Wādī al** *watercourse* Iraq/Saudi Arabia
151 B8 **Ube** Japan
167 E3 **Úbeda** Spain
214 C2 **Uberaba** Brazil
211 G7 **Uberaba, Lagoa** *l.* Bol./Brazil
214 C2 **Uberlândia** Brazil
154 □ **Ubin, Pulau** *i.* Sing.
167 D1 **Ubiña, Peña** *mt.* Spain
154 B1 **Ubolratna, Ang Kep Nam** Thai.
181 J3 **Ubombo** S. Africa
**Ubonrat, Angkep Nam** *resr* Thai. *see* **Ubolratna, Ang Kep Nam**
154 C2 **Ubon Ratchathani** Thai.
165 G5 **Ubstadt-Weiher** Germany
178 C4 **Ubundu** Dem. Rep. Congo
138 E5 **Üçajy** Turkm.
137 K1 **Ucar** Azer.
210 D5 **Ucayali** *r.* Peru
144 B3 **Uch** Pak.
**Uch-Adzhi** Turkm. *see* **Üçajy**
138 D1 **Uchaly** Rus. Fed.
140 C2 **Uchān** Iran
150 G3 **Uchiura-wan** *b.* Japan
**Uchkuduk** Uzbek. *see* **Uchquduq**
138 E4 **Uchquduq** Uzbek.
**Uchsay** Uzbek. *see* **Uchsoy**
138 D4 **Uchsoy** Uzbek.
165 G2 **Uchte** Germany
165 J2 **Uchte** *r.* Germany
146 F1 **Uchur** *r.* Rus. Fed.
161 H7 **Uckfield** U.K.
186 D5 **Ucluelet** Canada
197 H3 **Ucolo** U.S.A.
194 F2 **Ucross** U.S.A.
148 C2 **Ud** China
133 O4 **Uda** *r.* Rus. Fed.
173 H6 **Udachnoye** Rus. Fed.
133 M3 **Udachnyy** Rus. Fed.
143 B4 **Udagamandalam** India
144 C4 **Udaipur** *Rajasthan* India
145 G5 **Udaipur** *Tripura* India
145 E5 **Udanti** *r.* India/Myanmar
143 B3 **Udayagiri** India
159 J4 **Uddevalla** Sweden
162 D5 **Uddingston** U.K.
158 L2 **Uddjaure** *l.* Sweden
164 D3 **Uden** Neth.
143 B2 **Udgir** India
172 H2 **Udimskiy** Rus. Fed.
170 E1 **Udine** Italy
189 I2 **Udjuktok Bay** Canada
172 E3 **Udomlya** Rus. Fed.
154 B1 **Udon Thani** Thai.
146 F1 **Udskaya Guba** *b.* Rus. Fed.
143 B4 **Udumalaippettai** India
143 A3 **Udupi** India
146 F1 **Udyl', Ozero** *l.* Rus. Fed.
168 G4 **Ueckermünde** Germany
151 F6 **Ueda** Japan
124 C2 **Uekuli** Indon.
178 C3 **Uele** *r.* Dem. Rep. Congo
184 B3 **Uelen** Rus. Fed.
165 I2 **Uelzen** Germany
178 C3 **Uere** *r.* Dem. Rep. Congo
165 H1 **Uetersen** Germany
165 H5 **Uettingen** Germany
165 I2 **Uetze** Germany
132 G4 **Ufa** Rus. Fed.
165 I5 **Uffenheim** Germany
179 B6 **Ugab** *watercourse* Namibia
178 D4 **Ugalla** *r.* Tanz.
178 D3 **Uganda** *country* Africa
181 H5 **Ugie** S. Africa
146 G2 **Uglegorsk** Rus. Fed.
150 C3 **Uglekamensk** Rus. Fed.
172 F3 **Uglich** Rus. Fed.
170 F2 **Ugljan** *i.* Croatia
172 E3 **Uglovka** Rus. Fed.
150 C3 **Uglovoye** Rus. Fed.
139 J2 **Uglovskoye** Rus. Fed.
133 P3 **Ugol'noye** Rus. Fed.
133 S3 **Ugol'nyye Kopi** Rus. Fed.
172 E4 **Ugra** Rus. Fed.
139 H4 **Ugüt** Kyrg.
168 H6 **Uherské Hradiště** Czech Rep.
202 C4 **Uhrichsville** U.S.A.
162 B3 **Uig** U.K.
178 B4 **Uíge** Angola
152 D5 **Uijeongbu** S. Korea
152 C3 **Ŭiju** N. Korea
158 O3 **Uimaharju** Fin.
197 F3 **Uinkaret Plateau** U.S.A.
194 E3 **Uinta Mountains** U.S.A.
152 E5 **Uiseong** S. Korea
179 B6 **Uis Mine** Namibia
163 D4 **Uisneach** *h.* Ireland
181 F6 **Uitenhage** S. Africa
164 C2 **Uithoorn** Neth.
164 E1 **Uithuizen** Neth.
189 H2 **Uivak, Cape** Canada
151 D7 **Uji** Japan
151 A9 **Uji-guntō** *is* Japan
144 C5 **Ujjain** India
**Ujung Pandang** Indon. *see* **Makassar**
181 H4 **uKhahlamba-Drakensberg Park** *nat. park* S. Africa
137 I5 **Ukhaydir** *tourist site* Iraq
145 H4 **Ukhrul** India
172 J2 **Ukhta** Rus. Fed.
172 J2 **Ukhta** *r.* Rus. Fed.
127 J2 **Uki** Australia
196 A2 **Ukiah** *CA* U.S.A.
194 C2 **Ukiah** *OR* U.S.A.
185 J3 **Ukkusiksalik National Park** Canada
185 M2 **Ukkusissat** Greenland
159 N5 **Ukmergė** Lith.
173 D5 **Ukraine** *country* Europe
139 J2 **Ukrainka (abandoned)** Kazakh.
172 I2 **Uktym** Rus. Fed.
151 A8 **Uku-jima** *i.* Japan
180 D1 **Ukwi** Botswana
180 D1 **Ukwi Pan** *salt pan* Botswana
**Ulaanbaatar** Mongolia *see* **Ulan Bator**
148 D1 **Ulaanbadrah** Mongolia
146 B2 **Ulaangom** Mongolia
127 H4 **Ulan** Australia
148 C2 **Ulan** China
146 C2 **Ulan Bator** Mongolia
139 G3 **Ulanbel'** Kazakh.
148 C1 **Ulan Buh Shamo** *des.* China
173 H6 **Ulan Erge** Rus. Fed.
146 E2 **Ulanhot** China
148 D1 **Ulan Hua** China
173 H6 **Ulan-Khol** Rus. Fed.
148 D1 **Ulan Qab** China
148 C1 **Ulansuhai Nur** *l.* China
148 A1 **Ulan Tohoi** China
146 C1 **Ulan-Ude** Rus. Fed.
145 G2 **Ulan Ul Hu** *l.* China
136 F2 **Ulaş** Turkey
125 G2 **Ulawa Island** Solomon Is
141 E4 **Ulāy, Kūh-e** *h.* Iran
139 J2 **Ul'bi** Kazakh.
159 J4 **Ulefoss** Norway
126 E2 **Ulenia, Lake** *salt flat* Australia
159 N4 **Ülenurme** Estonia
139 F2 **Ul'gili** Kazakh.
143 A2 **Ulhasnagar** India
146 D2 **Uliastai** China
146 B2 **Uliastay** Mongolia
164 C3 **Ulicoten** Neth.
158 P1 **Ulita** *r.* Rus. Fed.
147 F6 **Ulithi** *atoll* Micronesia
152 E5 **Uljin** S. Korea
139 I4 **Ul'ken Aksu** Kazakh.
139 J2 **Ul'ken Boken** Kazakh.
139 K2 **Ul'ken Naryn** Kazakh.
139 H4 **Ul'ken Sulutor** Kazakh.
127 I5 **Ulladulla** Australia
162 C3 **Ullapool** U.K.
158 M3 **Ullava** Fin.
152 F5 **Ulleung-do** *i.* S. Korea
160 E3 **Ullswater** *l.* U.K.
168 D6 **Ulm** Germany
127 J2 **Ulmarra** Australia
164 E4 **Ulmen** Germany
159 K4 **Ulricehamn** Sweden
164 E1 **Ulrum** Neth.
152 E6 **Ulsan** S. Korea
158 J3 **Ulsberg** Norway
163 D3 **Ulster Canal** Ireland/U.K.
126 E5 **Ultima** Australia
207 G5 **Ulúa** *r.* Hond.
136 B1 **Ulubat Gölü** *l.* Turkey
136 C2 **Uluborlu** Turkey
136 B1 **Uludağ** *mt.* Turkey
139 H5 **Ulugqat** China
154 B5 **Ulu Kali, Gunung** *mt.* Malaysia
184 G2 **Ulukhaktok** Canada
136 E3 **Ulukışla** Turkey
181 I4 **Ulundi** S. Africa
145 G2 **Ulungur Hu** *l.* China
154 □ **Ulu Pandan** Sing.
124 D4 **Uluṛu** *h.* Australia
136 D1 **Ulus** Turkey
162 B4 **Ulva** *i.* U.K.
164 C3 **Ulvenhout** Neth.
160 D3 **Ulverston** U.K.
127 G8 **Ulverstone** Australia
159 K3 **Ulvsjön** Sweden
**Ul'yanovo** Uzbek. *see* **Dashtobod**
172 I4 **Ul'yanovsk** Rus. Fed.
172 H4 **Ul'yanovskaya Oblast'** *admin. div.* Rus. Fed.
199 C4 **Ulysses** U.S.A.
139 F2 **Ulytau** Kazakh.
139 F3 **Ulytau, Gory** *mts* Kazakh.
207 G3 **Umán** Mex.
173 D5 **Uman'** Ukr.
141 G4 **Umarao** Pak.
144 E5 **Umaria** India
144 D6 **Umarkhed** India
143 C2 **Umarkot** India
144 B4 **Umarkot** Pak.
194 C2 **Umatilla** U.S.A.
132 E3 **Umba** Rus. Fed.
203 H2 **Umbagog Lake** U.S.A.
124 E2 **Umboi** *i.* P.N.G.
158 M3 **Umeå** Sweden
158 L2 **Umeälven** *r.* Sweden
137 K7 **Umgharah** Kuwait
**Umhlanga** S. Africa *see* **uMhlanga**
181 I4 **uMhlanga** S. Africa
185 N3 **Umiiviip Kangertiva** *inlet* Greenland
184 H3 **Umingmaktok (abandoned)** Canada
188 E2 **Umiujaq** Canada
181 I5 **Umkomaas** S. Africa
181 I4 **Umlazi** S. Africa
137 J6 **Umma** *tourist site* Iraq
140 D5 **Umm al Qaywayn** U.A.E.
140 C5 **Umm Bāb** Qatar
177 E3 **Umm Keddada** Sudan
137 K6 **Umm Qaṣr** Iraq
177 F3 **Umm Ruwaba** Sudan
177 E1 **Umm Sa'ad** Libya
140 C5 **Umm Sa'id** Qatar
140 C5 **Umm Şalāl Muḥammad** Qatar
194 A3 **Umpqua** *r.* U.S.A.
179 B5 **Umpulo** Angola
144 D5 **Umred** India
144 C5 **Umreth** India
181 I5 **Umtentweni** S. Africa
176 C4 **Umuahia** Nigeria
214 B3 **Umuarama** Brazil
181 H5 **Umzimkulu** S. Africa
181 I5 **Umzinto** S. Africa
170 G2 **Una** *r.* Bos.-Herz./Croatia
214 E1 **Una** Brazil
136 F6 **'Unāb, Wādī al** *watercourse* Jordan
214 C2 **Unaí** Brazil
184 B3 **Unalakleet** U.S.A.
162 C2 **Unapool** U.K.
213 D2 **Unare** *r.* Venez.
136 E6 **'Unayzah** Jordan
142 B4 **'Unayzah** Saudi Arabia
137 G5 **'Unayzah, Jabal** *h.* Iraq
195 E4 **Uncompahgre Plateau** U.S.A.
181 H4 **Underberg** S. Africa
126 D5 **Underbool** Australia
198 C2 **Underwood** U.S.A.
172 E4 **Unecha** Rus. Fed.
127 G4 **Ungarie** Australia
126 B5 **Ungarra** Australia
188 F1 **Ungava, Péninsule d'** *pen.* Canada
189 G2 **Ungava Bay** Canada
173 C6 **Ungheni** Moldova
138 E5 **Unguz, Solonchakovyye Vpadiny** *salt flat* Turkm.
138 D4 **Üngüz Angyrsyndaky Garagum** *des.* Turkm.
172 I3 **Uni** Rus. Fed.
214 B4 **União da Vitória** Brazil
213 B4 **Unilla** *r.* Col.
210 F4 **Unini** *r.* Brazil
214 A4 **Unión** Para.
203 I2 **Union** *ME* U.S.A.
201 D5 **Union** *SC* U.S.A.
202 C6 **Union** *WV* U.S.A.
197 F4 **Union, Mount** U.S.A.
190 E5 **Union City** *OH* U.S.A.
202 D4 **Union City** *PA* U.S.A.
201 B4 **Union City** *TN* U.S.A.
180 E6 **Uniondale** S. Africa
201 C5 **Union Springs** U.S.A.
202 D5 **Uniontown** U.S.A.
191 F4 **Unionville** U.S.A.
140 D6 **United Arab Emirates** *country* Asia
132 E3 **United Kingdom** *country* Europe
192 D4 **United States of America** *country* N. America
187 H4 **Unity** Canada
203 I2 **Unity** *ME* U.S.A.
194 C2 **Unity** *OR* U.S.A.
144 C5 **Unjha** India
165 F3 **Unna** Germany
144 E4 **Unnao** India
152 C4 **Ŭnp'a** N. Korea
152 C3 **Unsan** N. Korea
152 D4 **Ŭnsan** N. Korea
162 □ **Unst** *i.* U.K.
165 J3 **Unstrut** *r.* Germany
145 G2 **Unuli Horog** China
151 F6 **Uonuma** Japan
143 D1 **Upar Ghat** *reg.* India
213 E2 **Upata** Venez.
179 C4 **Upemba, Lac** *l.* Dem. Rep. Congo
179 C4 **Upemba, Parc National de l'** *nat. park* Dem. Rep. Congo
153 C5 **Upi** Phil.
213 B3 **Upía** *r.* Col.
180 D4 **Upington** S. Africa
144 B5 **Upleta** India
158 O2 **Upoloksha** Rus. Fed.
**'Upolu** *i.* Samoa *see* **'Upolu**
125 I3 **'Upolu** *i.* Samoa
194 B3 **Upper Alkali Lake** U.S.A.
202 B4 **Upper Arlington** U.S.A.
186 F4 **Upper Arrow Lake** Canada
128 E4 **Upper Hutt** N.Z.
190 B4 **Upper Iowa** *r.* U.S.A.
203 J1 **Upper Kent** Canada
196 B2 **Upper Klamath Lake** U.S.A.
196 A2 **Upper Lake** U.S.A.
186 D2 **Upper Liard** Canada
163 D3 **Upper Lough Erne** *l.* U.K.
202 E5 **Upper Marlboro** U.S.A.
154 □ **Upper Peirce Reservoir** Sing.
189 I4 **Upper Salmon Reservoir** Canada
202 B4 **Upper Sandusky** U.S.A.
203 F2 **Upper Saranac Lake** U.S.A.
128 D4 **Upper Takaka** N.Z.
159 L4 **Uppsala** Sweden
188 B4 **Upsala** Canada
203 H2 **Upton** U.S.A.
137 K7 **'Uqlat al 'Udhaybah** *well* Iraq
137 K6 **Ur** *tourist site* Iraq
213 A2 **Urabá, Golfo de** *b.* Col.
140 E4 **Ūrāf** Iran
150 H3 **Urakawa** Japan
127 G4 **Ural** *h.* Australia
138 B3 **Ural** *r.* Kazakh./Rus. Fed.
127 I3 **Uralla** Australia
132 G4 **Ural Mountains** Rus. Fed.
138 B2 **Ural'sk** Kazakh.
**Ural'skiy Khrebet** *mts* Rus. Fed. *see* **Ural Mountains**
178 D4 **Urambo** Tanz.
127 G5 **Urana** Australia
127 G5 **Urana, Lake** Australia
214 D1 **Urandi** Brazil
187 H3 **Uranium City** Canada
127 G5 **Uranquinty** Australia
213 E4 **Uraricoera** Brazil
213 E4 **Uraricoera** *r.* Brazil
213 E4 **Uraricoera** *r.* Brazil
213 E3 **Uraucaima, Serra** *mt.* Brazil
197 H2 **Uravan** U.S.A.
140 B5 **'Urayq ad Duḥūl** *des.* Saudi Arabia
173 F5 **Urazovo** Rus. Fed.
190 C5 **Urbana** *IL* U.S.A.
202 B4 **Urbana** *OH* U.S.A.
127 J2 **Urbenville** Australia
170 E3 **Urbino** Italy
210 D6 **Urcos** Peru
172 I2 **Urdoma** Rus. Fed.
160 F3 **Ure** *r.* U.K.
172 H3 **Uren'** Rus. Fed.
132 I3 **Urengoy** Rus. Fed.
125 G3 **Uréparapara** *i.* Vanuatu
172 H4 **Urga** *r.* Rus. Fed.
138 E4 **Urganch** Uzbek.
**Urgench** Uzbek. *see* **Urganch**
141 H3 **Urgūn-e Kalān** Afgh.
136 E2 **Ürgüp** Turkey
139 F5 **Urgut** Uzbek.
158 N1 **Urho Kekkosen kansallispuisto** *nat. park* Fin.
213 B2 **Uribia** Col.
126 E2 **Urisino** Australia
159 M3 **Urjala** Fin.
164 D2 **Urk** Neth.
173 H7 **Urkarakh** Rus. Fed.
171 L5 **Urla** Turkey
163 D5 **Urlingford** Ireland
139 G5 **Urmetan** Tajik.
140 B2 **Urmia** Iran
140 B2 **Urmia, Lake** *salt l.* Iran
149 □ **Urmston Road** *sea chan.* Hong Kong China
**Uroševac** Kosovo *see* **Ferizaj**
139 G5 **Üroteppa** Tajik.
145 F3 **Urru Co** *salt l.* China
**Urt** Mongolia *see* **Gurvantes**
206 B2 **Uruáchic** Mex.
214 C1 **Uruaçu** Brazil
206 D4 **Uruapan** Mex.
210 D6 **Urubamba** *r.* Peru
211 G4 **Urucara** Brazil
211 J5 **Uruçuí** Brazil
214 D2 **Urucuia** *r.* Brazil
211 J5 **Uruçuí Preto** *r.* Brazil
211 G4 **Urucurituba** Brazil
212 E4 **Uruguaiana** Brazil
212 E4 **Uruguay** *r.* Arg./Uruguay
215 F2 **Uruguay** *country* S. America
146 A2 **Ürümqi** China
127 J3 **Urunga** Australia
173 G6 **Urup** *r.* Rus. Fed.
146 H2 **Urup, Ostrov** *i.* Rus. Fed.
173 H7 **Urus-Martan** Rus. Fed.
173 G5 **Uryupinsk** Rus. Fed.
139 J3 **Urzhar** Kazakh.
172 I3 **Urzhum** Rus. Fed.
171 L2 **Urziceni** Romania
151 B8 **Usa** Japan
172 I4 **Usa** *r.* Rus. Fed.
136 B2 **Uşak** Turkey
179 B6 **Usakos** Namibia
129 B6 **Usarp Mountains** *mts* Antarctica
212 E8 **Usborne, Mount** *h.* Falkland Is
132 I1 **Ushakova, Ostrov** *i.* Rus. Fed.
139 J2 **Ushanovo** Kazakh.
139 G4 **Usharal** Kazakh.
139 J3 **Usharal** Kazakh.
151 B8 **Ushibuka** Japan
139 I3 **Ushtobe** Kazakh.
212 C8 **Ushuaia** Arg.
165 G4 **Usingen** Germany
132 G3 **Usinsk** Rus. Fed.
161 E6 **Usk** U.K.
161 E6 **Usk** *r.* U.K.
145 E4 **Uska** India
172 C4 **Uskhodni** Belarus
165 H3 **Uslar** Germany
173 F4 **Usman'** Rus. Fed.
159 M4 **Usmas ezers** *l.* Latvia
172 I2 **Usogorsk** Rus. Fed.
146 C1 **Usol'ye-Sibirskoye** Rus. Fed.
139 I1 **Uspenka** Kazakh.
139 H2 **Uspenskoye** Kazakh.
166 F4 **Ussel** France
150 D1 **Ussuri** *r.* China/Rus. Fed.
146 F2 **Ussuriysk** Rus. Fed.
172 H3 **Usta** *r.* Rus. Fed.
133 L4 **Ust'-Barguzin** Rus. Fed.
173 G5 **Ust'-Buzulukskaya** Rus. Fed.
139 J1 **Ust'-Charyshskaya Pristan'** Rus. Fed.
173 G6 **Ust'-Donetskiy** Rus. Fed.
170 E5 **Ustica, Isola di** *i. Sicily* Italy
146 C1 **Ust'-Ilimsk** Rus. Fed.
146 C1 **Ust'-Ilimskoye Vodokhranilishche** *resr* Rus. Fed.
132 G3 **Ust'-Ilych** Rus. Fed.
168 G5 **Ústí nad Labem** Czech Rep.
168 H3 **Ustka** Poland
139 J1 **Ust'-Kalmanka** Rus. Fed.
133 R4 **Ust'-Kamchatsk** Rus. Fed.
139 J2 **Ust'-Kamenogorsk** Kazakh.
139 K2 **Ust'-Kan** Rus. Fed.
139 K2 **Ust'-Koksa** Rus. Fed.
146 C1 **Ust'-Kut** Rus. Fed.
133 O2 **Ust'-Kuyga** Rus. Fed.
173 F6 **Ust'-Labinsk** Rus. Fed.
159 O4 **Ust'-Luga** Rus. Fed.
133 O3 **Ust'-Maya** Rus. Fed.
132 G3 **Ust'-Nem** Rus. Fed.
133 P3 **Ust'-Nera** Rus. Fed.
172 I2 **Ust'-Ocheya** Rus. Fed.
133 M2 **Ust'-Olenek** Rus. Fed.
133 P3 **Ust'-Omchug** Rus. Fed.
146 C1 **Ust'-Ordynskiy** Rus. Fed.
132 J3 **Ust'-Port** Rus. Fed.
172 G2 **Ust'-Shonosha** Rus. Fed.
132 G3 **Ust'-Tsil'ma** Rus. Fed.
172 H2 **Ust'-Ura** Rus. Fed.
138 E1 **Ust'-Uyskoye** Kazakh.
172 G2 **Ust'-Vayen'ga** Rus. Fed.
172 H2 **Ust'-Vyyskaya** Rus. Fed.
172 G2 **Ust'ya** *r.* Rus. Fed.
172 F3 **Ust'ye** Rus. Fed.
172 F3 **Ust'ye** *r.* Rus. Fed.
138 C3 **Ustyurt Plateau** Kazakh./Uzbek.
172 F3 **Ustyuzhna** Rus. Fed.
151 B8 **Usuki** Japan
206 G5 **Usulután** El Salvador
207 G4 **Usumacinta** *r.* Guat./Mex.
172 D4 **Usvyaty** Rus. Fed.
197 G2 **Utah** *state* U.S.A.
197 G1 **Utah Lake** U.S.A.
158 N2 **Utajärvi** Fin.
140 C5 **Utayyiq** Saudi Arabia
159 N5 **Utena** Lith.
133 S3 **Utesiki** Rus. Fed.
154 B2 **Uthai Thani** Thai.
141 G5 **Uthal** Pak.
154 A2 **U Thong** Thai.
181 I4 **uThukela** *r.* S. Africa
154 C2 **Uthumphon Phisai** Thai.
203 F3 **Utica** U.S.A.
167 F3 **Utiel** Spain
186 F3 **Utikuma Lake** Canada
206 H4 **Utila** Hond.
181 F3 **Utlwanang** S. Africa
145 E4 **Utraula** India
164 D2 **Utrecht** Neth.
181 I3 **Utrecht** S. Africa
167 D4 **Utrera** Spain
158 N1 **Utsjoki** Fin.
151 F6 **Utsunomiya** Japan
173 H6 **Utta** Rus. Fed.
154 B1 **Uttaradit** Thai.
144 D3 **Uttarakhand** *state* India
144 D4 **Uttar Pradesh** *state* India
161 F5 **Uttoxeter** U.K.
125 G3 **Utupua** *i.* Solomon Is
**Uummannaq** Greenland *see* **Dundas**
185 M2 **Uummannaq Fjord** *inlet* Greenland
185 P2 **Uunartoq Qeqertoq** *i.* Greenland
158 N3 **Uurainen** Fin.
159 M3 **Uusikaupunki** Fin.
213 C4 **Uva** *r.* Col.
199 D6 **Uvalde** U.S.A.
173 G5 **Uvarovo** Rus. Fed.
138 E1 **Uvel'ka** *r.* Rus. Fed.
178 D4 **Uvinza** Tanz.
181 I5 **Uvongo** S. Africa
146 B1 **Uvs Nuur** *salt l.* Mongolia
151 C8 **Uwajima** Japan
177 E2 **'Uweinat, Jebel** *mt.* Sudan
161 G6 **Uxbridge** U.K.
148 C2 **Uxin Ju** China
207 G3 **Uxmal** *tourist site* Mex.
138 E1 **Uy** *r.* Rus. Fed.
138 E3 **Uyaly** Kazakh.
146 B1 **Uyar** Rus. Fed.
**Üydzin** Mongolia *see* **Manlay**
176 C4 **Uyo** Nigeria
212 C2 **Uyuni** Bol.
210 E8 **Uyuni, Salar de** *salt flat* Bol.
172 H4 **Uza** *r.* Rus. Fed.
137 J4 **'Uzaym, Nahr al** *r.* Iraq
138 E4 **Uzbekistan** *country* Asia
166 G4 **Uzès** France
173 B5 **Uzhhorod** Ukr.
171 H3 **Užice** Serbia
172 F4 **Uzlovaya** Rus. Fed.
172 G3 **Uzola** *r.* Rus. Fed.
136 C3 **Üzümlü** Turkey
139 G5 **Uzun** Uzbek.
139 I3 **Uzunbulak** China
137 K3 **Üzün Darreh** *r.* Iran
173 C7 **Uzunköprü** Turkey
173 D5 **Uzyn** Ukr.
139 I4 **Uzynagash** Kazakh.
138 E3 **Uzynkair** Kazakh.
138 F1 **Uzynkol'** Kazakh.


## V


159 N3 **Vaajakoski** Fin.
180 H3 **Vaal** *r.* S. Africa
158 N2 **Vaala** Fin.
180 F4 **Vaalbos National Park** S. Africa
181 H3 **Vaal Dam** S. Africa
181 H2 **Vaalwater** S. Africa
158 M3 **Vaasa** Fin.
**Vabkent** Uzbek. *see* **Vobkent**
169 I7 **Vác** Hungary
212 F3 **Vacaria** Brazil
214 A3 **Vacaria** *r. Mato Grosso do Sul* Brazil
214 D2 **Vacaria** *r. Minas Gerais* Brazil
214 C2 **Vacaria, Serra** *hills* Brazil
196 B2 **Vacaville** U.S.A.
172 G4 **Vad** Rus. Fed.
144 C6 **Vada** India
143 A4 **Vadakara** India
159 I4 **Vadla** Norway
144 C5 **Vadodara** India
158 O1 **Vadsø** Norway
168 D7 **Vaduz** Liechtenstein
158 K2 **Værøy** *i.* Norway
172 G2 **Vaga** *r.* Rus. Fed.
159 J3 **Vågåmo** Norway
170 F2 **Vaganski Vrh** *mt.* Croatia
158 □ **Vágar** *i.* Faroe Is
137 J1 **Vagharshapat** Armenia
158 L2 **Vägsele** Sweden
158 □ **Vágur** Faroe Is
158 M3 **Vähäkyrö** Fin.
140 E4 **Vahhābī** Iran
125 H2 **Vaiaku** Tuvalu
159 N4 **Vaida** Estonia
143 B4 **Vaigai** *r.* India
197 G5 **Vail** U.S.A.
164 B5 **Vailly-sur-Aisne** France
125 H2 **Vaitupu** *i.* Tuvalu
139 H5 **Vakhan** Tajik.
139 G5 **Vakhsh** Tajik.
143 C5 **Valachchenai** Sri Lanka
191 J2 **Val-Barrette** Canada
159 L3 **Valbo** Sweden
215 C4 **Valcheta** Arg.
170 D2 **Valdagno** Italy
172 E3 **Valday** Rus. Fed.
172 E3 **Valdayskaya Vozvyshennost'** *hills* Rus. Fed.
167 D3 **Valdecañas, Embalse de** *resr* Spain
159 M4 **Valdemārpils** Latvia
159 L4 **Valdemarsvik** Sweden
167 E3 **Valdepeñas** Spain
166 E2 **Val-de-Reuil** France
215 D4 **Valdés, Península** *pen.* Arg.
191 J3 **Val-des-Bois** Canada
184 D3 **Valdez** U.S.A.
215 B3 **Valdivia** Chile
191 I1 **Val-d'Or** Canada
201 D6 **Valdosta** U.S.A.
159 J3 **Valdres** *val.* Norway
137 I1 **Vale** Georgia
194 C2 **Vale** U.S.A.
186 F4 **Valemount** Canada
214 E1 **Valença** Brazil
166 G4 **Valence** France
167 F3 **Valencia** Spain
167 F3 **Valencia** *reg.* Spain
213 D2 **Valencia** Venez.
167 G3 **Valencia, Golfo de** *g.* Spain
167 C3 **Valencia de Alcántara** Spain
167 D1 **Valencia de Don Juan** Spain
163 A6 **Valencia Island** Ireland
166 F1 **Valenciennes** France
150 D3 **Valentin** Rus. Fed.
197 F4 **Valentine** *AZ* U.S.A.
198 C3 **Valentine** *NE* U.S.A.
199 B6 **Valentine** *TX* U.S.A.
153 B3 **Valenzuela** Phil.
159 J3 **Valer** Norway
213 C2 **Valera** Venez.
139 G1 **Valikhanov** Kazakh.
171 H2 **Valjevo** Serbia
159 N4 **Valka** Latvia
159 N3 **Valkeakoski** Fin.
164 D3 **Valkenswaard** Neth.
173 E5 **Valky** Ukr.
129 D4 **Valkyrie Dome** *ice feature* Antarctica
207 G3 **Valladolid** Mex.
167 D2 **Valladolid** Spain
159 I4 **Valle** Norway
213 D2 **Valle de la Pascua** Venez.
206 D3 **Valle de Santiago** Mex.
213 B2 **Valledupar** Col.
215 C1 **Valle Fértil, Sierra de** *mts* Arg.
210 F7 **Valle Grande** Bol.
207 E2 **Valle Hermoso** Mex.
196 A2 **Vallejo** U.S.A.
207 E4 **Valle Nacional** Mex.
170 F7 **Valletta** Malta
161 C4 **Valley** U.K.
198 D2 **Valley City** U.S.A.
194 B3 **Valley Falls** U.S.A.
202 C5 **Valley Head** U.S.A.
186 F3 **Valleyview** Canada
167 G2 **Valls** Spain
187 H5 **Val Marie** Canada
159 N4 **Valmiera** Latvia
167 E1 **Valnera** *mt.* Spain
172 C4 **Valozhyn** Belarus
188 E4 **Val-Paradis** Canada
214 B3 **Valparaíso** Brazil
215 B2 **Valparaíso** Chile
215 B2 **Valparaíso** *admin. reg.* Chile
206 D3 **Valparaíso** Mex.
190 D5 **Valparaiso** U.S.A.
166 G4 **Valréas** France
147 F7 **Vals, Tanjung** *c.* Indon.
144 C5 **Valsad** India
180 F3 **Valspan** S. Africa
158 O3 **Valtimo** Fin.
173 G6 **Valuyevka** Rus. Fed.
173 F5 **Valuyki** Rus. Fed.
167 C4 **Valverde del Camino** Spain
154 C3 **Vam Co Tây** *r.* Vietnam
159 M3 **Vammala** Fin.
145 E5 **Vamsadhara** *r.* India
137 I2 **Van** Turkey
137 I2 **Van, Lake** *salt l.* Turkey
137 J1 **Vanadzor** Armenia
199 E5 **Van Buren** *AR* U.S.A.
203 J1 **Van Buren** *ME* U.S.A.
154 D2 **Vân Canh** Vietnam
203 J2 **Vanceboro** U.S.A.
202 B5 **Vanceburg** U.S.A.
186 E5 **Vancouver** Canada
194 B2 **Vancouver** U.S.A.
186 A2 **Vancouver, Mount** Canada/U.S.A.
186 D5 **Vancouver Island** Canada
200 B4 **Vandalia** *IL* U.S.A.
202 A5 **Vandalia** *OH* U.S.A.
181 G3 **Vanderbijlpark** S. Africa
190 E3 **Vanderbilt** U.S.A.
202 D4 **Vandergrift** U.S.A.
186 E4 **Vanderhoof** Canada
180 F5 **Vanderkloof Dam** *resr* S. Africa
124 D3 **Vanderlin Island** Australia
197 H4 **Vanderwagen** U.S.A.
124 D3 **Van Diemen Gulf** Australia
159 N4 **Vändra** Estonia
159 K4 **Vänern** *l.* Sweden
159 K4 **Vänersborg** Sweden
202 E3 **Van Etten** U.S.A.
179 E6 **Vangaindrano** Madag.
154 D2 **Van Gia** Vietnam
**Van Gölü** *salt l.* Turkey *see* **Van, Lake**
199 B6 **Van Horn** U.S.A.
191 J3 **Vanier** Canada
125 G3 **Vanikoro Islands** Solomon Is
124 E2 **Vanimo** P.N.G.
146 G2 **Vanino** Rus. Fed.
143 B3 **Vanivilasa Sagara** *resr* India
143 B3 **Vaniyambadi** India
139 G5 **Vanj** Tajik.
139 G5 **Vanj, Qatorkŭhi** *mts* Tajik.
133 U3 **Vankarem** Rus. Fed.
203 F2 **Vankleek Hill** Canada
**Vanna** *i.* Norway *see* **Vannøya**
158 L3 **Vännäs** Sweden
166 C3 **Vannes** France
158 L1 **Vannøya** *i.* Norway
147 F7 **Van Rees, Pegunungan** *mts* Indon.
180 C5 **Vanrhynsdorp** S. Africa
159 K3 **Vansbro** Sweden
159 N3 **Vantaa** Fin.
125 H3 **Vanua Lava** *i.* Vanuatu
125 H3 **Vanua Levu** *i.* Fiji
125 G3 **Vanuatu** *country* Pacific Ocean
202 A4 **Van Wert** U.S.A.
180 D5 **Van Wyksvlei** S. Africa
180 D5 **Van Wyksvlei Dam** *l.* S. Africa
149 B6 **Văn Yên** Vietnam
180 E3 **Van Zylsrus** S. Africa
145 E4 **Varada** *r.* India
159 N4 **Varakļāni** Latvia
140 C3 **Varāmīn** Iran
145 E4 **Varanasi** India
158 O1 **Varangerfjorden** *sea chan.* Norway
158 O1 **Varangerhalvøya** *pen.* Norway
170 G1 **Varaždin** Croatia
159 K4 **Varberg** Sweden
143 B2 **Vardannapet** India
171 J4 **Vardar** *r.* Macedonia
159 J5 **Varde** Denmark
140 B1 **Vardenis** Armenia
158 O1 **Vardø** Norway
165 G1 **Varel** Germany
215 C2 **Varela** Arg.
159 N5 **Varėna** Lith.
170 C2 **Varese** Italy
150 C2 **Varfolomeyevka** Rus. Fed.
159 K4 **Vårgårda** Sweden
214 D3 **Varginha** Brazil
164 D3 **Varik** Neth.
158 N3 **Varkaus** Fin.
171 L3 **Varna** Bulg.
138 E1 **Varna** Rus. Fed.
159 K4 **Värnamo** Sweden
159 K3 **Värnäs** Sweden
172 H3 **Varnavino** Rus. Fed.
136 D4 **Varosia** Cyprus
158 N3 **Varpaisjärvi** Fin.
168 I7 **Várpalota** Hungary
137 H2 **Varto** Turkey
145 E4 **Varuna** *r.* India
202 D3 **Varysburg** U.S.A.
140 D3 **Varzaneh** Iran
214 D2 **Várzea da Palma** Brazil
172 H2 **Vashka** *r.* Rus. Fed.
172 H2 **Vasil'yevo** Rus. Fed.
159 N4 **Vasknarva** Estonia
169 M7 **Vaslui** Romania
191 F4 **Vassar** U.S.A.
159 L4 **Västerås** Sweden
159 K3 **Västerdalälven** *r.* Sweden
158 L2 **Västerfjäll** Sweden
159 L4 **Västerhaninge** Sweden
158 L3 **Västernorrland** *county* Sweden
159 L4 **Västervik** Sweden
170 F3 **Vasto** Italy
173 D5 **Vasyl'kiv** Ukr.
166 E3 **Vatan** France
162 A4 **Vatersay** *i.* U.K.
143 A2 **Vathar** India
171 L6 **Vathy** Greece
170 E4 **Vatican City** Europe
158 C2 **Vatnajökull** *ice cap* Iceland
158 C2 **Vatnajökulsþjóðgarður** *nat. park* Iceland
169 L7 **Vatra Dornei** Romania
159 K4 **Vättern** *l.* Sweden
195 F5 **Vaughn** U.S.A.
164 B4 **Vaulx** *tourist site* Belgium
213 C4 **Vaupés** *r.* Col.
166 G5 **Vauvert** France
**Vava'u Group** *is* Tonga *see* **Vava'u Group**
125 I3 **Vava'u Group** *is* Tonga
176 B4 **Vavoua** Côte d'Ivoire
143 C4 **Vavuniya** Sri Lanka
172 C4 **Vawkavysk** Belarus
159 K4 **Växjö** Sweden
154 B3 **Vay, Đao** *i.* Vietnam
143 B3 **Vayalpad** India
133 S3 **Vayegi** Rus. Fed.
172 H1 **Vazhgort** Rus. Fed.
179 E5 **Vazobe** *mt.* Madag.
154 B2 **Veal Vêng** Cambodia
165 G2 **Vechta** Germany
164 E2 **Vechte** *r.* Germany
165 H3 **Veckerhagen (Reinhardshagen)** Germany
143 B4 **Vedaranniyam** India
159 K4 **Veddige** Sweden
171 K3 **Vedea** *r.* Romania
173 H7 **Vedeno** Rus. Fed.
137 J2 **Vedi** Armenia
215 E2 **Vedia** Arg.
172 E2 **Vedlozero** Rus. Fed.
190 D5 **Veedersburg** U.S.A.
164 E1 **Veendam** Neth.
164 D2 **Veenendaal** Neth.
158 J2 **Vega** *i.* Norway
199 C5 **Vega** U.S.A.
187 G4 **Vegreville** Canada
144 C3 **Vehari** Pak.
159 N3 **Vehkalahti** Fin.
144 B3 **Vehowa** *r.* Pak.
144 B4 **Veirwaro** Pak.
165 H5 **Veitshöchheim** Germany
167 D4 **Vejer de la Frontera** Spain
159 J5 **Vejle** Denmark
213 B1 **Vela, Cabo de la** *c.* Col.
164 F3 **Velbert** Germany
171 J3 **Velbŭzhdki Prokhod** *pass* Macedonia
180 C6 **Velddrif** S. Africa
170 F2 **Velebit** *mts* Croatia
164 E3 **Velen** Germany
170 F1 **Velenje** Slovenia
171 I4 **Veles** Macedonia
213 B3 **Vélez** Col.
167 D4 **Vélez-Málaga** Spain
167 E4 **Vélez-Rubio** Spain
214 D2 **Velhas** *r.* Brazil
173 H6 **Velichayevskoye** Rus. Fed.
170 G2 **Velika Gorica** Croatia
171 I2 **Velika Plana** Serbia
172 I3 **Velikaya** Rus. Fed.
133 S3 **Velikaya** *r.* Rus. Fed.
172 D3 **Velikaya** *r.* Rus. Fed.
150 E2 **Velikaya Guba** Rus. Fed.
150 E2 **Velikaya Kema** Rus. Fed.
171 L3 **Veliki Preslav** Bulg.
172 D3 **Velikiye Luki** Rus. Fed.
172 D3 **Velikiy Novgorod** Rus. Fed.
172 H2 **Velikiy Ustyug** Rus. Fed.
143 B3 **Velikonda Range** *hills* India
169 P2 **Velikooktyabr'skiy** Rus. Fed.
171 K3 **Veliko Tŭrnovo** Bulg.
172 F3 **Velikoye** Rus. Fed.
172 F3 **Velikoye, Ozero** *l.* Rus. Fed.
172 G4 **Velikoye, Ozero** *l.* Rus. Fed.
170 F2 **Veli Lošinj** Croatia
176 A3 **Vélingara** Senegal
172 D3 **Velizh** Rus. Fed.
168 H7 **Veľký Meder** Slovakia
125 F2 **Vella Lavella** *i.* Solomon Is
143 B4 **Vellar** *r.* India
165 H5 **Vellberg** Germany
165 H3 **Vellmar** Germany
143 B3 **Vellore** India
165 I2 **Velpke** Germany
172 G2 **Vel'sk** Rus. Fed.
165 L2 **Velten** Germany
164 D2 **Veluwe** *reg.* Neth.
164 E2 **Veluwezoom, Nationaal Park** *nat. park* Neth.
187 I5 **Velva** U.S.A.
219 J8 **Vema Seamount** *sea feature* S. Atlantic Ocean
218 I5 **Vema Trench** *sea feature* Indian Ocean
143 B4 **Vembanad Lake** India
162 D4 **Venachar, Loch** *l.* U.K.
213 B3 **Venado Tuerto** Arg.
170 F4 **Venafro** Italy
213 E3 **Venamo** *r.* Guyana/Venez.
213 E3 **Venamo, Cerro** *mt.* Venez.
214 C3 **Venceslau Bráz** Brazil
166 E3 **Vendôme** France
172 F4 **Venev** Rus. Fed.
**Venezia** Italy *see* **Venice**
213 C2 **Venezuela** *country* S. America
213 C2 **Venezuela, Golfo de** *g.* Venez.
219 E4 **Venezuelan Basin** *sea feature* S. Atlantic Ocean
143 A3 **Vengurla** India
170 E2 **Venice** Italy
201 D7 **Venice** U.S.A.
170 E2 **Venice, Gulf of** Europe
166 G4 **Vénissieux** France
143 B3 **Venkatagiri** India
143 C2 **Venkatapuram** India
164 E3 **Venlo** Neth.
159 I4 **Vennesla** Norway
164 D3 **Venray** Neth.
159 M4 **Venta** *r.* Latvia/Lith.
159 M4 **Venta** Lith.
215 D3 **Ventana, Sierra de la** *hills* Arg.
181 G4 **Ventersburg** S. Africa
181 G3 **Ventersdorp** S. Africa
181 F5 **Venterstad** S. Africa
161 F7 **Ventnor** U.K.
166 G4 **Ventoux, Mont** *mt.* France
159 M4 **Ventspils** Latvia
213 D3 **Ventuari** *r.* Venez.
196 C4 **Ventucopa** U.S.A.
196 C4 **Ventura** U.S.A.
126 F7 **Venus Bay** Australia
206 D2 **Venustiano Carranza** Mex.
206 D2 **Venustiano Carranza, Presa** *resr* Mex.
212 D3 **Vera** Arg.
167 F4 **Vera** Spain
207 E4 **Veracruz** Mex.
207 E3 **Veracruz** *state* Mex.
144 B5 **Veraval** India
170 C2 **Verbania** Italy
170 C2 **Vercelli** Italy

158 J3 **Verdalsøra** Norway
215 D4 **Verde** *r.* Arg.
214 B2 **Verde** *r. Goiás* Brazil
214 C2 **Verde** *r. Goiás* Brazil
214 C2 **Verde** *r. Goiás/Minas Gerais* Brazil
214 B2 **Verde** *r. Mato Grosso do Sul* Brazil
192 E6 **Verde** *r.* Mex.
212 E2 **Verde** *r.* Para.
197 G4 **Verde** *r.* U.S.A.
215 D3 **Verde, Península** *pen.* Arg.
214 D1 **Verde Grande** *r.* Brazil
153 B3 **Verde Island Passage** Phil.
165 H2 **Verden (Aller)** Germany
199 E4 **Verdigris** *r.* U.S.A.
166 H5 **Verdon** *r.* France
166 G2 **Verdun** France
181 G3 **Vereeniging** S. Africa
215 G2 **Vergara** Uruguay
203 G2 **Vergennes** U.S.A.
167 C2 **Verín** Spain
173 F6 **Verkhnebakanskiy** Rus. Fed.
169 P3 **Verkhnedneprovskiy** Rus. Fed.
132 J3 **Verkhneimbatsk** Rus. Fed.
158 O1 **Verkhnetulomskiy** Rus. Fed.
138 D1 **Verkhneural'sk** Rus. Fed.
133 N3 **Verkhnevilyuysk** Rus. Fed.
172 D1 **Verkhneye Kuyto, Ozero** *l.* Rus. Fed.
138 D1 **Verkhniy Avzyan** Rus. Fed.
173 H5 **Verkhniy Baskunchak** Rus. Fed.
173 I5 **Verkhniy Kushum** Rus. Fed.
158 P2 **Verkhnyaya Pirenga, Ozero** *l.* Rus. Fed.
172 H2 **Verkhnyaya Toyma** Rus. Fed.
172 G2 **Verkhovazh'ye** Rus. Fed.
172 F4 **Verkhov'ye** Rus. Fed.
173 C5 **Verkhovyna** Ukr.
133 O3 **Verkhoyansk** Rus. Fed.
133 N3 **Verkhoyanskiy Khrebet** *mts* Rus. Fed.
139 J2 **Verkhuba** Kazakh.
164 B5 **Vermand** France
214 B1 **Vermelho** *r.* Brazil
187 G4 **Vermilion** Canada
190 C5 **Vermilion** *r.* U.S.A.
197 F3 **Vermilion Cliffs** U.S.A.
190 A2 **Vermilion Lake** U.S.A.
190 A2 **Vermilion Range** *hills* U.S.A.
198 D3 **Vermillion** U.S.A.
187 K5 **Vermillion Bay** Canada
203 G3 **Vermont** *state* U.S.A.
129 E2 **Vernadsky** *research stn* Antarctica
194 E3 **Vernal** U.S.A.
191 G2 **Verner** Canada
180 D5 **Verneuk Pan** *salt pan* S. Africa
186 F4 **Vernon** Canada
197 H4 **Vernon** *AZ* U.S.A.
203 G4 **Vernon** *CT* U.S.A.
199 D5 **Vernon** *TX* U.S.A.
197 F1 **Vernon** *UT* U.S.A.
201 D7 **Vero Beach** U.S.A.
171 J4 **Veroia** Greece
170 D2 **Verona** Italy
215 F2 **Verónica** Arg.
126 B4 **Verran** Australia
166 F2 **Versailles** France
165 G2 **Versmold** Germany
166 D3 **Vertou** France
181 I4 **Verulam** S. Africa
164 D4 **Verviers** Belgium
166 F2 **Vervins** France
164 C5 **Verzy** France
170 C3 **Vescovato** *Corsica* France
132 G4 **Veselaya, Gora** *mt.* Rus. Fed.
173 E6 **Vesele** Ukr.
173 G6 **Veselovskoye Vodokhranilishche** *resr* Rus. Fed.
139 J2 **Veseloyarsk** Rus. Fed.
138 F1 **Veselyy Podol** Kazakh.
150 D3 **Veselyy Yar** Rus. Fed.
173 G5 **Veshenskaya** Rus. Fed.
164 B5 **Vesle** *r.* France
166 H3 **Vesoul** France
164 D3 **Vessem** Neth.
158 K1 **Vesterålen** *is* Norway
158 K1 **Vesterålsfjorden** *sea chan.* Norway
159 J4 **Vestfjorddalen** *val.* Norway
158 K2 **Vestfjorden** *sea chan.* Norway
158 □ **Vestmanna** Faroe Is
158 B3 **Vestmannaeyjar** Iceland
158 B3 **Vestmannaeyjar** *is* Iceland
158 I3 **Vestnes** Norway
158 D2 **Vesturhorn** *hd* Iceland
170 F4 **Vesuvio** *vol.* Italy
172 F3 **Ves'yegonsk** Rus. Fed.
168 H7 **Veszprém** Hungary
158 M3 **Veteli** Fin.
159 K4 **Vetlanda** Sweden
172 H3 **Vetluga** Rus. Fed.
172 H3 **Vetluga** *r.* Rus. Fed.
170 E3 **Vettore, Monte** *mt.* Italy
164 A3 **Veurne** Belgium
168 C7 **Vevey** Switz.
197 F3 **Veyo** U.S.A.
140 C4 **Veys** Iran
166 E4 **Vézère** *r.* France
136 E1 **Vezirköprü** Turkey
215 B2 **V. Hermosa, Paso de** *pass* Chile
210 C6 **Viajas, Isla de las** *i.* Peru
211 J4 **Viana** Brazil
167 B2 **Viana do Castelo** Port.
164 D3 **Vianen** Neth.
**Viangchan** Laos *see* **Vientiane**
171 K7 **Viannos** Greece
214 C2 **Vianópolis** Brazil
170 D3 **Viareggio** Italy
159 J4 **Viborg** Denmark
170 G5 **Vibo Valentia** Italy
167 H2 **Vic** Spain
206 B2 **Vicam** Mex.
196 C5 **Vicente, Point** U.S.A.
206 D3 **Vicente Guerrero** Mex.
170 D2 **Vicenza** Italy
213 C3 **Vichada** *r.* Col.
172 G3 **Vichuga** Rus. Fed.
215 B2 **Vichuquén** Chile
166 F3 **Vichy** France
197 F5 **Vicksburg** *AZ* U.S.A.
199 F5 **Vicksburg** *MS* U.S.A.
214 D3 **Viçosa** Brazil
190 A5 **Victor** U.S.A.
129 D4 **Victor, Mount** *mt.* Antarctica
126 C5 **Victor Harbor** Australia
215 E2 **Victoria** Arg.
124 D3 **Victoria** *r.* Australia
126 F6 **Victoria** *state* Australia
186 E5 **Victoria** Canada
215 B3 **Victoria** Chile
206 H5 **Victoria** Hond.
170 F6 **Victoria** Malta
199 D6 **Victoria** U.S.A.
178 D4 **Victoria, Lake** Africa
126 D4 **Victoria, Lake** *N.S.W.* Australia
127 G6 **Victoria, Lake** *Vic.* Australia
145 H5 **Victoria, Mount** Myanmar
124 E2 **Victoria, Mount** P.N.G.
185 K2 **Victoria and Albert Mountains** Canada
179 C5 **Victoria Falls** Zambia/Zimbabwe
185 N1 **Victoria Fjord** *inlet* Greenland
149 □ **Victoria Harbour** *Hong Kong* China
184 G2 **Victoria Island** Canada
189 I4 **Victoria Lake** Canada
129 B6 **Victoria Land** *coastal area* Antarctica
178 D3 **Victoria Nile** *r.* Sudan/Uganda
128 D5 **Victoria Range** *mts* N.Z.
124 D3 **Victoria River Downs** Australia
189 F4 **Victoriaville** Canada
180 E5 **Victoria West** S. Africa
215 D3 **Victorica** Arg.
206 D3 **Víctor Rosales** Mex.
196 D4 **Victorville** U.S.A.
215 D2 **Vicuña Mackenna** Arg.
197 E4 **Vidal Junction** U.S.A.
171 K2 **Videle** Romania
171 J3 **Vidin** Bulg.
144 D5 **Vidisha** India
162 □ **Vidlin** U.K.
172 E2 **Vidlitsa** Rus. Fed.
169 M3 **Vidzy** Belarus
172 I2 **Vidz'yuyar** Rus. Fed.
165 K5 **Viechtach** Germany
215 D4 **Viedma** Arg.
212 B7 **Viedma, Lago** *l.* Arg.
165 J1 **Vielank** Germany
164 D4 **Vielsalm** Belgium
165 I3 **Vienenburg** Germany
168 H6 **Vienna** Austria
200 B4 **Vienna** *IL* U.S.A.
203 F5 **Vienna** *MD* U.S.A.
202 C5 **Vienna** *WV* U.S.A.
166 G4 **Vienne** France
166 E3 **Vienne** *r.* France
154 B1 **Vientiane** Laos
215 B3 **Viento, Cordillera del** *mts* Arg.
205 K5 **Vieques** *i.* Puerto Rico
158 N3 **Vieremä** Fin.
164 E3 **Viersen** Germany
168 D7 **Vierwaldstätter See** *l.* Switz.
166 F3 **Vierzon** France
206 D2 **Viesca** Mex.
159 N4 **Viesīte** Latvia
170 G4 **Vieste** Italy
158 L2 **Vietas** Sweden
154 **Vietnam** *country* Asia
149 B6 **Viêt Quang** Vietnam
149 B6 **Viêt Tri** Vietnam
153 B2 **Vigan** Phil.
170 C2 **Vigevano** Italy
207 H4 **Vigía Chico** Mex.
164 A4 **Vignacourt** France
166 D5 **Vignemale** *mt.* France
170 D2 **Vignola** Italy
167 B1 **Vigo** Spain
158 N2 **Vihanti** Fin.
159 N3 **Vihti** Fin.
158 N3 **Viitasaari** Fin.
144 C3 **Vijainagar** India
143 A2 **Vijayadurg** India
143 C2 **Vijayawada** India
158 C3 **Vík** Iceland
158 N2 **Vikajärvi** Fin.
171 K4 **Vikhren** *mt.* Bulg.
187 G4 **Viking** Canada
158 J2 **Vikna** *i.* Norway
159 I3 **Vikøyri** Norway
176 □ **Vila da Ribeira Brava** Cape Verde
**Vila de Sal Rei** Cape Verde *see* **Sal Rei**
176 □ **Vila do Maio** Cape Verde
**Vila do Tarrafal** Cape Verde *see* **Tarrafal**
167 B3 **Vila Franca de Xira** Port.
167 B1 **Vilagarcía de Arousa** Spain
181 J2 **Vila Gomes da Costa** Moz.
167 C1 **Vilalba** Spain
179 E5 **Vilanandro, Tanjona** *pt* Madag.
167 B2 **Vila Nova de Gaia** Port.
167 G2 **Vilanova i la Geltrú** Spain
176 □ **Vila Nova Sintra** Cape Verde
167 C2 **Vila Real** Port.
167 C2 **Vilar Formoso** Port.
143 B4 **Vilavankod** India
214 E3 **Vila Velha** Brazil
132 H1 **Vil'cheka, Zemlya** *i.* Rus. Fed.
158 L2 **Vilhelmina** Sweden
210 F6 **Vilhena** Brazil
159 N4 **Viljandi** Estonia
181 G3 **Viljoenskroon** S. Africa
159 M5 **Vilkaviškis** Lith.
159 M5 **Vilkija** Lith.
133 K2 **Vil'kitskogo, Proliv** *str.* Rus. Fed.
207 E4 **Villa Alta** Mex.
210 E6 **Villa Bella** Bol.
167 C1 **Villablino** Spain
215 E2 **Villa Cañás** Arg.
167 E3 **Villacañas** Spain
168 F7 **Villach** Austria
170 C5 **Villacidro** *Sardinia* Italy
215 E2 **Villa Constitución** Arg.
206 D4 **Villa de Álvarez** Mex.
206 D3 **Villa de Cos** Mex.
207 G4 **Villa de Guadalupe** Mex.
215 D1 **Villa del Rosario** Arg.
215 D1 **Villa del Totoral** Arg.
215 D1 **Villa Dolores** Arg.
207 F4 **Villa Flores** Mex.
215 F3 **Villa Gesell** Arg.
207 E2 **Villagrán** Mex.
215 E1 **Villaguay** Arg.
207 F4 **Villahermosa** Mex.
215 D2 **Villa Huidobro** Arg.
206 B2 **Villa Insurgentes** Mex.
215 D3 **Villa Iris** Arg.
167 F3 **Villajoyosa-La Vila Joiosa** Spain
207 D2 **Villaldama** Mex.
215 D3 **Villalonga** Arg.
215 D2 **Villa María** Arg.
215 E1 **Villa María Grande** Arg.
215 D2 **Villa Mercedes** Arg.
210 F8 **Villa Montes** Bol.
181 H1 **Villa Nora** S. Africa
213 B2 **Villanueva** Col.
206 D3 **Villanueva** Mex.
167 D3 **Villanueva de la Serena** Spain
167 E3 **Villanueva de los Infantes** Spain
212 E3 **Villa Ocampo** Arg.
206 C2 **Villa Ocampo** Mex.
206 C2 **Villa Orestes Pereyra** Mex.
170 C5 **Villaputzu** *Sardinia* Italy
215 C3 **Villa Regina** Arg.
215 B3 **Villarrica** Chile
212 E3 **Villarrica** Para.
215 B3 **Villarrica, Lago** *l.* Chile
215 B3 **Villarrica, Parque Nacional** *nat. park* Chile
215 B3 **Villarrica, Volcán** *vol.* Chile
167 E3 **Villarrobledo** Spain
170 F5 **Villa San Giovanni** Italy
215 E2 **Villa San José** Arg.
215 C1 **Villa Santa Rita de Catuna** Arg.
212 C3 **Villa Unión** Arg.
206 D1 **Villa Unión** Mex.
206 C3 **Villa Unión** Mex.
206 C3 **Villa Unión** Mex.
215 D2 **Villa Valeria** Arg.
213 B3 **Villavicencio** Col.
210 E8 **Villazon** Bol.
166 F4 **Villefranche-de-Rouergue** France
166 G4 **Villefranche-sur-Saône** France
191 H2 **Ville-Marie** Canada
167 F3 **Villena** Spain
166 E4 **Villeneuve-sur-Lot** France
166 F2 **Villeneuve-sur-Yonne** France
199 E6 **Ville Platte** U.S.A.
164 B5 **Villers-Cotterêts** France
164 D5 **Villerupt** France
166 G4 **Villeurbanne** France
181 H3 **Villiers** S. Africa
168 D6 **Villingen** Germany
143 B4 **Villupuram** India
187 G4 **Vilna** Canada
159 N5 **Vilnius** Lith.
173 E6 **Vil'nyans'k** Ukr.
159 N3 **Vilppula** Fin.
165 J5 **Vils** *r.* Germany
164 C4 **Vilvoorde** Belgium
172 C4 **Vilyeyka** Belarus
133 N3 **Vilyuy** *r.* Rus. Fed.
133 L3 **Vilyuyskoye Vodokhranilishche** *resr* Rus. Fed.
159 K4 **Vimmerby** Sweden
164 A4 **Vimy** France
196 A2 **Vina** U.S.A.
215 B2 **Viña del Mar** Chile
203 I2 **Vinalhaven** U.S.A.
167 G2 **Vinaròs** Spain
200 C4 **Vincennes** U.S.A.
129 D6 **Vincennes Bay** *b.* Antarctica
158 L3 **Vindelälven** *r.* Sweden
158 L2 **Vindeln** Sweden
144 C5 **Vindhya Range** *hills* India
203 F5 **Vineland** U.S.A.
203 H4 **Vineyard Haven** U.S.A.
154 C1 **Vinh** Vietnam
**Vinh Linh** Vietnam *see* **Hô Xa**
154 C3 **Vinh Long** Vietnam
149 B6 **Vinh Yên** Vietnam
199 E4 **Vinita** U.S.A.
171 H2 **Vinkovci** Croatia
173 D5 **Vinnytsya** Ukr.
129 B3 **Vinson Massif** *mt.* Antarctica
159 J3 **Vinstra** Norway
190 A4 **Vinton** U.S.A.
143 B2 **Vinukonda** India
170 D1 **Vipiteno** Italy
165 K1 **Vipperow** Germany
153 C3 **Virac** Phil.
144 C5 **Viramgam** India
172 F2 **Virandozero** Rus. Fed.
137 G3 **Viranşehir** Turkey
144 B4 **Virawah** Pak.
187 I5 **Virden** Canada
166 D2 **Vire** France
179 B5 **Virei** Angola
214 D2 **Virgem da Lapa** Brazil
197 F3 **Virgin** *r.* U.S.A.
191 H1 **Virginatown** Canada
163 D4 **Virginia** Ireland
181 G4 **Virginia** S. Africa
190 A2 **Virginia** U.S.A.
202 D6 **Virginia** *state* U.S.A.
203 E6 **Virginia Beach** U.S.A.
196 C2 **Virginia City** U.S.A.
205 L5 **Virgin Islands (U.K.)** *terr.* Caribbean Sea
205 L5 **Virgin Islands (U.S.A.)** *terr.* Caribbean Sea
159 N3 **Virkkala** Fin.
154 C2 **Virôchey** Cambodia
190 B4 **Viroqua** U.S.A.
170 G2 **Virovitica** Croatia
159 M3 **Virrat** Fin.
164 D5 **Virton** Belgium
159 M4 **Virtsu** Estonia
143 B4 **Virudhunagar** India
178 C3 **Virunga, Parc National des** *nat. park* Dem. Rep. Congo
170 G3 **Vis** *i.* Croatia
159 N5 **Visaginas** Lith.
196 C3 **Visalia** U.S.A.
144 B5 **Visavadar** India
153 B4 **Visayan Sea** Phil.
165 G2 **Visbek** Germany
159 L4 **Visby** Sweden
184 G2 **Viscount Melville Sound** *sea chan.* Canada
164 D4 **Visé** Belgium
171 H3 **Višegrad** Bos.-Herz.
211 I4 **Viseu** Brazil
167 C2 **Viseu** Port.
143 C2 **Vishakhapatnam** India
159 N4 **Višķi** Latvia
144 C5 **Visnagar** India
170 B2 **Viso, Monte** *mt.* Italy
171 H3 **Visoko** Bos.-Herz.
168 C7 **Visp** Switz.
165 H2 **Visselhövede** Germany
196 D5 **Vista** U.S.A.
214 A2 **Vista Alegre** Brazil
171 K4 **Vistonida, Limni** *lag.* Greece
169 I4 **Vistula** *r.* Poland
213 C3 **Vita** *r.* Col.
144 B3 **Vitakri** Pak.
170 E3 **Viterbo** Italy
170 G2 **Vitez** Bos.-Herz.
210 E8 **Vitichi** Bol.
167 C2 **Vitigudino** Spain
125 H3 **Viti Levu** *i.* Fiji
146 D1 **Vitim** *r.* Rus. Fed.
146 D1 **Vitimskoye Ploskogor'ye** *plat.* Rus. Fed.
214 E3 **Vitória** Brazil
214 E1 **Vitória da Conquista** Brazil
167 E1 **Vitoria-Gasteiz** Spain
219 G7 **Vitória Seamount** *sea feature* S. Atlantic Ocean
166 D2 **Vitré** France
164 A4 **Vitry-en-Artois** France
166 G2 **Vitry-le-François** France
172 D4 **Vitsyebsk** Belarus
158 M2 **Vittangi** Sweden
170 F6 **Vittoria** *Sicily* Italy
170 E2 **Vittorio Veneto** Italy
167 C1 **Viveiro** Spain
181 H1 **Vivo** S. Africa
126 B6 **Vivonne Bay** Australia
206 A2 **Vizcaíno, Desierto de** *des.* Mex.
206 A2 **Vizcaíno, Sierra** *mts* Mex.
173 C7 **Vize** Turkey
132 I2 **Vize, Ostrov** *i.* Rus. Fed.
143 C2 **Vizianagaram** India
172 I2 **Vizinga** Rus. Fed.
164 C3 **Vlaardingen** Neth.
169 K7 **Vlădeasa, Vârful** *mt.* Romania
173 H7 **Vladikavkaz** Rus. Fed.
150 D3 **Vladimir** *Primorskiy Kray* Rus. Fed.
172 G3 **Vladimir** *Vladimirskaya Oblast'* Rus. Fed.
150 C3 **Vladimiro-Aleksandrovskoye** Rus. Fed.
138 F1 **Vladimirovka** *Kustanayskaya Oblast'* Kazakh.
138 B2 **Vladimirovka** *Zapadnyy Kazakhstan* Kazakh.
172 G4 **Vladimirskaya Oblast'** *admin. div.* Rus. Fed.
146 F2 **Vladivostok** Rus. Fed.
181 H2 **Vlakte** S. Africa
171 J3 **Vlasotince** Serbia
180 D7 **Vleesbaai** *b.* S. Africa
164 C1 **Vlieland** *i.* Neth.
164 B3 **Vlissingen** Neth.
171 H4 **Vlorë** Albania
165 G2 **Vlotho** Germany
168 G6 **Vltava** *r.* Czech Rep.
138 F4 **Vobkent** Uzbek.
168 F6 **Vöcklabruck** Austria
172 F2 **Vodlozero, Ozero** *l.* Rus. Fed.
162 □ **Voe** U.K.
164 D4 **Voerendaal** Neth.
165 H4 **Vogelsberg** *hills* Germany
170 C2 **Voghera** Italy
165 K4 **Vogtland** *reg.* Germany
165 K5 **Vohenstrauß** Germany
179 E6 **Vohimena, Tanjona** *c.* Madag.
165 G3 **Vöhl** Germany
159 N4 **Võhma** Estonia
178 D4 **Voi** Kenya
176 B4 **Voinjama** Liberia
166 G4 **Voiron** France
159 J5 **Vojens** Denmark
171 H2 **Vojvodina** *prov.* Serbia
172 H3 **Vokhma** Rus. Fed.
172 D1 **Voknavolok** Rus. Fed.
194 F2 **Volborg** U.S.A.
215 B1 **Volcán, Cerro del** *vol.* Chile
146 G4 **Volcano Islands** Japan
139 J1 **Volchikha** Rus. Fed.
159 I3 **Volda** Norway
164 D2 **Volendam** Neth.
173 H6 **Volga** *r.* Rus. Fed.
190 B4 **Volga** *r.* U.S.A.
173 G6 **Volgodonsk** Rus. Fed.
132 F5 **Volgograd** Rus. Fed.
173 H5 **Volgogradskaya Oblast'** *admin. div.* Rus. Fed.
168 G7 **Völkermarkt** Austria
172 E3 **Volkhov** Rus. Fed.
172 D3 **Volkhov** *r.* Rus. Fed.
164 E5 **Völklingen** Germany
181 H3 **Volksrust** S. Africa
150 B3 **Vol'no-Nadezhdinskoye** Rus. Fed.
173 F6 **Volnovakha** Ukr.
139 G1 **Vol'noye** Rus. Fed.
133 K2 **Volochanka** Rus. Fed.
173 C5 **Volochys'k** Ukr.
173 F6 **Volodars'ke** Ukr.
173 I6 **Volodarskiy** Rus. Fed.
169 N5 **Volodars'k-Volyns'kyy** Ukr.
169 M5 **Volodymyrets'** Ukr.
173 C5 **Volodymyr-Volyns'kyy** Ukr.
172 F3 **Vologda** Rus. Fed.
172 G3 **Vologodskaya Oblast'** *admin. div.* Rus. Fed.
173 F5 **Volokonovka** Rus. Fed.
171 J5 **Volos** Greece
172 D3 **Volosovo** Rus. Fed.
169 O2 **Volot** Rus. Fed.
173 F4 **Volovo** Rus. Fed.
173 H4 **Vol'sk** Rus. Fed.
176 B4 **Volta, Lake** *resr* Ghana
214 D3 **Volta Redonda** Brazil
172 H1 **Vol'tevo** Rus. Fed.
170 F4 **Volturno** *r.* Italy
171 J4 **Volvi, Limni** *l.* Greece
172 I4 **Volzhsk** Rus. Fed.
138 B1 **Volzhskiy** *Samarskaya Oblast'* Rus. Fed.
173 H5 **Volzhskiy** *Volgogradskaya Oblast'* Rus. Fed.
179 E6 **Vondrozo** Madag.
172 G1 **Vonga** Rus. Fed.
158 D2 **Vopnafjörður** Iceland
158 D2 **Vopnafjörður** *b.* Iceland
172 B2 **Vörå** Fin.
169 L3 **Voranava** Belarus
172 I3 **Vorchanka** Rus. Fed.
172 E2 **Vorenzha** Rus. Fed.
219 J1 **Voring Plateau** *sea feature* N. Atlantic Ocean
132 H3 **Vorkuta** Rus. Fed.
159 M4 **Vormsi** *i.* Estonia
173 G5 **Vorona** *r.* Rus. Fed.
173 F5 **Voronezh** Rus. Fed.
173 F5 **Voronezh** *r.* Rus. Fed.
173 G5 **Voronezhskaya Oblast'** *admin. div.* Rus. Fed.
172 G3 **Voron'ye** Rus. Fed.
169 P3 **Vorot'kovo** Rus. Fed.
173 E5 **Vorskla** *r.* Rus. Fed.
159 N4 **Võrtsjärv** *l.* Estonia
159 N4 **Võru** Estonia
139 G5 **Vorukh** Tajik.
180 E5 **Vosburg** S. Africa
139 G5 **Vose** Tajik.
166 H2 **Vosges** *mts* France
138 D1 **Voskresenskoye** Rus. Fed.
159 I3 **Voss** Norway
**Vostochno-Sibirskoye More** *sea* Rus. Fed. *see* **East Siberian Sea**
**Vostochnyy Chink Ustyurta** *esc.* Uzbek. *see* **Sharqiy Ustyurt Chink**
139 J2 **Vostochnyy Kazakhstan** *admin. div.* Kazakh.
146 B1 **Vostochnyy Sayan** *mts* Rus. Fed.
129 C5 **Vostok** *research stn* Antarctica
150 D1 **Vostok** Rus. Fed.
123 I5 **Vostok Island** Kiribati
150 D2 **Vostretsovo** Rus. Fed.
132 G4 **Votkinsk** Rus. Fed.
214 C3 **Votuporanga** Brazil
164 C5 **Vouziers** France
166 E2 **Voves** France
172 I3 **Voya** *r.* Rus. Fed.
200 A1 **Voyageurs National Park** U.S.A.
158 O2 **Voynitsa** Rus. Fed.
172 F2 **Vozhe, Ozero** *l.* Rus. Fed.
172 G2 **Vozhega** Rus. Fed.
139 G1 **Voznesenka** Kazakh.
173 D6 **Voznesens'k** Ukr.
**Vozrovdenye** Uzbek. *see* **Kantubek (abandoned)**
**Vozrozhdeniya, O.** *i.* Uzbek. *see* **Vozrozhdenya Island**
138 D3 **Vozrozhdenya Island** *pen.* Uzbek.
**Vpadina Chagyllyshor** *depr.* Turkm. *see* **Chagyllyshor, Vpadina**
150 C3 **Vrangel'** Rus. Fed.
**Vrangelya, Ostrov** *i.* Rus. Fed. *see* **Wrangel Island**
171 I3 **Vranje** Serbia
171 L3 **Vratnik** *pass* Bulg.
171 J3 **Vratsa** Bulg.
170 G2 **Vrbas** *r.* Bos.-Herz.
171 H2 **Vrbas** Serbia
181 H3 **Vrede** S. Africa
181 G3 **Vredefort** S. Africa
180 B6 **Vredenburg** S. Africa
180 C5 **Vredendal** S. Africa
164 C5 **Vresse** Belgium
143 B4 **Vriddhachalam** India
164 E1 **Vries** Neth.
159 K4 **Vrigstad** Sweden
171 I2 **Vršac** Serbia
180 F3 **Vryburg** S. Africa
181 I3 **Vryheid** S. Africa
172 D2 **Vsevolozhsk** Rus. Fed.
171 H2 **Vukovar** Croatia
132 G3 **Vuktyl** Rus. Fed.
181 H3 **Vukuzakhe** S. Africa
170 F5 **Vulcano, Isola** *i. Isole Lipari* Italy
197 F5 **Vulture Mountains** U.S.A.
154 C3 **Vung Tau** Vietnam
159 N3 **Vuohijärvi** Fin.
158 N2 **Vuolijoki** Fin.
158 M2 **Vuollerim** Sweden
158 N2 **Vuostimo** Fin.
172 H4 **Vurnary** Rus. Fed.
171 I3 **Vushtrri** Kosovo
138 E1 **Vvedenka** Kazakh.
179 D4 **Vwawa** Tanz.
144 C5 **Vyara** India
**Vyatka** Rus. Fed. *see* **Kirov**
172 I3 **Vyatka** *r.* Rus. Fed.
172 E4 **Vyaz'ma** Rus. Fed.
172 G3 **Vyazniki** Rus. Fed.
173 H5 **Vyazovka** *Astrakhanskaya Oblast'* Rus. Fed.
138 A1 **Vyazovka** *Saratovskaya Oblast'* Rus. Fed.
172 D2 **Vyborg** Rus. Fed.
172 I2 **Vychegda** *r.* Rus. Fed.
172 H2 **Vychegodskiy** Rus. Fed.
172 C4 **Vyerkhnyadzvinsk** Belarus
172 D4 **Vyetryna** Belarus
172 E2 **Vygozero, Ozero** *l.* Rus. Fed.
172 G4 **Vyksa** Rus. Fed.
173 D6 **Vylkove** Ukr.
169 K6 **Vynohradiv** Ukr.
172 E3 **Vypolzovo** Rus. Fed.
172 D3 **Vyritsa** Rus. Fed.
161 D5 **Vyrnwy, Lake** U.K.
173 F6 **Vyselki** Rus. Fed.
172 G4 **Vysha** Rus. Fed.
173 D5 **Vyshhorod** Ukr.
172 E3 **Vyshnevolotskaya Gryada** *ridge* Rus. Fed.
172 E3 **Vyshniy-Volochek** Rus. Fed.
168 H6 **Vyškov** Czech Rep.
173 D5 **Vystupovychi** Ukr.
172 F2 **Vytegra** Rus. Fed.


## W


176 B3 **Wa** Ghana
164 D3 **Waal** *r.* Neth.
164 D3 **Waalwijk** Neth.
188 B3 **Wabakimi Lake** Canada
186 G3 **Wabasca** *r.* Canada
186 G3 **Wabasca-Desmarais** Canada
190 E5 **Wabash** U.S.A.
190 E5 **Wabash** *r.* U.S.A.
190 A3 **Wabasha** U.S.A.
191 E1 **Wabatongushi Lake** Canada
187 J4 **Wabowden** Canada
188 C2 **Wabuk Point** Canada
189 G3 **Wabush** Canada
189 G3 **Wabush Lake** Canada
196 C2 **Wabuska** U.S.A.
201 D6 **Waccasassa Bay** U.S.A.
165 H4 **Wächtersbach** Germany
199 D6 **Waco** U.S.A.
127 H6 **Wadbilliga National Park** Australia
177 D2 **Waddān** Libya
197 F5 **Waddell Dam** U.S.A.
164 C2 **Waddenzee** *sea chan.* Neth.
126 B4 **Waddikee** Australia
186 D4 **Waddington, Mount** Canada
164 C2 **Waddinxveen** Neth.
161 C7 **Wadebridge** U.K.
187 I4 **Wadena** Canada
198 E2 **Wadena** U.S.A.
164 E5 **Wadern** Germany
143 A2 **Wadgaon** India
164 E5 **Wadgassen** Germany
141 G5 **Wadh** Pak.
177 F2 **Wadi Halfa** Sudan
177 E3 **Wadi Howar National Park** Sudan
136 E7 **Wādī Ramm National Park** *nat. park* Jordan
177 F3 **Wad Medani** Sudan
196 C2 **Wadsworth** U.S.A.
152 B4 **Wafangdian** China
165 G2 **Wagenfeld** Germany
165 I2 **Wagenhoff** Germany
185 J3 **Wager Bay** Canada
127 G5 **Wagga Wagga** Australia
144 C2 **Wah** Pak.
196 □1 **Wahiawā** U.S.A.
165 H3 **Wahlhausen** Germany
198 D3 **Wahoo** U.S.A.
198 D2 **Wahpeton** U.S.A.
197 F2 **Wah Wah Mountains** U.S.A.
143 A2 **Wai** India
196 □1 **Wai'ale'e** U.S.A.
196 □1 **Waialua** *reg.* U.S.A.
196 □1 **Waialua Bay** U.S.A.
196 □1 **Wai'anae** U.S.A.
**Waianae Ra.** *mts* U.S.A. *see* **Wai'anae Range**
196 □1 **Wai'anae Range** *mts* U.S.A.
128 D5 **Waiau** *r.* N.Z.
168 G7 **Waidhofen an der Ybbs** Austria
147 F7 **Waigeo** *i.* Indon.
128 E2 **Waiharoa** N.Z.
128 E2 **Waiheke Island** N.Z.
128 E2 **Waihi** N.Z.
128 E2 **Waihou** *r.* N.Z.
147 D7 **Waikabubak** Indon.
128 B6 **Waikaia** *r.* N.Z.
196 □1 **Waikāne** U.S.A.
128 D5 **Waikari** N.Z.
128 E2 **Waikato** *r.* N.Z.
128 F2 **Waikawa Point** N.Z.
126 C5 **Waikerie** Australia
196 □1 **Waikīkī Beach** U.S.A.
128 C6 **Waikouaiti** N.Z.
196 □2 **Wailuku** U.S.A.
128 D5 **Waimakariri** *r.* N.Z.
196 □1 **Waimānalo** U.S.A.
128 C4 **Waimangaroa** N.Z.
128 F3 **Waimarama** N.Z.
128 C6 **Waimate** N.Z.
196 □1 **Waimea** *HI* U.S.A.
196 □2 **Waimea** *HI* U.S.A.
144 D5 **Wainganga** *r.* India
147 E7 **Waingapu** Indon.
161 C7 **Wainhouse Corner** U.K.
187 G4 **Wainwright** Canada
184 C2 **Wainwright** U.S.A.
128 E3 **Waiouru** N.Z.
128 E3 **Waipa** *r.* N.Z.
128 B7 **Waipahi** N.Z.
196 □1 **Waipahu** U.S.A.
128 F3 **Waipaoa** *r.* N.Z.
128 B7 **Waipapa Point** N.Z.
128 D5 **Waipara** N.Z.
128 F3 **Waipawa** N.Z.
128 F3 **Waipukurau** N.Z.
128 F3 **Wairakei** N.Z.
128 E4 **Wairarapa, Lake** N.Z.
128 D4 **Wairau** *r.* N.Z.
128 F3 **Wairoa** N.Z.
128 F3 **Wairoa** *r.* N.Z.
128 E1 **Wairoa** *r.* N.Z.
128 F3 **Waitahanui** N.Z.
128 B6 **Waitahuna** N.Z.
128 E2 **Waitakaruru** N.Z.
128 C6 **Waitaki** *r.* N.Z.
128 E3 **Waitara** N.Z.
128 E2 **Waitoa** N.Z.
128 E2 **Waiuku** N.Z.
128 B7 **Waiwera South** N.Z.
149 F5 **Waiyang** China
151 E6 **Wajima** Japan
178 E3 **Wajir** Kenya
151 D7 **Wakasa-wan** *b.* Japan
128 B6 **Wakatipu, Lake** N.Z.
187 H4 **Wakaw** Canada
151 D7 **Wakayama** Japan
198 D4 **WaKeeney** U.S.A.
191 J3 **Wakefield** Canada
128 D4 **Wakefield** N.Z.
160 F4 **Wakefield** U.K.
190 C2 **Wakefield** *MI* U.S.A.
203 H4 **Wakefield** *RI* U.S.A.
202 E6 **Wakefield** *VA* U.S.A.
**Wakeham** Canada *see* **Kangiqsujuaq**
123 F2 **Wake Island** *terr.* N. Pacific Ocean
139 H5 **Wākhān** *reg.* Afgh.
150 G4 **Wakinosawa** Japan
150 G2 **Wakkanai** Japan
181 I3 **Wakkerstroom** S. Africa
126 F5 **Wakool** Australia
126 E5 **Wakool** *r.* Australia
189 G2 **Wakuach, Lac** *l.* Canada
168 H5 **Wałbrzych** Poland
127 I3 **Walcha** Australia
168 E7 **Walchensee** *l.* Germany
164 C4 **Walcourt** Belgium
168 H4 **Wałcz** Poland
203 F4 **Walden** U.S.A.
168 F6 **Waldkraiburg** Germany
161 C7 **Waldon** *r.* U.K.
202 E5 **Waldorf** U.S.A.
161 D5 **Wales** *admin. div.* U.K.
127 H3 **Walgett** Australia
178 C4 **Walikale** Dem. Rep. Congo
190 B4 **Walker** *IA* U.S.A.
198 E2 **Walker** *MN* U.S.A.
196 C2 **Walker** *r.* U.S.A.
180 C7 **Walker Bay** S. Africa
201 E7 **Walker Cay** *i.* Bahamas
196 C2 **Walker Lake** U.S.A.
196 C4 **Walker Pass** U.S.A.
191 G3 **Walkerton** Canada
198 C2 **Wall** U.S.A.
194 C2 **Wallace** U.S.A.
191 F4 **Wallaceburg** Canada
127 I2 **Wallangarra** Australia
126 B4 **Wallaroo** Australia
161 D4 **Wallasey** U.K.
127 G5 **Walla Walla** Australia
194 C2 **Walla Walla** U.S.A.
165 H5 **Walldürn** Germany
180 B5 **Wallekraal** S. Africa
127 H5 **Wallendbeen** Australia
203 F4 **Wallenpaupack, Lake** U.S.A.
161 F6 **Wallingford** U.K.
203 G4 **Wallingford** U.S.A.
125 I3 **Wallis, Îles** *is* Pacific Ocean
125 I3 **Wallis and Futuna Islands** *terr.* Pacific Ocean
127 J4 **Wallis Lake** *inlet* Australia
164 B4 **Wallonia, Major Mining Sites of** *tourist site* Belgium
203 F6 **Wallops Island** U.S.A.
194 C2 **Wallowa Mountains** U.S.A.
162 □ **Walls** U.K.
187 H2 **Walmsley Lake** Canada
160 D3 **Walney, Isle of** *i.* U.K.
190 C5 **Walnut** U.S.A.
197 G4 **Walnut Canyon National Monument** *nat. park* U.S.A.
199 F4 **Walnut Ridge** U.S.A.
145 I3 **Walong** India
161 F5 **Walsall** U.K.
195 F4 **Walsenburg** U.S.A.
165 H2 **Walsrode** Germany
143 C2 **Waltair** India
201 D5 **Walterboro** U.S.A.
201 C6 **Walter F. George Reservoir** U.S.A.
126 F2 **Walter's Range** *hills* Australia
191 I3 **Waltham** Canada
200 C4 **Walton** *KY* U.S.A.
203 F3 **Walton** *NY* U.S.A.
179 B6 **Walvis Bay** Namibia
219 I8 **Walvis Ridge** *sea feature* S. Atlantic Ocean
178 C3 **Wamba** Dem. Rep. Congo
144 B2 **Wana** Pak.
126 F2 **Wanaaring** Australia
128 B6 **Wanaka** N.Z.
128 B6 **Wanaka, Lake** N.Z.
149 E5 **Wan'an** China
191 G2 **Wanapitei Lake** Canada
203 F4 **Wanaque Reservoir** U.S.A.
126 D5 **Wanbi** Australia
128 C6 **Wanbrow, Cape** N.Z.
126 D2 **Wancoocha, Lake** *salt flat* Australia
150 C2 **Wanda Shan** *mts* China
165 I4 **Wandersleben** Germany
165 L2 **Wandlitz** Germany
152 D6 **Wando** S. Korea
154 A1 **Wang, Mae Nam** *r.* Thai.
128 E3 **Wanganui** N.Z.
128 E3 **Wanganui** *r.* N.Z.
127 G6 **Wangaratta** Australia
126 A5 **Wangary** Australia
148 C3 **Wangcang** China
149 D4 **Wangcheng** China
165 F1 **Wangerooge** Germany
165 F1 **Wangerooge** *i.* Germany
152 A3 **Wanghai Shan** *h.* China
149 C5 **Wangmo** China
152 E2 **Wangqing** China
144 B5 **Wankaner** India
178 E3 **Wanlaweyn** Somalia
165 G1 **Wanna** Germany
149 E4 **Wannian** China
149 D7 **Wanning** China
148 E1 **Wanquan** China
164 D3 **Wanroij** Neth.
149 D6 **Wanshan Qundao** *is* China
128 F4 **Wanstead** N.Z.
161 F6 **Wantage** U.K.
191 G2 **Wanup** Canada
148 C3 **Wanyuan** China
149 E4 **Wanzai** China
164 D4 **Wanze** Belgium
149 C4 **Wanzhou** China
202 A4 **Wapakoneta** U.S.A.
190 B5 **Wapello** U.S.A.
188 C3 **Wapikopa Lake** Canada
186 F4 **Wapiti** *r.* Canada
199 F4 **Wappapello Lake** *resr* U.S.A.
190 A5 **Wapsipinicon** *r.* U.S.A.
148 B3 **Waqên** China
140 C6 **Waqr** *well* Saudi Arabia
144 A4 **Warah** Pak.
143 B2 **Warangal** India
126 F6 **Waranga Reservoir** Australia
144 E5 **Waraseoni** India
127 F8 **Waratah** Australia
127 F7 **Waratah Bay** Australia
165 H3 **Warburg** Germany
124 C4 **Warburton** Australia
126 B1 **Warburton** *watercourse* Australia
187 G2 **Warburton Bay** Canada
128 A6 **Ward, Mount** N.Z.
128 B5 **Ward, Mount** N.Z.
126 B5 **Wardang Island** Australia
181 H3 **Warden** S. Africa
165 G1 **Wardenburg** Germany
144 D5 **Wardha** India
144 D6 **Wardha** *r.* India
186 D3 **Ware** Canada
203 G3 **Ware** U.S.A.
161 E7 **Wareham** U.K.
203 H4 **Wareham** U.S.A.
164 D4 **Waremme** Belgium
165 K1 **Waren** Germany
165 F3 **Warendorf** Germany
127 I2 **Warialda** Australia
165 J1 **Warin** Germany
154 C2 **Warin Chamrap** Thai.
128 E2 **Warkworth** N.Z.
160 F2 **Warkworth** U.K.
164 A4 **Warloy-Baillon** France
187 H4 **Warman** Canada
180 C4 **Warmbad** Namibia
181 H2 **Warmbad** S. Africa
**Warming Island** *i.* Greenland *see* **Uunartoq Qeqertoq**
161 E6 **Warminster** U.K.
203 F4 **Warminster** U.S.A.
164 C2 **Warmond** Neth.
196 D2 **Warm Springs** *NV* U.S.A.
202 D5 **Warm Springs** *VA* U.S.A.
180 D6 **Warmwaterberg** *mts* S. Africa
203 H3 **Warner** U.S.A.
194 B3 **Warner Mountains** U.S.A.
201 D5 **Warner Robins** U.S.A.
210 F7 **Warnes** Bol.
127 J2 **Warning, Mount** Australia
144 D5 **Warora** India
127 I1 **Warra** Australia
126 E6 **Warracknabeal** Australia
127 I5 **Warragamba Reservoir** Australia
127 F7 **Warragul** Australia
126 C2 **Warrakalanna, Lake** *salt flat* Australia
126 A4 **Warramboo** Australia
127 G2 **Warrambool** *r.* Australia
178 C3 **Warrap** South Sudan
124 E4 **Warrego** *r.* Australia
127 G3 **Warren** Australia
191 G2 **Warren** Canada
199 E5 **Warren** *AR* U.S.A.
191 F4 **Warren** *MI* U.S.A.
198 D1 **Warren** *MN* U.S.A.
202 C4 **Warren** *OH* U.S.A.
202 D4 **Warren** *PA* U.S.A.
202 C4 **Warrendale** U.S.A.
163 E3 **Warrenpoint** U.K.
198 E4 **Warrensburg** *MO* U.S.A.
203 G3 **Warrensburg** *NY* U.S.A.
180 F4 **Warrenton** S. Africa
202 E5 **Warrenton** U.S.A.
176 C4 **Warri** Nigeria
128 C6 **Warrington** N.Z.
161 E4 **Warrington** U.K.
201 C6 **Warrington** U.S.A.
126 C3 **Warriota** *watercourse* Australia
126 E7 **Warrnambool** Australia
198 E1 **Warroad** U.S.A.
126 A5 **Warrow** Australia
127 H3 **Warrumbungle Range** *mts* Australia
126 D2 **Warry Warry** *watercourse* Australia
141 H2 **Warsaj 'Alāqahdārī** Afgh.
169 J4 **Warsaw** Poland
190 E5 **Warsaw** *IN* U.S.A.
198 E4 **Warsaw** *MO* U.S.A.
202 D3 **Warsaw** *NY* U.S.A.
202 E6 **Warsaw** *VA* U.S.A.
165 G3 **Warstein** Germany
**Warszawa** Poland *see* **Warsaw**
168 G4 **Warta** *r.* Poland
165 I4 **Wartburg, Schloss** *tourist site* Germany
127 J2 **Warwick** Australia
161 F5 **Warwick** U.K.
203 F4 **Warwick** *NY* U.S.A.
203 H4 **Warwick** *RI* U.S.A.
195 E4 **Wasatch Range** *mts* U.S.A.
181 I4 **Wasbank** S. Africa
196 C4 **Wasco** U.S.A.
198 E2 **Waseca** U.S.A.
141 F5 **Washap** Pak.
190 C5 **Washburn** *IL* U.S.A.
203 I1 **Washburn** *ME* U.S.A.
198 C2 **Washburn** *ND* U.S.A.
190 B2 **Washburn** *WI* U.S.A.
144 D5 **Washim** India

202 E5 Washington DC U.S.A.
(City Plan 113)
201 D5 Washington GA U.S.A.
190 B5 Washington IA U.S.A.
190 C5 Washington IL U.S.A.
200 C4 Washington IN U.S.A.
198 F4 Washington MO U.S.A.
201 E5 Washington NC U.S.A.
203 F4 Washington NJ U.S.A.
202 C4 Washington PA U.S.A.
197 F3 Washington UT U.S.A.
194 B2 Washington state U.S.A.
129 B5 Washington, Cape c. Antarctica
203 H2 Washington, Mount U.S.A.
202 B5 Washington Court House U.S.A.
190 D3 Washington Island U.S.A.
185 L1 Washington Land reg. Greenland
199 D5 Washita r. U.S.A.
141 G5 Washuk Pak.
140 B5 Wasī' Saudi Arabia
137 K5 Wasit tourist site Iraq
188 E3 Waskaganish Canada
187 J3 Waskaiowaka Lake Canada
206 H5 Waspán Nicaragua
164 C2 Wassenaar Neth.
180 C3 Wasser Namibia
165 H4 Wasserkuppe h. Germany
165 I5 Wassertrüdingen Germany
196 C2 Wassuk Range mts U.S.A.
188 E4 Waswanipi, Lac l. Canada
147 E7 Watampone Indon.
203 G4 Waterbury CT U.S.A.
203 G2 Waterbury VT U.S.A.
187 H3 Waterbury Lake Canada
163 D5 Waterford Ireland
202 D4 Waterford U.S.A.
163 E5 Waterford Harbour Ireland
163 C5 Watergrasshill Ireland
164 C4 Waterloo Belgium
191 G4 Waterloo Canada
190 A4 Waterloo IA U.S.A.
203 H3 Waterloo ME U.S.A.
202 E3 Waterloo NY U.S.A.
190 C4 Waterloo WI U.S.A.
161 F7 Waterlooville U.K.
181 H1 Waterpoort S. Africa
190 C2 Watersmeet U.S.A.
186 G5 Waterton Lakes National Park Canada
203 E3 Watertown NY U.S.A.
198 D2 Watertown SD U.S.A.
190 C4 Watertown WI U.S.A.
126 C4 Watervale Australia
203 I2 Waterville U.S.A.
187 G3 Waterways Canada
191 G4 Watford Canada
161 G6 Watford U.K.
198 C2 Watford City U.S.A.
187 I3 Wathaman r. Canada
165 I2 Wathlingen Germany
202 E3 Watkins Glen U.S.A.
199 D5 Watonga U.S.A.
187 H4 Watrous Canada
178 C3 Watsa Dem. Rep. Congo
190 D5 Watseka U.S.A.
178 C4 Watsi Kengo Dem. Rep. Congo
187 I4 Watson Canada
186 D2 Watson Lake Canada
196 B3 Watsonville U.S.A.
162 E2 Watten U.K.
162 E2 Watten, Loch l. U.K.
187 I2 Watterson Lake Canada
126 A2 Wattiwarriganna watercourse Australia
161 H5 Watton U.K.
190 C2 Watton U.S.A.
124 D2 Watubela, Kepulauan is Indon.
124 E2 Wau P.N.G.
177 E4 Wau South Sudan
190 D3 Waucedah U.S.A.
127 J3 Wauchope Australia
201 D7 Wauchula U.S.A.
190 D4 Waukegan U.S.A.
190 C4 Waukesha U.S.A.
190 B4 Waukon U.S.A.
190 C3 Waupaca U.S.A.
190 C4 Waupun U.S.A.
199 D5 Waurika U.S.A.
190 C3 Wausau U.S.A.
202 A4 Wauseon U.S.A.
190 C3 Wautoma U.S.A.
190 C4 Wauwatosa U.S.A.
161 I5 Waveney r. U.K.
190 A4 Waverly IA U.S.A.
202 B5 Waverly OH U.S.A.
201 C4 Waverly TN U.S.A.
202 E6 Waverly VA U.S.A.
164 C4 Wavre Belgium
190 E1 Wawa Canada
176 C4 Wawa Nigeria
190 E5 Wawasee, Lake U.S.A.
196 C3 Wawona U.S.A.
199 D5 Waxahachie U.S.A.
201 D6 Waycross U.S.A.
202 B6 Wayland KY U.S.A.
190 B5 Wayland MO U.S.A.
198 D3 Wayne U.S.A.
201 D5 Waynesboro GA U.S.A.
199 F6 Waynesboro MS U.S.A.
202 E5 Waynesboro PA U.S.A.
202 D5 Waynesboro VA U.S.A.
202 C5 Waynesburg U.S.A.
199 E4 Waynesville U.S.A.
199 D4 Waynoka U.S.A.
177 D3 Waza, Parc National de nat. park Cameroon
144 C2 Wazirabad Pak.
176 C3 W du Niger, Parc National du nat. park Niger
155 A1 We, Pulau i. Indon.
188 B3 Weagamow Lake Canada
160 E3 Wear r. U.K.
124 E3 Weary Bay Australia
199 D5 Weatherford U.S.A.
194 B3 Weaverville U.S.A.
191 G2 Webbwood Canada
188 C3 Webequie Canada
186 D3 Weber, Mount Canada
218 M5 Weber Basin sea feature Indon.
203 H3 Webster MA U.S.A.
198 D2 Webster SD U.S.A.
190 A3 Webster WI U.S.A.
198 E3 Webster City U.S.A.
202 C5 Webster Springs U.S.A.
218 B9 Weddell Abyssal Plain sea feature Southern Ocean
212 D8 Weddell Island Falkland Is
129 C3 Weddell Sea sea Antarctica
126 E6 Wedderburn Australia
165 H1 Wedel (Holstein) Germany
194 B3 Weed U.S.A.
202 D4 Weedville U.S.A.
127 H2 Weemelah Australia
181 I4 Weenen S. Africa
164 F1 Weener Germany
164 D3 Weert Neth.
127 G4 Weethalle Australia
127 H3 Wee Waa Australia
164 E3 Wegberg Germany
169 J3 Węgorzewo Poland
148 E1 Weichang China
165 K4 Weida Germany
165 J5 Weidenberg Germany
165 K5 Weiden in der Oberpfalz Germany
148 F2 Weifang China
152 B5 Weihai China
148 B2 Wei He r. Henan China
148 D3 Wei He r. Shaanxi China
148 E3 Weihui China
152 D2 Weihu Ling mts China
165 G4 Weilburg Germany
127 G2 Weilmoringle Australia
165 J4 Weimar Germany
148 C3 Weinan China
165 G5 Weinheim Germany
149 B5 Weining China
165 H5 Weinsberg Germany
124 E3 Weipa Australia
127 H2 Weir r. Australia
187 K3 Weir River Canada
202 C4 Weirton U.S.A.
194 C2 Weiser U.S.A.
148 E3 Weishan China
148 E3 Weishan Hu l. China
148 E3 Weishi China
165 I5 Weißenburg in Bayern Germany
165 J3 Weißenfels Germany
201 C5 Weiss Lake U.S.A.
180 C2 Weissrand Mountains Namibia
165 G5 Weiterstadt Germany
149 B5 Weixin China
148 B3 Weiyuan Gansu China
149 B4 Weiyuan Sichuan China
168 G7 Weiz Austria
149 C6 Weizhou Dao i. China
152 B3 Weizi China
168 I3 Wejherowo Poland
187 J4 Wekusko Canada
187 J4 Wekusko Lake Canada
186 G2 Wekweètì Canada
202 C6 Welch U.S.A.
203 H2 Weld U.S.A.
178 D2 Weldiya Eth.
196 C4 Weldon U.S.A.
178 D3 Welk'īt'ē Eth.
181 G3 Welkom S. Africa
191 H4 Welland Canada
161 G5 Welland r. U.K.
191 H4 Welland Canal Canada
143 C5 Wellawaya Sri Lanka
191 G4 Wellesley Canada
124 D3 Wellesley Islands Australia
186 B2 Wellesley Lake Canada
203 H4 Wellfleet U.S.A.
164 D4 Wellin Belgium
161 G5 Wellingborough U.K.
127 H4 Wellington N.S.W. Australia
126 C5 Wellington S.A. Australia
128 E4 Wellington N.Z.
180 C6 Wellington S. Africa
161 D7 Wellington England U.K.
161 E5 Wellington England U.K.
194 F3 Wellington CO U.S.A.
199 D4 Wellington KS U.S.A.
196 C2 Wellington NV U.S.A.
202 B4 Wellington OH U.S.A.
199 C5 Wellington TX U.S.A.
197 G2 Wellington UT U.S.A.
212 A7 Wellington, Isla i. Chile
127 G7 Wellington, Lake Australia
190 B5 Wellman U.S.A.
186 E4 Wells Canada
161 E6 Wells U.K.
194 D3 Wells NV U.S.A.
203 F3 Wells NY U.S.A.
124 C4 Wells, Lake salt flat Australia
202 E4 Wellsboro U.S.A.
128 E2 Wellsford N.Z.
186 E4 Wells Gray Provincial Park Canada
161 H5 Wells-next-the-Sea U.K.
202 B5 Wellston U.S.A.
202 E3 Wellsville U.S.A.
197 E5 Wellton U.S.A.
168 G6 Wels Austria
203 J2 Welshpool Canada
161 D5 Welshpool U.K.
165 L3 Welsickendorf Germany
161 G6 Welwyn Garden City U.K.
165 H6 Welzheim Germany
161 E5 Wem U.K.
181 H4 Wembesi S. Africa
186 F3 Wembley Canada
188 E3 Wemindji Canada
201 E7 Wemyss Bight Bahamas
194 B2 Wenatchee U.S.A.
149 D7 Wencheng China
149 F5 Wencheng China
176 B4 Wenchi Ghana
148 B4 Wenchuan China
165 J5 Wendelstein Germany
165 F4 Wenden Germany
197 F5 Wenden U.S.A.
152 B5 Wendeng China
178 D3 Wendo Eth.
194 D3 Wendover U.S.A.
191 F2 Wenebegon Lake Canada
149 C5 Weng'an China
148 A4 Wengda China
149 E5 Wengyuan China
148 F3 Wen He r. China
148 B4 Wenjiang China
149 B4 Wenjiang China
149 F4 Wenling China
190 C5 Wenona U.S.A.
139 J3 Wenquan China
149 B6 Wenshan China
139 J4 Wensu China
161 H5 Wensum r. U.K.
165 I1 Wentorf bei Hamburg Germany
126 D5 Wentworth Australia
203 H3 Wentworth U.S.A.
148 B3 Wenxian China
149 F5 Wenzhou China
165 K2 Wenzlow Germany
181 G4 Wepener S. Africa
165 J2 Werben (Elbe) Germany
180 E2 Werda Botswana
165 K4 Werdau Germany
165 K2 Werder Germany
165 F3 Werdohl Germany
165 F3 Werl Germany
165 K5 Wernberg-Köblitz Germany
164 F3 Werne Germany
186 C2 Wernecke Mountains Canada
165 I3 Wernigerode Germany
165 H3 Werra r. Germany
126 D5 Werrimull Australia
127 I3 Werris Creek Australia
165 H5 Wertheim Germany
164 B4 Wervik Belgium
164 E3 Wesel Germany
164 E3 Wesel-Datteln-Kanal canal Germany
165 K1 Wesenberg Germany
165 I2 Wesendorf Germany
165 H2 Weser r. Germany
165 G1 Weser sea chan. Germany
165 G2 Wesergebirge hills Germany
198 C4 Weskan U.S.A.
191 I3 Weslemkoon Lake Canada
203 J2 Wesley U.S.A.
189 J4 Wesleyville Canada
124 D3 Wessel, Cape Australia
124 D3 Wessel Islands Australia
181 H3 Wesselton S. Africa
198 D2 Wessington Springs U.S.A.
190 C4 West Allis U.S.A.
129 B4 West Antarctica reg. Antarctica
218 K6 West Australian Basin sea feature Indian Ocean
144 B5 West Banas r. India
136 E5 West Bank terr. Asia
189 I3 West Bay Canada
199 F6 West Bay b. U.S.A.
190 C4 West Bend U.S.A.
145 F5 West Bengal state India
191 E3 West Branch U.S.A.
161 F5 West Bromwich U.K.
203 H3 Westbrook U.S.A.
West Burra i. U.K. see Burra
127 G8 Westbury Australia
161 E6 Westbury U.K.
127 G5 Westby Australia
190 B4 Westby U.S.A.
216 E5 West Caroline Basin sea feature N. Pacific Ocean
203 F5 West Chester U.S.A.
203 G2 West Danville U.S.A.
191 F3 West Duck Island Canada
201 E7 West End Bahamas
196 D4 Westend U.S.A.
201 E7 West End Point Bahamas
165 F4 Westerburg Germany
164 F1 Westerholt Germany
168 D3 Westerland Germany
164 C3 Westerlo Belgium
203 H4 Westerly U.S.A.
187 H1 Western r. Canada
124 C4 Western Australia state Australia
180 D6 Western Cape prov. S. Africa
177 E2 Western Desert des. Egypt
143 A2 Western Ghats mts India
126 F7 Western Port b. Australia
176 A2 Western Sahara terr. Africa
164 B3 Westerschelde est. Neth.
165 F1 Westerstede Germany
165 F4 Westerwald hills Germany
212 D8 West Falkland i. Falkland Is
198 D2 West Fargo U.S.A.
190 D5 Westfield IN U.S.A.
203 G3 Westfield MA U.S.A.
203 J1 Westfield ME U.S.A.
202 D3 Westfield NY U.S.A.
164 C1 West Frisian Islands Neth.
164 E1 Westgat sea chan. Neth.
203 J2 West Grand Lake U.S.A.
165 I6 Westhausen Germany
162 F3 Westhill U.K.
198 C1 Westhope U.S.A.
129 E5 West Ice Shelf ice feature Antarctica
164 B3 Westkapelle Neth.
West Lamma Channel China see Sai Pok Liu Hoi Hap
202 B5 West Lancaster U.S.A.
128 B5 Westland Tai Poutini National Park N.Z.
161 I5 Westleton U.K.
196 B3 Westley U.S.A.
202 B6 West Liberty KY U.S.A.
202 B4 West Liberty OH U.S.A.
162 E5 West Linton U.K.
162 B2 West Loch Roag b. U.K.
186 G4 Westlock Canada
191 G4 West Lorne Canada
164 C3 Westmalle Belgium
216 E4 West Mariana Basin sea feature Pacific Ocean
199 F5 West Memphis U.S.A.
202 E5 Westminster MD U.S.A.
201 D5 Westminster SC U.S.A.
202 C5 Weston U.S.A.
161 E6 Weston-super-Mare U.K.
203 F5 Westover U.S.A.
201 D7 West Palm Beach U.S.A.
199 F4 West Plains U.S.A.
126 A5 West Point pt S.A. Australia
127 F8 West Point pt Tas. Australia
199 F5 West Point MS U.S.A.
203 F4 West Point NY U.S.A.
191 I3 Westport Canada
163 B4 Westport Ireland
128 C4 Westport N.Z.
196 A2 Westport U.S.A.
187 I4 Westray Canada
162 E1 Westray i. U.K.
191 G2 Westree Canada
164 F5 Westrich reg. Germany
186 E4 West Road r. Canada
132 J3 West Siberian Plain Rus. Fed.
127 G7 West Sister Island Australia
203 H2 West Stewartstown U.S.A.
164 D1 West-Terschelling Neth.
203 H4 West Tisbury U.S.A.
203 G2 West Topsham U.S.A.
203 G3 West Townshend U.S.A.
190 B4 West Union IA U.S.A.
202 B5 West Union OH U.S.A.
202 C5 West Union WV U.S.A.
190 D5 Westville U.S.A.
202 C5 West Virginia state U.S.A.
196 C2 West Walker r. U.S.A.
196 B1 Westwood U.S.A.
127 G4 West Wyalong Australia
194 E2 West Yellowstone U.S.A.
164 C2 Westzaan Neth.
147 E7 Wetar i. Indon.
186 G4 Wetaskiwin Canada
190 D2 Wetmore U.S.A.
165 G4 Wetter r. Germany
165 J3 Wettin Germany
165 G4 Wetzlar Germany
124 E2 Wewak P.N.G.
163 E5 Wexford Ireland
187 H4 Weyakwin Canada
190 C3 Weyauwega U.S.A.
161 G6 Weybridge U.K.
187 I5 Weyburn Canada
165 G2 Weyhe Germany
161 E7 Weymouth U.K.
203 H3 Weymouth U.S.A.
164 E2 Wezep Neth.
128 F2 Whakaari i. N.Z.
128 F2 Whakatane N.Z.
128 F3 Whakatane r. N.Z.
154 A3 Whale Bay Myanmar
186 B3 Whale Bay U.S.A.
201 E7 Whale Cay i. Bahamas
187 K2 Whale Cove Canada
162 □ Whalsay i. U.K.
128 E2 Whangamata N.Z.
128 E3 Whangamomona N.Z.
128 E3 Whanganui National Park N.Z.
128 E1 Whangarei N.Z.
188 E2 Whapmagoostui Canada
160 F4 Wharfe r. U.K.
191 F2 Wharncliffe Canada
187 I2 Wharton Lake Canada
190 A5 What Cheer U.S.A.
186 F2 Whatì Canada
194 F3 Wheatland U.S.A.
190 C5 Wheaton U.S.A.
195 F4 Wheeler Peak NM U.S.A.
197 E2 Wheeler Peak NV U.S.A.
202 C4 Wheeling U.S.A.
215 E2 Wheelwright Arg.
160 E3 Whernside h. U.K.
126 A5 Whidbey, Point Australia
194 B3 Whiskeytown Shasta Trinity National Recreation Area park U.S.A.
162 E5 Whitburn U.K.
191 H4 Whitby Canada
160 G3 Whitby U.K.
161 E5 Whitchurch U.K.
186 A2 White r. Canada/U.S.A.
199 E4 White r. AR U.S.A.
194 E3 White r. CO U.S.A.
200 C4 White r. IN U.S.A.
190 D4 White r. MI U.S.A.
197 E2 White r. NV U.S.A.
198 C3 White r. SD U.S.A.
190 B2 White r. WI U.S.A.
197 G5 White watercourse AZ U.S.A.
124 C4 White, Lake salt flat Australia
189 I3 White Bay Canada
198 C2 White Butte mt. U.S.A.
126 E3 White Cliffs Australia
190 E4 White Cloud U.S.A.
186 F4 Whitecourt Canada
190 A2 Whiteface Lake U.S.A.
203 H2 Whitefield U.S.A.
191 G2 Whitefish Canada
194 D1 Whitefish U.S.A.
190 D3 Whitefish r. U.S.A.
187 H2 Whitefish Lake Canada
190 E2 Whitefish Point U.S.A.
163 D5 Whitehall Ireland
162 F1 Whitehall U.K.
203 G3 Whitehall NY U.S.A.
190 B3 Whitehall WI U.S.A.
160 D3 Whitehaven U.K.
163 F3 Whitehead U.K.
161 G6 Whitehill U.K.
186 B2 Whitehorse Canada
161 F6 White Horse, Vale of val. U.K.
197 E1 White Horse Pass U.S.A.
199 E6 White Lake LA U.S.A.
190 D4 White Lake MI U.S.A.
196 C3 White Mountain Peak U.S.A.
203 H2 White Mountains U.S.A.
177 F3 White Nile r. Sudan/Uganda alt. Abiad, Bahr el, alt. Jabal, Bahr el
180 C1 White Nossob watercourse Namibia
197 E2 White Pine Range mts U.S.A.
203 G4 White Plains U.S.A.
188 C4 White River Canada
197 H5 Whiteriver U.S.A.
203 G3 White River Junction U.S.A.
197 E2 White River Valley U.S.A.
197 E2 White Rock Peak U.S.A.
195 F5 White Sands National Monument nat. park U.S.A.
202 B6 Whitesburg U.S.A.
132 E3 White Sea Rus. Fed.
187 J4 Whiteshell Provincial Park Canada
194 E2 White Sulphur Springs MT U.S.A.
202 C6 White Sulphur Springs WV U.S.A.
201 E5 Whiteville U.S.A.
176 B4 White Volta r. Ghana
190 C4 Whitewater U.S.A.
197 H5 Whitewater Baldy mt. U.S.A.
188 C3 Whitewater Lake Canada
187 I4 Whitewood Canada
127 G6 Whitfield Australia
161 I6 Whitfield U.K.
162 D6 Whithorn U.K.
128 E2 Whitianga N.Z.
203 J2 Whiting U.S.A.
161 C6 Whitland U.K.
160 F2 Whitley Bay U.K.
201 D5 Whitmire U.S.A.
191 H3 Whitney Canada
196 C3 Whitney, Mount U.S.A.
203 J2 Whitneyville U.S.A.
161 I6 Whitstable U.K.
124 E4 Whitsunday Island Australia
126 F6 Whittlesea Australia
161 G5 Whittlesey U.K.
127 G5 Whitton Australia
187 H2 Wholdaia Lake Canada
197 F5 Why U.S.A.
126 B4 Whyalla Australia
154 B1 Wiang Sa Thai.
191 G3 Wiarton Canada
164 B3 Wichelen Belgium
199 D4 Wichita U.S.A.
199 D5 Wichita Falls U.S.A.
199 D5 Wichita Mountains U.S.A.
162 E2 Wick U.K.
197 F5 Wickenburg U.S.A.
161 H6 Wickford U.K.
127 E7 Wickham, Cape Australia
163 E5 Wicklow Ireland
163 F5 Wicklow Head Ireland
163 E5 Wicklow Mountains Ireland
163 E4 Wicklow Mountains National Park Ireland
127 G2 Widgeegoara watercourse Australia
161 E4 Widnes U.K.
152 D6 Wi-do i. S. Korea
165 G2 Wiehengebirge hills Germany
164 F4 Wiehl Germany
169 I5 Wieluń Poland
Wien Austria see Vienna
168 H7 Wiener Neustadt Austria
164 E2 Wierden Neth.
165 I2 Wieren Germany
164 C2 Wieringermeer Polder Neth.
164 D2 Wieringerwerf Neth.
165 G4 Wiesbaden Germany
165 K5 Wiesenfelden Germany
165 I5 Wiesentheid Germany
165 G5 Wiesloch Germany
165 F1 Wiesmoor Germany
165 H2 Wietze Germany
165 H2 Wietzendorf Germany
168 I3 Wieżyca h. Poland
160 E4 Wigan U.K.
199 F6 Wiggins U.S.A.
161 F7 Wight, Isle of i. U.K.
187 H2 Wignes Lake Canada
161 F5 Wigston U.K.
160 D3 Wigton U.K.
162 D6 Wigtown U.K.
162 D6 Wigtown Bay U.K.
164 D3 Wijchen Neth.
164 E2 Wijhe Neth.
164 C3 Wijnegem Belgium
197 F4 Wikieup U.S.A.
191 G3 Wikwemikong Canada
194 C2 Wilbur U.S.A.
126 E3 Wilcannia Australia
165 K2 Wildberg Germany
187 I4 Wildcat Hill Provincial Wilderness Park Canada
Wildcat Hill Wilderness Area res. Canada see Wildcat Hill Provincial Wilderness Park
196 D2 Wildcat Peak U.S.A.
181 H5 Wild Coast S. Africa
165 G2 Wildeshausen Germany
190 C1 Wild Goose Canada
186 F4 Wildhay r. Canada
190 A2 Wild Rice Lake U.S.A.
168 E7 Wildspitze mt. Austria
201 D6 Wildwood FL U.S.A.
203 F5 Wildwood NJ U.S.A.
181 H3 Wilge r. Free State S. Africa
181 H2 Wilge r. Gauteng/Mpumalanga S. Africa
126 A3 Wilgena Australia
202 C4 Wilhelm, Lake U.S.A.
124 E2 Wilhelm, Mount P.N.G.
165 G1 Wilhelmshaven Germany
203 F4 Wilkes-Barre U.S.A.
129 C6 Wilkes Land reg. Antarctica
187 H4 Wilkie Canada
129 B3 Wilkins Ice Shelf ice feature Antarctica
186 D3 Will, Mount Canada
194 B2 Willamette r. U.S.A.
161 D7 Willand U.K.
126 F4 Willandra Billabong watercourse Australia
127 F4 Willandra National Park Australia
194 B1 Willapa Bay U.S.A.
202 B4 Willard U.S.A.
203 F5 Willards U.S.A.
197 H5 Willcox U.S.A.
165 H3 Willebadessen Germany
164 C3 Willebroek Belgium
205 K6 Willemstad Curaçao
187 H3 William r. Canada
126 E6 William, Mount Australia
126 B2 William Creek Australia
197 F4 Williams AZ U.S.A.
196 A2 Williams CA U.S.A.
190 A5 Williamsburg IA U.S.A.
202 A6 Williamsburg KY U.S.A.
190 E3 Williamsburg MI U.S.A.
202 E6 Williamsburg VA U.S.A.
201 E7 Williams Island Bahamas
186 E4 Williams Lake Canada
189 H1 William Smith, Cap c. Canada
202 E3 Williamson NY U.S.A.
202 B6 Williamson WV U.S.A.
190 D5 Williamsport IN U.S.A.
202 E4 Williamsport PA U.S.A.
201 E5 Williamston U.S.A.
203 G3 Williamstown MA U.S.A.
203 F3 Williamstown NY U.S.A.
202 C5 Williamstown WV U.S.A.
203 G4 Willimantic U.S.A.
180 D5 Williston S. Africa
201 D6 Williston FL U.S.A.
198 C1 Williston ND U.S.A.
186 E3 Williston Lake Canada
161 D6 Williton U.K.
196 A2 Willits U.S.A.
198 E2 Willmar U.S.A.
186 F4 Willmore Wilderness Provincial Park Canada
126 B3 Willochra watercourse Australia
186 E4 Willow r. Canada
187 H5 Willow Bunch Canada
202 E4 Willow Hill U.S.A.
186 F2 Willow Lake Canada
180 E6 Willowmore S. Africa
190 C3 Willow Reservoir U.S.A.
196 A2 Willows U.S.A.
199 F4 Willow Springs U.S.A.
127 I3 Willow Tree Australia
181 H6 Willowvale S. Africa
124 C4 Wills, Lake salt flat Australia
203 G2 Willsboro U.S.A.
126 C5 Willunga Australia
126 C4 Wilmington Australia
203 F5 Wilmington DE U.S.A.
201 E5 Wilmington NC U.S.A.
202 B5 Wilmington OH U.S.A.
203 G3 Wilmington VT U.S.A.
161 E4 Wilmslow U.K.
165 G4 Wilnsdorf Germany
126 C3 Wilpena watercourse Australia
165 H1 Wilseder Berg h. Germany
198 D4 Wilson KS U.S.A.
201 E5 Wilson NC U.S.A.
195 F4 Wilson, Mount CO U.S.A.
197 E2 Wilson, Mount NV U.S.A.
198 D4 Wilson Reservoir U.S.A.
203 H2 Wilsons Mills U.S.A.
127 G7 Wilson's Promontory pen. Australia
127 G7 Wilson's Promontory National Park Australia
164 E2 Wilsum Germany
190 B5 Wilton IA U.S.A.
203 H2 Wilton ME U.S.A.
164 D5 Wiltz Lux.
124 C4 Wiluna Australia
161 I7 Wimereux France
126 E6 Wimmera r. Australia
190 D5 Winamac U.S.A.
181 G4 Winburg S. Africa
161 E6 Wincanton U.K.
203 G3 Winchendon U.S.A.
188 E4 Winchester Canada
161 F6 Winchester U.K.
190 B6 Winchester IL U.S.A.
190 E5 Winchester IN U.S.A.
202 A6 Winchester KY U.S.A.
203 G3 Winchester NH U.S.A.
201 C5 Winchester TN U.S.A.
202 D5 Winchester VA U.S.A.
184 E3 Wind r. Canada
194 E3 Wind r. U.S.A.
126 B3 Windabout, Lake salt flat Australia
198 C3 Wind Cave National Park U.S.A.
160 E3 Windermere U.K.
160 E3 Windermere l. U.K.
179 B6 Windhoek Namibia
198 E3 Windom U.S.A.
124 E4 Windorah Australia
197 H4 Window Rock U.S.A.
190 D4 Wind Point U.S.A.
194 E3 Wind River Range mts U.S.A.
161 F6 Windrush r. U.K.
165 I5 Windsbach Germany
127 I4 Windsor Australia
189 H5 Windsor N.S. Canada
191 F4 Windsor Ont. Canada
189 F4 Windsor Que. Canada
161 G6 Windsor U.K.
203 G4 Windsor CT U.S.A.
201 E5 Windsor NC U.S.A.
203 F3 Windsor NY U.S.A.
202 E6 Windsor VA U.S.A.
203 G3 Windsor VT U.S.A.
203 G4 Windsor Locks U.S.A.
205 L5 Windward Islands Caribbean Sea
205 J5 Windward Passage Cuba/Haiti
201 C5 Winfield AL U.S.A.
190 B5 Winfield IA U.S.A.
199 D4 Winfield KS U.S.A.
160 F3 Wingate U.K.
127 I3 Wingen Australia
164 B3 Wingene Belgium
164 F6 Wingen-sur-Moder France
127 J3 Wingham Australia
191 G4 Wingham Canada
188 C2 Winisk r. Canada
188 C2 Winisk (abandoned) Canada
188 C3 Winisk Lake Canada
188 C3 Winisk River Provincial Park Canada
154 A2 Winkana Myanmar
187 J5 Winkler Canada
203 I2 Winn U.S.A.
176 B4 Winneba Ghana
190 C3 Winnebago, Lake U.S.A.
190 C3 Winneconne U.S.A.
194 C3 Winnemucca U.S.A.
196 C1 Winnemucca Lake U.S.A.
198 D3 Winner U.S.A.
199 E6 Winnfield U.S.A.
198 E2 Winnibigoshish, Lake U.S.A.
187 J5 Winnipeg Canada
187 J4 Winnipeg r. Canada
187 J4 Winnipeg, Lake Canada
187 I4 Winnipegosis Canada
187 I4 Winnipegosis, Lake Canada
203 H3 Winnipesaukee, Lake U.S.A.
199 F5 Winnsboro U.S.A.
197 G4 Winona AZ U.S.A.
190 C2 Winona MI U.S.A.
190 B3 Winona MN U.S.A.
199 F5 Winona MS U.S.A.
203 G2 Winooski U.S.A.
203 G2 Winooski r. U.S.A.
164 F1 Winschoten Neth.
165 H2 Winsen (Aller) Germany
165 I1 Winsen (Luhe) Germany
161 E4 Winsford U.K.
197 G4 Winslow U.S.A.
203 G4 Winsted U.S.A.
201 D4 Winston-Salem U.S.A.
165 G3 Winterberg Germany
201 D6 Winter Haven U.S.A.
203 I2 Winterport U.S.A.
196 B2 Winters U.S.A.
164 E3 Winterswijk Neth.
168 D7 Winterthur Switz.
181 H4 Winterton S. Africa
203 I1 Winterville U.S.A.
203 I2 Winthrop U.S.A.
124 E4 Winton Australia
128 B7 Winton N.Z.
161 G5 Winwick U.K.
126 C4 Wirrabara Australia
161 D4 Wirral pen. U.K.
126 B3 Wirraminna Australia
126 D6 Wirrega Australia
126 A4 Wirrulla Australia
161 H5 Wisbech U.K.
203 I2 Wiscasset U.S.A.
165 H1 Wischhafen Germany
190 B4 Wisconsin r. U.S.A.
190 C3 Wisconsin state U.S.A.
190 C4 Wisconsin, Lake U.S.A.
190 C4 Wisconsin Dells U.S.A.
190 C3 Wisconsin Rapids U.S.A.
202 B6 Wise U.S.A.
162 E5 Wishaw U.K.
Wisła r. Poland see Vistula
168 E4 Wismar Germany
161 I7 Wissant France
190 B3 Wissota Lake U.S.A.
186 D4 Wistaria Canada
180 C2 Witbooisvlei Namibia
161 H6 Witham U.K.
161 G4 Witham r. U.K.
203 G2 Witherbee U.S.A.
160 H4 Withernsea U.K.
164 D1 Witmarsum Neth.
161 F6 Witney U.K.
181 I2 Witrivier S. Africa
164 C5 Witry-lès-Reims France
181 G5 Witteberg mts S. Africa
190 C3 Wittenberg U.S.A.
165 K3 Wittenberg, Lutherstadt Germany
165 J2 Wittenberge Germany
165 J1 Wittenburg Germany
166 H3 Wittenheim France
165 I2 Wittingen Germany
164 E5 Wittlich Germany
165 F1 Wittmund Germany
165 K1 Wittstock Germany
124 E2 Witu Islands P.N.G.
179 B6 Witvlei Namibia
165 H3 Witzenhausen Germany
127 J1 Wivenhoe, Lake Australia
152 D3 Wiwon N. Korea
168 I3 Władysławowo Poland
169 I4 Włocławek Poland
203 H2 Woburn Canada
127 G6 Wodonga Australia
165 F6 Wœrth France
164 D5 Woëvre, Plaine de la plain France
165 G4 Wohra r. Germany
164 E5 Woippy France
147 F7 Wokam i. Indon.
150 B1 Woken He r. China
145 H4 Wokha India
161 G6 Woking U.K.
161 G6 Wokingham U.K.
190 D5 Wolcott IN U.S.A.
202 E3 Wolcott NY U.S.A.
165 L1 Woldegk Germany
164 F1 Woldendorp Neth.
186 C2 Wolf r. Canada
190 C3 Wolf r. U.S.A.
210 □ Wolf, Isla i. Galapagos Is Ecuador
210 □ Wolf, Volcán vol. Galapagos Is Ecuador
194 D2 Wolf Creek U.S.A.
195 F4 Wolf Creek Pass U.S.A.
203 H3 Wolfeboro U.S.A.
191 I3 Wolfe Island Canada
165 K3 Wolfen Germany
165 I2 Wolfenbüttel Germany
165 H3 Wolfhagen Germany
186 C2 Wolf Lake Canada
194 F1 Wolf Point U.S.A.
168 G7 Wolfsberg Austria
165 I2 Wolfsburg Germany
164 F5 Wolfstein Germany
189 H4 Wolfville Canada
168 F3 Wolgast Germany
168 G4 Wolin Poland
212 C9 Wollaston, Islas is Chile
187 I3 Wollaston Lake Canada
187 I3 Wollaston Lake l. Canada
184 G3 Wollaston Peninsula Canada
127 I5 Wollongong Australia
181 F3 Wolmaransstad S. Africa
165 J2 Wolmirstedt Germany
126 D6 Wolseley Australia
180 C6 Wolseley S. Africa
160 F3 Wolsingham U.K.
141 G3 Woluswālī Behsūd Afgh.
164 E2 Wolvega Neth.
161 E5 Wolverhampton U.K.
190 E3 Wolverine U.S.A.
164 C3 Wommelgem Belgium
164 F5 Womrather Höhe h. Germany
126 F3 Wongalarroo Lake salt l. Australia
127 H4 Wongarbon Australia
145 G4 Wong Chhu r. Bhutan
149 □ Wong Chuk Hang Hong Kong China
152 D5 Wonju S. Korea
126 E3 Wonominta watercourse Australia
152 D4 Wŏnsan N. Korea
126 F7 Wonthaggi Australia
126 B3 Woocalla Australia
124 D3 Woodah, Isle i. Australia
161 I5 Woodbridge U.K.
202 E5 Woodbridge U.S.A.
186 G3 Wood Buffalo National Park Canada
127 J2 Woodburn Australia
194 B2 Woodburn U.S.A.
190 E4 Woodbury MI U.S.A.
203 F5 Woodbury NJ U.S.A.
202 A6 Wood Creek Lake U.S.A.
196 C2 Woodfords U.S.A.
196 C3 Woodlake U.S.A.
196 B2 Woodland U.S.A.
195 F4 Woodland Park U.S.A.
154 □ Woodlands Sing.
125 F2 Woodlark Island P.N.G.
124 D4 Woodroffe, Mount Australia
194 E3 Woodruff U.S.A.
124 D3 Woods, Lake salt flat Australia
187 K5 Woods, Lake of the Canada/U.S.A.
202 C5 Woodsfield U.S.A.
127 G7 Woodside Australia
127 G6 Woods Point Australia
189 G4 Woodstock N.B. Canada
191 G4 Woodstock Ont. Canada
190 C4 Woodstock IL U.S.A.
202 D5 Woodstock VA U.S.A.
203 F5 Woodstown U.S.A.
203 G2 Woodsville U.S.A.
128 E4 Woodville N.Z.
202 E3 Woodville NY U.S.A.
199 E6 Woodville TX U.S.A.
199 D4 Woodward U.S.A.
160 E2 Wooler U.K.
127 J3 Woolgoolga Australia
127 J2 Wooli Australia
126 C3 Wooltana Australia
126 B3 Woomera Australia
126 A3 Woomera Prohibited Area Australia
203 H4 Woonsocket U.S.A.
202 C4 Wooster U.S.A.
161 F6 Wootton Bassett, Royal U.K.
165 I3 Worbis Germany
180 C6 Worcester S. Africa
161 E5 Worcester U.K.
203 H3 Worcester U.S.A.
168 F7 Wörgl Austria
160 D3 Workington U.K.
161 F4 Worksop U.K.
164 D2 Workum Neth.
194 F2 Worland U.S.A.
165 K3 Wörlitz Germany
164 C2 Wormerveer Neth.
165 G5 Worms Germany
161 C6 Worms Head U.K.
180 B1 Wortel Namibia
165 G5 Wörth am Rhein Germany
161 G7 Worthing U.K.
198 E3 Worthington U.S.A.
216 G6 Wotje atoll Marshall Is
147 E7 Wotu Indon.
164 C3 Woudrichem Neth.
198 C3 Wounded Knee U.S.A.
164 F5 Woustviller France
147 E7 Wowoni i. Indon.
133 T4 Wrangel Island Rus. Fed.
186 C3 Wrangell U.S.A.
186 C3 Wrangell Island U.S.A.
184 C4 Wrangell Mountains U.S.A.
184 D3 Wrangell-St Elias National Park and Preserve U.S.A.
162 C2 Wrath, Cape U.K.
198 C3 Wray U.S.A.
161 F5 Wreake r. U.K.
180 B4 Wreck Point S. Africa
165 I2 Wrestedt Germany
161 E4 Wrexham U.K.
194 F3 Wright U.S.A.
199 E5 Wright Patman Lake U.S.A.
197 G6 Wrightson, Mount U.S.A.
186 E2 Wrigley Canada
168 H5 Wrocław Poland
168 H4 Września Poland
148 D4 Wu'an China
148 E2 Wu'an China
148 D2 Wubu China
152 D1 Wuchang China
149 D6 Wuchuan China
149 C4 Wuchuan Guizhou China
148 D1 Wuchuan Nei Mongol China
148 F1 Wudan China
148 D3 Wudang Shan mt. China
148 C3 Wudang Shan mts China
152 A4 Wudao China
145 H2 Wudaoliang China
148 E2 Wudi China

149 B5 Wuding China
148 D2 Wuding He r. China
126 A4 Wudinna Australia
149 D4 Wufeng China
149 D5 Wugang China
148 C3 Wugong China
148 C2 Wuhai China
149 E4 Wuhan China
148 E3 Wuhe China
148 F4 Wuhu China
149 E6 Wuhua China
144 D2 Wüjang China
149 C6 Wujia China
149 C4 Wu Jiang r. China
176 C4 Wukari Nigeria
145 H3 Wulang China
144 C2 Wular Lake India
148 F3 Wulian China
149 B4 Wulian Feng mts China
146 C4 Wuliang Shan mts China
147 F7 Wuliaru i. Indon.
149 C4 Wuling Shan mts China
149 C4 Wulong China
149 B5 Wumeng Shan mts China
149 C6 Wuming China
165 H1 Wümme r. Germany
149 E4 Wuning China
165 G3 Wünnenberg Germany
165 K4 Wunsiedel Germany
165 H2 Wunstorf Germany
146 B4 Wuntho Myanmar
197 G4 Wupatki National Monument nat. park U.S.A.
149 E5 Wuping China
164 F3 Wuppertal Germany
180 C6 Wuppertal S. Africa
148 C2 Wuqi China
148 E2 Wuqiao China
165 H5 Würzburg Germany
165 K3 Wurzen Germany
148 B3 Wushan Gansu China
148 C4 Wushan Sichuan China
148 D4 Wu Shan mts China
149 C4 Wusheng China
149 C6 Wushi Guangdong China
139 I4 Wushi Xinjiang China
165 H3 Wüstegarten h. Germany
148 D2 Wutai China
124 E2 Wuvulu Island P.N.G.
148 E4 Wuwei Anhui China
148 B2 Wuwei Gansu China
149 D4 Wuxi Hunan China
148 F4 Wuxi Jiangsu China
148 C4 Wuxi Sichuan China
Wuxing China see Huzhou
149 C6 Wuxu China
149 C6 Wuxuan China
149 E4 Wuxue China
148 D3 Wuyang China
149 F4 Wuyi China
146 E2 Wuyiling China
149 F5 Wuyishan China
149 E5 Wuyi Shan mts China
149 E4 Wuyuan Jiangxi China
148 C1 Wuyuan Nei Mongol China
148 D2 Wuzhai China
149 C7 Wuzhishan China
148 C2 Wuzhong China
149 D6 Wuzhou China
190 B5 Wyaconda r. U.S.A.
127 G4 Wyalong Australia
191 F4 Wyandotte U.S.A.
190 C5 Wyanet U.S.A.
127 H4 Wyangala Reservoir Australia
126 F2 Wyara, Lake salt flat Australia
126 E6 Wycheproof Australia
161 E6 Wye r. U.K.
161 F6 Wylye r. U.K.
161 I5 Wymondham U.K.
124 C3 Wyndham Australia
126 F6 Wyndham-Werribee Australia
199 F5 Wynne U.S.A.
184 G2 Wynniatt Bay Canada
127 F8 Wynyard Australia
187 I4 Wynyard Canada
190 C5 Wyoming IL U.S.A.
190 E4 Wyoming MI U.S.A.
194 E3 Wyoming state U.S.A.
194 E3 Wyoming Peak U.S.A.
127 I4 Wyong Australia
126 D5 Wyperfeld National Park Australia
160 E4 Wyre r. U.K.
203 E4 Wysox U.S.A.
169 J4 Wyszków Poland
161 F5 Wythall U.K.
202 C6 Wytheville U.S.A.
203 I2 Wytopitlock U.S.A.


## X


178 F2 Xaafuun Somalia
138 A4 Xaçmaz Azer.
180 E1 Xade Botswana
145 H3 Xagquka China
144 D1 Xaidulla China
154 B1 Xaignabouli Laos
145 G3 Xainza China
179 D6 Xai-Xai Moz.
207 G3 Xal, Cerro de h. Mex.
207 E4 Xalapa Mex.
138 D4 Xalqobod Uzbek.
137 L1 Xaltan Aşırımı Azer.
148 C1 Xamba China
146 B4 Xamgyi'nyilha China
Xam Hua Laos see Xam Nua
147 C4 Xam Nua Laos
154 B1 Xan r. Laos
Xan, Xê r. Vietnam see Pe Cô, Krông
148 E1 Xanadu, Site of tourist site China
179 C6 Xanagas Botswana
148 B1 Xangd China
148 D1 Xangdin Hural China
Xangdoring China see Xungba
179 B5 Xangongo Angola
Xangyi'nyilha China see Xamgyi'nyilha
137 K2 Xankändi Azer.
171 K4 Xanthi Greece
210 E6 Xapuri Brazil
137 L2 Xaraba Şähär Sayı sea feature Azer.
137 L2 Xärä Zirä Adası is Azer.
145 F3 Xarba La pass China
148 F1 Xar Moron r. China
167 F3 Xàtiva Spain
179 C6 Xau, Lake Botswana
211 I6 Xavantes, Serra dos hills Brazil
Xa Vo Đat Vietnam see Đưc Linh
139 J4 Xayar China
139 I5 Xekargol China
154 C2 Xékong Laos
202 B5 Xenia U.S.A.
152 F1 Xiachengzi China
149 D6 Xiachuan Dao i. China
148 B3 Xiahe China
148 E2 Xiajin China
149 F5 Xiamen China
148 C3 Xi'an China
149 C4 Xianfeng China
148 D3 Xiangcheng Henan China
148 E3 Xiangcheng Henan China
149 F4 Xiangshan China
149 D5 Xiangtan China
149 D5 Xiangxiang China
148 D3 Xiangyang China
149 D4 Xiangyin China
149 F4 Xianju China
149 E4 Xianning China
149 D4 Xiantao China
149 E5 Xianxia Ling mts China
148 E2 Xianxian China
148 C3 Xianyang China
149 F5 Xianyou China
149 F4 Xianyuan China
148 D4 Xiaochang China
149 C6 Xiaodong China
149 D4 Xiaogan China
146 E1 Xiao Hinggan Ling mts China
148 B4 Xiaojin China
145 H2 Xiaonanchuan China
149 F4 Xiaoshan China
149 E5 Xiaotao China
148 E2 Xiaowutai Shan mt. China
148 E3 Xiaoxian China
149 B4 Xiaoxiang Ling mts China
Xiaoxita China see Yiling
149 G4 Xiaoyang Shan is China
148 D2 Xiaoyi China
149 F5 Xiapu China
152 A2 Xiawa China
148 D3 Xiayukou China
149 B5 Xichang China
148 B4 Xichong China
149 B6 Xichou China
148 D3 Xichuan China
149 B4 Xide China
213 D4 Xié r. Brazil
154 C1 Xiêng Lam Vietnam
149 C6 Xieyang Dao i. China
148 E3 Xifei He r. China
Xifeng Gansu China see Qingyang
149 C5 Xifeng Guizhou China
152 C2 Xifeng Liaoning China
148 C2 Xi Ganqu r. China
135 G4 Xigazê China
148 C3 Xihan Shui r. China
148 B3 Xihe China
152 A3 Xi He r. China
148 B3 Xiji China
149 D6 Xi Jiang r. China
145 G2 Xijir China
145 G2 Xijir Ulan Hu salt l. China
148 B2 Xijishui China
148 D1 Xil China
152 B2 Xiliao He r. China
149 B5 Xilin China
148 B2 Xilin Gol China
148 E1 Xilinhot China
148 A1 Ximiao China
148 C2 Xin China
181 J2 Xinavane Moz.
152 C3 Xinbin China
148 D1 Xin Bulag China
148 E3 Xincai China
149 F4 Xinchang China
149 C5 Xincheng Guangxi China
148 C2 Xincheng China
148 A2 Xinchengzi China
149 D6 Xindu Guangxi China
148 B4 Xindu Sichuan China
149 E5 Xinfeng Guangdong China
149 E5 Xinfeng Jiangxi China
149 E6 Xinfengjiang Shuiku resr China
149 E5 Xingan China
149 D5 Xing'an China
152 A4 Xingang China
Xingba China see Lhünzê
148 F1 Xingcheng China
149 E5 Xingguo China
135 H3 Xinghai China
148 D1 Xinghe China
148 F3 Xinghua China
149 F5 Xinghua Wan b. China
150 C2 Xingkai China
Xingkai Hu l. China/Rus. Fed. see Khanka, Lake
149 E5 Xingning Guangdong China
149 D5 Xingning Hunan China
149 D4 Xingou China
148 C3 Xingping China
149 B5 Xingren China
148 A3 Xingsagoinba China
148 D4 Xingshan China
148 E2 Xingtai China
211 H4 Xingu r. Brazil
211 H6 Xingu, Parque Indígena do res. Brazil
149 B4 Xingwen China
148 D2 Xingxian China
148 D3 Xingyang China
149 C6 Xingye China
149 B5 Xingyi China
149 E4 Xingzi China
139 J4 Xinhe China
148 E1 Xin Hot China
149 D5 Xinhua China
148 B2 Xinhuacun China
149 C5 Xinhuang China
149 D6 Xinhui Guangdong China
148 F1 Xinhui Nei Mongol China
148 A2 Xining China
148 E2 Xinji China
149 E4 Xinjian China
148 D3 Xinjiang China
145 D1 Xinjiang Uygur Zizhiqu China
145 E1 Xinjiang Uygur Zizhiqu aut. reg. China
148 C2 Xinjie Nei Mongol China
149 B6 Xinjie Yunnan China
149 B4 Xinjin China
152 B1 Xinkai He r. China
148 D2 Xinkou China
152 B3 Xinmin China
149 D5 Xinning China
149 A5 Xinping China
149 E5 Xinquan China
149 D5 Xinshao China
148 E3 Xintai China
149 D5 Xintian China
148 E4 Xinxian China
148 D3 Xinxiang China
149 D6 Xinxing China
148 E3 Xinyang China
148 D3 Xinye China
149 D6 Xinyi Guangdong China
148 F3 Xinyi Jiangsu China
148 F3 Xinyi He r. China
149 C7 Xinying China
149 F6 Xinying Taiwan
149 E5 Xinyu China
139 J4 Xinyuan China
148 D2 Xinzhou China
149 F5 Xinzhu Taiwan
167 C1 Xinzo de Limia Spain
152 B3 Xiongyue China
148 D3 Xiping Henan China
148 E3 Xiping Henan China
148 A3 Xiqing Shan mts China
211 J6 Xique Xique Brazil
148 C1 Xishanzui China
149 C4 Xishui Guizhou China
149 E4 Xishui Hubei China
149 F4 Xiuning China
149 C4 Xiushan China
149 E4 Xiushui China
149 E4 Xiu Shui r. China
149 C5 Xiuwen China
148 D3 Xiuwu China
152 B3 Xiuyan China
149 D6 Xiuying China
138 E4 Xiva Uzbek.
145 F3 Xixabangma Feng mt. China
148 C2 Xixia Ningxia China
148 D3 Xixia China
148 E3 Xixian Henan China
148 D2 Xixian Shanxi China
148 C3 Xixiang China
Xixón Spain see Gijón
149 F5 Xiyang Dao i. China
149 B5 Xiyang Jiang r. China
149 F6 Xiyuping Yu i. Taiwan
145 G3 Xizang Zizhiqu aut. reg. China
152 A4 Xizhong Dao i. China
138 D4 Xo'jayli Uzbek.
145 H3 Xoka China
Xom An Lôc Vietnam see An Lôc
Xom Dưc Hanh Vietnam see Đưc Bôn
139 H4 Xonobod Uzbek.
139 G4 Xovos Uzbek.
148 F4 Xuancheng China
149 C4 Xuan'en China
148 C4 Xuanhan China
148 B2 Xuanhe China
148 E1 Xuanhua China
154 C3 Xuân Lôc Vietnam
149 B5 Xuanwei China
Xuanzhou China see Xuancheng
148 D3 Xuchang China
138 A4 Xudat Azer.
178 E3 Xuddur Somalia
149 C5 Xuefeng Shan mts China
149 F5 Xue Shan mt. Taiwan
145 H2 Xugui China
145 E2 Xungba China
145 F3 Xungru China
148 C3 Xun He r. China
149 D6 Xun Jiang r. China
149 E5 Xunwu China
148 E3 Xunxian China
148 C3 Xunyang China
148 C3 Xunyi China
149 D5 Xupu China
167 F3 Xúquer, Riu r. Spain
145 F3 Xuru Co l. China
148 E2 Xushui China
149 D6 Xuwen China
148 F3 Xuyi China
149 B4 Xuyong China
148 E3 Xuzhou China


## Y


149 B4 Ya'an China
126 E5 Yaapeet Australia
176 C4 Yabassi Cameroon
178 D3 Yabēlo Eth.
146 C1 Yablonovyy Khrebet mts Rus. Fed.
148 B2 Yabrai China
148 B2 Yabrai Shan mts China
136 F5 Yabrūd Syria
152 E1 Yabuli China
213 C2 Yacambú, Parque Nacional nat. park Venez.
149 C7 Yacheng China
149 C5 Yachi He r. China
210 E6 Yacuma r. Bol.
143 B2 Yadgir India
193 J4 Yadkin r. U.S.A.
172 H4 Yadrin Rus. Fed.
177 D1 Yafran Libya
148 B1 Yagan China
219 E9 Yaghan Basin sea feature S. Atlantic Ocean
150 G2 Yagishiri-tō i. Japan
138 C5 Yagman Turkm.
177 D3 Yagoua Cameroon
145 E3 Yagra China
145 H2 Yagradagzê Feng mt. China
215 F1 Yaguari r. Uruguay
207 E4 Yagul and Mitla, Prehistoric Caves of tourist site Mexico
154 B4 Yaha Thai.
136 D2 Yahşihan Turkey
136 E2 Yahyalı Turkey
151 F6 Yaita Japan
151 F7 Yaizu Japan
149 A4 Yajiang China
136 F3 Yakacık Turkey
141 G4 Yakhchāl Afgh.
194 B2 Yakima U.S.A.
194 B2 Yakima r. U.S.A.
140 D3 Yakinish Iran
Yakkabag Uzbek. see Yakkabog'
139 F5 Yakkabog' Uzbek.
141 F4 Yakmach Pak.
176 B3 Yako Burkina Faso
186 B3 Yakobi Island U.S.A.
150 C2 Yakovlevka Rus. Fed.
150 G3 Yakumo Japan
151 B9 Yaku-shima i. Japan
186 B3 Yakutat U.S.A.
186 B3 Yakutat Bay U.S.A.
133 N3 Yakutsk Rus. Fed.
173 E6 Yakymivka Ukr.
154 B4 Yala Thai.
191 F4 Yale U.S.A.
207 G3 Yalkubul, Punta pt Mex.
127 G7 Yallourn Australia
149 A5 Yalong Jiang r. China
136 B1 Yalova Turkey
173 F6 Yalta Ukr.
173 E6 Yalta Ukr.
152 C3 Yalu Jiang r. China/N. Korea
152 C4 Yalujiang Kou r. mouth N. Korea
136 C2 Yalvaç Turkey
150 G5 Yamada Japan
150 G5 Yamagata Japan
151 B9 Yamagawa Japan
151 B7 Yamaguchi Japan
Yamal, Poluostrov pen. Rus. Fed. see Yamal Peninsula
132 H2 Yamal Peninsula Rus. Fed.
127 J2 Yamba Australia
127 E7 Yambacoona Australia
187 G2 Yamba Lake Canada
213 C4 Yambi, Mesa de hills Col.
177 E4 Yambio South Sudan
171 L3 Yambol Bulg.
132 I3 Yamburg Rus. Fed.
148 A2 Yamenzhuang China
151 G6 Yamizo-san mt. Japan
159 O4 Yamm Rus. Fed.
176 B4 Yamoussoukro Côte d'Ivoire
194 E3 Yampa r. U.S.A.
173 D5 Yampil' Ukr.
144 E4 Yamuna r. India
144 D3 Yamunanagar India
139 I2 Yamyshevo Kazakh.
145 G3 Yamzho Yumco l. China
133 O3 Yana r. Rus. Fed.
126 D6 Yanac Australia
143 C2 Yanam India
148 C2 Yan'an China
210 D6 Yanaoca Peru
142 A5 Yanbu' al Baḩr Saudi Arabia
148 F3 Yancheng China
124 B5 Yanchep Australia
148 C2 Yanchi China
148 D2 Yanchuan China
127 G5 Yanco Australia
126 D3 Yanco Glen Australia
127 F3 Yanda watercourse Australia
126 D3 Yandama Creek watercourse Australia
176 B3 Yanfolila Mali
145 H3 Ya'ngamdo China
145 G3 Yangbajain China
148 D3 Yangcheng China
149 D6 Yangchun China
148 E2 Yangcun China
152 D4 Yangdok N. Korea
152 E5 Yangdong tourist site South Korea
148 D1 Yanggao China
148 E2 Yanggu China
148 E1 Yang He r. China
Yangiabad Uzbek. see Yangiobod
Yangikishlak Uzbek. see Yangiqishloq
Yangi-Nishan Uzbek. see Yangi Nishon
138 F5 Yangi Nishon Uzbek.
139 G4 Yangiobod Uzbek.
139 F4 Yangiqishloq Uzbek.
Yangirabad Uzbek. see Yangirabot
138 F4 Yangirabot Uzbek.
139 G4 Yangiyo'l Uzbek.
Yangiyul' Uzbek. see Yangiyo'l
149 D6 Yangjiang China
Yangôn Myanmar see Rangoon
148 D4 Yangping China
148 D2 Yangquan China
149 D5 Yangshan China
149 D5 Yangshuo China
154 D2 Yang Sin, Chư mt. Vietnam
149 E4 Yangtze r. China alt. Chang Jiang, alt. Jinsha Jiang, alt. Tongtian He, alt. Zhi Qu, long Yangtze Kiang
178 E2 Yangudi Rassa National Park Eth.
149 D6 Yangxi China
148 C3 Yangxian China
152 E5 Yangyang S. Korea
148 E1 Yangyuan China
148 F3 Yangzhou China
149 C4 Yanhe China
148 D2 Yan He r. China
145 E2 Yanhuqu China
126 A4 Yaninee, Lake salt flat Australia
152 E2 Yanji China
149 B4 Yanjin China
176 C4 Yankari National Park Nigeria
198 D3 Yankton U.S.A.
149 D5 Yanling China
133 O2 Yano-Indigirskaya Nizmennost' lowland Rus. Fed.
213 D3 Yanomami, Parque Indígena nat. park Brazil
143 C4 Yan Oya r. Sri Lanka
148 E1 Yanqing China
148 E2 Yanshan Hebei China
149 E4 Yanshan Jiangxi China
149 B6 Yanshan Yunnan China
148 E1 Yan Shan mts China
145 H2 Yanshiping China
152 E1 Yanshou China
133 O2 Yanskiy Zaliv g. Rus. Fed.
127 F2 Yantabulla Australia
152 A5 Yantai China
126 E2 Yantara Lake salt flat Australia
169 I3 Yantarnyy Rus. Fed.
152 D2 Yantongshan China
149 A5 Yanyuan China
148 E3 Yanzhou China
176 D4 Yaoundé Cameroon
Yaoxian China see Yaozhou
154 A3 Yao Yai, Ko i. Thai.
148 C3 Yaozhou China
147 F6 Yap i. Micronesia
213 D4 Yapacana, Cerro mt. Venez.
147 F7 Yapen i. Indon.
147 F7 Yapen, Selat sea chan. Indon.
216 E5 Yap Trench sea feature N. Pacific Ocean
206 B1 Yaqui r. Mex.
213 C2 Yaracuy r. Venez.
124 E4 Yaraka Australia
172 H3 Yaransk Rus. Fed.
126 A4 Yardea Australia
136 C3 Yardımcı Burnu pt Turkey
137 L2 Yardımlı Azer.
161 I5 Yare r. U.K.
172 J2 Yarega Rus. Fed.
125 G2 Yaren Nauru
172 I2 Yarensk Rus. Fed.
213 B4 Yari r. Col.
151 E6 Yariga-take mt. Japan
213 C2 Yaritagua Venez.
139 I5 Yarkant He r. China
191 I3 Yarker Canada
144 C1 Yarkhun r. Pak.
145 G4 Yarlung Zangbo r. Asia alt. Dihang (India) conv. Brahmaputra
189 G5 Yarmouth Canada
161 F7 Yarmouth U.K.
203 H4 Yarmouth Port U.S.A.
197 F4 Yarnell U.S.A.
172 F3 Yaroslavl' Rus. Fed.
172 F3 Yaroslavskaya Oblast' admin. div. Rus. Fed.
150 C2 Yaroslavskiy Rus. Fed.
126 F6 Yarra r. Australia
127 G7 Yarram Australia
127 I1 Yarraman Australia
145 H3 Yartö Tra La pass China
132 J3 Yartsevo Rus. Fed.
172 E4 Yartsevo Smolenskaya Oblast' Rus. Fed.
213 B3 Yarumal Col.
145 F5 Yasai r. India
125 H3 Yasawa Group is Fiji
173 F6 Yasenskaya Rus. Fed.
173 G6 Yashalta Rus. Fed.
139 H5 Yashilkŭl l. Tajik.
173 H6 Yashkul' Rus. Fed.
138 D2 Yasnyy Rus. Fed.
154 C2 Yasothon Thai.
127 H5 Yass Australia
127 H5 Yass r. Australia
140 C4 Yāsūj Iran
210 C4 Yasuní, Parque Nacional nat. park Ecuador
136 B3 Yatağan Turkey
125 G4 Yaté New Caledonia
199 E4 Yates Center U.S.A.
187 J2 Yathkyed Lake Canada
151 F7 Yatsuga-take vol. Japan
151 B8 Yatsushiro Japan
161 E6 Yatton U.K.
149 □ Yau Tong b. Hong Kong China
210 D5 Yavarí r. Brazil/Peru
206 B2 Yávaros Mex.
144 D5 Yavatmal India
137 H2 Yavi Turkey
213 D3 Yaví, Cerro mt. Venez.
173 B5 Yavoriv Ukr.
151 C8 Yawatahama Japan
145 E1 Yawatongguz He r. China
145 H5 Yaw Chaung r. Myanmar
207 G4 Yaxchilan tourist site Guat.
140 D4 Yazd Iran
141 F3 Yazdān Iran
136 G2 Yazıhan Turkey
199 F5 Yazoo r. U.S.A.
199 F5 Yazoo City U.S.A.
159 J5 Yding Skovhøj h. Denmark
171 J6 Ydra i. Greece
154 A2 Ye Myanmar
126 F6 Yea Australia
161 D7 Yealmpton U.K.
139 I5 Yecheng China
206 B1 Yécora Mex.
201 D7 Yeehaw Junction U.S.A.
126 A5 Yeelanna Australia
172 F4 Yefremov Rus. Fed.
137 J2 Yeghegnadzor Armenia
139 I2 Yegindybulak Kazakh.
139 G2 Yegindykol' Kazakh.
173 G6 Yegorlyk r. Rus. Fed.
173 G6 Yegorlykskaya Rus. Fed.
150 E2 Yegorova, Mys pt Rus. Fed.
172 F4 Yegor'yevsk Rus. Fed.
177 F4 Yei South Sudan
148 E4 Yeji China
132 H4 Yekaterinburg Rus. Fed.
139 H2 Yekibastuz Kazakh.
173 G5 Yelan' Rus. Fed.
173 G5 Yelan' r. Rus. Fed.
127 I2 Yelarbon Australia
138 E5 Yelbarsli Turkm.
173 F4 Yelets Rus. Fed.
176 A3 Yélimané Mali
162 □ Yell i. U.K.
143 C2 Yellandu India
143 A3 Yellapur India
148 E2 Yellow r. China
190 B3 Yellow r. U.S.A.
202 D4 Yellow Creek U.S.A.
184 G3 Yellowknife Canada
127 G4 Yellow Mountain h. Australia
152 B6 Yellow Sea Pacific Ocean
194 F2 Yellowstone r. U.S.A.
194 E2 Yellowstone Lake U.S.A.
194 E2 Yellowstone National Park U.S.A.
194 E2 Yellowtail Reservoir U.S.A.
162 □ Yell Sound str. U.K.
Yeloten Turkm. see Ýolöten
173 D5 Yel'sk Belarus
139 J3 Yel'tay Kazakh.
185 J1 Yelverton Bay Canada
139 J3 Yemel' r. Kazakh.
178 C7 Yemen country Asia
172 G2 Yemetsk Rus. Fed.
172 G2 Yemtsa Rus. Fed.
172 I2 Yemva Rus. Fed.
158 O2 Yena Rus. Fed.
176 C4 Yenagoa Nigeria
173 F5 Yenakiyeve Ukr.
145 H5 Yenangyat Myanmar
145 H5 Yenangyaung Myanmar
145 H6 Yenanma Myanmar
149 B6 Yên Bai Vietnam
139 I2 Yenbek Kazakh.
149 B6 Yên Châu Vietnam
127 G5 Yenda Australia
176 B4 Yendi Ghana
178 B4 Yénéganou Congo
137 K3 Yengejeh Iran
139 I5 Yengisar China
136 D1 Yeniçağa Turkey
136 E3 Yenice Turkey
171 L5 Yenice Turkey
136 D2 Yeniceoba Turkey
136 B1 Yenişehir Turkey
132 K4 Yenisey r. Rus. Fed.
132 K4 Yeniseysk Rus. Fed.
132 K4 Yeniseyskaya Ravnina ridge Rus. Fed.
132 I2 Yeniseyskiy Zaliv inlet Rus. Fed.
149 B6 Yên Minh Vietnam
173 H6 Yenotayevka Rus. Fed.
152 D5 Yeoju S. Korea
144 C5 Yeola India
152 D6 Yeongam S. Korea
152 E6 Yeongcheon S. Korea
152 E5 Yeongdeok S. Korea
152 D6 Yeonggwang S. Korea
152 E5 Yeongju S. Korea
152 D6 Yeongsan-gang r. S. Korea
152 D6 Yeongsanpo S. Korea
152 E5 Yeongwol S. Korea
152 D6 Yeosu S. Korea
Yeotmal India see Yavatmal
127 H4 Yeoval Australia
161 E7 Yeovil U.K.
206 B1 Yepachi Mex.
124 F4 Yeppoon Australia
138 D5 Yerbent Turkm.
133 L3 Yerbogachen Rus. Fed.
137 J1 Yerevan Armenia
139 H2 Yereymentau Kazakh.
139 H2 Yereymentau, Gory hills Kazakh.
173 H6 Yergeni hills Rus. Fed.
196 C2 Yerington U.S.A.
136 E2 Yerköy Turkey
143 A2 Yerla r. India
220 A1 Yermak Plateau sea feature Arctic Ocean
206 C2 Yermo Mex.
196 D4 Yermo U.S.A.
173 I5 Yershov Rus. Fed.
139 H1 Yertis Kazakh.
Yertis r. Kazakh./Rus. Fed. see Irtysh
172 G2 Yertsevo Rus. Fed.
Yerushalayim Israel/West Bank see Jerusalem
173 H5 Yeruslan r. Rus. Fed.
152 D5 Yesan S. Korea
138 B2 Yesbol Kazakh.
139 I4 Yesik Kazakh.
138 F2 Yesil' Kazakh.
139 F1 Yesil' r. Rus. Fed.
136 E2 Yeşilhisar Turkey
136 F1 Yeşilırmak r. Turkey
136 B3 Yeşilova Turkey
138 C3 Yeskene Kazakh.
139 H4 Yespe Kazakh.
173 G6 Yessentuki Rus. Fed.
133 L3 Yessey Rus. Fed.
161 C7 Yes Tor h. U.K.
127 I2 Yetman Australia
146 B4 Ye-U Myanmar
Yeu Myanmar see Ye-U
166 C3 Yeu, Île d' i. France
137 K1 Yevlax Azer.
173 E6 Yevpatoriya Ukr.
148 D3 Yexian China
173 F6 Yeya r. Rus. Fed.
145 E1 Yeyik China
173 F6 Yeysk Rus. Fed.
172 H1 Yezhuga r. Rus. Fed.
172 D4 Yezyaryshcha Belarus
215 F2 Yí r. Uruguay
149 B4 Yibin China
145 F2 Yibug Caka salt l. China
149 D4 Yichang China
148 D4 Yicheng Hubei China
148 D3 Yicheng Shanxi China
148 D3 Yichuan China
146 E2 Yichun Heilong. China
149 E5 Yichun Jiangxi China
149 E4 Yifeng China
148 D3 Yi He r. Henan China
148 D3 Yi He r. Shandong China
149 E5 Yihuang China
148 C3 Yijun China
150 A1 Yilan China
171 L4 Yıldız Dağları mts Turkey
136 F2 Yıldızeli Turkey
149 B5 Yiliang Yunnan China
149 B5 Yiliang Yunnan China
149 D4 Yiling China
149 B6 Yilong Hu l. China
149 B5 Yimen China
152 E1 Yimianpo China
148 F3 Yinan China
148 C2 Yinchuan China
152 C2 Yingchengzi China
149 D5 Yingde China
149 C7 Yinggehai China
148 E3 Ying He r. China
152 B3 Yingkou China
148 B2 Yingpanshui China
149 E4 Yingshan Hubei China
148 C4 Yingshan Sichuan China
148 E3 Yingshang China
149 E4 Yingtan China
148 D2 Yingxian China
139 J4 Yining China
149 C5 Yinjiang China
145 H5 Yinmabin Myanmar
152 C1 Yinma He r. China
148 C1 Yin Shan mts China
145 H3 Yi'ong Zangbo r. China
149 A5 Yipinglang China
178 D3 Yirga Alem Eth.
148 F2 Yi Shan mt. China
148 F3 Yishui China
154 □ Yishun Sing.
152 C2 Yitong China
152 C1 Yitong He r. China
146 B2 Yiwu China
152 A3 Yiwulü Shan mts China
149 E4 Yixian Anhui China
152 A3 Yixian Liaoning China
148 F4 Yixing China
149 D4 Yiyang Hunan China
149 E4 Yiyang Jiangxi China
149 D5 Yizhang China
149 C5 Yizhou China
159 M3 Yläne Fin.
158 M3 Ylihärmä Fin.
158 N2 Yli-Ii Fin.
158 N2 Yli-Kärppä Fin.
158 N2 Ylikiiminki Fin.
158 O2 Yli-Kitka l. Fin.
158 M3 Ylistaro Fin.
158 M2 Ylitornio Fin.
158 N2 Ylivieska Fin.
159 M3 Ylöjärvi Fin.
139 G2 Yntaly Kazakh.
199 D6 Yoakum U.S.A.
150 G3 Yobetsu-dake vol. Japan
155 D4 Yogyakarta Indon.
186 F4 Yoho National Park Canada
177 D4 Yokadouma Cameroon
151 E7 Yokkaichi Japan
177 D4 Yoko Cameroon
151 F7 Yokohama Japan
151 F7 Yokosuka Japan
150 G5 Yokote Japan
150 G4 Yokotsu-dake mt. Japan
177 D4 Yola Nigeria
138 E5 Ýolöten Turkm.
207 E4 Yoloxóchitl Mex.
154 B2 Yom, Mae Nam r. Thai.
176 B4 Yomou Guinea
152 D5 Yŏnan N. Korea
151 G6 Yonezawa Japan
126 C4 Yongala Australia
149 E5 Yong'an China
148 A2 Yongchang China
148 E3 Yongcheng China
149 F5 Yongchun China
148 B2 Yongdeng China
149 E5 Yongding China
148 E2 Yongdinghe Ganqu r. China
149 E5 Yongfeng China
149 C5 Yongfu China
145 H3 Yonggyap La pass India
152 D4 Yŏnghŭng N. Korea
152 D4 Yŏnghŭng-man b. N. Korea
152 D2 Yongji China
149 F4 Yongjia China
148 B3 Yongjing China
148 D2 Yongjin Qu r. China
149 F4 Yongkang China
152 C3 Yongling China
148 E2 Yongnian China
149 C6 Yongning China
149 A5 Yongren China
149 C4 Yongshun China
149 F5 Yongtai China
149 E5 Yongxin China
149 D5 Yongxing China
149 E4 Yongxiu China
149 D5 Yongzhou China
152 D3 Yŏnhwa-san mt. N. Korea
203 G4 Yonkers U.S.A.
166 F2 Yonne r. France
213 B3 Yopal Col.
139 I5 Yopurga China
124 B5 York Australia
160 F4 York U.K.
198 D3 York NE U.S.A.
202 E5 York PA U.S.A.
201 D5 York SC U.S.A.
124 E3 York, Cape Australia
160 F3 York, Vale of val. U.K.
126 B5 Yorke Peninsula Australia
126 B5 Yorketown Australia
160 E3 Yorkshire Dales National Park U.K.
160 G4 Yorkshire Wolds hills U.K.
187 I4 Yorkton Canada
202 E6 Yorktown U.S.A.
206 H5 Yoro Hond.
176 B3 Yorosso Mali
196 C3 Yosemite National Park U.S.A.
196 C3 Yosemite Village U.S.A.
151 C8 Yoshino-gawa r. Japan
151 D7 Yoshino-Kumano Kokuritsu-kōen nat. park Japan
172 H3 Yoshkar-Ola Rus. Fed.
136 E7 Yotvata Israel
163 D6 Youghal Ireland
202 D5 Youghiogheny River Lake U.S.A.
149 C6 You Jiang r. China
127 H5 Young Australia
215 F2 Young Uruguay
126 B3 Younghusband, Lake salt flat Australia
126 C5 Younghusband Peninsula Australia
129 B6 Young Island i. Antarctica
202 C4 Youngstown U.S.A.
149 D4 You Shui r. China
176 B3 Youvarou Mali
149 F5 Youxi China
149 D5 Youxian China
149 C4 Youyang China
150 B1 Youyi China
148 D2 Youyu China
139 G5 Yovon Tajik.
127 F1 Yowah watercourse Australia
136 E2 Yozgat Turkey
214 A3 Ypané r. Para.
214 A3 Ypé-Jhú Para.
Ypres Belgium see Ieper
194 B3 Yreka U.S.A.
138 E2 Yrgyz Kazakh.
138 E2 Yrgyz r. Kazakh.
Yr Wyddfa mt. U.K. see Snowdon
164 A4 Yser r. France
164 D3 Ysselsteyn Neth.
159 K5 Ystad Sweden
161 D5 Ystwyth r. U.K.
Ysyk-Köl Kyrg. see Balykchy
139 I4 Ysyk-Köl salt l. Kyrg.
162 F3 Ythan r. U.K.
133 O3 Ytyk-Kyuyel' Rus. Fed.
154 A1 Yuam, Nam Mae r. Myanmar/Thai.
148 D4 Yuan'an China
149 C5 Yuanbao Shan mt. China
149 D4 Yuanjiang Hunan China
149 A6 Yuanjiang Yunnan China
149 D4 Yuan Jiang r. Hunan China
149 B6 Yuan Jiang r. Yunnan China
149 F5 Yuanli Taiwan
149 D4 Yuanling China
149 A5 Yuanmou China
148 D2 Yuanping China
148 D3 Yuanqu China
196 B2 Yuba r. U.S.A.
196 B2 Yuba City U.S.A.
150 G3 Yūbari Japan
149 C4 Yubei China
207 G4 Yucatán pen. Mex.
207 G3 Yucatán state Mex.
204 G4 Yucatan Channel Cuba/Mex.
197 E4 Yucca U.S.A.
196 D3 Yucca Lake U.S.A.
196 D4 Yucca Valley U.S.A.
148 E2 Yucheng China
133 O4 Yudoma r. Rus. Fed.
149 E5 Yudu China
149 C4 Yuechi China
124 D4 Yuendumu Australia
149 □ Yuen Long Hong Kong China
149 F4 Yueqing China
149 E4 Yuexi Anhui China
149 B4 Yuexi Sichuan China
149 D4 Yueyang China
149 E4 Yugan China
132 H3 Yugorsk Rus. Fed.
172 J2 Yugydtydor Rus. Fed.
149 F4 Yuhuan China
148 E2 Yuhuang Ding mt. China
149 E4 Yujiang China
149 D6 Yu Jiang r. China
133 Q3 Yukagirskoye Ploskogor'ye plat. Rus. Fed.
136 E2 Yukarısarıkaya Turkey
178 B4 Yuki Dem. Rep. Congo
186 B2 Yukon admin. div. Canada
184 C3 Yukon r. Canada/U.S.A.
137 J3 Yüksekova Turkey
138 D1 Yuldybayevo Rus. Fed.
201 D6 Yulee U.S.A.
149 F6 Yuli Taiwan
149 D6 Yulin Guangxi China
149 C7 Yulin Hainan China
148 C2 Yulin Shaanxi China
197 E5 Yuma U.S.A.
197 E5 Yuma Desert U.S.A.
213 A4 Yumbo Col.
139 J3 Yumin China
136 E3 Yumurtalık Turkey
136 C2 Yunak Turkey
149 D6 Yunan China
148 E3 Yuncheng Shandong China
148 D3 Yuncheng Shanxi China
149 D6 Yunfu China

149 B5 Yungui Gaoyuan plat. China
149 F4 Yunhe China
149 D6 Yunkai Dashan mts China
148 D4 Yunmeng China
149 A5 Yunnan prov. China
148 D4 Yun Shui r. China
126 C4 Yunta Australia
149 D6 Yunwu Shan mts China
148 D3 Yunxi China
148 D3 Yunxian China
149 E6 Yunxiao China
148 D3 Yunyang Henan China
148 C4 Yunyang Sichuan China
149 C5 Yuping China
149 F4 Yuqian China
148 E1 Yuqiao Shuiku resr China
149 C5 Yuqing China
127 J2 Yuraygir National Park Australia
146 A1 Yurga Rus. Fed.
150 G5 Yurihonjō Japan
210 C5 Yurimaguas Peru
213 E3 Yuruán r. Venez.
213 E3 Yuruari r. Venez.
213 C2 Yurubí, Parque Nacional nat. park Venez.
144 E1 Yurungkax He r. China
172 I3 Yur'ya Rus. Fed.
172 G3 Yur'yevets Rus. Fed.
172 F3 Yur'yev-Pol'skiy Rus. Fed.
206 H5 Yuscarán Hond.
149 F4 Yushan China
149 F6 Yu Shan mt. Taiwan
148 D2 Yushe China
172 E1 Yushkozero Rus. Fed.
152 D1 Yushu Jilin China
146 B3 Yushu Qinghai China
172 I3 Yushut r. Rus. Fed.
173 H6 Yusta Rus. Fed.
137 H1 Yusufeli Turkey
148 E3 Yutai China
145 E1 Yutian China
148 C2 Yuwang China
149 B5 Yuxi China
148 E2 Yuxian Hebei China
148 D2 Yuxian Shanxi China
149 F4 Yuyao China
150 G5 Yuzawa Japan
172 G3 Yuzha Rus. Fed.
146 D1 Yuzhno-Muyskiy Khrebet mts Rus. Fed.
146 G2 Yuzhno-Sakhalinsk Rus. Fed.
173 H6 Yuzhno-Sukhokumsk Rus. Fed.
173 D6 Yuzhnoukrayins'k Ukr.
138 E1 Yuzhnoural'sk Rus. Fed.
173 G6 Yuzhnyy Rus. Fed.
132 G2 Yuzhnyy, Ostrov i. Rus. Fed.
139 G4 Yuzhnyy Kazakhstan admin. div. Kazakh.
138 D1 Yuzhnyy Ural mts Rus. Fed.
148 B3 Yuzhong China
148 D3 Yuzhou China
Yuzkuduk Uzbek. see Yuzquduq
138 E4 Yuzquduq Uzbek.
168 C7 Yverdon Switz.
166 E2 Yvetot France
154 A1 Ywathit Myanmar
Yylanly Turkm. see Gurbansoltan Eje


## Z


Zaamin Uzbek. see Zomin
164 C2 Zaandam Neth.
137 I3 Zāb al Kabīr, Nahr az r. Iraq
137 I4 Zāb aş Şaghīr, Nahr az r. Iraq
146 D2 Zabaykal'sk Rus. Fed.
140 B2 Zab-e Kuchek r. Iran
142 B7 Zabīd Yemen
141 F4 Zābol Iran
141 F5 Zābolī Iran
138 B3 Zaburun'ye Kazakh.
207 G5 Zacapa Guat.
206 D4 Zacapu Mex.
206 D3 Zacatecas Mex.
206 D3 Zacatecas state Mex.
207 E4 Zacatlán Mex.
138 B2 Zachagansk Kazakh.
171 I6 Zacharo Greece
170 F2 Zadar Croatia
154 A3 Zadetkale Kyun i. Myanmar
154 A3 Zadetkyi Kyun i. Myanmar
145 H2 Zadoi China
173 F4 Zadonsk Rus. Fed.
137 K4 Żafarābād Iran
167 C3 Zafra Spain
140 E3 Zaghdeh well Iran
137 L5 Zāgheh Iran
170 D6 Zaghouan Tunisia
170 F2 Zagreb Croatia
Zagros, Kūhhā-ye mts Iran see Zagros Mountains
140 B3 Zagros Mountains Iran
145 G3 Za'gya Zangbo r. China
141 F4 Zāhedān Iran
141 H3 Zāhidābād Afgh.
136 E5 Zahlé Lebanon
138 E5 Zähmet Turkm.
141 G4 Zahri Nur Gama Pak.
Zair Uzbek. see Zoir
Zaïre country Africa see Congo, Democratic Republic of the
171 J3 Zaječar Serbia
Zakhmet Turkm. see Zähmet
137 I3 Zākhō Iraq
177 D3 Zakouma, Parc National de nat. park Chad
171 I6 Zakynthos Greece
171 I6 Zakynthos i. Greece
168 H7 Zalaegerszeg Hungary
168 H7 Zalai-domsag hills Hungary
167 D3 Zalamea de la Serena Spain
169 K7 Zalău Romania
172 F3 Zales'ye Rus. Fed.
177 E3 Zalingei Sudan
169 L6 Zalishchyky Ukr.
172 D3 Zaluch'ye Rus. Fed.
136 E2 Zamanti r. Turkey
153 B3 Zambales Mountains Phil.
179 C5 Zambeze r. Africa alt. Zambezi (Angola)
179 D5 Zambezi r. Angola alt. Zambeze
179 C5 Zambezi Zambia
179 C5 Zambia country Africa
153 B5 Zamboanga Phil.
153 B5 Zamboanga Peninsula Phil.
141 F4 Zamīndāwar reg. Afgh.
210 C4 Zamora Ecuador
167 D2 Zamora Spain
206 D4 Zamora de Hidalgo Mex.
169 K5 Zamość Poland
148 A3 Zamtang China
213 C2 Zamuro, Punta pt Venez.
213 E3 Zamuro, Sierra del mts Venez.
144 D3 Zanda China
181 K2 Zandamela Moz.
164 C3 Zandvliet Belgium
202 C5 Zanesville U.S.A.
139 I5 Zangguy China
144 D2 Zangla India
140 C2 Zanjān Iran
137 K3 Zanjān Rūd r. Iran
144 D2 Zanskar r. India
144 D2 Zanskar Mountains India
Zante i. Greece see Zakynthos
178 D4 Zanzibar Tanz.
178 D4 Zanzibar Island Tanz.
149 D4 Zaoshi China
176 C2 Zaouatallaz Alg.
148 D3 Zaoyang China
146 B1 Zaozernyy Rus. Fed.
137 I3 Zap r. Turkey
172 E3 Zapadnaya Dvina Rus. Fed.
172 D4 Zapadnaya Dvina r. Rus. Fed. alt. Daugava (Latvia), alt. Zakhodnyaya Dzvina, conv. Western Dvina
171 J4 Zapadni Rodopi mts Bulg.
Zapadno-Sibirskaya Ravnina plain Rus. Fed. see West Siberian Plain
139 H4 Zapadnyy Alamedin, Pik mt. Kyrg.
138 C3 Zapadnyy Chink Ustyurta esc. Kazakh.
138 C3 Zapadnyy Chink Ustyurta esc. Kazakh.
138 C4 Zapadnyy Chink Ustyurta esc. Kazakh.
138 B2 Zapadnyy Kazakhstan admin. div. Kazakh.
158 P1 Zapadnyy Kil'din Rus. Fed.
135 G1 Zapadnyy Sayan reg. Rus. Fed.
215 B3 Zapala Arg.
199 D7 Zapata U.S.A.
213 B3 Zapatoca Col.
213 B2 Zapatoza, Ciénaga de l. Col.
158 O1 Zapolyarnyy Rus. Fed.
173 E6 Zaporizhzhya Ukr.
144 E2 Zapug China
137 K1 Zaqatala Azer.
145 H2 Zaqên China
145 H2 Za Qu r. China
136 F2 Zara Turkey
Zarafshan Uzbek. see Zarafshon
139 G5 Zarafshon Tajik.
138 F4 Zarafshon Uzbek.
138 F5 Zarafshon r. Uzbek.
139 F5 Zarafshon, Qatorkŭhi mts Tajik.
213 B3 Zaragoza Col.
195 F6 Zaragoza Chihuahua Mex.
206 D1 Zaragoza Coahuila Mex.
167 F2 Zaragoza Spain
141 H3 Zaraḩ Sharan Afgh.
140 E4 Zarand Iran
136 E6 Zaranikh Protected Area nature res. Egypt
141 F4 Zaranj Afgh.
159 N5 Zarasai Lith.
215 E2 Zárate Arg.
213 D2 Zaraza Venez.
Zarbdar Uzbek. see Zarbdor
139 G4 Zarbdor Uzbek.
137 K1 Zärdab Azer.
158 O2 Zarechensk Rus. Fed.
137 L4 Zāreh Iran
186 C3 Zarembo Island U.S.A.
144 A3 Zargun mt. Pak.
176 C3 Zaria Nigeria
173 C5 Zarichne Ukr.
140 B2 Zarīneh Rūd r. Iran
141 F3 Zarmardān Afgh.
137 K5 Zarneh Iran
171 K2 Zărnești Romania
140 D4 Zarqān Iran
140 D3 Zarrīn Iran
150 B3 Zarubino Rus. Fed.
168 G5 Żary Poland
138 D2 Zarya Oktyabrya Kazakh.
213 A3 Zarzal Col.
177 D1 Zarzis Tunisia
158 O2 Zasheyek Rus. Fed.
Zaskar r. India see Zanskar
Zaskar Mountains India see Zanskar Mountains
172 C4 Zaslawye Belarus
181 G5 Zastron S. Africa
165 K2 Zauche reg. Germany
Zaunguzskiye Karakumy des. Turkm. see Üngüz Angyrsyndaky Garagum
179 D6 Zavala Moz.
140 D3 Zavāreh Iran
171 H2 Zavidoviči Bos.-Herz.
146 E1 Zavitinsk Rus. Fed.
139 K1 Zavodskoye Rus. Fed.
139 J1 Zav'yalovo Rus. Fed.
148 A2 Zawa China
169 I5 Zawiercie Poland
139 K3 Zaysan Kazakh.
139 J2 Zaysan, Lake Kazakh.
Zayü China see Zhigang
168 G6 Žďár nad Sázavou Czech Rep.
173 C5 Zdolbuniv Ukr.
159 J5 Zealand i. Denmark
137 J3 Zēbār Iraq
181 H2 Zebediela S. Africa
164 B3 Zedelgem Belgium
164 B3 Zeebrugge Belgium
127 F8 Zeehan Australia
181 G2 Zeerust S. Africa
164 B3 Zeeuwsch-Vlaanderen reg. Neth.
136 E5 Zefat Israel
165 L2 Zehdenick Germany
124 D4 Zeil, Mount Australia
165 I4 Zeil am Main Germany
164 D2 Zeist Neth.
165 K3 Zeitz Germany
148 A3 Zêkog China
139 H1 Zelenaya Roshcha Kazakh.
158 P2 Zelenoborskiy Rus. Fed.
172 I4 Zelenodol'sk Rus. Fed.
159 O3 Zelenogorsk Rus. Fed.
172 F3 Zelenograd Rus. Fed.
172 B4 Zelenogradsk Rus. Fed.
173 G6 Zelenokumsk Rus. Fed.
172 H3 Zelentsovo Rus. Fed.
139 G2 Zelenyy Gay Kazakh.
168 F7 Zell am See Austria
165 H5 Zellingen Germany
164 B3 Zelzate Belgium
148 A3 Zêmdasam China
172 G4 Zemetchino Rus. Fed.
178 C3 Zémio Cent. Afr. Rep.
167 G5 Zemmora Alg.
207 E4 Zempoala, Pirámides de tourist site Mex.
207 F4 Zempoaltépetl, Nudo de mt. Mex.
149 D6 Zengcheng China
152 E2 Zengfeng Shan mt. China
196 A1 Zenia U.S.A.
171 G2 Zenica Bos.-Herz.
161 B7 Zennor U.K.
196 C2 Zephyr Cove U.S.A.
139 I5 Zepu China
Zeravshan r. Uzbek. see Zarafshon
165 K3 Zerbst Germany
139 G1 Zerendy Kazakh.
164 E5 Zerf Germany
165 I1 Zernien Germany
165 K2 Zernitz Germany
173 G6 Zernograd Rus. Fed.
173 G7 Zest'aponi Georgia
Zêtang China see Nêdong
165 F1 Zetel Germany
165 J4 Zeulenroda Germany
165 H1 Zeven Germany
164 E3 Zevenaar Neth.
146 E1 Zeya Rus. Fed.
146 E1 Zeya r. Rus. Fed.
140 D4 Zeydābād Iran
141 E4 Zeynālābād Iran
146 E1 Zeyskoye Vodokhranilishche resr Rus. Fed.
167 C3 Zêzere r. Port.
169 I5 Zgierz Poland
172 C4 Zhabinka Belarus
139 F2 Zhaksy Kazakh.
139 G2 Zhaksy-Kon watercourse Kazakh.
138 E3 Zhaksykylysh Kazakh.
138 E3 Zhaksykylysh, Ozero salt l. Kazakh.
138 F3 Zhalagash Kazakh.
139 J2 Zhalgyztobe Kazakh.
138 B2 Zhalpaktal Kazakh.
139 G2 Zhaltyr Akmolinskaya Oblast' Kazakh.
139 I2 Zhaltyr Pavlodarskaya Oblast' Kazakh.
138 B3 Zhaltyr, Ozero l. Kazakh.
138 E2 Zhamanakkol', Ozero salt l. Kazakh.
138 C3 Zhamansor Kazakh.
139 G3 Zhambyl Kazakh.
139 G3 Zhambylskaya Oblast' admin. div. Kazakh.
139 J3 Zhameuka Kazakh.
139 G3 Zhanabas (abandoned) Kazakh.
138 B2 Zhanakala Kazakh.
138 B2 Zhanakazan Kazakh.
138 E3 Zhanakentkala tourist site Kazakh.
139 F4 Zhanakorgan Kazakh.
138 E3 Zhanakurylys Kazakh.
138 F3 Zhanala tourist site Kazakh.
139 H3 Zhanaortalyk Kazakh.
138 C4 Zhanaozen Kazakh.
139 I4 Zhanatalan Kazakh.
139 G4 Zhanatas Kazakh.
138 E3 Zhanay Kazakh.
138 B3 Zhanbay Kazakh.
148 E1 Zhangbei China
152 E1 Zhangguangcai Ling mts China
152 B2 Zhanggutai China
148 E2 Zhang He r. China
149 F5 Zhanghua Taiwan
149 D4 Zhangjiajie China
148 E1 Zhangjiakou China
148 B3 Zhangla China
149 E5 Zhangping China
149 E5 Zhangpu China
152 B2 Zhangqiang China
149 E4 Zhangshu China
148 E2 Zhangwei Xinhe r. China
152 B2 Zhangwu China
148 B3 Zhangxian China
148 A2 Zhangye China
149 E5 Zhangzhou China
148 D2 Zhangzi China
152 B4 Zhangzi Dao i. China
148 F2 Zhanhua China
138 A2 Zhanibek Kazakh.
149 D6 Zhanjiang China
139 I3 Zhansugirov Kazakh.
138 C3 Zhanterek Kazakh.
149 B5 Zhanyi China
149 E6 Zhao'an China
149 B4 Zhaojue China
149 D5 Zhaoping China
149 D6 Zhaoqing China
139 J4 Zhaosu China
152 B2 Zhaosutai He r. China
149 B5 Zhaotong China
148 E2 Zhaoxian China
152 C1 Zhaoyuan China
149 D6 Zhapo China
139 J3 Zharbulak Kazakh.
145 F3 Zhari Namco salt l. China
138 D3 Zharkamys Kazakh.
139 J3 Zharkent Kazakh.
172 E4 Zharkovskiy Rus. Fed.
138 C4 Zharma Mangistauskaya Oblast' Kazakh.
139 J2 Zharma Vostochnyy Kazakhstan Kazakh.
139 J3 Zharsuat (abandoned) Kazakh.
139 J2 Zharyk Kazakh.
173 D5 Zhashkiv Ukr.
148 C3 Zhashui China
Zhaslyk Uzbek. see Jasliq
145 F2 Zhaxi Co salt l. China
144 D2 Zhaxigang China
139 G2 Zhayrem Kazakh.
Zhayyk r. Kazakh./Rus. Fed. see Ural
148 E3 Zhecheng China
149 F4 Zhejiang prov. China
139 H2 Zhekezhal Kazakh.
132 H2 Zhelaniya, Mys c. Rus. Fed.
139 H1 Zhelezinka Kazakh.
173 E4 Zheleznogorsk Rus. Fed.
139 H3 Zheltorangy Kazakh.
138 C3 Zhem r. Kazakh.
148 C3 Zhen'an China
148 C3 Zhenba China
149 C4 Zheng'an China
148 E2 Zhengding China
149 F5 Zhenghe China
148 C3 Zhengning China
148 E3 Zhengyang China
148 D3 Zhengzhou China
149 F4 Zhenhai China
148 F3 Zhenjiang China
148 B3 Zhenjiangguan China
149 B5 Zhenning China
148 D3 Zhenping China
149 B5 Zhenxiong China
148 C3 Zhenyuan Gansu China
149 C5 Zhenyuan Guizhou China
173 G5 Zherdevka Rus. Fed.
149 F5 Zherong China
172 I2 Zheshart Rus. Fed.
138 C4 Zhetybay Kazakh.
138 E2 Zhetykol', Ozero l. Rus. Fed.
135 F2 Zhetysuskiy Alatau mts China/Kazakh.
149 D4 Zhexi Shuiku resr China
139 F2 Zhezdy Kazakh.
139 F3 Zhezkazgan Karagandinskaya Oblast' Kazakh.
139 F3 Zhezkazgan Karagandinskaya Oblast' Kazakh.
139 F3 Zhezkazganskaya Oblast' Kazakh.
149 D4 Zhicheng China
148 C2 Zhidan China
145 H2 Zhidoi China
146 B4 Zhigang China
133 N3 Zhigansk Rus. Fed.
145 G3 Zhigung China
149 D4 Zhijiang Hubei China
149 C5 Zhijiang Hunan China
149 B5 Zhijin China
173 H5 Zhirnovsk Rus. Fed.
138 E1 Zhitikara Kazakh.
173 H5 Zhitkur Rus. Fed.
137 K4 Zhīvār Iran
172 D4 Zhlobin Belarus
173 D5 Zhmerynka Ukr.
144 B3 Zhob Pak.
144 B3 Zhob r. Pak.
133 Q2 Zhokhova, Ostrov i. Rus. Fed.
139 J2 Zholnuskau Kazakh.
139 G2 Zholymbet Kazakh.
145 F3 Zhongba China
148 B4 Zhongjiang China
148 B2 Zhongning China
129 E5 Zhongshan research stn Antarctica
149 D6 Zhongshan Guangdong China
149 D5 Zhongshan Guangxi China
Zhongshan China see Liupanshui
148 D3 Zhongtiao Shan mts China
148 B2 Zhongwei China
149 C4 Zhongxian China
149 E5 Zhongxin China
149 F6 Zhongyang Shanmo mts Taiwan
Zhongyicun China see Gucheng
149 D7 Zhongyuan China
138 F3 Zhosaly Kazakh.
148 E3 Zhoucheng China
148 C4 Zhou He r. China
148 B2 Zhoujiajing China
148 E3 Zhoukou China
149 F5 Zhouning China
149 G4 Zhoushan China
173 E5 Zhovti Vody Ukr.
152 B4 Zhuanghe China
148 B3 Zhuanglang China
139 G3 Zhuantobe Kazakh.
148 F3 Zhucheng China
152 C1 Zhuchengzi China
149 F5 Zhudong Taiwan
148 B3 Zhugqu China
149 D6 Zhuhai China
149 F4 Zhuji China
148 F4 Zhujing China
172 E4 Zhukovka Rus. Fed.
148 E2 Zhulong He r. China
148 E3 Zhumadian China
138 B3 Zhumysker Kazakh.
149 C4 Zhuo He r. China
148 E1 Zhuolu China
148 E2 Zhuozhou China
148 D1 Zhuozi China
139 G2 Zhuravlevka Kazakh.
138 D2 Zhuryn Kazakh.
139 H3 Zhusandala, Step' plain Kazakh.
148 D3 Zhushan China
148 C3 Zhuxi China
149 D5 Zhuzhou Hunan China
149 D5 Zhuzhou Hunan China
173 C5 Zhydachiv Ukr.
138 C2 Zhympity Kazakh.
138 B3 Zhyngyldy Kazakh.
173 C4 Zhytkavichy Belarus
173 D5 Zhytomyr Ukr.
141 G4 Ziārat-e Shāh Esmā'īl Afgh.
169 I6 Žiar nad Hronom Slovakia
137 I3 Zībār Iraq
148 F2 Zibo China
148 C2 Zichang China
141 E2 Zīdar Iran
168 G5 Zielona Góra Poland
165 H3 Zierenberg Germany
165 K2 Ziesar Germany
136 C6 Ziftá Egypt
137 L1 Zığ Azer.
145 H5 Zigaing Myanmar
145 G2 Zigê Tangco l. China
149 B4 Zigong China
176 A3 Ziguinchor Senegal
159 N4 Žīguri Latvia
148 F2 Zi He r. China
206 D4 Zihuatanejo Mex.
149 E6 Zijin China
164 E2 Zijpenberg h. Neth.
136 E5 Zikhron Ya'aqov Israel
138 D1 Zilair Rus. Fed.
136 E1 Zile Turkey
169 I6 Žilina Slovakia
146 C1 Zima Rus. Fed.
207 E3 Zimapán Mex.
207 E4 Zimatlán Mex.
179 C5 Zimba Zambia
179 C5 Zimbabwe country Africa
140 B3 Zīmkān, Rūdkhāneh-ye r. Iran
176 A4 Zimmi Sierra Leone
171 K3 Zimnicea Romania
173 G6 Zimovniki Rus. Fed.
136 E4 Zimrīn Syria
141 F3 Zindah Jān Afgh.
176 C3 Zinder Niger
176 B3 Ziniaré Burkina Faso
197 F3 Zion National Park U.S.A.
188 B3 Zionz Lake Canada
213 B3 Zipaquirá Col.
145 H2 Ziqudukou China
141 F4 Zirah, Gōd-e depr. Afgh.
165 I5 Zirndorf Germany
145 H4 Ziro India
149 D4 Zi Shui r. China
168 H6 Zistersdorf Austria
207 D4 Zitácuaro Mex.
168 G5 Zittau Germany
137 J3 Zīveh Iran
149 E5 Zixi China
148 E2 Ziya He r. China
138 D2 Ziyanchurino Rus. Fed.
148 C3 Ziyang Shaanxi China
149 B4 Ziyang Sichuan China
149 D5 Ziyuan China
149 C5 Ziyun China
149 B4 Zizhong China
171 K3 Zlatitsa Bulg.
168 H6 Zlín Czech Rep.
173 D4 Zlynka Rus. Fed.
139 J2 Zmeinogorsk Rus. Fed.
173 F5 Zmiyiv Ukr.
139 I2 Znamenka Kazakh.
139 I1 Znamenka Altayskiy Kray Rus. Fed.
172 E4 Znamenka Orlovskaya Oblast' Rus. Fed.
138 D1 Znamenskiy Rus. Fed.
173 E5 Znam"yanka Ukr.
168 H6 Znojmo Czech Rep.
180 D6 Zoar S. Africa
137 K4 Zobeyrī Iran
164 C2 Zoetermeer Neth.
137 J4 Zohāb Iran
148 B3 Zoigê China
138 D4 Zoir Uzbek.
144 C2 Zoji La pass India
181 G6 Zola S. Africa
164 D3 Zolder Belgium
173 E5 Zolochiv Ukr.
173 C5 Zolochiv Ukr.
173 E5 Zolotonosha Ukr.
139 G1 Zolotorunnoye Kazakh.
173 F4 Zolotukhino Rus. Fed.
179 D5 Zomba Malawi
139 G5 Zomin Uzbek.
136 C1 Zonguldak Turkey
145 G3 Zongxoi China
149 E4 Zongyang China
170 C4 Zonza Corsica France
165 K3 Zörbig Germany
176 B3 Zorgho Burkina Faso
139 H5 Zorkŭl l. Afgh./Tajik.
176 B4 Zorzor Liberia
164 B4 Zottegem Belgium
177 D2 Zouar Chad
148 E3 Zoucheng China
176 A2 Zouérat Mauritania
148 E2 Zouping China
149 D4 Zoushi China
171 I2 Zrenjanin Serbia
165 L4 Zschopau Germany
165 K3 Zschornewitz Germany
213 D2 Zuata r. Venez.
140 A4 Zubālah, Birkat waterhole Saudi Arabia
215 D3 Zubillaga Arg.
172 G4 Zubova Polyana Rus. Fed.
176 B4 Zuénoula Côte d'Ivoire
168 D7 Zug Switz.
173 G7 Zugdidi Georgia
168 D7 Zuger See l. Switz.
168 E7 Zugspitze mt. Austria/Germany
Zuider Zee l. Neth. see IJsselmeer
164 E1 Zuidhorn Neth.
164 C2 Zuid-Kennemerland Nationaal Park nat. park Neth.
167 D3 Zújar r. Spain
213 B2 Zulia r. Col.
164 E4 Zülpich Germany
179 D5 Zumbo Moz.
190 A3 Zumbro r. U.S.A.
190 A3 Zumbrota U.S.A.
207 E4 Zumpango Mex.
176 C4 Zungeru Nigeria
148 F1 Zunhua China
197 H4 Zuni U.S.A.
197 H4 Zuni Mountains U.S.A.
149 C5 Zunyi Guizhou China
149 C5 Zunyi Guizhou China
149 C6 Zuo Jiang r. China/Vietnam
148 D2 Zuoquan China
148 D2 Zuoyun China
137 J2 Zūrābād Iran
137 K5 Zurbāţīyah Iraq
168 D7 Zürich Switz.
141 H3 Zurmat reg. Afgh.
164 E2 Zutphen Neth.
177 D1 Zuwārah Libya
172 I3 Zuyevka Rus. Fed.
159 N4 Zvejniekciems Latvia
172 I4 Zvenigovo Rus. Fed.
173 D5 Zvenyhorodka Ukr.
138 F1 Zverinogolovskoye Rus. Fed.
179 D6 Zvishavane Zimbabwe
169 I6 Zvolen Slovakia
171 H2 Zvornik Bos.-Herz.
176 B4 Zwedru Liberia
164 E2 Zweeloo Neth.
164 F5 Zweibrücken Germany
181 G6 Zwelitsha S. Africa
165 L3 Zwethau Germany
168 G6 Zwettl Austria
165 K4 Zwickau Germany
165 K3 Zwochau Germany
164 E2 Zwolle Neth.
165 K4 Zwönitz Germany
133 Q3 Zyryanka Rus. Fed.
139 K2 Zyryanovsk Kazakh.



## ACKNOWLEDGEMENTS

Maps, design and origination by Collins Bartholomew Ltd
HarperCollins Publishers, Glasgow

Population statistics: UN Department of Economic and Social Affairs Population Division

Earthquake data: United States Geological Survey (USGS) National Earthquakes Information Center, Denver, USA

Köppen classification map: Kottek, M., J. Grieser, C. Beck, B. Rudolf, and F. Rubel, 2006: World Map of the Köppen-Geigerclimate classification updated. *Meteorol. Z.*, 15, 259–263. http://koeppen-geiger.vu-wien.ac.at

*Climate Change 2007: Impacts, Adaptation and Vulnerability, summary for Policymakers*, Intergovernmental Panel on Climate Change

Population map: Center for International Earth Science Information Network (CIESIN), Columbia University

International Food Policy Research Institute (IFPRI); and World Resources Institute (WRI). 2000
Gridded Population of the World (GPW), Version 3. Palisades, NY: CIESIN, Columbia University
Available at http://sedac.ciesin.columbia.edu/plue/gpw

## IMAGE CREDITS

**Pages 4–17**
Blue Marble: Next Generation. NASA's Earth Observatory

**Pages 18–19**
Landsat Image Mosaic of Antarctica (LIMA) Project and Blue Marble: Next Generation. NASA's Earth Observatory

**Pages 20–21**
IKONOS image courtesy of GeoEye.

**Pages 22–23**
NASA/GSFC/METI/ERSDAC/JAROS, and U.S./Japan ASTER Science Team

**Pages 24–25**
IKONOS images courtesy of GeoEye. Copyright 2008. All rights reserved

**Pages 26–27**
IKONOS image courtesy of GeoEye.

**Pages 28–29**
NASA/GSFC/METI/ERSDAC/JAROS, and the U.S./Japan ASTER Science Team

**Pages 30–31**
NASA image created by Jesse Allen, using Landsat data provided by the University of Maryland's Global Land Cover Facility.

**Pages 32–33**
Shutterstock/Jarno Gonzalez Zarraonandia

**Pages 34–35**
Image courtesy of GeoEye.

**Pages 90-91**
Haiti earthquake: © United Nations Development Programme. Licensed under the Creative Commons 2.0 Attribution License.
Mount Bromo: ©Manamana/Shutterstock

**Pages 92-93**
Hurricane Sandy: NASA Earth Observatory image by Robert Simmon with data courtesy of the NASA/NOAA GOES Project Science

**Pages 94-95**
McCarty Glacier: NSIDC/U. S. Grant. (top);
NSIDC/Bruce F. Molina (bottom)

**Pages 96-97**
Hong Kong, China: testing/Shutterstock

**Pages 100-101**
Lake Eyre: MODIS/NASA
Mississippi: ASTER/NASA
Caspian Sea: MODIS/NASA
Madagascar: MODIS/NASA

**Cover**
Mt Everest, Himalayas, Nepal © Vadim Petrakov/Shutterstock

GeoEye www.geoeye.com
NASA earthobservatory.nasa.gov
NASA rapidfire.sci.gsfc.nasa.gov
NASA asterweb.jpl.nasa.gov/index.asp
TeleGeography www.telegeography.com
United States Geological Survey www.usgs.gov

# KEY TO THE MAP PAGES

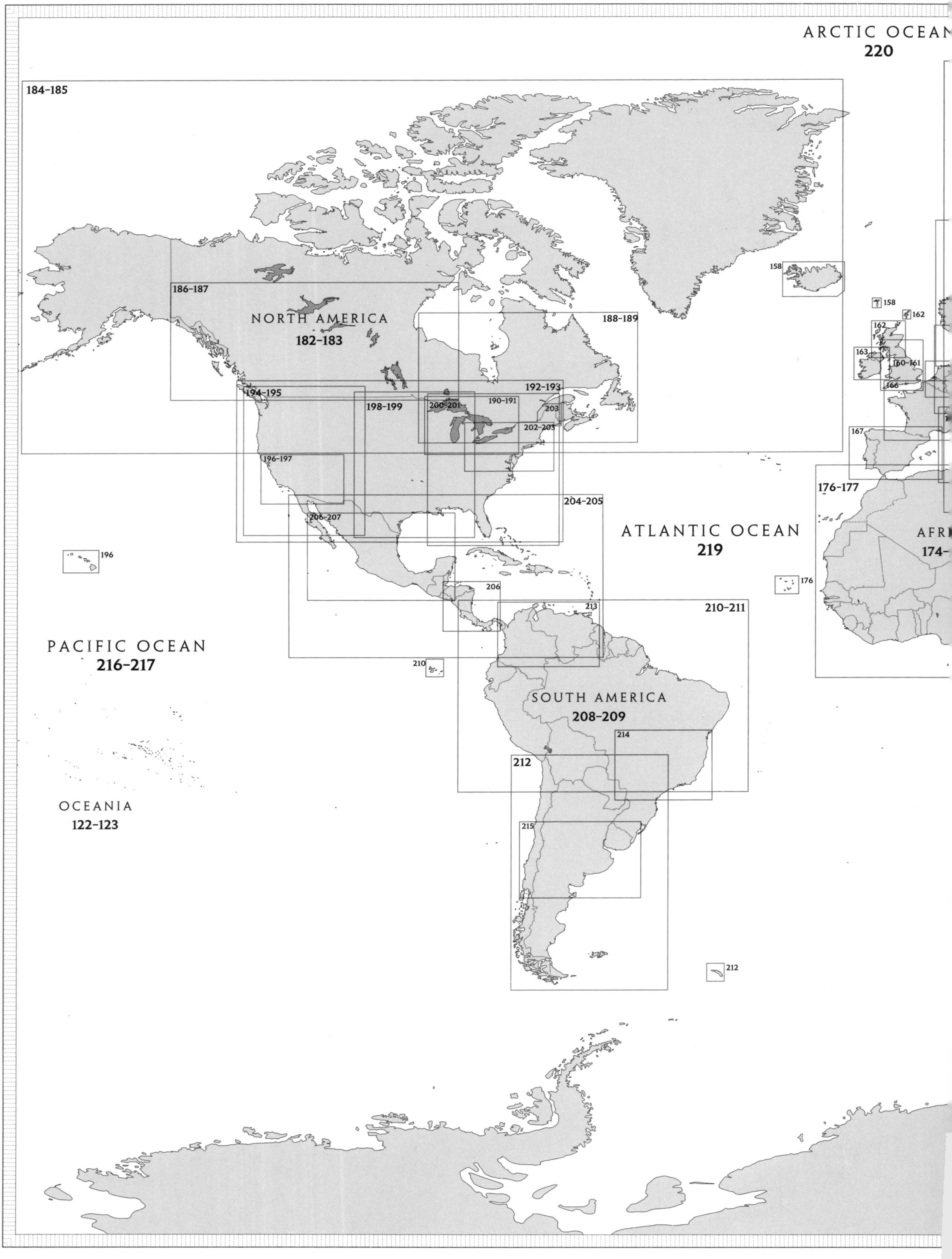